Contemporary Literary Criticism

Contemporary Literary Criticism

Excerpts from Criticism
of the Works of Today's
Novelists, Poets, Playwrights,
and Other Creative Writers

Dedria Bryfonski
Editor

Gale Research Company
Book Tower
Detroit, Michigan 48226

STAFF

Dedria Bryfonski, *Editor*

Phyllis Carmel Mendelson, *Contributing Editor*
Laurie Lanzen Harris, *Associate Editor*
Laura A. Buch, David J. Szymanski, *Assistant Editors*

Sharon R. Cillette, *Production Editor*

Linda M. Pugliese, *Manuscript Coordinator*
L. Elizabeth Hardin, *Permissions Coodinator*
Thomas E. Gunton, *Research Coordinator*
Jeanne A. Gough, Jean C. Stine, Carolyn Voldrich, *Editorial Assistants*

Special acknowledgment to Gerard J. Senick, *Editor,*
and Sharon R. Cillette, *Associate Editor,* **Children's Literature Review**

Contents

Preface vii

Conrad Aiken 1

Nelson Algren 4

José María Arguedas 8

Elisaveta Bagryana 11

Beryl Bainbridge 15

Imamu Amiri Baraka 18

John Barth 21

Samuel Beckett 24

Saul Bellow 36

John Berryman 45

John Betjeman 52

John Bishop 54

Robert Bly 54

Jorge Luis Borges 63

Ray Bradbury 68

Melvyn Bragg 71

William Bronk 73

Olga Broumas 76

John Brunner 77

John Buell 81

Basil Bunting 83

Anthony Burgess 86

Frederick Busch 91

Paul Vincent Carroll 95

Hayden Carruth 100

Paul Celan 101

John Ciardi 104

D. L. Coburn 107

Ivy Compton-Burnett 108

Richard Condon 111

Julio Cortázar 112

Donald Davie 120

C. Day Lewis 125

Don DeLillo 134

Peter De Vries 136

Philip K. Dick 138

James Dickey 139

Isak Dinesen 144

J. P. Donleavy 153

Ed Dorn 155

Margaret Drabble 162

T. S. Eliot 167

Lawrence Ferlinghetti 174

E. M. Forster 178

John Fowles 183

Marilyn French 191

Robert Frost 192

Christopher Fry 199

Carlos Fuentes 204

William Gaddis 209

Gabriel García Márquez 214

John Gardner 218

Jean Genet 224

Penelope Gilliatt 229

Édouard Glissant 230

William Golding 231

Nadine Gordimer 239

Lois Gould 241

Juan Goytisolo 243

Chaim Grade 246

Pete Hamill 251

Dashiell Hammett 252

Peter Handke 254

Mark Helprin 260

Ernest Hemingway 262

Rayner Heppenstall 271

George V. Higgins 273

Richard Howard 274

Langston Hughes 278

Uwe Johnson 283

D. G. Jones 285

James Jones 289

Mervyn Jones 294

Preston Jones 296

Thomas Keneally 298

John Oliver Killens 300

John Knowles 302

György Konrád 304

Jerzy Kosinski 305

Reiner Kunze 309

Pär Lagerkvist 311

Doris Lessing 313

José Lezama Lima 317

Louis MacNeice 323

D. Keith Mano 327

John P. Marquand 328

Michael McClure 331

Carson McCullers 334

José Rodrigues Miguéis 340

Arthur Miller 342

Marianne Moore 346

Toni Morrison 354

Alice Munro 356

Lorine Niedecker 360

Flann O'Brien 362

Flannery O'Connor 364

Kenzaburō Ōe 372

Juan Carlos Onetti 374

Boris Pasternak 382

Alan Paton 387

Octavio Paz 388

Katherine Anne Porter 394

Ezra Pound 399

Anthony Powell 408

David Pownall 418

Manuel Puig 420

James Purdy 421

Salvatore Quasimodo 427

Raymond Queneau 429

Piers Paul Read 434

João Ubaldo Ribeiro 436

Alain Robbe-Grillet 436

Jill Robinson 438

Claudio Rodríguez 439

Gabrielle Roy 440

Muriel Rukeyser 442

Ernesto Sábato 444
William Safire 446
Carl Sandburg 447
William Saroyan 452
Nathalie Sarraute 457
John Sayles 460
Delmore Schwartz 462
Erich Segal 466
Anne Sexton 467
Ahmad Shamlu 469
Wilfrid Sheed 472
Alix Kates Shulman 474

Alan Sillitoe 476
W. D. Snodgrass 477
Aleksandr I. Solzhenitsyn 478
Susan Sontag 484
Stephen Spender 487
Hollis Summers 492
Mark Van Doren 495
Mario Vargas Llosa 496
Gore Vidal 501
Vladimir Voinovich 504
Edward Lewis Wallant 511
Robert Penn Warren 517

Michael Weller 525
E. B. White 526
Thornton Wilder 531
P. G. Wodehouse 537
Larry Woiwode 540
James Wright 542

Cumulative Index to Critics 553
Cumulative Index to Authors 605
Appendix 611

Preface

Literary criticism is indispensable to the layman or scholar attempting to evaluate and understand creative writing—whether his subject is one poem, one writer, one idea, one school, or a general trend in contemporary writing. Literary criticism is itself a collective term for several kinds of critical writing: criticism may be normative, descriptive, interpretive, textual, appreciative, genetic. Conscientious students must consult numerous sources in order to become familiar with the criticism pertinent to their subjects.

Until now, there has been nothing resembling an ongoing encyclopedia of current literary criticism, bringing together in one series criticism of all the various kinds from widely diverse sources. *Contemporary Literary Criticism* is intended to be such a comprehensive reference work.

The Plan of the Work

Contemporary Literary Criticism presents significant passages from the published criticism of work by well-known creative writers—novelists and short story writers, poets and playwrights. Some creative writers, like James Baldwin and Paul Goodman, are probably better known for their expository work than for their fiction, and so discussion of their nonfiction is included.

Contemporary Literary Criticism is not limited to material concerning long-established authors like Eliot, Faulkner, Hemingway, and Auden, although these and other writers of similar stature are included. Attention is also given to two other groups of writers—writers of considerable public interest—about whose work criticism is hard to locate. These are the newest writers (like Robert M. Pirsig, Erica Jong, and William Kotzwinkle) and the contributors to the well-loved but unscholarly genres of mystery and science fiction (like Georges Simenon, Agatha Christie, Robert Heinlein, and Arthur C. Clarke).

The definition of *contemporary* is necessarily arbitrary. For purposes of selection for *CLC,* contemporary writers are those who are either now living or who have died since January 1, 1960. Contemporary criticism is more loosely defined as that written any time during the past twenty-five years or so and currently relevant to the evaluation of the writer under discussion.

Each volume of *CLC* lists about 150 authors, with an average of about five excerpts from critical articles or reviews being given for the works of each author. Altogether, there are about 1100 individual excerpts in each volume taken from about 50 books and several hundred issues of some one hundred general magazines, literary reviews, and scholarly journals. Each excerpt is fully identified for the convenience of readers who may wish to consult the entire chapter, article, or review excerpted. Each volume covers writers not previously included and also provides significant new criticism pertaining to authors included in earlier volumes.

Beginning with Volume 10, *CLC* will contain an appendix which lists the sources from which material has been reprinted in this volume. It does not, however, list every book or periodical consulted for the volume.

A Note on Bio-Bibliographical References and Page Citations

Notes in many entries directing the user to consult *Contemporary Authors* for detailed biographical and bibliographical information refer to a series of biographical reference books published by the Gale Research Company since 1962, which now includes detailed biographical sketches of about

50,000 authors who have lived since 1962, many of whose careers began during the post-World War II period, or earlier.

Beginning with *CLC,* Volume 5, the method for referring to pages in the original sources has been standardized. Page numbers appear after each fragment (unless the entire essay was contained on one page). Page numbers appear in citations as well only when the editors wish to indicate, with an essay or chapter title and its *inclusive* page numbers, the scope of the original treatment.

Acknowledgments

The editors wish to thank the copyright holders of the excerpts included in this volume for their permission to use the material, and the staffs of the Detroit Public Library, Wayne State University Library, and the libraries of the University of Michigan for making their resources available to us.

A

AIKEN, Conrad   1889-1973

Aiken was an American poet, novelist, short story writer, critic, editor, and playwright. He was influenced by the intellectual movements of the twenties; his interest in the work of Freud is reflected in the psychological probing characteristic of his poetry. Aiken's work stresses the primacy of content over form: for him thematic and philosophic unity took precedence over structural coherence. (See also *CLC*, Vols. 1, 3, 5, and *Contemporary Authors*, Vols. 5-8, rev. ed.; obituary, Vols. 45-48.)

CAROLYN HANDA

Conrad Aiken remains firmly established in his exalted position as one of America's most neglected contemporary writers. (p. 375)

Artistically, [Aiken's short story] "Impulse" is finely-constructed, so carefully molded that its structure and imagery adhere tenaciously to its theme, lending this theme an appropriate form and serving as more than adequate vehicles of expression. Aiken constantly welds images and overall design to reinforce his point of view: that "civilization is only skin-deep"; once shaved of that paper-thin skin of civility, mankind shows itself to be "criminal, ex-post facto." The imagery, consequently, relates to shaving and the breaking of bonds, and the form the story takes—that of the "'V' turned upside down" mentioned in its first paragraph —assumes significance for this tale of a man defeated by exposing his inherently criminal nature. . . .

Giving form to this story is Aiken's idea that civilized nature is only a thin veneer beneath which every human feels similar impulses, and which, when punctured, releases man's anti-social tendencies. Once aware of the theme, we immediately begin to see juxtaposed the "civilized" and "uncivilized" actions in the story. The idea that civilization is only skin-deep provides the chief thrust for the story's main action. In addition, Aiken heaps level upon level of irony since we realize that except for civilization, the men would not be contemplating impulse in such a cerebral manner. . . . (p. 376)

Aiken's structure consists of an upward movement towards a peak situation, followed by an immediate reversal of the previous action. Michael begins at a low point made comfortable by illusions, rises in his comfort due to an increase of illusions, then performs his impulsive, catalytic act which triggers a series of confrontations that bring him back to a most painful reality. The second half of the structure thus complements the first through its reversed movement (we see the coming down of what went up), and reversed perceptions (reality follows illusions; what was flatly literal assumes a deeper figurative cast).

As we might expect, Aiken's imagery follows and accentuates the structure of the story while reinforcing the "civilization is only skin-deep" theme. One of the primary sets of images centers around the "civilized" ritual of shaving. Aiken emphasizes this action subtly and first depicts Michael shaving—literally: "Michael Lowes hummed as he shaved, amused by the face he saw." . . . Structurally, we can place Aiken's first reference to shaving at the foot of one side of the inverted-V shape of the story. The next reference to shaving occurs in the scene at the apex of the inverted-V where Michael acts to bring about his downfall. Here Michael receives his fatal impulse to steal the very instrument used in the act of shaving: "a *de-luxe* safety-razor set, of heavy gold," . . . —in other words, a *shaver*. Aiken includes no final direct reference to shaving, but does infer, indirectly, to the state of a "shaved" man in the last scene. We see Michael Lowes sitting on the edge of his bed in his cell, thinking of his past life—his childhood, his college years, his days as a husband and a father. By the final line of the story, Michael realizes: "It [that whole life] had all come foolishly to an end." . . . He is now figuratively a shaved man. His theft has erased his entire previous life and leads him back down, in the structure of the story, to the second low point of the inverted-V. Just as Michael's movement from the peak of illusion to harsh reality places him in a more painful situation than his first low illusory state, this shaving is more drastic than Michael's first ritual action, because it exposes that lower side of his human nature which lies beneath civilization's thin skin. Finally perceiving his degradation mirrored in [his wife] Dora's last glance, Michael guesses she is probably "wondering what sort of people criminals might be. Human? Sub-human?" . . . And through that one short reference to sub-humanness, we can sense Aiken wondering how far mankind has indeed developed since its cave man days.

The less obvious imagery of the card game is also noteworthy. The four men are playing bridge, and, more specifically, contract bridge. Aside from their use as card game titles, both ''bridge'' and ''contract'' suggest attempts to overcome some type of abyss separating human beings, and Aiken plays with these definitions through his tale. The noun and verb forms of ''bridge'' denote times, places, means of, or attempts at connection or transition. In the first half of the story, Michael feels that he has achieved reasonable connections in many of his relationships; but this first half, we remember, shows Michael's growing illusions about himself, and we can see that he is just as deluded in his belief that he has established any true relationships with others. (pp. 378-79)

The second half of the story exposes Michael's ''insubstantial bridgework'' for all its flimsiness, and follows the V-structure of the story, just as the shaving imagery did. Both images are pictured as literal actions in the first half of the story; the second half, however, reveals them in a reversed, figurative, and more disastrous light. Thus Michael begins with the act of shaving, but ends figuratively shaved; he also begins playing a game of bridge, but by playing the wrong cards in life, ends up destroying all his bridges to the present point. (pp. 379-80)

Aiken leaves us with no doubts about Michael's downfall in this story. The author's imagery shows his character shaved and isolated, and his structure brings the man to a lower point than ever before. Once Michael had seen the inverted-V in the mirror, he should have known that the hand his human nature had been dealt contained sufficient points only for defeat—not victory. (p. 380)

> Carolyn Handa, '''Impulse': Calculated Artistry in Conrad Aiken,'' in Studies in Short Fiction (copyright 1975 by Newberry College), Fall, 1975, pp. 375-80.

BERNARD WINEHOUSE

This article was prompted by the reading of Carolyn Handa's analysis of Conrad Aiken's ''Impulse'' in *Studies In Short Fiction* [see excerpt above]. As I see it, Miss Handa interprets this story in a manner diametrically opposed to the spirit and the form of its conception. She describes ''Impulse'' as a ''tale of a man defeated by exposing his inherently criminal nature''; civilized and uncivilized elements in the story are juxtaposed and Michael Lowes, the protagonist is criminally arraigned as uncivilized. Michael's act of stealing is, according to Miss Handa, illustrative of ''man's anti-social tendencies'' and that it is Aiken's purpose in this story to show mankind as ''criminal ex-post facto''. The structure is described in terms of an inverted ''V'' in which Michael, after a faint upward swing of illusion, falls to ignominy and defeat. I find that Miss Handa's discussion of rather peripheral symbolism such as the inverted ''V'', the bridge game and the act of shaving lead us into an analysis which moves away from the central concerns of the story; these concerns in fact call upon the reader to make an almost total identification with Michael Lowes, a character whom Miss Handa would make the villain of the piece. I will illustrate Aiken's ''calculated artistry'' in terms of point of view, characterization and biblical allusion, all of which serve in ''Impulse'' to exonerate rather than condemn the protagonist.

The point of view in ''Impulse'' makes a very clear call for sympathy with Michael Lowes. The technique of third person limited omniscience allows the events of the story to be seen almost entirely through the prism of Michael's thought

—with surprisingly little ironic intrusion, explicit or implied, on the part of the omniscient narrator. No moral condemnation of any kind is made by the narrator. The reader's insight into Michael's mind reveals a bored little man in a lonely and hideously alien world who seeks cheap palliatives for his condition. Michael himself is seen to evince a considerable degree of self-knowledge as to the realities of his situation. . . . His repeated choice . . . of words like ''little'' and ''real'' suggests that he understands his motives [for stealing] quite clearly. In fine, point of view, whether in the reporting of thought process or in the exercise of the narrator's privilege of comment, consistently refuses to apportion any criticism to Michael's behaviour.

A vital complement to the psychological realism embodied in the third person (central) limited omniscient point of view is the use of peripheral characterization to underscore questions of theme. Such characterization in ''Impulse'' delineates a world in which self-knowing neer-do-wells such as Michael Lowes are decidedly preferable to any of the time-serving or establishment figures who betray and outlaw him. Without exception, there is no character in the story who is in any sense ''reliable,'' who would suggest in terms of the fictional world created, a valid criticism of Michael. (p. 108)

But the most persuasive signposting of all . . . is found in the central, expanding allusion in the story to the myth of Eden. . . . This pattern of allusion is first made evident in the course of the card game which precedes the theft. The conversation during the game and Michael's thoughts are punctuated throughout with a connotatively precise group of words: ''impulse,'' ''temptation,'' ''stealing,'' ''caught, by God,'' ''opening . . . eyes wide,'' ''Christ,'' ''hell,'' ''yield,'' ''fascinating,'' ''thrills.'' . . . Likewise there are four references in the conversation of the card players to woman's temptation of man. Michael's theft of a ''snakeskin box,'' ''a delicious object'' which contains a ''gold razor'' is a clear reference to the theft of Eve . . . , and his attempts to escape from the detective recall those of Adam and Eve as they hid amongst the trees of Eden. The prelapsarian world of Michael appears to have the beauty and the blessing of God: ''The lights on the snow were very beautiful. The Park Street Church was ringing, with its queer, soft quarterbells, the half-hour.'' . . . His exit in the custody of the detective, after the theft, is described in very different terms. What we have here is a parody of the exit from Eden: ''. . . he was firmly conducted through a back door into a dark alley at the rear of the store. It had stopped snowing. A cold wind was blowing. But the world which looked so beautiful fifteen minutes before, had now lost its charm. They walked together down the alley in six inches of powdery snow, the detective holding Michael's arm with affectionate firmness.'' . . . Michael's direct appeals to God and the God-like lieutenant at the police station ''writing slowly in a book'' serve to expand the allusion further. (p. 109)

The quiet close of this story of maturation takes the form of an epiphany in which Michael Lowes realizes clearly that his past life, which had been composed of ''trivial and infinitely charming little episodes,'' . . . had come to an end. Michael will or will not change but he is now a wiser man. But the central theme of this story is concerned with the frightening tedium of the human condition which can be relieved only by an occasional act of "impulse" made for "kicks"—as that Americanism puts it. Often the richness of allusion allows a literary work to make a comment on the source of the borrowing. Aiken says, perhaps, that God overacted in dooming the inhabitants of Eden to expulsion, just as society overacts in this story by betraying Lowes for a very ordinary piece of human behaviour. Aiken implies that the reader should not commit the same act of betrayal for Lowes is a mirror of our own being. "What would be more human," asks Michael as he begins to see himself as a "Columbus of the moral world." . . . Impulse is a momentary circumvention of the stabilizing Ego, a hubristic refusal to accept the dictates of "a cockeyed world" . . . of boredom and routine, the disciplines of life's Eden. Lowes "remembers his mother always saying, 'Michael, you *must* learn to be orderly.'" The First Sin was and still is the Sin of all mankind; the extended biblical allusion of this story and the clear functional thrust of point of view and characterization persuade us that indeed "impulse" is a "universal human inclination." (p. 110)

> Bernard Winehouse, "'Impulse': Calculated Artistry in Conrad Aiken," in Studies in Short Fiction (copyright by Newberry College), Winter, 1978, pp. 107-10.

MALCOLM COWLEY

[Aiken] was a poet essentially, but he was also the complete man of letters, distinguished for his work in many forms of verse and prose. The unity was there, however, and in every form he spoke with the same candid, scrupulous, self-deprecatory, yet reckless and fanciful New England voice. (p. 231)

[Candor] was close to being his central principle as a man and a writer, particularly as a poet. The principle evolved into a system of aesthetics and literary ethics that unified his work, a system based on the private and public value of self-revelation. No matter what sort of person the poet might be, healthy or neurotic, Aiken believed that his real business was "to give the low-down on himself, and through himself on humanity." (p. 233)

"Look within thyself to find the truth" might have been his Emersonian motto; and it had the corollary that inner truth corresponds to outer truth, as self or microcosm does to macrocosm. Aiken believed that the writer should be a surgeon performing an exploratory operation on himself, at whatever cost to his self-esteem, and penetrating as with a scalpel through layer after layer of the semiconscious. That process of achieving self-knowledge might well become a self-inflicted torture. . . . Let him persist, however, and he will be rewarded by finding—here I quote from a letter—"what you think or feel that is secretly you—shamefully you—intoxicatingly you." Then, having laid bare this secret self, which is also a universal self, the writer must find words for it, accurate and honest words, but poured forth—Aiken says in a Prelude—without reckoning the consequences: "Let us be reckless of our words and worlds, / And spend them freely as the tree his leaves." Here enters the public as opposed to the merely private value of complete self-revelation. By finding words for his inmost truth, the writer—especially the poet—has made it part of the world, part of human consciousness. (pp. 233-34)

The writer must divide himself into two persons, one the observer, the other a subject to be observed, and the first must approach the second "with relentless and unsleeping objectivity." The observer-and-narrator must face what Aiken calls "that eternal problem of language, language extending consciousness and then consciousness extending language, in circular or spiral ascent"; and he must also face the many problems of architectural and sequential form. The words that depict the observed self not only must be honest; they must be "twisted around," in Aiken's phrase, until they have a shape and structure of their own; until they become an "artifact" (a favorite word of his) and if possible a masterpiece that will have a lasting echo in other minds. The "supreme task" performed by a masterpiece—as well as by lesser works and deeds in a more temporary fashion—is that of broadening, deepening, and subtilizing the human consciousness. Any man who devotes himself to that evolving task will find in it, Aiken says, "all that he could possibly require in the way of a religious credo."

His name for the credo was "the religion of consciousness." It is a doctrine—or more than that, a system of belief—to which he gave many refinements and ramifications. Some of these are set forth, with an impressive density of thought and feeling, in two long series of philosophical lyrics, Preludes for Memnon (1931) and Time in the Rock (1936); Aiken regarded these as his finest works. But the doctrine is a unifying theme in almost all the poetry of his middle years, say from 1925 to 1956, and in the prose as well. It is clearly exemplified in his novels, especially in Blue Voyage (1927) . . . and Great Circle (1933). . . . Self-discovery is often the climax of Aiken's stories, and it is, moreover, the true theme of his autobiography, Ushant (1952). (pp. 234-35)

In American literature there is nothing to compare with it except The Education of Henry Adams, which is equally well composed, equally an artifact . . . but which gives us only one side of the author. In Ushant the author writes in the third person, like Adams, and maintains the same objective tone while recording not only his "education" but also his faults and obsessions, his infidelities, his recurrent dreams, his uproarious or shabby adventures: in short, while trying "to give the lowdown on himself, and through himself on humanity." (p. 236)

Without in the least abandoning his religion of consciousness, Aiken's poems of the fifties and sixties introduced some new or partially new elements. One of these was a note of ancestral piety, with allusions to earlier Aikens, but more to his mother's connections, the Potters . . . and the Delanos. The note is already audible in "Mayflower," written in 1945. It is a poem partly about the ship (on which two of the poet's ancestors had been passengers), partly about the flower, and partly about the sandy shores of Cape Cod, where the Pilgrims had landed before sailing on to Plymouth. In other poems there is frequent mention of what might be called ancestral scenes: New Bedford and its whaling ships; the Quaker Graveyard at South Yarmouth, on the Cape, where Cousin Abiel lies buried; Sheepfold Hill, also on the Cape; and Stony Brook, where the herring used to spawn by myriads. There is also talk of "godfathers" and tutelary spirits: among the poets Ben Jonson, Shakespeare, Li Po, and among historical figures Pythagoras and William Blackstone, the scholar and gentle heretic who built a house on the site of Boston before the Puritans came, then moved away from them into the wilderness.

Blackstone becomes the hero of Aiken's cycle of poems about America, *The Kid*. (p. 239)

Another new or newly emphasized feature of the later poems is something very close to New England Transcendentalism. Its appearance should be no surprise, except to those who have fallen into the habit of regarding Transcendentalism as a purely historical phenomenon, a movement that flourished from 1830 to 1860, then disappeared at the beginning of the Civil War. On the contrary, it has been a durable property of New England thinking, a home place, one might say, to which some poets return as they grow older. (pp. 239-40)

Is consciousness, for Aiken—the consciousness of mankind as shared by each individual—close to being an equivalent of the Over-Soul? That might be stretching a point, and indeed, I should be far from saying that among twentieth-century New England writers there is any complete Transcendentalist in a sense that might be accepted, for instance, by Margaret Fuller. (p. 241)

[Bold] in his development of certain Trancendental notions, [Aiken] also, rather late in life, found them confirmed by ancestral piety and especially by the writings and career of his maternal grandfather. (p. 242)

When the poet came to read Grandfather Potter's published sermons, he was impressed by their bold speculations about the divine element in men. He wrote an admiring poem about his grandfather, "Hallowe'en," in which he quoted from the journal that Potter had kept during his early travels in Europe. A quoted phrase was ". . . so man may make the god finite and viable, make conscious god's power in action and being." That sounds the Transcendental note, and it is also close to phrases that Aiken himself had written: for example, in the 1949 preface to one of his Symphonies, where he says that man, in becoming completely aware of himself, "can, if he only will, become divine."

There is another point, apparently not connected with Grandfather Potter, at which Aiken comes even closer to Transcendentalism. . . . Aiken, with his senses open to the tangible world, often speaks of [the correspondence between the physical world and the human mind], which sometimes becomes for him an identity. (pp. 242-43)

Aiken is . . . clearly Emersonian . . . in what is almost the last of his poems, *THEE*, written when he was seventy-seven. Though comparatively short . . . , it is indeed one of his major works. First, one notes in it that the poet has changed his style and that—as, to a lesser extent, in some of the other late poems—he has abandoned the subtle variations and dying falls of his earlier work. *THEE* is written in short, galloping lines with rhymes like hoofbeats:

> Who is that splendid THEE
> who makes a symphony
> of the one word
> be
> admitting us to see
> all things but THEE?

Obviously THEE is being used as the Quaker pronoun: "Thee makes," not "You make" or "Thou makest." Aiken may well have learned that usage from the Potter family. As for his question "Who?" it sends us back once more to Emerson. Just as Aiken's "consciousness" at times comes close to being the Emersonian Over-Soul, so

THEE is the spirit of Nature itself as defined in Emerson's essay. "Strictly speaking," the essay says, ". . . all that is separate from us, all which Philosophy distinguishes as the NOT ME, that is, both nature and art, all other men and my own body, must be ranked under the name, NATURE." Aiken's name for it is THEE, but has a different connotation. Whereas Emerson's Nature is admired for revealing in each of its parts the universal laws that wise men obey, Aiken's THEE is a pitiless force that nourishes and destroys with the divine indifference of the goddess Kali. Also and paradoxically, it is a force evolving with the human spirit. . . . (pp. 243-44)

[Where] Emerson celebrates the power of the indwelling spirit, Aiken gives a twist to Transcendental doctrine by stressing, first, the indifferent power of THEE, and then the dependence of THEE on the individual consciousness—with which it must "meet and mate," from which it learns to become more truly itself, and with which, perhaps, it must die. The speculation seems more imaginative than philosophical, and yet one feels that—along with the whole religion of consciousness—it finds a place in the Transcendental line.

In Aiken's beginnings, he had been poles apart from Emerson. He had been atheistic and pessimistic, not optimistic and Unitarian. He never had been impressed by the German Romantic philosophers or by the Neoplatonists, let alone by Sufism and Brahmanism; instead, his intellectual models had been Poe first of all, then Santayana, Freud, and Henry James. . . . Nevertheless, at the end of his long career, he had worked round to a position reminiscent of that which Emerson had reached in 1831, before he had published anything. (p. 246)

For the neglect of his work by the public, one can give several explanations, though none of them seems adequate. In the early days when he was writing a book-length poem every year, Aiken's poetry was too modern and experimental for him to share in what was then the enormous popularity of Amy Lowell and Vachel Lindsay; then in the twenties it seemed not experimental enough, or at least not eccentric enough. In the thirties it was condemned as having no social or revolutionary meaning; in the forties it wasn't rich enough in images (most of his work is musical rather than visual, and music was becoming the lost side of poetry); in the fifties it was condemned again as not being "close enough in texture" to suit the intensive reading methods of the new critics (but what about the *Preludes?*); and in the sixties it was disregarded as being written mostly in iambic pentameter, a measure that had fallen out of fashion. Aiken followed his own fashion, and his work developed by an inner logic which was not that of the poetry-reading public. (p. 247)

Malcolm Cowley, "Conrad Aiken: From Savannah to Emerson," in his –And I Worked at the Writer's Trade: Chapters of Literary History, 1918-1978 (copyright © 1978 by Malcolm Cowley; all rights reserved; reprinted by permission of Viking Penguin Inc.), Viking Penguin, 1978, pp. 231-48.

*   *   *

ALGREN, Nelson   1909-

An American novelist, short story writer, and editor, Algren

creates a fictional world peopled with society's underdogs. The strength of his work lies in his impressionistic evocation of mood and scene, rather than in character or plot development. Algren is concerned with the lack of tradition in American letters and his work consistently reflects his search for a definitive vision of America. Two of his novels, *The Man with the Golden Arm* and *A Walk on the Wild Side,* have been made into films. (See also *CLC*, Vol. 4, and *Contemporary Authors*, Vols. 13-16, rev. ed.)

GEORGE BLUESTONE

Nelson Algren is known as a Chicago novelist, but he is only secondarily an urban writer. He has chosen, rather, to explore the theme of death and survival among our *Lumpenproletariat.* Of his four novels, all of one and two-thirds of another are set entirely outside Chicago. In *The Neon Wilderness,* his collection of stories, at least one third take place outside the urban world. In brief, only slightly more than half his published fiction is centrally concerned with Chicago....

Somebody in Boots, Algren's first novel, is the most uneven and least satisfying, but in some ways the most revealing of his books. It is a tale of wandering during the depression of the late twenties and early thirties. Cass McKay is a yokel from the border town of Great Snake Mountain in West Texas where earth is parched, townsmen poor, and Cass's life unpromising. (p. 27)

[Nancy, Cass's sister, and Norah Egan provide] Cass with temporary relief from his primitive wandering, the hope of something more than sheer survival. Nancy offers innocent love; Norah profane love. The two climactic movements of the book center around the destruction of both relationships. (p. 29)

There are weaknesses, of course. The narrative is episodic without consistent structural justification. The style is erratic, often uncertain of its mood and emphasis. The parenthetical broadsides against a thinly disguised *Chicago Tribune* (for blind encomia to a local World's Fair while half the city starves) are purely didactic intrusions. At the same time, Algren reveals certain inclinations which will become more important later on: the choice of fallen, barely articulate characters; a narrative sensibility aware of verbal complexity; a prose appropriation of poetic devices; a piecing together of previously published pieces (no less than seven magazines are acknowledged); a central concern with love and survival in the face of loneliness and death.

Never Come Morning, Algren's second novel, is located entirely in Chicago, but more than setting has been unified. Instead of a single character going through a wide variety of adventures, Algren gives us a small, relatively homogenous group of characters, a more tightly knit conflict to trigger Bruno Bicek's fate. Once a character appears, he remains fixed, reappears frequently to carry out his appointed role.... This time the narrative events are spare, more cleanly delineated. Bruno Lefty Bicek, a tough eighteen-year old who has decided to become a heavyweight fighter, seduces his girl, Steffi Rostenkowski. Later, under the combined pressure of his own cowardice, his spurious code of manhood, and his friends' clever threats, he permits his gang to "score" with Steffi, too, in the sordid shadows of an abandoned warehouse underneath the El. Bruno's frail humanity is overwhelmed.... Bruno's sense of sin makes

him homicidal. The rest of the book is merely a logical and inevitable working out of Bruno's destruction. (pp. 30-1)

What appears here ... is an emerging structural pattern which is characteristic of Algren's fiction: first the destruction of a love relationship, then a physical defeat or death. The pivotal acts constitute a kind of double reference, a dual climax, and both are somehow preordained from the moment the conflict appears.... Between the crucial acts of broken love and brute destruction occur a number of events which scarcely affect the central character at all, a series of frozen images in which development and consciousness seem to be arrested. In such interludes, waking seems a kind of living death, and death seems like relief.... [In] Algren's central vision, self-destruction becomes operative only after the destruction of some loved object. The moment a central character becomes responsible for such ruin, he is irrevocably doomed. That "irrational, destructive force," then, is the impulse to destroy love which is tantamount to death.

It is the *manner* in which the pattern is rendered, however, that gives Algren his special idiom and identity. In *Never Come Morning,* Algren's characteristic symbolism and indirection endow the action with pity and concealed prophecy. (pp. 31-2)

[We] find here, woven into the matrix of the prose, those haunting images of deserted cities, symbolizing the characters' life-in-death, which becomes increasingly typical of Algren. (p. 32)

Such moments illustrate the way in which Algren is able to sustain a narrative in the frozen moments between pivotal events. Supplementing these moments is Algren's skill with humor and physical action. He becomes a master of digression.... [Through] all of this ... the impression of frozen life persists, as if the characters had become mere puppets, performing by rote or ritual. Because these sequences do not have any real effect on either Steffi or Bruno, the reader soon finds himself watching the performance for its own sake. Any one of these acts could easily stand alone. After Steffi's climactic fall, only the thinnest of narrative threads stitches them together. More important than any plot or character development is the general doom implicit from the start. Only the powerful voice behind the events insists on our attention.

This view of the book helps explain, I think, a certain dissatisfaction with most of the stories in Algren's collection, *The Neon Wilderness.* For if in the root-pattern of the prose a crucial fall is followed by an interlude of frozen change before a death or final loss, then a short story which fails to encompass such a mechanism is liable to seem more like a sketch than a story. It is true that the stories, like meditative finger exercises, explore situations and characters that have already become familiar. The drug addicts, petty thieves, prison inmates, small-time fighters, corrupt police, dypsos, winos, hobos and prostitutes—all are here.... As in Balzac's world, or Faulkner's, a character, once created, can crop up anywhere. But the stories, like the novels, are bound not so much by a common cast of characters as by a general background of disorder. The characters have a curious kind of horizontal mobility, capable of changing their physical location without ever changing their status. What makes this change impossible is less the entrapment of poverty than the destructive forces unleashed by the failure of love.... [Whatever] the origin, love's destruction breeds a terrible kind of spiritual stasis, a curious kind of dreamlike, empty marking time for which terminal death is the only cure. (pp. 32-4)

In *The Man With the Golden Arm,* all of Algren's exploratory motifs merge for the first time to form a satisfactory whole. The humor, the incantatory style, the graphic eye, the poetic imagery all elucidate a central pattern. The reasons for this success, however, are not easily fixed. True, the characters are more clearly etched than ever before.... True, Algren combines the leisurely, episodic narrative of *Somebody in Boots* with the spare, more tightly unified structure of *Never Come Morning,* lending the novel new tension and density. (p. 35)

The real center [of the novel] ... lies in an advancement of the love-death theme we have traced before. More specifically, it lies in the complex relationship between Frankie and Sophie on the one hand, and between Frankie and Molly on the other....

Haunted by his own destructive past, hunted by the police, Frankie is driven out into the deserted streets to loneliness and suicide. Frankie's destruction of Zosh has made Molly's love impossible. It is this double focus in Frankie's identity that gives the digressions, the mood pieces, and the reveries their structural significance. (p. 36)

[The] figure of the altar ... represents a recurrent thread which Algren has suggested in his previous work but has never before so fully woven into his texture: an inverted use of Christian myth to comment ironically on the action.... This ... level of inverted Christian imagery functions ironically because in Algren's world there is no hope of an afterlife. In themselves, the Christian terms would be no more significant than other recurrent images if they did not have a special meaning. This secular appropriation of religious ritual is pertinent to Algren's central theme. For in this novel, Algren's prose approaches a very individualized kind of incantation, like the chanting of ritual itself. The incantatory style continually makes implicit judgments on the action. If, as Algren makes abundantly clear, morality is not to be found in the law, the church, in criminal ethics, in social struggle, in any normative standards for success, then where is the moral authority? Only in love. But if love is doomed by the social milieu, or by some inexplicable destructive instinct, where does redemption lie? In the stubborn ingenuity that guarantees these characters' survival? Yes, to some extent, Algren seems to say. The details of this drama can be very funny ... but surely mere survival is not enough. Then is redemption to be found nowhere at all? The peculiar intensity of Algren's prose seems to support the harsher judgment. If man is deprived of salvation in an afterworld, if he must make his way in this world or not at all, then life is truly harsh. Indeed, Algren's final image, despite the humor, despite the intensity, despite the struggle to survive, is one of hopelessness and desolation. In this world, death is inescapable.

What possible approaches are open to the narrator who wishes to communicate such a vision? He can laugh; or he can lament. Algren does both supremely well. But the laughter is edged with bitterness; before the reality of death, it sadly falls away. (pp. 37-8)

The lament, on the other hand, becomes at once a threnody of pity and a defense against terror. It enables Algren to

look at his Medusa without turning to stone, as if the act of writing itself had become an amulet for evil. For Algren, then, the incantatory style is a surrogate for prayer.

A final word about the structure of this novel, since much has been made of its weakness.... [Not] only is a very real theme sustained, but that the structure is the only one really suited to it.... If the novel gives the impression of separate pieces of cloth loosely stitched together ... it is simply because no other scheme will do. If Algren is concerned with the living death that follows love's destruction, then one can understand the succession of timeless moments, each indistinguishable from the rest, like a series of stills in which action is both palpable and frozen. Postures succeed each other without correlative shifts in consciousness. Only moments of love—or love's destruction—can create new states of being. What lies between these points is the echoing wind of death. Everyone meets death at the end; the loveless meet it sooner. (pp. 38-9)

The meaning of all the digressions is precisely in their pointlessness. A more conventional development, conforming to traditional standards of plot, crisis and resolution would constitute a different kind of novel. To reject Algren's structure, then, is to reject his central vision. When his vision changes, then his structure, too, will change. He is too careful a writer to have it otherwise. (p. 39)

[In his book of non-fiction, *Chicago: City on the Make,*] Algren's impressions of Chicago are typical of a new and sympathetic look at urban life which goes beyond recoil and horror. Much of what we have seen in the stories and novels appears here, too: a pervasive sense of loss and loneliness, an image of urban desolation, an eye for graphic detail, incantatory prose. In the slender arc-lamps which "reveal our backstreets to the indifferent stars," there is still an implacable universe indifferent to human suffering. But there is also something here we have not seen in the novels and stories. In ranging out beyond the world of the *Lumpenproletariat,* the author implies a certain dissatisfaction with his own past work. The highly articulate voice which narrates the book possesses more knowledge than is ever allowed to enter the circumscribed world of the novels. Algren knows politics and business; knows the history of the town; knows Darrow and Masters, Lindsay and Sandburg, Dreiser, Altgeld and Debs. This outside information gives his prose an historical perspective which the fictive characters cannot possibly possess, yet manages to avoid the didactic intrusions of *Somebody in Boots.* This author knows that in urban society there is vertical as well as horizontal mobility, that Skid Row is merely the ugliest manifestation of tendencies embedded in all strata of city life. It is this mind that accounts, perhaps, for the curious turn in Algren's latest work.

At first glance, *A Walk on the Wild Side* seems to be a mere rewriting of *Somebody in Boots....* From the point of view of Algren's entire output, however, it represents a fascinating reappraisal of his central theme. Again we have a country yokel from a Texas town who is propelled into the world by broken love and finds his education in depression year adventures. Like Cass McKay, his earlier cousin, Dove Linkhorn discovers that there is no more hope of redemption in the outside world than there is in Arroyo, the town where he was born. Again the structure resembles a patchwork, or mosaic, the pieces loosely worked together. Again episodes are borrowed. (pp. 39-40)

Ultimately, the differences between the two books are more striking than the resemblances. The first and most startling difference appears in Algren's tone. The narrative alternates between a mood of savage tenderness and one of broad burlesque, but this time the comic mood is strongest. The tenderness, to be sure, appears at important intervals, carrying out the obsessive pattern of the earlier books.... Again there are moments of sweet redemption; again the breaking up of love leads to violence.

The broadly comic tone, on the other hand, instead of endowing the intervening acts with the aura of living death, transforms them into moments of high, acetic comedy. (pp. 40-1)

At least one reason for the change in tone is apparent in the love affairs. Unlike Frankie and Bruno, Dove Linkhorn has not been destructive. Terasina and Hallie reject him, not the other way around. Both women have been maligned by men before the story opens. Without Dove, neither one degenerates. The corruption of female innocence ... is completely absent here.... Within this scheme of things, even death itself is parodied. During a raid on Finnerty's brothel, Dove is thrown out. This leads two policemen to the mistaken conclusion that the blow has truly killed him. A colloquy between them on what to do about the corpse is rudely interrupted. Dove pops up to answer for himself. The joke is on the law. Dove's playing possum is the first and only instance of mock death in all of Algren's work. The author, it is clear, has learned to laugh at his most sacred cow. Instead of living death, we have a new and indestructible vitality.

The main point, however, is more serious than this. For Dove has injured someone after all. In running off with Hallie, he has deprived Legless Schmidt, Hallie's lover, of *his* one redeeming love. A personage of grace and power (certainly not a freak!), Legless Schmidt is not one to be deprived. And so punishment is bound to follow after all. We realize that although Dove himself is free of death's obsession—only the lonely memories of Terasina rise up to distrub him—Algren's prose is not. Like a distant tocsin, the warning sounds continually between the lines. In a coal picking scene at the beginning, a child is inexplicably destroyed.... The second section ends with Hallie's desertion; the third with a weird barroom brawl in which Legless Schmidt reduces Dove to a mass of cartilege and bone, only to be pushed to his own death by a mob of sadistic spectators. In the very last scene ... a blind and humbled Dove comes home to old Arroyo.

Dove's innocence, then, becomes a kind of moral blindness which precipitates his fall.... He must pay the price of his eyes to learn that love, trust and giving are, after all, the only graces in this world and that one tampers with them at one's peril. (pp. 41-2)

The picture of blind Dove stumbling toward Terasina's chili parlor, still struggling to live and to love despite his defeat, is something new in Algren. Unlike so many Algren characters, Dove is not condemned to true or living death.... He becomes the first major character to accept defeat, to return home, and to continue looking for love in this world. The innocent yokel has been redeemed, chastened, changed; he has learned to do penance for his sins. If the ending does not quite come off (the comic tone is never fully integrated with the passages of sadness and de-

feat; no rendition of Dove's new awareness matches the superb barroom brawl), it does at least show Algren working his way to new levels of thematic consciousness, and, at the same time, to a unified story structure....

If Algren ever felt the efficacy of social amelioration, he both posed and rejected it in his first book. If, on the other hand, he is mainly concerned with the problem of death, one can understand his popularity with those French Existentialists who see in him a continuation of the Symbolist tradition. It is not by accident that where Algren's earliest epigraphs are taken from Marx, his later epigraphs are taken from Baudelaire and Kuprin. For out of the poetic exploration of this marginal, half-lit world there emerges the image of a universe in which human action must inevitably seem absurd. And yet, within that world, there co-exists a real belief that human action can have validity and meaning. Not only can the human condition be redeemed through love; it can also be altered by the very existence of Algren's incantation. (p. 43)

In his long and impassioned lamentation on death, Algren has surely learned how to sing. It remains to be seen whether the song will now become a dirge or dithyramb. (p. 44)

> *George Bluestone, "Nelson Algren," in*
> The Western Review *(copyright 1957 by* The
> Western Review*), Autumn, 1957, pp. 27-44.*

RALPH J. GLEASON

A Walk on the Wild Side ... deserves to be read by every *Catch 22* and *Cuckoo's Nest* freak just so they can find out what opened the door for two novels that had the same kind of effect on the changing American consciousness that Bob Dylan has had. It's not only that before Heller and Kesey there was Algren. It's that Algren is where they came from, and the fantasy/reality, inside/outside paradoxical view of the inversion of the American Dream that is central to their books was first laid out by Algren in *A Walk on the Wild Side*.

Algren got to where he was when he wrote that book by discovering, during the depths of the Depression, that the whores and the pimps and the junkies and the thieves (even before the Bonnie & Clyde/Robin Hood mythology) dealt with the reality of America, and in their dealing exposed the hypocrisy of the whole social structure....

Up until Algren, no American writer had really combined a poetic gift for words and a vision of the truth about the textbook democracy. He saw it, gradually or all at once makes no difference, and he put it down in the one novel which blew the minds of hundreds of other writers and had the effect—very specifically on Kesey and Heller—that Robert Johnson had on the Cream and Mick Jagger.

And when he had said it all ... he tried for a while to do other things, turning, like Mailer, to journalism and then finally, like Dylan, turning off to a private world. It is an odd relationship, the literature of Algren and the song/poetry of Dylan. They cover the same territory, see the same images with or without different faces and different names, and no one familiar with the inhabitants of the night world where Algren took his wild side walk was startled to meet the images of Dylan's apocalyptical visions....

When he wrote *A Walk on the Wild Side,* Algren did not

really believe that the whole thing had gone out of control. He believed in a kind of goodness indigenous to the American scene or at least possible in the American scene. He believed, too, in a kind of non-secular God, I suspect.

> *Ralph J. Gleason, "Perspectives: Is It Out of Control?" in* Rolling Stone (© *1970 by Straight Arrow Publishers, Inc.; all rights reserved; reprinted by permission), Issue 64, August 6, 1970, p. 9.*

ROSS MACDONALD

I have never quite met Nelson Algren—we talked on the phone once—but he has been a continuing influence in my life. He is the poet of the sad metropolis that underlies our North American cities; I was among those millions who caught an early chill there. Reading Algren didn't dispel the chill, but it did teach us to live with it and to look around us with deepened feelings and thoughts.

Algren's Chicago and the people who live in its shadows are still there. Algren is their tragic poet, enabling those who can read him to feel pain. And nearly everyone can read him. He writes with a master's clarity about the complex troubles of simple people, and not so simple people. Bruno Bicek and Frankie Machine and Steffi "with the new city light on her old-world face" appear to be simple because Algren presents them with such understanding.

Algren came into the full use of his talent in the early years of the Second World War, which promised to open the way for a reassessment of our society. In full knowledge of the lower depths which had to be redeemed, Algren asserted the value of the people who lived in those depths. The intensity of his feeling, the accuracy of his thought, make me wonder if any other writer of our time has shown us more exactly the human basis of our democracy. Though Algren often defines his positive values by showing us what happens in their absence, his hell burns with passion for heaven. (p. 62)

> *Ross Macdonald, in* The New York Times Book Review (© *1977 by The New York Times Company; reprinted by permission), December 4, 1977.*

*   *   *

ANTSCHEL, Paul
    See CELAN, Paul

*   *   *

ARGUEDAS, José María   1911-1969

Arguedas was a Peruvian novelist, short story writer, poet, and ethnologist. He began his literary career as a regionalist, writing in the "indigenista" tradition of Latin American writers who sought to create a native culture free of European intellectual domination. His later work, however, surpasses that of his fellow regionalists through his mastery of literary technique, particularly in the areas of point of view, language, and characterization. He took his own life in 1969.

PHYLLIS RODRIGUEZ-PERALTA

For more than three decades José María Arguedas steadily wove new colors into his work. He produced a Peruvian mosaic which reflects the nuances of changing literary, sociological, and philosophical thought. It is this constantly flowing creative process which stands out in the total literary production of Arguedas. . . .

The brooding presence of Arguedas's native Andean environment hovers over his first writings: *Agua*, 1935, a simple collection of three stories. At the same time his deep sensibility and his anger against feudal repression place him immediately with writers of social protest, even if his initial literary efforts could not keep pace with his determination to denounce the injustice. (p. 225)

The crest of Peru's regionalism belongs to the years 1930 to 1945, and in his initial stage of literary development, Arguedas struck the dominant chords of contemporary literature in his country. He used the primary elements of local settings and social protest, to which he added his own complete identification with the Quechua mind. His stories from *Agua* possess dramatic force, particularly because of the personal involvement of the narrator; at the same time these early attempts suffer from an overflow of intensity which the young Arguedas does not temper by control of the structure. In *Yawar fiesta*, written as a traditional exterior narrative, Arguedas holds the shuttle more firmly as the threads form their design. Dialogue is interspersed by descriptive passages; plot unfolds in measure; bitter anger at the Indians' plight is held in check so as to permit greater insight into the general picture. Based on local customs and life styles, *Yawar fiesta* is the Arguedas work which fits most easily into the mold of accepted regionalism.

Still cautious in assessing his own abilities, Arguedas proceeded on a slow and winding course. He carried along with him the seeds of his early regionalism, husbanding them during a long pause which lasted into the next decade. . . . Two decades have added polish and facility to the writing, and [*Diamantes y pedernales*] serves as a transition piece, as though the current is picking up momentum just before it flows into new environments.

After years of anticipation, Arguedas reached the culmination of his artistic creation in *Los ríos profundos*, 1958. Fundamentally autobiographical, the interior world of a sensitive boy is the author's main material, but he goes effortlessly from inner contemplation to participation in the erupting violence of the surroundings. (pp. 225-26)

The omnipresence of the Andean environment is fragmented through the style that Arguedas has developed. Making use of dissociation of time techniques, the novel flows easily. Free from structural difficulties, the dialogue, the action, and the fluid thoughts of the boy's nostalgia are kept in balance. (p. 226)

Los ríos profundos, while still an "indigenista"-regional novel, has moved at the same time into the realm of an interior novel. . . . No Peruvian work in this vein touches the fiber of *Los ríos profundos* with its interior vision, its constant flow of the subconscious that mingles with reality.

At the height of his artistic power Arguedas chose to deviate from this literary route and to shift to political deliberations. *El Sexto*, 1961, is a journalistic novel—like so many in Latin American literature—although Arguedas attempts to balance the reporter's details with art. (pp. 226-27)

In *El Sexto* Arguedas tried to paint a humanity capable of triumphing over surrounding brutality. Unfortunately, faceless prisoners, the constant cacophony of political dissension, and the obvious division of art and politics lessen his success. It is clear, however, that Arguedas intends to enter new currents of literary endeavor. The material for this novel was blocked out years beforehand, but Arguedas did not write the definitive version until 1961. Like *Diamantes y pedernales* before the polished *Los ríos profundos,* the limited sphere of conflict in *El Sexto* is a rehearsal for the all-encompassing *Todas las sangres* of 1964.

Arguedas' last novel is a vast sociological document which focuses on the latent unrest in all social strata of Peruvian society. . . . *Todas las sangres* is the completion of Arguedas' social mission. Originally cast in the regional mold, his work has retained only its outlines as Arguedas follows the path of Peruvian reality. (p. 227)

It is evident that Arguedas wished to present his socio-philosophic study with artistic care and to avoid the separation between art and politics of *El Sexto*. Perhaps this accounts for the extensive use of stylized pageantry which often produces a stilted artificiality at odds with the author's purpose. . . .

Todas las sangres goes beyond tragedy to explore solutions. To emphasize his intent, Arguedas suppresses the intimate, nostalgic air of past works. The novel is explicit and penetrating. . . . (p. 228)

Arguedas did not enter the sordidly vicious, chaotic world of current Peruvian novelists. He returned to the genre of the short story in his final publication, a collection called *Amor Mundo y todos los cuentos,* 1967. The familiar Andean environment provides a backdrop—with the exception of one narrative—but dialogue is often the structural base. How succinct these stories are in comparison to those of earlier collections! The technical ability of Arguedas, which followed a progression of "cuento" to short novel to successive forms of the novel itself, flourishes in these later short stories. . . .

Nurtured almost exclusively in Peruvian soil, Arguedas was able to absorb the changing attitudes circulating in his environment, and thus, to transcend the confines of his original regionalism as he moved into considerations of contemporary Peru. Over the years his writing shows a gradual suppression of the regional in favor of the racial and the social. But the evolving perspectives of his prose must be understood in the context of his regional roots.

An eventual adjustment to the Indian reality is a thread which runs through all his writings. It is based on his deep affection and respect for the race. The Indian as focal point . . . belongs to the "indigenista" literature. . . . The figure of the Indian coexisting with nature is always present, even though this has become less dominant in the recent works of Arguedas. [Arguedas deplores] the aspects of feudalism which bind the Indian, and [he paints] his rejection from the life of his own country in vivid and in muted colors. (p. 229)

[Arguedas] deals with [the Indian's] suffering realistically and stresses [his] unspoiled greatness. He calls for the reader's admiration and respect but not his commiseration. And he delves ever deeper into the sociological and economic reasons behind the Indian's plight. . . .

There is a distinct feeling in Arguedas' last three novels of having emerged into contemporary times. This is due as much to style as to content. . . .

The presence of nature has always been an inherent part of Peruvian literature, and Peru's finest regional writers have mirrored the cosmic mystery and grandeur of the Andean panorama. Arguedas' use of telluric imagery which links the forces of nature and man reflects the influence of this descriptive style. . . . (p. 230)

While the descriptive passages of Arguedas offer great beauty, they also indicate a continuous change in perspective. Indeed, Arguedas' modulations in handling his description provide another thread for following his transition into the stream of contemporary literature. Initially in his stories he interspersed paragraphs of description in the expected manner, although he was never the omniscient author describing the contemplation of the Indian. (pp. 230-31)

Towering over all Arguedas' prose is his belief in the creative capacity of the Quechua people and the beauty and richness of the Quechua language. . . . His constant preoccupation with the speech of the Indians in his literary works emphasizes his love of authenticity in language. For the bilingual Arguedas it was impossible to convey the essence of the Indian in either traditional Spanish or in a dialect concocted for picturesque effects. Indeed his laborious search for a valid style of speech inserts a unique tone in his writing. . . . By the time Arguedas reaches his major novels, the intertwining of Quechua and Spanish is handled so magnificently that the reader himself is aware of the psychological and artistic distinctions of the language. . . . (p. 231)

In his early works [Arguedas] exhibits the primary weakness of the Latin American regionalists who concentrate on the "paisaje" or on the action at the expense of any character development. Conversely, *Los ríos profundos,* while still in the frame of an "indigenista"-regional novel, is actually based on character portrait. The first-person format and the exquisite use of techniques of interior vision give an intimate picture of the sensitive, intense Ernesto. . . . However, when Arguedas reaches the epic proportions of *Todas las sangres,* with its vast mural of multiple characters, there is an inescapable tendency toward mass anonymous figures, and the detailed political analyses obscure characterization even more. The purpose has taken precedence over the literary.

Throughout the changing patterns and perspectives of his translucent prose, Arguedas has interpreted the social turmoil of his time. The measure of the man's spirit shows itself in his ability to clothe his urgent message in coeval folds, and thus he remains contemporary from the 1930's to the present without sacrifice of his originality. (p. 232)

Phyllis Rodriguez-Peralta, "The Literary Progression of José María Arguedas," in Hispania (ⓒ*1972 The American Association of Teachers of Spanish and Portuguese, Inc.), May, 1972, pp. 225-33.*

WOLFGANG A. LUCHTING

[*El zorro de arriba y el zorro de abajo*] refers to *indio*-mythology (cf. *Dioses y hombres de Huarochiri,* tr. by Arguedas, where this specific myth is given). "Above" and "below" are Coast and Sierra. "Below" is Chimbote, the fecund, mad, hectic, pernicious and crude new town, a harbor north of Lima where the fishmeal industry has come to have its capitalistic paroxysms. To it flock the unemployed *indios* from the Andes, as well as others who try, founder, die—or succeed—at the cost of losing what Arguedas considered their essential purity and goodness. "Above" is little touched upon (*El zorro* can be considered the counterpart of Arguedas's *Yawar fiesta* or *Todas las sangres:* the Coast reached up into the Sierra; here, the Sierra comes down). Ultimately, this novel describes the destruction of the very myths that have always been the substance of Arguedas's fiction: the noble *indio* who possesses a *patria* versus the rootless minor or major capitalist, domestic or foreign, *mestizo* or *blanco.*

The book alternates between diaries Arguedas kept—on the novel, his life, literature, Peru, et cetera (they contain the famous attack on Cortázar's cosmopolitanism)—and the narrative parts, some of them astounding in their fascination, scenes one could never have imagined. Yet, there are also incoherences that leave the reader blinking and groping in desperate attempts to follow, *to understand.* The novel is incomplete, of course—the last diary is called "Ultimo diario?"—yet I believe it to be the best Arguedas wrote (together with *Yawar fiesta*). An epilogue comprises his last letters, to publisher, university, friends and his acceptance speech when receiving the Inca Garcilaso Prize in 1968.

Julio Ortega has made the best observation: this is a novel written to defeat death; but death won. All in all, a novel replete with defects, as is all Arguedas's fiction, but defects one feels ashamed to point out, for one feels that by criticizing one again destroys life, that of the author's memory

and perhaps of a vital myth. *El zorro* is in parts deeply moving and disturbing: it proves that writing can be living, or even death. Arguedas was a very great man, and this book proves it. (p. 630)

Wolfgang A. Luchting, in Books Abroad *(copyright 1972 by the University of Oklahoma Press), Vol. 46, No. 4, Autumn, 1972.*

M. E. DAVIS

The time spanned by [*Relatos completos*] reveals Arguedas perfecting the art of revealing contradictory emotions. The total effect of each story is the result of a series of antitheses stable throughout Arguedas's prose. Through the eyes of an orphaned child or alienated adolescent the reader participates in a reality at once magical and cruel. Although each Andean village is controlled by a vicious landowner, the Indians inject the consciousness of another mode of being in which the environment contains gods who are themselves artists. Just as Arguedas contrasts the beauty of music with death, he also presents a narrative world in which the consummation of love is as possible as its betrayal. (pp. 72-3)

M. E. Davis, in World Literature Today *(copyright 1977 by the University of Oklahoma Press), Vol. 51, No. 1, Winter, 1977.*

B

BAGRYANA, Elisaveta (also Bagrjana; pseudonym
of Elisaveta Belcheva)   1893-

**Bagryana is a Bulgarian poet, editor, translator, and writer
of books for children. She projects an exuberant love of life in
her verse, expressing the joys and sorrows of freedom as an
artist and as a woman. She has collaborated with Ioran Vasi-
lev on biographical works and has translated her own work
from Bulgarian into French.**

ERIKA KNUDSEN

For many years Elisaveta Bagrjana was identified with the
concepts of her first collection, *Vechnata i svjatata* (1927)
—taken as categories of woman's love—but her later works
have changed fundamentally the view of this great Bulgarian poet. Bagrjana was considered, and by some still is, the
exponent of the emancipated woman, primarily because of
her concept of love, and her poetry has, therefore, usually
been interpreted simply as love lyrics. For this reason the
main core of the poetic confessions of Bagrjana has been
overlooked, the extreme tension between opposite attitudes
and emotions, between the dreams and expectations of life
on one hand, and, on the other, their accomplishment, or
even more often, their non-accomplishment. (p. 353)

There is a definite trend from optimism to pessimism in
Bagrjana's poetry . . . although her faith in the future and
her enchantment with life are never completely crushed,
and in her poems of recent years this faith appears to be
reborn. Her new confidence is an acknowledgement of the
human values compiled throughout life, as well as by the
simple joys of everyday life; its opposite pole is the now
constant presence of her own death.

In the early poetry of Bagrjana, the lyric self indulges in
bold and ambitious dreams of her future, a passionate,
dramatic surrender to man's love. Everything seems possible and attainable. Her strength and her will can cope with
any demand, and can overcome any obstacle. (pp. 353-54)

The opposite extreme in Bagrjana's first book [*Vechnata i
svjatata*] is represented by the complete despair of the ''Re-
quiem'' (1927).

The up and down movements of Bagrjana's frame of mind
are marked clearly by the choice of words and the structure
of the sentences. . . . Uncertainty and doubt are revealed
by the many questions, often initiated by ''dali'' (I wonder)

or ''nima'' (could it be?). Dreams and yearning are emphasized by the use of the future tense, . . . and the optative
clause with ''da.''

This means of expression, always pointing forward, gradually yields to terms which indicate a growing assurance
and an immediate mental and physical activity. . . .

Bagrjana meets the challenges of life with a defiant ''neka''
(let it be so). But then comes a sharp break from cheerfulness to despondency. The future perspective and the present satisfaction vanish and give way to the backward
glance, to the return to memories. (p. 354)

The incongruity between her expectations of life and life as
it actually unfolds . . . can be called the *fundamental theme*
in almost all of Bagrjana's poetry. It determines the underlying tone of her verse, irrespective of its main themes
which are love and individual freedom, the lust for life and
for the whole world, the devotion to Mother Earth and
above all to her own country. . . . *Most,* containing poems
from the years 1937-44, indicates the establishment of a relation between opposite points, and could be interpreted as
the comprehension and acceptance of the contradictions of
human existence, a theme repeated once more in the latest
book *Kontrapunkti* (1972).

Bagrjana's tribute to time and history, *Pet zvezdi* (1953),
famous for the cycle ''Suvetski khora,'' does not quite fit
into the pattern of her total work. These poems, on a broad
scale, reflect the struggle of man for a rich life full of meaning, that is, an interest which matches a fundamental stirring in the progressive mind of the poet, but the work
seems inferior compared to the major part of Bagrjana's
production. The reason may be a lack of real personal engagement, without which art remains sterile. Still, part of
Pet zvezdi, especially the cycle ''Sluntse nad poleto,'' has
much in common with the later Bojana cycle, fascinating
the reader by its ease and lyricism.

The tension between unreconcilable extremities, so significant in Elisaveta Bagrjana's poetry, is recognizable in all of
the individual themes.

The love theme in Bagrjana's poetry is very complex, reflecting the never ending struggle for individual freedom
and, at the same time, an unrestrained enjoyment of everything life can offer. (pp. 354-55)

Love as a spell, as a natural and inescapable instinct, harmonizes neither with the ethics nor with the free will of Bagrjana, the defender of free love and independence. (p. 355)

In poems like "Poslushnitsa" and "Ljubov" the involvements of the suffering Jesus and of the seductive Mephistopheles suggest that the loving woman is in conflict with her Christian belief. . . .

These discrepancies exclude, it would seem, the interpretation of Bagrjana as a pioneer of free love and believer in the total emancipation of women. Her confessions are entirely personal, and the presentiment of the price she will have to pay for her unprecedented courage, in "Kukuvitsa" and "Potomka," for example, preclude the slightest note of propaganda. (p. 356)

The very consequence of her struggle for personal freedom, her full devotion to human love, excludes this very freedom. . . . These are the extremes of her love and her life: the necessity of being independent, and the dependency of the relations created by herself.

In Elisaveta Bagrjana's lyrics, love is a fascinating unity of purity and passion. (pp. 356-57)

Though dominant, love is only one of the spheres where Bagrjana's general craving for personal freedom and self-realization are reflected. Her conception of life as a whole bears the impress of this personal combat. Intoxicated with her own power and possibilities, her mind starts on high-levelled flights, borne by the dashing horse of the "Amazonka" (1922) or by the sea and the wind ("Stikhii," 1925). . . . The conflict between individual revolution and established order is intimated in the designation of herself as "nepokornata." Only too well does she anticipate the difficulties she may encounter in life, but she will not or cannot curb the fatal instinct of nature within herself. (p. 359)

Again it should be pointed out that there is a very personal and individual element in the attitude of the lyric self which does not match the conception of Bagrjana as a pioneer of women's liberation. In the poem which is often referred to in this connection, "Zovut na moreto" (1931), it is true that she says that if she were not a woman, she would abandon everything and go out as a sailor. But she does not really reveal any actual desire to take over man's work, but rather the urge to flee from the complications of her own life, to seek new friends and new surroundings, that is, to travel *like* a mariner, not *as* one. . . . What was characteristic of her experience of love, applies to her total existence, spent in conflict between the expectations and dreams of the lyric self and reality. "I laugh and I cry when I think of what I expected, and what I obtained," she confesses ("Zhivotut . . ."). This conflict, which ranges from the last poems of *Vechnata i svjatata* to her latest works, displays all the shades of despair and hopefulness, and encompasses the surrender to sorrowful memories and new manifestations of life and activity. (p. 360)

A turning point is signalled by the poem "Vurni me" from "Parashut" (1938). Here the attention of Bagrjana embraces the whole wide world, not as the focal point of journeys, but as a continent of people who are worth her concern. . . .

The inner drama of Bagrjana's verse is created mainly by the movement from one extreme to the other, by the tension between revolt and acceptance, victory and defeat, youth and old age, life and death. Both poles, the positive and the negative, may function as starting points. (p. 361)

The call of foreign places and the fondness of the intimate and familiar are equal in intensity, and evoke the unique atmosphere of Bagrjana's poems of travel which originate from the tension between the opposite movements, departure and return. . . . It is a kind of physical necessity, similar to that of the tide, that draws the lyric self of Bagrjana out into the world by a magnetic power and casts her back again on to her shore, though not to stay! (p. 362)

The origin to which she will always return encompasses her personal relations as seen in ["Ptitsata s motornoto surtse"], in "Korab ot Ispanja" and "Slovenski vecheri," the latter even underlining the sadness of her life at home, haunted by memories and the monotony of everyday life. And it may be seen in her ethnic rooting in Bulgaria, in its history and in its soil. (p. 363)

Bagrjana's travelling urge is linked organically with her personality as a whole, with her philosophy and her practice of life, in the sense of recklessness of prejudices and consequences. . . .

In most of Bagrjana's travel poems it is obvious that the focus of attention is not directed from the visual experience to the observer's mind, but vice versa; the lyric self picks out the impressions, things, and colours which best reflect her mood. . . .

In more than one sense the Venetian cycle (1930) is an exception. Here the consciousness of the poet has yielded to an extraordinary perception of visual impressions. The result is a symphony of colours, ranging from the faintest pastel to brilliant and saturated shades, and of an artistic level which places it among the best of its kind in world poetry. Usually Bagrjana is economical in her use of colours. She often prefers the contrast of black and white, arranged in winter landscapes or in starry nights, expressing a thought or a mood which reflects the contrarieties of life. . . . Green shades symbolize a sense of quiet harmony, and all the red and golden colours, which are without doubt the most characteristic ones in Bagrjana's poetry, are the signs of the climax of love and life. (p. 364)

Though one could not call the nature in Bagrjana's poetry descriptive, yet it is to a high degree illustrative. The philosophic contemplations of the poet generally originate with concrete observations and experiences, from actual situations which evoke thoughts and emotions. They are always put forward in simple, understandable words and contexts. The external occasion may be a natural phenomenon—a landscape in its entity or represented by a detail, the weather, a season as in the poems of the cycle "Kushta v poleto" (1936). Thus the picture of the sea always induces feelings of restlessness and longing for freedom and independence.

Technology also evokes the philosophical contemplations of Bagrjana. . . . It becomes . . . more important for Bagrjana to emphasize the eternal human element as being superior to technology. "Which seismograph," she asks, "could possibly measure the disastrous bore of despair, threatening to suffocate a poor human heart?" ("Seismograf na surtseto," 1936). One of the most suggestive poems within this problematic field is "Industrija" (1963), in which the horrified poet proposes the idea that art is submitted to mass fabrication, that is, put into the piston engine of unification.

The theme of technical progress influences Bagrjana's vocabulary. A quick glance at the titles of her later poems reveals this fact ("Radio," "Seismograf," "Industrija," "Letishta," "Grumootvodite," "Budilnikut," "Radar"), and a thorough study of the idioms used confirms it. Some times the dead material is connected with life in a very poetical way such as the "bird with the motor-heart," or the "parachute" which symbolizes the rescue of a human heart. At other times the technical device is used to underline the unpoetical reality of life and the inability of technology to relieve the mental sufferings of man ("Radio," "Seismograf"). Mostly, the technical idioms form parts of metaphors and comparisons in order to give a more explicit formulation to thoughts and moods. . . . It is indeed, a matter of taste whether or not one appreciates this technical concretion of abstract ideas and mental conditions. Its aesthetic value is, in some cases, doubtful, but the sober-mindedness and cogency of this technique accentuate, in return, the ethic scope of this kind of verse. (pp. 364-66)

Another reflection of modern times, in the sense of technical revolution and growing disharmony in the world, can be seen in the increased use of free verse and the use of a diction which approximates prose. This trend is notable in Bagrjana's poetry from the end of the twenties and throughout the thirties; it later yielded to a more frequent use of syllabic-accentual verse.

Though the poetry of Elisaveta Bagrjana is rich in contradictory elements, it would be wrong to say that it lacks harmony. Her special harmony which holds the extremes of all her urges and frustrations, her hopes and disappointments, her joy and grief, lies in the recognition of the eternal cycle in Nature, the only secure basis which gives gravity to life. She is aware of this continuity, one might say, from the beginning of her existence as a poet, and her conception of it extends to the change of generations as well as to the regular shift of the seasons. (p. 366)

Bagrjana's latest poems show a still substantial tension between the irreconcilable sides of nature such as life and death, but this tension is governed by the acceptance of their equal future possibilities.

The discrepancy between the high-set expectations and the harsh reality of life has shrunk to an unsentimental survey of "black and white days," viewed without regret, as the necessity of "the paths she chose, or the path which chose her" ("Parola" in *Kontrapunkti* 1972).

The most fascinating part of this supreme wisdom of Bagrjana's is that it does not tend towards resignation. Her love and her sorrow are as deep as ever, and she carries her memories not as a disturbing ballast, but as the beauty and synthesis of her life. (p. 369)

> *Erika Knudsen, "The Counter-Points of Elisaveta Bagrjana," in* Canadian Slavonic Papers, *Autumn, 1974, pp. 353-69.*

EDWARD MOŻEJKO

In general, when reading Bagryana's poetry, one cannot withstand the impression that whatever she has written or accomplished bears the features of a well-prepared, systematic and well-disciplined esthetic activity. . . .

Bagryana's first collection of poems, entitled *Večnata i svjatata* (The Eternal and the Sacred), appeared in 1927 and became a literary *événement*. Without going into detail, one could say that the novelty of this volume consisted in a clear rejection of the hitherto dominating streams in Bulgarian literature and an acceptance of the exceptionally rich traditions of national oral folklore as a source of artistic inspiration. What Bagryana inherited from this tradition was simplicity and directness of expression. The poetic world of Bagryana is built up of objects and phenomena which surround us. By its concrete character, the early poetry of Bagryana was a reaction against symbolism; by its personal tone, it contrasted with the revolutionary rhetoric of Khristo Botev . . . and the old-fashioned patriotism of Ivan Vazov. . . . If anything, Bulgarian poetry moved more easily in the world of politics, in the world of heroic actions, in the world of war and revolution than in the inward world of intimate confessions. The turnabout accomplished by Bagryana was twofold in its consequences: the intimate tone of her poetry has manifested itself not only in a turn toward the internal feelings of man, toward his spiritual "I"; this tone also dominates where the theme seems to befit a more pathetic and objective presentation. Irrespective, however, of whether Bagryana speaks of her fatherland (as is the case in her latest poems) or talks to God, she never exceeds the limits of her own personal experience and does not relate these themes to a "cause of higher order."

It is possible to delineate four major motifs in Bagryana's poetry: woman, love, traveling-space and life as a biological phenomenon. The degree of intensity with which these motifs appear in her poetry varies from one collection of poems to another, but it is impossible to discuss them in separation because they are constantly intertwined and constitute a homogeneous and typically Bagryanian whole. (p. 216)

Bagryana enters the scene of Bulgarian poetry as an advocate of women's emancipation. The word "emancipation," however, is far too faint to render the depth and perspicacity with which the whole problem is approached in her poetry. To say that woman revolts against existing social and moral conventions would be nothing but a shallow statement. The question does not concern woman historically conditioned by a definite cultural and social epoch. The title of the first volume does not leave any doubt: the words *večnata i svjatata* mean "the eternal and holy woman." To present woman in such dimensions, Bagryana refers to various archetypal images of women known from ancient, Christian and pagan mythology. (pp. 216-17)

The Bagryanian woman possesses two principal characteristics: revolt and love. All other desires and dreams are offshoots of these two passions. When we say "revolt," the question is: against what or whom? It is the revolt against women's submissiveness, humility and surrender. This revolt does not arise from social considerations or a growing awareness of women's position in society; it grows organically out of unfathomable layers of the past. The poet feels very close blood ties with her ethnic past, that is, with the heritage of her Thracian, Slavic and Turkish ancestors. . . . [We] can interpret her "revolt" as the call of the blood, as a constant recurrence of some atavistic necessity. . . .

What Bagryana values most are the primitive and primordial elements in human nature. The return to the primary origins of our existence is combined with the biological joy of life, enabling woman to break prejudices about her situation, to free herself from seclusion and humiliation. In other words, these rebellious qualities reside within woman herself and burst the ossified crust of prejudice from inside. . . . In its impetuous revolt Bagryana's lyrical "I" does not hesitate to question such sacred institutions as marriage.

From the time Bagryana first began to write, to the latest poems in the sixties, her poetry resounds with a cry for love (note some typical titles of her poems: "Vik," or "Cry"; "Zov," or "Call"). Without this feeling our world would be poor, sad and gray. Moreover, the degree of woman's liberation, her real equality with man, can be measured in terms of love and by the relation of both sexes to love, which the poet calls "the conscience of earth" ("Kato slunce," or "Like the Sunshine"). Again, mythological analogy can be drawn upon: Bagryana's treatment of this motif reminds us of the love tale "Amor and Psyche" by Apuleius. (p. 217)

["Intérieur"] is typical of Bagryana's poetry for two reasons. Firstly, there is a clear reversal of roles: it is not man but woman who seeks gratification of her passions in additional adventures. On the contrary, man appears as the guardian of ideal love, and he is utterly faithful; for woman, seclusion within the four walls of the home is unbearable. Secondly, we can perceive here a leitmotiv which underlies many of Bagryana's love poems: the lust for love is so great that one love cannot fulfill our desires. The heroine of Bagryana's poetry wants to experience love in its complete fullness. She wants to love many and to be loved by many. . . .

In poems devoted to women's emancipation we come across the word *skitnica,* the feminine form of "wanderer"; and in those where love reaches its climax, the lovers dream about an unknown and fantastic land, as in "Unes" (Exaltation). Both motifs usher in the myth of the Great Odyssey. At the bottom of this motif lies the lust for life. As in love we cannot confine ourselves to one person, so in life we should not be limited to one place alone. Movement by various mechanical means (train, airplane, ship) disenthralls dreams and is associated with a sense of freedom. Travel is a kind of challenge which both verifies and enriches mankind. . . . The myth of the Odyssey is probably the most all-embracing motif in Bagryana's poetry. At any rate, it constitutes a permanent component of all her poetry devoted to women and love. . . .

Beginning with the second collection of poems, *Zvezda na morjaka,* we can observe . . . a gradual retreat from a somewhat naïve enthusiasm and a voluptuous spontaneity in favor of a more subdued poetry which reveals a more tangible disposition for intellectual discipline and reflection. The latter is not based on abstract speculations but grows out of everyday observations; it is entrenched in the fullness of life so much admired by the poet. Bagryana's third volume of poetry, *Surce čoveško* (The Heart of Man; 1936), includes a cycle of poems entitled "Kolelo" (Circle). Whether the symbol of the circle appears in primitive sunworship or modern religion, in myth or dreams, in the mandalas drawn by Tibetan monks, in the ground plans of cities or in the spherical concepts of early astronomers, it always points to the single and most vital aspect of life—its ultimate wholeness. If we read Bagryana's poetry from this

vantage point, we see how much she is preoccupied with this theme. In "Kolelo" Bagryana wants to embrace life in all its manifestations and to follow it in all directions. . . . (p. 218)

In general, from the beginning of the thirties Bagryana shows an acute interest in man's position vis-à-vis modern civilization. This subject is treated with an amazing originality and sagacity in "S.O.S." Bagryana perceives the threat of civilization to her countrymen in their lack of preparation to cope with it. There is a dangerous gulf between the still unspoiled primitiveness and sentimentality of her people on the one hand, and the civilization of skyscrapers on the other. The whole poem is a chain of basic oppositions: East-West, past-present, contemporaneity-poetry.

It is not difficult to note that whenever Bagryana speaks of the present, distrust or irony slip into her poetry, and both express a sense of forboding. The menace of civilization consists in the fact that man is lost in it, that he is someone "without a face." In "Klounut govori" (The Clown Speaks), from the cycle "The Big Circus," she employs a synecdoche which indicates in a forceful manner the tragedy of our age. The circus ring gradually extends its boundaries and finally covers the whole earth, where clowns appear as hypnotists who hypnotize the masses and lead them to self-destruction. If earth is a circus, then the city is a hell where innocent people suffer and die. Is there a way out of this cul-de-sac? Bagryana does not belong to the spectrum of poets who tend to formulate political or social programs of salvation, but some of her poems seem to suggest a moral solution in that they call for a return to nature, to the primitive, to the source of all life—earth itself. In her recent poems this motif has found its most vehement manifestation in "Kladenec" (The Well). (pp. 218-19)

Her poems written immediately after the war, that is, in an atmosphere of increasing Stalinism and under the imposition of socialist realism, are typified by a withdrawal from the hitherto familiar tone of reflection in favor of a more bombastic and politically motivated style of poetry. Fortunately, Bagryana realized soon that this road of artistic endeavor was foreign to her nature and esthetic beliefs. Consequently, we observe in her last two volumes of poetry a return to the original interests and preoccupations, though perhaps with more attention now being paid to the motif of her fatherland and its nature. The style of her poetry becomes even more simple and direct. . . .

It is interesting to note that it was in the sixties that she wrote her poem "Poèzijata" (Poetry), in which she clearly spelled out her esthetic program and recapitulated, as it were, her poetic experience. The question "What is the goal of poetry?" was posed as early as 1931, in the poem "Poèt," and reoccurred in the poems devoted to modern civilization. The role of the poet is seen here as being very modest and limited. In the humdrum and turmoil of contemporary civilization the task of a poet is to reveal his heart. A few years later, in the cycle "Seizmograf na surceto" (Seismograph of the Heart), Bagryana broadens this definition of poetry by saying that it should discover the inner experience of the "man in the street," who is lost in the modern "inferno" of civilization. This subjective attitude becomes even more evident and intensified in "Poèzijata." Here it is dealt with on the level of a highly subjective relationship: the "I" versus poetry. To Bagryana, poetry means the joy of an unusual perception of the world, the source of joy and richness of her personal life and the source of personal strength. All three stanzas of "Poèzijata" speak of nothing else but this: poetry is a very personal and subjective experience.

In the course of more than fifty years Bagryana has enriched the treasury of Bulgarian and world poetry without drawing much attention outside her own country. If she were to be placed in a certain line of literary development in twentieth-century poetry, she would definitely not fall into the category of the so-called "intellectual" poets. Bagryana represents the other wing of the twentieth-century avant-garde, that is, poets who draw their inspiration from the abundance of folklore and primitive art. It is here, perhaps, that we must look for an explanation of the epic and narrative framework of her lyrics (note her preference for writing cycles of poetry, a device developed to such an extent that some poems can be understood only in the context of other poems). Bagryana's spontaneous and lively temperament has been subordinated to a strong creative discipline. She has achieved such a degree of assertiveness and classical lucidity of expression that when we read her verse, the form itself appears unobtrusive or "invisible." What remains visible, however, is the unusual wisdom, warmth and perspicacity of her poetry. (p. 219)

> Edward Możejko, "The Private World of Elisaveta Bagryana," in World Literature Today (copyright 1977 by the University of Oklahoma Press), Vol. 51, No. 2, Spring, 1977, pp. 216-20.

*   *   *

BAINBRIDGE, Beryl   1933-

Bainbridge is an English novelist, playwright, and essayist. Her fictional world is a drab, claustrophobic one, peopled by unhappy, unlucky denizens of the lower middle class. The dreariness of subject and setting is, however, relieved by her satiric wit and spirited dialogue. (See also *CLC*, Vols. 4, 5, 8, and *Contemporary Authors*, Vols. 21-24, rev. ed.)

JULIA O'FAOLAIN

Muting her technique to match her subject, [in "A Quiet Life" Beryl Bainbridge] works with the sly precision of a trap. Early on she plants a foreboding that something explosive is stirring beneath the surface of her characters' lives. They are a family of four living on the west coast of Britain shortly after World War II. There are still undetected mines in the woods and father wears his air raid warden's uniform for doing odd jobs. The obsolete gear draws ironic attention to the difficulties of parrying crossfire on the domestic front.

Events are seen through the eyes of Alan, the high-strung 17-year-old son, whose defense against unwelcome news is a refusal to hear. "I don't want to know," he says. "Shut up." "I'm not listening."

But secrets trickle out. Because the reader knows only what Alan knows, learning things in driblets, he shares the boy's sense of shock. . . .

These are quiet lives and she portrays them without narrative pyrotechnics. Tragedy comes in subdued guise and brings no sense of release. What happens is that Alan's father dies of a heart attack brought on partly by marital jealousy, partly by his family's indifference and, most im-

mediately, by Alan's exasperated lapse into candor to tell him that mother has no lover and only leaves the house at night to sit in the station waiting room. "'She can't stand being in the same room with you,' cries Alan. . . . 'You make her flesh creep.'" . . .

Murderers in Mrs. Bainbridge's novels are never brought to book. This time she goes further than before in stripping down the murder-story mechanism until all that is left is the build-up of suspense and suspicion that goads readers to try assigning blame. But censoriousness boomerangs. Responsibility here is too diffuse to be pinned on anyone unless we set up standards by which it would be uncomfortable to live. The author's trap closes as neatly on the reader as it did on Alan. Moral murders like that of his father must be common in quiet lives.

The novel itself is quiet: a feat of concealed craft. It is hard to deal with semi-articulate people without either short-changing them or boring the reader, and it must have been harder still to tell the story through the consciousness of someone as fact-shy as Alan. Mrs. Bainbridge turns the disability into a tool. Alan's flinching apprehension speeds the pace and gives it a life-like rhythm. His strobe-light vision allows sharp focus, flashes of intelligence and believable returns to bewilderment. Clothes define their wearer: trays of paste jewelry for sad, aspiring mother; impenetrable vests for the girl with whom Alan fails to find passion in the woods; the incongruous old A.R.P. uniform for father to die as he lived, a misfit. Twenty-five years later, when Alan has become a replica of his parents, the anarchic Madge, still refusing the bonds of adulthood, turns up in a school coat.

Such devices help Mrs. Bainbridge catch the essential selves of her lower middle-class people, while respecting their reticence. Her ear for speech seems to me perfect. Her 1940's are authentically drab but returning to them in her company is a delight. She is a subtle and protean writer.

> Julia O'Faolain, "Getting Away with Murder," in The New York Times Book Review (© 1977 by The New York Times Company; reprinted by permission), March 20, 1977, p. 6.

CLAIRE TOMALIN

Binny [protagonist of *Injury Time*] . . . , mother of three, husbandless, in her mid-forties, is not the first Beryl Bainbridge heroine to be afflicted with an indignant sense that her life is not under control—her own or anyone else's. At times indignation rises to terror though more often it's bad temper; except when drink or, less often, a moment's off-guard tenderness releases her, she is usually trembling, alert to some imminent slight or outrage. She can't go shopping without seeing or suspecting nastiness of one kind or another. (p. 57)

We know by now the deadly striking power of the Bainbridge sentence, the exactness of her social horror show. This is as good as ever: the jokes are funny in the 'I could have died' style. Indeed, 'I could have died' lurks inside each of the overburdened, slightly malfunctioning frames she has given her middle-aged characters. I'm not entirely carried away, though, by the move towards plot—or perhaps it is a device for turning a novella, just, into a novel. Binny, Edward and their friends are thrust into real adventure, risk and violence: 'I could have died' begins to look like an outside threat, as a group of gunmen invade the house, pursued by the police. Of course it gives her a chance to have some satirical fun about television sociologists' attitudes to criminals, and her local effects are as sharp as one could wish. A rape evokes one large tear from the left eye, a rather distant sense of responsibility and 'she wasn't even young enough . . . to feel sorry for herself'. It's believable, if not what women are currently supposed to come up with. But the fact is criminals do remain ineffectual stereotypes and although they inconvenience their victims they don't advance very far into the reader's imagination: they are clearly a device, and a device that is going nowhere. And so the book loses momentum. (p. 58)

Claire Tomalin, "Trite Finish," in The New Review *(© The New Review Ltd., 11 Greek Street, London W1V 5LE), November, 1977, pp. 57-8.*

JAMES BROCKWAY

[It's] from *Harriet said . . .*, the first to be written, back in the Fifties, and eventually published . . . in 1972, that the Bainbridge *oeuvre* as we know it today begins.

Six almost slim volumes . . . of a surprising uniformity. . . . In the Seventies Miss Bainbridge seems to be repeating what Mrs Spark was doing in the Sixties, giving us one brief, beautifully turned book after the other.

This year the product is entitled *Injury Time,* which immediately demonstrated the authoress's feeling for the mood of the day, her perfect ear for its idiom: a term derived from the twentieth century's chosen religion, football, here very effectively and outrageously applied to the middle age of human beings of the western urbanised, upper-lower-middle-class, bruised-but-still-battling-on variety, whom Miss Bainbridge has made it her speciality to portray. . . .

Perhaps Binny and her Edward epitomise Western society itself, but however that may be, here Miss Bainbridge, again sensing exactly what's wanted, has them and their dinner-party guests taken hostage in Binny's house by a gang of bank-robbers who are being chased by the police. What topic more topical? I wrote 'however that may be', but it occurs to me that this makes it all the more likely still that this dilapidated, illicit, ill-assorted, ever-warring, internecine couple, Binny and Edward, does, whether the author intended it or not, symbolise All Europe Now. Or, at very least, a bewildered Britannia and John Bull.

Miss Bainbridge would be the last novelist in London to be portentous or to appear for one moment to be coming along with a message and writing a series of novels on a Grand Theme. Yet the more I read her the more I suspect that the grip her work has taken on us, the ease with which she has won us, the enthusiasm with which the critics (most of them) greet her work,—the more I suspect that this is not merely due to her being an exquisite entertainer—a star performer, in fact, who can get away with anything, Grand Guignol included, a deliciously preposterous humorist and a very, very clever writer, but also to the powerful *subconscious* appeal of her subject matter: our present parlous postwar condition.

So far these six novels fall into two groups: *Harriet said . . .* (1) *The Dressmaker* (2) and *A Quiet Life* (5) are set in a grey and grubby Lancashire in the war and early postwar years, the era of Bainbridge's girlhood; while the other three: *The Bottle Factory Outing* (3) *Sweet William* (4) and now *Injury Time* (6) are set in tatty London in our own tatty time. Yet there are thematic links (the main one: the psychological warfare perpetually proceeding among humans), while the action is always more or less the same: frustration within the confines of lower-class would-be respectability which must sooner or later lead to violent eruption; and the setting too, whether in Lancashire or London: a family, or environment, either bursting at the seams with pent-up emotion or already in ruins, with the characters fighting it out frantically among the rubble. It's a shambles. It's a battlefield.

Here I am reminded once again of Muriel Spark, especially in Bainbridge's London novels, and particularly of the title of an early short piece of Spark's: *You Should Have Seen the Mess.* Again like Spark, who has often taken press reports (of rapes, murders, kidnappings, swindles) as the framework or departure point of her novels, Bainbridge, in this new novel, makes use of the taking of hostages in their humble homes, but not, of course, for the interest inherent in such a situation but to illustrate, by means of it, her characters' psychology and the absurdity of their reactions. Our absurdity. . . .

[*Injury Time*] has the ingredients and set-up for a satirical social comedy and, since it is in Bainbridge's hands, for a very knock-about comedy too. There is a very great deal of knocking-about in this *oeuvre.* Not only do nervous agitated lovers tend to bark their shins on bicycles propped up in narrow hallways, but people have even been known, when not hurling abuse at one another's heads, to switch to throwing stones, while, if need be, assault and battery are taken as far as manslaughter. Frustration must out, so violence is in.

In *Injury Time* there are a few signs, as in the immoderately praised *The Bottle Factory Outing,* of invention and ingenuity proceeding beyond the bounds of the likely or credible, signs here and there of strain, but on the whole the story is handled with resource, gusto and a marvellous adroitness. That it ends abruptly merely illustrates that it is not the story and situation which matter to Bainbridge but the opportunity they offer her to display the comic absurdity of her characters and to satirise the society which has produced both them and the situation they find themselves in.

It is in her use of language, however, that Beryl Bainbridge's main strength lies, the hawklike, devastating accuracy with which she swoops down on always the exactly right word. Laugh if you will, but I think she is our 1970s Oscar Wilde. Not so preposterous a comparison, after all, when one considers that he was the beaming satirist of the class which was in power in his time, while she is the poker-faced satirist of the upper-lower-middle-class in power today.

James Brockway, "Penalty Areas," in Books and Bookmen *(© copyright James Brockway 1977; reprinted with permission), December, 1977, p. 52.*

GILBERTO PEREZ

The limited point of view of a character can be a tiresome device, especially when it is used ironically by an author who clearly knows better than the character we are limited to. The character we are stuck with in another new English novel, Beryl Bainbridge's *A Quiet Life*, is a boring adolescent boy, a conformist to the absurdly genteel standards of his family, while the more interesting character, his rebellious younger sister, is off somewhere on the beach most of the time.... My feeling reading this book was that I wanted to get out of there, out of that house where the parents quarrel all the time, out of that boy's point of view.... This book might have been more interesting if it had been done in the first person, Faulkner-style, in the fumbling words of a repressed adolescent; as it is we get the author's knowing third-person prose. (pp. 610-11)

> *Gilberto Perez, in* The Hudson Review *(copyright © 1977 by The Hudson Review, Inc.; reprinted by permission), Vol. XXX, No. 4, Winter, 1977-78.*

EDITH MILTON

Beryl Bainbridge's *A Quiet Life* [is a success]. The quintessential family novel, its tiny world is confined to Mother, Father, and daughter Madge. It is son Alan through whose flawed vision we see the rest of the family. Madge, by an obscure miracle of valor and will, has managed to rescue a small part of honesty, feeling, and humor from the tight prison of the childhood which Alan recalls in his memoir of a dreary, postwar Lancashire seaside town. Poverty and dishonor are both personal—the result of Father's unsound business practices—and the general lot of the country at large. The family is locked inside its middle-class gentilities; yearning for better things, for romance, new hats, social status, money, a bit of fun, a bit of love, its members jangle hilariously against each others' suspicions and expectations. The father is frantic with a passion of jealousy for the mother, who escapes it, and at the same time keeps it alive as the only romance in view, by reading novels in secret at the railway station.... When Mother and Father accompany Alan and his girl-friend Janet for a walk,

> [Mother] took Father's arm at first, leaving Alan and Janet to walk behind, but she was moved by a show of daffodils.... She stepped backwards, neatly severing the two of them asunder and clung to Janet's arm, pointing at the yellow flowers stiffly bordering the patch of lawn.
>
> "Look at them," she cried. "Oooh, look at that hydrangea." Haltingly they proceeded down the lane towards the railway crossing. "Winter's dying," she proclaimed, tilting her bright face to the sky and stumbling in her high-heeled shoes.

The lyric mixture of Freud and histrionics which structures the passage pervades the whole novel, a satirical, understated memento of the pathetic poetry of the characters' attempts to escape the obsessions which govern them. In its cool look backward, *A Quiet Life* informs the cause of feminism.... Madge can embrace her freedom, as she could embrace her brief, illicit passion for a German prisoner-of-war, only outside the confines of respectability and therefore outside the confines of the novel. In their eccentricities the characters are touching; in their childlike behavior, their isolation, their pain. (pp. 262-63)

> *Edith Milton, in* The Yale Review *(© 1977 by Yale University; reprinted by permission of the editors), Winter, 1978.*

JOHN MELLORS

Beryl Bainbridge writes horror-comics. She is ruthlessly funny about drab, even squalid, lives which are interrupted and changed for ever by some unexpected event—a violent death, an unsuitable love affair, or, as in *Injury Time*, a kidnapping. Her dramas are played on an untidy, cluttered stage where dishes are piled high in the sink, where ashtrays or, more likely, saucers, are overflowing, and where neither vacuum cleaner nor carpet sweeper can be relied on to work properly. Her male characters are often bombastic, ineffectual and insensitive. Her women tend to be zany, easily deceived and sluttish: they are capable of making perceptive, imaginative comments about love, marriage, old age and death, but they may well have forgotten to change their underwear for several days and they will almost certainly not have cleaned the oven in the cooker or de-frosted the fridge for months.

Bainbridge is at her most successful, I feel, when she disciplines her inventiveness and does not allow too much to happen. In *The Bottle Factory Outing* she got carried away. In *A Quiet Life* she kept her talents under control, and the result was far more credible. Credibility is maintained in *Injury Time* until just into the second half; after that, weak refereeing by the author lets the game get out of hand. (p. 93)

To be fair, if *Injury Time* had been Bainbridge's first novel one would have greeted it with enthusiastic acclaim. She is a writer who creates her own special climate. For Binny, 'the world was menacing and full of alarms', and that is Bainbridge's world, too, the world of the menopause when 'all the big issues were over and done with.' ... (p. 94)

> *John Mellors, in* London Magazine *(© London Magazine 1977), January, 1978.*

EDITH MILTON

Macbeth's was perhaps the most memorable, but from the time of Hrothgar's, which lasted several nights, to the time of Gatsby's, which went on till dawn, the disastrous dinner party has been as much a cliché of dramatic and narrative literature as it is an unfortunate fact of social life. I suppose the fictional violation of our most amiable ritual serves to emphasize the horrors of less amiable impulses, as the son is served up in a ragout, the warming-cover lifted to reveal the severed head or the pet budgerigar.

More frequently still, disaster at the table is merely funny, a forceful image of our ineptness as social beings.... We know, before it appears, the destination of the banana cream pie. Nor are we surprised, in Beryl Bainbridge's *Injury Time*, to find the chops overdone and the dessert, inside a plastic bag, fallen behind the fridge. She has chosen a time-honored vehicle for her comedy.

But she has also chosen a dessert which is not a pie; it is instead, foil wrapped, raisin stuffed apples, as yet unbaked, one of which becomes, in due course, a missile for her protagonist's frustration. *He* wanted pie. And the image of him heaving an apple across the room like a grenade is one of many examples of the book's fascinating marriage of the two traditions of dining disaster: the Gothic tradition of violence invading an intimate ceremony of comfort and friendship, and the comic tradition of the bumbling hostess and the guests who are not what they pretend to be.

The hostess in this case is Binny, a divorcée on the threshold of menopause, who has persuaded her married lover, Edward, that it is time for him to invite some "close friend" to dinner. Agreeing in principle, but far too conventional to risk even distant friends, Edward asks a business acquaintance whose wife he has never met. Edward, who is a tax accountant, is dismayed by the dishevelment in which Binny lives, her casual housekeeping, her tremulous upbringing of three adolescents, her middle-aged skin, but he tends to pretend that his disapproval is really being felt by someone else. . . .

The scene is familiar enough; halfway between Wycherley and "I Love Lucy." But is played on a stage set for a larger, darker drama, with a backdrop of Northwest London in decay, and, beyond that, rumors of a world disrupted by violence. Television brings the themes and temper of the times into Binny's living room. "Between placing the kettle on the gas and water coming to the boil, whole cities disintegrated, populations burned. A thousand deaths, real and fictional, had been enacted before her eyes." Binny is poorer than Edward and less educated, and her resentment of his exploitation of her, sexual and social, echoes a resentment common to our day. (p. 27)

All day, as she prepares her middle-class, three-course dinner, for which neither her talents nor her world are suited, violence and anarchy hover in the corner of Binny's perception. They are implicit in the eggshells strewn over the hedge, and the neighbors fornicating behind the dustbins; they are explicit in a robbery which goes on quietly as Binny draws money from the bank. Finally they burst full upon her, in the shape of the four desperadoes who, the bank job accomplished, have failed to meet at the appointed rendezvous, and now find themselves regrouping in Binny's kitchen. They arrive, needless to say, already pursued by the police, in the middle of her dinner party, and immediately seize the four diners as hostages.

In their roles of criminals, they are having difficulties of their own which pretty much parallel the difficulties their hostages have playing good citizens. . . . It is apparently as hard for the thieves to behave with appropriate criminality as it is for their victims to adhere to the spirit of the laws of England. (pp. 27-8)

Younger than their hostages, the criminals play their game by slightly different rules. Ginger, who is shocked by Edward's connubial hypocrisy, takes sex, like cash, the most direct way, without any unnecessary intervention of work, emotion or pleasure. He is the emanation not only of London's decay, but, in spirit, the child of the middle-aged people gathered at Binny's table, the inevitable man of the future. Above all, he is the "wayward young man in westerns and gangster movies and war films," the message of television made flesh.

For clearly the world of Binny and her guests is past, and the game with these desperadoes, the footloose, feckless present, already lost. Still, they try to play on. But what is the game, and what are the rules? Binny compares their lives to a football match, already decided, in which the players, "Short of breath and flecked with mud, trembling in every limb," wait for the final whistle. The rules of marriage, affairs, raising children, keeping house, seem not to have worked. Edward, trained by a life of cricket and tax evasion, plays better than the others, and at one point organizes a ping-pong match at the lighted window of Bin-

ny's bedroom, to convince the police watching outside, that inside all is well.

But inside all is not well. There is, to begin with, no ping-pong ball. The match is mere illusion, its purpose so obscure as to escape all sense. The characters, desperate for a *modus vivendi,* or a *modus ludendi,* tend to put their trust upon delusions and on what they think other people think of them. Television is believable, but Binny finds reality quite unconvincing. And all of them have forgotten entirely what they really feel, or if, indeed, they ever really felt it. . . .

[It] becomes obvious that there is no game. There are no rules. And there is, in their lives as on the ping-pong table, no ball to play with. The only reality, after all, is the final whistle which blows in the novel's last sentence.

The book ends without resolution, mid-violence, so to speak. It opens with a joke without a punch line, which, still without a punch line, is repeated later. Beryl Bainbridge, a witty and spartan stylist . . . , has written a very funny, very complex dialogue between life and art; or, more exactly, between life and bad art, bad jokes, the reproduction of the Last Supper on the wall, the repetition of last generation's gangster movies on the tube. "'I keep thinking I'm watching television,'" says Binny. "'There doesn't seem to be much difference.'"

Bainbridge explores what difference there is. The setting, the characters, the situation, like the disastrous meal itself, are almost trite; almost the stuff from which serials are made. She mocks at the same time our lives' drab imitation of fiction, and our fictions' bright imitation of life. Though her impact is that of satire, and though her joke is really very good, her method has the purity of certain photographs, where a closeness of focus, a magnification of detail, turns organic confusion and the ugliness of the familiar into geometry. When the laughter is over, what remains is almost an abstraction, a rather novel view over a well-known landscape. The scale and clarity of its perspective are astonishing. (p. 28)

> *Edith Milton, in* The New Republic *(reprinted by permission of* The New Republic; © *1978 by The New Republic, Inc.), March 25, 1978.*

*   *   *

BARAKA, Imamu Amiri   1934-

Baraka, formerly known as LeRoi Jones, is an American poet, playwright, short story writer, essayist, jazz critic, and editor. Baraka's subject is the oppression of blacks in white society and his work an intense emotional response to this condition. He received acclaim for his first professional production, *Dutchman.* **His subsequent work for the theater has provoked both praise and controversy. His poetry and prose are characterized by difficult syntax, often obscuring the logic, but never the purpose, of his thought. Having rejected white values and white society, Baraka strives to create art with a firm didactic purpose: to forge an Afro-American art that reflects the values and sensibilities of the black community. (See also** *CLC,* **Vols. 1, 2, 3, 5, and** *Contemporary Authors,* **Vols. 21-24, rev. ed.)**

RICHARD HOWARD

LeRoi Jones is already familiar to New Yorkers as the au-

thor of some sensational little plays, and to readers of poetry as the author of some sensational little poems, and if
his book [*Blues People: Negro Music in White America*]
fails to be sensational, it is not because he has tried to keep
it from being so, but because his accommodation of his subject has been couched—bedded down, in fact—in that language of all languages most refractory to sensationalism:
the latest jargon of the social sciences. It is almost French,
Mr. Jones's enterprise, if we think of the ways Parisian intellectuals have of investing a complex popular phenomenon like the movies with whatever intellectual forces they
happen to have lying around; and though Mr. Jones's tone
is one of letting the chips fall where they may—off his or
anyone else's shoulders—his effort is analogously stren-
uous. . . . (p. 403)

The undertaking has less, evidently, to do with information
than with public speaking. . . . Yet this fancy-talk of the
social sciences is not used to describe or even to analyze,
but to condemn and to despise. There are times when the
belief in original virtue, a concept Mr. Jones has invented
to oppose the original sin of being Black in White America,
sounds either histrionic or professional, and in *Blues People,* for all its clever discussions of Armstrong and Beider-
becke, Bebop and Swing, Cecil Taylor and Ornette Coleman (the way out, these last, of "overused Western musical
concepts"), Mr. Jones does little more than attempt to create a system or dogma of evil and innocence by sheer classroom oratory. Unfortunately he makes this attempt in the
very language of the "deadeningly predictable mind of
white America". (pp. 403-04)

> *Richard Howard, in* Poetry (© *1965 by The
> Modern Poetry Association; reprinted by
> permission of the Editor of* Poetry), *March,
> 1965.*

M. L. ROSENTHAL

[Baraka's] poems and plays have explored the subjective
effects of the dominant whites' violation of black mentality,
and at the same time have acted out psychologically and in
fantasy the politics of intransigeant confrontation. No
American poet since Pound has come closer to making poetry and politics reciprocal forms of action. That is not necessarily a good thing. When the reciprocity comes out of
the very nature of the language and feeling that engage the
poet, when it amounts to a discovery as of the awakening of
the senses, then we have to do with an accomplishment
whose moral and aesthetic character are inseparable values:
as in *Hamlet* or *Coriolanus* or, less grandly, in Shelley's
glorious chorus in *Hellas:* "The world's great age begins
anew." In such work the quality of the poet's engagement
with truth makes him incapable of using language dishonestly. But in part of "BLACK DADA NIHILISMUS"
Baraka's political rhetoric cheapens his poem and dilutes its
intended but merely contrived barbaric ferocity. His catalogue of names, for example, places Lumumba in the same
category of race victims as characters in American comic
strips and radio serials, nightclub performers, and prize-
fighters, so that he weakens and at last loses the poem's
original incantatory force.

Even in this poem, however, . . . Baraka has not betrayed
himself entirely through an oversimplified rhetoric. He is
the victim of his own best human qualities, a man who refuses to let himself slide out from under the burdens of less
privileged black Americans. The psychological and political

dangers of his position are obvious, for his own problems of
poetic perspective are almost engulfed by the demands of
his insistent militancy. Many of his poems are the deliberate invention of an intellectual poet setting out to internalize the violence of the poor blacks' experience and convert
it into an equal and opposite reaction, and one just about as
acceptable as a promise of national enlightenment. But in
his best work he is guided by the subjective pressures underlying this process. (pp. 62-3)

It is easy to slip from the rigorous truthfulness of "An
Agony. As Now." to the easy political tendentiousness of
most of "BLACK DADA NIHILISMUS" and of the
many imitations of Baraka's work by younger black poets.
Understanding the *poetic* problems involved is essential to
do something more sustained in its achievement than Baraka has yet done. (p. 64)

> *M. L. Rosenthal, in* Salmagundi (*copyright*
> © *1973 by Skidmore College), Spring-Sum-
> mer, 1973.*

BARBARA MACKAY

[*Sidney Poet Heroical* is] a slick, semi-musical satire of
Sidney Poitier. In fact, Baraka's play attacks all blacks who
"make it big" in white society, forget their roots, and begin
to think, talk, and live "white." Much of Baraka's characterization is funny and effective: his portrait of Sidney's
egotistical, ruthless buddy and mentor who prances across
the stage in knee-high boots, skin-tight pants, and shirts
invariably open to subnavel levels, and his white she-devils
in glittery make-up, women propelled by extravagant sexual
and economic tastes, are clever exaggerations of America's
fortune-hunters and culture vultures.

But *Sidney Poet Heroical* . . . overworks the contrast between the bizarre, surrealistic white world and the more
realistic scenes from black life. The down-to-earth black
chorus that chides Sidney, warning him not to sell out, becomes predictable and tedious. So does the dizzy white
nymphomaniac, who continually shinnies up poor Sidney as
if he were some great phallic monument available to public
climbers.

Eventually, what begins as a witty analysis of human appetite (not specifically black or white) dwindles into a simplistic morality tale, resolved as if by magic. All Sidney has to
do is put on Black Muslim gear and chant a Muslim chant,
and the evil that threatened him disappears, the girlfriend
he abandoned when he married a white woman comes back
to him, and all is well in Sidney's little heaven. The Black
Muslim religion may be a potent force in the unification of
black people, but at the end of a theatrical farce it makes
for an incredible, heavy *deus ex machina.* (p. 52)

> *Barbara Mackay, in* Saturday Review (©
> *1975 by Saturday Review/World, Inc., re-
> printed with permission), July 12, 1975.*

CARLL TUCKER

Maybe humanism is not an adequate stand from which to
review Amiri Baraka's political diatribe "S-1." Maybe
devotion to a just perspective, temperate weighing of evidence, and fairness are luxuries that can no longer be afforded in our oppressed and ravaged society. . . .

But if the situation in America were as bad, or even potentially as bad, as Baraka suggests, then there would be no

call for this critique or this critic: We would have lost the battle for civility, compassion, and toleration that the American enterprise is all about and would have to relapse into silence or join the ranks of the shriekers.

Ordinarily, a piece of political claptrap like "S-1" would not be worth your attention. . . . With a message so powerful and persuasive, original packaging or marketing is presumed unnecessary. Since style evinces individuality, it is anathema. Stylelessness (itself a style; an automaton's style) is a virtue. The more execrable your art, the more absolute your faith.

Ordinarily . . . the fact that an Amiri Baraka wins high grades for faith and correspondingly low grades for art would be of no interest. But once, in a former life, Baraka was LeRoi Jones and scoring the reverse. Skeptical, angry, eloquent, with an active and original intelligence, Jones was a playwright and poet on whom not just blacks and militants, but all lovers of art were putting their faith and their bets. For a moment he radicalized our vision in the only way possible, by making us see in a new way a truth we've known but never recognized. But then LeRoi Jones died and comrade Baraka was born and even though one read occasionally about his political activities in Newark, one trusted that, if he chose, he could resume the path toward greatness as an artist.

Except for one brief moment in "S-1," when the children of an arrested couple, presumed innocents, turn out to be their parents' collaborators, Baraka's political concerns have abolished his dramatic sense. . . .

Baraka's problem as an artist is that, not hurt as much as he wishes he were, he must invent his affronts, fashion paper oppressors whom he can heroically oppose. LeRoi Jones wrote out of real, Amiri Baraka out of postulated hurt. The really hurt do not cry out in isms.

> *Carll Tucker, "You Don't Know, Mr. Baraka," in* The Village Voice *(reprinted by permission of* The Village Voice; *copyright © by The Village Voice, Inc., 1976), August 30, 1976, p. 83.*

SHERLEY ANNE WILLIAMS

Fifty years from now when negroes and others take "English," . . . they'll read: LeRoi Jones (aka Amiri Baraka) was at the cutting edge of mid-twentieth century American literature. Black Arts and Black Consciousness and Black Liberation will be explained away in a footnote like Harlem (a Negro area in New York) in the *Norton Anthology of Literature.* The process of cultural cannibalism, until now confined to black music, speech and dress, will have been extended to Afro-American literature.

Baraka's early association with the Beat poets, the finality with which, in his poetry, he shook off the dry husks of Pound, Williams, etc., and his political conversion to Marxist-Leninist-Maoist thought do place him within the tradition of Western literary radicalism. But cannibalism has become such an ingrained part of the American Way, that to say this seems . . . to exclude Baraka from an equal place in Afro-American experience. That is, the literary achievement of Baraka the radical, the black militant, is used to glorify what Stevie Wonder aptly calls "That Bad Luck Way." (pp. 435-36)

The major tension in Afro-American poetry has been the dialectic between the Euro-American literate tradition—the cultural assumptions as well as the body of texts which are based on those assumptions—and Afro-American oral culture—music, speech and the patterns of living out of which they are created. This tension is symbolized in the two "dialects" Afro-American poetry, the one based on standard English, the other on black vernacular speech. . . . [In] their drive toward technical excellence, Afro-American writers never really confronted the paradox that plain English and its literary traditions are vehicles of cultural domination. Thus, Afro-American writers were always in the position of unconsciously affirming their cultural inferiority even as they protested consciously and often vehemently against economic, political and social oppression. (p. 436)

If Baraka were ever haunted by the spectre of technical inferiority, it doesn't show up in his work. The classic volume of poetry, *The Dead Lecturer,* is a clear statement of his recognition that mastery of the standard English idiom has a political as well as an aesthetic dimension. In the "Crow Jane" sequence, the brilliant and biting attack on the decay of the West, his mastery of the idiom becomes a repudiation of the literary tradition as well. In "A Poem for Willie Best" and "*An Agony. As Now.,*" he inverts the symbolism of the mask, for the persona looks out at a third world of sun and cool air, separate from his inner world (the world which the iron mask of white society puts on the black mind). Still, the persona is inside the white world, "inside someone who hates me," perhaps inextricably bound to it. The mask becomes a metaphor for the black situation in this country, and for the black who, steeped in Western culture, comes to hate his own blackness because it is not white.

All this, of course, is a part of the more comprehensive analysis which gave rise to the black political movements of the sixties. But Baraka's impact on our literature might have gone unnoticed amongst us had it not been for his political activities, his consciously militant actions and his articulation of the philosophical system behind them. In combining theory with action, Baraka became our Malcolm and our DuBois, the bad man and the intellectual, now made one as writer. As one of the founders and chief movers of the Black Arts Movement, the movement whose central thesis is that art by Afro-Americans ought to contribute to the cause of black liberation, he continues to influence a whole generation of writers.

Here is the man who liberated our language, getting down in the streets, coining the phrases that fired the cities. And this was thunder to us. His wasn't the only voice raised, nor the only voice we listened to. But we hung in there long after Malcolm's other brothers—Carmichael, Cleaver, Brown, *et al.*—had been driven or retreated into exile or murdered. And, as a writer, he came closest to articulating a necessary fusion of politics and aesthetics, making that fusion a potent political force. The cosmetic features of Black Consciousness—dress, hairstyle, catch phrases— were merely a reflection of deeper changes taking place within our collective psyche. Baraka now rightly repudiates the regressive excesses, the sheer lunacy of the extreme positions which he helped to dignify in the name of liberation and "Pan-African" morality, but his work remains a testament to our recognition that we exist as a people in our own literary and intellectual tradition. (pp. 436-37)

> *Sherley Anne Williams, "Anonymous in*

America,'' in boundary 2 *(copyright* © boundary 2, *1978), Winter, 1978, pp. 435-42.*

P. J. LASKA

Hard Facts is a self-consciously communist poetry book, right down to the red cover with the silhouettes of Marx-Engels-Lenin-Stalin-Mao on the back. Baraka's consciousness is committed to class struggle and his poetics is materialist, but it too often falls short of dialectics. . . . [There] is the bad mouthing of the phonies with a hot stream of scream-of-consciousness hip talk mixed with revolutionary exhortations. All of which breaks our ear rather than sings to our needs. An atheist preacher is still a preacher, and one wonders how much respect for the multinational masses is really there. I'm reminded of a line from Baraka's earlier *Preface to a Twenty Volume Suicide Note:* ''Nobody sings anymore.''

Song is what's missing from Baraka's list of what the people need from poets.

Wedged in between the revolutionary rhetoric there are a couple of poems that let you know Baraka is still a major poetic voice. (p. 115)

A problem for political poetry is that of achieving an abstract statement raised up from the materials and linked dialectically with the content. A political poet runs the risk of assertion. Baraka's assertion has the fierce intensity characteristic of left-wing sectarian attitudes. (p. 116)

P. J. Laska, in The Minnesota Review *(© 1978 by* The Minnesota Review*), Spring, 1978.*

*   *   *

BARTH, John   1930-

Barth, an American novelist and short story writer, is a skillful parodist, satirizing language and literary style, the tools of his craft, as well as social and moral conventions. Fascinated with literary theory, Barth explores in his novels the complexities of myth and the traditional concept of the hero in literature. (See also *CLC*, Vols. 1, 2, 3, 5, 7, 9, and *Contemporary Authors*, Vols. 1-4, rev. ed.)

JOHN HAWKES

[Barth's] awareness of the right word and manipulations of ''voice'' are brilliant and sometimes devastating. Barth's wit—his word-play, his verbal parody, his subtle ridicule of everything pretentious, banal, ignorant, pedestrian—is clearly inseparable from his basic fictional impulses. The word ''flabbergasting'' is appropriate to Barth himself as fiction writer, but it is not appropriate to me as fiction writer. On the other hand, my own heavier cadences and ''darker'' voice—''coldness, ruthless determination to expose, ridicule, attack''—do not seem to me to be at all appropriate to Barth. . . .

If Barth and I are not concerned with realism, not even with psychological realism, nonetheless we are both working with psychic substance or substance of the mind, are both starting with the materials of psychic or cerebral derangement in our efforts to arrive at ''aesthetic bliss.'' Barth's imagination *is* in fact a kind of higher-fi system out of which he creates new landscapes of mental existence. . . . (p. 20)

[To] me Barth's desire to ''re-invent the world'' as opposed to my own desire to ''create a world,'' means that he is a writer who perceives the threatening irrationality of total consciousness, whereas I am a writer who perceives the threatening ''rationality'' of the unconscious. Barth's total consciousness is comic nightmare, my sometimes comic nightmare creates its own frightening sense.

As soon as we turn to [Barth's] *The Floating Opera* . . . and to [my] *Second Skin* . . . , we discover once more a catalogue of alarming parallels. Both novels are told in the first person, both are comic treatments of death, both are concerned with derangement, unreality and the pain of sexual experience. Both novels are about the imagination and about the writing of novels, and both end, finally, as grudging or sardonic or tenuous or hard-won affirmations of life. (pp. 20-1)

The Floating Opera and *Second Skin* are both novels that deal compulsively with physical desire, sexual impotence, and sadism. Both novels represent a facing down of suicidal impulses, both are told by morally reprehensible narrators and yet, at the same time, represent satiric treatments of conventional morality. In each case the writer knows more than his narrator, of course. But in each case these two narrators may be taken as comic representations of the writers themselves, and the differences between *The Floating Opera* and *Second Skin*, and between Barth and myself.

These differences are evident in the story-telling purposes as well as in the personalities of the two narrators. That is, as *lawyer* Todd Andrews tells his story in order to make sense of it, or in order to exemplify the ''reasoning'' (an excitingly ''demented'' reasoning, to be sure) which accounts for the actions and decisions of his life. In *Second Skin*, however, Skipper is talking, reconstructing his past life, not for the sake of ostensible understanding but in order to keep himself alive, is compulsively attempting to talk himself literally into continued existence, and this emerges as an historionic sensibility. The ''thinking'' Todd Andrews, however, emerges as a colloquial, controlled, legalistic, clever, sometimes sadistic, sometimes demented jokester, the kind of man who, speaking of his heart trouble, can say that ''each soft beat my sick heart beats might be my sick heart's last.'' His rational narration is a mixture of serious thought, intellectual game, sardonic rhetoric, and satire on the function and value of logic. For Skipper there is no logic, except the ''logic'' of violent coincidence and purely sensuous association. (p. 22)

[There] is a decided refraction between Barth's non-fiction voice and Todd's poignant or outrageous flights of rhetoric. But at any rate, the ''flabbergasting'' plot of *The Floating Opera* supports the assumption that Todd's three peach baskets full of notes are in fact a parody of Barth's own view of the ordering process in fiction. This plot, depending as it does on knowledge of law and legal machinations, and on knowledge of philosophy and complicated systems of logic, further supports the idea that Barth's novelistic intelligence—whatever else we may say about it—is encyclopedic. Figuratively speaking, Barth's ''notes'' cover every subject from boat-building to courtroom procedure; the plot of *The Floating Opera* is a plan as careful and elaborate and shockingly humorous as, say, the plan of the anarchists who, in Conrad's time, attempted to blow up the Greenwich Royal Observatory. . . .

The Floating Opera/ plot/total consciousness (artifice); *Second Skin/* association/dream (vision)—in this way we might phrase these two novels as "polar opposites." To do so is to "point up" differences which in turn suggest analogy and bring us back to the dominant working requirement revealed in *The Floating Opera* and *Second Skin*. That is, both of these novels centralize "the shadow of the self-inflicted death of the father," and for all their differences (or because of their differences) everything within these novels functions toward this end. (p. 24)

[There is] the evident creative pleasure Barth takes in his plot. Were it not for the fact that Barth's "tuning up" of plot also amounts to a "tuning up" of his narrator's voice, the Harrison Mack "inheritance" sub-plot might well be no more than comic idea. But when Barth contrives the resolution of this sub-plot so that it hinges on a hundred and twenty-nine pickle jars filled with the bodily waste of Harrison Mack Senior, he transforms law, philosophy, death, money, reason and unreason into a palpable scatological reality that sets up a sudden new melodic reverberation in Todd Andrews' voice. (p. 26)

To extend and withdraw, to engage and alienate, to open and close the stops of his language—surely this . . . exemplifies the true pitch of Barth's method as he first discovered it. . . . Barth's creative thrust, we feel, was all in terms of . . . conscious tactic which is, again, aimed at the gross unsettling of consciousness (or of rationality). . . . Barth's truly artistic "reach" is toward the abstraction and incongruity of the narrator's . . . statements: "One doesn't concern oneself with trifles at one's father's grave. One is concerned with reasons." The first statement is true. The last, of course, could not be more unreasonable. . . . [It] pleases me that Barth should return to childhood when attempting to uncover the worst of all fears, since obviously childhood is the true world or source of imaginative strength. And yet I quicken as well to the glazed excitement of what appears to be the deepest of Barth's fictional purposes: to extend fiction into a realm of pure and lively and fearful paradox, to cloak abstractions of the human voice in the comic clothes of humanity, to reinvent the world's language. He has gone nearly this far, I think, in his novel *Giles Goat-Boy.* (p. 28)

> *John Hawkes, "'The Floating Opera' and 'Second Skin',"* in MOSAIC: A Journal for the Study of Literature and Ideas *(copyright © 1974 by the University of Manitoba Press; acknowledgment of previous publication is herewith made), Vol. VIII, No. 1 (Fall, 1974), pp. 17-28.*

JAMES F. WALTER

The theme of interior disorder and illness caused by a division between human faculties which naturally complement each other in the act of knowing is, of course, a common one in Western literature; a certain vein of that literature, however, which extends to us from the satires of a Syrian Cynic named Menippus, takes this theme as its primary obsession. Thus we must place *Giles Goat-Boy* among the works of that vein, including *The Satyricon, Gargantua and Pantagruel, The Praise of Folly, Don Quixote, Gulliver's Travels,* and *Tristram Shandy,* in order to understand and evaluate it. *Giles Goat-Boy* is neither novel, tragedy, romance, or epic, nor is it a simple allegory; although it shares much with works in these traditional genres, it re-

mains aloof from all of them, primarily through an extravagant spirit of parody which holds nothing sacred finally except the integrity of its hero's vision, arrived at through an epic glut of experience and ideas ranging across the vast spectrum of possibilities.

An essential characteristic differentiating the Menippean satire from the novel is its attempt to reach the extreme limits of human experience—physical and intellectual, farcical and serious, obscene and sacred, comic and tragic—at the same time. . . . Menippean satire aims at the tranquil stability in knowledge and experience possessed by "kindergarteners," but it is a stability to be enjoyed only on the far side of the doubts, divisions, conflicts, and dead ends experienced by men fully wise about the world. (pp. 395-96)

The growth of George Giles, hero of *Giles Goat-Boy,* into the wisdom of the middle way is long and painful, carrying him from mindless childish innocence to a tested stoic wisdom. (p. 396)

George's westward quest is probably the richest in allegorical parody of any in the Menippean tradition. His quest is that of Everyman to find his place. But Barth enhances the significance of his journey by allusions to nearly all of the great quest literature in the Western tradition. George is at the same time a representative of the Israelites crossing the River Jordan into the Promised Land and one of the Billy Goats Gruff passing the Troll into greener pastures. The Quixote parallels are obvious as are those with Dante's descent. George is Sir Galahad faced with perilous ordeals, as he is Pilgrim faced by the Wicket Gate. And he is Aeneas dallying with Dido, as well as Odysseus the external adventurer. These parallels function not only to extend the imaginative resonance of George's quest; since many of them are conscious in the mind of the hero, they are also symptomatic of the bookishness of his knowledge and, hence, of his naïveté about getting along in the human way. George's deficiencies as a Grand Tutor, it is clear, are not merely goatish, they are also godlike: imagining that the world he has prefabricated in his mind is the real one, he operates on the dangerous assumption that the external world will readily conform itself to his will. (p. 398)

Besides being an important actor, WESCAC [the computer] is one of Barth's most complex symbols in the satire. As an arch element in modern technology, the computer is a natural symbol for the whole urban, industrial, bureaucratic way of life that this technology supports. Thus WESCAC symbolizes on a psychological level the abstracting, analytical powers of the agent intellect and the expansion of the natural sciences which has made this way of life possible. But in a more universal psychological dimension it represents simply the searching, conceptualizing, discriminating powers of the mind which have been essential to all great human achievements and civilizations. . . .

WESCAC also has a historical symbolic dimension since in the last century or so it had "cut the last cords to its progenitor and commenced a life of its own." In this dimension it represents a habit of mind bequeathed by Descartes, a working assumption that the clear and distinct categories of science are the only valid ways of knowing truth. Consequently, as a means for the systematic and "scientific" categorization of all human concerns, the nearly absolute hegemony of WESCAC (and its less sophisticated twin, EASCAC) is proof of the loss of the imaginative faculty in modern man; its domineering presence is both result and cause of man's failure to respond wholly to the objects of his experience, with his senses and heart as well as his mind. Modern man, the satire suggests, has generally lost that spiritual vision of the passive intellect by which the existential mysteries of the heart are intuited directly, as a landscape is taken in by the eye. (p. 399)

Yet in spite of its limitations and its active trollery at times WESCAC is not finally the archdemon of the satire. In the satire's topography, which is an allegory of the human soul, WESCAC is shown to be dependent for its energy on Maurice Stoker's Power Plant. . . . Stoker's Power Plant . . . , besides being an emblem of the tremendous forces in physical nature, also represents the subconscious psychic energies, often lawless and destructive, in man. George's journey into that region is a parody of all similar epic and romance descents, which ritualistically enact and signify the hero's coming to terms with the various parts of the self —the evil and the good, the flesh and the spirit, the light and the dark. (p. 400)

The real dragon of George's quest . . . is not any single human faculty, person, or institution; rather it is an intellectual attitude which creates schisms among things and acts which are parts of a whole.

These schisms start in the individual soul when the WESCAC in each of us deracinates itself from natural feeling and holistic intuition in an attempt to become the sole censor of truth. The result is a rejection of what our hearts and spirits know, particularly the knowledge of value, which alone gives meaning and purpose to our lives. As this schism spreads to the social order, it manifests itself in a variety of ways: in religion it is the proliferation of sects, secular and otherwise, which rush in to fill the moral vacuum once faith has been lost; in education it is the bureaucratization of curricula into increasingly specialized and exclusive departments, each with its own method, even when the subject of study, the nature of man, remains unitary; in politics it is the conflict of the urban intellectual against the rural folk; in economics it is capitalism's glorification of private greed against socialism's glorification of public greed; and in personal relationships it is the harsh scrutiny of all motives by the method of psychological analysis and the consequent formulation of individuals into types.

The knowledge of self that George initiates in Stoker's Power Plant is not by any means brought to its maturation there, nor can it be; his descent, like Dante's into hell, is not so much for knowledge of the good as for knowledge of human sin and internal deficiency. (pp. 400-01)

[Because] of its multiplicity and ever-changing variety, the Menippean scene is one impossible to grasp from a point of immersion within it; and yet it defies analysis and understanding by the aloof who are inexperienced in its ways. Whoever would come to terms with it must first enter the whirlpool and become its victim before emerging its victor. Or, in another figure, it is, like Dante's hell, one of those dragons into whose bowels one must first descend before ascending into light.

George enters into this whirlpool by stages, through a steady accumulation of experiences. (p. 402)

This tragic theme of moral insight gained through suffering,

clarified despite the burlesque terms of its presentation, is important to what follows in Barth's satire. Although George Giles does not have to become blind to see, several of the other characters are so limited in self-knowledge that the introspection forced by blindness is their only way to wisdom. All of the characters, including George, have to suffer some sort of tragic fall as the means to growth. (p. 403)

[Suffering] which brings the victim deeper into the hollows of the self is not alone the key to spiritual and imaginative maturity. Indeed suffering is useless if it is not accompanied by a reach beyond the self in love. This is the significance of Anastasia (her name means literally "of the resurrection") in the satire. Besides being a simple female person, her couplings with an epic variety of characters suggest that she embodies a universal principle of being: she is the eternal feminine, foil to the self-aggrandizing impetus of WESCAC. The duty she imposes on George, consequently, is somehow to mediate between the masculine and feminine forces, a polarity common in satirical allegories. (p. 406)

The symbolic measure of George's understanding of [the] "female elements" within himself, and hence of the health of his imagination, is his increasing empathy with Anastasia. (p. 407)

Except for a few personal discoveries, *Giles Goat-Boy* ends pretty much where it began. Studentdom in general has refused to reform, and the old chaotic order that preceded George on the Campus Mall will continue. . . .

[The] controlling current in the satire is tragic. But it is more stoic than cynical: in spite of the losses and the decline there is a gain, signified by Anastasia's pregnancy after her long sterility among men too diseased to make her fertile. There is also a newfound, almost childlike joy in the imagination's rediscovery of the world's body. . . .

Barth's world, finally, is the one described in Max's cyclological theory "founded on such correspondences as that between the celestial and the psychic day, the seasons of the year, the stages of ordinary human life, the growth and decline of individual colleges, the evolution and history of studentdom as a whole, the ultimate fate of the University, and what had we." . . . As always, life and death follow one another in their fated, ineluctable circle. (p. 408)

There are many flaws in *Giles Goat-Boy*. . . . [Tedious] repetition . . . bloats a good deal of it. The Christian reader must find its unrelieved stoic irresolution and the private, muted tone of its celebration deficient. In aesthetic terms, this irresolution, heightened by questions raised in the "posttape" and "postscript to the posttape," suggests uncertainty in the author's intention; but this is to judge the work by the criteria of the novel. Menippean vision sees a world always in process so it admits of no resolution within that world. Also, the allegory throughout is flat, the characters absurdly two-dimensional. But stylized characters are of the essence of the genre. They are not so much to be rejected as to be sublimated by the art of the maker, and this Barth generally achieves simply by the epic range of his imagination and a continuous interlacement of his two-dimensional characters in complex three-dimensional situations. Finally, the first-person narration, especially as it is adjusted to the confining terms of the beast-fable, leaves doubtful the authenticity of the hero's growth. Too often his interior changes are simply reported and do not seem to have any necessary relation to dramatic incident. But again, these are more the limitations of the genre than of the particular work. Most Menippean satires, because they are concerned primarily with intellectual attitudes and interior order, depend on the first-person narrator point-of-view. And the goat-fable is what is most charming about *Giles Goat-Boy*, lending the specific quality to its world.

Barth's satire, then, like the WESCAC that "read it out," is indeed a monster—but no Troll. The only way to come to terms with it is to imitate its hero re-placing the Founder's Scroll: you must eat it "shard by shard" until it lives within you. That is of course the only way that any literature, including the vast body of it that *Giles Goat-Boy* parodies, ever lives. (p. 409)

> James F. Walter, "A Psychology of Lust in the Menippean Tradition: 'Giles Goat-Boy'," in Twentieth Century Literature (copyright 1974, Hofstra University Press), December, 1975, pp. 394-409.

ROBERT MARTIN ADAMS

The sequence in [*Lost in the Funhouse*] leads us from the meditations of a sperm through the boyhood adventures of Ambrose to the mythical life history of an anonymous Homeric bard marooned on a desert island and forced to create a life-work out of his own life. From infancy through childhood, and then to the province of the mythical, Barth seems intent on writing large that wonderful sentence of Joyce's, "God becomes man becomes fish becomes barnacle goose becomes featherbed mountain." One thing is largely omitted, to be sure; that is the development of the individual sensibility. We leave Ambrose before he has become much more than a very embryonic artist; and what takes his place in the latter part of the book is simply the narrative process itself.

In playing the games of self-consciousness, Barth is in his own sportive element; he delights in sound-box, mirror, and echo effects, which turn every story into a wry questioning of its own processes. He raids an imaginary textbook on fiction for comments on the fiction that's being told, takes over the mind of a writer complaining about the process of writing, or enters into a story bewailing the mode of its own existence. His mythological fables are contaminated by an awareness that they are already mythological, but they are also cast, not just linguistically but motivationally, in the mode of the present. Most of Barth's mythological figures are in fact self-conscious writers, mocked by their own clichés and trapped by their own narrative reflexes. Character thus diminishes into the jokes and paradoxes of a quick-trick dialectic that's always pretty much the same, whatever the name attached to it. It's a spry and elegant kind of funny; but it's often very private too, and there's a lot of protesting—half dramatic, half quite personal as I hear it—against the narrow twists and turns of thought compressed by its own means of expression.

In fact Barth makes use of mythology, when he does so—in *Chimera* as well as *Lost in the Funhouse*—for ... limited and defined purposes. ... He feels the classical world, or that of the Arabian Nights, as decisively distant and different from the casual, colloquial American dialect in which his retellings are cast. He sometimes puts so much new wine in his old bottles that they bulge alarmingly, and comi-

cally, far out of their original shape. ... Barth is a joker who gets most of his jokes from cross-cultural incongruities. In the process not only the original fable but the identity of the reteller is remarkably attenuated. There's little that's positive about Barth's artist-in-the-making. He is programmed to run through the funhouse of his own personality, as through the museum of the world's cultures, more in terror and anxiety than in delight. He is also afflicted with a terrible sense of *déjà vu*. The funhouse has been here a long time, we have visited it before, and it's a closed experience in any case, because it always bends the story-teller back into the corridors of his own story. (pp. 185-86)

[Barth] seems to prefer mythological skeletons that we have known very well on the formal pages of Bulfinch, so he can set them to jigging by means of his own nervous syncopations. Indeed, the big pastiche- and burlesque-novels—*The Sot-Weed Factor* and *Giles Goat-Boy*—are more spacious and outward, but over the long run they fall into another trap, when the capering narrator outwears his welcome. It's an old complaint, that a narrator who walks in front of his puppets splits the reader's interest, and risks making his story or himself seem intrusive. In the shorter fiction, there is really no center of interest apart from the story and its teller, who are one. But in the big fictions, the novelist is perceptibly present behind his capering creations, yet he isn't present enough to be felt as a deepening of the story. (p. 186)

Barth is a serious comic novelist, with more interest in language than in character, a performer and even a bit of a clown. ... [And] he gives evidence of a careful reading of Joyce. His prose, in its rhythms and concentrated impressionism, reminds one of Joyce again and again: its rendering of experience, by slipping from object into mind and back again, is exactly similar. And yet there's one great difference, as a result of which one leaves Barth ... with a sense of thinness and insubstantiality. His books seem written to be read at a rapid canter, catch as catch can, take it or leave it. Even Barthian puzzles aren't heavily elaborated like Joycean labyrinths; reading them the second or third time over is like reading them the first. It's not to be expected, of course, that a man will write in palimpsest who doesn't see the world in palimpsest; Barth isn't worse as a writer because he's less weighty—only different. My own sense is that miniatures constitute his best work so far—and that, in its own terms, is praise. (p. 187)

> Robert Martin Adams, in his AfterJoyce: Studies in Fiction After "Ulysses" (copyright © 1977 by Robert Martin Adams; reprinted by permission of Oxford University Press, Inc.), Oxford University Press, 1977.

*   *   *

BECKETT, Samuel   1906-

Beckett is an Irish-born playwright, novelist, poet, critic, essayist, short story writer, and translator who now resides in Paris and writes predominantly in French. In Beckett's drama, the traditional literary concepts of time, place, dramatic language, and character are suspended, as the playwright explores the meaning of existence and its presentation. The viewer is presented with fragments of sentences in the place of dialogue, and characters whose identities and even names remain in question. The recipient of the Nobel Prize in 1969,

Beckett continues to influence contemporary drama and to inspire critical exegesis as perhaps no one else has in contemporary literature. (See also *CLC*, Vols. 1,2,3,4,6,9, and *Contemporary Authors*, Vols. 5-8, rev. ed.)

ALAIN ROBBE-GRILLET

The human condition, Heidegger says, is *to be there*. Probably it is the theater, more than any other mode of representing reality, which reproduces this situation most naturally. The dramatic character *is on stage*, that is his primary quality: he is *there*.

Samuel Beckett's encounter with this requirement afforded a priori, an exceptional interest: at last we would see Beckett's man, we would see *Man*. For the novelist, by carrying his explorations ever farther, managed only to reduce more on every page our possibilities of apprehending him. (p. 111)

Thus all these creatures which have paraded past us served only to deceive us; they occupied the sentences of the novel in place of the ineffable being who still refuses to appear there, the man incapable of recuperating his own existence, the one who never manages to be present.

But now we are in the theater. And the curtain goes up. . . .

The set represents nothing, or just about. (p. 112)

This is called *Waiting for Godot*. The performance lasts nearly three hours.

From this point of view alone, there is something surprising: during these three hours, the play *holds together*, without a hollow, though it consists of nothing but emptiness, without a break, though it would seem to have no reason to continue or to conclude. From beginning to end, the audience follows; it may lose countenance sometimes, but remains somehow compelled by these two beings, who do nothing, who say virtually nothing, who have no other quality than to be present.

From the very first performance, the virtually unanimous critics have emphasized the *public* character of the spectacle. As a matter of fact, the words "experimental theater" no longer apply here: what we have is simply theater, which everyone can see, from which everyone immediately derives his enjoyment.

Is this to say that no one misjudges it? Of course not. *Godot* is misjudged in every way, just as everyone misjudges his own misery. There is no lack of explanations, which are offered from every side, left and right, each more futile than the next.

Godot is God. Don't you see that the word is the diminutive of the root-word *God* which the author has borrowed from his mother tongue? After all, why not? Godot—why not, just as well?—is the earthly ideal of a better social order. Do we not aspire to a better life, better food, better clothes, as well as to the possibility of no longer being beaten? And this Pozzo, who is precisely *not* Godot—is he not the man who keeps thought enslaved? Or else Godot is death: tomorrow we will hang ourselves, if it does not come all by itself. Godot is silence; we must speak *while waiting for it*: in order to have the right, ultimately, to keep still. Godot is that inaccessible *self* Beckett pursues through his entire *oeuvre*, with this constant hope: "This time, perhaps, it will be me, at last."

But these images, even the most ridiculous ones, which thus try as best they can to limit the damages, do not obliterate from anyone's mind the reality of the drama itself, that part which is both the most profound and quite superficial, about which there is nothing else to say: Godot is that character for whom two tramps are waiting at the edge of a road, and who does not come.

As for Gogo and Didi, they refuse even more stubbornly any other signification than the most banal, the most immediate one: they are men. And their situation is summed up in this simple observation, beyond which it does not seem possible to advance: they are *there*, they are on the stage.

Attempts doubtless already existed, for some time, which rejected the stage movement of the bourgeois theater. *Godot*, however, marks in this realm a kind of finality. Nowhere had the risk been so great, for what is involved this time, without ambiguity, is what is essential; nowhere, moreover, have the means employed been so *poor;* yet never, ultimately, has the margin of misunderstanding been so negligible. (pp. 114-16)

What does *Waiting for Godot* offer us? It is hardly enough to say that nothing happens in it. That there should be neither complications nor plot of any kind has already been the case on other stages. Here, it is *less than nothing*, we should say: as if we were watching a kind of regression *beyond* nothing. As always in Samuel Beckett, what little had been given to us at the start—and which seemed to be nothing—is soon corrupted before our eyes, degraded further, like Pozzo who returns deprived of sight, dragged on by Lucky deprived of speech—and like, too, that carrot which in the second act is no longer anything but a radish. . . .

"This is becoming really insignificant," one of the vagabonds says at this point. "Not enough," says the other. And a long silence punctuates his answer.

It will be evident, from these two lines, what distance we have come from the verbal delirium [found in theater before Beckett]. From start to finish, the dialogue of *Godot* is *moribund*, extenuated, constantly located at those frontiers of agony where all of Beckett's "heroes" move, concerning whom we often cannot even be certain that they are still on this side of their death. (pp. 116-17)

As for the argument, it is summarized in four words: "We're waiting for Godot"—which continually recur, like a refrain. But like a stupid and tiresome refrain, for such waiting interests no one; it does not possess, as waiting, the slightest stage value. It is neither a hope, nor an anguish, nor even a despair. It is barely an alibi.

In this general dilapidation, there is a kind of culminating point—that is to say, under the circumstances, the reverse of a culminating point: a nadir, an oubliette. . . . There is nothing left on stage but [a] wriggling, whining heap, in which we then observe Didi's face light up as he says, in a voice almost calm again, "We are men!" (pp. 117-18)

Thought, even subversive thought, always has something reassuring about it. Speech—beautiful language—is reassuring too. How many misunderstandings a noble and harmonious discourse has created, serving as a mask either for ideas or for their absence!

Here, no misunderstanding: in *Godot* there is no more

thought than there is beautiful language; neither one nor the other figures in the text except in the form of parody, of *inside out* once again, or of corpse. (p. 118)

Over seventy centuries of analysis and metaphysics have a tendency, instead of making us modest, to conceal from us the weakness of our resources when it comes to essentials. As a matter of fact, everything happens as if the real importance of a question was measured, precisely, by our incapacity to apply honest thinking to it, unless to make it retrogress.

It is this movement—this dangerously contagious retrogression—which all of Beckett's work suggests. (p. 120)

[Despite the disintegration around them, the] two tramps remain intact, unchanged. Hence we are certain, this time, that they are not mere marionettes whose role is confined to concealing the absence of the protagonist. It is not this Godot they are supposed to be waiting for *who has "to be,"* but they, Didi and Gogo.

We grasp at once, as we watch them, this major function of theatrical representation: to show of what the fact of *being there* consists. For it is this, precisely, which we had not yet seen on a stage, or in any case which we had not seen so clearly, with so few concessions. The dramatic character, in most cases, merely *plays a role,* like the people around us who evade their own existence. In Beckett's play, on the contrary, everything happens as if the two tramps were on stage *without having a role.*

They *are there;* they must explain themselves. But they do not seem to have a text prepared beforehand and scrupulously learned by heart, to support them. They must invent. They are free.

Of course, this freedom is without any use: just as they have nothing to recite, they have nothing to *invent* either; and their conversation, which no plot sustains, is reduced to ridiculous fragments. . . . The only thing they are not free to do is to leave, to cease *being there:* they must remain because they are waiting for Godot. . . . They will still be there the next day, the day after that, and so on . . . *tomorrow and tomorrow and tomorrow . . . from day to day* . . . alone on stage, standing there, futile, without past or future, irremediably present.

But then man himself, who is there before our eyes, ends by disintegrating in his turn. The curtain rises on a new play: *Endgame,* an "old endgame lost of old," specifies Hamm, the protagonist.

No more than his predecessors, Didi and Gogo, has Hamm the possibility of leaving to go elsewhere. But the reason for this has become tragically physical: he is paralyzed, sitting in an armchair in the middle of the stage, and he is blind. Around him nothing but high bare walls, without accessible windows. Clov, a kind of attendant, half-impotent himself, tends as well as he can to the moribund Hamm: he manages to take him for a "turn," dragging the latter's chair on its casters around the edge of the stage, along the walls.

In relation to the two tramps, Hamm has therefore lost that ridiculous freedom they still possessed: it is no longer he who chooses *not to leave.* When he asks Clov to build a raft and to put him on it, in order to abandon his body to the ocean currents, it can this time only be a joke; as if

Hamm, by immediately abandoning this project, were trying to give himself the illusion of a choice. As a matter of fact, he appears to us somehow imprisoned in his retreat; if he has no desire to emerge from it, he now does not have the means to do so either. This is a notable difference: the question for man is no longer one of affirming a position, but of suffering a fate.

And yet, within his prison, he still performs a parody of choice. . . . (pp. 120-22)

[Even in the] final image, we come back to the essential theme of *presence:* everything that is *is here,* off-stage there is only nothingness, nonbeing. It is not enough that Clov, up on a ladder to get to the tiny windows that open onto the outside pseudo-world, informs us with a phrase as to the landscape: an empty gray sea on one side and a desert on the other. In reality this sea, this desert—invisible, moreover, to the spectator—are uninhabitable in the strictest sense of the word: as much as a back cloth would be, on which might be painted the water or the sand. (p. 123)

[Everything] is present in time as it is in space. To this ineluctable *here* corresponds an eternal *now:* "Yesterday! What does that mean? Yesterday!" Hamm exclaims several times. And the conjunction of space and time merely affords, with regard to a possible third character, this certitude: "If he exists he'll die there or he'll come here."

Without past, without place elsewhere, without any future but death, the universe thus defined is necessarily deprived of sense in the two acceptations of the term in French: it excludes any ideas of *direction* as well as any *signification.*

Hamm is suddenly struck by a doubt: "We're not beginning to . . . to . . . mean something?" he asks with feeling. Clov immediately reassures him: "Mean something! You and I, mean something! *(Brief laugh.)* Ah that's a good one!"

But this waiting for death, this physical misery which grows worse, these threats Hamm brandishes at Clov ("One day you'll be blind, like me. You'll be sitting there, a speck in the void, in the dark, for ever, like me. One day you'll say . . . I'm hungry, I'll get up and get something to eat. But you won't get up . . ."), all this gradual rot of the present constitutes, in spite of everything, a future.

Whence the fear of "meaning something" is perfectly justified: by this accepted consciousness of a tragic development, the world has thereby recovered its whole signification.

And in parallel, before such a threat (this future simultaneously terrible and fatal), one can say that the present is no longer anything, that it disappears, conjured away in its turn, lost in the general collapse. (pp. 123-24)

[Finally] Hamm is driven to the acknowledgment of his failure: "I was never there. Clov! . . . I was never there . . . Absent, always. It all happened without me. . . ."

Once again the fatal trajectory has been made. Hamm and Clov, successors to Gogo and Didi, have again met with the common fate of all Beckett's characters: Pozzo, Lucky, Murphy, Molloy, Malone, Mahood, Worm, etc.

The stage, privileged site of *presence,* has not resisted the contagion for long. The progress of the disease has occurred at the same sure rate as in the narratives. After having believed for a moment that we had grasped the real man, we are then obliged to confess our mistake. Didi was only an illusion, that is doubtless what gave him that dancing gait, swaying from one leg to the other, that slightly clownlike costume.... He, too, was only the creature of a dream, temporary in any case, quickly falling back into the realm of dreams and fiction.

"I was never there," Hamm says, and in the face of this admission nothing else counts, for it is impossible to understand it other than in its most general form: *No one was ever there.* (pp. 124-25)

> *Alain Robbe-Grillet, "Samuel Beckett, or Presence on the Stage" (1953 and 1957), in his* For a New Novel: Essays on Fiction, *translated by Richard Howard (reprinted by permission of Grove Press, Inc.; copyright © 1965 by Grove Press, Inc.), Grove Press, 1965, pp. 111-25.*

GERMAINE BRÉE

Samuel Beckett's fictional world, especially *Watt*, contains a quasi-Rabelaisian parody of all the rhetorical and logical devices that have permitted Western man, like Beckett's Ubu-esque creation, the "man-pot" Mahood, to hold a "partially waterproof tarpaulin" over his skull. Describing, reasoning, discussing, examining—Beckett's characters never tire of these activities, though no two of them proceed in exactly the same way. They share our "deplorable mania" not only for "when something happens wanting to know what" but furthermore for wanting, like Watt, to know why. Beckett is thus something of a contemporary Faust who, through the agency of his characters, indiscriminately, and with ferocious humor, undermines all our past and present attempts to give reality an intelligible structure, to "think out" our human situation. (p. 74)

Like Joyce, perhaps still more than Joyce, Beckett seems marked by the scholasticism of his philosophy classes at Trinity College. We can find many traces of it in his imaginary world. Descartes and Geulincx are perhaps given an important role in his early novels because they broke with the great intellectual tradition which from Plato to Thomas Aquinas, via Aristotle, conceived creation as a moving hierarchy of creatures oriented toward a perfect and definitive form, a final cause, God. Descartes thus unintentionally prepared the way for Beckett's "great articulates"—creatures whose special articulation, in body, thought or speech, even though sadly defective, makes them forget that they are really "frightened vagabonds," willy-nilly dragging aimlessly along, dying by degrees, while words and images spin round and round inside their bony white skulls. Skulls, jars, rooms, or other habitations, and the monotonous surrounding "country" form the two inseparable and rhythmically alternating settings for the adventures of Beckett's great articulates: beings who travel, or rather wander, toward some illusory "home" or "refuge," telling each other their adventures, while their dual disarticulation proceeds insidiously, "by direct route."

Beckett's characters seem to parody the pre-Copernican theory that all incomplete and abortive forms move toward that which perfects them by completing them. They are strangely intent on travel if only in spirit, even when bedridden or "in jars," or on relating their travels; they seek one another and form unstable couples when, for a few brief moments, one seems to appear in order to complete the other.... Identified with each in turn, yet each time reemerging, modified by the contact, just as the different characters emerge from one another, there always finally remains he who is known only by his voice, a voice which, as a matter of fact, is not his own, the nameless one who is "alone here, the first and last" and nonetheless is never there, the animator of this verbal cosmos and source of its Logos, like the God of Genesis.

Murphy, tied to his rocking-chair by seven scarfs, attempting to attain perfect repose through an increasingly frenetic rocking can hardly fail to remind us, however vaguely, of certain Thomistic categories: that, for example, of celestial beings halfway between God and terrestrial beings who, since they are endowed with essential forms, know no other kind of movement than that of movement in repose. Murphy's ignominious fall, hindside foremost—which does not in the least discourage Murphy himself—is but the first of a whole series of falls precipitating Beckett's characters, one after the other, into any and every muddy ditch. Beckett thus brings out both the pathos and absurdity of our mental postures by grossly simplifying them and turning them into concrete situations which his characters act out physically: Pim (whose identity merges with that of the narrator of *How It Is*), his shoulders firmly encircled by an arm whose hand plunges into his bag, crawling in the mud with a can opener, his main educational toool, between his buttocks, is the latest, and strangest, of Beckett's fantastic inventions. (pp. 75-6)

A Beckett character's means of locomotion is a piece of factual evidence, a *donnée* such as might be discerned by an inhuman eye observing the successive variations each infinitesimal character brings to the continuous, irresistible movement carrying it along into the interior of an unchanging countryside.

Beckett's cosmos retains a few traces of the medieval sky, "a world up there" occasionally glimpsed "in the blue," far from the mud and excrements. Although the episodes in *Murphy* are located, with Joycean precision, in London and Beckett's early environment near Dublin, where *Watt* also begins and ends, the scenes of the succeeding novels become progressively vague.... [After] *Watt*, Beckett's characters evolve in a setting which is, on the whole, more in the tradition of Dante or of Milton; we sense a familiar metaphysical vision beyond the imaginary structure. (pp. 77-8)

All Beckett's characters, including Murphy, are victimized by words, and all, beginning with Watt, must contend with that voice, "qua-qua," presiding over the birth of characters and scenery which accompanies the reader as faithfully as Virgil accompanied Dante. Unlike Virgil, however, it has a wide range of tones, according to whether or not it asks, or answers, all the questions. (p. 79)

Speech is the animating principle of Beckett's comedy which, as such, is very far removed from that of Dante. Unlike Dante's tortured victims, Beckett's characters discuss their miserable and repugnant situation very calmly; they find it not only tolerable but, on the whole, fairly good and, primarily concerned over the possibility of eviction, accept its inevitable deterioration in good spirit. When it comes to describing this situation, enumerating its advantages, discussing its resources, effecting certain improvements hanging on, they could hardly be excelled. (p. 80)

If, however, these characters are commanded to tell a story or relate their own adventures, panic inevitably ensures. Molloy, Moran, Mahood, and others assume voices and forms as best they may, appear and disappear without ever being completely born; they die piecemeal, departing this life feet first as all must do, but without ever ceasing to disappear; meanwhile "the other," the nameless narrator who, after *Watt,* always begins the story in the first person, speaks on and on. . . . A sort of anguish hovers over the human comedy, the drama of a creation continually menaced by abortion, an unsuccessful enterprise, situated somewhere between darkness and light, which must always be re-begun.

Beckett's fiction, committed to failure, thus apparently stems from a very personal experience: this onerous obligation to speak—an activity of vital importance, inspired by a force that comes from "elsewhere," and frightens him because it threatens to plunge him down into the eighth circle of hell with the falsifiers in words—he who would have been so well satisfied with Belacqua's rock. In order to name "the unnamable," say "the unspeakable," he must resort to the "jokes," "fairy tales," and "lies" that will enable these specters to make their way toward light. At the same time Beckett is also faced with the cruel necessity of destroying his fable in order to protect himself, as best he can, against the possibility of being alienated (depredated, expropriated, dispossessed, dislodged, displaced) by "the other" that he has created. He is thus obliged to flout the forms emerging from his story by every possible means. He must annihilate everything susceptible of being annihilated; everything, in other words, that is part of himself. Beckett is not inclined to "upholster" the truth. He does not wish to add anything to reality, he does not wish to transform anything. This is why he has so little patience with those who attempt to reduce his "fables" to a system of clear ideas. As the narrator of *The Unnamable* remarks, with somewhat exaggerated eloquence: "Perhaps I shall be obliged, in order not to peter out, to invent another fairytale, yet another, with heads, trunks, arms, legs, and all that follows, let loose in the changeless round of imperfect shadow and dubious light." . . . The "others" who "pass by" the narrator are thus able, by dispossessing him, to "pass for" him, abandoning him, nameless, before an empty, "immeasurable" stretch of time which—sand, mud, water or whatever—insidiously suffocates him. These confrontations of narrator and character; the substitutions, during the course of the story, of one protagonist for another; the emergence, from nothingness, of one or several characters—sometimes an infinite series of new and *sans imprévu* "representatives," "agents," "surrogates," or "avatars" of "the unnamable"—these all give rise to considerable confusion, agitation, and also anguish. At such times Beckett's style begins to pant, take on incantatory overtones, produce a sense of uneasiness, while, both in contrast and in defiance, countering and neutralizing the incantation, irony, parody, and occasionally coarseness intervene, and the author begins to multiply his admonitions to himself: That's enough, no, not that; something went wrong here. During the whole course of the story the narrator comments on its developments: "Well, well, I wasn't expecting that"; "This will all have to be rewritten in the pluperfect"; "Now that we know where we're heading, let's go"; "What a bore"; "I'm fed up with all this make believe." He also occasionally addresses the reader: "I'm

using the present tense, it's so easy to use the present tense when you're dealing with past events. It's the mythological present, don't pay any attention to it." It is up to us to decide which of the various "I"'s is presently speaking, to keep up with the various verbal tricks and traps which often fit into existing patterns of rhetoric. Beckett here turns Joyce's devices to his own ends: puns, subtly dislocated quotations of prose or poetry, unexplained allusions, unfamiliar words taken from the technical language of philosophy, medicine, or natural history. In this respect he is nearer to Queneau than to any other contemporary writer. Since Beckett is extremely learned, no existing lexicon or encyclopedia would be adequate for those seeking a precise definition of every term or explanation of each allusion. These are all undoubtedly procedures characteristic of the epic form—negative, as it were anti-heroic, epics unfolding in an "immeasurable time"; "badly" told, taken up over and over again by the voice that animates the characters— characters vaguely aware that they are yet once again about to make gestures they have already made several times before. The evolving presence in Beckett's world is not so much the scenery and characters, "conveniences" that can easily be renewed, as the quality and behavior of this voice. Beckett sometimes indulges in surprisingly facile effects, lingers over puerile jokes; the voice idles along, fading into an interminable plashing sound; the same ironic dialogue monotonously recurs; the reader yawns. But the writer never abandons his hand-to-hand combat with language, his unceasing struggle to subject it to an "unnamable" truth resuscitated by this very combat and by-passed as soon as it is named, his own past-present.

Beckett's often brutal descriptive realism, which links him with the expressionists, should not obscure the specifically "fabulous" character of his novels. *Murphy,* despite the strangeness of its hero, is, from this point of view, still close to the familiar adventure story genre, solidly anchored in everyday reality. But beginning with *Watt* and the visit to Mr Knott, the strange and monstrous depths of Beckett's universe increasingly tend to absorb the characters who are part of himself. One is reminded of Odilon Redon's disturbing creatures; of the bizarre, although innocent, monsters Dubuffet seems to mold out of mud; or of Michaux's "properties." [As revealed in his article "Samuel Beckett and the Sheela-na-gig,"] Vivian Mercier, who is also Irish, considers Beckett's combination of the grotesque and the macabre a form of Irish humor that is also found in native legends and fairy tales. Beckett's characters remind him of "sheela-na-gig"—figurines with bald heads, emaciated bodies, crooked legs, and enormous mouths and genitals. According to Mercier they reflect primitive man's anguished reaction to the process of sexual reproduction, a form of death, and expulsion from the maternal womb, a prefiguration of his expulsion from life. It would indeed appear that Beckett's characters stand, as it were, between himself and the "murmur" of a voice situated in nothingness, forming a sort of barricade against dread.

The stories told are, moreover, strikingly similar, unfolding according to a cyclical epic pattern, frequently pointed out by Beckett, which becomes increasingly simplified: voyage, quest or encounter, combat, separation, return; sometimes, especially in the early novels, the patterns are complicated by secondary episodes, pauses in sheltered spots and love affairs in deceptive refuges, for example—that are "seen" retrospectively and seem to parody certain types of fiction.

The characters, no less than the stories that they tell, have a certain air of family resemblance, and a whole network of reminiscences—encounters, objects, words—are carried over from one novel to the next. Everyone wears the clownlike Beckett uniform, or what remains thereof: for the hats, long, stiff coats, odd shoes, and ill-fitting, cast-off garments of the "human envelope" may vanish one after the other; there still remains the long white hair, dirty and matted, the accumulated filth of centuries. As a matter of fact we soon begin to realize that, from *Murphy* to *How It Is,* it is doubtless the same adventurer that goes his way and gives birth, from book to book, to the unpredictable and inevitable book that follows.

Beckett thus follows his own adventure on the trail of "that little creature in numerous disguises" who haunts him. Each stopping place along the way appears to be the last but always turns out to be "next to last" or the "penultimate." He too, like his own characters, must set out again, proceeding from west to east, against all natural forces and the underlying order of the cosmos. His own adventure thus rejoins that long, monotonous human enterprise that is based on written language, as old as man himself and never finished. And so the annihilation of Samuel Beckett proceeds along its course. (pp. 81-5)

With *Texts for Nothing* Beckett, undermining the existing structure of both plot and syntax, had already started moving toward the unfamiliar yet entirely intelligible form of *How It Is.* Beckett seems to be attempting, in every domain of his work, to reduce speech to an underlying pattern that is nonetheless easily grasped. From now on, with a systematic use of ellipses, he eliminates everything that the reader himself is able to supply. (p. 85)

With *How It Is* Beckett seems to have emptied his imaginary world of all that is not essential to a fundamental image of man's fate, arriving at a sort of diagram of his own intimate drama: a dumb mortal committed to physical disintegration, headed for death, but who is at the same time possessed by a voice, "not his own," which he is unable to annihilate. *How It Is* is hardly any longer a novel; it is rather a fable, channeled into a very carefully controlled form. Nothing, this time, has been "left to chance." The words stream along fluently and easily, evoking everything that is no more once it has been; everything that is imperfect and committed to nothingness from the outset—images, memories, feelings, thoughts. They extricate everything that gets stuck in the mud during the slow slipping down toward death which constitutes Beckett's time: hair, buttocks, can opener, incongruous as they may seem—just as Pim's education, situation and song may seem incongruous—here find their significance in a very natural way. This unity of incongruities is an exact image of the intimate contradiction which the novel illustrates without resolving. At the same time, however, nothing here throws any light on the nature of a future novel, if such there is to be, by Samuel Beckett, or the means he would use to impose once more a form and limits on "the Unnamable" that dwells within him. Amid the "qua-qua" of the rumor of words that splashes around and within him, what word (his-own-and-not-his-own) will he now extort from himself? (pp. 86-7)

Germaine Brée, "The Strange World of Beckett's 'grands articulés'," translated by Margaret Guiton, in Samuel Beckett Now, *edited by Melvin J. Friedman (© 1970 by The University of Chicago), University of Chicago Press, 1970, pp. 73-87.*

JOHN REES MOORE

Beckett's humor seems inseparable from dead seriousness. All his best jokes depend on a double-edged attitude toward the fact of human creation. In order to laugh, the joker partly identifies with a God's-eye point of view, detached and "scientifically" neutral; yet we know and the speaker knows how devastating the consequences of the joke are for the speaker. In *Happy Days* Winnie says, "How can one better magnify the Almighty than by sniggering with him at his little jokes, particularly the poorer ones . . . ?" The "sniggering with him" has just the right touch of sneaky and obsequious appreciation of His point of view, but the jokes are criticized with an alarming audacity as though Winnie were an all-licensed Fool, presuming on her occupational immunity from reprisal. To be born a sentient, struggling creature merely to suffer a certain amount of frustration and pain and then be no more—what could be funnier than that? Such a life is a triple offense to even the rudimentary philosopher: against logic, against esthetics, against formal design, a denial of human value. Yet Beckett's humor is never merely a technique for deflation. It is, rather, integral to his structure of meaning. It is necessary to the action, and the suspense of his plays depends on it. (pp. 74-5)

[The] "problem" in Beckett's pieces for the theater is intellectual only in a special and limited sense. What is so impressive is the almost intolerable unity of his work. From eating a carrot to relieving oneself to crying out against the inscrutability of the cosmos, every action and thought proceeds from a common center: the necessity and impossibility of "going on". Once born, we are committed to existence and everything we do is charged to our account no matter how trivial it is. We are forced to wonder, Are even our deepest and noblest thoughts anything but trivial? Perhaps no other author has brought into such sharp focus the possible insignificance of mankind—and his adamant refusal to accept that insignificance. (p. 75)

[As] Beckett witnesses in his early story "Dante and the Lobster," the question of pain (a simpler version of the problem of evil) extends at least as far down the evolutionary scale as lobsters. In that story the narrator's aunt assures him that lobsters suffer no pain from being plunged in boiling water. But out of nowhere at the very end of the story the authorial voice contradicts the aunt and assures us (the readers) that they do. The ability to suffer or to inflict pain may not qualify a creature for the moral life, but the *knowledge* that you may increase or reduce the amount of pain in the world, once acquired, irreversibly places you in a moral posture. . . . Pain is our most reliable indicator that something is wrong, and morality is the weapon man has devised to fight back. The guilty must, or ought to be, brought to judgment. If guilt did not exist, man would have to invent it for dignity's sake.

So in *Waiting for Godot* we see how the process works. Starting from sensations that prick them into the interrogative mood, Gogo and Didi bat the conversational ball back and forth, orienting us and inevitably leading to the overwhelming question: Is there a Father who can answer all his children's questions? And if so, will he ever make himself available? The old question about justifying God's ways to man looms in the background, but Gogo and Didi are really not up to asking anything so grandiose. If only Gogo could stop having nightmares of being beaten, if only Didi could speak to whoever is watching him. The ennui is terrible, but the hardest thing of all is to figure out what to do with hope. Each moment of existence inexorably carries them toward the Void, and they can only twiddle their thumbs. If they could give up hope, that would at least be restful. If they could be strong in faith, their fretting would be over. They can do neither. (p. 76)

[No] one questions Mr. Godot's existence. In fact, [Godot's messenger] says just enough about his master to make him seem real and no more. . . .

The characteristic condition in this play, as in other Beckett plays, is a state of suspended animation, and the scene collaborates in producing this effect. The tree too is waiting. It orders the space around it, providing a mysterious center, but it depends on the attitudes of Didi and Gogo for its meaning. It is a very humble tree in itself. Though it does have enough creative energy to put forth a few green leaves. When Gogo and Didi think of hanging themselves, the tree seems to provide the opportunity. But whether the tree is special or just another tree remains unsettled. Sometimes simply to exist in Beckett's world seems arduous enough without the added burden of meaning something. (p. 77)

In [*Endgame* and *Godot*] gamesmanship is important, but just as chess is a more demanding and aggressive game than poker (though in both the stakes may be all or nothing), so the "play" in *Endgame* is more abrasive and unyielding than in *Godot*. Though Hamm controls almost every move that Clov makes, directly or indirectly, Clov is "free" to do otherwise, in theory at least. The agony between them is a contest not only of wills but of roles. Hamm conceives himself as an archetypal father appointed (so to speak) to do penance for all fathers. Since to become a father is to compound the original sin of existence, Hamm's logical reparation is to put a lid on the existence of all life for which he is responsible. Yet every father (on the model of God) has an obligation to take care of his family. Hamm is torn between these opposite duties, and the tension has contributed to his present condition. Clov, in the role of dutiful son, ought to do everything possible to aid and comfort the father. Yet to do the father's bidding is to deny the meaning of his own being, for Hamm deliberately forces Clov to act as collaborator in Hamm's scheme for self-destruction. (p. 80)

Lack of pity assures the ultimate loneliness that is such a terror to Hamm. He prophesies that one day Clov will find himself "like a little bit of grit in the middle of the steppe" because he has pitied no one. And with no one left to pity. But Clov has that dependable Beckettian reply: "It's not certain." Unlike Lucky, Clov is a son and not a slave. Whether this is worse or better is not certain. The burden Clov has to carry is not so fatally predetermined as Lucky's, but Clov's spiritual freedom, such as it is, makes the anguish sharper. (p. 81)

The story that Hamm calls his "chronicle" epitomizes both the artist's struggle to master his materials and Hamm's supreme effort to come to terms with himself. (p. 83)

The relationship between the couple [in *Happy Days*] has the usual ambiguity of Beckett's pairs—an amalgam of shared memories, hostility, affection, and cross-purposes—but is complicated by the peculiar tensions and differences of marriages. This is the first time Beckett has given us a detailed dramatic portrait of a woman, though in the hell of *Endgame* we got premonitions of the special strengths and weaknesses of the woman's point of view, and in the Mrs. Rooney of *All That Fall* what we might call a womanly sense of the burden, perfectly combining physical and spiritual heaviness, of being among the fallen. (p. 85)

Beckett never backtracks: each play is a further advance into the restricted territory he has cut out for himself. All the plays present characters hampered in their freedom of movement, but Winnie [of *Happy Days*], so solidly fixed in place, is paradoxically freed from all those decisions that require some power of locomotion. (p. 86)

[Winnie's and Willie's] positions—back to back—until almost the end of the play tell louder than words the condition of their relationship. Though Winnie seems to dominate, her actual power is ambiguous. As in other Beckett twosomes, the question who is the stronger is an underlying, subtly moving, and finally unresolved riddle. (p. 87)

In a superficial sense we might infer that one thing cancels another out, that Beckett's irony is a device for showing disintegration. And it is true that the constant rebuffs meted out to hopeful expectation are funny and sad. What saves them from becoming mechanical is the larger irony that such a state of compensation may indeed be characteristic of the best of all possible worlds, with a gain for every loss as well as a loss for every gain. The reduction of possibilities as time passes gives a heightened value to whatever remains—as long as there is room for any freedom at all. Beckett has found a way to dramatize the old question of free will and determinism with unprecedented eloquence by reducing every movement of body or mind—from the most trivial to the most consequential—to a problem in moral weight-lifting. However helpless the victims of a cruel world may be, we are forced to reflect on the question, What *can* they do? because the characters themselves make such an effort to keep "crawling" on. They may say or think that they are stuck, but in spirit they cannot help resisting this conclusion any more than they can disencumber themselves of their bodies. There are no quietists in Beckett's drama. (pp. 87-8)

Unlike Beckett's earlier endings where the final impasse seems a logical coming to "rest" when the possibilities of diversionary action have been exhausted, the ending of *Happy Days,* where the potential for action seems nearer the zero point than ever, introduces a new complication with (for Beckett) melodramatic suddenness. True, the final tableau has the customary fixity, but its meaning tingles with awakened life, like a numb limb that has been asleep. Both Willie and Winnie are allowed to reach a climax of fulfillment that, for all its painful ambiguity, suggests astonishing resources of animation latent in their relationship. For Beckett it is surely an "upbeat" ending. (pp. 92-3)

Beckett's even-handedness is extraordinary. He makes us feel the pity and terror of life—the literal sense in which to die is to lose one's life—with uncanny precision. His victims have every right to scream. At the same time, no intruder from outside appears to bedevil them, or judge them, or execute them. They carry their own woes with them. . . . Each member of the pair needs the other to reveal fears and aggressions, loves and concerns. The pressure of human dependence is "terrific" because the loneliness outside is absolute. As Hamm puts it, "Nature has forgotten us." Even nature! In the plays, especially in *Endgame*, nature is either a horror because it is the source of life (though we find piercing evocations of a more romantic time in the past when the beauties of nature could console, even lead to a kind of ecstasy), or nature is a kind of machine whose effects are best registered by instruments. At any rate, it is no friend of man. We are always reminded of the dividing line between the "old days" when nature, whether smiling or frowning, at least allowed mankind to feel at home in it, and the present of the play in which humanity is at odds with the physical environment. And if Mother Nature is dead, how much more inaccessible is what lies beyond nature. (pp. 93-4)

[There] is no getting away from psychology in Beckett, though the psychology is made somewhat bizarre by the removal of large areas of ordinary experience. Getting and spending, whether of power, pleasure, success, or money belong to a past outside the plays, recalled in story perhaps but irrelevant to the task that faces the characters. Technically, Beckett's "point of attack" is very late. Lives are set. What chance do his people have of significantly altering the shape of things to come? Nevertheless, having "mislaid" the answers to the metaphysics exam, they show us in every speech what it feels like to be babes lost in the intellectual woods. One of their great charms, in fact, is their infantilism. They react with transparent egoism to the pains, frustrations, and satisfactions of the moment. But they are children forced to be adults, which means they are unceasingly trying to reason everything out. Beckett's famous pauses suggest the effort involved as well as the doubtfulness of the answers. (p. 94)

But no matter what is lost, "a part remains," as Winnie says of her classics. To lose one's mind is to lose something so wonderful it ought to be immortal. The last indignity is never to have been. So, through *Happy Days* at any rate, the soul struggles to keep glowing like a coal in the dark. Nothing in the inexorable movement of the world indicates any consciousness, much less any sorrow, that creatures of such intelligence, such sensitivity, such endurance are buried forever in the sands of time. Yet the creatures themselves cannot get rid of the intuition that they are objects of attention, that they are being watched, by some kind of intelligent consciousness. The effort to make contact, however, is somewhat like trying to establish communications with beings in outer space. One strong link with the religious past that remains is guilt, and these descendants of the Western tradition "accept" their fall into individual consciousness. Guilty of having identified themselves with the cult of reason, at however distant a remove, they insist on *understanding,* and when that is denied them they are left with paradox (or perhaps we should say the audience is). They can go neither forward nor backward. (pp. 94-5)

Beckett has said, "What is the good of passing from one untenable position to another, of seeking justification always on the same plane?" Yet that is what his characters seem to be doing. Though the action that encloses them is unstoppable, it is never final; for finality would falsify a process that never stops. In place of an Aristotelian action with beginning, middle and end, Beckett gives us an action of starts and stops, a kind of stuttering ramble around the

"old questions, old answers." In the space occupied by the gods in Greek tragedy Beckett puts a "nature" heavy with implication but apparently barren of specific meaning. It is at once inescapable and inscrutable. The characters venture to its edges, peer at it, feel its pressure and temperature, speculate about it. They are subject to its majestic rhythm. But they are continually turned back on themselves in their struggle to carve a personal destiny out of stony Fate. . . . Boxed in by a set of "laws" that severely limit their freedom, Beckett's people succeed in demonstrating all the more persuasively the *uncertainty,* the indeterminacy, of the human mind. Unlike the Naturalist who maintains a considerable intellectual distance between himself and his characters, implying that they are unconscious agents of a force the author understands far better than they do (owing to his scientific knowledge), Beckett assumes no such superiority. As he once said, if he knew who Godot was he would have told us. (pp. 95-6)

So no final release of tension, no catharsis, occurs. On the contrary, the action is suddenly frozen as the curtain descends. The play reaches its climax as the silence descends, and we are left with the peculiar sensation of witnessing the end of something that nevertheless still goes on. The thrust of the ending is to "throw out" at the audience the unresolved ambiguities at the heart of the play. Beckett has gone on to explore even further subtleties of his theme, but on the evidence of these three plays we can say that his haunting power comes from the way he brings extremes together. Moral honesty and esthetic playfulness appeal at once to what is most naive and most sophisticated in his audience. (p. 96)

> *John Rees Moore, "The Exhilarating Mr. Beckett," in* Shenandoah *(copyright 1977 by Washington and Lee University; reprinted from* Shenandoah: The Washington and Lee University Review *with the permission of the Editor), Spring, 1977, pp. 74-96.*

ALICE and KENNETH HAMILTON

The title *How It Is* suggests that an answer is being given to the question, "How is it in the world, in this human life of ours?" That interpretation seems the more certain because of the nature of the narrative. The nameless narrator tells how he moves painfully through a world of warm mud. We hear that he meets another like himself, tortures him, and then finds that his victim has moved away in the mud. The narrator proceeds to speculate at large upon life in the muddy world. He draws up theories about his own experience being only part of a series of similar encounters in the mud, where pairs of beings are continually meeting; where each one plays in turn the part of the torturer and the tortured; and where the transition is made by the victim of the encounter crawling away to find some one else to torture, while his torturer lies supine awaiting the arrival of some new ex-victim to torture him. Perhaps (so he speculates) the population of mud-dwellers may be in millions. Yet, finally, the narrator confesses that what he has said is all a lie. He never met anyone in the mud. All that he knows for certain is the mud and himself lying in it.

For the most part, *How It Is* has been taken to be an imaginative presentation of Beckett's view of human existence. As several critics have pointed out, the work indeed contains most of the "basic ingredients" of Beckett's previous fiction. And it is undeniable that portraying the pain and meaninglessness of human life has been a central concern in all Beckett's writings. (p. 2)

[The] supposition that *How It Is* delineates the world of the artistic imagination rather than the world of human existence in general is one that opens up much in the text that otherwise seems obscure. Moreover, there are some pointers to such a hypothesis being at least a possible one.

To begin with, there is the title of the work. The pun evident in the original *Comment c'est* is necessarily lost in the English translation. *Commencez*! This command relates to every artistic performance, where the artist must embark upon his chosen theme and continue until his creation is brought to an end satisfying to the imagination. Commentators upon *How It Is* have noted with some surprise that Beckett's narrator promises a narrative in three parts and actually completes what he promises. Beckett's heroes so often mention some subject which they intend to write about—and then forget to do so. Beckett has said that the task of the artist today is "to find a form that accommodates the mess." If *How It Is* is concerned with the imaginative form created by the artist confronted with "the mess" of raw experience, then the prominence given to the structure of the work is not so surprising. (pp. 2-3)

It is well known that Beckett found himself in an impasse after completing the third novel of his trilogy. With *The Unnamable* he had reduced his fiction to a voice crying in a void, and there seemed to be no further reduction possible and nowhere else to go. *How It Is* was an artistic breakthrough. The nature of Beckett's achievement can be understood when we turn to look at Beckett's beliefs about the dynamics of the artistic vision. (p. 3)

For Beckett there are two levels of vision. On the first or surface level the sensory eye sees a multitude of familiar objects. On the second or deeper level the eye of the imagination sees only unvarying mud or muck—cosmic excrement. The poet strips off the "fleshly" surface vision. Thus Estragon, who rejects with vehemence the idea that he sees scenery, asserts equally vehemently that he is a poet. (pp. 3-4)

Moreover, the world of *How It Is* is a world of darkness. . . . While the sensory eye demands light in order to see and while it shuns the dark, the imaginative eye must (in Beckett's thinking) cultivate darkness in order to find its proper vision. In *Krapp's Last Tape* Beckett has explored this theme, for his play shows Krapp to be a man who has betrayed his artistic calling through his refusal to leave the world of light. Because the narrator of *How It Is* has descended into the darkness we may conclude that he, unlike Krapp, has not turned away from the artist's obligation to express under the conditions of powerlessness and negativity. Knowing only an environment of featureless mud, he has reached that state which Beckett says that art should prefer, namely, the expression that there is nothing to express. It is true that into his consciousness come "rags of life in the light" . . . ; yet these memories of the world "above" are so fragmentary that they succeed most of all in accentuating the surrounding darkness. (p. 4)

Beckett believes that the descent into the darkness is obligatory for the artist, because the artist must understand that his empirical self cannot be his real self. A self more basic than the individual called Samuel Beckett exists in the 'virtual beneath' and can be caught momentarily by listening to

its murmers. The narrator of *How It Is* says that his task has been to communicate the murmurs that reverberate in the dark, even though the act of communicating what he hears is impossibly hard. He begins by confessing, "I say it as I hear it." (pp. 4-5)

The text of *How It Is* reflects on the page the manner in which the narrator hears the murmuring both as scraps and also as a flow of words: "unbroken no paragraphs no commas not a second for reflection." . . . In the book there is no punctuation, and the telescoped syntax of the phrases making up the narrative suggests the hurrying pace of the voice. . . .

Form, beginning with the form of words on the page, is clearly of the utmost importance in this book. But that is not to say that here Beckett is interested in form rather than in content, that he has cut away the picture and is concerned only about the frame. What Beckett praised most in Proust and Joyce has always been his own ideal: the unity of form and content. While *How It Is* in form stands closer to the prose poem than to the novel, it tells a quite definite story. The story is about one who has descended into the dark and about his efforts to record truthfully "how it is" there. (p. 5)

Mud, darkness and the recording of voices heard in the dark; these are all ingredients found elsewhere in Beckett. But only in *How It Is* are all three ingredients central. It is this fact that indicates how the book is about the artist and the genesis of his art.

The starting point of the story (not surprisingly, where Beckett is concerned) seems to have been found in Dante. In the seventh canto of the *Inferno* Dante describes the Marsh of Styx. There the Wrathful continually assault one another; while the Sullen, lying deep in the black mud, cry out incoherently—being unable to form whole words. Thus Dante has given Beckett the world of "primeval mud impenetrable dark." . . . He has given him as well the inhabitants of the Marsh, naked figures either actively tormenting others or passively accepting their fate. Most important of all, the *Inferno* has suggested the painfulness of speech. In Dante the broken words of the Sullen simply reflect their situation in the mud. But Beckett makes his active character attack a passive one, giving his victim a carefully calculated training through the method of stimulus-and-response. In *How It Is* violence is no longer aimless, and suffering is inflicted for no other purpose than to elicit speech. This is the wholly new element introduced by Beckett, and it is one which transforms totally the original source upon which he has drawn.

In *How It Is* words seem to flow abundantly. Yet the narrator is continually concerned with the difficulty of forming words and also of the extreme importance of maintaining speech. In Part I he says:

> . . . it's here words have their utility the mud is mute
>
> . . . I strain with open mouth so as not to lose a second a fart fraught with meaning issuing through the mouth no sound in the mud

> (pp. 5-6)

These statements about words convey much of Beckett's understanding of the significance of the writer's art. The "fart fraught with meaning issuing through the mouth" may be no more than a rudimentary attempt to form a word, yet it is enough to restore dignity to the one who originates it. For Beckett, the socially unacceptable fart is a fitting image for the creation of the writer. Farting and word-forming alike mock at artificial conventions and assert the basic conditions of existence. The writer does not write to please society but because of an inward compulsion. Words are at one and the same time his glory and his torment. Also, the more he explores their use, the more he finds them eluding his control. He alone is responsible for selecting them, nevertheless they seem not to issue from his conscious choice but to be dictated to him. . . . The result of this conviction is that he distrusts fluency, so that (as has been often noted) his writings have become increasingly spare and have steadily moved in the direction of silence. (p. 7)

Honesty and singlemindedness in expression, the painfulness and the compulsive nature of speaking, and "the infinite futility—for the artist—of all that is not art" . . . : these are matters of immense concern to Beckett. And they are matters that have shaped the narrative of *How It Is*.

The seventh canto of Dante's *Inferno* describes Dante's arrival at the boundary between Upper and Nether Hell at midnight on Good Friday. . . . A constant theme in [Beckett's] writings is that of all men being suffering Christs condemned to walk the *via dolorosa* of life without respite. Yet, although there is no escape from the long crucifixion that is existence, the coming of night at least makes the phenomenal world less all-encompassing. Particularly in the early poetry Beckett speaks of the night as an interval when the harmonies of art dispel for a moment the discords of the day.

Thus, on two counts, the source in Dante fits Beckett's personal mythology. It points to the suffering of Good Friday and to the night-hour at which imaginative perception is most intense. Both themes are omnipresent in *How It Is*.

The narrator certainly moves painfully through the chaotic world of the living which is the world of muck. . . . Like Estragon in *Waiting for Godot* he knows, "it's the same kingdom as before a moment before the same it always was I have never left it it is boundless." . . . But he knows also the achievement of being able to say something to himself. Of course, nothing he can say will alter his condition. . . . (pp. 7-8)

In Part 3 the narrator confesses that his encounter with Pim and all the rest of his story (except himself lying in the mud) is a complete lie. Yet already in Part 1 he admits that Pim is no more than a fiction created in order to explain the possibility of imaginative expression. . . . Pim is the creature of his fancy, a figment given shape for the purpose of accounting for the "murmur in the mud" which the writer is able to capture in his art. The narrator, then, speaks of capturing Pim and of forcing him to express meanings through words; and this process becomes the substance of the "events" recorded in Part 2. Behind the fantastical account there lies a factual basis, namely, that the imaginative work of the artist is carried on in the darkness below the sensory world and that it is made possible through suffering.

When the narrator begins to "quicken" Pim he torments him by digging his nails into Pim's flesh so that he cries out. Soon Pim learns that his tormentor is not satisfied with cries, and he begins to sing. In the songs are heard "a word

or two eyes skies the or thee" . . . , encouraging the narrator to teach Pim to articulate spoken words. After further painful lessons Pim responds to questions carved upon his back in roman capitals. Most troublesome of all is the lesson to teach Pim his name. (p. 8)

The name may have been chosen at random, yet there is a real possibility that it may stand for the name Christ. The likelihood of the latter explanation being the correct one is indicated by the narrator's insistence that his own name, too, is Pim. When Pim is utterly confused by this information, the narrator allows himself to be called Bom, explaining, "Bom he can call me Bom for more commodity that would appeal to me at the end and one syllable the rest indifferent." . . . Since all men are thought by Beckett to be Christs on the Good Friday road to crucifixion, the name Pim (or Christ) is the proper name for all dwellers in the mud of existence. If, however, the multiplication of the same name is misleading, at least all names can be monosyllabic (as in *Christ*) and carry as a constant the thirteenth letter of the alphabet. For Beckett, who is known to his friends as Sam, thirteen means especially the day of his birth, Good Friday. So long as this central link with the crucified Christ is kept in the names of his characters, what the other letters in the names happen to be matters not at all. . . . The essential knowledge is the knowledge that life is always a slow crucifixion.

Pim's first attempt at artistic expression is song. When he puts words to music they are words about the sensory world (*eyes, skies*) and the individual objects (*the* or *thee*) found in it. Pim is following the easy path of popular artists with their routine of familiar subjects and hackneyed rhymes. Bom will have none of it. He make Pim stop by thumping him on the back of the head. This action, as he observes, drives Pim's face right into the mud. . . . A true artist, as distinct from a crowd-pleaser, must first of all learn that the phenomenal world is nothing but muck. Bom's torture of Pim is so severe that at one point he thinks his victim may have died. Yet Bom insists, "I am not a monster," and he justifies his severity by saying, "but words could be involved in the case of Pim a few words." . . . No suffering can be too great if the result is a few words manifesting imaginative truth and spoken out of the darkness in which alone genuine art can find its material. (p. 9)

Because *How It Is* has its focus in the artistic experience, it is a narrative of suffering and boredom has almost no place in it. Yet *How It Is* is not only a work about the suffering through which the artist comes to experience his creative powers. The book also describes the special suffering of the artist that is caused by his artistic vocation, namely, loneliness.

In *Proust* Beckett wrote about the necessity laid upon the artist "who does not deal in surfaces" to reject friendship:

> Because the only possible spiritual development is in the sense of depth. The artistic tendency is not expansive, but a contraction. And art is the apotheosis of solitude. There is no communication because there are no vehicles of communication.
>
> (p. 10)

Although it is only in the last few pages of Part 3 [of *How It Is*] that the narrator explicitly repudiates the truth of the story he has been telling, his narrative provides plenty of indications throughout that the story is an invented one and not a transcript of actual experiences He constantly says that there is only one voice, a voice which is his alone yet not his. The questions that he scores with his nails upon Pim's back, too, bring answers affirming that nothing can be either affirmed or denied, except consciousness of lying flat in the mud . . .—in short, his own final confession.

The invention of Pim, therefore, is simply a device on the part of the narrator (and, through him, of Beckett) to find a form that accommodates the mess, to communicate the impossibility of communication, to expose the contradictions resulting from the attempt to describe (in terms of "the light above") the consciousness that has its being in the darkness. Part of the same formal device is the three-fold division of "how it was" before Pim, with Pim, and after Pim: "divide into three a single eternity for the sake of clarity." . . . Beckett has always scorned the traditional division of artistic composition into a beginning, a middle and an end, since this form assumes the reality of an ordered universe. The narrator of *How It Is* explains . . . how his narrative gives only three parts of what he has been describing as a four-part play. His story states that, when a crawler through the mud meets and tortures his victim, the victim then crawls away to find *his* victim to torture, leaving his torturer lying to await the arrival of one who shall now torture him. This sequence—seeker, torturer, abandoned, tortured—assumes an eternal vicious circle, a four-sectioned wheel that can never cease turning. Yet, while the four-fold form expresses eternity, it does not express eternity's singleness. Hence the narrator explicitly disowns all the elements in his story so that the imaginative constructions he has made shall not be taken for a literal transcript of reality. (p. 11)

[In *How It Is* no] answers are given to questions rendered unnecessary by the darkness surrounding the artist who "damns the life of the body on earth as a pensum." . . . No explanations are looked for by the one whose concern is with the murmur in the mud, neither natural nor super-natural explanations—and especially not supernatural explanations or supernatural comforts. (p. 12)

Alice and Kenneth Hamilton, "The Process of Imaginative Creation in Samuel Beckett's 'How It Is'," in MOSAIC: A Journal for the Study of Literature and Ideas *(copyright © 1977 by the University of Manitoba Press; acknowledgment of previous publication is herewith made), Summer, 1977, pp. 1-12.*

LAURA BARGE

Stylistically and thematically, [*First Love, The Expelled, The Calmative,* and *The End*] mark what is probably the most distinct transition in the entire [Beckett] canon. Shifting from the English third person (of *More Pricks Than Kicks, Murphy,* and *Watt*) to the French first person, Beckett creates a fictional hero and environment so uniquely and consistently characteristic that they are recognizable (although often changed in certain particulars) throughout the remainder of his published prose. The hero is no longer undecided, as the earlier heroes Belacqua, Murphy, and Watt are, between life in the macrocosm of the outer world or in the microcosm of the mind—his choice is the microcosm, a descent inward toward the core of the self. . . . This descent becomes a quest which, fully defined in the

trilogy and developed ever more intensively in the subsequent fiction, undergirds all of Beckett's work as a dominant theme, the quest for whatever constitutes metaphysical reality, for the essence of human experience. That this reality can finally be described only as nothing, as a Plenum-Void that never yields any substance but continually recedes into infinity, does not negate the centrality of this quest in Beckett's oeuvre. The failure of the quest does, however, negate anything that might be called development of character. Neither in these stories nor in the fiction that follows does a protagonist show real gain or make progress beyond his initial state. Thus the hero is frozen into a definite shape that is little changed beyond this point. He is in exile but longs for a home . . . and is abused by nearly all the elements that make up his world. Consequently, his repsonses become those of abuse or loathing, although he is haunted by a yearning for companionship. Like Watt, he is hindered by a failure to understand or to communicate, but unlike Watt, he feels no real compulsion to do either. Instead he is content to relate countless fictional episodes, to use words only because words are all that he has been given to fill space and time. He regards these fictional episodes with the contempt he feels they deserve. As for his body, it is rotting away and loathsome with sores and disease (also with disability in the later fiction). Detached from this body, his mind is likewise deteriorating—even to a state of uncertainty as to whether it exists in a condition of life or death.

Although a sequence of events takes place in each story (and a general sequence, with much repetition, in the four stories as a whole), these happenings can hardly be labeled as plot because they are parts of a futile circle, a rigmarole, ending where it begins. Thus Beckett has abandoned even the sardonic plots of his earlier novels (Watt may not have accomplished anything, but he does learn something—even if the something he learns is that he can learn nothing) and is anticipating the circular endlessness of the trilogy. (pp. 333-34)

It is also in these stories that the ill-defined "they" make their appearance. Resembling some malignant god or Kafkan high official who delights in tormenting his creatures without known reason, these obscure and mysterious personages (or personage), although never explicitly said to exist, are sensed by Beckett's heroes as being those ultimately in charge of the miserable and absurd affair known as life on the planet Earth. (p. 334)

If the first-person narrator of the stories can be said to retain his personhood (after Belacqua, Murphy, and Watt, Beckett almost ceases to create persons; each hero becomes Everyman), he is nevertheless in the process of becoming only a voice still bodied at the beginning of the trilogy but disembodied by its end, who is an indistinct blend of protagonist, narrator, and author. This blending of roles results in another change in the stories—a subtle difference in Beckett's use of irony. Through *Watt* Beckett remains reasonably close to the conventional use of literary irony. In such use, two levels of ironic awareness are in operation—the narrator's description of the ironic scene or object and the reader's awareness that this description is ironic, that is, that the material that the narrator is presenting is deliberately falsified from what he actually intends the reader to perceive. But a third level of ironic awareness appears in the stories and reappears throughout the remaining fiction. Because there is a blending of the consciousness of the narrator and the protagonist (who is playing the role of narrator by relating the tale), the protagonist often becomes aware, in a subtle, undercover way, of the ironic implications of what he is relating about himself with a straight face. He becomes cognizant of the falsity of his own statements or actions. (pp. 334-35)

Of all the specifics indicating these stories as a point of transition, none is more significant than the permeation of the tales with the concept of mortality. Not that Beckett has not been obsessed with mortality before, both Belacqua and Murphy are fascinated by death as a possible state of "embryonal repose" in which they can possibly escape the frustrations of life in the macrocosm. But oddly enough, the fact that they do die (a release Beckett never again gives any hero) and find death to be nothing other than annihilation robs these early works of the existential anguish, *Angst,* associated with mortality in the subsequent fiction. Watt does not die, but following the failure of his epistemological quest, his existence becomes a continuing crucifixion. It is not some character's death, then, but the fact of death that begins overtly to overshadow Beckett's fiction in the conclusion of *Watt* and in the stories.... Beckett conceives of mortality as the abnegation of all value in life and begins to define life itself as an event of death. (pp. 335-36)

Breaking his usual pattern of reticence in offering comment on his work, Beckett has said that the experiences of the protagonists of these stories can be taken as three phases of one existence—"prime, death, and limbo." We cannot, however, be certain which phase designates which story. (p. 336)

The difficulty of trying to separate the stories into states of life or death is a small part of the larger dilemma encountered in attempting to define the word symbols *life* and *death* as used by Beckett, not only in the stories, but also in all the fiction that follows. Because Beckett conceives of physical life as an experience of dying and because he suspects that human consciousness or being does not end with physical death, the meanings of the words merge—life becomes death, and death is a continuation of life.... The equating by Beckett of life with light and salvation, and of death with darkness and damnation is strongly reminiscent of the defining of life by the Apostle John, although presumably Beckett's equations have no theological implications. Beckett explains that it is because man is faced with the dual existence of both light (life) and darkness (death) that the human "situation becomes inexplicable." That is, innately aware of the desirability of qualities such as truth, love, justice, beauty, and happiness, man confronts a universe in which the realization of such qualities is simply not possible. (pp. 336-37)

[The] symbolizing of death by darkness rests on the association of death with something that is inexplicable (or absurd) or that causes distress. It is dying without ever having lived that is associated with the idea of death here. (pp. 337-38)

Although Beckett's comments in *Proust* are primarily about Proust and should not be uncritically applied to Beckett's own work, certain observations in this criticism are relevant at this point. The anguish associated with death is not directly related to a fear or dread of death per se. Because of the numbing effect of what Proust calls Habit, unless

death is made concrete by being forecast at some particular point in the future, it has no meaning in the present because its "possibility" remains "indistinct and abstract." ... Instead, the anguish derives from the impermanence of any given moment before the onslaught of time.... The real villain of Proust and of Beckett is not death ... but time— "that double-headed monster of damnation and salvation" that makes each passing day a "calamitous day" by continually destroying and recreating for further destruction its "victims and prisoners." ... Having reached such a conclusion, we can make the further statement that, beginning with the stories, physical death becomes for Beckett a metaphor for the existential anguish of sensing infinity in a finite world, of longing for selfhood in a universe of continual change that denies the possibility of being.

In spite of his sick humor (which nevertheless succeeds in being funny) and detached irrationality (he has either five or six feet, none of which function properly), the protagonist of the stories suffers acutely from a dislocation with his universe defined in terms of exile. When the hero of *The Expelled* is thrown out of his childhood home, he is *expelled*—either from some undefined state before birth or from some Paradise that exists only as an intuitive consciousness of a world that should be. However the haven is defined, the hero is evicted, and all subsequent events become what the earlier protagonist Murphy has called "a wandering to find home" ... —a search for an ending of exile, for a place of belonging, a sanctuary for the human spirit. (pp. 338-39)

Beckett's hero is Heidegger's man being "thrown" and left in a world not of his own making. He is man without a resting place for his heart in Nietzsche's nihilistic universe, and Sartre's man, forlorn and orphaned in an alien environment where he can never be at home. Or, in a more limited sense, Beckett's tramp is Camus' Meursault, a stranger so imprisoned within himself that whether he is actually behind prison walls is of little significance in determining his alienation. More definitively, the tramp's exile can be likened to the estrangement of the prodigal son of Luke's gospel, who is separated both from his father and from his father's house. Although, unlike man as described by Nietzsche and Sartre, Beckett's hero is not consciously aware of any need for a missing God, and although, unlike the prodigal son, he has made no choice that has caused his homelessness, the hero is nonetheless existentially estranged. ...

It is ... this suffering of dislocation that is expressed as a metaphorical undercurrent in the stories by images or events of death. In the first three stories, death appears either as an inconsequential mentioning of some object, as a chance remark or thought of the narrator, as the meaning of some symbol, or as an integral part of the episode that is being related. Making up a disjunctive collection, the death references in these stories are parallel in form to the loosely structured narratives of the stories themselves. The references to death in the fourth story, *First Love,* exhibit a pattern corresponding to the tighter structure of this story—the references occur at specific points in what might ironically be called the cycle of life or of love. (p. 340)

Death appears symbolically in references throughout the first three stories to the sea. Leaving the cabman's stable (he has had enough of the horse's company), the tramp of *The Expelled* comments on his habit of following the rising sun and states that in the evenings he continues to pursue the sun's path below the horizon of the sea until he is "down among the dead." . . . Irresistibly drawn toward the sea, the protagonist of *The Calmative* nevertheless fears it as a "dead haven. . . . the black swell was most perilous, and all about me storm and wreck. I'll never come back here." . . . (pp. 341-42)

Repeating the theme of exile, *First Love* defines love as a banishment ("What goes by the name of love is banishment" . . .) and the cycle of human life as a cycle of death. Thus, as in the first three stories, death becomes a metaphor for the suffering of existence, which is by definition an exile. As such a metaphor, death presents itself in some form at each significant point in the life cycle of the hero. His comments concerning the place of his birth center upon his father's death and the cemetery where his father is buried. The hero enjoys this spot of earth because he does "not find unpleasant"—in fact he finds "infinitely preferable to what the living emit"—the "smell of corpses, distinctly perceptible under those of grass and humus." . . . A more obvious image of death is the hyacinth . . . that Lulu places in the room of the hero after they come to live together. The hyacinth looks as if it might live but instead dies and begins to smell "foul." He refuses to allow it to be removed from the room, and the day Lulu announces the impending birth of their child (possibly the child is theirs; Lulu is a practicing prostitute while married to the hero) one of her eyes (she is cross-eyed) seems riveted on the remains of the hyacinth. . . .

When the birth cries of the child banish the protagonist from the house of his marriage ("they pursued me down the stairs and out into the street"), the "leaves were falling already," and he remarks that he dreads the winter. . . . Thus nature, which traditionally joins love with life in spring, joins it instead with death in winter, and Beckett's tale becomes not a life cycle but a cycle of death. The cries of the new-born infant pursue the hero relentlessly to the grave, apparently never to cease, and thereby are defined as the cries of death. . . . (pp. 342-43)

If life becomes an event of death, then it is possible to conceive of death as simply a continuation of this death-in-life. What Beckett is doing is to distort John Donne's triumphant assertion that death shall die into the terrifying possibility that life shall live—a mystery that in Beckett's world is reason enough for despair. For Beckett, the play or story can never be finished, and a significant aspect of the hell that his protagonists endure is that existence goes on and on. The reason his heroes cannot experience the release of death is because they have never achieved being in life. . . . This inability of matters to end finally, of everything to come to a close, is introduced into the Beckettian canon in the stories. Life and death become so merged in a cycle of continual flux that neither can be defined as a beginning or as an end. (p. 343)

That the stories parallel events and images associated with physical death with existential anguish defined in terms of exile is obvious, but the question remains whether this significance assigned to death begins in the stories and whether it continues as a strong emphasis in the fiction that follows. To answer this question we must examine *Watt,* which directly precedes the stories, and the trilogy, which directly follows. In *Watt* nothing other than foreshadowings of Beckett's obsession with mortality occurs. No major

character dies or is anxiously concerned with death, nor does the idea of death exist as a metaphorical substratum beneath the flow of surface narration. The only dominant treatment of death is the portrayal of Watt in the asylum garden as a crucified Christ figure. . . .

Other than this scene, only minor references to death occur, two in the closing episode of the novel. As Watt waits to make his final journey to the asylum, where he continues life as a crucified existence, he smells a peculiar odor in the waiting room of the train station. He identifies this smell, "exceptionally foul, and yet at the same time in some way familiar," as the odor of death—that of a "decaying carcass of some small animal," perhaps hidden under the stone floor. (p. 345)

Once we have crossed over the bridge of the stories and reached the trilogy, . . . we are dealing no longer with suggestions but with a full development of Beckett's concept of mortality. Death, with all of its Beckettian ramifications, is a dominant theme throughout the trilogy. . . . Animals and insects die (Lousse's dog and Moran's hens and bees), secondary characters die (Moll and the unfortunate family of Mahood), and persons are murdered (Moran's unidentified victim in the forest and the two sailors hacked to death by Lemuel). Furthermore, an obsession with death figures prominently in each book of the trilogy. Molloy considers suicide, Malone is undergoing the ordeal of dying, and the Unnamable longs for but is unable to attain the release of death (unless, ambiguously enough, he is already dead).

This presence in the trilogy of the motif of mortality can be traced to its beginnings with unmistakable echoes of the stories. In a futile effort to finish his tale, Malone refers to what is obviously the death scene at the close of *The End:* "absurd lights, the stars, the beacons, the buoys, the lights of earth and in the hills the faint fires of the blazing gorse." . . . (p. 346)

Because life is a quest for a haven that can never be found, it becomes a death, and because death is a continuing consciousness of exile, it does not end the suffering of life. We are reminded of Beckett's drama *Breath,* which consists solely of a stage scattered with rubbish, certain lighting effects, an instant's sound of a baby's cry, a breathing in and out of a single human breath, and then a final cry, identical to the first. It is in the stories that these cries of birth and of death are first defined as one and the same. (p. 347)

Laura Barge, "Life and Death in Beckett's Four Stories," in South Atlantic Quarterly *(reprinted by permission of the Publisher; copyright 1977 by Duke University Press, Durham, North Carolina), Summer, 1977, pp. 332-47.*

*   *   *

BELCHEVA, Elisaveta
See BAGRYANA, Elisaveta

*   *   *

BELLOW, Saul   1915-

A Canadian-born American novelist, short story writer, playwright, essayist, editor, and translator, Bellow is considered by many to be the most important novelist now writing in America. His fictive concerns are revealed in his protagonists, who consistently reject the absurdist philosophies of our

time and strive instead to forge a humanistic personal ethic. Bellow mingles suffering with joy, pessimism with survival of the self, as his characters seek a balance between individuality and moral responsibility. He has received both Nobel and Pulitzer prizes for his work and is a three-time winner of the National Book Award. (See also *CLC*, Vols. 1, 2, 3, 6, 8, and *Contemporary Authors*, Vols. 5-8, rev. ed.)

JOHN BERRYMAN

[*The Adventures of Augie March*] is dominated by a recurrent allusiveness to masters of Greek, Jewish, European, and American history, literature, and philosophy. Sometimes their deeds or opinions are mentioned, sometimes they rule the imagery. We might call them Overlords, or Sponsors. ("If you want," Augie says at one point, "to pick your own ideal creature in the mirror coastal air and sharp leaves of ancient perfections and be at home where a great mankind was at home, I've never seen any reason why not.") The Overlords have a double use. They stand as figures of awe and emulation to Augie (one of whose favourite authors is plainly Plutarch)—corresponding in this to the heroes of his actual experience, such as Einhorn. And they create historical depth, the kind of legendary perspective that our naturalism has deeply desired; a portrait on the scale of Einhorn's would be impossible without them. Replacing the vague merciless forces invoked by Dreiser, they remind me of the marvelous vast heads of statues in some of Watteau's pictures, overlooking his lovers. They are bound to irritate some readers as pretentious or hand-to-mouth, or a mannerism, because they are a new element, a new convention, in our fiction; new conventions are likely to irritate at first.

Along with these differences goes a decisive change in theme from the naturalism we have known, which dealt as a rule with success, and was likely to be tragic. Augie does not aim at success, and his story is a comedy, having for theme the preservation of individuality against the pressures in American life (modern life) toward uniformity, the adoption of socially acceptable roles: pressures exactly toward success, or at any rate security. The pressures are dramatized by Bellow as "recruiting," everybody's attempts to get Augie to serve their ends. Augie is all risk, he always consents; but then he always withdraws, because, experimental and aggressive, he is trying to refuse to lead a disappointed life. The insistence upon having one's own fate we might relate to the divorce now between parents and children, in (as W. H. Auden has put it) "a society where the father plays as minor a role as he plays in America." Augie has no visible father (he is illegitimate) and can hardly follow in his father's footsteps.

The novel, then, because of the recruiting, has the form of a theme-and-variations, and because of the search for a fate good enough, it has also the direction of a "pilgrimage"—Bellow's word late in the book. The first is more important than the second, but I don't quite understand Clifton Fadiman's regarding it as "undirected." Another critical mistake seems to me to be Warren's when he wishes that Augie "had been given the capacity ... for more joy and sorrow." Surely he suffers and rejoices enough for several books. Possibly Warren read *The Adventures of Augie March* too much in the light of Bellow's earlier, constricted novels, which strike me as interesting now chiefly in relation to this one. Both the stunning wit and the emotional range are new here to Bellow. Wit has not been a character-

istic of our twentieth-century naturalists, either. At the same time, notwithstanding these differences, *Augie March* does clearly belong on the Dreiser side, inclusive and tidal, as against Hemingway's and, in its insistence that what is widespread shall also be intense, may help to foster a fresh dimension for naturalism. (pp. 222-24)

> *John Berryman, "A Note on Augie" (1953), in his* The Freedom of the Poet *(reprinted with the permission of Farrar, Straus & Giroux, Inc.; copyright © 1940, 1944, 1945, 1947, 1948, 1949, 1956, 1959, 1961, 1964, 1966 by John Berryman; copyright © renewed 1972 by John Berryman; copyright © 1951, 1953, 1960, 1965, 1966, 1975, 1976 by Kate Berryman; copyright © renewed 1973, 1975, 1976 by Kate Berryman), Farrar, Straus, 1976, pp. 222-24.*

CAROL M. SICHERMAN

The linguistic lowpoint of Saul Bellow's brief novel *Seize the Day*—and one of its comic delights—is Dr. Tamkin's poem, deliciously entitled "Mechanism vs Functionalism: Ism vs Hism." The very paper on which Tamkin has typed his poem (it has "ruled borders in red ink") warns us to expect a student production, and Bellow exceeds expectation by delivering a classic non-poem by someone who thinks that rhyme and sing-song iambs, archaically decorated with inversions and the ungrammatical second-person singular, are the vital constituents of poetry.

In the poem, Tamkin, self-described as a "psychological poet," ... advises his audience: "Why-forth then dost thou tarry ... Seek ye then that which art not there." Small wonder that Bellow's bewildered protagonist, Tommy Wilhelm, cannot get beyond his initial reaction: "What kind of mishmash, claptrap is this!" But Tommy, who remembers Literature I at Penn State as the "one course that now made sense," ... respects poets and poetry, and he answers politely when Tamkin asks his opinion of the poem: "I'm trying to figure out who this Thou is." To his shock, Tamkin replies, in another capsule of comic grammar: "Thou? Thou is you." ... "The main idea," he explains, "is *con*struct or *de*struct;" but there is no way of divining this interpretation from the poem itself. (pp. 1-2)

Bellow is not merely having fun at the expense of portentously obscure and vacuous poetry, of timid critics who dare not say aloud what their common sense whispers, and of teachers justly suspected by their pupils of plotting to trap them. He is pursuing in a comic interlude a topic which seriously and centrally concerns him throughout the novel, from the title onward: the breakdown of language as a common bond among men. (p. 2)

Wilhelm's reflections on the unfathomable Tamkin lead him to [an] extended speculation on language and society, one which encapsulates many of the ideas of the novel:

> Every other man spoke a language entirely his own.... If you wanted to talk about a glass of water, you had to start back with God creating the heavens and earth ... up to Einstein; then war and Lenin and Hitler. After reviewing this and getting it all straight again you could proceed to talk about a glass of water. "I'm fainting, please get me a little water." You were lucky even then to make

yourself understood. And this happened over and over and over with everyone you met. . . . The fathers were no fathers and the sons no sons. . . .

Increasingly alone, Wilhelm talks to himself; in the novel's last pages, "past words," he cries to himself, a full realization of his isolation finally affording him the release of tears.

Before that moment, however, Wilhelm has fought isolation with words, always futilely. He and his father, as he confesses to Tamkin, "had words," but not the words either wants. . . . When his father talks, Wilhelm rightly thinks he means something other than he says; beneath the exterior affability lies a censorious dismissal. When Wilhelm talks, his father either shuts him out by not listening or wrongly surmises that Wilhelm means something other and worse than he says; Wilhelm cannot "speak his mind or ease his heart to him." . . . Wilhelm in fact reveals his anguish more than he wishes, more than his father can stand or his own dignity bear. (pp. 3-4)

The problem of words is general, as the example of Tamkin suggests. The divorce lawyers representing Wilhelm and his wife "talk and send me bills," getting nowhere. . . . Wilhelm and Rubin, the newsstand keeper, know a great deal about each other's concerns, but inexplicably none of this "could be mentioned, and the great weight of the unspoken left them little to talk about." . . . (p. 4)

The title [*Seize the Day*] declares clearly Bellow's principal means of organizing his analysis of human isolation in mid-twentieth-century New York: the hoary injunction *carpe diem*. The novel deals, expectedly and appropriately, with only a few hours of a single day in late spring, but Bellow uses his motif in a thoroughly ironic way. Concerned with dramatizing not merely the loneliness of individual New Yorkers but also their social milieu and cultural assumptions, he details the manifold discordances between Wilhelm's world and the literary world evoked by his title—the world, say of Robert Herrick's "Corinna's Going a-Maying." (pp. 4-5)

In the world of *Seize the Day* the human cycle has been disrupted. Not only is there Wilhelm in his infinitely protracted adolescence. There is his father, nearly eighty, wearing an "unseemly, monkey-striped shirt" bought in a college shop. . . . There are the old guests in the hotel lobby who, past seizing anything but money, have "nothing to do but wait out the day." . . . There are the old ladies with faces grotesquely marked in rouge and mascara who "stared at you with expressions that did not belong to their age." . . . In this world the way to seize the day is not to imitate the intense fragile beauty of the rose; instead of the rose, Tamkin advises, contemplate what is before you, "a man in a brown suit" and "corduroy shirt." To do so is to obey these commands: "Be in the present. Grasp the hour, the moment, the instant." . . . (pp. 5-6)

By transmuting "seize the day" into "here-and-now" Tamkin turns a crisp imperative into a mumble. Rappaport, the nearly-blind ex-chicken merchant, finds Wilhelm on the street; "he commanded him, 'Take me to the cigar store'" —and this command Tamkin interprets as "another instance of the 'here-and-now,'" a request for help. . . . To make such a man's "Take me to the cigar store" equivalent to *carpe diem* is unutterably to debase human language.

Bellow exploits his title most extensively to suggest radical contrasts in tone: Herrick's Renaissance celebration of youth, modulated finally by the remembrance of inevitable death, versus Bellow's morose neutrality enlivened by the gentle sad cynicism of the culminating funeral. Technically bright and sunny, the weather in the novel is in fact terrible: "the gassy air was almost motionless under the leaden spokes of sunlight." . . . Instead of Herrick's verdant countryside . . . the landscape is urban: "the mouth of midtown stood open and the skyscrapers gave back the yellow fire of the sun." . . . (pp. 6-7)

[Bellow] counters Herrick's delight in the seasonal harmony of man and nature . . . by observing again and again the irrelevance of the seasons, indeed of all nature, to money-ridden New Yorkers who play spring-time financial games with "futures"—with November wheat, July soybeans, and December rye. . . . Nature means nothing to New Yorkers; wheat, soybeans, eggs, the lard and rye which Wilhelm watches rise and fall, all are abstractions. But their meaninglessness means something to Bellow, who knows that the significance of *carpe diem* depends on dominant and inevitable natural cycles which relate intimately to human life. Behind the artificial birds caroling the rise and fall of December rye in the spring, Bellow hears Renaissance resonances—the song in *As You Like It* celebrating lovers who lie in spring "between the acres of the rye" (real rye), the voice of Titania deploring alteration in the tradition model of the seasons. . . . (pp. 7-8)

Natural sex suitable to spring becomes in Bellow's novel the furtive affair of a middle-aged man and a mistress who makes him talk with her disapproving priest. Wilhelm and Olive are not, like Herrick's speaker and his Corinna, "in our prime;" they are out of kilter with the cycle of human life. (p. 10)

Debasement of language is, I have suggested, a principal theme of the novel. Bellow's subtle and pervasive use of the *carpe diem* motif is typical of his procedure, as he sets barren, incommunicative New York speech against the evocative richness of literary language of the past—language, indeed the only language, which speaks to Wilhelm in the present. Shakespeare and Milton, Shelley and Keats, come to him by "involuntary memory" . . . and Bellow reinforces Wilhelm's allusions with others of his own—to the Bible, Emerson, Yeats, Spenser. These literary references harmonize with the major reference, *carpe diem*, and like it are used with irony. (pp. 10-11)

Repeatedly Bellow juxtaposes what Wilhelm calls "corny" (cheaply emotional, self-dramatizing, hackneyed) language with the paradoxically fresh language of the Renaissance so as to sharpen at once the corniness and the freshness. What Bellow admires and Wilhelm confusedly desires is the impersonal, controlled, and deeply moving expression of Milton and Shakespeare. After a painful interview with his father, Wilhelm thinks: "And finally sink beneath that watery floor—would that be tough luck, or would it be good riddance?" . . . The American colloquialisms jar ironically with Milton's simple grandeur, revealing the impossibility of realizing Milton's meaning in Wilhelm's world. Wilhelm's alternative interpretations of drowning—"tough luck, or . . . good riddance"—are both, according to Milton, incorrect. Milton's point in the turn of his poem is that "*Lycidas* your sorrow is not dead, / Sunk though he be beneath the wat'ry floor;" understanding that Lycidas is "mounted high" in heaven, "the Shepherds weep no more." . . . But Wilhelm cannot imitate the shepherds in relinquishing sorrow, in part because he lacks Milton's religious structure. (p. 12)

The line from "Lycidas" connects with a profusion of images related to water, images suggesting (as in Milton) both death and resurrection. From the first page to the last, Wilhelm has a sinking feeling; Bellow brings the cliché alive. The novel begins with Wilhelm in an elevator which, instead of elevating, "sank and sank;" he emerges into an oceanic lobby where (in a parody of Homer's "wine-dark sea") "the great dark red uneven carpet . . . billowed towards Wilhelm's feet." (pp. 12-13)

Again in the last paragraph of the novel he has a sinking feeling, as in the first paragraph, but this time differently: ". . . the heavy sea-like music [of the funeral he happens into] poured into him. . . . He heard it and sank deeper than sorrow," although one cannot be sure that he has understood that "*Lycidas* your sorrow is not dead."

In putting the weight of his conclusion on a submerged metaphor, in playing with Wilhelm's sinking feeling, Bellow is asking his water imagery to float a large meaning, and to some extent we have to take Wilhelm's final movement "toward the consummation of his heart's ultimate need" on Bellow's say-so. That need, the novel implies, is for self-forgiveness, for sympathy, for love; yet it is a little hard to accept the seeming epiphany at the funeral of an anonymous man as any more genuine than that "blaze of love" in the subway tunnel, which afterwards seems no more than an "involuntary" gush of feelings. Wilhelm's tears at the end (more salt water) are also involuntary—"He could not stop"—and Bellow's earlier irony leads one to apply the epiphany in the tunnel to the one in the funeral home, seeing Wilhelm's sour dismissal of his first "onrush" of feeling as predictive of a parallel dismissal once his tears have dried. Perhaps Bellow means to leave Wilhelm in a transforming ecstasy, but if so he undercuts his purpose by his previous delicate and forceful ironies and even, at the end, by directing Wilhelm "toward" but not "at" the "consummation." It may well be, whether or not Bellow willed it, that the final ironic touch is the omission of Wilhelm's inevitable come-down from the ecstasy of tears; the blank space after "consummation" may even suggest the "sorrowing dulnesse" which Donne (in "Farewell to Love") and his colleagues believed to follow upon the act of love. (pp. 13-14)

True to Emerson, Wilhelm in the end goes "past words" to the action of weeping, and thereby maybe approaches the truth he seeks. His wish to escape his ordinary condition may be compared, Bellow hints, with Yeats' impetus in "Sailing to Byzantium" to escape from old age in Ireland. Yeats takes actions ("And therefore I have sailed the seas") in order to achieve the condition, past words, of a golden bird singing upon a golden bough "Of what is past, or passing, or to come"—a song about time which encompasses and surpasses *carpe diem*. Watching the commodities figures move birdlike on the broker's screen, Wilhelm is, in Yeats' words which Bellow appropriates, "sick with desire." . . . But in *Seize the Day* the desire is not for wise teaching from Yeatsian sages but for a tip on December rye from Rappaport. . . . (p. 17)

[The] main reason Tamkin appeals to Wilhelm is that "I am a sucker for people who talk about the deeper things of life, even the way he does." . . . (p. 21)

Wilhelm's inarticulate accusations of himself and his world provide a clue to both his virtues and his vices. "Whenever at the end of the day he was unusually fatigued," he would exclaim "in his heart:" "Chicken! Unclean! Congestion! . . . Rat race! Phoney! Murder! Play the Game! Buggers!" . . . Each separate exclamation is a cliché; and yet by separating each from the other, by not developing or making connections among them, Wilhelm half-redeems the clichés. Bellow completes the redemption, using Wilhelm's terms to describe the rapaciously money-hungry Rappaport and Tamkin, thus implying that Tommy's perceptions apply less to himself than to others. . . .

That Wilhelm should fall for such an evidently suspicious redeemer demonstrates the depth of his desperation, of his passionate need to "know why he exists." In his yearning for Truth—about Life, about himself Wilhelm is typical of Bellow's heroes, all of whom, in the hackneyed phrase of Joseph in *Dangling Man*, seek to "know what I myself am," to answer the question "How is it possible today for a good man to live?" In other respects he is different, as this short and modest novel is different from and superior to Bellow's longer and more pretentious works—novels seemingly designed to prove Bellow's distance from the majority of contemporary novelists, whom he condemns as "strangely reluctant to use their brains or to give any sign that they have brains to use." (p. 23)

"The greatest achievement possible in a novel of ideas," Bellow has said, is to allow "the views most opposite to the author's own . . . to exist in full strength." *Seize the Day,* alone among his novels, succeeds in fulfilling this prescription. . . . By treating his great talker as a fraud and by making his hero inarticulate and ill-educated, Bellow insures against the danger of his characters' walking away with him, as Mr. Sammler, Herzog, and the rest tend to do.

No one in *Seize the Day* speaks for Bellow—that is, no one except Shakespeare and Milton, Emerson and Yeats, and the poets of *carpe diem*. For what Bellow does is invoke, and transmute into his own prose, the formal control of Shakespeare's sonnets and Milton's blank verse, along with the interlocking intellectual and emotional structures of Renaissance thought. Instead of boasting about his literary knowledge, he uses it to give the novel a discreetly concealed and solidly placed foundation. Through his spare juxtapositions of Spenser's gorgeous court of Gloriana with Broadway's faded Hotel Gloriana, he says or implies more substantial truths, and elicits more justified and complex sympathy for his "corny" hero careening out of control, than he is able to do in any of his more ambitious works. Reaching past polluted Broadway in the 1950's to a timeless world of "Dew-bespangling Herbe and Tree," Bellow methodically and splendidly fulfills the promise of his title. (pp. 23-4)

> *Carol M. Sicherman, "Bellow's 'Seize the Day': Reverberations and Hollow Sounds,"* in Studies in the Twentieth Century *(copyright 1975 by Stephen H. Goode), Spring, 1975, pp. 1-31.*

ROGER JONES

What make [*Mr. Sammler's Planet*] worth writing about, I feel, is its level of artistic organisation, a significant achievement for Bellow, already considered by many to be among America's finest writers. In two sections, one on *meaning*, the other on *form*, I shall highlight distinctive features of this compact work. . . .

First of all, the reader's approach to the book. Are we to take Bellow's feelings about life and society as identical with Sammler's?

There is a tendency to regard fictional protagonists as if they are a direct embodiment of their creator's life and attitudes. Some writers, not properly understanding *Mr. Sammler's Planet*, have criticised Bellow for showing more interest in the dying than in the living because of Sammler's preoccupation with the dying Elya Gruner and his own close escapes from death. In fact there is scant evidence that Bellow shares the weariness of life Sammler has. (p. 138)

In reading *Mr. Sammler's Planet* one is left in little doubt that Bellow is presenting a vision of contemporary society. But I believe a useful key (and Bellow seems to agree with me in this) to the interpretation of the book is found in a paper by Bellow entitled 'Skepticism and the Depth of Life.' . . . (pp. 138-39)

In 'Skepticism and the Depth of Life' Bellow, listing three literary tendencies he sees in this century, gives as the third "The rejection of sentiment and antagonism to human qualities which seemed to interfere with the supremacy of consciousness . . . which has the support of many contemporary psychological developments." . . . [He continues,]

> It seems . . . that intelligence has reached a point of extreme skepticism about this human carrying-on. It is with this skepticism that the writer today has to deal. It gives readers and spectators great satisfaction to see these old dramas of personality, love, duty, beauty, family, "heroic will", exposed. . . . The modern public has developed a curious spectator-passivity and detachment from things formerly felt and believed. . . . A withdrawn, musing anti-self watches the emotional circus.

From this quotation . . . we may infer Bellow's position: he sets out to deal with, to combat and to cure a destructive scepticism about the depth of life. So withdrawn musing Sammler is not Bellow. It is Bellow's way of reaching a public he fears epitomise a "withdrawn, musing anti-self (watching) the emotional circus" with cynicism. Bellow's work gives, then, a view of society, not of self. (pp. 139-40)

[There appears little enough significance in the bare events of the novel.] Yet Bellow's narration makes the book dense with meanings. And though little happens in the conventional sense the book is a wholly convincing reading experience, for much of the meaning is conveyed without abstract intellectualisation and the book remains novelistic, evoking a sense of real life. This, in a novel of ideas, is a significant achievement. (pp. 140-41)

Various critics have suggested it as a flaw in Bellow's earlier work that, in supposedly naturalistic works with intendedly full characters, the important element of a dynamic reciprocal relationship such as exists between real individuals was missing or poorly done. This sort of relation between characters is similarly absent from *Mr. Sammler's*

Planet yet it is not missed there. Perhaps this is partly because the book is wholly the consciousness of Sammler, a man in any case distanced from others. There is a form of relationship between characters, though, and through this a great deal of the significance is conveyed. It is not an existential relationship but a static relation of marriage or blood, or relative function in society, or trend or generation represented. Such relationships convey meaning immediately because this is how we tend to identify characteristics in daily life. This is often how characters are cast in films and plays. As types. By age, job, race, family status.

So the organisation of the characters in the novel parallels the shape of the meaning Bellow conveys. Sammler is the focal point and he is related to most of the characters directly or by marriage. Were a genealogy drawn for all the book's characters and in place of their names was written what they are made to represent, the genealogy would be a picture of the recent historical forces shaping this society, as Bellow sees it. And the notable thing is the way it works without the reader realising or being jolted from the world of the book by abstract comment extraneous to the fiction.

We can see the process in Sammler's own characteristics. Bringing together details revealed gradually in the course of the narrative, we see Sammler as a tall, ruddy-faced old intellectual, a Polish Jew of monied parents, brought up as a gentleman, first interested in culture by his mother, becoming like a 'Britisher' by imitation, living in the Bloomsbury of the thirties and taking pride in knowing H. G. Wells. (p. 141)

The name Uncle Sammler—a European Jewish Uncle Sam (USA). The imitation of British culture: and the multi-level meaning of his having one eye and knowing H. G. Wells. Some connections are evident, others more uncertain. It may be, for example, that his first name, Artur, is not only after Schopenhauer but is in one passage an allusion to *Art* as an activity. When Sammler is trying . . . to report a theft he has seen on the bus the policeman calls him "Art" several times. . . . The policeman has no time to spare and the conversation displays the irrelevance of the individual in an over-stressed society. But the conversation may also be a poignant metaphor for the artist like Bellow ("Art . . .") trying vainly to convey his perception of how something of deep value to us is being 'stolen', while most of us are, as Bellow has said elsewhere, too busy with other priorities to heed. (p. 142)

Sammler has only one eye. This not only serves to set him apart from others and convey the awful time he had in the war (as representative of a whole generation and race), it suggests an inner eye that looks to deeper knowledge. For his damaged eye does distinguish light and dark. Good and Evil? And the references to H. G. Wells (his optimistic view of how life would develop by our time ironically contrasted with the reality) calls up Wells's short story 'The Country of the Blind'. If we do not already know the story Bellow, with characteristic reflexive awareness, makes Sammler mention the connection whilst talking with Dr. Lal. In Wells's story, instead of the one-eyed man being king in the country of the blind, as the proverb foretells, he is almost persuaded that his is the faulty perception and is about to agree to be blinded, when he regains confidence in his vision. Bellow's use of Sammler's one-eyedness is manifold. But one significance seems ironically to invert Wells's view of scientific enlightenment.

This touches only a few of the connections Sammler's characteristics suggest. As we pass from Sammler to Shula, his "loony" daughter, we can see her as representing the meaningful cultural attitudes of the parent generation emptily mimicked by the children. The daughter is a cultural scavenger. Any information or education, religious or cultural, she soaks up but is unable to respond to or use in her life. (pp. 142-43)

If we see Shula-Slawa as the confused cultural manifestation of a generation originating in the thirties, her relationship with her husband Eisen, from whom she is separated, comes to be a comment on the relationship between a generation and its artists (or some of them). Eisen is about to become recognised as an artist. Previously he has been a reasonably competent craftsman. His art is absurdist art. And as he beat Shula till she finally left him, so absurdist art beats society till its audience deserts. Eisen's art, which makes those it portrays hideous and deathlike and ridiculous, may exemplify the destructive art referred to in Bellow's essay on scepticism previously quoted.

This Eisen downs the princely negro by swinging at him from behind with a bag of iron sculpture. Mad Art crushes the noble thief who here seems to represent man's last sense of his own barbaric nobility. The negro thief is "probably a mad spirit". But he is "Mad with an idea of *noblesse*." And that even this corrupt nobility should be destroyed by degraded, absurd Eisen is one of the most sad and shocking moments in the book.

Feffer the student-entrepreneur is unintentionally involved in the destruction of this mad nobility. Feffer seems to personify the insatiable curiosity of Americans, the get-up-and-go, the time-and-energy-for-everything syndrome. He has scores of crazy schemes. His curiosity and his desire to *use* the sight of the pickpocket at work leads him into a struggle with minor evil that he cannot win. A struggle Sammler (personifying the old culture) is powerless to save him from without calling upon the culture of the next generation, mad Eisen, to 'save' him in a way almost more awful than the fate he otherwise faces. (pp. 143-44)

Many threads like this can be followed up to yield an analysis of recent and contemporary society. Almost every detail of each character works to convey a sense of real individuals *and* this larger pattern. With so many functions for each to fulfil, it is perhaps no wonder that we do not notice the characters' lack of 'relations' in Mailer's sense.

Unifying these socio-historical details is Sammler's worldview, a metaphysical stand brought out mainly through conversations with the Indian Dr. Lal.

Sammler sees personality types as particular "forms taken by spiritual striving." They are not fully developed, merely alluded to, but the idea seems to be that what is perceived and explained is but the form taken by the underlying 'thing-in-itself' as mind imposes its own form upon it. Behind 'appearances' is 'spirit' which endures unchanged, 'appearances' including man's nature and the perceptual world. Sammler apparently believes that individual personality is an innovation, comparatively speaking, in man's history. And that the bitterness at the suffering the failure to find a viable individual personality has caused gives rise to such things as the Theatre of the Absurd (I take this from Bellow's essay). Sammler tells the story of mad King Rumkowski as an example of the process. This 'king' was

an absurd failure, set up as puppet king over the Jews of Lodz by the Nazis, to rule even as his people were loaded for Auschwitz. This 'king' acted out a king's old functions with pageants, ceremonies, government; he even printed money and stamps. He terrorised his 'people'. It was a reality for them, yet entirely set up by the Nazis. One might think of it as a Monty Python programme played with real people. In seeing the abasement of human beings in failed forms of humanity the Germans took great delight.

Sammler sees this failure of personality not as an intrinsic failing of human beings but only as a failure so far "to produce a human figure of adequate stature" to match the obscure whisper of intuition, the often unheeded demands of the spirit. But he sees depths beyond our present awareness, something more than the scientifically discoverable make-up of man, and this is what the book seeks to evoke at the end. (pp. 145-46)

So far I have left out one slant of all Sammler's thought: his mistrust of explanations. "All will explain everything to all, until the next, the new common version is ready", Sammler thinks ironically.

Yet paradoxically this book contains much explanation, of various sorts, from insights to fictionalisation of abstract points. Bellow's work could be regarded as a novel of ideas of explanations. And yet of mistrust of explanation. Talking with Dr. Lal, Sammler says "One must live with all combinations of the facts." And indeed this seems to be what Bellow is doing.

In practice the volume of explanation in his work makes it futile for him to express mistrust. (p. 146)

Saul Bellow's previous novels have been criticised for the weakness of his narratives which were seen to have dramatically unjustified resolutions and characters not fully realised. He has been criticised for presenting a solipsistic world, and for failing to create a convincing spatial world. In *Mr. Sammler's Planet* Saul Bellow transcends these limitations, for he makes features that had been limitations work for him. The solipsistic tendency in most of his work becomes justified in the book since it is intentionally restricted to the consciousness of one man. *Story* is relegated so far into the background that we hardly see it sufficiently to become aware whether it is dramatically justified or not as the rapid flow of thought and image holds attention.

And as for the world of space and time found in conventionally naturalistic works, in this work we are aware of almost no sense of space and time. There is *compression of time*. By transitions from inner world to dialogue with the external world Saul Bellow dislocates the time and space sense of the reader (without causing discomfort) and creates a literary world where the flow is not experienced as time flow. (p. 148)

It is worth highlighting here the manner in which, by virtue of Bellow's great self-awareness of the act of writing, the book becomes an explicit commentary on its own processes. I have already mentioned several places where an implicit characteristic is pointed up in the narrative. For example, the connection between Sammler's one eye and the H. G. Wells story. Bellow's *in medias res* may have been his view of the form of the book. Or he may have meant it at face value, just as describing Feffer. With hindsight, his earlier works can be seen working their way towards this form. *Herzog* already manifested many aspects of it. But *Mr. Sammler's Planet* is the purest example yet. It is as if the writer has realised the direction and potential of a naturally developing form and consciously clarified it. In referring to Joyce he is acknowledging his debt; indeed we already suspected from the name Moses Herzog, the name of a minor character in *Ulysses,* that Bellow had been dipping into Joyce's writers' manual.

The important thing is that Bellow succeeds in using this self-awareness without throwing the reader out of the fictional world into an awareness that he is not 'in' the story but merely reading a writer's excrescence. (p. 149)

Bellow is on record as disapproving of *imposing* form on the novel. It is likely, then, that the form *in medias res* arises from the effort to express his vision. . . . Though *Mr. Sammler's Planet* is a mixture of various things, novelistic in parts, elsewhere philosophical, essay-like, sometimes speechifying, aphoristic, speculative, these are unified as an expression of Bellow's vision of contemporary reality, so that the separation of meaning and form in discussing the book is just a critic's simplifying device which has no reality in the book. The meaning is in the very structure of the sentences, the paragraph and subject changes, the way characters are introduced, and dialogue, and in the rhythm of events.

By referring to details in the narrative I shall attempt to show more precisely the nature of this form.

One aspect is the quality of flow. This is a *lateral* flow, by association of ideas as Sammler moves from one thought to something laterally—rather than sequentially or logically—related. The flow is kept unbroken by an interesting device: when a character is about to appear or an event occur (this is only noticed in retrospect) some small reference to it is made within the flow. Not only does this stop disparate events diverting the flow; it puts us into the middle of things before they happen, which is what the form demands. (pp. 149-50)

These are things that dislocate our sense of clock time within the book, dissolving the separation between mind and external reality. Consequent upon this creation of a timeless, spaceless literary world the flow of Sammler's thought is no indication of time passing. We have few reference points to indicate whether moments, hours, or days have passed between successive emergencies from Sammler's inward thought into his witnessing of an external event. The mode of flow by association rather than time-flow by sequence of event, the mode most commonly found, is broadly similar to that used by Henry Miller; though Bellow has said that to his knowledge he is not influenced by Miller.

One striking occurrence of the compression of time is pointed up—with Bellow's characteristic awareness, and confidence—when Sammler asks himself, "Feffer's lecture, twenty-four? forty-eight hours ago?" A question most readers will be unable to answer immediately. For in accordance with the form (mirroring Bellow's sense of the ways consciousness moves in its layers?) we have been thrown from day 1 into day 2 without our being aware of it and without being able to say precisely *where* in the book it occurred. (pp. 151-52)

Not everything in the book strikes me as harmonious. The most severely jarring parts are the comparatively long passages detailing Sammler's Second World War experiences. I find their quality unconvincing. Perhaps it is my failing, for I do not understand what function Bellow intends these passages to fulfil. It is true that people had such experiences, and they were certainly awful. (p. 152)

The fact that such events happened does not justify their inclusion in fiction. Perhaps part of their unconvincing quality is in the essaylike nature of these descriptions, out of character with the quick flow and turn of Sammler's other thoughts. It is more like someone writing a report. Part dispassionate, yet with just enough of a touch of sensationalism to remind one uncomfortably of the cheap romanticism of poor films and women's magazine stories.

Bellow has Sammler deny any romantic value. "To some people, true enough, experience seemed wealth. Misery worth a lot. Horror a fortune." This disclaimer almost disarms us but it finally fails to dispel the association with cheap romanticism. One can continue to speculate on Bellow's intent, moral, symbolic, as a correction to seeing suffering as glamorous. But contextual justification failing as it does by the nature of the piece, there can be no other justification.

Finally, I am not sure that the vision of society Bellow presents is true of society as a whole. Perhaps all America *is* like that. To me the vision looks like that experienced by only a very small sector of humanity, living a certain sort of big-city life. Or it is a generalisation of the image presented by glossy magazines, weekly tv mags, and a substantial part of the national media. The greater part of society is moved by far more real values and desires than are Shula, Margotte, Feffer, Wallace, and Angela. (pp. 152-53)

> *Roger Jones, "Artistry and the Depth of Life: Aspects of Attitude and Technique in 'Mr. Sammler's Planet',"* in The Anglo-Welsh Review, *Spring, 1976, pp. 138-53.*

RITA D. JACOBS

It is . . . [the] seemingly paradoxical currents in Bellow's work, the dignity of life and the comic accident that we exist at all, that are so exhilarating. Like the true comedian, the one who shows the truths of life, Bellow discards the easy laugh in favor of the deeper, cosmic laughter which responds to the human condition. . . .

The ghetto feeling, the feeling of being set apart and yet making a kind of virtue of this separateness, is strong in Bellow's work. His characters are often outside the mainstream of society and go through internal conflicts about whether this is a condition that is imposed or chosen. In a sense, this ghetto image is a metaphor of alienation not only for the Jew but for modern man. (p. 194)

In speaking about his novel *Herzog* Bellow has said that "any Bildungsroman—and *Herzog* is, to use that heavy German term, a Bildungsroman—concludes with the first step. The first *real* step." In this sense all of his novels are Bildungsromane. Throughout the novels his major characters are striving to "be," rather than to exist in a state of "becoming." In the Bellovian world the first real step is made when one stops becoming and starts to be. . . .

All of Bellow's characters wander, physically or mentally, until they take their first real steps.

This agony, this intense desire to be and in that be-ing know a true direction, is Bellow's depiction of the crisis of modern man. This desire is constantly thwarted by all of the alternatives and stimuli, the cacophony of modern life. The strident and self-announcing possibilities of the modern world, of technology, of urban life, of sexuality, are often overwhelming and prevent his characters from finding a truth about themselves. Hence they spend much of their time relishing their consideration of alternatives and at the same time feeling the burden of choice imposed by the presence of alternatives. (p. 195)

[A theme that occupies] Bellow throughout his career [is] man's difficulty in reconciling his desire for individuality and greatness with his desire for community and love. It is only when harmony is achieved that his characters can take the first steps. But for modern man, and especially for Bellow's intellectualizing, rationalizing men, the knowledge that although these desires appear to be contradictory they can be accepted as complementary and compatible is hard to come by. In essence, the battlefield is within the self, the struggle is between head and heart. The individual resides in the head. Indeed, Bellow's characters are among the most intelligent and articulate in American literature, and the communion comes with a balance of head and heart.

But there are many things that distract Bellow's modern men from finding a balance. They test and try the alternatives and sometimes get swept away by the sheer variety confronting them. . . .

The city for Bellow is representative of distraction, of the modern striving for originality and the concomitant exhibiting selves that clamor for attention. As Herzog says, "The question of ordinary human experience is the principal question of these modern centuries." But where is that ordinary experience to be found? Certainly not in the glass and steel structures known as our modern cities. What is found in the cities is condemned as ultimately uninteresting. (p. 196)

Bellow's characters go in search of reality instructors, models or teachers who can help them make their choices. Henderson finds the African king, Tommy Wilhelm listens to the pseudo-psychologist Dr. Tamkin, Herzog takes instruction from his ex-wife Madeleine and his onetime best friend and Madeleine's current lover, Gersbach, and Charlie Citrine tries to learn through his antagonistic encounters with a small-time hoodlum, Cantabile. But these reality instructors are foils. They have no glimpse of any reality but their own, and Bellow's central characters eventually learn that reality is indeed nothing that can be taught but something that must be known for itself. It is true that everyone in the city speaks his own language and that each one sees his own world. Bellow's protagonists finally know that they can never accept anyone else's reality until they have accepted their own. Henderson's innermost self continually screams, "I want, I want," but it is only when he can identify what it is that he wants that he can hear the other people—the "he wants," the "she wants"—who surround him.

Lest it seem that Bellow's world is only one of agonizing thought and self-recrimination leavened by puns and costumes, it must be stated that his characters and their adventures are lusty and humorous. The characters pursue sensuality and sexuality and are often prone to pratfalls for passion's sake. Bellow's female characters are never as fully characterized as his males and are often overly bitchy or overly sensual, but they are not cartoons or caricatures. (pp. 196-97)

Bellow's women are often one-sided for argument's sake, but he always gives us at least a glimpse of them in other contexts where they display fuller character traits. . . . He does not create women as central characters but as foils, in much the same way as the reality instructors are portrayed. Bellow's men cannot find their own realities through the women, but they cannot exist without them; and much of the humor in his novels emerges from this very human conundrum. Ultimately it is the reality and the intensity of the self that Bellow's characters hunger for and find. It is the self that the intellectual, the city dweller, the man burdened with the history of civilization and confronted by the ambiguities of modern forms can only come to by working through and then past the questioning, always seeking mind. . . . [The] only way to find the truth is to intensify, to feel intensely and not to attempt to make sense of it, not to interpret but to welcome it as a gift.

For Henderson and Herzog the buried poetry of America is brought to the surface by Whitman. . . .

There is a coming-of-age quality about Bellow's work that has nothing to do with chronology but rather with the achievement of a harmonic balance of self. Balancing the head and the heart and ceasing to have to prove oneself, not seeking success but embracing dignity and humor, appreciating history but breaking free of its shackles—there is about all of these notions a peculiarly American quality. It is an American goal—to be born anew with the lessons and riches of the past clearly present in the minds of the founders alongside the belief that here, at last, the past will no longer be a burden but a liberation. Bellow tells us we can make it if we only allow ourselves to be what we are. Bellow has not been afraid to say that "the mystery is too great." Yet unfailingly and with great skill he has followed his own notion that "novelists are wrong to put an interpretation of history at the base of artistic creation. . . . It is better that the novelist should trust his own sense of life." (p. 197)

Rita D. Jacobs, "'Truths on the Side of Life': Saul Bellow, Nobel Prize 1976," in World Literature Today *(copyright 1977 by the University of Oklahoma Press), Vol. 51, No. 2, Spring, 1977, pp. 194-97.*

JOHN CHEEVER

Saul Bellow is the living author I most admire. Since having read his description of a woman washing window-glass in "The Dangling Man" so many years ago I have found him the most interesting author I know writing in English, which is the only language I can read with ease these days. Saul's virtuosity, his keen sense of the perils of his vocation and the architecture of his accomplishments seem to me peerless. (p. 3)

John Cheever, in The New York Times Book Review *(© 1977 by The New York Times Company; reprinted by permission), December 4, 1977.*

CYNTHIA OZICK

[Bellow is] amused by a crucifix (as if it were a toy without a history); and about sex he's a baby. But beyond this, one reads him with the seriousness one brings to the redemption of the garbage pile of one's own life. He mixes recklessness with a primordial awe, and his philosophic whine concentrates mainly on the petty, where we live. His perception of the unity of the human mind doesn't wash out its diversity. He uses language like a gill. Our worst writers (even when they are, in language, our best) write as if their own being were a one-shot affair, instead of an instance of a continuing history; solipsists, who want to be "original," bore because they don't believe in evil. Bellow, even when he is on the run from history, believes in history; and his whole fiction is a wrestling with the Angel of Theodicy. It's uncomfortable to read him because he doesn't allow a distance (as Chekhov does) between the rumpled spirits of his fiction and the reader, and because in this sense he isn't a "modern"; also he is argumentative and nags after a victory. All this means he is a real Voice.

What, in literature, is a Voice? A presence—a corpus of fine size—that can speak to its own generation because it has itself been spoken to by the generations before. (p. 66)

Cynthia Ozick, in The New York Times Book Review *(© 1977 by The New York Times Company; reprinted by permission), December 4, 1977.*

GLENN A. KINDILIEN

Saul Bellow's "Looking for Mr. Green," which records social worker George Grebe's attempt to deliver a relief check in a Chicago ghetto, is typically and correctly read as a search for the real self. But why is the object of the search called Mr. *Green?* Wouldn't any other name serve this theme as well? The answer is no. Green is used because the story is about more than a search for the self; it is also about how the self in modern society is defined.

The story says, in effect, that the self is created by money. Rather than detract from the search-for-the-reality-of-the-self theme, however, this idea gives greater depth to the theme by defining the nature of that reality. To understand this process it is first necessary to become aware of the identity between the name "Green" and money.

"Mr. Green" is a common courtroom code-word, one that would be familiar to social workers like George Grebe and authors as well versed in the law as Saul Bellow. If an attorney's client fails to pay his bill, the lawyer normally asks for a postponement of the case. He begins his request by addressing the bench as follows: "Mr. Green is not here." To laymen it simply means that a key witness has not appeared; to insiders the attorney has signalled the judge that he wants a delay because he has not received his client's money (his "green"). The client is left without counsel, and until he pays his bill, he doesn't (in the court's view) even exist. Once the payment is made, he will again be represented by counsel as a "real" person.

This process is also at the heart of what happens in "Looking for Mr. Green." Here too "Mr. Green" defines a state of non-being; here too money is the passport (or pass*word*) to identity. Grebe's search may lead to Mr. Green, but until Green actually accepts the check he doesn't really exist. His reality is determined by money—because that is how identity is determined in the modern world.

In the story the money-identity equation is defined by Winston Field, another of Grebe's check recipients. His scheme to create a series of Black millionaires "by subscription" states the central truth of the story: " . . . the only big thing is money. . . . "

Winston Field thus knows that a person cannot be respected by society until society recognizes his existence, and that in the modern world he exists who has sufficient capital to participate as a competitive consumer; he does not exist who lacks that capital. This is the assumption upon which society (and the story) operates: money precedes identity, precedes respect. (pp. 104-06)

The lawyer's client is an anonymous "Mr. Green" until he pays his bill; Winston Field's people are non-beings until they become, also through money, participating members of society; Bellow's Mr. Green is likewise without identity until he receives his check. The name "Green" is thus the very substance of the search-for-the-self motif, clarifying the definition of self and offering insight into an economic system that uses money as a measure of character. (p. 107)

Glenn A. Kindilien, "The Meaning of the Name 'Green' in Saul Bellow's 'Looking for Mr. Green',' in Studies in Short Fiction *(copyright 1978 by Newberry College), Winter, 1978, pp. 104-07.*

JOHN GARDNER

[Bellow] is actually not a novelist at heart but an essayist disguised as a writer of fiction. In *Seize the Day, The Adventures of Augie March,* and *Henderson the Rain King,* Bellow makes serious use of fictional techniques, but even there the essayist-lecturer is always ready to step in, stealing the stage from the fictional characters to make the fiction more "important."

Bellow's self-indulgence takes various forms. On occasion it appears as stylistic fiddling—as language designed mainly to show off Bellow's gifts as philosopher, poet, mimic, or Jewish humorist—not aimed, as it should be, at clarifying action and character or at controlling the reader's attention and response, heightening his pleasure and understanding. When Bellow is feeling self-indulgent, his language, instead of sharpening effects, distracts the reader, calls attention to the writer and thus away from the story unfolding like a dream in the reader's mind. Fiction should go after understanding by creating characters who subtly embody values and who test them. with clear but inexpressible results, in action. Discursive thought is not fiction's most efficient tool; the interaction of characters is everything. But Bellow can almost never handle more than one character at a time (an exception, perhaps, is his creation of both Humboldt and Citrine in *Humboldt's Gift),* and that one major character, Bellow's surrogate, has always an inordinate love of talk. At every opportunity, Bellow leans his characters and action on some doorframe, turns off his fiction's clock, and from behind the mask of his hero expatiates. When the essay voice begins, we are asked to appreciate, mainly on the basis of the speaker's charm, a set of prejudices and opinions, or shrewd observations—that have nothing to do, directly, with the progress of the action or the values under test.

Bellow may sometimes get away with his intrusions, partly because of his comic gift and his gift for finding powerful symbols—for instance the symbol of the moral individual buried alive in *Mr. Sammler's Planet*—and also because his opinions often strike the reader as carefully thought out and wise. Certainly his stand is boldly opposed to those trashy popular philosophies we so often encounter in other writers' work—cynical nihilism or the winking, mugging despair of Thomas Pynchon (Bellow counters with a theory of faith and responsible love); self-regarding existentialism (Bellow offers, instead, a theory of universal relatedness in which animals and people have certain common woes); tyrannical Marxism and a whining hatred of "American business" (Bellow offers, instead, a view of people—even naïve Communists and crass business people—as individuals, of suffering as universal and a thing to be dealt with, and of history as a moral search). And it is true, too, that though Bellow's intrusions offend, they nevertheless prove that Bellow can still feel unabashed concern. But the fact remains that his novels come off in the end as sprawling works of advice, not art. (pp. 30, 32)

> *John Gardner, in* Saturday Review *(© 1978 by Saturday Review Magazine Corp.; reprinted with permission), April 1, 1978.*

*   *   *

BERRYMAN, John   1914-1972

Berryman was an American poet, biographer, and editor. Along with Robert Lowell and Sylvia Plath, he led the confessional movement in modern poetry and is considered one of the twentieth century's most important poets. A striking feature of his verse is the combination of a strict stanzaic pattern with idiosyncratic language, a lively poetic voice, and emotionally intense, highly personal themes. Berryman's Dream Songs, which he worked on from 1964 until his death, are generally considered his most outstanding poetic achievement. The poet took his own life in 1972. (See also *CLC*, Vols. 1, 2, 3, 4, 6, 8, and *Contemporary Authors*, Vols. 15-16; obituary, Vols. 33-36, rev. ed.; *Contemporary Authors Permanent Series*, Vol. 1.)

JOHN HAFFENDEN

Reading and rereading these essays [in *The Freedom of the Poet*], I am struck forcibly by their consistency of attitude and expression, and by their interrelatedness, even though they were written over a period of three decades, some as lectures, some for a college textbook, others as introductions, another to be broadcast over the radio. The style can be muscular, dense with clauses and parentheses, occasionally self-indulgent—as in the famous, vexing, but engrossing analysis of Lowell's "Skunk Hour," which Lowell told me he found interesting (as I do) as a parallel to the poem. All the same, I would not wish away any of Berryman's *obiter dicta;* every sidelight—impious, erudite, arrogant—is revealing. Equally delightful are his deft and incisive characterizations, and such attributions as that Cummings and Williams, "loaded with merited honours," were "impenitent, irregular, mannered," and that Pound's verse is "discrete and suave."

For the stories: here are "The Lovers," an enigmatic, evocative piece which John Crowe Ransom considered "brilliant"; the masterful "Wash Far Away," first penned in 1947, often revised, twice rejected by *The New Yorker,* one of Berryman's best . . . ; and "The Imaginary Jew," a startling, autobiographical tale which Delmore Schwartz compared to Turgenev's, and which even Ezra Pound admired, but which now strikes me as perhaps too program-

matic: but this is not to undervalue its candor and impact. It was written in 1945, when modern civilization first knew itself naked. Given time and occasion, Berryman would have rewritten the ending. "Thursday Out," a meditation of the Taj Mahal, stands curiously, but correctly, with the fiction. Like some of Hemingway's journalism, it is not purely expository, since Berryman sees himself in the picture. It is more an invocation, an exploration of a mystery, figured by a person in a tale. It stands comparison with Henry Adams's writing on Chartres; I can only add that the reader owes such celebrations to himself. The evidence of this volume renews one's sadness that Berryman was not able to, in his own phrase, reassemble his gift. (pp. 298-99)

> *John Haffenden, in* The Yale Review *(© 1977 by Yale University, reprinted by permission of the editors), Winter, 1977.*

WILLIAM PRATT

As he was transforming himself from an imitative young poet into the inimitable later fantasist of the "Dream Songs," Berryman was developing a comparable critical style that was provocative, erudite and humorous. His nearest counterpart was Randall Jarrell, a poet-critic with whom he had much in common, including the lamentable suicide; and it may be said of both writers that their wit was costly, since it placed them at a measurable distance above most of their contemporaries and may have contributed to their sense of desperation. But there is no desperation [in *The Freedom of the Poet*], and in fact the collection shows all the best sides of Berryman and little of his worst. As a critic, Berryman can be enjoyed for the sheer pleasure of his discoveries, often made in the reading of very familiar authors. Perhaps his most original piece of criticism is on "Shakespeare at Thirty," a tour de force in which, by looking closely at the earliest works, he brings Shakespeare to life as a young man starting out on the greatest of literary careers. Not only does Berryman achieve a remarkable identity with the mind of Shakespeare, but he does equally well with modern poets as different as Stephen Crane and Ezra Pound, establishing the wide range of his critical sympathies.

Good at throwing new light on accepted authors, he can also be illuminating about minor authors, especially in essays on "*The Monk* and its Author" and on "Thomas Nashe and *The Unfortunate Traveler*," and he provides some excellent examples of literary exegesis in short pieces on Hemingway's "A Clean, Well-Lighted Place," on "The Sorrows of Captain Carpenter" and on "Prufrock's Dilemma." He plunges off the deep end of symbolic interpretation only once, in a highly Freudian reading of Conrad's *Heart of Darkness;* but even in the midst of murky speculations about sexual innuendo he can flash forth with a memorable aside about his own motives for criticism:

> One works out of a desire to *know*—or perhaps boredom or habit—but I think the first cause is paramount. Just to know for oneself. Then, as to writing out and printing, I feel myself that we should trade all accessible information on important works of art.

We can be glad that John Berryman often felt the need to write out and print what he knew about literature, since it adds to the sum of what we all know. (pp. 286-87)

> *William Pratt, in* World Literature Today

(copyright 1977 by the University of Okla-homa Press), Vol. 51, No. 2, Spring, 1977.

HELEN VENDLER

The charm and vivacity of Berryman's apprehension of the world, even in his last unlivable years, stayed alive in his poems. Berryman was a consummate entertainer, and there is scarcely a song which is not, however horrible its subject matter, entertaining—"the natural soul," as he says here, "performing, as it will." The most endearing of talkers, he can make even Baudelaire's "hypocrite lecteur" light-hearted. . . . (p. 85)

The alternations of exhaustion and gaiety, self-loathing and affection, witticism and sorrow, flicker like a light-show through [*Henry's Fate*], as through his other songs. "Even in this last *Dream Song*," says Lowell in his elegy for Ber-ryman, "to mock your catlike flight / from home and classes." That last song, written "within forty-eight hours of his death" according to [John] Haffenden [the editor of the collection], imagines the full scenario for the suicide—"unless my wife wouldn't let me out of the house, / unless the cops noticed me crossing the campus / up to the bridge / & clappt me in for observation." This full self-knowledge of the impractical man, sure he cannot plan even his own suicide so that it will come off, exhibits that part of Berry-man that was always coldly aware of his escapades. The torture of the contemplative self watching the errant self lies behind the elaborate and successful literary charade of Henry Pussycat, the alter ego enabling the poems, more often than not, to escape that lyric soddenness so evident in the "Morning Prayer." *Sotto voce,* under all the Henry poems, we hear the lyric that would be breathed out by the despairing self if it were to speak straight. The poems about alcoholism and family here are often written directly by the despairing self, and they lack the comic flexibility contrib-uted by Henry, who served Berryman like an arrangement of mirrors to see around corners when a view of his own face in a glass would have undone his language. Oddly enough, for all their affectation of chattiness, the Dream Songs are poems written to be read on the page as well as heard aloud; though their meaning "explodes" (to quote Hopkins) when read with the proper conversational empha-sis, their careful shapeliness is visible only on the page. (pp. 85-6)

Helen Vendler, in The Yale Review *(© 1977 by Yale University; reprinted by permission of the editors), Autumn, 1977.*

PETER STITT

The popular conception of John Berryman that one most often encounters is that he was a boozehound and skirt-chaser who chose to reveal his personal life in verse. This legend was fostered in part by Berryman's late poems, in part by semi-salacious discussions of him as a *confessional* poet, and in part by his own unfortunate attempts . . . to project an image as the *poet maudit*. This popular concep-tion has unfortunately tended to obscure the serious and intellectual nature of Berryman's writings. Nowhere is this seriousness more evident than in his literary criticism, now happily collected into a single volume entitled *The Free-dom of the Poet. . . .* As we might have expected, Berry-man's criticism shares many traits with his poetry—it is se-rious and playful, it is scholarly and personal, it is consistently intelligent—and it is good.

That Berryman was deeply serious about literature is proven on every page of this book. He has as much con-tempt for nonserious writing, for "the popular boys," as he has admiration for the real thing—and the real thing is, by its nature, intellectual: "It is no exaggeration to say that the slick writer wishes to make the reader forget himself and the serious writer wishes to make him *think*." . . . Berry-man makes this heavy demand of every work he considers—either it has something important to say or it is nothing, either it appeals to the intellect or it is nowhere. (pp. 368-69)

One of the most impressive things demonstrated by this collection is how well and how completely Berryman did his homework. In areas which I can judge, the record is striking. For example, in a review of some books about Henry James first published in the *Sewanee Review* in 1945, Berryman takes time to instruct the uninitiated in how to read James's works, and suggests the order in which they should be read. (p. 369)

It has been observed, by Hyatt Waggoner and others, that New Criticism, with its emphasis upon nuance and tech-nique and its de-emphasis of biography, history, sociology, and psychology, was the appropriate approach for modern-ist writers to take to literature. Berryman is in another camp; just as his poetry is post-modernist, his criticism is post-New Critical. The most common complaint we find him making in this volume is against what he calls "T. S. Eliot's intolerable and perverse theory of the impersonality of the artist." Berryman's tack is quite different—he chose to place the question of personality, usually of his own per-sonality, at the heart of his major poems. In his criticism, likewise, he never forgets the writer behind the work, and is quite willing to refer questions of interpretation and em-phasis back through the author's writings to his life. His general position is explained by this statement, made in ref-erence to Robert Lowell: "One thing critics not themselves writers of poetry occasionally forget is that poetry is com-posed by actual human beings, and tracts of it are very closely about them."

Berryman's reliance upon the life and personality of the author is evident in small issues as well as in large ones. . . . The method is sometimes revealing about Berry-man's own poems—as when he points out the semiautobio-graphical basis of the *Cantos* (in *The Dream Songs,* Berry-man took Pound's method a step further)—and sometimes the method is poignant. The brilliant essay "Shakespeare at Thirty" gains much of its power from Berryman's implicit identification with his subject, whom Berryman imagines in 1594—forced out of London by the closing of the theaters because of the plague—as frustrated and stalled, aware of his powers but uncertain of his future. (pp. 370-71)

Berryman does not always handle his version of the bio-graphical fallacy with such skill. . . . Berryman's knowledge of Freud serves him well in *The Dream Songs,* but turns ["Conrad's Journey"] . . . into an unintentional mockery. It is typical of Berryman, however, to proceed authorita-tively and with élan, even when he is marching into a swamp. Like everything that he wrote, this book is domi-nated by his voice and personality, and generally the effect is entirely positive.

For one thing, the book is witty. . . . Intellectual playful-ness is present throughout the volume—it is what allows

Berryman, for example, to analyze the style of Broad's eulogy for McTaggart. . . . (p. 371)

More striking, more personal, even more confessional are the opening sentences of the essay of Anne Frank: "When the first installment of the translated text of *The Diary of Anne Frank* appeared in the spring of 1952, in *Commentary,* I read it with amazement. The next day, when I went into town to see my analyst, I stopped by the magazine's offices—I often did, to argue with Clem Greenberg. . . ." Berryman was a master at the use of this kind of intimate, irritating detail.

I notice that this sort of thing is much more common in Berryman's later criticism than in his earlier, the point of change coming in the middle fifties. When he wrote *Homage to Mistress Bradstreet* in 1953 and began *The Dream Songs* in 1955, Berryman ceased being a rather uninteresting disciple of Auden and Yeats and firmly adopted his own individual voice. That this voice is distinctly personal has already been established—and the self-preoccupation that this implies is reflected in the criticism—and the fiction—written after this time. But, while Berryman's poetry was strengthened by this change, his work in other genres was weakened, and the later essays are valuable more, perhaps, for what they reveal about Berryman's own poems than for what they say about the literary work under consideration. His best essays are generally those written between 1945 and 1953. (p. 372)

If this book has a serious weakness, it is its structure. Berryman's most interesting—and ultimately most important—essays are those on modern American poetry and modern American fiction. These, however, are placed near the end of the book in favor of Berryman's excursions into the British Renaissance. . . . [These] lead-off essays are intelligent, scholarly, insightful, and illuminating—but there is no way the reading public of today is going to find them more interesting than what comes later. (pp. 372-73)

In general, the essays which Berryman wrote for publication and saw into print are polished and well organized. The others were mostly written as lectures, and it is clear that Berryman intended to revise them before letting them appear in this book. Now that he is dead, the necessary editing and polishing has been left undone. We find unnecessary repetitions, awkward sentences, and unfulfilled promises. I would single out, in particular, the pieces on Marlowe (which opens the book on an especially weak note), Conrad, and Cervantes. (p. 373)

However, I don't wish through this carping at editors to diminish the ultimate radiance that emanates from this book. As a teacher, Berryman was known for the enthusiasm for literature which he was able to generate in his students. The same quality is present in his criticism. . . . Berryman's criticism has authority and freedom. He lets himself and his knowledge go, and does not equivocate. This is an entertaining, a captivating thing for a critic to do —we admire his brave ventures away from safe ground, even when he fails. A critic need not be correct to be enlightening—often he does his job best just by asking the right questions.

Finally, one hopes that this book will help to correct and fill out the picture too many people have of Berryman. The excellence of his achievement in three major genres—fiction, poetry, criticism—places him in the company of our finest men of letters. One thinks of comparing him with his friends and contemporaries Randall Jarrell and Delmore Schwartz. The similarities among these men's lives are astonishing and frightening, to be sure. But their careers are also remarkably similar. Of the three, Berryman consistently shows the greatest intensity, especially in poetry and criticism. (pp. 373-74)

> *Peter Stitt, "John Berryman's Literary Criticism," in* The Southern Review (*copyright, 1978, by Peter Stitt*), *Vol. XIV, No. 2, Spring, 1978, pp. 368-74.*

EMMA FISHER

Berryman's life of tortured bardic alcoholism, and the piercing eye he turned on himself and (sometimes) the world, have aroused respect, if not reverence, among reviewers and critics. (p. 22)

[Under the languid exterior of a Dream Song from *Henry's Fate and Other Poems*] seethe images of Henry as a soul in hell; a Doubter, like Thomas; a clock-like, unnatural man, kept going only by drugs; a junkie waiting for his fix; a crucified thing like Christ and the clock. At suggesting torment the poem works better than it deserves.

Apart from the useful personification device, Berryman has the poetic equivalent of 'it', which seems to reside in his language: colloquial, compressed, jerky, cute, unpompous. He also has a drunkard's fatal charm. One would always have bought him another drink. A peculiarity of the Dream Songs is that they are so informal and repetitive (Berryman apparently once said he kept on writing them 'just out of habit') that individual ones give an impression of depth and concision because oblique references can be made to things the reader knows from the others. They are interdependent and do not have to stand on their own. The thought of hundreds more still unpublished is daunting, but one looks forward to them as to brilliant letters from an unstable friend. (p. 23)

> *Emma Fisher, in* The Spectator (© *1978 by* The Spectator; *reprinted by permission of* The Spectator), *April 1, 1978.*

EDWIN MORGAN

Berryman is a noted example of the poet who is hard to like and equally hard to forget. He drags his reader protesting almost continuously through a landscape of intense, jagged, contorted, often obscure, often touching subjectivity; no one conveys better the sheer *mess* of life, the failures and disappointments, betrayals and jealousies, lust and drunkenness, the endless nagging disjunction between ambition and reality. If it is dangerous to let life cohabit too lovingly with art, Berryman revels in taking up that danger and brandishing it bizarrely, like a gorgon's head, to mesmerise the audience. . . .

[What] gives body and weight to the dream songs as a whole is their underlying intimation of the wider discontents and anxieties, whether of the modern world or of man in general. Unlike Pound, he does not easily intellectualise the wider themes, but they keep surging up, explosively, savagely, sadly, through references to writers' suicides, through comments on America and on other countries, through gropings towards the consolations of philosophy or religion. (p. 552)

[The new dream songs published in *Henry's Fate, and Other Poems*] are not, for the most part, among his best.... It is curious how, in their relative straightforwardness but frequent flatness, they have the effect of throwing the reader back towards the idiosyncrasies, grotesque though they might be, of the earlier dream songs. The style of a Berryman, whether he writ no language or not, has to be swallowed whole, and probably the gristly bits are more functional than we like to suppose. (p. 553)

Edwin Morgan, "Struggle and Surrender," in The Listener *(© British Broadcasting Corp. 1978; reprinted by permission of Edwin Morgan), April 27, 1978, pp. 552-53.*

GARY Q. ARPIN

To say that John Berryman's poetry is controversial is to state the obvious. Few poets—and none that I can think of since Pound—have aroused such varying and often violent responses. A. Alvarez has written that one either loves or loathes Berryman's work, and that seems to be the case. This should not be a matter of great surprise. For one thing, Berryman's work—especially *The Dream Songs*—is difficult, difficult in a way that most recent poetry is not. At a time when American poetry is moving away from the Eliotic modern, Berryman's work seems to be a throwback, if a self-conscious one, to an earlier age, bringing poetry, to paraphrase Williams's remarks on *The Waste Land*, back into the classroom. (p. 3)

[There is] a tendency in much of Berryman's mature work which in the best light might be called reticence, in the worst light gamesmanship—a certain toying with the reader. Berryman spoke in interviews of his "trade secrets," and implied that there were secret meanings in *The Dream Songs* that would challenge scholars for years. His work is highly allusive, and he obviously enjoyed this aspect of the difficulty of his work, as lines from *The Dream Songs* indicate:

> I feel the end is near
> & strong of my large work, which will appear,
> and baffle everybody.

This is partially a way of poking fun at the literary establishment, a *blague* directed at the academic community with which Berryman enjoyed a distinct love-hate relationship (compare his portrait of the MLA convention in *77 Dream Songs*). More frequently, though, the allusiveness of Berryman's work is intended to serve a serious function. Berryman was an enormously well-read man, and in his work, especially *The Dream Songs,* he used that knowledge both to create a world and to give the effect of a man ransacking our culture in an attempt to find a way of living in that world. This is not a new use of allusion, obviously; it is firmly in the modernist tradition. The effect of both the playful and the serious uses of allusion, however, has been harmful in some cases, irritating some readers and obscuring more important aspects of his work. *The Dream Songs* is not an intellectual game, but Berryman managed to convince several critics that it was. "After working out the double crostics," wrote Mary Curran of *77 Dream Songs,* "there is only the feeling of dissipation and boredom."

Let us add a further element of difficulty before going on: style. The words "Berryman's style" call up a host of adjectives: idiosyncratic, eccentric, quirky, willed, perverse, in ascending order of disapproval. Style: a use of

language that so impresses itself upon the mind that subject and meaning are all but lost. Randall Jarrell's early criticism, in a review of *The Dispossessed*, was prescient: "Doing things in a style all its own sometimes seems the primary object of the poem, and its subject gets a rather spasmodic and fragmentary treatment." The quotation, selectively applied to Berryman's work, even his major work, is accurate—most accurate when the verse is weakest, for the assumption behind the criticism is that style is not intended to hide meaning but to express it, an assumption with which I agree. (pp. 3-4)

What is centrally important about *The Dream Songs* is that [to quote Martin Dodsworth in *The Survival of Poetry*] "despite all appearances, these poems are not hermetic in intention; they seek to *expose* the poet's most remote level of consciousness, to present the reader with the kind of experiences Berryman believes and feels to be behind the superficies of life, but which we are ordinarily content to ignore." This emphasis on experience in the poem proves it to be anti-Symbolist, despite its surface resemblance to a work in the Symbolist tradition.... The poem appears to be modernist, but the style is not explicable by ordinary means. Therefore, the style must serve some other, extraordinary purpose. In [Peter] Dale's view, it serves to obscure a lack of substance. [See *CLC*, Vol. 2.] In Dodsworth's view, the language of the poem is intended to emphasize the importance of experience. What Mr. Dodsworth calls "the *superfluous oddity*" of Berryman's style "is calculated, I think, on the supposition that what is superfluous to the conventional demands of literature may establish a means of personal expression and communication with the reader, something that cannot, as yet, be contaminated by the student's desire to incorporate all literature into some vast and inoffensive system of conventions."

"Superfluous oddity," in the example that Mr. Dodsworth discusses (dream song 33), refers principally to the use of "ah" and "ha," especially their emphatic use as rhyme words. It is not necessary to posit a new poetic to come to terms with this oddity, however. In song 33, the *ah*s and *ha*s are the outbreak of Henry's own powerful emotions aroused by the story of Alexander and Clitus; both the violence and the form it takes of chopping are aspects of Henry's own character that he can barely control, as song 29 makes clear. They are thus not superfluous here; they are rather an indication of the enormous difficulty Henry is having in telling the story. The oddity comes principally from not reading the song as part of a larger whole. I must hasten to add here that I don't think every sample of distorted or mannered language can be justified, or seen as adding to the poem. When such distortions cannot be justified, it seems to me, the language has failed; I do not think that it is necessary (or reasonable) to make of these failures a success. Berryman was a daring poet who pushed the language to its limits and sometimes beyond the limits. (pp. 5-6)

I do not think *The Dream Songs* is a radical break with the Symbolist tradition any more than I think it is a radical break from Berryman's earlier poetry. There are some important differences between Berryman's work and the work of the Symbolist and modernist poets who wrote before him, and there are some crucial differences between his major work and his earlier work; but there are also important similarities, ones that should not be ignored. Berryman was, in fact, always a modernist poet, although at different stages in his career different aspects of that modernism were of primary importance to him. The history of his career may indeed be seen as an attempt, or a series of attempts, to discover which aspects of what we have long called the tradition were appropriate to his own vision. And the two things which come immediately to mind, for they were the two areas that were of greatest importance to Berryman's work, are language and the image of the poet.

The origins of Berryman's style have been the subject of a great deal of speculation, largely in terms of a search for a presiding influence. It is not unreasonable to look for such an influence. Berryman's early work was so heavily indebted to the work of Yeats and Auden, and Berryman was always such a bookish poet, that we can expect to find important stylistic influences on his major work as well. Hopkins is most frequently mentioned in this context, although Berryman denied that Hopkins had much influence on him. Cummings has also been mentioned, as have Dylan Thomas, Crane (Hart and Stephen), and Stevens. I would add Milton and especially . . . Tristan Corbière, whose work Berryman was reading during the time of his own greatest stylistic development in the mid-1940s. (pp. 6-7)

Berryman's style evolved not just through the reading and influence of a few other poets, but in response to an aesthetic implicitly accepted, but never explicitly expressed, the aesthetic of Symbolism, with its insistence on creating a new language that, in Rimbaud's words, "would be of the soul, for the soul, containing everything, smells, sounds, colors; thought latching onto thought and pulling." In this context, I mean by "aesthetic of Symbolism" not the idealistic foundation for that aesthetic, but the necessity it imposes of expanding the language, and the technical liberation that it implies. There is a certain amount of the idealist-aesthete in Berryman, especially . . . in his early work, but in his major work he is, as Mr. Dodsworth quite correctly points out, concerned above all with living in the world. The language that he found, which we could well describe as containing everything—even some things which some Symbolists would have excluded—served as a means of describing and living with the absurdity and pain of that world.

Berryman's style—but not his interest in style—changed greatly over the course of his career; his thematic concerns changed to a lesser extent. His subject was, as he described Pound's subject matter, "the life of the modern poet," and virtually everything he wrote revolved around that theme. Berryman's image of the poet, though, changed through the years. The poet figure of the early poems is usually sensitive, committed, alienated, and above all aloof. . . . (pp. 7-8)

There is much in this image of the poet that would remain as a part of Berryman's later work. Berryman's later poet figures—especially, of course, Henry—tell our story, indeed live our story, but remain rejected by the rest of us, apart from us, *poètes maudits* who find it increasingly difficult to find anything that makes the suffering worthwhile.

Berryman's style, as I have noted, derived from the Symbolist aesthetic, with the very important difference that it was intended to create a language that would enable us to express and thus survive, perhaps even triumph over, the absurdity and pain of our lives. Berryman's suffering poet figure is the result of a similar transformation of an element of the Symbolist tradition. He undergoes the suffering that Rimbaud said the poet should undergo, hoping to find not so much the "unknown" or some ideal realm but a strategy for living in a world filled with all-too-real difficulties. . . . The attempts to deal with [these difficulties], the emergency adaptations of the Symbolist notions of the poet and of language recorded in Berryman's work—especially *Homage* and *The Dream Songs*—are what make Berryman's poetry memorable. The problem is living in the world, a problem that became in Berryman's work increasingly insistent, increasingly intense. (pp. 9-10)

[If] one were looking for Berryman's "confessional verse," [*Berryman's Sonnets*] would be the place to start. It is clearly unreasonable to assume . . . that Berryman entered the post-*Life Studies* "confessional movement" with *77 Dream Songs* in 1964. On the contrary—throughout his career, from the earliest Yeats imitations on, Berryman experimented with various ways of turning personal experience into art. At the same time he was constantly aware of the need for his poems to "leap into myth," to move out from the personal to the general. And in the *Sonnets,* which is one of Berryman's most personal works, there is a similar attempt to "leap into myth." The original problem, as he makes clear in the preface, was not the affair, but the more general problem of "whether wickedness was soluble in art." In the *Sonnets* he attempted, through adopting an old convention, to put his specific and particular character in a general situation—to portray, as he portrays in his other work, the life of the representative man, the modern poet who bears the burdens of his culture.

Nevertheless, *Berryman's Sonnets* cannot be said to be a completely successful attempt, precisely because these poems do *not* "hunt the whole / House through," at least not very convincingly. When Berryman restricts himself, as he does in most of the *Sonnets,* to "fidelity-infidelity" and the ramifications of that theme, mostly Freudian, in the culture, the poems are generally effective. But Berryman is not successful—as he is in his later work—in expanding this central theme to include broader considerations. Sonnets which attempt to relate his particular situation to political or metaphysical themes are generally flat and unconvincing. This is not because the form of the sonnet sequence is not flexible enough to handle a variety of themes—it is—but because Berryman was discovering themes that he didn't yet know how to handle. (pp. 42-3)

Homage to Mistress Bradstreet is in many ways Berryman's central work, the breakthrough that fulfills earlier promises of genius and makes new promises for the future. This is true of both the language of the poem and its thematic elements. In *Mistress Bradstreet* Berryman brought together several concerns that he had touched on in his earlier work and which would be of increasing importance in his later work: loss, rebellion and submission, the importance of the family. He also brought up, through the voice of Mistress Bradstreet, that difficult word which he had mentioned briefly and to no apparent purpose in the *Sonnets,* but which he would use frequently in later works: God. *Mistress Bradstreet* is an ambitious poem, but it attempts less than *The Dream Songs* and, because it is more coherent, is more successful. (pp. 47-8)

It is tempting to say that *Homage to Mistress Bradstreet* is

Berryman's Sonnets writ large, but this would be a bit misleading. Let us say, rather, that in the *Sonnets* Berryman discovered an important theme, adultery, which was closely related to his major thematic concern, the relation between the poet and his culture, but—perhaps because he was too close to the actual experience—Berryman didn't quite know what to do with it. *Berryman's Sonnets* is an attempt to generalize his experience but, finally, not a successful one. Berryman was unable to include everything he wanted to say. What he needed was a form that would allow both the lyric voice of the sonnet sequence and the scope in subject matter of the epic. What he needed, indeed, is what every ambitious poet since Wordsworth has needed—a form that doesn't exist. *Homage to Mistress Bradstreet* and *The Dream Songs* are Berryman's two attempts to create a narrative form that would include both history and the personal voice. In *Homage to Mistress Bradstreet* he faced the problem of form by yoking two forms together and creating what might be called a love poem containing history, a poem in which the muse and heroine are one. . . . (p. 48)

[Anne Bradstreet's] only claim to Berryman's interest would seem to be that she was the first American poet, and thus the stuff that myths are made of. But Berryman, unlike Hart Crane, whose *Bridge* has often been compared to *Mistress Bradstreet,* is not primarily concerned with creating American myth. *Mistress Bradstreet* is concerned with more particular relations—relations between individuals and between individuals and society. (p. 49)

As the [writing of *The Dream Songs*] grew and the years wore on, the line between Berryman's poem and Berryman's life became at times a very fine one. At times, indeed, individual songs simply became vehicles for the expression of Berryman's peeves about minor aspects of his life. If Berryman had trouble with the mail, for example, Henry complained about it. Trivial experiences *can* make good poetry, of course, but frequently in *The Dream Songs* —especially in the latter sections of the poem—they do not; they remain records of trivial experiences. There is, it seems to me, no question that this reduction of Henry and his experiences harms the poem. At the same time let me emphasize that this doesn't happen so often that *The Dream Songs* dwindles into the expression of a series of merely personal grumblings. (p. 61)

From evidence in the poem it seems quite clear that Henry is intended to be a representative figure. He is yet another of Berryman's poet-heroes, taking "immortal risks" and bearing "in the fading night our general guilt." Berryman's subject is the life of the modern poet, and that subject is not only personal but also national and metaphysical; it is absolutely necessary that Henry be a broad enough character to be able to contain all these concerns. The obvious precedent here is *Song of Myself,* with the important difference that in *The Dream Songs* the poet is united with the rest of us not through a transcendental vision, but through suffering. In song 242, which begins "About that 'me,'" Berryman describes a woman visiting Henry's office and breaking into tears. He cries with her and at the end of the song says "I am her."

Saying this in one song does not make it true for all the songs, of course, but it clearly states Berryman's intention. When this characterization of Henry is successful, we are given a picture of a comic poet-hero, taking upon himself

our suffering, and bodying it forth in song, saying, with Jeremiah in Lamentations, "I am their musick." When it does not work, as in "Henry's Mail," mentioned above, we are merely given a picture of Berryman. (pp. 61-2)

The Dream Songs is different in form from *Homage to Mistress Bradstreet,* but in theme it is similar. In many respects *The Dream Songs* is of longer and more complex treatment of the themes Berryman had explored in the earlier poem. Like Mistress Bradstreet Henry rebels against his environment, his family, himself, and God. Like Mistress Bradstreet Henry ultimately finds in his family the values necessary for survival in and, indeed, triumph over, a hostile world. At the center of Henry's world, though, is an element that figures only peripherally in the earlier poem —loss. . . . (p. 63)

To a certain extent, the conditions of the modern world are the cause of much of the despair of *The Dream Songs.* The world of the poem is not very different from the world of "The Dispossessed," in which "no hero rides. The race / is done." This fear that the end of the race is imminent, that we are at the end of a long decline, and that "Man has undertaken the top job of all, / *son fin*," . . . occurs periodically in the poem. It is viewed in relation to the other deaths and losses of the poem, fulfilling the pattern. But if Henry's difficulties are more intense than they would have been in the past, at bottom his problems are not new, nor are they merely the product of twentieth-century life. . . . The problem is less twentieth-century life than it is life itself, the attempt to live right in a world that makes it very difficult. . . . (p. 65)

The title of *The Dream Songs* allows Berryman a great deal of linguistic freedom. . . . The dreamer is an inveterate punner and player with language. But "good poets love bad puns," and we do not really need the title to describe (or defend) the language. The title refers in the first place to dreams as we have learned about them from Freud—the welling up of repressed material in a disguised fashion in sleep. Dreams are caused by a conflict that is of great importance in *The Dream Songs,* the conflict between instinctual needs and the needs of the culture. Indeed, dreams are the battlegrounds of that conflict, for the instinctual material which would conflict with the needs of the culture is allowed in dreams a harmless release. So the title refers to both the purpose and the method of dreams. (p. 79)

Randomness, although it is certainly present in *The Dream Songs,* is more the lack of structure than a structural principle. At the same time, as tantalizing as the thought might be, there seems to be no tightly knit but hidden or "secret" structure to *The Dream Songs.* . . .

I think that this could safely be said about the other books in the volume and about the volume as a whole. It has a beginning and an end and a general development from beginning to end; it is loosely unified by theme, subject matter, imagery, and, of course, Henry, but many individual songs could be juggled around without affecting that loose unity. (p. 81)

The Dream Songs is not a completely successful poem. *Homage to Mistress Bradstreet,* more compact, more coherent, is a more successful work. There is not enough narrative in *The Dream Songs* to hold such a long work together, and what narrative there is is often confused. The methods of organization which are essentially lyric—recurrent images and language—are not developed consistently enough; there is just enough development to force us to read the poem as a whole, but not enough for us to see it as a totally coherent whole. The poem was too available to the daily events of Berryman's life, perhaps. The attempt to turn his life into myth succeeds best when Berryman abstracts himself from Henry, by putting him in a fictive environment—up a tree, or dead, or even simply bored—or by treating him ironically or humorously—showing us Henry hungering after a woman in a restaurant, or suffering the effects of a "truly first-class drill" in a dentist's chair. Unfortunately, this attempt does not always succeed. But despite its faults, the poem remains a considerable achievement; Henry, his dream world, and his language remain in the mind after reading, indelible. (pp. 85-6)

[*Love & Fame*] is structurally more satisfying than Berryman's major long poem, *The Dream Songs,* for there are few obtrusions into the narrative, and the story told is fairly clear. That story is not very different from the stories told in Berryman's other works. The book describes the development of a poetic sensibility struggling against both outer and inner obstacles. In his earlier work, though, much greater attention is paid to the outer obstacles—the mad culture the poet finds himself a part of—than is paid here. In *Love & Fame* there are some poems about American society, but what is most important about that society is Berryman's isolation from it. (pp. 88-9)

Love & Fame is far from being the aesthetic botch that most reviewers found it to be. But this is not to say that it is Berryman's finest work. There is a problem with this "wiping out" strategy, for after the sensibility of the early poems is wiped out, there is very little left. There is very little stylistic attraction in the first two sections. Had the young Berryman been presented as a slightly more despicable character, the volume would have been improved. One will return to the unpleasant Berryman of "Damned" as one returns to some of Browning's monologues, for the monstrousness and the unattractive vitality of the poem; but most of the early poems present a sensibility without vitality. Young Berryman is not evil enough to attract, and, once or twice read, the anecdotes lose much of their power. The poems are necessary—the second half of the book depends upon them—but they are too often simply straw men, put up in order to be knocked down. The structure of the volume is satisfying, but the early components of that structure, by and large, are not.

In *Delusions, Etc.,* published posthumously but seen through proof by Berryman, there is a thematic unity of a sort, but no clear overarching structure. When poems fail, and quite a few do, they do so on their own, without any narrative compensation. It is true that section 4, the only section with a title, is called "Scherzo," but I would hesitate to claim a symphonic or sonata structure for the book. Individual sections are fairly well unified, but beyond that the book is more of a collection than were Berryman's earlier volumes. The full title of the book is *Delusions, Etc. of John Berryman,* but the delusions are not Berryman's alone. The chief delusion is man's thinking—the pride he takes in his rational faculties. Berryman's work had always been romanticist, and here that romanticism is quite blatant, but curiously mixed: at times Berryman sounds like Emerson, at other times like Melville.

"I don't try to reconcile anything," Berryman had approv-

ingly quoted Ralph Hodgson, "this is a damned strange world"; and that is how Henry had ended, looking to Ralph Hodgson and not trying to reconcile "things and the soul." But the conflict that he had ended for Henry did not end for himself. Berryman *did* try to reconcile things: reason and faith, science and religion, the existence of evil and the notion of a benevolent God, and *Delusions, Etc.* is largely a record of that attempt. Hence, the Emersonian-Melvillian contrast: in some poems Berryman does seem to have reconciled these things, in others he recognizes, with pain, that he cannot. (p. 94)

There are . . . some very weak poems in this collection. The book has been compared favorably with *Love & Fame,* in both reviews and criticism, but I must believe that this is due less to the poetry than to the attitude Berryman seemed to strike in each volume. In *Love & Fame* Berryman appeared to be a bragging oaf and the appearance hid the poetry. In *Delusions, Etc.* Berryman is "properly humble," and this too seems to have hidden the poetry, for the best one can say of the volume is that it is very uneven. The chief failure of the book, moreover, is not one of sensibility, but one of language—it is not that Berryman is too "confessional" or that his conversion is not convincing, but that his artistic experiments too frequently do not succeed. (p. 98)

There is a distinction that must be made, even in these late, personal poems, between poet and man, between maker and subject. Berryman the poet has not been subsumed by Berryman the man. In all of these poems the emotion is worked, given form and order. Berryman was never a poet of "raw expression" (indeed, critics linking him with the Beats have overlooked this obvious fact), and even in *Delusions, Etc.* one must allow for the essential distinctions between the personality of the poet-in-the-poem and the personality of the poet. They are not completely discontinuous, but neither are they identical, and it is dangerous to argue across the barrier between them.

One fairly popular conception of the dangers inherent in confessional verse is that the poet, by seeking out the unsettling and self-destructive in himself, succeeds, not in controlling those feelings and putting them to the service of his art, but in allowing those feelings to control him. At least part of the responsibility for the rash of recent poet suicides, then, is to be laid both to the type of material the poets were concerned with and to the ultimate failure of their art. This might be true in certain cases, and one may look at *Delusions, Etc.* in this manner, but such a view would seem to me to be a great oversimplification. One must be very careful of the post hoc fallacy here. The relation between life and art—or at least Berryman's life and Berryman's art—is too complex to fit such a matrix. I cannot prove this, of course. To do so it would be necessary to conduct what scientists call a thought experiment—working out in one's mind (or in computer simulation) all of the results of all of the causes of both the life and the art. Nevertheless, I hope I have indicated enough evidence of the complexity of the relationships between Berryman's life and his art—even in these late poems—to call such a simple explanation into doubt.

There are both failures and successes of art in these late works. Despite the successes, however, both *Delusions, Etc.* and *Love & Fame* are overshadowed by the accomplishments of *Homage to Mistress Bradstreet* and *The*

Dream Songs. It is hard to see how it could be otherwise. But I cannot argue from the weaknesses of many of these poems to a failure of life, or even a failure of talent, as many critics have—there are poems enough here to attest to the continuance of Berryman's gift. Moreover, what problems there are here are what might be termed positive problems—attempts to do with the language more than the language will successfully allow. Thus his failures here are not failures of character or even the failures of a dried-up talent, but those of the experimentalist that Berryman was until the end, pushing the language around at times quite roughly, to use it in ways in which it had not been used before. (pp. 99-100)

> *Gary Q. Arpin, in his* The Poetry of John Berryman *(copyright © 1978 by Kennikat Press Corp.; reprinted by permission of Kennikat Press Corp.), Kennikat, 1978.*

*   *   *

BETJEMAN, John   1906-

Betjeman, an English poet, essayist, and critic, was knighted in 1969 and became Poet Laureate in 1972. His verse, which frequently warns of the dangers of technological development, is uncomplicated both in form and content. His prose writing is devoted almost exclusively to architectural criticism and history. (See also *CLC*, **Vols. 2, 6, and** *Contemporary Authors*, **Vols. 9-12, rev. ed.)**

G. M. HARVEY

[Although] he writes from within the essentially middle-class tradition of English liberal humanism, Betjeman has been a consistently subversive force in modern English poetry, and it is clear from his latest poems that his criticism of English society has taken on an angrier tone. A second element in his writing is the increasingly powerful note of spiritual anguish, a deepening of the religious doubt and despair which was evident in an earlier poem, 'Tregardock', in his volume, *High and Low* (1966). . . . In his later poems it is the urgency of Betjeman's social anger and spiritual anguish which seem to me to characterise his response to life as it really is, but the depth of his personal commitment does not hinder the poetry from exploring some of the fundamental issues of twentieth-century life and expanding into an accurate general statement of the human condition.

In an important sense, his subversive attack on the values of contemporary society is a corollary of his profound reverence for places. Betjeman insistently questions the validity of the notion of progress, in the headlong pursuit of which the modern world heedlessly destroys both the community and the natural environment. (pp. 112-13)

Betjeman's technique of contrapuntal points of view serves to stress once more the paradoxically dehumanising effect of human progress. . . .

Betjeman's concern for the preservation not merely of fine buildings but the human frame of things which they represent is not reactionary but, ironically, in modern society with its commitment to size, growth and change for their own sakes, economically and politically subversive. (p. 114)

Betjeman's consistent, remorseless probing of the weaknesses of English social institutions includes the church. 'Lenten Thoughts of a High Anglican' is a quietly whimsical poem, which on closer reading turns out to be subtly

and powerfully subversive. Fundamentally it challenges not only the church's doctrines but the whole relevance of institutionalised religion. (p. 117)

[In 'Lenten Thoughts of a High Anglican'], the poet's wise innocence and imagination quietly confound bureaucratically guarded knowledge, with its emphasis on mystery, the arduous search for God, the centrality of church ritual and the discipline of the instincts symbolised by Lent. For Betjeman the church provides quite inadvertently the context for worship of an instinctive and spontaneous kind. His God frankly embraces femininity, sexuality and emancipated modernity, and there is a subdued zest in his kicking over theological and ecclesiastical traces in order to illuminate a spiritual truth.

Most of his later poems which deal with religious themes are governed by his deepening horror at the facts of life and death, by a sense of doubt and loss. 'Aldershot Crematorium' is a truthful and compelling response to the modern way of death. Sandwiched between the swimming-pool and the cricket-ground, the crematorium creates a dominant image of the casual interpenetration of life and death, but this is only fully experienced in the shock of seeing the smoke from the furnace chimney:

> And little puffs of smoke without a sound
>   Show what we loved dissolving in the skies,
> Dear hands and feet and laughter-lighted face
>   And silk that hinted at the body's grace.

This brutal juxtaposition of the vital solidity of the flesh with the air into which it dissolves enforces our true reverence for the human body, particularly because our sense of another's identity depends so much on purely physical attributes. More importantly, perhaps, the hideous incongruity of the transformation, like a grotesque conjuring trick, denies death its proper human dimension and baffles our natural responses. (p. 118)

[Betjeman] makes the whole situation of the poem focus our attention on its central paradox. Cremation emphasises so insistently the incontrovertible reality of a merely material universe that simple but profoundly human questions about the nature of resurrection and the possible form of a new spiritual identity become, for the modern sceptical age, irrelevant. Modern man seeks to escape his fear in the temporary oblivion which materialism affords, but for a believer, like Betjeman, death presents a constant challenge to his own sense of spiritual identity: "'*I am the Resurrection and the Life*': / Strong, deep and painful, doubt inserts the knife."

Betjeman's anguish at being trapped in the vacuum between faith and doubt proceeds from an often appalling sense of cosmic isolation. In 'Loneliness' he explores the personal paradox of his simultaneous belief and unbelief. In tone and feeling he frequently recalls Matthew Arnold, in 'Dover Beach' for instance, but his confrontation with his personal hell of doubt and despair is more dramatic and urgent. The poem proceeds on two levels in a vain attempt to relate the natural and metaphysical worlds, symbolised by nature and the Easter bells; but the poem's organising symbol is an infinitely expanding and contracting universe, which bewilders and terrifies the poet and which gives the poem its emotional tautness. (p. 119)

The season of natural and spiritual renewal only deepens

the irony of his terrifying isolation. The bells represent for Betjeman what the Dover sea did for Arnold, but unlike Arnold he can find no consolation either in human love or in the natural universe.

These later poems of Betjeman are important because they deal with large issues, although they are often located in the local and familiar, and like Arnold's, Betjeman's personal crises expand into a poignant general statement of the human condition. (p. 120)

Betjeman's clinging to a particular place where time has been contained and ordered [as in 'On Leaving Wantage 1972'], where this peculiar synthesis has in a real sense created and sustained human identity, is an attempt to find a temporary refuge from time manifested outside place which, for the sceptic, becomes an impersonal abstraction and a force of dissolution. (p. 121)

Behind the covert horror of so much of Betjeman's later writing there also lies a hard-won equilibrium of temper. It is this Augustan sense of balance between private and public, imagination and reason, commitment and detachment, sympathy and irony, which marks the fundamental sanity of his poetry. (pp. 121-22)

In Betjeman's poetry his commitment to life as it really is is balanced by his insistence on the need to maintain a comic stance towards it, and in this he is, I think, closer to the Augustans than to the Victorians or the moderns. In his early poetry comedy was a form of social celebration, but in his later writing it has also become both an instrument for satire and for personal defence against the horrors of age and death. . . . The humanising quality of comedy allows Betjeman to transcend the anger and anguish of life, and his choice of laughter to help him towards death testifies to his profound belief in the importance of human scale and human values. It is this fundamental commitment to life as it really is that makes Betjeman a truly significant poet. (pp. 123-24)

> *G. M. Harvey, "Poetry of Commitment: John Betjeman's Later Writing," in* The Dalhousie Review, *Spring, 1976, pp. 112-24.*

KELLY CHERRY

[Betjeman] is the poet of *rus in urbe*. A good thing, too: the inherent contradictions of the suburb (not to be confused with Academia) too seldom receive a hearing in contemporary literature, despite the number of writers who must live in one. Betjeman celebrates "old brick garden walls" and "the mist of green about the elms / In earliest leaf-time." Alas, mortar crumbles, and leaves fall, and though he's gentle or even affectionately comic in his recording of these changes, Betjeman's celebration is always a kind of elegy. There is a touch of something Roman in his poetry, as if he were a senator following the custom of releasing a dove for luck—and knowing it flies only for itself. Betjeman's great talent is to hold two opposing attitudes together without technical distress. . . .

In the same way, he simultaneously eulogizes and scolds, pities and mocks and adores the people who inhabit his places. . . . Betjeman's deliberate rhythms reduce the poet's anger to a manageable wryness.

Readers who are interested solely in the unmanageable will know by now to bypass Betjeman: nothing in a Betjeman poem is ever out of control, and yet everything is more than likely to stray—by design—slightly off-course. (p. 325)

A Nip in the Air is a slight volume; a number of the poems are occasional pieces—souvenirs for royalty or memoranda to friends—and a few are little more than doggerel, but now and again Betjeman hits his old stride. . . . [Any] Betjeman poem is just what it is, and therefore he is loved even where he isn't admired; there is no pretense or guile in his work. As for his technique, as usual, it can't be faulted, whether he's working with gimmicky rhymes . . . and seven-stress lines . . . , or with the sonnet . . . , or with blank verse. . . .

Nothing very serious or argumentative is attempted in any of these poems, but that is part of their charm. They give a reader, in these days of fraught confessions, a chance to relax. Betjeman is the most amiable of poets. If we take the distinction between poetry as song and poetry as speech, we must somewhere make a separate, special corner for Betjeman, the poet as conversationalist. (p. 326)

A good Betjeman poem . . . lasts and will last because it is *made;* it *is* art, and artifice, that holds its shape against the buffetings of time and critics alike. (p. 327)

Betjeman survives, then, because he is himself. His poems have discernible outlines, his sentiments are never vague or confused with those of the times. A reader might as well ask Betjeman to be Eliot or Auden as insist that all the members of an orchestra should play the same instrument. (p. 328)

> *Kelly Cherry, in* Parnassus: Poetry in Review *(copyright © by Poetry in Review Foundation), Spring-Summer, 1977.*

WILLARD SPIEGELMAN

Sir John Betjeman is now England's Poet Laureate, and the recent brouhaha over his silver anniversary poem to the Queen is a sign of the dangers of being *too* public a poet (still, it always seemed to me that if he had to use an adverb to modify her blue eyes, "profoundly" would do as nicely as anything else). But *A Nip in the Air* proves him to be . . . an accomplished writer of light verse, with a gusto for ordinary life and an affection for odd angles of vision. Once again we have somber themes amiably treated. Hardyesque horrors rise from seasonal descriptions:

> What misery will this year bring
> Now spring is in the air at last?
> For, sure as black thorn bursts to snow,
> Cancer in some of us will grow.
>
> (pp. 311-12)

Although contentment sometimes comes dangerously close to Tory smugness [Betjeman has been called too content], Betjeman redeems himself by nimbly mixing personal and public occasional poems. In "A Ballad of the Investiture, 1969," he confesses the difficulties of dealing with his subject: "For years I wondered what to do / And now, at last, I've thought it better / To write a kind of rhyming letter." The verse epistle is an ancient, honorable form; here, its informality counterpoints the solemnity of the occasion. In fact, the poem skirts its main subject by cunningly focusing on preparations, the scene, the surprising intrusion of television cameras, and by mentioning only in passing the somber moment itself. Betjeman's wisdom in so doing allows him not only to avoid the trap of self-satisfied mysticism or self-conscious patriotism, but also to emphasize the irreversibility of the single, transient moment. . . .

The [volume's] longest and most serious poem, "Shattered

Image,'' an internal dramatic monologue in blank verse, shows how Betjeman can turn his attention to social and moral dilemmas (in this case, an older man is charged with pederasty, and faces the hostility, condescension, and disbelief of friends and employers), without sacrificing the condensation of language which is poetry's *sine qua non*, and without succumbing to either preacherly moralizing or in-depth psychology which a ''heavier'' treatment of the subject might have demanded. Like all writers of light verse, Betjeman understands his limits. (p. 312)

Willard Spiegelman, in Southwest Review *(© 1977 by Southern Methodist University Press), Summer, 1977.*

*   *   *

BISHOP, John

Bishop is an American playwright.

CLIVE BARNES

There is always a fascination about the failure of a hero, a fascination possibly more intense when the failure concerns a hero who could never have made it. Most of us identify with the special seediness of unfulfilled glory. And there are simply geniuses who have no cause for worry. John Bishop's play ''The Trip Back Down'' . . . is about a stock-car racer approaching his last lap. . . . He is desperately gallant, an all-time loser who knows the value of losing.

At the end of the play he is able to retort to a detractor: ''Let me tell you one thing about losing—you have to be in the race to do it.'' In that one line you just about have the interest and the value of Mr. Bishop's play. . . . [It] is an in-built cliché. It is the kind of remark that confirms and massages potential losers rather than challenges and disturbs potential winners. This is not necessarily bad. But it is simplistic.

It is not even certain that the concept of a stock-car racer as a hero is a very good one for the theater. Could not the movies do it better? . . . Perhaps it doesn't matter. I think it does. Drama should stay away from areas where it is locked out and the movies have all the keys. . . .

[Mr. Bishop] does not really write like anyone else. He writes in the glib, empty vernacular of TV serials. The sort of language that echoes a language rather than transforming it. . . .

The story line has an obviousness to it, yet Mr. Bishop is nobody's fool. He can write certain scenes . . . with a loving awareness blunted by the obviousness of the way people are expected to feel.

Clive Barnes, ''A Bad-Trip,'' in The New York Times *(© 1977 by The New York Times Company; reprinted by permission), January 5, 1977, p. C17.*

BRENDAN GILL

''The Trip Back Down'' . . . is a well-written and well-constructed play, serious in its intentions and yet often effectively comic in tone. . . . I hope that no readers will deduce from this rather grim-sounding preliminary ruffle of drums that I am recommending the play because it will prove, in some obscure, puritanico-educational fashion, ''good'' for them to see—or, for that matter, ''good for

Broadway,'' whatever that pious cant phrase may be thought to mean. John Bishop . . . is an ambitious man as well as a talented one, and his play has certain valuable speculations to offer about the nature of winners and losers in contemporary middle-class life. . . . I found it always interesting, if not exhilarating, to be in Mr. Bishop's presence. . . .

Brendan Gill, ''The Loser as Winner,'' in The New Yorker *(© 1977 by The New Yorker Magazine, Inc.), January 17, 1977, p. 47.*

JULIUS NOVICK

I, personally, have no direct knowledge either of the racing-car circuit or of blue-collar towns in Ohio, but [*The Trip Back Down*] convinced me that Mr. Bishop knows both kinds of life very well. Bobby Horvath, a tense, touchy, violent character, is both believable and sympathetic. I respect Mr. Bishop for avoiding the suicidal-car-crash ending I thought I could see coming a mile off (though his actual ending leaves too much unresolved). And Mr. Bishop is quite good at things like bristling confrontations, drunken confessions, funny sidekicks.

But there are plenty of bristling confrontations, drunken confessions, and funny sidekicks in other plays. The stock-car-racing life, as seen in *The Trip Back Down*, is not unlike other kinds of competitive, high-tension, you-can-be-a-star ways of life that have been on view elsewhere, and ordinary, drab, American Mansfield, Ohio, is similar to ordinary drab American other places. There is not really much new about *A Trip Back Down*: it is another solid, decent, realistic-with-flashbacks American drama. . . .

Julius Novick, ''A Vroom of One's Own,'' in The Village Voice *(reprinted by permission of* The Village Voice; *copyright © by* The Village Voice, Inc., *1977), January 24, 1977, p. 75.*

*   *   *

BLIXEN, Karen
See DINESEN, Isak
*   *   *

BLY, Robert   1926-

Bly is an American poet, translator, essayist, and editor who through his rebellion against rhetoric and his development of the ''deep image'' has greatly influenced contemporary poetry. Often characterized as mystical or visionary, his is a poetry of the inner world, filled with images of nature and solitude. Bly was a founder of ''American Writers against the Vietnam War.'' A 1968 recipient of the National Book Award, he donated the prize money to aid young Americans in defying the draft. (See also *CLC*, Vols. 1, 2, 5, and *Contemporary Authors*, Vols. 5-8, rev. ed.)

HOWARD NELSON

[There] was a radical shift between [Robert Bly's] first and second books, *Silence in the Snowy Fields* and *The Light Around the Body*. Since then, however, Bly has not put aside one style or mode to take up another, as some other poets have tended to do. Rather, he has taken the discoveries made in the first two books and used them to write different sorts of poems simultaneously, and has mingled the ways of writing explored there in new ways. The result has been a fascinating body of work, a voice as distinctive as any we now have in our poetry. (p. 2)

A quietly revolutionary book, [*Silence in the Snowy Fields*] has had an important influence in American poetry in the years since [it appeared]. The snow, fields, barns, lakes, and trees, presented so plainly and precisely, yet seeming to resonate, to glow, with some deep, moving mystery; the quiet declaratory tone; the open expressions of pleasure (there must have been a refreshing, freeing feeling then in writing lines like: "There is a privacy I love in this snowy night" and "I love to see old boards lying on the ground in early spring"); the unexpected leaps of metaphor; the silence, the sense of solitude, the poetry "in the blank spaces between the stanzas"; the rich subjectivity of it all;—all went to make a book that was strikingly original, and that tapped resources that had long been turned away from, for the most part, in American poetry: silence, subjectivity, association, the unconscious, a limpid style. Bly was not alone in his interest in this kind of poetry, but *Silence in the Snowy Fields* was one of the crucial examples of its re-emergence. More important, it was and is a beautiful and moving book of poems. I think it still stands as Bly's best single collection. The critic who reviewed it in 1963 and said that the poems were less effective read grouped together was dead wrong; the repetition of images, phrasings, and feelings enriches the book—artful repetition being one of the oldest keys to poetry—and in a way holds it together as if it were a single long poem. As an expression of a deep marriage between the inner and outer worlds in one man's life and place it is in the line of *Walden*. I imagine that it will stand, in spite and because of its limitations, as a small (i.e., 60 pages) classic in American poetry. (pp. 2-3)

While there is of course some continuity between [this and *The Light Around the Body*] (most notably interest in what is now well-known as the "deep image"), the change from *Silence* to *The Light* was a jarring one. *The Light* doesn't have the clarity, the purity, of *Silence;* instead it is woolly with surrealism and wild associative leaps. The remarkable evocations of the motions of the soul in peaceful solitude are replaced—nearly obliterated—by political and social rage and despair: the Vietnam War, "The Great Society," America's "Hatred of Men With Black Hair." It is an angry, uneven, powerful book, and clearly with it Bly made a major contribution to the growth of an American poetry which is truly political and truly poetry.

After *The Light*, the question was: what sort of poetry would Bly write now? Inward pastorals, or barrages of wild imagery and political passion? As I've said, the answer has been to abandon neither, to open himself to the energies, and risks, of both. So in Bly's most recent book, *Sleepers Joining Hands*, we find together his most ambitious political poem, "The Teeth-Mother Naked at Last," a surrealistic, wildly associative poem like "Hair," and the quiet, brief, haunting meditations of "Six Winter Privacy Poems."

The single most important word with regard to *Sleepers* is association; it is the dominant principle throughout the book. Bly has written a good deal about association in his essays; an entire issue of his magazine *The Seventies* (#1) was devoted to it. While it doesn't detract from the self-sufficiency of the poetry or the value of his stimulating essays, it is obvious that with Bly, as with Poe (and probably every other writer who has written both poetry and critical essays), a knowledge of the criticism is an important aid in getting a fuller understanding of the poetry.

When he speaks of association Bly seems to have three things in mind. First, association is a structural principle.... Second, association has to do with speed, the speed with which a poet is able to move from one image, feeling or idea to another, from "the known part of the mind to the unknown part and back to the known." ... Third, association means being able to travel a long way from an initial, literal subject into subjectivity and the unconscious, and still be talking about the original subject.... Taken together, the result of these three ideas—the absence of connectives or "natural" order, rapid leaping, and moving the poem far from the objective world—is poetry which is demanding: the reader must be able to fly along with the poem, without the supports we rely on during most of our waking lives. The effect of this highly associative kind of poetry can be breathtaking ... or, if the energy doesn't flow and ignite just right, the poem can be merely busy and muddled. In *Sleepers,* there are passages near both ends of the spectrum.

The book's major poem, the title piece, is a long dream odyssey in five sections, streaming choruses of fantastic imagery, a Jungian extravaganza; it is, I suppose, about as highly associative as a poem could be. It is a poem of cumulative effect, and that effect is strong. (pp. 3-4)

That "Sleepers" is flawed work is obvious. But we shouldn't allow the weaknesses to blind us to what is interesting and effective in the poem.... Like the book as a whole, "Sleepers" is uneven and given to excess; it is poetry that we respect for its ambitions and excellent moments and emotional drive rather than for any purity or perfection of craft or spirit. The poem shares its major problems with the collection as a whole: the tendency toward bombast and self-righteousness, images which are more bizarre than right, stumbles in the language, associative leaps that are manic rather than exciting. The strengths are the same also: images that do penetrate the psyche, leaps that do connect us with a new intuitive intelligence and release emotion, an imagination which is lavish and swift. (pp. 5-6)

Sleepers is Bly's only full-sized collection since *The Light*. His best recent work, however, is to be found in slim volumes from small presses and in the little magazines, and has been done primarily in two forms: the very short poem, and the prose poem. (pp. 6-7)

Bly had several very short poems in *Silence;* the simplicity, the suddenness and surprise of the form, were central to what he was working for there. But those poems, and the book as well, lacked any humor. If *Silence* created an impression of purity in the reader's mind, that purity was in part the result of an austerity, in tone and in what was and was not allowed to enter the poems. The poems in *Silence* seem somehow chastened—"artificial"—when compared to [his best recent poems]. The poems in *Silence* have a sense of ritual about them, while the more recent poems seem more spontaneous. It is probably because of this subtle artificiality in *Silence* that some critics praise that book, but shy away from the more recent work: the greater feeling of spontaneity in the new poems makes them uneasy—it is too open, too much like notations of the mind in motion, rather than perceptions worked patiently into poems. How the poems were actually composed is irrelevant. The point is that Bly's voice has grown warmer and more varied: more fully and believably—and likably—human. He can still write a brief poem full of a haunting silence, but now he also gives us poems that are impulsive, energetic, with a gaiety reminiscent of Issa. (pp. 9-10)

The same warming and opening of the voice which I've tried to point out in the tiny poems is a central source of strength in Bly's prose poems as well. (p. 10)

Reading Bly's prose poems, Roethke's phrase "a steady storm of correspondences" constantly comes to my mind. Even in small, quiet poems, there is an excited imagination, sensing totally unexpected connections.

All metaphor tacitly acknowledges interconnectedness in the universe, a great web of relationships. For some poets the relationships are primarily interesting for their stylistic uses; for others, like Bly, the ability to see the connections has a deeper importance: it is part of staying spiritually alive, part of one's involvement with the universe.

The imagination we find in these poems has an odd heaviness and substance to it, but with a feeling of lightness at the same time—like a large, solidly built man who is also very nimble. Some of the correspondences which Bly discovers are amazing. One thing that makes them so is a way Bly has of playing with the pathetic fallacy; it is another technique which he has used since *Silence,* and now uses with marvelous ... nerve.... There is an eccentricity [in these poems], but eccentricity is no fault where there is imagination as well. As to the use of the pathetic fallacy, the mingling of the natural world and the world of human emotion can be explained by saying that when Bly writes a line like "the black ducks that fly desolate, forlorn and joyful over the seething swells," he is projecting his own inner world onto the natural world. That's true, but it is also true that Bly, unlike many of us, is not offended by the suggestion that beings other than humans might possess a spiritual life.

It is interesting that so many of the prose poems deal with the seashore.... The sea and the land, the inner world and the outer, the unconscious and the conscious mind—Bly is always concerned with such meeting places. A rich, creative relationship between the inner and outer worlds might, in fact, be called his central theme.

To return to the idea of imaginative leaping, it seems to me that it is in the prose poems that Bly realizes these leaps with most exhilaration and grace. For myself, I find the leaps in them usually more effective than those in the stream-of-consciousness poems in *Sleepers* because in the prose poems the leaps are made from concrete setting and objects, which tends to put more energy and surprise (and the sheer surprise, the marvelous unpredictability, of the metaphoric insights of these poems is one of the main sources of their vitality) into the flights into the unconscious or through time and space. The imagination here is capable of collapsing millions of years quite casually, and without the strain that sometimes occurs when, say, a mammoth appears out of nowhere in a passage of free association (pp. 11-12)

We also see in the prose poems the kind of integration of the techniques and styles represented by *Silence* and *The*

Light that I've been referring to. There are the quiet, mundane, concrete situations, the attentive eye, and clarity and simplicity of language that characterize *Silence,* but also the wildness, the freedom and energy, of sudden surrealistic images and profuse, quick associative shifts that were first fully utilized in *The Light.* (pp. 12-13)

There is something in Bly's combination of mysticism and intuition and passion and didacticism that is reminiscent of D. H. Lawrence. Or perhaps it is better to say Whitman than Lawrence: Bly's criticism and political poems often have Lawrence's curtness and fervor, but the central enterprise of the poetry is more akin to Whitman, who was essentially concerned with helping (rather than analyzing) the growth—the deepening and unfolding and transcendence—of the self. (p. 14)

> *Howard Nelson, "Welcoming Shadows: Robert Bly's Recent Poetry," in* The Hollins Critic *(copyright 1975 by Hollins College), April, 1975, pp. 1-15.*

JULIAN GITZEN

Robert Bly's poetry owes its appeal in part to vivid descriptions of the region around Madison, Minnesota, where he has spent much of his life. The chief concern of his verse, however, is not the objective portrayal of external nature but, rather, the presentation of various states of mind. Natural surroundings assume importance for him either as influences contributing to thoughts or emotions or as media of symbolic expression. Along with James Wright, James Dickey, Robert Kelley and others, Bly has argued for the writing of poetry of increased subjectivity, with emphasis upon the poet's personal vision.... He shares significant ground with the surrealist André Breton, particularly in his fondness for images generated by powerful feelings in the poet's unconscious and designed to appeal to the unconscious of the reader. Although he lacks Breton's Freudian faith in "the omnipotence of the dream," dreams and dream-images do appear in his verse. Similarly, while his art is much more consciously constructed than the automatic writing or "pure psychic automatism" prized by the surrealists, it does contain such notable imagistic departures from objectivity as "moles with golden wings" and Arabic numerals "dressed as bankers and sportsmen," images which are solidly in the surrealist tradition.

In accordance with his attraction to subjectivity, Bly's typical authorial stance is emotional, as reflected in titles like "Three Kinds of Pleasures," "Unrest," "Depression," "Melancholia," and "Written in Dejection near Rome." Despite the predominant gloominess of these titles, the emotion most often expressed in the poems is not sadness but delight. Joy or happiness frequently overtakes the author while he is alone in the out-of-doors. He is both comforted and inspired by solitude, not only because it facilitates the reflective and meditative moments which are vital to his well-being but also because is frees him to develop a mental intensity out of which poetry may issue. Bly refers to the artist's psychic potential as "desire-energy" and explains that during periods of solitude this desire-energy accumulates until it overflows into expression.... (pp. 231-32)

Since Bly's verse depends heavily upon dominant images, it is essential that the most important images be carefully examined. Among his most frequently repeated images is darkness. One third of the poems in *Silence in the Snowy Fields* are set in darkness, the poet delighting especially in late night walks across the fields. No doubt darkness attracts him partially because it is conducive to solitude. Furthermore, it serves as a convenient emblem of the unconscious, an important realm to this poet who, like the surrealists, wishes "to open new corridors into the psyche by association." . . . For Bly, as for generations of other poets, darkness also represents death. Such observations as: "the darkness of death," "The farmer looks up at the paling dome reminding him of death," and "We are falling, / Falling into the open mouths of darkness," combined with the juxtaposition of darkness and death in poems such as "Night" and "Riderless Horses" provide conclusive evidence of Bly's intentions.

Frequently linked with darkness (as in the quotation above from "Return to Solitude") is the image of water, occasionally described by Bly as itself "dark." . . . Having an easily penetrable surface and variable depth, water is uniquely appropriate as an image attached to the related conditions of sleep and death, both of which Bly associates with a fertile strangeness and inwardness. Somewhat as a sleeper falls away from surface consciousness into the depth of the unconscious, so the newly dead literally descend beneath the earth's surface and figuratively break through the surface of conscious existence and into a mysterious, unfamiliar realm. The imagistic usefulness of water in such contexts is self-evident.

Bly's aspiration to escape the tyranny of rational consciousness, experiencing instead the inward state and its richness, is expressed through a water-image in "After Drinking All Night With a Friend . . .". The poet acknowledges that his experiences have been essentially conscious, that his have been the same interests which, as he says elsewhere, have caused American poetry to cling at unprofitable length "to the surface of life." Like the boat in which he is seated, he has simply drifted above the depths, but he yearns to go underwater. . . . (pp. 232-34)

Like darkness and water, snow is a favorite Bly image associated with sleep and death. As with darkness, he is employing a traditional, even archetypal, image because of its proven suggestive power. In his preference for snow he joins a symbolic tradition among whose modern representatives are James Joyce's "The Dead" and Robert Frost's "Stopping by Woods on a Snowy Evening." Like Joyce and Frost, Bly prefers to link snow and darkness, thereby intensifying if not actually doubling the evocative powers of the images. (pp. 234-35)

Frequently associated with snow, water, or darkness in Bly's poems is moonlight. To fully understand its place in his imagistic realm, it is first necessary to review his relation to the German mystical theologian Jacob Boehme (1575-1624), whose writings have furnished epigraphs for both *Silence in the Snowy Fields* and *The Light around the Body*. The poet's choice of epigraphs, such as, "We are all asleep in the outward man," indicates his approval of Boehme's distinction between materialism (associated with greed and selfishness) and spiritualism (associated with godlike love). Boehme accounts for creation in terms of the gradual emergence from the Divine Will of three contending wills or principles, which he identifies as: light, darkness, and bitterness. These three compete in the shaping of all living matter, including man, and the degree to which one principle dominates a specific act of creation determines the unique form which the living matter will assume. During its formation matter passes through distinctive evolutionary stages. The most important of these is the fourth form, Fire, for any matter which reaches this stage acquires self-consciousness (identified with Fire). Self-consciousness, the feeble light of the outward or external man, consists of greed, wrath, and pride.

Although Fire-man is still dominated by the principle of darkness he has been introduced to the light, and it is within his power to elevate himself to the fifth form, Light, which will manifest to him the inner world of the Divine Will, permitting him to escape the Fire of "self" which consumes and to be guided instead by the Light of Divine love. By emulating the life of Christ, men may reach the fifth form, but only by following Christ in rejecting the world, the flesh, and the devil. True peace and harmony are attained only by those who achieve understanding of the Divine Will. . . . Bly's matching conception of a sharp division between the selfish materialism of the outward man (whose animalistic greed is imagistically represented by "the hairy tail" that "howls in the dirt") and the humility, charity, and love of the inner man, as well as his persistent longing to escape from the material to the spiritual world are apparent in such poem-titles as "Smothered by the World," "In Danger from the Outer World," and "Moving Inward at Last."

Since Boehme assumed that the male is temperamentally more aggressive and self-serving than the female, he described the fire-source as the masculine element, conceiving of the light-source as feminine. Obviously Bly has adopted these distinctions to the extent that in "A Man Writes to a Part of Himself," he addresses his inner spirit as a forsaken wife "starving, without care." Again in "The Busy Man Speaks," which opposes spiritual activities to material counterparts, spiritual affairs such as love, art, and sorrow are associated with "the mother," while material concerns, characterized by righteous conduct and "the Chase National Bank," are assigned to "the father." (pp. 235-37)

By following Boehme in the association of women with the spirit and with light, Bly is once more adopting a traditional literary device, particularly when he invokes the archetypal feminine image of moonlight. Typifying his use of moonlight imagery is the opening stanza of "Solitude Late at Night in the Woods":

The body is like a November birch facing the full moon
And reaching into the cold heavens.
In these trees there is no ambition, no sodden body,
   no leaves,
Nothing but bare trunks climbing like fire!

The trees set us an example in stretching their branches toward the light, the source of spiritual illumination. Their exemplary behavior resides not simply in their aspiration to light but in their prior shedding of leaves or "sodden body." (p. 237)

Sleepers Joining Hands . . . adds an additional dimension to Bly's spiritual quest. While essentially a book of poems, it contains an essay, "I Came Out of the Mother Naked," in which the author argues that prehistoric human societies were matriarchal and that "what we call masculine consciousness is a very recent creation." He identifies the spirit presiding over the lives of primitive men as that of the Great Mother, of whom he distinguishes four types: the Good Mother or procreative force, whose interest is in abundant life; the Death Mother, whose "job is to end everything the Good Mother has brought to birth"; the Ecstatic Mother, who ministers to mental and spiritual development; and the Stone Mother or Teeth Mother, who opposes the Ecstatic Mother, dissolving consciousness, "dismembering . . . the psyche," as the Death Mother destroys life. While not arguing that Father-consciousness is evil, Bly does associate it with logic, and he senses an increased weariness with reasoning, resulting in an arising interest in the intuitive mode of Mother-consciousness. It appears that the Great Mother (and particularly the Ecstatic Mother) constitutes for Bly the mythical extension of the feminine spirituality which he found in Boehme. For him as for his fellow poet Robert Graves the feminine myth offers a tangible and profound expression of spiritual forces. Not surprisingly, Bly finds two of the Mother's favorite images to be "the night" and "the moon," images which, as we have noted, dominate his verse. His immediate affinities are with the Ecstatic Mother, or Muse, of whom he observes, "When a man or woman is joyful alone, the Ecstatic Mother is there." Given Bly's preference for creative solitude and his poetic emphasis upon solitary joy, it is apparent how fully he has committed himself to the Ecstatic Mother.

Whether or not his own interest in the unconscious led him to this myth, Bly certainly assumes that the path to its rediscovery lies through the unconscious. (p. 238)

The need to rediscover the Great Mother is urgent, for our modern contempt for spirituality has engendered a dangerous imbalance. Poems like "The Teeth Mother Naked at Last" indicate Bly's conviction that the destructive Death Mother and Teeth Mother, perhaps aided by overwhelming Father-consciousness, are threatening us. It is vital to restore favor to the Good Mother and the Ecstatic Mother. Although in his essay, Bly claims to be encouraged by finding "in my own poems and in the poems of so many other poets alive now fundamental attempts to right our spiritual balance, by encouraging those parts in us that are linked with music, with solitude, water, and trees, the parts that grow when we are far from the centers of ambition," his recent poetry, nevertheless, is permeated by a tone of frustration and by prophecies of doom, underlining his belief that capitalism and materialism have triumphed at the expense of essential human qualities.

He mourns the disappearance of kindness and sympathy as Americans discover the selfishness and attendant brutality which are their birthright. A terrible disillusionment is evidenced by "the light in children's faces fading at six or seven." Conscience and humane feelings are not easily trampled, however, and, if scorned, may eventually take revenge. Bly is convinced that a large-scale surrender to greed and selfishness has in turn generated a suicidal self-hatred, a guilty yearning for death. Among those most susceptible to self-destruction are the most tender and conscientious, and leading the suicides are "ministers who dive headfirst into the earth." "Hurrying Away from the Earth" portrays various horrible forms of suicide, indicating the dreadful extent to which people are willing to go to escape from a world in which "the poor, and the dazed, and the idiots" are neglected and abused. (pp. 239-40)

Bly's version of the Waste Land is set forth in nightmare-images appropriate to the heightened emotionalism and intensity of his gloomy prophetic tone, images marking a transition to genuine surrealism. "Now the whole nation starts to whirl, / the end of the Republic breaks off" as the godhead of empiricism, "the ghost of Locke," continues to preside "above the railroad tracks." Human servants of the materialistic ethic are "black spiders, / having turned pale and fat." Violent self-destructiveness abounds as "the body tears off its own arms and throws them into the air" and "The sheriff cuts off his black legs / And nails them to a tree." Swallowed by a black selfishness which shuts out the spiritual light, the population is ripe for death, and "The grave moves from its ambush, / Moving over the hills on black feet," while "Some shining thing, inside, that has served us well" strives to escape. Bly's vision is conveyed with an urgency reminiscent of the British poets of the Thirties. As a social critic he invites comparison with Auden, whose moral viewpoint resembles his own. Auden's line, "We must love one another or die," sums up the impulse behind much of Bly's recent poetic effort. (p. 240)

> *Julian Gitzen, "Floating on Solitude: The Poetry of Robert Bly," in* Modern Poetry Studies *(copyright © 1976, by Jerome Mazzaro), Vol. 7, No. 3, Winter, 1976, pp. 231-40.*

MICHAEL ATKINSON

In *Sleepers Joining Hands,* Robert Bly offers his readers a various weave of the personal and the public, the psychological and the political modes of experience. Each mode illuminates the other, though . . . the collection is most fundamentally and formally psychological. The layout of the book is pleasantly indirect: two dozen pages of poems, ranging from haiku-like meditation moments to longer poems of protest. Then there is the essay, a short course in the Great Mother, an analysis of the disturbing but finally nourishing configuration of feminine archetypes in the collective unconscious. And finally we have the oneiric title sequence: four poems and a coda, written at different times and published in different places, but here offered as a single structure, a whole.

The poems on either side of the essay seem to point back and forth to each other. And so naturally we ask: what is the relation of the earlier poems to the later sequence? What is the final shape of the book?

The essay points the way. Like most poets who pause to explain themselves, Bly works obliquely. His essay focuses on the work of Bachofen and Neumann; yet the pattern of the book rests firmly on the thought of a successor to the first and the teacher of the second—Carl Jung. The essay coordinates the variety of anima archetypes which inhabit our subconsciousness: the Good Mother who gives us life, the Death Mother who takes it away; the Ecstatic Mother, muse of joy, and the Stone or Teeth Mother who reduces us to the stupor of psychic annihilation. But the title sequence, which is the key to the book's integrity, focuses on two other Jungian dream archetypes—the shadow and the Self.

The symbols of the earlier poems gain resonance in the schematic context of the later sequence: imagist poems move toward plotted action, oracles toward ritual, archetypes toward myth. Here, I would like to present the scheme of the sequence and show its relation to the shorter poems, delineating the system of archetypes that coherently applies throughout the book, linking Biblical allusions to contemporary consciousness and connecting dream images with myth. (pp. 135-36)

In Jung's overall schema, the personality striving for full individuation or integration has four aspects, which are personified in our dreams: (1) the ego (or persona), that person (or role) we consider ourselves to be in normal waking consciousness; (2) the shadow, that figure of the same sex as the ego who embodies negative or positive traits which might have been conscious but which have now been repressed; (3) the anima, the woman within the man, that feminine consciousness with which he has to come to terms —or the animus, the man within the woman, representing the male consciousness with which the woman must reconcile herself; and finally, (4) the Self, that perfect wholeness which the individual can become, when he has reconciled himself with his shadow and anima (or she with her shadow and animus) and become his own potentiality for being.

The first poem of the "Sleepers" sequence hearkens back to the time the ego became split from its shadow by repression, and is appropriately entitled "The Shadow Goes Away." It records the fragmentation of the questor, chronicles his separation from that lost aspect which he must again come to recognize in himself. Until he incorporates his shadow, he is powerless to act effectively. We feel his powerlessness as we gaze with him upon "The woman chained to the shore," Andromeda-like, and hear him express his fear of going into the ocean to fight for her, to liberate her. (In mythic compression, the woman *is* the ocean —la mer, la mère—the womb from which he must be reborn whole.) He fears the sea. Juxtaposed to his feeling of impotence is its cause: his loss of the shadow.

Often—perhaps most frequently in dream and art—the shadow is a figure that embodies the negative aspects of the personality; the negativity provides the reason they are repressed. Thus we have Jekyll's hidden Hyde, Dimmesdale's Chillingworth, Gatsby's Wolfsheim, and the like. But, as Jung notes, we may just as easily deny parts of ourselves that—grown wiser—we would consider good. Because something about them threatens the fragile, narrowly defined persona or ego, they too may be repressed. But ultimately they must be admitted to our consciousness and assimilated, or the results will be disastrous. Ishmael's savage Queequeg, Willy Lowman's Charley, Macbeth's Banquo: each contains "values that are needed by consciousness, but that exist in a form that makes it difficult to integrate them into one's life."

The protagonist in Bly's poems has a shadow that is protean but consistent. (pp. 136-37)

The questor's shadow—and, the poem suggests, ours—is the natural man, the primitive, at home in the world of nature and the unconscious. The pillagers of the tribal village and the Marines who appear late in the poem are intended to remind us how we have duplicated our oppression of the Indian in the bombing of Vietnam. Equations that seem both familiar and strained in political rhetoric are here given greater coherence and vitality in a psychological connection. In each case we have attempted to destroy (or repress) the people who best exemplified the very qualities we most need to acknowledge and cultivate in ourselves— positive shadows.

"The Shadow Goes Away" gives a larger context for a number of the other poems—poems, already integers themselves, now resonate within the larger pattern. "The Condition of the Working Classes: 1970" is blamed not on those above them, but on those they have trod under—blamed not on the oppression that workers might suffer, but on the repression of their shadows, inwardly and outwardly. (p. 138)

As the repression intensifies, so does the terror of living with it. Denying the shadow drives us into the maw of "The Teeth Mother Naked at Last." Here the horror hits its highest pitch and an unfamiliar list toward stereotype and stridence appears. Maybe it is unavoidable—so many have spoken out against the war for so long that even the most telling analysis has deteriorated into formula and finally come to rest in cliché. Bly's poem cannot shake itself free of stereotypy, even though it has considerable power. The power comes not just from its imagery . . . but from the analysis of cause and effect that is given in the hard terms of imagery which will not allow the luxuries and niceties of rationalization. These cause-effect concatenations generate both the strengths and weaknesses of the poem. I suspect each reader will find different equations effective. But when they work, they work; when they don't, they grate. (pp. 138-39)

[Bly's Teeth Mother] is naked and terrible. But at least we can see her now, as our forebears perhaps could not. In the terror of Vietnam she has become clear to us, our own creation. As Bly explains in his essay, the Teeth Mother "stands for numbness, paralysis, catatonia, being totally spaced out, the psyche torn to bits, arms and legs thrown all over." . . . "The Teeth Mother Naked at Last" offers a diagram of despair, a brittle anatomy of agony with only a gesture to indicate the possibility of healing, of wholeness.

Here, then, is a picture of the U.S. at our most culturally destructive, annihilating our own shadows—Indians, Blacks, Vietnamese—with whom we must be reunited if we are to have psychic fullness and dimensionality; if we are to be solid enough to cast shadows. Concern for oppression of our shadows pervades the book, essay and poems. But it is neither a continuing accusation nor an extended *mea culpa* that Bly chants, as "Calling to the Badger" shows. This poem, like all of Bly's work on the shadow, is pervaded by a "sadness that rises from the death of the Indians," and that is a sadness for our own loss. . . .

This backward look over the shadow poems that begin the book can help define the conditions that apply as the title sequence opens. As in most myths (whether the king be impotent, the land waste, or the virgin guarded by a dragon —all of which conditions more or less obtain as we return to the opening of the "Sleepers" sequence) the call to the quest begins with a perception of a lack, an imbalance. Whereas the earlier, shorter poems mainly expressed despair at the loss, "The Shadow Goes Away" proceeds from recognition to restorative action. Our fugitive imaginations are personified in the protagonist who, too, calls to the badger and otter, animals still in touch with the renewing waters of psychic life, the stream that emerges from beneath the ground. (p. 141)

Bly's seeker goes in search of his shadow, which hides in all dark peoples, Negro, Eskimo, Indian, Asian. The equation between past and present betrayals, between Indian and Asian wars, is now complete, clear to the protagonist as well as the reader. Refusing to continue the old path of inner denial and outward oppression, he turns from the zeal of battle to view the littered land with primitive consciousness and compassion. He has begun to assimilate the consciousness of the shadow, and can now continue his journey of integration.

The second poem of the sequence finds the dreamer momentarily awake, noting but not yet comprehending the femininity of the earth on which he finds himself: "fragments of the mother lie open in all low places." But his task here is "Meeting the Man Who Warns Me," and the substance of the warning is that he may not understand, may not proceed further without realizing from a transcendental viewpoint where he has already been.

Dreaming again, the sleeper experiences everywhere the death of the father. . . . The dreamer experiences absolute separation from the presence of the father because he has seen the father only as external; he has not yet recognized the father-energy as a part of himself, waiting to be actualized.

But now that vision can change, for in the paradoxical logic of myth, once the shadow figure has become visible, the light may be seen. (p. 142)

Quite strikingly, as the protagonist of the poem 'sees the light' and realizes that "The energy is inside us," he immediately encounters a personification of the Self:

> I start toward [the light], and I meet an old man.
> . . . .
> And the old man cries out: "I am here.
> Either talk to me about your life, or turn back."

When the protagonist pauses for breath and begins to account for his experience, the rendering is most startling; for it comes from a greater completeness, and a greater mythic awareness than either reader or dreamer knew he had. He begins by announcing his own shadow-including nature and proceeds to recount a mythical journey which neither we nor he knew he had taken. (p. 143)

The synoptic recollection of the journey of the protagonist, which appears in the last lines of "Meeting the Man Who Warns Me," is expanded in "Night Journey in the Cooking Pot," which is a flashback composed of reflections on the experience and meaning of his immersion, of the dark, still uncomprehended part of his quest. Here, again, a problem of continuity confronts us; but the apparently confused and confusing emotional swings of "Night Journey" can be understood once we see that the poem divides itself into two movements, describing two phases of the mythic journey: the departure into the realm of mystery and also the return to the ordinary world. As the seeker begins to reexperience and rearticulate his journey retrospectively, we hear a familiar pattern: "I was born during the night sea journey." That he "love[s] the whale with his warm organ pipes" is less expected, but perfectly consonant: for Bly, this going-out is an *ecstasis*, a standing-outside-of the ego, an ecstasy; it is the return to the world of ordinary men and affairs that proves the difficult leg of the journey.

The departure into the water is a journey into ego-dissolving solitude, a necessary prelude to finding a path of effective action in the ordinary world: "I float on solitude as on water . . . there is a road" (Bly's ellipsis). The poem's first

movement explores his privacy, which for Bly is sister word to privilege, not privation. Here we see the rejuvenating exhilaration of going a little crazy in private, deprived of human contact in the "womanless loneliness." The enthusiasm for isolation expressed in "Night Journey" is reinforced and clarified by several of the book's earlier poems. (pp. 145-46)

Finally, of course, this privacy is the solitude of the womb, for the voyage he recalls in "The Night Journey in the Cooking Pot," is the night sea journey in the womb of la mer, notre mère. The cooking pot of the title, like the oven and hearth as Bly explains in his essay, is the province of the woman and symbol of the womb. In the opening movement of "Night Journey" images of rebirth abound: "I feel . . . / the baby whirling in the womb," and "Nuns with faces smoothed by prayer peer out from holes in the earth." (p. 146)

In the second movement of "Night Journey" [the seeker] faces the difficulty of returning to the world of ordinary experience. Like Buddha, whose ultimate temptation was simply to stay in the oceanic trance of nirvana, like the silent Lazarus and other such questors, this seeker sees how difficult it will be to communicate the joy of going beyond the ego, the personality, the boundaries of our daily round. But like Whitman in "Crossing Brooklyn Ferry," he urges us to realize that we are not separated from him, but united by a common experience we sometimes forget.

> I am not going farther from you
> I am coming nearer,
> green rain carries me nearer you,
> I weave drunkenly about the page,
> I love you,
> I never knew that I loved you
> Until I was swallowed by the invisible.

Here, in his protagonist's plea for understanding, it would seem that we have Bly's apologia for his own method. By writing in the language of dream and vision, he does not hope to remove himself from our experience, for we are all dreamers, and can eventually intuit the scheme of our dreams. . . . Though he acknowledges that the poem's oracular words may seem skew and difficult, he assures us that when he emerges from the water (night, mother, chaos, unconscious, dream) his speech will be straight as the branch—a promise, as we have seen, difficult to fulfill. (pp. 146-47)

But such a conclusion is far too optimistic, or else many would have returned and spoken, and redemption would be daily for all men. Bly realizes that—and in the second movement of "Night Journey," the questor suffers the inexorable difficulty of returning to the realm of ordinary experience while preserving his vision. (p. 147)

He is ashamed looking into the limpid pool of his dreams. The poem has moved fully from the ecstasy of the journey to the restrictions of the return. And those restrictions include the difficulty of making the poem "good enough."

In the fourth poem, Bly spells out the nature of the journey as explicitly as possible:

> Here is some prose
> *Once there was a man who went to a far country*
> *to get his inheritance and then returned.*

This, of course, is (in the phrase of James Joyce and the system of Joseph Campbell) the "monomyth" in its briefest form: the story of the hero who is called from the ordinary world of experience into the realm of the mysterious, where he battles various foes, conquers or converts them, and gains a boon, his "inheritance," a life-restoring elixir with which he recrosses the threshold and with which, after some readjustment, he transforms the world or his vision of it. (pp. 148-49)

There is a nascent realization, a new Self, "another being living inside" the poet: "He is looking out of my eyes. / I hear him / in the wind through the bare trees." (p. 150)

As Ginsberg ended *Howl* with a joyous footnote—not as a palinode, but to affirm the divinity of the horror he chronicled—so to this strange and often painful oneiric journey, Bly appends "An Extra Joyful Chorus for Those Who Have Read This Far." In several ways the chorus alludes heavily to Whitman. Its closing lines (and indeed the very title of the entire "Sleepers Joining Hands" sequence) bear strong resemblance to the opening of the last section of Whitman's poem "The Sleepers." ... Yet, though both poems record psychological night sea journeys, and though both close with affirmations, the similarities between the poems are not continuous. Bly borrows from Whitman for his own ends, as we shall see.

And so with technique. The "Joyful Chorus," Bly's chant of polymorphous identity which echoes and goes beyond his handling of the protean shadow in "The Shadow Goes Away," also recalls Whitman's chants of universal identity. Here again, there are some important differences to balance the similarities. Whitman's sympathetic identifications are usually directed toward the commonplace and the possible, encouraging the reader to follow along.... Bly, on the other hand, opts to include the fantastical and folkloristic along with the ordinary and credible, which encourages the reader to relate these elements to other symbolic quests or to translate them into his own terms, but not to engage directly in the protagonist's own identification:

I am the ball of fire the woodman cuts out of the wolf's
    stomach,
I am the sun that floats over the Witch's house,
I am the horse sitting in the chestnut tree singing.

While both poets work within the tradition of the psychic quest, Bly is also *referring* to it, and asking the reader to refer to it, schematically.

Like Whitman, Bly makes use of the transcendent power of the aggregate. The catalogue of beautiful and ordinary and terrible beginnings which dominates the first sixty lines of section 15 of "Song of Myself" yields the aggregate exhilaration of Beginning; in "The Sleepers" the catalogue of actor, nominee, stammerer and criminal in an averaged aggregate of sleeping humanity allows Whitman to say

The soul is always beautiful
The universe is duly in order. . . . every thing is in its
    place. . . .
. . . .
The diverse shall be no less diverse, but they shall flow
    and unite . . . they unite now.

For Bly's protagonist the transcendent aggregate is the experience of the completed quest: its component parts, no matter how painful, finally become redeemed because of their place in the whole. Even "fleeing along the ground like a frightened beast" or being "the last inheritor crying out in deserted houses" become fit matter for a "Joyful Chorus" when the protagonist realizes that he is at every moment "an eternal happiness fighting in the long reeds." Each act contains the imprint of all others, and of the completed sequence. Bly's questor images his life everywhere at once and at all stages simultaneously. Perhaps most summatively he is "the man locked inside the oakwomb, / waiting for lightning, only let out on stormy nights." He is that core of life in the tree of the Self, drawn from subterranean waters and waiting, now that the old foliage has died, to manifest himself in the new spring. He is everyone and "no one at all" simultaneously, for he is prior to personality. Thus, in the womb, aching to deliver himself, he can paradoxically say:

I love the Mother.
I am an enemy of the Mother, give me my sword.
I leap into her mouth full of seaweed.

For he honors the womb of the unconscious and arational which he has reentered as embryo, and he honors the rational and masculine desire to translate that primeval wholeness into the articulate world of forms—water to leaves, sea to sword.

Further, he sees and feels the archetypal nature and universal possibility of his experience—new incarnations and new Bethlehems for all men who attend to their dreams:

Our faces shine with the darkness reflected from the
    Tigris. . . .
The panther rejoices in the gathering dark.
Hands rush toward each other through miles of space.
All the sleepers in the world join hands.

(pp. 150-53)

Michael Atkinson, "Robert Bly's 'Sleepers Joining Hands': Shadow and Self," in The Iowa Review *(copyright © 1976, by The University of Iowa), Vol. 7, No. 4 (Fall, 1976), pp. 135-53.*

ALAN HELMS

The experience of reading *Sleepers Joining Hands* . . . is a bit like slogging your way through a violent storm.

The book begins in deceptive calm, with "Six Winter Privacy Poems." . . . Bly's central theme, beautifully rendered: the duality of inner and outer worlds, the deep duality of a consciousness often conflicted but existing here in a momentary state of peaceful coexistence. It's the American haiku, fully and quietly accomplished. . . . [However,] the final, frenetic Whitmanesque catalogue of wildly various identifications [in "An Extra Joyful Chorus for Those Who Have Read This Far"] should give you some idea of the bumpy ground Bly travels in *Sleepers Joining Hands*.

Bly's troubled yearning to achieve the condition of a Whitman most shows in passages of "The Night Journey in the Cooking Pot." . . . Whitman's influence is everywhere. . . . Whitman was not, so far as I can recall, ever ashamed sitting on the edge of his bed, nor did he ever announce a decision in his poetry that "death is friendly." For Whitman, death was a fact of his condition, not a subject for debate. Whitman's belief became the condition of his poetry, not the occasion for it.

No, "this is not the perfect freedom of the saints" for it lacks the saint's bedrock of belief; the result is a poetry of claim instead of conviction. . . . (pp. 284-85)

How difficult it must be to cultivate this special brand of solitary sensibility ("inwardness, inwardness, inwardness, the inward path I still walk on") and still hope for the kind of reader community Bly writes about, in this book but especially in his criticism. He's accomplished this job in the past, it's true—by shunting between inner and outer worlds, writing "private" poems of quiet, mystical meditation on the one hand and "public" poems of scathing political and psychological analysis on the other. *Sleepers Joining Hands* is an attempt to come to terms with the inner outer dichotomy, to integrate them or at least to lead them toward integration. (p. 286)

There is however one calm, searching eye in the midst of this storm. The prose center of the book, "I Came Out of the Mother Naked," explores the arguments of Bachofen, Neumann, and Jung that matriarchies only gradually gave way to patriarchies, and that "the Great Mother can best be understood as a union of four 'force fields.'" In working through his exciting "psychic archaeology," Bly achieves with his prose what he hopes for in his poetry: establishment of community created through an imaginative reading of the history of his own consciousness and the culture in which it lives, works, suffers, and sometimes exults. The essay focuses the energies dispersed throughout the poetry; it also provides Bly with a possible mythology. But it is as archeologists in search of a community that we finally come to read the poetry, discovering here a flying turtle, there a cooking pot, picking our way slowly through a littered maze of Jungian psychology and Great Mother imagery, backwards in the order of literature down to the foundation of Bly's theory which gives us the clues we need to reconstruct the poems. Though he will hate the comparison, Bly's latest poetry is written like almost all of Ransom's, in the service of a theory.

Says Valéry, ". . . there is no theory that is not a fragment, carefully prepared, of some autobiography." Bly has given us a lot of his autobiography, including these rearranged quotations . . . :

> For my own generation of poets the whole problem of the community has been an agony. . . . When I publish a book. . . . I try to give something to the community. . . . the more the weak function in the writer is developed, the closer the writer comes to the community, or to "humanity.". . . . my weakest function, feeling, is still poorly developed. . . .

It follows that if Bly is to develop what, in his view, is his weakest function, thereby resolving his agony of the community, he should write fragmented poems full of feeling. That's just what he's done in the past, giving us poems of intense feeling in which discreetly marked fragments sit comfortably together, held by the power of his extraordinary imagery. (pp. 286-88)

[The] essential shift in Bly's recent poetry, as distinct from his prose [is] a turn from charting and chanting the geography of America's psychological and moral landscape, to mapping and mourning the battered terrain of his own fragmented sensibility. And coincident with this development,

from having been our critic who most successfully demolished the confessional mode, he's recently opted for it himself: "O yes, I love you, book of my confessions." Insofar as that "book of confessions" is synonymous with his latest actual book, Bly's performance is sloppy and self-conscious, as if he could suddenly hear himself thinking, and out loud at that. (p. 288)

> *Alan Helms, in* Partisan Review *(copyright © 1977 by Partisan Review, Inc.), Vol. XLIV, No. 2, 1977.*

HUGH KENNER

Robert Bly's prose poems have a parallel hallucinatory quality [to the drawings by Gendron Jensen that illustrate "This Body Is Made of Camphor and Gopherwood"]. . . .

"My beloved is to me as a cluster of camphor," we read in the Song of Solomon (1:14); and the Ark, God told Noah (Genesis 6:14), was to be made "of gopherwood." The Ark was by some accounts an allegory for the body, and that's all the explanation you're going to get in these pages about what it's like to be alive in a body; in it, yet through it mysteriously part of everything else material. . . .

Bly is attempting to write down what it's like to be alive, a state in which, he implies, not all readers find themselves all the time—certainly not all readers who lack the luck to live in rural Minnesota, where a voice isn't always trying to sell you something. (p. 10)

> *Hugh Kenner, in* The New York Times Book Review *(© 1978 by The New York Times Company; reprinted by permission), January 1, 1978.*

JAMES FINN COTTER

Nowadays, everything Bly touches becomes a holy cause and reason for another book. [In *This Body is Made of Camphor and Gopherwood*] he consecrates "the often neglected[?] medium of the prose poem." Like the snail in the book's twenty-one drawings by Gendron Jensen, Bly has crept into the shell of his own meditations and remains absorbed in Sufi poetry, Rilke, protozoa, animals, woods, and fog. The pilgrim's mecca is a small black stone, mysterious and impenetrable. One may admire such pure isolation, but the poet does not help us to share it. The result is not mysticism but solipsism, and we are left out in the cold by passages like this one from "The Pail"; "So for two days I gathered ecstasies from my own body, I rose up and down, surrounded only by bare wood and bare air and some gray cloud, and what was inside me came so close to me, and I lived and died!" In earlier collections—especially *Sleepers Joining Hands*—Bly could convince us of a mystical experience by imagining and hinting at its beauty. Too often these poems are overwrought and pretentious. The one delightful piece here describes the poet's children and their friends preparing to put on a play. Except for this "Coming In for Supper," a reader would not know a family existed or, rather, mattered in the poet's hermetic world. Even the love poem that closes the volume, "The Cry Going Out over Pastures," appears to be too rhetorical to be moving, talking more about the poet than the loved one: "I first met you when I had been alone for nine days." A strange way to greet someone you love. (pp. 214-15)

> *James Finn Cotter, in* The Hudson Review *(copyright © 1978 by The Hudson Review,*

Inc.; reprinted by permission), Vol. XXXI, No. 1, Spring, 1978.

*   *   *

BORGES, Jorge Luis   1899-

Borges is an Argentine short story writer, poet, essayist, critic, and translator. He is one of the most important and original figures in contemporary literature, best known for his *Ficciones.* **Developing archetypal concepts of myth through fantasy, Borges creates a fictional world without the constants of time and reality, searching not for "truth" but for a polysemous quality of vision. He was influenced early in his career by the** *ultraísta* **movement in Spain, and brought this influence, with its emphasis on metaphor, to Latin America. Borges has collaborated with Adolfo Bioy Casares under the pseudonyms of H(onorio) Bustos Domecq and B. Suarez Lynch. (See also** *CLC,* **Vols. 1, 2, 3, 4, 6, 8, 9, and** *Contemporary Authors,* **Vols. 21-24, rev. ed.)**

ROBERT SCHOLES

Borges needs neither praise nor explanation from me or anyone else. My discussion of him, then, must be neither of these, though it may partake of both. It is a personal statement in the form of a modest fiction: the creation of a character named Borges, based on certain documents that have appeared in the English language bearing that name. The title of this performance might have been even more presumptuous—"Borges and I"—or, most presumptuous, "My Borges."

My Borges writes English, of course, though he has gone to some lengths to disguise this fact. Sometimes his works appear as translations made by people with patently fictional names like Norman Thomas di Giovanni. On other occasions he has published poems, designating these English texts as translations made by some of the finest poets of our day. (pp. 12-13)

The ingenuity of Borges in disguising his true situation can hardly be credited. He has gone to the incredible length of planting different versions of his English texts, sometimes so strikingly at odds that mere error can hardly account for the differences. Let me cite an instance of this, in which he has clearly overplayed his hand. In a book called *Other Inquisitions,* in a text bearing the possibly spurious dateline Buenos Aires, December 23, 1946, he writes of a supposed ancestor who

> left Argentine letters some memorable poetry, and who tried to reform the teaching of philosophy by purifying it of theological shadows and exposing the principles of Locke and Condillac. He died in exile; like all men, he was born at the wrong time. . . .
>
> (p. 13)

The clinching case for the Anglicism (whether British or North American) of this elusive author may be found in the writers he alludes to most frequently. There are in his works, of course, a few perfunctory references to Cervantes, Quevedo, and Unamuno, designed to provide a sort of literary local color, and there are even pseudo-allusions to South American authors who are probably inventions of Borges himself, like the notorious Honorio Bustos Domecq and B. Suarez Lynch. But the authors he returns to most often are a relatively small group of British men of letters

who were prominent at the end of the last century: G. K. Chesterton, Robert Louis Stevenson, Oscar Wilde, G. B. Shaw, Rudyard Kipling, and H. G. Wells. He knows these writers better and reads them more sympathetically than most English teachers do. Can you imagine an English professor saying of Wilde, "He was an ingenious man who was also right"? . . . It is even harder to imagine an Argentine writer saying it. After all, not even the French, who dare to admire Poe, have gone so far as to admire Wilde. Even Gide only pitied him. But Borges is clearly steeped in the work of these British writers. They, along with the North Americans, Poe and Hawthorne, and a few Europeans like Kafka and Valéry, are his true literary ancestors. (p. 14)

By sketching for you a factually false version of Borges, I have intended to raise some questions about the relationship between fiction and reality which he has considered himself and upon which he has shed as much light as any living writer. And I have also intended to warn you that in my less obviously false presentation of Borges in the remainder of this essay, there will also be a certain measure of fiction. But now I propose to consider what Borges has had to say about the fact/fiction relationship, beginning in a very humble way by considering some of the instances of the word "reality" in his texts. My first set of illustrations will be taken from his essays on other writers collected in *Other Inquisitions,* where he takes up this problem on many occasions, with different emphases that are often quite illuminating.

Writing of Quevedo, he introduces a persistent theme in his critical work. He says of one sonnet, "I shall not say that it is a transcription of reality, for reality is not verbal. . . ." This opposition between language and reality, the unbridgeable gap between them, is fundamental to the Borgesian vision, and to much of modern epistemology and poetic theory. In particular, the notion of a lack of contact between language and world is a characteristic of those schools of critical thought that are usually called "formalist." . . . It is frequently assumed that Borges is a typical formalist, who holds that language is self-contained and self-sufficient—self-referential, in fact. But this is simply not the case. Let us return to that statement about the Quevedo poem. In presenting it to you the first time I actually cut it off in mid-sentence. Here is the whole thing:

> I shall not say that it is a transcription of reality, for reality is not verbal, but I can say that the words are less important than the scene they evoke or the virile accent that seems to inform them. . . .
>
> (p. 15)

Poems are made of words and reality is not, yet there is something here between the words and the reality which is important. In this case there are actually two things: a "scene" evoked by the words and an "accent" that seems to inform them. This scene and this accent, then, are mediations between language and world. Born of words, they have nevertheless moved beyond words toward experiences. The words suggest a speaker with a virile accent; they imply a human being of an order of reality greater than their own. And they also present a scene which is realer than language, though it falls short of reality. These fictions or inventions, then, move language *toward* reality, not away from it. Artful writing offers a key that can open the doors of the prison-house of language.

Borges develops this idea further in his philosophic discussion, "Avatars of the Tortoise":

> It is hazardous to think that a coordination of words (philosophies are nothing else) can have much resemblance to the universe. It is also hazardous to think that one of those famous coordinations does not resemble it a little more than the others, if only in an infinitesimal way. . . .

The term "coordination of words," of course, applies equally well to philosophies and stories. They are all fictions because they are verbal and the universe is not. But again comes the qualifying notion. Some of these coordinations catch more of the universe than others. And Borges adds that, of those he has considered in this context, the only one in which he recognizes "some vestige of the universe" is Schopenhauer's. Reading this, we are permitted, or even obliged, to ask by what faculty Borges or anyone else is capable of recognizing vestiges of the universe in a mere coordination of words. I don't want to pause and consider this question here. Or you might say I can't. But Borges's statement seems to imply that we are in touch with reality in some way, either through valid perceptions or through intuitions which are non-verbal. (pp. 15-16)

Borges suggests that allegory fails when its fictions are reducible back to single word-concepts, but succeeds when its fictions function as complex signs moving away from simple concepts toward the "ungraspable reality." For Borges the tendency in language toward logic is a movement away from reality. The more precise and fixed the terminology, the more inadequate it must become. Thus allegory, at its best, is thinking in images, intuitive, and open to truth. Whereas logic is a kind of game, often admirable, but not likely to catch much of the universe in its play. (p. 17)

In discussing the writer to whom he is most justly generous, he elaborates this notion further, making his illustrations concrete and specific. Having discussed the excellence of H. G. Wells as a storyteller, and recounted with amusement the reaction of Jules Verne to Wells's *The First Men in the Moon* (Verne "exclaimed indignantly, 'Il invente!'"), Borges suggests that Wells's achievement rests on something even more important than ingenuity:

> In my opinion, the excellence of Wells's first novels—*The Island of Dr. Moreau,* for example, or *The Invisible Man*—has a deeper origin. Not only do they tell an ingenious story, but they tell a story symbolic of processes that are somehow inherent in all human destinies. The harassed invisible man who has to sleep as though his eyes were wide open because his eyelids do not exclude light is our solitude and our terror; the conventicle of seated monsters who mouth a servile creed in their night is the Vatican and is Lhasa. Work that endures is always capable of an infinite and plastic ambiguity; it is all things to all men, like the Apostle; it is a mirror that reflects the reader's own features and it is also a map of the world. And it must be ambiguous in an evanescent and modest way, almost in spite of

the author; he must appear to be ignorant of all symbolism. Wells displayed that lucid innocence in his first fantastic exercises, which are to me the most admirable part of his admirable work. . . .

(pp. 17-18)

This is one of the most perceptive and succinct paragraphs of literary criticism that I have encountered, and it takes us to the heart of Borges's notion of literary reality. Wells's work is a "*mirror* that reflects the reader's own features and it is also a *map* of the world." I wish to suggest that the two images employed here were not chosen lightly. Mirrors and maps are two highly different ways of imaging the world around us. They are also images that Borges returns to again and again in his own fiction. They are, of course, pointedly non-verbal signs of reality, and they are signs of different sorts. Mapping is based on a sign system that is highly arbitrary in its symbols but aspires toward an exact iconicity in its proportions. Mirrors, on the other hand, are superbly iconic in their reflections of reality, but patently artificial in at least three respects. They reduce three dimensions to a plane surface of two; they double distance and reduce size (our face in a mirror is only half its true size), and most significantly, they reverse right and left.

The distortions of maps and mirrors, because they are visible and comparable with the reality they image, are obvious. With language, however, the distortions are less obvious and therefore more sinister. Thus fiction, which gives us images of human situations and actions, is superior to philosophy, which tries to capture these things in more abstract coordinations of words. Like Sidney, like Shelley, and other apologists for literature, Borges is answering Plato's charge that poets falsify the universe. But this is a more total answer and a stronger one for two reasons. Unlike the others it does not weaken itself by accepting the Platonic premise. Borges does *not* argue that literature points toward some eternal realm of perfect ideas. His argument concerns a complex human reality. And furthermore, he uses this complexity as the ground for an attack on philosophy itself. (p. 18)

Returning now to the passage on Wells, there is yet one more aspect of it that must be considered. The notion that art is a mirror is not a new one. . . . But Borges's mirror is . . . modest, and does only what ordinary mirrors do. We see in it not nature or the world but only ourselves: "it is a mirror that reflects the reader's own features." Of the world, art is merely a map, but it is a map that points accurately to things that are there in reality. In Wells's image of the invisible man we recognize "our own solitude and our terror"; and in the "conventicle of seated monsters who mouth a servile creed in their night" we see an image of "the Vatican" and "Lhasa." Such mirroring and such mapping take us deeply into reality though the images are obviously fabulations rather than transcriptions. And this is a major point. Reality is too subtle for realism to catch it. It cannot be transcribed directly. But by invention, by fabulation, we may open a way toward reality that will come as close to it as human ingenuity may come. We rely on maps and mirrors precisely because we know their limitations and know how to allow for them. But fiction functions as both map and mirror at the same time. Its images are fixed, as the configurations of a map are fixed, and perpetually various, like the features reflected by a mirror, which never gives the same image to the same person. "Work that endures," says Borges, "is capable of an infinite and plastic ambiguity."

The world that Borges maps for us in his own fictions seems at first to be as strange an image of reality as the work of a medieval cartographer. It is a world populated mainly by gauchos and librarians, men of mindless brutality and others of lettered inactivity. These extremes meet, of course, in the figure of the detective, who both acts and ratiocinates. But for the most part the extremes are what Borges chooses to present to us. His map of the world excludes much of the middle ground of life. He concentrates on the fringes, where heroes and monsters, warriors and demigods, meet and interact. And his map abounds in cartographers, busily making their own maps and titling them "Reality." For Borges the ultimate futility is that of the creature in "The Circular Ruins" who hopes to "dream a man . . . with minute integrity and insert him into reality"— only to discover that he is himself a fiction in someone else's dream world, and not in "reality" at all. This vertiginous notion that the world may be a dream is perhaps what most people think of when they hear the name Borges. But I am trying to suggest that this notion is not a value held by him but a fictitious position assumed by him to provoke reality into showing itself. Unlike the figure in "The Circular Ruins," Borges is in reality himself and knows it. (pp. 19-20)

The problem for the writer is not to "represent" his own time. This he cannot help but do. The problem is to be like the apostle, all things to all men. To reach beyond reality to truth, beyond the immediate and contemporary to those aspects of the real which will endure and recur. No dream tiger ever becomes a real tiger, but the image of a man of letters struggling to capture the tiger's reality is an image that may still be valid when both men and tigers are extinct and replaced by other forms of life. The writer seeks this kind of durability for his work—against great odds. . . .

Pierre Menard, author of the *Quixote*, . . . is in one sense Borges's greatest hero and in another his greatest fool. By acting on . . . feelings of futility . . . , Menard has refused the possibilities of literary creation. He has sought to defy time by plunging backward through it toward seventeenth-century Spain. But his work, because it is *his* and to the extent that it is *his*, must be read as that of a *fin de siècle* Frenchman affecting an archaic style. He is as tied to his time as Flaubert, even though he sought to avoid the curse of temporality by hiding in the past and assuming the voice of Cervantes. Either he has no reality, and is absorbed into the voice of the dead Spaniard, or he has his own, that of a contemporary of William James and the friend of Valéry. Readers will see him as "brazenly pragmatic" or hopelessly relativistic. Borges is reminding us in this tale that there is no meaning without a meaner. Language itself always assumes a larger context. It can never be self-referential, because in order to interpret it we must locate it in a frame of reference which is ineluctably temporal and cultural. The world is real and Menard, alas, is Menard.

There is a further paradox here, which I have only hinted at so far, but which Borges himself has clearly articulated. Reality itself is real, is in time and subject to the same consuming fires as the creatures and things which constitute it. (p. 21)

Thus reality itself is a thing which fades into mythology with the passage of time. Or rather, most of reality fades into obscurity, and what endures is transformed into mythology. Truth vanishes. Fiction endures if it partakes of that reality beyond reality, which enables it to survive as myth. The real reality is that which has not yet happened but is to come. In one of his finest essays, "The Modesty of History," Borges encourages us to consider this situation. He begins by remarking on the way that governments try to manufacture or simulate historical occasions with an "abundance of preconditioning propaganda followed by relentless publicity." . . . But behind this fraudulent facade there is a "real history," which is "more modest," he suggests, with "essential dates that may be, for a long time, secret." He cites as one instance an occasion which passed with no chronological marker but certainly altered the world of letters—the date when Aeschylus is said to have changed the shape of drama by introducing a second actor upon the scene. (p. 22)

[Politics], wars, exchanges of words and sword-thrusts, are saved from oblivion by the historian who turns them into instances of heroic myth, and by doing so offers us a glimpse of a humanity beyond nationalistic pride. . . .

History, for Borges, is a matter of witnessing as much as a matter of doing. The forms of the past are preserved in frail human vessels which are themselves destined to die—and these deaths, too, are historic though unrecorded. (p. 23)

Far from being self-referential or a labyrinthine cul-de-sac, poem and story exist to bridge the gap between people and things—and between one person and another. In this connection it is interesting to observe that Borges's poem ["Limites"] bears a startling resemblance to a fugitive piece written by Johnson himself—*Idler* 103, the closing paper in the *Idler* series, in which he speculates on the phenomenon of finality. . . . (p. 24)

I do not mean to suggest that Borges, like Pierre Menard, has been trying to rewrite Dr. Johnson. Quite the opposite. For, though their subjects are quite similar, they are each irrevocably of their time, in style and emphasis, and in those unspoken values that inform style and emphasis. What links them despite these differences is reality itself, and in particular the human condition of that reality. And Johnson, I am sure, would applaud Borges's most succinct statement of his position in this matter. Literature, he has said, "is not a mere juggling of words." . . . It requires that a writer have what Chesterton called "everything." A notion which Borges glosses in the following way:

> To a writer this everything is more than an
> encompassing word; it is literal. It stands for
> the chief, for the essential, human experi-
> ences. For example, a writer needs loneli-
> ness, and he gets his share of it. He needs
> love, and he gets shared and also unshared
> love. He needs friendship. In fact, he needs
> the universe. . . .

And the universe—the universe of men and women at any rate—needs the writer. We need him to say the big things, of course, but also the little ones: things like, "Perhaps a bird was singing and I felt for him a small, birdlike affection." . . . And when I say the writer I mean specifically the one who is called Jorge Luis Borges, for whom many people in many lands feel a strong human affection, and of whom it is very appropriate to speak in precisely the same language in which he spoke of H. G. Wells. Referring to Wells's early scientific romances, Borges wrote:

> I think they will be incorporated, like the fables of Theseus or Ahasuerus, into the general memory of the species and even transcend the fame of their creator or the extinction of the language in which they were written." . . .

So be it. (p. 25)

> *Robert Scholes, "The Reality of Borges," in* The Iowa Review *(copyright © 1977, by The University of Iowa; copyright © 1978, by Robert Scholes), Vol. 8, No. 3 (Summer, 1977), pp. 12-25.*

ROBERT MARTIN ADAMS

Borges appears before us with the modest but cheerful demeanor of a stage-magician performing small acts of leg-erdemain with rapid confidence. Linguistically his surfaces are plain, not to say ordinary; his mode is eminently common-sensical, or at most owlish and scholarly. Far from being the mad scholar beloved of fiction-writers since Rabelais, he is reluctant and skeptical. But the train of his investigation leads as abruptly as may be to a logical crux, impasse, or surprise, involving more often than not a second order of nature, a cunning imitation of nature, or an esoteric order in nature.

Apart from Borges himself, there are few characters in his stories who amount to more than stick-figures. Like Erik Lonnrot the detective in "Death and the Compass," they tend to be wholly without background or features; or else they are unidimensional, like Vincent Moon in "The Shape of the Sword"; or they are purely mythological, like the metempsychosing hero of "The Immortals." Very often Borges dispenses with characters altogether, and quite as often with the merest pretext of a story; his essays are fantastic speculations, his stories speculative fantasies—it would be a bold man who tried to draw a straight line between the categories. The fact is that Borges is a gymnast of rationalism. He does not seem to have any deep feeling for the irrational, as it takes the form of deep feeling or private association or mental disease. Even his irrationals are alternative rationalisms. His favorite game is with public systems of counter-logic. The archetypical story in this context is "Tlon, Uqbar, Orbis Tertius," in which one small anomaly in one copy of one volume of a well-known encyclopedia gradually expands into a whole new and intrusive cosmos. The Kabbalah, the Zahir, the Lottery in Babylon are other instances of an occult system of relationships that intrude on "real life" in such a way as to supplant a long-accepted structure. They are often barbaric or mysterious, but that is because the normal occupants of the established system, including our pedantic friend the narrator, don't have a proper key to the new system; when they start seeing the new system from the inside out, resistance fades. (pp. 190-91)

[He] often brings [his] mystifying author directly onstage to demonstrate that he not only mystifies us, but is himself a victim of his own questioning, mystery-spinning mind. An intriguing parallel here is with the remote figure of Sir Thomas Browne, who like Borges is ostensibly concerned with pseudo-learning—the more copious, intricate and eso-

teric, the better. Both in this sense are structuralists, in that they are fascinated by arrangements and patterns of belief, symbolic systems which have an inherent delight far beyond the matter of their truth or falsity. And thus both, under the guise of scholarship and science, are really engaged in an exploration of their own temperaments, their own equivocal positions in the world.

The model for self-consciousness is an infinite recession of self-reflecting mirrors, and Borges as the central figure of his own magic-show reserves the mystification-vocabulary and mystification-syntax (rhetorical questions are highly favored) very largely for the question of his own identity. He is not only elusive here but illusionistic, his figure of Borges resists definition by multiplying definitions. Hardly anyone who asks, in the course of a fiction, who he really is, really wants to be told. In Borges's case, the question gives depth and resonance to the labyrinths that surround it, as no specific answer to it could possibly do, for it suggests a receding sequence of labyrinths, the last of which are a mystery even to the labyrinth-maker himself. (p. 192)

The very concept of a labyrinth implies an antagonistic relationship between the artist as mage or adept, and his disciples; they will be such only as long as he stays ahead of them, so that his position in the fictional relation rises as theirs is depressed. This alone is enough to set Borges apart from Chesterton or Wells. As does Joyce, Borges often gives us nuts to crack that are more shell than kernel; and of course the atrophy of narrative is apparent in both. But the whole visionary-symbolic side of Joyce, which leads us to sink under the surface of his language, and exposes us to painful and wracking violence wrought on our most intimate phonemes, is absent from Borges. Joyce harrows, Borges at his best hypnotizes, so that even his self-division and self-questioning are felt to take place at a distance and on a stage. Even if we feel ourselves moving from labyrinth to deeper labyrinth, it's deeper within Borges, not within ourselves, nor in any sense on an outward spiral. (p. 193)

> *Robert Martin Adams, in his* AfterJoyce: Studies in Fiction After "Ulysses" *(copyright © 1977 by Robert Martin Adams; reprinted by permission of Oxford University Press, Inc.), Oxford University Press, 1977.*

ROBERT MAGLIOLA

[The main concern of this article will be] a structuralist treatment of *Dr. Brodie's Report.* Structuralist analysis can do either of two things: it can expose the semantic and morphological syntaxes which combine the elements of a story into a whole, or it can show how structuralist intuitions, many of them philosophical in nature, illuminate what a writer is doing. I shall choose the second of these options; in the long run an exposition of the second kind better serves the general reader, since it can be applied with equal validity to everything Borges has written. The first premise of structuralism is that the human mind comes into the world with an a priori structure, and that this structure requires that all data be combined in terms of binary opposition. Each human being perceives the world in binary opposition, or, to be more accurate, he sees the world in terms of millions of binary combinations. (pp. 26-7)

For this reason, Borges loves to present us with characters who combine unique content. The first story in *Dr. Brodie's Report* is entitled "The Gospel According to Mark," and in it we confront a hero who "worshiped France but despised the French," who thought "little of Americans but approved the fact that there were tall buildings, like theirs, in Buenos Aires," and who believed "the gauchos of the plain to be better riders than those of hill or mountain country." Notice that the combinations are all oppositional, and only the content is unique (and, I might add, comical at that). Binary opposition also controls relationships between individuals: notice how almost every story in *Dr. Brodie's Report* is about two people fixed in some sort of dramatic opposition to each other. To name a few, the stories entitled "The Meeting," "Juan Muraña," "The Unworthy Friend," "The Duel," "The End of the Duel," and "Guayaquil." Combinations build upon combinations, and certain basic contents of combination characterize the collective culture of a whole people. And here, one cultural syntax is as good as another. Thus Borges loves to shock us by postulating alternative cultures. (p. 27)

A second structuralist premise is that the pool of content is finite, so that the sophisticated patterns of one culture will sooner or later recur. Tracking down these recurrences, and often creating fictional ones, is a central preoccupation in Borges. It explains that omnipresent "mirroring" technique. In "Afterword" Borges tells us "the essential stories of man's imagination have long since been told, and . . . now the story telling craft lies in rethinking and retelling them." In "The Gospel According to Mark," we are told the fanaticism of the Calvinist and the superstition of the pampa Indian recur in the behavior of the Gutre family; the crucifixion of Christ recurs in the crucifixion of the protagonist, Balthasar Espinosa; and in the tale entitled "The Unworthy Friend," we find an ironical recurrence of the Judas myth. In "Rosendo's Tale," Borges offers an intriguing variation, what the French call the technique of *dédoublage*. Here Rosendo distances himself from his double, —he catches his own reflection in the mirror, as it were—, and decides to convert, lest he end the way his erstwhile double had ended. *Dédoublage* often functions as a mediating mechanism. (pp. 27-8)

The third premise is that a valid comprehension of historical structure is synchronic. The history of past civilization can be adequately understood only if it is spatialized, and to spatialize it is necessarily to regard all of it as a simultaneous event. Past history should be seen as one sees in dreams, which are, in Borges's words, "a more complex state spanning at one and the same time past, present, and future." Or, as Borges explains in the "Afterword," history should be seen with a sense "of all things being already there." The structuralist thinker attempts to place himself at an Archimedean point outside of time. In short, he practices meta-history. He is like Dr. Zimmerman in the story "Guayaquil," whose "words . . . make of the future something as irrevocable as the past." Another structuralist premise is that causality as such cannot be demonstrated, so we lack sufficient reason to posit it as an operating principle. The most we can validly posit is a principle of transformation, namely, that phenomenon A becomes phenomenon B, or perhaps is followed by phenomenon B, but not that A causes B. In *Dr. Brodie's Report*, Borges begins his attack on causality with the remark "I no longer know whether the events I am about to relate are effects or causes." Then, using an old nihilist tactic, Borges proceeds to give examples of reversed causality, so as to shake our naive belief in causality as such. In the tale entitled "The

Meeting," a knife-fight takes place. The point of the story is that the antagonists do not control their knives. Their knives control them. And finally, in the title story, we find the aboriginal tribe described by Dr. Brodie has no notion of causality at all. We are told the tribe is not a primitive but degenerate one. And this is very, very important. Michel Foucault, the prominent structuralist, makes clear that structuralism is a degenerate vision, that is, a vision which explains a culture that has lost contact with the *Ding-an-sich*, with the thing-in-itself, with Being in other words. The degenerate Amazonians of the story become types of the modern man.

All this brings us to the next structuralist premise, that language as we know it is not referential; rather, it is a self-sufficient structure: words just refer to other words. In *Dr. Brodie's Report* we find repeated descriptions of language severed from what Borges calls "the sordid facts," severed from the solidity of the real, if you will. In the story "Juan Muraña," the facts of Juan's actual life and death have evaporated. What has taken over is the ongoing myth as it is told by his countrymen, often with many contradictory variants. And myth, propagated by language, takes over again in the stories "The End of the Duel" and "The Elder Lady." Perhaps this premise explains, too, Borges's fascination with the frame tale. A story enframing a story which in turn enframes a story is at a far remove from the actual facts. Language is contextual. Words derive their import not from an isolated intrinsic value nor from their referents, but rather from a system of relationships. (pp. 28-9)

But language does even more. Man doesn't use language. Language is a precedent followed by an inevitable subsequent. . . . The subsequent is that man inevitably operates as language does, and this is the next structuralist premise. . . . [The] individual *cogito* dissolves in the collective syntax of language. If we were able to put aside the usual structuralist rejection of causality, we could put it even more bluntly: language *uses* man. Borges complains in the "Afterword" that his weakest pages are those in which "conscious self has to intrude." In "Rosendo's Tale," Rosendo is totally conditioned by the oral tradition. Rosendo admits "For years I tried to *live up to the part* of the outlaw Moreira, who in his time—the way I figure it—was probably trying to *play the part* of some other gaucho or outlaw" (italics mine). In "Guayaquil," language likewise strips the two historians of their own identities, and makes them into the military generals of a century-old myth. And so too it kills the "elder lady," whose own identity is controlled and then effaced by a myth about her forebearer.

The last structuralist premise I will demonstrate is an extension of the preceding one. This last premise is not common to all structuralists. . . . It argues in effect that since the individual *cogito* is dissolved in language, the human personality can be best defined as an *intersection* of relationships, and not as an ego. Borges seems to demonstrate this in the tale entitled "The Duel," where the two women artists, Clara and Marta, define themselves exclusively in terms of their mutual relationship. (p. 29)

Thus far I have explicated *Dr. Brodie's Report* in terms of structuralist insights. I now devote some space to possible reactions to Borgesian fiction, and structuralist fiction in general. First, I distinguish between two critical roles that we as readers can exercise,—the esthetic and the philosophical. The literary critic as such should, in my opinion, limit himself to esthetic evaluation. That is, he should judge and only judge how successfully the author in question verbalizes a possible way of experiencing the world. In other words, the literary critic should judge how effectively a subjective truth, i.e., truth to the author, is "made present" in language. . . . If we grant that *Dr. Brodie's Report* is a structuralist work, we must conclude, I think, that it is esthetically successful. With grand *éclat* the book manifests a world wherein man's primordial contact with Being has been lost. (p. 30)

> Robert Magliola, "Jorge Luis Borges and the Loss of Being: Structuralist Themes in 'Dr. Brodie's Report'," in Studies in Short Fiction (*copyright 1978 by Newberry College*), Winter, 1978, pp. 25-31.

*   *   *

BRADBURY, Ray   1920-

Bradbury is an American novelist, short story writer, playwright, poet, children's author, and editor. He is the leading writer of the school of science fiction and fantasy that is concerned with the human implications of futurism, rather than in the wonders of advanced gadgetry. His fiction is based on the inhumanity, apathy, and technology of modern society. Bradbury is essentially optimistic, however, in his portrayal of the importance of human values and the imagination. (See also *CLC*, Vols. 1, 3, and *Contemporary Authors*, Vols. 1-4, rev. ed.)

KINGSLEY AMIS

[Despite Bradbury's] regrettable tendency to dime-a-dozen sensitivity, he is a good writer, wider in range than any of his colleagues, capable of seeing life on another planet as something extraordinary instead of just challenging or horrific, ready to combine this with strongly held convictions. . . . The suppression of fantasy, or of all books, is an aspect of the conformist society often mentioned by other writers, but with Bradbury it is a specialty. (pp. 106-07)

[There] is about Bradbury, as about those I might call the non-fiction holders of his point of view, a certain triumphant lugubriousness, a kind of proleptic *schadenfreude* (world copyright reserved), a relish not always distinguishable here from satisfaction in urging a case, but different from it, and recalling the relish with which are recounted the horrors of *Nineteen Eighty-Four* and a famous passage that prefigures it in *Coming Up for Air*. Jeremiah has never had much success in pretending he doesn't thoroughly enjoy his job, and whereas I agree with him, on the whole, in his dislike of those who reach for their revolver when they hear the word "culture," I myself am getting to the point where I reach for my ear-plugs on hearing the phrase "decline of our culture." But in this respect Bradbury sins no more grievously than his non-fiction colleagues, whom he certainly surpasses in immediacy, for *Fahrenheit 451* is a fast and scaring narrative. . . . The book emerges quite creditably from a comparison with *Nineteen Eighty-Four* as inferior in power, but superior in conciseness and objectivity. (p. 109)

Bradbury's is the most skilfully drawn of all science fiction's conformist hells. One invariable feature of them is that however activist they may be, however convinced that the individual can, and will, assert himself, their pro-

gramme is always to resist or undo harmful change, not to promote useful change. (pp. 109-10)

> *Kingsley Amis, in his* New Maps of Hell: A Survey of Science Fiction (*© 1960 by Kingsley Amis; reprinted by permission of Harcourt Brace Jovanovich, Inc. and A. D. Peters and Company Ltd.*), Harcourt, 1960.

RUSSELL KIRK

Ray Bradbury has drawn the sword against the dreary and corrupting materialism of this century; against society as producer-and-consumer equation, against the hideousness in modern life, against mindless power, against sexual obsession, against sham intellectuality, against the perversion of right reason into the mentality of the television-viewer. His Martians, spectres, and witches are not diverting entertainment only: they become, in their eerie manner, the defenders of truth and beauty. (p. 117)

[Bradbury] thinks it . . . probable that man may spoil everything, in this planet and in others, by the misapplication of science to avaricious ends—the Baconian and Hobbesian employment of science as power. And Bradbury's interior world is fertile, illuminated by love for the permanent things, warm with generous impulse. . . .

Bradbury knows of modern technology, in the phrase of Henry Adams, that we are "monkeys monkeying with a loaded shell." He is interested not in the precise mechanism of rockets, but in the mentality and the morals of fallible human beings who make and use rockets. He is a man of fable and parable. (p. 118)

Bradbury is not writing about the gadgets of conquest; his real concerns are the soul and the moral imagination. When the boy-hero of *Dandelion Wine*, in an abrupt mystical experience, is seized almost bodily by the glowing consciousness that he is really *alive*, we glimpse that mystery the soul. When, in *Something Wicked This Way Comes*, the lightning-rod salesman is reduced magically to an idiot dwarf because all his life he had fled from perilous responsibility, we know the moral imagination.

"Soul," a word much out of fashion nowadays, signifies a man's animating entity. That flaming spark the soul is the real space-traveller of Bradbury's stories. "I'm alive!"— that exclamation is heard from Waukegan to Mars and beyond, in Bradbury's fables. Life is its own end—if one has a soul to tell him so. (pp. 118-19)

[The] moral imagination, which shows us what we ought to be, primarily is what distinguishes Bradbury's tales from the futurism of Wells' fancy. For Bradbury, the meaning of life is here and now, in our every action; we live amidst immortality; it is here, not in some future domination like that of Wells' *The Sleeper Awakens*, that we must find our happiness. (p. 119)

What gives [*The Martian Chronicles*] their cunning is their realism set in the fantastic: that is, their portrayal of human nature, in all its baseness and all its promise, against an exquisite stage-set. We are shown normality, the permanent things in human nature, by the light of another world; and what we forget about ourselves in the ordinariness of our routine of existence suddenly bursts upon us as fresh revelation. (p. 120)

In Bradbury's fables of Mars and of the carnival [in *Some-*

thing Wicked This Way Comes], fantasy has become what it was in the beginning: the enlightening moral imagination, transcending simple rationality. (p. 123)

The trappings of science-fiction may have attracted young people to Bradbury, but he has led them on to something much older and better: mythopoeic literature, normative truth acquired through wonder. Bradbury's stories are not an escape from reality; they are windows looking upon enduring reality. (p. 124)

> *Russell Kirk, "The World of Ray Bradbury" and "Depravity and Courage in Modern Fable," in his* Enemies of the Permanent Things: Observations of Abnormity in Literature and Politics *(copyright © 1969 by Arlington House), Arlington House, 1969, pp. 116-20, 120-24.*

TOM BRADFORD

[*Dandelion Wine*] has no more reason to end than it has to begin. Its cause and effect relationship is a spontaneous one, for which A leads to B, and Z again to A. It is a brief glimpse on a crowded street of a stranger one can never forget and always love. It has the drug color vividness of black and white photography, giving the honest shade and contrast of face stories at moments removed from motion, from time, from definition. But, in the same breath, it has a prescribed structure, with Douglas, his brother Tom, his friends, his senses, all acting under the assumed reality which the freedom of fantasy offers. *Dandelion Wine* is fantasy, in the most boundless sense of the word. It is the fantasy which is always at hand, known to us all—not the thirty-five cents a copy world of escapism and plasticity, but the unrigid, free, real world of the mind's expectations. Though one may not have logical inference patterns to make, conflicts to resolve, or character types to establish, there is a single, though all encompassing direction, a "place" to go, an exercise to perform. In effect, this unavoidable and necessary element of imposition requires expansion, and passionate devotion to this mental growth. When Bradbury sets his stage, much like a theatre director, an animated world appears in which the *facts* of the imagination become as acceptable as the facts of reality. (p. 161)

Bradbury proves his fantasy by this reaching through the senses, this *creating* of real life. We believe, really believe, only that which is proven artistically, employing both the aesthetic criticism of the intellect and the senses. Only the latter is nearly infallible, as the virgin innocence of sensual intuition either refuses to accept or trustingly incorporates the devil deceptions of illusion's mists. . . . To write successful fantasy, to employ successful imagination, elements of the real world must be among the constituent ingredients of the mental exercise. Only then can the mind feel secure in its journey. (pp. 162-63)

What can threaten this sensual stage which Bradbury sets? His worlds of fantasy, his circus balloon journeys up and out, incorporate in their very nature a fastening line to the ground, a kinship with the realistic, cold visioned animal appraisal of life and death. And, to be sure, Douglas reflects off his first glimpse of death's impersonal reality, and looks forward to winter's harvestings of the dandelion wine. . . . But what can be done with the last breath finality of death; what can be done with the inescapable fact that we really don't want Douglas Spaulding to ever die? (p. 163)

What can fantasizing do to soften the blue steel edge of pain and aging and decay? Can one merely accept death as an inexplicable force, a cellophane haze of gradual dying lasting as long as life? And can the mythology of religion, of art, of *Dandelion Wine* satisfy us, explain to us perhaps, the mystery of death with the same force it uses in portraying the wonder of life? Bradbury asserts that fantasy is a way of dealing with the monster death, driving a cedar stake through a werewolf's heart, killing it, vomiting it out. (pp. 163-64)

In analyzing Bradbury's "style" one must carefully avoid scholastically rigid interpretations, if only for the sake of greater enjoyment. The beauty of his work, the personality of his written words, can best be appreciated by the innocent ears of readers who are not aware of archetypes and genres and styles. If one looks for contrived style in Bradbury's works, he is likely to sacrifice the full satisfaction of the experience. Of course, one does find in *Dandelion Wine* a conscious effort to *be* Bradbury throughout, to always be the fellow with the magic citric mind. Art is its process, and *Dandelion Wine* is the product of artistic creation, unique only in its virgin beauty, an experience that needn't be looked back upon and analyzed. This critique itself shows what happens when one reviews a Bradbury work; its beauty enslaves one to the point where the best picture seems to be the one with maximum Bradbury and minimum reviewer. Perhaps one sacrifices a context for interpretation, blurring the intrinsic uniqueness which is self expressive. It is remarkably simple to like Bradbury, to know and feel his style and perspective on life, without really being able to define them.

Air like water, scented with thyme . . . this is what Bradbury wants. Prose with rhyme and color vivid, poetry at all times. Children's newly-planted awareness, untarnished copper, untarnished eye. Spells, seconds, births, deaths, where you can

> hold summer in your hand, pour summer in
> a glass, a tiny glass of course, the smallest
> sip of children; change the season in your
> veins by raising glass to lip and tilting summer in.

His is world of truth, a world of children, a world whose history recalls being born. It is a world free of burning fire's intentions, tragedy's grimace, and downhill falls. It is such a fine, honest world that it risks being classified as contrived, inflated literature. He almost seems to cheat. When he gets mad at death, he drives a stake through it. And when his heroes do wrong, they can erase the past with a life time. It is a world of real supermen. It is a material commodity in which buying and selling are nothing more than juggling, trading a perfect red ball for a perfect blue ball. He never gets mad, and he is always beautiful, and one gets jealous. (pp. 164-65)

> *Tom Bradford, in* Chicago Review *(reprinted by permission of* Chicago Review; *copyright © 1971 by Chicago Review), Vol. 22, Nos. 2 and 3, 1971.*

A. JAMES STUPPLE

[Of] all the writers of science fiction who have dealt with [the] meeting of the past and the future, it is Ray Bradbury whose treatment has been the deepest and most sophisticated. What has made Bradbury's handling of this theme distinctive is that his attitudes and interpretations have changed as he came to discover the complexities and the ambiguities inherent in it. (p. 175)

Bradbury's point [in *The Martian Chronicles*] here is clear: [the Earthmen] met their deaths because of their inability to forget, or at least resist, the past. Thus, the story of this Third Expedition acts as a metaphor for the book as a whole. Again and again the Earthmen make the fatal mistake of trying to recreate an Earth-like past rather than accept the fact that this is Mars—a different, unique new land in which they must be ready to make personal adjustments. Hauling Oregon lumber through space, then, merely to provide houses for nostalgic colonists exceeds folly; it is only one manifestation of a psychosis which leads to the destruction not only of Earth, but, with the exception of a few families, of Mars as well. (p. 177)

[Despite] the fact that it cannot be called science fiction, *Dandelion Wine* closely resembles *The Martian Chronicles* and much of Bradbury's other writing in that it is essentially concerned with the same issue—the dilemma created by the dual attractions of the past and the future, of stasis and change.

In *Dandelion Wine* Bradbury uses the experiences of his adolescent protagonist during one summer to dramatize this set of philosophical and psychological conflicts. At twelve, Douglas Spaulding finds himself on the rim of adolescence. On one side of him lies the secure, uncomplicated world of childhood, while on the other is the fascinating yet frightening world of "growing up." (p. 178)

[In *Dandelion Wine*] Bradbury seems to be reiterating what he has said in *The Martian Chronicles*—that the past, or stasis, or both, is enticing but deadly, and that Douglas, like the colonists, must forsake the past and give himself up to change and progress. But it is not so simple and clear-cut. . . . [What brings Douglas] out of his coma is a swallow of a liquid . . . concocted out of pieces of the past (such as Arctic air from the year 1900). With this development, Bradbury's thesis seems to fall to pieces, for Douglas is saved for the future by the past. He is liberated from a static condition by bottled stasis. The ambiguous nature of his recovery is further compounded by the strange, anti-climactic nature of the last chapters of the novel in which Bradbury indulges in a nostalgic celebration of old-fashioned family life. This conclusion so detracts from the story of Doug and his rebirth that one can only conclude that the author was confused, or more probably ambivalent, about these past-future, stasis-change dichotomies.

It is evident, then, that in *Dandelion Wine*, Bradbury began to become aware of the complexity of his subject. Where in *The Martian Chronicles* he seemed confident in his belief that a meaningful future could only be realized by rejecting the past, in this later novel he appears far less certain about the relative values of the past and stasis. Perhaps in this regard Bradbury can be seen as representative of a whole generation of middle class Americans who have found themselves alternately attracted to the security of an idealized, timeless, and static past (as the current nostalgia vogue illustrates) and the exciting, yet threatening and disruptive future world of progress and change, especially technological change. (p. 181)

[This] stasis-change conflict, besides being a function of Bradbury's own history and personality, also seems to be

built into the art form itself. What distinguishes Bradbury and gives his works their depth is that he seems to be aware that a denial of the past demands a denial of that part of the self which is the past. . . . [He] has not been able to come to any lasting conclusion. Instead, he has come to recognize the ambiguity, the complexity, and the irony within this theme. (p. 182)

Bradbury had discovered through his years of working with this theme, the past is not one-dimensional. It is at once creative and destructive. It can give comfort, and it can unsettle and threaten. (p. 184)

> *A. James Stupple, "The Past, the Future, and Ray Bradbury,"* in Voices for the Future: Essays on Major Science Fiction Writers, *Vol. 1, edited by Thomas D. Clareson (copyright © 1976 by The Popular Press), Bowling Green University Popular Press, 1976, pp. 175-84.*

WILLIS E. McNELLY

If Bradbury's ladders lead to Mars, whose chronicler he has become, or to the apocalyptic future of *Fahrenheit 451*, the change is simply one of direction, not of intensity. He is a visionary who writes not of the impediments of science, but of its effects upon man. *Fahrenheit 451*, after all, is not a novel about the technology of the future, and is only secondarily concerned with censorship or book-burning. In actuality it is the story of Bradbury, disguised as Montag, and his lifelong love affair with books. (p. 169)

"Metaphor" is an important word to Bradbury. He uses it generically to describe a method of comprehending one reality and then expressing that same reality so that the reader will see it with the intensity of the writer. His use of the term, in fact, strongly resembles T. S. Eliot's view of the objective correlative. Bradbury's metaphor in *Fahrenheit 451* is the burning of books; in "The Illustrated Man," a moving tattoo; and pervading all of his work, the metaphor becomes a generalized nostalgia that can best be described as a nostalgia for the future.

Another overwhelming metaphor in his writing is one derived from Jules Verne and Herman Melville—the cylindrical shape of the submarine, the whale, or the space ship. It becomes a mandala, a graphic symbol of Bradbury's view of the universe, a space-phallus. Bradbury achieved his first "mainstream" fame with his adaptation of Melville's novel for the screen, after Verne had aroused his interest in science fiction. (pp. 169-70)

Essentially a romantic, Bradbury belongs to the great frontier tradition. He is an exemplar of the Turner thesis, and the blunt opposition between a traditionbound Eastern establishment and Western vitality finds itself mirrored in his writing. The metaphors may change, but the conflict in Bradbury is ultimately between human vitality and the machine, between the expanding individual and the confining group, between the capacity for wonder and the stultification of conformity. These tensions are a continual source for him, whether the collection is named *The Golden Apples of the Sun, Dandelion Wine,* or *The Martian Chronicles.* Thus, to use his own terminology, nostalgia for either the past or future is a basic metaphor utilized to express these tensions. Science fiction is the vehicle.

Ironic detachment combined with emotional involvement—

these are the recurring tones in Bradbury's work, and they find their expression in the metaphor of ''wilderness.'' To Bradbury, America is a wilderness country and hers a wilderness people. (p. 170)

For Bradbury the final, inexhaustible wilderness is the wilderness of space. In that wilderness, man will find himself, renew himself. There, in space, as atoms of God, mankind will live forever. Ultimately, then, the conquest of space becomes a religious quest. The religious theme in his writing is sounded directly only on occasion, in such stories as ''The Fire Balloons,'' where two priests try to decide if some blue fire-balls on Mars have souls, or ''The Man,'' where Christ leaves a far planet the day before an Earth rocket lands. Ultimately the religious theme is the end product of Bradbury's vision of man; the theme is implicit in man's nature.

Bradbury's own view of his writing shows a critical self-awareness. He describes himself essentially as a short story writer, not a novelist, whose stories seize him, shake him, and emerge after a two or three hour tussle. It is an emotional experience, not an intellectual one; the intellectualization comes later when he edits. To be sure, Bradbury does not lack the artistic vision for large conception or creation. The novel form is simply not his normal medium. Rather he aims to objectify or universalize the particular. He pivots upon an individual, a specific object, or particular act, and then shows it from a different perspective or a new viewpoint. The result can become a striking insight into the ordinary, sometimes an ironic comment on our limited vision.

An early short story, ''The Highway,'' illustrates this awareness of irony. A Mexican peasant wonders at the frantic, hurtling stream of traffic flowing north. He is told by an American who stops for water that the end of the world has come with the outbreak of the atom war. Untouched in his demi-Eden, Hernando calls out to his burro as he plows the rain-fresh land below the green jungle, above the deep river. ''What do they mean 'the world?''' he asks himself, and continues plowing.

Debate over whether or not Bradbury is, in the end, a science fiction writer, is fruitless when one considers this story or dozens like it. The only ''science'' in the story is the ''atom war'' somewhere far to the north, away from the ribbon of concrete. All other artifacts of man in the story—the automobile, a hubcap, a tire—provide successive ironies to the notion that while civilization may corrupt, it does not do so absolutely. A blownout tire may have brought death to the driver of a car, but it now provides Hernando with sandals; a shattered hubcap becomes a cooking pan. Hernando and his wife and child live in a prelapsarian world utilizing the gifts of the machine in primitive simplicity. These people recall the Noble Savage myth; they form a primary group possessing the idyllic oneness of true community. The strength of Hernando, then, is derived from the myth of the frontier; the quality and vigor of life derive from, indeed are dependent upon, the existence of the frontier.

Yet irony piles on irony: the highway—any highway—leads in two directions. The Americans in this fable form a seemingly endless flowing stream of men and vehicles. They ride northward toward cold destruction, leaving the tropical warmth of the new Eden behind them. Can we recreate the past, as Gatsby wondered. Perhaps, suggests Bradbury, if we re-incarnate the dreams of our youth and reaffirm the social ethic of passionate involvement. And nowhere does he make this moral quite as clear as in *Fahrenheit 451.* (pp. 171-72)

Fahrenheit 451 illustrates his major themes: the freedom of the mind; the evocation of the past; the desire for Eden; the integrity of the individual; the allurements and traps of the future. At the end of the novel, Montag's mind has been purified, refined by fire, and phoenix-like, Montag—hence mankind—rises from the ashes of the destructive, self-destroying civilization. '''Never liked cities,' said the man who was Plato,'' as Bradbury hammers home his message at the end of the novel. '''Always felt that cities owned men, that was all, and used men to keep themselves going, to keep the machines oiled and dusted.''' . . . (p. 173)

[The] vision of the future which Bradbury provides at the end of *Fahrenheit 451* shows his essentially optimistic character. In fact, Bradbury seized upon the hatreds abroad in 1953 when the book was written, and shows that hatred, war, desecration of the individual are all self-destructive. Bradbury's 1953 vision of hatred becomes extrapolated to a fire which consumes minds, spirits, men, ideas, books. (pp. 173-74)

Bradbury has proved that quality writing is possible in [a] much-maligned genre. Bradbury is obviously a careful craftsman, an ardent wordsmith whose attention to the niceties of language and its poetic cadences would have marked him as significant even if he had never written a word about Mars.

His themes, however, place him squarely in the middle of the mainstream of American life and tradition. His eyes are set firmly on the horizon-Frontier where dream fathers mission and action mirrors illusion. And if Bradbury's eyes lift from the horizon to the stars, the act is merely an extension of the vision all Americans share. His voice is that of the poet raised against the mechanization of mankind. (p. 174)

> *Willis E. McNelly, ''Ray Bradbury: Past, Present, and Future'' (originally published in a different version in* CEA Critic, *March, 1969), in* Voices for the Future: Essays on Major Science Fiction Writers, *Vol. I, edited by Thomas D. Clareson (copyright © 1976 by The Popular Press), Bowling Green University Popular Press, 1976, pp. 167-75.*

*   *   *

BRAGG, Melvyn   1939-

Bragg is a British novelist, screenwriter, essayist, broadcaster, and producer. His film credits include the screenplays for *Isadora* **and** *Jesus Christ Superstar.* **(See also** *Contemporary Authors,* **Vols. 57-60.)**

Once again Melvyn Bragg has written a novel about rural life in Cumberland [*The Hired Man*], and once again it is earnest, worthy and sometimes a struggle to read.

Melvyn Bragg is a good novelist but his narrative is clogged by heavy phrasing, especially when trying to report the self-communication of his characters. When he tells what they said, what they did, how they and their environment appear to the author, he is consistently successful.

This novel is largely concerned with the changing attitudes among working men during this century towards being 'hired'—or employed, exploited, used. John's grandfather had 'worked as if he was made for nothing else in the world: he called by "sir" and "master" those "set above" him'. The movement of [John's brother] Seth and, later, John into the pits involves them in corporate action against those set above. But there is another life-style hanging over from older times, that of the third brother Isaac, who lives for sport, like a free man—changing his job frequently, leaving his wife for weeks on end, dealing with horses, dogs, fighting-cocks, boxing and gambling. . . .

[In a scene depicting a confrontation between the three brothers and a group of miners] the reader may wish that [the characters'] thoughts had been put into words which the men might really have used. If the author had recorded their dialogue, which he can write so well, the situation would have been enlivened. . . . The result of the fight is important. John had been planning to leave the pits but it is now 'impossible to think of working anywhere in that town but with those he had fought'. It is a similar sense of what is fitting that impels him to meet his brothers soon afterwards and volunteer for the First World War. There is enough in this theme to make a good novel; but Melvyn Bragg says a great deal more, as if challenged by the largeness of his subject-matter—the working class.

"Habits of Work," in The Times Literary Supplement (© *Times Newspapers Ltd. (London) 1969; reproduced from* The Times Literary Supplement *by permission), October 23, 1969, p. 1225.*

VICTORIA GLENDINNING

[*The Silken Net*] is a traditional novel of a particularly English kind. Words could be used linking Melvyn Bragg with Hardy, Lawrence and Bennett in the Grand Chain: that he belongs there is indisputable. The intensity of the writing leads Mr Bragg into occasional linguistic clumsiness. In the interests of grace (if grace interests him) he might have edited himself . . . more severely. . . . One could argue about the strengths, the weaknesses and the implications of *The Silken Net* all night. (p. 229)

Victoria Glendinning, in New Statesman (© *1974 The Statesman & Nation Publishing Co. Ltd.), August 16, 1974.*

JOHN MELLORS

In his novels, Melvyn Bragg has always shown complete disregard for the 'modern' and the 'experimental' in fiction. He writes as if Joyce, Virginia Woolf and Hemingway had never been. In style, structure and content he is closer to the traditional 19th-century novelist than to most of his contemporaries. Like Hardy, he places his characters in a particular rural and small town setting—in his case, Cumberland—and chronicles the tensions and conflicts between different generations of the same family, between husband and wife, between individual and society. He believes that an author should take into account the usefulness of his book to its reader. The first-person narrator in . . . *The Nerve* says that 'where possible, fiction, like all imaginative writing, should be helpful; the very best is beautiful *and* truthful and instances of those aspects of life are all the help we need.'

Bragg is most helpful in making you see the importance of work, as something either satisfying or soul-destroying. . . . [He] has the knack of bringing to life the handling of tools and materials. . . . This, I had thought, together with his accurate picture of the country between the Lake District and the Solway Firth, was his main achievement. His characters had never seemed as interesting as what they did or where they were.

The Silken Net is Bragg's best book yet; at last he is as successful with people as with place. (pp. 253-54)

John Mellors, in The Listener (© *British Broadcasting Corp. 1974; reprinted by permission of John Mellors), August 22, 1974.*

CLANCY SIGAL

Speak for England [an oral history of a small market town] has the flat, unpatronizing power of Bragg's Cumbrian novels, such as *The Hired Man* and *A Place In England*—and also their undercurrent of anger, even bitterness, against the centuries-old class system that has darkened the lives of his people for so long. Yet the major flaw in this work is that it is too nice, too filial. There are no scoundrels, no black sheep. The author has given us a sincere, unmalicious, and perhaps oversimple tribute to a place he can always safely return to. (p. 24)

On the whole, Bragg's Wigtoners don't complain. This may partly reflect the traditional stoicism of the working class in northern England. But the even, placid tone of Bragg's informants also owes much to his method of screening out the "characters" and big talkers. He admits that he "itched to embroider and take off gossip," but he forced himself not to fictionalize or dwell on unpleasantries. It's our loss. . . .

The reluctance of Bragg's "speakers" completely to let their hair down makes the absence of town characters and compulsive talkers all the more glaring. For all their exaggerations, it is such eccentrics who might have injected a useful dash of grit, even of violence, into this suspiciously well-balanced group portrait.

Bragg's discretion is pardonable, because he knows that the poeple he loves are vulnerable to the continual, nagging prejudice built into the English class system. But by being needlessly protective, Bragg denies his friends a certain human fullness, and this unwittingly plays into the hands of the condescending critics whom Bragg rightly resents.

My other worry is the author's claim that his book is "a representative record of English life during this century." Though I, too, came to admire Bragg's neighbors almost as much as he does, not for a moment was I convinced of their universality. . . .

Still, readers who carefully pick their way through these interviews will be richly rewarded with a fascinating saga of personal memoirs that do, in fact, add up to the kind of "people's history" that (as Bragg correctly asserts) almost always gets left out of the academic books and tourist guides. (p. 26)

Clancy Sigal, "Pilgrim's Progress in Wigton," in Saturday Review (© *1977 by Saturday Review Magazine Corp.; reprinted with permission), February 19, 1977, pp. 24, 26.*

*   *   *

BRONK, William   1918-

Bronk is an American poet and essayist concerned with the themes of time, space, and the nature of reality. With a pared-down simplicity of line and an often imageless clarity, he creates a poetry of place, a poetry of statement. Often meditative and experimental, his work has been compared to Wallace Stevens's in its use of form and recurring motif.

ROBERT D. SPECTOR

More than most collections of poetry, William Bronk's *The World, the Worldless* . . . possesses an unbroken thematic unity. Existential anguish links poem to poem, so that lines from one might easily be coupled with those of another. It is not, however, a poetry of despair, for it begins with an acceptance of the fact that "We are here. We are here," and it recognizes our need "to make / a world for survival . . . ," since "One is nothing with no world." But Bronk will not settle for man's comfortable, conventional falsities and pretenses. For religious orthodoxy and promises of salvation he holds no hope: "Nothing is coming but what is already here"; and yet, for all the uncertainties of human existence, there is one truth: "we are, somehow we are." Whether or not we find satisfaction in Bronk's philosophy, his poetry of statement impresses with its clarity and precision of language; it manages to make metaphysics a subject of human emotion rather than a grand abstraction. (p. 47-8)

> *Robert D. Spector, in* Saturday Review (©️ *1965 by Saturday Review, Inc.; reprinted with permission), February 13, 1965.*

RICHARD ELMAN

["The New World" is a collection of] essay-meditations on the architecture and algebra of space and time of the Incan and Mayan religious temples at Machu Picchu, Tikal, Copan, Palenque, . . . by one of our finest—though largely uncelebrated—poets. Lucid, precise, abstract, capable of infinitely slow movement and graceful, careful observation, the prose here is of a high order of excellence, a celebration of mystery and wonder, but human in its scale and its syntactical arrangements. It permits an excursion into the mysteries of Time and Space and Numbers. . . .

In all his poems as well as here, Bronk's sensitivity is generated through his contemplation of architecture and habitation, by the details of a grand concept as well as the space it encloses. It's as if he has found and written, always vitally aware of the relationship between the sashes and beams and lintelings of his mill life and the seemingly more obdurate ideas in stone of the Mayan craftsmen. One of his finest early poems in the collection "The World, the Worldless" . . . considers his grand Victorian Hudson Valley town mansion. . . .

Every new volume of his poems is engraved with terse statement, a high seriousness and strong uncluttered feeling. With each new volume he seems to be determined to make his utterance all the more specific, determined and quiet, as if he wrote his poems in the voice and with the mind in which we all truly sometimes think, beautifully and sublimely, through our perceptions. . . . (p. 12)

Publication of these essays, for themselves, as well as for the attention they may give to some of Bronk's books of poems, should put to rest his favorite persona as the withdrawn homespun, a man of simple eruditions and pleasures. It's true that some of Bronk's best work is crafted in a homely way (in the best sense one can give to that word), without any irrelevant prettiness or gratuitous display for the eye or the ear, but he is among the most sophisticated of contemporary writers, almost arcane. . . . He has thoroughly ingested such late Romantic influences as the Imagists Wallace Stevens and William Carlos Williams, and become so completely versatile at rendering process in his freely cadenced, often ruminative language that he could then go on to the much harder task of being totally honest while remaining entirely sensate.

But if Bronk's poems of late have become increasingly brief, staccato and, when meditative, even somewhat dissociated, these essays, written a few years ago . . . commence the prospect of a new world for Bronk in which he can be highly speculative, extrapolating, hypothesizing, adventuresome and explorational; the great Mayan monuments to life as experience becoming occasions for Bronk to encounter and consider life as we permit ourselves to live it now. (pp. 12, 14)

In "The New World" William Bronk ruminates brilliantly, but to little practical purpose, one might say; his prose, at times, is so connected to the process of observation, inspection and perception that it almost feels as if we are proceeding with him hand over hand among the ruins, though, in the end, "Our responses are presences that tower around us, seemingly solid as stone." Of course such really close writing happens to be a joy of itself. By starting to encounter something so specifically it cannot help but yield insights in an unforced way about so much else that is human and mysterious. There is, additionally, the wonder and sense of beauty one shares when a first-rate mind considers the world impinging on it, shares in the meditation of perception with an informed, factual syntax, and indulges in the splendors of one of the finest intact prose styles one may encounter anywhere in America. (p. 14)

> *Richard Elman, in* The New York Times Book Review (©️ *1975 by The New York Times Company; reprinted by permission), March 9, 1975.*

FELIX STEFANILE

William Bronk writes about time and space; he writes about motion, the "motion" of interrelationships: people, places, objects, ideas. Like Wallace Stevens, a poet whom he resembles in some respects, he writes about the mind's motion, the processes of cognition. And he writes about these matters over and over again. . . . Like most major talents he holds on to a few ideas, and makes of them, over the years, his "quarrel with himself." (p. 222)

Over the years Bronk's diction has become sparer, his forms both more experimental and more crabbed—he is now writing quatrains and tercets—but the deft syntax, the mastery of "pause" and effect, the easy amplitude of statement, rarely too much or too little, and the refusal to yield imagery over to discourse . . . , are evidences of this ruminative poet's unvarying stance. Bronk is remarkably even, and remarkably urgent. Our poet is a poet of argument.

Bronk's concern, as that of Stevens, is for reality. In Bronk's case, however, and it is an inevitable distinction, the attention is for the actual *physis* of metaphysics. . . . Fictions and tentative orders are not so much contemplated as they are assailed. The result is not an act of imagination as will, but—in language that seems to do its own thinking, bare, hesitant, probing—a finally resolute recognition of, and concession to, Mystery. . . . Bronk does not pray . . . , but his surrender, in poem after poem—''On Credo Ut Intelligam,'' for one, from *That Tantalus*—comes as close to meditation as it can without becoming forthright prayer. He examines his consciousness the way some people examine their conscience. (pp. 223-24)

Time must be spent comparing Bronk with Stevens because no appreciation of his work can ignore the affinities between the two poets. Bronk himself states the problematic nature of influence, in his interview with Robert Bertholf, in *Credences*. ''I stopped reading him (Stevens) entirely. Not because I disliked him or had grown tired of him, but simply I didn't want just to be a Stevens imitator.'' (p. 224)

Both poets are heroes of consciousness. Both poets delight in the exercise of a fugal intelligence that harries a subject, sniffs around it, seems to proceed by fits and starts, turns it over, seems to let it go, and then quickly retrieves it. The repetition of a key word, for instance, that sends it caroming, like a motif, through the whole poem, is characteristic of the style of each man. Both poets, in our seemingly ''innovative'' day, keep up the good work for the five-stress line, using it in intricate, clever, and effective ways. There are places Bronk defies the standard foot, and like Hopkins' sprung rhythm, really returns to Anglo-Saxon accent verse, five-stress lines where each stress is associated with irregular syzygies of unaccented syllables. The variations make for great drama and emphasis. Most importantly, the dramatic situation of their poems—Bronk *talks* and talks to someone much more often than he describes—makes for an identity authentically presented from poem to poem, from book to book.

There is no gallicism to Bronk, however; he lacks the easy *blague*, the sense of intrigue for the subject. Humor exists, the bitter humor of Melville, perhaps, whom Bronk has studied. Melville wrote about the whiteness of the whale; Bronk writes about the irreality of reality. His feeling of history, as he roams the American continents, reminds me of Hawthorne a bit. Like Hawthorne, and like few North American writers today, he senses, and responds in organ tones, to the American past, the past of *both* Americas, the past before the white man, the pre-Columbian past—Hawthorne would not have called it that—and like another poet obsessed with the primordial past, Neruda, Bronk has gone up to Machu Picchu, and dreamed of time. . . . (pp. 224-25)

Bronk is American of a kind closer to Neruda and Paz, in their equating of man and time in the continuum of man's fate, than to Charles Olson, who also visited the Yucatan peninsula, and for whom, too often not to be noticed, locale and ''polis'' took precedence over the individual. Bronk sees the Incas, and the Mayans, names them in poem after poem and prose after prose, and he sees himself. . . . [For] Bronk ancient mountains and modern cities coexist in the flux of time and space in which man is trapped. That is why his startling connections are always so utterly contemporary, and personally relevant. Man is not man-in-history, or man-as-savage, but *man*. No other poet in the United States is quite like this. Gary Snyder comes to mind. William Carlos Williams came near in his essay on Benjamin

Franklin, his essay on Alfred Stieglitz, but the cause of Williams was the lost chance, the American Dream. . . . Bronk's emphasis is on how *same* man can be. Bronk takes the human condition out of the time-frame of possibilities and probabilities, and beyond the nostalgia of other poets. . . . (pp. 225-26)

In *To Praise the Music*, perhaps Bronk's most experimental book, these concerns with the nature of time, with reality, all come together. That he encases these concerns, in poems all of fourteen lines, many of them sonnets, sets up a formal drama worthy of his insistent mind. (p. 227)

Like Robert Lowell, Bronk uses the fourteen-line unit to create a battery of statements about his experience, some of which join in clusters and contexts, some of which stand out. No need to push the resemblance of these two poets except to state that they have both brought life to the supposed ghost of a form. In Bronk's case the fourteen-liners, when they are delivered as purely formal sonnets, sometimes offer an effect of playful virtuosity. Lowell does not try to do this, preferring to hack away at his stanzaic hunks. Bronk gives us not narrative, but, as always, lyrical meditations. They take many shapes: unrhymed Petrarchan sonnets, tercets closed off with a couplet, again unrhymed, quatrains and tercets together, seven-line stanzas as in the poem above, and two that look, and ring, suspiciously like unrhymed Shakespearean sonnets. Occasionally the poems carry a rhyme or two. The line is sinewy, lively, tricky. . . . (pp. 228-29)

The poems are in standard Bronkian garb, the sturdy, gray glamour of a quiet poet. But the poem is artifact as well as utterance; the poet, finally, does *make*. The poem is not only heard and felt; it has heft, shape, construction. There are such matters as line lengths, breath units, iterations, rhythmic combinations, the way we *use* speech. In this interpretation of Bronk's sensibility, the dance of technique, the uses of it, in *To Praise The Music*, is but an extension of his obsession with the futility of saying anything, and then going on to say. The result, in terms of form, content, whatever, is plain mockery. Or, to put it more exactly, Bronk is not a poet who says, but—and his syntax shows this—a poet who is trying to say. . . .

Bronk is a poet who is forever trying to *say his world*. But, as Bronk's poems tell us, ''It is unspeakable, that which exists.'' All serious poets become, in one way or another, poets for whom language is the theme. It is the attempt that is the celebration. In our dim region of lost certitudes this is the problem of contemporary art. (p. 230)

We are left, finally, in any consideration of Bronk, with a number of seemingly negative things that can be said of him, and that, from time to time, have been said. It has been charged that his world is loveless. Bronk seems to be responding to this charge in his poem ''Yes: I Mean So OK —Love'' from *That Tantalus*:

> Some people say, ''Well good,
> now you write about love.''
>
> ''Yes,'' I say, ''what else,
> I always have; what else?''
>
> ''You don't understand,'' they say,
> ''I mean love; that's what it's about.''
>
> ''Yes,'' I say, ''about love,
> but that's not what I mean.''

The poet will have his own terms. It has also been said that he is curiously apolitical and unengaged. This essay has been at some pains to deal with *that*. Then, too, he celebrates his failure, he gives us large doses of pessimism, skepticism. If, however, we were to use a word like poverty, instead of failure, in discussing Bronk's situation in art, we come closer to the truth, for Bronk, in his poems, is the artist who *empties himself*. The religious resonance of a word like *kenosis* for what is meant here does not make a Holy Roller or a saint out of Bronk. But if one considers, even in the work as presented in these pages, the plain speech, the quietness, the declarativeness that prevails over the decorative—Bronk insists somewhere that his poems are "statements"—the simplicity of diction, the refusal, under great pressure, to trail off into the circumambient gas, the deliberate stripping down of all the paraphernalia poets can muster to make the work more acceptable, we are confronted by a language, and a poetic stance, that presents us with the naked utterance: bare spirit. We are a long way from Lessing's dictum, always in danger of being misapplied, of making the Ugly beautiful. Failure? Poverty? Bronk's poetry tells us that whatever it is we must do, this time, this present, we must start from where he has started, nowhere, and with no cover. It is a radiant place. (p. 231)

His essays are as beautiful and as measured as his verse and, as Richard Elman pointed out, . . . superb prose [see excerpt above]. They provide, without striving to, insights into his poetry; as we have seen, in the few excerpts provided here, though they are not the poems, they are part of the man.... There is a versatility of effort in *Light and Dark,* his "first" book, that is its own strong recommendation, and offers the poet, already fully blown. Bronk's development is not so much from youthful enthusiasm to serene maturity as it is the forging of a style for what he has to say. By the time of his second book, *The World, The Worldless,* that style has arrived.

The language, as has already been observed, has become barer. Bronk has become a master of the short, imageless poem. . . . (pp. 231-32)

The imagelessness is distinct from Objectivist intent: there is little reliance on ellipsis, and no fooling with the "look" of the lines on the page. No aesthetic issue is involved, only Bronkian statement. Be all that as it may, the ground Bronk walks today is the same ground he walked a generation ago. He is a poet of cosmopolitan interests and yet he remains, also, a remarkably local poet, writing about anything to hand, house, street, whatever, as a glance at some titles from the book *My Father Photographed With Friends* will reveal—"Hudson Street," "The Gulls At Longbird Island," "The Woods, New York," "Home Address." Like Kenneth Rexroth and Hayden Carruth, he is difficult to classify, not out of a "school," not on to a topic or fashion. It is easy enough, at first glimpse, to say Stevens, when reading Bronk, as it might be to say Frost, when reading Carruth, but as this review has tried to discover, this is not saying much. He makes this writer think of some old Americans, Hawthorne, and especially Edward Taylor and Melville, Melville's bravado of syntax, his swoon of language, and Taylor's obsessive parsing of images and ideas; like these mentors Bronk is a genuine inimitable, and will breed no followers.... Despite the loneliness of his position, his work remains at the center of things, for his poems constantly identify the "work" to be done at this stage of crisis in contemporary poetry. To say we have many poetic universes today is, in certain essential respects, to say that we have none. The whole Bronk canon is a search for form, for style, for language; his poems, important in themselves, are clues to our problems, which is one of the reasons he is one of our very best poets. (pp. 232-33)

Felix Stefanile, "Praising the Music," in Parnassus: Poetry in Review *(copyright © by Poetry in Review Foundation), Spring-Summer, 1977, pp. 222-33.*

MICHAEL HELLER

In "Light and Dark," . . . William Bronk's first book of poems, . . . some anxious children in a car ask, "Where are we now?", to which the poem's narrator replies, "Pretty soon, pretty soon," suggesting that the answers we would like to hear are not always there. The narrator goes on, in this poem entitled "Some Musicians Play Chamber Music for Us," to instruct us that the worlds we seem to share are created worlds; like pieces of music, they are "composed, oh wholly and well composed." The tone is muted, the language spare, unable to alleviate either curiosity or uncertainty, yet the voice compels, even consoles; it is a strangely humane whistle in the dark.

Such an effect pervades the entire corpus of Bronk's poems and essays, for Bronk's is a poetry of the epistemological limit, a message formulated by a border guard on the outer reaches of our shared assumptions. The natural world, Bronk would insist, is a world we can never know; it is, as he notes in "My Father Photographed With Friends," another early collection, the "stuff of stubborn stuff // indifferent to what we do / or fail to do."

Against this recalcitrance, Bronk has fashioned a remarkable body of work, one which suggests that the recognition, the taking in of this fundamental estrangement, illuminates and clarifies the human situation. To make clear such an understanding, Bronk employs, with great tact, a language of logic and paradox, a language which eschews imagery in favor of direct statement of thought, of the unadorned mediations of experience which look on the page, particularly in the most recent poems, like the clean syllogisms of a logician. There is implied a distrust of the usual devices of ornament or analogy, of metaphor, of anything which might remove the reader from the exacting and naked process of realization. "Language," Bronk warns, "is the hypnotist" ready to lull us into a trance, against which there is only the poet's refusal to falsify, uncomfortable as it may be. As he puts it in "The Inability" in "Finding Losses":

She wants me to say something pretty to her because
we both know the unabettable
bleak of the world. Make believe, she says,
what harm? It may be so. I can't. I don't.

And yet Bronk's austere view of human limitation is neither solipsistic nor pessimistic. Instead it offers another way of looking at our common humanity, not in some imagined concurrence of shared knowledge, but in our need to construct and reconstruct worlds, in our attempts to appease a common metaphysical hunger. This, the poems show mainly by indirection; their terms of conflict, be it love or language or the natural world, are subsumed in a voice which seems as compassionate in its registrations as it is clear.... (p. 28)

Bronk's essays in "The New World," ostensibly observations on Inca and Mayan ruins which render with great descriptive power the sites of Machu Picchu, Tikal and Copan, are yet further reflections on the themes of the poems. In an impassioned meditative prose, Bronk writes of his encounter with these older alien civilizations, seeing in their otherness, as he remarks with great precision, not resemblances so much as identifications which "strike at a community of aspiration and value.".... These essays, the themes of which are our own identities, stand out in sharp distinction to the fashionable cultural relativism of much present-day writing and, in particular, to the contemporary urge to ransack and exploit cultures other than our own. But more than that, by forcing us to an act of self-reflexion, by reminding us that our own images are but masks of cultural and social roles, they aim at something liberating beyond our easy humanism.... (pp. 28, 30)

Bronk's work has been appearing now for over 20 years, quietly obeying its own laws and necessities, singularly persistent in its investigation of how our deepest truths are those which are almost unsayable. Such work must point away from the quick answer or surface attitude, away from the clever modernisms of alienation; indeed, the very clarity of Bronk's work seems to indict them in their shallowness. For these poems and essays are not unlike the stone pillars the Incas fashioned, the "intihuatanas," literally the posts-to-tie-the sun, meant to drive the sun back on its course after the solstice. Bronk's work in its refusal to "say something pretty" in the honesty of its presentation, is yet an anchor in our uncertainty; what he has said of the posts could be said of his own body of work: "It is that almost unique thing, an understated monument." (p. 30)

> *Michael Heller, in* The New York Times Book Review *(© 1977 by The New York Times Company; reprinted by permission), September 18, 1977.*

*   *   *

BROUMAS, Olga   1949-

Broumas, born in Greece and now living in the United States and writing in English, is a poet who presents themes of lesbianism, feminism, and eroticism in poetic language that is frankly physical. She was the recipient of the 1977 Yale Younger Poets Award.

LORNA SAGE

The salty, shifty, tidal atmosphere Olga Broumas inhabits [in her *Beginning with O*]—with its bodies plugged with seaweed stoppers and fingered by starfish lovers—is no longer particularly creepy or eccentric. Rather the reverse. The roll of honour she calls ("Anne. Sylvia. Virginia. Adrienne.") is dauntingly familiar, as is her motherly jibe at male poets "stroking their fragile beards" while the one-time Muses go off and share their inspiration among themselves.

She celebrates her derivation from the first sex ("straight from your hollowed basket / into the midwife's skirts") as purely as if she had been cloned.... The only curbs on her tongue and her sex are made to seem mechanical, external as scolds' bridles or clitorectomy. And though there is vio-

lence in her writing ("Gnaw back the fork to its simple crotch") she is more, much more preoccupied with caressing the "excised part" than with images of mutilation. She feels, as her style shows, cushioned and surrounded by benevolent poetic stepmothers who have hollowed out a place for her. She first heard the old fairy tales in their new versions.

The poems fall, roughly, into three kinds, not all equally confident, though to begin with the studied surface-life of the language—"crustal, striated with sweat"—conceals their unevenness. The first group, "Aspects of God", work least well.... [Even] the fact that Olga Broumas is Greek (though she writes in American) doesn't really rescue her mythy beings from unreality. Only when these poems overlap with the other two kinds, the love poems and the revised Hans Andersen (via Anne Sexton's *Transformations*), do they stop being pious illustrations....

It's this that she does best. Her finesse with syntax and line-endings acquires considerable relish when she's talking about the unstable social world of sisters who may or may not be lovers, the cups of tea or glasses of white wine shared in the kitchen, which only serve to put a bitter emphasis on the erotic event that hasn't happened.... This special area of embarrassment between women, now that they're exhorted to love each other (how literally?) is something that hasn't been written about much. She catches it very exactly.... The myth-making palls because of its sameness, but the failed love affairs have a different rhythm with the tensions of prose....

However, her voice is not (yet) a distinctive one. You notice her lack of definition especially in the third part of the book, not mainly or only because the poems are in the tradition of liberated bedtime stories, but because the main fairy-tale character rehabilitated is Mother.... *Beginning with O* is of course her first published volume, and neither its hesitancies nor its ready-$-eness are very important compared with the fact that she can write. She comes out of a fertile and invigorating context, full of ideas, formal as well as political. Stepmothers may still smother, for all that.

> *Lorna Sage, "Sappho on the Seashore," in* The Times Literary Supplement *(© Times Newspapers Ltd. (London) 1977; reproduced from* The Times Literary Supplement *by permission), June 24, 1977, p. 758.*

ROB COLBY

It is heartening to read a young woman poet who has not joined the Erica Jong Singalong. Olga Broumas ... is one —a poet of fluid, complex, and urgent voice, who attempts the elucidation of inner, primal feelings.

Most of these poems are love poems, erotic and lesbian. (p. 41)

The images ebb and flow, returning always to water as native element. With the sure skill of an ocean denizen, she leads one through the traversable waters of her loving. In and out, among the weedy shallows and dark caves of her womanhood, she finds the images for sexuality, birthing, and motherhood. She sets out to plumb unconscious domains and brings her finds to light with a deft combination of poetic musicality and the declarative tone of the spoken word. Her poems embrace a teasing and everpresent conflict: always aware of the primordial depths in which she sees her source and her continued rebirth, at the same time she struggles for the opposing modes of craft and insight to reveal and facilitate the experience. She tells us that this is her struggle as a poet, and when, in her poems, the reconciliation occurs, the poems are very good indeed. (pp. 41-2)

Unwilling to join the ranks of confessional wordmongers who assume that a primitive cacophony will do well by itself on the page, and that their private worlds need no elucidation, Broumas approaches the expression of instinctive and basic forces with at least a small supply of the effective tools of her trade. Occasional internal and end rhyme, a fine consonance of meter and content, and a vividly sirenic imagery certainly raise her free verse out of the realm of the merely personal and random.

But one wishes for something larger from her. She does well with her themes of eroticism, womanhood, and her own oceanic depths, but there are further complexities of love and civilization I would like to hear about from her. I hope she will broaden her thematic scope and master further aspects of prosody with the fluency she now shows.

There are some aspects of her content with which she cannot yet deal adequately. Her rare stabs at humor, for instance, are just that—stabs, unincorporated. . . . Broumas's marvelously fluid voice can encompass more than it does. She is clearly working toward this further mastery and, though it may be tempting to say that the conflict between chaos and definition can best be described by the personal poetics of one engaged in that struggle, Broumas knows that an illuminating artistry will make her world accessible. . . .

The best poems in [*Beginning with O*] are . . . love poems. Most of them—"Innocence" is particularly memorable— are fine examples of the power of the sustained image. . . . —a light that she struggles for, to show us the dark caves and photic depths of her love's home. (p. 42)

> *Rob Colby, "Caves of Sexuality," in* The Village Voice *(reprinted by permission of* The Village Voice; *copyright © by The Village Voice, Inc., 1977), August 29, 1977, pp. 41-2.*

HELEN VENDLER

Olga Broumas, wishing to avoid timidity, falls into the pit of a desperately uncertain tone [as evidenced in *Beginning with O*]—sensational, full of bluster, pretentious, sentimental, callow. The callowness appears in her schoolgirl catalogue of respect: she wants to say "Great spirits now on earth are sojourning," but the sentiment comes out as self-conscious attitudinizing in a chapel full of niches. . . .

All art, needless to say, is founded on what is juxtaposed to what and how the whole is composed. Broumas falls into a jumble of incompatibilities, where juxtaposition in haphazard and composition is that old Romantic cliché, the mount toward climax. (p. 72)

[The] transcription of feeling into stilted compliment is representative of Broumas's inability, as yet, to find a viable voice. (p. 73)

> *Helen Vendler, in* The Yale Review *(© 1977 by Yale University; reprinted by permission of the editors), Autumn, 1977.*

CHARLES BERGER

[Broumas'] poems, as everyone will remark, are frankly homo-erotic. I would also add that they are innocently erotic, amazingly unshadowed by guilt, remorse, or even by loss. The innocence comes from her sense of wonder in the presence of her lovers, her women. . . . Broumas watches and watches other women. This is especially clear in the . . . opening sequence [of *Beginning with O*], a group of lyrics entitled "Twelve Versions of God." "Twelve Versions" was written in conjunction with a series of paintings by Sandra McKee. The gods are goddesses, Greek goddesses, and for each one, Broumas (and McKee) have used ordinary women as models, have imagined contemporary equivalents for the classical and pre-classical myths. The sequence works brilliantly. The close of "Circe" is a gem, tough and witty, as Broumas pictures herself in her skirt of wine, walking past a construction site, turning men into swine.

Broumas writes with great clarity, with great natural feeling for how lines must begin and end. Her poetry is both compressed and clear, tied to the seen thing but also sharing and communicative. There is an element of chantlike stasis to the movement of some of her lines, a reciprocity between speaker and audience: "One would know nothing. / One would begin by the touch / return to her body / one would forget . . ." Not surprisingly, sometimes the lines grow overly taut and then the reader wishes that Broumas would open up a little more, grow more discursive, *talk*. But she has a strong sense of craft, not to mention of subject matter, and she will do as she must. (p. 18)

> *Charles Berger, in* New Boston Review *(copyright 1978 by Boston Critic, Inc.), Summer, 1978.*

*   *   *

BRUNNER, John   1934-

Brunner is a British author of science fiction novels, short stories, and poetry. His themes are humanistic, centering on the continuity of the human condition, and the psychological and physical survival of ordinary man. Brunner is a satirist, utilizing humor that is both playful and sardonic. Even at his most bitter or ironic, the events, atmospheres, and attitudes he describes have definite parallels with reality. Formerly a pilot, Brunner participated for several years in the British nuclear disarmament movement, an experience which has colored some of his works. Brunner is occasionally criticized for letting social protest override his literary sensibility, but he is generally recognized as one of science fiction's most controlled and realistic writers. (See also *CLC*, Vol. 8, and *Contemporary Authors*, Vols. 1-4, rev. ed.)

JAMES BLISH

The protagonist [of *The Whole Man*] is a man who, though physically handicapped himself, has telepathic powers which he uses for healing other people. . . . [The] novel showed powers of insight and compassion previously unsuspected . . . in this author—the powers of an artist, not just the technician. . . .

These powers were promptly shown again in almost unbearably concentrated form in "The Totally Rich," a novelette. . . . Ostensibly the story's subject is longevity vs. death, but filtered through the Brunner sensibility it turns out to be about love, and the overall effect almost approaches high tragedy. (p. 5)

These same powers are now abundantly evident in his recent work, and most particularly in his present penchant for choosing protagonists the reader can barely like at the outset and making them grow into full-fledged human beings worthy of love as well as respect. This was implicit in ''The Totally Rich''; it reaches full maturity in the 1972 novel *The Sheep Look Up*, along with much else. (pp. 5-6)

[Two aspects of The New Wave] relate directly to John Brunner: a dominant concern with the problem of today rather than the far future; and freedom to try any stylistic experiment no matter how wild (or, in the mainstream, old hat). John Brunner had shown an intense social consciousness before, both in his writing and in his personal life. It fused with stylistic experiment in the monumental *Stand on Zanzibar*. . . . The following novel, *The Jagged Orbit,* is also stylistically idiosyncratic—for instance, it is divided into a hundred ''chapters,'' two of which consist of single syllables—but though Brunner did not pioneer this freedom in modern science fiction, he remains to date one of the very few . . . who has subsumed it to artistic purpose.

The ultimate issue we have seen is *TSLU* [*The Sheep Look Up*], surely his finest work thus far. It is again a sociological science fiction novel, but one with the sea-change of immediate concern with imminent social problems. It is technically brilliant, not only experimentally but in the way it does not scorn the old pulp ideal of tight plotting and beyond that the older ideal of being well-made and in balance. It is long, but not a word is wasted—on the contrary, it is one of those novels like Gaddis's *Recognitions* where as the pages left to be read dwindle the reader regrets that it does after all have to come to some end. (It is not the masterwork *The Recognitions* is—Brunner has yet to give us that. . . .) There are scores of characters, all vividly brought to life and treated with sympathy, even the obvious villains. And it has nevertheless the most merciless happy ending I've ever encountered: the burning down of the entire United States. This may not strike you as happy at all, but it is the inevitable solution for the multiplex problem posed, and the only one. The work has beauty, compassion, power, precision, and immediacy. It is not science fiction as we used to know it, but we are all the better off for that. (p. 6)

It cannot be said fairly, in my view, that [John Brunner] has fulfilled his early promise, because very little promise was visible at the beginning; but once he found his real voice, the outcome was not so much a promise as a sort of aesthetic explosion. (p. 7)

James Blish, ''John Brunner: A Colleague's View,'' in The Happening Worlds of John Brunner, *edited by Joe De Bolt (copyright © 1975 by Kennikat Press Corp.; reprinted by permission of Kennikat Press Corp.), Kennikat, 1975, pp. 3-7.*

WILLIAM P. BROWN

Government is a key ingredient in Brunner's recent work. He develops his major theme, human survival, around it. He directly comments on it as part of his social criticism and frequently makes it a determining factor in his novels. This is certainly the case in [his most politically orientated novels,] *The Squares of the City, Stand on Zanzibar, The Jagged Orbit,* and *The Sheep Look Up.* All are first-rate political novels because they tell the reader something significant about politics—the activity of government. . . .

Brunner's use of politics differs from more typical political novels like *The President, All the King's Men,* and *Advise and Consent.* They deal with the institutional decision-making centers of government, which Brunner conspicuously avoids; his analysis focuses instead upon the actual failings of government and the motives behind such failures. (p. 130)

The failure of policies, not the failure of institutions, are Brunner's concern. Readers are left with someone to blame but aren't shown exactly why they ought to blame him. They just never see politicians at work.

Of course, Brunner is not a political scientist objectively attempting to explain reality and predict the future. His function is, in fact, diametrically opposed to such a role. His is value-oriented in intent and purpose. Brunner writes fiction and defines actuality as he desires. He writes of the future, which provides additional freedom to lead the reader wherever he wishes. In addition, his dystopian novels are oriented toward developing negative images of the future. Thus, the ultimate failure and subsequent demise of society is his concern. . . . He is no more writing *about* politics than he is *about* science. It is merely one element in his social analysis. . . .

These novels are especially valuable for speculative purposes because Brunner does not play runaway games with his images of the future. Almost everything about them is closely related to the present. There is no escape into a Buck Rogers future where amazing new techniques influence behavior or where man has been transformed into a different creature. Brunner's plausible scenarios and characters can be taken seriously.

The dominant political themes of the novels are . . . predicated on contemporary dilemmas. (p. 131)

Brunner's political objects and events also extend from present actuality.

In short, Brunner's novels are relevant to an understanding of politics. He writes about its failures in a manner that allows us to reflect on what tomorrow could be like. At the same time, the immediacy of his speculation adds a dimension of believability to his analysis that forces us to contrast government's present activities with those in the novel. Brunner conveys the message that we could be headed for disaster because government is not performing its function well.

Brunner in these four novels follows a pattern that can be loosely interpreted as an explanatory model. This model is quite simply and easily outlined:

1. Government is a dangerous institution because it fails to order society and provide for its future.

2. It does not better the state of human affairs for most people nor even provide them any assistance in leading comfortable lives.

3. It does, in fact, consistently take action that makes matters worse.

4. These conditions hold because government officials are both self-serving and short-sighted. The reasons for this are many, but the most important ones are undue emphasis on nationalism, close ties between industry and government, and a corresponding lack of concern about real human problems.

5. The government that emerges is a callous politics of self-interest. The self-interest of governmental elites and of the masses are distinctly different because elites relate to preferences that are unrepresentative of the long-range needs of the whole society. (pp. 132-33)

Throughout these books, government troops and officials murder young people, persecute reformers, tacitly support arms dealers who prey on the populace, and continuously destroy people both physically and psychologically by prying into the most private portions of their lives. In each instance, the actions reward or save political influentials. (p. 134)

It would be a mistake to conclude that Brunner's commentary provides only a point of comparison for use in questioning actual and specific government programs that might resemble them. Brunner seems to be challenging far more than the acceptability of individual policies as they apply to sets of problems. His campaign is not a simple one for environmental protection or population control; he is asking the broader and more generalized question: "Is government doing its job?"...

In essence, the real job of government is to order society and provide for its future. It can only achieve such ends by bringing predictability to personal relationships and to the utilization of social resources. Assurances must be made that individuals will not be subject to unexpected pressures from others and to shortages that abruptly threaten life.

The governments portrayed in these novels do neither. Brunner presents a society composed of people and groups who depend on one another and share the same resources, but no rules exist either to limit or define behavior. (p. 135)

The "response-failure" political model accounts for governmental ineptness but it does not explain it. In the first place, the causality implied in the model is only assumed. Brunner presents no evidence to substantiate this claim except to note that governmental policies consistently reward powerful interests. Second, there is no explanation as to why these interests should be served by government officials. Since the decision-making system is never revealed, government officials are never portrayed as receiving or using any benefits or rewards that could have been derived from such coalitions.

On the contrary, political leaders are portrayed as inept or foolish, and perhaps these factors account for their *response* to special interests.... [The] United States president always responds out of misguided sympathies for business. Politics, as presented here, is not shown as a bargaining game where trade-offs and exchanges are necessary. Instead, it resembles the world of C. Wright Mills's *The Power Elite* where government is captured and dominated by wealth. But again, no concrete reasons for capture are provided, at least none that relate to the special significance of wealth.

Brunner presents no evidence or information to suggest that this model, or the political system it represents, is self-sustaining. Rather, this system seems to perpetuate both itself and governmental failure because society is at fault. Citizens fail to take the steps necessary to provide direction for governmental officials, and wealthy interests come to power in their absence. (p. 136)

[There] is no political force in these four novels to stop

[citizens who] are willing to assume the personal cost of participation. However, citizens fail to do so because their social relationships and the environment which they structure militate against active participation in any constructive endeavor. Government may be discouraging participation, but the languid behavior of the citizenry makes any such actions relatively unnecessary. In short, Brunner tells the reader that he has little faith in popular control.

Brunner's treatment of popular participation in politics is far more sophisticated than in most speculative fiction. Most authors of this genre, including those of *Brave New World* and *1984,* portray humanity as perfectly manipulable. Huxley's and Orwell's citizens are subject to such total control that their best efforts to assert individual preferences are easily crushed by direct government action. Thought police and television surveillance are sufficient explanations for their subjugation.

Such factors are insufficient for Brunner. Government may indeed attempt control; but when it does, it is by clever trappings rather than forceful techniques. The preferred means of control is propaganda devices intended to promote citizen agreement. Subliminal perception employed by the regime in *SOTC* [*The Squares of the City*], for example, redefines viewer images according to the needs of the government. Heavy-handed domination would only promote animosity and hostility, leading to avoidance and resistance.

The implication is that citizens are free to think and act if they want to. They just don't. As a result, officials not only propagandize through the media, they also manipulate symbols through the policies they enact and the citizen actions they encourage. (p. 137)

However, this manipulation does not fully explain the lack of political participation. People restrict themselves as much as does government. Propaganda techniques, Brunner reveals in a rather subtle and implicit fashion, would never work in a society where people share a sense of community and actively engage in its pursuits. They work only because people are willing, even anxious, to accept them. Citizens want to believe. The inhabitants of these novels are too drug-oriented, too selfish, too concerned with material affluence, and too much without any sense of values to revolt against government's manipulation. They could be, and are, conned by anyone. This is the easiest route for them to follow.

At the heart of Brunner's political world is a weak society. Ineffective government only exists because its citizens allow it. Society, not politics, is the source of the problem and the subject of most of the author's criticism. (p. 138)

Those of Brunner's characters occupying positions of political power are distinguished only by their eminence. They, too, are selfish, visionless, and paranoid.... To Brunner, they're as ignorant as the next person and can't be expected to succeed. But this is only part of the problem.

Greater difficulties arise after people arrive in official positions. At that point they are confronted with an interplay of technical innovations, economic interests, and governmental forces that combine to determine future behavior. Big government and big business are portrayed as a collusive, almost singular force, operating together for some common purpose. In Western countries this purpose is financial profit, while in underdeveloped and non-Western countries, like *SOZ*'s [*Stand on Zanzibar*'s] Yatakang, the motivation is industrial growth. The end product of both is political power which can be utilized to exercise even greater control over already acquiescent subjects.

In short, the political world of these four novels is little more than an unrestricted power grab in which citizens see little reason for taking part. Brunner shows the need for coordinated governance by noting its absence. Beyond that, very little is revealed about political decision making. If indeed there is collusion, we don't know how or why. The biases of government policies are obvious, but the reasons for them are not. . . . Brunner doesn't say. . . .

This seems to be the only solid clue that suggests collusion between Brunner's government and his large economic interests—government manipulates citizens but not wealth. Manipulation to retain power and avoid difficult policies is expected of any government. The absence of manipulation, on the other hand, suggests that it is unnecessary because these interests are apparently vital supporters of government. Still, we don't know how or why.

Brunner wisely could devote considerable attention to this void in these novels. He could proceed best by developing the point that these two forces come together through material need. (p. 139)

Brunner's novels could obviously have been developed more fully by further applying compatible interpretations of actual conditions rather than halting with the simple assertion that governmental responsiveness is dangerous. The reader never understands the nature of the danger, and Brunner's presentations become half-truths in terms of the probable.

Other things that Brunner suggests about governmental process are far-fetched. His portrayal of the president of the United States is especially shaky. All authority is too carefully placed in the hands of the chief executive, who moves other officials at will. (p. 140)

Brunner touches on some very real problems in [the] areas of international relations. . . . But again, Brunner's presentation is incomplete. Nationalism is indeed a problem similar to what Brunner describes, but it is not unchecked by economic factors. Brunner misses the multinational corporation whose profit motives overstep the boundaries of any one country. . . .

Despite some problems with his analysis and the omission of some important explanatory factors, Brunner constructs some intriguing interpretations of the political process and why it fails. He begins with the society and its support of government and details a plausible explanation of the general reasons why important problems are not solved by governing institutions. On the whole, his accounts are quite well done. They not only concur with many elitist interpretations of politics but they also offer explanations for the existence of the elites. (p. 142)

Brunner's political insights make for eventful study. . . . The satire that characterizes Brunner's political writing also contributes to the readability of this material. His points are often made with such bitter irony that readers cannot help but be jolted by the significance of the action. (p. 143)

William P. Brown, "Government and Poli- *tics in Selected Works of John Brunner," in* The Happening Worlds of John Brunner, *edited by Joe De Bolt (copyright © 1975 by Kennikat Press Corp.; reprinted by permission of Kennikat Press Corp.), Kennikat, 1975, pp. 130-44.*

MICHAEL GOODWIN

Far too often, SF writers with no taste for homework set their cautionary tales in so distant a future that the *process* of shattering an ecosphere becomes a side issue.

John Brunner never tells us exactly when *The Sheep Look Up* is taking place, but it seems to be no later than 1980 or 1990—the very point at which all the "minor" environmental crises are beginning to converge into a disaster. It's the process that concerns Brunner, because an ongoing process can be stopped. *Sheep* has more political punch than any other ecological disaster novel I've read, precisely because its concrete details suggest concrete action.

Brunner has done his homework, and the novel's background is scrupulously built up from a collage of current data and careful extrapolation. (p. 63)

That the environment is delicately balanced is hardly a new insight. Yet Brunner scatters characters and climaxes in every direction—there's always someone, or something, near at hand to serve as a horrible example of what happens when you mess with Mother Nature. Hence, for a didactic novel, *Sheep* is virtually free of sloganizing.

The one problem is that, given the cast of hundreds (most of whom are locked into ideological functions), very few characters can be portrayed with much depth. Still, individuals are no more the focus of this book than a single oil spill. Brunner works with statistical extrapolation, and his large sample makes *The Sheep Look Up* utterly convincing. (p. 64)

Michael Goodwin, in Mother Jones *(copyright © 1976 by the Foundation for National Progress), August, 1976.*

DEREK de SOLLA PRICE

John Brunner's best work is related to the tradition of literary naturalism. His fictions offer projections into the relatively near future—a few decades—of trends that are clearly detectable in the present. He works with large canvasses, building worlds out of many individual lives. He himself has expressed his indebtedness to John Dos Passos for his naturalistic blend of fiction and documents from the communications media, but he has altered the technique of Dos Passos in several crucial ways. First, by attempting to "document" the future he has set himself a task which is more demanding and more interesting than documenting the present. Put simply, documenting the future requires imagination as well as some skill at social science.

But even more important, a naturalism of the future radically alters the deterministic quality that makes literary naturalism so oppressive and even unesthetic. Brunner gives us a fictional world in which the lives of characters are limited or destroyed by cultural decisions enacted before their time. This world is highly deterministic. But the fictional world which is so oppressive is emphatically not our own world. We are in fact presently making the cultural decisions which will either bring into being the dreadful world of Brunner's fiction or prevent these horrors from being visited upon us. As Brunner puts it, his books are intended as signs reading DO NOT GO THIS WAY. Thus he replaces the numb inertia and helpless pity required of readers by traditional naturalistic texts with a direct appeal to the conscience of the reader. This is most concretely realized in his last novel, *The Shockwave Rider* (1975), which ends with a ballot upon which the reader is invited to mark his or her choice for the culture.

In *The Shockwave Rider* the fictional world is thus left open for salvation. But in Brunner's greatest and most sombre novel, *The Sheep Look Up* (1972), there is no such choice for his fictional characters. Still, the choice for the reader is presented with stunning power. The title echoes lines from Milton's "Lycidas" about the abuse of power and the spread of moral poison, starvation and pollution. The novel is about these things also, but it is literally about the spread of physical poison, pollutants. . . . It is impossible to say of this book that fact ends here and fiction begins there. Every day headlines turn Brunner's fictions into fact, and the nightmare comes closer. And Brunner's novel teaches better than anything else in print what may happen if we pass certain points in the spread of pollutants, after which an irreversible process will set in. It is a beautifully made and horrifying vision, in its all too plausible solidity. . . . Brunner paints a picture of the future, clear as Brueghel or Bosch, along with that little sign: DO NOT GO THIS WAY. (pp. 38-9)

> *Derek de Solla Price, in* The New Republic *(reprinted by permission of* The New Republic; © *1976 by The New Republic, Inc.),* October 30, 1976.

*   *   *

BUELL, John   1927-

Buell is a Canadian novelist, short story writer, essayist, and playwright. (See also *Contemporary Authors*, Vols. 1-4, rev. ed.)

ROGER BAKER

[*The Shrewsdale Exit* is a] neatly compelling reworking of a not unfamiliar theme: how the insider becomes the outsider. Joe Grant is an ordinary, clean-cut middle-American in his thirties. He has a matching wife and a dolly six-year-old daughter. On holiday their car is attacked, on the highway, by three motorcyclists—Hells Angels types. The women are raped and murdered, Joe survives. But, there being no witnesses to the incident, and a minimum of evidence, no case can be brought against the three freaks. Stunned and appalled by the apparent inability of the law and its processes to deal with the gang, Joe takes on the business of revenge himself.

This is just the beginning, and John Buell achieves a writing style that relates strongly to a film. The way in which he sets up the opening scene of violence is creepy and brilliant; not giving away too much, but just enough to scare the reader with anticipation. . . . [Buell uses a] simple, detached technique. Joe fails in his revenge and finds himself in prison for attempted murder. . . .

With Joe's own imprisonment, the book changes gear a little. . . . [We] now find a picture of a man moving from the interlocked security of society into the position of outsider.

Joe is cool in prison and is soon selected to make up a breakout party, and the novel moves into its final stages of re-birth through an assertion of simple human values: not the highly organised structures of society, but the wholesomeness of a rural, farming community.

Undoubtedly the tension with which the novel opens, slacks off. And it is replaced with a not particularly convincing portrait of Joe's re-emergence; unconvincing because the move from skilled documentary style to sensitive fiction underscores the novel's own move from possibility to the speculative. And the golden rays of hope with which the saga ends seem contrived and, in fact, render suspect the hitherto fairly rigid and consistently critical view of society projected. Not to worry . . . it was only a story, really. . . . (p. 102)

> *Roger Baker, in* Books and Bookmen (© *copyright Roger Baker 1973; reprinted with permission), October, 1973.*

IRA HAUPTMAN

[*Playground*] is a novel about man and nature. The man is pretty close to nobody in particular—which by the logic of some novels is supposed to make us see ourselves in him—and the nature, though a carefully identified segment of primeval Canada, is really any old conveniently featureless wilderness of water and trees.

The human half of this well-worn dialectic is Spence Morrison, who [crash-lands in the wilderness and] . . . spends most of the novel alone with his descriptive powers.

Well, not quite alone. To guide him there emerges from his subconscious a know-it-all inner voice that sounds like an impeccably starched straightman talking his way toward a pie in the face. Unfortunately, it's supposed to be the whisper of latent resourcefulness. The voice helps him dry his clothes, and later look for food, and in general is as helpful as Robinson Crusoe's Friday and also eats less and doesn't want to beat him at checkers.

He survives nature for three weeks, tells himself he's learned something, and then is rescued just in time, when *Playground* has stumbled through as many ironic permutations of his two lives as it can conceive. . . .

Playground is a dutiful novel in a fussy way, and gives the impression that it's recording what it has to more than what it wants to. . . . Writer and reader seem locked in some obligatory dance that neither of them can lead.

Buell's prose accomplishes the difficult task of being businesslike and flaccid at the same time. In its runny fashion it just wants to get on with things. No spaces for our response are granted or required. . . . Buell excels in anticlimatic explanations of the obvious that I probably shouldn't criticize but just send in to *The New Yorker*, followed by a little "oh," for the bottoms of their columns.

The reader can find for himself such delights as booby-prize chapter beginnings that reward us with heavy underlinings of what we've just had to plod through in the last chapter, the use of "yeah" to indicate manly perception, and such similes as "contradictions tugged at him like turbulence."

Although he tries hard to make it all mean something, Buell ends up describing events for their own sake, not as pressures on the consciousness of his hero. The novel is filled with physical actions that never become experiences.

What's missing, among other things, is the alchemical magic of sensuousness. . . .

Buell's hero . . . unfortunately brings to the woods the sensory sweep of a kitchen sink.

Buell drops plenty of hopeful suggestions about the meaning of his novel. They're grand but inchoate, and seem randomly placed, difficult to relate to anything we've read. Of course when you haven't made anything happen, the trick is to pretend something really big has happened. ''I've come to know . . . things. I'll tell you about it when I'm ready. If I ever can.'' (p. 28)

Ira Hauptman, in The New Republic *(reprinted by permission of* The New Republic; © *1976 by The New Republic, Inc.), July 3 & 10, 1976.*

WILLIAM BAUER

The settings for John Buell's first three novels, *The Pyx, Four Days,* and *The Shrewsdale Exit* are vaguely identifiable as Montreal in the first two and northern New York state in the third. But these places are kept unspecified with such deliberate care that readers cannot help noticing the artful dodging. In Buell's grim and violent novels characters move about in spaces so familiar to themselves that a reader who wants a sure fix on the North-American map is unprovided for. He can recognize, of course, the urban, the suburban, the smalltown, and so on, but these are more conditions than places, and he begins to suspect that he is being nudged toward conclusions that have to do with ''the human condition,'' or some other such major abstraction. Above all, he is never allowed to imagine that political boundaries, regional cultures, or local traditions make any difference in what really matters. (p. 77)

It is momentarily surprising, then, to find that his fourth novel, *Playground,* is peppered with so many specified and exact Canadian locations as to invite the curious to confirm their accuracy with roadmap and atlas. His hero does not merely travel from a city to the great woods as might Joe Grant of *The Shrewsdale Exit.* Spence Morrison [travels a route very carefully delineated by Buell]. . . . This selection of detail from the first few pages of the novel . . . seems to exhibit Buell making up for prior deficiencies, perhaps with hyperbolic irony.

But the change is only apparent. It is Buell's character, Spence Morrison, a prosperous, suburban, middle-aged executive—hooked on efficiency, planning, route markings, brandnames, clock-readings and the like—whose mind demands the assuring specificity of time and place, and though this Morrison, the technology-ridden modern man, operates out of Montreal, he is of a type to be found, one supposes, in any modern metropolis. His story is a story because of the proximity to a wilderness large enough to be lost in, and once that happens all this needless clamor for putting novels in Toronto or Toledo is revealed for the shallow matter it is. The Canadian North could be a fiefdom of Paraguay for all it will help Spence Morrison. We eventually get even the irony that Canadian bills are more valuable as ignitable kindling than as currency to [this] poor fellow whose plane goes down in uninhabited terrain; and for all his maps, charts, and mental doodads, Morrison comes to feel that when he is lost he isn't ''even at a real place.'' . . . (pp. 77-8)

Buell's main character, Morrison—to all intents and purposes the only one in the novel, whose consciousness is continuously reported to us throughout—. . . assumes [after the airplane crash] a vitality and plausibility that was lacking before. Because the work is a kind of allegory, we must accept the Morrison who amid the complexity of social intercourse and economic conditions had manipulated the details of that existence with 100% efficiency. Though no such grotesque paragon or horrid perpetual winner can be imagined to exist, there is no harm in the invention—especially since all of Spence's technology and his assurances sink to the bottom of the northern lake in the downed Cessna.

Morrison's real game, survival without the continuities of society and culture, is brilliantly rendered by Buell. His struggles with the exigencies of hunger, thirst, and the need for shelter are engrossing in themselves, but more important is the portrayal of Morrison's mind, alerted to emergency keenness and aware of its own need to maintain its balance and worth. Efficiency now becomes redefined by the new context: conservation of physical energy and mental equilibrium. . . . It seems fair to say, since Spence tells his wife after his ordeal that he has ''come to know . . . things,'' that some of those things have to do with what has been reported to us tellingly—the play of mind for all the chips in this wilderness playground—that the pithy philosophic insights uttered internally under the duress of primal danger have application and value to those of us who have never quite been derailed from our delusory sure routes and routines.

Thus the reader of *Playground* cannot be blamed for seeing Spence Morrison as Buell's attempt to give us a twentieth-century Crusoe, for the comparison involves more than just a man-alone-against-nature story. Like Defoe, Buell seeks truth by prying man out of his social context and out of his ordinary contingent existence. When Crusoe searches his wild island and his panicked mind for markers of an ordered divine providence, Spence Morrison meets his wilderness by exploring his own resources of mind and body, and alone, makes whatever operable and responsible psychological and philosophical order he can against the chaos. Though the quests may differ, the assumptions are the same: human truth is known through an analytical separation of man from the states where he is usually to be found. In this respect it is interesting to note that Buell's earlier novels, like many of Defoe's, portray the criminal—another sort of character who can be imagined as operating beyond boundaries and having to make his own alert and crucial moves, moment by moment.

It is possible, of course, to quarrel with Buell's assumptions by suggesting that such inventions, insofar as they seem to deny the integral importance of cultural places and conditions—these are certainly not invariably soporifics—are unnecessary melodramas. But Buell and we, like those in Defoe's age, live in a world in which the weight of social reality lies heavy upon us; we can hardly be blamed for enjoying the murdering to dissect, and playing with the fiction that our separated man alone encounters, most dramatically, truer truth.

Playground, especially in its middle portion, once Morrison's presumed ordinary life is shucked, is probably Buell's best writing to date. It has intensity and moment found rarely enough in any novelist, though he has perhaps matched it before in portions of *Four Days*. It should be observed here, as it has been before, that Buell is an excellent craftsman indeed—above all, a serious novelist. He is, perhaps, the kind of serious novelist who ought to have his leg pulled now and then, but as Spence Morrison discovered when jokes kept popping into his mind in the boondocks, one has to wonder about the usefulness and pertinence of them in a sobering dangerous existence. Most of the jokes worth repeating are those that are made by an earnest fellow observing grim absurdities in the human condition. (pp. 78-9)

William Bauer, "John Buell's Playground," in The International Fiction Review (© copyright International Fiction Association), January, 1977, pp. 77-9.

*　　*　　*

BUNTING, Basil   1900-

An English poet and journalist, Bunting is considered an important literary descendant of Ezra Pound. His work, which is imagistic in style, also shows the influences of Eliot and Zukofsky. It incorporates many musical qualities, not only in the cadence of individual lines, but also in its formal structure. He has entitled one group of poems "Sonatas," another "Descant on Rawley's Madrigal." Bunting often mingles historical and personal elements, creating complex poetry that is both lyrical and dense. *Briggflatts* is generally considered his most important work. (See also *Contemporary Authors*, Vols. 53-56.)

ANTHONY SUTER

Bunting's poetry [deals] in the structure of meanings and, moreover, the meanings are organised according to a musical architecture—that of sonata form. . . .

For some years Bunting sought the kind of musical structure he required for his poetry, but he must have fixed his choice very early on the sonata, rather than on the more impressionistic prelude, for example. His first published long poem, *Villon* (1925), is based on simple sonata form, although he had embarked on more complicated variants at first. . . . (p. 47)

Villon (1925) is a very good example of how the poet's elementary sonata technique works. In fact, it has a pure, simple sonata structure that Bunting never bettered, if one considers that the later "sonatas" are much more complicated in form and often go far beyond the ordinary sonata because of the complexity of the themes involved. . . . Not only does each individual part have a beautifully structured development, but also the total structure of the poem moves through two parallel statements of themes to the final resolution of Part III. (p. 48)

A significant indirect influence on the development of the sonata was a poem that does not belong to this category at all, *Chomei at Toyama* (1932). This long poem shows Bunting making natural ideogrammic juxtapositions within a skeleton framework of narrative, so that the life of the work comes from within.

As the sonata becomes more complex, it does so from the inside, from Bunting's own development of sonata form. He took a fixed model to begin with, but when he found that model too limiting he did not seek a more complicated one that was ready-made for him (such as a Beethoven so-nata): he sought to expand and experiment the basic form he had chosen in the beginning. Therefore, there is a development from a fixed form artificially imposed from the outside (—that is why *Villon* and *Aus dem zweiten Reich* seem so neat, almost *too* neat) to an organic growth of that form. *Attis* and *The Well of Lycopolis* represents a sort of testing ground, because instead of the simple, parallel structures of *Villon* and *Aus dem zweiten Reich,* the movements of these works have a complex interweaving of themes and a growth from movement to movement that foreshadow *The Spoils* (1951) and *Briggflatts* (1965).

The earlier of these two poems is obviously intended to make thematic material of the range of *Attis* and *The Well of Lycopolis* fit a structure nearly as simple as that of *Villon*. (p. 50)

The sonata element A B A is present in the two outer movements [of *The Spoils*] and in the total design of the poem. Also, all the various themes are in reality theme clusters, different manifestations of the central notion of "the spoils" (the spiritual treasures Man can gain on his journey through life), so that there is a development from movement to movement, more and more significance being added to the theme stated at the beginning of the whole work.

This is partly a preparation for the method of *Briggflatts*, except that the latter treats its thematic material in reverse. Whereas *The Spoils* states its theme at the beginning like a classical symphony, *Briggflatts* hides the real nature of its central thematic ideas until the end. . . . Fragments of theme—death, love, time, nature and the cosmos, artistic expression and experience—are presented throughout its five parts. . . . (p. 51)

Different fragments of the same theme gradually gain in significance as they are repeated and as the reader relates them together. The basic sonata elements of statement, recapitulation and development, are certainly present, but they do not come in strict parallels as in some of the very first sonatas. Rather, they are organising elements within the poem which is, paradoxically, both very tightly knit and loosely structured. It is tightly knit because every element has its particular place within the total design; without this the thematic centres would not progress as they do. . . .

The design of *Briggflatts* is further enhanced by symbolism of a musical nature. The most far-reaching example is the slowworm, a figure which appears in unexplained fashion at various climactic points in the poem and takes on a different significance according to context, being phallic symbol, and also associated with death, and with an attitude of quiet resignation. This is symbolist writing of the purest kind. The slowworm not only has a different "value" each time it appears, it is the kind of "object" that, I think, can have no "a priori" significance for the reader. This enhances its effect as an essentially "neutral" symbol: "neutral" emotionally for the reader, it can absorb into itself the feelings created by the circumstances of the poem. At the same time its inherent mystery introduces a kind of climactic hush, making the reader sense a moment of great importance, even if he cannot define the nature of the moment. Thus a pure symbolist manner achieves the condition of music. (p. 52)

Anthony Suter, "Musical Structure in the Poetry of Basil Bunting," in Agenda, Spring, 1978, pp. 46-54.

PETER DALE

One has in the past done one's darndest to persuade oneself that Bunting does not really mean what he says when he argues, if it can be called argument, that poetry is pure sound. (p. 56)

The analogy of poetry with music is a dangerous one for two basic reasons: first, poetry has severe limits in pitch, key, tone, and range; nor can it orchestrate; second, it does not have notes devoid of referrents as music largely does. Words mean—if the poet discards their meaning the hearing mind puts them back, just as it picks up echoes of its own tongue in an unknown foreign speech.... Another thing that makes it a dangerous analogy is that users slip between two aspects of music: one as a set of scale-systems of sounds, the other as a set of structural principles like sonata-form. This use of musical form is ultimately a mere metaphorical usage. There's a touch of both aspects in *Briggflatts*. In general, the musical approach is nearly always a form of anti-rationalism. (p. 58)

My feeling is with *Briggflatts* ... that both in its use of sound and its gesture towards musical structure it is rather obvious and not a little contrived. For in insisting on musicality it invites comparison with some of the finest poets who naturally excelled in that field: Chaucer; Shakespeare; Milton; Tennyson; Pound and Eliot, the closest comparison actually being *The Four Quartets* which clearly by contrast illustrates a coarsening in *Briggflatts* of the musical tradition.

The most obvious way in which *Briggflatts* is no step forward in the tradition is the poverty of its use of syntax. The poem is tediously dominated by the simple sentence, extended by appositional developments to subject and object. In addition to this the custom of English in excising a repeated subject pronoun makes this appositional effect sound worse. Along with these appositions goes a considerable reliance upon present participles.

This may be defended by the musical argument that the present tense must be used to make the narrative time of the poem appear to match the duration of the piece as music. That may be so but the danger of syntactical boredom should have been averted. (p. 62)

What is ultimately the objection to the musical approach is that it is used as an excuse or cover for a growing distance from speech and the continued use of rather bardic poetic devices like apostrophising an untenable tenor bull. It is also an uneconomic way of writing. *Briggflatts* seems longer than its matter requires.

Briggflatts errs away from Eliot's suggestion that the music of poetry must arise out of speech. (p. 64)

[Bunting's] peak diagram, his Scarlatti, and his insistence upon music have been ways to enable him to extrude the matter of *Briggflatts*, some of which, he suggests in interview, lies too deep in the subconscious for his rational explication. Such crutches have their uses. Bunting's error is his persistence in trying to give poetry the same crutches. *Briggflatts* is a failure as a musical poem of any stature and a poor foundation on which new poets might build. (pp. 64-5)

In opposing Bunting's theory of the music of poetry, pure and simple, I am not opposing the idea of musical verse. Of course poetry must be musical but it must be more than just music—as that alone it is left standing by music proper. (p. 65)

> *Peter Dale, "Basil Bunting and the Quonk and Groggle School of Poetry," in* Agenda, *Spring, 1978, pp. 55-65.*

ANTHONY SUTER

While not having the significance and originality of musical sound and structure in his poetry, Bunting's use of image and symbol is an important aspect of his work and worth considering in its own right. In his mature work he employs a post-"Symboliste" technique to striking effect. Also, one never loses sight of the idea of music, for Bunting's most highly developed symbolism has an analogy with this form of art. (p. 82)

Particularly noteworthy in Bunting's pictorial imagery is his insistence, nearly to the point of obsession, on the physically disgusting. (p. 83)

Various other images that recur through Bunting's work are often connected with his main preoccupations. As is natural in a poet who is not only a lover of music but also the exponent of a particularly musical form of poetry, references to this art abound. "Seeing" in terms of sound and music imagery comes as naturally to him as it did to Spenser. The poetic utterance is described as sound reaching an ear: "My tongue is a curve in the ear." (p. 84)

More important are the musical parallels Bunting makes in *Briggflatts,* where he frequently sees a musical pattern in nature, whether it be the polyphonic design formed by bull's song and the river Rawthey, lark and the mason's mallet ... or the attribution of musical forms to fish, birds and animals.... (p. 85)

This is Basil Bunting's imagination informing his very strict observation of nature, and while it cannot be classed as a pattern of symbolism, ... it is significantly indicative of a poet's vision. (pp. 85-6)

Bunting's description of nature make his preference for country over town quite obvious, especially where nature is in relation with art as in *Briggflatts,* and with the life of a civilisation as in *The Spoils*. Urban life, as accurately described in *Attis* and *Aus dem zweiten Reich,* Bunting views with intense dislike. Thus, there is the traditional symbolic opposition between town and country, that is ... one of the guide lines of *Chomei at Toyama*.

Further images with a definite function are the frequent references to sculpting or chiselling and writing, which support the theme (so important in Bunting) of the difficulties of artistic expression and creation....

Such images abound in *Briggflatts,* where the mason working at his marble tombstone (partly symbolising the artist) is one of the important figures of the poem. (p. 87)

This imagery is developed through further associations ("a name cut in ice" and "name in soft slate"), to include not only the act of writing—which is furthermore evoked at other points in *Briggflatts,* for example: "Wind writes in foam on the sea:". . .—but also the page:

> It looks well on the page . . .

and the book:

The sheets are gathered and bound,
the volume indexed and shelved,
dust on its marbled leaves. . . .

So the book is connected up again with the marble tombstone, one of Bunting's ways of building images into patterns.

Thus, in a poem such as *Briggflatts*, recurring and associated images provide links to bind the whole together. The
same purpose is served by the imagery drawn from urban
and country settings in *Chomei at Toyama*. This is raised
to the level of a symbolic opposition, basic to our understanding of the poem. (pp. 87-8)

Recurring images, especially as employed in *Briggflatts*, go
a long way to creating symbolic patterns similar to those
Bunting fashions out of references to sex and to the sea.
Sexual images stand half-way between those which just
happen to recur and are employed in a fairly conventional
manner, and the rare example of sea imagery that builds,
across the poems, into a pattern of very personal symbolism.

Sex also has a personal meaning for Bunting in that it is often used to signify artistic activity. It is also mainly employed in a negative way to refer to artistic sterility. . . . In
attacking what he considers to be T. S. Eliot's poetic failure after his adoption of orthodox religion and right-wing
politics, Bunting represents him as the eunuch, Attis, and
employs such deliberately ambiguous terms as "ithyphal-
lic" to describe the poet's technique. . . . Poetry, love and
nature are seen engaged in the same acts:

>Infamous poetry, abject love,
>Aeolus' hand under her frock
>this morning. This afternoon
>Ocean licking her privities.
>Every thrust of the autumn sun
>cuckolding
>in the green grain of late-flowering trees. . . .

The sex imagery is particularly significant and more far-
reaching in this poem, because it unites Bunting's two main
subjects, love and poetry.

The symbolic functions of sexual imagery here can all be
interpreted in a quite straightforward manner. Examples
from different poems can be viewed together for convenience, but do not gain in subtlety for that. When fulfilling a
symbolic rôle, they form a consistent pattern, rather than
the very complex design made by all the references to the
sea in Bunting's poetry. Seen as a whole, they become a
strikingly original way of showing the poet's struggle,
"stubborn against the trades" . . . , against a philistine society.

The sea in Bunting's poetry shows how the boundary between image and symbol is sometimes ill-defined. Also, it
indicates that his symbolism is not referential in a facile
way: it is definitely post-"Symboliste". It avoids, however,
obscurity, because the context of the long poem informs
symbol (and vice versa). Sometimes the whole of a poem
becomes a symbol. (pp. 88-9)

Even the long poem, *Briggflatts*, could be considered in its
totality as a pure symbol in that it is the autobiography of
any artist, just as the whole of a Shakespeare play, such as
King Lear or *A Winter's Tale*, can be seen as a symbol of
the total human condition. Basil Bunting has said that one
could compare *Briggflatts*, the poem, to the Quaker hamlet
in Yorkshire after which it is named. Like the Quaker
meeting house where the believer waits to be "moved", the
reader enters the poetic structure in which he lets experiences, emotions, ideas, happen to him.

Basil Bunting's use of imagery and symbolism becomes
more and more personal as his work develops, so that the
most striking examples of all are to be found in the very late
work and especially in *Briggflatts*. One very idiosyncratic
use of imagery is for "shock" effect. Bunting delights in
shocking the reader by creating a bisociation between his
habitual reaction and the function of the image in the poem.
(p. 92)

Intellectually, this procedure can be viewed as similar to
René Char's shock associations of words. In Bunting, it
probably developed from his insistence on images of foul-
ness and decay in the earlier poems.

A similar, but subtler "shock" image is that of the rat in
Briggflatts. [Like the vulture in *The Spoils*], this animal
usually disgusts the onlooker. Not so Bunting, who compares the situation of a trapped rat to that of the poet in a
hostile, uncomprehending world. . . . The image is subtle
because Basil Bunting is playing on our usual reaction, so
that we feel what the "normal" representative of society
feels, as well as being conscious that Bunting admires the
rat. (p. 93)

[The mason in *Briggflatts*] is not a fixed symbol of one particular thing, but has different associations according to his
appearances in the poem. At first he is a rather sinister,
dehumanised character, associated with death. . . . He is
also an artist, creating a monument to the dead; and
through him are proclaimed the processes of nature. . . . As
artist he assumes the guilt of one who is unable to express
the burden of his experience in his work. . . . (p. 95)

Even though the mason does not appear directly in the rest
of the poem, the reader feels his presence by association,
when Bunting talks of "White marble stained like a urinal"
. . . and of "marbled leaves." . . . Thus, through its previous use—death, art etc.—the mason figure fulfills the
same kind of rôle as a Wagnerian "leitmotif" at its most
sophisticated, that is to say, it is not a motto for a particular
emotion or idea, but is modified with each appearance,
while at the same time remaining recognisable.

A more extreme example of this kind of technique is the
slowworm figure in *Briggflatts*, which has even fewer fixed
associations than the mason. . . . Like the blind beggar in
Madame Bovary or the sinister station porter in *Anna Ka-
renina*, the slowworm is a mysterious, deliberately unexplained presence at certain points of the action. It appears
as part of the polyphonic pattern Bunting weaves out of the
bull's song and dance, the "lark's twitter", the mason's
mallet and the grave. . . . In the furrow (a deliberate parallel with the grave) it is associated with death. It then reappears as a phallic symbol in the love scene between the two
children. . . . (p. 96)

It comes again in Part III. After a description of the failure
of Alexander's journey because of the essentially corrupt
nature of humanity, the reader is presented with a man at
his weakest, near death, poisoned by an adder. The slowworm makes its sudden, mysterious appearance on this
scene:

Heart slow, nerves numb and memory, he lay
on glistening moss by a spring;
as a woodman dazed by an adder's sting
barely within recall
tests the rebate tossed to him, so he
ascertained moss and bracken,
a cold squirm snaking his flank
and breath leaked to his ear:
I am neither snake nor lizard,
I am the slowworm. . . .

We are led away from the association with death. The passage develops into the slowworm's song and a new entry into the world of nature. . . . Finally, the tone becomes hushed and religious, under the effect of the slowworm's presence. . . . A brief, final "rappel" of the slowworm in Part V makes it an element in the new pattern, of stars, light, love, literature and time, that Bunting creates towards the end of his poem:

> . . . . light from the zenith
> spun when the slowworm lay in her lap
> fifty years ago. . . .

The phallic symbol of Part I again, therefore, but transmuted, by its new context.

Transformation, according to poetic context and the active reaction of the reader's mind, raises the slowworm—with the rat, [and] the mason . . .—to a level where language transcends its immediate function and becomes a kind of music. (pp. 97-8)

> *Anthony Suter, "Imagery and Symbolism in Basil Bunting's Poetry," in* Agenda, *Spring, 1978, pp. 82-98.*

G. S. FRASER

There is verse which is directly melodic, which seems to sing rather than speak. Basil Bunting is a master of this. . . .

Bunting perhaps excels all living poets in expressing emotional complexity through apparently simple—not so very simple—melodic artifice.

But there is [another] sense in which poetry can be musical, in imitating not the sound but the structure of music. . . . Bunting's most famous song poem, *Briggflatts,* is . . . constructed this way in five sections. The first two, spring and summer, mount to a false climax; there is a high and narrow real climax in the non-seasonal third; in the fourth and fifth, autumn and winter, the climaxes gently decline. The conception was not merely abstractly musical, but had in mind the expressiveness of music. . . .

What is clear is that, however much he feels that sound comes first, Bunting is incapable of writing a syntactically incorrect sentence or a meaningless one. He is not evading sense or even wit, his images are startlingly vivid, and he is ready to comment on them. . . .

The poet who puts musical expressiveness rather than total sense structure first may leave us, in the end, with a sense of even the musical pattern unresolved. Where should it stop, where should it start? What is it that answers expectation and what, by deliberate dissonance, seeks surprise? If the pattern we start from is not clear enough we cannot trace the deviations from the pattern. . . .

In an interview . . . Bunting expresses his admiration for

Wordsworth, a fellow northerner, and one who had, at his best, a wonderful ear (as in the best of the Lucy poems, which have like Bunting's a power of implying more meaning than can be laid out flat). Yet *saying* something very important to him, at great length, is central to Wordsworth. Perhaps the admiration is that of the fox for the hedgehog. Perhaps Bunting knows "one big thing" but I do not know what it is.

> *G. S. Fraser, "Sound Before Sense," in* The Times Literary Supplement (© *Times Newspapers Ltd. (London) 1978; reproduced from* The Times Literary Supplement *by permission), May 5, 1978, p. 496.*

* * *

BURGESS, Anthony   1917-

Born John Anthony Burgess Wilson, Burgess is an English novelist, editor, translator, essayist, composer, and critic. A remarkably prolific writer with a wide range of subjects, he frequently uses his knowledge of music and linguistics in his fiction. Burgess's fascination with languages is evident in many of his novels, most notably *A Clockwork Orange*. In this linguistically sophisticated novel, Burgess creates a slang which has the effect of drawing the reader into his fictional world. Terming himself a "renegade Catholic," Burgess explores free will versus determinism in his novels, most frequently arriving at the position of a latter-day Augustinian. He has published under the pseudonym of Joseph Kell. (See also *CLC*, Vols. 1, 2, 4, 5, 8, and *Contemporary Authors*, Vols. 1-4, rev. ed.)

JEAN E. KENNARD

[For Anthony Burgess], as for Joyce, "The artist is a Promethean figure who ends by usurping the place of Zeus." Burgess writes in *Re Joyce:* "The fundamental purpose of any work of art is to impose order on the chaos of life as it comes to us; in imparting a vision of order the artist is doing what the religious teacher also does (this is one of the senses in which truth and beauty are the same thing)." It is not surprising that of twentieth-century fantasy writers Burgess most admires Nabokov and Joyce, because his use of fantasy is for their purposes. . . . Burgess, like Joyce, is "a free-thinking fabulist." He needs his reader to be detached and observing, and so he needs fantasy rather than the techniques of realism, but he does not finally alienate his reader.

Burgess, like Joyce, wishes to manipulate "the commonplaces of language into a new medium that should shock the reader into a new awareness." His language has infinite reverberations. The important thing for Burgess is to keep the reader observing the pattern, yet involved, willing to fit the pieces of the jigsaw puzzle together, and then to believe in the picture. He does not take the reader towards nothingness, but towards an image of all-inclusiveness, where "everything is there at once." His purpose, like Joyce's, is the "atonement, at-one-ment, of contradictions." Burgess writes novels of nightmare. (pp. 131-32)

Although almost all of Burgess's fiction illustrates the same basic philosophic stance, the kinds of fantasy he employs vary considerably. . . . [These] five novels . . . illustrate most clearly both Burgess's answer to the Post-existential dilemma and his basic method of conveying it: *A Clockwork*

Orange, The Wanting Seed, Tremor of Intent, Enderby, and *MF.*

Burgess's novels deal with the same metaphysical questions as those of Heller, Barth, Purdy, and Vonnegut: the purpose of human existence, the nature of identity, the value and significance of language; but his answers—and he, unlike [them], has answers—are not the Post-existential ones. As comments in various interviews and many of his novels indicate, Burgess is directly answering Sartre's and Camus' notion that there is no essential pattern in the universe and that the relationship between man and his universe is therefore irrational.

MF, perhaps, demonstrates most clearly that Burgess is answering the Post-existential view. The protagonist, Miles Faber, believes he can define himself through acts of will, create his own identity in the way Sartre suggests. He imagines he is completely free and seeks for the poems of a little-known writer in whose work he hopes to find "Words and colors totally free because totally meaningless." . . . He learns, however, that "Nobody's free. . . . choice is limited by inbuilt structures." . . . Burgess reveals his interest in Existentialism also in his comments about his novels. For example, in an interview . . . , Burgess has stated that the central theme of *A Clockwork Orange* is "the idea of free will. This is not just half-baked existentialism, it's an old Catholic theme."

If Burgess's answer is the Catholic one—and he says himself that he "will not allow Catholicism to go over to the converts" nor "allow the Protestants to attack it," that what he writes "looks like Catholic writing"—it is certain only some Catholic doctrines interest him. Like Hillier, the hero of his novel *Tremor of Intent,* Burgess seems to have an Augustinian belief in the existence of evil and a sense of "what a bloody Manichean mess life is." . . . Duality is the key to Burgess's view of reality; the essence of reality for him—and there are essences in Burgess's scheme as opposed to Sartre's—is its double nature. "Ultimate reality," says Hillier, "is a dualism or a game for two players." . . . In religious terms this means that good and evil cannot exist without one another, "There is truly evil lying coiled in the good." But as Burgess realizes, "we don't believe in good and evil any more"; we need new terms. Each of the five Burgess novels illustrates this duality in new terms: *A Clockwork Orange* in psychological terms; *The Wanting Seed* in historical/sociological terms; *Tremor of Intent* in political terms; *Enderby* in aesthetic terms; *MF* in terms of the relationship between society's structures and those of language.

The basic method of each Burgess novel is to present the reader with two visions, sometimes two antithetical world views, sometimes two apparently opposed aspects of one personality, and to invite him to make a choice. The choice often proves to be a false one; the two visions are a double vision, a dualism, inseparable parts of the one reality. The true choice lies elsewhere, between this duality and another negative value. The great evil in Burgess's view is to see life as unstructured and therefore capable of being completely controlled by man. The world is not neutral, not simply there. Burgess's use of the double vision is reminiscent of Vonnegut's, but there is an important difference between them. Vonnegut . . . allows each vision to undercut the other, leaving the reader with nothing; Burgess . . . shows how the two visions are really one, leaving the reader with unity.

In *A Clockword Orange* Burgess presents a concept of human nature quite different from the Sartrean view that there is no essential human nature and that man is free to create his own identity. His view, like the Catholic one, is that there is a permanent and universal essence to man. Free will for Burgess, as for all Catholics, is the choice of "whether or not to realize a given essential nature. Sartrean man invents his own essence." (pp. 132-34)

Burgess's fable is constructed on a series of doubles: there are two characters called Alex; two visits to the old men in the library; two visits to the house of the author; two views of Alex's friends, as criminals and as policemen. The clarity of the pattern forces us to make comparisons. But Burgess's aim is our involvement. His use of the title of his own novel as the title of the author's book, which . . . might have served to alienate us by means of the self-conscious art technique, is employed here to suggest that Burgess is F. Alexander, "another Alex," and therefore partakes equally of the violence. Throughout the novel Alex addresses his readers as "O my brothers," a phrase with obvious implications of complicity. Finally the teenage slang, Nadsat, that Burgess invented for the novel, serves to include us also. Initially strange, the words of the language are learned by the reader as he learns any language by being constantly exposed to them. He is, in fact, conditioned as Alex was; the effect of Nadsat on the reader functions as an ironic comment on the novel itself. (p. 137)

Burgess stated that *The Wanting Seed* is a Catholic book: " . . . it's a very Catholic book. It's a total vindication of the encyclical [on birth control]. You know, of course, what the encyclical leaves out of account is the acceptance of natural checks, you know, is fact Malthusianism. Malthus has always been condemned by the church, yet the church will now accept Malthusianism, at least tacitly. What's going to happen to our excess population? 'Well, Nature will take care of it,' As Malthus said, in other words, wars and pestilence, earthquakes."

If the novel functions as a defense of the encyclical on birth control, it is also a defense of Burgess's own view of reality as duality. In the book Burgess expresses his view as a defense of the Augustinian against the Pelagian doctrine, this time in terms of history rather than those of psychology. (p. 138)

The Wanting Seed, like *A Clockwork Orange,* is constructed on obvious doubles: the day versus the night, "Pelagian day, Augustinian night"; . . . twin brothers Derek and Tristram, the Pelagian and the Augustinian, later repeated in Beatrice's twins also called Derek and Tristram; "The human dichotomy. The division. Contradictions. Instincts tell us one thing and reason tells us another." . . . The structure of the novel forces us to compare the separate journeys of Beatrice and Tristram. . . . Just as in *A Clockwork Orange,* Burgess has presented us with two unattractive visions and through the relentless logic of the fable method forced us to prefer his view of a dual reality over neutrality.

Tremor of Intent is not a fantasy novel in the same sense as *A Clockwork Orange* and *The Wanting Seed.* It is not science fiction, but takes place in a world very definitely that of the cold war period of postwar Europe. It is a spy-thriller, of the kind practiced by Ian Fleming and E. Howard Hunt, fantasy only to the extent that Burgess has deliberately exaggerated some of the characteristics of the form. (p. 140)

But Burgess explodes the spy-thriller form by relating its essential characteristic, sensationalism, to the evil of the book, Mr. Theodorescu. Hillier, who describes himself as subject to satyriasis and gluttony, a duality he claims tends to cancel itself out, sacrifices both at the end of the novel. The novel, with its surface story of spy intrigue, is actually the account of Hillier's spiritual regeneration after a mock death. . . . (pp. 140-41)

Hillier is associated with St. Augustine and shares with Burgess an Augustinian pessimism and a belief in the fundamental sinfulness of human beings. (p. 141)

Hillier's true enemy is not communism or Pelagianism but those qualities represented by Mr. Theodorescu. Mr. Theodorescu is a neutral "in the pay of no power, major or minor." . . . He is homosexual, and homosexuality here, as elsewhere in Burgess's novels, is used to suggest a denial of life, a denial of the great duality. Like Hillier, Theodorescu has used gluttony and self-indulgence as a way of avoiding real commitment. For Hillier . . . is, he discovers, a neutral too. (pp. 141-42)

This neutrality, as in *A Clockwork Orange* and *The Wanting Seed*, is the real evil. (p. 142)

The concept of the game is important to this novel and Hillier's progress is marked by a change in his attitude to the significance of the war he is fighting. . . . Hillier's final realization is that . . . the game on the floor of the world is a copy of the big war and as such must be taken seriously.

As in *A Clockwork Orange*, Burgess sets up a false choice and then reveals the true one. The pattern is again made obvious through the striking use of doubles: death must be compensated for by the other half of the duality, procreation. . . . The structure of the novel is a series of double scenes. . . . Burgess forces upon us the necessary degree of detachment so that we can perceive the metaphysical fable underneath the spy thriller. Form echoes theme brilliantly for the spy-thriller form here is an imposture, a game version of a metaphysical fable, just as the war between good and evil on earth imitates that in Heaven.

Part of *Enderby* was originally published as *Inside Mr. Enderby* under the pseudonym, Joseph Kell. The novel *Enderby* as it now stands in the edition published in the United States presents two visions of a poet. In the first and last parts, posterity, through a fantasy visit of a schoolmaster and a group of unappreciative school children, is watching the sleeping Enderby. Only in this way does the reader learn that Enderby has become a major poet, whose poems are assigned as set books for national examinations. Ironically, in becoming important Enderby has become an object; the children have to be reminded that he is "not a thing to be prodded; he is a great poet sleeping." . . . "Thingness" is what Enderby, whose life is seen from his own point of view in the rest of the novel, has been avoiding all his life. While living he is a minor poet, not included in the anthologies, hardly known, with only the slightest intimation of the fantasy visit of posterity which he apprehends as a dream.

The part of the novel concerning Enderby's life seen from his point of view is fantasy only in the sense that the action is exaggerated, possible but improbable. Nevertheless, in

spite of the fact that the exaggeration serves primarily to make this a very comic book, . . . and the fact that the skeleton of Burgess's fable is much more fleshed than in the earlier novels, the same basic theme is here. Art depends on a choice of the duality of life over the neutrality of non-life. (pp. 142-43)

The dual nature of Enderby's life in [the] first part of the novel, composed of dirt and beauty, is summed up in the image of the lavatory, Enderby's "poetic seat." His poetry is written here, partly to suggest the function of art as time's cleanser and cathartiser, partly to suggest "a cell, smallest unit of life" . . . which is all that is necessary for art. Most of all, though, it conveys that duality which to Burgess is the essential nature of reality. The reader's associations with excrement and poetry are obviously in opposition to one another. (p. 144)

Although the end of the novel doubles the beginning . . . there is less emphasis in *Enderby* on the duality of reality, which this doubling has dramatized in other Burgess novels. It is implied, however, in Enderby's need for disorder to create order. Although *Enderby* offers the usual Burgess choice between life and no-life of the earlier novels, three important themes here—incest, the mysteriousness of reality, and the nature of bad art—point towards his next novel, *MF*. (pp. 145-46)

MF is an incredibly difficult book. . . . Burgess has dared to put the reader in the position of solving a whole series of riddles, not just those which Miles has to solve, but the riddles of the book itself. The reader is obviously intended to be placed in a position parallel to that of Miles, just as in *A Clockwork Orange* Nadsat conditioned the reader much as Alex was conditioned. *MF* is full of scraps of foreign languages . . . of conundrums, some of which Burgess has invented and some of which belong in folklore, of palinlogues, of every possible kind of word game.

To understand what Burgess is attempting here it is helpful to refer to two comments in his book on Joyce, who, after all, practiced many of these games before he did. The first concerns the significance of riddles and talks of the relationship between the mysteries of the cosmos and those of language. To Burgess, as to Joyce, there is more than a metaphorical connection between them: "The difficulties of *Ulysses* and, very much more, of *Finnegans Wake* are not so many tricks and puzzles and deliberate obscurities to be hacked at like jungle lianas: they represent those elements which surround the immediate simplicities of human society; they stand for history, myth, and the cosmos. Thus we have not merely to accept them but to regard them as integral."

The second is a comment about himself and the relationship between languages:

> Waking literature (that is literature that bows to time and space) is the exploitation of a single language. Dream-literature, breaking down all boundaries, may be more concerned with the phenomenon of language in general. . . .

In *MF* Burgess uses many languages as an indication of a fundamental structure basic to all languages. The fact that the reader does not need a translation is itself an illustration of Burgess's point. (pp. 146-47)

As the novel progresses Burgess expects the reader to solve them himself, but invariably gives the answer obliquely in the following sentence. For example, three riddles, the answers to which are Breath, Mouth, and Heart, are followed by the sentence, "The breath grew sour in my mouth, and my heart pumped hard." ... This is one of Burgess's methods of keeping the reader parallel to Miles, in the same relation to the experience of the novel. (p. 150)

Like all novelists of nightmare, Burgess takes us towards the mystery of infinity not the nothingness of the void. He answers the Post-existential premise that the world is irrational by a leap of faith that what we see is mystery not muddle. Each novel is constructed on a pattern of doubles to suggest a patterned, and therefore meaningful universe. His technique forces the reader to reconstruct the pattern, to fit the pieces together in an all-inclusive picture. The act of reading a novel of nightmare, like the act of writing it is, then, itself a way of transcending the Post-existential dilemma. (p. 154)

> Jean E. Kennard, "Anthony Burgess: Double Vision," in her Number and Nightmare: Forms of Fantasy in Contemporary Fiction (© 1975 by Jean E. Kennard), Archon Books, 1975, pp. 131-54.

BRUCE M. FIRESTONE

Mr. Burgess likes to portray the universe as a "duoverse," that is, a cluster of contending opposites which agitate against moderation. "The thing we're most aware of in life," he writes, "is the division, the conflict of opposites—good, evil; black, white; rich, poor—and so on." And since living in the center of this conflict is, to use Mr. Burgess's illustration, like trying to picnic in the middle of a football field, we gravitate naturally (and gratefully) toward any ideology which is able to convince us that this conflict is actually an illusion, that in fact there *is* somewhere an ultimate unity in which all extremes resolve themselves. To this end the Church proffers God; socialism, the classless society; and the artist, his art.

"Art," according to Burgess, "is the organization of base matter into an illusory image of universal order." The artist is an alchemist, drawing on the inherent disorder and dissonance of the human experience and somehow transmuting them into a dazzling display of order and harmony. Contending forces which divide our allegiances in the real world are tamed and reconciled in the artistic creation, or at least seem to be, and the illusion of unity is the final product of this creative process.

Yet though most people, according to Burgess, are possessed by the need to unify, they generally accept solutions rather than work out their own. How many Calvinists are there, after all, for every Calvin; how many Marxists for each Marx? Only the sexual division, the thing that makes a man different and apart from a woman (and vice-versa), is actually resolvable on an individual and thoroughly *active* level. This ritual, *grâce à Dieu*, is the exclusive possession of no one class or profession—there is, one assumes, no sexual aristocracy—and it may serve the artist as well or as poorly as it does anyone else. But it is of particular importance in Burgess's novels about artists because, as another means of achieving confluence, sex is closely allied with the creative act. It is, in fact, consistently used to reflect the condition of the less democratic syntheses which his artist-characters pursue.

Sex and art, then, serve as two separate though related expressions of the same drive, and because Burgess's protagonists in *Nothing Like the Sun* and *A Vision of Battlements* resort frequently to both, the two provide a good perspective on the conflict and confluence theme which figures so prominently in the ever-burgeoning Burgess canon. (pp. 46-7)

[In *A Vision of Battlements*] "the rock" looms like a threatening deity over the affairs of Sgt. Richard Ennis, Burgess's half-fictional protagonist who finds himself posted in wartime Gibraltar as instructor in the newly formed "Army Vocational and Cultural Corps." The unit is divided into two branches: the forward-looking "Vocational," which goes about training men to build a new world when the war is over; and the backward-looking "Cultural" (Ennis's), which is supposed to inculcate an appreciation for the arts, but languishes instead in the inattention of what C. P. Snow was to call the New Men. Ennis wants to make it in this new world, for his own sake as well as for his wife's (she eventually runs off with an American—the new world personified), but finds himself irresistibly attracted to the old: to his art, to the ancient culture of the Spanish and the Moors, and to his Spanish mistress, Concepción.

Burgess's description of the dilemma is characteristically direct: "Ennis had become a manichee, at home in a world of perpetual war. It did not matter what the flags or badges were; he looked only for the essential opposition—Wet and Dry, Left Hand and Right Hand, Yin and Yang, X and Y. Here was the inevitable impasse, the eternal stalemate." ... And down the line the alliances form. Ennis's English wife, Laurel, is cool, refined, aseptic; Concepción is rich, warm, fragrant. While Laurel is the England of the Norse gods and the briny sea, Concepción is Spain, the ancient mingling of Latin and Moorish cultures, the stronghold of the Catholic Church—not the defensive, displaced Catholicism of Ennis's (and Burgess's) Northern England, but the proud, entrenched faith of Mediterranean Europe. And while Ennis is portrayed as sexually impotent with his wife ("Really, you *are* impetuous"), he is seen to enjoy a quite satisfactory relationship with Concepción, the product of which, predictably enough, is conception. (pp. 47-8)

The dichotomy, of course, brings to mind Shakespeare, particularly the Shakespeare of the sonnets, who serves, if somewhat posthumously, as the subject of Burgess's *Nothing Like the Sun*. Fair England and dark Africa once more compete for the allegiance of the artist, and once more, it is the very delicate, refined beauty of the aristocratic North balanced against the rich and passionate allure of a black woman. In *Nothing Like the Sun* Concepción reappears as the dark lady, an East Indian woman of mysterious background whom Will woos and wins for his mistress; and Laurel's place is taken by young Harry (WH), Earl of Southampton, patron and sometime object of Will's hypergamous affections.

The important distinction between the two pairs, however, is not so much that the fair image turns male, but that the hostile/reverent attitude which characterized this relationship in *A Vision* takes on the added aspect of sexual attraction. With Laurel, Ennis is unable to achieve any sexual compatibility; rarely, in fact, does he think of her in sexual terms. But with young Harry, Will manages to express both his hostility and his admiration through the ambivalence of their homosexual relationship. Sex serves as a vengeance as well as a pleasure, and as a result, the role of the fair image in this novel becomes much more complex and much more vital.

Burgess carefully adumbrates the relationship which is to develop between Harry and the poet by inserting early in the narrative a number of passages which establish Will's homosexual leanings. (p. 48)

In the light of Burgess's concern with artistic synthesis, particularly synthesis as it carries over into sexual activity, homosexuality certainly seems a distortion of the drive to unite the male/female division. In *A Vision,* this is partially explained by the notion of channeling the energy which derives from the tension of conflict out of the natural heterosexual solution into the more demanding but ultimately more satisfying possibilities of art. The greater the sense of division, the more potent (and productive) the drive to unite it. When Ennis talks about transmuting lust into creative energy, it is to this that he is referring. The "calm epicene atmosphere" of Julian and his circle serves to dam the energy which might otherwise dissipate in lesser (i.e., sexual) activities.

But the relationship between the creative and the sexual impulse is much more complex than this simple equation of psychodynamics suggests, primarily because other factors enter into the process. For Ennis, as well as for Will, sexual excitement becomes almost a necessary condition for the creation of art. Time and again these artist/protagonists find themselves composing, often against their own will, at the height of their sexual passion. (p. 50)

In a sense, sexual heat becomes the *muse,* the inspiration to create. This is certainly the case in *Nothing Like the Sun,* where the entire narrative is built up around the conviction that the sonnets Shakespeare wrote stemmed from his bisexual entanglements. (p. 51)

But neither the homosexual nor the heterosexual relationship endures through the maturing of Shakespeare's own artistic abilities, and by the time he is ready to begin the period of the great tragedies both have virtually expired. Love ceases to be his goddess—fair or dark—and, simultaneously, love ceases to be his muse. The venereal disease which he contracts (Burgess speculating here) represents the product of his love, just as the miscarriage and death of Concepción in *A Vision* represent the end result of Ennis's love. Heterosexual love proves not only unproductive, as is the homosexual, but *destructive,* a force which is capable of inspiring the soul to create, but which in the process exacts a terrible price. The goddess is no longer one of love and sweet verse, as the early comedies certainly suggest, but an embodiment of the evil which shackles the lives of good men in the tragedies. Scabrous and near death, WS perceives that the disease which has come of his love is a metaphor for the evil that dominates all mankind, that ". . . the great white body of the world was set upon by an illness from beyond, gratuitous and incurable. And that even the name Love was, far from being the best invocation against it, often the very conjuration that summoned the mining and ulcerating hordes". . . . In both novels then the movement is away from this form of inspiration, and toward deeper and more personal wells of creative energy. Sexual love reveals itself to be far more destructive than it is procreative, and the division between man and woman, so al-

luring in its promise of synthesis, yields only to the confluence of the protagonist's art. (pp. 51-2)

> *Bruce M. Firestone, "Love's Labor's Lost: Sex and Art in Two Novels by Anthony Burgess," in* The Iowa Review *(copyright © 1977, by The University of Iowa), Vol. 8, No. 3 (Summer, 1977), pp. 46-52.*

ROBERT MARTIN ADAMS

[Like] Joyce, and like no other novelist in English, Burgess is fond of using language harmonically or impressionistically, and not just in nostalgic moods—he likes to strip words of their representational values and use them for their tonal values. This was apparent almost from the beginning. Without its special dialect, *A Clockwork Orange* would be not only a sparse but a muddled book, with its bare bones in evident disarray. (p. 166)

But the dialect of the novel performs several services for this rather crude fable. Being relatively opaque, it absorbs a lot of attention in its own right; it's a rich mixture of Russian conflated with English, Romany, rhyming slang, and Burgess-coinages, so that initially a lot of the meanings have to be guessed from the contexts. The reader is thus kept well occupied, not to say distracted; a good deal of his attention goes simply to the surface of the novel. Reading the book also involves a lot of back-and-forthing—that is, a word used in one context is given further meaning by its use in another context further on, which reflects back on its first usage. All this to-do on the linguistic surface of things blurs one's attention to the overall shape of the novel, and the scenes of gleeful sadism work to reinforce that desirable superficiality. It's a flat novel written in a thick, impasto style. The theme of music is integral to the novel, defined in this way; it makes for tonal unity on an immediate and impressionistic level, which is just another way of saying that the book is put together more like a movie than like a novel.

It is also a book, like those of Joyce, largely unconcerned with morality in any form. No doubt this was part of the reason for its popular success; it was an authentically cold book, at which a reader was entitled to shiver. Partly this was because of the society that Burgess envisioned, but partly also it derived from a personal artistic option within the book. One can almost feel the pathetic, beseeching figure of Poetic Justic imploring the novelist for admittance to his book and being roughly shouldered away. (p. 167)

Music in this novel . . . doesn't work in any logical way on the narration, nor is it an integral part of the plot, yet it's no less functional. In conjunction with the language, which is a major source of the book's vitality, it suggests a sphere of instinctual and uncorrupted response, . . . which contrasts with the asphalt jungle of the book itself. It's this intimation of the primeval and healthy barbaric, if only as a possibility within the corrupt, sick barbaric of the city slumster, that's distinctively Burgess and at the same time strongly Joycean.

Even more marked is the application of Joycean prose in a pure entertainment like *Tremor of Intent.* Burgess, like Joyce, is delighted by the linguistic patterns that form in the fading shadows of unconsciousness; and in this wholly implausible thriller, the most impressive and inventive passages are those where various characters . . . wander off for one reason or another into gaga-land, letting words, their sounds, and their associations take over for the common order of discourse, or imposing on them a whole new order of non-meanings. . . . [Though] it's only a dash of Joycean seasoning on books which are of a pretty common order, Burgess unmistakably uses that garnish, and not by any means to contemptible effect. . . . Burgess at the high point of his fictions escapes *into* Joycean language. (pp. 168-69)

> *Robert Martin Adams, in his* AfterJoyce: Studies in Fiction After "Ulysses" *(copyright © 1977 by Robert Martin Adams; reprinted by permission of Oxford University Press, Inc.), Oxford University Press, 1977.*

*　　*　　*

BUSCH, Frederick　1941-

Busch is an American novelist, short story writer, critic, and editor. His self-professed major concerns in writing are characterization and point of view, and his fiction has been praised for its precise use of language and uncluttered prose style. The basic, elemental aspects of life, particularly family relationships, form the subject matter of much of Busch's fiction. (See also *CLC,* **Vol. 7, and** *Contemporary Authors,* **Vols. 33-36, rev. ed.)**

RICHARD ELMAN

Domestic Particulars is a story of unspectacular martyrdoms, senseless sacrifices, of the endurance of long subway rides that end up nowhere except in front of dimly lighted houses behind shrubbery, of the cold of the marriage bed, and the stoicisms of a depression-minded generation, the specific betrayals of energy and excitement that result from the squandering of lives for caution's sake. . . .

Domestic Particulars is not an exhaustive treatise but a series of primary scenes, rich in incident and feeling, that seem to give the temperature of lives, and show the way they have been turning. Busch, who is one of our finest short story writers, is not ashamed of what his characters talk about and say. If they have any dignity it is because they are allowed to speak out of their feelings. (p. 468)

This novel has many . . . moments when its characters do things we almost wish for the sake of decorum they would not do, and then we realize that it is the same humanness that made them such victims which has now provided them with the gestures to express their victimization. It is an honest, angry, compassionate work, written with all the specificities of technique of the new novelists, but nowhere simply doing things for the sake of showing off. *Domestic Particulars* is committed to its strong subject matter, like people in a hostile integration, and to the air and light of particular days in Brooklyn, or on the upper West Side, to the look of the hills at sunset in upper New York State, or the complaining inner voice of Claire as she remembers a friend from her Greenwich Village days. . . .

This is not just another family novel; we do not come away from it feeling reconciled, or at peace with ourselves. What is radical to the work is its insistence on the separateness of these three lives, its painful understanding that so much was self-inflicted in an indifferent world not out of love but lovelessness, its awareness of bitterness and defeats, without redemption, and its sense of the littleness, the pettiness, the meanness of these characters that does not, oddly enough, demean them but gives them whatever stature they may have.

Publication of this work should bring Busch the larger audience he deserves. Of novelists under 40 in this country, he is one of the very few active practitioners who can combine an astonishing use of language with a really first-rate memory; he is brilliant, imaginative, and more often than not, just. (p. 469)

> *Richard Elman, "Specific Instances of Pain," in* The Nation *(copyright 1976 by the Nation Associates, Inc.), November 6, 1976, pp. 468-69.*

DONALD J. GREINER

[Busch's] first books, *I Wanted a Year Without Fall* (1971) and *Breathing Trouble* (1973), will become known as apprentice fiction, books in which he begins his tentative explorations of unspectacular lives surviving small but numbing crises. They are serviceable fictions that will be discussed and analyzed in future years as introductions to what may develop into a significant canon. With *Manual Labor* (1974) and *Domestic Particulars* (1976), however, Busch shows his mastery of familial frustration, his control of the sacrifices, misunderstandings, and love which make up the daily routine for most of us. The metaphors are convincing, the reading experience painful, the prose precise yet poetic. (p. 101)

Manual Labor is a novel about rebuilding a marriage, the sheer effort involved in renovating two lives. Physical work and emotional energy are expended, and the toil is exhausting. The title becomes a metaphor which reflects not only the work by Phil and Anne Sorenson to restore an old house but also the labor of bearing children. . . . What gives the novel its power is that the Sorensons are literally hoping to create their future lives out of the bloody losses of their immediate past. . . .

The distinction between Anne's terror of death [in childbirth] and Phil's fear for the death of their marriage is crucial, one that reflects on their attitudes toward the manual labor. Anne says that the work is a duty; Phil insists that it is for "us." In the opening pages Busch suggests, through the structuring metaphor of renovating the building, that their future together is as precarious as their dilapidated house. . . . (p. 102)

Following . . . introductions of pain and loss, Busch turns to the two sustained points of view which structure the novel. Anne's is an interior monologue couched in the form of a never-sent letter to his mother who, she thinks, pressures her for grandchildren. Busch lets her describe her own despair, and the effect is telling. Crazed with fear and grief, she loses the ability even to talk with Phil: "How could we say what couldn't be said?" So she writes letters she will not mail; Phil composes poems he refuses to send out; and their communication drowns in mental anguish and physical loss. The point is that the tension is never overtly stated. It remains, as it were, between the lines, accumulating as the novel progresses. Yet through all, through silence, solitude, and despair, their insistence on living is tenacious. Anne briefly considers and then rejects suicide as something that "sounds like medicine. Something you clean clogged drains with." . . . She wants order, not further chaos.

Busch narrates not the necessity of anything so melodramatic as physical suicide but the sheer effort involved in recovery from spiritual collapse. He parallels Anne's hesitancy about the manual labor on the house with her fear to take chances with creative literature.... Busch is especially good with little touches of domestic suffering, and we understand that the breakdown in the daily routine chronicles the collapse into a quagmire of pain and discord. Surviving but not living, [Phil and Anne] nevertheless wait for recovery. (pp. 103-04)

Busch encourages our concern for Anne with the sustained monologue; developing the perspective from her point of view, he narrows the distance between reader and narrator and convinces us to sympathize. We realize that instead of reading about a wife indulging in suffering while her husband renovates their marriage, we are witnessing two quiet acts of heroism: her determination not to kill herself and his commitment to showing her how the ordering act of physically rebuilding a house can transfer to the restoration of their lives. . . .

Sitting in a shack following a day of manual labor, [Phil] begins a journal. Anne writes to explain despair, but Phil creates to sustain life. His narration is an act of faith, a way of imposing, even creating order in the midst of their grievous losses. (p. 104)

What makes Phil's point of view so effective is that he struggles as much with the narrative as he does with the marriage. Aware that both are interwoven, he comments directly upon the novel he is composing. Rather than fear literature as Anne does, Phil resolves to create it. (p. 105)

Similar problems face the family in *Domestic Particulars*. Perhaps the heart of this moving novel can be found in Harry's explanation about "the flesh tearing away, the language less than adequate, the madness of continuing." They hang on because they care. Despite the pain and the misunderstanding, despite all the frustration and death, they continue to live and love. As we read, we follow their efforts to sustain themselves as a family from 1919 to 1976. Some readers may call *Domestic Particulars* a cycle of tales because the chapters vary points of view and time frames, but the book has the continuities of character, narrative concern, and mood which might not be expected in an unconventional novel. (p. 106)

Busch's touch is so light and yet so sure. Situations which might become maudlin here show up moving and true. Dressing his characters for life, he brings them through domestic particulars to the point where they no longer hope for fulfillment but demand it. How do mother and father adjust to a son who grows up "because families are—write it down, it's a definition—what you finally have to leave?" . . .

The heroics of hanging on; Busch convinces us to care about these little lives. An omniscient narrator oversees the final two chapters and shows us Harry checking *The Book of Fascinating Facts*, a childhood gift from his parents, for a comment on "Can Dreams Come True?" Apparently they can, explains the compiler, but Harry is not so sure. Still in search of his memories, he pays a last visit to an old friend of the family to ask, "do you remember my life when I was young?" He has so little, he explains, only a few facts. Mrs. Miriam cannot fill in the missing "it" that he longs for, but she does give him some advice: "It's done and put away and you should leave it. . . . Leave it where it is." . . . The end of the novel hints that he does just that. Although ambiguous, the final paragraphs detailing Harry's

deliberate motions as he drives away suggest his decision to live not with his ghosts but with himself. (p. 110)

In *Manual Labor* and *Domestic Particulars*, Busch expresses the tension between family misery and the desperation to continue living. Where does Frederick Busch go from here?—a question bound to be asked about a thirty-six-year-old author of four books of fiction. Chances are that his narrative voice will change, that his sense of fiction will include other concerns. . . . What matters, finally, is how Busch's novels confirm that American fiction is alive and well, revitalizing the language while shoring up our lives. (p. 111)

> Donald J. Greiner, "After Great Pain: The Fiction of Frederick Busch," in Critique: Studies in Modern Fiction (copyright © by James Dean Young 1977), Vol. XIX, No. 1, 1977, pp. 101-11.

JOHN ROMANO

[Something] exciting is going on in Busch's work that isn't going on anywhere else. Some of his virtues are old-fashioned enough: he's a superb storyteller, and he makes up people he cares about greatly. But finally his talent is anomalous, and the nature of his achievement is peculiarly hard to describe.

One way to begin is by taking note of a paradox that virtually rules contemporary taste in the arts. As an afternoon of gallery-going or a week of off-Broadway will show you, the approved formula for a new work, according to this paradoxical law, is that it should contain inverse proportions of emotional intensity and representation. In other words, great intensity is okay, if the art isn't descriptive or realistic or "about" anything real; whereas representational art, even a certain brand of realism, is okay, if its level of feeling is low enough. (p. 23)

So we have this curious divorce of feeling from the things that cause feeling, and the rarest artist, these days, is the one who, like Frederick Busch, is both mimetic *and* intense, and succeeds at the same time in sounding contemporary. His prose forswears the cool machinery of recent literary styles, as announced plainly on the first page of . . . *I Wanted a Year Without Fall* (1971):

> Listen to an old-time lay: I am adrift, and no one now can say by whom and by what smoky light and in which acid waters I am going to be found, as Leo found me, once upon a time of night and five flights up off Charles Street, summer ripening too fast for fruit, a sweet and nasty sense of rot already in the air, and on the pavement and in my rooms. I was in underwear and sweating through. I was in darkness on the bed, listening for roaches, or listening for the sound of sweat, or listening for the song that blood sang when I turned my face to the pillow and held it there until I insisted on breath.

What's anti-chic here is that the words don't quite consent to flow; the writing is lyrical but it's awkward, too, mimicking the body's discomfort, the labor of trying to breathe on a summer night that's too hot and still. Effort, labor, breath that comes hard: there's a collection of stories by Busch called *Breathing Trouble* (1973), and a novel called *Manual Labor* (1974).

Manual Labor, by the way, is Frederick Busch's best work to date—indeed, it's one of the most powerful contemporary novels I know.... The book is a sort of recitation for three voices, the fetus and its parents, their words almost woozy with pain and grief and loss. But what finally staves off morbidity, and keeps the writing on its feet, is Busch's unshakable specificity of physical imagery—the blood in the *linoleum* hallway, the "crimson slush"—so that it is not just a ghoulish hallucination of a miscarriage but somehow an actual event, with textures and contours that limit it. Again, the unfashionable synthesis: intensity *and* realism. (pp. 23-4)

It's significant that Busch, in his verbal onslaughts, wrings an almost bodily response from the reader, because a distinctive mark of his stories is their terribly intelligent concern with what might be called the plight of having a body.... Frederick Busch revives, in drastically reconstructed terms, the old romantic dilemma of being simultaneously, conflictually both spirit and flesh.

A figure that recurs in Busch's work is the man who's so fat he almost can't breathe. In the story called "Breathing Trouble," the fat man drives away his wife and child, whom he loves infernally much, and then stuffs himself with food to assuage his guilt and loneliness: "Do you understand," he says, "that I am being squeezed to death by calories. Another bite and my breathing stops.... Give me enough time, the heart will harden up and turn off-yellow and fall into my stomach and break me in half. Man, thirty years old, crushed by own heart. Too much fat too soon, say M.D.s." ... The protagonist of "Breathing Trouble" resembles Harry, the protagonist of "The Trouble with Being Food": big with appetites that he feeds without pleasure, almost literally taut with irony and self-hatred. There's a pent-up-ness about these characters that has something to do with the very aesthetic of Busch's stories, in which strong draughts of emotion are trapped, confined in brief, terse forms—in Busch's own phrase, "like a pattern of explosion caught and kept." Maybe it is true in a general way, as John Crigler says in a study of Faulkner, that the best short stories are over-stuffed, that they show signs of resenting the smallness and insufficiency of their size, and spill over messily in protest; coughing, sweating, and claustrophobic, like Busch's fat men, who are so fleshy that they give off steam, but are not at home in their flesh. For all of the characters in Busch's world, comfort is impossible. They move and speak and write with that excessive, deliberate, and defensive grace which is really the reverse of ease and belonging. Busch's achievement is to have scrutinized, with sympathy and guts and humor, the internal places of such ineluctable discomfort. It's there he's planted the ladders of his art.

As for ["The Trouble with Being Food"], it might prove an unfortunate introduction to this writer, suffering, as it does, from his chief pitfall: he's an indulgent writer, and gives us, as a rule, too much. It's a vice I'm inclined to be merciful toward, because what he gives us too much of is that emotional actuality which most contemporary writers leave us hungry for. But the excess—in this case, an excess of sympathy for a finally repugnant triangle of lovers—muddies the presentation of a potentially dramatic situation. *Domestic Particulars,* from which the story is taken, describes itself as a "family chronicle," episodes from the lives of three generations of Brooklyn Jews, literate, liberal, and poor. In shaping relationships among them, Busch pursues to an extreme one of the themes of *Manual Labor:* that one of the tricks of our nature is that we continue to love and need people whom we've ceased to understand, or have never understood, and that a helpless, inarticulate pathos attaches to such bonds. This hurtful impasse is the special provence of *Domestic Particulars,* and, as usual with Busch, it's the hurt that's most interesting. But the family members in their isolation are too alike within. You don't feel, as you do in the earlier novel, that in changing narrators the writer leaps from one world of consciousness to another, but rather that everyone is trapped in the same downward drag. And the flirtation in *Domestic Particulars* is not with morbidity, but with self-pity.

Against these reservations should be set the unavoidable sense that Frederick Busch is immensely what the doctor ordered. As a worker with words he is abundantly self-conscious and adept, but the streets are full, alas, of qualified paragraph-makers. His importance, which is already considerable and can be expected to grow, lies elsewhere: he is one of a small party who are resuscitating an ancient use of words, to connect us to our feeling, to refresh our vulnerabilities, to waken in the mind the prospect of an edifying pain. (p. 24)

> *John Romano, "Frederick Busch: Mimesis and Intensity," in* New York Arts Journal *(copyright © 1978 by Richard W. Burgin), February-March, 1978, pp. 23-4.*

NICHOLAS DELBANCO

[*The Mutual Friend*] is a venturesome novel, a substantial achievement, and it should be widely read. For the author of *Manual Labor* and *Domestic Particulars,* this new work represents a change. The previous books were in some sense family documents—intensely personal texts, charged with contemporary discourse and present problems. Busch seemed a kind of poet of claustrophobia. Whether writing of the city or farm, in Brooklyn or New England's hills, he stayed very close to the bone. His characters had *Breathing Trouble,* as in an early title; he cut tight, constricting circles, and had his people leashed.

Now the circles have enlarged. *The Mutual Friend,* as its name should suggest, owes a great deal to Charles Dickens. It starts with Dickens in America, on a reading tour, and ends with the end of the 19th century, in a London charity hospital.... Busch's erudition has been put to fruitful use. The scholarship is unobtrusive yet always germane. His habit of disjunction (the stock-in-trade of a short-story writer, perhaps) seems formally appropriate: the novel has six separate units....

Whole sections of the novel are lifted from Dickens; his will is transcribed verbatim, as are swatches of the scenes —Nancy Sykes's murder, for instance—he read to such acclaim....

[The] risk, of course, entails the great original; why should the reader not disregard Busch and turn again to Dickens? (p. 26)

Somehow, however, *The Mutual Friend* manages to gain from and yield nothing to *Our Mutual Friend.* This has much to do with the narrative device. Dickens is a ghostly presence in the charity hospital, enduring in remembrance and "written" by Dolby and Moon.... There's a certain archness in these visions, and revisions, and whether it's Dickens or Dolby or Moon seems sometimes just a self-reflexive game. (pp. 26-7)

Yet the whole has resonance. Dickens as "A Man of Parts" has stamped himself indelibly on every page; those who witnessed him cannot forget or exorcise the ghost. Therefore they spell him, in several styles. And the pastiche accumulates, at last, into something reverential: almost as if the unsayable name has been said, the voice from the whirlwind transcribed. Such referents are intentional; the book is about one writer's God. . . .

Eliot, in "Tradition and the Individual Talent," speaks of the way the present artist must engage the past. There's a vibrant rearranging—a kind of nexus established between those masterpieces that inform our culture, and our culture's need to continue. Such dialectic when successful has a double power: we lose sight neither of our origins nor the notion that art is original. *The Mutual Friend* seems to me to demonstrate this doubling conjunction—Busch has profited from Dickens, and the reader profits equally.

If an artist's reach is circular, as suggested above, then as his reach and grasp extend we come to be included. The concentric circles that surround this novel are large indeed —implicating by extension the very root of tale-telling: a twice-told story become familiar, subject to interpretation, and all the more welcome for that. *The Mutual Friend* is first-rate. (p. 27)

Nicholas Delbanco, in The New Republic *(reprinted by permission of* The New Republic; © 1978 by The New Republic, Inc.), *March 25, 1978.*

ROGER SALE

The subject of Frederick Busch's intelligent, careful, often brilliant, but inert novel ["The Mutual Friend"] is Charles Dickens, the driven dying Dickens of 1867-70 as summoned up by Dolby, his tour manager and companion, as he himself is dying 30 years later, a charity case in a Fulham hospital. . . .

It is a serious and scrupulous fiction Mr. Busch has concocted. . . . There are no elaborate set pieces of Victoriana, no huggermugger "vivid sights and sounds" where we might expect to find Oliver Twist or Pip walking down the street. Nor does Mr. Busch attempt to do a version of the Victorian novel, à la "The French Lieutenant's Woman." This is a contemporary American novel, written by a man who once wrote a book about John Hawkes. . . .

The most striking positive virtue of "The Mutual Friend" is Mr. Busch's way with Dickens's voice, as speaker and occasional narrator. For Mr. Busch to try to make Dickens speak just as he wrote would have been folly, because that would make Mr. Busch both a competitor and a writer of pastiche. But it would have been equally foolish to have tried to imagine Dickens speaking in a way that had nothing to do with the way he wrote. It is a ticklish task, and on the whole Mr. Busch handles it admirably.

Roger Sale, "Not Quite Dickensian," in The New York Times Book Review *(© 1978 by The New York Times Company; reprinted by permission), April 9, 1978, p. 10.*

C

CARROLL, Paul Vincent   1900-1968

An Irish dramatist and short story writer, Carroll once said of himself, "I write as Ibsen did. I take the life of a small village and enlarge it to encompass all human life." He developed what he termed "that unquenchable love of the drama" at Dublin's Abbey Theatre, where his first plays were produced. While teaching in Glasgow, Carroll discovered the writings of Jonathan Swift. Although profoundly influenced by Swift, Carroll never became as bitter in his satire or as bleak in his philosophy as his master. He also wrote movie scenarios and television scripts, and was a founding director of the Glasgow Citizens' Theatre. (See also *Contemporary Authors*, Vols. 9-12, rev. ed.; obituary, Vols. 25-28, rev. ed.)

SISTER ANN GERTRUDE COLEMAN

It was Paul Vincent Carroll who gave to the stage several portrayals of the Catholic priest in plays which not only dramatize the position of the priest in Catholic Ireland's national life, but also question the relation of religion to the daily life of the people. Carroll, up to the present time, at least, has neither peer nor imitator in this kind of Irish play. The figure of the Catholic priest has appeared frequently in modern Irish prose fiction, but only occasionally and incidentally in plays. (p. 87)

Irish-born Paul Vincent Carroll . . . wrote several plays, as distinctive as those of any of his great predecessors in the Abbey Theater, in which he frequently dramatized the conflict between the liberal and the illiberal wings of Catholicism in Ireland, often showing a sensitive concern for the plight of the rebel against oppressive convention imposed from within or from without. In two of his best-known plays, *Shadow and Substance* and *The White Steed*, he sets a type of obtuse Irish priest in opposition to a type of intransigent liberal, and at the stupidities of everyone involved, whether cleric or layman, he hits very hard indeed.

In a youthful tragedy entitled *Things That Are Caesar's*, presented at the Abbey Theater in August, 1932, Carroll broods over the spiritual decay in the family life of an Irish Catholic home. The play is unrelieved by even a little hope; nor does any character in it reveal the brighter side of the Irish nature, such as one finds in his more mature plays. Apparently Carroll later moved toward a more profound insight and a broader, deeper sympathy, for in *The Strings, My Lord, Are False*, produced just ten years later, the priest becomes a symbol of Christian heroism and many characters exemplify some of the finest traits in the Irish disposition.

One of Carroll's most significant plays is *Shadow and Substance*. . . . It is a deeply felt play about life, religion and education in one of the hill towns of County Louth, where Carroll was born. (pp. 88-9)

The penetrating analysis of Irish Catholic life in *Shadow and Substance* is more complex than that in any other Carroll play. The structure of the plot rests on two main personalities, each utterly unlike the other, yet closer in love and understanding and spiritual affinity than are any other characters to either of these or to each other. . . .

In Carroll's next play, *The White Steed*, . . . he again brings into focus the ugly differences between the shadow and the substance of true Catholicism by bringing together some remarkable character contrasts in both clerical and lay life. The play attacks pride, cruelty, stupidity, and the type of mind that identifies the Church with certain modern corruptions in art and piety.

Confined to his wheel chair, Canon Matt Lavelle, wise, tolerant, understanding, watches his administrator, Father Shaughnessy, bring into the parish fanaticism, intolerance and cruelty. The dramatic conflict resolves itself into a combat between benevolence, charity and tolerance on one hand and harshness, tyranny and terror on the other. (p. 90)

In the struggle of humanity against tyranny, which is chiefly what *The White Steed* is about, the canon states the case against religious feeling infected by puritanism and zealotry. Implicitly he pleads for a return to the mystical spirituality permeated by the spirit of St. Francis, which had beautified Ireland's religious faith in the old days of her monastic glory.

This evident affection for Franciscan spirituality is also present in a less-well-known play of Carroll, *The Wise Have Not Spoken*. . . . The play takes its title from a fragment of Padraic Pearse's poem, "The Fool":

> Since the wise have not spoken, I speak
> Who am only a fool. . . .

The only attractive character in this dark, hopeless, bitterly tragic play about Ireland is Tiffany, the silenced priest. He has a deep and gentle love of Holy Church and a tender anxiety for her welfare, but his notions of the brotherhood of man are judged to be so evangelical as to be considered dangerously radical. (pp. 91-2)

Carroll continues to hammer away at human corrosives in a Christian society in his war play, *The Strings, My Lord, Are False.* . . . As in *The White Steed*, there is in this play a lovable, largehearted canon who opens the crypt of his church and his own house as shelters during the Clydeside air raids. . . .

The canon's simple love of humanity, his gentle forbearance with human frailities are set against the religious intolerance and hypocrisy of some among his flock who hide their viciousness behind a façade of respectability as they mercilessly condemn a "fallen" woman of the parish. The central situation of this play provides Carroll with the occasion for his angriest invective, directed at those Christians who, even in the most savage war in history, would sacrifice the safety and preservation of people to their own gains. (p. 92)

In just about every play that Paul Vincent Carroll has written, he seems to have a twofold critical purpose: to hold up to reprobation certain very unpleasant habits of thought and conduct in Irish Catholic life—or any Catholic life—and to provide a corrective in the character of one or two admirable persons in each play, excepting *Things That Are Caesar's*, which is unrelievedly bleak. Carroll's plays, however, are not solely caviling; they are also a plea for the restoration of those virtues which infused and vitalized the spiritual life of an older Ireland, particularly the virtues emanating from the monastic spirit on which Irish spirituality was formed long ago and which writers like Carroll seem to believe have become obfuscated by laziness, unworthy ambition, materialism and mediocrity, which have overgrown the soil of Irish life.

Although Paul Vincent Carroll has castigated the clergy and the merchant class for waxing rich or powerful, or both, on the outcome of civil war and national independence; although he has written a stinging exposé of Catholic Ireland's school system; although he has created a portentous picture of religious hypocrisy, fanaticism, bigotry and the mob spirit they can let loose, in no sense can Carroll be said to be either anticlerical or anti-Catholic. His most lovable priests are eminently worthy priests, and they usually carry the weight of the play's meaning. And if in some of Carroll's plays there is the shadow of gloom, there is finally the substance of Christian hope.

Nevertheless, there is an abundance of fine satire in Carroll's plays (as well as wit and mysticism . . .), and it is generally directed against pietism in which there is neither innocence nor enthusiasm, but cunning and self-interest. At the heart of some Catholic family life Carroll sees and attacks all the bleak pharisaical bitterness and jealousies; he sees and deplores spiritual pride born of a narrow concept of religion, vindictiveness hidden under the show of duty, a combination of vulgarity and insincerity, and a mad pursuit of material prosperity in which every standard is thrown aside except success. (p. 93)

> *Sister Anne Gertrude Coleman, "Paul Vincent Carroll's View of Irish Life," in* Catholic World *(copyright 1960 by The Missionary Society of St. Paul the Apostle in the State of New York), November, 1960, pp. 87-93.*

PAUL A. DOYLE

Unquestionably, Carroll suffered because he lacked the charisma of O'Casey or Behan, yet in any sensible estimate of modern Irish drama, Carroll must be rated the most important dramatic talent in the Irish theatre since the early writings of O'Casey. (p. 15)

[The title, *Things That Are Caesar's*,] epitomizes the basic thematic motifs found in most of Carroll's early writing: the conflict between God and Mammon, Church and State, and Flesh and Spirit. Carroll became intrigued by observing these particular forces at work in each individual and determined to ponder the divisions, torments, and tragedies that resulted from such opposing elements in the nature of man. (p. 20)

[*Shadow and Substance* is] presented in the Ibsen formula of a tightly constructed play with intensely probing character revelation. But Carroll's ability with dialogue is his own gift. The conversation is quick-paced, concise, sharp, and frequently ironic, satiric, and humorous. Several of the dialogue exchanges are as keen and as lively as any conversations conceived by a modern dramatists. . . . The drama critics, who enthusiastically applauded the play, used such comments as "passionate eloquence," "probing power," "spiritual beauty," and "tender and sensitive," but the play is also masterly for its adept use of satire and irony. It possesses an astringency that both bites and purifies.

Like O'Casey in his anti-clericism and like Synge in his attack on Irish characteristics, Carroll tried to capture all that he found distasteful in Ireland and to present these aspects on the stage. (p. 36)

While the play has aspects that are rather peculiarly Irish, it is not simply an Irish play. . . . It establishes that pride, violence, intolerance, and similar abominations are false and vicious shadows compared with the essential substance of fundamental faith and humanity. (p. 37)

Carroll [in his conception of heroism is similar] to Yeats, Joyce, AE, and numerous other modern Irish writers who were obsessed with the desire for heroism in an unheroic world. *Kindred* demonstrates that Carroll was well-acquainted with a concept stressed in several of Yeats's plays; viz., that the gods must have human assistance before they can achieve their purposes. Furthermore, *Kindred*'s search for a new leader reflects the general Messianic ideal among Irish writers who were preoccupied with the heroic personality and with heroic ideals for Ireland. . . . In his portrayal of heroism and heroic qualities—in various forms—Carroll returns again and again to this theme in several of his plays, *Kindred* being his most philosophically grandiose statement of such conceptions.

Unfortunately, both for Carroll's high thinking and for his career, *Kindred* fails as a play—for several reasons. It is too often melodramatic, artificial, and stagey—at times almost wooden. (p. 47)

The majority of Carroll's stories can be classified as tales of humor, character sketches, and ghostly sagas—all of which usually inculcate some moral point, sometimes too obtrusively, at other times with just the precise amount of understatement and subtlety. Rarely does he venture to write the type of short story which is intended to be read and reread for additional insights and perceptions. When he does attempt such a purpose, as in "Home Sweet Home," his most artistic narrative, he demonstrates an ability to handle his material skillfully. (p. 93)

"Home Sweet Home" lingers long in the memory and repays endless readings. It stirs thoughts of man's deepest instincts, of love-hate relationships, and of the perpetual conflict between his need to be free and the demands of conformity, between man's highest aspirations and earthbound requirements.

Carroll's short stories are generally credible in plot and are marked by a deft handling of dialogue and local color. He captures fully the flavor and atmosphere of the scene about which he writes, sustains narrative interest, and with relatively few strokes, brings his characters to life. His narratives never fail to be entertaining. On the other hand they lack symbolic depths and, except for "Home Sweet Home," the intriguing interplay of memories, reflections, and internal perceptions which are the hallmarks of the best modern short stories.

The stories do illustrate many of the elements found in Carroll's plays: his gift for humor, satire, and irony; his talent for character revelation and inventive plotting; and his fundamental moral concerns. The preachment aspect basic in many of the narratives is reminiscent of Carroll's early playwriting while the more amusing tales link closely with the later period when his reforming zeal decreased but never completely vanished. (pp. 94-5)

Any overall estimate of Carroll's career must indicate that he well deserves a permanent place in contemporary Irish and English drama with his two finest achievements (*Shadow and Substance* and *The White Steed*), with two highly enjoyable satirical comedies (*The Devil Came from Dublin* and *The Wayward Saint*), and with three plays which have faults but which are talented works (*Things That Are Caesar's, The Wise Have Not Spoken,* and *Goodbye to the Summer*). In addition, Carroll has created the most convincing portraits of clergymen and clerical life yet to appear on the Irish stage. . . . Since the clergy enjoy such a dominant role in the life of the people, in-depth portrayals of their character and activities are fundamental in understanding Ireland. In the enthusiasm for the accuracy of such portraits as Canon Skerritt, Canon Lavelle, Father Shaughnessy, and curates like Fathers Kirwan and Corr, it should not be forgotten that Carroll has created memorable characters from all walks of life. (p. 108)

At his best Carroll is one of the wittiest and talented masters of dramatic satire and irony twentieth century drama has produced. Although his two non-reforming extravaganzas abound in humor and ironies, he demonstrated a born genius for these qualities throughout most of his career. Quite central to his work was his realization that at heart the Irish character is filled with mysticism. Carroll once said that an Irishman "knows he is the lost child of some celestial hall of high splendors." He wrote that deep spiritual stirrings are inherent in the Irish nature and quoted AE's line, "You cannot all disguise the majesty of fallen gods." . . . [This quality] gives most of Carroll's plays a universality and depth lacking in less thoughtful and perceptive Irish writers and further increases the lure his work holds.

With all his accomplishments and abilities, it is distressing that Carroll did not, particularly in the 1940s, achieve his potential. Curiously enough, his career in one basic respect

parallels O'Casey's. They both successfully started with a gripping realistic play—*Things That Are Caesar's* and *The Shadow of a Gunman;* then they experienced two hit dramas, and then a decline from their two most important works. Unlike O'Casey, however, Carroll did not possess the lyrical and poetic qualities that would have given his secondary work more distinction. But, like O'Casey, he became caught up and waylaid by the siren call of symbolism and allegory and also, like O'Casey, he became too message-and-thesis conscious so that with the advent of *Kindred,* instead of the themes emerging subtly from the play, they too often seem to be the principal reason for the play's existence.

If Carroll is not so great a dramatist as he should have been, these are the reasons why. He came to allow his heart to rule his head, to preach almost unceasingly the nobleness of, and need for, love, dignity, tolerance, and understanding at the expense of retaining consistent dramatic control, clearness, and firmness. To say this, however, is not to ignore the fact that as long as the modern English theatre exists, Carroll's best dramas will be played, and these works, and the characters existing therein, are sufficient reason indeed for placing him in the pantheon of significant modern playwrights. (pp. 108-10)

> *Paul A. Doyle, in his* Paul Vincent Carroll
> *(©1971 by Associated University Presses,*
> *Inc.), Bucknell University Press, 1971.*

ROBERT HOGAN

The great strength of *Shadow and Substance* lay primarily in the juxtaposition of two beautifully drawn and brilliantly contrasted characters. . . . Based vaguely on Carroll's interpretation of the character of Jonathan Swift, [the character Cannon Skerritt] actually reflects those facets of Swift with which Carroll himself most identified—the intellectual pride, the arrogance, the austerity, the savage contempt for folly. But if Canon Skerritt represents a stern and cold facet of Paul Vincent Carroll himself, these qualities were superbly balanced in the play by the Canon's young serving-girl Brigid. In Brigid's mysticism, simplicity, warm humanity and spiritual humility, another and probably more significant side of Carroll's own character was evident. These opposed contrarities combined to create one of the most solidly built, bitingly caustic and deeply moving plays to emerge from the remarkable dramatic movement of modern Ireland.

There are, I think, two reasons for Carroll's inability to create other plays as thoroughly memorable as *Shadow and Substance.* Although *The White Steed* was nearly as fine, and although his jeu d'esprit *The Devil Came from Dublin* really only needs a final polishing and tightening, in most of his other plays he was unable to achieve quite the same excellent balance of his own clashing character traits. In most of his other work, he seemed either totally Swiftian or totally Brigid-like. When he swung toward the Swiftian pole, as in *Things That Are Caesar's,* or *The Wise Have Not Spoken,* or *Farewell to Greatness!,* he was not always able to keep his savagery, his ferocity, his satire and his contempt for folly within reasonable bounds. To an appreciable extent, each of these plays is strident, harsh and a bit unbelievable. In *The Wise Have Not Spoken,* for instance, he describes the modern world as "a tower of Babel where fools, puritans, and scoundrels shout each other down. . . . a warping, killing, crookening rat-trap where the human mind and spirit are driven mad.'' In *Farewell to Greatness!*, his *saeva indignatio* takes a sexual bent, and Swift's detestation of Vanessa becomes so ferocious that it is simply inhuman and psychopathic.

When, however, Carroll veered, as he most often did, around to the Brigid point of view, he usually became too simple and too saccharine. In plays like *The Wayward Saint, The Old Foolishness* and the unpublished *The Lady from Nowhere-at-All,* he lacks the restraining critical brake of satire. In *The Wayward Saint,* he romanticizes goodness; in the nearly successful *The Old Foolishness,* he romanticizes romance itself; in *The Lady from Nowhere-at-All,* he amazingly romanticizes sexuality. The final effect of each play is no more convincing than his solely cold and critical plays.

A second reason for Carroll's inability to create other plays as integrated as *Shadow and Substance* is that as an artist he was largely untouched by the great political and social movements of his time. Only one play, *The Strings, My Lord, Are False* [about the bombing of Glasgow in World War II], has as its subject any of the notably traumatic events of the century. (pp. 3-4)

Carroll did, of course, react to his world, but the reaction was almost entirely through a personal, local vision. Even *Strings* was not played out on an important world stage, but in a backwater of the war. (p. 4)

When Carroll did write about social problems, they were ones limited to a quite particular area, a cultural neighbourhood that he knew well, that he had personally experienced. His *Goodbye to the Summer,* for instance, is about the depopulation of rural areas in Scotland and the relocation of people in urban tenements. Although it contains much craftsmanlike work, the play simply does not transcend its milieu. . . . *Green Cars Go East,* however, a play about the social waste of the Glasgow slums, almost does manage to transcend its faithfully evoked time and place. . . . Only finally, in its last act, does the play fail, and it fails because of the author's intrusive humanity. His Brigid self took over and destroyed the critical balance. He became too compassionate for his beleaguered characters, and so he tampered with his brilliantly established reality and imposed an artificially happy ending.

Most of Carroll's plays are about Ireland, and this fact also testifies to his personal vision. . . . His view of Ireland . . . is in the early plays based upon the quite personal reaction of a very young and very bright man to the stultifyingly bigoted and provincial society of his home town of Dundalk. Out of this memory of his formative years came the best of his early work—*Things That Are Caesar's, Shadow and Substance* and *The White Steed.* It has sometimes been remarked that Carroll, like Ibsen of the middle plays, seemed to be writing about the same people. There almost seemed a Paul Vincent Carroll stock company, whose leading members were the Young Girl, the village Canon, the village Schoolmaster, and the chorus of gossips. Of course, this was quite true, for he was writing out of his own youthful experiences, and his early horizons were closely limited by the mountains of Mourne.

In the later plays, when the memory of his own experiences began to fade, . . . Carroll turned . . . to fantasy, to a private embroidery of his remembrance of things past. . . . [The later plays, such as *The Old Foolishness, The Way-*

ward Saint, and *The Devil Came from Dublin*] are either genial daydreams about Carroll's own past, or romanticizations of what Ireland should be. Although none of them is thoroughly successful, all have moments of great appeal. . . . Carroll's strength was in his accurate eye and ear, rather than in his imagination. He needed . . . a real world to react to. (pp. 4-5)

There are compelling, droll, beautifully observed passages in nearly everything he wrote. And in two or three plays when he put everything together, all of his qualities—his caustically critical eye, his astonishing sympathy, and his command of realistic stagecraft—then he wrote nobly and movingly and, I think, lastingly. (p. 5)

> *Robert Hogan, in* The Journal of Irish Literature *(copyright © 1972 by Proscenium Press), January, 1972, pp. 3-6.*

MARY HAMILTON and DIANE ROMAN

During the ten year period preceding his dramatic debut [in 1930], Carroll wrote more than thirty stories. Apart from their somewhat nebulous literary value, these stories present valuable documentation of the writer's creative process, and of his early and deep concern for the indomitable spirit of the Irish. In the stories, as in the plays, there is no real thematic consistency, but the germ of his later method of handling theme, language and characterization is clearly visible. In ''The Treasure of Gold'' and ''The Stranger's Kingdom'' we find an ethereal mystical motif so evident in *Shadow and Substance* and *The Old Foolishness.* His portrayal of types such as the Irish rogue, the shrew, or the gossip in ''Terrible Man, Barney'' and ''Ould Biddy—The Newsmonger'' appear at a later date more finely drawn in *Things That Are Caesar's* and *The Devil Came From Dublin.* Many of the delicate, lilting descriptive passages apparent in all of the plays are scattered throughout the stories, but are particularly notable in ''The Unreturning Footsteps'' and ''The Little Old Woman.'' In ''The Loser'' and ''The Deeper Lesson'' we see a dichotomy of character similar to that of Swift in *Farewell to Greatness!* (pp. 72-3)

> *Mary Hamilton and Diane Roman, ''Paul Vincent Carroll's First Fiction,'' in* The Journal of Irish Literature *(copyright © 1972 by Proscenium Press), September, 1972, pp. 72-84.*

JOHN D. CONWAY

It is often remarked that there exists among Irish dramatists a natural impulse toward social satire. Playwrights such as Sheridan, Goldsmith, Wilde, and Shaw often outraged the English theatre with their satiric wit. During the Dramatic Revival in Ireland the satiric impulse found convincing expression in Synge, the early O'Casey, and Lennox Robinson. Hence it comes as nothing of a surprise that Paul Vincent Carroll, a man who deeply admired Swift, should have found a natural Celtic impulse irresistible.

Although there is bitter religious and social satire in Carroll's earliest published plays, *Things That Are Caesar's* (1934), *Shadow and Substance* (1937), and *The White Steed* (1939), it was not until the appearance of *The Wayward Saint* (1955) and *The Devil Came from Dublin* (1958) that he published plays actually designated as satires. (p. 13)

[*The Devil Came from Dublin*] crackles with witty dialogue, bizarre happenings, and a joyous atmosphere. It is at once the happiest and maddest play Carroll ever wrote; and although the major characters do espouse differing positions, the play does not wind down into a verbal dialectic better suited to a debating society than a theatre. If Carroll does not have the reach and the wit of a George Bernard Shaw, neither does he have the excesses. *The Devil Came from Dublin* is an engaging satire of Irish mores charged with a frivolous spirit, and it is primarily a play, not moral propaganda. However, it does contain some of the latter. Furthermore it has that intangible quality seemingly essential for successful drama: a playwright's natural sympathy for his subject matter. . . .

The work, which the author describes as "a totally irresponsible satirical extravaganza in which everyone is quite mad," is charged with an atmosphere of uproarious hilarity present in no other Carroll play. . . .

Carroll's approach to his material in *The Devil Came from Dublin* is not bitter; it is more Horatian than Juvenalian. He holds up a number of characteristically Irish foibles before his audience and invites a hearty and sympathetic laughter. In spite of his intense admiration for Jonathan Swift—an admiration especially evident in his play about Swift's private life, *Farewell to Greatness!* (1970)—his two dramas published as satires are good-humored and engaging, totally lacking in the invective and moral indignation suggestive of Swift.

However, it should not be assumed, even from Carroll's lighthearted manner, that he is simply concerned with the ephemeral in *The Devil Came from Dublin*. The play elicits something more than chuckles and grins about "the indomitable Irishry." Partially concealed amidst the laughter are glimpses of a country and a people delightfully out of step with a regimented, documented, bound, stapled, and mutilated 20th-century. (p. 14)

There is an insistence running throughout Carroll's plays from *Things That Are Caesar's* (1934) to *Goodbye to the Summer* (1971) that what really counts in the human experience is love. Whether it be through a peasant visionary, an elderly priest, or an indomitable redhead. Carroll's dramaturgy, even in the best of the children's plays, makes explicit the necessity to love. (p. 17)

Unquestionably, *The Devil Came from Dublin* is Carroll's best satirical work. It puts into motion a representative and credible group of Irishmen and little by little reveals the elemental condition of their lives: they are a romance-starved people similar in temperament to those peasants who listened with such rapture to the boasting of Christy Mahon in Michael Flaherty's public house. Indeed, there is ample evidence to suggest that perhaps more so than in any other Carroll drama *The Devil Came from Dublin* comes closest to what Synge believed essential for the stage—a reality rooted in joy. Carroll demonstrates that the popular imagination that Synge termed "fiery and magnificent and tender" is still capable of giving an audience what is superb and wild in reality.

Carroll is not the poetic dramatist Synge is, but that can be said for the vast majority of Irish playwrights. Nevertheless joy abounds in *The Devil Came from Dublin,* and the residents of Chuckeyhead, especially Rita Ronan, bear striking resemblance to the peasants in *The Playboy of the Western World*. In both plays the poetic imagination of the local people flourishes and flavors much of the dialogue. In both

plays the love theme is based upon what Ignatius Farrell calls "the breathless combination of the romantic and the heroic." . . . Finally, in both plays there is a spirit of abandonment amongst a people starved for activities commensurate with their dreams. (pp. 18-19)

In structure *The Wayward Saint* is similar to *Shadow and Substance* and *The White Steed*. The entire action takes place in the sitting-dining room of Canon Daniel Mc-Cooey's rectory in the small village of Kilkevin, near the Northern Irish border; and Canon McCooey, the wayward saint, is the central figure in the play. The other characters, including his lordship the Bishop of Oriel, are defined by their relationship to the Canon. In mood, however, *The Wayward Saint* shares a joy more characteristic of *The Devil Came from Dublin* than of *Shadow and Substance* or of *The White Steed*.

Yet, the joy in *The Wayward Saint* is quieter and more subdued than it is in *The Devil Came from Dublin*. At any rate, after an absence of almost twenty years from Broadway, Carroll had returned again to working with that material which had given him his greatest moments in the theatre. Portraits of the Irish clergy are plentiful in Irish fiction, as every student of Moore, Joyce, O'Connor, and O'Faoláin knows. Portraits of the same clergy in Irish drama, however, are something of a rarity. Certainly there is no other Irish playwright who has worked so well or so often with the Irish clergy as Paul Vincent Carroll, and his portrayals are as diverse as his subjects: the Skerritts are contrasted with the Kirwans and Corrs, and the Shaughnessys with the Lavelles. Hence when Carroll built *The Wayward Saint* around Canon Daniel McCooey, a latter-day Francis of Assisi, there must have been a modest hope among theatre people of another triumph by the Irish playwright most remembered for his portraits of the clergy.

But, a happy and frivolous comical satire, *The Wayward Saint* never rises above the level of mere entertainment. Canon Daniel McCooey, an aging and white-haired priest who seems to be on a first-name basis with most of the animals in his parish, is the principal issue in the play: his bishop wants to be rid of him, and Satan has sent a special envoy to capture his immortal soul. (pp. 19-20)

The difficulty with *The Wayward Saint* is not in Carroll's delineation of Canon McCooey. After all the Canon does have irresistible charm, infectious manner, and natural innocence, even though life in a rectory with him would be something of a hazard, what with two donkeys, several birds, and an escaped lion not only enjoying free access to the premises but also friendly camaraderie with a saint. No, the difficulty with *The Wayward Saint* is not Canon McCooey; it is in making the Canon the principal issue. . . .

[Opposition] between a Canon such as McCooey and his bishop scarcely provides substance for three acts, even with the assistance of a witless housekeeper, Miss Killicat; a vagabond friend, Pedar the Puck; a troubled Irish girl, Maura; and an ubiquitous menagerie. (p. 20)

Another less damaging but nonetheless real criticism of *The Wayward Saint* concerns a disturbingly large portion of its dialogue, which is often as lifeless as the struggle for the Canon's soul; when contrasted with the robust language of *The Devil Came from Dublin*, it seems tame indeed. (p. 21)

If there is anywhere in *The Wayward Saint* a brief hint of

the playwright who wrote *Shadow and Substance* and *The White Steed,* it comes in the final act. Even in his less successful dramas Carroll demonstrates his skill in *crescendo* writing. (pp. 21-2)

In spite of the flourish in Act III and an occasional well-placed barb or two, the chief impression one receives from reading and rereading *The Wayward Saint* is that Carroll went to the same well once too often. The material that worked so effectively in *Shadow and Substance* and *The White Steed* sputters in a comical satire of limited reach and even more limited appeal. Even in the United States a "Going My Way" mentality does not last indefinitely. There are, after all, limitations as to how much dramatic mileage a playwright can get out of canons, housekeepers, peasant girls, bishops, and an occasional jackass or two. . . .

As a satirist Carroll is most impressive in three plays: *Shadow and Substance, The White Steed,* and *The Devil Came from Dublin;* and of these plays only the last was designated a "satire." Although *The Devil Came from Dublin* is an engaging work and far superior to *The Wayward Saint,* those parts of *The White Steed* revealing the bitter and bigoted nature of Father Shaughnessy represent Carroll at his satiric best. Nowhere else in his dramas is the perspective so unflinching or the sting so acute. (p. 23)

> *John D. Conway, "The Satires of Paul Vincent Carroll," in* Éire-Ireland *(copyright Irish American Cultural Institute), Autumn, 1972, pp. 13-23.*

＊　　　＊　　　＊

CARRUTH, Hayden　1921-

Carruth is an American poet, novelist, critic, and editor. His poetry is versatile in mood and verse form, rich in language, and often autobiographical. Strongly influenced by Yeats, he creates eloquent poetry, noted for its control and lyricism. Carruth calls his philosophy a "radical secular existentialism." Though considered overly formal and academic by some critics, he is praised for the sustained power and emotional intensity of his long poems. (See also *CLC*, Vols. 4, 7, and *Contemporary Authors*, Vols. 9-12, rev. ed.)

PAUL RAMSEY

Hayden Carruth's beautiful "To Artemis" . . . is a poem of formal address to the moon goddess. . . . The poem is dignified, sharply perceived, thoughtful, translucent, and reverent. It is in free verse with irregular sections. Carruth has a good and practiced ear, and has worked in accentual-syllabic meters as well as free verse. The following passage is exciting in motion, sound, interworkings:

> flakes of light whirling away, a shower—
> moonflakes, sparks
> scurrying through dark trees.

The section stands out of context because it, like the section beginning "Snow lined," is in a different kind of free verse from the rest of the poem, which is soberly conversational, having no base but several times moving toward or into rising pentameter or trimeter, as in the beautiful ending:

> Whatever we are, these reflections, let us
> change them now, let us be silent, cold,
> let us be autonomous, bright,
>
> in this place so remote and altered.

The metrical convention of the poem is successful but just a little soft. The two kinds of free verse do not quite accord, though transitions are graceful. The long-line free verse is not so precise an instrument for feeling and meditation as iambic pentameter, as focusedly intense as the best short-line free verse, or as powerful in its surging as the best long-line free verse.

Both in convention and thought the belief in the value of the experience is intense and genuine, seeking with stoic unsuccess for an ontological foothold. The poem illustrates something of the limits good contemporary poets are held by and resist. (p. 396)

> *Paul Ramsey, in* Sewanee Review *(reprinted by permission of the editor; © 1974 by The University of the South), Spring, 1974.*

DAVID BROMWICH

More a document than a poem, *The Bloomingdale Papers* is a meditation on the several months of lost time Hayden Carruth spent in a mental institution during the early 1950s. It was written in conditions of extreme isolation: on a typewriter, in the ward, as the author's way of helping his doctors to understand him. Now it is offered, out of context, to the "candid reader" of a different age, who can know little of the peculiar and personal circumstances that gave it a more than clinical meaning. The overall effect is jarring and yet, it must be said, moving. This is after all a report from the front. Nothing in it shines so clearly as the plain desperate need to communicate: it is this that makes Mr. Carruth's case more than a case and imparts to his predicament, for a moment, the sense of something vital and shared. Revived after a lapse of years, his lines occasionally have the offhand analytic truth and hardness of a patient-of-the-world whose trouble is that he knows the world and himself far too well. (pp. 1021-22)

An observant nature together with a sense of humor must have been what kept Mr. Carruth going through the painful journalistic task he set himself. His prose introduction, a simple but thorough act of recollection and self-scrutiny, testifies as well as anything in his book to the gift of endurance that saw him past the ordeal. (p. 1022)

> *David Bromwich, in* The Georgia Review *(copyright, 1976, by the University of Georgia), Winter, 1976.*

DAVID SHAPIRO

Hayden Carruth's mottled document, *The Bloomingdale Papers,* opens with an appropriately horrifying apologia in prose that works: "Part of my illness was a need to do what I was told (in anger and under protest), so I did it. One of my doctors suggested that since I called myself a writer I should write something that might be helpful to him and his colleagues in their consideration of my case . . ." This, then, is a form of prison poetry, a genre we must not deprecate since . . . we are all a part of it. . . . (p. 228)

[Carruth] lucidly defends [the volume's] collagiste format from the reductionist label of "confessional" and underlines most vigorously its ambition and *topos:* "the inner condition of exile as the experience *par excellence* of the mid-twentieth century''.

The poem begins with a blasted landscape out of Stevens: ''It all begins on this November day. / The wintertime realities are thin.'' A dazed nostalgia reigns in a present anarchy: ''Only an image ago huge puffs of green, / Tribes of birds, cities of crickets and ants, / And the tumbling sun made jocund all our eyes.'' An Eliotic meditation follows, in a verse well furnished with Jacobean stridency and darkness: ''Our lives are close and iron-girt; we thread / Among the phantoms of this narrowed world, / We trolls and banshees . . .'' It is an allusive and self-reflexive hysteria in the grand style: ''. . . seeing what the guru sees in his / / Embracing stare? 'There is a pleasure sure / In being mad which none but madman know.''' What one appreciates here is the joy of a randomness made shapely under inordinate pressure of the will to form: ''And randomly / My thoughts revolve to form this comedy.''

The poetry is filled with polemics concerning poeisis, and Carruth has noted that the poem's intended first audience were his captors—or the doctors, not to speak too melodramatically. The poetry has something of that clumsily convincing schizoid quality that the recent novel *Zen and the Art of Motorcycle Maintenance* at the least showed. There is a jocular sermonizing style, from late Pound, no doubt, and Olson, perhaps, but effective here as additional texture, a critical interpolation in a life so drastically interrupted if not altered. . . . The prose often shows a posture of more self-reliance than the poetry; its realism seems often the more confident perspective. The poetry, nevertheless, sometimes achieves a success in a style that might be called diagnosis without prognosis. . . . Though I cannot be sanguine concerning the success of the whole fractured form, I am certain of its sanity. (pp. 229-30)

> *David Shapiro, in* Poetry *(© 1976 by The Modern Poetry Association; reprinted by permission of the Editor of* Poetry*), July, 1976.*

*   *   *

CELAN, Paul (pseudonym of Paul Antschel) 1920-1970

Born in Rumania of Hasidic Jewish heritage, Celan is generally regarded as the finest lyric poet to write in German since Rilke. His parents were victims of the Nazi extermination, and Celan himself was interned in a forced labor camp from 1942 to 1943. The anguish of the Holocaust can be felt in his work, often manifested in a dark, melancholy imagery; this is especially evident in his most famous poem, ''Death Fugue.'' Celan's is surreal, lyrical poetry, often elusive and dreamlike. His images are unusual, his diction pure. Also a translator of French and Russian, Celan adapted the works of Mandelstam, Rimbaud, Valéry, and Char. He committed suicide at the age of forty-nine.

DIETHER H. HAENICKE

Celan is the author of the most famous poem written after the war, ''Fugue of Death,'' which treats the atrocities of the concentration camps in a remarkable montage technique that seems to transcend the possibilities of linguistic expression. His early volumes, *Mohn und Gedächtnis* (*Poppy and Memory,* 1952) and *Von Schwelle zu Schwelle* (*From Threshold to Threshold,* 1955), capture impressions

of his chassidic background and reveal the influence of French surrealism on his poetry. The untranslatable titles of the next volumes, *Sprachgitter* (1959), *Die Niemandsrose* (1963), *Atemwende* (1967), and *Fadensonnen* (1968), show Celan's attempt to dissociate his poetry from conventional imagery. Bold oxymora and daring catachreses characterize his pursuit of new linguistic tools. His images often seem to be ciphers of his complex existence rather than mere visual impressions. (p. 396)

> *Diether H. Haenicke, in* The Challenge of German Literature, *edited by Horst S. Daemmrich and Diether H. Haenicke (reprinted by permission of the Wayne State University Press; copyright © 1971 by Wayne State University Press),* Wayne State University Press, 1971.

GUY DAVENPORT

Celan's poetry [in *Speech-Grille and Selected Poems*] reminds me of that of the English poet Christopher Middleton. The words in it tend to stand away from each other and be little poems in themselves. The images are startling and in perfect focus, yet the whole poem is like something one has never seen before, a machine dreamed up by Kafka, or a painting by Ernst or Klee. . . .

Here is the beginning of a poem by Celan:

> Lichtgewinn, messbar, aus
> Distelähnlichem:
> einiges
> Rot, im Gespräch
> mit einigem Gelb.

Mr. Neugroschel [Celan's translator] records the English equivalents of these strange words:

> Light-gain, gaugeable, from
> something thistle-like:
> some
> red, conversing
> with some yellow.

A riddle? It turns out that the poet is looking at the rubble in a vacant lot beside train tracks, and the rest of the poem discloses what we encounter often in Celan. He is writing not so much with words as with anguish. It will be remarked, I think, that words became *things* to a whole school of late twentieth-century poets. The scholars [of the future] will trace this metamorphosis back to Mallarmé and the *Dadaistes,* but they will have an aesthetic problem of some intricacy when they try to account for the hardware-like brilliance and distinctness of words in such a poet as Celan.

Nouns dominate Celan's poetry, and verbs tend to be negligible or so surrealistic as to abandon their dictionary meaning. An eye weeps stones. Voices are nicked in the green. Nothingness is borne into windfalls (*Nichts in den Windbruch getragen*).

Celan is undoubtedly a distinguished poet. His distinction, however, puts him severely beside or perhaps ahead of his time. Kafka in 1910 was speaking to the Europe of 1940. Celan's angular, odd precision with things beyond a sense of the precise may well be written for lonely readers in pressure-chamber outposts in the anthrax forests of Mars. (p. 701)

Guy Davenport, in The Hudson Review (copyright © 1972 by The Hudson Review, Inc.; reprinted by permission), Vol. XXIV, No. 4, Winter, 1971-72.

JERRY GLENN

The Germans are not the only objects of scorn in Celan's poetry. The traditional God of Judaism and Christianity is another, and these objects of scorn—I hesitate to say hate, although it would perhaps be valid—are certainly quite closely related to each other.... Celan's pessimism cannot be explained in terms of a general post-Nietzschean conviction that God is dead; it is rather a very specific form of theological thinking found in a number of contemporary Jewish poets and philosophers.... Celan's poems sometimes display an awareness of the role of Christianity in the historical development of anti-Semitism. The poem "Spät und tief" ..., for example, while alluding to Jewish "guilt" in the death of Christ, denies the possibility of the Resurrection, in effect reversing or refuting the Christian symbolism contained in the poem. Much of Celan's verse is profoundly pessimistic and correct interpretation is facilitated if the poems are approached with the historical background in mind. (p. 26)

[An important technique used by Celan in his hermetic poetry] is based on an apparently arbitrary succession of images and exclamations, a kind of stream-of-consciousness, often marked by verbal associations and word plays....

The complexity of the word associations is considerable, as is the significance of their implications. The word *Mandel* in this poem is applied to the Jewish people, to the hair of the Jews killed in concentration camps, to a Jewish eye (which is contrasted with the Christian eye viewing the picture), then to the Christian halo and, by way of the picture of Christ within it (or rather, which was formerly within it), to Christ himself, ironically a Jew in whose name the Jews have been persecuted....

The single line "Judenlocke, wirst nicht grau" [Jewish hair, you don't get gray] is rhythmically set apart and the same holds true for the final two lines. These two, furthermore, comprise a rhymed couplet. Such couplets are extremely rare in Celan's later poetry and when they do occur they usually have a bitter tone.... Celan was forced to write his poetry in German, the language of the Nazis.... Celan was in fact very personally aware of the dilemma, and specifically of the implications of the German rhyme. For this reason rhyme is sparingly used in his poetry and for this reason the places in which it is used tend to be intense and bitter. (p. 29)

Celan's works are not universally and unambiguously pessimistic, but the affirmative aspects have been stressed by critics to great excess. The similarities between Celan and contemporaries such as Elie Wiesel are overlooked because Celan, unlike Wiesel, never discussed his own personal fate or his personal reaction to it. The lasting psychological effects of the Holocaust, of which Wiesel and others openly speak, were surely felt by Celan and are indirectly reflected in his poetry. There is a decided pessimism in many of his poems, a result of his Jewish experience, which we see corroborated in life by his suicide. (p. 30)

Jerry Glenn, "Manifestations of the Holocaust: Interpreting Paul Celan," in Books

Abroad (copyright 1972 by the University of Oklahoma Press), Vol. 46, No. 1, Winter, 1972, pp. 25-30.

CORBET STEWART

Poetic language, in [Celan's] view, has become a rescuing device, a mode of speech barely audible and yet of sufficient intensity to wrench the poem back from the verge of its self-abolition in the realm of silence.... [When] Celan speaks of the poem's tendency towards silence he is speaking not in terms of an aesthetic absorbed from outside ... but in terms of the more immediately commanding dictates of personal emotion.

For silence, in Celan's work, is felt not only as a negative situation, but also as a force.... [The premise of the early poem 'Chanson einer Dame im Schatten' is that the] man who speaks too soon is ruined and a mysterious silence triumphs: and hence, despite the poem's obvious sexual implications, it is impossible not to read it as being to some extent also a metaphor of the poet's situation—that the spoken word must ever yield to the potency of what Celan will later term 'das erschwiegene Wort'.... Rilke's consciousness of the overwhelming force of 'das Unsägliche'; Valéry's 'tumulte au silence pareil'; Eliot's concept of the 'inarticulate' on which the poet is compelled to make continual raids—from none of these does Celan ... seem very far removed. But to say this is to ignore an all-important component of Celan's region of silence—the role, therein, of violence.... The specific sorrow to which Celan's poems most constantly refer is that caused by the Nazi death-camps, and he returns by frequent implication to the inadequacy of words to render the magnitude of this theme.... The word sought, the word 'nach dem Bilde des Schweigens', is thus one which will be commensurate with the horror it expresses and which will yet at the same time, transform it. At its simplest level silence, in Celan, implies death and the majority of his poems are in fact explorations into the realm of the dead. But here, of course, is the paradox—that the poet can explore silence only by means of its opposite condition, words. And thus silence is both desired and feared, desired as the region in which the beloved dead have their being, and feared because, by its very nature, it constitutes a threat to the poet's sole means of ingress. Hence, if the poet's attitude to silence fluctuates, so does his attitude to words. (pp. 127-29)

In Celan's third collection of poems, *Sprachgitter* (1959) there occurs an obvious change in, or refinement of, poetic technique. Characteristic of the earlier volumes, *Mohn und Gedächtnis* (1952) and, to a lesser extent, *Von Schwelle zu Schwelle* (1955) is a strong element of incantation, a somewhat *sotto voce* incantation of overtly hypnotic effect. But in *Sprachgitter* this element has receded: and although the final poem in the collection, *Engführung* (the German term for the *stretto* of a fugue) explicitly evokes a musical parallel, the music of these poems is much closer to that of, say, Webern, than to any incantation—sparse, intensely compressed and glacially beautiful: the product, one may feel, of a resolution that the poet's themes shall not become 'wild / überwuchert von Worten'.

Yet this paring down of the poet's means of expression is accompanied by an increased preoccupation with the range of expressive power which language possesses—and, concomitantly with this, with its expressive limitations. This last phrase is ambiguous, and I mean it to be: for it is characteristic of the paradoxical temper of Celan's poetic mind that ideas or situations which logically would be regarded as contrarieties can co-exist and even fuse with each other on the same linguistic plane. Hence it isn't simply playing with words to state that the phrase 'expressive limitations' implies in addition to its primary meaning the suggestion that the very limitations of language may themselves be expressive. 'Words, after speech, reach / into the silence' Eliot has it: and it is this realm, extending from the insufficient spoken or written word to the territory of silence, that Celan's poems have it as their immensely difficult task to explore. The word is the product of the living, silence that of the dead; the word may affirm, silence may negate the affirmation. Yet, as any careful reader of Celan will testify, this negating effect of silence presses heavily upon the poet's consciousness, acting, indeed, as a kind of challenge. It seems, in fact, mysteriously to affirm something: and hence language, at the very point where its limitations become most perceptible, may, precisely in those limitations, be expressive of a possible larger affirmation. And it is perhaps at some such situation as this that the word 'Sprachgitter' hints: a 'Gitter' may impede progress or cut us off from a world outside, but it does not impede vision: one can look out from between the bars.

One of the central themes of Celan's work is, as is well known, his preoccupation with the dead and the ways in which their absence affects the consciousness of the living. His search for what has been called 'das transzendentale Du' has been unremitting, and the world of his poems is thus peculiarly one in which affirmation and negation meet: and, for the exploration of this mental territory, many of the *Sprachgitter* poems adopt a similar technique. A great many of them open with the simplest form of affirmation, the naming of an object . . . , or of an object followed immediately by an adjective. . . . This is frequently followed by the naming of a second, associated object . . . or by the presentation of some motion or action set in train by the object first named. . . . There then occurs a gradual associative multiplication, the introduction of further images and a technique of statement, rejection, contradiction, restatement, etc. . . . (pp. 129-31)

[The poem *Blume*] is a tentative exploration of the possibilities inherent in the paradox 'Blume—ein Blindenwort', which stands, significantly, at the exact centre of the poem: a word which, though it be the product of vitality and abundance ('das den Sommer heraufkam') will yet somehow include within the scope of its reverberations the opposite condition best described perhaps by John Donne—'absence, darkness, death; things which are not'. The attempt at such a reconciliation is, of course, a theme by no means peculiar to Celan: it is also, for example, a major theme of Rilke's. We have only to think of Rilke's Orpheus, the singer-god to whom the 'beide Bereiche' of the living and the dead are indistinguishable, to see the resemblance; to realize also that in one important sense Celan is a poet of the Orphic tradition. But there is a significant difference in that Celan, unlike Rilke, discards the trappings of the myth. . . . Moreover, in discarding mythical accoutrements, Celan also implicitly discards their frequent concomitant, the vatic tone. Rilke's triumphant annunciations in the Elegies and Sonnets—the note of 'Rühmen'—give place in Celan to a quality of probing, a delicate exploration of symbolist landscapes—strange *venues* for a projected encounter between the poet's consciousness and the reality of the dead.

'Projected' encounter—the qualification is important. Rilke's vision of 'das erweiterte Ganze' was an optimistic one, a promise, in a world barricaded by the exigencies of time, of an infinite spatial freedom. In Celan's poems, however, there is no sense of freedom or exhilaration. Most of the poems in *Sprachgitter* are uncommonly slow-moving, imbued with a sense of the tentative: the 'du' is rarely reached, the encounter remains no more than the simultaneous symbolization of a desire and its non-fulfilment. (p. 132)

The opening, untitled poem in *Sprachgitter* . . . consists of eight sections, of which the first seven are concerned with the annunciations of various mysterious voices. Their messages are expressed in imagery which is largely drawn from water and from various types of vegetation. Two main areas of preoccupation seem to emerge—a situation of being emotionally *in extremis* and, linked with this, a close scrutiny of moments of disturbed time. These elements culminate in the evocation of two sets of incidents drawn from Jewish mythology; and the final section concerns the silence which remains when the 'Stimmen' have died away and which is perhaps more potent than any of them. (p. 134)

The 'Stimmen' poem traces . . . the emergence of meaning from terrible fragmentation, or, if this formulation suggests too smoothly operating a process, the intuiting of the latent meaning which inheres in fragmentation. Celan's final stanza, I think, makes no greater claim than this. We are not intended to observe the Poem, rising like Minerva from the head of Jupiter, nor do we witness a hope born of despair. We hear, simply, a paradoxical silence: no directing voice, but a 'Spätgeräusch', an excited whispering of incipient creativity.

The 'Stimmen' poem, then, culminates in the speech-silence paradox which is the theme around which most of the *Sprachgitter* poems turn. Even the most cursory glance through Celan's volumes is enough to reveal the weight attached to the word 'Schweigen' together with its derivates and synonyms—'schweigsam', 'verschweigen', 'stumm', 'verstummen', etc. But the implications of these terms—what we may call Celan's 'modes of silence'—are shifting. Roughly, and without any over-literal intention to claim that one category need necessarily exclude overtones of the others, we may, I think, divide these modes into four main groups. (a) Silence as purely negative, a silence which arises either because there is nothing to consummate or because there is no means of communication. . . . (b) At other times silence masks mystery, either of the beloved or of the dead. . . . And with the mystery goes a sense of significance which on occasion . . . is pitted against the purposeless proliferations of speech. . . . (c) But the mystery may be more than simply a generalized sense of the inscrutable: it may be the more specific mystery of that which is both figuratively and, ultimately, literally, unspeakable . . . : the dead, expressive silence of the death-camp victims. . . . Just as here fertility burgeons from non-existence, so expressiveness may flower from silence. . . . [This] brings us to the final implication of 'Schweigen', (d) the stirrings of the creative impulse. (pp. 138-40)

There is, of course, a tradition of silence in Western poetry:

a tradition which contains both negative elements (as in Dante's despair of the power of words to render the effect of the Beatific Vision) and, in a more positive light, the fascinations which silence has exerted over poets whose preoccupations have taken them to 'die letzte Ortschaft der Worte', the ultimate borders of the expressive powers of language. Celan, as we have seen, has inherited and used both attitudes. But he is also, and with equal relevance, heir to a more localized and specific tradition, that of East European Hasidic Jewry.... (p. 140)

> Corbet Stewart, "Paul Celan's Modes of Silence: Some Observations on 'Sprachgitter'," in The Modern Language Review (© Modern Humanities Research Association 1972), January, 1972, pp. 127-42.

JERRY GLENN

Dreams and dream imagery constitute an important, if far from pervasive theme in the postwar German lyric....

At first glance, Celan seems to stand in the surrealist tradition.... Celan's own poetry of the first three postwar years abounds in images and stylistic devices which have a close affinity with those typical of surrealistic verse....

Celan's dream imagery is puzzling. In many cases individual images and entire poems at first defy explication. At the risk of seeming to oversimplify this complex problem, I propose that the following three theses provide the necessary basis for gaining access to the enigmatic dream world of Celan's poetry: 1) Celan ... is a Holocaust poet, and the dream world in his early poetry is related to the phenomenon, often noted in literature on the Holocaust, that for the victims reality had become a nightmare; 2) many of Celan's early poems, whether the word *dream* is explicitly mentioned or not, resemble the images of a dream, and on the basis of the first thesis, these dreams are nightmares; 3) Celan's use of dream imagery did not remain constant but underwent one significant break (in 1948) and a series of subsequent gradual modifications....

Accounts of the Holocaust, autobiographical as well as scholarly, contain frequent comparisons between life in the camps and a nightmare. Especially interesting is a comment by Terrence des Pres [from *The Survivor: An Anatomy of Life in a Death Camp*]: "The first weeks in the camp were literally unreal and embedded in a nightmare." ... Not only the fact of the nightmarish nature of the experience is significant, but also the language used in a scholarly work in attempting to describe the experience: *literally unreal*....

[This illustrates] Celan's dilemma. In his early poetry dreams often directly reflect experience. The images are distorted and defy rational explanation, not because the poet was concerned with some theory of language and the relationship between dreams and reality, but primarily because the experience itself, though a fact in his life, was "literally unreal."

A cursory reading of Celan's poetry written in the years 1944-47 leaves the impression that dreams are associated with evil and danger, by virtue of the contexts in which *dream* (in various noun, verb and adjective forms) appears. For example, it is associated with weapons ("daggers of dream," ...), blood ..., the grave ..., weapons and the grave ..., insanity ..., and appears in other less specific

contexts which evoke a feeling of anxiety or uneasiness. Only on very rare occasions does the word *dream* seem to carry clearly affirmative connotations such as one often finds in poetry of earlier eras (one example: "Where dream is and lovers are reclining ... " ...). (p. 522)

An examination of portions of two poems in which the word *dream* occurs and dreamlike imagery is prevalent will elucidate the nature of the nightmarish world of Celan's early poetry. In "Der Einsame" (A Man Alone ...) the contents of the first stanza could with no difficulty be taken for a report of an actual dream: Autumn, who loves the speaker (the dreamer) more than it loves the dove and the mulberry tree, gives the speaker a veil, on which it has embroidered "Take it [the veil] for dreaming" and "God is also as near as the vulture." Although differing in specifics, psychological theorists—Freud and Jung, for example—are in agreement that some dream symbols are based on personal experience and others are common to all—or most—people and also that a dream can only be adequately interpreted in relation to the experiences of the dreamer. The juxtaposition of normal behavior and events and bizarre symbols and situations is also typical of dreams. In the present poem the vulture might seem to be a universally recognizable symbol of death, which is counteracted by the nearness of God. The presence of a personal symbol, however, precludes the possibility of the second part of such an interpretation. In the poem which follows "Der Einsame" in *Der Sand aus den Urnen* (The Sand from the Urns; 1948) Autumn is again personified, here being the messenger who brings to the poet the news of his parents' death in a camp. Autumn, then, is a personal component of the dreamer's nightmare, and nightmares are the sort of dream elicited by the veil. Furthermore, as one sees elsewhere in Celan (e.g., "Tenebrae" ...) and in several other Holocaust writers, God's nearness is not necessarily a blessing.

A second poem in which the word *dream* is mentioned in the context of imagery reminiscent of a nightmare is "Marianne." ... The first three stanzas contain dream imagery suggesting a love relationship and conclude with the words "we sleep." The destruction of the idyll is foreshadowed in the second line ("The cloud moves from eye to eye, like Sodom to Babel") and completed in the final stanza, where the beloved who is addressed in the poem is interred, and "Now the hard coin of dreams clinks on the tiles of the world." Like a nightmare the dream of love ends in the burial of the beloved. The final line suggests not only awakening from the dream, but also, as best language can, the identity of "dreams" and "the world"—reality. (pp. 522-23)

> Jerry Glenn, "Nightmares, Dreams and Intellectualization in the Poetry of Paul Celan," in World Literature Today (copyright 1977 by the University of Oklahoma Press), Vol. 51, No. 4, Autumn, 1977, pp. 522-25.

*   *   *

CIARDI, John   1916-

Ciardi is an American poet whose poems are marked, according to Josephine Jacobsen, by "a refusal to play safe." As a writer of books for both adults and children, his ambition is to have his poetry appeal to a general audience; he does so with poems that are perceptive, witty, and tough. Ciardi, an influential critic, has also been a teacher, editor, and translator. (See also *Contemporary Authors*, Vols. 5-8, rev. ed.)

M. L. ROSENTHAL

[John Ciardi's] war poems generally, and his love poems and political and satirical pieces, make him a graphic spokesman for the liberal and literate mind today, a mind in touch with earthy reality and even a certain redeeming crudeness, and also alive to the world of thought. (p. 250)

> *M. L. Rosenthal, in his* The Modern Poets: A Critical Introduction *(copyright © 1960 by M. L. Rosenthal; reprinted by permission of Oxford University Press, Inc.), Oxford University Press, 1960.*

JUDSON JEROME

No one (least of all, I imagine, John Ciardi) would call "In Fact," his ninth collection of poetry, a great book or even a particularly important one. But it is damned enjoyable reading—a statement that can rarely be made about any new book of poetry. It gets in some good licks at evil and awakens our response to joy.

It is a day-by-day sort of book—often as familiar as the bulletin board in the suburban Co-op. None of the poems are particularly ambitious, as are those in Ciardi's other volumes. Some are outright jokes with only an overtone of larger meaning, such as "Vodka," which is "upwind from all other essences" because it doesn't stay on the breath, yet "Like poetry, vodka informs any thing with which it is diluted." . . .

Perhaps the greater number of the poems bear on suburbia directly, sometimes with joy, more often with bitter wonder about how we can learn to live with our prosperity. (p. 78)

[The] pathetic need of the fortunate living within commuting distance of madness to see and believe anything, even to hear the glad birdsong while waiting for the train, is one of the book's preoccupations. The final, and most moving, poem of the book, "Letter to a Wrong Child," recommends a trip to Europe, where one may lose oneself in the Babel and misery of the race, as an alternative to suicide for

> my martyr, my poor, alas, white
> protestant middle-class wept goose
> of this prosperous wrong paved
> barnyard.

The key terms of the book are mercy and self. It celebrates giving in spite of all reason and justice and boundaries; national flags the poet would "gladly waive." The self itself needs mercy "for whatever / you did dark in some Keokuk . . . of the soul." But self and mercy come together most frequently in bed. Love needs magic in order not to be a "relationship," and the poems work at intimacy, tenderness, and escape from analysis and judgment. On this theme Ciardi is sometimes too much like Cummings. . . .

The book raises questions that I am sure Ciardi wanted to raise: How about a kind of poetry of hearty honesty and directness, poetry that is just plain good reading, sane, funny, delighting in words, images, patterns, socking out with opinions and ribaldry, with no philosophical pretension and no *Weltschmerz*? Well, it's fresh air, surely, and edifying reading for suburban neighbors. It is a crosswind to current intellectual lanes, it will ruffle a lot of prejudices. The spirit is ancient—that of the classical epigrams. But is it finally enough?

The answer is that no one said it was final or claimed sufficiency. It seems a rather casual book, and it fills a lot of casual but demanding needs. (p. 79)

> *Judson Jerome, "The Wedding of Mercy and Self," in* Saturday Review *(© 1963 by Saturday Review, Inc.; reprinted with permission), March 23, 1963, pp. 78-9.*

LAURENCE PERRINE

I read [Ciardi's "Tenzone"] as a competition in which both [the Soul and Body, the poem's speakers,] attack the Soul: the Soul first attacks itself; then the Body joins in and finishes the job. But the poem *is* a debate, though the Soul does not realize it. The question at issue is "Which writes the poetry?"

The Soul begins with a wryly ironical description of the poet as a performer on the lecture circuit, inspired, witty, well-paid, lucent—"a gem of serenest ray"—and then confesses sadly that this gem of the lecture circuit "is, alas, I." In the following stanzas the Soul describes the poet as his critics see and judge him—a view and a judgment which the Soul tends to share. But since the Soul has already identified itself with the poet, it is, in describing him, frankly describing and judging itself. . . .

When the Soul calls the poet a "greedy pig," it is not calling the Body names, it is calling itself names. Or, rather, it is doing two things at once: it is reporting the kind of thing that others . . . say about the poet, and it is agreeing with their judgment, which is a judgment against itself. The accusation that the Soul brings against itself is that it has sold itself out to the Body, has therefore, in effect, reduced itself to the level of the Body, has itself become nothing but a "belly" and a "greedy pig." (p. 19)

In judging itself so harshly, however, the Soul has implied its own importance. It has assumed entire responsibility for the poetry that has and has not been written. In the second part of the poem, the Body strips it of this importance. The Body begins with a wryly ironical description of the poet as a poet—grave, secretive, ignorant—"flaming and fire-freed"—and then says deliberately that this aspirant writer of poetry is "not wholly you," i.e. not wholly the Soul. The Body has a share in writing the poetry too. . . . The Soul is unsubstantial—a "glowworm," a "spook," a "wind" (though also a monkey on the Body's back)—and it writes poor poetry: it blows on ashes that won't catch fire. For, after all, good poetry is "belly and bone"—it is written out of physical and sensuous experience. The Body, not the Soul, is the true poet. The Soul is as dead as "yesterday's squall," but the Body knows how to savor "today's air." It lives and likes and thrives on the sensuous, the physical, and the material.

Thus the poor Soul gets it from both sides. The Soul, assuming its own importance, gives itself up because of its self-betrayal. The Body, denying the Soul's importance (the Soul is no more than a "burp"), gives the Soul up, feeling it can do better on its own: write better poetry and enjoy life more fully. But the poem that Ciardi has written says more than either of its two speakers. What *it* says is that Body and Soul are inseparable: Soul lives off of Body and can do nothing without it. Poetry is written by Body *and* Soul. (p. 21)

> *Laurence Perrine, "Ciardi's 'Tenzone'," in*

The Explicator (© *copyright, 1970, by* The
Explicator), *May, 1970, pp. 19, 21.*

JOHN W. HUGHES

Like Sinyavsky, Ciardi has been deemed a subversive by
certain mealy-mouthed inquisitors, but his true subversive-
ness eludes the wranglings of House committees. For *Lives
of X* strips away the "old lies" to reveal the rag-and-bone
shop that surrounded the youthful poet's growth to manhood:

> As I was born—
> To dim red glows I sensed but could not read
> except to know there are Presences, and to learn
> the first of everything is a lunacy
> whose chatter starts before us in the dark.

The Orphic voice is subversive in that it breaks down the
subject-object distinctions of the Cartesian mind, puts us in
touch with the chattering lunacy (the curling sea that circled
the rim of Achilles's shield) that precedes us in the dark.
Ciardi follows Wordsworth and Frost in molding the blank
verse to the flowing immediacy of his remembrances, and
in so doing explodes some of the mind-forged manacles that
shackle modern poetry. There is no modish trifling with
chaos and madness here, none of the Cartesian gimmicks of
the Symbolist élite. Ciardi, like Robert Lowell and Stanley
Kunitz and a few others, has recovered the Romantic sense
of existential subjectivity that lay buried under T. S. Eliot's
strictures about the "objective correlative" and Ezra
Pound's notion that the poem must present "an intellectual
and emotional complex in an instant of time . . ." Time in
Lives of X is never a frozen instant, but becomes instead a
vehicle for the existential encounter between poet and
world. The moments of epiphany, Wordsworth's "spots of
time," embody the crisp sensations of a Hemingway or
Joyce short story:

> I took my drink
> at clammy soapstone round a drain of stinks
> and slid back into bed, my toes still curled
> from the cold lick of linoleum.

The central theme is the growth of the poet's consciousness
through time, his eventual turning away from the "mad histories" of his Italian immigrant family. But the madness is
set in a social context, a vicious Irish South Boston of tenements and bigoted priests, and the turning away is accompanied by a powerful outflow of sympathy for his earthy
proletarian family. Unlike such trendy Poundian irrational-
ists as Michael McClure and Gregory Corso, Ciardi refuses
to glorify (or simplify) insanity and regression—he establishes a profound dialectic between Id and Ego, lunacy and
Orphic order. (p. 31)

Ciardi shows that [the I-Thou relation between poet and
world] is "ahead of thought"—it is the ground of human
feeling upon which a healthy rationality can be erected. All
forms of primitivism (including the fascist variety) are, in
fact, a kind of debased *thought,* a manipulative objectification of the living universe. All objects have "inscape," in
the words of Gerard Manley Hopkins, and every poet must
"deal out that being indoors each one dwells." A Hopkin-
sian intensity is captured by Ciardi in "The Graph," probably his most successful poem to date, in which the erudite
Italian-American youth is suddenly transformed into a
World War II airman:

> By time and after, where the guessed-at dead

> curled in, unborn, and charred before they hit,
> or blew to gases when their tanks cooked off,
> or only passed forever through one cloud;
> we manned wired systems, and the diagrams
> wavered on blue mirages like decals
> washed off a sunken panel, whole but warped.

The jet-stream currents of Ciardi's imagery coalesce into an
intense awareness of dehumanized brutality. The graph that
totals up the number of enemy dead becomes a symbol of
this "wired" brutality, the manipulative Cartesian cruelty
of modern life. The symbol is at all points inseparable from
the poet's experience; it is never imposed *on* that experience (what Erich Auerbach calls "figural symbolism").
After an apocalyptic air raid we are left with the poet writing "what I remember of the dead, / our duplicates and
their own in the globing moon." This is an appropriate vision of the humanism that pervades *Lives of X.* (pp. 31-2)

John W. Hughes, in Saturday Review *(©
1971 by Saturday Review, Inc.; reprinted
with permission), May 22, 1971.*

EDWARD CIFÈLLI

Ciardi possesses an authentic poetic voice with a technical
mastery of his craft to match his spiritual affinity for it. (p.
21)

[Ciardi] focuses with remarkable clarity on the elements
upon which one builds a theme into a poem. Ciardi is passionate about *writing* poetry; he recognizes full well the
axiom that it is the poem which gives the theme its force.

It is in the poetic handling of his subjects (i.e., the
"rhythm, diction, image, and form") that Ciardi reveals his
poetic principles most clearly, and here we find him very
consistent. He most often uses, for example, a closed
"form." That is, his poems are normally tightly contained
in traditional stanzas, although he frequently spreads syntactical units from one stanza to another. Containment of
this sort extends from individual stanzas to entire poems,
creating an unmistakable sense of completion, but completion in a Ciardi poem is built of other elements as well. His
ideas, for example, are developed within standard grammatical constructions, using normal word order more frequently than inverted forms. As to "rhythm," Ciardi's aim
is to achieve natural speech patterns and to reflect a "living" language; he uses what he calls a "sensitively trained
memory" of iambic pentameter, "the norm of English metrics." . . . (pp. 21-2)

Another key element of Ciardi's poetic principles is his desire to be understood. . . . Ciardi's poems occasionally fail
because they are *too* understandable. . . . Stated differently, the accumulated effect of predictability in stanzas,
grammar-patterns, and rhythms has a kind of logical
sturdiness—and the expectation of it—which is, too often,
an implicit threat to the metaphorical logic of the poem. Yet
this is but an occasional failing, and it is important to remember that Ciardi never intended to sacrifice the logic of
metaphor. . . .

Ciardi's verse is intensely personal, introspective, and self-
revealing. His poems reflect the quiet considerations of a
thoughtful, sensitive man. They are not white-hot representations of emotion: Ciardi more often *thinks* about passion.
His "diction" is less emotionally charged than it is intricately patterned. Frequently passion emerges in Ciardi

"imagery" only after it has been filtered through the poet's sense of the ironic or comic. . . .

The theme that exemplifies the great diversity of Ciardi's talent is poetry itself. Such poems as "The Gift," "On the poet as a marionette," "The Poet's Words," "A Guide to Poetry," "Why don't you write for me?" and "Vodka" clearly reveal his great poetic inventiveness. Each poem is about poetry, but no two poems are alike: they are, in turn, meditative, spiritual, despairing, cynical, arrogant, and humorous. From a technical standpoint, Ciardi has altered his handling of "rhythm, diction, image, and form" to meet the specific needs of the various poems. (p. 22)

["The Size of Song"] is one of Ciardi's marvelous small achievements. It consists of two equal movements of eight lines each and deals with the symbolic connection between birds and the creative or poetic spirit. Birds to Ciardi are always something special. They represent pure song, perfect, freedom, prayer in motion, and aesthetic experience. Ciardi develops this poem along literal and figurative lines simultaneously. At the literal level, of course, the details are physically right: the smaller birds sing the prettiest songs while the larger birds can neither sing nor fly. . . . Figuratively, however, "bird" becomes the symbol for "poet," and the poem may be read as a commentary on the "successful" poet.

The argument of "The Size of Song" is simply that, in the first place, smaller birds sing the best songs, and, in the second place, larger birds eventually lose their power not only to sing but also to fly. The size of the poem is consistently small which, in a passing sort of way, makes the poem reflect its content through its form but, more importantly, adds intensity to the symbol. . . .

The opening lines of stanza one contain a simple statement as well as a delicate image of a tiny, songful bird. "Some rule of birds kills off the song / in any that begin to grow / much larger than a fist or so." . . . The lines have no punctuation except the final period, and this lack of punctuation combines with certain sound values—smooth liquids, sliding sibilants, and open long vowels—to create a sense of unimpeded motion. The effect of motion is perfect as it prefigures the image of flight which will soon be developed. (p. 23)

The final three lines of the first stanza are divided into two sentences, almost identical in length. In the first, "Bird music is the tremolo / of the tremulous," there is a delicate turn on the bird image. In these lines the bird-poet connection becomes a bit more insistent. The word "song" back in line 1 is a shortened form of "bird song" (on the literal level), but "bird music" in line 6 is not quite the same thing. The word "music" implies *artistic composition,* coming from the Greek *mousikos,* meaning "of the Muses." The sounds of birds are "bird songs," never "bird music." This is an important poetic addition as it begins to develop the poem's primary symbol. The words "tremolo" and "tremulous" play perfectly on each other, suggesting at the same time human sound and weakness while being physically apropos of birds as well. (pp. 23, 26)

Metrically . . . both stanzas create a sense of speed and motion, altered at the end for a special effect. Through its metrics, its sounds, and its strong sense of freedom within form, the poem actually reproduces a flight-like motion. And the motion is made even more bird-like by the kind of floating pause between stanzas, possibly intended to re-create the momentary pause that birds take as they drift or fall free for an instant in time.

"The Size of Song" is a considerable poetic achievement. The image of the bird-poet is neatly built and expanded on both levels while at the same time the poem is structurally the embodiment of both rules of birds: it is small and it flies.

"The Size of Song" is also a good example of Ciardi's poetic principles in action. The poem is a "journey to itself," and at the same time it is a self-revealing journey into the poet. Moreover, the treatment of his subject in this poem is representative of Ciardi's attitudes and techniques. . . . It has, for example, the type of tight closure which Ciardi tries for, and it may be noted here that the poem's containment is less box-like than it is circular. In point of fact, the poem is most like the figure eight in that it captures a sense of fluid motion which seems to turn in and out at the same time, always turning back on itself to reach its point of origin. Grammatically and rhythmically the poem is typical of Ciardi's work; the atypical sentence fragment with which he ends the poem achieves some of its effectiveness because the reader receives it with surprise. The short line at the very end is also a break with the metrical pattern of the poem, effective, in part, because of its very difference.

Finally, it may be noted that "The Size of Song" is ultimately a poem with a reflective tone. The poet recalls in a series of observations a set of relationships which he believes to be true of the poet and his art. He engages us more intellectually than passionately, and the result is that we are able to gain an aesthetic perspective which is, to me, worth having—and sharing. (pp. 26-7)

> Edward Cifelli, "The Size of John Ciardi's Song," in The CEA Critic (copyright © 1973 by the College English Association, Inc.), November, 1973, pp. 21-3, 26-7.

*   *   *

COBURN, D(onald) L(ee)   193?-

Coburn, an American dramatist, won the 1978 Pulitzer Prize in Drama for his first play, *The Gin Game*.

BRENDAN GILL

["The Gin Game"] itself hints at the author's youth: by a readily understandable paradox, old playwrights tend to write about the remembered splendors of the past (and tend to get them all wrong), while young playwrights tend to write about the imagined horrors of the future (and tend to get them pretty nearly right). Mr. Coburn is telling us about a couple of miserable inmates of an old people's home, whose plight he observes with an astringent clarity and about whom, at the same time, he manages to be very funny. . . .

Mr. Coburn is also lucky in having the limited action of his play—we are present at four increasingly irascible bouts of gin rummy and at nothing else. . . . The dramatic function of the buffetings exchanged by the couple are, by the way, curiously old-fashioned; they are the Ibsen-like means of peeling off layer after layer of their earlier lives and holding them up to the still unbearable light of truth. The last notes struck in the play are unalleviatedly despairing, and it is one of the most precious mysteries of the theatre that, having heard these notes struck, we should go up the aisle and out onto Broadway with happy hearts. (p. 93)

> *Brendan Gill, in* The New Yorker (© *1977 by The New Yorker Magazine, Inc.), October 17, 1977.*

HAROLD CLURMAN

The first "straight" play of the Broadway season is *The Gin Game*....

It is nicely written and sympathetic in feeling. Two elderly people—the play's only characters—meet in a home for the aged. Their chief mode of contact is through the card game of the title. Through this, the author manages to suggest the loneliness of old age, the competition between the sexes or perhaps only the competitiveness of most human exchanges, the difficulty of people, even when they have very much in common, to arrive at a reasonably full accord.

In the hands of a Chekhov or a Schnitzler, the play's scheme might prove an apt means to achieve true poignancy. The exemplary American tonality of the play, with its two altogether ordinary characters whose personal backgrounds are only thinly sketched, leaves it rather slight. There is, especially in the first act, too much reliance on the sheer comedy of the game, more entertaining to those familiar with it than to others. (p. 445)

> *Harold Clurman, in* The Nation (*copyright 1977 by the Nation Associates, Inc.), October 29, 1977.*

CATHARINE HUGHES

[*The Gin Game*] takes place in an old-age home where two people who have recently met engage in a series of gin rummy games....

Coburn asks us to believe—and it is a perfectly honorable request—that these two, the one the embodiment of cantankerousness, the other a fairly typical prude who all her life has driven away those she most wished to keep, are lonely and alone not because of the divorce and estrangement suffered in their marriages but because of their temperaments. That, in a sense, they have always been lonely if not always alone, unable to rectify the flaws or characteristics that have made them so.

Perhaps a more experienced dramatist could have made more of what is, after all, an affecting and not uninteresting —if also not especially original—theme. What Coburn has made of it is a bit too predictable, a bit too clichéd and more than a bit too static to sustain an evening. (p. 334)

> *Catharine Hughes, in* America (© *America Press, 1977; all rights reserved), November 12, 1977.*

STANLEY KAUFFMANN

The gin games [in *The Gin Game*] are presumably meant as double symbols: first, as a geriatric substitute for courtship-and-sex, in which [the female protagonist] is unwelcomely, even unwillingly, dominant; second, as an x-ray exposure of [the two main] characters, revealing darknesses in both, beneath the cozy old-folks exteriors.

The only really interesting aspect of this play is that there's another play lurking within it. The author, D. L. Coburn, whose first play this is, may be delighted with this produc-

tion for all I know, but it occurred to me while watching it that the very same text could be legitimately used to less conventional ends. *The Gin Game* is now being done in (let's call it) the Paddy Chayefsky-Neil Simon vein: "We are ruthless modern truthtellers who scrape a whole fat millimeter below the Norman Rockwell surface, and we prove our *bona fides* by not giving you the hand-in-hand sunset-trail ending you expected." But this script could, I think, be played so that the ending is not a surprise, but inevitable, so that the intent is not to put a stinger at the end of a bittersweet piece of candy but to strip away some of the sentimental prerogatives of old age. If these two old people exploited their age, as stupid or vicious or spoiled elderly people often do, knowing even with each other—that they were claiming wisdom and respect the way one claims a pension, just because one has reached the right age; if it were the intent to show that age, not patriotism, is the last refuge of scoundrels, this might have been a moderately scathing play.

But it wouldn't have been a hit. So we get a "realistic" play instead of a real one. (p. 24)

> *Stanley Kauffmann, in* The New Republic (*reprinted by permission of* The New Republic; © *1977 by The New Republic, Inc.), November 12, 1977.*

* * *

COMPTON-BURNETT, Ivy 1892-1969

A prolific British novelist who wrote exclusively of the late-Victorian upper middle class, Compton-Burnett is numbered among the best English women writers of her generation. Her work consists of psychological novels that deal with murder, incest, and forgery, and avoids the melodramatic or sentimental. Rather, she exposes, with cool, cynical wit, the cruelty and complexities of families and the tyranny of personal relationships. Though concerned with moral values, she allows wickedness to go unpunished and the good to suffer. Description is minimal in Compton-Burnett's novels, with plot revealed almost entirely through lengthy dialogue. (See also *CLC*, Vols. 1, 3, and *Contemporary Authors*, Vols. 1-4, rev. ed.; obituary, Vols. 25-28, rev. ed.)

MALCOLM PITTOCK

[The] non-conversational parts of [Compton-Burnett's prose] have the brevity and quality of stage directions....

The dialogue itself has certain obvious characteristics: each of the characters expresses himself or herself in the same elevated, stilted, and sententious diction . . . and in a formal fluently staccato speech rhythm which is itself removed from the rhythms of normal conversation. (p. 44)

The brief descriptions of action are deliberately reminiscent of stage directions because Miss Compton-Burnett wished to stress that her characters are not behaving naturally: they are acting: and each is acting not only for the benefit of the others but for himself or herself. The dialogue is un-individualised because it is thus capable of embodying the author's sense that the consciousness of self issuing in the individual's desire to act a part is a central truth about civilised man and underlies what she sees as superficial differences of temperament and character. A more naturalistic mode of dialogue would have brought the differences between people into prominence whereas it is the similarities that she wishes to emphasise. The formal elevation of the dialogue can also be explained as a means of conveying to us that it is civilisation which, constraining our egotism and our conflicts with others within a formal code of behaviour and speech, prevents us from expressing them directly while allowing us to do so obliquely, and provides us with a variety of roles to play. (pp. 44-5)

Ivy Compton-Burnett's constant theme . . . is what civilisation does to people: the way in which the necessity to act according to a code of behaviour imposes an artificial pattern on human relationships, thus enhancing conflicts which it still further exacerbates by ensuring that they are expressed obliquely in a manner that puts a premium on our concealing or distorting what we really feel the better to deceive ourselves and/or manipulate others. Paradoxically it is civilisation which allows us to give the worst side of ourselves full play: if only we obey the rules or appear to obey them, we can, emotionally speaking, get away with anything. It is no wonder that secret crime makes a constant appearance in Ivy Compton-Burnett's novels, for it is a symbol of the festering violence and passion which the distorting effects of civilisation produce.

It is because this is her theme that her novels are always set among Edwardian families of the upper middle class, for we would agree that in these a more than usually rigid code of behaviour was accompanied by a corresponding degree of conscious or unconscious hypocrisy in the expression of conflict—a conflict which was itself exacerbated by the extreme artificiality of the socially endorsed pattern of family relationship. And in making some of the members of her Edwardian families actual criminals she is only making symbolic capital out of the fact that many such families had a skeleton of one kind or another in the cupboard. But, of course, for her Edwardian family life is a convenient paradigm of civilisation as a whole.

In her own way, then, Ivy Compton-Burnett reflects that distrust of civilisation, that sense that it is at least an ambiguous good, which is a wide-spread pattern of feeling, appearing in many novels superficially so different from hers. In her novels it is, however, represented with a narrow intensity which complements the diagrammatic stylization of her chosen mode. Ultimately, her work is unsatisfactory—an unsatisfactoriness manifesting itself as a thin repetitiousness—for though she presents with great force an interpretation of society she has not a flexible enough art to convey any real sense of its haecceity. (p. 46)

> *Malcolm Pittock, "Ivy Compton-Burnett's Use of Dialogue," in* English Studies (© *1970 by Swets & Zeitlinger B.V.), Vol. 51, No. 1, 1970, pp. 43-6.*

MALCOLM BRADBURY

It was in *Pastors and Masters* in 1925 that [Compton-Burnett's] main work began, and you might say that like William Faulkner with *Sartoris* she discovered a universe of her own which she was always to continue populating. She . . . started publishing under the reticent name of "I. Compton-Burnett", sexually confusing to some of her readers, and most of the main sequence came out as slimmish, economical and very abstemiously-presented books, . . . all appearing very much kin among themselves, and all having a universe and a tone in common. The universe was reassuring, but the tone not. It was savagely aphoristic and

ironic, and touched the world she handled with sensationalism and a devastating moral exposure which was less an attack on it than on life itself. The mixture of reticence and sensationalism, of nostalgia and irony, attracted much attention, and this finally became a high reputation. . . . However, the books were, and remain, ambiguous. One could see in them a kind of essential artlessness, or else a very high kind of artistic management, a precision of control both moral and technical of the most eminent sort. One could read them as an elegant camp game played with life, or as a harsh and cruel, almost a tragic, vision of experience. And one could find them either basically reassuring novels, nostalgic under the wit and malice, or else profoundly disturbing works. These questions raise others about the entire tone of her feelings about life, and about her technical assurance and her general contribution to the modern novel, in which she has undoubtedly played the part of a goad and an influence. (pp. 71-2)

I. Compton-Burnett is—in the very strict sense of the term—a conventional writer; she writes, that is, to her own made convention. . . . [She] early saw the uses of a persistent underplaying of explicit character detail, generating a drama of mystification in which the clear characteristics of persons are often subordinated to the total intercourse of the particular group or scene of which they are a part. But more important is the fact that the novels are set in a distinctive world of motives, principles, and experiences, a very sparse and cruel one, which is manifested in every novel as a single social world. In its historical place, this world can be dated and fixed: this is England, its landed gentry, in the period around 1880-1910, a period roughly coinciding with the author's birth and reaching (on occasion) through toward her maturity, though usually stopping short. It is an historically arrested world, one kept very pure by the author. . . . (p. 72)

I. Compton-Burnett not only makes but isolates a society. The convention is in some ways very fictional indeed, a recourse to a world established in other, and much earlier novels. . . . Her novels . . . don't so much belong to a period as conventionalise a historical phase suitable to her temper, her interests, her sense of human nature, and her feelings about the arena in which the basic aspects of human action are most really exposed. This arena is the family, within whose limits most of the action is confined, and the historical period she uses is one when the family was at its apogee, reinforced not only by that apparatus of servants, governesses, family solicitors and inheritance laws which she draws on for her cast and her plots, but also by concepts of power and patriarchy themselves profoundly interwoven with religious beliefs. This makes family life a total functional milieu. But it is also notable that she sets her book right on the edge of this phase of things, for the attack on the family in this solidly institutional form was already active in the late Victorian age she writes of—often conducted, especially in novels like *The Way of All Flesh* and *Father and Son,* through the instrument of a high agnostic irony showing the moral threats to egotism of this closed world. I. Compton-Burnett's novels act as if they were synchronic with such books; but the difference is that her world is that much more artificial, much cooler, more distant, and given in the distilled hard manner of more modern novels. In this way they turn into timeless works, novels about the Laingian politics of the unhappy family, seen above all as a struggle for power, precedence and affection in a world of self-knowing agents capable of arbitrary or half-revealed emotions, sudden emotional shifts and peccadilloes, and legal violations of every kind up to incest and murder. (pp. 72-3)

Miss Compton-Burnett, conventionalising a society and in her way universalising it, creates a world of grand self-awareness, where characters are capable of seeing themselves both in the light of their own egoism and in large schemas of power, precedence and affection, where even children know and utter the telling conditions of their own tenure . . . , and where the outright laws of the emotional jungle prevail. . . . The result is a fiction that seems to cross the regal courts and dynastic houses of tragedy with the sexual ambiguities and variations of French farce. The recurrent principle or paradox is a comic one—the profoundly exercised restraint of the novelist, paring down the telling in the direction of dialogue, simplified character-presentation and rapid plot-motion, interacts with the enormities of murder, incest, and an emotional promiscuity verging on the insane in persons capable, as all are, of high reason and self-knowledge. And it is telling because it is essentially anguished. . . . (pp. 73-4)

You could say that Miss Compton-Burnett ignores all the possible emotional gains in the pleasure of exposing, like some familial Marxist, the substructure of interest. Her irony has a moral passion to it, but it is in the end very carping and modern; it is this that helps bring her work into relation to other great contemporary novels. (p. 74)

> *Malcolm Bradbury, "Unhappy Families Are All Alike: New Views of Ivy Compton-Burnett," in* Encounter *(© 1973 by Encounter Ltd.), July, 1973, pp. 71-4.*

R. J. MacSWEEN

Ivy Compton-Burnett seems to be one of the undoubted classics to have emerged from the modern period. (p. 25)

Like anyone else, she had to learn her craft by experience, and her first book, *Dolores* (1911), is a dolorous thing indeed. It is stolid, conventional, without the imprint of Ivy's own peculiar nature. It could have been written by a dozen other beginners in the field of fiction. Time passed by until 1925 when *Pastors and Masters* appeared before the public. It, also, is not really vintage Ivy and is distinctly a minor work, but the book has the Ivy quality—the dry dialogue, the probing for secret motivations, the revelation of man's evil in the average mind, and, above all, an aphoristic turn of phrase. From then on Ivy is the wielder of the scalpel, the feared investigator of secret crime. (p. 26)

Reading a novel of Ivy's, one gets the impression that La Rochefoucauld is on the loose again, but this time he has taken to fiction. His salon is replaced by the closed family circle; his eye and ear monitor modern man; the impact of his maxims is diffused into the fictional matrix, and the blows come without the same quality of surprise. In fact, Ivy's famous syntatical control resembles that of a person who has labored assiduously over every word and phrase. This is the secret of her style; as we read we sense a listening group, acute and critical, who wait with amused expectation the hammer of a perfectly turned phrase. That is why her novels have been compared with eighteenth century comedy, as they could as well be with the comedy of Oscar Wilde. (pp. 28-9)

Ivy presents us with a series of unusual plots, sprung like monsters from the basements of genteel houses. We find in those claustrophobic enclosures all the terror of worldly power and crime. There is simply no place for escape. In her small world everyone must suffer or exploit suffering. There is every form of tyranny, every form of betrayal, every form of deceit and dishonesty. It is the contrast between the every-day ordinariness of the setting with the crime that makes the monsters so monstrous. The fathers and mothers, the children, the kept relative, the butler and the maid—everyone seems waiting either in expectation of a blow (generally verbal) or in the act of giving one. It is a world of fear, of passive suffering, of painful aging, of resentful poverty. (pp. 29-30)

> *R. J. MacSween, "Ivy Compton-Burnett," in* The Antigonish Review *(copyright 1975 by R. J. MacSween), Winter, 1975, pp. 25-30.*

JULIAN MITCHELL

The novels of I Compton-Burnett, as she always styled herself on the title-page, are quite unlike anyone else's, and she was proud of it—indeed, she was very scornful of critics who tried to compare her with other writers (usually Jane Austen, Euripides and Henry James). But her originality for many years repelled as many readers as it attracted. Though she was very much admired by a few, it was, to begin with, only a few. The main difficulty that readers had, and have, is that the books are written almost entirely in highly stylised dialogue. The conversations are so full of nuance and subtlety that it takes a new reader several chapters to get the hang of them, and sometimes he gives up in despair. There is no internalisation, no 'he thought' and 'she wondered', to help him understand what's going on or what the characters' motives are. Nor is there much description: each person is given a detailed portrait on his or her first appearance, but after that there is almost nothing. There is no description of landscape, either, or of the houses and rooms in which the characters talk and talk and talk. And, greatest difficulty of all, the characters seem at first reading, and sometimes at second, all to talk alike. This is an illusion: once one's ear is trained to Compton-Burnett one can hear that everyone speaks quite differently and individually. But new readers often get lost, can't work out who's speaking, and have to go back several pages and start the whole conversation again. Ivy said herself that once you'd put one of her books down, it was hard to pick it up again.

But it you get past these initial—one might say initiation—difficulties, the novels are wonderfully rewarding. They almost all concern the goings-on of large gentry families who live in the country at the turn of the century. Ivy's opinion of people was, on the whole, low. Dudley Gaveston, . . . in *A Family and A Fortune* . . . , says: 'It is a pity we have to be human. Human failings, human vanity, human weakness! We don't hear the word applied to anything good. Even human nature seems a derogatory term.' All Compton-Burnett novels are full of weak and vain humans failing spectacularly to behave well. The plots are often highly melodramatic, though the action is brief and only briefly described. Its function is to allow the characters to discuss the new light it sheds on everyone's motives, past and present, and how it affects their opinions of each other. The discussion is both dazzlingly witty and painfully truthful. All the families have tyrants who dominate them; truth is the only weapon the oppressed have to defend themselves. Long before R D Laing, Ivy Compton-Burnett had shown over and over again that the family unit could be an extremely destructive force. . . .

Plots didn't interest Ivy. She said they were like clotheslines—very necessary, you have to hang the washing from *something*—but it was the washing that mattered, not the line. As a result, there is often something arbitrary about her plots, and though that is perfectly acceptable within the novels, it makes most of them unsuitable for the stage. They are melodramatic rather than theatrical. (p. 8)

Ivy allowed her characters every possible variation on each theme. . . . The way Compton-Burnett characters examine everything minutely, never missing a possible nuance, gives Ivy's readers their greatest pleasure. (pp. 9-10)

> *Julian Mitchell, "On Adapting Ivy," in* Plays and Players *(© copyright Hansom Books 1975), April, 1975, pp. 8-10.*

* * *

CONDON, Richard   1915-

Condon is an American novelist, screenwriter, and playwright who currently resides in Ireland. His work attacks the absurdity and clichés of modern culture, especially concerning organized crime, motion pictures, corruption, and violence. Inventive and entertaining, his humor is based on exaggeration and excess. But it is a painful humor, undercut with despair and concern for moral values. A highly readable author, Condon is gaining popularity, attracting an almost cult following. (See also *CLC***, Vols. 4, 6, 8, and** *Contemporary Authors***, Vols. 1-4, rev. ed.)**

HERBERT GOLD

Richard Condon has tireless wit (though sometimes it fatigues the reader) and must enjoy what he is doing without necessarily believing it. And what he does can be fun—Nabokov without tears. (p. 10)

From internal evidence, one judges that [Condon] knows full well what he is doing, even if he might prefer to be doing something wise rather than shrewd. He bills ["Bandicoot"] as the companion to "Arigato," which is one I missed; but burrowing "as fast as a man can dig"—as in the description of the Australian rodent, the bandicoot, printed in the front of the book—I seemed to make sufficient sense, or nonsense, of an entertainer's latest entertainment.

Here . . . we have world travel, the famous and the rich, the powerful and the wicked, plus the usual food, drink and girlish meat-strudel of a Condon concoction. A certain megapop tic limits any commitment. We suspend both belief and disbelief. Is Richard Condon too smart for the novel? One wishes he didn't fall back on clever tics. Names are dropped or pulled in for laffs. Sometimes the burlesque gets the laugh he wants, as when an Olympic freestyle sexual event ends with: "Bitsy's frequent outcries were so piercing that they were taken for small craft warnings by fishing vessels.". . .

Mr. Condon's people at least allow us to believe in ourselves; we remain alive though reading. One wishes fairly steadily now that he would not waylay us with show-biz

puns and characters named after real people familiar to those who followed Cholly Knickerbocker's columns.

"Bandicoot" is a confection that amuses. It might be better if, in his self-delighted way, Mr. Condon made another stab at living up to the ringing proclamation of his essay on The Novel in Harper's: "When we want to understand grief beyond grief, or the external confrontation of man and woman, man and God, man and himself, we go to the novel." Failing grief beyond grief and eternal confrontations, we can here at least take pleasure in some frequent and piercing offhand funning that will hardly disturb any fishing vessels. (p. 39)

> *Herbert Gold, in* The New York Times Book Review *(© 1978 by The New York Times Company; reprinted by permission), March 12, 1978.*

WILLIAM COLE

Condon is a romper, and [*Bandicoot*] is one of his wilder and funnier romps. The plot? Forget it! The story concerns a gambling-mad ex-British naval captain, Japanese industrialists (they stretch their Rolls-Royces a few feet to make them the world's longest), oil deposits under Australia's Great Barrier Reef. Unlike other writers of improbable derring-do, Condon gives lots of little side essays on such things as ballooning, opal mining, haute cuisine, and sexual positions.

> *William Cole, "A Romper," in* Saturday Review *(© 1978 by Saturday Review Magazine Corp.; reprinted with permission), March 18, 1978, p. 55.*

RICK DAVIS

Satire is always difficult to write and often is difficult to understand. We have read the works of many authors who have failed in their attempts; not Condon. He's a master at it. . . . In a very funny, wild chase across the Australian outback—including a flight in a balloon—Condon pulls out all stops [in *Bandicoot*]. Condon deals in impossible situations but he makes them very plausible—and funny. (p. 31)

> *Rick Davis, in* West Coast Review of Books *(copyright 1978 by Rapport Publishing Co., Inc.), Vol. 4, No. 3 (May, 1978).*

ANTHONY R. CANNELLA

[*Bandicott*] has some very funny redeeming qualities: Yvonne Bonnette, the hero's mistress, has the body of "a ripened Nereid every square inch of whose skin was an erogenous zone." In the boudoir, when not otherwise engaged, she plays the saxophone. . . . Such humor, however, is sporadic in *Bandicoot*. And even when it surfaces, sometimes with rib-tickling effect, it is undermined by Condon's complete lack of restraint. A less experienced writer could be excused for this overkill of mirth, but one expects more from the veteran author. . . .

Condon stuffs [this novel] with humor—outrageous, more outrageous, most outrageous—until . . . it explodes and sputters into oblivion. (p. 101)

> *Anthony R. Cannella, in* Best Sellers *(copyright © 1978 Helen Dwight Reid Educational Foundation), July, 1978.*

CORTÁZAR, Julio   1914-

Cortázar is an Argentine novelist, short story writer, translator, and poet. Like his fellow Argentine and mentor, Borges, Cortázar creates a fictional work in which fantasy and reality are indistinguishable. In this bewildering dream world his characters are portrayed as victims both of their delusions and of the fantastic world around them. Cortázar's short story "Las babas del diablo" was made into the film *Blowup*. (See also *CLC*, Vols. 2, 3, 5, and *Contemporary Authors*, Vols. 21-24, rev. ed.)

DAVID I. GROSSVOGEL

Like most of Cortázar's short stories, ["Las babas del diablo"] is primarily a tale about the impossiblity of *telling* and about the frustration of *seeing*—twin expressions of the ontological dilemma that defines man, for Cortázar, as an irreducible separateness that recognizes similarly hermetic presences, without ever being able to establish more than a surface contact with them, without being able to *assimilate* them through either perception (sight) or definition (telling). The dramatic tension of Cortázar's stories derives from the exacerbation of their people's attempts to cancel and transcend their ontological sentence. They fail, but their efforts are sometimes of such magnitude as to alter forever the order of the natural world in which they previously dwelled.

Michel is a translator: his job is to understand *telling* and to make it *intelligible* to others. . . . But as a consequence of his unearthly adventure Michel will sense that his plight resulted from a desperation to see beyond the surfaces that limit human sight, and that even beyond existence (for the people of Cortázar are afflicted with the same curse as Beckett's people: death does not still their metaphysical questioning) the problem remains one of *telling*.

Michel's dilemma is that however he focuses on the objects of his world, those objects remain separate from him and alien; his focusing instrument—the camera, the typewriter, the word—cannot *bite* on those objects, is irremediably inert. . . . (p. 50)

As the virulence of the ontological sickness intensifies, the victim's urge to escape into, and possess, his vision increases his need to voice the sense of his proximity to this vision and the sense of his frustration at not being able to cancel the forever remaining distance. He must *tell* his state of being. . . . Just as the still photograph subverts the life it intends to reproduce, the very act of telling subverts the substance of what is to be told. . . . But in Michel, as in so many of Cortázar's protagonists, the ontological exacerbation is sufficient to affect the fourth dimension of his universe; like that of a latter-day Pygmalion, Michel's relentless desire to possess the object of his sight informs the photographic blow-up with the life of that desire and that life is sufficiently powerful to draw him into its own truth. He crosses over to another ontological dimension (retracing, in a sense, the steps of the surrealists drawn into their metaphysical mirror) and, in so doing, forever affects the natural balance of his universe without allaying the need that precipitated the metaphysical calamity.

Whatever else the parable may convey about the human condition, Cortázar's fable comments upon the Mallarmean need and frustration of the writer whose work is tensed between his unbounded vision and his unequal capacity to express it. Cortázar makes a literary point from the very first. . . . Like Michel, the artist can neither tell as he knows he must, nor can he accept *not* to tell, or tell inadequately. He must possess through words (if he is a writer) the objects of his world (and his sense of those objects), but the words have an opacity equal to his own ontological encapsulation: he cannot *be* the other and therefore he cannot *tell* what that other is, and the failure of telling extends to his inability to tell in its fullest the failure of telling. His attempts end in fiction. The writer is doomed to live out the double anxiety of his failure to achieve or voice the intensity of his questioning, but through a process of world reversal, his anxiety becomes the parafictional substance of his character. Michel's hunger and his agony are those of Cortázar—the writer attempting to deliver himself of that "tickle" in his own stomach and of which Michel is only an irremediable fiction. Michel's hopeless journey is the desperate groping of his creator. (pp. 50-1)

In the Cortázar story, Michel so desires his inadequate artifact to be more than its inadequacy that the artifact is ultimately loosed from the bonds that normally keep it within the phenomenal world and becomes, ironically, the object that *possesses* him. (In a similar way, the hero of Cortázar's "Axolotl" is so fascinated by the salamanders in the aquarium that his exacerbated need to *know* them projects him within the object of his desire: it is as an axolotl that he can finally see the desireless part of him losing interest in, and leaving, the aquarium.) When this intensity to know turns the characters into the representation of the one who conceived them (and the reason for that conception), the characters can no longer tolerate the artifact that has come to stand as an opacity between them and their artistic sense of the world. But they must also be the evidence of the unbridgeable distance that persists between artistic desire and expression: they must enter, without ever penetrating it, the object of their creation. . . . (p. 52)

> *David I. Grossvogel, in* Diacritics *(copyright © Diacritics, Inc., 1972), Fall, 1972.*

LANIN A. GYURKO

Many of the short stories of Julio Cortázar present situations that appear to be absurd or fantastic. . . . These stories of the bestial and the demonic may be interpreted on two different levels. One is the purely fantastic or supernatural, in which time is cyclical and the self has avatar identities. Metempsychoses occur not only between two human souls but between human and animal spirits. Demonic forces are conjured up, sometimes by a weird pagan ritual and at others by a type of extrasensory process or mental telepathy. Yet another, equally convincing tack of interpretation, and one that attests to the complexity of the short fiction of Cortázar, is to view him as a realist author and to interpret the bizarre experiences that plague the lives of his characters as due to the operation of their own disturbed consciousnesses. Their minds are invaded by subconscious impulses which they initially can suppress but which finally increase in power and overwhelm them. Thus the world of the short stories of this modern Argentine author becomes one of delusions, hallucinations, and nightmares—powerful fantasies that at times have the strength to kill and that frequently destroy the minds of the afflicted characters. If seen as inhabiting a realm constantly invaded by the supernatural, Cortázar's characters are pawns of fate, suborned by demons that they struggle against but whom they are compelled to obey. But if viewed in realistic, psychological terms, in most instances Cortázar's characters destroy their own selves. Fate becomes an inner force, the relentless action of the obsessed and tormented consciousness.

Most all of Cortázar's characters are prone to absorption into fantasy worlds because they are narcissistic, socially alienated, and emotionally unstable. They have no strong or meaningful outer lives to counterbalance the awesome power of their delusions. These individuals are studies in deficiency. Many lack will, courage, professional role, social relationships, and, often, even a name. (p. 988)

Fantasy worlds are experienced with a conviction and an intensity that make them real for the characters. External reality, on the other hand, recedes to the level of the unreal. (pp. 988-89)

Cortázar's narrative art is one of paradox, ambiguity, and ironic reversal. Throughout his short fiction there is a subtle blending of reality and illusion, nightmare and waking consciousness, man and beast, self and other, present and past, terror and humor, myth and fact, art (visual, verbal, musical) and life. Neither time nor space, psychic identity nor social role remain certain. In many stories reality is a mere façade that masks the demonic. . . .

The protean quality of Cortázar's world is particularly evident in the schizophrenic nature of many of his protagonists. (p. 989)

The unstable identities of the characters are often given a structural expression within the stories. Some are narrated in constantly shifting panels of present and remote past, reality and nightmare. The protagonist of "El otro cielo" rotates between experiences within the bourgeois world of Buenos Aires in the 1940's and adventures within his secret fantasy zone of Paris of 1870. His imaginative life is narrated with the same if not greater sense of authenticity as is his life in the real world. The story "La noche boca arriba" constantly oscillates between the twentieth century identity of the protagonist as a victim of a motorcycle accident and an oneiric self as an ancient Moteca Indian being pursued by Aztec warriors as a victim for blood sacrifice. The delirious mind of the guilt-stricken girl Wanda in "Siestas" confuses memory and nightmare, perception and hallucination. The molester with the hand of wax, initially a nightmare, finally materializes for the stricken girl, who has been driven insane. The hellworld created by the solipsistic consciousness is stylistically dramatized in many of Cortázar's narratives through a third-person indirect interior monologue or modified stream of consciousness technique. "Bestiario," "Las armas secretas," and "Siestas" combine this technique with sentence-pyramiding at the climactic moment of the narrative. The bewilderment and terror of the characters are strikingly conveyed through use of this onrush of thoughts that endows the narratives with high dramatic tension.

Many of the narratives use the labyrinth as the symbol *par excellence* of the mind in crisis. In Cortázar's first major work *Los reyes* (1949), a dramatic dialogue that is a variation on the myth of Theseus and the Minotaur, the labyrinth is not only a physical structure but also a symbol of the mind. (p. 990)

In addition to the labyrinth, another factor in many of the narratives that contributes to their air of unreality is that the protagonists are often artists—writers, photographers, musicians—or they are endowed with febrile imaginations easily influenced by artistic expression. Yet, ironically, the creative experience turns out to be a destructive one for most of the characters. (p. 991)

A third factor that undergirds the unreality of Cortázar's stories and which emphasizes the fatalism of his vision is his use of classical myths. . . . Cortázar also uses myths of destruction and of blood sacrifice in his novel *62: Modelo para armar* (1968). The will of Juan is negated by his being situated within a mythic time of misfortune and terror. He is compared with Acteon, torn apart by the hounds of Diana for having dared to look upon the goddess while she was bathing. Diana is the frigid Hélène, adored by Juan but who herself is a victim. Hélène is also linked with Iphigenia, the daughter sacrificed by Agamemnon. (pp. 991-92)

The fantasies of Cortázar's characters can be categorized into two major kinds, both predominantly negative: destructive and ironically redemptive. The destructive fantasies of the characters have their basis in fear, guilt, jealousy, or a thanatos instinct. Most of them initially are subconscious and are manifested in dreams and nightmares, but they rapidly become conscious and pervade the waking hours of the characters. These obsessive fantasies undermine the will and the integrity of the protagonists and often lead to their insanity, death, or both. Ironically redemptive fantasy can itself be divided into three types: premonitory, deceptive, and positive but unrealizable. Premonitory fantasy always adumbrates disaster or death. It is ironically redemptive in that although the characters are warned, often repeatedly, of their fate, they prefer to dismiss or to suppress these adumbrations. Instead they nurture another form of fantasy—their own illusions of self-exaltation. While destructive fantasies are afflictive from the start, deceptive fantasies initially seem to hold the promise of self-transcendence for the characters. . . .

Deceptive fantasies, initially reinforcing the characters, turn destructive. Positive fantasies, which do not change, are visions of paradisiacal worlds, most often on the conscious level of reveries or daydreams. Marini in "El otro cielo" nurtures his dream of an island paradise; the narrator of "Silvia" is entranced by the vision of the beautiful and enticing dream girl. These positive fantasies act as a compensation for the identity or fulfillment that the characters are unable to find in the real world. Detaching themselves from emotional involvement with others and shunning a professional reality that they see as tedious, constricting, and incapable of being changed, they become passive rebels, withdrawing into their own solipsistic paradises of the imagination. Yet they cannot achieve salvation through submersion in their fantasy realms. The delight, wonder, exhilaration and sense of freedom that they experience are all fleeting. At the end they are defeated from without by an adverse and dominating reality that often leads to their brutal disillusionment. (p. 992)

Destructive fantasies are most often the result of guilt feelings that work on the febrile imaginations of the characters. (p. 993)

Destructive fantasies are also a manifestation of the thanatos instinct that afflicts many of Cortázar's characters. The creative search that Johnny Carter in "El perseguidor" consciously undertakes for a higher plane of existence is a desperate reaction to a more powerful, subconscious urge to destroy himself. . . .

In many of the stories of destructive fantasy, the nightmares and delusions of the characters are linked with a past that is primitive, savage, and demonic. The maniacal Somoza in "El ídolo de las Cícladas" deliberately conjures up the primitive spirit of blood sacrifice that is the goddess Haghesa. (p. 994)

Like destructive fantasies, premonitions serve to underscore the determinism present in Cortázar's fictional world. Premonitory fantasies in some instances have a diabolical power of their own—Hélène in *62: Modelo para armar*, Alina in "Lejana" and the recluse in "Relato con un fondo de agua" experience visions that not only foreshadow their fate but that impel them toward actualization of it by their insistent and alluring quality. (p. 995)

It is ironic that many of Cortázar's protagonists who seek liberation through their fantasies are finally abased or enslaved by them. . . . The deluded Alina Reyes at the moment of unity with her double feels that she is liberating herself. But at the end of her experience she remains imprisoned within the identity she has loathed, dominated by her masochistic impulses and also succumbing to madness, a state that she has predicted for herself.

The attempts made by these characters to gain the salvation through fantasy that they cannot achieve in the real world always collapse. . . . Positive fantasies, like deceptive and destructive ones, are undergirded by irony and loss.

Fantasy in Cortázar is a complex, paradoxical phenomenon. Many times linked with the demonic, it also acts as a moral force, deflating vanity and destroying pretense. It often compels the characters to acknowledge or to confront a reality that they have refused to accept. (pp. 995-96)

Fantasy often represents truth. Although frequently seeming to be antithetical to the personality or life-style of the character, it often reflects his inner or subconscious life. In "La caricia más profunda," the delusion that the protagonist suffers of slowly sinking into the ground while neither family nor friends note any change, is but the grotesque exaggeration of his strong feelings of social alienation. The failure of these outsiders to see his abnormal physical state is symbolic of their unwillingness to comprehend him psychologically. At the end of the story his fantasy becomes their reality. Although his fiancée previously could not see any difference in him, now she cannot see him at all as she stands above her suitor who has sunk entirely into the ground. . . .

Fantasy in Cortázar is both communal or contagious and intimate. Often the porous, unstable identities of the characters facilitate the transference of delusion. (p. 997)

Cortázar's art has a subtle ethical basis. The negative fate of almost all of his characters demonstrates the danger or the impossibility of giving oneself up to fantasy worlds which hold only the spectre of salvation. The fantasy consciousness many times is the result of characters who wish to gain fulfillment through exalting the self rather than through meaningful relationships with other human beings. But the fantasy paradise created by the narcissistic self either is unsustainable or it becomes converted into a hellworld. . . .

At times characters withdraw into self instead of communicating guilt or anguish to others. The fear of humiliation keeps them from confiding in one another. But, ironically, their fantasies increase in strength precisely because they are repressed instead of exorcised. Self-isolation instead of diminishing the problem renders the solipsistic self more vulnerable to defeat. (p. 998)

Cortázar's characters cannot gain redemption either within reality or within fantasy. Self-centered characters who are frustrated in their relationships within the real world and who readily become drawn into a fantasy zone are those in *62: Modelo para armar*. In reality, they cling to inauthentic or meaningless relationships—Juan with Tell, Nicole with Marrast. . . .

Lured by the promise of freedom, happiness, and self-exaltation and fulfillment, the characters of Cortázar give themselves over to fantasy realms. Yet the inevitable result of this thrust within—into reverie, dream, and delusion—is disillusionment, insanity, and, sometimes even death. The most genuine relationship found in Cortázar, one grounded on a reality of sharing and of mutual concern, is that between Talita and Traveler in *Rayuela*. Both characters gain fulfillment, redeeming the self not through narcissistic expansion, as Alina Reyes, the protagonist of "Carta" and the narrator of "El otro cielo" attempt to do and fail, but through self-negation and selfless love. (p. 999)

> Lanin A. Gyurko, "Destructive and Ironically Redemptive Fantasy in Cortázar," in Hispania (© 1973 The American Association of Teachers of Spanish and Portuguese, Inc.), December, 1973, pp. 988-99.

ROBERTO GONZÁLEZ ECHEVARRÍA

It would be a naïve and predictable undertaking to show that self-referentiality occurs in Cortázar, since *Hopscotch* has already become a classic of self-referential writing. But it is precisely in self-referentiality that the mythology which I intend to isolate manifests itself. . . . [Self-reflexiveness] is a regressive movement, a circular journey back to the source. In literature self-referentiality is a return to origins in order to take away from conception its claim of originality, of constituting a single, fresh moment of beginning, an ordering principle and principium. Rather than the joyful game that it is often taken to be, self-referentiality is a deadly game in Cortázar, a violent ritual where Cortázar is at stake. *Los reyes,* the first book that he signed with his own name (as is known, an earlier work had appeared under a pseudonym), presents, under the guise of the Theseus myth, this ritual. By the reenactment of this ritual, Cortázar's writing labors to define itself, to cope with the opposition of the individual/original versus the general/collective, in short, the issue of generation. Who writes?

The most superficial consideration of *Los reyes* immediately leads to the issue of individuality and origin. The very appeal to classical mythology, to the dawn of Western literary tradition, is suggestive of a concern about the beginning of writing. The recourse to classical mythology is in itself hardly original, but rather a characteristic of the modern tradition: Nietzsche, Freud, Joyce, Pound, Unamuno; all take recourse to classical figures. In Latin America there is a strain of classicism of this sort that runs from Lugones and Borges through Reyes, Carpentier and Paz. It is not a neoclassical spirit that leads these modern writers to the classical tradition, since they do not imitate classical models, but instead (particularly in Nietzsche and Freud) a philological quest for a mythology of origins.... There is throughout Cortázar's work a recurrence of classical motifs and figures that answers to this general philological trend.

All myths, as we know, appear in many versions; but if one reads the most complete account of the Theseus myth, that of Plutarch, one is struck by the confusing number of contradictory accounts extant of this particular story. The charm, in fact, of Plutarch's rendition is his juggling of so many different versions in one and the same text, versions that cancel each other and blur or abolish altogether the possibility of a master version. To read Plutarch is to realize that the myth, while organized around a certain implied narrative core, is not a fixed text but a set of superimposed narratives. Thus we already have in the myth chosen by Cortázar the outlines of the question of conception: while being set at the dawn of Western tradition that classical mythology represents, the myth cannot claim originality in the sense of constituting a single source. (pp. 549-50)

What we find in *Los reyes* is . . . necessarily not a version but a subversion of the myth of Theseus. To begin with, as Cortázar himself has emphasized on many occasions, his Ariadne gives Theseus the clew only in order to free the Minotaur, once the monster has killed the hero.... *Los reyes* contains a "double tragedy." Instead of a triumph, Cortázar's version offers a mutual defeat: Theseus's quest leads not to heroic distinction, but to indifferentiation. The Minotaur, who would represent such indifferentiation and thus be the victor, is dead. Theseus's pursuit of individuation is thwarted from the start: he constantly recognizes himself in others, not only in the Minotaur, but also in Minos. What is emphasized in Cortázar's version is the violence that Theseus commits against himself in defeating Minos and killing the Minotaur. Instead of the erection of individual presence, Theseus's regressive voyage creates a vacuum at the center; the Minotaur is dead, Theseus has fled. (p. 551)

Whereas previously the labyrinth was inhabited by the "lord of games" (the Minotaur), it now stands as an empty gallery of winding walls. Theseus's victory has led to that other labyrinth suggested by Borges: the labyrinth of total indifferentiation, the desert, the white page. The I, the you and the we float in a space without perspectives and dimensions, as interchangeable masks of primeval chaos and apocalypse.

This confrontation of the monster and the hero constitutes the primal scene in Cortázar's mythology of writing: a hegemonic struggle for the center that resolves itself in a mutual cancellation and in the superimposition of beginnings and ends. The very image of man unborn, the Minotaur is the possessor of the immediate but naïve knowledge of man before the Fall. His speech is the incoherent, symbolic language of a savage god. Theseus, on the other hand, is not only a dealer in death, but is the very image of death. His linear, cogent language is temporal, discursive—it is discourse. In his enclosure the Minotaur speaks a perishable language that is not temporal but that is reinvented every day. The words he utters are, even if momentarily, attached to the things they represent.... If in other versions of the myth the birth of reason, morals or politics is at stake, what we have in *Los reyes* is the violent birth of writing. The catalogue of herbs that the Minotaur "tastes" is a

series of disconnected words, without syntactical and therefore temporal structure, linked to their individual origin through their "stems." By killing the Minotaur, Theseus attempts to replace the perishable sound of individual words with the linear, durable cogency of discourse, a cogency predicated not on the stems of words but on their declensions, on the particles that link them in a structure whose mode of representation would not be sonorous but spatial—writing. The irony, of course, is that once writing is instituted, Theseus does not gain control of the labyrinth but becomes superfluous and flees. Because writing cannot be dimmed like the stars with each dawn, because it is not a memory whose traces can be erased, Theseus is not needed to reinvent it, as the Minotaur reinvented his nomenclatures every day. Writing is the empty labyrinth from which both the Minotaur and Theseus have been banished.

This primal scene appears with remarkable consistency in Cortázar's writing. I do not mean simply that there are monsters, labyrinths and heroes, but rather that the scene in which a monster and a hero kill each other, cancel each other's claim for the center of the labyrinth, occurs with great frequency, particularly in texts where the nature of writing seems to be more obviously in question. (pp. 551-52)

The title of "All Fires the Fire" is drawn from Heraclitus and suggests the indifferentiation obtained when all things return to their primal state and ends and beginnings resolve into one. The story is in fact two stories that reflect each other, being told simultaneously. (p. 552)

As in *Los reyes,* there is no victory at the end of "All Fires the Fire," but rather a mutual annihilation. The fight between the Nubian retiarius and the gladiator is resolved when both fall dead upon each other in the sand. The mutual killing and the sand, which suggests the desert, prefigure the fire that kills everyone at the end, the fire that destroys the arena and which also levels the apartment building where, centuries later, Roland and Irene have fallen asleep on each other, like the dead gladiators, after making love. The stories merge at the end, not only on the level of the action but also at a conceptual level; love and war, presumably opposites, mingle to evoke the topic of the *ars amandi, ars bellandi*. Like the two gladiators and the lovers, the two stories have a common end that abolishes their difference and returns the text to the indifferentiation of origins—all texts the text. (p. 553)

Cortázar plays [his] philological game, more often than has been suspected, to undermine the notion of individuality. A clear instance of this . . . is Francine in *Libro de Manuel,* who so obviously stands for France and French values that she becomes an ironic abstraction. Not as obvious, though here the literary device is much more traditional, is Andrés, the protagonist of that same novel, whose name means, of course, everyman, or man in general. One might further note in this connection that the *o* plays a key role in the names of many of Cortázar's characters: N*o*ra, W*o*ng, *O*liveira, R*o*land, R*o*mero, R*o*bert*o*. That *o*, or zero, is the grapheme that designates an absence, a dissolution of individuality, a sphere demarcating nothingness. (p. 555)

It is not by accident that Cortázar's mythology of writing, as I have represented it here, should bear a Nietzschean imprint, since it is a Nietzschean problematic that seems to generate it. "Who writes?" is an essentially Nietzschean question. The struggle between the Minotaur and Theseus is analogous to that between Dionysus and Apollo in *The Birth of Tragedy*. In "The Pursuer" this Nietzschean quality is particularly evident. Johnny, whose musical instrument is a direct descendant of the Dionysian *aulos*, exists as if in harmony with the vast forces of the universe—with truth and actuality—and suffers as well as experiences joy for it. Bruno, on the other hand, the Apollonian seeker of light, deals in illusions; his aim is to domesticate Johnny's savage wisdom. The birth of tragedy, according to Nietzsche, is generated by the confrontation of these two figures, a birth that signaled the victory of Dionysus over Apollo, for tragedy could only emerge when the god of reason spoke the language of the god of music. In Nietzsche there remains a vestigial theodicy that confers meaning to the death of the hero. It would be reassuring to be able to say the same about Cortázar. But the analogy between the birth of tragedy and Cortázar's version of the birth of writing can only be carried so far, and beyond that point is where Cortázar emerges. Nietzsche, still the philologist in this early work, traces a curve that represents the birth of tragedy and its gradual decline, a decline provoked by the counter-offensive of Apollonian powers. Not so in Cortázar, where, as we have seen, each confrontation leads to a mutual cancellation, each conception carries with it its concomitant death. Writing in Cortázar must be born anew in each text; the whole of writing must emerge with each word, only to disappear again—not an eternal return, but a convulsive repetition of construction and deconstruction. A formal reflection of this might be found not only in the heterogeneity of Cortázar's longer texts, but also in their reliance on dialogue.

Cortázar emerges, then, at the point of the cancellation, of the negation. He must therefore be read whole, establishing no generic distinctions nor privileging either the fictional or the expository texts. Each text must be read as if it were the totality of Cortázar's production, given that each begins and ends in a question so fundamental as not to be transferable from one to the other, but must rather be repeated in each text and in each reading—a kind of spasmodic eschatology. Only the double thrust of the question can be retained. Holistic criticism is not a process of accumulation whereby details are gathered, stored, to construct with them the image of an author, but instead one where the impossibility of assembling the fragments in a coherent whole can provide a glimpse of totality.

There is an ultimate meaning to Cortázar's mythology of writing that belies its negativity, one that is performative rather than conceptual. What Theseus's self-reflexive quest shows is that literature, in the long run, cannot say anything about itself. The countermodernist position that decries literature's purity, its refusal to signify something other than itself, fails to recognize that, on the contrary, literature is always having to signify something else, and to implicate someone else. And indeed here we are reading, talking, writing about Cortázar, or better yet, reading, talking, writing Cortázar. Minotaur, Theseus, Johnny, Bruno—we as readers also drift into our own textual journeys, to turn reading once more into the ritual confrontation where you and I and we share for one moment, in each other, the illusion of meaning. (pp. 556-57)

Roberto González Echevarría, "'Los reyes': Cortázar's Mythology of Writing,"

in Books Abroad *(copyright 1976 by the University of Oklahoma Press), Vol. 50, No. 3, Summer, 1976, pp. 548-57.*

MARTHA PALEY FRANCESCATO

It is always Oliveira, Juan, Andrés that we hear about [in studies of Cortázar's works]. Why not La Maga, Hélène, Ludmilla? Or is the reader supposed to accept the term "man" as meaning "human being," which would also include woman? I don't think so. When Cortázar refers to the "new man" he means precisely that: man. And the term does not include the woman, although Cortázar himself has insisted he refers to both the man and the woman. On the other hand, why *not* only "new man"? A writer—a man—who writes in a world dominated by men, does not have to give woman equal importance. Or should he? In the course of the following discussion, I propose that we forget Cortázar the man. All references will be to Cortázar the writer. And in Cortázar's fictional world, I want to try to understand, and to emphasize, the actions and relationships of the characters, men and women—and children. Yes, we must not forget the latter: there is also Manuel, whom everybody wants to help get into a different cycle, at the same time salvaging for him some remains of the total shipwreck. Manuel—the newest new man.

As for La Maga, it is not in her head that her center lies; she is always clumsy and absentminded: "Even Perico Romero had to admit that, for a female, La Maga really took the cake." For a female. On the one hand, the treatment given to her is condescending; on the other hand, Horacio frankly admires her. Horacio's search cannot exist without her, in the same way that he later needs Talita. Although the two women act as Horacio's Vergil, the protagonist, the axis and center of the action is still Dante, Horacio, *the man*. (p. 590)

Hélène [in *62: A Model Kit*], on the surface, is . . . emancipated, sure of herself, admirable. When the Tell-Juan-Hélène triangle is completed, she too becomes an object, and incredibly, she is happy in that role. . . . An obedient object. Is it possible that, deep down, Hélène wishes a man to put her in her role as an object, which—who knows?—makes her feel more of a woman? And this woman is precisely the one who is apparently stronger, more independent, less insecure and more decided.

While Juan "objectifies" his two women, perhaps helping them, in his way, the other masculine characters of *62* give us other visions of women: "'Women are always bloodthirsty,' said Calac with a background of grunts of approval from Polanco and my paredros"; or "'There is nothing like women,' says Marrast, 'whether a heart is beating or not, the only thing they see is a gold lock.'" (pp. 590-91)

It's all right [that Marrast pronounces all women bitches]: Marrast is drunk; he is a Frenchman. . . . But why "bitch"? Why are *all* women bitches? Just because he is drunk, sad, in anguish? The fact of *being*, of *being a man*, implies that the woman is a bitch: "a man because of bitch only because of that." . . . (p. 591)

According to Marcos [in *Libro de Manuel*],

> Women don't lack the ability to exert themselves, but they tend to apply it to the negative, that is to say that when they don't like something, or everything goes wrong in poli-

tics or in the kitchen, then they are capable of such rage, such indignation, such eloquence that you would laugh at Stokely Carmichael. They have their motor accelerated the wrong way, I mean that they are champions when it comes to putting on the brake, I don't know if you follow me. . . .

Another reference that Andrés makes on this subject shows a paternalistic tone, the assuredness of a man who knows women well and can explain their behavior: "I, for instance, don't expect a woman to go crazy over a painting by Max Ernst or over a musical piece by Xenakis; they have their own metabolism, brother, and besides, how are we to tell whether at bottom they are not more enthusiastic than we are, only that you shouldn't confuse exercises with emotion.". . . That is, one shouldn't expect from women certain reactions that belong only to men. (p. 592)

Woman, in her established and accepted role, is more an observer than a participant; she is more passive than adventurous, and much more repressed than man in expressing herself. . . . Marcos observes that, with the exception of the Chilean *pico*, which is a rare example of masculinization, all the Latin American or Argentine terms for the male sexual organ are feminine in grammatical gender. This linguistic peculiarity could partially explain man's aggressive feelings. The fact that the part of him that makes him a *man* should be designated in feminine terms could explain an unexpressed resentment, a grudge that he holds against woman. All women, even a man's mother, are therefore guilty of feminizing his virility.

Women take a step forward and are placed in a more salient position in the two most recent works by Cortázar. In "Homage to a Young Witch" (1972) the writer discovers Rita Renoir through a road that leads him to the world of the comic strips. In that world he discovers Valentina, yes, "pretty Valentina, Valentina all thighs and breasts, of course I'm joking and I'm not placing you on the shelf of Emma Bovary and not even Scarlett O'Hara.". . . Valentina shares a special section along with other heroines such as Barbarella and Phoebe Zeit-Geist, but she is obviously above them, in the same way that Rita Renoir surpasses them all. Cortázar, without having even seen her personally, already admired her "for intellectual reasons," having seen some photographs in a magazine which led him to say to himself "but then this woman, this consumer's object from the Lido and the Crazy Horse.". . . Then he goes on to describe the experience of seeing Rita Renoir on a stage, a shuddering experience in front of an uncensored body, while she danced and made love to an invisible devil. . . . As he is witnessing the most daring of stripteases, the writer feels the birth of the new man through this experience: "The man, yes, old emblem of the phoenix rising from the ashes of an error of twenty centuries; yet no longer another phoenix but a different bird, another way of looking at oneself." . . . (pp. 593-94)

Rita Renoir surpasses shy Valentina: "Rita Renoir, sick and tired of the conventional striptease, goes beyond the apparent limits of the erotic toward the obscene, knowing that this road against all convention is equivalent for her and, hopefully, for others, to the abolition of the limits, to the denunciation of its deepest lie.". . . It is a question now of trying to understand what is happening on the stage if something of the old man has been destroyed, of learning to love the body in its entirety, of learning to look at it with the look of the new man. But which body is it we are looking at? *It is the body of the woman,* even though the writer mentions "our body and all bodies." It is the body of the woman on the stage which has motivated the writer to express what he has witnessed, to find the new man this time through an erotic experience. As a conclusion to the text, Cortázar says: "I don't like easy praise, I'm just saying that, since two nights ago, I have a respect for Rita Renoir that I don't always have for many women who are dressed from head to toe.". . . The writer feels the need to communicate his experience to the readers, to the male readers especially. It is not a question of women's being passive females or of their being shocked by the description or of their not understanding it. It is not that. I simply ask: Can a woman feel a rebirth as a "new woman" after such an experience as the one narrated, or is this rebirth reserved only for men?

We also find another woman in Cortázar's recent *Fantomas contra los vampiros multinacionales.* Because of the mysterious disappearance of books and the burning of the libraries all over the world, Fantomas gets in touch with the greatest contemporary writers. The narrator wonders who they are. The answer lies in an order Fantomas gives to his secretary Libra. (Once more, the roles fit in with tradition: the master is a man, the secretary a woman; the master commands, the secretary obeys.) The greatest contemporary writers are Julio Cortázar, Octavio Paz, Alberto Moravia and Susan Sontag. Although listed last of the four, at least a woman is included among the best writers. And when she happens to be the only one who has found out the true conspiracy, the men do not understand what she is talking about. They need to arrive at the discovery of truth through reasoning; Susan has arrived through her own means (intuition?) before anything else. The men, although they do not understand, accept what she proposes to them. "The matriarchate makes itself felt and I obey," Julio explains to Alberto. Woman does not need to explain her actions, and man does not require her explanations. It is the obedience to a group that every day is asking for more of what rightfully belongs to it; screaming more and more loudly, it makes itself heard, and it is the one entity that can find the truth.

At the end of this narration there is a small blond boy sitting on the curb. Like Manuel, he symbolizes the utopia that can be fulfilled in the future, the newest of new men, with the morning sun shining on his blond hair, a new man in the dawn of the new day. And the woman? (pp. 594-95)

Martha Paley Francescato, "The New Man (But Not the New Woman)," in Books Abroad *(copyright 1976 by the University of Oklahoma Press), Vol. 50, No. 3, Summer, 1976, pp. 589-95.*

MALVA E. FILER

Hands are the members of the human body most actively involved in the individual's psychological and emotional life. They are a source and instrument of pleasure; they can give love and affection. They can also, however, hurt and kill. Within the individual, popular tradition has identified the right hand with the rational, the left with the irrational or instinctive aspects of the psyche. From there it is a short step to having a hand represent one of the conflicting forces that strive to achieve control of the self. The literary possibilities of this inner conflict, as a subject, are without boundaries, for this is the main preoccupation of any human being. And Cortázar has found many imaginative and daring ways of expressing this conflict in his fiction. (p. 595)

In Cortázar's fictional world [a] routine life is the great scandal against which every individual must rebel with all his strength. And if he is not able or willing to do so, extraordinary elements are usually summoned to force him out of this despicable and abject comfort. In this respect it would be enough to recall "Casa tomada" (The House Taken Over) or "Carta a una señorita en París" (Letter to a Young Lady in Paris) from *Bestiario*. On the other hand, "Tema para San Jorge" (Theme for Saint George) from *La vuelta al día* shows his contempt and hatred for routine. In *Historias de cronopios y de famas* Cortázar expresses his rebellion against the objects and persons that make up our everyday life and the mechanical ways by which we relate to them. At the same time, he cannot help admitting that it is very tempting to accept this world, already organized for us, and to respect the established function of each one of its objects. The five fingers that destroy the man with the blue pullover [in "No se culpe a nadie"] seem to perform a role equivalent to the materialized obsessions or doubles in his other stories. What is attacked is the imprisoned, mechanized or overly domesticated self. Only here the attacker is a part of the individual's own body, and the punishment is nothing less than total destruction.

Hands are very noticeable in Cortázar's novels, especially *Rayuela* and *62*. The hand, for Oliveira, would intercede to provide an escape from the limits of reason and find access to the "center," the object of his desperate search.... Chapter 76 of *Rayuela* makes insistent reference to Pola's hands. Oliveira had not had a chance to find out her name, when Pola's hands were already the object of his obsessive attention. In fact, Oliveira meets Pola through her hands. And here again we find the idea of the hand as intercessor: "You moved that hand as if you were touching a limit, and after that a world against the grain began."

The introduction of Frau Marta in *62* is also made through references to her hands: "From an early stage our attention had been fixed on Frau Marta's hands.... Those hands had ended up by obsessing us." There is a similarity between the description of Frau Marta's hands "riffling through an ancient black purse" and Pola's opening her purse, which gives Oliveira "the feeling that the clasp is guarding against an entry into a sign of the zodiac." In both cases the hands symbolically open the way to some kind of mystical experience. (pp. 597-98)

The obsession with hands, clearly stated in *62*, finds a new expression in "Cuello de gatito negro." The situation includes, however, some significant new elements. The inner conflict is seen from outside, through the main character, whose only role is that of a catalytic agent. This time it is a woman who presents us with a split self. Her hands move on their own, totally free of any control or inhibition, causing her extreme anguish and embarrassment. (p. 598)

If we try to summarize the different roles that hands play in Cortázar's fiction, we find that they seem to symbolize instinct, intuition, imagination and, in general, the irrational. Their presence is connected with different attempts at liberating the individual from the limitations of reason, moral

convention and the mechanization by routine. However, the liberation of instincts which the author's characters have rationally advocated, particularly in *Libro de Manuel*, is nevertheless a source of anxiety at a deeper level. In fact, there seems to be sufficient reason to believe that Cortázar's characters are torn between the conscious desire to free their repressed instincts and the intensive fear and distrust of anything instinctive and irrational. They want to break the bars built by reason and morals but are at the same time extremely fearful of doing so. The struggle within the self often leads, as is shown above, to different degrees of aggression and self-destruction. If the interpretation proposed here were to be accepted as correct, it would help us to understand why the hand in Cortázar's fiction is an ambivalent if not altogether threatening presence. (p. 599)

> *Malva E. Filer, "The Ambivalence of the Hand in Cortázar's Fiction," in* Books Abroad *(copyright 1976 by the University of Oklahoma Press), Vol. 50, No. 3, Summer, 1976, pp. 595-99.*

DAVID WILLIAM FOSTER

One of the outstanding characteristics of [*Libro de Manuel*] is the blending of fictional narration and journalistic clippings, based on the organizing motif of a sort of baby-book for a revolutionary child compiled as the legacy of his parents and mentors. The novel moves back and forth between being the process of compilation and being the baby-book itself. The result is a noteworthy blurring of the distinction between fiction and documentation, using the materials of popular culture, both highbrow and yellow journalism.

Cortázar's present effort [*Fantomas contra los vampiros multinacionales*] is an even more radical step and bespeaks eloquently the concern of the contemporary writer in Latin America to produce a literature that addresses itself to the masses rather than to the educated elite, without being simply a modish and chic exploitation of big-market mass culture. *Fantomas* is a *historieta* both in graphic format and in narrative texture. It incorporates cartoons that directly, cleverly and satirically imitate large-selling strips such as *Superman* or *Batman* (both examples of American cultural imperialism that have been widely denounced in Latin American). But the cartoon strips that appear in the text contribute to the second-order configuration of a comic book which uses such drawings along with other graphic material and narrative text to make up a unified if defiantly ageneric text. Moreover—and it is in this sense that the structural features of the *nueva narrativa* are present and attest to the serious preoccupations with literary composition—the text narrates a series of events that occur in the "inner" comic book text as well as in the "outer" reality of the text that describes the former....

[There is] clever satirizing of the Fantomas figure and, in what really amounts to the same context, of the Western writer who is too bound up with his elitist cultural models to be able to distinguish between writing *about* the problems of the people and writing *for* and *at* them. Cortázar's incomparable blend of demythifying humor and a slang that deflates the most serious of cultural pretensions is the major narrative vehicle.

Fantomas is basically documentary in nature and reminds one of the valuable role played by *Supermachos* and *Los agachados* in Mexico in the consciousness-raising of their mass audience. (p. 66)

> *David William Foster, in* World Literature Today *(copyright 1977 by the University of Oklahoma Press), Vol. 51, No. 1, Winter, 1977.*

D

DAVIE, Donald 1922-

A British poet, critic, editor, and translator, Davie writes accomplished, stylized verse. His is a disciplined, technically polished poetry that is often both elegant and compressed. As a critic, he admires the structure and purity of eighteenth-century literature, and is against certain modernism, as well as the Romanticism of the forties. Often considered overly academic, Davie has shifted among various schools of poetic thought. He has recently experimented with confessional poetry and with looser verse forms. (See also *CLC*, Vols. 5, 8, and *Contemporary Authors*, Vols. 1-4, rev. ed.)

CALVIN BEDIENT

Of all the first-rate poets of the age, Donald Davie is the most notably reactionary. If only with some strain, we might see him, to advantage, as mining in the great ascetic vein of contemporary art, where the classical spirit thins away—as in Rothko, Bresson, Sarraute, Beckett, Cage—in ever starker forms. And yet Davie stands far to the right of most of his fellow ascetics—indeed, within hailing distance of the eighteenth century. In tone, diction, and verse form, he often recalls the late Augustan poets, of whom he has written well and whom he has also anthologised. Above all he has tried, like the Augustans, to be urbane: to voice (in words he quotes from Matthew Arnold) "the tone and spirit of the center." This is reactionary indeed. For of course there is no longer any center. Or the center is but a maelstrom, a contention. (p. 66)

[It] is just the poet's voice, and only this, that we hear speaking in Davie's poetry. It could not be otherwise. "To make poetry out of moral commonplace," Davie notes, "a poet has to make it clear that he speaks not in his own voice (that would be impertinent) but as the spokesman of a social tradition." . . . [To] "make poetry out of moral commonplace," as Davie tries to do, when the commonplace itself seems damaged, indeed marooned—indeed, *forlorn*—does require something like impertinence; and rapping on roving knuckles with yardsticks borrowed from old classrooms, impertinently using the word "impertinence" with its haughty assumption of determinate absolutes, what Davie himself exemplifies, we may feel, is not "the tone and spirit" of any center, but something more courageous and significant, not to say lonely: the individual man working out the necessities of his conscience. More-over, what really fires this conscience, we may feel, is not at all being at the center, whatever that may happen to be in any age, but being right: right about the need for civilized restraint, for faith in the idea of civilization itself. We hear in Davie's poetry a voice that *will* speak out in spite of its knowledge of the indifference or incredulity that awaits it—a voice consciously coming, not from the center of contemporary culture, but from out on the edge, in a kind of nagging nostalgia for an austerer day, when men lived and died by Nonconformist lights, or for Reason, Loyalty, Restraint, the Right. It is the voice of a conscience that—protestingly—finds itself left behind.

Davie's conscience is . . . more complex than I have yet suggested—or than he himself seems quite to have grasped. Almost dramatically self-divided, it contains its own principle of self-correction. It is larger and wiser, as it were, than Davie himself, since Davie, at any one time, embodies but half of it. There is, however, some justice in emphasizing its jaundiced and vigilant side; for there can be no doubt that Davie himself is partial to it. Indeed, it often seems that Davie has taken it as his peculiar role among contemporary poets to be perversely pure and dour—to knock on the ceiling shaken by the reckless goings-on of the present with the broom of the Puritan (or simply the reasonable) past. And if he has made too much of this, cramming himself into a niche that is really too small for him and from which, now and again, he has had to break out and stretch his limbs and take the air, still the niche is of his own carving—is in its measure congenial to him. And, having assumed it so often, he has indeed inclined us to regard him as the poet of "urbane" and reactionary admonitions, partial as this identity must seem in a final view. And certainly he has assumed it often enough to force us to ask what effect it has had on his art. (pp. 66-7)

[To] be an "urbane poet," if one is indeed a poet, is to be out of line with oneself, and out of line with poetry. The chief effect of Davie's attempt to be urbane—and not only in the Arnoldian sense but in the root sense of "civilized, polished, refined, witty"—has been a waste of his poetic abilities, a silencing while lesser instruments are played. In much of his work, Davie has gone through the motions of poetry, and given the result its name; but the rope he has walked has been utilitarian clothesline, its height but a little way above the ground, and the performance, accordingly, altogether lacking in that power to astonish which genuine poetry always displays. . . .

[In] one way Davie has indeed achieved, within poetry, a notable urbanity: an urbanity, not of voice or position, but of language. Linguistic urbanity lies (in a phrase Davie quotes from T. S. Eliot) in "the perfection of a common language." Here as elsewhere, the urbane principle is, of course, that of enlightened modesty: the intelligence, the sheer sociality deposited in a language seems so large, the poet's own inventions, his own ego, so small. The urbane mind scorns the folly and fears the vice of all private perspective; it trusts in the justice of the general. Accordingly, the ideal style, to it, is a style without style, as clear, unmarked, and compliant as water—and like water, wholesome, easy to assimilate, and used by everyone. . . . (p. 67)

What confronts us in [the examples of Davie's finest "urbane poetry"] is language rather than style—the common language filtered and purified. Impossible to parody: it would be easier to take hold of the air. Fleeing from a "distinctive" voice as from the very principle of evil, Davie, it is true, in a sense achieves one: in the midst of voices with a signature, his stands out by virtue of its choice impersonality. But clearly its intention is otherwise: Davie's is a language, as it were, surprised and found, not forged and made. If his words distinguish themselves, it is not by their manner, but by their "good manners," their social finality, their intention to communicate. . . . [It is from] the heart of the perfected common language, that Davie writes his poetry. And if he fails to make it seem the *necessary* place for poetry, still he proves it to be one of the positions of excellence.

And yet, to repeat, there has also been unhappy waste in this insistence on urbanity—unnecessary limitation and futility. The temptation to slight the real, unpredictable, and slovenly body of experience, to keep it at a polite and useful distance, to talk and civilize and "purify" the language rather than to write poems, has been more than Davie has been able to withstand. . . . And he has been, in consequence, a poet only when he has escaped from his theories —when he has opened the door, quietly so as not to waken the urbane guards, and stepped out into the surprising world. (pp. 68-9)

Toward the primal energy of poetry, which is evolving feeling—imagination intently migrating, arriving, arrived— Davie is in the position of the man who would rather not acknowledge a disreputable family connection. And yet there is, after all, no poetry without it; there is only prose. (p. 69)

Davie's ambition lies in "a poetry of urbane and momentous statement." Yet what Davie actually writes in such a piece as "Portrait of the Artist" is not poetry at all, but versified prose discourse—in brief, *verse*. Verse is poetry that we name as such only by grace of its *turning* rhythm and lines: it is the form of poetry without the substance, and so we call it, justly, by its vehicle alone. (p. 71)

What is troublesome [about verse] is the way it trifles with, and lowers, a form potentially great and beautiful. . . . [The] matters we find in Davie's verse are matters which prose does as well. Witness "Hypochondriac Logic," of which I give the final stanza:

So poets may astonish you
With what is not, but should be, true,
And shackle on a moral shape
You only thought you could escape;
So if their scenery is queer,
Its prototype may not be here,
Unless inside a frightened mind,
Which may be dazzled, but not blind.

Nothing here is so delicately conceived or organized, so dependent on feeling for its force, that it needs to be set off from the loquacities of prose. Indeed, Davie's lines cry out for prose—for freedom from their uncomfortable corset, their distracting jungle and bounce. (pp. 71-2)

[There] is reason to deplore Davie's conviction—strong at first, then slack, and now renewed—that he is obliged to write verse. In view of what Davie is able to do, he has not done enough, or he has done too much of what is little in itself. When he could have been mining gold, he has been mining coal or, at most, a little silver. Whereas most versifiers strain to become poets but fail to make it, Davie is a poet who chooses, much of the time, to write verse. . . . [It] would seem that it has all been done at the behest of fallacious theories.

Davie's ruling passion is not for the aesthetic but for the moral—or, more accurately, for the two in one, for a *moral style*: Davie is a man in love with noble restraint. And so long as he has been able to work the "common language" into something chaste and chastening, it has been almost a matter of indifference to him whether the anvil, much less the result, were poetry or verse. Nevertheless, his nature— deep, responsive, strong—veers toward poetry; and, left to itself, it might well have worked all its moral passion into poems. But it has not been left to itself. (p. 74)

Just south of conscience-stricken urbane verse there lies a temperate region that, following Bagehot, we might agree to call "pure art." Here we find art that employs the fewest strokes necessary for its purpose—a nobly restrained art, of jealous economy of means. . . .

It is to art of this chaste and temperate kind that almost all Davie's best poetry belongs. (p. 75)

"Creon's Mouse" is . . . poetry and not verse because it burns with a finite reality. And yet its status as poetry may leave us somewhat uneasy. How close it is, throughout, to the dry bones of verse! How set it is on recoiling from the crush of life to wisdom! The poem seems to begrudge having to glance at a particular reality at all. Giving us only just barely, with not a stroke to spare, the amount and kind of detail necessary to become a unique and absorbing experience, it leaves itself no aesthetic margin whatever, refuses to rest in itself, distrusts and nips its own fierce beauty. Yes, the author of this poem (we might find ourselves reflecting) is certainly a poet; but, a rock skipping over tense water, how little he seems to trust the poetic element! (p. 77)

[The] more one reads Davie, the more the unexpected element rises like a mist and discloses a serene and stable geography, as of an old and well-ordered country: it is just that the country is equally divided between a Northern and a Southern state, and that Davie now tours one, now the other. The fact is that, though almost always one as a poet, namely a pure artist, Davie is of two minds as regards the value of life. Righteously at arms, in some poems, with the way existence falls out, in others he embraces it—and not at all because he is slumming, but because he finds it *right* to embrace it. There are, then, two consciences within Davie, antipodean; and each has its own poise, its own authority.

One of these consciences, cold, dour, Northern, we have already seen in full force. For obvious reasons, the verse is its opportunity, its pet. But, as "Creon's Mouse" exemplifies, its weather blows, it finds its place, in the poetry as well. . . . And with perverse pride, this conscience believes in morality. What else, it might ask, is there to believe in? It rests on itself as the single substance between the void "God" and the void nihilism. Yet it is not at all metaphysically minded, or even self-reflecting. It simply asks of life, as of style, that it be clean, lifted free from the mess of existence: it is, in truth, a sensibility as much as it is a code. Candor and restraint, austerity, courage, fidelity and conviction—for the most part, it flies these flags without attempting to say why, and without caring to. . . . Davie's belief in morality scarcely waits for a pretext; it exceeds all occasions, amounting to a faith. (p. 78)

This Dissenting conscience, so queerly and attractively laced by the cosmopolitan, also turns, of course, to people, to human character—turns on them, as in "Creon's Mouse." It even turns on Dissent itself, because it is a church "based on sentiment"—as, too, on the Evangelist with his

> Solicitations of a swirling gown,
> The sudden vox humana, and the pause,
> The expert orchestration of a frown . . .

It is, as this suggests, a conscience hard to get around—in fact, so very skeptical that, leaving itself nothing to hang on to, its only resource is to be clasped upon itself. Known chiefly by what it does *not* permit, its purpose is to bind human nature. Hence, when it oppresses Davie himself, as now and then it does, his sense of it is understandably rueful, informed by bleak familiarity and by longing to get out. . . . (p. 80)

The other conscience in Davie, distinctively modern, is vital, instinctual—it asks, not "How can I organize or rectify existence?" but "How can I protect life, enhance it?" . . . It is a conscience that rests on what has been given, judging that it truly is a gift. Almost wholly reverential, it is made up of wondering acceptance, of submission to life's lilt. Even at lowest ebb it finds existence absorbing. It reacts with pain, with horror, to the waste of life. And just for that reason, it has reserves of reaction, and will quarrel with energy even when it finds an ideality in it. (pp. 81-2)

Such . . . are the two consciences of Davie's art, each possessing its own territory, indeed its own trophies, among the poems—the one nobly surrendering to life, the other taking life nobly to task. Their disjunctive arrangement is efficiently neat, like an agreed upon division of labor. Though it is natural to suspect it of convenient simplification, the poems . . . do not read like simplifications—they say fully and fairly what they have to say, shooting straight from the angle at which they find themselves, and at which, for the moment, they find it right to be. (p. 85)

In "Woodpigeons at Rahenny," there is, by distinction, a succession from one point of view to the other, oneness with the world giving way to gaunt divorcement from it. The poem begins in almost mesmerized immersion in a scene.

> One simple and effective rhyme
> Over and over in the April light;
>   And a touch of the old time
> In the serving-man stooping, aproned tight,
> At the end of the dappled avenue
> To the easy phrase, "tereu-tereue,"
> Mulled over by the sleepy dove—
> This was the poem I had to write.
>
> White wall where the creepers climb
> Year after year on the sunny side;
>   And a touch of the old time
> In the sandalled Capuchin's silent stride
> Over the shadows and through the clear
> Cushion-soft wooing of the ear
> From two meadows away, by the dove—
> This was the poem that was denied . . . . . .

Davie here conveys, through an enchanting circularity of sound, a lulling timelessness. In keeping with the touch of the old time in the present, the poem closes on itself in a gentle volley of echoes. A scene luxurious with repetitions has awakened in the poet a desire for that most consummate of repetitions, the reduplication of the world by art— the harmony of the setting seeming to invite, to seek augmentation in, the profounder harmony of poetry. But abruptly this further harmony is denied. The ascetic figure of the Capuchin—a reminder of mortality—breaks the illusion of a *circular* time, shows time to be but death-boned and linear. Estranged alike from time and eternity (a monk without God, a natural creature without a trust in nature), the speaker is overcome by that modern malaise, the experience of *dislocation:*

> For whether it was the friar's crime,
> His lean-ness suddenly out of tune;
>   Or a touch of the old time
> In the given phrase, with its unsought boon
> Of a lax autumnal atmosphere,
> Seemed quaint and out of keeping here,
> I do not know. I know the dove
> Outsang me down the afternoon.

Accordingly, the very music of the poem diminishes, wasting into boniness of syntax, and thudding upon "I do not know." If the earlier stanzas out-sing the last, it is, then, because they are innocent. Recapitulating English poetry from the age of Keats or the April side of Tennyson to its present day of lean music and still leaner faith, "Woodpigeons at Rahenny" gives us, marvelously, both the poet Davie might have been and the poet he feels he has to be.

As we have seen, Davie was not always to feel—what in the course of this early and perfect poem he comes to feel— a sort of Capuchin out of tune with the natural world. But whether enmeshed with or at odds with life, he was always to sing as one who finds it fitting that a contemporary song be lean. This leanness, this commitment to the pure style and to pure art, may prompt us to feel that, when Davie does come to praise life, his song is stinted, the "given phrase" too thin and pale. And yet there is an integrity in Davie's leanness that, the more one reads him, the more one admires. If his work cannot overwhelm us through a powerful excess, neither can it spoil. And how remarkable it is that, for all his leanness, Davie, like a long-distance runner, has covered so much of life, paused at the equator as well as at the Pole. The combination of his lean style and his rich, elastic nature has produced a body of work rare in character: pure art with a broad range. (pp. 86-8)

> *Calvin Bedient, "On Donald Davie," in*
> The Iowa Review *(copyright © 1971, by*
> *The University of Iowa), Vol. 2, No. 2*
> *(Spring, 1971), pp. 66-88.*

BERNARD BERGONZI

[Davie's *Collected Poems, 1950-1970*] shows that Davie soon moved on from the quasi-Augustan formality he had cultivated in the fifties, and since then has written in many styles and been open to a wide range of poetic influences, mostly American and Continental European. (p. 345)

[That Davie is an interesting writer] arises less from the character of Davie's poems, taken separately, than from the total impression one gets from all his writing of a powerful literary personality struggling with obsessions and endeavoring, with unexpected success, to balance or combine attitudes usually thought of as contradictory. Thus, Davie is emphatically a moralist, imbued with the rigorous spirit of the Cambridge English school of the forties and fifties. His first critical book, *Purity of Diction in English Verse* (1952), found admirable moral qualities in the lexical restraint and controlled syntax of eighteenth-century poetry and was offered as a lesson in the neoclassical virtues to Davie's contemporaries. In his own poetry Davie embodied this lesson in the sharp, cool, ironic observations of *Brides of Reason*. Yet he is also an aesthete, who believes with Henry James that "it is art that *makes* life, makes interest, makes importance." He was unable to remain satisfied for long with exclusively moral and social criteria for poetry; its significance, in the end, was ontological:

> The metaphysicality
> Of poetry, how I need it!
> And yet it was for years
> What I refused to credit. . . .

Davie's ideal in these matters is that pure realm where art and morality become indistinguishable. Few of us, however, can inhabit it for long.

In one allegiance Davie is, unashamedly, a provincial Englishman, strongly attached to his Yorkshire roots and the nonconformist religious tradition in which he was brought up, even if he is no longer a believer. This allegiance is personally exemplified in his affectionate memory of his father, to whom he has devoted several poems. In poetic terms it shows itself in Davie's admiration not just for minor eighteenth-century poets in general, but for hymn-writers such as Isaac Watts and Charles Wesley, in particular. Against this aspect of Davie—English, provincial, traditionalist—one must set quite different allegiances, which are cosmopolitan, global, and modernist. It is this, above all, which soon marked Davie off from the unambitious poetics of the Movement. He admires and imitates Pound and Pasternak, and is drawn to the heroic style, in life and art, of the early masters of modernism. However much his imagination is rooted in Pennine landscape, it constantly turns to the large unpeopled spaces of America and Russia. . . . Pasternak's short lines, regular but not stiff stanzaic forms, and frequent exclamations are a noticeable feature of *Events and Wisdoms*.

Pound's influence on Davie is more pervasive. . . . Davie reveres Pound for taking the art of poetry with true seriousness, as opposed to English amateurism. He finds, too, in Pound's imagist poetics a regard for the integrity of nature, seen and respected as something nonhuman, and accepted in its quiddity. He finds forerunners of this attitude in Ruskin and Hopkins and Hardy, and prefers it to the symbolist procedures of Eliot, in which the world of things is swallowed up in the all-embracing consciousness of the poet.

Pound's influence is explicitly and happily evident in two extended sequences adapted from existing literary sources: *The Forests of Lithuania* (1959) and *A Sequence for Francis Parkman* (1961). . . . [The] plains and forests of Eastern Europe and Russia form an integral part of Davie's mental and emotional world, fed partly from experience, partly from his reading of Polish and Russian literature. As he writes in "Behind the North Wind," recalling his service in northern Russia in 1942:

> More than ever I need
> Places where nothing happened,
> Where history is silent,
> No Tartar ponies checked, and
> Endurance earns repose. . . .
>
> (pp. 346-48)

Davie reveals a similar feeling about North America in *A Sequence for Francis Parkman*, which, as he acknowledges, draws heavily in a Poundian way on Parkman's *France and England in North America*. . . . The last poem is not adapted from Parkman but is wholly original; it points to a fascination with the alienness of North America that has remained a major preoccupation with Davie:

> But I only guess,
> I guess at it out of my Englishness
> And envy you out of England. Man with man
> Is all our history; American,
> You met with spirits. Neither white nor red
> The melancholy, disinherited
> Spirit of mid-America, but this,
> The manifested copiousness, the bounties. . . .

This is a key passage for understanding Davie's development and his later obsessions, both as poet and critic. The *Sequence* is a very successful result of the fusion of separate elements of experience: Pound's demonstration of the possibility of making one's own poetry out of other people's prose; the reading of Parkman; and a first visit to America. (pp. 348-49)

From the early sixties Davie became increasingly concerned with America as a poetic subject. Like his Russia, Davie's North America was something of a landscape of the mind: empty, vast, silent, uncluttered with humanity—the pristine vision of the first explorers rather than the contemporary USA. He envied the American poets their freedom of imagination, reversing the traditional American envy of Europe for its cultural achievements and possibilities. . . . In some recent poems Davie's concern with England is less ideal or metaphysical, and more overtly political. . . . His distaste for contemporary England has a heroic-modernist basis and is directed at many things: the drab complacency of postimperial Britain; an industrialized and polluted landscape; social egalitarianism; civic philistinism; and the fatuities of the "Swinging London" cult of the sixties. (pp. 349-50)

Poetry is an imperfect, even misleading guide to a man's actual opinions, and Davie's poems of the sixties tend to dramatize attitudes rather than develop arguments. (p. 350)

[Davie] is much concerned with English culture and its fate, but from the vantage point of chosen expatriation and exile.... [He] moves on, reads many literatures—though returning constantly to Pound, the master voyager of modernism—and longs for the heroic and the imaginatively possible, as well as what is actually and inescapably there.

Davie likes and cultivates the "open-ended" poem that does not return neatly and predictably to its starting point but moves onward and outwards like an arrow-shower or a river flowing into the sea. (pp. 359-60)

> *Bernard Bergonzi, in* Contemporary Literature *(© 1977 by the Board of Regents of the University of Wisconsin System), Vol. 18, No. 3, Summer, 1977.*

BLAKE MORRISON

Rationalism, scepticism, fastidiousness, fair-mindedness: the qualities which Donald Davie has claimed for himself over the years are not the qualities we have been taught to expect of a poet. Part of Davie's task has been to persuade us, and himself, that we have been wrongly taught—that our conception of the poet as a daring and passionate outsider is historically foreshortened, and that a broader, pre-Romantic conception of the poet could be profitably restored. From the earliest poems Davie has presented himself as an opposite, or anti-type, of the Romantic poet: as a "bride of reason", a "winter talent", "an even tenor", a "good fellow" but "pertinacious to a fault". Occasionally stung by suggestions that he is too cerebral and academic in his poetry, he has been troubled by self-doubt: in 1957 he accused himself in a note of failing to be "a natural poet", and as recently as 1975 admitted to being one of the "steely trimmers" whose suspicion of pretension in art is not always distinguishable from mean-mindedness. But on the whole Davie has felt confident enough to assert that the characteristics prized in academic circles can also be the characteristics of the poet....

The publication of *The Poet in the Imaginary Museum,* a selection of Davie's critical writings between November 1950 and October 1977, is the best opportunity we have had so far to observe the relationship between the concerns of the critic and the achievement of the poet.... With the exception of a discussion of Beckett's fiction, all the essays are concerned with poetry. They are arranged in chronological order, allowing Davie's development to be clearly discerned, and they have been preserved in their original form—there is no tampering with the historical record....

The first thing to note is that Davie is far more than, and sometimes far less than, the rigorous rationalist which his self-caricatures might imply. There is in his criticism a use of rhetoric, a readiness to take speculative risks, and an appropriation of other writers which makes it clear that there is as much a poet in the critic as there is a critic in the poet. This is not to say that Davie's criticism altogether lacks the qualities of "steely trimming"; far from it. The bluff commonsense tone which was the mark of several critics in the 1950s, John Wain in particular, is evident in "Remembering the Movement" (1959).... The desire to steer a sensible middle course (trimming of another kind) can be seen in "The Translatability of Poetry" (1967)....

And a distrust of irrationalism underlies his essay on the criticism of R. P. Blackmur, "Poetry, or Poems?" (1955)....

These essays are consistent with the image of Davie as a pragmatist with a high regard for close textual analysis and careful weighing of evidence. Some of his favourite phrases —"On this showing...", "It begins to look as if...", "If this is true, then..."—create the same impression of a man moving tentatively from analysis to conclusion.

In fact, such phrases are nearly always a sign that from meticulously gathered evidence, Davie is about to move to some highly speculative and quite undemonstrable theory. A famous example is his connection between Pound's fascism and his handling of syntax: "one could almost say, on this showing, that to dislocate syntax is to threaten the rule of law in the community". This is a challenging but surely untenable equation of poetic and political behaviour: it suggests how interested Davie is in the political implications of poetic form, but would be difficult to uphold. Similarly questionable is his suggestion that the unreliability of Yeats, Eliot and Pound as historians has forced subsequent poets to turn their attention to topography: "it begins to seem as if a focus upon scenery, upon landscape and the areal, relations in space, are a necessary check and control upon the poet's manipulation of the historical record". This, like many of Davie's critical theories, originates in his own poetic development; and it confirms that Davie likes to situate his own work by reference to earlier poets....

Davie admits that his readings of other poets are often readings of himself: "I am my own favourite author and often when I seem to be studying another writer, it's myself I'm studying really."...

The Poet in the Imaginary Museum provides important clues about Davie's poetic development. In the earliest essay, "The Spoken Word" (1950), he recommends to "the young English poet resentful of the tyranny of the 'image'" the poetry of Yvor Winters and his followers, and makes large claims for a "renewed poetry of statement"; the essay reads like an early manifesto for the Movement poets with whom Davie was to be associated, and whose main target was the "tyranny of the image" imposed by Dylan Thomas. "The Poetic Diction of John M. Synge" (1952) ... and "Professor Heller and the Boots" (1954) ... are further important texts for this period.

"Common Mannerism" (1957) is a turning point: Davie rejects the "ugly" and "philistine" Movement tone, and in the title essay of the same year develops Malraux's idea that what distinguishes the modern artist from his predecessors is a freedom (created by technological advance) to wander through an imaginary museum containing art from all ages and cultures. For Davie this means that poetry must become more pluralistic: "the modern style in poetry is the arrangement in new patterns of the styles of the past". At the time, Davie's thesis that the poet simply "picks and chooses" from all manner of styles aroused considerable controversy.... But perhaps the chief importance of the essay is its indication that Davie was broadening his scope: in the late 1950s and early 1960s there is a greater concern with translation, an exploration of the relationship between poetry and other arts, and a new respect for poetry which concentrates on the non-human world "bodied over" against us.

Davie has maintained these interests, but it is possible to detect a third phase in his career dating from the late 1960s. "Poetry and Other Modern Arts" (1968) qualifies the imaginary museum thesis by suggesting that poetry has remained a conservative art, unaffected by many of the technological changes which have influenced painting and music; and another essay of that year, "Landscape as Poetic Focus", shows a new sensitivity to topography in poetry and to the open forms of Charles Olson and Edward Dorn. Davie has always been interested in American poetry (the 1953 essay in which an "austere" Davie measures up to the "panache" of Wallace Stevens is another useful piece reprinted here), but in recent years he has become more conscious of the need for someone to act as a negotiator between British and American cultures.

Attention to a steady development in Davie's work can be misleading, however, if it conceals the ebb and flow of his critical judgments. Nowhere in his criticism is there a parallel to Leavis's change of heart about Dickens or to Eliot's about Milton. Rather than dramatic reversals, there is a constant pulsing between acceptance and rejection, admiration and detestation. . . .

The postscript to his discussion of *Hugh Selwyn Mauberley* (1961) warns that "I by no means preclude the possibility that, after three attempts to give an account of it, I may some time venture on a fourth!" The failure to provide a consistent perspective may look perverse, even self-indulgent, and there are moments when honest and instructive uncertainty about a writer's worth threatens to dissolve into confusion and self-contradiction. But for the most part Davie's arguments with himself are meaningful and useful: he has the power to identify the key issues of the modern era, to put the case of both sides, and to provide temporary solutions. Here again rhetoric is a key weapon, Davie's means not only of persuading his readers but of dispelling his own doubt. Davie is a more volatile critic than he pretends, and one of the virtues of *The Poet in the Imaginary Museum* is that it enables us to observe his fluctuations more clearly than before. . . .

The sharpness of Davie's insights in this collection reassures one that complaints about omissions are worth making: we do need a record of all that he has written. . . . He has helped radically alter our views of Hardy, has put questions about Pound which those too busy taking sides have forgotten to ask, and has struggled with most of the major figures in the modern period. Above all, he has kept his options open, responding to new developments in poetry while so many of his contemporaries remain entrenched. The price for this is occasional waywardness in critical judgment, but so long as his poetry continues to renew itself this should be a price we are willing to pay.

> Blake Morrison, "A Voice of Even Tenor," *in* The Times Literary Supplement (© Times Newspapers Ltd. (London) 1978; reproduced from The Times Literary Supplement *by permission*), January 6, 1978, p. 15.

DEREK MAHON

What a pity that Donald Davie is less interesting as a poet than as a critic. Picking up the *Collected Poems*, as I not infrequently do, I find myself returning constantly to the earliest volumes, *Brides of Reason* (1955) and *A Winter Talent* (1957). Here, it seems to me—in 'The Garden Par-

ty', 'Remembering the Thirties', 'Hearing Russian Spoken' and 'Rejoinder to a Critic'—he wrote with a confidence and poise that he has never (in verse) quite managed since. The early poems are full of quotations: 'Yet irony itself is doctrinaire', 'A neutral tone is nowadays preferred', 'Abjure politic brokenness for good', 'Appear concerned only to make it scan'.

Note, however, that each and every one of these lapidary pentameters concerns the practice of poetry itself; even at this stage Davie was already the critic, or at any rate the discerning reader. The poems bristle with the names of the great. . . . If we didn't know that Davie was Barnsley born and bred, we might be forgiven for thinking that he was nurtured in the imaginary museum of his title [*The Poet in the Imaginary Museum: Essays of Two Decades*]. 'Nobody wants any more poems about philosophers or paintings or novelists or art galleries or mythology or foreign cities or other poems. At least I hope nobody wants them.' Thus, of course, Kingsley Amis, in a much quoted proscription of 1955; but Davie, despite certain 'Movement' attitudes ('Appear concerned only to make it scan'), was never really a Movement poet at all; cultural exhibits have always been part of his stock-in-trade. As Barry Alpert remarks in his foreword to this collection, the title, liberally interpreted, 'might embrace most of what Donald Davie has written during the past 25 years'. . . .

One of the most attractive features of Davie's criticism is his generous openness to the unfamiliar and the idiosyncratic. He once accused himself of being 'one of the steely trimmers whose suspicion of pretension in art is not always distinguishable from mean-mindedness'; but this does him less than justice. True, his characteristic tone is fastidious, even pernickety—how unpleasant to meet Dr Davie!—but it is deployed in the service of a fervent devotion. While recognising and repudiating pretension in art, no less than painful modesty, he insists on the validity and importance of art's large and rightful claim.

> *Derek Mahon, "Exhibit A," in* New Statesman (© 1978 The Statesman & Nation Publishing Co. Ltd.), February 24, 1978, p. 256.

*   *   *

DAY LEWIS, C(ecil)   1904-1972

Day Lewis was an Irish-born English poet, novelist, translator, and children's author who was linked with the Oxford poets of the 1930s, Auden, MacNeice, and Spender. Although generally regarded as a minor talent (even though he was Poet Laureate of England), Day Lewis was a serious artist, throughout his career concerned with the search for selfhood, whether reflected in the overtly political poems of his early career or the pastoral lyrics of his maturity. He also received popular acclaim for the many mystery novels he wrote under the pseudonym Nicholas Blake. (See also *CLC*, Vols. 1, 6, and *Contemporary Authors*, Vols. 15-16; obituary, Vols. 33-36, rev. ed.; *Contemporary Authors Permanent Series*, Vol. 1)

JOSEPH N. RIDDEL

Literary history has come to consider Day Lewis almost exclusively in terms of his association with Auden and Spender, as a member of the so-called Auden Group. And while the group image, as we shall see, overstates the actual homogeneity of the three poets and detracts from the individual talent of each (in particular, Auden's), the tendency to associate Day Lewis with a collective point of view and an impersonal poetry reveals a crucial truth about his work. From the ''Auden Group'' to the Poet Laureateship, Day Lewis has sought in poetry to realize the self, or to discover a self, through self-effacement. His political and his personal poetry alike are of a piece, in that each begins with the vision of the disintegration of the self as mirrored in the disintegration of society. At the heart of Day Lewis' poetry is the search for a new society and thus a new language of human relationships; for language is not simply the medium of a culture but its infrastructure, and the self, if it is not to disappear, must be reconstituted in that structure. The fact of Day Lewis' belonging, if only figuratively, to a school or ''Group'' of poetry at the very time he emerged as a significant poet may be taken as an index to his career. (pp. 17-18)

The need of these poets for an impersonal poetry, while it derives theoretically from the argument set forth by Eliot in 'Tradition and the Individual Talent,'' testifies in fact to another view toward history. Their ideal past, unlike Eliot's, was not the tradition as embodied in the venerable institutions—of Church, Crown, literature—but a time that, figuratively at least, antedates history and its time-haunted systems. They sought a *time* of some pastoral ideal, in which man's elementary relations to others and to nature were realized in coherent communities. Thus the Marxist future, with its ideal of a retrieved unity, became for them a kind of pastoral vision—the past recoverable in the future. Their occasional return to archaic form (the ballad and its recall of the oral tradition; Anglo-Saxon patterns) suggests the essentially counterrevolutionary thrust of a poetry that seeks to transcend the history of progress and its progressive dualisms. (p. 21)

In the Preface to *Oxford Poetry, 1927,* written in collaboration with Auden, and then in *Transitional Poem,* some of which had appeared in the earlier anthology, Day Lewis first revealed the analytical spirit which later manifested itself in dialectical poetics. Nature, in these poems, lost her magic and became the self's nonhuman antithesis but remained the immediate ground of being. The perennial philosophical question of mind's relation to matter was easily extended into that of the poet's relation to society. The departure from his adolescent Georgian world was socially analogous to the metaphysical death of God; all coherence disappeared with it, leaving mind rootless, a nothingness, disembodied. Thus, the divided self. . . .

It is indicative that his first major poem emerged from his investigations of what role the poet might, and must, play in the modern world; for Day Lewis' immediate heritage from the past was an image of disorder. The question was whether the poet could, or must, manage a new synthesis— or build a new ''system'' out of the fragments of old ones— since synthesis, rather than analysis, was the poet's traditional function. The new synthesis, whatever else it might be, must incorporate the old order, and hence be true to tradition and its language. Or better, the deconstruction of an old system can only be made in the language of that system, since the new world and its language do not exist. The poet like the synthetic philosopher is dedicated to building his new world out of the fragments of the old one. In this sense alone could the ''tetragonal/Pure symmetry of brain'' . . . be a manifestation not of the private will but of the

''collective consciousness,'' and the poet be both the agent and the instrument of the dialectical will of history. (p. 27)

In *The Buried Day,* Day Lewis has remarked how Lawrence ''got mixed into my Marxism'' because each indicted a ''system'' (capitalism) which prevented the ''full flowering of individual personality'' and hence ''affected the relationship between man and woman, poisoning it with false idealism that encouraged only the self-conscious and cerebral sides of our nature.'' . . . The impact of economic turbulence on individual relationships was the subject of Day Lewis' three legitimate novels written in the mid-1930's, though in them he could follow neither the strict Marxian nor the rigid Lawrencean line; and the blurring of the two only reflected the hopeless mixture of two irreconcilable philosophies. The full flowering of the individual personality implied for Day Lewis the submission of the private will to the wholeness of the love relationship and thus an escape from the ''negative inversion'' of the will. (p. 28)

Auden's intellectualism had its ambiguous impact on Day Lewis' style. Auden's poetry moves from idea to reality— or it moves from an experience that is largely intellectual to a contemplation of ideas which admits their rich and often comic impingements upon life. Life renders the idea problematic, throwing it into comic relief. For Auden language is a human mean, and logos an illusion. Day Lewis' natural mode was lyrical; his primary thematic concerns are with the harmony of the emotional life. His attempt in *Transitional Poem* not only to impose the ''tetragonal/Pure symmetry of brain'' on modern chaos but to contemplate the implications of that urgent necessity (in a poem presumably both analytic and synthetic) had stylistic consequences that set his art in conflict with his sensibility. His development in the 1930's and early 1940's can be said, in effect, to have altered the ratio of idea to experience in his poetry but not to have changed his basic theme: the divided self, in which emotion and reason are at odds. Even as he moved more and more toward a public and a committed poetry, he was moved, as he later acknowledged, not by intellectual but by emotional convictions. (pp. 29-30)

In contrast to Auden, the distracting quality of Day Lewis' work throughout the 1930's is its schizophrenic dedication now to social change, now to emotional conservatism, which manifests itself in poems like *From Feathers to Iron* in a technological language used to evoke basic emotional responses to change and death. . . .

His search for a myth or a ''system'' by which to order experience and to make history coherent was, as it developed, his way of escaping from the labyrinth of his own internal conflict—of turning his inner life outward into the social sphere. His was an attempt to escape the romantic will, to transcend the self in impersonality; but he did so by asserting that man's only method of self-transcendence lay in creation—begetting the children, new societies, or poems —and thereby in sacrificing the private self to the future of community and order. (p. 30)

The revolutionary poets of the 1930's . . . found the kind of philosophical and meditative paralysis that afflicted their great predecessors, Yeats and Eliot, impossible. Having to take sides, they had to assume the role of actor, both in history and against history. Even in surrendering the individual self to the revolutionary will and process, they participated as a force in history. And their radical poems, especially Day Lewis' apparently political poems, are really about that role: the paradox of creating that which subsumes the creator. The lack of focus in those poems—their dependence on traditional forms or "moulds," yet their impatient search for a modern language; their often artless attempt to employ deeply personal experience as a metaphor or archetype for prescribed social changes, as in the incessant journeys—is in effect a blurring of the poet's role. They are poems intent on projecting the vision of a future, but their primary function is the deconstruction of a moribund present.

The real subject of these poems is themselves—the poet taking a double look at his role as at once the maker and the victim of history. The struggle toward impersonality—which manifests itself technically in a thoroughly metaphorical poetry wherein all analogies are horizontal and thrust themselves toward an ever receding future—only serves to call attention to the poet's self-transcending act in assuming his role. When he sacrifices his individual self to the role of poet and also to the inspirational force which not only preserves the immutable forms of the past but provokes changes of heart, he becomes more than a person. He becomes a part of the human will for rebirth, incarnating itself in the vision of a new society. But it is a society he can never realize actually, except that he possesses it in his own dream of self-transcendence manifest most intensely in the conditions of love. (pp. 34-5)

To celebrate the creative self is to celebrate the superhuman; and, as Day Lewis would claim in his later books of criticism, long after the need to reconcile his poetics with Marxism and revolution had passed, every poem strives to confirm man's superhumanity. The poem, that is, is a reaching toward wholeness; hence it reaches beyond the individual to the "communal experience." . . .

After 1938, Day Lewis' poetry seems to become . . . more his own: it is less ambitious, more introspective, inevitably less topical, and more nostalgic. But the old preoccupations remain; indeed, their implications are even more apparent. Day Lewis' search in the 1930's for a tradition and a language—a "system" which preceded the self and confirmed it—was destined to fail because it was based on historical nostalgia. The collapse of the last ultimate "system" forced him to revaluate the tradition within which the poet works. And what he discovered was that tradition is the "illusion" of wholeness the poet holds to as he lives in the present and points himself toward the future. Tradition is a myth or totalization that attempts to answer man's desire; thus, poetry would become his myth. (pp. 36-7)

As he has failed to be an original poet (he was that, perhaps, only for a brief time), he has found the true necessity of his vocation: poetry is a spiritual exercise in self-renewal and in self-transcendence, the method whereby the individual self survives in a world from which all systems had defected and only love was cohesive. In the illusory wholeness of the poem man possesses himself as timeless, at "home," and thus located in the interstices rather than the flow of history. (p. 37)

Dualism (the divided self) remained his theme. It translates itself into a variety of schisms, which provide Day Lewis with his own creative dialectic: the discontinuity of past and present, which is manifest in the alienation of the present generation; the schism of language, reflected every-

where in its connotative and denotative functions; the divided self, whose unconscious is at war with its conscious; the self's sense of its fall from wholeness into desire which was both creative and destructive. (pp. 37-8)

Day Lewis may serve us today as a relevant example of the poet-in-history as opposed to the poet-on-Parnassus. He is one of the few instances we have of an artist whose work was catalyzed by ideology into being better than it might otherwise have been. But, if this is the case, it is so only because that ideology spoke emphatically to emotional truths he already held and enforced them as historically objective. . . . Today we see not Marx in Day Lewis' early poetry but the perennial emotional food of a faith in telic order that affirms self-identity and man's creative role in history. For Day Lewis had discovered that man is language and thus is condemned to interpret himself repeatedly. He is condemned, that is, to seek his own origin and his own end because he is enmeshed in a network of relations that forever obscure origins and ends. (p. 38)

The divided self is Day Lewis' theme from beginning to end—hence the essential journey. If *Transitional Poem* brought the self into its intellectual majority, confirming the primacy of mind (collective mind) in the evolution of cultural order, it divorced the self from its ancient and timeless home—from the ideal of community only faintly hinted at in the disintegrating memories of childhood security and in his nostalgia for tradition. (p. 60)

The journey in . . . Day Lewis has two stages: (1) expulsion from the old order, from falling Eden and from suffocating womb; (2) the precarious, existential search through an alien and threatening landscape toward some vaguely sensed new order, a rebirth of the isolated self into some new community. The second and most significant stage of the journey is always away from the ugly familiar toward the mysterious, evanescent ideal: from complexity and conflict to simplicity and order, from city to country, from fear to faith. But the journey is never complete; its life is in its psychic moral immediacy. (p. 61)

It is revealing that *Transitional Poem* does not develop linearly but like its concluding image of the hawk, circles in upon its theme. *From Feathers to Iron,* on the other hand, is deliberately and consciously linear, though the line leads back upon its own beginning. The difference is that the earlier poem is a philosophical exploration (analysis) of the fall into consciousness, into selfhood—of what it means to be "well out" of Eden. The fall did not occur *in* time, but *into* time—that is, the fall had no duration; and its meaning is not manifest in historical or dramatic event but in the movement of self-discovery. But, once in time, the self's acts are circumscribed by history, just as the self is sacrificed to it. Creative self-sacrifice, indeed, is the preeminent theme of *From Feathers to Iron. . . .* (p. 63)

The structure of the poem is overtly and consciously archetypal: moving from autumn to spring, from time through the nascence of death of the self to rebirth, it bridges time's divisive flux; and it celebrates the self's (and mind's) role in the natural and necessary process of birth-death-renewal. In analogy with the process of the child's birth, the mind must seek in the iron world of the present—in the technological landscape of the modern world—those evidences of organic process and vital renewal which nature once provided the Romantic imagination. Thus once again Day

Lewis conducts his poem along multiple and discrete levels to the point where it often threatens to become patently allegorical. (p. 64)

The important fact . . . is that the political issues remain predominantly indirect; the larger issue of the new world is felt not in ideological but in intimate terms. The new world is an imperative in the wake of the fragmentation of the old, a pressure urgently felt on the level of the new family and manifest in the evolution of the poem itself. (pp. 64-5)

The political dimensions of this poem are mainly latent, for the primal dislocations of the self in its act of passion and the moral readjustments of self to other (mate), looking toward a future community (the family), are featured in its predominant movements. Love resolves anxiety and desire by generating anxiety and desire. Hence, we have the recurrent motif: over the health of the fetus, the wife's suffering within the proximity of death, the uncertainty of the new world beyond the "frontier," which is to be the heritage of his son and not his own. . . . The poet is suspended in anxiety but released by hope; and the alternation of moods creates a resonance by which alone the theme progresses. In other words, the themes constitute the act of creating the poem itself, for that is the ultimate implication of creative responsibility. (p. 67)

In *A Time to Dance,* which appeared in 1935, two titles, "The Conflict" and "In Me Two Worlds," signify not only two overtly political poems but provide explicit metaphors for the deep-seated division of personal loyalties that characterizes bourgeois Leftist poetry in the 1930's. Guilt, strangely enough, the very thing communal involvement is supposed to resolve, is the animating force. How to be concurrently an activist and a poet, how to reconcile the civic with the esthetic, was Day Lewis' burden. . . . Thus we have the guilt and also the search for a style that might move poetry toward action: not as propaganda or rhetoric but as a voice of the heroic future; not a poetry forecasting magnetic mountains but one evoking their immanent presence concealed in the chaos of history.

In a sense, we might say Day Lewis was searching for his own true style. . . . These poems of narrative action, which are, ironically, nonpolitical, eschew abstraction and the philosophical base of the earlier long poems; above all, since they are not allegorical, they do not subordinate narrative to a moral or symbolic purpose, though they were conceived as exempla of heroic action and sacrifice. These poems focus on the flesh and blood of man's little heroics, orchestrating as it were the rhythms of an action; and, with quiet eloquence, they affirm the possibility of a successful action and heroism in an antiheroic time. . . . Day Lewis sets this narrative style against the lyrics of guilt as he sets the instinct of hope against conscious despair in a dialogue which seeks to join the isolated self with the struggling society. (pp. 76-7)

An Italian Visit, Day Lewis' longest single poem, is another transitional piece. Published in 1953 as a single volume, it serves not only to introduce a third phase of his poetic career but to compose those fragmentary, fugitive explorations of the divided self which preoccupied him in the 1940's. . . .

An Italian Visit returned momentarily to the ambitious and contrived poems of Day Lewis' earlier invention and turned away from the lyrical mode toward which his style

had been developing. In this sense, the poem of intellectual accounting is self-consciously transitional, the kind of poem he seemed compelled to write at given intervals. As such, it returned to Day Lewis' earlier analytic mode, treating the self as a composite of abstractions, as the meeting point of three degrees of time consciousness. Yet despite its strategy, the poem is an attempt to move beyond this simplified view of self, to catch (in the image of a continuous dialogue) the interacting consciousness of historical man who is struggling to satisfy his appetite to live simultaneously in a world composed of immediate sensation, memory, and the a priori of received ideas or given language. (p. 109)

The three slim volumes of poetry (*Pegasus and Other Poems,* 1957; *The Gate,* 1962; and *The Room,* 1965) Day Lewis had published since *An Italian Visit* are in a sense his own surrender to the lyric impulse, a surrender, that is to say, to what of the old instinctual energy remains. But conscious surrenders are rarely total. The single obsession of his late poetry is "love" (which he had come to think of in *The Poetic Image* as "a kind of necessity by which all things are bound together and in which, could the whole pattern be seen, their contradictions would appear reconciled" . . .) against death. As early as *A Hope for Poetry,* he argued that the root of all human impulse was love and that love could only flourish in a social environment which made intimate contact among individuals possible. The poet must live among friends and speak the language that bound him ultimately to his living unit. Love, in other words, is Day Lewis' metaphor (or euphemism?) for a kind of primal (hence elementally social) unity. (p. 118)

The lyric . . . is for Day Lewis an escape from history, the abstraction of experience into its transcendent and eternal perspective. The ultimate temporality of music is synchronic rather than diachronic. (p. 119)

Day Lewis is not a purely lyrical poet, no more so in his later work than in his earlier; and so his poems turn out to be not pure lyrics but self-conscious speculations on lyric themes. The impurities with which, he argues, the mind has broken up the singing line of the original lyric remain at the center of his own poems: irony, self-conscious commentary, the overt moral. The pure image becomes metaphor, bearing its analogue of meaning to experience.

If the enervating conflict of modernism lies between the poet's desire to reinvoke the simple emotions and the complexities of a thought which will not trust simplicity, to use Day Lewis' own well-worn distinction, then his late poetry falls unceremoniously between the two. We might say that it yearns too powerfully for the purity of innocence, the simplicity of love, and the security of enclosed and remembered spaces. In other words, Day Lewis could not in the end face the consequences of his materialism, nor could he find an adequate belief in spirit—the "grace" of the lyrical impulse—to replace it. (p. 120)

[We] can more clearly understand Day Lewis' mystique of the poet's privileged moment in terms of restraint rather than of stimulation. The poems of recent years are anything but visionary breakthroughs, or even lyrics of innocence; they are, instead, the products of a disciplined reduction of experience to abstraction or to the substance of metaphorical insights. . . . The convenience of his orderly arrangements bespeaks his dependence on poetry as a way of containing, as opposed to transforming, the atoms of personal experience within the archetypal categories which make them appear universal. His journeys are no longer experienced ones, nor does the poetry manifest the urgency and immediacy of departure, dislocation, movement, or arrival. The maturity and the unstimulating sameness of Day Lewis' last poems are the pyrrhic victory of the poet over his self-doubts and the almost total submission of his material to a desired order. (pp. 121-22)

But Day Lewis remains a divided self—and a divided poet—torn between a willed innocence and an unremitting skepticism. The ''Moods of Love'' ... —the book's major poem, a sonnet sequence—indulges the illusory dream of innocence; but the ecstasy of moods depends upon a Keatsian double perspective, a negative capability. Unfortunately, Day Lewis' own negative capability does not afford him the Keatsian range of beauty within terror, but it is nevertheless the dialectic of illusion and skepticism, dream and history, out of which his last poems are composed. . . . (p. 125)

There has been no substantial development since *Pegasus*. The titles of Day Lewis' last two books of poems, *The Gate* and *The Room,* are metaphorically indicative of a poetry overwhelmed by deliberate limitation. The titles describe in a sense the kinds of desperate reduction Day Lewis was willing to make in order to achieve some kind of wholeness or order or perfection—some kind of perspective upon himself as person and upon his role, so often to himself problematic, as a man of letters. The books are filled with images of restricted space, spaces in which the imagination at last has control over the matter surrounding it. They are images, that is, of a poetic or artistically ordered space—of atomistic worlds finally composed, but only at the expense of severe reduction and at times ruthless condensation. (p. 126)

[Day Lewis is] a minor poet in the best sense of that phrase; and whatever reputation he has as a poet seems more the result of historical accident than of individual genius. He is a poet of the 1930's, the ''Auden Group,'' of ''Macspaunday,'' and though he has long since given up his allegiance to causes and groups, he has not really survived his ''group'' role nor become a force in modern poetry. (p. 131)

As inflexible as Eliot, Day Lewis set poetry against the reality of historical process; but unlike Eliot, he had no access to a ''system'' of belief which could adequately subsume process. And that lack, indeed, would appear to be the efficient cause of what original poetry (even that stylistically derivative from Auden) he wrote: his work in the 1930's. For the 1930's offered a severe challenge to his native conservatism, and it forced him again and again to confront the dynamics of historical change as a reality which denied the possibility of redeeming the past. Dialectical materialism, though it paid fit honor to the past, was not nostalgic. But, if Day Lewis became, as he later said, a ''future-fan,'' it was not really as a believer in the Marxist apocalypse. He was able to find within the Marxian ideal of a new community a reforming of the pastoral ideal. His view of history was ultimately circular, not linear or dialectical. But his being thrown so rudely into the contemporary scene did have the positive effect of forcing him to recognize its challenges. They brought him face-to-face with the inadequacy of any ''system,'' but did not allay his need of a ''system.'' The particular tension in his early poetry derives from the pull of past and future against the present because the experience of modern reality must be accommodated to some mythic order—the journey away from became the journey toward, the magnetic mountain being the same to all men who live in time and aspire to transcend themselves. (pp. 138-39)

Day Lewis' poetic career [is] a dedicated venture of escape from self and thus from the responsibility of his personal creative powers. He has tried to become impersonal by being a poet so deeply personal that his private identity would be subsumed by his communal role. His materialism, his Marxism, his search for ''ancestors,'' his desire for the impersonal, and his inveterate imitation of other poets—they all resolve into a strangely coherent poetics of a poet who fears to fall below his powers. . . . He has not been, like his modern ''ancestors,'' a revolutionary, and hence has not been a responsible caretaker of tradition. He has not extended the style he inherited, nor made a lasting impression in it. In this sense, he is properly the Poet Laureate, the voice of a community rather than a self.

It is the self-reflexive quality of his poetry, its recurrent self-examination of the problematic of language and thus of the myth of history, that characterizes his modernism. But he was never very comfortable with the role of modern poet, nor self-deceptive enough to think he could escape it. The self-consciousness of his poetry repeatedly indicates that he knew he had to ask more of poetry than it could deliver. In a universe otherwise without a fixed or vital center (without God), the human self must serve as the generating source of order; and the poet assumes his paradigmatic role as the caretaker of that creative energy. And yet the self as center portends an anarchy of selves, an atomistic world, and a terrifying isolation for the creative mind. It implies that the creative imagination is nothing but desire, insatiable desire. Day Lewis' traditionalism, as much as Eliot's traditionalism, testifies to that fear of the ultimate existential freedom and anarchy. Unlike Eliot, however, Day Lewis' world could afford no either/or commitment: neither self nor selflessness; for both, as he recognized of Eliot, denied the human and repudiated history. What Day Lewis demanded was some impossible reconciliation of the two. His poetry stands as evidence of the act of reconciliation—an act in which the problematic of creation, language, and order are the issue.

Day Lewis' poetry turns upon the theme of love, or the search for love. Love is sexual, social; it is communal; it is, above all, the ideal of order, a redeemed history. It is Unity. It is what the poem aspires toward; the wholeness of which the poem is the ''illusion.'' Day Lewis' poems, then, may stand as evidence of the act toward reconciliation; but we certainly do not expect that they achieve reconciliation. For all his distrust of history (that is, his yearning for ideal parts or consummate futures), his is ultimately the voice of a man who accepts change and hence has the precarious role of trying to define an ever changing self. If the weakness of Day Lewis' poetry is its nostalgia (an obsession with an earlier, buried self—that self which was whole, presumably), its strength is in its humility (its awareness that it is condemned finally to a present of change, and a future of death). Out of this sense emerges occasionally a poem poignantly aware of itself—a knowledge constituted in the face of necessity, which, as he predicted early on in *Transitional Poem*, makes him an ''orchard god'' who is ''Grounded in temperate soil.'' . . . (pp. 144-45)

Joseph N. Riddel, in his C. Day Lewis *(copyright 1971 by Twayne Publishers, Inc.; reprinted with the permission of Twayne Publishers, A Division of G. K. Hall & Co., Boston), Twayne, 1971.*

SAMUEL HYNES

The last notice of C. Day Lewis's verse to appear in these pages was a review of *The Whispering Roots* in 1970 [see *CLC,* Vol. 6]. . . . It was not so much a review, I thought, as a literary mugging.

Now that Day Lewis is no longer a living laureate, but simply a dead poet, perhaps the time has come to consider his work more temperately, to forgive him the great gifts that he did not have (and never claimed), and to value what he had, and what he achieved. . . . [He] was of Hardy's company, a decent minor poet in the same tradition.

If even Day Lewis's most friendly critics have not always seen him clearly in that tradition, they have had reasons for confusion. For one thing, he found his poetic place relatively late, after much searching and much imitating, and his earlier books are full of echoes of other poets, so much so that they often seem to have no more unity of style than an anthology of modern verse has. . . . [He] found it easier to speak in other voices than in his own: first the early Yeats and then the later, then Auden—all those kestrels and airmen—and after that Edward Thomas, Eliot, de la Mare, Frost, Hardy.

Day Lewis was quite aware that he was an imitative poet, though he sometimes tried to find a less pejorative way of putting it. . . .

The other principal obstacle to a just assessment of his achievement is, of course, his connection with the other principal poets of his generation. The swift emergence of a new generation of poets in the early 1930s blurred the differences among them, and did some damage to the individual reputations of all the poets concerned. . . . [Day Lewis, Auden, MacNeice, and Spender] were not a school; they were simply four poets, of whom the most gifted and most aggressive dominated the others. All of them (even Auden) cast off the early Auden influence eventually, but Day Lewis, because he had the slightest individual gift, and was the least sure of his own poetic identity, was the most influenced, and the last to break free.

For him, and I think also for most of his generation, the coming of the Second World War was a profoundly liberating experience. The decade of the 1930s had been a time when political action seemed, urgent and unavoidable, and every poem was a political act. Day Lewis entered that political world more completely and more naively than most of his contemporaries, and wrote some very embarrassing verse. . . . In later years he was inclined to minimize this part of his early work: "During my so-called political period", he wrote in the 1950s, "most of my poems were in fact about love and death." In a sense this is true, but the point is that in the 1930s all private experience and feelings, even love and death, were touched by public issues. A fair example is Day Lewis's own sequence of poems, *From Feathers to Iron* (1931): "For me", he wrote, the sequence "expressed simply my thoughts and feelings during the nine months before the birth of my first child"; but "the critics, almost to a man, took it for a political allegory." To a de-

gree the critics were right; the sequence does contain politics, because everything did then.

The war changed all that, and made it possible for Day Lewis to be what he had always been at heart—a private, lyric poet. Perhaps the simplest way to describe the nature of that transformation is to say that the coming of war changed the poet's relation to time. To be political is to be concerned with the present and the future, with, one might say, public time. But in a war the present is beyond any man's control, and the future does not exist. And so the poet was freed to turn backward, to the past, the time in which we live our most private lives. . . . As a source for the materials of poetry, the private past had replaced the public present.

Most of Day Lewis's best poems were written during this period of wartime liberation and just after. This was also the time when the many influences on his poetry became mainly one. . . . We may for convenience's sake call it the Hardy tradition, since Hardy has been its principal transmitter to the twentieth century, but it obviously has a history that is older than Hardy, that includes, for instance, Wordsworth and Clare, and has its roots in medieval lyrics. It is a tradition with many variations, but its constants seem to me to be these: it is English, and is primarily concerned with actual nature in the English countryside, and with man's relation to it; it is physical, not transcendental; it is descriptive, not symbolic; it is rooted in time, not in history; it is retrospective, often regretful and melancholy, but also ironic and stoic. Formally, the tradition is conservative, but inventive: Hardy played endless variations on inherited stanza forms, and rarely repeated one, and Day Lewis was the same sort of craftsman: in *Whispering Roots,* for example, there are thirty-seven different stanzas in thirty-four poems, and only one is repeated. . . .

Day Lewis is clearly in this tradition, and it was when he had found his place there in the neighbourhood of Hardy that he could begin to write his best verse. That he had freed himself from other influences only to assume a single and more powerful one is not to his discredit: it is characteristic, and indeed definitive of good minor poets that they depend on major ones. If they are fortunate, they find a stronger voice that is enough like their own to permit them to speak through it in their own accents. When such a poet finds the right tradition, his voice will sound true, not because it is his, but because it is the tradition's: when he chooses unwisely, he will simply sound like a bad imitator. Day Lewis's efforts to write like Auden fail both as imitations and as poems; but his poems in the Hardy tradition succeed, and though they remind us of Hardy, they retain their own individuality, they are not imitations but new poems. (p. 129)

By the time . . . *Poems 1943-1947* was written, Day Lewis was easy enough with his place in the tradition to celebrate some of its members by name. . . . There are also many fluent poems in the traditional manner, poems that show his confidence in his ability to use it. . . . Like *Word Over All,* the book has a unity of tone that none of the earlier collections had.

After the poems of the 1940s the Hardy tradition is less clear in Day Lewis's poems, though it never fades out entirely. In the later poems, irony melts into nostalgia, the past overshadows the natural present, and the tone becomes quietly reflective and meditative. . . . [In] Day Lewis's later work one feels a kind of easing of poetic tension, a relaxing into retrospection. A paradigmatic poem for this state is one in which the aging poet looks at an old photograph and recalls past emotions. There are several such poems . . . [which depend] on the instant nostalgia that old photographs create. . . . Another characteristic occasion (one that Hardy also exploited in poems of his old age) is the return to scenes of childhood; all the poems in the first part of *The Whispering Roots,* his last book, are about Ireland, where he was born. They are not exactly the poems of a revenant; Day Lewis was only two when he left Ireland, and he returned, as he says in a poem, with ''no drowned memories''. They are, rather, the poems of an elderly man in search of a past, one more step in that search for identity that had led him through other men's styles and other men's subjects, and finally back into himself.

Other late poems are records of ordinary occasions . . . , each moulded into a single metaphor, of vision or of loss. This kind of poetry, the habitual casting of commonplace things into verse, becomes inevitably a kind of autobiography, told with reticence (that too is in the tradition), but none the less an essentially personal record. Day Lewis's whole life is in his poems: childhood, adolescent love, marriage, the births of children, politics and the end of politics, the break-up of a marriage, later love, his own last illness. In cases like his, the life's work is really a single poem, and individual parts do not stand out from the whole. (pp. 129-30)

Nevertheless, one might propose a list of the poems in which the essential poet could best be discovered. It would be easy, first of all, to decide what to exclude: all the political and public poetry of the 1930s; all the poetic forms that he could not manage well—dialogue (so nothing from *Noah and the Waters*), narrative (neither *A Time to Dance* nor *The Nabara*), dramatic monologue; almost every poem of any considerable length. One would be left with only one kind of poem, the kind for which his talent was best suited —the personal lyric. Of the early verse, this means only the poems of *From Feathers to Iron,* the only one of his long sequences that is essentially private. From *Overtures to Death* (1938), the volume in which the turn away from political subjects is first apparent, I would take two poems: ''Regency Houses'' and ''A Happy View''. In *Word Over All* (1943), his best single volume, the essential poems seem to me to be ''The Album'', ''Departure in the Dark'', ''Cornet Solo'', the sonnet sequence ''O Dreams, O Destinations'', and the two fine poems of countrymen in wartime, ''The Stand-to'' and ''Watching Post''.

Poems 1943-1947 contains the tender poems of marriage and the end of marriage—''Marriage of Two'', ''Married Dialogue'', and ''The Woman Alone'', as well as a number of very Hardy-like poems: in addition to those I have mentioned above they are ''The Unwanted'', ''The Housewarming'', ''Is it far to go?'', and ''Chrysanthemum Show''. *Pegasus* (1958) has two of the photograph-poems (''The House Where I was Born'' and ''Father to Sons''), ''George Meredith, 1861'', and ''Lot 96''.

The Gate (1962) is the weakest of the later volumes, and one might skip it entirely, or perhaps single out the title poem and ''An Upland Field''. But the volume that followed it only three years later, *The Room,* is one of the best, with ''On Not Saying Everything'', ''Seven Steps to Love'', ''Derelect'', ''The Fox'' and ''Stephanotis''. *Whispering Roots* contains the series of Irish poems, most of which are sensitive and touching (though characteristically, the only poem that attempts a public theme, ''Kilmainham Jail'', fails), and so are the little poems of ordinariness: ''A Skull Picked Clean'', ''A Privileged Moment'', and ''Merry-go-round''. And finally, of the latest, previously uncollected poems, there is the deathbed poem, ''At Lemmons'', a small masterpiece—reticent and calm, and very moving.

This list-making may seem a tedious kind of sub-criticism, but in the case of Day Lewis it is necessary. . . .

Day Lewis needs no apology at all. He worked steadily and honestly at his craft, and he wrote poems—a good number of them—that will give pleasure and the sense of a shared emotion to sympathetic readers, and that deserve to survive. ''The writing of poetry'', he once wrote, ''is a vocation, a game, a habit, and a search for truth.'' His life's work was all of these, and something more; for by finding and writing in the English lyric tradition, he helped to keep that tradition alive, and earned his place with Hardy in Stinsford Churchyard. (p. 130)

Samuel Hynes, ''The Recovery of Privacy,'' in The Times Literary Supplement (© *Times Newspapers Ltd. (London) 1977; reproduced from* The Times Literary Supplement *by permission), February 4, 1977, pp. 129-30.*

SAMUEL HYNES

Transitional Poem is a conventional young man's statement of the transition from adolescence to manhood, with the particular poetic themes customarily associated with that passage: love and lust, philosophic doubts, mind and imagination, pride and ambition, the power of poetry—all the subjects that young men write poems about. The four 'aspects' that Day Lewis enumerates are not, to my eye, at all distinct: the metaphysical and psychological sides of the problem interweave throughout the poem, and the ethical is scarcely apparent at all.

More fundamental to the structure than transitions are oppositions: mind/body, ideal/real, infinite/finite, love/fear, eternity/time. Day Lewis' use of these terms often echoes Yeats very closely, indeed the whole sequence is heavy with Yeatsian borrowings, and it is not surprising that Day Lewis used Yeats' word for such oppositions: he is dismayed, he says early in the poem, 'by the monstrous credibility / Of all antinomies'. But Yeats was content to live with his antinomies; Day Lewis was not, and one can see, from his restlessness here, that he would be an easy convert to an Hegelian system that would offer synthesis. *Transitional Poem* is not a political poem, and no political philosophy could possibly be inferred from it; but it expresses a need for certainty, for which 'single-mindedness' is Day Lewis' term, that would make dogmatic political belief attractive, and would later draw Day Lewis' unpolitical lyric gift in didactic directions. (pp. 43-4)

Day Lewis did thrust images of modern civilization—gramophones, pitheads, loop-lines—rather randomly into his private lyric moods, and this suggests that he had at least recognized that one aspect of the new poetic situation was a changed relation between private and public experience.

But [*Transitional Poem*] does not show that he had found a satisfactory formal way of dealing with it. . . . Certainly the most striking thing about *Transitional Poem* is how conventional it is, how well it attaches itself to the English tradition: the verse forms are regular, the allusions are classical, the natural details are Romantic. Romantic, too, is the constantly present 'I', the poetic sensibility focussed always upon its own condition. None of these qualities is deplorable in a poet, and none is really surprising in a twenty-four-year-old poet writing in 1928. What is surprising is that the poem was taken as a break-through into a new modernism.

It does, however, have one quality that points toward later and better works of the 'thirties: its thrust toward action. . . . But the action here is put in very crude terms: 'pure symmetry of brain' versus disorder without suggests a too-easy confidence in the power of the mind to alter reality by thinking about it. Just how this is to be done the poem nowhere makes clear. . . . One gets a general sense, throughout the poem, that a past is being discarded and replaced by a mature understanding of existence, but the particulars of this process are not specified.

Transitional Poem anticipates later poems in another, more explicit way: in it Day Lewis creates—though only briefly and in passing—a mythology of his own generation. This device may owe something to Yeats, who made his own mythology out of the people he knew, but it is a persistent feature of 'thirties writing, and I take it to be another aspect of the generation's separation from its own past. . . . Here begins what Louis MacNeice called 'the myths of themselves'; here also begins the clubbishness, the view of the modern movement as private communications among friends, that is an irritating aspect of the whole generation.

Still, it is only a beginning: the title is right, the poem is transitional, between the Georgians and the poets of the 'thirties. Though it connects with what came after, it communicates very little sense of the generation's unique situation; Day Lewis did not yet feel that situation clearly or strongly enough to get it down. He felt disorder in the world, the chaos of values that [T. S. Eliot] and [I. A. Richards] had taught, and he tried to deal with it, but he gave to his theme no public dimension and no sense of urgency. The problem as he saw it then was primarily a private one, a crisis of belief that had no direct relation to the public world. So that world enters the poem not as a pressure, but as a set of details, gramophones and charabancs stuck in here and there, like raisins in a pudding; such details are not enough to locate the poem in contemporary time, to make it a piece of immediate history.

Most of all, the poem is not an alternative world. Day Lewis did not apparently feel the need to re-order reality entirely to conform to a new vision, and so his individual lyrics are like a series of commentaries or footnotes to the way things are—or, to be more precise, the way things *subjectively* are. The private life is the subject, and it remains private; it does not become, as later versions of private lives do, a parable. (pp. 44-7)

[Day Lewis' second long work, *From Feathers to Iron*,] is, like *Transitional Poem*, a series of more or less formal lyrics on a personal, young man's theme—the gestation and birth of his first son. The dominant mode is pastoral; the poet had in fact just moved to a country cottage, and the poem records his delight in country living. . . . The growth of the unborn child and the mother's changing states are systematically related to cyclical images of nature and the seasons. . . . By this account, the poem sounds traditional and private, a poem that could have been written by any young Georgian, or indeed in another century. But it is in several ways a topical poem, marked by its time and by the public world. It is, first of all, framed by the dominating presence of Auden. . . . [There] are scattered so many 'contemporary' images, often borrowed directly from Auden, that one could use the sequence to make an inventory of Auden Country: frontiers, passes, railheads, engines, turbines, and mine workings; and climbers, soldiers, airmen, and miners. Such images do not coalesce into a pattern—the image-line that carries the poem remains the natural, seasonal set—but appear only as decorations, like illuminated letters in a manuscript. . . . The initial image [in one poem, for example,] is of a railway journey (an important mode of transportation in Auden Country), with a change at the frontier, and even a refreshment room; but Day Lewis turns immediately away from it, to the birds and the primroses and the natural image-world in which he is more at ease, and on which the theme of the poem depends.

Why, then, are these images in the poem? Partly because Day Lewis was imitating Auden. Partly because he wanted to be a poet of his generation, and that seemed to require contemporary materials. But also partly, I think, because he felt, though not yet very clearly or precisely, that the contemporary world of industry and action, of frontiers and dictators, was a hovering threat to his private world, and had to be acknowledged, that a poem would not be a version of immediate reality that did not include some such references. (pp. 72-3)

In 'The Poet and Revolution', Day Lewis had said of the revolutionary poet: 'If the capitalist system is dead, his poetry will expose the fact . . . If there is new life about, you may be sure he will catch it.' When he wrote those words he was in the midst of writing *The Magnetic Mountain,* and it is clear that that sequence of poems was intended to do just what he said: it was to put the dead life and the new life together in one poem, and by doing so to demonstrate that poetry and revolution were compatible. (p. 117)

[In *The Magnetic Mountain*] Day Lewis was trying for something . . . ambitious—a parabolic whole made of individual lyric parts, comparable, perhaps, to *The Orators*. And the sequence, taken together, *is* a parable in form: that is, it has a non-realistic narrative line that carries a central moral meaning. (pp. 117-18)

The Magnetic Mountain addresses Auden directly in two poems, and is dedicated to him; and well it might be, for one can see at once . . . how much it owes to Auden's work. The journey is a recurrent motif in Auden's early poems, a trial occurs in *Paid on Both Sides*, and the Enemy is from *The Orators*. The tone of voice that Day Lewis adopts is also frequently Auden's. . . . Day Lewis had been under Auden's influence since their Oxford days, but this time, as one critic put it, he had completely surrendered. (p. 118)

Still, to imitate Auden is not to *be* Auden, and *The Magnetic Mountain* suffers a good deal by comparison with *The Orators*. Auden's work is wilfully obscure and private, but it nevertheless succeeds in convincing a careful reader that it deals justly with its theme. . . .

The Magnetic Mountain is another matter. In it the oppositions that Auden saw to be complex have been simplified and hardened. Day Lewis has set dead life against new life, and Us against Them, and these antitheses are polar and absolute; death and corruption belong entirely to one side, and life and virtue to the other, and the speaker of the poem knows which is the good side, and is on it. In Auden's own terms, *The Orators* is a parable art, but *The Magnetic Mountain* is a work that attempts parable, but succeeds only in being propaganda. (p. 119)

Formally, the poem is an uneasy mixture of modes—propaganda trying to be parable, parable becoming escape, lyric sliding into polemic, and polemic lapsing into lyric. The lyric-polemic problem is partly a consequence of the form of the poem: the series of short lyrics encouraged Day Lewis' most pronounced poetic gift, and worked against his political intentions. The roots of lyric verse are in private experience, and cannot easily be cut off; in trying to use the lyric tradition for public subjects Day Lewis was putting two sides of his consciousness in conflict, and the resulting poem oscillates uneasily between a Georgian simplicity and histrionics. In the end, one must conclude that it was a poem written by the time, and across the grain of the poet's natural gift. (p. 122)

[Day Lewis' *Hope for Poetry*] is not a particularly good, or a particularly original book, but it is the first to be written on the Auden generation by a member of it, and like many rather pedestrian books it is helpful for what it tells us of the commonplaces of its time. In the course of explaining his generation, Day Lewis repeats and fixes a number of the terms by which the generation had come to define itself. (p. 154)

Of all his poetic generation, Day Lewis was the one who most wanted to believe in the communist faith. But he was an honest, intelligent man, and a self-consciously dedicated poet, and his doubts and criticisms creep in. . . . (One should add that the best example of this ambiguity is Day Lewis' own *Magnetic Mountain*.) (pp. 156-57)

Day Lewis was the only critic of his time to see [the] interpenetration of public and private as a natural poetic process, and an understandable consequence of the post-war social situation. But, as [he] implies, it was also a problem; there is something wrong with the critical environment in which a poem about the gestation of a baby can be taken by *all* the critics as a political allegory. It is no solution of the problem simply to assume that all private references are public ones, though that was the common 'thirties response.

The hope for poetry that Day Lewis felt is not very explicitly defined in his book: when he got down to explanations, he reverted to what he really was as a poet, a sentimental Georgian who could talk about the nature of poetry in terms of 'the angel seen at the window, the air of glory'. As a contribution to Marxist literary theory the book is negligible, but it must have been reassuring to those traditional-minded readers who had feared that the young revolutionaries were bent on destroying English poetry. For what Day Lewis did was to place his own poetry, and Auden's and Spender's, at the end of a poetic line that runs back to the great figures of the past. In his criticism, as in his poetry, one can see a traditional sensibility, holding traditional ideas about poetry and poets, though he clothes them in the language of revolution. (p. 158)

Among the young writers [of the mid-'thirties], Day Lewis was the most committed to polemics, as he was the most publicly committed to politics. Since the *New Country* days he had been the most active propagandist of his generation: he had been the first to write on 'Poets and Revolution', and he had defended his contemporaries in *A Hope for Poetry* and the more militant *Revolution in Writing*. By 1936 he, more than any other writer, was *the* communist poet and propagandist, and propaganda was taking up a good deal of his time. . . .

Day Lewis' principal poetic work of 1936 was *Noah and the Waters*, a political parable in the form of a mediaeval morality play. (p. 199)

Noah is a parable about an abstract political decision: the bourgeois intellectual's decision to join with the revolution. But it is also a personal poem about Day Lewis' personal dilemma, and his feelings about political commitment. The most convincing passage in the poem is the one in which the burgesses warn Noah of how the workers (that is, the Flood) will treat him, in terms that reveal the anxieties of a private, middle-class poet in a threatening political situation. (p. 200)

In the end, Noah accepts the Flood. But then, we knew all along that he would—how could he not? For the Noah myth allows no choice, and contains no conflict: Noah is God's chosen survivor, and the flood is God's irresistible punishment. It is a parable of obedience, not of choice. And so the myth in Day Lewis' hands becomes not so much an expression of the issue that Day Lewis intended, as a confirmation and endorsement of the choice that he had already made. (p. 201)

Day Lewis . . . has made the natural image of destruction into something personal, the story of a man chosen by God for the small part of the ruling class that breaks away. His parable, in the end, is a form of self-congratulation.

Noah and the Waters has other faults as well. . . . Day Lewis had not found an adequate parabolic form for the political meaning that he wanted to put into it. (p. 202)

The dilemma that *Noah and the Waters* really expresses is not Noah's, but Day Lewis': not the problem of political choice, but the problem of how to make poetry a form of political action, and yet preserve the integrity of the poetic act. The poem is an example of a poem consciously used to impose political pressure (Day Lewis admits as much in the Author's Foreword when he says that the drama derives from the weight and imminence of the issue, not from the construction). But it is also an example of the way that pressure turns back upon the poet himself, and of the poetic consequences.

The poem is a failure and, it seems now, a violation of Day Lewis' natural gifts. What he could do, and did in places even in this bad poem, was to write about the English countryside with deep and convincing feeling. . . . But in the circumstances of 1936 that was not enough, and instead of good pastoral he wrote bad parable. (p. 203)

Like the earlier collections of his short poems, [*Overtures to Death*] shows the two conflicting sides of the poet's mind: his Georgian, nature-poet sensibility, and his political militancy. But it also contains a third kind of poetry—poems of passive waiting for disaster that one might call his 'post-political poems', such as 'Bombers', 'Newsreel', and the long title poem. The effect of the whole is more sombre, and more private, than the earlier Day Lewis had been; even the political poems seem less strident (the longest poem, 'The Nabara', a narrative account of a Spanish sea-battle, has [a] retrospective, historical quality . . .). (p. 335)

Day Lewis . . . spent the first year of the war like an old soldier retired from the battle, living in a Devon village and translating Virgil's *Georgics*. Both the retirement and the translation were political acts; he had physically withdrawn from his commitment to the Communist Party, and from politics in general, and he had underlined that change by choosing to work on Virgil's country poems, thus acknowledging that his true poetic place had always been in the tradition of natural, pastoral poetry, a tradition that seemed to him profoundly English. The foreword that he wrote for his translation, dated 'June 1940', makes this point very clearly; it is both a celebration of and a commitment to the tradition:

> The fascination of the Georgics [he writes] for many generations of Englishmen is not difficult to explain. A century of urban civilization has not yet materially modified the instinct of a people once devoted to agriculture and stock-breeding, to the chase, to landscape gardening, to a practical love of Nature . . . In our love of domestic animals, in the millions of suburban and cottage gardens, we may see the depth and tenacity of our roots in earth today.

Politics is not mentioned at all (though the vision of English rural life is essentially a Tory vision); the war enters only as an event which might lead in the end to a decentralization of industry, and thus a new 'rural-urban civilization'. By the end of the first paragraph it is clear that Day Lewis had come home.

As a preface to his translation Day Lewis wrote a set of 'Dedicatory Stanzas' addressed to Stephen Spender—the last example of that network of cross-dedications and cross-references among members of the generation that Mac-Neice called the 'myth of themselves'. It is an appropriate dedication, for the verses that follow are a valedictory assessment of the generation and its decade, seen from a point beyond the end, from a new decade and a new war. . . . [Day Lewis implies that] the failure of the political hopes of the 'thirties justifies the poet in turning inward, away from politics, toward poetry itself (which becomes not simply a medium for the expression of ideas, but a value). (pp. 389-90)

The most surprising thing about the 'Dedicatory Stanzas' is the tone in which Day Lewis deals with the present. If the poem was written at the same time as the foreword—and it must have been—then while the poet wrote France was falling before the German armoured columns, and the British were desperately withdrawing from Dunkirk. Day Lewis wrote about this moment in history like this:

> Meanwhile, what touches the heart of all, engrosses.
> Through the flushed springtime and the fading year
> I lived on country matters. Now June was here
> Again, and brought the smell of flowering grasses
> To me and death to many overseas:
> They lie in the flowering sunshine, flesh once dear
> To some, now parchment for the heart's release.

One is tempted to be ironic about this passage. . . . But this attitude toward death in battle, though it seems naive after Wilfred Owen, is in keeping with Day Lewis' commitment to an apolitical pastoral tradition. This is the way men have died in verse before; it is not an original stanza, or even a very good version of the old words, but it is another expression of Day Lewis' return to the subjects, the language, and the customary emotions in which he felt secure. And the very fact of the difference between this kind of poetical dying and the things that Spender and Cornford had said about the Spanish dead is another way of saying that for Day Lewis the 'thirties were over. (p. 391)

> *Samuel Hynes, in his* The Auden Generation: Literature and Politics in England in the 1930s *(copyright © 1976 by Samuel Hynes; all rights reserved; reprinted by permission of The Viking Penguin Inc.), Viking Penguin, 1977.*

*   *   *

DeLILLO, Don   1936-

DeLillo is an American novelist who writes satirically of contemporary events. Often compared to Thomas Pynchon, he has portrayed the chaos of society under the guises of football, science, rock music, and urban sophistication. (See also *CLC*, Vol. 8.)

WILLIAM KENNEDY

[With dialogue that gives] homage to the vapid ironies of Beckett and Pinter, . . . Don DeLillo's remarkable new novel of menace and mystery, *Players*, [is] a fastidious rejection of the modern age. (p. G1)

The book opens with an allegorical prelude DeLillo calls "The Movie," which collects all the story's principal characters, none of them named yet, on an airplane, watching a movie of a band of terrorists slaughtering several golfers on a fairway, a vicious scene accompanied by tinkly piano music suitable for a Buster Keaton movie. The contrast of blood and piano steeps the scene in "gruesomely humorous ambiguity, a spectacle of ridiculous people doing awful things to total fools."

When the scene ends we are thrown into the real story—Lyle's and Pammy's empty lives—and the book threatens to become another witty send-up of hard-core sophistication. But . . . while Lyle is seducing a secretary from the office, he sees in her apartment a photo of her with a man who was recently shot on the stock exchange floor. Also in the photo is the man who shot him. The story instantly assumes a tantalizing new dimension in keeping with the prologue. . . .

DeLillo is a spectacular talent, supremely witty and a natural story-teller. (He has written four other novels: *Americana*, his first, *End Zone, Great Jones Street*, and *Ratner's Star*.) From his first book it was also clear that his control of the language was of a high order. The difference between that first book and the latest is what he leaves out. *Players* is half the size of *Americana*, but just as dense with implication of the meaning of the lives it presents to us.

Lyle and Pammy are hastily defined, sketches really. But unforgettable sketches, like Lautrec's. How did they get the way they are? Who cares? There they are. Dig them. The entropy of bumblebees. And the flowers are all poison. (p. G4)

William Kennedy, "The Flowers Are All Poison," in Book World—The Washington Post (© The Washington Post), *August 21, 1977, pp. G1, G4.*

THOMAS LeCLAIR

Players is a fascinating little subtracting machine, a precision calculator of spiritual entropy. Like Renata Adler's *Speedboat*, DeLillo's novel is a New York book—sets by *The New Yorker*, people by Barthelme, fears by the *Daily News*. . . .

What makes this familiar material fascinating is DeLillo's dual perspective: he is a sensor inside the characters and a distant scientist converting signals into information. While Lyle and Pammy process (and reduce) a world they're trying to enlarge with adventure, DeLillo decodes both actions. The prose knows how experience turns into abstraction and how people become channels, how plot fades to probabilities and place empties into space, how little becomes less. DeLillo isn't writing sociology or satire, but the equations for what one character calls "the sensual pleasures of banality." His is no easy investigation, yet *Players* is both original and final, a new formula for the familiar. (p. 32)

Thomas LeClair, in Saturday Review (© *1977 by Saturday Review Magazine Corp.; reprinted with permission), September 3, 1977.*

CELIA BETSKY

Terrorism, one always assumed, springs from perverted idealism or protest overstepping rational bounds, and explodes under intolerable political pressures or its own heavy rhetoric. Recently, though, a third element has become discernible: Terrorism is now the stuff of diversion, merely another means of experimenting with "the uses of boredom."

The phenomenon is explored in Don DeLillo's fine new novel, *Players*. Lyle, apparently the perfect young stockbroker, is competent, smooth, happily married, on top of his part of the New York scene. But inside he harbors hostility, dissatisfaction and a crippling *ennui*. Sitting alone at night, he watches television for hours, switching channels every few seconds so that only the picture burns into his indifferent brain. Like David Bell, the hero of DeLillo's first novel, *Americana*, he is moved solely "by the power of the image" and suffers from a numbness of mind and soul that tinges the book with a quality of things that are sighted but not seen.

Through a sexual liaison with a colleague's secretary, Lyle gets involved with a terrorist organization bent on blowing up the New York Stock Exchange. This escape is typical of DeLillo's work; it is a journey into self-exile, a need to drop out just to see what it is like to challenge a self not held in the highest esteem. Lyle decides to exacerbate complexity by playing the double agent.

His wife Pammy, a staff writer for a company with the unlikely name—and business—of Grief Management Council, tries an alternative solution. She wants to simplify, to rediscover some "tokens of authenticity." Her response to boredom is a trip back to nature in Maine with two homosexual friends that ends in an ugly suicide. (pp. 22-3)

The plot is propelled by performers and performances, DeLillo being a great believer in the deceptiveness of appearances: Identities are disguises; although terrorism is "calculated madness," the so-called real world is insanity uncontrolled. In DeLillo's slightly skewed presentation, terrorism and revolutionary acts are a matter of perspective: Conspiracy and organized crime exist on both sides of the political fence; the "philosophy of destruction" expounded by the terrorists is no more irresponsible than the doctrine of gain practiced on the Stock Exchange. It is the flip side of corporate America.

DeLillo's players act in a movie, a silent film we watch them pantomime at the same time that they watch themselves. . . .

The characters move like people under water—slowly turning and twisting in an element more resistant than our own. With no past to define them and little future to speak of, they swim into view and away again, leaving hardly a trace. When they catch planes, cars and buses, they are in transition not from one place to another, but from dream to nightmare and back.

One-person dialogues are common here; internal and private, they nevertheless add to the visionary drift of the action. Fractured images and lives are beautifully controlled by DeLillo's extraordinary use of language. The simultaneity of divergent events underscores how Pammy and Lyle start to pass each other by. . . .

[The] doomsday message contained in DeLillo's earlier work becomes a *fait accompli*, not a prophecy. Still, if he is proclaiming apocalypse now, he does it movingly and well. A crisp, cool, observant writer, he chronicles irresolution and leaves people with their dilemmas open-ended in a way that is a solution in itself, because it is so pitiful and so true. Involvement and commitment are pointless without something worth committing oneself to, and at present, DeLillo seems to say, there is nothing. (p. 23)

Celia Betsky, "The Perils of Boredom," in The New Leader (© *1978 by the American Labor Conference on International Affairs, Inc.), January 2, 1978, pp. 22-3.*

JOHN UPDIKE

Don DeLillo seems determined to nail modern America down, and he may yet. His previous novels have tackled football ("End Zone"), pop music ("Great Jones Street"), and science ("Ratner's Star"), and in "Players" . . . he takes on terrorism. Terrorism of an attenuated, urbane sort; the book is really about sophistication, or at least nothing is as clear about it as the sophistication of the author, who combines a wearily thorough awareness of how people pass their bored-silly lives in New York City with a (in this novel) lean, slit-eyed prose and a pseudo-scientific descriptive manner. . . .

[The] drastic unlovableness of Lyle and the very tepid appeal of Pammy discourage the considerable suspension of disbelief necessary to follow them into their adventures as they break loose from connubial anti-bliss. (p. 127)

Don DeLillo has, as they used to say of athletes, class. He is original, versatile, and, in his disdain of last year's emotional guarantees, fastidious. He brings to human phenomena the dispassionate mathematics and spatial subtleties of particle physics. Into our technology-riddled daily lives he reads the sinister ambiguities, the floating ugliness of America's recent history.... But the very intensity of Mr. De-Lillo's wish, in this novel, to say something new about the matter has evaporated the matter, leaving behind an exquisite ash-skeleton of elliptic dialogue and spindly motivation. (p. 128)

> *John Updike, in* The New Yorker *(© 1978 by The New Yorker Magazine, Inc.), March 27, 1978.*

*   *   *

DeVRIES, Peter   1910-

DeVries is an American novelist, short story writer, poet, and editor known for his witty caricatures of upper middle-class American life. Raised in a strict Dutch Calvinist home, DeVries often combines comedy with religious and moral questions to create social satire with pessimistic, tragic undercurrents. Melvin Maddocks has called his work "Kafka crossed with the Keystone Kops." DeVries employs farce, parody, burlesque, and, especially, puns in his novels of manners. Several of his works have been adapted for film and stage. (See also *CLC*, **Vols. 1, 2, 3, 7, and** *Contemporary Authors*, **Vols. 17-20, rev. ed.)**

D. KEITH MANO

DeVries' writing is forty years old—Benchley, Woollcott, immature Kaufman—it dates from humor columns in the *Evening Mail*. And, when he isn't indulging in long words, modifying his modifiers, DeVries will preposition and pronoun and article you to death.... DeVries writes as grad students in sociology write: for other grad students in sociology. Enough to syntax anyone's patience.

Let me use DeVries' prose style: it's a serviceable metaphor: it apes his comic formula. Nouns exist for their adjectives: so, too, protagonist for cameo walk-ons; plot for digressions. The orgy scene [in *I Hear America Swinging*], say, is less momentous than one of its dangling participants: for example, DeVries' hunky woman wrestler, who will attack an orgasm as she would a pin. This is the nature—one nature, anyhow—of comedy: reemphasis, misemphasis. A bridge in DeVries' plot will be written cursorily—like those pronoun—article—preposition sentences— to get it out of the way. Which is why authors prefer black comedy. Not because they're morose by disposition, but because white or pure comedy is, no contest, the most exacting art form. A dull scene in black comedy might pass for one with some sort of opaque significance. In white comedy you can be too damned good for your own good. A real knee-slapper on page ten will orphan page nine and page eleven. Critics love the word "uneven"; its their favorite put-down. A white comic has to be consistent as a bomb-squad defuser.

DeVries is pretty even. If his prose has a coy and slipshod sound, his EKG report graphs the American beat. DeVries knows us: how we eat, pray, make love, appreciate art. He has an affection for affectation. There's the religious service that will end, not with coffee hour, but with a thing called "après church." Just right: coffee hour in 1976 has become part of the liturgy....

Comedy will take things to an extreme. Not DeVries: DeVries will take them to Iowa. He has re-established the New York swing set—its mores and feeding habits—in Dubuque-like Middle City. Overexaggeration can jeopardize humor. But this shrewd place-swap serves as a deductible clause in DeVries' comic insurance. It's safe to say that anything New York done in Iowa will have natural, riskless exaggerations. Notably when a farmer tries to use "brittle dialogue." That is: patter made up of quotations, fey rejoinders, name-dropping, and puns. And puns. And puns.

"He's keen on urban affairs—not that he doesn't have a thing or two going in the country as well."

> *D. Keith Mano, "No Rx for Menopause," in* National Review *(© National Review, Inc., 1976; 150 East 35th St., New York, N.Y. 10016), August 20, 1976, p. 906.*

MAX BYRD

The Mackerel Plaza ... is at once Peter DeVries' funniest and most characteristic novel, the loveliest jewel in the whole remarkable strand of his achievement. Immensely successful among mere readers, DeVries' work has been conspicuously overlooked by academicians and by the more solemn ideologists of contemporary literature. What he offers, however, that is missing from such celebrities as Thomas Pynchon or John Hawkes are modesty, humor, warmth, intelligibility. What he may be thought to lack in comparison is high seriousness (and perhaps a certain gratuitous obscurity). Like all genuinely funny writers, DeVries lulls our critical instincts. Nonetheless he projects a vision no less complete, no less interesting, no less insistent for being also comic.

The opening of *The Mackerel Plaza*, for example, sets briskly in motion a number of themes—the forward-thinking, back-sliding minister; the collision of literary styles like billboards and sermons; the irritably rational communication of males undercut by women; the displacement of religious values by what he elsewhere calls "Freudianity"—and as the book proceeds, we realize, they continue to swim mysteriously in and out of view, circling constantly and effortlessly, like fish in a bowl. Most followers will recognize these themes as typically DeVriesian.... Where Thurber's women loom menacingly above his cowering males, shrewish commandos dressing down the craven-hearted, DeVries' women dominate more subtly. They allure, they fascinate, they contrive. Emphatically sex objects—" She was naked except for skin, blouse, underthings, stockings, and shoes," Mackerel observes—they provoke his men to involuntary, fatalistic wooing, and the plots of his novels tend to suggest *Walpurgisnacht* in suburbia, an off-beat but rhythmical dance of approaches and retreats.

His men like to court with language. Parodies, quotations, aphorisms are their plumage, and everyone thinks of DeVries' novels first in terms of their wisecracks: "She was a thin, frail bulldozer of a woman." "Horticulture is nine-tenths destruction." "He's one of those doctors that think ninety percent of their patients are quacks." But his women, despite their inattention, reveal an even more remarkable, perverse power of language, a malapropulsion that leaves the men gasping in alarmed admiration: a sexual free-lancer is "AM-FM"; according to Miss Calico's mother, "when we speak of putting down roots we don't mean sticking in the mud"; suicide is "not a viable alternative." And that mothers and mothers-in-law so often produce these cliches only underscores our impression that some earthy, exclusively female creativity is at work.

Moreover, these women often release in De Vries' men a stream of surrealistic fantasy that he likewise shares with Thurber. . . .

The other-worldliness of such women suggests one reason why De Vries' men fail to find common ground with them. It also suggests how closely women are associated with the religious turmoil that permeats his novels. (p. 30)

The wisecracks, too, may be associated with De Vries' religious musings. Their unusual condensation, their zany luxuriance remind us that in Freudianity jokes are like dreams, which clear our way briefly, tantalizingly into forbidden areas of consciousness. Puns, jokes, fantasies and dreams are momentary, inconstant structures imposed upon the ordinary real world, as Mackerel might philosophize; they organize it temporarily much as religion organizes our world and intermittently gives it meaning. . . . De Vries' striking habit of metaphor, a figure of speech that reconciles incongruities—he "popped from the door like a slice of bread from a toaster"—further impresses us with how deeply his concern for organization, for design, reaches, and how fragile such order necessarily is. Similarly, his plots curl gracefully, confidently through their serpentine complications, only to break free at the end with a gasp, dashing past us like a hare from the woods. (pp. 30-1)

Like most modern comic novels, *The Mackerel Plaza* grows less and less funny toward the end. The drama of Mackerel's defrocking makes us squirm; public disgrace, paranoia, even accusations of murder darken the scene; an interview between Mackerel and his doctor in the People's Liberal psychiatric clinic creates the same dimly humorous unease we feel at Malvolio's imprisonment in *Twelfth Night*. De Vries lacks that offhand kind of seriousness which permits Auden to remark casually somewhere that God is a bore. His sense of potential disaster gives his humor, like Evelyn Waugh's and sometimes Kingsley Amis', an indistinct quality of apprehension. . . . Rare is the universe like P. G. Wodehouse's where the threats of comedy never slip their leash. De Vries' novels, however, are always turning imperceptibly into tragic ones, in which the laughing fates hunt down his characters remorselessly; not for nothing is he inclined to take his titles from Romantic poetry. . . .

De Vries' most characteristic effect is of detonation, of order flung violently apart—an effect found not simply in the tension of his inimitable wisecracks, but also in the explosions with which this beautiful book subsides.

But *The Mackerel Plaza* concludes in safety, in a classic renewal through marriage and, bringing its two major themes together, an ironic comparison of a designing woman and a designing God. And if Mackerel has lost his faith (a matter no more serious, he confesses, than losing a wooden leg in an accident), like every husband he has gained a mystifying and irrepressible goddess: "Her body against me was like a bursting star." (p. 31)

> *Max Byrd, "Reconsideration," in* The New Republic (*reprinted by permission of* The New Republic; © *1976 by The New Republic, Inc.*), *October 23, 1976, pp. 29-31.*

WILLIAM B. HILL

Peter De Vries has a talent which is almost unique, a talent which has made him the cleverest parodist of our time: the ability to put on those mental characteristics which give a writer or performer his style. He exhibits this talent for many pages at the beginning of [*Madder Music*] as his protagonist, Robert Swirling, suffers under the delusion that he is Groucho Marx—well, suffer is scarcely the word, since Swirling finds the life of Groucho most congenial. Eventually, he is cured—and when circumstances drive him into a relapse, he reappears not as Groucho but as W. C. Fields.

In between the marvelous imitations runs the story of Swirling's chaotic life. The redemptive force saving him from his first aberration is also the force which drives him into his relapse. Like other De Vries heroes, he is drawn from a splendid wife into a series of awkward adulteries which destroy his marriage. The incidents are not so humorous as the near-misses of the early De Vries novels; Swirling is sometimes too pitiful to be laughable. . . .

There are no cosmic overtones such as one has come to expect of De Vries, except in some slick summaries of attitudes towards sin. Yet there is much deft irony as the author lands his hero in one ludicrous situation after another, each of them showing one of the little follies which men take seriously. The book is slightly painful in that Swirling is ultimately frustrating: the reader must sympathize with him, and he turns out to be utterly ineffectual.

Here, as elsewhere, De Vries lets the reader look through his cold and penetrating gaze; the vision is clear, funny, and a little frightening. (p. 339)

> *William B. Hill, in* Best Sellers (*copyright* © *1978 Helen Dwight Reid Educational Foundation*), *February, 1978.*

STUART SUTHERLAND

The opening chapter of *Madder Music* . . . is as sustained a piece of comedy as anything De Vries has ever achieved. His effects cannot properly be conveyed by quotation since the dazzling edifice he builds depends upon his unique capacity to pile one witticism precariously on top of another. Like Oscar Wilde he believes a good remark is worth repeating, but there is enough fresh material for the reader to overlook such lapses as "she was one of those women you don't give a book because they've already got one". Just occasionally he reveals too much of the stage machinery: a character called Betty Tingle remarks to the hero as he fondles her breasts "You're making Betty Tingle"—worth it for the triple entendre?

Madder Music is the story of the events that forced the hero to escape into the character of Groucho Marx. De Vries makes play with those reversals of the natural order of things that occur so often in everyday life. . . . As in his previous novels, De Vries delivers numerous homespun insights . . . into the curious workings of the human mind: they are always expressed with deft economy—"nothing will make a man a model husband faster than infidelity."

De Vries's satire is as accurate as ever: he successfully derides many contemporary American institutions, including modern art, psychiatry, the real estate business and of course current sexual mores. But his satire lacks passion—and one suspects he would not really wish the world very different from the way it is for then there would be less to laugh at.

In some of the novels of his middle period, such as *Reuben Reuben*, Peter De Vries combined a feeling for the comedy of the human situation with genuine feeling for its victims. *Madder Music* and its immediate predecessor, *I Hear America Swinging*, revert to the style of earlier novels such as *Mackerel Plaza*. The characters are mouthpieces for DeVries's own witticisms—a nice device for disclaiming a bad joke. He has moments of sympathizing with them, but even then he holds them at a considerable distance: his hero is "unfit for either marriage or adultery, being restless in the one and remorseful in the other". When DeVries's verbal inventiveness flags, his lack of serious interest in his characters makes for the occasional dull page, but he remains one of the most stylish of living novelists and much, much the funniest.

Stuart Sutherland, "The Groucho Syndrome," in The Times Literary Supplement (© Times Newspapers Ltd. (London) 1978; reproduced from The Times Literary Supplement by permission), March 24, 1978, p. 337.

*   *   *

DICK, Philip K(indred)   1928-

Dick is an American science fiction novelist, author of short stories, and screenwriter. His interest in music and sociology and his fear of radical political trends are thematically reflected in his work. He has stated that his major philosophical concern, an attempt to define reality, is manifested in his literary exploration of varying states of consciousness. *The Man in the High Castle* won the 1963 Hugo Award for best novel. He has collaborated with Roger Zelazny on the novel *Deus Irae*. (See also *Contemporary Authors*, Vols. 49-52.)

ROBERT J. RAFALKO

[*Deus Irae*] may well be the worst book I have ever read. It struck me as something Tom Wolfe might produce if he were to crossbreed Walter M. Miller's *Canticle for Leibowitz* with a twisted version of *Pilgrim's Progress*. *Deus Irae* centers around a pilgrimage to find God, the God of wrath, and the pilgrim in the book encounters many portents and has many visions as he sticks to the straight and narrow: hence the resemblance to *Pilgrim's Progress*. Furthermore, the book describes monastic life in a period after a nuclear holocaust has left a charred and deformed world behind: hence the resemblance to Miller's *Canticle for Leibowitz*.

The search is for the God who could permit such devastation to occur, the Deus Irae. Thus, the story is a take-off from the Scholastics' traditional problem of evil: If God is omnipotent, then nothing can exist unless God wants it to exist. Therefore, either God wants evil to exist, or God is not omnipotent. Yet, to state this syllogism as the theme of the book, and to cite the influence of much finer authors on [co-authors] Philip K. Dick and Roger Zelazny, would be to lend much greater credence, suggest much greater depth and worth than *Deus Irae* has to offer. The authors don't seem to have the patience to adequately develop the ideas they conjure or the skill to combine their talents well. They dilly-dally with profundity, they substitute psychedelic whirlygigs for hard description, and at times they even seem to include whole chapters and parts of chapters as an afterthought.

What is especially disappointing, I think, is the fact that each of the two authors is individually capable, but when they work together, as they have done here, the product is

less than the sum of the two parts. This is a novel by committee, and I got the impression that one of the authors wanted to write a comedy while the other held out for a tragedy. The result was neither, and *Deus Irae* is hardly worth a reader's time or dime. (p. 244)

Robert J. Rafalko, in Best Sellers (copyright © 1976 Helen Dwight Reid Educational Foundation), November, 1976.

J. G. BALLARD

Martian Time-Slip ... describes a desolate, end-of-the-century Mars inhabited by doomed clairvoyants, an obsessed tycoon and an autistic child-hero who together move through a landscape that uncannily resembles southern California perceived through the glaze of some deep psychosis. ... [The] novel is full of incident, fusing terror and comedy in a unique way. More than any other SF writer, Dick is able to convey the sense of everyday reality as totally threatening. (p. 879)

J. G. Ballard, in New Statesman (© 1976 The Statesman & Nation Publishing Co. Ltd.), December 17, 1976.

RIAZ HUSSAIN

[*A Scanner Darkly*] treats one of the major problems of our society today, namely drug abuse, but is written as science fiction set in the near future. I wish the author had treated his main theme with realism, describing the situations and events more accurately, but instead everything tends to be vague and uncertain. ...

Unfortunately the things are described so vaguely that the situation gets quite illogical. I suppose the license of the science fiction writer allows him to present the ideas ambiguously without filling in specific details, and in this case the author has taken full liberty with his license. The result is a story which is formless, slow moving, and repetitive. (p. 37)

Riaz Hussain, in Best Sellers (copyright © 1977 Helen Dwight Reid Educational Foundation), May, 1977.

ERIC KORN

Philip Dick and Roger Zelazny's co-production, *Deus Irae*, lavishly strews wheezes, rather than ideas. Post-atomic, fragmented, monster-laden world; sardonic religion, the Servants of Wrath, idolizes Carl Lufteuful, the man who pressed the ultimate button; limbless painter sent on pilgrimage on cowpowered cart to find the Holy Face; various encounters with weird philosophical beasts, machines, mutants and metaphysics. Much irony about the relativism of religion and morality, somewhat in the style of James Branch Cabell. Vigorous, jumpy, startling, unflaggingly inventive, and rather a bore. (p. 820)

Eric Korn, in The Times Literary Supplement (© Times Newspapers Ltd. (London) 1977; reproduced from The Times Literary Supplement by permission), July 8, 1977.

PATRICK PARRINDER

Philip K. Dick's *A Scanner Darkly* begins as a standard American nightmare. It is California, 1994, and society is divided between the straights in their fortified apartment complexes, and the acid-heads who are hooked on a new drug of unknown origin, substance D (for Death). Most of the detritus of the 1970s survives unchanged but surveillance technology has been advanced by the invention of the "scramble suit", which reduces the appearance of the wearer to a nebulous blur, and is compulsory uniform within the bounds of police headquarters. Thanks to this garment the hero, a narcotics agent turned addict, is sent on a full-time assignment to spy on himself.

From this point paranoia radiates outwards, taking us through a bewildering series of conspiratorial world-views in search of the ultimate distributors of substance D, who (the theological strain in Dick's work is becoming more marked) appear to be nothing less than the executors of the divine plan. At another level, the novel is a frightening allegory of the process of drug abuse, in which some of the alternative realities experienced are revealed as the hallucinations of terminal addicts.

In a moving author's note at the end of the volume, Dick reflects on his own drug experiences and the deaths of several of his friends. He offers the novel as a record of the whole "bad decision of the decade, the sixties, both in and out of the establishment". Despite this, the loose ends of the plot are feebly tied up by a heroine who is by turns teenage drug-pusher, federal agent, metaphysician and angel of mercy, able to materialize and dematerialize at will. *A Scanner Darkly* is halfway between a contemporary nightmare and an allegory of absolute good and absolute evil. Although far from the best of Dick's novels, it may yet be instrumental in converting his distinguished career into a legend. (p. 83)

> *Patrick Parrinder, in* The Times Literary Supplement (© *Times Newspapers Ltd. (London) 1978; reproduced from* The Times Literary Supplement *by permission), January 27, 1978.*

*   *   *

DICKEY, James   1923-

Dickey is an American poet, novelist, critic, screenwriter, and essayist. His poetry possesses a strong rhythmic pattern, expressing his concern with the cycles of love and death and the interaction of man and nature. Dickey has enjoyed acceptance in both the popular and academic worlds. He received the National Book Award in 1965 and has served as the Consultant on Poetry in English to the Library of Congress. Dickey's novel *Deliverance* was made into a successful film. (See also *CLC*, Vols. 1, 2, 4, 7, and *Contemporary Authors*, Vols. 9-12, rev. ed.)

PAUL G. ITALIA

Perhaps [the patterned brutality in *Deliverance*] is nothing more than a macabre symmetry, a grimly humorous instance of "poetic justice," in which each of the perverted primitives gets what he deserves where he deserves it. But there is something more; the neatly ironic balancing of sin and retribution, of crime and counter-crime, is transcended by the mystery formed between the civilized hunter and the primitive one. What results from this whirlwind weekend courtship with death is love. (p. 204)

There are perversion and fantasy present in [the love scene between Gentry and his wife, a] scene of "civilized" love: it has one other important element in common with the climactic hunt—dreams and dreaming. For night (with its fantasies, inversions, dreams) constitutes the "atmosphere" of both the love-episode and the hunt-episode. Indeed, the scene that describes Gentry's embrace of his wife opens with his musing upon dreams. . . . Gentry defines wakening as the attempt to "get clear of" where he had been. Dreaming becomes another vehicle to illustrate his struggle to escape death and find "another life." Gentry's definition of dreaming takes us out of the bedroom and into the wilderness, out of the love-scene and into the hunt. And the dream ends in each episode with deliverance. A close look at that hunt furnishes the perspective needed to view this collage of night, dream, fantasy, and perversion.

The hunting episode begins with Gentry's climbing a steep gorge to reach the cliff where he suspects the bushwacker is hiding. This scene, too, begins with a dream. In fact, the whole episode might be called a dream sequence. Gentry's stalking of the backwoodsman begins just before dawn, as does the bedroom scene, and his difficult climb is reminiscent of the "dragged upward" sensation he always experiences in his attempts to struggle free of his dreams. . . . The sexuality becomes clearer as the hunt proceeds. "Then I would begin to try to inch upward again, moving with the most intimate motions of my body, motions I had never dared use with Martha, or with any other human woman. Fear and a kind of enormous moon-blazing sexuality lifted me." . . .

This hunt is a primal union with "mother nature," the intimacy of which is greater than marriage. And, as in the love-scene, something obtrudes upon his intimacy with his wife. But the strongest link between this passage and the earlier episode is the fact that Gentry manages to climb out of his dream and up the rock-face to eventual deliverance because an "enormous moon-blazing sexuality" lifted him beyond the abyss.

Gentry's sense of suspension during the climb strongly resembles that of the dream state. And, as in a dream, his thoughts during the hunt are a kind of fantasy. He thinks of his deadly accurate plan to trap the hunter as a daydream; indeed, the whole situation has the finality and matter-of-factness that dreams give to extraordinary events. . . . Sex, as well as murder, is the object of Ed Gentry's fantasy, of his "wet dream." (pp. 205-06)

The hunt, itself, is clearly sexual in [D. H. Lawrence's short novel] *The Fox*, perhaps less so in *Deliverance*. Dickey's use of sexuality in the hunt is subtle, but it is there: "We were closed together, and the feeling of a peculiar kind of intimacy increased," says Gentry. . . . And as he lined the woodsman up in his sights, he noted that "There was something relaxed and enjoying in his body position, something primally graceful; I had never seen a more beautiful or convincing element of a design. I wanted to kill him just like that. . . . Wait till he lies down, I said far back in my throat." . . . Finally, this chase ends in a whirlwind climax in which both hunters, feeling a sudden blast and finding themselves turning and twisting and falling, perform a macabre parody of sexual union.

The hunt, then, is a sexual one in *Deliverance*. But to end with this observation is to miss Dickey's point—and Lawrence's. . . . Lawrence's is the more explicit: . . . "He was a huntsman in spirit. . . . And it was as a young hunter that he wanted to bring down March as his quarry, to make her his wife." . . . The hunt is sexual, but the point of it is to bring love out of the perverseness of man's desire, to bring another life out of the quarry's death. Gentry's kill is no dodge of cleverness. But only gradually does it become clear that love is involved in the slaying of the woodsman. Dickey quietly injects the possibility of love into the chase when he slips into Gentry's mind the observation that "If Lewis had not shot his companion, he [the man he is tracking] and I would have made a kind of love, painful and terrifying to me, in some dreadful way pleasurable to him, but we would have been together in the flesh, there on the floor of the woods." . . .

The sexuality in the hunt is a function of the fantasy in the hunt. The fantasy dictates that he shoot the hillbilly in the back, as, earlier, he took his wife in the "back," and as the older backwoodsman got Trippe in the "back." . . . When fantasy ends reality takes over: the arrow pierces the mountaineer's throat and not his back. (pp. 207-08)

Earlier, Gentry regretfully noted that the hunted hunters could have "made a kind of love," could have "been together in the flesh." Yet, they do become one: each inflicts a wound in the other at the same moment, and their blood flows and mingles together just as their minds "merged" and "fused" during the chase. At the height of that climax both sex and death are transcended. They become "one flesh"—but not in the manner Gentry has fantasized. . . . Gentry escaped the backwoodsman's sexual fantasy, and he eludes Gentry's. The novel's treatment of sexuality makes the point that, like hunting, sex is a deadly struggle. But Dickey's treatment of hunting and sexuality indicate that love can result from the battle.

When now we return to Gentry's "struggle" with his wife, we can appreciate the function of dream and fantasy in that love-scene from the perspectives furnished by the hunt. Gentry's catching sight of his quarry's face turns the scene from exploitation to identification, from rape to love. The same thing occurs at the climax of Gentry's embrace of his wife. . . . Gentry's fantasy-girl does not usurp his wife, for the sudden reality of the girl's face (both during the photography session and the love session) and the "otherness" of her golden eye cause the unnatural and potentially exploitive fantasy to dissolve and become a genuine act of love.

Although Dickey clearly rejects the fantasy element, he does not dismiss the entire dream experience. In fact, the dream situation, when taken as a whole (all that precedes the climax both in the love-scene and in the hunt-scene), predicts and creates the essential truth in each experience. Life is like a dream, suggests Dickey, but each dream contains omens and illusions. The two major episodes in *Deliverance* are constructed as dream sequences. The illusion in each is precisely the same: Gentry's fantasy of sodomy and the power and pleasure it promises. The truth in each dream is similar: the "promise of . . . another life, deliverance." . . . The fantasy promises pleasure and power, but is death; the omen promises struggle, and yields new life.

Life is like a dream. Yet we can never distinguish between truth and illusion until the dream comes to its climax and we waken. The novel tells us that we are condemned to feeling our way in the dark, to finding truth through dreams like Penelope in the *Odyssey*. Defenseless, unable to touch or make contact with our own environment, surrounded by hypocrites, we live in a world of shadows and half-lights. By definition, mortals cannot distinguish between the

dream and the fantasy; but when dawn ends and day triumphs in its primal struggle with night, then mortals may know the truth. And, in *Deliverance*, the dreams do occur at dawn, just as in the *Odyssey*. (pp. 208-10)

If we say that the backwoodsman and the city-boy come together at the climax of the struggle, that in their identification the hillbilly becomes Gentry's "double," then what dies there is Gentry's other self. He has killed the predator in him by becoming a predator. Gentry has shucked off that part of himself that might kill or rape anything that turns its back on him. He becomes truly civilized by destroying the slackjaw hillbilly in himself. Thus, the death of the backwoodsman is not wanton exploitation: it is "in some dreadful way" a creation of something new—Gentry's freedom and love. (pp. 210-11)

The climax of the hunt (and the novel) is a kind of *liebestod*. It displays a union of the primal tensions of human existence, just as the dawn displays the brief union of night and day. Love and death are identified, and as inextricable as day from night or the hunter from his quarry. But Dickey's romance does not end with this *liebestod*. His conception of romance differs from the fin-de-siècle European version by being at once much tougher and more optimistic.

Dickey is not a decadent. The hunt may have its esthetics, but it is also a philosophy: the display of paradox and antithesis must be productive. And here again the sexuality in the novel furnishes some clarity. In *Deliverance*, love is the point; sodomy is the exaggeration that makes the point—sex as an end in itself is a dead end. Sodomy is a vicious exploitation, here, in which (biologically as well as ethically) "another life" cannot be produced. But if the minds "merge" and "fuse" and the eyes make contact and see, then the partners can be "together in the flesh." This merging happens to Gentry in bed with his wife and in the wilderness with the backwoodsman. If love is not brought out of the climax, if the miracle is not delivered out of the muddle, then the *liebestod* becomes a "mind-rape."

But what does the book say about sex apart from its function as a metaphor? I think Dickey is saying that sex is the energy that shapes all life. . . . (p. 212)

> *Paul G. Italia, "Love and Lust in James Dickey's 'Deliverance',"* in *Modern Fiction Studies (copyright © 1975, by Purdue Research Foundation, West Lafayette, Indiana, U.S.A.), Summer, 1975, pp. 203-13.*

ROBERT PENN WARREN

["The Zodiac"] is consistently demanding, characteristically eloquent and often in an original way, and sometimes magnificent. I can think of no poem since Hart Crane's "The Bridge" that is so stylistically ambitious and has aimed to stir such depths of emotion. Like "The Bridge" (and most works of man's hand) this poem has certain limitations and defects that may provoke quarrel: for instance, the structural principle of progression for the first seven or eight sections is not always clear, and there is again some sort of structural blockage in the last two sections—defects in, we may say, the dramatic pivots. But the audacity of imagery, assemblage of rhythms, the power of language redeems all—in a period too often marked by a delicate hovering over the fragile merely because it is fragile and the prosy because it is prosy, the celebration of sensibility as such, polite or academic scrupulosities, self-pity in a cruel world, craven free verse lacking basic and projective rhythms.

In one sense "The Zodiac" can be said to be about the over-ambitiousness of poetry—even as it celebrates its ambitiousness. . . .

The poem is a metaphysical poem, one that with passion, rage, eloquence, and occasionally hysterical yammer asks a metaphysical question as a form of poetry. If for nothing, it would be memorable for the passage that seals the end. . . . (p. 8)

> *Robert Penn Warren, in* The New York Times Book Review *(© 1976 by The New York Times Company; reprinted by permission), November 14, 1976.*

HAROLD BLOOM

Dickey, after the lapse of his later poems, . . . ventures everything in *The Zodiac,* a longish poem of some 30 pages loosely based upon a modern Dutch original. Dickey's "drunken and perhaps dying Dutch poet" speaks for Dickey's own will-to-power over language and the universe of sense, a will so monomaniac as to resemble Ahab's, rather than Melville's. *The Zodiac* is obsessive and perhaps even hysterical verse, and after a number of readings I am helpless to say whether, for me, it works or fails. I cannot say whether Dickey has mastered his own language here or not, but I will have to keep going back to this poem, as will many other readers. It ends as strongly as anything in the Orphic and Promethean demi-god Dickey: "So long as the spirit hurls on space / The star-beasts of intellect and madness." (p. 22)

> *Harold Bloom, in* The New Republic *(reprinted by permission of* The New Republic; *© 1976 by The New Republic, Inc.), November 20, 1976.*

STANLEY BURNSHAW

"[*The Zodiac*] is based on another of the same title by Hendrik Marsman", Dickey explains, and "with the exception of a few lines, is completely my own." "Based" is the warranted word. Part I of Dickey's poem is almost as long (414 lines) as the whole of Marsman's (422), Parts II-XII even longer. But the telling difference grows out of the two conceptions of the hero: "A drunken Dutch poet who returns to his home in Amsterdam after years of travel and tries desperately to relate himself, by means of stars, to the universe." . . . (p. 120)

[The] two works . . . are fairly close in story but in other ways vastly apart. Marsman's narrator describes and interprets the hero's thoughts, feelings, acts; he philosophizes, he exclaims—and all in verse of conventional patterns: spare, condensed, restrained. In Dickey's poem the hero himself speaks, moans, shouts, questions, streams with visions, spits out four-letter words, curses his soul and God. Dickey disposes the words on the page as a prosody music-score, the margins and spaces reflecting the twists, turns, leaps of a man half-drunk, half-mad, half-supersane: a more-than-lifesize creature torn between whisky and stars. (pp. 120-21)

Mallarmé sought "the secret's answer" on earth ("Things already exist . . . we have simply to see their relationships"); the Dutch poet reads it in the sky. But for both, humanity's salvaging power is the same: the "creative" answer. Mallarmé calls for "composing the Book, the Orphic explanation of the earth . . . attempted by every writer." Dickey's speaker goes further, affirming that man will not fail himself so long as he is able to conceive the world imaginatively—

> So long as the hand can hold its island
> Of blazing paper, and bleed for its images:
> Make what it can of what is:
> So long as the spirit hurls on space
> The star-beasts of intellect and madness.

The avowal is no useless fancy. Poetry's "re-enactment of unification" (as *The Seamless Web* sought to make clear) overcomes the divisiveness within ourselves, among ourselves, and between ourselves and the universe. Poetry thus can no longer be viewed as a cultural ornament. Rather by providing as it does the fulfilment of a need of our nature, poetry serves as an instrument for human survival.

In *Sorties,* a book which I urged on my fellow-judges for a National Book Award, Dickey declared "I want my poem to devour the reader, so that he cannot possibly put it down as he reads it, or forget about it." *The Zodiac* sets a new height in this writer's achievement. It is surely the most disturbingly remarkable booklength poem in decades, charged as it is with the "raw vitalism", "the convincing speech", the insights, the visions, the unflagging intensity that Dickey attains in the finest works of his art. Let the reader make himself ready to roll with this poem as it draws him into its vortex of search and light. (pp. 123-24)

> *Stanley Burnshaw, "James Dickey" (originally published in a different version as "Star-Beasts of Intellect and Madness," in* Book World—The Washington Post, *November 21, 1976, p. E1; reprinted by permission of William McPherson), in* Agenda, *Winter-Spring 1977, pp. 120-24.*

RAYMOND J. SMITH

[The] protagonist of Dickey's [*The Zodiac*], a Dutch poet who uses the expression "Old Buddy," is a drunk. One would have hoped that the romantic image of the whiskey-poet had been finally smashed by Berryman's suicide. Not so. Alcohol and creativity go hand in hand for this poet. . . .

More of a tour de force than the mesmerizing "Falling" or the brilliantly Gothic "May Day Sermon," *The Zodiac* marks a new departure for Dickey in that it is derivative. . . . (p. 96)

Dickey has divided his poem into twelve parts (related only numerically to the signs of the zodiac), each of which focuses upon a particular episode in the life of a man who after many years of travel has returned to his home town (Amsterdam), where he tries to order his life. . . . (pp. 96-7)

Specifically Dickey's is the drunkenness of the protagonist, as well as an appropriate openness of style (marked by an infusion of the colloquial) and form (the words sprawl drunkenly across these pages which [have been] widened for Dickey's purposes), which was anticipated by his previous book, *The Eye-Beaters, Blood, Victory, Madness, Buckhead and Mercy.* At its worst, the openness leads to something like this:

> Son of a bitch.
> His life is shot   my life is shot.
> It's also shit.   He knows it.   Where's it all gone off to?
> The gods are in pieces
> All over Europe.
> But, by God, not *God*—

Dickey's main contribution to *The Zodiac* is his development of the protagonist's interest in the stars, which Marsman (wisely, I think) only touched upon. This, indeed, is the focus of the later poem, which is about a man who (as Dickey puts it) "tries desperately to relate himself, by means of the stars, to the universe." (p. 97)

The fiction here is similar to that of the deeply stirring "Eye-Beaters," where desperate, blind, orphaned children beat their eyes to create sparks—a kind of internal zodiac. Here the poet, rather than turning inward for consolation, to tribal memories, the caveman artist drawing the life-giving animal ("the deer, still wet with creation"), turns outward to the macrocosm, the star-beasts of the zodiac—projecting in each case an imaginative pattern on space. The fiction is an intriguing one. But the whiskey-poet, who expresses a great deal of familiarity for his fellow-artist God ("Listen you universal son-of-a-bitch, / You're talking to a poet now, so don't give me a lot of shit"), attempts to link his drunkenness and creativity by taking on the role of God's bartender—"What'll it be?" goes the refrain. And in this role, he can try to serve up something life-giving to take the crab Cancer's place in the zodiac—a "healing lobster."

The Zodiac does manage to transcend the banal and ludicrous, especially in the last section.... The poet's concluding prayer begins:

> But now, *now*
> Oh God you rocky landscape   give me, Give
> Me drop by drop
> desert water at least.
> I want to write about deserts
>
> And in the dark the sand begins to cry
> For living water that not a sun or star
> Can kill, and for the splay camel-prints that bring men,
> And the ocean with its enormous crooning, begs
>
> For haunted sailors   for refugees putting back
> Flesh on their ever-tumbling bones
> To man that fleet,
> for in its ships
> Only, the sea becomes the sea.

In such a way does Dickey resolve the antinomies—art/often following [his predecessor] Marsman quite closely. Here is the Dutch poet's (or his translator A. J. Barnouw's) version of the passage just quoted:

> And in the dark the desert made its plaint
> For living water that no heat will dry,
> And for the footprints of a caravan.
> And the ocean's siren song begged for a crew
> To man its waves with a high-riding fleet,
> For without ships the sea is not a sea.

Although Dickey insists in his preface that the poem is "in no sense a translation," close correspondences such as this seriously limit its originality. We are left, indeed, with not much more than the boozy ranting and ludicrous fiction of the poet bartending for God. (pp. 97-8)

Raymond J. Smith, "'Bartending for God'," in The Ontario Review *(copyright © 1977 by The Ontario Review), Fall-Winter, 1977-78, pp. 96-8.*

DIANE A. PARENTE

As a reviewer, I find myself somewhat intimidated, even awed by this beautiful, ambitious concert of effort. Artist (Marvin Hayes) and Poet (James Dickey) have combined talents to produce [*God's Images*] a new vehicle through which to experience the Bible.

Biblical events and personalities come alive in a series of fifty-three striking etchings, each accompanied by a reflective, poetic meditation....

The verbal images will evoke a ... varied response from those who pause to read and reflect. Diversity is the key word here, the author's personal reactions to the Biblical passages illustrated—now it takes the form of a poetic retelling of a Biblical event modernized by expanded imagery, then there are the first-person reactions of a Biblical character as he or she confronts his moment of truth, and scattered throughout are the gem-like reflections which provide insight and inspiration for the reader rather than simply expanding his experience of the Bible. (p. 283)

Diane A. Parente, in Best Sellers *(copyright © 1977, Helen Dwight Reid Educational Foundation), December, 1977.*

RICHARD FINHOLT

Leonard Lutwack, in *Heroic Fiction*, has stated that Melville's *Moby-Dick* introduced "unequivocally the spirit of the epic to American fiction by daring to endow native materials with qualities of the heroic past." ... James Dickey's *Deliverance* ... fits the ancient pattern more closely than any of the novels Lutwack chooses to discuss (it seems, in fact, an almost perfect embodiment of Joseph Campbell's "monomyth"). (p. 128)

In a time when the suspicion begins to grow, as Mailer puts it, that "nothing is nailed down" or, as Lewis puts it, that "nothing 'stays put,'" Dickey would take us back across time to the time before man had a sense of history but did, instead, take "for granted" his place in the natural cycle of birth and death. The country people in *Deliverance* seem grotesque and simple-minded to city people like Bobby, Drew, and Ed, but Lewis Medlock tells Ed that "we're lesser men" ... than they, because they live the kind of natural existence that city-bound men have lost over the civilized centuries.

Lewis Medlock is cut from the mold of the "primitive" epic hero, the champion of a "less sophisticated way of life" who is as ready to "plunge outside of history" as Ellison's Tod Clifton. As Odysseus was the man "never at a loss," Lewis is, according to the narrator Ed Gentry, "the only man I knew who could do with his life exactly what he wanted to." ... "He was not only self-determined; he was determined." The obligatory epic description of his "prowess" reads: "He was one of the best tournament archers in the state and, even at the age of thirty-eight or -nine, one of the strongest men I had ever shaken hands with." ... Ed Gentry, the quintessential contemporary American, a soft and overweight suburbanite, finds himself nonetheless "of the chosen" ... of Lewis. If this is not exactly the honor of being chosen by Odysseus to man the voyage to Ithaca, it is at least as good as being asked by Papa himself to join him on the ''tragic adventure'' of fishing the swamp on the big two-hearted river. And since Lewis's river happens to flow through just such a dreaded underworld, his weekend canoe trip takes on an epical significance demanding an American-bred heroism that is at least Hemingwayesque, if not Homeric.

The tragedies and triumphs of Homeric epic, according to C. S. Lewis, were played against a ''background of meaningless flux,'' played against the sense of the ''permanence, the *indifference*, the heartrending or consoling fact that whether we laugh or weep the world is what it is.'' . . . The action of *Deliverance* is played against the Homeric background. As Ed says in a moment of revelation during his climb up the side of the cliff, ''The river was blank and mindless with beauty. . . . I beheld the river in its icy pit of brightness, in its far-below sound and *indifference*, in its large coil and tiny points and flashes of moon, in its long sinuous form, in its uncomprehending consequence.'' . . . The experience of *Deliverance* is a return in time (symbolized by the line Ed describes between the urban South and rural South . . .) to pre-Christian era to match that of our ''post-Christian America'' (Saul Bellow's phrase, *Herzog*), a return to a time much like our own when values were grabbed on the run and meaning was where you found it, to a time when the hero's role was not diminished by the indifference of the cosmos to his actions but heightened thereby because heroism was *all*. The final difference between meaning and meaninglessness was the hero's ability, versus his inability, to act when the necessary time came (Mailer's ''existential edge''). This is the nature of Ed's discovery after undergoing an initiation rite into heroism on the death climb up the cliff: in an indifferent universe governed by no laws except natural forces (the metaphor of which Ed sees in the running of the river . . .) ''Who knows what might not be possible?'' (pp. 129-31)

Deliverance is something other than just an epic; it is a *Bildungsroman*, a novel of Ed Gentry's education, playing Telemachus to Lewis's Odysseus, in the mysteries of heroism. Ed begins by being amused by Lewis's atavistic faith in the body as the ultimate source of human survival. . . .

In a cerebral society in which all bodily functions have been reduced to a complex of sublimations, and a dominant male threatens other submissive males with transfer to the branch office in Juneau rather than with physical harm, vanity is perhaps the principal reason a man can have for developing his muscles. But while society may nurture narcissism . . . , the wilderness teaches humility; a man of the wilderness develops his body as a hedge against its proven vulnerability. (p. 132)

Hemingway dead by his own hand, Gatsby the victim of the ''foul dust'' of industrial society that ''floated in the wake of his dreams''; these are the real-life and fictional embodiments of the American frontier spirit, reverse-scapegoats fighting not for the chance to ''light out for the territory'' but against the social mechanisms that threaten to cut off the individual from his last lingering sense of source. As Lewis teaches Ed, a man must never let his social role obscure his natural identity. . . . (p. 133)

The would-be contemporary American epic hero must learn first of all that his own life can have epic or mythic implications, but only if he bears the responsibility for his own deliverance that he would rather leave on the stronger shoulders of Odysseus, Victor Mature, or Lewis Medlock: ''The assurance with which he had killed a man was desperately frightening to me,'' Ed says of Lewis, ''but the same quality was also calming, and I moved, without being completely aware of movement, nearer to him. I would have liked nothing better than to touch that big relaxed forearm. . . . I would have followed him anywhere. . . .'' . . . Now Ed finds himself miscast as the epic hero in a classically defined kill-or-be-killed confrontation, and the thought makes his ''tongue thicken at the possibility.'' . . . (pp. 135-36)

Dickey uses archery to dramatize, and symbolize, the epic struggle of mind to master matter and of will to master fear. The arrow becomes the extension of the hero's will, and the rightness of its flight to the target mirrors the straightness of the archer's mind. (p. 136)

Lewis stands at full draw for a full minute, a demanding situation for an archer because the steadiness of his aim ebbs away with his strength, waiting for the right moment to shoot the man holding the shotgun on Ed. The man, of course, is ''center shot.'' We expect this steadiness and psychological ''cool'' from Lewis, as the ancients expected it from Odysseus, who made his incredible shot through the axe heads, Homer tells us, having never bothered to get up from his banquet seat. But we do not know what to expect from Ed, the ''dumb brute'' common man, when his time comes. This is the essence of the American epic: Will the common man, given his opportunity for deliverance, be able to conquer the hysteria that stalks us all? The reader is apprehensive because earlier Ed had ''exploded . . . high and wide'' . . . when he tried to shoot a deer. With this scene in mind, the reader waits for Ed's resolve to fail. It does, at his first glimpse of the mountain man, and pity and fear flood the hearts of all those readers in suburbia who suspect the same deeply rooted cowardice in themselves. . . . (pp. 136-37)

Dickey's use of the archery shot as the symbol and dramatization of the hero's balance of body and mind, instinct and intellect, that signals his resonance with the forces of nature is reminiscent of another American contribution to the mystique of epic heroism, that of Fenimore Cooper's frontier scout, Natty Bumppo. . . . Lewis would seem to have the same moral affinity with natural forces that made Natty so invincible. (pp. 138-39)

Ed's ''grace under pressure'' when the time comes that he must hit his target, or die for missing, is surely meant to signify his achievement of the moral secret of ''true aim.'' During his climb up the cliff he undergoes the renewal of his basic instincts and achieves the return of his unconscious to its physical source. (p. 139)

The real climax of the story occurs when Ed purifies his body enough to gain the capacity to discover or possibly to create the crevice which saves his life; in ecstasy he declares, ''I had both hands in the cliff to the palms, and strength from the stone flowed into me.'' . . . This may sound like mysticism, but its truth is attested to by such observers of the human being in combat as Robert Graves and Erich Maria Remarque. (p. 140)

For Ed the purification of the body leads to a purification of the mind, which is demonstrated by his discovery that ''the river was running in my mind, and I raised my lids and saw exactly what had been the image of my thought." . . . The secret strength of the hero is now his. His body has brought his mind into touch with nature's ways. His understanding of the human situation is now in balance with the existential reality of natural law. His aspirations are running in harmony with his expectations. His once fear-ridden imagination . . . is vibrating in concert with the way things are. And his nerves steady with the realization that human actions were never intended to matter very much, that there are no eternal cosmic repercussions, only momentary thrashings about. His mood comes to reflect the all-pervasive tone of the universe that he had seen reflected in the river: "It was not that I felt myself turning evil, but that an enormous physical indifference, as vast as the whole abyss of light at my feet, came to me: an indifference not only to the other man's body scrambling and kicking on the ground with an arrow through it, but also to mine." . . . (p. 141)

Dickey takes his epigraph from [an] Old Testament prophet, Obadiah: "The pride of thine heart hath deceived thee, thou that dwellest in the clefts of the rock, whose habitation is high; that saith in his heart, Who shall bring me down to the ground?" (Obadiah 3, KJV). Critics have wondered if Dickey meant this as a condemnation of the mountain men or of Ed and Lewis. But Dickey does not mean this as a condemnation at all but as a formula for salvation, the lesson of humility leading the man who learns it to "Mount Zion," infinitely higher than the highest human habitation, where, according to Obadiah, "shall be deliverance." . . . (p. 142)

Perhaps Dickey's choice of epigraph serves as a warning that Lewis's mystique is not as pure as it should be. "Lewis wanted to be immortal," Ed tells us in the beginning, but by the end, having resisted the pull of the river and having been wounded for it, Lewis learns that "he can die now; he knows that dying is better than immortality." . . . With this knowledge Lewis can return to his society and, like Nebuchadnezzar, live at peace with it. There is no longer any desperate need to "light out for the territory." He can sit by the man-made lake with Ed watching the water skiers, secure in his hard-won feeling for "the true weight and purpose of all water." . . . (pp. 142-43)

Lewis and Ed have learned the indifference to their own lives which is the secret to putting one's body and mind in touch with all life, that is the secret of the hero's power to save lives and to make this salvation the way to a life more abundant. They have learned that deliverance lies *down*river, that a man has only to give himself up to the primal pull of natural forces. So, Ed concludes, "Let the river run." . . . (p. 143)

> *Richard Finholt, "Dickey's American Epic," in his* American Visionary Fiction: Mad Metaphysics as Salvation Psychology *(copyright © 1978 by Kennikat Press Corp.; reprinted by permission of Kennikat Press Corp.), Kennikat, 1978, pp. 128-43.*

*   *   *

DINESEN, Isak (pseudonym of Karen Blixen) 1885-1962

A Danish short story writer, novelist, poet, dramatist, and essayist, Dinesen is best known for her tales which reveal an intricate and unique prose style, sometimes baffling in its complexities. She spent seventeen years living on an estate in Kenya, an experience reflected in her published reminiscences, *Out of Africa* and *Shadows on the Grass*. She did not begin her writing career until her return from Africa in 1931, publishing her stories in both English and Danish. Dinesen's pseudonym derives from the Hebrew word for laughter, Isak. (See also *Contemporary Authors*, Vols. 25-28; *Contemporary Authors Permanent Series*, Vol. 2.)

THOMAS R. WHISSEN

It may seem . . . [that Isak Dinesen is] merely moralizing and that she conceives of art merely as the expression of some traditional religious doctrine. . . . It would be closer to the truth to say that she is offering art as a substitute, rather than as an apology, for religion. No one has been able to assign her beliefs to any single known religion. All that can safely be said is that she believed in a creative force which, for the sake of convenience, she called God. (p. 8)

[There is] an unmistakable religious feeling behind her stories, a feeling which carries over into her critical thinking. It is a pervasive, albeit vague, religiosity. . . . (pp. 8-9)

What interests her is an attitude which she finds compatible with what life and art have taught her. . . . [She] does not make art justify religion but religion justify art. This idea is central to Isak Dinesen's thinking; . . . it explains those heretical inversions of doctrine that shock the reader of her tales into sudden awareness. (pp. 9-10)

Isak Dinesen sees the artist as one who, in surrendering himself to God's will, becomes an implement (bow) in God's hand whereby the divine origin of art (Logos) is manifested in the work of art (Mythos) which will leave in the mind of the audience an impression (blank page) that will reflect the divine origin of the art. (p. 11)

Isak Dinesen is constantly relegating the artist to an inferior position by referring to him in such terms as *servant* and *implement*. . . . In the sense that the artist is a "go-between," it can be said that, as Isak Dinesen conceives of him, he goes between God and man—or, more accurately, between Logos, the divine source of his creativity, and the blank page, the residual effect that the audience infers. (pp. 11-12)

In the sense that [the artist] absorbs from God the creative impulse, he is master; but he is also God's medium. God and the artist share the role of creator, but the artist alone is the medium of creation; and the stringed instrument on which he both plays and is played is the means whereby Logos becomes Mythos.

The artist is mute until "played," but then, too, so is the stringed instrument. Not until the latter is played upon does it send forth all the music that it contains. And even this music is inferior to the idea that produced it. . . . What emanates from Logos, then, is not the same as Logos but an approximation of it—an imitation of it—what Isak Dinesen means, apparently, by the term *Mythos*. (pp. 12-13)

Mythos, as the earthly reflection of heavenly existence, is synonymous with art and can be applied to any visible or audible manifestation of the Logos by which, as the poet says, *all* things were created. (p. 13)

[Within] the tales themselves Isak Dinesen is intensely concerned with the artist, even though the ultimate obligation of the artist is to disappear from the scene, to return to the state of the "mute implement" and let silence speak.

This [deliberate] contradiction between a preoccupation with the artist within many of the tales and an emphasis on effect as the purpose of the tale can be resolved, I think, if we make a distinction between the artist as subject matter and the artist as intruder. . . . The effect of the eloquent blank page will not be achieved if the artist intrudes himself into the work, draws attention to himself, or in any way interferes with his function as the "bow of the Lord." When the bow is drawn across the strings, it is not the bow that is to be noticed, nor even the strings; it is the music— and beyond that, the effect of the music which is something other than the music itself. Isak Dinesen, therefore, is concerned that the artist remember his modesty and allow nothing to hinder the communication between the Logos and the blank page.

To retain such modesty he must remain loyal to the Logos, or story, as I think Isak Dinesen defines it. "Be loyal to the story," says the old hag in "The Blank Page" to her story-teller daughter. ". . . Where the storyteller is loyal, eternally and unswervingly loyal to the story, there, in the end, silence will speak. Where the story has been betrayed, silence is but emptiness. But we, the faithful, when we have spoken our last word, will hear the voice of silence." (pp. 15-16)

In a little play, *Sandhedens Haevn* (*The Revenge of Truth*), written long before she was to achieve fame with her first collection of tales, Isak Dinesen expresses an idea that most critics have interpreted as the governing principle behind her attitude toward life and art. Early in the play, the witch Amiane comes forth to state this idea in a speech which is also included in "The Roads Round Pisa" [*Seven Gothic Tales*] as the central motif of that story.

> The truth, my children, is that we are, all of us, acting in a marionette comedy. What is important more than anything else in a marionette comedy, is keeping the ideas of the author clear. This is the real happiness of life. . . .
>
> (p. 19)

The author to whom the witch refers is specifically the human author of the marionette comedy, but it is obvious . . . that she is also referring to God as the author of life. The fusion of the two meanings in the single word is the beginning of Isak Dinesen's critical thinking, for stemming from this comparison between God and the artist are all the principles by which she judges art. . . . The artist is, himself, a character in God's greater story, and as such he is as much obliged as anyone else to "keep the ideas of the author clear." (p. 20)

["The Cardinal's First Tale," in *Last Tales,* expresses] not only the Apollonian-Dionysian tension in both artist and priest but also [reveals] how both share, along with the aristocrat, a separation from ordinary society as well as an obligation to a destiny that differs significantly from that of the rest of mankind. In fulfilling their own destinies, these are the only persons who consciously lead others to fulfill theirs. In a world where all destinies were obvious, the artist, the priest, and the aristocrat would have no reason to exist.

Because his back is to God and he serves as God's mouthpiece, the artist, as well as the priest and the aristocrat, must share something of God's loneliness and risk; and he is denied certain advantages that other men are free to enjoy, among these the possibility of remorse and the possession of honor. (p. 21)

The person best equipped, it seems, to perceive the masks that pervade reality is the artist; and it is his function, as the arbiter on reality, to make these masks apparent as masks, in a way that leads not to any explicable truth behind the masks, but rather to an acceptance of the presence behind the masks of a truth which we are not privileged to understand. Thus, mask stands between truth and reality, and the art that makes these masks apparent is a higher reality because it is closer to truth. (pp. 22-3)

In Isak Dinesen's concept of the artist there is a trace of the diabolical, and Louis E. Grandjean points out in *Blixens Animus* that she shared with Nietzsche the belief that the satanic are preferable to the good who do not create, since the diabolical create more than they destroy. (p. 29)

The artist's job, as she sees it, is not to show man how to live but to heighten his consciousness of the life he is already living. (p. 31)

In "Ehrengard" and "The Immortal Story" only the perpetrators [of the evil of exceeding the limits of art] suffer, but in "The Poet" the suffering extends to others. In the confusion of mask and reality, the innocent lovers become murderers. The true artist knows that masquerade and reality are antithetical, and he strives to keep them separate by infusing his masquerade with a higher reality that is in direct contrast to the reality of the senses. (p. 33)

Isak Dinesen is fond of dealing in antithetical terms . . . ; she looks upon opposites as locked caskets, each of which contains the key to the other. The dialectic of pride and humility is one of her most profound concepts, for the artist's relationship to these poles determines what he shall do with the part of God's nature which he shares. Pride, as Isak Dinesen sees it, is understanding the work of God as being the "right arrangement"; humility is understanding that within this arrangement God has no favorites. She excludes no man from the possibility of sharing in God's nature; she says simply that the man who is most sensitive to the rightness of things, who is equally proud and humble before such rightness, is the man we call an artist. (pp. 34-5)

[She is concerned with] the temptation to believe that the creative talent carries with it its own assurances of success and its own protection from despair. As she sees it, such an attitude can only lead to despair and failure, for it misleads the artist into expecting certain benefits without suffering— or into interpreting his suffering as a promise of forthcoming benefits. In renouncing faith and hope at such moments of temptation, the artist is putting himself in a position to be "inspired." (p. 36)

The artist who considers himself favored is, in effect, presuming that he knows God's plan in advance. It is one thing to believe that there is a plan and that it is right, but quite another to believe one can anticipate that plan; or, sensing at any given moment one's part in that plan, to assume that that part will not change. Such foreknowledge would violate the mystery of existence, and certainly, as Isak Dinesen conceives of it, the function of the artist is not to violate but to vindicate the mystery. (pp. 36-7)

Isak Dinesen believes firmly in inspiration as the transmission of the will of God to the artist by means of the Holy Ghost. In "The Deluge at Norderney" she implies that art is the book of the Holy Ghost, and in "The Cardinal's First Tale" . . . she describes the Holy Ghost as the sire of the artist. "I am not blaspheming, Madame," Cardinal Salviati tells the lady in black, "when I express the idea that any young mother of a saint or great artist may feel herself to be the spouse of the Holy Ghost." (p. 41)

In the tales of Isak Dinesen, the artist is the consort of loneliness and longing and is excluded from the society of common humanity in that he cannot enjoy the benefits either of honor or of remorse. Denied most of the prerogatives of either God or the devil, he is forced, nevertheless, as a man, to wear their immortal masks in a theatrical that lacks even the dignity of tragedy. . . . Isak Dinesen holds that those who function on this earth in lieu of God (artist, priest, aristocrat) can never be truly tragic figures. Tragedy is the privilege of ordinary mortals alone, and the gods and their agents must never condescend to be pitied; for to pity them is to annihilate them. . . . (pp. 49-50)

Denied the pleasures of ordinary human intercourse, the artist can find compensation in the creation of works of art; but there is a longing of the sort that leads beyond human existence and which can only be described in terms of a longing for a union with God, a oneness with the essence of creation. (p. 51)

Honor [being based on remorse] and remorse are irrelevant qualities to the artist; he has no need of them. But adversity and distress, poverty and sickness, even the harshness of his enemies, are the realities of which he is arbiter. Here, if anywhere, can be seen the peculiar power of Isak Dinesen's theory of submission. It is gay and glorious and not the least craven. We get from life, she says in one of her tales, both what we ask for and what we reject. Both are gifts, and the artist, in not separating them, acquires dominion over them. (p. 55)

Aside from personal preference, she revered the tale as a pure and original genre. She saw in it, I believe, an unbroken link with man's prehistoric beginnings. By reminding us, as she does so often, that in the beginning was the story and that stories have always been *told,* she is, in effect, placing the tale first in the ranks of literature and on a level with those art forms which anthropologists have traced to prehistory and which they have designated as spontaneous, archetypal expression—dance, music, drawing.

Isak Dinesen tried her hand at just about every literary genre—drama, poetry, novel, essay; but it would be foolish to say that she returned to the tale because she thought it superior. She returned to it, without a doubt, because she excelled at it. (p. 63)

To Isak Dinesen, God is not a painter or a poet or a musician. He is above all a teller of tales. *The* divine art is the story, the primary pattern of all art. Creation is a story, and we are told this story step by step, as the story progresses. There is a beginning and a middle and an end (the seventh day), and the characters appear in the story on a given day.

It is the unfolding that is important to Isak Dinesen. What matters is not what happens to man so much as the way in which it happens. It is only in the working out of the story that all men participate. There can be no story without man, yet man is subordinate to the story. . . . As the means

whereby creation is unfolded, the story, it seems, is the artistic counterpart of creation, and the other art forms are but parts of this greater art.

The elevation of the tale to the highest art form is a departure from the romantic tendency to exalt music above all other art, but Isak Dinesen still [has] . . . the romantic fondness for using musicians as serious subjects for literary treatment. . . . It is interesting to note . . . that the one character in her tales who bears the most obvious resemblance to herself is Pellegrina Leoni, a renowned opera singer. In [*Winter's Tales*], the first story in which Pellegrina Leoni appears, her identity is deliberately confused as she moves in and out of the story in a succession of widely varying disguises. One purpose of the story seems to be an attempt to show that the personality takes on meaning only in the context of the role it is playing—when, in other words, character is subordinate to plot. (pp. 65-6)

Her settings and characters are idealized; they are seen not through the distortion of a mirror but through the perception of a mind which orders things to conform with the dictates of a higher reality—a higher imagination. They are, in a word, dreamlike in that they seem to have had an existence even though they could never really have existed.

The relationship between art and dream figures importantly in Isak Dinesen's attitude toward reality. In *Shadows on the Grass* she writes: "For we have in the dream forsaken our allegiance to the organizing, controlling and rectifying forces of the world, the Universal Conscience. We have sworn fealty to the wild, incalculable, creative forces, the Imagination of the Universe." I think it can be shown that this statement is far from a cry for artistic anarchy. Anarchy lies in the opposite direction from such concepts as identity and metamorphosis, submission and destiny, that [are] as central to Isak Dinesen's thinking. The organizing, controlling, and rectifying forces mentioned in this passage are simply the bourgeois virtues that [Erik] Johannesson lists as sincerity, security, and being true to one's own self. These are the ingredients of the universal conscience and have nothing to do with art, which puts the mask above sincerity, uncertainty above security, and loyalty to the story above loyalty to one's self. The wild, incalculable, creative forces are the daring, passion, and imagination of the Word that Adam praises in "Sorrow-Acre" [*Winter's Tales*]. They are the principle of art, not the law; and when one swears fealty to them, he is yielding to authority, not anarchy—he is being loyal to the story and keeping the ideas of the author clear.

The imagination of the universe is the source of art, not the structure. When, farther on, Isak Dinesen speaks about shifting over "from the world of day, from the domain of organizing and regulating universal powers, into the world of Imagination," she is talking, I think, about a movement away from bourgeois values toward divine ones. The domain of organizing and regulating universal powers, since it is contrasted with the world of imagination, obviously refers to the sort of worldly reality by which we may mistakenly judge art. The dream can neither be argued not explained. It must be accepted on its own terms. And if this dream, which derives from the imagination of the universe, is reflected in art, then art must also be accepted on its own terms. This is a plea, I think, not for disorder in art, but for order of a kind different from that of reality.

The order of reality excludes compression and expansion. Every moment is of the same duration as every other, and one moment inexorably follows another. The order of art, like dream, lengthens some moments and shortens others. The relationship of one event to another is dictated by the inner logic of the work and is not bound by chronology. (pp. 71-2)

Isak Dinesen allows that dreams may have nightmarish qualities, but she does not believe that there is a place for nightmare as ultimate vision in art. . . . For her, apparently, . . . nightmare can only be a partial vision. . . .

By assigning the dream an exalted position, Isak Dinesen is moving away from the interpretation of dreams as a means to a better understanding of the human personality and in the direction of dream as myth, as collective unconscious, and, therefore, as a basis for art and for the understanding of art. (p. 75)

God's art, and the art of those who are loyal to God's art, is, in contrast to human art, the art of continuance. In change only will it find its value; and its truth, reality, and order will be concealed within the mask, dream, and disorder that argue change. This means, apparently, that there can be no absolute truth, reality, or order in art except the absolute truth, reality, and order of change. Art that implies anything else, it seems, is false—or human—art.

This concept of the absolute value of change is an important affirmation of the value of an organic theory of art. If each separate work of art contains its own truth, reality, and order, then there is no external standard that can be brought to bear upon it other than the condition that the work of art conform to its own standards and not suggest that those particular standards are applicable to any other work of art. This is an assertion of the uniqueness of individual works of art, for duplication would be not only unnecessary but contradictory. This is why Isak Dinesen cannot talk about the specific nature of the mask, dream, or disorder that might appear in a work of art. All she can do is to insist that these elements be taken on their own terms, and that whenever they appear, they affirm the value of change. (pp. 76-7)

Isak Dinesen makes a distinction between tragedy and comedy which is similar to the one she makes between the novel and the story. Tragedy, like the novel, is a human art; comedy, like the story, is a divine one. . . .

According to this distinction, tragedy cannot be an earthly reflection of the divine creative force unless it is considered as a part of comedy—much as Isak Dinesen considers nightmare as an incomplete dream. Northrop Frye has said that we reconcile ourselves to tragedy because it leads by implication to comedy. This implication Isak Dinesen would call the comic vision, I think; and I think she would insist that it be present before a work with tragic elements could truly be labeled the highest form of art. (p. 91)

Tragedy, then, can be defined, according to what Isak Dinesen has said, as a human phenomenon in which man, out of a sense of honor, rebels against the conditions brought about by the Fall by contrasting them with the Edenic ideal in an attempt to regain his innocence. Or she might prefer to say, simply, that tragedy is the imitation of lost destiny. Man cannot regain this lost destiny, as Isak Dinesen sees it, through tragedy alone, however. The ultimate purpose of

all art is to reflect cosmic intent, and the ultimate effect is to regain naiveté through submission to destiny. Neither this purpose nor this effect can be achieved except through the comic vision. (pp. 93-4)

Isak Dinesen's one truly tragic figure is Councilor Mathiesen in "The Poet" [*Seven Gothic Tales*] and it is to him that we can look for some illumination on the question of tragic flaw. His idyllic life is interrupted by the knowledge that he can never be the poet he has always dreamed of being. The necessity of being something else he finds tiresome, and as a countermeasure against this dull condition, he undertakes to arrange the lives of others in accordance with a plan which will afford him a vicarious success as a poet. This decision to meddle in his own destiny—and the destiny of others—to appoint himself as the best judge of what should be, is . . . his fatal mistake. . . . [On] the basis of Isak Dinesen's insistent comment on the subject, I would suggest that a tragic hero commits his tragic error at the moment when he takes destiny into his own hands. (p. 94)

It is in keeping with Isak Dinesen's general philosophy . . . to say that those who willingly submit to their destinies are comic figures and those who do not are tragic figures. Such a definition does not afford tragic figures the exalted station that Aristotle assigns them. Isak Dinesen's tragic hero is more pitiful than pitiable. For one thing, she excludes the nobility from the role of tragic hero; and for another, she specifies no moral qualifications. "Here on earth," says the old lord in "Sorrow-Acre," "we, who stand in lieu of the gods and have emancipated ourselves from the tyranny of necessity, should leave to our vassals their monopoly of tragedy, and for ourselves accept the comic with grace." Pity, for Isak Dinesen, is a degrading emotion, not to be directed, it would seem, towards God or His mouthpieces. "In pitying, or condoling with your god," says the old lord, "you deny and annihilate him, and such is the most horrible of atheisms." Moreover, the effect of an action differs between those who stand in lieu of the gods and their vassals. "Indeed," says the old lord, "the very same fatality, which, in striking the burgher or peasant, will become tragedy, with the aristocrat is exalted to the comic." (p. 95)

The part which Isak Dinesen assigns to the audience in the realization of a work of art is as demanding as that which she assigns the artist. It is not surprising, then, that the listeners in Isak Dinesen's tales are usually storytellers themselves, for to participate fully in a story, a listener must be able to involve himself in it as deeply as the teller, to assist the teller, as it were, in the creation of the story—just as man assists God in the creation of the world. The point at which the interdependent roles of author and audience merge is that point beyond the work of art which Isak Dinesen calls the *blank page*. It is at this point that the story which has been properly told will unfold its deeper meaning in the mind of the audience—will, in the silence that speaks, bring about the reconciliation of opposites which is the highest effect of art. (p. 101)

The concept of interdependence is one of Isak Dinesen's most fundamental and far-reaching attitudes towards both life and art. We [note] its importance in the relationship between God and artist, pride and humility, reality and dream, truth and mask, Logos and Mythos; and we have seen it offered as a clue to the understanding of the paradoxes of life and death, man and woman, rich and poor, artist and public. [Further,] interdependence culminates in reconciliation—that grand effect to which Isak Dinesen insists all art should, and great art does, aspire. (p. 115)

If the work of art is successful, it will convey intact the sense of the unity and necessity of all things in such a way that the audience will recognize and accept the truth of this unity and necessity without asking why it is so or why it must be so. In fact, if harmony has been achieved and transmitted through the work of art, the audience will feel that such harmony is right and proper and is itself the answer to the seeming diversity and whim of isolated experiences. It will understand that "everything, even the pain and the evil, is esthetically necessary." (p. 119)

However it is given to us, balance must be present in a work of art, it seems, before we can respond to it. We know that balance has been achieved once we see that opposites are interdependent. Out of this interdependence arises a concord that makes alternatives unimaginable. Once we have reached this point, we have arrived at the moment of reconciliation—the blank page. This is the moment in which the half that we have been given unites with the half which we can project, and question and answer become one. (pp. 120-21)

It is the rebellious tendency of romanticism to posit art at the extreme opposite of existing concepts of sensually perceptible reality. Isak Dinesen is merely reaffirming this tendency by constantly dealing in terms of paradox and resolution, in terms of thesis, antithesis, and synthesis. Nowhere are such terms more applicable or more appropriate, it seems, than in this ultimate achievement of art—to join with reality in a reconciliation that transcends both. In her own life and art Isak Dinesen repeatedly insisted on an equal acquaintance with art and reality for this very reason, and not on an understanding of one by means of the other. (p. 122)

Thomas R. Whissen, in his Isak Dinesen's Aesthetics *(copyright © 1973 by Thomas R. Whissen; reprinted by permission of Kennikat Press Corp.), Kennikat, 1973.*

JOAN PALEVSKY

[*Carnival, Entertainments and Posthumous Tales*] are of a piece with her already published works. But, since they are the last we shall have of Dinesen, certain observations come to mind about her and her art. All has probably been said already; yet we cannot leave it at that. She is too good a writer.

It is striking, for example, how at home Dinesen was in the past. In this volume, the stories go back and forth between Holland, Italy and France in the early 19th Century to Denmark and England in the 20th. Why the past? Because, of course, the past lends itself to strange happenings and odd personages. And also to violent passions. Dinesen was, in many respects, a true Romantic.

Yet in Dinesen, paradoxically, there is a kind of old-fashionedness in the modern tales and a timelessness in the tales of the past. One realizes that Dinesen actually created a world unto herself, a world of her peculiar shadow and light, a literary world as much her own as Proust's was his. To do this requires, if one thinks about it enough, an immense fund of general culture, of historical background, of literary instinct above all, to be able to write so convincingly of past times in countries foreign to one's own. . . .

The adjective "gothic" which clings to Dinesen's memory is supremely apt. There is an underlying mysteriousness in her tales . . . , subtly suggested by innocent, off-hand remarks about her characters. Thus, her characters tend to be contradictory and not easily dismissed at the end of the story as totally explained.

There is often an uneasiness in the reader's mind about motives and even about events in a Dinesen tale. In "The Bear and the Kiss," in the present volume, the eeriness of Northern Norway and a deserted island contribute certainly to the mystery, but the characters themselves—Joshua and his Finnish wife—have been given mythical and mystical qualities long before we meet them. . . .

Even more harrowing, in a modern sense, is "The Ghost Horses," set in an unsinister England of the 20th Century. The tale deals with a nice, middle-class child who refuses to recover from an illness. Her uncle believes he is leading her back to normal life until he discovers the real cause of the child's reluctance to leave her shadowy world. After the reader had been lulled into feeling that in this comfortable milieu all will end happily, he is shocked (and puzzled) by the story's last paragraph. The story is every bit as gothic as those of the Frozen North, perhaps even more so for its familiar setting. One realizes, too, that Dinesen is not only poking ironic fun at the pat diagnosis of the doctor . . . but reminding us also, we post-Freudians, that there are sinister elements at work in children. Here is Dinesen at her very best.

Lest one remember only the dark side to Isak Dinesen, it is good that this volume includes a youthful "entertainment" called "Uncle Theodore." Set in France in the early part of this century, it is a light-hearted story, with its characters given appropriately humorous names like *Vieusac* and *Petitsfours*. The juvenile vicomte is sympathetically portrayed with the affectionate irony of a Colette. Indeed, the story in its setting and treatment reminds us very much of the French writer . . . , yet this is not a Gallic work. A sober note underlies the story. But what is so rare and so appealing is its lack of sinister elements and its happy ending. It is a tale so well told that it is difficult to remember that it was written . . . at the beginning of Dinesen's career when she was just discovering her talent. (p. 20)

This brings us to the question of the style of these tales and of the famous, published ones. One might think that the stilted, old-fashioned language was that of a foreigner writing in English. But we know from *Out of Africa* that Dinesen was capable of writing perfectly modern English. . . . One realizes then how suitable the style is which she created for the tales of fantasy. It was a perfectly conscious way to bind them into a unity in their various geographical and chronological settings. . . . The style is very personal (as, again, was Proust's) to fit that personal literary world of her imagination. It is really a kind of never-never language in a never-never world.

It is, nevertheless, vigorous and rich in strong images. If the reader were not told who had written these tales, he would still know from the very first lines, so identifiably special is Dinesen's manner. The first paragraph of "The Last Day" in this collection could be used as a textbook example of the superior art of establishing a mood for the narrative that follows. (pp. 20, 36)

Joan Palevsky, "Tales of the Past," in

Books West (*copyright* © *by* Books West Magazine *and Book Fair, Inc.*), *Vol. 1, No. 7, 1977, pp. 20, 36.*

THOMAS WHISSEN

Dinesen lovers will rejoice over *Carnival*, a collection of eleven Dinesen stories that either have been out of print or never before published.... The stories, spanning half a century of creative effort, are of mixed quality, but all bear the inimitable Dinesen touch. All the familiar Dinesen themes are there: the double, the reality of the imagination, sorcery, the fusion of impulse and action, and above all, the joyful surrender to merciless destiny.

Two stories written in 1909 anticipate Dinesen's skill at plot twists. "The de Cats Family" develops the idea that a respectable family needs a black sheep to keep it respectable, and "Uncle Theodore" tells of an impoverished young nobleman who "invents" a rich uncle who turns out to be real. Both stories have a charm and clarity that is unfortunately missing from "Carnival," the title piece. This story of eight people who pool their incomes and then draw lots so that the winner may live for a year as he pleases is too contrived and digressive.

Probably the best tale of all, in terms of sheer storytelling, is "Anna." Set in Sicily in the last century, this story has everything—sharply defined characters, intrigue, romance, mystery—everything, that is, but an ending. Dinesen left it unfinished, but those who know and love Dinesen may prefer it that way. She herself has suggested that the last page should be blank, for upon the blank page all is revealed.

Two stories in the collection pose problems for Dinesen enthusiasts. "The Ghost Horses," one of her "dreaming child" stories, reinforces the suspicion some have that she was obsessed with royalty; and "The Proud Lady," the story of a persecuted aristocrat at the time of the French Revolution, tries but fails to justify tyranny in the name of divine necessity. "The Bear and the Kiss" is more of a puzzle than a problem. A curiously obscure story, it lacks the power but not the imagination of her *Seven Gothic Tales*.

The volume ends with the very last tale Dinesen ever wrote, "Second Meeting," a lean and moving story of Lord Byron's second meeting with his double, just before Byron is about to go off to Greece to die. It is Dinesen at her best and fitting conclusion to a collection of tales that rank among her best. (pp. 77-8)

Thomas Whissen, in The International Fiction Review (© *copyright International Fiction Association*), *January, 1978.*

MICHAEL IRWIN

Fifteen years after her death Isak Dinesen seems to be little read in this country. She has become a cult figure without a cult. Few modern writers of comparable status can have been so neglected. No doubt her work has proved hard to place because it is eccentric in kind. But more than that, the stories on which her reputation must rest, while superficially accessible, demand, if they are to be properly understood, a degree of attention and interpretative effort only likely to be accorded to a writer of acknowledged "importance"....

[Dinesen's short stories] can differ greatly in emphasis and effect, but they tend to be roughly similar in mode. The opening sentence will be a fine romantic flourish.... The characters will be exotic: princesses, cardinals, poets, actors, painters, singers, seafarers. But the developing tale will lack the simple narrative thrust that these elements seem to promise. An extravagant plot, plainly metaphorical in intention, is made to accommodate interpolated stories, poetic descriptions of nature, and stylized conversations, heavy with aphorism.

The most obvious critical problem posed by Isak Dinesen does not concern interpretation, though her meaning is often obscure, but rather a seeming discrepancy between means and ends. Can a tale so elaborately wrought, so resolutely artificial, shed light, as the author manifestly intends, on some fundamental theme—justice, love, sex, religious belief, social organization? She poses the question herself in the title *Anecdotes of Destiny*. The risk she runs is that her stylized fictions might seem no more than portentous whimsicalities....

[Robert Langbaum] speaks of her taste for "the extremely natural and the extremely artificial", and claims that she herself categorized her work accordingly: "Isak Dinesen considered that her stories fall into the two classes of Gothic and Winter's tale, which seem to divide along the lines of art versus nature—with the Gothic tale on the side of art: witty, extravagant, cosmopolitan; and the Winter's tale, Danish, provincial, natural." Up to a point the distinction is a useful one; but in fact most of the individual tales express both tendencies, and are centrally concerned with the need to reconcile them....

"Sorrow-acre" is one of a number of stories by Isak Dinesen that seem to celebrate a pre-democratic mode of life, in which people could guide their actions by ancient certitudes. It was chiefly the survival of such patterns of response that she found appealing in the life of her African natives. But she was not content to celebrate times past....

[Isak Dinesen carried the romantic] tradition a step forward by showing how selfconscious, analytical modern man can regain his "lost unity of perception". He is to regain it through artifice. By seeking to impose a pattern on his own life, or on the lives of others, however arbitrarily, he is daring God to frustrate him, and in doing so to grant him a glimpse of that greater, divine pattern that informs creation....

Isak Dinesen's philosophy poses two main problems. One concerns the character of the playful, unpredictable God that we are invited to laud and to emulate. (p. 25)

The greater problem, however, because it ultimately affects one's response to the very technique of her stories, concerns the nature or status of the artifice that she recommends. In *Out of Africa* she shows an attractive admiration for the dandyism of ... derelict characters.... She celebrates their proud individuality. But how, within an intricate fiction, is a writer to make sense of the changing whims of a wayfarer or drunkard? Frequently, as in "Sorrow-acre", Isak Dinesen implies that the dandyism she is describing is not merely random because it expresses a tradition. The whims of aristocrats are somehow special. This is not a sympathetic idea; and occasionally it seems to betray Isak Dinesen into a surprisingly crass kind of snobbery. But it makes for coherence within a given story.

Since the seemingly arbitrary elements of the tale in fact derive from, and disclose, a basic social and psychological pattern, the tale itself, for all its extravagances, can be patterned. Without this implication of structure the story and its moral must fall to pieces. The point is more important than it may at first appear. For Isak Dinesen the story-teller himself enacts the process she recommends. His artifice mimics God's artifice. His control over his tale suggests God's control over his world. But whence does the story-teller derive his authority? Only from the power and persuasiveness of his narrative.

This reflexive argument poses again, in rather different form, the problem of the artificiality of Isak Dinesen's stories. Characteristically a moral story, or fable, tends to gain power from the simplicity that implies general applicability, general truth. This would hold true of "Sorrow-acre", which was apparently based on a Danish folk-tale. But I was unable to provide anything like a full explication even of "Sorrow-acre"; and the great majority of Isak Dinesen's tales are far more allusive. For all the extremity and artificiality, every detail is calculated and relevant. Her stories are all meaning. . . . [In] fact it would be virtually impossible to discuss Isak Dinesen without painstaking synopsis. If you subtract the "meaning" almost nothing remains. Yet it is the story that must persuade you that the meaning matters. (pp. 25-6)

I have mixed feelings about the stories. Several of them—notably "Babette's Feast"—are brilliant. Most of them include notable flashes of wit and passages of exquisite description. But some of the literary substance, some of the pseudo-archaism, seems to me mere plastic or tinsel. And above all I do not see how most of her stories, however much they entertain or intrigue the reader, could move him. The dandyism can impress but it rarely persuades. A typical tale by Isak Dinesen is a complex, very personal statement: the lovingly articulated skeleton of a purely private truth. (p. 26)

> *Michael Irwin, "The Pattern of Creation," in* The Times Literary Supplement (© *Times Newspapers Ltd. (London) 1978; reproduced from* The Times Literary Supplement *by permission), January 13, 1978, pp. 25-6.*

MAUREEN HOWARD

The best of Dinesen's tales have always held a fine balance of a storytelling method derived from literary models—sagas, fairy tales—and her own piercing sense of psychological reality. In "Anna," to my mind the finest piece in [*Carnival*], there is a remarkable interlocking set of stories like an intricate puzzle toy that is pleasurable to the touch and equally pleasing to decode. (p. 183)

When the sentiment works in Dinesen's fables as it does in "Anna" she achieves the simplicity of line that we admire in good story ballet. It is her rhythms, her pairings, her quick character studies that support the romance and never let it go soft at the center. (pp. 183-84)

> *Maureen Howard, in* The Hudson Review *(copyright © 1978 by The Hudson Review, Inc.; reprinted by permission), Vol. XXXI, No. 1, Spring, 1978.*

ELIZABETH ELY FULLER

As one would expect in a collection of this kind, most of the tales [in *Carnival: Entertainments* and *Posthumous Tales*] do not compare in vision and quality with the collections for which Dinesen is rightly best known: *Seven Gothic Tales, Out of Africa, Winter's Tales,* and some of *Last Tales.* Yet they are of interest because they give us new insight into her best work, some by showing us her beginnings and the context of her art, and some, when they break off unfinished or sound a false note, by showing us the directions her art could not take once she found her true beginnings.

The true beginning of Isak Dinesen's art is where the art of many modern writers end. Two of Dinesen's earliest works, "The de Cats Family" and "Carnival" (in *Carnival*), in their very different ways, show the earliest starting points of her art. They are both characteristically outrageous, but delightfully so. In "The de Cats Family," the author incisively marks out the territory of her future art by way of negative reference. The opening lines clearly raise the issue of art's purpose and method: "Dear readers, I should not like to trick you into reading anything which you would later deplore. Here is a story which has no other merit than its excellent moral." Spurred by these words, the story proceeds by a simple strategy almost devoid of style and characterization, to beguile the reader into believing a moral he or she would initially have deplored. . . .

The moral of the story on the face of it is that vice can be an excellent thing. But the way in which the de Cats family explain this principle to themselves and accept it—that to collect the guilt of many onto one and condemn him to save the rest is a sound business principle; that scapegoating is the guarantor of virtue and, indeed, the foundation of Christianity; and that one must do one's duty—points to another moral: most of the tenets we live by are colossal lies. . . .

"The de Cats Family" is purely literary in that it proposes no meaning of its own but serves as a tool to destroy swiftly and economically what Dinesen sees as a limited notion of the law held by what has become a predominantly bourgeois world. It is as if Adam, ariving in Paradise, found the animals already named, incorrectly; and before he could name them he had to say ceremoniously to each: Thou art not named this, not named that. . . . In one sense the members of the de Cats family are level-headed bearers of Dinesen's ironic message that truth and morality do not work the way we think they do. In another sense, being a bourgeois family themselves, that they prudently turn their revelation to coin and only a certain kind of virtue is a further irony.

Having so clearly accomplished its purpose, this demolition strategy does not reappear as the focus of later works, but is absorbed into her style: sudden and quick turns of plot and dialogue take us through seeming improbabilities to reach a world with unfamiliar, though strict, laws of its own. . . .

Unlike "The de Cats Family," "Carnival" has a very loose structure. Set in 1925 the characters of the story are a group of contemporary young Danish men and women, wealthy and bored, who have come from a masquerade ball to the house of two of the characters for a midnight supper before returning to the ball. The supper becomes a symposium on various topics that soon focus on what will be Isak

Dinesen's three principal themes: love, the meaning of life, and art. In the course of their discussions, they express in germinal form ideas that will be central in her mature work. For example, an old painter's theory about black will become her theory of tragedy: the disillusionment that besets the younger generation stems from their ignorance of the color black. (p. 14)

Instead of providing a harder mask for the character's soft faces, the story turns the moment of real harshness—the real face that opposes their pink and blue masks—into simply a pastime of the decadent lives lived by what have now become indistinguishable as masks or faces. The story doesn't work because it has not found its true beginning, and therefore ends by simply stopping.

But "Carnival" is interesting because it provides the contemporary context for the Gothic settings of Dinesen's later work. The contemporary world is pink and blue and needs black, but in this world, the only act recognized as harsh is a bloody one. Therefore she must go back to past ages to find tools for her expression, to find a harshness that, cast in a fantastic past, avoids the question of real violence. This strategy may be interpreted by some as an act of cowardice, but the dilemma is real. (pp. 14-15)

In Dinesen's latest and best works, the carnival or mask principle is replaced by the principle of the obstacle. For the mask is not really a principle, but a strategy. It doesn't do any good, in Yeats's words, "To set your chisel to the hardest stone" ("Ego Dominus Tuus") if you are not driven to do it, if you are merely bored and restless. "The de Cats Family" is a strong story because it is destroying a false mask. But "Carnival," though more creative, lacks a strong and focused impulse. And here, in a word, is the problem of the modern writer: what impulse can he fashion or find to inform his art? . . .

It is in the principle of the obstacle, or destiny, that Isak Dinesen finds her true beginning. To put it one way, her theme is the consummation to be found in unconsummated or unrequited love. To put it differently, it is that tragedy is the principle of joy. Or, it is that a young girl, pondering as she dresses for a ball on the choice between comfort and beauty, will choose beauty because she knows that it will offer her perhaps a greater comfort, and if not, then a greater joy. Power, grace, and truth proceed only from a confrontation to the death with a force greater than oneself. The force may be loss, pain, or refusal. It may be honor. It may be love itself. . . .

For Dinesen, as seen most clearly in the first Gothic tale, "The Deluge at Norderney," the true God is a charlatan. "There never was a great artist who was not a bit of a charlatan; nor a great king, nor a god. The quality of charlatanry is indispensable in a court, or a theater, or in paradise." The problems of the modern world stem not from the fall of man but from "a fall of the divinity. We are now serving an inferior dynasty of heaven."

It is Dinesen's conception of God, destiny, and man's relation to them that explains her conception of the aristocratic. Her frequent choice of aristocratic themes, settings, heroes, and heroines is not a consequence of social snobbery or political views but of spiritual and artistic convictions. The aristocrat in her stories is a superior human being because only he and his servants truly understand the principle of service. The greatest servant proclaims the greatest master, and the aristocrat is the greatest servant because he serves a prince or master without considering questions of justice and virtue. He serves a creator.

As many of Isak Dinesen's characters say, and as her art form demonstrates, it is not the character who is primarily important, but the story. . . .

Even the body itself is a work of art, not a personal concern. The beautiful Heloise in "The Heroine" (*Winter's Tales*), trapped in a German inn with the group of French and English travelers at the outbreak of the Franco-Prussian War, is offered by the young commanding Prussian officer her freedom and the freedom of the others if she will show herself to him as the naked Venus. She refuses. Enraged, the officer orders their execution at dawn. At dawn, however he sends a letter of permission for the group to cross into Luxembourg and to Heloise a large bouquet of roses with the message: "[my] compliments to a heroine." . . .

In her tales after "The Deluge at Norderney," Isak Dinesen shows that death is not the only obstacle; destiny, like honor, comes in many other forms with almost equal power. As her storytelling gift sharpens and strengthens, she makes us feel the power and pain of these many forms of destiny. . . .

As the old lord in "Sorrow Acre" explains to his young nephew, Adam, the highest art is comic. The art of the gods is comic, and the art of the aristocrat must also be comic. Tragedy is a noble phenomenon, nobler than the art of the bourgeois, but still only human. The tragic artist and the tragic vision are bound by strict laws, but the comic artist has a freedom as unbounded as that of the gods, as long as he accepts the comic situation with grace. This acceptance demands the acceptance of tragedy, and the grace not to interfere in another's tragedy, and even, at times, the acceptance of being or providing the obstacle that will set the stage for another's tragedy. Thus Heloise risked her life and the lives of others to allow for a tragedy that would have been spiritually superior to what would have been in their eyes the low comedy of buying life cheaply.

If the informing principle of Isak Dinesen's art is that it is destiny that forces from us an exertion that will yield us tragic stature on the one hand or comic freedom and joy on the other, the confrontation between the tragic and the comic is an equally important theme; indeed the first principle depends on it. In the perspective of our yearnings, the obstacle is unnecessary, and therefore tragic—painful. In the perspective of the high comic, it is the absoluteness of the obstacle—its illogicality and its pain—that exalts comedy to its heights and saves it from low comedy. . . .

Though it may be impossible to give priority to either tragedy or comedy, it is possible to give a high priority to the issue itself. Thus the function of many of Dinesen's tales is to raise their characters out of innocence or low comedy by confronting them with a passion or yearning powerful enough to lead them into the tragic dilemma. Thus, for some characters passion itself is the obstacle to an inferior complacency. (p. 15)

The stories, and the collection as a whole, are constructed like a complex kaleidoscope. Each character and each event works as a little bit of mirror reflecting another character or event, and then turning slightly to catch some other reflection. To reinforce this overall plot structure, Dinesen uses mirror images and similes repeatedly as the characters muse on their own nature and on their relation to others. To any one of them, the story may make no sense, but taken as a whole, the stories, like a piece of music or a minuet, form a complete pattern of movement. This structure is similar, in concept and form, to some of Borges's stories. In "The Garden of Forking Paths," for instance, two plots and two notions of time are proposed and are so fit together through the action and thought that follow that at the end the reader is left puzzling which conception is the container and which the contained.

Although the struggle between human tragedy and divine comedy is never in any real sense resolved, there are moments in Isak Dinesen's tales when the characters seem to attain a point of release from their conflicts, a higher state, short-lived though it may be, in which they leave the personal perspective behind to unite with the very forces of existence themselves. This is a liquid state in which the substance and fixity of ideas, ideals, and social and personal forms have each yielded into their truer substance— force and energy. It is as if they have confronted and embraced the obstacle itself with such strength that it assumes clarity and liquid movement. It is a kind of reversal of Odysseus' wrestling match with Proteus. In these moments, the sea under Charlie's boats and the flood waters at Norderney have become spiritual principles: water is not outside but inside. Thus Lincoln loves Pellegrina because of the great strength she has attained in her new second life: like a well-sailed ship, she has not resisted but rather "allied herself with all the currents and winds of life. . . . There never seemed to be to her much difference between joy and pain, or between sad and pleasant things. They were all equally welcome to her, as if in her heart she knew them to be the same."

For Isak Dinesen, the reality of change is a truth and a principle of art, but as we have seen, not always an ecstasy. Perhaps, if we do not consummate our consciousness of the truth by so fully yielding to the forces of love that we drown in the literal waters of the sea, the only way, as beings both human and divine, that we can live in consonance with the truth is by alternating between what in our state must be two truths: between the flow of yearning and the obstacles of pain and denial.

Isak Dinesen's vision and art are expressed in their fullest maturity in *Seven Gothic Tales* and *Winter's Tales*. On either side of these two collections, so to speak, stand *Out of Africa* and her later tales. *Out of Africa*, though written after *Seven Gothic Tales*, looks back to a time in Isak Dinesen's own life when the two principles informing her work, a liquid oneness and confrontation, somehow seem magically to coexist or even reinforce each other.

We have the sense not of returning to our first paradise but of stumbling into a second paradise where the acceptance that God and the devil are one and that both love change has destroyed the low comic obstacles civilization has erected to kill the truth rather than risk the tremendous power of its joys, and has thus returned us to a more conscious innocence not separate from evil but somehow served by it. Both the passivity of the Kikuyu and the arrogance of the Masai allow them to bypass the efforts and laws that would prevent them from enjoying and experiencing the underlying unity that is Africa, though her manifestations may be eccentric and wrenching.

In facing the harshness of destiny, Dinesen found the creative principle that had been lacking in her early tales—she found her beginning. Forced to experience the extreme vision that Africa gave her—that God and the devil are one— she brought this truth, her sole possession, back to Europe and to European literary forms, and wrote her masterpieces, *Seven Gothic Tales*, *Out of Africa*, and *Winter's Tales*.

The tales she wrote after these three works, among them *Last Tales* and many of the selections in *Carnival*, seem to fall away from her central vision. There are exceptions: "A Country Tale" and "Converse at Night in Copenhagen" in *Last Tales* and "Second Meeting" in *Carnival*. But many of these later tales become Gothic in the usual sense of the word, what might be called bourgeois Gothic—shrill, like "Echoes"; grotesque, like "The Cardinal's Third Tale" and "The Blank Page"; intellectualized, like "The Cardinal's First Tale"; or confused and overly personal, like "Copenhagen Season" (all in *Last Tales*).

Yet reading these tales makes clearer the truly magical quality of Dinesen's best work. A story such as "The Cardinal's Third Tale" might be a brilliant statement of the doctrine that the story is more important than the characters, but is no more than a heartless doctrine if we have not read "The Roads Round Pisa." A story such as "The Fat Man" (*Carnival*) is perhaps a brilliant piece of psychological realism and a deftly told tale, but psychological realism and an ending with a twist are poor fare if we have read "The Monkey" or any number of her other tales. "Copenhagen Season" might be romantic and touching, but after reading "Sorrow Acre" we find the conception of the tragic in the later work unconvincing, a rationalization of a failure of nerve. "The Caryatids" and "The Bear and the Kiss"— except for its inner story, "The Glove"—might be appealing as thrillers of witchcraft and incest in the true Gothic vein, but the forces in Isak Dinesen's best tales are not those of witchcraft, but of the spirit. In these later tales, destiny seems to have lost its own destiny. (p. 16)

> *Elizabeth Ely Fuller, "Isak Dinesen: A Tale of Beginnings and Endings," in* New Boston Review *(copyright 1978 by Boston Critic, Inc.), Spring, 1978, pp. 14-16.*

ROSEMARY DINNAGE

Throughout [Dinesen's tales] runs a theme of common humanity surrendered in exchange for something else— pride? power? above all for the ability to turn life, with its muddle and pain, into art—exquisite where life is confused, heartless where life is passionate. (p. 15)

In *Carnival* and in *The Angelic Avengers* . . . we have the sweepings of Dinesen's work: the former made up chiefly of stories she discarded as not good enough for publication, the latter an "entertainment" written under a pseudonym during her time in Nazi-occupied Denmark. . . . [For] those who find the ruthlessness of her more serious work oppressive, *The Angelic Avengers* is a delightful romp, a Daphne du Maurier novel rewritten by Hans Andersen. The sultry presence of evil is there, as usual. . . . There is a touch of voodoo, a pact with Beelzebub, and some cannibalism; it is a romp nevertheless, for virtue triumphs, the charity of a virgin exorcises evil. . . . More seriously, the fact that it moves with pace and feeling, unlike some of Dinesen's more ambitious work, might be because she found herself happy with a fable about the redemption of the corrupt, i.e., the syphilitic [Dinesen suffered from syphilis]. The effect of her illness on her view of the writer as a dedicated being, yet cut off from common humanity, surely cannot be overestimated.

Carnival is chiefly for the Dinesen devotee, since most of the stories in it were rejected by the fastidious author. The usual ingredients are there, but often without the imaginative fusion of her best stories. The first two, however, written in Danish before she married, are interesting in showing that her early attempts at writing were fully in the vein of her later work: both are lightweight, ironic fables with the barest touch of cruelty. (pp. 16-17)

Will Blixen/Dinesen . . . come to be known more for her life than for her works? Of the books, *Seven Gothic Tales* and *Out of Africa,* the one with its extreme artifice and the other with its directness, will probably last the longest. But the pattern of her life is at least as remarkable a creation. . . . The survivor—*quod fecit, fecit*—is sometimes more frightening than the suicide. (pp. 17-18)

Rosemary Dinnage, in The New York Review of Books *(reprinted with permission from* The New York Review of Books; *copyright © 1978 NYREV, Inc.), May 4, 1978.*

* * *

DONLEAVY, J(ames) P(atrick) 1926-

Donleavy is an American-born Irish novelist, dramatist, and short story writer. Critics differ sharply on their assessment of Donleavy: some consider him a serious and original artist, others accuse him of continually mining the same vein that proved successful with his first novel, *The Ginger Man*. Most would agree, however, that his work is distinguished by its exuberant, idiosyncratic prose style, lusty, nonconforming anti-heros, and concern with finding peace and reason in an absurd world. (See also *CLC*, Vols. 1, 4, 6, and *Contemporary Authors*, Vols. 9-12, rev. ed.)

CHARLES G. MASINTON

[In] his most recent book, *The Unexpurgated Code: A Complete Manual of Survival and Manners* (1975), [as in his preceding works, Donleavy's] chief interest lies in exploiting for humorous effect the circumstances of the unpedigreed but desperately eager individual who seeks to join the ranks of the social elite. . . . Indeed, *The Unexpurgated Code* is the kind of book that the zany, non-conforming protagonist of *The Ginger Man,* Sebastian Dangerfield, very well might have written . . . had he decided, in rakish middle age, to reveal the rules by which he has managed not only to survive but also to prosper in a cutthroat society. (p. 210)

[Donleavy] uses his burlesque book of etiquette primarily as a vehicle for the expression of his great scorn for *all* elements in society—both ''high'' and ''low.'' The society he depicts—usually British in its demarcations of caste but sometimes suggesting an American milieu—is a freakish and sardonic distortion of the one we know, a cruelly comic caricature of the conventional social world. . . .

Donleavy's anger and disgust, which have always been a part of his humor, recurrently manifest themselves here in an impulse to scourge and satirize, though the impulse lacks

intellectual discipline and consistency and is, therefore, not fully realized. The bizarre social arena of the book mirrors a number of the follies and vices of humankind, and Donleavy concentrates his attack especially on those that either result from or help to preserve distinctions of class and rank. Moreover, his comic distortions are meant to reflect not only the anxiety that torments the socially inept but also the urge to dominate that so frequently underlies the desire for social prominence. (p. 211)

Quite clearly, and with gleeful malice aforethought, he has turned the standard book of etiquette on its head. Instead of treating distinctly proper matters with delicacy, in a manner that reflects well-received opinion, Donleavy examines subjects that range from the mildly sleazy to the utterly abominable and expresses, with arch disdain, attitudes about these seamy topics that harshly ridicule conventional society.

In its own terms, as a work of satiric low comedy, *The Unexpurgated Code* often succeeds marvelously well. It has laughter-provoking passages that display Donleavy's considerable powers as a sharp-eyed observer of human folly with a unique gift for creating droll scenes and funny dialogue. The pseudo-solemnity with which he approaches his deliberately inane or offensive material, and the modulations in tone that he manages to extract from this basic stance, in themselves demonstrate that this book issues from talent of a fairly high order. But in many instances the humor of *The Unexpurgated Code* flatly misses the mark and sharply disappoints.

One of the reasons is that Donleavy's comic routines have become too repetitious. . . . [*The Unexpurgated Code* is] a digest (randomly, randily set down) of the anxious antics that make it possible for Sebastian Dangerfield, George Smith (the protagonist of *A Singular Man),* Beefy (Balthazar's alter ego in *The Beastly Beatitudes of Balthazar B*), and Cornelius Christian (the central figure in *A Fairy Tale of New York*) to stay alive and preserve a sense of dignity or style in a vicious world. (pp. 212-13)

A second reason for serious shortcomings in the humor of *The Unexpurgated Code* is Donleavy's uncritical acceptance of inferior elements in his work. Too often he rests content with sophomoric jokes, uninspired name-calling, and rambling or irrelevant remarks on ''problems'' or situations that do not easily lend themselves to comic rendering (meditation, body odor, throwing food, dandruff, and the like). Naturally anything at all *might* be made amusing, but Donleavy's characteristic lack of intellectual detachment from or control over his material—that is, his failure to depend on the rational perception of limitations beyond which an action or gesture ceases to be funny—sometimes produces flat, heavy-handed attempts at humor that have no more wit or cleverness than the smirking solemnities of Ann Landers. His commentary on visiting the chiropodist or robbing banks, for instance, strains clumsily toward witty casualness but remains dull and inert.

The driving energy and originality, as well as the therapeutic rage and vulgarity, of *The Ginger Man* have never been equalled in Donleavy's later productions, quite possibly because he tends to rely on the fading impulses and feelings that inform that novel rather than on fresh experiences or new ideas. He has, however, matched its high level of performance in many chapters and scenes of succeeding books and has written three other generally excellent works of fiction: *A Singular Man, The Saddest Summer of Samuel S,* and *The Beastly Beatitudes of Balthazar B,* the last of which shows weaknesses only in the monotonously passive nature of the protagonist and in the excessive length of many sections of stream-of-consciousness narration that focus on his character. Deftness and control, clarity and restraint, and a sense of proportion—all implying esthetic and intellectual distance—are not the most salient or essential features of Donleavy's art. But the obvious need for a greater measure of these qualities in each book since *Balthazar* (*The Onion Eaters, A Fairy Tale of New York,* and, to a lesser degree, *The Unexpurgated Code*), without some wondrous inspiration like the one that shapes *The Ginger Man,* predictably means trouble for a writer whose forte is comedy. (pp. 213-14)

Donleavy normally proceeds by means of instinct, inspiration, and intuition—the tools of a romantic artist. He aims to produce belly laughs and (in the fiction) a sympathetic response to his chief characters; he does not set out to impose order and rationality on experience. And instead of elevated language (which he often parodies quite effectively), he records with great skill an earthy vernacular full of both comic and lyric possibilities.

But even on the level of farce and slapstick, and even with his taste for fictionalizing the chaotic Dionysian urges in preference to a spirit of Apollonian serenity, such aesthetic properties as clarity, formal control, and restraint qualify as artistic assets. If the first novel is buoyed up by an intensity of emotion and a matchless sense of discovery that make it consistently lively and explosively funny, the works that follows show signs of flagging energy and reveal an unfortunate habit of repeating its successful formulas. Since his art evolves primarily from feelings, which cannot always be held at a genuinely creative pitch, rather than ideas or concepts, which are longer-lasting if less immediately inspiring, this kind of literary entropy might well be inevitable. (pp. 214-15)

[This latest] uneven book will be read with a mixture of admiration and exasperation, for its flaws grow out of Donleavy's typical unwillingness to excise the amateurish portions of his writing.... If his talent is not to degenerate into self-parody, Donleavy would do well to acknowledge the need for a more rigorous critical attitude toward his future work and perhaps to consider whether or not he has exhausted the store of feeling and sensibility so richly present in *The Ginger Man.* (p. 215)

> *Charles G. Masinton, "Etiquette for Ginger Man: A Critical Assessment of Donleavy's 'Unexpurgated Code',"* in The Midwest Quarterly *(copyright, 1977, by The Midwest Quarterly, Kansas State College of Pittsburg), Winter, 1977, pp. 210-15.*

THOMAS LeCLAIR

Almost 20 years ago, before Ken Kesey's McMurphy, before Joseph Heller's Yossarian, "Dangerfield Lives" was on blackboards and toilet walls. Sebastian Dangerfield had scurried out of "The Ginger Man," J. P. Donleavy's first novel, into existence as the patron cad of the collegiate underground. His latest hero, Reginald Darcy Thormond Dancer Kildare, will never make the graffiti. The Donleavy hero hasn't grown up, just become more respectable, the

gentleman Dangerfield pretended to be in his homemade Trinity College rowing blues. Darcy Dancer lives, all right, but he is contained in this novel, where he won't be inspiring belief and attracting followers.

Create a cult hero and readers expect another one every time out or mistake their attraction for high art. So novels since "The Ginger Man" have been occasions to bemoan Donleavy's revisionism or debilities. But "The Destinies of Darcy Dancer, Gentleman" is not very different in quality from that first novel, when it is re-read and not just fondly remembered. While sensibility is sharper in "The Ginger Man," it and "Darcy Dancer," along with Donleavy's five other novels, are essentially literate entertainments, unpretentious picaresques with flaws that shouldn't be taken any more seriously than their pleasures. Repetition, simple-mindedness, even sentimentality are evident in Donleavy's previous works and here in "The Destinies of Darcy Dancer, Gentleman," too; they are part of the deal we have to make for the comedy and stutter-step prose. Like an ice show or circus, it's a good deal every two or three years. ("The Onion Eaters" excepted.)...

"The Destinies of Darcy Dancer, Gentleman" is a *bildungsroman,* though the succession of japes and scrapes makes one forget it. (p. 15)

In Donleavy's world luck and coincidence are destiny; energy rules. Places are pictures and names are jokes. The self is "I" one minute, "he" the next. Aristocratic codes are fabricated for the fun Donleavy has turning them against gentry and peasants alike. Property, food, drink and talk are the certainties. Especially talk: the humped syntax of farmers; the ecclesiastical intonations of retainers; the pukka formality of aristocrats—all are deflated by their own long hiss or the carefully chosen vulgarity.

Darcy's early moonings are just silly, but his reveries while being chased by huntsmen or while making love have a fine comic irrelevance, a mixture of accents and odd perceptions. The big set pieces go off well. (p. 20)

> *Thomas LeClair, "Bildungsroman Irish-Style,"* in The New York Times Book Review *(© 1977 by The New York Times Company; reprinted by permission), November 6, 1977, pp. 15, 20.*

RUTH MATHEWSON

When J. P. Donleavy's first novel, *The Ginger Man,* was published ..., it created something of a stir, especially among young readers who saw its hero, Sebastian Dangerfield, as an attractive representative of their generation. Less impressed were some critics, who found the book at best a celebration of adolescent wishfulfillment. They would not be surprised by the shallowness of Donleavy's seventh novel, *The Destinies of Darcy Dancer, Gentleman....*

I, on the other hand, now see in *The Ginger Man* an unfulfilled promise. Dangerfield, a GI in Dublin, a Yank in Trinity, was an interesting new hero.... And it seems to me that Donleavy had seized upon a valid idea—to place in Dublin, where the average citizen feels "like an outcast from life's feast" (Joyce's phrase is implicit in the book), a man with an insatiable appetite; a man who, observing that "67 per cent of the population have never been completely naked," is himself, for reasons of bohemian poverty or sexual activity, seldom clothed. Yet the full possibilities of the concept were unrealized. There was no real reciprocity between Dangerfield and the Irish, or any recognition that it was lacking. Perhaps the model for *The Ginger Man* was Henry Miller's *The Tropic of Cancer*—sexual acrobatics, brutality to women, cadging, flight, and all. Donleavy used Ireland as Miller used France, as a backdrop for enacting a dream of sexual freedom.

Darcy Dancer shows us that his heroes have never abandoned this dream. But it is difficult to determine whether this mock-innocent account of the young squire's sexual adventures on his Anglo-Irish country estate and in Dublin is meant to produce the effects of an old-fashioned pornographic novel, or merely to parody them. Parody—or at least imitation—is suggested, too, by the fact that Dancer, like Tom Jones, is a bastard. . . .

As in Donleavy's earlier books, nature and atmosphere are often vividly conveyed, and the author provides some sharp, funny talk when Dancer is cast out of his estate to wander the countryside and find work in the stables of a newly-rich family. On the whole, though, this "bawdy," "lusty," "gamy" novel is a bore. Sebastian Dangerfield at least stirred strong feelings pro and con. About Darcy Dancer, Gentleman, regrettably, it is impossible to care. (p. 17)

> *Ruth Mathewson, in* The New Leader (© *1977 by the American Labor Conference on International Affairs, Inc.), December 19, 1977.*

KEN LAWLESS

[*The Destinies of Darcy Dancer, Gentleman*] affords the reader all the delights of a master working at the top of his form. No literary artist working in English today is better than J. P. Donleavy, and few merit comparison with him. . . .

This new work is an important part of a significant oeuvre. The Donleavy eye for sensual detail is sharp as ever, the ear for idiomatic dialogue still perfect. The Donleavy themes—friendship, the family, loneliness—make up in importance what they lack in fashion. The chapter ending poems are as wonderful as ever. . . . It is too late to be discovering that J. P. Donleavy is a very great writer, although this . . . book is ample proof. It would be an interesting stunt to review a Donleavy work without mentioning "The Ginger Man" because even without that book his achievement would put him in the first rank, but it is time to realize that "The Ginger Man" did not place this artist in a sort of permanent Sophomore Slump. To state this in plain terms—the author of "The Ginger Man" has written yet another wonderful book with many of the virtues of that comic masterpiece and some interesting variations. (p. 128)

> *Ken Lawless, in* The Antioch Review (*copyright © 1978 by The Antioch Review, Inc.; reprinted by permission of the editors), Vol. 36, No. 1, 1978.*

NICHOLAS MOSLEY

It is difficult to write a life-affirming novel nowadays: too much is known about the tawdriness and shams of almost all levels of society, and a novel that does not have a social context is exposed to the sterilising rays of subjectivity. It is J. P. Donleavy's great achievement to have created both

a style of writing and a subject-matter [in *The Destinies of Darcy Dancer, Gentleman*] that are exuberantly in praise of life, and yet not too fantastical to seem true. . . .

J. P. Donleavy's last book was the extremely funny *The Unexpurgated Code: A Complete Manual of Survival and Manners*: this new novel is an even funnier (and much more touching) illustration of this code. It is picaresque in that it rambles on in the manner of some 18th-century novel about rogues: sometimes its extravagances drop over into the realm of fantasy. But what seem to me to be truly and uniquely life-affirming about it are the connections that exist between the story, the style, and what life seems to be about.

In Donleavy's writing there is an almost magically potent blend of the vulgar and the elegant, the grotesque and the lyrical, the archaic and the lewdly up-to-date. The vulgarity is part of the stuff of life: what is also part of life is the elegance and nobility with which human beings can, sometimes, handle the other, darker part—can come to terms with it and even love it. These opposites are held together in Mr Donleavy's writing in the person of the narrator in a quite self-conscious way: the narrator writes of himself now in the first person and now in the third—as if he were naturally aware of himself as in part foolish and helpless, and in part detached and with some possibilities of control. His sentences, his repartee, in the way they bring the vulgar and the elegant together, are often weirdly witty—as if in this there is authority and potency. Other characters with whom he has sympathy come to talk in his style: it is as if life-affirmation were held in an elaborate network of human wittiness. . . .

Donleavy ends each of his chapters with one of those brief four- or six-line poems that have become a hallmark of his writing. These, too, seem to be distillations, like pearls or tears, of all the stresses and strains that have gone before. They seem to say: in life, there is a lot of dross, yes; there are also small bits of gold and diamond, which, if you find them, are worth more than all the rest put together.

> *Nicholas Mosley, "Bits of Gold," in* The Listener (© *British Broadcasting Corp. 1978; reprinted by permission of Nicholas Mosley), May 11, 1978, p. 618.*

* * *

DORN, Ed(ward) 1929-

Dorn is an American poet, short story writer, critic, novelist, essayist, and editor. He was a student at Black Mountain College and his work shows the influence of Charles Olson and the techniques of projectivist verse. Lyrical and loosely structured, Dorn's poetry often explores patterns of American life: in particular, the frontier, the culture of the American West, the primitivism of the Indians. Considered in many ways political, his writing varies from the allegorical and humorous to the philosophically complex.

PETER ACKROYD

Edward Dorn is one of the two or three best American poets now writing. . . .

Dorn *is* very much an American poet, and he has created a distinctively American idiom. . . . [*Gunslinger* is] a specifically American work, using a dissonance which jars the European ear and a melodramatic virility which used to be characteristic of "the frontier" myth. The poems [in *The Collected Poems, 1956-1974*] show this language in the making; the earliest in the book are placed within that blank landscape, and within some long, emphatic lines which go right back to Whitman. . . . But Dorn sometimes makes his points too well:

> In America every art has to reach toward
> some clarity. That is our hope from the
> start.

English poets have also practised clarity, with varying degrees of success, for some centuries now; in fact, it is a general mistake of American writers to confuse clarity with sincerity. As Dorn puts it:

> It is a *real* mystique, not a
> mystique. A mystique of the real.

Statements like this, which have nothing very much to do with his achieved poetry, have often led to Dorn being confused with such poets as Robert Creeley or Gary Snyder; they also believed in "the real" but for them it was all mixed up with a tacky orientalism and a wheedling, hysterical adolescence. Clap your hands if you still believe in Allen Ginsberg.

From the start, Dorn had too firm an ear and too clear a vision to become involved with all that fiddle. The "real" in his early poetry is natural without being in the least sentimental, and this book marks the strength of his poetic progress from collection to collection—until he can now turn his poetry to a reality both more public and at the same time more intractable. The language is harder, the rhythms less fluent, and the whole exercise more individual than his earlier work. . . . (p. 17)

This is, if nothing else, a poetry of statement and with verse like this Edward Dorn has become the only plausible, political poet in America. Political poetry has nothing whatever to do with the extent of the poet's political knowledge, his *savoir faire,* or even the 'side' he takes; it has to do with the quality of his response to public situations, not whether that response is 'right' or 'wrong'. Dorn has created a lyrical, descriptive language which can effectively convey that quality. . . . What the "real" comes to mean for Dorn is the identity of the speaker and what is spoken, with something like an Orphic spirit, and in a culture which depends for its most splendid effects upon various forms of separation . . . this stance is in itself very much a political one. And this sense of connection—whether it be between the self and its proper place, or between the object and its exact role— leads Dorn to some very clear observations:

> All the children
> were taught the pledge of Allegiance, and
> the land was pledged
> to private use, the walnut dropped in the
> autumn on the ground
> green, and lay black in the dead grass in the
> spring.

This is a direct but not an unmusical language; its harmony comes from the specific depth of the words, rather than from assonance and polyphony: in other words, the lines cling to a simulacrum of truth, to a true and local voice.

The 'truth' of poetry can sometimes, of course, be painfully banal and there are certain poems in this collection which

are marred by amateur historicism and by a rhetorical use of the language of economics. . . . Dorn's proper achievement has been to create single-handedly a language of public reference, and to have brought within the sphere of expressive language and poetic experience objects and feelings which had been, literally, *unimaginable* in those terms. It is in this context that he is one of the masters of our contemporary language. (pp. 17-18)

> *Peter Ackroyd, "In Public," in* The Spectator *(© 1975 by* The Spectator; *reprinted by permission of* The Spectator)*, January 10, 1975, pp. 17-18.*

MARJORIE PERLOFF

Like his shape-shifting protagonist Gunslinger, that archetypal hero of the Wild West who also happens to be a Greek Sun God and a sophisticated New Philosopher expounding on Heidegger . . . , Edward Dorn has been unrolling the map of locations for some 20 years now, and the publication of [*The Collected Poems: 1956-1974* and *Slinger*] should finally earn Dorn the reputation he deserves as one of a handful of important poets writing in America today.

If Dorn has never been widely known . . . , the reasons are not hard to find. Dorn began his career at Black Mountain College in the shadow of Charles Olson, his acknowledged master. . . .

Yet despite such thematic links, Dorn is really quite unlike Olson; he is, for that matter, quite unlike any poet writing today. To call him a "regional poet" (he refers to himself as "a poet of the West—not by nativity but by orientation"), misses the mark, for his central concerns are metaphysical and have, finally, nothing to do with his chosen region, the American West. . . . [Despite] his use of drugworld *argot* and political invective, his poetry is decidedly more tempered, more detached, more humorous than that of, say, Allen Ginsberg. Finally, and most important, Dorn, as he himself insists, is a narrative poet—an unusual condition today when the norm tends to be the fragmented lyric or open-ended sequence. (p. 22)

"The Rick of Green Wood" (1956), which opens *The Collected Poems,* contains most of Dorn's typical stylistic traits. It begins:

> In the woodyard were green and dry
> woods fanning out, behind
>   a valley below
> a pleasure for the eye to go.
>
> Woodpile by the buzzsaw. I heard
> the woodsman down in the thicket. I don't
> want a rick of green wood, I told him
> I want cherry or alder or something
>   strong
> and thin, or thick if dry, but I don't
> want the green wood, my wife would die
>
> Her back is slender
> and the wood I get must not
> bend her too much through the day.
>
> Aye, the wood is some green
> and some dry, the cherry thin of bark
> cut in July.
>
> My name is Burlingame
> said the woodcutter.

> My name is Dorn, I said.
> I buzz on Friday if the weather cools
> said Burlingame, enough of names.

Compare this to Frost's famed "The Woodpile" and Dorn's originality becomes apparent. What begins in low key as a narrative about the purchases of some firewood is made new by Dorn's idiosyncratic syntax and lineation, his off beat rhymes, his peculiar mixture of high and low styles, of realism and fantasy. It makes no sense, for example, for the poet to say, "I don't / want the green wood, my wife would die," especially since he is himself obviously drawn to it. But the non sequitur underscores Dorn's theme, which is the "pied beauty" and fragility of this special moment in November, before the cold sets in, before things "bend." (pp. 22-3)

Dorn is less successful when he tries to incorporate history into his poems. . . . His is the lyric of geography, not of history. Accordingly, his overtly political poems are often simplistic and one-dimensional. . . .

Yet in the same years that Dorn was writing . . . angry political poems, he also composed some of the freshest, most natural love poems of our time—lyrics full of warmth, wit and gentle self-deprecation. . . .

But charming as Dorn's short lyrics are, in terms of scope and accomplishment, they must take second place to *Slinger,* Dorn's four-part epic poem begun in 1968, which is, I believe, one of the masterpieces of contemporary poetry. . . . [Plot] and characterization are subordinated throughout to Dorn's theme, which is the opaqueness of language, the mystery of human identity, the impossibility of getting meaningful answers to one's questions. (p. 24)

[Dorn's] feat is that he incorporates his phenomenological esthetic into the frame of the familiar Western. (p. 25)

Homonyms, puns, nonsense words, coinages, archaisms, jingly rhymes, ballad tunes, guitar notes, abstract nouns embedded in prepositional phrases—*Gunslinger* is a collage of all these things. . . . The poem's form perfectly embodies Dorn's theme that nothing is what it seems to be. (pp. 25-6)

[There] are inevitably some dull stretches, particularly in "The Cycle" (Book III), which often seems too abstract, too clever in its parodies of Blake, and its allusions to modern physics and Parmenides. Dorn himself recognizes that the later books are more abstract than the first, which is filmlike in its intensity. But *Slinger* is surely one of the most ambitious and interesting long poems of our time, a truly original cowboy-and-Indian saga, rendered in the most ingenious mix of scientific jargon, Structuralist terminology, junkie slang, Elizabethan sonneteering, Western dialect, and tough talk about kicking "a gorilla in the balls." Indeed, the real hero of *Slinger* is neither Gunslinger nor the curious "I" but language itself, the language of our time, refracted, distorted, heightened, but always recognizable as the jumble of speech we hear around us and see in print. When, at the end of the poem, Slinger announces his departure:

> But it grieves me in some slight way
> because this has been such fine play
> and I'll miss this marvellous accidentalism

the reader can only agree. The "fine play" of *Slinger*—its "marvellous accidentalism"—is quite literally *horse play,*

but horse play so learned and witty that it makes most of our long poetic sequences, with their obsessive confessional momentum, look like child's play. (p. 26)

> *Marjorie Perloff, in* The New Republic *(reprinted by permission of* The New Republic; © *1976 by The New Republic, Inc.), April 24, 1976, pp. 22-6.*

BILL ZAVATSKY

Dorn, who notes that his work is "theoretical in nature," is vehemently not in search of the well-crafted poem, though his best work [in "The Collected Poems: 1956-1974"] needs no avant-garde disclaimers to support it. (pp. 32, 34)

Despite his esthetic caveat, Dorn is best when most focused, and the zeroing in comes when he speaks clearly of what is directly in front of him, either in memory or in landscape. His longer works like "Idaho Out" blur with rhetoric when the poet begins philosophizing, and sharpen instantaneously when he moves us with the portrait of a woman in a bar:

> So there you are. She is
> as ripe and bursting as that
> biblical pomegranate.
> She bleeds spore in her
> undetachable black pants
> and, not to make it seem too good
> or too unlikely near
> she has that
> kind of generous smile
> offset by a daring and hostile look. . . .

Dorn's shorter poems retain this clarity, particularly those lyrics he has chosen to group throughout the book under the rubric of "Song."

With Dorn's move to England in the mid-60's, his work for a time grew overtly political, that is, preachy. . . . His (perhaps temporary) need to slam his reader over the head with politics is unfortunate, for all of Dorn's work is inherently political, needing no soapbox. . . .

Dorn's poetic strength has rested not on the "dazzle of learning" he admits to loving but on his capacity to feel with language the lives and the life of the land he knows best. . . . When in "Like a Message on Sunday" he speaks of his town's "forlorn plumber" and the man's daughter, and bids that "their failure be kindly, and come in small unnoticeable pieces," he touches the world that all of us can feel. (p. 34)

> *Bill Zavatsky, in* The New York Times Book Review *(© 1976 by The New York Times Company; reprinted by permission), October 17, 1976.*

DONALD WESLING

Dorn writes in his Preface (1974) to the *Collected Poems* that for him the work is ratiocinative, not bardic: "From near the beginning I have known my work to be theoretical in nature and poetic by virtue of its inherent tone." . . . [This] affiliates Dorn, in this regard only, with more recent figures such as Stevens and Ammons, with Olson of course, and with the open-field poetry which represents in its sequences of syllables and perceptions the act of the mind. Both in theory and in tone, particularly in the managing of transitions, the drive of thought in an extended meditation like "The Land Below," the declarative qualities are Wordsworthian. . . . [As] a writer whose work is theoretical in nature he wants us to respond to the cogency, precision of detail, and political credibility of his account of American reality. (pp. 142-43)

The end-and-cover maps on some of Dorns's books are symptoms of the need to make the geographical relations particular, while images of a detonator, grenades, revolvers on at least three covers suggest one central concern: the marvellous American competence, in its benign use so humane and liberating, is also an energy that can be deflected into violence that is swift, even scientific, aesthetic. In a poetry that proposes to itself such a degree of inclusiveness, the themes which absorb other American writers —the nature of poetry; landscape and perception; heightened states of consciousness; primitivism; fraternity and sexuality—are by no means de-emphasized; they are merely secondary. At its largest stretch the theoretical concerns are political and economic. . . . The hiddenness of contemporary power, which makes all of us victims in some measure and which has brought into much recent American history and writing the theme of the unseen assailant, becomes matter for comedy in the characters' quest for "an inscrutable Texan named Hughes" in *Gunslinger:* "Howard? I asked / the very same / . . . . He / has not been seen since 1833." Yet it would be wrong to conclude, from any review of such themes, that "theoretical in nature" means the defecated-to-a-transparency free-verse style of a starved diction and predictable syntax. (pp. 143-44)

The adequate theory realizes its own limits. For Dorn as for other Black Mountain writers theory, like the poem, is not enough: not commensurate with politics, the world, or experience itself in its "presyntactic metalinguistic urgency." (That phrase from *Gunslinger* II, a joking contradiction, demonstrates how Dorn can shoot academic phrases with the best). Hence a certain sadness, and an ethical and prosodic assignment. (p. 144)

Peter Ackroyd, in an accurate short review [see excerpt above], argues Dorn's poetry of statement makes him "the only plausible political poet in America," and then goes on to say political poetry "has nothing whatever to do with the extent of the poet's political knowledge, his *savoir faire,* or even the 'side' he takes; it has to do with the quality of his response to public situations, not whether that response is 'right' or 'wrong.'" The first reaction to Ackroyd, not my own, is the question: what, then, is so special about Dorn's response that makes it qualitatively superior to Lowell's, Ginsberg's, or Bly's? One answer to that would be to show the nature of Dorn's analysis of the way things work, which moves very often on the level of world-systems and commodities as well as the level of personal experience; to a greater extent he situates the psychological and individualist possibilities within a larger frame of reference. . . . As against the élitist pseudo-theology of poetry, which is always in our century associated with reactionary politics, Dorn belongs *in the direction* of Lautréamont. It is not the first time (I think of Wordsworth, Whitman, and Mayakovsky) that a poet writing for all the people had a certain degree of difficulty for some of the people.

The people: not the masses, and certainly not the public. Thus "for America" in my title, and thus Dorn's transfiguration of the genres of popular culture in his writing. (pp. 146-47)

The trouble with setting up as people's poet in North America . . . is, in one of Dorn's images, that so many of one's fellow citizens are complicit constabulary driving pickups with shotgun racks. (p. 147)

Collected Poems includes a book of 1967, *The North American Turbine,* the most penetrating attempt any American poet has made at an inquiry, in and through imaginative thinking, into the world system of trade, control, and oppression. . . . It can only be asserted here that the six parts of the *Turbine* poem "Oxford," enabled by a lyrical line of great prosodic interest and variety, move through paradox and humor to an analysis (idiosyncratic but highly searching) of multinational capitalism and of reasons why the American poet needn't be overwhelmed by the weight of European culture. . . . We may call this socialist or populist poetry but it tends in a certain direction, and must freeze out a certain readership of those who are unnerved by any attempt to analyze and denounce. Yet those who are willing to follow an argument wherever it goes, who can accept that a political poetry can also move by zaniness, hesitation, wit, laconicism, sudden bursts of speed, metaphorical leap, as well as by statement and denunciation, will find the arbitrariness justified. (pp. 148-49)

Turbine includes "An Idle Visitation," a strange and dazzling poem which does not fit with the others there, and which becomes the germ of *Gunslinger.* . . . This long laughing anti-epic of the American Southwest is a kind of comedy of dogmatism, parodic and even self-parodic, the evanescence of space and time relations and even of capitalism, and the entrance into the new dimension of what he has called *intensity.* (A difficult term, related to a shift in the focus in Dorn's writing: from the particularity of place to the power of analytical theory which enables the poet, like the scientist perhaps, to reduce empiricism.) One's initial response to it is a kind of excited apprenticeship, of the sort which must have greeted the appearance of Williams's *Paterson,* and the politics of the thing are so far under the surface that we cannot even estimate the extent of the complexities before us. (p. 150)

The allusions: from Parmenides to Heidegger, Lévi-Strauss, the drug culture, the oil industry, the Lone Ranger, Delmore Schwartz, a heap of arcane and obvious cultural clutter. The language: "derives from a combination of western soap opera, newspeak, rock-and-roll lyric, scientific-cybernetic argot, Shelleyan rhapsody, and comic strip dialogue" (Michael Davidson). The allegory: finally, I suspect, this repeats in a finer tone *Turbine's* interest in money's fundamental unreality as metal and paper and trust, and the way this is combined with absolute power by virtue of being *turned into* labor and commodities, creating here a Hughes, there a "Scarcity Industry." (p. 151)

Gunslinger, though, tends to resist description. It is "about" how and why we spend money and words in this "cosmological" place; about, and enacting through puns, surreal imagery, personifications, the texture of jokes, the paradoxical aspects of thinking; about how a narrative line snares attention despite or because of derangements; and about how a self or voice can be differentiated into a cluster of other selves, which then have a quasilife of their own as voices-in-recitative. [In an interview for *Vort,* Barry] Alpert asked: "Where's your personal presence in *Gunslinger?"* Dorn: "Omnipresent. It's omnipresent, absolutely omnipresent. . . . Actually I'm absolutely uncommitted except to what's happening.'' So the first person singular, in an apotheosis of the dramatic monologue, is first eliminated (we remember the death of the character ''I''), and then reintroduced as an omnipresence by a poet who in the same interview says he believes in ''the shared mind.'' This is not, in my experience of the poem, in any way contradictory, but it makes for a very high degree of opacity as we struggle, in the absence of nearly all clues of punctuation or quotation marks, to find which of the particular voices is speaking at a given moment. That frustration is built in, intentional, and one of the pleasures of the poem when you finally discover the mechanism. Dorn in this poem followed the freedom of his *donnée,* and that that was good and necessary should become clearer the longer we live with and in the poem. Eventually an account of *Gunslinger* will demonstrate how, without contradiction, those complexities of matter and perspective, now so forbidding and, yes, disturbingly Eliotic in the seeming absence of a center, are really clarifying developments of a consistent lifework which is populist and ''for America.'' . . . (pp. 152-53)

Dorn's interest in the American Indian [and in primitivism] reaches back at least as far as the ending of his long poem of the early sixties, ''The Land Below.'' . . . The *Collected Poems* refer to native Americans often, to their ancient rites and, like the ''Sacagawea wearing a baseball cap, eating a Clark bar,'' their present condition. (p. 153)

Three books, though, are the cynosures of Dorn's thinking here: the 1965 Berkeley lecture, *The Shoshoneans,* and *Recollections of Gran Apachería.* The first two, in prose and dealing with modern Shoshonis who live in reservations in the basin plateau surrounding the Great Salt Lake, are essential not only in their themes but also in the combined manner of simple declaration and arctic indirection which is the substance of all Dorn's poetry as well. *Recollections* is a gathering of twenty-seven poems which present the nineteenth-century history of American vs. American Indian encounter with the fierce Apaches, whom Dorn considers ''noble / not in themselves / so much as in their Ideas.'' (p. 154)

Dorn's writing partakes of the style of a school, and exploits and focuses a language similar to that of Olson, Creeley, Blackburn, Duncan, Jonathan Williams. The loosely-collected group style known as Black Mountain may be generally indicated in its premises by Robert Duncan's phrase ''mind is shapely,'' or William Carlos Williams' ''the poet thinks with his poem.'' . . . ''The Rick of Green Wood,'' from 1956 and the first item printed in *Collected Poems,* shows Dorn completely capable with free verse techniques, and this from the beginning at a higher level than Olson. . . . Dorn's lines [in *Gunslinger*] are not anything like parcelled-out iambs in blank verse, or like Whitmanic one-line units, and yet they do have an equality of length that is (despite other frustrations, and there are many) reassuring. The long poem's intent to develop a narrative, mostly by means of dialogue, meant retracting somewhat in prosodic format from the earlier, forbidding masterworks.

In *Gunslinger,* the reader's difficulties are not primarily formal but in the hip metaphysics of point of view, voice, and concept. Yet the poem's prosodies enact its play of ideas and wit, and so doing are a summation of many of Dorn's own achieved stylistic gestures as well as Black

Mountain's. For instance, the lowly equivalence of the pun, so often an isolated effect in Olson or the spring of a whole poem in Jonathan Williams, is here made part of the speech of imagined characters in the continuous texture of a paradoxical discourse:

> Just then a Drifter carrying
> a divine guitar
> passed by our table and the guise
> inlaid around the string cut hole
> pulsated as do
> stars in the ring
> of a clear night
> Hi! Digger
> the drifting guitarist greeted
> the Bombed Horse
> who was in his saddle bags
> rummaging
> Heidigger? I asked . . .

As a local effect, too, it shares in the whole poem's pervasive ambiguity of languages and selves, wherein the talk floats between nodes of the shared mind. (pp. 155-56)

The dictions are multiple, then, and to match them the syntax is duplicitous: I waive illustration by quotation, and merely urge that the book be opened anywhere so that the reader may be pleasurably lost in a fabric where relations merge, where punctuation is deliberately sparse, and where the very pages are unnumbered. These are all prosodic categories in the large sense, and not least the punctuation, salient by the functional ambiguities it creates in its absence, and very beautiful in its design when present in dashes, caps, italics, or adorned or outsized typefaces. . . . Irresolution, the creation of cognitive frustration, is on this showing the intent of both form and meaning in the poem.

Dorn justifies the arbitrariness of his measures in rant (''The Cosmology of Finding Your Place''), redundancy (''Thesis''), witty social exploration (parts of ''Oxford''), nostalgia (''The Air of June Sings,'' ''Hemlocks''), tribute (''From Gloucester Out,'' ''Sousa,'' ''Mourning Letter''), and the love song, among other generic-prosodic types. Close inspection turns up a rich working of rhyme-effects, almost always as instance rather than anterior-to-the-poem or line-end design. . . . Typically, the attractiveness of the sounds in his ''Rick of Green Wood,'' or in a line like ''The banding of her slightsmiling lassitude,'' is always poised against the wryness of the thinking. Among Black Mountain writers he is the master of the singing line, and the use of that skill of prosodic speed and accuracy in the service of ambitious public concerns makes for his real distinctiveness. (pp. 156-57)

[Dorn's] is, then, a political poetry which, in addition to being declarative and with no diminishment of theory, is philosophical, affectionate, subtle, singing, and humorous. Dorn writes in ''Idaho Out'': ''My desire is to be / a classical poet.'' He is. (p. 158)

> *Donald Wesling, ''A Bibliography on Edward Dorn for America,''* in Parnassus: Poetry in Review *(copyright © by Poetry in Review Foundation), Spring-Summer, 1977, pp. 142-60.*

WILLIAM J. LOCKWOOD

Ed Dorn is one of the most clear-minded and consistently

serious poets in the contemporary scene. A firm conviction that underlies his work is the belief that because the New World of the North American continent offers to the poet a new set of materials, a new set of possibilities for poetry becomes available to him. If he is aware of that truth, he will refuse "look[ing] back as the sluggish beast europe / at a residue of what was merely heaped up." Rather, Dorn suggests, "Our possibility is to sheer off what / is only suggested," meaning, as I take it, to objectify ("sheer off") what lies implicit in a scene or an occasion. By that route he will go on to forge a new art out of new materials. . . . (p. 58)

Dorn has given very careful thought to the idea of subject matter in his writing. Two statements, one in the form of an epigraph to "Idaho Out" in 1965 and the other a remark made during an interview in 1974, attest to his persistent thoughtfulness in this regard. At the beginning of "Idaho Out" he makes Carl O. Sauer's words a declaration of his own conviction: "The thing to be known is the natural landscape. It becomes known through the totality of its forms." (p. 59)

Dorn's idea of art based on new materials brings up the larger question I should like to raise in the course of this discussion . . . : that is, the question of the relationship between ideas of artistic integrity and the need to involve the reader in the experience of the poem. Matters of personality and stance arise, and the question is intensified by the problems inherent in writing the kind of long poem Dorn is drawn to and which, before the creation of *Gunslinger*, he attempts in "Idaho Out."

Before addressing that question, however, it will be instructive to examine the nature of Dorn's materials—the range of his landscape and the dynamics of human movement within it that concern him. In the prose pieces collected in *Some Business Recently Transacted in the White World,* we find something equivalent to William Carlos Williams' *In the American Grain.* Fascinating in themselves, they exhibit the whole range of Dorn's territory—territory here conceived of both as a physical entity and as a conceptual field. They range geographically from the remote northeastern corner of the American continent through the Midwest out to the westernmost reaches of the northern Great Plains, and express Dorn's concern for the fate of the men and women who live their lives in those places.

"A Narrative with Scattered Nouns" takes us to the northern coastal region of Massachusetts and opens with a miscellany of notes about the speaker's process of acculturation there. (p. 60)

The idea of place is not simply a sentimental one here; rather it involves, for Dorn, a truly sympathetic involvement of mind, one that allows the phenomena of that place to be understood as a totality. Beneath the mimetic surface of his writing lies a Platonic concern not with landscape so much as with landforms, not with men so much as with their mindforms, and this becomes evident in his "Of Eastern Newfoundland, Its Inns and Outs." . . . Here a closed-off, harsh world is revealed, a world closed off especially in the minds of the people who inhabit it. (p. 62)

The wide range of Dorn's transactions in *Some Business Recently Transacted* is intriguing, and in all cases "transaction" seems to be the correct word. Instead of an egocentric travelogue, one discovers here an attempt to understand the "singularity" of each place he visits. This activity of mind does not simply proceed out of the "bird's-eye view" of a Burke or a Goldsmith recounting his travels through foreign lands; rather it is an intensive survey and outward projection, a kind of open letter from a guerilla-like explorer of the unnoticed territory of one's own native continent. (p. 63)

"C. B. & Q.," like the other letters or reports, strongly suggests this larger purpose of informing most of us parochial white Americans of the geographical and cultural totality of which we are a part. But it also projects a set of images and a system of human dynamics in terms of which we may see ourselves actually mirrored—both in the vague rootlessness we feel and in the impulse toward irrational behavior we may believe we have successfully domesticated in our social lives. The piece begins by locating a restaurant called Tiny's in a small, remote, and unnamed town seven miles west of Belle Fourche, South Dakota. Dorn's northern Plains setting consists of a grain elevator standing behind the restaurant on a half desert which extends west to Montana, though in the minds of the railroad workers who hang out at Tiny's location is less firm, their talk being dominated by references to more exotic places like Denver, Kansas City, Wichita, and even Tucson and Albuquerque. Across the scene thus established moves Buck, a drifter and off-and-on section worker.

The complex narrative of this piece, taking place in three different, intersecting time periods—time present, time past, and ongoing time present—serves as a vehicle for Dorn's exploration of the dynamics of the nomadic pattern of American life. The flashback, within the time present narrative framework as defined by the opening Plains backdrop, gives us the journey that brought Buck to South Dakota from Kansas City. (p. 64)

This, then, is the range of Dorn's "territory," a spatial and a conceptual field for his "sheering off" the forms implicit in the landscape and in the lives of the men who live there. Equal to its extensive and intensive dimensions is the mind of the poet himself, who declares of his own Illinois hometown, "It is my place but not my time. Any place can be mine. Time is irrelevant." . . . A unique standpoint thus emerges in Dorn's work. It is not, as Donald Davie acutely observes, a fixed point: "It is a moving point, the continually changing standpoint of a man who is on the move across continents and oceans. Thom Gunn exhorts us to be "on the move," but Dorn *gives us* this man moving . . . his standpoint changing as he moves, yet conditioned by the terrain it moves through and over, as much as the consciousness which occupies the moving point." . . . Dorn manages to create a poem that sustains the objectivity and intensity of this standpoint, yet succeeds in involving the reader's sympathetic imagination in the experience of it. . . . (pp. 66-7)

We approach a long, asymmetrical poem that attempts to project into a spatial field the totality of forms that lie between Pocatello, Idaho and Missoula, Montana. It records, through the loose narrative of a drive by car, images of the landforms of the area and also the mindforms imposed on that space by the history of human habitation in it. (pp. 67-8)

Through the sheer intensity of the rendered images, Dorn draws the reader into the experience of the poem. . . . And despite the hostile electricity in the atmosphere, that vitality and feeling for the place is powerful indeed. (p. 68)

In "Idaho Out," . . . Dorn's strings are attuned to a tough-minded questioning. His song is harsh and alive as it names the rocks, celebrating them even as the occasion forms itself in the mind of the speaker as journeyman. His very setting out comes to involve an idea of responsibility for the place—which is, finally, one's own—and for the distinctive features of it, good and bad. For Dorn as poet, Idaho possesses a singularity that he has in a sense been commissioned to explore by way of its discrete and observable phenomena. Consequently, we learn that our own role as fellow travelers in this journey is not that of the tourist, but of the discoverer; this role involves our instruments of intellection, by the operation of which we begin to acquire a knowledge of the totality of forms present here. But we also find that the totality is shadowed and complex. Its discovery involves not simply intellection but intuition as well, that is to say an alteration of consciousness produced by the experience of the journeying motion itself. (p. 69)

The remarkable success of "Idaho Out"—in its own terms and perhaps also as a pattern of possibility for other contemporary poets—is that it overcomes the dangers while preserving the virtues and qualities of Dorn's idea of a poem. It remains "an instrument of intellection" whose singular qualities may be located in its remarkable intensity and clarity; and it sustains the integrity of the poet's stance as a non-bourgeois man of moderation, self-possession, and temperance. But, without relying upon easy, possibly distorting rhetorical techniques, Dorn has also succeeded in involving the reader in a kind of Homeric experience: first by the choice of the narrative form, using it to supply a large visual field, one that, in itself—given the physical topography of the journey—supplies clear bearings for the audience; and next, by establishing within it a vital, undulating, asymmetrical rhythm in terms of which the projected images are comprehended in an essentially human context. This combination—of a large visual field and, within it, an anticipation of recurrences—allows the reader, initially caught in the impetus of the setting out, to cooperate in the transfer, to his own mind, of the discrete images the poet ideally perceives. Dorn thus persists in his allegiance to a tough-minded and rigorous art, uncontaminated by worries about conventional manners or ideas of usefulness. But in "Idaho Out" he succeeds (as he does not always succeed) in establishing a close and fruitful relationship to his audience, one that implies the pattern of realized and unrealized human bonds defined in the poem itself. (pp. 74-5)

Since the publication of *Gunslinger, Book I*, in 1968, Dorn seems to have adopted the American Southwest as his "home" territory, and has made the exploration of interior rather than linear space the chief business of his poetry. The southwestern landscape would seem to supply to his creative imagination those elements of brightness, clarity, and austerity that correspond to the forms of his own mind and appear as the distinctive qualities of the best of his early poems. (p. 75)

The Southwest's spare and open, almost surreal landscape . . . offers an agreeable setting for that kind of exploration which is Dorn's deliberate concern in the *Gunslinger* poems. In them, he traces the episodic and apparently random wanderings of the Gunslinger, a sublime drifter mysteriously connected with the gods, traveling in the company of ordinary mortals by horse and carriage from Mesilla, an old Spanish village on the Rio Grande in southern New Mexico, north along the river's valley. He pauses in a city that sounds like Albuquerque and continues on through an increasingly abstract landscape, engaged in a mission that is only hinted at, a mysteriously purposed search for Howard Hughes. As with "Idaho Out," if in a more elusive and free-wheeling way, the journey narrative soon becomes a vehicle for reflection on, even a diagnosis of, the state of the American soul.

It is in the mind that our limitations—which is to say our orientation toward a condition of stasis—exist. As he declares in "Driving Across the Prairie," "that crippled stem of this country is made with the mind. There must be a way to stop it." . . . Thus Dorn seems to have come to the conviction that the crucial business of the poet is to put a stop to that crippling heritage, to create poems with the power of altering the reader's consciousness in such a way that his mind may be freed. Out of that conviction, I believe, arises the singularly ecstatic style of Dorn's *Gunslinger* poems.

A glance back at the writings examined earlier suggests that this style and outlook is not wholly new, but actually represents a natural and continuous evolution of Dorn's lifelong concern with the fate of men living on this continent. (pp. 75-6)

I think that Dorn's performance [in the *Gunslinger* poems] best matches his intention when he succeeds in engaging his audience in the poem's experience through a skillful combination of elements: a heroic presence of mind, a use of southwestern landforms, and a broad sense of humor.

"The Sheriff of McTooth County, Kansas" . . . contains the elements of the *Gunslinger* poems in miniature. This piece stands as a mirror of Dorn's creative imagination since the first of the *Gunslinger* poems and reveals the underlying seriousness of purpose that can be traced back to Dorn's earliest work. It appears here in his "sheering off" the forms of power and violence that underlie the typically placid surface of small-town (western Kansas) America. At the same time, the rollicking humor of the tale evidences Dorn's affection for the vitality and independent-mindedness of American frontier life. In what we may think of as a miniaturized epic of American life, a kind of bicentennial *Easy Rider*, the patriot heroes follow up their policies with a concession to the myth of the West:

> What about the Mustangs? Jim
> asked, there's gonna be some pressure
> there, that's a big symbol, the West
> dig it.
>   Don't worry about it they're gonna
> be a special event I'm gonna select
> some volunteers to drivem straight
> off the roof of the McEldridge Hotel,
> that's the highest building in town
> of any historical connection. . . .
>
>   (pp. 77-8)

In *Slinger*, especially in the early books, high-jinks and bravado of this kind engage the reader's imagination and involve him in the poem's experience. Here, however, the reader is drawn onto a larger, more heroic plane of action and finds himself involved in a more complex design. For Dorn's ecstatically humorous style in *Slinger* is modulated by the sense of decorum appropriate to the presence of a hero who is possessed of a demigod's essential seriousness while engaged in the business of carrying out his mission. The reader himself, as a participant in this heightened world, thus begins to find his self-consciousness altered toward a more open and less inhibited view of the universe and of his place in it. Indeed, we begin to perceive a repossession of that condition of harmony in the world that the original inhabitants of this continent appear to have possessed, a consciousness untrammeled by the destructive force of pure ego. And it is precisely for this reason, I think, that Dorn establishes "I" in the poem but makes him one of the secondary characters. "I," that likeable but green dude from the East, is assigned the role of initiate in the poem, learning wisdom at the side of the Slinger; and his death, reported in Book II as a sad but not tragic event, has the effect of dispelling the reader's own subjective identity, thereby leaving him in the direct presence of the serene and mysterious hero and of the objects of the universe that he seems remarkably comfortable with.

Although the footloose vitality of "C. B. & Q." and "Idaho Out" persists in Dorn's recent imaginative journeying, the impulse toward anarchy as a response to a static culture is here transformed into a search for that kind of vitality and wholeness that is found in harmony and self-possession. At any rate that is the ideal Dorn pursues in his recent poems—the latest versions of his "mystique of the real"—and it is clearly consistent with his earlier convictions about what constitutes new material for the poet living in a new continent. The broad humor of Dorn's writing, moreover, which might be viewed as a concession to the conventional expectations of a middle-American audience, is in fact an aspect of his strategy, adopted since "Idaho Out," of involving the reader in a transaction. It is a transaction, moreover, that does not compromise Dorn's ruling idea of intensity. Like Carl Sauer and Charles Olson before him, Dorn has thus earned a distinctive and distinguished place among the great geographers of the North American soul. And his muse shows no sign of deserting him. (pp. 78-9)

> William J. Lockwood, "Ed Dorn's Mystique of the Real: His Poems for North America," in Contemporary Literature (© 1978 by the Board of Regents of the University of Wisconsin System), Vol. 19, No. 1, Winter, 1978, pp. 59-79.

*   *   *

DRABBLE, Margaret   1939-

An English novelist, biographer, essayist, screenplay writer, and former actress, Drabble achieved acclaim with her first novel, *A Summer Bird-Cage*. Her early novels were private, interior pieces, while her more recent works reflect her concern for social and political issues. As an author of screenplays, Drabble has adapted her novels for film. (See also CLC, Vols. 2, 3, 5, 8, and *Contemporary Authors*, Vols. 13-16, rev. ed.)

PATRICIA SHARPE

Drabble's novels, particularly their conclusions, are structured to expose the narrowness and inadequacy of ... moral judgments by upsetting our expectations. As conditioned novel readers we anticipate conclusions which will confirm our values and sympathies, rewarding the hero or heroine with success and marriage. Throughout *Thank You All Very Much*, for example, we await Rosamund's declaration to George of his paternity and their subsequent union; therefore we are ... initially frustrated by her silence. Yet the final lines of the novel demonstrate that our taste for traditional happy endings may tempt us to misunderstand Rosamund's action. It proceeds not from frigidity, neurosis or the expectations of others, but from Rosamund's developing acceptance of her unique self. She opts for a relationship with her child alone because Octavia is all she wants at this point. She recognizes that this choice is a bad investment but reminds us that most other passionate choices are as well.... [For] that moment Rosamund has "lost the taste for half-knowledge," and in choosing according to her inclinations Rosamund better displays the emotional growth which has accompanied her motherhood than she would by taking a husband as she has taken escorts, because she believes it is expected of her. Rosamund's joy in her immediate, instinctive love for Octavia, the first of her life, is also her first experience of feeling "what all other women feel." Discovering this capacity for common human experience frees Rosamund from the need for her pretense of ordinariness. It permits her to accept her idiosyncratic but not totally private nature. Such non-judgmental accommodation to circumstance and to self-knowledge is common to Drabble's various conclusions.

It can be perceived in the heroine's return to a difficult relationship with her husband that concludes *The Needle's Eye*.... [It is] a disappointing alternative either to Rose's continued heroic solitude or to her loving union with Simon, the novel's male protagonist. In fact Rose's decision challenges such expectations for a clear solution. It represents the uneasy compromise Rose makes when her custody suit forces her to acknowledge the conflicting aspects of her nature.... Like Rosamund, Rose comes to know herself better and attempts to shape her life in accordance with her nature. The difference between their choices indicates these characters' differing natures, not the moral superiority of one. The salvation which inheres in the discovery of one's identity is subject only to personal measurement.

The heroine's "nature" is not, then, purely instinctive for Drabble, and need not be represented in an acceptance of sex. In fact the sex offered Rose or Rosamund is a debased effort at contact. Like the sterile politeness and legal dealings of *The Needle's Eye*, sex becomes a medium of human interchange in the absence of genuine ties and feelings.... Drabble's conclusion idealizes neither Rose's return nor the possibility of a romantic relationship with Simon. Instead Drabble demonstrates the superiority of true contact between individuals independent of physical contact or the legal institution of marriage. (pp. 227-28)

To the audience devoted to Drabble's more contemplative, considerate and self-effacing characters, Frances Wingate of *The Realms of Gold* seems unappealingly hearty, drinking too heavily and littering her belongings lavishly around large hotel rooms. While Rose had trouble feeling justified in occupying any space and consequently allowed herself to be encroached upon, Frances seems a potential encroacher.... Frances enjoys sex, has a warm relationship with a man despite his being married to someone else, and the novel concludes with her marriage to him. This conventional novelistic resolution so uncharacteristic of Drabble does not proceed from a conviction of the superiority of such a heroine, but from the irrational energy for living which just happens to be Frances's nature.

The novel's concluding with her happy marriage is one of the improbable surprises with which the whole work abounds. Drabble's abrupt uncharacteristic authorial intrusions also testify to the existence of situations which she as individual cannot fully comprehend or accept. (pp. 228-29)

The novel implies that . . . human impenetrability inheres in the multiplicity and diversity of individual human natures. Drabble's minor characters, always vivid and human, here offer an astonishing panorama of individual choices and solutions. . . . More often other people's actions, even convenient ones like Karel's wife's decision that she is lesbian, remain alien, mysterious. Drabble attributes our astonishment at them to our deluded expectation that others must act as we would. (p. 230)

Survival, Drabble implies, is just another possible outcome of confronting one's nature.

This realization astonishes the reader, initially disappointed with Frances, who values Drabble for her compassionate vision of troubled victims. For in displaying the breadth of her own imaginative sympathy Drabble exposes the instinctive narrowness of ours. Thus *The Realms of Gold* reenacts the drama of discovery found in Keats's poem from which its title comes. Like Keats Drabble uses metaphors of physical exploration, of geology and archaeology, to demonstrate the capacity of art to overwhelm our expectations and reveal new ways of perceiving. (p. 231)

> *Patricia Sharpe, "On First Looking into 'The Realms of Gold',"* in The Michigan Quarterly Review *(copyright © The University of Michigan, 1977), Spring, 1977, pp. 225-31.*

MAUREEN HOWARD

One of the astonishing feats of "The Ice Age" is the way in which Drabble incorporates the ever-increasing junk pile of current public disasters into a thematic background that never appears journalistic. The danger is, of course, that we all know about the economic plight of England, about the loss of hope, vision, empire, and that the facts she gives us may become a repeat of the evenings news. There is much open discussion in the novel about the "terrible times." A crude South African besieges Alison Murray, once a great beauty, with shallow attacks on her country. In the past Alison has always been able to escape hard facts by turning to her mirror, but that comfort is gone: "The country was growing old. Like herself. The scars on the hillsides were the wrinkles around her own eyes: irremovable. How could one learn to grow old?" Such direct and simple equations between the private and public world are frequent in "The Ice Age" and, surprisingly, they are not strained. The parallels between an ailing individual and the ailing society are acceptable because Margaret Drabble has given them full thematic and emotional support.

In the case of Alison Murray we know that she has sacrificed her first daughter, Jane—now a sullen, self-destructive young woman, to her second daughter, Molly, an eternal child with cerebral palsy, who "could not even sit tidily." . . . Like England she is listless, bankrupt, aging. "Alison has Molly. Her life is beyond imagining. It will not be imagined, Britain will recover, but not Alison Murray."

Here, in the final words of "The Ice Age," is a recapitulation of one of Margaret Drabble's main themes: if we are honest with ourselves, freedom is an illusory proposition. We are as trapped by our options as we are by our limitations. (pp. 7, 40)

One of the great pleasures of "The Ice Age" is the cast of minor characters, each embodying an alternative mode of survival. . . . And England itself is a presence, beautifully portrayed—the run-down railroad stations and littered streets, the inhuman highways and Government housing projects, the lethargic spirit of a demoted power. It is a dying country in possession of an almost comic *deus ex machina*—those oil fields in the North.

It's inevitable that "The Ice Age" will be referred to as "the new Drabble." That is a danger that prolific writers run. It is a remarkably fine book that takes its life from the best traditions of the 19-century novel: elaborate plotting, coincidence, meaningful resolution—and it has a surface vitality that comes from Margaret Drabble's pure, old-fashioned narrative skill. In the best of her previous novels, "The Realms of Gold" and "The Needle's Eye," she has come across as a bit of a schoolmarm, lecturing us on the role of the narrator and the machinations of her story. Here such defenses are used lightly. She assumes an authority that puts her reader entirely at ease. Yes, we say, the social context is like Hardy, the interlocking lives she's borrowed from Dickens, the chain of circumstances from Charlotte Brontë. In a way, it is all very self-conscious, but Drabble's technique is to admit to the difficulties of a self-conscious art. She respects literary conventions as riches of the past, and so gives that outmoded form, the novel, new life. Her structure does not have the energy of Thomas Pynchon's, nor her inventions of coincidence the imaginative delight of Nabokov's, but she shares their belief in the form. Hers is not an apocalyptic vision: the world survived the Ice Age, after all, and in that epoch is recorded the rise of man. (p. 40)

> *Maureen Howard, "Public and Private Games,"* in The New York Times Book Review *(© 1977 by The New York Times Company; reprinted by permission), October 9, 1977, pp. 7, 40.*

FRANK GRANVILLE BARKER

Clearly we are meant to take *The Ice Age* seriously, not as a diversion, and readers must indeed be prepared for a good deal of moralising as they follow the adventures of a collection of singularly unsympathetic characters. Since she is writing about England in the Seventies, Miss Drabble is presumably making her ice age symbolise the current period of economic stagnation, and if her grim-faced prose is anything to go by, moral stagnation too. She does not, alas, give any hint as to the direction in which our economic and moral recovery will move when the eventual thaw takes place, contenting herself with the glib assurance in the final sentence that 'Britain will recover'. This cliché, which is inevitably perpetrated at every political party's annual conference, seems a feeble punch-line for a novel so ambitious in scope. . . .

Predictably perhaps, Miss Drabble focuses her spotlight on a small group of property speculators, a human type which, though pretty despicable, is certainly capable of providing a satirist's field-day. . . . By choosing to restrict her cast-list to the exploiters, ignoring their victims altogether, Miss Drabble sacrifices the essential dramatic and moral validity of her subject. She brings personal conflict into the novel by way of her male characters' wives and mistresses, displaying a considerable degree of feminine masochism in her portrait gallery of women playing out their trivial fringe activities.

There is also a strong masochistic streak in the principal character, Anthony Keating, not only because he moves from the BBC to ITV, and from arts to current affairs, not even because he gives up an interesting career for the shady boredom of property speculation. One can't help wondering at this point exactly what the author is trying to say. 'He would wake up in the middle of the night', we are told, 'and think: is this it? Is what what? In short, he was underemployed, bored, and not at all happy in his relation to his work, his country, or the society he lived in: ripe for conversion, to some creed. A political creed, but there wasn't one: a religious creed, but he had had God, along with his father and life in the cathedral close. So what would happen to the vacant space, in Anthony Keating? What would occupy it?' Are we really expected to believe that property speculation could fill this need, that it could satisfy any man's desire to serve his country and the society he lived in, that it could provide a god-substitute? Either Miss Drabble is very naïve or her wit is very heavy-handed. . . . Anthony, it is claimed, has always been something of a wit as well as a successful television personality, yet the tone of his conversations with his friends makes the kind of annual speech by a typical Rotary Club treasurer seem positively Wildean. . . . (p. 40)

Anthony's sudden transformation from passive sufferer to heroic man of action and religious visionary seems equally implausible, if only because Miss Drabble does nothing to prepare us for it. There are some striking touches of dark comedy in his recruitment as an agent to rescue Jane, Alison's utterly tiresome daughter, from her imprisonment in the shadowy Iron Curtain country, but it is difficult to believe that anyone should choose such an ineffectual man for the mission. This weakness may well result from the author's sudden increase in narrative pace towards the end of the novel, as though she had become afraid her stock of typing paper were running out. (pp. 40-1)

The saddening thing is that Margaret Drabble has such abundant basic talent. She has the rare ability to move a considerable number of characters over a wide canvas without losing touch of continuity. Here, for instance, she displays immense skill in her description of the way in which the different men and women spend their Christmas. She handles the time element with expertise, too, falling down in this respect only towards the end of the novel. She also holds her readers all the way, even a reader like myself who rebels against her choice of characters. All this is achieved, moreover, in spite of writing which seems deliberately clumsy, as though she scorns elegance of expression with a perverse Puritan pride. Her style, if that is not too strong a word, is at once laboured and slipshod: although her sentences are obviously constructed with care and forethought, far too many of them are verbless and far too many open with the words 'And' or 'But'—indicating that she is a born *Daily Express* feature writer. Miss Drabble is so clearly superior to this category, and she is a novelist with such wide vision, that one is left bewildered that she should have

passed *The Ice Age* over to her publishers in the form in which it has appeared. It could have been much better, and she has the talent to have made it so. Even as it stands, it is a novel to be reckoned with, a novel worth giving up several hours of one's time to read. I doubt, on the other hand, that many people will find it worth reading a second time. (p. 41)

> *Frank Granville Barker, "Before the Thaw," in* Books and Bookmen (© copyright Frank Granville Barker 1978; reprinted with permission), January, 1978, pp. 40-1.

BEN YAGODA

[In *The Ice Age* it] is Drabble's design to portray the public plight of her country through the personal tribulations of a handful of characters, almost all of whom have experienced a catastrophe of one form or another as the novel opens. . . .

The single remotely happy person we encounter is Len's irrepressible secretary/companion, Maureen Kirby. Everyone else is feeling the effects of the chill, both physical and spiritual, that pervades this wintry tale. Their central concern—and by extension, that of the author—is why they have been afflicted. . . .

Perhaps they are being tested, like Job, or are simply the innocent victims of what Len's crazy prisonmate believes to be the reason for all the trouble—that nuclear waste has suddenly thrown the laws of chance out of whack. Alison is probably nearer the truth, though, and certainly closer to the spirit of a Freudian era, in thinking "There is no such thing as an accident," and glimpsing "for a moment, in the dark night, a primitive causality so shocking, so uncanny" that she shivers.

Drabble's previous novel, *The Realms of Gold*, posited the importance of coincidence and accident; *The Ice Age* suggests the opposite. Anthony may be undergoing punishment for what he has done to the land or for a form of hubris; Kitty for being good to the point of blinding herself to the existence of evil; Alison for ignoring Jane in favor of Molly.

Assuming this conception of causality applies to nations as well, England must have committed a pretty grave offense. As depicted here, the country is in a mess from which neither the *deus ex machina* of North Sea oil nor the marginally improved fortunes of the pound sterling offers much of an escape. In fact, nearly every facet of mid-'70s British life comes under fire. . . .

Why all this has happened to Milton's "noble and puissant Nation" is difficult to say, and Drabble does not ease the way. . . . England, the author seems to be telling us, had taken too much on itself, had eaten too richly; now . . . it must follow a strict regimen.

Implicit in this view, of course, is the probability that eventually the tide will turn once more, and Britain will again rise to its feet. That is indeed the hope of some of the characters. . . . But Drabble refuses to openly commit herself on what she thinks, heeding her caution in *The Realms of Gold* that "omniscience has its limits."

> *Ben Yagoda, "The Trouble with England," in* The New Leader (© 1978 by the American Labor Conference on International Affairs, Inc.), January 30, 1978, p. 21.

MAUREEN HOWARD

The Ice Age by Margaret Drabble has an authority about it that is new to her work. In *Realms of Gold* she began to assume that the large designs of the English novel were there for the taking but allowed herself to get caught up in imitations of Murdochian games. In *The Ice Age* she handles an intricate plot with confidence and creates a cast of characters meant to reflect a range of attitudes toward modern day Britain.... *The Ice Age* is an extraordinarily open work with elegiac passages that create a public background for the enactment of private lives.... [Control] of history and acceptance of the facts is one pole of the novel. The other is a cinematic odd-angled view of the trashy modern improvements in a heartless urban landscape of cement, steel, lurid hotel interiors and cheap goods that reveal the anxiety of everyday life. Alison, traveling home, finds herself in an unfamiliar train station with no services, walking through a concrete tunnel which leads illogically to a dangerous traffic island. There, an injured dog with its side ripped to the raw flesh finds its way with dumb persistence through the cars. It is a terrifying vision that remains with us throughout Drabble's description of the passive depression that overcomes Alison Murray when she is safely home. Though she can endure her personal tragedy, the world is too much for her, too disturbing as it can often be for any one of us.

The careful patterns of accident opposed to intention in *The Ice Age* come directly from a novelistic tradition that demands solutions. Margaret Drabble is accomplished at finishing off the design: the little secretary who fell in with the ruthless real-estate man becomes a distinguished business woman associated with an architect who still maintains views of a humane cityscape; Alison's sullen, drop-out daughter is chastened by the example of the decent adults around her and studies to be a nurse. The characters who can never be transformed by events are the defective child and a hopelessly optimistic woman "determined as she is to ignore the implications of reality." It is only with Anthony Keating that Drabble goes wrong. Imprisoned, this ordinary man discards his personal life and enters into a spiritual state that justifies his suffering. He reads Boethius' *Consolation of Philosophy* and like that medieval philosopher finds comfort "more in philosophy than faith." In a novel that refers to the over-arching myth of apocalypse so movingly, Anthony Keating's conversion to heroic stature by way of a superior inner life seems contrived, theoretical —like the mysticism Doris Lessing resorts to at the end of *The Four Gated City*. The finale of *The Ice Age* relies too heavily on what Maragret Drabble calls a *necessary* imagined future for Anthony Keating. (pp. 184-85)

> *Maureen Howard, in* The Hudson Review *(copyright © 1978 by The Hudson Review, Inc.; reprinted by permission), Vol. XXXI, No. 1, Spring, 1978.*

JAMES GINDIN

[For] epigraphs to *The Ice Age,* Drabble chooses to quote a long selection from the famous passage in Milton's *Areopagitica* that begins "Methinks I see in my mind a noble and puissant Nation rousing herself like a strong man after sleep ..." and to follow it with some lines from Wordsworth's stirring sonnet on Milton. The title of the novel is a metaphor for the economic and social "freeze" of 1974-75, during which most of its events take place, the novel focusing on Anthony Keating.... Anthony muses about the "terrible times we live in" and "the sense of alarm, panic, despondency which seemed to flow loose in the atmosphere of England." For Anthony, at this point, such musings are certainly understandable, but the author's voice supports him without equivocation. Instead of qualifying Anthony's point of view, Drabble uses its intensity as typical, gains complexity by anatomizing all the various responses (despair, perverse enjoyment of austerity, shabby official indifference, political opportunism) to the "freeze," as if to assume that the metaphor is a perfect representation of the condition of England. Other imagistic connections also seem too heavy, too obvious. For example, Anthony frequently thinks of his owning a long, spiky gasometer (a gas holding tank) that came with some property he had bought from the Gas Board and planned to re-develop, a gasometer that reaches far into the sky, as his "finest achievement." He connects the gasometer, in linear reach and in social contrast, with the spire of the cathedral in the shadow of which he, the son of a cathedral schoolmaster, grew up. The grandiose suggestions of England changing from allegiance to cathedral spires to allegiance to gasometers are repeated throughout the novel, as if we all leap from one grand vertical obeisance or apocalypse to another with no qualifying horizontal space or muted achievements.

To dwell solely on the exaggerated metaphors of *The Ice Age* would be to miss a great deal that is valuable, suggestive, and intelligent in the novel. The development of Anthony's background, from schoolboy and early marriage through television work to the excitement of property speculation, is both convincing as the depiction of an individual and perceptive about a generation.... At her best, Drabble can summarize historical directions, social issues, and the fortunes of her characters.... (pp. 230-31)

In addition, many of Drabble's other historical metaphors are comically qualified or carefully particularized, not left in the stark simplicity of the change from cathedral to gasometer. The legendary British lion, for example, now "shabby, mangy, old," its tail easily tweaked, is seen sometimes as pathetic, sometimes as emitting a humane gesture, sometimes as petulant. (p. 232)

[At the point of Anthony's] resolve toward recovery ... the novel fails to carry conviction. The recovery, like some of the extreme metaphors of the "ice age," seems only gesture, something pasted on, not earned through the development of the characters and events in the novel. Although Anthony is given sufficient choice to make a conscious recovery plausible, other characters are not, and the detailed, socially interrelated, referential nature of the novel, the sense of Britain, works against a reading that could establish Anthony as the single changing human being in a fictional world of stereotypes that represent possible choices or traps for him. Rather, the novel, in its texture, is dependent on complex and changing relationships; yet what we are given, for all the characters except Anthony, is a set of inflexible determinations. (p. 233)

The Ice Age also indicates a shift in Drabble's perspective, one that has, perhaps, been growing in recent years. In what, to me, are still her best novels, those of the middle and late sixties, *The Millstone, Jerusalem The Golden,* and *The Waterfall,* her perspective could be characterized as a knowing, sensitive, and obdurate refusal to judge her characters. In these novels, depicting young girls struggling to define themselves against rigid northern backgrounds or easily permissive cosmopolitan parents, wondering about the responsibilities involved with lovers, husbands, and children, and invariably chronicling the social world surrounding the characters, Drabble maintains a sense of hard and focused insight that never damns or sentimentalizes. *The Ice Age,* in contrast, allowing people fewer choices, establishing a world in which, except for Anthony, most human action is predetermined, also, quite inconsistently, scatters judgments. . . . The tone throughout the novel sustains this judging perspective, a constant ascription of "proper" or "not proper" to characters' actions, a constant sense, from the author's perspective, that characters in various situations are behaving well or behaving badly. I am not here objecting to the perspective of authorial judgment in itself, certainly judging his or her own characters is part of any author's prerogative; rather, I am saying that the perspective of judgment when combined with a world in which the nature of most people is determined, in which choice is severely restricted or non-existent, makes the possibility of "recovery" all that much more tenuous, more a matter for the fantasies of shoot-em-up foreign adventure and the fiction of fictions. (pp. 235-36)

> *James Gindin, in* The Michigan Quarterly Review *(copyright © The University of Michigan, 1978), Spring, 1978.*

E

ELIOT, T(homas) S(tearns)   1888-1965

Eliot was an American-born poet, dramatist, essayist, critic, and publisher who became a British citizen in 1927. A neoclassicist who had a profound effect on twentieth-century poetry and literary criticism, Eliot endeavored to re-educate his readers through the use of allusions drawn from the past: classical, biblical, and mythical allusions inform his work. He used classical literary structures and experimented with musical forms in his poetry, as evidenced in his *Preludes* and *Four Quartets*. The theme of death and rebirth, central to *The Waste Land*, is found throughout Eliot's work, as is his preoccupation with man's place in a world governed by the exigencies of time. Eliot received both the Nobel Prize and the British Order of Merit in 1948. (See also *CLC*, Vols. 1, 2, 3, 6, 9, and *Contemporary Authors*, Vols. 5-8, rev. ed.; obituary, Vols. 25-28, rev. ed.)

HARRY PUCKETT

Almost every poem Eliot wrote is dominated by one or more traditional epistemological concerns—knowledge and belief, memory and perception, forgetting, recognition, and precognition. But his poetry is also dominated by prophets and prophecies, magi, choric forebodings, people who know but cannot see or speak, or if they speak are not heeded. His people are surrounded by a world of talking birds, cryptic messages, telling images, and words unheard; and what his people come to know is what they should have known or do know already. Knowing is, for Eliot, an act of recognition or *re*-cognition. . . . The silent message, the word unheard—an image, a gesture, an atmosphere—is often associated with issues of life and death. Those who hear the word live; and those who do not, die. (pp. 179-80)

The word unheard . . . takes various forms. It may be knowledge in the possession of one who cannot speak. It may be knowledge embedded in an image not noticed. It may be an open warning, openly ignored. It may also be a silent gesture, like the nod of the Lady's head in *Ash-Wednesday,* fully acknowledged and acted upon, as Sweeney wisely acted among the nightingales; Eliot's word unheard is not always unregarded. But the word unheard appears most strikingly in such diverse figures as Philomel, the infant Christ in "Gerontion," and J. Alfred Prufrock—all unable to speak, and sure to be unheeded if or when speech becomes possible.

The knowledge that matters most in Eliot's world is not discursive and discovered, like scientific knowledge, but revealed, recovered, recognized. Eliot's world is much like the subconscious worlds described by Jung and Freud, each in a different way, and both different from Eliot's, yet all having in common the idea of knowledge latent, veiled, or hovering, often in some sense silent or unheeded, commonly available only through images. Common to all is the idea of knowing as an act of recovery or recognition, of being able to know in some sense without really knowing; and finally the idea of superficial knowledge as an evasion of deeper knowledge. . . . (p. 181)

One thing that frequently happens to people in an Eliot poem is that they pay insufficient attention to feelings and the felt whole. And one thing Eliot himself does in writing a poem is to preserve and convey a generous portion of the felt whole—images and sounds—compelling the reader to do much of the abstracting, if he wants abstractions. The importance that Eliot attaches to the felt whole sets up a common bond between him and the Imagists. But Eliot is obviously not presenting merely images in his poetry; he presents patterns of images and concepts, built together into a feeling or even a pattern of such feelings. His ultimate obligation as a craftsman is not to the image but to the feeling. Moreover, he regards pure perception and purely immediate experience as impossible, because all our perceptions are guided, or filtered through, various concepts and preconceptions. . . . (p. 182)

[The] main trend in the English and American schools throughout Eliot's era was toward analytic philosophy; and, given the advantage of hindsight, we can see that Eliot's epistemology leads rather directly away from that kind of philosophizing and toward poetry, the traditional province of feeling (in several senses of the term, including Eliot's). (p. 183)

Just as Eliot's epistemology leads from the writing of philosophy to the writing of poetry, so the particular kind of poetry he writes is a reflection of his attitude toward knowing. Knowledge is made available to his magi in images; it is also made available to his reader in images. Knowing is an act of recognition for the women of Canterbury; so it is for the reader. Knowledge hovers in Eliot's poetic world. It hovers also in his real world. Hence his poetry is built on image, myth, and allusion. His poetry conveys knowledge;

but it is knowledge the reader already has, in a latent state of one sort or another. As in the Jungian and Freudian constructs, it may be recovered only through struggle or crisis —in this case, struggle with the poetry.... By means of image, allusion, and myth ... Eliot conveys to his reader certain knowledge that the reader already possesses but does not readily recover. The poem thus draws on the subconscious, and it draws on archetypal memories, yet Eliot's poetry is not especially Freudian or Jungian. With those constructs it has only a common ancestor in ancient myths —Homer's Oxen-of-the-Sun incident, the Oedipus myth, the Adam story—where men know, but know darkly, and so die. One of the primary differences between the kind of knowing in Eliot's poetry and the kind postulated by Jung and Freud is that Eliot need not speculate: he need not postulate concepts of archetype or libido. Although he may use such concepts as "feeling" and felt whole in some of his prose, his poetry gets along well without them. The knowledge recovered by Eliot's poetry exists, not in a racial memory or a superego, but in tradition; and Eliot's allusions are a kind of documentation.... The knowledge that poetry recovers exists in time, and Eliot's attitude toward knowledge is thus closely linked to his attitude toward time —a relationship explored at length in *Four Quartets*. It is here, at the end of "East Coker," that Eliot achieves his most concise and explicit definition of poetry:

> the fight to recover what has been lost
> And found and lost again and again. . . .

A few lines later his idea of poetry and his idea of life merge into one:

>   Not the intense moment
> Isolated, with no before and after,
> But a lifetime burning in every moment
> And not the lifetime of one man only
> But of old stones that cannot be deciphered. . . .

The word unheard, as a symbol of the nature, process, and function of poetry, is generally referred to most explicitly in Eliot's later work, beginning with *Ash-Wednesday*, and more particularly the opening stanza of Section V . . . , which marks an important development. Prior to 1930 in such poems as "Gerontion," *The Waste Land*, and "Journey of the Magi" Eliot dwells primarily upon man's failure to hear and heed the word which is plainly, sometimes loudly or blatantly, set forth. During this earlier period the other aspect of the word unheard—the silent word silently heeded—ironically appears in only one important poem, "Sweeney Among the Nightingales," where Sweeney acts on the "felt whole" as Agamemnon did not. But in *Ash-Wednesday* both of these aspects appear together, and achieve full integration in Section V. Here, the fact that the silent Word does exist at the center is seen not merely as a consolation but also as something like a condition for the whirling of the unstilled, unhearing world:

> If the lost word is lost, if the spent word is spent
> If the unheard, unspoken
> Word is unspoken, unheard:
> Still is the unspoken word, the Word unheard,
> The Word without a word, the Word within
> The world and for the world;
> And the light shone in darkness and
> Against the Word the unstilled world still whirled
> About the centre of the silent Word. . . .

The pun on "still" is characteristic, with its multiple reference to time or duration, motion, and silence. The integration achieved in this poem is later developed and concentrated into a single image: "the still point of the turning world." As the geometer must postulate something he calls the "point"—a thing having neither depth nor breadth nor any dimensionality, yet somehow necessarily existing— without which he can have no geometry, so the unstilled world itself presupposes the geocentric still point, and for that matter the geotropic poet as well. Beginning with *Ash-Wednesday*, and no doubt due in part to the integration achieved there, Eliot sounds less like the prophet warning men against their obtuseness, more like the psalmist seeking his way into the silent center. He seeks that way, paradoxically, through words. *Four Quartets* is the continuation and culmination of that search, and a resolution of that paradox. Both the search and the resolution proceed through indispensable form. . . . [This] reliance on form as a way of redeeming words and music is reasserted, but redemptive form is now more explicitly Incarnation. . . . (pp. 184-87)

[Despite] the importance of the integration achieved in *Ash-Wednesday* and the elaboration of that achievement in *Four Quartets*, the word unheard is most successfully turned into poetry in the earlier work, where it is not explicit; the height of Eliot's achievement is *The Waste Land*, which is distinctly superior because more catholic, recovering more, from lost vegetation myths, the *Upanishads*, Greek drama, the Hebrew prophets, St. Augustine, Dante, the Elizabethans. Moreover, the function Eliot assigns to poetry is also a major function of literary criticism and scholarship: the recognition, recovery, or revelation of the word unheard. And *The Waste Land* is almost as much a work of criticism and scholarship as it is a poem—in this sense, too, an extraordinarily catholic work.

It is here, then, in *The Waste Land* that Eliot incarnates his word in the form likely to be most distinctly unheard by the modern ear. For it is here that the identification of tradition and the self, and the relation of tradition to redemption of the self, is most fully developed. The Cumaean sibyl in the epigraph is, as oracles traditionally have been, a source of information that does not fully inform, of knowing that often constitutes, in one way or another, not-knowing. As gatekeeper of the underworld in Vergil's *Aeneid* she also supplies Eliot with a symbol for the epic descent into Hell, which for Eliot as for Dante, represents a descent into the lower reaches of the self and the spectral images and the spectral knowledge waiting there—such a descent as in fact *The Waste Land* is—a descent through tradition, which is also a descent through the crowded sordid images of which the self is constituted. This identification of the self with the past is embodied in the ancient and virtually interminable self of the sibyl. In the main body of the poem this identification of self and past is achieved in the figure of Tiresias, presiding consciousness of *The Waste Land*. . . . (pp. 188-89)

"The Burial of the Dead" closes with an image of disinterment—a dog unearthing a corpse—that suggests the unearthing of buried truth. The allusion to Baudelaire's *Les Fleurs du Mal*, the disinterment of a consciousness, supports this suggestion—and so, in particular, does the charge of hypocrisy, implying the corpse in every man's garden. . . . Voices, prophecies, images, and incarnations hover throughout [*The Waste Land*] carrying knowledge, but somehow silent, or unheard, or latent, or ignored. In some form or other the word unheard is everywhere present. And it is everywhere associated with death, the dominant imagery in Part I: the Cumaean sibyl, the handful of dust, the man who knows nothing looking into the silence, the Hanged Man and death by water respectively unseen and foreseen by Madame Sosostris, the buried corpse. The association is sometimes sinister, sometimes comic, always ambiguous, uncertain. The only kinds of knowing in Part I are virtually identical with not-knowing, and both are akin to death. Here and throughout *The Waste Land* true knowledge, vital knowledge, redemptive knowledge is everywhere latent but one way or another inoperative.

The poem thus suggests the importance that Eliot assigns to ''feelings'' and ''the felt whole,'' which people in *The Waste Land* consistently overlook or ignore. But Eliot transcends such philosophical and pseudo-philosophical terms to integrate dramatically his epistemology with his concern over human failure and redemption. It is this concern that . . . puts him in touch with the problem of knowledge as it typically appears in Greek epic and tragedy, Hebrew prophecy, and modern works in the same tradition, most notably Dante's *Commedia*. (pp. 189-91)

[The] most striking symbol in Part II is Philomel . . . , evoking the theme of lust. Raped and mutilated, she cannot speak what she knows; transformed into the nightingale, she sings, but the world will not hear. In the myth she reveals what she knows with a woven image, hence the characteristic pun on ''still'': ''And still she cried, and still the world pursues.'' . . . [The words that are neither heard nor felt by the object of Prufrock's love song] are, of course, heard and felt by the reader, insofar as the poem is effective and the reader receptive. Prufrock's love song is, in this sense, really a love song. In the very process of not achieving that ultimate expression he longs for, he does achieve it. The poem he speaks is very nearly as musical as *Four Quartets,* and it does convey that total despair and alienation associated with the I-want-to-die genre of conventional love songs. Prufrock's word is, in fact, heard—just to the extent that his absurd private torment is transmuted into significant public poetry. (pp. 191-92)

Eliot commonly uses apparent nonsense to convey sense, as Shakespeare does in both comedy and tragedy. The effect of this technique might very aptly be described as moving the hearers to ''collection,'' and recollection. (p. 192)

The Waste Land is radically different from ''The Love Song of J. Alfred Prufrock,'' but the tones of melancholy, prophecy, and hysteria are as conspicuous in the voice of Prufrock, knowing it will not be heard, as they are in the voices of *The Waste Land*. (p. 193)

The closing lines of ''The Fire Sermon'' allude to St. Augustine's *Confessions*—first to Book III, in which Augustine recounts his chase after abstruse knowledge on two continents, like Eliot's, ending in a rejection of the academic for the religious, while nonetheless retaining an academic orientation. The substance of his confession in Book III is his failure to see the immanent God: ''These things I then knew not, nor observed; they struck my sight on all sides, and I saw them not.'' Book X, to which Eliot also alludes here, is an involved epistemological dissertation on memory, which Augustine regards as the source of his knowledge of God; but how a knowledge of God reached

his memory is a question he finds mysterious. He concludes that the Truth of God is all about him: ''Everywhere, O Truth, dost Thou give audience to all who ask counsel of Thee, and at once answer all. . . . Clearly dost Thou answer, though all do not clearly hear.'' And God, of course, is equally immanent. . . . Here is Eliot's emphasis on the ubiquity of truth, but its evasiveness, and man's extraordinary capacity for evading it—even when he appears to seek it most diligently. Here, too, is Eliot's emphasis on memory, and the act of knowing as an act or recognition. (pp. 194-95)

''What the Thunder Said'' is surely among the noisiest poetry in the language—faces sneering and snarling, singing grass, the cicadas, the hermit thrush, ''maternal lamentation,'' ''falling towers,'' ''whisper music,'' bats whistling, voices out of cisterns, the cock on the roof. The only interruption of this bedlam is the walk to Emmaus. In this incident two of Christ's disciples walk together discussing the strange events of the first Easter; Christ appears to them, unrecognized by his two followers, and enquires what they are talking about. . . . Their response to him is a masterpiece of dramatic irony that Eliot might have envied: ''Are you the only man living in Jerusalem who does not know what has been happening there these last few days?'' Then his disciples tell the risen Christ of his own crucifixion, expressing disappointment that he had not redeemed Israel. Still unrecognized, he rebukes them for not heeding the prophets, and soon after, at dinner, a recognition-scene occurs, but then he disappears. The whole incident epitomizes the kind of knowing-but-not-knowing—the virtual suppression of knowledge, or the fear of seeing and seizing the redemptive knowledge always close at hand—characteristic of Eliot's world. Yet in *The Waste Land* this knowledge is not exclusively Christian but goes back to the oldest of the Indo-European scriptures, the *Upanishads*. The final stanza recapitulates the entire section, and in large measure the poem itself—a jumble of noise, madness, hysteria, weariness, longing, climaxed by three words from a dead language, containing the sum of all redemptive knowledge, and a benediction. . . . Eliot fully expects his words to go unheard, as the tradition itself from which they come has gone unheard for up to several thousand years.

Yet ignorance of the word is death, and knowledge is redemptive. Despite his pessimism, Eliot thus exalts knowledge to an extent unsurpassed and hardly equaled by any other modern poet. In response to the ancient question, whether poetry conveys knowledge, Eliot's answer is positive. To be sure, the knowledge it conveys is knowledge we already have; yet for lack of it we go to perdition. (pp. 195-96)

> *Harry Puckett, ''T. S. Eliot on Knowing: The Word Unheard,'' in* The New England Quarterly *(copyright 1971 by* The New England Quarterly*), June, 1971, pp. 179-96.*

MICHAEL WOOD

Eliot's views on personality in poetry seem to have two phases . . . but offer no serious contradiction. The impersonality of the poet creates a set of poems which add up to a distinct and significant personality: the poems have the personality. The first half of this proposition, the purging of ''all the accidents of personal emotion'' from the poem, is not much cherished these days. . . .

Few critics are now as eager as Eliot was to separate "art" from "the event," "the mind which creates" from "the man who suffers."

Indeed, Eliot himself is supposed to have said that *The Waste Land* was "only the relief of a personal and wholly insignificant grouse against life; it is just a piece of rhythmical grumbling." But then he may have meant only that he thought *The Waste Land* was *not* a great poem, and while there are poets we must simply disfigure or dismiss if we look at them through Eliot's theory, there are others, Eliot included, whose achievement needs to be understood, not as a conquest of emotion, but as the translation of emotion into another key.

Eliot's unhappiness lies behind "The Love Song of J. Alfred Prufrock," but it is not *in* the poem, even as a source or a shadow. In the later work, the unhappiness appears more clearly, but it is still disciplined and displaced, so that the apparently confessional *Four Quartets* remain impersonal in Eliot's sense. Like the poetry of Yeats, and unlike the poetry of Hardy, Hopkins, Lawrence, or Pound, they inhabit a zone beyond personal anguish. In yesterday's aesthetic, this would have been a sign of the greatness of Yeats and Eliot and the inferiority of the others. I'm not sure we need to make such choices, but we do, clearly, need to recognize the differences of poetic mode.

The second phase of Eliot's views on the subject—the notion that greatness in poetry is measured by the dimensions and integrity of a whole oeuvre—seems more dubious.... Eliot would be a great poet if he had written nothing more than the last section of *The Waste Land*. Eliot's thought here seems to answer a moral or metaphysical need for wholeness, a quest for what he himself called "character," rather than a real critical requirement....

We gain something by taking the long view of Eliot, by tracing out a career rather than studying separate poems. But we probably lose more than we gain.... We can usefully place [*The Waste Land*] in a continuum, but it is more "fully itself" when we see it as a poem and not as an item in Eliot's spiritual progress. (p. 15)

Even so, any perspective which misses the abrupt discontinuities in Eliot's work has missed too much, for such discontinuities are the life of the poems. It is not simply that Eliot is a "poet of fragments," as Spender says, or that he sees the world as broken in pieces. Eliot specializes in putting fragments together in such a way that we see the wholeness that we lack:

> The nightingales are singing near
> The Convent of the Sacred Heart,
>
> And sang within the bloody wood
> When Agamemnon cried aloud,
> And let their liquid siftings fall
> To stain the stiff dishonoured shroud.

The accidental nightingales, merely singing in two different places and times, the brave flourish of the implausible connection ("And sang") offer a perfect picture of what it means not to be able to put things together. Of course the perfection of the picture, while not a solution to the problem, is a relief. Things are together in the poem, however violently they have been yoked to each other. It is striking that when Eliot writes of the last canto of Dante's *Paradi-*

so, he shows an almost exaggerated interest in Dante's sudden introduction of the pagan Neptune into the highest circle of the Christian heaven:

> I do not know anywhere in poetry more authentic sign of greatness than the power of association which could in the last line, when the poet is speaking of the Divine vision, yet introduce the Argo passing over the head of wondering Neptune.

This, Eliot says, "is the real right thing, the power of establishing relations between beauty of the most diverse sorts; it is the utmost power of the poet." The leap from the contemporary Convent of the Sacred Heart to the classical scene of Agamemnon's death is a parody of such power. It establishes a relation only in the poem, not in the world, and it is a relation between sorts of betrayal not sorts of beauty. But the parody has an authority of its own, and ... parodied revelations in Eliot often lead to the truth, which is not easily distinguished from its travesty. The point is that Eliot has found in Dante not only a model of lost unity, but also a poet who at a later date might have written *The Waste Land,* introducing the voice of Ezekiel, say, into Baudelaire's desolation.

The Waste Land itself is not the ruin of a whole poem pulled down with Pound's aid, but a selection of the best fragments from a larger bundle of fragments. (pp. 15-16)

The Hollow Men and *Ash-Wednesday* are not entirely successful attempts to point fragments toward a larger meaning, and the *Four Quartets* reflect the triumphant discovery that *that* is Eliot's enduring subject: how to join fragments into a poem; how to live out one's life in the long lulls between the fragmentary moments of illumination—"the moment in the rose-garden, / The moment in the arbour where the rain beat, / The moment in the draughty church at smokefall"—which represent our only chance of a victory over time. The *Quartets* record a sporadically successful, finally failing tussle with *temps perdu;* and their distinction lies not, I think, in their claims for religion or in their remarkable lyric passages, but in the unfolding enterprise itself. They are the poem of the mind's quarrel with the insufficiencies of language, where language at times, miraculously, is found to be sufficient after all. (p. 16)

Eliot's prose seems in its way as reticent as the poetry, and yet it does give us more glimpses of the man who suffered. Stray phrases in all kinds of sentences communicate an abiding sadness: "the eternal message of vanity, fear, and lust"; "the burden of anxiety and fear which presses upon our daily life"; "the fact that no human relations are adequate to human desires"; "the disorder, the futility, the meaninglessness, the mystery of life and suffering." The tug of those phrases helps us to understand Eliot's religion, I think; and his use of a formula like "the ecstasy of assent," and his attachment to Dante's line (always slightly misquoted), *"E'n la sua volontade è nostra pace."* Against such profound and extensive misery, perhaps only external agencies are any use at all: God, dogma, a harsh old law, our peace underwritten by His will. "I am really shocked by your assertion that God did not make Hell," Eliot wrote to a friend. "It seems to me that you have lapsed into Humanitarianism.... Is your God Santa Claus?" "Only Christianity," Eliot wrote earlier, "helps to reconcile me to life, which is otherwise disgusting...."

Eliot, especially in the years immediately following his entry into the Anglo-Catholic communion, could fall into a shrill moral snobbery. . . . Still, one can dislike Eliot's religion and his heartless high Tory politics without disliking Eliot, whose integrity survives his shrillness. (pp. 16-17)

> *Michael Wood, "The Struggles of T. S. Eliot," in* The New York Review of Books *(reprinted with permission from* The New York Review of Books; *copyright © 1976 NYREV, Inc.), May 13, 1976, pp. 15-18.*

CHRISTOPHER CLAUSEN

As a major poet T. S. Eliot began in the Waste Land and ended at Little Gidding. That both places are associated with chapels is no accident: even in the depths of the tradition [of Victorian and twentieth-century English poetry] . . . , the way out is symbolized for believers and unbelievers alike by religious buildings, real or legendary. Since it is in Eliot's later work that major English poetry emerges from its fixation on lost childhood and its spiritual paralysis, we naturally look for reasons that will explain his ability to reverse or (better) to complete the journey that had begun at Tintern Abbey. In *The Waste Land* (1922) there is already a spiritual prescription for modern man: give, sympathize, control. It is not until his culminating work twenty years later that we see fully the meaning and fruits of this advice.

"Burnt Norton" (1937), the first of the Four Quartets, begins with the observation, today almost hackneyed from frequent quotation that

> Time present and time past
> Are both perhaps present in time future,
> And time future contained in time past.

In our context this is a pregnant assertion, though its possible meanings are not clarified at this stage of the quartets. At least it raises the possibility that the past to which we look back nostalgically may be fulfilled in some future which is neither visionary nor unbearably distant. That past is "our first world" of leaves and roses and children's voices; but there is something amiss in it, and we cannot stay. The roses, as one might equally say of Wordsworth's performing daffodils, "had the look of flowers that are looked at." Their naturalness, and our own insofar as we *try* to be childlike, is deceptive. . . . What follows is adult life, a life of evasions. It contains at every point the possibility of transcendence, but only if we are willing to face reality. (What that means is also less than clear at this point.) Meanwhile, like Eliot's predecessors, we are left with spots of time, flashes of shame and nostalgia. . . . (pp. 417-18)

The pilgrimage to Little Gidding (1942) is clearly a voyage of recovery, but it is not made in the eager expectant frame of mind that one might anticipate. This is partly because spiritual purposes are never quite clear to those for whom or in whom they are accomplished, nor are they ever carried out in precisely the way one intends. The egotism that leads us to suppose we are either of great importance or in control of our own lives is one of the things we must lose in order to find ourselves anew. . . . We are reminded of several things about Wordsworth and children. First, Wordsworth went to Tintern Abbey in the first place as a refuge from traumas connected with the French revolution. . . . The purpose was refuge and, on the second trip, a slightly

self-indulgent revisiting. Second, and equally important, Eliot's is a more genuinely childlike position than anything we have seen so far. For the most striking fact about children is not that they are innocent but that they are helpless: they have little control over their own lives or purposes. To Wordsworth, being childlike meant something quite different from allowing oneself to be controlled by events not of one's own making, or by the will of another. . . . Eliot's pilgrimage is dominated above all by a discipline that excludes sentimentality and self-assertion. Unlike, say, Wordsworth's or Arnold's journeys, it is undertaken neither as an escape nor as a form of self-indulgence, but as a duty.

> You are not here to verify,
> Instruct yourself, or inform curiosity
> Or carry report. You are here to kneel
> Where prayer has been valid.

One thing that never occurred to Wordsworth at Tintern Abbey, or to Arnold at the Grande Chartreuse, was to pray. (pp. 419-20)

"Little Gidding" is, unlike "Tintern Abbey," both a war poem and a meditation on history. . . . The way to deal with history is not to flee from it but to open oneself to all of its crises and participants without refighting its battles. . . . History, like life at any stage, "is a pattern/Of timeless moments." Thus analyzed and accepted, nostalgia becomes something other than itself: it too is redeemed in a larger pattern. . . . Desire too must go—not only the desire for wealth, fame, comfort, but also the desire for liberation itself, peace, wholeness, indeed the achievement of any of our own purposes whatsoever.

That this austere, almost medieval form of self-denial is unlike anything proposed or practised by any of our other poets except Hopkins is obvious. That in it lies, for Eliot, our only salvation is evident from all of his major works. "Little Gidding" is in this as in other senses his masterwork, and it is not surprising that after it he wrote no more poems. Yet the reward that the "classicist" offers us at the end of this most romantic of nineteenth-century searches would have made Wordsworth and most of his successors nod their heads. It is, in truth, the achievement of their quest and the way out of their dilemma, even though the disciplines by which it is achieved are alien to all of them.

> And the end of all our exploring
> Will be to arrive where we started
> And know the place for the first time.

We shall know it as only adults can know, but we shall be at home in it as only children and those who have given up the desire that their desires should rule can be at home anywhere. (pp. 420-21)

> *Christopher Clausen, in* Sewanee Review *(reprinted by permission of the editor; © 1976 by The University of the South), Summer, 1976.*

ROBERT MARTIN ADAMS

Whether *Ulysses* had such overpowering influence on *The Waste Land* that the latter is in effect a parody of the former is a point that need not be decided here; Joyce thought it did, but he was touchy in these matters, and even if he was right, hardly anyone connected the two works till many years after both were published. The basic fact that *Ulysses* made a tremendous impression on Eliot is beyond question, and nobody did more to make it clear than Eliot himself. His friends were amazed; for the first time in their experience, he was openly enthusiastic about a contemporary book. He not only talked up *Ulysses* among his acquaintance, he wrote, in November 1923, a most influential notice for *The Dial* under the heading "Ulysses, Order, and Myth"; this statement served for many years not only as a landmark of Joyce criticism, but as a credo for advocates of myth as a structural principle in modern writing.

In fact, Eliot's essay in *The Dial* applies more directly to the use of myth in *The Waste Land* than to the use of myth in *Ulysses*. The Grail legend as interpreted by Jessie Weston really serves as a structural principle on which Eliot hung (with the help of Pound) his observations of contemporary London. (pp. 37-8)

> *Robert Martin Adams, in his* AfterJoyce: Studies in Fiction After "Ulysses" *(copyright © 1977 by Robert Martin Adams; reprinted by permission of Oxford University Press, Inc.), Oxford University Press, 1977.*

SAMUEL HYNES

[The] war book above all others in the 'twenties was *The Waste Land,* and no account of the forces that formed the 'thirties generation would be accurate that neglected that powerfully influential poem. Eliot had an acute sense of what he called 'the immense panorama of futility and anarchy that is contemporary history', and he put that sense of history into his poem. And in 1922 contemporary history meant vestiges of the war: hence the two veterans who meet in the first part, and Lil's husband, who has just been demobbed, in the second, and the shouting and crying in part five, which Eliot's note identifies with the Russian Revolution. But beyond that, the world of the poem, with its heaps of broken images and its shocked and passive and neurasthenic persons, is a paradigm of war's effects, and of a world emptied of order and meaning, like a battlefield after the battle. And the *manner* of the poem—its ironic tone, its imagery, its lack of heroes and heroism, its anti-rhetorical style—is also a consequence of the war, an application of war-poet principles to the post-war scene. (p. 25)

To Eliot's young admirers, *The Waste Land* was the essential vision of the post-war world, and the generation's *donnée.* It is worth noting that the generation involved here includes both the friends of Waugh at the beginning of the 'twenties, and the friends of Auden at the end. . . . [In] the 'twenties, when the two groups overlapped at Oxford, they were one post-war generation, sharing a view of society as decadent and emptied of values. And Eliot's poem seemed an immediate and authoritative expression of what they saw.

From its first appearance, *The Waste Land* was read as a work of primarily social and moral import, a public poem on public themes. It is possible, now, fifty years later, to see it as the private nightmare of a young expatriate having a nervous breakdown in Zürich or, in Eliot's own terms, as 'the relief of a personal and wholly insignificant grouse against life . . . just a piece of rhythmical grumbling', but in the 'twenties such readings were not current, because they were not useful to a generation living in the shadow cast by the late war. The poem was about the consequences of the war, and when influential young critics wrote about it, they dealt with it in essentially public terms, as a sentence

passed by the poet on post-war society. And by writing as they did they helped to fix this reading as the orthodox one.

I. A. Richards, then a young don at Cambridge, was especially influential, for he seemed, to the young men he taught, to occupy roughly the same place in post-war criticism that Eliot did in post-war poetry. (pp. 27-8)

Richards was the first English critic to develop a theory of modern poetry in terms of which *The Waste Land* was an important poem. [He wrote]:

> [Mr. Eliot] seems to me by this poem, to have performed two considerable services for this generation. He has given a perfect emotive description of a state of mind which is probably inevitable for a while to all meditative people. Secondly, by effecting a complete severance between his poetry and *all* beliefs, and this without any weakening of the poetry, he has realised what might otherwise have remained largely a speculative possibility and has shown the way to the only solution of these difficulties. 'In the destructive element immerse. That is the way.'

It is, I think, a crucial passage: it claims the poem as a philosophical support for a certain philosophical attitude—what Richards elsewhere in the book calls 'the neutralisation of nature'; and it links the poem with the post-war generation, as a perfect account of an inevitable state of mind. Henceforth, if one did not feel a sense of desolation, if one did not immerse in the destructive element, one was not a meditative person. For young people, this is surely the way beliefs, and feelings about beliefs, are often formed. And if this is so, then the creation of a received view of *The Waste Land,* and of the poem's connection with a post-war state of mind, was a significant part of the formation of the 'thirties generation.

The interpretation of the poem that Richards urged was not an eccentric one; it simply ignored the private meaning, what Eliot meant when he called it a personal grouse against life. He was encouraged to read it as he did by Eliot's own critical writings, by the famous defence of difficulty in 'The Metaphysical Poets', for example, and more specifically by Eliot's review of *Ulysses,* published in 1923. The essay is a justification of what Eliot calls 'the mythic method', and a transparent defence of the way *The Waste Land* is put together; the method, he says, 'is simply a way of controlling, of ordering, of giving a shape and a significance to the immense panorama of futility and anarchy which is contemporary history'. Such a vision of history separates the post-war world from all the past, and from past ideas of order and value; it must have both confirmed and helped to form Richards' understanding of Eliot's poem, and, more importantly, it must have helped to form the post-war generation's sense of its isolation from the world before the war. (pp. 28-9)

[All] through the 'thirties Eliot—classicist, royalist, and Anglo-Catholic though he proclaimed himself to be—managed to be both a model and a patron to the radical young. (p. 47)

> *Samuel Hynes, in his* The Auden Generation: Literature and Politics in England in

F

FERLINGHETTI, Lawrence   1919 (?) -

An American poet, editor, playwright, essayist, novelist, and translator, Ferlinghetti was a leader of the Beat movement and the American poetry revival of the fifties that aimed to bring poetry to a wider reading public. Much of his work is political and satirical, portraying reality as fragmented and protesting violence. Strongly influenced by French existentialism and the surrealists, he has been compared with Jacques Prévert, Paul Eluard, and e.e. cummings. Ferlinghetti's poetry is often improvisational, with the spontaneous quality of jazz. He uses flexible, spoken rhythms, as well as frequent allusions to literature and art. (See also *CLC*, Vols. 2, 6, and *Contemporary Authors*, Vols. 5-8, rev. ed.)

JASCHA KESSLER

Ferlinghetti has always been addicted to spiritual posturings, to invoking the names of the gods, saints and bards in phrases such as Time magazine uses for captions, and to digging their ineffable incarnations in the apparitions of old men and boys, misfits and thugs and flowers and bums. This is San Francisco-style sentimentality, largely his own creation.

He writes merely endless sentences of flat prose, with here and there a Tibetan or Arabic formula, a prayer phrase, and breaks them up into panting lines. Headlines, that is, blown up and made to sound as significant, as portentous as headlines shouted or keened out over a mike in concert with amplified sitars and bongos and young people rocking and whining, delirious with noise and smoke and bemused by the desire to trip along. Public poetry, publicly performed.

Everywhere today the voice of the inauthentic is heard in the land, and Ferlinghetti is its prophet. [The] six poems [in ''The Secret Meaning of Things''] wander lonely as a cloud through Boston, San Francisco, Germany and Russia, offering visions reminiscent of the first 15 seconds of TV commercials, before the product comes on, visions of blurbs commented on sententiously by an egotistic trifler, never a phrase or idea or rhythm original with himself.

> *Jascha Kessler, ''Sentimental Trifles in Frisco Vein,'' in* The Los Angeles Times *(copyright, 1969, Los Angeles Times; reprinted by permission), July 20, 1969, p. 49.*

CRALE D. HOPKINS

[Lawrence Ferlinghetti deserves] disentanglement from the old Beat-poet characterization. His poetry cannot be dismissed either as protest polemic or as incoherently personalized lyric. His craftsmanship, thematics, and awareness of the tradition justify a further consideration. (p. 60)

By the time his later works were published, Ferlinghetti had been firmly fixed by and large in the Beat school an‹ received little more individual attention. (p. 61)

The subject of the doctoral thesis Ferlinghetti wrote at the University of Paris was ''The Symbolic City in Modern Literature.'' His poetry reflects this acquaintance with modern European and American literature, and this constitutes the first point at which Ferlinghetti departs from the Beat stereotype. . . . [In] Ferlinghetti's poetry there is no bitter anti-intellectualism [as some critics found in Beat poetry] but rather a knowledge and appreciation of traditional literary materials which are integrated into his own verse.

A second generalization has it that all Beat literature is either crippled by disengagement and a poverty of feeling. . . . Ferlinghetti, however, wrote some of the most sensitive lyrics of the last twenty years. In *A Coney Island Of The Mind*, Poem 19 . . . is in part a criticism of the usual Beat stance, bemoaning

> this unshaved today
> with its derisive rooks
> that rise above dry trees
> and caw and cry
> and question every other
> spring and thing

(pp. 61-3)

The first published work, *Pictures Of The Gone World*, is largely composed of poems of lyric observation. The word ''gone'' in the title implies in its 50s slang sense that they are ''hip'' or ''groovy'' visions of the world, but it also suggests the past, the world that is gone. Thus there is one group of poems that deal with novel insights into the world. . . . Others are surrealistic portraits, which can be quite penetrating:

> Yes Dada would have died for a day like this
> with its sweet street carnival
> and its too real funeral
> just passing through it

                    with its real dead dancer
                              so beautiful and dumb
                    in her shroud
                              and her last lover lost
          in the unlonely crowd
                              and its dancers darling baby
               about to say Dada
                         and its passing priest
               about to pray
                         Dada
                         and offer his so transcendental
          apologies
Yes Dada would have loved a day like this
                         with its not so accidental
               analogies

Characteristically this poem, 23, uses the short broken lines alternatingly to slow the eye and produce a detached ironic effect emphasized by the alliteration and internal rhyme. The poem ends tellingly on the dangling word "analogies," beautifully preceded by "apologies" and the completed multiple rhyme of "transcendental-accidental." These devices, and the puns on Dada, are typical of Ferlinghetti's method in presenting an ironic insight into the incongruities of life. (pp. 65-6)

The poetry of Ferlinghetti's second, and most famous collection, *A Coney Island Of The Mind,* is more surrealistic and has more satiric social observation. The ultimate surrealist vision of the failed American Dream is in Poem 3 . . . :

     America
               with its ghost towns and empty Ellis Islands
     and its surrealist landscape of
                         mindless prairies
                         supermarket suburbs
                         steamheated cemeteries
                         cinerama holy days
                         and protesting cathedrals
     a kissproof world of plastic toiletseats tampax and taxis
          drugged store cowboys and las vegas virgins
          disowned indians and cinemad matrons
          unroman senators and conscientious non, objectors
     and all the other fatal shorn-up fragments
     of the immigrant's dream come too true
                    and mislaid
                         among the sunbathers

Some might object that this is not really poetry; it is by any definition an effective piece of work in the Dadaist-surrealist tradition, showing considerable craft. The accuracy of the items heaped together is telling; again, the mocking alliteration (toiletseats tampax and taxis) and the multiple rhyme (prairies-cemeteries) underscore the satire. The puns on drugstore, vestal virgin, and cinema underline the pattern of those lines, which name two merely foolish types (drugstore cowboys and vestal virgins) now become disgusting; then two more, one no longer dignified figure and one never dignified character; then two who are the opposite of two desirable types. The last four lines include an allusion to Eliot (shorn-up fragments) using Eliot's method, which Ferlinghetti does frequently in this collection.

A number of poems take up the theme of illusion and reality—of surrealism itself—and the role of art in that scheme. (p. 67)

Ferlinghetti's last poems on this theme are in *Starting From San Francisco.* "Flying Out Of It" . . . is a vision of spinning past heaven among the galaxies: "Death swings / its dumb bell / I'll catch it? . . . Ah there's a slit / to slither through / into eternity / . . . cannot make it / Pied Piper's cave / clangs shut." The abstract diction, cold tone, and short, three or four word triple-spaced lines combine to suggest that the failure to pierce through is due to a lack of that super realism, that mad north of introspection. . . . ["He" is] a portrait of a prophet of the ultimate reality, the surrealist who has achieved "the mad eye of the fourth person singular." The "fourth person singular" is the position above reality, seeing you, him, and himself also. (pp. 68-9)

Related to reality and the fourth person singular is the problem of love. A great deal of Ferlinghetti's poetry deals with that subject in one way or another, and it early involves the question of reality, the ideal versus the actual. . . . [In Ferlinghetti's novel *Her*] the story concerns the inability of the central character to achieve the viewpoint of the "fourth person singular," the position above reality that affords insight. (pp. 69-70)

The person with the viewpoint of the "fourth person singular" realizes that the world is "unreal" because it is not permanent—and there is nothing beyond. The values to be cultivated in this "unreal" world are therefore of paramount importance, love perhaps being the most important. The problem is to realize this and to comprehend love in its fullest sense. (p. 70)

[Most] of Ferlinghetti's poetry is concerned with his perceptions of the "unreal," ephemeral world and the kind of love that he sees as the only salvation. "After the Cries of the Birds" in *The Secret Meaning Of Things* . . . is in part an apocalyptic vision of the triumph of that true love. The vehicle for these ideas, the poetry itself, must be viewed in the proper perspective. The more lyrical pieces, such as Poem 20 of *A Coney Island Of The Mind,* discussed previously, use the traditional devices of rhyme, metrical arrangement, and harmonious alliteration. Rhyme, particularly multiple rhyme, and exaggerated alliteration are employed often in the satirical pieces for mocking and ironic effect. Other than the utilization of these basic poetic effects, though, Ferlinghetti's poetry departs sharply from conventional verse. (p. 72)

Ferlinghetti's poetry receives much of its force from its diction. The more lyrical poems avoid conventional poetic language and use common speech arranged to achieve its effect through unique juxtapositions and striking but hauntingly familiar images. The more declamatory poems mingle bizarre words, vulgar colloquialisms and literary tags to create a surrealistic, multi-dimensional quality: "pantomimic parrots pierrots castrate disaster / . . . while cakewalkers and carnival hustlers / all gassed to the gills / strike playbill poses." . . . Ferlinghetti finally introduces most popular four-letter words into his poetry, carrying Wordsworth's dictum to its logical conclusion. It should be said that they are not used for shock value or cheaply, but as they play a part in the day-to-day speech of many people. (pp. 73-4)

This poetry is striking, powerful, and convincing. It cannot be judged by conventional literary standards, however. Whether or not it is indeed poetry can only be answered when a comprehensive definition of that word is agreed upon—a situation not yet achieved. Ferlinghetti's work is not "message" writing, that must have your assent to receive your appreciation. Like all good imaginative writing it is its own justification: the interplay between statement, image and metaphor, surface meaning and plurisignation fuse and become, not state, its meaning.

It should also be realized that a considerable amount of his work is social poetry. While I don't feel that Ferlinghetti sees himself as a prophet, he clearly has an immediate sense of audience that many other modern poets do not. . . .

Ferlinghetti's poetry finally should be seen as a small but significant strain within the contemporary tradition. He shares with the more well-known modern poets a reaction to the "academic" poetry of Eliot and Pound but differs in his radical techniques, language, and social orientation. Many individual poems are valuable and significant achievements and the body of his work as a whole must be recognized for its sincere and sensitive cultural perceptions. (p. 74)

> Crale D. Hopkins, "The Poetry of Lawrence Ferlinghetti: A Reconsideration," in Italian Americana (copyright © 1974 by Ruth Falbo and Richard Gambino), Autumn, 1974, pp. 59-76.

C. R. METZGER

Ferlinghetti's "Autobiography" [one of seven "oral messages" in *A Coney Island of the Mind*] is a highly and mockingly-learned riddle poem. . . . [It] is a witty testament to Ferlinghetti's seriously held poetic faith. . . .

[One] cannot fully appreciate the poem without knowing that Ferlinghetti has written a "pied" or medley poem after the riddling manner of the ancient Celtic unofficial bards or minstrels, and that it contains allusions not only to ancient Celtic poetic history, but also to even more ancient pre-Cymric, old-Goidelic, myth. These are suggested by the presence of individual lines in Ferlinghetti's poem which are taken exactly from English translations of three ancient Celtic riddle poems. These three poems are 1) the *Hanes Taliesen* (*The Tale of Taliesin*), 2) the *Câd Goddeu* (*The Battle of the Trees*), and 3) the *Song of Amergin*. (p. 25)

[It is necessary] to explain what these lines "plagiarized" from translations of three ancient Celtic poems are doing in Ferlinghetti's "Autobiography," a poem presumably, and indeed actually, about Ferlinghetti himself, as person, and as poet. I suggest that the explanation lies in the nature and circumstances of these three ancient poems themselves, more particularly as they relate to the bardic tradition of thirteenth century Wales, and to the antecedent traditions of Celtic bards in the sixth century, and beyond that to the tradition of the Druid-Bards , or *Derwyddvierdd*, and to the *Beirdd*, who preceded them, dating back as far as 1268 B.C. . . . , and more than likely to some time anterior even to that date. (pp. 26-7)

[His] reference . . . to Joyce's "silence, exile, and cunning" is not only appropriate to a description of a portion of his own life, but also suggestive of the cunning and secretive nature of his own poem, as well as the similar nature of the *Song of Amergin* from which he does pirate. (p. 28)

It so happens that Ferlinghetti's "Autobiography" demonstrates [the] kind of deliberately pied, riddling poetry which

[Robert Graves describes in *The White Goddess*]. It demonstrates equally the kind of poetry which the Druid in the *envoi* at the beginning of the *Song of Amergin* called for: cunning, incantatory, extensively learned, mocking, and crystal clear to sufficiently well educated fellow poets. The crystal is no less clear, one might add, for having been cut with many facets; it merely reflects more light, more images. (p. 30)

Ferlinghetti's poem reads most richly and waggishly comprehensible when read in terms of Graves' *White Goddess*. . . .

[Of] the eighteen or more writers that Ferlinghetti either quotes, paraphrases, or alludes to in his 302 line poem (all but three are poets), the one poet that Ferlinghetti refers to most often, although never directly by name, is the thirteenth century Welsh bard whom Graves calls Gwion. It is to this Gwion that Graves ascribes the authorship of the versions of the *Câd Goddeu* and the *Hanes Taliesin* that appear in the *Romance of Taliesin*. And it is this Gwion whose lines, translated into English, appear in Ferlinghetti's poem. (p. 31)

Ferlinghetti identifies with this eponymous and Protean "Gwion-Taliesin." To remain ignorant of this identification is to run the serious risk of misunderstanding not only what the "Autobiography" is all about, but who the speaker is in that poem—the *I* who has "been leading a quiet life," who has "ridden boxcars, boxcars, boxcars," who is "a tear of the sun," who was "in Asia with Noah in the Ark."

Graves' Gwion, the poet that Ferlinghetti alludes to most heavily (excepting possibly Graves himself), is actually a composite of persons, all quite "real," but in different and complementary ways. First of all Graves' Gwion was an historical person or persons who wrote the thirteenth century poems contained in the *Romance of Taliesin*. Graves argues, from internal evidence, that this same poet wrote both the *Hanes Talieslin* and the *Câd Goddeu*. He argues further that it is this poet, or at least poets like him, that Phylip Brydydd (c. 1220-30 A. D.) referred to in describing a controversy between himself and "certain vulgar rymsters." . . . These rymsters, he charged, "had no honor," *i.e.,* (says Graves) "did not belong to the privileged class of Cymric freemen from which the court bards were chosen, but were unendowed minstrels." . . . (pp. 31-2)

This thirteenth century controversy between Graves' Gwion, or poets like him, and Phylip Brydydd, and official poets such as he, is important to readers who would clearly understand Ferlinghetti's "Autobiography" because it is one of at least four poetic controversies (or battles) suggested by the lines pirated from ancient Welsh poetry and pied into Ferlinghetti's poem. (p. 32)

The last and most recent of these controversies, I suggest, is that celebrated in Ferlinghetti's own poem, "Autobiography." It is the controversy between the author and other true poets like himself, on the one hand, including ancient partially mythical, eponymous poets such as Graves' Gwion (the thirteenth century opponent of Brydydd), including the sixth century Gwion, Elphin's bard (the opponent of King Maelgwin's bards), including Gwydion ap Dôn (the opponent of King Anwn), all these at least, not to mention more recent poets such as John Keats, Matthew Arnold, Walt Whitman, T. S. Eliot, Ezra Pound, James Joyce, and Robert Graves—all of these true poets, ancient as well as modern, standing in opposition to craven, sycophantic and ignorant academic, *i.e.,* official poets in general. (p. 33)

Graves' Gwion, from whom Ferlinghetti quotes, and in whose voice he speaks part of the time at least, is simply one of the latter-day thirteenth century versions of the bard as priest-hero of poetry. And Ferlinghetti himself, I suggest, is a more recent version or incarnation of this Gwion—he in company with fellow true poets such as Eliot, Williams, Ginsberg, and Graves, among others. (pp. 34-5)

[Ferlinghetti's allusions to Graves are] at least as significant to our understanding of Ferlinghetti's deeply held poetic faith as are his direct quotations from the poetry of the various Gwions-Taliesin.

Graves asserts that the true poets' sole mission in life is to celebrate through inspired and often riddling poetry, the true source of inspiration as well as death, the White Goddess, who according to pre-Christian Celtic religions is at once the mother, the lover, and the layer out of the corpse of true poets. She is the ultimate source of both inspiration and death. She is the night-mare whose nest is strewn with the bones and entrails of poets. She is Ceridwen in the *Tale of Taliesin.* She is at once Diana, Artemis, the Sow Goddess, the Mare Goddess, the three witches in Macbeth; she is at once mother, nymph, and hag. In her more attractive form she is the lady without mercy; she has yellow hair, a chalk-white face, lips like rowan berries.

One might reasonably expect, in view of what I have been arguing heretofore, to find reference to her in Ferlinghetti's "Autobiography." And it is there. (pp. 38-9)

One has reason to suspect that Ferlinghetti's references earlier in his poem to the Laughing Woman at Luna Park . . . , to the Venus Aphrodite, to the siren singing at One Fifth Avenue, suggest versions of his muse. It is the White Goddess, I suggest further . . . , who appears in the Statue of Saint Francis poem in the same collection with "Autobiography." It is she, I suggest further, who is the principal object, if not subject, of Ferlinghetti's novel *Her.* (p. 39)

Ferlinghetti adds in *Her* that the poetic imagination is begotten and inspired by *Her,* his version of the White Goddess, in Ferlinghetti's case by his mother, his phantasy lover, and the crone selling coquelicots, ultimately the layer out of his corpse. (p. 40)

In the "Autobiography" Ferlinghetti's assertion of the secret meaning of the poem, of his role as a latter day Gwion-Taliesin, of his avowed worship of the White Goddess, is guarded, hidden, and disguised by the pieing into the poem, along with the lines taken from Graves' Gwion, apparently superficial and gratuitous pirating of lines from, as well as references to, relatively recent writers such as Wordsworth, Keats, Matthew Arnold, Browning, Yeats, Joyce, Thoreau, Hawthorne, Melville, Whitman, Twain, Wolfe, Hart, Crane, Pound, Hemingway, and Eliot, among others.

These writers to whom Ferlinghetti alludes in one way or another have in common with Ferlinghetti and Graves' Gwion-Taliesin one important thing—they have been all, I suggest, during at least part of their careers true poets. To my knowledge Ferlinghetti never alludes to an academician-poet teaching in a university, sitting in an endowed chair. (pp. 40-1)

C. R. Metzger, "Lawrence Ferlinghetti as Elphin's Bard," in The Midwest Quarterly *(copyright, 1974, by* The Midwest Quarterly, *Kansas State College of Pittsburg), Autumn, 1974, pp. 25-41.*

MICHAEL SKAU

In his prose volume, *Her,* Lawrence Ferlinghetti explores the dynamics of artistic consciousness and control. He posits as his protagonist Andy Raffine, who is seeking his own unique identity, symbolized by his search for the enigmatic "her" of the title. His quest is frustrated by his reluctant recognition of his role as a fictional character and by his vulnerability to the forces of illusion. In addition, Ferlinghetti allows the relationship between the author and his creation to image his view of the relationship between God and man. (p. 40)

Her focuses on the interrelationship of three figures—the author; a theoretically unique and autonomous literary character; and the hybrid character resulting from the imposition of the author's experiences, fantasies, and language on the "pure" character. . . . The pattern of Ferlinghetti's approach closely resembles Robbe-Grillet's description of his own literary technique: "Not only is it *a man* who, in my novels for instance, describes everything, but it is the least neutral, the least impartial of men: *always* engaged, on the contrary, in an emotional adventure of the most obsessive kind, to the point of often distorting his vision and of producing imaginings close to delirium." Raffine is in precisely this delirious stage, occupying a *carrefour* where reality and illusion intersect and impinge on one another. Manifestations of fantasy and actuality become devices used by Ferlinghetti to explore and delineate a conceptualized reality. Deliberately elongated prose-rhythms and hypnotic dream-sequences are placed in sharp, contrasting juxtaposition with abruptly banal statements. Cinematic figures of speech also function to emphasize the indeterminacy of a chiaroscurist world. In addition, *Her* is seeded with images of a static, frozen world, as though actions were caught at a still moment, the time-suspended world of a painting or a photograph.

Given the complexity of Ferlinghetti's purpose, the reader may often be confused about the identity of the speaker as *Her* progresses. Ferlinghetti confronts such possible response by incorporating the confusion itself into the texture of his work: he allows Raffine to question whether the character's role in the plot and action is one of participant or audience. Since the central issues of *Her* involve artistic creation, many of the arts are called upon to provide imagery illustrating Raffine's uncertainty. He repeatedly finds himself unable to determine whether, to use his own cinematic image, he is an actor playing a role in a movie or simply a member of the audience watching the movie. Indeed, he suspects that he is continually shifting between these positions. Similarly, Raffine suggests that he may be an extra or a member of the audience who wanders onstage and perhaps becomes part of a dramatic production. . . . The arts of painting and sculpture also provide appropriate images of identity confusion. (pp. 40-1)

The artistic images appearing most frequently in *Her* spring from literature. The language, action, and emphasis of much of the last two sections of the book reflect off a cento passage derived from a prose work by H. D., *Palimpsest,* principally the first story, "Hipparchia: War Rome (*circa*

75 B.C.),'' portraying a woman named Hipparchia, whom Marius, her lover, feels may be "after all, a creature entirely of his imagining." The very image of a palimpsest is, of course, valuable to the focus in *Her* on how the author writes over his fictional character: Raffine at one point characterizes every human being as "a perambulant palimpsest." . . . In addition, Ferlinghetti provides numerous allusions and parodies of familiar passages from famous writers. The parodies, together with the numerous examples of paronomasia, offer evidence of verbal sabotage. Word associations, Joycean multilingual puns, Dylan-Thomas-like word harmonies, and sight-and-sound puns abound in *Her,* providing continual proof of liberated fancy and the associational capacity of the human imagination. Raffine sees the verbal medium as one of the chief factors in the creation of illusion and attacks its undermining effect: "words, in their quest for Attic verity, were the real destroyers, the real preventers, each a little fence." . . . (p. 42)

Her confronts the problem of illusion at another remove: Raffine, who rebels against imagination, is himself a creation of the imagination. . . . The tension that *Her* portrays is between autonomous self-depiction by the created character and creative invention springing from the author's own experiences. Raffine cries out desperately for autonomous purity, while recognizing his dilemma as "the same creepy nowhere hero making his mushy exiled rounds the same walking cliche never able to break away into the free air of underivative creation." . . . With eminent clarity, he identifies his function as that of a *"poupee interieure"* . . . but refuses to surrender to that state. Instead, he struggles against associations, misapprehensions, and stylized behavior. . . . *Her* thus begins to comment on itself and its own creative elements. The illusion of unique creativity is punctured by the barbs of realistic execution. (pp. 42-3)

Woman is both antagonist and ideal for [Raffine], because he realizes that the phantom figure of "her" is largely a product of his imagination, "capable of stretching into any form I imagined." . . . "Her" encompasses all women: mother, the Virgin, Dante's Beatrice, Helen, Mona Lisa, and Heidi, as well as all those encountered in the past, present, and future, with "the various women I've known all adding up to flash in a composite image all leading up to this moment in some lost connection with this Virgin's place." . . . Thus, while Raffine passionately pleads for his own independent identity, his associational eye deprives the entire female sex of precisely that uniqueness. Crucially, Raffine's view of women characterizes them all indistinguishably as incomplete, unfinished, uncommitted, and unawakened. (p. 44)

Raffine's quest for "her" is symbolic of his search for his own completed self. What he finally craves is synthesis of the elements of his character. . . . Raffine turns from flesh to spirit, from corporal concerns to ideational ones. Throughout *Her,* he seeks to free himself from his cumbersome body. . . . Flesh represents for him the form of illusion which masks or distorts reality, "the fleshpaint skin I hid in like painters hiding behind their paint, authors behind their words." . . . Liberation from the flesh, then, would parallel liberation from the word, which Raffine can achieve only when freed from the novelist's control, at the conclusion of the novel. . . . (pp. 44-5)

In the final section of *Her,* the relationship between the author and his character reveals itself as emblematic of more than literary concern. Religious imagery asserts itself. . . . Raffine's rebellion thus takes on the dimension of man's revolt against control by his Creator, in Whose likeness he is fashioned. The narrative voice would seem at this point to return to Ferlinghetti himself, rebelling against the chains of humanity and mortality. The rebellion is, of course, fruitless, as hopeless as Raffine's revolt against his author. Reluctantly, Raffine finally adjusts to his literary essence. . . . He recognizes "this site of myself made into the reassuring form of a story" . . . and submits to being caught by God.

Ferlinghetti's *Her* provides an exploration of life and letters on several different levels. The relationship between the author, frustrated in his attempt at autobiography, and his created character, prevented from asserting a measure of autonomous independence, symbolizes Ferlinghetti's view of the human predicament. He shows man as the inadvertent operator of the machinery of associations, frustrated in his attempts at "underivative creation." As victim of the illusions generated by those associations, man becomes a helpless puppet, energized by cliches and uncontrollable, repetitive behavior. Finally, the latter circumstance is used to portray man's helplessness in the hands of his Creator, with questionable free will and limited spontaneity, destined to re-enact perpetually the eternal movie of man in this world. (p. 45)

Michael Skau, "Toward Underivative Creation: Lawrence Ferlinghetti's 'Her'," *in* Critique: Studies in Modern Fiction *(copyright © by James Dean Young 1978), Vol. XIX, No. 3, 1978, pp. 40-6.*

*   *   *

FORSTER, E(dward) M(organ)   1879-1970

Forster was an English novelist, short story writer, essayist, and critic. His concept of humanism, reflected in all of his novels, was forged through an understanding and acceptance of both traditional and modern interpretations of the term. That is, he was concerned with both the study of classical texts and with the philosophy of human relationships and values. He rejected the precepts of Christianity, as is evidenced in his most famous work, *A Passage to India*, where the central principle of Hinduism, that of total acceptance, is posited as the greatest unifying force for mankind. *A Passage to India*, published in 1924, was Forster's last major work, followed only by essays and small minor pieces. Critics speculate that his inner struggle with his homosexuality (revealed only after his death) prevented Forster from adding to a collection of work that marks him as a major twentieth-century author. (See also *CLC*, Vols. 1, 2, 3, 4, 9, and *Contemporary Authors*, Vols. 13-14; obituary, Vols. 25-28, rev. ed.; *Contemporary Authors Permanent Series*, Vol. 1.)

FRANK KERMODE

Mr. Forster is a kind of Symbolist. He declares for the autonomy of the work of art; for co-essence of form and meaning; for art as "organic and free from dead matter"; for music as a criterion of formal purity; for the work's essential anonymity. Like all art, he thinks, the novel must fuse differentiation into unity, in order to provide meaning we can experience; art is "the one orderly product that our muddling race has produced," the only unity and therefore the only meaning. This is Symbolist. But there are interesting qualifications to be made; they bear on the question of differentiation, of stresses within the unity. . . . (pp. 90-1)

The first qualification arises from Mr. Forster's celebrated insistence on the point that the novel tells a story. . . . In the novel, the matter which seeks pure form is itself impure. This sounds like the old Symbolist envy of music; but we soon learn that Mr. Forster really values this impurity. . . . He agrees with [H. G. Wells] that "life should be given the preference, and must not be whittled or distended for a pattern's sake." If "life" in this sense is pattern-resisting, impure, nevertheless our direct revelation of reality, pure as it is, must somehow include it. One thinks of Valéry, who said that no poem could be pure poetry and still be a poem. Unity implies the inclusion of impurity.

The second qualification again brings the French Symbolist to mind. "Organic unity"—art's kind of unity—has to be produced by a process coarsely characterised by Mr. Forster himself as "faking." "All a writer's faculties," he says, "including the valuable faculty of faking, do conspire together . . . for the creative act." "Faking" is the power he so greatly admired in Virginia Woolf. (p. 91)

In this sense of the word, a novel not only fakes human relationships but also, working against muddle and chance, fakes an idea of order without which those relationships could have no significance. The fraud committed is, in fact, a general benefaction of significance. . . . I must have some sort of a shot at the task of illustrating how, in *A Passage to India,* where it is almost inconceivably elaborate, the faking is done. The events it describes include the coming of Krishna, which makes the world whole by love; and the novel's own analogous unity is achieved by faking.

One can start at the opening chapter, indeed the opening sentence. "Except for the Marabar Caves—and they are twenty miles off—the city of Chandrapore presents nothing extraordinary." Easy, colloquial, if with a touch of the guide-book, the words set a scene. But they will reach out and shape the organic whole. Or, to put it another way, they lie there, lacking all rhetorical emphasis, waiting for the relations which will give them significance to the eye of "love." But they are prepared for these relations. The order of principal and subordinate clauses, for instance, is inverted, so that the exception may be mentioned first— "except for the Marabar Caves." The excepted is what must be included if there is to be meaning; first things first. First, then, the extraordinary which governs and limits significance; then, secondly, we may consider the city. It keeps the caves at a distance; it is free of mystery till nightfall, when the caves close in to question its fragile appearance of order—an appearance that depends upon a social conspiracy to ignore the extraordinary. Henceforth, in this novel, the word "extraordinary" is never used without reference to the opening sentence. It belongs to the caves. The last words of the first chapter speak once more of "the extraordinary caves." Miss Quested's behaviour in relation to the caves is "extraordinary."

It is a characteristically brilliant device; the word occurs so naturally in conversation that its faked significance cannot disturb the story. The characters say "extraordinary" but the novelist means "extra-ordinary." . . . The caves are the exception that menaces the city, the city of gardens and geometrical roads made by the English, the Indian city of

unholy muddle. And sometimes it is possible to exclude them, to ignore them like the distance beyond distance in the sky, because, like God in the song of the beautiful ecstatic girl, they are without attributes.

In a sense, they *are* God without attributes; because his absence implies his presence. Therefore, says the Professor, we are entitled to repeat to Krishna, "Come, come, come." Without them there is no whole by which we may understand the parts. Fielding rejects them, and will never understand; he believes in "thought." Mrs. Moore accepts them, seeing a whole, but one in which love is absent; all distinctions obliterated not by meaning but by meaninglessness, the roar of the Marabar echo. Including the excepted does not necessarily result in felicity. But when we know the worst of Marabar—that it is of the very stuff of life, flesh of the sun, thrusting up into the holy soil of Ganges— we still have to observe that the last explicit mention of Marabar in the book, at the end of a petulant remark of Aziz, is drowned in the noise of rejoicing at Krishna's coming. An ordinary conversational remark, of course, with its place in the story, bears the weight of this piece of faking. Similarly, in the last pages, the rocks which, as in a parable, separate the friends Aziz and Fielding, are thrust up from the Indian earth like the fists and fingers of Marabar. Story, parable, coexist in the wholeness of the revelation.

Privation, the want of wholeness, may entitle us in life to say "Come, come, come"; but in the novel this appeal has also to be faked. Godbole first uses the words at the tea-party, after his statement concerning Marabar. In his song, the milkmaid asks Krishna to come; but he neglects to come. At Marabar the need of him is absolute; and even the road to the caves, where everything calls out "Come, come," remains what it is because "there is not enough god to go around." Resonant with the absence of Krishna, it confuses distinctions like that between love and animal feeling; so Miss Quested discovers. But it is not only Marabar; nothing is proof against the god's neglect. . . . The lack of this coming is felt by the guests at the party who heard Godbole's song; they are unwell, with some malaise of privation; they are suffering from a deficiency of meaning, which cannot be cured until Love takes upon itself the form of Krishna and saves the world in the rain. The unity he makes is an image of art; for a moment at least all is one, apprehensible by love; nothing is excepted or extraordinary. The novel itself assumes a similar unity, becomes a mystery, a revelation of wholeness; and does so without disturbing the story or the parable.

But after this, does it, like the rejoicing at Krishna's coming, "become history and fall under the rule of time"? Like the birth of the god, the novel is contrived as a direct revelation of reality, of meaning conferred by a unifying and thought-excluding love; as—leaving gods out of it—the one orderly product. But does it still fall under the rule of time? Perhaps this mystical conception of order in art *was* more accessible to Mr. Forster than to his younger contemporaries. (pp. 91-4)

The feeling that a work of art, a novel for instance, must be in this exalted sense orderly, survives; but, for whatever reasons, it seems less potent now. Perhaps you cannot have it very fully unless you have that "conviction of harmony" of which the Cambridge philosopher McTaggart used to speak in Mr. Forster's youth. For him, too, all meaning depended upon oneness. He had an argument to prove that it could never inhere in inductive thought; on the contrary, it depended upon what he called "love," meaning not sexual love nor benevolence nor saintliness nor even the love of God, but something like full knowledge and the justice and harmony this entails. McTaggart even allows the possibility of one's experiencing a mystic unity which is not benevolent, not indeed anything but "perfectly simple Being" —without attributes—"difficult, if not impossible, to distinguish from Nothing." He is thinking of Indian mysticism. Marabar is perhaps Being under that aspect; however, Godbole can distinguish between presence and absence, and it is Mrs. Moore who cannot, and who therefore becomes a saint of Nothingness.

These remarks about the intellectual climate at the relevant period are meant to be suggestive, but not to suggest that Mr. Forster as a novelist is a conscious disciple of any philosopher. I do think, though, that the wonderful years at Cambridge enabled him to prepare the ground for a creation of order—gave him the secure sense of organic unity that made possible those feats of faking, and allowed him to see that, properly viewed, the human muddle could itself be mystery. Only in some such way can I account for the marvellous ease with which story, parable and image here coexist. There was a "conviction of harmony," a belief in order. Perhaps that has fallen under the rule of time.

We, in our time, are, I think, incapable of genuinely supposing a work of art to be something quite different from *A Passage to India;* it is, in this sense, contemporary and exemplary. In another sense, though, it does fall under the rule of time, because any conviction of harmony we may have will be differently grounded. Of these two facts, the first seems to me of incomparably greater importance. It is a consequence that we cannot know too much about the remarkable *inclusiveness* of the book. We continue to have our illusions of order, and clever faking; but this book reminds us how vast the effort for totality must be; nothing is excepted, the extraordinary is essential to order. The cities of muddle, the echoes of disorder, the excepting and the excepted, are all to be made meaningful in being made one. This will not happen without the truth of imagination which Mr. Forster calls "love"; love cheats, and muddle turns into mystery: into art, our one orderly product. (pp. 94-5)

Frank Kermode, "The One Orderly Product (E. M. Forster)" (1958), in his Puzzles and Epiphanies: Essays and Reviews, 1958-1961 *(copyright © 1962 by Frank Kermode; reprinted by permission of the Chilmark Press and Routledge and Kegan Paul, Ltd.), Chilmark, 1962, Routledge and Kegan Paul, 1962 (and reprinted as "Mr. E. M. Forster as a Symbolist," in* Forster: A Collection of Critical Essays, *edited by Malcolm Bradbury, Prentice-Hall, Inc., 1966, pp. 90-5).*

MALCOLM BRADBURY

Recent criticism of Forster has tended to take a different approach [from earlier commentaries]; in a variety of ways it has demonstrated that Forster's intellectual and technical character is a good deal more complex and more modern than the earlier view allows. What has been shown to us clearly over recent years is—among other things—the complexity and resource of Forster's fictional method, particularly in *Howards End* and *A Passage to India,* his last two novels. . . . On the other hand, the balance of criticism has

now turned so far in favour of regarding Forster as a modern symbolist that we are sometimes in danger of forgetting the important fact about him that many earlier critics never got beyond—that he is a comic social novelist, a writer of comedy of manners, a man who manifests and is attentive to the social and historical context out of which he derives. This is not the whole Forster, but it is a Forster who never ceases to be present in all the novels, short stories, travel books, and essays.

There is another view of Forster—associated with the opinion that his fictional manner is Victorian—which has also tended to fade. This is the view that he is *intellectually* a Victorian, that he is visibly the child of English middle-class liberalism, a liberalism that has an evident historical location in the heyday of the advanced, but wealthy, intellectual bourgeoisie. To locate a writer like this is often an effective means of limiting him, a means of suggesting that his work has not transcended its determining situation, that it is not universal. . . . Certainly Forster does derive much from the Victorian intellectual tradition. . . . And this means that he derives substantially from the Romantic debate which continued through the nineteenth century and into the twentieth. Forster himself has made such debts quite plain; and he clearly does espouse many of the attitudes of nineteenth century romantic and political liberalism. But he also confronts an essentially modern disquiet; the generous and positive optimism about the future that one finds in the nineteenth century is already uneasy in Forster before the First World War, which challenged that optimism so very radically. Forster, in *Howards End,* is one of the first novelists who portrayed in depth the struggle of the modern intelligentsia to define its alliances, who depicted both its disquiet about its independence and the principles that determine that independence. . . . When we call him a liberal humanist, then, we must be aware of his impulse to mysticism, on the one hand, and his sense of the difficulties of liberalism and openness of view on the other. He is prepared to assert a reconciling, enlarging, invisible quality in the "unseen," and thus to challenge his classical rationalism; at the same time, his visions, though they may suggest an order or unity in the universe, are defined in terms of the anarchy that they must comprehend, and therefore they are never fully redemptive; there is always something they may not account for. In *A Passage to India,* for instance, the novel moves toward but never achieves a visionary resolution.

Forster, I am suggesting, is much closer to Bloomsbury than to nineteenth century liberal optimism; but we cannot quite take him as fully representative of that group either. . . . That Forster is, in a positive way, a "representative" of a culture, or of several cultures, that he is a novelist much fed by his place and circumstances, is evident enough; what recent criticism has shown is the complexity of his position. (pp. 2-5)

The early books, though social comedies, lack the social dimension of the two last novels; they are also much more overtly comic, in the sense that the author's whimsy and his interest in the conduct of particular persons in particular situations of manners are more directly engaged. In all his novels, but particularly in the two last, one is aware of an urgent attempt to achieve some kind of reconciling and poetic vision, to approach through emotion, through the developed heart, those sensations of body and spirit that not only create a full life in the living but give a meaning to life, afford a visionary understanding of it. Forster's distinctive mixture of social comedy and "poetic" writing—his concern on the one hand with domestic comedy and quirks of character, and on the other with the unseen and the overarching—make him a difficult writer to read and to define. The modern emphasis on Forster as a symbolist has, as noted earlier, caused critics to overlook some of his distinctive features. The emphasis upon technical experimentalism and symbolist procedure has tended to obscure both the presence and the value of an interesting balancing of traditional and modern elements within his work. By asking aesthetic and technical questions, critics have been able to define him as a deeply modern writer; but this means that some of his particular and distinctive excellencies are not always recognised in their quality and centrality—I mean, for instance, the way he has developed the English tradition of the socio-moral novel into a world of experience not usually found within its capacities; his positive sense of culture, and his awareness of its significance for the individual, and for individualism; his concern with the social dimension on a national or a world scale; and his sense of scrupulous integrity which drives him beyond any simple or conventional account of an event or experience toward scepticism and irony. Because these qualities do involve him in paradoxes and ambiguities, it is not surprising that much of the early criticism of Forster was concerned with trying to reconcile two apparently disparate elements—the novelist of society and manners, and the mystic. It is around this issue that much of the uncertainty about Forster's reputation and literary character has turned. (p. 6)

[Though] Forster must be recognised as a major novelist, we must accept that his difficulties are often due to ambiguities within himself. . . . Nobody has yet resolved even the divergent accounts available of the meaning of *A Passage to India*. Is it—the case may be simply put—a novel which, after attempting to reconcile the differences between races, religions, social creeds, nature and man, asserts failure?— or is it a novel which, reaching beyond accepted faiths and accepted interpretations of the mysterious, the unseen, asserts a positive vision of unity? Is Forster in his last two— best two—books a spiritual and social optimist; or are his conclusions those of pessimism and defeat? It is, perhaps, because of the difficulty of estimating these last two books that Forster's reputation is less fully achieved, even now, than those of some of the early twentieth century novelists. . . . *Howards End* . . . is a remarkable and complex work; and *A Passage to India* is surely a major novel by any measure. (pp. 13-14)

> *Malcolm Bradbury, in his introduction to* Forster: A Collection of Critical Essays, *edited by Malcolm Bradbury (copyright © 1966 by Prentice-Hall, Inc.; reprinted by permission of Prentice-Hall, Inc., Englewood Cliffs, New Jersey), Prentice-Hall, 1966, pp. 1-14.*

FREDERICK P. W. McDOWELL

Forster's chief failure in *Maurice* is his conception of his protagonist. It is not that Maurice Hall does not possess life; rather, it is the kind of life he possesses that is disconcerting. In order for him to illustrate the difficulties that an average man would face if he were to express homosexual urges, Forster drastically limits Maurice as a human being.

He never expands, therefore, to the point that he threatens Forster's austere control of him, never expands to the point that he runs away with his author as Forster's best characters tend to do. In order to keep his homosexual subject matter in full prominence, Forster seems to have felt that he must downplay his central character, that he must conceive someone "completely unlike myself or what I supposed myself to be: someone handsome, healthy, bodily attractive, mentally torpid, not a bad business man and rather a snob.". . . To establish Maurice's mediocrity, Forster is, on the one hand, excessively tolerant of a type of individual that he does not like and, on the other hand, he is unnaturally condescending toward him and hypercritical of him. It is difficult, then, for us to feel much empathy with someone so lackluster as Maurice Hall. (p. 46)

The character fails to support the author's projected values because the author has not supported the character fully enough in the first place. Can an exceptional problem be accorded compelling literary treatment when the protagonist is so unexceptional as Maurice? Forster only too conclusively demonstrates, I think, that it is not possible to do so. Perhaps he was still fearful of adverse reaction and did not dare envisage as protagonist a man for whom most readers would care greatly, no matter what his sexual preferences might be. This fearfulness of arousing reader hostility dates the novel more than the details of social and intellectual milieu which act, as in other Forster novels, to give them a charm and authority of their own. . . .

It is curious that Forster describes Maurice as "obscene" when he indulges in sexual fantasies and auto-erotic activity, as though Forster shared Victorian hysteria about "self-pollution." There is something cringing, too, in Maurice (or in Forster) in his references to himself as "one of the unspeakables of the Oscar Wilde sort." The phrase, it seems to me, implies an unconscious concurrence with the prejudices against which Maurice and Forster are personally aligned. (p. 47)

A tepid, vacuous, complacent Maurice prevents our sympathizing to the full with him as he encounters his trials upon entering the Valley of the Shadow of Life (which is for him, really, the Valley of the Shadow of Death until he can renounce his class). We are not likely, either, to accept Forster's evaluation of Maurice's situation and his conflicts after Clive breaks with him and he must reorient his whole existence. . . . [It] is rather difficult to shake off the consistently nurtured impression that Maurice is pretty pallid or to believe in his moral strength any more than in his intelligence. He doesn't do much in his spare time even, except play games or do settlement work in London. . . . It seems to me, however, that Maurice's principal deficiency is a failure of insight and of intelligence . . . , until late in the novel anyway. Maurice is only sympathetic when he is completely denuded, when in the loss of Clive's love he has lost everything, when he is overwhelmed by absolute loneliness, when, but for a sense that love does somewhere exist, he would have ended his life, "a lamp that would have blown out, were materialism true." There is much poignancy and justified despair, when after the affair with Clive, Maurice seeks help from others and finds only dead silence. . . . (pp. 48-9)

As for Maurice's adventures and disappointments in love, Forster is as greatly indulgent as he is critical of his spiritual nature and intellectual equipment. To the extent that

Forster as homosexual expresses too directly his own pre-dilections and frustrations in *Maurice*, he is guilty of emotional overemphasis. We are informed, though hardly convinced, that Maurice has fused his brutality and idealism and found love—for Clive—as a result. Forster is overly anxious about Maurice's private life. Only occasionally does he treat Maurice and his problems humorously or recognize that homosexuality or any other form of human emotion may be no great matter under the eye of eternity. The element of distance is lacking between Forster and Maurice, as it is admirably preserved, say, between himself and Rickie Elliot in *The Longest Journey*. Then, too, the descriptions of feeling between himself and Clive are overwrought, because, for one reason, Maurice has been presented all along as a man insensitive to poetry. . . . (pp. 49-50)

There are other defects in Forster's novel. Too much is told to us instead of being dramatized, especially in the early chapters; and rather too much time in Maurice's life passes perfunctorily in too few pages. Too few of the early situations induce the later reverberations which such situations induce in other Forster novels. Maurice's lament for the dismissal of George, the garden boy from the lower class, while Maurice is still innocent of his own nature is meant to prefigure his involvement with the primitive and low-born Alec Scudder but it does not do so with unmistakable authority. . . .

But *Maurice* is finally not inconsiderable. Its strength lies in Forster's conception of Clive Durham and Maurice's relationship with him, and, to a lesser extent, in Forster's conception of Alec Scudder, Clive's gamekeeper, and Maurice's involvement with him. Clive Durham is interesting as the type of man who, in literature and in life, sublimates homosexual love. . . .

The affair with Clive is certainly the deepest (or the only deep) experience in Maurice's life, at least until he meets Alec Scudder. For this reason, of course, Maurice is shattered when Clive discovers that he no longer covets Maurice and has become oriented toward women. Forster arbitrarily motivates this change, I feel, and presents Clive's development as a volte-face rather than as a displacement in emotional focus. Clive may not realize the truth of his situation, but Forster ought to have done so, in order to make Clive's deconversion as credible as it ought to be. . . . Clive's absolute renunciation of Maurice and his complete physical revulsion from him are just possible; but, as it is, the change is too entire for the greatest possible number of elements of conflict to be effectively present. The relationship between Maurice and Clive ought to have been as absorbing in its termination as it was in its inception and growth, but it does not turn out to be so. Forster seems to have undergone, as he admits, psychic recoil from Clive after the deconversion.

Clive would have been a richer creation, if he had still felt some residual attachment for Maurice; if he had expressed a more intense involvement with Anne (whose sexuality ought also to have been stronger in order for it to neutralize most effectively Clive's passion for Maurice); and if he had been able to express with greater force the values of heterosexual love, especially as it aligns with western social and literary tradition, with racial continuance, and with fertility as opposed to the biological barrenness of homosexuality. (p. 50)

As for Alec Scudder, I find the sensual encounters between him and Maurice persuasive. . . . The conflict, furthermore, is genuine in *Maurice* when he tries to adjudicate between the claims of family and class and the claims of emotion and individual fulfillment. (pp. 52-3)

Alec Scudder is ambiguous enough as a human force to cause Maurice discomfort: whether he is to be comrade or devil, Maurice cannot quite fully predict. The connection between them does, in fact, demand this ambiguity, and it should possibly have been expanded. The presence of this psychic split in Alec argues, moreover, that Maurice's continued life with him could hardly have been harmonious. What is false in their relationship is the stated happy outcome and the direct rendition of passion, not the encounter itself and its equivocal aspects. The conflict in *Maurice* between convention and passion, though genuine, is perhaps underdeveloped: too little sense of the fact that, for both good and ill, Alec is Maurice's double, the "friend" for whom he has always searched but a demon lover also, a passionate rather than a kind man. (p. 53)

If *Maurice* partly fails because direct summary exceeds a dramatization of issues, there are yet many truly Forsterian scenes. (p. 55)

As in the other prewar novels Forster satirizes middle-class values, implicitly when Maurice at first unthinkingly embraces them and explicitly when, in moments of perception, he criticizes his compeers for specific defects. (pp. 55-6)

Maurice is the only one of Forster's novels which satirizes the Edwardian landed gentry, in the tradition of Carlyle's *Past and Present,* Chekhov's *The Cherry Orchard,* and Shaw's *Heartbreak House.* The satire represents Forster at his best in the novel; and the scenes at Penge, the Durham family seat, are some of Forster's most excellent and characteristic. In decline Clive's family connotes the decadence of the aristocracy which, along with the materialism of the middle class, has loosened the fabric of English life. Penge is a symbol of an England in decline: ". . . both house and estate were marked, not indeed with decay, but with the immobility that precedes it." The leaking roof is emblematic of the inefficiency of this class, its internal decay, its fecklessness, and its lack of will. The rain, as it comes in unchecked from the outside, may also symbolize the intrusion of nature, a life-giving element, an unwelcome reality. Maurice comes to feel that Clive's class is no longer fit to exert power, "to set standards or control the future"; and Clive himself, Maurice thinks, has deteriorated from the open, honest, forthright, idealistic pagan prince he once had known. The disintegration of his class parallels this personal decline and may have contributed to it. With Clive, in the years since Cambridge, respectability rather than life has triumphed; the result is Clive's "thin, sour disapproval, his dogmatism, the stupidity of his heart," when Maurice tells him of his love for Alec. (p. 57)

The succinct statements by which Forster criticizes society, with measured irony and understatement, he again uses in characterization, particularly for his minor figures. Sometimes his people tell us themselves what they or other people are like; more frequently, Forster is the omniscient commentator who sharply outlines his people for us. Many of his minor characters are vivid by virtue of Forster's ability to isolate the idiosyncrasies of an individual or a type. Mr. Hall, Maurice's deceased father, who figures in passing, is seen in terms of the complacency and sexual hypocrisy, native to the Edwardian business class: he "had supported society, and moved without a crisis from illicit to licit love." (p. 58)

In short, *Maurice* is not a perfect novel; and I would be the first to admit that it is inferior to the five novels that Forster published in his life time. But it is better than all but a few of the stories, and it has more of literary merit than most of its critics have been willing to concede. It is a worthwhile, if minor, accretion to the Forster canon. It has much to fascinate and to delight, and its full flavor comes through only after one has become accustomed to Forster's unusual subject, his directness of narrative line, and his suspension of irony toward his protagonist. The lack of complication in *Maurice,* its constricted scope, and its limited perspective detract from its stature, to be sure. But Forster's detached manner, his sustained compassion, his sporadic displays of insight, and his stylistic powers all assert that *Maurice* is his novel. (pp. 58-9)

> *Frederick P. W. McDowell, "Second Thoughts on E. M. Forster's 'Maurice',"* in Virginia Woolf Quarterly *(copyright © 1972 by Aeolian Press), Fall, 1972, pp. 46-59.*

GORMAN BEAUCHAMP

Forster's novella *The Machine Stops* established the essential outlines of the dystopian parable. It is set, of course, in the future, at a time when men have abandoned the surface of the earth to live in massive underground cities resembling air-conditioned anthills. Here, in a completely controlled and artificial environment, they are removed from all contact with Nature. . . . (p. 90)

In this story . . . Forster has anticipated most, if not quite all, of the themes of subsequent dystopian novels: the horrors of a society "perfected" by technology; the totalitarian face of a regime deifying "reason" in all its regulations; the denial of the body, the passions and the instincts, and the consequent automatization of man; and the lone rebel's attempt to escape from his mega-civilization and return to Nature. As in the classic dystopias, the rebel fails, crushed beneath the juggernaut of the Machine; but here the Machine fails too. One day the Machine stops. And in a few elegiac pages, Forster movingly chronicles the death of a world. (p. 91)

[Many contend that] *The Machine Stops* lacks the immediacy of the trio of important dystopian novels that follow it —*We* (1924), *Brave New World* (1932), and *1984* (1948)— because "it concentrates on the technological aspects of Utopianism and pays scant attention to its social and political implications." I would argue, however, that precisely this concentration on the technological characterizes all these dystopian works as well as other significant examples of the genre: C. S. Lewis' *That Hideous Strength* (1946), Kurt Vonnegut's *Player Piano* (1952), Ray Bradbury's *Fahrenheit 451* (1953), David Karp's *One* (1953), L. P. Hartley's *Facial Justice* (1961), Anthony Burgess' *The Wanting Seed* (1963), and Ira Levin's *This Perfect Day* (1970). Forster early on grasped the truth that the Machine creates its own politics, its own sociology, its own rationality, its own epistemology, its own axiolocy and, indeed, its own theology. Modern totalitarianism—the political phenomenon that [George] Woodcock sees as providing the historical impetus for dystopianism—would itself be impos-

sible without a highly complex technological apparatus. In any case, by depicting in *The Machine Stops* a society that depends on the omnipotence of the Machine to realize the millennial dreams of a Bacon, a Bellamy, or a Wells, Forster may be said to have founded the first anti-technological dystopia. His *mythos*—the rebel rejecting a mechanized mega-civilization—is the typical dystopian *mythos;* his fear —the mechanical abolition of man—is their fear; and his alternative—a return to Nature—is their alternative. (pp. 91-2)

> *Gorman Beauchamp, in* Extrapolation *(copyright 1977 by Thomas D. and Alice S. Clareson), December, 1977.*

* * *

FOWLES, John   1926-

Fowles is a British novelist, short story writer, translator, essayist, and poet. His work is a blend of classical and mythical allusions presented in a modern idiom; *The French Lieutenant's Woman,* **for example, is Victorian in story and style, but innovative in narrative technique and in its examination of the concept of time. Fowles consistently scrutinizes the importance of history in his novels, exploring how the past can inform the present. Recurring in Fowles's fiction is the idea that woman, because of her inherent "otherness," is fundamentally incomprehensible to man. Fowles uses this theme to analyze what man can know, and, further, what the artist, with the limitations of his perception and his ability, can reveal about the human condition. (See also** *CLC,* **Vols. 1, 2, 3, 4, 6, 9, and** *Contemporary Authors,* **Vols. 5-8, rev. ed.)**

DWIGHT EDDINS

One of the central concerns of metafiction from Borges to Barth—or perhaps, more accurately, from Laurence Sterne to Barth—has been the reanimation and expansion of the commonplace that each man's life is a novel of which that man is the author. If the commonplace is accepted, it follows that almost all novels are about "novels"; and that a novel in which the problem of fictiveness becomes explicit will be required in order to satisfy the thirst of the ironic consciousness for an adequate complexity of treatment. John Fowles's brilliant exploration of these ideas and their ramifications in his three novels points to a very complex and sophisticated view of the relation between "art" and "life." (p. 204)

[Frank Kermode's concept of the modern novel states that in] order to make sense to his reader, in order to present a humanized perception of existence, the novelist must fall back upon "eidetic images—illusions persisting from past acts of perception, as some abnormal children 'see' the page or object that is no longer before them. . . ." It is obvious that "eidetic," in this sense, must apply to almost all of the generalizations and patterns by which we organize our sense perceptions. The very act of using these images, however, belies the contingency and the perpetual flux of reality. This dilemma of the novelist obviously derives, by analogy, from the existential dilemma of achieving authenticity—of avoiding Sartrean *mauvaise foi.*

The two dilemmas, however, have a much deeper and more integral connection than mere analogy. This becomes clear in a relevant passage from an essay by Ortega y Gasset, cited by Kermode: "It is too often forgotten that man is impossible without imagination, without the capacity to invent for himself a conception of life, to 'ideate' the character he is going to be. Whether he be original or a plagiarist, man is the novelist of himself.'' Ortega y Gasset also refers to man the self-creator as '''a secondhand God.''' The problem facing this novelist-god is reconciling his own ideations with the fortuitousness of existence. In humanizing this world he lies; in trying not to lie he is threatened by incoherence and chaos. A corollary dilemma is that an extreme of ideation imprisons a given man inside his own fictional presuppositions, a character at the mercy of an omniscient author. Utter contingency, on the other hand, implies an author who has lost all control over his character, and a character without any real identity.. . . . [These] existential quandaries form a sort of ontological metastructure for the struggle between Collector and Liberator in the novels of John Fowles, and . . . Fowles looks for whatever degree of resolution is possible by examining existence as an exercise in creative artistry.

The Collector, as Fowles envisages him, imposes a static system of images on the world and then proceeds to live inside that system, denying the existential implications of contingency. The system is the result of accretion—a cumulative calcifying of social and political attitudes, aesthetic constructs, emotional responses, and (most insidiously) self-image. As author, the Collector is bound to his character in the mutual servitude of master and slave. At the other extreme the Liberator has fully realized and incorporated into his existence the behavioral implications of ''hazard.'' Fowles defends this state of bounded contingency as ''the best for mankind'' because: ''everywhere, below the surface, we do not know; we shall never know why; we shall never know tomorrow; we shall never know a god or if there is a god; we shall never even know ourselves. This mysterious wall round our world and our perception of it is not there to frustrate us but to train us back to the now, to life, to our time being.''

The movement of protagonists from Collectors toward Liberators is essential to all three novels [*The Collector, The Magus,* and *The French Lieutenant's Woman*]; but considerations already set forth should make it clear that this movement is a complex and paradoxical one. Some form of ''collecting'' is essential for communication and comprehension; language itself is, after all, eidetic, as are the patterns of logic. Also, the very concept of authorship implies some degree of conscious manipulation, as the concept of ''character'' implies at least vestigial identity. The mind cannot coalesce with pure contingency—at least, not the sane mind. It must have its fictions, and its fiction writer.

The problem facing the seeker of authenticity thus reveals at least two facets: reducing the gratuitous fictiveness of his necessary fictions, and reducing the element of ideational tyranny in the author-character relationship. Fowles's answer lies in creating an author who will keep his fictions open toward contingency, perpetually modifying them and continually admitting their provisional, fictive nature. Malcolm Bradbury [in ''The Novelist as Impresario: John Fowles and His Magus,'' in his *Possibilities: Essays on the State of the Novel*] traces the need of Fowles and other modern novelists to present their ''fictions as fictive'' to the lack of ordering ''communal myths.'' It is not necessary to quarrel with this conclusion in order to assert that, in Fowles's novels in particular, the fictiveness of fiction also has a more explicit thematic function.

To achieve his ends, Fowles involves his characters in initiations designed to make them the existentialist authors of their own lives. Each initiation centers upon a set of artistic constructs consciously engineered by a player of the ''godgame,'' which Fowles describes in *The Aristos* as governing ''by not governing in any sense that the governed can call being governed; that is, to constitute a situation in which the governed must govern themselves.'' . . . These constructs coalesce into various psychodramas that are related and overlapping, and to which I refer collectively as the ''Masque'' of a given novel. The Masque begins with patent artifice, combining the flamboyant and the horrific in various degrees. Charmed or shocked—or both—into a sense of new possibilities in experience, the protagonist is made to relate this sense to the offerings of reality as hazard. This transference is made possible by a gradual modification of the Masque's constructs. These shade from the ''artificiality'' of art into the ''naturalness'' of quotidian existence, without losing the power to generate the excitement of adventurous encounter. The premise upon which the modification rests is, of course, that creative existence *is* an art—in this case, an existentialist art.

Having reached a certain plateau of initiation, the protagonist is now qualified to play the godgame himself; and in particular, to take over responsibility for the ''novel'' of his own life from the initiates who have guided him. (pp. 204-07)

From the standpoint of structure, the stages of a given initiation form a series of Chinese boxes, with each stage subverting the eidetic images of the previous stage in favor of more contingent images. It is important to see that the sequence of novels itself constitutes an analogous structure: *The Magus* subsumes *The Collector,* and is in turn subsumed by *The French Lieutenant's Woman.* I am, of course, aware that the first draft of *The Magus* preceded the writing of *The Collector.* It is the order of the published novels that concerns me here. The process of subsumption is at work not only in the elaboration of specific motifs such as the Collector, the anima, or time-travel, but, more significantly, in terms of point of view. If *The Collector* is crystallized and unself-conscious ideation, a fiction pretending to autonomous existence, then the next two novels represent a progressive iconoclasm that proclaims the fictiveness of their own enterprises. This heightened self-consciousness, with its rich ironic implications, is accomplished partially by Fowles's use of an author-persona, a godgame player, who obtrudes more and more. This figure is used by Fowles to infuse contingency into the very structure of the novels, individually, and as a sequence, thus accomplishing at least three things: the relation between existential authorship and the search for authenticity is given a new dimension; the eidetic ''falsehood'' of the novel as genre is lessened; and the reader is forced to participate directly in an initiation into hazard.

Turning specifically to *The Collector,* we find its Masque composed of two psychodramas, both of which are focused on Miranda as novice. . . . The first psychodrama—Clegg's ''collection'' of Miranda—both precipitates and contains the second, which is a congeries of remembered experiences with the artist ''G. P.''

The element of artifice that characterizes the early stages of the Masque is provided here by the bizarre, aberrant circumstances in which Miranda finds herself, and by her position as an *objet d'art* in Clegg's collection. Forced to become part of an artistic arrangement that has replaced the familiar version of reality, she finds herself in a reciprocity typical of Fowles's fiction. Not only is she the spectacle for Clegg, he is the spectacle for her. Staring at him, she realizes that he is an artist engaged in "shaping" her just as G. P. was; and that she, too, has played a part in this shaping. The result is her shocking recognition of Clegg as a psychological double. She, also, has played the Collector by her smug accretion of upper-class values and assumptions that shut out the vitalizing powers of hazard. Her painting reflects this tendency toward mindless accumulation. . . . (pp. 207-09)

Both the awareness of this perversion, and the way to escape it, are suggested by the godgame as G. P. plays it. A painter dedicated to authenticity in his life and his art, he "collects" Miranda as beneficently as possible; i.e., in the interests of her eventual autonomy. . . .

From a Jungian perspective, G. P.'s role in Miranda's initiation may be described as that of the constructive animus. He provides her with an existential Logos that deepens her capacity for reflection and self-knowledge, without turning her into a dogmatist. She, in turn, is recognized by him as the anima. . . . (p. 209)

The functioning of archetypes obviously has a very special relation to G. P. and Miranda in their capacity as artists. Jung, it will be remembered, asserts that "the creative process, insofar as we are able to understand it, consists in an *unconscious animation of the archetype,* and in a development and shaping of the image till the work is completed." Returning, then, to the notion of life as existential artistry, we should have—if the ideal were fully realized—G. P. as the animus who strives for form and definition in Miranda's psyche; in other words, the determinative aspect of the internal author, supplanting the Clegg-figure. Since an aspect of Miranda as internal character is her anima role, a creative dialectic would be set up. Inspired by the changing images and the impetus that stem from the anima, the existential animus would attempt to keep from imposing forms that stifle, while the anima, seeking realization in form, would strive to avoid sterile entrapment. Though "collection" in the form of eidetic crystallization must occur in the very nature of things, its life-denying properties would be continually minimized by the dialectic. (p. 210)

Miranda, beginning in naiveté, never has time to gain a comprehensive perspective on the inner changes that she is experiencing, and Clegg is incapable of such perspective. But these are the only two narrators of the novel. The author-persona—a crucial ramifier of levels of consciousness in later novels—is represented here by the shadowy G. P., present only at the remove of memory. The result is a naively "realistic," one-leveled novel—in this case, one that deals thematically with transcending simple ideation, but does not make the transcendental movement in its own structure.

The movement to *The Magus,* then, is one into complexity of conciousness with respect to point of view. The voice of the narrator, Nicholas Urfe, is a much more mature and philosophical one than that of Miranda. And, since he is describing his initiation in retrospect, he is able to give us some perspective on its various stages. Even more important, perhaps, is the palpable and obtrusive presence of the

author-persona, Conchis. This presence is the result of at least three factors, one of them being simply the dominant part Conchis plays in the events described. Also, since the entire account is "remembered," Conchis has equal ontological footing with the Nicholas who is undergoing initiation. Finally, Conchis' presence is embodied in the very structure of the novel, which depends almost entirely upon the stages of the psychodrama that he arranges.

This third factor is crucial to the structure of *The Magus,* which is made up not only of the psychodrama that Nicholas experiences, but of the psychodrama experienced by the reader of the novel. . . . [The] eidetic remove between Nicholas and the reader is a part of Fowles's structural plan. . . . What happens is that the player of the godgame manipulates, indirectly, the pawns who are holding the novel in their hands. Faced with his own recurring gullibility the reader is thus forced to admit his tendency to "collect," to seize upon convenient "solutions" that are nothing more than screens hiding the next mystery. All of this is, in one sense, nothing more than the normal apparatus of the suspense novel as genre; but it is precisely Fowles's larger context of hazard that raises the machinery of melodrama to self-consciousness and lends it thematic significance. The result is the active initiation of the reader into awareness of the provisional nature of his own constructs, and the vagaries of hazard.

The reader's self-consciousness about the very act of reading is given yet another dimension by Conchis' assertions that "the novel is dead"; that one day he burned every novel he possessed, including a manuscript of his own; and that "words are for truth. For facts. Not fiction." The paradox presented by embodying these anti-novelistic views in a novel symbolizes yet again the tension that must exist between the necessary fictions of eidetic images and the urge to truthfulness about contingent reality. Art must continually undermine its own artifice if it is to maintain its dialectic with the reality that provides its elements. If it pretends to ontological autonomy, it becomes the enemy of its own vitality and authenticity. (pp. 211-12)

The other aspect of the Masque, the psychodrama of Nicholas' initiation, is much more complex than the psychodramas involving Miranda precisely because his consciousness is more complex than hers. Not only is he sophisticated, blasé, and cynical, he is very much aware that he is all three. It is exactly this ironic self-consciousness that is at once his hope for escape from imprisonment in a stultified persona, and the intricate barrier that makes escape a difficult and hypersubtle matter. To put it briefly, he is a sort of existentialist dandy who prides himself on his premature nihilism. His habitual exercise of the very irony and skepticism that are indispensable for breaking out of eidetic traps has led him to believe that no mystery can resist dissolution by his analysis; and this crystallized belief has itself become an eidetic trap. . . . Deluded into believing that he is constantly choosing "himself" in freedom, he has in fact fallen in love with a static image of himself. He is not existentially inside his "chosen" freedom. The result in Nicholas' case is a seemingly endless succession of ironic poses behind which he can hide from recognizing his personal inadequacy in the face of infinite freedom and potentiality.

To deal successfully with this labyrinth of evasiveness Conchis must mount an even more intricate attack. As the author-god creating a universe according to Fowles, his task is to construct a convincing model of hazard—one that will drive home to Nicholas at the deepest level of his consciousness the redeeming mystery and uncertainty of existence—that will make him, in Robert Scholes's apt phrase, "ultimately hungry for reality." Thus Conchis engineers the scheme already referred to, with the seemingly solid ground on which Nicholas stands after "seeing through" one deception turning into the next deception in an infinite series of eidetic destructions and reconstructions. The movement of the series is from obvious artifice or vivid past history—or a combination of the two—to insidiously realistic and subtle trickery that involves Nicholas' most basic emotions. Intrigued by the psychodrama's cleverness and flamboyance, and by his ability to see through these, Nicholas is led step by step toward real existential engagement. But this is precisely the movement of art at its best. A striking pattern of images diverts and intrigues us by its fictive but clever reshaping of reality; but on a deeper level this pattern is modifying the basic ideation by which we live, changing our conceptual "vocabulary" forever. Here again, the godgame is revealed as another name for authorship, and Conchis—in Nicholas' words—as "a sort of novelist *sans* novel, creating with people, not words." . . . (pp. 212-14)

The changes toward openness in Nicholas' anima construct are directed toward the same end as the other changes engineered by Conchis—that Nicholas himself should become the existentialist author, the freedom-affirming player of the godgame. Conchis makes it clear that "no good play has a real curtain. . . . It is acted, and then it continues to act." . . . The corollary is that the existentialist author equips his characters for ultimate independence of him. (p. 215)

We receive an important indication of Nicholas' victory over [his] "despot" at the beginning of chapter seventy-eight. The speaker has a tone of authorial intrusion that strongly suggests the voice of Fowles himself. Unless we are to posit such an intrusion—anomalous in this novel—we are forced to consider a narrator who has acquired a godlike perspective on that "plot" of his own life that he has been recounting. He sees himself at once as the "anti-hero" of the narration in progress, and as the real-life modern whose existence reflects that of the anti-hero. (p. 216)

Nicholas, achieving the plateau of Conchis, writes an account of that achievement. Then, having become the existentialist author of his own life, he is entitled to give a virtuoso demonstration of how this authorship must function, in the style of Conchis. *The French Lieutenant's Woman,* with its historical-philosophical perspectives and its technical exhibitionism, finds its origins in just this sort of sophisticated consciousness. I do not wish to suggest that Nicholas himself is the author-persona of the novel; but merely that such a novel is the logical new dimension of someone who has reached his degree of initiation. Alternatively, it represents the development of the author-persona from figment of memory through pervasive presence to spokesman, with the attendant ramifying of levels of consciousness.

As in *The Magus,* the Masque of *The French Lieutenant's Woman* is composed of the psychodrama which the author arranges for the reader, and that which he arranges for his characters. The relation between the two initiations, however, is much more complex and suggestive in the later novel. *The Magus* had intimated a basic level of self-con-

sciousness, fiction aware of its fictiveness, by indirect means: the reader "overhears" Conchis' remarks and "shares" Nicholas' disillusionments. Fowles's use of a parodic structure in *The French Lieutenant's Woman,* including the introduction of direct communication between the author-persona and the reader, means that it is possible for him to write a piece of fiction concerned with fiction as genre; i.e., a "Victorian" novel that is a contemporary novel "about" the Victorian novel. The reader is thus made vividly aware of multiple removes of eidetic imagery —a situation that makes an ideal showcase for dramatizing the dialectic of this imagery with contingency. (p. 217)

[The] parodic structure forces the reader to come to terms with the relation between himself, the author-persona, and the characters; with the relation between Victorian history and contemporary realities; and with the overlapping of these two relationships. To deal with the first of these, we must examine the implications of authorial intrusion in the Victorian novel. By speaking in the role of expositor within the boundaries of a fictional framework, the author becomes a character within that framework—but so does the reader, insofar as he is the conception of the author. While these two personae are obviously an eidetic remove closer to "reality" than the characters in the plot proper, they are an eidetic remove away from the human beings to whom they correspond. The net result of the "omniscient" Victorian intrusion was to narrow the latter remove and broaden the former. The characters were shown as puppets dancing for the amusement of a puppet master and an audience who reveled in ontological superiority and freedom of will. Ironically the reader-persona was also at the mercy of the author-persona's ideational tyranny—a fact that tended to diminish the status gained by the latter's sharing of "confidences."

Fowles, parodying such intrusions, introduces an existentialist author-persona who reverses almost every effect described above. Claiming to be no more than a recorder of his characters' independent whims and caprices, "the freedom that allows other freedoms to exist," he consistently narrows the remove between himself and the characters— and thus between the reader-persona and the characters. Both author and reader as personae, however, are pulled deeper and deeper into the fictive web of the novel, and farther from their respective positions in "reality." . . . Fowles's claims of ontological equality between author, characters, and reader are all arrant sophistry . . . , but of a dramatically instructive sort. With the barriers temporarily down, the reader-persona is able to identify with the author-persona insofar as he shares the later's dilemma over how to give his characters the maximum degree of freedom; and with the characters insofar as he must also fall victim to the beneficent manipulations of the author-persona. These manipulations are, of course, designed to effect an initiation into hazard for both reader-persona and characters. In terms of *The Magus,* it is as though the reader-persona were not only duped and enlightened along with Nicholas, but made privy to Conchis' inmost scruples and concerns as the initiation proceeds. Finally, of course, it is the reader who must play author-god in deciding which of the endings will be chosen. His choice will reveal the degree to which he has absorbed the harsh lessons of contingency and will serve to decide whether he is now qualified as an independent player of the existential godgame.

Since both author and reader as personae find their fates entangled with the fates of characters separated from them by over a hundred years, it is obvious that the mechanics of this "time-travel" have an integral relation to the mechanics of the structure described above. The author-persona has a perspective on the Victorian author. But this perspective is, after all, nothing more than hindsight; and his apparent near-omniscience cannot tell him with certainty what a given Victorian character would have done in a given set of circumstances. These patent-enough observations have important symbolic consequences with respect to the novel's concern with eidetic imagery as such. They remind us that such imagery is based upon hindsight, the crystallizing of past experience into conceptual patterns; and that this imagery has severe limitations as the lens through which we must bring our present experience into focus as it is presenting itself.

To the extent the reader-persona shares the perspective of the author-persona, he is aware of these theoretical considerations; but insofar as he is a manipulated character of this author, he must undergo the gradual initiation into existential experience that these considerations suggest. (pp. 217-19)

The aim of this "time-travel" is to seduce us to full and authentic membership in our own time, and, as might be expected, the principal seductress is the anima. In the person of Sarah she is given a historical dimension that cuts across the parodic structure. For one thing, she must be seen not only as the anima in Charles's life, but that of the author-persona as well. . . . She also transcends her role in the Victorian metaphor by being conscious of her historical position, in particular of her existential relation to the future. Consciously breaking Victorian convention in the name of individual freedom, she is the harbinger of twentieth-century openness; yet she retains the air of mystery and remoteness essential to the anima's hold on the imagination.

It is significant that this air impresses most of her Victorian contemporaries as a pathological one, even to the point of suggesting insanity. (p. 220)

Sarah's "madness," like Hamlet's, may be seen as part of a machinery of deception in this case, the machinery of the psychodrama of which she is not only an instigator, along with the author-persona, but a beneficiary. The basic fiction—that she has given herself to a French officer—is designed to free her from expectations of conventional behavior, as she finally admits. She is thus duping the Victorian age in an escape that is also a mockery of the age's imprisoning forces. . . . The decision to use certain stratagems and even to manipulate people is made precisely in order to achieve an authenticity involving freedom from being manipulated by society's artifice. Thus Sarah, gripped by a real-enough loneliness and alienation, turns to Charles for emotional support, consciously using her assumed role as an "outcast" in order to enlist that support. In love with him, she nonetheless uses him as a test case for her self-image, and abandons him—in the ultimate ending—when he has become a threat to her existential growth.

Sarah, then, has become the existentialist authoress. She mercilessly excises and reshapes the materials of her own life according to criteria of contingency and freedom. . . . It is Sarah who has incorporated this distinction [between a static, closed ideation and one which is open toward hazard] into the very fabric of her mental processes who must decide what is to be done with Charles. If she is to remain true to her existentialist premises, she must make the choice most consonant with perpetual becoming—the ultimate ending. And if the author and reader as personae are to keep faith with these premises, they must "let" Sarah do the choosing—which is to say no more, perhaps, than that they must allow the anima to motivate continuously the "novels" of their own lives.

In keeping with the by-now-familiar sequence of Chinese boxes, Charles may be viewed as Sarah's "character," and his liberation as a by-product of her own more self-conscious liberation. Drawn into the psychodrama by artifice in the guises of mystery, pathos, and madness, he is led toward real existential discovery. With Sarah's final rejection of him, he is forced to come to terms with the paradox of the anima's perpetual attractiveness and recession. He thus achieves "authorship" himself, joining—within the framework of Fowles's ontological sophistry—Sarah, the author-persona, and the reader-persona. (pp. 220-22)

No matter what degree of freedom the author as Logos allows, he cannot—by definition—escape certain modes of manipulation. And, by the same token, the character as Eros cannot achieve definition without the shaping influence. What Fowles's three novels suggest, however—both individually and as sequence—is that the individual must strive for a maximum internalization of the dialectic. The dictates of the externally-oriented superego must give way to a creative interplay between the necessity to shape and the spontaneous impulses that drive life on. Only death stops the dialectic—the literal death of Miranda, or the death-in-life of Clegg. Nicholas Urfe, Sarah, and Charles must work continually toward the merger of existentialist author and autonomous character without ever fully effecting the merger. The tantalizing open-endedness of *The Magus* and *The French Lieutenant's Woman* symbolizes not only hazard's uncertainty, but the perpetual modification of the eidetic image as it tries to incorporate the flux of reality. (p. 222)

Dwight Eddins, "John Fowles: Existence as Authorship," in Contemporary Literature *(© 1976 by the Board of Regents of the University of Wisconsin System), Vol. 17, No. 2, Spring, 1976, pp. 204-22.*

JONATHAN KEATES

John Fowles has never been at ease with fiction. Even in so neat a package as *The Collector* we had the sense, here and there, of one or other of the author's intellectual concerns awkwardly protruding from the surface of the narrative. *The Magus,* probably the best thing he has ever done, used the machinery of fiction like a hydro-electric dam adequately to contain and direct his sometimes overpowering conceptual flow. In *The French Lieutenant's Woman,* an archetypally late 1960s morsel of rediscovered Victoriana, the wall finally collapsed and a flood of Fowles's Patent Notions came washing over us. I wasn't, I suspect, the only reader irritated at having to endure a drenching from a mixture of archly self-conscious detachment, toe-curling patronage, and a set of opinions, stated or implied, on the Victorians which I didn't share. . . .

His aim, a sufficiently laudable one, seems always to have been towards extending the range of possibilities within the traditional framework of the novel—take, for example, the experimental endings of *The French Lieutenant's Woman*. We can feel a certain gratitude, besides, to a writer who so gamely takes his reader's intelligence for granted. His chosen style, in *Daniel Martin*, is honest and plain enough. He has clearly noted the figures and types necessary for convincing us with each one of his small cast of characters. There is the additional interest of imagining, in a novel entirely devoid of a story and given over to the perceptions, doubts and speculations of its placid, almost bovine protagonist, that this just might be an autobiography.

The best sections are those in which Fowles relaxes Daniel's self-awareness in favour of straight, old-fashioned topographical sketching, a specifically English art in which he has few rivals. The opening account of a Devon harvest, the scene-setting in New Mexico and Egypt . . . are done with an arresting concern for the movement and placing of words and an engaging eye for surfaces and colours.

Such a considerable range of skills doesn't, however, go to make a novel. Given the length, we deserve more than Fowles seems able to offer. Initially well drawn as his supporting figures may be, they fail to grip, perhaps because Daniel himself appears to be so detached from them. Conversations, already enfeebled by the dialogue's endemic limpness, grow repetitive to the point of impelling us to look elsewhere in the book for their originals. Robbed thus of the more commonplace comforts of fiction, we turn expectantly towards the eponymous hero. (p. 58)

Fowles's philosophical ideas are doubtless fascinating and possibly new, but, clotted with such a degree of flat, formulaic expression, they form a tiresome ballast which we would gladly jettison to save something of whatever novel remains. (p. 59)

> *Jonathan Keates, in* The New Review (©
> *The New Review Ltd., 11 Greek Street,
> London W1V 5LE), November, 1977.*

DENIS DONOGHUE

Daniel Martin is a love story that might take place anywhere: indeed, it mostly takes place in circumstances which liberate hero and heroine from any involvement in society, politics, or ideology, on a trip to Egypt, the Nile, Abu Simbel, Palmyra, Lebanon. The relation between social structure and individual feeling is a major theme in itself, but it does not exert any pressure upon *Daniel Martin*. Fowles evidently wanted to exhibit the mutual bearing of society and individual, but the design does not go any further than the device of making Dan an English writer temporarily doctoring scripts in Hollywood. . . .

Fowles's native theme is more accurately indicated in the epigraph to *The French Lieutenant's Woman* (1969), a sentence from *Zur Judenfrage* in which Marx says that "every emancipation is a restoration of the human world and of human relationships to man himself." Much of the significance of *The French Lieutenant's Woman* arises from the conditions of that emancipation: social and personal relations are shown not as separate constituents of reality but as interconnected systems of motives, values, and actions. But if we are to think of Fowles's theme as it is displayed in his several novels and stories, we must define it more narrowly. He is preoccupied with the habit by which we turn

other people into objects and take possession of them. . . . Fowles's characters turn one another into objects, and then complain when they find their possessions missing, stolen, lost. . . .

Ostensibly, the theme of *Daniel Martin* is the possibility of undoing the damage, releasing our possessions to become people again, persons, presences. Ostensibly; because the possibility has more to do with Providence than with Gramsci, Buber, or the self-portraying Rembrandt invoked on the last page of the novel. The rhetoric of the book asserts that the process involves learning to feel again, practicing responsiveness as if it were a craft. But Providence supplies the conditions and provocations. Dan is divorced, his wife has married Andrew, he is on the loose in Hollywood, Jenny is hardly more than a casual possession. Jane's husband, dying of cancer, kills himself to make her free for Dan. The new idiom of responsiveness, understanding, and feeling is genuine, a series of spiritual exercises to be practiced until their knowledge is carried to the heart. These exercises are practiced in the second, serious part of *Daniel Martin;* the first part merely shows why they are necessary, allows Providence to make them possible, and entrusts their future to Dan and Jane.

I have no fault to find with Jane: she is capable of anything that is required of her. The inadequate penitents are Dan and his creator, John Fowles. Dan is simply not up to the job, he is smeared with the triviality of his experience. Nothing in the book persuades me that Dan is capable of the conversion to gravity that is ascribed to him. . . .

Fowles is to be blamed, of course: or rather, his language, which is just as defective as Dan. T. S. Eliot once said of Thomas Hardy's style that it sometimes achieved the sublime without ever having passed through the stage of being good. Nothing in *Daniel Martin* is sublime, but even the fine things in it are surrounded by pages of relentless falsity. . . . Someone in "Poor Koko," one of the stories in *The Ebony Tower*, refers to "hopeless *parole* in search of lost *langue*," and there are many other signs that Fowles keeps up with recent lore about language. His books regularly stop to make some comment on narrative problems, plot as Destiny, alternative endings, and so forth. "Language is like shot silk," one of the narrators says in *The French Lieutenant's Woman;* "so much depends on the angle at which it is held."

But Fowles's sophistication in the theory of fiction is compatible, I am afraid, with naïveté in the discrimination of styles. (p. 45)

Am I saying that Fowles has no merit? Or that *Daniel Martin* has none? Not quite, in either case. *The Collector* seems to me a decent novel, and moving in its presentation of Frederick and Miranda, their different experiences and values. The title story in *The Ebony Tower* is excellent, though one has only to compare it with nearly any of James's short stories about the artistic life to see the difference between the two writers in range and exactitude of implication. *The French Lieutenant's Woman* is Fowles's best work because he found for that occasion a major theme of great historical and personal importance, and he commanded a language at least adequate. I don't regard the alternative endings of that novel as more than a conceit; they merely represent Fowles's somewhat wide-eyed discovery that much depends on the angle at which a story is held.

But *Daniel Martin* puts in doubt the claim that Fowles, in addition to being an interesting writer, is also an artist. The new novel is a big, laborious book, but I have found in it no evidence that Fowles trusts his art sufficiently to be an artist. Richard Blackmur once invoked "the principle that the intelligence must always act as if it were adequate to the problems it has aroused." Fowles's intelligence does not act in this spirit or with this verve: he rarely trusts his vision enough to let it disappear in the work. That is why *Daniel Martin* contains so many pages and chapters which have not been given the authority of vision at all: odds-and-ends which have shaken loose from the work because they were never attached to it by force of faith to begin with. (p. 46)

> *Denis Donoghue, in* The New York Review of Books *(reprinted with permission from* The New York Review of Books; *copyright © 1977 NYREV, Inc.), December 8, 1977.*

TOM PAULIN

John Fowles's opening chapter [in *Daniel Martin*] is rich and promising. His stated aim is to offer "an exploration of what it means to be English", and his epigraph from Antonio Gramsci ("The crisis consists precisely in the fact that the old is dying and the new cannot be born; in this interregnum a great variety of morbid symptoms appears") promises an objective diagnosis of English decline. Succeeding chapters set in California and Oxford seem to have a fairly sure grasp of cultural realities and limitations—Los Angeles is described as "those famous hundred suburbs in search of a city", and Oxford is "not a city, but an incest." But then [a] feeling of too-familiar recognition . . . begins to deepen. . . . [The] trouble is that Fowles's narrative technique is so self-conscious it seems like a form of self-abuse—it's reminiscent of Isherwood's unbearably narcissistic *Christopher and His Kind*—while the characters it manipulates are a series of talkative transparencies who join Daniel Martin in numerous seminars on all those human emotions and motives we're meant to credit them with possessing. It's quite incredible that Fowles should present his celluloid fiction as an illustration "of an unfashionable philosophy, humanism." His vaguely theoretic and occasionally mystic imagination is in no sense humanist. . . . [The] illusion of participating in a deeply intellectual narrative is adeptly created. It is, unfortunately, only an illusion. This doesn't mean that John Fowles isn't intelligent—he is very intelligent—but his attitude to ideas is essentially that of a cultivated collector. Just as his botanising protagonist likes "looking for women who would interest him, for new specimens", so Fowles has culled a number of occasionally interesting ideas about contemporary society from various sources. However, in merely collecting those ideas he has reduced them to the status of intellectual curios—they are fixed and dead, like objects in a museum. (p. 69)

Daniel Martin is a brilliantly bogus structure, a mock-pyramid on a film set, a dead monument to what Samuel Johnson, in one of the sources of Fowles's novel, called "that hunger of imagination which preys incessantly upon life." (p. 70)

> *Tom Paulin, in* Encounter *(© 1977-1978 by Encounter Ltd.), January, 1978.*

WILLIAM H. PRITCHARD

After arising some days later from finishing the [revised version of *The Magus*], one feels—as is usually the case in reading Fowles—ambivalent. Doubtless "The Magus" is too long, but, as with the recent "Daniel Martin," that seems a dull thing to say. Sentences and paragraphs have been recast into a generally less sporadic if not clearly superior narrative. The erotic scenes have been developed and extended, though to no new point of revelation. And the same big, un-English ideas are kicking around: Hazard, Freedom, Infinity and those other concepts, which in "The Aristos: A Self-Portrait in Ideas" (1964) Mr. Fowles went on about so solemnly in so many aphorisms for so long. Those who, unlike this reader, were bored or annoyed by the speculation and argumentation in "Daniel Martin" will not find any more to their tastes the intellectual content of the revised "Magus."

Yet it is a remarkable tour de force, and not just as a promising writer's first novel. (pp. 7, 41)

What the reader consents to if he goes beyond the first 50 pages of the book (very good pages, the writing about London is first-rate) is an ambiguous alliance with the hero-narrator, Nicholas, who for our entertainment as well as his own presumed good is teased, fooled, lied to, and in one way or another seduced by Conchis and his minions—the revised version makes many analogies with "The Tempest." At the same time, we must indulge our annoyance and skepticism, as does Nicholas, at the stagy theatrics, the chicanery and charlatanry of this dubious "godgame" (a rejected title for the novel) made up out of old poems, old movies, old mythologies.

Meanwhile, the resulting entertainment is often satisfactory in the extreme, and it may do Mr. Fowles more credit to think of him as perhaps the best novelistic entertainer writing today (he has recently acknowledged a debt to Raymond Chandler) than as a ponderer of modern crises, the death of the gods or the novel, and the rule of "hazard," or as a psychological penetrator of great authority and acuity. At least there are long stretches, particularly in Conchis's narrative of his life—his experience in World War I, his later confrontation with the Nazis on the Greek island in World War II—which are no more nor less than masterful storytelling. Like Hemingway, Mr. Fowles is better on war than on sex; at least to me, Nicholas's extended pursuit of the marvelous Julie, Conchis's creation, seems the least inventive, most conventionally written (even though rewritten) part of the book. On the other hand, the climactic trial scene, with its echoes of the Circe section from Joyce's "Ulysses," is both spectacular in conception and finely ironic in effect, as a hoard of psychoanalytic babble and erotic humiliations is dumped on our hero's unbowed head. (p. 41)

> *William H. Pritchard, "Early Fowles," in* The New York Times Book Review *(© 1978 by The New York Times Company; reprinted by permission), March 19, 1978, pp. 7, 41.*

JAMES GINDIN

John Fowles is, in his recent novel *Daniel Martin*, as he was in his preceding novel, *The French Lieutenant's Woman*, . . . explicitly conscious of his attitude toward his own characters. . . . Fowles is fond of almost all of [them], sometimes, perhaps, excessively fond. . . . Man's brutality toward other creatures, in Fowles's world, is endemic, established in the first chapter, an account of a summer day during which Daniel Martin, the narrator and the subject of a long search for himself, worked helping out on a farm in Devon in 1942, a day on which he saw the mower, moving through high grass, slice the legs off a concealed rabbit and then saw the German bombers rip the skies on their way to Exeter.... [Fowles's use of animal imagery], like his use of the rabbit, is never heavy or melodramatic; rather, it is understated, part of a dense texture of detail, conversation, description, and experience.

The recovery of Daniel and Jane is . . . , both implicitly and explicitly, the recovery of their generation, what Fowles calls the last generation "brought up in some degree of the nineteenth century, since the twentieth did not begin till 1945." The whole story of Daniel and Jane, the love and its immediate denial, the resolution of the complexities of emotional attachment by punishing the self, is itself a standard Victorian Romantic story.... The initial conversations between Daniel and Jane, at Oxford in 1950, are part of their belated Victorian time, the ironies that constantly deflate themselves, their excessive consciousness in post-war Oxford of living at a momentarily idyllic time and place, of wondering whether or not they are "real." . . . The origins of the sense of loss are not merely Victorian but particularly English as well, the result of a national ethos of sitting grimly uncomfortable in railway carriages rather than asking the man who has opened a window to close it, a nation of people sometimes "happier at being unhappy than doing something constructive about it. We boast of our genius for compromise, which is really a refusal to choose." All these qualities, focused in both time and place, lead Fowles to both develop and satirize his own generation's "pandemic of self-depreciation," for it is a generation that can always laugh at itself, is always self-conscious about its own postures. Yet, as Fowles recognizes clearly, the laughter is itself part of the problem, part of the easy means of attractive evasion. (pp. 236-39)

Daniel Martin is full of the author's speculations, some of which are not connected as closely to issues central to plot and character as are those concerning loss and recovery.... Often, Fowles is at his best in describing landscape and its connection with people. He writes well about the blues and purples of the stark New Mexican mountains, also of the soft, rainy contours of Devon held in various greens and greys. A parochial quality is conveyed through the loyal Devonian couple who tend Daniel's house there, yet the couple is never sentimentalized.... The speculations and generalizations are not always on the same level, for Fowles sometimes does descend to the stereotype, waste images on the supposed insularity and silence of the English, fulminate about the stupidity of Americans in always missing conversational "undertones." . . . Daniel sometimes worries his Englishness into repetitive triviality, having himself called a "most English Englishman" for some universal reaction, and he is fond of illustrating the nature of the American with a series of bad jokes derived from television comics. Illustrations of Arab humor and Jewish humor and German humor are drawn out in long lists of presumably funny stories that simply purvey ethnic stereotypes. For the most part, Fowles's narrative method shifts effectively between the first person and the third, between Daniel telling his own story and the author telling Daniel's, a means of enabling the author to treat his character with both immediacy and distance, to slide the focus

close-in and move it back. But Fowles also punctutates the narrative with speculations about novel writing, about how a novelist deals with his characters and novels of the "open" ending. The speculations are often intelligent in themselves (particularly some of those about the differences between the novel and the dramatic form, differences between the author as dramatist and author as novelist), but they lack something of the freshness and probity many of the same speculations had in *The French Lieutenant's Woman*. In the earlier novel, the insistence on a discussion of novelistic technique was part of the novel itself, a necessary means of approach to a partially unfamiliar subject that involved the ambiguities of time, change, and history; in *Daniel Martin*, however, the technical discussion is more digressive and exterior, more easily and immediately assumed because the subject is dramatized in the ambiguities and complexities of self. (pp. 239-41)

History is always both a projection of the self, as the only way to know and feel anything, and a recognition of otherness, of difference. Fowles demonstrated the same process of understanding history in *The French Lieutenant's Woman*, but, there, the area was much more limited in both space and time, almost all confined to England (a few minor leaps to France and America) and all held to a single century. In *Daniel Martin*, in contrast, the need to understand and assimilate covers much more of the world over a considerably longer time. And, to present its similarities and differences, its identities and its otherness, to write of the history that is part of us and not part of us with conviction and particularity, Fowles requires a great many words. His words, for the most part, are justified, achieve history, and avoid the sense of generalization as gesture or as abstract exaggeration.... (pp. 242-43)

Fowles's sense of the past is literary as well as historical. His treatment of Devon explicitly acknowledges the influence of Thomas Hardy's treatment of neighboring Dorset, "an obscure amalgam of rain, landscapes, pasts, fertilities, femalenesses," and the theme of Victorian guilt in Daniel is often connected with Hardy's work and life, as it is in *The French Lieutenant's Woman*. (p. 243)

The recovery in the novel, however, remains centrally personal, achieved, in particular, only through Daniel and Jane.... The recovery also assimilates parts of the social, historical, and literary environment.... (p. 244)

Another way of looking at what Daniel and Jane achieve can be seen in a distinction Fowles establishes between Anthony and Daniel early in the novel. Both collect orchids, the shared hobby on which their friendship was originally based. Anthony, with vastly greater knowledge of species and classifications, is much better at "looking at" them, at analyzing, separating, breaking down; Daniel, however, is more interested in "looking for" them, able to find, almost accidentally, the rare example among the muddled fields. Anthony's whole career is "looking at," a career of academic linguistic analysis, and it rests, permanently, on a religious faith that is always assumed. He pursues exact knowledge and once pronounces that "the metaphor is the curse of Western civilization." Daniel's sometimes aimless career is "looking for." He does not "find" Jane for a quarter of a century, his art is only gradually beginning to expand away from his guilts and grudges and he may never finish the full novel, but he can, increasingly, deal with metaphor, deal with the tenuous connections between people and pasts and histories. He recognizes, too, that part of the appreciation of metaphor, part of the recognition of all the tenuous connections of experience, is a matter of human effort as well as a matter of understanding. (p. 245)

> *James Gindin, in* The Michigan Quarterly
> Review *(copyright © The University of Michigan, 1978), Spring, 1978.*

*   *   *

FRENCH, Marilyn   1929-

French is an American novelist, critic, and short story writer. Her work seeks to clarify human values of the past, portraying their importance and influence on modern thought. She draws upon her experiences of marriage, motherhood, and divorce in her work, perhaps most notably in *The Women's Room*. She has written under the pseudonym Mara Solwoska. (See also *Contemporary Authors*, Vols. 69-72.)

BRIGITTE WEEKS

The trouble with feminist novels is that politics gets in the way of fiction, and sorting out the resulting reactions is like extracting Brer Rabbit from the briar patch. In this respect *The Women's Room* is no exception. The novel's basic thesis—that there is little or no foreseeable future for coexistence between men and women—is powerfully stated, but still invokes a lonely chaos repellent to most readers. In almost every other way, though, the novel is exceptional; and despite its length, for a novel of ideas it is easy to read.

Its characters are engaged in demonstrating a premise most of us are unable and unwilling to accept, yet we care for them, sympathize with them and give them our support. It does not deal with a single, recognizable crisis, such as a woman discovering a new identity, but with a whole era— three decades and a generation of women. Most important, in its ungainly groping way it touches a painful chord, extracts an unwilling realization that its women speak at least a part of the truth about themselves and how our society has treated them.

It has not treated them well. But the book avoids melodrama or self-pity, concentrating instead on the constant, grinding details of life which turn the psyche bitter and the conscience cold. . . .

This long and disturbing book has no complex, honed structure. It quite simply follows 40 years in the life of one woman. (p. E1)

If what happened along the way was a reenactment of the battle between the sexes, the author playing a new set of variations on a theme of Adam and Eve, we could be interested, beguiled and reassured. But what we see, paralyzed like a rabbit before a snake, is the polarization of the sexes. The cracks under the microscope become crevasses, the crevasses widen to chasms.

It is easy to "tut, tut" about the limitations and the emptiness of a New Jersey suburb in the '50s. The new women, thank God, have escaped all that. They have cast it aside as have their men. But, in the book, self-satisfaction is short-lived. It changes to hurt and some surprise when the bright young men of Harvard, the graduate students and husbands of graduate students, go through the same collection of blindnesses and cruelties.

At this point the reader becomes more deeply involved, pulled away from the novel as literature, forced to agree or disagree with the author's grim view of men and women in conflict. The book is extreme, the portrait is skewed, but its cumulative strength lies in the large and diverse collection of women it gathers together. The uncovering, layer by layer, of the tiny bitternesses in what the book calls the struggle to be taken seriously, rings pervasively true.

As a polemic the book is brilliant, forcing the reader to accept the reactions of the women as the only possible ones; closing firmly every loophole that might lead to a better understanding of women by men. But standing back for a moment from the overwhelming political issue, *The Women's Room* has an amateurish air as fiction. It lacks craft. The narrative seems out of control, characters appear and disappear, loose ends abound, nothing is omitted, and little attempt is made to characterize the men who provide the catalyst for the women's development. The author seems to revel in her lack of control over her narrative: "Do you believe any of this?" she demands brusquely of the reader at one point. "It is not the stuff of fiction. It has no shape, it hasn't the balances so important in art." This lack of shape and economy tends to strengthen the book's political impact but lessens its achievement. Bullied by the author, the reader approaches it as autobiography, looking for documentation, not creation.

The author's unerring sense of women's hearts and minds betrays her only once, but that on a crucial question. Val, the free spirit, the Cambridge feminist who is used as a yardstick to measure the women's progress, is the novel's Achilles heel both artistically and politically. She has the author's love and sympathy and yet she is a wooden mouthpiece for rhetoric that contrasts oddly with the message the book builds so carefully from the tiny details of daily life. Val's speeches, her visions of Utopia, her idealism, are clumsily integrated into the narrative like uncooked dough. Her final commitment to a kind of sexual apartheid—the result of her daughter's rape—and then her own violent death leave us strangely uncaring. If she is the ideal, we would settle for less.

But flaws aside, *The Women's Room* is a wonderful novel, full of life and passions that ring true as crystal. Its fierceness, its relentless refusal to compromise are as stirring as a marching song. The reader, a willing victim, becomes enmeshed in mixed feelings. Perhaps that is why I resented *The Women's Room* in a way I have never resented a novel before. It is a novel that lacks grace, restraint, good manners, an acceptance of the realities and pleasantries of life. It forces confrontations on the reader mercilessly. (pp. E1-E2)

> *Brigitte Weeks, "Separating the Men from the Women," in* Book World—The Washington Post *(© The Washington Post), October 9, 1977, pp. E1-E2.*

ANNE TYLER

[Mira, the heroine of "The Women's Room,"] starts out submissive and repressed, anxious to live up to other people's expectations of her. She ends up liberated but lonely, painfully adjusting to a new kind of life. It's the period in between that make the book so interesting. (p. 7)

The details of suburban life accumulate: balky ice-cube trays and Cub Scout meetings interlace with adulteries, attempted suicides and enforced stays in mental institutions. It's the small events that make the large events ring true, that remove from them any hint of the soap opera. Some shattering dramas occur in this book, but they're nearly always believable; we're willing to accept them as part of normal life.

Mira feels herself to be a victim, and stories told by victims tend to be long and narrow, as if strung through a funnel of suffering. "The Women's Room" is, in fact, very long and very narrow. Everything that happens—marriage, pregnancy, childbirth, the most mixed and mingled of occasions— seems almost purely negative, viewed with the glassy eye of belated resentment. There is no "equal time" offered; the men are given no chance to tell their side of the story. Compared to the women—each separate and distinct, each rich in character—the men tend to blur together. They're all villains, and cardboard villains at that.

But this narrowness is, I believe (or hope), intentional. The bias of "The Women's Room" is a part of the novel. It's almost the whole point. When Mira, acting as narrator, fails to give us any clear description of the man she marries, we first suspect her of careless storytelling. But it proves later to have been deliberate—Marilyn French's own very careful way of telling us something important about Mira. . . . The problem, she feels, is that the white middle-class male is really hollow: a sort of walking uniform, making the expected jokes, maintaining the expected postures. No wonder it's hard to describe him.

In fact, what victimizes Mira is not men, but the chasm that she perceives between men and women—the mistrust, incomprehension and exploitation. Whether or not we agree that this chasm exists, it exists for *her;* it affects her whole life. With a narrator like Mira, a certain bias in the telling is not merely forgiveable; it serves a clear purpose.

We have more trouble accepting the polemics that creep in as the new Mira, divorced and liberated, begins to discuss with her friends the injustices done to women. Each character contributes her philosophy in great chunky paragraphs. We've stumbled into a seminar, it seems. But even these later, awkward sections serve as a kind of document—living witness, however discomfiting, to a stage that a multitude of women are certainly experiencing.

Think of it this way: Marilyn French has written a collective biography of a large group of American citizens. Expectant in the 40's, submissive in the 50's, enraged in the 60's, they have arrived in the 70's independent but somehow unstrung, not yet fully composed after all they've been through. Like those exhausting Russian novels in which quarrelsome and demanding families quarreled with *us,* made demands upon *us,* "The Women's Room" strains our patience, argues, wears us down. But it's proof of Marilyn French's abilities that we can finish this book feeling genuinely hopeful for some kind of happy ending, someday, for Mira. (pp. 7, 38)

> Anne Tyler, "*Starting Out Submissive,*" in The New York Times Book Review (© *1977 by The New York Times Company; reprinted by permission), October 16, 1977, pp. 7, 38.*

Enthusiastic reviewers in the daily and weekly press have called Marilyn French's polemic the major novel of the

women's liberation movement, and they have a point. The book does have an impact; this male reviewer found himself embarrassed for his sex. It is scarcely a surprise that women have suffered indignities for generations just because they are women, but it takes works like Ms. French's to make us realize just why that has got to stop. For those women who do not submit in a male-dominated society, life can be hellish, as Ms. French's heroines (she would reject the term) prove. Rape is not pretty, even when the act is committed with looks alone. (p. 68)

> *Virginia Quarterly Review (copyright, 1978, by the* Virginia Quarterly Review, *The University of Virginia), Vol. 54, No. 2 (Spring, 1978).*

*   *   *

FROST, Robert   1874-1963

An American poet, Frost described poetry as "a little voyage of discovery." The setting for his poems is predominantly the rural landscapes of New England, his poetic language is the language of the common man. His work has often been criticized for its uneven quality, as well as its simplistic philosophy and form. However, Frost's best poems explore fundamental questions of existence, depicting with chilling matter-of-factness the loneliness of the individual confronted with an indifferent universe. (See also *CLC*, Vols. 1, 3, 4, 9.)

YVOR WINTERS

Frost has been praised as a classical poet, but he is not classical in any sense which I can understand. Like many of his contemporaries, he is an Emersonian Romantic, although with certain mutings and modifications . . . , and he has labeled himself as such with a good deal of care. He is a poet of the minor theme, the casual approach, and the discreetly eccentric attitude. When a reader calls Frost a classical poet, he probably means that Frost strikes him as a "natural" poet, a poet who somehow resembles himself and his neighbors; but this is merely another way of saying that the reader feels a kinship to him and likes him easily. Classical literature is said to judge human experience with respect to the norm; but it does so with respect to the norm of what humanity ought to be, not with respect to the norm of what it happens to be in a particular place and time. The human average has never been admirable . . . , and that is why literature which glorifies the average is sentimental rather than classical.

Frost writes of rural subjects, and the American reader of our time has an affection for rural subjects which is partly the product of the Romantic sentimentalization of "nature," but which is partly also a nostalgic looking back to the rural life which predominated in this nation a generation or two ago; the rural life is somehow regarded as the truly American life. I have no objection to the poet's employing rural settings; but we should remember that it is the poet's business to evaluate human experience, and the rural setting is no more valuable for this purpose than any other or than no particular setting, and one could argue with some plausibility that an exclusive concentration on it may be limiting.

Frost early began his endeavor to make his style approximate as closely as possible the style of conversation, and this endeavor has added to his reputation: it has helped to make him seem "natural." But poetry is not conversation, and I see no reason why poetry should be called upon to imitate conversation. Conversation is the most careless and formless of human utterance; it is spontaneous and unrevised, and its vocabulary is commonly limited. Poetry is the most difficult form of human utterance; we revise poems carefully in order to make them more nearly perfect. The two forms of expression are extremes, they are not close to each other. (pp. 58-9)

Frost has said that Emerson is his favorite American poet, and he himself appears to be something of an Emersonian.... In Frost, [however,] we find a disciple without Emerson's religious conviction: Frost believes in the rightness of impulse, but does not discuss the pantheistic doctrine which would give authority to impulse; as a result of his belief in impulse, he is of necessity a relativist, but his relativism, apparently since it derives from no intense religious conviction, has resulted mainly in ill-natured eccentricity and in increasing melancholy. He is an Emersonian who has become sceptical and uncertain without having reformed; and the scepticism and uncertainty do not appear to have been so much the result of thought as the result of the impact upon his sensibility of conflicting notions of his own era—they appear to be the result of his having taken the easy way and having drifted with the various currents of his time. (pp. 60-1)

[Certain] poems throw more light on Frost as a whole, perhaps, than do any others, and they may serve as an introduction to his work. I have in mind especially three poems from *Mountain Interval:* the introductory piece entitled "The Road Not Taken," the post-scriptive piece entitled "The Sound of the Trees," and the lyrical narrative called "The Hill Wife." ... These poems all have a single theme: the whimsical, accidental, and incomprehensible nature of the formative decision; and I should like to point out that if one takes this view of the formative decision, one has cut oneself off from understanding most of human experience, for in these terms there is nothing to be understood—one can write of human experience with sentimental approval or with sentimental melancholy, but with little else.

"The Road Not Taken," for example, is the poem of a man whom one might fairly call a spiritual drifter; and a spiritual drifter is unlikely to have either the intelligence or the energy to become a major poet. Yet the poem has definite virtues, and these should not be overlooked. In the first place, spiritual drifters exist, they are real; and although their decisions may not be comprehensible, their predicament is comprehensible. The poem renders the experience of such a person, and renders the uncertain melancholy of his plight. Had Frost been a more intelligent man, he might have seen that the plight of the spiritual drifter was not inevitable, he might have judged it in the light of a more comprehensive wisdom. Had he done this, he might have written a greater poem. But his poem is good as far as it goes; the trouble is that it does not go far enough, it is incomplete, and it puts on the reader a burden of critical intelligence which ought to be borne by the poet. (p. 61)

["The Sound of the Trees"] has the same quality of uncertainty and incomprehension as "The Road Not Taken"; it is written with about the same degree of success, with about the same charm, and with about the same quality of vague melancholy. In considering either of these poems, especially if one compares them even to minor works by sixteenth- and seventeenth-century masters, one will ob-

serve not only the limitations of intelligence which I have mentioned, but a quality, slight though it may be, of imprecision in the rendering of the detail and of the total attitude, which is the result of the limitations.... [Frost] is mistaking whimsical impulse for moral choice, and the blunder obscures his understanding and even leaves his mood uncertain with regard to the value of the whole business. He is vaguely afraid that he may be neither wrong nor right. (p. 63)

["The Hill Wife"] has an eerie quality, like that of dream or of neurosis, but it has little else.... And one might mention also the poem from *A Witness Tree* entitled "A Serious Step Lightly Taken": the serious step in question is merely the buying of a farm; but the title is characteristic, and the title implies approval and not disapproval—it implies that serious steps ought to be lightly taken. But if serious steps are to be lightly taken, then poetry, at least, is impoverished, and the poet can have very little to say. Most of the world's great poetry has had to do with serious steps seriously taken, and when the seriousness goes from life, it goes from the poetry. (pp. 63-4)

[In "The Bear" Frost] is satirizing the intelligent man from the point of view of the unintelligent; and the more often one reads the poem, the more obvious this fact becomes, and the more trivial the poem appears. (pp. 64-5)

The idea in ["To a Thinker"] is the same as that in "The Bear," but is even more plainly stated; we have the commonplace Romantic distrust of reason and trust in instinct.... The poem is badly written, but one couplet is momentarily amusing:

> I own I never really warmed
> To the reformer or reformed.

Yet when we examine it more carefully, there is something almost contemptible about it. There are, of course, reformers and reformers, and many of them have been ludicrous or worse. Frost is invoking the image of the soap-box politician or the street-corner preacher in order to discredit reason. But the word *reform* can be best evaluated if one separates the syllables for a moment. To reform means to re-form. And the progress of civilization has been a process of re-forming human nature.... Frost endeavors to gain his point by sleight-of-hand; he endeavors to obscure the difference between St. Thomas Aquinas and Pussyfoot Johnson. (p. 65)

["The Egg and the Machine" presents] several familiar Romantic attitudes: resentment at being unable to achieve the absolute privacy which Frost names as a primary desideratum in "Build Soil," the sentimental regard for the untouched wilderness (the untouched wilderness would provide absolute privacy for the unique Romantic), and the sentimental hatred for the machine.... Frost's real objection to the machine, I suspect, is its social nature; it requires and facilitates cooperation, and Frost is unwilling to recognize its respectability mainly for this reason.

There have been other literary works dealing with resentment at the machine and the changes it has introduced; the resentment I believe to be foolish, but in certain settings it may have a tragic if barbarous dignity.... The trouble is again that the symbols will not stand inspection.... (pp. 68-9)

The carefully flippant tone [of "A Mask of Reason"] ...

belongs to the tradition of Romantic irony which . . . is used to make the ideas seem trivial. The ideas and the tone together express the Romantic ennui or disillusionment which is born of spiritual laziness, the laziness which is justified by the Romantic doctrine that one can best apprehend the truth by intuition and without labor. . . .

There is no understanding of good and evil in themselves, of the metaphysical questions involved. Good is submission to an anthropomorphic and undignified God and is made to seem preposterous. Evil is made equally preposterous, and for similar reasons. The poem resembles "The Bear," but is on a larger scale. If these concepts of good and evil were the only concepts available, or if they were the best concepts available, then Frost's satire would be justified. But they are not, and in reading the poem one can only be appalled at Frost's willful ignorance, at his smug stupidity. (p. 72)

[Frost] is a poet who holds the following views: he believes that impulse is trustworthy and reason contemptible, that formative decisions should be made casually and passively, that the individual should retreat from cooperative action with his kind should retreat not to engage in intellectual activity but in order to protect himself from the contamination of outside influence, that affairs manage themselves for the best if left alone, that ideas of good and evil need not be taken very seriously. These views are sure to be a hindrance to self-development, and they effectually cut Frost off from any really profound understanding of human experience, whether political, moral, metaphysical, or religious. The result in the didactic poems is the perversity and incoherence of thought; the result in the narrative poems is either slightness of subject or a flat and uninteresting apprehension of the subject; the result in the symbolic lyrics is a disturbing dislocation between the descriptive surface, which is frequently lovely, and the ultimate meaning, which is usually sentimental and unacceptable. The result in nearly all the poems is a measure of carelessness in the style, sometimes small and sometimes great, but usually evident: the conversational manner will naturally suit a poet who takes all experience so casually, and it is only natural that the conversational manner should often become very conversational indeed. (p. 75)

The great poet judges the tragic subject completely, that is, rationally and emotionally. . . . But Frost advises us to turn away from serious topics, and for the greater part he confines himself to minor topics. The major topics impinge upon his personal experience, however, for after all they are unavoidable; but his treatment of them is usually whimsical, sentimental, and evasive; and in his later years his poetry is more and more pervaded by an obscure melancholy which he can neither control nor understand.

Yet Frost has a genuine gift for writing, . . . and this gift emerges more clearly in his later work than in his earlier, though still hesitantly and momentarily. The view of human nature which we have seen Frost to hold is one that must lead of necessity to a feeling that the individual man is small, lost, and unimportant in the midst of a vast and changing universe. . . . The nostalgic love for the chaotic and the dream-like, which Frost inherits from the Romantic tradition, along with an habitual but unreasoned hesitancy or fear, which is the heritage of the earlier New England, keeps Frost looking two ways, unable to move decisively in either direction. He is neither a truly vigorous Romantic

. . . nor a truly reactionary Classicist. . . . He cannot decide whether to go or to stay, and the result is uncertainty and increasing melancholy. . . . [He] puts on the reader a burden of critical intelligence which ought to have been borne more fully by the poet; and if the reader is not capable of the necessary intelligence, the poem is likely to draw him into a similar state of mind. (pp. 76-7)

"Acquainted with the Night" . . . seems to me one of the two or three best poems that Frost has written. Superficially, the poem deals with the feeling of loneliness which one has when walking late at night in a strange city; but symbolically it deals with the poet's loneliness in a strange and obscure world, and the clock which tells him that the time is neither wrong nor right is a symbol of the relativism which causes his melancholy. The understanding of his predicament appears to be greater in this poem than in most of the others; he knows, at least, that it is a predicament and realizes the state of mind to which it has brought him. In the seventh volume, *A Witness Tree*, there is an even more impressive piece entitled "The Most of It." This poem represents a momentary insight into the vast and brute indifference of nature, the nature toward which Frost has cherished so sentimental a feeling through so many poems. . . . [The] style combines descriptive precision with great concentration of meaning and at the same time is wholly free from decoration, ineptitude, and other irrelevancy. The poem gives one some idea of how great a poet Frost might conceivably have been, had he been willing to use his mind instead of letting it wither. In this poem especially, and to some extent in "Acquainted with the Night," the poet confronts his condition fairly and sees it for what it is, but the insight is momentary: he neither proceeds from this point to further understanding nor even manages to retain the realization that he has achieved. (pp. 78-9)

["The Vindictives"] is probably the only poem in Frost in which one can find anything resembling heroic action; the poem is motivated by a simple and honest hatred of brutality and injustice so obvious that they cannot be overlooked. The hatred in question, however, can be justified only by certain ideas, the ideas of Christian and classical philosophy, which, although they are a part of Frost's background and influence him to this extent, he has during all of his career neglected or explicitly maligned. The poem is a little loose in construction and is occasionally careless in style; but it has an honesty and a controlled violence which make it very impressive. . . . "Come In" is a memorable lyric, but perhaps it contains too much of Frost's professional and somewhat sentimental charm. (pp. 79-80)

Frost is at his worst in didactic writing, in spite of his fondness for it: his ideas are impossible and his style is exceptionally shoddy. Furthermore, although Frost is frequently very skillful in the handling of short rhymed forms, he is extremely inept in managing blank verse; in blank verse his theory of conversational style shows itself at its worst—the rhythms are undistinguished and are repetitious to the point of deadly monotony. But it is in these poems that Frost states his ideas most unmistakably, and it is necessary to understand the ideas to form an estimate of him at all. He is at his best, as regards style, in the short rhymed lyric, but his short lyrics are less explicit in stating their themes, and unless one comes to them with a clear concept of Frost's principal themes one may overlook the themes or mistake them. Frost is at his best in such poems as "The Most of

It'' and ''Acquainted with the Night,'' in which he seems to be more or less aware of the untenability of his own position and to face his difficulty, or as ''The Vindictives,'' in which as the result of a fortunate accident of some kind he is able simply to ignore his usual themes and write as if he had never heard of them. The bulk of his really memorable work, however, is to be found among the symbolic lyrics, of which ''The Last Mowing'' and ''Spring Pools'' are excellent examples, lyrics in which the descriptive element is beautifully handled, in which the feeling is communicated with a sufficient degree of success to make them unforgettable but with so great a degree of imprecision as to make them curiously unsatisfactory. For the feeling does not arise merely from the contemplation of the natural objects described: if it did so, it would be too strong and too mysteriously elusive for its origins; the feeling arises mainly from the concepts of which the natural objects are the symbolic vehicles, and those concepts . . . are unacceptable, and when one tries to project them clearly into terms of human action are unimaginable. Frost's instinctualism, his nostalgia for dream and chaos, are merely the symptoms of sentimental obscurantism when, as in Frost's work, they are dealt with lightly and whimsically, but if taken seriously, as in the work of Crane and Pound, they may lead to more serious difficulties. They do not lead toward intelligence, no matter how far the individual devotee may travel in their company; they lead away from intelligence. They lead away from the true comprehension of human experience which makes for great, or even for successful, poetry. The element of the unimaginable, and hence of the imprecise, which lurks in the theme of ''The Last Mowing'' will make it forever, and in spite of its real and extraordinary virtues, a very imperfectly successful poem. . . . (p. 81)

He is in no sense a great poet, but he is at times a distinguished and valuable poet. In order to evaluate his work and profit by it, however, we must understand him far better than he understands himself, and this fact indicates a very serious weakness in his talent. If we do not so understand him, his poetry is bound to reinforce some of the most dangerous tendencies of our time; his weakness is commonly mistaken for wisdom, his vague and sentimental feeling for profound emotion, as his reputation and the public honors accorded him plainly testify. He is the nearest thing we have to a poet laureate, a national poet; and this fact is evidence of the community of thought and feeling between Frost and a very large part of the American literary public. The principles which have saved some part of Frost's talent, the principles of Greek and Christian thought, are principles which are seldom openly defended and of which the implications and ramifications are understood by relatively few of our contemporaries, by Frost least of all; they operate upon Frost at a distance, through social inheritance, and he has done his best to adopt principles which are opposed to them. The principles which have hampered Frost's development, the principles of Emersonian and Thoreauistic Romanticism, are the principles which he has openly espoused, and they are widespread in our culture. Until we understand these last and the dangers inherent in them and so abandon them in favor of better, we are unlikely to produce many poets greater than Frost, although a few poets may have intelligence enough to work clear of such influences; and we are likely to deteriorate more or less rapidly both as individuals and as a nation. (p. 82)

Yvor Winters, "Robert Frost: Or, the Spiritual Drifter as Poet," in his The Function of Criticism: Problems and Exercises *(© 1957 by Yvor Winters; reprinted by permission of The Swallow Press, Chicago), Alan Swallow, 1957 (and reprinted in* Robert Frost: A Collection of Critical Essays, *edited by James M. Cox, Prentice-Hall, Inc., 1962, pp. 58-82).*

MARION MONTGOMERY

The casual reader of Frost's poetry is likely to think of Frost as a nature poet in the tradition of Wordsworth. In a sense, nature is his subject, but to Frost it is never an impulse from a vernal wood. His best poetry is concerned with the drama of man in nature, whereas Wordsworth is generally best when emotionally displaying the panorama of the natural world. "I guess I'm not a nature poet," Frost said . . . in the fall of 1952. "I have only written two poems without a human being in them." (p. 138)

[We] may recall the epitaph Frost proposes for himself in ''The Lesson for Today'': ''I had a lover's quarrel with the world.'' This lover's quarrel is Frost's poetic subject, and throughout his poetry there are evidences of this view of man's existence in the natural world. His attitude toward nature is one of armed and amicable truce and mutual respect interspersed with crossings of the boundaries separating the two principles, individual man and forces of the world. But *boundaries* are insisted upon. . . . [Even in] moments of affinity, or ''favor,''] we shall always find the barriers which cannot be crossed. . . . Man is never completely certain that the earth, the natural world, returns his love.

From the publication of *A Boy's Will* down to the present time Frost has indicated a realization that nature, *natura naturata*, not only will, but sometimes seems intended to, hurt those who love it. The immediate natural world even seems to be moving toward chaos, intending to take man along with it if he isn't careful. But man has an advantage. . . . To sustain such injuries as nature inflicts ''It's well to have all kinds of feeling, for it's all kinds of a world.'' And Frost expresses his all kinds of feeling toward the natural world. . . . [At] times he writes of the natural world in a cavalier fashion which Wordsworth would consider heretical. ''You know Orion always comes up sideways,'' he says in ''The Star-Splitter,'' and he pokes fun at the seasons in ''Two Tramps in Mud Time.'' It is no spirit of nature which sends Frost's rain or wind; he never sees in the natural world the pervading spirit which Wordsworth saw. . . . Frost makes his attitude toward nature clear when he says in ''New Hampshire'' that ''I wouldn't be a prude afraid of nature,'' and again rather flatly, ''Nothing not built with hands of course is sacred.''

Frost at times speaks directly to objects in nature, as Wordsworth did. But what is high seriousness in Wordsworth is fancy or humor in Frost. Frost goes on at length in a Polonius-to-Laertes speech to his orchard, which he is leaving for the winter. Watch out for the rabbits and deer and grouse; they will eat you. And if the sun gets too hot before the proper season, you won't be bearing next summer. The final word is ''Goodby and Keep Cold.'' . . . [Even in] instances of direct address, . . . we never suppose that Frost feels the kind of brotherhood for natural objects that Wordsworth expresses through much of his poetry.

Always, to Frost, man differs essentially from other features and objects. . . . [There] is motion of natural objects and not emotion, human simile but not human feeling. In "A Considerable Speck" Frost says, after examining the microscopic creature, "Plainly with an intelligence I dealt." And in "Departmental" he seems to be interpreting the ants in human terms. But we make a mistake if we suppose that he would ascribe mind to the "microscopic item" in the first poem or human behavior to the actions of the ants in the second. The truth is that in each of these poems Frost is preparing the way obliquely for direct statement. In "A Considerable Speck" we have the final "No one can know how glad I am to find / On any sheet the least display of mind." And "Departmental" ends with the comment on the ants, "How thoroughly departmental." In the more direct poem, "The Bear," we find "The world has room to make a bear feel free; / The universe seems cramped to you and me." Whenever Frost talks directly to or directly of natural objects or creatures, we feel that he is really looking at man out of the corner of his eye and speaking to him out of the corner of his mouth. In all these poems Frost is describing the animal and vegetable natures in man, not reading man's nature into the animal and vegetable worlds, as Wordsworth was inclined to do.

If Frost feels, as he seems to, that the natural world is impersonal, unfeeling, and at best animal creation, what does he think of its creator? In his early poetry he, like the people he refers to in "The Strong Are Saying Nothing," holds his silence. He does not choose to make any sweeping statements about God any more than he does about nature or man. This has occasioned the belief among some critics that Frost is at best agnostic. (pp. 138-41)

Frost's hesitancy in speaking dogmatically on the subject of the supernatural is due more to his acceptance of man's limitations and the acceptance of mystery in existence than to agnosticism. . . . He is quite ready to believe that which is appealing *if* it is also reasonable. Then he will express opinion. At the same time he is not willing to discard completely the appealing if it fails to be reasonable, knowing the fallibility of reason. He rather reserves judgment. Experience comes early, understanding later.

In his later years Frost, feeling more sure of what he thought was true, has spoken more freely of his views of God, as of man and the natural world. An indication of his broadening scope appeared in his book *A Further Range,* published in 1936, and finally, he has come to devote two of his latest works, *A Masque of Reason* (1945) and *A Masque of Mercy* (1947), to the question of man's relation to God. In *A Masque of Reason* Frost attempts to justify God's ways to man, which justification is that none is necessary. In this work Frost presents God in a rather familiar fashion, and this presentation of a somewhat undignified God has occasioned difficulty for many readers. (pp. 141-42)

But Frost's presentation of a cavalier God is a deliberate device which points up the theme of the masque. . . . In this picture of God given in *A Masque of Reason* he is showing us not lack of reason or justice in God, but rather man's stubbornness and lack of understanding. It is like man, especially in our day, to see God "pitching throne with a ply-wood chair." It is like man to exclaim with Job's wife, "It's God. I'd know him by Blake's picture anywhere." As it has been the human error to read man into

nature, so is it the human error to read man into God: and Frost's poem, satirical in its shrewd observation on this human fallibility, is concerned with this problem. Is man's reason sufficient to overcome the wall between himself and God? Job and Job's wife are after a rational explanation of man's predicament which will clarify everything and bridge the gap between the finite mind and the infinite. The theme of the poem, then, is that understanding is dependent not only upon reason, but upon faith as well, a faith which helps the finite mind accept the mystery its reason will not completely explain. (pp. 142-43)

To Frost, the mindless world, despite its laws and patterns of cause and effect, lacks completeness. "There Are Roughly Zones," the title of a poem says, but understanding man is created so that he may try to make the world complete. Man's hands and mind bring order to himself to the world around him. Having all kinds of feelings for this all kinds of a world, he is able to bring order to the natural world "by making a garden and building a wall. That garden is art." And the man who erects the wall and makes the garden is in the world for that purpose, not that he may expect to bring permanent order but that he may work out his own salvation. Frost's consistency in this view from early to latest publication is shown by the two masques and by a poem from his first publication, *A Boy's Will.* "The Trial by Existence," which appeared in *A Boy's Will,* suggests that it is futile to attempt a complete explanation of why there are so many difficulties to prevent man's taking in and building his garden in the world. Man's real virtue, it argues, is to dare, to seek to build the wall which allows the garden to flourish for a time. Frost concludes that it is not important in the final reckoning whether or not one has actually succeeded in erecting a great or small wall or in raising a great or small garden; man is not measured by his works. (p. 143)

Man, like Job, continually repeats, "The artist in me cries out for design," and design man tries to discover. The barrier between creator and created is maintained. God will not let man see completely into the life of things. To this barrier are added the limitations imposed on man by his reason, or mind, and his desire, or heart. Yet reason and desire arouse the complementary faith which helps man accept his situation and grow from that point of acceptance. For here is true understanding in man, the recognition through reason, and acceptance through faith, of man's limitations and of the belief in God as "that which man is sure cares, and will save him, no matter how many times or how completely he has failed," as Frost said in 1916.

Frost considers this would be a pretty desperate and meaningless situation but for man's own ability to erect and destroy barriers. . . . This concern with barriers is the predominant theme in Frost's poetry. The barriers fall into several categories. First of all there is the great natural barrier, the void between man and the stars, a barrier which man continually, and sometimes foolishly, tries to bridge in his attempt to escape his limited haunt. The very stars, because of their remoteness, reduce man if he confuses distance and size with his own nature. (p. 145)

But the remoteness of the stars is also something which man may lean his mind on and be stayed. What is more disturbing to man than the barrier of space is the barrier between man and the immediate natural world, for it is in this realm of desert places that most of man's "gardening" takes place. This is where the ''breathless swing between subject matter and form'' becomes most apparent. And it is the struggle in this sphere which reveals what men are. (pp. 145-46)

Wordsworth in his early poetry tended to deny all barriers in his effort to become one with the great moving spirit of things, the soul of the world. He wanted to achieve the ''abstract high singular'' that Job's wife disparages in Frost's masque, to concern himself with the general idea rather than with the physical world. His approach was transcendental in that he denied the existence of barriers. For Frost there can be no such simplification of the problem of spirit and matter. Despite the necessity of maintaining one's garden against nature and of advancing it, there are certain limits which man cannot overstep, and one of them is the nature of physical existence. Frost has made no Platonic crosscuts to separate form and matter as Wordsworth did between 1798 and 1805. Existence is form plus matter to Frost, and any conflict in the world is conflict between such existences—form-and-matter man against form-and-matter world.

There is a fourth category of barriers in Frost's poetry—those between man and man. To Frost these barriers serve as framework for mutual understanding and respect. It is because of barriers that we understand each other, and, far from striving to tear them down as is the modern tendency, Frost insists on recognizing them. He even builds them wherever they seem necessary. The conflict caused by friction of personal barriers, ''human nature in peace and war,'' is the subject of his most dramatic poetry. (pp. 146-47)

The reader might suppose from [''Mending Wall''] that Frost does not particularly hold with the need for fences, but note that it is the narrator who ''lets his neighbor know'' when time comes to do the work. The narrator questions the necessity of the wall in an effort to make the neighbor think and come out of the darkness of mind he is walking in. Both men know that good fences make good neighbors, but only one of them knows why or that the wall is more than a barrier between neighbors. Something in the world doesn't like a wall between a man and the world or between a man and his neighbor. Something wants all walls down so that individual identity may be destroyed. The wise person knows that a wall is a point of reference, a touchstone of sanity, and that it must be not only maintained but respected as well. (p. 147)

Man's tendency, once he has brought what he understands as form to the semichaos of his world, is to try also to impose the form he understands on the mind of his fellow-men—to insist that they see as he sees. Since each man is an individual intended to discover his individuality by revealing or restoring order through his peculiar art—whether that art be the splitting of birch logs, the making of ax-helves, or the writing of poems about these activities—one thing he must remember: each man reveals form which is indwelling in the material with which he works. There are roughly zones which limit man's gardening, his restoration of order in his own image. The wood which the ax-helve is made from has its grain, and the artist reveals form within the limitations of that grain. If he does his job well, the ax-helve will bend in use without breaking. All the helve-maker may boast of is his ability to reveal the form he has discovered in a particular piece of wood; his understanding

of the form and his dexterity in revealing it mark his accomplishment. But when man imposes what he thinks should be the form of an ax-helve on a piece of wood whose grain will not allow the form, the first solid whack will split the finished helve. By showing the difference between a good and a bad helve, the French Canadian in ''The Ax-Helve'' argues against one man's imposing what he finds himself to be upon another man. The Canadian, it finally appears, is arguing that his children ought not to be forced to go to public schools where they will have themselves ground down to a form which is not in their nature.

Frost's view of man's nature, then, is consistent throughout his poetry. Each man is, in a sense, a stranger in this world, and so he remains. His is not to question why he is alone or why the world seems to be against him. He is to begin the breathless opening and closing of the mind, the hand, the heart, the eye upon the world, growing as he does so. As he grows he understands himself more, and as he understands himself he also understands more of the world and of his fellows. With understanding comes love which makes him respect the chaos of the world with which he is in conflict, the material with which he works. The same love makes him respect and accept differences between men also. He respects others' individual differences and expects that others will respect his. And he knows that those differences are not to be overcome by the ''tenderer-than-thou // Collectivistic regimenting love / With which the modern world is being swept'' (''A Considerable Speck''). That would be to reduce man to a numerical and animal problem, to make him no more than the other creatures who share the world of nature with him. . . . Scientific man has made so bold as to demonstrate the infallibility of natural laws and then has proceeded to measure himself against them. As long as there was man's fallibility, as long as he could bow to natural law, there was some distinction in being man. (pp. 148-49)

In arguing man's distinction, Frost will not go to the two extremes offered by the philosophy of Plato on the one hand or the science of Democritus on the other. He will not accept pure spirit or idea as an explanation of man and a way out of the universe, nor will he accept the scientist's materialism measured with microscope and telescope as an alternate. Unhappy man tries both like a bear in a cage [in ''The Bear'']:

> He sits back on his fundamental butt
> With lifted snout and eyes (if any) shut,
> (He almost looks religious but he's not),
> And back and forth he sways from cheek to cheek,
> At one extreme agreeing with one Greek,
> At the other agreeing with another Greek.
>
> (p. 149)

Once more [in ''A Masque of Mercy''] Frost affirms that what is most important is the courage and not the accomplishment, the attempting and not successful completion. . . . St. Paul, the spirit of the New Testament, finally convinces Keeper that man is saved only by God's mercy, which man receives for having labored under injustice, his inability to overcome completely the barriers imposed upon him and the temporal nature of those barriers which man himself may erect. This is the only way to man's salvation, for if he had not labored thus his limitations would not allow that salvation. To Frost, God is still ''that which man is sure cares, and will save him, no matter how many times or how completely he has failed.''. . . Justice, Frost says, is only to the deserving, but mercy is for the undeserving. And those who demand justice because of the limitations imposed upon them will receive justice; those who with courage in the heart move toward understanding through faith and reason may expect God's mercy. (p. 150)

> Marion Montgomery, "Robert Frost and His Use of Barriers: Man vs. Nature Toward God," in South Atlantic Quarterly (reprinted by permission of the Publisher; copyright 1958 by Duke University Press, Durham, North Carolina), Summer, 1958 (and reprinted in Robert Frost: A Collection of Critical Essays, edited by James M. Cox, Prentice-Hall, Inc., 1962, pp. 138-50).

HAYDEN CARRUTH

What one finds upon reading [Frost's] Collected Poems is a relatively small number of first-rate pieces and a much larger number of unsuccessful ones. I don't mean the failures are "bad poems"; a few are, but scores and scores of them are poems that almost make it—almost but not quite. Usually they contain fine descriptions, pointed imagery, apt and characteristic language; but then at some point they turn talky, insistent, too literal, as if Frost were trying to coerce the meaning from his own poetic materials. And in fact I think this is exactly what he was trying to do. Call it vanity, arrogance, or whatever: Frost came to distrust his own imagination, and believed he could *make* his poems do and say what he wanted them to do and say. His best poems, nearly all of them from his first two or three books, were poems in which meaning and feeling had come together spontaneously in their own figures and objects. They were esthetically functional creations in the fullest sense. Frost saw that this had happened, and presumably he wanted to make it keep happening, but he ended by coercing his poems in formulaic and predictable ways. He ended not with poems but with editorials. (pp. 37-8)

["Stopping by Woods on a Snowy Evening"] is not Frost's best poem. . . . But it is a good poem, to my mind quite genuine, and its meanings and feelings, larger than any stated in the poem, do emerge indirectly but unmistakably from the arrangements of images, rhythms, sounds, and syntax; we all know this, and Frost knew it too. The story is told that he wrote the poem at dawn in a state of near-exhaustion, after working all night on a longer poem that wasn't going well. He wrote it easily and quickly. And it turned out to say more than he knew he was saying, which is just the experience that all of us who write poems recognize and long for. Frost longed for it too. He longed to repeat it. But his longing drove him to attempt the coercion of the experience by means of contrivance and conscious control. (p. 38)

I am certain that "Stopping by Woods" sprang from an actual experience of stopping by a woods, while ["For Once, Then, Something"] was entirely a studio performance with only a consciously contrived connection to any experience, probably a remote experience, of looking down a well. . . . [My] feeling is distinct and forcible. Perhaps in part it comes from the exact hendecasyllables, which are uncharacteristic of Frost and which usually convey a feeling of artifice in English. Perhaps also the well metaphor is simply too pat, too sentimental. But the poem itself reveals more, its strongest part is the opening sentence, really quite

a good one, the syntax and sound patterns cast tellingly against the basic meter; which leads me to suspect that the poem's real, though hidden, occasion lay in those "others" —I wonder who they were?—who taunted Frost with his solipsism. That was the impetus; but it petered out, and after the first sentence the poem goes downhill rapidly. It becomes tendentious, almost peevish. . . . Then in the last line everything goes to pieces. The poet, in despair, *names* what his poem is about, "truth," thus committing the poet's cardinal sin; and at once the poem is destroyed, the labored metaphor of the well collapses. What lies at the bottom of the well is—is—is . . . but of course it *cannot* be named, that is the whole point, any more than the meaning of the snowy woods can be named. Yet Frost did it. He pushed and pressed and tried to coerce his poem. And he did it over and over again in other poems, many of them more substantial than this one.

"Two Tramps in Mud Time," another well known poem, is a case in point. It opens with the poet as wood-splitter in the thawing time of late winter, suffering the interruption of two unemployed loggers; this is good localized description, the kind Frost was master of. But then he appears not to know what to do with his opening. The poem wanders into further unnecessary description: the April day, the blue-bird, the snow and water; and then it ends in four stanzas of virtually straight editorial matter. The two tramps and the mud-time are left utterly stranded. When one thinks how Frost would have used these figures at the time when he was writing his earlier dramatic and narrative poems, one can see clearly, I believe, how he had deserted his own imagination and how he tried to make up the deficiency through conscious manipulation and force.

One point remains to be made—an important one—which is that although many of the failures are poems associated with Frost's deliberate optimism, many others are products of his darker intuition, just as his successes, too, are distributed, though unevenly, on both sides of the spectrum. . . . What else should we expect? After all, Frost's talent and his vanity both were functions of the whole man; they had to be. And if I think that in his whole career his vanity overcame his talent, and that he produced in consequence far more failures than a poet of his gifts ought to have produced, his successes still remain intact—such poems as "Mending Wall," "The Black Cottage," "A Servant to Servants," "The Hill Wife," "Acquainted with the Night," and others. These are fine poems, and I think some of them have doubtless already taken on the quality of greatness, as that term is used by historians. . . . To be concerned with his weakness is, now, a form of compliment. And to be instructed by him about our own weakness is a greater compliment. I see Frost's error repeated again and again in the work of other poets, including my own. I think all of us who labor in vanity have this to learn from him: that only a poet who remains open to experience—and not only open, but submissive, and not only to experience, but to the actual newness of experience here and now—only such a poet can hope to repeat his successes. (pp. 39-41)

> Hayden Carruth, "Robert Frost," in Parnassus: Poetry in Review (copyright © by Poetry in Review Foundation), Spring-Summer, 1975, pp. 35-41.

GEORGE MONTEIRO

Despite Frost's expressions of interest in Emily Dickinson, his critics have said nothing about the ways in which his reactions to Dickinson's poetry might have contributed to the shape of his own early poetry. . . . [There are numerous] affinities and interrelated differences discernible in Frost's early poems, principally that handful published between 1894 and 1901, and the first Dickinson poems published in the 1890s. . . .

In the spring of 1892, during his final months at Lawrence High School, Frost discovered the poetry of Emily Dickinson, just out in two small volumes, *Poems* (1890) and *Poems, Second Series* (1891). He was immediately taken with her, discovering in her poetry the voice of a kindred New England soul. "Although her terse, homely, gnomic, cryptic, witty qualities appealed very strongly to him," writes Lawrance Thompson, "he was again fascinated to find that his new author was also 'troubled about many things' concerning death. . . . [The] poems which cut deepest for him were those which expressed her doubt whether any reasons fashioned by the mind concerning life in heaven could compensate for the heart's passionate and instinctive regrets over the transience of earthly bliss." (p. 371)

Frost's "The Birds Do Thus" can be read as a reply to [a Dickinson poem]. Her anxiety is countered by his whimsy. If, as she decides plaintively in her twelve-line, three-stanza poem, that "earth is short" (meaning, of course, that what is short is one's stay on earth), then Frost in his poem of the same length disagrees by answering that "Life's not so short." If, for Dickinson, "anguish is absolute," then Frost's advice is to sleep away "the unhappy days." Even Frost's use of the short line coincides with Dickinson's customary practice, but with a difference. While Dickinson moves from two-foot to three-foot lines and back again, Frost stubbornly sticks to the greater regularity of the two-foot line. (pp. 372-73)

Between Frost's ["My Butterfly"] and [Dickinson's several "butterfly" poems] there are thematic correspondences—particularly the importance of flight and journey, the butterfly's dalliance with immortality, and the ephemeral nature of the individual's life cycle. There are also differences, and they suggest the difference between the accomplished poet and the talented apprentice. In two important respects "My Butterfly" is less modern than Dickinson's [poems]. First, its diction is slightly archaic, at best early Victorian—"thine," "thee," "frighted," "oft," "wist," "dist," "o'er-eager." Second, and more characteristically, is Frost's propensity to adapt his poetic symbol to an explicitly personal allegory. In the third stanza Frost presents rather discursively his allegorical application of the butterfly's fate to his own biography. Emblemized morals subjectively presented remained common in Frost, though he would learn to handle them with great skill. (pp. 375-76)

[In his poem "In White"] Frost moves away from the Dickinsonian idea of heroic extinction into a white immortality to his own emphasis upon the fated, designed convergence of whiteness and death. Echoing Dickinson's preoccupation with the color itself, "In White" . . . works back through "My Butterfly" to Dickinson's "From the Chrysalis" (1890). . . . At best, in ["My Butterfly" and "In White"] at least, Frost answers Dickinson's trace of bright optimism with his own version of end-of-the-century naturalism.

Dickinson's customary view of the butterfly's ephemeral day as a flight of ecstasy, rather than as a tragic rush toward death, provided Frost with the core of still another poem. His "Pod of the Milkweed" builds on her most panegyric celebration of the ephemeral butterfly's total freedom. The poet begins by "Calling all butterflies of every race / From source unknown but from no special place," and he continues in a vein that recalls Dickinson in her most festive mood. . . . In their sinless intemperance Frost's butterflies play out the ironic boasts of Dickinson's "I taste a liquor never brewed," and the ecstasy of these "ephemerals" again links Frost's poetry to Dickinson's. Significantly, Frost's poem does not end at this point. It swerves away from Dickinson's climactic treatment of the exuberant, soulful butterfly, to the notation that the broken milkweed and exhausted butterfly are, after all, the sum and residue of that day's singular activity. . . . (pp. 378-79)

Emily Dickinson's poetry was useful to Frost in various ways. It constituted a source for congenial images and themes. (p. 380)

That Emily Dickinson's poetry was often in Frost's mind during his first decade as a poet can be established in still another way. Even when the primary source of a poem was not Dickinson, Frost still tended to cast his poem in Dickinsonian terms. (p. 382)

Judging by whatever success Frost had in placing his poetry in his first dozen years of trying, one is struck with the fact that it was his handful of Dickinsonian poems which first achieved print. Her example had shown him the way to the kind of poetry he then wanted to write and that, to a modest extent, his editors wanted to put before their readers. Throughout his long career he would continue to deal lyrically with certain themes that Dickinson had first put into poetic focus for him, but early on he had discovered the characteristics of a personal voice which took him in the direction of his major work. Yet to Frost, Emily Dickinson's poetry never ceased to be an example, a resource, a warning, a challenge, and, above all, a threat. He did not name her but one suspects that Frost had Dickinson in mind when late in life he insisted that one of his reasons for writing "eclogues" was "to do something women have never succeeded in doing." (p. 384)

George Monteiro, "Emily Dickinson and Robert Frost" (© by George Monteiro), in Prairie Schooner, Winter, 1977-78, pp. 369-86.

*   *   *

FRY, Christopher 1907-

Born Christopher Fry Harris, Fry is a British dramatist, screenwriter, translator, critic, and children's author. Using the form of the verse play, he mingles drama and poetic language, humor and tragedy, metaphysics and wit in an Elizabethan richness that invites comparison with Shakespeare and T. S. Eliot. Also Elizabethan is his incorporation of verbal ornament into the actual meaning of the play, creating an elegant view of reality. The unconscious effect of poetry and word sounds is drawn upon for dramatic impact. Fry celebrates life in his work, often using religious and historical

themes. His optimism has been criticized by some as escapism. (See also *CLC*, **Vol. 2, and** *Contemporary Authors*, **Vols. 17-20, rev. ed.)**

J. WOODFIELD

Fry's plays concentrate on a group of closely related themes: the redemptive power of love, both *eros* and *agapé;* the wonder, paradoxes and unity of existence; the cycle of life, death and renewal; the operation of necessity and the nature of individuality; and man's relationship with the universe and with God. Several of his plays—*The Boy with a Cart* (1939), *The Firstborn* (1949), *Thor, with Angels* (1948), and *A Sleep of Prisoners* (1951)—are overtly religious, but the secular plays, through their distinctly religious sub-structures, also pursue, in Fry's own phrase from *A Sleep of Prisoners,* "an exploration into God." A few examples of such sub-structures are the ritual death and rebirth patterns in *A Phoenix Too Frequent* (1949) and in *The Lady's Not for Burning* (1949), the process of love, sacrifice and redemption in those plays and in *Venus Observed* (1950) and *The Dark Is Light Enough* (1954), and the sacramental nature of Rosmarin's human relationships in the latter.

It is not surprising, therefore, that Fry should be drawn to the near-mythical contest between Henry II and Becket over the respective demands of Church and State. Their struggle exemplifies the clash of the secular and the spiritual and, although unresolved historically except by death, invites the artist to explore its shape. Fry's exploration in *Curtmantle* takes the path of a dual quest. One aspect is "the progression towards a portrait of Henry, a search for his reality," which is indicated in the play by Richard Anesty's repeated question at the end of the Prologue: "Where is the King?" Structurally, this theme is explored in a series of episodes which are linked by the process of history and by the controlling consciousness of William Marshal's memory. The other half of the quest is also firmly established in the Prologue: the search for "Law, or rather the interplay of different laws: civil, canon, moral, aesthetic, and the laws of God; and how they belong and do not belong to each other." . . . This second quest is inextricably allied with the artist's desire to find form: just as Henry's energy "was giving form to England's chaos" . . . , so Fry is attempting to structure action, character and language in a form that will express the "permanent condition of man" and will yield meaning for the modern audience from the barren facts of history.

The controlling framework of the play is William Marshal's mind. The memory device is not used as in *The Glass Menagerie* to explore the narrator's experience, but to endow Marshal with a choric function which enables him both to recount the action "[doing] away with time and place" . . . as Fry intended, and to comment on its significance. Marshal's name suggests his function: he is a high official of the court close to the king; he marshals the facts in order for the audience; and he records the passing of time and events. Another function is to manipulate the response of the audience in favour of Henry, a role which is an important corrective to history, especially as recorded in the dramatic interpretations of Tennyson, Eliot and even Anouilh, where the dramatic focus, and inevitably sympathy, lie with Becket rather than Henry. Marshal respects Henry's energy and his determination to replace anarchy with order on behalf of the people he governs. His respect

and that of the common folk indicate the range of the governed, and give a reference point for the facts of church exploitation that lead to the division between Church and State, Becket and Henry. Marshal's mind and attitudes express the "Pugnacious reality" . . . that lies behind the facts of history.

Another structural means of exploring this inner reality is through the use of expressionistic and cinematic devices which reject the surface reality in favour of a stylized, or even distorted presentation of the stage action and its setting. Both the turbulent action and the storm setting of the Prologue indicate the chaotic state of the kingdom to which Henry is attempting to bring order. Paradoxically, it shows disorder under Henry's very nose, and thematically the storm foreshadows the turbulence of his reign. There is a smooth scenic transition into Act I, when the wind drops to a calm and the darkness changes to light. Anesty's final question at the camp, "Where is the King?" . . . is answered by Marshal in Westminster: "The King's arrived in the yard. . . ." . . . This non-realistic merging of time, place and action characterizes the sequences of the play, and helps to produce tight dramatic unity. (pp. 307-08)

The telescoping of historic events leads to an exciting dramatic pace which asserts the inevitability of Henry's tragic downfall. Once he decides to appoint Becket Archbishop, and "co-ordinate the two worlds" . . . of Church and State, all subsequent decisions partake of the same quality of *hamartia*. The combination of the device of memory and the technique of expressionism, by enabling Fry to escape the limitations of a realistic chronological approach which would break the action, carries the audience through a sequence of decisions and outcomes that drive Henry inexorably down the path of tragic descent. The episodes, which lend themselves to a Brechtian Epic treatment of disjunction, are thereby bridged rather than broken, and the plot unfolds in one continuous movement interrupted only at the end of Act I at a climactic point where Henry squares for a fight, and at the end of Act II where an appropriate pause occurs at Becket's death. As tragic hero, Henry fulfils the classical Aristotelian pattern of the great man of wasted potential whose fall, brought about by *hubris* and flawed decisions, involves his realm, which sinks in power and prestige with its king. . . . [Henry progressively] assumes the role of divinity ascribed to him by his subjects, and it is this defiance of the ontological order that constitutes his major crime. Henry's gradual—and unconscious—movement towards this self-concept is skilfully dramatized by Fry in both language and action. Henry possesses a charisma not unlike that of the Countess Rosmarin, yet more positive than hers. In *The Dark Is Light Enough*, Fry endows the human Countess with divine attributes: in *Curtmantle*, he humanizes the mythical king who is credited with, and assumes, divinity. . . . Henry's action of appointing Becket to the dual post of Chancellor and Archbishop in order to reconcile the conflicting interests of Church and State to his own advantage, is one which Becket warns him is

> a kind of intrusion on the human mystery,
> Where we may not know what it is we're doing,
> What powers we are serving, or what is being made of
> us.

By his action, Henry sets up a counter movement against himself which is exemplified in the rise in the fortunes of

Louis, whom Henry despises. Fry repeatedly draws parallels and comparisons between the two kings. (pp. 309-10)

A further confirmation of the tragic pattern is found in the concatenation of events. When the events and their outcome are known, the dramatist who wishes to do more than merely chronicle them must seek some inner dynamic within the historical context. Just as in *The Firstborn* Fry creates a tension between necessity and the desires of the characters to provide this dynamic and an alternative to plot suspense, so in *Curtmantle* he creates a similar tension between the declared aims of his characters and the grip of events which once initiated take on an autonomous inevitability. . . . Men become the tools of destiny and although they may rage and defy, as Henry does, they eventually succumb. Paradoxically, it is this refusal to bow down before the inevitable, even when as guilty as a Macbeth, that is one of the chief characteristics of the tragic hero, and here Fry's Henry shares tragic aspects with such figures as Oedipus and Lear. Another shared characteristic is loneliness: Henry is successively separated from or deserted by friends and family, except for his Kent, Marshal, and his Cordelia, Roger, until he dies completely isolated. He descends from the role of quasidivine ruler to that of an expelled *pharmakos*, ritualistically stripped of his possessions in the catalogue of reparations demanded by Philip . . . and in the actions of the two peasants who strip his body. . . . The pattern of renewal that justifies the suffering and waste of tragedy is not strongly asserted, despite a gesture in that direction by Roger who attempts to rally his dying father by urging him

> Sir, believe what you have accomplished.
> Your laws are fixed on England . . . accepted
> As a source of strength. . . .

The play follows the pattern of Henry's concern as expressed by Marshal, "beginning and ending . . . with the people he governed" . . . , but in both the Prologue and the last scene he is shown to be their scourge rather than their benefactor. The full tragic cycle, therefore, is not completed in *Curtmantle*, but here the author's respect for the facts of history does impose a certain limitation. Fry's search for the King reveals a complex man of paradoxes, as the Foreword states . . . , but subsumes these complexities within the tragic mould. Henry's struggle becomes an expression of man's struggle with forces in the environment that oppose any attempts by man to define his own destiny in defiance of the higher powers.

The second theme, or quest of the play is that of Law, which is dramatized primarily in the conflict between Henry and Becket, which in turn represents that of State and Church, physical and spiritual, and ultimately Man and God. . . . In the struggle between Henry and Becket it is the dramatic conflict of character, the way each presents his argument rather than the respective merits of each side, that expresses the dichotomy in a dialectic of minds: the practical and realistic *versus* the philosophic and idealistic. (pp. 311-13)

Henry's affirmative way clashes with the negative way of Becket who "realizes the essential instrumentality of man's will as, at its highest form, wholly submissive to the ways of providence." Eleanor appears to be acting as Fry's spokesman when she urges Henry to "Consider complexity, delight in difference" . . . , and later when she asserts that

> The true law hides like the marrow of the bone,
> Feeding us in secret. And this hidden law may prove to
>   be
> Not your single world, not unity but diversity.

Eleanor's own "Love Court of Poitou" which makes "laws for sport and love" . . . , is almost a parody of Henry's courts. Her position is one of balance rather than polarity where the tension of oppositions stimulates the creative force. "Oh, never define!" . . . , she cries, and although later guilty of attempting to "define the world of woman / And man" . . .—and despite the dubious evidence of her court—her declarations affirm Fry's recurrent theme of the essential multeity of existence.

The dialectic of *Curtmantle,* therefore, takes on a familiar thesis-antithesis-synthesis form. The synthesis is weak because the two main protagonists remain polarized, and the synthesis proposed by Eleanor is inadequately structured dramatically, although strongly expressed verbally. Because Henry is the common factor in all the conflicts—against Becket, Eleanor, his sons, and Louis—and because he receives Marshal's approbation the dramatic balance lies with him. However, the tragic form adumbrates the lost opportunity: "if only. . . ." If only Henry and Becket could have seen how in fact they sought a common goal, as Merchant suggests, and if only they could have attained the flexibility advocated by Eleanor, then a resolution of their differences would have been possible. It is thus that the dramatic form, the shape of tragedy plus the shape of the ideas expressed asserts the writer's meaning. (pp. 313-14)

In *Curtmantle* Fry's language attains a degree of clarity, economy and flexibility rarely equalled in his earlier plays. *In The Dark Is Light Enough* he had begun to move away from the excessive verbal decorations of *Venus Observed*, using figurative language sparingly, and the direction is continued in *Curtmantle* without going to the extent of Eliot where, in *The Elder Stateman* particularly, verse all but disappears. He uses interwoven clusters of images: light and darkness; cold and hot, especially fire; water in various forms; animals, particularly horses; building; and the journey. There is a general movement in the metaphors of both language and action from darkness to light, through fog, back to darkness, and a parallel movement from cold, through warmth and intense heat, back to the icy cold of death. The Prologue opens at night with the Juggler's cry for light paralleling the kingdom's need for illumination of its darkness. At the end of the scene, the increasing light heralds the glow of warmth and optimism at Becket's successful return. The second act opens in fog. . . . The fog becomes a symbol for both the confused state of affairs and for the states of mind of the protagonists. (pp. 314-15)

Henry's life as a journey is established in the Prologue, in which Anesty pre-figures the King in his quest for truth, law and order, and the action exemplifies the restless, desperate quality of Henry's search. Fry's compact structure gives a vivid sense of movement as the journeys and errands of a lifetime are compressed into a single action. Henry has an almost compulsive belief in the efficacy of movement and pursuit: "providence," he declares, "is a great maker of journeys / And whoever refuses to go forward is dropped by the road." . . . (pp. 315-16)

[Both] the images used and the language in which they are expressed are direct and forceful. The rhythms of the verse are almost colloquial, but at points of high emotion or when the occasion demands a ritualistic incantation, Fry's blank verse achieves a noble eloquence. Becket's affirmation of anti-Sartrean existentialism is an example:

> What a man knows he has by experience,
> But what a man is precedes experience.
> His experience merely reveals him, or destroys him;
> Either drives him to his own negation,
> Or persuades him to his affirmation, as he chooses.

Prose is utilized in the Shakespearian manner mainly for the speech of "low" characters, but also where Fry intuitively feels that the action demand it—as in the addresses by Marshal to the audience, where natural prose sets him apart as their link with the action, and in the final scene where the departure from the controlled rhythms of verse is a correlative for the disintegration of Henry's life and work.

Commenting on Henry's appointment of Becket to Canterbury, Marshall recalls the hope of stability, prosperity and unity at that time, but "the whole significance of unity was not debated, nor what fires can forge a diverse multitude into one mind" . . . , Fry's plays, and *Curtmantle* in particular, constantly explore these questions, and he finds the significance in the diversity which encompasses him in life. In the Preface he declares, "pattern and balance are pervading facts of the universe" . . . , and this perceived unity is an expression of the inner mystery which contains the significance—or meaning—of creation. Ritual can "give shape to the mystery revealed / Yet as a mystery" . . . : art also aims to express "the creative order contained in the apparent anarchy of life . . . the form of the hidden order." In *Curtmantle,* because Fry succeeds in subordinating time, place and specific issues to the tragic pattern and to the timeless quest for identity, law, order, truth and meaning, and because the elements of language, action and character are so integrally structured, he succeeds in eloquently expressing his own sense of this mystery through the medium of his form. (p. 317)

> *J. Woodfield, "Christopher Fry's 'Curtmantle': The Form of Unity," in* Modern Drama *(copyright © 1974, University of Toronto, Graduate Centre for Study of Drama; with the permission of* Modern Drama*), September, 1974, pp. 307-18.*

STANLEY M. WIERSMA

Any mature understanding of violence and pacifism must begin with an acknowledgement of the violence in one's own heart, and in *A Sleep of Prisoners* . . . Fry had defined the progression from the recognition of violence within to a complete pacifism. That play begins with the personal violence of Cain and Abel, moves through the political assassination of Absalom by Joab but condoned by David, progresses to the sacrificial offering of Isaac by Abraham, and concludes with Daniel's friends in the fiery furnace, the flames being the inescapable violence of the human condition, which the pacifist must learn to endure without being violent in return.

Although *The Dark is Light Enough* is three years later than *Sleep,* no other play intervened, and this paper assumes that Fry's perceptions of violence and pacifism remained constant during the interim. The chief difference between the plays is the surrealistic, lyrical organization of *Sleep,* in the writing of which Fry was still discovering his

own position on violence and pacifism, and the cause-and-effect plot of *Dark,* in which Fry is expressing what he has discovered earlier.

Though the literary form of the two pieces is very different, the intellectual content is much the same: violence as self-assertion, violence as loyalty to the state, violence as loyalty to God, and, finally, violence to be endured but not to be inflicted. (pp. 4-5)

The theme of the duel is fascinating to trace through [*Dark*]. Just at the point that Jakob is using Belmann's hell-bound agnosticism as his pretext for not fighting the duel, Stefan takes up the duel with Gettner. Both Jakob and Stefan are sure that they are issuing challenges in the cause of honor. Still, whether duels are fought or not has less to do with the moral necessities of honor than with the murkier necessities of violence. Violence is like an infection with its own irrational necessities. The violence in the situation and within the people is moving toward a duel; who fights it or against whom is beside the point.

The hostile attitude of Jakob, Belmann, and Kassel against Gettner, the hostile attitude of Jakob toward the other guests, and Stefan's vacillating attitude toward Gettner suddenly fixing itself on violence are all like the hostilities of the war between Austria and Hungary raging outside. (p. 9)

Like *Sleep, Dark* embodies violence as self-assertion; both plays, also embody the idea of violence as loyalty to the state. The permissive violence of David and the active violence of Joab against Absalom in *Sleep* is justified in the minds of the instigators because it is intended for the good of the state.

Likewise, Janik in *Dark* also justifies his violence because it promotes the justice of the Hungarian claims against the Austrian tyranny. (pp. 9-10)

The inadequacy of a strictly military identity is evident when Janik, who before as a soldier condemned the Countess for sheltering Gettner from the Hungarians, returns to the Countess, at the play's end and after his defeat, as a private person, expecting the same kind of treatment as she gave Gettner before.

A military self is never enough, not even on the just side of a war. For even just wars are fought by military establishments which institutionalize violence, justify violence as the only means to freedom, and measure patriotism by the energy of the violence. Violence for the honor of Hungary or Austria is only a little less selfish, a little less narcissistic, than violence for personal honor.

In addition to violence as self-assertion for honor and violence as loyalty to the state, *Sleep* and *Dark* embody violence for God's sake. The honor of God is the motivation for Abraham's willingness to sacrifice Isaac in *Sleep;* his willingness to sacrifice Isaac is a combination of performing violence and enduring it, of activity and passivity.

The honor of God is at once Peter's consolation and his cause. When the Hungarians are completely broken, Peter consoles himself with the fact of the Incarnation. . . . The Incarnation is for Peter a redefinition of the concepts *God* and *man,* which cannot be altered by any circumstances, a sure basis for confidence. But the Incarnation is also a process: a learning to become both a son of man and a son of

God, along with Jesus Christ. Whatever else being a son of man means, it certainly means taking pains choosing the most Christlike alternative in a muddled situation. Whatever else being a son of God involves, it involves being permanently conditioned against disillusionment in failure. (p. 11)

But Peter never reaches serenity, for at heart he remains an overbalanced activist. Stefan sends for him and he rushes to Rosmarin's house "the moment / He could manage to get away." . . . Taken captive by the Hungarians, he fights valiantly on their side. Making up with Gelda in Act III, he can stay only briefly; he must rush off to Austria because the victorious government is "shooting and hanging / Every Hungarian of note who fought in the war." . . . The concept of betrayal keeps coming up, for Peter is never sure he has done the right thing:

> You make me think
> I shall betray something either way,
> Staying or going. If I stay, I think
> Of nothing but getting to Vienna. If I go,
> I think of nothing but what you have said to me. . . .

Peter lacks a single workable criterion by which he can make moral choices and then, for good or ill, rest in them. Peter is that humanly understandable but logically contradictory phenomenon: the militant pacifist. He fight for peace the way Jakob fights for the honor of the Countess and the way Janik fights for Hungary, but in the cause of peace one should not fight at all. (pp. 12-13)

All three learn something about the violence within themselves. Jakob sees it is not an isolated instance of outraged honor which drives him:

> One always thinks if only
> One particular unpleasantness
> Could be cleared up, life would become as promising
> As it is always promising to be.
> But in fact we merely change anxieties. . . .

The military Janik returns defeated, he for whom the Hungarian cause had become everything. He must be coaxed by the Countess to sing a bawdy song of the soldiers. Only after he sings does the Countess comfort him:

> Child,
> I know your cause is lost, but in the heart
> Of all right causes is a cause which cannot lose. . . .

The unselfishness in Janik's devotion to Hungary must grow into Peter's devotion to God; God is the only cause which cannot lose, though Janik will need to become a child to know that. Peter overcomes some of the snobbery inherent in any pacifist's scorn for the military, when he fights with Janik against the Austrians. . . . Jakob, Janik, and Peter all acquire insight into the violence which drives them, although they do not change significantly within the play. But their insight into the violence which drives them is essential if they are going to overcome the problem of violence, if not in the play then outside of it, if not in time then outside of it. (pp. 13-14)

The plots of *Sleep* and *Dark* embody the ideas of willingness to endure violence and unwillingness to inflict it. In the last dream in *Sleep* Daniel's three friends in the fiery furnace of life are joined by the son of man under God's command, a *figura Christi*. None of the four are naively shocked at the violence that comes with living, all of them are willing to endure it, and none of them will inflict it. It is the position of the Countess in *Dark*.

She too is a *figura Christi*, surrounded as she is by her rock-like Peter, who "treads the earth more surely / And reassures more instantly / Than any other man" . . . , her James (Jakob = Jacobus = James), and her John (Janik): the three characters who acquire insight into their own violence, although they do not change within the scope of the play. Besides, the Thursday "at homes" are reminiscent of Maundy Thursday, the Thursday of the footwashing, the Lord's Supper, and the new commandment "that ye love one another." That the Countess leaves her nine guests in order to hunt up Gettner in spite of a blinding snowstorm and at great risk to herself is reminiscent of Christ's parable of the good shepherd, in which ninety-nine sheep are left for the sake of one. . . . But simply to label the Countess a *figura Christi* is to make her into a static icon. . . . To freeze the Countess into a *figura Christi* is to make the play into a static allegory and is to ignore the dynamic interplay between human and divine. . . . The Countess is a believable person and inhabits a world we recognize as our own. (pp. 14-15)

In many ways the Countess is like Peter. When Gettner calls to her to save him, she puts her own world down and takes his up, just as Peter responds to Stefan's call. . . .

One great differece between Peter and the Countess is that the Countess is not at all militant about her pacifism. She has learned long ago that violence cannot be organized or fought out of existence. The only effective locus for effecting the victory of peace over violence is the individual human heart: one's own. (p. 16)

The Countess completely bypasses the intricacies of politics in pursuing peace. . . . In the darkness of the human condition, where degrees of comparative guilt and the causes for a particular act of violence are impossible to discern, only one criterion functions: the least violent alternative is always best, no matter how unreasonable and unjust it may appear. . . . She is, from the perspective of the audience and reader, an amazingly complete pacifist. (pp. 16-17)

Outside of time she will be able to love all people, even the unloveliest. Her present inadequacy in love—her awareness of the violence remaining within her—is her continuing impetus for growth.

Hence, the Countess has none of the moral superiority which the others demonstrate. (p. 18)

The stance of the Countess is the stance of the play. When Peter as a Hungarian on the Austrian side temporarily is taken with the Hungarian cause and fights against Austria, we applaud his high spirits and his impartiality. But then we begin to ask whether he is so different from Gettner, the Austrian who enlists on the Hungarian side and then deserts. Not judging by the results but by the condition of heart that produced them, is the denial of Peter very different from the betrayal of Judas? In fact, Fry has Peter use the Judas word, *betrayal,* about his own moral dilemma in another situation. . . . Untangling good from evil is next to impossible, given the complexity of the human heart. Judging the violence in others is a venting of our own violence. Seeing the violence in other people as our own makes self-righteous condescension disappear. Then the best and worst seem not very different from each other. (pp. 18-19)

For the moral ambiguity which the Countess and the play recognize, the blinding snowstorm is the symbol. The snow is white, yet produces a darkness as effectively as any blackness. The white snow is dark enough to make the journey difficult. But the dark produced by the snow is also light enough, given the divination of the Countess, for her to reach her destination. . . . The darkness of the moral situation is always light enough with the one absolute moral principle of the Countess: the least violent alternative is always best. (p. 19)

Like the butterfly [in the epigraph to the play], the Countess finds the darkness light enough, which is to say that she finds warmth enough in the winter of our discontent, goodness enough in a wicked world, life enough in death.

That the darkness is light enough to enable the Countess to pursue her non-violent way non-violently is one important difference between the Countess and Peter. The other difference is that only in her presence do "Lives make and unmake themselves . . . / As nowhere else." . . . There are two people particularly who "would have been remarkably otherwise / But for her divine interference" . . . : Gelda and Richard Gettner.

Gelda's problem is pride, the root of all other sin and violence. Violence increases in proportion to one's blindness to the violence within himself, which blindness is pride. (p. 22)

Just as the complete pacifism of the Countess supercedes the incomplete pacifism of Peter, so Gelda achieves a new willingness to look inside herself for pride and violence, and hence she becomes more humble and nonviolent. . . .

Gettner begins hostile and humble, hostile and passive, which is to say indifferent. He must progress toward a loving pride, which is to say self-respect, and toward a loving activity. His progress throughout the play runs counter to that of the other characters. The reason he is so disliked by the others is not only his hostility, but his pilgrimage toward wholeness running so incomprehensibly counter to theirs. (p. 23)

The change in Gettner is the conversion of Judas. For you are the life you pray for when you pray for Judas—or Hitler. A pacifism which makes an exception of Judas and Hitler is not complete. The conversion of Judas makes the play aesthetically as satisfying as it is satisfying intellectually and religiously, for it provides a motion contrary to the rest of the play, and yet the contrary motion is curiously appropriate to the rest of the play since it can all be analyzed by the same categories. It is a complete play.

The changes in Gelda and Gettner . . . demonstrate how the pacifism of the Countess supercedes Peter's. Not only does the Countess pursue non-violence non-violently, but the result of her non-violence is that in her presence "Lives make and unmake themselves . . . / As nowhere else." . . . But making that point, one admires the aesthetic wholeness of *Dark*. Even the servants reinforce the theme. Bella's concern for the honor of the Countess justifies her lying and justifies her belittling Willi; Willi cannot lie, understands perfectly why Bella lies and forgives her for it, and does not mind being made the fool for the sake of the honor of the Countess. . . . Bella tends toward Jakob and Janik's end of the violence continuum, and Willi toward Peter and the Countess's end. *Dark*, even to the incidental characters, is organized by theme.

That idea, the progressive stages toward peace, is the same idea as *Sleep*. Are the two plays the same? (pp. 25-6)

The absence of indifference in *Sleep* and its presence and redemption in *Dark* is . . . one way in which the scope of *Sleep* is narrower than *Dark*. Already in *Sleep* Fry had distinguished the stages in the ascent through the creatures, but these stages are juxtaposed without transition; the stages are barely discernible in *Dark* because how one stage folds into another, in Gelda's case for instance, is part of the flow of life. In *Sleep* all four characters progress to the next stage simultaneously; in *Dark* all the characters are at different stages from each other. Gelda goes through all four stages, Gettner travels all four stages by a contrary route, and the Countess has well-nigh arrived at the beginning of the play. For all its brilliant surrealism, the dream form of *Sleep* remains abstracted from life. No viewer would ever think that four soldiers would really dream these four dreams in such eloquent succession. The illusion of reality is not even attempted in *Sleep*. The evocation of life during wartime in the court of the Countess in *Dark* provides, if not an everyday setting, at least a recognizable one, in which recognizable people hanker after God while they are awake—even though not all of them realize what they are hankering for. Fry knew a great deal about overcoming violence in writing *Sleep*, but he had not yet experienced it sufficiently, or if he had experienced it, he had not had time to assimilate and articulate the experience. In *Dark* Fry knows what he knew in *Sleep*, but he knows it better and he knows more. The form of *Dark* is less splendidly experimental than the form of *Sleep*, but it does not need to be. In *Dark* man's soul thirsts for God in the very world we live in, which Fry evokes rather conventionally; what is unconventional here is Fry's evocation of the experience of that thirst. *Sleep* communicates the idea of the ascent to God through the creatures, *Dark* the experience.

Sleep has "become renewed, transfigured, in another pattern." *Sleep* and *Dark* are and are not the same play. (pp. 27-8)

Stanley M. Wiersma, "Christopher Fry's Definition of the Complete Pacifist in 'The Dark is Light Enough'," in Ariel *(copyright © 1975 The Board of Governors The University of Calgary), October, 1975, pp. 3-28.*

*   *   *

FUENTES, Carlos   1928-

A Mexican novelist, playwright, short story writer, screenwriter, essayist, and critic, Fuentes creates a prose noted for its innovative language and narrative technique. His concern for establishing a viable Mexican identity is revealed in his use of the history and legends of the Mexican past, from the myths of the Aztecs to the Mexican Revolution, which he uses allegorically and thematically in his narratives. (See also *CLC*, Vols. 3, 8, and *Contemporary Authors*, Vols. 69-72.)

JUAN GOYTISOLO

One of the usual tactics of critical terrorism (whether or not it is legitimized by the power of the State) is to create a scarecrow-image, either of the author . . . or of the work, making it out, for instance, to be an impenetrable, confused, chaotic hodge-podge . . . so that the potential reader comes to associate it in his mind with the label "unreadable." The ambition, difficulty, and deliberate excesses inherent in *Terra Nostra* thus make it the ideal candidate for transformation into a scarecrow-image of a work, which is quoted from (in order to tear it to pieces) but not read, and the mausoleum of an author whom the penny-a-liners would like to see interred in it once and for all. But these over-eager grave-diggers forget that *Terra Nostra* belongs to that category of novels that, like *Ulysses* or *Under the Volcano*, little by little create, through the text alone, an audience of fanatically devoted readers. (p. 6)

Fuentes alternates the expression of a historical pessimism on the part of his characters and a much more nuanced vision which, while taking into account the repeated failures of the past, nonetheless does not resign itself to fatalism or passivity.... From the point of view of the narrators, the repetition of the cycles of history is not necessarily absolute or inevitable: the need for revolution, for the material and moral progress of mankind continues, as strong as ever, despite the failures, the errors, the blood baths that it has everywhere left in its wake. To call them to mind is not a sign of helpless resignation, but precisely the contrary. As one narrator, Guzmán, remarks: "... nothing is forgotten as quickly as the past, nothing is repeated as often as the past." The awareness of this is therefore an indispensable step to be taken on the steep, arduous path that will one day permit history not to repeat itself. (p. 8)

The ideological debate that runs through the pages of *Terra Nostra* cannot leave us indifferent, inasmuch as it takes up many problems that those of us who believe in the ideals of justice and progress must necessarily confront. The attentive reader will glimpse between the lines a subtle denunciation of the compensatory mechanisms employed by those who justify today's avoidable evils in the name of imaginary future paradises. Over and against the familiar—and false—assertion that "new worlds are born only through sacrifice" and "that there have always been men who have been sacrificed," there rings out, like a cry of hope, the impassioned invocation of the *hic et nunc* by the rebel leader: "... my history, neither yesterday nor tomorrow, I wish today to be my eternal time, today, today, today." Justice and freedom here and now, won painfully, step by step, without allowing a single inch of them to be given up in the name of some supreme later perfection; taking as the point of departure the fact that the real, concrete man is irreplaceable; living and glorifying the instant, through the daily struggle for an immediate terrestrial heaven that does not waste and destroy human beings for the well-being of future generations; abandoning the Christian notions of guilt and sacrifice in favor of the reappropriation of the body and the attaining of a social order whose aim is to promote physical, material, and moral well-being for all rather than the conquest and monopoly of power for the benefit of the few.... The historical thought in which the events of the novel are steeped —set forth from the shifting, contradictory points of view of the various characters who alternately take on the role of narrator—appears to oscillate ... between two diametrically opposed ideas—the necessity and the failure of revolution—without ever definitely opting for either one. (pp. 9-10)

The novel is above all a cruel and penetrating vision of Spanish history and its prolongation in the New World through the Conquest. Here too the accusations of pessimism and fatalism—reality seen as a "sick dream"—that have been leveled against Fuentes would appear to have

some foundation.... According to the novelist's detractors, Fuentes paints far too dark a picture. But let us consider a few examples and judge for ourselves. The history of Spain: "the chronicle of inevitable misfortunes and impossible illusions"; Spaniards: "heroes only because they would not disdain their own passions but rather, would follow them through to their disastrous conclusion, masters of the entire realm of passion but mutilated and imprisoned by the cruelty and the narrowness of the religious and political reasoning that turned their marvelous madness, their total excess, into a crime: their pride, their love, their madness, their dreams—all punishable offenses"; our appointed destiny over the centuries: "to purify Spain of every plague of infidels, to tear it out by the roots, to mutilate her limbs, to have nothing left save our mortified but pure bones"; the ideal of our leaders: "servitude, slavery, exaction, homage, tribute, caprice, our will sovereign, that of all the rest passive obedience, that is our world"; ... Hispanic America: "the same social order translated to New Spain; the same rigid, vertical hierarchies; the same sort of government: for the powerful every right and no duty; for the weak, no right and every duty." ... (pp. 10-11)

When *Terra Nostra* was published in 1975 the panorama offered by the Spanish-speaking world was not one that inspired much hope.... A national awareness of their wretchedness on the part of the Spanish-speaking peoples is not a recent phenomenon: to limit ourselves to the Hispanic Peninsula, the work of our best writers, from Blanco White and Larra to Cernuda and Luis Martín-Santos is steeped in it and nourished by it. (p. 11)

To scoff at Fuentes's historico-poetic vision as being evasive and unrealistic is to fall into the error of accepting the canons of a shallow and mechanistic realism which continually confuses life and literature, thus demonstrating that it does not understand either of them very well. (p. 12)

As the reader makes his way through [*Terra Nostra's*] fascinating hall of mirrors that reflect both the world and each other, he never loses sight of real history. Though the novelist has thoroughly assimilated the admirable precept of Goya and put it to striking use, he nonetheless remains scrupulously faithful to the rational and objective vision of the historians. Even though it takes on the appearance of a dream or madness, his historical nightmare never employs these latter as a substitute for real past history. At each step of the way the reader is able to return to real history, and then plunge once again into the novelist's deliberately distorted and often grotesque perception of things. Even in the most delirious and most dreamlike passages—the magnificent scenes, for instance, in the rotting-chamber of the Hapsburgs with the Madwoman, the dwarf Barbarica, and the doltish Prince—there appear, at times as a sort of sudden brief powder-flash, at times in the form of parody or incantation, reminders of a real and specific history with which the novelist—as well as the Spanish reader—is perfectly familiar.... "History shares the methods of science and the vision of poetry," Octavio Paz has written. This fundamental vision or intuition of Castro's has demonstrated its seminal power not only in the field of historiography but also in that of literary creation. When I say this, the first case that naturally occurs to me is my own, but that of *Terra Nostra* is even more obvious. In no way does the novelist's stimulating and unconventional method of confronting our past, his interpretation of tradition, at once critical and creative . . . , preclude our interpretation of real history. . . . (pp. 12-13)

It goes without saying that the novelist can allow himself to take a number of liberties with the past that would be unthinkable in the case of the historian. Hence *Terra Nostra*'s author performs sleight-of-hand tricks both with chronology and with the real-life existence of historical figures. (p. 13)

For Fuentes history and literature become one: history can be read as literature and literature as history. By weaving the fabric of his novel with threads from both, the novelist demonstrates to us "his wish to use, with no exceptions and no scruples, all of reality as a work tool." . . . The liberties that Fuentes takes with our cultural patrimony are the sign of an omnivorous creative appetite. His imaginary museum impartially houses novels and chronicles, paintings, legends, sciences, myths. But these liberties are much less gratuitous than they might appear to be at first glance. The normal relation with history, we repeat, is always present as a point of reference, in the form at times of what would seem to be the most trivial novelistic details. . . . All the precepts of realism are applied with great felicity in the novel, though they are incorporated and juxtaposed in such a way as to be unrecognizable to those who refuse to stray from the well-worn path of tired literary convention. Fuentes' meticulous reconstruction of historical reality takes as its point of departure not only chronicles and annals but also literary texts and above all certain major or minor Spanish, Flemish, and Italian paintings. We will find the best example of this "unreal realism" . . . in the extensive passages in the novel devoted to the necropolis of the Escorial and the hallucinatory cortege of the specters of kings and queens of the dynasty and the fierce, monstrous, or ridiculous figures in their retinue.

The cult of death, the fatalism disguised as serenity of spirit, the stiffness of movement, the frozen, motionless ceremonial in which the Hapsburg dynasty slowly immures itself, are described by Fuentes with the pen of a master. . . . [What] might be taken to be a lugubrious invention of the novelist is in fact the literary expression of a historical reality. (pp. 13-14)

[The] Spanish past frequently defies all reason and surpasses our powers of imagination. The monarchs of the Hapsburg dynasty appear to have had a secret obsession: to build "a hell on earth" in order "to ensure the need of a heaven" to compensate themselves and their wretched subjects for the paralyzing horror of their lives. . . . We thus discover that as in Goya's painting of Charles IV and María Luisa, Fuentes has not used too dark a palette at all: sheer fidelity to reality has permitted both painter and novelist to enter the realm of the fantastic and the hallucinatory. (p. 15)

Fuentes' historical imagination is not simply an oneiric game that masks reality and perpetuates myths, as our incorrigible defenders of a superficial, one-dimensional reading have written of García Márquez's *One Hundred Years of Solitude*. Many crimes have been committed in the past, are being committed today, and will be committed in the future in the name of ideology, and perhaps the gravest and most infamous of them lies in the fact that—just as patriotism is the last refuge of scoundrels and the priesthood frequently that of fools—it is used as a shield or a bunker by

zombies in order to conceal from the eyes of the public their abysmal lack of ideas and their insufferable lack of sensibility.

Fuentes' creative imagination—like that of Lezama in *Paradiso*—is often nourished by a vast imaginary museum of oils, frescoes, engravings. Some of these are readily identifiable: El Greco's "Dream of Philip II," Signorelli's "Last Judgment," Hieronymus Bosch's "Garden of Delights," Goya's "Royal Family of Charles IV." Others belong to that common heritage or store of memories shared by all of us whose daydreams or reconstructions of our history were first inspired by the plates and reproductions that customarily illustrate grammar-school textbooks. Once again, the novelist's pen, sketching in as it does a wealth of minute detail intended to create an "unreal realism," succeeds in portraying a series of unforgettable scenes in which the prose appears to take on the concrete texture of a fabric, becoming a canvas saturated with color, light, movement, sensuousness. (pp. 16-17)

Fuentes' pictorial prose, his appeal to the visual memory of readers are particularly noticeable in the hunting scenes and in his many evocations of a bestiary whose plastic values are once again mindful of the genius of Lezama: portraits of the mastiff Bocanegra lying at the feet of the Lord and Master; of a pack of famished hounds, "a river of glistening flesh, with tongues glowing like sparks"; of the Lady's mind-haunting falcon: "Such is the union of the avian feet with the woman's gloves that the birds's talons appear to be an extension of the greased fingers of the gauntlet." In other passages, the phantasmagorial discourse of the narrator transports us to the canvases of Velázquez and El Greco, to Goya's *caprichos,* and to Buñuel's films. . . . (p. 17)

One of the most striking and most successful devices is the abrupt shift in narrative point of view (at times without the unwary reader's even noticing), passing from first-person narration to second, and even to a personal narration (since in the final analysis that is what the recounting of events from the point of view of the novel's "he" is equivalent to), and simultaneously rendering objective and subjective reality in one and the same passage with patent scorn for the rules of discourse that ordinarily govern expository prose. . . . (pp. 17-18)

[This] pluridimensional narrative that situates us simultaneously inside and outside the consciousness of the characters . . . achieves its greatest success and reaches its high point in the pages devoted to the rebellion of the *comuneros*—a multidimensional space in which different voices come together and speak in turn, assuming one after the other the task of relating events from different perspectives. . . . The multiple perspective, the story that reflects itself and appears to contemplate itself brings us back once more to Velázquez, whose seminal influence is transparent in one of the most highly charged and meaningful moments of the book—the sequence entitled "Todos mis pecados" ("All My Sins"), devoted to the contemplation of a painting from Orvieto (in reality Signorelli's "Last Judgment"). . . . The novel, like the friar's composition in the style of Valázquez, is a hall of mirrors in which the intruder—the reader—is reflected and lost in the vertigo of an infinite duplication of his own image. (p. 18)

The rich repertory of narrative resources that Fuentes sets before us with such bravura is almost never employed gratuitously: the novelist does not dissociate what (for mutual understanding though with little conceptual rigor) we ordinarily term "form" and "content" by resorting, as do so many mimetic avant-garde writers, to the use of complex narrative devices to express simplistic ideas devoid of either daring or vitality. *Terra Nostra* is a synthesis, achieved by a form of writing that makes no distinction between the two terms: a work that emerges and takes shape, as Pere Gimferrer notes in his discerning review [in *Plural*, July, 1976], through the active intervention of a literary architect of a new type: the *voyeur*, the intruder, the reader. . . .

Fuentes' ambitious novelistic exercise is a deliberate exploration of the literary space opened up by Cervantes. The man from La Mancha, Fuentes reminds us, is not only a hero in a novel born of the reading of novels of chivalry: he is also the first character in fiction who knows that he is read and who changes his behavior as a function of this reading. (p. 19)

Like *Paradiso*, *Three Trapped Tigers*, and other works that are clearly descendants of *Don Quixote*, *Terra Nostra* contains numerous references and statements of the author regarding the structure of the novel that he is writing—a characteristic which, as we have said elsewhere, distinguishes literary language from everyday language governed by norms that we automatically obey. . . . The narrative space of *Terra Nostra* is a free space, open to dialogue and the intervention of the reader aware of the fact that "nothing is beyond belief and nothing is impossible for poetry, which relates everything to everything." Like García Márquez and the authors of novels of chivalry, Fuentes believes in the pleasure of improbable fantasies. . . . Metamorphoses, transformations, anachronisms that instead of controverting the order of the real, confirm it and enlarge it —a "total" realism, in the sense in which Vargas Llosa employs the term: objectivity and subjectivity, acting and dreaming, reason and miracle. (p. 20)

Fuentes engages in a systematic "sacking" of the whole of Spanish culture. For one thing, he borrows entire phrases from Fernando de Rojas, Cervantes or the chroniclers of the Indies and incorporates them in his own narrative (a trick typical of the author of *Don Quixote*); for another, he transforms the world of the novel into an imaginary museum in which the paths of all manner of disparate literary characters meet and diverge (thus bringing us back once again to *Don Quixote*). . . . In his literary voracity, Fuentes does not scorn the use of age-old devices characteristic of storytelling in all times and places, but—and herein lies the difference as compared to conventional novelistic narration —he employs them to weave a radically new overall pattern, a sort of dizzying *summa* of storytelling. Manuscripts found in a sealed bottle are used, for just one instance, to interpolate a story of the same type as . . . inserted by Cervantes in *Don Quixote;* and above all there is Fuentes' vast gallery of story-tellers, whose function consists of extending to infinity the Chinese-box technique of the story within a story within a story. . . .

As in *Don Quixote* once again, the one possible reading offered by traditional works of fiction is superseded by alternative or multiple interpretations that preserve our freedom of choice and judgment, thus conferring on what would appear to be merely an esthetic undertaking a profound moral justification that quite obviously goes beyond the limits of literature. (p. 21)

The beginning and the end of *Terra Nostra* . . . represent the working-out of a curse or a prophecy whose fulfillment is at once the cabalistic key of all of history and the organizing principle of the novel. I am here anticipating the outcry that will be forthcoming from ideologues who cling to the certainty that time is progressive, linear—as they have a perfect right to do. But to scornfully dismiss the "circularity" imposed upon real history for the purpose of constructing a work of literature that "bites its own tail"— an artistic convention likewise employed most effectively by García Márquez in the final pages of *One Hundred Years of Solitude* and by the author of the *Divine Comedy* long before him—as simply an attempt to "erase from the reader's mind all recollection of reality" and to "perpetuate ignorance and myth," as has been written of the Colombian novelist's work, is to be hopelessly blind to the distinction between reality and novelistic technique. . . .

As Carlos Fuentes says by way of one of his characters: ". . . every human being has the right to take a secret to the grave with him; every storyteller reserves the right not to clear up mysteries, in order that they may remain mysteries; and anyone whom this displeases may ask for his money back." (p. 24)

> *Juan Goytisolo, "Our Old New World," translated by Helen R. Lane, in* Review *(copyright © 1976 by the Center for Inter-American Relations, Inc.), Winter, 1976, pp. 5-24.*

SELDEN RODMAN

Carlos Fuentes' . . . ambiguous [and] wide-ranging historical panegyric, *Terra Nostra*, is an [easy] read but . . . inconclusive. There is the Old World (Spain), the New World (Mexico) and the Next World (Revolutionary). All are drawn with poetic license and give no clues to the mechanics of power politics.

History for Fuentes is not linear but circular. He ruminates at length on the mystic number three: father, son and spirit; mother, father, child; white race, black and red; fire, water, air; Moses, Christ, Apocalypse—the third element required to bring unity to the duality of thought and matter. Like the eternal triumvirate, the book is divided into three parts: Past, Present and Future, separated into segments yet melded into one. . . .

Fuentes' characters—incarnated in each of his three worlds with identical names but (presumably) different identities— long for a world free of servitude, illness, sin, and God. They do not really believe, though, that it is attainable. If life is an endless repetition, one cannot hope for improvement. All effort is an exercise in futility. . . .

The book is so full of symbols that the reader may see what he wants, believe what he chooses, or . . . catalogue symbolisms without drawing any conclusions at all. (p. 8)

[The] Marxist writer comes . . . to the recitation of his polemic. He idealizes the new world of constant change, sensual awareness, love and solitude, freedom of body and mind, tolerance, doubt, and life. The old world we know (carefully weighted) consists of nothing but changelessness, extermination, ignorance, power, repression, and death.

To an American, the equation of sexual and personal liberty with Communism is an affront to reason. The Communist regimes we know not only deny freedom to the individual but are incredibly puritanical. To a Mexican (or Colombian) intellectual it may make some kind of sense, for their culture identifies the sexual repressions of the Church with the mindlessness of unrestricted capitalism. But the Latin American masses, in the few instances where they have been given any choice, have not been so naïve. Maybe it is time for Latin America's political novelists to stop focusing so relentlessly on the depravity of their rulers and devote some of their admirable talents to analyzing the conditions that support such monstrous tyrannies. (p. 9)

> *Selden Rodman, in* The New Leader (© *1976 by the American Labor Conference on International Affairs, Inc.), December 6, 1976.*

JOHN BUTT

Terra Nostra exploits every possibility in the language to make a truly memorable denunciation of the Hispanity symbolized by the Inquisition, the rape of the New World, the Valley of the Fallen and the Escorial palace, the plunder of Flanders, Philip, Franco and their Latin American inheritors. The central theme is, in fact, how a Roman culture pledged to a murderous unity of faith and obedience has waged war on the notions of diversity and fertility. Caught in a sterile dualism—right/wrong, good/evil, God/Devil—Hispanity, to use the novel's curious language, has failed to come to terms with the unity in harmony symbolized by the number Three, a cabalistic emblem Fuentes uses to express a trinity of life in potential which Imperial Spain has everywhere conspired to destroy. . . .

Only knowledge of what could have been can release us from history's repetitiveness: the fantasy in the novel is designed to show us the infinity of unrealized potential that Hispanity's oppressively single-minded development has neglected. But Fuentes's inexhaustible, cloying exuberance and his encyclopedic knowledge of the paraphernalia of sorcery and mythology submerge the book in a mass of detailed extravagances and horrors which will test the patience of readers incurious about what might have been had reality not been what we all know it was.

Unfortunately, two of the novel's themes hold no water. The black legend beloved by progressives is a caricature: Spanish imperialism is different only in effect and not in spirit or morality from other imperialisms. . . . The ideal of Threeness, on the other hand ("Three aspire to oneness", an Aztec sage tells us), is never realized artistically, duality never superseded. As a result the novel falls into two bits: powerful historical satire on the one hand and obscure private mythology on the other. It is sometimes said that in novels of this kind language is reality, form is free, the novel discovers its own arbitrariness—why narrate this rather than that? But the real themes of the novel are too concrete and pervasive: no amount of shuffling and blurring and depersonalization of the characters and narrators can conjure the book's links with real life out of existence.

> *John Butt, "Down with Hispanity," in* The Times Literary Supplement (©*Times Newspapers Ltd. (London) 1977; reproduced from* The Times Literary Supplement *by permission), July 15, 1977, p. 849.*

ROBERTO GONZÁLEZ ECHEVARRÍA

Fuentes is the most ambitious and deliberate of Latin America's "new" novelists, and *Terra Nostra* is clearly an effort to produce a *major* work. Whether he has succeeded or not, only time can tell, though I fear that he has not. Fuentes's greatest flaw as a novelist, his intellectualism and hastily gathered erudition, is magnified in *Terra Nostra,* a huge and unreadable volume that endeavors to recover Mexico's (and by extension Latin America's) Hispanic past.

If readers of Fuentes's earlier novels could find in *La nueva novela hispanoamericana* (1969) a compendium of his theoretical and literary biases, *Terra Nostra* comes with a companion volume all its own, *Cervantes o la crítica de la lectura.* This latter book concludes with a bibliography to cover both works, but the reader need not get that far to find that the volume is a combination of apology for and explanation of *Terra Nostra.* As criticism, *Cervantes o la crítica de la lectura* is as thin as *La nueva novela hispanoamericana.* If in the earlier book Fuentes attempted to capitalize too quickly on structuralism, in the more recent one Derrida appears to be his latest discovery. But it is a Derrida too lightly read and adapted to some of Fuentes's old hobbyhorses about "original words" and improbably mixed with Juan Goytisolo's recent efforts to draw political blood by wielding Américo Castro's theories on Spanish history. Fuentes, it seems to me, misses the point completely about both the *Quijote* and *Finnegans Wake.* There is no rejoicing in origins in those works, but a gleeful celebration of their demise. This crucial misunderstanding is at the core of *Terra Nostra,* giving it the solemn, massive verbosity of a funeral rite, not the gaiety of Joyce's *Wake. Terra Nostra* is a stony monument to that original word which never quite comes to life in 800 words of effort. . . .

As an intellectual venture, *Terra Nostra,* with its effort to approximate the Spanish Baroque and the modern tradition, is the culmination of efforts begun by Hispanic writers in the twenties. I am thinking not only of the Spanish Generation of '27 poets, but of more recent works by Alejo Carpentier and Severo Sarduy. *Terra Nostra* is in this regard not only a culmination but also a compendium. The most original contribution of the book in this regard is to make Rojas's *Celestina* the origin of this trend in a more explicit manner than Sarduy's *Cobra.* . . . Fuentes's error is to privilege Celestina as origin, not to take into account that she is the very negation of origins, given that precisely her major occupation is to restore virginities, to offer the new as patchwork.

Perhaps Fuentes intended this to be the point of his work and the Latinate title is to be taken ironically to mean that there is no earthly mother in the textual world, but only the indiscriminately disseminating old whore who presides over his novel. Still, the voluminous, erudite, trite and solemn nature of his work nearly buried this reviewer. (p. 84)

> *Roberto González Echevarría, in* World Literature Today *(copyright 1978 by the University of Oklahoma Press), Vol. 52, No. 1, Winter, 1978.*

G

GADDIS, William 1922-

An American novelist, Gaddis has tackled themes of hypocrisy, greed, and alienation in two highly complex, large-scale works of fiction. Echoing Joyce, James, and Gide, he employs multiple levels of meaning and intricate allusions in his portrayal of the confusion and pain of human interaction, the despair and purposelessness of the human condition. He won the National Book Award in 1975 for *J.R.* (See also *CLC*, Vols. 1, 3, 6, 8, and *Contemporary Authors*, Vols. 17-20, rev. ed.)

PETER WILLIAM KOENIG

[Few] outside of a coterie of devoted followers have read or even heard of *The Recognitions*.... We have now had, however, access to some of Gaddis' manuscripts, which may help *The Recognitions* find its rightful above-ground reputation. (p. 61)

To understand Gaddis' relationship to his characters, and thus his philosophical motive in writing the novel, we are helped by knowing how Gaddis conceived of it originally. *The Recognitions* began as a much smaller and less complicated work, passing through a major evolutionary stage during the seven years Gaddis spent writing it. Gaddis says in his notes: "When I started this thing . . . it was to be a good deal shorter, and quite explicitly a parody on the FAUST story. . . . (p. 64)

[When] Gaddis read James Frazer's *The Golden Bough*, . . . the novel entered its second major stage. Frazer's pioneering anthropological work demonstrates how religions spring from earlier myths, fitting perfectly with Gaddis' idea of the modern world as a counterfeit—or possibly inspiring it. In any case, Frazer led Gaddis to discover that Goethe's *Faust* originally derived from the Clementine *Recognitions*, a rambling third-century theological tract of unknown authorship, dealing with Clement's life and search for salvation. Gaddis adapted the title, broadening the conception of his novel to the story of a wandering, at times misguided hero, whose search for salvation would record the multifarious borrowings and counterfeits of modern culture. . . . Thus from a limited Faust parody, his novel expanded into an epical, theoretically limitless pilgrimage of recognitions parodying the immense *Recognitions of Clement*. (pp. 64-5)

The Recognitions examines the complex problem of salvation, a problem with Gaddis sees as stemming from the "Modernism heresy," . . . the rationalist interpretation of history, which does not allow for meaningful suffering or redemption. Science, according to Gaddis, works against recognition of the need for suffering, as does its therapeutic extension, psychoanalysis. Religion tries to work toward salvation but fails, because like science, it is only a counterfeit of an earlier impulse and ability to wonder and believe. Modern art too, with its worship on the one hand of the past, and on the other of unbridled originality, has forgotten its earlier, painstaking function of recording genuine wonder and dread. Thus all of our modern occupations, institutions, and amusements seem in Gaddis' parody to be the counterfeit secrets of a pagan Egypt, where mere magic replaces true mystery and renders belief impossible. (p. 65)

Far more suggestive and full of potential, but deluded and a counterfeiter like the rest, Wyatt thinks of himself as an alchemist, recognizing that alchemy "wasn't just making gold," . . . but was originally the search for the redemption of matter. For Wyatt it represents a spiritual quest such as medieval alchemists made when they saw "in gold the image of the sun, spun in the earth by its countless revolutions, then, when the sun might yet be taken for the image of God." . . . Gaddis' search for the ideal goes back to what he calls in his notes "those perfect forms of neo-platonism," and in *The Recognitions* "a time before death entered the world, before accident, before magic, and before magic despaired, to become religion." . . . Wyatt chooses the alchemist—part magician, part priest, part scientist—to reunite all these fragmented modern approaches and go back as far as possible to original truth. (p. 66)

Clearly, the world around [Gaddis' characters] is not conducive to the survival of any ideal, it is so full of unhealthy and dangerously impermanent counterfeits, of unordered spiritual, sexual, and creative impulses.

Through this unhealthy, uncertain world, Wyatt attempts to journey from the counterfeit to the genuine, from sin to redemption, chaos to design. The structure of Gaddis' novel symbolizes voyage and return, dislocation and reestablishment, lost recognitions and found. Gaddis felt that "It should be 'apparently' broken up, because that is the nature of the problem it attempts to investigate, that is, the separating of things today without love." . . . To make the novel "'apparently' broken up," Gaddis employs montage or broken narrative, skipping from place to place without connections, consciously imitating a film. But the fragmentary scenes return at strategic points in the novel, producing surprises by recurrence, and an overall sense of completeness.

Gaddis' symbolic use of structure in fragmenting and then reuniting his fictional world is best exemplified by his treatment of the martyr-saint theme, the most important one in the novel. The major authentic martyr-saint is Wyatt, the main subplot the making of a counterfeit saint out of a dead Spanish girl. Whereas the original *Recognitions* of Clement describes the making of a true saint out of Clement, Gaddis shows the preposterous difficulties involved in Wyatt's becoming a saint through martyrdom in the twentieth century. He does this by creating a structural model of modern, secular chaos. (pp. 67-8)

Wyatt's father offers him a . . . model of sainthood in the person of the martyred Saint Clement, who died by drowning with an anchor tied to his neck. Years later Valentine cynically predicts Wyatt will be drowned . . . , as he is—by his guilt, and by the chaotic world in which he lives. (p. 69)

[Near the novel's end] Wyatt reveals a pair of earrings, presumably his mother's, which he wishes to give to someone, possibly to a daughter by the prostitute Pastora, whom he met in Spain. Gaddis originally planned to make this ending explicit, as his notes indicate:

> I say I don't want the end to seem trite, an easy way out; because I don't want it to sound as though Wyatt has finally found his place in company with a simple stupid and comparatively unattractive woman who loves him. . . . I simply want the intimation that, in starting a drawing of his daughter, Wyatt, seeing her in her trust and faith (love), is *beginning*. He may not yet understand, but the least we can do is start him, after all this, on the right way, where the things that mattered, not simply no longer matter, but no longer exist. . . .

Gaddis finally decided, however, that even this ending would be facile and left only hints of it in the final version. He chose instead to emphasize Wyatt's drowning, Clement-like martyrdom. . . . Thus in the final pages, all the suggestions of Wyatt's martyrdom and possible salvation coalesce, briefly and fragmentedly, as Wyatt believed from the first that recognitions occur. (pp. 69-70)

Gaddis considers himself "a religious person" on one hand, and a blasphemous nihilist on the other. Like his hero Wyatt, he is an artist of religious concerns in a nonreligious age. This explains what is most puzzling about *The Recognitions*—why Gaddis opens his novel with an epigraph about nothing being vain or without significance as concerns God, and then attacks every form of religion and faith. He believes that all their myths fail to give meaning to modern life and that he must hasten the collapse, lay bare the emptiness, "to betray the lack of pattern and still its final, if seemingly fortuitous persistence." He uses *Recognitions of Clement* to symbolize a lost spiritual integrity, a personal search for redemption. *The Recognitions* itself is a search for redemption, in which Gaddis seeks to avoid his

characters' "hazardous assurance," . . . and to "unfold, not the pattern, but the materials of a pattern, and the necessity of a pattern." The novel offers no final answers to the questions it raises, but its questions do penetrate "so deeply that the doubt it arouses is frightening and cannot be dismissed." The very suggestiveness and structure of his questioning constitutes a partial answer.

Like Alexander Solzhenitsyn in *The First Circle*, Gaddis seeks to produce a consciousness of Heaven through a massive recognition of Dantesque Hell. (pp. 70-1)

[In *City of Words: American Fiction, 1950-1970,* Tony] Tanner summarizes the importance of *The Recognitions* by stating that "the problems Gaddis raises and the themes he explores seem . . . to be at the heart of American Literature, and in looking back to Hawthorne while it looks ahead to Pynchon, his novel reminds us of the continuities which we might otherwise, perhaps, overlook." [See *CLC*, Vol. 3]. Gaddis deals with Hawthorne's problems, permanently rooted in the American consciousness, of too much guilt and not enough morality. In showing how intertwined are the confidence men and the innocents in American life, Gaddis also places himself directly in the tradition of Melville. . . . Certainly *The Recognitions* is among the first, along with the novels of Nabokov, Nin, and Hawkes, to deal in an original way with the post-war world. It is one of the first "cold war novels," in which the hero never appears or the battle never takes place, and yet one feels that great tensions are abroad and enormous consequences are at stake. In this it foreshadows the novels of Pynchon, as well as many others, a masterfully crafted prototype of contemporary American fiction as well as a satirically prophetic picture of American life. (pp. 71-2)

> *Peter William Koenig, "Recognizing Gaddis' 'Recognitions'," in* Contemporary Literature *(© 1975 by the Board of Regents of the University of Wisconsin System), Vol. 16, No. 1, Winter, 1975, pp. 61-72.*

CHARLES LESLIE BANNING

In Gaddis' as well as Heller's and Pynchon's novels there is always apparent an ominous vertical structure of society, which finally appears to leave the individual completely at the mercy of its manipulative powers and with no human in control. But Gaddis, it seems, is much more of a Romantic than either Heller or Pynchon: there is individual triumph, and the inherent possibility of it, though necessarily of a very localized nature. Wyatt Gwyon in *The Recognitions* does reject finally the superficial and impersonal determinants of society, just as Edward Bast in *JR* rejects J R—the sixth grader who becomes a corporation tycoon—and his tyrannical financial manipulations; Bast goes off to write his opera unmindful of his material well-being. It is as though Gaddis shows us the primacy of "counterforce," whereas Pynchon wants to establish an *inevitable* transformation of "counterforce" into "Counterforce" into "They."

Moreover, Gaddis believes, like William James, that the world is essentially chaotic and furthermore that there is no ontological hierarchy. He sees that the multiple imposition of formal structures upon the chaos results finally in chaos, too. (pp. 153-54)

The tension which underlies Gaddis' work can be seen as one created by the antithetical perceptions of human existence by the individual and by Society. The individual is aware of his body and his bodily needs: Edward Bast tells the students, "here's [a letter Mozart] wrote to a girl cousin about the time he was writing his Paris symphony he says, he apologizes to her for not writing and he says "Do you think I'm dead? Don't believe it, I implore you. For believing and shitting are two very different things." Society, operating as it does in an abstract and inhuman realm, is interested in individuals in only a formal manner. Society in our time has tended toward technological efficiency, in the course of which it has demanded that we ourselves become technologically efficient—that we be predictable, that we be consistent. . . . It is within [the] framework of the institutionalization of inhumanism that Gaddis creates his fiction. He wants to place the onus of our inhumanness squarely on the shoulders of Society, specifically "masculine" society.

Gaddis in both *The Recognitions* and *JR* sees the rejection of physicality and the repression of physical needs as a culturally induced situation. In his first novel he saw the dynamics as inherent in New England Calvinism and the Pauline doctrine as enunciated in Galatians 5.24: "And those who belong to Christ Jesus have crucified the flesh with its passions and desires." The world of New York and Paris, of business and jurisprudence, is seen as the direct result of this; it is the world prophesized by God through "the Greek Clement: I am come to destory the work of the woman, that is, concupiscence, whose works are generation and death." Thus *The Recognitions* is a sterile and impersonal world of "poses become life." Fortunately there is a more balanced assortment of characters in *JR*—a result, I believe, of the more "restricted" vision of the book. (pp. 154-55)

In *JR* . . . we see the demands of society that bodily passion and desire be rejected; only this time rather than developing these demands in terms of the metaphysical and religious tenets of the American experience, Gaddis simply drops us into the American educational system, a system operating within a technological imperative to teach skills, viewing human beings as little machines. The running look at J R Vansant's school provides the backdrop for the future structure which will result from the programmatic demands of business and industry for persons who are "trained" and "taught" the proper answers, not how to think. (p. 155)

Coach Vogel . . . is one of the prize teachers in the school; he has come out to this Long Island institution from New York City. Asked to create a sex-education film for the students, the future inventor of the Frigi-Com and Teletravel processes for a subsidiary of J R Corp. comes up with a show befitting the "man: the incredible machine" metaphor. (pp. 156-57)

J R, the sixth-grade mastermind of J R Corp., is a product of this environment; he is himself as dehumanized and mechanical as the various images that barrage him throughout the day at school—it doesn't seem illogical to him that the museum diaramas of Eskimo life should have "stuffed Eskimos." Having no appreciation of even the forms he is seeking out and copying in order to succeed in the American Way, it is not surprising that he has no appreciation for nature or music (or literature or painting). (p. 157)

Edward Bast . . . is never really interested in playing the game in the first place; he gets drawn in by a seemingly innocuous meeting he has for J R with the stock broker Mister Crawley. . . . Bast just floats around; unable to decide what to do next, he does what J R arranges for him. (pp. 158-59)

In a sense, their relationship epitomizes the numerous relationships throughout the book, for those whose only satisfaction is playing the game and following the rules are supported by those who lower themselves to their level and support the game through the suppression of their own creative efforts and desires. The novel actually ends on a note of rejection by some of the characters, such as Edward Bast, Jack Gibbs and Thomas Eigen, of the meaningless games being played by the others. (pp. 159-60)

The various formalizations of human activity which society imposes on the individual rest upon language. The areas of human activity such as school administration or the stock market perpetuate themselves by creating discourse which not only establishes the rules for moving within the game, but which finally becomes itself the object for manipulation. The most important individuals in the company structure are the lawyers and the public relations personnel because they know how to use language most abstractly and, hence, most meaninglessly. Every statement and every transaction coming out of J R Corp. offices must go through the hands of the company lawyer, Piscator.

The resulting disembodiment of language from meaning—induced especially by advertising—which appears to be the "absolute" result of the swelling discourses, was a central concern for Gaddis in *The Recognitions*. Though the constant mimicry and repetition of each other's speech may have certain prescriptive foundations in the Calvinist deprecation of originality as articulated by Aunt May, there is a general atmosphere of meaninglessness which plagues both Otto the playwright and Esme the poet. Otto is reduced to writing his play by putting together the scraps of conversation he collects from those around him; whereas Esme retreats to "intuition," using words for their sound and shape only—"What does it *mean*. It just *is*," she tells Otto about her using "effluvium" in a poem.

The dialogues at the parties and on the Paris sidewalk throughout *The Recognitions* are reduced to images of what Piaget has termed "collective monologue." There is no desire to communicate with one another, rather the individuals just seek to be part of the cacaphony, thereby affirming their own existence. Moreover, the general problem of the meaninglessness of language is not restricted to the characters themselves; due to Gaddis' own existence in such a community of discourse, and given his penchant for philosophizing, *The Recognitions* itself became a search on the part of the author/narrator for meaning and significance and answers to meaningless questions.

Gaddis in seeking, or in seeking to expose, the symbolic nature of words and images in the text itself, was caught up in a necessarily frustrating search through all realms of discourse. Like Melville's futile search for the "meaning" of the whale's whiteness, Gaddis in his first novel proceeded to reduce semantics to syntax, to hide meaning behind structures. Not only the words of the text but the characters as well become merely the sum total of their possible contextual definitions; not only do the characters deny their physicality, but Gaddis' manipulations *tend* to deny the characters their necessary physicality. We are left, often, with caricatures and types which exist only within a general abstract framework, the novel. The characters in *The Recognitions* become player-piano players with no possibility of being pianists—they are simply role-players.

This is not the case for *JR*. Here, Gaddis has not tried to elucidate recurring images or to encompass them in a general abstract system. He allows them to simply exist in all their ambiguity and meaningfulness within the various discourses established by the characters themselves. Furthermore, the characters' discourses rather than being speculative and metaphysical are the discourse of everyday life. The characters are, for the most part, not concerned with impressing others with their knowledge of arcana or in pondering philosophical truths; they use language as "communication."

To call their speech "communication" requires some explanation. It is to a great extent like the collective monologues in *The Recognitions;* however, there is an underlying illusion that their speaking will have an effect upon other people, which is lacking in Gaddis' earlier novel. Whereas in Gaddis' earlier work there were few people (notably Esther) who believed that speech could somehow effect things, in *JR* the dialogue again and again moves with the illusion on the part of the speakers that somehow what they say will have ramifications elsewhere, that speech is communication even though it gets permuted and lost along the way. Like the man sent by the Teletravel process through the telephone lines, however, there is no guarantee that what was sent will ever be located, let alone be recovered, again. Thus language becomes tyrannical. It is only a "writer" like Jack Gibbs—or an artist like Bast—who recognizes that the discourses are all incomplete attempts to control the underlying chaos of reality. With such recognition, Gibbs is able to easily move from one language game to another; he can carry on the discourse of the classroom or of the administration or of the financial world with equal ease without getting sucked under and drowned in the detritus of language with its nonexistent goals and meaningless valuations. (pp. 160-62)

Yet the vast majority of the characters cannot get out of the discourses they are caught in; they cannot see how life is other than the abstract concepts controlling the discourse they have been raised in. They subjugate themselves to such non-entities as "patriotism," "the American way," "profit," and "business" without realizing that the terms only have meaning (and the game only exists) while *they* are repeating and utilizing them, that the terms and games are inherently vacuous.

But, what does have meaning then? Briefly stated: physical action or the possibility of it is the meaning of language. Those terms which cannot and do not signify possible action by human beings can (and do in *The Recognitions*) float away in abstract meaninglessness. Meaning is restored to language through its direct connection to a sensible reality, and it is this connection of the dialogue to human action and to the objects of such action which makes it meaningful, and which gives the characters such immediacy and physicality. Gaddis, for whom the meaninglessness of language was such a problem in his earlier novel, avoids the dilemma altogether by relying upon the failure of others to communicate for his own communication. Gaddis has, in *JR*, overcome the ambiguity of language not, as some writers would, through parody but by making such discourse the object (or constituent) of his discourse. By reposing

narrative within the characters' discourses rather than trying to formalize the chaos himself, Gaddis not only avoids the semantic dilemmas which plagued him earlier but succeeds in creating a viable and intense reality of human action. (pp. 162-63)

Charles Leslie Banning, "William Gaddis' 'JR': The Organization of Chaos and the Chaos of Organization," in Paunch (© 1975 *by Arthur Efron), December, 1975, pp. 153-65.*

JAY L. HALIO

William Gaddis' tour de force, *JR,* attacks many . . . perversions of the American Dream, above all the materialism of Franklinian man. Adapting a stream of consciousness technique borrowed from Joyce and contemporary telephone conversation, Gaddis mercilessly lays bare the greed and essential mindlessness of those for whom wealth has become an end in itself—an obsessive end. His satire is particularly effective since he uses as his primary vehicle a twelve-year-old school boy who has mastered all of the jargon and methods of a Wall Street wizard constructing immense paper empires inevitably and fatally vulnerable to strangulation by the very tape which once held it together. But missing from Gaddis' overlong satirical saga, and its radical defect, is any sense or hint of a redeeming virtue. There is no music in his America, no poetry, despite the fact (or rather revealed by it) that one of his major characters is a composer desperately trying to finish a cantata. The world's distractions, epitomized by stock options, puts and calls, tax loopholes, telephone calls, educational TV, legal suits, and all the other paraphernalia of today's urban centers, are triumphant. The poet or artist cannot cancel them; he is canceled by them. (p. 840)

Jay L. Halio, in The Southern Review *(copyright, 1977, by Jay L. Halio), Vol. XIII, No. 4, Autumn, 1977.*

SUSAN STREHLE KLEMTNER

While the fictional achievement of William Gaddis is massive, both in importance and in sheer volume, the critical reception of his two novels has been skimpy and uncertain. (p. 61)

The uncertain reception of Gaddis's novels is understandable; the reviews indicate common problems in both for a casual reader: complexity of event and structure, unusual treatment of character, a difficult narrative surface. Gaddis self-consciously anticipates his lack of an audience in both works. . . . If Gaddis's novels have achieved only a very small audience because of their difficulties, they deserve a much larger one because of their importance. In particular, *JR* is an extraordinary achievement—richly funny and powerfully accurate; it is more successful in several ways than *The Recognitions*. (pp. 61-2)

One of the most extraordinary qualities of *The Recognitions* is its ambitiousness. It is vast in scope, covering a span of some thirty years and ranging from New York to Europe. It is encyclopedic in knowledge; the literary sources and references include not only Joyce but Augustine, Saint John of the Cross, Thoreau, Melville, T. S. Eliot, and dozens more. In tracing its religious themes, the book explores Catholicism, Calvinism, various forms of mysticism, and Mithraism, the worship of the sun. The scientific lore contained in the novel ranges from counterfeit mummy-making to counterfeit money-making to the method for analyzing the date of a painting. Several levels of discourse are included: from graffiti to sermons, from inebriated party chitchat to serious debates of aesthetic principles. The novel left several reviewers with the uncomfortable sensation that Gaddis had poured everything he knew into it. . . . (pp. 62-3)

One reason for the heavy literary allusiveness of the novel is its presentation of artistic creation as an act of atonement; art has metaphysical significance in *The Recognitions*. Several characters experience artistic creation as a kind of transcendental perception of truth. The recognitions evoked in the title are revelations of religious certainty, when the fragmentation and chaos of modern culture are stripped away to reveal simplicity, necessity, and love. . . . Art, as the fragments of past creations, the creations of the characters, or Gaddis's novel itself, has redemptive power in *The Recognitions*.

Gaddis's first novel is a profoundly serious exploration of aesthetics and religion, with some moments of comic relief. As recognitions are treated with earnest respect in the novel, failures of recognition become ridiculous. . . . Rich in humor as it is, the novel is primarily concerned with an earnest exploration of aesthetic recognition, and the comic failures form a minor counterpoint to the dominant theme.

While *JR* shares a similar preoccupation with art, it is a very different novel in several respects. Its protagonist, Edward Bast, is not as heroic as Wyatt Gwyon; while he shares Wyatt's innocence, he is successfully manipulated throughout the novel. (pp. 63-4)

JR is far more limited in scope than *The Recognitions*. The time covered in the narrative is only three or four months. . . . The novel opens as the leaves have begun to turn and closes before Christmas; the seasonal decline with no Nativity reflects the sterility of the natural and civilized world in the book. . . . Relatively few . . . allusions . . . are used; while aesthetic fragments could redeem the damaged world of *The Recognitions,* the world of *JR* is ruined past redemption.

The creation of art appears in *JR* as a worthy action, with no ability to save or redeem the world. Like *The Recognitions,* the novel includes a great many plagiarists and failed artists. . . . Unlike *The Recognitions*, however, *JR* includes no truly successful artists. . . . (pp. 64-5)

Art fails to redeem in the novel because its audience is incapable of exaltation—or even appreciation. . . . Because American culture as it is presented in the novel is incapable of awakening or exaltation, the artist's problem becomes one of motivation: if his creation is considered worthless by his audience, can it have any worth? In *JR* art has no culturally redemptive power, but it can achieve worth "for a very small audience."

JR is far more concerned with failures of recognition than with moments of religious or aesthetic perception; thus the novel assumes a tone of sustained black humor. Where Gaddis's first novel suggested solutions to the problem of despair in the perception of simplicity, necessity, and love, his second novel admits, in a tone of desperate glee, that the problem cannot be resolved. (p. 65)

Gaddis jokes about the destruction of language and ideals,

about human inadequacy and death, about the cosmic absurdity of his characters' quest for order and beauty in a world of squalor and chaos. His jokes suggest that he finds neither a solution nor a fully adequate response to despair.

While both of Gaddis's fictional worlds are characterized by a "sense of disappointment, of something irretrievably lost," . . . Gaddis radically shifts the way he defines the problem. The source of loss and despair in *The Recognitions* appears as the fragmentation and separation of a once-unified world; in *JR* these symptoms are traced to the entropic decline of a chaotic and random world. While fragments can be collected and ordered, to reverse the enervating process described in the second law of thermodynamics is impossible: Stanley manages "to get all the parts together into one work," but Bast cannot turn off the flow of hot water that represents a pointless loss of energy. . . . As the loss of energy, the decline toward inertness, and the increase of disorder, entropy dominates the world of *JR*.

One important manifestation of the entropic process, as it appears in the fiction of both Gaddis and Thomas Pynchon, is the loss of communication. *JR* is made up almost entirely of spoken words, with very little narrative description or authorial comment, yet for all the speaking that occurs, little communicating is accomplished. Most of the dialogues in the novel become monologues because one character dominates and cuts the other off; *JR* is full of interruptions and sentence fragments. But even when both characters manage to complete their sentences, misunderstandings proliferate. (pp. 66-7)

As human communication is lost and energy declines, inert things come to dominate the settings of *JR*. Two of the most important locales in the novel, the Long Island school and the Ninety-sixth Street apartment, literally fill up with objects so that people can no longer move about. . . .

Several recurring motifs reinforce the notion of entropic decline and also unify the novel. Among these, the most significant is a repeated pattern of spilling, falling, and scattering; these actions increase randomness and disorder. (p. 68)

All of the spilling and scattering underscores Gaddis's more explicit suggestion that order is imposed perilously "on the basic reality of chaos."

People are similarly afflicted by the manifestations of chaotic randomness in another recurring motif: injuries and accidents are prevalent throughout *JR*. . . .

[The numerous] "walking wounded" reinforce the accidental quality of experience in an advanced entropic state.

Because they live in a chaotic world without a sense of history or culture, most of the characters respond by seeking the ordering power of money. Money lifts one about the entropic process; it gives one the power to control inert objects, to manipulate other people, and to create constellations of order around one's own central importance. (p. 69)

JR himself is at once the chief symbol and the most pathetic victim of the drive for money and power. (p. 70)

But for all his undeniable greed, JR is also a touchingly helpless product of the world around him. . . . In all his corporate exploits, he has simply been trying to find a purpose, "trying to find out what I'm suppose to do," and he has quite naturally looked to the adults around him and imitated them. At several points he has even quoted from John Cates, Whiteback, Hyde, and others in justifying his actions. While we never learn what his initials actually stand for, they clearly suggest "Junior," as his character clearly suggests a junior reflection of his elders. If this eleven-year-old's obsession with money is ominous, it is also typical of every one of his peers. . . . (pp. 70-1)

JR's empire is constructed of paper, and while he becomes a millionaire on paper he never appears one in reality. He never uses his paper money, not even to replace the torn sneakers or sweater. By the novel's end, money is clearly not only lifeless but an agent of lifelessness; its worth is called into question at the beginning, and its worthlessness firmly established by the end.

The search for some form of worthy activity preoccupies most of the sympathetic characters in the novel; like Wyatt Gwyon in *The Recognitions*, they realize that "looking around us today, there doesn't seem to be much that's worth doing." . . . For Schramm, Eigen, and Gibbs, worthy art must redeem the insignificance of the artist and the illiteracy of the audience; their efforts are doomed to failure. For Bast and for Gaddis, art may be worthy without being able to redeem anything; *JR* creates its worth out of the tacit admission that experience cannot be turned "into something more than one more stupid tank battle." (pp. 71-2)

For Bast, as perhaps for Gaddis, his art was and continues to be worth creating, whatever the condition of his audience. He does not expect to win fame or money, as he does not expect others to recognize the worth of his creations. In a conversation with Eigen as the novel ends, Bast says of his new composition, "I mean until a performer hears what I hear and can make other people hear what he hears it's just trash isn't it Mister Eigen, it's just trash like everything in this place." . . . Bast's heavily ironic statement can also be taken as a final comment on *JR;* the audience of both works may be small, but neither creation is "just trash." Both works stand on their own, with or without recognition, proving the worth of the art and the artist. (p. 72)

> *Susan Strehle Klemtner, "'For a Very Small Audience': The Fiction of William Gaddis," in* Critique: Studies in Modern Fiction *(copyright © by James Dean Young 1978), Vol. XIX, No. 3, 1978, pp. 61-72.*

*   *   *

GARCÍA MÁRQUEZ, Gabriel   1928-

García Márquez is a Colombian novelist, short story writer, journalist, and screenwriter. Effectively combining imagination and corrupt reality, his novels often occur in a setting of political oppression and conflict. His invention of the town Macondo with its function as microcosm, and his use of interior monologue often elicit comparison to Faulkner. (See also *CLC*, **Vols. 2, 3, 8, and** *Contemporary Authors*, **Vols. 33-36, rev. ed.)**

LINDA B. HALL

When the first edition of *One Hundred Years of Solitude* was published . . . , there was an immediate storm of critical attention and acclaim which has not yet subsided. . . . *One Hundred Years of Solitude* brings to the novel form a deep exploration of aspects of solitude, from the loneliness

of power to sexual anguish, drawing heavily on the earlier ideas which had been suggested by Paz and Borges.

García Márquez's novel takes place in Macondo, a mythical town in Colombia, and the one hundred years represent both the life of the town from its founding to its collapse and the survival of the Buendía dynasty—from its founders, José Arcadio and Ursula, to the death of the last Aureliano Buendía. . . . García Márquez uses all the techniques of magic realism to give his town an enchanted yet real aspect: the Buendía family lives, dies, works, but is surrounded by ghosts, especially that of Melquiades, the old gypsy who first introduced them to the outside world. Melquiades has brought with him parchments, which off and on fascinate certain male members of the family, but are indecipherable to them. Only the last member is able to read them, and that in the moment of ultimate destruction.

In many ways, García Márquez's characters are embodiments of the aspects of solitude which Octavio Paz has pointed out in his essays. In "The Dialectic of Solitude," published in his work *The Labyrinth of Solitude,* Paz says, "Solitude is the profoundest fact of the human condition. Man is the only being who knows he is alone, and the only one who seeks out another. . . . Man is nostalgia and a search for communion." García Márquez's characters, particularly the series of male members of the family named Aureliano, have a profound sense of their solitude and vacillate between an attempt at communion and a return to total absorption in themselves. (pp. 254-55)

For both Paz and García Márquez, the deepest form of communion and the closest antidote to solitude is sexual love. . . .

The most fascinating parts of García Márquez's work are those which describe in a kaleidoscopic fashion many aspects of love—as communion, as frustration, as a breaking away from accepted patterns. The love which furnishes a release from solitude is always a love which defies society and leads to ultimate destruction and the return of solitude. In *One Hundred Years of Solitude,* loves which are forbidden between members of the same family, between individuals of varying ages, between people of different social classes, are endowed with universal, mythic qualities. (p. 256)

But if love cannot permanently relieve solitude, what then is left? Paz believes that the essence of the feeling of solitude is "a nostalgic longing for the body from which we were cast out, . . . a longing for a place." The ancient belief, common to many peoples, is that that place is the center of the earth, "the navel of the universe." Usually this place is identified with the group's point of origin, real or mythical, and in turn with paradise. The path to this place is frequently viewed as a labyrinth. The labyrinth therefore fulfills a mythic need in a people: if the key to the labyrinth can be found and the labyrinth penetrated, redemption from solitude is at hand.

This connection between the labyrinth and solitude has been explored by another of the major thinkers of Latin America, Jorge Luis Borges, who, like Paz, is one of the major influences on García Márquez's work. In Borges's short stories, the deciphering of the labyrinth is a frequently recurring symbol for the search for redemption from solitude. But in Borges's stories the inhabitant at the center of the labyrinth is still locked in solitude, and the penetration of the maze may bring destruction to both the one who penetrates and the one whose solitude is violated. This solitude is not viewed as the desperation that is felt by those seeking to invade the labyrinth, but as a vague disquiet, a waiting. (p. 259)

The labyrinth in García Márquez's book is [the] set of unintelligible parchments. . . . (p. 261)

Aureliano grows to manhood as the family collapses and the house decays, finally to fall in love with the only remaining member of the family, Amaranta Ursula, whom he believes to be his sister but who is actually his aunt. Their child is born with a pig's tail. This circumstance does not disturb the parents greatly, as the child seems otherwise healthy, but the mother suddenly hemorrhages and dies. Aureliano flees the house and returns to find the child consumed by ants. It is at this moment that the parchments become clear to him. He realizes that the entire past of the family has been leading to this moment, fulfilling the prophecy written in the epigraph of the documents: "The first of the line is tied to a tree and the last is being eaten by the aunts."

He realizes that he and Amaranta Ursula had been seeking each other through the generation of the Buendía family "through the most intricate labyrinths of blood until they would engender the mythological animal that was to bring the line to an end." The center of the labyrinth is precisely this mythological animal, this child, the last of the Buendía line, who dies horribly and symbolizes the complete destruction of the family, rather than the hoped-for release from solitude. Aureliano desperately tries to finish deciphering the last page of the parchments as their prophecies are simultaneously coming true, "as if he were looking into a speaking mirror." He realizes, though, that he will never leave the room,

> . . . for it was foreseen that the city of mirrors (or mirages) would be wiped out by the wind and exiled from the memory of men at the precise moment when Aureliano Babilonia would finish deciphering the parchments, and that everything written on them was unrepeatable since time immemorial and forever more, because races condemned to one hundred years of solitude did not have a second opportunity on earth.

Gabriel García Márquez has indeed created in his novel Jorge Luis Borges's labyrinth. The labyrinth is confined in time to one hundred years of one family, and the repetition of family names in various generations is a way of working out various possibilities in various futures, a "garden of forking paths." But the novel . . . achieves internal coherence through the seemingly chronological passage of time, although the reader is aware that he is seeing over and over the mutations and interactions of only a few personalities. These interactions permit García Márquez to show us dozens of variations of solitude and to reveal to us what Borges and Paz had suggested: that man is always alone. (pp. 261-63)

> *Linda B. Hall, "Labyrinthine Solitude: The Impact of García Márquez," in* Southwest Review *(© 1973 by Southern Methodist University Press), Summer, 1973, pp. 253-63.*

KESSEL SCHWARTZ

García Márquez' mysterious caudillo, perhaps a composite or a specific individual like Juan Vicente Gómez, symbolizes the abuse of power as traditionally practiced in novels from *Amalia* to Carpentier's current *El recurso del método*. In his novel, which resembles *El gran Burundún Burundá* of his countryman Jorge Zalamea, García Márquez copies his own verbal mythology to describe a dictator whose life extends beyond a hundred years. Combining erotic fantasies, mystery and nightmare visions, both real and imagined, he uses the oneiric, symbolic, temporal and atemporal to obfuscate his "reality." He uses plural address, interminable sentences, multiple person changes and points of view to reflect the bits and pieces of the rambling memory of the dying dictator.

Part of the recall involves a series of horrific scenes. His bosom companion, Rodrigo de Aguilar, who had once saved his life, is cooked and fed on a platter to his fellow conspirators. The dictator's wife and son are eaten by a pack of attack dogs trained for that specific purpose. Children, used in a scheme to win lottery prizes for the *patriarca,* are dynamited at sea.

A series of women affect his life. Leticia Nazareno, a novice nun spared from a general exile when the Church refuses to accept the sainthood of his mother, Bendición Alvarado, becomes his only wife and love. Newly wed Francisca Linero, whose husband the dictator has sliced to bits so he can enjoy her, lives to be ninety-six and is buried with honors, though he cannot remember why. . . .

García Márquez mixes horror with black humor. The dictator dips food in private parts to add flavor and defeats a series of deposed dictators at dominoes. So great is his power that when he asks what time it is the reply is: "las que usted ordene mi general. . . ."

García Márquez' vision of the lonely old dictator who dreams, sweats, and recalls serves him as a kind of exorcism. But, however sincere, the novel, a self-repetition, offers us one more version of the idle jabber which characterizes the latest works of many of the greatest Spanish American novelists of the day. (p. 557)

> *Kessel Schwartz, in* Hispania *(© 1976 The American Association of Teachers of Spanish and Portuguese, Inc.), September, 1976.*

PAUL WEST

What is supremely interesting [in *The Autumn of the Patriarch*], and more so than anything in *One Hundred Years of Solitude*, is García Márquez's *modus operandi*, which a merely cursory description would have to call a voluptuous, thick, garish, centripetal weaving and re-weaving of quasi-narrative motifs that figure now as emblems, now as salient samples of all the stuff from which the world is made (at least the Caribbean one), now as earnests of a dominant presence who might be the dictator's wife Leticia, the dictator aping his double, the double aping the dictator's aping the double or the dead head of either or schoolgirls, or even an indeterminate chorus of voices all of whom have something to contribute to the burgeoning mythos of one distended career. . . . (pp. 76-7)

Hyperbole is the keynote, of course; even when it isn't on stage it is hovering, off, ready to be exploited. But what lodges in the mind after finishing the book is a technique I'd call horn-of-plenty bravura, not so much hyperboles amassed as Caribbean phenomena keenly registered non-stop, so that what you read is a flood, a crop, a spate, all the more poignant because, as often as not, it's the general's vision of "life without him," by and large going on as if he had never been. . . . A great deal of García Márquez's book, therefore, is construable as posthumous present, with the constant implication that, insatiable as it is, the observing eye takes in the merest fraction of available phenomena and has to make do with, in fact, next to nothing.

Such is my own reading of this technique, at any rate. Crammed with data, the book is a bulging elegy for the unseen, the not-experienced. . . . The evoked theme is ancient, a fusion of *carpe diem* and Husserl's "More than anything else the being of the world is obvious." Not that García Márquez lists things; he does, but he assembles them in such a pell-mell fashion that the movement from one item to the next becomes almost a narrative kinesis in its own right, while the items themselves, far from being mere entries in a stock-book, are epitomes of action: people, animals, plants, waves, clouds, captured in moments of characteristic and definitive doing. The effect is extraordinary, creating a textural narrative to counterpoint (even abolish) the story line. . . . Try to figure out what is happening and you end up with a better knowledge of event's context than of event itself. It just isn't that kind of novel. Its point is its precision-studded vagueness. Its content is a mentality, a sensibility. Its power is that of what I think radio technicians call side-band splash, when to receive one thing you must receive another. And that means the novel is all accretions, almost like a language being spoken century after century until, at some point, one asks: *What was Indo-European like? When?* What follows those questions is the work of sheerest hypothesis; such a proto-language must have been there spoken by such and such a people. . . . Much the same applies to the plot of this novel: you have to move toward it through what it has generated, and when you get there it has gone, and you are encountering an hypothesis of your own. (p. 77)

García Márquez's forte is that he always provides enough material in the next twenty syllables, and always in greater detail than most novelists can muster. Something Keatsian is going on here, in that he not only loads every rift with ore, he also evokes an obsolescent Hyperion trying to figure out why one set of gods has to give way to another. The book is an ode to "the uncountable time of eternity" that always comes to an end, whether we call it autumn or the general's reign. . . . At almost any juncture in the book there are . . . many different things going on; the compound ghost of the narrator speaks with mouth full. An effect of marmoreal amplitude is what you end with, not least because this is a book of no paragraphs, few sentences, and many, many commas, all toward a cumulative surge of the whole, Beckettian in rhythm yet full of all the stuff that Beckett leaves out, Nabokovian in its appetizing abundance yet quite without his mincing, dandyistic sheen.

It is such a book as, at the lowest level, would teach a fiction student how to write, what to keep on doing; every sentence, every phrase, *has enough* in it. At a much higher level, it's a book which raises the ghost of something truly unnerving: the chance that, after all is said and done, literature has nothing to say, no message, no interpretation, no answer, but only a chance to catalogue what the senses find and cannot do without. (pp. 77-8)

Paul West, "The Posthumous Present," in Review *(copyright © 1976 by the Center for Inter-American Relations, Inc.), Fall, 1976, pp. 76-8.*

RONALD DE FEO

Though he is one of the wittiest and most exhilarating of contemporary Latin American writers, García Márquez has repeatedly created characters who live, to varying degrees, in a state of solitude. From the earliest work, *Leaf Storm*, to the wonderful novella *No One Writes to the Colonel*, to the masterwork *One Hundred Years of Solitude*, we find people existing not only in spiritual isolation but in physical isolation as well: Macondo, the author's miraculous mythical town—the setting of much of his work—has been "condemned" to solitude, and indeed is so remote from the rest of the world that it possesses its very own laws of nature and logic.

The Autumn of the Patriarch . . . is García Márquez' most intense and extreme vision of isolation. In this fabulous, dream-like account of the reign of a nameless dictator of a fantastic Caribbean realm, solitude is linked with the possession of absolute power. The author has worked with this theme before—notably when tracing the career and increasing loneliness of Colonel Aureliano Buendía in *One Hundred Years of Solitude*—but here it receives the grand treatment.

Yet the book is in no way a case history or a psychological portrait of a dictator. It is, rather, a rendering in fantastic and exaggerated terms of a particular condition of might and isolation. As such, it is essentially plotless, though it is stuffed with enough anecdotes and incidents for several novels. When, at the beginning of the book, an unidentified party breaks into the decaying presidential palace and discovers the lichen-covered body of the patriarchal general who has governed the country for well over two centuries, a flood of memories of his incredible reign is released, and it is these memories, both collective and individual, flowing in free-associative, temporally jumbled repetition, that form the entire novel. (pp. 620, 622)

No summary or description of this book can really do it justice, for it is not only the author's surrealistic flights of imagination that make it such an exceptional work, but also his brilliant use of language, his gift for phrasing and description. As with *One Hundred Years of Solitude*, the reader is repeatedly surprised by the grace and ease with which an image is recorded, a phrase is turned.

And yet one must note, regretfully, that for all its brilliance *The Autumn of the Patriarch* is a difficult book to stay with for an extended length of time, difficult not because of the sentences that run on for pages or the absence of paragraphs, but because of an overabundance of riches. At times, the marvelous details accumulate so rapidly that the reader is simply overwhelmed by them. He seeks relief, a subdued passage in which to rest, but the author does not accord him that opportunity. At times, García Márquez' passion for inflation causes him to create a tale that is, even in a fantastic context, a shade too strained and whimsical—such as the account of the two thousand children kidnapped by the government to prevent them from revealing their role in the general's crooked lottery.

Still, of course, it is that very same passion for the absurd and the exaggerated that is responsible for the innumerable grand, witty passages we find—for example, the general discovering the hidden sentiments of his staff through the graffiti in the palace bathroom, or the account of a traitor who is served as a main course to the general's staff ("Major General Rodrigo de Aguilar entered on a silver tray stretched out on a garnish of cauliflower and laurel leaves ... embellished with the uniform of five golden almonds for solemn occasions"). Here and elsewhere throughout this unique, remarkable novel, the tall tale is transformed into a true work of art. (p. 622)

> *Ronald De Feo, "The Solitude of Power," in* National Review *(© National Review, Inc., 1977; 150 East 35th St., New York, N.Y. 10016), May 27, 1977, pp. 620, 622.*

WENDY McELROY

The Autumn of the Patriarch translates into words an image that haunted Gabriel Garcia Marquez. It was the image of an old man wandering aimlessly through the wasting rooms of a palace. It was an image of death and decay. The Patriarch is an ancient dictator whose exact title is General Of The Universe even though his domain is a poor Caribbean country, dependent upon the charity of world powers. His Autumn is the personal decay that preceeds his death. And his death is the focal point with which the novel begins, returns and ends. Each chapter begins with a different stage of discovering the general's corpse and backtracks to a different stage of the moral/physical decay that leads to such an end. . . .

The Autumn of the Patriarch is a novel of style. And it is a style that I generally dislike. A style in which sentences run on for three pages, and in which there are no paragraphs. Dialogue is not indicated by quotes. Pronouns change in mid-sentence. And the narrative point-of-view is in constant flux. I used to think that I disliked this style because it seemed to violate principles which make English intelligible to no apparent advantage. I have come to think that it is an extremely difficult style and this is the first time I have seen it handled properly.

Gabriel Garcia Marquez ignores many conventions of the English language which are meant to provide structure and coherence. But he is so skillful that his novel is not difficult to understand. It is bizarre; it is disorienting. But it is not difficult. Moreover, it is appropriate to the chaos and decay of the general's mind and of his world. (p. 3)

The narrative is predominantly from the general's point-of-view but it drifts in and out of other people's thoughts and reactions with a change in pronoun indicating this drift; "'. . . she sat down on the sofa opposite him, where the gush of his fetid body odor would not reach her, and then I dared to look at him face to face for the first time spinning the glow of the rose with two fingers so that he would not notice my terror . . .'" Just as people do not think in sentences and paragraphs, but in trains of thought that conclude and springboard into related trains of thought, so the sentences of the novel flow. They do not express a single idea, but a single chain of ideas and resemble a highly contrived flow-of-consciousness. (pp. 3, 10)

As you would suspect from the style, *The Autumn of the Patriarch* is a psychological portrait. Or, more accurately, it is a psychological expose. It is the expose of a fascist dictator. . . .

This portrait is a particularly successful one. Much of the narrative takes place in the general's mind; it wanders through what he thinks and what he sees. It does not describe how he sees the world; it *is* how he sees the world. From here, the point-of-view shifts to other people's reactions to him. In other words, the general is a specimen, x-rayed and viewed from all sides. On the whole, it is an objective view. He is not seen as an evil or good person. He is just seen. . . .

It would be redundant to say that *The Autumn of the Patriarch* presents the general as a symbol. But few writers are as blatant about it as Marquez. He presents the general as a plains person, born far from the smell of the sea—the sea being a universal symbol for life. His greatest treachery is selling that sea to the gringos in exchange for the security of his power. Symbolically, he is selling, betraying life itself. And, in particular, he is betraying the life of his country and of its people. Unless you accept this symbolically it will make little sense to you. . . .

The plot is insignificant. What there is consists of episodes from the general's life that are out of time sequence and that focus on the psychologies involved rather than on the events. It records the inevitable decay of the general. But simply because it is inevitable, there is little mystery or suspense.

There is one caveat. Although *The Autumn of the Patriarch* is not difficult to understand, it can be difficult to read. The style is dense and rich. It is packed with "uselessly precise detail', uselessly complete descriptions and repetition. The repetition is particularly rampant. It sometimes seems that every few pages the general takes time out to wander through his palace checking the locks. Even the imagery, which is quite striking (tiptoing like an evil thought, soft boiled dreams, a postcard heart), is overdone. The result of all this resembles a cluttered closet. (p. 10)

> *Wendy McElroy, in* World Research INK, *11722 Sorrento Valley Road, San Diego, Calif., September, 1977.*

JOHN STURROCK

Since ["One Hundred Years of Solitude"] and since its successor, "The Autumn of the Patriarch," ... García Márquez has felt doubts about what he is doing. His is the old quandary of the "committed" writer: should he continue to luxuriate in exile, writing books mocking the stagnation and repression of his native continent, or would it not be more honorable to attempt something practical in order to remove them? García Márquez hankers after political activism, to make propaganda for the many as against an exclusive art for the few. But literature needs him. He will do more good for his socialist cause by continuing to write fiction, guilty conscience and all, than by demagogic pamphleteering. He is one of the small number of contemporary writers from Latin America who have given to its literature a maturity and dignity it never had before. That in itself is good propaganda. . . .

["Innocent Eréndira"] is in García Márquez's most beguiling manner: ruthless, fantastic and eventful. The stories [which form the remainder of the collection], on the other hand, mostly are not. They are makeweights here, the ambitious but as yet uncertain and over-abstract tales of a writer too young to recognize that even the most imaginative fiction needs to be filled with things as well as strange thoughts. Indeed, García Márquez's own imagination is now at its most prodigious when he allows his characters no obvious thoughts at all. . . .

["Innocent Eréndira"] is about exploitation and what makes exploitation so distressingly easy—the subhuman resignation that has much to answer for in García Márquez's unhappy world. Eréndira [the story's protagonist] is criminally passive. She has the family gift of being able to work even in her sleep and is victimized by nature and human nature alike, being in every sense too dumb to tell the difference.

John Sturrock, "Shorter Márquez," in The New York Times Book Review (© *1978 by The New York Times Company; reprinted by permission), July 16, 1978, p. 3.*

* * *

GARDNER, John 1933-

Gardner, an American novelist, short story writer, essayist, critic, biographer, and children's book author, is also a scholar of medieval literature. As both an artist and a critic, Gardner believes that art should serve a moral purpose, that essentially art is "a game played against chaos and death." The subject of his work is often drawn from myth and legend. Admitting an indebtedness to Chaucer, Dante, and Walt Disney, Gardner is consistently drawn to the fairy tale for the source and style of his writing. The breadth of his learning is revealed in the wealth of allusion from the entire spectrum of Western literary and philosophical tradition found in his work. (See also *CLC*, Vols. 2, 3, 5, 7, 8, and *Contemporary Authors*, Vols. 65-68.)

SUSAN STREHLE

[*The Resurrection* and *Nickel Mountain*, two novels from the "very early" phase of Gardner's career,] resemble each other in several ways. They share an upstate New York setting, which Gardner will replace with more fabulous realms in the later novels. They share an omniscient narrator, presenting plausible characters who speak convincing dialogue; Gardner will use self-conscious and unreliable first-person narrators in the later novels. They share a conventional chronological structure, which will be modified to more experimental forms in the last three novels. *The Resurrection* and *Nickel Mountain* share a large, philosophical focus on the question, posed bluntly and emphatically to James Chandler, *"What is the meaning of life?"* . . . Gardner will rephrase the question and alter the simplicity with which the answer is achieved, but he will not change the affirmative tone of his answer.

Just as the first two novels share similar themes and techniques, they also share a similar flaw. At their worst, they are sentimental; the affirmations made by the protagonists are not earned nor are they fully credible. . . . If sentimentality forms the implicit trap for the affirmative vision, Gardner will avoid it in his last three novels through the use of self-consciousness and humor.

Gardner's last three novels are his best and are distinguished from the first two by their inclusion of the figure of the alien, developed to its fullest in *Grendel*. Gardner's three most compelling characters are aliens: the Sunlight Man, Agathon, and Grendel. Each is an eccentric, estranged from a society he improves through the biting wit of his alienation; each is pitted against righteousness and complacency; each is an artist of sorts: the Sunlight Man with magic, Agathon with fictionalized narrative, and Grendel with poetic myth. Finally, each is a joker, a sad clown, whose jokes emerge like black humor from a mood of despair.

The Sunlight Dialogues and *The Wreckage of Agathon* share a similar theme, in which the metaphysical focus of the earlier novels is replaced by a social focus. Both novels are about the inadequacy of law and the need for justice, the narrowness of codified rules and the need for a broader human understanding. (pp. 87-8)

Though both novels suggest the kind of affirmative vision that remains constant through Gardner's career, its locus is changed from the protagonists' celebration of life to the legacy of understanding they leave for others. (p. 89)

[The] prison cells of both novels are fundamentally alike in spite of the differences of time and space, and the cell works as a controlling metaphor for human experience in both novels. In form, each of the novels replaces the realistic conventions of the earlier works with more experimental techniques. Both play with contrasting narrative perspectives; *The Wreckage of Agathon* contrasts the first-person accounts of mentor and disciple, and *The Sunlight Dialogues* shifts among the consciousnesses of several major and minor characters in the third person. Both works are dialogues of a sort between opposed perspectives on the same events: the Sunlight Man's dialogues with Clumly are echoed in Agathon's dialogues with Peeker.

Finally, both works are self-conscious about their status as fiction. . . . In these two novels, artificially constructed truths survive and, indeed, benefit from the authorial admission of the lie. (pp. 91-2)

While the novels in Gardner's second phase presented the alien figure in dialogue with a member of the society he mocked, the alien Grendel provides the only voice in his novel. His alienation shapes the narrative. (pp. 92-3)

In spite of his view of life as accidental and art as a "gluey whine of connectedness," Grendel becomes an artist. Gardner has commented that "at the end of the novel Grendel himself becomes the Shaper. . . . At the end, Beowulf slams Grendel into a wall and demands that he shape a poem of walls. Grendel responds with an original poem that blends motifs from the Old English alliterative tradition. . . . Not only has Grendel achieved a successful poetic form, but he has arrived at a vision of time as both destructive and creative. His poem is about time's destruction of the walls of Hrothgar's hall and their simultaneous survival through the creative process of art: "these towns shall be called the shining towns" because artistry, the *Beowulf* epic or Grendel's own narrative, connects them in a meaningful vision of human experience. Though he dies by accident, "Blind, mindless, mechanical," Grendel has also arrived at the fortuitous accident of poetry, and as he dies he wonders, *"Is it joy I feel?"* . . . (p. 93)

[The] novel affirms the human ability to learn nobility and dignity through suffering imposed by the alien.

In form, *Grendel* is the most experimental of Gardner's novels. Its twelve chapters follow a year's cycle, and each chapter is keyed to an astrological sign. . . . The chapters are also identified with what Gardner termed "the main ideas of Western civilization." Each chapter presents a spokesman for one of the ideas, which include imperialism, mysticism, materialism, solipsism, and anarchism. As single-minded claims to truth, these ideas appear limited and are meant to be rejected in favor of the seasonal cycle which provides the frame of the novel.... The poetry functions, like the diary entries in *A Portrait of the Artist as a Young Man,* to turn the form of the narrative into a metaphor for its concerns; as Grendel becomes the heir of the Shaper's vision, he also becomes the heir of his craft.

Like *The Wreckage of Agathon* and *The Sunlight Dialogues, Grendel* is a self-conscious novel, but its self-consciousness takes on a more literary, parodic quality and works more successfully for sustained humor. *Grendel* is, first, a literary inversion of the epic *Beowulf*.... The epic is humorously inverted, for Gardner takes the limited viewpoint of the monster, who cannot see the larger meaning of the events he narrates because he lacks an epic perspective. A literary echo of Frankenstein's monster is also made comic by this monster's self-conscious awareness of his own ludicrousness.... Another comic inversion is of Camus's Sisyphus: a mountain goat climbs up to Grendel's mere while Grendel throws stones down at him; the animal, absurdly, refuses either to die or quit climbing, so Grendel continues throwing. While one must imagine Sisyphus happy, one witnesses Grendel simply frustrated.

Out of the self-consciousness of his alien narrator Gardner generates most of the novel's superb, if black, humor. Grendel mocks himself, just as he mocks human society.... Not only is his twentieth-century perspective incongruously comic in the eighth-century setting, but his consciousness of his own ridiculousness is also delightfully humorous.

Gardner has said that "what art ought to do ... is to celebrate and affirm.... Of course, a beautiful affirmation is meaningless if it doesn't recognize all the forces going against it." In his last three novels, Gardner successfully found a way to make the affirmation while acknowledging the forces going against it. His solution came through the figure of the alien, developed at its best in Grendel, who improves the world through the bitter humor of his alienation. Not an affirmer himself, the alien makes possible the affirmation of maturity, complexity, and understanding by other characters. Such a process of growth, Gardner has written, provides the solid truths accessible to the novel.... (pp. 94-6)

Susan Strehle, "John Gardner's Novels: Affirmation and the Alien," in Critique: Studies in Modern Fiction *(copyright © by James Dean Young 1976), Vol. XVIII, No. 2, 1976, pp. 86-96.*

JUDY SMITH MURR

The best key, although a reductive one, to John Gardner's fiction is the narrator's question in *Jason and Medeia:* "Is nothing serious?" In his fiction Gardner engages us in a search for the answer to this question, a search to determine if life is nothing more than a series of comical, meaningless exercises. A representative of order and one of disorder, an adherent to forms and a believer in magical chaos, conduct the quest through a series of bizarre confrontations.... Mythic and quotidian realities inevitably merge in Gardner's work. The answer to his question lies in the

merging of contradictions: "the true measure of human adaptability is man's power to find, despite overwhelming arguments, something in himself to love." Man is ridiculous, his actions are absurd; but such perception and his ability to love regardless grant man his seriousness.

Gardner is, of course, telling us nothing new. He recreates new forms and revitalizes old ones for a new perception of the often-conducted search for meaning. His astoundingly visual prose, his reworking of myths, and his resurrection of old forms (pastoral novel, epic poem) shock us out of our complacency about the nearly exhausted question and its equally repetitive answer. His use of magic and deformity, of the mythic and the common, and his insistence on the positive power of love transport a tired search into an active playground.... Gardner lets us laugh precisely because we are laughable, and only in our ability to laugh can we approach our seriousness. The ridiculous and the serious are inseparable in his fiction; operating simultaneously with and against each other, they bring us into Gardner's funhouse and out into his gravity.

The ridiculous is emphasized by a special kind of deformity, based on the ludicrous.... Antagonistic non-order and protagonistic order repeatedly merge in Gardner's fiction; the deformity of the one merges with and defines the conformity of the other. He brings them together and concerns himself with articulating the result of the confrontation.... Disparate at first, the deformed anarchists and the conformed heroes of law and order are inextricably joined, not without pain and not without healing.... What matters in these meetings is not who wins but what fusion can occur. Both sides are right and wrong; order is as ridiculous as non-order. In their fusion, in the interstices between contradictions, lies the meaning.

Accident necessarily plays a large part in Gardner's fiction; fusion depends on accident as much as anything else, but it is not negative; it rings with the positive value of chaos. (pp. 97-9)

The world of *Grendel* is the mythic stage which occupies half of Gardner's fiction. Absurdity abounds in his legendary retelling, and accident, meaninglessness, and chaos are its bywords. By retelling the myth from the monster's point of view, Gardner places us with Grendel in the underground.... Emphasizing the anarchistic quality of Grendel, Gardner prepares us for the paradoxical fusion of the monster's chaotic world and the ordered world of man. The underground world of Grendel is dark, terrifying, and chaotic, but it is no less frightening or disordered than the above-ground world of man....

Even absurdity, Gardner informs us, must have a focal point for articulation. (p. 99)

His efforts to find order and meaning, to rail against the ultimate truth that all is nothing, haunt Grendel and impel him toward ultimate absurdity. He is ridiculous, his battle is idiocy, but the fight against foolishness is as necessary as its recognition. (pp. 100-01)

"Poor Grendel's had an accident": his closing words are haunted and dignified by the fact that he "could laugh if it weren't for the pain." ... Horribly caught by accident, by the joke he established as truth, the Destroyer finds his dignity in his indignity, his seriousness in his absurdity. Myth is dismissed, order made as laughable as disorder, but what emerges is the truth that the striving toward order is necessary and that our only hope in a world of meaningless non-pattern is the realization of our comical madness. . . .

Grendel, in a sense, is an introduction to Gardner's most complex opposition of order and disorder. *The Sunlight Dialogues* brings both the comic and the grave to extremes and creates a terrifying sanity in a world of preposterous absurdity. Grendel gains self-recognition, and we join with him in serious laughter; the Sunlight Man also learns the truth, but we merge with him in serious laughter and a poignant, loving acceptance of the lunacy of it all. (p. 101)

Gardner alleges, without pejorative judgment, that we are bizarre, deluded, and have meaning only in the momentary fusion of contradictions which is inevitably madness; but our seriousness is in our celebration of our piddling lunacy and the buzzing chaos which surrounds us. Order and disorder are one and the same madness, but they are all we have. In the face of such sparsity, love and laughter are the eternal verities Gardner constructs as our salvation. (p. 107)

> *Judy Smith Murr, "John Gardner's Order and Disorder: 'Grendel' and 'The Sunlight Dialogues'," in* Critique: Studies in Modern Fiction *(copyright © by James Dean Young 1976), Vol. XVIII, No. 2, 1976, pp. 97-108.*

STEPHEN J. LAUT, S.J.

[In *The Life and Times of Chaucer* Gardner] shows both his scholarship and his imaginative talent. Many external facts about Chaucer's life are available; little can be discovered about his inner life, nor about many of the important events of the times. Gardner furnishes what has been learned over the years, and uses his novelist's skill for the rest. Some of this works; some doesn't.

Perhaps the chief problem with the book is that Gardner never aims at a specific audience. The general reader will find out far more than he wants to know. . . . All the dubious data of Chaucer's career are mentioned: his uncertain date of birth, his education, employment, patronage, the questionable details of his marriage and fatherhood, his jobs and places of residence, his financial successes and failures. No place in all this is there certainty. Gardner has to fill in much of his account with "Probably," or "It seems likely that . . ." and "It would be pleasant to think that. . . ." As a result, much of the book is too detailed and too full of minutiae to please the popular audience. As for the scholar, there is too much summary recounting of well-researched commonplaces to be of real appeal. Surprisingly, for a novelist of Gardner's stature, the tone and style of the work is spotty, moving from pedantic to chatty without warning.

As any competent scholar, Gardner has his own axe to grind in many of the details he furnishes and the conclusions he draws. One need not agree with them; however, one must be challenged and provoked to reconsideration by the ideas Gardner puts forward. . . . He finds explanation of much of the poet's art in his encounters with Nominalism, then a great issue at Oxford. Gardner makes a good case for tying the "Marriage Group" of Tales together as a discussion of government. His insights into the personal meaning of many lines of Chaucer's verse is quite persuasive and ingenious. Gardner set himself a formidable task in this book; let us rejoice that he has succeeded as well as he has. (p. 121)

Stephen J. Laut, S.J., in Best Sellers *(copyright © 1977 Helen Dwight Reid Foundation), July, 1977.*

JAY L. HALIO

[*October Light* is a] strange but often beautiful and touching account of two lonely, elderly people, caught up in their memories, their convictions, and their prejudices. . . . *October Light* examines American culture and values retrospectively and, at least at the end, prospectively. Some of those values, embodied in these two sturdy Vermonters and their friends, seem in danger of extinction, about to be swept away by a crasser, younger generation that, paradoxically, they themselves have bred. The title of the book and much of its writing seems to indicate that even in Vermont, or especially there, we are witnessing the twilight of our civilization—a sad, briefly exhilarating period that will relentlessly pass into a dark, wintry time. There are many signs of decadence and degeneration. For example, . . . Sally reads a paperback novel that her grandnephew found in the pigstye and accidentally left behind. Though torn and soiled, with frequent gaps of missing pages, it provides a fascination for her, and she reads the whole thing. An ostensibly cheap thriller filled with sensationalistic accounts of attempted suicides, dope smuggling, sexual license, and other tawdriness, this novel-within-the-novel contrasts and compares with the main events and, in part, offers an oblique running commentary. At one point Sally glimpses that the thriller she is reading is about Capitalism, about the same values her brother holds dear—"An Hour's Work for an Hour's Pay, and Don't Tread on Me, and Semper Fidelis!" If so, it is an utter parody of that system and its values, although how conscious or deliberate a parody she is not sure, and at times Gardner's writing of these episodes rises well above the level he is apparently mocking. Both stories portray more or less unflatteringly the Rugged Individual of a former age, but the alternative of an effeminate dependency is hardly more attractive.

What emerges, then, from James's experience—intolerance of his sister's modern notions, a drunken rampage, his daughter Ginny's almost fatal accident—is a sense that while many of the values he holds dear are still worth preserving, they need not exclude others that may be more compatible with his own than he had previously thought. (p. 841)

[Descriptive passages throughout the novel] show Gardner at his lyric best, a poet really in tune with America's rural music which complements and is older than her urban poetry. (p. 842)

Jay L. Halio, in The Southern Review *(copyright, 1977, by Jay L. Halio), Vol. XIII, No. 4, Autumn, 1977.*

JOSEPH MILOSH

The plot of *Grendel* is based on that of the Old English poem *Beowulf*, though not in an especially straightforward way. The main action of *Beowulf* breaks into four parts: the Grendel episode . . . ; the subsequent battle with Grendel's mother . . . ; the return voyage . . . ; and the dragon fight. . . . In the original, each major conflict concludes before the next begins, and a fifty-year successful reign by Beowulf separates his fight with the dragon from his conquest of Grendel and his mother. Gardner's novel opens with Grendel ravaging Hrothgar's meadhall and men, and ends immediately after the fight with Beowulf, Grendel's death being imminent: this episode represents only about one-fourth of the Anglo-Saxon poem. Both Grendel's mother and the dragon appear, but Gardner assigns them new functions, as well as departing from the chronology of the original.

Gardner's restructuring of the Anglo-Saxon original, which strikingly alters the epic material, points to further literary sources, but the advice of a medieval author, Hugh of St. Victor, should be taken: "Do not strike into a lot of by-ways until you know the main roads: you will go along securely when you are not under the fear of going astray." Concentrating on Gardner's alterations in character, theme, and rhetoric will provide a structure for beginning the task of explicating the art of *Grendel*. (pp. 48-9)

In *Beowulf,* the character Grendel is static. He enters as an evil force, enraged by the music of men and associated with Cain. Like many a pagan in later medieval romance, he appears to require little motivation for his malicious activity. Once on the scene, he is predictable: he will return regularly to find his human dinner, his strength and intent will be invariable so that there is no hope of overpowering him or stirring his pity, and his horrendous deeds will become increasingly terrible in the minds of men because of their repetition. . . .

Gardner's Grendel, on the other hand, is anything but a static character. He grows, passing through several initiations, evolving more than many a modern hero. Grendel begins as an unseen observer of men, reporting their actions and difficulties and threats. He comes into contact with them because he is forced to, and he then seeks to proceed from observation to communication and understanding. . . . (p. 49)

Grendel's response to their violence results in the quick retreat of his attackers and, for the monster, an increasing awareness of his power, particularly his ability to toy with men. The joy which Grendel feels in the destruction of men is itself another indication of his growth and understanding. Ravaging is not merely a vendetta, as it is for Grendel's mother in the original poem. It brings awareness: "I had *become* something, as if born again. I had hung between possibilities before, between the cold truths I knew and the heart-sucking conjuring tricks of the Shaper; now that was passed: I was Grendel, Ruiner of Meadhalls, Wrecker of Kings!" . . . This bloody baptism, intensified by the reference to the reversal of Christian tradition, marks spiritual development just as surely as does the orthodox sacrament it parodies. Grendel is searching for truth, however, so that one step climbed leads but to another on his ladder of imperfection. (pp. 49-50)

In his searching and changing Gardner's Grendel is very like man, again in contrast to the original. His initial contacts with Hrothgar's followers stem from pity for exiles or a desire for friendship . . . , and poetry brings out his tenderness. . . . He knows fear and trembles before the teachings of the dragon . . . , and he responds to beauty with a passion akin to love. . . . (p. 50)

The humanizing of Grendel is necessary to Gardner's portrayal of the absurdity of war. In the original poem, struggle is inevitable, but noble and glorious as well. In *Beowulf,* drinking, boasting, swearing of oaths to serve, and ringgiving are the meadhall counterparts to courage and loyalty on

the modern battlefield: reciprocity strengthens. Conversely, in *Grendel* war loses its nobility and contaminates whatever is associated with it. (pp. 50-1)

Accompanying the humanizing of the monster and the antiheroic war theme is a comment on the poet's role. In Anglo-Saxon society, the scop held a place of honor, bringing dignity to a lord's meadhall. Poems about the scop, like "Widsith" and "Deor," attest to the knowledge of the scop, and his need for a lord. *Beowulf* itself stands as a monument to the Anglo-Saxon poet and his domain, the heritage and actions of great men.

Grendel is an altogether different literary monument. The scop or "Shaper" here is indeed skillful, so skillful that Grendel himself is moved. . . . But the skill is a technical one only, and even then so entirely a product of tradition and convention that the scop himself merits little credit. . . . The motivation of the scop is belittled as much as his conscious artistry. Instead of participating in a lord-retainer relationship with reciprocal benefits and dignity, the scop works simply "for a price," . . . "for pay, for the praise of women—one in particular—and for the honor of a famous king's hand on his arm." . . . When he ceases to please or is displaced, the scop acts like any other entertainer out of work and looks for "refuge in the hall of some lesser marauder." . . . The superficiality of such motivation produces an expected result: he lies. (p. 52)

The changed character of Grendel, the treatment of the theme of war, and the small worth of the poet's art are sufficient indicators of the changes John Gardner has made. The original *Beowulf* has been classified in many terms, all serious, including Tolkien's "heroic-elegiac." *Grendel* is hardly susceptible to those classifications, precisely because it is much more than "the Beowulf legend retold from the monster's point of view," to crib from the cover of the paperback edition. Presented with Gardner's creation, critics have responded variously—understandably enough. (pp. 52-3)

Attempting to resolve, or at least to put into perspective, . . . diverse critical possibilities, a reader might well want to consider what kind of source or analogue provides a framework that can bear all that Gardner achieves and suggests. With a novelist-scholar like John Gardner, looking to the Middle Ages might be productive. *Grendel* is in many ways more like a medieval exemplum than anything else. But that label also says too little, for the contrasts already analyzed are complemented by a certain tone, a tone inconsistent with the simple and serious morality of a typical exemplum. This tone makes *Grendel* a work that eludes categorization. In tone and effect *Grendel* is like a later and very different medieval work, an elusive masterpiece itself, Chaucer's *Nun's Priest's Tale.*

The story of Chauntecleer and Pertelote, the fable of the cock whose prideful singing leads him into the fox's mouth, is merely the core for the exercise of Chaucer's high art of embellishment. The satire of traditional wisdom in the discussion of dreams, dreamlore, and Pertelote's prescription of a laxative for a bad dream; the absurdity of pride in a vulnerable rooster; and the limitation of a world view drawn not from Boethius but from a barnyard—all function together to jest with and undercut the seriousness with which man seeks to understand himself. Gardner's *Grendel* jests with the same seriousness in much the same way.

Traditional wisdom, whether presented pretentiously by the poet or uttered ironically by the dragon, does not help the inquiring Grendel, for it turns out to be neither consistent with reality nor wise. Grendel's struggle to understand this wisdom, judge it, and reject it indeed causes him pain, but it is the pain of a monster who insists upon knowing as truth what was constantly disputed by medieval clerks. The reader can sympathize, but always from a distance, which permits a concurrent smile. So too with the scop, or poet. Like Chaucer's Chauntecleer, Gardner's scop wants to sing with a sense of nobility and dignity, but like Chauntecleer he produces only the sonorous and evanescent, not truth—not even for himself. Further, the scop's desire "for the praise of women—one in particular." . . . is as overtly sexual as Chauntecleer's, and the scop's female audience is remarkably similar to Chauntecleer's entourage of seven admiring and willing hens and his love of one in particular, Pertelote. Finally, the barnyard setting which contains and constrains all this in Chaucer has a direct analogue in *Grendel*. When the monster ponders Hrothgar with amazement, he remarks, "His power overran the world," a questionable enough extrapolation for the greatest of kings, even without the rest of Gardner's sentence: "from the foot of my cliff to the northern sea to the impenetrable forests south and east." . . . Boethian limitations on worldly glory become delightfully amusing, though not necessarily less serious, when transformed into a few square miles of actual terrain and the naïveté of the untraveled observer. Not as strong as flat disrespect or as critical and incisive as satire, the effect of such toying with traditional wisdom is a slightly skeptical questioning.

A second aspect of the tone of *Grendel* grows from Gardner's self-conscious parody of rhetoric. The literary play in *Grendel* demands attention, but with an appreciative grin—unlike the serious rhetoric of the original poem, but very much like the overblown debate rhetoric, the mock-epic epithets, and the incongruous courtly descriptive detail in the *Nun's Priest's Tale*. In *Grendel*, alliterative phrases like "fire-forged" . . . and "squeal and screech," . . . etymological reconstructions like "bone-fire" instead of "bonfire," . . . and litotes like "I am no stranger here," referring to Grendel's eleven years of devastating visits to the meadhall . . . , contribute to the rhetorical density and Anglo-Saxon atmosphere of the work. But juxtaposed against the rhetoric are a reminder of the ignoble work it inflates and a confession of conscious artifice: "No more the rumble of Hrothgar's horsemen, riding at midnight, chainmail jangling in the whistling wind, cloaks flying out like wimpling wings, to rescue petty tribute-givers. (O *listen* to me, hills!)." . . . Intensifying the allusive richness of the lines is the reminiscence of Chaucer's "gynglen in a whistlynge wynd" from the portrait of the superficially attractive Monk, which serves to heighten the contrast between the splendid rhetoric and the self-gratification it admits. The same kind of self-conscious rhetoric undercuts the process of Grendel's learning. At one point he decides to kill the queen for pedagogical purposes, but reconsiders: "I changed my mind. It would be meaningless, killing her. As meaningless as letting her live. It would be, for me, mere pointless pleasure, an illusion of order for this one frail, foolish flicker-flash in the long dull fall of eternity. (End quote.)." . . . Occasionally proud, yet humorous admissions of conscious artistry force the reader to query the tone of all the embellishment in *Grendel*, and consequently to rethink what and how it modifies.

The skepticism resulting from the undercutting of traditional wisdom and from the self-conscious rhetoric, the questing character of Grendel, the antiheroic war theme, and the deception practiced by the poet are of a piece. Questions about truth arise and remain, since answers are at best temporary, but humor keeps despair in abeyance even to Gardner's masterful last chapter.

Grendel's fastidious decision to wear a napkin around his neck for what will be his final meal, his humiliating struggle with a Beowulf who demands songs from the monster tantamount to the schoolyard surrender of "enough," and Grendel's consciousness of dying in full view of animals "evil, incredibly stupid, enjoying my destruction" . . . are Gardner's additions to the Anglo-Saxon original. These scenes provide the background for Grendel's final assessment of his experience, the last lines of the book: "'Poor Grendel's had an accident,' I whisper. *'So may you all'*." . . . Death without nobility, in fact with little more than a whimper, and evidently the result of the capricious goddess Fortuna, provides no answers for the inquiring monster. The curse, understated as it is, gives the reader nothing concrete to fear. Perhaps the final sentence is not a curse at all, but a Boethian observation meant to remind man that he is not in control. Whatever the case, the offhand presentation of this serious lack of resolution is striking. Yet it is perfectly consistent with what Gardner has created, even in the lack of an explicit moral, of clear "sentence." In its final elusive words, *Grendel* is again like Chaucer's masterpiece *The Nun's Priest's Tale*. After the playful telling of the cock-fox story, with its attention to fortune and free will, the Nun's Priest advises, "Taketh the fruyt, and lat the chaf be stille." But Chaucer's tale and its embellishments have been jests, and so *may* be the directive to find truth there. We do not know for sure. John Gardner's *Grendel*, very much a Chaucerian achievement in narrative manner, humor, and rhetorical technique, leaves us in the same quandary—whether to delight in the literary art and not concern ourselves with the ambiguous and elusive morality, or to see our own inquiring minds through Grendel's. Perhaps the very quandary is the curse: *"So may you all."* The answer *may* be significant. (pp. 54-7)

Joseph Milosh, "John Gardner's 'Grendel':
Sources and Analogues," in Contemporary
Literature *(© 1978 by the Board of Regents*
of the University of Wisconsin System), Vol.
19, No. 1, Winter, 1978, pp. 48-57.

MAX APPLE

There is a paragraph toward the end of *On Moral Fiction* in which Mr. Gardner tells us about the kind of frustration which must have led him to publish his beliefs about art in this form.

> . . . I've been in conversations where no one seemed to care about the truth, where people argued merely to win, refused to listen or try to understand, threw in irrelevancies—some anecdote without conceivable bearing, some mere ego flower. A thousand times I have heard some person—some casual acquaintance about whom I had no strong feeling—cruelly vilified, and have found that to rise in defense of mere fairness is to become, suddenly, the enemy. I have witnessed, repeatedly, university battles in

which no one on any side would stoop to
plain truth.

The strength of Gardner's argument comes from his conviction that this "plain truth" is before our eyes. It is the argument of the prophet, the one whose vision is not clouded by the ephemera of his particular time. And such righteous indignation is a strong rhetorical device. The mere force of Gardner's conviction carries a lot of weight. His model seems to be Tolstoy who also sought the "plain truth" and found it in what he called "Christian Art." Gardner has substituted the secular idea of the "moral" to salvage for art among other things, Tolstoy's novels. . . .

He believes that there is some common understanding of how people ought to behave, an understanding that might as well be called "right reason" or "common sense" as any of the more elaborate philosophical terms. It is a feeling that is clear and "moral" and as "old as the hills." Thus Gardner is amazed that most contemporary art, especially fiction, strays so far from this "plain truth."

The particular enemies to the truth as Gardner sees it are the *"merdistes,"* the nay-saying offspring of Sartre affecting nausea in the house of culture. After chastising the "existentialists" Gardner's anger moves to the "trivializers." In this category he seems to include most living fiction writers except John Fowles. (p. 462)

Because Gardner's anger is honest and wholesome the criticism of his contemporaries never descends to mere vindictiveness or gossip. He simply knows what he likes and why he likes it and is ready to share his beliefs. His straightforward sincerity mingled with his certitude make it difficult to detach oneself from his opinions. Here is a respected and popularly acknowledged novelist getting hold of you the way only a skillful essayist does, whispering the "truth" in your ear. It seems almost rude to reject truths offered with such enthusiasm and good intention, but when Gardner moves from the general to the specific it is sometimes as easy to say no to him as it is to the missionary on the street corner. When he tries to ground his argument in the framework of aesthetic theory he is solemnly tedious. When he uses the "touchstones" of Homer or Shakespeare to judge rightly a Ron Sukenick or a William Gass he is indulging in the sort of comic exaggeration he criticizes. Mr. Gardner has the big guns of antiquity in his hip pocket and is quick to use them. His essays on Homer and Dante are splendid interpretations quite apart from their argumentative use in the book. But it sometimes seems as if his admirable sense of the past has distorted his notion of time. The bulk of the argument on literary values concerns fiction written in the past fifteen years. Mr. Gardner is busy judging writers still in the midst of their careers as if they were the "mute inglorious Miltons" of Gray's *Elegy*.

Furthermore, we have the odd circumstance of a serious writer whose own fiction has received acclaim and wide popular acceptance finding threats to the nature of art in the mists of "experimental" fiction where the audience is small enough to fit under Mr. Gardner's fingernail. (pp. 462-63)

The main technique of the trivializers is what Mr. Gardner calls "texture," "fiction as pure language." They create what he calls "linguistic sculpture." They focus "their attention on language, gathering nouns and verbs the way a crow collects paper clips sending off their characters and action to take a long nap." . . .

The failure to see the reality within the exaggeration, the moral within the "trivial," may be Mr. Gardner's literary blind spot. No fiction writer ever has immunity from the charge of being a "trivializer." . . .

When Gardner is making the grandiose claims of art in simple language he is most eloquent. "Art asserts and reasserts those values which hold off dissolution . . . rediscovers, generation by generation what is necessary to humanness." He knows that often writers settle for the tricks of style, and that critics tend to fall into the bureaucracy of their diction. His indignation and the general truths he represents should shake us even when the specifics of his argument do not. (p. 463)

> Max Apple, "Merdistes in Fiction's Garden," in The Nation (copyright 1978 by the Nation Associates, Inc.), April 22, 1978, pp. 462-63.

WEBSTER SCHOTT

In *On Moral Fiction* Gardner pronounces virtually all contemporary art defective. To correct the situation he gives us this "attempt to develop a set of instructions, an analysis of what has gone wrong in recent years with the various arts." It's a thoughtful, amusing, and arrogant little book designed to pick fights, and may get more of them than Gardner can handle. . . .

John Gardner is isolated, idealistic, and ever so gently totalitarian. There is more to art than is accounted for in his philosophy.

Gardner doesn't like what contemporary art does because it's not uplifting. It doesn't inspire. It doesn't celebrate. . . .

Gardner operates a closed system of art. No darkness. . . .

Gardner's attacks on dozens of writers, a particular sculptor, Rauschenberg, and one composer, John Cage, are pertinent chiefly because they show us why Gardner can't win his case.

Partly it's because he is uninformed. He knows a lot about European and American fiction. He knows little of painting, sculpture, and music. And he seems to know almost nothing about anthropology, logic, psychology, and sociology—or he forgets how they impinge on what we call art. How can you construct a field theory of art on such a foundation? Beyond recent literature, mostly in English, Gardner can't extend his proposition that "art instructs" and that "moral art tests values and rouses trustworthy feelings about the better and the worse in human action."

But finally Gardner's proposition won't stand because he can't demonstrate it and history won't support it. Just the contrary, I think. Art does not change us. We change art. The Nazis who murdered Jews at Auschwitz listened to Beethoven at night after their day's work was done. The Russian aristocracy that read Gardner's beloved Tolstoy and Chekhov kept serfs and waged war for sport. Not artists but ideologists like Lenin and Trotsky altered Russian consciousness and social structure.

The way to read *On Moral Fiction* is as a statement of what Gardner likes to see in literature, what many of us wish were true and no one can prove. Art is the expression of the human imagination. It may affirm. More often it protests. It may exist only to be consumed. It may have no measurable utility. Art rises directly from the complexities of the culture that produces it. To assert a dogma of art as another form of religion is to throw history into reverse. Gardner can't give us a theory of art that rises from modern knowledge, so he makes one based on discarding the very art this knowledge has created. If you can't join them, beat them.

> *Webster Schott, "The Sound and the Fury," in* Book World—The Washington Post *(© The Washington Post), April 23, 1978, p. E3.*

*   *   *

GENET, Jean   1910-

Genet is a French novelist, dramatist, and poet. An abandoned child, he spent his youth in prisons and reform schools. Instead of reforming him, he claims, these institutions led him to defy society and to dedicate his life to the pursuit of evil. In his quest for identity, Genet aligned himself with criminals and homosexuals, choosing them as his heroes and their world as his. He posits that evil is superior to good because it is nothingness expressed in its purest form. Susan Sontag wrote of him that "only a handful of twentieth-century writers, such as Kafka and Proust, have as important, as authoritative, as irrevocable a voice and style." (See also CLC**, Vols. 1, 2, 5, and** Contemporary Authors**, Vols. 13-16, rev. ed.)**

JERRY L. CURTIS

Genet's originality stems from the fact that he has cogently chosen to refuse society's values and has set about to reverse, if only for himself, the moral code of our time. His "Jansenism of Evil," as Sartre calls it [in his illuminating study *Saint Genet*], is, in reality, a search for identity in an atmosphere of uncertainty. For Genet, as for Shakespeare, the world is a stage, and you and I, the players.

In his massive biography of Genet, Jean-Paul Sartre states that the key to understanding this admired criminal's self-imposed bastardy can be found in an incident taken from his adolescence: discovered with his hand in a purse, the youthful Genet was market for life by the accusation: "You are a thief." At least he became convinced, according to Sartre, that he should become *"Another than Self."* Since this child of ten did not view himself as an *absolute* criminal yet was extremely intimidated by the unflinching judgment of others, he chose for himself a mode of being which posits its justification in the look of others. . . . [Genet] seems to view literature as a fabric of lies which veil the truth. By means of the mystification called literature, he is able to swindle and rob the public. Genet abandons himself to literature because the fictional world he creates becomes the evasive object of an often credulous body of admirers. He thereby confirms, both to himself and to us, that the world is a stage. The most salient confirmation of his views on the subject, as one might expect, is to be found in his theatre. For his plays, as Leonard Pronko has rightly observed, are rituals where "Genet's characters perform their sacraments." The images we find there are indeed alarming; for they are meant to unmask the duplicitous nature of man's behavior, to reflect our grimaces and masks back to us. (pp. 33-4)

[Genet endeavors to show] the public that the spectator is as deeply involved with role-playing as the actors on the stage. Carried to its logical conclusion, this means that one cannot differentiate between the world outside the theatre and the world within. Genet's theatre must then be seen as an image, or, more exactly, as the reflection of the world. His characters are puppets whose actions are controlled and whose existence can be defined only in terms of the roles assumed, or the function the actors fulfill with relation to each other. For Genet, we, like his actors, are no more than the image or reflection which we see in the eyes and opinions of others. (p. 34)

In assuming the ecclesiastical, judicial and military images of society as their own identities, the three clients [of the brothel in *The Balcony* who travesty a Judge, a Bishop, and a General] find themselves in a situation very similar in nature to the illusory and pleasurable task they fulfilled in the brothel. Now, rather than using prostitutes as the foil of their imaginations, they can rely on the whole of society. The General will have his soldiers, the Bishop his sinners, and there will be criminals for the Judge. The thus-prostituted world becomes a stage where the travestied plays enacted in Irma's brothel are to be re-enacted on a social plane. It is the Bishop who grasps the idea: "As long as we were in the bedroom of a house of prostitution, we belonged to our own fancy: for having exposed it, for having published it, here we are bound together with all men . . . and compelled to continue this adventure according to the laws of visibility." . . .

The so-called "laws of visibility" are precisely those rules by which we exist. The dilemma of man, it is implied, is that he cannot exist as an individual in society, for in order to remain in society, man must relinquish his individuality. This is so because we are what others see in us. They exist, on the other hand, because we see and recognize the roles they play. We *expect* them to act in a given way and they, in turn, act according to our expectation. This *Jeu de glaces* is nothing other than the condition of man.

Genet's theory, in summary, is this: "Those things which are most beautiful on the earth, we owe to masks." . . . While we dispose of two sources of information by which we know things and ourselves—our intimate sense, which furnishes us with subjective information, or the persons around us, who furnish all other information—most of us are satisfied with living in a manner which others expect of us. . . . Thus the theatre of Genet poses the basic question of man's existence—not with relation to the universe, since there is no search for God or transcendent meaning in life—but rather with regard to man's complicitous relationship to man. Genet's theatre leads us to question whether we, any less than the clients of Irma's brothel, are impersonators in a world of dreams and phantasmagorial convention. (pp. 35-6)

Genet's theatre stresses the thesis that because the world is a stage and life itself an inescapable hall of mirrors, one must reveal one's own being, as well as that of all men, as duplicitous or multifarious. In Baudelairean fashion, Genet consents to be trapped by the look of mankind, if only to reflect that look, now deformed and hideous, back to its source. (p. 40)

> *Jerry L. Curtis, in* Modern Drama *(copyright © 1974, University of Toronto, Graduate Centre for Study of Drama; with the permission of* Modern Drama*), March, 1974.*

HARRY E. STEWART

From the very beginning, Genet has been preoccupied with flower imagery and flower symbolism. The two titles, *Notre Dame des Fleurs* and *Miracle de la Rose,* plus the abundance of flower references in all of Genet's works give ample evidence of his interest in, and knowledge of flower symbolism. . . . [There is] a relationship (in Genet's mind) between flowers, crime, and solitude. (pp. 87-8)

An accumulation of the references to lilacs in *Haute Surveillance* reveals a tally of sixteen "lilacs" in the 1949 version, and twelve in the 1965 version. This represents only a count of the nouns and does not include pronouns even when they clearly refer to lilacs. The high frequency of references is immediately significant since it suggests that the lilac symbolism is definitely not fortuitous. However, the frequency of references is less important then the dramatic use of the lilacs as esoteric symbol which explains and supports the meaning and action of the play.

In the 1949 version Genet first establishes a relationship between lilacs and the tomb, that is between lilacs and the general concept "death." This is a traditional relationship found in the majority of folk legends involving lilacs. . . . Genet then develops a sometimes ambiguous symbol pattern in which there exists a confusion between the flower-death-criminal-sex symbol and the lilac-death-murder-fate-betrayal-criminal-sex symbol. Genet, aware that his symbols do not correlate as exactly as he wishes, clarified the symbol pattern in the 1965 edition by changing the word "lilacs" to "flowers" . . . , thus establishing a dichotomous symbol pattern in which both lilacs and flowers correlate to criminals and sex, but only the lilac equates to murder.

The above distinction between murder and death is necessary because death is not the major theme in this play that it is, for example in *les Bonnes* or *le Balcon.* Murder is important because it provides the linking element between the criminal and the saint, and because it is the common denominator in determining the level of attainment in the religious-criminal hierarchy. . . . The central theme of the play is Lefranc's desire to advance in the religious-criminal hierarchy from mere petty thief-supplicant . . . to murderer-saint. One function of the lilacs, which are involved in both Yeux-Verts' murder of the girl and Lefranc's murder of Maurice, is to force the comparison between Yeux-Verts' essentially accidental and unwanted murder and Lefranc's consciously chosen crime in order to illustrate that Genet's sympathy lies with Lefranc.

In both versions of the play, Genet moves from the lilac-flower-death symbol to a flower-criminal symbol. (pp. 88-9)

In both French and English there are various slang expressions in which the word flower is a sexual euphemism—for example, to "deflower." Genet, in *Miracle de la Rose,* uses the word "effleuré" (note the root of the word is "flower") to mean "one who is buggered," and in *Notre Dame des Fleurs* he compares the male sex organ to a lily. In describing Harcamone's murder of the ten or eleven year-old girl, Genet says that Harcamone "ne pouvait garder plus longtemps sa fleur," a clear reference to his virginity. Since Harcamone is the prototype for Yeux-Verts, and since Yeux-Verts' murder is patterned after Harcamone's, it seems likely that the lilac reference here means that the girl followed Yeux-Verts because she wanted his sex. Furthermore, Yeux-Verts demonstrates that his nickname—

"Paulo les dent fleuries"—is indeed appropriate for he had a bunch of lilacs between his teeth when he attracted the girl. (pp. 90-1)

The progression toward a climax continues with Lefranc's announcement that he has finished with flowers, that he intends to create his own flowers. . . . Lefranc's statement is related to the fact that he has written letters for the illiterate Yeux-Verts, and on these letters Lefranc has sketched flowers and doves. It must be noted that Lefranc also has a penchant for sketching false tattoos in imitation of famous criminals, and, in the criminal hierarchy, there is a unique symbolism attached to these tattoos. . . . It is not the flowers, nor the tattoos themselves that fascinate Lefranc-Genet, it is their symbology, their mythical aspect. When Lefranc says he has finished with flowers, he means that he has finished with vicarious experience, with sketching flowers for other people, with trying to live someone else's myth. When he says that he will create his own flowers (a reminder of Genet's intention to so bedeck his convicts with flowers that they will become gigantic and new flowers), he means that he wants to establish his own myth. . . . (pp. 92-3)

By killing Maurice and by involving the lilacs in the gesture . . . , Lefranc seeks to create his own myth as "The Lilac Murderer" (to "become a flower, a gigantic and new one"), and to advance in the criminal-religious hierarchy from petty thief to murderer. (p. 93)

Unlike most flowers, there is no biblical or even Christian symbolism connected with the lilac, quite simply because the lilac is not mentioned in the Bible and because it was not introduced into Europe until the sixteenth century. Thus Genet was quite free to find "therein the many meanings I wish to find." Generally, in the so-called "language of flowers," the lilac is a symbol of the first emotions of love, which is not without ironic implications in so far as Harcamone's murder (the probable source of *Houte Surveillance*) of the ten or eleven year old girl is concerned. Furthermore, it is traditional in England and in Germany that it is "unlucky to bring lilacs in the house, but elsewhere only the white, which will cause a death in the household." It would seem that Genet began with a basic symbol, that is, it is unlucky to take lilacs into a house for they will cause a death, and then expanded this symbol to include the basic themes of the play—murder, betrayal, fate, sex, and the criminal-religious hierarchy. (pp. 93-4)

> *Harry E. Stewart, "The Case of the Lilac Murders: Jean Genet's 'Haute Surveillance',"* in French Review *(copyright 1974 by the Association of Teachers of French), October, 1974, pp. 87-94.*

GAY McAULEY

In [*Les Nègres*] the characters are masks, they exist as appearance only, and the black skin of the negroes is as much a mask as the grotesque white masks of the actors who mirror us, the white audience, and our society; the dramatic action is presented as performance, and the ritual qualities of this performance are emphasized by incantations, chanting and dancing as well as by echoes of rituals which are central to our christian civilisation: the *litanie des blèmes,* the music of the *dies irae* chanted at the time of the ritual murder, etc. (p. 51)

The printed edition of Genet's play is prefaced by the following note: . . .

> One evening an actor asked me to write a play for an all-black cast. But what exactly is a black? First of all, what's his colour?

This most accurately sums up the whole tone of the play, for Genet has taken the "colour" or "race" problem, and has used it as an image for an even wider theme. As he presents it, all identity is a matter of mirror reflections, you define yourself in relation to other people, you know who you are through the reflection of yourself that you see in other people's attitudes to you. This means that personal identity becomes very much a social question, intimately concerned with the power structure of society and with relations of dominance and submission.

The blacks see themselves as defined by their colour; as Neige says, . . . "My colour! Why, you're my very self!" . . . They have no separate, individual identity for the whites but are first and foremost *black* . . . and so they accept the definition and even reinforce it to emphasise their identity: at the beginning of the play, Félicité, the black queen, mother of the black race, ceremonially blackens the face of Village (the negro who will commit the ritual murder of the white woman). (p. 52)

[The] one thing that [the blacks] can do, is to ensure that the image in which they as individuals have been drowned, is one which will terrify their white creators. . . . Hence the ritual murder of the white woman, the systematic reversal of all white values, the glorification of hatred and ugliness.

We are confronted, then, with two groups: the dominant, grotesque whites on their raised platform, spectators like us, and the subservient blacks, performing for their masters, acting out the horrible role allotted to them by the whites, committing murder. . . . Genet shows us that the dominance of the whites is only apparent: they are spectators, not performers, and so are in fact on the receiving end. When the white Queen finally confronts Félicité in the jungle, she realizes that they are Blacks (that is to say, not the niggers of white invention, but something else, not a mere opposition to white, but something positive. . . . As Félicité puts it:

> . . . we were Darkness in person. Not the darkness which is absence of light, but the kindly and terrible Mother who contains light and deeds. . . .

So the whites depend for their identity on the blacks, just as much as *vice versa,* and in this way Genet carries his theme beyond the social implications of the central images, and raises questions about reality and identity as such. (p. 53)

Genet . . . uses singing throughout *Les Negres:* the play begins and ends with the incongruous dignity of a Mozart minuet, there is the recitative as they smoke around the corpse, the lullaby as they reject Diouf, the elemental tribal rhythms of the dance after the whites are massacred, and the echoes of the christian mass. . . . In all of these instances, Genet is drawing attention to the performance as performance and to the ritual qualities of the play (both of which are important thematically), and at the same time playing on various incongruities, contrasts and oppositions that continually emphasize the duality which is clearly such an important part of the central image. (pp. 57-8)

Genet has his pseudo-white audience on stage, facing the real white audience in the auditorium, thus forcing the spectators to be aware of themselves, both as spectators and as whites, in the spectacle of the grotesque, distorting mirror that faces them, and . . . drawing attention to the simultaneous existence of stage and auditorium. (p. 58)

In *Les Nègres,* the curtain is drawn to reveal what is apparently a coffin, draped with a white cloth and covered with flowers. This coffin is the central focus of all the action, the body of the murdered white woman is present, as they prepare to re-enact the murder and be judged for it. When judgement is about to be pronounced, it is revealed that the coffin is not a coffin at all, and that the cloth covers only two chairs, chairs that really belong to the Valet and the Bishop, and that they have been complaining about throughout the play. This lends visual reinforcement to the idea that the whites are dependent for their identity on the blacks, and if the blacks do not play the game, then they, the whites, risk begin swallowed up in a gulf of nothingness. . . . The two chairs become a kind of visible scandal, an insolent reminder that power is also powerlessness, that everything contains its opposite, a reminder also of the nothingness, "le vide," that threatens all appearance. At the end of the play, Ville de St. Nazaire, significantly the one who has been the link with the off-stage trial, the "real" trial, comes on with another coffin, and the set up is as it was in the beginning, and the minuet starts again. But this time we know that the coffin is not just a cloth draped over two chairs, for we have seen the box carried in, but our faith in reality has been so undermined that we hesitate to claim it as a real coffin. The fact that it is Ville de St. Nazaire who brings it in, adds further ambiguities: he is the one who may be expected to have access to a corpse (as there has been an execution off stage), but the body will be that of a negro traitor, not a white woman; however, the white victim of the performance is played by Diouf, the black considered by the others to be a traitor, because of his acceptance of white religion. And so we go round and round again, led on by Genet in this way, too, to discover only layer upon layer of appearance or illusion or performance instead of the truth or reality we seek. (pp. 60-1)

In *Les Nègres* the blacks have a certain individual reality, their off-stage existence, as prostitute, curate, etc., has some bearing on the part they play in the performance and on their attitude to it; however, we are not presented with individuals, and the whole message of the play is that their real off-stage reality is their blackness, this is what defines them and denies them individual existence. (p. 61)

[*Les Nègres* uses the device of the play within the play] intensively, and indeed it is central to the whole action: the blacks perform for the pseudo-whites on stage, but all are performing for another audience, not physically represented on stage, so as to mask the fact that there is a real trial going on elsewhere, and of course the implications are there for the "real" white audience, sitting there and being entertained (or distracted) by the real black actors. . . . Performance within performance, audience within audience, play within play—all these are images of the multiple levels of reality or appearance that Genet is concerned with, and his play is structured in such a way that all the levels of performance cut into one another, undermine one another, and together undermine the whole concept of reality. (p. 63)

Gay McAuley, "The Problem of Identity:

Theme, Form and Theatrical Method in 'Les Negres,' 'Kaspar' and 'Old Times'" (a revision of a speech originally delivered at the University of New South Wales in August, 1973), in Southern Review (copyright 1975 by Gay McAuley), March, 1975, pp. 51-65.

ALBERT BERMEL

Genet's plays, like Pirandello's, have become a treasure house for the rococo critical imagination. As the visitor basks in the heady atmosphere—the mirrors, the screens, masks, grandiose costumes and *cothurni,* the role-playing, verbal efflorescence, and paradoxes—he burbles about the undecipherable nature of levels, dimensions, contexts, multiple images, loci, ritualism, and infinities of reflections. . . .

Genet takes for granted [in *The Balcony* the] confusion between sexual and social obsessions. In the brothel's studios the devotees abandon themselves to sexual consecration; the house of pleasure is a house of worship. In it each man finds a contrary, double satisfaction: he acquires a feeling of potency from the clothes and the role he puts on; at the same time he abases himself in that role. Or rather, he abases the role and its clothing in order that it may serve his sexual satisfaction. There is then an element of masochism in each of the aberrants' personalities. . . .

From the first Genet intermingles sexual and religious ceremonies. Scene One sets the tone by introducing us to the Bishop in a studio set that represents a sacristy. He wears robes of exaggerated size so that he looks larger than human, like a principal in a Greek tragedy. (p. 268)

Now, although we are led to believe that this Bishop is played by a gas man, we never see the gas man, only the Bishop. There may be a gas man in the story but there is none in the action; and if a gas man in Bishop's apparel differs dramatically from a bishop in bishop's apparel, Genet declines to show us the difference; if we insist that this is a gas man *metaphorically* wearing a bishop's mask, that mask then has the same lineaments as the face behind it—or else it is transparent—or else it is not a mask any longer but has become a face. . . .

[The other patrons of the brothel] seem to don roles the way some tribesmen assume charms, as a plea to heaven for virility and safety. But Genet shows us only the roles. These roles *are* the characters. (p. 269)

In [Pirandello's] *Six Characters in Search of an Author,* the six characters are actually in search of an audience. An author may dream up the Father, but it takes a spectator to recognize him as that character. . . .

Genet introduces something like this reciprocity into the action of *The Balcony.* To be the Bishop, the character needs an "opposite," a penitent, somebody who will confess to him and whose sins he will absolve, somebody who will certify him as the Bishop. . . . But if the function of the opposites is to take the kinkies seriously and attribute roles to them, the girls seem unable to take themselves seriously *as opposites.* They keep breaking out of their parts and virtually winking at the audience: in the Judge's scene the Executioner does "exchange a wink with the Thief." These girls are never anything but whores.

Later in the play the opposites become dispensable. When the Envoy asks the kinkies to drive through the city in a coach as the "real" Bishop, Attorney-General, and General, they feel nervous about abandoning their brothel scenarios and translating themselves from private images in Irma's studios into public images in the world at large. . . . When their public performance begins, the only doubt that arises is whether they will sustain their parts convincingly or look like kinkies.

At this point, in the absence of the brothel girls, the task of being a collective "opposite" or role-confirmer falls to the general public. We do not see this public, but we do learn subsequently that it accepted the Bishop, Judge, and General for real, without question. Possibly the public was blinded by the "gold and glitter" that surrounded the dignitaries. In any event, it responded favorably; it threw flowers and cheers at them; it even blew them kisses. And why not? We, the other "general public," have already attributed these roles to the kinkies; to us they have *become what they pretended to be.* (p. 270)

Irma is another case in point. The Envoy asks her to stand in for the missing queen. . . . Irma is not impersonating the queen, but extending her own personality. She is playing *herself,* and the Envoy, who later says she made a first-rate queen, functions as her opposite. As though to underscore this conclusion, at a certain point in the text Genet drops her name and starts calling her the Queen; it is the most natural thing in the world for this procuress to assume royalty.

What does Genet mean by this demonstration? That life is all pretext, appearances, theatre? I think he is driving us toward a narrower, sharper, and more satirical conclusion: bishops, judges, and generals are kinkies; queens are procuresses; opposites (the public) who take these figures at their dressed-up value and serve them are whores: revolutionary slogans and symbols (Chantal) are whore-mongering.

Genet likens this state of affairs to the performance of a play. But Irma's much-quoted final speech, which compares her brothel with a theatre, has been frequently misunderstood:

> In a little while, I'll have to start all over again . . . put all the lights on again . . . dress up. . . . *(A cock crows)* Dress up . . . ah, the disguises! Distribute roles again . . . assume my own. . . . *(She stops in the middle of the stage, facing the audience.)* . . . Prepare yours . . . judges, generals, bishops, chamberlains, rebels who allow the revolt to congeal, I'm going to prepare my costumes and studios for tomorrow . . . You must now go home, where everything—you can be quite sure—will be even falser than here. . . .

She is not saying that life is less "real" than Genet's theatre (or her brothel) is. To claim this on his behalf would be to deprive the play of its application to life. She is insisting that there are more disguises and pretense in life than in the theatre, and that in life the disguises are harder to discern. A play can show us, more clearly than a scrutiny of life can, what life is really about. It can reveal kinks and shams for what they are. It can do a sorting job, bring life into focus. It can make us laugh at these characters . . . until we realize that we are laughing at ourselves. For if we have accepted what the play says, we are the people who make bishops, judges, and generals out of kinkies, and queens out of whore-mistresses.

Most of the criticism of *The Balcony* fastens on to other aspects of it, in particular the rituals, disguises, and mirrors, which are constantly held up as prima-facie evidence of Genet's contempt for reality: his masks beneath masks, reflections within reflections, screens behind screens, and other infinite recessions. (pp. 271-72)

What is a ritual? It is a prearranged ceremony. A church service is a ritual; so is a public parade. They go according to form, according to plan. There are no serious hitches, no divergences from the timetable or program. If a horse in a parade kicks an onlooker or if one of the ceremonial figures passes out, that part of the ritual resembles theatre. But ritual is the opposite of theatre, just as the girl who plays the Penitent is the opposite of the Bishop. She defines him, and ritual defines theatre; it marks one of theatre's boundaries by being what theatre is not: predictable, self-contained, formal. (p. 272)

[The screens, disguises and mirrors] are part of a device that Genet uses theatrically, not ritualistically. And far from telling us that nothing is real, they tell us that in the brothel, as in the playhouse, everything is adaptable. . . .

Irma thoughtfully provides a mirror for each studio. The Bishop gazes into his and is smitten with his image. . . . Up to now he has not tasted the power of being a bishop; he uses the image in the mirror for erotic stimulation, yet even as he does he appeases his power-lust by profaning the robes and "destroying" their "function."

The Judge, too, has a mirror available to him, but does not use it. Instead he looks at beefy Arthur, the male whore, and talks lovingly to him as though to an idealized version of himself, heavy wtih tangible musculature. . . . (p. 273)

The mirror in the General's studio has the same purpose again. Admiring his image in it, the General sees shining back at him an historical validation: he is the hero of Austerlitz, Napoleon vanquishing the Austrians. . . . As in the two previous scenes, the kinky loves his image in the mirror because what he sees there is *himself transfigured.*

As an element in the stage design, the mirrors have a further purpose, suspense. Each one is angled to reflect to the audience part of Irma's room. We will not see that room until Scene Five, but the mirrors forecast it. They alert us to Irma's omnipresence as the brothel's grandmistress, and they hint at the immensity of the premises. (pp. 273-74)

By reflecting the studios and Irma's room to each other, they enlarge the brothel and unify the scenes. They also enlarge the studios: mirrors make a room look artificially bigger.

Genet's language serves as another means of enlargement and ratification. The Bishop says, "We must use words that magnify." And most of the characters do. Their speeches move effortlessly out of conversation and into clusters and imagery. Genet sometimes handles images the way a writer like Shaw handles logic, with comic hyperbole. By exalting the dialogue, raising it beyond simple meanings, he frees it from the constraints of everyday banter and attains a language that can cope with complicated states of consciousness. (p. 274)

The brothel . . . seems to resemble a vast, rotating movie lot with the sound stages distributed around the hub of Irma's office. Genet does not provide a full list of the studi-

os, but if we visualize each one as a miniature of some activity outside the theatre and brothel, the brothel is a miniature of society as a whole. The mirrors in each scene reflect the world to itself. (p. 275)

As a satire of society, *The Balcony* laughs at men in authority as they seek for images of themselves that they can love. It laughs more bitterly at men without authority who defer to those images (attribute them) and even worship them. Both groups are taking part in a game. X names himself a judge or bishop or general. He drapes himself in an awesome outfit, grows confident from the feeling of being dressed up and from the sight of his magnified reflection, and so enlarges himself artificially in the eyes of other men. His old self or personality fades away.

These games are what gives the play its unity of tone, games such as I'll-be-bishop-and-you-be-penitent. But they are games played in earnest; games propelled by desperate intentions; games that are liable, because of their peculiarities, to invoke the unexpected; games of life and death.

Now, games are play and the gerund *playing* has two principal meanings: it means enjoyment, as in a house of pleasure; it also means mimesis. . . . The Bishop begins by masturbating or "playing" with himself; he ends by wishing to play with other men's lives, to move them about like pieces: "Instead of blessing and blessing and blessing until I've had my fill, I'm going to sign decrees and appoint priests." (p. 276)

Theatre, as an arena for games, plays by heightening its effects. In his playhouse-brothel Genet takes this heightening to a personal extreme. He pours into his drama a sumptuous language, bulks out his conceptually big characters with padded costumes; and seizes other theatrical opportunities, such as keeping visible that token of the post-Renaissance, indoor theatre, the chandelier.

As part of the heightening procedure he plants contradictions in the characters' desires: they feel pulled between playing games of sex (the mastery of themselves) and games of authority (the mastery of others). Genet marries the contradictions, without trying to resolve them, in an ingenious way: he implies that power over oneself and power over others can be achieved simultaneously by playing games of death.

In the early scenes he seems to show us the brothel as a theatricalization of life, of real life, with a real bishop, judge, and general giving rein to their all-too-real kinks in order to live at the top of their bent. But there are plenty of hints that death is a more attractive game for them to play than life is. . . .

At last it is the turn of the gaudiest character in *The Balcony* to play the game of death. He is the Police Chief, Georges by name, the ultimate provenience of power in the state. (p. 277)

Genet's exquisite irony intensifies. Georges decides that his ideal memorial, his death-in-life, would be for somebody to impersonate him in the brothel. While the impersonator mimics him, he will mimic death by disappearing to "wait out the regulation two thousand years," the equivalent of the Christian era. The two millennia will sanctify him, much as the Church (the Bishop), the Law (the Judge), and the Military (the General) have been sanctified by the two millennia since the death of Christ and the decline of Rome.

He will, we assume, mimic resurrection too when he feels like it, and re-emerge as top dog in the state. (pp. 277-78)

Fortunately for Georges, Roger the defeated revolutionary comes into the brothel expressly to impersonate him. No sooner is he inside a studio (which is got up to look like a mausoleum) than Roger is awarded his "opposite," a slave, to attribute to him the role of Police Chief. But Roger is still secretly a rebel. And in him the revolution twitches its final, futile defiance.

He ends his scenario by making "the gesture of castrating himself." With this gesture he hopes to mutilate the image of the Police Chief as a man of power.... For the purposes of the play, he is dead. And his gesture has gone awry. Trying to discredit Georges, he has succeeded only in becoming Georges' opposite, an impotent, and in confirming Georges. (p. 278)

Georges, Genet's most savage portrait in the play, is so unmanned that he cannot play out his own fantasies. He must wait until somebody does the job for him by proxy—anybody, no matter who, an avowed revolutionary if necessary—just so long as he does not get hurt. Now he can go into his two-thousand-year hibernation. A studio has been prepared. It is a mocked-up replica of a tremendous piece of architecture still in the planning stage. It incorporates law courts, opera houses, railroad stations, pagodas, monuments.... But this edifice is no less than a magnification of the brothel, right down to the mirrors. Like the brothel, a floating balcony, it will "sail in the sky" on top of its mountains. Here Georges's image will live on with its wound, while he plays the game of death in a brothel mausoleum. The image will evoke the images we retain of other symbolically castrated heroes: the shorn Samson, the blinded Oedipus, Philoctetes and his rotting foot, Christ crucified.

A magnified image in a magnified brothel. So much, says Genet, for your saints and heroes. (pp. 278-79)

> *Albert Bermel, "Society as a Brothel: Genet's Satire in 'The Balcony'," in* Modern Drama *(copyright © 1976, University of Toronto, Graduate Centre for Study of Drama; with the permission of* Modern Drama*), September, 1976, pp. 265-80.*

*　　　*　　　*

GILLIATT, Penelope　1932-

Gilliatt is an English novelist, short story writer, film and drama critic, screenwriter, and editor. Critics have praised her attentiveness to detail, her sophisticated use of word play, and her ear for dialogue. (See also *CLC*, Vol. 2, and *Contemporary Authors*, Vols. 13-16, rev. ed.)

ABBY ANN ARTHUR JOHNSON

In *Nobody's Business* ... Gilliatt criticizes those who would organize life on scientific principles, who would use the computer to make sense of erratic human nature. In the face of computer analysts and efficiency experts, Gilliatt turns to that which celebrates the diversity and dignity of human life. (p. 322)

Throughout the collection, Gilliatt suggests that interpersonal communication deteriorates when computers and machines gain pre-eminence. This emphasis reaches its fullest expression in "Property," a story reminiscent of Samuel Beckett's *Endgame*. Confined to their individual beds, wired to separate electrocardiographs, a triangle of two men and one woman endure a hellish existence. The threesome understand neither themselves nor each other, as the absurdist dialogue indicates.

The machines are powerful, but the mechanical way of life is not inevitable. The final lines of the concluding tale, "Nobody's Business," summarize the heart of Gilliatt's statement. Emily Prendergast, who writes for the radio "the most popular low comedies of the century," expresses her understanding of life: "Nobody can do what he can't ... Unless he has a terrific wish to.... Then I expect he could." Earlier in the volume, the "dispossessed"—a schizophrenic woman, a crippled young man, a bastard born to a British gentleman and a poor Indian—say much the same.

Gilliatt makes her point by using wit and understatement. In all the nine stories, she advances humor as a weapon mighty in a confrontation with the mechanical and standardized. Speaking for Gilliatt, and for her "dispossessed" heroes and heroines, a character asserts that "one comes to rely on one's bit of fun." Perhaps the best wit appears in the last selection, which particularly shows Gilliatt's gift for comedy. While swimming with her husband, a former suitor, and two young archivists, Emily Prendergast nearly drowns, seized with a fit of convulsive and unexpected laughter. She is saved by her seventy-four year old husband, apparently only an adequate swimmer. The two archivists are excellent at the butterfly stroke and therefore totally ineffective in the crisis. Imbued with scientific methods, they are merely good at retrieving obscure bits of information. To the very end of *Nobody's Business,* then, Gilliatt maintains her unity of theme and her appealing sense of humor. She thereby offers to the public a book which should be the "business" or concern of those readers interested in contemporary short fiction. (pp. 322-23)

> *Abby Ann Arthur Johnson, in* Studies in Short Fiction *(copyright 1974 by Newberry College), Summer, 1974.*

ANATOLE BROYARD

[The stories that compose "Splendid Lives" are] resolute in forcing the reader to make up his own mind as to what he is supposed to feel after finishing them. I suppose that a virtuoso of exegesis might apply an almost unlimited number of interpretations to them, for, God knows, they are wide open to the winds of doctrine.

I propose to attempt only one, to resist the seduction of supererogation. It is possible to read "Splendid Lives" just as the title suggests, as stories about people who are not constricted by convention or economic considerations, who are free to follow their impulses and to need nothing more than impulse to satisfy themselves. This is not an altogether unrealistic depiction of a certain style in contemporary life. While the stories have what might be called the authority of eccentricity, I wish that they had more literary security—better-turned sentences, apter invention, more appealing or dimensional characters, a behavioral curve that pleases the mind as an agreeably contoured landscape pleases the eye.

In my reading, the stories work—if they do work—by virtue of their texture, relying on the unexpected or incongruous to keep the reader from growing restive or bored.

When we do finally grow restive under such unremitting stimulation, the stories break off. Discontinuing in the middle of things, they baffle us, and this bafflement acts as a depressant that quells impatience. You have to concede that it's all very ingenious.

A writer who opposes the fatigue of the ordinary, who suggests a liberating gratuitousness as a counterpoint to riveting purpose, who lets air—even if it's hot air—into our lives, ought to have some claim on our gratitude. I take off my humdrum metaphorical hat to Miss Gilliatt. (p. 12)

> *Anatole Broyard, in* The New York Times Book Review *(© 1978 by The New York Times Company; reprinted by permission), January 29, 1978.*

SUSAN WOOD

[The stories in *Splendid Lives*] are amusing, even at times hilarious, in a quiet, British sort of way. Still, one doesn't quite know what to make of them beyond that; the stories seem to end at an arbitrary point, leaving one wondering what the point in fact was. I suspect that Gilliatt doesn't intend to make one, and that has its own virtues, though one wishes that behind the charming surface the characters had more dimension, more resonance.

The way to read *Splendid Lives* is one story at a time, delighting in its ingeniousness, expecting nothing more. (p. E5)

> *Susan Wood, in* Book World—The Washington Post *(© The Washington Post), March 12, 1978.*

EILEEN KENNEDY

Gilliatt is a comic writer with a piercing eye for the zany, the bizarre, the eccentric, but she lacks the intellectual energy and philosophical breadth, the penetrating view that's true of [Iris] Murdoch at her best. . . . Gilliatt is as witty, glib, as tangy, but thin as peanut brittle. Mistress of dialogue, of the flashy remark and the unusual situation, she seems to be afraid of exploring a situation, of developing a character, of examining the serious emotions. . . . She's quick, a phrasemaker, an evoker of fleeting attitudes, a conjurer-up of domestic situations, where frequently the women are strong, monolithic, and loving, and the men passive, ineffectual cadgers.

[The nine stories in *Splendid Lives*] are billed as English and American, but Gilliatt's American settings lack verisimilitude. Her grasp of American idiom is tenuous. . . .

Gilliatt has the potential to explore human comedy and human tragedy, as in the best story of the lot, "Catering," which treats mother love, fidelity, caring, fertility, and abortion. But the wonderful mother in this story is never fully developed, is only sketched in through a hilarious, yet almost painful, description of her meagre house as she home-caters a wedding for 125. We want to know the mother better, but Gilliatt makes her too inarticulate, too much like a dumb beast of burden, to be able to carry the tragic dimension. Another potentially fine story, "Fleecing," fails to touch the emotions, though the tutor-boy relationship is well done, because the author skimps on developing the climactic moment. . . .

I suspect that because the short story demands much more verbal analysis than a film—where the visual carries so much of the meaning—Gilliatt errs in applying film-writing techniques to fiction. The House of Fiction does have many doors, but Gilliatt has yet to earn her place there. (p. 6)

> *Eileen Kennedy, in* Best Sellers *(copyright © 1978 Helen Dwight Reid Educational Foundation), April, 1978.*

JAMES BROCKWAY

In *Splendid Lives*, Penelope Gilliatt skates brightly on the surface . . . , whether in England or the States, but there is a humour, a critical discernment and a keen, satirical mind at work here, which make for more briskness and more fun.

These lives are far from splendid, although the satire in the first story, about an elderly English bishop, cossetted and materially secure—in fact everything His Lord said he should not be—is so velvet-gloved, you might miss it at first. . . . The social observation . . . is sharp-sighted, the writing alert, the dialogue true to (awful) life. The stories tend, however, to be shapeless, to end abruptly, as though the authoress didn't know where to go from there and didn't much care, either. . . . But despite their brisk, modern air and their satire, these stories are not really funny any more than these modern lives are splendid. All rather sad, really. (p. 51)

> *James Brockway, in* Books and Bookmen *(© copyright James Brockway 1978; reprinted with permission), April, 1978.*

*   *   *

GLISSANT, Édouard   1928-

A Martinican poet, novelist, playwright, and editor, Glissant explores in his fiction the condition, culture, and history of West Indians. His first novel, *La Lézarde*, won the prestigious Renaudot Prize.

BEVERLEY ORMEROD

Among those who have sought beyond *négritude* for a more realistic approach to the problem of Caribbean identity, perhaps the most assured and convincing is the Martinican author Édouard Glissant. (p. 361)

In place of *négritude*, Glissant offers in his poetry, novels, and theater a new world view, of which the Caribbean is the center. Africa remains present in his system of thought, but not as a metaphor for black beauty or vanished dignity: Africa is, for Glissant, an instructive actuality, a paradigm of social cooperation. The African pattern of sharing, the prizing of the community above the individual, is opposed by Glissant to the European cult of personality and free will which militates against the concepts of participation and universality. (p. 362)

Poetry, in European tradition the most arcane of arts, is seen by Glissant as an obligation to explore *and reveal,* to understand the nature of things and to share this understanding. Where the conventional European lyric was content to immortalize an "anecdote"—a moment of joy or suffering—modern poetry should be concerned with man and his destiny, not with men and their personal concerns. (pp. 362-63)

The idea of history is omnipresent in Glissant's work: much of his poetry is devoted to what he has called "a prophetic vision of the past.'' Glissant shares with many West Indians a desire to restore and elucidate the vast areas of the Caribbean past which have been ignored by European historians or else recorded with an unjust bias. . . .

[History] is viewed optimistically as a possible means of arriving at prescriptions for the contemporary situation. But history is also viewed in a wider context, as a particular obsession of those born in the Americas, who are impelled by the urge to define their own heritage and to establish a tradition apart from Europe. (p. 363)

[Underlying] all of Glissant's works is a deep political commitment to the concept of Martinique's independence from France. This concern is evident not only in the themes of his novels, but in the painful descriptions of Caribbean aimlessness and improvisation, and in the familiar dichotomy of brilliant nature and abject humanity which recurs in much of his poetry. Among the many poetic symbols in Glissant's work, the one which seems above all to encapsule the predicament of Martinique is the symbol of the serpent. For Glissant the serpent is an icon of historical ambiguity: potentially beneficent (in Africa a tutelary spirit associated with the mythology of creation, in Europe the symbol of knowledge), yet in fact deadly in Martinique, which is infested with poisonous snakes. (In a certain tradition of despair and resignation, the belief is held both that the European colonizers imported snakes deliberately and set them against the runaway slaves, and that at the same time the snakes of Martinique represent Africa's revenge on her Caribbean descendants for having rejected their ancestry.) (pp. 366-67)

Glissant's ultimate message seems to point the way beyond the present impasse, to come to terms with the twin serpents of alienation from Africa and intellectual dominance by Europe. It is interesting to recall that the phallic symbolism of the snake is present in both cultures, in the Ashanti myth of procreation as well as in *Genesis,* and Glissant's solution is bound up with the phenomenon of cultural synthesis. (pp. 367-68)

Glissant's attitude to cultural synthesis is . . . directly related to the social realities of the Caribbean and to the vexed question of *métissage* (race mixing). He sees *négritude,* a reaction to white cultural supremacy, as paradoxically defined and limited by reference to, and comparison with, European culture. This simple black-white opposition fails to take into account the undeniable fact of the extent to which the races have mingled in the French Caribbean. Glissant proposes an undramatic acceptance of this fact and a willingness to move forward naturally along Caribbean—that is, culturally mixed—lines. In place of profitless anxiety to establish an instant local culture, he proposes that the Caribbean should permit a *métis* way of life, a mixed culture, to shape itself naturally and gradually, with no frantic seeking after roots outside the Caribbean area. For too long the *métis* has been the outcast of all the ''pure'' races, the unwanted bastard of the Caribbean. For Glissant, West Indians are unquestionably *à mi-chemin des races,* halfway between the races, as he says in *Les Indes.* They are, in fact, a symbol of racial synthesis, and the anthropologist who speculates as to whether the juxtaposition of so many races, customs, and ways of looking at the world can possibly lead to any form of unity can easily find his answer in the living presence of individuals such as Glissant himself. Pride in *métissage* has always been un-

dermined by racism, and the complex racial neuroses of the Caribbean are perhaps colonialism's most lasting legacy. Glissant, however, calls on us to see racism not as an absolute but as a phenomenon with certain motivating factors—social, economic, and political—which must be brought to light and resolved. (pp. 368-69)

> *Beverley Ormerod, ''Beyond 'Négritude': Some Aspects of the Work of Édouard Glissant,'' in* Contemporary Literature (© 1974 by the Board of Regents of the University of Wisconsin System), Vol. 15, No. 3, Summer, 1974, pp. 360-69.

JURIS SILENIEKS

Glissant's third novel [*Malemort*] may be viewed as a polymorphous narrative as well as a compendium of the author's aesthetic and ideological tenets. Like most of his writing, *Malemort* deals with the condition of Glissant's homeland, Martinique, and therewith ramifies into a multidirectional search for a definition of Antillanité, a concept that Glissant wants to substitute for the much exalted and maligned Négritude. Among other things, Antillanité is predicated on the recognition of a collective consciousness of the Caribbean peoples, still to be distilled and instilled. If, by and large, Glissant's Renaudot-prize-winning first novel, *La Lézarde,* can be considered as an exploration of Martinican space in its dichotomous opposites of mountain/plain, sea/land, country/city, his second novel, *Le Quatrième Siècle,* is laid out on a predominantly temporal matrix, evoking ''une vision prophétique du passé,'' the past which has been lost and is to be reconstituted from folkloric legends and recollections by means of historic research and creative sublimation. *Malemort* attempts a further integration of Martinican space and time, which are intricately enmeshed in the experience and consciousness of the Martinican people. Thus, there is no chronological plot line as the narrative scans back and forth between 1788 and 1974. 1788 is the year when a slave ship brought over from Africa Glissant's ancestors and the first rebels fled to the hills to become *marrons.* The fictional locus likewise encompasses a whole range of Martinican *paysages* that offer startling contrasts of geographic features, a lush rain forest, an arid salt plain, a volcanic landscape, fertile agricultural fields, etc., that Glissant's descriptions render vibrant: authenticated by his intimate knowledge of the island's fauna and flora; infused with his love for that ''Eden potentiel'' endowed with natural splendors and plagued with human miseries; impassioned with his anguish to see the island being destroyed by developers and promoters of tourism. . . . Along many facets, the novel, though imbedded in a very specific locale, dealing with endemic problems, transcends its topicality to reach a level of universal significance. The novel's stylistic and structural forms are disconcertingly complex, its language being couched in a very idiosyncratic idiom that occasionally flaunts grammatical improprieties and borrows from creole. (p. 826)

> *Juris Silenieks, in* French Review *(copyright 1976 by The American Association of Teachers of French), April, 1976.*

*   *   *

GOLDING, William   1911-

Golding is a leading British novelist, short story writer, playwright, poet, and essayist. He writes what Samuel Hynes

terms "unusually tight, conceptualized, analogical expressions of moral ideas," novels which chart the struggle of good and evil in man. Essentially optimistic despite the grimness of much of his fiction, Golding writes out of a desire to assist people "to understand their own humanity." (See also *CLC*, Vols. 1,2,3,8, and *Contemporary Authors*, Vols. 5-8, rev. ed.)

PETER M. AXTHELM

In contrast to [Arthur Koestler's] *Darkness at Noon*, which introduces one complete system, examines its collapse, and then tentatively offers another one, Golding's *Free Fall* presents only fragments of systems. Its hero begins with no system at all and ends with only a hint of one. Yet, in describing man's approach to meaning rather than his scrutiny of its elements, Golding examines [an] important aspect of the modern confession.

Superficially, the hero of the novel is a success, a boy from the slums who has become a famous artist and now lives on Paradise Hill. Yet he calls himself "a burning amateur, torn by the irrational and incoherent, searching and self-condemned." . . . Unlike most confessional characters, who are never sure what kind of perception they will find, Sammy Mountjoy clearly defines the goals of his self-examination. Foremost among them are the questions which are introduced at the beginning of the second and third paragraphs and repeated throughout the novel—"When did I lose my freedom?" and "How did I lose my freedom?" The lost quality of freedom is described as a tangible element, like "the taste of potatoes," yet it stands for broader philosophical problems than Sammy admits, directing his confession toward a fuller consideration of the meaning of sin and guilt.

In addition to seeking this one point in his life, "the decision made freely that cost me my freedom," the hero of *Free Fall* is approaching a kind of personal religion. In the disintegration following the loss of freedom, "all patterns have broken, one after another. Life is random and evil unpunished." Sammy wants to rebuild a pattern and restore order and justice; in doing so, he hopes to give meaning to his divided existence, to find "the connection between the little boy clear as spring water, and the man like a stagnant pool." . . . Like all confessional heroes, Sammy Mountjoy seeks a perception which is deeply personal; he is concerned with an internal system of order. (pp. 113-14)

After the tightly organized presentation of the central goals and themes of his confession in the opening pages, Sammy Mountjoy begins the examination of his past. He ranges back and forth through what he calls the "shuffle fold and coil" of time, often juxtaposing events from his innocent childhood with others that occur after his "fall." As the grey faces of his past take on shape and color, he approaches the discovery of his moment of sin. Five times, after the accounts of events in his youth, Sammy asks, "Here?" Each time he answers himself, "Not here." After the final perception of the moment in which he lost his freedom, Sammy repeats his question; it is followed by a profound silence.

The method in which Sammy describes his early childhood recalls the explanation of Saul Bellow's hero, Augie March, that "All the influences were lined up waiting for me. I was born, and there they were to form me, which is why I tell you more of them than of myself." As a boy growing up in the slums, Sammy is innocent and happy, being shaped by

external forces. . . . Even as he emphasizes the depth of his happiness, however, Sammy sees the shadow of the sin to come. . . . (pp. 115-16)

In the next stage of his life, which centers around the rectory and the school, Sammy's outlook becomes more cautious, his perception more sophisticated. His new guardian, Father Watts-Watt, repels him ("Talking with him was like a nightmare ride on a giraffe"), but, for the first time, Sammy shows the ability to resist the influence of another person. . . . Father Watts-Watt represents the antithesis of the confessional hero, a man struggling to avoid the reality of his being. In addition to this contrast to the hero, however, he is also a kind of double. "He was incapable of approaching a child straight because of the ingrown and festering desires that poisoned him," says Sammy. . . . In this, he reflects the dark and confused drives which plague the hero in the events leading up to his fall. (p. 117)

The "nationless words" of Dr. Halde cut Sammy loose from all his remaining ties with order. Halde is clearly a double of the hero. He implies that he, too, has sacrificed his own freedom by choosing Nazism and emphasizes the price of such a sacrifice: "I made my choice with much difficulty but I have made it. Perhaps it was the last choice I shall ever make. Accept such international immortality, Mr. Mountjoy, and all unpleasantnesses are possible to man." . . . (p. 121)

Halde is more than a reflection of the hero's life, however. His psychological powers allow him to claim, "I can get inside your skin"; and it is only from within that perception can reach Sammy. Halde's power over his prisoner becomes vividly clear as the interrogation progresses. When the Nazi first describes his theory of "international immorality," Sammy hastens to deny its relevance to his own condition: "What's all that got to do with me?" Within moments, however, his mind has accepted Halde's thought as its own: "I could see this war as the ghastly and ferocious play of children who having made a wrong choice or a whole series of them were now helplessly tormenting each other because a wrong use of freedom has lost them their freedom." . . . This striking progression illuminates the full meaning of Sammy's statement that he "was given the capacity to see" by Dr. Halde. When the interrogation ends, Sammy walks out of the office "in an awful trance of obedience" and is led to his cell. (pp. 121-22)

In the early stages of his experience in the cell, it appears that Sammy will follow Ivan's path into madness; but in his resurrection he emerges with a vision that is, in some ways, even more hopeful than that of Rubashov [the protagonist of Koestler's *Darkness at Noon*]. For Sammy is not at the end of life. He has time to use the "new mode of knowing" which Halde has given him and to apply his newly discovered "vital morality" to the reconstruction of meaning in his own life. If he succeeds, he may place a living reality where Rubashov could see only a dream of the future. On this promising note, Golding directs our attention back over Sammy's life to seek a positive "pattern" amid the disintegration.

However, Golding . . . denies his hero the fulfillment of his momentary religious perception. The blazing hopes of the prison camp resurrection are tempered by an ironic reality. Sammy probes deeply into the "two worlds" of his existence and achieves a clear perception of both, but the crucial missing element of his pattern eludes him. "There is no bridge," he admits on the final page of the novel.

A closer examination of Sammy's "two worlds" elucidates both the pattern he seeks and the true nature of his fall. He is painfully aware of the split which robs his life of meaning: "I can love the child in the garden, on the airfield, in Rotten Row," he says, "because he is not I. He is another person." . . . That child is innocent; the adult Sammy is tainted with guilt. They are thus relegated to two separate worlds.

The impossibility of crossing back into the first world is shown most emphatically in Sammy's attempt to contact the central characters of that child's world. Like Michel in Gide's *The Immoralist,* Sammy confronts utter futility in his effort to retrace the course of his earlier actions. (pp. 122-23)

Almost every proper name in *Free Fall* implies something about the character it identifies, but none is so crucial as "Beatrice Ifor." The girl is, as Gregor and Kinkead-Weekes suggest [in their article "The Strange Case of Mr. Golding and His Critics"], "a *fusion* of the spirit and the body . . . both Beatrice and I-for''; in other words, she is the potential bridge between Sammy's two worlds. But the young boy, torn by the contradictory worlds of his two teachers, each of whom denies the existence of the other's system, cannot see the possibility of fusion; he sees Beatrice in the light implied by another reading of her name, "If-or" and thus feels compelled to choose one of the two worlds. Repelled by Miss Pringle and attracted to Nick, who finds "no place for spirit in his cosmos," he ignores the spiritual side of the girl and grasps only the "I-for," the self-centered, exploitative lust. He upsets the balance and destroys the bridge.

Herein lies the full significance of his loss of freedom. He has chosen to shut out a part of the complex world and embrace a simplified half-truth as a substitute for the full consciousness of existence. One dominant theme of the confessional novel is the inadequacy of such "simple solutions"—from the Grand Inquisitor through Jean-Baptiste Clamence, from Ivan Karamazov through the "defective saints" of Rubashov's party. Golding does not spare Sammy Mountjoy from the effects of his error—the denial of freedom and the "fall."

Ultimately, the reader of *Free Fall* is challenged to find another bridge—a reconciliation of the blazingly affirmative vision of the prison camp with the final bleak realization that "There is no bridge" in Sammy's existence. Golding offers one clue to this solution on the final page of the novel. Sammy walks out of his cell expecting to meet his judge but finds pity instead. Halde has been replaced, and the commandant apologizes for Sammy's punishment. A soldier asks, "Captain Mountjoy. Have you heard?" and he answers, "I heard." What he has "heard" is the voice of his own being and perhaps also a voice of absolution. He is an image of fallen man, unable to undo his sin; but he has suffered for it and sees a hope of redemption.

The position of *Free Fall* in the context of all Golding's work also illuminates the religious vision of the novel. His first two novels, *Lord of the Flies* and *The Inheritors,* are parables portraying the evil inherent in man's nature; in them, the author employs images of man's origins, in childhood and in prehistory, to illustrate man's swift and inevita-

ble loss of innocence. *Pincher Martin* turns from the nature of evil itself and focuses on its spiritual consequences. The hero, shipwrecked on a barren rock, seems to survive for several days through a monumental assertion of will. "I will impose my routine on this rock," he says. On the last page of the novel, we learn that he has been dead all along, and the routine he has imposed is a self-created hell. The final page emphasizes the terrible irony of Martin's earlier conversation with his "hallucination" of God (a striking derivation from Dostoevsky's hallucinatory doubles). In that exchange, the hero shouts, "I have created you and I can create my own heaven." The old man answers, "You have created it."

The idea that man creates his own hell is carried into the prison cell of *Free Fall.* "Why do you torment yourself?" Sammy says. "Why do you do their work for them?" . . . But Sammy Mountjoy is given the power to escape from the hell he creates and even, "between the understood huts, among jewels and music," to glimpse at heaven. Although the heaven fades and he can never regain the innocence that preceded the fall, he can return to an existence enriched by "a new mode of knowing." (pp. 124-26)

[Golding] applies his hero's religious perception to a reexamination of life. In such a reexamination, the pentecostal brilliance is dimmed by the reality of sin and weakness, but it is never extinguished. Although Sammy is denied the last bridge that would complete his pattern, Golding affirms the possibility that such a bridge can exist in the world, that the effort to reconstruct a pattern is indeed worthwhile. Such a pattern is rare (like "the taste of potatoes, element so rare that isotope of uranium is abundant by comparison"), and it is elusive, for it can be lost forever in one act. But it does exist, like a religious goal, heralded by a "flake of fire" and forever compelling modern man to sincere and passionate self-scrutiny. (p. 127)

> *Peter M. Axthelm, in his* The Modern Confessional Novel *(copyright © 1967 by Yale University), Yale University Press, 1967.*

JEAN E. KENNARD

It is untrue that Golding's novels leave us without answers, as [some critics] suggest. Golding admits that he cannot subscribe to any particular religion, but insists that he is a fundamentally religious man. . . . [His] faith in a pattern that transcends man is not the only difference between Golding's position and that defined in the early work of Sartre and Camus, but it is the basic one. . . . [It] is this belief which underlies all other aspects of his philosophy and determines the techniques of his novels.

It is because "man hasn't seen this" that he is in trouble, according to Golding. Golding sees man as trapped in himself, "islanded," a condition he appears to believe comes inevitably with consciousness of self, with the loss of innocence. . . . All Golding's major characters—Sammy Mountjoy, Pincher Martin, Dean Jocelyn—are men who have created the world in their own image, who turn everything into themselves. (p. 177)

Golding suggests, most clearly in *The Inheritors,* that man in a state of innocence is an integral part of his universe. The separation of man from the rest of his world through consciousness is apparently Golding's way of defining original sin. At this point man is islanded. . . .

Golding believes man's salvation lies in a recognition of the macrocosm in which he is a microcosm; man must find a bridge off the island of himself into an outer reality. (p. 178)

Each novel is a microcosm of a greater whole: in *Lord of the Flies* the innate violence of the children alone on the island is a version in miniature of the adult world represented by the officer with his cruiser; the prehistoric world of *The Inheritors* is one episode in a history repeating itself in every man, as each loses his innocence; Pincher Martin, actually centered on his own nagging tooth, is living out in miniature the story of his whole life; *Free Fall* is closely related to *The Inheritors* and again deals with each man's loss of innocence in terms of one man, Sammy Mountjoy; Dean Jocelyn's obsession with building a spire is revealed as every man's drive to find meaning. Each islanded situation is gradually seen to incorporate more significance until one has the feeling that Golding has incorporated everything. (p. 180)

The experience of expansion the reader goes through in Golding's novels happens with every aspect of his technique: his characters, first recognizable as individuals, are seen to function also as allegorical figures; the patterning of the plot gradually adds increasing significance to each episode as its place in the overall scheme becomes clearer; each novel is related to earlier books by other writers, . . . and thus is seen to be part of a larger culture; and, perhaps most importantly, Golding's language is so densely metaphoric that the reader is constantly given the sense of one thing's relation to another. These techniques are, of course, Joycean, and in many ways serve the same ends. They are, in fact, the defining characteristics of the novel of nightmare. (pp. 180-81)

The decline of the children's society [in *Lord of the Flies*] and the gradual revelation of evil is paralleled to the boys', particularly Ralph's, increasing self-consciousness. He begins to have a recurring "strange mood of speculation that was so foreign to him." . . . Self-consciousness is, of course, the separation of self from the not-self, the outside world, and it is in terms of a breaking up of an initial harmony that Golding defines evil in the novel. . . . Finally each boy is alone, an island, afraid of everyone else. (p. 182)

If human nature is innately violent and selfish, then what hope does Golding offer us? Not much in *Lord of the Flies*. In various interviews and essays he has suggested a possibility of curbs voluntarily imposed by individuals upon themselves, though he does not talk very optimistically about the likelihood of this. (p. 183)

Although Golding suggests the harmony of an ideal society, he does not indicate any faith in its creation. If man is to be helped, he appears to need help from God, represented in this novel, not altogether successfully, by Simon, the boy Golding himself has called a saint. More sensitive, more farseeing than the others, Simon has visions and attempts to communicate them to the others, only to be murdered by mistake as the beast. Golding . . . [has said] that Ralph should have been weeping for Simon at the end of the novel, not Piggy. . . . Simon represents for Golding a supernatural world which does exist. As long as it exists, then, there must be hope that we can recognize it, unless to Golding's God we really are as flies to wanton boys. The later novels at least reject this concept of God. (pp. 183-84)

The reader is constantly being drawn to compare his disappointment, his horror at the boys' savagery, with the institutionalized savagery of his own world.

The action of the novel is a gradual expansion. Each event foreshadows another or, to put it another way, eventually becomes the event of which it had earlier been an imitation or representation. Everything is, then, seen to be an integral part of everything else, as in all novels of nightmare. (p. 184)

Golding's ability to create characters which function both realistically and allegorically is illustrated particularly well in *Lord of the Flies*. It is necessary for Golding to establish the boys as "real" children early in the novel—something he achieves through such small touches as Piggy's attitude to his asthma and the boys' joy in discovering Piggy's nickname—because his major thesis is, after all, about human psychology and the whole force of the fable would be lost if the characters were not first credible to us as human beings.

Increasingly, though, Golding shows the children responding differently to the same object or event and the highly patterned nature of these episodes makes it clear that the reader is intended to read them as allegory. . . . The strength of Golding's characterization lies in the fact that while the reader is led out from the reality of individuals to a wider significance, his initial sense of real people is not lost. When, for example, at the death of Piggy the reader recognizes this is the death of reason or logic, he nevertheless retains the sense of horror at a child's being murdered by other children.

The allegorical aspects of the characterization and the action lead the reader imaginatively into other worlds of the cultural macrocosm. There are, as so many critics have pointed out, innumerable Biblical associations with the Eden myth and many political implications in the democracy/fascism opposition represented in Ralph and Jack. [Critics have related the novel to] Ballantyne's boys' adventure story *Coral Island* . . . [and] to classical Greek literature, particularly to Euripides's *The Bacchae*. These critics are, of course, illustrating the same point about Golding's work, that one of its important aspects is its relation to a cultural whole he wishes the reader to perceive.

The final and perhaps most important way in which Golding's techniques dramatize his theme is the metaphorical density of the language itself. Golding describes everything in terms of something else. This is particularly true of his descriptions of natural phenomena. (pp. 185-86)

The ability to use metaphor and simile, to perceive relations, is an essential characteristic of the loss of innocence, as Golding makes clear in his second novel, *The Inheritors*. But even though one must perceive things as separate before one can compare them, the act of comparison, of course, is a putting together and thus a sign of hope, of possible salvation from the prison of oneself.

The Inheritors, like *Lord of the Flies,* is concerned with the fall of man and with the loss of innocence. Set in prehistoric times, it tells of the destruction of a Neanderthal tribe and particularly of one member of it, Lok, by a group of "new" men, homo sapiens, led by Tuami. But the new men are not superior to the Neanderthals in much that Golding feels matters; Golding has reversed the notion of history as progress to suggest the notion of history as spiritual decline. The notion he rejects is that represented by H. G. Wells in his *Outline of History,* that Neanderthal man was bestial, hairy, gorilla-like, with possible cannibalistic tendencies. (pp. 186-87)

Like the boys in *Lord of the Flies,* at the opening of the novel Lok's people are innocent. They live in a harmonious world, in which, whatever its physical dangers and difficulties, they are one with each other. (p. 187)

They do not need language to communicate but use a form of telepathy or shared pictures. Language apparently carries implications of the separation of name and object, of distortion, that Golding does not wish to assign to the state of innocence. The pictures they share may be less exact, in some ways less useful than language, but they undoubtedly indicate a closer communication. The early scenes of the novel are full of such remarks as: "[Fa] did not need to speak"; . . . "as so often happened with the people, there were feelings between them"; . . . "without warning, all the people shared a picture inside their heads." . . . The pictures not only transcend the barriers among people, but also those between present and future. . . . Lok's people are totally responsible for one another and provide that sort of warmth and acceptance of each other contemporary sensitivity groups attempt to imitate. (pp. 187-88)

[The] "other" is frightened and greedy, not at one with his world as are Lok's people. Unlike Lok's tribe, "new" people kill and eat meat; their sexuality is a form of rape. . . . Tuami's people have already lost their innocence. They are afraid of the darkness. . . . Tuami's people, then, in their inability to see beyond themselves, in their sense of being surrounded by a frightening darkness, have in Golding's terms lost touch with the macrocosm which is the unity of God.

Lok gradually takes on the characteristics of the "new" people. Their existence forces him into self-consciousness. He discovers metaphor. There are now two parts of Lok, inside-Lok and outside-Lok. . . . The "new" people with their intelligence, violence, and strength supersede the Neanderthals by literally destroying them, but it is also clear that their characteristics are dominant anyway; "Neanderthalness" is dead in Lok before Tuami destroys Lok's people.

The Inheritors is a pessimistic book in the sense that Golding does not show the way to salvation for fallen man. (pp. 188-89)

The Inheritors is a microcosm of the whole of human history. What happens here is repeated in every child as he grows to maturity. Read this way, Golding's view is Wordsworthean in its stress on the loss of childhood vision through self-consciousness, although *The Inheritors,* less than *Lord of the Flies,* emphasizes the paradisical elements of innocence. Lok's integration with his world is, however, no different in kind from the boy Wordsworth's in *The Prelude.* (p. 189)

For the reader the plot is an opening out; his view is, for much of the novel, as limited as Lok's. Golding forces the reader to leap ahead guessing at what Lok cannot see, placing him in the macrocosm of human history. At the end, when the reader suddenly sees Lok from the point of view of Tuami, "a red creature," and "it," he has passed beyond Lok and Tuami both, since he is able to compare them with each other. The novel allows the reader, then, to make the relationship necessary in Golding's view, to transcend the Fall, even if it is not possible for Lok or Tuami. (pp. 189-90)

Is *Pincher Martin* an Existentialist novel with Pincher an heroic, Promethean figure standing out against death, forging his own identity with his intelligence? Are we to take as good in a Sartrean sense Pincher's awareness that he can have no "complete identity without a mirror," . . . that he has created God in his own image, or not? Certainly it is hard to believe Golding is not consciously concerned with Existentialism here. The passage in which Pincher analyzes his feeling of lost identity, his comments on the way he used mirrors to watch himself as if he were watching a stranger, his use of others to assure himself of his own existence would not be out of place in *The Myth of Sisyphus* or in *Being and Nothingness.* It is difficult, too, for the reader not to feel some respect for the tenacity and courage Pincher displays. Nevertheless, Golding does not think Pincher heroic but presumptuous; critics who judge the experience by Existentialist criteria have, as James Baker points out, "made a hero out of Golding's villain." (p. 191)

"To achieve salvation, individuality—the persona—must be destroyed," Golding has written elsewhere; and it is his individuality that Pincher refuses to surrender. He is physically and spiritually islanded, clinging to his own identity as to his rock. Relieved to find his identity disc around his neck, he shouts, "Christopher Hadley Martin. Martin. Chris. I am what I always was!" . . . ; he survives by shouting, "I am! I am! I am!" . . . , knowing only that he "must hang on." . . .

He is nothing but greed, as the flashbacks to his past life reveal; his role of Greed in the morality play is type casting. Everything and everyone is food to feed Pincher Martin. . . . He is guilty of Golding's greatest sin, self-obsession; he turns everything into himself, just as he has created his own purgatory on the rock. A recurring image in the novel, that of the Chinese box, in which a fish is buried and gradually eaten by maggots who subsequently eat each other is obviously intended to reflect Pincher's experience. . . . (p. 192)

Although there are various clues to the fact that Pincher is inside his own head, it is really only on a second reading that this becomes clear. The discovery in the last chapter that Pincher was dead all along comes as a shock, not as a confirmation of suspicions. The clues are frequently in the form of metaphors: Pincher compares his experience to lying "on a rim of teeth in the middle of the sea" . . . ; he feels as if "the pressure of the sky and air was right inside his head." . . . Much of the metaphoric density of the novel lies in this set of images. But in order for the reader to see these comments as ironic, he already has to know the truth of Pincher's situation. Other clues come in the form of Pincher's dawning awareness of the familiarity of the rock. He resists recognizing the truth, refuses to connect himself with a reality beyond his illusory world, but the awareness comes to him anyway. At the end of the novel his realization of the nature of his own character, his place in the pattern of his experiences, is paralleled to his realization of the truth about the rock: he "understood what was so hauntingly familiar and painful about an isolated and decaying rock in the middle of the sea." . . . (p. 194)

In piecing the separate worlds together, the reader and Pincher come to realize that he is indeed what he always was, and that "an hour on this rock is a lifetime," . . . all the experiences of the book have happened in a moment, but a moment which is the microcosm of a whole life.

The techniques of characterization Golding uses in this novel are very similar to those he used in *Lord of the Flies;* the characters function midway between realism and allegory. . . . But in brief snatches of description or dialogue Golding keeps every character functioning on the human level also, even as the reader is beginning to see the allegorical pattern. (pp. 194-95)

Through allegorical characterization Golding makes the reader relate his microcosmic world of Pincher on the rock to Christian mythology, and through references to Prometheus to Greek mythology also. (p. 195)

Many critics have commented that the title of Golding's fourth novel, *Free Fall,* has both a theological and a scientific significance, but Golding himself has, as usual, expressed it best: "Everybody has translated this in terms of theology; well, okay, you can do it that way, which is why it's not a bad title, but it is in fact a scientific term. It is where your gravity has *gone;* it is a man in a space ship who has no gravity; things don't fall or lift, they float about; he is completely divorced from the other idea of a thing up *there* and centered on *there* in which he lives." Sammy Mountjoy, narrator of *Free Fall,* has more insight and perhaps more conscience than Pincher Martin, but basically his is Pincher's problem. He is islanded, trapped in himself, "completely divorced from the other idea of a thing up there."

There are images of cells everywhere. The whole novel can be read as taking place in a prison cell where Sammy is held by the Germans in World War II. . . . Since he recognizes no reality beyond himself, for Sammy, as for Pincher, other people are merely objects for his use. He knows the way out is to make contact with something beyond himself, to build a bridge. . . . (pp. 195-96)

The novel is Sammy's attempt to build the bridge, to find his place in a reality beyond himself. One way in which he attempts this is to search for the pattern of his own life, particularly for the moment when he lost his freedom. As in *The Inheritors,* loss of freedom is equated with loss of innocence, with self-consciousness. . . . (p. 196)

Although *Free Fall* resembles *Pincher Martin* in that the physical situation of the central character, here a prison cell, is a microcosm of his spiritual life, it is only in terms of its time scheme a fantasy novel. It takes place in recognizably modern times in familiar English places. The novel has been criticized for its lack of a controlling myth. . . . It has been criticized also for the extent to which Sammy comments on his own experience. This, surely, is perfectly defensible given Golding's thematic concerns in this novel. Sammy's desperate desire to communicate, to find a link with an outside reality, is dramatized very well in those passages of commentary directed to the reader. They are not in fact comments upon the action, but rather the essential action of the book itself. As the book progresses and the reader comes closer to Sammy in sharing his search for a pattern, they become fewer in number. Sammy no longer tells the reader at the end, "we share nothing but our sense of division." . . . Sammy's communication with the reader is in itself a sign of health, a bridge built.

For there is a pattern in Sammy's experiences as related in the novel. . . . The experience of reading *Free Fall* is, like that of reading Golding's other novels, a piecing together of a puzzle, a working from the microcosm to the macrocosm. Each scene of the novel illustrates a paradox: the world of feeling is not parallel to the rational world. (pp. 197-98)

The existence of a pattern is underscored by parallel events and characters the reader is invited to compare. The boy Sammy laughs at the retarded girl, Minnie, who urinates on the classroom floor; the man Sammy mourns Beatrice who does the same thing on the floor of the hospital. (pp. 198-99)

The language of *Free Fall* is as dense metaphorically as that of the earlier novels. Here too Golding gives one the sense in which this particular situation is all inclusive; the reader is taken to worlds beyond the novel and is left with the feeling that these worlds may well be infinite. As in other novels of nightmare the reader moves towards infinity. (p. 199)

The metaphorical implications of Jocelin's spire [in *The Spire*] are multiple, but the most important is the significance of the spire as a symbol for man's reaching towards another world, in religious terms Heaven, in an attempt to understand it. The building of the spire, then, is a metaphor for Camus' premise that man seeks meaning. (p. 200)

It is not that the search for meaning is in itself wrong in Golding's terms, but the motive for the search is all important. It may be vision, a true search; it may be presumption, mere will. Jocelin believes he is fulfilling a mission that began when he was first chosen Dean by God. The action of the novel questions this assumption: Jocelin's position as Dean was in fact given him as a sort of joke by his aunt, then mistress of the king; the spire may have inadequate foundations. (pp. 200-01)

Jocelin clearly comes to realize his folly. He recognizes that God is indeed love—"If I could go back, I would take God as lying between people and to be found there". . . — and at the end, dying, apparently calls upon God for help as do Sammy and perhaps, although not willingly, Pincher. In this novel Golding answers the problem critics raise about *Free Fall,* that Sammy himself does not fully recognize the unity he seeks. The answer he gives is that . . . some mystery is both inevitable and necessary. "God knows where God may be," . . . says Jocelin at the end. He may indeed mean, as the critics believe, that man cannot find where God is. But the words can also be read more optimistically to mean that even though man does not know where God is, God indeed does.

The confirmation of God's existence comes finally in the vision of the apple tree given to Jocelin before he dies. . . . [The] tree is an apple tree and must carry overtones of the Garden of Eden. The transformed apple tree is a perfect image for Golding's concept of salvation. Man, a child, lives alongside the apple tree in innocence; adult, he eats of its fruit and falls into sin as he gains self-consciousness and knowledge. But knowledge is also the way forward to salvation; man must see that he is part of a macrocosm, that the tree touches earth and heaven. In this way the original sin may be transcended, the tree transformed. (pp. 201-02)

Golding refutes the Sartrean view of man as an alienated being in absurd relation to the universe with what amounts to a leap of faith. He believes that there is meaning, unity, but recognizes this is unprovable. Redemption from the Post-existential dilemma, nevertheless, lies in each man's recognition of his place in the universal scheme. . . . [He] frequently defines this recognition as love. What convinces his reader is not the logic of his argument, but his techniques, those of the novelists of nightmare. He forces the reader outward from the island of a particular situation over the bridges that lead in all directions. Only from the macrocosm can one see that the island is a microcosm of everything else. (p. 202)

> *Jean E. Kennard, "William Golding: Island," in her* Number and Nightmare: Forms of Fantasy in Contemporary Fiction *(© 1975 by Jean E. Kennard), Archon Books, 1975, pp. 176-202.*

AVRIL HENRY

On the merely narrative level, flashback in *Pincher Martin* is the natural result of Martin's isolation and illness, and is the process by which he is gradually brought to his ghastly self-knowledge. This process is quite distinct from the flashbacks' effect on the reader, who sees each memory both in relation to all the other memories presented in the book, and in relation to the physical circumstances of Martin's life on the rock. Neither relation is simple: they constitute the main device by which the writer characteristically obliges his reader to pay more than casual attention.

In *Free Fall* and *The Pyramid* this control of attention is achieved by the use of flashback in an elaborate time-structure. In *Pincher Martin*, however, events in flashback are not precisely dated, as in *The Pyramid*, or even clearly placed in a sequential biography, as in *Free Fall*: we have to struggle to place them accurately in Martin's past. . . . It is not possible to construct a precisely ordered "real-life" sequence of events behind the fragmented sequence we meet in *Pincher Martin*. In *Free Fall*, in *The Spire* to a degree, and certainly in *The Pyramid*, it is not only possible to do this, it is essential if a dimension of meaning is not to be missed: the time-structures are part of the novel's meaning. . . . The novel works in terms of related images, not formal time-structure. (p. 3)

[In *Pincher Martin*, the] writer's attention is on presenting the same image in different contexts rather than making intellectual play with a clear time-structure. . . .

If there is any device here which compels attention it is the sheer obscurity of the references when we first meet them. With hindsight, however, we can see their unifying significance. . . . (p. 5)

The thematic reason for presenting . . . events in scarcely-comprehensible form [in a flashback sequence early in the novel, presenting a series of images which reoccur with greater significance later] is that in retrospect it makes us think about the treatment, in the novel as a whole, of the exposure of selfishness and hypocrisy. This is to take us to the heart of the matter, since Martin's entire experience is a self-induced act of will to avoid any truth that is not himself. The progress of physical exposure, memories and metaphysical experience is an unsuccessful "divine" attempt to persuade him to abandon the mask of his own ferociously defended selfishness which is a false identity. The experience provided is an attempt to penetrate a moral blindness so extreme that it regards only outcome, ignoring motivation. . . .

Mr. Golding was not very interested in the strict order of events in this novel as a whole, let alone in this flashback. It might be objected that in this he has simply observed accurately: the human memory does not recall sequentially. . . . [Since] in a fictional biography even the arrangement of linear biographical details is artificial, it robs the writer of a mode of drawing attention to patterns of ideas. If a writer can establish a sequential norm from which he then departs, the points of departure will provoke thought. But as we have seen, there is no reliable sequential norm in *Pincher*. (p. 7)

It is usually, but not always, possible to relate events recalled in flashback to the general stages of Martin's life. Where it is not possible, the flashbacks must carry their relevance with them, in near-isolation, or fail. Their overall function is the gradual revealing of a man whose admirable qualities, courage and ingenuity, are apparent only on the rock, not in flashback. . . . Perhaps it is a symptom of misplaced ratiocination to look for any further coherence in these images than the context gives them. In any case they are, as already suggested, evidence that Mr. Golding's attention is not on merely logical cohesion, which would perhaps be inappropriate in a work so informed by the workings of an inflamed imagination, whether fictional or not. (pp. 8-9)

[In fact, the] flashbacks function in several ways. First, the flashbacks relate to each other and to the varied forms in which they themselves are repeated throughout the book; second, they relate also to the details of Martin's "survival" on Rockall. . . . Third, they relate to the six-day structure of the whole experience: the structure which is superficially a temporal check for us and Martin in the otherwise timeless and distorted events on the rock and in the mind, and at a deeper level is a horrible parody of the six days of Creation. What we watch is an unmaking process, in which man attempts to create himself his own God, and the process accelerates daily. (p. 9)

"Day and Night One" extend through the first four chapters. Let us consider first the relation of their flashbacks to each other. The first image of all, the little glass sailor suspended in a jam jar, occurs four times in this period; in each of the four main flashbacks . . . [the] jam jar is not a "constant" symbol: its implications vary with its context. At first it is related explicitly to the drowning man:

> The delicate balance of the glass figure related itself to his body. In a moment of wordless realization he saw himself touching the surface of the sea with just such a dangerous stability, poised between floating and going down. . . .

It becomes, almost at once, a metaphor of Martin's will—at this stage, a metaphor of his control over himself, at the moment when his force of will creates a world to inhabit:

> The pleasure of the jar lay in the fact that the little glass figure was so delicately balanced between opposing forces. . . . By varying the pressure on the membrane you could do anything you liked with the glass figure which was wholly in your power. . . .

The jam jar is clearly a general metaphor of Martin's condition: not only his physical condition, poised in the water, but his spiritual condition, poised at the point of every man's last decision, to choose possession of himself or acceptance of a greater than himself. (pp. 9-10)

[The jam jar also] forms part of a group of events presenting Martin observed at a disadvantage. It next occurs, not at the beginning, but at the end of a sequence:

> Under the side of his face the pebbles nagged. The pictures that came and went inside his head did not disturb him because they were so small and remote. There was a woman's body, white and detailed, there was a boy's body; there was a box office, the bridge of a ship, an order picked out across a far sky in neon lighting, a tall, thin man who stood aside humbly in the darkness at the top of a companion ladder; there was a man hanging in the sea like a glass sailor in a jam jar. There was nothing to choose between the pebbles and the pictures. . . .

The image here is not simply the jam jar but specifically a comparison of himself, suspended in the sea between worlds, and the sailor. The effect of the image's occurring at the end of the sequence is to suggest that this condition somehow results from the preceding details, as we later learn it does. It represents the manipulator himself manipulated by superior forces. (p. 11)

One might imagine that the unfolding significance of the flashbacks could be inserted with equally telling effect into almost any points in Martin's battle with exposure, so powerful is the tension between his undoubted courage and the sheer nastiness of his slowly displayed character. There is effective contrast also between the careful, physically detailed account of the minutiae of daily survival—live mussels and stale water, bowel-movements and sunburn—and the fragmentary, unpredictable flashes of memory. But with characteristic economy the novelist exploits his form to the full. Rock and recall are related to each other with great care not only in chapter four, . . . but on every occasion. (p. 14)

"The Second Day" . . . contains no flashback. It is wholly concerned with the detailed mechanics of survival which are so acutely observed and logically undertaken that at this stage they seem unrelated to any memories the survivor may have. . . . The contrast between this admirably practical, courageous man and the miserably self-regarding, inefficient officer we have just been watching on duty is not only effective in that each view makes the other more powerful, but in the way these two apparently irreconcilable views of one individual are subsequently show to be indivisibly part of the same person. This is one of the main purposes of interweaving survival and flashback.

"Day Three" begins with Chapter Five and ends with Chapter Six. At the beginning of Five, experience on the rock and painful memories are linked by the imagery of fire: the metaphorical fire of pain in Pincher's limbs; the sudden vision of the sun itself, invisible on the other side of the earth which is still in darkness; and the earth's central, unattainable fire. (p. 16)

["The Fourth Day"] marks a departure from the obviously controlled use of flashback employed so far. On the naturalistic level this is accounted for by three factors. Martin

has spent a sleepless night, afraid to lose consciousness and so expose to the violence of "the ultimate truth of things" the "hoarded and enjoyed personality." . . . Secondly, the sickness of body evident in previous chapters worsens, and thirdly, the sickness of mind first apparent in the previous chapter, when he became too afraid to name half-recognized impossibilities in his environment, also worsens. . . . These are the ostensible reasons why the day begins with a remarkably disjointed series of pictures which "changed, not as one cloud shape into another but with sudden and complete differences of time and place." . . . The structural reason for the apparent confusion is that from now on a dual tendency is present in the flashbacks. On the one hand, some hitherto cryptic images are presented in explanatory detail; on the other hand, the fragmentation and accumulation of small pictures increases. . . . The passages explaining hitherto cryptic images thus occur in the second half of the novel, set in effective contrast with a proliferation of nervous, short memories. (p. 18)

The disjointed series of pictures and this ambivalent vision are effectively followed by a long narrative flashback of linear construction, the passing of time and the oscillation of the remembered mind being stressed by the precautionary Zig, Zag of the tacking destroyer. In this seventh chapter (central to the thirteen chapters of "consciousness") Martin comes to the innermost of his Chinese boxes, the most secret of the carved ivory ornaments: conscious formation of his intent to murder. As if to emphasise the deeply interior quality of this section . . . , the motive for the planned murder is revealed in flashback within flashback. . . . (p. 19)

Chapter Ten (Night Five) is above all concerned with the rape of Mary. . . . This chapter, almost all of it flashback, begins and ends with reference to the sky: summer lightning —the flash without thunder suggesting metaphorical "illumination"—links rock experience to remembered rape, and at the end of the chapter Martin, having dreamed through the night, sits in the sun, and feels "pressure of the sky and air." . . . The lightning will return, in "negative" at the end of the book, when it splits his world apart like a cosmic crack in his pathetic scenery: then, the sky's thunder will be heard as well, sounding like a spade on his tin box.

"The Sixth Day" has already begun by the end of Chapter Ten. It is the last day described, because in the parody of the six days of creation: "On the Sixth Day he created God . . . In his own image he created Him." . . . Chapter Eleven is without flashback, perhaps because Chapter Ten showed the rise and fall pattern just described: Martin's pitiful victories followed by his defeats at last acknowledged, as it were, by his consciousness. . . . It is also without flashback because reality emerges with the "pattern": the rock is recognised as a product of his own mind. Once the ground under Martin's feet has begun to move—the chunk of rock has fallen from the trench-side, revealing its tree-like pattern of black lightning—the real nature of the existence Pincher has chosen begins to appear, and all the imagery of solitude, the essence of his condition, physical and spiritual. He tries to act the part of a madman since that is less terrible than acknowledging he is unreal. (pp. 21-2)

The end of the novel may say something powerful about the state we call Hell. The structure of the novel says something equally powerful about the nature of responsibility. The constant juxtaposition of survival-struggle and flashback works in many ways, flashbacks as we have seen being related to each other and to the informing symbols, in particular to one or two main themes running throughout, such as acting and exploitation. The pattern cleverly reveals the paradoxes of a nature simultaneously seeking to communicate and isolate itself—to be and exclude other people. But in not giving us the pattern of increasing self-knowledge and repentance that we might expect from the very harshness of the superfically "purgatorial" experience of Rockall, it also underlines another paradox. Responsibility grows with knowledge. Acknowledgement of wickedness is no excuse for wickedness: indeed the guilt of a nature brought to understanding of itself is increased unless that self is rejected. (p. 23)

The novelist succeeds in making us share Martin's double vision of himself. We deplore the destructive man but come near to tolerating him for his courage and "creative" energy. If the island-life is Martin's "creation" he belongs among the artists around whom Mr. Golding's later novels are built— . . . certainly with Jocelyn in *The Spire*, whose lightning-like apple-tree is also a symbol of the inextricable entanglement of selfishness and vision. Yet *Pincher Martin* does not attempt to present a man who can really confuse his evil with aspiration. His character is "static not dynamic": his art is for himself alone and nothing is learned from it, as under-lined by the constant relating of survival detail to flashback. Pincher's weakness is the novelist's shaping strength. (p. 24)

> *Avril Henry, "The Pattern of 'Pincher Martin',"* in Southern Review *(copyright 1976 by Avril Henry), March, 1976, pp. 3-26.*

LAWRENCE R. RIES

William Golding has taken exception to the neohumanists and the prophets of despair. He rejects their view of mankind: "I believe that man suffers from an appalling ignorance of his own nature. I produce my own view, in the belief that it may be something like the truth." His novels are exceptions to the socio-realistic novels of his contemporaries, and Golding himself has characterized them as "myths." His goal is always the nature of man, and this can be examined as well under prototypical conditions as in the contemporary environment. Current affairs are merely a gauge by which to measure the basic human condition. While examining man's ferocity and brutality, he distinguishes himself from many of his contemporaries by showing this to be a universal condition, not merely the result of immediate social conditions. His first two novels, *Lord of the Flies* and *The Inheritors*, are studies in human nature, exposing the kinds of violence that man uses against his fellow man. It is understandable why these first novels have been said to comprise Golding's "primitive period."

Lord of the Flies presents a world removed from normal adult and civilized forces. The boys at first gradually and then quickly recede into a world of primordial violence. It is important to understand that Golding describes the human condition as one of aggression and hostility, in which the stronger rise up against and destroy the weaker. Piggy, the spokesman for rationality and intelligence, is ineffectual in a world governed by force and violence. Sam and Eric are the ordinary people who eventually succumb to the influence of the stronger. The boys, like modern man, are

ignorant of their own nature; as Golding has said, "I think, quite simply, that they don't understand what beasts there are in the human psyche which have to be curbed." The appearance of the captain of the cruiser at the end reasserts the issue of man's inclination to violence. Golding has summarized the theme as "an attempt to trace the defects of society back to the defects of human nature." (p. 29)

In discussing how he came to write *Lord of the Flies*, Golding said that his own twentieth-century vision "had been seared by the acts of superior whites in places like Belsen and Hiroshima." The same quality in human nature is explored in *The Inheritors*. Lok and Fa are terrorized by the new people, who are more civilized but also more brutal and destructive. Modern man enters the world by crushing his immediate predecessors. Golding's aim is ultimately moral, to expose man's violent nature so that he will learn the necessity of restraint, and in this way he stands between the neohumanists and those who embrace violence. He acknowledges the violence in the world and the necessity to come to terms with it; he would not deny the place of assertiveness and aggression in human nature as the neohumanists seek to do. (pp. 29-30)

> *Lawrence R. Ries, in his* Wolf Masks: Violence in Contemporary Poetry *(copyright © 1977 by Kennikat Press Corp.; reprinted by permission of Kennikat Press Corp.), Kennikat, 1977.*

* * *

GORDIMER, Nadine 1923-

Gordimer is a South African novelist, short story writer, and essayist. Many of her works deal with the political and social ramifications of the apartheid system in South Africa, and with its recurrent problems of alienation and despair. (See also *CLC*, Vol. 3, 5, 7, and *Contemporary Authors*, Vols. 5-8, rev. ed.)

PAUL BAILEY

In several of her novels—*A World of Strangers, The Late Bourgeois World, The Lying Days* and *The Conservationist*—Nadine Gordimer implies that the insulted and injured make substantial ghosts, haunting a society whose survival depands on the maintenance of insult and injury. Indeed, "He's dead but he won't lie down" could serve as an appropriate epigraph to much of her fiction. The South Africa she describes in affectionate, glowing detail is a country in which an abandoned corpse is a common sight. . . . That body by the roadside, waiting to be disposed of by the "proper channels", has taken on a frightening symbolic vitality—for Miss Gordimer, he is an underground man in more senses than one; he has staked a claim on the earth he will soon inhabit.

Over the thirty odd years of her writing life, Nadine Gordimer's vision has become bleaker and her art more confident. The increases in quality in her work disproves the currently fashionable maxim that only mediocrities develop. The difference between an early book like *A World of Strangers* (1958) and, say, *A Guest of Honour* (1971) is immediately striking. In the latter the ideas are contained, given a satisfying aesthetic shape, expressed through character and incident, but in *A World of Strangers* the ideas displace the characters whose mouths they are put into, with the result that the reader occasionally feels as if he's being lectured. It's a lecture worth paying attention to, of course—her comments on the easiness of liberalism are especially salutary—but the best fiction demonstrates and insinuates rather than explains. The trouble with *A World of Strangers* is that the novelist uses the ignorance of her principal character, Toby Hood, a well-to-do young Englishman from a cause-espousing family, as a means of informing the ignorant about the precise nature of South African life in the 1950s. A great deal of information is undeniably conveyed, but not without effort: Toby's gradual accumulation of knowledge lacks that sense of messy actuality, of confusion, which so often hinders the progress of spiritual growth.

Conversely, there is far too much in this ambitious novel about the trivial people whose long weekend parties Toby honours with his ironic presence. They are recognizable types, certainly, but the shallowness of their conversation, faithfully recorded, eventually becomes exasperating.... Miss Gordimer doesn't quite sustain the necessary balance between the cocktails-on-the-veranda flippancy which she sets in contrast to the furtive trips to shebeens Tody makes with his black friend, Steben Sitole, where the atmosphere of surface gaiety conceals suspicion and desperation. And yet, with all these faults, *A World of Strangers* is a book of deep intelligence—an apprentice work by a novelist of real stature.

The Late Bourgeois World, written almost a decade later, is a shorter, more assured performance.... Less wide-ranging than *A World of Strangers*, it succeeds by concentrating fiercely on a few individuals, whose failures of communication have an everyday authenticity about them.

For the greater part of her career, it has been a critical commonplace to say that Nadine Gordimer is happier with the short story form than with the novel. In a superficial sense, it is an accurate judgement, as the selection *Some Monday for Sure* make clear: her quiet, unforced skill was evident from the start; and didacticism has never affected her stories as it sometimes has her novels. Yet the fact remains that with *A Guest of Honour* and *The Conservationist* she has created works of fulfilled ambition. Miss Gordimer's development as a novelist has been a long and painful one, not unlike Conrad's. She has fought her way into the front rank of contemporary writers by taking risks, and the flaws in her early fiction were a necessary factor in that daunting development.

> Paul Bailey, "Unquiet Graves," in The Times Literary Supplement (© Times Newspapers Ltd. (London) 1976; reproduced from The Times Literary Supplement by permission), July 9, 1976, p. 841.

FRANK KERMODE

[*Selected Stories*] is full of pondered, significant details, the symptoms of [the] dementia—the bureaucratic and social combinations that make everybody ill, white and black alike. The stories are not all about race relations and the stresses they place on people who suffer, enforce, try to mend, or even to live with them; some are about the restricted lives of the whites themselves, their self-imposed and paralyzing mental suburbanism. Gordimer splendidly observes the remnants of persons beneath the repulsive stereotypes, an imaginative effort paralleled by her view of Africa itself, its extraordinary beauty showing through the

obscene mess that has been dumped on it. So here . . . is a fiction of protest; and here too the sense that the truer the protest the more certainly it will end in death. . . .

Gordimer is always an artist, within but never of the society she writes about. After holding this difficult position for so long she is able, in her preface, to speak interestingly about it. It was as a woman, she says, that she most belonged to the culture into which she was born: "Rapunzel's hair is the right metaphor for this femininity: by means of it, I was able to let myself out and live in the body, with others, as well as—alone—in the mind." Thus, she claims, she was able to achieve solitude without "alienation," two conditions she wants to distinguish, while remaining aware of "the serious psychic rupture between the writer and his society that has occurred in the Soviet Union and South Africa, for example. . . ." . . .

She is, I think, by nature a short story writer, and some of the best things in the novels are episodes "held" in the manner of the story; for example, the seven pages in *The Conservationist* describing a furtive sexual adventure in an airplane. The stories lack the heavy self-consciousness that occasionally oppresses the reader of the novels. But by and large Gordimer's work, never raucous, always subtly considered, gives one the sense of an educated imagination focusing on the exemplary issues her intelligence presents to it; it includes and transcends the world of constriction and distortion. (p. 43)

> Frank Kermode, in The New York Review of Books (reprinted with permission from The New York Review of Books; copyright © 1976 NYREV, Inc.), July 15, 1976.

BRUCE KING

Gordimer has been developing into a major novelist, and *The Conservationist* is one of the best novels of recent years. While it lacks the flashiness and topicality that have made some commonwealth novels fashionable, its perfection and depth are bound to bring it recognition as one of the most accomplished works of our time. Thickly textured poetic prose, in which narration, memories, fantasy, and dialogue perform an elaborate dance, evokes a sense of character and place comparable to that found in nineteenth-century fiction. Gordimer's previous novels have often had at their center a sensitive liberal who is overwhelmed by the crude violence of modern Africa. In the South African police state, or in the chaos of modern independent Africa, good intentions are often naive, leading to despair. By focusing her narrative on the mind of a progressive successful businessman, Gordimer has avoided the literary traps common to the liberal novel since E. M. Forster. Ideas do not form part of the novel's texture, although they are implied through the son and mistress whom Mehring rejects. Perhaps the only fault of *The Conservationist* is that the ideas and character of Mehring's left-wing mistress are given a crudeness that seems inappropriate to his own sensibility. We could read the book in various ways—for instance as an illustration of Fanon's theories of the colonial mind on the eve of national liberation. But any such reading is an imposition on the rich, finely grained life portrayed.

In the introduction to her *Selected Stories*—an intelligent discussion of the artist's sense of reality and fiction—Gordimer speaks of the interplay between the writer's engagement and the society that is portrayed. She illustrates this through her use of the words *native, African,* then *black,* which reflect the changing social, moral, and political realities of modern Africa. Her claim is that a writer's subject is *"the consciousness* of his own era. How he deals with this is, to me, the fundament of commitment." This is different from the usual demand for political engagement, and it shows Gordimer's awareness that over the years she has been creating for her readers a sense of how Africa has changed. The selections from her five volumes of stories included in the present collection illustrate both her growth as an artist and a society in rapid transition. . . . Gordimer's fine intelligence, shaped by the Cape liberal tradition, attempts to express the sensitivities and fears of her characters, whether they are those with whom she has affinities or those whom we expect to be her enemies.

Most noticeable is the growth and deepening of her art. Many of the early stories treating of sexual initiation, adolescent alienation, and explorations of the frontiers that separate the races are pat and contrived, often ending on a note of irony. In their portraits of sensitivity wounded and in their tight reversals, they are too much illustrations of a fixed position. In the later stories Gordimer has learned to write monologues that feel natural and unforced. They, however, spread out to a wider range of situations and explore new areas of feeling which cannot be defined accurately within the length of a short tale. The stories from the last volume, *Livingstone's Companions,* although realistic and powerful, are disturbing in their lack of rational definable conclusions. . . . On the basis of *The Conservationist* and her recent stories it would seem that Gordimer has outgrown the short-story form and, by projecting her own feelings of alienation and solitude onto those unlike herself, has learned to avoid the weaknesses that have marred the conclusions of her previous novels. (pp. 127-28)

> *Bruce King, in* Sewanee Review *(reprinted by permission of the editor;* © *1977 by The University of the South), Spring, 1977.*

*   *   *

GOULD, Lois   1938(?)-

Gould is an American novelist, journalist, and former magazine editor. Her protagonists are contemporary women facing the complex problems of freedom in a society of shifting mores and values. (See also *CLC,* **Vol. 4, and** *Contemporary Authors,* **Vols. 77-80.)**

ANNIE GOTTLIEB

["A Sea-Change,"] a weird, "Persona"-esque fable about power and sexual identity, is what will be called controversial. Freudian analysts, if there are any left, will call it penis envy. Feminists (and lesbians) will call it reactionary. It will also be called racist, and maybe even sick. Apart from all *that,* does it work on its own terms? Is it a good book? . . .

There is considerable suspense in "A Sea-Change," but surely not in the sense the author intended. One reads on not to see what Gould is going to do, but whether she will be able to figure out what she wants to do. In this murky psychological fable, swirling and swelling with inchoate forces, the writer seems as uncertain of what will emerge as the reader. And so bewildering is the product that this reader *still* feels uncertain what Gould intended, to what extent she is identified with her bizarre solution, to what extent distanced and in control.

At a crucial threshold in the development of women's writing and women's awareness—a threshold no one knows quite how to cross—Gould, like many others, seems to be feeling her way, blind and thoughtful, trying to think with the body. Fine. But what apparently happens is that she gropes up against a barrier—made of ambivalence, of fear of the unknown?—and turns back in the guise of going forward. A book which could have been about the dawning of female power, *whatever that is,* is instead about the capture and magical appropriation of male power, which is defined as the only kind of power there is. It's a frightening, yet oddly cozy, crawl back and deeper into the sadist//masochist trap Gould delineated so well in "Such Good Friends" (and more blatantly and less well in "Final Analysis"), a burrowing for the very roots of it. And yet, far from being a questioning, an exploration of that trap, it winds up feeling like a strange embrace and acceptance of it. Gould finally seems unable to see the world in any other but power terms. . . .

What is astonishing here is that vulnerability and masochism are consistently associated not only with the female role, but with the female anatomy. . . . Conversely, the symbol of power and invulnerability is not even the phallus —that's too human. . . . [But] that perfected phallus, the gun. . . .

Power grapples, deep and bloody, into submission. And power is male and submission is female. I've tried letting Gould off the hook by saying maybe this is meant to be an ambivalent study of psychopathology, of the psychic inextricability of the sexes—a way of saying we are as possessed by the cultural image of the male as gay males are by the exaggerated female. But it just doesn't wash. Irony and distance are missing; Gould seems to take her dichotomy seriously and to confuse the cultural cliché with the underlying and unknown nature. (p. 33)

One can't tell a writer what to write, or prescribe ideological guidelines. . . . It's the inner inconsistency of "A Sea-Change," its midcourse shift of direction, that disturbs me, with its implication that the end product of women's most turbulent transformations is—a man! After reading "Such Good Friends" and "Final Analysis," I wondered where Gould would take the pent-up rage and witty desperation of her believably masochistic heroines. . . . In "Final Analysis," though it's not a very good book, hopeful flashes emerge: the brief clear taste of self experienced in a women's group, or alone as a writer. Here Gould's heroines enter a brief and giddy free zone, only to plunge, midway through "A Sea-Change," back into "identification with the oppressor." After Gould's female tempest, as before, anatomy is more or less destiny, and power grows out of the barrel of a gun. (p. 34)

> *Annie Gottlieb, "Female Power: It's Male, Black, and Shoots," in* The Village Voice *(reprinted by permission of* The Village Voice; *copyright* © *by The Village Voice, Inc., 1976), August 30, 1976, pp. 33-4.*

ANNE TYLER

In Lois Gould's third novel, "Final Analysis," the almost ludicrously masochistic heroine eventually straightened herself out by withdrawing alone to a deserted beach cottage to write a book. It was a curiously sudden sort of resolution—perfunctory, vague, as if the author herself were not entirely convinced of its feasibility.

Now in "A Sea-Change," Lois Gould's fourth novel, we find another woman withdrawing to another beach cottage —maybe hoping to get it right this time.... [We're] back with the heroines of "Final Analysis" and "Such Good Friends"—women who feel a sense of disgust for themselves and who are drawn to men who share that disgust. (p. 4)

The purpose of Jessie's withdrawal is to accomplish a transformation—from victim to aggressor, from soft and yielding to hard and controlling. She grows flat-chested, angular; she wears a tool belt slung low on her hips that gives her an athletic stride. In her dealings with Kate, who becomes her lover, she adopts a brutal, condescending tone while Kate turns whining and supplicating. It's the ultimate metamorphosis: woman to man. Except that we're going by a stunted definition of woman here, and an even more stunted definition of man....

[As] a story, "A Sea-Change" will while away an evening nicely. (Though it's not meant for the squeamish.) It's crisply written, hard-edged, and it demonstrates Lois Gould's special skill in selecting the solitary detail that speaks volumes. But there are broad hints throughout that this is less a story than a statement—a generalization on the very nature of male and female. Generalizations of any kind tend to arouse a reader's suspicions; generalizations of *this* kind (men are brutal, and women love it) arouse out-and-out irritation. It's a plot best left in the singular case: ignore the polemics, read it as a bizarre fantasy about one mild woman transformed by rage, and let it go at that. (p. 5)

Anne Tyler, in The New York Times Book Review *(© 1976 by The New York Times Company; reprinted by permission), September 19, 1976.*

ELLA LEFFLAND

If this novel had been written ten years ago, I doubt that it would have been published. Bad writing in itself never kept a book from print if its subject was hot, but what audience in prelib days would have been thought ready for an oppressed woman who at the climax of a hurricane turns into the gunman she was raped by? Supernatural sex change could be entertaining (*Orlando, Turnabout*), but what would one make of the subject drenched in mythology and awash with symbols, a dark churning vehicle for the sufferings of Woman in a male-dominated world? ...

Once an idea's time arrives, the novels rush forth in droves to meet the demand. Some meet it creatively; too many, like *A Sea-Change*, can only bore their readers and litter the milieu with paste figures and message-scrawled placards. (p. 92)

Jessie is supposed to typify the submissive woman of yesterday—"She was, after all, not a new woman, but an 'old' woman in a new time"—while yet possessing enough spark to show potential. This might have been achieved if the author had made the effort, but her method of creating characters is to tack on statements about them as she goes along, as if posting announcements on a bulletin board. A quarter of the way through the book, for instance, we're puzzled to read that Jessie is "a strange and wonderful creature, full of discomforting insights and improbable passions," since we've seen no hint of this creature on previous pages. Nor is it possible to reconcile the statement that Jessie is too lax and timid to order for herself at a res-

taurant or to learn to drive, with the statement that she walked out on a lover of long standing one night, without a suitcase, to marry someone else. Lois Gould is much less interested in fusing the disparities of her heroine than in getting on with her sea-change. With no emotional fullness at its disposal, the change takes place in a vacuum.

The change is one from helplessness to control, with a long convoluted way to go before Jessie emerges as B.G. (black gunman).... [We] wonder in retrospect why Jessie couldn't have gone from point A to point B.G. without all the goddesses and natural phenomena in between. But then what would the author have done for symbols?

These are so abundant and explicit that they deal the death-blow to any hope of verisimilitude the story might have possessed.... [Virtually every name in the novel is symbolically significant—we] have been given carte blanche to play word games in the margin.

Diane [Jessie's daughter] and her younger sister are the prime source of symbols, engrossed in a collection of foreign dolls from which they have ousted all male representatives.... (pp. 92-4)

All the author's concern seems to have gone into this allegorical network, leaving nothing for the writing itself.... [Gould's stylistic] clumsiness bespeaks an indifferent attitude to readers who might conceivably expect more than a scribbled first draft. The tone, as well, has a slipshod quality. Dealing with earthbound matters in her first chapter, the author speaks unjarringly in what is probably her natural writing tone, one of brittle irony; but faced by a sea-change rich and strange, her voice slubbers around, becoming in turn lugubrious, indignant, and pedantic. We have no sense of a writer seized by an idea and wrestling with it to the best of her ability; rather, the writer seems to have looked for a surefire project and pulled out occult feminism. Good, a bag of symbols, sex thrown everywhere, and a hurricane for excitement. The tone can be figured out along the way—and, if possible, the meaning.

If Ms. Gould has figured out the meaning of her mishmash, I haven't. Control is clearly the book's pivotal idea, and there clarity ends. I know that a great deal more has been thrown into the pot than the concept of exploitee-turning-exploiter, but that is the most I can make out. As an idea, it is a good one, psychologically valid.... There is perhaps nothing so terrifying and tragic as the passion for safety that compels the oppressed to become oppressors, and, handled without abracadabra, Jessie Waterman might have had some literary value as one of these—a woman who abruptly sees her entire past as a gang rape, and becomes, herself, a psychological rapist. A more literal change than that should be attempted only by a writer with the sensibilities of Robert Louis Stevenson.

Presented as it is, *A Sea-Change* comes across vulgar, meretricious, and pointless. Whatever its inflated symbols may be up to, it never rises above the level of this characteristic scene: her house about to collapse on her, her daughter swept out to sea and presumably dead, Jessie finds the time and inclination for sexual experimentation with Surfman Leo on the floor. (p. 94)

Ella Leffland, "Heavy Weather," in Harper's *(copyright © 1976 by* Harper's Magazine; *all rights reserved; excerpted from the*

October, 1976 issue by special permission), October, 1976, pp. 92-4.

JUDITH VIORST

At the end of this witty and intelligent collection of essays ["Not Responsible for Personal Articles"] Lois Gould wonders what has happened to what she terms "the old ethical feminism." "We used to come together from very different places," she writes, "and we came not to judge, destroy, appease or lie to each other, but to find the connective tissues, without ever disowning our differences. Therein used to lie our strength."

Whether or not that strength has been lost to the women's movement . . . there is plenty of connective tissue in this book, which takes a feminist look at the meaning and morality of everything from ERA to Bloomingdale's. And, while readers may find themselves—as I did—differing strongly with Lois Gould on this or that point, I imagine that they will also find themselves—as I did—more interested in the connections than in the divisions. . . .

But if I am moved to argument, surely that's part of what makes this book worthwhile. For by challenging readers to think through old positions and consider new ones, it encourages us to distinguish reason from rote. And by offering us an essentially quite sane and humane point of view, it offers the hope that even after the lines of division are drawn, we still can find ourselves on the same side.

> Judith Viorst, "How Costly Is a Held Door?" in The New York Times Book Review (© 1978 by The New York Times Company; reprinted by permission), February 26, 1978, p. 13.

* * *

GOYTISOLO, Juan   1931-

Goytisolo is a Spanish novelist known for his works of ideological social comment. A child during the Spanish Civil War, he often reflects his experiences with a powerful, violent realism in works that are documentary in character. Considered part of the Spanish new wave, he has earned the reputation of the best Spanish novelist of his generation. (See also CLC, Vol. 5.)

MARY E. GILES

Juegos de manos [*The Young Assassins*] . . . reveals a . . . consistent and coherent treatment of the theme [of the scapegoat figure].

The narrative of *Juegos de manos* is structured into five main parts, formalized as chapters; these in turn are subdivided into cinematographically presented episodes. Through each of these five parts the scapegoat motif gradually takes shape as the characters assume appropriate archetypal roles. . . . [The] scapegoat motif effectively clarifies the universality of the novel's specific vision of man. . . .

The novel as a totality forcefully portrays the alienation and lack of purpose in a group of bourgeois Madrid youths. . . .

Each member of the group dramatically particularizes the collective anguish and lack of commitment. (p. 1021)

The archetypal function of chapter one is to establish an analogy between the anguish and disorientation of these youths and their counterparts' two thousand years ago. As man at that time lived in moral and physical despair without positive commitments, so, too, do the young people in Goytisolo's novel blindly and anxiously look for a meaning to existence. Man now, as then, uncertainly awaits redemption.

The many fragments of conflict—youth against society, against one another, against their own fears and insecurities—which fleetingly appear in chapter one coalesce and solidify in the second part. . . .

The scapegoat motif in this part unfolds in two ways. First the decision to have one person assassinate the politician on behalf of the group sets up the role of scapegoat. Second, Luis' actions and words about David suggest another main role, the betrayer. The chapter in its entirety, then, brings the action onto a more immediately personal level by defining roles and suggesting players: David, the scapegoat; Luis, the betrayer. (p. 1022)

[There is a] possibility of a third major role in the archetypal story, to be played by Agustín Mendoza. . . . Agustín appears in scenes from part three as a figure of real and potential evil in relation to David. His evil is real because his pernicious hold over David causes the once obedient, industrious youth to abandon his studies, reject his family, and foolishly accept Agustín's negative values. The potential of evil emerges from ominous contrasts between David and Agustín: Agustín is strong, David, weak; Agustín, the leader, David, the follower; Agustín is dark (archetypal symbol of evil), David is blonde (symbol of good). (p. 1023)

Although the fourth chapter is the briefest of the five, its exclusive concentration on David's conflict vis-à-vis his scapegoat role makes it crucial in the development of the motif. Its very brevity combined with the intensity of David's emotional crisis creates a sense of urgency which is esthetically apposite to this climatic moment in the narrative. In these pages David consciously (interior monologue) and subconsciously (stream of consciousness) recalls his childhood, adolescence, and futile student years in Madrid. As he reflects upon himself in relation to his friends and society in general, through three separate but inter-connected divisions of the chapter, his archetypal function is brilliantly clarified.

The chapter opens with a scene of David seated contemplatively in his room. He picks up the pistol to be used in the assassination and invoking a mental litany, tries to visualize himself a killer. . . . But seeing the Bible open on the table, he recognizes his cowardice. . . . These initial paragraphs underscore his hesitancy and fears.

The camera next focuses on David reading in a notebook some childhood reminiscences in which he depicts himself as a sick, lonely child. . . . (pp. 1023-24)

The use of stream of consciousness to present his psychological conflict in the third episode of the chapter is technically consummate. Through his subconscious runs a conversation in which he looks at the Bible and [questions] his grandmother. . . . The reference [in this passage] to the iniquity of the Egyptians *and* their children might be interpreted on a Judaic-Christian level as an allusion to man's original sin, in which case it would be reasonable to associate that concept with the idea of salvation through a redeemer. The conversation could then be seen as a means of anticipating the role which David will play later. . . .

These three episodes in chapter four represent the victim's spiritual preparation before entering public life. For just as Jesus spent forty days in the desert preparing himself, so must David endure these moments confronting his own weaknesses and fortifying himself for his commitment. (p. 1024)

David's role as scapegoat is fairly consistent, although there are some questionable areas in the analogy between him and Christ. Clearly David resembles Christ insofar as he willingly and knowingly allows himself to be chosen the scapegoat for the group. The following details strengthen the fundamental similarity between David and Christ: preparation for public life which for Christ is his three year ministry and for David the assassination attempt; the failure of each to succeed in terms of his colleagues' standards (for Christ's followers, success would have been the establishment of a kingdom on earth, not just in heaven; for David's friends it would be the assassination completed); the spiritual fortification before each is killed; the actual "crucifixion."

David's motives for accepting the scapegoat role, however, do not parallel Christ's in that he is prompted less by altruistic concern for his fellow man than selfish desire to prove himself a hero. . . . A resuming difference between the two figures . . . is that in the one story love is demonstrated positively through the unerring example of the scapegoat, whereas in the other that value is to be inferred from the actions of a less than perfect propitiatory victim. (pp. 1026-27)

Christ, David, and Agustín are scapegoats who assume a collective responsibility and guilt and in so doing clarify a universal truth—that love is the value by which man can best authenticate his humanity. Christ and Agustín demonstrate this truth through the extreme examples of their own actions, Christ's example being consistently and thoroughly positive, that of Agustín, consistently and thoroughly negative. David occupies an intermediary position in which the negative example of his initial acceptance of hate combines with the positive example of first rejecting that value and then sacrificing himself. (p. 1028)

Neither evading nor capitulating to the harshness and cruelty of reality, [Goytisolo] universalizes and humanizes the specific world of these Spanish youths so that we feel intensely the need to re-examine our own values in relation to our fellow man while at the same time hoping that out of this revaluation will come a renewed commitment to self-respect, compassion, and the dignity of man. Analyzing the novel as a predominantly negative example of the archetypal motif of the scapegoat is one means of bringing this universality dramatically into focus. (p. 1029)

> Mary E. Giles, "Juan Goytisolo's 'Juegos de Manos': An Archetypal Interpretation," in Hispania (© 1973 The American Association of Teachers of Spanish and Portuguese, Inc.), December, 1973, pp. 1021-29.

REED ANDERSON

Señas de identidad [*Marks of Identity*] is the detailed and intimate, yet broad and panoramic exploration of a personal crisis. Álvaro Mendiola, the author and protagonist (or perhaps Unamuno's term "agonist" would be more appropriate) portrays his own experience as a member of a specific generation of young Spaniards who were born during

the thirties, and for whom the Civil War is one of their childhood memories. He is the descendant of a tradition-bound family of industrialists and landowners whose values he despises. . . . The complex contradictions between these profound roots in a reactionary and dying social class, and Álvaro's conscious efforts to align himself sincerely and integrally with progressive social and political causes are what impel him toward the crisis of conscience that he attempts to explain and understand in this extensive self-examination. (p. 3)

Álvaro writes this complex autobiography as he looks back upon the experience of acute crisis he describes. He takes the reader with him through three August evenings and into the morning following his "breakdown". But the novel's real substance is the highly elaborated flashbacks that reveal all that has led up to Álvaro's most anguished hours of confusion and paralysis.

In order to examine his experience and judge whether it is or is not integral to forming an authentic notion of his own identitiy, Álvaro, as narrator, objectifies that experience as he writes. In a rather literal sense, he "goes out of his mind" so that he may see his experience more clearly. In narrative terms this objectification is achieved through the perspective adopted by the author: Álvaro Mendiola is actually looking back on not one, but several versions of himself. (p. 4)

[The] narrator is never, up until the final two pages of the novel, able to refer to himself using the pronoun "I" (yo). Instead, there are two main autobiographical subjects here: one is referred to as "you" (tú), and the other as "Álvaro," or simply "he" (él). It is as though the use of the "I" would assume an integration, a wholeness and unity of self that Álvaro is simply incapable of achieving as he looks at himself. The committed, definitive and integrated "I," therefore, has no place in his vocabulary as he examines his experience.

When referring to either of these subjects (tú or él) of his autobiography, Álvaro is referring to aspects of himself which he sees as somehow distinct from one another, and distinct from the person who is described as suffering this crisis of identity. At the same time, whether the narrator uses "tú" or "Álvaro" as his subject implies in either case an attitude toward that subject or aspect of himself which he is describing in the past. "Tú" conveys a sense of intimacy and identity, while not necessarily implying affection. The implicit relationship with this "tú", in fact, may be one of intense love and hatred at the same time. In contrast to the more intimate "tú", "Álvaro" or "él" as subject, implies a more objectified view of that aspect of the narrator's personality in the past. A sense of estrangement, of personal distance and even a lack of recognition is introduced where the experience of "Álvaro" rather than "tú" is the narrative's subject. (pp. 5-6)

"Álvaro" seems most basically to be a witness, an observer, a person through whose eyes and consciousness we understand the historical and human context of the narrator's past experience. (p. 6)

In the biography of "Álvaro," subject of . . . flashbacks in the third person, we [see] an example of a "novela testimonial," the biography of a young bourgeoise intellectual that traces his abortive attempt to escape the moral chaos of his own social class (seen in his family and his friend, Sergio), and, as an intellectual, to involve himself in a committed way to a struggle for social justice. But this biography of "Álvaro" is actually an autobiography, and the Álvaro we have seen so far is also the "tú" we encounter so often in this narrative. (p. 9)

If "Álvaro" embodies the narrator's capacity to bear witness to and chronicle the events of his life and his circumstances, then "tú" represents his affective capacities; when using "tú" as his subject, the narrator is elaborating his past experience at a subjective and more intimate level. From this perspective, the narrator touches upon the most elemental and unchangeable aspects of his own character. (p. 10)

In isolation, the portions of the novel narrated in the second person singular have a distinctly negative tone. They relate the profoundest and most permanent aspects of the narrator's subjective experience. Beneath the surface of the testimonial of "Álvaro" runs the deeper current of an impassioned confession (tú). The two currents most often run counter to one another. There always seems to be an ironic distance between "Álvaro" and "tú." Emotions and hatred clash with ideals, intuitive impulses and needs contradict conscious moral convictions, deep-rooted personal rebellion clouds his ability to see objectively, and action finally becomes impossible for him.

Álvaro's lack of personal integration is the novel's very subject then. Its coherence as a narrative rests in the process through which the author analyzes his own emotional and intellectual experience, which grows out of and contributes to that same lack of integration. It is the process of self-analysis and the experience so minutely analyzed that is central here, and not the sort of synthesis or philosophical view of that experience that we might expect to find in a more traditional confessional autobiography. (pp. 15-16)

[In] the final pages of his chronicle, having declared himself a pariah, the living contradiction of all that the official order of Spain has come to stand for, Álvaro has enabled himself to finally use the first-person as subject, to refer to himself with the committed and now definitive "yo."

The voices which opened the novel condemning Álvaro after his exile in France return now to assert the permanent victory of their moral and social order, and to send him once again into exile.... The novel ends with an ambiguous and melancholy tone. Álvaro seems to have derived a new sense of personal identity out of his crisis. But his rebellion as he finally expresses it here, seems puerile, the product of a personal rage that will again fail to find expression through effective channels. If Álvaro cannot formulate and realize his rebellion in social terms, it will remain private, eccentric and hermetic, easily dismissed by those he would attack, and posing no real threat to the order he opposes so vehemently. This final problem finds no resolution in *Señas de identidad*.

The only link that continues to unite Álvaro with Spain is the beautiful language they have in common. He now sees that even the language has become enslaved to the self-sustaining interests of the established order and its mythology.... It is the language itself, then, and its inherent function as the transmitter of the ruling class' mythologies and values that perpetuate the hated order and determine the crippled consciousness of Spain—this language will become both the medium for and the object of Álvaro's attack as a

writer in exile. In *Señas de identidad*, there is little indication of the direction Álvaro will take; but out of his new sense of personal identity as outcast and writer in fierce rebellion, *Reivindicación del Conde Don Julián* (Goytisolo's subsequent novel, 1970) is offered as the definitive annihilation of Álvaro's roots in the bourgeoise culture of Spain, and the most devastating of attacks on that culture, its values and its mythologies. (pp. 18-19)

> *Reed Anderson, "'Señas de identidad': Chronicle of Rebellion," in* Journal of Spanish Studies: Twentieth Century *(copyright © 1974 by the* Journal of Spanish Studies: Twentieth Century*), Spring, 1974, pp. 3-19.*

V. S. PRITCHETT

[The subject of exile] was established in "Marks of Identity" and "Count Julian;" now "Juan the Landless" ... completes a trilogy.... [Goytisolo's] novels are a sustained skirl of love-hatred for the country he derisively calls "Sunnyspain" of the travel brochures, or "the foul Stepmother." He has the traditional Catalan contempt for the central power of Castilian government and culture, its stagnant bureaucracy, monkish fanaticism, and cruelty—the lifeless formality and obedience to custom which put a lasting puritan gooseflesh on the famous Spanish stoics and saints and on the spontaneous sexual life of the natural man.... Savage digs at the Castilian classics are among the farcical passages of "Count Julian." ... The book was less a novel than a kind of anti-psalm—a chanted autobiography and a work of offensive travel.... There was an exhilarating scorn in that book. In "Juan the Landless," exhilaration turns to pain in the raw.

It is notoriously difficult to know how to sustain the force of a trilogy in its final volume. A scream will turn into a sob unless one can transpose it into thunderous orchestration, all drums going hard. To end not with a bang but a whimper may have suited the twenties, but it is useless now. There are alternatives: one of them is to give one's personal noise a wider geographical and historical territory. Goytisolo plays the dangerous game of solving his problems by enlarging them—as H. G. Wells did—to make them sound global. The danger is that generalized hate becomes vague and loses the force of the specific, and it must be said that in Goytisolo's final volume rhetorical generalities have weakened the force of his destructive fantasy and wit. To offset this, he, like other modern satirists with a revolutionary turn, has fallen back on obscenity. Here his masters are the homosexual Genet and the fashionable Marquis de Sade—sex and the scatological have their anarchic uses. Politically, the exile turns to Beckett for the *clochard*, the outcast and pariah, and finds a sort of anti-hero in T. E. Lawrence, whose sexual aberrations were a private revolt in the desert. Here Goytisolo is a neo-romantic celebrating the nonchalant freedom of the vagrant Arab sodomite. There are also references to Swift's obsession with excrement and gross sexuality....

"Juan the Landless" is really a book about the exile's imagination. (p. 146)

Although Goytisolo is rubbing our noses in his disgusts, he is also lashing himself, for the journeys and scenes he makes so physically vivid may not have occurred.... [The] joke is that he is imagining it all in his bleak North African room and is really writing about the imagination peculiar to exile; the exile's only capital, his only luggage, is his language. For the artist, language is "the splendid prerogative of our disguise": language dictates his "protean ever-shifting voices," as it certainly did in another of Goytisolo's masters, James Joyce. His North African room is, intellectually, in the Boulevard Saint-Germain. . . .

I trust [Goytisolo] in the streets of Fez, in all his ferocious caricatures, and in his satire on brochures, travelogues, and corrupt historical films. I trust his laughing phrases: "the double row of sphinxes pierced like sieves by the cameras of sightseeing tours," and "baritone sightseeing guides . . . recite names, dates, limp spaghetti-like bits of serpentine erudition." I admire his "protean voice" when he is sardonic. But when he is evoking T. E. Lawrence and I see "The Seven Pillars of Wisdom" on his table I know the tortured prose of that work will infect him. I prefer Goytisolo's tricks. I admire his ingenuity as an original narrator who addresses himself as "You," as if "You" were a kaleidoscope he is shaking, or were the half-mocking yet self-entranced audience of his schizophrenia. . . . [At the trilogy's end] Goytisolo returns to the pain of his remark that an exile's only luggage is his language. The pain is real, and he has made it real to us. . . . But when we find him ending his trilogy with a tormented avant-garde manifesto about the staleness of the realistic novel, the fraud of character drawing, the autonomy of the literary subject as a verbal structure, his incantation falls as flat as a lecture. (p. 149)

> *V. S. Pritchett, "An Exile's Luggage" (©*
> *by V. S. Pritchett; reprinted by permission*
> *of Harold Matson Co., Inc.), in The New*
> *Yorker, March 20, 1978, pp. 146, 149.*

*   *   *

GRADE, Chaim   1910-

Grade, a Lithuanian novelist, poet, short story writer, and essayist now living in the United States, is considered one of the greatest contemporary Yiddish writers. The setting for his work is the Eastern European Jewish ghetto prior to the ravages of the Second World War.

ELIE WIESEL

[The] work of Chaim Grade, by its vision and scope, establishes him . . . as one of the great—if not the greatest—of living Yiddish novelists. Surely he is the most authentic.

If we take as premise that for the contemporary Jewish writer to write means to testify, then we may affirm that Chaim Grade fulfills his mission with much talent and devotion. His . . . poetry and prose depict a world that is no more. (p. 5)

Every literary creation aims to correct injustice. In this case to remind the killer of his crimes, to affect the memory of the onlooker, to rebuild communities murdered and burned to ashes. What other writers have done for Warsaw or Sighet, Grade does for the town of his childhood: Vilna. His tales, his obsessions, his experiences always lead back to it—for that is where his roots are. Vilna, this fabulous and dazzling city that was so Jewish that it was given the surname of Jerusalem of Lithuania. And that is where the action of "The Agunah" unfolds. The time: some 15 or 16 years after World War I, when, far away, the reign of the executioner is about the begin. (pp. 5-6)

Will the uninitiated non-Jewish reader understand this so profoundly Jewish novel? I hope so.

True, Grade's universe seems closed to external events; it offers no opening to the outside world. All his characters, even the least important, are Jewish: the house-painters, the grave-diggers, the beggars, the revellers, the ladies' men, Grade's gaze never leaves them. I hope the reader will follow him; Vilna transcends Vilna. As is the case for many artistic endeavors, this singularly Jewish novel becomes universal because of its very singularity.

Furthermore I believe that in this particular work the absence of external history is deliberate. One can almost feel the killers' ominous shadow loom on the horizon. As though the author wished to tell us that while Jewish scholars engaged in passionate discussions over the faithful interpretation of a divine law, 3,000 years old, on the other side of borders, entire peoples readied themselves to solve the question of Jewish solitude and waiting—and all other questions—in their own way: by erecting an altar of flames, the darkest in history. (p. 6)

> *Elie Wiesel, in The New York Times Book*
> *Review (© 1974 by The New York Times*
> *Company; reprinted by permission), Sep-*
> *tember 1, 1974.*

RUTH R. WISSE

Yiddish literature, which flowered a century ago in Eastern Europe as an impulse of modernization, has now become largely commemorative, bearing favorable testimony to the world of traditional feeling and practice which Yiddish writers once rejected and sought to reform. This change is not simply a matter of nostalgia for the irretrievable past, but the result of a distinct inversion of values. Western modernity once held out to the Yiddish writer perspectives of individual freedom and a richness of spirit not to be found within the constraints of the Pale of Settlement or the code of Jewish law; yet that same constrained past, seen from this side of the Holocaust, now appears to offer a compelling image of a relatively hopeful, morally robust, and genuinely *better* world. To write of East European Jewry is thus today a means not of expressing but of repudiating a tragic vision of mankind.

The work of Chaim Grade, one of the finest contemporary Yiddish writers, is a powerful instance of this altered view. . . . His single most ambitious work, *The Yeshiva*, . . . returns to the obsessive subject of Grade's best poetry and prose—his years in the yeshivas of Vilna, Valkenik, Bielsk, and Bialystok. But the atmosphere that was once represented in Grade's work as harshly oppressive now appears almost luminous and bracingly fresh. . . .

Among the many outstanding Yiddish writers who came to adolescence in Vilna before World War II, Grade was the only one thoroughly trained in talmudic and rabbinic sources. . . . [In] his teens Grade attended one yeshiva after another, where he came under the decisive influence of the *mussarists,* followers of Rabbi Israel Salanter.

The *mussar* movement developed in response to two perceived dangers: on the one hand, the threat of the Haskalah, or Enlightenment, that was weaning Jews from religious observance; on the other hand, the stultification of Jewish religious experience, which was hardening into ritualism. (p. 70)

The title of his first book of poems, *Yo* ("Yes"), confirmed the affirmative dedication of his verse, which was now channelled to national themes. The poet, said Grade, "must learn from the prophets who in times of brazen impudence warned of impending danger, and in time of ruin, when all lay waste, foretold the resurrection of the dead."

Nevertheless, Grade's single most powerful work of the 1930's was neither prophetic nor an affirmation. *Mussarniks,* a long narrative poem of thinly-disguised autobiography, was Grade's first attempt to dramatize the conflicts that drove him from *mussar* but continued to claim the deepest regions of his mind and soul. In the poem Chaim Vilner, the author's fictional self, looks back from a distance of seven years to the autumn of 1930 when he felt himself torn between the punishing moral rectitude of Reb Aba, his fiery headmaster, and the attractions of secular books and ideas. (p. 71)

A book of poems dedicated to his dead wife, *With Your Body Upon My Hands,* [written after the destruction of Grade's family, friends, and neighborhood] inflicts as cruel a self-punishment on its author as one would wish the murderers to have suffered. Memories of his mother and of their teeming Vilna neighborhood stirred up yet wilder despair. Perhaps in the hope of finding a new artistic equilibrium, Grade turned to prose, for him an untried medium and one that appeared to offer both a lower level of intensity and a more relaxed pace.

From the perspective of Paris, where he began to reconstruct his postwar life, Grade returned to his struggle with *mussar.* "My Quarrel with Hersh Rasseyner" is a singular story, the first to make Grade's reputation in English; it dramatizes the fortuitous reunion in the Paris metro of Chaim Vilner and his fellow *mussarist,* the antagonist of the story's title. Utterly free of the then-prevalent tendency toward romanticization, the story takes up the old argument with surprising acerbity as the two survivors, one now a well-known Yiddish writer, the other a *mussarist* teacher, oppose one another in unrelenting debate.

The brilliant confrontation between Jewish believer and Jewish secularist is heightened by the play of a third participating presence: time. The Holocaust, recognizing no distinction, has with crushing irony ravaged Vilner and Rasseyner alike. They, however, resist its undiscriminating reductivism.... There is in this story a remarkable exhilaration, deriving not only from the tension of the debate—which remains a draw—but from the combined victory of the debaters over time and circumstance....

It is this same argument that Grade takes up again in *The Yeshiva,* the grandest of several novels he wrote after settling in America....

The Yeshiva, set in Poland in the 1920's, is a superabundant work, charged with a moral obsessiveness like Dostoevsky's and the bereaved lover's passion to record every remembered moment of the past. Grade goes straight to the heart of the matter, choosing for his protagonist the rigid *mussarist* headmaster, Reb Aba, here in the somewhat suppler form of Tsemakh Atlas.... (p. 72)

From [the time that the author's familiar projection, Chaim Vilner, is introduced], the book goes off into many byways, with every minor figure introducing a subplot of his own, all with a similar tension: the harsh competition between passion and continence in the forging of human identity.... Tsemakh's determination to uproot evil by force creates a

web of hardship and resentment, and his attempt to will away temptation, humbling himself and others into submissiveness, ends only in misery, in ever deepening depression, Chaim Vilner turns from the punishing joylessness of *mussar* to a milder master, Reb Avraham-Shaye Kosover. (pp. 72-3)

One might have expected Grade, working in the greater amplitude and leisure offered by the novel as a form, to develop his old subject in any number of new ways.... Yet Grade ... [restricts] his canvas once again to the internal Jewish world, and within that to the ethical and moral dimensions of its religious culture. There is greater psychological depth in this work than in any of Grade's earlier prose, but even here he stays within his single context, probing underlying motives and subconscious desires—just as *mussar* does—not in the interests of an integrated personality but as part of the search for true moral perfection. Despite the more ambitious genre, the concentration is as exclusive as ever, and two familiar types still occupy center stage: Tsemakh Atlas, the *mussar* activist, and Chaim Vilner, in many ways his younger counterpart, equally lustful and stubborn by nature, at first unable and later unwilling to subjugate his feelings to his will.

Grade's major thematic innovation in *The Yeshiva* is Reb Avraham-Shaye, the man of seemingly effortless goodness and wisdom, who steps into the lives of the two main characters, and into the breach between them, bringing the same harmony he has achieved in himself. Unfortunately, though the modest sage is a particularly memorable figure, in his capacity of spiritual cornerstone he blunts some of the novel's force. Where *Mussarniks* and "My Quarrel with Hersh Rasseyner" bring conflict to a pitch and leave it suspended there, *The Yeshiva* attempts a wistful resolution that is dramatically unconvincing and historically dubious.

This becomes clearer, and correspondingly, more problematic, in Volume II.... It is as if Grade were suggesting that a truly wise man could not only resolve the perplexities of yeshiva students, but even find a way to pacify a process of personal, interpersonal, and communal upheaval that was beginning to reach, in the period the novel describes, the proportions of a cultural earthquake. The influence of Reb Avraham-Shaye over the more compelling fictional personalities of Tsemakh Atlas and Chaim Vilner is not psychologically convincing. More importantly, the quickened pulse of one of the most fractious periods in Jewish history, which Grade brilliantly evokes, is artificially slowed by the presentation of the "good Jew" as an effective principle of conciliation.

It is clear from a comparison of Grade's several treatments of his subject over the years that he has grown more protective of the past with each successive work....

Grade's greatness lies in confrontation. When the voices of husband and wife, father and son, teacher and pupil, Zionist and anti-Zionist, are raised in a flush of disputation, *The Yeshiva* grows charged with narrative energy that regenerates the past and brings it a rare immediacy. Grade's imagination—honed in talmudic dialectic, nurtured by the contradictions of his youthful environment and by the warring impulses within himself—finds its most satisfying expression in debate, the defiant clash of opposing convictions.

It is only when an understandable deference to the culture

that produced him prompts Grade to wrap his characters in kindly resolution or proclaim their greatness as fact that his work loses its fire, becomes elegaic, and, rather than keeping the past alive, helps lay it softly to rest. At such moments Grade seems almost to have entered into a silent complicity with today's reader, for whom *all* of the East European experience—religious and secular, radical and Zionist, Yiddishist and Hebraist, and each of the contending factions in between—is likely to be bathed in the same historical glow, and to whom both those who accepted God and those who rejected Him now seem equally "pious." As a definitive corrective to just such leveling notions stands the work of Chaim Grade at its corrosive best. Indeed, there is probably nothing in literature that more vividly confirms the vanished culture of East European Jewry than the rhetorical splendor of Grade's intellectuals and marketwomen when they remain triumphantly unreconciled, fixed in attitudes of animated opinion. (p. 73)

> *Ruth R. Wisse, "In Praise of Chaim Grade" (reprinted from* Commentary *by permission; copyright © 1977 by the American Jewish Committee), in* Commentary, *April, 1977, pp. 70-3.*

MOSHE MOSKOWITZ

From its inception, the theology of Rabbinic Judaism has been that of a beleaguered community whose classic institutions were under constant attack. In reshaping and restating the principles of a normative Judaism at the critical moment when the political and judicial responsibility for the community first passed into their hands, the Rabbis' main effort was directed at keeping the Torah supreme. They reasoned that adherence to the highest discernible meaning of the Torah would keep the community together and, at the same time, promote the higher life of the Jewish people. Nevertheless, the early teachers of the Torah were superlatively practical and what they enjoined was not blind and automatic obedience, but, rather, a reasonable adherence to the Law in keeping with Hillel's principle of "practical benevolence."

It is this traditional principle, in conflict with the self-damning dogma of ascetic Musarism, which forms the background of Chaim Grade's sweeping and masterful Yiddish novel, *Tsemakh Atlas*, the first volume of which is [an English translation entitled] *The Yeshiva*.

Grade's novel begins at that point in Jewish history when the Musar movement had begun to fail as a constructive religious reaction to the Haskalah. Founded by Rabbi Israel Salanter in 1840, it sought to counter the centrifugal effects of the Haskalah by stressing Torah study, good deeds, compassion, and critical self-examination, all within the fraternal bounds of a cohesive Jewish community. Some of Salanter's later disciples, however, contributed to the eventual inefficacy of the movement by accenting a harsh and masochistic asceticism, thus forgetting the practical view of the founders of normative Rabbinic Judaism who, many centuries earlier, had recognized both human weakness and potentiality and had decreed that "no ordinance is to be laid on the people unless the majority of the people are able to bear it."

Placing the action of his novel in the environs of Vilna, Poland, after the first World War, Grade spins an alternately moody and volcanic tale which is not only breathtaking in its polychromatic effect, but which also gives visible evidence of the profound and compassionate understanding of man's vulnerability to his own instincts.

It is the milieu of the Musarist yeshiva—its students, supporters, enemies, and its particular flavor—which is the focal point of the novel. For those to whom the word *yeshiva* conjures up arcadian visions of pale and sensitive young Jews forever preoccupied with matters of Torah and other heavenly thoughts, Grade's portrayal comes as a rude shock. The paleness is there, but the sensitivity is frequently replaced by lust, greed, and a vicious concern for self-glorification. These yeshiva students often evince a pettiness which is at the furthest remove from the intent and spirit of the Torah. (pp. 115-16)

The novel bristles with characterizations, and there are fascinating portraits of some of the parents of the yeshiva students as well. These portraits and vignettes are never flat, or black and white. Each of the characters, negative though he may be, seems caught up in the turmoil of his feelings, and in the feelings of those about him. The ultimate effect is that of an East European Jewry rocking on its emotional heels, clawing its way to some inscrutable goal. . . .

In addition, Grade's profiles of pious and love-hungry Jewish women, as well as of scheming adolescent girls bent on snaring a husband, are drawn with skill and sympathy. The most memorable feminine portrait is that of Slava, the protagonist's wife. (p. 116)

All of these characters, however, appear as peripheral rapids churning about the maelstrom that is the central character, Tsemakh Atlas. There has seldom been a more powerful characterization in all of Yiddish literature than that of the brooding and guilt-ridden Tsemakh, who, to shift the figure of speech, hovers over the pages of the novel like some gigantic Promethean vulture ready to swoop down and devour its own liver. (pp. 116-17)

Although Tsemakh's self-punishing behavior often seems exaggerated in the light of modern morality, in Grade's skillful delineation he emerges as an impressive and tragic figure. This is so because his nature, though it appears within the Jewish context of a religiously sanctioned socialized masochism, is, nevertheless, universal. Tsemakh is not self-destructive merely because he is an adherent of the Musarist philosophy. On the contrary, the Musarist yeshiva offers him the convenient framework within which he can inflict the needed punishment. (p. 117)

Tsemakh's disposition contains both of these elements. When faced with the prospect of moderate comfort, as in his betrothal to Dvorele Namiot, he flees into the arms of the dubious and flighty Slava. When finally presented with the opportunity of becoming a settled, wealthy, and possibly philanthropic merchant through his marriage with Slava, he destroys that relationship and becomes involved with Ronya, with whom he will not permit himself even a modicum of pleasure. Thus, his life becomes a long series of punishments and failures which, to his mind, are richly deserved and which provide him with a certain measure of perverse enjoyment: "Though he had found no answer during his solitude, he spent every free hour there and took pleasure in tormenting himself." . . .

Why this overriding inclination for self-negation and humiliation? Perhaps it is precisely because he feels so deeply the animal part of his nature. It is certainly no accident that most of the characters in this novel are described in animal terms. Thus, Vova Barbitoler looks like a man "who had crawled out of a forest cave," or else he is described as a "wild beast sunning his face." Volodya Stupel, Tsemakh's brother-in-law, is compared to "a bear with an upraised paw," and Slava herself is pictured as a cat: "She clambered over to a deep chair, folded her legs beneath her again, and stroked her knees with both hands." In addition, there are numerous descriptions stressing the dark, animal-aspects of Tsemakh's nature. (p. 118)

Tsemakh despises himself for these animal features.... The buried lust hidden within himself, Tsemakh feels, must be extirpated by resorting to a religious masochism.

There are two aspects of these "buried lusts" that bear remarking upon. One is that they cannot possibly refer only to Tsemakh's feelings for the bizarre and inaccessible Slava, for these lie on the surface, as do his hesitant gropings for Ronya. Instead, it is quite likely that Tsemakh is actually punishing himself for those infantile lusts and desires which are "buried" in the unconscious and which have surfaced again with merely a change in characters: it is no longer the forbidden mother who is desired, but a Slava or a Ronya.

Secondly, it is not incest that the rabbis regard as the ultimate sin, but, rather, the wish to do away with God. The son not only wishes to possess the mother but also to replace the father. Throughout the novel, Tsemakh is tortured by doubt.... Thus, Tsemakh punishes himself not only for his fantasies of forbidden women, but also because of his ambivalent feelings toward God the father. In so doing, he indulges in even more sinful self-aggrandizement: to Grade's brilliant imagery of Tsemakh as a bird of prey must be added another image—that of Tsemakh as a sinister avenging angel who steals God's wrath and turns it against himself.

These latter remarks, which may seem to be a kind of psychoanalytical *divertissement*, are perfectly fitting in view of the therapeutic aspects of another wonderful Grade characterization—that of Reb Avraham-Shaye, referred to in the novel as Mahaze Avraham. This imposing but radiant figure, who is based on one of the author's early teachers, Rabbi Abraham Isaiah Karelitz, also known as Hazon Ish, counters the fierce gloom which emanates from Tsemakh Atlas. He calms the emotional storms raging about Tsemakh and soothes the self-inflicted wounds of the *Musarnikes* with patient listening, a deferential smile, and gentle aphorisms which point the way to right conduct. (pp. 118-19)

Mahaze Avraham never proposes a general moral laxity, nor does he advocate a secular humanism with little or no connection to the basic customs and practices of traditional Judaism. On the contrary, though he espouses social and artistic sublimation, he does so within the context of the foundation of Rabbinic Judaism: "The strength that can lift man up is inherent in the acquisition of wisdom.... Hence studying Torah is the only sure way...." (p. 119)

It should be noted that behind the technical device of animal imagery, Grade's art remains essentially humanistic and imbued with a sense of high seriousness. Through its use of multiple plots and characters *The Yeshiva* conveys an atmosphere teeming with the thickness of Jewish life.... In its total effect, Grade's *The Yeshiva* not only communicates a brilliant illusion of life and reality within the Jewish context and at a particular point in Jewish history, but it also imparts Grade's essential message: it inveighs against the excessive achievement of a self-defeating heroism, and restates the traditional Jewish belief in an inward principle of tolerant order. (pp. 119-20)

> *Moshe Moskowitz, "Contra 'Musar'," in* Judaism (*copyright © 1978 by the American Jewish Congress*), *Winter, 1978, pp. 115-20.*

MORTON A. REICHEK

Chaim Grade is a major author in what has tragically become a minor language, Yiddish....

"Masters and Disciples" is the second part of Grade's two-volume epic novel, "The Yeshiva."...

"The Yeshiva" is a saga about Talmudic students and their teachers, and is laced with plots and subplots involving brooding moralists consumed by guilt and doubts and religious scholars grappling with secular temptations. It presents a panorama of life in Eastern Europe's yeshivas, or Talmudic academies, that has never been depicted before in fiction.

Like all of Grade's novels, "The Yeshiva" eulogizes the pre-Nazi world of Jewish religious scholars and functionaries in the ghetto towns of Poland and Lithuania, and resurrects in literature a society that was destroyed in World War II. Written in a quaintly old-fashioned style and brimming with an extraordinary gallery of *shtetl* personalities, it is concerned with the ethical considerations of Judaism and the confrontation between religious faith and secular values....

"The Yeshiva" is a powerful and complex novel that demonstrates why Grade ranks as a literary heavyweight among Yiddishists, and it helps explain why the translation of his writing has been so long delayed.

Comparison of his work with Singer's is inevitable. Singer is a highly gifted storyteller who disclaims any concern with social or philosophical messages. His mystical and often erotic tales appeal to modern tastes and his exotic color is relatively easy for an outsider to absorb. Grade's work is markedly different. The Jewish particularism is much stronger in his writing. In focusing so clinically on Jewish ethics, Grade is immersed in more formidable themes and makes considerably greater demands on the reader. He is less immediately accessible to the non-Jew, and to Jews who are unfamiliar with Orthodox religious ritual and Talmudic dialectic....

Though Volume II is self-contained, familiarity with Volume I enriches it. It continues the story of Tsemakh Atlas, a man of fierce piety and terrible secret doubts....

A supreme moralist, Atlas is tormented because neither he nor the people around him can live up to his own extremist code of behavior.... His is the tragedy of a man who cannot do the good he wants to do and who performs the evil that violates his own conscience....

This remarkable book will make rewarding reading for anyone willing to cope with an unfamiliar cultural and religious terrain, for he will encounter an exceptional literary talent and a provocative treatment of the universal theme of man in conflict with his own religious beliefs.

Morton A. Reichek, "Talmudic Temptations," in The New York Times Book Review *(© 1978 by The New York Times Company; reprinted by permission), January 8, 1978, p. 10.*

H

HAMILL, Pete 1935-

Hamill is an American journalist, novelist, editor, and screenwriter. *Flesh and Blood* is his third novel. (See also *Contemporary Authors*, Vols. 25-28, rev. ed.)

CHRISTOPHER LEHMANN-HAUPT

"Flesh and Blood" is a powerful story. For one thing, Mr. Hamill's boxing material seems unusually savvy and authentic, though it's hard to say whether this is a purely technical achievement or the result of Mr. Hamill's having thinly disguised several actual figures in the profession. . . . Whatever the case, the boxing passages are a good deal more sophisticated than they are in most fiction of this sort. For once we can really believe it when Caputo tells his young charge, "You're not a fighter. You're a bum. An Irish bum . . . But I can make you a fighter." And he does. (p. C29)

> *Christopher Lehmann-Haupt, in* The New York Times (© *1977 by The New York Times Company; reprinted with permission), November 18, 1977.*

ELIOT ASINOF

Blond blue-eyed Bobby Fallon is a tough Brooklyn Irish kid with a hunger to slay dragons. His fists hit like a mule kicking downhill. When he throws a punch, a scream bellows his rage, for his world is an endless chain of enemies.

The torment of Pete Hamill's hero [in "Flesh and Blood"] is an erotic passion for his mother Kate, a beautiful half-Shoshone woman of 36 with a poignant, enigmatic smile. Kate, in turn, miserably lonely at the desertion of her dashing husband Jack, transfers her love to Bobby. In this savage novel there are no priests to condemn their sinning, nor are they tormented by conscience. Son and mother love and make love repeatedly, dominated by their irrepressible need for each other. . . .

Hamill writes through the voice of his hero, sometimes in the first person, sometimes in the second—stark staccato sentences designed to sting, building suspense that is rooted in character, relentlessly knifing through Bobby's ferocity.

In prison for punching out a cop in a barroom brawl, Bobby punches out his frustrations: "I lived in a world where being white was being alone. It was different from the oth-ers. They were all black or Puerto Ricans. They had each other. But I was white. Being unbeatable was my only edge." Later, a reporter writes that he boxed "like a man imprisoned in solitude, unaware of the crowd, unaware of anything but the presence of an enemy." And Bobby says of himself: "I made every fight a war . . . because if I lost . . . I was in terrible trouble. I would become nothing again." And through it all, Hamill gives us the jargon: a knocked-out fighter, for instance, is "a tomato can." (p. 15)

Hamill's hero is brought to the final crucible, fighting for his soul, in combat with everyone . . . and, most of all, himself. Hamill takes us down to the hard sweaty canvas with him, and there's nothing pretty about it.

If you like such fables of the fight game served up tough and sordid with the lyrical strains of "Danny Boy" to sweeten the anguish of Oedipus, here is a taut, punchy read that makes "Rocky" seem like a fairy tale. (p. 46)

> *Eliot Asinof, "Some Oedipus, Some Danny Boy," in* The New York Times Book Review (© *1977 by The New York Times Company; reprinted by permission), November 20, 1977, pp. 15, 46.*

ROBERT STEPHEN SPITZ

Pete Hamill's previous novels (*A Killing for Christ, The Gift*) have been cogent, mannered vignettes about Brooklyn life. In *Flesh and Blood*, Hamill has unfortunately succumbed to the ignoble television-bred myth that the public will respond positively only to recycled pulp. However, despite its commercial obeisance, this book illuminates the author's ability to capture with stylized brio the nuances of the aching underbelly of society. That sensitivity in itself warrants a modicum of respect, with a cautious eye to the future. . . .

Flesh and Blood is an engrossing enough study of the lineal knot that becomes slowly untied. It travels the *Rocky* road, and while it "coulda been a contenduh," it emerges as only a pretender to the crown. (p. 40)

> *Robert Stephen Spitz, in* Saturday Review (© *1978 by Saturday Review Magazine Corp.; reprinted with permission), January 7, 1978.*

HAMMETT, (Samuel) Dashiell   1894-1961

An American novelist, short story writer, and author of scripts for film and radio, Hammett is known for his development of the realistic crime novel. A former detective himself, he is perhaps most famous as the creator of Sam Spade. His use of dialogue and terse literary style are often compared to Hemingway's. (See also *CLC*, Vols. 3, 5.)

STEVEN MARCUS

[The complex, ambiguous, and problematic] permeate Hammett's work and act as formative elements in its structure, including its deep structure. Hammett's work went through considerable and interesting development in the course of his career of twelve years as a writer. He also wrote in a considerable variety of forms and worked out a variety of narrative devices and strategies. At the same time, his work considered as a whole reveals a remarkable kind of coherence. In order to further the understanding of that coherence, we can propose for the purposes of the present analysis to construct a kind of "ideal type" of a Hammett or Op story. Which is not to say or to imply in the least that he wrote according to a formula, but that an authentic imaginative vision lay beneath and informed the structure of his work.

Such an ideal-typical description runs as follows. The Op is called in or sent out on a case. Something has been stolen, someone is missing, some dire circumstance is impending, someone has been murdered—it doesn't matter. The Op interviews the person or persons most immediately accessible. They may be innocent or guilty—it doesn't matter; it is an indifferent circumstance. Guilty or innocent, they provide the Op with an account of what they know, of what they assert really happened. The Op begins to investigate; he compares these accounts with others that he gathers; he snoops about; he does research; he shadows people, arranges confrontations between those who want to avoid one another, and so on. What he soon discovers is that the "reality" that anyone involved will swear to is in fact itself a construction, a fabrication, a fiction, a faked and alternate reality—and that it has been gotten together before he ever arrived on the scene. And the Op's work therefore is to deconstruct, decompose, deplot, and defictionalize that "reality"·and to construct or reconstruct out of it a true fiction, i.e., an account of what "really" happened.

It should be quite evident that there is a reflexive and coordinate relation between the activities of the Op and the activities of Hammett, the writer. Yet the depth and problematic character of this self-reflexive process begin to be revealed when we observe that the reconstruction or true fiction created and arrived at by the Op at the end of the story is no more plausible—nor is it meant to be—than the stories that have been told to him by all parties, guilty or innocent, in the course of his work. The Op may catch the real thief or collar the actual crook—that is not entirely to the point. What is to the point is that the story, account, or chain of events that the Op winds up with as "reality" is no more plausible and no less ambiguous than the stories that he meets with at the outset and later. What Hammett has done—unlike most writers of detective or crime stories before him or since—is to include as part of the contingent and dramatic consciousness of his narrative the circumstance that the work of the detective is itself a fiction-making activity, a discovery or creation by fabrication of some-thing new in the world, or hidden, latent, potential, or as yet undeveloped within it. (pp. 370-71)

When a fiction becomes visible as such it begins to dissolve and disappear, and presumably should reveal behind it the "real" reality that was there all the time and that it was masking. Yet what happens in Hammett is that what is revealed as "reality" is a still further fiction-making activity—in the first place the Op's, and behind that yet another, the consciousness present in many of the Op stories and all the novels that Dashiell Hammett, the writer, is continually doing the same thing as the Op and all the other characters in the fiction he is creating. That is to say he is making a fiction (in writing) in the real world; and this fiction, like the real world itself, is coherent but not necessarily rational. What one both begins and ends with then is a story, a narrative, a coherent yet questionable account of the world. This problematic penetrates to the bottom of Hammett's narrative imagination and shapes a number of its deeper processes—in *The Dain Curse*, for example, it is the chief topic of explicit debate that runs throughout the entire novel.

Yet Hammett's writing is still more complex and integral than this. For the unresolvable paradoxes and dilemmas that we have just been describing in terms of narrative structure and consciousness are reproduced once again in Hammett's vision and representation of society, of the social world in which the Op lives. . . . There is a kind of epiphany of these circumstances in "The Golden Horseshoe." The Op is on a case that takes him to Tijuana. In a bar there, he reads a sign:

> ONLY GENUINE PRE-WAR AMERICAN AND
> BRITISH WHISKEYS SERVED HERE

He responds by remarking that "I was trying to count how many lies could be found in those nine words, and had reached four, with promise of more," when he is interrupted by some call to action. That sign and the Op's response to it describe part of the existential character of the social world represented by Hammett.

Another part of that representation is expressed in another kind of story or idea that Hammett returned to repeatedly. The twenties were also the great period of organized crime and organized criminal gangs in America, and one of Hammett's obsessive imaginations was the notion of organized crime or gangs taking over an entire society and running it as if it were an ordinary society doing business as usual. In other words, society itself would become a fiction, concealing and belying the actuality of what was controlling it and perverting it from within. One can thus make out quite early in this native American writer a proto-Marxist critical representation of how a certain kind of society works. Actually the point of view is pre- rather than proto-Marxist, and the social world as it is dramatized in many of these stories is Hobbesian rather than Marxist. . . . In Hammett, society and social relations are dominated by the principle of basic mistrust. As one of his detectives remarks, speaking for himself and for virtually every other character in Hammett's writing, "'I trust no one.'"

When Hammett turns to the respectable world, the world of respectable society, of affluence and influence, of open personal and political power, he finds only more of the same. The respectability of respectable American society is as much a fiction and a fraud as the phony respectable society fabricated by the criminals. Indeed he unwaveringly represents the world of crime as a reproduction in both structure and detail of the modern capitalist society that it depends on, preys off, and is part of. But Hammett does something even more radical than this. He not only continually juxtaposes and connects the ambiguously fictional worlds of art and of writing with the fraudulently fictional worlds of society. He connects them, juxtaposes them, and sees them in dizzying and baffling interaction. He does this in many ways and on many occasions. One of them, for example, is the Maltese Falcon itself, which turns out to be and contains within itself the history of capitalism. It is originally a piece of plunder, part of what Marx called the "primitive accumulation"; when its gold encrusted with gems is painted over it becomes a mystified object, a commodity itself; it is a piece of property that belongs to no one— whoever possesses it does not really own it. At the same time it is another fiction, a representation or work of art— which turns out itself to be a fake, since it is made of lead. It is a rara avis indeed. As is the fiction in which it is created and contained, the novel by Hammett. (pp. 372-74)

[There] is a paradoxical tension and unceasing interplay in Hammett's stories between means and ends; relations between the two are never secure or stable. (p. 376)

It is through such complex devices as I have merely sketched here that Hammett was able to raise the crime story into literature. He did it over a period of ten years. Yet the strain was finally too much to bear—that shifting, entangled, and equilibrated state of contradictions out of which his creativity arose and which it expressed could no longer be sustained. His creative career ends when he is no longer able to handle the literary, social, and moral opacities, instabilities, and contradictions that characterize all his best work.... Yet for ten years he was able to do what almost no other writer in this genre has ever done so well— he was able to really write, to construct a vision of a world in words, to know that the writing was about the real world and referred to it and was part of it; and at the same time he was able to be self-consciously aware that the whole thing was problematical and about itself and "only" writing as well. For ten years, in other words, he was a true creator of fiction. (p. 377)

Steven Marcus, "Dashiell Hammett and the Continental Op," in Partisan Review *(copyright © 1974 by Partisan Review, Inc.), Vol. XLI, No. 3, 1974, pp. 362-77.*

H. H. MORRIS

Along with Raymond Chandler . . . Hammett was one of the giants who established an American voice and style that stood in opposition to the British-dominated country-house school. His criminals were habitual wrongdoers, not insane spinsters, vicars, or retired colonels. His detectives were hardworking professionals, not gentlemen amateurs solving murders for lack of a more edifying hobby. He wrote about killings committed with the weapons men routinely use for murder, not exotic poisons or knives made of ice. Most importantly, Hammett set his crimes in a believable and recognizable environment.

This use of environment makes Hammett worthy of discussion as a serious American novelist and short story writer. His achievements in crime fiction have tended to obscure his genuine literary talents.... (p. 196)

Hammett's vision of America was that of a man staring at a vast wasteland. He shared with Sinclair Lewis the belief that the nation's traditional leaders lacked integrity, that the balance sheet had replaced ethical codes of conduct. Like F. Scott Fitzgerald, Hammett saw the children of the rich as spoiled seekers after illicit thrills. With Faulkner, he wrote of society's dregs, the misfits condemned to live out a nightmare existence with no hope of escape. Hammett was one more writer of the 1920's and 1930's who took the naturalism of Dreiser and Norris as a received fiction technique and applied it to life around him.

None of these comparisons should suggest that Dashiell Hammett belongs among the giants.... His writing is flawed. He fit too well into the *Black Mask* ambience. His strained metaphors and thieves' argot come across as stylized and artificial.... Hammett's characters are often flat, distinguished from one another only by colorful nicknames, physical descriptions, and police records. Because pulp fiction demanded lots of action, his plots dominate all other story elements.

There are many points for comparison between [John] Gay and Hammett. They lived in different centuries and different cultures; one wrote for the stage, while the other wrote mass fiction, yet both found incontrovertible proof that the seamy underbelly of society is an honest reflection of the dishonest upper stratum.... Hammett's attack on his corrupt society was part of an honorable literary tradition.

Nonetheless, Hammett was unique to his time and place. In choosing to write hardboiled crime stories and novels, he committed himself to producing works that would please a mass audience unwilling—or unable—to search for subtleties. As a crime writer he had but two choices: to create a milieu that matched the conventions surrounding certain romanticized characters (Robin Hood, A. J. Raffles, Sherlock Holmes), or to set his stories in an environment that readers connected with reality.... Hammett chose recognizable reality.

He could have stopped with genuine criminals pursued by hardworking cops who considered the third degree a routine investigative method. This alone would have sufficed to make him important in crime and detective fiction, for his literary abilities were far above the standards demanded of the subgenre's practitioners. Hammett went far beyond this safe point, however. He saw—and wrote about—a culture in which petty criminals went to jail while the truly big crooks ran for Congress. When he wrote about this phenomenon, his readers recognized it as the story behind the headlines in their local newspapers. (pp. 197-98)

The importance of [Hammett's] attitude lies less in his influence on subsequent crime writers than in his success in a mass audience subgenre. A writer who aims his work at the uneducated or unsophisticated must reflect their perceptions and beliefs. Hammett succeeded by assuming that his readers perceived the wasteland as clearly as did the literary and intellectual elites....

He wrote always about greed. Both wealth and power corrupted his characters. Dishonest cops and politicians were the norm. Nick Charles and Sam Spade, the two detectives whom the moviemakers turned into pallid, posturing imitations of Hammett's harsh originals, found the desire for easy wealth a temptation too great to overcome. (p. 200)

In Hammett's environment, the law itself was often at fault. This, too, came from reality.... Society's strictures had become absurd, and a free man could only resist them. If there is any Romantic element in Hammett's worldview, it is the glorification of every individual, the passionate commitment to personal freedom that underlies the American myth of the frontier. (pp. 200-01)

This view of a corrupt universe is what makes the comparison of Hammett to Lewis and Fitzgerald so accurate. All three wrote in a conservative style. All three assumed that their readers comprehended the impulse to gain material wealth—and that these same readers recognized the impulse's potential for destroying those who followed it. None of them posited an America where the people fully believed in the pious public virtue so ostentatiously professed by politicians and preachers. Hammett, however, carried the idea of public despair over and disenchantment with American life much further than did the other two. Lewis strove for outrage. By exposing corruption and hypocrisy he hoped to anger his readers into action. Fitzgerald wanted a bittersweet sadness. He made his sad, rich young men suffer from their sins, so that readers could feel sorry for them. Hammett gave his readers credit for more intelligence. He assumed that they would suffer the full numbness of helpless recognition.

Recognition began with real criminals and detectives who couldn't spell nobility, let alone practice it.... The sum of Hammett's work is a powerful jeremiad indicting virtually all of American society.

His world was as much the wasteland as London/Limbo, the "Unreal City / Under the brown fog of a winter noon." ... But while Eliot holds out the hope of the impending rescue by Parsifal, Hammett never suggests that any man can enter the ruined tower and find the Holy Grail. The rain will never come. Hammett's Wasteland will remain parched and sterile, a place where human evil and corrupt leaders will reach out to blight every level of society. (pp. 201-02)

> H. H. Morris, "Dashiell Hammett in the Wasteland," in The Midwest Quarterly (copyright, 1978, by The Midwest Quarterly, Kansas State College of Pittsburg), Winter, 1978, pp. 196-202.

* * *

HANDKE, Peter 1942-

Handke is an Austrian-born novelist, playwright, poet, and essayist writing in German. He is considered a major innovator in contemporary theater for his experiments with language. One of Handke's major themes is the inadequacy of language as a means of communication. This is perhaps best illustrated in his "Sprechstücke," or "speak-ins," Handke's own theatrical creation. Lacking the structure of traditional drama, these plays are basically language exercises in which the actors are speakers rather than characters. Instead of dialogue the speakers engage in cliché-ridden, fragmented monologues, thus conveying to the audience the way language impedes true expression. (See also *CLC*, Vols. 5, 8, and *Contemporary Authors*, Vols. 77-80.)

GAY McAULEY

Handke presents us with a clown [in *Kaspar*]—the visual impact of Kaspar, with his unco-ordinated gestures and bizarre costume, is clown-like, his name suggests that he is a puppet, and he is, of course, manipulated by language, just as a marionette is manipulated by strings; but he is also Kaspar—a person—and his mask is so like a face that the audience only gradually becomes aware that it is, in fact, a mask; the set represents nothing but itself—a stage, and there is no dialogue, let alone conversation, merely the voices that condition and torment Kaspar and his responses to them. (p. 51)

In Handke's play we see Kaspar, the non-person, undergoing his "Sprechfolterung" (speech torture), and being transformed by language into a model citizen who will accept the system, keep the rules and play the part demanded of him. Handke demonstrates a diabolical process whereby everything "useful" that Kaspar is taught is paralleled by some propaganda for the system the voices belong to, the system that invented the language, no doubt.... Violence is as natural a part of life as grammar and syntax....

> You beat the dust off your pants: you beat
> the thought out of your head ...
> The table is standing. The table is not standing, it was placed there. The corpse is lying.
> The corpse is not lying, it was placed there....

This clearly gives the play a very pronounced social and political emphasis. However, the process to which Kaspar is subjected is also a search for his own identity: his entrance onto the stage, struggling to find the slit in the curtain that will let him through, and unaware even that there is a slit, that there is a "through," is an image of the birth process. The one sentence he is "born" with— ... "I want to be a person like somebody else was once"—reveals a need to be someone, to be other than he is, a need to have a self and be aware of it. Kaspar does not seem to understand the words he is saying, which is perhaps Handke's way of suggesting that the need expressed is not a conscious or rational one.

Language teaches him the difference between "you" and "I," and when the voices finally tell him he has been "aufgeknackt" ("You've been cracked open" ...), he is immediately confronted with another Kaspar, identical to himself. The proliferation of Kaspars represents, in visual or theatrical terms, his awareness of his self or selves, and also his awareness of others as separate from, and yet ultimately the same as himself. In this way, Handke is raising the question as to whether they are the same as Kaspar because they, too, are created by language—the same language. (pp. 53-4)

At the end, he realizes that he was trapped by language with his very first sentence ..., i.e., before the prompters started to programme him. This shifts the emphasis from the social system the voices represent to language itself. However, he also realizes that language is not all powerful: just as the word "snow" is not the snow, so the word "I" is not his self, and language has not brought him knowledge.... The ultimate meaning of the play seems to be that you cannot find or know yourself without language, and yet language reveals only a social self, that it has itself created. Kaspar knows he is trapped, he knows he has not found his "ich," and that language cannot lead him to it, but that it can make him aware of the lack. (pp. 54-5)

Handke emphasizes that the stage should appear to be nothing but a stage, a representation of itself, so it becomes, in a sense, a non-place, a purely theatrical reality: this is obviously relevant thematically, as it reinforces our awareness of Kaspar as a non-person, a creature of the theatre. However, Handke is also drawing our attention to two off-stage spaces. The existence of the wings is emphasized by the fact that the sofa is half off-stage, half on-stage; it is only fully drawn onto the stage when Kaspar has learnt order (i.e., with the assimilation of his lesson, something from the unknown place off-stage is being closed off). It is significant that it is from the wings that the other Kaspars appear, and it is from there that they bring their mysterious parcels. That is to say, then, that the other selves, or the aspects of Kaspar's self that revolt and disagree, come from there, a place the voices implicitly reject, and they bring their means of revolt (the files in the parcels) from there. So we have visual reinforcement for the idea that the voices do not control every part of existence. The second offstage area is back stage, the place from which Kaspar himself comes. The back curtain is the same size and colour as the front one, which is open revealing the stage, so the suggestion is implanted that there is perhaps another stage back there, or another reality, as valid, or as invalid, as this one. When the play ends and the front curtain closes, we are confronted with the exact replica of the back stage curtain, but now the focus has shifted, and the "stage" is now the auditorium. So Handke is able to emphasize the relevance of Kaspar's situation to us, the audience, and at the same time to provide another image for the idea that any reality contains another, or possibly several other realities, and further, that all these "realities" might be merely appearance or theatre. (p. 58)

In Handke's play the wardrobe is used in such a way that it lends visual reinforcement to the underlying implications that the whole process Kaspar is undergoing is a search for authentic existence, a search for something within. The wardrobe is closed when Kaspar struggles onto the stage, but in his unco-ordinated stumbling around he kicks it, accidentally at first, and then intentionally, and the doors swing open. So the door is "cracked open" with violence, just as he is "cracked open" by the speech torture of the prompters. In the wardrobe are many colourful garments—possible identities, or possibilities of choice and action, for him; to emphasize this interpretation, it is from the wardrobe that he selects the "correct" jacket to go with his trousers, when the voices have taught him the need for order. When the cupboard door is closed, it necessarily conveys the idea of an enclosed space, another space within the enclosed space of the stage, like the enclosed space of the mind. The voices only start when he has kicked open the door, and the indication here is that the gesture is a sign that he is ready and open to receive the voices. It is significant that the open door remains something that frightens him; he uses it as the model for all that frightens and hurts. . . . (p. 59)

Kaspar, besides being merely a clown/puppet/mask or purely theatrical being, is not complete in himself, but has a number of identically dressed and masked Kaspars, which represent other aspects of himself; although the social and political implications are strong in this play, the figure of Kaspar, together with his fellow Kaspars, represents less a social or personal reality than a philosophical one. (p. 61)

In *Kaspar,* Kaspar is performing for the voices (he is their little puppet or Kasperle) and in a different way he is performing for the audience; at the end, he is performing for the other Kaspars, and he seems to have taken over the function of the voices, but the nonspeaking Kaspars are not little puppets and are not manipulated, nor are they a docile audience; however, the question of whether their revolt is a victory over language or a despairing admission of defeat is left deliberately ambiguous. Here . . . the performance within the performance device structures the action, making it reflect ironically on itself. (p. 64)

> *Gay McAuley, "The Problem of Identity: Theme, Form and Theatrical Method in 'Les Nègres,' 'Kaspar' and 'Old Times'" (a revision of a speech originally delivered at the University of New South Wales in August, 1973), in* The Southern Review *(copyright 1975 by Gay McAuley), March, 1975, pp. 51-65.*

JAMES WOLCOTT

Gregor Keuschnig, the protagonist of [*A Moment of True Feeling*], awakens one morning from uneasy dreams to discover that he has not been transformed into a gigantic insect. His "large and intricate" Paris apartment shows no signs of convulsion, the leaves of the trees outside his window flutter tranquilly, his wife and daughter are peacefully asleep; still, the dream—in which he murdered an old woman—has cataclysmically cracked open his life. "[He] felt as though he were bursting out of his skin and a lump of flesh lay wet and heavy on the carpet." As Keuschnig goes through the day—drudging away at his Austrian Embassy job, coupling with his mistress, feverishly wandering the streets—he lives on the edge of transformation and then, at a small dinner party, the molecules begin to dance. "[Keuschnig] felt himself to be something BLOODCURDLINGLY strange . . . a monstrous, unfinished bag of skin, a freak of nature. a MONSTROSITY. . . ."

Kafka, of course. However, Keuschnig's metamorphosis never really takes place: those molecules were only jitterbugging in his imagination. Early in the novel it becomes apparent that the existential mandarins hover near, and that *A Moment of True Feeling* is yet another ramble down Nothingness Boulevard. . . . With all its Pop-violent effects . . . *A Moment* is comic-strip Sartre, with the ooze of Nausea blurring the edge of every panel.

As always, Peter Handke is concerned with the perimeters and possibilities of language. In his great play *Kaspar* . . . language is used tyrannically to control a puppet-victim who enters the world armed only with the sentence, "I want to be a person like somebody else was once." All through *A Moment*—as in his novels *The Goalie's Anxiety at the Penalty Kick* and *Short Letter, Long Farewell,* and the memoir *A Sorrow Beyond Dreams* . . . Handke describes the breakdown of connections with the world as a disassociation of language and consciousness. When Keuschnig first reels from the void-opening meaninglessness of his life, he tries to maintain equilibrium through "a frantic effort to think in complete sentences."

Like so many passages in *A Moment,* this parallels the moment in Sartre's *Nausea* when the narrator Roquentin, in his own existential swoon, says that "things are divorced from their names. . . . Alone without words, defenseless, they surround me, are beneath me, behind me, above me."

Without language one becomes unmoored from reality, set adrift on Cubistic debris-strewn seas of incomprehensibility. Characteristically, Handke spikes the narrative by making language call attention to itself; capital letters blaze like neon above the busy streets of Handke's prose. . . .

Handke has also proved that he has an operatic gift for denunciation. . . . The liveliest pages of *A Moment* are those in which Keuschnig rails all around him with the wrath of a comic Coriolanus. . . .

Yet for all its commotion, snaking humor, slapstick, and Road Runner pacing, the book skids and scrapes along for pages upon PAGES of screeching tedium. I don't really understand what spurred Handke to undertake this novel; from the very first page it hits a tinny chord. The narrative is prefaced by a quotation from the founder of the Frankfurt School, M. Horkheimer, which asks, "Violence and inanity—are they not ultimately one and the same thing?" No, M., they are not. And as a burlesque of modernist angst (as represented in the work of Beckett, Sartre, Kafka), *A Moment* seems about as pertinent as a send-up of proletarian literature—why bother? Compared with the brooding, somber prose of his previous work, *A Sorrow Beyond Dreams,* the writing here seems artificially wired up—it has an amphetamine breathlessness.

A Moment of True Feeling is a curiously unfelt book. I don't much care for *Goalie's Anxiety* . . . , but *Short Letter, Long Farewell* and *A Sorrow Beyond Dreams* are works of a strong original intelligence, and both have autobiographical reverberations. . . .

Though *A Moment* has its personal echoes—the protagonist, like Handke, is Austrian, the protagonist's doppelganger is a writer, and a dateline informs us that the novel was written in Paris—it lacks the tension, texture, and hard grain of veracity that make his other narratives so compelling. It's more of a performance than a novel, and a hoarse-voiced performance at that. Since Handke is perhaps the most influential young writer in the West today, one hopes that this is a work that needed to be spat out so that he could clear a space in his life for the next endeavor.

> James Wolcott, *"The Critic's Anxiety at Kicking Peter Handke,"* in The Village Voice *(reprinted by permission of* The Village Voice; *copyright © by The Village Voice, Inc., 1977), June 6, 1977, p. 84.*

BONNIE MARRANCA

Handke's body of work is chiefly concerned with language and behavior, a major interest with central European writers. (p. 272)

Kaspar, perhaps Handke's most praised play, is a major dramatic work of the contemporary theatre. Drawing on the absurdist influences of Beckett and Ionesco it is, nevertheless, Handke's personal critique of society which regulates reality by means of its language structure. In it Handke attempts to show his audience the difference between a world shaped by consciousness and one burdened by platitudes.

Any serious playwright writing in the German language is forced necessarily to undergo a comparison between himself and Bertolt Brecht, if not technically, at the very least in terms of engagement. Handke's plays resemble Brecht's dramaturgically in their "estrangement" of the audience,

their use of a nonliterary language, popular forms of entertainment, and social [gestures]. Significantly, however, the dramaturgy of Handke and Brecht is comparable more in its means than its ends.

Handke has consistently refused to use the drama for his own political statements, or to demonstrate solutions to political problems. (pp. 272-73)

[*My Foot My Tutor*] has . . . to do with what Handke refers to as "pre-political sensations"—those feelings which eventually lead to political acts. *My Foot My Tutor* is concerned with behavior and attitude; it focuses on surface realities and the ordinary poses of the individual.

In *My Foot My Tutor* surfaces and appearances are of utmost importance. Handke's theatrical exploration of non-linguistic modes of communication and presentation provides a sensory experience rarely accessible in today's theatre. That the theatrical text of this play is semiotic rather than verbal [it is a play without words], compels one to concentrate on movements, sounds, and gestures. *My Foot My Tutor,* like all modernist works, demands of its audiences an alternative, radical way of approaching the theatre event.

My Foot My Tutor is a highly stylized silence play . . . comprised of ten scenes which are variations on a central theme: power. . . . The multiple choices of meaning—political, social, aesthetic—subtly exposed in the play are varied and variable; it is an exercise in metaphors.

Handke's wordless, plotless play which articulates every action in great detail, exists in the realm of pure naturalism, inviting the audience to investigate with great awareness all of its non-semantic elements: movement, sound, music and light. (p. 274)

My Foot My Tutor illustrates Handke's fascination with the act of creation. That the playwright's enthusiasm has sired a kind of literary authoritarianism is evident in his anticipation, and at times coercion, of the reader's "justifiable" reaction. . . .

The text specifies directions for the presentation of the play and directives to the audience/reader concerning the most comprehensible approach to it. Like Handke's earlier "speak-in," *Offending the Audience,* it is written virtually as a dialogue with the audience. . . .

Early on in *My Foot My Tutor* Handke establishes an observing technique by which one learns to be responsive to the play's non-verbal elements. This fundamentally cinematic technique compels the viewer to deflect his eyes from the gravitational center of the action and to focus instead on other events and objects in the same scene. (p. 275)

Handke also calls attention to the producedness of the play (his *Offending the Audience* is entirely about the theatre and the theatre-goer) by referring intermittently to the props on the stage, to the introduction or withdrawal of light or music in a scene. . . .

All of Handke's work for the theatre is concerned with language and behavior. . . . Like Ionesco, Handke believes that language is incapable of functioning as an absolute mode of communication.

In *My Foot My Tutor* Handke disregards language as a prerequisite system of meaning by eliminating words altogether in favor of a semiotic text. In the non-verbal world of sound, gesture, and movement are to be found the suggestions for meaning in the play, and the variations of the play's themes. The play is, in effect, a series of tropisms. (p. 276)

My Foot My Tutor examines the banality of ordinary actions, just as the Sprechstücke ["speak-ins"] concern themselves with the platitudes of speech. The minimalist technique employed by Handke exposes both man and object as subjects for observation, as though theatre were a laboratory. Man becomes a specimen under a microscope, to be focused in close-up, medium shot, long shot. Handke's language is sparse and unequivocal, without stylistic flourishes, unemotive. There is only what is; nothing more, nothing less. . . .

My Foot My Tutor is Handke's most eclectic work for the theatre, borrowing heavily from artistic and scientific developments. The play reflects the technical innovations of progressive music, film, art, and the novel while also revealing a scientific orientation.

The concept of subtraction is a dominant feature of the play. Continuing in the direction of many artistic modernists, Handke has "subtracted" himself from his work, and become an objective reporter of events instead. As avantgarde composers rebelled against the tyranny of the music score, Handke (for production of the play) has rebelled against the tyranny of the dramatic text. Hence, the subtraction of dialogue.

Psychological reference to the Ward and Warden is also lacking in the play. The impersonality of the characters makes it impossible to define them in psychological-historical terms. The characters inhabit a world of the continuous present; they have no past. The play manifests movement minus time, sound minus language, character minus personality. The barren landscape of the play emphasizes the void that defines the lives of the two men, alone in a farmhouse away from civilization.

Handke's method of constructing the scenario for the production approximates cinematic technique. His approach is that of a film director who is setting up a "shot." One may think of the entire play as a series of "shots" or stills. . . . (p. 277)

The text of *My Foot My Tutor* is written in the manner of a novel, a continuous body of sentences and paragraphs, narrative in form. It reflects the anguish of Beckettian characters and the minimal technique of both Beckett and Robbe-Grillet. Influenced by the French new novel and the new cinema of Antonioni, Resnais, Straub, Handke's main occupation in *My Foot My Tutor* is the meticulous narration of surface realities. His novels demonstrate the same techniques, and show the same concerns for the existential realities of his characters.

In addition to cinematic and literary influences, the play has a scientific base, namely in its reliance on probability. (p. 278)

[Textual references given in the play] are the literary counterparts of mathematical theories of probability which are rarely explored in contemporary theatre. The tautological structure of the play—for instance, "see above" is a textual directive, ditto marks appear four times under a line in the text—mirrors the mathematical principle of infinity, and in-

finite sets of numbers, a concept often examined in modern art, poetry, and music, but not in theatre.

There are other features which reflect the play's focus on time (stasis). . . . The Ward is leading a "still life." He is in an advanced state of entropy; his literary counterparts include many of the most famous characters in modern literature, among them those created by Kafka, Sartre, Camus, Beckett. The time metaphor is reinforced in . . . [another scene:] the fitting Beckettian image at the end of the play—sand slipping through the fingers of the Ward. *My Foot My Tutor* is, in effect, Handke's *Endgame*.

In *My Foot My Tutor* Peter Handke has gone farther than any other contemporary experimental playwright in his exploration of behavior patterns in the interactions of individuals. By stripping away dialogue, he gives us only the image, forcing us to see—to confront—two men enacting a series of metaphors of contemporary reality. It is their silent ritual that "speaks" to us in a language we of the 20th century can recognize . . . to our misfortune. (p. 279)

> Bonnie Marranca, "Peter Handke's 'My Foot My Tutor': Aspects of Modernism," in The Michigan Quarterly Review (copyright © The University of Michigan, 1977), Summer, 1977, pp. 272-79.

FERDINAND MOUNT

[Handke] uses all the old-modern tricks. In one of his plays not a single word is spoken. In another, the characters are to be given the names of the actors who play them. These devices are intended to disorient the spectators, to deny them the familiar naturalistic illusions, the comforts of character and narrative. By now these distancing effects are as stale as any of the conventions of the well-made play and have built up their own expectations in the audience. The confections of their originators—Jarry, Brecht, Ionesco, Beckett—seem . . . stagey . . . and enjoyable. . . . [You] soon pick up the resonances of Ubu or Godot in *They Are Dying Out* or *The Ride Across Lake Constance*. But just because Handke derives his *techniques* from so many of the standard modern sources, it may be easier to isolate the individuality and consistency of his *themes*.

Handke is preoccupied with domination, with the systematic ways in which one human being acquires and wields power over another and the ways that this shapes the behaviour, aspirations and prejudices of both owner and owned. In *My Foot, My Tutor*, the two characters are actually called *Ward* and *Warden* and they carry out an elaborate silent pantomime of copying and modifying one another's gestures and actions. (p. 33)

Everything we say and do, however apparently noble, touching, loving or courageous, is in reality the end-product of social processes which are based on the domination of one human being by another. We must not be deceived by the glitter of quartz crystals into endowing them with divine properties or supreme value; they are merely geological formations. And it is essential above all that we should realise this, we should not wrap up unpleasant realities in false emotion. This is the first rule, and the second, which follows from it, is to accept only the evidence of your own feelings here and now. You must not let memory or external authority play tricks with you. . . .

This distrustful egoism is the attitude of the narrator of

Handke's second semi-autobiographical novel, *Short Letter, Long Farewell.* . . .

He says that "often in the past I had been overcome by confusion and disgust at the thought that someone was different from myself.". . .

The reality for Handke is that relationships *are* fraudulent and ephemeral. Human beings do not and cannot belong to each other. Each man belongs only to himself, and is answerable only to his own consciousness. Even nature cannot get him "out of himself.". . .

The narrator . . . justifies his egoism by a political argument. His grievance against the social system permeates his view of nature; his melancholy and disgust are legitimised and ennobled by his perception of political injustice. (p. 34)

This trick of overworking the sense of injustice, of politicising the whole visible universe for literary effect is again employed in *A Sorrow Beyond Dreams,* Handke's fictional memoir of his mother. Here the narrator builds up a grim picture of life in rural Carinthia and implies that the grimness is a consequence of all the decent land in the neighbourhood belonging to the church or to noble landowners. For practical purposes, life is just as hard as it had been before the formal abolition of serfdom in 1848. Life, particularly for women, is run on tramlines. The narrator's mother was high-spirited and would not tolerate this predictable, cramped existence. . . . Her attempts to get away in body or in mind demonstrate the suffocating tyranny of an apparently idyllic mountain village. Finally she kills herself. Her son writes this memoir to shake off the dull speechlessness with which he reacted to the news of her suicide. It is the system of property relations which grinds people down, robs them of themselves, deprives them of the capacity or even the wish to talk about themselves, to articulate their feelings and aspirations. (p. 35)

A still bleaker picture . . . is to be found in *The Goalie's Anxiety at the Penalty Kick.* Joseph Bloch, unemployed building worker, formerly a goalkeeper, picks up the cashier at the cinema, sleeps with her and then strangles her, apparently for no reason. He then makes his way to a country inn where he lies low, spending his time watching the trivial, purposeless routine of village life. He is obsessively aware of his own sensations and of each tiny sight or sound that they record. Yet he shows very little interest in his own fate and hardly seems conscious of what he has done.

Consider for a moment the salient elements in these three fictions: the unattached hero recoiling from emotional attachment, his indifference to morality, his lack of overt reaction to his mother's death, the girl he picks up casually (either a stranger or passing acquaintance), the apparently motiveless murder of another person. Is there not something familiar about them? Mix them all in together and you have Camus' *L'Etranger* very nearly in its entirety. I do not adduce this coincidence, remarkable though it is, in order to stress how derivative Handke's themes are or to deny his undeniable qualities as a writer. At its best, his writing is haunting and intense. But *L'Etranger* remains the classic literary study in alienation; it lacks Handke's vulgar Marxist gloss and it has the further advantage for critics that Camus left us in no doubt as to what he intended. (pp. 35-6)

We are instructed to admire Meursault [in *L'Etranger*] for his authenticity, his refusal to surrender to the pieties or to suppress his feelings. Handke's protagonists are by contrast primarily the victims of social processes. And yet it is surely intended that we should admire them too for their exercise of inner freedom, their refusal to slip into the fraudulent slime of human relationships, the dignity, however pitiful, of their solitude. For their apparent refusal to ask for sympathy or affection, we are to accord them both. From Werther to Handke, the low-spirited egoist has been tugging at the intelligentsia's heartstrings. A touch of the psychopath has only intensified his farouche charm. (p. 36)

To say that Peter Handke's mother had a sad life because she did not understand her social situation is both to patronise her and to trivialise her fate. These slick elisions between the life of an individual and the structure of a society are anything but humanist, in that they take man to be such an easily degradable substance.

The young Handke no less than the young Camus demonstrates in his work that his concept of the individual is both inconsistent and dishonest. To accept Mersault's one virtue —his refusal to lie about his own feelings—as a proof of his authenticity is to accept a pathetically shrivelled view of "a free man." If that phrase is to carry any real force, it must surely entail the idea of man as a responsible agent, not a being whose only free actions are the honest expression of his impulses but one who also stretches his consciousness to take account of the consequences of his actions and the relationship between them.

It is of the essence of what we mean by a free agent that he should know what he is doing. If a man lies or murders without having a reason "of his own", that suggests that he is acting in accordance with the reasons of others. He is under the compulsion of biology, or society, or another person. The supposedly gratuitous act is gratuitous only in the sense that the reasons for it are not the conventional ones. The "gratuitous" murderer may have one of several reasons—desire to demonstrate his indifference to bourgeois morality or his coolness of nerve, wish to revenge himself on the world as a whole rather than on the particular victim which entails random selection of that victim, pleasure in killing and so on. But to describe a person who has *no* reasons of his own for his action as "free" is to rob the term freedom of any meaning. Freedom is inseparable from the idea of agency. (pp. 36-7)

The reader's sympathy is abused not because Handke taps it on behalf of people who feel cut off from the ordinary worlds of thought and feeling and who find themselves unable to make natural and authentic connections with other people. The abuse lies in the way he exploits that real and specific pathos to illustrate and strengthen political morals which may not properly be derived from it. . . .

Handke's . . . radical critique of society rests on evidence which is tangential, fragmentary, and equivocal. The bold outlines of a political manifesto cannot be given dramatic form by a cast of vague and elusive characters. The appeal of the cryptic, bitter melancholy which Handke's writing at its best exhales cannot, with any degree of integrity, be pressed into the service of the modish crudities of a New Left. (p. 37)

Ferdinand Mount, "Peter Handke, and 'Alienation-Fiction': The Sorrows of Young Outsiders," in Encounter (© *1978 by Encounter Ltd.), March, 1978, pp. 33-7.*

OLAF HANSEN

Taking the strained relationship between philosophy and fiction seriously, [Handke] has with single-minded stubbornness developed his own artistic form at the core of which lies the effort to reconstruct the truth of fiction. Description of reality becomes the creation of meaning. For Handke, the truth of fiction does not lie in a realm of imagination where symbols and metaphors are artistically combined to achieve the reality of literature. He does not intend to reveal the previously unknown. Instead, Handke is preoccupied with the world of conventionalized knowledge. His critical intention is to expose everyday reality as one that is known by heart, so to speak, a lost reality that has become a predictable succession of petrified experiences. Meaningful experiences are not to be found *beyond* the surface of common life but have to be wrested from it: Handke, therefore, is obsessed with realistic details of stale knowledge. Writing for him is the act of opening the forgotten scars of original recognitions, which have become encrusted by layers of stereotyped experiences. The restoration of truth as an act of destruction makes *A Moment of True Feeling* a philosophical novel *sui generis,* to be distinguished from the novel of ideas. . . .

When novels and poems became sociological case studies presenting the individual as a victim of his social environment, Handke tried to rescue for his heroes a realm of contemplation. Handke, in short, did not believe that writing could be seen as political action; he did insist, however, on the poet's responsibility to destroy established conceptions of reality. The writer's political commitment, as he saw it, was not fulfilled by pledging allegiance to a cause, but by creating an intellectual space which would first of all allow to *imagine* any kind of allegiance. . . . Handke's own notion of intellectual space was, of course, derived from his belief in the ultimate power of aesthetic experience; hence his attempt to create literary models which would allow him to trace the destructive mechanisms of society by describing their impact on the very subjective experience of the individual. Extreme subjectivity became Handke's starting point in his attempt to justify his idea of poetic truth. The literary model, turned into a tale, worked as a narrative redemption of language as a medium for true perceptions. . . .

Handke knows of course that the mystical experience of true feeling can at best be an aesthetic vanishing point, unless art embraces ideology, and accordingly in *A Moment of True Feeling* he uses various traditional literary devices to guide his hero Gregor Keuschnig toward his epiphany. . . . In *A Moment of True Feeling,* the epic transcendence of ordinary life, where the trivial assumes unknown dignity and the hero achieves a hitherto unknown unity with the world around him, presents itself as a well known topos: that of sudden change.

The image of sudden change, at the beginning of a novel, is a promise of revelation. . . . In *A Moment of True Feeling* the sudden change in the life of Gregor Keuschnig results from a dream: "Who has ever dreamed that he has become a murderer and from then on has only been carrying on with his usual life for the sake of appearances?"

That Keuschnig's sudden change of identity from *pressattaché* at the Austrian embassy into the role of a murderer results from a dream is an important deviation from the traditional literary formula of sudden transformation. . . .

Keuschnig's transformation has no social or historical explanation, nor does it imply any immediate promises for the future. . . .

Handke's strategy of reducing the historical and psychological past of his hero to a moment of sudden transformation works as a radical emphasis on poetic experience. The text leaves no room for external interpretation: Keuschnig's fate does not lend itself to an analysis of the individual's alienation in modern society; the explanatory dimension of the hero's biography is left untouched. Handke's literary achievement, therefore, lies in successfully assimilating both the reader's and Keuschnig's imagination. There is, literally, nothing before or beyond the text. (p. 5)

Right from the beginning of Keuschnig's transformation, Handke has . . . limited the hero's potential range of experience. Keuschnig's realization that there is nothing in store for him but a rediscovery of his own self reduces the epic formula, by depriving of any social relevance the hero's walks through Paris and his encounters with the people around him. The immediate result of his transformation is a kind of dialectical negation of his former identity: old attitudes and habits persist as meaningless shells, becoming a threatening duplication of their original state. . . .

Keuschnig's loss of social identity is, however, experienced as an absolute *loss:* there is no relief for him by assuming new roles. He does not become the classical observant outsider or stigmatized clairvoyant; instead, the absence of meaning throws him into a painful state of double consciousness. . . .

To conceive of fiction as poetic thought necessarily implies a certain amount of programmatic concern. The ontological status of fiction as a body of imagined occurrences, related to reality by mimesis is, however, essentially alien to philosophical systems. . . . Handke's *A Moment of True Feeling* resolves the epistemological differences between philosophy and fiction at its best where the poetic process assimilates the particular with the general, where the disturbing contingencies of reality become part of the poetic whole. His epic intention to describe the world by an approximation of feeling and object eventually results in the conscious literal reconstruction of this approximation itself. At this point, the technical problem of reconciling the modal differences between poetic and philosophic discourse in fiction inexorably becomes one of content.

The novel has to be *about* something and its most extensive epic expansion is to deal with its own concern. *A Moment of True Feeling,* thus, is a novel about the legitimacy of fiction. . . .

Making the legitimacy of fiction the concern of his novel, Handke has avoided both the didactic fallacy of experimental formalism and epigrammatic composition of a moral statement, disguised as a tale. His epic intentions are, instead, achieved by using the existing patterns of familiar ideas and emotions. Handke's literary exorcism of reality takes as a point of departure the characteristic grammar of customary language as it constitutes the substance of the spurious and ideological components of human experience. For the poet exorcising reality means purifying language of those elements which camouflage reality, give it false shape, reproduce appearances at the cost of the essential. The poetic merger of vision and reality has to be achieved against the resistance of language itself. . . .

Handke does not primarily attempt a restoration of language as a medium of truthful expression. . . . We have to enter . . . its contemplation, comprehending the concrete alternative of aesthetic patience to the latent violence of analytical attribution. For Handke, the attitude of aesthetic patience is by no means an esoteric one; it does not indicate a withdrawal from common reality. . . .

[Handke's] conviction that it is only by rediscovering the extremely individualistic rudiments of private experience that the poet can express something which is relevant for all of us stands out against the current literary trend. Against the present tendency of fiction toward the biographical and historical modes of thinly disguising reality, *A Moment of True Feeling* reaffirms the cognitive authority of fiction. (p. 6)

> Olaf Hansen, "Exorcising Reality," in New Boston Review (copyright 1978 by Boston Critic, Inc.), Summer, 1978, pp. 5-6.

WILLIAM KAKISH

In *A Moment of True Feeling*, Peter Handke deals with [the Kantian] problem of the perception of the world, crystallized in the problem of identity of Gregor Keuschnig. . . . In his private life, Keuschnig identifies himself on the basis of his perception of his image in public life. Others know him from their perception of that image. But one morning Keuschnig awakes to discover that that image by which he identifies himself and by which the world identifies him is out of sync with his own true existence. The world has collapsed on him and he can no longer know without doubt who he is. He has dreamed he is a murderer. But is he? So begins an odyssey into everyday occurrences, into the realms of perception and existence, treated with wit, humor, and irony. . . . [The reflex actions of the day's work] remain as background and reference to the true action of the novel which goes on in the isolation of Keuschnig's own being. These reflex actions and the struggle in Keuschnig's being become punctuated by moments of insight into the essence of true being—the tension within a branch, the sign in the Metro, the dripping of wax from a candle. The only person who realizes that there has been a change in Keuschnig is the writer invited to dinner at Keuschnig's apartment, who by chance has been stalking him all day. With such a structure, let the reader beware. The author (Handke) utilizes a writer (Handke?) who perceives a change in Keuschnig (Handke?—by way of biographical similarities), who in turn perceives the action of his existence as different from that which it really *is* (Handke on Handke?); and one must remember that this is fiction (don't get carried away with Handke). The novel piles level on level, filter on filter, lens upon lens, and then as is typical of Handke, ends as abruptly as it began. There is no resolution. As we are told in the opening sentence, the action is still going on. Reading such a novel can be a very frustrating endeavor, a frustration only alleviated by several readings. (pp. 166-67)

> William Kakish, in Chicago Review (reprinted by permission of Chicago Review; copyright © 1978 by Chicago Review), Vol. 29, No. 3, 1978.

*   *   *

HELPRIN, Mark   1947-

Helprin is an American short story writer and novelist. A student of Middle Eastern culture who has served in the Israeli army, Helprin in his work often portrays the struggle of the modern Jew. (See also *CLC*, Vol. 7.)

JULIA O'FAOLAIN

Mark Helprin has points in common with [Isaac Bashevis Singer]. He too writes for the *New Yorker*. His characters are nearly all Jewish and his settings range from Rome and Sicily to Paris, Tel Aviv and the western United States. His dust jacket [for *A Dove of the East and Other Stories*] . . . claims that he is a 'born teller of tales'. After reading the first story, 'A Jew of Persia', I was inclined to agree. . . . The tale is colourful and resonant and the use of the supernatural is adroit. Clearly, when Helprin has a tale to tell he can tell it. Unfortunately, in the rest of this thin, uneven book, he fails to come up with another. There is some effective writing in the title novella but the structure is weak and Helprin lets words run away with him. The rest of his book makes one wish for him that he, like Singer, had had the benefit of a sceptical mother whose ghost he might have felt the need to placate by wit and wile. He is dangerously lacking in these qualities without which a story-teller is as vulnerable as a hero in a folk tale. Helprin is more vulnerable than most because his subject is love—not, as in cannier writers, the obstacles surrounding it, but love itself, which is perhaps the trickiest subject since, at the heart of love, as at the heart of tragedy, there is no individuality but only a transcendency which cannot be described and so must be rendered by a shrewd deployment of metaphor and plot. (pp. 59-60)

Although he seems to have lived in many places, the impression left by his writing is that he might as well have stayed home because he homogenises whatever he describes and one guesses that he was blear-eyed throughout his travels as a result of overdoses of Hemingway, *Hiawatha* and Roget's *Thesaurus*. . . .

[This is] why Helprin's characters are so ectoplasmic, all the same and curiously unalive: they are dream projections of the author. What we have here is not writing in the normal sense. It is wish-fulfilment. We are being treated to fantasies projected onto dream landscapes often animated by that old fantasist's standby, pathetic fallacy, so that trains grow 'tired' and the land 'beckoned' men 'challenging them to make their mark'. Of course wish-fulfilment can be an element in writing. Stendhal and Dante indulged in it, but only after they had looked outside themselves, seen what was out there and learned to render it in its untidy reality. Reality is always a bit jagged-edged and different from what one might expect. Pastiche, instead, is smooth: an object which has passed through too many hands. (p. 60)

> Julia O'Faolain, in The New Review (© The New Review Ltd., 11 Greek Street, London W1V 5LE), June, 1976.

JOHN MELLORS

In *Refiner's Fire*, Mark Helprin makes his adventurer several sizes larger than life and eschews realism for a prose charged with romantic extravagances and purple rhetoric: as if *The Odyssey* had been updated and rewritten by Dylan Thomas in his less sober moments. While still a schoolboy, Marshall Pearl hunts down Rastafarian brigands in the Jamaican jungle, outshooting professional soldiers. He sails and even swims through a hurricane, makes 'perfect love' to 'the most beautiful woman he had ever seen', and as a recruit in the Israeli army shows a grasp of strategy that could have put Dayan out of business.

Occasionally, Helprin's imagery is strikingly apt. Pearl's Harvard contemporaries 'spoke with a's so flat that they could slide them under doors'. Too often, he lurches haphazardly from simile to simile and metaphor to metaphor, obscuring where he should be clarifying. In Brindisi harbour, 'miscellaneous unkempt craft . . . nestle against a cruiser or a minesweeper, not quite in the manner of a calf leaning on its mother but rather like the flies which settled on carcasses in the horse butcheries.' Which were they like, calves or flies? Or 'not quite' like either? When in doubt, leave out, Mr Helprin. *Refiner's Fire* is partly redeemed by the account of the build-up to the Yom Kippur war and of the first few days' fighting on the Golan Heights, in which the author disciplines himself to let his story come before his verbal excesses; but even that is spoiled by a melodramatic, back-from-the-dead epilogue in Hospital 10. (p. 223)

> *John Mellors, in* The Listener *(© British Broadcasting Corp. 1978; reprinted by permission of John Mellors), February 16, 1978.*

JOHN RYLE

Aleister Crowley once planned an epic poem in which he proposed to "celebrate everything in the world in detail". Mark Helprin's lengthy [*Refiner's Fire*] reveals something of the same aspiration. . . .

[The] story takes on some of the lineaments of a bildungsroman and slips awkwardly from genre to genre as the hero moves from continent to continent and woman to woman. Mr Helprin takes this all very seriously. He has given his tale the classic ingredients of romance: a mysterious birth, a long-lost childhood sweetheart, military heroism and intimations of higher things. Marshall has a thing about light. He's very sensitive to it. So was his mother, whom we first see in the throes of a vision in an abandoned cathedral. The image of this God-struck Jewish woman is rather impressive, though he uses it to usher in a peculiarly uncomfortable metaphor ("she lay in painful intercourse with the spectrum"), but Marshall's hyperphotosensitivity is not a sufficient substitute for the lack of character development or properly sequential plot.

Refiner's Fire is appropriately judged by traditional standards of this kind because it is an essentially old-fashioned book. Mr Helprin's symbolic use of light is a revealing archaism in a time when the labyrinth of the word has replaced the white radiance of eternity as the central metaphor of consciousness. He cannot resist modernism entirely and sometimes seems to be mustering his forces for a new exploration of the genres he is working with: Marshall tries to catch some fatal illness to conform to the stereotype of the romantic valetudinarian and there is a hint, since his mother was raped by gentiles in a pogrom, that he may not be his supposed father's son after all, but this simply weakens the plot. The hero still does his best to live out his idea of a heroic life against the shapelessness of history, an irony that goes unexploited, as most of the potential ironies in this book do. . . . When Marshall is on the point of meeting the man who saved his life and sent him to America as a newborn child, we are told that he "was about to satisfy an overwhelming curiosity which though unknown to him until this very moment had directed his entire short life". It is symptomatic of the author's uneasy relation to the dynamics of the plot that this moving force should be revealed only retrospectively.

The romantic impetus is weakened but the sensibility remains unexamined. Female characterization is almost nonexistent. . . . It is the old story of Love and Death in the American novel, the ideal-type women who never come alive. . . . The novel glimmers with unresolved symbolism and unassimilated influences, false promise and fool's gold, which despite the alchemical flash of the title it fails to transmute into the real thing.

> *John Ryle, "Beyond Saturation Point," in* The Times Literary Supplement *(© Times Newspapers Ltd. (London) 1978; reproduced from* The Times Literary Supplement *by permission), February 17, 1978, p. 185.*

ROGER SALE

Mark Helprin's *Refiner's Fire* is a long ambitious novel of almost spectacular arbitrariness. . . .

[Various episodes in the novel] might have comic possibilities but Helprin's tone is cool and unamused. A pattern does begin to form, and damned if it doesn't seem designed by Ayn Rand, all about the light of the West, the refining energy of a naturally endowed aristocracy: "There was nothing greater, thought Marshall, than men like this who had lasted, who were old, whose passions had been refined in fire and in ice and yet whose love was solid and gentle and true." . . .

Marshall is a Jew, and must be got back to Israel somehow, where perhaps he will find a new heaven and a new earth. But Helprin does not seem interested in Jews and his Israel is positively distasteful. Marshall is thrown into an Israeli regiment of criminals, idiots, sadistic officers, and a few others like himself, though what fifty pages of suffering do for him is unclear, because we don't know if or how much Marshall has been refined before or during it. He ends up on the Golan Heights, and we can presume he has become refined at the very end when, wounded, in the hospital, he pulls the tubes from his body and says, twice, "By God, I'm not down yet." . . . [Is *Refiner's Fire*] subtler and more carefully worked than I think it is? If the pieces can be made to fit, they will turn out to be held together, I suggest, by a dreamy romanticism of a silly and bigoted kind. (p. 42)

> *Roger Sale, in* The New York Review of Books *(reprinted with permission from* The New York Review of Books; *copyright © 1978 NYREV, Inc.), February 23, 1978.*

PETER ACKROYD

Refiner's Fire is a rather old-fashioned novel. It receives impressions of the outer world without cynicism or the self-confessed failure to understand, and Mark Helprin is so sure of his own narrative skills that the novel glows with his permanent presence. In other hands, this could all become breathless and boring, but Helprin escapes fatuity by being genuinely talented. It needs a kind of genius, I think, to accept orthodoxy and, by accepting it, to make it live again.

In other words, Helprin hasn't trod doggedly in the footsteps of other and older novelists. Everyone under the age of thirty-five now seems to be imitating the dry, toneless and wry manner of a Roth or an Updike: forgetting that if you imitate American writers who burned and faded in the 'sixties, your own writing will be so far out of sight in the 'seventies that it will be practically invisible. Mark Helprin has turned his back on all of that and if, in his awkward position, he can sometimes be clumsy or bathetic, he can also reach moments of lyricism which are as satisfying as they are unexpected: 'That night in his bunk Marshall felt as if all the mountains and the heights of the sky were in him . . . and that night in Colorado the moon came up so bright that even sheep and horses could not sleep, and stood in the fields staring upwards as confused as the first astronomers.'

Marshall Pearl, the absurdly romantic figure here, is clearly some sharp image of Helprin himself . . . and that can pose peculiar difficulties. When the author is intimately involved with one character, everything in the book becomes a mirror for their double-reflection. Pearl is squarely at the centre of the narrative: born on an immigrant ship, by a mother he never sees, he is adopted by an American family and that whole continent becomes the geography of his obsessions. He is invaded by physical distress, adolescent love, and also by mysterious fits of epilepsy which leave him weak and unguarded. In a sense epilepsy dominates the book, since the plot itself centres around mysterious moments of violent activity, stupor and acts of monumental self-control. . . .

Refiner's Fire's most important, and attractive, quality is its absence of realism on every level. The book is wonderfully egocentric; Helprin trusts his perceptions enough to transcribe them directly, without the benefits of realism. The language is affective rather than descriptive, floating among adjectives and adverbs which, if you were to examine them too closely, would blur and dissolve. The book might easily have turned into a spectacle of one person's personality, as trials are overcome and escapades successfully completed, if it weren't for the fact that Helprin can always turn outward to problems of plot and perspective.

It could have meant, for example, that the novel could become over-determined as the author struggles toward some kind of grand and permanent self-expression. But then Helprin's vitality reasserts itself: he has a great capacity for telling stories, twisting the plot this way and that, and forgetting the boring questions of 'tone' and of message. . . . It is part of his self-assurance—part of his ability to abandon all the readily available methods of writing a modern novel —that he can control his novel with great fluency and invention. He is so self-assured, in fact, that he can employ some powerful but generally outmoded ideas without embarrassment. There are references to 'the race' (in this case the Jewish race), to 'history' and to an idea of 'the West'. This attitude takes its toll—it means that the book is rarely funny, which is a pity—but there is nothing wrong with orthodox writing as long as it stays interesting. 'Realism' is no longer interesting; fashionable American writing is no longer interesting; 'modernism' is no longer interesting. Vast egotistical longings, magical panoramas, and an ability to contort the language into unusual shapes, still are. And this is where *Refiner's Fire* makes its mark. . . .

> Peter Ackroyd, "Ranging," in The Spectator (© 1978 by The Spectator; reprinted by permission of The Spectator), February 25, 1978, p. 23.

JOHN CALVIN BATCHELOR

With *Refiner's Fire*, Mark Helprin . . . risks more than most novelists dare in 10 years. Helprin writes like a saint, plots like a demon, and has an imagination that would be felonious in all but the larger democracies. That *Refiner's Fire* is his first novel (though second book) humbles me, and that Marshall Pearl, his Odysseyan protagonist, went to Harvard and yet still emerges as a likable soldier of fortune stuns me. Ivy Leaguers are supposed to be no longer eligible for veneration. (p. 72)

But, back to the beginning, for Helprin's nature is starkly exemplified in his first book, *A Dove Of The East* (1976). Here, in a collection of generally competent short stories . . . Helprin practiced sketches of his heroic temperament. There are no antiheroes in *Dove*, of course, but there are young men torn between the fantastic and the desperate. . . . [There] is, in the title story, a mythical Jewish cowboy tending a cattle herd on the Golan Heights. The cowboy's soul mesmerized me; his sad history as a Jewish survivor of the Holocaust come to a redemptive victory with a dying dove in the Levant must have permanently shaped Helprin's fiction. At heart, Mark Helprin is a noble Jewish cowboy.

For it is the state of Israel—the idea of the state of Israel, the romance of the state of Israel—that Helprin preaches with an eloquence that may be unmatched since, well, 1947, the year of Marshall Pearl's birth. *Refiner's Fire* can be read as an adventure story, but it can also be read as an allegory of the profounder sort. Marshall Pearl becomes the state of Israel. And this is not the Judaism of the schlemiel, so familiar in much modern Jewish fiction but the Judaism of the Torah. Marshall Pearl is not Philip Roth's *Professor of Desire*. He is Judah's David. (pp. 72-3)

His experiences are more metaphorical than perhaps need be (this sort of fiction can stumble into fairy tale). Pearl is precocious beyond measure. . . .

I will not deprive you of the glamour of reading Marshall Pearl in the Israeli army by mentioning particulars. It has as much Heller comedy as it does Mailer pathos. And Helprin makes the battle for the Golan Heights so transcendant that, momentarily, lost in the firefight between the Israeli Centurions and the Syrian T-62s, I considered enlistment myself. (p. 73)

> John Calvin Batchelor, in The Village Voice (reprinted by permission of The Village Voice; copyright © by The Village Voice, Inc., 1978), March 6, 1978.

*   *   *

HEMINGWAY, Ernest   1899-1961

An American novelist and short story writer, Hemingway received the Nobel Prize for Literature in 1954 and the Pulitzer Prize in Fiction in 1953. The ultimate truths that face man in Hemingway's world are pain, disillusionment, violence, suffering, and, above all, death. For Hemingway's characters, value and purpose in life can be found in confrontation, in the bullfight, for example, and meaning can be gained through manly action, strong friendships, and, most importantly, through a relationship with nature. (See also

CLC, Vols. **1, 3, 6, 8,** and *Contemporary Authors,* Vols. **77-80.**)

D. H. LAWRENCE

[*In Our Time*] does not pretend to be about one man. But it is. It is as much as we need know of the man's life. The sketches are short, sharp, vivid, and most of them excellent. (The "mottoes" in front seem a little affected.) And these few sketches are enough to create the man and all his history: we need know no more.

Nick is a type one meets in the more wild and woolly regions of the United States. He is the remains of the lone trapper and cowboy. Nowadays he is educated, and through with everything. It is a state of *conscious,* accepted indifference to everything except freedom from work and the moment's interest. Mr. Hemingway does it extremely well. Nothing matters. Everything happens. One wants to keep oneself loose. Avoid one thing only: getting connected up. Don't get connected up. If you get held by anything, break it. Don't be held. Break it, and get away. Don't get away with the idea of getting somewhere else. Just get away, for the sake of getting away. Beat it! "Well, boy, I guess I'll beat it." Ah, the pleasure in saying that!

Mr. Hemingway's sketches, for this reason, are excellent: so short, like striking a match, lighting a brief sensational cigarette, and it's over. His young love affair ends as one throws a cigarette end away. "It isn't fun any more."—"Everything's gone to hell inside me."

It is really honest. And it explains a great deal of sentimentality. When a thing has gone to hell inside you, your sentimentalism tries to pretend it hasn't. But Mr. Hemingway is through with the sentimentalism. "It isn't fun any more. I guess I'll beat it."

And he beats it, to somewhere else. In the end he'll be a sort of tramp, endlessly moving on for the sake of moving away from where he is. This is a negative goal, and Mr. Hemingway is really good, because he's perfectly straight about it. . . . [He] doesn't love anybody, and it nauseates him to have to pretend he does. He doesn't even *want* to love anybody; he doesn't want to go anywhere, he doesn't want to do anything. He wants just to lounge around and maintain a healthy state of nothingness inside himself, and an attitude of negation to everything outside himself. And why shouldn't he, since that is exactly and sincerely what he feels? If he really *doesn't* care, then why should he care? Anyhow, he doesn't. (pp. 93-4)

> *D. H. Lawrence, "'In Our Time': A Review," in his* Phoenix, *edited by Edward D. McDonald (copyright © 1936 by Frieda Lawrence; copyright © 1964 by The Estate of the late Frieda Lawrence Ravagli; all rights reserved; reprinted by permission of Viking Penguin Inc.), Viking Penguin, 1936 (and reprinted in* Hemingway: A Collection of Critical Essays, *edited by Robert P. Weeks, Prentice-Hall, Inc., 1962, pp. 93-4).*

MARK SPILKA

One of the most persistent themes of the Twenties was the death of love in World War I. All the major writers recorded it, often in piecemeal fashion, as part of the larger postwar scene; but only Hemingway seems to have caught it whole and delivered it in lasting fictional form. . . . Hemingway seems to design an extensive parable. Thus, in *The Sun Also Rises,* his protagonists are deliberately shaped as allegorical figures: Jake Barnes and Brett Ashley are two lovers desexed by the war; Robert Cohn is the false knight who challenges their despair; while Romero, the stalwart bullfighter, personifies the good life which will survive their failure. Of course, these characters are not abstractions in the text; they are realized through the most concrete style in American fiction, and their larger meaning is implied only by their response to immediate situations. But the implications are there, the parable is at work in every scene, and its presence lends unity and depth to the whole novel. (p. 127)

[His] fear of emotional consequences is the key to Barnes' condition. Like so many Hemingway heroes, he has no way to handle subjective complications, and his wound is a token for this kind of impotence.

It serves the same purpose for the expatriate crowd in Paris. In some figurative manner these artists, writers, and derelicts have all been rendered impotent by the war. Thus, as Barnes presents them, they pass before us like a parade of sexual cripples, and we are able to measure them against his own forbearance in the face of a common problem. Whoever bears his sickness well is akin to Barnes; whoever adopts false postures, or willfully hurts others, falls short of his example. This is the organizing principle in Book I, this alignment of characters by their stoic qualities. But stoic or not, they are all incapable of love, and in their sober moments they seem to know it.

For this reason they feel especially upset whenever Robert Cohn appears. Cohn still upholds a romantic view of life, and since he affirms it with stubborn persistence, he acts like a goad upon his wiser contemporaries. As the narrator, Barnes must account for the challenge he presents them and the decisive turn it takes in later chapters. . . . [Tokens] of virility delight [Cohn] and he often confuses them with actual manliness. (p. 128)

Cohn's romanticism explains his key position in the parable. He is the last chivalric hero, the last defender of an outworn faith, and his function is to illustrate its present folly—to show us, through the absurdity of his behavior, that romantic love is dead, that one of the great guiding codes of the past no longer operates. . . . [For] this generation boredom has become more plausible than love. . . .

Of course, there is much that is traditional in the satire on Cohn. Like the many victims of romantic literature, from Don Quixote to Tom Sawyer, he lives by what he reads and neglects reality at his own and others' peril. But Barnes and his friends have no alternative to Cohn's beliefs. There is nothing here, for example, like the neat balance between sense and sensibility in Jane Austen's world. Granted that Barnes is sensible enough, that he sees life clearly and that we are meant to contrast his private grief with Cohn's public suffering, his self-restraint with Cohn's deliberate self-exposure. Yet, emasculation aside, Barnes has no way to measure or control the state of love; and though he recognizes this with his mind and tries to act accordingly, he seems no different from Cohn in his deepest feelings. . . . No, at best he is a restrained romantic, a man who carries himself well in the face of love's impossibilities, but who seems to share with Cohn a common (if hidden) weakness. (p. 129)

With a man's felt hat on her boyish bob, and with her familiar reference to men as fellow "chaps," [Brett] completes the distortion of sexual roles which seems to characterize the period. For the war, which has unmanned Barnes and his contemporaries, has turned Brett into the freewheeling equal of any man.... [She] survives the colossal violence, the disruption of her personal life, and the exposure to mass promiscuity, to confront a moral and emotional vacuum among her postwar lovers. With this evidence of male default all around her, she steps off the romantic pedestal, moves freely through the bars of Paris, and stands confidently there beside her newfound equals.... But when men no longer command respect, and women replace their natural warmth with masculine freedom and mobility, there can be no serious love. (p. 130)

[The cripples who appear in Book I] are all disaffiliates, all men and women who have cut themselves off from conventional society and who have made Paris their permanent playground. Jake Barnes has introduced them, and we have been able to test them against his stoic attitudes toward life in a moral wasteland. Yet such life is finally unbearable, as we have also seen whenever Jake and Brett are alone together, or whenever Jake is alone with his thoughts. (p. 131)

[In a footnote, Spilka states: Hemingway's preoccupation with death has been explained in various ways.... Yet chiefly the risk of death lends moral seriousness to a private code which lacks it. The risk is arbitrary; when a man elects to meet it, his beliefs take on subjective weight and he is able to give meaning to his private life. In this sense, he moves forever on a kind of imaginative frontier, where the opposition is always Nature, in some token form, where the stakes are always manliness and self-respect, and where death invests the scene with tragic implications. In *The Sun Also Rises,* Romero lives on such a frontier, and for Barnes and his friends he provides an example of just these values.] (n., p. 133)

[The encounter between Cohn and Pedro] is the highpoint of the parable, for in the Code Hero, the Romantic Hero has finally met his match. As the clash between them shows, there is a difference between physical and moral victory, between chivalric stubbornness and real self-respect. Thus Pedro fights to repair an affront to his dignity; though he is badly beaten, his spirit is untouched by his opponent, whereas Cohn's spirit is completely smashed. From the beginning Cohn has based his manhood on skill at boxing, or upon a woman's love, never upon internal strength; but now, when neither skill nor love supports him, he has bludgeoned his way to his own emptiness.... [Where] Cohn expends and degrades himself for his beloved, Romero pays tribute without self-loss. His manhood is a thing independent of women, and for this reason he holds special attractions for Jake Barnes.

By now it seems apparent that Cohn and Pedro are extremes for which Barnes is the unhappy medium. His resemblance to Pedro is clear enough: they share the same code, they both believe that a man's dignity depends on his own resources. His resemblance to Cohn is more subtle, but at this stage of the book it becomes grossly evident. Appropriately enough, the exposure comes through the knockout blow from Cohn, which dredges up a strange prewar experience:

Walking across the square to the hotel everything looked new and changed.... I felt as I felt once coming home from an out-of-town football game. I was carrying a suitcase with my football things in it.... It was like that crossing the square. It was like that going up the stairs in the hotel. Going up the stairs took a long time, and I had the feeling that I was carrying my suitcase.

Barnes seems to have regressed here to his youthful football days. As he moves on up the stairs to see Cohn, who has been asking for him, he still carries his "phantom suitcase" with him; and when he enters Cohn's room, he even sets it down. Cohn himself has just returned from the fight with Romero: "There he was, face down on the bed, crying. He had on a white polo shirt, the kind he'd worn at Princeton." In other words, Cohn has also regressed to his abject college days: they are both emotional adolescents, about the same age as the nineteen-year-old Romero, who is the only real man among them. Of course, these facts are not spelled out for us, except through the polo shirt and the phantom suitcase, which remind us (inadvertently) of one of those dreamlike fantasies by ... Franz Kafka, in which trunks and youthful clothes are symbols of arrested development. Yet there has already been some helpful spelling out in Book I.... [Cohn], urged to say what comes into his head first, ... replies, "I think I'd rather play football again with what I know about handling myself, now." (pp. 134-35)

The first thought to enter Cohn's mind here has been suppressed by Barnes for a long time, but in Book II the knockout blow releases it: more than anything else, he too would like to "play football again," to prevent that kick to his head from happening, or that smash to the jaw from Cohn, or that sexual wound which explains either blow. For the truth about Barnes seems obvious now: he has always been an emotional adolescent. Like Nick Adams, he has grown up in a society which has little use for manliness; as an expression of that society, the war has robbed him of his dignity as a man and has thus exposed him to indignities with women. We must understand here that the war, the early football game, and the fight with Cohn have this in common: they all involve ugly, senseless, or impersonal forms of violence, in which a man has little chance to set the terms of his own integrity. Hence for Hemingway they represent the kinds of degradation which can occur at any point in modern society.... [The] whole confluence of events now points to the social meaning of Jake's wound, for just as Cohn has reduced him to a dazed adolescent, so has Brett reduced him to a slavish pimp.... Barnes has no integrity to rely on; he can only serve her as Cohn has served her, like a sick romantic steer. (p. 135)

These are decadent times in the bull ring, marred by false aesthetics; Romero alone has "the old thing," the old "purity of line through the maximum of exposure": his corruption by Brett will complete the decadence. But mainly the young fighter means something more personal to Barnes. In the bull ring he combines grace, control and sincerity with manliness; in the fight with Cohn he proves his integrity where skill is lacking. His values are exactly those of the hunter in "Francis Macomber," or of the fisherman in *The Old Man and the Sea.* As one of these few remaining images of independent manhood, he offers Barnes the comfort of vicarious redemption. (p. 136)

[When] Brett refuses to let her hair grow long for Pedro, it means that her role in life is fixed: she can no longer reclaim her lost womanhood; she can no longer live with a fine man without destroying him. This seems to kill the illusion which is behind Jake's suffering throughout the novel: namely, that if he hadn't been wounded, if he had somehow survived the war with his manhood intact, then he and Brett would have become true lovers. The closing lines confirm his total disillusionment:

> "Oh, Jake," Brett said, "we could have had such a damned good time together."
>
> Ahead was a mounted policeman in khaki directing traffic. He raised his baton. The car slowed suddenly pressing Brett against me.
>
> "Yes," I said, "Isn't it pretty to think so?"

"Pretty" is a romantic word which means here "foolish to consider what could *never* have happened," and not "what can't happen now." The signal for this interpretation comes from the policeman who directs traffic between Brett's speech and Barnes reply. With his khaki clothes and his preventive baton, he stands for the war and the society which made it, for the force which stops the lovers' car, and which robs them of their normal sexual roles. As Barnes now sees, love itself is dead for their generation. Even without his wound, he would still be unmanly, and Brett unable to let her hair grow long.

Yet according to the opening epigraphs, if one generation is lost and another comes, the earth abides forever; and according to Hemingway himself, the abiding earth is the novel's hero. Perhaps he is wrong on this point, or at least misleading. There are no joyous hymns to the seasons in this novel, no celebrations of fertility and change. The scenic descriptions are accurate enough, but rather flat; there is no deep feeling in them, only fondness, for the author takes less delight in nature than in outdoor sports. He is more concerned, that is, with baiting hooks and catching trout than with the Irati River and more pleased with the grace and skill of the bullfighter than with the bull's magnificence. In fact, it is the bullfighter who seems to abide in the novel, for surely the bulls are dead like the trout before them, having fulfilled their roles as beloved opponents. But Romero is very much alive as the novel ends. When he leaves the hotel in Madrid, he "pays the bill" for his affair with Brett, which means that he has earned all its benefits. He also dominates the final conversation between the lovers, and so dominates the closing section. We learn here that his sexual initiation has been completed and his independence assured. From now on, he can work out his life alone, moving again and again through his passes in the ring, gaining strength, order, and purpose as he meets his own conditions. He provides no literal prescription to follow here, no call to bullfighting as the answer to Barnes' problems; but he does provide an image of integrity, against which Barnes and his generation are weighed and found wanting. In this sense, Pedro is the real hero of the parable, the final moral touchstone, the man whose code gives meaning to a world where love and religion are defunct, where the proofs of manhood are difficult and scarce, and where every man must learn to define his own moral conditions and then live up to them. (pp. 136-38)

Mark Spilka, "The Death of Love in 'The Sun Also Rises'," in Twelve Original Essays on Great Novels, *edited by Charles Shapiro (reprinted by permission of The Wayne State University Press; copyright © 1958 by The Wayne State University Press), Wayne State University Press, 1958 (and reprinted in* Hemingway: A Collection of Critical Essays, *edited by Robert P. Weeks, Prentice-Hall, Inc., 1962, pp. 127-38).*

LEON EDEL

Hemingway has not created a Style: he has rather created the artful illusion of a Style, for he is a clever artist and there is a great deal of cleverness in all that he has done. He has conjured up an *effect* of Style by a process of evasion, very much as he sets up an aura of emotion—by walking directly away from emotion!

What I am trying to suggest is that the famous Hemingway Style is not "organic." And any style worthy of the name must be, as the much-worn, but nevertheless truthful *mot,* that *Style is the man,* testifies. Is Hemingway's Style the man? At the risk of a pun, I would answer no, it is the mannerism! It is an artifice, a series of charming tricks, a group of cleverness. Gertrude Stein taught Hemingway that one can obtain wry effects by assembling incongruities, and Hemingway really learned how to juxtapose these with high skill. (pp. 169-70)

What of the substance? . . . [His] is a world of superficial action and almost wholly without reflection—such reflection as there is tends to be on a rather crude and simplified level. It will be argued that all this is a large part of life and thus has validity in fiction. Of course. It is my contention merely that such surface writing, dressed out in prose mannerisms, does not constitute a Style and that the present emphasis on this quality in Hemingway tends, in effect, to minimize the hollowness of his total production. Hemingway has created a world of Robinson Crusoes, living on lonely islands, with bottle and gun for companions, and an occasional woman to go with the drinks. (p. 170)

He has contrived, with great cleverness, some very good novels. He is at his happiest, in reality, in the short story. The short story by its very nature demands simplification; characters need not be developed, plot and drama need not be created—a mood, a nostalgia, a moment of experience, suffice. Hemingway is an artist of the small space, the limited view. And I am not sure that what I have called "evasion" in his work will not be borne out if we search for its roots in his life, from which, after all, an artist's work always springs. To be able to cope with emotion only by indirection, or to write prose which seeks surface expressly to avoid texture—is this not a little like escaping from life by big-game hunting or watching violence in a bull ring or daydreaming through long hours of fishing? These are all fascinating pursuits for our hours of leisure or when given a proper perspective and taken in proper proportion (unless indeed one earns one's living by fighting bulls or is a career-fisherman). When they become a substitute for other forms of life—and granted that they themselves are part of life and partake of it—they can become an evasion of life. (pp. 170-71)

Leon Edel, "The Art of Evasion," in Folio *(copyright 1955 by the Department of English, Indiana State University; reprinted by*

permission of the author and Folio), *Spring,
1955 (and reprinted in* Hemingway: A
Collection of Critical Essays, *edited by
Robert P. Weeks, Prentice-Hall, Inc., 1962,
pp. 169-71).*

TONY TANNER

One could easily list the particular moments that Hemingway chooses to focus on in his short stories and nearly always they will be found to be moments of crisis, tension and passion. This is not to say that they are epiphanies in Joyce's sense, but rather that they deal with moments of pain, shock, strain, test, moments of emotional heightening of some kind. It may be an ageing courageous bull fighter facing and succumbing to his last bull, it may be a man listening to his wife say that she is leaving him to go off with a woman: the subject matter varies widely, the emotional pitch of the characters is almost uniformly high. And it is at such moments that the details of the encompassing world seem saturated with relevance in an unusually intense way. They do not become symbolic, it is a weakness in the later Hemingway that he pushes them too far in that direction: they can be full of mute menace (as rain, for instance, always is in his stories): but usually they function as the recipients of the characters' intense attention. The character's emotion and the surrounding concrete details interpermeate. In *A Farewell to Arms* there are at least three detailed accounts of meals, detailed to an extent which would be boring if they were simply meals taken by habit for sustenance. But they occur—immediately before the hero is bombed; while he and Catherine are enjoying a snatched few moments of ecstasy away from the war; and while he is waiting to hear the result of her fatal delivery. In the first case the vividness is retrospective: the moment frozen and etched in the memory before the shattering upheaval. In the other two cases the mundane minutiae are included because the intensity of the hero's emotions has so sharpened his sensory faculties that details are elevated from the mundane to the significant. It is as though anything he touches or smells or sees becomes a temporary reflector, even container, of his emotion. The scrupulous registration of details will give the most accurate morphology of the feeling. . . . What the hero of *For Whom the Bell Tolls* ponders to himself is in some way relevant to [all Hemingway's major characters]: 'I know a few things now. I wonder if you only learn them now because you are over-sensitized because of the shortness of the time?' Most of Hemingway's characters (and a very large number of major characters in American fiction) exhibit this 'over-sensitization' in the face of the world. In Robert Jordan's own case it is the danger of his mission and the love of Maria that sensitize him, prompting his senses to an almost awed alertness and efficient clarity. . . . The book abounds in . . . brilliantly perceived particulars: it is because the sights, smells, sounds and tastes are recorded with such resonant accuracy that the book has such a rich surface texture. It is because it contains little more than that that it lacks any overarching structure. It is interesting to see how Hemingway tries to give his material an externally derived historical significance which the book in fact belies: 'that bridge can be the point on which the future of the human race can turn' argues Jordan to himself to invest his task with a sense of purpose. But Hemingway's and Hemingway's heroes' interest lies elsewhere. They are not interested in the capillary movements of history, in progress, in the slow erosions

and rehabilitations of time, in the fall and survival of societies. They are committed to their own moment-by-moment experience and what Jordan says of his relationship with Maria could be said by all of them of their relationship with the world: he intends to 'make up in intensity what the relation will lack in duration and continuity'. And they would agree that if your senses are properly attuned and at work 'it is possible to live as full a life in seventy hours as in seventy years'. And because of this belief in the great truth and value of the intense momentary sensory experience the Hemingway hero is committed to 'the now'. 'You have it *now* and that is all your whole life is; now. There is nothing else than now. There is neither yesterday, certainly, nor is there any tomorrow.' Such an attitude is at bottom indifferent (though not hostile) to the large palpable social historical stirrings around it. . . . And of course it is this elevation of intensity over continuity, the 'now' over history, and the evidence of the senses over the constructs of the mind that determines the whole point of view and strategy of Hemingway's prose and explains his essential preoccupation with what we might call the 'oversensitized hero'. (pp. 231-34)

Abstract concepts only have any meaning for Hemingway if they are translated into sensory particulars. Hemingway's prose is based, among other things, on a 'nausea of untruth' and for him the only verifiable truth is the evidence of the senses. Hence his prose is calculated to resist any tendency towards abstract words which somehow suggest that qualities and meanings have a super-personal life of their own, irrespective of individual incarnation and sensory recognition. Hemingway denies the Platonic idea of 'Courage'—but there is a certain smell to a brave man, an unmistakable odour to his actions which he will testify to and describe by comparing it to other natural sensations. This, of course, avoids any theoretic analysis of the quality, and it is this avoidance of analytic explanation which is one of the striking aspects of Hemingway's style. Meticulous description takes its place. . . . For Hemingway . . . description is definition. (pp. 234-35)

[For] Hemingway, Existence is an incomprehensible void inhabited by concrete particulars perceptible to the senses. In place of vague consoling speculations about the meaning of the infinite nothingness which surrounds human life, the Hemingway hero prefers to overcome his horror of vacancy by a ritual of orderliness and cleanliness in small things. In the living, in the writing. Only this will give him any meaning. . . . No spillage, no sloppiness, no outcry or mess [at the point of death]: rather, a continuing attachment to that essential ritual of meticulousness in practical details which compose the only aspect of life on which the Hemingway hero can pin his faith. You don't know where you're going, but you shut the door cleanly behind you. Under the circumstances—the circumstances of vanished belief—it is all you can do.

Death is the dissolution into nothingness. As the dying writer in 'Snows of Kilimanjaro' discovers: 'And just then it occurred to him that he was going to die. It came with a rush; not as a rush of water nor of wind; but of a sudden evil-smelling emptiness. . . .' The moment of death, for the Hemingway hero, is the testing moment when he is agonizingly poised between the wondrous plenitude of the world and the oncoming smell of black emptiness. The only way he can maintain himself is by orienting himself in the world just as he had done during his life. . . . [As Jordan awaits death] he regains control of himself. 'He was completely integrated now and he took a good long look at everything. Then he looked up at the sky. There were big white clouds in it. He touched the palm of his hand against the pine needles where he lay and he touched the bark of the pine trunk that he lay behind.'

That last act of communion is one of the most moving things in Hemingway: the senses taking their farewell from all the truth they have ever known; the wounded individual, his dignity unimpaired, preparing himself for the slide into nothingness with a final feel of the earth. Jordan takes death 'straight', without religion, his attitude to life summed up with poignant simplicity as he says to himself: 'It is only missing it that's bad.' This is all far more eloquent than the slangy metaphysics of the justifiably outraged hero of *A Farewell to Arms:* 'They threw you in and told you the rules and the first time they caught you off base they killed you.' In thinking like this the hero has detached himself from the only certainties, the certainties of the senses. He speaks more profoundly than he realizes when, earlier in the book, he decides: 'I was not made to think.' Thought has a way of spiralling up and away from our concrete surroundings. That is why at various key points in *The Old Man and the Sea* the fisherman fights against the onset of thought.... A basic distinction must be made between the ordinary intelligence which interprets difficulties, formulates intentions, and modifies actions, etc.; and the sort of vague speculation, metaphysical or theological, etc., which the fisherman is countering. It is, of course, only this latter form of thought which the Hemingway hero tries to avoid.... The point is that for the Hemingway hero only concrete things are 'true' and only practical tasks efficiently undertaken and rigorously seen through offer any meaning and salvation: salvation from the crippling and undermining sense of nothingness which is his perpetual nightmare.... Life, for Hemingway, is all too often a 'spectacle with unexplained horrors': think of the amount of sheer physical suffering and human damage and cruelly capricious disaster there is in his work. The ambition, the necessary thing, is to try and make it, momentarily at least, 'something that was going on with a definite end'. (pp. 236-39)

[In *The Sun Also Rises*] Jake is meditating to himself on the meaning of the world. 'Perhaps as you went along you did learn something. I did not care what it was all about. All I wanted to know was how to live in it. Maybe if you found out how to live in it you learned from that what it was all about.' That last sentence reveals more of a philosophy than is at first apparent. It points not only to the particular Hemingway ethic—'grace under pressure'—but also suggests that the only meaning to be found lies in the relationship of man to the environment he is immersed in. And to learn how to *live in it* it is essential first of all to learn how to *look at it*. (p. 240)

Hemingway makes use of ... Nick's 'first chastity of mind' [in the Nick Adams stories] which wonderingly notes the details without being tempted away into the blurring habits of theorizing. If there is a symbolic 'first man in the world' hidden inside the name 'Adams' it is only because Nick retains that essential integrity of the senses even when confronted with the most brutal disillusioning scenes. He is the ideal Hemingway 'eye' and if, for example, you look at the first few paragraphs of 'A Way You'll Never Be',

which offer a scrupulously and horrifyingly detailed picture of a battlefield, you will notice that they are prefaced by the phrase 'Nicholas Adams saw'. The essential virtue of this sort of eye is best expressed in Jordan's admonition to himself while he awaits his death. 'Keep it accurate, he said. Quite accurate.' Accurate in the parts, we might add, accurate as far as the senses can honestly testify. No further. The rest is nada.

This explains, from another angle, why so much of Hemingway's prose is restricted to scenery and environment, for this is the one known and knowable quantity in any situation: this the unprejudiced eye can quite properly assimilate, whereas there are no senses which can so surely annotate the dubious internality of the people involved in the scene. Hemingway wrote in *The Green Hills of Africa:* 'But if I ever write anything about this it will just be landscape painting until I know something about it. Your first seeing of a country is a very valuable one.' The scenery—the first seeing: a lot of what is really good in Hemingway is based on these two factors. It is interesting to recall that both of Hemingway's last ageing heroes [the colonel and the fisherman] indulge in reveries connected with a feeling for 'place'.... Given Hemingway's philosophy it follows that for him only concrete things, perceptible manifestations of nature, have certain value: 'the earth abideth forever' is the most important phrase from Ecclesiastes which prefaces *The Sun Also Rises*. Thus when any Hemingway hero starts to indulge his memory it instinctively seeks back, not for episodic continuity or vague congenial atmospherics, but simply for things the senses had registered and then stored away.... (pp. 242-43)

Only what the isolated self can do on its own is valuable, only what the isolated ego can perceive for itself is true. To have any significant experience the Hemingway hero must, in one sense or another, for one reason or another (a wound for instance), be 'beyond all people'. Any peace he makes with the world will be personal rather than social, not communal but 'separate'. (p. 246)

[Hemingway's] prose makes permanent the attentive wonder of the senses: it mimes out the whole process, impression by impression.... This pursuit of the exact progress of the senses is everywhere in evidence in Hemingway, even in his earliest work, as for example in the story 'The Three-Day Blow'. 'They stood together, looking out across the country, down over the orchard, beyond the road, across the lower fields and the woods of the point to the lake.' Out, down, beyond, across—as the eye shifts its direction and focus, the prose follows it. As a result the prose very often has recourse to the words 'then' and 'and', and participles: these become important structural factors. They serve to thrust the reader much closer to the actual moment. (p. 247)

Hemingway's practice of unravelling the instant, of hugging the details of a sequence with his whole attention, is not merely the developed habit of a graphic news reporter, no matter how much Hemingway owes to his early journalism. It is a reflection of his faith in the ultimate veracity of the attuned and operating senses and the unsurpassable value of the registered 'now'. As Jordan realizes: '*Now*, it has a funny sound to be a whole world and your life.' A moment is 'a whole world': this is why Hemingway explores its geography with such delicate care. Perhaps we can understand why Hemingway's prose always works to extract and arrest the significant fragments from the endless continuum of sense impressions which constitutes experience. His unflagging efforts to discover and hold 'the real thing, the sequence of motion and fact which made the emotion' constitute a creed and not a gimmick. Hemingway's style has been called 'matter-of-fact' as though its laconic understatement was its main achievement: but we could more accurately rephrase that and say his style was after the facts of matter, those items of the material world which prompted and provoked the attention of his characters. In this he could be compared with Thoreau who, we recall, also made it his aim to 'front only the essential facts', to ascertain 'the case that is'. And it is surely significant that in Hemingway's later work the facts tended to become fabulous, to expand into myth—just as Thoreau asserted they would do if seen properly. (pp. 247-48)

Hemingway valued perception more than inflated self-generated excitement in writing: his interest was not in the subjective self which makes a world of its own, but in the objective world which makes and moves the outward-looking self. This is not to say that he was a mere positivist with no values or illusions to mobilize his attention: the aim is rather to continually check what we believe in against what we can see. (pp. 248-49)

His concern, then, with edge, clarity, distinct contours, and accuracy is profoundly connected with his whole attitude towards life. It is no mere coincidence that we can find the best clues to Hemingway's ideal of 'style' in his descriptions of the bullfighter and the fisherman.... If we ... bear in mind [the comments on bullfighting and] the old fisherman who does everything 'as cleanly as possible', who elevates 'precision' into an ethic and who asserts 'It is better to be lucky. But I would rather be exact'—then we have a sufficient vocabulary to discuss Hemingway's prose. Without any strain the bull and the fish can be seen as representative of the experience of the world which the artist has to confront and master—beautiful, powerful, and dangerous; sometimes fatal to the challenger, the man seeking to dominate through his 'craft'. Those who do manage to kill the bull, land the fish, must employ cleanliness and precision (we should here remember the old man in the café for whom these virtues were the sole source of consolation in life [in 'A Clean, Well-Lighted Place']: there must be no false histrionics, no mere flourishes, no eye-catching exhibitionism. Every gesture must be absolutely focused on the job in hand: every move must be unhurried, unhampered, and controlled. The beauty and vitality of a work of art will depend on the maximum exposure of the artist to experience, the linear clarity and purity with which he gradually asserts his control over the experience, and the exhilarating cleanliness and exactitude with which he finally demonstrates his mastery over his material in 'the kill'. The idea of maintaining a 'purity of line through the maximum exposure' applies equally to Hemingway's prose and Romero's bullfighting. (pp. 249-50)

[There is a] sort of journalism which when, for instance, writing up a train crash, selects one or two 'moving' details to achieve a quick front-page pathos. No one questions the truth of it, but somehow we feel our emotions are being too crudely roused, we resent the facility with which we are shocked, we feel that the very material which makes us feel sick is being cheapened by such improper synecdoche. For there is certainly a way of making the part stand for the whole which is debasing. Hemingway is not guilty of this, but there is that in his style which occasionally moves in that direction. It is a risk any writer must run if he refuses to avail himself of complex conceptual thought and the whole range of analysing, comparing, and placing powers which the fine intellect has at its disposal. It is an honourable risk, but the hazards are very real; not only for the artist trying to write, but also for the man trying to live. This is not the place to discuss Hemingway's code, his scale of values, his ethics: but if there is a simplifying tendency to them, if we feel human conduct cannot be so easily assessed and reduced as Hemingway's categories will allow, part of the reason must be that he tried to attend only to his senses. The disregard of mind not only sharpened those senses until they were a miraculously sensitive instrument, it also imposed a great strain on them, with the result that the range of his emotional response stayed small—either sensuous contentment (fun, ecstasy) or a sort of stunned shock and disillusioned horror which just manages to conceal itself behind the compacted concrete details of the prose. This combination of wonder and horror is very common in American literature. (pp. 252-53)

[The swamp in 'Big Two-Hearted River'] is the dark barren place, the earthly terrain of nada, the opposite of the clean well-lighted place which, in this case, is not a café but simply the sun-drenched world offering its sharp and well-lit particulars to the disciple's reverent eye. It is this patch of dismal foreboding shadow in the story which gives a sort of retroactive enhancement to the concrete details of the world which Nick has been so lovingly appropriating with his sensitized attention.... Because of this ineradicable surrounding threat, Nick seeks to establish contact with the concrete world, by careful touch and by careful sight. In this way he manages to 'give concrete filling to the empty "mine"' in Hegel's terminology, i.e. he fills the mine of consciousness with the positive stuff of existence. By limiting himself to a sort of scrupulous sense-certainty Nick revitalizes his senses, he refurnishes his mind, he replenishes his consciousness with a rich concrete content which will keep the void at bay. And this is why he so carefully relishes and even prolongs, every sensation that nature offers him. 'Nick climbed out onto the meadow and stood, water running down his trousers and out of his shoes, his shoes squelchy. He went over and sat on the logs. *He did not want to rush his sensations any.*' [my italics] That last sentence is one of the most important in the whole of Hemingway. It explains the conduct of his main characters, it explains the structure of his prose, it even hints at his total philosophy. Our sensations of the phenomenological world are the most precious, the most truthful, the most necessary things we have. We must not rush them. That is why, to stress it again, Hemingway's prose is essentially outward-looking, close to the ground, acutely alert in the face of the texture and contours of the objective world, reverently sensitive in its notation of the perceptions of the senses.... Hemingway's syntax works to disentangle each precious single sense impression: it is if you like the syntax of sensation. His prose attempts to establish and preserve 'everything a human being can know at each moment of his existence and not an assembling of all his experiences' as Stein put it. By deliberately not hurrying his sensations Hemingway wonderfully attests reality and finds a way of orienting and stabilizing man in a world which is, after all, only a teeming flux surrounded by a gaping nothingness. (pp. 255-56)

A proper reverence for the world precedes intellectual understanding; indeed, attempts to understand it, to reduce it to reason, may lead to a loss of that reverence, a dulling of the sense of beauty. Similarly the concrete natural world is best seen and arranged according to its original topography: man's reworking interference, literally with machines and metaphorically with certain kinds of art, is ultimately a desecration. Ultimately man, civilized man, is the fallen part of a beautiful world. The old fisherman respects the great fish as 'more noble and more able', if less intelligent, than himself: he feels that 'Man is not much beside the great birds and beasts'. (p. 256)

Hemingway wanted to follow Huck into unspoiled mythical territories, but for the race as a whole that is no longer possible: as Clemens had felt before him. But Nick Adams, like Huck, has moments when he reachieves that fading rapport with nature, and then the prose of their creators sheds all complexity of thought and follows the naive, wondering eye as it enters into a reverent communion with the earth that abideth forever. (p. 257)

> *Tony Tanner, "Ernest Hemingway's Unhurried Sensations," in his* The Wave of Wonder: Naivety and Reality in American Literature *(© Cambridge University Press), Cambridge University Press, 1965, pp. 228-57.*

FRANK W. SHELTON

Hemingway's books may seem to lack entirely that most primary group to which every individual belongs, at least initially, the family.

However, with the posthumous publication of *Islands in the Stream* and *The Nick Adams Stories,* the importance of the family to Hemingway becomes increasingly clear. In *Islands in the Stream,* Thomas Hudson's loss of his sons in part causes his final deep despair. Placing the Nick Adams stories in chronological sequence, as the recent volume does, also highlights how so many of them deal, at least obliquely, with Nick's relationship with and attitude toward family and marriage.

As a child Nick is never closely tied to anyone for a long period of time. In the previously published stories, we see at best an ambivalent picture of Dr. Adams in "Indian Camp," although the newly published fragment, "Three Shots," emphasizes Dr. Adams' sympathy for Nick's fear of the woods. Other stories, especially "The Doctor and the Doctor's Wife" and "Ten Indians," suggest the inadequacy of both Nick's parents, particularly when one compares the coldness and constraint of the relationship between Nick and his father in the latter story to the warm, relaxed atmosphere surrounding the Garners, a true family unit. It is surely no accident that, in the stories of Nick's childhood, Hemingway never presents father, mother, and son all together at one time.

The inclusion in the posthumous volume of "The Last Good Country" is particularly relevant to the family theme. Certainly the most important addition in this story is Nick's sister, who plays a central role. With their father absent and mother untrustworthy, Littless and Nick *"loved each other and they did not love the others. They always thought of everyone else in the family as the others."* The type of family life they have experienced is suggested by Littless' comment, *"'I'll go back whenever you tell me to.*

But I won't have fights. Haven't we seen enough fights in families'." ... The close brother-sister relationship, despite the disparity in their ages, is extremely important to both of them, for in effect they constitute a family of two who must be self-sufficient. His sister's presence prevents the loneliness Nick fears if he is forced to flee by himself, and he is very solicitous of her welfare throughout. The hint of something unnatural in their relationship is a striking and unsettling element. Nick thinks: *"He loved his sister very much and she loved him too much. But, he thought, I guess those things straighten out. At least I hope so."* ... This uneasiness is augmented by their fear of being caught, but in contrast to their apprehension is the sincere love and devotion they feel for one another. In the light of the strikingly inadequate family experiences Nick has had heretofore, this brother-sister relationship demonstrates the potential support close family relationships can provide.

The stories of Nick's maturity shift in emphasis to his attitude toward marriage and possible voluntary association in a family unit he can himself originate. Leslie Fiedler feels Hemingway treats the whole idea of marriage unfavorably: "In Hemingway the rejection of the sentimental happy ending of marriage involves the acceptance of the sentimental happy beginning of innocent and inconsequential sex, camouflages the rejection of maturity and of fatherhood itself" [see *CLC,* Vol. 1]. Some of the Nick Adams stories appear to reject marriage and fatherhood, especially "Now I Lay Me," "In Another Country" and "Cross-Country Snow." But Fiedler errs in identifying Nick's opinions with Hemingway's. In particular the additional material in this volume and the chronological ordering of all the stories suggest that Nick's attitude is not constant but changes in the course of his career. Thus Nick's determination not to marry in "Now I Lay Me" can be seen as his extreme reaction to the tension in his parents' relationship. In the same light the major's extreme stance against marriage in "In Another Country" shows that his marriage must have been the most positive influence in h:s life.

When Nick returns from the war, he continues to avoid marriage and women. In "The End of Something" he rejects close ties with women in favor of male comradeship. In a newly published story, "Summer People," Nick definitely does not shun association with women; in fact he welcomes and needs Kate's company. But he remains determined not to marry, here because he wants to preserve the freedom he needs to be a writer. Getting married would permit another to make demands on him which might prevent his artistic fulfillment.

Of course Nick does marry, though his wife is only a shadowy presence in the later stories. Certainly he is the first to admit that marriage has meant the end of particular aspects of his life. In "On Writing" he realizes that *"when he married he lost Bill Smith, Odgar, the Ghee, all the old gang. . . . He lost them because he admitted by marrying that something was more important than the fishing."* ... Yet Nick does not resent this loss. In fact he is able to remember with amusement *"the horror he used to have of people getting married. It was funny. Probably it was because he had always been with older people, nonmarrying people."* ... [By] the time Nick has been married for some time, his previous adolescent attitude toward marriage has been replaced by a more mature acceptance of the institution and his need for it.

"Fathers and Sons," the final story both in the volume of Hemingway's collected stories and *The Nick Adams Stories*, shifts the focus back to Nick's relationship with his father and his own son. Nick, through the presence of his son, can forgive his father's failures, recognize his own share of the blame for those failures and reaffirm a love of and appreciation for him. Nick's son, who wants to visit the tomb of his grandfather, senses and communicates to his father a relationship spanning three generations.

Thus in the Nick Adams stories Hemingway clearly deals with the role the family should play in relation to the individual. Nick learns as he matures that individuals, in the face of a chaotic and brutal world, must band together for protection and emotional comfort. Family relationships can be the source of great pain, as Nick well knows, but through them the individual can prevent isolation and despair. (pp. 303-05)

> *Frank W. Shelton, "The Family in Hemingway's Nick Adams Stories," in* Studies in Short Fiction *(copyright 1974 by Newberry College), Summer, 1974, pp. 303-05.*

JOHN BERRYMAN

This short, almost desperate, and beautiful story ["A Clean, Well-Lighted Place"] is an unusually fine example of a very special kind of story which is not anecdotal at all. If you were asked by somebody, "What happens in this story?" you would have to reply, "Nothing." Now *nothing* is exactly what the story is about: Nothing, and the steps we take against Nothing. The fact that there is no plot is part of the story's meaning: in a world characterized by "Nothing," what significant action could take place? The two waiters are only very gradually distinguished from each other; their voices in the beginning are choric, just two men talking, any two men. Of the old man in the café we learn very little, and of the barman at the end, nothing. The older waiter is clearly the most important person in the story, but we do not really learn very much about him, either. You could hardly say that the story is *about* him. The part usually played by plot and characterization is left in this story largely to setting and atmosphere.

Hemingway's style is famous for its simplicity—short, common words, short sentences—and is said to be realistic or naturalistic. Is it realistic? "I am of those who like to stay late at the café," the older waiter says. "With all those who do not want to go to bed. With all those who need a light for the night." Surely this is elaborately rhetorical, nobody actually talks this way, and one of the reasons (though only one) for the Spanish setting of the story is the author's desire to achieve from time to time this highly poetic and unnatural tone (as he can do by pretending to be translating from Spanish into English) without its seeming inconsistent with the curt talk, rapid description, and coarse and bitter material of the story. Hemingway's style is very complicated; even where it appears simple, it is not very simple. Look at the first two sentences:

> It was late and every one had left the café except an old man who sat in the shadow the leaves of the tree made against the electric light. In the day time the street was dusty, but at night the dew settled the dust and the old man liked to sit late because he was deaf and now at night it was quiet and he felt the difference.

Then we learn that this old man tried to kill himself last week, even though he has plenty of money; in short, he is *in despair,* and the phrase is used by one of the waiters. That is why he is drinking himself drunk, as he does every night. Even in themselves Hemingway's opening sentences are rather stylized—the rhythms are insistent, alliteration is employed (dew . . . dust . . . deaf . . . difference), even rhyme (night: quiet), and "late" is repeated in a choric way. But as the opening of *this* story, which is to come to a climax in a violent parody of the Lord's Prayer, clearly these sentences have already begun the symbolism which is the reason for the story's being. It is *late,* not only on this evening, and in this man's life, but *in a tradition*—a religious tradition, specifically the Christian tradition (we are in a Catholic country, Spain); so late that the tradition cannot support or console, and suicide invites. There is thus a second reason, besides the physical debility that awaits all of us at the end of life, for the old man's being deaf: he is deaf to the Christian promises, he cannot hear them. He is *alone,* isolated, sitting in the "shadow" left by nature in the modern artificial world. All the light desired in this story is artificial, as if nature had abandoned man, and anything he may want he has to get for himself—precariously and briefly. (pp. 217-18)

This is not just a sour joke, though it is that, too. We have to hear "Nothing" also as *something very positive,* the name given in this story to the modern condition of moral vacancy and meaninglessness which the old man feels, and so he tried to kill himself, and the older waiter feels, and so he suffers from insomnia: "It was a nothing that he knew too well. It was all a nothing and a man was nothing too. It was only that and light was all it needed and a certain cleanness and order. Some lived in it and never felt it but he knew it all was nada y pues nada y nada y pues nada" (nothing and then nothing and nothing and then nothing).

It is *feeling* this condition of nothingness, not the nothingness itself, which is Hemingway's real subject. His deep sympathy with the two sensitive men, the old man and the older waiter, is the story's strongest feeling. Neither is a passive victim. The old man has his "dignity"—a key word for Hemingway. When the younger waiter says, "An old man is a nasty thing," the older waiter, without sentimentalizing or denying the general truth of this (very unpleasant) remark, defends the honour of this particular old man with precise observation: "Not always. This old man is clean. He drinks without spilling. Even now, drunk. Look at him." And when the impatience of the younger waiter has pushed him out, he walks away "unsteadily but with dignity." It is not much, human dignity, in the face of the human condition of nothingness, but it is what we can have.

The older waiter's symbol for it is *light*—here a man-made device to hold off the darkness, not permanently, but as late as possible, and *in public,* as if man's essential loneliness were less intolerable where the forms of social life have to be observed, where one's dignity is called on. (The specific danger of being alone is, of course, suicide.) He formulates this, as it were, on behalf of the old man, and only gradually do we become aware that *his* plight is similar, he is an *older* waiter. . . . More and more distinctly he has become the story's spokesman, the younger waiter being unfitted for this role by his insensitivity (in one of his very rare value judgments, Hemingway implies that he is "stupid") and the old man by being too completely isolated. (pp. 218-19)

Light, cleanness, order, dignity: to hold the Nothing at bay. The reason these things are necessary is that everything else has failed. The parody of the Lord's Prayer has a deliberate effect of blasphemy, and thus explains why these symbols have been used—and why this story, for that matter, has come into existence. Notice how brilliantly the narrative is handled. Turning the light off in the café, he continues the conversation with himself. We are given no indication that he is moving, much less going somewhere else. The parody ends: "Hail nothing full of nothing, nothing is with thee. He smiled and stood before a bar with a shining steam pressure coffee machine." Without our knowledge he has been moving, while blaspheming, and the Lord's Prayer has brought him—where? Precisely where you cannot be with dignity, standing at a bar. Religion is a cheat. You might as well worship this sudden apparition, the shining steam pressure coffee machine, as the Christian God or *nada.*

When the barman asks what he wants, he answers, "*Nada,*" meaning, "Nothing is all that is possible, so that is what I'll have." The barman does not understand, of course ("*Otro loco más*" is One more lunatic, another joker). The lack of understanding of the barman is the point of the end of the story. Insensitive, like the younger waiter, the barman leaves the older waiter isolated with his knowledge that all is *nada.* . . . The last two sentences of the story come like a lash, ranging him again, in his loneliness and desperate need for dignity, with the large class of human beings ("I am of those who . . .") who feel and suffer man's desertion by God—an invented God. (One of Hemingway's little poems takes a different tone with the same theme:

> The Lord is my shepherd.
> I shall not want
> Him for long.)

This essential human ordeal is for all men, but it is only recognized, the story suggests, in age; so that this is what our journey is toward. This, miserably, is what wisdom is of: *nada.* Perhaps no story in English has ever been built so obsessively around one word (the volume of stories in which it originally appeared was called by Hemingway *Winner Take Nothing*).

The angry desolation of the story has its roots in Hemingway's disillusion during the First World War, best expressed shortly in a famous passage of his novel *A Farewell to Arms.* An Italian and the hero are talking, and the Italian says, "We won't talk about losing. There is enough talk about losing. What has been done this summer cannot have been done in vain." "I did not say anything. I was always embarrassed by the words sacred, glorious, and sacrifice and the expression in vain. . . . I had seen nothing sacred, and the things that were glorious had no glory and the sacrifices were like the stockyards at Chicago if nothing was

done with the meat except to bury it. There were many words that you could not stand to hear and finally only the names of places had dignity. Certain numbers were the same way and certain dates and these with the names of the places were all you could say and have them mean anthing. Abstract words such as glory, honor, courage, or hallow were obscene beside the concrete names of villages, the numbers of roads, the names of rivers, the numbers of regiments and the dates.'' In the light of this passage, it is clearer why the older waiter has such difficulty in saying what it is that he hates—*nada*—and what it is that he sets against it—dignity—and why he has to use symbols to express his malignant dissatisfaction with the Christian universe. (pp. 220-21)

> *John Berryman, "Hemingway's 'A Clean, Well-Lighted Place'" (originally published in a different version in* The Arts of Reading, *edited by Ralph Ross, Allen Tate, and John Berryman, Thomas Y. Crowell, Inc., 1960), in his* The Freedom of the Poet *(reprinted with the permission of Farrar, Straus & Giroux, Inc.; copyright © 1940, 1944, 1945, 1947, 1948, 1949, 1956, 1959, 1961, 1964, 1966 by John Berryman; copyright © renewed 1972 by John Berryman; copyright © 1951, 1953, 1960, 1965, 1966, 1975, 1976, by Kate Berryman; copyright © renewed 1973, 1975, 1976 by Kate Berryman), Farrar, Straus, 1976, pp. 217-21.*

*   *   *

HEPPENSTALL, (John) Rayner   1911-

Heppenstall is an English novelist, poet, critic, short story writer, playwright, editor, and translator. Often autobiographical, his work reflects the influence of Yeats, Blake, and the French symbolists, as well as the French New Novelists. *The Blaze of Noon* is considered Heppenstall's most successful novel. (See also *Contemporary Authors*, Vols. 1-4, rev. ed.)

DEREK VERSCHOYLE

The Blaze of Noon is a remarkable and original book. It is the story of a phase in the life of a blind man which, though it is an astonishing *tour de force,* possesses a depth and certainty of the kind which one does not associate with books whose distinction lies in their brilliance. It is a book of which, whether one likes it or not, time will not change one's opinion, for it is not tied to the tastes of a decade; unlike the average English novel of today, written and read within defined social boundaries, it might as effectively have been written in another language and given an alien setting, it will not date, and a reader coming to it in ten years' time will be in just as good a position to appreciate it or criticise it as a reader now. . . . The originality of the book lies not in the exploitation of unusual material, but in its fresh approach to ordinary experience. . . . [The] life, both inner and social, of the particular man who is the central subject of the examination is revealed with absolute consistency and vividness. It is a remarkable achievement.

The book's chief faults, which are irritating rather than crucial, are didacticism and—particularly towards the end—a sense of obsession which creeps through the cool and lucid prose. . . . It is possible to be irritated by the arrogance with which he makes his statements; it is possible to see in what is presented as realism no more than a disguised form of romanticism; it is possible to object on theoretical grounds to any emphasis being placed in this context on physical love, since it is of human activities the one where in practice the visual element generally counts for least. But it simply is not possible to pretend that the book bears the slightest taint of pornography. The world abounds with books containing passages of an equal "frankness," the majority of them too trivial to penetrate beyond the underworld of the circulating library. It is safe to say that to palates formed on such a diet this distinguished and austere book will seem notably lacking in flavour.

> *Derek Verschoyle, "A Blind Man," in* The Spectator *(© 1939 by* The Spectator; *reprinted by permission of* The Spectator*), December 15, 1939, p. 878.*

GEORGE DANGERFIELD

Louis Duncan [the blind protagonist of "The Blaze of Noon"] experiences life with four intensified senses, the fifth being absent; and since he is the narrator, everything in the book is felt not seen.

Certainly Mr. Heppenstall (presumably by shutting his eyes and discovering what it feels like) has done an admirable job of describing a blind man's emotions when he enters a strange room, meets a strange person, takes a walk in an unknown garden, or swims in the sea. But this is not a novel about blindness but a novel about Love—Love as propounded by Louis Duncan—Love without any visual descriptions to aid it. . . . [The] fact remains that the novel is an obstinate entity; it demands the creation of acceptable characters; and Louis Duncan comes very short of this simple ideal. He is, in fact, rather tiresome. He speaks of Love as if he were a gymnastic instructor, and Love an exercise that must be conducted without gaiety or humor. He is a bit of a prig, and more than a bit of a bore.

> *George Dangerfield, "Obstinate Entity," in* Saturday Review *(© 1940 by Saturday Review, Inc.; reprinted with permission), May 25, 1940, p. 22.*

RICHARD WHITTINGTON-EGAN

Heppenstall, the lately arrived criminal historian of murder *à la môde Française,* [reminds us in *Bluebeard and After*] that while we may have our *Jacques l'Eventreur,* our Crippens, Seddons, Heaths, Haighs and Christies, in the words of Sterne, 'They order . . . this matter better in France.' Or if not, strictly, better, at least statistically they are our superiors, being on average rather more than twice as murderous as ourselves.

Taking Landru as a kind of sinister marker, Mr Heppenstall proceeds to range about him the grand assassins of three decades—the twenties, thirties and forties. . . .

The account of the misdeeds of all these anti-heroes is set against the march of political, social and cultural events within France, and contrasted with coeval criminalities in other countries. This treatment, while providing a most effective panoramic view of the chronologically unfolding record, does have the intrinsic disadvantage of making for very dense reading, and the result is not one of those books which can be picked up and put down. It requires sustained and concentrated effort on the part of the reader. But the effort is worth making, for there is certainly no better ac-

count available of the art and artifice of the practice of murder in the fair land of our new common market partners. (p. 103)

> *Richard Whittington-Egan, in* Books and Bookmen *(© copyright Richard Whittington-Egan, 1972; reprinted with permission), May, 1972.*

ANTHONY HOLDEN

[George] Orwell pointed to the brutalising effects of war. Rayner Heppenstall, unconsciously showing how murder is absorbed into the fabric of an increasingly violent society, reaches a remarkably similar conclusion after noting sectarian killings in Ulster: 'One began to wonder whether old-fashioned murders took place any more.'

And that's really an epitaph on his own kind of book [*The Sex War and Others*] (subtitle: *A Survey of Recent Murder, Principally in France*). In the criminology stakes, Heppenstall is a pro: to him, a buried corpse is not decomposing, it is 'falling to pieces', cremation is 'incineration', a psychopath is 'a nut'. But no post-Freudian criminologist can afford, as Heppenstall thinks he can, simply to chronicle atrocities for the wide-eyed or moist-lipped. With a brief this broad, conclusions are only avoided by those out for not very gentlemanly relish; Heppenstall's impressionistic approach leads merely to some rather splendid (and possibly libellous) non-sequiturs, for example: 'As Sir John Hunt's expedition toiled up the lower slopes of Everest, the bodies were discovered at Rillington Place.'

The book is a thinly disguised manifesto for the return of capital punishment. (p. 589)

> *Anthony Holden, in* New Statesman *(© 1973 The Statesman & Nation Publishing Co. Ltd.), April 20, 1973.*

ERIC KORN

[*Two Moons*] is a carefully constructed, defiantly random paste-up of *faits divers*—homicides, road accidents, the goings and comings of heads of state, weather reports, and a sports round-up, observed by a mandarin-in-the-moon. . . . [The] duplex narrative line [is] neither as difficult to follow nor as interesting as you might think.

Gradually, from the sandstorm of occurrences, preoccupations . . . , charming speculations . . . , and uncharming prejudices . . . , a focus and a narrator appears: Harold Atha, a writer preparing a television programme on bell-ringing, whose son has had a disastrous accident. . . . Depressingly, [Harold] concludes that "traditional astrology may sometimes adumbrate a pattern where all, at first, seems meaningless", and we are subjected to a barrage of lunations, conjunctions, aspects, and sextiles. For the sceptical reader, for whom fictional events are not evidence, it remains meaningless, though Mr Heppenstall, despite the obstacles he puts in his own path, rarely writes without clarity and sensibility. (p. 682)

> *Eric Korn, in* The Times Literary Supplement *(© Times Newspapers Ltd. (London) 1977; reproduced from* The Times Literary Supplement *by permission), June 3, 1977.*

NEIL HEPBURN

The two moons of Rayner Heppenstall's title [*Two Moons*] are not the astronomical bodies that might imply a descent into Anglo-Vonnegutism, but those more familiar as patronising approximations of 'savage' speech—the periods of time that we call lunar months or lunations. The two in question are consecutive, those of August and September 1972; their phases frame the events of this extraordinary novel without restricting its temporal scope, which easily accommodates 50-year-old memories, as well as a 'writing present' about a year after the main events.

These events are not in themselves outstandingly strange or momentous. They concern the consequences of an accident —a fall in Croydon—to Lewis Atha. . . . [There is] a parallel personal tragedy, in which a young bellringer is killed travelling from work.

The method—presenting in close focus a series of fictional events against a background of real ones in long focus—is not new. Dos Passos's *USA* provides a precedent if not a provenance. What I think is new, in English fiction, is the way Mr Heppenstall has used this method to overcome the problems of representing in literary form Bergson's idea that 'the past is continually organised with the present'. To say that the two moons are consecutive is misleading: in *Two Moons*, they are concurrent, and represented as such by running the narrative and apparatus of the first lunation only on the left-hand pages of the book, and those of the second only on the right-hand pages, with the intention that they should be read in parallel. By reading, first, all-left, and then, all-right, you can frustrate this intention and produce a conventionally linear story.

The results are astonishingly successful. The contexting of Lewis's tragedy within a pattern of mundane violence produces a continually changing perspective on both; and this is again modified by the bringing into focus of the young bellringer's death, by the contingent interest developed by Harold Atha in campanology and by the detailed descriptions of astrological configurations at crucial points in the narratives. The apprehension of the interdependence, if not the simultaneity, of past, present and future is overwhelming. (p. 254)

> *Neil Hepburn, in* The Listener (© *British Broadcasting Corp. 1977; reprinted by permission of Neil Hepburn), August 25,1977.*

*　　*　　*

HIGGINS, George V(incent)　1939-

Higgins is an American novelist and short story writer. A criminal lawyer who has been an assistant U.S. District Attorney and assistant Attorney General, he is known primarily for crime novels which paint a realistic, deglamorized picture of the criminal subculture. His work is characterized by suspense and humor, with action portrayed largely through dialogue. Recent novels have moved into the realm of Washington politics. (See also *CLC*, Vols. 4, 7, and *Contemporary Authors*, Vols. 77-80.)

STEVE OWNBEY

Here's a tip on how to read *The Judgment of Deke Hunter*. Read only Chapters 5, 10, 12, 14, 16, 19, 21, and 22, and you'll enjoy an exciting, colorful, funny, clever, and rather provocative novelette about a bank robbery trial. . . .

So much for the good parts. The rest of the book, as one of George V. Higgins' characters would put it, sucks.

The female characters . . . aren't worth knowing. Higgins seems to think he'd be branded naïvely romantic if he depicted a happy marriage. Every scene involving a married couple shows them bickering, and reading them is as much a waste of time as watching *The Honeymooners*. The fact that Higgins' audience is (probably) mostly male is ironic, since so much of his book is soap opera. (p. 1302)

Higgins has comic talent; you wonder why he doesn't settle down and write something non-serious. His comedy is broad, but with surprising touches of subtlety. . . . But the laughs are too scattered. For every line that is both dirty and funny, like "He just isn't your basic hard-nosed desperado, that eats nails and fishhooks for breakfast and washes them down with horse piss," a hundred other lines are just dirty, not funny. (pp. 1302-03)

Higgins' famous "realistic dialogue" is often excellent. . . . But too much of it is tedious, unnecessarily filthy, and pretentiously florid. (p. 1303)

> *Steve Ownbey, "Adam-and-Eve-12," in* National Review (© *National Review, Inc., 1976; 150 East 35th St., New York, N.Y. 10016), November 26, 1976, pp. 1302-03.*

IVAN GOLD

["Dreamland"] is George V. Higgins's sixth book since 1972, when "The Friends of Eddie Coyle" appeared. Seven books in five years—clearly an oeuvre in the making, and in "Dreamland" Higgins works to extend the range, leaving the tightly plotted, swift-moving netherworld of Eddie Coyle for the denser, more literary air of Boston Brahmins, high finance and international skullduggery. . . .

I found the intricacies of the plot—and the relationship between Compton and Andrew—ultimately baffling, and the issue of whether or not Wills senior was a Government spy of no great moment. Compton's narration is turgid at times, mannered at others, with echoes of Faulkner, Conrad, James. Yet the book has a consistent appeal, powered as it is by a determined intelligence and filled as it is with lore: There is much of interest on the workings of the legal profession, on sailing, on politics, on the lives of the rich, on trade secrets of investigative reporting and much else. Compton (or Higgins) knows a great deal, and if the narrative is not exactly seamless, it is filled with moving scenes and sharp observations of character that keep reader involvement high. Perhaps one is not meant to take the plot involutions very seriously but, rather, to respond to the book's amplitude and to the spectacle of a good, established writer stretching and enlarging on his talent, and moving on. (p. 15)

> *Ivan Gold, in* The New York Times Book Review (© *1977 by The New York Times Company; reprinted by permission), September 11, 1977.*

MICHAEL MASON

Dreamland can . . . be thought of as something of a compromise between thriller and political novel. Its main theme is the hero's reluctant discovery of some facts about his deceased father's personal and professional life, which are dug up in the course of a journalist's pursuit of a story. So the book is structurally a novel of mystery, moving towards exposure and explanation. There are, however, no corpses in the cellar. The exposed truths are mostly non-criminal acts of espionage and international diplomacy.

Another category which *Dreamland* fits into is the American novel of conspiracy, a new genre which has flourished in the 1960s and 1970s for reasons that need not be enumerated. In fact this is probably the more correct way to regard the component of mystery in *Dreamland*, for its clarifications and discoveries are ambiguous and incomplete in the way that the exposure of conspiracy has been in American fiction and reality alike recently. At the end, the reader will still be partly in the dark not only about who done it, but also about what "it" was in the first place.

This admittedly clever attempt to mirror the haziness of history may have been carried too far by Mr Higgins. At points the narrative is so allusive and oblique that it ceases even to be tantalizing. And then it is additionally muffled by the great importance given to direct speech in the novel —speech both as narrative event and as narrative medium. . . .

Mr Higgins has remained very loyal to the spoken word in his novels through all their changes of direction. Dialogue is almost as prominent in *Dreamland* as it was in *The Digger's Game*. In addition, the narration is a first-person one by the hero, Compton Wills. . . .

He creates a definite idiom for both Compton and many of his acquaintance which is impressively different from the Boston underworld dialect, but less successful. This pompous, circumlocutory style harmonizes nicely with the book's themes of façade and genteel fraud, and on Compton's lips it expresses well his resistance to half-recognized truths about himself and others. But the author's hunt for a mealy-mouthed, arcane diction often leads him into implausibility and solecism. The villain—if that's what he is—is an Englishman who uses phrases such as "Pause yet awhile". It most be a very long time since any crook, even an English one, has talked like that.

> Michael Mason, "The Dirt on Daddy," in The Times Literary Supplement (© Times Newspapers Ltd., 1977; reproduced from The Times Literary Supplement by permission), November 4, 1977, p. 1285.

JOSEPH McLELLAN

After some sidetrips into the less congenial field of Washington fact and fiction, the author of *The Friends of Eddie Coyle* and *The Digger's Game* is back in his old, familiar territory: criminals and those who pursue them, in and around Boston. [In *The Judgement of Deke Hunter*, as] in the past, [Higgins's] eye for detail and his ear for dialogue are precise and vivid, his story plain and believable, his characters realistic to the point that they would be banal in less skilled hands. This time, the focus is on the family and professional problems of a detective sergeant rather than a petty criminal, and the moral seems to be that hunters and hunted are members of the same animal species. (p. E6)

> Joseph McLellan, in Book World—The Washington Post (© The Washington Post), March 12, 1978.

*   *   *

HOWARD, Richard   1929-

Howard is an American poet, critic, translator, and editor.

His poetry is highly structured, with definite meter and carefully chosen language. Considered neoclassic by some critics, Howard's work is often historically inspired. His use of narrative verse and dramatic monologue has prompted frequent critical comparison to Browning. He received the Pulitzer Prize in Poetry in 1970 for *Untitled Subjects*. (See also *CLC*, Vol. 7.)

ROBERT K. MARTIN

Richard Howard's verse is elegant and cultured, tasteful and erudite. A man of learning and a connoisseur, he brings to his poetry a mind trained in the rigors of French poetics and an ear attuned to the rhythms of Ronsard as well as those of Browning.

In these days of vatic pronouncements and True Confessions, he remains a voice of civilization, a man trained in an older tradition. His poems speak clearly of his commitment to the mind and to precision of expression.

I can think of no other living poet who writes with such elegance. Only Richard Wilbur among Americans seems to come close. It is perhaps worth noting that both Wilbur and Howard are skillful translators steeped in the somewhat more controlled atmosphere of French poetry. (p. 109)

[Richard Howard] has clearly defined his own notions of poetry, and his practice reveals his fidelity to those standards of rigor. His danger is of turning in the direction of academic verse, where technical precision is matched to essentially torpid matter.

[*Two-Part Inventions*] is marked by a sense of High Wit. Its keynote is its urbanity: Howard rarely ever missteps. He has a clear voice of his own. The question remains: what does he have to say with that voice?

Two-Part Inventions consists of six relatively long poems . . . , all more or less dramatic dialogues. The form is surely Howard's own, although it derives somewhat from the Renaissance body-soul dialogue and the Victorian dramatic monologue. The title, we are told, is meant to be taken in its musical sense as "two voices . . . each developing a single idea."

The poems are also inventions, that is to say, fictions. Each of the meetings is more or less imaginary, although based on actual events and characters. A large part of their appeal will derive from our general desire to gossip about the famous and frequently scandalous. Sex, madness, and death recur as topics, always, however, carefully modulated by the tones of drawing room or polite correspondence. (p. 110)

The topic of homosexuality is one which recurs frequently in this volume: it is one of the bases of the conversation between Walt Whitman and Oscar Wilde in "Wildflowers" and of the conversation between Rodin and the unidentified traveler in "Contra Naturam." In the Victorian and Edwardian world of which Howard writes, the unmentionable crime remained barely beneath the surface, frequently giving rise to art, but remaining still unacknowledged—ashes to be carefully deposited in ash trays, or tidied away under the rug, never to be strewn about on the public thoroughfare. (p. 112)

The world of Edith Wharton, Henry James, and Marcel Proust has been marvelously recaptured in its bitchiness, its short-sightedness, its hypocrisy, and its genius. After 16 pages of verbal sparring, Howard gives us his own "turn of the screw": this meeting, so telling for the two participants, has been arranged by the sadistic Henry James. But they manage yet another turn, by agreeing never to tell Mr. James what has passed between them: silence "is the one / telling punishment." It is a magnificent *trouvaille.*

This meeting, like all the others Howard invents, is a confrontation with truth, naked and cruel. Most of his characters refuse to hear what they are told. . . . The poems are verbal *tours de force;* they display Howard's easy mastery of free forms. There is rarely a wrong note, even in this collection which demands so many different voices. His "Wildflowers" has a brilliant counterpoint between the exuberance and self-dramatization of Wilde and the homeliness of Whitman.

Wilde: I shall cross that bridge
          after I have burned it behind me

Whitman: Kiss me,
          and catch your trolly, I've lectured long
     enough. You must read the writing on the wall,
               or the page, or on the face,
          by yourself, Oscar

Such stylistic pyrotechnics can only come from a man to whom a poet or any artist cannot exist except through his words.

If one cannot fault Howard's taste or his reading, one can still wonder if he will ever give us his own voice. There is no doubt of his ability to hear and recreate, to translate from language to language, or from age to age, but we must still ask . . . whether he is finally a poet or an author.

The present collection offers the reader many selves; but it does not make clear the choice to be made among them. One finds oneself in the position of Rodin's fellow-traveler in "Contra Naturam" who assures the artist "You have been, from the first, the inspiration / of us all" and who looks for a profession of shared faith, an acknowledgment of what he sees in Rodin's work, "pleasure rises to the pitch of vision." But the voice of Rodin is that of a tired man who feels himself "slowly, inevitably / flowing toward death." . . . One suspects that Howard can sympathize with Rodin's desire to remain private and his fear of the naked moment.

To have ten voices is perhaps to have none. The intelligence that created these poems is too great to be spent only in exercises. Howard's poetry is not academic in the sense of a sterile conformity to a set of rules; but it runs the risk of looking only backward, of eternally recreating the past. Ours is clearly an age of museums; a time for recouping the forces. No one can perform this task better than Richard Howard.

But his work also gives every sign of knowing the sources of authentic art:

Whitman:

     Without the boys—if it had not been for the boys,
               I never would have had the *Leaves,*
          the consummated
          book, the last confirming word.

Rodin's traveler:

          it is neither Jacques nor Jean
     I look at, once they are naked before me,
               but Endymion
     who stands, momentarily illuminated
               in a clearing

Hölderlin:

               We have come too late
          for [the gods]. It is the world which is divine now,
          and that is why there is no God. The divine
          has no name, only the gods are named, like these,
                    and they change their names.

It is these qualities which we miss: a certain carnal truth which is at the same time divine; a sense of the immediacy of experience. The world of which Howard writes has as ineluctably vanished as the Greek world for Hölderlin.

Howard sees civilization as the last barrier against encroaching madness and death. And yet it is the balance of the two which creates artistic tension, just as it is the balance of body and soul, of self and Doppelgänger which is so precariously at stake in these poems. The voice of convention and the voice of folly: Howard knows that the two are finally inextricably wound up together. (pp. 113-15)

Robert K. Martin, "The Unconsummated Word," in Parnassus: Poetry in Review *(copyright © by Poetry in Review Foundation), Fall-Winter, 1975, pp. 109-15.*

ROBERT PHILIPS

Fellow Feelings contains some of [Richard Howard's] most impressive work. These include "Venetian Interior, 1889," a remarkably full rendering of the sad world of Pen Browning; "Decades"; and "The Giant on Giant-Killing." The latter two utilize Hart Crane's history and Donatello's bronze of David, respectively, to illumine Howard's own life. Both poems openly explore homosexuality: indeed, the book is the most out-of-the-closet collection since Howard's own *Two-Part Inventions.* Rather than being sensational, Howard's poems convey tenderness, and seek understanding. He movingly pictures both himself and Crane as on "permanent short-leave from the opposite sex." In "The Giant on Giant-Killing" we are given a defense of homosexuality, yet are reminded that the name Goliath, while meaning *destroyer* in Assyrian, means *exile* in Hebrew. Throughout the volume there is a feeling of singularity and alienation.

Howard's most felicitous gift is for the well-turned epigram. Some are worthy of Wilde: "Ripeness is hell"; "The tiny is the last resort of the tremendous"; "Kissing is not cosmetic, merely cosmic"; "We are what we see"; "The sacred and the suburban often coincide;" etc. The danger Howard risks is that he displays too much wit. Verbal pyrotechnics call attention to themselves, rather than to the meaning they are employed to convey. . . .

Yet all wit and wordplay are employed to extremely serious ends. If the book has two misfires ("Compulsive Qualifications" and "Howard's Way"—poems in which questionable subjects seem paraded rather than contemplated), it also has many direct hits on fascinating and difficult targets. Howard is one of our most original poets. (p. 597)

Robert Philips, in Commonweal *(copyright © 1976 Commonweal Publishing Co., Inc.;*

reprinted by permission of Commonweal Publishing Co., Inc.), September 10, 1976.

JOHN R. REED

More than ever, Richard Howard's poems convey the sense of personal history transformed into a fable that is worth hearing. There is a powerful personality behind the poems of *Fellow Feelings,* and the individual pieces, from the opening poem "Decades," to "Howard's Way" and "Compulsive Qualifications," to "The Giant on Giant Killing" and "Vocational Guidance," convey this personality with a clarity that relates it to something larger, for the poems of *Fellow Feelings* are also about art, and thus the personal history that colors them becomes part of the larger story of the modern artist. It is a familiar story of wounds that must be turned to profit, of inspiration that comes mysteriously and cannot be denied, of achievement which solves nothing but makes the need to persist more acute.

The three finest poems in the volume are in the third section of the book, devoted mainly to works of art. All three poems demonstrate the insinuation of narrative into an essentially lyric poem. In the first of these, "The Giant on Giant Killing," inspired by Donatello's bronze statue of a sensuously appealing David, we have Goliath's account of how David defeated him. The basic story is familiar to us all, but Howard's version is surely unusual, for it suggests that Goliath was willingly defeated in order to be near the beautifully young David for whom he had conceived a strong passion. "In "Vocational Guidance," the subject is Simone Martini's *Annunciation.* Again the story is familiar, assuming we know that an angel appeared to Mary announcing that she was to be the mother of Christ. Once more the story is transformed, for Howard finds in the details of the painting parallels with his own case, and with the case of any artist who feels inspiration come like an angel bearing the questionably welcome news that he must bring to birth a work of art. (p. 88)

"*Purgatory* formerly *Paradise,*" gives us a clearer idea of the method employed in these poems. The poem opens with the lines "*He used—these are his words—to wander about / in his pictures at will. . . .*" What follows is Howard's wandering in Bellini's *Sacred Allegory* . . . , creating from it a story apparently related to his own life. The painting itself is an allegory that specialists have still not entirely explained, but Howard's story requires no academic solution, for it is his wish to create from others' artworks his own works of art that gain their strength from the fellow feelings one artist shares with another. . . .

Richard Howard creates his narratives from works of art in *Fellow Feelings,* just as he created narratives from imagined biographies in *Untitled Subjects.* But the narrative remains only a structure to convey a personal statement that transcends that narrative. (p. 89)

John R. Reed, in The Ontario Review *(copyright © 1976 by* The Ontario Review*), Fall-Winter, 1976-77.*

HENRY SLOSS

Like Good and Bad Angels, two spirits of very different kinds are at work in Richard Howard's six books of poetry to date. One is genial and generous, and shows itself in the two best known of the volumes, *Untitled Subjects* (1969) and *Two-Part Inventions* (1974). . . . [The] measure of the

heights to which the books rise can best be taken in terms of *pleasure.* There is an ampleness about the books that is perhaps the sine qua non of pleasure itself. For the reader of the poetry entire, however, the surest guide to their genius (or angel) is the relief felt in coming to them, particularly since we cannot help but sense that this feeling was the poet's before it was ours—his Good Angel was at work. . . .

But the two books are haunted by their successors, *Findings* (1971) and *Fellow Feelings* (1976), the fourth and the sixth of the volumes, in which the Bad Angel shows itself. These two are demanding where the other two are openhanded, compelling where the others are attractive; if we sense the poet's ease in *Untitled Subjects* and *Two-Part Inventions,* we will feel the constraints under which he works in *Findings* and *Fellow Feelings.* The measure of the depths to which the latter two sink, as it is perhaps the Bad Angel's name, is *will.* (p. 85)

But *Findings* and *Fellow Feelings* are no less accomplished than their predecessors in the oeuvre; their success is different in kind. . . . [For] the reader, the delight in pleasure should be no less enjoyable than the admiration of will. . . .

The line of the oeuvre is clearest if we see the six books in three pairs and note the movement in each: the rising from *Quantities* to *The Damages,* and the falls from *Untitled Subjects* to *Findings* and from *Two-Part Inventions* to *Fellow Feelings* respectively. . . . But before attempting to follow these ups and downs through the six volumes, it will be helpful to have some idea of the landmarks to be met with along the way. [There are six landmarks which occur as major themes throughout the poetry. They are: water, twilight, paradox, preconception, contra-naturam (art and homosexuality), and the past.] (p. 86)

[Water:] The Brenta's paradox, that it moves and stays the same, is just what interests the poet, as the sea's rising and falling interest him for the analogy to sex and to inspiration in art. . . .

[The] edge of the sea is the site of metamorphosis and realization. . . .

[Twilight:] The twilight in Richard Howard's poetry is often literal, a favorite site or situation for the poems, but it is more often figurative: the poems take place in "the day between" two opposing states, usually late in the day of the one with the night of the other coming on. The setting for the love poems is as the love itself is setting. . . . (p. 87)

Between sickness and recovery is another of the twilights in which the poetry finds a congenial locus (and the reader finds another paradox). Since recovery must be to another and perhaps more devastating illness, the normal everyday sickness of self, getting better is also getting worse. . . .

But the most interesting of the twilights is semantic. Most markedly after *The Damages,* the poems proceed almost as a consequence of the connotations and etymological suggestions that gather about a preceding phrase or word; qualification seems always to be compulsive in Richard Howard's poetry. (p. 88)

[Paradox:] Change is the subject of Richard Howard's poetry; to contain change is its project. No rhetorical device better suits each than paradox, however little the paradoxes are themselves rhetorical.

Most if not all of the paradoxes turn on the impossibility of having what is possessed, perhaps because one is possessed by it as well, so that losing something is the one way to know that it had once been had. . . .

In the way that a paradox contains change within itself, so will the many emblematic poems, for they defy change by being incomplete (in the sense that only what is complete can be changed): their application needs to be discovered again and again. . . .

In general, there is about the poetry what I can only think to call a kind of self-destruct mechanism, for the art seems to ask that the made fail before the unmade, the particular disappear into the exemplary, and the conceived call attention to the anterior conception. (p. 89)

[Preconception:] Richard Howard usually works from a model. The poems begin with something that is already *there*—a life, a painting, a poetry, a quotation, or a model (or models) draped and posed by the poet himself (as in *Untitled Subjects* and *Two-Part Inventions*). A favorite form, then, is the epistle where the boundaries of the correspondence are carefully defined by the stated subject matter and the relationship between the correspondents.

The power of the given or preconceived is perhaps the dominant characteristic of the poetry, for the poetry works *from* something rather than *toward* something and finds its satisfactions or dismay *within* a situation rather than in its sequel. . . . The poetry is dramatic, not narrative; comedy, not tragedy. (pp. 89-90)

[Contra-Naturam (art and homosexuality):] Richard Howard's verse sets itself in opposition to nature. As often as not, experience in the poetry is the experience of art, in the same way that the oeuvre might better be described as a criticism of art than as a criticism of life. So thorough-going is the poet's antipathy to nature, workaday experience, and life "as it merely passes" ("Waiting for Ada") that even the art upon which he lavishes his attention is non-representational, non-mimetic.

Implicit in the poetry is an analogy between art, as a second and superior nature, and homosexuality; the basis for the comparison is that both are unnatural, where nature is anything but ideal. . . . [Perversity's] definition in Richard Howard's poetry is precisely denial of one's nature. (pp. 90-1)

[The past:] The past as burden and the past as relief; the past as "all that exists" ("A Phenomenon of Nature") and the past as non-existent . . . ; the past that yields the accomplishments of *Untitled Subjects* and *Two-Part Inventions* and the unyielding past that exacts the accomplishments of *Findings* and *Fellow Feelings;* the past that is at the heart of the paradox of possession and loss and that is the core of identity; the past is as much Richard Howard's preoccupation as it was Proust's. Or, say, as much as it is the preoccupation of the highest strain of American verse and fiction. (p. 91)

Where all else is uncertain [in *Quantities*] the poet keeps these short, painstakingly crafted poems to the high road of formal achievement (almost inevitably it seems); he has not yet found his stride. But if the poems are less the poet's own than those in *Findings* and *Fellow Feelings*, the poems in the three of these volumes (the unaccented syllables in the poetry's line) share characteristics first found in *Quanti-*

ties: the poems are brittle, individual, definitive—as though each of them were the last poem instead of the next poem. (p. 92)

"Loss" (like "rot") is an uncooked word in *Quantities*, an absolute that renders all else relative; the question to which the poems answer, or which exacts those answers that are the poems, is how to survive loss. (pp. 92-3)

The more loss costs, that is, the more survival does. Take "At Bluebeard's Castle" and "The Shepherd Corydon": poems at once feral and admonitory that reckon the costs of survival at any cost with an unashamed honesty worthy of Andrew Undershaft himself. It is all very well to 'be a survivor', . . . but these poems show that surviving tells *against* the survivor; for to overcome loss is to repudiate the lost—it is to make a grand refusal. The two poems contain, in addition to their images of the sexual demonic and the post-coital monstrous, a portrait of the artist as something less or more than human (a monster, a god), and they argue an equivalence between the impersonality of lust and that of art. In the harrowing conclusion to "The Shepherd Corydon," there is what amounts to a preview of the desolation of *Findings* and *Fellow Feelings* in which inspiration, however much it was demonic possession, is known by its having passed. In those late books as here in Richard Howard's first, the key to survival is will—but a will that one must almost dare to have. . . . Richard Howard's is a poetry of unease and, often, disease. It is a questing, Faustian, perhaps even Satanic poetry where the search is for knowledge and power, the power over loss that can only come from knowledge.

Probably a more important than a brilliant beginning, *Quantities* strikes many notes, and authoritatively, that resound throughtout the poetry; some of these unknown quantities will become the familiars of the later and more unexceptionably fine work. (pp. 93-4)

In terms of the oeuvre, then, *The Damages* is decisive in two respects. It passes a negative because silent judgment on some of the lyric impulses in *Quantities* and undertakes the exploration of the poet's past about which the first book was itself silent. . . . And, as for the second respect, *The Damages* points the way for the later poetry. In "A Far Cry After a Close Call," the letter "To Aegidius Cantor," and "Bonnard: A Novel," it uncovers the subject matter and, more crucially, the forms that some of the subsequent poetry's highest realizations revolve upon. Finally, when Richard Howard turns to the Twentieth Century's past in *Untitled Subjects,* it is because he has learned in *The Damages* that his past is not as vital as our past. (p. 94)

If what the poet will find in *The Damages* is that he cannot live in his past however much it lives in him, the lesson can only be learned by his having plunged into it. . . .

In *The Damages*, the past is turned to in the hope of making sense of the present. (p. 95)

Released from a Freudian version of the significant past, just because it so little signifies, Richard Howard goes on in *Untitled Subjects* to his century's past (or, what is more significant still, his century's art's past) because he has discovered in *The Damages* that we are

> much less individuals
> than we hope or fear to be.

("Bonnard: A Novel")

[*Untitled Subjects*] gives me pause. I think that the overriding *fact* of the book is its greatness, but it is just greatness in a work of art that is unaccountable. (pp. 96-7)

For their accessibility to the reader and what is perhaps their inaccessibility to criticism, then, the poems in *Untitled Subjects* ask for little commentary.

What is at issue in the volume is identity in one of its most fascinating respects, that as between the life of the artist and his living (on) in the art. As an artist's work may be taken as a realization of his or her life, it takes the life from them as well—one of Richard Howard's twilit paradoxes. (p. 97)

In *Untitled Subjects,* Richard Howard's "aspiring memory" seeks and succeeds in finding a means for resuscitating the lives of artists that have been absorbed by and lost sight of in the work we know them by. . . .

As explicitly retrospective in its title as *The Damages, Findings* . . . is the most moving of Richard Howard's books of poetry, perhaps because what it looks back on are prospects that have been foreclosed. Not the least of these is the claim staked and mined by *Untitled Subjects*—the past. . . . The poetry in *Findings* is wrung from the want of those resources—an abundant past, an abundant language —that had been the poet's on the heights of *Untitled Subjects.* Cast down, the poetry will arise from resistance in the first part of *Findings,* from acceptance in the second part. (p. 98)

In *Findings* and *Fellow Feelings* where the world is closed to the poet, language is open to him; lexicography and linguistics take up when afflatus leaves off. . . .

The world that is closed, or foreclosed, opens a world in art. Art in *Findings* and *Fellow Feelings* is entered into, and is the more lively for the world's deadliness. (p. 99)

Power is the characterizing preoccupation of American verse since World War II—not the acquisition of power, but its renunciation once had. In Richard Howard's work, the giving over begins in *Findings* . . . and continues through *Fellow Feelings.* . . . But *Two-Part Inventions* . . . contains its most brilliant images, in Edith Wharton's surrender of Gerald Mackenzie's ashes and Sandro Fiore's exultation in the loss of his art, and its most explicit expressions. . . . The prerequisite to relinquishing power is admitting that it is not yours, and still less yours to *have,* so the great work of *Two-Part Inventions* will be the admission of the Other. (p. 100)

From the unions of *Two-Part Inventions,* the poet has been returned to the isolation of self. Others are just what he lacks and all that he seeks to find in *Fellow Feelings,* for alienation is monstrous.

Now we can see, retrospectively, that what the characters in *Two-Part Inventions* had to give each other seems to have been offered from within the circle of self, as though over walls that finally closed the characters off from one another, for the end of each poem is or anticipates a separation. But we should never have noticed but for the "coming-to" in *Fellow Feelings.*

The poet turns to the worlds in language . . . and in art . . . , exactly as he turned to these resources in *Findings.* . . . But the others most sought after are people.

So he calls them up and calls on them (Larbaud, Magritte, Proust, and Cornell face to face, Toulouse-Lautrec, Simone Martini, Giovanni Bellini, Robert Browning, and Randall Jarrell increasingly obliquely). (p. 102)

As often as the poet has turned from life to art, when art turns into life he flees—alienated and therefore on his way to the notion that art is Purgatory not Paradise. Seeking others, the Other finds him.

Appeals of an altogether different kind are made to Auden and Hart Crane, for of each Richard Howard asks and receives a paternity. (pp. 102-03)

In "Decades," the image of paternity is . . . more explicit. As Hart Crane found his father in Walt Whitman, Richard Howard finds his in Crane: "Take my hand / as you gave yours to him." Brilliant in the poem is the degree to which the artistic lineage is so inevitable that it seems even more natural than nature. (p. 103)

> *Henry Sloss, "'Cleaving and Burning': An Essay on Richard Howard's Poetry," in* Shenandoah *(copyright 1977 by Washington and Lee University; reprinted from* Shenandoah: The Washington and Lee University Review *with the permission of the Editor), Fall, 1977, pp. 85-103.*

*   *   *

HUGHES, (James) Langston   1902-1967

Hughes was a black American poet, novelist, short story writer, playwright, children's book author, editor, and translator. Original, insightful, and musical in his verse, he became the "poet laureate of Harlem" during its literary renaissance of the twenties. A poet of the city, he wrote of racial injustice, social struggle, and interracial relations in poetry which has its roots in jazz and the blues. Hughes's style is simple and colloquial in its use of slang, dialect, and humor. Many of his poems have been set to music. (See also *CLC,* Vols. 1, 5, and *Contemporary Authors,* Vols. 1-4, rev. ed.; obituary, Vols. 25-28, rev. ed.)

JULIAN C. CAREY

If, as other critics suggest, [Simple, the protagonist of Hughes's *The Best of Simple,*] is the universal black man in the street, the average and typical Afro-American, the cause of his (their) problems is not his lack of cultural awareness of his misdirected efforts to champion his *négritude:* "White folks is the cause of a lot of inconveniences in my life." White America has tried to give him a false sense of culture and to replace his black pride with a desire to be white. In both instances, Jesse B. Semple, the prototype for black Americans, has repulsed white America's efforts. (pp. 162-63)

If Langston Hughes's character has any shortcoming it is that while Simple is laughing to keep from crying, most of his readers are only laughing—laughing and failing to recognize the tragic ethos that Simple symbolizes. His efforts to acknowledge the cultural, social, and political assets of *négritude* are challenged by lovers, friends, states, and institutions. Nevertheless, he perseveres, he endures. He refuses to believe that Negroes are "misbred, misread, and mislead." He is not sophisticated enough to diagnose the racist psyche, but he does know that he is not the problem. Simple is not made for defeat. He is just simple, and in his simplicity and compassion and bufoonery he exposes his soul, truly hurt by a racist country; he illustrates, sometimes too humorously, the reason he is lonesome inside himself. He knows he is equal; what he wants is to be treated equal. He prays a prayer that we learn to do right, that we learn to get along together because he "ain't nothing but a man, a working man, and a colored man at that." (p. 163)

Julian C. Carey, "Jesse B. Semple Revisited and Revised," in Phylon, *XXXII (copyright, 1971, by Atlanta University), Second Quarter (June), 1971, pp. 158-63.*

STANLEY SCHATT

Langston Hughes is generally acknowledged to be the major Afro-American poet of the twentieth century, yet the myth persists that despite his over nine hundred published poems he was more an entertainer than a serious poet. . . . Because so many of his early volumes are out-of-print and available only in rare book collections, the general public and many critics are unaware of the vast number of revisions Hughes has made over the years.

These changes vary from minor alterations in punctuation to additions of entire stanzas reflecting changes in Hughes's philosophical stance. (p. 115)

Selected Poems contains twenty-two revised poems from *The Weary Blues* and *Fine Clothes to the Jew,* Hughes's first two volumes of poetry. In most cases the revisions consist merely of eliminating commas preceding dashes at the end of lines. Another revision found often in poetry from these two volumes is the elimination of a Dunbar-like dialect that Hughes had enjoyed using in his late teens and early twenties. In his autobiographical *The Big Sea* Hughes revealed that the first real poems he wrote were "little Negro dialect poems like Paul Lawrence Dunbar's and poems without rhyme like Sandburg's. . . ." (pp. 115-16)

Many of Hughes's revisions reflect his realization that certain passages had become outdated and obscure. (p. 116)

Often Hughes's changes make his poems more specific. In "Sinner" . . . Hughes describes the sinner as "Po' an' bowed." In *Selected Poems* this is changed to "Po' and black," more nearly reflecting Hughes's experience with the black evangelical churches in Harlem. (p. 117)

One of Hughes's most controversial poems is "Christ in Alabama." . . . Hughes indicates in *I Wonder As I Wander* how he barely escaped with his skin because of [this] poem which described how Christ would be accepted if he were born in the South of a Negro mother. In *The Atlanta World* of December 18, 1931, Hughes declared, "Anything which makes people think of existing evil conditions is worthwhile. Sometimes in order to attract attention somebody must embody these ideas in sensational forms. I meant my poem to be a protest against the domination of all stronger peoples over weaker ones." . . . At the time Hughes wrote the poem he was extremely angry about the Scottsboro Nine, but viewing it again from the perspective of thirty additional years he decided to shift the point of view and remove himself from the poem. It is still a social statement about the black man's plight in the South, but the revision makes it universal and less personal. (p. 118)

Some of Hughes's other revisions also reflect changes in his philosophy; during the 1960s his poetry came to reflect the new black consciousness. "Elderly Politicians" first appeared in 1958. It lambasted those who were "old . . . cautious . . . over-wise" and who were more concerned with clutching "at the egg / Their master's / Goose laid." . . .

[In a poem in *One Way Ticket,* Hughes] reflects the black man's plight in the early fifties: powerless physically and politically, religion seemed to offer the only possible balm for amelioration from the pain inflicted by a Jim Crow society. . . .

[In his revision of the poem in *The Panther and the Lash*] he indicates the enormous change in political climate that has taken place during the eighteen years between the two books. Instead of ending on a despairing question, the new ending suggests not only a certain cynicism about trusting in the Lord to solve all black people's problems, but it also suggests that the speaker is willing and able to take some action of his own if necessary. (p. 119)

As Hughes matured as a poet, he became more and more concerned with the limitations of language compared to the range of emotion that could be expressed through music. During the fifties and early sixties he experimented with jazz poems (*Ask Your Mama*) and with a book-length poem that formed a musical montage (*Montage of a Dream Deferred*). Hughes included *Montage of a Dream Deferred* in his *Selected Poems* and did not change a single line. In a way his experimentation during the fifties and early sixties is similar to his experimentation with blues melodies during the twenties. In both cases Hughes apparently moved away from the problem of the relationship between music and poetry as political conditions drew more and more of his attention. The political poems found in *A New Song* (1938) can be compared to the political poems in Hughes's posthumous *The Panther and the Lash.* Stalin and Lenin are replaced by Malcolm X and Stokely Carmichael. While much of Langston Hughes's political poetry is ephemeral, many of his poems are beautifully compressed works of art—the result in some cases of forty years of revision. (p. 120)

Stanley Schatt, "Langston Hughes: The Minstrel As Artificer," in Journal of Modern Literature (© *Temple University 1974), September, 1974, pp. 115-20.*

CARY D. WINTZ

The most outstanding feature in [*The Weary Blues*] was the use of Negro music as a model for a number of poems. The blues and jazz, the distinctive music of Negro life, provided the form for the title poem and several others. This stylistic experimentation was one of the major elements in Hughes's work. In this first volume the young poet also introduced the two major themes that would characterize his poetry throughout his long career. First, he expressed a deep commitment to the Negro masses. . . . His verses reflected a keen insight into the life of the Negro masses, including a vivid picture of the poverty and deprivation of their life. (p. 60)

The second theme that Hughes introduced in his first volume of poetry was Harlem. Although he depicted Negro life in the rural South, and occasionally in his native Midwest, Hughes was essentially an urban poet, and life in the Negro metropolis was a basic element in his work throughout his career. (pp. 60-1)

More clearly than most other Renaissance writers he saw that beneath Harlem's glitter was an oppressive, melancholy slum; the excitement of jazz contrasted sharply with the weary blues. . . . (p. 61)

As Hughes developed his portrayal of the black lower classes and their ghetto environment, he became more and more preoccupied with the question of the Negro's racial identity. Hughes had begun his search for the meaning of the racial experience in America shortly after he graduated from high school. In his first mature poem, "A Negro Speaks of Rivers," he found an analogy between the river that flowed through his native Midwest and the ancient rivers that watered the lands where his race was born. . . . (pp. 63-4)

Hughes continued this investigation in several directions. First, like many of his contemporaries, he looked to Africa, where he found few answers but a great many questions. . . . In his poetry Africa became a symbol of lost roots, of a distant past that could never be retrieved. . . .

As one who had grown up in America's heartland [Hughes] seemed content with his conclusion that American blacks were Americans, not Africans, and consequently he focused his attention on the Negro's identity problems in this country. In particular, on several occasions he looked into the role of the mulatto in American society. . . . Very quickly, very directly, Hughes moved beyond anger and resentment to expose the isolation that was the real tragedy of the mulatto in a racist society. He followed [the early poem "Cross"] with an equally dramatic, but a more bitter examination in "Mulatto." Here he wove together two themes, an angry confrontation between an illegitimate youth and his white relatives, and a taunting description of the violent act of miscegenation. . . . (p. 64)

Given Hughes's interest in the problems of the lower classes and his attempt to uncover the difficulties of being black in the United States, it is not surprising that he occasionally turned his pen against racial and social injustice. Fortunately his protest poetry did not succumb to bitterness. . . . Instead, he approached the subject of racial oppression through satire, understatement, or wry, sardonic humor. The poem "Cross" was a clear example of his ability to expose an extremely controversial subject in a cool, matter-of-fact fashion. In "Mulatto" his language was angry and even inflammatory, but the impact of the poem remained controlled and powerful. This was also true of his most controversial protest poem, "Christ in Alabama," which he wrote at the height of the Scottsboro case. . . . Hughes described this piece as "an ironic poem inspired by the thought of how Christ, with no human father, would be accepted if he were born in the South of a Negro mother." Its power, like that of most of his poetry, came through using inflammatory images to produce a cool, controlled anger.

Perhaps the most interesting feature of Hughes's poetry was his innovative style. Throughout his literary career he experimented with adapting black musical forms to his work. . . . As a result, he emerged as one of the few truly innovative writers to come out of the Harlem Renaissance, and in the process he uncovered a poetic style that was adaptable to a variety of circumstances. The blues form, for example, with its repetitive reinforcement, was a very effective technique to impart a subtle sense of suffering and despondency:

When I was home de
Sunshine seemed like gold.
When I was home de
Sunshine seemed like gold.
Since I came up North de
Whole damn world's turned cold.

. . . .

Weary, weary,
Weary early in de morn.
Weary, weary,
Early, early in de morn.
I's so weary
I wish I'd never been born.

It is difficult to imagine a literary form that could capture the exhaustion and despair of the working class more effectively. (pp. 65-6)

Hughes used jazz rhythms and the tempo of black work music to achieve different effects. In "Brass Spittoons," for example, work rhythms set the pace of the poem and captured the feeling of menial, methodical labor. In jazz he found a particularly fertile area for experimentation. . . . Hughes took this music with its choppy, breathless, almost chaotic tempo and recreated the bustling rhythms of city life and the boisterous atmosphere of the ghetto at night. . . .

He refined his technique in his post-Renaissance poetry and applied it most successfully in his Harlem epic, *Montage of a Dream Deferred,* where he used jazz models to capture the full essence of Harlem life. (p. 66)

The weaknesses of [Hughes's novel *Not Without Laughter*] are fairly obvious. Sandy [the protagonist] is never fully developed as a character, while the more interesting figures, Harriet and Aunt Hagar, remain on the periphery. The plot is also weak—in fact the novel essentially consists of a series of unrelated episodes in Sandy's life. Nevertheless the novel does have its strong points. The characters, while not fully developed, are believable. More importantly, Hughes's description of small town Negro life is unsurpassed. (pp. 67-8)

Not Without Laughter was the only serious attempt Langston Hughes made to examine the experience of blacks in the Midwest. After he completed the novel in 1930, his career changed dramatically. He continued to write prodigiously, but not about his own childhood, and he disassociated himself from the declining Harlem Renaissance. (p. 68)

Hughes's poetry also shifted to the left during the 1930's. Although he always had been concerned with the problems of blacks and of the poor, during the depression years he moved closer to Communism in his personal beliefs, and his poetry became angrier and more inclined toward propaganda. Unfortunately, as Hughes became more political, the quality of his work declined. . . .

Fortunately, along with his other accomplishments Langston Hughes took the time at least once in his career to examine the Negro's life in small-town America. (p. 69)

Cary D. Wintz, "Langston Hughes: A Kansas Poet in the Harlem Renaissance," in Kansas Quarterly *(© copyright 1975 by the* Kansas Quarterly*), June, 1975, pp. 58-71.*

WILLIAM PEDEN

The short fiction of Langston Hughes . . . —from *The Ways of White Folks* (1934) to *Laughing to Keep from Crying* (1952) or *Something in Common and Other Stories* (1963), and particularly the Simple pieces, *Simple Speaks His Mind* (1950), *Simple Takes a Wife* (1952), *Simple Stakes a Claim* (1957)—is in my opinion the best and most likely to endure body of work about Blacks—and Whites—by an American Black prior to the beginnings of the new, varied, and vigorous Black literature of the sixties and seventies.

Hughes's narrative method tends to be relaxed and leisurely; he is at his best in his own combination of traditional short story, essay, and autobiographical reminiscence. He tends to be gentle rather than violent, more good natured than bitter, but his stories are deadly serious and highly provocative beneath their smooth surfaces. . . . [His] stories suggest as much or more about the nature of intolerance and atavistic reactions to Black-White relations as the more militant and often savage work of the James Baldwin-LeRoi Jones-Eldridge Cleaver-Ed Bullins era; at the same time, they constitute a plea for tolerance and understanding with which the average White is most easily able to identify. (p. 233)

> *William Peden, in* Studies in Short Fiction *(copyright 1975 by Newberry College), Summer, 1975.*

LLOYD W. BROWN

In his poem, "Children's Rhymes," Langston Hughes offers a brief but rewarding glimpse of Black children at play on city streets, complete with jingles that have been improvised out of the Black experience to replace more innocent ditties:

> What's written down
> for white folks
> ain't for us a-tall:
> "Liberty and Justice—
> Huh—For all."

The contrast which Hughes offers here is familiar enough: it is the well known contradiction between the American promise of "liberty and justice," on the one hand, and on the other hand, the political and socio-economic disadvantages of the Black American. But, looked at more closely, Hughes' poem is interlaced with additional ironies. . . . [The] ironic ambiguity of Hughes' poem implies that if Blacks have been excluded outright from the American Dream, White Americans have also denied themselves the substance of those libertarian ideals that have been enshrined in the sacred rhetoric, and history, of the American Revolution. Liberty and justice, he seems to suggest, have been "written down" for, but not actualized by, White Americans. . . .

To return to the provocative nuances of that phrase, "written down for white folks," Hughes is also invoking a *time* reference—a reference to that period, the American Revolution, in which certain notions of liberty, justice and equality were cited, justified, and of course, written down, in various guises, in the Declaration of Independence and later in the Constitution of the United States. So that in effect the doubts which Hughes' irony casts on the substance of liberty and justice in American history also extend to the American Revolution itself: the essential limitations, or insubstantiality, of revolutionary rhetoric about freedom raise questions about the substance of the Revolution. In other words, how revolutionary *was* the American Revolution? The identity of the speakers in Langston Hughes' poem is crucial here. The image of children at play and the traditionally innocent connotations of children's rhymes seem deliberately to invoke an image of innocence upon which Americans have always insisted in their cultural history—an innocence defined by allegations that the American War of Independence was not simply a rebellion but a revolution. . . . But, to repeat, Hughes associates these revolutionary notions with only an *image* of childhood innocence. It is manifest that the children of his poem are not innocent in a behavioral sense (they are noisy, rambunctious window-breakers), and as their knowing sneers about nonexistent liberty and justice imply, they are not innocent in the sense of ignorance or inexperience.

Altogether, their own lack of innocence and their archetypal roles as deprived outsiders have the effect of stripping away their society's complacent mask of innocence: the American Revolution is not an indisputable historical fact, but part of America's myth of innocence. (p. 16)

Langston Hughes [explores] the nature of . . . revolutionary inclinations in order to determine whether they are fundamental revolutions against the majority dream and culture as a whole, or whether they are actually rebellious attempts to break down barriers to their realization of the majority dream.

On the whole Langston Hughes' poetry inclines towards the latter direction. Hence, to take a work like "Children's Rhymes," he ironically invokes the myth of the American Revolution, with its attendant dream of equality and socio-economic fulfillment, and then pits these against the Black American condition of deprivation and rebellious impatience. For there is nothing inherently revolutionary in the poem's emphasis or assumptions. The acid reminders of a tradition of revolutionary rhetoric are really taunts directed at the majority culture rather than some species of exhortation aimed at Black Americans. Here, too, the child-identity of the poem's protagonists is revealing. Their truant sidewalk games and their destruction of neighborhood property are presented as rebellious acts of frustration (i.e. protest) rather than as the result of some calculated revolutionary posture. The child-identity minimizes the possibilities of such a posture, at the same time that it emphasizes the Black American as child-heir to the American dream-legacy of freedom, equality, and individual fulfillment. . . . [The] expose of the failure of the American Dream in Black America is, simultaneously, an implicit challenge to America to make its tradition of revolution or socio-political reality rather than a semantic imposture. Altogether, Hughes' poem explores the essentially *rebellious disposition* of the disinherited Black American while at the same time implying the very real possibilities for revolution in the *situation* of Black Americans: their situation as the dispossessed heirs to a mythic revolution encourages an intensely partial interest in the threat of a genuine American Revolution. (p. 17)

Hughes does not explore this legacy of revolution in any exhortatory sense. That is, he obviously identifies with the Black rebel-heirs to the American Dream—indeed their rebellion is the very essence of his own poetic protest—but he does this without necessarily espousing any concept of a radically transforming revolution. And here we are brought face to face with a basic ambiguity in some of Hughes' "dream" poems: on the one hand, his satiric expose of the deferred dream in Black America is invariably couched in terms which taunt White America about the essentially non-revolutionist nature of *its* Revolution; but, on the other hand, his identification with the Black American's rebellion does not go beyond protest to any revolutionary ideology of his own. . . .

The poetic insights of Hughes' "Freedom's Plow" insist on a frank, if unflattering, admission of the gulf between the artist/intellectual and the masses, a gulf which Hughes as poet deliberately crosses in order to share a popular faith in the American Dream. On the other hand, the current trend in Black revolutionary literature [exemplified in the work of LeRoi Jones] assumes a rather easy identification of the artist with some mass revolutionary taste, a taste, one should add, that is often postulated but never really demonstrated as fact. Hughes' admission may very well irk the revolutionary enthusiasts among us; but in the absence of any obvious enthusiasm for radical revolution (as distinct from rebellious impatience) among those masses, one is left with the suspicion that Hughes is perhaps more realistic about the actual relationships between the Black American masses and the American Dream and that, conversely, Jones' prophetic vision of Black people as Black poets, Black poem as Black world is another dream legacy—that is, another revolution as dream. (p. 18)

> *Lloyd W. Brown, "The American Dream and the Legacy of Revolution in the Poetry of Langston Hughes," in* Studies in Black Literature *(copyright 1976 by Raman K. Singh), Spring, 1976, pp. 16-18.*

BAXTER MILLER

[The] image of home unifies *Not Without Laughter*. Hughes works within a long tradition, ranging from Homer to Baraka (Jones) in verse. . . . [The literature of this tradition attempts] to define home and man's relationship to it. This effort indicates a movement from innocence to experience. It implies alienation, happiness or despair. (p. 362)

Not Without Laughter emphasized *home* and the three levels on which this image has meaning: the mythical, the historical, and the social. . . .

From an initial situation of home, the reader moves first to a disintegration of the Williams family and then to a process of the family's re-creation. (p. 363)

The structure of *Not Without Laughter* reveals a continual process of venture and return. The first chapter strikes a biblical tone. To this, the implied author will return at the end, but then Sandy will understand more about life. Simple narrative merges with mythic symbol. (p. 364)

In *Not Without Laughter, home* does more than reveal biblical myth: indeed, it implies racial history. To the ideal reader, wandering connotes four hundred years of enslavement. (p. 365)

The functions of *home* unify *Not Without Laughter*. The implied author can shift easily from a mythic level to a historical plain—to a social setting of character, or to any combination of the three. He can portray first the Williams family, then its disintegration, and finally its re-creation. (p. 369)

> *Baxter Miller, "'Done Made Us Leave Our Home': Langston Hughes's 'Not Without Laughter'—Unifying Image and Three Dimensions," in* Phylon, *XXXVII (copyright, 1976, by Atlanta University), Fourth Quarter (December), 1976, pp. 362-69.*

J

JOHNSON, Uwe   1934-

Johnson, a novelist, was born in East Germany and has lived in West Berlin since 1959. His novels portray the conflict of a divided Germany, focusing on people lost between two worlds and two generations. Johnson strives for journalistic objectivity and clarity in his work. (See also *CLC*, Vol. 5, and *Contemporary Authors*, Vols. 1-4, rev. ed.)

W. G. CUNLIFFE

Uwe Johnson has an assured place in the history of modern German literature as the novelist of divided Germany. When *Mutmassungen über Jakob (Speculations about Jacob)* appeared in 1959, commentators were quick to appreciate that Johnson's was the first serious treatment of a strangely neglected theme, and *Das dritte Buch über Achim (The Third Book about Achim)* of 1961 confirmed Johnson's position as the writer of the two Germanies. All such comments are true enough, but need qualifying, for, as the reader soon notices, Johnson's theme is not so much the two German states themselves, as the fact of their separation. In other words, he does not compare the two systems nor does he discuss or evaluate their differences, but rather points insistently to the gap separating them. It is, he claims, an unbridgable gap. (pp. 19-20)

It is plainly not Johnson's aim in his novels to promote discussion, to present an issue or attack abuses. Rather he is interested in the clash of opposites that denies the possibility of reconciliation or compromise. In other words, his approach to the German question, as reflected in his novels, can fairly be described as anti-liberal. . . . (p. 20)

The theme of separation runs constantly through all the novels. In the first novel, *Jakob*, however, this separation is but one aspect of a prevailing lack of comprehension that separates man from man and makes truth inaccessible. Human motives are shrouded in fog, and the novel demonstrates this fact in its structure, for it proceeds by a series of conjectures and suppositions, so that it is often uncertain whose thoughts or words are being recorded. All the minor conjectures that go to make up the novel are finally gathered into the conjecture as to the ultimate cause of Jakob's death, when crossing the railroad tracks in a fog. The death may well be a case of suicide, motivated by Jakob's secret despair at his position, torn between East and West, but this is deliberately left uncertain.

The subsequent novels are far more vehement in pointing to the gap separating the two Germanies and far less inclined to stress the isolation of the individual. In *Achim* the separation is no longer shrouded in fog, but concretely represented in a central symbol, the inability of the Western journalist, Karsch, to write the biography of the East German bicycle racer, Achim. The separation is here quite plainly a matter of opposing ideologies. Achim's achievements as an athlete increase the prestige of the East German state, and any book about him must support this overriding purpose. An East German official, Herr Fleisg, explains to Karsch what his book must be about—the construction of a new economy, and a new contentment in life, and the spectators waving flags at the edge of the racetrack.

Herr Fleisg's views of the function of literature are never discussed, but the reader is still, so to speak, invited to comment. . . . In *Zwei Ansichten (Two Views)* of 1965, East and West never meet but are handled in alternating chapters concerning a man, B, from the West and a woman, D, from the East. The principle of separation is embodied in the very structure of the novel, so that even the possibility of discussion between the parties is removed.

Yet even the first novel, *Jakob*, for all its undogmatic speculativeness, is far from taking a liberal, detached view of the two Germanies. It is misleading to assume that Johnson is taking some independent stance, attacking tyranny impartially in the tradition of the Western man of letters. Johnson is not an heir to this tradition, although commentators on *Jacob* are sometimes inclined to believe that he is. Johnson shows the readers where his preferences lie by showing the allegiance of Jacob, the wholly admirable hero, to the East German cause. (pp. 20-1)

In Johnson's novel the liberal cause has no . . . robust representative. On the contrary, with a conspicuous absence of liberal fairplay, the liberal opposition is characterized by the feebleness of its representative, Jonas Blach, who is unable even to muster enough decisiveness to move to the West. (p. 22)

With such a creature, enfeebled by consciousness of thoughtcrime, there can be no question of discussion. . . . Johnson's novel . . . presents such an anti-liberal, Marxist front that one critic was able to compare it with novels of the "social realist" school, in which there is a popular hero and a weak and wavering intellectual. Yet the whole is overshadowed by a question-mark, and veiled in the mists of speculative uncertainty. Is the hero as fully in accord with the regime as he appears to be on the surface, or is his death a case of suicide based on despair? The pervasive doubts give Johnson's first published novel an air of undogmatic liberalism.

The next novel, *Das dritte Buch über Achim,* shows a distinct movement away from this suggestion of liberalism. (pp. 22-3)

Even though nobody in *Achim* speaks up for the West, Karsch's helpless neutrality invites the reader to discuss and argue on his behalf. In the story "Eine Reise wegwohin 1960", Karsch ceases to be neutral and turns neurotic and querulous. Moreover, the story describes, as the novel does not, Karsch's return to the West, and this develops into an attack on the West. (p. 23)

Johnson seems to combine rejection of the West with a keen interest in the American scene, evinced in his latest novel *Jahrestage,* which has an American setting. This combination of rejection and interest is strongly widespread among German intellectuals of Johnson's and younger generations. (p. 25)

> *W. G. Cunliffe, in* MOSAIC: A Journal for the Study of Literature and Ideas *(copyright © 1972 by The University of Manitoba Press; acknowledgment of previous publication is herewith made), Vol. V, No. 3 (Spring, 1972).*

PEARL K. BELL

[Johnson's] methods of exploring and integrating a narrative so defy conventional realistic ideas of sequence that he has been labeled "difficult" by well-intentioned critics, and this putative encomium has inevitably been confused with "incomprehensible" and "obscure." . . . Johnson is not a difficult novelist in the sense that Henry James and Melville, Nabokov and D. H. Lawrence can often be difficult, and Tolstoy, George Eliot and Mann are not. In difficult fiction the words on the page suggest much more than they specifically denote; one intuitively understands that the writer has in mind an equation of meaning and consequence going beyond the language itself, and uncoverable only through a metaphoric, deliberately uncharted, collaboration between reader and writer. Uwe Johnson's meaning, on the contrary, is consistently lucid, hard and immediately accessible. This is as it should be, since the matrix of his novels is politics—the all-too-clear politics of a divided, defeated nation.

It is no accident that Johnson's titles usually are flat declarations of unequivocal intent. They announce investigations into the human archeology of political conflict, narratives *about* an East German railroad worker, Jakob Abs, whose mysterious death needs to be explained, or an East German bicycle champion, Achim, whose biography is being written by a journalist. The titles are mockingly Teutonic in their earnest pedantry—the *third* book, *two* views (of a politically menaced love affair). Numbers become Johnson's ironic refutation of *alles in Ordnung.*

Everything in order, except for the untidy human beings who refuse to conform, who don't want to atrophy in the Socialist utopia of the DDR, who scheme their crazy plots

to leap over the Wall (even before there actually was a Wall), who refuse, like Jakob, to collaborate with Soviet agents, who are foolish, impulsive, irrational, reckless, burning with a chaotic rage to be free. For Johnson, the psychological truth of German politics cannot be presented through the traditional device of a detached and omniscient narrator. Rather, it must be painstakingly stitched together in a collage of deceptively disjointed remarks, a person's stammering conversations with himself, the intrusion of objects and events on the perpetual inner movement of longing, memory and fantasy.

Yet for all the apparent eccentricity of his technique, Johnson is a remarkable storyteller, and never more so than in *Anniversaries.* This work carries the complex tale of Gesine Cresspahl and her lover, Jakob, begun in *Speculations,* forward into an American future of 1967-68, and back to a past that is every contemporary German writer's inescapable theme—the Hitler era. . . .

It is through Gesine's and Marie's passionate devotion to New York as haven and safe harbor—the one city in America that can absorb two refugees from Europe without destroying their foreign particularity, without scorning them or ignoring their dark burden of memory—that Uwe Johnson pays his own affectionate tribute to the city. He has written a beautiful book, somber and joyous, about the complex idea of home. (pp. 16-17)

> *Pearl K. Bell, in* The New Leader *(© 1975 by the American Labor Conference on International Affairs, Inc.), March 17, 1975.*

P. N. FURBANK

The metaphor sustaining [*Anniversaries*] is the dossier or data-bank. The reader is given an excess of data, from which he must learn to select; and sometimes the novel (showing that it is alive after all) will positively buttonhole him upon the irrelevant. With this goes an 'affectless' tone; the novel may start numbering its statements. . . .

[The novel, further, has a] fondness for the 'finding-out-about-someone' plot (to which, of course, the dossier-like form is appropriate). Someone is trying, across the years or the political frontiers, and from questionable, or perhaps deliberately falsified, data, to reconstruct another person's life and deeds; or perhaps several different people are doing it for different motives; or someone is doing it for some third person's benefit. . . .

Two stories emerge and are pursued in parallel—the story of what led up to, and the story of what followed, the events in Uwe Johnson's first novel, *Speculations about Jakob.* (p. 318)

As in *Speculations about Jakob,* one soon finds Johnson's expressionless, 'mechanical' form to be, after all, expressive. The 'mechanism of events' is not an idle phrase to Uwe Johnson. We are a long way from the Victorian novelist's 'Character is destiny'; destiny, here, is every kind of fact or pressure, none singled out as privileged. There is expressiveness, too, in telling the story discontinuously, with suppressions and withholding of information. . . . And even the insistence on irrelevant details recalls life under totalitarianism, where survival may depend on diverting attention from your significant actions.

So—much praise to Uwe Johnson, who has devised a powerful fictional method, by which he makes us feel much and think much. . . . But that method not only depends on a metaphor, it is itself a rhetoric. It dawns on us that these modern German novels are providing something that the English novel has long renounced—I mean, pattern heroes and heroines.

What we are to glean, through all the objectivity of presentation, is that Heinrich Cresspahl and his daughter, Gesine, are very good persons indeed: they are paragons, models for us all. And this, in itself legitimate, is made a little suspect by the contrivance of the 'finding-out-about-someone' plot. The unspoken meaning of this kind of plot is that heroic deeds have an audience, not merely in the shape of us the reader, but in someone in the book itself. And this dangerously resembles our daydream fantasies of having an ideal friend or witness.

There begins to seem a cosiness, a mutual admiration society in that triangle of [Gesine's daughter] Marie, Gesine and Gesine's dead father. Johnson, for all his 'mechanical' form and 'affectless' tone, is a sentimental writer. . . . (p. 319)

> *P. N. Furbank, in* The Listener (© *British Broadcasting Corp. 1977; reprinted by permission of P. N. Furbank), March 10, 1977.*

*   *   *

JONES, D(ouglas) G(ordon)   1929-

Jones is a Canadian poet and critic. (See also *Contemporary Authors*, Vols. 29-32, rev. ed.)

PHYLLIS WEBB

The poems in Jones' [*The Sun Is Axeman*] depend delicately from the top of the page, reminding me of that excellent poem which opened his first book, *Frost on the Sun*, with the question, "Do poems too have backbones?" In that book, D. G. Jones explained that his poems were

> . . . attempts to apprehend and understand fragments of experience . . . to capture and suggest the sense that the universe is a vast pool, globe, or continuum of energy—mysterious and potent—in which the individual thing or creature participates, changes, or dies.

The dominant sun of his poetry symbolizes that continuum of energy, with its creative and destructive potential. The sun *is* axeman, "it crashes in the alders," but it also produces dazzling protective revelations. . . . (p. 58)

The sun and weather, birds and girls are centring images in this carefully crafted work. The clarity, control, and music of these poems reveal the benevolent influences of W. C. Williams and Pound, influences which have been absorbed and used towards a personal utterance. . . . (pp. 58-9)

For a poet whose imaginative range is somewhat limited, Jones appears remarkably at home in . . . longer poems. The reasons for this security are not hard to find, for his poetic aims are as lucid as his poetic line:

> So let my mind
>   be, like this river,
>   thin as glass
>   that thunder, dark clouds, rain,
>   the violent winds, may pass
>   and leave no lasting darkness in their
>   wake. . . .

Occasionally the fear of leaving a "lasting darkness" results in a dodge into coyness. "Clotheslines", for instance, which begins with a tone I can describe only as a normal nobility, promising Williamsesque truths from common things, drops down into coy self-consciousness. . . . The overall achievement of *The Sun Is Axeman* results in a distinctive voice, a poetry of lovely assonances, syllabic grace, of insights glancing from a landscape "in which the birds or trees / Find all their palpable relations with the earth." (p. 59)

> *Phyllis Webb, in* Canadian Literature, *Spring, 1962.*

E. D. BLODGETT

Beside the meteoric flash of such writers as Leonard Cohen and, now, Margaret Atwood, Jones's subtle brilliance seems a pale fire indeed. This is because Jones is a poet who is penetrating with care and delicate concern many of Canada's more troubling aesthetic preoccupations. He is a poet of courage whose surfacing is always deceptive and often misleading in a country where the search for self and heritage can be so exhausting that most poets would prefer to settle for any mode of irony that would both expose the mysterious folly of self-discovery and, also, prevent whatever fulfillment of exploration might be possible.

This is the poetry of an imagination that was early formed, and such changes as occur are those of a style deepened only by tragic events. It should be remarked, nevertheless, how the centre of Jones's circles of radiation is placed in his first book. As a poet who seems only minimally ready for statement, he enunciated an almost consuming passion in his first poem in *Frost On The Sun* entitled "John Marin". Jones's passion is for art, form and the artist's ambiguous relation to the world present to the eye. Every volume of his poetry has, in fact, begun with meditations on this problem. *The Sun Is Axeman* opens reflecting upon Anne Hébert; *Phrases From Orpheus* moves confidently into the same kind of aesthetic dimension. By the third book, however, the self is no longer a spectator of a simple other; there the spatial order of his early work yields to an interplay, suggested in the course of the second book, of kinds of perceptual events where

> The cries of children come on the wind
> And are gone. The wild bees come,
> And the clouds.
>
> And the mind is not
> A place at all,
> But a harmony of now,
>
> The necessary angel, slapping
> Flied in its own sweat.

The transmutation of "place", which was so much a part of design for the poet to whom Jones here almost to his undoing boldly alludes, is where the ambiguity of speech and its mode of visual revelation focus in his poetry. But Jones, unlike Stevens, never teaches explicit. . . . The Canadian poet's persona is every part, no part, a picture and absence. . . . Conjoined, finally, to a love for art and the world seen as theatre, is a need for masks, either tragic or Edenic, whose rôle is to reflect upon how the place of tragedy—a disharmony of then—is at once present, illusory and quick with death.

If it is true that an exceedingly refined notion of art resides at the centre of Jones's consciousness, it is the sense of the visual relations of things and their deceptions that shades both the imagery and form of the poems. In its approximation to visual art, his poetry in fact illuminates imagery which is by its nature and in its effect illusory and deceptive. Similar to any image cast upon a screen, the "place" where it reflects is a blank, a reminder and menace of absence. The mechanics of beaming light is complicated *a fortiori* by the poet's ability to blend images. Jones's arrival at such aesthetic positions does not seem to be through an interest in film but rather *via* an obsession with photographs and painters, not only Marin, but also Klee, Chagall, the Hour Books of the Duke of Berry, Cézanne, Matisse, Hokusai and Chinese art in general. . . . These interests are [most] likely only aspects of an intensely visual imagination, and a peculiar bent for the way things come and go before the eye. (pp. 159-61)

[This idea is demonstrated in the poem "Antibes: Variations on a Theme".] It has been remarked that this is a kind of nineteenth-century travel poem. Among its few faults, this need not be numbered. Its faults are more technical: an occasional failure of cadence, an unnecessary use of "very" in the next to last line. Its virtues, emerging like flotsam in many of the stanza's final lines, should suggest that little is being described in this poem, but much is thrust delicately into our purview and then removed. The poem has no background other than the repetition of the word "Antibes". The speaker is a demonstrator; his rôle is to thin out the three or four dimensional world to a screen where action is naught, where, "under fallen stars", gods are aligned with "trivial flesh", creation becomes "reproduction", and where all process is a silent corruption. The strength of the poem is not the apparent idea, but the skill with which emptiness becomes a mirror against the reader's eye. The action of the poem has nothing to do with either the speaker or the figures he indicates. The action depends upon a random superimposition of accidentally related images. But the modulation of imagery relentlessly urges upon us the fact that fantasy, memory, noon, night, Nicolas de Staël's suicide, an older painting of Picasso—that all these show us how the world becomes picture steadily emptying itself of centre and depth: time, deceptions of memory, fallen gods, necrosis become positions and azimuths of the visual world.

As a paradox working against the persuasive order of the poem's stanzas, we are urged to believe in the momentary and exclusive validity of every point of reference. . . . To proportion visual interest is precisely Jones's rôle in the poem. Against the depth-creating properties of line, colour and form, the poet juxtaposes time, plays with the irony of language, remembers the images of other men and, without any suggestion of continuity, allows Antibes to die at noon, at evening and at night, while somebody eats ice-cream. (pp. 163-64)

[For Jones] the form of a poem, particularly a longer one, is a spatial composition in which the tonalities of margins, masks and fragmentary implosions create an interplay of voices whose perspectives mix "background" and "foreground" which, for the unwary, seems inhuman. The persona of these poems may indeed have no precise outline, but the effort to project a shape, to cast a "profile in the birdless air", to shadow forth the labyrinth of the human spirit in the formal design of the poem is what distinguishes Jones from the unexamined romanticism of his contemporaries. The persona, finally, is a creation of a poem's design.

What always characterizes Jones's levelled manner of speech is its reflective pitch. It is at once a meditation and an argument; it surrounds the world witnessed over the shoulders of both Narcissus and Li Po, the Chinese and the classical . . . pool of the mind playing one reply against another. Sometimes the poet's attitude emerges dry and pure, as in the image chosen as the title for his recent study of themes and images in Canadian literature, *Butterfly On Rock*. But the larger poems brood almost bizarrely over the water illusions of Narcissus's pool, a place of expected dissolution in expansion, and unforeseen restoration into depth. . . . (pp. 164-65)

Of façades [in Jones's poetry], the simplest is the mask. But the pathos of masks, as the poet asserts in the form of most of his poems, is their totally amorphous capability: they droop from branches like Dali's dead time-pieces. . . . Mask is modulation—it is in the same order of phenomena as a visual proportion. Hence their adoption by Jones is neither classical nor archetypal. . . . [They are] attuned to the mortal and transitory. The woman is often Eve and often Persephone; and the speaker, when not Orpheus, Orestes, Odysseus, Phosphor, can assume even the guise of Michael the archangel in a curious peripheral allusion to the dissolution of his first marriage ("To Eve In Bitterness"). The paradox of Jones's use of the mask is such that while it evokes some of the playfulness of Cocteau and Giraudoux posing past against present (the foreground and background of time), he seems to have abandoned the stability that past can provide in the mask. The past seems totally over in Jones, a blurred background. Yeats would recreate past; Jones's touch seems to make it more remote. To that extent the past belongs to the visual presence of time:

> The osprey disappears, dissolves,
>
> Banked at another angle on the wind. And so all things
>
> Deliquesce, arrange, and rearrange in field.
>
> ("Mr Wilson, The World")

As I have suggested, to find in these poems, even when no mask is employed, a unified voice similar to a unified vision, is not necessary. Jones's strategy is field composition. . . . [In "Soliloquy to Absent Friends", Jones creates] a surprising and intricately structured panel description of the month of February in the *Très riches heures* of the Duke of Berry. Everything is there, the magpies who "drop sounds like barley in the muted yard," haystack, wood, axeman and drover, village and cold that "has cast a greenish glow / On the dissolving hills." Even in late mediaeval France, dissolution stood upon the margins, but within the frame there is "No distance, no abyss". Here art plays the rôle of the monitory mask and screen reminding us of that we have lost. The fact that it is ancient art transformed to word only underscores the elegaic character of the image.

It is a poignant intrusion of the Ptolemaic order upon a world where "abyss is infinite." Its only consolation is the scant cheer of a pictorial presence. . . . But no one can live in or by an illuminated book, and the poet's advice is only sufficient for that poem. We may, in fact, consider the didactic hortations of the last section ("Let us be bare, / Let us be poor") is simply a shift of mood to suggest a variation of proportion. (pp. 165-68)

Of the longer poems, the most achieved is the title poem from *Phrases From Orpheus,* whose stature and originality arise at once against the kind of technical tradition in which Jones participates and the modern treatment of the Orpheus story as it has developed in Europe. In this poem the poet plays off in a disturbing manner Eliot's "voices" of soliloquy and direct address. It is disturbing for he adopts, among others, the mask and mythological hints of Orpheus; he then speaks across the mask in another voice, more modern, approaching probably his own, and this voice speaks to its own, and not the mate of Orpheus, Euridice. Weaving through these voices is heard the voice of literary allusion; and that voice speaks contrapuntally against a kind of voice of no time and no body, which can be considered a parody of what Eliot calls the impersonal voice. This final voice gives shape to the modern drive to make the world an image and then to seize it as image. It is the voice of illusion, despair and loss *made visual.* Taken together, the four dimensions of the poem turn with varied response and intensity upon the several descents that the ancient myth evokes, and as the poem proceeds, its profoundly self-reflective character reminds us that Orpheus's need as a singer was intimately involved with the loss of the substantive world. He falls into the pool of Narcissus. Jones stamps his understanding of the fluid tangent of word and thing by an almost terrified response to the visual dissolution of things in time, such as one observes—and there are a number of poems that contain this mystery—in the punctuation of the "present" through an old photograph. Hence, Jones puts on the mask of Orpheus not to return the reader to a mythic past where there will be "no distance [and] no abyss", but rather to open into the shared abyss because it is more courageous, as he suggests, to embrace mortality than to embrace the image which is beautiful only. The poem becomes Jones's most sustained effort to probe his consuming passion for art and the dark it aims to lighten.

This poem, to an extraordinary degree, employs margins to define masks, and the technique exemplifies in verse the proportioned play of visual interest. . . . Language, of course, participates in the normal curve of the Orphic story: it is a katabasis of recessive backgrounds. It should also be observed that going beyond Eliot, Jones has split his voice to play off the problem of the gnomic (and, hence, suggestively Orphic) against the blankness of death. It is a technique characteristic of the whole. Its function is to point the central attitude that the gnomic must partake of an awareness of death. To seek the substance of gnomic realities dissociated from morality is to court a kind of total dissolution. . . . The place that Jones evokes is [a prison] . . . of several superimposed dimensions deliberately unfocused, as opposed to "clear". The epigraph to [*Phrases From Orpheus*]—"each in his prison / We think of the key" —points directly to this fact; and so also the poem's shape and central metaphor bear upon the closure of prison and death. But if our existence is a *huis clos,* some prisons are

better for us than others, hence the dialectic employed between illusion and mortality. At the core of death the new life is possible. In that regard, Jones is paradoxically Dantesque, despite his efforts in [*Butterfly On Rock*] to persuade us otherwise. (pp. 168-73)

Most modern poetry runs the risk of becoming merely cosmopolitan. This poem runs not only that risk, but also that of being rooted in a sensibility that is normally taken for granted between the contending views of British and American writing. Canadians have made a virtue of remaining parochial within the blown universe. This poem's particular risk is that it assumes that the Orpheus myth, contrary to the usual assumption, is not a pattern for Gnostic modes of salvation. It is enough simply to hang on through death's winter that "descends like a glacier into the soul." By suggesting that literary allusion and image-making are metaphors for sterility, a kind of life without the definition of death, Jones is then able to persuade us that the Orpheus story, a major monument of our literary tradition, participates in illusion as well. Thus the myth subserves the poet's central preoccupation with visual art whose eye-play is the place of our awareness of mortality. Pure perception against a screen of non-death would be otherwise senseless. By so envisioning the myth as a dramatization of illusion and death, he strips the myth of its general character as a pattern or order. The myth's ambiguity is displayed everywhere in the poem's ambiguity. It projects deception as the only place where the self can be identified as an event capable of death. Along with other major modern views of the pattern, "Phrases For Orpheus" constitutes an important revision. Jones's burden is not that there is immortality in song, despite the ironies of language, but that survival is a visual craft. But such a burden is fundamental to his art, apparent from the poem that opens *Frost On The Sun,* and traceable through all the kinds of *trompe-l'oeil* that his poems hit upon. (p. 173)

It is [the shorter poems, however,] that distil the kinds of technique I have pointed to. They are not simply lyrical; they press carefully against their form at the edge of evanescence. . . . From the outset, from *Frost On The Sun,* Jones has sought a voice and a persona that without becoming cosmic would dramatize the problem of the world's conflicting claims. In "Phrases From Orpheus" a kind of resolution occurs in which the persona plays against other voices. The risk of the persona has less to do with language and silence than with the visual and non-visual presence of background and foreground. Absence in Jones is not silence but disappearance. Hence, as he remarks in "For Françoise Adnet", "Time is space, it glows." The longer poems seek such a spatialization of event; the best of the shorter poems employ such a technique by superimposing imagery in a manner suggestive of theatre. (pp. 173-74)

Some objects lose substance by being seen too much. Or, to put it another way, a frequency of modified images suggests the same kind of ambiguity as several voices emerging from different levels of awareness. (p. 175)

To seize mortality in the form of art—it can only fail as an endeavour. Had Orpheus been a painter, many things would have been "lost in light" and dark. Jones seems haunted by this: if art cannot possess anything by illusion, what can? . . . In [a] poem entitled merely 13/3/72 he speaks of the effort to make art mortal so as to overcome death. . . . Jones is rarely so spare: art is simply fine stone;

mortality, thy flesh, with all the ambiguity that demands. Loss is broadly spatialized into a crumbling field. As in "Phrases", the action of actualization is dialectical for the speaker moves "a travers" as if to foil absence by becoming its foreground, by becoming finally the act of art, and so dramatizing an illusion played against the eye of death, "pour 'naître' enfin".

I would avoid any conclusion that would call Jones a romantic. I would say rather that I have been endeavoring to sketch aspects of a Canadian, of a classical Canadian, poetry. (p. 176)

[Jones broods upon the past, but] it is a past that has become untimed and makes the present difficult to perceive. It is an ambiguity peculiar to Canada, and Jones has observed it as well in public papers in which the American that explodes from Whitman to Ginsberg is welcomed as a continental possession, but the Pentagon is condemned as simply "European". Jones's response to the predicament is natively elusive, but it is as centrally Canadian as the work of Lampman to whom I have referred, and to Lampman's contemporary Charles G. D. Roberts. . . . (p. 177)

> E. D. Blodgett, "The Masks of D. G. Jones" (copyright © by E. D. Blodgett), in Poets and Critics: Essays from "Canadian Literature" 1966-1974, edited by George Woodcock, Oxford University Press, 1974, pp. 159-78.

GEORGE BOWERING

The typical setting for a poem by D. G. Jones, in 1953 or 1973, is some rural place in the Canadian Shield at that time of year when it is still winter but perhaps beginning to be spring. The difference between the 1953 poem and the 1973 poem lies in where the poet is situated. In the earlier poems Jones is the interpreter of the landscape. In the later ones he is part of the landscape. It is as difficult as that. To put it another way: during his early career he seemed faced with a dispute—shall he be "realistic" or "mythic"? Later he succeeded in discarding both poses, in favour of being actual. He learned to listen to his own body, the music it was (forced) to make in its environment, and there is the body of his later work, as beautifully trim as any we have heard in this country.

Jones has a reputation as an "intellectual" poet. . . . Certainly he has always distinguished himself from the majority of Canadian lyric poets writing in English, they who are satisfied to tell you how they are feeling right now about some occasional perception. Jones has always wanted to know that, plus: what does it mean. . . . [A] consecutive reading of his work reveals that he has always been looking for a world-view that would seem sensible given his perceptions and emotions. (p. 7)

Jones embodies the spirit of the Anglo-Saxon poet in a strange wintery land, the first morning outside Eden. For that was the European Eden, not so much a garden as a garrison, where the animals were paraded in front of you and you were allowed to name them and subject them to your use. The consistent development and improvement of Jones' writing has come about as the words seeped through the walls, as the man became resolved to living the rest of his life in his own wilderness, himself as explorer, with memories, maybe, of "home". (pp. 7-8)

[*Frost on the Sun* (1957)] exhibits the early lines of the conflict in Jones' poetics. In the introductory poem, "John Marin" . . . the poet announces that he wants to make poems as particular and interdependent as the rest of nature; that is, not poems *about* nature, but poems to take their place *in* nature. . . . So the poem begins with a smart identification of strophe with plant and bird, themselves difficult to separate:

> Do poems too have backbones:
> stalks of syntax on which sway
> the dark
>   red
>   or blue images—
> a flock of red-wings
>   swaying in the alders—. . . .

Compare some lines written in 1970, where the urgency to fabricate metaphor has been overcome, and the poet simply submits to his own functioning in the place and poem:

> I am led into the winter air
> by certain nameless twigs, as bare
> as we are. I would find
>
> them also in our mouths
>
>   (pp. 8-9)

He gets observably more interesting as the forms assert themselves over the structures—in that way Jones became a most serious and worthwhile demonstration of the great leap forward in postwar Canadian literature.

There is a great deal of energy being exercised in that first book, so much being tried out, so much desire on the young poet's part to meet, perhaps, the cosmos, especially the portents in its immediate manifestations, birds, the sun, snow. Hoping to be equal to the real itself, Jones brings to the poetry-making act all the tricks of poem-writing. He is performing them—lay a Greek name on the landscape here, a simile there, a couplet beside that. But the poem, not the poet, is made to live in that scene. (p. 9)

It is a curious (subjective?) thing that you can *feel* Jones' mind moving more than you can most poets', and thus you can feel the difference between the tangled lines that try to feed rime-schemes, and the others that attempt to re-enact perceptions. (pp. 9-10)

The centre of Jones' work tries to resolve the dialectic between . . . pessimism and that hope. The influence of Robert Frost can be guessed at here, and the worlds of the two poets are not all that far apart, vestiges of Puritan New England and U.E.L. Canada. The reader can't help noticing that in these early poems Jones views nature from and in his solitude. . . . The early loneliness outside of Eden is met by an earth, nature that endures, and Jones consistently shows it enduring despite men's depredations. (p. 10)

[*The Sun Is Axeman*] shows a desire on Jones' part to compose longer poems, to get beyond the lyric, and beyond the stasis imposed by presentation of a mind willing only to reflect upon a universe. (p. 11)

The English [influence], with the voice of Auden somehow heard along the line, seems to have produced two essentially "academic" features: the fact that so many poems work upon extended metaphors, and the pose of the detached sensibility. . . . Perhaps the best example of the detached and academic poem is "Antibes: Variations on a

Theme'', wherein abstract noun-phrases lie dead where one wants to find verbs or where the lyric with its unlikely verbs sags into reflection, a reflex of the cortex wanting to respect itself. Often the abundant similes are used to connect the natural scene with the Hellenic one in the teacher-poet's head, leaving in our museum a picture of the academic back home on the family farm.

The problem, of course, is Jones' decision to appear as observer, to keep himself hidden from any eyes looking back. . . . I think that Jones instinctively distrusted the mode but found that he had to punch his way out of its bag with its gloves on his hands. Moments of clarity and actuality are shared when he is not concerned with sustaining a metaphor or structure. (pp. 11-12)

One can't help feeling gratified to find that once again [in *Phrases from Orpheus*] the clear attention to voice as the base for form opens for the reader a clear vision of the materials and thought presented. A naked strophe takes its place in the field beside a sunlit rock. The particulars of the verse imitate human speech, and speech *is* nature, to advantage undressed if you like. I am suggesting that Jones' welcoming of life (his argument, what it *means*, etc.) depends upon the bright (candid) sharp profile of his line and stanza in these poems—I don't think that anyone could read them aloud and be confounded by the voice that is articulated. It is the clarity of Yeats, Pound, and Williams, the music of the human voice that makes the sun rise in the morning.

Part of the advance is made by the class of the language. Academic inversions and circumlocutions are dropped in favour of highly vocal exclamations that remind one of Williams—"What a ruckus!" Authentic personal slang finds its way in now, and brings the poems home, so that after the poet refers to a "two-bit creek," one feels with him "a new respect for / Metals, rare-earth, salt." But most of the advance is in the integrity of the syllable, line and stanza, particulars that respond to the rhythms of a voice, part feeling, and once into print, part ideogrammatic. (pp. 16-17)

[The] items of nature are no longer pathetic, but joined and celebrated. That change, as it involves the poet and his poems, is the source or energy of hope, or at least hope of reconciliation. The poems are still set in winter and before hovering spring, but now "We shall survive / And we shall walk / Somehow into summer." Somehow—there's resolution and qualification in that word. The earlier poet Jones was, with his detachment and brainy irony, an idealist, and a stoic. Now he is a stoic, but he says "I thought there were limits to this falling away, / This emptiness. I was wrong." His poetry is now a part of that process, not its opposite, not its dreamy redemption. Poems are not finite, but constantly metamorphose themselves. They are not signs of the poet's control over (his) nature; being inside nature, they are process. . . . (pp. 18-19)

As in his earlier poems, in [*Phrases from Orpheus*] Jones records many images of rural nature—seasons, weather, soil, growth. But now there are so many images of nature denuded, bare branch, stone, the great naked Canadian Shield that does not provide welcoming habitat for furze or figure of speech. Feelings, like signs of life, must be tenacious and carefully searched for, "deep in the silence / Which is continuous sound."

The image of nakedness has special emotional meaning for someone writing out of the Anglo puritan and academic backgrounds. It bespeaks strong and once-infibulated desire. But it is the way to join rather than observe the earth. . . . (p. 21)

Butterfly on Rock (1970) can tell us much of the place that Jones the poet has come to by the end of the sixties. At the same time as the book is the most convincing symbolic reading of our literature we have seen recently, it states in prose many of the principles the poet has come to as his own due to the Orphic voyage.

Paramount among these is the replacement of the ego. It once peered over the battlements of the stockade—now it is looking for an explorer's way across the uncharted continent. . . .

It is not surprising . . . to note that the word "courage" has become as important to Jones as the word "candour" once was. . . . The emphasis is on heart and discovery, thus mortality—and such realization calls for its representation in the form of the verse. Jones' verse becomes, around this time, open and vocal, responsible and vulnerable to changes in the weather, exterior or interior. (p. 22)

The poems written since *Phrases from Orpheus* are songs of a man who is once again above ground and now at home there. The lines and stanzas are more thoroughly integral, fully used, than ever before, and they are shaped by the poet's full physical faculties, as inevitably authentic as the interreactions of wind and tree-stand.

The scenes are still generally winter, or the last days of winter, but now winter rimes with the rest of the year and not allegorically with poet's gloom:

> The climate of the flesh
> is temperate here
> though we look out on a winter world
>
> (p. 23)

There are lots of people in these new poems. They are addressed in title and poem; they are simply in the world. The snow now has signs of people in it, their tracks that mess up a perfect quatrain and let us follow—who is to say that their steps are not ours as we put our feet into them? Jones is no longer the idealist. He is at home now. In fact the house has become a very important image. He is living there, with other people, no longer a spectre on the rise of the landscape. (p. 25)

At home in the flesh, at home in the land, at home in the number one, after all the enumeration in Eden and on the Ark has become only rumoured history. D. G. Jones is proof that there is a tradition of English-Canadian poetry, and that the tradition is going to be here. (p. 27)

> *George Bowering, "Coming Home to the World," in* Canadian Literature, *Summer, 1975, pp. 7-27.*

*   *   *

JONES, James   1921-1977

An American novelist and short story writer, Jones is best remembered for his candid, realistic portrayals of military life and the horrors of war. His first novel, *From Here to Eternity*, secured for Jones an international reputation, but his following works have often been criticized as crude and

simplistic. *Whistle*, **on which he was working when he died, was completed from his notes by his friend Willie Morris. He won the National Book Award in 1952. (See also** *CLC*, **Vols. 1, 3, and** *Contemporary Authors*, **Vols. 1-4, rev. ed.; obituary, Vols. 69-72.)**

IRWIN SHAW

Jones wrote out of his obsession with the condition and fate of [the] doomed men [who made up the ranks of enlisted men in the years before the democratization of the Army]. His important works are really one long book. Jones considered it a trilogy, starting with "From Here to Eternity," going on to "The Thin Red Line" and the book he had almost completed when he died—"Whistle." . . . By adding his "The Pistol" I would prefer to call the work a quartet. . . . (pp. 3, 34)

Speaking of a work of another writer—"Golden Boy" by Clifford Odets—the director of the play, Harold Clurman, once said, "It is a play about the conflict between the fiddle and the fist," meaning, of course, the conflict between art and savagery, civilization and barbarism. In the case of Jones, we might say his work is about the conflict between the gun and the bugle. It is no accident that Jones's hero in "From Here to Eternity" is both a boxer and a bugler, and renounces boxing.

Now the last notes have been played and we can ask of the player, What was the call we heard and how was it played?

It was a song about valor and sorrow, a cry of exile, of pride in adversity, of comradeship and hatred, of resignation to organized injustice, a speaking up for men too inarticulate to speak up for themselves, a song of outcasts, of men who did the dirty work that others shunned. And how was it played? Clearly, unsentimentally, bluntly, knowingly, with a craftsman's hard-earned skill. It came from a group of men who spoke plainly, without euphemisms, using words about death and sex and cowardice and chicanery and despair that before Jones had rarely been seen on the printed page in this country. By "talking dirty," as children say, Jones helped clean up our ideas of permissible language and enlarged the boundaries of our literature. Among his other accomplishments Jones removed the asterisk from our novels. What we know we now can describe, making the novelist's world more solid and credible in the process. Along with the war he celebrated, Jones made his own war on cant and dishonesty. From the stink of the battlefield and the barracks came a bracing, clear wind of truth. To use a military term, he walked point for his company. (pp. 34-5)

The future will classify us all, and there are surprises in store for even the wisest of us. If we believe now that Stephen Crane's "The Red Badge of Courage" will endure in American literature, we must believe that James Jones's four-volume book of men at war will endure with it. (p. 35)

> *Irwin Shaw, in* The New York Times Book Review *(© 1977 by The New York Times Company; reprinted by permission), June 12, 1977.*

KRIM

Of the four main protagonists of *Whistle*, two are suicides, one is murdered in a bar fight, and the last goes mad. All are medal winners for heroism during the U.S. South Pacific campaign of World War II. That was Jones's final verdict on the war he himself had tried to fight honorably and found there was no honor; there was only self-survival, which became contaminated by meaningless death on every side and led to the most profound despair on the part of every man with a shred of conscience.

It might be appropriate to give a newer generation a quick sketch of what made Jones unique. Unlike radical intellectuals and practicing Christians who also condemn war—as a matter of fact, who doesn't today?—Jones began as a romantic, hard-nosed war lover. . . . There was something so basically up-yours American male in his appetites that he spoke for hundreds of thousands in his first, most widely read novel, *From Here to Eternity*, which ended with the attack on Pearl Harbor.

A decade later came *The Thin Red Line*, which examines with a kind of brooding contempt the murder and monstrosity on Guadalcanal during the campaign against the Japanese in '42 and '43. Any male romanticism that Jones might have had about testing himself in the ultimate contest had long since fled. What makes the book extraordinary is the tremendous calm and self-discipline with which he opens a door on hell; no shrieking, no hysteria, but instead a very level and unrelenting examination of what modern warfare is like. . . .

Whistle brings this big, sad story of the American fighting man and the so-called last great war to its final ghoulish resting-place. The four characters who dominate the book have all been wounded in some fashion during the fighting on the Pacific Island of South Georgia, following Guadalcanal. They are all sent to an army hospital in "Luxor," Tennessee, to mend. . . . The hospital and the town become the final stage for the deterioration of the four men.

Three of the four we have met before under different names. Mart Winch was the sardonic and masterful 1st/Sgt. Warden in *Eternity* and 1st/Sgt. Welsh in *Red Line:* Bobby Prell was the defiant bugler Pvt. Prewitt (really the young Jones) in *Eternity* and Pvt. Witt in *Red Line*, and John Strange was the amiable Mess/Sgt. Stark in *Eternity* and Mess/Sgt. Storm in *Red Line*. (p. 70)

All have deep mental wounds as well as physical ones, revolving around the men they have deserted on South Georgia. One must recall that the war is still going on, getting ever more fierce. Loyalty to the company and the division is their only patriotism. Even at the hospital this bond makes the surgeon think twice before amputating Prell's festering leg, almost as if these vets would lynch him if he added to their humiliation. But as Mark Winch sneeringly predicts—and they look to him as their father figure, a role he can't abide—the bond is going to fray. They have all seen too much and been through too much to take unquestioning comfort in each other. (pp. 70-1)

The odor of death permeates this last book in a sharp, unflinching way that distinguishes it from its predecessors. Jones had the first of several heart attacks in 1970, when he was beginning the final rewrite on *Whistle*, and one can't help but be aware that this knowledge of foreshortening mortality colors the book. To Mart Winch, the oldest, wisest, and most disillusioned of the four, Jones gives his own weakening physical symptoms and much of his mature outlook. If Prewitt was the persona of Jones's roaring young manhood, Winch is the used-up lion of his middle age. . . .

This is a sadder book than the others because there is no relief from the starkness. Whether it is the most profound of the three is an arguable point. Jones fought to keep his humanity to the end—and a novelist without humanity becomes a propagandist—even though one feels at moments that the author wants to sit the reader down on his knee, like a naive child, and lecture him about the insanity of the human race. But Jones keeps this impulse under tight control for the most part and goes about his business as a conscientious, if sometimes nose-thumbingly raw, craftsman. Yet there is little contrast in the emotional coloration of the novel.

It is very realistically written, with all that gorgeous, snickering love of army detail that Jones knew down to his fingertips. But the four leading figures have in one sense already died when they are shipped back to the States. They are almost ghost figures compared to their earlier personifications in *Eternity* and *Red Line*. We know they are doomed, and that we can do nothing about it. It is painful and frustrating, and sometimes we feel that Jones is sadistically prolonging the agony when he could have ended it with a blunt literary pistol shot—made it half as long, half as painful.

And yet one still roots for him all the way to wring every drop of spleen out of his heart about the one subject he knew better than any other writer in the country. The art may have suffered, the suspense is that of a mystery in which we know whodunnit in the first chapter—but the bulldog snarl of the man is heightened by his refusal to let us off easy. This is what American war has done to American man, he is saying, and it is all a revolting crock of shit. Look at it. Feel it. Goddam—eat it, you foolish civilians who cloak the dead meat of a generation in judicious abstractions. You are the pitiable ones! . . .

Jones didn't want to let us off the hook of his grim final vision one little inch, especially at the mutual windup of his life and art. It will take time for the just rank and worth of this soldier-scribe to emerge from the journalistic gunfire of our time, but if you squint through the haze you can see Stephen Crane and Hemingway waiting at the barracks door to welcome a tough soul brother home. He was an equal. (p. 71)

> Krim, "In a Bulldog Snarl: War Is a Crock," in The Village Voice (*reprinted by permission of* The Village Voice; *copyright © by The Village Voice, Inc., 1978*), March 6, 1978, pp. 70-1.

L. J. DAVIS

There are a number of excellent reasons why James Jones's last novel shouldn't work, none of them particularly new. Jones was neither a psychologist nor a stylist; his characterizations lack both depth and complexity and his prose is serviceable at best, although there is, as always, rather a lot of it. His notions about sex are frequently preposterous, and his ideas concerning American womanhood are egregious when they are not positively insulting. His protagonists are unpleasant. His plot is a symphony based on a single note. His earnestness resembles that of a man trying to thread a needle in boxing gloves.

These qualities have inevitably proven fatal to most if not all of Jones's civilian fiction, but in *Whistle*—as in its predecessors in the trilogy, *From Here to Eternity* and *The Thin Red Line*—they are either moot or, what is more remarkable, they are improbably transmuted into virtues. What his characters lack in depth is more than made up for in resonance. The interminable clumsiness of the prose, the sexual naiveté, and the unidimensional eroticism of the male-female relationships cease to function as crippling liabilities and become instead badges of authenticity.

Jones as a writer had mastered a single subject: World War II as perceived and experienced by the proletariat of the military slum, the common professional soldiery. If his words do not possess the suppleness, wit, and majesty brought to that struggle by enthusiastic amateurs, they also lack the innocence; Jones, like his protagonists, worships in a different church. . . . With its peculiar crude power, James Jones's voice is the best and truest one they will ever have. (pp. E1-E2)

Jones at his best—and he is at his best [in *Whistle*]—was neither a cynic nor a romantic; he possessed none of Hemingway's power of self-delusion. It is tempting to extract a facile metaphor of the human condition from his vision of battle, but he will not allow us to do so. His integrity would not permit him to treat combat as a bad roll of the dice; it is an unendurable proposition for which no preparation is adequate, a situation unspeakable in its horrors. . . . [This] is an important book, and it completes a monument that is certain to endure. It may very well be the only major body of American fiction to come out of the war. If, as Mallarmé would have it, the novelist is a mirror walking down the road of man, James Jones accepted the challenge, and in the last analysis he proved more than equal to the task. (p. E2)

> L. J. Davis, "G.I. Jones: The End of the Epic," in Book World—The Washington Post (© The Washington Post), *March 12, 1978, pp. E1-E2.*

PEARL K. BELL

Throughout his career as a novelist, James Jones . . . was a self-willed anachronism out of step with his literary generation. . . . After 1945, when other ex-soldiers lusting for literary glory began spinning the ephemeral exploits of war into the relative permanence of fiction, Jones doggedly set out, in *From Here to Eternity*, to write not about combat but about the pre-war, peacetime Regular Army. . . . Not until 1962 did Jones get around to publishing *The Thin Red Line*, drawn from his combat experiences in a rifle company that fought on Guadalcanal and New Georgia.

Characteristically, Jones wrote *The Thin Red Line* oblivious to all the signs that the advance guard of intellectual opinion about war and venerable American ideals had begun to turn with radical hostility against the exultant mood of victory now more than fifteen years in the past. Only a year earlier, Joseph Heller, in *Catch-22*, had provided the decade with a startling new attitude toward the World War and all war. . . . Yet while Heller's savage mockery of army bureaucracy and the shibboleths of war became the absurdist epiphany of the 1960's, Jones was choosing to celebrate such old-fashioned virtues as bravery under fire and the warm solidarity of men at arms. . . .

Not that *The Thin Red Line* was merely a gung-ho glorification of combat. If one side of Jones's imagination strove to apotheosize warfare as "the greatest" of all human endeavors, he was also capable of rendering with blunt power the charnel-house brutality and mutilation and senseless death that await soldiers in battle. . . . [Jones] needed to believe that the reality of war, however nightmarish and bloody, was in the end something other than Heller's lunatic farce. (p. 90)

The Thin Red Line was the last work of sustained literary merit that Jones wrote. . . . It was as if his idea of the fearlessly aggressive virility that distinguishes men from boys had become frozen for the rest of his days by the army's unyielding maleness, which ritualized not only the soldier's performance of his duty and the punishment of his derelictions, but his drunkenness and whoring, his obscenity, his deeply private longings and distemper. If the army was the only milieu in which Jones felt at home as a writer, it was because that fine-tuned machine of war, that honeycomb of rules and traditions and ranks and regulations, provided him with a rigidly stable point of personal, sexual, and social reference, the unalterable measure by which he could grasp and judge the world at large. Indeed, the army *was* the world—the great American cross-section of rubes and city slickers, leaders and lackeys, bullies and men of honor, fags and he-men, pillars of society and Dead End kids, redneck louts and visionary rebels. (pp. 90-1)

The numbing regimentation and the jungle violence, the mindless tedium and primitive integrity of the barracks world was Jones's singular experience, his sole claim to originality. In his first book, *From Here to Eternity,* he had made the most of it. Investing all his imaginative energy in "the cult of experience," Jones relived his peacetime-army years with such seductive authority, such a torrent of unforgotten detail, that, rereading the book after more than twenty years, I found myself drawn helplessly back into its raw vitality. . . .

But of course all the weaknesses of the redskin writer also stand out like bayonets in *From Here to Eternity*—the sentimentality and the half-baked mysticism, the puerile rejection of human and cultural attachments. Thus, Robert E. Lee Prewitt, the Harlan County miner's son who blows the sweetest and purest bugle ever heard, and whom Jones portrays, *à la* Natty Bumppo, as one of nature's doomed noblemen, yearns with restless nostalgia for the boundless freedom and undemanding male fraternity of hobos on the open road. . . .

Like Thomas Wolfe, whose woozy ah-life rhetoric had made Jones decide to become a writer after he left the army, Jones had a bad habit of confusing incantation with thought, particularly if the big pseudo-philosophical bubbles came from a self-taught rolling stone like (in *From Here to Eternity*) the charismatic ex-Wobbly Jack Malloy, who becomes Prewitt's mentor while the two of them are doing time together in the stockade. Ideas were in fact alien and threatening to Jones's imagination and temperament. Although he did not come by his devotion to "naturalness" altogether naturally . . . , Jones did feel an instinctive affinity for the "basic artless simplicity" of unlettered hillbillies strumming mournful and lonely songs on cheap guitars. (p. 91)

If Jones's commitment to the cult of experience paid off handsomely, in every sense, in *From Here to Eternity* (and rather less so in *The Thin Red Line*), it proved a literary disaster when he applied his "technique" of total saturation to postwar civilian life in the Midwest (*Some Came Run-*

ning, 1957) and, foolishly rushing in where Hemingway had dared to tread, to the sporting life (*Go to the Widow-Maker,* 1967). Without the organizing framework and moral architecture imposed by a military setting, Jones rambled and limped, pelted his readers with fatuous pseudo-profundities about art/life, and told them everything they didn't want to know about spearfishing, skin-diving, and sex, especially sex.

In his first two novels, Jones had been forced to cut out yards of sexual explicitness and foul-mouthing of the kind that was then considered impermissible. But when the repressive walls came tumbling down, it turned out that he had nothing different to offer, just a great deal more of the same. His male characters in *Go to the Widow-Maker* think of women no differently from the Schofield Barracks soldiers who crowd Mrs. Kipfer's whorehouse in *From Here to Eternity.* His women are either neurotic wives who don't know what they're missing or jolly hookers who love their line of work so much, they will even do it for nothing. Indeed, the anything-goes society of the 1960's proved more liability than liberation for Jones. (pp. 91-2)

After the clobbering he took for his one Paris novel, *The Merry Month of May* (trying to cope with intellectuals caught up in the Sorbonne riots of 1968, he was completely out of his depth), Jones sensibly turned again [in *Whistle*] to the military past where he belonged. . . .

Four soldiers from the same infantry company make the long and painful journey together to Memphis (Jones calls it Luxor), and three of them, Jones reveals in an introductory note, are old friends, renamed from *From Here to Eternity.* . . .

In the opening chapter of *Whistle,* an intensely charged meditation on the soldier's allegiance to his company, Jones writes with a passionate assurance that had evaded him for years, but after this splendid start, the novel disintegrates along with the company. When sex rears its head, as it does with paralyzing redundancy in *Whistle*—Memphis in wartime, as Jones remembers it, had an inexhaustible supply of doxies only too eager to please—everything else is obliterated, and the tedium becomes lethal.

Yet if one can manage to overlook his obsession with the mechanics of fornication, Jones is clumsily trying to explore in *Whistle* a phenomenon that no other contemporary American novelist I know of has touched upon. This is the atavistic force of male bonding. . . . That male bonding does exist in modern society is unarguable, however, and James Jones portrays its power in the fears of his wounded soldiers that the collapse of their company, that masculine confraternity of *cojónes* and valor and comradeship, will leave them vulnerable to a lonely and destructively separate fate. . . .

An unregenerate anachronism to the last, Jones was immune on this issue, as on every other, to the promptings of the *Zeitgeist.* What the paleface considers unmentionable, this redskin did not hesitate to say. Jones had learned from experience that men can feel bereaved when army solidarity comes to an end, and what he had learned from experience was the only truth he knew. (p. 92)

Pearl K. Bell, "The Wars of James Jones"
(reprinted from Commentary *by permission;*
copyright © 1978 by the American Jewish

Committee), in Commentary, *April, 1978,
pp. 90-2.*

LEONARD KRIEGEL

From his first appearance on the literary scene with *From
Here to Eternity* in 1951 . . . , Jones presented himself, and
was viewed by critics, as a writer in whom art and life had
synthesized. He possessed a distinct, if limited, talent as a
novelist, and asked that his readers accept the honesty of
his observations. . . .

Jones was a late arrival in the ranks of those Philip Rahv
labeled the "redskins" of our literature. Unlike their "paleface" rivals, the redskin writers were so distinctly American, so much the product of this culture, that even their
harshest criticism could be easily absorbed into the American way of looking at things. . . . For Rahv, the redskin
was "a self-made writer in the same way that Henry Ford
was a self-made millionaire. On the one hand, he is a crass
materialist, a greedy consumer of experience, and on the
other a sentimentalist. . . ." Jones is the very model of the
redskin writer. . . . Our major redskin writers—Twain,
Dreiser, Hemingway, Steinbeck—draw their metaphors
from biology rather than literature. . . . But the situations
one discovers in redskin novels are public and irremediable,
even when they deal with the private individual. The redskin writer tends to see man as part of an inevitable process, ground down by fate or accident.

The limitations in James Jones's work are similar to those
in Dreiser. Everything his critics have pointed to as weak is
readily observable. He was unable to create concise
scenes; he almost always portrayed reality as an affair of
surfaces; he was nearly pre-Freudian, despite the awkward
textbook psychologizing about life and sex that clots his
work; his dialogue could be as wooden and repetitious as
Dreiser's . . . ; his women never get beyond the sexual fantasies of an adolescent glued to the pornographic quies-
cence of his own musings . . . , and what passed for thought
in his fiction invariably lacked complexity, yet it was presented as if Jones had struggled to arrive at insights which
the reader considers hackneyed. Add to all of this problems
of narration (the point-of-view and the narrative voice in
Whistle shift for no apparent reason, at least none that I
can see) and a deadly seriousness even in the face of the
obviously comic and the case against Jones seems rather
formidable. . . .

With all that he could not do as a writer, Jones possessed a
command of the novelistic situation that few contemporary
writers possess. And he remains admirable for the persistence with which he forced a skeptical world to read him.
Like his redskin ancestors, he insisted that we encounter
life as the process that he had observed, and that we face,
as honestly as he had faced, the absence of choice. . . . It
was this stubborn insistence on putting down what he saw
which makes him a serious writer, one whose work deserves the attention he demanded.

Jones's true subject was not the army but American masculinity. The army provided the most obvious examples of
that subject, but in his better novels and stories he caught
the ways in which an entire generation of American men
thrust themselves against the world. Jones understood the
manner in which the individual man was isolated, a solitary
voice speaking to the nation's demands. . . . Jones never
abandoned such individualism, not even in his best novel,

The Thin Red Line, where the individual seems swallowed
up in the collective movement of the army. But the movement is not really collective; it is, rather, the herding instinct of men who share only the terror of potential annihilation. (p. 405)

Whistle is a novel in which the army and the war exist
merely as the setting in which men see themselves. The
novel is about the consequences of manhood in America
and the army hospital in which most of the action takes
place simply indicates that Jones was unwilling to let go of
the surfaces that knowledge of army life gave him. The
hospital is like a battlefield in what it provides the novelist
—a self-contained male world. (pp. 405-06)

We know that [Jones's four protagonists] are doomed from
the start, and it is a further tribute to Jones's honesty, along
with his refusal to manipulate his readers, that he does not
really want us to feel sympathy for any of these men. . . .
Taken together, the four men have the stamp of a collective
authenticity, for they embody not individuals but conditions
of existence. . . .

Like Hemingway and Crane, Jones codified existence. The
characters in *Whistle* have survived combat through
wounds which are both physical and psychological. They
struggle to hold on to their integrity as men. It is an integrity which can be defined by the individual alone, but they
are forced to define themselves as a group, those who have
been crippled in combat, because it is the only definition
which separates them from the rest of the American
world. . . .

[*Whistle*] is a novel which contains all of [Jones's] characteristic weaknesses. At times, it is rhetorical, overblown,
and sententious. It is filled with self-conscious profundi-
ties. . . . And yet, as often happens in a novel by James
Jones, one [is] . . . willing to forgive even such prose for the
sake of an honest novelistic vision. For there is so much
else that James Jones gave us. Few other novelists were as
capable of facing up to the exigencies of the situations they
created. And few other novelists were as capable of taking
American men on their own terms. Jones understood those
aspects of life in America which forced men to redefine
themselves constantly, to measure up or be damned. Like
Hemingway, he was fascinated by the ability to endure
pain; in *Whistle,* he invokes it almost as a religious value. . . .

In this last of his novels, James Jones painted himself into a
corner. But that seems characteristic of the man. Unlike
many of his contemporaries, he lacked the capacity for literary irony and, fortunately for us, he never gave in to the
temptations of rhetoric for very long. (p. 406)

> *Leonard Kriegel, "From the Infected
> Zones," in* The Nation *(copyright 1978 by
> the Nation Associates, Inc.), April 8, 1978,
> pp. 405-06.*

THOMAS R. EDWARDS

James Jones may have been the last prominent American
novelist to suppose that fiction should be a virtually unme-
diated presentation of life, that material counts for more
than craft. . . .

Certainly the last and most important question one asks of
a novel is not How is it done? but What does it know? To
this extent Jones struck the right note when he wrote of

Whistle, his last and not quite finished novel, that "it will say just about everything I have ever had to say, or will ever have to say, on the human condition of war and what it means to us, as against what we claim it means to us." But even if Jones was a novelist who aimed for, and often enough achieved, something beyond mastery of technique and style, no assessment of *Whistle* can avoid saying that it is a very badly written book. . . .

Except for Landers, these are not characters who could be expected to be very eloquent or even articulate about what they know and feel, and Jones relies a great deal on explanatory narrative that stands close to their thoughts without purporting to reproduce them verbatim. But even with Landers the method keeps muffling or confusing the consciousness it means to explain to us:

> But Landers knew there was something more. Something inside him. Aching to get out. There was something inside him aching to get out, but in a way that only a serious fight or series of serious fights would let it get out. Anguish. Love. And hate. And a kind of fragile, short-lived happiness. Which had to be short-lived, if he was going out of this fucking hospital and back into the fucking war. It had just built up in him.
>
> There was no way on earth to explain it to anybody, though. Not without sounding shitty. There was no way to say it.

Here a method that means to be plain and unobtrusive becomes an obtrusion itself. There are indeed states of mind, complex or confused ones, that are hard to put into words, but in the text of a novel, an "it" that means both love and hate, anguish and happiness, looks lame. The passage may reproduce a credible human muddle, but it doesn't provide any way of examining and understanding it. "There was no way to say it" sounds as true of the author as of Landers.

Nor, if we recall the pungent, closely recorded passages of soldier-talk that provided the major excitement and pleasure of *From Here to Eternity,* is dialogue in *Whistle* very remarkable. There's not much of it, and what there is usually sounds lifeless. . . .

Unlike *From Here to Eternity, Whistle* tries to conceal the presence of an impersonal narrator who is verbally more adroit than any of the characters, and Jones has to keep struggling with the problem of believable speech. . . . [The] major characters, whose minds the novel stays close to until the end, can't credibly be as articulate as the book sometimes needs them to be.

Again and again Jones stumbles over, and then usually backs away from, his need to say things that his characters could not have thought. (p. 30)

A curious kind of homogenizing seems to take place in *Whistle.* Along with their supposed differences in temperament, the characters come from different parts of the country—Winch from New England, Strange from Texas, Prell from West Virginia, Landers from the Middle West. Yet their speech and thought show scarcely a trace of regional accents and idioms. They think alike, they talk alike, they come to similarly dreadful acts of self-destruction. . . .

Whistle is dedicated "to every man who served in the US Armed Forces in World War II," and it sustains this generously collective note by stressing what the characters have in common—their violent impulses, their hostility to noncombatants, their edgy concern for each othbr, the conflict between their fear of being killed and their deep, unexaminable need to "stay in," to keep on soldiering rather than return to a civilian world that doesn't need or understand them. This is a kind of madness, as Jones tries to show. . . .

This fusing of identities in madness should not be dismissed as mere technical ineptness. Maybe the experience of war does challenge our rather complacent belief that the best, most important meanings are personal, private, individual ones, our insistence that collective selfhood is somehow inauthentic. For bookish civilians to try to think otherwise is an interesting exercise, if not a very cheering one. But it remains true that this novel's two most powerful moments of understanding are private and personal ones, and that both of them are given to the clerkly, introspective Landers and not to the less self-conscious professional soldiers he admires and tries to be like. . . .

[All] the soldier's values as Jones represents them—professional competence, concern for comrades, pride in fighting, drinking, making love—matter only because they don't finally matter, because one does them freely, without caring or hoping for a return.

When *Whistle* tries to go beyond this sense that nothing matters in the end, a sense whose language is usually simple and confident, it gets soft and sentimental. We are too often invited to feel more for these soldiers than they would want to feel for themselves, as in the novel's bathetic ending (supplied by Willie Morris . . .), where the drowning Strange imagines that he's swelling up to oceanic, planetary, even galactic proportions and "taking into himself all of the pain and anguish and sorrow and misery that is the lot of all soldiers, taking it into himself and into the universe as well."

One hopes that had he lived to revise, Jones would have thought better of this. But there are enough other moments of rhetorical and philosophical inflation, moments that seem too conscious of an audience with literary expectations, to suggest an author who often mistrusted his own understanding of things. This is sad but not decisively so. Jones has surely to be counted as a minor novelist, one with a single subject and a limited control of his craft; but he knew what he knew wonderfully well, and in *From Here to Eternity* and *The Thin Red Line,* and intermittently in *Whistle,* he told us much about how the military life shapes and marks those who follow it. He can't be blamed for having had larger ambitions too, but these are not what he will be remembered for. (p. 31)

> *Thomas R. Edwards, "Something about a Soldier," in* The New York Review of Books (*reprinted with permission from* The New York Review of Books; *copyright © 1978 NYREV, Inc.), May 4, 1978, pp. 30-1.*

*   *   *

JONES, (Everett) LeRoi
See BARAKA, Imamu Amiri

*   *   *

JONES, Mervyn   1922-

Jones is a British essayist, editor, short story writer, and

novelist. His novels often deal with political issues from a leftist perspective, and he has written a carefully researched fictional account of the life of Joseph Stalin, *Joseph*. (See also *Contemporary Authors*, Vols. 45-48.)

Don't be put off by the cadaverous title [of ''Twilight of the Day.''] This is not a tearjerker about an autumnal Philadelphia love affair; it is, rather, a sophisticated and lively chronicle of a London working-class family from the turn of the century to the present. The very real personal dramas of the Wheelright family . . . are so successfully interwoven with the major social upheavals of the period—the abortive general strike, the Depression, the two World Wars—that the result is a novel as fascinating for its social history as for its characterizations. More than we realize, most of us inherit our idea of how the English working class lived and lives from Dickens, D. H. Lawrence, and those self-conscious films of the sixties in which women were always called ''birds'' or ''dollies'' and men usually referred to one another as ''mate'' or ''bloke,'' and both were invariably treated as bits of comic (or tragic) exotica. Mr. Jones neither glamorizes nor caricatures his characters but shows us how several generations of people who lived in a now defunct sort of East End community led and thought about their daily lives. (pp. 97-8)

> The New Yorker (© 1975 by The New Yorker Magazine, Inc.), January 20, 1975.

VALENTINE CUNNINGHAM

Today the Struggle is the kind of undauntedly capacious, generation-spanning novel to which British writers of our time seldom nerve themselves. So bulky that the book is a bit of an effort to pick up, it is also so engrossing that it's hard to put down. In it the fortunes of a persistently (often surprisingly) related lot of families are followed from mid-Thirties, through mid-Fifties, to the mid-Seventies. The generations are closely scrutinised, swirling and settling about their points of crisis, the epicentral moments of an apocalypse that's always just coming and never quite does: the Spanish Civil War, the Ban-the-Bomb movement, and the present financial lows. . . .

It's bound, of course, occasionally to seem a bit too schemed-for, too shrewdly schematising. The recurring locations (homes and houses, Liverpool Street Station), seasons (Easter, Christmas) and events like picnics all come on naturally enough. A lot, though, does look less excusably pat. . . . Inevitably, not all the events and characters are equally known to the author nor made equally knowable to us. There are some intriguing hops and yawns, and some blank spaces just tarted over with stereotypes; while items put in just for the record (journalist Sophie beds JFK; Mervyn Jones is mentioned) can seem sorely obtruded.

But these are midget grouses. Many of the people are wonderfully believable in themselves . . . ; they are, what's more, placed most convincingly in their time. The set-pieces keep coming off too: the CP branch meeting, the anti-Fascist demo, the Committee of 100 sit-downs. And above all there's the irrefutably steady slide into Seventies apathy, the ironically bleak future that Thirties communists and Fifties protesters never dreamed of, the unending grey of our economic distress. (p. 227)

> *Valentine Cunningham, in* New Statesman (© 1978 The Statesman & Nation Publishing Co. Ltd.), February 17, 1978.

D.A.N. JONES

This long family chronicle [*Today the Struggle*] seems to have all the qualities desired by readers of family chronicles, except the conservative values. . . .

Mervyn Jones rattles on, with incident after incident, for forty years of this century, almost at the pace of Henry Fielding—but rarely pausing to settle on a scene or character, or to philosophize in Fielding's manner, until the final third of the book. . . . The first two-thirds seem designed for the family-chronicle reader to enjoy, slowly, in bed, on long winter evenings, getting to know the characters with their ever-changing relationships and kinship patterns. But the pace of the novel is such that it resembles a very long synopsis for a very long-running television serial. . . .

If we did not know Mervyn Jones's career as a committed left-winger, we might suppose this book to have been written by an uncommonly broad-minded Conservative, gently attempting to expose the follies of well-meaning left-wing idealists over the past forty years. But in fact, surely, he is struggling with the politics and society of the present, and that is why his final chapters are so much more alive than the earlier. Hindsight makes him bland about the past. He finds ''today'' more of a struggle, and it brings out his best.

> *D.A.N. Jones, "Keep the Red Flag Flying Here," in* The Times Literary Supplement (© Times Newspapers Ltd. (London) 1978; reproduced from The Times Literary Supplement *by permission), February 17, 1978, p. 185.*

PAUL ABLEMAN

The struggle referred to in [*Today the Struggle*] is, broadly speaking, the struggle to enlarge, or even merely to preserve, political decency in a world perpetually besieged by barbarism. The actual struggle fought out in its pages is to use the classical resources of the novel to examine what Mr Jones takes to be key episodes in recent history. I don't think he succeeds. Nor do I think anyone else could. It is not a matter of talent, or vision, or research, or noble intentions. It is simply that the dynamics of our scientific-technological culture can no longer be exposed by exploring the interaction of fictitious individuals. . . .

Today the Struggle certainly tries. It is an ambitious work of five hundred tightly-packed pages and is divided into three main sections. These concern the Spanish Civil War, the Campaign for Nuclear Disarmament and what, lacking an official title, one might designate the Present Struggle for Economic Survival. Marginal treatment is accorded other contemporary campaigns, the women's movement, black liberation etc. In Mr Jones's view, these are, of course, all facets of the same, unending struggle. His book concludes with a reminiscence of a brave lady called Marie Durand who, at the time of the Huguenot persecutions in France, spent forty years in a cell rather than renege her faith. In that cell one can still read the inscription: *résister*.

And most of Mr Jones's characters, throughout most of the book, are honourably engaged in resisting. . . . The trouble is that they are not free simply to resist and fade into history. Their fictional life must endure the length of the book. Thus while a few of them perish the rest get caught up in the most extraordinary web of coincidence. Selected initially to provide representative figures of the mid-twentieth century—idealistic working class, decaying aristocracy, culture-oriented bourgeoisie—they can only be penned into the same narrative by cavalier manipulation of the laws of probability. Thus, if one of them has a minor car crash in the South of France, the other driver will inevitably turn out to be an old acquaintance. . . .

But apart from the coincidence-logged lives, necessary to preserve the appearance of unity in a work essentially devoid of it, the characters are pathetic. Not because of their innate nature—at least as conceived, if rarely achieved, by the author—but because they are swamped by History. We perceive them as castaways, glimpsed through smoke and flame, clinging to spars of reason, huddled together on life-rafts of sanity, as the battle thunders about them. At least, the intention is that it should thunder. In melancholy fact, Mr Jones's bland journalese thunders as little as it sings. . . .

There are, in fact, two distinct sets of characters in the book: the fictitious and the real. These are juxtaposed but hardly ever interact, other than by report. . . . Had Mr Jones endowed his real characters with a fictitious life within the novel then, presumably, they would have been forced onto the same plane of reality as the fictitious characters and might indeed have enhanced the verisimilitude of the book. But by merely seeding his text with their names, the author stresses the huge disparity between say, a real, and great, man called Bertrand Russell and the docile figments of his imagination.

Here and there, Mr Jones achieves an artistic evocation of scene and character. Strangely enough, he is more successful with women than men. There is a convincing and touching account of the revulsion, fused with the martyr's suppressed exaltation, felt by a girl demonstrator as she is manhandled by bullies. And by far the most striking passage in the whole book describes the rape of a sensitive schoolgirl by a gang of school toughs. Here, briefly, the prose rises to the occasion and we smell the rotting house and endure the horror felt by the victim. But, in terms of his obsessive theme, of what value is this episode to the author? Can poor Francesca's struggle be considered a province of *the* struggle? Since it is involuntary, clearly not. And so Mr Jones hastily returns us to the world of the great causes and the plastic people.

> *Paul Ableman, "Plastic People," in* The Spectator (© *1978 by* The Spectator; *reprinted by permission of* The Spectator), *February 18, 1978, p. 24.*

*   *   *

JONES, Preston   1936-

Jones is an American playwright, actor, and director. His first play, *A Texas Trilogy,* reveals him to be a regional playwright, with characters and settings drawn from the rural Southwest. (See also *Contemporary Authors,* Vols. 73-75.)

BRENDAN GILL

Plainly, [Preston Jones] is an ambitious man. It is his good fortune to be making his début on Broadway with three plays instead of one; it is his ill fortune that Broadway, on hearing of the plays' rapturous reception out of town, and

with its usual tendency toward overexcitement, came to regard his advent as the Advent. If the triple début ["A Texas Trilogy"] is unprecedented, the plays are not; they are specimens of a kind of domestic comic melodrama long familiar to our stage and must be dealt with as such. Mr. Jones is talented and has an excellent ear, but at the moment his stagecraft is more nearly carpentry than marquetry —when two characters are required for reasons of plot to have a private conversation, he is not above sending a supernumerary character forcibly off to the bathroom. When he must handle more than two or three characters at a time, the effort shows. Nevertheless, we are lucky to have him among us, and not least because he is able to make us laugh. (p. 75)

> *Brendan Gill, in* The New Yorker (© *1976 by The New Yorker Magazine, Inc.), October 4, 1976.*

HAROLD CLURMAN

Eugene O'Neill once said that the United States was the greatest failure in history. It had entered the world arena with every possible advantage—a new land, noble ideals, few hierarchical burdens—but it had muffed its opportunity by overlooking the Bible's challenge, "For what shall it profit a man if he shall gain the whole world and lose his own soul?" In its rush toward material power, America had lost all valid faith. On this premise O'Neill planned a nine-play cycle to be called *A Tale of Possessors, Self-Dispossessed.*

That cycle would undoubtedly have been a tragic work. But imagine if someone today undertook to compose a similar series as farce. Might it not resemble Preston Jones's *A Texas Trilogy* . . . ?

Mr. Jones does not seek to prove anything. As for O'Neill's "thesis" he might respond with a four-letter expletive signifying "Perish the thought!" His trilogy is "simply" a depiction of citizens in Bradleyville, a tiny Texas town from 1953 to 1973. It is an unsentimental comedy and much of it is very funny. (p. 348)

It has been said that when history repeats itself, it does so as farce. *A Texas Trilogy* is not farce; it is a genre piece in three parts . . . which, to begin with, has the appearance of minute realism that gradually turns to something close to savagely hilarious grotesquerie. Though [several comparisons can be suggested] it is an *original* work. It fits into no single, obvious category. Jones writes with a keen ear for the speech of a particular locality as if he were only bent on recording it for fun, but we soon realize that *he* is not laughing, but making us laugh, so much so at times that we are hardly aware of what we're laughing at.

We forget that, whether Jones meant it to be so or not, Bradleyville is not just a remote rural town but a microcosm. Something more is being achieved in the trilogy than an inside view of the kind of place we big-city folk know very little about. The play's sights point to domains beyond Texas or the South.

Bradleyville is spiritually void. Most of its vital impulses have dried up or evaporated; their presence for the most part is expressed in spastic jerks. (p. 349)

There is much repetition, which adds to rather than detracts from the play's mood and meaning. There is not much "plot," but that hardly matters: the play *exists* and takes hold as very few new American plays these days have done. (p. 350)

Harold Clurman, in The Nation *(copyright 1976 by the Nation Associates, Inc.), October 9, 1976.*

ALAN RICH

What Mr. Jones has created most notably in [*A Texas Trilogy*] . . . is a series of verbal tone poems about empty lives in an empty setting, a decaying small town somewhere in west Texas. As a fledgling author (with, to be sure, a considerable background in other aspects of theater, as an actor and a director), his command of both tone and poetry is remarkable. His models aren't difficult to fathom: popular fiction of the *Peyton Place* variety for the sense of creating and interweaving of character; William Inge's better plays for the technique of relating character to setting. But Mr. Jones has one talent that far surpasses either of these dubious sources: a gift for the indigenous, if not always ear-tickling, individualities in language.

Inasmuch as the plays are given without the customary amenity of a printed glossary or translator-earphones, perhaps I'd better tell you a little more about this language. Texas is a rather large state, and one effect of this size is that words tend to sprawl out to fill the surrounding space. Unlike people in, say, Rhode Island, Texans have room to carry around double names, like Billy Bob or Martha Ann. One-syllable words also tend to stretch out into two syllables or more; vowels, similarly, ooze out into diphthongs. Extra words, sometimes mildly profane, sometimes get added to sentences, simply as ballast. That old paradigmatic sentence becomes, in Texan, "Whar's muh ay-unt's bah-God pay-in?"

Mr. Jones loves his language, and when he dips his pen into it that instrument is transformed into a paintbrush. That is both the joy and the sorrow of *A Texas Trilogy*, that the author has somehow transformed human action into the elements of still-life or landscape painting. Two of his most appealing characters are a pair of mule-headed old codgers who, apparently, spend most of their lives together at checkers or horseshoes, each convinced that the other is a monstrous swindler. They spray each other with ferocious verbiage, their lives hanging on the knowledge that the combat will never, *can* never, be resolved. . . . [What] we finally see is not character but horizon, a line of language stretched out toward infinity. . . .

There is some nice observation [in *Lu Ann Hampton Laverty Oberlander*, the best of the three], but no real play. Whatever action there is has taken place between acts offstage; the stage itself is a triptych of flat canvases full of interesting perspectives that state little more than that time goes on. . . .

The other two plays are built around a character who could, under better circumstances, provide Mr. Jones with some semblance of motive power. Colonel Kinkaid, an old soldier living out his last hours in a raging senility that is punctuated by flashes of rational recollection, is hardly an original conception, but Mr. Jones uses him with sure and obvious affection. . . . (p. 88)

Mr. Jones has been hurt, I think, by the hoopla his plays have generated. . . . [These] plays are obviously not going to outlast their initial news impact, and that can do our tenderfoot playwright a lot of unwarranted harm. There is much to be said, judging from the evidence at hand, for coming up slowly through the ranks. (p. 89)

Alan Rich, in New York *Magazine (copyright © 1976 by the NYM Corporation; reprinted with the permission of* New York *Magazine), October 11, 1976.*

K

KENEALLY, Thomas 1935-

An Australian novelist, Keneally is an ex-seminarian of Irish-Catholic descent. Best known for his *Blood Red, Sister Rose*, a retelling of the Joan of Arc legend, Keneally has been praised both for his realistic characterizations and his use of history. (See also *CLC*, Vol. 5, 8.)

ROBERT E. McDOWELL

In the course of doing research for a World War I film script, the Australian Thomas Keneally was, fortunately for novel readers, sidetracked into an exhaustive study of the members of the Armistice Team. The result of his effort is *Gossip from the Forest*, a gripping evocation of the tensions of the time and of the men who made the Armistice. . . .

All of the shortsighted military arrogance in the story arouses mainly disgust in the reader. What the politicians and military officers did there at Compiègne to end their war games is not presented as either very intelligent or very important. This is one sense, at least, in which the story amounts, ironically, to mere gossip from the forest. That Marshal Foch and his attendants, in forcing their terms on Germany did little more than "weave a scab over that pit of corpses four years deep" seems painfully clear now. (p. 157)

In probing the murk of personality, Keneally demonstrates that the men who made the event are more compelling than the event itself. He examines the characters' private and public lives in detail—through their dreams, through comments of the men about each other, through copious conversations, through reminiscences about lovers and home and family.

Atrocities, both military and civilian, and the brutal execution of power are commonplace in Keneally's books, as readers of *Bring Larks and Heroes, The Chant of Jimmy Blacksmith* and *Blood Red, Sister Rose* are aware. But with *Gossip from the Forest* Keneally has succeeded better than in any of his previous books in lighting the lives of historical figures and in convincing us that people are really the events of history. (pp. 157-58)

> *Robert E. McDowell, in* World Literature Today *(copyright 1977 by the University of Oklahoma Press), Vol. 51, No. 1, Winter, 1977.*

GEORGE STEINER

Thomas Keneally is frequently spoken of as "the other" major Australian novelist. But in the present instance comparison is unfair. "Season in Purgatory" . . . is entertainment with only intermittent and infelicitous pretensions to anything more. (p. 132)

[One] asks oneself just why Mr. Keneally, whose previous novels show an oddly costive but unmistakable stylishness and adultness, should turn out this purple tripe. He is obsessed by the sensual texture of history, by the immediate impress of political and military drama on the nerve and marrow of those involved. Like Patrick White, this novelist out of a new, almost "nonhistorical" continent is immersing himself in the dense, equivocal European past. His immediately preceding book, "Gossip from the Forest," a highly schematic, allegorized portrayal of the Compiègne armistice talks of 1918, was an interesting failure. "Season in Purgatory" is a boring success. (p. 134)

> *George Steiner, in* The New Yorker *(© 1977 by The New Yorker Magazine, Inc.), May 23, 1977.*

PETER ACKROYD

Although the publishers describe [*A Victim of the Aurora*] as 'Thomas Keneally's first detective story', it effectively marks the demise of that debased and flatulent genre. . . . It is set at the close of the sticky Edwardian era and so, theoretically, it might be described just as easily as an historical novel—but, like all of Keneally's work it actually subverts European history . . . by bringing to it alien and more vigorous perceptions. . . . In Keneally's hands the historical novel is redeemed as the raw materials of the past are turned into a kind of fable.

These blinding metaphysical matters don't mean that Keneally is forgetful of technical considerations. He astutely aligns the imaginative content of historical fiction with the pert structure of the detective thriller, and by conflating them creates a new thing. (p. 19)

But this is not a weak-kneed or vapidly ironic handling of the techniques of English fiction. . . . Thomas Keneally is a powerful and subtle writer, whose simplicity of style must never be confused with simplicity of meaning. He actually uses the Polar Expedition as a way of breaking several historical codes, as the Edwardian age vanishes as mysteriously as the aurora itself. . . .

The book is full . . . of extraordinary images and implications. In all of Thomas Keneally's work there is an attempt at what I have called the subversion of received European history by rendering it both more exactly—his sense of place is remarkable—and more luridly. It is part of the strange darkness of the Australian imagination. The colour, the vivid imaginings, the rhetorical simplicity of his evocation of the past have to do with Keneally's own manner, but also with a quality in Australian writing: its bleakness and its blank pessimism. . . . (p. 20)

> *Peter Ackroyd, "Burning Down," in* The Spectator *(© 1977 by The Spectator; reprinted by permission of The Spectator),* September 3, 1977, pp. 19-20.

NEIL HEPBURN

There is no more diligent soothsayer than Thomas Keneally, forever poking about among the entrails of the European past for some clue, previously missed, to the development of a present that no rational seer before about 1950 could have predicted. His last three books have drawn attention to significant stages in the attenuation of the old European chivalric virtues, and their replacement by bloodthirst, vengeful greed, and the tyranny of the majority. Now, in *A Victim of the Aurora,* he focuses on two related aspects of that corruption—the ease with which old-fashioned virtues like loyalty can be manipulated for bad ends by charismatic leaders, and the willingness with which even their victims will co-operate. (p. 382)

Mr Keneally's most immediately striking achievement in this new book is to make you simply want to know what happens next. *A Victim of the Aurora* is an excellent whodunit and a splendid adventure story, with the atmosphere of its Antarctic setting most brilliantly evoked and sustained. But its importance does not lie in these undoubted virtues, uncommon and enjoyable as they are. It lies in Mr Keneally's clear-sighted view of how vulnerable conventional men are to the poisoned authority of great leaders, and of how calmly the best of us can be led to sanction abominations in the name of the common good. (p. 383)

> *Neil Hepburn, in* The Listener *(© British Broadcasting Corp. 1977; reprinted by permission of Neil Hepburn),* September 22, 1977.

VIVIAN FUCHS

The early years of this century were the heroic years of Antarctic exploration and it is in this period that *A Victim of the Aurora* is set. The pity is that, unreal though the novel is, it defiles the historical events and characters from which it derives. Thomas Keneally has chosen to use clearly recognizable episodes from the past as a backdrop for homosexuality, murder, execution and other unworthy practices and qualities ascribed to characters who are imaginary, yet many of whom would seem easily identifiable to anyone with a vague general knowledge of polar exploration. . . .

Today it is commonplace for writers to seek to destroy idols of the past. All sorts of ideas and motives are thought up for them and adjectives are judiciously chosen which will denigrate a person without the need to make a direct

statement which could be refuted. Thomas Keneally achieves this result in an original way. All the characters in his who-done-it have something discreditable to hide. They also suffer from obscure and complex processes which would be unlikely to get them past even the most naive selection board. Indeed, one becomes somewhat confused by their odd mentalities. . . .

The inaccuracies of fact and the silly idea of a lone survivor living the life of a hermit in some ice cave can be forgiven, the misrepresentation of what is for many a way of life cannot.

> *Vivian Fuchs, "Polluting the Ice-Cap," in* The Times Literary Supplement *(© Times Newspapers Ltd. (London) 1977; reproduced from* The Times Literary Supplement *by permission),* October 14, 1977, p. 1185.

JONATHAN YARDLEY

You can read [*Victim of the Aurora*] on several levels, all of them entertaining and provocative. It is an adventure story, the tale of an expedition to Antarctica in the years just before World War I. It is a mystery in the classic British style, complete with a murder most foul, a large cast of plausible suspects, and a narrator who fits together all the pieces of the puzzle. And it is a thoughtful novel about the corruption of innocence, the unending burden of guilt, and the perpetuation of official deceit. . . .

[Keneally's] depiction of Edwardian innocence and stuffiness crashing against the Antartic void is superb, as is the manner in which each member of the expedition is pressed to bear the burdens of his own past. The introduction of the theme of homosexuality into a small world of men alone is natural and sensitively handled. And considering that Keneally has a rather large cast of characters in a rather small book, he brings them all to life with remarkable clarity and distinctness. . . .

[Keneally's] fascination with violence sometimes comes close to veering out of control. Here his story is tightly reined: terse, ironic, reflective. *Victim of the Aurora* is entertaining and, more than that, it is interesting.

> *Jonathan Yardley, "Murder on Ice," in* Book World—The Washington Post *(© The Washington Post),* March 26, 1978, p. G3.

ANNE TYLER

[It] almost seems that Thomas Keneally, on a slow day, picked up a copy of "The Survivor"—his earlier Antarctic novel—turned the plot over in his mind awhile, and decided to rework it with a few new twists. In "The Survivor" a middle-aged man reflected upon the disaster that overcame the leader of his South Pole expedition, and tried to deal with his own guilt, which grew out of his brief affair with the leader's wife. In "Victim of the Aurora," an old man in a nursing home refelcts on the disaster that occurred to *his* South Pole expedition (this time a murder). But at the periphery, once again, is a leader troubled by his wife's infidelity with one of his men; and the man is consumed with self-reproach.

The shift of emphasis has changed a story of character (of the effects of guilt, the averted gaze of the conscious mind, the crazy selfishness of the true explorer) to one of action. When you get right down to it, "Victim of the Aurora" is a murder mystery. Like most murder mysteries, it's fascinating reading; you want to know what happens next. But also like most murder mysteries, it lacks a sense of depth. The characters tend to be puppets, conveniently performing whatever acts will speed the plot along. And the narrator, for all he says about how this story has changed his view of the world, shows no real signs of being affected. As nearly as we can tell, he returns from his expedition to lead a normal life forever after. (pp. 12-13)

> *Anne Tyler, in* The New York Times Book Review *(© 1978 by The New York Times Company; reprinted by permission), March 26, 1978.*

*   *   *

KILLENS, John Oliver   1916-

An American novelist, Killens writes realistically of the black experience in America in fiction structured with a rich fabric of black folklore and the blues. (See also *Contemporary Authors*, Vols. 77-80.)

DAVID LITTLEJOHN

John Oliver Killens has written two long, detailed, humorless, artless, almost documentary race novels, *Youngblood* (1954) and *And Then We Heard the Thunder* (1963). The first is a sort of Negro family epic, the expected tale of two generations of long-suffering blacks and their sadistic white masters in a Georgia town. The second tells the interminable story of Negroes (and whites) in wartime, where the ordeal of World War II seems less harrowing, in the long run, than the race war inside it. It runs through pages of somber "graphic realism," i.e., pages of vapidly obscene barracks chatter and hard-boiled crudeness of description: that's the way it was. Both books are sincerely well intended, and packed to bursting with details of Negro (Southern, army) life, episode after episode, as detailed by a careful, intelligent, unimaginative Negro with absolutely no sense of the art of fiction. They represent the kind of novel most Americans with great stocks of experience would probably write, if they had the will and were Negroes. The books are useful, and, to readers who make no great demands on their novelists, mildly moving and exciting. (pp. 143-44)

> *David Littlejohn, in his* Black on White: A Critical Survey of Writing by American Negroes *(copyright © 1966 by David Littlejohn; all rights reserved; reprinted by permission of Viking Penguin Inc.), Viking Penguin, 1966.*

WILLIAM H. WIGGINS, JR.

In his first three novels, John O. Killens makes traditional and structural use of black folktales. A careful re-reading of *Youngblood, And Then We Heard the Thunder*, and *'Sippi* reveals Killens' literary progression, from the former to the latter. *Youngblood* and *And Then We Heard the Thunder* have black folktales incorporated into their story line to invoke humor and also to embellish the dominant theme of all three novels: black manhood. This ornamental use of black folktales is traditional—the most common use among black writers. Killens adheres to this method of writing in the two earlier novels. The folktales embedded within them are not inextricably woven into their plots. They could either be replaced by some of Killens' prose or other folk-

tales from the black community which are funny or convey the theme of black manhood. Killens extends this traditional usage to a higher and much more sophisticated level in *'Sippi*. Like its two predecessors, *'Sippi* includes folktales for humorous effect and as variations on the theme of black manhood. However, in addition to this customary use, Killens breaks new literary ground among black novelists by using both the structure and dynamics of a black folktale as the basic outline of his novel: Unlike the other folktales which appear in these novels, you cannot remove the "'Sippi" folktale from the novel *'Sippi;* they are basically one and the same. (p. 92)

In a real sense, Killens' three novels form an historical trilogy which chronicles the black American experience from 1900 to the present. Black manhood and the Negro race's century-long struggle for human dignity in America are the major and minor themes of these books. The three heroes, Robby Youngblood in *Youngblood*, Solly Sanders in *And Then We Heard the Thunder*, and Chuck Chaney in *'Sippi*, are all black men valiantly struggling against white racism in America. *Youngblood* deals with the crippling effects of "the southern way of life" on Negroes from 1900 until World War II. *And Then We Heard the Thunder* concerns itself with integration and the Negro's mid-fifties push to enter the mainstream of American life. *'Sippi* begins after the Second World War—the date of the Supreme Court's ruling on integrating public schools, May 17, 1954, to be exact—and reveals through its hero, Chuck Chaney, the disenchantment of many blacks with the American dream and a growing enchantment with black pride, race awareness, and separatism. (p. 93)

While developing these characters, Killens made great use of black folklore. Basically an item of folklore has three characteristics. First, it is traditional. . . . Second, folklore is communal. It must be shared by a group. . . . Third, genuine terms of folklore must be communicative. They must convey, to member and non-member alike, the thinking of the people from whom they have come. (pp. 93-4)

Black manhood is the dominant theme of both Killens' three novels and the majority of the black folktales he incorporates into them. (p. 97)

The tabooed white woman is also a theme of one of the black folktales selected by Killens. Sexual relations with a white woman is the cardinal sin for black men in the south. The John cycle of tales has one about the slave putting his hand under the dress of a master's wife—while it was still hanging on the clothesline. (p. 99)

Killens has made the customary literary use of this folklore genre; he uses them, that is, to invoke some response from his readers, such as humor or social protest. In many of his folktales humor and social protest are combined. In *'Sippi*, he not only uses the message of a traditional folklore genre, but more importantly, he uses the structure of the folktale as a formal outline for his novel. Hence, it is not possible to remove the "'Sippi" folktale from Killens' novel and have the same book: the novel *'Sippi* is a bigger and much more sophisticated offspring of her folktale father. . . .

There have been other instances in which traditional black folktales have been closely integrated into the fabric of a novel beyond the use for comic effect or to register a social complaint. Richard Wright and Cecil Brown are two authors in point. (p. 100)

In *'Sippi*, Killens goes further than either Wright or Brown in his use of the black folktale. The tale that he selected for this innovative act was very popular during the early and middle sixties. . . .

> Negroes getting mean now. They ain't taking no more stuff off the white man. Like this mad Negro who went up to these white folks that he's worked for all his life and said, 'Ain't gon be no more Mister Charlie. It's just Charlie from now on.' Then he looked at his wife and said, 'Ain't no more Miss Ann. It's just plain Ann from now on." After saying this the Negro turned in a huff to leave. But when he got to the door he turned again and said, 'And another thing! Ain't no more Mississippi! It's just plain 'Sippi from now on!'

The title, *'Sippi*, is one of several clear indications that Killens has brought about the perfect marriage between the folktale and the novel. For *'Sippi* obviously refers to the above black folktale. (p. 101)

Basically the structures of [the] "'Sippi" folktale and John O. Killens' novel *'Sippi* are the same. In the first place, both the novel and the folktale are built upon the same theme, namely that black people, black men especially, will no longer passively accept southern racism. Both the novel and the folktale proclaim that the time has arrived in American history in which black people will be actively engaged in the task of changing this social system. The folktale begins with the black hero breaking a "southern custom" by entering the front door of a white home and concludes with him re-affirming his newly found manhood by shouting:

> Ain't no more Mississippi!
> Ain't no more Mississippi!
> It's jes' 'Sippi from now on!

In short, his closing words articulate what his bold initial action implied. Killens repeats his novel's basic theme of black manhood in his prologue and an epilogue. Secondly, the flow of Killens' novel is similar to [the] folktale; that is, it moves from the black hero's confrontation and rejection of: (1) the racial southern custom, (2) the white man, (3) the white woman, and (4) the violence which white southern society meters out to Blacks who get out of their "place." In the process of developing his central hero, Chuck Othello Chaney, Killens has him meet and pass all four of these trials.

In addition to these similarities in structure, Killens also develops both the stated and implied themes of the "'Sippi" folktale in his novel. . . . Black pride and black manhood are the two implied themes that Killens . . . develops throughout his novel. For both Chuck Othello and the nameless folktale hero are men in the eyes of black Americans because they both stood up to the white man and, by so doing, affirmed their own worth as Blacks, their independence from whites and their culture and an identification with fellow Blacks and their shared African and Afro-American cultures.

My research has . . . revealed the similarity of Killens' literary style with some stylistic devices of African and Afro-American oral tradition. . . . I was able to identify three stylistic devices which are both an integral part of black storytelling in all of these areas and Killens' *'Sippi* as well.

The first jointly used stylistic device is repetition. Like black storytellers in Africa and the Black Diaspora, Killens uses repetition to develop his novel. First of all Killens repeats throughout *'Sippi* the key names which appear in the black folktale. By re-reading his novel I was able to find fifteen references to the name "Mr. Charlie," sixteen to "Missy Anne," sixteen to "boy," fifty-seven to "nigger," and forty-seven to the book title, "'Sippi." By repeating the title of the novel, Killens is not only able to keep the attention of his reader but also constantly remind him of the dominant theme of both folktale and novel: "Black folks today are in no mood to humor white folks. We have no patience any longer." . . . Killens uses "'Sippi" as an effective symbolic shorthand which constantly reminds his readers of this fact. (pp. 102-04)

Violence is another theme that Killens repeats throughout his novel. Like the "'Sippi" folktale, Killens attaches covert and overt violence to any action of Blacks which challenge the "southern tradition." (p. 104)

Black manhood is the theme Killens repeats the most throughout his novel. It begins and ends his novel. From the prologue to the epilogue Killens introduces courageous black men who, like the hero in the "'Sippi" folktale, have stood up to "Mr. Charlie." . . . Killens also attaches the theme of black manhood to the recently assassinated Malcolm X. One of Killens' characters sobs upon the knowledge of his death: "He was the last hope that black folk could achieve manhood." . . . Next Killens returns to the Malcolm X device and introduces other contemporary examples of black manhood: Martin Luther King, Jr., John Lewis . . . , Julian Bond, James Foreman, Stokeley Carmichael . . . , LeRoi Jones, Bill Branch, Loften Mitchell, Larry Neal and Bill Kelley. . . .

Against the background of this combined real and fictional geneology of black manhood Killens traces the development of Chuck Othello Chaney from boyhood to black manhood. (p. 106)

Parataxis is the second stylistic device Killens borrows from African and Afro-American folklore. Ruth Finnegan noted it among the Limba of West Africa and she defines it as being a style of narration in which "sentences flow on one after the other as parallel formulations complete in themselves rather than making up long periods of complex subordinate clauses." Some American ballad scholars have noted the same practice among Afro-American ballads. For example, N. I. White described the composition of Negro ballads in this rather revealing manner: "There is hardly any such thing as a stanza belonging particularly to one song and to that alone. Generally speaking, practically any stanza is at home in practically any song." LeRoi Jones has also noted an exchange of "classical lines of blues verse in the Black American's blues tradition." Killens skillfully uses parataxis by his constant restatement of the four basic motifs of the "'Sippi" folktale he introduces in his novel's prologue. In the main, his novel is composed of independent episodes which are basically restatements of the folktale's motifs concerning the black man who bravely confronts: (1) southern custom, (2) the white man, (3) the white woman, and (4) the covert and overt violence that such "out-of-place behavior" brings to the black American who tries it. By charting the appearances of these four motifs in the novel I have been able to isolate eleven cycles in which the four motifs of the folktale are bunched together by Killens in the writing of his novel. There is no standard sequence in which Killens introduces these themes, but one thing is certain: he has built his novel around this four-motif structure of the "'Sippi" folktale.... Perhaps the best explanation of why Killens makes such extended use of these four basic motifs in the development of his novel is the fact that each one of them serves as a major area of cultural concern for the Afro-American community. Great collections of folklore have developed around the four motifs of black Americans confronting (1) southern custom, (2) the white man, (3) the white woman, and (4) racial violence.

But more than this, the dynamics of both the 'Sippi novel and folktale can be traced to their painfully accurate reflection of the black experience in America's southland. (pp. 107, 110-11)

In addition to the front door and "Miss Ann" motifs, both the novel and the folktale are centered around black men who are the antithesis of the stereotype smiling and docile black man. (p. 112)

Parallel phrasing is the third and final black storytelling device that Killens has used in the development of his novel. Ruth Finnegan describes parallel phrasing as a method of narration in which objects or events of the story "are often recited with a conscious air of comprehensiveness or climax." She also noted that rhythm too plays a major role, for as the climax of the story is reached the rhythm of the folktale is increased. These twin characteristics of climactic ending and change in rhythm are reflected in the chant sermon of the black American preacher. Both Bruce A. Rosenburg and William Pipes have noted this stylistic device in their studies of the sermons of black American preachers. The blues also has many examples of parallel phrasing. (p. 113)

Both the "'Sippi" folktale and 'Sippi novel are composed with parallel phrasing in mind. Like the stained glass of a cathedral window which begins with soft yellows at the window sill and climaxes with bright reds at the top, behind the cross, the movement of the folktale and the novel is from the lesser to the greatest denial of white superiority. The hero of the folktale has these actions of social protest phrased in a climactic parallel fashion: (1) he breaks with tradition by entering the front door of a white home; (2) he breaks with tradition by refusing to call the white man "Mr. Charlie"; (3) he refuses to call the white woman "Missy Anne"; and (4) he refuses to be intimidated by the violence which inevitably results from a black man's refusal to passively accept the customs of Mississippi, that is, the "southern tradition." Each of these four motifs are arranged so that they build to a climax. Killens has written his novel in exactly that same manner. Like the folktale, it ends on the climactic note of Blacks expressing their refusal to tolerate the racism of white people any longer.

Killens skillfully builds the twin themes of violence and the black man's seduction of the white woman to final climaxes in his novel. Taking the latter theme first, there are numerous examples throughout the novel in which the white woman confronts the black man. For example, Chuck and Carrie Louise play "momma and poppa" while they are children; they are caught by Chuck's mother and Chuck is given a brutal whipping.... During adolescence a nude Carrie Louise saves Chuck from drowning.... Ron, Chuck's roommate, disrupts an interracial party by dancing

with a blond white girl and telling the story about his refusal to join the Black Muslims because he could not give up his white women.... This sexual theme is climaxed with Chuck's seduction of Carrie Louise.... Killens adds a stylistic device from the blues when he has Chuck seduce Carrie Louise twice. In a real sense it resembles an enlarged AAB blues pattern. (pp. 113-14)

Killens also alters the rhythm of his novel as he carries his reader along to its climax.... Killens has woven the four motifs of the folktale into his novel. But, in the main, these episodes are short in nature, some being only a page in length and others not more than four or five pages long. However, as Killens draws 'Sippi to a close he begins to lengthen the treatment of some of these motifs. In fact, several of them are given chapter length treatment, beginning with chapters 6 and 7 in Part Three. Both of these chapters deal with Chuck's seduction and humiliation of Carrie Louise Wakefield. Black Pride receives a similar treatment in chapter 5 of Part Four. In this chapter, Killens devotes the entire chapter to David Woodson's Mississippi speech, which extoled black pride and the need for black Americans to challenge and change the white racism of Mississippi. Racial violence and all of the despair and frustration which accompany it is the subject of chapter 6 in Part Four. In this chapter David Woodson is assassinated as he begins to address a Civil Rights rally in his native state of Mississippi. And, finally, Killens restates the major theme of black manhood in his epilogue. In this final section, Chuck has become a man in the tradition of his father and all of the other fictional and real-life black men that Killens has constantly paraded before his readers during the telling of the novel. This creative use of rhythmic changes is reflected in many genres of Afro-American folklore. Creative use of rhythm is seen in the toast, the chant sermon, and the music of the black Americans.

Killens ends his novel in a fashion, the twist ending which is among the stylistic devices of Africans and Afro-Americans.... Killens' ending is reminiscent of the ending of a black sermon. In most instances, the black preacher will conclude his oration with a quotation that the congregation knows and serves as a summation of the sermon. It may be a song or a quotation from some well-known book, like the *Bible*. In the case of the former the congregation takes up the words and ends the sermon by singing it through to its conclusion. And in the case of a quotation, the people may also join in with the preacher in a sort of concluding litany. Killens ended 'Sippi with Paul's quotation of manhood. In a real sense it reflects the preaching style of Dr. Martin Luther King, Jr., who had the penchant for ending his sermons with a summarizing.... John O. Killens has brought the same emotional fire and style to the ending of 'Sippi. (pp. 114-16)

> *William H. Wiggins, Jr., "The Structure and Dynamics of Folklore in the Novel Form: The Case of John O. Killens," in* Keystone Folklore Quarterly (*copyright by the author*), *Fall, 1972, pp. 92-117.*

*   *   *

KNOWLES, John   1926-

An American novelist, short story writer, and travel writer, Knowles is noted for his sensitive portrayals of the problems and joys of youth. Best known for his novel *A Separate Peace*,

Knowles has received critical acclaim for his brisk, unaffected style and his adept use of imagery. (See also *CLC*, Vols. 1, 4, and *Contemporary Authors*, Vols. 17-20, rev. ed.)

MICHAEL DIRDA

In 1960 *A Separate Peace* catapulted Knowles both to international prominence and to life as a full-time novelist. Unfortunately, with each succeeding work ... Knowles has gradually been relegated to the gloomy circle of those who fail to realize their initial promise. Sad to say, *A Vein of Riches* will not restore him to public and critical favor.

John Knowles's latest book chronicles the fortunes of the Catherwood family of Middleburg, West Virginia from the early 1900s to the mid 1920s. . . .

To be a work of art a novel requires an inventive use of language, a meaningful design, and a compelling vision of life. *A Vein of Riches* lacks all of these. Knowles's prose is generally competent, but it can easily turn embarrassing or trite. At one point, Doris Lee reflects on her husband's lovemaking: "Virgil. He had possessed her as naturally as a stream flows down to the river, as clear and swift and exhilarating as a fast-flowing mountain stream." Lyle gushes that "Tot's biscuits were really the next best thing in this world to Canadian whiskey." Such sentences are set off by dialogue that resembles a catechism: When Lyle earnestly propounds solemn questions, his parents answer in brief soliloquies.

Many of the story elements of *A Vein of Riches* are so disturbingly familiar that one may suspect claim jumping. Several incidents strongly echo *All the King's Men*, Minnie's feeling of transience recalls Cather's *A Lost Lady*, the miners' struggle evokes the Steinbeck of the '30s, and Tot appears a first cousin of Faulkner's Dilsey. Virgil Pence's crucial and untimely end seems a weak homage to that masterly surprise death of Gerald in Forster's *The Longest Journey*. Even the name Catherwood is irritatingly close to that of Cowperwood, the hero of Dreiser's robber baron trilogy.

Knowles's treatment of his characters proves equally fragmented and unsatisfying. Minnie reveals some interior life, but she virtually drops out of the action after the first 60 pages. As may be appropriate to a man of affairs, Clarkson is viewed only from the outside, but nowhere are his business operations convincingly described. Lyle, who is intended to be the sensitive hero, comes across as merely insecure, shallow, and ignorant. . . .

A long panoramic novel connecting business, social progress, and family life should achieve a certain grandeur. Yet the mystical religion of Minnie leads only to a snug little farm; the miner's ordeal results not in any transformed social consciousness, but in a love affair; the father and son's potentially tragic desire for the same woman is undercut by a fairy tale ending in Washington's Rock Creek Park. In brief, *A Vein of Riches* moves not with the inexorable rightness of art, but with the obvious contrivedness of the merely literary. It is a perfectly readable novel—R. F. Delderfield comes to West Virginia. But it should have been more.

> Michael Dirda, "Mining the Delderfield Vein," in Book World—The Washington Post (© The Washington Post), *February 19, 1978, p. E4.*

JONATHAN YARDLEY

Up to now John Knowles has been something of a miniaturist, his novels and stories set in close quarters: the boarding school of "A Separate Peace," the Yale campus of "The Paragon." At their best these short, intense novels are quite fine; in particular, Knowles has displayed a sensitive and unsentimental appreciation of the real and imagined agonies of young men as they go through the rites of passage.

But "A Vein of Riches" is something else again. . . . It pains me greatly to say so, but the novel does not possess a single redeeming virtue. Its characters and situations are clichés. Its irony is hamhanded. It is utterly lacking in subtlety, grace or wit. It is talky, obvious and boring. . . .

It's an old story, and all Knowles's ingredients are old: the domineering, insensitive, sexually frustrated father; the dreamy, wispy, yet unexpectedly resilient mother; the son [Lyle] frustrated by his father's indifference, desperately seeking his own identity; the widow whom the son adores but who becomes the father's mistress; the dogged, feisty miners and the blacks reeking with natural integrity. There isn't a spark of life or originality anywhere in the novel.

As if that weren't bad enough, Knowles's depiction of Lyle's adolescent maunderings has none of the clarity and subtlety of his earlier work. He wavers uncertainly between sarcasm and melodrama; sometimes he seems to regard Lyle as a drooling idiot, at others as the conscience of Catherwood castle. He makes Lyle bear too much of the novel's thematic burden, and it isn't long before Lyle—like the reader—collapses under it. . . .

Whatever the occasional failures of his earlier books, they are all honorable, scrupulous—and serious. "A Vein of Riches" is windy and graceless. I'm sorry Knowles wrote it.

> Jonathan Yardley, "Mined Out," in The New York Times Book Review (© 1978 by The New York Times Company; reprinted by permission), *February 19, 1978, p. 15.*

JOHN McINERNEY

Most people remember John Knowles as the author of *A Separate Peace*, a brief, enormously popular novel which searchingly studied the lives of two boys on the brink of adulthood. The writing was low-keyed, but it seemed to capture perfectly the quicksilver mental atmosphere of that stage of adolescence. In *A Vein of Riches*, Knowles turns to a different subject—the expansion and collapse of the "King Coal" industry in West Virginia from 1909 to 1924—and to a new genre—a Dreiserian chronicle of people and power. He seems very knowledgeable about the subject and rather uncomfortable with the form. . . .

[The southern coal industry is portrayed] through the adventures of the Catherwood family, one of the small dynastic groups at the pinnacle of this terribly American boom society, and they are, unfortunately, transparent devices. . . .

Further, the narrative point of view shifts often and abruptly from one character to another so that each person can show us yet another phase of the special world the author wants us to explore. In the same vein, Knowles drags in other awkward storytelling tricks: like the series of implausibly analytic, informative letters supposedly written by one minor character to his wife.

The result is a readable but rather flatly ordinary tale that somehow seems like the prospectus for a "docudrama" series on public television. Finally, one gets the impression that Knowles would have preferred to settle down with one of his characters and get on with the kind of personal probing he does so well. *A Vein of Riches* might have been a better book if he had. (p. 7)

> John McInerney, in Best Sellers (copyright © 1978 Helen Dwight Reid Educational Foundation), April, 1978.

*   *   *

KONRÁD, György   1933-

Konrád is a Hungarian novelist and social worker. *The Case Worker* is his best known translated work, gaining its power, according to Irving Howe, "from Konrád's gift for the vignette, the suddenly snapped picture, as if taken from a slightly overfocused camera." (See also *CLC*, Vol. 4.)

NEAL ASCHERSON

The Case Worker, a first novel by the young Hungarian writer George Konrád, has been widely praised in the West.... *The Case Worker* is horrific, and Konrád possesses both the power to see and the power to describe what he sees. But there is much to make reservations about: his violent, remorseless battering of the feelings causes monotony, his rhetorical seizures which spatter the reader with a hundred hot adjectives in a few sentences are, it seems to me, the easy but wrong way to the effect he wants....

What is memorable about the book is neither its narrative structure nor its tirades: Konrád's real achievement is, in fact, his evoking of a "case," the brilliant, economical creation of a character in a trap. He is a very talented writer, but *The Case Worker* is the sort of abreacting, subjective novel which does not yet prove him a gifted novelist and which, by its nature, can't be repeated in variation or developed upon. Konrád's next work will probably tell us more.

> Neal Ascherson, in The New York Review of Books (reprinted with permission from The New York Review of Books; © 1974 by NYREV, Inc.), August 8, 1974, p. 16.

IVAN SANDERS

With the skill of a social scientist, the compassion of a humanist, and the stylistic pyrotechnics of the avant-garde, Konrád [in *The City Builder*] outlines the political, social and economic history of an unnamed East European city....

Much of *The City Builder* reads like an extended essay, although it is profoundly literary. Its ideas arrive in language of extraordinary power and plasticity. Moreover, by constantly condensing and telescoping events, Konrád manages to pack a number of potential novels into his text. Alfred Kazin has said that novels cannot be written anymore, only scenarios. Eastern European novelists and film makers are particularly adept at schematic, elliptical modes of composition. Konrád merely hints at the specifics of time and place, yet each hint is crucial, for it evokes a state of mind and a way of life. The true protagonist of the novel is

the city, whose main square, with its impressive public buildings and statuary, is a memorial to mock heroism and real suffering. The narrator finds his city at once cozy and confining, irreplaceable and detestable—"an Eastern European showcase of devastation and regeneration" that "can welcome its enemies with salt and bread and, having taken crash courses in the art of survival, change its greeting signs, statues, scapegoats—its history."

In his much-praised first novel, *The Case Worker*, Konrád already proved his stylistic agility. *The City Builder* is another bravura performance, though here, too, the verbal abandon, the stunning fusion of abstract and concrete, the tricky interplay of reality and fantasy add up to more than a self-conscious tour de force. Konrád has evidently learned a great deal from Joyce and the French nouveau roman, but like many technically accomplished East European avant-gardists, he eschews the impersonality of modern fiction. In *The City Builder*, cynicism and quiet despair yield periodically to anguished litanies, appeals, exhortations....

For all his humanist sensibility and reformist zeal, Konrád excels at constructing scenes of concentrated cruelty. The highlights he offers from his city's history culminate invariably in sieges and slaughters. His main character as well as other figures who flit in and out of the narrative are survivors of various ordeals who like to think they have been chastened by their harrowing experiences but who realize with horror that they have only been brutalized by them. (p. 504)

> Ivan Sanders, "Human Dialogues Are Born," in The Nation (copyright 1977 by the Nation Associates, Inc.), April 23, 1977, pp. 504-06.

JASCHA KESSLER

George Konrád's first book, "The Case Worker," was a fictive essay built with blocks of grotesque realism: the daily horrors of the lives of the poor and helpless, the deficient, abandoned, crazed and rejected.... Its thesis was that our urban culture grows more vacant of humane values in proportion to our power to process masses of people through a machinery designed to give them well-being....

Still, "The Case Worker" accepts love, is drenched in compassion as it offers a traditional humanist solution of the problem of human imperfection. Konrád sees that it is just the problem—the intolerable evil inherent in our defective human condition—that spurs the revolutionist, and infuriates the utopian planner. The source of our delusions, it perverts our brief residence here to a hell on earth. This becomes the theme of "The City Builder." Its narrator, the anonymous incarnation of our 20th-century's contradictions, reflects upon the fate of his nameless city—recognizably in Hungary.

The 10 chapters of "The City Builder" are a set of meditations composed with an unusual metaphorical density. They project a surreal compound of decades of brutal history evoked by the inexpugnable memories of the citizens of the city. This is a work of poetry, in fact. There are no characters; there is no plot. The sentences (amounting in the end to a sentence of damnation), are uttered by the architect, a social engineer whose thoughts portray the consciousness of conscience itself, within the span of four generations. (p. 13)

It is interesting to note that the women during these four generations wither and vanish from the private consciousness, to be replaced perhaps by a "you" to whom the narrator addresses his most poignant wishes and regrets. God being absent from our world, Konrád's persona has no choice but to speak to that now dead woman, one among the many suicides that haunt the living.

The City Builder's ruminations are essentially an outcry against the hypocrisy and murderous careerism of state bureaucrats who live under terror from above, against the absurdities of utopian dictatorship and the utterly immoral pretension of speaking in the name of the people.

But the importance of this brilliant book is not polemical. For Konrád, socialism is "what we live in; it is what was and is—not a goal, a disaster, an ideal, a law, or an aberration, but an East European present tense, a neatly proportioned order, an unfolding drama, the power play of interests, endowments, self-delusions and self-exposures, trials and failures. . . . We don't know it but live it. We programmed a system and it programmed us." (pp. 13, 21)

"The City Builder" is a beautiful, brave book, a work of the stoic imagination. It could only have come from a nation of ironists and visionaries who, in their impenetrable language, have built a great arena for themselves in their consciousness alone. Always crushed by despotisms of the Right and the Left, external and internal, somehow they have managed to speak not only to each other, but to us as well. (p. 21)

Jascha Kessler, in The New York Times Book Review *(© 1978 by The New York Times Company; reprinted by permission), January 22, 1978.*

SUSAN LARDNER

"The City Builder" is written as an interior monologue delivered by a city planner—a Socialist bureaucrat who lives and works in an "East-Central European city.". . .

The namelessness of speaker and city—besides possibly indicating a diminished individuality owing to East-Central European political circumstances—emphasizes the general pertinence of Konrád's theme, which is the bitter disappointments of middle age. East European Socialist middle age, true; but readers of diverse persuasions will recognize, if they don't also share, the planner's close attention to his aging body, his feeling of private and professional failure, his absorption in thoughts of death and of the sexual joys of the past. In fact, to an American reader the most exotic aspect of "The City Builder" is not its distant setting or its narrative eccentricity but the combination of a lavish metaphorical style with the structural forms and devices of classical rhetoric. . . .

[The book consists of] interwoven fragments that range in tone from grim irony to nostalgia, and include reminiscence, indecipherable dreams, panoramic description, invective, and exhortation. Although he opens the book with daybreak and winds it up with a New Year's celebration, Konrád otherwise observes the conventions of interior monologue. Time doesn't move clockwise, and transitions are abrupt and often mysterious. (p. 141)

Konrád shows a taste and talent for the good old rhetorical devices (epanaphora, antistrophe, antithesis, antimetabole, and paradox . . .). . . . [As] a method of controlling his

flight from ordinary ways of saying things the traditional formulas work well. . . .

[Whatever] its roots in the notably unsteady geography and history of Hungary, Konrád's mercurial prose has a likely and more immediate source in his belief in the destructiveness of worn-out words and ideas. . . . [The] following items, pulled apologetically out of context, may give a sense of how Konrád works his way through the platitudes of literature and life—successfully, I think, more often than not:

> the crocodiles of the unconscious
> shock troops of light
> locusts of my vanity
> the gladiolas of early-morning lucidity
> the latrine of the here and now
>
> (p. 142)

At times, I think, the accumulation of images leads to an impression of waste and windiness. At times, an abstraction seems stubbornly to resist a valiant assault. . . . Toward the end of his utopian oration—"The fragile structures of the city are regularly repeated messages from a misshapen void, aimed at our incorporeal mother who in the hall of possibilities plays a cheap little ditty about time and space"—it sounds as if Konrád had not completely defeated the cliché; or perhaps the messages from the void, the cheap little ditty reflect the hazards of translation. (p. 143)

Susan Lardner, in The New Yorker *(© 1978 by The New Yorker Magazine, Inc.), April 10, 1978.*

*   *   *

KOSINSKI, Jerzy   1933-

A Polish-born American novelist and sociologist, Kosinski is a controversial artist, drawing both praise and condemnation for fiction heavily laden with sex and violence. Despite the sensationalism of his subject matter, he is a serious artist, making a strong statement on themes of communication and morality. He won the National Book Award in 1969 for *Steps*. He has written under the pseudonym Joseph Novak. (See also *CLC*, Vols. 1, 2, 3, 6, and *Contemporary Authors*, Vols. 17-20, rev. ed.)

GERALD BARRETT

Kosinski's novels consist of many . . . episodes, self-enclosed stories that reflect two of the novel's most traditional interests, the telling of interesting tales and the description of how something is done. His stories of psychological manipulation strike, unfortunately, a responsive chord in us all, just as his descriptions of how to make and use the hardware of our culture is closer to us than, say, a description of how to catch and cook a whale.

But rather than *Moby Dick, Cockpit* will remind the reader of *The Confidence Man,* Melville's unfinished story of a man of many disguises who manipulates people for complicated reasons. (pp. 356-57)

[A] quality found in all of Kosinski's novels [is] a dispassionate rendering of the human condition, sometimes for the sake of possible correction, sometimes for the sake of simple understanding. One of the most fascinating outcomes of reading the modern parables that make up *Cock-*

pit is our insight into the ambiguities of the self. The very title, *Cockpit,* serves to point up man's ambiguous state. An actual airplane cockpit, the heart of a controlling mechanism designed to destroy people, appears only once in the entire novel, but one finds it a number of times in disguise. From that high perch, Tarden [the protagonist] can look down upon the rest of mankind; he considers himself to be free because everyone is his potential victim. He can act rather than be acted upon. On the other hand, the word "cockpit" is a sexual pun which ultimately suggests Tarden's entrapment in the human condition, part of which is death. (p. 357)

Tarden's romantic career simply establishes a modicum of logic, causality, and believability that is needed in order to draw the reader into the experience and meaning of the forty or so episodes and memory fragments that make up the novel. Although Tarden is involved in all of them, time and space are in flux because placement within *Cockpit's* structure is governed by memory, another ambiguous cockpit which simultaneously offers a means of survival, a human identity, and a loss of control over the self.

Tarden's first concern is for his survival, and he chooses to involve himself in the lives of others in order to stir his blood, giving him the energy to live. He is amazed that so few notice themselves and the things around them, and he makes use of this knowledge to stimulate himself.... Tarden reflects his own ambiguous state in his use of people and their lives as mirrors of himself. With Tarden, images of auto-eroticism flow hand-in-hand with images of the manipulation of others. (p. 358)

Early in *Cockpit,* Tarden learns that memory is "much more accurate and explicit" than photographs, and, in spite of his desire to be free, to be in control, he is excited because he has no control over his memory.... Memory gives *Cockpit* its energy, its freshness, because no matter what Tarden does, his memory of the past bursts from him and plays havoc with his programmed freedom.

According to Kosinski, the act of remembering operates in uncontrollable spurts with little linkage. He once suggested that one can create a montage of memories in much the same way that one can create a montage of celluloid shots. He noted that "the cinematic image has become the key to modern perception." In *Cockpit,* the Eisensteinian theory of montage, shot A plus shot B creates a shot C of the imagination, is what the author counts on to structure both the novel and our recognition of its truths. (pp. 358-59)

> *Gerald Barrett, "Montage," in* Michigan Quarterly Review *(copyright © The University of Michigan, 1976), Summer, 1976, pp. 356-59.*

LEE T. LEMON

Because Jerzy Kosinski has given us several important novels, the temptation is to talk about *Cockpit* as if it were significant. I could say all the things that other reviewers have said and will say—*Cockpit* is a metaphor of modern life, a study of the depersonalization that threatens from within and from without, a biting satire on what the cold-war-detente state makes of its brightest, a warning of the danger that threatens our lives and our sanity, and so on. But I would not believe it because *Cockpit* just does not work. Despite the overall slickness of presentation, the reason is at least partly technical; it is a failure in that cru-

cial area where a failure of technique is also a failure of theme.

One of the sounder clichés of modern literary criticism is that a genuine work of art earns its meaning. That is, it not only presents a set of values, it places them in situations where they are harshly, definitively, tested. The writer builds into his work a counter-voice, a set of powerful and carefully wrought forces antagonistic to those the author is testing. Technically, the problem is one of balance: a protagonist needs a worthy antagonist; values need effective opposition, even if that opposition must eventually lose; ideas need struggle in order to test their ramifications....

Nowhere [in *Cockpit*] is there a worthy antagonist for either the protagonist or his values. The result is a document with all the fascination of a trip through a carnival freak show, but with neither social nor human significance. (pp. 172-73)

> *Lee T. Lemon, "Freak Show," in* Prairie Schooner *(© 1976 by University of Nebraska Press; reprinted by permission from* Prairie Schooner*),* Summer, 1976, pp. 172-73.

WILLIAM PLUMMER

Jerzy Kosinski's second novel, *Steps* (1968), is made up of a series of vignettes set in Poland during and after WWII, and in "the West." Always the setting is exotic; always we sense, in Thoreau's phrase, that we are immersed "in dreams awake." The protagonist-narrator of *Steps* is alternately the dark-complected boy of Kosinski's first novel, *The Painted Bird* (1965), and that same boy as an adult. He is variously a waif, soldier, photographer, waiter, day laborer, servant.

In whatever guise, he is—when not merely the witness to enormity—that agent of a malignity so darkly inscrutable that, by comparison, Shakespeare's Iago seems the Man from Glad. The only absolute in the world of *Steps* is the self of the protagonist-narrator—an utterly solipsistic Self for whom the Other is no more than an occasion for the fulfillment of outrageous fantasy....

The vignettes have to do with murder, disease, rape, sodomy. Some register only slight readings on our internal Richters; most achieve palpable hits....

Yet the rehearsal of the details of the vignettes testifies only partly to the power of *Steps*. Each is a two-handed engine, and it remains to say something about Kosinski's language....

Apart from his genius at deconstructing and recodifying the grammar of our tainted desires, Kosinski knows to keep his language plain and unobtrusive.... The language is deliberately antiseptic, devoid of reference; it awaits possession, demands inhabitation by the reader's Self. Monotone, Kosinski knows, stimulates prurience and ensures complicity.

Steps was (and remains) powerful because it was not "literary." It offered none of the usual facilities and reliefs, there was no beginning-middle-end, no story at all, no likable character to feel for and with, no recognizable narrative voice, no conventional moral center. Its vision was not developmental but incremental; it did not grow to a point but hammered its point over and over again, It was a better book than *The Painted Bird*, even though the images in the first book were as stunning, because its knife-thrust form better suited its obsessive interests.

Yet *The Painted Bird*—a bildungsroman complete with sentiment and moralizing—enabled the achievement of *Steps*. The reader knew *Steps* was not literature because he knew (or felt he did) that Kosinski's own experience was that of the boy in *The Painted Bird*.... Kosinski had been there, we felt. He had suffered and survived. He was the exemplary modern artist—authentic, not literary.

It was dismaying, therefore, to read *Being There* (1971), the third novel, for it was not only slight but recognizably a "moral" fable to boot....

Every writer must be allowed a bad book or two, but what was most disturbing about *Being There* was Kosinski's option for that musty "literary" tandem—instruction and delight. In spinning his cautionary tale, he had forsaken his more serviceable, certainly more subversive allegiance to the repulsive and the outrageous. (p. 77)

The next novel, *The Devil Tree* (1973), was an out-and-out disaster, even with the critics who admired *Being There*. Interestingly, the new novel discovered Kosinski trying to make rhetorical hay out of the sissified generation he so despised. (pp. 77-8)

Cockpit (1975) reads like the out-takes of *Steps*. The novel is narrated by Tarden, a former intelligence agent for something called "the Government." Tarden would no more be welcomed on Walton's Mountain than would the protagonist of *Steps,* but this time Kosinski added a new wrinkle. The predatory intentions of his protagonist are implemented not so much by physical force as by the gathering and manipulation of "intelligence." In a typical episode, the narrator happens to see a woman slip and fall before an oncoming taxi. He shoots three rolls of film of her being hit, dragged, and removed. After the accident he offers two different sets of photographs to the cabbie and the woman, each set establishing the recipient's innocence. Time and again in *Cockpit* Tarden insinuates himself into similar positions of trust; repeatedly he gains access to privileged information through both primitive and sophisticated means—rifling bureau drawers, penetrating data systems. The new mode of Selfishness serves to put friends and strangers at one another's throats.

Despite mixed reviews, *Cockpit* may have retrieved some of Kosinski's old audience. But it is the new book, *Blind Date,* that seems more telling about Kosinski's progress....

The new novel revolves around George Levanter.... Like most of Kosinski's works, the novel moves freely back and forth in time and is, as usual, really a collection of vignettes —but with a difference. *Blind Date* is tonally the least integrated of Kosinski's fictions.

The title episode is familiar stuff: the "blind date" refers to a particularly brutal mode of rape practiced by one of Levanter's boyhood pals and tried out successfully by Levanter himself. The rape is as potentially appalling as any in *Steps,* but Kosinski has added a new element: Conscience. The Kosinski hero is no longer the unbridled Self viewed externally and chronicled in monotone but rather an ordinary man whose range of antisocial desires and social and moral checks mirrors our own. He is a sympathetic character who, by his own anxieties, relieves us of taking an active

role in the vignette. Thus, the reader's part is reduced to voyeurism, to taking keyhole delights.

Levanter's odyssey is, of course, marked by violence, yet the violence is no longer gratuitous. It is enervated by purposefulness. (p. 78)

The handling of sex and disease no longer constitutes a radically disturbing statement about the life force but degenerates to kinkiness. Levanter picks up a gorgeous hitchhiker in Switzerland who, it later turns out, is a transsexual; Levanter is her first man. In a similar episode in *Steps* the reader is jolted by the intimations in the situation of masturbatory narcissism. In *Blind Date,* Levanter is torn: "He was crushed to think of the helplessness of her condition, yet he knew that at the moment he must consider himself" —a dilemma that would never have arisen for the rapacious protagonist of *Steps*. (pp. 78-9)

Towards the end of the novel, Levanter discovers a woman from the early pages—a woman who has never achieved orgasm. In an episode that pales beside Norman Mailer's famous story, "The Time of Her Time," or Harold Brodkey's "Orra Perkins's First Orgasm," Levanter brings her to ecstasy. But what is most interesting is the effect on Levanter himself: "A sudden current ran through her like lightning; then just as suddenly, the tension that gripped her dissolved. He lost the feeling of his own shape; in the ultimate moment, when his vision shrank, he heard her whisper, Yes!"

What is extraordinary here is that the heretofore utterly solipsistic, rapacious Kosinski hero is subordinating his own to another's pleasure and, in the process, producing the first truly erotic occasion in Kosinski's fiction. For the goal of Eros, the heretofore great dread of the Kosinski hero, is the dissolution or transcendence of self and the merger with another. Still more stunning, Levanter "lost the feeling of his own shape" through performing oral sex and receiving no physical stimulus himself.

It must be that Levanter, like all the great lovers since Isolde's Tristan, is in love with love itself. To say the least, the Kosinski hero is a much different man from his counterpart in the early works. It is obvious that Kosinski has become an altogether more palatable author. His new geniality, however, has cost him much of his power. (p. 79)

William Plummer, "In His Steps: The Mellowing of Jerzy Kosinski," in The Village Voice *(reprinted by permission of* The Village Voice; *copyright © by The Village Voice, Inc., 1977), October 31, 1977, pp. 77-9.*

ANATOLE BROYARD

Jerzy Kosinski calls George Levanter, the hero of his novel "Blind Date," a "small investor." But to me he is more like a claims adjuster in the ambiguous morality of the modern world. Among other things, Levanter is a skier and, as the West declines, he finds sport on its slope....

When Levanter rapes a beautiful young girl whom he might legitimately have won, he does it simply because it is admissible in his morality. [Here] one feels that the author is dealing in cynical homiletics. There is a considerable proportion of sexual activity in "Blind Date," and most of it can only be understood as a search for something other than pleasure. Levanter is obsessed, for example, with a prostitute who kills an anonymous chauffeur who seems intent on killing them with his driving. She stabs him in the neck with a sharpened comb and later his blood, which spattered over Levanter and herself, serves as an aphrodisiac. I hesitate to try to explicate this passage. To ascribe it to simple sadism does not do justice to Kosinski's sophistication, yet it seems far fetched to interpret it as the just deserts of a reckless driver.

Kosinski is a poet of morbidity. We meet a young woman in a baby carriage who is almost all head and no body and it goes without saying that Levanter desires her. . . .

Kosinski means to shock. He wants very much—too much, perhaps—to make a statement of some sort about ethics and values which belong to man and man alone. As a result, "Blind Date" sometimes verges on being a jeremiad. Levanter rarely turns up any of the benign aspects of the new morality whose dangerous Don Quixote he appoints himself.

In his two best books, "The Painted Bird" and "Steps," Kosinski was admired for the intensity with which he evoked a world that had broken loose from its moral moorings. In "Blind Date," Levanter's cool detachment, all too reminiscent of Clint Eastwood, tends to congeal not only the passion of the author's vision, but his high seriousness as well, so that incidents meant to evoke horror often come across as merely lurid. Without the melding intensity, Kosinski's discontinuous panorama sprawls and disintegrates.

In his mistrust or dislike of the ordinary, Kosinski runs the risk of pretentiousness, the social disease of much current fiction. The resources of art can go a long way toward softening an author's assault on the reader's credulity, but the author of "Blind Date" seems to have lost faith not only in morality, but in art as well. Like blind anger, "Blind Date" simply asserts itself, with little attempt at persuasion. The author's prose is stoical, his structure random, his characterizations incurious. (p. 14)

> *Anatole Broyard, in* The New York Times Book Review *(© 1977 by The New York Times Company; reprinted by permission), November 6, 1977.*

TOM PAULIN

Kosinski's fantasy world is a place of such barren superficiality and murderous frustration that it often reads like the case-history of a vindictive neurotic. For all its dreams of positive action and complete power, *Blind Date* is an ignorant account of [a] drab hell. . . . The trouble is that he actually believes he's writing fiction. . . . (p. 194)

> *Tom Paulin, in* New Statesman *(© 1978 The Statesman & Nation Publishing Co. Ltd.), February 10, 1978.*

PETER ACKROYD

There are certain great moments in fiction, when the vast mists of the world suddenly part; *Blind Date* has one of them: 'Levanter could not speak. Mute, dispirited, he started the engine. Without pausing to look back, Jaques Monod walked away. As he started to climb the steps to the house, the last rays of the setting sun wrapped him in their glow.' I haven't come across such a potent combination of effects since I last opened an American novel, but the mixture here of name-dropping, cheap romance and

rather precious fictionalising succeeds mainly by being worse than anything that has come before it. *Ragtime* turned this particular tone into an industrial process. It consists of saying as little as possible in the largest possible space—while at the same time convincing the reader that he is part of an amazing and genuinely historical experience. But the flatness of the writing here is peculiarly un-American; Kosinski himself is of European origin, and so he tries hard to avoid the flashiness of his contemporaries. He provides the emptiness, but without the rhetoric.

The tone of the book is unsettling: at one moment we dive into the wide-eyed breathlessness of conventional romantic fiction (where girls are girls, and 'Levanter studied the shadows her lashes cast on her cheeks . . .'), and at the next we're in the City of the Night where Levanter, the 'hero' of the novel, cuts through the undergrowth like a chainsaw. . . . It is always easy to load one character with . . . many meretricious blessings, but it's difficult to make him interesting as a result. Characters fade in a novel unless they are comprehensible or sympathetic: Levanter is a creature of fantasy and, like all fantasies, he becomes quickly and irredeemably boring. . . .

Kosinski must realise this in part, since he has divided the novel into a number of separate but unrelated episodes, so the reader can switch off at any point without actually missing very much. . . . But none of it really adds up to much, and the narrative flaps and crawls along the ground as the fictional puppets are introduced alongside Charles Lindbergh, Monod, and even Svetlana Alliluyeva. Kosinski has clearly included everyone and everything he can think of, on the principle that bad writing abhors a vacuum—even when it is one of its own making. But when real figures jostle beside fictional characters, narratives become troublesome and ambiguous; fantasies can be disastrous if the line between life and art isn't carefully measured and maintained.

In fact that line is blurred only for suspect purposes, when the imagination is not strong enough and life is not real enough. And in order to confer a solid identity upon Levanter, this creature of his imaginings, Kosinski has had to create a two-dimensional world which will act as a support. One dimension stretches into some fantasy of sexuality and virility, where all the usual cliches are brought into play, and the other wanders out into some half-real world where Levanter meets important people and thereby becomes important himself. It is the usual alchemy of false writing.

And so the novel founders on unreality; since Kosinski doesn't recognise, let alone acknowledge, the ambiguities that surround his central figure, Levanter simply becomes a vehicle for grey fantasies and brutally prurient acts. . . .

Living people—that includes you and me, who have to read the stuff, . . . —are diminished and cheapened by a book which treats everyone as an object of prurient fantasy. The fact that Kosinski drags in real human suffering almost as an after-thought—he deals at some length, and inexplicably, with the Sharon Tate killings—only makes his attempts at significance and 'meaning' all the more gratuitous and unpleasant. Death is the easiest merchandise for a bad writer. And *Blind Date* makes *Mein Kampf* seem like a miracle of good taste.

> *Peter Ackroyd, "Prurience," in* The Spectator *(© 1978 by* The Spectator; *reprinted by*

permission of The Spectator), *February 26, 1978. p. 20.*

XANA KAYSEN

I have been mulling over the sense of dreariness [Kosinski] provokes—a dreariness quite separate from that conjured up by his venomous outlook on life. He presents a brutal, anarchic world, where only the man who takes things into his own hands is commendable. His famous flat tone has been interpreted as an emblem of the flatness of modern life. The trouble is that the symbolism fails; the books refuse to produce the overtones that dozens of reviewers (and the author) have hopefully and earnestly sought to find. My own feeling of dreariness came from reading badly written, sadistic hocus-pocus, and not from being overwhelmed by a convincing view of life-as-crap.

To begin with mechanics, Kosinski's prose, which is so easy to read that it is unnoticeable, turns out to be a string of clichés. . . .

The writing is simple enough and clear enough to read with minimal attentiveness; the brain can hop from verb to verb undisturbed by extraneous words. . . . These novels could be read almost without thinking, but for the jerkiness of the story line. The books do not have plots. They consist of a series of vignettes taken in haphazard order from the protagonists' lives. One may find Levanter, the hero of *Blind Date,* sunning himself in France in one paragraph, and disemboweling somebody in London the next. The movement from one situation to another is abrupt and disturbing, and is similar to the movement of the TV camera in police adventure serials. In fact, the atmosphere of the books, particularly *Cockpit* and *Blind Date,* reminded me of the type of TV show that deals with five unrelated disasters in twenty-two minutes.

This comparison should not be surprising. Both Kosinski's novels and cop shows feature a loner good guy bucking the system, and both portray the system as a bureaucratic malevolence embodied by superior offices—the Supreme Court, Party officials, or simply the constraints of civilization. The police officers complain that they are restricted by the law; if they didn't have to spend time reading criminals their rights and gathering acceptable evidence against them, our cities would be safe. Kosinski takes this argument one step further by placing his heroes outside the law. They can cheat, forge checks, kill, and blackmail with impunity, because their cause is right.

The clichéd phrases and the narrative technique of eliminating motivation and sequence seem to me to be stylistic efforts to keep the reader worrying about what will happen next and to deflect any possible concern for why things happen, or for what anyone thinks about what happens. If Kosinski is not interested in those two questions, why then does he write?

Kosinski has an idea about the world that he is eager to communicate. He believes that life is a series of encounters with a vicious but disinterested "fate" or "chance" and that each encounter offers a man (never a woman) the opportunity to take control of events. This idea of control includes a violent, manipulative drive for power. . . . The message appears to be that by emulating fate, that is to say, amorality, one becomes a real man. . . .

The book most likely to have been read by anyone who has read Kosinski is his first, *The Painted Bird.* This story of a child abused by adults, rats, winter, and war is apparently an autobiography. That fact is well known, and Kosinski has never taken any pains to keep it a secret. If he was ill-treated even a tenth as much as the child in the book, he has good reason to take a dim view of people. But there is something suspicious in the way he wields his suffering. . . . I believe that a good part of Kosinski's success with the critics comes from their dual wish to placate, or somehow "make it up" to him, and to prove that they can take what he's dishing out. His popular success, on the other hand, is probably due to his readability and his sex-and-violence themes. . . .

But the morals of this Moralist are not good. He is a misanthropist, who gleefully expects the worst of everyone, and like most misanthropists, he majors in misogyny. Kosinski's heroes move from one faceless woman to another without establishing (or looking for) either friendship or love. Only the women who are unfaithful, unobtainable, or deformed are fleshed out. . . .

On more general moral issues, Kosinski seems to think in a manner similar to the CIA. He has an obsession with cleaning things up, even when there are no ostensible messes, by means of secrecy and electronic arrangements (there is a great deal of bugging and taping and picture taking in his books) and by imposing his idea of Right, with force if necessary. In fact, his heroes are one-man CIAs, suspicious, alert, looking for a way to provoke a mix-up in order to kill in the name of justice. This would be a believable, if depressing, symbolic spoof of the modern world, but for Kosinski's lack of distance from it. With a straight face, he presents his Robin Hood heroes making the world safe for democracy. There seems to be no realization on the author's part that his creations are vile. (p. 18)

I don't like to venture into the land of dream interpretation criticism, but what is omitted in the novels means as much as what is chosen, and, beyond that, there are no "unloaded" choices. Kosinski's pretense that he has dispensed with an outlook on his characters only means that he doesn't object to them. He has refrained from "injecting the moral" because the moral is there, clear as day. These books are not unbiased reports from an eyewitness in Hell; they are propaganda for one of mankind's most disreputable ideas: might is right. Kosinski has modified this slightly into: might is right when used for Our Cause, and is a moral outrage which must be punished when used by Them. The trouble with this, as everybody knows, is that using Their methods tends to blur whatever differences there may have been between Us and Them.

The purpose of art may not be to make us feel good, but surely it is obliged to extend us in some way. Kosinski's books are numbing, diminishing, anti-human. They are dreary in a pointless way. What they give rise to is the feeling that all is indeed wrong with the world if a writer who is so inhumane can be touted as a humanist. (pp. 18, 22)

Xana Kaysen, "Kosinski: Rapist as Moralist," in New Boston Review *(copyright 1978 by Boston Critic, Inc.), Spring, 1978, pp. 18, 22.*

*   *   *

KUNZE, Reiner   1933-

Kunze is an East German poet and novelist now living in

West Germany. He was recently expelled from his country for the West German publication of *The Wonderful Years*, a novel quietly caustic about life in East Germany. This novel won the 1977 George Büchner Prize, West Germany's most important literary award.

DIETHER H. HAENICKE

The student of East German literature is painfully aware of the fact that the preponderance of all poetry originating in that country must still be labelled versified propaganda. There are few writers whose poetry deserves our attention and respect. Without any doubt Reiner Kunze belongs in this category. A poet of the younger generation, he chooses to live in the Communist part of Germany identifying himself with the Marxist doctrine, however not necessarily with the government of the country in which he resides. His new volume of poetry [*Zimmerlautstärke*] is weighty, though small, containing only some forty poems, which are grouped together in four major division. Kunze's poems, with very few exceptions, all reflect in one way or another the political conditions in his country: intimidation through government officials, the monotony of the party celebrations, travel restrictions imposed on the citizenry by the government, the iron curtain, and so on. Toward Peter Huchel and Wolf Biermann, East German poets dissenting from the official party line, Kunze courageously shows his reverence in three poems. Although all poems are supposed to be spoken in *Zimmerlautstärke*, (with turned down volume) one must assume that it takes intrepidity to write and to publish them.

Kunze's style is laconic, terse and concise. He often reduces his poems to one observation followed by a very brief reflection or comment. Thus, some poems consist of only three or four lines. This extreme economy lends his verse an epigrammatic character which settles it in the familiar neighborhood of Brecht's "minimal" poems. Given the limited freedom of expression he finds in his country, Kunze's latest book of verse is a most remarkable and noteworthy document of contemporary East German poetry. (p. 139)

> *Diether H. Haenicke, in* Books Abroad *(copyright 1974 by the University of Oklahoma Press), Vol. 48, No. 1, Winter, 1974.*

ROGER GARFITT

Reiner Kunze's . . . writing is spare, outward in its address, but quick with character, with a strange blend of urgency and philosophic calm, giving very sharply the sense of a life lived, in the face of severe restraints, almost entirely out of its own vitality. . . .

Kunze is one of the wittiest critics of repressive aspects of the East German regime, and he makes some telling points against the logic of that repression. . . . At the same time, the poems make it clear that to write means to live not only with frustration, but with fear. Under these conditions, even their aims as Socialist poets suffer violence. Minimal poetry takes on a new sense, not what survives the critical process, but simply what survives. This is movingly expressed in 'Like Things Made Of Clay.' . . . (p. 107)

> *Roger Garfitt, in* London Magazine (© London Magazine *1974), June-July, 1974.*

MARTIN GREENBERG

["The Wonderful Years" is a] little collection of quiet-voiced sketches and anecdotes about the gray oppressiveness, the dead-faced brutality of life under the East German Communist régime, with its policemen and its police dogs. . . .

Reiner Kunze's book is an act of heroism. As a piece of literature it is quite modest, and modest in its manner. It is not entirely free from sentimentality about the young. Perhaps a certain delicacy it has suffers in translation; but it will not do to overpraise it. . . . How one hates the roar of publicity which envelops these heroic works. I think of the overpraised "Dr. Zhivago," of the overpraised novels of Solzhenitsyn. By all means let us praise the courage of these writers. But literary truth is important too.

> *Martin Greenberg, "Everyday Misery in East Germany," in* The New York Times Book Review (© *1977 by The New York Times Company; reprinted by permission), April 24, 1977, p. 15.*

L

LAGERKVIST, Pär   1891-1974

Lagerkvist was a Swedish poet, playwright, and novelist. Known as an Expressionist in his early days, Lagerkvist is best known for his *Barabbas*, which was one of the first novels to deal with a biblical subject in a realistic manner. Known for his spare, haunting prose style, Lagerkvist won the 1951 Nobel Prize for Literature. (See also *CLC*, Vol. 7, and *Contemporary Authors*, obituary, Vols. 49-52.)

ROGER RAMSEY

Lagerkvist has apparently called himself a "religious sceptic." His novels have a curious unfinality about them, for their characters never come to their proper reward, never gain the solace suffering is supposed to bring. In manifestly Christian fiction, the main characters seem completed by their faith, whether that faith has temporal reward or not. In explicit existential fiction, generally the protagonist achieves some sort of pride, even happiness, in his incompleteness. But for the religious sceptic, like Lagerkvist, there is neither fulfillment nor pride. Humility, very human love, tenuous community, striving—these are the "rewards" of such a world. They are universal conditions, but they are not rigidly defined. In other words, they do not congeal into dogma. In the Lagerkvist scheme of things there are no conclusions, no party lines, no givens. As near to Christian as the basic tenets are, they are not locked into doctrine. In *Barabbas,* the Christian enclave ignores and then purges Barabbas, the truer seeker. Christ himself is said to have cursed Ahasuerus in *The Death of Ahasuerus.* And the Christians in *The Dwarf* are generally materialistic and vicious beings, even sadistic in their faith. Lagerkvist consistently attacks those who are so meager of spirit that they accept the narrow word and in consequence reject the spirit of religious law. (p. 98)

As a brief against the acceptance of dogma, *The Dwarf* holds no truth as self-evident. The misapprehension of events by the dwarf serves the important literary purpose of portraying insubstantial knowledge directly; no other technique could as well have evoked the reader's dissatisfaction with answers and judgments. We cannot trust the dwarf, just as we cannot trust the evidence of this world or the "evidence" of an otherworld. . . . Like Henry James and Vladimir Nabokov in some of their fictions, Lagerkvist has created a narrator whose conclusions leave the reader ill at ease. The brilliant use of the memoir format in *The Dwarf* accomplishes the sceptical attitude in the most immediate, almost visceral way by encouraging doubt in the reader himself. In effect, the unreliable narrator *is* the meaning of the novel.

Even though the dwarf's narration veils some of the actuality in the novel, there will be agreement on a number of his characteristics: his ugliness, his misanthropy, cynicism, pride, shallowness, his love of war and of killing. The common denominator of these is not, however, undifferentiated evil, as Alrik Gustafson avers in *A History of Swedish Literature*. He states that "in many ways" the dwarf is "the very incarnation of evil," and thus far the commentators have agreed. But the dwarf is too closely drawn, too *specifically* malicious to represent all evil. Furthermore, to designate the dwarf as evil incarnate is to imply metaphysical manicheism, a rather simplistic duality which certainly would not appeal to a modern sceptical mind. *The Dwarf* is full of realistic detail unusual for Lagerkvist's novels, and the first-person narrator is also unique; the consequence of these techniques is that we may be confident of determining the dwarf's precise nature. The "evil" is really an overwhelming egoism, a selfishness raised to the highest power, an I-ness such as that touted by the existential philosopher. The dwarf denies any values outside himself; he retreats within, where fickleness, vacillation, and ephemerality have reign. His judgments begin and end in himself, referring at every instance to his own self-serving. So extreme is his egoism that he convinces himself of his authority in the court, though he obviously has none, and of the continuing reliance of the Prince on him, though he is chained in a dungeon. Since his character emanates from the vicissitudes of the "I" he is arbitrary and changeable in his opinions. He adores his Prince but turns against him bitterly; he taunts the Princess and brings about her death although he confesses his love for her; he has unlimited admiration for the leader of the mercenaries and then denounces him. The dwarf's only consistency lies in the inconstant and incontinent ego. His resources located only within himself, and those proving to be insubstantial, the dwarf's career exposes the insipid egoism of the self-ish, in effect a parody of the existential. The "evil" of the dwarf is his inversion of values. (pp. 99-100)

The dwarf's "freedom" throughout the novel is a parody of existential freedom. For Sartre, as he describes it in the famous essay, "Existentialism and Humanism," the final stage of recognition is the knowledge that each man is condemned to freedom, condemned to utter freedom of choice. This is literally true of the dwarf. But Lagerkvist asks further, who condemns man to this lonely freedom? And the answer is, man does, when and if he choses to do so. As criticism, by means of parody, of the existential position, *The Dwarf* presents the alienated hero limited in vision (the dwarf cannot see the stars which others guide by), shrunken in stature and self-serving. He is, of course, also sterile. (p. 101)

Any bridging of the existential abyss which separates people evokes his malice, for the dwarf's view of life disallows communion, sharing, being together, communication. Ironic in the portrait of the dwarf himself, *The Dwarf* here partakes of olympian irony: as a deliberate writer of his own memoirs, the dwarf is in the very process of communication. In thus sharing his experience, in the very intent of offering his life and views to others, he ridicules his own attitude and parodies every "existential" view he holds.

This is the purpose of the form of *The Dwarf*, unique in the Lagerkvist canon. It turns on itself, just as the dwarf's egoistical pretense to freedom of action in the palace and to authority is ironically subverted by his actual status. He is living a lie which he has made dogma. The existential conception of life is just as dogmatic and blind, Lagerkvist suggests, as the most canonical law of any religion, for it invents absolute premises and erects a superstructure of demands onto them. The idea of "existence before essence," first premise of existentialism, is only a possibility; "But perhaps it is not thus." But a dogmatist rushes to aver or argue. The dwarf is quick to accept the idea that "life itself can have no meaning. Otherwise it would not be." He exposes both his basic existentialism and his egoism: "Such is *my* belief" (italics his). Of course, *The Dwarf* is fiction, not a disquisitory refutation of a system of ideas. As Richard Vowles, the first appreciator of Lagerkvist in English, has said, "Lagerkvist is always the artist, seldom the philosopher." In the character of the dwarf is embodied the perversion of truth which dogmatic adherence to existential premises can cause; the novel is a warning from the north of Europe that humanistic scepticism and breadth of vision are endangered by this new dogma.

Neither is *The Dwarf* Christian apologetics. It is frustrating to hear critics and students speak of existential elements in Lagerkvist, although his early pessimism and constant subject, the isolated man, might account for this. No less erroneous is it to ascribe to Lagerkvist doctrinaire Christian principles, although the settings and spiritual questings in his novel might again lead easily to such a conclusion. It is likely that the popularity of the fiction among the general public in America has something to do with this misapprehension.... But a more acute perception of the settings shows that they suggest an atmosphere of turbulence, of conflicting loyalties and insecure commitments.... [All] of the characters are pilgrims, seekers, in the chaos of the sea.

Except the dwarf, Renaissance Italy is a superb selection of setting to invoke the spirits of feudal authority structures and of the rise of liberating humanism. The dwarf calls himself a Christian, and in a sense he is. We have seen that his misanthropic alienation is anti-Christian, in the larger sense, but his dogmatism corresponds to that of a Church at the zenith of its power.... Like the existential dogma,

religious dogma is here parodied as untrue even to itself, toadying and arbitrary. In the Lagerkvist world, rigorous execution of Church law is no less binding to the human spirit than militant egoism, and no less false at its very source. (pp. 102-03)

For a religious sceptic like Lagerkvist, even the misguided and dogmatic Church will not deter the proper religious spirit from expressing itself in the people. As always, in literature at least, this truth is discovered only after intense suffering, after war and siege and plague. Man's proud and pretentious character must bow before the ultimate mystery, wherein is located the true spirit of religion. (p. 103)

Even in *The Dwarf*, perverse and unreliable as the point of view is, we may find the positive values that inform all of Lagerkvist's fiction. Dogmatism is antithetical to the human spirit, evidenced in the cruel and severe oppressiveness of the Renaissance Church, machiavellian deviousness, and existential egoism.... In *The Dwarf*, Lagerkvist isolated a particular kind of evil, one that paralleled the groundswell of totalitarianism in politics; existentialism was as dogmatic as legalistic Christianity and power politics. All of them blind and blinker man's capacity for thought and investigation, a capacity which has as its only reward the pleasures of incompleteness, tentativeness, pursuit. This is man's lot; like Keats' lovers on the Grecian urn, Lagerkvist's heroes are forever searching, never to find, "forever panting" after truth. And this is the beauty man can achieve. Only a dwarf can convince himself that he is happy and whole. His negative example reminds us of the consequences of immediate commitment, the kind that the Pope, the Macchiavel, and the Sartre demand. No commitment is vital or vitalizing in a world ungraced by truth, and so in recognizing the evil of dogmatism, incarnated in the dwarf, we may recoil from it and take refuge in scepticism, affirmative scepticism. We may, with Bernardo, question the meaning of existence and be humble before its silence. (pp. 105-06)

Roger Ramsey, "Pär Lagerkvist: 'The Dwarf' and Dogma," in MOSAIC: A Journal for the Study of Literature and Ideas (copyright © 1972 by The University of Manitoba Press; acknowledgement of previous publication is herewith made), Vol. V, No. 3 (Spring, 1972), pp. 97-106.

IRENE SCOBBIE

Throughout most of his creative life Pär Lagerkvist has given artistic form to an inner conflict, a struggle between on the one hand a pessimistic view of life and man, and on the other a belief in man's ability to overcome the restrictions imposed upon him by life and gradually evolve into a truly spiritual being. (p. 128)

In many respects *Mariamne* (1967) reads like the antithesis of the Pilgrim trilogy, *Ahasverus död* (1960), *Pilgrim på havet* (1962) and *Det heliga landet* (1964).... [Lagerkvist shows in the Pilgrim trilogy] that it was a woman's pure and gentle love that guided Tobias to his ultimate goal. In *Mariamne* the influence of a pure and gentle woman is again shown, but the results on this occasion may appear on first reading to be little more than complete desolation.

The man with a troubled soul is this time Herod, an example of the "desert" man so often encountered in Lagerkvist's works, most notably in *Barabbas*.... Like Barabbas he inhabits geographically and metaphorically the desert bordering the Dead Sea, and like Barabbas he is wholly isolated, a captive of his own egocentricity.

Lagerkvist depicts Herod as man in his early stages of development. He is less primitive than the Dwarf, that demonic human figure physically almost as ancient as Apeman although spiritually in his infancy, but he has much in common with him. (pp. 128-29)

Herod is a man of primitive urges, a point Lagerkvist underlines in his characterization, by his references to blood and fire. (p. 129)

Lagerkvist's story deals with the point in Herod's life when he comes into contact with Mariamne, his antithesis in every respect. She is fair, gentle, fragile, sensitive and unselfish to the point where she sacrifices herself for others. . . . The fire of Herod's passion is contrasted to the cool, silvery light that radiates her whole being. If she is unable to satisfy Herod's sexual appetite, he is even less capable of fulfilling her need for gentleness and tenderness. . . . She is a representative of human goodness, an aspect of man that for Lagerkvist is the divine form that can lead man's spirit forward to some kind of eternity. (p. 130)

It is Herod's tragedy that, being confined within the wall of his own selfishness, he cannot allow his desire for Mariamne to develop into true love. Like all Lagerkvist's evil characters, he is sterile, so that even his love is converted into hatred or suspicion, and leads to isolation and death. (p. 132)

The conflict between good and evil, as enacted in the relationship between Herod and Mariamne, seems to remain unresolved, for although Herod causes Mariamne's death and reverts to his cruel, dissolute life, he can never rid himself of her strange fascination or of his memory of her, and he dies with her name on his lips. Mariamne's qualities of purity and goodness match those of the woman who loved Tobias, but Herod's death is a far cry from the peaceful scene by the sacred stream when Tobias breathed his last. An awful desolation pervades the last pages of the book, and the dying Herod's cry of 'Mariamne!' is filled with anguish.

However, if we examine the symbolic use Lagerkvist makes of his characters what emerges is not such a far cry from *Det heliga landet*. Mariamne is a secular *mater dolorosa*, through whose suffering the symbol of goodness is introduced into Herod's desert. . . . [At the sight of Mariamne mourning the death of her kinsman at the hands of Herod] Herod falls down at her feet and begs her forgiveness. His change of heart is short lived, but by her continued suffering Mariamne helps to introduce human love into the desert of the human soul. (pp. 132-33)

[A child born at the time of Mariamne's death] is given three gifts by the wise men, a pebble, a thistle shaped like a royal sceptre and a jar containing water from a miraculous spring in the desert. Here is Lagerkvist's version of the nativity, but we must remember that for Lagerkvist Christ is not the son of God but of man. He epitomizes human love and suffering, a positive force in man's spiritual evolution. (p. 133)

It seems that through the purity and the suffering of Mariamne it has been possible for Christ (i.e. the Lagerkvistian Christ) to be born into Herod's waste lands. . . . Herod

outlived Mariamne in a very limited sense, but the final message would seem to be a positive one. There will be suffering and sacrifice, admittedly, but ultimately "desert" man will be superceded by "spiritual" man. (p. 134)

> *Irene Scobbie, "An Interpretation of Lagerkvist's 'Mariamne'," in* Scandinavian Studies, *Spring, 1973, pp. 128-34.*

ROBIN FULTON

Although Pär Lagerkvist will no doubt remain best-known for his fable-like fictions, his poetry is an important part of his output and it is a pity so little has been done to make it accessible to English readers. To that extent we should welcome the British edition of *Aftonland* [*Evening Land*]. . . . As the title suggests, the awareness of approaching age is present (Lagerkvist was sixty-two) but this should not lead us to expect any simple form of resignation, for his exploration of the enigmas of God, eternity, human fate and loneliness is as probing and kaleidoscopic here as it was throughout his writing life. As Östen Sjöstrand stressed in his inaugural address as Lagerkvist's successor in the Swedish Academy, a certain inner dynamism characterizes all of Lagerkvist's work: it can be sensed behind the quietest tones and at times it can break through the wrought surface. . . .

Lagerkvist's poetry, often because of its surface simplicity, can be very resistant to translation. The worst we can do to Lagerkvist is make him appear banal—yet, given his lifelong probing of "timeless" enigmas, given his fine ear for the musicality of certain unexportable Swedish cadences, and given his reliance, in his earlier work especially, on relatively simple and at times rather four-square literary models inherited from his early pietistic environment, the trap of banality yawns wide for the unwary translator. . . .

Aftonland generally avoids . . . closed forms and [translator W. H. Auden] wisely keeps clear of acute rhyming problems. But when we look at the texture of his versions, there are many pages where lithe Swedish has become stiff English, as if Auden felt too bound by the literal versions from which he was working, so that some of the grammatical mechanics of the Swedish show through.

> *Robin Fulton, "The Eternal Enigmas," in* The Times Literary Supplement (© *Times Newspapers Ltd. (London) 1978; reproduced from* The Times Literary Supplement *by permission), March 10, 1978, p. 291.*

*   *   *

LESSING, Doris   1919-

Lessing is a British novelist, short story writer, essayist, playwright, and poet who was born in Persia and raised in Rhodesia. Her work is informed by an overriding concern for racial justice and autonomy for women in a white male-dominated society. Lessing began her career as a realist, and her early novels exhibit a fervent belief in communism, which she later renounced. Primarily a novelist, Lessing has also written some well-received short stories, many of which revolve around her African experiences. (See also *CLC*, Vols. 1, 2, 3, 6, and *Contemporary Authors*, Vols. 9-12, rev. ed.)

ROBERT S. RYF

[*Briefing For a Descent Into Hell*] seems to me to be an

important synthesis of central aspects of *The Golden Note-book* and *The Four-Gated City* and in some ways to consti-tute [Lessing's] most mature vision thus far of the ultimate nature of human experience. (p. 193)

To center initially on the question of mental disturbance is natural enough for both reviewer and reader; after all, Charles is a patient at a mental hospital throughout the novel. But to remain centered on this aspect of it, or on the related needs for understanding, compassion, and reform is, it seems to me, to miss the central import of the novel and the position it occupies in Lessing's major fiction.

Her own cryptic description of the book may have been misleading. In an interview while she was at work on it, she described it as "a mad, dreamlike book, completely differ-ent from anything I have done before."

Yes and no. Certainly it is different from her other novels in plot and in its use of several media through which to bring us the story. Yet as one moves through the book and, in particular, contemplates it afterward, one is aware of important resonances. For one thing, this novel, as do her other two major ones, stands squarely in the context of twentieth-century literature, and reflects, as do they, most of the principal concerns of the literary consciousness of our time, concerns shared, in various particulars, by most major modern novelists. The nature of the self and of con-sciousness, the gulf between inner and outer states, the emphasis on myth and archetypal patterns of experience—these are familiar enough landmarks. Additionally, the con-cerns Lessing has shown, elsewhere and here, with the dehumanizing aspects of society, with conditioning as a result of political structures, and with the consequent diffi-culties of surviving as persons, place her in the mainstream of the contemporary tradition. More particularly, her con-centration, in *Briefing,* on the nature and problem of lan-guage itself, its use as subject as well as vehicle of commu-nication, its inadequacies, the paradox of the use of language to get us beyond language, the attempt to commu-nicate what is recognized to be incommunicable, these lat-ter considerations relate her closely to such twentieth-cen-tury poets as Eliot. It is surely more than a coincidence that Charles finds himself more than once beset by Sweeney's problem: "I gotta use words when I talk to you."

But what connects *Briefing* importantly to her other two major novels, and what reflects her most mature vision, it seems to me, is the movement beyond ideology, which takes shape in the emerging opposition to and final rejection of categories, and the recognition of the primacy of expe-riential insights and values as against abstract knowledge and norms. (pp. 194-95)

[The] circularity of structure [in *Briefing For a Descent Into Hell*] embodies both good and bad news about human experience. The great cycles of moon, myth, and man are reassuring, but there is no escape from them. Indeed, a central portent of the book seems to me to be that there is no Utopia, no magic place. We must somehow make it where we are.

Structure also embodies central motifs. The theme of de-scent of course pervades the book. The descent of the gods implies the divine element of man, but it is a divinity stifled by man himself, and by his institutions. Charles, one of these descended gods, is stifled by society, here repre-sented by the hospital. We learn much later that he has

given lectures on the education of children, whose trailed clouds of glory have been quickly dissipated by schools. Whether child or man, both school and mental hospital want the same thing: docile child, tractable patient. Institu-tional messages to each correspond: to the child, sit still; to the man, cooperate.

Descent is also evident in Charles's archetypal journey through the forest, subtly analogous to that of Conrad's Marlow, penetrating the heart of darkness. It is a journey through consciousness, out of time, or back to the begin-ning of time. But time, as history, reasserts itself, and the descent becomes a deterioration as Eden-forest yields to city, and the innocence of the lone traveller to the rapa-ciousness of the meat-eaters whom he joins. It is a descent into the hell of the rat-dogs and monkeys, whose bestiality forms a circle of imprisonment around him. (p. 196)

Serving as a link between the circles of inner and outer worlds, the Crystal, perhaps a symbol for thought itself, gives occasion to his vision of unity and harmony. But the vision does not hold for long, and his descent from its heights is inevitable. And of course the white bird descends also, first to pick him up, but secondly and inevitably, to bring him back down again.

Closely associated with these themes is that of the quest. His entire journey through consciousness and time seems bent first toward Utopia, but, that never reached, toward perhaps a heightened vision of man. If as just noted, that vision does not hold for long, it does at least offer a mo-mentarily intense vista of unity, in which each infinitesimal creature "struck a note, made a whole," in cosmic har-mony "in the great singing dance, everything linked and moved together." Yet even in the midst of this moment, "that very ancient weight, the cold of grief" persists; it may be the weight of estrangement, the grief of aloneness. There is, we are reminded again, no Utopia, no collective Eden.

A major preoccupation of the novel is with language, not only as vehicle of meaning but as subject. Charles's journey is also a journey into meaning. . . . Charles, . . . even in his most disoriented state is sensitive to language and to its associative possibilities. . . . Although Charles, like Swee-ney, realizes on more than one occasion that he must use words to communicate, he is, unlike Sweeney, particularly sensitive to the sounds of the words as well. . . . (p. 197)

Charles's journey [includes an] . . . assault upon our com-pulsive attempts to compartmentalize experience. The world of ideology and structure is an either/or world; Charles, however, inhabits, at least in part, a both/and world, a realm of existence free from the strictures of closed systems. Language is such a system; if not com-pletely closed, at least relatively so. And Charles is con-scious of its limitations as a system, its inability to get at the reality that it symbolizes. "Doctor," he says, "I can't talk to you. Do you understand that? All these words you say, they fall into a gulf, they're not me or you. Not you at all. I can see you. You are a small light. But a good one. God is in you, doctor. You aren't these words." But the doctor does not understand the import of this, and gives Charles the traditional stultifying prescription: "Rest then. Lie down and rest." (p. 198)

[Language], in Charles's experience, constitutes . . . [a] barrier, and the only "meanings" that can be gotten at through its use are those circumscribed half-truths permitted by the system itself.

This recurring sense of the inadequacy of language and the system of logic which undergirds it must be seen, it seems to me, as applicable to any ideology, and it is at this point that the relationship among *The Golden Notebook, The Four-Gated City,* and *Briefing For a Descent Into Hell* emerges most clearly. In each of these three novels there is a major attack upon categories and ideology, in one form or another. In *The Golden Notebook,* the separate notebooks, representing as they do Anna's attempts to compartmentalize her life, prove to be finally inadequate, and the Anna who tends them is sterile, blocked. It is only the golden notebook, a synthesis, which is finally operative, and the golden notebook comes into being only because Anna and the American writer, Saul Green, have experienced a kind of collapse together. As Lessing has directly pointed out in her preface to the second edition of this novel, the "breakdown" which the two characters experience is in effect a breaking down of categories, a breaking down unto each other. Each is thus able to reach out and strike through to the other, and to give the other a new start as a writer. (p. 199)

[In *The Four-Gated City*] Martha's whole construct of self begins to dissolve, as she merges herself with the life around her. She becomes, in effect, a secular saint, for it is her selflessness that informs her final identity. Instead of continuing the process of constructing a self and life for her own purposes, she has been used by life for its own cryptic purposes, and our final vision is not of her immobilization but of her goodness, and, it may be, of her triumph.

It is the case that in each of these three novels, the movement beyond categories or compartmentalization is involved with mental illness or emotional collapse. I think, however, that it is a gross oversimplification to conclude that Lessing's purpose is simply to follow Laing in proclaiming that in a special sense only the insane are sane, or to mistake her clear sense of the "special knowledge" apparently available to the disturbed as her main point. Nor do I think that the eloquence of her implicit plea for understanding and compassion is quite the heart of the matter. What she seems essentially to be showing is breakdown or collapse as a desperate and agonized attempt of the self to escape those very categories or ideologies that have entrapped and fragmented it. The implication, then, is that society should not only seek to increase its understanding of its victims, but of the reductive compartments it has erected which are central causes of the victimization. (p. 200)

Charles seems to have been "cured" during the course of [*Briefing*]; he returns at the end to his post; his concluding letters seem quite "normal." Is this, then, simply the story of the triumph of psychiatry, another ideology after all, over the person? Has Charles been shriven and bereft of his visions, and returned to the constrictive world of our customary habitation? Perhaps. And yet there is, I suggest, quite another possibility, and it is at this point that we must take into account Lessing's interest in and knowledge of Sufism. This elusive and eclectic configuration of thought and belief, communicated largely through parable and aphorism, contains a number of teachings which seem to be of direct relevance to the conclusion of *Briefing.* Prime among these is the exhortation to be in this world but not of

it. It may be that this is Charles's final condition. . . . [He] might announce himself as "cured" in order to maintain his inner vision free from further assaults by society, to be operational in the "real" world while at the same time maintaining the freedom and richness of his inner life, here symbolized by his archetypal journey in all its ramifications. He might be calling into play those weapons which Stephen Dedalus proclaimed as the artist's defense against the world: silence, exile, cunning. He might, in short, be in this world but not finally of it.

This possibility gains further credibility when we recall Charles's insistence on a both/and mode of thought, rather than the either/or postulations of external reality. The both/and mode is of course more compatible with eastern than with western thought, and is thoroughly consonant with being in the world but not of it. (pp. 200-01)

In all three novels we can see an evolution beyond ideology toward existence, a recognition of the primacy of experience itself over attempts to categorize it, a conviction that abstractions ultimately give way to the on-going and inscrutable processes of life itself. Lessing is ultimately concerned with the survival of the spirit, with the hope of living compassionately in the world but not as a victim of its reductive categorizations. She affirms the possibility of maintaining untrammeled the inner life and therefore of being, even as fallible mortals in a finite world, finally, transcendently, free. (p. 201)

> *Robert S. Ryf, "Beyond Ideology: Doris Lessing's Mature Vision," in* Modern Fiction Studies *(copyright © 1975, by Purdue Research Foundation, West Lafayette, Indiana, U.S.A.), Summer, 1975, pp. 193-201.*

CELIA BETSKY

[*The Memoirs of a Survivor*] is about the future, where now the "ordinariness of the extraordinary" has taken hold. Yet in the chaos of this imagined future, in the hiatus between two eerily unspecified disasters, Lessing takes a definite, if disillusioned, stand on a number of issues she has made vital before: the lot of women, sexual relations, the problem of community, the problem of social behavior and personal morality, the price of maturity, the plight of the individual. For Lessing, this book of speculation about the years to come is an occasion for ruminating on traditional roles and assumptions. Life will go on as the world falls apart. . . .

In Lessing's future, the group mentality has spawned bands of roving teen-agers, later joined by adults, all willing to shirk responsibility for mass action and mass destruction. . . . It is rule by the horde, and terrorization, an extension of perceptions articulated in Lessing's other books. . . .

The collapse of communication is also exacerbated by the circumstances of tomorrow. Incomprehension reigns between different segments of the population, and between them and the authorities. . . . Language is the casualty in the game the narrator sees everyone playing, a charade against a hated power structure—and against themselves. The only thing shared is the premonition that some terminal event is at hand, a pall of anticipation. The fragmentation of the English language, emblematic of the class distinctions Lessing has persistently taken to task, has exploded into open hostility and class warfare. . . .

In the midst of a confused time lives a woman, Lessing's narrator. Afflicted with disorientation, she is anchored by the sudden presence of responsibility. A young girl, Emily, is one day brought to her apartment by a stranger and left there. In dealing with this child-woman's struggles, Lessing too achieves a bleak stability. (p. 184)

Having explored the poignancies of adolescence in so much of her autobiographical fiction, Lessing draws here a tragi-comic portrait of that stage, accelerated as she thinks it will be by the disturbed tempo of the times. . . . [Emily] learns from life, but that life is bankrupt. For her, responsibility is a burden, not a blessing. She is an "anachronism," with her drive to save and salvage, to help and protect others. This urge restores to her guardian a sense of humanity, as it has made of Lessing a somewhat unwilling patron saint to people (especially feminists) everywhere. Caring for others can be debilitating as well as restorative; Emily is the most recent in a long line of stoically self-destructive Lessing heroines. Watching her suffer under and give into the demands of love, the narrator sees decades of feminism contradicted and finally reversed; observing the girl's forays into the outside world, she realizes that the tyranny of the majority has usurped the place of cooperation. Lessing passes sad judgment on the future of such cherished causes as feminism and socialism. (pp. 184-85)

[Lessing's] view is entirely pessimistic. The future is the nullification of all progress; even her own work has circled back on itself, for the conditions she rejected in her childhood have grown nightmarish in the future. Lessing can envision only a mystical escape from that existence—a flight into an ambiguous paradise of annihilation. . . . Whether she is foreseeing this world or the next, Lessing leaves the "end" vague. She forces upon us the most harrowing of apocalypses: the necessity of creating out of our fears an end that we must imagine and face on our own. (p. 185)

> *Celia Betsky, "Intimations of the End," in* The Nation *(copyright 1975 by The Nation Associates, Inc.), September 6, 1975, pp. 184-85.*

RENE KUHN BRYANT

Complex character creation, spell-binding plot-spinning, delicate character interplay, bright dialogue—none of these has been regarded as Mrs. Lessing's forte in earlier novels, and *Memoirs of a Survivor,* alas, is no exception. In those earlier writings, her choice of fiction as a vehicle for her ideas seemed almost accidental and perhaps irrelevant. Her weaknesses as a novelist were beside the point since, despite them, she was an intellectually stimulating, philosophically provocative social commentator. In *Memoirs of a Survivor,* however, her indifference to the demands of fiction becomes both obvious and oppressive. Although Mrs. Lessing follows the same patterns she has traced before, the result here is nightmare rather than revelation. And the principal trouble with nightmares is that their terror and meaning, so real to the dreamer, diminish to the vanishing point in the telling.

> *Rene Kuhn Bryant, "Mrs. Lessing's Vanishing Point," in* National Review *(© National Review, Inc., 1976; 150 East 35th St., New York, N.Y. 10016), April 30, 1976, p. 462.*

ROBERTA RUBENSTEIN

[*Stories*] offers Lessing's most characteristic voices, moods, preoccupations. Stories such as "The Habit of Loving," "The Other Woman," "A Man and Two Women," "How I Finally Lost My Heart," reveal by their titles the emphasis on the remorses and dislocations of desire. The tone is never strident, often acutely ironic (though rarely humorous), as Lessing details the subtler losses attendant upon growing up, growing old, shedding the illusions of love, and confronting the limits of passion. Her "love" stories are anti-sentimental, wry vignettes that often focus on somewhat curious groupings—people who simply don't dovetail in the traditional pairings. (p. G5)

The stories in this mood yield insights into the social rituals that frame relationships between the sexes and the generations. . . .

Not all of these stories are about failures of illusion or affection. Several explore important rites of passage. . . . The singular science-fiction story, "Report on the Threatened City," conveys—through the perspective of extraterrestrial beings visiting earth to warn of catastrophe—the author's more recent apocalyptic voice, which expresses her impatience with the myopia of human beings who ignore the signs of their culture's destruction. . . .

Reading these stories, one can locate the themes and qualities that make Doris Lessing a central figure in this generation's fiction. Her oblique vision provides ironic, psychologically astute, and unsparing exposures of the social masks and false expectations governing human relationships; of the critical moments in the slow growth of emotional knowledge through experience; and of an essentially tragic, sometimes even weary sense of despair that life is so intractable. Her always credible characters, both male and female, are defined by longing, by the emotional compromises constructed to bridge the gap between illusion and actual experience.

The emotional pitch of the stories in this volume is understated but utterly persuasive. Lessing's fiction evokes neither laughter nor tears; instead, it makes you feel the blunt ache of knowledge paid for by loss that only occasionally yields solace. (p. G8)

> *Roberta Rubenstein, "Disturber of the Peace," in* Book World—The Washington Post *(© The Washington Post), May 14, 1978, pp. G5, G8.*

DIANE JOHNSON

It is not Mrs. Lessing's fault that, among the many secrets she knows, her knowledge of women's anger and aggression, even more than of their sexuality, took people by surprise and categorized her. That is the fault of our times and of history. But ["Stories"] should repair any misunderstanding of her timelessness, the breadth of her sympathy and range of her interests and, above all, the pleasures of reading her. Rereading these stories is like returning to a Victorian novel one loves, and affords the same delightful feeling of self-indulgence combined with self-improvement.

Mrs. Lessing is the great realist writer of our time, in the tradition of the major Continental novelists of the 19th century, particularly Stendhal and Balzac, but also Turgenev and Chekhov—a masculine tradition with which she shares large moral concerns, an earnest and affirmative view of human nature, and a dead-eye for social types. . . . She has remained faithful to the difficult realist esthetic (no recourse to graphics or muddle) and also to the obligation of ethical judgment, which her fictional predecessors believed to be inarguably the writer's right and duty, but which many writers since have refused. She has never been fooled into the kind of moral determinism that characterizes the resolution of much 19th-century fiction. She never confuses what should be with what is, and that is a very forbearing thing in a moralist. . . .

For dealing with the subtlest nuances of the human personality she has a style so plain it is almost affectation—has, it seems, something like disdain for figurative language, and her plainness includes the deceptively forthright way of telling a story from beginning to end with nothing left out, in the author's particular, somewhat chilly and omniscient voice. . . .

The people in her stories make their own mistakes, but it is clearly Mrs. Lessing who takes responsibility for singling them out. Hers is a real authorial presence, with the welfare of real readers in mind. . . .

Collections of stories are often praised for their variety, their range of technical effects, the versatility of the writer; and certainly Mrs. Lessing is various and versatile. But what is impressive about these stories is a cumulative coherence. They have, even as they particularize human experience, almost the gathering suspense of a novel—a novel of sensibility, about itself as much as about the nearly arbitrary (it seems) subjects whose stories the author has chosen to tell. . . .

To each of the small and great subjects—gardens, nameless grief—Mrs. Lessing brings that rarest of narrative gifts, the ability to fascinate. (p. 7)

On sex Mrs. Lessing has few equals in understanding not only desire, but the rest—boredom, disappointment, erotic fury. Perhaps vanity is at bottom her great subject, but on every subject there is a selfless, composed quality about her writing, a special combination of indignation and compassion. She uses her own life with the dispassionate relish of an evangelical after new converts to her world view, and in hers we recognize ours.

Of course, in the long run, it really isn't possible to anatomize genius. Mrs. Lessing is the great novelist of the unspoken thing, of the part a husband and wife cannot tell each other, of the mysteries that have no name and the little things people are simply reluctant to talk about—disapproval, grudges, vague longings, disappointments, the promptings of the self in all its guises. . . . [Taken] together, her work is suffused with a calm charity that reassures, heals and encourages. (pp. 7, 56)

> Diane Johnson, "Equal to the World," in The New York Times Book Review (© 1978 by The New York Times Company; reprinted by permission), June 4, 1978, pp. 7, 56.

*   *   *

LEZAMA LIMA, José   1910-1976

Lezama Lima was a Cuban poet, essayist, and novelist. A disciple of the baroque poet Góngora, Lezama Lima is best known for *Paradiso,* a complex, experimental novel about a Cuban family. His work is out of favor with the Castro regime for its rejection of revolutionary themes. (See also *CLC,* Vol. 4; and *Contemporary Authors,* obituary, Vols. 69-72.)

CLAUDIA JOAN WALLER

An exotic narration of family history, the theme of adolescent friendship, homosexualism, mythology, and world scriptures, *Paradiso* embraces what may well be Latin America's greatest literary testimony to universal man's intellectual and spiritual evolution.

Within a complex narrative of Gongoristic imagery, disguised allusions, and vague limits of external reality, the enigmatic significance and symbolic themes of *Paradiso* represent the work's greatest difficulty. A careful examination of the novel's highly philosophical content, revealing a concentrated focus on religious systems of the orient and the various symbols associated with them, led to my investigation of the eastern philosophies. An analysis of the concluding chapter of *Paradiso,* the culmination of Lezama's symbolism, revealed that many images logically corresponded to the metaphorical code and emblems of the Atma-Buddhic system. Based on the symbols of this philosophy, it is possible to recreate a symbolic spiritual journey of the protagonist, José Cemi, in his rise from the level of Natural Man to the Archetypal Man or World-soul and higher realms of Wisdom, Truth, and Love of the Atma-Buddhi (designated as "Paradise").

An examination of the rest of the novel affords the possibility of a further application of the Buddhic symbols, particularly with regard to the characters' association with and search for light and clarity, the Buddhic essential for all knowledge. If one accepts the Buddhic idea, this theme of light provides a major element of thematic unity in the novel and logically prefaces the spiritual resurrection of the protagonist to the state of higher consciousness or Paradise.

Paradiso's apparent symbolic portrayal of man's inner nature incorporates an emblematic language based on a universal code underlining the multiple systems of world scriptures. (pp. 275-76)

In *Paradiso* four metaphorical concepts emerge from the overall structure of the illumination motif, establishing thematic prefigurations of the protagonist's spiritual resurrection to the higher Self of the Atma-Buddhic planes: (1) an attempt to attain the most difficult, (2) the search for the hidden and secret, (3) the idea of completeness and unity, and (4) the concepts of a higher consciousness: happiness, Truth and Wisdom. (pp. 276-77)

Factors of symbolic illumination, represented most frequently by elements of "estrellas," "claridad," "luz," and "iluminación," are made manifest in an occult descent through three major character divisions: (1) the Cemí and Olaya families, (2) Ricardo Fronesis and Eugenio Foción, who form a triad of adolescent friendship with the protagonist, and (3) Oppiano Licario, José Cemí's mysterious spiritual guide and protector, charged to him by the Coronel.

Doña Mela, Cemí's great-grandmother, initiates a possible association of the illumination motif with the Buddhic function in a cosmic dream, the significance of which emerges from a series of symbolic elements. . . . (p. 277)

Within the Atma-Buddhic system stars are metaphorical representations of the Divine Sparks or Monads of Life (the planes of atma-buddhi-manas or Archetypal Man) which descend to the Monads of Form (the planes of manas-kama-sthula or Natural Man) to be linked with them, thus preparing to manifest their forms and qualities in the souls of humanity. . . . In Doña Mela's dream, the "estrella," an illuminating element of happiness ("para alegrar") and possible buddhic symbol of the ideal qualities, descends from the higher planes to the realm of Natural Man. The image of the star as a "balón plateado" restates its symbolization of the buddhic cosmos ("balón" [sphere] = cosmos; "plateado" = buddhic . . .). The emblematic significance of the dream (if one accepts the application of the buddhic theory) emerges as one of the novel's striking displays of the buddhic function as a thematic preface to José Cemí's final resurrection to the higher Self of the Atma-Buddhi.

Upon hearing Mela's description of the symbolic vision, Cemí's father, El Coronel, continues a possible reference to the buddhic theme in a search for light and Truth where the element of "claridad" brings forth the concept of a higher consciousness and correlates with the idea of completeness. . . . (pp. 277-78)

The Coronel's [comment] . . . attains significance within a symbolization termed the "mysteries of light," referring to the raising of the consciousness to a higher level and designating the higher nature suffused in the light of Truth, which is a mystery to the lower mind. . . . The figure of the Coronel . . . appears drawn from an exotic region of myth and ceremony ruled by light, a buddhic symbol of the essential condition of all knowledge. . . .

[The Coronel's reference to] (1) *dancing* in the (2) *light ray* represents: (1) a symbol of mental and buddhic activities exercised harmoniously and in accordance with (2) a Divine mode of functioning bringing illumination from the Spirit to the aspiring soul. . . . The Coronel thus aspires to attain the Truth and Wisdom of a higher consciousness evidenced in an apparent desire to incorporate: (1) the "mysteries of light," (2) elements of "claridad" (Wisdom) and "fuerza secreta," and (3) the exercise of mental qualities ("diálogo") in order to perfect the soul.

The premature death of the Coronel transports the theme of light to the destiny of his wife, Rialta. . . .

Rialta imparts the concepts of the higher Self to her son, José Cemí. . . . The ascent to light and Truth radiates from a superior destiny of the Cemí and Olaya families. . . . (p. 278)

The descent through the Cemí and Olaya families of a thematic search for light and clarity, conceivably representing the Atma-Buddhic concept of the higher consciousness of Truth and Wisdom, now centers primarily in the destiny of José Cemí.

The triad of adolescent friendship formed by Cemí, Ricardo Fronesis, and Eugenio Foción marks a second major division of the light motif and its direction toward the protagonist. . . . The attraction of José toward Fronesis as an ideal of light and higher qualities (Lezama states that "Fronesis" among the Egyptians signifies wisdom . . .), finds reinforcement in Cemí's relative disassociation with Foción, whose homosexual instincts place him within the depths of Hades,

symbolic of the lower nature and darkness. . . . Foción's self-destructive love for Fronesis converts the latter into a symbol of darkness. . . . The contradictory characterization of Fronesis as a symbolization of both light and darkness . . . effectively enhances Cemí's direction toward the higher qualities of the light motif. (pp. 278-79)

[Light] is most effective only when it illuminates the darkness. Cemí's "claridad" of instincts, emerging from a "confusión" of ideas characterizing the realm of Natural Man, thematically foreshadows his instinctive motivation to reach the higher planes of the Archetypes.

Cemí's last years of adolescence witness a sudden disappearance of Fronesis and Foción, . . . who are replaced mysteriously by the magical figure of Oppiano Licario. . . . Licario emerges again in the last two chapters of the novel, incarnating a key symbol within the illumination motif and Cemí's spiritual resurrection. . . .

[Licario] represents for Cemí a spiritual guide or protector in the struggle of the mental qualities to attain Wisdom and the higher consciousness. In the final chapter of *Paradiso*, seemingly impelled by the spirit of Licario, Cemí appears to undertake a symbolic journey through a surrealistic realm of light and darkness, destined to draw him to the death bed of his protector. Representing the commencement of Cemí's spiritual resurrection to the Atma-Buddhic planes, it is here that Lezama Lima reaches the epitome of symbolic expression. The prelude to Cemí's journey of light conducts him through a twilight zone of darkness. . . . (p. 279)

[In that] passage, the description of two nights, that of the stellar night, indicating a divine realm which remains to be clarified . . . , and the subterranean night, representing Hades or the Lower Nature, situates Cemí between the regions of the lower consciousness and the higher planes of the unknown. The total image evokes a symbolic presentation of the struggle of the lower emotions to attain the higher mental qualities. . . .

The appearance of the lighted house describes a possible symbolic prefiguration of the arrival of the soul on the Buddhic plane of consciousness. . . .

Cemí finally enters the house, and [is] greeted by the sister of Oppiano Licario. . . . The interassociation of Licario and the theme of light, symbolic of the Buddhic concept, culminates in its direction of José Cemí toward the attainment of what appears to be his spiritual resurrection to the higher consciousness of the Atma-Buddhi, symbolically structured in the closing passage of the novel. . . . (p. 280)

The closing image of the "Onesppiegel sonriente," a German compound meaning "without" ("one" = German "ohne"), "mirror" ("sppiegel" = German "spiegel"), or without reflection (without ego), symbolizes the realization of Cemí's spiritual resurrection: freedom from the egoism and desires of the lower nature (Natural Man) and attainment of the Archetypal Man and blissful state of consciousness on the Atma-Buddhic plane designated as "Paradise" . . . , in which the soul is suffused in Wisdom, Truth and Love.

Paradiso's narrative framework of a possible spiritual evolution based on the Atma-Buddhic system incorporates the motif of light, the Buddhic symbol of knowledge, as a major element of thematic development and coherence. . . .

The novel extends a vision far beyond the author's own troubled Cuban society. Unlike the majority of new Latin American novels today where the idea of "esperanza" remains obscured by themes of existentialism and despair, the quest of *Paradiso*'s main characters for clarity and light, and the spiritual resurrection of José Cemí to the higher consciousness of the Archetypal Man, appear to indicate a hope for the future. (p. 281)

> *Claudia Joan Waller, "José Lezama Lima's 'Paradiso': The Theme of Light and the Resurrection," in* Hispania (© *1973 The American Association of Teachers of Spanish and Portuguese, Inc.), April, 1973, pp. 275-82.*

PETER MOSCOSO-GONGORA

[The] real subject of *Paradiso* is *style*. The grouping of *hautes bourgeoises* Cuban families, their illnesses, deaths, petty preoccupations, are pegs on which to hang a series of elaborations. The triad of young sons growing to manhood, José Cemí, Fronesis, Foción, and their discovery of the subterfuges of Eros, achieves some reality, though less in their human dimensions than as a sort of chess problem. Sensuality and intellectual puzzles, character and incident, the real and the imagined whirl away in the rush of a verbal storm that wishes to concentrate on itself. The lack of stylistic demarcation between the various speakers and the narration is an indication that the aim of *Paradiso* is exaggerated artifice, not verisimilitude. Words are not transparent tools for the creation of the work, but the work itself. This poses the problem of a novel not concerned with its presumed subject, but with sustaining a lyricism of intertwining allegories, none of which is fully decipherable. One remains suspended above the story, viewing it through a prism, a bank of clouds.

With José Lezama Lima's *Paradiso* the battle will be waged between those who feel that elaboration has deracinated and dispersed the characters, the action, the static, tableau-like story, and those who feel the elaboration and story are here one and the same. But the issues will be obscure to the reader of this translation.

Lezama Lima is one of Cuba's leading poets and, one assumes, is attempting here to create a unified vision that would shatter if individual voices, characters, scenes were given a momentum of their own. The characters explain one another in lyrical accounts that establish no identity other than the fantasy of *Paradiso*. Scene flows into scene, apparently for considerations of style only. Cemí, Fronesis, Foción, conversing philosophically on the university steps, are interrupted by a bloody clash between police and students, and the narration rushes on without taking notice, without change in mood. The several deaths in the book are equally rushed through, beneath an elaboration that will not halt its pace.

"A Proust of the Caribbean," Lezama Lima has aptly been called. His erudition, the novel's breathless coda echoing *The Past Recaptured,* the recurrence of temporal images—peeling white-washed walls, white ants, empty patios, the moon, swaying lanterns, silent houses—symbols of death and resurgence, evoke Proust directly. Proust, in the opaqueness of language; in the asthma of the main character, José Cemí, and its visionary consequences; in Boldavina, the housekeeper, a chthonic Françoise, immersed in

timeless archetype. In Marcel's asparagus become Cemí's "sweet yolks." In Foción, an adolescent Charlus, and his inversion, accounted for in a manner reminiscent of the "botanical" lesson which begins *Sodome et Gomorrhe* (Foción, unlike Charlus, heading for insanity rather than longevity). In Lima's fascination with homosexuality, precisely his fascination with artifice, the self-created act, out of whimsy, petulance, simple negativity, which flies in the face of the obvious and can blatantly threaten it. Without this suspension of the laws of actuality, Lezama Lima says, art is impossible.

The animism of Proust's harmonious French countryside and the childhood room by the sea becomes a sinister animal in *Paradiso*. One feels in José Lezama Lima . . . the dichotomy between a stylized life of French cultivation, and an island teeming with the gods of the Congo, where venomous lianas creep toward the Flemish tapestries. This contradiction between the chthonic ("A Caribbean Zend-Avesta," as one of the novel's characters puts it), and a cultural refinement achieving the effete is the source of a brilliant Cuban literary renaissance.

The repeated references to Velásquez in *Paradiso* inspire the question of whether Lezama Lima might not be a painter of profound superficiality. The answer is found in the discussions of Góngora in the novel; it is on Góngora's ground that *Paradiso* ultimately succeeds. As in the case of that great poet, the obscurity vanishes when one grasps the essential intention—that the action is occurring through a shadow, in a reflection, on a tapestry.

Gongorisms abound: the verbal density and the literary conceits are Góngora through and through, as is the pretext of a story, and the erotic passages. These last have achieved a deserved renown; they sustain an astonishing balance between elaboration and subject.

Paradiso must be read as a fable. Judged as a story, it cannot be deemed a success. But even on the novel's own terms, the task of deciphering the final coda may be too much to ask of most readers. A pity. The wonder of *Paradiso* is the rediscovery of the world of words, not as a tool but as an art form in its own right. The rediscovery of an ancient and profound need, the solace of language. The novel's characters remain indistinct, philosophical arguments at loose ends. One has no idea what is occurring contemporaneously in the world outside these pages. Yet *Paradiso* triumphs as a work of pure aestheticism, of absolute digression and linguistic tour de force, in which, as with Góngora, everything is subsumed—sometimes soundly abused—in favor of the word. (pp. 600-01)

> *Peter Moscoso-Gongora, "A Proust of the Caribbean," in* The Nation *(copyright 1974 by the Nation Associates, Inc.), May 11, 1974, pp. 600-01.*

GUSTAVO PÉREZ FIRMAT

[While] there exist significant parallels between elements in [*Paradiso*] and certain symbols of Eastern philosophy, the preponderant correlative is the *Divina Commedia*, after which Lezama has patterned not only the structure of the novel but also the climactic last scene. . . .

[Cemí's] attainment of paradise entails a concomitant affirmation of his homosexuality; within the novel's symbolic corpus, this affirmation constitutes a descent to the Underworld. Unlike Dante the Pilgrim, Cemí simultaneously ascends and descends, entering Paradiso as he enters Inferno. His enigmatic polar movement can be understood as the ritual component of a process of androgynization. . . .

[Like] Dante in the *Divina Commedia*, [Cemí] is continuously a wayfarer, *un caminante*. . . . As in the *Divina Commedia*, the act of walking (Dante opens his poem with the line "Nel mezzo del cammin di nostra vita") becomes a metaphor for the spiritual journey of the soul. In the course of this journey, Cemí, like Dante, will undergo revelatory experiences which will result in a final epiphany. Like Dante, he will not be alone, but accompanied and guided by two mentors: Rialta, his mother, the "centro, justificación y fertilidad" of his existence . . . , and Oppiano Licario, the sapient and mysterious man . . . he meets in a bus.

While a comparison of Rialta and Beatrice on any except the most general grounds might, at first sight, seem anomalous, it is entirely in order. The problem posed by Rialta and Cemí's consanguinity is easily overcome if one considers that their relationship has a definite Oedipal coloring. . . . Furthermore, Dante's behavior throughout the *Divina Commedia* is that of a timid child who, at every turn, must seek his mother's advice and care. (p. 247)

With considerable simplification, Beatrice's role in the *Divina Commedia* may be described as follows: like Rialta, she is the center and justification of her protégé's existence. . . .

Rialta is also Cemí's comforter and guide and, as with Beatrice, these qualities, which are transmitted *sub specie lucis*, reside in her eyes and in her smile. (p. 248)

Like Beatrice, Rialta is depicted as an incorporeal being who obeys a higher calling. . . . Similar to Beatrice's constant encouragement of Dante is Rialta's advice to Cemí that he should attempt the most difficult. . . . In each case, the ultimate goal is a vision of eternity.

Similar parallels can be established between Virgil and Oppiano Licario. Dante is entrusted into Virgil's care by Beatrice. . . . Cemí's father, El Coronel, recommends his son to Licario in like manner. . . . Subsequently, Dante meets Virgil at nightfall when, in the middle of his journey through life, Dante has strayed from the true path. . . . Cemí also meets Licario at nightfall. . . . Both Virgil and Licario are poets and, within each work, they symbolize knowledge and reason. (pp. 248-49)

When the [last scene of *Paradiso*] opens, Cemí is walking in a "noche verdosa sombría," burdened with "un temor incipiente." . . . He sees an illuminated house which lures him, but, before reaching it, he crosses an amusement park and a forest. As the *Divina Commedia* begins, Dante is wandering inside a dark wood when he sees a "pleasant mountain." . . . [The] house in Lezama's novel is a symbol of Paradise, and the amusement park and the forest, of Hell and Purgatory respectively. Cemí, like Dante, must first pass through Inferno and Purgatorio before he can climb to Paradiso. (p. 249)

Like Charon, [the old man who guards the amusement park] is white-haired . . . , dresses sloppily and possesses a repugnant appearance. . . . Just as Charon will receive into his boat only those who have the passage money, the old man will admit into the park only those who have paid for the rides. . . . The machines inside the amusement park are also depicted as Hellish contraptions. . . . (pp. 249-50)

Having crossed the amusement park, Cemí's advance becomes increasingly difficult. . . . He is now passing through Purgatory. Like Dante's, his toilsome progress is hampered by the fog which, in the *Purgatorio*, is so thick that it prevents one's eyes from opening. . . . While Dante is on the Fifth Terrace of Purgatory he feels a tremor that shakes the entire mountain. . . . The [trembling] that Cemí feels, then, is an indication that he is ready to ascend to the Earthly Paradise and, from there, to the Heavens. . . .

Once he has progressed through Hell and Purgatory, Cemí enters Paradise, represented in the novel by the house. . . . Like Dante's Paradise, its outstanding characteristic is its luminescence. . . . Even the conceptualization of paradise as a house may be said to be Dantean, since the *Paradiso* is modeled on the theological concept of the Mansions of Beatitude. (p. 250)

Inside the house, Cemí gradually ascends by a stairway. The mention of an "escalera" . . . is once again reminiscent of Dante's poem, where the ladder of Jacob appears leading from the Seventh Sphere to the Empyrean. . . . On the topmost floor he notices a room which emits an inordinate amount of light. . . . Cemí has achieved the beatific vision. The image which Lezama employs is identical to that which appears in the *Divina Commedia*: the whirling motion of luminous circles around an invisible point which is God. . . . Like Dante, Cemí has progressed from the darkness to the light, from the "noche sombría" to the "fiesta de luz." . . . (pp. 250-51)

But Lezama's cosmology is not as homogenously structured as Dante's. There are no visible boundaries dividing the realms of the Other World. . . . This ambiguity points to an essential structuring principle of *Paradiso*: the intricate web of heliotropic imagery is counterpoised by an equally intricate network of geotropic images. His Dantean ascent notwithstanding, Cemí is the focal point of this network of geotropic imagery, by means of which his homosexuality becomes evident. . . .

[One] of the principal themes of *Paradiso*, the definition of Cemí's sexuality, unfolds on a mental and figurative level. The novel, as it follows Cemí from childhood through adolescence and into young adulthood, documents and delineates his sexual crisis, one which will be resolved symbolically in the last scene.

The attitude of José Cemí toward homosexuality is equivocal. (p. 251)

The psychoanalytic background of Cemí's sexual ambivalence is well-defined. . . . Cemí, a frail and asthmatic child, is resented by his father, a colonel in the artillery corps who considers his son's ailment a mark of shame. . . . [On one occasion] the Coronel, exasperated by his son's asthma, tries to effect a cure by immersing him in a tub of icy water. When Cemí begins to turn blue, his mother, Rialta, revives him with "fricciones de alcohol." Typically, in this situation it is the father who inflicts the pain and the mother who soothes.

Cemí's family constellation is illustrated by a dream he experiences the night following the bath. . . . This dream enacts the ultimate consequences of Cemí's Oedipal fixation: the desire to copulate with his mother. . . . The dream ends with the transfiguration of Rialta, which serves a double purpose: it shows Cemí's quasi-religious adoration for his mother and it allows him to avoid guilt-feelings by removing his affections to a neutral object.

As the novel progresses, Cemí becomes conscious of his homosexual tendencies. . . . [Throughout] the novel homosexuality is equated with descent. In order to describe the sodomitic union of Baena Albornoz and Leregas, Lezama —borrowing a motif from one of Verne's novels—compares their copulation to a voyage to the center of the earth. . . . Anal intercourse, then, consists of the union of the shadow and the crater and the subsequent descent. This imagery occurs repeatedly. . . . [The] network of geotropic images is also linked with Rialta. In the aforementioned dream Cemí sees in the floor of the ocean "un boquete infernal . . . *que parecía buscar el centro de la tierra*" (italics added . . .). When he nears the "boquete" he discovers the smiling face of his mother. . . . Expression and etiology coalesce; appropriately, the symbol of homosexuality is associated with its principal cause.

With this imagery in mind, the significance of Cemí's encounter with Foción becomes evident. The latter's avernal feast . . . represents the homosexual alternative which Cemí must accept . . . ; otherwise, his sexual deviance will still surface, but on "tierra apesadumbrada."

The conclusive *auto da fé* takes place in the last scene of the novel. Cemí, accosted by several doubts, is walking uncertainly in the night. . . . As he walks along he feels two different nights: one, a phallic subterranean night . . . ; the other, an astral night. . . . These two nights represent the contending forces in Cemí's personality. The "noche subterránea," which descends as it spins a web around Cemí's genitalia, embodies his homosexual urges; the "noche estelar," his tendency to repress these urges. The struggle between these two forces constitutes the leitmotif for this scene and is sustained throughout.

While still under the influence of the two nights, Cemí sees the house which stands out in the dark like "un bloque de luz" [a block of light]. . . . The house, which in the previous section was seen as a figuration of paradise, may also be interpreted as a hypostasis of Cemí's turbulent sexual consciousness: it is both luminous and geotropic. . . . (pp. 251-54)

In the last paragraph of the novel, after Cemí has left the house, the narrator comments (italics added): "Lo acompañaba la sensación fría de la madrugada *al descender a las profundidades, al centro de la tierra* donde se encontraría con Onesppiegel sonriente" [The cold sensation of the dawn accompanied him *in the descent into the depths, to the center of the earth* where he would meet with the smiling Onesppiegel]. . . . Cemí's development culminates with this statement, which places him definitely within the novel's network of homosexual behavior, at the same time recalling his fixation on Rialta, who in the dream was seen smiling from the center of the earth. Cemí's realization is substantiated by the fact that as he enters a cafeteria he hears a tinkling which brings to his mind the "ritmo hesicástico." As Oppiano Licario explains, hesicastic rhythm denotes "equilibrio anímico" [psychic equilibrium]. . . .

Foción, during his discussions with Fronesis and Cemí, contends that primeval man was an androgyne and that the differentiation of the sexes did not occur until later, being reinforced through "un posible error por la costumbre" [a possible error on the part of custom]. . . . (p. 254)

Interpreted in this light, Cemí's homosexuality can be considered a conscious regression to an androgynous past (or a projection into a postulated androgynous future) directed toward recovering (or attaining) paradise. His descent to the center of the world *becomes* his ascent to Paradise. This interpretation is supported by the fact that throughout the novel homosexuality and androgyny are identified. . . . It is further supported by the erotic suggestiveness of the house which assumes both heliotropic and geotropic qualities, that is to say, which embodies both Paradiso and Inferno. (pp. 254-55)

[Myths] of androgyny reflect man's need to see the cosmos as a totality, a Grand Unity, a sphere, a cosmic egg, a One. On a human level, the primal man is envisaged as possessing both sexes, as being, like the cosmos, undifferentiated and self-sustaining. Cemí's twin trajectory is an attempt to regain this primordial totality by, once again, co-joining heaven and earth, ascent and descent, light and darkness. This juncture of opposites effectively accomplishes Cemí's transfiguration into an androgyne. . . .

Both of these interpretations, which share as an axis the concept of androgyny, are upheld by a reading of the final paragraphs of the last scene. Having ended his journey through the night, Cemí [has a vision]. . . .

[This] vision comes together as an exteriorization of the process of androgynization which Cemí is undergoing. The tiger revolving around the fire represents the fusion of the female and male principles, of the vagina and the phallus. Indeed, the image suggested is that of a phallus projecting out of a vagina. The flames and the tiger are, in turn, each aspiring toward the One: the flames reach toward the celestial embryo; the tiger licks the medulla. Once the fusion has been achieved, Cemí's mind becomes the mirror of the Taoists in which the distinction male-female is obliterated: the fire has been quenched by the fountain; the white tiger continues its revolutions, but choked by its own tail. Licario's words . . . provide the cipher with which to unravel the complicated structure of *Paradiso*: Cemí does rise and descend, and in so doing comes to know the celestial egg, Taoist conception of the primordial unity of the universe. (p. 255)

Gustavo Pérez Firmat, "Descent into 'Paradiso': A Study of Heaven and Homosexuality," in Hispania (© 1976 The American Association of Teachers of Spanish and Portuguese, Inc.), May, 1976, pp. 247-57.*

ROBERT MARTIN ADAMS

[The] polyphlusboious richness of *Paradiso* is to be sensed on every page; it may be chiefly a verbal phenomenon, but that's far from implying a sense of impoverishment. Like Joyce, Lezama has a gift for mingling the obscene with the erudite, for phantasmagorizing gobbets of realistic detail, for deep-plowing the subconscious. The various miscellaneous ingredients of the fiction are never held under such strict control that one can't envision them exploding or spiraling off into separate nebulae. From the beginning, it's an anxious, a high-tension performance; and after the disappearance from the book of Fronesis and Foción (abrupt and inconclusive, hardly mitigated at all), the orbits widen still further, the narrative chunks whirl through vaster and more evident distances of empty space. Characters become detached from their surroundings, their names, the laws of nature, even from a consistent set of pronominal references (*he* and *we* are particularly apt to get interchanged), and the prose becomes even more remotely metaphorical, more fragmented syntactically, than before.... Actually, the final pages come close to being disembodied writing—image generating image, as in a poem by Yeats, without explicit reference to a hypothetical speaker or even an ostensible subject.

In this liberation of language to its own inner energies, Lezama surely represents the fulfillment of a major Joycean potential, one that we're more likely to associate with the *Wake* than with the *Portrait;* one, too, that transcends all questions of influence and even inspiration, but can only be intimated under the loose formula of affinity. One doesn't pass very confident judgment on a novel such large parts of which are, and are likely to remain permanently, indigestible; but there's enough fascination in *Paradiso*, even for a relatively uninformed reader, to give it a major place among the books that have fulfilled and extended lines that Joyce first began to trace. (pp. 183-84)

> *Robert Martin Adams, in his* AfterJoyce: Studies in Fiction After "Ulysses" *(copyright © 1977 by Robert Martin Adams; reprinted by permission of Oxford University Press, Inc.), Oxford University Press, 1977.*

M

MacNEICE, (Frederick) Louis   1907-1963

An Irish-born English poet, critic, translator, playwright, radio scriptwriter, and novelist, MacNeice was connected with the left-wing literary movement of Auden and his circle in the 1930s. He was much praised for the fine sensory and visual qualities of his poems. (See also _CLC_, Vols. 1, 4.)

T. BROWN

MacNeice's interest in allegory and dream is most developed in his series of Clark lectures which comprise _Varieties of Parable_. This work is a broad survey of allegorical writing in English. A sensitive book, perhaps its most interesting aspect is its treatment of modern allegory, since this throws light on some of the poet's own experiments in the form.... MacNeice sees allegory as the exploration of an image, the creation of a 'special world' with a relationship of meaning to the real. Traditionally this relationship was fairly simple—image embodied concepts familiar to most readers, while the image was comprehensible to them since it received its significance from cultural authority, as, for instance, Bunyan's imaginative world in _Pilgrim's Progress_ depends for its meaning upon the received cultural and doctrinal traditions of Puritan religion. With cultural pluralism the situation, as MacNeice sees it, becomes much more complex. Allegory and parable become much less didactically clear, since the poet has no accepted tradition of concepts and related imagery within which he can work.... By comparison with traditional allegory the modern parable is ambiguous, obscure. Its relationship with reality is conceptually vague.... The meaning of modern parable, the structuring and ordering of the work is, according to [MacNeice's] view, implicit within the work itself, not imposed upon it from beyond itself. The meaning is not imposed from without, by a necessarily ordered, meaningful reality, or by an intellectual system. The writer of a modern parable explores an image, creates a special world, self-consistent, yet tantalizingly without simple conceptual meaning. His 'conceit' is indeed a 'dark' one.

Throughout MacNeice's poetic career and particularly since about 1940, poems appear which have to be understood [as MacNeice suggests we understand the modern parable].... They explore an image that ambiguously suggests a relationship of meaning to our world, but they do not make it explicit.... [In 'Order to View', for example,

there is] a peculiarly unreal atmosphere. There is a strange fusion between subjective and objective experience as there is in a trance or delirium.... It is a special landscape, an image explored, a new disturbing world which we must attempt to interpret. Another poem of this semi-allegorical nature is 'The rest house'. This also opens in a haunting, dreamlike landscape: 'The thick night fell, the folding table unfolded ...' The scene is nightmarishly alive, objects have an unpleasant, spontaneous life of their own. The description which follows: 'The hissing lamp had hypnotised the lizards / That splayed their baby hands on the wired window.' is particularly suggestive of nightmare experience. This seems to be no natural landscape, but an inner imaginative world. (pp. 18-20)

In MacNeice's later poems, such interior, mental landscapes and dream experiences become more frequent—perhaps as his interest in parable became greater. One of the best of these poems is 'After the crash'. The first stanza of this perplexing poem moves with the assured illogic of a dream:

> When he came to he knew
> Time must have passed because
> The asphalt was high with hemlock ...

But in the dreamworld we accept such logic without quibble. The last stanza suggests an allegorical vision of judgement, but its meaning remains unstated and ambiguous.... Yet the poem, although conceptually inexplicable in any fully satisfying way, has a haunting, memorable power. Oblique and ambiguous, the irreducible image fixes gruesomely in the mind.... [In] 'After the crash' ... we feel that the nightmare world tells us something of our own. We live after a crash, after some cosmic catastrophe.... Overhead are the gigantic scales of judgement, ominous in the dead calm. We live after the fall, and for this we are to be judged and found wanting. But we must not overinterpret. The poem may be an allegory of original sin and judgement, or it may not. The image is explored by the poet in the hope that it will by an indirect means reveal some truth which no simpler approach could discover. Yet the poem in its ambiguity resists all rational explanation. It is a modern parable of the variety MacNeice identified in his lectures at Cambridge.

Yet MacNeice, in areas where cultural concensus still exists, was perfectly capable of writing convincing traditional allegories. Some of the best of his late poems are of this kind [although some of these attempts must be adjudged failures]. The discovery of Romantic love is a theme MacNeice treats allegorically with some success. 'The Burnt Bridge' is an assured, economical and convincing allegory of a traditional kind. The hero, in a dream landscape, journeys to find a 'shining lady' (surely suggested by the Shining Ones of *Pilgrim's Progress*).... Not every image in the poem of course has a conceptual correlative. Much of the detail, as in Bunyan, provides imaginative flesh to the allegorical skeleton. The hero moves through a mysterious landscape where the feared dragon dwells in a creaking wood until he, against all odds, meets his shining lady and they walk hand in hand by the side 'Of the sea that leads to nowhere . . .'. Love in our world must be striven for against great odds, but once discovered our life achieves its spiritual dimension, partakes of mystery. (pp. 20-3)

MacNeice in his late poetry also demonstrates his ability to write convincing short semi-allegorical poems, when he organizes them round a central motif or ikon.... The effect of these poems is related to the fact that he uses traditional imagery and iconography deeply engrained even in our fragmented culture. The poems communicate without explanation. 'The tree of guilt' is an allegorical presentation of the well-known fact that we pay for our weaknesses. At times of self-indulgence the tree of guilt (obviously suggestive of the tree in Eden which wrought our fall) seems lush and green, utterly without danger; but time passes for the hero:

> Till he finds later, waking cold
> The leaves fallen, himself old
> And his carved heart, though vastly grown,
> Not recognisably his own.

Another poem which is very similar in technique is 'The habits'. This uses the motif of the ages of man. In each stanza enervating habits enter like allegorical personifications of the vices in a medieval morality play; they tempt and destroy the hero.... Each stanza is a dramatic representation of temptations appropriate to particular stages of life—games, bonhomie, woman, and alcohol—until in the last stanza 'Everyman' (for this is what the simple 'he' suggests) is left with nothing but death. The poem is extraordinarily effective, with its dark, sombre tone and trenchant honesty. A traditional allegory in technique, it proves the genre to be a living form in modern verse. MacNeice, when he died, was perfecting this kind of poem, and from a passage in *Varieties of Parable* we know that this was the realm he wished to continue to explore. . . . (pp. 23-4)

> T. Brown, "Louis MacNeice and the 'Dark Conceit'," in Ariel (© A. Norman Jeffares and the University of Calgary, 1972), October, 1972, pp. 16-24.

WILLIAM T. McKINNON

'The Pale Panther' is one of the 'thumbnail nightmares', as MacNeice called them, in his last collection, *The Burning Perch*. It is not only one of the most terrible of the nightmares, but also one in which the mood of bleak despair is not balanced by any of his old sardonic optimism (though there is bitter wit), or any of the stoical determination of, say, his last-published poem, 'Thalassa', with its courageous message:

> Our end is Life. Put out to sea.

Our end is anything but Life in 'The Pale Panther'. Worse, it is not even Death.

MacNeice confessed he was 'taken aback by the high proportion of sombre pieces' in this collection, but could only say that 'they happened'.... If he was the spokesman for the '30's in ['An Eclogue for Christmas'], he was no less the spokesman for the '60's in 'The Pale Panther' and similar poems. (pp. 388-89)

I should like to glance at a useful comment of MacNeice's about what he called the 'properties' and the 'images' in a poem, especially in relation to their symbolic role, since the word 'image' has been upsetting some people almost as much as the word 'symbol'. In his chapter on imagery in *Modern Poetry* he wrote:

> The properties are the objects which enter a poem by their own right, as flowers enter a poem about a garden, whereas the images enter a poem by right of analogy, as flowers entered Plato's descriptions of his mystical and abstract Heaven. But, conversely, the properties themselves may be, in the ultimate analysis, only symbols. Was, for example, Wordsworth's celandine really all celandine and nothing but celandine?

Now, in 'Experiences with Images' MacNeice warned that in some of his poems the images 'carry the weight of dream or of too direct an experience', and so 'will require from the reader something more—or less—than reason'. As 'The Pale Panther' is obviously very much a poem of this kind, where property and image merge into each other, and celandine is anything but just celandine, I hope I may use expressions like 'image', 'symbol' or 'emblem' without arousing hostility.

There is no image in this poem that is not pulling its load of double meaning. Several of these are favourite emblems of MacNeice's in contexts where he is dealing with similar themes. The poem is dominated, for instance, not by the pale panther and its death-spring so much as by the sun, that Heraclitean emblem of renewal, so dear to MacNeice from the start. (One must of course assume, though in emblematic rather than strictly visual terms, that the sun *is* the pale panther.) Above the elaborate interplay of images hangs the sun—pale and lifeless in the first stanza, the morning sun of a 'late and lamented / Spring', too weak and too late to renew the present dying cycle of creation; blazing at noon in the second stanza, but in a blaze of death, stirring to life only the death-dealing microbes; low on the horizon in the third, casting the long shadows of evening, not giving enough light to continue play. Thus it binds the poem, in terms both of structure and theme.

The sun not only dominates the poem, but is integrally connected with almost all the other images.... The untamable black panther had already represented elsewhere 'the brute Other', uncontrollable destiny, as he explained in 'Experiences with Images'. In 'Coal and Fire', in his first collection, *Blind Fireworks*, it was a 'coal-black sphinx', identified both with the blazing flames and with riddling, inscrutable destiny; and in 'Homage to Clichés' it was dreaded as the irresistible, impending movement of fate. MacNeice's mood in these poems was, in the first, excited acceptance of destiny and its puzzle, and, in the second, awe and dread, mingled with a thrill of apprehension. Now that the panther has made its threatened spring, it seems to have become, like the sun, old and weak. . . . The prevailing mood in the first stanza is 'too late': destiny should have struck sooner, when we were fit for death, before we had declined to the bleak, dim end of our generative cycle. This is the sense in which, in 'After the Crash', it was 'too late to die', and in which, in 'Charon', the ferryman said coldly, 'If you want to die you will have to pay for it'. (pp. 389-91)

This first landscape has the wavering physical aspect of a modern zoo, but its property/images, the ribs (of the cages), the giraffe-necked lamp posts, the (animal) excrement, the discarded newspapers, the tiny tractor, the fence (electrified or not), might just as well be the features of any unspecific industrial conurbation, or, more specifically, airport, or defence installation. They are the endlessly adaptable, because undifferentiated and colourless (even if, in the case of the electric fence, restrictive and forbidding) features of the landscape in which modern man, and the animal creation he dominates and corrupts, have their being. (pp. 391-92)

The cause of the slow-down, and then the full-stop, in our cycle of creation that MacNeice tirelessly emphasized was the familiar one that we have sought knowledge without understanding. There is no wisdom behind our technological skill, which is, moreover, quite unreliable as a skill: the stalled engine, caused by incompetent or absent-minded manipulation, is also used in other poems—for instance 'Hold-Up'—to symbolize the involuntary full-stop. It is, for MacNeice, the end of a process that goes back at least as far as an uncollected poem 'Utopia'. . . . The spark is now extinguished. Nor is there any wisdom to be found in the newsprint over which we bend blindly or myopically. Linked here, in syllepsis, with excrement, it is one of MacNeice's routine symbols for the merely phenomenal, as, for example, in 'The Stygian Banks', where 'the end of the news' is 'the beginning of wisdom'. Our spiritual myopia is the very cause of our spiritual death. Nor, as he constantly stressed in the later poems, is there any more hope for animal instinct than for human will. Elsewhere, however, it is generally the confinement (here symbolized by the electric fence) or the perversion of animal instinct that is the evil; but now the animal is struck down along with the man. The full-stop is complete.

The rapid cut to the image of the milkman and the empties develops, with appropriate switch in tone, the theme of the first stanza, on a new note of bitterness. The milkman appears to be a savagely banal version of MacNeice's dreaded Charon figure, and we are the empties to be collected. . . . While I agree [with Auden] that judgement—not necessarily the last—is an important part of the theme, I still think the overall theme [of 'The Stygian Banks'] is failed renewal; as in the whole group of poems in *The Burning Perch* to which it belongs. The implied cry is surely the one he makes in 'Spring Cleaning': 'Let someone soon make all things new'.) A relevant gloss on the empties jiving in the sun is provided by MacNeice himself in the early 'Ode', where he says that 'bottled time turns sour upon the sill' (which in the holograph draft was even closer to the later image as: 'bottled time left out in the sun on the step is . . .'). The whole image, indeed, seems to be a deliberate contradiction of his extravagant optimism at the end of Canto XXV of *Autumn Sequel,* where 'a new sun is rising'

as 'the pails / / Ring with the new day's milk'. There follows an abrupt, but quite congruous, cut to the airport, with its 'Runways in rut, control / Towers out of touch', which thematically continues the warning to milkman, now airman, Charon of the consequences of delay. This theme, too, has been recurrent in the later poems, with many emblematic variations suggestive of lost control. There is also powerful ambiguity in 'rut', which personifies as stags grown savage in rut the rutted runways of a waterlogged airport, such as he may have seen in West Africa. It is on a level of Düreresque macabre with the empties jiving on the steps. . . . As we are the empties jiving on the steps, whose bottled time has turned sour, so we are also the 'broken test tubes', whose search for knowledge without understanding has led away from life. We are also 'shards / Of caddis', the discarded remains of the mayfly that has already flown and enjoyed, in the words of the early 'Mayfly', 'One only day of May alive beneath the sun'. The mayfly, which 'Goes up and down in the lift so many times for fun', was a favourite Heraclitean emblem of MacNeice's for the constant upwards and downwards movement, for glad acceptance of the life of the moment in the endless cycles of creation. (pp. 392-94)

The final landscape of the golf course green in shadow is connected with the opening one by the tiny tractor that stalled when failing light stopped play. The tiny tractor pulling the mower is a familiar feature of the golf course landscape, which he uses elsewhere as an emblem for the merely temporal. . . . Life played in terms of a game was one of his recurrent delusions, which he latterly rejected. . . . And the stalled engine, as we noted, symbolizes incompetent, involuntary stoppage, caused by removing foot pressure when the engine is still in gear—upward and downward gear changing being another of his emblems for Heraclitean upwards and downwards movement. (p. 394)

[The warning that it is 'too soon / To order replacements' for the empties] is in fact the crux both of the poem and of our metaphysical predicament, the culminating agony. The new cycle of creation does not begin immediately the death-blow is struck. There must be an interval of decay and disintegration before the empties are finally disposed of, and the replacements may then be ordered, the new cycle begin. It is in this interval we are now living. Hence the despairing appeal, both in this poem and in several of the other best and most moving in the collection, to 'someone' finally to sweep away the broken vestiges of the old and 'make all things new'. Hence, too, the stoical encouragement of 'Thalassa', in whose timeless perspective 'late' and 'soon' are One.

Although MacNeice considered that the successful lyric is 'above all, symbolic', he certainly did not neglect the other two features, the dramatic and ironic. By these he meant that the lyric should be a monodrama, with the lyric poet alone on the stage, deliberately choosing his tone of voice, but indicating by appropriate changes of mood, diction, imagery the presence of a latent content. It is clear that MacNeice is alone on the stage here, speaking a dramatic-descriptive prelude in the first stanza, and directly addressing two symbolic figures in the second and third. (p. 395)

MacNeice noted that in many of the poems in *The Burning Perch* there was 'a conscious attempt to suggest Horatian rhythms', as the formal counterpart of his mood of 'Horatian resignation', and an effort to 'get out of the "iambic" groove which we were all born into'. Thus his natural tones, suitably dramatized and varied, are superimposed on the formal metric of the poem in a well-modulated counterpoint. (p. 396)

Although there is no system of end-rhyme, there is some near rhyme, ghost rhyme, half-rhyme and assonance, both end and internal (bent/print, sun/burns, soon/green, runways/rut, shards/caddis), and an elaborate pattern of alliteration. Repetition is also used, both as a binding and an emphasizing device ('your empties', 'tractor stalled', 'play'). He uses enjambment to the same end, notably in the 'lamented/Spring' at the beginning, and the 'tractor/Stalled' at the end. The relevance of all this sound effect to the theme is obvious, suggesting as it does a very tenuous and sporadic order of unity and the menacing finality of another and a different order.

MacNeice's own description of the relation between form and content in these poems could not be bettered:

> When I say that these poems 'happened', I mean among other things that they found their own form. By this I do not, of course, mean that the form was uncontrolled: some poems chose fairly rigid patterns and some poems loose ones but, once a poem had chosen its form, I naturally worked to mould it to it.

He 'naturally worked'. Indeed he did, with a force of imaginative insight and a shaping command over it that have been undervalued for quite long enough. Yet, when all is said, MacNeice did well to stress the importance of the symbolic aspect. It was, we remember, Aristotle's axiom that command of metaphor is the real mark of poetic genius, as it was Coleridge's that one of the basic qualities of the creative imagination is its power of dissociating the normal image connections, subordinating them to cohere in a new and startling unity. This is the power that mainly characterizes the best of MacNeice's late poems, such as 'The Pale Panther', and it is the power that will probably have to be decisive in slowly raising his reputation from the dreary flats of taken-for-granted where it still seems incredibly to languish. (pp. 396-97)

> *William T. McKinnon, "MacNeice's 'Pale Panther': An Exercise in Dream Logic," in* Essays in Criticism, *October, 1973, pp. 388-98.*

SAMUEL HYNES

MacNeice had always been the least political writer of his generation, and his play [*Out of the Picture*] articulates a mood of the time unaffected by political ideas. The main plot-line concerns an indigent painter named Portright, whose only completed picture, 'Venus Rising', is seized by bailiffs for debts and auctioned off to a film star. Portright represents the artist and the individualist, and his painting, and Moll, the model for it, stand for art, love, and life. The film star and her psychoanalyst-adviser are the other side—society's parasitical life-deniers, the locus of money and power.

In these terms the play is simply another version (rather a conventional one) of the relationship of the artist to modern society. But it contains another theme that is of equal importance and of greater originality. The play begins with a

news announcement of the failure of a peace conference, and as the action unfolds war is 'about to be declared', and then is declared; Paris is bombed, and the play ends in an air-raid on London. Portright, in a fit of rage, shoots the Minister of Peace who has precipitated the country into war, and is then poisoned by Moll to save him from prison or the army.

It is not a very good play. . . . Nevertheless, it has two interesting aspects. The first is the way in which MacNeice treats war. War enters the play in two forms: as announcements on the radio, and as a Minister of Peace. The first gives to war a remote, invisible, but imminent power that is beyond human resistance; the second gives to government the same sort of power, for the same sort of destruction. There are no soldiers in the play, no armies, and no political issues; there is only war itself, approaching like a pestilence. When it comes, it comes first as news of destruction elsewhere . . . and in the final scene as an air-raid on stage. The destruction is not done by visible hands or for any expressed cause; it is simply destruction, which cannot be opposed or altered. What occurs is not so much the beginning of a war as the end of a civilization. . . . (pp. 293-95)

What is lost, as war comes, is commonplace reality, the pleasures of simply living. MacNeice had always been a celebrant of ordinary things; his self-proclaimed role of common man was a kind of substitute for political commitment, a way of being apolitical with a good heart. 'I am all against the rarefying effects of good taste,' he said. . . . This love of commonplace, particular life appears in the play in an elegiac naming of things that will be lost in the world of war. . . . It is that sense of what is coming—the Apocalypse that will transform life or destroy it—that makes *Out of the Picture* so much a parable of its moment, a sad, bitter, passive goodbye to all that. (p. 295)

Modern Poetry is an 'education in the 'twenties', and an explanation of how the 'thirties generation evolved. MacNeice's account is less self-centred than [*Lions and Shadows, The Road to Wigan Pier*, and *Enemies of Promise*], for though he was a sentimental man, he was also a reticent one, but it is nonetheless an important part of the record. His very sentimentalism is the source of one kind of value that the book has; for he was able to step back from himself and to describe the sentimental bases of his generation's attitudes. (p. 332)

Of the poets of his generation, MacNeice was the most isolated, and the least political. He was never involved in movements, and he remained outside the political-literary cohorts of the period. . . . Living in the time that he did, he accepted left politics as necessary, but commitment went against his nature. . . . He was, he cheerfully admitted, a snob; but then, so was everyone else. 'All the people I know,' he wrote, 'have been conditioned by snobbery.' The people he knew were mainly his own generation, and this is a generalization about the whole lot; the only difference was that MacNeice accepted his snobbery, and so found it easy to confess it. But his vestigial class feelings, and his political unease must have been shared by many of his contemporaries.

MacNeice published four books in 1938—*Modern Poetry, I Crossed the Minch,* a book on the London Zoo, and *The Earth Compels,* a volume of poems. All are to some degree autobiographical, and all are touched by the same strains—

his nostalgia, his melancholy sense of the present, his apprehensiveness about the future. The world that he wanted was a world of ordinary pleasures, suited to the ordinary, sensuous man-in-the-street that he liked to imagine he himself was, and wished all poets would be. . . . But he did not expect to find that world in the near future; he expected a crisis that would silence the poetry and suspend the pleasures. Until that crisis came he would go on writing poetry, but the poetry that he wrote was autumnal and melancholy. Some of this quality was no doubt the tone of the professional lachrymose Irishman; but it was also the tone of the time, of living in the late 'thirties. (pp. 333-34)

[Even] in times of crisis the private life goes on, and MacNeice's achievement in his poem [*Autumn Journal*] was to interweave the constituent part of his life, and to show how those parts acted upon each other: how the past affected his responses to the present, and how the present forced him to judge the past; how the public world invaded private life, and how private losses coloured his attitude toward public crises. It is a poignant last example of that insistent 'thirties theme, the interpenetration of public and private worlds.

The poem takes its primary structure from the chronology of public events. . . . But there is also another chronology, less causal and less consequential—the sequence of private occasions and private feelings of a man living an ordinary lonely life. In less critical times one might expect that these two chronologies would exist separately—what have politicians to do with a man's loneliness?—but in the autumn of 1938 they intermingle, seem to become analogies of each other. MacNeice is very good on this relationship; he was always a poet of private living, but in this poem he counterpoints private and public circumstances in a way that creates the mood of crisis as it must have been felt by men like himself.

For example, a principal theme of the poem is his lingering love for his first wife, who had left him and had married another man. Some passages of *Autumn Journal* are love poems to that lost love, and they are intimate and moving; but the mood is the mood of England in that critical autumn, the private loss is an analogue of public loss, and the poet's helpless misery is an appropriate response to the public situation as well as to the private one.

The relation works in the opposite way, too—public events echo private feelings. . . . So public and private interweave, and have one theme—loss: the loss of a by-election, the loss of a dog, the loss of Czechoslovakia, the loss of love, all together composing the mood of the autumn of 1938. (pp. 368-69)

[A] good deal of *Autumn Journal* is retrospective autobiography. I have called such backward glances nostalgic, and they are very much that in MacNeice's case; his habitual sentimental melancholy was especially suited to nostalgia. But the autobiographical passages are more than that: they are also judgments of the past imposed by the disastrous present. . . . [Somehow] that life of careless love in the careless early 'thirties is made to share responsibility for the way things are at the end of the decade, for the general loss. (pp. 369-70)

Each [part of his early life] is treated with nostalgic affection, but also with the ironic knowledge that it is irrelevant to the present crisis. (p. 370)

[Like] everyone else, MacNeice took the war against fascism as already determined; the only question was how to confront it.

Perhaps it was because of that question that MacNeice travelled to Barcelona in December 1938, and made the record of his journey there, and his night thoughts of New Year's Eve in that beleaguered city, the substance of the closing sections of his poem. The presence of the Spanish War gives the poem an oddly anachronistic quality, for by the time it was published Barcelona had fallen, and the war was over; *Autumn Journal* must be the last poem written in which the struggle in Spain functioned as a symbolic event. . . . [The poem] is an indictment that seems more than personal, that spreads out from the poet to involve his class and his generation, and the postures of the 'thirties. On the last night of 1938, MacNeice was acknowledging the end of a time.

The poem ends, not with a call to action, but with an invocation of love and life that is like a blessing, or a prayer. . . . Like other works of the time, this is Literature of Preparation: the die is cast, and there seems a kind of relief in that knowledge. What is coming will be terrible, but less terrible, perhaps, than waiting for the end.

Autumn Journal is a passive poem, a record of a private life carried on the flood of history. It has no personal momentum, no important decisions are made; the most positive thing that MacNeice does is to work in an Oxford by-election (which his candidate loses). Nor does it propose any positive values, any programme for confronting the future; England has come to the end of *laissez faire*, but MacNeice has no alternatives to offer, beyond a vague solidarity of resistance against the common enemy. I don't wish to suggest that the poem *should* have these elements in it in order to be excellent, but simply that the state of mind that MacNeice recorded in his journal did not include them, and that MacNeice, who was honest about his feelings even when they were self-pitying and sentimental, would not falsify what he had felt. In an introductory note to the book, he acknowledged inconsistencies and over-statements, but refused to alter them; he was not, he said,

> attempting to offer what so many people now demand from poets—a final verdict or a balanced judgement. It is the nature of this poem to be neither final nor balanced.
>
> (pp. 370-72)

Autumn Journal is the best personal expression of the end-of-the-'thirties mood. (p. 373)

> *Samuel Hynes, in his* The Auden Generation: Literature and Politics in England in the 1930s *(copyright © 1976 by Samuel Hynes; all rights reserved; reprinted by permission of The Viking Penguin Inc.), Viking Penguin, 1977.*

*   *   *

MANO, D. Keith   1942-

An American novelist and critic, Mano is best known for *Bishop's Progress*, which, like most of his fiction, reflects his deep concern for the state of Christianity. (See also *CLC*, Vol. 2, and *Contemporary Authors*, Vols. 25-28, rev. ed.)

D. Keith Mano's novel, *Bishop's Progress* . . . , details the twelve-day wait of Whitney Belknap, famous Episcopalian bishop, for major heart surgery to be performed by Dr. Snow, an equally famous surgeon. The impersonal life of the hospital and Dr. Snow contrast with the bishop's concern for Love in his book, *A God for Our Time,* but the bishop, though trying to relate to others, is as impersonal and loveless as his scientific counterparts. The twelve days become tedious before they are over, and the bishop's leaving the hospital before the performance of surgery, though intended to be a noble gesture, seems foolhardy. (p. 365)

> Prairie Schooner (© *1969 by University of Nebraska Press; reprinted by permission from* Prairie Schooner), *Winter, 1968-69.*

Horn is set in the future, at a time when Black militancy is strong. Harlem is run by George Horn Smith, a Negro who has a freakish eleven-inch horn jutting from his forehead, and who, according to his autobiography, tackled incredible adversity before becoming middleweight champion of the world and, finally, a leader of the Black revolution in the United States. The narrative is provided by Calvin Beecher Pratt, a mild, fat, understandably frightened Episcopalian priest, who elects to take a parish in Harlem after reading of Horn's life. The stand-off between these two men—their crass dissimilarity—provides Mr. Mano's theme, which is to show that, despite everything, they are not so unalike.

There are some very clever things in *Horn:* the high rhetoric and gaucherie of Horn's autobiography (excerpts are slotted, rather leadenly, into Pratt's narrative) is well judged, occupying a position somewhere between the embarrassing and the frightening. Similarly, John Meeker, a priest also, and a Harlem veteran, is finely characterized as a liberal whose desire for identification with and acceptance by, the black population of Harlem has pushed him to almost psychotic extremes; and Pratt's fear of physical violence—and his ultimate subjection to it—is conveyed with a fitting intensity and tells us as much about the potential hatred of a tormented race for its persecutors as about Pratt's personal timidity.

The book's length, though, proves a major drawback. There is too much space for the tension to spread into, and become absorbed; too often, this is what happens. (p. 642)

> The Times Literary Supplement (© *Times Newspapers Ltd. (London) 1970; reproduced from* The Times Literary Supplement *by permission), June 11, 1970.*

PATRICIA MEYER SPACKS

Colonel Mint provides a pleasant donnée: an astronaut in action sees an angel and says so. Most of the novel concentrates on the torments subsequently invented to force him to recant. One can surmise why the author might have thought it funny: long ago men suffered for their divergences from religious faith; now the state's destruction of deviants is as certain as the Inquisition's; such parallel and reversal is the stuff of comedy.... This is supposed to be an "extravagant comic novel," but the experience of reading it is simply depressing. For one thing, there's the quality of the prose: "I know who you think I am. A handy man, that's all. Husband, father—dead from the neck up. But I'm more than that. Shit, shit, yes. You want me to be like all the rest of them." And the quality of the mind behind it, manipulative, exploiting the sensational, apparently devoid of serious thought. (pp. 503-04)

> *Patricia Meyer Spacks, in* The Hudson Review *(copyright © 1972 by The Hudson Review, Inc.; reprinted by permission), Vol. XXV, No. 3, Autumn, 1972.*

MARTHA DUFFY

Mano is still a writer of more promise than achievement. His strengths are energy, earnestness and a tough intelligence. But he is a stiff writer, not especially imaginative, and his overdrawn characters tend to be mere mouthpieces for ideas.

Part of Mano's success may stem from a frankly religious outlook. In these cynical, pragmatic times, nearly everyone is eager to admire religious faith—particularly if it is someone else's. Mano, an Episcopalian, is a specifically Christian novelist. In his books, God is a respected familiar; eternity is a definite place on the map. There is always an old-fashioned metaphysical confrontation. In his first novel, *Bishop's Progress,* the bishop and a surgeon angrily reshuffle old arguments about Christian charity. In *Horn,* a priest and a black leader dispute ethics. Now, in the new book [*The Bridge*], a fashionable venture into futurism, the author yokes a world-weary priest and a profane Noah who repopulated a ravaged world.

The Bridge is set in New York State a millennium hence, with a prologue and epilogue that occur 600 years beyond that. These short sections show a society struggling back to some kind of sufficiency after the human race has committed mass suicide during the Age of Ecology. Though comfort is meager and government insanely harsh, man is glorified as the Lord of Creation.

Excepting science fiction, novels set in the future almost always turn out to be traps for writers. Mano may have intended to make some comment on the tyranny of liberalism—or ecology—run wild, but he fails to get beyond the mechanical business of detailing the societies he envisions.... Mano has always been obsessed by the functions and malfunctions of the body, but in earlier works like *The Life and Death of Harry Goth,* his prose has been funnier and more focused. In the new book he finally runs out of energy, one quality he never seemed to lack before.

> *Martha Duffy, "Lost Worlds," in* Time *(reprinted by permission from* Time, The Weekly Newsmagazine; *copyright Time Inc. 1973), September 10, 1973, p. 91.*

*   *   *

MARQUAND, John P(hillips)   1893-1960

An American novelist, Marquand primarily dealt with the upper and upper middle classes of Boston and New England. Essentially a novelist of manners in the tradition of Ellen Glasgow, Marquand was an adept satirist with a gift for capturing the details and atmosphere of life in a vanishing American aristocracy. (See also *CLC*, Vol. 2.)

C. HUGH HOLMAN

Marquand was not an extensive or dedicated experimenter with the art of fiction, but a practitioner of the novel of social realism as it had been developed in the nineteenth century. He tried to represent man in his social milieu and to reveal man's character through his conduct and the choices he made in his society, rather than through the exploration of the inner self....

What he knew best when he began his career as a serious novelist was the Boston of the patrician classes, the New England of the upper middle classes, and the New York of commercial fiction and advertising. (p. 6)

The impact which democracy makes on manners converts the novelist from being a tester of character by established standards to a portrayer of character under the persistent impact of change. The social novelist's subject becomes mutability rather than order, and his testing cruxes occur when change rather than stasis puts stress on the moral values of his characters. "Social mobility," a term which he borrowed from the social anthropologists, thus becomes a recurrent condition, even in Boston, in Marquand's novels. (p. 7)

In his serious novels, Marquand drew extensive, accurate, convincing, and often uncomplimentary pictures of the world he knew best, writing of it with an ease that masked the penetration of the study which he was making. In his polished and patrician way, he defined the ambitions, the intentions, and above all the frustrations of the average moderately successful middle-aged citizen with an acuteness that made many of his readers meet his characters with a shock of self-recognition.

Although he was probably as impatient with the young existentialists as he clearly was with those who prate in Freudian terms of "free social guilt," his major novels define a moral and spiritual emptiness, a sense of loneliness and quiet despair, that is not far removed from Kafka and Sartre. . . . Yet this pessimism is usually masked behind a gently ironic tone, and these characters are handled with the wry detachment of the novelist of manners and not, except in a few cases, in tragic terms or with bitterness. (pp. 7-8)

In Mr. Moto [Marquand's Japanese intelligence agent and main character in six novels] Marquand had found a fictional character that seemed to lend himself to extensive and highly remunerative elaboration, and a plot situation that utilized his knowledge of far places. . . . It is a mistake to call Mr. Moto a detective or to call Marquand a writer of detective stories or even of mysteries in the traditional sense. These books are spy thrillers of a very high order, but they lack the tight construction of the detective story. (pp. 18-19)

[*The Late George Apley, Wickford Point,* and *H. M. Pulham, Esquire*] form a kind of triptych, defining in three sharply contrasting panels Marquand's view of Boston. *The Late George Apley* is a portrait of old Boston and its tradition, which had flowered in Concord in the mid-nineteenth century. In *Wickford Point* Marquand turned his satiric attention to a decaying family loosely bound to the Transcendentalists and themselves the possessors of a very minor nature poet in the family tree. *H. M. Pulham, Esquire* is a self-portrait of a contemporary Bostonian, a post-World War I businessman, whose ineffectual revolt against his class fails and who now believes himself to have a happier and better life than, as the reader knows, he actually does have. Taken together these three panels constitute a complex and varied definition of an attitude which dominates one segment of America and which probably is, as Mr. Marquand insisted, not unique to Boston but is to be found wherever society begins to allow the past to establish firm controls over the present. (pp. 20-1)

Neither of Marquand's two novels dealing with wartime America, *So Little Time* and *B. F.'s Daughter,* is completely successful, perhaps because Marquand was writing of experiences too recent for him to have achieved the necessary detachment and perhaps, also, because he was attempting some very limited experiments with new fictional techniques. But both books are serious attempts to deal with the frighteningly fast changes that war makes. In the New England satires, the enemy appeared to be a caste-conscious society failing to respond to change. In *So Little Time* and *B. F.'s Daughter* not society but time itself is the great villain, social change is time's inevitable manifestation, and war is an accelerating device which destroys too rapidly the structure and tradition of society. (pp. 22-3)

[*Point of No Return*] is unique in the thoroughness with which Marquand functions as a sociological analyst. For his interest is now centered not so much in Charles' personal dilemma as in the world that has made him, in the pattern of social gradation and of change in Newburyport and in New York. In his analysis of the social forces of Clyde, Massachusetts, Marquand produces a significant commentary on one segment of American society. (pp. 23-4)

Probably no other American novelist since Sinclair Lewis has examined the class structure of a small American city with the accuracy and illuminating insight that Marquand employed in this novel.

After *Point of No Return,* he was to produce three major novels. Although his earlier work clearly adumbrates these books, each of them represented a significant variation from its predecessors. Each was a study of success—its costs, its joys, and its deprivations—whereas the earlier novels had been essentially portraits of defeat. And each of the last three novels varied significantly from its predecessor in technique.

Melville Goodwin, USA (1951) is an ironic picture of the professional soldier and of the quality of the "opinion molders" who make him a kind of demigod. The professional soldier, his courage, and his code were persistent themes throughout Marquand's whole career. . . . The novel is told by Sidney Skelton, a nationally famous radio commentator, who represents unconsciously much that is sentimentally mindless in contemporary American life. . . . *Melville Goodwin, USA* has the most skillfully ironic use of an unreliable narrator that Marquand ever attempted. (pp. 24-5)

In 1955 he published *Sincerely, Willis Wayde,* a devastating picture of the big business promoter and the Marquand book that is most nearly in the mode of Sinclair Lewis. In *Willis Wayde* Marquand for the only time in a serious novel avoids extensive use of the flashback, and centers his attention directly on his satiric butt, Willis Wayde. The result is a harsh and unsympathetic picture of a lower-middle-class boy who succeeds, through unremitting effort, in becoming what his father calls "a son of a bitch." This most pitiless of Marquand's books echoes situations which he had earlier treated with sympathy. For Wayde alone of his protagonists Marquand has contempt. (p. 26)

[*Women and Thomas Harrow* (1958), a] story about the three unsuccessful marriages of a very talented and successful playwright, is a kind of ironic *The Tempest* to his career. Upon its publication [Marquand] declared it to be his last novel, and the book has a twilight sense of putting away the players and closing the box in the mood of an embittered Prospero. When Tom Harrow looks back over the skillful and successful use he has made of his great dramatic powers, it is with a sense of nothingness that makes the book finally very dark indeed. (pp. 26-7)

In dealing with experience, Marquand was anxious to record what he called "the extraordinary panorama of society, the changes in life since the horse and wagon days." Yet in portraying that panorama, he turned, as many writers of the social novel have, to the novel of character. . . . [It] is the man, revealed through the impact of [the] environment upon him, that is the central interest of Marquand's serious novels.

One of the obvious clues to the centrality of character in his work is the looseness and, it sometimes seems, the nonexistence of plot. Even his early adventure stories and his Mr. Moto tales have relaxed construction, and his major novels so far concentrate on character rather than event that they may seem to the casual reader to be formless, flowing with the narrator's whim. (p. 28)

[Seven] of his nine novels of manners deal not with plots in any conventional sense but with crucial situations—what Marquand calls taking "a man facing the crisis of his life" and "show[ing] how he got there"—with the protagonist looking backward in memory to his formative years. The exceptions to this backward movement as the controlling structural pattern are in *The Late George Apley,* where an "official" biographer is writing about a deceased friend, and *Sincerely, Willis Wayde,* where the sequence of events is presented in a straightforward fashion, from childhood onward. In *Willis Wayde,* despite this chronological sequence of events, the actions are viewed from an undefined vantage point in the present. This vantage point that establishes a relationship between past and present for the chief actions through their presentation by backward looks was a hallmark of Marquand's fiction from *The Unspeakable Gentleman* onward. It is very effective in pointing up the contrast between past and present, whether it is used to create the romantic nostalgia of his historical fiction, best seen in *Haven's End,* or to explore the methods by which the actions and the environments of the past make and control the present. . . . These nine novels attempt not to recreate that past but to picture that part of it which survives in the memories and impression of the present. (p. 29)

The basic method of *The Late George Apley* is that of parody, an aping of the diction and attitudes of editors of what Marquand called the "collected letters of V.I.P.'s in Boston (and elsewhere) . . .". Willing, vain, pedantic, and smug Boston "man of letters," is editing the correspondence of George Apley, a very proper Boston Brahmin. . . . Style, it has been said, is the man; but in *The Late George Apley* it becomes a device for social criticism. The use of Willing to tell the story of Apley results in a double view of the Brahmin type and in a double portraiture that gives depth to the study. . . . (pp. 30-1)

Although the time sequences had been handled loosely in *Apley,* Marquand's next novel, *Wickford Point,* represented an apparently even looser use of time, but one which, on closer examination, is very artful. The story is presented through the reminiscences of Jim Calder, a writer of popular magazine fiction, as a series of events in the brief forward motion of the story trigger his recollections of

the past, within which most of the significant action is to be found. (p. 32)

Jim's diction and sentence structure are those of the professional writer, and, although ostensibly relaxed, they have a directness, a clarity, and an accuracy that Willing's had lacked. . . . Each book is, in a sense, a stylistic tour de force. But the publication of *H. M. Pulham, Esquire* revealed what many had not fully understood—that Marquand had a finely discriminating ear for American speech, a sensitivity to the significance of word choice and sentence structure that probably has not been surpassed in American writing since Mark Twain. Willing's narrative might have been a parody of a literary form, requiring sensitivity to the printed page; Calder's might have been Marquand's own voice. But Pulham's first-person narrative is a triumph of stylistic exactness. The language and attitudes of a Boston investment counsel are perfectly caught and are used successfully to portray Harry Pulham, as he reveals himself through contemplation about the writing of his "class life" for the twenty-fifth reunion of his Harvard class.

This ability to capture the very accent of American upper-middle-class and upper-class speech, to employ its jargon with authenticity, and to know the precise degree of exaggeration to use in order to point out its absurdity and pretension, Marquand was to use with increasing ineffectiveness. (pp. 33-4)

There is basically little that is new in Marquand's fictional methods. They are those of the realist, employing an unreliable narrator who tells the story through retrospection and in the language and attitudes of the profession, class, and locale from which he comes. But the skill with which Marquand employed this method is quite unusual, and the subtlety with which he uses it for satiric portraits should never be underestimated. Command of the tools of the trade does not make a novelist great—that is a function of many factors, including the things upon which the tools are used—but such command does make a novelist a fine craftsman, and that Marquand certainly was. His clarity, sureness of touch, firmness of structure, and wit are all of a high order.

Since he centered his attention in these books on character shaped by environment and on the tension between self and society which defines the value systems of people and the context of social structures, the test of Marquand's ultimate importance in the American novel must rest with the people he created and the problems he gave them. No other American novelist since Sinclair Lewis has had a sense of the significant social detail that is as great as Marquand's. (pp. 35-6)

Marquand's major theme is the defeat of the self by society, and he intends this theme to have a broader basis than might appear if we think of it as the defeat of the self by a special society at a special time. One of the illuminating things about his Boston trilogy is that he covers a very broad span of years. The powerful thing that is Boston society slowly embraces the young whenever you find them, and its iron claw may express itself in various ways at different times but never painlessly.

When we look beyond the remarkable virtuosity of Marquand's narrative point of view to the central characters whose portraits he draws, we find him less a satirist than we had expected. The world he describes with all its foibles and fools is one in which he is finally comfortable if not contented. His protagonists are pleasant to meet, with few exceptions admirable to do business with, and delightful golfing companions. If they are surrounded in large measure by fools and pour out their efforts fruitlessly on unfertile soil, their lot seems to him little different from that of most "American males." If they seek but never find "the ideal woman" they partake, he feels, of the common experiences of our world.

The crucial event in most of these novels occurs at a point where the opportunity for personal choice has already passed. It does not change the character's position in the world, but rather confirms it. Titles like *So Little Time* and *Point of No Return* underscore this position. The standard Marquand hero in the past once faced the forks in Frost's yellow wood and took the road most traveled by. At that moment of choice each of them had tried to rebel without success. And now in his backward searchings each is seeking to understand the point in time when his choice of roads became irrevocable. (pp. 36-7)

But if Marquand's protagonists ultimately find themselves strangers and afraid in a world of vast change, they still lack tragic proportions, because they are too easily betrayed. (p. 40)

Marquand seems to be saying that a staid and backward looking society can best be portrayed by what it stifles in able, good, but weak men. Thus these various protagonists become finally, not tragic figures, but standards for measuring their society. This is comedy rather than tragedy because the men and their goals lack tragic magnitude, because, deserving what they get, it becomes satirically appropriate that they should get it—and that their own recognition scenes should be wry rather than wrathful.

A great deal of the delight in reading Marquand comes from the many satiric pictures of the minor characters. . . . In these minor characters a world is created with great success, its very tone and quality caught in the amber of precise language. In portraits of these people Marquand's comic powers are shown and his novels become witty representations of ourselves, viewed in the steel glass of the satirist.

Furthermore, Marquand is a social historian of considerable magnitude. He has caught the language, the cadence, the attitudes, and the absurdities of upper-middle-class America. (p. 41)

He confessed once that he had never been able to write poetry or to keep rhythm in his head. And the element of poetry is missing in his work; never does he try to use this world to suggest a more ideal reality. . . . His work is not designed to lift the spirit or to translate the immediate into the eternal. . . . (p. 42)

The actual society which he knew was his subject, and he valued it for itself, not as symbol or metaphor for transcendent truths or abstract ideals. (p. 43)

Maxwell Geismar once said, "Mr. Marquand knows all the little answers. He avoids the larger questions." The statement, although true in a sense, is more witty than wise. Denied the soaring reaches of transcendental thought or poetic elevation, he dealt with the little answers in large part because the people of whom he wrote were people who asked little questions of life, except in those confused moments when they merely raised frightened cries. . . . (p. 44)

The life, world, and times of these people who are so obsessed with the material trivia of their daily deeds, the stifling formulas of their caste and class, the busyness of making money, and the confused personal diplomacy which their marriages demand are indeed unflattering but very amusing pictures of ourselves. . . . [Marquand] examined the social condition of our lives with irony and grace, and his "badgered American male" captures in his recurrent problems and poses, not only how we behave, but also how hollow our lives often are at the core. He speaks both to our social historical sense and to the unslacked spiritual thirst which our aridity creates. To our age, at least, he speaks with ease and skill, with irony and wit, but above all with the authority of unsentimental knowledge. (pp. 44-5)

> *C. Hugh Holman, in his* John P. Marquand *(American Writers Pamphlet No. 46; ©* *1965, University of Minnesota), University* *of Minnesota Press, Minneapolis, 1965.*

LEO GURKO

I confess to being an uncompromising admirer of John P. Marquand's novels. *The Late George Apley, Wickford Point,* and *H. M. Pulham, Esquire* are splendid books. The later works, from *So Little Time* on, contain many remarkable passages, and even the last novel, *Of Women and Timothy Harrow,* holds up well. I herewith make the following extravagant claims for Marquand: as a recorder of the upper-middle-class scene he is the equal of Edith Wharton; as an explorer of nostalgia, he can stand comparison with F. Scott Fitzgerald; as an ironist, he ranks with Thackeray, to whom, for plain reasons, he has been frequently linked. (p. 696)

> *Leo Gurko, in* American Literature *(reprinted by permission of the Publisher; copyright 1973 by Duke University Press, Durham, North Carolina), January, 1973.*

*   *   *

McCLURE, Michael   1932-

McClure is an American poet, playwright, and novelist. His poetry is noted for its combination of words and phonetic phrases which are intended to be read or even growled aloud in order to provide a sensory experience. McClure is concerned with communication in his works: he believes that only by direct and personal communication can art be effective in providing personal revelations. David Kherdian says, "Michael McClure is that rarity, a writer who invites the reader to seek pleasure as the antidote to depression and ennui." (See also *CLC*, Vol. 6, and *Contemporary Authors*, Vols. 21-24, rev. ed.)

RICHARD GILMAN

The basic dramatic proposition [of *The Beard*] is arresting enough: to bring Jean Harlow and Billy the Kid together in eternity, face to face in the sort of other-worldly middle-class room which Sartre employed for very different purposes in *No Exit,* and have them go at one another. . . . [The first line spoken by the Harlow character:] "Before you can pry any secrets from me, you must first find the real me. Which one will you pursue?"

This ritual phrase runs throughout the play, often to good effect, and is the verbal mode and talisman of one plane of its operations. The other verbal procedure may be conveyed, in what is literally its minor key, by Harlow's snarling remark a little later on: "You're a sack of shit!" This vocabulary is undeniably as "dirty" as anything the American stage has ever known . . . yet it is in no real sense shocking, which is to say morally disconcerting. . . . For it is there to release and embody most of the action between the pair, to *be* their central encounter in all but a few respects (crucial ones however), and as such it has to be judged for its dramatic value and effectiveness.

The ferocious lewdness is, in other words, never prurient but structural, one constituent of the play's attempted life as drama. For these two American legends, the cinema queen and the outlaw, are engaging in a duel to a certain kind of death and possible resurrection, a knock-down ballet of sexual thrust and parry, of desire and defense, come-on and come-down, with Billy's hard rapist's momentum running up against Harlow's satiny, wised-up, hands-off, daydream sensuality, her fixed and legendary position as shiny unavailable temptress. Or rather . . . such mythic-sexual-sociological dimensions are what McClure is trying, with only partial success, to fill. (pp. 184-85)

As sexual clash and combat, and as an exhibition of voluptuous fantasy being released into theatrical actuality, the play is obviously mostly untrammeled and hard-driving. But, as I have said, it aspires to much more than this, and it is the failure of this aspiration which keeps it from being more than fitfully engrossing even on that *Who's Afraid of Virginia Woolf* level. McClure is continually trying to move past psycho-sexual boundaries into realms of metaphysical and cultural-philosophical recognition. The whole point of the couple's being dead and legendary is that they may now serve as exemplary figures of the American confusion between orders of being, of our perpetual conversion of sexuality into one kind of art—the popular mythology of archetypal surrogates, the blonde bombshell, the steely outlaw—and the consequent depletion of the sexual by being turned into emblem and shady metaphor. The hard insistent urge, beyond good and evil and beyond social "value," which sexuality continues to be at bottom is what McClure is attempting to liberate from its prison inside *culture*.

To this end Billy is given the task of trying to convince Harlow that they are both "divine," "immortal," and that this means they are free to do what they want to do, if anyone is free. "There's nobody *here*!" he keeps insisting; no one is watching them, they are beyond the social order, which has to fit sex in among other considerations and repress its amoral ambitions while exploiting it for purposes of civic and economic morale. Yet this theme is never more than stated, never made an integral element of the dramatic movement, a source of transformation for its explicit harshness and ponderable assaults against what we already know. And this is mostly because Billy is its sole proprietor; while between scatological expletives he goes on reminding her of their wonderful status, she stays on the ground of her portrait as a dumb, foul-mouthed blonde, with the result that her naturalism pulls away from his half-incantatory and poetic task. And that poetry is never acute or interesting enough to work as a kind of yeast bringing the rest of the material to a rise despite itself. (pp. 185-86)

Everything . . . mounts up to a perspective on *The Beard* as occupying that foggy ground of contemporary culture where new energy hasn't yet found a distinct shape and revolutionary sounds outstrip the creation of revolutionary substance. (p. 187)

Richard Gilman, "With Harlow in Hell," in his Common and Uncommon Masks: Writings on Theatre 1961-1970 *(copyright © 1971 by Richard Gilman; reprinted by permission of Random House, Inc.), Random House, 1971, pp. 183-87.*

MICHAEL LYNCH

Charles Olson's parenthetical admonition in his "Human Universe" seems—as if he wanted to avoid the charge laid against, I think, Camus, that he was a "human racist"—at least self-directed: "It behooves man now not to separate himself too jauntily from any of nature's creatures."

Michael McClure has taken Olson's parenthesis to heart. He wrote an essay once about Gerard de Nerval's "The Black Spot," and praised Nerval for "showing us our kinship with all creatures." He made this poem a rallying cry for a new consciousness: "LET US THROW OUT THE WORD *MAN*! Such poems as this translation of Nerval remind me that I am MAMMAL! . . . The poem makes me see the surge of life. . . . We become Mammals as we were once Men." Others of McClure's *Meat Science Essays* develop this mammalism (which can slide, in that famous treatise on Jayne Mansfield, into mammaryism). As Mammals we "bring the universe to life." Intellect as we know it subsides and mammalian intelligence—acknowledgement of the senses as organs of knowing—returns. Restrictive, constrictive rationality is replaced by true "REASON!"—a part of the body by which we are "connected to the universe." Mammalian Reason is the "revolt of all the senses against regulations that dull them." "All that is experienced, without being twisted into the shape of preconceptions, is REASON." It accepts time, chance, luck, and leads to freedom, to "the fullness of being a mammal."

The exponent of this hip zoological primitivism saw his poems first published nationally in the January, 1956 issue of *Poetry*. . . . These poems were, with the exception of several quirks, settled. Two villanelles in iambic pentameter, dedicated to Theodore Roethke, echoing in tone "The Waking" and in imagery Roethke's mystical biology. . . . Even the quirks . . . seemed recognizably Rimbaud and sang along in key. Nestled between poems by John Hollander and Ricahrd Howard—it was Howard's first *Poetry* appearance as well—"2 for theodore roethke" were not out of place.

Now, nearly two decades later, "Mike" [as he signed earlier] is "Michael" and his style rests more than a continent away not only from Howard and Hollander but also from his mentors Roethke and Olson. . . . He reigns widely as a culture prince with a considerable coffer of prose (besides the *Essays*, several novels and *Freewheeling Frank*), plays (besides *The Beard*, about a dozen), and poems (at least nine volumes and many broadsides) in print. It is inviting to read his poems as dayglow excrescences of a distinct subculture and let them go at that, but this prince wants to be read as a poet. He evokes, variously, Anacreon, Blake, Shelley, Keats, Rimbaud, Roethke, and others as if to insist: read me in their line.

[Despite his poetry's] rather skilled play of syntax . . . it remains talk about sensation, not sensation evoked. McClure's language operates much as his fellow Californian Professor Hayakawa sees language operating: it is a map which but points to something beyond itself. This gives the lie to his, McClure's claim that "poetry is not a system but is real events spoken of, or happening, in sounds." They are spoken of, yes, but only rarely happen.

His poems seldom give us mammals but do give us Mammal. Have you ever seen or felt "Mammal?" Of course not, and that is what ties McClure's poems to his prose: both are meat *science*, "bioalchemical investigations," proclamations and not presentations. Mammal reason seldom appears in them because thought seldom disappears. . . . McClure's poems give the banner, the editorial comment or the lab hack's technicolor diagram, not the "real events" themselves.

His idiosyncratic language is thus appropriate to his poems, not to his usual accounts of his poems. Like the banner of the politician or the excited journalist, it seeks to eliminate resonance, subtlety, freshness, precision. . . . It incorporates the technicolor blow-up of pop art:

> GRUNTS HURLING FRAG GRENADES. Monk
> tranked at his piano.
> Dreamers in the painted caves.

gross thuds of reference and phrase:

> Like Dante, we're really
> down to it!
> THIS IS OUR DARK WOOD, OUR LEOPARD!
> LION! WOLF.

self-conscious archaisms to devivify speech for hymnal use:

> HAIL THEE WHO ART ME BURNING
> BLOSSOMING TRANSMUTING.

and self-conscious rhyme to distance it from live idiom. . . . It revels in the surrealist's stark juxtaposition of dissimilar entities—"Pink elephants and cherubim holding purple plastic flowers"—which, fairly or un-, may keep reminding one of what Wallace Stevens wrote for the surrealist magazine *View:* "To make a clam play an accordion is to invent not to discover." It accomplishes a curiously indeterminate tonality that laughs weakly at itself even as each headline is proclaimed. . . . (pp. 160-62)

None of these qualities seem unintentional; McClure has sought not so much to derange his senses systematically . . . as, simply, to tin his ear and cap his eye in order to preserve the programmatic against the senses' incursions.

In "We," a longish poem in *Blackberries*, McClure programs himself for a vision within this inferno of darkness. It is not, he declares, vision like Blake's or Boehme's, occurring in some "THERE," but here, insistently here where "WE / STAND / WITH / MEAT / AT / THE / BOTTOM / OF / EACH / FOOT," where we may pass beyond the "LIVING BLACKNESS" in which "pictures fall away within the brain" to another blackness: "the kind we whirl around in—before / we even touch the earth." By pointing towards this latter primordial blackness, "We" opens the way for McClure's Long Poem, *Rare Angel*, which does accomplish, at points, a "THINKING, THOUGHT-LESS" poetry beyond meat science.

Rare Angel is an act of manifold stretching out: to the "surge" of universal expansion, the energy of construction and destruction in the modern city, the edges of knowing—to the Rare Angel muse herself who emerges from these. . . . The recurrent image of a flashlight playing over a concrete wall in darkness aptly figures the poem's imaginative probing.

Although much plasticene rhetoric still burdens the Pleistocene vision—McClure upholds his ability to avoid any lyrical lines—many of the images are convincingly mysterious and the play of the mind's flashlight almost muscular. In the length and speed of the poem, then, McClure accomplishes a sensation of energy which none of its details do by themselves. For once he has not forsaken structure and proportion but has used them—a middle degree of dramatic progression is clear—as launching pads for the Whoosh he seeks in poetry.

Rare Angel even recognizes a tradition to blast away from: that of *Song of Myself*, where a fluid "I" rehearses the variety of individual "I's" and—here's the surprise—*Notes Toward a Supreme Fiction*. Stevens was ever happy to have a poem resist the intelligence almost successfully. . . . Stevens' struggle was with a faulty figure for the major man, the apostate Canon Aspirin who had to be rejected: "Angel, / Be silent in your luminous cloud." McClure's struggle is more like Whitman's—with the difficult implications of a too-easily assumed identification with everything.

Rare Angel's outcome is a reenactment of the bison-mammoth kill in which the "I" is both the slayer and the slain. In isolation the final rhetoric—"HE IS I AND I AM HIM"—may invite one to add a Lennonesque GOO GOO GOO JOOB, but it is largely validated because of the largely realized scene:

> The monster's deep-set eyes look at the sky.
> Branches of creosote hang from the mouth as he drinks.
> The coppery horsehair snake writhes by . . .
> Mosquito larvae dive, the painted men
> almost giggle
> in the rushes.
> The sound of water being swallowed in a giant throat.

These flashlit moments in the mind come closer than anything else in the poem to fulfilling its claimed program: "Real Poetry / comes in moments like the dawn / or instances of thoughtlessness / made bright by rich and blank / sensoriums." But for the bulk a gap remains between claim and accomplishment. A sunny pleasure dome with caves of ice—and *Rare Angel*, carving a "VAST CAVERN . . . OUT OF THE ICE," evokes a visionary poet whose "Kinky hairs float in sunny wind"—requires a directness which no broad silk banner of meat science can provide. *Rare Angel* refers only once to "MAMMAL-MAN," and that at the very end where it quickly dissolves into the hunt sequence. Perhaps McClure is beginning to accomplish his mammalism by attending to the lesson from Charles Olson which heretofore he has slighted:

> The meeting edge of man and the world is
> also his writing edge. If man is active, it is
> exactly here where experience comes in that
> it is delivered back, and if he stays fresh at
> the coming in he will be fresh at his going
> out. If he does not, all that he has inside his
> house is stale.

(pp. 162-65)

Michael Lynch, "A Broad Silk Banner," in Parnassus: Poetry in Review *(copyright © by Poetry in Review Foundation), Spring-Summer, 1976, pp. 156-65.*

McClure is acclaimed for a poetry infused with science and mysticism. [The poems of *Antechamber, and Other Poems*], resplendent with a humanistic approach, are no longer preoccupied with "mammalian" themes, that irritant from other works. Their broad sweep suggests that Mc-Clure has challenged his own ideas about relationships; their energy is, as always, amazing. (p. 1407)

> Booklist (*reprinted by permission of the American Library Association; copyright 1978 by the American Library Association), May 1, 1978.*

*   *   *

McCULLERS, (Lula) Carson   1917-1967

An American novelist, short story writer, poet, and playwright, McCullers is considered one of the most skilled authors of the southern gothic tradition. Noted for her fine dramatic sense of detail, McCullers dealt thematically with concepts of alienation and loneliness. *The Heart Is a Lonely Hunter* is her best known work. (See also *CLC*, Vols. 1, 4, and *Contemporary Authors*, Vols. 5-8, rev. ed.; obituary, Vols. 25-28, rev. ed.)

IRVING H. BUCHEN

McCullers images the artist as a screen on which is projected a series of emerging and expanding stills whose flickering breaks dislocate the continuity of causality; or because the artist sees and is seen, he is the eye of a golden bird as well as the observer of the reflections of that golden eye. Such a state is tyrannically relationless and unwilled, for nothing is translated or translatable into anything except itself. Things tenaciously remain things, feelings, feelings; and nothing is symbolic of anything, yet. If any conversions do occur they do so only under the melding power of the unconscious to animate things with feelings and to concretize feelings with things. The initial creative process then to McCullers is the special art of dreaming while awake.

Significantly, that semi-awake state is for McCullers predominantly musical and visual, not verbal, and seems to flourish at the dawn of time or pre-consciousness. Although for McCullers and for some of her more complex characters, that is but the first stage of a developing progression, for many it is their initial and only one. Not accidentally, her preference for children and adolescents as well as for child-like adults like Spiros and Leonora is of a piece with her preoccupation with states of mind that are closer to the unconscious than the conscious, more involuntary than willed, more pristine than sophisticated. The result is a host of characters who are curiously incomplete, only half-formed, half-human. Perhaps the most dramatic example of an arrested child is Ellgee Williams whom McCullers describes as having the "strange, rapt face of a Gaugin primitive" . . . :

> The mind is like a richly woven tapestry in which the colors are distilled from the experiences of the senses, and the design drawn from the convolutions of the intellect. The mind of Private Williams was imbued with various colors of strange tones, but it was without delineation, void of form. . . .
>
> (pp. 530-31)

It is crucial at this point to recall that Williams is a voyeur

and that the theme of voyeurism appears as persistently in McCullers' work as that of art. Ellgee's voyeurism is comparable to dreaming while awake; he takes in or projects the images of Leonora's naked flaming body on the screen of his mind and patiently waits for those stills to achieve the coherence of design. The unformed mind, indeed, equals unformed art; and the cohesive power of art appears as the cohesive power of love. Indeed, John Tucker in *The Square Root of Wonderful* speaks about his loveless life in the same way McCullers speaks about Ellgee's undefined mind. Tucker tells Mollie that before he met her, "'there was no back or front to my life . . . No back or front or depth. No design or meaning'". . . . Before art, there is nothing; without love, life is nothing. The great terror for McCullers is the void; or as Philip puts it: "'nothing resembles nothing. But nothing is not a blank. It is configured hell'". . . . In short, McCullers' aesthetics and characterization focus on the redemption of the void by form—hence, her enormous emphasis on what precedes not what follows consciousness—on what invites design not so much on what enriches or extends it. The considerable care and energy that a Henry James expends on sensibility and consciousness are shifted by McCullers to what constitutes the foundations of both. In the process, what is clearly established is not only McCullers' receptivity to the child as the emblem of the unconscious, but also her recognition that the child is permanently alive in the adult as the agent of the unconscious. Her adult freaks and grotesques actually represent mangled shapes born of the disparity between the child and the adult, for in McCullers' world wholeness is defined by all the characters who never achieve it. (pp. 531-32)

[What] McCullers' pervasive use of dreams in both her artistic theory and her actual works makes clear is the extent to which her entire vision is rendered obliquely, through a glass darkly or more appropriately bathed in the reflected golden light of a bird's eye. Moreover, McCullers' dreams tend to make use of brilliant colors and forms; movement tends to be orchestrated or choreographed. In other words, for McCullers, dreams tend to be closer to music and the plastic arts than to literature. It is therefore not accidental in this connection that none of her artists or artist-figures is a writer. They are predominantly musicians, a few are painters and sculptors, and one is a dancer. It is the musical and visual that dominate not only her dreams but also McCullers' mode and characterization. Indeed, to the extent that the imagination and mind of both the musician and the plastic artist are closer to the unconscious and more reluctant to employ analysis or conceptualization, then one can better understand why McCullers, aside from her substantial early training in music, has placed such enormous emphasis on dreams in her work and has created an artistic theory which forces literature to be subservient to the other arts. In any case, for McCullers, dream is the natural ally of art. It is ancient and permanent and yet new and transient; it is situationally personal and yet mythic. It also adjusts the mystery of existence and the mystery of art in that while the meaning may be obscure or even finally unknown, the effect is gripping and ultimately possessing. Above all, in its final flowered form dream offers the promise of a closed circle; or as Frankie Addams puts it, "the telling of the wedding had an end and a beginning, a shape like a song". . . . How it acquires that final shape, especially one of song, requires a consideration of the contribution of the intellect and of God to the creative process.

Although the "writer by nature of his profession is a dreamer", McCullers insists, however, that he is finally a "conscious dreamer".... Although McCullers takes great pains to secure the priority of the imagination for the artist, as in her works she strives for love for the dreamer, the intellect under wraps does make a crucial contribution at the closing arc of the creative process.

The intellect introduces tension and sets in motion an interplay between hard thought and soft imagination to produce the ideal of lyrical realism. In other words, the dream must meet the pressure of surviving in this world; and the intellect serves as the mid-wife assisting the dream in its rites of passage into reality. (pp. 533-35)

[In] McCullers' world all the larger patterns of later life are already available in miniature form in childhood or adolescence. Existence can thus be defined as a series of repetitive arcs, each one duplicating the drama of a dream reaching for its flowering form but withering on the vine. How deep-seated this notion of imperilled wholeness is in McCullers appears in an experience she recalls from her own childhood and with which she significantly begins her essay on "The Flowering Dream":

> When I was a child of about four, I was walking with my nurse past a convent. For once, the convent doors were open. And I saw the children eating ice-cream cones, playing on iron swings, and I watched, fascinated. I wanted to go in, but my nurse said no, I was not Catholic. The next day, the gate was shut. But, year by year, I thought of what was going on, of this wonderful party, where I was shut out. I wanted to climb the wall, but I was too little. I beat on the wall once, and I knew all the time that there was a marvelous party going on, but I couldn't get in....
>
> (p. 537)

The touchstone of both McCullers' artistic theory and work is thus rooted in the child's exclusion from paradise because he is not one of the elect.... Moreover, because that experience is not limited to childhood but reverberates throughout life, childhood establishes the tyranny, if not of original sin, then of original exclusion. The permanent drama then for McCullers is that of incompletion or as John claims in "The Sojourner": "There's nothing that makes you so aware of the improvisation of human existence as a song unfinished".... Indeed, unfinished melodies abound in McCullers' work as musical accompaniment to all the unfinished characters. (pp. 537-38)

McCullers' preoccupation with children, freaks, adolescents (normal freaks) and artists is all of a piece. They all act out in different forms the initial and permanent trauma of their dreams being in excess of existence. As a result, they never really change; they only exchange partners. The original dreaming child never really dies; he remains alive in the adolescent and in the adult in the form of a legacy of incompletion. Partial or distorted adults like Spiros, Leonora, Honey Brown and Ellgee Williams are basically children in adult bodies or as McCullers calls them "stunted giants". The old assortment of midgets and dwarfs represent the most flagrant versions of arrested growth, for aside from their grotesquerie they underscore that the movement of existence is not progressive but recurrent. In short, the persistence of dreams and of childhood are really one and the same.

There is one final yield that emerges out of and summarizes McCullers' aesthetic metaphysics. Not accidentally it, too, has its roots in the child. One of the most striking and recurrent patterns in all of McCullers' work is her preoccupation for odd pairs—for the small and the tall, the dwarfs and the giants, the talkative and the reticent. Judge Clane in *Clock Without Hands* notes: "'Ah, the patterns of life, both the big and the small'"... But as noted in McCullers the big is to be found in the small. (p. 538)

McCullers regularly employs a dualistic style which is alternately or contrapuntally leisurely and rapid, soft and hard, lyrical and mean. Clearly, her rhapsodic style in her artistic theory is allied to poetry; her realistic style to prose. Moreover, the rhapsodic style by its incantation has a natural affinity for dreams and achieves its ultimate refinement when poetry is rarified into music or silence. In contrast, the realistic style embodies the unyielding antithesis of the intellect and mercilessly becomes the agent of violence which abounds in her work as recurrently as yearning adolescent dreams. To be sure, that violence is adjusted in obedience to the analogous planes of the square root. The violence may be essentially verbal and escalate from the hurting meanness of Mick Kelly to the raging ferocity of Jake Blount. More often, however, it is actual, and in contrast to the rhapsodic, deflective style, its appearance, as Frankie notes, is sudden. Indeed, every single violent scene in McCullers' work—and there are many—is rendered with such immediacy and power that it is impossible to separate the impact of death from the impact of her language. Destruction is so super-efficient, so precise . . . , that its aim is infallible. (pp. 539-40)

Big and small—violent and paradisaical—these are the converging modes and styles that create the poles of tension that strain and sustain the artistic theory and work of McCullers. The supreme issue is whether a harmony born of divine collusion will bring art or love; or whether discord will dominate and the divine presence will be cut off from a world now severed from redemptive visitation. No one situation more fully reflects the alternatives of promise and failure than the archetypal one of the party. Significantly, when Frankie Addams shows some signs of being less "greedy and big" and becoming more loving. Berenice promises her a schizophrenic party. One is to be an elegant bridge party with dainty olive sandwiches set properly in the living room. The other is to be rowdy and boisterous with hot dogs as the fare and set outside in the backyard.... Like the party which started out sweet and ended up violent in *The Heart is a Lonely Hunter;* and like the seminal party from which McCullers was excluded as a child, Frankie's party symbolizes in McCullers the permanence of dualism and imperfection in existence no matter how strongly art fights for the possibilities of heaven on earth.

Growing up does not resolve the intense dualities of childhood. Rather, it only magnifies the extent to which the dream may be shattered. It is in fact significant that every major and minor work which contains an artist-figure also is sustained by an ideal which glows like a heavenly possibility. In *The Heart is a Lonely Hunter* silence and music embody the notion of perfect communication. Captain Penderton's ideal is "To square the circle". Frankie's is to be a member of the wedding. Amelia's is to move within the warm, magic circle of a well-lit cafe. John Tucker's is to find design through love. In *Clock Without Hands,* it is the dream of homosexual love as a symbol of race relations. But if the above ideals represent the promises of childhood and the dreams of heavenly beginnings, McCullers regularly concludes with terrible endings, arrested children, grotesque adults, and freakish odd couples. (pp. 540-41)

The only ideal not shattered is that of art. The mature artists in her work, though few and zany, are the only ones who achieve any kind of wholeness. The price they and their art play for such an achievement is that their art to be true must record failure. Nevertheless, art is justified in being called divine by McCullers and her aesthetics, her metaphysics because art alone provides the flowering dream by which to measure and to portray the permanent drama of paradisaical exclusion. If art is indeed born of divine collusion, then it alone serves as the square root of heaven on earth. (p. 541)

Irving H. Buchen, "Divine Collusion: The Art of Carson McCullers," in The Dalhousie Review, *Autumn, 1974, pp. 529-41.*

NANCY B. RICH

Although Carson McCullers referred to her novel, *The Heart is a Lonely Hunter,* as "an ironic parable of Fascism," critics have not taken her statement seriously, either because it seems too general a reference to the social and economic conditions of the novel or because it appears too restrictive in terms of the theme of isolation. Considerable evidence, however, suggests the probability that politics was a motivating factor in the genesis of the novel and that the parable is a key not only to broader implications in the theme but also to the tight construction McCullers claimed and reviewers have so often questioned. (p. 108)

Perhaps the most logical way to approach this novel is as a parable, for its context clarifies such mysteries as the function and meaning of Antonapoulos, its structure is clear, and its theme is specific. The parable has a conventional protagonist pitted against specific forces, but develops in thematic patterns rather than in traditional plot formation, treating successively the ideas of the nature of government, the failure of democracy, and the condition of freedom. The thematic patterns are delineated by situation and setting and dramatized through character and action. The parable's theme is an affirmation of the democratic process, but its implications are the universal problems of illusion versus reality and the nature of man himself. It not only supports but also greatly strengthens the theme of isolation. Far from being restrictive, it extends the dimensions of pathos already perceived. . . . Government in this parable . . . is represented by a deaf mute, and the instrument of oppression is the sound of silence, an image which McCullers introduces in her opening chapter where no word is spoken.

The author's decision to objectify the negative force of government as John Singer was the turning point in the construction of the novel, for it provided a means of dramatizing the image of silence and created a concrete symbolic structural device for the parable.

Singer, who is seen by most reviewers as the pivotal character of the novel, achieves that status because the eye of every other character is on him. Minor characters who

remain nameless except as they are associated with various ethnic, business or agricultural groups, think he is one of them, and major characters believe him sympathetic to the social, economic or political interests they pursue. The accuracy of their assumptions remains moot, for Singer neither confirms nor denies. In fact, aside from walking the streets, visiting Antonapoulos, and eating at Biff's café, Singer does almost nothing in the novel. He appears prominent, but in reality he is little more than a memory or an expectation in the minds of the other characters during a major portion of the action. The few specific acts which essentially define his character suggest democracy at work, for he takes in the homeless, gives money to the poor, and brings technology (the radio) within the reach of all. But his chief characteristic is his muteness, which is the mark of his distance from others. Moreover, the accessibility which brings others to him gradually diminishes as the novel progresses, so that as a symbol of government, Singer clearly exemplifies its ineffectuality. He welcomes people to his room at first because they relieve his solitude and sorrow, but in chapter seven of Book II, which is the mid-point of the novel, he comes to grips with the fact that these people "do not attend to the feelings of others"; feeling "alone . . . in an alien land," he gradually withdraws. . . . [As] the figure of Singer gradually fades into the background, the parable shows that for all practical purposes government has become defunct.

Its absence is clearly manifest in the official silence which follows each successive act of violence (the violence begins in earnest in chapter seven and continues to become worse). . . . [It] is not what people do that is incredible; it is the fact that nobody does anything. It is the sound of silence. This is, after all, not Fascist Germany but the land of the free. This is the Sunny Dixie Show (which incidentally "wants" a mechanic) with its "bright lights . . . and lazy laughter" where, in a strange Kafkaesque way, everything seems normal. . . . Jake senses something "sullen and dangerous" . . . under the deceptively bright Dixie Show, and this something is the insanity of imagining that everything is fine when reality clearly shows that it is not. "America," says Jake, is a "crazy house" . . . and in fact it is a grotesquely distorted world where people seem oblivious to reality.

To clarify this point and dramatize her image of insanity, McCullers presents us with a king who rules benignly over a lunatic asylum.

Like Singer, Antonapoulos is a deaf mute, which signals that his role in the parable is associated with government; also like Singer, who used to be able to talk and was functional in the beginning of the novel, Antonapoulos was originally sane and a part of the work force in the town. But unlike Singer, Antonapoulos has always remained just out of view of the major characters. Singer is the arm of government, which is symbolized in chapter one by his continually trying to move the chess men around. But Antonapoulos is puzzled by the practical business of the game; he does not understand the female figures and prefers whites over blacks, an analogy to the historical confusion of how these minority figures should be treated in a free democratic society. The "dreamy Greek" is impractical because he symbolizes an ideal. His strange pagan/Christian aura is not really strange at all; it signifies his role in the "ironic parable of Fascism" as the representation of that combination of Greek democracy and Christian idealism which constitutes the basis of the American political system. (pp. 111-13)

Except for Biff, who remembers him vaguely, no one in the town he leaves even thinks about him but Singer. As Singer rides through the American countryside, he associates the "abundance of growth and color" somehow with his friend, and in all his dreams, "Antonapoulos was there." In the dream tableau, which defines the relationships of characters, Antonapoulos stands at the top, holding something above his head. This something is the Constitution of the United States, and Singer is fascinated by it, but unfortunately it exists only in his dream, and even then it remains just beyond the sight of the American people who are behind him in the dark; while he watches, the whole vision collapses. This tableau is indeed central to the novel, and it is a crystallization of the situation of the parable. (p. 113)

Mick represents both the white population in general (Lucille says she lives in a "common" neighborhood) and most women. This is why most reviewers "see Mick as the central personage of the novel" [as evidenced in Edgar E. MacDonald's "The Symbolic Unity of 'The Heart is a Lonely Hunter'"]. But like Singer, she is a negative force—a "silent" majority—for although she has within her a song or dream, and might therefore restore the dream (Antonapoulos) to Singer, she does not know exactly what the dream is all about. The dream-song is entitled "THIS THING I WANT, I KNOW NOT WHAT." . . . Thus as the collective mind of the majority, she represents the real causes of the failure of democracy.

The tendency of reviewers to blame Mick's failure on social and economic factors has resulted in some critical vagueness with regard to her character, but her flaws are just as relevant to her personal tragedy as they are to her symbolic role. In the parable, she represents public apathy; its causes, which appear to be immaturity, immorality and irrationality, are manifest in her behavior. These traits may seem incongruous with our generally sympathetic view of Mick, but if we are deceived about her true fibre, it is because she is deceived about herself. Both the deception and the qualities are demonstrably major aspects of her character delineation.

Mick seems at first to be a nonconformist. . . . Since at the end of the novel she joins their ranks, the original image of her is deceptive. . . . (pp. 114-15)

Judged by her actions, Mick is selfish, dishonest and prejudiced. (p. 115)

Mick is not entirely the "selfless seeker after love" she seems to be. In every respect except for her dream of music, she seems to exemplify that condition in America which Swedish philosopher Myrdahl labeled the "American dilemma," which is to say that she thinks she embodies both Christian and democratic principles, when in fact she practices neither. (p. 116)

Critics who interpret the novel without considering the parable see the dream tableau as a key to character relationships and conclude that Singer is a God figure and the other major characters are of equal stature in a row behind him. But in the parable, Singer represents the government, and what the tableau means is that theoretically all men are equal in relation to and in sight of government, and not to

each other, since these characters are in no way alike. Neither the radical reformer nor the Negro nor the woman nor the conformist is going to change political systems in the thirties or for a long time to come. That leaves only Biff Brannon.

An unlikely candidate for hero, Biff has no special talent; he is not particularly "aware," as is indicated by his watching "from a distance" when Copeland comes into his café and is insulted. Neither is he equipped with any special knowledge, for he continually asks questions, some of them not very astute. Nor is he possessed of "vision," as some critics have asserted: when Blount talks of soul brotherhood, for instance, Biff thinks he means the Masons. . . . (pp. 117-18)

Biff is clearly an average, middle-class American; therefore, he is the most important character in the parable, for its central question is concerned with the survival of freedom under a democratic political system. (p. 118)

Measured by conventional standards of plot construction, which are discernible in the parable, Biff is clearly the main character. The opening chapter introduces a situation which defines the two major images of silence and lunacy. Except for the two figures who symbolically dramatize these ideas, no other character but Biff appears in this chapter. Although specific clues as to the causes of the situations reflected in the images appear in the picture, Biff is remote from them in terms of his position in the chapter, the implication being that he is surrounded by things of which he is unaware. And yet these clues are the kinds of things an observant man like Biff should have seen or known or read about. Some of these are the power of capitalism (Charles Parker), racial and sexual prejudice (the chess men), and disregard for law (in the escapades of Antonapoulos).

The final chapter again evokes the images of silence and madness. Biff is alone in the "peaceful silence of the night," except for the sound of a radio voice which is describing Hitler's evil schemes in Danzig. But this time there is a difference, for Biff labels this lunacy a "crisis," and his own voice rings out through the quiet. In this chapter Biff dominates the scene and the emphasis is on his thoughts. He has not yet put together the pieces of the "puzzle of Singer," but he is thinking about Willy, whom the law maimed, and Mick, who had "grown older," and himself; and he has decided "money" and "profit" are not important to him. (pp. 119-20)

[What] Carson McCullers is saying is that the average man's biggest problem is that he deceives himself. But he does have the intellectual and moral possibility to be better than he is, and there are some grounds for optimism in a man like Biff who at least knows what he wants to be, and in whom, as [Ihab] Hassan has noted, is to be seen "an image of clumsy endurance, a will for right action which no excess of hate or suffering or disenchantment can wholly suspend." The fact that this will is exerting some influence on Biff is demonstrated by the slight change in him between the first scene and the last. When Biff first looks at himself in the mirror in chapter two, his eyes are "cold and staring," and all his image tells him is that he needs a shave. In the last chapter, however, one eye is looking into the past and the other into the future; thus he is beginning to get perspective on things. Furthermore, he is frightened by the image and reacts by almost forcibly pulling himself together to take one positive step in the present.

McCullers commented that her heroes are "not the only human beings of their kind. Because of the essence of these people . . . they will someday be united and they will come into their own." History has proved that she was right. Biff is only one man, and the time was not ripe, which accounts for the seemingly pessimistic ending of the novel. But he is "a sensible man"; in contrast to the discord outside, his café "is serene." Somewhere, soundless in the background is the Negro he has hired. He is still working on the "puzzle of Singer." The door of his café is never closed through the dark of night, which is the present; and one day, the parable implies, he will unite with others like himself to put a new image of government before the people, just as surely as he puts fresh flowers in his display. The implications of Biff's character thus suggest that the failure of democracy is itself an illusion—that the nature of the democratic process is like that of Biff, slow, and the condition of freedom is perseverance. (pp. 121-22)

> Nancy B. Rich, "The 'Ironic Parable of Fascism' in 'The Heart is a Lonely Hunter'," in The Southern Literary Journal (copyright 1977 by the Department of English, University of North Carolina at Chapel Hill), Spring, 1977, pp. 108-23.

LOUIS D. RUBIN, JR.

I think it is not without importance that the all-night restaurant in Carson McCuller's first novel, *The Heart is a Lonely Hunter,* is called The New York Cafe. In the small-sized Southern city in the late 1930's, when the story takes place, there is little doing at night and none of the people involved in the story is either very contented or very hopeful; the New York Cafe is the only place for them to go, and its forlorn hospitality is indicative of what is barren and joyless about the lives of those who go there. From Columbus, Georgia to New York City is a long way.

Biff Blannon's restaurant is presumably called the New York Cafe because of the ironic contrast between what it is and what its name signifies. . . . Set in the backwaters of civilization (as Carson McCullers's imagination saw it, anyway), the pathetic name given the all-night restaurant mocks the romantic dream with its commonplace actuality. . . . [The] inappropriateness of the name New York Cafe is meant by the author to convey a sense of cultural starvation, the provincial dreariness of the kind of city where the sidewalks, as they used to say, are rolled up each night at ten o'clock. As well call it the Café de Paris.

Is that what Columbus, Georgia was like? I suppose it depends upon the viewpoint, and Carson McCullers's viewpoint at the time she was writing *The Heart is a Lonely Hunter* was not exactly that of the Nashville Agrarians, or even of William Faulkner or Eudora Welty. Frankie Addams's view of Columbus and her own, she once remarked, were identical. (pp. 265-66)

In neither McCullers nor [Thomas Wolfe] is the hold of the Southern community upon characters very real. Neither is very much involved in the kind of historical tradition or community identification that writers such as Faulkner and Welty use for the stuff of their fiction.

A major difference between McCullers's South and Wolfe's is that there is no sense of Wolfe himself feeling trapped in it. He is going to leave. Carson McCullers's people are there to stay, and their yearning for something better and finer and more fulfilling has a kind of painful *angst* about it. Their yearning for the metropolis, as has often been said, is like that of Chekhov's provincial Russians for Moscow: for a place of impossible fulfillment that is too far off in time and space to represent anything more than a forlorn hope. (pp. 267-68)

In [*The Heart is a Lonely Hunter, Reflections in a Golden Eye, The Ballad of the Sad Cafe,* and *The Member of the Wedding*], produced over a period of less than a decade and while the author was still in her twenties, we have a very impressive body of fiction indeed.

That was all. Nothing that she wrote in the remaining two decades of her life adds much to her achievement. *Clock Without Hands* was an artistic disaster; only her most devoted admirers could say much for it. Whatever it was she had in the way of a gift, she had lost it. When she died in 1967, I doubt that anyone felt that she was leaving good books unwritten.

We are dealing, therefore, with certain works of fiction written and published during a period of intense and often brilliant creativity, by a young writer, a *wunderkind* as it were, one who did not develop or extend her range afterward. I think it is important to remember that. Whatever the faces and tensions that were central to her life and art, and which ultimately destroyed both, they attained, during this period, an equilibrium that made her fiction possible. (p. 268)

The McCullers fiction, I believe, has at its center a fundamental premise: which is, that solitude—loneliness—is a human constant, and cannot possibly be alleviated for very long at a time. But there is no philosophical acceptance of that condition, and none of the joy in it that one finds in, say, Thomas Wolfe or even Hemingway. The solitude is inevitable, and it is always painful. Thus life is a matter of living in pain, and art is the portraying of anguish. Occasionally, a character of hers knows happiness, but never for very long. (p. 270)

Mrs. McCullers explains it by her remarks on love, which she says involves the lover and the beloved, who come from two different countries. There is no way that such love can be shared, for one of the two must love and the other be loved; no reciprocal relationship, whereby one both loves and is loved in turn, is possible.

Obviously love in this definition involves possession. The lover, she says, "is forever trying to strip bare his beloved. The lover craves every possible relation with the beloved, even if this experience can cause him only pain." For this reason, she points out, it is much more desirable, and most people wish, to be the lover rather than the beloved, since the "beloved fears and hates the lover" who is trying to possess him. . . . Carson McCullers not only declares that it *must* be that way, but that the very nature of being loved, which is to say, wanted and needed by another, is intolerable.

Such of course is the scheme of *The Heart is a Lonely Hunter.* "In the town there were two mutes, and they were always together." Singer is the lover, Antonopoulos the beloved. Antonopoulos accepts Singer because it is convenient and comfortable for him to do so, but then he loses his intelligence and also his need for what Singer can provide, since as a vegetable he requires nothing outside himself. So Singer is left, bereft, loveless. As long as he could retain the illusion that Antonopoulos had a place for him in his affections, he could cope; Antonopoulos's very inchoateness and lack of awareness were an advantage, since they permitted Singer to believe in the fiction that his love understood and returned.

Singer's self-deception in turn makes possible the self-deception of all the others. . . . So long as Singer will sit and listen to them speak their troubles, they can for a time at least function. Singer understands them only imperfectly; he depends upon lip-reading. The fact that he cannot answer back, cannot carry on a dialogue, is what makes him so satisfactory, for in that way the others are enabled to believe that he understands, sympathizes, and accepts all that they say and feel. In this respect, Singer fills the role of the beloved; he allows himself to be loved, because he is insulated from the demands and the possessiveness of love by virtue of his deafness. If he were not deaf, and thus solitary in a world of talkers, he could never tolerate the others, of course, and this not because he is selfish or mean—he is neither—but because he is a human being. Thus Singer serves the others as the object of their love (which obviously is self-love), while Antonopoulos fills a similar role for him, and the self-deception works—until Antonopoulos dies, whereupon the occasion for Singer's love collapses and he shoots himself, and the others are left stranded. The artistry is in the pain—Mrs. McCullers has never let us participate in the deception; we have witnessed it at all points for the ruse that it is, and when the arrangements collapse we perceive only the inevitable outcome of what we have seen developing all along. Again [as the narrator says in *The Ballad of the Sad Cafe*], you might as well go listen to the chain gang—which is pretty much what as readers we have been engaged in doing. (pp. 271-72)

[What I find most remarkable about *The Heart is a Lonely Hunter*] is that a writer whose imagination is so subjective, whose art is so suffused with emotional coloration and is based upon the capacity to convey the endless sameness of human suffering, could at the same time see and record and catalogue so much, with such clear specificity and concrete objectivity of detail. For one whose view of the human condition is so thoroughly pessimistic to be able to combine that with the kind of knowledge of people and things outside of her that surely stems from a considerable fascination in observing the varieties of experience seems odd, to say the least. (p. 273)

Carson McCullers focuses upon her maimed, misfitting, wounded people not as a commentary upon the complacent "normality" of the community which would term them freakish, but as exemplars of the wretchedness of the human condition. It isn't that freaks are commentaries or criticisms on normality; they *are* normality. Their physical grotesquery merely makes visible and identifiable their isolation and anguish; "normal" people do not confront these on quite such immediate and inescapable terms, perhaps, but they are really no better off, no happier. Everybody that is human is on the chain gang; on some the stripes and chains are merely more readily visible.

The particular vision of Carson McCullers, the capacity for recognizing and portraying and sympathetically identifying

with pain and loneliness, could arise only out of a social situation [as in Southern communities] in which the patterns and forms and expectations of conduct and attitude are very firmly and formidably present, so that the inability or failure to function within those patterns seems crucial. If everything is permitted and expected, then there is no need to feel pain or frustration because one's own behavior and inclinations are different from those of others. But if there is a strong set of expectations, and one is unable to fulfill them and yet be oneself, then one searches out for kindred sufferers, in order to feel less lonely through assurance of their pain as well. Thus the portrait gallery of Carson McCullers' "freaks"—i.e., of those who must accept being set apart. And the conviction that this is the way the world goes, and no genuine human sharing is possible.

The appetite of Mrs. McCullers for viewing and identifying the details of human life, and the accuracy with which she was able to create so many sharply delineated people, then, was not exactly a joy in the richness and variety of experience, so much as a hunger for possession. It wasn't enough to see and identify; she had to demonstrate that, despite the varied surfaces and individually realized characterizations, they were really all alike, and what lay at the core of each was suffering and pain deriving from loneliness. One is reminded of a writer that Mrs. McCullers very much admired: Marcel Proust—significantly, a homosexual, as Mrs. McCullers was a lesbian. In that brilliant and profound panorama of men and women who appear in the seven volumes of the *Recherche du Temps Perdu*, each individual struggles to possess and to use others. . . . [At] the core of each one is the unsatisfied desire to possess, to use, to pleasure oneself through or upon (never with) others, and it is all doomed, for life in human time is meaningless, since everything changes and nothing remains. Only the art that derives from personal, involuntary memory can achieve meaning; art is *not* life, but its subjective recreation in the possessive imagination of the artist.

Something like this, I imagine, is what the writing of fiction was for Carson McCullers; art was a way of possessing. It was the creative act of taking what she saw and molding it, transforming it beyond identifiable shape into the form of art, so that it represented her kind of world. And I am tempted to say that, in the tension between the observed authority of the recalcitrant materials she drew upon and the powerful, possessive will to shape them to her desired meaning, the artistic equilibrium came that made her best work possible. Her first book, *The Heart is a Lonely Hunter*, produced the most convincing and richest of all her characters, Dr. Benedict Maby Copeland, the black physician, and this is because, more so than with any of the others, there was a kind of palpable and inescapable social integrity in the material itself. With the other characters in the novel (and all have their individual integrities), the pain and loneliness were personal, subjective; with Dr. Copeland, there was added a specific and very formidable social deprivation. . . . Dr. Copeland is an educated, talented black man in the segregated society of southwest Georgia; any chagrin, mortification, rage he feels requires no dependence upon personal, subjective sensibility. Thus the kind of sensibility with which Mrs. McCullers invests him—the loneliness and anguish—blends so completely with the social outrage that the one gives body to the other. Each time I reread *The Heart is a Lonely Hunter* I am the more impressed with the characterization of Dr. Copeland. He is masterful, one of the reasons I . . . [feel] that the first novel is the best of all her full-length works.

I say this despite my admiration for so much of *The Member of the Wedding*. Frankie Addams is the most appealing of Mrs. McCullers's people; I like her better than Mick Kelly because she is less strident—less written, I think, to a thesis. She is what Mick Kelly would perhaps have been, had there been room for her to have a whole book of her own. In *The Heart is a Lonely Hunter*, the "Mozart" motif always seemed a bit incongruous and sentimental to me, as if it were somewhat forced upon the characterization. Frankie Addams has the same sensibility without the extraneous element, as I see it, and her struggles with pre-adolescence are entirely convincing and wondrously done—up to a certain point. That point is reached when, two-thirds of the way through, Frankie's sensibility moves beyond that inherent in her situation and becomes something bizarre and genuinely distorted—when the piano tuner goes to work and Frankie and Berenice have some kind of surrealistic, mystic vision of pain and misery. After that point, I cease to believe fully in the meaning Mrs. McCullers is (as it now seems) forcing upon Frankie. That's not Frankie as we have known her, and she never recovers. The novel, in other words, goes beyond the pain of pre-adolescent awkwardness and becomes truly aberrant; it drops off the deep end into distortion for the sake of distortion. The death of John Henry, for example: he seems to be killed off gratuitously, in order to provide more misery. And in the epilogue, when Frankie enters full adolescence, becomes Frances, and is made into a "normal" teenager, it seems too arbitrary, too pat. That isn't Frankie, either. (pp. 275-79)

[Her] two important artist figures, Mick and Frankie, cannot go beyond the point of incipient sexual awakening and yet remain consistent with their characterizations. These young girls, both with masculine names, remain fixed in pre-adolescence; when they have to become women, as they must, they are, as characters, all but destroyed. (p. 279)

Instead of her characters representing aspects of Carson McCullers's sensibility, they seem to have *become* her sensibility. Not only was the gap between life and art erased; the fantasy, and the suffering it embodied, were allowed to become the reality. Whatever anchor to everyday life had existed before, in the form of her childhood identity, her early experience, the necessity of having to fit into and live in a world beyond and outside her emotional needs, ceased to hold. The pain, the suffering, the yearning, no longer a commentary upon experience, were now the experience itself. (p. 281)

She could not draw from the pain and loneliness the truths that, in Proust's words, "take the place of sorrows," since "when the latter are transformed into ideas, they at once lose part of their noxious effect on the heart and from the very first moment the transformation itself radiates joy." For Carson McCullers this never happened. "She was never an intellectual," a onetime friend said of her; "she only felt." If so, she had reached a stage at which the perception of pain was not enough, if she was to go beyond the early fiction. But that was all she knew. There was, for her, no Recapture of Lost Time, but only *Clock Without Hands*.

Like certain other of her contemporaries, Carson McCullers, it seems to me, constructed her art out of the South, but not out of its history, its common myths, its public values and the failure to cherish them. What is Southern in her books are the rhythms, the sense of brooding loneliness in a place saturated with time. Compare *The Heart is a Lonely Hunter* or *The Member of the Wedding* with, say, *Winesburg, Ohio,* and the relationship with the region is obvious. Sherwood Anderson's grotesques are more simple; a few clear, masterful sentences and we get their essential quality. Carson McCullers must show her misfits, whether spiritual or physical, in an extended context; there is plenty of time for everything. The Southern quality is unmistakable, in the unhurried fascination with surfaces, the preoccupation with the setting in which the characterization reveals itself. Character is not for McCullers, any more than for Eudora Welty or William Faulkner or Thomas Wolfe, an idea, but a state of awareness. To repeat, there is plenty of time . . . and when the violence comes, as it so often does, it erupts in a place and a context, and it jars, queerly or terribly or both, the established and accustomed patterns. Before and after, there is lots of waiting, lots of time to think about everything. (pp. 281-82)

Southern literature is filled with depictions of characters who, set for one reason or other on the outside, contemplate the intense coming and going of a community life from a private distance. . . . [This] is an essential element in Southern fiction, and in no other Southern author's work is it more essential than in the fiction of Carson McCullers.

Surely this situation lies at the heart of her relationship with the South, and nowhere is it given more pathetic rendering than by her. This is what one takes away, most of all, from Carson McCullers's people in their time and place: the way that it feels to be lonely.

That is why her people do and say what they do. That is the source of the pain. That is why the New York Cafe keeps open all the time: "the only store on all the street with an open door and lights inside." And that is why her best work may survive. (pp. 282-83)

> *Louis D. Rubin, Jr., "Carson McCullers: The Aesthetic of Pain," in* Virginia Quarterly Review *(copyright, 1977, by the Virginia Quarterly Review, The University of Virginia), Vol. 53, No. 2 (Spring, 1977), pp. 265-83.*

*   *   *

MIGUÉIS, José Rodrigues   1901-

Miquéis, a Portuguese short story writer and novelist, centers his work around specific notions of class structure, the nobility of work and love, and principles of neorealism.

GERALD M. MOSER

On the surface [*O milagre secundo Salomé*] revolves around a sentimental plot: a poor country girl exploited in the city and forced into prostitution is rescued by a rich old bachelor, himself a country boy. Bored with luxury, the girl runs off, finding true love with a poor but talented and ardent young writer, who discovers she has conserved her purity! Their fortuitous encounter in a nocturnal Lisbon street tops a series of unlikely coincidences. But reserve your judgment: in fact, the sequence of idylls, fulfilled yearnings and shattering nightmares forms a dream world which contrasts ironically with the realism of the psychological insights, Portuguese settings (chiefly in Lisbon) and historical events. . . .

Following an old penchant for mystery novels, Miguéis hints early at a strange connection between Dores, known as Salomé since her brothel days, and Our Lady of Sorrows (*Dores*), known universally as the Virgin of Fátima. (p. 84)

The sincerity and intensity of feeling inherent in good autobiography inspire the best chapters of the *Milagre,* beginning with the one on the arrival of the inexperienced country boy in Lisbon. Only one other Portuguese novelist has tried to give a panoramic view of contemporary Portuguese society, Joaquim Paço d'Arcos, who brought to the task familiarity with the life of the upper class and a mocking spirit. Miguéis has a better grasp of the life, feelings and thoughts of the lower classes, richer emotion and an unsurpassed mastery of subtle, precise language. (p. 85)

> *Gerald M. Moser, in* World Literature Today *(copyright 1977 by the University of Oklahoma Press), Vol. 51, No. 1, Winter, 1977.*

JOHN AUSTIN KERR, JR.

The novelette "Léah" by the well-known Portuguese writer José Rodrigues Miguéis has attracted a considerable amount of published comment, but it has been reviewed almost exclusively in terms of the larger work of which it now forms a part. . . . [However], the story was first published separately in 1940, nearly two decades before its appearance in *Léah e Outras Histórias.* . . . (p. 220)

As might be expected from Miguéis's earlier works, "Léah" is replete with social problems. Many of them are familiar. There is, for example, the problem of the modest means of the protagonist. Carlos's genteel poverty has its effect in many ways, but with relation to the plot it is particularly important to note that it is his lack of money that first brings him to Mme Lambertin's *pensão,* where he takes a room which is far from being luxurious and is only passably clean. It is at the *pensão,* of course, that he meets and falls in love with Léah. Then, as Carlos and Léah's love affair progresses, it is primarily his impecuniousness that stops him from accompanying Léah to her native France, where she hopes they can marry and settle down. Thus poverty, or at least a certain lack of affluence, not only leads to Carlos's meeting his lover but also militates against the couple's regularizing their relationship. . . .

[The poverty in] "Léah" has many ramifications and several levels of complexity. The protagonist's poverty can logically be ascribed to his years of study as well as to his travels abroad. His lack of affluence is thus a result of positive personal decisions, of an investment in his future, as it is often put, however much it may weigh upon him at the moment. [Other characters are in an analogous financial position for different reasons]. . . . In this way Miguéis has highlighted certain aspects of a life of poverty through contrasting perceptions of reality. And finally, it is apparent that, even though the author has discussed the problem of poverty before and has dealt with it elsewhere from various points of view, it appears in "Léah" as yet another example of his complex treatment of a problem beneath the surface of a seemingly simple presentation.

[While there is a wide range of other social problems which the author brings to the reader's attention in "Léah" the main social problem] consists of the whole complex episode centering about the fact that a man from a relatively higher socioeconomic class falls in love with, seduces and then abandons a girl from a lower socioeconomic class. As usual, Miguéis does not present the situation in simplistic terms, for in Carlos and Léah's case the process of falling in love and being seduced is a mutual affair. But in the end it is Carlos who abandons Léah. This is a very old theme in Miguéis's writings. . . .

Typically, too, Miguéis prepares the way for Carlos's final act of abandonment by pointing out early in the story the differences in social class that exist between him and Léah. These are due primarily to education, which Léah lacks almost entirely. This facet is given a neat, rationalizing twist, however, to obscure this basic incompatibility between the two lovers: Léah's lack of formal education is seen initially as a virtue because it results in her having a refreshing candor. In this manner Léah's innate attractiveness has been enhanced at the beginning of the episode, while the seed of future dissension and drawing apart has also been planted, all but unnoticed. Thus it can be seen that the author's subliminal infiltration, observable in such earlier works as *Páscoa Feliz,* continued to be an important part of his literary technique. . . . (p. 222)

[Carlos] is not intentionally an evildoer, for he at least thinks he has been in love with Léah and is left with a sense of permanent loss. . . . Carlos is . . . typical of the ordinary mortal, neither weak enough to be entirely evil nor strong enough to master all of life's temptations. He is, in sum, a very human character. . . .

There is . . . a group of psychological problems which is both central to the development of the plot of "Léah" and is observable in many other works by the same author: that is, the problems a foreigner has in adjusting to his new surroundings, which are manifested in Carlos by his disillusionment with his Belgian surroundings, a recurring sadness and loneliness and a longing for home. He is dissatisfied with life and even with his own compatriots. In this respect, then, Carlos is in a position analogous to that of the protagonist of "Cinzas de Incêndio": in many ways he could be the latter's twin except that he has scientific rather than artistic tendencies. Like his counterpart, Carlos is ripe for an amorous adventure—hence the importance of these problems to the story's development.

There are other psychological problems apparent in "Léah," such as the fact that Mme. Lambertin's husband does not seem to care about anything that takes place around him, M. Albert's mental retardation and the emotional effects of a girl's loss of virginity prior to marriage. None of these, however, is as important to the progress of the story as those preparing the way for, and arising from, Carlos and Léah's love affair. And of course these have their social as well as their psychological importance: it is an added dimension which furnishes yet another bit of evidence that Miguéis is a writer of major talents.

Finally and perhaps most importantly, because one can note this point of view in earlier writings—as, for example, in *Páscoa Feliz* and "O Acidente"—the most striking of the various complementary aspects of "Léah" which come to the fore is the author's depiction of the worker as an essentially noble being. . . . The theme of the nobility of work itself is incorporated into that of the nobility of love between man and woman as well. . . . [This] aspect is hedged with rhetorical doubt and melded into a dream of a fuller life. But it is there, and it was perhaps one of the reasons why a critic of the stature of Adolfo Casais Monteiro could place on Miguéis's brow the perhaps unwanted laurel of being the true, if unacknowledged, mentor of the Portuguese neo-realist movement. (p. 223)

> *John Austin Kerr, Jr., "Some Considerations on Rodrigues Miguéis's 'Léah'," in* World Literature Today *(copyright 1977 by the University of Oklahoma Press), Vol. 51, No. 2, Spring, 1977, pp. 220-23.*

* * *

MILLER, Arthur   1915-

Miller is an American playwright. A moralist who has often been charged with didacticism, he poses questions for which he gives no answers, instead seeking a state of "heightened consciousness" for his heroes and audience. (See also *CLC*, Vols. 1, 2, 6, and *Contemporary Authors*, Vols. 1-4, rev. ed.)

C. W. E. BIGSBY

In many ways . . . *The Price* seems to mark a return to the world of Joe Keller and Willy Loman. Once again, it appears, we are invited to witness the struggles of a man who has "the wrong dreams" and who embraces too completely the ethics of a society intent on success at any price. But . . . since *Death of a Salesman* Miller has become aware of more fundamental influences than those exerted by Horatio Alger Jr. and while he continues to expose the vacuity of the American dream he is more concerned with probing the nature of human freedom than with exposing the social charade. [*The Price*], therefore, owes more to *After the Fall* and *Incident at Vichy* than to *All My Sons* and *Death of a Salesman*.

The line between *Incident at Vichy* and *The Price* is disturbingly direct. Miller has said that he is fascinated by the Nazi era because it constituted a turning point in man's perception of human nature. The war and the Nazi occupation of Europe produced not merely "a chilling of the soul by the technological apparatus" but also "the obstruction of the individual's capacity for choosing, or erosion of what used to be thought of as an autonomous personality." (p. 16)

As in *Death of a Salesman* and *After the Fall* we are at a point in time when the main characters are made suddenly aware of the futility of their lives thus far. For Willy Loman it had been an imperfect perception—a dull sense of insufficiency and failure. For Quentin it was a sudden realisation that his life had been dedicated only to self-interest. In *The Price* the crisis emerges from a meeting between two brothers. Both men are at a crucial stage in their own lives. Victor, a frustrated and bitterly disappointed policeman, looks back over his life and sees no meaning and no hope for his remaining years. He is poised. He lacks the courage to retire because this means that he will be forced to acknowledge his failure to create anything worthwhile through his career. Likewise he lacks the will to start again—to change a destiny which he has already rationalized away as the consequence of the economic determinism of the nineteen-thirties. His brother, Walter, is in a similar position. Al-

though successful he can find no purpose or meaning behind his frenzied pursuit of wealth and fame. His personal life is in ruins, his professional integrity compromised. But after a serious nervous breakdown he feels at long last that he has begun to understand himself and as the play progresses it becomes apparent that he is determined to put this new, imperfect, knowledge into practice. For the first time he feels genuinely alive to the possibilities of a life built on something more substantial than mutual recrimination and obsessive guilt. Seized with a naive excitement he struggles against his old nature and fights to explain his new perception to his brother. (pp. 16-17)

What [Walter] now understands and tries to convey to his brother is that human failure can be traced not to some indefinable hostility in the universe or to the destructiveness of a particular social system but to the failure of individuals to recognise the paramount importance of some kind of genuine human relationship. The misery of their own family life, for example, was not a sign that "there was no mercy in the world" but rather that there was "no love in this house . . .". (p. 17)

[Miller failed], in many of the early plays, to trace moral and social failures to their source in the human character. In the person of Chris Keller, in *All My Sons*, he demonstrates the cruelty of the idealist without attempting to understand its cause while in the same play he draws a picture of a war-profiteer without questioning a human nature which could evidence such cruelty and deceit.

Again, in *Death of a Salesman*, he seems uncertain as to whether Willy is the victim of his own weakness or of a brutally simple-minded society. We know, finally, that Willy is fatally illusioned but discover little about the true nature of reality or the potential freedom of moral or social action which depends not only on Willy's state of mind but on the nature of the human situation. . . . [At] this time Miller was himself confused as to the reality of human nature. At one moment he could declare that "there are people dedicated to evil in the world" and regret not having made Judge Danforth, in *The Crucible*, more of a villain; while in the same breath he could say that "man is essentially innocent" and that "the evil in him represents but a perversion of his frustrated love." (pp. 18-19)

With *After the Fall* and . . . *The Price* he has probed not only behind the bland facade of success but also behind the social and psychological rationalisations of earlier plays. Discovering somewhat belatedly an existential ethic he recognises the imperfection of human nature but insists on man's responsibility for his own fate. Earlier he had said that "The great weight of evidence is upon the helplessness of man. The great bulk of the weight of evidence is that we are not in command." But significantly, even then, he felt constrained to add that "we surely have much more command than anybody, including Macbeth's Witches, could ever dream of and somehow a form has to be devised which will account for this. Otherwise the drama is doomed to repeating and repeating *ad nauseam* the same pattern of striving, disillusion and defeat." In spite of this panegyric in favour of man's power to act few playgoers can have seen much evidence of this in Willy Loman's sure progress towards death or even in Biff's belated and untested declarations of faith in a realistic future. Even *The Crucible* proved only that men could be brave in the face of their fate, not that they could do much to avoid unjustified persecution. To recant or to remain obdurate was still to be subject to circumstances not of one's own making. It is only with his most recent work that Miller has been able to reconcile man's freedom to act with the determining factors of his own nature. In *After the Fall* and in *Incident at Vichy* he draws, with Sartrean finesse, the lines which connect individual choice with social injustice and immorality. He probes, for virtually the first time, the real nature of evil and the human origin of cruelty and deceit. (p. 19)

Miller spent the war years in America, safe from any threat of invasion and thus direct persecution and remote from the incomprehensible brutality of Nazi terror. With the end of the war he was left to face a number of paradoxes and his attempt to resolve them is the story of his development as a writer. The treachery and brutality of the war years forced him to reassess his vision of human nature. The naive optimism of the pre-war world, the pathetic faith in political solutions bowed before the realities of Auschwitz and Hiroshima. The world was open to ambiguity again and Miller was sensitive enough to reflect this.

As a Jew who had survived and indeed suffered little inconvenience he felt an ill-defined sense of guilt. This guilt appears throughout his work in a sublimated form. . . . To many critics he seemed to be consciously avoiding specifically Jewish characters while continuing to use a Jewish idiom. Only with *After the Fall,* his painfully autobiographical work, do we discover the real source of this guilt as Quentin, Miller's protagonist, confesses to feeling the "guilt of the survivor." To be a Jew and to have survived is to be inexplicably favoured and hence to be a hostage to the past. This play, then, resolved many of the problems which had vexed Miller throughout his writing career. It served to exorcise his personal sense of guilt but, more significantly, provided evidence that he had finally evolved a consistent concept of the relation between human freedom and human limitations. (pp. 19-20)

In these most recent plays . . . man is unequivocally in control of his own destiny. If he chooses to see himself as a victim this is evidence of his failure of nerve and not of the impossibility of positive action. Man's absurdity, in other words, is of his own making. (p. 20)

The paramount need to accept the consequences of one's actions: the need to "take one's life in one's hands," as Holga had put it in *After the Fall,* is underlined in *The Price* by Solomon. At eighty-nine he had thought his life finished until contacted by Victor. Now, faced with the prospect of disposing of the furniture, he seems to get a new lease on life. He is suddenly aware that there are "more possibilities." This, indeed, is the very heart of the play. Victor has been living his life as though there were no alternatives. . . . The furniture itself, stored for sixteen years in a single room and left untouched, is in many ways an appropriate image for Victor himself. When Solomon says of the furniture that its main drawback lies in the fact that it has "no more possibilities" the comment could obviously apply equally well to Victor's own self-image. But even after the need for some kind of positive action had been demonstrated both by Solomon and Walter he is still unwilling to concede the truth of Esther's comment that, "You can't go on blaming everything on . . . the system or God knows what else! You're free and you can't make a move." (pp. 21-2)

[In *Death of a Salesman*] the two brothers, Happy and Biff, . . . reflect the two sides of Willy's warring personality. Happy values only material things. He looks for some kind of consolation in his relationship with women and, though vaguely conscious of some insufficiency, measures himself solely by reference to his success in business. Biff, on the other hand, is aware of other values than the purely material and is capable finally of the kind of genuine humanity which Willy only approaches in moments of rare sensitivity.

In *The Price* Miller makes use of a similar device. The two brothers represent profoundly different approaches to life—approaches which not only coexist in the world but which constitute the basis of most individual lives. This is the significance of Walter's remark that "we're brothers. It was only two seemingly different roads out of the same trap. It's almost as though . . . we're like two halves of the same guy. As though we can't quite move ahead—alone." (p. 22)

Victor is revealed as a weak and irresolute individual, unwilling to concede responsibility for his own life and consciously avoiding painful realities by retreating into illusion. Walter, on the other hand, is a man who, like Biff, has gradually come to recognise the inconsequence of wealth and success and who now tries to pass his insight onto others. He recognises the need to acknowledge the reality of human weakness and to accept responsibility for one's own actions. (pp. 22-3)

[The] conflict is not simply defined by the individual brothers in some kind of moral polarity. If Walter has a clearer understanding of reality and the need to accept responsibility for one's actions he lacks Victor's moral sensitivity. Yet the struggle is to find an interpretation of existence which depends neither on a naive endorsement of human perfectibility or a cynical pose of alienation. The real problem lies in acknowledging the imperfection of man and the inadequacy of society and yet continuing to place one's faith in human potential. In the words of the wise Solomon, "it's not that you can't believe nothing, that's not so hard—it's that you've still got to believe it. *That's hard*. And if you can't do that . . . you're a dead man." . . . As a piece of moral philosophy this is no different in kind from Quentin's final perception, in *After the Fall,* that it is perhaps enough to know that "we meet unblessed; not in some garden of wax fruit and painted trees, that lie of Eden, but after, after the Fall." To accept imperfection in individuals and in society is not to capitulate before despair. Rather it is the first stage in the reconstruction of meaning and purpose. But there is a price to pay for such a revaluation. It means granting the death of innocence; it necessitates the acceptance of responsibility for one's actions. However, the price for ignoring the challenge is even greater. It involves the destruction of human relationships and the erosion of identity—a price paid by both Victor and Walter. At the end of the play, however, purged of all illusions and forced to face the reality of their lives they have at least a chance to recreate not only themselves but also the society which they in part represent. In this way the social element of Miller's work is traced to its origin in the nature of individual experience and the essence of the human condition. (p. 23)

The Price marks a sharp improvement over his last two plays. It avoids the pretentious dialogue of *After the Fall* and the simple-minded manipulation of *Incident at Vichy*. It acknowledges, too, a sense of ambiguity lacking even from his earlier successes. Despite the somewhat contrived nature of the debate between the two brothers and the unconvincing nature of the minor characters—Solomon and Esther never become anything more than caricatures—there is some justification for feeling that Miller has at last emerged from the personal and artistic difficulties which he has experienced since the mid-fifties. (p. 25)

> *C.W.E. Bigsby, "What Price Arthur Miller? An Analysis of 'The Price'," in* Twentieth Century Literature *(copyright 1970, Hofstra University Press), January, 1970, pp. 16-25.*

BARRY GROSS

[Of the failures of *All My Sons*, most] notable is what might be termed its failure in mode, a serious flaw in methodology: simply and baldly stated, the play is too insistently "realistic"—which is, of course, what Miller meant it to be—to accommodate Chris' fine speeches or to give any weight or resonance to their words. In the narrow and pedestrian setting of the Keller back yard they announce themselves as speeches, in this mundane place the words ring loud and hollow.... The realistic mode is adequate to *All My Sons* as long as the play is dominated by the family relation; it is not adequate to the social relation Miller requires the play to represent, nor does Miller attempt to express that social relation in another, less realistic mode. The problem is clearly illustrated in the case of appropriate stage speech:

> When one is speaking to one's family one uses a certain level of speech, a certain plain diction perhaps, a tone of voice, an inflection, suited to the intimacy of the occasion. But when one faces an audience ... it seems right and proper for him to reach for the well-turned phrase, even the poetic word, the aphorism, the metaphor.

Chris' speeches fall flat because they violate our sense of suitability, our sense of context. They are made at the wrong time in the wrong place to the wrong people. (p. 22)

All My Sons does not burst out of the living room, or, more precisely, the back yard, and yet Miller insists that his characters confront non-familial, openly social relations and forces which exist only beyond it. The result is that same tension Miller feels in *The Cocktail Party*, that "sense of ... being drawn in two opposite directions." In Eliot's play, Miller argues, the tension is created by the language, or, rather, by "the natural unwillingness of our minds to give to the husband-wife relation—a family relation—the prerogatives of the poetic mode," whereas no such problem existed in Eliot's more successful *Murder in the Cathedral* which "had the unquestioned right to the poetic" because its situation was "social, the conflict of a human being with the world." It is, of course, Miller's thematic and philosophic intention to draw us in two opposite directions in *All My Sons,* to dramatize the polar conflict between the familial and the social. But he fails to counter the natural unwillingness of our minds to give to the social relation the prerogatives of the prosaic mode. We grant *All My Sons* the unquestioned right to the prosaic as long as its situation is familial, but if the situation is also to be social, then Miller must extend his play to the poetic, not just in language but also in concept.... [The] foreground the Keller family

occupies looms too large, so large as to obliterate any other context which might or should be behind or around it.

The absence of the larger context does not represent a failure in technique alone—it also represents, and more unaccountably, a failure in content.... [For] its stated intentions, the play is not straightforward enough.... In *All My Sons* Miller is not guilty of presuming to teach, or even of presuming to preach, but of not doing it with sufficient force and directness, of not pinpointing with sufficient sharpness Chris' amorphous and formless sentiments. *That* the world should be reordered is not at issue; *how* it should is.

"Where the son stands," Miller says in "The Shadow of the Gods," "is where the world should begin," but this does not happen in *All My Sons* anymore than it does in the "adolescent" plays Miller criticizes. It is undeniably true that "the struggle for mastery—for the freedom of manhood ... as opposed to the servility of childhood—is the struggle not only to overthrow authority but to reconstitute it anew," but by this token Chris has achieved neither mastery nor manhood by the play's end.... If we are to take Chris' stated sentiments about the men who died so that he might live seriously, then he is in the position at the beginning of *All My Sons* that Miller ... [as revealed in an article] sees the Jewish psychiatrist in at the end of *Incident at Vichy:* his is "the guilt of surviving his benefactors" and whether he is "a 'good' man for accepting his life in this way, or a 'bad' one, will depend on what he makes of his guilt, of his having survived." By that criterion, Chris Keller is a bad man when *All My Sons* begins and he is no better when the play ends. (pp. 22-4)

> *Barry Gross, "'All My Sons' and the Larger Context," in* Modern Drama *(copyright © 1975, University of Toronto, Graduate Centre for Study of Drama; with the permission of* Modern Drama*), March, 1975, pp. 15-27.*

STANLEY KAUFFMANN

Death of a Salesman contains the idea for a great play, and I would maintain that its immense international success comes from the force of that idea prevailing over the defects in execution. The force takes hold with the very title, which is highly evocative, and is amplified by the opening sight of Willy Loman coming in the door. That sight is a superb theater image of our time, as unforgettable an icon as Mother Courage and her wagon (another traveling salesman!): the salesman home, "tired to the death," lugging his two heavy sample-cases, rejected by the big milk-filled bosom of the country from which he had expected so much nourishment.

The force of the play's idea continues fitfully to grasp at us: the idea of a man who has sold things without making them, who has paid for things without really owning them; an insulted extrusion of commercial society battling for some sliver of authenticity before he slips into the dark.

But to see the play again is to see how Arthur Miller lacked the control and vision to fulfill his own idea. First consider the diction of the play, because a play is its language, first and finally. *Salesman* falters badly in this regard. At its best, its true and telling best, the diction is first-generation Brooklyn Jewish. ("Attention, attention must be finally paid to such a person.") But often the dialogue slips into a fanciness that is slightly ludicrous. . . . When Miller's language is close to the stenographic, the remembered, it's good; otherwise, it tends to literary juvenility, a pretended return from pretended experience.

Thematically, too, the play is cloudy. It's hard to believe that, centrally, Miller had anything more than muzzy anti-business, anti-technology impulses in his head. Is Willy a man shattered by business failure and by disappointment in his sons? . . . The figure that comes through the play is not of a man brought down by various failures but of a mentally unstable man in whom the fissures have increased. Willy is shown to be at least as much a victim of psychopathy as of the bitch goddess. When was he ever rational or dependable? Is this a tragedy of belief in the American romance or the end of a clinical case? . . .

What we are left with is neither a critique of the business world nor an adult vision of something different and better but the story of a man (granting he was sane) who failed, as salesman and father, and who made things worse by refusing to the end to admit those failures, which he knew were true. That is one play, and possibly a good one if it were realized; but it is quite a different one from a play that, in its atmosphere and mannerisms, implies radical perception about deep American ills. (p. 20)

> *Stanley Kauffmann, in* The New Republic *(reprinted by permission of* The New Republic; © *1975 by The New Republic, Inc.),* July 19, 1975.

IRVING JACOBSON

Arthur Miller's short stories "Monte Sant' Angelo" and "I Don't Need You Any More" share a supplementary relationship to his essay on "The Family in Modern Drama." All develop themes that prove essential for an understanding of Miller's imagination, and all deal with man displaced from the enveloping context of the family. The meaning of this displacement includes the loss not only of mother, father or brother but also a psychological state of being, a cultural and religious inheritance, a position in the community and in human history. "I Don't Need You Any More" illustrates the process by which a child becomes isolated from his family, losing that state of equilibrium, identity and completeness that Miller defined in his essay as man's fundamental state of satisfaction. "Monte Sant' Angelo," however, presents a set of experiences by which an adult comes to feel himself at home in the larger world outside the family structure, reconstructing that earlier state of satisfaction with later materials and experiences. . . .

[In "Monte Sant' Angelo"] Appello maintains his identity as an American but also enjoys status as a "son of Italy" with an assured place in a long family line of some prominence. He can trace that line from town to town [in Italy] and receive immediate recognition for the very fact of his name. (p. 507)

Dissociated from an historical past, [his friend Bernstein] senses himself dissociated from a personal past as well. Just as Martin, in "I Don't Need You Any More," when asked to demonstrate his spelling to his family "could not bear the indignity, the danger, that lay in having to produce something in exchange for their giving him a place among them," so Bernstein feels insecure in not being able to assume that his place in the world is his by birthright, an absolute posi-

tion from which he might expand his resources with freedom and ease. (p. 508)

Mauro di Benedetto functions as a catalyst for transformation in Bernstein's life. The similarity between his own neglected and Benedetto's vestigial Jewishness forms an emotional bridge between him and Europe. Revitalizing a positive sense of his own family past, the common ethnic background between Bernstein and Benedetto functions as Bernstein's equivalent for Appello's family line, releasing his capacity for excitement and giving him a new sense of placement in the world. (p. 509)

Bernstein's deduction that the man is Jewish accounts for part of this. Although it is not entirely clear from the story itself why Bernstein reddens when Benedetto says he sells cloth, it seems possible that Bernstein associates the trade with being Jewish. . . . Jews in Europe were traditionally active in interurban trade because of special legal and social factors. Also, Appello translates the name, Mauro di Benedetto, as Morris of the Blessed, or Moses. Further, the man says that he follows the same route and pattern his family has followed for generations, making certain he is home by sundown each Friday night—the beginning of the Jewish Sabbath. But the key factor that leads Bernstein to a conclusion about Benedetto, and the one that draws the most direct lines of connection between them, is the meticulous way the man unknots his bundle and then wraps a loaf of bread in it. This makes Bernstein announce to Appello, with "a new air of confidence and superiority in his face and voice" that Benedetto is Jewish. He explains: "It's exactly the way my father used to tie a bundle—and my grandfather. The whole history is packing bundles and getting away. Nobody else can be as tender and delicate with bundles. That's a Jewish man tying a bundle." . . . (pp. 509-10)

Yet not only is Benedetto unaware that he is Jewish, but he hasn't the vaguest idea what the two Americans' eager questions about his background mean. . . . [He] has no knowledge of what a Jew or Hebrew *is*. In that sense, he can be called a vestigial Jew, maintaining in his life pattern remnants of behavior that had religious significance for someone in the past but which have become merely a "manner of the family," an eccentric set of habits.

Thus, some part of the intensity with which Bernstein responds to Benedetto might be explained by *his* being a vestigial Jew, almost as unconscious of his own background as Benedetto. The encounter brings him to the realization, at the end of the story, that "his life had been covered with an unrecognized shame," a denial of his own religion and, with that, his own access to history. . . . (p. 510)

The effect of the experience is to remove Bernstein from an isolation that has been, in part, self-imposed, and it places his life in the kind of context within which he can form relationships. He can both understand what he had once called Appello's "ancestor complex" and feel that the past [is] his own as much as Appello's. . . . This new sense of belonging makes it possible for him and Appello to achieve a new kind of rapport, a new commonality of spirit. . . . (pp. 510-11)

Bernstein's experience in Monte Sant' Angelo makes it possible for him to yield to his own emotions. In Miller's story there is a sense in which Appello represents the emotional and expressive aspects that are lacking or repressed in Bernstein's personality. . . .

Bernstein comes to feel "at home" in the larger world outside the family structure. Significantly, the means by which he accomplishes this relate intimately to his own sense of family. Mauro di Benedetto is not only a Jew but one, more specifically, who reminds Bernstein of his own father and grandfather. By association, he can be interpreted as a paternal figure—not merely an interesting or admirable man who also seems Jewish, but a kind of father. Suitably, then, he is both Jewish, like Bernstein, and Italian, like Appello. (p. 511)

In both "I Don't Need You Any More" and "Monte Sant' Angelo," the isolated ego, incapable of thriving alone, seeks to strengthen itself through relationships with other men. Given his father's concern and approval, Martin, if only temporarily, feels supported by a community of manhood. (p. 512)

> *Irving Jacobson, "The Vestigial Jews on Monte Sant' Angelo," in* Studies in Short Fiction *(copyright 1976 by Newberry College), Fall, 1976, pp. 507-12.*

ROBERT A. MARTIN

When *The Crucible* opened on January 22, 1953, the term "witch-hunt" was nearly synonymous in the public mind with the Congressional investigations then being conducted into allegedly subversive activities. Arthur Miller's plays have always been closely identified with contemporary issues, and to many observers the parallel between the witchcraft trials at Salem, Massachusetts in 1692 and the current Congressional hearings was the central issue of the play.

Miller has said that he could not have written *The Crucible* at any other time, a statement which reflects both his reaction to the McCarthy era and the creative process by which he finds his way to the thematic center of a play. If it is true, however, that a play cannot be successful in its own time unless it speaks to its own time, it is also true that a play cannot endure unless it speaks to new audiences in new times. The latter truism may apply particularly to *The Crucible,* which is presently being approached more and more frequently as a cultural and historical study rather than as a political allegory. (p. 279)

The Crucible has endured beyond the immediate events of its own time. If it was originally seen as a political allegory, it is presently seen by contemporary audiences almost entirely as a distinguished American play by an equally distinguished American playwright. As one of the most frequently produced plays in the American theater, *The Crucible* has attained a life of its own; one that both interprets and defines the cultural and historical background of American society. Given the general lack of plays in the American theater that have seriously undertaken to explore the meaning and significance of the American past in relation to the present, *The Crucible* stands virtually alone as a dramatically coherent rendition of one of the most terrifying chapters in American history. (p. 290)

> *Robert A. Martin, "Arthur Miller's 'The Crucible': Background and Sources," in* Modern Drama *(copyright © 1977, University of Toronto, Graduate Centre for Study of Drama; with the permission of* Modern Drama*), September, 1977, pp. 279-92.*

JUNE SCHLUETER

When the twentieth century is history and American drama viewed in perspective, the plays of Arthur Miller will undoubtedly be preserved in the annals of dramatic literature. Few will dispute that Miller's plays, along with those of O'Neill and Albee and Williams, constitute the "best" of American theater. This may, however, be more a comment on the state of American drama than on the excellence of Arthur Miller, for, in a larger perspective, there is little in Miller's drama other than well-plotted social and psychological realism, coming decades after the form was established by Ibsen and Shaw.

When Miller defends such realism in his "Preface to an Adaptation of Ibsen's *An Enemy of the People*" (1951)—one of 23 essays and three interviews collected in [*The Theater Essays of Arthur Miller*]—one experiences a déjà vu and wonders why what by then was a donnée of the modern theater needed defense. . . .

With a few exceptions, the essays and interviews which constitute this book are singularly unnoteworthy. Miller's views on the state of the theater reflect a professional's, not a literary critic's, awareness; his ideas concerning form are anachronism offered as innovation; and his prefaces, while helpful as such, are incomplete in isolation. The exceptions are Miller's two anti-Aristotelian documents, "Tragedy and the Common Man" (1949) and "The Nature of Tragedy" (1949). . . . (p. 345)

> *June Schlueter, in* Best Sellers *(copyright © 1978 Helen Dwight Reid Educational Foundation), February, 1978.*

*   *   *

MOORE, Marianne   1887-1972

Moore was an American poet, translator, essayist, and editor. Her poetry is characterized by the technical and linguistic precision with which are revealed her acute observations of the human character. Indeed, her role as "observer" is evident in the remarkable attention to detail found in her poetic descriptions, whether of an object, an animal, or the human condition. The later poems reflect a sense of moral judgment, in contrast to the objectivity of the earlier work. Although her early work has often been connected with the Imagist school, her independence of style and vision have established her as a poet unlike any other. (See also *CLC*, Vols. 1, 2, 4, 8, and *Contemporary Authors*, Vols. 1-4, rev. ed.; obituary, Vols. 33-36, rev. ed.)

STANLEY KUNITZ

Miss Moore is unique, and she never argues. Like peace she is indivisible, and of her verse it can be said that nothing resembles it so much as her prose. Not the least of her accomplishments is that her readers, unprovoked to question her definition of poetry, accept its premises implicitly, without supererogatory judgment or comparisons, because it is their pleasure to do so. . . .

One would like to be able, if only as a reciprocal gesture, to describe Miss Moore's peculiar faculties with the same exactness of detail, founded on the microscopic patience of the eye, with which she delineates the antic physiology of a reindeer, an ostrich, a butterfly, a paper nautilus, or the elaborate pangolin. . . . (p. 220)

Miss Moore's metrics must be classified *sui generis*. Few of her poems—the stately title-piece of [*What Are Years*] is an exception—move on the flood of an internal rhythm. Since her rhythms, by design, are generally extensions of prose rhythms, with frequent word-breaks as run-overs to contradict the line-divisions, Miss Moore's intricate rhyme-schemes and stanzaic structures are actually extra-prosodic and contribute little or nothing to the ear. (The eye, of course, is thankful for white spaces.) Miss Moore even goes to the painful extreme of syllable-counting. But if these are devices to tempt and test her creative spirit, it would be ungrateful for us to cavil. "In writing," she has said, "it is my one principle that nothing is too much trouble." And elsewhere, in one of those quotations that stud the "hybrid composition" of her poems: "Difficulty is ordained to check poltroons."

For obvious reasons, modern poetry is largely a cry of confusion and anguish. The face of Miss Moore's poetry is serene. Shall we look into her mind for signs of travail? The mind of Miss Moore is astonishingly clean. Cluttered, to be sure, like your grandmother's attic; but with everything dusted and in place, labeled, catalogued, usable. The tensions are in the things themselves. The poetry is not in the self-pity. . . . (pp. 221-22)

> *Stanley Kunitz, "Pangolin of Poets" (originally published in* Poetry, *November, 1941), in his* A Kind of Order, a Kind of Folly (© *1941, 1975 by Stanley Kunitz; reprinted by permission of Little, Brown and Co. in association with the Atlantic Monthly Press),* Atlantic-Little, Brown, 1975, pp. 220-22).

WALLACE STEVENS

Somehow, there is a difference between Miss Moore's bird [the ostrich of "He 'Digesteth Harde Yron'"] and the bird of the *Encyclopaedia*. This difference grows. . . . The difference signalizes a transition from one reality to another. It is the reality of Miss Moore that is the individual reality. That of the *Encyclopaedia* is the reality of isolated fact. Miss Moore's reality is significant. An aesthetic integration is a reality.

Nowhere in the poem does she speak directly of the subject of the poem by its name. She calls it "the camel-sparrow" and the "the large sparrow Xenophon saw walking by a stream," "the bird," "quadruped-like bird" and

> alert gargantuan
> little-winged, magnificently
> speedy running-bird.

This, too, marks a difference. To confront fact in its total bleakness is for any poet a completely baffling experience. Reality is not the thing but the aspect of the thing. At first reading, this poem has an extraordinarily factual appearance. But it is, after all, an abstraction. Mr. Lewis says that for Plato the only reality that mattered is exemplified best for us in the principles of mathematics. The aim of our lives should be to draw ourselves away as much as possible from the unsubstantial, fluctuating facts of the world about us and establish some communion with the objects which are apprehended by thought and not sense. This was the source of Plato's asceticism. To the extent that Miss Moore finds only allusion tolerable she shares that asceticism. While she shares it she does so only as it may be necessary for her to do so in order to establish a particular reality or, better, a reality of her own particulars: the "overt" reality. . . . Miss Moore has already found an individual reality in the ostrich

and again in its egg. After all, it is the subject in poetry that releases the energy of the poet. (pp. 108-09)

The gist of the poem is that the camel-sparrow has escaped the greed that has led to the extinction of other birds linked to it in size, by its solicitude for its own welfare and that of its chicks. Considering the great purposes that poetry must serve, the interest of the poem is not in its meaning but in this, that it illustrates the achieving of an individual reality. (p. 110)

> *Wallace Stevens, "About One of Marianne Moore's Poems" (1948), in his* The Necessary Angel (copyright © *1948 by Wallace Stevens; reprinted by permission of Alfred A. Knopf, Inc.), Knopf, 1951 (and reprinted in* Marianne Moore: A Collection of Critical Essays, *edited by Charles Tomlinson, Prentice-Hall, Inc., 1970, pp. 107-11).*

CLEANTH BROOKS

[The] soundest account of the general function which Miss Moore's birds and beasts perform in her poetry [is that] they provide the perspective through which to see our (and her) finally human world. Birds and beasts have, of course, performed such general functions in literature from the time of Aesop down to the time of Walt Disney. Miss Moore's use of them is a variant of this general function, for all that Miss Moore's variant is peculiarly her own.

It is, however, so peculiarly her own that the superficial reader may easily be baffled. . . . Confronted with, and perhaps overpowered by, the complex and edged detail with which the "vehicle" is treated, the reader may conclude that there is no "tenor" at all—that he is dealing, not with a metaphor, but with a thing presented, almost scientifically, for its own sake.

Yet, of all men, it is the poet for whom man must be the measure of all things. In Marianne Moore's poetry, man is the measure ultimately. Her beasts give her, as they have given other poets, a way of breaking out of the conventionally human world—or, to put it more accurately, a way of penetrating into her human world, as it were, from the outside. All of which means that Miss Moore's animals are not conceived of clinically and scientifically even though they are not treated romantically or sentimentally. The latter point is to be emphasized. For Miss Moore's animals do not become easy caricatures of human types that we know. The poet does not patronize them. Not even the more furry, tiny ones ever become cute. Instead, she accords them their dignity; she accepts them with full seriousness, and they become the instruments by which man is judged and known. (pp. 201-02)

She is willing to be whimsical, and even witty. She is constantly alive to the humorous collocations which the shapes and habits of her creatures set up. But the whimsy, when it occurs, is never a sniggering human-being-before-the-monkey-house kind of humor. It is as solid as that displayed by Alice toward the birds and beasts of Wonderland, and as little romantic. (p. 203)

> *Cleanth Brooks, "Miss Marianne Moore's Zoo" (originally published in* Quarterly Review of Literature, Special Moore Issue, *edited by José Garcia Villa, 1948), in* Quarterly Review of Literature (© *Quarterly*

Review of Literature, *1976), Vol. XX, Nos. 1-2, 1976, pp. 201-08.*

WILLIAM CARLOS WILLIAMS

[Marianne Moore's] is a talent which diminishes the tom-toming on the hollow men of a wasteland to an irrelevant pitter-patter. Nothing is hollow or waste to the imagination of Marianne Moore. (p. 112)

A statement she would defend, I think, is that man essentially is very much like the other animals—or a ship coming in from the sea—or an empty snail-shell: but there's not much use saying a thing like that unless you can prove it.

Therefore Miss Moore has taken recourse to the mathematics of art. Picasso does no different: a portrait is a stratagem singularly related to a movement among the means of the craft. By making these operative, relationships become self-apparent—the animal lives with a human certainty. This is strangely worshipful. Nor does one always know against what one is defending oneself. (pp. 112-13)

I don't think there is a better poet writing in America today or one who touches so deftly so great a range of our thought.

This is the amazing thing about a good writer, he seems to make the world come toward him to brush against the spines of his shrub. So that in looking at some apparently small object one feels the swirl of great events.

What it is that gives us this sensation, this conviction, it is impossible to know but that it is the proof which the poem offers us there can be little doubt. (p. 113)

> *William Carlos Williams, "Marianne Moore (1948)," in his* Selected Essays *(© 1948 by William Carlos Williams; reprinted by permission of New Directions Publishing Corporation), New Directions, 1969 (and reprinted in* Marianne Moore: A Collection of Critical Essays, *edited by Charles Tomlinson, Prentice-Hall, Inc., 1970, pp. 112-13).*

PAMELA WHITE HADAS

Throughout my study of Marianne Moore's poetry I have found myself coming back again and again to two particularly intriguing questions that are intimately bound up with all the questions of style and mystery, confusions and morality, which the figure of Marianne Moore poses and persuades us to care about. One is her answer to her own question, "What is more precise than precision?" to which she answers, "Illusion." The other is her question, asked in the late poem "Saint Valentine," "Might verse not best confuse itself with fate?" The answer to this one is strongly implied: yes. The precise illusions that substantiate the humanity of all of us and certain uncertain affirmations of what is too much with us at the same time as it is quite beyond us, are the real subjects of this book. Without "efforts of affection"—those of the poet foremost, and those of the critic not far behind—it is doubtful that we would get very far with them. William Carlos Williams affirms the confidence we have that Marianne Moore generously provides conclusions as well as questions that are worth our efforts, that "the quality of satisfaction gathered from reading her is that one may seek long in those exciting mazes sure of coming out the right door in the end." (pp. xi-xii)

Marianne Moore is a sightseer of virtuosity; she sees what is hidden from the casual scan, including importantly those things that are hidden by their obviousness, and she shares her inspections with wit and grace. Virtuoso definitiveness is often the subject of her verse, as well as its object [as in "An Octopus"]:

> Neatness of finish! Neatness of finish!
> Relentless accuracy is the nature of this octopus
> with its capacity for fact. . . .

Marianne "Octopus" Moore has a grasp for the detailing and numbering of things: the eight whales on the beach in "The Steeple-Jack," the nine nectarines painted on a plate, the nine eggs a dragon must lay (in order to have the mythologically prescribed nine sons), the six shades of blue in an artichoke, and so on, and it is not frivolous. It leads to the counting of invisible things—the lines and spaces and syllables that give form as it were breath; it leads to reliance on faith in what we do see. She offers us quotations from travel pamphlets, sermons, and *The New York Times;* she gives us footnotes and revisions of visions, all toward the greater precision of life and probity. "We are precisionists, / not citizens of Pompeii arrested in action," she says in "Bowls." Precision requires a constant activity of the eyes in perception, a constant flow of syllables in expression, and, in affairs of thought and affection, the constant readjustments of a living thing in response to its environment. The octopus-response is to grasp. But one who is determined to be a precisionist of the spirit as well as of the letter and of the thing must inevitably come up against mysteries that are beyond her evidence or her grasp. These mysteries, as well as letters and forms, must somehow be borne by the style of the writer. (p. 7)

The subjects of Marianne Moore's poems are often objects, and these objects are held in an attitude that is close to that of the scientist, where the subject is often an object, and the ultimate objective is truth. . . . If the object she observes happens to be a porcupine of particular splendor, then her subject, first of all, is the particulars of its appearance and its observable existence; the metasubject is simply splendor. When an animal or an El Greco exists in itself and is "brimming with inner light" that is able to be shared, the accurate description of that object shares its truth. (pp. 8-9)

Just as we shall note again and again in Moore's most successful poems the correspondence between rhetorical and psychological structures, we shall note the correspondence between the apparent object in its unlikeliness and the hidden objective in its profundity. It is a "personal affair" that includes the reader; as unpretentiously announced idiosyncrasy can invite a precise illusion of intimacy, one treasures the special knowledge of another's predilections, shared or not. This is the basis of many a conversation, many discoveries. (p. 9)

She is in complete agreement with Ezra Pound's conviction that technique is a measure of sincerity in poetry, and that "the touchstone of an art is its precision.". . . Abstraction is earned in Moore's poetry and her inspirations are owed to accumulations of detailed intricacy rather than to a *coup de main* by some muse of universals. Her imagery is not a "correlative" for feeling in the sense that Eliot's imagery is. In her poetry the correspondences between psychological and rhetorical, between obvious and hidden, or between things and their emotive possibilities are the products of an "unconscious fastidiousness." "The hero does not like some things," and she does like others. She has general feelings about the things she sees, but the things themselves, especially the "rock-crystal" things, always precede the poet's state of mind. They are there to be responded to, gifts; they are responsible; they represent the choices of responsibility. (p. 12)

The objective of a poetry that would possess the power of divination is to find subjects, or images, which are complete in themselves, or which have the power of continuing in themselves *as* units of thought, and *as* vision, not as mere illustrations or "objective correlatives"; they are *evidence*, not truths imagined incarnate. (p. 13)

There are two predilections pervading and informing Marianne Moore's work at every level. One is poetic wonder, the need for a near-magical communication with the objects and objectives of nature, and the other is a detached curiosity which demands precise and intelligent observation of these. It is important to see how her subjective enchantment and her objective devotion to facts work together to produce those particular celebrations that we recognize immediately as those of Marianne Moore. They are the elements of her style. If the ways of making poetry can be divided into the way of the self and the way of the not-self, we may say that in her poetry these ways are not only identifiable, but often identical. (p. 16)

Style for Marianne Moore is most proper when "uncursed by self-inspection"; she finds herself near the ideal in the simple recitation of dancers' proper names in the poem "Style." . . . (p. 21)

Every poem, as a living organism, survives partly by what it has inherited and partly by its individual adjustments to its environment. For every word we might say the same. Marianne Moore's art of survival is mimetic, directed nominally toward the world, prescribing imitation of artifact, animal, or artifice for the survival of art. Her style is what it does, filling space so that what was inert may become living. "That was framework." But for style, "There is no suitable simile," she says, having uninsisted on various ones in the poem called "Style." And in a review of Pound's *Cantos* she reminds us that "to cite passages is to pull one quill from a porcupine." (p. 30)

Style is the offspring of machine and wishing-cap, the general thrust of life made specific. In Marianne Moore's work one may discern four types of this general thrust of life or style: one to be identified with survival, on the premise that expressing is being; one to be identified with conversation —persuasion or exchange, on the premise that individual moral choice and differentiation (sometimes opposition) are essential to expression; one to be identified with discovery, on the premise that deep silence, in the shape of a question mark, asks creation continually to find new forms for the obliteration of that particular silence; and one to be identified with selfhood as a process of vision and revision, on the premise that words are not simply identified with life, but with its uniquest reincarnations. Style stresses what words simply express. (p. 31)

[The] conception of style and its survival *as* style *in* style is a major concern of Marianne Moore, who is careful to preserve in inverted commas any stylistically striking agglomeration of words, strikingly resetting them herself like gems in her own stylistic framework. Reaching farther back, she integrates the unsigned masterpieces of style preserved as proverbs and mottoes into her own style as well, often imitating their aphoristic succinctness to halt and/or regenerate a flow of less concision. On a purely lexical level Moore takes pains to admit the playful music of polysyllables little used in the lyric poetry of her time, and she encourages words to flower by attending to their roots. She has a special affection for proper names, as the most accurate of designations, and she arranges these to set off their precise music much as she arranges her eccentrically gathered quotations and other verbal memorabilia. She . . . [submits] her own use of language to a proper (proper in the sense of personal as well as appropriate) ordering of the subject at hand, the subject most often being how to survive along with a particular means to that end, a protective and submissive style. (p. 32)

Marianne Moore's attitude toward the language she has inherited in both cultural and individual forms is chiefly a protective one. . . . Certain words—some more than others —are treasures to be protectively displayed; their spirits must not be injured and their new poem-bodies must be sufficient armor against natural enemies—time and iconoclasm. Both versatility and specialization are essential as each word-as-survivor, each germinal phrase, each animal, and each artifact in Moore's poetry is uniquely co-responsible with the poetic environment. Padraic Colum has said of Marianne Moore that she "can place a word in a way that gives it the effect of a rarity." (p. 33)

In the work of Marianne Moore we are reminded again and again that the abilities to communicate, to listen, to be interesting, to learn, and to be generally socially acceptable are moral abilities that show themselves nowhere as clearly as in one's conversation. For the poet who can say, offhand and sincerely, of poetry, "I, too, dislike it" ("Poetry"), style must aspire to the conversational state to be of use. . . . [Ultimately] in the poetry and prose of Marianne Moore, conversation will be seen as a moral fabric of personal persuasions and eccentric yarns. Education, goodness, and reciprocity are, all of them, moral affairs and all of them are displayed in "conversation" in its largest sense, including its archaic meanings as "an abiding" or "a manner of living or conduct" as well as its most common meanings as social intercourse or just friendly talk. Marianne Moore means highest praise when she says of T. S. Eliot's prose, "I detect no difference between it and conversation." (pp. 62-3)

One justification, and by no means the least important one, for Marianne Moore's extensive use of quotations in her poems and essays and reviews is that both listening and talking are implicit in them. Quotations are the fruit of audition and the seed of further talk. (p. 65)

Moore's poems might reasonably be described as systems of utterances with a social and moral purpose. They are not, however, as [Hugh Kenner] thinks, "oddly depersonalized system[s] of analogies" or, quoting Williams, "thing[s] made, not said." Marianne Moore's poems *are* said, are full of sayings and personal quirks, quandries and informations in the manner of superior conversation, not neatly programmed machinery. (p. 67)

The constant informing of the self by the self and the self-conscious hesitance of Moore's style are important to the defeat of the egocentricity from which refuge is sought. . . .

She would discover a selfhood in style that is beyond self-enclosed choppy reiterations. Mirror, mirror on the wall, she speaks into her poem "A Face":

> I am not treacherous, callous, jealous, superstitious,
> supercilious, venomous, or absolutely hideous:
>   studying and studying its expression,
>   exasperated desperation
>   though at no real impasse,
>   would gladly break the glass;
>
> when love of order, ardor, uncircuitous simplicity
> with an expression of inquiry, are all one needs to be!
>   Certain faces, a few, one or two—or one
>   face photographed by recollection—
>   to my mind, to my sight,
>   must remain a delight.

The first two lines of this poem are a desperate catalogue, informed by that self-mocking humor which is humorous simply because it is an evasion of the directness of suffering. In saying she is not treacherous, callous, jealous, or any of those things, she is telling us she has considered those possibilities; but, as she rightly sees, the problem goes beyond simple excuses for unhappiness. Having considered and discarded them, she is still "studying and studying" with "exasperated desperation" like somebody trying to revise a neatly finished but superficial poem in the direction of profundity without spoiling the form. There's "no real impasse," yet she is ready to efface the image of herself altogether, break the glass. The two tones of the first stanza—the first grievingly joking, the second puzzlingly grieving—give one the sense that the real block to feeling or knowing how to describe one's own face is self-consciousness supreme. The only way out is to remind oneself, after those "intermingled echoes" of adjectives mockingly listed in the first stanza, that "love of order, ardor, uncircuitous simplicity / with an expression of inquiry are all one needs to be!" Failing in depth, then, the revision is to be toward greater superficiality, pleasant to everyone. If one can accept plain and polite words, one need not need to be a complexly describable self at all, but simply to be, to love and inquire. On one level this is glib, but on another level, familiar to Marianne Moore, praising and questing are the only real substantiation of being. The face that is closed to itself, ignored in favor of other faces that are loved, or one other particular face, solves the critical problem of self-image with a sight-delight rhyme. The solution, as in many of Moore's poems, is part avoidance and part displacement to other issues, and it is, if technique is a true measure of sincerity, a heartfelt one. The poem does not, however, satisfy the appetite for phonological delicacies dressed with despair that the style of the first stanza arouses. It is as if we were offered a crazy salad only to have it puréed before our eyes.

"When plagued by the psychological," Moore says to a giraffe, "a creature can be unbearable." She intends to direct her own conversation toward the outside, toward the other face, toward the feats of the Gentlemen of the Feather Club, and toward the survival in the real world of peculiar creatures, only some of whom write poems, but all of whom merit them. Her preoccupation with the psychological always betrays itself, however, in coming to terms with words that have obvious psychological import even if they do not epitomize egocentricity as she fears they might. (pp. 90-1)

In saying certain things in a way that is peculiar to herself and calling attention to the construction rather than to the deep meaning, Moore means to divert us—to entertain with a purposeful distraction. She likes to incorporate phrases in quotation marks into her poems to convince us that her interest in what is being said is just as much in the *how* as in the *what*. Perhaps this is why the whole of the last part of "Novices"—about the terrible passion and force of the sea—is in sets of inverted commas. "The chrysalis of the nocturnal butterfly" has resonance with images of butterflies and nocturnal flying things in other of Moore's poems. We may be diverted from its intense personal meanings by the sense that its being in quotation marks gives us, that it was said by somebody else and picked up by a passing fancy. Far from it—this mention of the nocturnal butterfly is necessarily related to the courtship and loss of the strange butterfly in "Half-Deity," the spooky thing that flies out at night to frighten "The Hero," and the "pest" that alights on the poet's wrist to arouse wonder and anger in "Armor's Undermining Modesty." Quotation marks in Moore's work are an important gesture of modesty as well as a diversion. She is well aware of their protective use, and in her essay on the work of Sir Francis Bacon she comments on her own technique: "The aphorisms and allusions to antiquity have an effect of formula; quoted wisdom from Greek, Roman, Hebrew, and Italian sages tending to excuse attention as much as to concentrate it."

One of the odd things about Marianne Moore's self-protective style is the aggressiveness she occasionally attributes to it, and the real though muted aggressiveness that we feel is behind it. "The staff, the bag, the feigned inconsequence/ of manner, best bespeak that weapon, self-protectiveness." . . . It is the *rhetoric* of humility that is the real wedge—between her and us, us and a deep understanding of her poems. (p. 93)

Marianne Moore obviously has mixed feelings about acceptance and rejection, and also about the protectiveness of her language, which is seen by her on one hand as an asset, and on the other as a liability insofar as "efforts of affection" are involved. (p. 94)

We may regard the tone of abstraction in Moore's poems as an aspect of her verbal armor in that it displaces our attention from the level of personal desires and quirks to a level of civilized, social, or religious aspiration. (p. 96)

At no time are we directly exposed to the deepest level of motivation in Moore's poetry, but are continually exposed to different *attitudes* of protectiveness which reveal it indirectly. Moore protects her readers from direct statements of her suffering, knowing that "when plagued by the psychological / an animal can be unbearable" . . . , and she withholds aggressiveness also—"everything crammed belligerent / ly inside . . . a tail-like, wedge shaped engine." . . . There is danger in too much precision concerning feeling, but there is danger in illusion, also, and the poetry of Marianne Moore, taken all together, may be regarded as an illustration of the tension between two modes of confronting experience: a scientistic and particularized observation and an aesthetic, illusive fabrication of the human self drawn from observation. It is as if she admits, "I must look and be seen to be looking to be convincing at all, but I must be seen only indirectly, in the 'mirror-of-steel uninsistence' of my own vision." (p. 97)

There are, roughly, five themes which bind Moore's animal poems together, all of which are related to those poems not centrally about animals and to her style in general. They are: *survival,* which may be seen as a metaphor for the survival of any individual in a world that conspires against one at the same time as it nourishes one; *"delicate behavior,"* an expression of integrity with regard to the world, an attitude for fitting conversation with it; *judgment* with regard to ethics and aesthetics; *art* devoted to animals and the turning of animals into art, a loving petrification; and *magic,* the discovery in animal nature and the self of the ability to enchant and protect a supernatural vision. All these themes are drawn together by the poet's pervasive interest in "capturing" them, saving them from the danger of extinction through ignorance, classifying and preserving them. It is a magical prevention against loss of life and art as well. (p. 107)

The poem "Marriage" is permeated with the wickedness of mundane aspirations, the most thoroughly pessimistic work Marianne Moore ever produced for public consumption. It admits the attractiveness of earthly affection, of the idea of love, of the possibility of a new world, a paradise that "works," but love is damned in every instance by false affection, by affectation and insincere speeches, by the "savage's romance." Marianne Moore does not say that there is another kind of love in this poem, unless it is love of art; but the earthliness, the "faulty excellence" of this love too is undercut, here as in other poems of hers.

"Marriage" appeared in 1923, one year after T. S. Eliot had shown the literary world what could be done with a fragmented experience in *The Waste Land....* "Marriage" is seldom, if ever, mentioned in connection with what have come to be known as the standard long poems or neo-epics of the present century, including *The Waste Land,* the *Cantos,* certain long poems of Stevens, Crane's *The Bridge,* and Williams' *Paterson.* Though Marianne Moore's "Marriage" is not as flamboyant as some of them, not perhaps as painstakingly conceived (though one may have doubts about this), or as successful, it shares with these poems certain origins in late nineteenth-century (French) and twentieth-century poetic speculations, and certain "originalities"—disjunctiveness, obscurity, implied criticisms and cynicism about modern society, a free combination of poetic styles. The relations these poems bear to each other and to literary and social traditions are expressed not by logical or continuous argument, but by glancing allusions and sly parataxis. It is helpful to think of Moore's "Marriage" in relation to these poems, as an experiment partly influenced by other experiments in poetry and partly by the social and literary *Zeitgeist* that influenced them all. She refers both to marriage and to Adam's mishap as "experiments," and almost certainly she considered her poem as a similar consciousness-expanding experiment. Experimenting is, after all, something one does when one is not satisfied with the way things are and wants to find something better; an experiment is also often a bid for power, whether it occurs in Eden or in a fallen world.

"Marriage" may be seen as a woman's bid for power in a man's world, or a poet's bid for power in a prosaic world. Yet "Marriage" was never acclaimed as the men's experiments were. It was perhaps felt too strongly that a woman could not propose it. When she did, there was an embarrassing silence. Somebody blushed to imagine "a wife / with hair like a shaving brush." Years later T. S. Eliot chose to admire "The Jerboa." Marianne Moore is best known for her elegant and eccentric descriptions of harmless animals. Her passion was for baseball. No one until lately has thought of her in connection with marriage. But enough of that. (pp. 174-75)

The institution of marriage, certainly, is as flexible an image for the joining of disparate elements, in self or society or both, as is the bridge, the growth of a city-man, a general quest in a wasted land, the journey of a comic Crispin or blue guitarist. The concept of "marriage" is as abstract as the basic concepts of any of these. The poem "Marriage," proposes, as the other long poems do, to investigate rather abstractly, through all its imagistic and rhetorical particulars, the possibility of joining, of making sense of bits and scraps of experience—a past there, a present here, and so forth. These go forth to some implied future and have no small pretensions to a kind of prophecy. Whether it is the clairvoyance of a Madame Sosostris, the babble of the falls in *Paterson* that contains history and prefigures the future, or the statue of the failed statesman at the end of "Marriage," all look to some difficult future, some further fall of man which, like past falls, may not be without its rewards (mainly for sensibility, one suspects), but which is somehow without epic, or even true or traditional poetic dignity.

So, after the long-range ineffectiveness of everything, what is left? "The statesmanship / of an archaic Daniel Webster" seems to be all. The victim of lingering sorrow in Moore's poem says, "I have encountered it." Love? The grasp of opposites? The birth of a nation? The God-exploited storm? The sorrowful world has encountered a language of "cycloid inclusiveness," as the sorrowful poet has, which can transform hopeless complexity into simple statements, a language that can arrange marriages between entities that are as fundamentally opposed as North and South. The summary: "Liberty and union / now and forever." Liberty is not union and now is not forever, but one can say it; it sounds nice and people want to believe it, and they do. They even say "I do." Marianne Moore ... finds this remarkable, and the poem "Marriage" may be regarded as her series of remarks on this very peculiarity of language, its ability to persuade.

I find the last two lines of "Marriage" devastating in their anticlimactic oddness and complacency: "the Book on the writing table; / the hand in the breast pocket." After all that! After a poem of such strange complexity, after all the wit and the rich allusiveness and elusiveness of style, we are left with a cold statue, paralyzed. The Book on the writing table is naturally the Bible. That must be all that is left if the world has failed one utterly: hypocrisy and self-satisfaction punished, heaven promised. The hand in the breast pocket is not the hand given in "Marriage," or, if it is, it has been retracted to the self in a stiff pose, for the sake of an image really. And what is in the breast pocket that the hand should go after it? Is it love, or money? If "Marriage" is to be seen ultimately as an act of statesmanship, a record of articulate language and worldly calculation, which is worth its while whether it works or not, this, I suppose, is a good way to end. (pp. 175-76)

"The Hero" describes the qualities that to Marianne Moore's mind inform an heroic style and vision. The hero is cautious; she needs to be so to survive her human frailty. The hero needs to understand social orders and manners;

she has to be able to converse with them. The hero needs to discover things; she looks intently for the "rock-crystal thing." The hero needs to know about her self, origin, and end. The poem begins by asserting childlike and instinctive predilections rather than those of intellect. This approach . . . is for Marianne Moore essential to the most genuine criticism of art and life. The poem goes on to consider the inherent unfairness of the world and the tolerance one must learn in order to have an heroic integrity. The hero must have "reverence for mystery" along with an inclination to seek and share profoundest visions—of the "inner light" of things, of invisible power. This poem shows that the energies needed for creation and criticism of creation are the same, instinctual or intuitional, and integral. We are asking for trouble when we ask the adult question, "What does it mean, literally?" There are intensities of mood, flashes of being. That is all. We should not ask if this is enough for a poem or not. It is obviously enough for "The Hero," poem and person both having retained or gained a healthy disrespect for artificial congruity. (p. 202)

Uncertain meanings, uncertain words, uncertain sounds— all are stipulated by the human predicament, all equally plagues and blessings for the poet-hero. . . .

The hero, as a person of heightened sensibility, is more susceptible to [the] loveless warning-sounds (or are they love-making?) of nature than an ordinary person. (p. 203)

> The decorous frock-coated Negro
> by the grotto [who]
>
> answers the fearless sightseeing hobo
> who asks the man she's with, what's this,
> what's that, where's Martha
> buried, "Gen-ral Washington
> there; his lady, here"; speaking
> as if in a play—not seeing her; with a
> sense of human dignity
> and reverence for mystery, standing like the shadow
> of the willow.

The crux of ["The Hero"] is contained in this grotesque stanza, in the very discrepancy between the innocent omens on its surface and a profound need underlying them, the need to discover true even if uninnocent origins. The "hobo" is a wanderer like Pilgrim, mentioned earlier, but a wanderer importantly with no destination in mind. She (and her gender is somewhat of a surprise, adding disgrace if anything to the description of her) is "fearless." She has a lot to learn about history and herself. The "hero" is, on the other hand, full of fears and rightly so. The casualness of the female "hobo" is in direct contrast to the decorousness of the "frock-coated Negro." Although he is obviously the costumed and "official" guide to the place of sightseeing, the hobo ignores him and asks her also-ignorant companion to explain the historic grave. She wants to know where Martha is buried. She is, although perhaps touchingly ignorant of the fact, looking for her mother, the mother of her confusing country. The guide points out the positions of both Washingtons. The irony is implicit and dramatic. The Negro plays the role of guide at the site of America's buried parentage, its primal scene, its conception of "freedom." This is the very conception by which he has, like an unequally blessed son, been made to suffer inhumanly. He is not blind, but he doesn't look at the hobo. *He* knows the undeviating headstones; *he* knows where the spirit of free-

dom and equality is buried, lost. And he has too much dignity to stare at the undignified curiosity of the staring woman. His personal dislike for her, for her irreverence for mystery, for the superficiality of her wanting to peek at the position of the parents in their last bed, is an heroic dislike. The hero must realize loss and mystery. He stands like the shadow of the willow because the willow is a traditional symbol of loss and mourning. He is a knower who *is* what he knows.

Here, strangely and without power, are all the themes of loss, mystery, kingship, magic, marriage, and vision that Moore explores separately and together in all the major poems of her life. They are deeply buried, but they are there as surely as the plumet basilisk is alive there in his cocoon of living green, and it is the business of the hero to discover them for herself. Not only must she bear the knowledge of the burial place herself, but the ignorance of other people, which can be just as painful. The mysterious noises and metaphysical terror of the hero's introduction to the world make up her primal scene. She may be curious but she knows that according to the rules of a civilized society she may not look at some things. The hobo would see literally where the parents lie in relation to each other, but hers is not the truest curiosity or the truest discovery. Yet she is on her way, making the only sort of pilgrimage she can think of to make. She may be on her way to becoming a hero, and her travels in this direction are part of the mystery. Perhaps all heroes start as hoboes. The accomplished hero will allow all the mystery, and discover reverence. (pp. 205-06)

One cannot easily generalize about the meaning of jewels and the crystal-like substance in Moore's poems, but these images do all share an important quality, and that is that they both represent and preserve a moral integrity in the thing looked at or in the eyes that are doing the looking. Praise, good sense, punctuality, tough individuality, all partake of a rock-crystal nature. (p. 210)

Marianne Moore is not an original thinker. Her "message" of freedom through sacrifice could not be more commonplace, as she herself would agree. Yet she may make it strike us with an original force because it is arrived at in the poems themselves only through difficulty. It is hard for her to sacrifice silence. Then again, it is hard for her to sacrifice speech. Sacrifice alternates with sacrifice, and the freedom with which we are able to put them together, reclaiming both speech and silence "in / the name of freedom" and as a taboo against psychical oppression, is the freedom of Moore's verse. We may take freedoms with her verses because she has given them to us. She covets nothing that she has let go.

What is commonplace as idea is not necessarily commonplace as a personally held and acted-upon conviction; in fact, commonplace, as Marianne Moore embraces it, is rare. It is for the intensely personal valuation that Moore has performed upon the common places as well as the exotic places of the world that we feel gratitude and enlightenment, if we are able to feel them. "In Distrust of Merits" shows us commonplace abhorrence of war and the Self who participates by not participating, yet it has a felt intensity, a "mountainous wave" of unconscious fastidiousness "that makes us who look, know depth." "He / sees deep and is glad, who / accedes to mortality" ("What Are Years?"). It is an easy thing to *say,* but difficult to *see.*

Moore's essay "Humility, Concentration, and Gusto" ends with a motto of importance to anyone interested in those three famous qualities of hers: "The thing is to see the vision and not deny it; to care and admit that we do." To admit to the self, to admit to the core of the self and others—everything—is perhaps the hardest thing. To admit that the hardest thing—the devalued commonplace—is true, is to see the hardest thing, the rock crystal thing, invisible in its prevalence, powerful with the "power of the invisible." (p. 213)

Marianne Moore's work is a lifelong exposition of paradox, and no matter how much careful observation she lavishes on the objects that illustrate her various paradoxes, no matter how much precise illusion is given shape through her disarming rhetoric, the paradoxes still remain and are always interesting. Perhaps paradox itself is the rock crystal thing that the hero is seen to see. It is accuracy and mystery well married; it is naked in its objective transparence, but armored in the untouchable axial law that made it.

The desire for the purity of the rock crystal is an impulse toward criticism that is not self-congratulatory or other-abasing. . . . The task of the hero as critic is to make her way through the false complexities of the world and her fear of them to the rock crystal thing. (pp. 216-17)

In Marianne Moore's world, as in most other people's worlds, there is no heroism without efforts, specifically efforts of affection, because the world is basically a disaffecting place, a disordered and disturbing place. One who can forge style, honor, and conscience out of such a given mess of materials, who can, moreover, move comfortably between the precisions and specificities of objects and the abstractions which pertain to one's self, is heroic. Marianne Moore does not always seem to move comfortably between the extremes of particulars and abstractions in her poems; she does not always succeed in pulling an order and a clarity out of a bag of disorder and obscurity, yet the efforts of affection for the world and for the other minds in it are always in evidence, and a great amount of heroism is to be found in those efforts themselves, just as a great amount of poetry is to be found in unconscious fastidiousness. This is true even when a poem as a whole is judged to be something less than whole. (p. 220)

[Images of a king or of kingship recur] in Moore's poems, but it is to be noted also that the king is never the hero by virtue of kingship alone. The king is more often a person in absentia. "The king is dead" ("No Swan So Fine"), or he is at the bottom of Guatavita Lake ("The Plumet Basilisk"), or he is, as he is to any working knight, somewhere distant, at the place of the quest's origin and the place to which the knight hopes to return. The king is a father, an origin, or a Father, an end, that we know only through rumor or on faith. He does not play a real part in the acts of the hero, or in the poems of Marianne Moore, but we feel the presence of some high or far mind to which the poems must be submitted for approval, a sort of ur-editor.

The king may represent the spiritual poise within us whose center we cannot locate because it is essentially everywhere, but whose presence is felt as possibility. The circumference of "spiritual poise" is of course nowhere; there is always another circle of reference to be drawn upon in any figure of reality. It is between the extremes of an inner center and an infinity of complexions outside the self, that

the style and the heroism of Moore's poems move. She is ever self-conscious and ever self-effacing. We can never hope to locate the exact center of this self of which she and we are conscious, nor can we begin to set limits on just what in the miraculous abundance of the world her self will see fit to take to itself. There is a mechanism of "picking and choosing" that activates any poem of hers (or anyone's), but the mechanism itself is dark. The world from which this particular self can pick and choose is infinite, or infinitely light, including everything that can be seen or imagined and any combination of these.

Unconscious fastidiousness is the critical apparatus of the hero, and it would be far less than realistic to demand consistency from it as well as honesty. (pp. 220-21)

We shall always come back to "science" in the work of Marianne Moore, because science was to her a method of knowledge indispensable to her comprehensively evaluative mode of poetry. Moral sense may be uppermost, but it must be informed with the greatest possible exactitude about the state of things in the physical world. In order to make spiritual acknowledgment of creation, it must make technical acknowledgments—how it was done, how it is to be done. This technique links the past and the future as well as the matter and the spirit of all worldly phenomena. If "science" is accurate observation of the world's developing, temporary balance, and eventual dissolution, and "prophecy" the accurate observation of those processes on a spiritual level, then poetry, if it is to contain the truest of all observations, must put them together. The confusion is accurate and necessary. Confusion, submitted to poetry by unconfusion, confusion affectionately admitted, leads to the development and expression of the whole soul. It must acknowledge the desolation and loss described in such poems as "The Fish" as well as the "plan / deep set within the heart of man" ecstasy of "Sun." It must see how the pangolin walks strangely on the edges of his feet and how the icosasphere is welded together. It must see [in "The Pangolin"]:

> Sun and moon and day and night and man and beast
>   each with a splendor
>   which man in all his vileness cannot
>   set aside; each with an excellence! . . .
>   (pp. 223-24)

An acknowledged multiplicity may be disturbing to some, yet it gives us the choice of our lives where literature is concerned. . . . Picking and choosing among the figures our age has given us, we may be refreshed to encounter Marianne Moore, whose still, small, and relatively unexploded voice somehow comes through all the shared confusions of intelligence to give us not only choice but also conviction with humor. . . . (p. 226)

Pamela White Hadas, in her Marianne Moore: Poet of Affection *(copyright © 1977 by Syracuse University Press), Syracuse University Press, 1977 (poetry excerpts from* Collected Poems *by Marianne Moore, copyright 1935, 1941, 1951, 1969 by Marianne Moore; copyright 1963 by Marianne Moore and T. S. Eliot; reprinted with permission of Macmillan Publishing Co., Inc.).*

MORRISON, Toni   1931-

Morrison is an American novelist and editor. Noted for her sensitive portrayals of black families, Morrison has been praised for her stylistic freshness and authentic dialogue. (See also *CLC*, Vol. 4, and *Contemporary Authors*, Vols. 29-32, rev. ed.)

CHIKWENYE OKONJO OGUNYEMI

Toni Morrison's *The Bluest Eye* is a novel portraying in poignant terms the tragic condition of blacks in a racist America. In her criticism of American life, she has structured her work in triadic patterns beginning with the reproduction of a passage three different times as the first three paragraphs of the work. Other triadic patterns emerge in her presentation of the tragedy of black life in relation to blacks, whites, and God or existential circumstances worked out through her thematic approach involving the problems of sex, racism, and love (or the dearth of love); in the aspect of ritual expressed through the scapegoat mechanism with the cat, the dog, and the girl, Pecola, as agents; and in the typology in the characterization affecting the three black family women—Geraldine, Mrs. MacTeer, and Mrs. Breedlove—and the three black prostitutes—The Maginot Line, China, and Poland. The pattern is concretized by the dictum that is generally accepted in the social milieu of the novel, a dictum which is clearly expressed by Calvin Hernton: "if you are white you are all right; if you are brown you can stick around; but if you are black . . . get back."

The opening paragraph of the novel in its simplicity and clarity could have been taken from a primer. The paragraph deals, quite ironically it turns out, with a white American ideal of the family unit—cohesive, happy, with love enough to spare to pets. It is a fairy-tale world, a dream world, childlike in extreme—it is desirable, but for man, particularly the black man, it is unattainable. (p. 112)

After the orderliness of the first paragraph, the same passage is reproduced as the second paragraph but without punctuation marks. The lack of punctuation shows some disorder in a world that could be orderly; however, the world is still recognizable. . . .

The third paragraph is a repetition of the first but without punctuation and without word division, and it demonstrates the utter breakdown of order among the Breedloves. Thus we have three possible family situations: first Geraldine's (a counterfeit of the idealized white family), further down the MacTeers', and at the bottom the Breedloves'. They are all manifestations of the social concept of the family, just as the first three paragraphs are identical except that circumstances have changed the premise implicit in the ideal of the first paragraph. The Mother-Father-Dick-Jane concept is finally transmuted to the Mrs. Breedlove-Cholly-Sammy-Pecola situation. The transmutation is Morrison's indirect criticism of the white majority for the black family's situation and for what is taught to the black child in school, as evidenced by the primer paragraph, that in no way relates to the child's reality. The black man is attacked emotionally from childhood, living in two impossible worlds: the fairy tale world of lies when he is in contact with the white world and the equally incredible, grim world of black life.

The first section of *The Bluest Eye*, "Autumn," opens with a sentence which reflects the disorder and moral chaos of the novel: "*Nuns* go by as *quiet* as *lust,* and *drunken* men with *sober* eyes *sing* in the lobby of the Greek hotel" (emphasis added). Here "nuns" with an appropriate attribute, "quiet," are juxtaposed to "lust," a word not usually associated with nuns. Furthermore, the "drunken men" "sing" (a not unusual event) but their eyes are surprisingly "sober." The sentence opens up a strange world, one where expectations remain unfulfilled and contradictions are rife. These incongruities exist either because of man's oppression of irresponsibility against man or else because of existential circumstances. (p. 113)

The Bluest Eye has a structural resemblance to Baldwin's *Go Tell It on the Mountain.* Just as Baldwin does not deal only with John, the protagonist, so Morrison does not deal only with Pecola. She is the centripetal force bringing all the different characters together, as John does in *Go Tell It on the Mountain.* (p. 114)

In handling the narrative, Morrison has put her literary heritage to very good use. One notices the influence of black writers in her arrangement and her material. Cholly's terrible life is in the tradition of Ellison's Trueblood. His surname, Breedlove, becomes an irony, since, deprived of love by his parents and society at large, he is expected to cultivate love. (p. 115)

Running through the novel is the theme of the scapegoat: Geraldine's cat, Bob the dog, and Pecola are the scapegoats supposed to cleanse American society through their involvement in some violent rituals. Pecola is associated with the black cat with blue eyes, whose eyes in the moment of death were transformed into "blue streaks of horror." . . . (p. 116)

Most characters in the novel are made typical, as are Geraldine, Mrs. MacTeer, and Mrs. Breedlove. Geraldine has been cast as an old black bourgeoisie; Hernton's description tallies with her role in the novel: "[They] share the same contempt and stereotyped views about 'lower-class' Negroes as the outer society. And when it comes to sex, the orthodox middle-class Negro woman is far more rigid, repressed, and neurotic than any other female in America." Her attitude towards lower-class blacks is dramatized in her brief encounter with Pecola when she permits her venom to erupt. (p. 118)

Another strong point in the novel is the intricate weaving of Pecola through the plot and her portrayal as a scapegoat with its implicit ambivalence. In the plot, however, Morrison ran into some difficulties with Pecola; although she tried to establish in two sentences a genetic factor for Pecola's madness, one feels the madness is a *deus ex machina.* One has a feeling that Morrison has fictionalized those sociological factors discussed in Hernton's *Sex and Racism in America* without first distancing herself enough from that work. (pp. 119-20)

[For] a first novel *The Bluest Eye* is appealing. In her simplicity of style and sentence structure, Morrison sometimes recalls Hemingway; with the themes of blindness, invisibility, incest, racism, she belongs to the tradition of Ellison; in the structure of the work she suggests Baldwin. What she has done, in essence, is to present us with old problems in a fresh language and with a fresh perspective. A central force of the work derives from her power to draw vignettes and her ability to portray emotions, seeing the world through the eyes of adolescent girls. The patterns that emerge in her handling of the novel demonstrate that she executed her work after careful planning. (p. 120)

> *Chikwenye Okonjo Ogunyemi, "Order and Disorder in Toni Morrison's 'The Bluest Eye',"* in Critique: Studies in Modern Fiction *(copyright © by James Dean Young 1977), Vol. XIX, No. 1, 1977, pp. 112-20.*

VIVIAN GARNICK

[*Song of Solomon*] moves slowly, but with gathering momentum, into the heart of that myth-making impulse, pressing ever deeper on the human pain that is its motive force....

As readers of her previous novels, *The Bluest Eye* (1970) and *Sula* (1974), know, Toni Morrison is an extraordinarily good writer. Two pages into anything she writes, one feels the power of her language and the emotional authority behind that language. The world she creates is thick with an atmosphere through which her characters move slowly, in pain, ignorance, and hunger. And to a very large degree Morrison has the compelling ability to make one believe that all of us (Morrison, the characters, the reader) are penetrating that dark and hurtful terrain—the feel of a human life—simultaneously.

Unfortunately, in *Song of Solomon,* Morrison's ability is not exercised to the *largest* degree. At a certain point one begins to feel a manipulativeness in the book's structure, and then to sense that the characters are moving to fulfill the requirements of that structure. Once this happens, the plausibility of Milkman's search into the mythic, magical heart of the fear of leaving childhood—the book's central metaphor—begins to disintegrate. Revelations seem to be set up like pieces on a chessboard, and the "magic" loses its ability to command suspended disbelief.

With any other writer, this could be fatal. But it is not with Toni Morrison. There are so many individual moments of power and beauty in *Song of Solomon* that, ultimately, one closes the book warmed through by the richness of its sympathy, and by its breathtaking feel for the nature of sexual sorrow.

It seems to me that the source of the artistic trouble in *Song of Solomon* lies with Morrisons's choice of Milkman as protagonist—instead of with one of the women in the book. Milkman never really comes to life.... There are a few pages describing the blossoming love affair between [Milkman's sister] First Corinthians and a traumatized handyman that are filled with such astonishing pain and beauty that a book dominated by such descriptions would have been a masterpiece. These pages turn on Morrison's sure, hard knowledge of the inside of that woman's life: the grotesque anguish beneath the surface of a stifled existence....

Song of Solomon does not, in my view, achieve wholeness because it suffers from a misdirected angle of vision. But it is the work of a real writer and, as such, cannot fail to yield up moments of rich life, no matter what the direction of its vision.

> *Vivian Garnick, "Into the Dark Heart of Childhood,"* in The Village Voice *(reprinted by permission of* The Village Voice; *copyright © by The Village Voice, Inc., 1977), August 29, 1977, p. 41.*

REYNOLDS PRICE

Toni Morrison's first two books—"The Bluest Eye" with the purity of its terrors and "Sula" with its dense poetry and the depth of its probing into a small circle of lives—were strong novels. Yet, firm as they both were in achievement and promise, they didn't fully forecast her new book, "Song of Solomon." Here the depths of the younger work are still evident, but now they thrust outward, into wider fields, for longer intervals, encompassing many more lives. The result is a long prose tale that surveys nearly a century of American history as it impinges upon a single family. In short, this is a full novel—rich, slow enough to impress itself upon us like a love affair or a sickness....

"Song of Solomon" isn't, however, cast in the basically realistic mode of most family novels. In fact, its negotiations with fantasy, fable, song and allegory are so organic, continuous and unpredictable as to make any summary of its plot sound absurd; but absurdity is neither Morrison's strategy nor purpose. The purpose seems to be communication of painfully discovered and powerfully held convictions about the possibility of transcendence within human life, on the time-scale of a single life. The strategies are multiple and depend upon the actions of a large cast of black Americans, most of them related by blood. But after the loving, comical and demanding polyphony of the early chapters ..., the theme begins to settle on one character and to develop around and out of him.

His name is Macon Dead, called "Milkman" because his mother nursed him well past infancy. (p. 1)

The end is unresolved. Does Milkman survive to use his new knowledge, or does he die at the hands of a hateful friend? The hint is that he lives.... But that very uncertainty is one more sign of the book's larger truthfulness (no big, good novel has every really ended; and none can, until it authoritatively describes the extinction from the universe of all human life); and while there are problems (occasional abortive pursuits of a character who vanishes, occasional luxuriant pauses on detail and the understandable but weakening omission of active white characters), "Song of Solomon" easily lifts above them on the wide slow wings of human sympathy, well-informed wit and the rare plain power to speak wisdom to other human beings. A long story, then, and better than good. Toni Morrison has earned attention and praise. Few Americans know, and can say, more than she has in this wise and spacious novel. (p. 48)

> *Reynolds Price, "Black Family Chronicle,"* in The New York Times Book Review *(© 1977 by The New York Times Company; reprinted by permission), September 11, 1977, pp. 1, 48.*

DIANE JOHNSON

[*Song of Solomon*] and to an even greater extent Morrison's earlier novels *The Bluest Eye* and *Sula,* ... entirely concern black people who violate, victimize, and kill each other.... No relationships endure, and all are founded on exploitation. The victimization of blacks by whites is implicit but not the subject. The picture given by ... Morrison of the plight of the decent, aspiring individual in the black family and community is more painful than the gloomiest impressions encouraged by either stereotype or sociology....

Song of Solomon is a picaresque and allegorical saga of a middle-class northern black family, the Deads, in particular of the son Milkman Dead, but also of parents, sisters, aunts, cousins, and, when Milkman eventually travels south in search of treasure and family history, of numerous distant connections. The resemblance to *Roots* is perhaps the least satisfying thing about the book; the characters are apt at any moment to burst into arias of familial lore less interesting than their immediate predicaments. . . .

Here, as in Morrison's earlier and perhaps more affecting work, human relationships are symbolized by highly dramatic events. In *Sula* a mother pours gasoline over her son and lights it, and, in another place, a young woman watches with interest while her mother burns. But the horrors, rather as in Dickens, are nearly deprived of their grisliness by the tone. It might be a folktale in which someone cuts someone else's heart out and buries it under a tree, from which a thorn bush springs, and so on. Morrison is interested in black folklore, but in fact the influences of the Bible, Greek myths, and English and American literature are more evident, as in the work of other American writers.

There is a sense in which the use of myth is evasive. Morrison's effect is that of a folktale in which conventional narrative qualities like unity and suspense are sacrificed to the cumulative effects of individual, highly romantic or mythic episodes, whose individual implausibility, by forcing the reader to abandon the criteria of plausibility, cease to matter. In this way, the writer can imply that hers are not descriptions of reality but only symbols of a psychological condition. Yet if her tales are merely symbolic, the reader can complain of their sensationalism. If they are true, her view of a culture in which its members, for whatever reasons, cannot depend for safety and solace on even the simplest form of social cooperation is almost too harrowing to imagine. (p. 6)

> *Diane Johnson, in* The New York Review of Books *(reprinted with permission from* The New York Review of Books; *copyright* © *1977 NYREV, Inc.), November 10, 1977.*

MAUREEN HOWARD

Song of Solomon by Toni Morrison is a fine novel exuberantly constructed and stylistically full of the author's own delight in words. Morrison has a strong narrative voice and much of her novel's charm comes from an oral tradition, the love of simply telling, for example, how places and people got their names and how these names—Not Doctor Street, Ryna's Gulch, a boy called Milkman, Mr. Solomon, women known as Pilate, Sing and Sweet—contain history. There is an enchantment in Morrison's naming, a heightening of reality and language. Though each name is almost mythical it can be explained factually. . . . In *Song of Solomon* lives are as strange as folk tales and no less magical when they are at last construed.

Toni Morrison has written a chronicle of a black family living in a small industrial city on the shores of Lake Michigan, but the method of the book is to enlarge upon the very idea of family history, to scrape away at lore until truth is revealed. (pp. 185-86)

Song of Solomon is so rich in its use of common speech, so sophisticated in its use of literary traditions and language from the Bible to Faulkner, that I must add it is also extremely funny. Toni Morrison has a wonderful eye for the

pretensions of genteel blacks and the sort of crude overstatements made by small time revolutionaries. Like many fine artists she dares to be corny—there is a funeral scene worthy of Dickens in which a crazed old woman sings "Who's been botherin' my baby girl" over her daughter, a poor deluded creature who has died of a broken heart. And like many great novels at the core it is a rather simple story of a boy growing to maturity. . . . As for myth, Toni Morrison knows it's dead material unless you give it life—that's art. (p. 186)

> *Maureen Howard, in* The Hudson Review *(copyright* © *1978 by The Hudson Review, Inc.; reprinted by permission), Vol. XXXI, No. 1, Spring, 1978.*

*   *   *

MUNRO, Alice   1931-

Munro, a Canadian short story writer and novelist, is known for her precise recording of personal experiences. Her stories chart the search for personal freedom in nostalgically rural settings. (See also *CLC*, Vol. 6, and *Contemporary Authors*, Vols. 33-36, rev. ed.)

FREDERICK BUSCH

Alice Munro . . . writes stories you have to call "well-made." . . . They are journeymen's work. But they are no more than that, and by now . . . we ought to demand that a volume of stories delivers the thrilling economy, the poetry which makes the form so valuable.

Alice Munro's subject matter is ordinariness—disappointment, the passage of time—but she doesn't bring to her stories what, say, John Updike or Tillie Olsen do: extraordinary language, a mind in love with the everyday but able to exalt it so that we feel the magic in what is usual. Most of the stories [in "Something I've Been Meaning to Tell You"] concern the past, hidden from others but told to us . . . and the stories do seem formulaic.

The book is filled with lots of information on who did what to whom, and when, and where, but there is little emotional tension arising from the events. Everything is thought out, decided upon. Most of the dialogue, even, seems there for the sake of information, not for its own sake. And much of the writing seems to be designed to win our love rather than stun us with character or prose. . . .

When the narrative voice of the story doesn't use winsomeness as a strategy, it takes refuge in Art: "I invented loving you and I invented your death. I have my tricks and my trap doors, too. I don't understand their workings at the present moment." Such a dependency on our sense of the artful paradox of contemporary writing—while the author permits herself to cease responsibility for her characters—is close kin to the childishness of "I wouldn't have looked in her drawers, but a closet is open to anybody. That's a lie, I would have looked in drawers, but I would have felt worse doing it and been more scared she would tell." In both cases, as in most of these stories, there is the kind of innocence of tone that can make you grin, but the way you grin at someone else's charming child: already forgetting. (p. 54)

> *Frederick Busch, in* The New York Times Book Review *(© 1974 by The New York Times Company; reprinted by permission), October 27, 1974.*

RAE McCARTHY MACDONALD

[In Alice Munro's vision there] are those of "the world," of society, of the accepted norms, and those "from the other country" . . . , people such as Miss Marsalles [in the title story of *The Dance of the Happy Shades*], whose innocence has made her, at the best, a fondly tolerated anachronism and, at the worst, a social embarrassment. Miss Marsalles, with [a] terrible *faux pas,* has placed herself in the same category as idiots, seniles, eccentrics, criminals, and the fatally ill, all of whom are uncontrollable, unpredictable, and, therefore, painful, embarrassing, and plainly unacceptable by "the world." (pp. 366-67)

The prevalence . . . in Munro's work, of idiots, senile old people, suicides, the fatally ill, and that recurring image of the mother who is attacked by Parkinson's disease are guides to her controlling vision. Munro sees society and life as cruel and deforming. Those who appear to adapt or cope and survive are, in her eyes, more deformed in an internal, spiritual way, than those who are clearly retarded or maimed and unable to enter the struggle. In some stories, the obviously defective people seem better off and freer than those who have found acceptance in a "normal" world. In most cases, they work as a symbol or externalization of the suffering and deformity of the apparently healthy and adjusted characters. They are also a deflecting release valve for the tension that builds up from the reader's sense of repressed pain in Munto's world. (pp. 368-69)

In *Lives of Girls and Women,* no one idiot, invalid, or suicide externalizes the suffering of any one character; rather, they all reflect each other and compositely suggest the hidden illness of the apparent survivors. (p. 370)

Something I've Been Meaning To Tell You reveals the same divided universe as do *Dance of the Happy Shades* and *Lives of Girls and Women.* And it asks Munro's characteristic questions. "Walking on Water" and "Forgiveness in Families" both play with the old question, "Who or what is mad?" In "Memorial," the central character, who has been confronted anew with the rigidly defined world of her sister, thinks "the only thing we can hope for is that we lapse now and then into reality." . . . (p. 373)

Alice Munro's work bears the marks of a distinctive, vital, and unifying vision. Though this vision shows itself more complex and subtle with each of her books, the basic terms remain unchanged. Man finds himself divided into two camps, and the price of this division for both sides is loneliness and pain. The external deformities and violences of "the other country," the place of outcasts, are simply transferences of the unseen, hidden disfiguration of "the world," place of "survivors." Which group suffers most is a question without significance in a universe where men, the pathetic victims of chance, offer each other not kindness or encouragement, but suspicion and hate. (pp. 373-74)

Rae McCarthy Macdonald, "A Madman Loose in the World: The Vision of Alice Munro," in Modern Fiction Studies *(copyright © 1976, by Purdue Research Foundation, West Lafayette, Indiana, U.S.A.), Autumn, 1976, pp. 365-74.*

PATRICIA BEER

[*Lives of Girls and Women*] is not, the author says, autobiographical except in form. In fact, in form it more closely resembles a series of short stories, and it is no surprise to see that the author won a Canadian award in this genre. Each chapter of *Lives of Girls and Women* is virtually self-contained; characters who appear in more than one are nearly always reintroduced, however well we might reasonably be supposed to remember them. Yet each protagonist is closely connected with the central family; Del Jordan, the daughter, is the narrator throughout and though she is not the heroine of every episode it is very much her story. The first chapter, it is true, is set at a decided angle to the main narrative line; its hero, Uncle Benny, appears only peripherally in the later chapters—and his vicious mail-order bride never—but the effect is intriguing rather than confusing.

The title is accurate, for the book presents not only the growing up of a girl, her relationships with her family and her approaches and eventual introduction to sexual experience, but also the histories of her female contemporaries and older relatives, especially her mother. In other words, we are in *Kinflicks* country, but whereas *Kinflicks* tries, too hard for its artistic good, to be a, or even the, Great American Novel, *Lives of Girls and Women* obeys its own natural range and scope and is consequently much more successful. Neither does it fall flat into the long, lush grass of so many British autobiographies and novels about country adolescence. It is an honest book. . . .

The beginnings and endings of some of the chapters weirdly recall, if not the exact voice of *Penguin New Writing,* a good parody of it: "We spent days along the Wawanash River, helping Uncle Benny fish." . . . The best of the sexual scenes are completely explicit; their straightforwardness is necessary and the reverse of bawdy. . . . Alice Munro knows when not to be explicit; the often puzzled loves of the young are more reticently portrayed.

The book draws a clear distinction between youthful and adult emotional attitudes even when exactly the same things are happening. . . .

One of the few criticisms that can be made of the book is that it often explains too much. The writing is in fact good enough to rely much more on implication than it allows itself to do.

Patricia Beer, "Beside the Wawanash," in The Times Literary Supplement (© *Times Newspapers Ltd. (London) 1978; reproduced from* The Times Literary Supplement *by permission), March 17, 1978, p. 302.*

HALLVARD DAHLIE

[Alice Munro is] a writer who has quietly and firmly established herself over the past decade. In a very real sense, she occupies [two] fictional worlds: her fiction is rooted tangibly in the social realism of the rural and small town world of her own experience, but it insistently explores what lies beyond the bounds of empirical reality. Though she has said that she is "very, very excited by what you might call the surface of life," the substance of her fiction to date suggests that this excitement must also derive in part from her intuitive feeling that there is something else of significance just below that literal surface. This may be one reason why to date she has been more attracted to the short story than to the novel. . . . [That] more concentrated fictional form probably allows her to explore in a more imaginative and intense way the intangible aspects of her world:

those shadowy and shifting areas between the rational and the irrational, between the familiar, comfortable world and sudden dimensions of terror, and between various facets of uncertainty and illusion.

These metaphysical concerns find their aesthetic and formal complements in the structures of her fiction, where a similar illusory balance operates between the conventional fictional elements of plot and character on the one hand, and on the other, a kind of psychological or even psychic verification or resolution of a particular dilemma. Though emanating from a recognizable sociological reality, the situations that are characteristically depicted in her fiction frequently transcend the literal bounds of our conscious realizations, and leave us with a residual uncertainty, puzzlement, or even despair. (pp. 56-7)

Something I've Been Meaning to Tell You . . . essentially picks up on the same themes and concerns as [Munro's] two earlier works, *Dance of the Happy Shades* and *Lives of Girls and Women*. In most of this fiction, Munro is the chronicler of a particular region, that of south-western Ontario. . . . (pp. 57-8)

Alice Munro's fiction could profitably be examined in terms of the themes of isolation and rejection, which unfold in situations where human relationships are rarely cemented or consummated. . . . [For example, in the short story "The Peace of Utrecht," home], the past, family ties —forces which are conventionally interpreted as positive forces—are . . . dramatized as disturbing elements, and the narrator even defines "home" as a "dim world of continuing disaster." . . . (p. 58)

It is [the] intangible or irrational impulses between the protagonist and some other element—other characters, the past or childhood, a code of morality or behaviour—which give Munro's fiction its haunting and disturbing quality. . . . In Munro's first two books, the emphasis was on the youthful protagonist trying to come to terms with the adult world, but in her latest collection it is frequently the other way around: grandmothers trying to understand granddaughters ("Marrakesh"), elderly sisters trying to make sense out of their common past ("Something I've Been Meaning to Tell You"), a sensitive old man just failing to come to terms with the younger generation around him ("Walking on Water"). (pp. 61-2)

[There is] an underlying element in Munro's fiction in general, and [it] is an irony which both enlarges the possibilities of experience and helps define her characters' specific attributes that operate within a given situation. In some cases, the irony is delightful and benign, as in "How I Met My Husband," which is not without its touches of an O. Henry or Somerset Maugham ending: inevitably combined with moral relief. (p. 65)

A more complex and essentially unresolved effect of irony and ambiguity is reflected in such stories as "Tell Me Yes or No" from her latest collection, or "The Office" from *Dance of the Happy Shades*. In this latter story, all the circumstantial evidence convicts the landlord right off: Mr. Malley is unpleasant, deceitful, dishonest, and perhaps even lecherous, in his dealings with the narrator, a writer who simply wished to use the office as a creative refuge away from her domestic demands. But there are many other layers of meaning here, and we are drawn into the basic dilemma about the nature of reality. The narrator, as

a writer, rearranges words to create her version of reality that takes its authority through the workings of imagination; the landlord, as a hostile commentator on the whole idea of a woman writing outside the home, re-arranges or manipulates facts to create another version of reality, one that to the outsider is as credible as any work of fiction. What we have in this story is the simultaneous creation of two imaginative worlds, and in this process, Mr. Malley manages to transform his outrageous distortions into some semblance of truth. "I arrange words, and think it is my right to be rid of him," . . . muses the narrator, but it is clear from the unresolved conclusion of this story that Mr. Malley's violations of her version of reality cannot be easily dismissed. (pp. 65-6)

[There is] a recurring pattern in Alice Munro's fiction: the dramatization of the conjunction of existential terror or desperation and existential possibility within a total vision that is much closer to faith than it is to despair. Worlds are always qualitatively changed at the conclusions of Munro's stories, and though the causal changes have contributed to the unsettling of her protagonists, they characteristically point to an enlargement of possibilities rather than a restriction, or they imply a resolution already attained. . . . There is a strong sense of amazement at the human condition in Munro, a quality that seems to be born of a recognition that ordinary people have an intangible talent or gift: not necessarily for goodness or truth or beauty, though that happens, too, but more frequently for lucking it out, for intuiting a move or an action which will get them out of a present predicament. At times, her characters appear to drift into salvation rather than consciously elect it, and their emergence into new possibilities is frequently accompanied by [a] kind of amazement. . . . This kind of realization constitutes what can be defined as an existentialist resolution, a phenomenon particularly relevant to the twentieth-century comic protagonist, to which category Munro's characters can essentially be said to belong. (pp. 67-8)

The total evidence in Alice Munro's fiction ultimately dictates that she cannot easily be categorized, and to say that she writes essentially in the comic mode, or that she is moving consistently beyond realism, reveals only part of the complexity of her art and vision. Her accomplishments offer gratifying evidence that fiction of significant substance, of careful craftsmanship, and of sympathetic treatment of the complexities of human relationships, is very much alive in Canada. All this is of course very much in the tradition of the realism of George Eliot or D. H. Lawrence or Robertson Davies, and as I indicated at the outset, Munro's fiction is strongly rooted in the realism of region and time. But in the Epilogue to *Lives,* [the protagonist] Del, by now an aspiring novelist and recorder of Jubilee's stories, recognizes the problems that she faces, as she visits Bobby Sherriff, out temporarily from the Asylum, and the last person she sees in Jubilee. "No list could hold what I wanted, for what I wanted was every last thing, every layer of speech and thought, stroke of light on bark or walls, every smell, pothole, pain, crack, delusion, held still and held together—radiant, everlasting." . . . But Bobby from the Asylum reminds her—and us—that there is another world that is not so decipherable, as he suddenly rises in a graceful-grotesque manner and looks at Del in such a way that she construes his action "to be a letter, or a whole word, in an alphabet I did not know." . . . In a very real way, this unknown or irrational world has been as much a concern of Alice Munro as have any of the things she can list, and her very substantial contribution to our fiction lies in the successful way she has addressed herself to this dilemma, with the authority of the artist and the astonishment of the seer. (pp. 70-1)

Hallvard Dahlie, "The Fiction of Alice Munro," in Ploughshares *(© 1978 by Ploughshares, Inc.), Vol. 4, No. 3, 1978, pp. 56-71.*

N

NIEDECKER, Lorine 1903-1970

Niedecker was an American poet. *Blue Chicory* is her best known work. (See also *Contemporary Authors*, Vols. 25-28; *Contemporary Authors Permanent Series*, Vol. 2.)

Miss Niedecker is a modest, cheerful writer whose publisher has served her ill in *North Central* with an oversized format and lopsided layout, confusing the beginnings, middles, and ends of her poems. She finds her theme in the relation between a region and its people. Natural history and local history are drawn together in short, breath-long lines of free verse. The three-stepped line of W. C. Williams supplies the form of several poems, especially the last and longest, "Wintergreen Ridge", in which the book culminates. Miss Niedecker often tries to let the succession of images carry so much implication that a few discursive touches and cool hints of her own attitude will point us to the generalizations on her mind. The method is like [Basil] Bunting's in *Briggflatts* but less erudite and pretentious—though not more reliable. While we move hesitantly from the level of rock formations and the time of the early explorers to the urban present, Miss Niedecker speaks more freely, recommending the wildness of mountain landscape, creatures, and flora as life-giving and sacramental. Natural human ties strengthened by these associations assert themselves against the death-directed impulses of industrial capitalism and war. The argument is hardly startling, but Miss Niedecker avoids oracularity. . . . (p. 212)

> The Times Literary Supplement (© *Times Newspapers Ltd. (London) 1969; reproduced from* The Times Literary Supplement *by permission), February 27, 1968.*

TONY HARRISON

[In 'Poet's Work', Niedecker typifies her poetic activity as 'condensery.' It is an] activity that, at its worst, is much like that of the white ants' mandibles nibbling away Sappho's full-bodied poems into so many passionate haiku. There is a sense of strain in much of her condensery, of observations nipped timidly in the bud, of a cut out detail of a print framed as a genuine miniature, of the lopped top few inches of a fir passed off as a bonzai. She admits to having Basho on her mind and has a section called 'In Exchange for Haiku', and as one follows the other, generously displayed in appropriate white spaces, one has the feeling of

mounting panic like watching a child go blue in the face from holding its breath too long, a sort of Black Mountain hara-kiri. Some of the shortest poems are of a folksy banality stripped to essentials as though Robert Frost had grown suddenly tight-lipped on saki. . . . (pp. 166-67)

Sometimes Miss Niedecker goes in for very awkward rhyming in short poems of very short lines, so that they sound like tumbling Skeltonics decapitated in mid-air. Sometimes a desperate alliteration props up her Zukofsky/WCW triplets:

> there the light
> > pissed past
> > > the pistillate cone

There are a few successes even among the palimpsests, like 'Museum' and other fragments in 'Wintergreen Ridge' and 'Paean to Place' where memories of her dead parents help her to sustain her landscape by water long enough for it to have a human presence. (p. 167)

> *Tony Harrison, in* London Magazine (© *London Magazine 1971), April-May, 1971.*

JAMES NAIDEN

Lorine Niedecker's new collection, *Collected Poems 1968: My Life by Water,* is a part of a rather long period in contemporary American life, from 1936 to 1968. Many of these poems are reflective of a spare genius, not without occasional impatience with what rankles at the soul—the very personal, yet sociable, tendencies in the life of any artist. Lorine Niedecker's poems reveal a most compassionate awareness of those elements that either impair or sustain the poet's vision in an hour of great turmoil. . . .

The concerns are always close to home and personal in ways peculiarly feminine, yet not in the least precious or "endearing"; above all, there is a good humor, with the eye always alert. . . . (p. 119)

> *James Naiden, in* Poetry (© *1972 by The Modern Poetry Association; reprinted by permission of the Editor of* Poetry), *May, 1972.*

THOMAS MEYER

". . . Am I the American indeed—I can't be entirely content, it seems, without some puzzlement, some sharpness, a bit of word-play, a kind of rhythm and music in however small a way. . . ." Lorine Niedecker wrote Cid Corman the fifteenth of December 1966. (p. 85)

The New York Times daily crossword and Lorine Niedecker, however far from one another, occupy points on the same language circuitry. Words in both instances are devices used for amplification, switching, and detection—each one, in short, a transfer resistor or transistor. (p. 86)

Anyone who reads more than three poems by Lorine Niedecker will not fail to feel a need satisfied, or at least resolved. Perhaps only her own, but the work is of that order. The poems are short and relatively few, not so much perfected as complete in themselves. We know from her letters to Cid Corman she was slow before the task a poem exacted, careful to trust only what absorbed her, almost Carthusian in that act of silence she demanded her poems be. . . . Apart from the awe we sense in the animal, vegetable, or mineral her poems fed on, what feeds us in her work?

> The radio talk this morning
> was of obliterating
> the world
>
> I notice fruit flies rise
> from the rind
> of the recommended
> melon

Obviously a woman well enough read that we can't rule out the possibility of Bashō's informing such a poem. Yet it seems impossible that our idea of Japanese poetry should be so vitally present in the way the words play such a precise music on *flies, rise, rind,* ending their run on *melon* via *recommended.* We can only speak of affinity, or the slave-boy Socrates was able to exact the theorems of geometry from without the kid's knowing he knew them. Amazingly, there is something so authentic, American, about the poem we are relieved of seeking pedantic sources. . . . She wrote Jonathan Williams in December 1965, "My inclusion in *A Test of Poetry* in the folk category under general heading Recurrence pleased me and he [Zukofsky, editor] said in a general way: 'The less poetry is concerned with the everyday existence and the rhythmic talents of a people the less readable that poetry is likely to be.'" The "readable" for Lorine Niedecker meant "one person to another, spoken thus, or read silently." In a lifetime she exercised little direct influence upon her generation or the next, making almost no disciples, yet producing work which, it is already clear, exerts a masterly influence.

[In a letter to Cid Corman, she wrote:] "I think this is it—the ultimate in poetry . . . —and it's done largely by the words omitted. Stark, isolated words which must somehow connect with each other and into the next line and the sense out of the sound.". . . The last poems (section two of *Blue Chicory*) are largely "portraits," longer works about other people's lives: Darwin, William Morris, Thomas Jefferson. (Ruskin and Hopkins occasion some poems but no sequence.) What an oddly touching trio. . . . "Wintergreen Ridge," the last in *Collected Poems 1968,* was by her standards a long poem and accomplished apparently what she wanted from a poem with herself as subject for more than a single page. Herself as subject though isn't quite right. Her world perhaps, but it was always hers and fully possessed, be it Linnaeus' Lapp drum or the new electric water pump. Otherwise it wouldn't do as poetry. Whatever alerted her,

alerted her need of complete possession. "Know thyself and nothing in excess," Apollo taught. In fewer words, she condensed emotion. The shadows in her poems are all cast by daylight. She is Artemis who thinks with eyes and fingers, measures and distills, dissects, discerning those aliances between tide and strawberry, pebble and ripple. (pp. 87-9)

How does she go about the labor these huge public lives give her? By honing in, seining the frailest detail. From Morris' letters to his wife, Jane, she arrests

> I work in the dye-house
> myself

amid all the toils he feels concerning socialism, paternalism, "art," "craft," and the "workers.". . . Apparently it isn't what we do with our attention or to perception, but the perceived attention itself that creates vision. (pp. 89-90)

It's as though these poems, this work, tricked language itself into becoming a poem, like using beer cartons for seed flats. No waste, nothing left over but the resonant sense of having done it oneself with what was at hand. Also, of having gone no further than one's own backyard. The concentration it took to transistorize language into a poem came from within. Lorine Niedecker was no pupil of any Zen Master nor did she attend conferences at The Naropa Institute. She stayed home, read a little Swedenborg. She exercised her faculties. Deeply troubled by her own longer poems, afraid she'd abandon the short ones, she wrote, "don't feel I shd. leave what's been a part of me all these years." Not because it became an issue between herself and Zukofsky or anyone else, but because it became an internalized matter. At the end of her life her work was changing proportions. Still very much in control, she nonetheless was disquieted: ". . . I always feel kind of faded out —my way of writing—compared to some parts of the *Cantos.* I'm the piece of wash that has hung too long in the sun!" Nor is it out of any sense of failing she says this. This is a clear reflection. The beauty of the wash she hung out is there, but it is interesting, perhaps, to note how the color for her was going at a time when she was doing something slightly different. In poetry of this scale the slightest difference or hint of departure magnifies itself. . . . Those few critics she's had up to and since her death . . . have either praised her without reservation or have been baffled by how the poems work, if not why. She herself said it was the simple speech of nursery rimes, the laconic snatches of conversation. Yet the poems, while they are laconic and rime, are neither simple nor conversational. How and why are ways of finding out, they can describe as much as they explain.

Blue Chicory is quite a book, just as object. The poems. Corman's "Editorial Note" in a few, but not hasty words, suggests and unfolds the attendant problems of a poet's last works, the executor, the texts, the archive, a forthcoming *Complete Collected Works.* . . . The title, though, fascinates me most, *Blue Chicory.* In all this spare and careful exercising of attention, are we seeing with some new eye the blue flower of the Romantics? That deepest need of oneself within, met with as though it were the flower's. . . . (pp. 90-1)

Thomas Meyer, "Chapter's Partner," in Parnassus: Poetry in Review *(copyright © by Poetry in Review Foundation), Spring-Summer, 1977, pp. 84-91.*

O

O'BRIEN, Flann (pseudonym of Brian O Nuallain, also known as Brian O'Nolan) 1911-1966

An Irish novelist and journalist, O'Brien tempered nearly everything he wrote with a lyricism that echoes the style of James Joyce. His subjects were usually fantastic, and he frequently burlesqued other Gaelic writers. He wrote an immensely popular column for the Irish *Times* under the name Myles na gCopaleen. (See also *CLC*, Vols. 1, 4, 5, 7, and *Contemporary Authors*, Vols. 21-22; obituary, Vols. 25-28, rev. ed.; *Contemporary Authors Permanent Series*, Vol. 2.)

'When a writer calls his work a Romance', Hawthorne said in the preface to *The House of the Seven Gables,* 'it need hardly be observed that he wishes to claim a certain latitude, both as to its fashion and material, which he would not have felt himself entitled to assume had he professed to be writing a Novel.' Flann O'Brien claimed the latitude without bothering to give his books a generic title. . . .

It is customary, on the strength of *At Swim-Two-Birds,* to place O'Brien in the Joycean tradition in Irish literature. The reasons are clear enough: a delight in verbal nuance, farce, parody, ostensibly fierce disputation, the implication that 'words alone are certain good'. . . . But it is not at all certain that these are the right lines. *The Third Policeman* has for nearest neighbour *The Dalkey Archive.* Indeed, Sergeant Pluck's obsession with bicycles is to be found, ascribed to Sergeant Fottrell, in the *Archive.* These two books throw a different light upon *At Swim-Two-Birds,* and suggest that the proper place for Flann O'Brien is the tradition of modern Irish fantasy and romance in which the definitive figure is James Stephens. Reading O'Brien now, one is reminded far more vigorously of *The Crock of Gold, The Charwoman's Daughter,* and Stephens's stories and sketches, than of Joyce in any of his manifestations. The elaborate discussions, the pedantry, the consecration of time to reverie: these are Stephens, not Joyce. Keep talking, and it won't happen: this is a motto applicable not only to Stephens but also to the tradition which goes on from Stephens to Eimar O'Duffy, Flann O'Brien, and Brinsley MacNamara's *Various Lives of Marcus Igoe.*

> *"Tall Talk," in* The Times Literary Supplement *(© Times Newspapers Ltd. (London) 1967; reproduced from* The Times Literary Supplement *by permission), September 7, 1967, p. 793.*

WILLIAM SAROYAN

To those who know O'Nolan's writing, ["Stories and Plays"] is a treasure. To those who don't, it is an excellent introduction, for every type of thing that he did in English is here, in brief, and in a rich assortment: the unfinished novel, "Slattery's Sago Saga," or "From Under the Ground to the Top of the Trees" is pure wild O'Nolan wit. "The Martyr's Crown" is one of the world's greatest short stories of comic intelligence. The two plays "Thirst" and "Faustus Kelly," do not contribute anything new in the technical sense to the play form, but they are perfect for reading. . . . (p. 7)

And finally there is a piece called "A Bash in the Tunnel." This is a mixture of literary criticism, a portrait of an Irish eccentric, a self-portrait of the writer as an ageless dog, and a short story: "A better title of this piece might be: 'Was Joyce Mad?'" (pp. 7-8)

> *William Saroyan, in* The New York Times Book Review *(© 1976 by The New York Times Company; reprinted by permission), March 28, 1976.*

JOAN KEEFE

In O'Brien's early writing the surface brilliance of his invention is underscored with an affectionate concern for "the plain people of Ireland," but a harshly bitter quality seeps into his later work, probably because of professional and personal disappointments. He can be compared to Joyce, Beckett and James Stephens. All of them display an obsession with physical details of ludicrous discomfort vividly presented, often to comic effect. O'Brien always angrily rejected the comparison to Joyce, but certainly he shares what he himself described as "Joyce's almost supernatural skill in conveying Dublin dialogue." His method of creating a grotesque reality heightened by details of surpassing ordinariness can be compared to Beckett's, while his use of fantastic Irish mythological motifs has some of the poetic wit of Stephens. Add to these the intricately constructed bilingual dimension of his work, and a unique comic genius emerges. (p. 141)

Certainly O'Brien is accessible to readers of English, in

which language he is a superb stylist with an uncannily true ear for usage. That he had the same gifted way with Irish must be taken on trust by many. (pp. 141-42)

Joan Keefe, in World Literature Today (*copyright 1977 by the University of Oklahoma Press*), *Vol. 51, No. 1, Winter, 1977.*

ROBERT MARTIN ADAMS

[There's] such a swirl of mostly fantastic activity inside [*At Swim-Two-Birds*] that the external torpor of the nameless [lie-abed] novelist is more than justified. But of course none of this is visible to the [author's mean-spirited] uncle, any more than the various marks by which the book's characters are distinguished are apparent to readers for whom the author hasn't bothered to describe them. O'Brien seems to have put some effort into the ancient wheeze that language was given to man in order to conceal his thoughts.

Much as he resembles Beckett's figure of Murphy, who was born just the year before, O'Brien's somnolent author is not yet psychotic, he is simply distracted. The Greek motto at the head of the book declares that "All things naturally draw apart," and under the analytic gaze of the author (who helpfully provides many sections of his book with solemn descriptions of their rhetorical modes), that's exactly what they do.... The hero of the book is not the story, ... partly because O'Brien sets so many stories going, and the characters involved in them start so many counter-stories, that none of them really gets told. Here language itself is the hero or villain, language which is able not only to transform and then reflect itself, but to give events and ideas and objects instantaneous new characters—often in a surprisingly literal sense. Language itself is the first mover, under whose impulse "all things naturally draw apart." (pp. 187-88)

As the innermost story collapses, the outer ones are resolved: sweetness and light seem to prevail. But the *Conclusion of the book, ultimate,* which the author appends, is a curious and very beautiful prose poem after the manner of Robert Burton, on the fragility of the human mind, its frightful susceptibility to its own *idées fixes*. Two images predominate: Mad Sweeny, a prophetic bag of bones hung in a tree between heaven and earth like a starved bird or a sibyl, listens to the barking of dogs, a creaturely noise that only deepens his sense of the infinite immensity of space: and a man run mad on the number three goes home and cuts his throat three times, scrawling with his blood on the mirror a last note to his wife, "good bye, good bye, good bye." As an ending to a comic novel, it is as grim a passage as the ending of *The Sound and the Fury,* which is also a novel about the mind's inability to keep things from falling apart.

At Swim-Two-Birds is a Joycean novel, but it's Irish as well, and fantastic in addition; there's no way of saying very clearly where one element leaves off and the other begins. The trial scene, the burlesques of epic tradition, and the derisive report of a learned conversation between three villainous pub-crawlers (they are as full of solemn, disjointed, useless miscellaneous information as the "Ithaca" section of *Ulysses*) are among the passages that stand out as directly derivative. Then there's an area where without the Joycean precedent O'Brien perhaps wouldn't have written just as he did, but where the resemblance is too general to justify talk about "influence." The knack of rendering colloquial speech is only to be picked up by listening to colloquial speech, but with *Ulysses* beside him, O'Brien evidently found certain rhythms and certain hard, funny vulgarisms within easy range of his discourse, as earlier practitioners of vulgar Irish English had not. The contemptuous hash made of narrative, the drying out of description, the intrusion of the author as stylistic manipulator—all these conventions, with some others, mark O'Brien as a *post*-Joyce if not wholly *propter*-Joyce writer. The elements of fun and play are purer in him than in Joyce, the labyrinth of the author's language is less intricate and perhaps less oppressive: for all its illusionistic entanglements, the story comes closer to being a story than anything in Joyce. But the evidence of influence is too strong to need further emphasis. (pp. 189-90)

Robert Martin Adams, in his AfterJoyce: Studies in Fiction After "Ulysses" (*copyright © 1977 by Robert Martin Adams; reprinted by permission of Oxford University Press, Inc.*), *Oxford University Press, 1977.*

TERENCE WINCH

O'Brien was an eccentric writer of tremendous comic spirit. His work reveals an impressive knowledge of science, philosophy, literature, and theology. But his attitudes are always playful and satiric. Like Swift, who made fun of the Royal Society in *Gulliver's Travels,* O'Brien had a talent for making the principles of science seem ridiculous. The Sergeant in *The Dalkey Archive,* for example, explains the "Mollycule" theory: "Now take a sheep. What is a sheep only millions of little bits of sheepness whirling around doing intricate convulsions inside the baste." This is all by way of explaining that people who spend too much time on bicycles, according to the Sergeant, "get their personalities mixed up with the personalities of their bicycles." In the same novel, the crazy genius and fraud De Selby invents a substance to "abolish air" and destroy the world. He calls it DMP (after "The Dublin Metropolitan Police") and it brings to mind Kurt Vonnegut's "ice-nine."...

O'Brien's "better-class journalism," as he called [the writing he did for the Irish Times after 1953,] is largely work that seems to ride on the coattails of his talents as a novelist: the journalism is a little too close to, and not quite as good as, his fiction.... O'Brien's newspaper work is more a run-off from his fiction. The fiction of Flann O'Brien bleeds into the journalism of Myles na Gopaleen]....

[He] almost never wrote "out of the depth" of his feelings. This refusal to be serious is at first a relief from the high-minded self-importance of many artists. But after hundreds of pages of jokes, put-ons, puns, satires, and parodies, the reader starts to become ravenous for something more directly from the heart. The constant humor, like the pseudonyms, is a way of disguising the "real" O'Brien, or O'-Nolan, or Myles, or whoever this man is, providing him with some very effective, self-protective distance from his audience....

What is strikingly present in the work of Flann O'Brien is his intelligence, anger, and wit. He called himself "an accomplished literary handyman," but he was more than that. He produced a body of work that is funny, innovative, and all his own.

Terence Winch, "The Comic of County

Tyrone," in Book World—The Washington Post (© *The Washington Post), March 12, 1978, p. E8.*

V. S. PRITCHETT

[At] every point [in "At Swim-Two-Birds"] there are satirical glimpses of Dublin life. If the whole were simple, broad farce, it would soon pall. What transforms it is the great, if often maddening, influence of Irish pedantry—the comedy of hairsplitting—and O'Brien's ear for the nuances of Irish talk: above all, for its self-inflating love of formal utterance and insinuation. His humor . . . depends on the intricacy of its texture. Language is all: he is a native of a country of grammarians, thriving on the perplexities of a mixed culture, and creating, as Joyce did, vulgar or scholarly myths.

To say this is not to underrate O'Brien's superb invention in broad farce—in, say, "The Hard Life.". . . O'Brien's extravagant mock encounters with Joyce (who is heard saying that "Ulysses" was smut written by American academics) and with Keats and Chapman paralytically drunk in a pub after closing time (when the landlord has to declare that the illegal drinkers are all his uncles and nieces) are fun of a journalistic order. (pp. 153-54)

The curious theme of death kept at bay by the invention of conceits underlies "The Third Policeman," the posthumously published version of the early novel that had failed. It seems to have begun as a mock detective story, in which the author is forced to commit an appalling murder by a man who has enslaved him and robbed him of his property. This is a dark and disturbing tale. O'Brien's work is rich in distracting episodes, and here we come upon a conceit that seems to point to something obsessive in his inward-turning mind. The conceit reminds one of Borges and of those figures who multiply in a series of reflections in retreating mirrors. In O'Brien, the object is a box that contains a box containing boxes, getting infinitely smaller, until they are invisible. It seems that O'Brien put off doom by retreating into a metaphysical solitude. But the scene becomes macabre. Ridiculous policemen arrive. The narrator is arrested and hears being built, plank by plank, the scaffold on which he will be hanged. Bicycles—another of O'Brien's obsessive subjects—confuse the tale, for he cannot resist an idea. But there is no doubt of his laughter and unnerving melancholy. (pp. 154, 157)

> *V. S. Pritchett, "Flann vs. Finn"* (© *by V. S. Pritchett; reprinted by permission of Harold Matson Co., Inc.), in* The New Yorker, *May 15, 1978, pp. 151-54, 157.*

*   *   *

O'CONNOR, (Mary) Flannery   1925-1964

O'Connor was an American short story writer, novelist, and essayist. A Roman Catholic from the Bible Belt, she liberally laced her fiction with material from each of these religious backgrounds to create a unique, highly personal vision. Her vision is a chilling one, reflected in a world characterized by sudden, bizarre violence and peopled with grotesques whom she sees as mirrors for men fallen from grace. O'Connor is considered one of the important figures of the Southern Renascence. (See also *CLC,* **Vols. 1, 2, 3, 6, and** *Contemporary Authors,* **Vols. 1-4, rev. ed.)**

PATRICIA D. MAIDA

Vision functions as the dynamic principle in Flannery O'Connor's fiction. From her first novel *Wise Blood,* through *The Violent Bear It Away,* and in both collections of short stories, O'Connor portrays characters who are morally blind. Her people project their true selves through the physical qualities of their eyes—through color, shape, and intensity. And their perception of the world is controlled by their limited powers of sight. The reader enters this world through the eyes of the characters, experiencing an environment fraught with extraordinary signs in the form of natural imagery. Among the recurring images a triad dominates: the treeline, the sun, and the color purple. Essentially, the tree-line suggests a delineation between the known and the unknown; the sun reflects light or enlightenment; and the color purple indicates bruising and pain. But on the metaphysical level, this triad represents an existential awareness and a spiritual process. (p. 31)

The focus on the eyes of the characters not only provides greater insight for the reader, but it also increases the reader's awareness of the conflict between individual perception and truth. . . . By assuming the objective point of view, O'Connor the narrator focuses closely on the telling details, especially the eyes of the characters and other elements that will inform the reader. . . .

Vision controls not only the way a person views himself and others, but also the way he perceives nature. One of the recurring images O'Connor employs from the natural environment is the "tree-line," a demarcation of what is immediate to a character's experience and that which lies beyond. Sudden consciousness of the tree-line on the part of a character foreshadows an impending crisis. (p. 32)

Sun images work along with the tree-line images to convey impending light or enlightenment. In an O'Connor story the intensity of the sun is most acute at the point where the hero is suddenly enlightened, having experienced a moment of truth—a process like James Joyce's epiphany. . . . The strength of the sun is not only a reflection of the illumination occurring in the psyche of the character; it also highlights the source of power—truth and Divine intervention. (p. 33)

The red-golds of the sun contrast with the purple tones of the imagery surrounding the moment of enlightenment. Purple suggests bruising, pain, and self-abnegation—it is always part of the process of change depicted in an O'Connor story. . . . The classical idea of suffering as a prelude to knowledge as well as the irony operative in classical tragedy permeates O'Connor's fiction. If illumination is to occur, the individual's defenses must be shattered in a kind of shock therapy. The outcome is a collision with truth —a metaphysical experience.

The totality of the natural imagery that reflects this metaphysical experience represents ultimately a spiritual process basic to O'Connor's orientation. The juxtaposition of earth and sky, the role of the sun, the use of the color purple portray the process of Redemption. Representing infinity and the omnipresent Divinity, the sky hovers over the earth separated by the horizon or tree-line. The barrier is penetrated by the rays of the sun—the influence of God called grace. The sun causes a purpling effect or a form of self-abnegation on the part of the individual that prepares him for change. The color purple is traditionally used in Christian liturgy to symbolize penetential seasons. The fact that the occasion for the moment of illumination arrives unexpectedly, often ironically, indicates the unique power of Divine intervention.... All of O'Connor's works are concerned with Christian values, even though some of her short stories do not touch upon religion directly. She manages to evoke a sense of the redemptive process throughout her works, however, by reinforcing the moment of truth with symbolic imagery. (pp. 33-4)

The momentum of Flannery O'Connor's fiction is basically hopeful in assessing man's limitations amid the constant possibility of redemption. Although man is thwarted by his lack of vision, the light remains a hovering presence—ready to pursue, if necessary, the recalcitrant. The process of enlightenment, so basic to O'Connor's works, is reinforced by natural imagery.... The fusion of character, situation, and imagery culminates in a unique experience, a metaphysical awakening, a spiritual illumination. (p. 36)

> *Patricia D. Maida, "Light and Enlightenment in Flannery O'Connor's Fiction," in* Studies in Short Fiction *(copyright 1976 by Newberry College), Winter, 1976, pp. 31-6.*

DAVID AIKEN

[In "The Enduring Chill"] four explicit references to Joyce are only the most obvious of an elaborate series of correspondences between Asbury Porter Fox and the Stephen Dedalus of both *Portrait* and *Ulysses:* correspondences involving not only major events and images but even details of diction and syntax and providing the basis for a sharply satiric portrait of the self-conscious artist-hero. O'Connor frequently uses satire as an instrument of moral judgment, but "The Enduring Chill" is unique among her stories because its satiric object is a specific literary character. Taking Stephen's distinguishing characteristics and exaggerating them to create a caricature of the modern hero who vows to serve nothing except art, O'Connor presents her view of the would-be artist as a personal failure. By revealing her attitude about Joyce's artistic techniques and about the young Stephen as a cultural hero, "The Enduring Chill" becomes an important index of O'Connor's own central esthetic tenets.... (p. 245)

Like Stephen Dedalus, who for the sake of his vocation adopted a *non serviam* stance against country, family, and church, Asbury perceives his home, his family, and his religious tradition as constricting limitations which he must defy in the name of art. (p. 246)

One of the Achaean backslappers, Mr. Dedalus was most at home in a bar with his drinking companions; and Asbury is convinced that his "old man," who has been dead for twenty years, would also have been one of the "courthouse gang," no more intelligent or sensitive than anyone else in the rural wasteland. Like Stephen, however, Asbury rebels most vigorously against his mother. Compared with the pious, sentimental, and possessive Mrs. Dedalus, who appears as a suffering, victimized woman, Mrs. Fox is industriously independent, proud, mannered, and indulgent toward her children, especially the younger, Asbury. But even though the two women are very different, Asbury's rebellion against his mother is an exaggerated reflection of Stephen's *non serviam* toward his. (p. 249)

In one of her critical essays, O'Connor remarks that "There is no excuse for anyone to write fiction for public consumption unless he has been called to do so by the pres-

ence of a gift"...; Asbury clearly lacks both call and gift. (p. 251)

Ultimately, O'Connor identifies Asbury's failure (and, by implication, Stephen's) not with his failed art but with his flawed character, the result of his peculiar mind-set and one of the most important objects of O'Connor's satire. Asbury's temperament and attitude are exaggerated reflections of Stephen's distinguishing personal characteristic, his coolly aloof and seemingly disinterested disposition.... (pp. 251-52)

In *Portrait* Joyce painted not a moral picture, but a portrait of the artist as defined by his own awareness and social situation.... In *Ulysses,* however, Joyce intimates that Stephen's art is no consolation for his personal failure.... As Bloom emerges, Stephen recedes as the focus of attention, fading out, as it were, before his moral and spiritual superior. (p. 253)

Omitting the epiphany of vocation in order to emphasize the revelations of self-knowledge, [O'Connor] settles the question of her hero as an artist before the story even begins, thus creating not a portrait of the artist as a young man but a portrait of a young man using art for his own purposes. Whereas Joyce maintains a dual, if uneven, focus between Stephen's vocation and personality, O'Connor focuses almost entirely on the childish self-centeredness of her protagonist.

The nature of Asbury's disposition, which is no secret to anyone except himself, is revealed in his "irritable," "ugly," and "fretful" voice. Whereas he sees himself as an artist defiant against a stupid, insensitive world, O'Connor satirizes him as merely an indulged child who was insufficiently disciplined when growing up. (p. 254)

Cherishing a protective image of himself as a type of Joycean hero, Asbury has used the modern role of the sensitive artist at odds with his materialistic and unknowing surroundings to justify his own egocentricity. But O'Connor's character of petty defiance is not who he thinks he is: he is not part of the intellectual and artistic vanguard of society; and he is not Stephen Dedalus. His adoration of exile is more a manifestation of his willful character than an artistic transcendence over a crass and squalid world; his *non serviam* defiance is mere petulance. Having erected a pseudointellectual wall as protection from true self-knowledge and exposure to maturity, he has both prolonged and glorified his self-centeredness by worshipping it as dedication to art. In O'Connor's terms, what Asbury must recognize is that he is not the artist at odds with a philistine society, but that in his egocentric childishness he is simply at odds with everyone and everything ... and most of all with himself and with God. Before Asbury gains true self-knowledge, however, he has to be kicked by a cow; ridiculed by his sister; scorned by the blacks; prodded and examined by a country doctor; in his dreams licked in the face by a spotted cow as if his head were a block of salt; accused and judged by a one-eyed, partially deaf priest; and attacked by both the fevers of nature and the purifying chill of the Holy Ghost.

Unlike Stephen, Asbury returns from exile not to his mother's death, or even to his own as he expects, but rather to the death of his hallowed, false self-image. Only at the end of the story, after Asbury learns the true source of his fever, does he with "shocked" eyes take back the key to the drawer containing the letter to his mother. At this point his wall of egocentricity has been breached, his old self-image is crumbling, and he sees himself as he truly is—thereby, in O'Connor's vision, opening himself to the mysterious power of the Holy Ghost. Like the younger Stephen, Asbury experiences an epiphany which is "the call of life"...; but whereas Stephen's epiphany is vocational, Asbury's is the vehicle of potential personal transformation. O'Connor presents this revelation in figures of violence and natural catastrophe—"earthquakes," "gunshot," "whirlwind," and a "purifying terror"—emphasizing the natural resistance of Asbury's old self, which can be destroyed only by a vastly superior force. In her world such a power is necessary to overcome the natural man's barrier of self-protection. (pp. 255-56)

The conclusion of "The Enduring Chill" is flawed by O'Connor's heavy-handedness. By blatantly entering the story herself and identifying her epiphany with the Holy Ghost, perhaps she wished to confess that all epiphanal experiences are God-centered rather than man-centered events. (p. 257)

The objects of O'Connor's satire in "The Enduring Chill" are many. She portrays Asbury in his childish "foolishness" as a ludicrous and comic figure. But in deflating Asbury's self-image, she also satirizes the youthful type that rebels against his tradition and alienates himself from his family in the name of absolute dedication to art. She is, then, addressing those artists and intellectuals who see Stephen Dedalus not just as the young artist but as the model of the hero most precious. They, like Asbury, fail to perceive Joyce's ironic treatment of the youthful errors of the sometimes maudlinly romantic adolescent and instead identify with the young defier, seeing in his alienation from family, country, and religion a personal model of behavior for artistic and intellectual freedom, a model which should be gospel for all knowing persons. O'Connor is, then, satirizing the popular reading of Stephen Dedalus as a cultural hero, an image which she—like many others—derives from a limited understanding of Joyce's attitude toward the character of Stephen, especially in *Ulysses.*

O'Connor felt that a narrative was flawed if the author failed to reveal a clear moral judgment.... [She] did not realize that Joyce's attitude toward Stephen and the nature of his exile for art shifted considerably in *Ulysses;* nor did she recognize the similarity of her criticism of Stephen with Joyce's own criticism of his young hero.... [Both] religiously informed writers ultimately see egocentric exile from the world as loveless and sterile; both ridicule extreme hyperborean defensiveness, making it the source of personal failure. At any rate, ...O'Connor provides the clear judgment and comment which she thought Joyce failed to offer. If anything, in her zeal to correct what she considered a Joycean flaw she errs in the opposite direction and overwrites. One of the few times that O'Connor lost control of her fine tension between seeing and believing was surely the result of misreading.

Satire is the sword thrust O'Connor uses to puncture her reader's defensive worldly values, in this case the general adoration and emulation of a hero who, at least in her eyes, makes art a rival to God. Resembling the younger Stephen's hawk-god, the fierce bird in O'Connor's world is not art but the Holy Ghost, which stands in stark contrast to the huffy bird that is Asbury's emblem. O'Connor does

not, of course, reject art; but the old priest, in his response to Asbury's affirmation that "the artist prays by creating," is surely her mouthpiece. For O'Connor art is indeed "Not enough": she clearly confesses that God, not art, is the mysterious source of creativity and the foundation of fulfilled personal existence. In her theocentric world, even to the young artist, the last word is God's. (pp. 257-59)

> *David Aiken, "Flannery O'Connor's Portrait of the Artist as a Young Failure," in* Arizona Quarterly *(copyright © 1976 by the Arizona Quarterly), Vol. 32, No. 3, Autumn, 1976, pp. 245-59.*

ANDRÉ BLEIKASTEN

[No] reader can fail to discern the permanence and seriousness of [O'Connor's] religious concerns. Fall and redemption, nature and grace, sin and innocence—every one of her stories and novels revolves around these traditional Christian themes. It is hardly surprising that O'Connor should have acknowledged close affinities with Hawthorne. Her fiction is of a coarser fabric than his, less delicately shaded in its artistry and far less muted in its effects, but it belongs without any doubt to the same tradition of American romance: characters and plots matter less than "the power of darkness" one senses behind them; symbol, allegory, and parable are never far away, and with O'Connor as with Hawthorne, the accumulated mass of allusions and connotations derives in a very large measure from the rich mythology of Christian culture. The temptation is therefore great to decipher works like theirs through the cultural and hermeneutic codes which the Christian tradition provides, and in O'Connor's case it is all the more irresistible since we have the author's blessing. (pp. 53-4)

O'Connor's public pronouncements on her art—on which most of her commentators have pounced so eagerly—are by no means the best guide to her fiction. As an interpreter, she was just as fallible as anybody else, and in point of fact there is much of what she has said or written about her work that is highly questionable. The relationship between what an author thinks, or thinks he thinks, and what he writes, is certainly worth consideration. For the critic, however, what matters most is not the extent to which O'Connor's tales and novels reflect or express her Christian faith, but rather the problematical relation between her professed ideological stance and the textual evidence of her fiction.

Ideologically O'Connor was an eccentric. Her commitments were definitely off-center: antisecular, antiliberal, antiindividualistic, and she had as little patience with the cozy assumptions of conventional humanism as with the bland pieties and anemic virtues of its fashionable Christian variants. What counted for O'Connor was not so much man as his soul, and perhaps not so much his soul as the uncanny forces that prey on it. Hers is a world haunted by the sacred—a sacred with two faces now distinct and opposed, now enigmatically confused: the divine and the demonic. Hence, we find in most of her characters the double postulation noted by Baudelaire: one toward God, the other toward Satan.

In accordance with this dual vision, the human scene becomes in her fables the battleground where these two antagonistic powers confront each other and fight for possession of each man's soul. To judge from O'Connor's hellish chronicle, however, the chances hardly seem to be equal. To all appearances, Evil wins the day. Or rather: Satan triumphs. For in her world Evil is not just an ethical concept; it is an active force, and it has a name, personal, individual. In the middle of the twentieth century O'Connor, like Bernanos, was rash enough to believe not only in God but also in the Devil. And, like the French novelist, she had the nerve to incorporate him into her fiction. In *The Violent Bear It Away* we first hear his voice—the voice of the friendly "stranger" who accompanies young Tarwater during his tribulations; then we see him in the guise of a homosexual sporting a black suit, a lavender shirt, and a broad-rimmed panama hat. (pp. 54-5)

But the Devil does not have to strut about the stage to persuade us of his existence and power. Reflected in the implacable mirror O'Connor holds up to it, the whole world becomes transfixed in a fiendish grimace: mankind has apparently nothing to offer but the grotesque spectacle of its cruel antics. At first glance, it almost looks as if all souls had already been harvested by the Demon. For, despite O'Connor's firm belief in the existence of immortal souls, her world strikes us most often as utterly soulless. There is indeed little to suggest the "depths" and "secrets" of inner life which are the usual fare of religious fiction. The ordinary condition of most of her heroes is one of extreme emotional exhaustion and spiritual numbness, and from that catatonic torpor they only emerge to succumb to the destructive forces of violence or insanity. Moreover, in their deathlike apathy as well as in their sudden convulsions, O'Connor's characters are ruthlessly stripped of any pretense to dignity. People, in her fiction, suffer and die, but pettily, just as they are pettily evil. Wrenching from the Devil the dark, handsome mask afforded him by romantic satanism, O'Connor exposes his essential banality and restores him to his favorite hunting ground: the everyday world. The color of evil, in her work, is gray rather than black—a grim grayness set off by lurid splashes of red. Its face is difficult to distinguish from that of mediocrity, and its most characteristic expression is meanness. The banality of evil is what brings it within range of mockery: insofar as it thrives on human folly and wretchedness, it becomes laughable.

Yet with O'Connor laughter is never harmless, and her savage humor seldom provides comic release. It is not an elegant way of defusing horror. Far from dissolving evil in farce, it emphasizes its demonic character, and calls attention to its terrifying power of perversion and distortion. Woven into the fabric of everydayness, evil becomes trivial, but at the same time the world of common experience is defamiliarized and made disquieting through its contagion by evil. Under Satan's sun the earth spawns monsters. O'Connor's tales drag us into a teratological nightmare, a ludicrous Inferno partaking at once of a hospital ward, a lunatic asylum, a menagerie, and a medieval *Cour des Miracles*. Like a Brueghel painting or a Buñuel film, the stories of *A Good Man Is Hard to Find* invite us to a sinister procession of freaks and invalids. . . . (p. 55)

O'Connor's penchant for freaks, idiots, and cripples, her fascination with the morbid, macabre, and monstrous, are traits she shares with many southern writers. The same gothic vein can be found to varying degrees in Erskine Caldwell, Eudora Welty, Carson McCullers, William Goyen, and Truman Capote, as well as in William Faulkner.

Like them, she belongs to the manifold progeny of Poe. Yet the primal function assumed in her art by the grotesque cannot be explained away by fashion or tradition. Nor can one ascribe it merely to the gratuitous play of a perverse imagination. O'Connor used the grotesque very deliberately, and if it became one of her privileged modes, it was because she thought it fittest to express her vision of reality. As she herself stated, its meaning in her fiction is closely linked to her religious concerns; in her eyes, the grotesque can no more be dissociated from the supernatural than evil can be separated from the mysteries of faith. The grotesque has the power of revelation; it manifests the irruption of the demonic in man and brings to light the terrifying face of a world literally *dis-figured* by evil. The derangement of minds and deformity of bodies point to a deeper sickness, invisible but more irremediably tragic, the sickness of the soul. Gracelessness in all its forms indicates the absence of grace in the theological sense of the term.

This, at least, is how O'Connor vindicated her heavy reliance on grotesque effects and how she expected her readers to respond to them. Yet her vigorous denunciation of spiritual sickness is not devoid of ambiguity, and its ambiguity partly proceeds from the very rage with which she fustigates man's sins and follies. . . . Between her and her characters (with a few notable exceptions) lies all the distance of contempt, disgust, and derision, and it is the very harshness of the satire that arouses suspicion. . . . With methodic thoroughness and almost sadistic glee, O'Connor exploits all the resources of her talent to reduce the human to the nonhuman, and all her similes and metaphors have seemingly no other purpose than to degrade it to the inanimate, the bestial, or the mechanical. Like Gogol and Dickens, she possesses a weird gift for deadening people into things while quickening things into objects with a life of their own (Hazel's rat-colored Essex in *Wise Blood*, the giant steam shovel in "A View of the Woods").

Hence a world both frozen and frantic, both ludicrous and threatening. O'Connor's landscapes—her fierce, fiery suns, her blank or blood-drenched skies, her ominous woods—are landscapes of nightmare. . . . Yet, even though O'Connor defended her use of the grotesque as a necessary strategy of her art, one is left with the impression that in her work it eventually became the means of a savage revilement of the whole of creation.

Questions then arise on the orthodoxy of her Catholicism. For Barbey d'Aurevilly, Catholicism was, in his own phrase, an old wrought-iron balcony ideally suited for spitting upon the crowd. It would be unfair, certainly, to suggest that O'Connor used it for similar purposes. Yet one may wonder whether her Catholicism was not, to some extent, an alibi for misanthropy. And one may also wonder whether so much black derision is compatible with Christian faith, and ask what distinguishes the extreme bleakness of her vision from plain nihilism. (pp. 56-7)

If we are to believe the Christian moralists, one of the Devil's supreme wiles is to leave us with the shattering discovery of our nothingness and so to tempt us into the capital sin of despair. From what one knows of O'Connor's life, it seems safe to assume that this was the temptation she found most difficult to resist, and it might be argued that her writing was in many ways a rite of exorcism, a way of keeping despair at a distance by projecting it into fiction. Small wonder then that in her work the demon of literary creation, as John Hawkes so judiciously noted, is inseparable from the Demon himself. When, as in *The Violent Bear It Away,* O'Connor makes the Devil speak, his sarcastic voice sounds startlingly like the author's. (p. 57)

Yet it is not enough to say that O'Connor was of the Devil's party. Many ironies and paradoxies interact in her work, and exegetes of Christian persuasion would probably contend that in its very abjection O'Connor's world testifies to the presense of the divine, the fall from grace being the proof *a contrario* of man's supernatural destination. O'Connor's heroes live mostly in extreme isolation, yet they are never truly alone. However entrenched in their smugness or embattled in their revolt, they find no safe shelter in their puny egos, and sooner or later, by degrees or—more often—abruptly, some invisible force breaks into their lives to hurl them far beyond themselves. They are *called*—called by whom? By what? How can anyone tell if the calling voice is God's or the Devil's?

A major theme in O'Connor's fiction, the enigma of *vocation*, is nowhere more fully explored than in her two novels. As most critics have pointed out, *Wise Blood* and *The Violent Bear It Away* offer very similar narrative and thematic patterns. Their heroes, Hazel Motes and Francis Marion Tarwater, are likewise obsessed by their vocation as preachers and prophets, and in both of them the obsession is significantly embodied in the figure of a despotic old man, the more formidable since he is dead: a fanatical grandfather, "with Jesus hidden in his head like a stinger" . . . for Hazel; a great-uncle no less single-minded and intolerant for young Tarwater. . . .

Prophets or false prophets? The question is not easy to answer. Many of O'Connor's backwoods preachers are simply frauds, and for a sincere Christian there is perhaps nothing more scandalous than religious imposture. . . . Satirizing southern evangelism, however, was obviously not O'Connor's main concern. Her preachers and prophets are by no means all vulgar charlatans. Nor are we supposed to regard them as lunatics. The reader is of course free to dismiss characters such as Hazel Motes or the two Tarwaters as insane, and to interpret their extravagant stories as cases of religious mania, but it is clear that this is not how the author intended them to be read. As a Roman Catholic, O'Connor must have had her reservations about the fanatic intolerance and apocalyptic theology of primitive fundamentalism. Yet, as she herself admitted on several occasions, its integrity and fervor appealed to her, for she found them congenial to the burning intransigence of her own faith. Her fascination with the southern evangelist—whom she came to envision as a crypto-Catholic—is not unlike the attraction Bernanos and Graham Greene felt for the priest figure. (p. 58)

In O'Connor violence rules man's relation to the sacred, just as it rules his relation to other men. Nothing here that suggests "spirituality": the word is too smooth, too polished, too blandly civilized to apply to the compulsions and convulsions of these savage souls. For Motes and Tarwater as well as for the "Misfit" of "A Good Man Is Hard to Find," God is above all an idée fixe, and the divine is primarily experienced as an intolerable invasion of privacy, a dispossession—or possession—of the self. What torments O'Connor's heroes, at least at first glance, is not their being deprived of God, but rather the fact that their obsession with Him cannot be escaped. Religious experience, as it is

rendered dramatically in her fiction, comes pretty close to Freud's definition: a variant of obsessional neurosis.

God is the Intruder. Therefore the first move of O'Connor's "prophet freaks" . . . is to resist or to flee. (p. 59)

Rebellious children, O'Connor's heroes assert themselves only by willful transgression of the divine order, as if only the certainty of flouting God's will and of doing evil could give them an identity of their own. Their revolt springs essentially from a refusal to submit, to alienate their freedom and have their fate coerced into some preestablished pattern. In their stubborn striving for autonomy, they commit what Christian tradition has always considered to be the satanic sin par excellence: the sin of pride.

Yet pride is not the only obstacle to the fulfillment of their spiritual destinies. Soiled from birth by the sin of their origins, how could these fallen souls hoist themselves up to God's light? They do not know God; they experience only his burning absence. For the theologian and the philosopher God is a matter of speculation; for the mystic he may become the living object of inner experience. For O'Connor's Christomaniacs he becomes "the bleeding stinking mad shadow of Jesus." . . . Their God is above all a haunting specter, a power felt and feared in its uncanny emptiness, and this ominous power they can only apprehend anthropomorphically through the incongruous phantasmagoria of their guilt-ridden imaginations. There is apprehension, but no comprehension. Their notion of the godly is not exempted from the distortions of the corrupt world in which they live, and therefore the divine gets so often confused with the demonic. In its extreme form, this rampant perversion comes to manifest itself as radical inversion. Everything, then, is turned upside down, and the religious impulse is subverted into its very opposite: desire for God is transformed into God-hatred, prayer into blasphemy, and the quest for salvation turns into a mystique of perdition.

Nothing exemplifies this inversion better than the *imitatio Christi* in reverse which O'Connor presents us in *Wise Blood.* After turning himself into the prophet of the Church Without Christ (the negative of the Church of God, the very image of the "body of sin" referred to by St. Paul), Hazel Motes ironically becomes a Christ without a church, an anonymous, solitary pseudo-Christ or anti-Christ. His disciples are morons and mountebanks, his preaching meets only with indifference, and his calvary at the close of the novel ends in a seemingly pointless death. Worn out by self-inflicted pain and privation, he is clubbed to death by two fat policemen. Motes dies like a dog, and his atrocious end reminds one strongly of the last pages of *The Trial,* when two men appear and lead Joseph K. to the outskirts of the town to kill him. The life and death of O'Connor's hero appear likewise as an absurd Passion. (pp. 59-60)

Christian references and Christian parallels abound in O'Connor's fiction, and more often than not they strike us as ironic. In *Wise Blood,* especially, parodic overtones are so frequent that the whole novel might almost be read as sheer burlesque. A "new jesus" appears in the guise of a shrunken museum mummy; a slop-jar cabinet becomes the tabernacle to receive him, and Sabbath Lily Hawks, a perverse little slut, cradles the mummy in her arms as if she were the Madonna. O'Connor's penchant for travesty is likewise reflected in the eccentric ritualism of many of her characters: baptismal drownings (in "The River" and *The*

Violent Bear It Away), rites of exorcism (Tarwater setting fire to his great-uncle's house), purification rites (Tarwater firing the bushes where the rape occurred), initiation rites (Enoch Emery's shedding of clothes in *Wise Blood* and Tarwater's in *The Violent Bear It Away*), sacrificial rites (Motes's self-blinding), etc. In their appalling extravagance, these ritual actions are likely to shock any reader, whether Christian or not. But here again, if we are prepared to accept the premises of the author, we shall avoid mistaking them for mere fits of madness, for to her, in a desacralized world like ours, these savage and sacrilegious rites paradoxically assert the presence of the sacred through the very excess of its distortion or denial. (pp. 60-1)

O'Connor's satiric stance, her penchant for parody, her reliance on the grotesque, and her massive use of violence—the features of her art we have examined so far all contribute to the subtle interplay of tensions and ambiguities through which it comes alive, and they resist alike reduction to a single interpretative pattern. The same irreducible ambiguity also attaches to another significant trait of her fictional world: the enormous amount of suffering and humiliation which is inflicted on most of her characters, and the inevitability of their defeat and/or death. Hazel Motes's destiny probably offers the most telling example of this process: after an active career in sin and crime, all his aggressiveness is eventually turned against himself, driving him to a positive frenzy of masochism and self-destruction. He blinds himself with quicklime, exposes himself to cold and illness, walks in shoes "lined with gravel and broken glass and pieces of small stone," . . . wraps three strands of barbed wire round his chest, and when his baffled landlady protests at so much self-torture, Motes replies imperturbably: "I'm not clean," or again "I'm paying." . . . (p. 61)

According to the prototypal Christian pattern, the hero's journey leads in both novels from sinful rebellion to the recognition of sin and to penance. O'Connor would have us believe that her protagonists are responsible for their fates, that they possess freedom of choice, and are at liberty to refuse or accept their vocation. . . . But her readers, even those who sympathize with her Christian assumptions and are willing to make allowances for the mysterious working of grace, will hesitate to take her at her word. For in the text of the novel there is indeed little to indicate that Motes or Tarwater could have made a different choice and that events might have followed another course. Her heroes are not allowed to shape their destinies; they only *recognize* fate when it pounces upon them. . . . O'Connor's heroes are . . . like sleepers: they traverse life in a driven dreamlike state, and with the sense of impotence and anxiety one experiences in nightmares. They go through the motions of revolt, but their violent gestures toward independence are all doomed to dissolve into unreality. They are nothing more than the starts and bounds of a hooked fish. Tarwater and Motes both act out scenarios written beforehand by someone else. (p. 62)

On the face of it, [the novels] develop in accordance with the three major phases of the *rite de passage*: separation, transition, and reincorporation, but they give no sense of moving forward in time and no evidence of psychological development. Instead of inner growth, there is a backward circling which takes O'Connor's heroes inexorably back to where they started. *Wise Blood* and *The Violent Bear It Away* both follow the same circular and regressive pattern,

made conspicuous by the close similarities between opening and final scenes. In *Wise Blood* Mrs. Hitchcock's fascination with Hazel's eyes in the initial train scene anticipates Mrs. Flood's perplexed watching of his burnt-out eye sockets at the close of the novel. In much the same way the punishment he inflicts upon himself at ten—walking through the woods, his shoes filled with pebbles—prefigures the penitential rites preceding his near-suicidal death. In *The Violent Bear It Away*, on the other hand, the parallelism is emphasized by the use of the same setting: the novel starts with Tarwater's departure from Powderhead and closes with his return to it. "I guess you're going home," . . . Mrs. Hitchcock says to Hazel Motes on the train; in symbolic terms, his journey is indeed a journey home, and Tarwater's is quite literally a homecoming. These repetitions, to be true, are repetitions with a difference, and one could say that the movement is spiral-like rather than circular: there are intimations that through his harrowing ordeals Motes has moved toward a state of saintliness, and his physical blindness may be taken for an index to the spiritual insight he has at last achieved. It is obvious too that in *The Violent Bear It Away* the fire symbolism of the closing scenes reverses the meaning it was given in the first chapter. And it might be argued finally that recurring situations, settings, and imagery are part of the author's elaborate technique of foreshadowing.

But this is perhaps precisely where the shoe pinches: O'Connor's foreshadowing is so dense as to become constrictive; the signs and signals of destiny clutter so thickly around the protagonists of her novels that no breathing space is left to them. The author plays God to her creatures, and foreshadowing becomes the fictional equivalent of predestination. Everything propels her heroes toward submission to their predetermined fates and, at the same time, pushes them back to their childhood allegiances. Not only does their rebellion fail, it also ends each time in unconditional surrender to the parental powers from which they had attempted to escape.

In *Wise Blood* the prophetic mission is anticipated in the haunting figure of the grandfather, but Hazel's backward journey is essentially a return to the mother. The return motif is already adumbrated in the remembered episode of his visit to Eastrod after his release from the army. The only familiar object Hazel then found in his parents' deserted house was his mother's walnut chifforobe, and before leaving he put warning notes in every drawer: "This shiffer-robe belongs to Hazel Motes. Do not steal it or you will be hunted down and killed." . . . In the claustrophobic dream touched off by this reminiscence, the chifforobe is metamorphosed into his mother's coffin, while the coffin itself is fused with the berth in the train where Hazel is sleeping. What is more, Hazel, in his dream, identifies with his dead mother. . . . This dream is significantly related to another one, in which Motes dreams that he is buried alive and exposed through an oval window to the curiosity of various onlookers, one of whom is a woman who would apparently like to "climb in and keep him company for a while." . . . Furthermore, these two coffin dreams relate back to the traumatic childhood scene of Motes's initiation into evil: the disturbing sight of a nude blonde in a black casket, exhibited in the carnival tent where the ten-year-old boy had secretly followed his father. At his return from the country fair, his mother (whose image he superimposed mentally on that of the woman in the casket) knows, after one look at him, that he has sinned, and it is her accusing look that induces his first penitential rite. In the visual symbolism of the novel, the urge to see and the fear of being seen are recurrent motifs, and in this scene as in several others they both point to sin and guilt. What also appears through the interrelated imagery of these oneiric and actual scenes is the close conjunction of sex and death. But the most remarkable feature is that the themes of sin and guilt, sex and death, all coalesce around the mother figure and its surrogates. Motes's mother, while being deviously linked to his sordid sexual experiences, is at the same time a haunting reminder of the demands of religion: when he goes into the army, the only things he takes with him are "a black Bible and a pair of silver-trimmed spectacles that had belonged to his mother." . . . (pp. 62-4)

In *Wise Blood* Motes is finally reabsorbed into his mother. In *The Violent Bear It Away* Tarwater is likewise reabsorbed into his great-uncle. Raising the orphan boy to be a prophet like himself, the tyrannical old man has molded him in his own image and conditioned him for a destiny similar to his. When he dies, young Tarwater does his utmost to assert his own separate self through repeated acts of defiance, but what the novel seems to demonstrate is that there can be no escape from the self-ordained prophet's posthumous grip. In the concluding scene the repentant boy submits to what he so fiercely rejected, and his act of submission reminds one of the etymological origin of "humility" (humus = soil): prostrate on old Tarwater's grave, smearing his forehead with earth from his burial place, he acknowledges at last the absolute power of the past over the present, of the dead over the living or, to put it in terms of kinship, of the father over the son. The story comes full circle: otherness is resolved into sameness, difference into repetition. Having forever renounced his desire for autonomous selfhood, young Tarwater is now willing to become a faithful replica of old Tarwater, and in all likelihood his ulterior fate will be nothing more than a reenactment of the dead prophet's.

For neither protagonist of O'Connor's novels, then, is true separateness possible. Nor can they ever achieve true relatedness. Theirs is a demented mirror world of doubles, where the self is always experienced as other, and the other apprehended as a reflection of self. The schizophrenic dilemma they are both confronted with is either the madness of extreme isolation or the deadness of total engulfment. In both cases, the failure to define a viable identity leads ultimately to complete self-cancellation; in both cases, the inability to grow up provokes helpless surrender to an omnipotent and all-devouring parent figure. (pp. 64-5)

For almost all of O'Connor's characters there is a time for denial and a time for submission, a time for sin and a time for atonement. The passage from one to the other is what she has attempted to describe in her two novels, but as we have seen, she shows relatively little interest in the continuities and intricacies of inner growth. Her heroes do not change gradually; they progress—or regress—in fits and starts, through a series of switches and turnabouts rather than through a slow process of maturation. What engages most deeply O'Connor's imagination—and this, incidentally, may account for her feeling more at home in the short story than in the novel—is not so much time as the sudden encounter of time with the timeless: the decisive moments in a man's existence she would have called moments of

grace. . . . Grace plays indeed a major part in her novels as in most of her stories, especially the later ones, and as a religious concept it forms the very core of her implicit theology. Left to his own devices, man, as he appears in her fiction, is totally incapable of ensuring his salvation. Whether it degrades itself in grotesque parody or exhausts itself in mad convulsions, his quest for the holy is doomed to derision and failure from the very start. Grace alone saves, and even that is perhaps going too far: reading O'Connor's tales, one rather feels that grace simply makes salvation possible. (p. 65)

The impact of grace, as evoked by O'Connor, is that of a painful dazzle; it does not flood the soul with joy; her characters experience it as an instantaneous deflagration, a rending and bursting of the whole fabric of their being. For the revelation it brings is first and foremost self-revelation, the terrified recognition of one's nothingness and guilt. As each character is brutally stripped of his delusions, he sees and knows himself at last for what he is: "Asbury blanched and the last film of illusion was torn as if by a whirlwind from his eyes.". . . Not until the soul has reached that ultimate point of searing self-knowledge does salvation become a possibility. (p. 66)

In O'Connor, grace is not effusion but aggression. It is God's violence responding to Satan's violence, divine counterterror fighting the mutiny of evil. The operations of the divine and of the demonic are so disturbingly alike that the concept of God suggested by her work is in the last resort hardly more reassuring than her Devil. In fairness, one should no doubt allow for the distortions of satire, and be careful to distinguish the God of O'Connor's faith from the God-image of her characters. Her handling of point of view, however, implies no effacement on the part of the narrator, and her dramatic rendering of spiritual issues as well as the imagery she uses to evoke the actions of grace, provide enough clues to what God meant in her imaginative experience.

O'Connor's imagination is preeminently visual and visionary. Like Conrad's, her art attempts in its own way "to render the highest kind of justice to the visible universe," and far from clouding her perception, her sense of mystery rather adds to its startling clarity and sharpness. It is worth noting too how much of the action of her stories and novels is reflected in the continuous interplay of peeping or peering, prying or spying eyes, and how much importance is accorded throughout to the sheer act of seeing—or not seeing. *Wise Blood* is a prime example: a great deal of its symbolism springs from the dialectic of vision and blindness, and a similar dialectic is also at work in *The Violent Bear It Away* and in many of her stories. For O'Connor seeing is a measure of being: while the sinner gropes in utter darkness, the prophet—in O'Connor's phrase, "a realist of distances"—is above all a seer. In God the faculty of vision is carried to an infinite power of penetration: God is the All-seeing, the absolute Eye, encompassing the whole universe in its eternal gaze.

The cosmic metaphor for the divine eye is the sun. Through one of those reversals of the imagination the sun, in O'Connor's fiction, is not simply the primal source of light that makes all things visible, it is itself capable of vision, it is an eye. In *The Violent Bear It Away* there are few scenes to which the sun is not a benevolent or, more often, malevolent witness. After the old man's death, while Tarwater is reluctantly digging his grave, the sun moves slowly across the sky "circled by a haze of yellow," . . . then becomes "a furious white blister" . . . as he starts listening to the seductive voice of the "stranger." (pp. 66-7)

O'Connor's sun is both cosmic eye and heavenly fire. It thus condenses two of her most pregnant symbol patterns in a single image. For fire imagery is indeed as essential in her symbolic language as eye and sight imagery: incandescent suns, flaming skies, burning houses, woods, trees, and bushes—hers is an apocalyptic world forever ablaze. Fire is the visible manifestation of the principle of violence governing the universe, and the ordeal by fire is the *rite de passage* all of O'Connor's heroes are subjected to. A symbol of destruction and death, and a reminder of hell, it is also the favorite instrument of divine wrath and, as the old prophet taught young Tarwater, "even the mercy of the Lord burns.". . . Associated with purification and regeneration as well as evil, fire is the ambiguous sign of the elect and the damned, and its voracity is God's as much as Satan's.

That eye, sun, and fire are all emblems of the sacred is confirmed by another symbolic figure which both unites and multiplies them in animal form: the peacock. In "The Displaced Person," instead of being associated with human pride and ostentatiousness, the peacock becomes a symbol of the Second Coming, evoking the unearthly splendor of Christ at the Last Judgment. His tail, in O'Connor's description, expands into a cosmic wonder: ". . . his tail hung in front of her, full of fierce planets with *eyes* that were each ringed in green and set against a *sun* that was gold in one second's light and salmon-colored in the next." . . . (p. 68)

Immensity, brilliance, splendor, a dizzying profusion of eyes and suns, such are the features O'Connor chooses to celebrate God's power and glory. And one can hardly refrain from the suspicion that power and glory are in her imagination if not in her belief the essential attributes of divinity. In cosmic terms, her God is sun and fire. . . . Small wonder then that the spiritual errancy of O'Connor's heroes turns into a paranoid nightmare: aware of being watched and scrutinized by the relentless eye of the almighty Judge, they are unable ever to see their remote and silent persecutor. Not until grace descends to seize and possess their tormented souls is the infinite distance separating them abolished. Now the celestial Watcher, now a God of prey; first hovering, motionless, above his victim, then swooping with terrible speed to devour it.

One might have expected so fervent a Catholic as O'Connor to focus her fiction on the figure of Christ. In a sense, to be true, she does: whether in prayer or profanity, his name is obsessively referred to, and the question of whether Jesus suffered and died for our sins is indeed of vital concern to many of her characters. Yet her work is not so much Christ-centered as Christ-haunted. Unlike T. S. Eliot's later poetry, it is by no means a reaffirmation of the Christian mystery of the Incarnation. O'Connor's divisive vision perpetuates the idealistic cleavage between spirit and body, eternity and time, God and man, and Christ is likewise split into two irreconcilable halves. His image in her work constantly oscillates between the extremes of radical humanity and radical divinity. Now he is the mythical paradigm of human suffering, as Christ crucified and recrucified, now he appears in the plenitude of his

majesty as Christ the King, most startlingly represented in the image of the Byzantine Pantocrator tattooed on Parker's back. Or, to put it otherwise, he is alternately the impotent victimized Son and the omnipotent Father. These are images quite common in Christian literature and iconography. The point is that in O'Connor they never meet and merge in the dual unity of Christ, the God become man, the Word become flesh. The mediating function associated with Jesus by the Christian and particularly the Catholic tradition is hardly acknowledged, and what characterizes O'Connor's fictional world is precisely the absence of all mediation, of all intercession. On the one hand, there is the utter darkness of evil, on the other, the white radiance of divine transcendence. Between the two: man, battered and blinded, the victim of Satan or the prey of God, doomed to be defeated and dispossessed whatever the outcome of the dubious battle fought over his wretched soul. (pp. 68-9)

O'Connor envisioned the writer's relation to his work on the same pattern as God's relation to his creation, as if art were simply the fulfillment of preexisting intentions, the embodiment of a fixed vision prior to the writing process. In defining herself as a writer, she failed to acknowledge the insight so admirably dramatized in her fiction: that the self is not even master in its own house. For the writing self is certainly not exempted from the common lot: its imaginative constructs escape its mastery both in their deeper motivations and in their ultimate effects.

The truth of O'Connor's work is the truth of her art, not that of her church. Her fiction does refer to an implicit theology, but if we rely, as we should, on its testimony rather than on the author's comments, we shall have to admit that the Catholic orthodoxy of her work is at least debatable. O'Connor is definitely on the darker fringe of Christianity, and to find antecedents one has to go back to the paradoxical theology of early church fathers like Tertullian, or to the negative theology of stern mystics like St. John of the Cross. Pitting the supernatural against the natural in fierce antagonism, her theology holds nothing but scorn for everything human, and it is significant that in her work satanic evildoers (the "Misfit," Rufus Johnson) are far less harshly dealt with than humanistic do-gooders (Rayber, Sheppard). What is more, of the two mysteries—or myths—which are central to Christianity, the Fall and the Redemption, only the first seems to have engaged her imagination as a creative writer. Gnawed by old Calvinistic ferments and at the same time corroded by a very modern sense of the absurd, O'Connor's version of Christianity is emphatically and exclusively her own. Her fallen world, it is true, is visited by grace, but is grace, as she evokes it in her last stories, anything other than the vertigo of the *nada* and the encounter with death? And who is this God whose very mercy is terror?

It may be argued of course that these are the paradoxes of faith, or that O'Connor's rhetoric of violence was the shock therapy which her benumbed audience needed. There is little doubt that there will be many further exercises in exegetical ingenuity to establish her orthodoxy. Yet her work is not content with illustrating Christian paradoxes. It stretches them to breaking point, leaving us with Christian truths gone mad, the still incandescent fragments of a shattered system of belief.

Flannery O'Connor was a Catholic. She was not a Catholic novelist. She was a writer, and as a writer she belongs to no other parish than literature. (pp. 69-70)

André Bleikasten, "The Heresy of Flannery O'Connor," in Les Américanistes: New French Criticism on Modern American Fiction, *edited by Ira D. Johnson and Christiane Johnson (copyright © 1978 by Kennikat Press Corp.; reprinted by permission of Kennikat Press Corp.), Kennikat, 1978, pp. 53-70.*

*   *   *

ŌE, Kenzaburō   1935-

Ōe, one of Japan's most popular novelists, is a leading member of his country's "new left." His wide knowledge of Western literature is evidenced in his fiction, which shows Occidental influences in both its philosophy and style. Ōe is also an editor, short story writer, and critic.

JOHN BESTER

Ōe has been accused, with some justice, of writing Japanese that reads like a translation from a Western language. His long and complex sentences have neither elegant simplicity nor effortless flow, but are knotty challenges for the mind to unravel. Crammed with adjectives and similes, they consciously—occasionally almost self-consciously—prod the reader along, constantly forcing him to make unexpected associations, or emphasizing the author's analytical self-awareness.

In a sense, perhaps, the Japanese language is being made to do something for which it was never intended; one can well imagine some Japanese readers finding the style overladen or self-assertive. But though it is obviously to the literatures of the Western languages—their syntax, vocabulary, analytical approach—rather than to the Sino-Japanese heritage that Ōe looks to enrich the expressiveness of modern Japanese, what is still more important is that the ideas and, even more, the imagery are consistently and unmistakably his own. The density is an essential part of Ōe's artistic fiber, the sense of strain intrinsic to his themes.

A similar density is to be found in the structure of his works. In *A Game of Football,* each chapter is organized solidly and intricately; the narrative moves to and fro in time and space, tied by a close web of inter-relationships to what has preceded and what is to come. Great use is made of leitmotifs—repeated references to incidents, constantly recurring imagery, repetitions of actual phrases—that gradually lead the reader, almost against his will, into the world of the author's sensibility.

On their first appearance, the references are sometimes unexplained, their part in the whole structure only becoming apparent as one reads on. Not only does this serve to heighten the interest—the ingenuity of the work's structure is in some ways reminiscent of the detective story—but it also maintains a special interplay between the incidental and the essential, between bizarre fantasy and the actual world.

The constantly recurring images are at once concrete and highly symbolic, a combination that creates an almost hallucinatory quality. In the world that the author painstakingly constructs, human society, natural landscapes, the minor characters are presented in concrete, recognizable terms yet remain somehow—and especially in relation to the human immediacy of the central characters—curiously

remote, seen through the subtly distorting mirror of the intellect-emotions. Even the natural landscapes are landscapes of the mind, vivid in their details yet always in a sense "subjective"; as such, they inevitably afflict the reader at times with a sense of claustrophobia.

The duality of concrete and symbolic in particular images is paralleled in the novel as a whole by the fine balance maintained between allegory and story-telling. Thus the misfortunes that afflict the hero might seem almost comically over-emphasized if they were not so obviously symbolic of the general condition; on the other hand, the novel might seem over-intellectualized and over-organized were one's interest not involved at an early stage by the humanity of the main characters, and one's imagination captured by its extraordinary, if repellent, atmosphere.

The relationship between these two aspects is subtle. Although one could point to various general themes underlying the novel—the quest for identity and the sense of alienation, the tyranny of the physical world, the problem of commitment, the failure of tradition—I suspect that the work as a whole would resist any over-literal interpretation: that it succeeds, in short, as a work of the creative imagination, fusing a consideration of universal problems with poetry in the broadest sense and an act of emotional purgation for the author. That this last aspect is a continuing process in Ōe's work may be inferred from, for example, the prevailing "sick" quality of the imagery, which is too consistent to be inspired merely by intellectual (such a distinction, of course, is ultimately false) anxiety or disgust, and must surely stem from very particular and personal experiences.

Torn by distaste for the world, Ōe continues to write. Surrounded by violence both physical and intellectual, his hero continues to survive. It may be that the very fact of survival offers (as John Nathan suggests in a note to an earlier translation) a key to the problems plaguing him. Either way, the account of his tribulations is a work of formidable richness and intellectual power. . . . (pp. 428-29)

> *John Bester, in his translator's note to "A Game of Football" by Kenzaburō Ōe, in* Japan Quarterly *(© 1973, by the Asahi Shimbun), October-December, 1973, pp. 428-29.*

WAYNE FALKE

When Bird [protagonist of *A Personal Matter*] makes his final choice [to reject an adventurous life in favor of tedious domesticity], he is fulfilling, not [an] imported nineteenth-century romanticism, but an attitude native to Japan for almost as many centuries as [Westerners] have taken the attitude that action is intrinsically good, that rebellion is under a number of circumstances virtuous, particularly if it allegedly gives greater individual freedom, that fighting to the death against insurmountable odds carries with it its own honor. Bird and Ōe reject these convictions. Japan has a long tradition of accepting the inevitable which, in the West, is called resignation, which like "derivative," is an earnestly prejudicial term. For the Japanese, to assume the responsibilities imposed upon one by one's superiors, by filial piety and the like, is an act of virtue. To maintain existent orders is preferable to change, and certainly the subjugation of the individual to a wide structure of relationships and responsibilities is considered right and honorable. Meeting demands and fulfilling obligations are required.

Bird, therefore, is commendable in his actions from a Japanese perspective. By doing all the wrong things from a western point of view, he succeeds from a Japanese point of view by making the hard decision to stay within his social structure. The decision is for him the hard way and not, as with us, the easy.

The Japanese ability to settle for less than the ideal, not even to hope for some platonic ideal, seems to occidentals a seditious doctrine. Nurtured on striving for perfection (or at least progress) we are disarmed by a character who does not ask for much, who decides that the best solution is to learn to live with things as they are, to make do, hopefully, but not grandiosely. Our reflexes reject the man who decides to give in, not to struggle. Such cowardice is discomfitting, particularly when he seems pleased with his decision. In the West, we accept resignation as a solution only when it carries with it total despair. A more or less cheerful acceptance of circumstances is beyond our comprehension. We are in sympathy with Bird as he is frantic, anomic, behaving outrageously, but when he behaves reasonably, we condemn him and his creator. (pp. 50-1)

Bird cannot escape acceptance any more than we can escape admiring frantic struggle. (p. 51)

Superficial technological westernization does not mean loss of tradition. The implication that Ōe is necessarily echoing western thought is unjust: only our continental provincialism prevents a just appraisal of a novel that reflects the best and worst of probably the most international of cultures. (p. 52)

> Wayne Falke, "Japanese Tradition in Kenzaburō Ōe's 'A Personal Matter'," in Critique: Studies in Modern Fiction (copyright © by Critique 1974), Vol. XV, No. 3, 1974, pp. 43-52.

FREDERICK RICHTER

On the surface it is paradoxical that Ōe Kenzaburō . . . , a spokesman for the Japanese New Left, admirer of Mao, and student of Sartrean Existentialism, should give thematic treatment to anything quite so traditional as the notion of "shame," a complex emotional response to a variety of situations in Japanese society. Although very much the modern writer and liberated from many of the complexes that burdened older literary figures such as Tanizaki Jun'ichirō and Mishima Yukio, Ōe, in the short story "Sheep," directly confronts the experience of shame with power, subtlety, and insight. Whereas other major Japanese writers generally deal with shame as incidental to their primary thematic concerns, only as part of the psychological makeup of their characters, Ōe pushes his creations headlong into shameful situations where reader and characters are afforded a deeper insight into the nature of shame, and at times a full-fledged revelation occurs in which the self is strengthened and achieves a new identity through the ordeal. The originality of Ōe's achievement in his young career lies in the fusion of shame in its traditional setting, calling for a traditional interpretation, with an understanding of shame informed and shaped by Sartrean Existentialism, with its implications for the self in the world. (p. 409)

The soldiers . . . use the young man and his fellow victims as a means to an end: that of venting their anger and as an object of amusement. This is a constituent in the structure of shame, to become an instrument of possibilities that are not our possibilities. But what is crucial in the case of the soldiers is that the incident begins and ends spontaneously. While the humiliated victims existed as objects for them, . . . the motivation for their behavior does not extend beyond the simple emotions of amusement and anger. . . .

The school teacher perceives the victims as a means to a loftier end, a moral aim. The "innocent" spontaneity of the incident disappears [with his effort] to communicate the shame to the world at large. . . . The desire on the part of the victim to hide what has been revealed, to hide what one is at the moment, conforms to our own experience and [is] . . . peculiar to the nature of shame. Any threat to this desire to remain hidden is normally an occasion for unpleasantness. Thus the teacher has done violence to the nature of shame, as one insensitive to its implications, and has oddly turned out to be the "villain" of the piece, although some readers may have divided sympathies. The desire of the school teacher to expose the young man's shame in a broader context is likewise linked to what Sartre calls l'esprit de serieux in that values are considered as "transcendent givens independent of human subjectivity." The teacher ignores human subjectivity and seeks to manipulate the young man in order to assign a value to the incident that ultimately derives from an abstraction external to the concreteness of the situation: that of social justice. (p. 413)

Imagery [in the story] not only creates atmosphere, but also functions structurally, as a dynamic element clustering around and anticipating attitudes and actions within the narrative. The abstract framework of the story, however, is dualistic; and this is seen in its composition, where the story naturally falls into two parts: events involving the soldiers and then when the teacher begins his attempt to impose his will on the young man. The brief stasis when the soldiers have left forms a natural hiatus before the second half of the story begins. Also, as has been suggested, the Sartrean dualistic view of consciousness may be inferred as a basis of analogy for the dualistic structure. The interplay of opposites is also seen in the Japanese vs. the foreign soldiers, victims vs. observers, passivity vs. activity, and also quite importantly in the divided sympathies of the reader. The teacher appears in a negative light, and although to a certain degree we share his moral outrage, our emotional sympathies are with the young man and the second ordeal he is forced to undergo at the hands of the teacher. The last and most pregnant pairing of opposites involves Japan vs. the outside world. The story as an allegory pointing to Japan victimized and humiliated during the Allied Occupation cannot be overlooked. But what is represented is more the psychological climate of the times rather than a political call-to-arms. (pp. 414-15)

> Frederick Richter, "Circles of Shame: 'Sheep' by Ōe Kenzaburō," in Studies in Short Fiction (copyright 1974 by Newberry College), Fall, 1974, pp. 409-15.

CORNELIA HOLBERT

Teach Us to Outgrow Our Madness is the best of [Ōe's] novels. Among those who will highly value it are parents, especially parents of retarded or autistic children. For doctors and other health-care personnel, it is prescribed as part of continuing education. The I-Thou experience, and beyond it the feeling for what Philip Berrigan calls Equal Jeopardy . . . are here exquisitely clear. As the courtroom scene in Wilder's Heaven's My Destination is a classic short comedy, the ophthalmological consultation in *Teach Us* is a drama of classic power.

The existential problem of stigma is met by Ōe as it is met by John Gardner, Bellow, Maxine Kingston: met, recognized, and then transcended. A man is fat to the point of disgust, blind, hypochondriacal. A child is moronic or autistic or blind or all three. The man is beautiful. The child is beautiful. . . .

Ōe is a sophisticated and unerring writer, a great thinker and lover, not to be missed. (p. 198)

> *Cornelia Holbert, in* Best Sellers *(copyright © 1977 Helen Dwight Reid Educational Foundation), October, 1977.*

EMIKO SAKURAI

Kenzaburō Ōe [is] the most talented writer to emerge in Japan after World War II. Like his previous publications (*A Personal Matter*, 1968, . . . and *The Silent Cry*, 1975), [*Teach Us to Outgrow Our Madness*] is certain to surprise some Western readers who have come to expect delicate prose and exquisite imagery from a Japanese novelist. Having learned his craft from postwar American authors such as Norman Mailer and French existentialists such as Jean-Paul Sartre, rather than from *The Tale of Genji*, Ōe writes fiction that is more brutal and savage than exquisite or quaint. . . .

"Prize Stock" [one of four novellas that compose the collection] is a tightly knit tale of a black American flier's captivity in a mountain village during the War. Ōe referred to it as a "pastoral." But what a pastoral! Ōe superimposes a mythic, primeval society on the village and reveals the nature of man and conditions of human existence through a densely woven pattern of animal images. . . . It is a powerful story that exploits all the elements of fiction. (p. 345)

The four novellas vary in technique and style as well as subject matter but are alike in the theme of alienation . . . , in their absurdist, ironic, black-comic view of life and the use of anti-heroes. Artistic excellence characterizes all four. . . . *Teach Us to Outgrow Our Madness* is a book that should be read by everyone interested in contemporary fiction, for Ōe is as important a writer as Mailer or Updike. (pp. 345-46)

> *Emiko Sakurai, in* World Literature Today *(copyright 1978 by the University of Oklahoma Press), Vol. 52, No. 2, Spring, 1978.*

*   *   *

ONETTI, Juan Carlos   1909-

Onetti is a Uruguayan novelist and short story writer. His concern with the disintegration of language is reflected in his fragmentary style and episodic narrative form. The episodes that constitute Onetti's fiction, especially *A Brief Life*, are often unrelated fantasies of the narrator, effecting a quality of detached obscurity. (See also *CLC*, Vol. 7.)

BEVERLY J. GIBBS

Although a reflection of conditons . . . in Uruguay and Argentina, Onetti's novelistic world transcends geographical bounds and is in essence the fictionalized spiritual landscape of contemporary man, a spiritual world that can be situated in the black-literature tradition of Céline and Sartre

and that owes a largely technical debt to Dos Passos and Faulkner. . . .

Onetti's work is marked by a fundamental ambiguity that appears in a variety of guises: as doubt, uncertainty, enigma, vagueness, obscurity, inexplicability, indistinctness, unreality, fantasy. (p. 260)

On the surface *El astillero* is structured around one basic narrative thread: Larsen's return to Santa María after a five-year time lapse, his involvement in Puerto Astillero in the Petrus shipyard and the parallel development of a relationship with the shipyard owner's mentally defective daughter, his inability to maintain his position as general manager of the shipyard, and his ultimate abandonment of Puerto Astillero in one of two ways and with one of two consequences. Events in this main narrative line are arranged, on the whole, in linear succession, and time encompasses a sharply limited interval. . . . The spatial setting is likewise closely restricted as far as the primary narrative is concerned, with key developments in Larsen's present occurring in five locations [which are used as section headings in the novel]. (pp. 260-61)

The foregoing description of the novel's structure is accurate, but incomplete, since this seemingly tightly knit whole is so run-through with ambiguity that the result is one of almost total fragmentation.

The book opens with an immediate temporal reference to certain events that happened some five years ago to a man called Larsen or Juntacadáveres, as we are told immediately in a parenthetical remark by the narrator. . . . The reader . . . knows that something serious occurred, but he remains totally ignorant of any details. The note of mystery injected into the novel by this *in medias res* beginning is never eliminated or the enigma clarified. If anything, the mystery is deepened by obscure references throughout the novel to people, places, and events inexplicably connected with Larsen's past of five years ago. . . .

[Contributing] to the ambiguity of the novel are isolated details, presented as thoughts of individual characters or as descriptions of the narrators, whose significance in terms of the main plot line is unclear. The meaning or implication of an event, action, thought, or whatever, is either initially obscure and elaborated upon subsequently to the point where some of the reader's questions are resolved, or the significance is forever hidden. In the latter case, narrative details are not just suspended or withheld temporarily; they are totally and deliberately omitted. (p. 261)

Not only does the reader find himself compelled to supply his own interpretations of the thoughts and actions of the characters, he is also in the position of having to furnish dialogue transitions that are lacking. . . . The justification for [the] use of juxtaposed, disconnected dialogue is that the characters not only talk past one another, but they fail to make contact in other senses and continue each isolated in his own world.

Further contributing to the ambiguity of *El astillero* and the collaborative task of the reader is the utilization of variant conclusions to the novel. . . .

The variant ending of the novel is related to flexibility in arrangement of narrative material and to the unimportance of any specific sequential structure. . . . [Whatever] course Larsen attempts to set for himself (whatever role he plays) is doomed to end in failure and in the completely individual and real phenomenon of death, (hence his full name in the hospital records). This is the fixed point, and how one reaches it or in what sequential arrangement of events is relatively immaterial. (p. 262)

The work has an over-all plot line that focuses on Larsen and progresses through certain identifiable states to a fixed conclusion. Except for the certain specific episodes that of necessity precede or follow other events and thereby create the sensation of the novel's temporal lineality, incidents are presented randomly as a series of enigmatic, isolated fragments, juxtaposed against each other in a montage technique that serves to fragment narrative structure.... The reader is thrown into a world where significant events have already transpired, but whose detail is forever cloaked, partially or completely, in mystery. Allusion is made to events, and then their elaboration is delayed or omitted. Statements are made by characters and about them that omit the key to motivation and interpretation. Gaps or blanks in information alternate with enigmatic details, speculative remarks, cryptic utterances, and different versions of the same event. Rather than being advanced logically step by step, the narrative is developed in fits and snatches, backward to the past, forward to the future, or it seemingly stagnates in a static present.

Scrutiny of the book's table of contents or recall of its section headings reveals another significant fact. Specifically, that placement of incidents and episodes in *El astillero* has a spatial rather than a temporal orientation. The five sections (Santa María, El astillero, La glorieta, La casilla, and La casa) receive their titles on the basis of where key incidents in Larsen's development occur. Allusion is made, for example, to "the scandal" in "La casilla-I," but the episode is developed, of *spatial* necessity, in "El astillero-V" where the key events took place. Linking incidents to space reinforces the separateness of events and allows freedom and flexibility in their arrangement, making for increased fragmentation. When most incidents happen is secondary to the fact that they do occur in a particular place at some or any point in the novel. The effect of this treatment of plot arrangement is to blur or obscure the structural design of the work and to leave the reader without his customary guideposts or supports. Such atemporal structuring, which negates sustained cause-effect plot (in this case character) development, creates in large part, the paralytic or static sensation that is characteristic of Onetti's novels. (pp. 262-63)

[There] exists in *El astillero* a reality-fantasy plane that results from the interweaving of the real and the imaginary (no less "real") and that is another major source of ambiguity in the novel, as becomes apparent when space, time, and character are analyzed.

Although often realistically detailed ..., space is more important as atmosphere and stage setting against and on which the drama of personality is portrayed....

This, then, is a nightmare world, very real in its absurdity. But as in nightmares, space has a tendency to lose its real properties. Of basic importance in *El astillero* is the inner world of the characters, and the qualities that typify spatial settings of the novel are a direct reflection of the situations, perceptions, and traits of specific individuals, particularly Larsen. (p. 263)

Complementing the note of mystery produced by the deliberate withholding of information is the sensation of strangeness and unreality evoked by personification of natural and abstract elements.... The effect of this animation and humanizing of objects coupled with immobilization of people in a reflective state is to invert customary reality and give the novel an "aire de leyenda," a phrase used in the work itself to describe one of the settings....

Time gives the appearance of functioning in what might be called its usual manner; that is, it seems, on the surface, to progress chronologically and bring about change.... Some temporal blurring is evident when attention is called to time that is indeterminate.... It becomes especially vague at those points in the novel when the narrator-creator admits and discusses his uncertainty regarding the temporal placement of events.

Looking beyond the surface factors that give the novel an appearance of chronological progression, the reader encounters a number of ways in which time is made a substance that reinforces the subjectivity and unreality or fantasy of the spatial setting. In the first place, *El astillero* is a work that concentrates fanatically on "la peripecia interior" with Larsen as the principal focus. Experienced from his perspective, time becomes a subjective substance that can be reversed as the character's thoughts turn to the past, advanced as awareness of failure and premonition of doom foreshadow his end, and halted as his gaze lingers, for example, on an object. (p. 264)

Also a major factor in destroying the appearance of chronological progression is the fact that the novel goes beyond Larsen's present, the period of involvement with the Petrus shipyard, and encompasses events in his past and future. When this is linked to the multiple-narrator structure used by Onetti in this work and the movement of narrators within some or all of these three temporal dimensions, the net result is non-linear arrangement of incident.

In addition, the forward progress of time is halted by the narrators through numerous reproductions (in quotes) of characters' thoughts. Time's flow is stopped and then reversed by several interpolations of parenthetical commentary by a collective narrator and an impersonal omniscient consciousness. It is further distorted by the variant conclusions to Larsen's life which cover the same time span twice. Additional distortion results from recurrent references to the same event (such as, Larsen's departure from Santa Maria five years prior to his reappearance in that city and "the scandal" involving Angélica Inés in Larsen's office at the shipyard), since such references carry the narrative from other points in the temporal flow to that point when the events in question occurred....

With the effect or result predetermined, not only is the temporal thrust of the novel inverted, but time additionally fails to fulfill its customary function in that it brings little or no change in surroundings (atmosphere) or in characters, all of whom resemble each other in superfluousness....

Without doubt the principal emphasis in *El astillero* is character, and its treatment contributes significantly to the establishment of this novel on the ambiguous reality-fantasy plane. Elements of the unreal are immediately apparent in the almost continual depiction of the inner reality of individuals locked in their own subjectivity. This continual portrayal of the main characters through privileged narration

and their quoted thoughts attests to the existence of a contrived reality, a reality of fiction. (p. 265)

Additional sensations of acute unreality that result from
treatment of character are related to dehumanization of the
individual. Among the methods employed to achieve this is
the not uncommon description of a person in terms of an
animal (insect) or a thing. . . . Individuals are also dehumanized by descriptions that single out a particular personal detail and dwell on it to such an extent that the detail
comes to replace the person. A woman in a cafe, for instance, becomes her face . . . , Angélica Inés, her laugh
. . . , Petrus, his mouth. . . . Or a mannerism is more vividly presented than the individual and substitutes for the
whole person or is, at least, an integral part of him, as in
the case of Larsen's clicking his heels when walking. In
addition, repeated references are made to individuals using
relatively the same descriptive phrase that becomes a kind
of epithet to which their identifiable reality is reduced. . . .
Recurrent usage of the same or similar words to identify a
character when identification is no longer needed smacks of
purely mechanical repetition, and such repetition plus reduction of characters to single traits makes them wooden
and stick-like. . . .

The line between reality and fantasy is further obscured by
the impression that the characters are actors play-acting on
stages that are more theatrical than real. They have their
own farces . . . , their own dramas, their own roles (*juegos*)
with themselves as doubles. Although seeming to represent
parts that they themselves have chosen, the suggestion is
clear that they (and man in general) are only inventions acting out roles assigned them by the author. . . . Everyone is
"una frase," an invention, a fiction. The creation of another and with his fate predetermined, man becomes a robot whose steps follow a random pattern to a fixed end. (p.
266)

When the ambiguity is stripped away from *El astillero*, several certainties seem to remain. Seen with Larsen as the
point of reference, although in truth Man is the focus, the
conclusions to be drawn are that the individual's authentic
self (E. Larsen) is hidden behind a mask worn by a double
(Junta, Juntacádaveres, Larsen of *el astillero*), and the copy
(*reproducción*) or other self engages in creating a role or living a farce that for a time challenges the predetermined fate
(*condena*) of the true self. Collision with reality (the falsified documents and Gálvez's denunciation of Petrus) puts
an end to the farce or drama, and having realized his symbolic death, the character assumes his robot existence mechanically carrying out the necessary acts that lead ultimately (in variant two) to his literal death, with the hospital
now recording his full, real name. . . .

[These] actors condemned to a predetermined fate struggle
to free themselves. To live, in fact, is to so struggle, is to
play a game or to invent roles, but doing this is also to deceive one's self in a game already lost.

There appears to be the suggestion that the only possible
escape in all this, either for Onetti's characters or for the
author himself, is to invent fictions, to create another reality. . . . One suspects, nevertheless, that his "escape" is
only another deception, since, as Onetti's created world
reveals, all men are superfluous in terms of the fate that
awaits them, or as Borges suggests, the world, unfortunately, is real, and there is no escape for any man. (p. 267)

*Beverly J. Gibbs, "Ambiguity in Onetti's 'El
Astillero'," in* Hispania *(© 1973 The Ameri-
can Association of Teachers of Spanish and
Portuguese, Inc.), April, 1973, pp. 260-69.*

M. IAN ADAMS

Many of [Onetti's works] fall into the territory between
novel and short story. The relative complexity of theme
and the quantity of subjective elements associated with it
. . . seem to be reasonable criteria to separate short novels
from short stories. Thus *El pozo,* although of few pages, is
in Onetti's novelistic mode because of the presence of
many themes and because of the subjective, ambiguous
presentation of these themes. "El infierno tan temido" is
structured around one action and its consequences and is
very limited thematically. "Jacob y el otro" is of greater
length than the other stories, but is again characterized by
simplicity. A future action, a wrestling match, is the cause
of all of the story's movement, and there are few complications of imagery or subjective content.

Complexity and ambiguity are the major characteristics of
Onetti's novels. (p. 38)

Readers of Onetti know that Santa María is a creation,
because they were present at its birth in *La vida breve,*
where it is an invention of the main character, Brausen.
The major difference [between this and Faulkner's Yokna-
patawpha County is] that Onetti's world is centripetal. The
external features serve only as a frame for internal chaos.
All the characters fall toward this center point, and individuals do not stand out as they do in Faulkner. Onetti himself, in *Juntacadáveres,* has best described his typical character in Santa María: "He isn't a person; he is, like all the
inhabitants of this strip of the river, a determined intensity
of life molding itself in the form of his own mania, his own
idiocy."

Alienation is a major feature of Onetti's internalized world.
(p. 39)

Onetti's artistic manipulation of [what has been called a]
schizophrenic experience (or the experience of extreme
alienation) produces a unique imagery and an unusual sensation for the reader of participation in an alienated
world. . . .

The protagonist of *El pozo,* Eladio Linacero, is one of the
best examples in contemporary South American literature
of the completely alienated man. (p. 40)

The story is, however, built not around the solitude of the
protagonist but, rather, around his attempts at communication. The time elapsed, less than one day, is limited to how
long it takes Linacero to write his first-person narrative.
The author-protagonist gives the reader fragments of past
and present personal history and an ostensibly complete
picture of his emotional life.

Based on the nature of the attempts at communication, the
novel divides itself into two parts. The first is concerned
with the narrator's presentation of his present situation, the
beginning of the act of writing, a statement of purpose that
is . . . both aesthetic and emotional, and, finally, the first
attempt at written communication, directed toward the
reader. The second part is primarily a description of past
frustrated attempts at communication with other people. In
each case the hidden content of these efforts reveals more
of the narrator's condition than he is aware of presenting.

The result of the narrative is that Eladio Linacero reaches a crisis of self-hate, induced by a confrontation with his own existence. The novel ends at the moment of his maximum desperation. (pp. 40-1)

The room is important as the boundary of the narrator's physical solitude and as the setting for the entire story. It is also the only place left to the narrator in his retreat from the world. At the beginning of the narration, the room has been a fixture and a delimitation of his life for some time, to the point that he is no longer aware of its existence. Yet, upon starting an attempt at communication, he sees it again, with new perspective. The inference is that he is entering into a new relation with his surroundings, no matter how reduced they are, caused by the act of creation. (pp. 41-2)

[When] he is looking at the room as though it were for the first time, he does not generalize on what he sees. Instead he describes isolated parts, substituting them for a totality of vision.

This form of vision emerges more clearly in his first description of a person, a prostitute. . . . Two fragments—fingers and a shoulder—serve to represent a human being. The narrator remembers nothing else about her.

The function and meaning of this type of vision do not become evident immediately. It is only through the additional information given by the narrator and through contrast with another kind of vision present in his dreams that the reader can begin to define their importance. (p. 42)

Onetti often uses two levels of repeated actions: habitual actions and repeated meaningless actions. They have as a common ground repetition, but habitual actions are meaningful in that they reflect and define the existence of the person involved. Repeated meaningless actions are external to the character of the person but may have meaning in relation to the book. An example of habitual action is seen in *Los adioses;* the protagonist is most frequently seen in the act of drinking, and this act is his major connection with the narrator.

In addition to the function of these two types of action with respect to the description of characters, they also are major structural elements. In *Para una tumba sin nombre* the action of smoking a pipe is used to separate the narrative sections and to represent the narrator's periods of communication. It has a similar function in *La cara de la desgracia.* Habitual action is raised to the level of ritual in *Tan triste como ella,* where it is central to the understanding of the protagonist's suicide. When she can no longer struggle against the vegetation in her garden, life ceases to have meaning for her. In *El astillero* repeated meaningless action, reading former business transactions, becomes a defensive ploy in Larsen's fight to endure.

One of the significant differences between Onetti's novels and his short stories is the relative lack of repeated action patterns of both types in the latter. "El infierno tan temido" initially seems to be built around repetition, the sending of pornographic photographs, but the action is really cumulative rather than repetitive: it is the vengeance taken by the wife for damage done by her husband. The stories probably lack these patterns because they are concerned with one action and its immediate consequences, whereas the other works emphasize an expanding series of possibilities, conflicts, and ambiguities arising from any situation or action.

The aesthetic result of this technique is a fragmentation of the character or characters involved. The repetition destroys what would be a normal process of development and response, so that, instead of gaining recognition and familiarity with the literary figure through cumulative exposure, the reader is constantly thrown back to the uncertainty and ambiguity of his first contacts with the character. Onetti's frequent use of a narrator separated from the protagonist would also seem to indicate his intention to distance the reader from his characters. In effect this is planned alienation of the reader from the content of the work.

El pozo is atypical of Onetti's works in that the first-person narration has an immediacy and a directness not seen in most of the others. (pp. 44-5)

[The] reader should be aware that he cannot take the declarations and judgments of the narrator at face value but must instead search for evidence of other interpretations. . . .

As a literary device the deceitful narrator poses several problems. First of all, the reader must not have a sense of being manipulated by the author. Onetti avoids this problem by making deceit an integral part of the narrator's character and an essential part of the meaning of that which is narrated. (p. 46)

Another problem is the possibility of excessive distancing of the reader from the character, with resultant loss of interest in the entire work. This possibility is also avoided because the detection and evaluation of the deceit become a necessity. Thus, although the reader is separated from the protagonist, he participates in the work because of the independent judgments he has to make. . . .

It becomes apparent that the only satisfactory life [Linacero] has takes place in his dream world. His attempts at communication fail because people either reject his dream world or see the true motives behind it that he is unwilling to accept. The division is so important that it is reflected by the novel's imagery. Each world is characterized by its way of looking at people and objects. (p. 47)

The picture of alienation that [emerges] from the study of what the narrator relates and what can be seen behind his words is one of almost total withdrawal and isolation, made even more intense by repeated efforts at communication. The underlying causes of this alienation are rooted in the character of the narrator and are not due to any outside social pressures. The essence of Linacero's personality is an irrational disgust for all aspects of living. This disgust is coupled with self-hate that seems to arise from his adult sexual life. However, the origins of these features remain largely conjectural. Onetti has limited himself to presenting the condition without going into the causes of it.

The dominant technique used in the development of the protagonist's personality is that of the deceitful narrator. The reader, although distanced from Linacero, participates in the work because he has to make judgments about it that affect the meaning of the entire story. (p. 54)

[The] use of habitual or repeated action, does not play a very great role in *El pozo,* although several times the act of smoking carries the true meaning of what is being narrated. Of much more importance are the vision and visual images described by the narrator. A fragmented imagery is characteristic of all that he describes in the real world. The dream world contains coherent vision and imagery. . . . [Linacero] obviously has a totally split personality in that his emotional life takes place in his imaginary world. His external "real world" personality is permeated by his fantasy self. Neither part functions satisfactorily. The visual fragmentation is schizophrenic, offering a broken surface with no depth coherence. An example of this depthless vision is the lack of sexual connotations of the parts of the female body described in the "real world." Only in the fantasy world is there something behind the imagery.

Thus, in order to convey the experience of extreme alienation, Onetti has created a schizoid form of vision and made it coincide with the split personality of the protagonist. On a different plane he has fragmented normal action patterns, emphasizing repeated or habitual actions. The result of this technique is to give the entire work a schizoid atmosphere. The personality of the protagonist is, however, the determinant for the techniques used to create alienation. This is not the case in many of the later works of Onetti, in which the personality becomes lost in a web of objects, actions, incongruous emotions, and partially understood symbolism. (pp. 54-5)

[There] is a symbolic plane in *El pozo,* but it is weakly developed and serves only as background to the narrative. All the important action, real and imaginary, takes place in small enclosed areas. On the real plane this setting is indicative of the isolation of the protagonist, but in the imaginary world these enclosed areas, "the log cabin," above all, become indistinct sexual symbols. All the imagery related to the cabin has sexual overtones on an oneiric Freudian level.

The theme of artistic creation introduced at the beginning of *El pozo* is seen to be determined and formed by the personality of the narrator. The content of his dreams is a manifestation of emotions and desires that he conceals from himself in the real world. The dreams also serve as sexual stimulants. The reader is able to judge the extent of alienation by the schizoid form it forces upon the images and actions of the protagonist. In contrast to this process of creation of imagery from within the person, in . . . *Tan triste como ella,* the images come from outside the protagonist and are projected inward. (pp. 55-6)

[*Tan triste*] is the clearest statement in Onetti's writing of man's radical inability to penetrate life and to communicate with other human beings. It shows what Onetti's characters do when there is no evasion, only struggle with their crushing concept of reality. Their alienation is clear and total.

Tan triste is also the most symbolic of all Onetti's works. Many of them can be interpreted symbolically, the best example being *El astillero.* In this novel both the action and the situation have strong symbolic overtones. In *Tan triste* there is a profusion of objects and actions that have only symbolic meaning and that impinge upon the protagonist. . . . [The] symbolism of *Tan triste,* like that of the images in *El pozo,* is of a special nature to meet the needs of the author in his expression of extreme alienation.

The outstanding difference between *El pozo* and *Tan triste como ella* is the latter novel's complexity. While in *El pozo* ambiguity is restricted to the true motives of the protagonist, in *Tan triste* it extends to all aspects of the work: its structure, symbolism, and meaning.

In broad outline the novel has a cyclic structure, beginning and ending with the same image. The first part is a symbolic dream that at the end becomes reality with the suicide of the female protagonist. . . . [To] characterize the world as one of phallic obsession [as Emir Rodríguez Monegal does] is an over-simplification. The obsession is sexual. It will be seen that almost all the symbols are sexual, but only a part of them are phallic. The symbolic meaning of the form of suicide is definitely phallic, but too much emphasis should not be put on it by itself.

At the level of action, very little takes place in the novel, which is the examination of a marriage in the last stages of disintegration. The focus is the woman, whose personal collapse matches that of the marriage. (pp. 56-7)

Another feature of *Tan triste como ella* that distinguishes it from most of Onetti's other novels is the presence of the author. Onetti's most common technique is the use of multiple narrators, one of the functions of which is to completely mask the presence and thoughts of the author. . . . Onetti's figures are openly manipulated, either by the narrator-character or by the reader himself, because of the choices he must make about their actions and motives. The lack of the author's presence thus has to be significant. It is a form of alienation, a desire not to be responsible for or to have lasting visible control over one's actions. Many critics have assumed that the narrator's viewpoint is also that of Onetti. This assumption seems to be supported by the uniformity of tone throughout. However, the deception or ambiguity characteristic of these narrators indicates the need for additional evidence before any view can be assigned to the author. *Tan triste* provides some of this evidence.

The reader is made aware of Onetti's presence before the work begins by an introductory letter whose outstanding characteristics are ambiguity and evasion. The letter is to "Tantriste," and there is no indication if Onetti is addressing a person or, as an artist, his creation. The terms are predominantly personal; the time has come to break an intimacy and to separate. There is a declaration of mutual alienation and defeat. . . . [There] is also, in whatever context, a declaration of evasion and of a desire to keep the self hidden.

The letter . . . offers a problem of interpretation. There is no conclusive evidence for either of two possibilities: the letter could represent a personal or a literary position. Because both seem to be valid they must be accepted. . . . Both possibilities express alienation in the form of radical solitude, evasion, and withdrawal. But, because of the ambiguity, it is impossible to make any inference as to the extent of the author's personal revelation.

Another aspect of the ambiguity of the letter deserves attention. The uncertainty as to meaning is coupled with vague references to actual events, "the intimacy of the last few months," "the failure," and "the happy moments." The effect, implied certainty joined to ambiguity, destroys any deep meaning. The emotions presented suggest a depth of feeling that is vitiated by the form. The result is an emotional surface with nothing behind it. The emotional experience arising from this depthless surface is schizoid in nature. (pp. 57-9)

The initial reaction of the reader to the [opening] scene is the same as his reaction to the letter. There is an emotional surface that suggests depth but that on examination is seen to cover nothing. (p. 60)

Within the [woman's] dream,. . .there is a two-level presentation of [her] alienation. On the rational plane her solitude and despair are visible. The more complex irrational level symbolically presents her own attitude toward her body, in sexual terms. She is divorced from her feminine sexuality, for reasons unknown, and, more importantly, she seems to be self-destructive. The dream could be viewed as a fulfillment of a death wish in light of its connection with her suicide at the end of the novel.

The protagonist's alienation, then, is total at the beginning of the novel. The symbolic message of the dream also has a structural function in outlining the trajectory of the protagonist from despair to destruction. *El pozo,* starting at the same emotional point, ends in the protagonist's desolation without self-destruction. In *Tan triste,* by the elimination of the first-person narration, the despair, desolation, and destruction seen at the end of the work are generalized into the human condition.

The failure of the marriage is presented first from the masculine viewpoint and is due to the same reasons found in *El pozo:* inevitable loss of innocence and transformation from girl to woman. "He had loved the small woman who prepared his food, who had given birth to a creature that cried incessantly on the second floor. Now he regarded her with surprise; she was, fleetingly, something worse, shorter, deader than some unknown woman whose name never comes to us.". . . This attitude, because of its persistence through all of Onetti's work, can certainly be considered as a basic attribute of the author. He does not deny the existence of human happiness through love. Instead, he believes in the inevitability of a transformation into unhappiness because of the nature of life. The emotional result of the form of this belief, a movement from positive to negative, assures a maximum degree of suffering both for those who undergo the experience and for those who believe it is a fundamental truth. In terms of alienation and loss of self the view has several functions. It can be a defense of the alienated, withdrawn individual in that it provides a reason not to participate in life. It can also be a symptom of an extensive dislocation of self through self-hate. The person who hates himself, as does Eladio Linacero, frequently punishes himself. Linacero's attempts at communication are a form of self-punishment. Another form, seen in many of Onetti's characters, is the adherence to a pain-causing belief. (pp. 61-2)

[Of Onetti's main characters, only] Larsen in *El astillero,* because of his desire to endure despite misfortune, seems to have found something positive and irreducible at the corrupt core of life. But because of the persistence and pervasiveness of this disgust with life in all of Onetti's writing it must be considered as a basic element of his personality. Its context . . . is always that of evasion and ambiguity, and its existence must frequently be deduced from secondary evidence. Thus it is essentially an emotional perspective rather than an articulated philosophical stance. It is the medium in which Onetti and his characters live rather than the meaning of their existence. Their reaction to it is essentially that of irrational evasion. (p. 64)

For the sin of living one receives either "pay, recompense, or punishment," but they are all the same and have no separate meaning. The root of this ambiguity is alienation. If life is viewed with repulsion, the viewer is already radically separate from it, and whatever forms it assumes are equally distant from the nonparticipating self. (p. 65)

[The] garden seems to be an ambiguous symbol for feminine sexuality in conflict with masculine sexuality. Nevertheless, although the symbol's general nature is moderately clear, its meaning for the woman and her struggle with it are not. Even the additional information that the garden has provided the only true happiness the woman has known since infancy, and that the husband discovered in it the only thing that was of true importance to her, seems to be unimportant. However, if one considers that the novel is built around total sexual polarization, as is indicated by all its symbolism, then two possibilities suggest themselves. The first is that, because of the garden's importance in the woman's youth, the feminine sexuality it represents is that which is uncontaminated by contact with masculinity. Onetti's interest in and repetition of the theme of the loss of purity and the loss of virginity would tend to support this interpretation. The other possibility is that the symbolic pleasure resulting from the struggle with the garden is erotic. In the context of a completely feminine sexuality this pleasure would mean symbolic masturbation. Again, either masturbation or autostimulation is a theme seen in Onetti's work. It is important in *El pozo.* In all cases it results in self-punishment and self-disgust. The fact that as the garden is destroyed the woman turns to promiscuous sexual activity with the men who are physically destroying it would give some support to this interpretation. The central feature is, however, that because of lack of direct evidence and due to intentional ambiguity the meaning of the symbol remains conjectural. The result is a fragmentation of imagery on a deeper level than has been seen in other works by Onetti. Surface fragmentation is evident in *El pozo,* with a consequent lack of depth. In this central image in *Tan triste* the vertical dimension of the fragmentation is greatly extended. There is neither rational nor irrational, conscious nor subconscious coherence. This is not to say that Onetti has abandoned the techniques seen in *El pozo.* The broken surface imagery is evident in the description of the well-diggers, where only parts of their bodies—their arms and chests—are described. The only total presentation of a human body occurs in the woman's dream. These techniques are merely extended into areas where they were not seen before.

The form and nature of the woman's alienation are directly related to the symbolic presentation of the conflicts that drive her to suicide. That she experiences these conflicts symbolically is the measure of the separation of her self from direct experience. In addition the ambiguity of the nature of the conflicts reflects the fragmentation of the self. She is estranged from her body and in conflict over the nature of her sexuality. Heterosexual activity in the form that she has known it is a threat to her personality. This fact is evident in her relation to her child, who should be regarded as a fulfillment of married sexual life. Instead she hates him for being male and shows absolutely no emotional bond with him. She expresses the wish for a female child, who would have been an affirmation of her flawed sexuality and could not be related to the masculine threat she fears. (pp. 66-8)

As the novel nears its end the symbolic plane comes to the foreground. The reasons for the woman's suicide are presented entirely in this plane. The major element that pushes her toward self-destruction is the failure of the ritual in the garden. . . . Her reaction to the loss of the garden shows that her self has also been destroyed. She no longer has any contact with reality, and her actions are completely separate from her. "Everything was a game, a rite, a prologue.". . . (p. 69)

There are [in her suicide] several possibilities. The first is that the woman's suicide is an act of surrender to masculinity and a destruction of the feminine self, made more complete by the perverted nature of the action. This interpretation is supported by the symbolic context of the story and the male-female polarity that develops from this symbolism. The other possibility is that the form of the action indicates only partial surrender to heterosexual drives. The essence of the woman's femininity does not participate. (p. 70)

[The] woman's alienation and loss of self, like Eladio Linacero's, are due to personal factors, the foremost of which is a defective sexuality. The woman's being is polarized or split, and heterosexuality becomes destructive. Her fear of masculinity is so great that she is unable to feel anything but hate for her son. She needs love but can attain only promiscuity.

Her life is presented through a series of symbols with a common feature, ambiguity. In most cases the images show surface coherence with increasing fragmentation as deeper levels of meaning are sought. Several images seem to reverse the process; they show surface fragmentation and lack of meaning but have significance at depth. The result is the same as that of the techniques of imagery in *El pozo*: a quantitative and qualitative reproduction of a schizophrenic world, but a world much more extensive than that in *El pozo*.

In addition, a few of the author's fundamental attitudes are visible in *Tan triste como ella*. The most revealing is a belief in the destructive force of life, in the inevitable unhappiness caused by living. Other attitudes may be inferred from the themes common to *Tan triste* and *El pozo*. The loss of innocence that comes with sexual awakening, with resultant unhappiness, is the clearest of these. (p. 71)

[Of] the four suicides [in Onetti's works]—Elena Salas in *La vida breve*, the woman in *Tan triste*, Julita in *Juntacadáveres*, Risso in "El infierno tan temido"—three are women. The only thing these figures have in common is their failure to avoid unacceptable reality through evasive activity. Elena Salas and the woman in *Tan triste* make no attempt at evasion and thus cannot tolerate life. Julita evades through insanity, but when this evasion no longer serves she kills herself. Risso is forced by a woman into a situation in which he has no power to evade. At the other end of the spectrum, Larsen, the man who endures, does so because he is an artist of evasion. Thus evasion per se in Onetti's novels becomes a life-giving force. . . .

[The] most characteristic form of evasion seen in all Onetti's works is the ambiguity surrounding all actions, images, and attitudes. In the sense that this ambiguity separates the author from his work, the reader from the content, and the characters from themselves, it is another form of alienation. (pp. 71-2)

An initial similarity exists between Brausen, the protagonist of *La vida breve*, and Eladio Linacero. Both men project their lives into imaginary structures, the marriages of both have failed for the same reasons that all marriages fail in Onetti's creations. Beyond these points of similarity resemblance diminishes. Brausen is a much more intelligent and

complex person than Linacero. He is highly articulate and, more importantly, shows a great deal of self-knowledge. The greatest difference between him and Linacero is that he is a man in society and is both conscious and critical of that society on an intellectual level, free from his personal necessities. In addition he is capable of action.

The clarity of Brausen's self-definitions and his frequent discussions of the meaning of his creation of other lives make the conditions of his alienation clear. His first definition locates him in terms of personal history and of society. "Meanwhile, I am this small and timid man, unchangeable, married to the only woman I seduced, or who seduced me, incapable not only of being another but even of the will to be another. The little man who disgusts as much as he causes pity, a small man lost in the legion of small men who were promised the Kingdom of Heaven. This one, me in the taxicab, inexistent, the mere incarnation of the idea of Juan María Brausen, a biped symbol of a cheap puritanism made of negatives." His alienation is measured by the distance he is separated from himself in order to have the perspective to make this description. It is also seen in his self-disgust. Further, emotional alienation is seen in his opinion of his own morality. It is also shown in his relation to his wife: he is separated from her to the point that he does not know the emotional nature of a pivotal action in their lives. (pp. 72-3)

The new element [in *La vida breve*] is the concept of mass man. Brausen sees himself as lost and faceless in surrounding humanity. (p. 73)

Brausen's alienation [at his job] is due to his being forced to play a part he despises and that is self-destructive. In addition, he has no control over the results of his actions; they are something separate from him that arises in response to the fear of losing his job.

Brausen's direct and indirect criticism is only a part of his social vision. He is specific in his condemnation of the artificiality of modern consumer society. . . .

Thus a large part of Brausen's alienation is due to the form of his society, and he recognizes this fact. He also sees social aspects in the deeper levels of loss of self. "Because each one accepts what he keeps discovering about himself in the looks of others, one is formed from living with others, and blends with what others suppose him to be, and acts according to what is expected from this inexistent being.". . . Brausen rejects this way of creation of self. Instead, he destroys the self that is associated with the life of Juan María Brausen. By separating from his wife, by being fired from his job, by ceasing to associate with his companions, and by isolating himself in his room, he eliminates his social and emotional self and attempts to construct other imaginary selves, believing that he retains that which is essential to his existence. (p. 74)

In *La vida breve* the author is trying to produce the totality of the schizoid experience. (p. 75)

It is Onetti who gives the novel a final ambiguous direction. Brausen disappears and the book ends with an adventure with Díaz Grey, who now has a life and personality of his own. He is no longer dependent on Brausen the creator. The ambiguity arises in the relation of Díaz Grey's autonomy to Brausen's conquest of self. No evidence is available to indicate the nature of the relation. The only certainty is that Onetti, as author-creator, has taken the place of Brausen, the creator of other lives. . . .

Onetti, through Brausen, makes a specific criticism of modern society and the conditions of impersonal labor, showing their destructive force on the personality. The other influence leading to alienation and destruction of self is the psychology of the character. The terms of this psychology are essentially the same as those seen in the other works studied: disgust with life, failure of marriage, desire for self-destruction. (p. 77)

Larsen, the protagonist of *El astillero,* is the opposite of Brausen, in that his life is concerned with the maintenance of self in the face of a hostile and overwhelming world. Díaz Grey describes the heroic side of Larsen's existence, calling Larsen "this man who lived the last thirty years on filthy money given him with pleasure by filthy women; who hit upon defending himself against life by substituting for it a treachery without origin; this man of toughness and courage, who used to think in one fashion and now thinks in another; who wasn't born to die but instead to win and impose himself; who at this moment is imagining life as an infinite and timeless territory in which it is necessary to advance and to take advantage." This heroic quality does not mean that Larsen is not alienated, because he is, but to a much lesser degree than Brausen. He maintains a functional self in the face of his alienation and failure. (pp. 77-8)

The relation between Larsen and the dead shipyard is the central feature of the novel. Larsen's entire personality is revealed in his attitudes and activities with respect to the shipyard. His relation to his job is much more complex than that of Brausen to his job in *La vida breve.* To begin with, he knows the job is meaningless, but he converts it into a defense against life. . . . Brausen, alienated by his work, flees from it. Larsen accepts the alienation and manipulates it, . . . "with the only aim of giving him a meaning and attributing this meaning to his remaining years.". . . The result of Larsen's efforts is the conversion of the shipyard into a separate world. He recognizes what has happened but is not worried by it.

The most important difference between Larsen and Brausen is that the former can act both in the real world and in the one ordered by his imagination, and the latter only in

his created world. In addition Larsen can function with full knowledge of his alienation from all that surrounds him, believing in the complete meaninglessness of his actions. (p. 78)

When Larsen is faced by total failure, without future, alienated from his body and his external existence, he still maintains a self that gives him the will to act in the face of meaninglessness. . . . The narrator, of uncertain identity, judges Larsen's existence at this point—"Thus nothing more than a man, this one, Larsen. . .". . .—indicating Larsen's reduction to his essential self.

Onetti does not allow Larsen's posture to remain unequivocal to the end. Two possible endings are given, the origins of which are unknown to the reader. In one Larsen leaves, defeated but intact. In the other he is destroyed—humiliated by the boatmen, incoherent; he dies shortly thereafter. The reader must choose. The ambiguity of the ending vitiates any generalization about the positive values represented by Larsen, as it is not certain to what extent he maintains them in the face of his failure. Thus any retrospective judgment of these positive values must be relative to their position in the novel and to their possible final collapse. (p. 79)

The use of the first person plural relates [the narrator] to the town of Santa María, as does his interest in events pertaining to the town. The scenes presented, on the other hand, make him omniscient. This omniscience in turn is confused by the equivocal nature of the ending. . . . One must suspect a deliberate attempt to cloud any positive interpretation of Larsen.

Nevertheless, what does emerge from *El astillero* is a pattern of alienation that does not seem to lead to loss of self. The will to act, although the actions be meaningless, preserves and defines the essential self. Because of this will to act the alienating conditions of society and life may be met and held at bay. (pp. 79-80)

M. Ian Adams, "Juan Carlos Onetti: Alienation and the Fragmented Image," in his Three Authors of Alienation: Bombal, Onetti, Carpentier *(copyright © 1975 by M. Ian Adams), University of Texas Press, 1975, pp. 37-80.*

P

PASTERNAK, Boris   1890-1960

Pasternak was a Russian poet, novelist, dramatist, essayist, translator, and autobiographer. Although Pasternak is best known in America as the author of the novel *Dr. Zhivago*, he is primarily recognized in Europe as a poet. There is a trace of mystical Christianity akin to that of Dostoevsky running through his work. His poetry has been praised for its dense imagery, highly personal nature, and its complex, yet close-knit, structure. Pasternak was awarded the Nobel Prize for Literature in 1958 which he declined under political pressure. (See also *CLC*, Vol. 7.)

ELLIOTT MOSSMAN

Pasternak in *The Blind Beauty* has sought to adjust the native laws of Shakespearean drama to the Russian historical stage. The adaptation is evident in the central importance accorded theatricality in *The Blind Beauty*, in the weight given to political and historical parallelism, in the range of characters from noble to peasant, in the themes of genealogical taint, institutional corruption, unchecked violence and predetermined restraints on freedom of action.

It is all the more evident the closer one looks at Pasternak's writing, most persuasively so in Pasternak's use of language in the play. If "language is half a cemetery," as Pasternak noted in connection with his studies of Symbolism in 1912, then each word has its history, each has its own tale to tell. In his notebooks for 1941-1942, when he was first translating Shakespeare, we find Pasternak recording: "The ingenuity of language lies not in its soaring poetic quality; it is much more: each element is a fable. The tale is put together from separate words, of which each one is a small fable. The charm of the common folk vocabulary lies in adages and riddles." This principle of artistic language, even if honored only seldom, is a central Shakespearean element in the drama of Pasternak. In *The Blind Beauty* it is the words which excite the historical as well as the histrionic imagination. Pasternak has consistently shunned the nineteenth century Russian *literary* language in favor of an unbookish spoken language. His Russian words are ones to delight and frustrate perusers of dictionaries, words retrieved from disuse and largely unheard on the Russian stage. (p. 239)

> Elliott Mossman, "Pasternak's 'Blind Beauty'," *in* Russian Literature Triquarterly

(copyright © 1973 by Ardis), Fall, 1973, pp. 227-42.

JANE GARY HARRIS

[Although] Pasternak's earliest images of life are feminine images, they are not associated with human incarnations of life, but rather with the personification of abstract forces: Nature . . . , the Life Force or Life . . . , both feminine nouns. Indeed, in [*My Sister, Life*], personification is a favorite device used to emphasize the poet's sense of personal involvement with Nature and Life. It comes as no surprise to find love poems and nature poems addressed to Life, for Pasternak's earliest love poetry is more often dedicated to the Life Force than to a human being. The few exceptions in *My Sister, Life* which are addressed to a woman portray her more as an object, as another natural phenomenon, than as a female person, as a woman with whom the poet can share his emotional life. And she is always associated with Nature: she is either imagined as (and transformed into) one or more natural phenomena, or she awakens to find herself in a natural environment which she does not fully appreciate. Her human qualities are ignored or even repudiated. Furthermore, Nature rather than a human female protagonist seems to serve as Pasternak's prerequisite for love. And, at least in this collection, love can be consummated only in nature, real or imagined, for there alone the poet can be at one with life. Life, moreover, is almost always presented through nature imagery, in particular water imagery—a raindrop, spring showers, flooding, pouring, splashing, rushing, etc. (pp. 390-91)

Human love relationships, on the other hand, are portrayed primarily as means to the poet's communion with the Life Force. In the poem, "Out of Superstition," . . . the poet views his beloved through the prism of nature, that is, in kissing her lips he finds "violets," in admiring her dress he hears it "chirp, like a snowdrop / To April: 'Hello!'" And, upon entering his tiny room, he finds it appears to him like "a box with a wild orange tree," its walls look brown as an "oak tree." In the final lines of this poem, the poet also comes to associate his beloved with the Life Force, for she reveals to him the essence of his own life. . . . Hence, in *My Sister, Life*, Pasternak's images of nature, life and love are intimately related. Love is presented as a means to achieving communion with Life; while nature or a natural environment is a prerequisite to love, and in turn, to communion with Life. (pp. 391-92)

[In] the poems of *My Sister, Life,* and in most of Pasternak's verse before *Second Birth* (1932), the poet's love is valued as a means of communion with the Life Force, but it is far from being considered Life's highest gift to man and woman, as that which unites two kindred souls in their mutual communion with each other and with Life. Love does not yet empower the poet's beloved to share his personal experience. He is alone. She remains but an object, on a par with the natural phenomena.

On the other hand, true love, and in particular, "a poet's love," is . . . presented as something extraordinary, as a force capable of transforming the world. In his poem, "Darling—it's frightening! When a poet loves . . ." . . ., Pasternak expresses his idea of true love as an elemental force, and as creative power. . . . It is here that we first encounter Pasternak's idea that true love is synonymous with poetic inspiration, with Life's highest gift to man, creative power.

What is more, the title poem of this collection, "My sister, life," although not as explicit as "Darling—it's frightening!", develops the idea of the poet's love for Life as synonymous with poetic creativity. . . . [The poet] alone can interpret Life's gift. (pp. 393-94)

[While] Pasternak has not yet developed a feminine image in *My Sister, Life* whose kindred soul can share the poet's ecstatic love for Life or serve as his source of creative inspiration, certain basic elements of his future feminine image are already implicit in this first major cycle of poems. Life is personified as "my sister, life," implying an intimate relationship between the poet and a feminine incarnation of Life, while true love, emanating from Life's extraordinary powers, is already presented as a prime source of creative inspiration.

Nevertheless, Pasternak's image of Life remains very abstract. It is but a personified metaphor, unrelated to a human being who has suffered and thus experienced life, to one who has freely sacrificed herself to the commands of Life and thus come to understand both its sorrows and joys. Indeed, in this collection, Life remains primarily a source of esctasy, of joy and beauty; ugliness and evil go almost unrecognized as a part of Life. The theme of death is also barely touched upon. In the poem, "English Lessons," . . . two feminine images of beauty and unrequited love, Desdemona and Ophelia, sacrificed their lives by merging with the "pool of the universe." The conception of death merging with Life is presented here in embryonic form based on the idea that the life cycle completes itself only to renew itself again. But this theme is not fully developed until *Dr. Zhivago.*

[When] Pasternak first tried his hand at creating an image of Life in prose, he not only introduced into his novella, *Childhood of Luvers,* the first traces of a humanized feminine image, but also began to include some of the less "poetic" themes until then barely touched upon in his poetry.

The two major protagonists in the novella are Pasternak's incipient feminine image, Zhenya Luvers, and his abstract metaphorical image of Life. In the character of Zhenya Luvers we literally follow the development of Pasternak's feminine image from childhood through adolescence to the threshold of womanhood. She is portrayed as an extremely sensitive child whose intuitive perception of the mysteries of Life and receptivity to the commands of Life are antithetical to the values ascribed to ordinary adults who

know how to shout and to punish, who smoke and bolt doors.

Many of the essential qualities of Pasternak's adult feminine ideal are inherent in her characterization. However, she still does not "represent Life," but in the course of the novella learns about her responses to Life, becomes aware of Life and her relationship to it.

Pasternak's metaphorical image of Life appears here not as his "sister," but rather as a purposeful, yet at times seemingly whimsical feminine spirit or Life Force with a definite, even eudemonic "plan" for the universe. "Life" uses all means to carry out her design, conjuring up various methods to "deflect" her subjects so that she may guide them properly and execute her ultimate purpose, Creation. Man, her most troublesome subject, is a major target, but all the phenomena in the universe are under her control since they are her creations. (pp. 395-96)

Sensitivity to Life's plan and receptivity to Life's commands are presented in *Childhood of Luvers* as synonymous with the highest form of human sensibility, with intuition, poetic consciousness or the poetic soul. Hence, Pasternak depicts the child Zhenya as at first bewildered by her experiences, ignorant of their cause, but aware of their mystery. Her intuition (or poetic soul) guides her in responding to her environment, to events which seem mysterious because they are not yet comprehensible to her as part of Life's design. (p. 397)

Pasternak's incipient feminine image is depicted as a developing human consciousness. By relating the child's first perceptions of change in herself and in her environment to later more "indelible" impressions, Pasternak indicates how experiences are acquired and how impressions are left on her soul which gradually make her more "aware" of Life's mysteries. Zhenya passes through several stages, each one perceived by her as wondrous, mysterious, and traumatic, each one leaving a strong imprint on her. The most significant impressions includes love for a friend, recognition of her mother as a woman and as the most precious being in her life, a growing awareness of her own approaching womanhood, and the realization of the idea of death as somewhat more than merely a "vaporized third being," as something which involves her total response to another human being.

According to Pasternak, such impressions "have no name" and are beyond the control of the person affected by them, for they are comprehensible only to those "aware of, or able to discern, what it is that creates, harmonizes and stitches them together." In a word, the highest possible stage of human sensibility, of human consciousness, is receptivity ot those seemingly mysterious occurrences which represent Life's commands and form an essential part of her plan.

Most significant, the indelible impressions left on Zhenya's consciousness pertain to relationships between people, to the moral concern of one individual for another, to the sense of communion between people, even though that other person may remain unknown in the usual meaning of the words "known-unknown." (pp. 397-98)

To Pasternak, the prerequisite for true love appears as pity or compassion, involving a deep sense of moral guilt and moral responsibility closely bound to the mystery or riddle of Life, or to the theme of Man's destiny. . . . Zhenya Luvers' free spirit or "free personality" is the result of her developing awareness and spontaneous receptivity to Life's commands, while her childhood suffering (bewilderment, fear, sorrow, guilt) and her intuitive acceptance of her role in life (joys as well as sorrows, in particular, "the idea of death" and its realization) may be interpreted as her growing awareness of the "idea of life as sacrifice."

But while the idea of compassion as a prerequisite to true love appears in *Childhood of Luvers* as feminine compassion for a man, from 1929 on, it is always associated with the sensitive man's or poet's vision of woman. It is hinted at in Pasternak's "novel in verse," *Spektorsky,* it appears as a significant element in his prose work, *The Tale,* as well as in the poetry of *Second Birth,* and it emerges as a fully developed theme in *Dr. Zhizago.* (pp. 398-99)

Although the relationship between love and compassion is tendered in *Spektorsky,* its most significant aspect is undoubtedly Pasternak's dual vision of woman, by which he opposes two feminine images based on their antithetical attitudes toward Life and love. While his active, passionate and practical woman attempts to dominate Life, to control the forces of history, of destiny, Pasternak's passive, sensitive, impractical and often confused woman expresses her receptivity to Life's commands and so experiences poetic freedom and genuine love. The hero's compassion for the latter leads to a genuine love idyll, while his equally strong feelings of fear, even repulsion, for the former makes true love impossible. (p. 399)

[Both Pushkin in his poem *The Fountain of Bachchisarai*] and Pasternak present a dual vision of woman by contrasting antithetical attitudes toward life and love; a passive hero exposed to both, expresses compassion for the more passive, acceptant, spiritually oriented persona. (p. 401)

[In *Spektorsky*] Marya Ilina becomes an image of the pure soul, the poetic spirit, of the poet destined to live in an alien social, political and cultural environment. Her love affair is a Pasternakian idyll, predestined in its inception as well as in its unexpected conclusion. Her love appears as a gift of Life, for in describing her romance with Spektorsky, Pasternak emphasizes their intimate union with nature and life. . . . [As] a poet, Marya Ilina is more closely associated with Life than the feminine images presented in Pasternak's early collections of verse, while as an adult representative of the human sensibility, she comes closer to Pasternak's ultimate conception of his feminine image than Zhenya Luvers.

To both Pushkin and Pasternak, love epitomizes the pure soul, a pure spiritual state. For Pushkin, the pure soul expresses itself through Christian love; for Pasternak, in *Spektorsky,* through human love, but in *Dr. Zhivago,* through both human and Christian love: "communion between mortals is immortal." And these forms of love all stem from a sense of sacrifice to a higher form of consciousness, to a state of mind receptive to the forces of destiny, history, and life, which in turn lead to salvation and immortality. (pp. 404-05)

[In] *Spektorsky* we encounter a more complex characterization of Pasternak's feminine image, perhaps influenced by Pushkin's Princess Marya [the heroine of *The Fountain of Bachchisarai*], or possibly merely a matter of the coincidence of poetic vision. Nevertheless, it is not until *Dr. Zhi-*

vago that Pasternak's feminine image is termed the "representative of life" and is empowered to inspire the poet, Yury Zhivago, to immortalize her image in his art. In the novel, love is presented as the highest calling of the feminine image; it is her gift of life to living man, the inspiration behind the creative urge, the source of art. And art is depicted as the highest calling of the poet, his means of communing directly with Life, his way of "helping" Life to carry out her ultimate purpose, Creation. (p. 405)

Unlike the image of the beloved in his earlier collections, Pasternak's feminine image in *Second Birth* helps the poet to understand Life. Love is difficult only because it involves the poet completely, not merely with his own ego, but with all of Life. As the "key to life," the image of the beloved unites their kindred souls and becomes the means of communing with Life.

Other poems in this collection present love as the inspiration behind the poet's art. Although this idea was hinted at in *My Sister, Life,* it involved only the poet's love for life, not the communion of poet and his beloved. (p. 406)

Pasternak elucidates his poetic intentions in *Spektorsky* by specifically denying any interest in a hero *cum* hero and in asserting the generality of his subject matter. . . . Pasternak was concerned with his hero only in so far as he appeared before him in that "radiant" or ray or illumination comprising Pasternak's subject, his vision of Life, that which included and made comprehensible all the various events, persons, ideas, and feelings—the details of Life—which the poet considered worth preserving through artistic transfiguration. (p. 408)

[In *Safe Conduct*] Pasternak strives to render intelligible his conception of creative power which he refers to as the "power" or ray of light sent forth by the poet to illuminate reality of life. The poet's soul or poetic consciousness which expresses the creative urge or force behind all art is empowered to send out its inner light or its "voice" into reality, into Life, to illuminate it. Furthermore, all art is born of the theme of creative power, for creative power alone can transform the characteristics of life into art. . . . (p. 409)

Pasternak's heroes are not intended to stand out from life, to be judged as independent actors against the background of reality or life. Rather, they are intended to reflect aspects of Life—Pasternak's major subject—in order to illuminate the interconnectedness of all of Life's creations, and so aid in the presentation of a vision of Life in artistic form.

But it is not until his "novel in prose" [*Dr. Zhivago*] that Pasternak achieves his poetic intentions as enunciated in *Safe Conduct.* Lara Guishar, the "representative of life," embodies the "ray of power [which] passes through [life]." Although her love may be her greatest source of "power," of illumination, her voice, her very being, her every act illuminates Life, for she is able to experience it completely and, what is more, she is empowered to convey its meaning to others. . . . Pasternak's image of Lara is his "record of the displacement of [reality]." Her image transforms or transfigures life or reality. . . . Pasternak touches on that characteristic of Lara's personality which distinguishes his ultimate feminine image: both the source of her femininity and the source of her "awareness" of Life stem from her acceptance of the "idea of life as sacrifice" enunciated by Nikolai Nikolaevich. (pp. 410-11)

[In] the very process of illuminating Life, Pasternak's feminine image becomes an artistic vision of Life. Lara is not merely a "heroine" in a novel, but has become that "image" of Life which Pasternak described in *Safe Conduct,* a new creation.... Similarly, Yury Zhivago ... is not merely a passive receptor of Life's commands. He appears as an "image" of "living man," as an active, intelligent thinker, writer, doctor, a compassionate human being. He accepts Life's commands as does Lara, but in his role as creative artist, he imitates Life, for his art is a mimetic form of Life's Creation; and in so doing, he is inspired by the "representative of Life." His art, like Pasternak's

> concerns itself with life as the ray of power passes through it ... [and] the characteristics of life become the characteristics of creation.

Indeed, in his "novel in verse," it is not the hero but the author, Pasternak, who must perform the artistic function of recording the "displacement" of reality, while in his "novel in prose," the role of artist is transferred to the hero. Pasternak than stands back as omniscient author, as teller of the tale of Life and Creation through the portrayal of the "representative of life," his ultimate feminine image, and the living human creator, the image of the poet. The poet, Yury Zhivago, meanwhile, creates yet another image of Life as Immortality symbolized by Mary Magdalene, the "reminder of life," and presents himself in the image of the Creator, as Christ.

In this way, both Pasternak's feminine image and his image of the creative artist attain their full development in *Dr. Zhivago.* But how do they function in the overall structure of the novel? Although the structure of *Dr. Zhivago* incorporates numerous elements of Pasternak's poetry and earlier prose efforts, it succeeds in combining those elements into a new artistic form. The novel's main subject, Life (as Creation and Immortality), retains the characteristics of the imagery of lyric poetry, while the major characters operate on two distinct but related planes of existence determined by the narrative structure of the work as a tale of everyday life and creation within a tale of Eternal Life and Creation. The major personae appear as hero and heroine of the novel and as symbolic images in Yury Zhivago's verse. The flexible narrative structure allows Pasternak's hero to elevate Lara, Pasternak's heroine and the "representative of life," to the universal metaphysical plane as Mary Magdalene, the "reminder of life," the "memory" of the mystery of Life, and simultaneously, to envision himself as Christ, the doctor become Healer, the poet-Creator. This elevation to the plane of pure poetry or pure creation may be viewed as a kind of esthetic resurrection of the idea of life as Immortality or Eternal Life. At the same time, the epilogue presentation of the story of Tanya, Lara and Yury Zhivago's daughter, serves as a more prosaic retelling of history as a more traditional, novelistic portrayal of the feminine image as the ultimate progenitor of life and creation, as the representative of the continuity of the life cycle: birth, death and renewal.

But here we must delve somewhat deeper into Pasternak's ideas about the relationship of art, life, history and Christian myth in order to achieve a clearer picture of the function of his feminine image in his overall esthetic vision. (pp. 411-12)

Pasternak, in attempting to indicate poetry's function [in *Spektorsky*], maintains that it must relate the unique or individual aspects of life to the universal, but never subordinate one to the other. This idea emerges in subsequent stanzas which include Pasternak's first efforts to polemicize against crude political directives demanding that poets and artists subordinate their individual esthetic and ideological values to those established by the political leaders of the Revolution. Pasternak cites the "mute heavens" as unwilling to accept such directives, for they refuse to agree "that the class be victorious over the individual," that is, that the individual or "free personality" submit to the universal against its will.

Nevertheless, in anticipation of the reader's confusion over political and historical events, Pasternak goes on to explain that although at first events cannot always be understood, suddenly, one day, "it's explained," for we come to realize that everything—all the phenomena in the universe—are interrelated. How? Through history. The abstract idea of Revolution as a moral imperative for change, as an inevitable force of history, receives a kind of cosmic justification here. (p. 413)

Pasternak views history not as justification, but as revelation: the discovery of fundamental, essential values, in particular, the realization of the idea of the interconnectedness of all the phenomena in the universe. Through history, man discovers the essence of life, the "naked" facts, including the idea of the continuity of basic human values, of the eternal verities. And through art, he discovers the "mystery" of life, the idea of the uniqueness of the individual as well as the idea of the interconnectedness of the individual and the universal aspects of life. Even more significant, art preserves history in that it records the idea of the "naked" individual and his role in Life.

In *Dr. Zhivago* this lyrical digression is extended and made more explicit through Lara's explanation of how she and Yury Zhivago, as unique individuals, as "naked" as Adam and Eve, were sent forth into the world to represent Life's mysteries or "marvels," and to record their memory. According to Lara then, their lives represent both the historical record, and the esthetic vision of Life.... (pp. 413-14)

Pasternak's narrative structure functions on two distinct but intimately related planes: the plane of history and the plane of art. The lives of his heroes represent both the continuity of the eternal verities through time and history, and the memory of the mystery of Life.

Furthermore, in *Dr. Zhivago,* Pasternak explicitly attempts to resolve the metaphysical question of the relationship between life and death through an esthetic presentation of his ideas on history, Christian mythology, and art. This is in contrast to his early work where he barely touches on this theme. (p. 414)

[At] the very beginning of the novel, when Pasternak's spokesman for his personal vision of Christianity, Yury Zhivago's Uncle Nikolai Nikolaevich, defines history, he refers to it as a means of overcoming death. He also associates it with art and the creative process in general....

[Man's] crude attempts to remake history or to "reshape life" go against history and against life, for they deny man's "spiritual equipment" and cause him to rebel against Life's plan. Rather, man is urged to attempt to understand and experience life through love, sacrifice and the search for genuine freedom. In the absence of these Christian ideals, man forgets that Life is constantly renewing itself, that Life is a cyclical proces which includes birth, death and rebirth. (p. 415)

[History] and life are not antithetical concepts. On the contrary, life contains history, and is the creative force behind all those events, persons, phenomena which history records. Through history man endeavors to understand and experience the "breath" and "heartbeat" or soul of life, to overcome the "idea of death" by recording the continuity of the eternal verities and the constancy of the life cycle.

In addition, Christian myth conveys Life's meaning to man through timeless, universal symbols: these are used in history to record man's communication with the past, the source of his being, his "naked" entry into the world, and in art to affirm man's idea of the future, his vision of Immortality, of Eternal Life. . . .

Pasternak's idea of Life does not merely include everyday life or reality, but encompasses all of Creation, that which relates the past (history) to the present (relations between living human beings on earth) and the present to the future (art).

Christianity, or at least those tenets of Christianity advocated by Nikolai Nikolaevich, echo throughout the novel. . . . In Pasternak's view, Christian symbolism serves to make historical facts comprehensible to the present generation, and the ideas of the present and past recognizable to posterity. (p. 416)

Lara, as Pasternak's ultimate feminine image, his "representative" of Life "born to understand its insane enchantment," expresses the "voice" or "presence" of everyday life in its most intricate details, for in her "the articulate principle of existence becomes sensitive and capable of speech." In the course of the novel, she enacts the entire life cycle, including birth, childhood, growth, love, sacrifice, death and rebirth. As a child she was "charged with electricity, with all the femininity in the world," as wife and mother and lover she expressed love as the ideal relationship described by Nikolai Nikolaevich: "communion between mortals is immortal," as the mistress to the image of evil incarnate (Komarovsky) she experienced the "idea of life as sacrifice," and as the poet's mistress she embodied the idea of true love, enacting the role of muse—the source of creative power. Moreover, transfigured by art and the Christian symbolism of Yury Zhivago's verse into the metaphysical vision of Mary Magdalene, she becomes the image of "memory," the "reminder of life," in which form she fulfills Yury Zhivago's poetic intention expressed in his grief at her departure from Varykino:

> I'll put my grief for you in a work that will endure and be worthy of you. I'll write your memory into an image of aching tenderness and sorrow . . .

And what more appropriate universal image could he have chosen than Mary Magdalene to reveal Pasternak's ultimate image of the feminine, of life as love and sacrifice and individual freedom?

Yury Zhivago, cast as life's companion, life's champion, life's celebrant, is Pasternak's ultimate image of living man. He is presented as a doctor or minister of compassion and

love for his fellow men, as a poet reflecting man's natural instinct to overcome death through the creative process and therefore as capable of accepting Life's greatest gift to man —creative inspiration, as a lover experiencing the supreme communion allowed in this life on earth between mortals. But transfigured by art and the Christian symbolism of his own verse to the metaphysical realm, he becomes the image of Christ, the Healer and Creator, the symbol of Resurrection and Immortality.

Furthermore, the union of Lara and Yury Zhivago represents

> [the] last remembrance of all that immeasurable greatness which had been created in the world in all the thousands of years between [Adam and Eve] and us . . .

while the communion of Mary Magdalene and Christ represents the supreme relationship between the Creator and Man, and in particular, between the Creator and Woman, as Sima Tuntseva revealed to Lara:

> What familiarity, what equality between God and life, God and the individual, God and a woman!

Indeed, it is this awesome and miraculous relationship which elevates Yury Zhivago's and Lara's extraordinary love to the metaphysical plane, to the plane of the miracle and mystery of Life. For if "communion between mortals is immortal," they are empowered to penetrate the mystery of Life, of Immortality.

What is more, this vision of the union of kindred souls is subtly interwoven into the fabric of the novel. Related to the theme of illness and death, it emerges both on the plane of life as everyday reality and on the plane of life as Immortality. And it is reinforced by the philosophical ideals first enunciated by Nikolai Nikolaevich and subsequently reiterated by Yury Zhivago, Misha Gordon and Sima Tuntseva. While Lara does not express these ideals verbally, as the "representative of life" she absorbs them and acts them out. (pp. 417-18)

At the very end of the novel, when Lara and Yury Zhivago are reunited for the last time over Yury's coffin, the metaphysical meaning of "The Turmoil" becomes explicit. The theme of Yury's imaginary poem is reflected in the actuality of Lara's presence at his coffin, in her joy and tears over their reunion, and in her attempt to shield his body with her own to return life to him. . . . The imagery of "The Turmoil" is reiterated in the imagery of spring, life and resurrection represented by the flowers, by Lara's physical presence, and by her embodiment of Mary Magdalene. The latter image is expressed both in Lara's declarations of remorse and repentance, and in her role of preparing Yury for his "entombment":

> "At last we are together again, Yurochka. And in what a terrible way God has willed our reunion . . . [But] it's so much our style . . . something big, irreparable. The riddle of life, the riddle of death, the enchantment of genius, the enchantment of unadorned beauty . . . Remember how we said goodbye . . . after that everything was ruined . . .

[The] images of illness and death in *Dr. Zhivago* serve as a major link between Pasternak's vision of life as everyday reality and his vision of life as Immortality or Eternal Life. Lara's words penetrate the very mystery of Life as Pasternak conceived it, in that they articulate the intimate relationships between life and death in the life cycle and in Pasternak's affirmative vision of Creation and Immortality, the major theme of his novel.

In this way, we come to see how in Pasternak's esthetic vision the poetic or artistic image combines with the metaphysical Christian symbol to unify the two planes of vision comprising the fabric of this complex novel. The ultimate theme of the novel—Life—emerges on the esthetic plane in Pasternak's vision of Life as Creation, and on the metaphysical (historico-Christian) plane in his vision of Life as Immortality. The novel as a whole thus becomes Pasternak's artistic explanation of how Life (through the feminine images of Lara and Mary Magdalene) and the Creative act or the Creator (through the images of Yury Zhivago and Christ) are related, or, in purely esthetic terms, of how the creative process is born. . . . (pp. 419-21)

> *Jane Gary Harris, "Pasternak's Vision of Life: The History of a Feminine Image," in* Russian Literature Triquarterly *(copyright © 1974 by Ardis), Fall, 1974, pp. 389-421.*

RIMVYDAS ŠILBAJORIS

According to Yevgeny Pasternak, the writer's son, the manuscript of "The Story of a Counter-Octave" came with a bundle of odd papers his father had asked him to burn for firewood in 1945. This unfinished story was written in 1913, at about the same time as "The Twin in Clouds," and it is a companion piece to the early prose works "The Sign of Apelles" (1915) and "Letters From Tula" (1918). It tells of a church organist, Amadeus Knaur, in a fictional Hessian town of the eighteenth century who became so engrossed in his improvisations on the organ after the Whitsunday service that he never noticed how his little son, who had somehow strayed among the mechanical workings of the instrument, was crushed to death by one of its levers. Years later Knaur came back to the town, possibly by an accident of Divine Providence, and asked to be reinstated in his old job, but was indignantly rejected. No one ever saw him again.

Once Pasternak wrote in a poem: "Our significance is in what we lose." Nevertheless, this early romantic and symbolic piece has some merit as a record of the writer's developing artistic devices in prose which constitute an unbroken line leading to his great novel *Doctor Zhivago*. One of these is an attempt to write of people and things, of the processes of nature, of changes in light with the passing of the day and of the movement of time itself as a single living entity, as continuum without qualitative dividing marks. The result is that people with their emotions do not come through as persons but rather as poetic images. Another device, following from this, is to establish a direct and meaningful correspondence between events in nature and crucial turning points in human lives in a manner which appears to move from strange coincidence to intimations of magic or, as the critics of *Doctor Zhivago* used to say, .o pathetic fallacy. In Pasternak's work this is not a false but a poetic logic, and one cannot say enough to emphasize the difference between the two. (p. 119)

> *Rimvydas Šilbajoris in* World Literature

Today *(copyright 1977 by the University of Oklahoma Press), Vol. 51, No. 1, Winter, 1977.*

*   *   *

PATON, Alan   1903-

Paton is a South African novelist and poet. A humanist and a moralist, he writes lyric novels that attack the racial situation in South Africa. (See also *CLC*, Vol. 4, and *Contemporary Authors*, Vols. 15-16; *Contemporary Authors Permanent Series*, Vol. 1.)

MYRON MATLAW

The emotional impact of *Cry, the Beloved Country* is achieved, first of all and most consistently, by Paton's stylistic understatement, by his use and reuse of a few simple, almost stilted, formal phrases. *Is it heavy?* Jarvis asks Stephen Kumalo when the latter haltingly and painfully reveals his identity as the father of the murderer of Jarvis' son. Kumalo's reply echoes and reechoes the adjective: *It is very heavy, umnumzana. It is the heaviest thing of all my years . . . This thing that is the heaviest thing of all my years, is the heaviest thing of all your years also. . . .* Similarly Mrs. Lithebe, whenever she is praised for her great generosity, repeatedly responds with a question that becomes something of a litany: *Why else were we born?*

In their stark simplicity, these and other phrases often suggest the biblical. Like the scripture readings . . . and the errant son's name (Absalom), they sometimes even echo the Bible directly. . . . Such phrases are so effective because their very understatement heightens the impact of what is clearly implied. They achieve yet greater power because they appear at climactic moments, . . .and they are repeated periodically. Thus their effect also resembles that of the incremental repetition of folk ballads.

Paton's selection of episodes and his narration and descriptions follow a similar stylistic manner. In these, too, understatement and repetition predominate, thus contributing to the desired effect. Almost conspicuously Paton eschews depicting—instead he merely alludes to or presents in the form of newspaper accounts—externally dramatic situations. This is true not only of the most consequential event of the novel—the murder itself—but also of such inherently dramatic situations as the abortive miners' strike or the confrontations between the novel's four sets of fathers and sons. . . . (pp. 262-63)

Instead of depicting violent scenes, Paton interweaves into the narrative events seemingly tangential to the main story line. These events are made interesting in themselves as history, but they are also made immediately pertinent to and revealing of the novel's action and characters. (p. 263)

Much of the story is seen through the eyes of an omniscient author whose tone ranges from reportorial objectivity to editorial evangelism. Parts of the story, however, are presented through the eyes of one or another of the characters, though this apparently limited point of view is controlled by the author to convey specific effects. Whatever the viewpoint, there are constant yet subtle shifts in tone, ranging from sympathy and hope through bewilderment, grief, and indignation.

The lyrical first paragraph of the brief opening chapter of Book I is identical, word for word, with the opening of

Book II: *There is a lovely road that runs from Ixopo into the hills . . . which are lovely beyond any singing of it . . .* Both openings describe the panoramic beauty and the lush vegetation of the hills. This is the home of Jarvis, and the opening description of Book II, which focuses on Jarvis, stops with the hills. The opening chapter of Book I, which focuses on Kumalo, continues with another and in all respects contrasting description, that of land that is barren and desolate, the valley in which Kumalo and the other blacks live. *The titihoya does not cry here any more,* for here there is insufficient food to attract even a bird. The tone becomes indignant as the green fecundity of the hills is contrasted with the red barrenness of the valley: *Stand shod upon it, for it is coarse and sharp, and the stones cut under the feet. It is not kept, or guarded, or cared for . . .* Finally, as we are shown the sterile land in which only the aged are left, the tone becomes elegiac: *. . .the young men and the girls are away. The soil cannot keep them any more.*

Even more explicitly 'editorial' are the sections that follow newspaper accounts and such other apparently journalistic digressions as the vignettes on the erection of Shanty Town, the panoramic view of Johannesburg's fear after the murder, and the descriptions of the discovery of gold and the miners' strike. In these chapters' terminal sections, the attitudes implied in the apparently objective narrative are made explicit. (pp. 263-64)

Understatement, deceptive simplicity, repetition, selectivity of narrative, episode, and setting, as well as the emotional charge of Paton's style—all these are manifested also in Paton's characterizations.

The novel's major character, the Reverend Stephen Kumalo, has evoked its readers' greatest compassion. Throughout his sufferings he remains an apparently humble, affectionate, kindly, simple, pious, God-fearing old man. Yet far from being simple or simply virtuous, he is portrayed in depth, as a flawed human being. Heroic in his ability to bear terrible private afflictions and tragedy, he is also able to continue to lead his parishioners out of communal suffering and tragedy. At the same time he is subject, too, to anger that manifests itself even in cruelty. . . . Kumalo is marred, too, by such lesser human flaws as jealousy . . . , vanity . . . , and pride . . . , and there is an allusion to an earlier episode that had nearly culminated in adultery with one of his parishioners. . . . Finally, though he is well aware of its futility, Kumalo cannot resist repeatedly nagging his already contrite and doomed son with recriminations and unanswerable or futile questions. All these attributes of Kumalo are shown rather than stated, and their manifestations are narrated with striking verbal economy and deceptive simplicity. (pp. 264-65)

Even some of the minor characters are portrayed in three-dimensional terms. The almost saintly Msimangu, as he himself says. . .is not flawless. . . . (p. 265)

[Carefully] and subtly and symmetrically wrought contrasts are achieved in the portrayals of [the] women just as they are in the portrayals of the Kumalo brothers, of Jarvis, and of Harrison—all members of the conflicting old order as well as fathers in conflict with their sons, proponents of differing new moral as well as new social orders. (p. 266)

Myron Matlaw, in Arcadia *(© 1975 by Walter de Gruyter & Co.), Vol. 10, No. 3, 1975.*

ROBERT L. BERNER

Knocking on the Door is a collection of short pieces written between 1923 and 1974 and hitherto unpublished or otherwise inaccessible. The chronological arrangement provides insight into the growth of Paton's moral vision, and the book is less valuable for the "creative" pieces, which are of minor importance in his canon, than for the articles and speeches, which are vital to an understanding of the tensions and contradictions which burden the life of South Africa and which provide much of the power of its best fiction. One piece, "Why I Write" (1974), is of great importance, not only as an expression of Paton's own artistic motives but as an expression of his sensitivity to the Afrikaners, who consider themselves Africans. It is a fact that anthologies or surveys of African literature almost never include works by white South Africans, who are apparently presumed to be European sojourners in a black continent. Paton provides a corrective: "When we talk of 'home' we mean the country in which [we] were born, which commands our affections, and excites our desire to write of what we know and understand." Paton knows that the real South African drama is in the souls of the whites, where fear must contend with love and justice; and a number of these pieces are designed to save that literary subject from those who seek simpler solutions in racial, political or economic theories.

Paton recognizes the conflict in himself between "the desire to write and the desire to do." As a writer he has resembled his Mr. Thomson in the story "The Hero of Currie Road" (1972), who argues that Mau Mau violence is no better than white violence and returns to his typewriter when he is booed by an audience of (black) Africans. As a man of action he spoke in 1968 on behalf of "the right to live under the rule of law"—scarcely a popular position with those who pervert words to justify violence; and his "Memorial to Luthuli" (1972) is an eloquent defense of "knocking on the door"—the act of either the artist or the political leader who demands admission to the hall of justice. (p. 492)

Robert L. Berner, in World Literature Today *(copyright 1977 by the University of Oklahoma Press), Vol. 51, No. 3, Summer, 1977.*

*   *   *

PAZ, Octavio   1914-

A Mexican poet, essayist, diplomat, and social philosopher, Paz also has written one play. Known primarily as an epic poet, Paz in his verse departs from traditional concepts of linear time, reality, and consciousness. Like Whitman, Paz uses the concept of the Self to merge metaphorically with other sensibilities and to make personal discoveries at a deeply psychic level. (See also *CLC*, Vols. 3, 4, 6, and *Contemporary Authors*, Vols. 73-76.)

JASCHA KESSLER

Octavio Paz stands in the first rank of poets on the world-scene today. I'd stress the notion world-scene because it won't do thinking of him as a local, a Mexican or even South American.

Paz's poetry, uttered in what seems a direct, even brutally vigorous language, derives its transcendental thrust and vision, its visual, aural, tactile power from the intellectual authority of the French Symbolists, from Surrealism during the 20s and 30s, from English and German romantic poets —all melded through the sonorities of 17th-century Spanish Baroque masters.

What results is a poetry cosmopolitan, truly international, often somewhat mystical in a realistic or materialistic way. Partly, it's the Latin American's situation that forces such development. . . .

The language that long ago was imposed on ancient native empires has worked to create a necessarily complex, irrational and tensely potent continuum, as is demonstrated in Paz's magnificent long chant, ''Sun Stone.'' . . .

[Paz] has recently gone from his erotic, world-seeing rapturous lyrics toward a structuralist and Buddhist view, via concrete poetry, and is exploring (and erring too, I think: see ''Blanco,'' a long poem) . . . the silences between words and sounds, the blank spaces between words.

Paz must emerge from this passage through theory; he has the power. He may be reacting against the way the world is being crammed with sheer noise, but it's no help to speak about the unspeakable, when the poet's task, finally, is to express it itself.

> *Jascha Kessler, ''Paz: An Ecumenical Poet,'' in* The Los Angeles Times *(copyright, 1971, Los Angeles Times; reprinted by permission), November 28, 1971, p. 20.*

DONALD SUTHERLAND

In spite of being a ''world'' poet, as glossily cosmopolitan as they come, [Octavio Paz] remains programmatically Mexican, not to say pre-Columbian; and in spite of being contemporary, so abreast of the very latest movements that he suffers, not gladly, the tag ''post-avant-garde,'' he is still acutely conscious of belonging to his own generation, far from a young one now. . . . (p. 5)

A Mexican, but what is a Mexican? . . . The question is not a simple one for Señor Paz himself, and his many prose works on all sorts of subjects, and many of his poems too, are indirectly or directly about it. (p. 7)

A great part of his being a Mexican poet is a variable and ambivalent relation to Spain and her literature, quite like our relation to England and her literature. As we have tended to loosen the colonial relation by adopting other cultures than England's for our literary uses . . . , Mexico, or rather Central America, has tended to adopt other cultures as counterpoises to Spain, mainly the French. . . . [For] Paz the French master is not a contemporary . . . but, of all people, Mallarmé, and this in spite of Paz's affinities with contemporary French surrealism and his friendship with André Breton. (pp. 7-8)

The connection or, as Paz would say, the ''correspondence,'' is surprisingly plain if you take Mallarmé in what has become his essential aspect, his use or expression of Nothingness. The full insistence on that aspect—on *Un Coup de Dés,* as against the Symbolist sumptuosities of *L'Après-Midi d'un Faune* or the syntactical fancy-work of such poems as the sonnet on Poe's tomb, which were Mallarmé in my youth—probably dates from about 1959, when Maurice Blanchot, himself a great specialist and virtuoso in Nothingness, published his essay on Mallarmé in a collec-

tion entitled, if you please, *Le Livre à Venir.* It is true that in 1939 Raymond Queneau had already invented the memorable and rather wicked formulation: *la mallarmachine à faire le vide,* but I imagine that was only a gag in passing, not a decisive reinterpretation.

Though Nothingness as a concept is prevalent enough in France, especially since Sartre's *Being and Nothingness,* and nihilism as an attitude is now, understandably, common among young Frenchmen, a strong sense of Nothingness as something substantial is far more Spanish than it is French. You can pretty well manipulate *le néant,* but *nada* gives no ground. As Spanish, it is to a degree Mexican, and to a high degree if you associate it closely with death. . . . In spite of the historical anomaly, which is not really an anomaly if you reject, as Paz does, ''linear'' history in favor of history as multidimensional and discontinuous, Mallarmé ''corresponds'' to French, Spanish, and Mexican realities simultaneously and even—if you follow Blanchot and not Queneau —to future poetry. Paz's poem *Blanco,* which uses blanks or white spaces in the manner of Mallarmé, looks like a supercivilized little stunt, and it is that, but it is much more real and weighty than that, to him, and to a contemporary Hispanic reader. It stands firmly on one of the prime intuitions of that culture and is furthermore backed, not so much by a Mallarmé revival, as by modern philosophy, which Paz takes as seriously, and as personally, as an earlier Mexican might take theology.

The Hispanic mind, however, loves to go by pairs of opposites, whether the opposites conflict, complement each other, alternate, or interact. Nothingness and its modes, such as death, emptiness, and silence, have to be countered with Being and its modes, such as life, plenitude, and sound, and all those things are usually made emphatic, peremptory, unmodulated. So that that other side of Mallarmé, his great richness and intricacy, is also to the Mexican purpose. Those qualities are certainly characteristic of Octavio Paz's mind, while he can also be, naturally simplicity itself. In *Blanco* they are at an extreme, in the dense interlocked passages, which counter the open-work passages on a ground of emptiness. (pp. 8-9)

Repleteness or congestion is a quality of most of his own work, poetry or prose. He may have got it from—or been confirmed in it by—the muralists [Rivera, Orozco, and Siqueiros], . . . but he seems to have felt they were old-fashioned political illustrators, and a more congenial source would have been the Baroque façades of Mexican churches and, still more, Aztec sculpture. One of his handsomest poems, ''Sun Stone,'' is a verbal version of the circular Aztec calendar stone, containing as many lines as that calendar has days: 584. The initial scheme is no doubt trivial, at best ritual, but the congestion of the poetic design, like that of the stone, has a rather terrifying force. . . . [He] can take on far more of the Occult, East and West, come Bodhisatvas, Boehme, or Blavatsky, without being for an instant (or for more than one ecstatic instant) befuddled by it all, than one would think possible. And he has the irrationalities of Surrealism quite in his pocket. And the devotional intellectualism of a Calderón or a Hopkins. The man is an orchestra. (p. 10)

Moving to and fro among the contrarieties of his own mind, those of his country, and those of his lifetime, political and artistic, he still keeps—or instantly recovers—his head and his balance. He goes at everything with a passion, with a voracity of interest, which threatens to carry him away, but he regularly plays a subject against its opposite—Duchamp against Picasso, Pound and Eliot against the European moderns of the same time, or against each other—and that keeps it all steady as well as dramatic. Incidentally, or alternately, he is excellent at elaborating finer distinctions than polar contrast. (pp. 11-12)

In *The Bow and the Lyre,* a vast and swarming panorama of the poetry of the world as he, a participant, sees it or lives in it, the "savage" or visionary figures, such as Blake or Hölderlin or Rimbaud or Lautréamont loom larger than usual. I see them smaller, but a reader more in sympathy with current poetry of the bardic and prophetic sort may feel, with joy, that Paz has got everything exactly in scale and place at last. I do, though intermittently, and when I do not I am still delighted with the beautifully conducted argument, in thought and style.

One disturbance, for me, comes in his handling of Greek epic and tragedy. Obviously, nobody can have gone through all the scholarship and speculation on those highly unsettled subjects, and if some prodigy had done so, exhaustively, there would be nothing left of his mind to make a generality with. Even the decently informed scholar, if he wants to treat Greek epic and tragedy as single and distinct genres—they are in fact maddeningly multiple and mixed—has to abstract and simplify in a very high-handed way. . . . At any rate, once he has set up his philosophical formulations of Greek epic and tragedy, he uses them with wonderful dexterity and imagination to distinguish other kinds of epic, the novel, and other kinds of tragedy, Elizabethan, French, and Seventeenth-Century Spanish. And so it goes, through a formidable range of forms, literatures, and ideas.

The *Bow and the Lyre,* though most of it is early (1956), is no doubt his big central work in prose. Later works are excursions or developments from it. *Conjunctions and Disjunctions,* while still concerned with modern man and his literatures, is occupied mainly with correspondences and differences in the Orient, especially with the sacred abominations of Tantric Buddhism. *Alternating Current* is a collection of fugitive and topical essays, brilliantly turned and fascinating to read, whether or not you know the larger work looming behind them. The prose works, together, constitute a monumental accomplishment, and, outside the Hispanic world, they may well outweigh his poetry, since they lose much less in translation. But what are they? Criticism? A few years ago, when I had read very little of him, I referred to him as "the eminent Mexican critic," which was miserably inadequate. Though I still like him best when he is bringing his manifold resources to bear on the analysis of a particular and difficult case, such as Duchamp or Pessoa, the criticism seems incidental to philosophy, as it is in Sartre. Does that make Paz a philosopher?

I think so, but of a kind that is a little strange to us. Our philosophers are not poets, except for Emerson, whereas Spain, from the end of the Nineteenth Century, has produced several philosophers of stature who are poets also, or novelists. . . . Paz has been compared with Ortega y Gasset, and owes a little to him, but Ortega was not a poet, and Paz is better associated with the others, especially with Machado, to whom, especially as a philosopher of Being and Not-Being, he owes a great deal. Not much, however, as a poet. (pp. 13-15)

In prose or poetry he is Unamuno's "man of flesh and bone" and then some. He carries a skeleton inside him (I owe that one to Machado) and has all the erotic fleshliness our fashion could ask. Moreover he celebrates the asshole, as fact and symbol. How complete can you get? A speculation of his on shit should interest us especially, even the Federal Reserve. Assuming the Freudian correspondence between gold (or capital) and the retention of shit, he proceeds to another correspondence, between gold and the sun, so that gold, not hoarded but invested and expended, becomes, like the sun and its light, the great productive source. I know of no better rationale for capitalism since Calvin, though the method is "savage" and poetic, not logical or theological as in Calvin.

That flight of Baroque imagination indicates, besides his energy and dash, the main terms of his world: man in the mortal flesh and an astronomical universe. That large view of the world need not exclude history, society, terrestrial nature, reason, taste, and other secular matters, but it certainly does subordinate and surround them. It corresponds to the view of Seventeenth-Century Spain and, I gather, that of the Aztecs, so that Paz comes by it naturally, but for him the religion that kept up the scale of Calderón's universe is gone, and the planet Venus is no longer Quetzalcoatl. The stars are now a "vain chess-game, once a combat of angels." You would think the universe would thus shrink to its foreground concerns, history and the rest; but, marvelously, it does not. The Calderonian spaciousness, in which man is "prisoner of the stars," is kept up. On what? Nothingness, largely.

Gertrude Stein one said that Spanish space has always to be "full, very full, of emptiness and suspicion." She was referring to pictorial space, but the remark may serve to account for Paz's cosmic space, which is full, very full—"replete"—with a *nada* substantial enough to support the constellations.

Though his philosophizing, savage and logical, ranges over everything that concerns him, small and large, myth and history, language and versification, his great distinction is, I feel, as a philosopher of temporality. Not of Time or of History so much as of the brutal changes in temporal orientation he and his generation have had to live in. . . . Hardest of all to deal with, for literary people, is the fact that modernism depends for its meaning on history, on getting on from the past into the future, and so does the avant-garde. The situation is intricate, to say the least, and worse, unconcluded, but Paz is magnificent in making it articulate, even in its indeterminations. What remains, through the shipwreck of historicism, is evidently the cosmos and the more-or-less nonconsecutive present, in Paz's version, a universe bounded by the stars and then the fulgurant or "eternal" moment of poetic vision. (pp. 15-17)

Renga is of very little interest in itself, as a book of poems. If you can read the four languages in which it is written it is an amusing exercise for your polyglottery, and the roughly surrealist manners, though rather belated, have some charming moments. But the importance of the work, if any, is in the theories behind it, questions of the author and his identity, single or multiple, of Language and languages, of the work as written or something lived. (p. 17)

Early Poems 1935-1955, on the other hand, can be enjoyed in a number of ways, with or without theoretics. The poems, though relatively "early" and preliminary to more impressive works like *Blanco* and *Sun Stone*, are not juvenilia, and already the main terms of his world are set. . . . [One] can spot motifs and manners from more recent predecessors, Machado, Jiménez, and perhaps Alberti, but these early echoings are, as I hear him at least, happily dominated by his own strong voice—not necessarily a shout, but round, full, and emphatic. There is also a delightful variety of forms in this volume, from short epigrams, with and without images, to rather long avalanches of metaphor, from very neat and complete things to long and short fragments, from the very plain to the very fancy. The book, though small, is a multitude.

Is there anything like him in English? He has something in common with Charles Olson, but really not much; with e. e. cummings in his typographical phase, but their differences are vast; with T. S. Eliot as a philosophical poet, but . . . [Hopkins] may well be our best approach to Paz, at least in his more Baroque stretches. Catholic doctrine apart, they have the same vast world, the same acute sense of the instantaneous and abrupt—in phenomena, but in their phrasing, too—and in both there is "the roll, the rise, the carol, the creation" in the thick of abounding imagery. Hopkins is an approach well enough but no thread for the labyrinth. For the ordinary reader, with little time, the short prose work, *Children of the Mire*, would be the best possible introduction. (pp. 17-18)

> *Donald Sutherland, "Excursions and Incursions and Returns of a Candy Skull," in* Parnassus: Poetry in Review *(copyright © by Poetry in Review Foundation), Spring-Summer, 1975, pp. 5-19.*

RICHARD C. STERNE

Octavio Paz wrote in 1953 his only play, a one-act re-creation of [Hawthorne's] "Rappaccini's Daughter." Re-creation, not simply adaptation. For while the Mexican poet does not tamper much with the plot, he significantly changes the atmosphere and meaning of the tale. Hawthorne contrasts love with "poisonous" sex, transcendent faith with imperfect empirical and rational knowledge. The tone and symbolism of "Rappaccini's Daughter" are influenced by the writings of such intensely moral allegorists as Dante, Spenser and Milton. Paz's chief concern, however, is metaphysical rather than moral; while he treats the human situation as "fallen," his idea of the fall is similar to André Breton's in *Nadja*: a loss of memory of a deep, original self. Like Breton, and unlike Hawthorne, Paz seeks reintegration, wholeness, through erotic love; but in *La hija de Rappaccini*, this love is undermined both by its external enemies—a sterile rationalism and a murderous will to power—and by the very differences between man and woman which draw them together in the first place. (p. 230)

Paz has much in common with Eastern thinkers. Specifically, the image in *La hija de Rappaccini* (and elsewhere in his poetry and prose) of "the other shore" ("la otra orilla") is closely related to the concept of The Other Shore in Buddhist texts. As Paz uses the term, its meaning differs from that of the "paradise" evoked by Hawthorne in that it implies not a washing clean of sin, but a reabsorption into the wholeness or nothingness from which we emerge at birth.

A third important difference in Paz's poetic drama from Hawthorne's story is a mythic perspective emphasizing cyclical rhythms rather than linear time. In *La hija de Rappaccini* as in the Aztec world view, death and life are complementary manifestations of one reality. (pp. 230-31)

[In Hawthorne's tale] Beatrice's body is as poisonous as the shrub, both having been nurtured by Rappaccini, [but] her soul is pure, like the water from the shattered fountain. The story is the most explicit condemnation of unhallowed sex that Hawthorne ever published. One passage, in which a smirking servant tells Giovanni of a "private entrance" into Rappaccini's garden, "where you may see all his fine shrubbery," . . . recalls the earthly delights of Hieronymus Bosch. No other Hawthorne fiction contrasts so clearly the "Eden of the present world" with a vision of paradise regained.

It is this kind of dualism which Octavio Paz considers to be typical of the "unhealthy" Western world view. In 1953, after returning from a stay in Japan and India, he contrasted the outlook of "primitives, Chinese Taoists, ancient Greeks, and others" whose "vision of chaos is a sort of ritual bath, a regeneration by immersion in the primal source," with the Occidental conception of the world: "It is moral. It isolates, divides, splits man in two. To return to unity of vision is to have done with the morality of duality." The central theme of *La hija de Rappaccini* is the quest of a lost unity, the effort to escape from the prison of individuality through love or—finally—through a leap to "the other shore." (pp. 232-33)

[Paz's] prologue prepares us to meet characters who are not, as in "Rappaccini's Daughter," individuals making choices weighted with moral responsibility, but types enacting patterns recurrent throughout history. And history, in *La hija de Rappaccini*, is a dream in which human beings catch occasional glimpses of a forgotten reality. The doomed erotic relationship between Juan and Beatriz is their almost somnambulistic effort to rediscover what each of them has lost. . . . Unlike Hawthorne's Beatrice, Beatriz does not construe Juan's eventual shrinking from her on account of her poisonousness as a lack of faith in her inner purity; rather, she accuses him of refusing to accept the mortal risk of love. (p. 234)

Paz's characterization of "el doctor Rappaccini" emphasizes the theme of sexual estrangement, for the scientist understands that man and woman seek in each other a lost unity. (p. 235)

Paz's treatment of Beatriz's death underlines the difference in his idea of Rappaccini from that of Hawthorne. When at the end of the short story Beatrice dies at her father's feet, he is "thunder-stricken," but this is all we know of his reaction. In the play, just after Beatriz has drunk the antidote (an act which her father has repeatedly pleaded with her not to commit, while Hawthorne's Rappaccini seems unaware of her intention), he cries out, "Daughter, why hast thou abandoned me?" This ironic echo of Jesus' last words emphasizes both Rappaccini's quasi-incestuous dependence on the daughter he has enslaved, and his despair as she leaves him forever. Hawthorne's scientist is an inverted Puritan, who sees Beatrice as a projection of his will to power. Paz's Rappaccini is an impassioned *caudillo* who would bind Beatriz to himself as well as to her lover.

Two relatively minor differences enhance the contrast between the Christian allegory and the pagan play. The Baglioni of Hawthorne's tale is a conventional and worldly academic who respects "the good old rules of the medical profession" and has social "habits that might almost be called jovial." . . . Since we're impelled when reading Hawthorne to assess the characters in moral terms, we would probably consign Baglioni to limbo. But Paz, whose categories differ from Hawthorne's, simply squeezes all the juice out of Baglioni: he becomes the "Hermit" of the Tarot deck, "worshiper of the triangle and the sphere . . . ignorant of the language of the blood, lost in his labyrinth of syllogisms . . . ". . . . He is a desiccated, sententious Cartesian, an enemy of the body as Paz's Rappaccini is an enemy of the spirit.

Consonant with his treatment of erotic love not as sinful but as a quest for a lost harmony is Paz's divergence from Hawthorne's idea of the pandering servant. The smirking Lisabetta of "Rappaccini's Daughter" is given a piece of gold by Giovanni as payment in advance for showing him the "private entrance" into the garden. In Paz's version, the servant Isabel obviously wishes to lead Juan to Beatriz, but she speaks of no private entrance, and Juan makes his way unaided to the girl.

Finally, the difference between Hawthorne's and Paz's major symbols reflects the dissimilarity of the writers' preoccupations. Hawthorne is particularly concerned to contrast the heavenly purity of water with the earthly impurity of the poisonous shrub; Paz, to oppose the idea of the "other shore," where mortal contradictions are resolved, to that of the "mirror"—a symbol of the imprisoned self. . . . Juan and Beatriz, incarnating the "Lovers" of the Tarot deck, fail to escape from the imprisonment of the self (given Paz's idea of sexual alienation, we may wonder whether love actually is a "choice," in the Messenger's words, of "life or death"), and Beatriz seeks re-integration into the "other world" from which she had received a "message" in the form of the bouquet of flowers given to her by Juan. . . . Her [dying] words, "I have made the final leap, I am on the other shore," echo language quoted elsewhere by Paz from the *Sutra Prajnaparamita:* "Oh, gone, gone, gone to the other shore, fallen on the other shore." But Beatriz's final words, "I do not touch the depths of my soul!" leave unanswered the question, What follows death? Unlike Hawthorne, who envisioned Beatrice in paradise, forgetting her grief in the light of immortality, Paz can only give expression to an ardent hope. As he says in his essay, "The Other Shore," "We scarcely know what it is that calls us from the depths of our being. . . . Do we truly return to that which we are? Return to what we were and foretaste of what we shall be . . . And perhaps man's true name, the emblem of his being, is Desire. . . ." Certainly it is the essence of *La hija de Rappaccini.* (pp. 235-37)

> *Richard C. Sterne, "Hawthorne Transformed: Octavio Paz's 'La hija de Rappaccini'," in* Comparative Literature Studies *(© 1976 by The Board of Trustees of the University of Illinois), September, 1976, pp. 230-39.*

RAYMOND D. SOUZA

[The] sense of motion created by "Exclamación" and "Juventud" . . . is a key to the dynamic process of both poems. However, neither work contains any verbs and the poet has succeeded in creating the feeling of motion without the use of a single verbal mechanism, and this is a remark-

able achievement. In "Exclamación" the skillful juxtaposition of contradictory statements produces a feeling of motion and both poems depend on the adept manipulation of words to enhance this sensation. The reader's imagination is activated and stimulated by the staccato lines and the contradictions in both poems.

"Exclamación" and "Juventud" portray an objective reality and there is little if any human presence in these poetic compositions. . . . [The] poetic voice narrates in an impersonal third person in both poems and this tends to enhance the sensation of human distance, at least in a personal sense. However, the reader becomes involved in the creative experience of both poems by participating in a process of discovery, and the trajectory of this experience moves him toward the attainment of an illuminating insight that transcends the limitations of material reality. Although the approach is depersonalized, it does not mitigate the reader's participation in the two poems, and this is testimony to Octavio Paz's mastery of poetic technique. The reader's subjective and limited view and the extensive visions offered by the poems are combined by a dynamic process, and this creative procedure causes the reader to experience the world in a new light. It is the reader's own subjective being rather than the poet's that merges and is incorporated into the objective reality portrayed in the poems. The poet stands aside and works his artistry on the reader and the world. In this regard, the poetic work is the point at which the subjective reader and the objective world meet. "Exclamación" and "Juventud" do not contain the anguished or highly emotional individual voice so frequently present in Paz's poetry, and one encounters in these two poems a contemplative serenity and an integration with the material world that impart a sense of harmony. Both poems emphasize a creative process of discovery rather than a static condition, and it is unlikely that a reader will see the world in exactly the same light after experiencing these poems. (pp. 121-22)

> *Raymond D. Souza, "Time and Space Configurations in Two Poems of Octavio Paz," in* Journal of Spanish Studies: Twentieth Century *(copyright © 1976 by the* Journal of Spanish Studies: Twentieth Century), *Fall, 1976, pp. 117-22.*

DORE ASHTON

[In the poems of Octavio Paz] I recognized the paradox which haunts us all, which makes of art criticism a perpetually unsatisfactory endeavor. I recognized that if the word springs ahead of thought, as Octavio said, and if it rises from the written page, and if, as he keeps repeating in all his poetry, the *presencia* arrives by means forever undisclosed, so does the painted image. What is true about the image, or *presencia,* is precisely what cannot be rendered through any other image, and especially not through that logic encountered at the circumference of experience. What I knew about visual art, I found confirmed by Octavio's poetry. (p. 32)

The mirrors and bridges and apparitions which course in the timeless currents of Octavio's creations, surfacing in the most unexpected moments to pose the paradox of creation itself, are finally justified by his faith in the *presencia*— which after all abides with the same durability in the works of the true visual artists. In those grand metaphors from which, by the very nature of perception, we cannot escape, finally lies the poet's power of salvage. (p. 35)

> *Dore Ashton, "Octavio Paz and Words and Words and Images," with translations by Andrée Conrad, in* Review *(copyright © 1976 by the Center for Inter-American Relations, Inc.), Fall, 1976, pp. 32-5.*

ARTHUR TERRY

Though [Paz's] account of modern poetry is deliberately selective [in *Children of the Mire*], there are many passages which a more systematic historian of literature might envy. As a Latin American poet, he writes with particular authority of the relation of *modernismo* to European romanticism and of the extent to which positivism, for nineteenth-century Latin American writers, implied an intellectual crisis similar in its terms, if not in its scope, to that of the Enlightenment in Europe. There are signs, too, that Paz is continuing to adjust his view of the romantic tradition: thus, his long-standing interest in Nerval now takes him back more profoundly than before to the German romantics, and in particular to Jean Paul Richter, the earliest proponent of the "death of God." Whether he is speaking of intellectuals like Marx and Fourier (one of the few writers, for Paz, in whom the possibilities of poetic thought and revolutionary thought coincide), or of the differences between Eliot and Pound, his judgments are invariably accurate and often memorable. (pp. 86-7)

Occasionally, what might have been a genuine insight remains at the level of a bright idea, as when he speaks of an "intimate relation" between Protestantism and romanticism, or of the possible link between accentual versification and analogical vision. More seriously, perhaps, there are moments at which the pattern is made to seem a little too neat, as when certain phenomena are said to be linked by a "contrary dialectic" or are described as "metaphors" of one another. Such verbal shortcuts are particularly frustrating in a writer of Paz's intelligence, since one inevitably feels them to be the result of overcompression, rather than of any basic failure of thought.

Having said this, one can only admire the scope and clarity of the rest. The final sections, in particular, contain some of Paz's most persuasive observations on the situation of the contemporary artist. Roughly, what he is saying here is that the whole conception of the avant-garde is becoming outdated, since, as he puts it, "modern art is beginning to lose its powers of negation" . . . ; or, in terms which deliberately echo the theme of the early chapters, "the present has become critical of the future and is beginning to displace it." . . . Thus poetry, like politics and ethics, is being driven back on the present, though the very idea of the present has by now taken on the sense of a return to the beginning. Where poetry is concerned, this means a return to the voice of language itself, to the "founding word," which is more permanent and less fortuitous than the utterance of the poet as individual.

These are difficult speculations, though all the more admirable since they offer no easy solutions. Yet, if Paz's account of modern poetry often has more of the quality of a fable than of objective history, his own recent poetic practice is there to provide the necessary body to his theories. Both as a profession of faith and as a subtle commentary on some of the most striking tendencies in the poetry of the last two hundred years, this is an impressive book, and one which could only have been written by a major poet. (p. 87)

> *Arthur Terry, in* Comparative Literature *(© copyright 1977 by University of Oregon), Vol. 29, Winter, 1977.*

CARLOS CORTÍNEZ

Why does the writer write? Paz once stated that this was the only valid question. He himself has been writing, as early as his classical *Labyrinth of Solitude* (1950) shows, in order to understand Mexico. In *Vuelta* he continues this commitment. A privileged moment is his return from the East (in 1969) that allows him—as happened before with Diego Rivera's return from Europe—to see the Mexican reality as if he hadn't seen it before.

Back in Mexico, Paz weeps not tears of love, as did Ulysses at the sight of his Ithaca, but of wrath, as did Moses descending from the Horeb. . . . Anger is all-powerful in the valley and contaminates the poet. Seeing Mexico's errors—those common to Latin America—allows him, forces him, to meditate on himself and the meaning of his vital adventure. . . . The autobiographical is another important thematic line of *Vuelta*, continuing the effort emphasized by his previous books *El mono gramático* (1974 . . .) and *Pasado en claro* (1975).

Paz has defined himself as a man in search of the word. . . . His fidelity to this destiny has been an exemplary one. Consequently he is beginning to be praised by the new generations of Hispanic readers. But this poet, finally consecrated by the literary establishment, does not permit himself to be deceived by this recognition. He knows that, in a real sense, he has not "arrived." . . .

In the uncertain path that the poet walks, in which the return to the fatherland is *not* the final journey, what is it that sustains Paz? First of all, in spite of his surrealistic flair, his lucidity. Neither slogans nor ideologies, nothing moves him but his own visions—poetry/language, woman/nature. Also, the existential certainty that "History is a mistake." . . . (p. 87)

Vuelta is written in four parts (four is the cipher of the universe for ancient Mexicans), and each part has a long central poem. There are others, shorter, mostly in homage to artists of words or images. Another constant of Paz has been his generous perception of the young artists around him. The poetry of Octavio Paz is not easy. There are neither sentimental effusions nor dazzling metaphors. He faces language with both vigilance and abandonment. Normally it is the mot juste, but sometimes a drunken freedom leads him to strange neologisms. . . . Like Huidobro, he plays, not always succeeding, trying to go through alliteration and paronomasia to new discoveries. Paz is primarily a poet of Poetry, one who looks at himself in the act of creation, one who never tires of reflecting on the mysterious and sacred nature of that "most innocent of all occupations" (Hölderlin).

Some of the passages of this skillful and refined book are unforgettable: the opening of the day over a grove, the snow falling among a river of cars, the sleeping wife "sculpted by her throbs," and the poet finally feeling himself alive—confident of the woman's "quiet flow." (p. 88)

> *Carlos Cortínez, in* World Literature Today *(copyright 1978 by the University of Oklahoma Press), Vol. 52, No. 1, Winter, 1978.*

PORTER, Katherine Anne   1890-

An American short story writer, essayist, and novelist, Porter is considered a technical master of the short story. The recipient of a Pulitzer Prize, Porter instills her work with profound irony, and her thematic considerations revolve around the workings of the heart and emotions, the difference between appearance and reality, and the consequences of self-deception. (See also *CLC*, Vols. 1, 3, 7, and *Contemporary Authors*, Vols. 1-4, rev. ed.)

M. WYNN THOMAS

[Katherine Anne Porter's] sense of what makes for an ending is similar to that found in Aristotle's definition of Greek tragedy; and that was an analogy that she was proudly conscious of, as she remarked. "Any true work of art has got to give you the feeling of reconciliation—what the Greeks would call catharsis, the purification of your mind and imagination—through an ending that is endurable because it is right and true. Oh, not in any pawky individual idea of morality or some parochial idea of right and wrong. Sometimes the end is very tragic, because it needs to be."

In terms of the act of writing, this can be put differently and very simply: the story must tell you, "I know where I'm going." And that is where Mr. Helton comes in. "He just clumped down his big square dusty shoes one after the other steadily, like a man following a plow, as if he knew the place well and knew where he was going and what he would find there." That's how Mr. Helton walks into the story "Noon Wine," and into Mr. Thompson's life. The story ends with Mr. Thompson walking out of his own life. As he says at the end of the story, "I still think I done the only thing there was to do" . . . ; and there is no doubt that unless this statement of his made some kind of sense to us Miss Porter would feel that the story had failed. (pp. 230-31)

"Noon Wine," then, is a story which shows us where a man is going and what he finds when he gets there. But this sense of a direction is not something that can be grasped simply: what the story shows is the complex nature of "direction" in human life. To reverse Miss Porter's dictum, if the story creates a sense of order it does so successfully only insofar as it recognizes and respects life's confusion. The direction of a man's life is not the same as the direction a man takes when following a plow, and any writer who mistakes the one direction for the other is liable to clump down his big square dusty shoes one after the other all over his "story." When, after reading the story, we re-read that opening passage which describes the arrival of Mr. Helton, we must not only be struck by the implications of this description, now revealed by our sense of the ending, but must also believe anew in the particularity and incidental quality of the metaphor. The "as if" must genuinely lead us to the way the man walks as well as to the strange sympathies and antipathies in the story that follows.

This palpable sense of a world is vitally important to the story's meaning. What happens is intelligible only in terms of the place where it happens. It is a matter not only of direction (which is one metaphor) but also of texture (a different metaphor). The murder Mr. Thompson commits is as much a matter of the heat as anything else. "Meantime the August heat was almost unbearable, the air so thick you could poke a hole in it. The dust was inches thick on everything." . . . The word "thick" is just right: it comes to

mean more and more from then on in the story. It is the word that describes Mr. Thompson's voice after he has struck Mr. Hatch down. . . . "Thick" becomes resonant, a word that explores all the bafflement and inarticulateness of the man, his dim sense of a world growing thick around him, until it becomes unbearable. . . . And yet that is the world which he had always felt as solidly familiar. (pp. 231-32)

The word "thick," in the phrase "thick hands," itself expresses and explains Mr. Thompson's helplessness. The same word used in the description of his Sunday suit makes us feel the solid respectability of the cloth, a respectability so important to the farmer and so stifling a part of his tragedy. Once the language of the story becomes familiar (and this need not involve noticing the repeated use of a word, of course), there seems a particular aptness and poignancy in Mr. Thompson's writing his lonely suicide note with "a stub pencil" and on "a thin pad of scratch paper" taken "from the shelf where the boys kept their schoolbooks." . . . It is then that he fully realizes and accepts his isolation. (p. 232)

What dominates and guides [Mrs. Thompson's] understanding of what happened is her fear and suspicion of male violence and physicality. And yet what the story, through the shape of its action and the shape of its language, makes clear, is that Mrs. Thompson's bitterness here, her frustration, is of the same order as the bitter indignation and frustration that leads her husband to kill Mr. Hatch. This is quietly brought out . . . : "Her thoughts stopped with a little soundless explosion, cleared and began again." . . . It is typical of Mrs. Thompson that her "explosions," compared to those of her husband, should be "little" and "soundless." One of the most distressing things about her husband is that he is big and loud. Mrs. Thompson is more liable to implode than explode. . . . (p. 234)

The measure of the difference between what the same scene means to Mr. Thompson and to Mrs. Thompson is beautifully and quietly brought out by the language of the two following passages. The first describes the slowly mounting anger that leads to Mr. Thompson's killing Mr. Hatch. "Mr. Thompson sat silent and chewed steadily and stared at a spot on the ground about six feet away and felt a slow muffled resentment climbing from somewhere deep down in him, climbing and spreading all through him." . . . Though he cannot find what other people would consider proper reasons for this, his sense of how things are is stronger than his sense of how they would look to other people; and in persisting to act according to his feelings he relegates everyone else to the situation of outsiders, lookers-on. When Mrs. Thompson appears, her reaction is also very much in character. "Mrs. Thompson sat down slowly against the side of the house and began to slide forward on her face; she felt as if she were drowning, she couldn't rise to the top somehow." . . . (pp. 235-36)

It is important that both of these reactions should be in character. Each does what he or she does upon coming to the end of thought, and something else takes over to resolve the matter. "Thought" is, in fact, an important word in the story, and part of the meaning of the story seems to move through its recurrence. It is not by any means the only word of such importance in "Noon Wine"; and of necessity these words pursue no solitary course through the narrative. They are centers of gravity, attracting and concentrating meaning. Or, to put it another way, they quietly intensify the language of the world of the story. Their relationships to each other become vital to the way they mean anything—as "thick" can be said to lead in the direction of the language of the end of the story.

The word "think" attains a similar life of its own: "Mr. Thompson couldn't think how to describe how it was with Mr. Helton. . . . It was a terrible position. He couldn't think of any way out." . . . This use of "think" is more than accidental. The problem of not being able to think is the heart of the tragedy, not least because thinking is a means of finding a way out through words. It is a process of understanding, a way of discovering, a form of knowing—and "knowing" is a word significantly related to "thinking" in this story. It is not only of his children that Mr. Thompson can feel, in the earlier part of the story, that he has succeeded in raising them "without knowing how he had done it." . . . [Mrs. Thompson says:] "I always say, the first thing you think is the best thing you can say." . . . [This] provides a good account of the embarrassment and real difficulty of sustained thinking for such people as these. Their minds work painfully slowly, bemused at the least disturbance of the limited vocabulary of their understanding. But because of this they come to stand for the real difficulties of thought and understanding. . . . Katherine Anne Porter is here able to bring [the complications of meaning and the halo that surrounds events] out through the fumbling ordinary speech of her characters. There is a distinct difference between bungling and fumbling. Mr. Thompson starts out as a potentially comic figure—a bungler: and this contributes all the more to the tragic figure he becomes, fumbling in his memory, trying to get things straight. And it is this that gives point and dignity to his death—to his fumbled suicide, all the more deliberate and meaningful because it is such a clumsy thing to do.

The word "think" leads, then, to some such understanding of the story as has been here suggested. But to say that an important part of the story's meaning seems to be expressed and explored through the use of a simple word is not, obviously, to say that every use of that word in the story is significant. Still, there are casual, unimportant uses of the word that become charged with at least a measure of irony when some of its meanings elsewhere are recalled. . . . The point need not be labored. All that is worth noting is [that a phrase like] "the more I got to thinking about it" becomes resonant with additional, ironic, bitter meanings, gathered from the rest of the story and the powerful history of the phrase. The intensity of "Noon Wine," the peculiar texture of its meaning, is created in this way. (pp. 236-37)

Mr. Thompson's suicide is committed as deliberately, as thoughtfully as he writes his final letter. Here he not only stops to think but thinks and then stops; here he takes his stand; and here, on the last page, many of the words that have taken on great strength of meaning throughout the story lend their strength and depth to this last scene. (p. 238)

[There] is dignity of a high order in Mr. Thompson's death. The key words in these final passages are "cautiously" and "carefully." . . . The details are right; Mr. Thompson's arrangements are careful and detailed. He does not rush on death, he approaches it deliberately, walking "to the farthest end of his fields" and in the direction to which the

whole story may now be seen to point. He does not drown thought in the roar of the gun. Though his suicide is clumsy, fumbled, movingly awkward, it is literally an achievement of the mind, an achievement of thought. . . . The story ends here, at the "logical" end of the plot: there is no other way out. The words Mr. Thompson speaks towards the end are words he "has to" speak. Though they come out of his deepest experiences, they are the simplest of words. The words with which he takes leave of his wife are charged with the whole meaning of his tragedy. He leaves her in the hands of the "boys," saying that he is just going out to fetch the doctor. . . . Though Mr. Thompson is not one to speak pregnant sentences, the sentence, "You'll know how to look after her," is nevertheless pregnant with meaning. It is full of his resignation—in all senses of the word: his sense of finally having to give up, to act out the inevitable, and the identification of this with "resigning" his wife, committing her to the care of those who know how to look after her. He no longer knows. And there is tragic irony here. During all his married life he has been devoted to her; a great part of the sense of his life has come from his care for Mrs. Thompson's delicate health. Moreover, this care and protection of his wife has sustained his sense of his own manliness, a manliness that has now been challengingly, almost threateningly, assumed by his sons. (pp. 239-40)

The fresh start he makes is very different from anything he had imagined only a short time previously. But it comes from the final complete understanding he has of how and where he stands. Everybody believes him a murderer: he believes that he is not. . . .

[He and his wife] are isolated by what they "don't know" as much as by what they know, and as such they become two witnesses on our behalf to the terrible mystery of life. The infinite chaos of their situation springs in part from their lack of imagination but much more from the unimaginable chaos of life. . . . What Mr. Thompson knows at the end of "Noon Wine" is the depth of his unfathomable world.

Something of this has been in the story from the first. Mr. Thompson has been prone to bafflement all along. . . . (p. 241)

"A stranger in a strange land": that perfectly sums up Mr. Thompson's situation at the end of "Noon Wine." Is it "God's world" . . . or is it "a strange land"? Are the phrases incompatible? Mr. Thompson, like Mr. Helton, talks wrong: "his words wandering up and down." . . . His accent is all wrong, he puts the emphasis in the wrong place, and his neighbors, even the Thompson family, can't understand him. . . . [The harmonicas are Mr. Helton's] speech, his language; they are what enable him to express himself, to understand himself, to survive. They bring order into his world. And this is what—metaphorically, not literally—the song Helton plays over and over to himself means. It stands for everything that people, in this story and out of it, cannot "put into words, hardly into thoughts." . . . Mrs. Thompson assumes that what the song means is in the words; and several critics have followed her, believing that the title of the story needs to be understood in terms of the words of the song. But this can be only partly true. Mr. Thompson learns through bitter experience what the song "means." At the end he knows that it means one man's being isolated with his understanding—the fateful privacy of meaning. (p. 244)

Katherine Anne Porter spoke of the shape of a story, the way it is brought to "a logical and human end." "Human" here is not an addition to the logic but the character of the logic: it is the logic of human experience. And that is what this essay has been concerned with exploring. It has tried to show the "direction" of "Noon Wine," which is of course "where it is going." "Direction" can be a misleading word—it is too linear in its implications; "shape" might be better, it can at least imply body, which allows for what here has been called the texture of the story. What this reading has tried to suggest is that feeling this is a matter of realizing how a certain language is characteristic of the story: the "logic" of "Noon Wine" is the same as its character.

What is remarkable is that the "plot" thickens to the extent that a reader masters the story in its ordinariness. A story creates a sense of order successfully only insofar as it recognizes and respects life's confusion. The order of "Noon Wine" is gradually sensed in the fine confusion of people's talk. It cannot be extracted: it must be left where it is. There is a depth and dignity of reticence to the story, and all the garrulity of explanation should finally rest on this.

The artist's task is to thicken language, to make it compact of meaning. There are ways and ways of doing this, since art knows no musts but only an infinite may. Katherine Anne Porter's way is that of a rich plainness. (p. 245)

[The] more one reads, re-reads, the more "the light thickens." And such thickening of the light in "Noon Wine" seems to be of the nature of that kind of intensity that is tragedy.... Her story is about ordinary people, all the more ordinary in being "strangers in a strange land." They are unaware that in their lives they act out the ceremony of fate. We, through them, are made aware of the fearful symmetry of a life. (p. 246)

> *M. Wynn Thomas, "Strangers in a Strange Land: A Reading of 'Noon Wine',"* in American Literature *(reprinted by permission of the Publisher; copyright 1975 by Duke University Press, Durham, North Carolina), May, 1975, pp. 230-46.*

JANE FLANDERS

Like so much American writing—particularly Southern writing—Katherine Anne Porter's stories of the Old South ("The Old Order" series and "Old Mortality") based on her family past in antebellum Kentucky and Texas during the Reconstruction Era offer a statement about the past and its impact on the present. At the same time, these stories provide a way of approaching Porter as a woman writer. Like Faulkner—also writing about the Southern past in the mid-1930's—Porter takes as her subject the artificiality and inhumanity of the Old Order, presenting it from the standpoint of the woman's experience. While Faulkner emphasizes slavery and racial injustice, Porter takes as her subject the rigidly circumscribed experience and sexual repression of the white Southern woman—kept like the blacks in submission and fear by the doctrines, taboos and social realities of a paternalistic culture.

This theme is not restricted to Porter's stories of her native South. The theme of woman's oppression, especially emotional and sexual inhibition, may be found in everything she wrote. A feminist critical stance is a primary element in her view of American society—a view confirmed by her experi-

ence as an expatriate living in Mexico during the 1920's. Compared with the vividness of Mexican life, particularly the simplicity and spontaneity of the Mexican Indians, American culture seemed emotionally impoverished, narrowminded and dishonest. The damage to women in such a society appeared even more obvious to her. During this period Porter frequently attacked the "puritanism" of American culture, joining in with other critics of the twenties, and along this line she began a fictional biography of Cotton Mather which portrayed him as a sanctimonious hypocrite whose wife suffered martyrdom under his tyranny—jointly condemning self-serving Puritan piety and male-dominated marriage. (pp. 48-9)

Woman's emotional frustration, sexual repression and subjection to the laws of a man's world constitute a major theme in Katherine Anne Porter's fiction. Female characters, who predominate in her work, are typically damaged by their experience. Family ties, marriage and love are threats to freedom; those women who attempt to escape are usually thwarted; and even those who gain independence achieve it at great cost. For many of Porter's heroines, like those of "Flowering Judas," "Theft," and *Pale Horse, Pale Rider,* escape takes the form of inner withdrawal from life. Although she has long maintained an enigmatic silence about herself, the insistence with which Porter returns to the themes of female entrapment and resistance, the damage of sexual inhibition and the failure of love in the lives of women, tempts one to speculate about the personal statement embedded in her work. Her autobiographical stories may provide us with some clues.

The stories of the Old South are central to Porter's *oeuvre,* illuminating the fiction leading up to them and following them. They are unusual in several ways: they are openly autobiographical; though written over the span of a decade, they fall into a pattern, being united around the heroine and called the "Miranda stories" (together with *Pale Horse, Pale Rider*); they present a wide variety of characters illustrating the kinds of feminine models Porter grew up with, thus providing insight into her ideas about herself and woman's role in society.

These stories make it clear that Porter's childhood experience offered her no acceptable models of womanhood. No "normal," happy young women, no satisfying or fulfilled marriage relationships are described in the Miranda stories. Closely following the author's own life, the stories tell us that Miranda's mother died when she was two, and her father is a shadowy figure. Men are usually weak, or absent characters; Miranda grew up in a matriarchal household dominated by [Sophia Jane] her grandmother, a figure (modeled on Porter's own grandmother who raised her from infancy) who stands in striking contrast to the many trapped and damaged females found throughout Porter's work.

Miranda's grandmother illustrates the only kind of freedom or self-sufficiency a woman could achieve in Porter's childhood world, yet she achieved it only after long obedience to the conventional role of wife and mother, slowly surmounting the limitations of that role, and finally freed from it only by her husband's death. A woman must be alone to be free. (pp. 49-50)

But the alternative roles are no better. Another, very different response to the woman's situation under the Old Order is exhibited by the spirited and flirtatious belle, Miranda's Aunt Amy; but Amy's capricious behavior became self-destructive, and she had died young. Amy had capitulated to the sexual role demanded of her in many ways. But she refused to relinquish her supremacy as a coquette, a sought-after object of male desire. She resisted marriage because it meant giving up her freedom.

Miranda's cousin Eva, a homely spinster, illustrates a third alternative: having failed in the sexual competition of her youth, never having found her "definition" in marriage and maternity, she had compensated by becoming self-supporting as a teacher and campaigner for women's rights. Yet Eva is bitter about her past: independence was thrust upon her because she did not succeed in fulfilling the expected feminine role. Indeed, none of these women fulfills that role —that impossible combination of beauty, charm, chastity and grace which flowers into the capable wife and devoted mother, upholding the moral, religious and cultural standards of the household, while remaining submissive to her husband and the traditions of society. Clearly, Porter finds the demands of "Southern womanhood" to be incompatible with actual experience.

Miranda's response, finally, is to reject all these roles, to reject family, even love. The basic theme of the Miranda stories is "growing up female," and for Miranda, growing up entails repudiation of her family and her past. Each story centers on a crucial event or revelation which marks a stage in Miranda's awakening to the world—as a child of five or six, or eight, nine or ten. At the end of "Old Mortality" we glimpse her at eighteen, having emerged from the secure yet limiting world of her youth, renouncing all ties, "loving and being loved," committed to resistance and flight. (p. 51)

Miranda finds it hard to reconcile her grandmother's rigid authoritarianism with the story of her youth. The grandmother she knows is the embodiment of order and security who strives to instill in her grandchildren discipline, obedience and proper manners. And yet that very grandmother had suffered great trials, had worked with her hands to raise the food with which to feed her family. Her story exhibits a model of self-sufficiency and defiance of the established order which could not fail to stir Miranda's young imagination. Life had been a battle from which Sophia Jane had emerged triumphant, but she did not win that battle by remaining submissive to any code of genteel femininity. (p. 52)

The sufferings of Sophia Jane's life, as Porter sees it, resulted directly from the moral and social values of the Old Order—values she associates with the men who dominated it. Porter exalts her heroine in proportion to her resistance to that order. Built on the immorality of slavery, locked in the unrealistic dream of a labor-free existence for the privileged rich, not only denying the humanity of an entire race, but denying women like Sophia Jane the natural fulfillment of their protective and nurturing functions, the Old Order destroyed human character.

Through the grandmother, Porter extols womanhood, and at the same time demonstrates through her story the weakness of the men corrupted by a dishonest society, as well as the obstacles that lay in the grandmother's path as she tried to express her character and virtues. Clearly it was largely by chance that Sophia Jane was forced to win her freedom.

Many other women of that hard time had not survived, among them her own daughters and her daughter-in-law, Miranda's mother, who died in childbirth. Whatever strength the grandmother had acquired was the result of a desperate struggle, and was not to be transmitted to succeeding generations. (p. 55)

The legend of Miranda's Aunt Amy, described in "Old Mortality," ... also comes out of the past. Amy was a beautiful belle excelling in every feminine grace; but, ailing and unhappy, she had gone unwillingly into marriage and had died six weeks later, perhaps by her own hand. Amy's whole life had been a struggle against confinement and convention, personified in her strict, repressive father who made life "dull" and unendurable. Yet her story comes down to Miranda clothed in the irresistible aura of romance.

Miranda understandably identifies with such a passionate and defiant spirit. Throughout the Miranda stories there are hints that the little girl recognizes the narrowness of the role she is destined to fill; she resents the tight solidarity of the family which surrounds her, lectures her and admonishes her, and she recognizes in her beloved grandmother the principal opponent of her freedom. She begins to realize that the restrictions placed on her have something to do with her sex. In "The Grave" (1935) nine-year-old Miranda learns the truth about her future procreative function when her brother kills and opens the belly of a pregnant rabbit. He swears her to secrecy: this is forbidden knowledge, and he should not have allowed her to see what she had seen. At last grasping the secret of her own sexuality, and the taboo accompanying this knowledge, Miranda senses a mysterious threat in her femaleness which will bind her still more closely to the rules of feminine decorum. (pp. 55-6)

"Old Mortality" describes how an ideal of femininity is communicated to the young Miranda—at ten, then at fourteen, acutely conscious of her approaching maturity. ... Miranda wants ... fervently to be like Aunt Amy, beautiful "as an angel," unequalled as a horsewoman, lighter and more delicate than any dancer before her time or since, remembered for her quickness of wit, her daring, and her devastatingly charming ways with men. (p. 57)

The romantic appeal of the legend is finally destroyed when eighteen-year-old Miranda returns home for a family funeral—her first visit home for more than a year. After she had run away from school to get married, her father had found it difficult to forgive her. Miranda meets her elderly Cousin Eva, a chinless old-maid schoolteacher and suffragist who had been tormented in her youth because of her homeliness. Eva presents a merciless view of the young girl's experience in the old days: the girls pitted against each other in desperate competition, their future contingent upon success in the marriage mart. "The rivalry ... you can't imagine what the rivalry was like," says Eva bitterly. "Those parties and dances were their market." And behind all the delicacy and coquetry, "it was just sex ... all smothered under pretty names ... their minds dwelt on nothing else." ... Eva particularly remembers Amy, who had mocked her because of her lack of chin: "Well, Amy carried herself with more spirit than the others ... but she was simply sex-ridden, like the rest." ... (pp. 58-9)

Although Miranda recognizes in Eva's savage account a

distortion of truth as romantic as all she had heard before, though she hears in it Eva's bitterness at her own failure in the sexual contest, Eva's suspicions destroy the fairytale legend Miranda had so long accepted. Miranda despairs of trusting anyone else's version of the past, and resolves not to be "romantic" about herself: "At least I can know the truth about what happens to me," she tells herself. . . . But she does not realize how far she has already been shaped by romantic traditions; in her rebellion she imitates many a spirited family heroine who resisted having to define herself in terms of men. Miranda vows to escape family bonds; though she had run away to marriage, she knows that she will run away from marriage, too. She will repudiate love, she says to herself; but what she does not know, "in her hopefulness, her ignorance," . . . is that it is too late. She cannot escape "loving and being loved," nor the grip of family and its legends, and she will never know the truth about herself.

Many ghosts out of the Southern past haunt Miranda, as they haunt her author-self as a mature woman. Katherine Anne Porter invests in the grandmother many qualities which constitute a womanly ideal; she stresses the grandmother's courage, her willingness to work, her commitment to her "natural" duty to protect and instruct the young, and her faith in nature's abundance—in short, her "natural" humanity and acceptance of life. But at the same time Porter realizes that this ideal had been purchased at a terrible price, and only by a painful resistance of men and a male-dominated world. It had maintained itself in the teeth of antagonistic forces so formidable as to make such self-sufficiency and courage impossible to imitate, difficult at times even to love. To carry out what she had to do, the grandmother had to become as strong, as absolute and inflexible as the men whose tyranny she had escaped.

Miranda will follow none of these women from her family past, except to follow them in rebellion. All three women had struggled in various ways to escape the restrictions of the role of Southern womanhood, and by the end of these stories we see Miranda, too, committed to flight, to withdrawal from experience and evasion of human ties—prominent patterns in Porter's fiction. But Miranda will never know the "truth about herself" because she cannot reconcile her need to express her own identity with any acceptable model of mature womanhood; she has never known one. As we may conclude from *Pale Horse, Pale Rider*—the last Miranda story—and from the bulk of her later work, Katherine Anne Porter's own experience was that of the failure of love and the death of the heart. Her stories of the South help to explain why. (pp. 59-60)

> *Jane Flanders, "Katherine Anne Porter and the Ordeal of Southern Womanhood," in* The Southern Literary Journal *(copyright 1976 by the Department of English, University of North Carolina at Chapel Hill), Fall, 1976, pp. 47-60.*

JOAN GIVNER

[In a speech given to a group of University of Maryland students in 1972, Katherine Anne Porter] said that all her fiction is reportage, it really happened, but she arranges it and it becomes fiction.

Her most ambitious attempt to explain her creative process was made at the invitation of Robert Penn Warren and ap-

peared as "'Noon Wine': The Sources" in *Yale Review* in 1954. In this essay she related the separate anecdotes which formed the basis of "Noon Wine," saying that the story was "true" in the way that a work of fiction should be true, created out of all the scattered particles of life she was able to absorb and shape into a living new being. (p. 217)

A comparison of the epistolary and fictional versions shows omissions which are as significant as the events either reported exactly or transmuted. The letters show that Porter was very interested in the political situation around her. (p. 220)

Porter's omissions do not indicate indifference, since both the letters and personal reminiscences of friends testify to her intense political and social awareness. . . . They show rather her ability to hold taut the thread of her theme. Porter was very sure of her theme's scope and ruthless about excluding all details, no matter how interesting, which did not bear on that theme.

In "The Leaning Tower" the political atmosphere was useful in providing texture, but subsidiary in its importance to theme. Closer to "Old Mortality" than to *Ship of Fools*, the story turns on the contrast between the imagined dream of paradise and the hellish reality of the present. Finding themselves stranded in Berlin, all the characters in "The Leaning Tower" dream of paradises past and future. For the barber it is Spain. For Hans, Paris, and for Rosa, the unreal Italy of her honeymoon. Tadeusz Mey wishes to go to London, but he dreams also of his childhood in Cracow, remembering the place as something between a cemetery and a lost paradise, with an immense sound of bells. Only Charles has actually attained his imagined paradise, and the story records his disillusionment as he discovers that Berlin does not merely fail to measure up to his dream of paradise, but is, in fact, a hell on earth.

When she described the genesis of "Noon Wine" Porter spoke of drawing heavily upon childhood memories. She draws equally heavily on them in "The Leaning Tower," filling out Charles Upton's past from her own childhood experiences. She describes Charles as growing up on a small farm, dreaming of Germany as his earthly paradise. Katherine Anne Porter likewise grew up in a small farming community, and her dream of paradise was also Germany. (pp. 222-23)

Throughout ["The Leaning Tower"] the horror of the time is balanced against the earlier point of view. The standard of comparison for every detail of life in Berlin is the Texas of Charles Upton's youth, evoked both in his memories and in his speech. When he sees Hans's *Mensur* scar he muses that people in San Antonio would think he had been involved in a cutting scrape with a Mexican. He thinks that Texas is full of boys like Otto and that Hans reminds him of Kuno. In the cold winter he thinks that in Texas he has seen northern travelers turn upon the southern weather with the ferocity of exhaustion. In his speech he uses American slang, especially later in the story, as if fulfilling Tadeusz's expectations of American speech. He thinks that his dancing companion in the cabaret is a "knock out," tells her that she's a "whizz," and says, "What say we give up the technique and let nature take its course."

Thus Porter juxtaposes past memories and present impressions; the laying bare of the sources of "The Leaning Tower" is as instructive as her own explanations of the sources of "Noon Wine" and "Flowering Judas." It shows the range and variety of experiences which she telescopes together, the immense compression and care which go into her selection of details, and the sure sense of the time necessary for the ideas to mature and assume their final perspective. (pp. 224-25)

On the subject of her symbolism Porter has been reticent, perhaps almost embarrassed. Possibly her attitude is the result of having seen her symbols overexplained and even on occasion reduced to a series of geometric diagrams. She has quoted more than once, each time registering horror, Mary McCarthy's story about a student advised by her creative writing teacher to finish her story by adding some symbols. Porter has said that she never in her life consciously took or adopted a symbol. What she means is that she never imposed a symbol upon a story but rather used the symbolic implications of actual objects.

"Flowering Judas" is an example of her method, for she has said that it was only on looking back over the finished story that the whole symbolic plan became visible. She did not invent the Judas tree or write it into the story, but saw it there in the Mexican patio she was describing. As she worked on the story over a period of ten years, the biblical and literary associations of the tree came into her mind. The final version gains its texture from the associations with the story of Judas Iscariot, with *The Education of Henry Adams,* and with Eliot's *Gerontion.* The Leaning Tower of Pisa functions in a similar way.

On the simplest level the replica is a cheap tourist souvenir, as fragile and insubstantial as the dreams of paradise of all the characters, particularly of Rosa for whom it represents a brief period of honeymoon happiness. (p. 225)

The Leaning Tower of Pisa . . . has sinister overtones from its association with Canto XXXIII of *The Inferno,* where Dante meets the traitors to their own country. The central figure here is Ugolino of Pisa who conspired with an enemy party of that city in order to defeat a rival faction within his own Guelph party. His treachery merely served to weaken his own party so that he found himself at the mercy of the very enemy with whom he had conspired. Imprisoned with his children and grandchildren in a tower (not the Leaning Tower, although the story is closely connected with Pisa through Ugolino's imprecation against that city), the keys thrown away, he was forced to watch them all die of hunger before he himself starved to death. . . .

The account of the chance-gathered occupants of Rosa Reichl's pension, all wanderers or defectors from their own native lands, is full of images emanating from Ugolino's story. The claustrophobic atmosphere of the pension in which they are all shut up, waiting for disaster and with no means of escape (only for Charles Upton is a ship coming from America), is conveyed in images of imprisonment, starvation, cannibalism, death, and hell. (p. 226)

Hell is the frequent expletive on many lips, the infernal references culminating in the smoky subterranean nightclub. Charles thinks that the pension is a "hell of a place really," and thinks of himself: "Hell, maybe I'm a caricaturist." When he feels hatred for Hans he thinks, "Hell, what of it?" Tadeusz hears him and gives back the echo: "I think so too, I think, hell, what of it?"

Like Ugolino, Charles experiences a series of warnings of danger, persecution, and death. Sometimes they are actual dreams, as when the groans of Hans evoke a terrible nightmare that the house is a blazing, towering inferno. Sometimes they are mere premonitions that surface in his waking consciousness. (p. 227)

For Charles Upton, no less than for those who must remain in Germany, the problem of what action a man of vision should take is a real one. In the Walpurgisnacht scene in the nightclub he becomes fully aware of the corruption around him. He sees clearly that Hans is the real villain, full of hostility and vengeance, and he is not deceived by Hans's statement—made as he lovingly fingers his scar—that he is not bloodthirsty. As Charles watches him turning into a visibly Satanic being, he is well on the way to recognizing the monstrous evil everywhere around him. . . .

At the end of the story there is no course of action immediately clear for Charles, and Porter does not force a resolution where she does not see one. There is no sudden departure as there is at the conclusion of "Hacienda," where the first-person narrator takes flight from the deathly situation. Nor, on the other hand, is there a sense of the character's bewilderment, as there is at the end of "Old Mortality," when Miranda asks, "What is truth?" and determines naïvely to find it. What Charles achieves is clarity of vision, the ability to face up to the situation unflinchingly and not take flight in any of the ways available—drunkenness, daydreams, self-pity—or in occupations good in themselves but bad if used as refuges from reality, such as work, art, or academic studies. Perhaps this is what Porter meant when she said once that the first responsibility of the artist in time of war was not to go mad. At the end of the story Charles's lost innocence and newly gained wisdom are summed up and conveyed in his speculations on the mended tower:

> It was mended pretty obviously, it would never be the same. But for Rosa, poor old woman, he supposed it was better than nothing. It stood for something she had, or thought she had, once. Even all patched up as it was, and worthless to begin with, it meant something to her, and he was still ashamed of having broken it; it made him feel like a heel.
>
> (p. 229)

The recognition of the significance of the tower with all its literary and legendary associations is as crucial to an understanding of the meaning and the technique of the story as it is to Charles Upton. It is the center around which all the themes, moral implications, and images converge, harmonize, and arrange themselves into a coherent whole; once its position is recognized the entire pattern of the story is revealed and completed. (p. 230)

> *Joan Givner, "'Her Great Art, Her Sober Craft': Katherine Anne Porter's Creative Process," in* Southwest Review *(© 1977 by Southern Methodist University Press), Summer, 1977, pp. 217-30.*

*   *   *

POUND, Ezra   1885-1972

Pound was an American poet, translator, and critic. His political sympathies at one time threatened to diminish his reputation as one of the most innovative and creative artists of his

generation. Influencing poetry before, during, and after his career as a poet, Pound was a secretary to Yeats, playing an important part in transforming that great poet's artistic vision during his last period. He is responsible for editing *The Waste Land* into the form that won Eliot world-wide acclaim, and his tenacious support of Joyce during a period of financial distress allowed the novelist to finish *Ulysses*. His Fascist sentiments during the Second World War and his subsequent confinement, first in an Italian prison and later in an American mental institution, shattered his optimism but not his artistic gifts. He was able to emerge from his experience with his poetic gifts intact, and continued to contribute to his monumental opus, the *Cantos*. Originally a proponent of the Imagist school, with the *Cantos* Pound established himself as a unique artist. In this long poem Pound draws from the historical and artistic wealth of the ages to tell the story of an Odyssean character journeying through time. The points of reference raised in the *Cantos* are often obscure, but they reveal Pound's vast knowledge of history and culture and his determination to use the past to explicate the present. (See also *CLC*, Vols. 1, 2, 3, 4, 5, 7, and *Contemporary Authors*, Vols. 5-8, rev. ed.; obituary, Vols. 37-40.)

MARJORIE G. PERLOFF

When *A Draft of XXX Cantos* appeared in 1930, William Carlos Williams remarked with characteristic insight: "A criticism of Pound's *Cantos* could not be better concerned, I think, than in considering them in relation to the principal move in imaginative writing today—that away from the word as symbol toward the word as reality." (p. 91)

To understand Pound's gradual shift from what Williams called "the word as symbol toward the word as reality," we might profitably consider Pound's debt to the late nineteenth-century French poet who, in the words of Delmore Schwartz, "tried out the whole century in advance" —Rimbaud. (pp. 91-2)

In referring us back to his *A Study in French Poets* of 1918, Pound reminds us that his initial interest in Rimbaud coincided with the first burst of activity on the *Cantos*, which got under way, after the abortive First Draft of Cantos 1-3 in 1917, with the publication of Canto 4 in 1919, and, more significantly, with the composition of the Malatesta sequence in 1923. These dates are important: in study after study, we read that *the* nineteenth-century French poet who influenced Pound was Gautier, but we look in vain in the *Cantos* for echoes of the Parnassian mode of *Emaux et Camées*—a mode that does stand squarely behind *Hugh Selwyn Mauberley*. It is my contention that after 1920, with *Mauberley* behind him, Pound turned more and more from Gautier and "the 'sculpture' of rhyme" to Rimbaud's particular brand of Imagism as model. Rimbaud's influence on Pound has gone largely unnoticed, no doubt because Pound paid no attention to Rimbaud's major works: The *Saison en Enfer*, the *Illuminations*, or even such late great poems as "Mémoire" and "Larme." But one must remember that Pound's interest in a given poet was almost always stylistic rather than thematic. Rimbaud's feverish self-conflict, his search for identity, his ambivalence about the Church or about sexual experience—these were matters in which Pound had not the slightest interest. What he could learn from Rimbaud, however, was how an American poet of 1920, brought up on Browning and the nineties, and having worked in close conjunction first with Yeats and then with Eliot, could escape from the Symbolist impasse. (pp. 92-3)

In the essay "Vorticism," . . . Pound took great pains to distinguish his own theory of poetry from Symbolist doctrine as he understood—or misunderstood—it. "Imagisme," he declares, "is not symbolism. The symbolists dealt in 'association,' that is, in a sort of allusion, almost of allegory. They degraded the symbol to the status of a word. . . . One can be grossly 'symbolic,' for example, by using the term 'cross' to mean 'trial'." What Pound objects to, in other words, is that Symbolism is still essentially a mimetic art, the image (*a*) standing for something else (*b*) behind it, as in Baudelaire's famed "correspondances" between the natural and the spirit world. Such dualism, Pound insists, is detrimental to poetry: "to use a symbol *with an ascribed or intended meaning* is, usually, to produce very bad art." . . .

One can object, of course, that in the poetry of the great Symbolists from Nerval to Eliot, there is never such obvious one-to-one correspondence between the image and its referents. But Pound is purposely overstating the case because he wants to replace the polysemous discourse of Symbolist poetry with the language of pure presentation. "If I had the energy," he says, "to get paints and brushes and keep at it, I might found a new school of painting, of 'non-representative' painting, a painting that would speak only by arrangements in colour." . . . This statement recalls a very similar comment made by Rimbaud in 1872: "We must root out painting's old habit of copying, and we must make painting sovereign. Instead of reproducing objects, painting must compel agitation by means of lines, colors, and shapes that are drawn from the outer world but simplified and restrained: genuine magic."

By 1916, then, Pound was actively campaigning for a new non-representational art. But theory is one thing and practice another, and I cannot quite accept [Herbert N.] Schneidau's assumption that the poetry of *Cathay* (1915) and *Lustra* (1916) is post-Symbolist. Take "The Jewel Stairs' Grievance," Pound's version of a Chinese lyric by "Rihaku" (Li Po), which Schneidau cites as an example of "reticence and presentational condensation." . . .

> The jewelled steps are already quite white with dew,
> It is so late that the dew soaks my gauze stockings,
> And I let down the crystal curtain
> And watch the moon through the clear autumn. . . .

Even without Pound's prose gloss, it is evident that this is a lament for lost love, spoken by a high-born lady. The "jewelled steps" symbolize aristocratic or courtly status; the dew-soaked white gauze stockings stand for the defeat of something precious and fragile, and the letting down of the crystal curtain suggests the coming on of night and despair. Surely in this poem, Pound's images function symbolically rather than presentationally; the principle of substitution (*a* stands for *b*) still operates. (pp. 93-4)

In 1918, the *Little Review* published Pound's *Study in French Poets*, a 60-page essay which provided the Anglo-American reader with an extensive, if rather biased, anthology of modern French poetry, interspersed with Pound's critical commentary. The *Study* contains a large selection from the poetry of Corbière, Laforgue, and Rimbaud, followed by shorter samples of twelve less well-known later poets such as François Jammes and Jules Romains. In his brief introduction, Pound says: "I do not aim at 'completeness.' I believe that the American-English reader has heard in a general way of Baudelaire and Verlaine and Mallarmé; that Mallarmé, perhaps unread, is apt to be slightly overestimated."

This remark provides us with an important clue to Pound's thinking. We must remember that for most Anglo-American poets from Arthur Symons to Wallace Stevens, Baudelaire, Verlaine, and Mallarmé constituted a kind of Holy Trinity, although individual predilections naturally varied. . . . If Pound had no use for these poets, it is surely because he dismissed their work as "Symbolist" without distinguishing between such minor neo-Symbolists as Fargue and Larbaud on the one hand, and a great creator of "clear visual images" like Baudelaire on the other. But dispassionate, objective judgment was never characteristic of Pound; he dismissed the Symbolists outright simply because he was looking for models who could teach him the rudiments of a non-representational art. "After Gautier," he thus announces airily, "France produced, as nearly as I understand, three chief and admirable poets: Tristan Corbière, perhaps the most poignant writer since Villon; Rimbaud, a vivid and indisputable genius; and Laforgue—a slighter, but in some ways a finer 'artist' than either of the others. I do not meant that he 'writes better' than Rimbaud. . . . Laforgue always knows what he is at; Rimbaud, the 'genius' in the narrowest and deepest sense of the term, the 'most modern,' seems, almost without knowing it, to hit on the various ways in which the best writers were to follow him, slowly." . . . (pp. 96-7)

[Pound] discovered in Rimbaud the qualities he most esteemed in poetry: directness of presentation, the image as the "poet's pigment," ideogrammic terseness, and the avoidance of adjectives and other "non-functioning words" in favor of straightforward subject-verb-object syntactic patterns. (p. 99)

Mauberley has a problematic place in the Pound canon. Throughout the twenties and early thirties, it was hailed as Pound's one indisputable masterpiece; thus Eliot declared in 1928: "I am quite certain of *Mauberley,* whatever else I am certain of. . . . This seems to me a great poem . . . a document of an epoch; it is . . . in the best sense of Arnold's worn phrase, a 'criticism of life.'" . . .

In recent years, as the greatness of the *Cantos* has come to be increasingly recognized, the pendulum has swung. It is now fashionable to argue that *Mauberley,* far from being unlike the *Cantos,* is to be seen as an early sketch for them, a slighter work containing in embryo many of Pound's later themes and techniques. (p. 100)

This is true enough with respect to what *Mauberley says.* But if we look at the way the poem *works,* a rather different picture emerges. Take, for example, III (Part I), which contains Pound's scathing attack on the bad taste of the modern age, whether in art, religion, or politics. It begins:

> The tea-rose tea-gown, etc.
> Supplants the mousseline of Cos,
> The pianola "replaces"
> Sappho's barbitos.
>
> Christ follows Dionysus
> Phallic and ambrosial
> Made way for macerations;
> Caliban casts out Ariel.

"To use a symbol *with an ascribed or intended meaning,*"

Pound had said in *Gaudier-Brzeska,* "is, usually, to produce very bad art." . . . Yet I count eight such symbols in these eight lines. Briefly, the "tea-rose tea-gown" symbolizes the vulgarity of modern dress in contrast to the delicate and beautiful "mousseline of Cos"—the Propertian tunic of Coan silk. The pianola, which reduces music to a punched sheet of paper to be played mechanically, is contrasted to Sappho's barbitos, that is, to the original lyre of poetry, which symbolizes, as Witemeyer puts it, "the ideal relationship between the musician and his music" as well as "the ideal relationship between music and poetry." . . . In the second stanza, Dionysus symbolizes the "Phallic and ambrosial" rites of pagan fertility, which have unfortunately been replaced by the "macerations" typical of Christianity. Ariel, the symbol of all that is delicate, airy, light, poetic, and spiritual, is cast out by Caliban, the symbol of earth, mindlessness, joylessness—the anti-poetic.

These rather facile contrasts between an idealized past and a vulgarized present continue throughout the poem as Pound produces symbol after symbol "with an ascribed or intended meaning." . . . One feels that Pound begins with an idea, not with an image, and then sets about to find an objective correlative for that idea. Caliban vs. Ariel, pianola vs. Sappho's barbitos—all these items could be replaced by others without a real change in poetic effect. Moreover, despite is allusiveness and ellipses, the poem moves sequentially and logically from *a* to *b*; it is not a collage of "super-pository" images or a "VORTEX, from which, and through which, and into which, ideas are constantly rushing."

The continuing controversy over the status of Mauberley (is he Pound? a persona who represents the failed aesthete? or sometimes Pound and sometimes this persona?) has obscured what seems to me much more important: that Pound was never quite at ease with the poetic materials of *Mauberley,* that he was trying too hard to write like Eliot. . . . No wonder Eliot preferred *Mauberley* to all of Pound's other poems, for *Mauberley* is the one poem of Pound's that Eliot might have written himself. It represents the height of the Laforgue and Gautier influence, filtered down via Eliot's "Prufrock," "Portrait of a Lady," and the 1920 quatrain poems. But whereas Eliot's symbols have great richness, suggesting a broad range of meanings, Pound's symbolic mode tends toward one-to-one correspondence, annoying in its schematic neatness. "Half-hose" (modern vulgarity) versus "Pierian roses" (classical splendor)—it all seems too easy.

The lessons of Rimbaud—or, for that matter, those of Fenollosa, Ford, and Flaubert—had not, then, been mastered by 1920. Practice had not yet caught up with the theory that the "proper and perfect symbol is the natural object." . . . We can see Pound's dilemma in the early Cantos, which contrary to general opinion, do not yet use the presentational method. I have already spoken of the conventional symbolism of Ur-Canto 1, but Canto 4, first published in 1919 in what was substantially its final version, illustrates the same points. Here is the opening:

> Palace in smoky light,
> Troy but a heap of smouldering boundary stones,
> ANAXIFORMINGES! Aurunculeia!
> Hear me. Cadmus of Golden Prows!

(pp. 102-03)

The opening of Canto 4 is often used as an example of Pound's superpository technique, his elliptical juxtapositions of words and phrases with no seeming logical connection or explanation, producing the effect of collage, of what Hugh Kenner has called "cultural overlayering." But despite the concentration and condensation of Pound's lines, one should note that he is still organizing his images according to Symbolist principles: the fall of Troy and allusion to Pindar make up one symbolic cluster which is then juxtaposed to a second one: "Aurunculeia" and "Cadmus of Golden Prows." Destruction is countered by rebirth. (p. 103)

From the opening motif of burning Troy to the dawn lyric about "choros nympharum," to the reference of light raining down "beneath the knees of the gods," the Canto's images function symbolically rather than presentationally. The description of the wedding torches as "blue agate casing the sky," for example, is hardly a case of what Pound called "constatation of fact"; in the context, the torches are clearly symbols of procreation just as the pines at Takasago traditionally connote long life and conjugal loyalty.

In short, Pound had not yet hit upon the presentational method. (pp. 104-05)

Canto 9—the future Canto 8—was a Malatesta Canto. Pound refers to it in a letter to his mother on August 20, 1922, and the four Malatesta Cantos were finished by the summer of 1923 and published in the July *Criterion*. Significantly, Pound's revisions of these Cantos for the 1925 book publication were minor, generally restricted to changes in lineation and occasional phrasing. "What is more important," says Slatin, "the design of the poem suddenly crystallized, perhaps partly as a result of the long and intensive labor which went into the Malatesta group. Within a month or perhaps two months of the publication of these Cantos, Pound had entirely revised the beginning of the poem and had come to the end of the composition of the first sixteen Cantos." (p. 105)

What caused this dramatic shift in Pound's style? We cannot attribute it wholly to the influence of Ford or Fenollosa, for Pound had been an ardent disciple of both for at least a decade, and yet, as we have seen, he continued to write, against his better judgment, a poetry of diluted Symbolism. The example of *Ulysses* is often cited, yet nothing could be less like Joyce's scholastically organized novel, that "Aquinas-map" in which each episode has its own Homeric analogue, symbol, technique, organ, color, and so on, than the *Cantos*, with their "constatation of fact," their cuts, their paratactic structure and autobiographical intrusions. *The Waste Land*, whose final form was, after all, largely determined by Pound's excisions and revisions, is a more plausible model, but Eliot's complex orchestration of water and fire symbols, of Hyacinth Garden and Unreal City, Game of Chess and empty Grail Chapel, is quite unlike the documentary, presentational mode of the Malatesta Cantos.

In 1923, just a few months before these Cantos appeared in the *Criterion*, Pound brought out, in the same journal, an article called "On Criticism in General." This was a rough sketch for the later essay "How to Read," in which Pound praised Rimbaud's "clean" images and phanopoeic "directness of presentation." Perhaps Rimbaud's example was one factor leading to the new mode of the Malatesta sequence. (pp. 105-06)

Much has been written on the background and themes of the Malatesta Cantos, and I don't wish here to go over familiar ground. (p. 106)

The portrait of Malatesta that emerges from these Cantos is ... hardly novel; it takes us back to Burckhardt's understanding of the Italian Renaissance as a time of incredible tension between sexual brutality and courtly love, physical violence and artistic delicacy. To paraphrase Samuel Johnson, "if you were to read the Malatesta Cantos for their thematic interest, your patience would be so much fretted that you would hang yourself." And this is precisely how some readers have responded. "'Reading,'" says Donald Davie, "is an unsatisfactory word for what the eye does as it resentfully labors over and among these blocks of dusty historical debris."

Yet on closer inspection, Pound's manipulation of these "blocks of dusty historical debris" exerts a peculiar fascination. It is not just a matter of "cultural overlayering" or of juxtaposing love letters to battle scenes and to lists of building materials. I would posit that Pound's basic strategy here—a strategy quite different from that of Canto 4 where thematically related myths are telescoped and aligned paratactically—is to create a flat surface, like that of a late Cezanne or Cubist painting, devoid of aerial perspective—a surface of linguistic distortions and contradictions that force the reader to participate in the poem's action. Just as Rimbaud invents cityscapes in which Swiss chalets on magic pulleys dissolve into Vesuvian craters and then into gorges spanned by little footbridges, so Pound dislocates language so as to create new landscapes.

The 1923 version of Canto 8 opens as follows:

> *Frater tamquam et compater carissime*
>   *(tergo*
>   . . hanni de
>   . . dicis
>   . . entia
> Equivalent to: Giohanni of the Medici, Florence)
> Letter received, and in the matter of our Messire
>   Gianozio
> One from him also, sent on in form and with all due
>   dispatch,
> Having added your wishes and memoranda.

Unlike the opening of Canto 4, with its juxtaposition of "ANAXIFORMINGES" and "Aurunculeia," this passage is not polysemous as D. S. Carne-Ross, in a general discussion of the *Cantos*, puts it, "the whole reverberating dimension of inwardness is missing. There is no murmuring echo chamber where deeps supposedly answer to deeps." But neither is the passage a rag-bag of dusty historical debris. Its strategy is best understood if we compare it to its source: a 1449 letter from Sigismundo to Giovanni di Medici. (pp. 106-07)

The lines, in short, do not convey information; rather, they take certain facts and present them from different linguistic perspectives (formal, florid Italian; broken Italian words; English translation) as if to undercut their historicity. Fact, in other words, is repeatedly transformed into fiction. Thus in the body of the letter, Pound takes Sigismundo's perfectly straightforward "Ho ricevuto vostra lettera" ("I have received your letter") and turns it into business English—"Letter received"—while the phrase "li preghi et recordi vestri" ("your best wishes and remembrances") becomes, by an absurd sleight-of-hand, "your wishes and memoranda," as if Rimini were dissolving into Wall Street.

Such linguistic indeterminacy is one of the central devices of these Cantos. Pound uses a variety of techniques to command our attention. Perhaps the simplest is condensation and modernization. In Canto 8, for example, Sigismundo's letter to Giovanni di Medici regarding his renewed alliance with Venice is a seven-line condensation of the original eighteen lines of prose, in which Sigismundo gives a formal explanation of the precise terms the Venetians have offered him, his military troubles caused by renewed flooding, and so on. (pp. 107-08)

Such updating of history would not in itself make the Malatesta Cantos unique; it is a device many poets have used. But Pound's forte is to take a passage like the one just cited and then suddenly to switch back to the voice of the Renaissance chronicler. . . . (p. 108)

Another common strategy is to set the original Italian side by side with a correct English translation so as to intensify and reinforce a central image; thus "*non gli manchera la provixione mai*" is followed by "never lacking provision," and the line "With his horsemen and his footmen" precedes "*gente di cavallo e da pie*." Or again, Pound may translate a given letter or document written in highly formal Italian so literally that it sounds like a parody in English. The best example of such satiric super-literalism is the letter of Sigismundo's five-year-old son, which Pound translates in Canto 9 with tongue-in-cheek pedantic fidelity:

> Magnificent and Exalted Lord and Father in especial my lord with due recommendation: your letter has been presented to me by Gentilino da Gradara and with it the bay pony (ronzino baiectino) the which you have sent me, and which appears in my eyes a fine caparison'd charger, upon which I intend to learn all there is to know about riding, in consideration of yr. paternal affection for which I thank your excellency thus briefly and pray you continue to hold me in this esteem. . . .

In English the endless "the which," "upon which," and "for which" clauses, the consistent circumlocution, and the involuted address sound wholly absurd, especially since the subject of the letter is no more than the gift of a bay pony. Translated thus literally, the letter has neither the status of fifteenth-century document nor twentieth-century adaptation; it remains a curiosity, removed from a specific time-space context. The introduction of the Italian phrase "ronzino baiectino" is particularly skillful: "ronzino baiectino" does mean "bay pony," but in the context it sounds more like a zoological specimen or a rare disease.

The Malatesta Cantos "cut" back and forth between such literal translation on the one hand and intentional mistranslation on the other. (pp. 108-09)

Closely related to such artful mistranslation is the purposely incorrect rendering of the Italian itself. (p. 109)

The Malatesta Cantos do not, then, recreate history; they decompose and fragment historical time so as to create a new landscape without depth, what Jean-Pierre Richard calls, with reference to Rimbaud, an "anti-paysage." . . .

The mode of the Malatesta Cantos is thus quite unlike that of *Mauberley* with its symbolic allusions to the "mousseline of Cos" and "Pierian roses." Pound is moving from a poetry of product to one of process, from an aesthetic of contemplation to one of participation. One could, for instance, study the shifting pronouns in these Cantos as one form of radical disjunction. Thus in Canto 9, Pound begins as chronicler ("One year floods rose . . . ") but suddenly switches in line 28 to the first-person plural—"And old Sforza bitched us at Pesaro"—adopting for the moment Sigismundo's own point of view." (p. 111)

The perspective is thus constantly shifting as in a cubist painting. One can see events, people, and things from many sides, simultaneously. Pound's definition of a VORTEX as "a radiant node or cluster . . . from which, and through which, and into which, ideas are constantly rushing" . . . is entirely applicable to the technique of the Malatesta Cantos. The poet is everywhere present, placing and displacing his figures upon a shallow screen; the reader enters that screen, constantly brought up short by shifts in language, levels of style, linguistic deformation, and so on. Pound discards tropes of similarity like metaphor and symbol for those of contiguity—individual images are related metonymically as parts of a mosaic that must be reassembled with the reader's help.

Pound's later Cantos do not consistently follow the pattern I have been describing with respect to the Malatesta sequence. Indeed, no poem the size of the *Cantos* can be entirely consistent. . . . I would like to suggest that the Pisan sequence (72-84), generally held to contain some of Pound's finest poetry, carries on the mode of the Malatesta Cantos and, indeed, brings that mode to its logical conclusion. Sharply-etched literal images composing flat surfaces, multi-linguistic perspective, syntactic and verbal dislocation —all these features recur in the Pisan Cantos, but now the fragmentation described earlier becomes more and more extreme; the basic unit is no longer the verse paragraph or group of lines as in Canto 9, but often the individual line, word group, or even the single ideogram.

I would not want to press the similarity between the *Cantos* and the poetry of Rimbaud. The differences between the two are all too obvious. Where Rimbaud is dreamlike, hallucinatory, incantatory, visionary, Pound is matter-of-fact, literal, documentary, down-to-earth. Nevertheless, I would argue that the *Cantos* are much closer to Rimbaud's poetry (especially to the *Saison* and the *Illuminations* which Pound pretended to ignore) than they are to, say, the *Odyssey* or the *Divina Commedia*. I realize that what I am saying is tantamount to heresy, that Pound's debt to Homer and Dante is accepted as a historical fact. But however much Pound may have thought he was influenced by Homer and Dante, his structures of decomposition and fragmentation have, formally speaking, almost nothing to do with the architectural design of the *Odyssey* or the "Aquinas-map" of the *Commedia*. Structurally, the Malatesta or Pisan Cantos may be said to fulfill Pound's aim: to forge a conscious aesthetic out of Rimbaud's random intuitions. (pp. 111-12)

Marjorie G. Perloff, in The Iowa Review *(copyright © 1975, by The University of Iowa), Vol. 6, No. 1 (Winter, 1975).*

IAN F. A. BELL

[We] need to know about the curious vocabulary used in the "Mauberley 1920" half of [*Hugh Selwyn Mauberley*] and, crucially, the problem of Mauberley's temperament remains an urgent issue in the reading experience. Professor [John J.] Espey established the formula [in his *Ezra Pound's 'Mauberley'; a Study in Composition*] for that temperament which, in one way or another, has characterised all subsequent commentaries:"... the relation is, I think, clear enough: the passive aesthete played off against the active instigator".

Such a formula seriously distorts the operation of the poem. One cannot deny that Mauberley *is* a minor artist, that it is right to see him quite firmly as a composite figure partaking of the whole range of aesthetic activities of a secondary nature prevalent during a particular period in English literary history. But is seems to me that the point of the poem is not simply to construct a debate about various kinds of creative behaviour: we can leave that within the sphere of "Imaginary Conversations". To play off one kind of imagination against another is not only too easy but to evade what was, for Pound, the actual situation of the artist, a situation to which he consistently responded in crisis terms. To recognise this situation, we have to get away from the idea of Mauberley as a passive "toy of circumstance", as the delicate diluter of what is potentially an aesthetic programme of some strength. He has to be seen as a more positive force who is painfully aware of his own crisis.

Part of the problem here is that what we actually have in the poem itself is only the end of Mauberley's life, his drifting, chaotic demise, and 'crisis' is perhaps the last epithet we would want to apply to such a life. There are, however, pointers which do suggest that 'crisis' may be meaningfully employed. I propose to focus my remarks on the first major term in the piece which defines Mauberley's situation—the word "phantasmagoria" in the second poem of the "Mauberley 1920" sequence:

> "He had moved amid her phantasmagoria.
> Amid her galaxies."

The word demands attention partly because of its unusualness; if we are already familiar with it before encountering Pound's usage, it is probably in the gothic context of the ghosts and ghouls of an insubstantial spirit world. But it has also a technical meaning and so takes its place in the general order of the highly problematic system of vocabulary that characterises the second half of *Hugh Selwyn Mauberley* as a whole. (pp. 361-62)

The technical meaning of the word allows us, in part, to relate it to the debate concerning the visual arts which predominates over much of the poem. It was first introduced into the English language by a Frenchman, Philipstal, to define an exhibition of optical illusions produced by means of a 'magic lantern' at the London Lyceum in 1802. (p. 362)

'Phantasmagoria' rapidly became associated with images of horror and the grotesque through contemporary usage shortly after the Lyceum exhibition. (p. 363)

[It is] the idea of time that is so destructive for Mauberley. His world is essentially that in which time becomes virtually suspended with all its attendant uncertainty and ultimate impotence. He is poised at the frozen moment of metamorphosis, like the "still stone dogs" that are fittingly "left him as epilogues"; the miracle of creative transforma-

tion is trapped at that high-point of stasis when the possibility of new form becomes manifest, but for Mauberley remains only a *possibility*. (p. 364)

The most obvious point about metamorphosis is that it demands a recognition of time as process; Pound notes in his 1917 essay on Arnold Dolmetsch: "The undeniable tradition of metamorphosis teaches us that things do not remain always the same. They become other things by swift and unanalysable process". (Early in *High Selwyn Mauberley* we are told ironically, "All things are a flowing, / Sage Heraclitus says;") Faced with "unanalysable process", Mauberley reaches the peak of his crisis and is at his most impotent, continually seeking that moment of stasis over which he has a measure of control. It is time above all else, in the sense of process and in the sense of the 'Age's Demands', that dominates Mauberley's final efforts at organisation. The auditory insistence of the polysyllabic line-endings in the second and third poems of the "Mauberley 1920" sequence return us to the effect imposed by the monosyllabic repetition of "time" in "Prufrock" where the central figure is similarly engaged by the problem of temporal succession. Prufrock finds a certain comfort in the deterministic properties of time, the way in which it helps to organise his social role (cf. the "public clocks" in "Portrait of a Lady"), and although he lacks Mauberley's sense of the pressure that time can bring to bear, he is aware of the interminable stretch of time that can fill a single minute during periods of crisis. The endings of both poems rely on literary images of the sea; the private imaginative worlds of Prufrock and Mauberley drown with a recognition of their social and artistic status. But the major point of comparison to be made between the poems occurs at that moment towards the end of "Prufrock" where the protagonist begins to look back on his experience and to attempt to rationalise his failure: "And would it have been worth it, after all," etc. The attempt is followed by his acute fear of exposure which is offered through a technical image of the phantasmagoria: "But as if a magic lantern threw the nerves in patterns on a / screen". (pp. 364-65)

The connection between 'phantasmagoria' and a private imaginative world enduring a phase of crisis in "Prufrock" suggests that larger implications are involved in the word's usage. The occurrence of the word after the initial excitement of its introduction into the language seems to me significantly to inform its appearance as a defining term for Mauberley.

Parallel to its atmospheric connotations for nightmare, 'phantasmagoria' retains its technical reference throughout the nineteenth century as a device for visual description. (p. 365)

The technical reference of the word . . . invariably informs its usage. The main point about this usage, in major texts of the nineteenth and early twentieth centuries, is that it provides a specific tradition for a private imaginative world of a particular kind: it occurs as a defining term for the crisis-point of the interaction between the private imagination and a public actuality. (p. 366)

The traditional usage of "phantasmagoria" associates the word and its field of reference with crises of inter-action between private imaginative worlds and the public phenomena that are inevitably at odds against such worlds. Within *Hugh Selwyn Mauberley* itself, "phantasmagoria" isn't left to stand on its own. It is not only part of the technical vocabulary whereby Mauberley attempts to organise experience through syntax; the sound of the word is picked up in Mauberley's delight with "the imaginary / Audition of the phantasmal sea surge" in the third poem of the "Mauberley 1920" part of the sequence.

Both Professor Espey and Professor Witemeyer have noted the Homeric source for these lines. . . . The Homeric source is the *Iliad,* I, 34; Chryses, priest of Apollo, begs Agamemnon to return his daughter to him, but Agamemnon refuses him rudely and sends him away: "Forth he went in silence along the shore of the loud-resounding sea". The word "polouphloisboio" is onomatopoeic, meaning literally 'any confused roaring noise'; in the *Odyssey* it is used to describe the sound of battle. It carries, therefore, a considerable weight of activity; Pound's version of it in *Mauberley,* "phantasmal", thus seems deliberately impoverished, suggesting merely the trap of auditory illusion, counterpointing the Sirens' song, "Caught in the unstopped ear", which traps E.P. in the opening "Ode Pour L'Election de son Sepulchre". But despite its apparent impoverishment, the word still carries echoes of its original source, and the point is that "phantasmal" in *Mauberley* isn't allowed to carry the ironic connotations of "polouphloisboious" in [Pound's] "Moeurs Contemporaines".

We need to go further by looking at Pound's customary use of "polouphloisboious" in his prose such as it occurs in an article which appeared three months after the first publication of "Moeurs Contemporaines." . . . Pound bemoans the problems that literary journalism, forced on him for financial reasons, were imposing on his poetry: " . . . I can not write six sorts of journalism four days a week, edit the *Little Review* three days a week, and continue my career as an author". . . . He continues:

> There are plenty of voices ready with the quite obvious reply that: nobody wants me to continue my hideous career as either author, editor, or journalist. I can, in imagination, hear the polouphloisboious twitter of rural requests for my silence and extinction. . . .

His use of the word is self-explanatory. Significantly, following directly on from this diatribe is Pound's reprinting of the Preface to *Germinie Lacerteaux* where he wearily proclaims: "I am tired of rewriting the arguments for the realist novel . . . The Brothers de Goncourt said the thing once and for all . . .". . . . Pound is continuing the battle he began in "The Serious Artist" of 1913. . . . Pound's use of the word is one of the more deliberate gestures of modernism against the contemporary situation during the second decade of the twentieth century. (pp. 378-80)

So, in *Mauberley,* we have "phantasmal" as a version of "polouphloisboio" partly to pick up an echo from "phantasmagoria" and partly, avowedly, to avoid the Marsden Hartley citronic horror at this order of language. But the latter effort stands as a rather sophisticated Poundian joke; the "neurasthenic" effect that Hartley had found painful in "the Pound-Eliot phraseology" is precisely that of the polysyllabic rhymes in the third poem of the "Mauberley 1920" sequence: "graduations", "exacerbations", "examination", "elimination", "consternation". One of the crucial words used to describe Mauberley's creativity in the preceding poem is "anaesthesis" which internally rhymes with "diastasis"; we now enter a different, although related order of terminology, that of biological science. Mauberley's evaluative lexicology is a gesture of protection against experience which, whilst attempting to organise experience syntactically, assumes the authority and sanction of scientific method. (pp. 380-81)

I have drawn attention to "phantasmagoria" in order to suggest how the fuller resonance of the word may be incorporated into an effort to re-align some of the assumptions that commentators have made in reading the poem. The effort is to see Mauberley as a more active figure whose "life and contacts" are the result of the kinds of crises with which the word has been traditionally associated. The technical meaning of "phantasmagoria" survives to perpetuate an active visualisation rather than a neo-impressionist receptivity of images. My attempt is part of a larger programme to restore to *Hugh Selwyn Mauberley* dramatic qualities which part of the critical discussion of the poem, in trying to locate specific sources as means of illuminating, and ultimately 'solving' the poem's problems, implicitly denies. Those problems, of voice, of the ambiguous presence of the figures informing the battles that *Mauberley* dramatises, are not there to be solved but to be recognised as setting up a series of tensions through which the poem operates and achieves its effectiveness as a portrait of a difficult literary situation. (p. 385)

> *Ian F. A. Bell, "The Phantasmagoria of 'Hugh Selwyn Mauberley'," in* Paideuma *(international copyright © 1976 by the National Poetry Foundation, Inc.), Winter, 1976, pp. 361-85.*

THEODORE WEISS

The two last poems of *Ripostes,* "The Return" and "The Alchemist," facing each other, offer a chance to watch Pound's genius quarrying out its resources. Both poems triumph in the skill with which they conjure up their particular moment: the return of the gods and the transformation of inferior—though lovely, alive—metals into gold. Both poems are miracles of equipoise. In "The Return" we must recognize the provisional, brilliant peace Pound has achieved between stone and wave. For the poem in its near Sapphic stanzas has a carved feeling indeed: cut out of a giant rock, broken off from a once mighty temple, vibrant as Valéry's notion of the dance. As with such great sculpture the poem is made wholly of movement: tentative waves, then swiftly hurtling breakers. In short, one element is composed of the other, rises out of the other: a permanent beauty out of the sea and the sea, its incessant flux, caught forever in that beauty. A frieze of a poem, it slowly thaws out and becomes frieze the more. It begins with a slow, accumulated series of waverings expressed in three-syllabled, hovering words: tentative, uncertain, wavering, half-awakened ("as half-" is echoed by the next lines "As if"), hesitant. In tune with this wavering, snow, a superb "natural" image of hesitant, late winter movement, hangs in air, murmurs, and half turns back. Then as the poem remembers what once these beings were, the mere thought of them discovers enough energy in itself to give us a moment of their powerful, ecstatic presence, not murmuring now but crying "Haie!" as they rush on "wingèd shoe" with swift hounds, sniffing not winter but blood. Then promptly, the past tense overtaking them, they dwindle again, from keen, swift "souls of blood" to leash-slow, "pallid" ghosts. Or no more than a frieze.

"The Alchemist," on the other hand, suggests a magnificent simultaneous expression of the love act, the moment of creation in the making of a poem, and actual alchemy, all done, since varyingly forbidden, at night. Beautiful mellifluous names of beautiful women, mythical as semi-goddesses and real, compose the chant, are the ritual words in a veritable catalogue of fair women. The attendant handmaids of beauty, each supplies, in her moving and her singing some basic ingredient or part . . . , almost metal already, yet alive (and perhaps already at their liveliest). . . . And in the bringing, the women and their gifts not only begin the transformation but perform it until "the golden artifice of eternity" is completed as they quiet the metal. Rarely has a more sumptuous, formal, yet performing poem been composed, hard lines of verse, welded, not fused. The ingredients are properly brought at night when they are free from the office of light which imposes rigid shapes and duties on them, free in alchemy's alembic or the fragrant darkness of the imagination. One recalls one of Pound's most radiant lines, "In the gloom the gold gathers the light against it." Then the mind can enjoy the quiddity of things.

Here Valéry's contention comes to mind that genuine poetry contains no inert matter, that, on the contrary, it all metamorphoses into vibrant form. On the side of the world, not of "shadows" and "dreams," but of the "shapes of power" and "men," Pound was resolutely anti-symbolist, with imagism a direct rejoinder to it. For this insistence as for other attitudes Pound again and again has been accused of being unoriginal, lacking a matter of his own; at best merely a translator. Perhaps simply another roundabout way of saying he was too bookish, with no fund of life to draw on. Pound would have scoffed at this separation of life and literature; for life was—and is—often at its best in some great ancient text. Nobody would deny that Pound believed and lived in literature as much as in anything else, was often at his liveliest in and through it, that he made past literature one of the most impressive vehicles of reality. (pp. 104-05)

Plainly developing out of and seeking to absorb the materials, external and internal, of his life, in a most complicated way [*The Cantos*] resemble, among other things, the journal, that most popular American "form," which sanctions one's right to a world of process and action. This mode's excitements and shortcomings for the kind of art Pound desired to produce should be clear. He could introduce anything and everything (part of his wish to reclaim for poetry domains appropriated by the novel), everything that happened to him or at least seemed important, no matter how outwardly trivial: an accidental encounter, a remark overheard, a quotation from a letter, a scrap of altogether local history involving private individuals, yet all providing evidence as Pound "read" them. This solipsism was for the material, not for Pound. Like the disparate poems of *Leaves of Grass, The Cantos* are kept together on the breath and by the skin of the poet.

Unfortunately now and then the form that resulted, rather than absorbing and using its materials, did appear "all surface and articulation"—the material too abruptly surfaced out of the general hurlyburly. Or it became a huge valise, jam-packed to bursting with all the valuables and not so valuables a traveler in a headlong rush might throw to-gether. Accordingly, artistry notwithstanding, Pound's words on Williams' work may prove most relevant to *The Cantos*:

> Art very possibly *ought* to be the supreme
> achievement, the 'accomplished'; but there
> is the other satisfactory effect, that of a man
> hurling himself at an indomitable chaos, etc.
>
> (pp. 112-13)

The Cantos may be fairly judged a mixture of both satisfactory effects. A poem that will not settle down, it changes in the varying light of the reader's awareness (this, of course, is true of most good poems, but nothing like *The Cantos*). Protean like Pound himself, it will not submit to total academicizing, no matter how many literary archeologists may be diligently digging away. The crucial troubles Pound heroically weltered in, magnificently or frantically, are in the poem and in our readings of it; thus it stays obstinately, thrashingly alive. (p. 113)

As the cantos came along, in operatic fashion they gathered up many leitmotifs. And with greater and greater frequency they play upon, glance off each other (or what he wished to restore: "the radiant world where one thought cuts through another with clean edge, a world of moving energies," one bird's flight cleaving in swift, sure shadow the flight of another) till, for the brevity and speed and frequency, one must read ever more slowly to supply room and time for recollection's resonance and for the turning up, in endlessly new combinations, of new gleaming facets. The cantos are often relentless in their saltancy, a seven hundred league leaping, far surpassing Yeats' or Eliot's, say, sometimes between sections of cantos, sometimes between two cantos, and sometimes even inside one canto. Some of these hurdlings it is hard not to regard as capricious, if not adventitious. The difficulties are obvious. In music we need not identify the leitmotifs (though identifying does intensify our pleasure); the music, an interwoven pattern moving along via its players and singers, plays on us. But in language, even poetic language charged with great energy, the analogy with music must break down. The vexing matter of meaning, of active understanding on the reader's part, unavoidably dogs us. How long can we hold our intellectual breath, submit to the battering waves lunged over our heads, or treat *The Cantos*, large sections of it, as an intriguing, wonderful-sounding foreign language?

Pound's was an incredible attempt to turn imagism, the epigram, and the ideogram, which by their very nature are meant for short, explosive flights, into a long epical poem. Consequently, more and more lamination ensued, images heaped on and twisted with images: a vastly intricate mosaic that does not too often compose one image or poem. At times, overseen from the distance—as from a plane—of rapid reading, details blend like tiny myriad flowers into one huge, golden-blazing field in the manner, say, of impressionist painting. At times. Elsewhere these leitmotifs become, no doubt for economy and drama, shorter and shorter phrases, sometimes a single word substituting for the whole text: a shorthand, a kind of code. Or allusions not altogether unlike those of Pound's chief *bête noire*, Milton. But Milton's allusions, in part because his audience was more homogeneous, were usually shared, not private or dependent exclusively on previous first mention, sometimes hundreds of pages earlier. Whatever pleasure Pound's method of composing may give initiates, elated with their sudden discoveries, it does seem to exact excessive labor from even the interested, intelligent, but non-professional reader. Yet, after the mine-fields of hieratic works like *Finnegans Wake,* how dare we complain? (pp. 114-15)

Like many others, until fairly recently I used to read in *The Cantos* for their lyrical moments, their sudden waterspouting into imagistic loveliness. Impatiently I leaped over much of the rest as undigested lumps, a flagging of Pound's creative powers, overridden by his other interests. But I have come to realize the importance of that rest to Pound—and to the poem. Like ideograms and other unique bits of foreign languages studding *The Cantos,* documents, passages of books, and chinoiserie become precious, sacred texts as Pound judged them the truth (therefore beauty). He must have been sorely tempted at times to reprint these texts *in toto* in *The Cantos,* claiming that the lyric moments would not have flowered without such soil. Endeavoring to remove the gap between content and form, fact and beauty, life and art, he kept insisting on their oneness. (p. 116)

Let us accept for a moment [his] challengeable assumption that [historically significant] letters are literature; but what of the many lesser documents, drossy history books, dreary pamphlets Pound felt called on to stuff *The Cantos* with? We have been taught in our time, happily at its best, to see everything as potentially poetic: either the gods live everywhere, live with and in everything or they do not live at all. But surely the word "potentially" means something. Unless that everything undergoes the sea-change Eliot expected how does it indeed become poetry? Or for that matter, if the text is already literature, who needs the poet?— What is his use? A mere collector? Unlike the collages of a Picasso and a Braque, say, with their browning newspaper scraps, Pound's inserts are often long and meant to be read, pondered, digested. How many of us bother or are expected to read the Picasso newsprint, despite his puns and jokes in choosing it? The newspaper's "reality" quickly becomes absorbed into the painting's ensemble, an additional, collaborative texture and color and—whatever pleasure of tension we may care to find in it, even in its origins— not an obtrusive hunk of "life." However much his inserts may now and then serve Pound by his skill, his passion, the pressures of the context, this "method" rarely works for others. Rather it has helped to prompt a spate of poems, mere notations and descriptions, astonishing in their casualness, their patent triviality. And "poetry concrete" notwithstanding, whatever love one may have for books, the letters on the page are not normally ideogrammic, not calligraphy in themselves. However strongly Pound may have wished for active picture-writing, the importance of print still principally resides, not in its physical look, but in its sound and sense.

The remarking of these difficulties and contradictions is not meant to demean Pound and his spending himself with a prodigality possible to very few of us. Instead it intends to underscore the richness, often bewildering, of the mixture and of his gifts, and the intelligence and enormous good will *The Cantos* requires to be dealt with sanely, judiciously, honestly. But the difficulties do reflect the dilemma of trying to arrive at a settled view of Pound and his work, a dilemma he shared. We may dismiss his last verdict on himself and his work as that of a disappointed, exhausted old man, readying for death, so naturally turning on his

past. Or the frustration, the sense of failure bound to descend on most of us, if we are haunted by perfection or at least by what we have yearned to accomplish. But we cannot wholly ignore his awareness of his mistake in assuming he was a Fortinbras, say, sent to set all right or, perhaps more accurately, Hamlet's father, from the start directing the play from the wings, when all the time he was—great wit, art, energy, grace, and all—much more Hamlet, much less certain or in charge of reality, than he knew. Also, perhaps, he saw at last the inadequacies of his tycoon-like puritanism: his relentless, if not rigid and monomaniacal seriousness; of his sense too not only of an ordered universe with a well-defined hierarchy, but of his belief in his mastery of that order.

Yet caught in *The Cantos,* like iridescent insects and monarch butterflies, shimmeringly, lovingly alive, stirred by our fascinated, ignited, and igniting breath, glimpses of the terrestrial paradise—its sunsets, its lightning-bright dawns— flare forth. Even to *The Cantos'* end, for Pound—like Homer's cicada old men, the Homeric loud in their dry rustling still, startled by the loveliness of Helen—the beauty of the seasons, of day and night, of change prevails. (pp. 116-18)

Theodore Weiss, "E.P.: The Man Who Cared Too Much," in Parnassus: Poetry in Review *(copyright © by Poetry in Review Foundation), Fall-Winter, 1976, pp. 79-119.*

DONALD E. STANFORD

As we read through the original verse of Ezra Pound (as distinct from his "translations") from the beginning of his career until the end, that is, from *A Lume Spento* to the final *Cantos,* we become convinced that Pound was a poet not for all time but for an age. We must hasten to add, however—what an age! The complexity, depth, and brilliance of the poetry written during the first six or seven decades of this century will rival that of any other period of comparable length in the history of English and American literature. And yet something went wrong. The Experimentalist Movement—of which Pound was the founder and leader—ended in the *Cantos,* many of which (let's face it) are unreadable, and in the prose of Joyce's *Finnegans Wake,* which for the most part is also unreadable.

The final failure of the Experimentalist Movement was, I think, brought about not so much by a lack of talent as by a mistaken attitude toward and theories about the nature of poetry. A study of the career of Pound, who theorized about poetry almost as often as he practiced it, will throw a good deal of light on the history of literature of our time. For such a study the *Collected Early Poems of Ezra Pound* . . . is indispensable. (pp. 643-44)

In this collection we can watch the eclectic young poet writing (not very well at first) under the influence of the Pre-Raphaelites, Browning, the early Yeats, Swinburne, and the Troubadours. There is page after page of precious, affected, archaic diction, but also there are several real achievements such as "Alba Innominata" in which the style of Rossetti and the spirit and subject matter of the Provençal poets are triumphantly fused. We can watch Pound's progress (still under the influence of the Troubadours) in the well known "Planh for the Young English King" and in the not so well known "Canzon: of Incense" and "Canzon: the Yearly Slain." . . . We have, then, in this volume an almost complete record of Pound's poetry through the year 1912, that is, up to the Imagist phase. We can see here also in its beginnings the result of a poetic theory which he took over from the Pre-Raphaelites and Pater, which dominated the Imagist period, and which was carried to the point of destruction in the *Cantos*. I am referring to the Pre-Raphaelite notion that the arts should be primarily concerned with the "charged moment," the experience of transitory intensity or even ecstasy which may be considered divine or semidivine. In his early critical statements in *The New Age* and elsewhere Pound called this experience "the luminous moment," "the flash of cosmic consciousness," or more formally in his definition of the image "an intellectual and emotional complex in the instant of time." Stated simply, the theory means in practice that a successful poem presents and communicates one or more of these luminous moments without comment and with a minimum of connecting links. The theory has affinities with Eliot's objective correlative and with Joyce's definition of the lyric as "the simplest verbal gesture of an instant of emotion" and with his notion that the first function of narrative writing is to present an epiphany or a series of epiphanies, that is, sudden insights into the nature of reality. We see the results of the theory (which of course has its roots in the Romantic movement) in *The Waste Land* as well as in some of Eliot's shorter poems. The theory has led to a great deal of intense, brilliant, but often irrational and obscure writing by the experimentalists of the Pound era.... There are weaknesses other than those I have mentioned in Pound's pre-Imagist verse—particularly his employment of obscure bits of erudition which become comprehensible only after an unacceptable amount of research. But there is a good deal of distinguished writing too in at least a dozen other poems including the famous translation from the Anglo-Saxon "The Seafarer," "Sestina: Altaforte," "The Return," and "Piere Vidal Old." (pp. 644-45)

> *Donald E. Stanford, in* The Southern Review *(copyright, 1977, by Donald E. Stanford), Vol. XIII, No. 4, Autumn, 1977.*

*   *   *

POWELL, Anthony   1905-

Powell is an English novelist and screenwriter. His twelve-volume fictional work "A Dance to the Music of Time," is gradually coming to be considered a masterpiece of modern fiction. The Poussin painting, from which the novel's title is derived, establishes and defines the pattern of the work. As in the painting, where the four seasons, represented as four dancers, move to the music played by Time, the novel explores the seasons of life and the cyclic nature of time. Powell's prose is characterized by formal elegance and subtle wit. (See also *CLC*, Vols. 1,3,7,9, and *Contemporary Authors*, Vols. 1-4, rev. ed.)

ARTHUR MIZENER

Despite Powell's inexhaustible interest in the highly competitive literary and artistic life of London, he has never shown the slightest desire to gain power for himself, a characteristic that helps explain the strange, almost anthropological interest with which he examines those men—of whom the power-hungry are the most obvious example—whose public image of themselves is so important to them that they subdue their whole natures to it.

With this insight into the folkways of men of will, Powell gives us an understanding of a fundamental distinction of character in twentieth-century life. His sense of its refinement is remarkable....

Powell is specially fascinated by the comic predicament of men of will who, though wholly engrossed by personal policy, are pitifully incapable of effective action.... (p. 80)

It is possible to work out the chronology of *The Music of Time*, but there are astonishingly few dates in it. It is the human sense of time rather than chronology that interests Powell, the shape of the feelings at a particular age, the characteristic tone of a period. He fixes our attention on "that feeling of anxiety ... that haunts youth so much more than maturity," or the "sense of guilt in relation to [marriage that] makes itself increasingly felt" as one approaches thirty.... (p. 84)

This representation of the shifts and changes in our consciousness of reality as both we and society change with the passage of time is made possible by the scope of *The Music of Time* and by the controlled variety of circumstances through which the dancers to this music move. But these conditions only make the effect possible; the effect itself has to be realized in the action of the novel or in Jenkins' comments on the action, and it may be that Powell's comparative lack of popularity is a consequence of the quietness with which Jenkins presents the action and comments on it. He never stops to point out to the reader the comic significance of such things as General Conyers' remark to the theosophist Trelawney, with his solemn superiority to Time and Space, "Off you go now—at the double," or to explain to him what he is to deduce from the many marriages of *Casanova's Chinese Restaurant*. He clearly has an instinctive dislike of what Henry James called "the platitude of statement," and it is only when the significant action is an event in Nicholas Jenkins' consciousness that something of what Powell is driving at becomes overt. (pp. 84-5)

Powell is a man for whom "in human life, the individual ultimately dominates every situation, however disordered, sometimes for better, sometimes for worse," and constitutes the operative center of energy and value in society, however complex the organization and immediately irresistible the conventions of society may be. Powell's awareness of society's power is very acute, but he never fails to suggest that it is both energized and used by the egos of individuals. (p. 85)

Powell, an expert on the rituals of British upper-middle-class life, is fascinated by the essential independence of those who sustain these rituals with such skillful concern for their own egos. (p. 87)

Of all the characters in *The Music of Time* Nicholas Jenkins is the most subtly and fully developed, but he is no more significant than a number of others. (p. 89)

Powell's sense of character is like his sense of time. Even Jenkins is almost always revealed to us by implication.... (p. 90)

Thus Jenkins' thoughts—and he is a thoughtful man—always effective and often brilliant as comments on experience in general, are always dramatic revelations of character. (p. 91)

[In] Powell's novels passages of speculation are always dramatic displays of the speculating character's motives for action as well as acute general comments on the life about him....

Powell's conception of [both the major and minor] characters and of their immensely complex interrelations has been clear since the opening pages of *A Question of Upbringing,* where, in a timeless prologue that may well describe the actual genesis of *The Music of Time,* Jenkins is reminded, by a London street scene, of the Poussin in the Wallace Collection called "A Dance to the Music of Time." ... (p. 92)

This beautifully disciplined comparison really tells us all we need to know about the design of *The Music of Time.* It proposes that we contemplate the interaction of these brief lives as constituting a loosely woven pattern within which parallels, contrasts, repetitions will occasionally occur, sometimes planned by the characters, sometimes unexpected by them. Its emphasis is on the relations of the dancers to the dance, and what it finds important is not what abstract meanings may be ascribed to the dance or to the melody by which the winged and naked greybeard guides it, but what response of the order evoked by Poussin it arouses.

The allusion to Poussin is not accidental. Powell's imagination is intensely visual and his deepest responses express themselves as images. It is characteristic of him to see loiterers outside a nightclub as "two Shakespearean murderers, minor thugs from one of the doubtfully ascribed plays." ... It is when, as here, such images are specifically drawn from the fine arts that we can be sure the controlling attitudes of Powell's imagination are asserting themselves. (pp. 92-3)

Images like these dominate *The Music of Time,* establishing and defining the pattern of feelings for the action. They make us feel—even as Charles Stringham leans over his school-room fire toasting a piece of bread on the end of a paperknife—the splendid but tragic melancholy that will ultimately destroy him. They give us a glimpse of Powell's deep, quiet sense of the twentieth century as a wrecked civilization grubbing along in the shadow of its greatness's ruins, a world nearly transformed by the Widmerpools though still haunted by the Stringhams. "Though ominous," as Jenkins puts it, "things still had their enchantment." This is the tone everywhere in *The Music of Time....* (p. 94)

It is the continuous triumph of *The Music of Time* to show us, in these ways, without resort to extravagance of representation or distortion of perspective, that "all human beings, driven as they are at different speeds by the same Furies, are at close range equally extraordinary" and that human affairs are therefore both absurd and sad. The title of Powell's first novel, *Afternoon Men,* comes from Burton's *Anatomy of Melancholy....* Like Burton, Powell assumes without argument that, despite some superficial appearances to the contrary created by social convention, men, seen close up, reveal themselves to be demented, driven by invisible but powerful spirits to behave in extraordinary ways. He is fully aware of the horror this is. What could be sadder than the life of Charles Stringham ...? What could be more frightening than the single-minded, unrelenting, inhuman drive for power of men like Wid-

merpool, the destructive anarchy of Audrey Maclintock's nature and of the scores of other characters like them in their self-regard if in nothing else?

Yet, however terrifying, these people are also ridiculous, "to reason most absurd," an endless source of comic enchantment. (pp. 95-6)

No doubt the hopeful generalization to be deduced from these observations of life would be some conviction of the temporary decline of our culture and the need for energetic reform, as the unhopeful generalization would be one of the more or less gloomy cyclical theories of history. But feelings in Powell never ossify into doctrine, which is associated in his mind with egotism and inhumanity; all his doctrinaires are men so egotistical as to be incapable of enough human experience to engage their feelings, who must substitute doctrine for understanding. (p. 97)

Like his sense of the absurdities of the human imagination —willful or not—Powell's sense of its sadness asserts itself as implication, a shadow behind the character's immediate responses and conscious intentions.... Even more remarkably, this sadness is evoked by the great comic egotists of *The Music of Time,* the J. G. Quiggins, the Uncle Gileses, the Widmerpools. It is a faint but persistent aftertaste of the comedy of their marvelous, unremitting self-absorption. In the end, despite their outrageous selfishness, one always sees the sadness of the defeat they have, from their own point of view so unjustly, suffered.

The heart of Powell's work is these brief lives, these beautifully realized characters, all moving within the pattern of Time's dance, but all moving in their own ways, and, as they suppose, at the dictates of their own desires, more or less ludicrous according to the extent to which their sense of reality has been distorted by the willful assertion of their public images of themselves, but—ludicrous or not—always a little sad. Every one of them is both a period piece and himself.... (pp. 97-9)

[Uncle Giles's] is a wonderfully ludicrous life, and it would be easy to be so amused by Uncle Giles as to miss his underlying pathos, for his is not a despicable life.... It is in this way that Powell makes his great egotists, for all their absurdity, something not essentially different from the rest of us; even Widmerpool, the most extravagant of them all, is not. However sublimely ridiculous he becomes, he continues to remind us, not so much, perhaps, of what we have done, as of what we have, in our time, known we might do. (pp. 100-01)

The effect of *The Music of Time* is a very remarkable one for the mid-twentieth century. It is as if we had come suddenly on an enormously intelligent but completely undogmatic mind with a vision of experience that is deeply penetrating and yet wholly recognizable, beautifully subtle in ordination and yet quite unostentatious in technique, and in every respect undistorted by doctrine. (p. 102)

> *Arthur Mizener, in his* The Sense of Life in the Modern Novel *(copyright © 1963 by Arthur Mizener; reprinted by permission of Houghton Mifflin Company), Houghton, 1964.*

JAMES TUCKER

Anyone wanting to give a general idea of Anthony Powell's novels will find himself talking pretty soon about an easily recognised prose style and a steady concern with the well-born, well-off and well-educated. As it happens, the writing changes sharply between the early books and [A Dance to the Music of Time (ADTTMOT)]; for that matter, there are changes within ADTTMOT. But a distinctive polish, restraint and wit do run through all, and touches of learning are fairly regular. As to class, a few books may glance at lowish, or even low, life but this is not typical. . . . (p. 1)

One further common quality needs to be mentioned early: a constant aim to be readable, to entertain, for the most part wonderfully realised. To draw the three elements together, one can say that much of this readability in ADTTMOT and in several of the earlier books comes from the elegantly deadpan treatment of liberated upper-class behaviour, and especially sexual behaviour: the lowdown on high life in charming undemonstrative prose.

If Powell's work went only this far it would be slight: no more than a slick and funny exposé of the privileged. That is not how it turns out. Certainly the novels occupy themselves at some length with shallow, possibly effete, lives and skilfully create the right drifting, inconstant, often anarchic tone of the society they inhabit. What seems to give the books their substance is this unflurried willingness to see high life as it is and accept its rough edges; while suggesting in a moderate, not too convinced manner that it is better on the whole to do things in a humane, temperate way free from self-obsession and from cruelty. . . . Tolerance, humanity, decency attend Powell's heroes and narrators and come through to the reader as the qualities most worth bothering about. (pp. 1-2)

One feels . . . a plea throughout Powell's books for the natural warmth and vitality of life to be allowed their expression. Bores and monsters get in the way. It is this belief which gives the platform on which Powell's humour, elegance and épatant disclosures rest, and which provide the books with the solid ground to support their charm. A reservation must be made here too, though. In many ways, Powell, like the narrator of ADTTMOT, has a classical mind and terms like warmth and vitality may sound purple; after all, the standard description of his style is cool. In addition, a conservative, if not Conservative, rationality pervades the books. . . . Yet, for all their attention to control, and their regard for decorum and what is proper . . . the books see further. (pp. 2-3)

The distinction of Powell's novels is that they engagingly look at surfaces and, at the same time, suggest that this is by no means enough. They will continually disturb the surface to show us much more. In their quiet way they direct us towards a good, practical, unextreme general philosophy of life. Where very specific admirable behaviour is implied by the irony the books are less assured: Nicholas Jenkins's radiantly unexceptionable marriage comes to seem freakish, given the surrounding sexual restlessness; what St John Clarke, during his Marxist days, would have called bourgeois. The assertions which really count in the book, though, are made through an overall generosity of outlook and a consistent advocacy of sound sense.

What, then, is Powell's stature? It can be unfair and dangerous to blame novelists for what they have left out: the critical focus has slipped on to infinity. All the same, one does feel conscious of large gaps in Powell's work. . . . [While] Powell believes in and extols feelings he is not good

at igniting them on the page so that the reader feels the heat; it does happen, but the moments are exceptional. The books fall particularly short on the emotional lives of women, and a disproportionate number of his females seem brassy, shallow, restless. When, during the later books of ADTTMOT, he attempts something more in Pamela Flitton he resorts to overcolouring. Yet Ortrud Mavrin, portrayed by Powell with such delightful warmth in what was only his second novel, [Venusberg (V)], showed a genuine understanding of women, and it is hard to know why he discarded it.

Possibly related to his failure to involve us in feelings is an inability, or disinclination, to deal with action as if it were taking place while we watch; the reader tends to view from afar, with the aid of first-class field-glasses, it is true, and an amusing commentary, but we are at times conscious of the distance. In Powell's work there is a general flight from immediacy, and notably in ADTTMOT where the narrative method is allowed to fuzz incident and situation. Often this is essential to Powell's intent, but the lack of definition and energy which can result is a disturbing weakness, just the same. (pp. 3-4)

What Powell has is a powerful sense of life through character, caricature and period; fine humour and invention; a largely humane point of view; and unequalled competence at setting down the ways of a small, deeply interesting class of English society. Technically, he has remarkably extended what can be done through the first-person narrative; and he has the control to mix comfortably within one volume very different modes of novel writing: naturalism, fantasy, comedy, farce, occasional tragedy. (pp. 4-5)

[Afternoon Men (AM)] is a book of continuously mannered style whose entertaining surface is broken now and then by the brief but clear sight of some enormously important theme; it is the early form of a method which Powell will follow throughout his work. Like leaping fish, big topics may glint for a second in AM before sinking again beneath the sea of inarticulate if not opaque dialogue. Fotheringham's insight that 'there must be something beyond this sex business' is central to the novel. But it must be spoken by a lightweight, hilariously disorganised character so that the book's sustained tone of farce and inconsequence will not be ruptured by prêchi-prêcha.

Yet the theme is constantly present and AM's apparent shallowness may at any time be touched by sadness and, to risk a more ponderous term, significance. The novel shows a group of mainly young people at a fairly undistinguished level of London society between the wars. (p. 9)

Consistently Powell avoids neatness, symmetry and well-fashioned motivation because these would clamp on to his glimpse of this social group an inappropriate system and order.

Many chapters end in farce or banality, particularly chapters where some deep, possibly poignant, matter has been hinted at. The technique is deliberate and, for the most part, highly effective. Powell is, of course, writing here and in most of his work about a group which conceals, plays down and even avoids feelings. But feelings cannot be entirely excluded from life, nor are they from the novel. (p. 15)

A discussion of style in AM must be mainly to do with dialogue. Powell abandons the heavy reliance on speech after this novel and in *ADTTMOT* conversation is comparatively sparing. *AM*'s dialogue is almost always laconic and, by intent, generally trite and laborious. Through it Powell conveys much of his amused criticism of this aimless and silly group.... [Sluggish] formula conversations excellently catch the pattern of such lives....

Frequently, too, he can use monosyllabic, repetitious conversation to say far more than appears, a skill crucial in realistic fiction.... (p. 16)

It would be untrue to say that all the writing of *AM* is pared down and simple. Once or twice Powell turns to a very complicated, parenthetic style, rich in multisyllable words; in fact, a style which foreshadows the prose of *ADTT-MOT*. (p. 17)

AM remains a book of remarkable qualities, despite signs of immaturity.... Above all, the novel is very funny, combining understated wit, farce and what might be called comedy of mannerisms. It also sounds a gentle but clearly heard note of sadness that things should be as they are. (pp. 17-18)

Like *AM*, Powell's second novel *Venusberg* (1932), also moves in something of an ironic, deflationary circle, its end similar in mood to its opening. Although *V*, too, is almost continuously funny, the flavour has become more subtle; and the novel's world is wider and harsher, its personnel socially more various, their lives less confined and less protected.

In a superficial sense the book may be seen as a love story. More conventionally plotted than *AM*, it contains no elaborate comic set-pieces and skilfully uses several minor characters in linking roles....

The book's irony is remarkably complicated, beginning with the basic agonies of those who yearn only for the lover they cannot have, and developing towards vast strokes of luck—good or bad, depending on who you are—in the conclusion. (p. 19)

The point Powell is making does not become entirely clear. One must beware of ... imposing weightily obtuse interpretations on a book where charm and delicacy of touch are so important. (p. 20)

Perhaps *V* can be criticised for overdoing the irony and becoming a little glib. It is worrying to see the regularity with which incident is shaped towards wryness; at times this seems as much a simplification as would be thraldom to romantic cliché. (pp. 20-1)

Unemphatic, oblique, deadpan, the narrative method of *V* looks forward to the way in which Powell will present *ADTTMOT*. Rarely does he seem interested in describing incident with force and immediacy; it is the results which concern him. (p. 22)

[In] a book whose theme is that we are creatures of circumstance there would be little place for a hero bursting with decisiveness. Lushington, on the whole, is someone to whom things happen, not who makes them happen; a character type common enough in twentieth-century fiction.

He is also, of course, an ironic observer and listener, something like Jenkins in *ADTTMOT*. Passive qualities are implied. Frequently there is not even need for Powell to de-

scribe Lushington's reactions: we sense them because we know what sophisticated and worldly values he stands for.... This is an admirably subtle technique but does require a central character here, as in [*What's Become of Waring (WBOW)*] and, above all, in *ADTTMOT*, with spectacular powers of self-effacement. Some readers find such shadowiness a let-down, particularly as it affects Jenkins.

Yet it is crucial to Powell's ironic campaign: an energetically intrusive central figure, seeking to set people and things to rights, would suggest more moral certainty than Powell wants to show. We are going to find throughout his novels a fascinating variety in his ways of presenting the narrative, and a thorough look at these methods will help us understand his aim, I think. (p. 24)

In general Powell keeps the style of *V* rigorously simple, sometimes to the point of flatness....

Overall ... the prose is a controlled, sensitive instrument capable of holding tragedy and farce in a single grip. (p. 25)

Bare survival is a theme of both *AM* and *V*: Atwater will keep going through mere habit, Lushington through a patched-up unecstatic love affair. *From a View to a Death* [*FAVTAD*] (1933) concerns itself with durability in a more positive, though not exactly more pleasant, sense. Having shown social hierarchies shifting or already flat in the earlier books, Powell here demonstrates that there are also instances when those with position can look after themselves very capably, even when backed by little money. (p. 27)

Zouch is not ... central to *FAVTAD* as Atwater and Lushington are to the previous books, not the 'eye'. He represents only a partial turn towards the dynamic hero. Powell shifts the narrative between several groups of characters and Zouch and his viewpoint disappear for sizeable stretches. It is this loosening of allegiance to one character which enables Powell to make Zouch a more complicated hero than either of his predecessors, and to excite contradictory reactions to him in the reader: the kind of indecisive response that tallies with our judgement of some people in real life. (p. 28)

Style has become less mannered [in *FAVTAD*] than in the first two books, a more straightforward instrument for telling a story: brisk, occasionally witty, still off-hand and antidramatic. As in *AM* there is some excellent terse conversation, but in this later book Powell manages now and then to touch surface ridiculousness with menace or sadness.... Overall *FAVTAD* reveals a growing range of accomplishment but lacks—deliberately avoids for the sake of other intentions—the charm and carefully maintained single flavour of *AM* and *V*. (p. 32)

It is not necessary to regard *ADTTMOT* as a kind of *Decline and Fall* of the English upper classes—as some do—to see these first three novels as early and variously emphatic treatments of disintegration, with *FAVTAD* the grimmest in tone and the most effectively ominous. The qualities which Powell prizes—tolerance, humanity, decency—have gone on leave for this novel, and he is showing us the dispiriting result. (p. 33)

As if to compensate for the sombreness of *FAVTAD* Powell gives each of his next two novels, *Agents and Patients* [*AAP*] (1936) and *What's Become of Waring* (1939), a light, almost inconsequential surface. These last novels before

ADTTMOT treat segments of English upper-middle-class and middle-class life with Powell's familiar wit and precision. *AAP* is often very funny; and *WBOW* has for at least three-quarters of the book a passably suspenseful and intricately shaped plot, something unique in Powell's novels. . . .

As the title suggests, *AAP* is concerned, beneath its humour and extravagances, with freedom. (p. 34)

Powell may mean that we are all prisoners of our personalities and will stay so, regardless of efforts to change. . . .

It is a harsh message and may reach out towards Wesleyan predestination. In its brighter, more mannered way the book is as pessimistic as *FAVTAD*. (p. 35)

WBOW is a very capable lightweight exercise and represents a pause in Powell's progress: it contains few of those deeper implications which can be felt now and then in the earlier novels and throughout *ADTTMOT*. (p. 37)

Near the start of [*A Question of Upbringing (AQOU)*] we get an explicit account of what Powell means by his overall title *A Dance to the Music of Time*.

> The image of Time brought thoughts of mortality: of human beings, facing outwards like the Seasons, moving hand in hand in intricate measure: stepping slowly, methodically, sometimes a trifle awkwardly, in evolutions that take recognisable shape: or breaking into seemingly meaningless gyrations, while partners disappear only to reappear again, once more giving pattern to the spectacle: unable to control the melody, unable, perhaps, to control the steps of the dance.

Life, then, has shape, method, pattern: it would be hard to imagine music or dance without. There is order. What sort? Not only are the dancers unable to control the melody but they may lack power over the steps they perform. (That late 'perhaps' is sizeable.) In Powell's title 'dance' does not evoke primarily rhythm, harmony, gaiety. Instead the word is at least ironic and possibly derisive, echoing the use in a phrase like 'led a dance'. The intricacy of the measure is sad and demeaning, not elaborately beautiful, since those engaged have no choice but to take part, and their responses are like those of a complicated machine. Their lives have some kind of meaning—are only 'seemingly meaningless'—but they do not know what and do not consciously express it. We hear of life as a 'ritual dance' in [*A Buyer's Market (ABM)*]. Ritual is metaphor so this, too, suggests underlying meaning. Yet it is the other, less heartening aspects of ritual which sound most strongly here, and once more the intent is ironic: people behave as if they can play fresh, original parts in life, whereas really the lines have been laid down from far back, and all the moves are inflexibly formalised, limited and repetitive. Life has some system but it is hard to find comfort in the fact. Patterns exist but they may be utterly destructive of those which people would wish for themselves. The human will can look very feeble. The contrast between how people might want to behave—or might have been expected to in view of upbringing and background—and the actual performance imposed as time calls the tune is a main theme. (pp. 77-8)

[We find] the insistent suggestion that people's lives may be linked in strange, unpredictable, often perverse fashion.

Time will secure these couplings, and break them. ('Partners disappear, only to reappear again.') Sometimes the results will be intriguing, sometimes droll, sometimes devastatingly harsh. This provides the 'meaning' of the dance: we shape and condition each other's lives in ways which may seem at the same time spectacularly random and ferociously intense. (p. 78)

Presumably . . . we are all as unreliable as Powell's narrator, Nicholas Jenkins, at reading the signs of how people will develop and how they will impinge on each other. This is an extension of Powell's view, and an important one: at least some indications of the future are available to us. . . . But we are often too blind, prejudiced, insensitive or ignorant to take it in; only hindsight makes things clear. . . . [Here] and there time will take on for a brief while characteristics of fate or chance or destiny: god-like qualities. That is probably as much as we can say. The degrees of contrariness, inevitablity, coincidence and determinism with which time works out its designs in *ADTTMOT* are so enormously and fascinatingly varied that it becomes dangerous to speculate beyond what we are directly told. Time rules.

We may see how in one of the books' chief relationships; the one between three characters we meet first as schoolboys in *AQOU*, four if we include Nicholas. They are Kenneth Widmerpool, Peter Templer and Charles Stringham. . . . Widmerpool [becomes] fixed in the minds of his contemporaries as a freak, to be treated with amusement or contempt. Against Stringham and Templer he seems particularly blighted. Although these two are graphically differentiated they have in common an aura of unquestioned superiority over Widmerpool. . . . The reader who takes the narrator's impressions for truth would foresee Stringham and Templer moving easily towards success in later life, while Widmerpool flounders in hard-working mediocrity, at best.

Fiction tends to avoid the predictable and the reversal of these expectations is total. Widmerpool eventually achieves such power that he may certainly be accused of causing Stringham's death; and is possibly also implicated—a far more sombre matter—in the death of Templer. Long before this Jenkins has been forced to see that his school verdict on Widmerpool was faulty. (pp. 78-80)

Powell . . . is telling us that in the affairs of Widmerpool, Stringham and Templer—and to a much smaller degree Jenkins—time has applied coincidence according to a flagrant and exact scheme. We are invited not to close one and a half eyes to unlikelihood but to watch, wonder at and learn from the ways in which life—the dance—will arrange almost unbelievably interlocked connections and events in order to ensure dizzy and often chilling alterations in fortune.

A qualification is needed. There is one sense in which time changes nothing. Careers and power are important but they are not everything, certainly not in novels. Regardless of what progress Widmerpool may make in business, the army or politics his basic rating as a character remains constant. He begins grotesque and is never anything other to Jenkins or—I think it is fair to say—to the reader: the more eminent the more ludicrous. (p. 82)

Essentially . . . the question is whether we can take certain cornerstone assumptions—often honestly and directly spelled out—on which *ADTTMOT* is built. The main one is that characters pass very closely related lives and that this will be true not merely in the limited geography of well-to-do London . . . but also in the worldwide setting of the 1939-45 war: to take only one instance, Nicholas's meeting with the South American husband of Jean at the Victory Day Service.

On the one hand these nicely fashioned surprises are the entertaining tricks of fiction, and let us be grateful for entertainment. They also represent, of course, elements in the dance thesis: further affirmations of another basic assumption of the books that links between people, once established, may well find ways of reasserting themselves. . . .

Powell has made an entirely believable whole of this. He (or at least Jenkins) holds as a further premise that in all our lives there is someone like Widmerpool who will reappear at crucial stages and around whom key events will form. I am not sure that many of us could think of such a person in real life. That is not the whole question, though. We demand that a fiction writer should by technique or art, and maybe both together, convince us that this is how the world as he sees it might behave. Through a number of skilfully employed devices Powell is able to make us accept the existence of a tight-knit, limited and very tangible world. He establishes, for example, a remarkably dense texture of resemblances and connections between characters by continually comparing their appearances, careers and dispositions. (p. 84)

Given time then truth will out, taking truth here to mean what people were bred up to, or what are their ruling passions. . . . [A striking instance of obsessive career progress] is seen in Widmerpool, the novel's major character development. He begins as an exemplar of vehemently willed ambition and ends, or at first appears to, deep in self-abnegation, seemingly contemptuous of everything that previously governed his life. Is this, then, one of time's swingeing ironies? Not quite. In fact, Widmerpool, naked, ill and in his sixties, dies while urging a group of cultists to greater speed while out on a ritual run in the early hours of one morning. Widmerpool draws ahead. 'I'm leading. I'm leading', he shouts. Even in self-abasement he had to be the top: time finally asserts what was always there. (pp. 86-7)

What strikes one first about the prose of *ADTTMOT* is its elaborate texture and seemingly cast-iron poise, qualities suiting the narrator's wisdom, favoured status, knowledge and assurance. Nicholas senior sets the past's uncertainties against the comparative—and only comparative—clarity of hindsight. Above all, the style is a generalising instrument, designed to bring apparently fragmented material into unity. By continually opening its focus wide the writing places incident and feeling of the moment in their background.

We may look at the first two paragraphs of *AQOU* for early evidence of Powell's method. The prose is smooth, belligerently sure of itself, measured and parenthetical. Simile abounds and especially simile not meant so much to make accurate parallels as to satirise through fanciful, even outrageous, allusion: 'as if', which appears twice in the first paragraph, is a favourite Powell device, often raised aloft when one of these jokes is on the march. It is a technique bringing great pictorial richness, along with a sense of amused, knowledgeable detachment: the writing sees beyond the obvious and actual and can appraise situations by

wide-ranging—free-ranging—standards. Only a little later than these opening paragraphs Jenkins describes his housemaster Le Bas standing 'as if he were about to leap high into the air like an athlete or ballet dancer; and in this taut attitude he seemed to be considering best how to carry out his threat, while he breathed heavily inward as if to inbibe the full savour of sausages.'

Colons do heavy duty in *ADTTMOT*. In these opening two paragraphs, and throughout, the prose is largely appositional: to borrow the mode, plain statement followed by commentary or modification or conjecture, so that the reader feels himself presented with a very wide choice of possible responses; the uncertainties of real life are caught. Colons give Powell the ferry between immediacy and perspective, between events and their interpretations. . . . (pp. 89-90)

[The] style of *ADTTMOT* helps establish the novel's basic duality: the poise of hindsight against the intransigence of fact and actuality. There is, of course, detachment and assurance, but they are not absolute; the prose can be high-flown but it will often be reeled in again pretty sharply. . . . This modulated dignity, mandarin with the skids under it, gives Powell's style its distinction. (pp. 90-1)

We will often meet this comic method in *ADTTMOT*: the presentation of fatuously trivial or even degraded subject matter in elevated language. (p. 91)

This contradiction of style by subject matter is one way towards deflation, perhaps the simplest. There are others. Throughout *ADTTMOT* we come across instances of highly-fashioned and, or, potentially dramatic and earnest prose tugged sharply back on the short leash. Jenkins first takes Jean Duport (Templer) in his arms during a drive along the Great West Road, in *TAW* [*The Acceptance World*]. The writing is intermittently sonorous and passionate; but both qualities are kept in check—at least that—by a description of the locale: an 'electrically illuminated young lady in a bathing dress dives eternally through the petrol-tainted air' as part of an advertising display. And there is an unglamorous doubt: were Nicholas and Jean thrown together by complicated psychological and emotional causes or by pot-holes in the road? (p. 92)

[The] first two books are the most liable to over-blown complexity; but the novel is never altogether free of it. . . . (p. 96)

Although occasional uneasiness with Powell's style on these grounds is inescapable, we do need to keep in mind what his intentions are. Perspective on what happens is as important to him as what happens; and he has evolved a prose which will quite calculatedly lower or even kill the impact of some potentially exciting situation for the sake of reflective comment or allusion. It is deflation . . . : a deliberate reduction of vivid, sharp, perhaps even pacey writing to the less lively language of analysis and interpretation. The technique is particularly apparent in Powell's treatment of love and sex, and one can see why. The overall attitude to love—Jenkin's marriage and a couple of others excepted—is anti-romantic and ironic. (p. 97)

The style is, then, trying to say in its texture what has to be said about love, and saying it on the whole honestly and effectively. Most of us would be prepared to concede that the fictional treatment of sexual love is habitually glamorised. Powell avoids that, while also avoiding cynicism, in a style shaped to suggest amusement, melancholy, pain and heartfelt uncertainty.

Although the writing can lose its balance, for the most part it is a subtly controlled means of setting against each other immediacy and retrospect, surface and substance, incident and theme, impulse and perspective, social poise and the signs of powerful change. (p. 99)

Powell's narrative method in *ADTTMOT* is, of course, crucial to the novel's shape, a uniquely subtle and complicated device. More than a little arbitrarily, I would like to break it into three elements . . . : the relationship of sheer, basic story-telling requirements to those of commentary and reflection; the personality of Nicholas, Powell's narrator; and the means by which Powell brilliantly widens, varies and extends what can be done within the 'I' formula.

Like most first person narrators, Nicholas Jenkins participates in the action; he observes and comments; and he reminisces, from a position often decades ahead. It is the degree of tilt towards comment and retrospective judgement which makes Jenkins exceptional. (p. 100)

We often find Jenkins as narrator looking back on Jenkins the protagonist looking back: both *AQOU* and *ABM* open like that, as if Powell wished from the start to give the 'present' of the book fluidity and a time context. . . .

The effect of such roving narration is, inevitably, to catch in the construction of the books the theme of time's sameness beneath seeming change. It is as if it does not much matter from which chronological point we view the incidents and characters. (p. 102)

The description of events as they occur tends to be less important than the placing of them in the overall scheme, a scheme we are constantly reminded about. It is only one of Powell's objectives to convey the flavour and freshness of a moment, and possibly not the chief objective. As a result, he needs a specially devised style, . . . a style which rarely strives for narrative pace, and which may down-play and blur the impact, edge and immediacy of events as they happen. He needs, also, of course, a carefully devised narrator. It is time to look at the character of Nicholas.

There is more than one Nicholas. Jenkins, the elderly narrator, is a lavishly developed character, opinionated, learned, prosy, philosophical, reflective and copiously articulate. There is also Jenkins a participant in the events recalled; though 'participant' may be putting it rather strongly. Jenkins senior keeps Jenkins junior pretty well battened down except for occasional exercise spells and airings. . . . [Very] important aspects of feeling and behaviour are left out almost altogether; Nicholas's relations with his wife, both before and after marriage, are treated with glaring economy, for instance. (pp. 102-03)

Where Jenkins is most alive, and then considerably and interestingly alive, is in friendship, in devotion to his work and art (though we should note that even this is muted: he speaks of 'that hard, cold-blooded almost mathematical pleasure I take in writing and painting'), in wit, in the gossip's curiosity about odd sexual habits (Sir Magnus's primarily), and in an occasional sharp animosity towards people he feels have fallen below standard. . . .

Nicholas, the participant, is then a character whose ac-

tions, thoughts, attitudes and emotions are given to us through the filter of retrospection and which are therefore short of vividness, actuality, suspense. The younger Nicholas will have some of the characteristics of an exhibit. On top of that, he is not by nature a raucous, swashbuckling or aggressive figure. Of a recognisable upper-class English type, he is endowed with considerable self-control and calmness and a notable taste for understatement. I say English. This restraint—so often used in lampoon portraits of, say, the Foreign Office man—does have its counterpart elsewhere. An Italian word—*sprezzatura*—best sums up Nicholas's qualities. (p. 108)

Inevitably there is a certain amount of tolerated duplicity in this kind of narrative stance. A man looks back over his life; many of the uncertainties and imponderables of a particular time are so no longer: he knows the upshot. But where the 'I' of the story is an active central figure we accept that he will recount his adventures as they unfolded for him at the time, with all the unknowns and obscurities of that period kept in. This the technique of, say *David Copperfield*, or *Jane Eyre*. Powell is not quite in this category, though. He is not telling an unfolding story. Although by and large the books advance in time and finish about fifty years later than the sequence began there is no straight, chronological flow from beginning to end as in a more conventionally plotted novel. . . . It is, in fact, crucial to Powell's purpose that the novel should be able to move about in time, so that he may show the complex relationships of one period with another. As Proust puts it in *Time Regained*, reality is a relation between sensations of the moment and 'those memories which simultaneously encircle us'. There will be flashes forward and back.

Another point: as we have seen, Jenkins is not in any simple sense the hero of this novel. He is an observer more than a participant; much more. He does not put before us simply a series of adventures in which he figures, but describes an incident or a relationship and reflects upon it, drawing from many sources, some of them natural to the Jenkins of the period we are seeing, some not. Many first-person narrators do this, it is true, but not on the same scale.

What this means is that we are given continual reminders that Jenkins is at once a participant in the events described, or, at least, a contemporary witness; yet someone, virtually omniscient, looking back from anywhere up to fifty years ahead. The result is a narrative method which is not completely logical—or to use a word more often applied to detective story writers—fair. (p. 109)

In Powell's hands the first-person narrative is, in fact, an extremely elastic and varied device. It is a form of storytelling which has, in principle, certain very obvious limitations: we are largely confined to the judgements and experiences of one person. . . . Powell very successfully skirts or utilises the limitations. One of his chief methods is explicitly to imagine Jenkins viewing events through the eyes and mind of someone else, and particularly through those of Uncle Giles, who becomes at times a kind of second-string narrator. This is a most remarkable technique. It is not simply a matter of augmenting the chief narrator's information by getting reports from temporarily better placed characters, which goes on all the time in first-person novels. Nicholas will actually surrender his point of view, his judgement, to Giles for a while. That, in itself, brings a notable complexity. It is more than this, though. 'To look at things through Uncle Giles's eyes would never have occurred to me.' Jenkins reflects in *ABM*. The book then, naturally, goes on to do exactly that: look at things as Giles might have assessed them, had he been present at the time; it would be difficult to get more notional. It is the mature—indeed, elderly—Jenkins who gives us what he takes to be Giles's way of judging matters, while pointing out that the younger Jenkins would never have considered such a stratagem. What we are getting here is a narrative viewpoint from fifty or so years on, based on a hypothetical version of what someone other than the story-teller might have felt about people and events he did not even see. (pp. 111-12)

This is fiction, so perhaps one should not speak of hypotheses as a departure from the rule. The whole world is make-believe and there is a sense in which the author can just as validly see matters as Uncle Giles as he can see them as Jenkins. Within the limitations which he has set himself, though—those of the 'I' narrative—this is a fascinating means for an author to secure himself more elbow-room. (p. 112)

It is worth spending a little time examining how Powell does make use of uncertainty and imprecision as a narrative aid. The aim, of course, is naturalness, realism: many of our impressions in life are fragmentary, partial, faulty, either at the moment of receiving them or in retrospect. Powell catches this quality. Jenkins will continually express doubts about his own reading of a situation or assessment of a character. . . . Where Jenkins requires to pass on others' impressions the possibility of mistake is greater still; tentativeness in the narrator's version becomes obligatory.

Powell gives Jenkins explicit, and far-reaching, reflections to make on the problem in [*Temporary Kings (TK)*]. Pamela Widmerpool has been discovered naked at night in Bagshaw's house, where Gwinnett was a lodger. Pamela was seen in what was probably the downstairs hall by Bagshaw's father, a short-sighted, elderly, retired insurance employee who had got out of bed to go to the lavatory. The description of this extraordinary event comes to us, then, from an original source of questionable reliability (Bagshaw we know to be older than Nicholas, who is in his fifties; so Bagshaw senior must be well on); via Bagshaw himself to Jenkins. . . . For a moment here Powell raises explicitly the whole question of how a novel is told, quoting Trapnel, as a matter of fact, though it could as easily have been Henry James or Percy Lubbock. Trapnel believes that every novel must come from 'a point of view'. Jenkins takes this thought further and says that the reader of a story, or the listener, must adjust his responses to the known or suspected prejudices of the teller. This is, of course, Powell commenting on his own method in *ADTTMOT*. If anything, Powell actually emphasizes the unreliability of his narrator's perceptions; and the continual eruption of comment from Giles, Barnby, Sillery and others is to stress Jenkins's limitations and partialities. Overall, the effect is of a naturally fallible, many-faceted presentation of truth. (pp. 115-16)

By recognising from the outset this possibility of uneasiness in the reader, Powell attempts to forestall criticism. It is another example of an author using his technique—tolerably, I think—to get things two ways. He wants the drama and comedy of the incident; at the same time he knows he is pushing us a little hard and so has Jenkins say that the

account is not put forward as what actually happened. The debate about truthfulness or not is conducted in weighty, solemn language . . . which, although possessing a facetious undertone, is also intended to distract the reader into wondering whether the incident was mechanically possible, rather than whether it is acceptably likely as a piece of serious writing. (p. 116)

[Two] of the most striking examples of what one might call second-hand narrative occur in *TK*, a book dominated by Pamela. She is unique to *ADTTMOT* in that she continually produces moments of lurid dramatic force. She carries her own purple patch with her. To accommodate such a character within the generally subdued tone of his novel Powell will distance her by deflected reports of her behaviour. He will blur her in doubts. It is a notably shrewd recognition of a problem, of a limitation, in fact; and a notably skilful way out. He knows himself to be not well equipped to deal with direct versions of forceful action and, in finding a means to compensate, has usefully extended the capabilities of the 'I' narrative. (p. 118)

Sexual passion is treated mainly from the point of view of an observer, not a participant, in *ADTTMOT*. Of course, the narrative method ensures this: Jenkins can tell us at first hand only about his own love affairs, and on those aspects of his life he tends to close up. It is not simply a matter of narrative method, though; or, to put it another way, Powell chose the method and with it the limitations: these include a distanced, ironic treatment of most characters' sexual behaviour, interest in the social effects of liaisons taking a higher priority with Powell than their emotional content. . . .

Although a few central established upper-class marriages seem to survive without the remotest menace—notably those of Jenkins and his father—they are small rocks of stability among acres of shifting sand. Such volatile relationships are basic to the music of time theme. . . . What one has to ask, I think, is how far sex—love might be putting it high—is utilised in the novel simply as a means of keeping the patterns of the dance in a constant, interesting state of change.

It is not by any stretch a simple question. For one thing, we have learned from the pre-war books that Powell's view of sexual love—the happiness it can bring, its stability, its authenticity—is sceptical. (pp. 119-20)

[One] result of Powell's fascination with the externals of fragile sexual relationships is that *ADTTMOT* offers a large number of women who, although of expertly differentiated personality, seem, as to their feelings, all made to similarly tough, shallow or even negative pattern. They move between men without showing what impels them; at least, what beyond mere acquisitiveness or whim. (p. 120)

Pamela Flitton [is] by far the most ambitious piece of female characterisation attempted by Powell and the only woman projected with the thoroughness of the novel's chief men. (p. 122)

Pamela emerges suddenly in [*The Military Philosophers (TMP)*] as a woman of exceptional sexual éclat and ruthlessness, the impression growing in the books that follow, until she dies in *TK*. As a means of contriving the extraordinary turns of time and the dance she is supreme. (p. 123)

Yet although her function as creator and tangler of relationships is so patent—even blatant—and although she shares with some of the other roving women a surface personality of startling toughness and consistent aggression, Pamela receives a degree of character development unequalled among other women. This is not to say that she is entirely convincing. The portrait is perhaps tinged with sentimentality and its psychology over-simple. But it has some very accomplished features. As a result, Pamela can hold some of our sympathy, and a good deal of our curiosity, even when she appears at her most pugnacious or sullen. She has enabled Powell to break away from what had become almost a female stereotype and create someone who is a complicated living woman with elaborate emotions. One feels blistering energy whenever she is present, combined with a sense that she is looking, hopelessly, for a fulfilling response somewhere in life, and chiefly through love. Her promiscuity is a symptom of despair, as is her marriage to Widmerpool. (pp. 123-24)

On the face of it then she is not merely of a pattern, but the most startling model produced from it. We are required to look deeper in her case, though. Her sexuality is part of the essence of her personality, not an incidental, and it is accounted for in both physiological and psychological terms. (p. 125)

Intimidating, poignant, honest, Pamela is a fine creation, particularly in *BDFAR* [*Books Do Furnish a Room*] (matters grow a little strained in *TK*). The relationship with Trapnel is treated like a real love affair, not as a symbolic, intriguing, passionless, jokey coupling. And yet it is symbolic and intriguing all the same. (p. 127)

[One] should recognise that sexual passion in *ADTTMOT* is treated with something other than absolute realism. In Powell's view, desire—for someone, for status, for the quiet domestic life, for change—transforms people; so sharpens and emphasises this one impulse that they become for that time single-dimensional characters, swift-moving counters on a board. These movements themselves may then be fascinating and exciting to watch; the causes, though, are secondary, banal, scarcely worth talking about: simply what the dice dictate.

There will be effective departures from this method, as with Pamela above all. And the method itself is generally all it needs to be in a work of irony, more concerned with social patterns than with feelings. When, though, as in Nicholas's and Isobel's case, a love affair is ostentatiously exempted that irony; and when this particular pair of counters do not speed separately around the board but settle together snugly in their square, we are bound to ask why this should be. (pp. 127-28)

AQOU circles, seeming to leave Nicholas pretty well where he started and this helps bring an almost emphatic shapeliness to the book. In the first chapter, Nicholas's Uncle Giles, nosy, aggressive, a little shady, calls on him at school to discuss family business, centred on the Trust from which Giles draws an income. . . . [Near] the end of the volume, he meets Giles again, this time in a London restaurant: once more the atmosphere lacks conviviality, once more the conversation is the Trust. (p. 129)

Between these two cheerless meetings, Nicholas has observed vivid changes in others and believes that 'a new epoch' is starting for himself. In those closing moments, though, as he eats with Giles, *faute de mieux*, at the Trou-

ville, we are most conscious of a similarity between the young man and the senior schoolboy, as we are meant to be. Like Salinger in *The Catcher in the Rye*, Powell has posted his hero to a transit camp: that painful, confusing, absurd, anxious and, for some, protracted waiting time between late youth and full adulthood. . . . As if to contradict [the] signs of change he turns to Giles again; but we are to take it that, while things may look the same, essentials have begun to alter: the surface seems as ever but in fact a great deal of water has gone under the bridge. Gradualism, tentativeness and occasional reversals attend Nicholas's development in a fashion which seems exactly right. (pp. 129-30)

It is, of course, the ambiguous advance of Nicholas—an impression of lingering childhood seen against signs of emergence as an adult—which makes *AQOU* seem at the same time symmetrical yet about to move into an enormous future: important attributes in a book which must be able to stand alone as well as provide the start to a sequence. . . . This first volume illustrates well the high skill with which Powell can give a book remarkable solidity of structure—a sense of entity and completeness—while suggesting that all has not been said. (pp. 132-33)

In other words, *AQOU* is put together with such architectural finesse that apparently tentative, imperfectly resolved matters can be comfortably accommodated and cause the reader no unease. We can see functioning within the comparatively small scope of the single volume Powell's theory of pattern and system in life, while sensing at the same time that these tendencies will show themselves over the full sequence. (p. 134)

We leave Widmerpool as we first met him, out on a run; vain, grotesque effort the chief quality now as then. During those clumsy jogs in *AQOU* he was trying for an athletic competence that would never come, though as an exercise of will his dogged sorties showed the kind of toughness that would help him later. Complicated ironies tie his final ludicrous, tragic sprint in [*Hearing Secret Harmonies (HSH)*] with our sight of him as a schoolboy hopelessly training in *AQOU*. Now, he is elderly, sick, naked, a dropout who has dropped as far as he could. Under orders, Widmerpool is running with a group from the commune who, with his permission, have moved into his house, and who seem to provide all he now seeks in life. (p. 188)

After *HSH* there can be no doubt that *ADTTMOT* is primarily about Widmerpool. Simply, he is the only character of any sizeable previous development left alive. There had seemed—to me, I mean—a chance that as the period of the novel approached the present the retrospective and contemporary Nicholases might coalesce, as images can in trick photography, and become a rather more positive force; though, of course, he is elderly by the time we reach this volume, not altogether in shape to emerge as a vivacious hero. If anything, he is less personally involved in *HSH* than during any of the previous books. His reporting duties have grown weighty. (pp. 188-89)

The chief secret harmonies . . . are those sounded now and earlier in Widmerpool's life. Time leaves him with his yearning for eminence still powerful. (p. 189)

We are to make of Widmerpool at the end of *HSH* what we have made of him all through: he is a fool, knave and bore. He sought treasure on earth for the wrong reasons and now gives it up for the wrong reasons. So much in Powell is contradicted, half-contradicted, left in doubt that it would be foolish to enunciate with any pretence at certainly what the whole novel is 'about'. . . . Looking at Widmerpool in *HSH* I think one can say that his course through these books demonstrates that an absence of style, moderation, sense and imagination, coupled with devotion to will, egotism and materialistic push, will result in at least fatuousness, possibly disaster, probably evil; 'so called right and wrong' not being illusory concepts at all. The world has beaten Widmerpool and driven him towards bizarre supernature because the natural is too much for him. . . .

Having said that much, though, we must then go on to recall that life has defeated others, too: Templer, Trapnel, Pamela, possibly Stringham. We do not find a thesis here that the decent or talented or imaginative or emotionally questing shall inherit the earth. As a matter of fact, though, the meek do seem to do pretty well, if we may use that word about someone as tough in outlook, though not in action, as Nicholas. (p. 190)

And Nicholas? At the end he is working peaceably in his garden and, one assumes, continuing his writing (we hear of 'all those books' he has produced), without too much worry; without in this volume even very much irony. Quarry developments are afoot near his home and these stir a brief token movement of self-assertion in him, the rural conservation thing, but nothing frenetic. If we look to Nicholas to tell us anything at the end of this sequence it is this: keep calm, keep steady, keep individual—that above all. Hear the secret harmonies if you can; listen to the music of time and observe the dancers. That will do. Otherwise, we should cultivate our garden. (p. 192)

> *James Tucker, in his* The Novels of Anthony Powell (© *James Tucker 1976; reprinted by permission of Columbia University Press and MacMillan, London and Basingstoke),* Columbia University Press, 1976.

WILLIAM B. HILL, S.J.

The pace of Anthony Powell's very graceful novels in *A Dance to the Music of Time* is almost imperceptible; by contrast, his autobiography, *Infants of the Spring*, is a kaleidoscope of jumbled figures, piled together, emerging like members of a very large cast taking individual bows. . . . (p. 278)

The book goes only to the end of Powell's Oxford days, though there are many flashes forward. It can be tedious and trying—especially the genealogical Appendix—but it can also be sprightly and amusing. It will have its strongest appeal for those who already know the time and the literary figures in it. (pp. 278-79)

> *William B. Hill, S. J., in* Best Sellers (*copyright © 1977 Helen Dwight Reid Educational Foundation),* December, 1977.

JOHN BAYLEY

It is one of Anthony Powell's most disarming characteristics that his anecdotes exist for themselves, at most illustrating some nuance in the custom and fashion of an epoch: 'the period flavour of the incident must excuse its triviality,' as he remarks in his leisurely way, or 'social hairs are the most enjoyable ones to split.' His fiction draws its subtle contentment from highlighting such trivialities, as in their different style do his current series of memoirs, [*Messengers of Day*]. . . .

Fascinating in themselves, Powell's memoirs suggest that, in shaping social acquaintance and episode for the uses of fiction, he never goes beyond the anecdotal, resisting any temptation to concoct figures at all 'representational'. Where most novelists who use real-life models elevate them vertically, as it were, into more than life-sized archetypes (Charlus, Natasha, old Karamazov), Powell manipulates his on the lateral plane, into a world of art in anecdote on the same scale as in life. Thus Constant Lambert moves sideways into Moreland, Aleister Crowley into Trelawney, an acquaintance called Basil Hambrough into Dicky Umfraville. One trouble with Widmerpool is that he is really a minor character whom the reader is apt to interpret as a major one—even one with 'representational' significance—and in the concluding volumes [of *A Dance to the Music of Time*] this may possibly occur with the connivance and encouragement of the author.

Powell's art depends on his own idiosyncratic shaping of the fact that life is lived mostly in the minor key, and this logically extends even into the artistic tastes of characters and narrator. Thus there are enthusiasts for Tourneur or Modigliani, never for Shakespeare or Cézanne; painter and composer characters are in some none the less colourful way not very good; quoted verses by de Tabley have more resonance than anything by Yeats or Tennyson could have. This helps to give the whole series its superlative coherence in terms of form, and in a chapter in *Messengers of Day* called 'Set Books', Powell throws light by commenting on his lukewarmness about Tolstoy, his admiration for *The Sun also Rises* and *A Hero of Our Time*, his preference for *L'Education Sentimentale* over *Madame Bovary*.

> *John Bayley, "The Artist as Raconteur," in* The Listener (© *British Broadcasting Corp. 1978; reprinted by permission of John Bayley),* May 11, 1978, p. 615.

HILARY SPURLING

'Reading novels needs almost as much talent as writing them' is a favourite saying of X. Trapnel's, and one perhaps specially appropriate to the work in which he figures. For one could hardly find a work of fiction which more clearly demonstrates what Trapnel himself calls 'the heresy of naturalism' than this sequence of novels in which, for the reader, the deepest satisfaction comes less from character and incident than from the structure that supports them both: a structure so contrived that, as it flows, straggles or jerks itself along, by turns farcical and grim, sombre, tumultuous, absurd, reaching out through almost infinite varieties of egotism to embrace the furthest shores of crankiness and melancholia, it seems not so much to shape as to contain the disorderly process of life itself. It is not for nothing that Nicholas Jenkins takes his first name from that specialist in rhythm and design, Nicolas Poussin, whose painting provides both the title and the model for *A Dance to the Music of Time*.

Time, in that painting, smiles a sinister smile as well he may considering that in life and art he has the upper hand. In fiction, or at least in this particular fiction, Time is to the writer what Space is to the painter. Time may be empty or so densely packed that the reader can barely take in more than a few sample details in a hectic corner of the canvas. Time may dawdle or work fast, stretching forward or doubling back to shift a perspective, change an angle, open up one vista, close another, superimpose a further twist on a design already loaded or tweak skew-whiff a whole connecting system of supports. It is Time who disposes of the characters, causing them to topple and collide, tangle, scatter and regroup in new and unexpected couplings. Almost any character will serve to illustrate Time's role. (p. xi)

[Not] the least disconcerting thing about *The Music of Time* is . . . its humorous tone. Jenkins himself notes at one point that Shakespeare found it necessary to alternate tragedy with comedy largely because people in everyday life will insist on acting without due regard for procedure; and any reader of Jenkins' own narrative will find again and again that events which seemed hilariously funny at the time become steadily less so in retrospect. A case in point is the scene at the Huntercombes' ball when Barbara Goring drenched Widmerpool with sugar: a surprise attack still sharply etched on Jenkins' imagination thirty years and nine volumes later. . . . [Humour] can go to almost any lengths, given that it works in conjunction with Jenkins' constant awareness of 'the tricks Time can play within its own folds, tricks that emphasize the insecurity of those who trust themselves over much to that treacherous concept'.

The combination governs every part of the design, above all the long series of jolts which make up Jenkins' relationship with Widmerpool. But it can be seen perhaps most clearly in the career of such a relatively minor figure as Stringham's stepfather, the polo-playing sailor, Lieutenant Commander Buster Foxe. (pp. xv-xvi)

Stringham . . . loathes Buster's guts; their rivalry supplies a minor theme in *A Question of Upbringing*, provisionally resolved in victory for Stringham. It runs underground for the next three volumes in which Buster disappears from view . . . , only to surface again in foul play at Mrs Foxe's party in *Casanova's Chinese Restaurant* which ends with game, set and match to Buster. But the origins of this feud are disclosed only long afterwards by Buster's old enemy Umfraville, telling the ghastly story of his life and incidentally of Buster's marriage in *The Valley of Bones*. So that it is not until well into the second half of the sequence that the reader is at last in a position to unravel the tensions sensed by Jenkins as a schoolboy. . . . (p. xvii)

[Jenkins' uneasiness] in Buster's presence changes to horror at his part in Stringham's disintegration, itself a prototype of the lives of other romantics—Roland Gwatkin, X. Trapnel, to some extent Hugh Moreland—shipwrecked in the gulf between their dreams and an obdurate reality. . . . Whatever the underlying cause of Stringham's troubles—a Hamlet-like temperament exacerbated by his mother's domination, by Buster's machinations, perhaps by the wrongs of his own divorced father—there can be no doubt that they exert a powerful pull on the whole structure of *The Music of Time*: so much so that it is something of a shock when the reader realizes on looking back that, as a friend, Stringham has effectively dropped out of Jenkins' life by the end of the first volume. His disillusionment, his captivating liveliness, his melancholy wit are already so securely established that though from now on he appears at greater intervals—and falls out altogether just over half way through the sequence—large stretches of the action will take place in his shadow.

If Stringham is one of several characters who define the basic framework, others, more often heard than seen, serve so to speak as filters, constantly available to change the lighting of a particular scene or modulate from one incident to another years before or still to come. (pp. xvii-xviii)

Indeed Jenkins himself may be seen in much the same way, as a convenient device for the adjustment of perspective. It is a device especially noticeable at the beginning of the sequence, where behaviour and events which caused Jenkins no small perplexity at the time—Mrs Andriadis' Hill Street party is one of many instances—are more clearly scrutinized in the light of an understanding arrived at only many years later. It means that the reader sees much of the action in the early volumes as it were in double focus, through the eyes of the narrator and simultaneously through the eyes of his naive younger self: a character hopelessly out of his depth in matters like sex, power and the literary life, equally at sea in his estimate of other people's motives, for ever stubbing his toe on mysteries he is unable to resolve, developments he hadn't anticipated, problems with which he can't begin to cope. The flexibility of this multiple approach is plain in the case of someone like the novelist, St John Clarke, to whom Jenkins' attitude veers through four successive phases (initial dislike, succeeded by a kind of adolescent infatuation which gives way first to the extreme intolerance of youth, later to a more complex mistrust), any or all of which may be called into play at a given moment in the narrative.

It is also perhaps worth noting that there is one unique element in this particular portrait, arising from Jenkins' account of the novelist's work: a technical analysis which in itself amounts to a short course in the art of writing as instructive as it is diverting. (pp. xviii-xix)

Jenkins writes somewhere that he takes a 'hard, cold-blooded, almost mathematical pleasure' in writing and painting. The reverse side of this pleasure is his attitude to Clarke's novels, a rejection framed according to the uncompromising laws of an aesthetic rather than moral or emotional system. It strikes a note not heard elsewhere in a work devoted to exploring, in all their painful and preposterous diversity, the workings of that general rule laid down at a fairly early stage in *The Music of Time*: 'All human beings, driven as they are at different speeds by the same Furies, are at close range equally extraordinary'. (p. xix)

> *Hilary Spurling, "The Heresy of Naturalism: Some Notes on Structure," in her* Invitation to the Dance: A Guide to Anthony Powell's "Dance to the Music of Time" *(copyright © 1977 by Hilary Spurling; reprinted by permission of Little, Brown, and Co.), Little, Brown, 1978, pp. xi-xix.*

*   *   *

POWNALL, David   1938-

Pownall is a British novelist and short story writer now residing in South Africa.

PETER ACKROYD

The Raining Tree War is a very funny first novel. It concerns a group of Ogden Nash savages who flash their pearly teeth, limbo, and worship Maud, Wife Of Our God, Woman Of Your Friend and Your Old Mother Herself. . . .

[Pownall] is not satirising the black races themselves, but rather the Western Idea of them. It is only in musicals, after all, that natives wear palm fronds, and sentences like ''I am a sensitive person and can feel that I will die before many days have passed,'' have come straight from the set of a Tarzan movie. (p. 22)

The improbable events of pastoral comedy have been transported to a more garish natural spot, where gigantism invades all things and improbable events become ever noiser and more unpredictable. But, like all comedy, it has a happy ending as nurture grudgingly gives way to nature in the irrefutable shape of Maud. Africa is the spot, of course, from which people are supposed to come and Pownall throws in a Tree of Life to keep everyone smiling. There is a touch of self-consciousness about this paradisaical manoeuvre, but I can forgive most things for a little black comedy. (p. 23)

> *Peter Ackroyd, in* The Spectator *(© 1974 by The Spectator; reprinted by permission of* The Spectator*), July 6, 1974.*

PETER ACKROYD

It never occurred to anyone that you could be funny about black Africans without being patronising or even bigoted; David Pownall changed all that with his first novel, *The Raining Tree War*, which turned Africa's 'Liberation' into the material of farce at the same time as it brought the native breed into a new and sympathetic light. *African Horse* goes back to this emerging world and makes it even more colourful, violent and awkward than before—and I have a feeling that Mr Pownall has created a comic landscape which will supersede Blandings Castle, Ambrose Silk, Lucky Jim and the rest of the old boys. . . .

The thing which keeps all of [the many] foreign elements together is the astonishing and sustained inventiveness of Mr Pownall's prose. The sexual, political and alcoholic adventures of Hurl Halfcock provide the tenuous story-line of the book, and its sheer linear force and the constant accumulation of new jokes and new situations place it close to the spirit to such narrative epics as *Tom Jones* and *Don Quixote*. In this sense, *African Horse* is not a particularly subtle or witty book, but it is an extremely funny one. I know that comic novels, deep down where it never really matters, are supposed to be profound or at least 'serious' but Mr Pownall never quite gets that far. There are, however, some moments of subdued lyricism, sharp polemic and blunt description which would do credit to a different kind of novel altogether, and there are some fast changes of tone and language to enforce the variety of moods which Mr Pownall creates around his adopted country. . . . This comic version of Africa, this ''Cradle of Man'', this ''Garden of Eden'', is both mother and spoiler, both violent and serene. *African Horse* is the only novel to bring this puzzling life into the light without pomposity or the slow, grinding tedium of 'serious' novels. (p. 113)

> *Peter Ackroyd, in* The Spectator *(© 1975 by The Spectator; reprinted by permission of* The Spectator*), July 26, 1975.*

H. B. MALLALIEU

[In] *African Horse* it is the style, Swiftian in its sharpness though contemporary in its influences, which keeps the reader interested: plus a very imaginative and vivid satirical view of an environment—the copper belt of southern Africa —with which he is so familiar. If an author should know three times more about his subject than is required for a particular work, Pownall is an example to others who have written more. . . . Despite a scenario acted out in the manner of the Marx brothers at their best, the author makes us believe that life is like this, larger and more eccentric than we think. . . . What [his characters] say and do may seem mad, or madly comic, but their accents ring bells. Haven't we ourselves come across such oddities, if oddities they are? There is a hero, Hurl Halfcock, whose search for his identity gives a narrative continuity, yet it is not so much him we remember as the atmosphere in an emergent black nation as self-seeking, as ridiculous, as incompetent as its former rulers. In spite of the craziness, the goonery, the cruelty even, a compassion comes through. If men are all villains, fools, or failures, for whom else can we have compassion? To make a precis of the book, if it were possible, would destroy the surprises and the fun. David Pownall has established himself as a writer in running for promotion to a major league. (pp. 73-4)

> *H. B. Mallalieu, in* Stand *(copyright © by* Stand*), Vol. 17, No. 2, (1976).*

NICK TOTTEN

In *My Organic Uncle*, David Pownall successfully carries off a remarkable eclecticism of place, class, theme and tone. The stories move from Zambia to Liverpool to the Mediterranean, from farce to realist fragment to macabre tragedy. The juxtapositions genuinely manage to convey, in a way that is neither cliché nor concealed cultural imperialism, the collective, unitive nature of human experience. There is no self-conscious theme; but there is a sense in which each story's emotion is a tributary to a single confluence, a pressure which emerges clearly in the last story, 'The Walls of Shimpundu'. The black miner, Golden, at the deathbed of the white foreman nicknamed Shimpundu, demands to understand his racism, the 'walled city' of whiteness inside his head. He gets no answer, but death: 'Shimpundu's eyes held nothing but a wide clear plain as broad as Africa itself, and the walls of Shimpundu lay submerged beneath the flood of red, forgiving waters'.

David Pownall demonstrates an unassuming competence which goes beyond itself. Only a few of these stories—'The Walls of Shimpundu', 'The Going-away Clothes', 'Buffs'— are individually very impressive; some of the others are pretty damp squibs. But there is a cumulative power: the power of a warm intelligence that brings together scraps of disparate experience into a surprisingly coherent fabric. (p. 22)

> *Nick Totten, in* The Spectator *(© 1976 by The Spectator; reprinted by permisssion of* The Spectator*), October 2, 1976.*

PETER PRINCE

God Perkins is formidable. At times it seems to contain as many characters as the telephone directory, but the plot, alas, has nothing in common with *A-D*'s austere restraint. I got lost well before the end. . . .

The theatre world is naturally so full of humour that it seems almost perverse of David Pownall to have written in such a frantically farcical style. So many people are being so busy all the time no single figure ever stands still long enough to establish himself. The only one to get close to doing so is the harried, sensuous, suicidal writer McHugh. It would have been nice to have known more about McHugh, and I cannot think why Mr Pownall let the other members of the cast get away with so much obstreperous upstaging. Still, Mr Pownall's approach throws up some merry quips—"we all know writers and directors have rows about interpretation, but I think McHugh is the first writer I have heard of who has brought the police in on his side" —and fans of freewheeling farce should certainly feel they have been taken a full fifteen rounds by *God Perkins*.

When he tries for satire, however, Mr Pownall is often decidedly shaky. We need to be able to trust a satirist's small, everyday perceptions—otherwise it is difficult to follow him confidently into his large fantasies. I am not sure Mr Pownall earns that basic confidence.

> Peter Prince, "Everyone on Stage," in The Times Literary Supplement (© Times Newspapers Ltd. (London) 1977; reproduced from The Times Literary Supplement by permission), March 11, 1977, p. 261.

*   *   *

PUIG, Manuel   1932-

Puig is a gifted Argentine satirical novelist whose usual target is vacuous middle-class romanticism. (See also *CLC*, Vols. 3, 5, and *Contemporary Authors*, Vols. 45-48.)

Boquitas pintadas is Manuel Puig's second novel, and it treads much the same genteel Chekhovian ground as his first book, *La traición de Rita Hayworth* [*Betrayed by Rita Hayworth*]. Sr. Puig describes an environment that has scarcely been touched in Latin-American fiction up to now, outside the photo-novel and the newspaper serial: the lives and loves of the self-respecting lower-middle-classes in the provinces. With a blend of cruelty and compassion, he listens in to the telephone conversations of teenage girls, and snoops in their hectically emotional diaries, photograph albums and private letters. Some of his characters—the pompous husband with a heart of gold, the wronged, pregnant maid—border on cliché. Yet the novel is so fertile in surprises and so humorously written that the clichés are forgiven—being perhaps a necessary part of the parody....

Much of *Boquitas pintadas* is, indeed, a parody of popular literature and music, the news media in the provinces and, in general, the considerable degree of inarticulateness of provincial Argentines, particularly when they are trying to impress. Though limited in scope, *Boquitas pintadas* emerges as one of the most delightful novels written in Spanish in recent years.

> "Provincial People," in The Times Literary Supplement (© Times Newspapers Ltd. (London) 1970; reproduced from The Times Literary Supplement by permission), November 6, 1970, p. 1306.

D. P. GALLAGHER

The most encouraging recent arrival on the Latin American literary scene has been that of Manuel Puig. His two novels, *La traición de Rita Hayworth* (1969) and *Boquitas pintadas* (1970, Painted Little Mouths) see to express the ethos of the provincial middle classes, an enterprise that

has not been successfully attempted before in Latin American writing. His characters are usually rootless sons of immigrants who, for lack of a viable tradition of their own, have relied on what to many may seem a curiously eclectic range of cultural models: the Hollywood film, the local woman's magazine, the *radionovela*, and the lyrics of the tango and the *bolero*. Puig expresses the ethos of the so-called *cursi*, the middle-class *parvenu* who lives according to the rules of what he imagines to be elegant in order to be thought elegant himself, but who is able only to display a grotesque imitation of the real thing.

Like [Cabrera Infante's] *Tres tristes tigres*, Puig's novels are very funny while at the same time deploying an underlying pathos: the pathos of having to project a borrowed identity, the pathos of being forced by admen to compete according to arbitrary norms, the pathos of being sensitive and intelligent, like Toto, the young hero of *La traición de Rita Hayworth*, amidst a disapproving environment concerned only with such 'normal' pursuits as material gain.

Above all, Puig has captured the language of his characters. He has recorded the gap that separates their public language from their private language, and the gap that separates their written language (a grotesque *performance* whose sole aim is to impress) from their more spontaneous spoken language. There is no distance separating him from the voices he records, moreover, for they are the voices that he was brought up with himself, and he is able to reproduce them with perfect naturalness, and without distortion or parodic exaggeration. That is not to say that his novels are not very polished and very professional. Like all the best Latin American novels . . . , they are structured deliberately as fictions. But the authenticity with which they reflect a very real environment cannot be questioned. . . . Puig's novels can be read on a complex level but are capable also of wide appeal: they are no doubt accessible to the secretaries, cooks, shop-assistants, and policemen that appear in them. (pp. 187-88)

> D. P. Gallagher, in his Modern Latin American Literature (© Oxford University Press 1973; reprinted by permission of Oxford University Press), Oxford University Press, 1973.

ROBERT ALTER

The Argentine writer, Manuel Puig, is one of the most consistently interesting novelists to have emerged anywhere during the past 10 years. "The Buenos Aires Affair," his third novel . . . is, like "Betrayed by Rita Hayworth" and "Heartbreak Tango" before it, a sustained bravura performance by a writer keenly conscious of how both the novel as a literary form and the kinds of people who are its best subjects have been caught up in the clichés of popular culture, especially in its Hollywood versions. Like Nabokov, Puig takes endless delight in contemporary *poshlost*—all the most shameless forms of trash masquerading as sublimity—while using it against itself to show how it deforms lives and how a cunningly crafted literary art can transcend it. . . .

What makes Puig so fascinating, here as in his two previous books, is the extraordinary inventiveness he exhibits in devising new ways to render familiar material. . . .

There are, by my count, at least 14 different narrative methods used in this novel, ranging from quasi-cinematic visual descriptions and documentary collages to interior monologues (in at least three separate varieties) to dialogues in which the speech of one of the two interlocutors is suppressed. All this is not just technical trickery because a narrative technique, certainly as Puig handles it, is a way of defining and making available for experience a human reality that would be inaccessible from other narrative angles.

Puig is, like Faulkner from whom he may have learned much, a master of occluded narrative. His strategies mislead, baffle, befuddle, tease us, finally to yield a meaning that can only be attained by experiencing ambiguities and perplexities. (p. 4)

> *Robert Alter, in* The New York Times Book Review *(© 1976 by The New York Times Company; reprinted by permission), September 5, 1976.*

* * *

PURDY, James   1923-

An American novelist and short story writer, Purdy is the author of various "black comedies," including *Malcolm* and *The Nephew*. Noted for his terse style and ironic tone, Purdy pictures a world similar to Samuel Beckett's in its grotesque emptiness and sadness. His works are designed to emphasize the sterility of modern American life, and his characters seem to simply exist with no discernible past and an ephemeral relationship with the physical world. (See also *CLC*, Vols. 2, 4, and *Contemporary Authors*, Vols. 33-36, rev. ed.)

FRANK BALDANZA

The structure of a typical Purdy short story has . . . [an epiphanic effect]: a selected moment or series of moments that body forth a spiritual or psychological state of exalted confrontation between one person who is *in extremis,* and an auditor who is deeply but always powerlessly perceptive. . . .

Of Purdy's twenty-two collected short stories in *Color of Darkness* and *Children Is All,* fourteen (roughly two-thirds) are . . . "duologues," conversational confrontations between two persons, and some of the longer works, like the novella "63: Dream Palace," are built up out of duologues, with only a rare scene involving three speakers. (p. 256)

The eloquently pervasive theme of all of Purdy's works is the failures of love, and these failures have their source in the orphanhood and half-orphanhood of children who, as adults, pass on the anguished, lonely legacy to their own offspring. Purdy's handling of the half-orphan situation employs the brief short story to represent the fetishism of one-parent children and the troubled anguish of deserted, sacrificial-possessive mothers; a frequent subtheme is the essentially epistemological problem of very young children's understanding of the listings and failures of adult love which victimize and deprive them. An almost equal number of stories, and two plays, present the problem from the mother's point of view, culminating in "Cracks," where the archetypal mother is seen as parallel to the God of Creation. In the earlier novels, the theme is largely implicit, subsidiary, or—in *Cabot Wright Begins*—absent; in the . . . novel *Jeremy's Version,* it becomes one of the dominant, major motifs as an exploration of the distortions visited on sons' and fathers' sexuality by matriarchal power. (p. 271)

[There is] a broad pattern in all his works, supported by varied, accurate, and deeply moving detail. . . . [An] examination of the half-orphan stories reveals the failure of human love in a pattern of reciprocal paradoxes: feminine sexuality is blasted by all the paradoxes of creation, because the immense sacrifices and devotion exacted by conceiving and nurturing offspring eventuate in a possessiveness which in turn distorts and cripples the masculinity of the son. His distorted sexuality renders him a grotesque who, as an adult, grants the same legacy to the next generation. Purdy's vision is somber and frightening, and it is to our own peril that we continue to ignore it. Certain of his more rabid partisans do both him and their readers a disservice in implying that his vision is absolute and exclusive, the only key to contemporary reality. If it were, even God could not help us. But it is a vision that touches, to some degree at any rate, the experience of every American family, and to that degree it deserves a far more serious consideration than it has received. (pp. 271-72)

> *Frank Baldanza, "James Purdy's Half-Orphans," in* The Centennial Review *(© 1974 by The Centennial Review), Summer, 1974, pp. 255-72.*

JEAN E. KENNARD

[The] world of James Purdy's novels is the Post-existential one of Heller's and of Barth's: the world has no meaning which can be rationally discovered; human beings have no innate identity; human action is futile. It is true, too, that although Purdy's techniques appear at first to be closer to realism than Heller's and Barth's, in the sense that fewer obviously impossible events take place and that his settings are familiar places—Brooklyn, Chicago, towns in the Midwest—his intention is usually theirs: to reject the reader, to destroy his illusions about the novel as a form, and hence to bring about in him the experience of the absurd. Most of Purdy's techniques are, in fact, those of the other novelists of number [Ihab Hassan's label for certain Post-existential fantasists, here including also Heller, Barth, and Vonnegut, whose language creates worlds of "pure and arbitrary order," which it then systematically destroys. This novelist of number] deliberately omits the motivations of his characters and indicates no causal relationship between events. His tone frequently conflicts with his subject; his dialogue has few logical connections.

Nevertheless, Purdy differs significantly from Heller and Barth in the effect that the Post-existential dilemma has upon him. For him it is cause for despair rather than for ironic laughter. The characters of Purdy's novels are human beings whose needs are desperate and whose agony is extreme. This agony is so apparent to us, perhaps, because of Purdy's emphasis on one aspect of the absurd dilemma: the failure of human communication which a purely subjective world and the lack of any innate human identity make inevitable.

The failure of communication is present in two forms in each of Purdy's novels. First, it is seen as a failure of all love relationships; for Purdy, love is primarily a matter of communication. . . . The progress in each of Purdy's novels is the same: it is a movement towards the loss of the hope of love. . . . (pp. 82-3)

The second, equally important failure of communication in Purdy's novels is the failure of art. More than any of the other novelists of number Purdy resembles Beckett in illustrating the concept of art as fidelity to failure.... Each of [Purdy's failed writers] fails to communicate through words, finding either that the truth, being subjective, escapes him, or that language is inadequate to express it. Purdy's own novels give us precisely that sense of attempted expression which fails, of art struggling against its own impossibility. Yet they exist, expressions of the paradox of their own existence. Like all novels of number they take the reader towards nothingness; each novel, like its reader, struggles but fails to make sense of the experience it records. (pp. 83-4)

The themes of "63: Dream Palace" [an early novella] are more fully developed in Purdy's first full-length novel, *Malcolm*. Using the picaresque novel pattern of a young man setting out to learn about life through a series of adventures, Purdy ironically tells the story of a young man who is used by everyone he meets and learns nothing.

Purdy stresses the "nothingness" at the core of his central character; Malcolm is an illustration of the non-identity of Sartre's being-for-itself. He looks like a "foreigner" and appears to belong "nowhere and to nobody." ... He describes himself as "a cypher and a blank," ... claims that he hardly feels he exists, and has no knowledge of such facts about himself as his date of birth. When he dies and is buried, it is rumored that there is no corpse at the funeral.

Malcolm is an orphan; at least, his father has disappeared and is presumed dead, but his relationship to his father, his need for him, is central to the novel. It is clear that Malcolm's father's absence is intended to represent the absence of God in the modern world. Whether God ever existed or was simply a creation of man's desire for meaning, as Sartre and Camus claim, Purdy never makes clear. (pp. 87-8)

In the absence of God man will seek to find his own meaning, and Malcolm sets out to do this through visiting a series of addresses provided by Mr. Cox, called significantly the astrologer. It is through communication with people, then, that Malcolm first tries to come to terms with life, but as always in Purdy's novels, this proves impossible. *Malcolm* can be read as an account of the failure of many types of love. Each character with whom the boy comes into contact is insulated from reality and genuine human communication by his own obsessive illusion, by his own particular perversion of love. (p. 88)

Purdy stresses the negative aspects of Sartre's theory that being-for-itself is nothingness, that we have objective reality only to others. Identity is elusive to all the characters in *Malcolm*, so they cling to labels.... Language, they appear to feel, can create reality; Purdy knows better. (p. 89)

[Malcolm loses] his illusions, his hope of his father's return. On his deathbed he desperately turns writer in the vain hope that language will make some sense of his experience. He attempts to record his conversations with those he has met. This too is a failure; he is writing in a foreign language in delirium. *Malcolm*, then, is a novel of a young man's initiation into disillusionment.... Malcolm dies because there is no new direction to take. He has run out of addresses.

Malcolm, like "63: Dream Palace," opens deceptively: "in front of one of the most palatial hotels in the world, a very young man was accustomed to sit on a bench which, when the light fell a certain way shone like gold." ... The effect of providing such details as the gold color of the bench, when nothing else is revealed, is to suggest that these details are highly meaningful, to raise the reader's expectations of discovering the significance. The point of them in Purdy's fiction seems to be simply that they are completely irrelevant: the aim is to frustrate the reader's expectations.

Similarly, the introduction of Malcolm himself, which takes place in the second paragraph, is a parody of similar introductions to be found in realistic novels where the reader is given the necessary information to place the protagonist in his background. The paragraph develops through a series of negatives; we learn nothing about Malcolm except what he is not: he "seemed to belong nowhere and to nobody, and even his persistent waiting on the bench achieved evidently no purpose, for he seldom spoke to anybody, and there was something about his elegant and untouched appearance that discouraged even those who were moved by his solitariness." ... It is as if the novelist were attempting to begin but finding little he can say for certain; art is struggling with its own impossibility.

Purdy's description of the subsequent meeting with Mr. Cox contains many sentences suggesting meaning when there is none or emphasizing in contradiction to the sense.... What Purdy is doing in the first few pages of *Malcolm* is to suggest by means of such techniques the impossibility of establishing reality through words. He is attacking our preconceptions about language, is pointing out that language is that "absurd structure of sounds and marks" Roquentin sees it to be in *Nausea*.

The failure of communication is dramatized in *Malcolm*, as in "63: Dream Palace," through conversations in which characters reply to each other in a series of nonsequiturs. Although the characters frequently continue as if they had fully expected an illogical reply, their mutual lack of comprehension is obvious to the reader. (pp. 89-91)

Just as individual sentences cancel each other out, so too the action of the novel progressively unmakes itself. All relationships disintegrate.... As Malcolm follows up the addresses, each interview cancels the one before it; the new characters defame the old, as if ... they feel they exist only by defaming others. There is progressively less relationship between the scenes, and Malcolm is eventually found drifting aimlessly from one place to another.

Each scene also tends to disintegrate, the characters becoming increasingly grotesque, the action more extreme. Purdy's method is to describe his characters only after we are used to their names and have been listening to their conversation. We are lulled into what we take to be a familiar scene and are then suddenly forced to recognize its grotesqueness.... It is not that these characters are impossibilities; they can be met elsewhere in life and in fiction. But Purdy has so many of them in one novel that he leaves the impression that the whole human race is distorted and grotesque in some way or another.

The struggle between the necessity to write and the impossibility of writing is clearly demonstrated in the final pages of the novel. The action, the langauge, the characterizations have all unmade themselves, and Purdy heightens the effect of this by adding some paragraphs which parody the neat endings of realistic novels. He demonstrates the impossibility of imposing form upon life by doing so in an exaggeratedly tidy way. He gives an account of what happens to each of the characters after the end of the novel. Kermit marries a wealthy film star; Eloisa and her husband take up social work; Estel Blanc runs an opera company; Girard Girard has six children; Melba marries Heliodoro, the Cuban valet; Madame Girard has a constant companion in a young Italian biochemist. Purdy has struggled towards a grotesquely happy ending.

In *The Nephew* Purdy extends the concept of elusive identity; the central character does not appear at all. Cliff Mason is missing in action in Korea when the novel opens and when it ends he is dead. We know nothing more of him at the end than at the beginning, in spite of the fact that the action of the book consists almost entirely of his Aunt Alma's attempt to write a "memorial" of his life. . . . Halfway through the novel Alma discovers "there isn't a thing she knows for sure about him," . . . and finally she puts the record book, which contains "only a few indecisive sentence fragments," . . . away in a drawer. The only evidence that does come to light about Cliff, the existence of four thousand dollars he had been given by Vernon Miller and some large photographs of him in Vernon's room, has implications that Alma prefers to ignore. Cliff is so elusive in this novel that his death . . . comes as a "mere corroboration to the public of the old suspicion that he had never existed at all." . . . (pp. 91-2)

Although *The Nephew* appears to be more realistic than either "63: Dream Palace" or *Malcolm*, it employs many of the techniques of the other two novels. Rainbow Center is peopled with grotesques. . . . These characters are reminiscent of Beckett's; their bodies are gradually disintegrating. Alma's and Boyd's increasing deafness is not perhaps as extreme a form of disintegration as Malone's, but it has much the same effect.

The action of the novel is a movement towards the void: Cliff, reported missing at the beginning of the novel, is reported dead at the end; Alma gradually realizes that she never knew anything about her nephew. Similarly, the reader is taken towards nothing as each piece of information gleaned contradicts what has gone before. (p. 93)

Purdy occasionally employs [a] technique used by Heller in *Catch-22:* he gives accounts of people or events at different places in the novel, and only in retrospect does the reader realize that they could not have happened as described. . . . The effect of this is to prevent the reader's being fully able to place the events in the novel [which resists] any chronological organization.

But in spite of this use of some of the techniques of number and in spite of Post-existential world view of the novel, *The Nephew* is not, perhaps, fully a novel of number. Purdy makes no use here of the language techniques important to the other works and there is no dramatization of art's struggle with its own impossibility. (pp. 93-4)

The world of *Cabot Wright Begins* is exactly the same world as that in Purdy's other novels. Here, too, everything is subjective . . . and each character has an illusory view of the next. . . . It is a world where identity is impossible to maintain and where the labels one attaches to oneself have no basis in reality. Thus Curt Bickle is a "writer," although he does not write, and Bernie can accept the promise Carrie [his wife] extends that he will be a famous novelist even though he has never done anything but sell

used cars. Human action is motiveless and purposeless in this world. Cabot Wright apparently rapes for no reason. . . . It is the Post-existential world again, where all absolutes are necessarily illusions and a life built upon them ends in failure. (pp. 94-5)

[Although] the themes of *Cabot Wright Begins* echo those of the earlier novels, the emphasis here is different. Purdy is less concerned in this novel with the failure of human communication and more interested in the relation between art, particularly fiction, and reality. Purdy suggests that the usual concept of art as an ordering and conveying of reality is simplistic. Bernie Gladhart is sent to Brooklyn "with a mission to get the story of Cabot Wright from the convicted rapist's own lips, and to write the truth like fiction." . . . This proves to be impossible because Cabot Wright has no recollection of the "truth" himself. He has read so much about himself that he can no longer distinguish reality from fiction. Cabot Wright wants Zoe Bickle, who has now taken over Bernie Gladhart's task, to tell him the truth, so that he can find out who he is. Zoe attempts to do this but the gratuitousness of reality, the impossibility of finding the meaning in such a diversity of events, prevents her from completing the job. She finds that "Cabot Wright's life . . . was a hopeless, finely-ground sediment of the improbable, vague, baffling, ruinous and irrelevant minutiae of a life." . . . Fiction cannot capture reality and make sense of it, claims Purdy; the world is irrational and has no inner meaning to be discovered. Life is no more real than fiction, for to find a pattern in a life is to fictionalize it. Art is impossible.

Cabot Wright's realization of this makes him give up the search for who he is and brings him finally to laughter. What is described at the end of *Cabot Wright Begins* is an experience of the absurd: for the first and only time in Purdy's fiction a character laughs the laugh of ironic detachment. . . . However, Cabot Wright does not move from this realization of absurdity to find a way of living in rebellion or freedom. . . . Cabot's solution, then, as far as one can determine, . . . is merely to continue, to live in the present, with the full realization that there is no meaning, no intrinsic value in anything, always before him.

The impossibility of writing is the subject of *Cabot Wright Begins,* and Purdy's techniques dramatize his theme. Language techniques dominate this novel. Purdy parodies the inadequacies of the styles of various forms of writing, each of which lays some claim to the truth. When Cynthia, Cabot's wife, breaks down in a supermarket, Purdy reports it as if writing for a newspaper. As in "63: Dream Palace" and *Malcolm* he shows us the relative insignificance of knowing the facts. . . .

In this novel, which is closest in tone to Heller's and Barth's novels, Purdy makes much use of that disparity between tone and subject they employ. An incongruous or ridiculous action is often mentioned obliquely in a sentence in which the main emphasis lies elsewhere. "It is doubtful if Mrs. Bickle would ever have been able to meet Cabot Wright or get one word or fact from him had she not, during a three-alarm fire, fallen through the skylight directly above his quarters," . . . Purdy tells us, and then goes on to describe Zoe Bickle's life before she came to Brooklyn. When we are eventually given the details of Mrs. Bickle's descent into Cabot Wright's apartment, the objectivity of the description and the introduction of such irrelevant facts as the kind of sofa she landed on cut against the violence of the action and render it absurd. This discrepancy between what and how events are described suggests, of course, the impossibility of language's capturing reality.

For the first time in any of his novels, Purdy makes significant use of coincidence to suggest the futility of human action. Since there is no reason why things happen as they do, it is possible for characters to appear suddenly in unexpected places. . . . In novels we do not expect coincidence; we expect events to be related to one another and to progress to a conclusion. Purdy's novels end where they began or, if they move at all, move backwards towards nothingness.

Another way of saying this is to say that the novel unmakes itself. In his later novels Purdy has employed those techniques of self-conscious art used by Barth in *The Sot-Weed Factor* and *Giles Goat-Boy*. He casts doubt on the validity of Cabot Wright's story by constantly reminding us that it is a version invented by Bernie, a novel within a novel. . . . Purdy ends *Cabot Wright Begins* with contradictory readers' reports . . . suggesting that art is as impossible to evaluate as it is to produce. There is no "true" version of the Cabot Wright story and, if there were, language could not describe it. (pp. 95-7)

[*Eustace Chisholm and the Works*] bears little resemblance to *Cabot Wright* in tone, is full of the agony of "63: Dream Palace" and *Malcolm,* but is concerned, like *Cabot Wright* with the dual failure of communication between lovers and between writers and their audience. It is the story of two men. The first, Eustace Chisholm, a pet, is scribbling a narrative poem on old newspaper. If the newspaper is our only version of reality, then how can one write a poem? But Eustace has second sight, knows in advance what will take place. Purdy appears to be hypothesizing: Supposing one could know the truth, he asks, would art be possible then? The answer is no. Eustace Chisholm burns his poem and says to his wife, "I'm not a writer, that's my news, never was, and never will be." . . .

The second character is Daniel Haws who cannot face his homosexuality and communicate directly with the boy he loves. Instead he visits him in his sleep. . . . [He] finally communicates with another human being, Captain Stadger, in a savage, sado-masochistic act that kills them both. Daniel's story is the story of all the minor characters in the novel. Each is in love with someone who does not return his love. . . . They are all, in a sense, sleepwalkers, an image Purdy picks up in his next novel, unable to touch each other. (pp. 97-8)

Amos Ratcliffe functions as the dream of illusion in which all the characters invest their lives. . . . There is a suggestion through metaphor that he functions as a symbolic representation of a debased deity, as Mr. Cox perhaps does in *Malcolm.* The important thing, though, is that Amos is not real to anyone. . . .

The stories of Amos and Daniel become the material for Eustace Chisholm's writing as for Purdy's novel, and Chisholm's failure is, of course, Purdy's own. The characters steadily disintegrate, though Purdy tries to pin them to the page with labels: "Clayton Harms, the electric-sign salesman"; "Daniel Haws, the boy's landlord.". . . Communication becomes worse among the characters as the novel progresses until, in the final section, people communicate only through letters. . . . (p. 98)

This is a minor example of the technique of self-conscious art which is Purdy's main way of unmaking this novel. Eustace talks of the life of Amos as chapters in a novel. "If anybody had asked Eustace which of the chapters in the life of young Rat he liked the best . . . he would have had to reply, "The Make-Believe Dance Hall," . . . says Purdy, and then proceeds to write the chapter. As Eustace waits to hear from Daniel, he is "as anxious to know the end of the Daniel-Amos story as a depraved inveterate novel-reader.". . . Purdy's increasing interest in the mutual incompatibility of various versions of one story is indicated in the titles given to the three main parts of *Eustace Chisholm:* "the sun at noon," "in distortion-free mirrors," and "under earth's deepest stream." It is an interest revealed in the title of his next novel, *Jeremy's Version.*

It is difficult to know Purdy's intent in this novel which is longer, closer to realism, and at the same time less interesting than his previous ones. The reader is informed on the jacket that it is the first of three independent works collectively titled *Sleepers in Moon-Crowned Valleys.* The image of uncommunicating people as sleepwalkers is only one of Purdy's major themes to appear here. . . . Once again Purdy links fiction with newspaper reporting. The story—the material—concerns two families, the Summerlads and the Ferguses, and the effect of their destructive relationship upon a subsequent generation. For the first time Purdy deals directly with the agony of family relationships. (p. 99)

Jeremy's Version does not unmake itself in quite the same way as the earlier novels. Purdy suggests, however, that he is once again interested in the incompatibility of the versions of one story. . . .

Purdy's work to date has been, with the possible exceptions of *The Nephew* and *Jeremy's Version,* a dramatization, primarily through language and action techniques and through self-conscious art, of the Post-existential dilemma. Art has been seen to fail many times. But the detached tone of Barth and Heller characterizes only some of Purdy's novels; his concern for human suffering tends to make itself known despite his intellectual assent to the notion of the futility of human action. It may be that the realism of *Jeremy's Version* indicates Purdy's intention to deal in the future in a more realistic way with the agonies of human experience in the Post-existential world. (p. 100)

> *Jean E. Kennard, "James Purdy: Fidelity to Failure," in her* Number and Nightmare: Forms of Fantasy in Contemporary Fiction *(© 1975 by Jean E. Kennard), Archon Books, 1975, pp. 82-100.*

JEROME CHARYN

"In a Shallow Grave" is a modern Book of Revelation, filled with prophesies, visions and demoniac landscapes. The moon appears to Garnet [the narrator] "by daylight, horned and angry and discolored." The novel itself is "horned" like Garnet's daytime moon. It holds us because we are stuck in the powerful, swaying rhythms of Garnet's voice.

This comes as a surprise, because Purdy's most recent novels, "The House of the Solitary Maggot" and "I Am Elijah Thrush," have been cranky, meandering exercises. The books tend to creak. They reflect in a sorry way the beautiful, ribbed dream world of "Malcolm," Purdy's first novel.

The new book perhaps will bring to Purdy the wider audience he deserves. Written in a sparse yet rough-edged style, it indicates the dilemmas of Purdy's writing. There have always been briers in his voice, as if he meant to tear at his readers with a kind of harsh music. Purdy is one of the most uncompromising of American novelists. Working in his own dark corner, he has collected his half-fables about a corrosive universe where children search for their fathers and are waylaid by endless charlatans and fools.

The very awkwardness of his lines, that deliberate scratching of the reader's ear, is Purdy's greatest strength. It allows him to mix evil and naiveté without spilling over into melodrama and tedious morality plays. There are no "legitimate" people in Purdy's novels, just fleshy ghosts like Garnet and Potter Daventry. Underneath Purdy's brittle language is a sadness that is heartbreaking, the horror of isolated beings who manage to collide for a moment, do a funny dance and go their separate ways. (p. 3)

> *Jerome Charyn, in* The New York Times Book Review *(© 1976 by The New York Times Company; reprinted by permission), February 8, 1976.*

KATHA POLLITT

Although its subject is physical passion, "Narrow Rooms" is strangely bodiless. There's almost no characterization, which makes it hard to remember who's supposed to be dominating and murdering whom—I tried to keep a running score, but I still don't get that bit about Gareth and Brian and the train. Clearly, James Purdy thinks his story is fraught with significance, but the four boys are so interchangeable that I found myself wondering as I read what all the fuss was about: Why didn't they just draw straws for one another's favors, or take turns?

Contributing to the general aura of implausibility and thinness is the complete absence of a sense of place. This is a real loss, because Mr. Purdy's last book, "In a Shallow Grave," rather beautifully evoked the seacoast of Virginia and its inhabitants. A touch of local color is provided by folksy old Doc Ulric (who, because he is given nothing to do, seems invented for that sole purpose), and the boys sometimes say "ain't" and "cain't," although a lot of the time they don't bother. For the most part, though, Mr. Purdy seems uninterested in grounding his fantasies in accurate, or even credible, detail. . . .

"Narrow Rooms" is well below the level of Mr. Purdy's past work, which has its witty moments (parts of "I Am Elijah Thrush") and even, in a bizarre way, its tender ones (the first half of "In a Shallow Grave," before the blood starts flowing). The abundance of clichés here—whereby a stopped grandfather clock is "the very embodiment still of Father Time" and West Virginia is continually referred to as the "Mountain State"—is puzzling in a writer whose prose has always been, if anything, too rarefied. Maybe the lackluster writing is a sign that even Mr. Purdy found his rural foursome a wearisome crew. (p. 46)

> *Katha Pollitt, in* The New York Times Book Review *(© 1978 by The New York Times Company; reprinted by permission), April 23, 1978.*

PAUL BRESNICK

For Purdy, Christ's message was the last great event—the critical idea—in the history of human consciousness: "love one another as I have loved you." But Purdy is also a Calvinist (by way of Presbyterianism); he's a firm believer in man's fallen state. . . . When you put Christ and Calvin together, you wind up with the conflict at the heart of Purdy's vision: Christ held out the *hope* for love; lapsarian man continually assures love's *defeat;* hence, *terror.*

So Purdy's books are love/horror stories. In a significant sense, they are typically American tales of love and death. . . . They are chronicles of thwarted, aborted, twisted, hopeless, failed love. Purdy examines aspects of eros that we'd rather not acknowledge: the part of love that is hate; love as a struggle for supremacy; love as a constantly shifting pattern of submission and dominance; lovemaking as an act of revenge, or as ritualized murder; loving as obsessive behavior—the uncontrolled urge to possess, to subsume, to consume another; love as cannibalism. Purdy's subject is the suffering, blundering *cruelty* of love—a cruelty arising from its very helplessness. And here, in the recognition of the innocent, helpless springs of love, is Purdy's surprising, affecting sweetness. As John Cowper Powys put it: "His insight into the diabolical cruelties and horrors that lurk all the time under our skin is as startling as his insight into the angelic tenderness and protectiveness that also exist in the same hiding-place." Christ, cum Calvin.

It should also be said, before we go any further, that Purdy writes about a specific category of love: the love between men. This is a crucial undercurrent in almost all his books . . . , but *Narrow Rooms* is clearly his most explicit, graphic treatment of this subject thus far. . . .

The violence, the perversion, the depravity [of the plot] sound perverted and depraved out of context, but there is a fine, inevitable emotional logic to the actions these characters take: they have to do the things they do.

Roy is the mesmeric, demonic center of the book. He cannot help acting out his inner psychic being, and he forces the others to play parts in his insane psychodrama. . . . Roy is the mad, evil genius, whose whole life is devoted to a single purpose: possess Sidney DeLakes. . . . Roy's is Ahab's story: his life, and the lives of all who come in contact with him, is devoted to a monomanical pursuit of an absolute—in this case, love. It is a quest that is doomed because absolute love, Christian love, is impossible in the post-Edenic universe. (p. 15)

Narrow Rooms is the most thorough, honest, *human* treatment of homosexual love by a writer of serious fiction in America. . . .

Purdy must be praised for having the courage to examine a hitherto ignored area of human experience in a serious novel—for illuminating these passions in a "bright book of life." If only for this, Purdy's novel deserves to be recognized as groundbreaking; revolutionary, even.

But there are certainly other reasons to praise this book. For one thing, Purdy has a remarkably accurate ear for American speech patterns—for the cadences and special flavors of the vernacular. . . . Purdy knows the importance of speech-rhythms. His characters are alive because their language is authentic.

They are alive, also, because we not only hear them speaking, but are intimately involved in their emotional lives as well. These people may be obsessed, crazed, murderous, drugged—in general, grotesques, freaks—but we understand their feelings. Purdy has the uncanny ability to compel us to experience emotional states we are thoroughly unfamiliar with. He alerts us to impulses we thought we had successfully murdered or buried. He sensitizes us to new (or rather, submerged) areas of our souls. . . .

This is the largest reward of James Purdy's fiction; that is, the unique, subterranean angle from which he sees America. . . . Purdy probes the underside of the American psyche. (p. 16)

Paul Bresnick, "Love in the Zone," in New York Arts Journal *(copyright © 1978 by Richard W. Burgin), April-May, 1978, pp. 15-16.*

DAVID BIANCO

[*Narrow Rooms*] is a tightly woven short novel set in a rural Southern landscape. . . .

Although there are some explicit love scenes between two men, Purdy's interest in homosexuality does not seem to be pornographic. Sidney, Brian, Gareth, and Roy are all misfits. In a sense, they are lost souls who have become victims of their own illusions. The strong drama of the four men is maintained by their obedience to an unspoken and unwritten code, making it seem as if they are acting out a predetermined fate.

The story is filled with moments of violence and passion. It is easy to become involved with the characters and share their hopeless frustrations, even as their twisted logic and odd behavior keep them distanced from us. No irrelevant details intrude into Purdy's concise narrative as it moves to its chilling, grotesque climax. (p. 71)

David Bianco, in Best Sellers *(copyright © 1978 Helen Dwight Reid Educational Foundation), June, 1978.*

Q

QUASIMODO, Salvatore   1901-1968

An Italian poet, translator, and critic, Quasimodo imbued his poems with lyrical, musical qualities underscored with a strain of sadness and anxiety. He believed that the artist could not remain separated from society, but instead must take an ethical, political stand on the events of his time. Quasimodo received the Nobel Prize for Literature in 1959. (See also *Contemporary Authors*, Vols. 15-16; obituary, Vols. 25-28, rev. ed.; *Contemporary Authors Permanent Series*, Vol. 1.)

LOUIS R. ROSSI

Salvatore Quasimodo has always worked to remove the barriers that prevent understanding between men. This preoccupation brought about a change in his poetic and critical orientations during the war. The time for engaging in "abstract modulations of one's own feelings," he insists, has come to an end. He believes that poetry must serve as a means of communication; the poet must address all men and speak out for truth and "not renounce his presence" in the world. But it would be a mistake to use his own words against him, to interpret them as a repudiation of his earlier poetry, and so to pass over the very personal and often involute poems in which he distilled his private anguish. (pp. 3-4)

While a number of the earlier poems may have seemed derivative, with echos of D'Annunzio and Pascoli and certain attitudes of despair reminiscent of Ungaretti or Montale, it was also apparent that Quasimodo had fused these elements in the alchemy of a personal style. The sensual music of his verse was not audible in any of his contemporaries, who were perhaps wary of the facile musicality of too much Italian poetry. Compared to the harsher line of Montale, for instance, the lush cadences of many of Quasimodo's earlier poems make him sound less "contemporary." To find the equal of his rich melody one must go as far back as Tasso. . . . But despite his musicality, Quasimodo shared with Ungaretti a sparse phrase reduced to the bare essentials of discourse, yet rich in suggestive power. Like Montale, his poems encompassed a vast and changing landscape over which moved the elemental forces of winds, tides and rivers, and he filled it with the sounds of nature and with things that stand as mute witnesses to the solitude of man. And like his contemporaries, but more than they, he discovered in this world stripped of illusion the presence of mystic signs.

A vision of a lost but still remembered blessedness pervades Quasimodo's wasteland, evoked in accents that recall Baudelaire, and more directly, the Italian Leopardi, especially where the evocation is bitter. . . . [Often], the poem becomes an incantation that for an instant suppresses time and dissolves all bitterness; a new power of illusion restores a moment of youth and hope once lost, lived on "Islands that I have inhabited / green upon immobile seas."

However, the obsession of a lost Eden and the crushing sense of an irremediable fall are themes older than Quasimodo, or Baudelaire. Ultimately, they are simply the themes of life and death, which, as must be, are the basic stuff of all poetry. Their affective power in Quasimodo's poems derives from their particular determination in the form of each poem. The contrasting themes are related in a changing oscillation that in some of the poems develops a structure of complex formal beauty. In its context, the words and sounds of the poem take on related values, and the contrasting themes are fused in the play of a verbal chiaroscuro. Obviously, these effects can only be observed in a close reading of some of his earlier poetry. (pp. 4-5)

"Ed è subito sera," the shortest poem of Quasimodo's first volume of verse (*Acque e terre,* 1930), embodies in its three lines the epigrammatic terseness that characterized much of the poetry he wrote in the Thirties.

> Every man stands alone on the heart of the earth
> pierced by a ray of the sun:
> and suddenly it is evening. . . .

Human life is telescoped into three successive instances: emergence, apogee, and decline. (p. 5)

The rigorous simplicity of the metaphysical geometry and its polar equilibrium along an armature of assonance and of alliterative sounds give the poem the form that makes it something more than a mere restatement of the "tragic human condition."

In some of Quasimodo's early poems, the descent in time is not a sudden extinction but a slow disintegration—a "minor curve." (p. 6)

[In "Curva minore" the] concept of becoming . . . includes both its positive and negative aspects in time: it is an or-

427

ganic maturation that is both growth and decomposition. But since only a minor curve is left, it is the aspect of deterioration that must dominate. (p. 7)

[Expressions] of hope or consolation are interwoven with the darker moods in varying patterns traced by Quasimodo's sensuously melodic line. The basic pattern of many of the poems is, however, the essential oscillation that we have already seen in "Ed è súbito sera" and "Curva minore"; a privileged moment or lost Eden is glimpsed, a possible evasion opens up; a moment of transport follows but then the way of escape is closed and there is a return to a real and painful present. But often in the longer poems a coda is added that recapitulates both themes, and a resolution is effected in which some of the consoling power of the vision is retained. The early "Vento a Tìndari" is perhaps one of the better examples of this full pattern. (p. 8)

"Vento a Tìndari" contains something of the mystic aura that surrounds Quasimodo's Sicily, magically resurgent in apocalyptic visions of winds, lands and waters and heavenly prodigies, a Sicily to which he has restored its ancient powers of myth and metamorphosis. (p. 11)

[The] mythic vision is often fused with very human memories of childhood and adolescence. (p. 12)

The poem ["L'Anapo"] is about the stir of life and the silence of death that inhabit the body of the eternal Adam-adolescent. (p. 13)

The poem is not simply a bitter comment on the tides of blood and the vain cycles of death. Its irony has a double edge: it also celebrates the moment of human laughter and the eternal recurrence of life preserved in immortal germ. (p. 14)

[With the appearance of *Giorno dopo giorno,* it] became evident that Quasimodo had worked a definite change in his style, and it was felt that his new idiom shared some of the qualities of his translations. The concentrated phrases had opened up, had become longer and more explicit and, in contrast to the fragmentary utterances of his first style, they were connected in a discourse of greater continuity. There were already indications of this change in some of the later poems of the volume *Ed è subito sera,* especially the longer ones, but perhaps even in the shorter "Che vuoi, pastore d'aria" ("What do you want, shepherd of the air?") the sententiousness of the earlier poems has dissolved in an almost idyllic tone; in the place of their compressed and richly melodic phrase there is a sustained but subdued rhythm. (pp. 14-15)

[Roles] for the man and woman in the alternation of dream and reality, and the man's acquiescence—if not his complete resignation—are expressed in "L'alto veliero" ("The tall sailing ship"). The tone also remains subdued—the dialog of a domestic idyll. (p. 15)

The memory of Sicily is also present in these poems, but it is invoked with new accents: the mythic grandeur and aura of miraculous power, once recalled in images "not human," are diffused in softer tones. There is, to be sure, a passage in which the south wind is envisioned as a creative force, like the Lucretian Venus infusing the stir of life in the land, but it remains a natural power. . . . (p. 16)

The poems contained in the volume *Giorno dopo giorno* (*Day after day*) recite the efforts of a heart enclosed in a "defeated christian pity" to overcome its rancor and to find the words and signs that could establish the dialog with other men: "the yearning to speak a word to you / before the sky closes again / upon another day." The anguish that before remained enclosed is now poured out in pity for the living and the dead. . . .

[In "The Snow," the] solitude and sense of estrangement remains, but the rancor has become *pietà,* a word now often repeated. It is more than pity; it is piety and love that seeks a means of breaking out of solitude, of surpassing a life that seems to have been reduced to a mechanical "play of blood." (p. 18)

The name of Christ and Christian images now appear in these poems, a Christ invoked because of his absence from the earth and from the hearts of men at war. . . . The human beings who inhabit this world can be loved only with a measure of ironic pity. (p. 19)

"Man of my time" is the closing poem of the volume *Day after day,* and with it we have reached the present term of Quasimodo's evolution as a poet. . . . [In three subsequent volumes] the content of the individual poems vary, but the same direct, emphatic voice and rhetorical attitude prevail. The change is deliberate and reflects Quasimodo's conception of the poet's necessary role in our time.

The wispy dream, the wavering flutes of the Mallarmean faun or the perennial Arcadia are now impossible pastimes. Absent is the passive or despairing attitude often assumed in Quasimodo's earlier poetry; the new activist of the word now assumes his social responsibility and his poems breathe a positive fervor. A decisive voice tells us that this is not a time for "closed mumbling of maledictions." The blank page must be filled and a reply must be given to the unanswered questions. (pp. 20-1)

The forcefulness of these two poems cannot be discounted as rhetoric. But very often the dramatic statement is overcharged, the image crude and emphatic. . . . Many Italian readers, conscious of the qualities of reserve and understatement recently recovered by Italian poetry, have not taken kindly to the later Quasimodo. He answered them in a "Discourse on Poetry" published in *The false and true green* (1956). The idiom of poetry, he proclaims, has no life apart from history. . . . The mode of poetry is determined by history, but in return, the real poet "modifies" the world. "The strong images of his creation beat upon man's heart" more powerfully than philosophy or written history. His poetry is transformed into ethics because of its very beauty; his responsibility is the direct consequences of its perfection. He opens a dialog with his fellow men that is more necessary than science or than treaties between nations. . . . (pp. 22-3)

Quasimodo takes himself—and life—with a terrible seriousness. He once said of his poetry:

> Your tremendous gift of words, O Lord,
> I pay out
> assiduously.

Such seriousness is not without presumption, and there have been moments when it seemed slightly ridiculous, at least to some. Quasimodo himself has allowed querulous comments to enter his "dialog," and one senses a professional rancor. But no one . . . would deny the expressive power and beauty of much of his poetry. They cannot deny, either, his sincerity, nor the basic soundness of his poetics, and the need for a new rhetoric. . . . Salvatore Quasimodo may not have succeeded in writing the poems implicit in his poetics. But there is something admirable in his intense and pained awareness. (p. 23)

> *Louis R. Rossi, "Salvatore Quasimodo: A Presentation," in* Chicago Review *(reprinted by permission of* Chicago Review; *copyright © 1960 by* Chicago Review*), Vol. 14, No. 1, 1960, pp. 1-23.*

FRANCIS GOLFFING

[Quasimodo's] voice is not only unique in contemporary European poetry but it is a voice of rarest distinction: absolutely free of rhetorical inflation, at once generous and fastidious, *un "fashionable"* yet representative of an entire generation. The formal perfection of his verse is matched by both solidity and urgency of matter; in other words, Quasimodo is the least vapid of poets, even as he is one of the purest by those exigent standards to which Mallarmé, Rilke, and Valéry have accustomed us, the dedicated readers and judges of lyric poetry.

Italian critics have made much of Quasimodo's changes of style, of his evolution from complete internality, or subjectivity, into a writer of verse that is public and largely available, because of his new concern with extra personal issues and relevancies. Provocative though they are, considerations of this sort tend to base themselves on psychological rather than artistic evidence. Unquestionably the late war brought on a crisis in Quasimodo's career as a poet: from 1940 onward there is less listening to the "inner voice," a marked shift from the personal to the general tragedy. Unquestionably, too, that shift of thematic attention has resulted in certain stylistic modifications, which I am the last to undervalue. But what strikes the reader most forcibly is the continuity of Quasimodo's work, not its discontinuity. I would even hesitate to speak of the later work as being richer, or more mature, or more complex, than the poems contained in *Ed è subito sera*. From first to last Quasimodo is an extraordinarily subtle but rather simple poet, compared with such writers as Montale, Eliot, Yeats. His poetic extensions have been lateral rather than in (intellectual) depth; his gains have been gains in technical mastery, made possible by the influx of fresh subject matter. Yet even in his latest work the prevailing mode is that of the *chant intérieur*, the continuous melodic line in the manner of Eluard or Reverdy. There are certain traits, too, which he shares with Montale: a strong distaste for the anecdotal conduct of the poem; his determination to allow the initial emotion to shape the occasion—not *of* the poem, but that occasion which *is*, itself, the poem.

The pieces contained in *Giorno dopo giorno* are his most formal compositions, Leopardian up to a point, at least in diction and the technical management of the hendecasyllable. Yet Quasimodo's sensibility is entirely different from this or any other predecessor. His nostalgia points to no Nirvana (Leopardi) or Platonic eros (*il dolce stil nuovo*), no Christian or pagan cosmic essence (Pascoli, Carducci). Rather, it seeks to relocate emotion in a primordial purity of perception and compassion, a paradisiacal state of radical innocence. That innocence is, most frequently, associated with nature, the basic vegetative conditions of the earth. . . .

While Quasimodo lacks the intellectual complexity and male power of Montale, he excels the latter in sheer lyrical intensity. That lyricism is sustained in poem after poem, throughout the body of his work. Passages of deliberate prosiness—there are many of those in his latest book—only serve to give further resonance, a subtler edge, to the welling up of music from within: They never contradict the song, nor do they destroy any "poetic illusion." For of illusion there is none in Quasimodo; every word means exactly what it says, even as it shades into the unsayable; every statement is authentic and involves, along with the poet's inwardness, the total constellation of this earth as we know it; as we can never forget it, save at our peril. For this earth is incomparable—*impareggiabile*—precisely because we and it are one; comparison can neither raise it in our esteem nor dwarf it. This co-extension of man and earth is, to me, the most significant—and most affecting—aspect of the poet's work. Quasimodo triumphs in the abolition of both facile dualism and mystical vagueness, in the resolute allegiance to what *is* and, since it can be, *will* be. (p. 17)

> *Francis Golffing, in* Books Abroad *(copyright 1960 by the University of Oklahoma Press), Vol. 34, No. 1, Winter, 1960.*

THOMAS G. BERGIN

Assaying [the letters of *Lettere d'amore a Maria Cumani*] collectively, the first thought that comes to mind is that they are truly and exclusively love letters. For the central theme throughout is the love inspired in the poet by the dancer: its mystery, its strength and its significance in his life and his art. Over the years this obsessive concentration endures. . . . The preface, by Davide Lajolo, suggests that the collection provides a kind of commentary on the literary world of the period, but I doubt the validity of this affirmation. . . . We do hear much about Quasimodo's own work of course—what he is planning, what he is writing, what kind of reviews he gets and the like. We get a clear picture of a man who has no doubts about the importance of his art nor about his own destiny. And of a man in love. The beauty and eloquence of many passages bear witness to the sincerity of his love, and they have their own irony in a way. For Quasimodo had a horror of being "romantic," yet, as he is obliged to confess, some of his outpourings of rapture are couched in the old romantic idiom. (pp. 103-04)

> *Thomas G. Bergin, in* Books Abroad *(copyright 1975 by the University of Oklahoma Press), Vol. 49, No. 1, Winter, 1975.*

*   *   *

QUENEAU, Raymond   1903-1976

A French novelist, playwright, poet, screenwriter, essayist, editor, and critic, Queneau was a master of colloquial speech, slang, and varied rhetorical devices. Like Joyce, he was concerned with the relationship between written and spoken language, and he continually toyed with the conventions of written French. Viewing literature as a category of speech, Queneau attacked traditional rhetoric through parody, and his works are imbued with the surrealist's taste for the ridiculous aspects of ordinary existence. (See also *CLC*, Vols. 2, 5, and *Contemporary Authors*, obituary, Vols. 69-72.)

ROBERT ALTER

Queneau's *Exercices de style* (1947) is an intriguing and at times immensely amusing book, but it is just what its title implies, a set of exercises; and to suggest, as George Steiner has done, that it constitutes a major landmark in twentieth-century literature, is to mislead readers in the interest of promoting literary "future shock."

The instance of *Exercices de style* is worth pausing over briefly because it represents one ultimate limit of the whole self-conscious mode. Queneau begins his book by reporting a banal anecdote of a young man with a long neck and a missing button on his coat who is jostled in a crowded bus. He tells this anecdote ninety-nine times, constantly changing the narrative viewpoint, the style, the literary conventions; going as far as the use of mathematical notation and anagrammatic scrambling of letters in one direction, and the resort to heavy dialect and badly anglicized French in the other; even rendering the incident in alexandrines, in free verse, as a sonnet, as a playlet. All this is extremely ingenious, and, I would admit, more than ingenious, because as one reads the same simple episode over and over through all these acrobatic variations, one is forced to recognize both the stunning arbitrariness of any decision to tell a story in a particular way and the endless possibilities for creating fictional "facts" by telling a story differently.

The controlling perception, however, of *Exercices* is one that goes back to the generic beginnings of the novel; and to see how much more richly that insight can be extended into fictional space, one has only to think of Sterne, where a "Queneauesque" passage like the deliberately schematic "Tale of Two Lovers" is woven into a thick texture of amorous anecdotes that critically juxtapose literary convention with a sense of the erotic as a cogent fact of human experience. Precisely what is missing from *Exercices de style* is any sense—and playfulness need not exclude seriousness—of human experience, which is largely kept out of the book in order to preserve the technical purity of the experiment. I don't mean to take Queneau to task for what he clearly did not intend; I mean only to emphasize that criticism need not make excessive claims for this kind of writing. Queneau, of course, has written full-scale novels of flaunted artifice, both before and after *Exercices de style,* that do involve a more complex sense of experience. (pp. 211-12)

Over against *Exercices* one might usefully set a novel like *Le Chiendent* (1933), Queneau's remarkable fictional farce in the self-conscious mode. At the center of this grand display of verbal highjinks, parodistic ploys, hilarious stylizations, and satiric illuminations, stands a death—that of Ernestine the serving-girl, which, for all its abruptness, improbability, and absurdity, has large reverberations in the novel. "When a tree burns," says Ernestine, dying on her wedding night, "nothin's left but smoke and ashes. No more tree. That's like me. Nothin left but rot, while the li'l voice that talks in your head when you're all alone, nothin's left of it. When mine stops, it ain't gonna talk again nowhere else." (p. 221)

[In] a final paragraph, Queneau dissolves his joined characters into separate and unconnected entities, concluding with a single silhouette, not yet a realized character, one among thousands of possible alternatives—which was precisely the image of the novelist-artificer's arbitrary choice in the making of fictions that began the whole novel. And yet the arbitrary invention is one that has been elaborated in order to reveal something about the real world. The whole farce is

in fact a sustained metaphysical meditation on the dizzying paradoxes of being and nonbeing, in life and in fiction; and that meditation culminates in these last two pages, where the characters are finally shuffled back into the shadowy pre-world of fictional beginnings. . . . (pp. 221-22)

> *Robert Alter, in* TriQuarterly 33 (© *1975 by* TriQuarterly), *Spring, 1975.*

ROBERT HENKELS, JR.

Raymond Queneau remains unclassifiable. It is as fruitless to group him with a single literary school as it is to reduce one of his intentionally bad puns to a single meaning. Recalling the Surrealists, Queneau rolls words like dice. Anticipating the "new novel," his plots come unravelled like scarfs caught on a snag. With the publication of *Le Vol d'Icare* and its translation, the "franc-tireur" of French literature has struck again, casting about the literary scene with thrusts of a rapier wit. It should come as no surprise that *The Flight of Icarus* is neither fish nor fowl, that it explores several topics, and dabbles with several genres all at once.

A light-hearted pastiche of the "new novels'" narrative austerity; a historical reconstruction of literary circles in the 1890s; a spoof of the clichés of the mystery story; and a novel about the novel told in the form of a play complete with stage directions and 74 scenes, Queneau's book is a heady literary cocktail which provides amusing reading. (p. 160)

For all of its sparkle and verve, or perhaps because of them, toward the end *The Flight of Icarus* often seems a bit forced and breathless, rather like an elaborate Peter de Vries joke-novel running down. Here, as in *Les Fleurs bleues,* Queneau's satirical target is to a large degree topical, and a reader unaware of the debate ranging in France in the '60s over the role of characters and plot may well miss some of the fun. Doubtless these effects are intentional, however, and they help focus attention on the plays on words and the juxtaposition of levels of language. On the positive side, Queneau remains the master of this kind of inspired juggling. . . . In short, *The Flight of Icarus* is a witty, contagiously funny treatment of literature and language whose humor palls as one realizes that all there is behind the character's flight and words themselves, "c'est du vent." (pp. 160-61)

> *Robert Henkels, Jr., in* French Review *(copyright 1975 by the American Association of Teachers of French), October, 1975.*

ROBERT W. GREENE

Morale élémentaire, while it holds few surprises for the reader familiar with Raymond Queneau's earlier writings, represents nonetheless an important and fascinating achievement. Surrealist, poet, mathematician, novelist, humorist, linguistic explorer, Queneau is most of these again in his latest book. It has three parts, a sequence of fifty-one identically constructed verse poems and two groups of prose poems, a series of sixteen texts followed by a series of sixty-four. With one exception (the last poem in part two), no text takes up more than a page. The prose texts blend the narrative with the descriptive mode in such a way as to keep the "moral" just beyond our grasp, and all are graced with Queneau's characteristic wit.

The verse texts, a stunning tour de force, give us Queneau

the student of linguistic production and the inventor of poetic forms at his best. Every text has precisely the same structure and appearance and can be read either from left to right, line by line from top to bottom (i.e., according to the usual procedure for reading a poem), or from top to bottom within each of the three columns that appear on the page. Each poem is fifteen lines long. Except for a part of the middle column (always the same part) which reads like a seven-line poem, the columns comprise only two words per line, a noun and its modifier. Each phrase so formed seems a variant of another such phrase in the text; a semantic element in one phrase appears to derive from or to engender another phrase by tautology, antithesis or metonymy. The miniature "poem" inserted in the middle column is as rudimentary in its way as are the noun-modifier phrases that literally surround it.

It is obvious that we are once again dealing with a kind of *exercises de style,* but this time everything is on a more elemental level, with the author more concerned with the production of writing itself than with narrative voice variations and thus more concerned than ever before, perhaps, with every writer's *morale élémentaire.* (p. 833)

> *Robert W. Greene, in* Books Abroad *(copyright 1976 by the University of Oklahoma Press), Vol. 50, No. 4, Autumn, 1976.*

LOUISA E. JONES

In all his novels, Raymond Queneau questions the process of history. Individual lives are drawn into historical disasters.... *Les Fleurs bleues* stands out as one novel in which history, as it relates individual and group experience, does not appear only in the dénouement....

Queneau makes no pretense to careful observation and recording of social mores. Rather, he examines the metaphysics of history, the rapport between general and particular circumstance, between event, experience and invention—his own, or that of his characters. Such problems inevitably lead him to be concerned with perception, both in life and in art, both conscious and unconscious. (p. 323)

Queneau's novels recognize none of the traditional criteria for *vraisemblance* except for that of cohesion. They shamelessly present pure fantasy instead of the judicious observation of verifiable realities. His adhesion to the actual instead of the abstract does not, for him, preclude gratuitous invention. He neither records history nor imitates it. How then does he make of it an element of major importance?

A similar paradox exists in Queneau's treatment of individual characters. Although interest in psychoanalysis is strikingly present in all of his books, his characters are never psychologically complex. They are never the case studies of realist novels, never individualized psyches through which he can reach more general problems of society and history. Instead they are simple, emblematic, almost allegorical at times. (p. 324)

It is ... the Duke's individual actions, spanning several centuries, that constitute linear time in the novel. Suspense demands on recognizing what period he is in at a given moment, anticipating the next stage and wondering about the outcome. In this sense, *Les Fleurs bleues* is teleological and corresponds both to earlier conventions of the novel and to the western concept of history.... Queneau carefully identifies the development of his story with the progression of history, all the more so since the Duke is directly involved in many historical events of each period. Each slice of history is characterized in the same ways: by its food, its monuments, its inventions and, most important, by the unique historical events in which the Duke takes part. (pp. 324-25)

We learn to expect this range of topics in each period. A recurrent pattern is thus set up. Yet at the same time, by contrasting the Duke's experiences in each age, we become sensitive to change and progression....

The focus remains clearly on society's changes, not on the Duke's. Even more important, it is because his character remains the same throughout that society's evolution stands out in contrast. (p. 325)

While linear progression is ... strongly established in *Les Fleurs bleues,* the very parallelism between [the Duke's and Cidrolin's] personal lives provides a fine example of Queneau's efforts to counterbalance linearity in his novel.... Such patterning has many functions. Its improbability constantly destroys narrative illusion, pointing up the novel's existence as a verbal construct. At the same time, like rhyme in verse, it reveals unsuspected meanings linking the two instances thus paralleled. For our purposes, however, its most important function, again similar to that of verse rhyme, is to break up the linearity of the novel's progression and to institute a strong sense of cyclical organization, both on the level of language and on that of represented action. (p. 326)

In *Les Fleurs bleues,* linear and cyclical time function as ... potential systems. At the same time, the many echoes suggest that somehow Queneau's heroes were united all along, in some other, nonlinear dimension. (p. 327)

Queneau's debt to Flaubert [is evident] in the depiction of banality in its link with progress, and *Les Fleurs bleues* continues the preoccupation of earlier novels, to some degree. Not only does Queneau create a strong sense of the meaningless proliferation of objects, language, and event familiar in so many writers since Flaubert, he also underlines in this way Cidrolin's loneliness and isolation....

Queneau's history shows us the individual more and more controlled by group opinion. Part of the modern "bêtise" Queneau denounces is the determination of values by general concensus, particularly with regard to normalcy. (p. 329)

Queneau suggests both the irrelevance of consciousness to events and on the tendency of the latter to become cyclical.... The linking of imagination with historical process, in Cidrolin's dreams and the Duke's acts, is established firmly at a level beyond logic and conscious perception.

Both of Queneau's heroes, however reprehensible their behavior might seem at moments, remain strongly sympathetic to the reader. Partly this is because of the schematic presentation of character which mitigates the Duke's violence in particular, giving it the effect of cartoon or comic strip action, but mostly it is because both men represent, in complementary ways, the creative power of imagination. In fact, both the heroes in this novel suggest the artist. For the Duke, art is a means of directly creating history—or the fiction of history, since his cave drawings will provide conclusive evidence that pre-Adamite man existed. Cidrolin, in his much more modest if equally self-directed art, is not only a painter but a writer, a graffitomaniac. Much has been made by critics of Queneau's famous games with language, his inventions of words, his mixtures of the conventions of written and spoken language, his imaginative use of naming and all the other techniques, so often catalogued. While a major function of such *exercises de style* is to point up the literalness of language and the status of fiction as a language construct, to increase the reader's awareness of the texture and matter of the medium, in *Les Fleurs bleues* these devices also underline language as an historical reality. (pp. 331-32)

Les Fleurs bleues creates a softened, . . . promising fatality, allowing greater possibilities for personal invention. . . . As for Cidrolin, . . . he need not be crushed by or even involved in history. His Ark comes equipped with a small rowboat in which he and Lalix set off on their own. . . . The contemplative hero safeguards his detachment when he "detaches" the rowboat. Again, of course, the narrative is metaphorical, almost allegorical, but the abstract term of the allegory remains open to many interpretations. Only the general tone is unambiguous: in this book, it is by no means disastrous. If *Les Fleurs bleues* remains Queneau's most affirmative novel, it is largely because of the close connection made between historical time, both linear and cyclical, and creative invention. History can be presented fantastically because it is itself a story, a fiction, a privileged balance between imagination and event. It is concrete and localized, like the intrigue of fiction, yet universal, like poetry. In *Les Fleurs bleues* time does not destroy the magic but creates it.

Queneau has obviously rejected the connection between writer and society, between language and event, that [Balzac wrote of in *La Comédie humaine*]. Far from being the expression of action, language is itself action; history, like an individual act, is a verbal construct. By showing us historical process and social behavior through the texture of language, Queneau underlines the creative potential of language as a kind of cultural index. . . . *Les Fleurs bleues* emphasizes its own existence in historical time, without sacrificing its status as created object. (pp. 333-34)

As presented in this novel, the cycle of history has no privileged origin, no central point of reference which gives meaning. The search for pre-adamite man and the Duke's phoney evidence sufficiently parody the nostalgia for beginnings and render it ridiculous. . . . Queneau portrays in his novel [in the words of Jean Hippolyte] "a history which no longer has anything to do with eschatological history, a history which loses itself always in its own pursuit, since the origin is perpetually displaced." The fiction, then, cannot be told but simply experienced. It is not a report on history but an historical construct. Movements towards awareness means growing realisation of the shaping role of language in consciousness; various equilibria between event and invention give more and more place to the texture of language, to relationships between *signifiants* as they both create and reveal our experience, rather than to those between *signifiés*. (pp. 334-35)

> Louisa E. Jones, "Event and Invention: History in Queneau's 'Les Fleurs Bleues'," in Symposium (*copyright © 1977 by Syracuse University Press*), Winter, 1977, pp. 323-36.

MICHAEL WOOD

Queneau confesses his debt to Céline and Joyce, but we probably ought to situate him closer to Nabokov than to either. There is a similar word-play, of course, but there are also similar touches of sentimentality, a similar aloofness, a similar elegance, and the same dim view of history. *The Sunday of Life* was Queneau's tenth novel, published in 1952, and if it doesn't quite have the verve of *Zazie,* it has almost everything else that makes Queneau such an appealing and elusive writer. . . .

If there isn't much room for high moral exploits in Queneau's world, it is not because he is a cynic, or because he wishes, as Barbara Wright suggests in her introduction to *The Sunday of Life,* to portray "humble characters" or to stay close to "the common man." It is because high morality is almost always spouted by frauds, and people who live in falling countries should not throw stones. . . .

Queneau's characters, like his eccentric spellings, are energetic alternatives to a false nobility, and their charm lies in their persistent intelligence and their absolute refusal of respectability. (p. 38)

> Michael Wood, in The New York Review of Books (*reprinted with permission from* The New York Review of Books; *copyright © 1977 NYREV, Inc.*), May 12, 1977.

WEBSTER SCHOTT

Nathaniel Hawthorne said that happiness is like a butterfly that evades you if you chase it and may light on you if you sit down. *The Sunday of Life* is a novel about a man whom happiness follows like Hawthorne's butterfly. The report of how this marvel occurs is so droll that one could read it as a . . . smile—which would miss the larger wonder of how playfulness turns serious, which we often call art. . . .

[Like] some of the better French wines, [Queneau's] fiction doesn't travel well. It has an ambiguous philosophic cast that doesn't square with conventional Anglo-Saxon morality.

Furthermore, Queneau doesn't really write stories. He writes points of view. He illustrates ideas, most of which come from Queneau's romance with Hegel. The essence of spirit is freedom. War defines mankind. We cannot reach truth without passing through contradictions. Some of this Queneau believes. Some he spoofs. Some he throws in to make sure we're paying attention.

Queneau's young hero, Pvt. Valentine Bru, glides through life as though demonstrating Freud's principle that pleasure is the absence of pain. Absurdity is visited on him without effect. Queneau has Bru look at life in odd pieces that bear no apparent relationship—new prime ministers and statues in a park, heavy necking in a tunnel of love and business failures. Yet the pieces must be integrated into a perception of the whole, regardless of how boring, undramatic, and perhaps pointless the whole may be. Such considerations plunge Bru "into an abyss of stupefaction." . . .

Queneau's novel is about all the things it appears to be about: being nobody, lost in history, but content; clouds of gloom with comic linings; the tranquilizer imagination; the struggle of doing good (the recalled Pvt. Bru tries sainthood and gets captured); and how time becomes the money of our lives. And it's about stretching the limits of the novel form. *The Sunday of Life* refracts philosophy into fiction. It bends ideas into jokes and characters that form a comic reconstruction of the philosophy. Valentine Bru is Charlie Chaplin posing as Hegel in a state of innocence. And the book leaves open other possibilities as well. After all, Queneau's favorite character in fiction was Dostoyevsky's Idiot. (p. K10)

> *Webster Schott, in* Book World—The Washington Post *(© The Washington Post), July 3, 1977.*

R

READ, Piers Paul 1941-

Read is an English author of both fiction and nonfiction. He is perhaps best known for *Alive*, his restrained account of what has been called the most arresting peacetime survival story yet told, the 1972 Andes air crash. He was the choice of the survivors to write their official story. (See also *CLC*, Vol. 4, and *Contemporary Authors*, Vols. 21-24, rev. ed.)

The severity of [*The Upstart*] is not immediately apparent. The opening chapters record the childhood and youth of a Yorkshire clergyman's son in a sharp but amusing way, so that the author might be congratulated on the "malicious" wit with which the boy's "agonies" of social embarrassment are presented. But, quite suddenly, words like "malice" and "agony" need to be used less lightly and loosely. The boy, Hilary Fletcher, might seem not unlike L. P. Hartley's Eustace as he diffidently tries to place his social position between the knowing children of the local aristocracy and the rough farmboys. Eventually, it becomes apparent that the boy has grown up monstrous. The calm, graceful prose which seemed so appropriate for a traditional social comedy about class is equally effective for describing young Fletcher's progress in joyless depravity. Finally he becomes a Roman Catholic, recognizes himself as evil, and repents. So it is, after all, rather like one of Hartley's novels—*My Fellow-Devils*, with its persuasive emphasis on Catholicism and evil. . . .

[There is a] melodramatic sequence of events [that] takes up most of the book. It is so lurid that it could have been ludricrous, but there is a grim, simple intensity in the writing which makes the story acceptable as a serious representation of evil. The narrator persuades through the apparent objectivity of his presentation of himself: it is like the cold, factual-sounding account that the agnostic Winterman gave of the sins and penitence of the hero of Mr Read's *Monk Dawson*.

> "Prodigal's Progress," in The Times Literary Supplement (© *Times Newspapers Ltd.* (London) 1973; reproduced from The Times Literary Supplement by permission), September 7, 1973, p. 1017.

NICK TOTTEN

Novels like *Polonaise* usually die at the outline stage. In skeletal form they impress everyone, not least the author; but as the appalling difficulty of actually writing them gradually emerges, there is a tendency to turn to other projects. Also, they fall uncomfortably between two stools: more than just another novel, but distinctly less than the masterpiece one will write some day. But there is a lingering attachment to the material—always a feeling that it could somehow be pushed and prodded into that vital inevitability which was promised in the original conception. So sometimes the writer buckles down to it.

Piers Paul Read has buckled down to it, and produced a novel not without conviction. It is about a writer, which is difficult enough; but much more so when the writer is a decayed Polish aristocrat involved in Communist politics between the wars. Stefan Kornowski is also a very particular kind of writer: he is and remains into middle age an adolescent nihilist, the kind who identifies dutifully with De Sade and picks interminably at the scab of his atheism. The characterisation is extremely accurate—in terms of a stage of development: many precociously intellectual young people enjoy this pose for a while, and can be seen any day promenading through the older universities with their black capes and other paraphernalia. It is at least an effective cover for sexual nervousness. But the idea of someone spending his life stuck like this—because the wind changed at the wrong moment?—is horrifying. It makes one worry about Mr Read. . . .

There's a great deal of plot in *Polonaise*, certainly, spun in endless strands of insubstantial candy floss. The historical background is solid, though, or at any rate plausible; and obviously something has to happen to fill the prolonged pause in Stefan's development. Clearly if anyone could keep this stuff up for a lifetime it would be a Slavic Catholic aristocrat: look at Nabokov. But why should we, or Mr Read for that matter, be interested? By the time Stefan makes his earth-shattering discovery that nihilism is a mistake (the whole tenor of the novel being that old Chestertonian nonsense about Christianity and nihilism as the only alternatives) I was watching the picture with the sound turned down. (p. 22)

> *Nick Totten, in* The Spectator (© *1976 by* The Spectator; *reprinted by permission of* The Spectator), *November 20, 1976.*

434

JOHN MELLORS

Stefan, ... [the] unheroic hero [of *Polonaise*], is a writer thwarted by 'the unreliability of his characters'. He persuades himself that he is a Marxist, but when he tries to write about 'positive heroes', his carefully constructed puppets run amok and shock even him, their creator. He concludes that his 'muse', his creativity, 'is irony, undiluted irony'. He rejects communism because communists still believe in the perfectibility of the soul; the Soviet Union 'is Holy Russia under another name'.

Stefan is a typical Read character, introspective, intelligent, determined to use self-knowledge in order to cultivate his true individuality....

Polonaise is a rich and resonant novel of ideas, saved from solemnity by the astringency of Read's style and his ability to make the most eccentric characters believable. Where it fails, as *The Upstart*, Read's last novel, failed, is in slipping at crucial points from drama into melodrama. (p. 688)

> *John Mellors, in* The Listener (© *British Broadcasting Corp. 1976; reprinted by permission of John Mellors), November 25, 1976.*

JAMES BROCKWAY

The sub-title of [*Polonaise*] should read: 'Or the Wreck of the Titanic'. Like the Titanic, the greater part of this book is a magnificent piece of engineering, a product of intelligence, great technical skill and hard work. Also like the Titanic, when the journey has almost been completed, in fact as late as page 343, Read's finely constructed artefact, of which its creator has every reason to feel proud, hits an iceberg of such shattering banality that the reader is left at the end like the survivors of the Titanic after she had plunged from sight for ever: surrounded by nothing else but flotsam and jetsam, a very cold feeling at the bottom of the stomach and the unanswerable question: Why did it have to happen?

Now, in his previous book, *Alive,* Read wrote highly successfully of the Andes air crash of 1972 and in the novel which preceded that, *The Upstart,* he showed how his cold-blooded hero wreaked havoc and destruction among those who had humiliated him during his youth. Could it be that the author has now been unable to resist the temptation to wreck one of his own creations, and just as ruthlessly?

What is *Polonaise* about? Stripped to its barebones, which Read has richly covered with some excellent writing, it recounts the fortunes of Stefan and Krystyna Kornowski, children of a dissolute and spendthrift Polish count who reduces his family to poverty and is very soon reduced to imbecility himself, after an absurdly unsuccessful attempt, à la Uncle Vanya, to slay the representative of the bank to which he has come to owe all he has....

It is Stefan with whom Read is chiefly concerned. We first meet him lying across a summerhouse table on his father's ruined estate, attempting to take *Cogito, ergo sum* a few philosophical steps further. He is a thinker, a cynic, an immoralist (God is dead, so why shouldn't Stefan Kornowski take over?). He is also an embryo Marquis de Sade and Jack the Ripper, who in his early writings is soon linking the ecstasy of sex to the ecstasy of inflicting pain. As for Poland, his attitude to his country is one of contempt. When he is successful as a fashionable playwright, founding the 'theatre of brevity', he sees his success as the triumph of Polishness over himself.

Of art he says: "what is art but artificiality . . . a fraud, a hallucinatory drug for those without the courage to live?"... His plan [to murder for pleasure] is frustrated by an unexpected opportunity to indulge his sensuality in another way—a nice example of Piers Paul Read's special brand of undercooled cynicism, his refrigerated sense of humour.

Indeed, it is partly because he makes of this monster, Stefan Kornowski, so fascinating a creature that the final disaster is so disastrous. But it is also because Read is a fine writer, so that about halfway through his novel, the reader, who has so far felt everything is proceeding pretty slowly, begins to feel he is on familiar territory—in fact, in the middle of a nineteenth-century novel such as Dostoevsky's *The Idiot* or Flaubert's *Education Sentimentale,* to which there is indeed a passing reference, without actually mentioning title or author.

By the time Stefan has just avoided committing his murder, Hitler has crossed the Polish border and Stefan, man of ideas and not of action, is then halfway across the Atlantic, on his way to America, where he stays for the duration.

The author then leaps twenty years (Whatever Happened to Baby World War II?) and the last part of his novel begins in Paris in the late Fifties. Here, Krystyna, escaped from the Nazis and now Madame de Pincey, takes into her home young Annabel Colte, daughter of the Earl of Felsted, whose seat is an unlikely manor on the north coast of Cornwall.

In Paris, young Annabel meets young Teofil [Krystyna's Polish son] but also Uncle Stefan.... Meantime the air is cooling and we are entering the iceberg zone. Soon all these disgusting Continentals are invited across to Cornwall to meet the English aristocracy, into which poor Teofil is going to marry. Icebergs are now already actually in sight, in the shape of Annabel's relatives. Then along comes the fatal iceberg. Uncle Stefan, wise to the game the dastardly English aristocracy are up to, to wreck the proposed marriage between their daughter and this piece of Polish riff-raff, Teofil, gets rid of the pawn the English aristos are using, by shoving him over a cliff.

The incident here is sufficient to annihilate everything the author has achieved up to page 343, just as that iceberg put paid to the Titanic. I have suggested the author may have done it deliberately. Out of contempt for the novel? Out of contempt for the reader, who hasn't the courage to live but uses the novel as a hallucinatory drug? Or was it to be able to end his novel somehow, any old how, because what had fascinated him, Polish society between 1929-1939, was now lost and gone for ever, anyway?

I have taken the risk of telling much of the story but have deliberately left many salient features out so as not to spoil the reader's enjoyment—for writing of this quality, which is fascinatingly unlike much other novel writing of quality in England at present, should be read. Piers Paul Read is an authentic personality as a writer and, icebergs in the offing or not, to read his novel is an authentic experience too and not to be equated with the taking of an hallucinatory drug. (pp. 22-3)

> *James Brockway, "Going Down Bravely,"*
> *in* Books and Bookmen (© *copyright James Brockway 1977; reprinted with permission), February, 1977, pp. 22-3.*

PETER VANSITTART

Admirers of the spare, intelligent *Monk Dawson* may be disappointed by *Polonaise*, an unexciting academic chronicle-novel.... A leading theme is the slow evaporization of oh young men oh young comrades into disillusion, self-interest, patriotism, common sense. There is the familiar amiable, soft-fibred intellectual whose ineffective good intentions and minor talents compete with a feeble sadism and a mordant temptation to see Hitler as the uninhibited artist in action. The Poles tend to cherish self-absurdity and national deprecation. The writing is clear yet makes somewhat plodding recapitulations. 'Capitalism is a necessary state in the development of Man's productive capacities ...'.... Read fills in everything to the last detail, his dialogue more earnest than compelling. He describes and explains too much. (p. 108)

Hitherto justly acclaimed for freshness, stylishness, inventiveness, Read here takes too few imaginative risks. He reminds us of serious matters in what is not quite a serious novel. (p. 109)

> *Peter Vansittart, in* London Magazine (© London Magazine), *February-March, 1977.*

* * *

RIBEIRO, João Ubaldo   1941-

Ribeiro is a Brazilian novelist and short story writer.

PHOEBE-LOU ADAMS

[*Sergeant Getúlio*] is a tale of heroic dedication to an ideal of conduct told entirely through the thoughts and occasional conversations of the dedicated hero who is, ironically, a very bad man indeed. Sergeant Getúlio is an ignorant, quarrelsome, foul-mouthed frontiersman, a policeman who moonlights as hit man for a crooked politician, a torturer if excuse arises, an abominable brute by any standard of decency.... It is Mr. Ribeiro's intention to make the reader accept this wretched fellow as intelligent, amusing, pitiable, and ultimately a true epic hero—an astounding project, brought off with brilliant, astounding success. (p. 93)

> *Phoebe-Lou Adams, in* The Atlantic Monthly (*copyright © 1978 by The Atlantic Monthly Company, Boston, Mass.; reprinted with permission), February, 1978.*

[*Sergeant Getúlio* is an unusual tale] of a grisly mercenary's fulfillment of a mission to transport a political prisoner despite the armies sent to stop him and even a retraction of his original orders. Employing the thoughts and conversations of Sergeant Getúlio in a stream-of-consciousness style, the story is broken midway with a dialogue. It is at this point, when Getúlio defies the new orders in an attempt to righteously pursue his goal, that he begins to turn from a ghastly, violent figure into a sort of moral hero. The novel, though difficult in style and steeped in violence, is a rewarding vision, touched with sardonic humor, of an age-old conflict. (p. 977)

> Booklist (*reprinted by permission of the American Library Association; copyright 1978 by the American Library Association), February 15, 1978.*

BARBARA PROBST SOLOMON

[In "Sergeant Getúlio," the] secret narrator is the Brazilian backlands. Nature is as much a force for Ubaldo Ribeiro as low town life is for Mr. Vargas Llosa.

The narrative takes place entirely in the crazed, childlike and savagely moral mind of Getúlio, who is a gunman for hire. (p. 11)

As Jorge Amado points out in his brief introduction [see excerpt below], "Sergeant Getúlio" is very much a novelist's novel. The book belongs neither to the dreary school of social realism from which Brazilian letters has long suffered nor to its now fashionable word-game elite. (p. 30)

> *Barbara Probst Solomon, in* The New York Times Book Review (© *1978 by The New York Times Company; reprinted by permission), April 9, 1978.*

JORGE AMADO

Among the works of fiction published in Brazil in the last decade, few have been as important as João Ubaldo Ribeiro's *Sergeant Getúlio* for the development of our fiction.

The importance of this novel is, among other things, that it makes possible the harmonious development of the literary art by preserving and deepening the most significant traits of a literature characterized throughout its history by its persistent concern with exposing both individual and social problems; in other words, a literature free of all gratuitousness.

Another reason for the novel's importance is the language of *Sergeant Getúlio*, the fruit of a literary idiom which has been taking shape for a long time, based upon creative work with the vital, popular, rich and free language that is Brazilian Portuguese, so distant from the Portuguese of Portugal in spite of their common roots. (p. ix)

Sergeant Getúlio is a novel that not only avoids the alienation process, but also points to the way in which Brazilian literature should evolve, experimenting and innovating. In developing an extremely rich narrative voice, the novelist makes use of his deep knowledge of the language spoken by the people, of the most profound reality of our people, and so his literary language is a fertile and powerful instrument of creation, competent and faithful in its artistic representation of the life of the Brazilian man....

The language in *Sergeant Getúlio*, artistically molded on the speech of the people, is often terse, hard, and cruel.... And this language gives very proper expression to the strong substance of the book, which is treated with extraordinary ability in original technical solutions. Among the mass of books published in Brazil in the last ten years, *Sergeant Getúlio* stands out as one of the few works contributing to the development of a literary art that is genuinely Brazilian. (p. xi)

> *Jorge Amado, in his introduction to* Sergeant Getúlio, *by João Ubaldo Ribeiro (copyright © 1977 by João Ubaldo Ribeiro; reprinted by permission of Houghton Mifflin Company), Houghton, 1978, pp. ix-xii.*

* * *

ROBBE-GRILLET, Alain   1922-

Robbe-Grillet is a French novelist, essayist, screenwriter, and critic. In 1964 he published *Pour un nouveau roman*, a work

which established the precepts of the New Novel movement. Rejecting traditional literary devices and theories as dishonest and misleading in their representation of the natural world, Robbe-Grillet proclaimed in his brilliant manifesto: "The world is neither significant nor absurd. It just is." He strives for complete objectivity in his writing and leaves the meaning intentionally ambiguous, for Robbe-Grillet wishes each reader to bring his own perceptive powers and life experiences to bear on his interpretation. Robbe-Grillet's theories and subsequent fictional works continue to be a center of controversy in literary circles. (See also *CLC*, Vols. 1, 2, 4, 6, 8, and *Contemporary Authors*, Vols. 9-12, rev. ed.)

VALERIE MINOGUE

In his first novel, *Les Gommes*, Robbe-Grillet deliberately exploits the potency of the Oedipus myth, while simultaneously undermining its pretensions to significance. Once the myth is planted in the text, a sculpture of a Greek chariot becomes fraught with meaning: station announcements become oracular, and snippets of news in the newspaper take on Delphic profundity. It is not only the central figure, Wallas, who is trapped, but readers too are caught in the snare of words. Readers determined to make sense of the latent symbolism of the Tarot cards, of the rue de Corinthe, the picture of Thebes, and so on, are likely to make of the novel a reworking of the Oedipus myth. But the fact that the image of the Sphinx, seen in a canal, is only a momentary configuration of bits of paper and orange peel should give us pause. . . . [The] inclusion of a report on the state of the potato crop in the newspaper "oracle" is discouraging to symbolic interpretation. The famous riddle of the Oedipus myth is here presented only as a muddled conundrum on the lips of a drunk. Robbe-Grillet is in fact both exploiting the myth, and simultaneously undermining the mythologising impulse. He draws attention to the insidious patterns of association as they arise, and from time to time renders them ludicrous by giving them an ironic pat on the head.

We seem here to observe language in the very act of generating associative series and systems: a mention of swollen feet or a whisper of Corinth generates a whole mythical infrastructure; a reference to espionage and the *Café des Alliés* evokes passages crediting Fabius with an exciting wartime past. . . . The repetitive and associative forces that are apt to influence narration are not here discarded or concealed but exhibited and exploited with considerable wit. Despite his explicit disengagement from moralism, Robbe-Grillet's aesthetic concerns lead him in fact to examine the processes of a kind of linguistic determinism from which only awareness can free us. (pp. 37-8)

He presents men in the grip of passions which disturb their perception and make them the victims of their imagination. . . . The unfortunate Wallas is everywhere tripped and trapped by the insidious patterns that interpose themselves between him and the world. Sadistic fantasies seem to leap —from iron rings, film-posters, or even bits of string—into the mind of Mathias in *Le Voyeur*. An obsessive picture of the world forms the substance of *La Jalousie*; *Dans le labyrinthe* elaborately unfolds the processes of observation, distortion, and creation in a tormented mind. In *La Maison de Rendez-vous* and *Projet pour une révolution à New York*, Robbe-Grillet turns to exploring the deviations and distortions, the recurrent motifs and obsessions of his own narrative imagination. (pp. 38-9)

[In the aptly named *Le Voyeur*], Mathias is primarily a seer, and what is more, a seer *seen*. We have no access to an inner coherent world in which smells, tastes, and feelings would take their place in an ordered structure presided over by a character. The reader too becomes a *voyeur*: our eye follows the eye of Mathias, and everywhere sees other *voyeurs*. Indeed, the vignette [is] repeated throughout the novel. . . . The world is full of eyes. . . . The figure-eight represents both the seer and the seen, the eyes that gaze, and the female figure that is the object of the gaze. And the *huit couché* is also the mathematical symbol for infinity, and thus an appropriate mark for this area of unlimited imagination. . . .

Mathias' hearing is [also] shown, like his vision, to be unreliable, selective, and subject to interpretations governed by his erotic fantasies. (p. 39)

All through the novel, neutral and geometrical descriptions stand in counterpoint to the heavily subjective and distorted world of Mathias, for whom all objects are evocative, and become part of recurrent and significant patterns. When I say *all* objects, I should of course say *all the objects he sees*. For his seeing itself is selective. . . . (p. 40)

[The] real and insistent counterbalance to Mathias' distorted perceptions lies in the meticulously neutral descriptions in which Robbe-Grillet has framed them.

The distorting—or creative—impulse reveals itself not only in Mathias' obsessed imaginings, but on a milder and everyday level in such banal inventions as the stereotyped image of the wayward girl, the precocious Jacqueline. . . . She has . . . moved out of *histoire* and into *histories*. She is already an invention. On the larger scale, the general mythomania is reflected in the promulgation among the islanders of an ancient legend . . . involving the sacrifice of a virgin in the Spring to appease the sea-gods. Like the Oedipus myth in *Les Gommes* it is an ironic reflection of the creative and distorting process of human narration. . . . The human narrative is always liable to pull down some handy myth or stereotype, ignoring the reality. . . . (p. 41)

In this novel, Robbe-Grillet reflects directly the distortions of perception in an obsessed man: scenes observed by Mathias change as they are fired by his imaginative response—"fired" is indeed the word, when the girl in the photograph begins to crackle and burn as the flames leap round her from Mathias' observing eye. . . . We see perception in the act of becoming imagination. The passionate attention which Robbe-Grillet has elsewhere given to parallels, reflections, and repetitions indicates the same conviction in the novelist that observation is creative. . . . As we can never enter the same river twice, so we cannot observe the same scene twice—or even continuously. We change, and it changes. The continually modified repetitions of *Dans le labyrinthe* make the same point as they illustrate the observing and the imagining processes at work, the one insidiously replacing the other, with no visible hiatus. (pp. 41-2)

> *Valerie Minogue, in* Forum for Modern Language Studies *(copyright © by* Forum for Modern Language Studies *and Valerie Minogue), January, 1976.*

ROBERT MARTIN ADAMS

Mathias, in Robbe-Grillet's *Le Voyeur*, sees and/or creates figure-eights wherever he goes. Seagulls form the pattern overhead, bits of string fall into it underfoot, iron rings on docks form it before his eyes, even his bicycle trip around the island falls naturally into two joined loops, a figure-eight. The murder which he may or may not have committed takes place on a blank page between Section 1 and Section 2; in the spatial context of the island and his trip around it, it takes place at the point where the line drawn in forming a figure-eight crosses itself, and in the first French edition that page is numbered 88. Mathias is of course an obsessed figure; what he is pre-programmed to see and do he sees and does. But some of these figure-eights never impinge on his consciousness at all, and most of those that he does notice don't tell us anything about his surroundings or him, except that there are a lot of free-floating figure-eights in the vicinity of both. In the classical economy of the novel, this kind of distraction would destroy a variety of author-reader relations, a shared trust which the author's proceedings and the reader's learned responses aimed to build. The new-style novel implies a measure of antagonism and mistrust to begin with; a fixed relation between author and reader is avoided, and the grid or pattern is a kind of pseudo-structure, serving to unsettle and complicate that relation. It is pseudo, not in terms of the author's beliefs, which may be utterly sincere, but in terms of the workings of the fiction, defined in the old way, of course, as action, character, representation. But as the reader's engagement with these old friends diminishes, so it becomes more involved with the texture of the author's construct—not with the author as public spokesman, but with the author's personal game. (pp. 46-7)

> *Robert Martin Adams, in his* AfterJoyce: Studies in Fiction After "Ulysses" *(copyright © 1977 by Robert Martin Adams; reprinted by permission of Oxford University Press), Oxford University Press, 1977.*

Intrepid admirers of M. Robbe-Grillet or of the "new" novel, or of both, might conceivably read "Topology of a Phantom City" with interest, but most readers will undoubtedly find its strained affectlessness crushingly soporific. Consider, for example, how M. Robbe-Grillet sets the stage for his imaginary city: "The first thing that is striking is the height of the walls: so high, so disproportionate to the size of the figures it does not even occur to you to wonder whether or not there is a ceiling; yes: the extreme height of the walls and their bareness; the three that are visible, constituting the back and two sides of the rectangular, possibly square (it is hard to say because of a powerful perspective effect), possibly even cube-shaped cell (which again raises the problem of the improbably existence of a ceiling) . . ." (p. 112)

> *The New Yorker (© 1978 by The New Yorker Magazine, Inc.), February 27, 1978.*

JOHN J. McALEER

Robbe-Grillet is a filmmaker and [*Topology of a Phantom City*] addresses itself to the eye almost exclusively. There is not a line of dialogue in the book. But there is endless scene setting—the same scene presented over and over again. In the opening pages we are asked to gaze upon the nude body of a young girl who lies in a spreading pool of blood. With a technique that is hard to differentiate from standard stream-of-consciousness, Robbe-Grillet brings us back to this scene again and again. . . . Eras change. We

move from the mythic past, to the now, to the hereafter. But the story is the same. We move round and round the event like a camera dollying circularly. We discover the book's real merit in this technique. We see things with an artist's eye. After a while, you may think you are Paul Signac ready to embark on a career of pointillism. Yet the imagery is, at times, as stark as Colette's, e.g., "When she got home next morning she was fit only to be thrown with the dirty rags, if that."

Robbe-Grillet's theatrical world is a narcissistic world, a world of mirrors endlessly casting back an image of itself, and of vampires ceaselessly seeking replenishment. As a film, *Topology* might stir our sense of wonder. As a novel, it is better calculated to induce vertigo. (pp. 373-74)

> *John J. McAleer, in* Best Sellers *(copyright © 1978 Helen Dwight Reid Educational Foundation), March, 1978.*

*   *   *

ROBINSON, Jill   1936-

Robinson is an American novelist and essayist. She is a frequent contributor to *Vogue* magazine.

NANCY LYNN SCHWARTZ

"Hollywood is both a small town and a magical kingdom," remarks an actor in Jill Robinson's novel *Perdido*. And it is precisely this tension, this contradiction between daily life and larger than life, which makes this Hollywood novel so interesting. It is hardly the steamy fan-mag *roman-à-clef* or the explicit memoir one might expect from the daughter of a one-time studio chief [Jill Robinson is the daughter of Dore Schary]. Rather, it's part *Our Town* and part epic, with Hollywood as the backdrop for an often haunting story of a young woman's search for her father.

The heroine is Susanna Howard, granddaughter of one of movieland's founding fathers, who lives with her extended, dynastic family in one of those mansions Hollywood's immigrant pioneers built, a sprawling American Versailles called "Perdido." Susanna's small adolescent obsessions are magnified against the opulent background of movieland aristocracy. (p. 473)

The best thing about Robinson's depiction of family life in a patriarchal kingdom is her illumination of the women in Hollywood: mothers, wives and daughters of actors, directors, producers, writers. The book conveys a perceptive vision of this distaff network of life-supporting appendages and indicates that the women are, for myriad reasons, the survivors, defying the beauty ethic that would seemingly make them this town's first casualties.

The epic, rather tragic flavor of *Perdido* is heightened by the fact that the story begins at the end of an era. The pioneer immigrants have mostly died out. Television and the cold war are laying siege to the kingdom in a slow war of attrition, breaking down the walls that can no longer isolate Hollywood from the rest of the world. Perdido, loss, lost. . . .

Perdido is overflowing with fascinating observations, but for all its richness it's a frustrating, often disappointing work. The witty, acute statements about Hollywood are made in passing but not pursued. So much that's good in this book is on the periphery, indirectly illuminated or glimpsed momentarily, but where the center should hold it fumbles.

The biggest problem, unfortunately, is that Susanna, the poor little princess, doesn't sustain the book. Robinson has attempted, for most of the book, to use one of the most difficult narrative voices—a precocious child speaking in the first-person present. Sometimes it works, sometimes not, and when it fails it's like an American primitive portrait of a child with a freakishly adult face. I am an ardent admirer of Robinson's autobiographical *Bed/Time/Story,* a beautifully written book which forces the reader to care about the characters and their fate. It seems almost as if Robinson retreated after such a cathartic, confessional work, but in distancing herself from her characters she has drawn back too far. The result is that apart from two or three characters who come vitally to life only to be snatched away too quickly, most of the characters in *Perdido* are curiously lacking dimension. In that way, *Perdido* is an impressive attempt to build a mansion which comes out resembling a movie set. It's a glorious, almost believable façade but you couldn't live there. (p. 474)

> Nancy Lynn Schwartz, *"She Lost It at the Movies,"* in The Nation *(copyright 1978 by the Nation Associates, Inc.), April 22, 1978, pp. 473-74.*

PEARL K. BELL

The liveliest moments in this very uneven novel ["Perdido"] are firmly rooted in Jill Robinson's abundant insider's lore of Hollywood opulence and vulgarity and the protective astigmatism that habitually blurred the line between projection-room fictions and unglamorous realities, such as blacklisting, television and box-office clinkers. (pp. 11, 45)

But it is one thing to have been reared in that phantasmagoric hothouse, to possess such an unweeded surfeit of scenes and plots and musical themes from hundreds of movies, and another to convert all this authentic detail into a serious novel. In the first half of "Perdido," Jill Robinson establishes her credentials for writing about pre-television Hollywood with witty intelligence, skewering its absurdities and artifice, its cutthroat anxieties about money and fame and power. But when she moves on to the story department, the tenacious grip of old movies proves stronger than literary originality, and she settles for a weary B-movie scenario that would have been a dud property 30 years ago. . . .

The harder Susanna runs [in search of her true father], the less Jill Robinson seems willing to bother with any irritating complexities of character, feeling, motive and experience. Indeed, she abandons Hollywood, the novel's indispensable locus, for so long that by the time Susanna defeatedly returns to Southern California, the popcorn and the patience have run out. Little that happens to the girl during her quest seems worthy of Mrs. Robinson's savvy wisecracking talent (as Susanna would put it: just like Rosalind Russell).

"Movie stars are different from real people," the Hollywood princess, now grown up and fretting at the reins of her dull marriage to a Hollywood prince, declares toward the end of the book. "If you ever saw one of the big ones you know what I mean." This is glib and lazy; it merely asserts what the novelist should long to portray with all the

dramatic richness and precision that memory and understanding can bestow. Instead, Jill Robinson has leaned far too heavily in "Perdido" on the facile and perfunctory slickness of the movie-fed mentality, and the result is another missed opportunity—not a good Hollywood novel but just another movie. (p. 45)

> Pearl K. Bell, "Hollywood Princess," in The New York Times Book Review (© 1978 by The New York Times Company; reprinted by permission), April 23, 1978, pp. 11, 45.

[In "Perdido,"] Perdido is the (loaded) name of the dream estate belonging to a Hollywood producer, and it is where this story of his stepdaughter's coming of age in the nineteen-fifties begins and ends. We join Susanna Howard—precocious, spoiled, and self-conscious—on page 1 in the first person and in the present tense, and we never leave her side as she caroms around the country in search of the actor Jackson Lane, a golden-haired idol whose relation to Susanna is the crux of the plot. At first, it is all a lot of fun. But the style and tone soon begin to wear; the naïve and bubbly voice of Susanna, the meticulous sameness of pace, and that damnable present tense as she feeds the action, like inches of film, out of her sensitive memory become maddening. Considering how many adventures, discoveries, and crises Susanna has had by the time she reaches the age of twenty-four, one can only wonder at how much she remembers and how little she has learned. (p. 145)

> The New Yorker (© 1978 by The New Yorker Magazine, Inc.), May 1, 1978.

* * *

RODRÍGUEZ, Claudio   1934-

Rodríguez is a Spanish poet.

ANDREW P. DEBICKI

Thanks to this volume [*Poesía 1953-1966*] we now have available the complete poetry to date of one of Spain's most important young poets. Like most of his contemporaries, Rodríguez . . . uses an everyday vocabulary and builds his poems around everyday scenes, common objects and familiar happenings. But his work is far from being merely descriptive or anecdotal: the reality which he presents us comes to embody and vivify basic human themes and concerns. By carefully controlling words, expressions and details, Rodríguez makes us discover in seemingly ordinary happenings the key patterns of our existence. . . . What gives success to this process is the poet's way of making us feel his theme without ever converting it into a mere message, without losing the sense of a concrete reality and experience.

In the first two books included in this volume, *Don de la ebriedad* (1953) and *Conjuros* (1958), natural scenes and events are contemplated by a speaker who draws wider implications from them. In the third book, *Alianza y condena* (1966), the process is tightened: the wider themes are implicit rather than explicit. Yet the perspective we have of the objects and events described always leads us beyond them. Like the earlier books, this one is written primarily in free verse, although the expression is more concentrated, the periods shorter and the surface tone less emphatic. The impact comes from the words themselves, not from the speaker's exclamation or the tone adopted. All of Ro-dríguez's books consider the quest for a fuller and purer vision of life, the desire to find one's place in life's patterns, the desire to transcend the limitations of self and of one's literal existence. What counts is that they make these themes meaningful. (p. 456)

> *Andrew P. Debicki, in* Books Abroad *(copyright 1972 by the University of Oklahoma Press), Vol. 46, No. 3, Summer, 1972.*

MIKE MUDROVIC

Claudio Rodríguez must be considered one of the foremost poets writing in Spanish today. It is little wonder that, for those of us who hold his poetry in such high esteem, the release of a new volume after an eleven-year silence should create immediate excitement.... The new volume [*El vuelo de la celebración*] is a much different experience than its immediate predecessor [*Alianza y condena*] but continues to demonstrate Rodríguez's fundamental and intriguing approach to the act of poetic creation.

In all of his books, Rodríguez not only writes individual poems, but fits these poems into a total pattern in the structure of the volume. *El vuelo de la celebración* presents a unified paradoxical experience, as evidenced by its structure. The first section of the volume, "Herida en cuatro tiempos," sets the atmosphere and the direction of the volume. Each of the four poems of this section then has a direct relationship with the four remaining sections of the volume. The experience this creates seems first to describe a serious loss suffered by the speaker and then to show the various ways in which he comes to grips with his subsequent situation. The spectrum of tones—all intimate and personal—is astounding. A few of the poems that immediately stand out are "Herida," "Arena," "Ciruelo silvestre," "Lo que no se marchita" and "Noviembre." Throughout the work there appears to be a constant struggle between desolation and hopefulness, as the title possibly indicates.

The final poem bears out this duality. The elegy is traditionally a lament caused by the death of an actual person or the poet's contemplation of the tragic aspects of life. But in this lament the poet also finds consolation in the contemplation of some permanent principle. Thus "Elegía desde Simancas" presents the paradoxical resolution of the poet's experience throughout the poems of *El vuelo de la celebración*.

This new volume appears to be a transitional work in the context of Rodríguez's lyric production. In spite of some obvious changes in style and tone as compared to his earlier works, *El vuelo de la celebración* maintains an intrinsic appeal that is exciting and fulfilling to discover. More and more, Claudio Rodríguez is rising to a preeminent position in Spanish poetry. (p. 88)

> *Mike Mudrovic, in* World Literature Today *(copyright 1978 by the University of Oklahoma Press), Vol. 52, No. 1, Winter, 1978.*

*   *   *

ROY, Gabrielle   1909-

A French-Canadian novelist, Roy was twice the winner of the Canadian Governor General's Award. Her fiction is nationalistic in character, treating themes such as the adverse effect of progress on Canada and its people. Although Roy writes in French, most of her novels have been translated into English. (See also *Contemporary Authors*, Vols. 53-56.)

PAULA GILBERT LEWIS

What Gabrielle Roy has ... accomplished in *La Route d'Altamont* is to place together in a close rapport a young and an old person, both of whom express a deep need to communicate and to understand one another. In the four "short stories" that compose what the author has classified as a novel, the reader sees a narrator, Christine, first as an eight-year-old child in her relationships with her eighty-year-old grandmother and then with the eighty-four-year-old Monsieur Sanit-Hilaire, and, in the final story, as a mature woman, desirous of communicating with her seventy-year-old mother. (pp. 457-58)

It is ... themes of memory and death which are so vivid to the characters of *La Route d'Altamont* and which Gabrielle Roy succeeds in rendering so vivid to her own readers.

There are several distinct levels of memory to be found throughout *La Route d'Altamont*. All of them, however, are closely interwoven into the circle of time where particular moments or experiences appear to be frozen into one instant equaling all time or where history is seen in a repetitive fashion. Such timelessness is accomplished either through one's own remembrances of oneself and of another or through heredity, the transmitting of certain traits from the old to the young. (p. 458)

In describing the varied attributes of memories, it is made clear that they are generally deep and intimate secrets in our minds and are activated in an instinctive and involuntary manner. In "La Route d'Altamont," for example, Christine, as an adult, accidentally discovers a road which passes through the sole mountain chain in Manitoba. The sight of these mountains causes Eveline, accompanying her daughter, to recall the mountains of the Province of Québec that she had so dearly loved during her childhood. What this "road through the town of Altamont" actually represents is the route to the past, accidentally or involuntarily discovered by youth on behalf of the old. When Christine tries consciously to find this road again, she has difficulty. Rediscovery is not within her will. (pp. 458-59)

Precisely because of their involuntary nature, memories need a key in order to be stimulated. Symbolically in "La Route d'Altamont," this key will be the town itself.... But even this key, as has been seen, must be involuntarily rediscovered. (p. 459)

It is inevitable that, with ... [an] emphasis on the themes of youth, old age, and memory, death also be presented strongly in *La Route d'Altamont*. In addition to the actual presence of death in the stories, that of the grandmother and those impending of M. Saint-Hilaire and of Eveline, Gabrielle Roy uses several symbols in order to describe or to underline the overriding power of death. After "Ma Grand-mère toute-puissante" and "Le Vieillard et l'enfant," both seen under the influence of death because of the age of the characters, "Le Déménagement" first seems to be out of place. It is the story of the young Christine's experiences when she accompanies a friend and her father on one of their daily trips as household movers. As François Ricard points out, however, this physical move is actually Christine's first contact with separation, with the leaving behind of stability and security. In this sense, what occurs in "Le Déménagement" is a metaphorical experience of what eventually will be the entrance into the realm of death.

The wagon upon which Christine sits with all of the old furniture represents, therefore, the chariot of death. It symbolizes death, in addition, in that it is a reminder of the dead past before the use of automobiles. Christine has the strange sensation of a mixture of time, past and present, as she moves along on the old wagon. She herself becomes the past.... In a circular motion, she returns to death, just as she is heading toward the future of life's experiences and of the inevitable end.

Death is seen, therefore, as a departure. It is an unknown route, involuntarily chosen, that leads either to past youth in memory and heredity or to the future end. (p. 463)

There are numerous examples throughout *La Route d'Altamont* of a belief in a circular structure to nature, life, and death. (p. 465)

The entire day spent by Christine on her momentous trip with the movers is ... circular. She departs on an old wagon that carries her both to past times and to new future experiences. But she eventually returns home to the security of her family. This particular trip, foreshadowing Christine's entire life, also reflects the great voyage made by her family from Québec to the new West of Manitoba. The return trip will be made by an adult Christine who desires to rediscover her origins not only in Québec, but also in the old world, in France....

The trip past the town of Altamont to the Manitoban mountains is likewise circular, both in the fact that a return trip is undertaken and that both visits stimulate a mental return to the past in the mountains of Québec. These mental wanderings are, of course, the most obvious circular trips in the book. Through memories, one is able to rediscover one's own lost past and youth, and a form of second childhood, both beneficial and dangerous, may result.

As has already been mentioned, there exists as well a round trip, toward the future and toward the past, through one's children, through heredity. It often happens that parents, who have aged and who feel that they have not accomplished what they had hoped to do during their youth, will attempt to relive a full life through their children.... The circular movement is toward the future in one's children and the past in one's youth, precariously relived. But the movement is even more complex.... While remaining an individual in the present, one is also linked to the past and the future, as part of the great circle of life and death.

Despite the constant presence of death, can one definitively state that this circle closes? With the concept of heredity and a form of eternity or immortality where one remains alive in the memory of another, does the circle not continue infinitely? Perhaps a more accurate description of Gabrielle Roy's emphasis on circular structures is that of a series of concentric circles, all within one large circle encompassing the birth and death of humanity, or perhaps of nature itself. Only in this way could the ultimate circle close. But until that time, at least some semblance of continued or rediscovered youth and life can be found either in the hereditary circle of families or in the constant departure toward the unknown roads of memory that pass through Altamont. (p. 466)

Paula Gilbert Lewis, "The Themes of Memory and Death in Gabrielle Roy's 'La Route D'Altamont'," in Modern Fiction Studies *(copyright © 1976, by Purdue Research Foundation, West Lafayette, Indiana, U.S.A.), Autumn, 1976, pp. 457-66.*

JULIA RANDALL

I have stolen the title of my essay from the *Dossiers de Documentation sur la Littérature Canadienne-Française*.... But my working title, in bad French, was "Gabrielle Roy: Chère Maître." Gabrielle Roy has nothing in common with Henry James except mastery and a deep concern with emerging national character. Her one short-term expatriate, Pierre Cadorai of *La Montagne Secrète*, dies of homesickness. Casting around for helpful comparisons, I thought of Flaubert—but Roy has sympathy. Of Willa Cather—but Roy has subtlety. Of Katherine Mansfield—but she has force. Of George Eliot—well, yes, but hardly canoeing down the Mackenzie. Finally I paused at Tchekov, and was rewarded when my research heard her say

> I lived part of my life under the secret charm
> of a nouvelle that I read when very
> young.... For a long while this early read-
> ing penetrated my thoughts, fashioned in
> me, so to speak, a way of seeing, of observ-
> ing and grasping the real.... A nouvelle of
> Tchekov, *The Steppe*.... Perhaps my pen-
> chant for uniting landscapes and states of
> mind (*âme*) dates from this time.

In the following introduction to Roy's work, I have grouped the novels and tales without regard to chronology: The City, The Plain, and the Territory are my categories, transected by the Innocence/Experience or Garden/City theme.... This grouping seems to be the commanding one, though other groupings suggest themselves. (pp. 2-3)

The City, in *Bonheur d'Occasion* and *Alexandre Chenevert*, is Montreal; in the former the French working-quarter of St.-Henri, which looks from the docks and the railroad-tracks up toward the more affluent and more English Westmount.... [*Bonheur d'Occasion*] is both compassionate and angry (though not in tone). It was denounced in a Montreal pulpit and sold to Hollywood. Though in every sense a novel, it marks the transition, I think, from Gabrielle Roy journalist to Gabrielle Roy artist....

[*Alexandre Chenevert*] is realistic, but its realism is touched by both humour and poetry. A sympathetic, unsentimental, unself-conscious imagination penetrates it; *otherwise*, in its clarity of observation and of style, it is very French. (p. 3)

Like *Alexandre Chenevert*, *La Montagne Secrète* concerns the inner journey, but this time the external one starts at the Green Lake [of *Alexandre Chenevert*] and ends in an unfamiliar city. The setting, except to the final scenes in Paris, is in fact the Garden—and what a strange forbidding Garden it is, from the Mackenzie across Saskatchewan and Manitoba to Ungava and Labrador: Canada North, already perishing with the caribou before our eyes. (p. 6)

[It is a simple story] as lightly drawn as [the protagonist] Cadorai's sketches. It is left to us to be surprised by the bare reality (old Gédéon, a Klondike relic, does not at first recognize his own likeness), or to draw further implications. One is reminded of that steamy journey to the heart of darkness, if only by contrast to this icy voyage to the heart of light.

In the arctic Eden, man is not yet fallen. Those who meet—Pierre and Nina, Gédéon, Steve, Orok—are brothers and sisters. They suffer bodily privation, they must kill to eat, they survive in a hostile or at best an indifferent Nature. Yet even here the worm of imagination is at work, and his image is communicated by Pierre across a continent. (p. 8)

Somewhere between the Garden and the City lies the Frontier. It may be way up in the northwest (*La Petite Poule d'Eau*), where, because she persuades the province to send a school-teacher to her island family, Luzina Tousignant loses them one by one to the civilized south. Or in the northeast (*La Rivière sans Repos*), where the white man's impact on Inuit life is dramatized by Elsa Kumachuk's struggle to bring up her half-white son. Or it may be as near as the back streets of Winnipeg—la rue Deschambault, three steps from the prairie. . . . The overwhelming impression is one of distance from home. (p. 10)

To have expressed in words the secret connections between Garden and City, hill and plain, youth and age, pioneer and pilgrim—such is the work of Gabrielle Roy. She has "given the regard" to her vast open-ended country—"beautiful, but only to those who know how to look at it." Like Virginia Woolf, she sees the novel not as a succession of events, but as "a succession of emotions radiating from some character at the center." The mistake of the amateur writer is to think that the emotions are, in themselves, valuable to art. An opposite mistake is to think that the object irradiated can be known in itself, without taking into account the organ of perception. Art, if not consciousness itself, begins in a mysterious co-operation. But beneath this world of "fitting and fitted," of internal and external, subject and object, seems to lie some universal unchanging underground, where, as Edwin Muir has it, all our most precious experience takes place. None of us exists wholly in the world which others see, and upon which our daily life is necessarily based. We exist also in that underground where the artist, when his regard is deep enough, can take us; where the life of men and beasts and stars is indivisible. Gabrielle Roy's books will appeal to proponents of the One Life in Canada and abroad. (pp. 11-12)

> *Julia Randall, "Gabrielle Roy: Grand-daughter of Quebec," in* The Hollins Critic *(copyright 1977 by Hollins College), December, 1977, pp. 1-12.*

*   *   *

RUKEYSER, Muriel   1913-

Rukeyser is an American poet, novelist, playwright, biographer, screenwriter, translator, and children's book author termed by Louis Untermeyer "the most inventive and challenging poet of her generation." She is noted for her ability to imbue all of her poetic themes—the historical, social, and political, as well as the personal—with an intensity derived from her subjective stance. (See also *CLC*, Vol. 6, and *Contemporary Authors*, Vols. 5-8, rev. ed.)

SUE ANN ALDERSON

One dominant subject of Muriel Rukeyser's *Breaking Open* is that life is one's attitude towards it, and the attitude Ru-

keyser promotes through these many and varied poems is positive affirmation without sentimentality. . . . Rukeyser's diction is often abstract, her imagery unadorned. Whatever the occasion for the poem (often autobiographical, as in the poems about her emotionally withholding parents or the many poems stemming from her experiences protesting the war in Vietnam), the important image-ideas are the need for stroking, touching, sharing, transforming, making. Her concerns are those of a mature Jewish intellectual woman writing in the American tradition (see "After Melville"), frequently in response to the Vietnamese conflict. At the same time, in many poems Rukeyser generalizes these concerns; as a Jungian, she is after the archetypal in the particular ("The Running of the Grunion," in which the image of the grunion procreating despite imminent death becomes a symbol of archetypal perseverence/creativity/life is a good example of this and a powerful poem). (p. 46)

> *Sue Ann Alderson, in* West Coast Review *(copyright © October, 1975 West Coast Review Publishing Society), October, 1975.*

WILLIAM MEREDITH

It is very hard to write the way Muriel Rukeyser does, using your life as the direct vehicle of apprehension, the poems the same thing as closest attention to your daily life. . . .

"The fear of poetry is the / fear," she wrote many years ago. In the new book she asks, "Do I move toward form, do I use all my fears?" Clearly the experience of poetry is the cutting edge of the life of someone who speaks like that.

If you are not used to thinking of poetry the way Muriel Rukeyser does, her work can be hard to read. The reader must acquiesce, perhaps more openly than with more conventional poems. Many people seem to have trouble with this beautifully voiced verse. . . .

When the Academy of American Posts recently gave her the Copernicus Award . . . , the citation started: "From her first book, 'Theory of Flight,' published when she was 21, through her recent collection, 'The Gates' . . . the work of Muriel Rukeyser has been committed to ideas of freedom." The concerns of her poetry and her life remain inextricable, as with a person who can only tell the truth and take the consequences. The poetry in ['The Gates'] moves toward form, using all her fears—it is crafted in that hard way.

> *William Meredith, "A Life of Poetry," in* The New York Times Book Review *(© 1977 by The New York Times Company; reprinted by permission), September 25, 1977, p. 26.*

ROBERT COLES

Upon reading Muriel Rukeyser's latest volume of poems, upon going through *The Gates*, one feels silent, sad, instructed, grateful. . . . We all struggle with the sin of pride; Muriel Rukeyser has been blessed with less narcissism than most of us—especially remarkable in such an introspective, sensitive, and self-aware person, who has for so long been committed to telling others what crosses her mind. She is save from self-centeredness by a compassionate concern for others, all over the world, and by a wonderful capacity for self-mocking irony: "Anne Sexton the poet saying / ten days ago to that receptive friend, / the friend of the hand held camera: / 'Muriel is serene'. / Am I that in their sight?'' And at another point: ''I'd rather be Muriel / than be dead and be Ariel'', an entire poem, and shorter than its title: ''Not to be Printed / Not to be Said, / Not to be Thought''.

Her poem ''St. Roach'' provides a beautiful lesson in the psychology and sociology of prejudice—worth dozens of social science articles or books. It is also an example of her capacity to distance herself from the self-serving demands of the ego. . . .

She reaches out for all that is part of this earth—for the distant past, even for inanimate matter in the present. In ''Painters'' she reminds us of the pre-historic men and women who etched animal forms on the walls of caves—an effort to make sense of things, a desire to represent, to show and tell. In ''Artifact'' she demonstrates an almost unnerving capacity for calm detachment. ''When this hand is gone to earth, / this writing hand and the paper beneath it'', she begins, and soon tells us what may be left, what may survive—tells us quietly, with no sense of triumph or satisfaction: an artifact—''This pen. Will it tell my? Will it tell our? / this thing made in bright metal by thousands unknown to me . . .'' . . .

She has a visionary side to her: ''There were poems all over Broadway that morning. / Blowing across traffic. Against the legs.'' In her hands New York City becomes a series of brief images that remind one of James Agee's short film ''In the Street''. She has a nagging, important historical sense—a side of her that can jolt the reader. . . .

A series of poems is subsumed under a larger thematic effort, titled ''Gates'', the book's title. ''The poet is in solitary'', she tells us in a prose prologue: ''the expectation is that he will be tried and summarily executed . . .'' Then another person is introduced, ''an American woman [who] is sent to make an appeal for the poet's life.'' This person ''stands in the mud and rain at the prison gates—also the gates of perception, the gates of the body.'' Again Muriel Rukeyser modestly places herself as an onlooker, a compassionate, aroused, decent person who is not quite the other poet whose ''stinging work—like that of Burns or Brecht'' has managed to get ''under the skin of the highest officials''. She is no Brecht, nor was meant to be. But she also shows her ideals through calls to brotherhood, sisterhood. . . .

Not that she blinks at the mean, ugly, corrupt, exploitative side of the world. In ''New Friends'' she makes clear her awareness of the terror many decent, morally honorable and outspoken individuals have to face, day after day. . . . Still, there are friends, friends of the poet, friends of all that is decent and just in the world, friends who may be ''unknown'' to the poet, to all who suffer for their goodness and kindness and sensitivity, but who deserve recognition —hence a book titled ''Gates'', hence poems about the ordinary, the undramatic, hence a salute to those standing near the gates, no Brechts but comrades, indeed, and possessed of their own special, considerable, necessary virtue: Muriel Rukeyser, chief among them.

Robert Coles, ''Muriel Ruckeyser's 'The Gates','' in The American Poetry Review *(copyright © 1978 by World Poetry, Inc.; reprinted by permission of Robert Coles), May-June, 1978, p. 15.*

S

SÁBATO, Ernesto   1911-

Sábato is an Argentine novelist, essayist, and critic. Like many Latin American authors, Sábato is concerned with the historical and social problems of his country. Many of his essays deal with the social and political climate of contemporary South America, and he has published a volume of correspondence with the late revolutionary leader Che Guevara.

RAYMOND D. SOUZA

The third section of *Sobre héroes y tumbas,* ''Informe sobre ciegos,'' is the most important of the novel's four parts. It is in this section that the reader enters the mind and world of Fernando Vidal, the novel's main protagonist. Most of the other characters in the work are secondary to Fernando, because he forms the vortex around which their existences revolve. All who enter into this sphere of influence are changed. Some (e.g. Alejandra) are destroyed while others (e.g. Martín) find in their lives the possibility of a purpose and meaning that did not exist before.

Fernando's existence serves as a synthesizing axis which combines all the destructive and creative forces found in human existence. It is Fernando's mission to explore the unrecognized and unadmitted elements of human life, the repulsive and ugly aspects, in order that an attempt can be made to reintegrate and coordinate the splintered self of contemporary man. It is this mission or function that explains why *Sobre héroes y tumbas* is a novel of extremes and why Fernando's existence is marked by a series of radical actions such as the incestuous relationship he maintains with his daughter Alejandra. . . . Fernando defies the laws of man and of nature, but, paradoxically, his evil acts produce good results. . . .

The malefic and sinister character of Fernando may seem at first glance to be an unlikely candidate for a hero's role, but close examination of *Sobre héroes y tumbas* reveals that the hero motif is one of the major elements of the novel. Joseph Campbell in his comprehensive study of the hero archetype, *The Hero with a Thousand Faces,* suggests that despite the many variations to be found in the lives of different heroes, there are certain basic similarities. Essentially, these can be seen in the hero's adventure which is divided into three major segments: the hero departs from his immediate surroundings, penetrates the primordial source of life, and then returns to the contemporary

scene to convey the wisdom he has gained. The hero usually appears during a time of great danger when a social order is in a state of disintegration. The knowledge that the hero brings to his contemporaries makes it possible for them to survive the crisis they are facing. Campbell suggests that the hero's actions result in the release of new energy within a cyclic process of emanations and dissolutions. Fernando's adventure is related in great detail in the ''Informe sobre ciegos'' and his story parallels that of the hero-archetype. In this section, presented in the form of a manuscript, the protagonist withdraws from his surroundings, narrates his encounter with the primordial source of existence, and returns and leaves his testimony.

In Fernando's case, however, what starts out as a struggle against the external world ends up as a major confrontation with the contradictory elements of his own being. . . . [Precisely like the modern heroes Campbell discusses, Fernando] perceives that the central enigma to be solved is in man himself and not in the world exterior to him. Sábato's novel contains episodes that allow the reader to view the differences between a contemporary hero who delves into his own being to find meaning and an earlier heroic figure who wages war with forces exterior to himself. (p. 241)

There is an exterior-interior movement in Fernando's quest. His struggle against the exterior world involves him with anarchists and bank robbers. He travels extensively and becomes obsessed with the idea that there exists a sinister international organization of blind people. His attempts to penetrate the sect of the blind provides the link between the world that is exterior to Fernando and his own being. . . . The concept of sacrifice or self-destruction is frequently associated with the hero-quest. Nietzsche has pointed out that the hero does unnatural things and breaks the laws of nature to discover or reveal wisdom. He has also indicated that the price paid by the hero in his quest for wisdom seems to indicate that knowledge is ''an unnatural abomination.'' If this is the case, it can be seen why evil acts can produce good results. Fernando's essential evil, therefore, is a prerequisite to the good that comes from his accomplishments, and the success of his mission is paradoxically linked to the degree of evil he can attain. (pp. 243-44)

Fernando's dream journey results in the dissolution of his own ego and the encounter with the origins and secrets of existence. . . . There occurs during the dream a synthesis of opposites, of the individual with the world, of life with death, of the finite with the infinite, and for Fernando existence has a meaning it did not have before, for he comprehends and feels integrated with the totality of all existing things. (p. 244)

Having discovered these secrets and a sense of integration with existence, Fernando awakes and returns to the mundane world of contemporary life. It now becomes his mission to convey to others the knowledge that he has found, and this explains the origin of the strange testimony "Informe sobre ciegos." Fernando's "Informe" is his link between the exterior and interior manifestations of existence, between reality and dream, between himself and his fellow man.

The possibilities for positive change that result from Fernando's accomplishments are seen in the transformation that takes place in Martín. . . . [Martín's] existence is like that of modern man's in that it is accidental and devoid of any positive tradition. Martín's parents represent a past from which he feels alienated and one that offers nothing to sustain him. Therefore, the family unit becomes a symbol of society's failure or inability to transmit to its youth a sense of purpose and meaning.

Martín's encounter with Alejandra and Fernando profoundly changes him. At the end of the novel he is no longer a passive individual terrified by the world he lives in. . . . Despite the extremes the novel deals with, it ends on an optimistic note. Or one could say that because of its extremes the novel offers the hope that once man has confronted the contradictory and negative elements that exist within him, he may find the capacity to live with himself and others.

In spite of the macabre and repulsive aspects of their lives, Alejandra and Fernando's existences have meaning and purpose which is reflected in the profound changes that take place in Martín. . . . Martín functions as both introduction and epilogue to the work's central theme—the hero-quest. (pp. 244-45)

Sobre héroes y tumbas is an extensive novel that attempts to fathom the meaning of existence by proceeding from an individual to a collective point of view. Sábato moves in his work from the finite point of view of the individual, utilizes an interiorization process to move to a consideration of the infinite, and returns at the end of the novel to the individual standpoint. The individual point of view, however, is different at the end of the novel from what it was at the beginning. It no longer closes in on itself in an endless process of self-contemplation that bears no results. Rather, it opens up to that which is exterior to itself. Fernando and Martín's lives appear to testify to the belief that the individual by reconciling the contradictions within his own being can find it possible to advance to a consideration of the relationships that exist between the finite and infinite. In its presentation of this view the work seems to suggest that paradoxes hide within their shrouds the seeds of solutions. (p. 245)

> Raymond D. Souza, "Fernando as Hero in Sábato's 'Sobre Héroes y Tumbas'," in Hispania (© 1972 The American Association of Teachers of Spanish and Portuguese, Inc.), May, 1972, pp. 241-46.

DAVID WILLIAM FOSTER

One aspect of Ernesto Sábato's sprawling *Sobre héroes y tumbas* (1962) concerns the implicit sympathy of the novelist with the "uncomplicated of human spirit," as represented by the central character Martín. In support of this sympathy the novelist contrasts Martín's intimate involvement with Alejandra with the detached preoccupation of the novelist manqué Bruno, and on another more pervasive level, common people are contrasted with the decaying Olmos family. But perhaps the most significant contribution in terms of Sábato's subtle panegyric of the simple folk is Olmos Vidal's "Informe sobre ciegos," a complicated and fascinating conceit that in the last analysis becomes an ironic burlesque of the ponderous interpretations of existence by the degenerate intellectuals.

Vidal's "Informe," the third part of the novel, is part diary, part confession, part exposé. Given the absurdity of Vidal's premises concerning the underground movement of the blind that is supposed to control the world, this part of the novel stands out as quite an autonomous document, and indeed was so published. . . . Nevertheless, so much interest has been invested in detailing Vidal's scribblings in terms of psychoanalysis and existentialism that not enough attention has been paid its relationship with the novel as a whole. The document is, of course, without a doubt a brilliant piece of "confabulación." Vidal's hypotheses are spell-binding in the elaborateness of detail that becomes a magnificent flight of fancy. (pp. 44-5)

The latter part of the document shifts dramatically in tone from the sardonic to the surrealistic. Supposedly, Vidal is under the influence of an agent of the sect about to execute the sentence imposed upon him for his curiosity. However, the reader realizes that this portion of the document corresponds to the final disintegration of the man's personality under the weight of his own inner "dragons" and that the She who appears with ever greater insistence and terror for Vidal is no blind executioner but in fact his own daughter, Alejandra. Although he has seduced and destroyed her with his own infernal evil, a sense of guilt that comes from we know not what dark corner of his being ultimately converts her in his eyes into the agent of his own destruction and expiation by fire for the original sins of his degenerate soul. We come to realize that, for reasons unknown, Vidal is a haunted and tortured man, that somehow he has communicated as a spiritual inheritance this burden to his daughter, and that by some accord, conscious or unconscious, that, like Martín, we are not privileged to know, they go to meet their self-inflicted destiny in the fiery holocaust of the decaying family mansion.

In another more profound sense Sábato is only executing in his handling of the personal stories of Alejandra and Vidal his implicit convictions concerning the over-intellectualization that easily becomes so uncontrollable a monster. If *Sobre héroes y tumbas* does indeed have a strong anti-intellectual under-pinning as I have suggested, then it is only appropriate that the novel, in both its diffuseness and its refusal to crystalize for the reader a transcendent, higher meaning of the central mysterious happenings, reflect this implied disenchantment with the power of intellectual reasoning to provide a salvation of man in his unknown disquietudes. (pp. 45-6)

An initial approximation to a deeper meaning is to be found in the superficial significance of Vidal's name, the etymon of which is of course Latin *videre*. Thus, he is the seer in both the sense of one who scrutinizes analytically what he perceives around him, as well as the one who is able to project his insight onto the level of vatic prophecy. Obviously, Vidal's "seeing" stands in metaphoric contrast to the physical sightlessness of the blind that he both pursues and, in his own sick mind, comes to be pursued and persecuted by. But what Vidal "sees" is not the literal shape of the world—this is available to anyone with eyes. He perceives, instead, an inner, cloacal meaning of the universe, and his is a seeing that becomes an interpretation of his own experience destined to be of value, an urgent warning, to be sure, to all non-blind mankind. One could go on here compounding the conceit of seeing. . . . (p. 46)

In their ingenuity and in their attention to a peculiar inner logic, the pages of the "Informe" constitute in the end one individual's attempt to make some sense out of the chaotic world around him. . . . [No] matter how deranged he is by the vague standard of our "normal" society, his document represents for him a carefully thought-out and executed exegesis of the mysteries of existence, a key that is to explain why and how things happen as they do: it is for Vidal all the design, not of an omnipotent God, but of an omnipotent Sect of the Blind. (p. 47)

[Like] the Christian mystic who is able to resign himself to a predisposed place in the Divine Plan, Vidal enjoys some sort of fearful confidence that he has come to the particular attention of the sect and has been accorded the special consideration of vengeful elimination for his interest in and comprehension of their activities. More than this man cannot demand of his god.

Vidal's "Informe," then, becomes an extended novelistic conceit for the search by the sensitive, intelligent individual after the meaning of the universe and the existence which it proportions to each man. As far as the novel is concerned, Vidal's apocalyptic illumination is a private one, destined for communication to the rest of mankind only after his sacrifice. Is it not only in this privateness that we can call the "Informe" the ravings of a madman, particularly when we compare it with other, even distinguished, metaphysics and theologies? Indeed, Vidal, in his role as prophetic seer and indefatigable pursuer of the secrets of the Sect, must have come to see himself as a sacrificial figure, a sort of Christ, for it is through the contributions of his investigations and the enormous burden of knowledge which he has accepted with resignation that mankind will be made aware of what has been hidden until now. . . . Vidal's calmness in the face of his fate is born of a satisfaction with the validity of his discoveries and conclusions. . . . The "Informe" is an example of the disastrous result of a man's superior intelligence when set free to elaborate an exegesis of the universe and human experience. It is within the overall anti-intellectual stance which *Sobre héroes y tumbas* comes to assume in its final pages that one must see Vidal's report. In addition to whatever it is on one level as a revelation of Vidal, on the higher level of the unity of the novel, it stands as an implied metanovelistic statement on the dangers of the overly creative, the overly fecund mind of man, the pseudo-philosopher, and the pseudo-novelist. For, if I am correct in my assessment of the two levels of meaning for the "informe"—vis-à-vis Vidal's soul and vis-à-vis man's compulsion, reflected to an enormous degree in his literature, to construct all-encompassing interpretations of experience—that the "Informe" should be the most memorable contri-

bution of Sábato's novel underlines in reverse the very point which he appears to be making in incorporating it within the overall structure of *Sobre héroes y tumbas.* (pp. 47-8)

> *David William Foster, "The Integral Role of 'El Informe Sobre Ciegos' in Sábato's 'Sobre Héroes y Tumbas'," in* Romance Notes, *Autumn, 1972, pp. 44-8.*

H. ERNEST LEWALD

The 125 captioned chapters of *Abaddón* offer the reader an unconvincing pastiche made up of the "flesh, blood, tears and thoughts" emanating from [Sabato's] previous writings. Thus we find Sábato playing himself, surrounded by a host of characters from his two previous novels . . . ; monologues on the function of literature, on the writer and his public and on literary genres and currents (anti-Robbe-Grillet but pro-Kafka) which are barely paraphrased statements taken from earlier works such as *El escritor y sus fantasmas* or *Hombres y engranajes;* and reminiscences of his early "scientific" years in Paris. Stylistically and thematically, Sábato appears as his own spokesman, at times under the guise of Quique delivering known diatribes against a rational universe and its crassest manifestations—the culture of the United States for instance—at times exploring the "humble" Buenos Aires in waterfront cafés or the Olmos cemetery as Bruno. Powerless to transcend his earlier periods, he is forced to witness a repetition of himself and his creations and thus finds himself playing the great man of letters who is recognized, followed and venerated on the basis of his own legend. Neither the creation of additional characters . . . , nor the inclusion of fragments from Che Guevara's diary are able to bring *actualidad* or a new focus on this *Gesamtwerk.* In fact, the many allusions to places and events taken from previous works create a cumulative effect of regionalism that undermines any claims to universality entertained by the author. The chapters dealing with Sábato's struggle against the irrational forces of evil—demons, the sects of the blind, Kafkaesque metamorphoses—fail to leave an emotional impact, perhaps because they have been so exhaustively preempted in the "Informe sobre ciegos" in *Sobre héroes y tumbas.* (p. 286)

> *H. Ernest Lewald, in* Books Abroad *(copyright 1975 by the University of Oklahoma Press), Vol. 49, No. 2, Spring, 1975.*

*   *   *

SAFIRE, William   1929-

Safire is a Pulitzer Prize-winning American journalist, essayist, and novelist. He was a special assistant to President Richard Nixon from 1968 to 1973 and has since served as a columnist for the *New York Times*. *Full Disclosure* is his first novel. (See also *Contemporary Authors*, Vols. 17-20, rev. ed.)

JOHN KENNETH GALBRAITH

On the very first page [of *Full Disclosure*] Safire makes the kind of mistake that gladdens the heart of the politically hostile reviewer—in an ostentatiously knowledgeable account of the origins of the Secret Service he tells us that it began during the Civil War when the banks were flooding the country with counterfeit specie. Specie is, in fact, just as good as gold (or silver), for that, precisely, is what specie is. Throughout, Safire is casual in his economics. . . .

In spite of these aberrations, I soon found myself very much involved in Safire's story, and, more particularly, with his people. . . .

I once before observed that the characters of amateur novelists are always called one-dimensional by the professionals. They will have trouble with William Safire, for his people are sharply and distinctively etched as to speech, political style and personal behavior. They are always interesting, they are frequently funny, and most are deeply unattractive. . . .

[The] author also brings to his effort a nice sense of excitement and suspense. Some, I am sure, will read into his story a heavy moral—a good man like Richard Nixon harried unmercifully by ingrates, traitors, the networks and The Washington Post. I would like to think that Mr. Safire had only entertainment in mind and if so, he succeeds.

> *John Kenneth Galbraith, "Can President Ericson Hang In?" in* The New York Times Book Review (© *1977 by The New York Times Company; reprinted by permission), June 12, 1977, p. 7.*

WILLIAM GREIDER

William Safire's columns in The New York Times occasionally sound like crank calls from a pun-crazed gag writer. He does have a weakness for word games. He also expresses outrageous opinions, sometimes persuasive and always provocative, even when wit dims his meaning. Safire is a gaudy flame on display in a gray museum, so every spectator pays attention.

Now comes Safire the novelist who is a compelling figure too. Improbable, occasionally offensive, but genuinely entertaining. The novelist has suppressed the polemical excesses of the columnist, though he still can't resist the aroma of a warm pun.

"Time wounds all heels," one character observes. The reader gulps. "I thought I heard a presidential seal bark," says another character. The reader thinks there is a fly in his soup.

Safire is not playing for cheap laughs, however. This is a serious Washington "what-if" novel, and given the limits of that genre, it is an entertaining story, sustained by marvelous plot complications and a feast of semi-believable character types. The mechanics are handled so adroitly, one admires the fictional house that Safire has built.

> *William Greider, "William Safire Strikes It Rich," in* Book World—The Washington Post (© *The Washington Post), June 19, 1977, p. K 1.*

CHARLES WHEELER

All too obviously, it is the aftermath of Watergate that has inspired this deadeningly long-winded political adventure story [*Full Disclosure*]. Like earlier masters of the genre, John Erlichman and Spiro Agnew, Mr. Safire has built a central character out of parts of recently rejected presidents, surrounded his hero with a type-cast set of aides, and fleshed out his novel with indiscriminate doses of intrigue, corruption, hunger for power, violence and sex.

> *Charles Wheeler, "Heads That Go Bump," in* The Times Literary Supplement (©

> *Times Newspapers Ltd. (London) 1977; reproduced from* The Times Literary Supplement *by permission), October 7, 1977, p. 1135.*

FARLEY CLINTON

This "novel" [*Full Disclosure*] is a long series of very bad sentences. The "characters" speak exclusively in stupid clichés. And he has a lot of trouble opening his chapters, poor Mr. Safire, which he copes with as best he knows how by being bright and snappy. In his White House, we feel that everyone has been chewing gum just before uttering the flat remarks that are his approximation of dialogue. That is all part of his cynical fabrication of a plot by which to convey his observations. But he has one or two authentic observations. They are of genuine interest. 1) Though this was not his intention, he makes one realize that even the White House no longer has a large staff of well-trained servants. . . . 2) Safire understands Nixon. (p. 106)

> *Farley Clinton, in* National Review (© *National Review, Inc., 1978; 150 East 35th St., New York, N.Y. 10016), January 20, 1978.*

* * *

SANDBURG, Carl   1878-1967

Sandburg was a poet, biographer, novelist, children's author, and folklorist who is often considered to have captured the essence of America in his works. He recorded and celebrated the history of the American people in such free-verse poems as "Chicago" and *The People, Yes*, works which reflect his respect and hope for the common man. Sandburg's own background provided a basis for his strong populist feeling. The son of illiterate immigrant parents, he traveled through the Midwest as a self-styled hobo, working a variety of odd jobs before becoming an organizer for the Socialist party and a Chicago newspaperman. Early in life Sandburg began to accumulate material on Abraham Lincoln, the result of which was an exhaustive, monumental six-volume biography for which he won a Pulitzer Prize in 1939. He wrote a novel, *Remembrance Rock*, and tales for children, *The Rootabaga Stories*, and also collected and performed national folk songs. Sandburg's second Pulitzer Prize was awarded in 1951 for his *Collected Poems*. In his poetry Sandburg often presented his images in the language of America, using colloquial and idiomatic lines and phrases which are both colorful and eloquent. Although his poetry has been criticized as being "subliterary," its readers have recognized themselves and their land in it. Sandburg was perhaps the most representative spokesman for Americans among the literary figures of his lifetime. In his eulogy, Lyndon Johnson said, "Carl Sandburg was more than the voice of America. . . . He was America." (See also CLC, Vols. 1, 4, and Contemporary Authors, Vols. 5-8, rev. ed.; obituary, Vols. 25-28, rev. ed.)

GAY WILSON ALLEN

A prominent theme in *Chicago Poems* is the longing of ordinary people for the beauty and happiness they have never known. This clutching at dreams was not a creation of Sandburg's fantasy, but a social phenomenon which he accurately observed. (p. 18)

A more cheerful theme in *Chicago Poems* is the laughter and joy workmen manage to find in spite of their toil and poverty. (p. 19)

In the use of slang and undignified language Sandburg achieved in actuality the theory which Wordsworth set forth in his Preface to *Lyrical Ballads:* to "present incidents and situations from common life . . . in a selection of language really used by men . . ." Sandburg's poems are also more realistic than Wordsworth's, or even naturalistic (in the Zola sense), as in "The Walking Man of Rodin," with "The skull found always crumbling neighbor of the ankles." Yet Sandburg is also just as definitely romantic in his ability to see beauty in the commonplace. "The Shovel Man," for example, is

> A dago working for a dollar six bits a day
>   And a dark-eyed woman in the old
> country dreams of him for one of the
> world's ready men with a pair of fresh lips
> and a kiss better than all the wild grapes
> that ever grew in Tuscany.

(pp. 19-20)

In his second volume of poetry, *Cornhuskers* (1918), Sandburg played less the role of the urban poet and wrote more about rural sights and sounds and his wider experiences during World War I. (p. 20)

In these poems Sandburg shows his fondness for elemental things: sky, moon, stars, wind, birds, and animals. He celebrates nature in all seasons, but especially late summer and autumn: the ripening corn, the yellow cornflower in autumn wind, the blue of larkspur and Canadian thistle, and red-ripe tomatoes. (p. 21)

Sandburg has often been compared to Whitman, and he frequently wrote on the same themes, but always with his own handling of them. The long verses of "Prairie" look superficially like Whitman's form, but the music is different. A major distinction is in their treatment of the theme of death. To Whitman death was always beautiful, an old mother crooning a lullaby from the ocean of immortality, but to Sandburg death is the final irony of life—stillness, nothingness. In "Cool Tombs" Abraham Lincoln and his assassin, Ulysses Grant and the "con men" who brought shame to his administration, lovely Pocahontas and "a streetful of people" are all equalized "in the dust . . . in the cool tombs." This is one of Sandburg's most beautiful lyrics, and most devastatingly ironic. In "Grass" the scars of World War I will be covered by the perennial grass, not in a Pantheistic transmutation of men into vegetation, but as nature erases the scars of human violation of life. (pp. 22-3)

There are intimations, almost premonitions, of Eliot's *Waste Land* and "Hollow Men" in some passages in *Smoke and Steel.* In "Four Preludes on Playthings of the Wind" the cedar doors are broken and the golden girls vanished from the city which thought itself "the greatest city, / the greatest nation: / nothing like us ever was." Now the black crows caw and the rats scribble their hieroglyphic footprints on dusty doorsills. (p. 25)

An important influence unconnected with the war which became obvious in *Smoke and Steel* was the Japanese haiku. Sandburg had already become more aware of images because of the Imagistic movement discussed and practiced by Ezra Pound and Amy Lowell in Harriet Monroe's *Poetry* [to which Sandburg himself had been a contributor as early as 1914]. . . . [The] haiku taught him to insinuate cryptic wisdom in an image. (p. 26)

Sandburg's third volume of poetry was followed not by another book of poems but by *Rootabaga Stories* (1922), stories he had made up to amuse his three little daughters. These stories have a fairy-tale sense of unreality, with transformations, actions that defy gravity, and the reduction of winds, moons, landscapes, and human actions to child-fantasy dimensions. But much of the fun is in the names and places, with their absurd sounds, outrageous puns, and comic imagery. (p. 27)

To reassert his faith in the common people and to help them regain confidence in themselves [after the Depression], he wrote and published *The People, Yes* (1936). An amalgam of folk wisdom and wit, verbal clichés, tall tales, preaching, slangy conversation, "cracker-barrel" philosophy, and Carl Sandburg cheerfulness, the book served its purpose, as Steinbeck's *Grapes of Wrath* did in another manner. It was wildly praised by people who liked Sandburg, and mostly ignored by those who did not. Mark Van Doren in a lecture on Sandburg at the Library of Congress in 1969 said, "*The People, Yes* is talk, nothing but talk." Van Doren did not mean this in a derogatory sense, and he was right. In this long talky poem we hear the voices of hundreds of Americans, and by listening we learn what kind of people they are, their ambitions, prejudices, superstitions, sense of humor, optimism, generosity, and sense of identity. But *The People, Yes* now seems repetitious and tedious. . . . (p. 31)

The whole structure of [Sandburg's novel, *Remembrance Rock* (1948)], if it may be so classified, is . . . obviously symbolical (its chief fault). . . . Some of the characters are historical and some are fictional, representing the earliest white settlers of America, the period of the American Revolution, the migrations into and across the Great Plains, the Civil War, and World War II.

As in all of his writings, Sandburg is facile with conversation in *Remembrance Rock,* but the reader is made too aware of what each speaker "stands for." The story has heroic people and epic action, yet the total effect is that of a patriotic pageant rather than a novel. (pp. 33-4)

[As] a reader and contributor to *Poetry* in its early years, [Sandburg] was aware of the arguments for and against "free verse," a form (or, as its opponents said, lack of form) in which the phrase is the prosodic unit and the words themselves create their own rhythms. More important than where Sandburg learned free-verse techniques is the fact that he had an excellent ear for the musical sequence of sounds, the balancing and counterpointing of phrase against phrase. Sandburg wrote for both the ear and the eye. His famous "Chicago" poem has an almost architectural structure, beginning with the short, pithy salutation epithets. . . . Both the line breaks and the accents in the phrases [of "Chicago"] play variations on the tempo, slowing or speeding up the sounds to add emphasis. The difference between these long lines and ordinary prose is in the skillful paralleling and accumulating of grammatical units (phrases and clauses). The resulting rhythm is grammatical, or rhetorical, rather than metrical. (pp. 36-7)

One of the many ways in which Sandburg's sense of rhythm became more subtle and sensitive was in his handling of syllabic weight, timbre, and vowel tone. This development culminated in the marvelous tone poem "When Death Came April Twelve 1945" [written upon the death of Franklin Roosevelt], which opens:

> Can a bell ring in the heart
> telling the time, telling a moment,
> telling off a stillness come,
> in the afternoon a stillness come
> and now never come morning?

The bell intones throughout the elegy, not mechanically as in Poe's "The Bells," but resonating the deep feelings of the nation grieving for its lost commander, and the sons lost in the South Pacific or on European soil, all now sleeping after toil and battle. The tones of the poem, reinforcing the images of stillness and silence, have the empathy of cleansing and calming the emotions of the readers (hearers). In every technical detail the elegy is almost perfectly ordered, timed, and developed. . . . (p. 38)

The longest and most ambitious poem in *Honey and Salt* is "Timesweep." The theme might be said to be the same as "Wilderness" (1918), in which the poet lyrically boasted of his kinship with foxes, wolves, and other wild animals. But "Timesweep" is both more genuinely lyrical and more philosophical, lyrical in the poet's empathy with the natural forces and creatures with which he feels a sympathetic kinship, and philosophical in his knowledge of his place in the cosmic scheme. (p. 42)

Sandburg's poem is more personal, less "prophetic" in tone [than Whitman's "Song of Myself," to which it has often been compared], more aware of human limitations, but the lyrical utterance of a sensitive man who enjoys the sights and sounds of his physical existence. . . . (p. 43)

Knowledge that some almost infinite (or perhaps infinite) chain of life begot him out of Nowhere to Somewhere gives Sandburg sufficient assurance of a *purpose* at work, however humanly unknowable. He will not worry about theology, or teleology. Yet "Timesweep" throws more light on Sandburg's philosophy than any other literary work of his. At the end of this last poem we find a summation of his humanism, rooted in his early socialism, and consolidated by a lifetime of effort to propagate the idea that the Family of Man is One Man:

> There is only one man in the world
> and his name is All men.

(pp. 44-5)

Gay Wilson Allen, in her Carl Sandburg *(American Writers Pamphlet No. 101;* © *1972, University of Minnesota), University of Minnesota Press, Minneapolis, 1972.*

DAVID PERKINS

[Vachel] Lindsay once said that "the people of America walk through me, all the people walk through my veins, as though they were in the streets of a city, and clamor for voice." But it was Carl Sandburg . . . , even more than Lindsay, who wrote the poetry whose underlying intention is suggested by these words. His legacies to later poets were his "report of the people," as William Carlos Williams called it, and his flexible, inventive, and scrapbook methods of presentation. His work provoked bitter controversy. To admirers he seemed to give poetry purpose and relevance and to liberate its technique. (p. 356)

The *Chicago Poems* were a shock to most readers. The title poem created a myth of the city as a strong man, a sweating worker, and rejoiced in his brutal strength. Other poems pictured the urban and industrial milieu. Sandburg underscored the contrast of the slums with the wealthy homes along the lakeshore; he pictured such sights as the skyscrapers looming in the smoke. . . . He tended especially to give portraits or brief accounts of typical characters. . . .

Here was a directly phrased poetry of the contemporary world. It gave sights and sounds. It showed people at work. It had something to say about the character and quality of their lives. It dwelt on the romance in the familiar and it enforced a political and social message by concrete contrasts. (p. 357)

Sandburg did not merely describe the people; he glorified them. He was the opposite of Eliot, who was repelled by "Apeneck Sweeney" and the "damp souls of housemaids." To Sandburg the picnicking Hungarians, the prostitutes, the shovel man, and the working girls were so many jewels, which his poetry exhibited. (p. 358)

The theme of his next volume, *Cornhuskers* (1918), was the prairie. Here he pictured farm people and their work. He also dwelled on the beauty and fatness, the mellow scents and sounds of the land. Social protest was not present in all his *Chicago Poems* nor was it absent from *Cornhuskers,* but most of the pieces in the latter, such as "Grass" and "Cool Tombs," were lyrics of a more traditional type, contemplating time, vastness, change, perenniality, and death. Sandburg did not wrestle very strenuously with these mysteries; neither did he find them very chilling. It is poetry of the agreeable kind, bland, relaxed, simply direct, and very fond of its subject.

Henceforth Sandburg's poetry tended to fall into one or the other of these loosely separate kinds: he either dwelled on the lives and qualities of the people or felt a "philosophic" pathos—he often did both in the same poem. There are also pleasant poetic impressions, such as "Fog." The effect of the 771 pages of his poetry is no test of his worth, but is may be remarked that his "philosophic" pathos becomes wearisome because it lacks energy. He recites fact with an absence or inarticulateness of feeling and with comparatively few thoughts in his head. The effect is of a quizzicalness or a slight wonder or a vague, momentary disturbance of mind, soon settling into calm. . . . Similarly, his poems of social protest are often no more than sketchy outlines in black and white. (pp. 358-59)

Better than any other poet, Sandburg represents the new style of the 1910s—the "modern" style before Eliot. . . . In Sandburg one sees what the age had to teach about writing. "Chicago" is an imitation of Whitman; some of the *Chicago Poems* might be one-deimensional versions of the Robinsonian portrait; some are Impressionist; some combine Impressionism with the sparer imagery of Japanese verse. As for Imagism, Sandburg said he had no connection with it. But his poems seek the concreteness and objectivity which the Imagists communicated to American poetry in general. He is not always simple or easy to understand, but the materials of his poetry—the facts, images, allusions—are never recondite.

The most striking thing about Sandburg's style is its flexibility and inventiveness, its freedom to use whatever means or methods seem appropriate. . . . His vocabulary is simple and seldom "poetic" or abstract but, with these limitations, it is flexibly ready to adapt to the subject. He exploits the diction of common speech when it suits him, and one finds slang and vigorous folk metaphors. . . . Usually, however, his diction has a precision that mitigates the impression of vernacular speech. His syntax can have the shapelessness of talk:

> And I saw a crowd of Hungarians under the
> trees with their women and children
> and a keg of beer and an accordion.

But he also makes much use of parallel syntax and repetition, and his effects can be decidedly rhetorical. He never uses meters. That is the only general remark that can be made about his versification, for everything depends on the effect he seeks, which may require a drumming, recurrent rhythm or a rhythmless sprawl. The principles of form that govern his poetry are simply the principles of effective thinking and presentation in general—revelance, economy, contrast, conclusion, and the like.

He was more gifted in sympathy than in synthesis. He enters, though not deeply, into characters, feelings, and objects over a broad range but takes them one at a time. . . . The objects accumulated or contrasted make a meaningful pattern, but they do not interpenetrate. . . . The list of associations is one of his main poetic forms. He picks a large, vague subject—"Prairie," "River Roads," "Band Concert," "Smoke and Steel," "Pennsylvania," "Hazardous Occupations"—and accumulates facts, thoughts, images, and poetic feelings about it. The effect is of a scrapbook. Its items convey the same general attitude of appreciation, social protest, or whatever. *The People, Yes* (1936), a heap of sayings, anecdotes, character sketches, dialogues, and the like, shows the method at book length; the subject is "the people" and the attitude is "yes." Sandburg's greatest weakness as a poet was the minimal demand he made of a poem. It was enough to render the sound of the wind ("Wind Song") or contrast the bustle of a street by day with its stillness by night ("Blue Island Intersection"). Or it was enough merely to make some bland observation, or evoke some pleasant object or feeling, or accumulate images without tension or wit. His example helped poets surrender to what Yeats called the greatest temptation of the artist, creation without toil. (pp. 359-61)

> *David Perkins, in his* A History of Modern Poetry: From the 1890s to the High Modernist Mode *(copyright © 1976 by the President and Fellows of Harvard College; excerpted by permission of the author and publishers), Cambridge, Mass.: The Belknap Press of Harvard University Press, 1976.*

LOUIS D. RUBIN, JR.

[Sandburg's] way of using language can be deceptive. It is much like prose in its syntax, and the colloquial vocabulary adds to an apparent casualness. In his best poetry Sandburg *uses* vernacular language, slang even; by this I mean that in Sandburg's instance it isn't the self-conscious employment of a "low" vocabulary to call attention to commonness, a vaunting of plebeian virtue (though later in his career Sandburg was prone to do just this, ad nauseam). An expression such as "the *crack* trains of the nation" is an organic part of his vocabulary, not an affectation, and he employs the adjective because it is simply the appropriate word to image what he wishes to convey about the train. As such it provides precisely the intensification of language, the heightened awareness of the texture of experience, that the best poetry affords.

I stress this because unless the way in which Sandburg employs vernacular imagery is properly recognized, his way of poetry will be misunderstood. If we compare, for example, "Limited" [in *Chicago Poems* (1916)] with another fine poem about a train, Stephen Spender's "Express," we can see the difference. Spender writes of "the black statement of pistons," portrays the train as "gliding like a queen," as "gathering speed" so that "she acquires mystery," and so on, until "like a comet through flames she moves entranced," and as conclusion: "Wrapt in her music, no bird song, no, nor bough/Breaking with honey buds, shall ever equal." Spender thus asserts in his poem that the train, an artifact of industrialism, is eminently worthy of the kind of aesthetic contemplation accorded to other objects that have traditionally been the subject of poems. He does it by applying to the train certain imagery and reference customarily ascribed to more familiarly poetic matter, and he ends his poem with the assertion that the beauty of the train is superior to that of most conventionally beautiful objects.

Sandburg might well have agreed, but in "Limited" he felt no occasion to assert the right of the train to such treatment. On the contrary he assumes it, as a matter of language. To refer to a "crack" train, to "fifteen all-steel coaches," to "diners" and "sleepers," to a man as being "in the smoker" is in his poetics all that the railroad imagery needed to make his point; and he will conduct his poem in such terms, without any feeling of self-consciousness in doing so, and without having to introduce traditional poetic imagery to justify the depiction of a train in a poem. This is what I mean about the language as being vernacular in an organic way, not as tour de force or demonstration. (pp. 182-83)

Of course there is no inherent literary virtue to using vernacular discourse in a poem, or for that matter any other kind of discourse. But given Sandburg's mastery of the vernacular, his ability *as a poet* to think in it without self-consciousness, it should be obvious that he enjoys certain advantages in dealing as poet with the kind of experience that he writes about. If you wish to write a poem about a railroad train, then if you can do so in the kind of documentary denotation that you and others customarily use to think about a train, without having to introduce for your purposes a different convention of language not customarily applied to it, you will be able to come closer to being able to reproduce your personal experience of the train. The same goes for other objects of Sandburg's experience. . . . And in the poems of Sandburg's best years he is able not only to invest that kind of experience with language that can give it the intensity of poetry but also to achieve the intensification within and through the rhythms, syntax, parallelisms, and imagery of the vernacular reference customarily employed to denote that experience. He is able, in short, to make the ordinary into the extraordinary on its own terms, without violating the everyday authenticity of the documentation.

The result is an enlargement of the range and nature of our poetic experience through his poems. Any good poet provides that; Sandburg's particular talent is that he opens up areas of our experience which are not ordinarily considered objects of aesthetic contemplation, through language that enables him, and us, to recognize such experience in new ways.

A great deal has been made of his work as being, in its subject and its language, essentially midwestern American, and this is quite true. It is not thereby the less general or sophisticated in its relevance, however; and the view of Sandburg as a kind of rude, untutored regional bard whose poetry achieves its effects through its presentation of novel subjects attendant upon the industrialization of the cities and towns of the Corn Belt hardly bears serious scrutiny. He is, at his best, a poet of much subtlety and sophistication; and it is through the skillful intensification of language, not fresh subjects alone, that he works his art. It is true that his language is much closer to the rhythms and word choices of vernacular discourse than what one normally encounters in verse, but it is precisely *through* that discourse that he works his poetry. . . . [It] is not the subject as such, so much as what Sandburg does with the language, that makes the poem. Sandburg's best poetry will survive, where the once popular *Spoon River Anthology* of Edgar Lee Masters has faded, because Masters placed his emphasis on subject, the "thought," while Sandburg at his best achieves it with language.

There is, of course, a built-in psychological hazard in such poetics, and by the early 1920s Sandburg succumbed to it. The best poems in *Chicago Poems* (1916), *Cornhuskers* (1918), and *Smoke and Steel* (1920) succeed because of the tension between the idiom and the subject; their impact lies in the resolution, through language, of that tension. But from using vernacular language to intensify everyday experience into poetry it is an easy, and a fatal, step for one to begin assuming that because the experience is ordinary and the language is of the earth earthy, they are therefore inherently Poetic. To depict in compelling and appropriate language a train moving across the prairie is one thing; it is another and a considerably less interesting matter to assert that because it is a train on the midwestern American prairie, and because the language is avowedly vernacular, the joint appearance within a poem constitutes the poetry. On the contrary the instant that the tension between language and object is slackened, what is produced is not poetry but rhetoric.

This is what begins happening to Sandburg as poet very early in his career; following the *Chicago Poems* his poetry shows an increasing tendency thereafter, in almost a kind of geometric progression, to substitute rhetoric about experience for evocation of his experience. Sandburg began to believe his press notices. He was now the Poet of Mid-America, and thenceforward he sought to live up to the title by cataloguing the everyday scene in the Midwest. His poetry had been likened to Walt Whitman's; now he proceeded to imitate the least attractive aspects of Whitman's verse, producing only hot air and chaff. You are parodying yourself, his friend Joseph Warren Beach warned him. This is precisely what he was doing, with the process culminating in *The People, Yes* (1936), in which democratic ideology is passed off as being Poetic merely because it is personified and documented. There is no tension, no discovery. There are no people in *The People, Yes;* all is abstract, "typical." The single, terribly glad fish crier of the *Chicago Poems* is more human and credible than all the varieties of abstracted Common Men catalogued in the 107 sections of *The People, Yes.*

It is clear that by the early 1920s Sandburg was no longer interested in writing poems. He had become increasingly involved in prose, in particular with the life of Abraham Lincoln. Had he continued to invest in poetry the emotional capital that now went into biography, he might have developed further as a poet. But he became occupied with what turned out to be a six-volume biography of the war president. Few persons who are properly familiar with his work on Lincoln, especially with the four volumes of *Abraham Lincoln: The War Years* (1939), can overly regret his defection from the muse, however. (pp. 184-86)

The practice among academic historians has been to dismiss Sandburg's biography as being "useful for its poetic insights"—which, coming from an academic historian, is not intended to be a compliment, since in such circles to be "poetic" is an euphemism for being unreliable and impressionistic.

There is a sense in which such criticism is valid for the two early volumes, *The Prairie Years* (1926), and in particular the first of these, which is developed out of sometimes scanty factual material. . . . But if Sandburg erred in dealing too imaginatively with the sparse source material available for writing *The Prairie Years,* he would seem to have taken to heart the criticism to that effect made by book reviewers at the time of publication, for the four volumes of *The War Years,* while written with grace and while unfailingly interesting in presentation, are solidly anchored in abundantly recorded fact; and they seldom drift into unsubstantiated hypothesizing. They are a remarkable portrayal not only of Lincoln himself but of all the major and many of the minor figures around him. . . . *The War Years* constitutes not only a perceptive biography but a magnificently detailed history of the United States during the civil war. Academic historians may fault the work because Sandburg did not bother to annotate his sources; to the general reader this is no stumbling block at all. At times repetitious, the work contains few factual errors and is never opinionated or unfair. I know no other work on nineteenth-century American history that can surpass it for its depiction of the times and its delineation of Lincoln. I read it through again recently and was more than ever convinced of its magisterial stature. Sandburg's biography of Abraham Lincoln is a classic of our language; it puts the other biographies of the man in the shade. (pp. 186-87)

For the remainder of his days Sandburg regularly indulged in grandiloquent Yea-Saying and celebrating of the *Volksgeist,* becoming and remaining a kind of professional Prophet of Democracy demonstrating (so far as I am concerned) impeccable political attitudes and insufferable intellectual allegiances. He participated in all the claptrap of midcentury middlebrow liberalism, blending invocations to democracy, pseudopopulist jargon, and commercialized aesthetics in a soufflé heavily flavored with cliché. (p. 187)

The language of discovery [became] the rhetoric of advertising. The early 1960s found him out in Beverly Hills, serving as consultant for a movie on the life of Christ!

Yet in 1952 he also produced a beautiful memoir, *Always the Young Strangers,* chronicling his childhood and young manhood, a book written with freshness, candor, without pose or glibness. Returning to the recollection of his early days, he seemed to have sloughed off all the hokum, pretense, and self-serving rhetoric, and found his integrity still undamaged and unabated. It is almost as if there were two Carl Sandburgs, one of them the private, sensitive artist, the other the public performer, self-important and pompous, willing to debase the language for gain. (p. 188)

In 1963, at the age of eighty-five, he brought out a new volume of poetry, *Honey and Salt*. Astoundingly he seemed to have regained his long neglected energy as lyric poet. Here was the old vision of the real world he inhabited, a trifle dimmed perhaps but once again depicting remembered experience in new language. . . . Compared with the best of the early poems, only a few of those in *Honey and Salt* quite manage to hold their own. But the verse in Sandburg's last book is in large part interesting, genuine, alive: once again, after many years, language is being put to work.

Those who chronicle and interpret American letters are bound ultimately to rediscover for themselves the excellence of Carl Sandburg. When that happens, the fine poet and masterful biographer will at last reemerge from the dumps. There have been other poets who have written and spoken silly things—things far sillier and sometimes considerably more sinister than ever he wrote or spoke—and who have woven a public image of specious rhetoric and role-playing about their reputations, and yet been remembered finally because at their best they wrote well. (pp. 188-89)

> Louis D. Rubin, Jr., "Not to Forget Carl Sandburg . . . ," in Sewanee Review (reprinted by permission of the editor; © 1977 by The University of the South), Winter, 1977, pp. 181-89.

* * *

SAROYAN, William 1908-

Saroyan is an Armenian-American novelist, short story writer, playwright, essayist, editor, and writer of children's books. During the Depression, Saroyan's sentimental fiction, with its nostalgia for a former, better time, was received with welcome relief by an American public who sought escape from the bleak reality of their lives. With the advent of World War II, however, the changing values and tastes of a more sophisticated readership rejected Saroyan's simplistic stories of optimism and the triumph of the American Dream. His refusal to adapt his fiction to the growth and change of a more complex society has prompted critics to dismiss his work as superficial and limited. He was awarded the Pulitzer Prize in Drama in 1940 for *The Time of Your Life*, but refused it saying that this play was "no more great or good" than the rest of his work. He has written under the pseudonym of Sirak Goryan. (See also *CLC*, Vols. 1, 8, and *Contemporary Authors*, Vols. 5-8, rev. ed.)

THELMA J. SHINN

Saroyan's philosophy is not a resolution of but a recognition and acceptance of the contradictions of life. He tells us that life is both funny and sad, both violent and tender, and that generally the contradictions are present in the same scene, the same person, at the same time. Consequently, critics could not define Saroyan's plays—to give one interpretation would conceal the other interpretations simultaneously maintained by the symbolism. This led many critics to reject Saroyan's works because they felt that the plays, in appealing to the irrational and to the emotional in the audience rather than to the intellectual and rational, could be dismissed as mere Romanticism. The more perceptive critics, however, suspected that there was more to Saroyan than sentimentality. (p. 185)

The nonplot symbolic dramas of Pinter, of Beckett, of Ionesco with their usually unrelieved pessimism are remarkably similar to the "romantic fantasies" of Saroyan. Saroyan displays the same disregard for spelling out meanings to the audience, the same freedom with scenery and plot, the same concentration on the individual. Much of modern drama is considered existential because the individual is trying to find for himself some meaning in this absurd universe—and the meaning, if any, appears to be within himself. In this sense, at least, the existential theme is precisely what most concerns Saroyan.

Saroyan's departure from modern theater, as well as from the theater of the 30's and 40's, is his remarkable—his critics say unrealistic—ability to find a note of affirmation, to testify finally to the rejected ideal of human dignity. (pp. 185-86)

The multiplicity of [critical interpretations of *My Heart's in the Highlands*] reflects the symbolic import of the play, a symbolism . . . exclusively American. Saroyan explores the themes of economic inequality, the plight of the artist, individual integrity, the search for beauty and the growth of awareness in a seemingly haphazard way in the simple international American stock of a small neighborhood. The Scotch bugler, the Armenian-speaking grandmother, the Polish grocer are all beautifully American. The setting is representative rather than realistic; the simple dialogue is intuitive rather than logical.

The economic inequality is implicit in the poverty of the family. . . . Saroyan's interest lies not so much in the inequality indiscriminately arising from the indifference of the external world as it does in the individual's ability to turn even this into a vehicle for the expression of human dignity. . . . Saroyan's play emphasizes the brotherhood of man and the dignity of the individual, the human relationships rather than the social "realities."

The plight of the artist theme is also treated in a universal manner by Saroyan. Though Johnny's father represents the artist, he is not alone. Saroyan recognizes the artist—the sensitive awareness to living—in each of the characters. . . . Saroyan identifies the artist as the man sensitive to the beauty which can be found in the world. His plight is in the rejection by the world of his attempts to express this beauty, and that rejection is equally wrong—or at least equally possible—whether the man is a first-rate or a tenth-rate poet. (pp. 186-87)

This search for beauty within the individual which Saroyan recognizes comes close to being the element of the divine in humanity. MacGregor, who achieves recognizable expression of beauty in his music, has his "heart in the highlands," and goes there at the end of the play. The townspeople implicitly recognize the divine origin of this gift when they bring the food as sacrifices to it. The father has created his successful poem in the person of Johnny and in himself—thus they are in this sense identical and thus MacGregor wants to come to their home to die because that is the closest he can come to the divine perception in this world.

It is Johnny's father who gains the most complete awareness of the value of the individual and of the search for beauty in this play. . . . Johnny himself, as he ends the play with "I'm not mentioning any names, Pa, but something's wrong somewhere," has only grasped half the truth—the easiest half according to Saroyan. His recognition of the injustice of a world that prevents good people from dwelling together peacefully in the goodness of the universe is the stopping point of most modern views of the world. Saroyan goes on to assert that man's search for beauty can carry him beyond the ugliness of the world to the divine within himself and within his fellow men. If this attitude must be romantic and sentimental, then Saroyan is both—and so is Emerson, Thoreau, Hart Crane, any artist who believes that man can transcend the injustice of the external world by looking within himself and that man can find a beauty within himself that is within each man. Saroyan tries to reach this inner beauty, and if he does not appeal to it with logical arguments, it may be because beauty is beyond logic. If he couches his appeal in what seems sentimental and romantic, it is because inner beauty is the source of whatever sentiment and romance man can know. Even this first play shows that Saroyan is not simply saying that life is beautiful and all men love each other. He says rather that in each man with any sensitivity there is a desire for beauty and that this desire should be followed and nurtured if there is to be any positive reality of beauty in this absurd world.

Saroyan's greatest success, *The Time of Your Life,* carries the same message as *My Heart's in the Highlands,* or messages rather, since the simple statement above can scarcely represent the levels of meaning presented in Saroyan's symbolic dramas.... The central set is a run-down bar where the central character sits drinking champagne and watching people. Every person (with the exception of Blick, the depersonalized symbol of the authority of the external world reminiscent of Kafka's bureaucrats) is seeking for beauty. However, it is not at all easy to dismiss this as romanticism either, even the most "apparently" romantic situation of the prostitute with the heart of gold who gets a new life through the sincere love of a man. The ingredients are romantic—because they deal with that desire for beauty within the individual which is the source of all romance—but Saroyan's treatment of the material reveals more perception than is usually attributed to him. The prostitute remembers the beauty of her childhood—when her childhood wasn't beautiful.... Here Saroyan's admiration for family ties is apparent, but most apparent is that the word "home" epitomized for Kitty her search for beauty. Her perception of the indefinable beauty of her family and her childhood—despite the trouble and the sadness—was her artistic achievement, her communication of beauty where it is not immediately discernible.... [This] attempt is infinitely better than the alternative, than the prostitution of the individual by the depersonalized destructiveness of the external world.

Saroyan's ending to this play, however, if not condemned as sentimentality, will have to be recognized as pure wish-fulfillment. (pp. 187-89)

[In *Hello Out There, Across the Board on Tomorrow Morning,* and *Death Along the Wabash,* all pessimistic plays,] Saroyan openly admits that his romantic individualists in their search for beauty do not always succeed—and this is perhaps why he said later that he repudiated *Hello Out There*—but the value of their attempts contrasted with the rest of the world still places them far above the other characters. The most romantic of these three is *Hello Out There,* where the young man says to the girl that with her he could be good—but in the light of Saroyan's other plays this can be raised above its typically sentimental interpreta-

tion. The young man's recognition of beauty in the girl makes her a symbol of his unique expression of beauty, of his poem or song, and therefore of the true goal of his restless search for beauty. (p. 190)

But we should avoid placing only one interpretation on Saroyan's symbols; the girl must also be seen in relation to Mr. Kosak of *My Heart's in the Highlands.* She is the one person who has listened to the young man, who has in a sense read his poetry and therefore given value to it. Thus at the end she blends with him through their shared perception of beauty and her last line is the same as his first line—"Hell—out there!"—which is both an attempt to communicate with the world and an acceptance of the alienation of the individual.

Across the Board on Tomorrow Morning is even more symbolic than *Hello Out There,* leaving realistic presentation far behind.... The most obvious theme is the conflict and identification of illusion and reality. Saroyan maintains in this play a precarious balance between the external and internal world, and the success of the play is that he doesn't reject either as illusory: in the delightfully drunken perception of Fritz the cab driver, "Illusion or reality, no illusion or no reality, one more drink before I go."

However, in attesting to the illusoriness of the external world at all, Saroyan is taking his stand for the internal world as before. Whether Kitty's dream of home is an illusion, whether each man's search for beauty is illusory, it is an illusion which many—Saroyan included—honor by such titles as divinity, as art, as inspiration. Simultaneously, for Saroyan at least, whether the external world is irrelevant and is going to disappear tomorrow morning or not, it is within the context of that world—with all its "delicate balance of despair and delight"—that inner reality must be expressed.... (pp. 190-91)

The final lines of the play, in which Fritz places a bet on Tomorrow Morning, show that Saroyan had passed beyond the wish-fulfillment he allowed himself in *The Time of Your Life....* Fritz's bet symbolizes Saroyan's willingness to gamble on the desire for beauty in mankind despite his realization that the odds are against him and that he has lost before.

Death Along the Wabash is the most pessimistic of Saroyan's plays. *Hello Out There* recognized the world's rejection of the artist's perception of beauty, but held out the hope that the search for beauty would still be carried on by the individual. In *Across the Board on Tomorrow Morning,* despite the lighter tone, the conclusion ... is even more pessimistic. This is only relieved by Fritz's willingness to continue betting on the losing horse anyway.

In *Death Along the Wabash,* no one is left to search for beauty anymore, and the world refuses to gamble on the individual. Instead, it destroys him, ostensibly because it is helping him to reach his goal—which is only attainable in heaven, or at least out of this world. The Hobo as the representative of the world is right when he says that he has destroyed the idealistic, Negro, escaped convict Joe in self-defense: a complete perception of the beauty possible within oneself does destroy the external irrelevancies for that individual, and in this sense Joe was threatening the Hobo's existence. (pp. 191-92)

This play, so reminiscent of Pinter, surpasses both the obvious theme of murder for materialistic satisfaction and the topical theme of racial discrimination—of the Hobo representing society's specific persecution of the Negro. It is the somewhat superficial concentration on the racial theme which weakens all three of [these plays]. . . . Saroyan transcends this in *Death Along the Wabash* because he is not so much trying to write as a black man as to portray the individual persecuted by the world, the individual searching for beauty who has been his main concern in the other plays. Consequently, portraying a hero that is black rather than a black hero enables Saroyan to point out parallels between discrimination against minority groups and discrimination against the individual. Except for the blatant exposition in Joe's first speech, the play is powerfully written. The speeches are generally longer and weightier than those usually found in Saroyan's plays, and the conclusion of unrelieved pessimism is hardly recognizable as the work of this affirmative playwright. . . . [The Hobo, a] powerful portrait of that portion of mankind which recognizes the external world as the only reality . . . and thus destroys the inner reality in others and in themselves, is especially significant because the Hobo's arguments appeal strongly to logic, to the rational perception of the world. Those critics who argued that Saroyan was not logical should read this play—they might note an undercurrent of resentment here of the artist who was critized for appealing to the heart. This play gives modern society what it claims to want—a realistic pessimism and the destruction of the idealistic and romantic in mankind.

In fact, the pessimism of this play strikes deeply because Saroyan's multi-level symbolism enables him to reflect parallels between many forms of persecution and discrimination and at the same time to show the close relationship between the persecutor and his victim. Saroyan not only realizes that, as in this play, the sensitive individual, the artist, the economically oppressed, the black man or Armenian in search of something beyond what society has allotted him, will more likely than not be destroyed by the world before he can reach his goal; but even more painful is Saroyan's recognition that this destruction is likely to be at the hands of the individual's own father—from another man who could have chosen to search for beauty or fight for freedom but who sold out to the world instead for materialistic reasons.

This is not a new discovery Saroyan made just before writing *Death Along the Wabash*. The world had always opposed his individuals; it is only that he has preferred to place his bet on beauty, on humanity, on tomorrow morning despite the odds. He reaffirms the value of the individual in . . . *The Cave Dwellers*, and if one reviewer derides it for imitating Beckett by calling it "an affirmative '*Waiting for Godot*'" it should be remembered that Saroyan was writing plotless symbolic drama many years before *Waiting for Godot* appeared in 1953. It is true that several of Saroyan's general situations reflect other plays—Wilder's *Skin of Our Teeth* is strongly recalled in *High Time Along the Wabash* and Hart and Kaufman's *You Can't Take It With You* provides the source for much of the merriment in *The Beautiful People*. Despite these recognizable influences, Saroyan's plays . . . are still very original and carry different messages from their models. This is equally true of *The Cave Dwellers*, where the characters resemble nothing so much as characters in other Saroyan plays. (pp. 192-93)

The Cave Dwellers, however, lacks the power of Saroyan's earlier works except in isolated moments. The ingredients are there, the intention is there, but somehow the use of romanticism has become an immersion in romanticism. Saroyan is pushing too hard: as Walter Kerr observed, "The sentence beginning 'Love is . . .' occurs more times in eleven scenes than I could count, try though I did." Critics have frequently argued that Saroyan tends to state his message rather than present it dramatically, and statements do detract from the effect of this play, anyway. In fact, Saroyan protests too much this time, perhaps because he had become increasingly more aware of the loneliness of his affirmative position and the difficulties of maintaining it in the face of current conditions. . . . [We] might validly wonder whom he is trying to convince in the *Cave Dwellers*, the audience or himself?

However, allowing for the intrusion of sentimentality and didacticism in *The Cave Dwellers*, on the whole Saroyan has succeeded remarkably well in using romantic material symbolically. To one who automatically identifies any affirmation with romanticism, he is a romantic. But to recognize the world for what it is, to admit the apparent hopelessness of an affirmation of the individual, yet still to be willing to gamble on human dignity because of the value of the attempt itself sounds more like courage than romanticism. (p. 194)

> *Thelma J. Shinn, "William Saroyan: Romantic Existentialist," in* Modern Drama *(copyright © 1972, University of Toronto, Graduate Centre for Study of Drama; with the permission of* Modern Drama*), September, 1972, pp. 185-94.*

EDWARD HOAGLAND

[Saroyan's] contribution has been to write from joy, which is in short supply lately, and sparse as a tradition in our literature anyway, unless one looks back to some of the founding figures, such as Walt Whitman, Emerson, Thoreau. He predates the glut of black humor and rancorous ethnicity, the literary theater of cruelty and the absurd, though part of the point about Saroyan which is so interesting is that he has been a profoundly, innovatively "ethnic" writer—one of the very first in America, one who has been a conscious spokesman for a people who survived a genocidal holocaust—but that throughout his life he has chosen to write not of despair and dadaism and devastation, but joy. . . .

The Saroyan working method—and it can seem repetitive—is to swing way out from the trapeze, do a somersault or two, and reach out flatly for our hands, trusting partly in us, and secure in the faith that if he misses there is a God somewhere to break his fall. He is an all-around believer; and of course there are, for example, the two ways to lay one's hand against one's face: either feeling the cheek, or feeling the skull—death—underneath the cheek. One can look at one's hand and see a mechanized, strange set of bending pincers, terrifying to contemplate, or see the hand as an elixir of the spirit. Because we can admire artists who lean toward either view, it's not a matter of shutting anybody out: only of insisting that both be heard.

> *Edward Hoagland, "A Master and a Master's Master," in* The New York Times Book Review *(© 1976 by The New York*

Times Company; reprinted by permission), August 15, 1976, p. 2.

KENNETH W. RHOADS

A careful reading [of *The Time of Your Life*] shows that Joe [the play's central character] may be seen as a valid Christ-figure—not a literal Christ, for *The Time of Your Life* is no Second Coming, nor even an allegorical Christ, but a type of Christ, essentially realistic and certainly very human—whose nature and behavior are completely consonant and who takes on stature as heroic protagonist within such a mode. Whether Saroyan consciously created Joe as Christ-figure is immaterial; this is the character which emerges and which the script projects—by allusion, by indirect revelation, by implicit scriptural parallel in Joe's motivations and the shape of his life, and by specific episodes whose relevance to the meaning of the play is carried by their symbolic content. (pp. 228-29)

Although, as with Christ, the facts of Joe's past essentially comprise a lacuna in his life up to the point of his ministry, he does reveal that—like Christ the young carpenter—he had once worked but ultimately gave it up. And the nature of that experience bears directly on his having rejected that life for his present endeavors. The commercial world brought him only disillusionment and a deep sense of guilt derived from his very success. For although he had learned how to make money, he found material success to be achieved only at the expense of others. . . .

Joe is a type of scapegoat for the sins of his fellow man. He distinctly bears a burden of guilt for those who exploit and hurt others, and suffers in full empathy with the injured and the have-nots. (p. 230)

A multitude of passing allusions and episodes augmenting the major motifs of the play pervades *The Time of Your Life*, contributing to an accretion of Joe's Christ-image. Throughout the play, with the exception of one brief scene in Kitty's hotel room, Joe spends his entire time seated at his table in Nick's euphemistically named Pacific Street Saloon, Restaurant, and Entertainment Palace at the foot of Embarcadero on San Francisco's waterfront. Thus, as Christ found his mission not in the houses of the rich patriarchs or the elite council of the Sanhedrin, but rather on the shores and in the fields among poor fisher-folk and sweating farmers, ministering to the leprous, the ill, the dying, so too Joe finds his greatest compatibility with the common people of his world. . . . (p. 231)

Joe seems to possess an uncanny perception, transcending time, into the future and the past, which suggests a supernatural omniscience. (p. 234)

Joe's obsession with the playthings of children thus reveals a poignant depth which goes far beyond the surface naiveté of ingenuous delight. He experiences the toys as metaphor for a tragically lost innocence in a world (basically wonderful but now gone corrupt from the unconscionable power of evil men) which cries out for redemption.

Here again a parallel with Christ is suggested. Jesus' love for children is frequently cited, and he also saw the innocence of childhood as a metaphor for the purity of soul necessary for spiritual salvation. (pp. 235-36)

Joe's essential quality . . . is his intense humanity—his awareness of other people and his sensitivity to their inner agonies as well as their outer struggles. This was also true

of Christ, but to have endowed Joe overtly with incarnate divinity would have shifted the grounds of the play and introduced an element incongruous with its dramatic and thematic premises. Thus, the hints of Joe's supernatural qualities, the suggestions that his realm of existence somehow transcends this material, mortal one, need not—should not—be taken literally. These hints and suggestions do, nevertheless, recur with frequency and insistency. Consequently, they function effectively to enrich Joe's character through meaningful ambiguity: an ambiguity which, by the very air of mystery it imparts, serves to establish Joe's awareness of a higher, spiritual level of existence and to augment his inherently Christ-like nature. . . . Within the realistic context of *The Time of Your Life* Joe is a vital human character with his share of the passions and the foibles that mark the human animal; at the same time he is endowed with a consummate humanitarian concern for all his fellow beings. Through meaningful ambiguity Saroyan manages to suggest the transcendent spiritual quality—the greatness of heart and soul—which sets Joe apart from other men, while he keeps him firmly rooted in the real world.

While structurally Joe's dramatic function is diffuse and varied (he seems at one and the same time to be objective observer of life, interested, even passionate, participant in the swirling action, dissociated chorus, perceptive commentator on life's pains and joys, father-figure, and ingenuous child) his connection with the plot action most specifically concerns Tom and Kitty and his ultimately successful maneuverings to bring about their physical and spiritual union and effect their escape from a hopeless past and present to a new life. . . . (pp. 237-38)

[Joe] is prime mover in the union of the two young people. Savior of both of them in a very literal sense, he also effects a kind of rebirth for them individually and in their new life together. Tom, educated and strengthened through Joe's tutelage, may now end his discipleship and go forth to a life of independence and self-achievement; Kitty, cleansed and released from the prison of her former life, may now realize the long-suppressed dream in the return of innocence. Together, now in this time of their lives, they will be fulfilled by the strength and purity of their mutual love. In short, they will have attained, through the power of Joe's love and compassion, both the inner peace and the outer joy in living which all the habitués of Nick's Pacific Street Saloon, Restaurant, and Entertainment Palace so desperately seek but so rarely find. (pp. 239-40)

It is true that Joe expresses no regret over Blick's demise, nor does he condemn Kit for his violation of the Fourth Commandment. This does not necessarily present an inconsistency. Since Blick has come to represent unrepentant evil, the Christ-impulse in Joe would not lament its eradication, and Kit's action might even be viewed—wryly, perhaps—as a minor harrowing of hell. At the same time, Joe does not expressly approve of the killing, nor does he participate in the general exultation which it precipitates. Again, he does not judge.

The final aspect of any Christ-figure is that his ending, whether it be in death or mere disappearance, is, like his origins, obscure. Joe's departure from Nick's bar similarly carries an aura of vagueness and mystery. (p. 241)

The Time of Your Life is a play of intense romanticism and unashamed sentimentality; one must, in fact, accept Saroyan here on his own grounds if the play's full potential for an affecting emotional involvement is to be realized. Saroyan is not for the cynic or the iconoclastic realist. The interpretation of Joe [as a Christ-figure] is not only consonant with such a dramatic mode, but it may be seen to gain therein considerable dramatic depth. Any Christ-figure—as in Christ himself—is highly romantic in concept. Everything that he is and symbolizes, and all that he does, is strongly stimulating to the imagination and the emotions, capable of communicating simultaneously intellectual, moral, and spiritual meaning. Certainly other interpretations of Joe may be validly advanced.... Nevertheless, Joe as Christ-figure is solidly grounded in the evidence from the script ... whose very bulk and pervasiveness seem to belie coincidence. Above all, seeing Joe as type of Christ not only removes critical ambiguities heretofore existing in the absence of an alternate viable rationale, but more importantly reveals a focal character of greatly augmented stature and meaning and increases immeasurably the ideative and emotional dimensions of the play. (p. 242)

> *Kenneth W. Rhoads, "Joe as Christ-type in Saroyan's 'The Time of Your Life'," in* Essays in Literature *(copyright 1976 by Western Illinois University), Fall, 1976, pp. 227-43.*

JOEL OPPENHEIMER

"Chance Meetings" is another of the familiar, loosely tied remembrances that [Saroyan] has done before but, as always, there are new and marvelously alive passages, and his wonderful, unconditioned people.... Years ago Mr. Saroyan postulated that there are two kinds of writers: those who run to meet death, and those who fight to keep it off. It's always been clear which side he's on, and so every person he's met, everything he's done, becomes cause for celebration.... (p. 11)

There is a particular theory about friendship in this book: "Brief friendships have such definite starting and stopping points that they take on a quality of art, of a *whole* thing, which cannot be broken or spoiled." Mr. Saroyan prefers these brief acquaintanceships, these chance meetings; he sometimes gets upset when the friendship extends past that wholeness; when, for example, the bookseller he's been chatting with for months suddenly realizes that his customer is *the* Saroyan. What Mr. Saroyan is talking about, I believe, is his own special ability to see a wholeness, a unity, in an episode. It is what makes him a great storyteller. His many short stories in that long list of published work stay with us; though they are each a tiny thing, they are *whole* and complete.

So I continue reading him, because he is worth reading. Forget the sentimentality that threatens to sink each line, forget the cloying sweetness that occasionally overwhelms; ride past it all, because at base, and solid, there is the story.

In a "chance meeting," he writes, "You have been thrown together accidentally, total strangers, in order to pass along ... the essence of your own story and reality. You are not there to acquire more story, to have more material to carry with the rest of the material that still hasn't been really understood, or certainly hasn't been used, and you are there anonymously." Because he is always there in this fashion he does acquire more stories, more material. Be-

cause he has the honesty to admit when he doesn't understand the material, he is able to pass it on to us, and to wonder.

For this, and for other strengths, we owe a great deal to Mr. Saroyan. He's never been ranked among the heavyweights, and yet he lasts, and he keeps writing. He matters. The stories (and the plays, which are extended stories) are the best of it. I wish there were more of those coming from him, and fewer memoirs, in which the stories get subsumed and lose their clarity a little. (pp. 11, 24)

The Saroyan voice is there because he's always been willing to listen and to talk. He never merely transcribes, as so many other prose writers do. That is the reason we have paid attention to him for more than 40 years: *because* he is discursive. And, curiously, some of those things we find have now come back into style: the wonderment, the fine appreciation of lunacy, the almost mystical acceptance of another person's arcane self. (p. 24)

> *Joel Oppenheimer, "Friendly People," in* The New York Times Book Review *(© 1978 by The New York Times Company; reprinted by permission), March 12, 1978, pp. 11, 24.*

D. KEITH MANO

So much for the omniscient observer. And the first-person narration. What you've got [in *Chance Meetings: A Memoir*] is the Ethnic Naïve. An Ethnic Naïve book will be less than two hundred pages long, with deep margins (for deep marginalia) and fat, blank chapter breaks. Also simple, sentence-length paragraphs that reveal simple-but-profound truth because, well, they're simple. (p. 599)

William Saroyan is our Great Wise Old Armenian (Black, Pole, Jew) Who Deigns to Favor You with Reminiscences of a Rich Long Ethnic Life. The reader had better show respect: in deference to age and Armenia. Being Saroyan, Saroyan can supply his own book-jacket propaganda. "*Chance Meetings* is as large as anybody who happens to read it." Some gall bladder there. An *ad hominem* attack in advance on his critics: those who don't appreciate *Chance Meetings* are not honest, authentic, heart-big enough. You may have caught on by now: *Chance Meetings* irked the lymph juice out of me.

"What is a story?" Saroyan asks. Right away I'm ticked off. That designation, "story," is arch and self-indulgent: affected. It implies a correspondence, doncha know, between Saroyan and the Primitive Bard, the Ancient Carrier-On of National Traditions....

And what does "story" mean? "It's a writer with his mind made up to tell a story. To remember something, or to invent something. (It comes to the same thing.)" Like hell it does. But accurate, artless remembering—or the presumption of such—has been indispensable to Saroyan's renown: to any Ethnic Naïve's renown. In comparison, consciously created art is like a plastic shoe: unnatural, unwholesome. Saroyan doesn't make, he finds. To criticize him is to criticize his past, even his race. This puts the reviewer right where Saroyan ... would want him: in a very uncomfortable spot.

The memoir genre, then, is automatic for Saroyan: an overt statement of what, in actuality, he has been doing—or pretending to do—since nineteen thirty-something. This, his eighth memoir, never achieves even "story" form: at best it's anecdotal; at worst it's just muttering. The kind of narrative you'd shake from a hearth-drowsy, cantankerous old man.... It's as if Saroyan were doing us a big favor. His book has the disjoint, uncoordinated wobble of new-born crane flies....

Saroyan, of course, has been richly overrated: his time ran out with *Vo-Mag*'s, with WPA murals and their peculiar bluff intenseness. He was always ethnic naïve, repetitive, sentimental, pompous. And, in that, *Chance Meetings* is involuntary self-burlesque.... Saroyan has written the Armenian *Snow White:* a Donald Barthelme performance. Remembering breaks down. Consciously or unconsciously the Ethnic Naïve has become the Ethnic Absurd. Which is, I guess, some small improvement. (p. 600)

> *D. Keith Mano, "Gnomic Naive," in* National Review (© *National Review, Inc., 1978; 150 East 35th St., New York, N.Y. 10016), May 12, 1978, pp. 599-600.*

NICHOLAS J. LOPRETE

Chance meetings, William Saroyan tells us, are sometimes memorable because they have a definite starting and stopping point and take on a quality of art, something concluded and whole, which cannot be improved upon. In [*Chance Meetings*] Mr. Saroyan proceeds to prove his thesis.... *Chance Meetings* is a sketchbook, a homily, a philosophy of the self written from a unique perspective about "the stragglers everywhere and all the time, from the very beginning of one's memory." ... (p. 121)

It is obvious that he is still having "the time of his life," and the undeniable charm of Saroyan the writer still exists, along with a sentimentality which threatens to sink the book. In less certain hands the danger would become reality, but Mr. Saroyan's warmth and irreverence save the day. "Human memory works its own wheel, and stops where it will, entirely without reference to the last stop, and with no connection with the next." (p. 122)

> *Nicholas J. Loprete, in* Best Sellers *(copyright © 1978 Helen Dwight Reid Educational Foundation), July, 1978.*

*   *   *

SARRAUTE, Nathalie   1902-

Sarraute, a Russian-born French novelist, essayist, playwright, and critic, is a leading figure in the New Novel movement. Like Robbe-Grillet, Sarraute believes that traditional literary theories are limiting, and that the novel must be in a state of evolution. Early in her career, Sarraute developed her theory of "tropisms" to explain the workings of the mind. Tropisms are presented in intricately woven monologues and images that reveal the constant flux of the subconscious and the involuntary responses to stimuli that govern our behavior. Sarraute believes that the New Novelists have little in common other than their mutual intent to abandon traditional literary forms and theories, and should be approached by reader and critic individually. (See also *CLC*, Vols. 1, 2, 4, 8, and *Contemporary Authors*, Vols. 9-12, rev. ed.)

DENISE GOITEIN

Clearly, the two paramount problems recurring throughout

Nathalie Sarraute's writings are those of communication and of truth. And it is no accident and no surprise to find that her only two plays [both originally written for radio] bear the titles: *Le Silence* and *Le Mensonge*. (p. 102)

In their content and approach the two plays are a logical extension of Nathalie Sarraute's novels, even if the dramatic form constitutes a departure from her other writing. In both plays a number of men and women, who seem to know each other well, are gathered for an evening, for no apparent specific reason. These men and women are not identifiable characters. In *Le Silence,* with one exception, they are not given any names. In *Le Mensonge* they have names, but names that confer no identity upon them. Both plays are set in motion in both cases by an utterance that has upset the usual order of things.

In *Le Silence* the man who appears to be the main character has committed a *faux pas* in evoking out loud a sentimental memory: a "dream-country" of his in the form of a village with little houses, fretwork trimming over windows, bits of colored lace, fences around gardens, and fragrant evenings perfumed by jasmin and acacia. The statement has been made in elemental form, unstyled and spontaneous, a part of himself handed over in crude form. In the sophisticated setting constituted by the gathering, this lapse causes quite a stir. Everyone pleads with the perpetrator: please, continue, how delightful. But do they really mean it? Are they on his wave length? Are they in tune with this lyrical part of himself, which he has inadvertently handed over? No, he feels, there is no real sympathy, no real communication; they just want to strip him naked. The poor man feels ridiculous, trapped—less, in the end, by the vocal insistence of those surrounding him than by the obstinate and oppressive silence maintained by Jean-Pierre. The latter breaks through his own terrible silence only to utter an occasional laugh or, once, even a whistle. The laughter and the silence both contrive to appear as unspoken criticism, a censorship all the more severe since true communication has been made impossible. Jean-Pierre's silence becomes unbearable to all, though it is felt most acutely by the more sensitive main character. It is he who in the end will restore order by attaching to a reiterated description of the dream village a number of factual objective details, pertaining to art history, and enunciated in a bold and clear tone. Jean-Pierre is then ready, to everyone's relief, to rejoin the conversation. The "subconversation" (the poetic lapse) which has caused the break (the silence) is covered over by logical, objective facts.

In *Le Mensonge* Pierre, unable to condone even a "white lie," has exploded and has told off an heiress who likes to play the pauper. The other characters, used to accepting the polite lies society is built on, are suddenly compelled to question their more habitual behavior. Only Jacques pleads for wisdom and good will—in other words, distortion of the truth, our daily fare. But the ball has been set in motion: they *must* try and define the nature and value of the truth. To this end they enter into a round of confession games (a kind of psychodrama, suggests one of the characters). The game becomes painful in the extreme when Simone starts playing in earnest. She insists this is no game; her story is true, though Pierre points out the glaring contradictions with a previous story of hers. We are back at Pirandello's *To Each His Truth.* Where is the game? Where is the truth? No one knows any more. Desperately seeking safety, they try to restore logic. They come on bended knees to Simone: please, tell us you were playing. She yields and thus restores accepted convention. Pierre, without deep conviction, pays lip-service to the renewed social contract.

In both plays silence and the truth represent elements which have come to disturb the established order. They appear as active beings, endowed with unsuspected force, capable of inflicting terrible tortures. Silence, such as the one imposed by Jean-Pierre on his surroundings, walls in human beings. Like a net, it traps them, so that they can neither reach out to others nor be reached by them. The author of the silence is only a sort of trigger, himself seemingly unaffected by the silence he imposes, while it is the silence itself which carries "some strange threat, some mortal danger." . . . [This is] the dilemma: silence kills, but the word, which can save, can also kill. So beware, use words with discernment. . . . [*Le Silence*] ends on an ambiguous note. The silence has indeed been broken, but only because what caused it (the *faux pas*) has been clothed afresh, respectably, so as to restore the former "normal" order. The malaise is dissipated, but a bitter taste lingers—"his silence," briefly evoked at the very end, and promptly dismissed ("what silence?"), swept under the rug. Let us all play according to the rules, otherwise life is too risky. The episode was nothing but an excursion into another reality. It proved painful; let us agree to terminate the interlude.

Like silence, truth appears as a living thing, gifted with a "force of expansion"—sometimes a beast, pressing hard, ready to spring forth. In most cases, in order to preserve "normal" social exchanges, people control the beast, they tame it, put it on a leash. But there are times when the more you hold it back, the more it swells, presses, and wants to come out. Then you feel like shouting out: "stop lying." If one does not explode, one is condemned to suffer, for truth that is never allowed out "sinks in and burns." . . . And so it is that Pierre, unable to bear it any longer, explodes, and in so doing creates a terrible uproar, for social living demands its dose of lying. Jacques is there to remind everyone of the social convention. We lie, we play, lo and behold, "we change the truth," rather than change ourselves. So what? We must. Absolute truth would make social living impossible. This appears to be a restatement of Molière's *Le Misanthrope*. (pp. 102-06)

Just as there are no recognizable characters, there is, in these two plays, no plot, no dramatic development in the ordinary sense. Some anonymous people are gathered together and they talk (or they refuse to talk). The play is set in motion by a particular utterance; it is resolved by another utterance. The power of the Word could not be underlined more clearly. At the same time, throughout the plays, we feel undercurrents and subconversations, expressed by a particular intonation (one of derision, irony, anxiety, etc.)—this because of a deep awareness of the inadequacy of words to express our deeper, more subtle feelings. . . . [There are] two main problems of the writer which recur in Nathalie Sarraute's works: the problem of communication ("I perceive only for myself, and not for others") and the ultimate value and efficacy of verbal expression.

Thus when words cannot or must not be used, either because of their inadequacy or inherent threat, they are replaced by tropisms. In the radio script these often come in the form of audible laughter. All this is not new for Nathalie Sarraute. The same preoccupation, intent, and technique are discernible in the novels. So, one may ask, why this excursion into drama, and more particularly into radio plays? It would seem that here was an opportunity to concentrate on one form of discourse, the dialogue, and dispense with inner monologues, description, and narration. On the one hand, the dialogue offers the best medium for stating the problem of communication; on the other hand, it provides the most convincing way of showing both the power and the inadequacy of words. This is particularly striking when we try to characterize the type of dialogue and drama which is put forth here. There is no exchange of ideas; the dialogue follows neither time sequence nor logical sequence. It is an instantaneous and a completely spontaneous dialogue, or, what matters more, it creates the illusion of spontaneity. Therefore the play is short . . . and circumscribed and circular in structure. It is not intended to engender any development. There are no sustained speeches, no arguments, no discussions; no one convinces anybody of anything, at least not by logical means. When things happen—for instance, when Simone admits she was playing or when Jean-Pierre breaks the silence—it is not as a result of a logical argument, a fiery speech, or an event that intervened; it is simply because certain gestures were made, certain sounds uttered, certain words spoken which created a favorable climate. (pp. 106-08)

This type of dialogue, being no exchange, espouses the slightest innermost movements of the psyche. Phrases, cuts, silences, words must . . . stick to the feeling. The discourse therefore defies syntax; it is chopped, disorderly. There are many examples of disjointed speech, particularly when a character is overcome with strong emotions, which the others cannot share or understand. (p. 108)

The radio play affords the only privileged situation where we have to be *all ears*, thus particularly attuned to the scintillation and reverberation of words, as well as to the inflexions and intonations of the human voice. (p. 111)

By giving the auditory preeminence over the visual and the dialectical, the author makes us exceptionally receptive to a pure verbal impact. Whereas Nathalie Sarraute's plays extend and continue the statement and discourse of her novels, the medium employed, if more limited, is more distilled and refined. And the communication established with the audience is of a subtle nature; the listener participates accordingly. (pp. 111-12)

> Denise Goitein, "Nathalie Sarraute as Dramatist," in Yale French Studies (copyright © Yale French Studies 1971), June, 1971, pp. 102-12.

VALERIE MINOGUE

Portrait d'un Inconnu is a novel concerned with its own composition. It draws on many fields of imagery—notably biological and zoological—but it is particularly the imagery of childhood, sustained throughout the novel, which introduces the reader to the core of the novel's preoccupations. . . . [A] systematic use of childhood imagery serves two related purposes.

First, it is a stylistic device for conveying the fluid sub-surface of consciousness to the reader, without falling into the pitfalls of psychological abstraction, or over-precise definition. . . . Nathalie Sarraute reaches down to the universal experiences of childhood in order to surmount the difficulties faced by the narrator, and to overcome the resistance of readers who may resent the unfamiliar matter.

Secondly, childhood imagery illuminates for the reader the uncertain situation of the narrator in relation to the world of his experience. This uncertainty is not peculiar to the narrator, but reflects the problematic areas involved in the creation of any narrative.... The defences and refusals which the narrator (whom we shall call N) encounters are at the same time those which adults might offer a questioning child, and which readers might offer a questioning writer. Through the figure of N, in his dual rôle as child and writer, we are able to observe closely the effort to submit a particular, non-authoritative version of human life to the reader, and persuade him to acknowledge it as his own. (pp. 177-78)

How is the novelist, stripped of authority and the traditional props, to sustain the interest of the reader? The answer lies in part in the fact that the abandonment of such props as plot and characterization is not entire. It is the gradually emergent figure of N himself that gives the novel its unity, and his attempt to establish reality—a narrative—is its plot. Although the external world appears decomposed and fragmentary, the framework of N's preoccupations presents a relatively stable world of consciousness. And in this world, N's situation as a quasi-child, baffled and questioning, elicits the reader's sympathy and focuses attention on N's simultaneously literary and existential quest. (p. 178)

We are allowed to observe the physical limitations of the narrator's viewpoint, and reminded that he is neither ubiquitous nor omniscient. We see his dependence on his own experience and imagination for his interpretation of people and events. Further, we are encouraged, by the tentative and self-correcting mode of the narration, to be aware of the difficulties of precise expression. N, in short, presents the drama of the individual mind trying to make sense of himself and the world, while lacking any absolute point of reference to confirm or deny his constructions. (p. 179)

A childhood universe of good and evil (in which the figures are often reversible) is always implicit, and provides the basic imagery in which the movements of emotional life are to be apprehended. Such imagery allows the novelist to reach down beneath the surface of cultural and social sophistication to an almost elemental level of feeling, since it permits rapid movement between the nuances of complex reactions and the tiny primitive elements of which the complexities are composed. It is by the use of such a technique that Nathalie Sarraute is able to present the fluidities of experience both in slow motion and in close-up, without falling into static analysis.

A further result of this technique is the exhibiting of a gesture or word in the very act of taking its place in N's world. It is N's habit to isolate a word or gesture in such a way as to communicate by metaphor or analogy the nature of his reaction to it.... [The] immediate recognizability of the image sharply evokes the lived quality of the experience, and stresses the permanence of childhood experience in maturity. Beneath the sophistication of adult social life, we are made aware of the continuance of a child world of aggression and defence, hope and fear. (pp. 180-81)

The imagery of childhood and childish games is also a means of expressing the moments when the gap between the inner and outer worlds reasserts itself, creating an unbridgeable gulf between the individual and his experience. The gulf is expressed by the crumbling of reality, and the reduction of whole areas of experience to the realm of childish fantasy. When there is a gap between the child's reality and the 'adult' reality acknowledged by the world, one of the two is at fault, and we see, in the course of the novel, each version of 'reality' in turn identified with a fantasy world of games and toys, a world of make-believe.... The imagery of childhood ... embodies a central question of the novel: is N giving an account of 'reality', or is his world merely the negligible product of his childish fantasies? N is constantly threatened by assimilation into the world of playthings and dolls, but when his confidence is firm, it is the world of the cliché and the commonplace that disintegrates into a dolls' house, furnished with make-believe.

The everyday world of the novel abuts at all points on the realm of fairy-land, and like images of childhood, references to fairytales recur from novel to novel in Nathalie Sarraute's work.... [The fairy-tale imagery] seems to express a permanent undercurrent of hope and fear, a constant total emotional involvement of the individual, moving so rapidly between defence and attack, withdrawal and expansion. And it has another function, which is to embody the longing to take possession of the world by incantation, or—in N's case—by the magical power of language. (pp. 183-84)

N's language betrays a constant impulse to escape into the *conte de fées*, where incantation and magic are all-powerful. The transposition into fairy-tale terms conveys the longing to create a world in which unpredictability is ultimately governable, and where the vicissitudes of life may be dominated by the magic of words—or talismans like the portrait of the unknown man. But when N finally uses the portrait as a talisman, in his encounter with the daughter, he finds it unavailing against the personal attack with which she responds. This failure anticipates N's ultimate failure to reduce the world to the dimensions of his chosen language.

The fairy-tale supplies N with a familiar and evocative imagery for the expression of his feelings about the world. If the eyes of the portrait are so intense and vital, it is because they are like the eyes of some creature in which the soul of a prince or princess is trapped by enchantment, and if N feels 'delivered' by the sight of it, he also sees himself as the 'deliverer'. In so far as he pierces the charm, and reestablishes his reality, he is both deliverer and delivered: he becomes the prince in command of magical forces.... It is similarly by the creative magic of his own language that N attempts his conquest of the world of his experience, though his language ultimately proves ineffectual against the obstinate strength of practical life.... At the end, having questioned the rules of the game, and having scrutinized the players, N is faced by defeat. He is forced to join the ring—a recurring image of child-subjection.... (p. 185)

Throughout *Portrait d'un Inconnu*, the efforts of the child-figure to exist in a world ruled by powerful and threatening adults coincide with the efforts of the novelist to create his own world. As the child strives after his freedom and his own values, so the novelist strives for his creative freedom, tries to find his own voice, and to impose that voice in a hostile world. (p. 186)

Valerie Minogue, "The Imagery of Child-hood in Nathalie Sarraute's 'Portrait d'un Inconnu'," in French Studies, *April, 1973, pp. 177-86.*

JOHN MELLORS

For over forty years Nathalie Sarraute has been writing about 'tropisms', the name she has given to what lies underneath the words, gestures and facial expressions that come to the surface when we communicate with others or react to their communications with us. . . . She will not be distracted by conventional ideas of character and plot. She tries to stay entirely in her world of 'the secret source'. It is interesting that among the writers whom Sarraute admires are Virginia Woolf (were 'the waves' tropisms?) and Ivy Compton-Burnett. In an essay in *Nouvelle Revue Française* in 1956 Sarraute praised Compton-Burnett for her conversations that 'are located not in an imaginary place but in a place that actually exists: somewhere on the fluctuating frontier that separates conversation from sub-conversation'. (p. 90)

What do the tropisms themselves look like? . . . In her first book, which she called *Tropismes,* and which she says she started writing in 1932, although it was not published until 1939, the tropisms are much as she later described them, like images from a slow-motion film:

> For a moment he believed he felt stronger, propped up, patched up, but already he sensed his legs and arms grow heavy, lifeless, become numb with this solidified waiting, he had, as one has before losing consciousness, a tingling sensation in his nostrils: they saw him withdraw into himself all of a sudden, assume his strangely preoccupied, absent look: then, with little pats on his cheeks—the Windsors' travels, Lebrun, the quintuplets—they revived him. But while he was coming to himself and when they left him finally mended, cleaned, repaired, all nicely seasoned and ready, fear formed in him again, at the bottom of the little compartments, of the little drawers they had just opened, in which they had seen nothing, and which they had closed.

In her latest book *'Fools Say',* Sarraute turns more often from that kind of imagery to the 'sub-conversations' she mentioned when talking about Compton-Burnett. There is much more speculative thinking, about identity, about subject and object, and about the temptations of solipsism. The tropisms have been intellectualized and lack something of the psychological authenticity of those in her first book: for example, 'He and I. Impossible to separate us. We are the two points of a comparison. We are the two terms of an equation. We are the two poles of an opposition.' The tropism is a valuable concept, and Sarraute's work is undeniably a 'Text', in the Barthesian sense, but the pleasure of the Text is, for me, diminished by its unrelenting solemnity. I am fairly certain that the tropisms behind my own words and gestures would include something of the ribald, the erotic and, even, the obscene. Nothing like that is allowed to sully the chaste pages in which Madame Sarraute charts her *'mouvements indéfinissables.'* (pp. 90-1)

> *John Mellors, in* London Magazine *(© London Magazine 1977), December, 1977.*

SAYLES, John   1950-

Sayles is an American novelist. His work is noted for its controlled prose style and its accurate reflection of American dialects. (See also *CLC,* Vol. 7, and *Contemporary Authors,* Vols. 57-60.)

GREIL MARCUS

[*Union Dues* is a] long, well-written, ultimately formless tale about a kid from a coal-mining family who in 1969 leaves West Virginia for Boston to find his brother, a burnt-out Vietnam veteran. The guts of the story concern the boy's haphazard entree into a radical Boston commune that defines itself somewhere between early Weatherman and present-day U.S. Labor Party. The desperation, pretentions, honesty and hopelessness of such politics are captured cleanly and without much condescension, which makes *Union Dues* virtually unique among the political novels of the last ten years. (p. 119)

> *Greil Marcus, in* Rolling Stone *(© 1977 by Rolling Stone Magazine; all rights reserved; reprinted by permission), Issue 247, September 8, 1977.*

BRUCE ALLEN

John Sayles's second novel [*Union Dues*] is a story of flight and search. . . .

The omniscient narration moves back and forth between the two protagonists' "searches." But several scenes are shown from the viewpoints of peripheral characters—who are about to meet up with Hunter or Hobie [the protagonists]. . . . [The] writer's ability to hear the way real people talk (also evident in Sayles's gritty first novel, *Pride of the Bimbos*) imparts a very special conviction to scenes involving mine- or factory-workers. There's a wonderful set-piece in a Boston saloon, where cronies rattle on about "pure, above-bawd patronage politics," and a lugubrious barfly mourns the passing of "poor Joe" (Kennedy). Sayles packs the book with irreverent, combative, funny and dirty songs and stories, as well as a flinty-eyed affection for the people who love to spout them.

The only real flaws show in Third Way's interminable "conferences." As Hobie observes, "argument seemed to be the language they spoke." I suppose the point had to be made, but Sayles overemphasizes their self-defeating absorption in round-the-clock talk and circular reasoning. It isn't credible: if the '60s radicals had been quite *that* disorganized, the Jesus Freaks and Young Republicans would have taken over the country, and buried them.

Besides, the ironies are manifest, and don't require authorial underlining. The people who try to share possessions and live simply are no match for the hardnosed materialists. . . .

The novel sets up its character's hopes (and ours), then firmly knocks them down. We sense a common purpose uniting Sayles's people; they're all fighting the same kinds of battles. (p. 40)

In the final fifty pages, the alternating stories bounce off each other with terrific cumulative force. . . . Everybody has to "pay dues" to the outfit he's managed to join. The book's last words are Hunter's hopeful optimistic ones—but we scarcely hear them (just as we disbelieve them), because of the sounds still reverberating from the penultimate scene.

Sayles's plot locks everything together tight. We believe things couldn't have happened any other way. Of course it can be said that this isn't, precisely, realism. The situations are carefully deployed, pitched to make us feel exactly what the author wants us to feel. The world of the novel is a trap, set to catch its characters.

The point is that Hobie and Hunter McNatt are so real, and we care so much for them, that it is painful to look at what we know is bound to happen to them. I could not keep myself from racing through the final chapter, even though I was afraid of the story's certain conclusion. Not many novels, or novelists, can overpower you that way. (p. 41)

> *Bruce Allen, in* The New Republic *(reprinted by permission of* The New Republic; © *1977 by The New Republic, Inc.), September 17, 1977.*

EDWARD McCONVILLE

John Sayles's *Union Dues* is a disturbingly well-written novel. I'll begin by praising the book's obvious merits, before I deal with what disturbs me so much about it.

The plot in itself should guarantee reasonable interest. A miner's son, Hobie McNatt, runs away from his home in desolate West Virginia coal country, in search (he thinks) of his older brother Dar, a burnt-out Vietnam veteran. He comes to Boston where he falls in with one of the "revolutionary collectives" that proliferated during the late 1960s. His father, Hunter McNatt, reluctantly leaves his buddies in Joseph Yablonski's insurgency against the United Mine Workers' Boyle machine to look for his son in the Brave New World of the Boston-Cambridge axis circa 1968-69: a good mix of materials—working-class hero meets the New Left.

Fortunately, Sayles is too serious and skillful a writer to succumb to the temptations of the facile and topical. He manages to create a compelling American tragedy, the dissolution of a family, and then to extend it to our nation's desperate search for lasting roots and personal ties. This theme is suggested on the book's first page with the description of a strip-mined hillside Hobie sees on his way out of town: "The trees were all gray up by the dozer-scraped highwall, tilted at crazy angles with their roots poking out into space." As the book continues, the theme takes root and spreads. . . .

Sayles, a Williams graduate who has worked at several blue-collar jobs, has written a realistic novel of working-class life. He understands the petty but intensely personal politics of the shop floor and the union local. He captures the physical sensations of moderately hard menial labor and he has an uncanny ear for the dialogue of diverse working-class subcultures. . . .

Hunter McNatt is a brilliantly wrought character, but Sayles is considerably less kind to the middle-class radicals who appear in his narrative. He captures their Movement jargon and their presumptions in devastating dialogue. (p. 408)

No one who was involved in the political activism of the 1960s will read this book without feeling a twinge of embarrassed nostalgia. The professional revolutionaries' blatant manipulation of their working-class "clients" is at once repulsive and realistic, and their attempts to relate to working people are often downright ludicrous. Sayles is good at this sort of satire, but the book's real strength lies in its portrayal of working-class life. *Union Dues* is, quite simply, the best book of its kind since Harvey Swados's *On the Line*. In many ways it is better than Swados's classic novel of the men of the assembly line. Its scope is much broader, Sayles has a better developed sense of humor and irony and, finally, *Union Dues* is more concrete and less analytical, relying more on incident and dialogue and less on an omniscient narrator to tell its story.

Nevertheless there is something deeply disturbing about this book, a misleading perspective it conveys to its readers. Literary critics generally argue that a novel should not be judged by its social "message," if indeed it is uncouth enough to have one. But Sayles's book, whether intentionally or not, bears an unmistakable message about political people and the very nature of political involvement.

I raise the question of intention because Sayles himself is not entirely judgmental toward most of the middle-class radicals he portrays. A songfest scene shows them able to laugh at their own political and moral pretensions, and an examination of one radical couple's motivations seems to absolve many of the book's New Left characters of insincerity and bad faith.

But these qualifications will be lost on many readers. (pp. 408-09)

In the eternal tension between the private and the public, the personal and the political, Sayles opts entirely for the private and the personal. He begins with the valid point that people are generally at their most effective when acting on behalf of people they know intimately, rather than for abstract ideas, causes, or faceless classes of people. Hunter joins the anti-Boyle movement not primarily out of concern for his fellow miners but for his son, whom he expects to join him in the mines. But when Hobie runs away, the rank-and-file insurgency "wasn't enough" for Hunter anymore. "There has to be something in it for me, something personal," he tells a fellow miner, "or it's not worth staying for. With Hobie gone I'd feel like an outsider, my heart just wouldn't be in it." When he is forced to recognize that his family is broken up beyond his power to bring it back together, Hunter forges new family ties with a South Boston woman and her children. Sayles's vision of apolitical bliss, as embodied in their new relationship, is appealing and persuasive, but also a bit deceptive.

Most people who have been able to maintain lifelong commitments to social change are people who have found a workable balance in their lives between their personal and political needs. In ignoring the need for such a balance, in implicitly but unmistakably counseling a return to privatism, Sayles is just as narrow at his own extreme as the "political heavies" of the 1960s who preached the complete denial of one's personal feelings in the service of impersonal ideological goals. (p. 409)

> *Edward McConville, "A Separate Peace," in* The Nation *(copyright 1977 by the Nation Associates, Inc.), October 22, 1977, pp. 408-09.*

STEPHEN FENDER

[*Union Dues*] is a bleak story, relieved only by occasional flashes of humour in the dialogue and by the (not wholly credible) possibility that Hunter may marry a sympathetic widow. It is also very much a book of the 1970s: which is to say that it reviews the 1960s as someone with a bad hangover might consider his binge the night before, applying to that decade the old-fashioned value judgments that prevail today. The cops are no longer pigs, though they do get a bit cheesed off now and then. The older generation, matured by their experience in the Second World War, care about their kids, in an inarticulate sort of way, and make the best of a bad job at work. By contrast those of the younger generation who have been to war have been unmanned by it, while their noncombatant contemporaries are stridently articulate and care for no one. Of course, these clichés of the 1970s are no more satisfactory than those of the 1960s. On the other hand, John Sayles never loses his grip on the dialogue, or his interest in the detail of people's work. Indeed, at times the reader seems to be chewing through great, enriched slabs of Studs Terkel's *Working*. The book jacket says that *Union Dues* "has a solidity nearer to that of nineteenth-century novels than to those of our day": this is right.

> *Stephen Fender, "Working Model," in* The Times Literary Supplement (© *Times Newspapers Ltd. (London) 1978; reproduced from* The Times Literary Supplement *by permission), April 21, 1978, p. 433.*

*   *   *

SCHWARTZ, Delmore   1913-1966

Schwartz was an American poet, playwright, short story writer, critic, and editor. He achieved critical success in his twenties with the publication of the short story, "In Dreams Begin Responsibilities." His subsequent work, however, did not match this early work in either substance or depth. There is a fatalistic and disillusioned quality in his work. The persona revealed in his writing is one of a tormented, egotistical sensibility. (See also *CLC*, **Vols. 2, 4, and** *Contemporary Authors*, **Vols. 17-18; obituary, Vols. 25-28, rev. ed.;** *Contemporary Authors Permanent Series*, **Vol. 2.)**

PHILIP RAHV

[Delmore Schwartz] was an exceptionally able literary critic. Far too sophisticated intellectually and too much at home with conceptual matters to turn himself into an exponent of any given exclusive "method," he also understood the pitfalls to which critical discourse is exposed when it oversteps its limits to indulge in philosophical or sociological divagations. Sound in his literary judgments, he wrote without pretension or solemnity and without ever divesting himself of his fine and highly original sense of humor.

But it is precisely as a critic that he was grievously underrated, and for reasons not too difficult to identify. In the first place, readers were mainly aware of him as a poet and short story writer, and only marginally as a critic; and, secondly, he himself put no particular emphasis on his critical work, conceiving of himself as primarily a creative writer. Yet in no sense can he be considered an amateur in criticism; he wrote a great deal of it, quite as much as he wrote fiction. (p. 19)

At the age of twenty-four he had already written some of his finest poems as well as "In Dreams Begin Responsibili-

ties," the most captivating and, in the judgment of most people who know his work well, the best short story he was ever to compose. What is even more surprising is that in that very year he also published what, in my view, are three superb critical pieces: "The Critical Method of R. P. Blackmur" is a definitive essay; another is the long and thoroughly cogent analysis of Yvor Winters's *Primitivism and Decadence;* and still another, entitled "John Dos Passos and the Whole Truth," is as fair in its argument as it is perceptive of that novelist's strengths and weaknesses—perhaps the most plausible single evaluation of Dos Passos as yet available to us.

Now while it is well-known that many poets have produced their best work in their early twenties, it is only very rarely that a critic has contributed anything memorable at that age. Usually it is not until their early thirties that critics are able to write anything really substantial exhibiting a mature cast of mind. And this is exactly where the paradox of Schwartz's precocity calls attention to itself in a striking way. The criticism he wrote even as late as 1953 (such as "The Duchess' Red Shoes," for instance, an essay on Lionel Trilling as notable for its humor as for its insight into that critic's social bias) has enduring value, while the poetry he published in his thirties and forties is clearly inferior to his earlier work in that medium. Thus the thematic richness as well as the diction, versification, and rhythmic range of the verse contained in *Vaudeville for a Princess* (1950) is almost embarrassingly feeble in comparison with such earlier poems in his first collection as "The Heavy Bear that Goes with Me," "In the Naked Bed, in Plato's Cave," or "Tired and Unhappy, You Think of Houses."

The same goes for his later fiction. In my reading of it only four of his stories are truly superior: "In Dreams Begin Responsibilities," "America! America!," "The Statues," and "A Bitter Farce," all written, I believe, before the age of thirty. Moreover, in the later stories, such as "The Child Is the Meaning of this Life" and those collected in his last volume *Successful Love*, the prose becomes flatter and flatter, the narrative movement slows down, dramatic impact is lost in tiresome repetitiousness; and in the novella *The World Is a Wedding* some of the characters are barely distinguishable from one another as they carry on a prolonged dialogue that is excessively, even compulsively, "literary" in the pejorative sense of that term. (pp. 19-20)

He was not endowed with the capacity to create a solid fictional world seemingly self-governing in structure and possessed of an energy supple enough to establish a necessary congruity between interior and external event and circumstance. In Schwartz's narratives the best writing (and effects) is mostly achieved in lyrical moments and in passages embodying the emotional and intellectual pathos of self-recognition or self-identification.

In other words, his fiction at its best is "personal" in a sense which seldom applies to good narrative prose. For this reason perhaps it is very revealing as biography, more so, it seems to me, than his poems, in which his obsessive search for his true self is transposed into a type of metaphor and image that tends to gloss over the specificity of the person writing in favor of a certain kind of indented generality about the human condition as a whole. . . .

Schwartz's intricate inner life . . . might be described as a kind of unremitting self-reflexive internal labor . . . to which I believe both the origin and the imaginative source of his most expressive stories can be traced.

Consider the climactic scene in "In Dreams Begin Responsibilities," where the protagonist, easily identifiable with the author himself, watching on the movie screen a series of incidents in the courtship of his future parents, stands up in the theater, much to the discomfiture of his neighbors in the audience, and loudly cries: "Don't do it. It's not too late to change your minds, both of you. Nothing will come of it, only remorse, hatred, scandal and two children whose characters are monstrous." This startling intervention by the dreaming protagonist is by no means to be taken as a literary flourish, a finely devised ending, or some kind of symbolic statement concerning the human condition. It is the writer's adverse yet most intimate confession, the one psychodynamic form open to him for attaining transcendence. . . .

Schwartz, in his more abstract musings, dreamed of a different kind of life, a life in which "the idea of love" held sway, but at the same time he was persuaded that "the ideas of success and failure are the two most important things in America." This distressing state of affairs, in which the real so crudely mocks the ideal, is among the more haunting themes of his creative work. (p. 20)

That he greatly admired Eliot's poetry goes without saying, but what struck me in his truly obsessive talk about Eliot was the note of suspicion it sounded, the elusive hints of literary politics and the gossipy stories that plainly had no foundation in fact about the man behind the career, a man, by the way, he had never known. There was something in these palpably absurd stories, abounding with "delusions of reference," to use a Freudian phrase, that contained in embryo the paranoia that later overwhelmed him. . . .

[As] he grew older his self-concern mounted, so much so that the tendency to ritualize, if I may put it that way, his own unhappiness became more and more marked in the later poetry and fiction. This may help to explain their evident flatness of style and debility of emotional force.

However, he did not falter to the same degree in his criticism. After all, the critical medium permits only a minimum of subjectivity. Moreover, in any case, regarding himself as a creative writer above all and therefore attaching no ultimate importance to articles and reviews, he was able to approach the writing of them with greater relaxation and, curiously enough, in a more disciplined spirit. On the surface his essays are marked by a kind of deceptive simplicity, yet an attentive reading cannot but verify their rare precision of statement and shrewdness of insight. (p. 21)

In his function as a critic Schwartz was far more disinterested than most of his contemporaries. Indifferent to "grand theory" and fashions in "methodology," he was singularly free of ideological prejudice. Also, he was sufficiently well-educated in philosophy to spot with ease the metaphysical presuppositions that some critics unknowingly let slip into their work. . . . Though highly sensitive to fallacies of discourse, he was never an unkind critic of the sort who is ever on the lookout for faults by way of displaying his superiority. Despite a certain moral insecurity that sometimes retarded his creative efforts, he not only understood literature thoroughly but also loved it passionately. (p. 22)

Philip Rahv, "Delmore Schwartz: The Paradox of Precocity," in The New York Review of Books *(reprinted with permission from* The New York Review of Books; *copyright © 1971 NYREV, Inc.), May 20, 1971, pp. 19-22.*

MICHAEL COLLIER

If the task of reading Delmore Schwartz's poetry seems more difficult than it should be, it may be that one finds it difficult to reconcile the reputation of the poet . . . with the poems themselves. I make this general and possibly incorrect remark to suggest that [the] recently published selection of Schwartz's poems *What Is to Be Given* might better serve to revive interest in Schwartz's work if Douglas Dunn's thorough Introduction had been placed as an Afterword. Schwartz's work needs to be properly placed, and the only way this seems possible is for a fair and unprejudiced reading of the poems; this is unlikely to occur if all we hear is, "'We poets in our youth begin in sadness; thereof in the end comes despondency and madness'."

Although Schwartz actually was one of the brilliant poets of that generation including Lowell, Berryman, and Jarrell, the reader may find very little to suggest a connection with these poets, so little that such a comparison seems to be made out of deference to certain friendships. The fact is that Schwartz was the first of this generation. We can see the influence of Schwartz on Berryman's early poems. Schwartz is overpowering in his unrelenting seriousness (seriousness not sincerity) and in asking the right questions for his generation. . . . (p. 118)

The questions that Schwartz asks do rank him with that generation already mentioned, but his style is obviously not as easily placed. Schwartz is the philosopher of that generation and his work never made the kind of surface and stylistic changes which Lowell and Berryman made. Neither the ironic flamboyant personality of Berryman, the historical energy of Lowell, nor the Frost-like monologues of Jarrell are found in Schwartz. Instead, Schwartz presents abstractions of philosophy through language charged with the hopeful energies of love and the annihilating pessimism of egotistical despair. (p. 119)

Michael Collier, in Agenda, *Winter-Spring, 1977.*

BONNIE LYONS

Schwartz's fictional aims are suggested in his criticism of other fiction writers. This fictional "credo" is clearest in "John Dos Passos and the Whole Truth," a review of *U.S.A.* which goes beyond its topical subject to make a general statement about the nature of fiction. . . .

This "whole truth" and "imagination" necessary for great literature enter fiction through a "multiscient individual," "the individual of the fullest intelligence and sensibility," who "in some one of many quite different fashions *transcends* the situation and the subject." . . .

What distinguishes *The World is a Wedding* from social history, what makes it meaningful today almost thirty years since its publication in 1948, is this transcendent "whole truth." Schwartz's fiction embodies this multiscient vision . . . especially in style and language.

Schwartz manipulates language to bracket his stories in

irony and to create a distance between the narrative voice and the stories themselves. It is in this tone and distance that the multiscient vision comes into play. (p. 260)

The title of the story I shall explore in some detail, "The World is a Wedding," suggests Schwartz's method, for it derives from conversation within the fiction. This is particularly fitting because Schwartz's stories are supremely cerebral, verbal pieces whose focus is thought—rembrance, analysis, verbal evocation—and the sharing and comparing of thought—conversation. They are highly internalized both in location (inside apartments) and in characterization. With minimal description of landscape or of the physical traits of characters, the fiction relies on internal analysis and conversation for revelation. To a large extent the events themselves have little significance except as their meanings are fully analyzed by the characters; the movement of the mind is the highest form of action. . . .

Section one [of the story's ten sections] displays the multiscience in both the complex style and in the ideas and beliefs which give direction to the work. The disarming first paragraph—"In this our life there are no beginnings but only departures entitled beginnings, wreathed in the formal emotions thought to be appropriate and often forced. Darkly rises each moment from the life which has been lived and which does not die, for each event lives in the heavy head forever, waiting to renew itself" . . . sets the tone immediately, for it must be taken on two levels which contradict each other but do not cancel each other out. The ideas are meant seriously; they suggest Schwartz's tortured sense of time and the perils of consciousness. (p. 261)

Through an artful combination of narrative summary (condensation and generalization) and the full embodiment of a few telling scenes, Schwartz suggests both the inevitable, generally unnoticed movement of time and a sense of timelessness, the revelation of a central moment: he achieves the building sense of development of the novel and the illuminating moment of the short story.

The layers of irony pile up dizzily as the narrator—and characters—peruse the events and other characters from every angle. It is as if the world were a prismatic sphere turned endlessly in the hands of some fascinated Supreme Intelligence. (p. 262)

Schwartz's somersaults of dialectic reach a climax at the final party of the circle [of friends, the characters of the story,] which is breaking up because Rudyard finally accepts a job as a drama teacher outside New York City. Bitter that she has been used by Rudyard and his friends, and particularly that she is still unmarried, Laura tells a distorted version of a Kafka story and compares herself to a cow eaten alive by a hunter and his horse (Rudyard and the circle). Trying to comfort her, Jacob explains "'all of us consume each other,'" and insists that the world is a wedding which means that "'the world is a wedding of God and Nature.'" . . . He says that Breugel's painting "The Peasant Wedding" exemplifies this notion: "'If you look at it long enough, you will see all the parts that anyone and everyone can have.'" . . . At this wedding "'if no one can play every part, yet everyone can come to the party . . . and anyone who does not know that he is at a wedding feast just does not know what is in front of him.'" . . . (p. 263)

[Beyond] the dialectic between Laura's conscience or consciousness and Jacob's idea of the joy of life is Schwartz's

ultimate irony: the fact that Laura's speech is more fitting for Jacob and vice versa. Here is a clear example of the multiscient function of ironic distance. Despite her negative speech, it is Laura who is *engaged* in the world, who plays a part at the wedding. . . . In contrast, the idealist Jacob is the true renouncer, the one who stands aside and watches without participating. Despite his life-praising words, he embodies conscience, and consciousness. (pp. 263-64)

This special kind of ironic tension between the "truths" of the characters and their own personalities is evident throughout. . . .

Arguing against a critic who declared that life was too various and vast to be brought as a whole within the compass of a novel, Schwartz once explained that "merely the whole truth about a part of life will suffice—and moreover the part can stand for the whole, the symbol being the very essence of literature." . . . In the short fiction of his first collection, *The World is a Wedding*, Schwartz has given us this whole truth about a part of life—and that is why his "social history" of the Jewish middle class in New York during the depression years is so much more than that. (p. 264)

Bonnie Lyons, "Delmore Schwartz and the Whole Truth," in Studies in Short Fiction *(copyright 1977 by Newberry College), Summer, 1977, pp. 259-64.*

DAVID ZUCKER

Even joyous passages, as in "The Kingdom of Poetry," are deeply tinged by fatalism. It is as if, true diagnostician that he was, [Delmore] was constantly remembering his depression in the midst of his mania, and vice versa.

This melancholy is deeply rooted in Delmore's view of history and the growth of self. For him, man is constantly shaped by unconscious or dimly perceived forces—as the melancholy commentators of *Genesis* and *Coriolanus* point out. Delmore never fixed on the precise ideology for this view of history: he had many different versions and the Choruses reflect them. What is clear from his work is that he believed that against History and the Unconscious the individual can claim only an illusory sense of freedom. Yet he *must* choose in order to assert his creative power, his dignity. The melancholy tone and theme lie in the tension between this determinism and the assertion of the necessity of freedom. The supreme act of freedom for Delmore was the creative act itself—which either flowed with manic excess or was squeezed painfully from his torpor. He was said to have remarked: "I write when manic, revise when depressed."

In one of his most lyrical poems, "Abraham and Orpheus," this melancholy determinism expresses itself in a form that is quintessentially Delmorean. There is in the poem a very simple lyric repetition which circles around a simple theme: the exhaustion of love and the heavy presence of time as a defeating force. The central image is of circular movement. Abraham and Orpheus (the moral and poetic imperatives, if you like) are presented as figures who act out of love, mystery, and ignorance of consequences. Although their actions are "the substance of care" they are "poised on nothing, weighted on the air," and they have an intuitive knowledge or faith in the rightness, or perhaps only the inevitability, of their actions. Thus the poet can invoke their "learned presence" as a comfort in his dilemma. That dilemma is never specifically named, and this vagueness is typical of Delmore's poems. Yet we somehow can intuit the situation: the evocation of loneliness, helplessness, philosophical and imaginative uncertainty, awareness of the infinite choices made in *time*.

In *Genesis* and *Coriolanus* these concerns are dramatized more concretely. But the resigned acceptance of the darkness and the ignorance of the Ego and Id are still present, as in "Abraham and Orpheus." The images in that poem, as in so many other lyrics . . . , have an uncertain focus, the dreamlike intensity of surrealism. (His stories, of course, develop this magnificently—"In Dreams Begin Responsibilities" and "The Statues" being two famous examples.) But I should guess that they derive less from "surrealism" than from the monumental symbolism of Yeats and the fragmented and allusive symbolism of Eliot. Typically, Delmore evokes images of the city that are both dehumanizing and terrifying but also form the backdrop for his heightened awareness of himself as vulnerable and fragile. They have [a] . . . disembodied, vacant quality. . . . They also express specifically Delmore's intense insomniac sense of the terrors of night and the qualified promises of early morning. (pp. 96-7)

[We note] his lyric evocations of solitude, of great imaginative masters, of obsession with being caught in a twilight world between past, present, and future. He is constantly dissolving the distinction between universal and personal history. Shadowy philosophers (Plato, Socrates, Marx, Freud, James, Whitehead, Aristotle) are evoked throughout his work to bear witness to events and moods that in themselves appear mysterious, impulsive, melancholy, retrospective. They are appealed to, in effect, to impose intellectual order on a patchwork and exhausted self that yet has immortal longings for beauty, tenderness, grace, and power. Yet these longings too often appear to disguise a brutish, angry, and resentful self. . . . [In "The Heavy Bear"] Delmore conceives of the self almost as a neo-Platonic spirit which begs release from the gross material (and the womb) enclosing it.

This imprisonment is found not only in the self but also in the family. The figure of the dominant but sinister father is everpresent, of course, in *Genesis*. But his symbolic presence is felt everywhere. He is softened in the philosopher-presences, but is still judging and overseeing. The mother is the soft, inviting figure for the child to hide in, to protect him from the father and the turbulent complexities of the outside world, especially the world of the city. Moreover, the family itself is connected to the concept of historical determinism, the family and history forming an intricate tissue that the poet cannot escape from, though he would like to. As in "The Ballad of the Children of the Czar," Delmore places the psychological issue clearly in the historical context: that of his own Rumanian grandfather, the events of the Russian revolution, and his family's uncertain place in America. . . . [The] antagonism between his tormented self—willful, impulsive, yet knowing his own psychological entrapment—and his view of history as "unforgiven," as a determinist force that he cannot escape, and of his family that he is inextricably if rebelliously part of, is the dominant theme of Delmore's work. He *is*—though the phrase is overworked—the Alienated Man.

Yet there is a strong countermovement to this alienation. It is his romantic lyricism, deeply melancholy but at the same time celebrating the transcendent power of the self over circumstance and the very determinism that oppresses him. This lyric transcendence is best expressed in the title of his selected poetry—*Summer Knowledge*. Specifically, it is the idea of *ripeness*, the full maturity of a moment of perception that sees life as beautiful and whole and precious. This reaches one peak in the prose interlude in *Coriolanus* called "Pleasure," in which he evokes the joys of being alive as a response to the tragedy of Coriolanus himself. Yet one should note that even here, in his manic phase, so to speak, Delmore knows that he must recall the everpresence of the deterministic and tragic.

> Pleasure believes in friends, pleasure creates communities, pleasure crumbles faces into smiles, pleasure links hand in hand, pleasure restores, pain is the most selfish thing. And yet, I know, all this is nothing, nothing consoles one, and our problem and pain are still before us.
>
> (pp. 98-100)

Delmore's lyric and romantic hope should be viewed as equipoised throughout his work against the despairing certainty of a deterministic and hopelessly entangled ego, itself caught within the net of history and family. The poet's task is essentially "a fixed hallucination / Made by the passion of imagination," as the Chorus finally comments on the plight of the "Sleepless Atlantic Boy," Hershey Green, at the end of *Genesis*. The central perception left in that poem is that all experience is passing and is to be held in deep suspicion at the same instant that it is relished. (pp. 100-01)

Much could be said negatively about Delmore's elaboration of commonplace ideas [in his criticism]. Yet the very fact that he takes pains to remind his readers of what they may take for granted is a sign of the importance the issues had for him. Modernism, in fact, is the condition which Delmore thought he must define and redefine, no matter if the subject be meter or metaphor, or the themes typical of the pre-Romantic or post-Romantic imaginations. . . . He argues with great precision and a sense of the importance of the commonplace, for instance, that from the "isolation of poetic sensibility the obscurity of modern poetry also arises." . . . [As] an extremely tactful essayist, he steadfastly avoids discussing himself or his own work. In this fastidiousness he is like his critical and poetic mentor, Eliot, whose authoritative detachment he consistently admired. (p. 101)

Delmore made [a conscious effort] as a critic to be generous to both the ideas and the particular forms that poets and poems took. He was faithful to his sense of history and to the infinite ways poets took in interacting with history. At the same time that he succeeded so admirably in the primary task of the critic to be a good elucidator and a generous spirit, he also succeeded in commenting indirectly on his own dilemmas as a poetic man. He saw his fellow artists as he saw himself—trying to find a language faithful to the particular torments of our time that his own life so tragically embodied. (pp. 102-03)

> *David Zucker, "Self and History in Delmore Schwartz's Poetry and Criticism," in* The Iowa Review (*copyright © 1978, by The University of Iowa*), Fall, 1977, pp. 95-103.

IRVING HOWE

The slyly clever stories that Schwartz wrote, as well as his rueful, contemplative poems, can leave some readers cold. These stories and poems are associated with the span of influence enjoyed by "the New York intellectuals" from 1937 to, say, 1960, an influence deriving from a special blend of opinion and sensibility: anti-Stalinist left, aggressively modernist, brashly high-brow, freeswinging cosmopolitan, uneasily Jewish. All in all, this adds up to a pretty stiff dose for certain kinds of American literary people. Especially stiff for the academic "traditionalists" straining for Anglo-Saxon attitude and the anti-academic redskins declaring themselves just folks. The New York sensibility had its moment, and that moment is over. . . .

[Embarrasment] regarding his cultural sources, his literary role, his large, awkward body is one of the persistent motifs in his work. . . .

When his remarkable story "In Dreams Begin Responsibilities" first appeared in *Partisan Review* . . . , they read it with delight persuaded that no previous American writer had caught so well the emotional costs of immigrant Jewish life. All the wordless griefs that the second generation felt about parents with whom its ties had been cut seemed to come pouring out in this story about a delusional courtship —and pouring out as art, not mere outcry. . . .

He became famous for his bumbling, erudite, impassioned flow of speech, bringing together mother-wit from ancestral sources and literary sophistication from European capitals. . . . He soon became part of the mythology of a literary-intellectual generation, and naturally enough, once the next generation came along, it did not hesitate to stress that the myth had partly been based on misapprehensions. . . .

Schwartz's literary ambitions, like the ambitions of an entire immigrant generation, brought together purity and craftiness, a love for the thing itself and an eye for the main chance. (p. 458)

[Schwartz left a] small body of work, not the sort that even intense admirers would claim to be "major", yet rich in the flavours of New York life, marked by a strong ironic intelligence, and in its sum making a difference in one's perception of things.

There are five or six first-rate stories, notably "In Dreams Begin Responsibilities", "America! America!", and "The Child is the Meaning of This Life". These deal with the comic pathos and hopelessness of the conflict between immigrant families and emancipated children, and the occasional recognition by the latter that they have left behind not only ghetto parochialism but a culture of value. Wry, depressed, insidiously ratiocinative, these stories have little visible plot but much entanglement of characters, stylized dialogue replacing action, and a major dependence on passages of commentary, deflated epigrams, and skittish ventures into moral rhetoric. There is a strong awareness of the sheer foolishness of human affairs, the radical ineptitude of our being, such as reminds one a bit of Dostoevsky's use of buffoonery. But there is also something rare in contemporary writing, and that is a shy aspiration towards spiritual goodness and nobility—perhaps an echo of immigrant voices. . . .

[Schwartz's verse] is flecked with humour, graced with modesty. At their best, these poems are both serious and funny on a high level of intellectual consciousness, bringing together declamation, lyric introspectiveness, and bits of vaudeville. (p. 459)

> *Irving Howe, "Purity and Craftiness," in* The Times Literary Supplement (© *Times Newspapers Ltd. (London) 1978; reproduced from* The Times Literary Supplement *by permission), April 28, 1978, pp. 458-59.*

*   *   *

SEGAL, Erich   1937-

Segal is an American novelist, playwright, librettist, screenwriter, editor, and classics scholar. He is far better known for his first novel, *Love Story*, than for his scholarly writing. Both *Love Story* and its sequel, *Oliver's Story*, were critically received as maudlin, simplistic depictions of contemporary romance. (See also *CLC*, Vol. 3, and *Contemporary Authors*, Vols. 25-28, rev. ed.)

RICHARD R. LINGEMAN

Erich Segal's "Love Story" was one of those perfect little pop entertainment machines, gears greased by schmaltz, purring and clicking as it delivered simulated sentiments like a Swiss townhall clock parading its figurines on the stroke of the hour. It served up a love affair between a rich WASP Harvard jock and a pretty, poor, dirty-talking diluted-ethnic girl, in dialogue that was glib, contemporary-collegiate and sometimes funny. At the end the heroine expired in a death scene that suggested Oscar Wilde's dictum that "One must have a heart of stone to read the death of Little Nell without laughing"—of a disease with the symptomology of a bad case of mono. Yet in the moment of bathos, most readers could no more resist tears than readers of "Jaws" could resist shivers. As Kurt Vonnegut said, the book was as hard to put down as a chocolate éclair. . . .

Erich Segal has now delivered up a sequel, "Oliver's Story," in which a still-grieving Oliver is discovered in the throes of a bad case of survivor guilt. He tries a shrink and jogging, but is unable to follow the advice of his menschy father-in-law, Phil Cavilleri, and find himself a girl. But then the gorgeous, athletic, smart, blonde Marcie Nash comes jogging around the Central Park Reservoir and into Oliver's life. (p. 6)

Actually, as a sequel, "Oliver's Story" is a decent enough job. Good marathoner that he is, Segal is trying all the way, but one senses him flailing about early in the course. He is handicapped by having done away with Jenny in his last book, and her wisecracks are sorely missed; Marcie is not all that entertaining—or involving—a love interest, and the reader doesn't care much whether or not Oliver works it out with her. Still, towards the end of the book Segal gets second wind, and his effort pays off. The closing scenes, such as the Christmas Marcie and Oliver spend at the Barrett mansion, work; and the ending, in terms of Oliver's ultimate fate, has a nice fitness about it. So one almost forgets the previous voguish cause-dropping and the style, which at times resembles the offspring of a marriage between Holden Caulfield and That Cosmopolitan Girl. "Oliver's Story" is no laurel winner, but Segal ran his own race, and I give him that. The philosophical question of the day is, had no "Love Story" existed, would it have been necessary to invent this book? (p. 7)

Richard R. Lingeman, "The Son of 'Love Story'," in The New York Times Book Review *(© 1977 by The New York Times Company; reprinted by permission), March 6, 1977, pp. 6-7.*

DOROTHY SINCLAIR

In these days when *tempus* has a way of so quickly *fugiting,* it scarcely seems seven years since Erich Segal taught us that love means never having to say you're sorry. Well, Oliver, of the ill-fated brief marriage of *Love Story,* apparently had plenty of time to *feel* sorry, and to do a little guilt-wallowing in the two years after the untimely death of his wife, Jenny. Segal picks his story up at that point, showing us [in *Oliver's Story*] a faithful, work-driven, dedicated-only-to-his-law-practice, Oliver. . . .

Segal has found the formula. Having created Love #1 as poor as a church-mouse, he elects to make Love #2 as rich as Croesus. The adorable Marcie matches Ollie, cashmere for cashmere, auto for auto, mansion for mansion. It all comes out, finally, in the Boston wash, and Oliver ends up with a real *purpose* in life, at last.

This critic must admit that Segal spins quite a tale and has a style that certainly works for this Hollywood-oriented genre. Witty rather than weighty, the novel provides a few hours of diversionary reading that should make Avon Paperbacks not one whit sorry for the price they coughed up for the rights. (p. 30)

Dorothy Sinclair, in West Coast Review of Books *(copyright 1977 by Rapport Publishing Co., Inc.), Vol. 3, No. 3 (May, 1977).*

H. T. ANDERSON

In an age of the spin-off and the follow-up, maybe it isn't too surprising that Erich Segal has decided to give us "Son of *Love Story.*" It's also no great revelation that it is a predictable book and easy to knock. Like its predecessor, *Oliver's Story* is mawkishly corny but infinitely more whining. (p. 73)

The reader, ironically, discovers a strange kind of truth. Witness some dialogue:

> Please (Oliver says) understand. We aren't "living together." Although it's been a summer of excitement. It's true we eat together, talk together, laugh (and disagree) together, sleep together under the same roof (*i.e.,* my basement). But neither party has acknowledged an arrangement.

This sounds like the kind of capricious absurdity found in fables, but it isn't. There are people who think like this. Perhaps Mr. Segal has unwittingly given us a mirror for the times. The book is filled with "right-on" issues and "right-on" people, bright people (legal and energetic and concerned) who punctuate with four-letter words and are covered with youth and honesty.

Mr. Segal does have his way with this sort of thing, but *Oliver's Story* is a soupy bore. (p. 74)

H. T. Anderson, in Best Sellers *(copyright © 1977 Helen Dwight Reid Educational Foundation), June, 1977.*

SEXTON, Anne   1928-1974

Sexton was an American poet, playwright, and author of books for children. Associated with the confessional school of poetry, Sexton was in fact a student of the confessional poet Robert Lowell at the beginning of her career. Her poetry explores dark and secret areas of the mind, revealing the fearful isolation that accompanies emotional anguish. The critical evaluation of Sexton's work, while acknowledging its energy and respecting its candor, has frequently found her poetry solipsistic and uneven in quality. Sexton won the Pulitzer Prize in 1967. She took her own life in 1974. (See also *CLC,* Vols. 2, 4, 6, 8, and *Contemporary Authors,* Vols. 1-4, rev. ed.; obituary, Vols. 53-56.)

DAVID BROMWICH

To mourn the woman [Anne Sexton] by telling less than the truth about the poet is to perform no service. She was, let it be said, a flawed poet who became more deeply flawed, as she made of her worst tricks a trade. I did not follow her career attentively. In a life filled with books to read and things to do, one may be excused for giving second place to a poetry that dwells irritably on the squalor of the everyday, without abatement or relief. Did no one acquaint this poet with Arnold's famous words?—that there are "situations, from the representation of which, though accurate, no poetical enjoyment can be derived? They are those in which the suffering finds no vent in action; in which a continuous state of mental distress is prolonged, unrelieved by incident, hope, or resistance; in which there is everything to be endured, nothing to be done. In such situations there is inevitably something morbid, in the description of them something monotonous. When they occur in actual life, they are painful, not tragic; the representation of them in poetry is painful also." The amused or wry tone of some of her poems was sheer ballast. She was sustained by a long argument, and a *private* one, which might well have been carried on in prose or in a diary, about whether life was worth its cost in suffering.

She decided not. And in her last book [*45 Mercy Street*], together with much ballast, there is an evil spirit brooding, and something more hateful than bitterness. It is hatred. A lover is addressed as "Mr. Panzer-Man". He is the Nazi, she the Jew. Sylvia Plath had used the same analogy, in her celebrated attractive-repulsive poem, *Daddy.* How far does it hold? Do fathers and lovers seek to exterminate women who are poets, is there a plan to wipe them out, are they hauled from their beds and beaten and killed? No, the poem has no source in experience, it is not authentic. But then, does the poet convince us that she experiences these things *in the poem*? No, it is not sincere. Perhaps the subject ought to be dropped; it is too disgusting. Confessional poetry, we must see, has come to us historically in two kinds. There is the terrible secret (Baudelaire) and there is the beautiful secret (Wordsworth). The newer confessional poets touched neither of these bases. "I am desperate," they were saying. "Others are responsible. The world has done this to me. Look!" *Life Studies* inaugurated the reign of a personal and debased mode of the poetry of grievances; [Robert Lowell] brought a few of his students with him; now they are gone, and his own poetry has grown indistinguishable from theirs. (pp. 170-71)

David Bromwich, in Poetry *(© 1976 by The Modern Poetry Association; reprinted by permission of the editor of* Poetry*), Decem-ber, 1976.*

DOROTHY RABINOWITZ

Anne Sexton's is, indeed, a poetic voice that seems, even when most intense, to lack heart. The falsification of feeling that is a prominent feature of her poems, including the most celebrated among them, emerges more often than not in the form of contrived metaphor, exercises in compression that are at once agile and empty of resonance. One of her most famous poems, called "Live" (1966), is as good a case in point as any, an "affirmation" that has more to do with eliciting approval, a skill at which she was adept when she wished to be, than with any profound realization of life's value:

> So I won't hang around in my hospital shift,
> repeating the Black Mass and all of it.
> I say *Live, Live* because of the sun,
> the dream, the excitable gift.

There were, to be sure, instances when emotional integrity triumphed, notably when her eye turned inward on her life's obsession, suicide, the impulses toward which had yielded her an identity as strong as, and possibly stronger than, any she had found as a poet. Indeed, it was when that identity was most available to her that she seemed to perform best as a poet:

> But suicides have a special language.
> Like carpenters they want to know *which tools*
> They never ask *why build.*
>
> (p. 76)

Among the letters collected [in *Anne Sexton: A Self-Portrait in Letters*], none is as strong and evocative as the one she writes her husband during a trip to Europe, in which she confirms her inability to function alone. For Anne Sexton, whose poetry Robert Lowell praised for its "swift, lyrical openness," was clearly all her life a stranger, like a good many other profoundly neurotic people, to the ordinary range of feelings and emotions. In some measure aware, as such people are, that there was something lacking in her relationship to feeling, she became a watcher, an obsessed observer, and sometimes a skilled imitator of the way other people deal with one another. (pp. 76, 78)

> *Dorothy Rabinowitz, "Death Watch" (re-printed from* Commentary *by permission; copyright © 1978 by the American Jewish Committee), in* Commentary, *March, 1978, pp. 76, 78.*

GAIL POOL

[By] the end [of Sexton's career her] work had deteriorated badly. But long before, the faults had been advertised, and like most advertisements the statements were only half true. The labels ("confessional") and the adjectives ("ostentatious") had come so early and had remained so permanently that no one really noticed when they didn't apply. The final, sprawling, entirely personal poems appeared like a self-fulfilling prophecy.

Yet one has only to look at those first five books, and in particular *Transformations,* which is really a tour de force, to realize how much of her work did not fall into the handy Sexton categories and that where she ended up was not where she had begun.

Sexton began in fact as a formalist, and rhyme and meter, the usual equipment of form, were an integral part of the early poems. In an early review of Sexton's work (*Poetry,* Feb., 1961), James Dickey complained not that the poems were too loose and rambling but that they were too artificial, too constrained, too conscious of themselves as poems. And he was right. In part, the problem was that of a beginner struggling with the mechanics of form: the too-obvious rhymes (head/bed, know/go) fall heavily at the ends of the lines, reducing some of the serious poems to farce. More important, Sexton had not yet, to use the cliché, found a voice; she had not yet discovered in poetry who she would be. And so we do not feel one clear personality emerging in those first books so much as we feel we are watching a series of performances.

But some of the performances are marvelous. Despite Sexton's problems with form and the many limitations of formalism which made her finally shift away from it, the use of structure served her well, and some of her strongest works are the short, highly structured poems found in the early books, such as "Starry Night," "Her Kind," or "The Black Art." In these, the imagery—always Sexton's strongest point, the area where she was most surely in touch with herself—takes center stage, while the tight form manages to keep the words in check, a problem in the longer poems which often seem unable to stop themselves. . . .

Sexton [succeeds] in creating an extraordinarily eerie effect in ["Her Kind"], as she does in "Starry Night," and "The Black Art"; eeriness, in fact, was the realm in which Sexton did best, where she managed most successfully to bring about an element of shock, the kind of shock one wants in poetry, and which her more "shocking" poems rarely effected. But while it is obvious that the form—which is the same for the three poems—helped her to control the material she was working with, it is also obvious that the material here lent itself to a definite form in a way that the more complex feelings she wanted to write about did not. (p. 3)

Too often Sexton didn't allow her poems independence. "Lullaby" achieves it in part because the poem involves an actual scene from which the poet can stand back to observe; it provides something external upon which her imagination can work. Many of the successful poems in *Live or Die,* such as "In the Beach House" or "Pain for a Daughter," depend upon the creation of concrete scenes. It is interesting that these are minor poems. In the more ambitious poems of the collection, "Live" or "Flee on Your Donkey," the external scene is much less well defined; essentially the poet is simply "speaking out." Perhaps in these works there was too much at stake—they were too close for Sexton to let go of them, to give them an external shape. But the cost is a loss of power. . . .

[Sexton] doesn't seem to have considered that even if poetry is essentially exploration of the self, the best method of exploration might be indirect; that one might learn more by bringing oneself to a subject than by being the subject; and that so long as one insists on remaining inside one's mind one will have to put up with all the messy attitudes that live there unless one is willing to exorcise them by discipline.

That kind of discipline was not one of Sexton's strong points, and she not only put up with the attitudes, she befriended them. There is a terrible sentimentality running through many of Sexton's poems that is ultimately what is most devastating to them. In poem after poem she really seems to have felt she deserved some special pity because her mother had died, no matter that everybody's mother dies. And the sentimentality is not only for herself, it is extended to others, it becomes a world view. In "For Johnny Pole, On the Forgotten Beach," about a young man's death, she suddenly asks: "Does he lie there // forever, where his rifle waits, giant / and straight?" But this is pure rhetoric; of course he doesn't—and that is what is awful. In "The Truth the Dead Know," she compares the dead to stone; but the dead are *not* like stone, and surely it is the disintegration of the body, not the loss of feeling, that is the awful component of death.

What is ironic, and also what is aggravating, is that these poems present themselves as very hard, declaring their awful truths. But to present the worst is not necessarily to confront the worst. In truth, harshness or violence about the self is a form of self-dramatization, which is comforting, a kind of evasion; the real hardness is to be anonymous. While these poems pretend to confront the awful and the terrible, what they are really showing us is only a portrait of Medusa; we may get shivers up our spines, but nobody is turned to stone.

Of course Sexton, as a poet, wanted the power to turn everybody to stone, and perhaps Sexton wanted it more than most: in addition to her concepts of poetry as art and as therapy, she had a humorous but nonetheless serious concept of poetry as witchcraft. And this undoubtedly contributed to the pleasure she took in writing *Transformations,* which begins: "The speaker in this case / is a middle-aged witch, me." (pp. 3-4)

The retelling of Grimm's fairy tales was an ambitious project, a brilliant conception unlikely to be achieved with success; but for Sexton it proved to be ideal. The tales offered a rich medium for her colorful imagery; the psychological complexity allowed her to move in and out of relationships, the distance of those relationships making room for wit; they existed in the realm of the eerie, the grotesque, where she had always been her sharpest; and their own structure provided the structure she needed and so often had difficulty imposing on her own work. At last she had found material to which she could bring her intelligence, her wit, all that she knew, and she created, in Stanley Kunitz's words, "a wild, blood-curdling, astonishing book." (p. 4)

In all, Sexton published nine volumes of poetry, and in each there were some first-rate poems. But nine was too many books. Going through them, one has the sense that here was a poet with talent to burn—and she was burning it, letting it go to waste on the poverty and mishandling of the material. . . .

This sense is confirmed by . . . *Self-Portrait in Letters.* There are few ideas about poetry here; in fact, few ideas at all. But then it may be that Sexton didn't view the letter as a vehicle for her thoughts about life or art. One wonders why, however, if the material did not bear directly on the work or thought of the author, the volume was published. To feed once again the nonreaders who want to know more about her life? The book is filled with gossip. But even from the personal point of view to which it is limited, it does not offer a flattering portrait of Sexton, and I think the editors, however well-intentioned, have not served her well by publishing it.

What remains to be done for Sexton is not biographies or criticism or collections but the publication of the selected works, including only the very best poems and the entire *Transformations*—the final editing that will bring to light how much she really did achieve. (p. 4)

Gail Pool, "Anne Sexton: Poetry and Witchcraft," in New Boston Review *(copyright 1978 by Boston Critic, Inc.), Spring, 1978, pp. 3-4.*

*   *   *

SHAMLU, Ahmad   1925-

An Iranian poet, critic, translator, and writer of books for children, Shamlu is one of his country's leading writers and intellectuals. As a young man, Shamlu developed an enthusiasm for classical music, but his poverty prevented him from pursuing a musical career. However, his love of music is evident in his poetry. Shamlu's poetry, noted for its linguistic experimentalism and grand imagery, reveals his commitment to freedom of expression. Shamlu has written under the pseudonyms of A. Bamdad and A. Sobh.

MASSUD FARZAN

The poems in [*Ebrāhīm dar'ātash*] reflect a consistently distilled quality which at times verges on obscurity. Yet almost always the imagery is breath-taking—fresh, bare and yet potent. The poem called "Mohaq," significantly dedicated to the novelist-playwright Gowhar Morad, is of shimmering lyricism and at the same time suggestive of caustic social criticism. It is primarily this latter aspect of Shamlu's poetry which has made his books widely popular among students and young intellectuals.

Poem after poem the author seems to cry out for a sense of human contact, for dignity and for beauty. A dominant note is that of near-despair as well as restlessness in the face of a life that is fleeting, passing away in paralysis or estrangement. . . . (pp. 839-40)

Massud Farzan, in Books Abroad *(copyright 1974 by the University of Oklahoma Press), Vol. 48, No. 4, Autumn, 1974.*

ESMAEEL RANJBARAN

Prolific as he is in various genres, Shamloo is a poet; the rest of his work, therefore, is important primarily for its relationship to his poetry. . . .

Shamloo understands well the advantages of the Western methodologies but has taught himself to adapt them to the Iranian context. Compassion, resistance, empathy, and technique become inseparable functions of his poetic process. . . . What Shamloo gives us is the lyrical expression of a spontaneous mood—a mood that grows out of immediate experience; this expression is then repeated, qualified and elaborated subconsciously until it becomes a metaphor and finally a representative state of mind. He writes the most graceful and delicate lyrics in Persian since Hafiz (1324-88); at the same time, he has developed a muscular free verse that suits his strong attraction to prophecy as the poet's major role. . . .

["Unfolding in Fog"] is wordy, vague and far inferior to his previous works. A decade ago, he was at the peak of his poetic powers and was the best poet in Iran. But now, it seems, he is declining poetically, although he is still enjoying accolades. (p. 180)

Esmaeel Ranjbaran, in Books Abroad *(copyright 1975 by the University of Oklahoma Press), Vol. 49, No. 1, Winter, 1975.*

AHMAD KARIMI-HAKKAK

In his recent visit to the United States, the leading Iranian poet Ahmad Shamlu told me, with a tone of sober reflection, that he would rather be remembered and judged as the poet of collections such as "Aïda in the Mirror," "Blossoming in the Fog," "Phoenix under the Rain," "Elegies of the Earth" and "Abraham in the Fire" than as the author of the earlier and much more famous poems, particularly "The Fairies" and "Poetry that is Life." To those who have always turned and returned to Shamlu's poetry as documents of political and historical significance, this statement may be surprising. However, for those who in the past thirty years have attentively watched the evolution of this free spirit in an increasingly unfree society, the poet's estimation of his own work may come as an illuminating revelation. At any rate, all those who are familiar with the development of contemporary Persian poetry will perhaps agree that Shamlu's long and successful career, both as a poet and as an intellectual, is inseparably linked with the social and political conditions in modern Iran. His life has paralleled the life of his country, inspiring its future direction, reflecting its ups and downs and at times even caught in the middle of such extrinsic conflicts as World War II and the turbulence of the early 1950s. (p. 201)

In the past twenty years or so Shamlu's poetry has gone through many stages of development. The variety of his experiments with the language, the diversity of his poetic music, the multifariousness of his imagery and the stubborn independence of his poetic ideas demonstrate his refusal to fall into any easily identifiable category. In recent years the world of the Iranian intellectuals has come under increasingly forceful demands for conformity from the political establishment. As the possibilities of independent thought and free expression shrink more and more, only polar alternatives remain available to a living Iranian poet. Shamlu's reaction to this situation has been a grand internalization of his poetic message and a growing attitude of ambivalence toward his public. The sparkles of protest are still prevalent in his poetry, but whereas in his early poems he tended to confront the social system, in his later poems it is the healing power of poetry which soothes the anxieties of the poet and the reader.

Shamlu began his poetic career at a time when Persian poetry had been remolded and given a new dynamism in the hands of a dynasty of men who gradually broke through the stagnating traditionalism and the consequent decline into which Persian literature had fallen in the nineteenth century. . . .

Following in [the wake of this dynasty of socially motivated poets] came Nima, a solitary man of unusual genius who, in his rustic simplicity, single-handedly challenged and systematically changed almost all the traditionalistic tendencies in Persian poetry. In his hands poetry became the most profound means of an artistic expression whose order is organic rather than plastic, imposed from within by the dictates of the poet's feeling rather than from without by the tradition of poetic precepts. The excellence of the poet is measured, according to Nima, not by the degree of his success in strict adherence to traditional ideas of diction, decorum, rhyme and rhythm, but by the sincerity of his expression. . . . Of all the disciples of Nima, none has put the words of the master into poetic expression as astutely as Shamlu in his "Poetry that is Life," a poem which he himself once considered his ars poetica. This is how the poem opens:

> The subject of poets of yesteryear
> was not of life.
>
> . . . .
>
> Today the theme of poetry is a different thing.
> Poetry today is the weapon of the masses.
> For poets themselves
>
> are branches from the forest of the masses,
> not jasmines and hyacinths of someone's
>   greenhouse.

(pp. 201-02)

What Shamlu owes to Nima above all is the ever-searching spirit of his poetry, always ready to plunge into new domains for the true poetic experience. . . . In [his] early collections, written before the poet could fully comprehend the message of the master, a bewildered young man constantly seems to be trying to manage the unmanageable. An uneasy language, uneven rhythmic patterns and cumbersome rhyme schemes create an enervating atmosphere in which the poet's indeterminate attitude toward his art hinders him from the noble intention of singing the suffering of the masses. By contrast, in later works, particularly in "The Fresh Air," "Aïda in the Mirror," "Phoenix under the Rain" and "Blossoming in the Fog," Shamlu is always in command. Whether in a folk-inspired work like "The Fairies" or in an entirely lyrical song such as "Aïda in the Mirror," or even in his meditative poems, the excessive emotionalism of youth has hardened into a romantic belief in man, a mature outlook on life and a genuine faith in love. The easy-flowing rhythm in these later poems follows the poet instead of dragging him along; the softened music of the lines eases the movement of the poem, and strongly visual images reveal a penetrating power of observation. Most importantly, a happy marriage between Eastern and Western mythology and symbolism often gives a universal character to his poetry. (p. 202)

Shamlu's poetry and poetic philosophy reflect an even more deeply-rooted Western influence than he can perhaps be conscious of. In many of his lines one can detect direct echoes of Lorca and Aragon. His images are sometimes as visual as Pound's, sometimes as abstract as Breton's. Like Éluard and Aragon, whom he has translated, Shamlu believes that poetry is first and foremost language, and as such nothing is more essential for the poet than to begin by trying the language on all its levels. Like Pound and Yeats, he considers the visual experience of the poet the base on which the poem is made to stand or fall. His belief in the profound will of poetry, in its deep memory and in action as the ordering principle underlying any poem links him with many of the great contemporary poets of our time such as Mayakovsky, particularly in his early poems.

Shamlu is one of the few Iranian poets who have read both the Bible and the Koran as poetry. His lyrical poems are remarkably influenced by the Song of Songs, which he also has rendered rather successfully into Persian. Christ's character and his Passion have always held a fascination for Persian poets. His life can easily be identified with the lives of thousands of nameless heroes who were betrayed and tortured because of their free spirits and their love of humanity. Shamlu's richly lyrical ''Death of the Nazarene,'' for example, pictures a Christ who is liberated from within by his own compassion and purity. In ''Tablet'' Christ is identified with the poet whose message goes unheeded, while at the same time the nature of his mission vis-à-vis modern martyrs provides the poet's basic view of history. (p. 203)

In his more tranquil poems Shamlu preaches love not as an eternal allegory with cosmic significance but as a moment of internal harmony. Here a balanced, harmonious form often becomes the mirror, reflecting the deep tranquility and nobility which love is capable of bestowing upon man.... Shamlu's love poems are many and varied. In some, notably the earlier love lyrics, the poet pursues a sunlit, joyous kind of love which refines and ennobles the lover. Its benefits and ill effects are supreme joy and sorrow. In others love prompts the poet to meditate on the nature of man, a process which often leads to thoughts of *vanitas vanitatum*. In more recent love poems the poet expresses his feelings with dazzling immediacy and memorable drama. As one reads these love poems, most importantly the Aïda cycle, one cannot help but notice a gradual movement toward simpler expression and, at the same time, an increasing desire for isolation which is occasionally accompanied by a disquieting attitude of condescension toward the outside world. Lately Shamlu has written a number of poems which on the surface appear to be love poems. However, a close reading of these in conjunction with the poems of the Aïda cycle reveals a movement from love to solitude, from essential harmony with the other to an existential loneliness. The poet desires complete imprisonment in the self:

> A fortification like an onion-skin,
> that with my solitude when I sit in secret,
> seven gates shall slam shut
> upon the body's longings and belongings.
> Shut may they be,
> Yes, shut may they be
> and shut may they stay,
> and on every gate
> seven heavy locks of steel.

Passages of this kind may indeed seem at best unlikely from the poet of such socially committed works as ''Poetry that is Life,'' ''The Daughters of Mama Sea'' and, above all, ''The Fairies.'' When it exploded on the Persian literary scene in 1956, ''The Fairies'' brought a great excitement to the literary community of Iran. Even disregarding the meaning of its story and simply looking at it as an exercise in language, bringing together the literary and the common modes of speech, it was a triumphant achievement. It stirred the minds of the avant-garde literati with its sweeping force and profound implications. Finally a way had been discovered to create literature of social significance in the language of the masses. (pp. 203-04)

''The Fairies'' remains a landmark in modern Persian poetry. In it dance, song, music and poetry merge, while a deceptively simple and childish story becomes the vessel containing a far-reaching allegory. The poem tells a story with an internal coherence of its own, almost entirely independent of its rhythmical variation. Thus the poem derives its unity from the story it tells and its diversity from the rhythmical structure. As an exercise with the capacities of

folk and popular language, it is a superb experiment—one that none, including Shamlu himself, could ever again equal. As an allegory of political change, it drives the point home despite certain ambiguities which tend to make it rather difficult to comprehend without a line-by-line dissection. The images of light and darkness, in their literal and metaphorical opposition, create a dimly lit atmosphere in which such polarities as legend and reality, master and slave, fairies and men assume allegorical significance. The fairies, alien to the world of historical realities, are completely timeless creatures. They are not characters but symbols whose existence is justified by their function. The journeying horseman, on the other hand, can only be seen in his movement through time and space. When he describes what is about to happen in the City of Slaves, he assumes a degree of historical specificity that no one slightly familiar with the contemporary history of Iran can fail to interpret as the prophecy of an imminent revolution:

> The slaves gather, torch in hand
> to burn the night off our land,
> to force the chain-maker out,
> chain him, drag him all about.

And it was, above all, a promise of such magnitude which made ''The Fairies'' a stunning success and perhaps one of the most lasting poems in the mind of the Persians. (pp. 204-05)

The structure and pattern of ritual, the meaning of the metamorphosis of the fairies, the imagery and symbolism of the poem and the mythical basis of the story each can be the topic of a separate study, to say nothing of the narrative and descriptive technique, the folk elements, the extraordinary diction and the hypnotic rhythm of the poem. To mention but one feature, the rhythm of this unusual work is designed to change in harmony with the movement of the narrative and consequently with the heartbeat of the reader. When events overtake the horseman, the rhythm quickens breathtakingly and the reader is made to gasp, whereas the moment the hero regains the mastery of his own mind, the poem changes pace and the reader is calmed down by the serenity of a peaceful rhythm.

''The Fairies'' was the product of a historical moment—one of those poems which cannot be created without the help of some indefinable magic, like that of the fairies themselves. As the political environment of the country turned more venomous, and as the establishment quashed the intellectual ideal of a democratic society more and more brutally, it became next to impossible for the poet—any poet—to reflect such dreams. In the past fifteen years or so Shamlu has published half a dozen volumes of poetry in which not a single attempt has been made to revive the language and the rhythm of ''The Fairies.'' To be sure, Shamlu has constantly been trying to create a harmonious world of the image and the idea in which the only music is the sound and the meaning of the word echoed in silence. It is a much more subtle, much more abstract poetry. Images such as ''the height of the abyss,'' the ''depth of solitude,'' ''silence speaking with a thousand tongues,'' ''the bloody tumbling of the dawn'' and many others of this kind abound in his later poems. Often the unity of the poem depends on the symmetry and parallelism of its stanzas. . . . The fleet-footed, sure-minded horseman of ''The Fairies'' has now been lulled into the flat-footed, still-minded man of [''The Dark Song''] in which silence reigns supreme. The poet's own feelings and emotions, which build and occupy many of his poems, have undergone a parallel transformation. (p. 205)

A possible misconception must be dispelled before this brief account of one of the most influential living poets of the Persian language is brought to a close. I do not intend to lead the reader to believe that the early Shamlu is a better artist. On the contrary, Shamlu's later poems are likelier to determine the future trends in Persian poetry than are his earlier ones. The degree of cohesiveness which Shamlu has achieved in some of his recent poems such as "The Song of Abraham in the Fire," "The Song of the Man of Light who Passed into Gloom" and "I am still thinking of that raven . . ." can only be compared to such poems as Mallarmé's "Le cygne," Yeats's "Sailing to Byzantium" and Alexander Blok's "The Twelve." His lyrical poems are already approaching Pound's most lyrical moments in the *Cantos* or Cavafis at his best; and the poet, one must remember, is still in mid-career. What this essay proposes is that, in a world of shrinking possibilities of expression, Shamlu has perforce been separated from his audience and made to turn inward. He has moved from action to reflection, from certainty to doubt and from quest to solitude. Many of Shamlu's latest poems remain completely within the domain of intense personal experience, hardly venturing outside the poet without becoming blurred and vague. The poet who once expressed the dreams and aspirations of his society now tends to distill them into intense and pure feelings which he hopes will signify to the reader the underlying vision which the poet can no longer express as freely as he used to. By telling his reader about his weariness and despair, he hopes to prompt us to inquire about the reasons behind them. Thus the mere expression of this despondency becomes a gesture of protest in itself.

Early Shamlu is a man of power, persuasion and determination; later Shamlu is very much a poet of pen, paper and deliberation. As such, while the verisimilitude of his early works demands a basically historical response, the abstraction of his later poems evokes a primarily imaginative one. He has come more and more to view poetry as a mirror which the thinking poet, in an uncertain world, holds up to his own soul. The sweeping energy of the young dreamer has gradually subsided into the brooding pessimism of the white-haired poet who knows—or believes he knows—that change will come only if thought accompanies action. His struggle, like that of his countrymen, now goes on below the surface. (p. 206)

> Ahmad Karimi-Hakkak, "A Well amid the Waste: An Introduction to the Poetry of Ahmad Shamlu," in World Literature Today (copyright 1977 by the University of Oklahoma Press), Vol. 51, No. 2, Spring, 1977, pp. 201-06.

* * *

SHEED, Wilfrid   1930-

An Anglo-American novelist, short story writer, critic, essayist, and editor, Sheed writes witty, satirical novels in which the bite is tempered by his compassion. A frequent target for his sarcasm is the contemporary obsession with self-analysis. (See also *CLC*, Vols. 2, 4, and *Contemporary Authors*, Vols. 65-68.)

JULIAN MOYNAHAN

"Transatlantic Blues" . . . is fictional autobiography structured as a general confession in the old-Catholic sense of the term. This confession is stimulated by a mid-life crisis or breakdown stemming from the hero's self-condemnatory conviction that the work he does is despicable and immoral, even a symptom of diabolism. Pendrid ("Monty") Chatworth is a television host-interviewer toiling for both a major American network and the BBC, specializing in celebrity interviewing of the pseudo-candid type and in "searching" documentaries. (p. 1)

"Transatlantic Blues," written in the familiar Sheedian vein of dark comedy, is worth reading for its wealth of insight into the two societies during and since World War II, an insight further developed by the unusual inside-outside vantage points available to the narrator. As a novel about family life, it tells a touching story of how four people, including the sister, Priscilla, whose struggles to achieve a viable identity are sketched with real poignancy, deal with fundamental dislocation and uprooting. And as a novel on religious themes it offers an unusual look at the endlessly complex ways Catholicism in both its New and Old World forms affects the lives of bright children growing up in an exceptionally religious household.

Yet Sheed's strongest suit, as it always has been, is his mastery of voice, of tone and of style. One wants constantly to quote him, and this seems to me important at a time when many ambitious novels come out that display ragged syntax and a sludgy style as though these disabilities certified the value of their contents. (p. 19)

> Julian Moynahan, "Anglo-American Attitudes," in The New York Times Book Review (© 1978 by The New York Times Company; reprinted by permission), January 15, 1978, pp. 1, 19.

JAMES WOLCOTT

Chalices, confessionals, crucifixes—every page of Wilfrid Sheed's new novel *Transatlantic Blues* . . . is sprinkled with strained jokey references to Roman Catholicism. Like the father in *Looking for Mr. Goodbar* who tears around the house in a Notre Dame jacket, narrator-hero Pendrid "Monty" Chatworth isn't merely intensely Catholic, he's *pathologically* Catholic—God is his co-pilot, and together they're strafing the countryside. The novel opens with Chatworth on a 747 flight above the Atlantic, boozily asking other first-class occupants to hear his confession. After a Jewish passenger sarcastically obliges him, Chatworth growls, "Fuck you, you secular pig. You had a great religion once. What'd you do with it? Boiled it down to make wisecracks." Isn't that what Wilfrid Sheed has done with his talent? *Transatlantic Blues* is nothing but wisecracks, a grinning swarm of locusts. . . .

As the name "Chatworth" indicates, Sheed's protagonist has exploited his conversational gifts to the fullest. He's a transatlantic TV celebrity, like David Frost or Alistair Cooke, and he prides himself on being a million-particled Machiavelli. Chatworth is a master of fine modulation: sincerity, integrity, gravity, all are projected into the television camera with creamy precision. Yet though wealth and fame are firmly his, he is a spiritually tormented creature, and he pours his God-haunted thoughts into a tape recorder that he has nicknamed Father Sony. It's a promising premise for a novel, and I hoped that Sheed would do in *Transatlantic*

Blues what poet Clive James did in his verse narrative *Peregrine Prykke's Pilgrimage:* take the reader on a satirical tour of highbrow Celebrityville.... Here, however, the story is monotonously single-voiced: Chatworth fancies himself as a cruelly proficient mimic but only *his* voice penetrates the static. Which isn't surprising since there aren't any characters in the book except the narrator. Chatworth's father is a vague pink cloud of benevolence, the women in his life are little more than skirts rustling by, and his schoolmates are *Welcome Back, Kotter* rowdies, ethnicity spurting from every pore.

As in every Sheed novel, there are jokes and metaphors and loopy insights that leap from the page like novelty-shop snakes. A quick example: "For all her transparent wackiness, Maureen [Chatworth's sweetie] had also frightened me a little about the interviews, and the ones I did in the East were like fake surgery: all white gowns and rubber knives. Candor was already in its decadence, and a display of flying elbows was all you needed." Flying elbows, rubber knives—his command of comic detail is often astonishingly sure. But despite Sheed's slangy, offhand style, the novel moves with a mastodonic plod....

What's most bewildering—and exhausting—about *Transatlantic Blues* is that Sheed has strip-mined so much of his earlier work. Chatworth—born in England, educated in America—feels displaced on both shores: a dilemma handled far more movingly in *The Blacking Factory* (Sheed's best fiction, I think). Later Chatworth uses his tweedy Englishness to outfox America, a tactic described at Trollopean length in *Office Politics* (his worst fiction, I think, though *Max Jamison* comes perilously close). And the animadversions about Selling Out seem to have been sifted not only from *Max Jamison* but from essays in *The Morning After*. Indeed, a stray sentence from that collection—"The syndrome of 'making it' is directly connected with the loss of personal immortality"—says immeasurably more about success and embattled spirituality than all of Monty Chatworth's fizzy soliloquies. Despite the sound effects—the whirrs, flashbulb pops, and flutterings of angelic wings—the book lacks orchestral design. *Transatlantic Blues* finally is an expression of pure writerly will, of Wilfrid Sheed's determination to produce a novel. Nothing is alive on these hundreds of pages except the author's desire to drag sentence after sentence from shadowy silence into the noisy world.

Yet this book, brimming with schmaltz and small amusements, will hardly bruise Sheed's reputation. (p. 68)

The truth is that Sheed's style—springy, alert, kittenish—isn't really suited to the novel; it lacks steel and music. As a critic, working with a text, he can be almost frighteningly observant, and his wisecracks are both stinging and illuminating. But in fiction he works in a self-created void: the characters are store-window mannequins, the scenery consists of painted back-drops. Nothing is at stake, no giddy risks are taken, so the jokes become only curlicues in his elegant doodling.... All through this latest novel Chatworth's father implores him to be "first-rate." As a critic Wilfrid Sheed is consummately first-rate, yet he's worrying away his time with thickly trivial fictions. That's the real sell-out of *Transatlantic Blues*. (p. 70)

> *James Wolcott, "Wilfrid Sheed's Stations of the Cross," in* The Village Voice *(reprinted by permission of* The Village Voice; *copyright © by* The Village Voice, Inc., *1978), January 23, 1978, pp. 68, 70.*

ROBERT TOWERS

I found it impossible to identify [*Transatlantic Blues'*] real subject or to guess the impulse that led to its writing. Much of the Oxford material reads like a retread of Sheed's first novel, *A Middle-Class Education* (1960). And the differences in English and American attitudes and style that so agitate the adolescent (and collegiate) Pendrid have been more poignantly dramatized in *The Blacking Factory* (1968). It is not helpful to think of the novel as a kind of *Bildungsroman,* since the central character undergoes no real development; he merely tries on a series of less than adequate identities. It is then the story of a sell-out, an anatomy of guilt? The portrait of a once zealous (if slightly phony) Catholic in a post-Vatican II world? A satire on the mindlessness of television, the meretriciousness of fame? It is all of these things but only sporadically and half-heartedly. Somewhere within *Transatlantic Blues* there is, I believe, a real and potentially moving story of fathers and sons. Pendrid's gentle, honorable, rather unworldly father is one of the few appealing characters, and his injunction—"Be first-rate"—continues to haunt his son throughout the novel. But this strand is never sufficiently disentangled or drawn out. The book seems to be caught in a rip-tide of cross purposes, and much of it, I am afraid, is tedious.

A large part of the problem lies with the way in which Monty-Pendrid is allowed to present himself. Sheed's male characters (and in a sense there are no others) have always been prone to extreme self-consciousness. Their lengthy interior monologues tend to alternate between self-analysis and self-accusation, with very little scope for the spontaneous or serendipitous. The unremitting commentary frequently stops the action in its tracks. Consequently, the novels read more like demonstrations than imaginative works of fiction.... His novels seem stronger in documentation than in invention and regularly give the *appearance* of autobiography only slightly transmuted—even when the characters and their circumstances are obviously "made up." They have trouble progressing beyond their initial premise or situation into a freely moving story, with the result that their denouements are often unconvincing (Max Jamison's reconciliation with his wife) or melodramatic (Jimmy's breakdown at the end of *The Blacking Factory*).

These characteristics of Sheed's fiction become especially obvious in *Transatlantic Blues.* Monty's confessional style is heavily facetious, falsely intimate, cute, and shrill. And the voice never lets up, even when it is sometimes attributed to one of the two alter egos, Plunkett and Snead, whom Monty invents to represent, respectively, the pious and profane sides of his personality. But since the piety is false, Plunkett gets very few lines and the squinty-eyed Snead ("the meanest sound in the language") does a fair amount of the talking. (pp. 17-18)

It seems unfair that a writer of Sheed's industry, intelligence, and experience has not yet been able to produce a novel that sustains the promise of its conception. One keeps hoping that the *next* one will finally clear the ground. But *Transatlantic Blues* is not the redeeming book. It unaccountably lacks the wit, the cleverness of phrasing, the eye for aesthetic and moral dilemmas that in the preceding novels have offered the reader a generous compensation for their inadequacies as works of fiction. (p. 18)

> Robert Towers, in The New York Review of Books (reprinted with permission from The New York Review of Books; copyright © 1977 NYREV, Inc.), January 26, 1978.

JOHN B. BRESLIN

As a satirical tour de force, *Transatlantic Blues* has its moments. Like Chatworth, Wilfrid Sheed is also a transatlantic personality and his barbs slash both ways, skewering British dilettantism and American pragmatism with equal gusto. Of British heroism: "Fearfully brave. Group commander at Dunkirk. Made tea while the bullets sang. 'Oh dear, they've ruined our best pot. I *am* vexed.' Stamps foot, giggles." Of American nomadism: "Americans are so good at being homeless, they must practice it at home." And yet I did not find it a very funny book. Like Chatworth himself, the humor is too contrived, too much like a talk-show monologue. The constant play of mirrors and echoes that makes the hero so unsympathetic also vitiates much of the book's comic purpose. In sum, a flawed performance by an important novelist. . . .

> John B. Breslin, "Confessions of an Ex-Non-Catholic," in Book World—The Washington Post (© The Washington Post), February 5, 1978, p. G3.

BERNARD McCABE

Chatworth's voice, shrewd, sardonic, reductive—he is on to himself and on to everybody else—presents the Anglo-American scene, and particularly the Catholic scene, afresh [in *Transatlantic Blues*]. . . . Class plays its usual murky role, and Chatworth's voice reaches new levels of satirical irony as he confronts and rings the changes on all the traps of American anglophilia and anglophobia, of English pro- and anti-Americanism. The voice gets sharper still as yet another excruciating Catholic struggle with sex is rehearsed. Cheerfuller comedy comes in his account of self-prostitution for the media. Chatsworth is too "vibrantly superficial" to engage in the trapped masochisms of a Mauriac or Greene protagonist; he is too buoyant for the sin of Despair. Yet the poles of his confession are self-hatred ("I satirize myself, a Catholic vice"), and self-esteem (once starved, but now well-fed by his audiences), and it becomes clear as his brilliant nervous gabble goes on that a more or less desperate search for a self is involved . . . with a real fear that once the onion is peeled away there will be nothing left.

For these are exercises in contrition as well as confession. Chatworth does not want psychiatrist couch stuff; sin is real. It is not only that, with his carefree TV specials on the world's trouble spots, he has publicly sinned against sincerity and authenticity. These true confessions provide a history of crushing private failures as well: failing his father and sister at crucial moments in their lives for example, or dishonestly wielding his thin Catholicism as a twisted weapon against his disturbingly honest lover (a brilliant chapter of dark comedy tells that story), and of course, failing himself, notably in relation to his father, who quietly dominates his conscience with his distant challenge of love. All these are failures of love, and a great success in this novel is the balanced way in which sympathies are involved. . . . (p. 248)

But wit is the general solvent. Chatworth's ultimate ironic blasphemy, for instance, is to use his light Catholic training, his "spiritual insights" to get ahead in his TV shows, becoming a kind of public father confessor. . . . Wit is never set adrift from feeling, though. In the most poignant moments it still controls feeling. I think here of Kingsley Amis, who from the English end, in *I Want It Now* (about a TV personality) and in *One Fat Englishman* (about transatlantic encounters) has profitably explored somewhat similar territory. Amis also uses satirical wit to explore feeling. Yet (and there is a large issue here about secular and nonsecular habits of mind) at the crucial moment he is likely to lower the cruel sword and let sentiment in. Sheed never lets this happen. The insistent hardmounthed control ("When the M.C. called me a wit with a heart, I broke into that silly grin again and it wouldn't go away") only underlines the novel's seriousness of purpose.

The last chapters make the point. As he completes his tapes Chatworth knows that, at the height of his success, he is on the brink of decline; in twenty years time he will be "a trivia question; and then if I still haven't taken the hint and died, nothing at all." The novel ends in serious black comedy. On a sort of private secular retreat in New Jersey he plays all his tapes to a young ex-nun, a visiting journalist. Baring his soul to her he also bares his body and in a climactic passage, with Father Sony still working away, with his dead father (expert in primal scenes) there in spirit, and perhaps his quick-witted sister hinted at in Sister Veronica, a Mailer-ish procreation take place. With whiffs of incense and incest wafting around Chatworth is reborn and reconciled. (pp. 248-49)

Sheed is better than ever in this novel, and funnier. Hard to single out examples, but I'll recommend the accurately savage encounters Chatworth has with an awful American TV journalist and another with an awful English Underground newsman. Sheed is uniquely expert at playing one dialect's incongruities off against its transatlantic opposite —though my wrinkled ear did catch a few slips. And, as for a moment I'm carping, "Father Sony"—the name—sounds a mistaken bit of whimsy to me. But it's no problem. There's another problem that really isn't a problem either. . . . Sheed has never cared much about cultivating a detailedly consistent point of view. Never mind. It doesn't matter. It never caused insoluble difficulties. By contrast in this complex novel the flashbacks and flashforwards the rapid sceneshifts and timeshifts, the movement from historic present to real present as we nip in and out of Chatworth's personality at various ages—in short the general jet-laggery—generates an atmosphere in which the fusion of past and present attitudes, of naiveté and sophistication, of confused half-lost boy and raddled successful middle-aged man, brings Chatworth to life in extraordinarily effective ways, a triumph of the Sheed method. (pp. 249-50)

> Bernard McCabe, "Bless Me, Father . . . .," in Commonweal (copyright © 1978 Commonweal Publishing Co., Inc.; reprinted by permission of Commonweal Publishing Co., Inc.), April 14, 1978, pp. 248-50.

*   *   *

SHULMAN, Alix Kates   1932-

Shulman is an American novelist, essayist, editor, and writer of books for children whose works reflect her strong commit-

ment to the feminist movement. Her major fictive concerns are with the problems of growing up female in America and with the political and social implications of the Women's Liberation movement as it enters its second decade. (See also *CLC*, Vol., 2, and *Contemporary Authors*, Vols. 29-32, rev. ed.)

LYNNE SHARON SCHWARTZ

Zane IndiAnna, the heroine of [*Burning Questions*]—ingeniously cast as the autobiography of a militant feminist—wants above all, in the words of Oliver Wendell Holmes, Jr., to "share the passion and action of [her] time." After much tedious floundering in aimless confusion, Zane achieves her goal. . . .

Burning Questions is actually, and problematically, two novels in one, unsuccessfully conjoined. One is the traditional *Bildungsroman*. . . . [Zane] undergoes the ordeals of the late fifties, sleeping around among the Beats, typing-pool jobs, retreat into a dull marriage, motherhood, and emotional deprivation until she discovers the Movement and changes her life. It is the oft-told tale, valid but uninspiringly repeated. The other novel, though, the second half of *Burning Questions*, is vastly more exciting and written with conviction and authority: the rebel's tract, merging the circumstances of the historical moment with Zane's personal destiny.

Shulman is at her best when describing with passion the young days of the Movement. . . . In this aspect, *Burning Questions* is an experiment in a form unfortunately fallen into disuse, the novel of ideas.

Shulman's formidable intelligence regrettably stands in the way of the more urgent demands of fiction. Every experience is presented twice—as it happens, and in Zane's analysis. (For example, a beautiful, taut moment of sexual desire in the unlikely dark of a police wagon is immediately marred by Zane's explanation of the complex forces that produced it.) This constant commentary on the action, along with the older Zane's hindsight, reflects the awkwardness of trying to have it both ways: how appealingly foolish I was and how mellow I have become. Justification of dubious acts (marriage, adultery) by quotations from the diaries of rebels is not persuasive motivation. (pp. 40-1)

The last section of *Burning Questions* gives a fine portrayal of the changes in the Movement from the late sixties to the mid-seventies. . . . Wisely, Shulman makes no premature judgments about this transition, but invokes the passage of time and the constant flux of radical impulses. One wishes she had delineated this ebb and flow in greater detail. (p. 41)

> *Lynne Sharon Schwartz, "'How Foolish I Was: How Mellow I've Become',"* in Ms. *(© 1978 by Ms. Magazine Corp.), March, 1978, pp. 40-1.*

ANNE TYLER

It's hard to go unprejudiced into [*Burning Questions*], which is yet another novel about how an ordinary, middle-class housewife becomes an ardent feminist. It's even harder when there's a bibliography at the end . . . and when the novel turns out to be, quite literally, a novel within a novel.

The puzzling thing about Zane's story is her extreme distance from her own life. She recounts it in a sweeping way,

categorizing, summing up. . . . Zane has a habit of offhandedly mentioning, a hundred pages late, that such-and-such an event has already occurred, more or less by the bye: her loss of virginity, her marriage, childbirth, two abortions, divorce. Experiences skim past her, as if happening to someone else.

But the surprise is that by the end of the book, we do care for Zane, however impatient we've been with her along the way. I think the reason for this can be found in the title. The "burning questions" are not, as I had feared, queries about women's victimization or men's supremacy, but about "how to live, how to be." What Zane is struggling for is a way of making the best use of her life. What she's struggling against, from childhood onward, is that cursory, pigeonholing glance that "places" her and forgets her; and who wouldn't sympathize with that? The most convincing scenes in the book are those where she attempts to involve herself in the causes of the '60s—signing petitions, joining marches—but is consistently excluded or ignored because she is a matron in sneakers, pushing a stroller: a middle-class white liberal woman, dime a dozen. . . .

She does avoid the temptation to end her story with the end of the '60s, on a note of glory; she admits that the '70s have seen a sort of slackening process. It is this new clear-eyed, steady view of hers that wins us over, finally. I started *Burning Questions* feeling edgy and suspicious, and some of my suspicions were confirmed; but I think that any book that so satisfyingly and believably portrays the altering of a character's life deserves to be read.

> *Anne Tyler, "After the Prom," in* Book World—The Washington Post *(© The Washington Post), March 26, 1978, p. G3.*

PEARL K. BELL

Will the women's movement survive its novelists? This question seems urgent in the wake of Alix Kates Shulman's new novel, "Burning Questions." Mrs. Shulman has undertaken to write not merely another of those vaguely fictionalized chronicles about the inchoate misery of a housewife-and-mother who finds her tongue and her freedom from patriarchal oppression after joining a consciousness-raising group; no, Mrs. Shulman aspires to loftier deeds than personal confession. With the story of a feminist leader who calls herself Zane IndiAnna (because she comes from Indiana), an early convert to women's liberation in the 1960's, she hopes to capture the apotheosis of radical feminism, an instructive exemplar who will be no less than the Representative Woman of our revolutionary times.

Mrs. Shulman has written "Burning Questions" in the form of Zane's autobiography so that her heroine will be endowed with prototypical stature. Its title ("My Life as a Rebel") and tone of didactic uplift are intended to echo the stirring autobiographies of such actual revolutionary women as Angelica Balabanoff (who also called her story "My Life as a Rebel"), Emma Goldman, Elizabeth Gurley Flynn, Mothers Bloor and Jones, Angela Davis, Vera Figner, and so on. At decisive moments of her narrative, Zane quotes her redoubtable predecessors as though to affirm her place in their legendary company, and when at the end of her book she provides a lengthy bibliography of these memoirs and other inspirational texts that changed her life (Marx, Engels, Lenin, Trotsky, Mao), she does not hesitate to include her own book. In her mind, it is now part of the gospel.

Zane seems to envision her liberated self as part Joan of Arc, part Emma Goldman, part Carol Kennicott, part Shirley MacLaine. Thus she is drawn and quartered. Not modest, she reminds us time and again that her grand design in recording the story of her life is "to reveal the causes and contours of our rebellion.". . .

Alix Kates Shulman spares her rebel girl not *one* of the currently fashionable lib-rad-fem simplicities and platitudes about politics and history, men and women. It is almost tempting to read "Burning Questions" as hilarious caricature, sly mockery of the radical feminist dedicated to a fault. But alas, Mrs. Shulman's earnest conviction is entirely unambiguous; she means every word of this ardent celebration of the women's movement. It is all straight from the heart, sentimental, doctrinaire and intellectually preposterous ("For a long time I hadn't read a single book by a male, though I knew I was probably depriving myself of several excellent works"), the sort of tract that could set back the cause of women's equality some 50 years and more. All unwitting, Mrs. Shulman has invented a heroine so irredeemably self-absorbed and simple-minded, so resentful and credulous, that she reinforces precisely those myths about women that she set out to demolish.

> *Pearl K. Bell, "Her Life as a Rebel," in* The New York Times Book Review *(© 1978 by The New York Times Company; reprinted by permission), March 26, 1978, p. 12.*

ELIOT FREMONT-SMITH

One of the burning troubles with [*Burning Questions*] is that it comes labeled "a novel." This makes one expect enticingly interesting character, artful movement of plot, efficiency of revelatory thought, etc.—all of which, along with a felicitous prose style, are missing. Humor isn't, but that's another problem. The book seems intended as a kind of way-we-are-now political statement—the saga of the development of a radical feminist consciousness over the last 20 years. One presumes that it is autobiographical. It is at times tongue-in-cheek. The heroine's name is Zane IndiAnna, and *Burning Questions* is her phrase, and this is meant to be her memoir and tract. But it is also, plainly, the author's—that is to say, it's serious business. This has the strange effect of making one feel out-of-line if one smiles, as if only the author could do that because she alone can do it in love of Zane, as if she alone can know precisely when Zane is being silly and when Zane is being brave. And, of course, it is at her direction. . . . It isn't a hateful book, and some will see it as intriguing, *clefy* history. But it isn't very good, either. As one of Zane's lovers notes (in a typically cute-macho way), Zane is "always thinking"; unfortunately, one's interest in the process depends somewhat on the quality of the results. Zane's are earnest but wanting—which makes me get irresponsible and giggly. But then ugliness sets in. For Zane's thoughts are only what Alix Kates Shulman has allowed; Shulman herself is off the hook (one can only guess what *she* thinks), and I am on. If winning players are always lucky, losers are set up—and *Burning Questions* is, for me, a losing game. I wish it hadn't been a novel. There is, of course, a lingering respect for the intentions of a plainer book, and for the hard-won consciousness

that this book is witness to. For the rest, sheepishly, with irritation, I must castle. (p. 69)

> *Eliot Fremont-Smith, in* The Village Voice *(reprinted by permission of* The Village Voice; *copyright © by The Village Voice, Inc., 1978), April 3, 1978.*

MICHELE TURIN

[*Burning Questions*] is a well-written and intelligent account of one woman's journey through befuddled and aspiring youth to satisfying and productive adulthood. In another way she reveals the saga of the women's movement—how we hope, how we struggle, how we survive, and even overcome. . . .

The book has its drawbacks. Many of the early pages' political references seem tedious. The main character has not been fully developed as yet, and much of this politicizing seems hollow pontification. . . . But these are minor points contrasted with Shulman's overall accomplishment.

She has written a forceful and articulate appraisal of one woman's transformation. It can be a guide to anyone slightly curious about the progress of the women's movement. It is bold, but it is thoughtful, too. (p. 109)

> *Michele Turin, in* Best Sellers *(copyright © 1978 Helen Dwight Reid Educational Foundation), July, 1978.*

*   *   *

SILLITOE, Alan   1928-

Sillitoe is an English novelist, short story writer, poet, translator, travel writer, playwright, screenwriter, and author of children's books. He explores in his fiction the violence born of futility among the working class. Society and its strictures are seen as a deadening force in Sillitoe's world, a theme that some critics have found to be handled in an overtly polemical and simplistic fashion in recent work. He has collaborated with his wife, Ruth Fainlight, on an adaptation of a play by Lope de Vega. (See also *CLC*, Vols. 1, 3, 6, and *Contemporary Authors*, Vols. 9-12, rev. ed.)

LAWRENCE R. RIES

Alan Sillitoe sees the violence of our present environment deriving from sociological conditions. His characters belong to the low classes and are in danger of losing what little identity they possess. Their lust for life throws them into open battle with the traditional elements of society—government, authority, middle and upper class people—and violence is a means of holding onto a world that is being destroyed. The individual feels himself the victim of technological production, impersonal war, governmental suppression. Violence, under these conditions, is a way for a person to demonstrate that he is still alive. (p. 30)

Sillitoe, more than any other contemporary novelist, sees violence as a valid and necessary expression in modern culture. . . . Because Sillitoe's heroes are trying to survive in a violent world, they react violently. The origin of their actions lies in sociological sources. (pp. 30-1)

> *Lawrence R. Ries, in his* Wolf Masks: Violence in Contemporary Poetry *(copyright © 1977 by Kennikat Press Corp.; reprinted by permission of Kennikat Press Corp.), Kennikat, 1977.*

GILBERTO PEREZ

[In *The Widower's Son*] Sillitoe sets up a metaphor which serves him throughout to tie together his story. It is the metaphor of life as battle, a man up against the world around him like a soldier facing an enemy. (p. 607)

[When William meets a woman at a party, he] drops all his tactics and makes a straight line for her, directly falling in love, proceeding to marry her soon afterwards. Getting the measure of that woman, Georgina, proves harder than charting any actual battlefield; the master gunner fails to keep his distance in the uncharted field of love, where secret forces he was unprepared to meet, assembled in a dead ground deadlier than he knew, wind up nearly destroying him. Strictly a male view, some will complain I suppose, this military metaphor with the woman cast as the enemy; but I found it a welcome change to have the break-up of a marriage, a subject mainly women write about these days, presented from the man's side. Sillitoe handles the point of view very nicely, staying with William most of the time but telling us just a little bit more about Georgina than William would know, so as to give us a sense of that ground hidden from him without dispelling its mystery. . . . It is not only the marriage which is seen as combat, but William's whole life, his upbringing by his soldier father, his actual fighting in the war, his civilian job running an entertainment center with a retired colonel's military efficiency, his facing in the end, as he loses the last battle against Georgina, the secret forces within himself. (p. 608)

> *Gilberto Perez, in* The Hudson Review *(copyright © 1977 by The Hudson Review, Inc.; reprinted by permission), Vol. XXX, No. 4, Winter, 1977-78.*

EDITH MILTON

The Widower's Son is . . . a novel about two generations of one family, and much of its main narrative covers . . . the period just after the war, which seems, for a great many English writers writing today, in its paradox of victory and decline, its upset hierarchies and devaluation of sacred trusts, to be a recognizable parallel for the aging and disillusionment of the individual. Certainly that is true of Sillitoe's novel, which traces the rise of William Scorton, grandson of a miner and son of an army sergeant, to the rank of Colonel, cuckold and madman on the easy path of the age.

Sillitoe . . . often writes about the isolation of the individual from society, and in a way *The Widower's Son* is about traveling too far and too fast from one's own origins. . . . The army, for Sillitoe, is the emblem of everything which tears men away from the earth, from nature, and from family. . . . [The] army divides [William] both from his historical place as a miner's grandson, earthy, lower-class, simple in his habits, and from his acquired position among the upper classes, educated into finer tastes, obsessed by his wife, Georgina. Though he loves his father and is in love with his wife, he understands neither.

In one scene, furious with Georgia, William punches her around "like a collier," in short, as his grandfather might have done. Throughout the novel there are references to historical cycles; to the past rising up to alter the perspective of the present. For William, the colliery is part of that past. But a more important part is his mother's death, which left him, while he was still a child, with only half a

history. *The Widower's Son* divides the world into two principles: a male principle of order, control, power, of which gunnery is an obvious and potent symbol; and a female principle of emotion, confusion, and passivity, of which Georgina is a rather extreme embodiment. (pp. 264-65)

Sillitoe's strength lies in making William and his father sympathetic and complex characters; in showing William's failings not as those of a martinet, though he speaks often of his own rigidity, but as an imbalance common to the species which one can recognize everywhere. Though Sillitoe tends to classify psychic qualities by gender, and though his novel centers on a struggle between the sexes, the incompleteness which causes that struggle is poignantly and quite comprehensively human. (p. 265)

> *Edith Milton, in* The Yale Review *(© 1977 by Yale University; reprinted by permission of the editors), Winter, 1978.*

* * *

SNODGRASS, W(illiam) D(e Witt)   1926-

Snodgrass is an American poet, critic, essayist, and translator. Although linked to the confessional school of poetry, Snodgrass prefers to view his work as a reaction against impersonal, intellectual poetry. His poetry, which is characterized by a straightforward poetic voice, is drawn from personal experience and frequently expresses anguish and despair. Snodgrass received the Pulitzer Prize in Poetry in 1960 for his first collection, *Heart's Needle*. (See also *CLC*, Vols. 2, 6, and *Contemporary Authors*, Vols. 1-4, rev. ed.)

GERTRUDE M. WHITE

Mr. Snodgrass's modest hope [for *In Radical Pursuit: Critical Essays and Lectures*]—"I hope my own essays lean toward a broader humanism (than that of the New Critics) —one less concerned with being right, and more concerned with enrichment"—[has] indeed been fulfilled. His personal involvement, his personal style, his conviction that "the world, and we ourselves, are far too complex to be accounted for in any political doctrine, philosophical doctrine, conscious ideation," his sense "that every important act in our lives is both propelled and guided by the darker, less visible areas of emotion and personality"—all [stand] triumphantly vindicated by the light he [sheds] on the processes of creation of literature and on the product of those processes, literature itself.

The "Four Personal Lectures" which make up the first section of this book are studies in how poetry achieves its effects. They deal with its nature, its material, and its aim; with its manipulation of words, of rhythms, of images to communicate the imaginative truth of experience with the greatest precision and power. Much of Mr. Snodgrass's material here comes from his own poems and the personal experiences which gave rise to them and which they reflect. With candor and sensitivity he discusses his own deepest feelings. With absolute integrity he uses these, not to exhibit himself or to comment on his own life, but to illuminate his subject; to show us how poetry is made, where it comes from, what it does and how. It is to make manifest this life of poetry that Mr. Snodgrass is concerned. His own life is merely a means to that end.

"Poems About Paintings," the last essay in this section,

seems to me an extraordinary achievement. I know of nothing quite like it. . . . What is really noteworthy is the poet's eye which sees the painting, the poet's sensibility which relates what he sees to his own deep, unconscious associations and motive, the poet's mind, cultivated, humane, wide-ranging, which links the painting and his own personal world to the larger world, outside, yet reflected in both. Art, history, philosophy, religion, psychology, the physical sciences: these brief thirty pages are a microcosm of the world in which we live, the world of thought and experience which shapes our perceptions and governs our lives, the world 'of which art, whether painting or poetry, is the expression and the revelation.

The essays which follow . . . are closer to what we usually think of as literary criticism. . . . But though the subject-matter is less personal, the point of view, the method, and above all the tone and manner remain unconquerably, and gloriously, Mr. Snodgrass's own. It is a manner that is personal without egotism, intimate yet objective, individual but obedient always to the facts, to the evidence of the text. In these studies the author draws on his own experience of psycho-analysis, on his insights into psychological truths, to illuminate levels of the work inaccessible to ordinary critical analysis. And the proof of point of view and method is that he *does* illuminate them, without distorting time-honored perspectives, without perverting plain sense and meaning. (pp. 373-74)

> *Gertrude M. White, in* Criticism *(reprinted by permission of the Wayne State University Press; copyright 1975 by Wayne State University Press), Vol. XVII, No. 4 (Fall, 1975).*

ROBERT W. DANIEL

The style of W. D. Snodgrass is not consistent enough to be readily categorized, and I am at a loss to account for his title, *In Radical Pursuit.* In a few essays, but not many, Snodgrass may be the pupil of, say, Ernest Jones. (p. xc)

In Radical Pursuit begins with "Four Personal Lectures" about contemporary poetry in general, and large parts of them concern the development of Snodgrass's own work. . . . Rightly defined, irony, in Brooks & Company's extended use of the term, is markedly similar to what Snodgrass praises as tact, in his essay "Tact and the Poet's Force." (pp. xci-xcii)

Six of the other essays in this collection plod their way through Roethke, Ransom . . . , Lawrence's "Rocking-Horse Winner," *A Midsummer Night's Dream, Don Quixote,* and the *Inferno.* I except the pieces on *Crime and Punishment* and on the gods in the *Iliad,* both of which quickened my interest and left me enlightened. Psychoanalytic criticism can be exasperating, applied to a work that is clear without it. But *Crime and Punishment* is a novel of perplexing motives and mysterious dreams; and Snodgrass, whose knowledge of Freudianism seems impressive at least to a reader with little of it, illuminates many of Dostoevsky's dark corners. . . .

These examples illustrate the miscellaneous nature of *In Radical Pursuit.* Literary criticism apparently is something for Snodgrass to dip into occasionally. (p. xcii)

> *Robert W. Daniel, in* Sewanee Review *(reprinted by permission of the editor;* © *1976*

by the University of the South), Summer, 1976.

HAROLD BLOOM

W. D. Snodgrass began in the shadow of Lowell's *Life Studies,* but with an individual lyricism that presaged a turn away from confessional verse. The turn is very evident in *The Führer Bunker* . . . , a cycle-in-progress of 20 dramatic monologues, spoken by Hitler, Goebbels, Eva Braun *et al.* . . . His audacity is more than matched by his astonishing skill in ordering his intractable material, and in combining his own inventions with the verifiable details of the last days of Hitler. Granted the immense difficulties he has taken on, Snodgrass demonstrates something of the power of a contemporary equivalent of Jacobean drama at its darkest. (p. 25)

> *Harold Bloom, in* The New Republic *(reprinted by permission of* The New Republic; © *1977 by The New Republic, Inc.), November 26, 1977.*

*   *   *

SOLZHENITSYN, Aleksandr I(sayevich)   1918-

A Russian novelist, short story writer, poet, dramatist, and critic, Solzhenitsyn now resides in the United States. His first novel, *One Day in the Life of Ivan Denisovich*, was the first exposé of Stalin's labor camps (in which Solzhenitsyn spent eight years) allowed published by the Soviet Central Committee. However, his persistent activities as a dissident and outspoken critic of literary censorship led to his expulsion from the Soviet Union in 1969 and the censorship of his subsequent publications in Russia. Rejecting the precepts of socialist realism, Solzhenitsyn writes from an unmistakably Christian point of view, depicting the suffering of the innocent in a world where good and evil vie for the soul of man. In this he is thematically linked to the great Russian writers of the nineteenth century. His writing, distinguished by its austere, simple style, is presented with compassion and moral concern. Solzhenitsyn continues to write in exile of the oppression in his own land, as well as to speak of his concern for the political and moral problems of the West. He received the Nobel Prize in 1970. (See also *CLC*, Vols. 1, 2, 4, 7, 9, and *Contemporary Authors*, Vols. 69-72.)

OCTAVIO PAZ

Solzhenitsyn is not only a critic of Russia and Bolshevism but of the modern age itself. What does it matter if that critique proceeds from presuppositions different from mine? . . . Solzhenitsyn speaks from another tradition and this, for me, is impressive: his voice is not modern but ancient. It is an ancientness tempered in the modern world. His ancientness is that of the old Russian Christianity, but it is a Christianity which has passed through the central experience of our century—the dehumanization of the totalitarian concentration camps—and has emerged intact and strengthened. If history is the testing ground, Solzhenitsyn has passed the test. His example is not intellectual or political nor even, in the current sense of the word, moral. We have to use an even older word, a word which still retains a religious overtone—a hint of death and sacrifice: *witness.* In a century of false testimonies, a writer becomes the witness to man. . . .

The Gulag Archipelago isn't a book of political philosophy but a work of history; more precisely, it is *a witnessing*—in the old sense of the word: the martyrs are witnesses.... (p. 7)

> *Octavio Paz, "Dust after Mud: Considering Solzhenitsyn" (originally published in* Plural *30, March 1974), translated by Michael Schmidt, in* PN Review (© *PN Review 1976), Vol. 4, No. 1, 1976, pp. 5-11.*

WILLIAM J. PARENTE

The temptation is to dismiss [*Prussian Nights*] as the mediocre poetry of a great novelist. Unlike Dante or Shakespeare, Solzhenitsyn is too concerned with catechesis to survive translation and transmutation into a culture significantly less friendly to poetry than the East European tradition from which he springs.

He has already tried his hand at other genre: two moderately successful plays, *Love Girl and the Innocent* and *Candle in the Wind,* as well as a number of short stories and prose poems....

What relates these secondary writings to the great novels and to *Gulag* is Solzhenitsyn's questioning of national and individual morality. He probes these problems much like a moral theologian pecking at a question of conscience or a surgeon sectioning a diseased organ....

Indeed, his pursuit of the problem of evil continues in Russian literature the tradition of Dostoyevsky and, in world literature, the tradition of the early Graham Greene and Böll.

The subject matter here—the Eastern front in January 1945—is related by irony and literary thread both to decisive events in Solzhenitsyn's life and to his previous *oeuvre.* His brief prose poem, "The Old Bucket," recalls but a moment during the War. His compelling short story, "Incident at Krechetovka Station," deals with the moral vagaries of war and a Soviet officer behind the lines. His *August 1914,* the first part of a historical trilogy climaxing in the Russian Revolution, which Solzhenitsyn has always regarded as his magnum opus, details the ebb and flow of life and death among German and Russian troops in East Prussia during a yet earlier war....

The work which most closely presages this present verse poem is the play, *Feast of Victors,* which depicts the behavior of Soviet troops toward German civilians during this 1945 period and which was suppressed by Solzhenitsyn himself for reasons which are still unclear but presumably pragmatic....

Prussian Nights is therefore more than merely an effort at sustained verse narrative. It touches on critical moments in the politicization of this mathematician-engineer with vague longings to pursue the study of history and eventually to become a writer of historical fiction.

The events described here apparently contributed greatly to Solzhenitsyn's revolutionary conclusion that personal morality transcended both nationality and ideology—a conclusion fatal to belief in either the pieties of Russian patriotism or the pretense of Soviet communism. The nights in Prussia seem to have been the beginning of the end of Solzhenitsyn as a Believer....

Solzhenitsyn typically sustains a ballad meter with alternating masculine and feminine rhymes throughout the 1500 lines, but variations are plentiful with meter and tempo changed for dramatic purposes.

Solzhenitsyn is no Dante—but then Solzhenitsyn's analysis of one-man government is considerably more sophisticated than *De Monarchia.* (p. 130)

> *William J. Parente, in* Best Sellers (*copyright* © *1977 Helen Dwight Reid Educational Foundation), August, 1977.*

JOHN BAYLEY

Can one imagine a famous British author bringing out a poem about his wartime experiences in the style of *Henry V,* or *Paradise Lost,* or *Childe Harold*? And having composed it while serving a ten-year prison sentence, committing it to memory, as he could not write it down? And, most unlikely of all, that it would be a marvellous poem, with some of the fiery freshness and energy of its great originals?

That, roughly speaking, is what Solzhenitsyn has done in *Prusskiye Nochi, Prussian Nights.* The title itself recalls Pushkin, who wrote a poetic fantasy called *Egyptian Nights....* And the metre is a freer version of Pushkin's agile rhyming octosyllabics that tear along like the wind, fiercely exultant, but with nothing crude or makeshift in the variety and flexibility of their rhythms. Solzhenitsyn is not a poet of today in the sense that Brodsky or Voznesensky are. He has no voice of his own. But his mastery of a common style and metre is so effective that it carries the reader irresistibly along. There is no trace of the synthetic tone, the inner failure of linguistic confidence, the usual mark of the amateur who avails himself of a traditional verse form....

It is the wild exhilaration of [the 1945 Russian advance on East Prussia] that is celebrated by ex-artillery-captain Solzhenitsyn, who rode along in it with his guns and the 60 men of his battery....

[Like] the beginning of the Gulag book, the poem stresses that to be with such an army was to have the illusion of getting away from the system and breathing the air of freedom. As Pushkin celebrated Russia in his matchlessly ebullient verses, and by doing so was able to ignore the dead hand of Nicholas I and his bureacracy, so Solzhenitsyn uses a similar style to celebrate the excitement of that advance to wreak revenge on the enemy's land....

But Solzhenitsyn's temperament is the opposite of Pushkin's or Blok's, and here his command of the verse is less serviceable, for though Pushkin can be reflective, even introspective, he is never in the least sententious, and to be so—in the best sense—is Solzhenitsyn's forte. He was not a novelist when he wrote the poem, perhaps he thought he was a poet—since *Evgeny Onegin* the two roles have always seemed to have a similar potential in Russia—and several episodes in the poem remind one of memorable things in his novels....

As the narrative proceeds, feelings of confusion and guilt become more evident amid the excitement, and the narrator strives to control or at least to rationalise them. A German communist baker brings bread and salt in a jubilant welcome to his liberators, and is promptly carted off by Field Security—no more trouble from *him.* Cows burn to death in a locked barn—*Ech milashi Vi ne nashi*—'poor dears, they aren't ours'. Civilians are casually shot down by seemingly amiable soldiers who sheepishly object, when remonstrated with: 'But Uncle, *krov za krov*—blood for blood—it's Moscow's order.' Finally, in a brilliant scene, the narrator's sergeant-major invites him to pick a woman he fancies from among the refugees in a barn. The NCO is crafty, paternal, guileful and yet respectable about it; the narrator shame-faced and uncertain. He takes the meek girl to bed and experiences the expected self-disgust:

> Have no fear . . . already
> Another's soul is on my soul.

There the poem abruptly ends. It bears all the marks of being autobiographical, the confused impression of a priggish, likeable and entirely comprehensible young man. . . .

And yet I am inclined to think this unexpected and fascinating poem is an interesting piece of evidence: it suggests that Solzhenitsyn is not really a born novelist, any more than he is a natural poet. He has a remarkable talent for making use of the rich traditional sources of Russian literature, in both fields; himself remaining—again in a Russian tradition—a polemicist and propagandist, prophet and voice of conscience.

> *John Bayley, "Marching through Prussia,"*
> *in* The Listener *(© British Broadcasting*
> *Corp. 1977; reprinted by permission of John*
> *Bayley), September 29, 1977, p. 400.*

ELIZABETH HARDWICK

In a small world, Solzhenitsyn sometimes appears too tall. I would not want to meet the striding Armageddon on the road, glowing as I imagine him to be with eschatological fires and accompanied by menacing dogs. Still, he is a great writer with great themes. The conditions of the retrograde Soviet Union, bad for the living writer, offer, in his case at least, a perverse propitiousness for the writing. There the world is, if nothing else, a *structure*.

I read again . . . two works. One fairly short, the beautiful story "Matronya's House" and the intense, brilliant "Cancer Ward"—a true novel, passionate, deep, in which the sufferings of the body and the punishment of the soul, the pain of private life and the diseases of political force are bound together by the knots of fate. An old-fashioned work of art, ruthlessly contemporary.

And all the others—the pyramids he has built of heavy stone, with the exquisite decorations hidden within. Solzhenitsyn's claim upon the spirit is immense, and I feel, as we used to chant in high school, "We needs must love the highest when we see it, not Lancelot, nor another." But Lancelot, still. (p. 3)

> *Elizabeth Hardwick, in* The New York
> Times Book Review *(© 1977 by The New*
> *York Times Company; reprinted by permission), December 4, 1977.*

LUELLEN LUCID

Western critics have been quick to analyze Aleksandr Solzhenitsyn's humanitarian concerns and brilliant development of the metaphorical novel. What has been lacking in discussions of Solzhenitsyn's works is an understanding of their relationship to Soviet literary tradition; his writings need to be placed in the context not only of the dissident movement but of Soviet literature as a whole. Solzhenitsyn's writings are neither simply an anachronistic return to critical realism with no relation to the Soviet literary experi-

ence . . . nor are they a natural development of "socialist realism." . . . (p. 498)

[The] Soviet literary experience of the thirties, forties, and fifties . . . had a profound, if negative, influence on Solzhenitsyn. Stalin's aesthetic doctrine of socialist realism, as established in 1932, embodies on a literary plane the social and political facets of Soviet life to which Solzhenitsyn is responding in his own fiction. A full appreciation of Solzhenitsyn must, therefore, take his reaction to the literary aspect of Soviet socialism into account. Moreover, it can be demonstrated that Solzhenitsyn's works evidence a strong concern with technical innovation; they constitute not only a "spiritual revolution" but also a rhetorical one. . . . [His] novels are a conscious reaction to Soviet literary doctrine, which they self-consciously subvert, satirize, and parody stylistically, structurally, and thematically.

Solzhenitsyn's rejection of totalitarian values and policies is conveyed in his novels not only by their explicit concern with the repressive nature of Soviet society and its "gulag archipelago" of prison camps but by a crucial displacement of the literary norms and conventions of socialist realism. . . . Estrangement from established literary form lies at the core of Solzhenitsyn's works, as his fiction depicts the conflict between the Soviet state and the political rebel through a stylistic examination of the literary conflict between socialist realism and critical realism.

The literary displacement accomplished by Solzhenitsyn is not a simple abandonment of the canons of socialist realism but rather a transformation of those principles. (pp. 498-99)

Socialist realism itself began as a rhetorical revolution designed to meet the needs of a socialist society. It displaced nineteenth-century realist literature and transformed Russian folk themes into a functional mythology that would further the ends of the revolutionary government. (p. 499)

Solzhenitsyn has achieved a revitalization of Russian literature by not only incorporating socializing modes of expression but baring them to show the tension which exists between the nineteenth-century novel and the montage techniques of twentieth-century fiction. He displaces the doctrine of socialist realism by "baring the device" which socialist realism has covertly employed, turning it against the Soviet regime stylistically and thematically. Through parody and contrast, he has exposed the totalitarian quality of its dicta and reversed its thematic content. While Solzhenitsyn's works follow the canons of socialist realism in their public intent and political subject matter, they effect a fundamental disruption of those canons in their thematic and stylistic reexamination of Soviet reality.

Socialist realist doctrine finds its counterpart in Solzhenitsyn's fiction, but crucially transformed. . . . Solzhenitsyn shares a sense of engagement in history with the exponents of socialist realism, but his works constitute an aesthetically expressed rebellion against their basic values. His art has the avowed intention of awakening the Soviet public to the truth about its reality rather than upholding the official version of social life. . . . Whereas socialist realism attempts to reduce complexity to simple-minded formulas and calls such art "proletarian literature," Solzhenitsyn deals with the complex issues of social life by depicting a microcosm of everyday Soviet existence. (p. 500)

The metaphorical quality of Solzhenitsyn's fiction resembles the mythologized portrayals of reality in works of socialist realism in its intention of drawing a personal response from the reader. (p. 501)

In order to address the social realities and political issues of his time, Solzhenitsyn utilizes literary forms associated with political action, but in contrast to socialist realism, Solzhenitsyn's objective is to negate the automatized conventions upheld by Soviet officialdom. His novels contain journalistic reportage, political statement, intellectual debate, and political satire, and the biting polemical and satirical style of his fiction lies at the core of Solzhenitsyn's rhetorical revolution against the Soviet state. Solzhenitsyn displaces a canon of socialist realism by reversing its intention. In place of the "Party line" type of political polemic offered by socialist realism, Solzhenitsyn provides a wide-ranging spectrum of political and philosophical positions, including the "Party line" itself.

The "positive heroes" of Solzhenitsyn's works are Russia's writers, who throughout its history have provided the Russian people with an "alternative government." . . . [The] writer-hero of Solzhenitsyn's works is depicted as an iconoclast, prophet, and truthteller; he is the ultimate and independent protector of human values and freedom. (pp. 501-02)

Although Solzhenitsyn's works have ideological concerns in common with those of socialist realism, they do not identify the author with any single character or point of view. This authorial estrangement from the characters and situations represents a displacement of socialist realism's mode of characterization and plot structure. The identification of author and hero that is made complete in socialist realism is reversed by Solzhenitsyn through a polyphonic structure which gives equal weight to each character as he appears rather than focusing on one particular character as "hero." The reader is forced to identify with a synthesis of the characters and hence with the author himself, who transcends them. In place of the "uplifting" plot of socialist realism with its "blank-faced optimism, decreed by officialdom," Solzhenitsyn's works are based on a dynamic of intellectual contestation where no easy answers or neat endings are provided for complacent readers. (p. 502)

Solzhenitsyn's revolt against the totalitarian nature of the Soviet state takes place on a linguistic level through his displacement of its slogans, clichés, and formulaic language. . . . For Solzhenitsyn, language that identifies truth with established truth and disavows its critical function is no longer capable of creating a literature. (pp. 502-03)

The German critic Theodor W. Adorno points out in *The Jargon of Authenticity* that "jargon reproduces on the level of the mind the curse which bureaucracy exercises in reality. It could be described as an ideological replica of the paralyzing quality of official functions." The "jargon" of socialist realism takes on exactly this symbolic role in Solzhenitsyn's works, linguistically expressing the repressive nature of Soviet society. . . .

The writer is particularly suited to the task of exposing Stalinist totalitarianism precisely because of the crucial role language has played in its perpetuation. . . . Solzhenitsyn defies the official discourse by using colloquial speech forms and depicting government policies in concrete human terms. (p. 503)

Solzhenitsyn's first novel, *One Day in the Life of Ivan Denisovich*, deals in an allegorical manner with the reversal of the individual from citizen to political prisoner. The Soviet prison camp serves as a microcosm of the society at large and metaphorically represents the repressive atmosphere which characterizes Soviet governance. All the features inherent in the automatization of Soviet life become explicit and obvious in the prison camp. The microcosm of the prison camp also demonstrates the ultimate similarity between "home" and "institution" in a society that has itself been turned into a prisonlike "total institution." Solzhenitsyn takes the socialist mythology of the "typical worker" and displaces it with the "typical prisoner" Ivan Denisovich, who at once typifies and exemplifies the characteristics of the Russian people. The reader is able to identify with the experiences of Ivan Denisovich whether or not he has himself been imprisoned, for the nonsensational, hour-by-hour description of the character's day suggests the institutionalized life of all Soviet citizens. . . .

The novel's portrayal of one "good" day in the life of a "typical" prisoner constitutes a reversal of socialist realism, which Solzhenitsyn underscores stylistically by referring to the prisoners familiarly through the consciousness of Ivan Denisovich while regarding the prison personnel and government officials impersonally as "they." By this stylistic device, Solzhenitsyn incorporates the reader into the world of the prisoners and alienates him from that of the officials. (p. 504)

Solzhenitsyn's use of prison slang also serves to estrange the reader from the established social order. Slang owes its origin and use to "the desire to break away from the commonplace, the stiff, or stuffy, the drab or trite, as imposed on us by the conventional community." It is the prisoners' symbolic protest against the status quo and the means for uniting themselves in their communal estrangement from the "normal" world. The language serves as a barrier between the prison-camp world and the "outside" world, and it puts a demand on the reader to enter into the prisoners' world on a linguistic level to share their dissociation from the "outside." Solzhenitsyn plunges the reader into the prison environment through this linguistic device and provides a contrast between the creative expressiveness of the prisoners and the formulaic language of the officials. Linguistically as well as thematically, the author has transformed the prison camp into an allegorical presentation of Soviet society and has provided a symbolic model of opposition to its dictates. (pp. 504-05)

As in *One Day in the Life of Ivan Denisovich*, Solzhenitsyn makes use of the folk idiom in *The First Circle* by presenting his moral opposition to Stalinism in the form of peasant wisdom. The peasant Spiridon possesses the most self-assured sense of individual conscience and communicates his instinctive ethical stance to the less self-confident intellectual Nerzhin, a fellow prisoner at the scientific institute. . . . Just as the simple-minded figure of Ivan Denisovich becomes elevated to the status of a Russian Everyman, Spiridon assumes the role of moral spokesman by providing the homely answer to Nerzhin's prolonged spiritual quest to comprehend and cope with Stalinism: the cannibal or "people-eater" who kills his own people indiscriminately is wrong, whereas the wolfhound who kills only what is wantonly destructive (the wolf) is right. Solzhenitsyn uses the word "people-eater" instead of using the normal Russian word for cannibal, which would only connote "eater-of-one's-own-kind," in order to emphasize the peculiarly inhuman nature of Stalinism. The peasant proverb thus displaces the "folk sayings" of socialist realism and provides a philosophy that justifies moral opposition to Stalinism. (pp. 505-06)

Solzhenitsyn introduces into [*The First Circle*] actual historical personalities, including that of Stalin himself, transforming the remoteness of history and public life into an accessible reality for the reader. To do this, Solzhenitsyn employs modes of political satire and parody, reenacting the mentality of the bureaucrats in their language and thereby exposing the falsity of their attitudes. Solzhenitsyn reproduces Stalin's manner of expression in which every sentence contradicts the next. . . . In a chapter entitled "Language Is a Tool of Production," Solzhenitsyn attacks the rhetorical fraudulence of Stalinism most explicitly by imitating Stalin's thought processes in a journalistic manner. He assumes that the evilness of Stalin's "ideas" is revealed by the rhetoric he employs to express them, so that the author need only "report" them factually for the truth to become apparent. (p. 506)

In *The First Circle,* a character states that "a great writer . . . is, so to speak, a second government." . . . The figure of the writer enters this novel as a crucial moral force that sustains the prisoners in their convictions and lends others the courage to listen to the voice of conscience. . . . The artist is a prototype of the two possible reactions to Stalinism and their consequences; acquiescence is shown to lead to loss of creative freedom and talent, while rejection brings loss of physical freedom but preservation of conscience and imagination. (p. 507)

Cancer Ward, even more than Solzhenitsyn's other novels, presents the everyday reality of Soviet life in a metaphorical setting with which the reader can easily identify himself. The characters, ex-prisoner and official, face the common enemy of illness, which behaves as a social leveler and unites those with divergent backgrounds and politics in a common struggle. The setting of the cancer ward, while it should not be construed as simply a metaphor for Soviet society, does supply the symbolic basis for a novel concerned with the political and spiritual "health" of a society that has recently undergone the grave "illness" of Stalinism. . . . The cancer ward functions symbolically as the tuberculosis sanatorium does in Thomas Mann's novel, *The Magic Mountain,* where the political inference is to Europe's "health" as it is about to plunge into the senseless conflict of the First World War. (pp. 508-09)

As in the previous novels, the artist functions as a positive moral force in *Cancer Ward.* A work of literature is shown to exercise a profound effect on the patients, particularly the terminal ones. The epicurean Podduyev finds the means for accepting his impending death in Tolstoy's *What Men Live By,* although previously he had been unable to "see the use of books in his everyday life." . . . Solzhenitsyn satirizes the "socialist realists" and contrasts the irrelevance of their "message" to people's real needs with the impact of Tolstoy's work on even the unliterary Podduyev. When a writer fails to relate his work to his reader's reality, it becomes a meaningless jumble of words. (p. 509)

Solzhenitsyn mimics the formulaic approach of the socialist realist in his portrayal of the writer Aviette. Aviette an-

nounces her main literary objective to be avoidance of any "ideological mistakes." . . . Solzhenitsyn's satire of socialist realism, while stylistically farcical and journalistic, is nonetheless composed of the very slogans and clichés mouthed by the Stalinists. . . . In his mimicry of socialist realism, Solzhenitsyn adopts its rhetorical style, just as he reproduced Stalin's rhetoric in *The First Circle* to expose the ruler's mentality. He has displaced its conventions simply by repeating them in a satirical context.

The socialist realist convention of the "positive hero" is undercut in *Cancer Ward* by Solzhenitsyn's creation of an "anti-hero," who provides a parallel to the characteristics of the Soviet hero. The character Kostoglotov serves as the embodiment of the aftereffects of Stalinism; his submissive attitude brought about by years of imprisonment and harsh treatment poses an ironic counterpart to the socialist realist ideal. (pp. 509-10)

The "uplifting" ending of socialist realism is displaced in *Cancer Ward* by its circular plot structure. Just as there is no resolution to the problems posed in Solzhenitsyn's other novels, *Cancer Ward* ends without having the "anti-hero" overcome his submissive state of mind. (p. 510)

As a documentary presentation of the effects of Stalinism, *Gulag Archipelago* contributes a new dimension to Solzhenitsyn's writings, but, like his fiction, it constitutes a displacement of the canons of socialist realism, in this instance, those applying specifically to nonfiction or "documentary" writing. . . . The thematic ambiguity of the fictional works and the complexity contained within their polyphonic form is missing from the tendentious tone of this documentary on the Soviet prison-camp system. . . .

Gulag Archipelago is a crucial displacement of the Literature of Fact ("literatura fakta") literary movement as practiced under socialist realism, which considers nonfiction writing, particularly the diary, autobiography, memoir, and journalism, to be a high literary form. The purpose of such nonfiction writing is to provide a "collective" history of the revolution and the progress of socialism; documentary writing has a duty to advocate a specific cause and organize the "facts" for a specific social purpose. The Literature of Fact movement initiated in the twenties emphasizes the importance of daily events as opposed to the "fanciful" and subjective concoctions of the artist. (p. 511)

In *Gulag Archipelago,* Solzhenitsyn makes reference to *The White Sea Canal,* written by thirty-six Soviet writers including Gorky, which is an example of the journalistic sketch of Soviet progress. Its aim is to glorify the use of slave prisoner labor in large construction projects and the "social rehabilitation" and "moral reformation" which the prison system exercised upon political prisoners and criminals alike. . . . Nonfiction socialist realism, like its fictional counterpart, is given the task of laying out the "objective" facts of the great social tasks of the day, and the result is a romanticized and polemical description of Soviet society.

Gulag Archipelago is not only a rebuttal of the Soviet documentary but makes use of its techniques and tone by turning prison memoirs and journalistic history into an exposé of the Soviet regime. In its use of memoirs and journalism, in its emphasis on the collective nature of the history, and in its polemical counter-documentation and argumentation, *Gulag Archipelago* clearly displaces the Literature of Fact movement much as Solzhenitsyn's novels displace socialist realism. (pp. 511-12)

Solzhenitsyn's documentary writing constitutes an extension of the historical basis of his previous works of fiction. He alternates between a "bird's-eye view" of his country's recent history, providing an extensive survey of how Soviet law developed, and an autobiographical "worm's-eye view" that authenticates the impersonal history with intimate testimony from himself and other prisoners. As in his fictional works, Solzhenitsyn organizes his historical material metaphorically, thereby personalizing it and making it more accessible to his reader. The book is unified by the image of the "archipelago," a series of "islands" strung out across Russia whose inhabitants are drawn—often arbitrarily—from all segments of Soviet society.... Throughout *Gulag Archipelago*, Solzhenitsyn emphasizes the image of the latrine bucket, "the symbol of prison, a symbol of humiliation, of stink." ... Unlike the unifying metaphor of *Cancer Ward*, with its Mannian overtones, and that of *The First Circle*, with its Dantesque aura, the pervasive use of the latrine metaphor undercuts in a caustic and naturalistic, almost brutal, manner the grandiose pretentions of the Soviet state.

As he does in his fiction, Solzhenitsyn stresses the collective nature of the history in order to incorporate the reader into the situation he is depicting and force him to assume moral responsibility for what happened. Solzhenitsyn offers his own personality through autobiographical references, making himself a surrogate for his entire generation.... Solzhenitsyn introduces his own memoirs as a typical example of the mass experience which his history documents, in contrast to the idealized abstraction of the "typical" worker in the socialist realist tract. The attention to personal pronouns takes on painful intensity in *Gulag Archipelago*, as "you" is not only directed at the contemporary Soviet reader but is also used rhetorically to fuse the reader and the victim being described. The pronoun "we" emerges with genuine force in joining the reader and writer in their mutual responsibility for shared guilt and moral duty; it is no longer acceptable simply to blame "them."

An ironic tension is maintained throughout the work by alternating between the "official" point of view and Solzhenitsyn's personally authenticated experience.... Solzhenitsyn resorts here to the rhetorical device of exaggeration in his contrast of Soviet and tsarist prisons, much as he did in *The First Circle*. Once again, his own account provides the rhetorical reverse image of the socialist realist perspective. (pp. 513-14)

Solzhenitsyn has transformed each of the canons of socialist realism through the themes, style, and structure of his writings. He accepts the socialist realist premise that art is a social act but posits a critical rather than conformist social function for it. In his use of folk themes and in the metaphorical quality of his works, he attempts to reach the Russian public with images and situations sufficiently limited and familiar to make a personal impact on the reader and spur him to a critical social consciousness. The premise that art should instill in the reader a sense of social interconnectedness is also implicit in Solzhenitsyn's works, as he explores both the negative and positive effects of this sense of community. On the one hand, he portrays the complicity of an entire society in the policies perpetrated in its name, and on the other hand, the necessity for communal acknowledgment of this complicity and acceptance of individual responsibility as the basis for a more honest and open political system.

As in the works of socialist realism, Solzhenitsyn achieves his social purpose by utilizing socializing modes of expression, and his writings share the polemical orientation of socialist realism. In place of the "positive hero" who mindlessly upholds the Soviet state, Solzhenitsyn provides the writer-hero whose role is to exemplify an ethical and independent outlook. He also creates an "anti-hero" who serves as an ironic parallel to the acquiescent "positive hero" of socialist realism. In contrast to the "uplifting" plot structure of socialist realism, the inconclusiveness of Solzhenitsyn's novels demonstrates the problematical nature of opposition to the regime. In both his nonfiction and his fiction, Solzhenitsyn maintains the values of truth, sincerity, and completeness in opposition to the standards set by socialist realism. On a linguistic level, Solzhenitsyn attacks the totalitarian quality of Soviet society through mimicry and parody of its literary and political discourse. The profound displacement which may at any time overtake the ordinary citizen and suddenly transform him into a political exile—a reversal Solzhenitsyn knows through personal experience—is conveyed through this displacement of Soviet literary norms and values to give us the world seen anew through that reversal. (p. 515)

> Luellen Lucid, "Solzhenitsyn's Rhetorical Revolution," in Twentieth Century Literature (copyright 1978, Hofstra University Press), December, 1977, pp. 498-517.

KONSTANTIN BAZAROV

[The Second World War] is the only major experience of Solzhenitsyn's life that has been conspicuously absent from his work. But it is the subject of *Prussian Nights*.... Poetically it is not very distinguished, so that as in Longfellow's poems the main interest is in the story, since the traditional metre does indeed carry the narrative effectively along....

[This] is the very reverse of a patriotic poem. While he was in East Prussia, Solzhenitsyn was arrested for criticising Stalin's conduct of the war, and sentenced to eight years' hard labour. Not, in the light of the horrifying events of this century which many millions of us have seen and endured, a particularly terrible experience to have to suffer. But it is the central experience which has moulded Solzhenitsyn's vision, so that Stalin and Communism have become for him the one great enemy. He ignores the far worse horrors of Nazism, and this is why the war is in fact the one major experience of his life that he has barely written about, since it cannot without total distortion be fitted into his picture of Stalin as devil. But the extraordinary thing about this war poem is that it completely reverses the actual situation, so that you would think that the Russians were invading innocent Germans instead of repelling a war of annihilation at the cost of enormous sacrifice. (p. 32)

Solzhenitsyn has often stressed the moral duty of the writer to tell the truth. And in this poem too he attacks Ehrenburg as 'senior ham of the lot.... If we win they'll neatly varnish the whole tale....' This then is Solzhenitsyn's claim, as it has consistently been in the past—that he is unique in giving us the past without *lakirovka* ('varnishing')—the plain unvarnished truth. But Solzhenitsyn's truth is a highly selective and one-sided one which can be refuted by consulting the work of any reputable German historian....

Solzhenitsyn thinks of himself as correcting a one-sided view of history. But to attempt to do that by offering an inverted but even more one-sided view of history is a contribution merely to polemic and invective. (p. 33)

Konstantin Bazarov, in Books and Bookmen *(© copyright Konstantin Bazarov 1978; reprinted with permission), April, 1978.*

*   *   *

SONTAG, Susan   1933-

Sontag is an American novelist, short story writer, screenwriter, essayist, film director, and critic. She is better known as a critic of contemporary art forms than as a writer of fiction. In one of her best known and most controversial works, *Against Interpretation*, Sontag established her precepts for the evaluation of art. She wrote that art must be responded to with the sensory, not the intellectual, faculties, with greater emphasis given to the form rather than the content of a work. This philosophy is reflected in her novels, notably *The Benefactor* and *Death Kit*. Sontag collaborated with Philip Rieff on *Freud: The Mind of the Moralist*. (See also *CLC*, Vols. 1, 2, and *Contemporary Authors*, Vols. 17-20, rev. ed.)

LOUIS D. RUBIN, JR.

Whatever became of Camp, both High and Low? A few years ago, before the Revolution became the fashion in New York, there was a period when just about all you heard out of our literary marketplace was talk of the virtues of Camp. The utterances of its high priestess Susan Sontag were being greeted with the kind of adulation previously reserved for such critics and sages as W. H. Auden, Marianne Moore, Simone de Beauvoir, and Norman Mailer. For a half-dozen years or so she had all the editors charmed with her particular brand of fashionable antiintellectualism. She could toss together a whipped syllabub of Robbe-Grillet, *Marat/Sade,* and Josef von Sternberg, garnished with phrases like ''the poetry of transvestitism'' and ''moral and aesthetic tact,'' that made her every printed observation a cultural event. But now the vogue for High and Low Camp has recessed into our cultural annals along with that for Krazy Kat and Significant Conversions. Ms. Sontag, I gather, has taken to writing novels, and the Beatles have long since been sprung for dope.

It is too bad, in a way. There was a delightful innocence about Camp and its followers that I found intriguing. It was determinedly and doggedly antiintellectual, in a very, very intellectual way. Its devotees were trying so hard not to seem Profound, though there was really no danger at all of that, and yet they couldn't help but intellectualize everything, because they knew no other mode of perception. Miss Sontag's program was very simple: she was against thinking. But she was not really antiintellectual. Indeed in a way she was the very epitome of intellectuality: she was all ideas, and her emotions were not so much felt as thought. She got her thrills out of abstractions, which she reified into attitudes. The kind of thinking she was against was the kind that attempted to make sense of ideas. She did not want to make sense out of anything: she preferred to revel in concepts, treating them as if they were form-fitting silken garments, to be enjoyed for the snugness and the sheen. What she affected to be for was emotion, feeling, texture; she wanted her art to reveal the Thingness of the world, she said. What she actually favored was an approach whereby one inserted an idea into a work of art like an aluminum mold onto an expanse of cookie dough. One then extracted

the thing, placed it in the oven to be baked and browned to taste, and what one got was a piece of shaped intellectual pastry which supposedly *was* the work of art. Well, it wasn't, because any work of art worth paying attention to isn't an expanse of malleable cookie dough to be cut into pretty shapes. To get anything worthwhile out of it one has to concern oneself with all of it, and not force one's own little idea-forms onto it. (pp. 503-04)

I would insist that, for all her dauntless talk, Susan Sontag is not really an exponent of pure feeling in the arts. Erotics aside she is purveying ideas, not emotions. They are not always complex ideas, to be sure; but Sontag is an intellectual all the way. (p. 508)

Miss Sontag [makes] the statement that taste is not ephemeral, subjective whim but compounded of intelligence and knowledge, and yet at the very next moment she is asserting that there is no kind of evidence that can be employed to prove it. The first statement is an idea, not an emotion. The second statement is an illogical contradiction of the idea. Miss Sontag is living by an idea, but it is not much of an idea, as such things go; still it *is* an idea.

That's what is wrong with so much of what she offers us in *Against Interpretation*. Her aesthetic, her approach to the arts are based on a few ideas, but once she asserts them, she gets emotionally excited over them, and goes about reifying them all over the place. In the reification she can be monstrously clever and most engaging, but when you get down to the text, all she is doing is—to quote what she says about some critics—mucking around in the sensuous surfaces. (p. 510)

Louis D. Rubin, Jr., ''Susan Sontag and the Camp Followers,'' in Sewanee Review *(© 1974 by The University of the South), Summer, 1974, pp. 503-10.*

WILLIAM H. GASS

[*On Photography*] is a thoughtful meditation, not a treatise, and its ideas are grouped more nearly like a gang of keys upon a ring than a run of onions on a string. (p. 7)

Every page of ''On Photography'' raises important and exciting questions about its subject and raises them in the best way. In a context of clarity, skepticism and passionate concern, with an energy that never weakens but never blusters, and with an admirable pungency of thought and directness of expression that sacrifices nothing of subtlety or refinement, Sontag encourages the reader's cooperation in her enterprise. Though disagreement at some point is certain, and every notion naturally needs refinement, every hypothesis support, every alleged connection further oil, the book understands exactly the locale and the level of its argument. Each issue is severed at precisely the right point, nothing left too short or let go on too long. So her book has, as we say, a good head: well cut, perfectly coiffed, uniform or complete in tone or color, with touches of intelligence so numerous they create a picture of photography the way those grains of gray compose the print.

Sontag's comments on the work of Diane Arbus are particularly apt and beautifully orchestrated, as she raises the level of our appreciation and understanding of these strange photographs each time, in the course of her exposition, she has occasion to remark upon them. But these six elegant and carefully connected essays are not really about individual photographers, nor solely about the art, but rather about the act of photography at large, the plethora of the product, the puzzles of its nature. (pp. 7, 30)

Instead of a text accompanied by photographs, Susan Sontag has appended to her book a collection of quotes, framed by punctuational space and the attribution of source. These are clipped from their context to create, through collage, another context—yet more words. And for a book on photography that shall surely stand near the beginning of all our thoughts upon the subject, maybe there is a message, a moral, a lesson, in that. (pp. 30-1)

> *William H. Gass, "A Different Kind of Art," in* The New York Times Book Review (© *1977 by The New York Times Company; reprinted by permission), December 18, 1977, pp. 7, 30-1.*

RICHARD KUCZKOWSKI

[In *On Photography* Sontag suggests that] photography is an aggressive, appropriating act (one shoots/takes a picture) which "makes reality atomic, manageable, opaque . . . denies interconnectedness, continuity . . . confers on each moment the character of a mystery." Alienating us from direct experience, the photo provides a more intense second-hand experience, an illusion of knowledge; essentially discrete, disjunct, mute, ahistorical, the photo cannot tell the truth that comes only from words and narration. Photography levels hierarchies, fosters seeing for seeing's sake. . . . Along with modernizing and surrealizing our perspective on reality, however, the camera also consumerizes it. The world becomes "a department store or museum-without-walls in which every subject is depreciated into an article of consumption, promoted into an item for aesthetic appreciation." And governments exploit the photographic image as another medium for capitalist ideologies. . . .

Sontag's six essays—really linked meditations or even prose poems—all take up these themes again and again, placing them in progressively more complex contexts, squeezing (now and then with visible strain) every bit of significance out of each disquieting aspect of the photographic image and its ambiguous but potent force in the modern consciousness. There are no illustrations here, just lean prose studded with tight-mouthed, provocative aphorisms (the intellectual's equivalent of the stand-up comic's one-liners): "All photographs are *memento mori*. To take a photograph is to participate in another person's (or thing's) mortality, vulnerability, mutability." . . . (p. 88)

A splendid performance—intellectual pinball on the French model where the goal is to keep a subject in play for as long as possible, racking up a brilliant score of cultural references and profound (if somewhat obscure) *mots*. Yet *On Photography* is less self-consciously self-advertising than that; more disenchanted with pure esthetics, less against interpretation than one might have expected. It is, finally, a moralistic (Marxist persuasion) indictment of our common lot as "image junkies." The last sentences of Sontag's book call for an ecology of images without specifying the meaning of that term. Rather than mindless delight and preservation (save the seals! save the snapshots!) or puritanical proscription (only the pure may survive!), *On Photography*'s analytical exposé of the dynamics and extent of our addiction should serve as a definition by example of such an ecology. (pp. 88-9)

> *Richard Kuczkowski, in* Commonweal *(copyright © 1978 Commonweal Publishing Co., Inc.; reprinted by permission of Commonweal Publishing Co., Inc.), February 3, 1978.*

GEORGE P. ELLIOTT

If photography were in fact the primary subject of [*On Photography*], one would be obliged to take exception to the many omissions and odd emphases to be found in it. Susan Sontag says everything worth saying about Diane Arbus's grotesquerie, almost nothing about Ansel Adams's photographs (though she does sneer at some of his prose), and nothing valuable about Dorothea Lange; she finds Richard Avedon interesting but does not mention Wright Morris (who in *God's Country and My People* combines words and photographs better than anyone else has ever done). . . . Moreover, if this book were really about photography one would look closely at some of the outrageous assertions she flashes about, in the manner of French intellectuals: "the way photography inexorably beautifies". Does it indeed? "Cameras are . . . a means of appropriating reality and a means of making it obsolete." A very jazzy notion. But since photography is secondary to the main theme of this book, such oddities as these are not lapses but strategies in an altogether other argument. . . .

Sontag observes that, after . . . Arbus killed herself, "the attention her work has attracted . . . is of another order [from what it had been before]—a kind of apotheosis. The fact of her suicide seems to guarantee that her work is sincere, not voyeuristic, that it is compassionate, not cold". This is an accurate observation of what in fact happened, and Sontag accurately "places" Arbus as a Surrealist, intense but very narrow.

However, note the "seems to guarantee" in the above quotation. Seems to whom—to the world at large, to Arbus's admirers, to all or some of those alert to current attitudes towards art and/or photography? More important, does it seem that way to Sontag herself? She is usually very slippery in this respect, as she is here, being able to claim or disavow ideas at her convenience so that, quite often, to pin her down is to appear ridiculous in the eyes of her camp.

When she comes to discuss a far more substantial photographer, Dorothea Lange, Sontag slurs her in a way she never slurs Arbus. . . . For Sontag, I believe, Lange's sin for which there can be no forgiveness was to go out of date; what Sontag despises as "humanism", all right in the 1930s, has become passé in the 1970s. . . .

Perhaps her interest in this book is only partly with the zeitgeist, as it is only partly with photography; perhaps she is out not to describe new trends so much as to promulgate a new doctrine.

In two areas she is absolute, is totally unironic: America is bad (except for the special few who like herself know both that and how it is bad), and revolutionary (as opposed to Soviet) Marxists are good. . . .

[She], who often in this book demonstrates her capacity to make fine aesthetic distinctions, also espouses what she calls the "modernist" view that "all art aspires to the condition of photography"—this after having argued that "the media blur, if they do not abolish outright", distinctions between authentic and fake, good taste and bad. . . .

Making distinctions is what thinking does. This book self-destructs. Reading it intensifies, gives the authority of high fashion to, that despairing, never-resting confusion which is endemic in this age, that moral perplexity, that cultural uncertainty. Sontag seductively encourages you to prefer the ugly to the beautiful, the trivial to the magnificent, slovenly workmanship to elegant. That this is fashionable, such a fad as punk rock leaves no doubt. Neither do I doubt that when such frenetic confusion becomes intense enough it can be allayed by no partial, compromising remedies but only by absolute, total ones. Indeed, there was a name for one such remedy: The Final Solution. In the *Partisan Review* for Winter 1967, she wrote: "The white race *is* the cancer of human history." There is only one thing to do about a cancer, right? Destroy it. Destroy or be destroyed. That is implicit in the metaphor. If Hitler or Idi Amin had said this, one would know how to take it, but since it was the High Priestess of the New Sensibility, one is supposed to think she did not really mean it that way at all. . . .

Sontag is right: America, the West, is spiritually in a bad way, its morale is dreadful. But by authorizing a nihilistic confusion for which a likely relief is totalitarianism (heavy drugs relieve it too), her writing becomes more than just analytic of what is wrong; it is symptomatic and causative as well.

Not always, however: at the end of an essay on the metaphorical uses of disease which appeared after this review was written (*New York Review of Books,* February 23), she accurately identifies the totalitarian implications of applying the cancer metaphor to social ills and reproaches herself for having done this in the sentence I quote. Furthermore, she identifies as her motive for doing this her intense distress over American involvement in Vietnam. If she were always as responsible in the use of her intellect as she is in this recent essay, High Fashion would be lucky to have her as its Queen.

> *George P. Elliott, "High Prophetess of High Fashion," in* The Times Literary Supplement (© *Times Newspapers Ltd. (London) 1978; reproduced from* The Times Literary Supplement *by permission), March 17, 1978, p. 304.*

MAREN STANGE

[Sontag] attributes her essays [in *On Photography*] to "my obsession with photography" and expresses herself often in the language of disease. She particularly favors "addiction" and "pollution"—"Industrial societies turn their citizens into image-junkies; it is the most irresistible form of mental pollution"—and "compulsive consumption"—"We consume images at an ever faster rate and . . . images consume reality." Evidently, her intention is to tell what she has learned from her own forced closeness.

In choosing to deal with what William Gass aptly calls "the act of photography at large," Sontag associates herself with a group of writers on photography that includes Hawthorne, Baudelaire, Oliver Wendell Holmes, Moholy-Nagy, James Agee, Richard Rudisill, and, of course, Walter Benjamin. A major difficulty in dealing with the subject defined at large, which can only increase as consciousness of the number and kinds of photography increases, is the tendency to look at photography as an abstraction. Such an approach treats the entire medium and craft process as if it

were simply a self-contained aesthetic object or performance functioning with reference to concrete purposes and situations.

Sontag, as her title suggests, takes this approach. But because of the number and variety of topics she addresses, however hastily, the result is not all bad. Some of her generalizations are very descriptive: a lot of photography *is* "class tourism." . . . But other of her generalizations do not succeed, at least for me. Photography does not "supply [my] pocket relation to the past," and I do not think the "act of taking pictures" is always "a semblance of rape." I expect that other people with opinions about photography feel the same way. Each of us likes and dislikes certain phrases, probably not the same ones. In Sontag's case, the abstraction of photography has the effect of insuring that approval or disapproval of her assertions remains on an arbitrary and subjective level. . . .

An irritating feature of the book is the dozens of thumbnail sketches of trivial yet unfamiliar aspects of popular culture —"For politicians the three-quarter gaze is more common: a gaze that soars rather than confronts." But the necessity for such banal descriptions faces any writer on popular culture.

More important, Sontag's actual topics are difficult to discern, so her arguments are hard to follow. Although her essays often seem to refer to traditional disciplines, especially history and aesthetics, they do not have a clear design or outline. Their structure is not the result of disciplined thinking.

For example, the second essay, "America, Seen through Photographs, Darkly," begins on a historical note with Walt Whitman and "photography's early decades [when] photographs were expected to be idealized images." It mentions Steichen, Stieglitz, Hine, and Evans and continues on to deal with more or less contemporary photographers. A discussion centered on Diane Arbus compares her "anti-humanist" images to the work of others, including Frank, Brassai, Buñuel, Steichen, and Lartigue. A reconsideration of "Whitman's discredited dream of cultural revolution" ends the piece. As historical account, this writing is very bad. . . . As history, the essay is at best superficial and at worst wrong. It bears little resemblance to the exacting discoveries offered by historical argument.

What of the aesthetics, art history, and epistemology? Sontag writes of August Sander's *Men Without Masks*, "his complicity with his subjects is not naive (like Carell's) but nihilistic. Despite its class realism, it is one of the most truly abstract bodies of .work in the history of photography." And, "The true modernism is not austerity but a garbage-strewn plentitude." And, "The photographer is willy-nilly engaged in the enterprise of antiquing reality, and photographs are themselves instant antiques."

Given Sontag's eminence, it is not unfair to compare these phrases to the painstaking and richly complex work on realism, class and otherwise, carried out by Linda Nochlin and T. C. Clarke, to Fredric Jameson's recent suggestions about new ways of understanding the relations among realist art, modernist art, and politics, and to Walter Benjamin's resolute efforts to place photographic form and content irrevocably in an adequate ideological context. But such comparisons only serve to suggest that Sontag is an intellectual who likes metaphors and photography but does not care about history or aesthetics.

Writers who accept the challenge of disciplined argument also receive, automatically, a universe of discourse in which they may exist. We trust them as we note their careful references that relate them to this shared universe. Sontag does not accept such limitations and definitions of her discussion. As a result, what momentarily seems brilliant and interesting in her language turns cloying and insipid, untrustworthy and banal. . . .

The language is derivative and full of fashionable jargon used for its own sake. It lacks the emphasis that might give resonance to complex terms like colonization and rationalization. . . . Sontag's style is without the integrity and moral clarity of Benjamin's critical effort.

My own frustration with *On Photography* is considerable. The history of photography in Western culture is little known and for the most part completely misunderstood. The tendency of virtually all twentieth-century photographic critics (except Benjamin's two or three relevant pieces) has been to "elevate" the photograph to the solitary eminence of an artwork. Criticism divorces the photograph from its text or caption, and thus from its original function and reality, in order to "understand" it. This reification of photography has distorted our understanding in such a way that only the historian's effort to reunite photographs with their original contexts and functions will right matters fundamentally enough to permit truly useful aesthetic, social, and historical discussion. This discussion, capable of posing many questions about photographic intention, function, and interpretation, can reveal photography as equally resonant, interesting and complex as any original and significant human endeavor. Despite its length and putative seriousness, Sontag's book does not initiate or prepare the reader for such critical efforts.

Sontag touches on many legitimate issues concerning photography. They are as current and fun to talk about as were television in the fifties and big American cars in the sixties. But to treat these, rather than take on deeper, more essential issues, makes for good journalism and not serious criticism. And, rather like a brilliant columnist, Sontag willingly confuses public and private, self and society, in order to achieve an adequate subject. Her essays are, ultimately, simply intellectualizations of her own responses. She can carry them off because she is an intellectual, but her status and eminence do not automatically validate them as useful work furthering the interests of a serious understanding of photography.

> *Maren Stange, "Susan Sontag: Recycling the Self," in* New Boston Review *(copyright 1978 by Boston Critic, Inc.), Spring, 1978, p. 12.*

MAGGIE SCARF

Sontag's *Illness as Metaphor* is a message sent to us from someone who has sojourned in what she calls "the kingdom of the sick." It is not, however, a personal statement about what can be learned by living there; rather, it is a plea from the ill to the healthy for nondiscrimination against the citizens who live there—specifically those people who happen to be suffering from cancer. In a careful, scholarly, and yet passionate argument, the author compares our own century's most dreaded and feared disease with the 19th century's romantic (often fatal) malady, tuberculosis. (pp. 111-12)

Sontag also takes short quotations from other writers and poets—Blake, Lermontov, Dostoevsky—that appear to support the thesis that most people believe that a person's character is the source of his or her cancer. The only scientific authorities she introduces are the controversial psychoanalyst, inventor of the Orgone Box, Wilhelm Reich; and Georg Groddeck, that odd contemporary of Freud's, who wrote *The Book of the It*. Both men were, of course, brilliant eccentrics, but Sontag writes as if the intellectual community took their opinions on these subjects with great seriousness.

That is just not the case. Reich and Groddeck may be enjoyable to read, but their reasoning—especially on this topic—is unscientific, and not supported by any known facts. (pp. 112, 114)

Is it really true, as Sontag maintains, that such stereotypic ways of thinking about people who suffer from cancer do exist and are widespread? I doubt it, because I have rarely heard such opinions expressed. . . .

Sontag is giving us a literary, not a scientific—or, indeed, completely realistic—analysis of the public perceptions of cancer and of the cancer victim. But she writes with curious ambivalence, accusing others of a form of prejudice which she herself seems to have entertained before the development of her own illness. She tells us that she now regrets having written "in the heat of despair over America's war in Vietnam, that 'the white race is the cancer of human history.' . . ." Such metaphors, she suggests, are a literary mode of further victimizing the victims of cancer. And that may be a point, for cancer victims may read the metaphor as referring to themselves and their disease—and therefore as something concrete and insulting. But this is a much smaller point than the all-embracing one that Sontag makes elsewhere: many people view cancer as a loathsome and ugly disease, and assume that the person who suffers from it is someone who has brought about (and therefore merited) his or her own punishment. (p. 114)

Sontag's gift to us, nevertheless, has been to begin a dialogue, on a dignified and philosophic level, between the kingdoms of the sick and of the well. She writes with her customary power, elegance, and authority. . . . (p. 116)

> *Maggie Scarf, "A Message from the Kingdom of the Sick," in* Psychology Today *(copyright © 1978 by Ziff-Davis Publishing Company), July, 1978, pp. 111-12, 114, 116.*

*   *   *

SPENDER, Stephen   1909-

Spender is a British poet, playwright, novelist, critic, short story writer, editor, translator, essayist, travel writer, and autobiographer. As a young man he was linked to the Oxford Marxist group which included Auden, Isherwood, MacNeice, and Day Lewis. Although he may on occasion use political and social issues as the fabric of his work, Spender is thematically concerned with self-knowledge and depth of personal feeling. (See also *CLC*, Vols. 1, 2, 5, and *Contemporary Authors*, Vols. 9-12, rev. ed.)

LESLIE M. THOMPSON

In his poem "Judas Iscariot," Stephen Spender depicts Judas's betrayal of Christ as an act of defiant individualism, and he further proposes that perhaps Christ betrayed Judas.

These unusual arguments, however, are not without precedent in twentieth-century literature, and there exists considerable evidence to suggest that Spender adapted to his own poetic purposes ideas that had already been given wide currency by Oscar Wilde, William Butler Yeats, and D. H. Lawrence. (p. 126)

"Judas Iscariot" expresses the same militant individualism, the same inadequacy in Christ that characterizes Wilde's, Yeats's, and Lawrence's use of this motif. Spender's poem affords an excellent study in literary inter-relationships, and it further reveals the unorthodox use of Christian myth in twentieth-century literature. (p. 130)

> *Leslie M. Thompson, "Spender's 'Judas Iscariot'," in* English Language Notes *(© copyright 1970, Regents of the University of Colorado), December, 1970, pp. 126-30.*

T. C. WORSLEY

It was Spender's *Poems*, 1933, which first made the general public aware that there was a new poetic generation born, and we can tell this from the fact that the popular press, borrowing a word from one of his poems, attached to the group the soubriquet 'The Pylon Poets'.... [It] was important, and particularly important (and deleterious) to Spender himself. He could have handled easily enough, with his habit of laughing at himself, the more vulgar role of spokesman for the group in popular interviews and such like. But he now became the chief pawn in the battle between the full-scale idealogues and the poets. ...

Spender was politically far the most knowledgeable of the group. He was certainly naive, in an admirable sense, as the poems show: but politically he was comparatively sophisticated. He was the son of an important Liberal journalist, an Asquithian high-up, and so knew what the others, and we rabid outsiders refused still to believe, that Stalin was as deeply dyed a barbarian as Hitler or Mussolini, even if less obviously so at the moment.

Enormous pressure was put on Spender to declare himself openly for the Communists, a pressure that only increased as the decade advanced. His sympathies were certainly with the Popular Front and he recognized that the Communist Party was the most effective and disciplined force in politics at the time. But he was not going to support Stalin's form of Communism, and he suffered much anguish in the struggle. ...

He was also, it must be remembered, fighting this battle on another front. It was his fixed and unshaken belief that poetry and art should never degenerate into propaganda. Auden (who drew alongside Spender the following year with his new volume, *Look, Stranger* which left the riddles of the last two books behind) was not troubled by these problems: he was ... not involved in politics on this level. But Spender was and was anguished by the decisions involved and in my view lost hereabouts some of that simplicity and 'naivety' which graced *Poems* 1933. ...

Some of this special Spender quality was, in fact, to reappear in the peculiarly touching and generous-hearted Spanish War poems. (p. 102)

I leave it to posterity to judge between us whether or not these poems are exceptionally fine. But, of course, they are in one unimportant sense written from the outside: Spender was neither a combatant nor a Spaniard. But much more importantly they were written from *the inside*, from the inside of a man who was rare among us rabble of rabid lefties in feeling and daring to acknowledge that Nationalist mothers and widows also wept for sons and husbands lost, and that our bombers killed children in the enemies' street just as Franco's did in ours. (p. 103)

> *T. C. Worsley, in* London Magazine *(© London Magazine 1976), October-November, 1976.*

SAMUEL HYNES

'From 1931 onwards,' Stephen Spender wrote, 'in common with many other people, I felt hounded by external events.' The date is not an arbitrary one: 1931 was the watershed between the post-war years and the pre-war years, the point at which the mood of the 'thirties first became generally apparent. (p. 65)

[By] 1931 many people in England certainly had begun to see the crisis in which they lived as more than a temporary economic reverse—to see it rather as the collapse of an inherited system of values, and the end of a secure life. (p. 66)

External events, if they are dire enough—a war, or the collapse of a society—challenge the value of private acts, and put the personal life to the test. For a young man (Spender was twenty-two in 1931) such a crisis, coming at a time when he was trying to define himself and his place in the world, must have been profoundly disorienting and disturbing.

When the young man is a poet, and the private act that he values is the writing of a poem, then a crisis in society becomes a literary problem. Is the role of a poet a defensible one in such a time? And if it is, what sort of poem should he write? Is the traditionally private content of lyric poetry, for example, appropriate to a time of public distress? In a situation that seems to demand action, can any poem be a sufficient act? These are all questions that imaginative writers faced throughout the 'thirties, and answered in various ways; they are the subjects of the best of 'thirties literary criticism, too, and they enter, colour, and sometimes distort many of the decade's best and most characteristic poems.

Spender wrote two poems in 1931 that show how these questions entered and disturbed his life: 'What I expected' ..., and 'I think continually of those who were truly great'.... The general subject of both poems is heroism—not brave deeds performed, but the young man's dream of valuable personal behaviour.... How exactly is one to act heroically in a time that is a 'chaos of values'? This is what the two poems are really about—the *problem* of heroic action; and in this they belong to their time.

'What I expected' is the more personal of the two, and the more negative. It deals with the disparity between the young man's dream of an heroic adult self, and his discovery of unheroic adult reality; this is, of course, a traditional subject—the disillusion of growing up. (p. 67)

['I think continually of those who were truly great'] is one of Spender's best known [poems].... It is also a young man's poem, a vision of heroism in traditional, romantic images. The vision is a noble and affirmative one, and the poem is very moving, and very youthful. Still, one must note that the vision is *retrospective:* the verbs are in the past tense, the truly great are gone. . . . So here again, though less directly, the separation of the present from the heroic past, and of the Self from the Hero, is made. (p. 69)

Neither of these poems could be called polemical or political or topical: neither urges a cause or proposes an action, or links its subject explicitly to immediate history. Language and imagery are entirely timeless, with none of the contemporary urban-industrial content that came to be the mark of the generation. . . . If they are nevertheless poems of their time, it is because they record a generation's state of mind. . . . (p. 70)

Spender's 'Poetry and Revolution' [an essay published in 1933] . . . is important because it is thoughtful, lucid, and honest (the qualities that his best poems also have). The problem that Spender deals with is one that every artist in the 'thirties had to face: what is the right relation between art and action? . . . Spender was the first of the young writers to address the question at length, and with critical and moral intelligence.

Spender's essay is an act of self-defence against an invisible but easily imagined antagonist—a hard-line communist, with a set of accusations and demands that are new to literary discourse. This new opponent argues that the bourgeois artist is an idealist and an individualist, and that what he writes is necessarily bourgeois propaganda, whereas it is the duty of the revolutionary artist to produce revolutionary propaganda and proletarian art. Spender opens his defence with a defiant sentence: 'Of human activities, writing poetry is one of the least revolutionary,' and goes on to argue the case for a traditional view of the artist, even in a revolutionary time. There is, he says, an inevitable relation between an artist and his culture: a bourgeois cannot choose to join the proletariat *as an artist,* because his imagination and his creative sources are formed, and will remain bourgeois; and in any case there is no proletarian tradition for him to attach himself to. But what he writes need not be propaganda for his own class; if he is truly an artist, his work will perform art's historic role of revealing to men the reality of the present and the past. So art will serve the revolution by telling revolutionaries the truth.

Spender argued that artists should not let themselves be 'led astray into practical politics'. He based his argument on the conviction—which he held throughout the 'thirties—that there is a deeper sense of *political,* beyond party politics, which is simply the truth about historic public issues, and which it is the artist's responsibility to reveal. This is a romantic notion of the artist, as a man with a superior morality and a higher responsibility . . . , but it is a strong defence against the demand for submersion of self in party. (pp. 104-05)

One can see [in the essay that there] is essentially an argument between language-as-art and language-as-propaganda, and that Spender, in urging the function of poetry as a preserver of pure meanings, was being conservative and counter-revolutionary, in spite of his expressed political sympathies. (p. 106)

Vienna is a poem not so much about the history of [the Austrian February Uprising] as about the mythology. It is not a narrative, though it includes narrative passages: it does not tell the whole story, it ignores chronology, and it does not explain. What Spender seems to have aimed at was the expression of his own personal sense of Vienna:

the poem includes, but is not limited to, the public events of the uprising, and it deals with even those events in a private way.

Formally, *Vienna* is rather like [Auden's] *The Orators:* the same division into dissimilar parts, the same mixture of modes, local obscurities, jokes, sudden shifts of tone, the same overlapping of political and sexual problems. Like *The Orators* it is concerned with a sick society and the need for action, and for a 'healer'. But there is one essential difference: by the time that *Vienna* was written, violent political events had occurred, a failed revolution had become history, and hence susceptible to re-telling and mythologizing. *Vienna* has the quality that Ezra Pound said all epics have: it is a poem containing history.

There is another difference, too: Vienna includes an 'I' who is not an invented persona (like Auden's Airman) but an experiencing self. Spender had gone to Vienna shortly after the uprising, and he had witnessed the public consequences of failed heroic action. He was young, and he was politically in sympathy with the workers' action, and one gets from his account his spectator's excitement at the drama of events. But he was also a young man living a troubled and emotional private life, and elements of that life are also part of the poem. This gives it, along with its epic side, something of the character of a long lyric poem, in which all events are filtered through a private sensibility.

A confused city, apparently shortly after the violent suppression of the uprising, and a confused young man—a stranger to the city and its people, troubled in his own life, desiring love, uncertain of his sexual identity: these are the constituents of the poem. The young man observes, records, and feels the public themes—the authoritarian rulers, the brooding unemployed workers, the political antagonisms—but he also feels his private troubles, and weaves his introspection through the poem. Between the public themes and the private ones there is no necessary connection, except the identity of the poet-observer, but the implication is . . . that history, *this* history of violence and betrayal, alters and inhibits love. The point is imperfectly made, and the poem remains in some ways fundamentally incoherent, but this assumption, which is so recurrent through the 'thirties, seems clear enough—that in a time of public catastrophe, private lives will be catastrophic, too. (pp. 145-46)

The problem is set entirely in psycho-sexual terms; sexual crisis seems to have been a crucial part of the Vienna experience.

But the solution that the poem offers is not set in sexual terms, but in vaguely revolutionary terms that seem to offer an alternative mode of action that will also be a cure for the 'desert' that the speaker feels in his breast. He imagines a stranger, another of those healing heroes who are central to the 'thirties myth, whose coming will drive out the sicknesses of the past, and all the introspective, self-regarding forms of love, the 'liars and buggers under the dark lid of centuries', and will integrate the creative, revolutionary forces that are already gathering, into a new life. . . . [The end of the poem is] visionary and positive, but without being very clear. Revolution apparently cures not only social sickness, but also private psychological sickness; the imagined stranger is at once a Leader and a Healer, and it is hard to say which the young man in the poem desires more.

Vienna is an unsuccessful poem, and one can see at once why it was likely to fail. Spender was attempting to mythologize immediate political events, to create an instant myth rather than allowing it to emerge; and at the same time he was trying to reproduce honestly his own feelings of the moment. So there is an uncertain mixture in the poem of politics and self, public and private, working in opposite directions, and obscuring each other. The problems of writing *personally* about public events in which one has played no part are very considerable (I can think of only one modern poet—Yeats—who has managed to do so successfully); there is an obvious temptation to make the self the subject and Spender did, so that, as one critic wrote of *Vienna,* 'we are led, on the whole, not only to pity for these Socialists, but also to a view of the poet himself in the act of being pitiful'. Beyond those problems, there was another that has to do with dramatic form: the February Uprising was a disastrous defeat, of the kind only appropriate to tragedy. But tragedy and revolution are surely not compatible. In Marxist terms, historical reversals are not tragic but simply inevitable parts of the dialectical process, to be acknowledged and incorporated into a 'correct' understanding of historical change. So Spender settled for defeat, with a bit of revolutionary hope at the end.

Spender is an acute critic, of his own works as well as of those of others, and his comments on *Vienna,* and the feelings behind it, are helpful to an understanding both of the poem and of the time. . . . [He wrote] that the effect of public violence was to undermine private feelings, that political emotions may overpower and mask private ones. So that the very failure of his poem has a political meaning. (pp. 147-50)

Both the sense of historical process and the critical defensiveness [of important critical writings of 1935] can be seen very clearly in Spender's *The Destructive Element,* published in [that year]. Spender had set out to write a study of Henry James, an enterprise that seems on the face of it more Bloomsburyish than revolutionary; but his idea of the book changed, as he thought about it, 'into that of a book about modern writers and beliefs, or unbeliefs; which turned again into a picture of writers grouped round the "destructive element", wondering whether or not to immerse themselves'. This three-stage change of mind corresponds to the three-part shape that the book finally took: first a section on James; then one on Yeats, Eliot, and Lawrence (in whom Spender saw the crisis of belief manifested); and finally a section on contemporary writers, for whom the fact of a world without beliefs is taken for granted as the base from which literary activity should begin. It seems reasonable to suppose that this form also corresponds to stages in Spender's own thinking about literature and belief, as his awareness of history grew during the early-'thirties years when he was writing the book. At any rate, the book he finally published is one in which the critical posture changes as the argument moves toward the present.

The 'destructive element' of the title is the phrase from Conrad's *Lord Jim,* but that is not Spender's immediate source. As he explains in his introduction, he took the phrase, and the argument of which it is a part, from [I. A. Richards' influential footnote on *The Waste Land,* advising poets: 'In the destructive element immerse. That is the way.'] (p. 162)

Spender's sense of . . . tradition, and his place in it, is very clear: he begins with James, whom he sees as a great writer forced by his attitude toward a decadent civilization to create an inner world of art; then Yeats, Eliot, and Lawrence —'Three Individualists', Spender calls them—all moralists aware of the 'destructive element', but each seeking an individual solution to his problem. . . . Spender's achievement was to demonstrate their common element of social criticism, and to claim them, on the basis of that element, as the true ancestors of his own generation. (pp. 163-64)

[His] insistence on the moral subject [necessary to art] is one of the principal motifs of Spender's book, and one of its strengths; but it is an argument for individualism—the *artist* decides what is moral—and one can see that it would offend the ideologues of the *Left Review.* The examples he cites, and his concern for the expression of non-realistic manifestations of the moral life, point to still another problem; Spender is defending the importance of literary form, the imaginative shapes that moral meaning may be given, and the right of the artist to follow his imagination, and to invent parables. . . .

[Spender argued] against ideology: a work of art that is concerned with a serious moral-political subject will have moral weight, but if it is really a work of art it will be translucent—its meaning will shine out, but diffused by the strategies of the formal medium. Spender throughout his book defends the parabolic impulses of art—the difficult, the avant-garde, the experimental, the visionary—all of those strategies by which the writer protects his complex vision from simplification; and he rejects dogmatic communism because

> it seems likely . . . that the Communist explanation of our society is not adequate to produce considerable art: it is adequate only to use art to serve its own purposes.

It is a difficult position to maintain, spraddled between revolution and tradition, and exposed on both sides; but Spender managed to do it, and to write a skilful and moving defence of the necessity of art in a revolutionary time. (p. 165)

[In 1937 Spender] went to Spain as a propagandist—he was to broadcast from Valencia—and both the propagandist role and the non-combatant status must have created problems. And so, surely, did his poetic sensibility, which was naturally lyrical and emotional, and not inclined to deal in history and abstractions. (pp. 248-49)

[Spender] separated individuals altogether from history and ideas. In his Spanish poems no distinctions are made between one side and the other, there is no enemy and no clear cause, there is not even, in most of them, an observing self. What remains is suffering individuals, and an overwhelming, unqualified compassion for them.

The poetry, then, is in the pity. Of all the English poets of the Spanish war, Spender was most clearly indebted to the example of Owen, and he was clearly conscious of his debt. . . . [Wilfred] Owen was not, for Spender, a technical influence . . . ; his example was a moral one, a matter of truth-telling. (pp. 249-50)

There is something missing from Spender's war poems, some authority for the right to pity; without that authority, which perhaps a poet must earn by sharing in suffering, pity becomes a patronising, distant attitude. Spender's experience of war had been compassion for those who fought, and anger for those who made propaganda, but these feelings had been distanced by the fact that Spender was neither a soldier nor a Spaniard. His compassion is in the poems, but so is the distance. They are, even the best of them, the war poems of a tourist. (p. 251)

[Spender's retreat from communism] occurred during 1937, just at the point at which he seemed to be most committed to [it]. During the latter part of 1936 he had been at work on a book which would express, as he put it, 'a personal attitude towards communism'. The book was announced in October under the title *Approach to Communism,* but when it appeared, in January 1937, the title had been altered to *Forward from Liberalism.* That change, from arrival to departure, is significant. For what Spender had tried to do in his book was to attach communism to the English liberal tradition, making it simply the latest and most contemporary expression of those values of individual freedom and justice that had been held by the great liberal idealists. . . . (pp. 261-62)

Forward from Liberalism is, as Spender said, a personal book, and it is valuable for that reason: it is the best testament that exists of the state of mind of a young literary man of good will in the mid-'thirties—eager to be active in the service of humanity, but jealous in defence of the privileges of art, and experienced only in the life and thought of his own circle. . . .

[But communists] attacked Spender bitterly for criticizing the conduct of the Moscow trials, and other communists joined in; the book was reviewed unfavourably in the *Daily Worker* ('It is clear that Spender has not come very far "Forward from Liberalism"'). . . . (p. 262)

Spender's response was to join the Party, and to recant his remarks on the trials in an article in the *Worker,* and then to leave for propaganda work in Spain. . . . [But] by the end of the year he was writing the defence of individualism . . . ; and when asked to contribute to the pamphlet, *Authors Take Sides on the Spanish War,* he replied:

> I support in Spain exactly such a movement
> in liberal and liberating nationalism as the
> English liberals supported in many countries
> still groaning under feudalism in the nine-
> teenth century.

So the *Worker* was right, Spender had not come very far Forward from Liberalism, or if he had, he had brought Liberalism with him. His belief in disinterestedness, justice, objectivity, and the aesthetic experience as an end in itself had not changed much from *New Country* to *Forward from Liberalism;* what had changed, that brought him briefly into the Communist Party, was history. And history took him out again. (p. 263)

The date of [Spender's *Trial of a Judge,* 1938,] is important, for it is a time when Germans might still have resisted fascism, and so the play is a cautionary tale for nations in which liberalism has not yet failed.

That is the principal theme of the play—the failure of liberalism and law under the pressure of fascism. (p. 303)

Spender called his play a tragedy. If it is one, it is a tragedy of liberalism; the principal line of action is the decline and fall of the Judge, who stands for the liberal faith in absolute justice and the rule of law, and who fails because his liberal values are weaker than the power of absolute, valueless evil. Certainly this is a shape that tragedy may take—the good man destroyed by his goodness, pulled down from his place by an antagonist that his values, however right and moral, are inadequate to deal with. The trouble with the play as a tragedy is that, though the Judge is the central figure, he represents no *power* in the play. (pp. 303-04)

The conflict is between fascists and communists, and in this conflict the values of liberalism are irrelevant.

But even that is not much of a conflict, for the fascists seem from the beginning to be an irresistible force. . . . The conquest of liberalism is so easy and inevitable that the play seems to be entirely about consequences. . . . [The] reality of the final scene is not a communist's vision, but a liberal's nightmare, of a world mastered by fascism, from which history has been abolished. (p. 304)

Intermingled with this political theme is another, which is a continual private accompaniment to statements of public terror . . . : the theme of the destruction of love by the power of hatred. . . . Fascism is the denial of love and life, and life-deniers are drawn to it. But personal feelings are also denied to those on the other side; in the conflict of Right and Left, it seems that there can be no place for private emotions: love, like liberalism and law, must wait for a time of peace.

By the force of its poetic langauge the play affirms the value of love, law, and justice; but its action demonstrates the power of barbarousness to destroy those values. . . . For Spender, the spirit of Europe was clearly the spirit of liberalism, which had created European civilization, and the force that opposed and destroyed it was not a European political force, but the total denial of what Europe means. Against this power of barbarism there seemed only one possible barrier—the power of the proletariat, organized by the communists. But communism in the play is no longer a movement forward from liberalism; it is discontinuous with that creating spirit, an alternate violent force that would exact its costs in love and justice, as fascism did. It is also discontinuous with the workers as they actually are in the world of the play. . . . By the time he wrote the play, Spender was no longer thinking like a communist (if he ever had); but more important, he was not *imagining* like a communist, and though his choruses assert the triumph of the workers, his play is really an elegy for the death of liberalism and of Europe. (pp. 305-07)

Spender was emotional, enthusiastic, naive, and quick to commit himself, but he was also intelligent and honest. He felt early in the ['thirties] the urgency of political circumstances, and he responded vigorously; but he also felt a deep and steady commitment to his vocation as a poet. Because he was naive, he believed, longer than most, that he could reconcile these two loyalties, not only to his own satisfaction, but to the satisfaction of other poets and other Marxists, and so he was continually criticized, by literary men for being too political, and by political men for being too literary. (pp. 359-60)

He had always found orthodoxy difficult, and he had always tended to take great issues personally, as though every public event were a potential lyric poem. And yet one side of his nature desired the sure solutions of orthodoxy—

hence the personal struggle that got confused with the class struggle.

There are evidences of this struggle in virtually everything that Spender wrote in [1938, the] last year of peace.... Even in his most militant political days Spender had not managed to still [his poet's] voice for long; in the last months of the decade it grew stronger, as the hopes of the Left grew weaker, and spoke with a sombre authority.

One name for that authority is the tragic sense. Spender had come to feel, as others had, that the good causes had suffered too many defeats, that it was now too late for any opposition except the disastrous opposition of war. That feeling is very clear in the introduction that he wrote for *Poems for Spain,* an anthology of poems of the Spanish Civil War that was published in March 1939. That was the month in which the Loyalists surrendered at Madrid, and though Spender's essay was written earlier, it is in the mood of that ending.

As so often in Spender's writing, [this essay] is a public statement about a political issue that is also a private confession of feeling. What Spender is recording here is the end of the Spanish struggle as an issue in history: it had been a cause that action might win; now, being tragic, it can only be a meaning to be understood.

In the face of such defeats, Spender drew back from political commitment, as Auden had done, to a defensive position from which poetry, at least, might be defended. *The New Realism,* a pamphlet published in May 1939, is his definition of that position. The point of view of the pamphlet is ostensibly socialist and revolutionary, but the principal arguments are not ones that Spender's Marxist acquaintances would have found agreeable, for they amount to a theory of disengagement from the world of action. 'The duty of the artist,' Spender writes in his opening paragraph, 'is to remain true to standards which he can discover only within himself.' ... But the artist himself may be a reactionary.... 'What is important is the analysis, and not the *means* of achieving the change, which is not the primary concern of art.' (pp. 360-62)

[Bourgeois] writers will have to go on analyzing what they know—that is, their own bourgeois world. On this point Spender attacks [Christopher] Caudwell, who had written in *Illusion and Reality* that the writer's only hope was to join the communist movement and identify himself with the interests of the working class. Spender rejects this notion entirely, and in so doing rejects the entire left-wing political commitment of his generation, including his own; the passage reads like a farewell to the hopes and illusions of the mid-decade, the years when action seemed possible.... (p. 362)

[In] personal terms it means that the artist accepts his inability to alter reality, and makes that inability his subject. It is, therefore, another aspect of that view of life which starts from the sense of human limitation—that is, the *tragic* view.

This separation of art from action is, like so many of Spender's utterances, a personal as well as a theoretical statement: it is a renunciation of his militant years, a confession of the failure of such effort. But it is also, more positively, a renewed commitment to art, not as an instrument of political change, but as a human value. This confessional note is especially clear in the final paragraph of the essay, in which Spender pleads for a new kind of criticism which would judge writers by the truth of their analysis rather than by their stated opinions.... Spender called this position 'The New Realism', but it was not new for him; it was rather a return to the position that he had taken in 'Poetry and Revolution' in 1933. And so this later essay seems a judgment, at the decade's end, of all the activist effort of the intervening years; poetically speaking, it had all been a mistake, a wasteful diversion of energies from the creative centre of his life to the political rim.

That image of centre and perimeter appears also in *The Still Centre,* the book of poems that Spender published in the same month in which *The New Realism* appeared. It was Spender's first collection since *Poems* in 1934, and he put into it all the work that he wished to preserve from the intervening five years; it therefore amounts to a record of Spender's ideas and concerns through those years, and is a parallel in poetry to the account of his career that he gives in *The New Realism.* (pp. 363-64)

'Darkness and Light', and the poems that follow it [in the last section of *The Still Centre*], are most interesting for what they exclude: there are no suffering poor here, no exiles, no heroes, and no politics. Spender takes his body as the world, and self as the whole subject. There are poems of childhood and of lost love, and introspective self-examinations, and even a poem entitled 'The Human Situation' is entirely concerned with subjective experience. Only in the last poem in the book does Spender return to the other, public world. It is an elegy for a Spanish poet, and is inevitably set in the context of the Civil War; but even that world becomes an inner landscape, a parable of the sense of personal loss.... The similarity between this poem and Auden's elegy on Yeats is unavoidable. It is not a matter of influence or imitation, but of a common occasion and a shared mood: a dead poet, a lost cause, a violent time, and a felt need to rejoice (the word occurs at the end of both poems) in spite of the darkness. They are poems of their time, *for* their time.

Together *The New Realism* and *The Still Centre* announced the end of Spender's uneasy alliance with communism.... Spender had reached the point of believing that poetry makes nothing happen, and to do so was to be confronted with the problem of finding a new subject matter. He had ceased to believe in the 'new world', or that he could make himself single-hearted by any possible effort. And so he turned back, as he said, to the personal; if the conflicts that he had felt in the troubled 'thirties could not be solved by action, then the best thing for a poet was to make those conflicts his subject, to re-enter the self and the personal past. (pp. 365-67)

> *Samuel Hynes, in his* The Auden Generation: Literature and Politics in England in the 1930s *(copyright © 1976 by Samuel Hynes; all rights reserved; reprinted by permission of The Viking Penguin Inc.), Viking Penguin, 1977.*

*   *   *

SUMMERS, Hollis   1916-

Summers is an American novelist, short story writer, poet, and editor. The setting for his work is often the socially constricting and stifling world of the rural South. In his work he

examines the role of violence in this tense and narrow environment. (See also *Contemporary Authors*, Vols. 5-8, rev. ed.)

ROBERT L. PETERS

Hollis Summers' dominant trait is a quiet clarity. His effects recall the painter Andrew Wyeth's steady melancholy, his whimsical affection for the mundane, and his strong shadows. The Sears Roebuck catalogue, soap stolen from hotels, calories, and a college commencement are among Summers' subjects. Like Wyeth also, Summers allows his forms a full display; their structures glow with vitality. The seven occasions for song he writes of [in *Seven Occasions*] are: singing for its own sake, discovering one's self in verse, celebrating sex, strengthening a delicate sensibility, venting one's anger and aggressions, warning of coming social and political horrors, and, finally, capturing quiet and containment. Summers' poetry appears to fit the last of his seven "occasions" best. It is mature verse with little experimentation: it satisfies within modest limits. (pp. 365-66)

> *Robert L. Peters*, in Prairie Schooner (© 1965 by University of Nebraska Press; reprinted by permission from Prairie Schooner), Winter, 1965-66.

MILLER WILLIAMS

Hollis Summers in *The Peddler and Other Domestic Matters* . . . takes us on a trip around the world to show us, not a fountain in Rome, but people. He deals mostly with the oneness of all who share the earth, and with our common mortality. He is writing, of course, about himself, because he is good enough to know that a poet cannot write about anyone else. . . .

Summers has an easy hand; he employs the devices of both conventional poetry and contemporary language without awkwardness. There is no stiffness, and no grand flourishes. The poems, in fact, are so quiet at times that the lines sink into the page until there is nothing there, nothing to resolve the poem but a shrug of the shoulders—whether the reader's or the author's I am not sure.

More than most poets working now, Summers is given to the abstraction, the direct statement. He cares little for—or, anyway, makes relatively little use of—the submerged metaphor and other indirect ways to meaning, and the objects with which he builds his images are usually what he calls them, with nothing hidden inside. This is not to disparage the plainer poems. The direct statement almost always does the job; but it is the lines rich with sense not immediately seen that are strongest. (p. 32)

> *Miller Williams*, in Saturday Review (© 1968 by Saturday Review, Inc.; reprinted with permission), March 9, 1968.

LON TINKLE

Although sensational happenings occur on each of the three Mondays [in "The Day After Sunday"], no single character involved is fundamentally changed. The days may not resemble each other, but each personality remains fixed, unaltered by experience. This is how a certain life-style in Lexington, Ky. (the author seems to say) has made existence resistant to shock and change, incurably sterile and mediocre, forever bourgeois in its devotion to ritual.

For the handful of characters Mr. Summers fully develops in his condensed and concentrated novel, the virtues of this life-style far outweigh its poverties of spirit and intelligence. These people settle for comfort, a cabalistic force in their lives. . . .

Clearly, their view of the Lexington life-style is not that of the author. He doesn't even impute the blame to Lexington. He has risked the toughest gamble for any novelist, to make mediocre and fundamentally unaware people interesting to the sophisticated mind. It is a measure of his power as a writer that he persuades us of the reality of these profoundly non-reflective characters as universal types.

> *Lon Tinkle, "Tomorrow and Tomorrow," in* The New York Times Book Review (© 1968 by The New York Times Company; reprinted by permission), July 21, 1968, p. 30.

DANIEL JAFFE

Hollis Summers's *Sit Opposite Each Other* . . . has the virtues of the best prose: economy, precision, and focus. Summers prefers cool to wild, wit and logic to exuberance. One can admire the restraint and skill, but the repetition of tactics and the narrow range of tonalities make this a limited even if a finely wrought book. It is a collection of intelligent observations, clear sentences, meaningful silences. . . . (p. 46)

> *Daniel Jaffe, in* Saturday Review (© 1971 by Saturday Review, Inc.; reprinted with permission), April 3, 1971.

MARTIN LEVIN

At first, Tom and Caroline seem as vital as Barbie dolls. Gradually, with rare skill, the author shifts from their surface mannerisms to their awareness of themselves and of one another. . . .

The magic of "The Garden" is that it makes a rhapsody of the commonplace. Hollis Summers's panoramic vision catches everything. From their meetings with strangers in an alien setting, Tom and Caroline achieve an almost painful isolation of their individual personalities. (p. 42)

> *Martin Levin, in* The New York Times Book Review (© 1972 by The New York Times Company; reprinted by permission), September 17, 1972.

"To make a sacred pageant," writes Hollis Summers, ". . . You do not need rock cliffs, / A walled city, a river running. / Start with a picture of where we live / Wearing what we're wearing." When Summers follows his own advice, writing about home, himself traveling, the small encounters of everyday life, he is at his best. Occasionally he tries something more nightmarish, and at times this approach leads to poems, like "The Doll," which depend too heavily on the intrinsic interest of their subject matter. To recount odd dreams in a matter-of-fact tone is not quite enough for poetry; what is needed is more attention to language's resources. But there are not many poems in [*Start from Home*] which fail as "The Doll" does. Most of them are wise, witty, and engaging, and remind us that a poet, if he only can stay alive, can function wherever he is. (p. xiii)

> Virginia Quarterly Review (copyright, 1973, by the Virginia Quarterly Review, The University of Virginia), Vol. 49, No. 1 (Winter, 1973).

HARRY BROWN

A great admirer of W. B. Yeats, Summers attempts balance not only in writing two genres; he shows a concern for balance and form at every level in his art, and the number three obsesses him as he orders. For example, he divided *The Day After Sunday,* his fourth novel, into three parts, each of which contains three sections. Each section in turn contains five chapters, one for each of the five major characters; each chapter is told from one major character's point of view. He has also arranged *Occupant Please Forward* into three parts. The poem "Occupant" opens the first section, and "Please Forward" is the second poem in the third section. Like his speaker in "Civilization," the poet "filled space with pattern." . . .

[For me the most important characteristic of Summers] is the Metaphysical quality of his poetry. An admirer of the English Metaphysicals as well as of later Yeats, he shows in his poems the subtlety, irony, ambiguity, elliptical quality, unusual figures of speech, and difficulty—in thought and syntax—that we often associate with Metaphysical style. (p. 251)

The poet in "The Marriage" and elsewhere uses sound patterns in a way that calls for careful reading. For example, although the speaker and his wife have had thus far a "sylvan" marriage, he knows the comfortable marriage can turn into a civil war. *Sylvan* may turn into *civil;* the change—in sound and subject—could occur easily enough. The middle section of the poem—seven couplets set between two sets of two five-line stanzas which open and conclude the poem —exhibits the poet's lyrical and elliptical manner as well as his use of balance and repetition of sound. . . . (p. 252)

"Tunnel," later in Part 1, uses another metaphor for marriage. Against the echo of the romantic and clichéd tunnel of love, the poet makes marriage a tunnel of laws and re-

strictions. The abstraction is older than Blake's "London," but Summers has wrought an original extended metaphor in this book of poems that emphasizes our small but lonely world of trains, planes, and freeways. . . . Although "Tunnel" like many of the poems in *Occupant Please Forward* portrays a strained relationship and hints loneliness, the poem concludes with, first, a hope for light and openness— "a curve of light"—however glimmering and far away; and, finally in any case, resignation.

Throughout *Occupant Please Forward* the poet balances need, loneliness, and loss against love, joy, and meaningful relationships. The title itself and the poem "Please Forward" set the book's tone. *Occupant Please Forward* says Out of Touch, but the title and the volume also say I reach —I yearn—and, occasionally, I touch. According to the opening tercet of "Please Forward," "I am not sure where you are, / I'm not sure if you are, / These days I am not sure." (pp. 252-53)

For the poet human beings matter and in spite of civil war, tunnels of marriage, and abrupt, impersonal departures, he makes a leap of faith to affirm meaningful human relationships. In "Figure," a very moving poem that takes opposition to the usually peripheral figure of Joseph in paintings and sculpture that represent the birth of Christ, the poet concludes,

> I know he held the child.
> I would remember him a father,
> If foster, tending.

With such faith Hollis Summers sends his book *Occupant Please Forward.* (pp. 253-54)

> *Harry Brown, "A Balanced Metaphysical," in* Modern Poetry Studies *(copyright 1976, by Jerome Mazzaro), Winter, 1976, pp. 252-54.*

V

VAN DOREN, Mark   1894-1972

Van Doren was an American poet, playwright, novelist, short story writer, editor, critic, historian, and author of books for children. Best known for his lyric poetry, he has been likened to Robert Frost for his portrayal of the natural beauty of rural New England and to the transcendentalists for his humanistic and idealistic concerns. Van Doren was awarded the Pulitzer Prize in Poetry in 1940. (See also *CLC*, Vol. 6, and *Contemporary Authors*, Vols. 1-4, rev. ed.; obituary, Vols. 37-40.)

MARGUERITE YOUNG

The poems of Mark Van Doren seem to be written in the rough music or muted undertone of a doubting intellect, the scraping, sad music of waves upon a rock barren of all but that dark music. But the imagery provides a mystical lighthouse evoking some altogether different world, even one which is acknowledgedly of the past, for many of the images relate to those things which, secular of nature, have disappeared or are about to disappear from a universe of the known objects into the unknown. Because of their being extinct in all but human consciousness which—if it is a poet's—has a remarkable power of retention and reproduction—or because they are already going, these most commonplace things are now rare, unique, lonely—and are hypostasized, in the poetry of Mark Van Doren, into a statement of divinity, an illusive substance more beautiful than the real and yet not unreal.

For it is humanized, existing in memory with such powerfulness that one may knock upon the door of a house which is already gone. The skeptic thus meets with the mystic, extreme opposite of being, and the two poles make the paradox of the poem. Van Doren is like that hero of whom he has written so well, the Don Quixote of the mournful countenance who continued to believe in a world of romance when it was gone.... [Realism] is a part of Mark Van Doren's poetic vision—but only that which ultimately collaborates with the fading vision of the ideal.

Things happen, in Mark Van Doren's poems, not in an objective time alone and not in the present but in a subjective past. *As long ago as earth, As long ago as evening, As bird time, as mirth* ... The mood is elegiac in every poem, so quietly stated that the sorrow is like an almost silent voice, more like the shadow of the falling leaf than the fall-ing leaf itself. In the poem "Like Son," for example, the people are intangible—they are window-people. *Our neighbors, at their little squares of glass Come suddenly to eye, then off again.*

A very complex urban intellect looks at that which is only delusively rural, since the rural is a mask for the death of beauty in time. In the poem "Uncle Roger," the poet tells of the memory of a train—*Of locomotives miles away ... He hears the whine of coming wheels, With desolate whistles overlaid ... Corroded gauges cloud his eye. So this is growing old and old, So this is what it is to die.*

In the poem "Old Whitey," we read that Old Whitey's hooves were noiseless ... that his were *weightless feet that, falling, tried to thud.* It is time to prove him dead, *this horse that once was flesh and then was cloud* ... and now is nothing. But can Mark Van Doren prove that he is dead who is a cloud or nothingness? The point of all his poems is that he cannot. Something always endures, even when translated into a cloud or the stone—as in "Private Worship" when he writes—*She lay there in the stone folds of his life Like a blue flower in granite.* This feminine figure may be, in Van Doren's poetic structure, Venus not sleeping but dead—through many poems, it is as if the child psyche mourns over the lost mother of the world.... [That] endures, in spite of all the odds and threats against it, is consciousness, even when the exterior image may be no more. (pp. 60-1)

The poems tell the history of fugitive things which ... have no history. They will be destroyed or snatched away, yet remain with some impression upon the mind or rock or cloud because they have been.... Reality may be hidden but is not lost—although the roads are nondirectional, and where they go may be forgotten by all but that perhaps cloud horse. (pp. 61-2)

Whatever Van Doren's Schopenhauerian sorrows are, there are also his Swedenborgian ecstatic visions illuminating darkness ..., every little leaf a sun, a wind flowering out of nowhere, horses falling like angels to this earth. For Van Doren is the redemptive Middle Westerner....

The themes of cosmic, mythic elegy in the lyric poems inform the narrative poems, also the short stories with their phantom people and under-currents of mystery which, even when they surface, remain mysteries and will disappear again, appear after all ends of time. (p. 62)

Marguerite Young, "Mark Van Doren: A Poet in an Age of Defoliation," in VOYAGES (copyright, 1970, by VOYAGES, Inc.), Winter, 1970, pp. 60-2.

MARJORIE PERLOFF

"Immortal," a typical poem from [Van Doren's second volume, *Now the Sky* (1928)], satisfies certain major New Critical criteria: it is an impersonal, well-crafted verbal complex, charactcrized by irony, wit, and organic metaphor. It impressed readers at the time as a characteristically "modern" poem; it displayed Frostian stanza form, diction, theme, indirection and understatement. But between *Now the Sky* and *Good Morning* almost fifty years intervene—years which have given us such seminal poems as *Four Quartets,* the *Cantos,* all of Stevens' post-*Harmonium* poems, Williams' *Paterson,* Crane's *Bridge,* Lowell's *Life Studies,* Plath's *Ariel,* O'Hara's *Lunch Poems,* Ginsberg's *Howl,* and Berryman's *Dream Songs.* Van Doren taught both Ginsberg and Berryman at Columbia, but as an artist, he seems wholly unaware that the bucolic, delicately ironic New England world of his early poems has become an anachronism. The counterpart of "Immortal" in *Last Poems* is "This Ground So Bare," which begins:

> This ground so bare, so beaten by winter,
> Suddenly sends up delicate green,
> Then blue, then yellow, and red, then white:
> Secrets it was saving for us,
> Wealth we didn't know we had.

Even the barest, most desolate winter landscape gives signs of returning spring. But unlike "Immortal," with its witty controlling metaphor, "This Ground so Bare" is straightforward statement. The poet doesn't present the process of discovering nature's "Secrets," he merely tells us they exist. And so the poem ends on a note of bathos:

> Oh, but the miracle from nowhere,
> Light out of darkness, gold out of poverty,
> Blessing beyond any unthinkable dream.

Even the poem's formal structure seems arbitrary. The division into three five-line unrhymed stanzas does not reflect a semantic division; fifteen continuous lines of blank verse would do just as well. Indeed, nothing in the sound structure of the poem suggests mystery or miracle. One senses, on the contrary, that the poet isn't fully engaged by his material, that he is reworking, somewhat mechanically, ground that has become all too familiar.

Throughout *Good Morning,* the "deceptive simplicities" of the earlier Frostian mode give way to the merely simplistic. The title poem, for example, begins "Good morning to the great trees / That bend above this little house; / Good morning to the wind that comes / And goes among the leaves and sings; / Good morning to the birds, the grass ..." and so on. A style that began as an accomplished adaptation of Frost has turned bland. The volume is redeemed only by a handful of poems that deal with the poet's premonition of his own death.... For a moment, at least, the poet does experience ... [in "Everything Went Still"] what it is like to be on the edge of the abyss. The sense of imminent death distinguishes such other poems as "The Time Has Come" and "Apprehension," but on the whole Van Doren's rendering of human experience remains shadowy and uncertain. (pp. 270-72)

Marjorie Perloff, in The Southern Humanities Review *(copyright 1976 by Auburn University), Summer, 1976.*

* * *

VARGAS LLOSA, Mario   1936-

Vargas Llosa is a Peruvian novelist, critic, journalist, screenwriter, and essayist. His writing is concerned with the hypocrisy and corruption of Peruvian society and politics. Violence is a recurring motif in his work, which Vargas Llosa believes reflects a society "where the social structures are based entirely on a sort of total injustice that extends to all aspects of life." His fictional works are noted for their structural complexity and innovative presentation of both time sequence and narrative structure. Vargas Llosa has collaborated with both José María Gutierrez and Rui Guerra on the screenplay adaptations of their novels. (See also *CLC,* Vols. 3, 6, 9, and *Contemporary Authors,* Vols. 73-76.)

WOLFGANG A. LUCHTING

[*Conversation in the Cathedral*] (together with [Vargas Llosa's] earlier novels) is a splendid and admirable proof of how three apparently disparate impulses—moral rage, authorial autoindulgence, and severe discipline—can combine into an harmonic whole of shattering power and icy autonomy. Read anything by Mario Vargas Llosa and you will be amazed by the contrast between the heat of the corruptions or perversions narrated and the formal and linguistic frost glittering over them....

The society described [in *Conversation*] is one of corruption in virtually all the shapes and spheres you can imagine: products and consequences of a dictatorship and the (human) instruments it employs to perpetuate itself. Yet, the language is—with the exception of a few passages that do not ignite—matter-of-fact, almost flat, without pressures of expression, almost casual—even in the most orgiastic and perverse moments! ...

[If] you can name it, *Conversation* has got it. And pervading it all, pulsating in *everything,* even in the most perverse parts of the spectrum of Peru's "quality of life," peeping from actions and reflections, there is masochism.... The tone and rhythm of the passages shaping such scenes stay cool. Yet the language never becomes diffuse or imprecise because this technique of a seemingly casual style is the apt expression of the underlying lament in *Conversation:* horror and terror, evil and hopelessness on the one, even virtue and courage on the other, the mutinous end of the power-stick, become stale in a society that has been "all fucked up."

"At what precise moment had Peru fucked itself up?" asks the second sentence of the novel. On ... the last page, we still do not really know the answer. Ultimately, because there is no definite answer, there is no "precise moment" either. (p. 13)

Similarly, the reader must decide who should be declared the protagonist of the novel.... Black Ambrosio might indeed be seen as the axis-character. If, however, you go by which character affects the greatest number of the other characters in the book, you will want to take Cayo Bermúdez as the center.... Finally, Zavalita himself might be considered the axis, for his is the story of an individual "fucking-up" that represents the Peru in the novel and, obviously, of much of Latin America, past or present.

Perhaps it is better to speak of a triangle, then, instead of axes. The three main characters are its angles; its contents, the fictional space of the novel. . . . [Even] this structure is too clean-cut, because all three men often act, or fail to act, for motives that remain ambiguous to the end. But, then, ambiguity is one of Vargas Llosa's specialties. (pp. 13-14)

[The] manifold actions of a multiple cast roll out and against each other, filling the expanding fictional reality in what José Miguel Oviedo has called "dialogue-waves." And these proliferating interactions precisely document the superb technical skill for which Vargas Llosa is famous, famous enough to have been called the Buckminster Fuller of novel-writing. . . .

Vargas Llosa still believes in telling a story (or possibly several). For Vargas Llosa, Walter Kerr's dictum of a few years ago—namely, that "aboutness is out"—or the French bit about "a text is a texture," are definitely not the essence of fiction-writing. On the contrary, he tells fascinating stories and tells them marvellously. True, they are often gross, stark, perhaps even melodramatic, and invariably full of sex; but so is the quality of life in Latin America. (p. 14)

[All] of Vargas Llosa's fiction is highly charged with sex. The present novel . . . deals with a wide variety of it; yet, sex is never used gratuitously. It is a determinant of many of the actions and embroilments the book narrates. What is more, the sexual corruption can be seen as a symbolization of the general corruption of the Peru of *Conversation.* Peru, Vargas Llosa appears to say, was a brothel at that time. And, indeed, a good number of the major characters at one time or another meet in or visit madam Ivonne's establishment. There is still more to this: in Vargas Llosa's fiction, sex is often the only satisfaction or fulfillment to be obtained any more. All other aspirations in Latin American lives either die or drag on in frustration and fear. (pp. 14-15)

This brings me to a controversial subject concerning *Conversation:* is it a political novel? I think it depends on what is meant by *politics*—and not so much on what a *political novel* is. If we leave the concept "politics" vague, relying only on the associations which probably come to most people's minds when they hear the word—the acquisition of power in order to change a given communal reality, combined with the wheeling and dealing that arises out of the acquisition—then *Conversation* is political only in the very crudest sense: the acquisition and retention of power by *violence.* . . . I believe that all [the political activities in the novel] only show an amazing political naiveté among the young people engaged in them. . . .

In *Conversation,* ironically enough, the non-violent, let's say ideological or theoretical politics, end in and with a love-story. *Conversation* in my mind is not a political novel in the traditional sense, especially if we except the ingredient of violence as a dimension of power. The novel is evidently a political *fact,* however: its very existence is a criticism of a past regime, and, implicitly (although hardly very implicitly), of such methods as the regime employed which may, perhaps, still be fashionable in Peru, in Latin America, or *anywhere* for that matter. (p. 15)

> *Wolfgang A. Luchting, "Masochism, Anyone?" in* Review *(copyright © 1975 by the Center for Inter-American Relations, Inc.), Spring, 1975, pp. 12-16.*

JOSÉ MIGUEL OVIEDO

[The appearance of military characters] is reiterated with insistence [in the novels of Vargas Llosa], almost in a manic way; they operate by means of saturation and concentration in narrative texts which, on the other hand, appear crammed full of characters, filled to the brim with entire human populations. Among that mass, however, the military stand out with an unmistakable brilliance which is not just that of their uniforms: they are there to tell us something, a great deal, about the author, his imaginary world, the key notions to his intellectual conduct. (p. 16)

What can explain this . . . seduction by the military and their hierarchies? Why do they captivate the author's imagination? What role do they play in the text and context of his works? In the first place, the world of the military appears to be ruled by the principle of rigor: military structure is a closed structure by nature, with its secret and self-sufficient codes, almost a freemasonry founded on symbols, values and purposes which the rest of society does not share or does not completely know. The military system is thus presented with an aura of prestige before the eyes of civilians and their institutions, whose principal weakness is a lack of unity and internal cohesion, a tendency to dissent. In the name of the sacred principle of order, the military society can always make the Spartan harshness of its rules even more severe: that will never destroy it; what can destroy it is, on the contrary, the excessive liberty of its members. Vargas Llosa's creative perception recognized this from the beginning. But in addition, the rigor of the military frequently would go beyond the limits of military statutes and reproduce itself, deformed and monstrous, on the other side of the social body. What allowed the military to survive destroyed the essence of civilian life, asphyxiating it under the hateful norms of imposition and supremacy that many times have been singled out as great regulators in the narrative world of Vargas Llosa.

Vargas Llosa's readers already know how the novelist's characters like to confront each other, disputing something very valuable one time, something contemptible at another, many other times nothing—except the bare fury and intensity of the challenge. Life has them confront each other; it throws them against each other, like dogs who fight over the prey, and it gathers them in perfectly recognizable groups. . . . Vargas Llosa's imaginary world assumes the form of a pyramid filled with people trying to find the top, ruining others or simply trying not to fall further down, heroically hanging on by their fingernails. The human contacts are casual but intense, more than a relationship, a friction on the vertical plane between those who are ascending and those who unfortunately are descending, perhaps forever. Even those who are not military personnel know in their own hearts that there are levels and ranks which are perfectly established in this life; to ignore them would be foolhardy, and failure to take advantage of them would be a weakness that would only result in more attacks and mistreatment.

The experience of that implacable net of impositions and hierarchies represented by military life leads to another which also exercises a special fascination for the inhabitants of the author's novelistic space: that of absolute power, which succeeds in converting a man into a master who, finally, does not have to submit to anyone else and is self-governing according to a code which makes others into his slaves. To reach the summit of the pyramid is everyone's secret ambition, but rarely does anyone realize it. In fact, reaching the top does not presuppose an escape from the iron rule of the pyramid but rather a confirmation of it; almost no one in Vargas Llosa's novels triumphs alone. That is why there are gangs, clans and violent fraternities: to be the master also implies, in a sense, being the best servant of the rule, feeding the pyramid's hierarchies with the systematic exercise of humiliation, exploitation and degradation. The Circle in *The Time of the Hero;* the champs, the fiefdom and harem of Fushía, and the rubber mafias in *The Green House;* Cuéllar's group in *Los cachorros* (The Puppies); the courtiers, bureaucrats, police and murderers of Odría's regime in *Conversation in The Cathedral;* and even Pantaleón's *visitadoras*—all are fraternities conceived and organized so that the pressure from the boss can be felt with equal force down to the lowest rung. (pp. 17-18)

However, in the novels by Vargas Llosa there are always individuals who enter into a fight with the hierarchies (military, political, religious), who try to disregard their rules and explore for themselves the tempting world outside. There are several traitors to the cause, but none ever enjoys his triumph; generally they are destroyed by the same act with which they intended to liberate themselves, or they are sadly reabsorbed by the hierarchy, degraded by their double abdication. Their gesture is consumed in the vacuum and in the end is valueless, like Jum's rebellion in *The Green House,* except to reinforce the system of abuses and to justify the hardening of the mechanisms of repression and defense. (p. 18)

Vargas Llosa's novels imply, in this manner, a subtle criticism of heroism. Perhaps for this reason the great figure who embraces and integrates all of these violators of the general norm, the most unredeemed, conflictive and contradictory character, is the *intellectual,* who, within the author's personal system of thought, is always defined as a marginal character, a sniper and perhaps as an undesirable who has lost all his rights in society. Intellectual figures exist in Vargas Llosa's works, but they are not very visible because they usually fail in the promise to be intellectuals and become frustrated. In reality, they are phantoms or aberrant parodies of intellectual conduct: their fight against the hierarchy of abuse and supremacy has left them indelibly marked, even in the middle of their rebellion.

It is very interesting to discover how the complex impact of military, religious and political reality has been produced in the key steps in Vargas Llosa's intellectual development, and how that hard experience has been reflected in the relation that exists in his novels between the bosses of the hierarchies and its most irreducible traitors, artists and intellectuals, whose dissidence appears signified by a ridiculously grandiose name. Each key experience in his life is marked by a fundamental experience with the hierarchies, and each one of them is expressed artistically by means of very characteristic figures. . . . (pp. 18-19)

[In *The Time of the Hero* the] fight against the militarized hierarchy is so intense and systematic at Leoncio Prado that the rebels have their organism, the well-known Circle, which also has its own hierarchy. . . .

[The] real traitor to the Circle is Alberto [the Poet], who never completely submits. . . .

Once in the school, Alberto creates a revealing mechanism

of defense: to survive among the corrupt, he generates his own source of corruption; this is a rather parodic manifestation of literary activity, a type of parody which is repeated throughout Vargas Llosa's works. (p. 19)

The adventures of the military hero (Gamboa) and the intellectual traitor (Alberto) end in a very similar fashion, diluted and blurred, in a form of moral stagnation: Gamboa loses his faith in his institution but resigns himself to continue serving it; Alberto silences his youthful rebellion in a bourgeois conformity which repeats the paternal cycle. . . . (p. 20)

Alberto asphyxiates (and makes a profit from) his rebellion by writing and selling pornographic novelettes; Zavalita [in *Conversation in The Cathedral*] also selects a substitute, something more decorous, for true action: journalism. That this activity is at the same time a falsification and a parody of literature is extremely suggestive. As he is told by Carlitos, the veteran newspaperman who knows him best, perhaps Zavalita is just a frustrated writer, a man whose world is words and the contradictions of reality which they bring forth: "You should have stuck to literature and forgotten about revolution, Zavalita." . . .

The incapacity of the intellectual to assimilate himself to a given order, his moral discomfort in the presence of the principles of the hierarchies, the link which is established between these orders (dictatorship, bureaucracy, military) and corruption, his problematic attitude and his bad conscience, the nostalgia of concrete action beyond his specific activity—all of this is pictured in a very moving way through the inquiry which the protagonist undertakes in *Conversation in The Cathedral.* (p. 21)

Pantaleón Pantoja is a singular case in Vargas Llosa's gallery, especially because he is a "constructive" character, an artist of action, a perfectionist of duty. In *Pantaleón y las visitadoras* the protagonist appears initially as a defender of the strictest order, of the blind subjection to rules and respect for superiors in the military hierarchy. . . . However, if we examine Pantaleón's conduct more closely and take note of the nature of the mission which he assumes, we can see that the author has left very obscure and profound clues in this character.

Pantaleón's task is a logical impossibility: introducing the pleasures of secular life inside the limits of the austere military life. The Servicio de Visitadoras is simply a prostitution service; under his impeccable appearance, Pantaleón is doing practically the same thing that Anselmo, from *The Green House,* was doing with his bordello in Piura: undermining the very foundations of a closed society. (pp. 21-2)

Pantaleón, with his manic professional zeal and his exclusive passion for perfection, is also a caricature of the intellectual as conceived by Vargas Llosa. His love of order and efficiency and the absorbing effort which he dedicates to his task make of this character a Flaubertian being who identifies completely with his duties, even to the point of metamorphosis. (p. 22)

Pantaleón's purpose implies (although it might not appear so) the total subversion of the system: where now an ideal of moderation and discipline rules, he and his *visitadoras* want to impose a sensual and Epicurean lifestyle. He is, after all, "the Emperor of Vice," . . . whose dream, according to Captain Mendoza, "is to be the Great Pimp of

Peru." ... Against Order, he promises Chaos, Orgy, Feast, Revolution. He does not write pornographic novelettes: he makes them reality for the users of the Servicio created by him.

In this, as in all the novels by Vargas Llosa, the orgiastic idea (the bordello) and intellectual dissidence (literature) interchange with each other and violently oppose the idea of a closed and autocratic order of the barracks, the convent or power. The Pantaleonistic language ... and the official rhetoric of the Peruvian regime are insidiously similar, for both conceal a falsification or a dangerous confusion: that of channeling the subversive impulse inside the restrictive framework of a bureaucratic and paternalistic order to whose needs for self-perpetuation and control all else is subordinated. ...

The profound conviction that neither author nor literature can ever be conformist is something the author has never abandoned, precisely because his life has been shaped under the constant pressure of repressive hierarchies, whose negating concept of what is human he has tried to picture first with passion, then with pathos, later and finally with humor. (p. 23)

> *José Miguel Oviedo, "The Theme of the Traitor and the Hero: On Vargas Llosa's Intellectuals and the Military," translated by Richard A. Valdés, in* World Literature Today *(copyright 1978 by the University of Oklahoma Press), Vol. 52, No. 1, Winter, 1978, pp. 16-24.*

J. J. ARMAS MARCELO

[Going] beyond the simple boundaries of a superficial reading of the plot [of *The Time of the Hero*]—in which "the city" and "the school" appear as the central spaces of the narration—other darker, more profound, more functional and more labyrinthine worlds emphasize the ambiguous characteristic of *duplicity* (personal, temporal, conceptual and functional), so that the same characteristic will be the center of contradiction, the grounds for two opposite poles, for two strata that fuse together and split apart simultaneously and constantly during the narrative process. This gives rise to a dual structure which is bipolar, oppositive and presented in a clear process of diminution that will continue fragmenting into two halves. ...

The *asymmetry* of the formal structure that Vargas Llosa utilizes in the novel has been pointed out with some insistence, as if—on managing as he pleases a great number of technical elements—the arbitrariness of the author exercised complete dominance over it and unbalanced the narrative discourse with marked anarchy. ... On the other hand, there are those who point out the constant presence of the author suffocating his creation, the actions of his characters and the way in which episodes and protagonisms are arranged within the novel. Nevertheless, it is here, at this exact point of conceptual confluence, that I see that Mario Vargas Llosa has tried to situate the narrative totality: *between ambiguity and determinism.* This conceptual duality accentuates even more the standard of bipolarity that sums up the novel at whatever level one tries to arrive at analytical dissection. (p. 68)

It is ... in that "mixture of two totally different philosophies: social determinism and existentialism," perceived by [George R.] McMurray, that the factor is rooted which forces the characters many times to configure as luck or ambiguity (but by their own will) those actions or reactions that function as key elements in *The Time of the Hero*. The same factor, independently of the strings that the author controls through the complicated mechanism of creation, forces each concept in *The Time of the Hero* (attraction or rejection, confinement or dissociation) to provoke its opposite, makes each concept function in the role of its opposite in order to contrast the problematic and maladapted personalities of the protagonists and to define them in bipolarity, in the symbiosis of violence and serenity, of appearance and secrecy, the fusion that marks within the novel the pendulum-like movement taking it from one concept to another, from one pole to its opposite. (pp. 68-9)

[Two] distinct worlds move within the novel: the world of appearance and the world of secrecy. ... These two worlds are within the same forge of the narrative structure of the work, shaping, to a greater or lesser degree, the symmetry or asymmetry of the elements that constitute the novelistic whole. ...

[The] proportionate, symmetrical, objective characteristics [of the first eight chapters] shape an interior world which responds to secret codes, to different readings of the world of appearance. As an inherent consequence of these same characteristics, there flows, in this first part of the novel, a fundamental concept ... : secrecy. If we examine part two of the novel, the second eight chapters, we will observe in it characteristics opposite to those indicated in the first part of the novel. Here reign subjectivity and spontaneity. ... [In] the first eight chapters the action is somehow moved along by a personal and collective consciousness which respects to the greatest extent those secret codes that shape the world of the cadets [from the military school, Leoncio Prado, the setting of the novel]. ... [Only the cadets] within their different personalities, can consent to and complete the secrets which they themselves offer in order to shape and constitute a different world, distant, opposed to that of appearance with rules imposed from without, at first from a familial basis and later from the school's military basis.

Consequently the code of values of the cadets is basically supported by *secrecy:* all the cadets are, to some extent, accomplices of all the clandestine acts of the Circle; they all participate in its benefits and its prejudices. But the cadets, as a group, merit a more profound study, in this case, with respect to their behavior. Without a doubt they are the group of actors that has the most meaning in the work. The world of *The Time of the Hero* is completely tinged by pressure from the cadets who act as the real, the only protagonists in the story. Around them revolve action and relationship; they direct the dynamism of the narrative discourse, marking the point of action and the counterpoint of relationship; they impose their perspective. Other characters in the work, who are many times only excuses to explicate the plot that connects the adolescents, are arranged in relation to the cadets and their behavior; they will be the ones actually responsible for their action, for the choice of their "situation." They are, finally, the authors of a secret code of values, of their secret world, a world closed, blind, without the solution of continuity, a world which connects them with a universe created by themselves. ... (p. 69)

[The] cadets, as a collective entity, not only carry out the complicated mechanisms of the content, nor are they limited to manipulating only the functionality of the anecdote: upon analysis, there exists a gradual parallelism between the internal coherence of the cadets' world—which, I repeat, is founded on secrecy—and the proportionality of the formal structure of *The Time of the Hero*. On attending the disintegration of the code of values they secretly invent and sustain in the Academy, we are attending the slow dissolution of the proportionality of the formal structure of the novel, still prevailing in almost all of part one. . . . [It] will be from the basis of the dissolution of those codes—which have made possible the union between the cadets and their secret world—that the proportionality, the certain regularity in the structural levels of the novel, disintegrates in order to give way to the formal incoherence of the structure. Thus it can be determined that the concept of secrecy exercises a structural function in *The Time of the Hero*.

When does the regularity, the structural proportionality of the novel, begin to crack? Two episodes mark the boundary of this rupture: first, for personal reasons, Ricardo Arana, "the Slave," denounces the theft of the chemistry test (part one, chapter six). The collective complicity breaks down, and, second, the same Arana suffers a fatal accident during military maneuvers (part one, chapter eight). But these are only conjectures, and only the collective complicity has broken down here. The cadets and the reader will not realize, until much later, that those two episodes are marking the beginning of the dissolution of the honor code. . . . It will be from the point of the news of the Slave's death (part two, chapter one) that the novel's plot, moving toward its denouement, shows us—to us the readers and to the officials of the school—the secret world of the cadets. Simultaneously that process of conceptual dissolution will influence directly the structural parameter of the work. The irregular behavior of the principal group of actors in the novel leads simultaneously to an irregular structure at formal levels.

This functionality of the concept of secrecy in the formal structure of the novel constitutes, without a doubt, one of the fundamental characteristics and, at the same time, one of the most outstanding stylistic features of *The Time of the Hero*. (p. 70)

> *J. J. Armas Marcelo, "Secrecy: A Structural Concept of 'The Time of the Hero'," translated by Mary E. Davis, in* World Literature Today *(copyright 1978 by the University of Oklahoma Press), Vol. 52, No. 1, Winter, 1978, pp. 68-70.*

JOSÉ MIGUEL OVIEDO

If writing about himself, exposing himself as in "una ceremonia parecida al *strip tease*" (*Historia secreta de una novela*), is what Vargas Llosa has done up to now under various disguises, then [*La tía Julia y el escribidor*] constitutes an exercise in boldness and brazenness. Half of *La tía Julia* is the account of an episode from the writer's youth . . . and the writer does not even hide behind a character: the protagonist is unmistakably named Varguitas o Marito, which introduces a perturbing element in the work of a novelist who has made Flaubertian objectivity a trademark in his writing. The other half of the novel (that which corresponds to the *escribidor* of the title) presents the story of Pedro Camacho, a picturesque type who earns his living as a writer of soap operas and whose "texts" are of a morbid and exaggerated unreality.

This bipolar structure (similar to that of *La ciudad y los perros* [*The Time of the Hero*]) has an appearance of simplicity at the beginning: a clear contrast between the episodes that we can call "autobiographical" (the odd chapters) and the "imaginary" episodes (the even chapters, with the exception of chapter twenty, and the conclusion), between the private life of one protagonist [Marito], and the outrageous fantasies of another [Camacho], encouraged and shared by a mass audience. . . . [The] autobiographical part of the novel is important, because it progressively connects —thanks to a favorite technique of the author (the *vasos comunicantes*)—with the world of Camacho, where everything is efficient and submitted toward an end: to feed the voracious public that listens to his soap operas. There is a comic paradox in the novel: on the one hand we see a writer who scarcely writes, who speaks of writing but engages in other activities; on the other hand we see someone who evidently does not have anything to do with literature but who is highly productive and enjoys all the status of that métier.

There are two basic elements in Camacho that make him a parody of the real writer: the *distortion* that his life suffers as a consequence of his writing, making everything appear as a stimulus for him to produce his stories; and the *methodological excess*, the endless fanatical devotion which he uses to write his lamentable scripts. . . . Through Camacho, Vargas Llosa not only has made a tragicomic and melodramatic portrait of the writer of novels; he has gone even further and has produced a criticism of realism in the novel, of *his* realism.

Throughout the book we are shown how the willingness of the narrator to remain strictly faithful to the episodes of his adolescence is inevitably impeded: the filtering of the novelistic structure changes the meaning of the real experience and transforms it into "literature," as if this linking with life were nothing more than an accident. And, at the same time, Camacho's world of fantasy, which appears disconnected not only from his life but from any contact with reality, shows fissures through which are revealed secret obsessions, aversions and perversions that allow us to view his soap operas as the story of his disturbed mind. A victim of the vicious activity of writing, ascetic in his morals but perverse in his dealing with reality, Camacho is the living incarnation of Vargas Llosa's well-known theory of the novelist and his *demonios*.

It is especially this level of autoanalysis by the writer in the act of writing, this operation by which fiction consumes itself, which makes *La tía Julia y el escribidor* interesting and which compensates in part for the absence of something which until now has been typical of the author: intense technical innovation. Curiously, more than his previous novels, *La tía Julia* should be read in light of Vargas Llosa's two books of criticism, *Historia de un deicidio* and *La orgía perpetua*, because it answers the same two questions: how and why someone writes a novel. (pp. 261-62)

> *José Miguel Oviedo, in* World Literature Today *(copyright 1978 by the University of Oklahoma Press), Vol. 52, No. 2, Spring, 1978.*

BARBARA PROBST SOLOMON

Mario Vargas Llosa has the ability to work on many different levels. On the one hand, he can produce a complicated study of Flaubert—"The Perpetual Orgy," published in 1975; on the other hand, he can write an uproariously slapstick novel ["Captain Pantoja and the Special Service"] that reads like a Peruvian "Catch-22" or "M*A*S*H." What Mr. Vargas Llosa borrows from Flaubert is his stylistic technique; in this case, the use of several third-person narrators and the device of making a place his central character: Flaubert's Paris becomes Mr. Vargas Llosa's Peru. Like Flaubert, he is fascinated by the shady role of the intermediary in society, the person who carries out commands and never questions why they are given. . . .

Clearly, Mr. Vargas Llosa is laughing at his native Peru [, satirizing its social clichés and sexual mores.] His wacky novel is well aided by the sleight-of-hand vernacular style of the translators, Gregory Kolovakos and Ronald Christ.

In his earlier, more somber works, "The Green House" and "Conversations in the Cathedral," Mr. Vargas Llosa was also obsessed by a cast of characters that included pimps, whores, shady journalists, scandal and a corrupt military. But neither in those novels nor in the present one are his whores tough Brechtian heroines waiting for the black ship to take revenge against the overstuffed bourgeoisie, nor is Captain Pantoja a rebel "outsider" like Joseph Heller's Yossarian. . . .

For North American readers to understand Mr. Vargas Llosa's preoccupation with whores and with intermediaries like Pantoja, they will need to be reminded of certain traumas that Latin American history has left behind. The psychic scar borne by Mexico and by certain parts of Latin America is the strong consciousness of being partially peopled by the illegitimate offspring of Indian mothers who were raped, shamed and converted into whores by the Spanish conquistadors. (p. 11)

> *Barbara Probst Solomon, in* The New York Times Book Review (© *1978 by The New York Times Company; reprinted by permission), April 9, 1978.*

*   *   *

VIDAL, Gore   1925-

Vidal is an American novelist, playwright, screenwriter, short story writer, essayist, and critic. His fictional subjects are often drawn from historical and political sources. In his work Vidal examines the plight of modern man, whom he sees as a victim of a valueless society and its corrupt institutions. His work in all genres is marked by his brilliant technique and urbane wit. Vidal has published detective fiction under the pseudonym of Edgar Box. (See also *CLC*, Vols. 2, 4, 6, 8, and *Contemporary Authors*, Vols. 5-8, rev. ed.)

FRANCIS X. JORDAN

Vidal says, "Of all tasks, describing the contents of a book is the most difficult." Such is certainly the case with [*Matters of Fact and of Fiction*], which presents the many glittering facets of a truly witty mind. Some will object to his recurrent use of epithets such as the "Great Golfer" and the "First Criminal" to refer to recent Republican presidents. Others will object to his incurable habit of name dropping, his penchant for sweeping generalizations, and his petulant tone of self-righteous superiority. Still others will object to feelings of being left in the dark as Gore recounts some of the cute goings on of his past in "Some

Memories of the Glorious Bird and an Earlier Self," an essay full of obscure allusions to events in his personal life.

In spite of these blemishes, the book holds up because its author is a man of wit and style. If you like paradox, you will find it: "After all, social climbing is one of the most exciting games our classless society has to offer." If you like puns, you will find them: "I fear that the best one can say of Solzhenitsyn is *goré vidal* (a Russian phrase meaning "he has seen grief")." If you like striking figures of speech, you will find them. Writing of Louis Auchincloss' position in a "literary society of illiterate young play-actors," Vidal observes, "Louis was indeed like a platypus in that farmyard of imitation roosters." If you like generous doses of cynicism directed chiefly at the academic critics of literature and the powers behind the power in our democracy, you will find this book an almost pure delight. (p. 122)

> *Francis X. Jordan, in* Best Sellers (copyright © *1977 Helen Dwight Reid Educational Foundation), July, 1977.*

JOHN ROMANO

[In an early essay Vidal wrote] that the shrinking audience for fiction was really a good thing, because it left the novel only "the best things: that exploration of the inner world's divisions and distinctions where no camera may follow." . . . (p. 1)

[In contrast,] "Kalki" is a potboiler: subspecies, disaster movie. Drugs, sex, espionage, apocalypse, even the morally damaged Vietnam Vet, who has become whatever-comes-after-ubiquitous—the synopsis reads, as in part the novel does, like a compendium of television specials. Recalling the language of Mr. Vidal's 1958 essay, it should be noted that this novel is careful *never* to go where the camera may not follow with ease. . . .

"Kalki" is so calculated, so replete with salable clichés that it raises in the sharpest way the question that must nag even Mr. Vidal's admirers: How can taste and intelligence so palpably superior spend themselves on such trendiness?

The question isn't rhetorical, and there are at least two ways to answer, sympathetic to Mr. Vidal; his quality as a critic earns him at least two benefits of doubt. The first is to say that Mr. Vidal isn't exploiting the trendy, he's parodying it. Consider Theodora "Teddy" Ottinger, who narrates "Kalki." Getting to know her, we're meant to have Erica Jong's "Fear of Flying" in mind. . . . [Teddy is] the world's best jet pilot, and the best-selling author of "Beyond Motherhood," about her "life and hard times as a flier, woman, mother, and would-be know-it-all." . . . Poolside at the Beverly Hills Hotel, just out of earshot of Merv Griffin, she is invited by a smarmy New York press lord to do a magazine piece on Kalki [a Vietnam veteran who claims to be a reincarnation of the Hindu god Vishnu], for much money, but quickly, so as to scoop Mike Wallace's "60 Minutes."

Handling such a scene, Mr. Vidal is, as it were, at poolside himself. He *clefs* away, or drops names outright: Joan Didion, Clay Felker. He is utterly beglamoured, and can't take his eyes off the passing stars. It's bitter social satire: of course, of course. But, as we know, there is a certain high intensity of attention that, however critical in tone, is tantamount to love itself. . . .

The novel is, however, critical and even harsh in tone,

mainly because we observe the world, which is coming to its well-deserved end, through the eyes of Teddy, who has steeped her mind in the mordant skepticism of Pascal. Rational and unsentimental to the point of superstition, she is the nastiest possible slur on the reconstructed woman of the 70's. Here she is on a visit to Earl Jr.:

> "I must have felt *something* for him once, I thought, staring through the martini's first comforting haze at my ex-husband's pale double chin.

> "Tears came to my eyes. There were tears in his eyes, too. Love? Tenderness? Regret? No. It was the red-alert smog, creeping up the Santa Monica Canyon. . . ."

Finding out that love is only air pollution is the sort of bland demystification that is found in the silliest feminist fiction. One expects that someone with Mr. Vidal's wit and social vision would detect the poverty of feeling in this humor; one expects that he would choose a narrator who detects the stereotype in herself. If she doesn't, or at least not consistently, perhaps it's because her sourness toward the emotional life is, without mitigation, her creator's own. (p. 22)

[When] we can't defend what is lurid and show-biz in Mr. Vidal's novels by saying that they're parodies, we can still take them seriously as the moral or philosophical allegories that they are ostensibly set up to be. "Kalki" is an end-of-the-world fantasy, resembling, according to the jacket copy, "Brave New World" and "1984." Its associations within Mr. Vidal's fiction, however, are with his two previous messianic novels, "Julian" and especially "Messiah." . . .

But as an allegory of the Last Things . . . , "Kalki" is worse than banal, it's irresponsible. Taken at its word, it is, after all, a big idea: big enough for Voltaire, or Pope. But Mr. Vidal cheats. He imagines an end to human life after showing us only the most tawdry and lamentable specimens. Who would regret such an end if the world were made up only of what we see in "Kalki": junkies on park benches, matrons bragging about their cancer operations, trash-minded media men from New York? Mr. Vidal doesn't portray people, or even caricatures, but, rather, insults of representation—condescending and unfelt. Not people, but cartoon figures die when Kalki dances. Dealing honestly with the significance of his theme would have required showing a fit sense, somewhere, of the greatness of the imagined loss. . . . Mr. Vidal lacks that sense, and lacks in general the humane fullness that the apocalyptic imagination of his story demands. (p. 26)

> *John Romano, "The Camera Follows," in* The New York Times Book Review *(© 1978 by The New York Times Company; reprinted by permission), April 2, 1978, pp. 1, 22, 26.*

ERIC KORN

The first task in reviewing Gore Vidal's new apocalypse [*Kalki*] is to write six paragraphs without using the obvious epithet "mandarin"; the next is to look at the book's relationship to its predecessor and prototype, *Messiah,* and see how the eschatology business has come along since 1955. Vidal, it is acknowledged, rewrites history to make it ap-

pear even less planned, formal and elegant. It cannot be that he revises his fictions with the same purpose. Nor is *Kalki* a resuscitation or a sequel—the *Myra/Myron* transform. Rather it is a restatement: in a word, the last days seem closer, grimmer, and more final. Sardony, however, is holding up well. . . .

Mr. Vidal is not averse to napalming a sitting duck, if it merits it. Among his sidelong targets, not all able to retaliate, thank heavens, are US senators ("not only sexually insatiable but impotent"), congress of all kinds, the Australian editor of a newspaper "dedicated to corrupting the morals of the lower IQs", and the White House, its furnishings and occupants recent, current, and potential. . . .

It's an ingeniously dusty fable, but uneven: tropes of virtuoso buffoonery ("The eyes were now as round as those Spanish gold doubloons that were found by two surfers north of Trancas last year. The doubloons turned out to be counterfeit. The surfers were for real") and tracts of slightly arid whimsy. Arbitrary it may be, but never unintentionally: it's all Lombard Street to a mandarin orange that that's the way the author meant it to be.

> *Eric Korn, "We Are for the Dark," in* The Times Literary Supplement *(© Times Newspapers Ltd. (London) 1978; reproduced from* The Times Literary Supplement *by permission), April 14, 1978, p. 405.*

DIANE JOHNSON

[*Kalki*] might originate from musings on [the] common intimation that immortality is wasted on gods. But it is also a novel by a singularly astute observer of human behavior and student of human history, who has noticed that so far no one, when given half a chance, has been able to avoid human mistakes. . . .

Is Kalki a god? He does destroy humanity; but his lack of malice, his serenity of character, seem godlike; also, his fit of pique, which leads him to kill the only other fertile male on earth, even when his own reproductive scheme has gone awry, is of the sort gods are given to. It is the narrator, Teddy Ottinger, who unwittingly distributes the sinister germ that drops the human race in its tracks. She spreads it around the world on a goodwill mission. . . .

It is art that accounts for this being a wise and charming, rather than a horrid book. Certainly horrid things abound in it: murders on television; followed by the death of billions; many unpleasant characters—senators, ex-husbands, ghost-writers—abound, at least until the end. But the swift, absorbing plot does not allow the reader to pause too long in painful reflection. And it is hard to resist the witty pragmatism of the narrator, whose unsparing view of the world as she finds it (as it is), reminds us that whether or not the world should be saved at all is very much an open question.

That it should be saved is the unspoken assumption of most apocalyptic literature. Perhaps that is what is unconvincing about novels of apocalypse. But utopian novels, from *Utopia* itself to science fictions of today, have uniformly failed to convince us on the other hand that alternative societies would be anything but worse. Amazingly, Vidal avoids the snares that beset novelists of utopia and apocalypse alike. He has more in mind than the doomsayer's wish to hector us into better behavior, has the historian's suspicion of progress. Has, in addition, a good novelist's ability to fascinate. One hears, it is true, the author's voice—he is saying "repent, repent"—but the message is tactfully faint while the tone, being, as usual, his own, is inimitably diverting.

Diane Johnson, "Gilding the Lotus," in
Book World—The Washington Post (© The
Washington Post), April 16, 1978, p. E3.

JOHN SIMON

Until now, Gore Vidal's fiction has mostly been wickedly clever. With his latest novel, *Kalki,* Vidal ascends into a new category: diabolically clever. I say "diabolically" rather than the more innocuous "devilishly" because what has increased is not the cleverness but the nastiness. *Kalki* is a hybrid: part social satire; part slick entertainment (in the Graham Greeneian sense); and part doomsday comedy in the manner of, say, Stanley Kubrick's cinematic black comedy, *Dr. Strangelove.*

Some of Vidal's diabolism manifests itself right away, in the plot's construction. For *Kalki* is a thriller, and by an ancient and honored custom, reviewers are not allowed to give away the main twist in a thriller's plot. What comes to their aid, however, is that the twist tends to be a single fact near the end of the book, one that the critique can easily sidestep. Here, however, the presumably unbetrayable twist comes much earlier and permeates and affects everything before and after it. . . .

Still, if I tell you that in *Kalki* the world does come to an end, I am not committing an unpardonable crime. For such is Vidal's cleverness that the suspense continues beyond Armageddon and hinges on such fascinating posers as "Will anyone survive?" and "If so, who?" and, above all, "Can a new race arise, and if so, what will it be like?" With such tricks still up his sleeve, Vidal can go on flaunting his mastery of suspense within suspense (p. 31)

[The novel's first problem lies in its heroine, Teddy Ottinger]: She is too multifarious to be a fully believable character. At the very least, she is distressingly twofold: the bright, enterprising, but also eminently fallible thirty-four-year-old female dilettante and the omniscient author of *Kalki.* . . .

Not only is Teddy at least two people, she also is at least two styles—perhaps rightly so for a bisexual, about whom one of her presumably favorite authors might have said, "The styles are the man-woman." Though much of what she sets down is sharp, pertinent, and virilely concise, she will also resort to the kind of sneaky shortcut appropriate to what used to be referred to with the now justly obsolete term "the weaker sex." At such times, Teddy (or Vidal) merely invokes a phrase like "as H. V. Weiss would have put it" and blithely plunges into blatant platitude. And even when she is not Weissianizing, Teddy fluctuates disturbingly between an enlightened best seller style (better, to be sure, than an unenlightened one) and an intermittent finer thing. Exactly what that is is hard to define; call it an American approximation of Evelyn Waugh—just as deadly, but a shade less funny.

Here enters the second problem. Vidal conceives of the novel as a receptacle for all of his personal gripes. Settling a personal score by dragging in a real person from left field seems needlessly bitchy. And not only bitchy but also something worse: essayistic rather than novelistic. There was, of course, a style of novel writing in the eighteenth century that could accommodate the odd essayistic excursus, but amid Vidal's fast, nervous forward movement even a clever disquisition on Jewish princes and princesses in fact and fiction feels inappropriate—to say nothing of a less skillful harangue against politicians. Moreover, Vidal often makes things too easy for himself, as when he describes Weiss as a "cliché master and structuralist" and demonstrates only the former sin. . . .

[*Everyone*] in the novel [is] a double agent of Vidal's—a pawn of his whimsy rather than a character real enough to dictate his own terms to the author, as truly successful fictional creations seem to be able to do. Here, however, a narc (a triple agent, but still a narc) will openly declare, "The single, nay, unique objective of the Bureau [of Narcotics] is the *increased* sale of every kind of drug all over the world," to which a demagogic senator running for the presidency will add that without international drug rings his richly funded Committee on Narcotics Abuse and Control "would wither away." (p. 32)

Satirist's privilege? Not so; in high gear, satire has its own crazy plausibility, as Vidal well knows. Thus when a television director for *60 Minutes* says about the interview in which Kalki announces the date on which he will end the world, "This segment will run ten, ten and a half, maybe eleven minutes, you know, an in-depth study," this is barely, if at all, tampering with the preposterousness of things as they are. Or take a doctor's urging Arlene "to give up tequila in the morning. He begged her to switch to a good, light, refreshing breakfast wine from the Napa Valley. He himself owned a share in a vineyard. He would sell her his own brand." Vintage satire, that. (pp. 32-3)

A man who can so easefully carry off such sardonic effects ought not to settle for less. Yet Vidal will stoop to the heavy and obvious. He writes: "Dr. Ashok looked so crazed that, for the first time, I thought him not only sane but possibly serious despite the essential frivolity of his alleged employer the CIA." Here both the facile paradox and the unduly propaedeutic tone of "the essential frivolity of his alleged employer" seem to me miscarriages of satirical justice. Yet Vidal can do worse. He will become pontifical and leave a good piece of satirical raw material uncooked: "This was a commonplace in that era: events were only real if experienced at second hand, preferably through the medium of the camera." Moreover, he will mix metaphors (and not deliberately—the speaker is his alter ego, Teddy): "the dark caravans of words that cross the pages of newspapers to invade and ravish the delicate house of memory like killer ants." It is unnerving to have camels shrink in mid-metaphor to ants, however deadly. . . .

But then, for a fastidious, indeed finicky, writer, Vidal can become remarkably sloppy. Thus the Hindu phallus is the *lingam,* not the *linga;* the Latin for duplicity is *duplicitas,* not *duplicitatem;* Chomsky's first name is Noam, not Noah; "imposter" is a vulgar error for impostor; "Myna birds" is a redundancy for mynas; "forthcoming" is not acceptable in the sense of communicative or outspoken; no Frenchman would write "de Vigny" for Vigny; "could not help but" is tautological; and so on.

But—and it is, as it is so often with Vidal, "but" time once more—there are also wonderful things in *Kalki.* There is at times a lightness of touch that nevertheless reduces the satire's butt to mincemeat: "I was able to read the odd page by Joan Didion, the even page by Renata Adler,'' which with the greatest gentleness makes both writers out to be unreadable. . . . And what about this splendid *reductio ad absurdum:* ''The Australian press was unusually aggressive. Apparently, they had once been able to drive Frank Sinatra out of Australia. This feat had made them overconfident.'' And, most devastating of all in its lethal concision: ''Ms. Brownmiller's book on men, and rape,'' where putting the declared subject last and what Vidal takes to be the real one (sour grapes rather than bitter rape) first is a masterstroke of ingenious—or insidious—ridicule.

But—again but—this meticulous writer is capable of such lapses as having a singular child on page 245 turn into plural children on the next page. Such things are disturbing. But more disturbing still is the ultimate question this novel raises: Can one really pardon the feeling one gets in reading *Kalki* that Vidal would welcome the end of the world? This slips out time and again: ''But then [if I were God] I would not have gone to the trouble of inventing the human race''; or ''I did not believe that Kalki would switch off the human race . . . as desirable a happening as that might be.'' Not even Swift, in all his *saeva indignatio,* went that far.

And yet, and yet—one cannot help savoring a master satirist able to put down a whole subcontinent with a mere description of arrival at New Delhi airport: ''The moon was still bright in the western sky. The dawn was pale pink. The air smelled of wood smoke, curry, shit.'' And who is able to dismiss the end of the entire world with, ''You cannot mourn everyone. Only someone.'' (p. 33)

> John Simon, ''Vishnu as Double Agent,'' in Saturday Review (© 1978 by Saturday Review Magazine Corp.; reprinted with permission), April 29, 1978, pp. 31-3.

MAUREEN BODO

Gore Vidal is rapidly becoming his own worst enemy, no small feat for a veteran of so many literary feuds and friendships that have gone sour. For years, Vidal has been railing against such abominations as the Non-Fiction Novel, the New Novel, and the University Novel. These literary forms, Vidal contends, may have some worth, but not as fiction. His own work, with one or two exceptions, has generally been in the traditional form exemplified by his favorite American novelist, Henry James. Since the publication of *Burr,* Vidal has enjoyed a reputation as one of the best novelists in the United States.

Lately, however, Vidal has begun to work against himself and his own best ideas by letting his novels become essays with stories wrapped around them. In the process, he is turning into the leading proponent of what might be called the Polemic Novel. In *Myra Breckinridge,* Vidal wrote, ''The novel is dead''; he later explained that he really meant the audience for the novel is dead. Since then, he has evidently started to worry about the death of audiences for the essay and the talk-show as well.

Having once admitted that he had ''nothing to say, only to add,'' Vidal seems to say in his latest novel, *Kalki,* that he now has nothing to add, only to repeat. (pp. 600-01)

The plot is clever, the story is well told, but it is all too easy. *Kalki* lacks the vision and conviction of Vidal's genuinely apocalyptic novel, *Messiah,* written 24 years ago. By comparison, the new novel seems a pale reminder of Vidal's prodigious but often wasted literary gifts.

There are echoes of voices from other works. Teddy Ottinger [*Kalki*'s protagonist] comes across like Myra Breckinridge in a leather flying jacket; when she offers her opinions on population control and bisexuality, she sounds like Gore Vidal doing his tiresomely familiar bit on the Johnny Carson show. Vidal treats us once again to the attack on the French New Novel, first mounted in *The New York Review of Books* ten years ago. This genre was satirized to death in *Myra Breckinridge;* now the corpse has inexplicably been exhumed for another trashing in *Kalki.* The parody has no purpose here, if parody it is. Vidal is becoming trapped in his own satire and has unconsciously adopted the style he dislikes. The tone here is too breezy, too flippant, and frequently awkward, a jarring shift from the cool, masterful prose praised by admirers of Vidal's essays.

Kalki seems to be one long process of self-cannibalization. Even minor characters are reminiscent of previous creations. . . .

Even worse, Vidal tries unsuccessfully to deal with ideas clearly suggested to him by other writers. Teddy Ottinger constantly remarks on the effects of entropy, laments that ''everything is running down,'' and throws in references to the Second Law of Thermodynamics for good measure. This has already been done, as Vidal points out in his essay ''American Plastic,'' by Thomas Pynchon in *V.* and *Gravity's Rainbow*. But where Pynchon makes intelligent use of scientific principles, Vidal makes pointless note of them and passes on.

For all of this, *Kalki* is not a bad novel. It is easy to read and frequently amusing; but it is also disappointing. One can only hope that in his next novel Mr. Vidal will stop stealing from himself and others and put his considerable talents and intelligence to better use. (p. 601)

> Maureen Bodo, ''His Own Worst Enemy,'' in National Review (© National Review, Inc., 1978; 150 East 35th St., New York, N.Y. 10016), May 12, 1978, pp. 600-01.

*   *   *

VOINOVICH, Vladimir   1932-

A Russian novelist, short story writer, and poet, Voinovich is a brilliant satirist. All of his fictional works deride social and political conventions in Soviet Russia and reflect his concern for the difficulty of maintaining an identity in a totalitarian society.

MARY ANN SZPORLUK

Voinovich's fiction as a whole reflects two main literary concerns. As a social critic and satirist, he wanted to create a world of caricatures and to develop his skill at building dialogue out of cliches and banalities. He also tried to create a new kind of hero, who would not only have the satirical function of contrasting with his predecessor, the Positive Hero, but whose behavior would also reflect a different morality. The responsibilities of the individual and the struggle of the free personality against manipulation by society emerge as major themes in Voinovich's most important works, and in these the characters are given clear moral tests.

These two sides of Voinovich, the satirical and the didactic, were difficult to synthesize artistically. To some extent he had tried out both approaches in *We Live Here,* but later he wrote two different types of stories. Those in which social satire is dominant take place in the provinces and use many stylistic devices favored by nineteenth-century Russian satirists. The two major stories with didactic tendencies have individualized heroes and urban settings and are told by first-person narrators in a more sophisticated, ironic tone, perhaps somewhat influenced by modern short stories from the West.

In Voinovich's best work, the novel *Chonkin,* he again mixes both aims. In *Chonkin* Voinovich places a thoroughly recast "positive" hero against a background of broad social satire. The peculiar nature of this hero, a product of Russian folklore as well as literary tradition, makes this mixture successful. *Chonkin* combines social satire and ethical judgments with fantasy and humor and is told in an easy narrative style which should appeal to a wide audience. (p. 101)

The novella *We Live Here,* his first published fiction, was written in 1960-61 and set in 1960. This work is interesting in light of Voinovich's later fiction, as it shows basic themes and approaches. In *We Live Here* Voinovich deromanticizes country life, makes fun of Soviet cultural myths, and offers the reader a young hero who questions the behavior of his society.

We Live Here describes the life of young people who are working on construction and agricultural projects in the country. Voinovich tries to examine their private emotions and hopes for the future, but the psychological analysis can only be appreciated when this work is contrasted to the literature which had dominated the preceding period.

We Live Here consists of a series of short scenes, most of which are chosen to illustrate an obvious shortcoming of some of its characters. . . . (pp. 101-02)

This first work has very definite heroes and villains, chosen and developed according to slightly more liberal principles than the heroes and villains from the immediate Socialist Realist past. . . .

In *We Live Here* Voinovich tried to free his hero from heroics and make him interesting as an individual. Goshka is similar to the hero-narrators of Voinovich's later stories in his honesty and concern with analyzing and judging his own behavior. Unlike Socialist Realist heroes, Goshka does not live according to a plan. . . . (p. 102)

Among the younger characters in the work, the main target of Voinovich's light satire is the idealistic and romantic Vadim. Vadim writes poems glorifying work on the kolkhoz, but the villagers soon learn that his work is all theory and no practice. The difference between life in the city and life in the country is an important theme in this work, and Voinovich's satire supports the view of those who work in the provinces. He shows there is nothing romantic about work on the farms and satirizes the accounts of country life written for those who live in the city. (pp. 102-03)

Although *We Live Here* satirizes cultural myths and contemporary morals, the work was not especially daring for its time in its social criticism. The book ends optimistically, even romantically; and as Goshka stands and proudly glances at the passing tractors, the worst seems to be over. As a literary work, *We Live Here* is structured rather clumsily and the characters are oversimplified. Yet the work shows Voinovich's concern with the problem of creating a

good, believable, and interesting hero while at the same time amusing the reader with social satire. In several places in the work there is good dialogue and we see some of the humor which Voinovich later uses so well. . . .

[In the story] "I Want to Be Honest," Voinovich uses a first-person narrator, a switch from *We Live Here* which allowed the hero to be presented more intimately and irony and sarcasm to be used more subtly. (p. 103)

The plot of "I Want to Be Honest" is structured around two moral decisions which the hero [Samokhin] must make. . . . Although the plot is a bit melodramatic, Voinovich's use of dialogue saves the story. Samokhin's winning ironic voice permits moral conclusions to be stated in an entertaining way.

The characterization in this story is again black and white. Most of the men connected with the work project are negative types, lazy, ready to compromise, afraid to disobey orders. . . . In addition to general dishonesty, Voinovich also satirizes the political meeting, drinking, Soviet incompetence (no one has the right materials at the right time), and Soviet journalism. (pp. 103-04)

The humor in this story is more sophisticated than that in *We Live Here* but the plot and characterization are too predictable. Voinovich was still trying to combine humor and social satire with the desire to create an individualized hero who could win some kind of moral victory over his society. The tone of this story is much less optimistic, though there is no direct criticism of the Soviet system as a whole. Voinovich's criticisms of Soviet life and its effects on the individual was in keeping with the general liberal spirit of many writers who were published in the early 60's.

In his story, "A Distance of Half a Kilometer," . . . Voinovich made greater use of folk humor and dialect. This story, told by an outside narrator, takes place in the country, but unlike *We Live Here* concentrates on types and has a somewhat burlesque comic tone. Voinovich was not so concerned with character development or individual moral problems here. In treating the realities of Soviet provincial life, he uses many devices found in nineteenth-century satires. (pp. 104-05)

The value of life in the face of death is questioned [in "A Distance of Half a Kilometer"], but this philosophical speculation is overshadowed by the humor in the tale. Voinovich experimented here with many devices he would later use successfully, such as awkward speech, the long rambling monologue, and dialogue built out of apparent nonsense, in the tradition of Gogol and Zoshchenko.

Village life is shown to be much more stupid and hopeless here than in Voinovich's first work. The most positive figure is a simple carpenter (reminiscent of some of Leskov's characters) who loves and gives names to the objects he crafts. Nikolai serves as a contrast to Ochkin [an army deserter and thief], who had preferred life in [labor] camps to work (at least it was free, and there were baths, concerts, and movies). Nikolai and his friend have a favorite argument: does the Bolshoi theater have six or eight columns? This forms their intellectual life; and when a visitor from Moscow gives Nikolai the answer, he decides not to inform his friend, for fear that they will have nothing to talk about. (p. 105)

[In "In the Compartment"] the male narrator relates a

conversation he had with a compartment-mate on a train ride from Moscow to Leningrad. This passenger, a prim and paranoic lady of thirty is (a bit too) afraid that the narrator will try to seduce her; therefore she sits up all night on guard. The woman, having lost all sense of reality, is unable to see that the narrator is not at all interested in her. Perhaps this sketch reflects Voinovich's growing interest in psychological loss of freedom; the woman has become a slave to a preconceived view of the world. Yet "In the Compartment" is above all a funny sketch whose humor again comes from Voinovich's well-constructed dialogue.

The best of Voinovich's stories to be published in the Soviet Union is "Two Comrades." . . . This story takes place in a city and concerns two adolescents who grow up there. The story is narrated, in retrospect, by Valery Vazhenin, who tells us of several incidents, and of one in particular which helped him to come of age. "Two Comrades" also examines concepts particularly important in this period of Soviet history—freedom and responsibility, friendship and loyalty. Although no direct attack on the Soviet system is made, there is a lot of Aesopian language and the basic moral argument of the story certainly bears on the current political scene. Nonetheless these criticisms were not strong enough to keep the story from being published; and Voinovich's primary interest was in the effects of the system on the individual psyche rather than on the nation.

In "Two Comrades" Voinovich develops the irony he had used in "I Want to Be Honest," but here the hero is an adolescent, and the dialogue is rich with adolescent city slang. Valery is Voinovich's most sensitive and intelligent hero, as well as his most successfully individualized one. He also has a dry sense of humor, does not take himself too seriously, and is unwilling to compromise with what he finds to be his own self.

The investigation of what defines friendship is very important in "Two Comrades." (pp. 105-06)

For different reasons and in different ways all of Voinovich's "positive" heroes are tested in ["Two Comrades"]. In light of the mass arrests and denunciations which occurred in the Soviet Union, the matter of loyalty was an important one.

"Two Comrades" also has more direct literary references than Voinovich's other works, and he enjoys satirizing the literary profession. (p. 108)

The last two works Voinovich had published in the USSR, the short story "Sovereign" . . . and the historical novel *Degree of Trust* . . . are not as good as "Two Comrades." It may be that with *Degree of Trust* Voinovich was still trying to work out a compromise whereby some of his unprinted works could be published as well. This historical novel tells the story of the revolutionary Vera Figner, but one feels that the author was more interested in her young, introspective, and likeable husband, whom she abandons one-third of the way through the work.

"Sovereign" bears some relation to *Chonkin* in its attempt to combine some structural and stylistic aspects of folklore with contemporary social problems and language. This story again shows Voinovich's tendency to mix moral messages with humorous dialogue and dialect, but in this case the mixture is not very successful. . . . The story ends with the death of both [the tale's] lovers, but the tragic elements

are not effective because the characters are not strongly developed.

The two works of fiction by Voinovich that were published abroad, the story "By Means of a Reciprocal Correspondence" . . . and the novel *Chonkin,* show an increasing concern with broad social satire and problems of social psychology and morality. Although the moral position of the hero still remains clear, Voinovich seems to have resolved the artistic conflict between individualized characters and satirical types, and his humorous and satirical side prevails over the overtly didactic. Yet Voinovich's continuing interest in the political and social importance of individual behavior is shown in these works. What kind of values and inner resources decide how men stand up to injustice? What is human about human behavior, what is normal, what is moral? (pp. 108-09)

Although "A Reciprocal Correspondence" is a study of relations between two individuals, it is hard not to relate its implications concerning loss of freedom and the psychology of tyranny to the culture at large. (pp. 109-10)

"A Reciprocal Correspondence" is the first work by Voinovich in which none of the major characters is more positive than negative. The foolish Ivan is a different Voinovich "hero" and is presented in a slightly grotesque manner. By the end of the story Ivan is a complete caricature; he becomes a puppet-like figure who is being beaten by his wife as the curtain drops. (p. 110)

In "A Reciprocal Correspondence" the world has become . . . cruel and depressing. The role of the hero has also changed. The reader is tempted to feel sorry for him, but why? The story deals with the psychology of tyranny and the loss of a freedom which Ivan did nothing to deserve. As the fictional world of Voinovich became more depressing and bitter, such a caricature was fit. In the novel *Chonkin,* however, Voinovich's aims were more complex. There we find a "foolish" hero cast in a positive role.

The Life and Extraordinary Adventures of Private Chonkin is also a study in delusion, but delusion on a mass scale. *Chonkin* further questions what man is, what men live by, who is sane and who is foolish. In this work Voinovich found the perfect form to combine his satirical and didactic aims. . . . Voinovich uses Ivan Chonkin's adventures as a means of revealing the absurdities of the Soviet system, but Chonkin is also a positive figure and is cast in a real hero's role. (p. 112)

By incorporating folk-tale elements into a satirical adventure novel, Voinovich created a framework which enabled him to combine heavy satire with a hero whose character was positive, familiar, and thus believable. From a totally incompetent soldier, who at first seems to be only a travesty of the traditional positive Soviet hero, Chonkin develops into a likeable human being. This change is opposite to that in "A Reciprocal Correspondence," where the hero turns into a complete caricature. Thus, in *Chonkin,* as in many folk tales, it is the "fool" who is wise and strong enough to slay the villain: following his own eyes, he distinguishes between truth and falsehood in a world of upside-down values. (pp. 112-13)

Among the different elements of Voinovich's style in *Chonkin* are contemporary slang, the jargon of the Soviet press and bureaucracy, nineteenth-century literary mannerisms and formulas and proverbs associated with folk tales. Such a mixture is very difficult to translate without loss of humor. (p. 113)

Chonkin uses and combines anecdotes based on contemporary events and political jokes, dream sequences with fairytale elements, and a great deal of everyday life . . . often told in a coarse manner. The coarseness forms an important stylistic element and supports the speculations on what is human. In Part I, for example, a long dream scene mixes Soviet political satire, folklore, the grotesque, and the love story of Ivan and Nyura. (p. 114)

The themes of respect for all life and loyalty to friends are found again in *Chonkin*. . . .

Voinovich's satire in *Chonkin,* especially in Part II, is both more broad and bitter. All important figures—the kolkhoz chairman, the head of the local KGB, the military commander, a leading woman activist—are complete scoundrels. . . . *Chonkin* is filled with examples of human stupidity, and Voinovich takes good advantage of the ridiculous situations made possible in such a system. (p. 116)

["An Incident in the 'Metropole'" and *Ivankiada*] are both satirical autobiographical accounts which relate, in an amusing manner, Voinovich's not so amusing confrontations with the authorities—the KGB in the former and the literary establishment in the latter. In both works the author is forced by events beyond his control to act as his own positive hero. These satirical pieces suggest that Soviet reality is often more fantastic than fiction (at least its own); for the world Voinovich presents seems to thrive on distorting its own rules. It is fitting, then, that "An Incident in the 'Metropole'" is subtitled "A True Story Resembling a Thriller," and that *Ivankiada* (subtitled "The Story of the Writer Voinovich's Installment in a New Apartment") is put into a mock-heroic framework. (pp. 116-17)

Ivankiada satirizes the methods by which the bureaucracy rules and reveals the discrepancies between official values and laws and real values and practices. . . . What is most effective about this satire is Voinovich's use of real names and authentic data (letters, memoranda, etc.). Again he condemns disloyalty to friends and man's readiness to rationalize this disloyalty. Friends who privately praised *Chonkin* seemed all too ready to censure it in public.

Voinovich uses dialogue very skillfully in *Ivankiada;* he is particularly good at capturing the ritualized formulas which are intended to discourage attempts to do business through official channels, and, indeed, discourage communication in general between Soviet citizens. (p. 118)

> *Mary Ann Szporluk, "Vladimir Voinovich: The Development of a New Satirical Voice," in* Russian Literature Triquarterly *(copyright © 1977 by Ardis), Winter, 1976, pp. 99-121.*

GEOFFREY HOSKING

As a "hero" [the title character of "The Good Soldier Chomkin"] springs from much earlier models: Chekhov's little men, Tolstoy's simple peasants, Leskov's eccentric and slightly ridiculous "saints" and, above all perhaps, *Ivan-durak,* the stupid peasant of Russian folk-tales, who leads a charmed life in close communion with animals and nature, and whose cheerful simplicity brings him miraculous victories over the rich, sophisticated and powerful of

this world. Literary and pre-literary echoes surround Chonkin. His very origins are mysterious: rumour has it that he may be the illegitimate son of the last Prince Golitsyn. On the other hand, his father may have been a shepherd. Who knows? But he clearly springs from a twilight world of the pre-revolutionary popular and literary imagination. The irruption of this unlikely yet ordinary figure into Soviet society provides the opportunity for a satire which reveals not only the absurdities of the system but also its deeper human mechanisms. . . .

Voinovich's first literary efforts were poems and lyrics for popular songs, one of which gained national fame because it was adopted as a kind of "cosmonauts' anthem" after Yuri Gagarin's flight in 1961. That is in a way appropriate, because his early career was a product of the Khrushchev period of cultural and scientific optimism. His first prose works, published in *Novy Mir,* were consonant with the general search at that time for personal integrity and more humane forms of community life. Writers were left relatively free to pursue this search in their own way, and Voinovich himself has testified that "the degree of freedom for literature in the Khrushchev period was sufficient for me personally". At that time his work could have been considered as part of a revaluation of Socialist Realism, and he himself certainly thought it consistent with the doctrine. His concern was with personal integrity and how it is, not ideally but actually, built up in the individual in the exacting and often corrupting circumstances of modern industrial and agricultural work.

His approach to the problem was, however, very different from that of the classical Socialist Realists. The heroes of his stories were vacillating young men not quite certain of themselves or their beliefs. This can be seen in all his works up to the *Two Comrades* of 1967. Voinovich was asking: what are the conditions in which principled action is really possible in everyday life? How is the good man formed and how does he live? In short, from the very start, he was reexamining the whole concept of the positive hero. . . .

[*We Live Here, I Want to Be Honest,* and *Two Comrades,* the] three early major works of Voinovich, all show the same preoccupation with the way in which human beings find themselves, the way in which they evolve a moral sense. But, significantly, what his characters find themselves seeking is not ideals but rather their own personal authentic existence. It is not correct ideals but only this individual discovery which can enable a human being to act morally in a consistent manner, Voinovich seems to be saying. Or, in grander philosophical terms: ontology precedes morality. The term "instinctive existentialism" has been used by Geoffrey Clive for Solzhenitsyn and for some of the nineteenth-century Russian novelists, and I think it applies just as well to Voinovich—who, moreover, has a lighter touch than most in his development of it.

It is this existential dimension which gives the satire in *Ivan Chonkin* its profundity. The fundamental absurdity which the novel brings to light is the inauthentic existence forced on everyone by an overbearing system of authority, the way in which the elaborate structures of this system come in extreme cases to replace the human personality itself. Chonkin is the ideal central character for this satire because, though he is subject to the external coercion as much as anyone else, he does not internalize it: indeed he does not even understand it, and in that way remains spiritually free from it. But when he stands up at a political education session and (goaded on by an unscrupulous colleague) asks if Comrade Stalin has had two wives, his naivety releases a pent-up complex of unmentionable subjects which reduces the political commissar to helpless and cross-pressured silence. He is the innocent fool who gets everyone at cross-purposes and in the process reveals their hidden motives. He is as good a catalyst for showing up the varieties of inauthentic existence as Chichikov in Gogol's *Dead Souls.*

In contrast to Chonkin the other characters stand out in clear relief. . . .

Gladyshev is the only person in the village who not only accepts the existing authority structure, but also accords it genuine devotion, out of belief in its progressive and scientific nature. The capacity people have for building their whole lives out of illusion is essential to this authority structure, as indeed to any totalitarian system, and it is a capacity which fascinates Voinovich and which he has investigated in other works. . . .

Obsession with a single idea and the capacity for boundless self-delusion characterize [many of his] characters. The story of Gladyshev shows how such people can become minor cogs in a huge machine of power.

Is there any "authentic existence" to set against all this? The answer is yes, in a way. Chonkin is, as I have said, not merely a satirical catalyst, but also a positive hero of a kind. But he does not function in any way like the classical Socialist Realist hero. No reader would actually wish to take Chonkin as a model for social behaviour. It is rather that Chonkin awakens the reader's humanity, and points to the essentials of human existence camouflaged by the gross and inflated inessentials of the system.

There is a further dimension to "authentic existence" here too. Like Gogol, Voinovich deliberately allows his usually realistic world to be penetrated now and then by the fantastic. One of Gladyshev's confident "scientific" assertions is that in the course of evolution the monkey became human by working. Chonkin is puzzled by this statement and contends that, if that is the case, then the horse would appear to have a better claim to human status. After this altercation, Gladyshev dreams (or *thinks* he dreams) that the farm pony has turned into a man and wants to go and make a career in the town. As the novel evolves, it becomes clear that this may not have been a dream at all, and this pony plays an important and semi-fantastic role in the development of the plot. The alternative to the generally accepted theory of evolution (the kingpin of positivist thinking) is thus, as it were, left open, and we are led back to fairytale and folk culture, as well as to non-scientific modes of perceiving the world, which, if they are fantastic, are at least harmless fantasies compared with those of the Gladyshevs and super-Gladyshevs of this world. (p. 93)

> *Geoffrey Hosking, in* The Times Literary Supplement *(© Times Newspapers Ltd. (London) 1976; reproduced from* The Times Literary Supplement *by permission), January 23, 1976.*

WALTER F. KOLONOSKY

"The Ivankiad" is a fitting sequel to Voinovich's "The

Life and Extraordinary Adventures of Pvt. Ivan Chonkin." . . . It is another example of satire at its best. . . . By coincidence, "The Ivankiad" appears at a moment when the roman à clef is flooding the US market. It is not exactly a roman à clef, but it is "the inside story" of an authentic Soviet apparatchik.

The term "Ivankiad" is rooted in Ivan'ko, at once a person with connections as well as a personification of connections. According to Voinovich, "He is legion." It is Ivan'ko who intrigues his way into the delicate layers of decision-making in order to obtain more living space: one half of a two-room apartment which has been lawfully promised to the narrator, Voinovich himself.

The theme of a ludicrous struggle for a Moscow apartment is not new, but in the hands of Voinovich it acquires a new dimension: documentation. Any resemblance to actual persons and places in the Soviet literary world is hardly coincidental, for the entire imbroglio actually took place in 1973, a year before Voinovich was expelled from the Union of Soviet Writers. . . .

In spite of the spread of Soviet satire, this literary mode is still rather risky; it is still possible to concoct an explosive mixture of candor, humor and wit. When Voinovich asks whether a saucepan can become a member of the Writers' Union, there is really no explosion—just a lot of noise in the kitchen. This time a US publisher has not acquired a manuscript written "for the drawer," but an extremely funny drama about authors who come face to face with the territorial imperative. (pp. 114-15)

> *Walter F. Kolonosky, in* World Literature Today *(copyright 1977 by the University of Oklahoma Press), Vol. 51, No. 1, Winter, 1977.*

THEODORE SOLOTAROFF

"I'd Be Honest If They'd Let Me" [is a story about an] ordinary Soviet citizen who is thwarted by the System and holds out against it in the name of his integrity as a man and a worker. . . .

This story . . . appeared in Novy Mir, just at the time Khrushchev was cracking down on the liberal writers, many of whom, like Voinovich, were trying to renovate socialist realism by replacing the standard "positive" hero with a human one whose true circumstances do not generally appear in Pravda. In the "cultural conferences" that were staged to call the liberals to account, "I'd Be Honest If They'd Let Me" was singled out by Ilychev, Khrushchev's chief ideologist and hatchetman, as being particularly odious and dangerous.

Voinovich's defense of the story claimed that though its hero finds himself fighting alone against "irregularities," its point was that "every human being has an aim in life in his own sphere, which means that he has something to devote himself to and to which he can sacrifice himself sincerely." This was not an evasive, noble sentiment but a bedrock conviction that had guided this *kolkhoznick* and carpenter to his vocation as a writer and was to sustain him in the difficult years that followed. . . .

From 1963 on, he had been writing his lifework, a long satirical novel about the encounters of a backward Army private with the Soviet system. In it he continued to draw upon his own experience and to explore his central abiding conviction that a man is what he does and hence should try to live in accord with his better nature and with the purpose he chooses to sacrifice himself for: in short, he should not become a hack. In "The Life and Extraordinary Adventures of Private Ivan Chonkin," he went much further in laying his truth directly across the public lie of the worker's state and the people's republic, to show how integrity and authenticity fare in the actual meshes of the Soviet system: not only the *kolkhoz* but the secret police, the Party and that Holy of Holies, the Red Army.

As a concession to the authorities he set the novel in the dark distant past of Stalinism, and as a strategy he chose a comic peasant hero and a tone of warm, ingenuous mockery and fantasy. The choice of a satirical mode was inspired, for it unearthed a first-rate comic talent that had been lurking beneath the sober gritty surface of his early realism and a new and powerful gift for rendering the transactions between reality and fantasy, the ordinary life haunted by the phantoms and phantasmagoria of the police state. (p. 6)

Voinovich is not widely known here, but he soon will be. For this is a stunning book as well as a brave one: a tender, hilarious piece of rural naturalism leavened by a pure imagination, and a stinging, far-reaching burlesque of institutionalized fear, stupidity, treachery, delusion and absurdity. Call it a masterpiece of a new form—socialist surrealism. Call it the Soviet "Catch 22," as written by a latter-day Gogol. (pp. 6-7)

One must bear in mind that the Red Army occupies about the same position in recent Soviet culture that Stalin did in his heyday. Every year another endless line of novels is cranked out about the heroes of "The Great Patriotic War." Voinovich slyly has his reader ask him why he didn't take his military hero from "real life, a tall, well-built, disciplined, crack student of military and political theory." He replies that he was too late, "all the crack students had already been grabbed up and I was left with Chonkin." (pp. 7, 24)

> *Theodore Solotaroff, in* The New York Times Book Review *(© 1977 by The New York Times Company; reprinted by permission), January 23, 1977.*

ANTHONY ASTRACHAN

Critics and blurb-writers have called [*The Life and Extraordinary Adventures of Private Ivan Chonkin*] a "Soviet *Good Soldier Schweik*" and a "Soviet *Catch-22*." They are right, but they leave out a dimension. *The Life and Extraordinary Adventures of Private Ivan Chonkin* is also a Soviet *Gulliver's Travels*. Vladimir Voinovich at 43 is not only the Soviet Hašek, the Soviet Heller, a 20th-century Gogol or Saltykov-Shchedrin. He is also the 20th-century Soviet Jonathan Swift, God help him.

I say "God help him" because his bitterness has not yet overwhelmed his humor and his tenderness, as Swift's did. But he lives in Moscow, where his telephone has been disconnected, where the bureaucrats who live by excreting the fear and stupidity and treachery that he burlesques will no doubt try to drown him in their excrement. Voinovich would appreciate the metaphor, I like to think; his book has many like it, part of the Swiftian flavor. Perhaps his surrealism will save him from the corrosion of bitterness. But it is not his surrealism. It is his characters', the surrealism of taking the absurd seriously and the serious with absurdity, of being totally unable to distinguish between them. . . .

[The] confrontation with a Jew named Stalin may be the funniest portrayal of Soviet officialdom ever written. ("Just why are you trying to pass yourself off as Comrade Stalin's papa?" "Because I am the father of Comrade Stalin. My son, Comrade Zinovy Stalin, is the most-well-known dental technician in Gomel.") The very idea of a Jew named Stalin is one of the funniest and most frightening ideas a Russian is likely to come across. That may be one of the problems an American reader faces with this novel. Its humor is universal, but the particulars may be hard to understand if one has neither lived in the Soviet Union nor studied its life. On the other hand, if you laugh at this book, you may be on the way to a more profound understanding of Soviet life than even reading Solzhenitsyn makes possible.

> *Anthony Astrachan, "Good Soldier Chonkin," in* Book World—The Washington Post *(© The Washington Post), February 6, 1977, p. F10.*

JOHN B. DUNLOP

The plot [of *Ivankiada*] offers a satirist more than a few opportunities to utilize his craft. To the service of his satire Voinovich brings a style which is a delight to read: ponderous Soviet acronyms and journalese rub shoulders with outlandish Americanisms and occasional archaic Slavonicisms; passages of devastating humour alternate with serious and even moralizing commentary. The tale is fast-paced, the transitions smooth. Voinovich dextrously mixes genres: "straight" narrative is interspersed with (or derailed by) selections from the author's diary, various letters of protest or declarations sent (or not sent) to Soviet officials, the tape-recording of a phone conversation, and extended fantasies about what Ivanko's thoughts would be in a given situation.

Voinovich also frequently engages in what the Russian Formalists have called "laying bare the device"—a deliberate toying with literary conventions. The narrator will break off his account to announce what he has just done or intends to do with the plot—the reader, of course, is well-advised to take such asides with a grain of salt. . . . Stylistically *Ivankiada* impresses me as superior to and exhibiting better control than the longer and more ambitious *Chonkin*, which has a tendency to sag and sputter in the middle sections, though its beginning and end are nonpareil. Voinovich appears still to be maturing as a writer; if his talent is not arrested, we can expect even better things from him in coming years.

While *Ivankiada* is obviously not written according to the canons of Socialist Realism, Voinovich has the norms and expectations of this doctrine very much in mind. (p. 1186)

Unlike a number of talented contemporary Russian writers —for example, Solzhenitsyn, Sinyavsky, Vladimir Maksimov—Voinovich is not a religious man, but there is what he calls a "moral factor" in his tale, and he shares the moral concerns of such authors. What matters, he shows, is not whether or not one wins a given battle, but how one lives. . . .

Vladimir Voinovich must surely be one of the best satirists of our time. His talent compares favourably with that of the late Mikhail Bulgakov, whose name is frequently mentioned in the pages of *Ivankiada* and whose *Master and Margarita* may have been given him some ideas on how to depict Soviet writers. (p. 1187)

> *John B. Dunlop, "The Invasion of the Ivankos," in* The Times Literary Supplement *(© Times Newspapers Ltd. (London) 1977; reproduced from* The Times Literary Supplement *by permission), October 14, 1977, pp. 1186-87.*

W

WALLANT, Edward Lewis   1926-1962

Wallant was a Jewish-American novelist and short story writer. Central to the four novels written during his brief career is the theme of suffering and redemption. Wallant believed it was the artist's role to see clearly and define life for a myopic public. (See also *CLC*, Vol. 5, and *Contemporary Authors*, Vols. 1-4, rev. ed.)

JONATHAN BAUMBACH

[Wallant's novels] are dark visions of disquieting, often apocalyptic seriousness, haunting, desolating books about the improbable possibilities of redemption in a corrosively malignant world. Each of Wallant's books is a kind of pilgrim's progress about those blighted innocents, who damned to disbelief, keep vigil at the gate.

Wallant's prose, at its best, seems to brush across the nerve of our feelings in fragile and uncanny ways. Even in his first novel, *The Human Season,* the least successful of the four, there are moments of rending insight, of agonizing perception of character. (p. 138)

Like all of Wallant's heroes, Sol [the title character of *The Pawnbroker*], in a delicate truce with survival, has of necessity shut himself off from his feelings. He is "sick and dying yet nowhere near the ease of physical death." The novel is about the Pawnbroker's slow return from the carrion sleep of numbness to the agonized awareness of pain, grief, and love—the torturous responsibilities of feeling.

If the Harlem pawnshop is our hell world in microcosm, Sol (the sun) functions in his realm as a kind of merciless god. In extension, then, Sol's grinding despair suggests the hopelessness, the death of possibility of the world; as a consequence, the problem of the Pawnbroker's survival has cosmic implications—the survival of the world, of human life itself, is at issue. . . . [The] pawnshop has the sacramental aura of a church, a place of penance and redemption, where Sol and his assistant Jesus dispense with ceremonial judgment, "in exchange for the odd flotsam of people's lives," small loans of cash—the artifact of grace. (p. 140)

As Sol assumes the "aggregate of pains" of his customers, Jesus, who patterns himself after the Pawnbroker, becomes an ingenuous conspirator in the strange church-hood of the store. The conspiracy of their relationship, its profane and sacred implications, is at the heart of the novel's experience. Jesus remains in Sol's employ for less actual money than he might earn elsewhere, in the hope of uncovering, as it seems to him, the secret wealth and power of the Pawnbroker's knowledge. For hope of undefined gain, he is Sol's apprentice, a sharer of his burden, though he misconceives until the end the true nature of such an apprenticeship. With an irony too deeply pitched for the boy's comprehension, Sol tells his helper that the only thing in the world he values is money. And so with a disciple's faith, the innocent boy conspires with three other Negroes to rob the Pawnbroker's shop. As Jesus sees it—his own bitter irony —in robbing Sol, he is merely putting into practice the lesson of the master. There are lessons and lessons, however. And at the end, with the instinct of a fit apprentice, Jesus enacts the deepest lesson of Sol's life, reteaches it to the Pawnbroker at the expense of his own. Ultimately, Jesus' sacrifice, a supreme act of faith, moves Sol into reassuming the responsibility of his own feelings, resurrects him from the death of spirit. The death of the son makes possible the salvation of the father.

The excess of contrivance of Wallant's allegory occasionally intrudes, though does not in any significant way deform the deeply perceived flesh and spirit of the novel's experience. The figure of the Pawnbroker looms through the work, a colossus of despair, carrying the burden of the world's horror in the dull pain of his spirit. He is an amazing characterization, one of the memorably dark heroes of our fiction. (pp. 141-42)

The fact of Jesus' sacrifice, an unlooked for miracle to Sol, brings the Pawnbroker back to sentient life. In the example of his assistant's humanity, Sol discovers the denied possibilities of his own. . . . In crying for his assistant he is able at last to mourn for the death of his family, for all his losses, for all his dead. In discovering the shock of loss, he discovers the redemptive and agonizing wonder of love.

The achievement of the *The Pawnbroker* is in its rendering, in the luminous insights of its prose. The novel is always on the thin edge of going wrong, of letting its allegory control its direction, of teetering into bathos. Yet it survives. Wallant succeeds in making credible as experience, through the artifice of art, turns of events that would seem in the circumstance of raw material merely willful contrivance. In fact, much of the power of the novel resides in the tension of its risk. The prose is the transforming instrument. Sol's sudden comprehension of the meaning of Jesus' death, for example, accepts every risk of sentimentality and manages at once to be moving and true. . . . (pp. 145-46)

All of Wallant's novels have a similar, ritual structure: a man cut off from the source of himself, in a delicate truce with the nightmare of survival, slowly, terrifyingly, at the risk of everything, rediscovers the possibility of feeling. Whereas *The Human Season, The Pawnbroker,* and *The Children at the Gate,* are almost airlessly intense, *The Tenants of Moonbloom* . . . is an attempt at treating the same dark concerns, the same human dislocations, with something like comic perspective. Where the others are indebted in tenuous ways to the fiction of Malamud and Bellow (and Dostoevsky), *The Tenants of Moonbloom* is, in the only way the term is meaningful, an original achievement. And since it shows another aspect of the resources of Wallant's vision, I think it worth the attention of close analysis. *Moonbloom* is also the most beautifully written of the four novels, an uncannily funny and discomforting book.

As Sol Nazerman is a figure of tragedy, Norman Moonbloom is clearly a comic hero. . . . Where the Pawnbroker is spiritually dead, Moonbloom has never quite been born. . . . *The Tenants of Moonbloom* is made up of a succession of comic and painful confrontations which work to push Norman across the "threshold of pain" into the exhilarating anguish of birth. The novel is about the awakening of Moonbloom and the quixotic implications of salvation. If it is Wallant's funniest book, it is also, as is the way with comic novels, his saddest and most pessimistic. (pp. 146-47)

The Tenants of Moonbloom moves uneasily across a delicate tight rope of risk between the comic and the pathetic. The last of Norman's renovations, the repair of Basellecci's swollen bathroom wall, serves to unify the two modes and to exemplify the profound, ambivalent sense of Norman's apparently senseless commitment. (p. 150)

None of Norman's repairs have any significant effect on the griefs of his tenants. Yet the terror of this knowledge only intensifies him in his purpose. His commitment exists purely for itself, without influence of gain. That his renovations are gratuitous endows them with a kind of special grace, an innocence of purpose. Norman's works of salvage are performed not for his tenants but for himself (the tenants have "entered him"), out of the deepest demands of his own need.

When Norman attacks the wall with a pickax, he becomes inundated by a "brown thick liquid," purging the building of all its corruption. . . . The joke of Norman covered with shit, announcing his birth, is cosmic and seems in context— Norman surrounded admiringly by his three drunken disciples—a revelation, a kind of miracle. . . .

The achievement of Wallant's four novels resides mostly, I think, in their revelation of character, in their ability to make sense of the dark extremes of human behavior we share in communal possibility, the best and worst of us. Out of the final depths of depravity and horror, Wallant's children of darkness discover the terrible luxury of feeling that provides, at the price of pain, the redemptive possibility of love. (p. 151)

> *Jonathan Baumbach, "The Illusion of Indif-*
> *ference: 'The Pawnbroker' by Edward Lewis*

Wallant," in his The Landscape of Nightmare: Studies in the Contemporary American Novel *(reprinted by permission of New York University Press; copyright © 1965 by New York University), New York University Press, 1965, pp. 138-51.*

THOMAS M. LORCH

[Wallant] pushes aside the glittering surfaces of modern society to write of the terror, suffering and mystery buried within. [*The Human Season*] describes one man's confrontation with the fact of death; although it states Wallant's major theme, the dilemma of the individual faced with the problem of evil, it contains little suggestion of the expanded historical and social dimensions created in the later three novels. A tragic chorus of the defeated, frustrated, helpless outcasts of society frequents Sol Nazerman's pawnshop, enters the hospital in *Children at the Gate,* and inhabits Norman Moonbloom's tenements. These unfortunates poignantly dramatize the ills of contemporary society, yet in the novels they function more as indices of the hero's development and his state of mind; the social and historical context derives its importance from its profound effects upon Wallant's primary interest, the individual's inner life.

The central character, therefore, dominates each of Wallant's novels; in only one, *The Children at the Gate,* does a second figure of comparable significance emerge. Before the action begins, Wallant's heroes have attempted to deaden themselves to their world in order to escape the evils dramatized by the chorus of outcasts. Yet the fact that they have been hurt indicates that within their protective shells they feel deeply, care about others, and long to develop their humanity and to love. They cannot repress their feelings fully or for long, and their return to life is measured by their gradual, agonized acceptance of the terrible, downtrodden figures. Each of Wallant's novels describes a form of rebirth, the process of returning to or achieving an affirmation of life. Thus, each novel contains both an effort to transcend the pervasive evils as well as the evils themselves, a movement toward hope and life as well as despair and death, and possibilities as well as limits. The novels derive much of their depth and tension from this conflict. The negation in the human environment seems all but overwhelming, yet Wallant effectively counters it with the extraordinary resources he finds within the human spirit.

Wallant immediately reveals himself as a highly skilled craftsman in *The Human Season.* He brings his characters alive, and by his selection of the most ordinary concrete details, gestures and actions he evokes a deeply moving human situation. The novel depicts Joe Berman, a fifty-nine year old plumber, during the summer after his wife's death. . . . Wallant develops the novel by juxtaposing Berman's present with his memories of the past. His present seems a terrible parody of his past. . . . As a result he turns to the past; almost every chapter contains a dated memory, each earlier than the preceding one. At first, reflecting his present state, his memories are of death and pain, but gradually memories of the joys of life begin to emerge intertwined with them. The general movement of his reminiscences is from death to life, but more important, his memories soon present joy and sadness mixed inextricably together: when his father died, for example, "his grief came out in a shape like beauty. He was filled with wonder, brimming with the peculiar beauty he felt like an inexplicable pain.''

Wallant describes these recollections in a smooth, pellucid, rhythmic style which differs markedly from the compressed, tense exchanges which characterize present time in the novel. Both the style and the imagery become increasingly lyrical as the memories reach back into Berman's childhood, and this lyricism contributes significantly to Berman's recovery.... The electric shock [which jolts him away from the past] remains a rather crude symbol, but Wallant's fusion of memory, imagery and style renders *The Human Season* a beautifully poetic yet richly human novel. (pp. 78-80)

[*The Pawnbroker*] derives much of its power from its shocking settings, characters and events. Yet at the same time *The Pawnbroker* is an intricately constructed, complex literary achievement. Significant patterns of things, words and images, of character relationships and interlocking actions enrich the novel's development. A number of verbal and image patterns surround Sol Nazerman. He is described as a stone, but one chipping away and developing cracks, and he is also described in images of precarious equilibrium or balance. He is called "uncle," by his niece and nephew, and because this is a generic term for a pawnbroker; but although his racketeer boss Murillio uses the term ironically, it gradually comes to denote a reality. Another term, prominent in *King Lear*, "nothing," echoes throughout the novel: both Sol and his assistant Jesus Ortiz try to convice themselves that the other means nothing to him, and both confront the various forms of nothingness. The echoes of *King Lear* are extensive enough to establish an unobtrusive but enriching parallel between the two works. Both Lear and Sol are strong men who are brought face to face with the realities of human frailty and human suffering; like Lear, Sol passes through a madness in which he becomes hypersensitive to the sight, sound and smell of mortality. Predatory animal imagery is also characteristic of both works. (pp. 80-1)

The revitalizing force of nature appears in still other images and patterns. A river which takes on connotations similar to those of the river in *The Human Season* frames the novel; Sol notes the disparity between its filthy surface and the insistent force beneath, and he is drawn to it. The names Marilyn Birchfield and Mabel Wheatly indicate that these women also offer a sustaining relationship with nature; both seek to save their men, Sol and Jesus, by providing love and hope.... Light images constitute the predominant image pattern in the novel. Repeatedly cruel and false artificial light is juxtaposed to sunlight. Sol seeks to evade sunlight just as he seeks to evade life itself. But Sol can never fully reject the sun, for as his name indicates, he in some sense is the sun; he has its life force within him, and eventually it will emerge.

The Pawnbroker also contains a vein of allegory, both in its settings and in its character relations. Its primary setting, the pawnshop, represents various aspects of Western civilization. It reveals the underside of man's dependence on things, both the pathos of his efforts to protect himself with things and the immense weights of things crushing in upon him. The shop is also referred to as a museum; thus it conveys also the weight of history, particularly of the failures of the past. Furthermore, Wallant carefully selects the specific objects he mentions in the shop and which people bring in to pawn: musical instruments, objets d'art, lights, means of communication, clothing and clocks predominate. Thus the things in the shop provide further evidence of the failure of art, culture, and refinement, the death of civilization which Sol feels was caused by the camps.

Wallant also employs the pawnshop to criticize materialism and the capitalistic system itself. The nature of the pawning transaction suggests that the Western economic system is based on exploitation and degradation; Sol's only defense of the business is that "poor people are always taken advantage of, and there could be no business in our society without that being so." Money itself exerts considerable force in the novel. Almost every human relationship in it has a financial basis; even those who have other interests find themselves forced to meet over money. Yet in spite of all this, things still have only the value people give them, and Sol's transactions retain a human dimension.... In an economically based social system, the economic transaction itself is forced to provide whatever human interaction that can be achieved.

Both the tightly interwoven structure and the allegorical dimension of *The Pawnbroker* are manifested in its character relationships. Directly or indirectly, all of these relationships focus on Sol Nazerman, and their allegorical dimension derives from the fact that most dramatize various facets of Sol's inner life. (pp. 81-2)

Like Levanthol the Jewish cop, the Kantors and Murillio have crossed over the line to become exploiters; they are presented as capable of acting as the Nazis did toward the Jews. These characters represent aspects of Sol himself to the extent that Sol also has moved in this direction (the name "Nazerman" is as close to Nazi-man as to Nazarene). Sol's fear of Robinson and his disgust at Murillio's mechanical voice, therefore, indicate his fear and disgust with himself; Sol instructively draws back from the logical results of his own repressions. His agonizing recovery begins when he realizes that his co-operation with Murillio is a form of complicity. (p. 83)

[Why] does Jesus sacrifice himself for Sol? The strength of the father-son relationship which develops offers one possible explanation. So also do Jesus's fundamental decency and innocence, as well as the practical considerations he mentions himself. Also, Jesus's (probably unfortunate) name and the religious imagery in the novel are too insistent to be ignored; and Ortiz does bring grace to Sol in the sense that he gives Sol something beyond Sol's reach. But Jesus is somewhat elusive as an independent character; he functions in addition in the novel as a secret sharer or alter ego of Sol, as another manifestation of an aspect of Sol's inner life. And in fact, the facet of Sol's personality which Jesus most accentuates is the capacity for love and sacrifice which Sol conceals so imperfectly throughout the novel. Not only does Wallant depict Jesus and Sol as very much alike, each also appears, and even functions, as a Christ figure for the other. *The Pawnbroker* is not a religious allegory; rebirth in it grows out of the resources of the human personality. (p. 84)

The Children at the Gate is an interesting but inferior reworking of *The Pawnbroker*. The skill, richness and allegorical depth which he exhibited in the earlier novel are still present, but almost invariably in less successful forms. In *The Children at the Gate*, the central relationship is reversed; the youth comparable to Jesus, a nineteen year old New Haven Italian named Angelo De Marco, becomes the person who has deadened himself in response to the evils which surround him, and he is brought alive by a fatherly Jewish orderly named Sammy who ultimately sacrifices his life, largely for Angelo. But . . . neither Angelo nor Sammy approaches achieving the immense force and personal depth of Sol Nazerman. Nor do De Marco's Pharmacy, lower class Italian life in New Haven, and the hospital ever achieve the resonance of the pawnshop, Harlem, and the camps. Like the pawnshop, the drugstore embodies materialism and the weight of things, and in selling fraudulent medicines and sending Angelo to work the hospital its owner, his uncle Frank, exploits others' suffering for financial gain. But this theme is not nearly so functional as in *The Pawnbroker,* for unlike Sol and Jesus, neither Angelo nor Sammy is at all attracted to money or power. In addition, particularly in its constant use of the children's ward and its dependence on the rape of a sick child which only indirectly involves either of the principal characters, the novel at times falls into the sensationalism and sentimentality which *The Pawnbroker* avoids.

The allegorical dimension of the novel grows out of Angelo's experiences at the hospital. Though less successful than the pawnshop as an image of Western civilization, the hospital is an effective image of the mind. His "labyrinthine journeys through the huge building" are to a significant extent descents into himself; he recognizes of what he fears at the hospital that "maybe it was in himself." . . . Most of the characters in the novel do not function as referents to Angelo's inner life; rather they act as false guides who can recommend only various forms of conformity to empty conventions. But Lebedov is an almost allegorical figure of desire; his first words to Angelo are simply "I *want*." The rape is presented as the outbreak of forces which can no longer be repressed, and Angelo recognizes his own complicity, in effect that Lebedov is an aspect of himself, in "terrible, erotic dreams" that involve his mother, his sister and the raped child. (In allegorical terms his feeble-minded sister represents his repressed emotions and affections; she dies gradually as he develops his capacities for feeling and love.) (pp. 84-6)

[Sammy] immediately establishes himself as one who speaks the truth with love; he examines Angelo like a judging but merciful God, and despite Angelo's resistance, develops a psychic, almost mystical power over him. Sammy represents the opposite of Angelo; he opposes mystery and art to Angelo's scientific rationalism; feeling, compassion, suffering, involvement and love to Angelo's coldness, indifference and detachment. Through his power over him, Sammy acts as a means of Angelo's development; he brings out these very qualities in Angelo. Yet Angelo's response to Sammy is only explicable as a response to something in himself. Thus Sammy also functions as Angelo's alter ego, as a manifestation of Angelo's hitherto suppressed but gradually emerging true self.

The relationship between Angelo and Sammy, however, not only leads Angelo finally to enter into life, it also contains the reasons for the novel's failure as a work of fiction. Fundamentally, Sammy's stature in the novel is at odds with his function. Structurally, *The Children at the Gate* is clearly intended to be Angelo's novel; Sammy is subordinate to him in that he acts as a means to Angelo's growth.

But Sammy is such a marvelous figure in his own right that he emerges as the more dominant and more interesting of the two. . . . But at the same time, the demands of the novel's structure force Wallant to undercut the characterization of Sammy upon which the novel comes to depend. . . . Too often differing requirements of theme and plot come in conflict; for instance, when for a moment Wallant wishes to leave Angelo in doubt as to whether Sammy committed the rape, he must make Sammy appear more indifferent to the girl's fate than his being a man of compassion should allow. Sammy remains a rich, extraordinary fictional figure, but he is asked to bear too much weight. *The Children at the Gate* is Wallant's least successful work. (pp. 86-7)

The Tenants of Moonbloom differs from [the earlier works] in two essential respects. For the first time Wallant depicts not only the process of rebirth but the hero reborn; Norman Moonbloom begins to enter into life less than a third of the way into the novel. Secondly, in marked contrast to his previous work, the tone of this novel is profoundly comic. Whereas the earlier novels described the struggle, *The Tenants of Moonbloom* portrays acceptance achieved, as well as the necessarily comic nature of this acceptance. . . .

The slums become images of reality; deceptive surfaces and the realities concealed within are repeatedly juxtaposed in the novel, and in entering the tenements Moonbloom penetrates beneath the surface for the first time. One function of his tenants is to represent mankind in all its variations (they also act variously as foils, sign-posts, guides and alter egos for Norman); thus, in the tenements Moonbloom is brought face to face with humanity. His awakening develops almost naturally, even inevitably, from this confrontation. As in Angelo's case, the transition is represented by an illness which is a metaphor for gestation, for the stripping away of his defenses and the emergence of human sensitivity. (p. 87)

Wallant adopts the view that the comic spirit possesses the ability to accept reality, even in its ugliest forms, and yet at the same time transcend it. *The Tenants of Moonbloom* contains a healthy sense of the limits placed on man, but these are limits upon man's capacity to act and understand, not of his capacities for sensitivity, creativity, acceptance, and love. (p. 88)

In the life of Norman Moonbloom, Wallant demonstrates that it is possible to transcend the limits of the human condition while at the same time remaining within it. This unique fusion is expressed in the novel in Wallant's paradoxical treatment of reason and madness, time and timelessness, and reality and fantasy. . . . Dreaming and "madness" . . . emerge as creative capacities; by comparing them with the senses Wallant suggests that they may be used to open up a richer, broader reality which subsumes but does not supersede the ordinary. At the end, perhaps too conceptually, Wallant states explicitly that man needs his dreams, illusions, or even delusions to supplement the harsher realities, and that these dreams have a reality of their own. . . . An extraordinary number of the tenants are themselves artists, and Norman gradually becomes one; his developing transcendent comprehension and acceptance come to constitute a creative artistic vision, and his repairs are his works of art.

The novel concludes with one of the finest comic scenes in literature, one which fully dramatizes comic transcendence.

Repairing the protuberance in Basellecci's bathroom has a quixotic quality about it, for Basellecci will, as Norman acknowledges, die of cancer anyway, alone, in terrible pain. But in repairing the wall Norman, his helpers and Basellecci achieve a joyous, truly beautiful and cleansing transcendent communion, which inevitable failure and death cannot destroy and which is the best that man who is doomed to die can hope for. Their transcendent communal experience provides the climax of the increasingly meaningful ceremonies which Norman's always ritualistic relationships with his tenants gradually become. The novel finally reveals itself as a comic celebration of man's capacity for love and joy.

Yet in spite of the comic genius of the novel, *The Tenants of Moonbloom* is less successful than *The Pawnbroker*. Comedy does not prove as effective a means of dealing with slums, suffering and evil. Wallant never quite convinces the reader of the immanent presence of hell in his comic world; thus *The Tenants of Moonbloom* lacks the tension of his earlier work. Furthermore, the novel's comic context somewhat vitiates the process of rebirth. Elsewhere this process involves terrible struggle, but here it is virtually painless; Moonbloom's past experiences offer no difficulties, nor is he pulled in several directions by various aspects of himself. Norman Moonbloom remains a less substantial figure than Wallant's other central characters. (pp. 89-90)

[There] remains a sense of mystery at the heart of each of his novels. How do rebirth and acceptance come about? how does one achieve them?—these questions are unanswered, because Wallant finds them ultimately unanswerable. In *The Human Season* Wallant employs lyrical symbols and style to describe Joe Berman's recovery, but he explains neither why nature has such healing effects nor why he experienced the joy he is able to remember. In *The Pawnbroker* and *The Children at the Gate,* the locus of mystery shifts from the central figure to the person who brings about his rebirth, to the mystery of man's concern for others, of human interaction and human love. What motivates Jesus and Sammy? As Sol says, "if it had been a mystery in the end to Ortiz, what right did he have to expect more." In *The Tenants of Moonbloom,* the mystery of rebirth becomes but a single instance of the final mystery of man's ability to accept the human condition. Why does Norman develop a compulsion to help others? And why is he able to embrace the comic spirit? . . . Each of Wallant's heroes seeks for a time to know and to understand why, but in the end they acquiesce in the mystery of life, that is, in a form of faith.

Rebirth and acceptance in Wallant's work finally derive from Wallant's abiding faith in man. He fully recognizes man's capacity to perform atrocities; yet in every man he finds redeeming qualities and impulses. . . . Wallant defines joy as the Romantic poets did, as an affirmation which includes but transcends pain; and joy proves irrepressible in Wallant's world. . . . At the same time that Wallant is all but overwhelmed by the horrors of modern life, he retains a deep awe and wonder at the goodness and beauty of man, and at the joy inherent in human existence. (pp. 90-1)

Thomas M. Lorch, "The Novels of Edward Lewis Wallant," in Chicago Review *(reprinted by permission of* Chicago Review; *copyright © 1967 by* Chicago Review*), Vol. 19, No. 2, 1967, pp. 78-91.*

NICHOLAS AYO

The human body in Wallant's world is a scandal. Mankind is portrayed in pain and ugliness, in the humiliation of a body that sweats, smells, runs over from glands out of control, ages and finally decays. The human situation exceeds the barrenness of Eliot's wasteland; it is a torture chamber, a garbage dump where people are buried alive and thrash around until they can no longer move. They wait for the peace of oblivion. "'Life is an avalanche—the little stones only bruise you, the big ones kill you. What's the sense getting excited?'" (p. 88)

Wallant's novels tend to maximize the vulnerability of the flesh, which is soft. It bruises, it tears, it can be crushed. Most of all, flesh can be pierced through by so many cutting edges. . . . Throughout Wallant the flesh is pierced, whether in punishment, like Sol ramming his hand through the spiked paperweight, or in celebration, like the tender anniversary intercourse between Berman and his wife, the woman who had been so reluctant to be entered on their wedding night.

Sex in the form of perversion, a love that is so desperate it becomes distorted, becomes another well of pain. Lebedov in *The Children at the Gate* molested the little girl recovering from her operation, and George Smith in *The Pawnbroker* "wished for a small, tender girl to appear so he could hurl himself on her as on a terribly beautiful stake." And yet, Lebedov loved butterflies, the symbols of beauty and resurrection of the flesh from darkness into sunshine, and George Smith loved nothing more than to ponder the spirit-filled ideas of the great minds of all time. Amazingly, Wallant can reverse the downward spiral of pain. (p. 89)

The puncture of innocent flesh is a recurrent image of the human condition. In Wallant's work, man's body is constantly entered. An electric shock revives Berman from his heart's sleep and he begins to feel again. Norman's loss of virginity with Sheryl initiates him into responsible manhood. *The Children at the Gate* is set in "Sacred Heart Hospital. Talk about Calvary." . . . In all the novels a heart is pierced, a heart that bleeds and finally leads to reconciliation. (p. 90)

Wallant's male protagonists, such as Sammy, Jesus, and Norman, would qualify as sinner-saints, somewhat like the whiskey priest in Graham Greene. The details of their life would invite comparison with Jesus of Nazareth, even if Wallant had not left a trail of lightly veiled allegory and even direct references to the cross of Christ. What one finally makes of the Christian symbolism, of course, will vary according to one's beliefs. For the believer, every man is called to relive Christ's passion and resurrection. For the non-believer, the references to the gospel operate at least on the level of allusion to a well-known and powerful myth of sacrifice and rebirth. (p. 91)

[Both] the sacred and the profane, both the sacred heart and the secular heart, can be viewed as related embodiments of a common ground, the human condition, where men are in agony, victims of the fact of suffering and the inevitable decline of mortal flesh. (pp. 92-3)

Wallant's fiction celebrates *radical incarnation.* So completely does a Sammy or a Norman identify with the human condition that their lives become "saintly" by merely becoming fully human. They accept the human body and the "slings and arrows of outrageous fortune." They consent to have their heart pierced with a vision of a suffering sea of humanity; they even agree to care, to love, to pour out their lives for other men. In a fragmentary character sketch Wallant concludes, "She can only learn pity and compassion and real love for others if she is brought to realize that she *does* exist as a human, learns *self-respect*!" This item is headed with a quote in caps: "You are irreplaceable and immortal." (p. 93)

What Wallant gives us is the shadow side of a dialectic, the "mystery of iniquity" rather than the "mystery of faith," the theology of garbage rather than the theology of creation. Ultimately, it is a plea that echoes the cry, "My God, why have you abandoned me?" As one critic put it, Wallant's heroes "believe in nothing and have faith in everything." There is a sudden reconciliation of opposites, and the stasis that is achieved by stating the case against life at its worst and moving from "breakdown to breakthrough" resolves, in a moment of insight and affirmation, the conflicts that beset us. (pp. 93-4)

> *Nicholas Ayo, "The Secular Heart: The Achievement of Edward Lewis Wallant," in* Critique: Studies in Modern Fiction *(copyright © by* Critique *1970), Vol. XII, No. 2, 1970, pp. 86-94.*

ROBERT W. LEWIS

[Wallant] achieves the dramatic by skirting the melodramatic; his characters tend to be drawn in outline or reduced to a few essential traits; his symbolism tends to be simple and straightforward, if not obvious; ... these aforementioned characteristics help to describe him as an American naturalist in the tradition of Dreiser and Norris.... [He] was interested in the difference between appearances and reality, and philosophically he was a meliorist determinist. Like the subjects that concerned the turn-of-the-century American naturalists, his subjects are contemporary social and personal problems; similarly, his characters live on the lower fringes of bourgeois society but are often distinguished by a certain native nobility, and his melodramatic stories are replete with violent death and gross sex. Also like some of the earlier American naturalists, Wallant incorporates symbolic and mythic elements into his novels. But the last novel written before his premature death, *The Tenants of Moonbloom* (1963), is an important exception to the naturalistic pattern in its comic treatment of similar subjects and ideas, in Wallant's movement toward an existential stance, and in his heightened, thorough-going use of mythic and symbolic elements. (p. 70)

His heroes have lost God, but they still keep room in their hearts where God once was, and each of [the earlier] three novels ends in a muted victory for traditional values like courage, love, friendship, and hope. (p. 71)

[Wallant's protagonists'] world is not as bleak as [in Hubert Selby's *Last Exit to Brooklyn*], but it is filled with enough horror to last us, and it has the further validation of apparent empirical test. The heroes have thought long and hard about life. That is, they are not merely reacting like Selby's erect beasts, but they are trying to live within the context of reason. Even a beautiful sunset is a delusion to Sol Nazerman. Appearances can be of beauty and kindness and mutual care, but beneath the surface, reality is coarse and brutal. (p. 72)

[Wallant] takes us with his tortured heroes through hell, but they finally "see" differently. They cannot curse God and die. They cannot find God irrelevant, let alone dead. They cannot be the pitiable sadistic or masochistic beasts of Selby's world, nor can they escape through narcosis. They must suffer, be crucified, and reborn.... In the Nazi concentration camp, Sol was forced to witness his wife's sexual abuse by an S.S. guard; his reaction was to go psychically blind—he *could not* see that which went beyond physical brutality and torture. But now that a cruel fate has preserved him, he refuses any human involvements or attachments that could again become avenues to feeling. He now *thinks* he sees clearly, without illusion. The East River that he and Marilyn Birchfield sit beside *appears* to be covered by "shimmering sequins" in the sun, but Sol knows what is in the greasy, filthy water: he thinks, "out of all the muck an illusion of brightness." Much of what Sol has seen has been the worst of humankind, and he tells the social worker that inhumanity is the standard. But then his vision begins to play tricks on him. "A customer would come up to the counter and it would seem the customer's face zoomed so close that Sol could no longer see the features, was blinded by the magnified surface of human skin."

And a half dozen more references to Sol's failing sight and insight come toward the end of the novel and precede the dénouement in which Jesus Ortiz in a Christly gesture lays down his life for Sol when he himself takes the robber's bullet intended for the pawnbroker. Then Sol truly sees, presumably in the way that Wallant sees, and the ending is swift and moving.... For Sol, Ortiz's black eyes are "dark openings into mysteries," and finally from his own eyes flood the cleansing tears, "drowning him, dragging him back to that sea of tears he had thought to have escaped ... of grief, of *grief*." His "anesthetic numbness" leaves him, and he is born again, born to raw wounds, born to love, born to the "ineffable marvel" of "the great mortal decay that was living because it was dying."

So similarly is Joe Berman of *The Human Season* reborn to hear the voice of children, a dog's bark, a plane's engine; so too is Angelo De Marco of *The Children at the Gate* revived after suffering and doubt. (pp. 73-4)

[His] strongly affirmative endings separate Wallant from the "new" naturalists, but while each of these three novels is interesting, it is the fourth of Wallant's novels, *The Tenants of Moonbloom,* that is most successful and pleasing.... Even though the themes and many of the motifs and images are the same as those of the other novels, ... it is different from the other three in its comic treatment, and it has a different kind of hero.... [*The Tenants of Moonbloom*] radically differs from them in the development and nature of the hero. While the first three protagonists acquire insight during the course of their crises, they are not initially innocents but need help and catharsis because they are "up tight," turned so completely inward. They have reacted to their griefs by forming shells around their wounded souls.... (pp. 74-5)

Norman Moonbloom, however, is an entirely different case, and speculating on the reasons for Wallant's creating a different kind of protagonist while keeping the same themes, will, I think, reveal a progression in Wallant's art and also in his understanding of meanings implicitly in those repeated themes.... [It has been suggested of *Moonbloom* that] comedy is inappropriate for the subject matter and less effective, vitiating "the process of rebirth."

. . . [However, it] is precisely in laughing at that which is serious *as subject* that we understand anew. (p. 75)

[In Moonbloom's] symbolic rehabilitation of his tenants' souls, he not only discovers responsibility; he also discovers his own soul in a series of encounters that are a hero's initiation to the mysteries of life. . . .

Norman Moonbloom is a low comic character, innocent, child-like, a *schlemiel* who is beset with no tragedy but with a series of petty irritations. (p. 76)

The heroes of the first three of Wallant's novels would not have had any doubt that they existed, and serpents sent by a vengeful god, or by faithless fellowmen, would have lashed round them. Indeed, Norman Moonbloom's world is also brought to change, and he initially conceives of it as chaos, ruin. A claw of life is reaching out to seize him, but we cannot take his anxiety too seriously. In spite of this thirty-three years, Moonbloom is merely suffering growing pains. (pp. 76-7)

[His] exultant howl of birth at the end of the novel means that he has come to spiritual as well as emotional life. He has been "baptized" and can now feel the joys of life as well as its pains, both of which he could not have felt in his fetal state. Like the imagery of symbolic birth, the religious imagery is also comic and is seen in such details as the "refectory furniture" and "phony arches" of the run-down apartments, and words like "angel," "altar," "jehad," "crusade," "benediction," and "transfiguration" that are used in profane rather than sacred contexts. (p. 77)

Norman is led to baptism and initiation to the mysteries of faith through learning how to feel, first for himself and then for others; through accepting responsibility for the needs and wishes of his tenants; through recognizing that rationality can be a tool of a profound ignorance of life; consequently, through developing the power of his imagination to see behind his own mask and the mask of others; and finally through discovering the holy trinity of survival: courage, dream, and love. (pp. 77-8)

In the other three Wallant novels, the rather conventional premise is that each of the heroes is hung up and must be cut down. But Norman Moonbloom's suspension is magical; no rope holds him to anything else until he learns to wallow in the wonderfully redemptive muck of life. . . . (p. 78)

Unlike his tenants and unlike the heroes of the earlier novels, Moonbloom has an irrelevant past and no hang-up, obsession, or dream until he undertakes his mad crusade. To be human is to be stupid and absurd, not rational like his successful brother Irwin whose commercial platitudes fog into double talk; to be human is to be animal, to bleed, to be cruel, desperate, hopeful, and kind. And above all, to be human and saved is to be able to laugh. (pp. 79-80)

Before Norman has his regenerative illness, his humor is "caustic" and humorless, "too silly" and "too ridiculous." This laughter early in the novel is merely "polite" or, as with the musician Katz who hangs himself, a deceptive mask. Early in Moonbloom's life, just as he had looked for God and found only theology, so the literalist Norman had been turned away from laughter because he had discovered that it could be cruel. Thus he and his tenants distort natural laughter. . . . But midway through the novel, Norman emerges from behind his mask with its humorless and false

smile to become susceptible to spontaneous, unconstrained laughter. . . . His tenants cannot understand why he would laugh when they tell him of their sorrow, but the laughter for Norman is pain, the pain of life that goes beyond mere sympathy. "Weeping and laughter, both expressed the irresistible, and pain and joy interchanged between them. How had he chosen laughter?" His mad, uncontrollable laughter makes Norman fear his own breakdown, but at the same time he feels that life is thus for the first time opening up for him, and he drives himself on in his holy war to redeem his tenants' lost dignities and joys. Though he had studied to become a rabbi, he had not believed in God, but his laughter becomes a devotion of "profound modesty and wonder and shyness." It contains "awe and terror." (pp. 82-3)

[Even] the dying Basellecci finally laughs with him. The first smiles were humorless and false, but at last the secret society of initiates simply smiles together, and Basellecci's smile is serene. When Norman finally discovers that he has earned a new name, crooning "to an infinite note of ache and joy," his response is both a thrill and nearly laughter. (p. 83)

Neither Wallant's style nor his ideas are new. He confirms the traditional values of self-awareness, love, and faith that are only won through a Dostoyevskian struggle of the hero with himself. Like his contemporary neo-naturalists, Wallant implies the irrelevancy of absolute moral and ethical judgments in a deterministic world. But in contrast to his serious approaches in the first three novels and the despair of the neo-naturalistic school of writing, Wallant's use of comedy and a parodied yet genuine myth of initiation in *The Tenants of Moonbloom* is an instructive variation on the theme of the hung-up hero and cause for grief at his premature death. . . . His last hero, Moonbloom, grows in the imagination to rival the great legendary heroes of myth, and he is a more successful champion than protagonists like the Pawnbroker *because* he is comic. (pp. 83-4)

> Robert W. Lewis, "The Hung-Up Heroes of Edward Lewis Wallant," in Renascence (© copyright, 1972, Marquette University Press), Winter, 1972, pp. 70-84.

*   *   *

WARREN, Robert Penn   1905-

Warren is an American novelist, poet, short story writer, playwright, essayist, critic, editor, and scholar. With major contributions in all these genres, Warren is considered one of the most distinguished men of letters in America today. He has consistently been in the intellectual vanguard of American scholarship: he was a member of the Fugitive poets and cofounder of the group's publication, *The Fugitive;* founding editor of *The Southern Review;* and one of the original and most influential of the New Critics. Warren's love of history, as well as the Fugitive conception of art as a vital force and means of expressing ideas and human experience, inform all of his work. Reflected in his writing are his strong moral values and persistent search for truth. He was twice recipient of the Pulitzer Prize, for fiction in 1947 and for poetry in 1958. He has also served as Consultant in Poetry to the Library of Congress. (See also *CLC,* Vols. 1, 4, 6, 8, and *Contemporary Authors,* Vols. 13-16, rev. ed.)

DENNIS M. DOOLEY

Through the three [long, personal digressions in *Brother to*

Dragons], Warren gives us the spiritual history of RPW, a spiritual history which parallels in many respects the spiritual history of Jefferson, the central concern of the poem, and which justifies the superior wisdom of RPW the commentator. (p. 19)

His cousin's butchering of [a slave was] a traumatic experience for Jefferson. Prior to this event, Jefferson saw man as standing between beast and God and aspiring to the divine. Evil was merely the blot of centuries of oppression, which could be erased within the context of the American Eden. In this context, man's basic nobility, goodness and innocence would assert themselves and man would fulfill his God-like potential. The slaying of George is such a traumatic experience for Jefferson that he reverses his philosophic position and denies that man is capable of any good. This is the Jefferson we encounter at the opening of the poem. (p. 20)

The three digressions in *Brother to Dragons* . . . can be seen to mark the three stages of spiritual growth of the persona RPW. In the first digression [like Jefferson], he is disillusioned, bitter and alienated. In his ascent of Rocky Hill, the second digression, RPW receives the truths necessary for spiritual growth from the images of his father, the mountain and the snake. The third digression marks the assimilation of these truths, which assimilation permits RPW to be reconciled to his father and to enter "the world of action and liability." The events within the digressions are all experientially prior to the "Any Time" reality of the central action of the poem and thus vindicate the mature spiritual wisdom which RPW displays in confronting Jefferson.

RPW's spiritual progress parallels the spiritual progress of Jefferson. (p. 29)

[The] digressions serve two other functions. First, the RPW episode functions as the traditional Warren device of the story within the story. . . . [The] RPW episode in *Brother to Dragons* provides a miniature working out of the ethical ideal of the main narrative action. Here the episode works more as a frame than a contained exemplum. After Jefferson has been introduced, RPW gives us his first digression. The second digression follows almost immediately while the third digression takes the final seventeen pages of the poem. Given the second digression, the third follows logically and organically. In the vast gap between the second and third digressions, Jefferson's confrontation and assimilation of spiritual reality takes place. Thus, the main action of the poem, Jefferson's conversion, is framed by RPW's conversion. This frame works in a second way. Warren says in his Introduction that the main issue with which *Brother to Dragons* is concerned is a "human constant." By having Jefferson's spiritual progress also acted out by RPW, the issue of the poem ceases to be simply an issue of the Nineteenth Century. By enclosing the past within the frame of the present, Warren is able to transcend mere past and present and to create his poetic "Any Time." (pp. 29-30)

> Dennis M. Dooley, "The Persona RPW in Warren's 'Brother to Dragons'," in The Mississippi Quarterly (copyright 1972 Mississippi State University), Winter, 1971-72, pp. 19-30.

DAVID B. OLSON

The internal level of action—the Jack Burden story with its moral-intellectual probings—which has surrounded the Willie Stark story is not concluded until the final twelve pages of [*All the King's Men*]. Here we find out what Jack has learned from all his efforts to piece things together. But these final pages are the conclusion of Jack Burden's story, and there is a feeling of anti-climax, not only because Willie is dead and settled but because the conclusion is the wrap-up on a character we have cared very little for from the start.

Yet the final twelve pages are also the conclusion, the all-important finishing touches, of the whole novel. It seems to me that if *All the King's Men* is a really good novel this ending must somehow contribute to the novel's success. . . . [Despite] some apparent weaknesses, the conclusion of the novel not only is successful but, in terms of Jack Burden's intellectual and psychological probings, is the consistent and the "right" ending for the novel. (p. 166)

[The] whole effect of the conclusion is one which suggests Warren's apparent confusion about what to do with the internal level of action in the novel. Both Jack's retreat to the past and his hope for the future suggest Warren really knew of no satisfactory way to resolve the course which Jack has followed throughout the novel. All of these present serious and threatening shortcomings for the novel's conclusion. But we can, I think, see the conclusion as not so unsatisfactory if we consider that in terms of the Jack Burden story the ending is quite consistent with the direction in which Jack's intellectual rationalizing and his incapacity for action have led him throughout the novel.

Early in the novel Willie Stark asks Jack what he thinks ought to be done about the embezzler, Byram White, and Jack caustically replies, "Thinking is not my line." . . . We know, however, that thinking *is* Jack's line, for at least half of the novel's action centers around Jack's intense intellectual probings. Much of the thickness and detail of the novel's texture, in fact, is the result of Jack's intense efforts to set down everything, to penetrate all actions, to delineate each shade of cause and effect, and to define and re-define every thought and feeling. While *All the King's Men* is spectacularly a novel of action, it is also very much a philosophical novel. And Jack is, despite his own disclaimer, the center of the novel's intellectual drama. Unlike Warren's other novels, *All the King's Men* quite effectively isolates and at the same time intertwines the dramatic and the philosophical impulses of the story. Jack's moral-intellectual inquiries ripple off of and around the events of Willie Stark's unequivocal course of action.

While this impulse of intense intellectual probing is present in Warren's other novels, in none of them does it spiral downward as deeply and acutely as in *All the King's Men*. In *Night Rider* and *World Enough and Time,* for example, both Percy Munn and Jeremiah Beaumont indulge in a good deal of self-scrutiny as they strive to define themselves through committing a purely unequivocal act. . . . But the introspection which Percy Munn and Jeremiah Beaumont exercise is not the kind of razor-sharp penetration that Jack Burden levels at himself and at the world. In their attempts at figuring out what makes them tick, neither Munn nor Beaumont perseveres in his probings the way Jack Burden does. Finding no intellectual answer to their problems, they capitulate to direct physical action. We might say that Jack Burden has more intellectual staying power. Warren can penetrate deeper with Jack because in *All the King's Men* the impulse of action is separated from the impulse of intellectual searching and defining. Unlike *Night Rider* and *World Enough and Time,* the novel contains, as Jack tells us, his story and Willie's story. With these two opposing drives isolated, Warren can focus more precisely and work more intensely on each. In *At Heaven's Gate* Warren attempts a similar process of separating out and isolating, but he has difficulty in controlling and unifying the separated strands of the novel. Perhaps there are simply too many detailed case-histories in the novel. (pp. 167-68)

While in abstract terms Jack proposes a belief in the "web theory" of history, he cannot commit himself to a total acceptance of it in the real, the personal world.... [He] obscures the parallel between Judge Irwin and Cass Mastern, for it will make too obvious a distasteful personal reality. Jack's escape mechanism is *not* really his Great Sleep or his Great Twitch theory. It is his power for intellectually qualifying and redefining, for creating alternatives. But unlike Percy Munn and Jeremiah Beaumont, Jack gets to the truth of things; he discovers the knowledge for which he strives so intensely. The only step remaining for him is to put the knowledge together and to *admit* that it is unequivocally true. Yet this would leave him no out.... [There] is a perilous balance between Jack's having the truth and his accepting it.... [His] rational probing in itself is what allows him to avoid the fall into irrational and compulsive action that destroys both [Munn and Beaumont]. Jack's intellectual staying power works in two ways: it goes deeper and it helps him pull back before self-scrutiny becomes self-destruction. (pp. 169-70)

The whole tone of Jack's thought in the novel has two contrasting levels which are present simultaneously. He is the cocky smart-aleck who overtly rationalizes through specious intellectual gymnastics, asserting, for example, that "thinking is not my line" or falling back on his complex definition of the Great Twitch. Or relying on his concept of Idealism:

> What you don't know don't hurt you, for it
> ain't real.... If you are an Idealist it does
> not matter what you do or what goes on
> around you because it isn't real anyway....

But Jack does not assume this fraternity-boy tone simply to be funny, just as he is not really "kidding" when he almost tells Sugar-Boy who killed Willie. Jack assumes the style of an intellectual wise-acre because it fulfills the serious function of tempering the threatening knowledge which he gains. Being the smart-aleck fulfills the same need that the mental gymnastics do in his overtly serious commentaries at the end of the book. Whether cocky or honestly serious, both impulses of his thought stem from the same need: rationalization.... And whether cocky or serious, Jack's intellectual style is one primarily oriented towards preserving some kind of mental health. Thus when Warren has Jack pull back in the final pages of the novel, it is consistent with the kind of rationalizing mental hygiene which has typified Jack's probings all through the novel. Jack ... remains a character who underneath it all is interested in adjusting before the breaking point. If we see this impulse of rationalization as central to the style of Jack's self-scrutiny, then it seems to me that his ambiguous regression at the conclusion is the consistent way out for him.

But though we recognize that Jack rationalizes in order to endure, we still cannot ignore the impulse in him that is attracted to action as a means of resolving rather than side-stepping problems. In fact, the two opposite drives in him —his tendency to intellectually qualify problems out of existence *vis-a-vis* his attraction to clear, "hot" action—generate the internal tension in Jack which, despite his annoying traits, ultimately involves us in his story. In spite of the mask of indifference which emanates from his continual "but if's," we are very much aware of his attraction to Willie's assertive personality. (pp. 170-71)

To follow Jack's metaphor, Willie is the surgeon ... who cuts sharply into Jack's passivity to give him vicariously the feeling of assertion. Anyone who is capable of committing the pure, "hot" action eventually gains Jack's admiration.... [Any] satisfaction Jack gets from action is achieved vicariously. Again, in spite of his disclaimer, thinking *is* his line. (pp. 171-72)

The ending of the novel concludes the internal action, the Jack Burden story, for Willie's story is over and settled. And from our look at the two impulses in Jack—his intellectual probing, with its qualifying, and his need for action, with its frustrating incapacity for action—we find that the pattern which dominates both impulses is one characterized by deep penetration and movement up to the verge of unequivocal consummation, and then a quick pulling back *before* consummation. There is in Jack's confrontation with himself and with the external world a rhythm: intense movement forward and inward, and a sudden retreat from the brink, repeating itself over and over.

This rhythm simply hits its final measure in the conclusion. After thinking about his two fathers and their relative strong and weak points, Jack tells us that he simply "quit trying to decide." And he later says something else which illuminates a good deal about the rhythm of his life and also about the way his story ends. "When the game stops it will be called on account of darkness. But it is a long day." ... Though ending a novel "on account of darkness" might seem less than effective, I cannot see that the Jack Burden story could end any other way. As we have seen, it is "in the nature" of Jack to pull back from any apex that would unequivocally conclude his story. (pp. 175-76)

> *David B. Olson, "Jack Burden and the End-*
> *ing of 'All the King's Men'," in* The Missis-
> *sippi Quarterly (copyright 1973 Mississippi*
> *State University), Spring, 1973, pp. 165-76.*

PETER STITT

On the basis of his recent work, I don't think it's an exaggeration to say that Warren is the best that we now have, the dean of living American poets, occupying the place left vacant at Robert Frost's death. If this ranking is accurate, it is not generally recognized....

It may be that Warren's versatility has had a detrimental effect on his reputation as a poet. Perhaps we assume that a truly fine poet must give his all to poetry, or that a writer can show true excellence in only one genre.... Another factor in the case, however, has to be the kind of poetry Warren writes, which must seem unfashionable to superficial readers. Poetry is a response to the world in which we live; since before the turn of the century, most poets have been convinced that the modern world is a terrifying, inhuman, and increasingly inhumane place in which to live. (p. 262)

Our poetry has been dominated for many years by despairing and negative voices, voices which have searched in vain for positive support in this world. . . . Warren's voice is markedly different, part of another tradition altogether. Throughout his career, he has been able to find at least the promise of something positive. Like Frost and Roethke, he has found it in nature; like his fellow Fugitive poets, he has found it in the past and in his native South; and like most poets throughout time, he has found it in an indigenous religious sense allied to nature, the land, and to the potentialities of man. Which is not, I hope, to suggest that Warren is a naïve yea-sayer. The sense he has of the final joyfulness of life exists with a full knowledge of life's many mysteries, including its tragedies.

At the center of Warren's poetry, holding everything together, are two closely related conceptions—of man, and of the self. Warren is careful to place man within nature, as an integral part of it. And yet there is a crucial difference, too, between man and the rest of the natural world. (pp. 262-63)

It is man's mind, his intellect and his imagination, that is celebrated in Warren's poetry, for it is man's mind that allows him to be "the form-making animal par excellence. By making forms he understands the world, grasps the world, imposes himself upon the world."

Also at the heart of Warren's recent poetry is the concept of a well-rounded self. In defining his concept in *Democracy and Poetry,* Warren laid special emphasis upon two elements—an awareness of time and a sense of moral responsibility: "continuity—the self as a development in time, with a past and a future; and responsibility—the self as a moral identity, recognizing itself as capable of action worthy of praise or blame." In his best poems, Warren ranges freely over time, accumulating memories, experiences, thoughts, which coalesce about a single personality, a single self. In *Incarnations* and *Or Else,* the self is that of the poet himself; in *Audubon* it is primarily the ornithologist but, through him, again the poet as well.

In *Incarnations,* as in *Or Else,* Warren has chosen to address himself to the largest questions facing man; questions concerning the nature of the world, the nature of man himself, and the meaning of time and eternity. Viewed from this perspective, *Incarnations* can be seen as a somewhat irresolute trial run for the later volume. I don't mean to deprecate the book, just to suggest that it does not contain the fullest flowering of Warren's wisdom. *Incarnations* is divided into three sections. Each of the first two sections revolves around its own major theme, while the final section tries (and I think fails) to supply an answer to the questions posed earlier.

The inspiring spirits behind the book are Ralph Waldo Emerson, to whom Warren once wrote a long poem, and John Henry, from whose folk ballad Warren has drawn one of his epigraphs. The title of the book suggests the major idea which Warren has adapted from Emerson—that the physical world which surrounds us and of which we are a part has at its heart a spiritual essence. The epigraph from the folk song ("John Henry said to the Captain, 'A man ain't nuthin but a man'"), suggests three things. First, it reminds us of man's humility—he is a natural creature subject to death. Second, and growing out of this, is a sense of the brotherhood of men, an idea which is reinforced by the other of the book's two epigraphs: "Yet now our flesh is as

the flesh of our brethren" (*Nehemiah,* 5:5). Third, we should remember that the folk song as a whole asserts the strength of man's will, his intelligence coupled with his determination. The themes of mortality and brotherhood are handled most deeply in Section II of the book. Of the two poems appearing there, one tells of the painful cancer death of a man in a southern prison, and the other tells of the humiliation suffered by a black woman in New York—after being slightly struck by a car, she lies on the pavement and pees in her pants while screaming at the top of her lungs. (pp. 263-64)

Although predominantly a philosophical poet, Warren does not write abstract poems; his thoughts are generally presented in terms of suggestive images drawn from the world of physical reality. Section I of *Incarnations*—a long sequence of poems titled "Island of Summer"—has a Mediterranean setting. The sequence celebrates the natural world and invests it with a spiritual dimension all its own. This spirituality is discovered at the heart of things, as beneath the surface of a plum, a peach, or a fig. . . . The effect of such thoughtful actions is always the same—penetrating to the soul of the physical world brings meaning to life. It is an action repeated many times in the sequence.

Involved in this action is a search, for certainty, for religious meaning in a seemingly chaotic world. . . . Over and over in the sequence Warren asserts that we must accept the world for what it is and for what it brings us; despite his will and his imagination, man cannot control the direction of his life. . . . (pp. 264-65)

All of this wisdom, of course, is concerned with time, the way man conducts himself on earth, rather than with eternity and the realm of death. Warren is careful to caution us in one poem that "The world means only itself." And yet he is deeply interested in the subject of eternity as well, though the knowledge here is much less certain. Eternity in Warren's work is generally associated with brightness, whiteness, the sun, the sky, the sea, snow—even at times with the cold light of the moon. We are cautioned in the sequence's first poem: "Do not / Look too long at the sea, for / That brightness will rinse out your eyeballs." The promise here is one of annihilation, not resurrection—a spiritual destiny is not to be achieved through an intense preoccupation with eternity: "for the sun has / Burned all white, for the sun, it would / Burn our bones to chalk." In that direction lies only the certainty of death. (p. 265)

And yet Robert Penn Warren is the poet of "Promises" and would not leave the answer to his question at such a point of terrifying emptiness. Though a concentration upon eternity leads only to a dead end, Warren suggests elsewhere in the sequence that a concentration upon the world itself may lead to fulfillment: "We must try // To love so well the world that we may believe, in the end, in God." The promise implicit in this statement is given its fullest treatment in the remarkable poem which occupies precisely the center of the sequence: "Myth on Mediterranean Beach: Aphrodite as Logos." The figure of Aphrodite here is an "old hunchback in bikini," "an old / Robot with pince-nez and hair dyed gold," whose "breasts hang down like saddle bags" and whose "belly sags" to balance her hump. This incredible figure walks along the edge of the beach, like a line of print across a page. The text, whether she realizes it or not, is religious, for "glory attends her as she goes"—she illustrates nothing less than "The miracle of the human fact." The promise implicit in her existence is suggested in the word which Warren attaches to her in his title—"Logos," the creative Word of God. Her progress has a destined end: "For she treads the track the blessèd know // To a shore far lonelier than this / Where waits her apotheosis." She is the oldest person on Warren's beach, and the most remarkable; all eyes are drawn to her as she progresses. She is an emblem, a pathmaker, and seems to embody Warren's ultimate hope: "The terror is, all promises are kept. // Even happiness."

The terror arises from the moment of passage, death, to be enacted on "a shore far lonelier than this." And despite these positive assurances, given in the form of promises, we must remember that the sequence as a whole ends on . . . less than promising lines. . . . At the end of the book a similarly uncertain note is also struck. The final poem, called "Fog," is part of a short sequence titled "In the Mountains." The landscape here is suggestively white—the speaker is surrounded by a white fog that has risen from the white snow at his feet. The poem (and the book) ends with lines that are almost an anguished cry. . . . In a moment redolent with suggestions of eternity and of death, the speaker does not salute God but cries out for the physical, the real, the utterly down to earth. If there is a promise of salvation, of resurrection, in this book, it obviously can come only through this world of ours: "We must try / To love so well the world that we may believe, in the end, in God."

Audubon differs from the other two works under consideration here in that it is much less a philosophical discussion and much more a pure celebration—of man, of nature. It also differs in form in that it is a single long poem rather than a long sequence of closely related, but still individual, poems. . . . Warren has chosen a few details and a few words from the writings of Audubon in an attempt to get at the essence of this mysterious man. And though Warren hints, through his choice of epigraphs, that he has failed to capture that essence, it seems to me that he has succeeded triumphantly. (pp. 266-67)

By placing his hero in the wilderness and on the frontier, Warren is allying himself with a venerable tradition in American literature, thereby adding to the reverberations called up by his poem. Audubon, however, is no Natty Bumppo—he is a consummate artist capable of transforming his environment into something magical.

Warren's poem, like Audubon's paintings, is transcendentally beautiful—and yet the world that each of them has recorded is often violent and ugly. (pp. 267-68)

The violence in *Audubon* goes further than that between men. There is also the predatory violence of nature, as exemplified by the hawk, the jay, "the tushed boar," and Audubon's own violence, seemingly against the natural world he loved. We must not forget how he acquired specimens of the birds he painted: "He slew them, at surprising distances, with his gun. / Over a body held in his hand, his head was bowed low, / But not in grief." It is perhaps ironic that Audubon should have been able to produce works of such beauty out of a world of such base violence. And yet, in this poem at least, such seems to be the nature of the world and the nature of art. The transforming agent is the human imagination, and it is this faculty which Warren chiefly celebrates in the poem. Immediately following the

lines just quoted, where Audubon slays the birds, Warren writes: "He put them where they are, and there we see them: / In our imagination." (pp. 268-69)

Perhaps the most admirable thing about *Audubon* is that, by virtue of Warren's artistry, the poem itself achieves the wonders for which Audubon is praised. We find here a re-creation and celebration of nature which, far from glossing over its violence and ugliness, transforms it as if by magic into beauty. . . .

At his best, Warren allows his meanings to speak through the world he describes rather than attempting to enunciate them directly. . . . The only adverse criticism I have to make on Warren's verse concerns his occasional violation of this excellent standard. Warren is sometimes too clever and too direct with his philosophical materials, as when he breaks into his concrete re-creation of the world to deliver a capsule of abstract speculation. (p. 270)

Such passages are, however, extremely rare, and do not seriously impair what I most admire about this poem—its loving re-creation, in all its multiplicity, of the texture and detail of the world's body. . . . [The poem's virtues include] a return to the usable past for a subject and a hero, an economy and density of expression, an exploitation of all the resources of the language to produce poetry of striking quality. *Audubon* is easily the finest long poem written by an American in almost twenty years, and as good as we are likely to get for at least another twenty. (p. 271)

Warren has been writing such poem sequences as [*Or Else—Poem/Poems 1968-1974*] since the middle fifties and is the acknowledged master of the form. Other poets have tried their hands at it . . . but none with the supple assurance of intention which Warren brings to his performances. Essentially, the form is an amalgamation of a book of individual lyrics and a single, coherent long poem. It may well be that the poem sequence has replaced the epic in the modern age. The epic depends upon a coherent world view for its basis; because our age lacks such a world view, we should expect its epic form to be somewhat disjointed as well. Whatever we call the form, however, it seems clear that *Or Else* is an ambitious attempt to enclose and explain a world and a life—the poet's own.

While the individual poems here may be viewed as discrete units, they obviously have a much greater meaning and impact when viewed in context. Warren seems to recognize this principle as relevant to the world at large; in one poem he begins by saying: "Necessarily, we must think of the world as continuous." The thought is carried on later:

> . . . if it were not so, you wouldn't know
> you are in the world, or even that the
> world exists at all—
>
>   but only, oh, on-
> ly, in discontinuity, do we
> know that we exist.

Discrete and individual events, recorded in single poems, prove the separate existence of the individual and reverberate with a sort of local meaning. Only when placed in a larger context, however, do these units show their larger meaning.

Or Else is composed of such events, memories, scenes, even visions, drawn from the mind and life of the author.

He puts them on the page in an attempt to understand their significance. The perspective which Warren adopts is that of an aged man nearing the end of his life. His mind is filled with questions about time and eternity as he tries to face the fact of his own future death. (pp. 271-72)

The sequence as a whole is an attempt either to fuse the two worlds governed by time and eternity—the concrete realm of earth and the abstract realm of sky and beyond—or to see how one of these realms could, at a certain point, melt into the other—obviously the concrete into the abstract, as at death. In order to understand this process—if there is one—Warren has accumulated a wide variety of discontinuous elements and placed them side by side in a search for continuity. He explains his method at the end of one of the longer poems here:

> All items listed above belong in the world
> In which all things are continuous,
> And are parts of the original dream which
> I am now trying to discover the logic of. This
> Is the process whereby pain of the past in its pastness
> May be converted into the future tense
>
> Of joy.

The direction the passage takes, of course, is by now quite familiar to us—in each of these books Warren tries to move through pain to a promise of joy.

The importance of the past in this sequence is at least twofold. First, there are elements drawn from Warren's own experience, each one of which, though existing only within time, bears somehow on the question of eternity. Second, there are memories which are directly concerned with eternity, as seen in other people's lives and deaths. (p. 272)

Most of the poems in the sequence can be treated almost as allegories, so suggestive are the stories they relate and the images they contain. In "Time as Hypnosis," one of the most striking poems here, Warren writes of a snowfall that occurred when he was a boy of twelve in Kentucky. The snow creates an unreal, almost symbolic landscape. The boy walks out in the morning and sees many things, including [a] scene of beauty and death.... The scene is carefully staged to make the strongest possible impact on both the boy and the reader; violence strikes through the gentle face of natural beauty.

This passage is followed by a suggestive description of the landscape in which the boy is wandering:

> There was a great field that tilted
> Its whiteness up to the line where the slant, blue ·
>   knife-edge of sky
> Cut it off. I stood
> In the middle of that space. I looked back, saw
> My own tracks march at me. Mercilessly,
> They came at me and did not stop. Ahead,
> Was the blankness of white. Up it rose. Then the sky.

Again the patterning is carefully controlled; surrounded by whiteness, the boy is trapped symbolically by the mystery of time—with a glimpse of eternity showing from his journey's end. Presented in the landscape is the mystery which the sequence as a whole sets out to investigate; at this point Warren can suggest no answer: "All day, I had wandered in the glittering metaphor / For which I could find no referent."

The solution, if there exactly is one, is gradually revealed through images which coalesce into a pattern as the sequence develops. These images are significant both spatially and in terms of color or tone; eternity is bright and above or far, time is dark and below or close. Often an image of time will be set against an image of eternity.... Elsewhere, an image of eternity will appear juxtaposed upon or growing out of an image of time.... (pp. 273-74)

Warren is most interested in finding his answer in nature and in presenting it through naturalistic images. This is not to say that he doesn't hint at it elsewhere. The concrete and the abstract are, for example, clearly united at the end of an amusing poem called "Remarks of Soul to Body": "But let us note, too, how glory, like gasoline spilled / On the cement in a garage, may flare, of a sudden, up // In a blinding blaze, from the filth of the world's floor." The most typical way for Warren to present such wisdom is through nature; he has, therefore, established several image patterns, all of which culminate in the final poem in the sequence. (p. 274)

The last poem in the sequence, titled "A Problem in Spatial Composition," is another carefully designed piece in which the images, either alone or in combination, are suggestive of a final promise. The poet looks westward through a high window, across a forest toward the setting sun. The time is late—late in the day, late in the year, late in the life. Although eternity is present in the bright distance of the sky, ... there is a suggestion of its mergence with earth in Warren's description of the mountains: "Beyond the distance of forest, hangs that which is blue: / Which is, in knowledge, a tall scarp of stone, gray, but now is, / In the truth of perception, stacked like a mass of blue cumulus." (p. 275)

[The] central and only player [in] the scene [is] a hawk.... The third part of the poem consists of a single line: "The hawk, in an eyeblink, is gone." The hawk's instantaneous disappearance from the scene is akin to man's disappearance from life at death. When he resumes his flight, the bird returns to the eternal realm of sky, having rested for but a moment on the time-bound earth. The hawk in this poem is analogous to the spirit of man, as birds so often are in English and American poetry generally. Through his choice and development of images, Warren has managed to suggest a solution to the problem which pervades the poem sequence. He does not tell us *how* man is able to transcend the physical realm at his death, but he does strongly suggest that it can be done. And this is as much of a promise as is needed: "For what blessing may a man hope for but / An immortality in / The loving vigilance of death?" This is the ultimate "definition of joy" which dominates so much of Warren's poetry, from "Promises" onward.... (pp. 275-76)

Or Else is a brilliant achievement; because it is Robert Penn Warren's finest poem sequence, it is the best such work to be found in contemporary American poetry. Warren's poems are a resounding testament to man, to nature, and to poetry itself. His devotion is to man as a natural creature, seen in conjunction with his environment and his God. Man is celebrated not for his solipsistic ego but for those qualities which unite him to the creative power of the universe—his intellect and his imagination. It is this very celebration that separates Warren from most of his contemporaries.... Among contemporary poets, it has been Robert Penn Warren's task to rediscover how the void at man's heart may be filled. Though revolutionary for our age, Warren's answer places him at the heart of the great tradition in

English and American poetry. Moreover, Warren has enclosed his wisdom in poems of consummate artistic skill. Beginning years ago with the traditional forms, Warren has evolved a style both relaxed and dense, as beautiful as it is individual. We must celebrate this man for what his long devotion to the sacred art of poetry has unquestionably made him—the greatest living American poet. (p. 276)

> Peter Stitt, "Robert Penn Warren, the Poet," in The Southern Review (copyright, 1976, by Peter Stitt), Vol. XII, No. 2, Spring, 1976, pp. 261-76.

CALVIN BEDIENT

With [*Selected Poems 1923-1975*] and his . . . novel *A Place to Come to* Robert Penn Warren continues to run both poetry and fiction toward the ring of Truth (often his ostensible, even ostentatious, subject). The race in unequal. His fiction is lame and always has been. And for a long time the poetry too was but fair-to-middling down the stretch. But as if more and more goaded by the cheers of death, it has gained speed, mass, power, grandeur. (p. 71)

The novels are dispiriting in every way—personally, morally, aesthetically. They are given over to a somewhat thin, raspy consciousness. The self-loathing of the male narrators glances up against things gracelessly. Something rotten in the South . . . some compensating "fine woman" worship. Throughout, the novels display what fiction can hardly tolerate, social awkwardness. They lack urbanity: the dialogue is a solopsist's rough copy, the tone is one long discomfort . . . the reader feels rather bound in. Then the arraignment of human failure before the "awful responsibility of Time" sits in the middle and palls. *A little more virtue* . . . the message dies of inanition. A regenerative vision must be radical after all, or it won't fire. Nor, finally, is there any poetry of approach or conception. A Faulkner pitches you toward his "subject" over and over with a tricky imaginative arm and the meaning, the poetry, is the alarmed getting-there. A Welty, even a Flannery O'Connor, transports. But on much the same country road Warren parks his battered Dodge and gossips a long piece about the mostly sordid ways of Man. There is no passage, only a foot-on-the-bumper presentation.

By contrast, the poetry at its best exhilarates. It is at once more sensuous and more philosophical, more impersonal and . . . more "gripping." Vulgar insecurity is here bouldered out by a massive yet intimate contemplation. And, no longer brook-busy, guilt deepens and broadens into elegy. Beauty and ugliness, pain and delight—in their all-but-unimaginable mingling they form almost a Southern province of sensibility: Faulkner, Agee, O'Connor, Welty being like Warren remote descendants of late Shakespeare, with something of his ripened astonishment of mind.

The poetry is about the saving and destroying beauty of contingency, as the fiction is about its moral stains. That "beauty" is the consecrating perception of mortal finality. What happened yesterday, what is happening now, may be either "accident" or "fate"—the equivocation tingles through the poems—but it must be cherished regardless; there is nothing else. In a translation of mind it appears at once grievous and beautiful, not intrinsically changed or forgiven and not changeable either yet no longer inadequate, indeed suddenly adequate beyond saying, having been consummated by the sorrowing intuition of the blas-

phemy its absence would be. This is "the appalling logic of joy."

Recurring in his work as a talisman, an existential absolute, and an insignia of his poetic authority, is the image of a soaring bird—gull, hawk, eagle—that takes the last light imperially or else as one receives a gift (the ambiguity is crucial): a measure of the limited yet thrilling venture of freedom within necessity, the realm thumbnailed in *A Place to Come to* as "gravity, time, and contingency." There, in the extreme reach of necessity, is the extreme reach of joy; there in truth is beauty. This is romanticism with the spikes of contingency in its feet and hands. Warren's is the opposite of a beached, platonic sensibility. He lives, "Man lives," by "images" that "Lean at us from the world's wall, and Time's." . . . For Warren, life, Time, the World, are the only things worthy of the polemical name of reality. And if their mix is painful it is magnificent.

Warren begins where every romantic begins, with the question, "what has been denied me?" and the conviction, "There is never an answer." . . . This search for what eludes "fulfillment-that-is-not-fulfuillment," this pending credulity of delight, is of course the mark of the romantic temper. As an American romantic Warren is peculiar, all the same, in his mature tolerance of limitation. He is our Keats, rather tough and raw-boned and fumbling as our Keats would be.

He has company, it is true, among his contemporaries; he typifies the current and further pulling-back of our romanticism. With Warren, Philip Levine, Louise Glück, John Ashbery—romantics all—a snail-like caution prevails, a waiting upon opportunity. Even A. R. Ammons humbles himself to the prosaic. Our romanticism is trying, within reason, to be honest. The watchword is, "Fall Back and Hold." Of all these poets Levine is the most like Warren, the two sharing a hunger for joy that prowls even through their most furious work. Yet none rivals Warren's combined nerve for limitation and largeness. Glück and Levine may be as pained and passionate, Ashbery at once as prosaic and extravagant, Ammons as lucidly impersonal, but none has Warren's broad normality and balance.

He is a poet of whom we have need. We want to know today the limits of an undeluded imagination. We want to know whether we are as unworthy of joy as we seem (and do not seem). We want to know how fully, if at all, a contemporary human being may sing of experience. What light we have moves in Warren now in a bold-to-harsh concentrated beam. (pp. 71-4)

Warren is valuable only as he is tentative—tentative till the hook catches, if it does, and then let him . . . tug in an access of belief. Unpreparedness is of his essence; he is a poet of surprise. A poet, moreover, of enfeebled self-judgment. He has failed to be ruthless toward himself, and his weaknesses loom oppressively in the reflected brilliance of his accomplishments. (p. 74)

Warren postures not only knowingness but a knowledge of the unknowable, that other intellectual chic. "Here is the shadow of truth, for only the shadow is true," he will write, missing paradox and hitting absurdity. Hungry for the food of the deep, he forces the clam. He sometimes insists on making us feel our ignorance—which can be a needlessly abasing emotion—while failing to examine how much he himself knows. (p. 75)

Just as from a researcher into truth we want the difficulty of truth, so from a researcher into joy we want joy, not fantasias of joy. To say that "In that bush, with wolf-fang white, delight / Humps now for someone: *You*" is to make rather a chimera of delight. And confronted by "*Seize the nettle of innocence in both your hands . . . and every / Ulcer in love's lazaret may, like a dawn-stung gem, sing–or even burst into whoops of, perhaps, holiness,*" we may prefer to stay corruptly sober. . . . So Warren sometimes tries too hard—indeed wants us all to try hard. . . . Something in Warren longs to lean against the sun, but such coyness does not suit him. His true sublimity is more temperate, a manliness touched to pain by the indifferent world of beauty.

Nor do we want from our heroic poet echoes of other poets, particularly grandiloquent echoes. The crisis of contemporary poetry is a crisis of pitch and can only be resolved in the moment, individually. Yet even advanced squawkers like Ted Hughes and advanced squeakers like Philip Larkin begin in their youth at the Renaissance, trying to outpurple or outhoney Shakespeare or Milton—as Warren himself did for instance in "Who saw, in darkness, how fled / The white eidolon from the fanged commotion rude?" Only youthful innocence can hide from intelligent poets the fact that the Romantics permanently injured eloquence (which was exalted in the Renaissance as a protest against necessity) by reducing it to a supporting role. . . . (pp. 75-6)

[For] four decades Warren wore distractingly, putting on and off haphazardly, the masks of Eliot, Hopkins, Auden, Yeats, Stevens, Pound. . . . (p. 76)

Warren has even today a barely exploited capacity for manipulating language. . . . Yet lately he has been taking the opposite path from Hopkins, a more privileged poet of joy, in favoring a certain downrightness. His mount is powerful but gentled and it travels. Though not one of those American poets who rather gullibly seek to surprise wonder from the ordinariness of language, he keeps his manner unencumbered. It has range and flexibility and a sufficient lack of self-awareness, as well as sensual positivity. There is never too much of it. He has tried to let a circumstantial ecstasy rise from his poems with a large-scaled directness.

It was not always so. Even apart from impersonating others, he postured in language as well as attitude. Syntax especially was for him a last refuge of Renaissance nobility. He fancied dignified dislocations, rearrangements of expectable order that, like a king's whim, demonstrated authority. . . . Occasionally too he delayed a monosyllabic verb till the end of the sentence, where it would fall with a base-note weight. Probably Eliot's fascinating "Nor knee deep in the salt marsh, heaving a cutlass, / Bitten by flies, fought" prompted the practice, and indeed it has resonance, but obtrudes. Then gradually Warren came to see what he was after. . . . A narrative, not a ritualized, line was what he needed. Directness and not gentility. His syntax surrendered its self-gatherings, as of garments lifted from the floor of the earth at the start of a dance. (pp. 76-7)

His style is now the opposite of, say, the willful Faulknerian rhetoric, so unregenerate, so fierce against nakedness. Where in retrospect the old, frequently rhymed stanzas seem safety belted, the new often walk out with their subjects, good for the distance. They are the space of an experience. In this they are abetted by his meliorated line, which, stripped of self-reflexive rhyme and meter, is forget-

ful, too, of any approximate length. Yet he favors the long line, having in fact gravitated toward a listing amptitude from the first. Like the very short line, which he also uses, the long lacks the self-sufficient air that the pentameter and even the tetrameter so readily possess. It runs forward, as it were, into experience.

Not that Warren is one of those sons of Whitman (like James Dickey) who are not so much writers as vatic sensibilities set loose in a field of words. His work is finished but, without diminishment, lacks gloss. (pp. 77-8)

Warren's humility of style and spirit is thus not what Yeats anticipated for us all in horror, a mirror-like passivity, but a way of assimilating himself to whatever adventures the world proposes. His aesthetic humility is at the same time an existential exploit—one might say quest. He lets himself go like the seeding cottonwood. Of course he thereby leaves himself open to confusion and incompletion too. "Rattlesnake Country" for instance is almost eloquent with the pain of inconclusiveness, of mixed evidence as to the blessing of life. Finally in fact the poem rather lets us down, as the remembered experience itself has let the poet down, though not without first raising us up, as it had raised him, and leaving us changed, as it has changed him: "And sometimes—usually at dawn—I remember the cry on the mountain."

It should be clear that Warren's humbleness partly entails and is partly entailed by a certain boldness, a lurking expectation of magnificence. The point at which his humbleness becomes indistinguishable from magnificence—of style, of spirit—is in fact the norm of his best poems. (pp. 78-9)

Warren's style has not really become meaner for having become plainer, and as for his spirit, it is bolder than ever, able to hold a level gaze with the horizon. Dense as their sensibility may be, the early poems take on only a little life at a time. The sublime crisis of the cruel unfinishedness of experience, with its joyful and surprising yield and alchemy of acceptance (of the kind grudging in Yeats, generous in the Melville of *Moby Dick*), has grazed but not pierced them. This crisis is the new greatness in Warren's spirit to which his broad, responsive manner lends a bonding force. More than ever, to be sure, he writes a poetry of question of which the only adequate answer would be the gorgeous totality of time. (p. 80)

The "wound" of "Time's irremediable joy" has become his obsessive subject—justified in this, that it subsumes and consumes all others. Still, the success of his poems waits on the right wild mix. In this he differs from Philip Levine, who, having found the same omnivorous subject, sounds it continuously as one terrible chord. . . . The need is like a saintly wound and rather sets him apart. Now Warren is considerably stauncher. He must be moved to sublimity out of his normal self-possession. The circumstantial imagination of time itself is his muse. (p. 81)

Warren has become more largely accepting without ceasing to be a modernist poet of assault—on recalcitrant reality, complacent reader, tired poetic convention. In fact, he has developed an aesthetics of the appalling—learning for instance to make the pronoun "You" less accusatory than absorptive, like a sudden draft into a vacuum. More and more he leads us on with dark and suspenseful intentions. . . . Warren piques the lyrical sublime with the grotesque, exposing a warp in "magnificence." He instances the modernist sensibility for the disturbed—a sensibility essentially primitive, interceding as it does against the threatening unknown by going half way to meet it. Still, his increasing fearfulness does not so much qualify as further define his peculiar sense of joy. After all, it was in a relatively early poem that he warned that the logic of joy is appalling.

Selected Poems thus comes to us as an implicit story of growth into existential humility, courage, awe. It is a story with its own degree of magnificence. (pp. 81-2)

This collection with its triumphant last third will doubtless avalanche a recognition of Warren's importance.... Of course we could wish that he were a more nearly faultless poet than even now he sometimes is. But with his ability to sustain a long poem in low whooshing partridge flight, his scale and openness of passion, his comprehensive sensibility, his many other virtues, he is almost certain to be placed in the pantheon of our poetry, where something of his raw air of the newcomer and latecomer, of the lanky, countrified talent, will no doubt dissipate in a compliant and universal acceptance. (pp. 82-3)

> *Calvin Bedient, "The Appalling Logic of Joy," in* Parnassus: Poetry in Review *(copyright © by Poetry in Review Foundation), Spring-Summer, 1977, pp. 71-83.*

HELEN VENDLER

Robert Penn Warren's poems [in *Selected Poems: 1923-1975*] are perhaps ... best described as those of a man of letters, novelist and critic as well as poet. His collections tend to follow poetic styles rather than to invent them, but within those inherited styles he can work consummately well.... Even [in early poems such as "Pursuit"] Warren had his storyteller's eye, his easy rhythm, and his feel for the horrible and the hopeful. The earlier poems are, like the later ones, alternately folksy and philosophical, swinging like ballads or tautly analytic, embodying a strange cohabitation, it might seem, of Whitman and Marvell, "Who saw, in darkness, how fled / The white eidolon" crossed with "Ages to our construction went, / Dim architecture, hour by hour." Among these influences there appeared, early on, Warren's own individual slant:

> Because he had spoken harshly to his mother,
> The day became astonishingly bright.

The rest of that young poem doesn't live up to its beginning, but the second line has the true surprise of an interior state clarified in language. Warren's essential self, early and late, appears not in the skillfully rhymed or fastidiously analytical poems, but rather in his long rambles and his short lyrical songs. (pp. 81-2)

The short lyric "Blow, West Wind," on the other hand, remains unmarred and unselfconscious. For its fine simplicity, one would want to put it in school texts, except that the young are not old enough to understand its brief symbols and its cheated bleakness.... On the whole, though, Warren's best work lies in the poems much too long to quote. The recent elegy for himself and his parents—"I Am Dreaming of a White Christmas"—has the gripping realism of vision as Warren sees, in a dream, his father sitting in his usual Morris chair, but dead; and then his seated mother, dead too; and the cold hearth; and a long-dead Christmas tree; and three presents under the tree; and three

chairs.... This kind of descriptiveness, like the song-rhythm of "Blow, West Wind," is a permanent resource of lyric. Warren continues, in these *Selected Poems,* some of the most firmly-based and solacing practices of poetry. (pp. 83-4)

> *Helen Vendler, in* The Yale Review *(© 1977 by Yale University; reprinted by permission of the editors), Autumn, 1977.*

*   *   *

WELLER, Michael   1942-

An American playwright now living in England, Weller writes of contemporary events with a brand of realism that is uncluttered and rhetorically fresh.

CLIVE BARNES

"Moonchildren" is a joyously funny (yes, funny-funny, as funny as the Marx Brothers) and yet unaffectedly profound play....

Mr. Weller's play traces, with a little more affection than remorse, the final year of a group of students about to embark on the mystery of graduation....

Vietnam and peace marches, love and grades, the entire aquarium-moment of student life is captured here. Mr. Weller's story—witty, absurd and touching—is not about any particular age group. He relates this period of transition to a special time—to his own special time—but it has a relevance to everyone who has grown up with strange people in a strange place.

Mr. Weller is punctilious in not having a story because he has settled on a theme. He gives us sketches of life on the turn, and it is not too fantastic to compare this with Chekhov's "The Cherry Orchard." The structure is almost identical, and the mood may have more in common than we can at present suspect....

Mr. Weller's skill is two-fold. He writes dialogue that is both believable and yet surprising, which is no easy trick. He also relates a man to his setting. There are a hundred and one stories in this play, but what is important is that every single character rings totally true....

"Moonchildren" is the rare kind of play that you go to, and you laugh a lot. But, rarer still, the next day your laughter has an aftertaste of immortality. Lines, scenes and attitudes stick with you and you suddenly realize that that harmless pile of jokes, interspersed with a few shards of reality, has really meant something to you. (p. 51)

> *Clive Barnes, in* The New York Times *(© 1973 by The New York Times Company; reprinted by permission), November 5, 1973.*

CLIVE BARNES

"Fishing" is a perceptive picture of a generation or at least one aspect of it....

Mr. Weller's ear for dialogue is as convincing as ever, and his good-natured wit (his characters are rarely waspish; irony or violence is the nearest they get to nastiness) is always appealing. Despite a slow, rather poor beginning, and a joking, pseudo-melodramatic ending that doesn't quite come off, the play is neatly constructed. You get to know the people and they are interesting.

The author's theme is one of survival. "Keep on," a character says at one point, "stay alive." They often talk casually of death, but do not wish it. I am not sure what kind of development this marks from "Moonchildren"—lateral perhaps—but Mr. Weller's writing, if not his dramaturgy, is more secure than ever. . . .

Mr. Weller does not seem to write gratefully for characters outside his central group—it was the same in "Moonchildren"—and the . . . monumentally stoned gravedigger and . . . the dying fisherman can never quite redeem for the author the basic shallowness of the characterizations.

After the first few moments of awkward angling, I thoroughly enjoyed "Fishing." It is certainly a revealing play. In 100 years time, if anyone is around, it will tell them something about us. Or some of us. (p. 41)

> *Clive Barnes, in* The New York Times (© *1975 by The New York Times Company; reprinted by permission), February 13, 1975.*

WALTER KERR

In "Moonchildren," a college generation adrift in a void and at a loss for identity devoted all of its crackling verbal powers to erecting far-out and very funny façades in order to conceal an emptiness. . . .

They were *performing* for others, creating alternate selves that lived only in the group imagination, making the hilarious most of lies that came within inches of persuading the unpersuadable. The device was called a "put-on" by this time, and was far more conscious than it had been. . . .

But [in "Fishing"] the little jokes are littler now, the antic urge to con the world gone flat. Flatness is an unrewarding thing to dramatize . . . and Mr. Weller has taken refuge in spelling out too plainly the ache that was formerly, gaily, implied. The remnants of that captivating college crew now speak of themselves, baldly, as "a lost generation in search of roles in a century without meaning," announce that "Life is a freak show, right?" (This of course gives the *whole* show away; we used to deduce such things, beneath the cock-crows, to our delight.) When one of the friends is told he's moody, he snaps "You're not supposed to notice, and if you notice you're not supposed to say anything, and if you say anything it's supposed to be a joke." In "Fishing" they *do* notice, and they *do* say, and it's not a joke.

> *Walter Kerr, "Poor 'Fishing'," in* The New York Times, *Section II (© 1975 by The New York Times Company; reprinted by permission), February 23, 1975, p. 1.*

JOHN SIMON

One of the main troubles with *Fishing* was that Weller had done it better in *Moonchildren,* itself only a very promising play. In *Fishing,* much the same young people who had cavorted through their final year of college in *Moonchildren* were seen, a handful of years later, still romping through life. This time they were trying to find themselves in the Pacific Northwest, the last American frontier abutting the *terra incognita* of myth—of clear air, good earth, and hard, clean living. . . .

Fishing is a play of texture. It captures accurately, I think, the sound and feel of whimsical, aimless, not yet uncontented lives, some of which will wander into usefulness, some into chronic dissatisfaction and dilettantism, and

some, perhaps, into suicide. But except for this texture, the play gives us little else. It is as if a tailor showed us an expertly woven and ingeniously patterned piece of cloth, but teasingly refused to comply with our request to cut it into a suit. (p. 78)

> *John Simon, in* New York *Magazine (copyright © 1975 by the NYM Corporation; reprinted with the permission of* New York *Magazine), March 10, 1975.*

CATHARINE HUGHES

None of [the characters in *Fishing*] really communicate with each other. They are caustic, sardonic, defensive, in their exchanges, as to a large extent were the young people in *Moonchildren,* but they are—with advancing age?—less spirited, less interesting. . . . Although the play frequently displays Weller's facility for adroit dialogue, it also abounds in exchanges that are heavily portentous. A little of such things as 'being on the ocean with no one to hassle you' and 'I feel there is some very negative energy between us' clearly goes a long way.

Yet, *Fishing* is not really a bad play. It seldom, except in a protracted opening scene, actually bores. . . . It does, however, rely far too heavily on dramatic tricks and, in a fake melodramatic conclusion, something bordering on a copout. Weller is a better playwright than that. . . . [Even] at his less than best, Weller is invariably worth watching. (p. 35)

> *Catharine Hughes, in* Plays and Players (© *copyright Catharine Hughes 1975; reprinted with permission), May, 1975.*

*   *   *

WHITE, E(lwyn) B(rooks)   1899-

White is an American essayist, poet, humorist, and author of books for children. His essays, characterized by witty and graceful prose, have appeared regularly in *The New Yorker* and *Harper's* for many years. He is well known for his children's literature, notably, *Charlotte's Web* and *Stuart Little.* White collaborated with James Thurber on a volume of essays entitled *Is Sex Necessary?* (See also *Contemporary Authors,* Vols. 13-16, rev. ed.)

LOUIS HASLEY

White has been a kind of national housekeeper and caretaker. He has gone on steadily and quietly, looking around and ahead, poking into public and domestic corners, defusing bombs, and brushing down cobwebs, caretaking whether anybody else cared or not (thousands cared that he cared); and hardly any literate American has not benefited from his humor, his nonsense, his creativity, and his engaging wisdom. White's readers can glean the astute observations and experiences of a dedicated denizen of megalopolis as well as of a sensible, serious dirt farmer living by an arm of the Atlantic Ocean down in Maine. White has managed to divide his time fruitfully between these two places, Manhattan and Maine. His concerns, however, are not merely tactile and local but ultimately transcendental. For the critical side of him is engaged with assessing the quality of life open to us in our time. He thus merits the title of philosopher although in no academic sense of the word.

Apart from his own unfaltering sophistication, White as

critic of our national life can be seen as a logical descendant of a whole line of nineteenth century American humorists, beginning with Maine's Seba Smith, whose character Major Jack Downing reported the doings, first, of the state legislature and then of the Congress in Washington. White, in no sense clowning his coverage, did hover over and provide enlightening political analysis during the painful birthing of the United Nations in San Francisco, as well as subsequently in New York. In these writings, however, the humorist is not strongly in evidence but appears only in the vital personal flavor that eases the underlying didacticism without destroying the objective validity of his argument. In his commitment to freedom and his belief in the necessity of world federation, White is persuasive and convincing. He is likely to leave the reader feeling that the only hope for survival of the human race is a 'one world' government, though like every other political architect he cannot furnish a practical blueprint for overcoming the stumbling block of nationalism.

It is principally in the genre of the personal essay that the humorist in White comes to the fore. . . . There must be little question that he is our best living personal essayist. His temperament is at once serious and funloving. His interests are broad—nothing, it seems, that is human is alien to him. His eye and his intelligence see what lies beneath the surface. His judgment about affairs of great moment is judicious, even when his expression is enlivened by the arresting metaphor or touched by zaniness. (p. 37)

The prose pieces of White show a remarkable range in both sensibility and subject matter. They run the gamut from the trivial and funny to the deeply serious and humorous. White's first book was a collaboration with James Thurber, *Is Sex Necessary?* (1929), to which the two writers contributed alternate humorous chapters. The resultant performance is a smooth job of dovetailing, and the book's overall quality is no drag on the humorous reputations that both writers went on to build.

Of the early work by White, readers will find *Quo Vadimus? or the Case for the Bicycle* the most diverting collection. The book contains no mention of a bicycle; yet there is point to the subtitle. We see White as a cautious critic of progress, fearing the loss of the precious sense for basic things. Science, technology, and business feel the edge of his satire, particularly because of the excessive complications they introduce in life. For example, in "Irtnog," he gives us a clever *reductio ad absurdum,* telling how, first the digests, then the digests of digests, heroically attempt to cope with the inundating tides of print that come from the presses. Finally, *"Distillate* came along, a superdigest which condensed a Hemingway novel to the single word 'Bang!' and reduced a long *Scribner's* article on the problem of the unruly child to the two words, 'Hit him.'" (pp. 38-9)

The most varied, the most imaginative collection by White is *The Second Tree from the Corner* (1954). Ultimately it contributes most to his bid for greatness. The shadow of World War II, which had hung over *One Man's Meat,* had somewhat dissipated, and while there is awareness of the "bomb shadow," the spirit here is less immediately constricted and more exuberant.

In *The Second Tree* there are excellent examples of all important genres that figure in White's literary reputation;

personal experiences ("Time Past"); pseudo-science stories ("Time Future"); notes on our times ("Time Present"); parodies and commentary on literary subjects; fifteen pages of verse; and experiences in the city and on the land.

The book is so richly varied that it defies any systematic attack in brief space. A random mention of the most outstanding pieces, however, with some indication of content, may be made preliminary to closer analysis of White's work for ideas and appraisal.

Here, then, is "A Weekend with the Angels," a charming account of White's experience of nurses while spending a wartime weekend in the hospital. "Farewell, My Lovely!" gives an animated portrait, nostalgia *par excellence,* of the oldtime Model T Ford. In "The Hour of Letdown" we meet, amidst foreboding humor, a machine that talks, drinks whiskey, corrects the bartender's English, drives a car, plays chess, and *cheats.* "Mrs. Wienckus" is an idea-profile, a laconic paragraph describing a modern, urban Thoreauvean woman who simplified her life by sleeping in empty cartons in a hallway despite possessing a healthy bank account. (pp. 39-40)

Like most men of balance, White is ambivalent about our civilization. Using the editorial *we* (which White once said was a device "to protect writers from the fumes of their own work") he stated his position.

> Half the time we feel blissfully wedded to the modern scene, in love with its every mood, amused by its every joke, imperturbable in the face of its threat, bent on enjoying it to the hilt. The other half of the time we are the fusspot moralist, suspicious of all progress, resentful of change, determined to right wrongs, correct injustices, and save the world even if we have to blow it to pieces in the process.

For White declared that "our goods accumulate, but not our well-being." He deplored the fact that "there is a great deal of electrically transmitted joy, but very little spontaneous joy." (p. 40)

White was well aware of the dictum of Mark Twain which holds that a humorous writer who wishes to live must both preach and teach though he must not do so professedly. White replied to this dictum, saying that he didn't think that humor needed to preach in order to live; rather, "it need only speak the truth."

Some of White's truth speaking has a cutting edge, though seldom is it as sharp as is his comment on the Christmas bonus, which he describes as "the annual salve applied to the conscience of the rich and the wounds of the poor." In the same connection he sees with dazzling clarity the trouble with the profit system—that it has always been highly unprofitable to most people, as "the profits went to the few, the work went to the many."

To use Robert Frost's memorable words, White too has had "a lover's quarrel with the world." He is no pessimist. His ideals may be labeled romantic or idealistic, as one prefers, but his vision is whole and realistic. The angelic hospital nurse who took his temperature "in the awful hour of a day born prematurely . . . personified the beauty and lunacy of which life is so subtly blended." In the Foreword to his 1962 volume, *The Points of My Compass,* he reiterates his love for the world and fervently declares, "I love it as passionately as though I were young."

It is clear from his writings that E. B. White is a religious man, though he falters when he tackles the subjects of his own beliefs and practices. In his first book of verse, the entirely negligible 1929 volume called *The Lady is Cold,* there are brief references to God and to St. Christopher. In view of the Vatican's 1969 consignment of St. Christopher to outer or at least dubious space, White's prayer to "the God I half believe in" might better have been directed to the lost patron of travelers. (p. 41)

Without question, the single piece of White's that is the richest embodiment of his ideas and temperament is the pseudo-science fictional story "The Morning of the Day They Did It," included in *The Second Tree from the Corner* (1954). He has pointed out elsewhere that "today's fantasy is tomorrow's news event." More than one phase of the story is no longer fantasy, especially that of electronic communication from a space vehicle to earth. But White has projected into this work so much of today's directional potential that the story's prophetic element should be fascinating for scores of years ahead.

"The Morning of the Day They Did It" is a first person parable carrying the now commonplace theme that science and its impact on human nature gravely forebode the destruction of the world. (p. 42)

Despite a pervasive irony, the narrator pays honest tribute to this country's "great heart and matchless ingenuity." Managing somehow to land, and survive, on another planet, he says that life there is more leisurely than it was on earth. "I like the apples here better than those on earth. They are often wormy, but with a wonderful flavor. . . . But I would be lying if I said I didn't miss that other life, I loved it so."

Objectively the events of "The Morning of the Day They Did It" are grim and the story ends in nostalgic pathos. But the tone is amiable and relaxed, reflecting the new peace which the narrator finds on his "inferior planet." The considerable irony is often light, and a good deal of humor emerges. (pp. 42-3)

White wrote no novels and only a few pieces that fall within the genre of the short story. Though he wrote a small number of other enchanting parables and prophecies, "The Morning of the Day They Did It" must stand as his finest achievement in fiction.

In an essay entitled "Poetry," White confessed that he would rather be a poet "than anything." We may readily concede him the title, but while his poetry is respectable, it is undistinguished and is greatly surpassed by his prose. Morris Bishop declared, in 1950, that E. B. White and a few others are creating a new mid-form between Light Verse and Heavy Verse. Contrary to wide current practice, they avoid pretentious obscurity, says Bishop, and aim at lucidity. That much is true of White's verse, which is ordinarily entertaining and competent, occasionally expert, but rarely of the stuff that draws the reader back to it again and again. In discussing his art, it will therefore be most useful to concentrate on his prose.

"To achieve style, begin by affecting none," White wrote in the chapter he supplied for . . . *The Elements of Style,*

by William Strunk, Jr. Further, as a writer becomes proficient in the use of langage, "his style will emerge, because he himself will emerge."

White's unselfconscious honesty shows in the statement just quoted. For in his work there is almost wholly lacking any special device, mannerism, or meretricious maneuver. "Words that are not used orally are seldom the ones to put on paper," he also cautioned. "Style takes its final shape more from attitudes of mind than from principles of composition." And: "The whole duty of a writer is to please and satisfy himself . . . an audience of one."

With the help of these precepts of style enunciated by White, we may see that, in the light of him as a person, his style is transparent and unobtrusive. With him, more than with most writers, the style is the man: careful, steady, sure, resourceful, concrete without flourish, capable of fun and even surrealistic fancy, and as often as not, expressing a deadly seriousness that may be richly compounded with humor. (pp. 43-4)

Most of his commentary on humor is unexceptionally perceptive. "Humorists fatten on trouble. . . . There is often a rather fine line between laughing and crying. . . . Humor, like poetry . . . plays close to the big hot fire which is Truth." Usually (he asserts wisely and for the most part contrary to his own practice) "the most widely appreciated humorists are those who create characters and tell tales." And "the subtleties of satire and burleque and nonsense and parody and criticism are not to the general taste." In writing of Marquis's *archy and mehitabel* he maintained that "to interpret humor is as futile as explaining a spider's web in terms of geometry." That essay, entitled "Don Marquis," is not without its measure of interpretation. Or is it that White's position, as stated, is hyperbolic and he does not intend a literal reading of his contention that essentially humor is a complete mystery? But he has also written: "The truth is I write by ear, always with difficulty . . . and seldom with any exact notion of what is taking place under the hood."

The fact that White writes by ear, and writes superlatively well, helps to explain the high quality of parody and burlesque of which he is capable. Any Whitman enthusiast (except Walt himself were he still hearing America singing) would be ecstatic over "A Classic Waits for Me," a satire on book club membership. (p. 44)

The *New Yorker* paragraphs, or mini-essays, are the twentieth century's distillation of absorbing personal experience and are justly a part of White's literary fame. They open without introduction, going forward with directness, concreteness, scrupulous economy, and ease. Often they occupy less than a single page, though they may run to several pages. The tone is quietly objective and curious, blending close and unstressed, unrhetorical observation with a wryly distinctive reaction of the writer, sometimes expressed, sometimes only implied. Excellent examples abound in both *One Man's Meat* and *The Second Tree from the Corner,* as well as in the earlier (1934) collection, *Every Day Is Saturday.*

White confesses that, in his early days, he was a graduate of the University of Mencken and Lewis, and admits to having been under the spell of Sandburg. Faint traces of the first two may be found in his work—the critical satire of Mencken (though rarely if ever holier-than-thou), and the clinical observation of Sinclair Lewis. More relevant, however, is his underlying kinship in political commentary with Finley Peter Dunne; his temperamental tendency to whimsy and oblique criticism of society as found in Don Marquis; and a frame of mind very often like that behind his all but worshiped *Walden,* product of that solid romantic, Henry David Thoreau. These are well deserved literary kinfolk, we conclude—good enough for any writer who rises above being a mere humorist. (p. 45)

> Louis Hasley, *"The Talk of the Town and the Country: E. B. White,"* in The Connecticut Review (© *Board of Trustees for the Connecticut State College, 1971), October, 1971, pp. 37-45.*

EDWARD C. SAMPSON

Although most of White's poetry is light verse, his best poems are not always his humorous poems, and his humorous ones often have an ironic twist or comment that gives them a serious tone. Those poems where humor is the chief or sole effect are apt to be too topical or too insubstantial to be effective; some, however, are successful. (p. 38)

By and large, we cannot claim a great deal for the poems in [*The Lady Is Cold*]; White is too restrained, and at times there is too much distance between the poet and the scene he describes; in most of these poems, he comments quietly on the daily routine of city life, its minor conflicts, its tensions. He describes late evening and early morning rambles, the chance appearance of a pretty face, and the brief contact with people that brings a transient sense of unity; taking a half-whimsical look at himself, he celebrates his minor victories, and is amused by his weaknesses.

A modest quality, as well as restraint, exists in many of these poems, almost as if White were afraid of being too serious, too involved—or perhaps too conscious of the danger of destroying his sensitive perception of life by putting it into words. . . . (pp. 39-40)

White experimented with a wide variety of poetic forms in *The Lady Is Cold,* but a kind of caution also appears; he is ultimately conventional. (p. 40)

One difference between the poems in [*The Fox of Peapack*] and those in the earlier one is that many in this begin with a newspaper comment and develop from it. This approach may tend to produce limited and topical poems but it also suggests that White was moving closer to his material. *The Fox of Peapack* has fewer lyrical poems, fewer bits of whimsy; it has, on the other hand, stronger and more vigorous statements. (p. 41)

White's poetry cannot be seen aside from White. If his real significance lies in his point of view, . . . then the ultimate significance of his poetry lies in how it helps to define what he represents. Since his prose defines that position far better than his poetry, his poetry must take a secondary role in any final assessment. (pp. 47-8)

White has been the great spokesman for what might be considered a mid-form, but a mid-form of ideas, of human warmth—the viewing of life not with cosmic seriousness but with tolerant affection. White speaks for this mid-form, not the mid-form of poetry. (p. 48)

[Almost] everything White wrote from 1927 to 1938 had some connection with *The New Yorker* and showed the spirit and attitude that he brought with him to the magazine, or developed while he was working for it. (p. 49)

[It] was *Is Sex Necessary?,* not [*The New Yorker*'s] "Notes and Comment," that first made White's name well-known. . . . The book was very much a part of the 1920's, and very much a part of White's early *New Yorker* days. In fact, we might say that the book, light-hearted spoof that it is, represents the maturity of White's first period of intellectual growth—if that is not too pretentious a way of talking about him. It is a humorous book, yet beneath its humor it makes a serious point, more serious than almost anything that White had said in *The New Yorker* up to that time. (pp. 50-1)

White, then, began as a poet and as a humorist, and it was as a humorist that he first attracted much attention. Although he never lost his humorous touch, a retrospective view of White suggests that humor is not his enduring quality. Serious themes emerge, and humor becomes more and more a means to an end, not an end in itself. (p. 53)

White was well on his way to becoming the spokesman for a literate, cultured minority. He could see the seriousness of the Depression; the follies and pretensions of politicians, ministers, and scientists; the growing threat to civilization posed by an impending second world war—he could see these things, and yet not lose his sense of humor, and not be drawn into a dogmatic or doctrinaire position. (p. 63)

The reader coming from *Quo Vadimus?* and *Every Day Is Saturday* to *One Man's Meat* is struck by White's greater sureness of material and expression, by his clearer thinking on many topics, and above all by his more penetrating moral purpose and his deeper conviction in attitudes and feelings. (p. 67)

Two topics run through many of the essays: often stated, often implied, they exist as a unifying pattern for *One Man's Meat.* One concerns war and internationalism, and the other domestic social and political problems. (p. 68)

The best essay in *One Man's Meat,* "Once More to the Lake," combines in rare form White's stylistic economy, which is essentially the stuff of poetry, with his skillful use of details, his gift for the evocation of the past and his feeling of the circularity of time; and, finally, his haunting awareness of the transient quality of life, the imminence of death. (p. 74)

We find in this essay much of the credo of E. B. White. Here is his simple love of nature; his nostalgia for the past, and along with that his inclination (never quite given in to) to reject the present (the tarred road, the outboard motors) in favor of the past; his preference for doing rather than thinking (the walking, the fishing, the boating); his feeling for the mystery outside the church, not inside it ("this holy spot," "cathedral stillness"); his vivid language, with his liking for the simple, natural figures of speech ("the boat would leap ahead, charging bullfashion at the dock"); his love for people, for his son, and his sense of identity with the young (which made him such a good writer, later on, of children's stories); and the everpresent sense of death that with White was sometimes whimsical [and sometimes intensely serious]. (p. 76)

Written over a period of three years, the editorials in *The Wild Flag* are White's only book-length discussion of a single topic. They form some of his best writing; because of the subject, however, they must be judged on somewhat different grounds from that of his other work—and judging them today is not easy. If the book seems naïve, the reader must remember the context—World War II—and the often naïve hopes many people had for world peace. If it is repetitious, he must remember that originally the editorials appeared at uneven intervals over an extended period of time. (p. 90)

Perhaps more serious than White's lack of historical perspective is the absence of any reference to the psychological and sociological aspects of war. (p. 91)

In "Across the Street and into the Grill," one of his best spoofs, White parodies Hemingway's novel *Across the River and into the Trees*. White chose his subject well; the novel, probably Hemingway's worst, deserves parody. White, I am sure, would grant that Hemingway's style at its best is beyond parody, but in a style like Hemingway's there is a thin dividing line between effectiveness and affectation—like the thin line between sentiment and sentimentality in much of Charles Dickens.

One of the functions of the parodist is to discover these fine lines and, by crossing them, to show the dangers and vulnerability of the style. With devastating skill White does precisely this, concentrating on chapters XI and XII of Hemingway's novel. His technique is to select certain words and phrases Hemingway used; placing them in a slightly different context, he pinpoints the foolishness of the original. (p. 124)

[It] is not in the specific word echoes that the greatest success of "Across the Street and into the Grill" lies, but rather in White's dead-pan parody of the fatuous, trivial tone of the whole scene in the novel. It is the posed and phony heroism, the pseudo-realistic, irrelevant details that White singles out for ridicule. (p. 125)

The essays in *The Points of My Compass* fall into what are now familiar patterns for White: national and international affairs, the idea of progress, the urban and rural scenes and, in two notable essays, the circularity of time—a theme in much of White's writing and one present by implication in a number of these last essays. In fact, the whole collection, ending as it does with an autobiographical essay that goes back to White's days in Seattle and Alaska, suggests the idea of circularity. Also, to many of these essays White has written postscripts containing "after-thoughts and later information." They add to the feeling of circularity.

We find also a curious sort of geographical circularity in the collection. . . . This "geographical distortion," as he calls it, seems to broaden the dimensions of the work; but it also underlines the importance of New York City to White. It was for him a microcosm, a center, and the four corners of the world could almost be contained within its emotional if not geographical limits. Geography *was* to White something of an emotional matter. . . . Without being pompous about it, we could say that the essays represent the culmination of White's experience, the farthest point of navigation—not quite to the heart of darkness, perhaps, but certainly to the heart of his message to his readers. (p. 132)

All of his reports of the past may not be in yet, all the points of his compass not yet revealed, but I suspect that his major themes have been stated; *The Points of My Compass,* in its subject and structure, is a fitting and impressive summation. In space, it is a microcosm of his world; in time, a symbol of the unity and coherence of human experience, where youth and age, city and country, past and present, come together. The book is ultimately White's plea for a vital life where the means do not become ends, where gadgets do not create more problems than they solve, where the "advances" of science do not destroy all possibility of real advance because they have destroyed life itself. (p. 148)

White's style . . . developed freely as an expression of himself and of all those forces, impossible ever to understand fully, that make a man a writer. . . .

If it is not easy to account for White's style, it is also not easy to describe it, though that must be my concern now. Certainly one key to its perfection is his choice of words. (p. 155)

Unlike some writers, White has few words or expressions that he keeps using. It is remarkable, for example, that for over a twenty-year period, while he was writing substantial parts of "Notes and Comment," there were only two or three instances when he opened a comment with the same word or phrase. And even those expressions or words of which he appears to be fond are used so rarely as to be scarcely noticed.

What is striking about White's use of words is not so much the individual choice but the context in which the choice appears—his brilliant use of contrast, his use of the specific word to make a generalization or an abstraction clear, his figures of speech drawn from clear observation of nature or daily life. (pp. 155-56)

[Over] the long stretch of White's work, the combination of seriousness and whimsy, or of the minute and the momentous, is effective, and at times profoundly true. Because human experience itself is a curious mixture of shifting tones and moods there is a basic honesty and wisdom in White's writing; he reveals himself as a man unafraid of surface contradictions or of simple and natural responses. (p. 158)

[It] must be admitted at the outset that White has not written great poems, great novels, great plays, or great short stories. As these are the genres most talked about and admired by today's critics, we might wonder what there was left for White to be. (p. 160)

Few admirers of E. B. White, however, would be content to let his significance rest on his connection with *The New Yorker*; or on his worth as a stylist; or as a writer of sketches, short stories, or children's books. He is equally important as the spokesman of our times for the right of privacy, a right threatened by the population explosion, by devices for snooping, and by repressive measures instituted through the fear of violence in our society. . . .

White is, in E. M. Forster's sense of the word, an aristocrat—one of the aristocracy of "the sensitive, the considerate and the plucky"— and he speaks for those like himself. (p. 163)

White speaks for those who have taken, like himself, the often lonely role of the true individualist. He gives strength to those who find the role difficult, who find it hard to resist putting on a badge or acquiring a label, but who do resist. Surely such a spokesman has a significant part to play in a society in which pressures to conform are great and in which even non-conformity turns upon itself and produces often the ultimate conformist. Although White may sometimes hold a middle position, his role is not that of the defender of compromise. But, unlike the professional liberal, or the professional conservative, he doesn't scorn the middle position; and, when he sees cause, he is not afraid to abandon whatever position he has taken. He embodies tolerance without condescension, understanding without over-simplification, individualism without eccentricity. (p. 164)

> *Edward C. Sampson, in his* E. B. White *(copyright 1974 by Twayne Publishers, Inc.; reprinted with the permission of Twayne Publishers, A Division of G. K. Hall & Co., Boston), Twayne, 1974.*

NIGEL DENNIS

One of the many interesting pieces in *Essays of E. B. White* is called "Some Remarks on Humor" and was originally the preface to an anthology of humor assembled by White and his wife and published in 1941. In it, White does his duty to the publishers like a man and talks about the essence of humor—why funny is so funny, what temperature the oven should be, and so on—but his heart is not in this unhappy duty; no man knows better that a dissertation on humor is bound to be worthless as information and painful as reading matter. So, he moves on smartly to the infinitely fascinating question, which nobody has managed to answer, of why Americans believe "that if a thing is funny it can be presumed to be something less than great, because if it were truly great it would be wholly serious.". . .

White shows that American humorists have accepted their secondary place in the scale of seriousness for many years. The greatest of them, Mark Twain, asserted that "Humor is only a fragrance, a decoration"; he himself was essentially a preacher, he said (how strange for a man to think that essence and fragrance are separable!). (p. 42)

Still the question remains: what seriousness can be expected of a man who can only write essays and is inclined to smile? White has smoothed out this question somewhat by the selection he has made for this book: there are a number of pieces, mostly about civil liberties, which would meet the serious test with perfect solemnity, even though they have no serious theories behind them and no serious clichés to push them forward. (pp. 42-3)

But the heart of the collection is the picture it presents of country life. A humorous undertow is running all the time, and the combination of this and the rural material is bound to startle the foreigner who depends not only on the press for his picture of America but on American writers who are first-class citizens with a vengeance. . . .

There are a few other things to be said in favor of White. In his old-fashioned way, he omits needless words and avoids a succession of loose sentences. He continues the old tradition which has made humor America's best ambassador. Though only an essayist, he makes definite assertions and says shortly what others say at length. He will never win the Nobel Prize and will certainly never approach a Great Work; but he will always make sense, which is an achievement too. To conclude that he should be ranked among serious writers would only give offense to those who are. . . . (p. 43)

> *Nigel Dennis, "Smilin' Through," in* The New York Review of Books *(reprinted with permission from* The New York Review of Books; *copyright © 1977 NYREV, Inc.), October 27, 1977, pp. 42-3.*

*   *   *

WILDER, Thornton   1897-1975

Wilder was an American playwright, novelist, essayist, and screenwriter. He seeks to explore the universal in the particular in his writing: his stereotypical characters and conventional themes reflect his belief that realism in the theater cannot adequately portray the human condition. The form and content of his novels also reveal his rejection of contemporary modes of literary expression. His fiction and his drama have thus been the subject of critical controversy for their lack of contemporary theme or exposition. Wilder was three times the recipient of the Pulitzer Prize: for his novel *The Bridge of San Luis Ray* in 1927, and for his plays *Our Town* in 1938 and *The Skin of Our Teeth* in 1943. (See also CLC, Vols. 1, 5, 6, and *Contemporary Authors*, Vols. 13-16, rev. ed.; obituary, Vols. 61-64.)

DOUGLAS CHARLES WIXSON, JR.

Wilder has known German since an early age. As a child he was sent to a German school in Hong Kong. Further, there is abundant evidence that he extended his knowledge of German and German literature with maturity: some of the lines in his early plays are in German; his first published collection of drama, *The Angel that Troubled the Waters and Other Plays*, published in 1928, is dedicated to Max Reinhardt; he visited Berlin in 1928, at the time when Brecht's plays were receiving considerable notice; much later, it might be added, Brecht and Wilder attempted collaboration on . . . a project which subsequently never materialized. But the main evidence is in the plays themselves. (p. 112)

Theatricalism as it applies to Brecht and Wilder restores the theater's reality as theater while destroying the illusion of reality. Instead of attempting to imitate reality it essays, more boldly than subtly, the perception of reality through symbol. The central idea, for instance, is suggested iteratively by a "succession of events." . . . Brecht's and Wilder's theater, then, is theater which draws attention to itself as theater.

Brecht's and Wilder's drama imposes itself upon its audience; the audience is forced to take a critical role. In this sense it is didactic. In didactic drama the dramatist has a tendency to speak in his own voice, rather than to dramatize his subject matter. Characterization is reduced to a minimum; it serves only to point up the underlying ideas embodied by the fable. "The myths, the parable, the fable," Wilder wrote, "are the fountain head of all fiction, and in them is seen most clearly the didactic, moralizing employment of a story." In order that the audience give their full attention to the lessons of the play it is important that their sympathies not be engaged. They must not, for instance, anticipate the dramatic climax rather than the underlying idea.

Brecht and Wilder rebelled against the naturalistic theater on grounds that it deprived the audience of any participation other than strictly emotional. . . . Wilder, in his *The Skin of Our Teeth* parodies the naturalistic theater he had known in his youth. Miss Somerset, an actress, unwillingly takes the role of Sabina in the author's play.... Later in the play, she refuses to continue her part, "Because there are some lines in that scene that would hurt some people's feelings and I don't think the theatre is a place where people's feelings ought to be hurt." (pp. 113-14)

Both dramatists set about to destroy dramatic illusion and insure detachment on the part of the audience.... Brecht's and Wilder's theater calls upon the imaginative participation of the audience. (p. 114)

Brecht's and Wilder's plays display a distinct self-consciousness; the dramatist's presence is felt along with his didactic purpose. For them the play is a means to convey those ideas in which the dramatist wishes to instruct his audience. For this purpose both dramatists frequently make use of a narrator.... [In *Our Town*, at] the point we begin to be "taken in" by the drama unfolding before us the Stage Manager appears to point the moral and shatter the illusion.... In Wilder's plays the Stage Manager actually arranges the props, directs the action, and takes different roles.... [The] effect is ... to provide interruption and digression in order that the audience not miss the significance of the action. The sequence of events in the play which constitute the narration is more important to Brecht and Wilder's dramatic purpose than exposition through character, for instance.

The importance of characterization, as a consequence, is minimized in Brecht's and Wilder's plays. The stage directions in Wilder's *Happy Journey* go so far as to prescribe that the Stage Manager read "from a typescript the lines of all the minor characters ... with little attempt at characterization, scarcely troubling himself to alter his voice, even when he responds in the person of a child or a woman." Wilder tends to portray types in his plays rather than individuals. Emily of *Our Town* is the small-town provincial girl; Ma Kirby in *Happy Journey* is the authoritarian but loving mother. Qualities are abstracted for the purpose of illustrating the human condition. (pp. 115-16)

Both Brecht and Wilder ... distinguish within the play between the character and the actor taking the part of the character.... Wilder wrote parts in his plays for the actor as both actor and character.... Wilder in his play *The Skin of Our Teeth* has the actress "Miss Somerset" perform the roles of Sabina and Miss Fairweather. In Wilder's *Our Town* the Stage Manager takes the roles, alternately, of four different characters.... [The] audience is not allowed to identify itself with the characters beyond a certain point. That point is determined by the author.... (pp. 116-17)

The intent of the two authors, Brecht and Wilder, is to portray social, viz., human characteristics which the audience has familiarity with and will recognize as being true once they have been pointed out. The effect of the interruptions in the action and changes in identity and self-consciousness of the characterization is to force the audience to confront the underlying arguments of the play, to recognize certain truths as a detached observer, and to engage its observations with intelligence. The actors alert the audience, preparing them in a sense for the author's desired interpretation of important incidents in the play. For example, an actor through a remark or expression makes an incident appear strange and astonishing. A stage direction in Wilder's *The Skin of Our Teeth* calls for Sabina to drop the

play suddenly and say "in her own person as 'Miss Somerset,' with surprise: 'Oh, I see what this part of the play means now! ... Oh, I don't like it. I don't like it.'" (pp. 118-19)

In *Our Town* the women go through the preparation of dinner in pantomime. The mimic action releases the commonplace event from the particular and reveals it as part of a generalized truth. (p. 119)

The reality of theater, in Brecht and Wilder's view, extends out beyond the stage to include the audience and life itself.... The audience is a participant in the reality of this kind of anti-illusionistic theater. On the one hand, characters in the play step out of their roles to address the audience directly. On the other, the audience is requested (symbolically) to take part in the action unfolding on stage. (p. 120)

Brecht's and Wilder's use of stage properties is in accord with their attempt to present reality symbolically.... The Stage Manager in *Our Town* serves to heighten our consciousness of the reality of what we observe on stage in pointing to properties which *do not exist*. Despite the absence of any visible representation of a railroad car we nevertheless "see" one through the actor's reactions to the swaying and lurching of Wilder's pullman car (*Pullman Car Hiawatha*). People leave the table and new faces join those remaining seated in Wilder's *The Long Christmas Dinner* in a symbolic presentation of generations dying and new ones taking their places. Since the stage is bare except for the dinner table, anachronism is avoided; the audience provides the setting with its imagination.

Brecht and Wilder each took delight in disintegrating the naturalistic stage.... Wilder parodies the conventional box-set of naturalistic theater in his *The Skin of Our Teeth*. Act One opens as a conventional box-set with a typical domestic of "old-fashioned playwriting" dusting the living-room. The walls suddenly flap, buckle and fly off. Sabina is "struck dumb with surprise." Her amazement calls the audience's attention to this remarkable incident which symbolically displays the disintegration of the conventional stage.... Wilder wrote: "... the box-set stage stifles the life in drama ... it militates against belief." His *Our Town* opens without curtain and scenery, the stage half-lighted. The Stage Manager enters and arranges a few tables and chairs for the convenience of the actors. Clearing the stage of ordinary scenery and props stresses the "pretense" of theater, while reminding the audience that they are spectators in a theater.... (pp. 121-22)

It is quite obvious that Brecht's and Wilder's staging makes demands upon their audiences' imagination, and even greater demands upon the actor's ability to present ideas which instruct as well as entertain. But the most difficult task befalls of course the two dramatists themselves who, working with the barest of stage materials, must elicit the audience's participation in a version of reality which is far more ambitious than the mimetic substitution for reality offered by previous naturalistic theater.

Finally, Brecht and Wilder both make use of an episodic structure.... While the episodic structure of Brecht's *Herr Puntila und sein Knecht Matti* implies the episodic nature of life itself and dramatizes the lack of continuity to life in terms of human emotions, the effect of the episodic (and cyclic) structure of Wilder's *The Skin of Our Teeth* is to suggest just the reverse. For Wilder what is significant throughout the history of mankind is that man's emotions and convictions have remained the same. Furthermore, it is this continuity in men's lives (as illustrated in the Antrobus family's everyday existence) which has maintained the survival of the human race: inventiveness in the face of adversity, and the determination under pressure to survive, as evidenced in the ordinariness of circumstances out of which profound convictions appear almost at the last moment.

An episodic plot has the effect of breaking up the flow of the play and alienating the audience from the action. Rather than the continuous narrative and unbroken illusion of naturalistic drama, what the audience views is a series of varying and broken scenes drawing attention to themselves as theatrical devices. . . . The repetitiousness of the episodes in Wilder's plays . . . reinforces his desire to show the importance of recurring commonplace experience and how this experience may illuminate the possibilities of life. But there is selection in these episodes also, for "Wherever you come near the human race, there's layers and layers of nonsense. . . ." The dramatist's task, in Wilder's view, is to strip the layers in order to reveal the meaning beneath the nonsense.

In between the publication of *The Angel that Troubled the Waters and Other Plays* (1928) and the publication of *The Long Christmas Dinner and Other Plays* (1931) a radical change took place in Wilder's dramatic technique. The new technique clearly followed many of the Brechtian rules for "epic" (or dialectical, as Brecht later called it) theater, including the shattering of dramatic illusion, the conscious role-taking of the actor, the symbolic use of stage properties in an effort to employ the reality that theater has as theater, the tendency to use parable as a basis of the narrative, the didactic intent, and the episodic structure. On the basis of internal evidence in the plays alone, some of which has been submitted here, we may conclude—without positive evidence—that some of the theory and techniques employed by Brecht worked their way into Wilder's plays published after 1928. Brecht himself implies it when, late in life, he wrote: "the term dialectical theatre has fulfilled its task if the narrative element that is part of the theatre in general has been strengthened and enriched . . . it has become almost a formal concept, which could equally well be applied to Claudel or even Wilder." (pp. 122-24)

> *Douglas Charles Wixson, Jr., in* Modern Drama *(copyright © 1972, University of Toronto, Graduate Centre for Study of Drama; with the permission of* Modern Drama*), September, 1972.*

EDWARD ERICSON, JR.

That an examination of Kierkegaard's influence on *The Eighth Day* will prove fruitful we have Wilder's own word. John Ashley, the hero of the novel, is repeatedly called a man of faith. Noticing what seemed to me striking parallels between Ashley and Kierkegaard's knight of faith in *Fear and Trembling,* I wrote to Mr. Wilder to inquire about the matter. In a letter addressed to me dated April 24, 1971, he responded: "Yes, indeed John Ashley is a sketch of Kierkegaard's knight. Once one has read S.K. he remains a part of one's view of life and I'd like to think that he appears and disappears throughout the book *even when I'm not aware of it.* Many have noticed also the presence of Teilhard de Chardin—very few have glimpsed S.K." This

compelling piece of external evidence is both sufficient encouragement to seek the internal evidences of Kierkegaard's thought in the novel and a *prima facie* case for their presence.

The purpose of this paper, then, is to locate as many of those places in *The Eighth Day* as we can where Kierkegaard "appears" and to indicate the nature of Wilder's debt. In general, we may note here that reference to Kierkegaard illuminates the main character of the novel, John Ashley, and the central theme of the book, living by faith, which is expressed most forcefully in the closing passage through the image of the tapestry of life. Other characters and secondary themes will also be clarified by an analysis in Kierkegaardian terms. *The Eighth Day* covers many issues which lie outside the scope of Kierkegaard's influence: the debate on heredity versus environment, the idea of progress, the concept of evolution, the influences of world religions, and others. Also, the novel presents a wide array of realized characters. We should not claim too much for Kierkegaard's influence. Nevertheless, an influence which explains the main character and the main theme must be considered the crucial one. (pp. 123-24)

The parallels are just the kind one might expect from a source which has been assimilated so thoroughly that its ideas have passed unobtrusively but firmly into the fiber of the author's own thought. Wilder is writing his own novel, not a fictional gloss on Kierkegaard based on slavish imitation.

Kierkegaard lists a variety of traits of his knight of faith, and Wilder echoes most, though not all, of them. The knight is not easily recognized as special by those around him. . . . John Ashley has the same kind of invisibility which comes from commonness. . . . Wilder describes men of faith primarily in negative terms. They are not afraid, not self-regarding, not interesting, not pathetic, not tragic, not articulate. "They have little sense of humor, which draws so heavily on a consciousness of superiority and on an aloofness from the predicaments of others." . . . (p. 124)

Kierkegaard contrasts his knight of faith, Abraham, with the tragic hero. Like the knight of infinite resignation, the tragic hero belongs to the ethical stage, while the knight of faith goes beyond this stage to the highest one in Kierkegaard's schema, the religious stage. . . . Ashley is a truly religious man, not one who lives in accordance with universally recognized precepts of morality. In fact, others consider him immoral because they do not understand the principles which motivate him. Like Kierkegaard, Wilder carefully distinguishes men of faith from tragic heroes: "Try as hard as you like, you cannot see them [men of faith] as the subjects of tragedy. (It has often been attempted; when the emotion subsides the audience finds that its tears have been shed, unprofitably, for itself)." . . . Ashley's whole life story is a sharp contrast from conventional tragedies. His death midway through the novel comes by mysterious accident, not from a tragic flaw. His life breathes a perpetual benediction on his family; there is no grief.

As the knight of faith is not a tragic hero, so "he is not a poet, and I have sought in vain to detect in him the poetic incommensurability." . . . Neither is Ashley poetic. He "had never distinguished a category of the beautiful." . . . (pp. 124-25)

The knight of faith, as a common man, belongs to the realm of the finite. . . . [Ashley is] a man conscious of no purpose other than the concrete, finite one of being a family man. Kierkegaard's knight "takes delight in everything." . . . Ashley is "constantly filled with wonder." . . . (p. 125)

[Like the knight of faith,] while Ashley gives the appearance of a carefree ne'er-do-well, he is as far from one as is the knight of faith. . . . Ashley's wife, Beata, remarks, "All Ashleys are happy, because we work. I'd be ashamed if we weren't." . . .

One of Kierkegaard's main themes is the limitedness of human rationality. For Kierkegaard existence imposes upon the individual the necessity to choose and to act. . . . Wilder speaks similarly: ". . . choice is the sovereign faculty of the mind." . . . For both Kierkegaard and Wilder, thinking about existence, trying to comprehend life's meaning and formulate it into dogmas, is insufficient. Reflection is a paltry substitute for action. . . .

Wilder makes a major point of the man of faith's inarticulateness and lack of reflection. His men of faith "are inarticulate, especially in matters of faith." . . . (p. 126)

However, inarticulateness does not mean ignorance. The man of faith knows much, and his knowledge is of the kind which comes by faith. (p. 127)

[The knight of faith's] self-knowledge does not come painlessly for John Ashley. It is through the sufferings which life imposes on him that he grows in wisdom. . . . But he does not succumb to despair. He keeps faith and grows through suffering. . . . Kierkegaard, too, spoke often of the relationship between faith and suffering. (pp. 127-28)

[Ashley's] exercises in self-understanding are, it should be clear, the result of experience, not abstract speculation. As such, they coincide with Kierkegaard's existentialism. (p. 128)

Kierkegaard realizes that it is impossible for the man without faith to fathom the leap of faith, because it embraces absurdity. . . . The knight of faith is fully as cognizant as the knight of infinite resignation of the impossibility, humanly speaking, of gaining his objective within the infinite order. Nevertheless, "he resigned everything infinitely, and then he grasped everything again by virtue of the absurd." . . .

If John Ashley is, as Wilder has said, "a sketch of Kierkegaard's knight" of faith, what impossibility does he gain "by virtue of the absurd"? Needless to say, the Kierkegaardian concept of the absurd is a difficult one to integrate into a realistic fictional plot, which generally depends on probability for its viability. It may be argued that such an effort is, in fact, impossible. Nevertheless, Wilder makes the effort. (p. 129)

While [Ashley] never stops planning his return to his family . . . , the mysterious circumstances of life never permit that cherished reunion to occur. It is, humanly speaking, impossible. Yet Ashley never loses faith that he will return to be a husband and father. And, "by virtue of the absurd," his faith is fulfilled.

Wilder's device for demonstrating Ashley's return as husband is a dream [of his return] which both he and his wife have. It is an important element of the novel, albeit a mysterious one. . . . Not only are these dreams mysterious and seemingly inappropriate in a realistic novel, but they are inexplicable apart from Kierkegaardian categories. John and Beata Ashley cannot possibly be reunited. Yet by faith, "by virtue of the absurd," they are reunited. John desires to comfort and encourage his wife, and through the vehicle to this shared dream, he does so. What he wants is, humanly speaking, impossible; yet he attains it. Apart from this Kierkegaardian interpretation, the likeliest reading is to consider these dreams a flaw in the novel, to be chalked up to unwarranted sentimentalism on Wilder's part. (pp. 129-30)

Ashley's desire to be a father to his growing children is also fulfilled, though less mystically and less dramatically. His son, Roger, asserts, "Maybe Papa's dead. But he's not dead for Sophia and me. He's alive in us even when we aren't thinking about him." . . . The subsequent deeds of his exceptional offspring are ample testimony to his continuing influence as their father. His continuing fatherhood is seen most clearly in the climactic passage at the end of the novel, when Roger accepts, by his own leap of faith, the meaningfulness of life with all its mysteries—and does so through the indirect agency of his father. . . . Despite the physical impossibilities John Ashley has fulfilled his earthly vocation of being both father and husband. (pp. 130-31)

While she does not attain her husband's heights, Beata Ashley is a woman of faith.

The Ashley children also resemble their father in ways which mark them as persons of faith, though only Roger approaches his father's stature. Wilder lists those traits which they had inherited, "particularly from their father." . . . (p. 131)

All of the Ashley children become famous except Sophia, who burns out early. Wilder links their later fame to certain traits of the person of faith. Lily shares "her father's inner quiet, his at-homeness in existence. This was the voice of faith—selfless faith." . . . Constance "possessed that rarer form of eloquence that arises from an absence of self-consciousness." . . . Roger "exhibited no signs of ambition; he effaced himself, unsuccessfully." . . . Like his father, Roger grows through the suffering inflicted upon him. While he gains enough wisdom to become fearful "that he would go through life ignorant—stump ignorant," . . . at that very time he has gained much of the maturity and insight which became his father's portion and which was mediated to him through his father's example. In Roger's case the result of his growth in faith is a reconciliation with the human community. . . . (pp. 131-32)

Sophia's main virtue is hope, a virtue which her father shared. . . . So while the novel does not discuss love, it does treat hope, and once again Kierkegaardian categories come into play. It is, like faith, a means of knowing. (p. 132)

John Ashley is one individual who successfully resists [what Kierkegaard saw as the modern] leveling, abstracting process. . . . Wilder and Kierkegaard share the anti-deterministic view that it is men who make history; they are individualists. (p. 133)

Wilder's denunciation of institutionalized religion is as vehement as Kierkegaard's. He speaks savagely of Roger's having "suffered the spectacle of his family being chewed up fine by a civilized Christian community." . . . Wilder does not denigrate Christianity or even all Christian assemblies. He praises the small church of Ashley's grandmother . . . and that of Indian believers on Herkomer's Knob. . . . However, these are disestablished "splinter" sects. The mainline churches, those with status in society, are the ones which come under his scathing fire, just as it was the established state church of Denmark which Kierkegaard attacked. (pp. 133-34)

[The] main influence of Kierkegaard on *The Eighth Day* (at least rivaling Wilder's use of Kierkegaard's knight) . . . [is] on the main theme of Wilder's novel, that of living by faith.

The central meaning of *The Eighth Day* is most clearly laid bare in the closing pages when the Deacon of the congregation at Herkomer's Knob shows Roger Ashley the old tapestry and uses it as an object lesson to give his view of the meaning of life. The rug has a complex mazelike design on one side, but "no figure could be traced on the reverse. It presented a mass of knots and of frayed and dangling threads." . . . The Deacon explicates: "Those are the threads and knots of human life. You cannot see the design." . . . After further explication of the tapestry image as it relates to Roger and the whole Ashley family, the Deacon adds, "There is no happiness equal to that of being aware that one has a part in a design." . . . In Wilder's own words, "History is *one* tapestry. No eye can venture to compass more than a hand's-breadth . . ." . . . . Life must remain an enigma to us because of our limited point of view. Only God, who in his omniscience can scan the whole tapestry of history in one glance, is in a position to assert with confidence that life is pervaded by a meaning which is objectively verifiable. We are left with the insoluble mysteries of suffering and injustice.

All this sounds strikingly like Kierkegaard. He does not deny that life has a system. He denies only that finite man is capable of viewing the system inherent in existence. But God has a vantage point which allows him to see it. (pp. 134-35)

Truth, for man, is always subjective and not objective, according to Kierkegaard. . . . One can attain this truth only by the leap of faith, which is executed in the face of the absurdity that the available evidence is insufficient for such a conclusion. . . .

Wilder urges faith. His men and women of faith in *The Eighth Day* attain just that kind of faith which is not fully supported by the facts of life. (p. 135)

It is only at the end of the novel that Roger—and the reader—learns of the religious principles which informed John Ashley's entire life. . . . [The] disclosure at the novel's conclusion casts a retrospective light over all of Ashley's life in the preceding pages. We see now that what underlay his nobility was not humanistic moralism but religious faith. We see now with full clarity why Wilder insisted on calling him a man of faith. (p. 137)

All of Wilder's persons of faith accept the meaningfulness of life despite its mystery. Eustacia Lansing meditates: "'We are our lives. Everything is bound together. No smallest action can be thought of other than as it is.' She groped among the concepts of necessity and free will. Everything is mysterious, but how unendurable life would be without the mystery." . . . She employs a metaphor strikingly similar to the tapestry image when she thinks, "Our lives are a seamless robe . . ." . . . . (pp. 137-38)

Why did [Ashley] die? Who can say? Can the reader find his share of that faith which Wilder extols and accept Ashley's death as part of the design which he cannot perceive from his finite vantage point? Or will he see it only as a *deus ex machina* which inexplicably rids the novel of its main character before it is half finished? Irrational faith may seem to some to be flimsy grounds for affirming that human life has meaning. But, say both Kierkegaard and Wilder, this is the best that we can do. We will affirm by rationally unsupportable faith, or we will not affirm at all. For understanding the ultimate issues of human existence, faith is all that we have. (p. 138)

> *Edward Ericson, Jr., "Kierkegaard in Wilder's 'The Eighth Day'," in* Renascence *(© copyright, 1974, Marquette University Press), Spring, 1974, pp. 123-38.*

JOHN SIMON

Wilder is obsessed with the notion of communality and identity of little people everywhere, but most particularly in middle America. They form, for him, a fictive *we*, the source and culmination of all that is enduring and wonderful about humanity, and most of Wilder's dramaturgy consists of brandishing this great, shaggy, unwashed lowest common denominator of a *we* as the tool, subject, and end product of playwriting. But lowest common denominators are too low and common for art: even Whitman, that other grassroots American, was saved by the rough idiosyncrasy of his *I;* Wilder sinks into the treacly morass of his *we*.

Philosophically, dramatically, and literarily I find *The Skin of Our Teeth* unpalatable. There is, first, the (all too or not enough) Joycean double or triple exposure of seeing the Antrobus family of Excelsior, N.J., as the prehistoric family—both the Biblical first family and early mankind inventing the wheel, the alphabet, the multiplication table, and such. What, except for a jejune jest, is achieved by this simultaneity? We learn nothing about the Stone Age, the Bible, or even New Jersey in 1942 except that Wilder considers them as interpenetrating and identical—interpenetratingly insipid and identically piddling. Next, we get Pirandellian reversibility: some of the characters revert periodically to the actors playing them, and a few minor members of the theatrical personnel also get briefly into the act. There is inconsistency here in that only Sabina is allowed much of this duality; George and Henry Antrobus get only one chance each, Maggie and Gladys none. Worse, though, is that the device serves only a very primitive purpose: to show that the players duplicate and continue the characters they are playing. . . .

Ideologically, there is—brace yourselves—more of this sameness. The point is that all men are alike and all women are alike: a couple of basic types, or stereotypes, constantly repeating themselves, without even the benefit of racy local variations. It follows that everyone is small. . . . Great writers have conveyed to us the greatness in some specific little people; Wilder, a mediocrity, merely conveys to us the littleness of great persons. . . .

The true failure, though, lies in Wilder's sentimentality and vapidity. . . . In Wilder's universe, catastrophe is a feeble joke, and evil only too willing to subside at a mere pat on the back. I could go on and raise such questions as why Wilder, the champion of all living creatures, is so callously ready to sacrifice those relatively harmless Atlantic City

Shriners and beauty contestants, not to mention the innocent and endearing mammoth and dinosaur. But let me say only that the trouble with this supposedly deeply humane and wise play is that it is only skin deep.

John Simon, "Epidermal Contact," in New York Magazine (copyright © 1975 by the NYM Corporation; reprinted with the permission of New York Magazine), July 28, 1975, p. 58.

VICTOR WHITE

[Theophilus North is] a story of a young tutor in the Newport of the 1920s, a mushy account of mild eccentrics and trivial complications and of a not very exciting young man's attempts at saintly midwifery and playing deus ex machina to bring to birth peace of mind in petty souls. In brief, sentimental drivel, [although] competent insofar as remembered craftsmanship and Wilder's memory of the 1920s were concerned. . . . The kindest thing one can say is that, just perhaps although there is no evidence of it, Wilder indulged himself in a playful pastiche—he always had a superb sensitiveness of style—of a "woman's novel" of the 1920s. (p. 76)

Inevitably one wondered whether one's own memory of The Bridge of San Luis Rey as a masterpiece was not the product of nostalgic falsification, whether it had really been all that good. . . . The only way to find out was to dig up an old copy—already listing seven printings a month after publication.

And, lo and behold, one is in for a pleasant surprise. Brilliantly constructed, wonderfully warm in spite of the terse style, witty, vibrant with startling insights into the darker corners of the heart, the book captivates one from the opening pages like the first few minutes with a fascinating woman. The device of Brother Juniper, who wants to make a scientific inquiry into the reasons of Providence for sending to their deaths just the particular five persons on the Bridge of San Luis Rey when it breaks, is significant. It frames what is really the story like two branches of some fanciful vine that embrace an initial in a medieval manuscript and burst into flower at the top. Delicate, barely noticeable tendrils of skepticism reach out from that inquiry and its foreknown futility and give tartness to the portraits of the characters Brother Juniper studies—reminders of a skepticism that is more of our time than of the giddy, self-confident 1920s, so that the whole tone of the book is surprisingly modern.

But it is the characters and their involvements with each other that compel admiration. Powerfully evoked, there, engrossing by their immediacy, each one a mine of idiosyncrasy and paradoxical verities, they are like Rodin sculptures no longer merely pregnant with life but come to life. . . . [Even if many of the characters were derived from other literary sources (or literatures)], those were the mere taking-off points of Wilder's characters, and every artist is the son of somebody—or, rather, of many somebodies.

It is what Wilder did with those possible suggestions for characters that is impressive. (pp. 76-7)

[The] originality that informs The Bridge of San Luis Rey is beyond challenge. . . . What is most astonishing, however, is Wilder's compassion and his grasp of the perverseness not only of things and Fate but of the human heart. One

would say they were those of a Dostoevsky with the years in Siberia and the long struggle against poverty and his passion for gambling behind him rather than the gift of a novelist who had had a rather easy time of it and was only in his late twenties when he wrote the book. (p. 78)

Yet more astounding even than the compassion is the mood of gentle skepticism which runs all through the book and anticipates by almost forty years the dominant mood of our time, when all certainties seem to have deserted us; that mood is a shining instance of the true artist's gift for seeing the future fruits in the present germ. Better than that, even, for, philosophically, Wilder in that book is even now ahead of us with the upbeat—not cheaply optimistic or vaguely pious, but convincingly realistic in its suggestion of the only way out of despair and doubt—on which he ends.

Yes, clearly a masterpiece. . . . (pp. 78-9)

Victor White, "'The Bridge of San Luis Rey' Revisited," in The Texas Quarterly (© 1976 by The University of Texas at Austin), Autumn, 1976, pp. 76-9.

GERALD WEALES

It is hardly surprising that Thornton Wilder, who found his immediate inspiration in the writers he admired and who turned to the Greeks as early as his third novel, "The Woman of Andros," should try to have his way with Alcestis. . . .

["The Alcestiad"] is certainly inferior to the major Wilder plays, but it is interesting as an example of the playwright's work and as another variation on the Alcestis story.

Although "The Alcestiad" is called "A Play in Three Acts," it is clearly intended as a trilogy in the Greek sense, three plays united by a common theme. . . . In Act II we get the traditional Alcestis story, unhappily without the tension and ambiguity that Euripides gives to both the sacrifice and the acceptance of it. In Wilder, the minor characters fall all over one another for a chance to die for Admetus, but Alcestis claims the honor, after the herdsman, who taught her in Act I that she best serves God / Apollo by responding to bits of him in her fellow humans, explains that there are two kinds of deaths—endings and beginnings. . . .

Since [Alcestis] is "the first of a great number that will not have that ending" [escaping her death], her translation to Apollo's grove suggests the Christian heaven; and Alcestis, like Chrysis in "The Woman of Andros," seems to embody Wilder's sense of a pagan world about to give birth to Christianity.

Wilder's trilogy, like its Greek ancestors, is followed by its own satyr play. "The Drunken Sisters" seemed a thin academic joke when it was published on its own in the centennial issue of The Atlantic Monthly in 1957. Here it has more point, but the comedic heavenly perspective on earthly tragedy would be more effective without Apollo's final cry of grief.

At this point I should say that "The Alcestiad," for all its faults, deserves a permanent place on the shelf of any Wilder enthusiast.

Gerald Weales, "The Wilder Shores of Love," in The New York Times Book Review (© 1978 by The New York Times

Company; reprinted by permission), January 1, 1978, p. 27.

* * *

WILSON, John Anthony Burgess
  See BURGESS, Anthony

* * *

WODEHOUSE, P(elham) G(renville)   1881-1975

Wodehouse was an English-born novelist, short story writer, playwright, screenwriter, essayist, and editor who emigrated to the United States in 1910. His fictional milieu is upper-class England, and his characters are the stock characters of this caste. He derides its social and moral conventions with a unique farcical genius. (See also *CLC*, Vols. 1, 2, 5, and *Contemporary Authors*, Vols. 45-48; obituary, Vols. 57-60.)

Future readers of Mr. Wodehouse's novels would be well advised to begin with those of his old age and work inwards towards those of his capacious prime. *The Girl in Blue*, for instance, is funny and well-written enough for anyone to start on, and in many ways it is characteristic of his work. Country house, hunt for disappearing valuables, strange butler, comic Americans, literary lady, benevolent aunt-like figure, village policeman, bohemian but athletic hero, trim and clean-cut heroine—they are all here. Addicts too will find it remarkably good, though what they look for in a new Wodehouse is something of much more specialized interest. First and foremost they are fascinated to see that this writer's gifts and productivity are still not exhausted. Then they watch for innovations: is the modern world making any impact on the traditional Wodehouse cosmography; have any of the old characters undergone interesting (if sometimes unintentional) new developments? Finally they note how and where the earlier books are most obviously superior.

In the present case the innovations are slight, and in some cases unsound. . . .

The main thing to strike the hardened reader is that the plotting is a bit flimsy, the adventures of The Girl in Blue (by Gainsborough) being nothing like as intricate or as neatly constructed as they would have been in the 1920s and 30s. But the slight feeling of dissatisfaction which this brings towards the end of the book is hardly likely to be felt by the unspoilt.

> *"Starter," in* The Times Literary Supplement *(© Times Newspapers Ltd. (London) 1970; reproduced from* The Times Literary Supplement *by permission), November 6, 1970, p. 1291.*

R. C. CHURCHILL

A writer like Wodehouse who published over a hundred books cannot have been a Flaubert or a James Joyce, but in his own style and idiom he was a connoisseur of the *mot juste,* as careful to get the precise nuance of every Bertie Wooster slang phrase—so artfully contrasted with the stately idiom of Jeeves—as Joyce was to catch the precise accent of the various inhabitants of Dublin on that June day in 1904. Wodehouse in translation, like Dickens in translation, must lose some of his appeal. Bertie, Jeeves, Ukridge, Mr. Mulliner and the Oldest Member belong to the English-speaking world as much as Sam Weller and Huckleberry Finn.

[The quotation which illustrates] Wodehouse's political innocence also illustrates (as it was meant to do) his superb command of the English language for his immediate humorous purposes. It is the opening of a story . . . collected in *Lord Emsworth and Others . . .*:

> The situation in Germany had come up for discussion in the bar parlour of the Angler's Rest, and it was generally agreed that Hitler was standing at the crossroads and would soon be compelled to do something definite. His present policy, said a Whisky and Splash, was mere shilly-shallying.
>
> 'He'll have to let it grow or shave it off,' said the Whisky and Splash. 'He can't go on sitting on the fence like this. Either a man has a moustache or he has not. There can be no middle course.'

Mark Twain himself, in his most solemn, deadpan manner on the professional jester's platform, could not have improved upon that opening. But Wodehouse's concentration on the growth or lack of growth on the Nazi dictator's upper lip was not intended to cover up the tyrannous nature of the Nazi regime, upon whose admirers in England he was to express his scornful opinion only a year or two later. The man who broadcast from Berlin in 1941 that in return for his freedom he was willing to hand over India and reveal the secret process of cooking sliced potatoes on a radiator was the same man who, in *The Code of the Woosters* (1938), had made pretty plain his opinion of Roderick Spode, 'founder and head of the Saviours of Britain, a Fascist organisation better known as the Black Shorts.'

Primed by Jeeves on Spode's shameful secret (under the trade name of Eulalie he designs ladies' underclothing), Bertie is emboldened to address him as follows: 'The trouble with you, Spode, is that just because you have succeeded in inducing a handful of half-wits to disfigure the London scene by going about in black shorts, you think you're someone. You hear them shouting "Heil, Spode!" and you imagine it is the Voice of the People . . .' The reference to Mosley and his Black Shirts could hardly have been more explicit. (p. 314)

Writers like Dickens, with a fundamentally serious view of the responsibilities of the comic art, can go on from a *Pickwick Papers* to a *Bleak House*, but writers with a smaller range and a more limited artistry, like Wodehouse . . . , would indeed be foolish if, having struck oil, they moved on to unfamiliar ground. The intricacies of Wodehouse's plots are often tiresome, but we don't read him for his stories so much as for his narrative style and his dialogue, both of which recall the early Dickens as well as *Huckleberry Finn* and *Three Men in a Boat*. It is nearly always the *early* Dickens from whom P. G. partly descends. One of the rare exceptions is Ukridge's sponsorship of Battling Billson in *Lord Emsworth and Others*. . . . (p. 315)

> *R. C. Churchill, "P. G. Wodehouse: 1881-1975," in* Contemporary Review *(© 1975 Contemporary Review Co. Ltd.), June, 1975, pp. 313-15.*

BARBARA C. BOWEN

Clearly Rabelais and Wodehouse are worlds apart, in many ways. For instance, Rabelais is primarily an intellectual and Wodehouse often aggressively anti-intellectual; Rabelais is deeply committed to the reform of religious, political and social institutions, while Wodehouse remains serenely aloof from society's problems; Wodehouse's novels are based on plot and its ramifications, while Rabelais' are based on ideas; Rabelais delights in unbuttoned comedy, while Wodehouse's is always decorous; nearly all Wodehouse novels are built around a romantic love story, while Rabelais is presumably not interested in romantic love, since he never mentions it. But equally obvious, both are great humorists, whose comic worlds are poised on the indefinable dividing-line between reality and fantasy, and it is not really surprising that they have techniques in common. . . . [The] intention of this article is not to claim influence of any kind by Rabelais on Wodehouse, but simply to compare a few of their common comic techniques, specifically in the domains of plot, characters, intellectual gamesmanship and use of language. I am not claiming either that no other comic writers use these techniques, but that they show us an astonishing, and instructive, similarity of literary method between a Renaissance Evangelical humanist and a twentieth-century English gentleman. (p. 63)

There are few fundamental plot similarities, though both repeat their plots. . . .

More importantly, both humorists' stories are at the same time authentic and parodic, and both derive from the epic. . . .

Most of Wodehouse's plots, like Rabelais', are concerned with "faicts heroïques," and the basic story line is hero-foils-villain, as it should be in an epic. Wodehouse's heroes, who unlike Rabelais' are usually foiling a villain in order to get a girl, are often presented as chivalrous knight-errants. . . . Comic references to chivalry are frequent in Wodehouse. . . . (p. 64)

Wodehouse's young men adhere to a feudal code of behavior, learned no doubt at their public schools (where many of them were football heroes), and even the unspeakable Ukridge never deliberately lets a girl down. There are done things and not-done things: Bertie may slide down a waterpipe to evade his Aunt Agatha, but he may not tell a ghastly girl that he doesn't want to be engaged to her. Gargantua and Pantagruel may in frivolous moments eat live bears or urinate on Parisians, but their relationship to father, God and subjects is always taken seriously.

We are, in fact, in a world of fixed class structures. People may change—Panurge from privileged companion to despised coward, or Bertie from vapid *boulevardier* to articulate philosopher—but the relative place of each man in society does not change. . . . And each author has his little list . . . of heroes and villains. Rabelais' villains are theologians, monks, doctors, lawyers and hypocrites; Wodehouse's include poets, newspaper proprietors, policemen, big-game hunters, successful financiers, all small boys, and most aunts. Or to put it more simply, both hate oppression, hypocrisy and smugness. And in both villains are usually unhappy—a basically Stoic outlook? . . .

Wodehouse's [heroes] are people who intrigue for the fun of it, ugly but kind young men, attractive nice girls, most butlers, most cats, and most members of the Drones Club. Both, moreover, despise humanity in the mass but are ca-

pable of great sympathy for individual members of it—as long as they do not try to step out of their place. (p. 65)

[Although] these two humorists have quite different attitudes to plot, there are certain resemblances worth noting. In each case a basically hackneyed plot outline is adorned with the zaniest kind of inventiveness. . . . Panurge's pranks are of the same undergraduate-rag type as those of the members of the Drones Club, Uncle Fred and Galahad. . . . [Wodehouse's characters] like Rabelais' . . . expend an extraordinary amount of effort for what seems like a trivial result. Perhaps Bobby Wickham is the best comparison to Panurge, since she creates havoc for the sheer fun of it, while Galahad and Uncle Fred are normally working, however deviously, toward a practical end. But in both authors action is often not 'real' action. . . .

[The] devious machinations . . . are often . . . pointless. . . .

Both authors make use of stock situations familiar to their readers. Rabelais' epic journey contains the regulation storm and fabulous monster, and Wodehouse's love stories the traditional misunderstandings and reconciliations. Both also enjoy turning a stock situation on its head. . . . (p. 66)

Both also like plots which turn on objects, to be defended, stolen or otherwise manipulated. . . .

The general atmosphere in both fictional worlds is also more similar than might appear at first sight. Rabelais' characters love enormous banquets and gallons of drink—but so do Wodehouse's. . . . Wodehouse also has plenty of violence, though his comedy is much less ferocious than Rabelais'. (p. 67)

All critics are agreed that there is no sex and no obscenity in Wodehouse. . . . [There are only two passages, one in *Jill the Reckless* and another in *The Prince and Betty,* in which physical arousal is indicated]: undoubtedly sex is usually left to the intuition of the reader. Obscenity, however, is quite often implied, though discreetly. . . . Euphemisms and periphrases, indeed, abound in both works. . . .

The gusto of Wodehouse's world may be rendered in more "classical" language, but is surely as vital and as infectiously enthusiastic as Rabelais'. Another general similarity is in the relationship between fantasy and reality. In both cases, improbable, even surreal, events occur in entirely realistic frameworks. . . . In both, time is similarly treated; though ostensibly linear, it is elastic enough to allow of lengthy flash-backs and improbably long pauses in the action. (p. 68)

I see a further similarity in each author's relationship with his readers. Rabelais often addresses his directly, and Bertie seems to do so even more than most first-person narrators. He worries about whether his regular readers will be bored by recapitulation of events they are already familiar with, and often asks rhetorical questions or appears to confer with his reader. Rabelais is often called a *conteur,* but he shares with Wodehouse the dramatic gift for staging a scene and creating characters by means of their speech. And both treat their readers as "customers" (Bertie's word) who have paid for the book and thereby acquired certain rights over it. (pp. 68-9)

Wodehouse's protagonists are [like Rabelais'] larger than life, although the techniques used to characterise them may be different. Lord Uffenham, with his enormous pear-shaped body, his eye-brows, huge feet and absent-mindedness, is typical; a few traits have been singled out for enlargement, so that the effect is of a two-dimensional caricature, as with Panurge's cowardice and Janotus de Bragmardo's self-satisfaction.

Both humorists have a fondness for truly horrible characters. . . .

[Surely] Roderick Spode, Stilton Cheesewright or Captain Bradbury invite comparison with Picrochole or Loup-Garou by their single-minded determination to destroy the adversary. Such characters often appear to be eight feet tall in moments of stress, and in other ways behave like the ogres of folklore. . . . Still more revolting characters, perhaps, are those who are not physically enlarged, but in whom the trait singled out for exaggeration is repulsive to start with, like Percy Pilbeam's pimples or Honoria Glossop's laugh like "the Scotch express going under a bridge."

Among both lists of heroes I should perhaps have included "men with inquiring minds." . . . Intellectual curiosity, though directed to very different ends, is a characteristic of both authors.

There are closer resemblances in the interaction between characters. The Bertie/Jeeves relationship is not unlike the Pantagruel/Panurge one in reverse: Jeeves is the omniscient, condescending Stoic Wise Man, and Bertie the incorrigible optimistic fool. Panurge, who has been critically compared to Hamlet as a problematic hero, is a good deal closer to Ukridge, who like him is totally irresponsible, especially about money, always convinced that the solution to his problem is just around the corner, incapable of seeing himself as others see him, and always straight-faced when everyone around him is laughing. And Galahad Threepwood and Uncle Fred are in many ways reminiscent of Frère Jean: always ready to rush with indefatigable energy into whatever fray is nearest, crushing the weaker-willed with scathing words, and creating mayhem always with the purest possible motives.

All Wodehouse people are "stock" characters in the sense that they are created to fill a certain function in the plot. They all behave consistently in recurring circumstances. . . .

Both authors assemble in one book an astonishing diversity of characters who apparently belong in quite different literary genres. This is not so striking in Rabelais, whose characters appear successively in successive chapters, as in Wodehouse, where the average country house party includes an absent-minded elderly aristocrat, an obnoxious interfering middle-aged female, a forceful but stupid business-man, a super-efficient secretary, a drooping heroine, a knightly hero, two unscrupulous criminals and a pig. The juxtaposition of the different languages spoken by all these characters is perhaps funnier than the succession of such languages in Rabelais. . . . (pp. 69-70)

The resemblance [concerning intellectual parlor-games] is very intriguing for it implies more intellectual kinship than we should expect between the Renaissance and the modern writer. We should remember that Wodehouse received an . . . education based on the Classics and including such obsolete exercises as writing Latin verse, which was closer to Rabelais' education than we might imagine. In particular, like Rabelais, he learned about literature from ancient

authors whose basic principle was not originality but *imitatio*—the imaginative use of *topoi*.

What do I mean by 'intellectual parlor-games'? First of all, the parody of literary traditions familiar to the reader. We have mentioned some aspects of their pastiche of the epic, and there are many others. They also make fun of courtly love conventions. . . . Wodehouse is often pastiching recent authors and literary trends unfamiliar to today's reader. . . . (pp. 70-1)

Such parodies are intellectual in-jokes, and so very often is the use of quotation, metaphor and cliché by both humorists. The only detailed discussion I have seen of Wodehouse's use of quotations does not even mention the essential fact that they are all to be found in a dictionary of quotations. Like Rabelais, he uses a compilation instead of the original source. . . . And in using these quotations both deliberately underline their nature as clichés or *topoi*. . . . Wodehouse, like Rabelais, delights in the juxtaposition of styles, and often in the combination of quotations from different sources into one sentence, which invites a type of guessing-game. (pp. 71-2)

Wodehouse's speciality is the mixed metaphor or simile, and the best of his are well up to Rabelais' standard. They sometimes take the form of straightforward juxtaposition of two metaphors ("locking the stable door after the milk has been spilt"). Or they may use startlingly eccentric description or comparison, like Wodehouse's "silent pool of coffee" or "sprung at it with the vim of an energetic bloodhound." . . . Still another variety dear to both is the quotation or cliché in lofty language which ends in colloquialism. (p. 72)

The intellectual gamesmanship here requires separating the constituent elements fast enough not to be held up in one's reading. Another aspect of the juxtaposition of styles is the disconcerting use of technical terminology in circumstances where the reader least expects it. . . . Wodehouse does it more often than one might think. Latin tags are frequent . . . , and we are sometimes treated to an enumeration of the Latin names of birds found in an English garden at dawn on a July morning, the technical names for the bacteria of milk, or the professional methods of distinguishing false pearls from genuine ones. And both are likely to slip Biblical quotations into almost any context, though of course Rabelais always does so with polemical intent, while Wodehouse's vicars and curates quote Scripture in order to impress their hearers and amuse the reader, and in other cases the quotation is so well hidden as to be almost invisible. . . . (pp. 72-3)

In all these cases: pastiche, quotation, metaphor and juxtaposition of styles, both novelists are playing games with a reader who is presumed to have the same kind of intellectual background and training which they have. A still more general resemblance is their use of cliché. . . . They are always conscious that language is composed of clichés, and they draw our attention to this fact in remarkably similar ways. . . . Often Wodehouse further underlines the nature of his clichés by pretending they are original (Lord Emsworth "was as blind, to use his own neat simile, as a bat"), or by pretending to get them wrong ("He is as rich as creosote, as I believe the phrase is"). This is a speciality of Bertie's, who often has to check with Jeeves that he has his clichés right. (pp. 73-4)

[Both] writers are debunking different levels of language in an analogous way, and expecting their reader to realise it. . . .

One of Rabelais' specialities is *fantaisie verbale,* and although Wodehouse is not a rival here he uses it superbly on occasion. . . . And listen to Wodehouse when he really wants to play with language: "A sort of gulpy, gurgly, plobby, squishy, wofflesome sound, like a thousand eager men drinking soup in a foreign restaurant." The inventive energy expended by Rabelais on synonyms for sexual activity is directed by Wodehouse toward insult. (p. 74)

Like Rabelais he enjoys taking words apart, or forging new ones. Everyone quotes the disgruntled man whom time had done nothing to gruntle, and Bertie is convinced that "already I am practically Uncle Percy's ewe lamb. That will make me still ewer." But such examples are rare; he prefers, again like Rabelais, the deformation of normal speech by people who are eccentric, or drunk, or merely foreign. (pp. 74-5)

As we might expect, hyperbole is a favourite device—one might say, a permanent habit of mind—of both authors. Characters are larger, and nastier, than life: meals are huge and so are reactions. In Wodehouse "a cascade of people falling downstairs" means two people, a startled woman's "eyes were now about the size of regulation golf-balls, and her breathing suggested the last stages of asthma," and Bertie when trying not to laugh "distinctly heard a couple of my floating ribs part from their moorings under the strain." Most of Wodehouse's characters habitually overreact, which helps to enlarge the trivial setbacks of their lives into disasters of epic proportions. In Rabelais only Panurge usually overreacts, and the comedy often consists in contrasting his overreaction with the normal behaviour of the others.

More surprisingly, Wodehouse is equally adept at litotes. He does not, like Rabelais, describe extraordinary scenes in a matter-of-fact manner, but he does sometimes juxtapose a genuinely horrific event and an underreaction. . . . The most regular user of litotes is Jeeves, who, when Bertie cries: "Jeeves! Hell's foundations are quivering!" will reply: "Certainly a somewhat sharp crisis in your affairs would appear to have been precipitated, sir." (p. 75)

A variety of periphrasis both are fond of is the comic use of irrelevant information to slow down the narrative or to annoy. . . . In Wodehouse this is one of Jeeves's specialities. He is forever holding up the action or breaking Bertie's train of thought by finishing quotations Bertie is not interested in, or providing information in too much detail. (p. 76)

[Despite Wodehouse's] constant parade of contempt for great literature and philosophy . . . , he is, like Rabelais, a profoundly intellectual writer in many ways. And finally, the basic resemblances between the two in all domains: plot and action, character and language, is that they are always debunking—pricking the balloons of tyranny, hypocrisy and pretention which threaten civilisation. Writing in anxious, turbulent times, they restore their reader temporarily to sanity, to a world where villains are foiled and purity of motive—and of language—must necessarily triumph. Evil is not ignored but exorcised by the comic techniques they share (and by many others they do not share), so that the final impression given is one of optimism, of confidence

that the powers of darkness will not destroy us. This is without doubt a kind of conservatism, and a comparison of the conservative aspects of both would be interesting. It is surely heartening to see that at least in this case the French Renaissance mind and the modern mind are not so far apart. (p. 77)

> *Barbara C. Bowen, in* L'Esprit Créateur: Special Issue—The French Renaissance Mind *(copyright © 1976 by L'Esprit Créateur), Winter, 1976.*

*   *   *

WOIWODE, Larry   1941-

Woiwode is an American novelist and poet who has been compared to Proust for his delicate, detailed chronicle of a midwestern family in *Beyond the Bedroom Wall*. He was awarded the William Faulkner Award for the best first novel in 1969 for *What I'm Going to Do, I Think*. (See also *CLC*, Vol. 6, and *Contemporary Authors*, Vols. 73-76.)

ROBERT V. DANIELS

Beyond the Bedroom Wall . . . , an enormously overlong tribute to the tender web of family relationships and the powerful endurance of the past in the present, is sometimes moving, more often exhausting. It is, basically, a conventional American epic of restless mobility and disappointed expectations, with the generations shifting from a secure rural environment imbued with faith and industry to the more unstable, relentless pursuit of change and displacement for their own sake. . . .

Rather than unfolding [his] family saga in a conventional linear narrative, Woiwode presents a series of frozen episodes and tableaux told in different voices, scrambling with harsh abruptness distant moments of time (Woiwode calls them still pictures from a family album) in a collage of childhood and maturity, joy and tragedy, life and death. The choppy dissociation of names and places and people, of scattered, deceptively isolated incidents, are meant as clues to the unspoken coherence making up one family's reality. Every piece is to contribute its crucial weight: photographs minutely described, job applications, pages from a young girl's diary, visions of a book that adumbrate the book we are reading.

But while some individual scenes are executed with a resonant beauty of human feeling and a genuine sense of place, the novel as a whole reles too primitively on the maudlin force of nostalgia. As one character remarks, seeming to speak for Woiwode: "Those days are best. I keep going over them and over them again and again . . . just like they were the only part of my life I really lived. . . . They never grow tiresome and I never run out of things to think about." For his readers, on the other hand, they do grow tiresome, because what is missing from *Beyond the Bedroom Wall* is a unifying, discriminating intelligence that might lend this family album some reflective meaning. . . . Woiwode gives self-indulgent voice to all the torrents of memory. As a result, the significance of the unforgotten is too easily lost in the dishevelling flood of detail, and he is forced to take refuge in the fraudulent certainties of sentimentality. (p. 16)

> *Robert V. Daniels, in* The New Leader *(© 1975 by the American Labor Conference on*

International Affairs, Inc.), October 13, 1975.

ROGER SALE

At his worst Woiwode is content to tell neat stories of children at hideous play that seem like many other *New Yorker* tales. But at his best he is marvelous, a real bringer of news, a writer in love with his world, who cares about the hurt it has given him as his inheritance, and honors and forgives it. *Beyond the Bedroom Wall* is a very long novel in which Woiwode has tried something unlikely and achieved something impressive.

He calls his book "A Family Album." . . . Woiwode's love for the Neumillers and for North Dakota—which is unashamedly a love for his own family and childhood home—is a matter of memory and reconstruction. He discovered at some point that he began to achieve his own life when his parents and grandparents achieved theirs, and an "album," a loosely connected series of pictures and episodes, is his way of honoring not only their achievement but his way of knowing it.

Does it sound a perfect formula for sentimentality? It is no more so than is "East Coker." . . . Like Eliot, Woiwode perceives a time for "the evening with the photograph album" and that "Love is most nearly itself / When here and now cease to matter." But where Eliot filtered and displaced his autobiographical sense of home and family, Woiwode succeeds by being personal, by putting his imagination at the service of memory, and by realizing in this way that love really is most nearly itself when the here and now cease to matter. (p. 31)

Woiwode is always evoking, but never in set pieces, and the links we get from episode to episode are never forced because they don't have to be. Home *is* where one starts from, and Woiwode's sense of home is strong enough to allow him to be relaxed and unself-conscious when he writes about winters and schools and sex and religion, and tries to make each one fully felt as lived. . . .

[When] Woiwode comes to his own experience he begins to falter, and much of his account of the boyhoods of Jerome, Charles, and Tim (who seems closest to Woiwode himself) reads like anecdotal *New Yorker* stories. . . . Earlier the fact that Martin is somewhat less distinct than Alpha seems nothing more than a reflection of his being less distinctly a personality, and none the less important as a person. Later, especially after Alpha dies, Martin's fuzziness begins to suggest a loss of control by Woiwode. . . .

Martin doesn't want to get ahead . . . , doesn't know why he wants to leave, and, we realize, Woiwode doesn't either, it seems. With this realization comes our first sense of the limits of Woiwode's making a novel out of a family album. The individual pieces that don't work, after all, are only that, and there are others right through to the end that are superb. . . .

[A] kind of nostalgia has obviously been at work in Woiwide, a much more interesting and hard-working kind, a nostalgia for his family and for North Dakota before he was born. In order to imagine or reconstruct or remember this world, he has had to lay aside simple reminiscence, to find a real and vivid use for this nostalgia, and he has done so wonderfully. The moment he comes to himself, as it were, to his own more direct memories, his novelistic hold slackens. . . .

I have no idea what "actually happened" to Larry Woiwode, or how much if any of this book is simply autobiographical. I am only trying to distinguish the impulses that seem to lie behind the two parts of his book, impulses that as I make them out seem related but crucially different. I want to make the distinction, furthermore, mostly out of gratitude to Woiwode for all he has achieved here. . . . Knowing how possessiveness and pride and fear were barriers to feeling, Woiwode breaks through the barriers and is able to feel and make us feel what those people experience. It may be one of the last books we'll get that can do this. (p. 32)

> *Roger Sale, in* The New York Review of Books *(reprinted with permission from* The New York Review of Books; *copyright* © *1975 NYREV, Inc.), November 13, 1975.*

ROBERT LEITER

[*Beyond the Bedroom Wall*] is a search for lost time, a book of remembrance, where desire, sleep, memory and death intertwine. (p. 38)

The novel's title reflects Proust's influence, mixing the wonder and fear of childhood with a dreamlike hint of the sexual jealousy Freud found basic to family life. . . . The North Dakota and Illinois of this work are like the terrain of dreams, a wide, continuous plain that seems forever cold or on the edge of winter. And for anyone who has lived there, this is the "reality" of the Middle West; one's life there is always remembered against a succession of gray skies whose clouds may break at any moment to reveal a deep blue as endless as the flat land.

But the similarity to Proust ends at this level. Woiwode does not try to duplicate Proust's grand "symphonic" design; his story is told from many points of view in an unembellished prose. Each of his major characters is given at least one chapter to narrate or oversee. And yet Woiwode's intention is far from, say, the cubist approach of Faulkner in *As I Lay Dying*. In fact, on the technical level, *Beyond the Bedroom Wall* is not particularly adventurous. Nor does it pretend to be. Woiwode does not jump about in time; he moves forward, from one year to the next in chronological order, from one major event to another, leaning heavily on ellipsis but keeping to a basically linear progression. Woiwode is more interested in the process of memory, in uncovering its depths and mysteries; and he gives his narrative a smooth, dreamlike flow by repeating a set of images and events and having his various characters respond to them, each in his particular way.

The first of these images is sleep. . . . To sleep and then awaken is to move from an illusion to reality, a distinction in Woiwode's province of memory that is, at best, tenuous. Revelation begins at the edge of consciousness and dreams are the connective tissue of memory. . . .

And then there is death itself. *Beyond the Bedroom Wall* tells a sad, sad story that is imbued with death. . . . The book's central experience is the death of Alpha, an event of such tragic weight (both for the characters and the structure of the book as a whole) that Woiwode divides it between two chapters, not to prolong but to banish the pain, to objectify and cleanse the past of its most tragic moments. . . .

[Like] Proust's great work [*Remembrance of Things Past*], Woiwode's novel should not be read quickly but rather in long slow draughts that will not blur its beauty and power. (p. 39)

> Robert Leiter, in The New Republic *(reprinted by permission of* The New Republic; © *1975 by* The New Republic, Inc.*),* November 29, 1975.

Rising young novelist Woiwode has made an impression with his ''Beyond the Bedroom Wall'' and ''What I'm Going to Do, I Think.'' That his poetic gifts are also of a high order is made clear by this first book of his poems [''Even Tide''], which surge and crackle with all the intensities of an immensely imaginative young man trying to recover from that first deep shock of his kind—separation from the woman he loves. These are poems of moods and phases, numbness and self-castigation, passion spent, remembered, transmuted. . . . Readers are not likely to be able to go all the way with this poet, who sometimes uses ''words that have been on my tongue so long they're mangled and broken.'' The curse of the crypto-confessional hurts communication, but readers who care will want to look in on even the self-lacerations of a genuine new young poet. (p. 55)

> Publishers Weekly *(reprinted from the October 31, 1977, issue of* Publishers Weekly*, published by R. R. Bowker Company, a Xerox company; copyright* © *1977 by Xerox Corporation), October 31, 1977.*

KAY LARRIEU

The judicious use of italics throughout [*Even Tide*] is part of the technique of creating a more distant voice speaking to the immediate, consistently strong ''I.'' This dialogue is extended frequently to others, sometimes simply ''you'' (meaning his wife, presumably, judging from other references), sometimes to named individuals whose identity is neither often specified nor necessarily relevant.

But addressing another does give an informal, conversational quality to the poems, which goes hand-in-hand with the varied tone of the collection. . . .

The choice of images is equally diverse. Such apt expressions as ''the kite tail of sin'' are testimony to the poet's skill in imagery. The many forces and faces of nature provide a metaphorical backdrop for many of the poems. The title of the work is evidently an extension of the many references to the sea.

Clearly, there is much to admire in this trove of poems. The studied technique (which admittedly goes astray occasionally in an annoying, but insignificant, abstruseness) compellingly conveys an important message, allowing the ensemble to serve as a welcome complement to more prosaic treatments of the same subject. Furthermore, the overall skillful treatment is a commentary on the ability and courage of an author (Woiwode has two novels to his credit) to extend himself in another literary genre. Finally, *Even Tide* is an appropriate application of W. H. Auden's definition of poetry as ''memorable speech.'' (p. 31)

> Kay Larrieu, in Best Sellers *(copyright* © *1978 Helen Dwight Reid Educational Foundation), April, 1978.*

WRIGHT, James   1927-

Wright is an American poet and translator. His poetry has gradually evolved in style from traditional to experimental verse, consistently reflecting strong lyric grace. Considered by many critics to be one of the finest poets writing in America today, Wright received the Pulitzer Prize in Poetry in 1972. He has collaborated with Robert Bly on a translation of Pablo Neruda's poetry. (See also *CLC*, Vols. 3, 5, and *Contemporary Authors*, Vols. 49-52.)

PETER A. STITT

Reading the *Collected Poems* of James Wright from the point of view of style is like reading a history of the best contemporary American poetry. One discovers a development which could be said to parallel the development generally of our finest recent poets. . . . [It is] a movement generally away from rhetoric, regular meter and rhyme, towards plainer speech, looser rhythms and few rhymes. . . . Not that the result is formlessness nor that the forms arrived at are alike. What one looks for is the individual voice, the distinctive style that is right for one poet but not quite right for any other.

James Wright has achieved such a style. . . . [Furthermore, his] poetry is sufficiently rich, both stylistically and thematically, to merit several voices. (p. 13)

Perhaps the most pervasive general theme in Wright's poetry—if theme it is—is that of separation. [In his first two volumes, *The Green Wall* and *Saint Judas*], separation appears in two guises—as the result of death and as the result of being at odds with one's society. There is a corresponding search for love as the ideal solution to the problem—but rarely is it a realised solution. The protagonists in these poems are loveless, either because they are outcasts from society or because death has separated them from the ones they loved. . . . I see such poems as attempts to overcome separation, alienation—attempts, of course, doomed to failure. (pp. 14-15)

The preoccupation with death in Wright's poems really reflects, at least [in some poems], the deeper preoccupation with and fear of separation, of alienation, of being completely alone. In other poems the emphasis on death will reflect a preoccupation with suffering, with the human condition as inevitably tragic, partially because of death.

The other side of separation—alienation from one's society—is reflected in Wright's constant concern with outcasts, down-and-outers—criminals, murderers, betrayers, lesbians, skid row characters, poets. Again, of course, Wright's sympathies are with the separated and not with the others, the ones who have cast them out. (p. 15)

''Saint Judas'' is one of Wright's best and most remarkable poems. . . . It is a poem of great compassion for man in general and for the outcast, and its title has puzzled for years those of a theological frame of mind. It really shouldn't be so puzzling because the poem itself explains and justifies its title. It would be hard to imagine a more universally reviled man in the western world than Judas, Christ's betrayer—he is the archetypal outcast. Wright takes him up after he had ''Bargained the proper coins'' and after he turned against himself and decided to commit suicide, and creates a situation that will test his humanity: "When I went out to kill myself, I caught / A pack of hoodlums beating up a man." His instinctive reaction is the right one—he tries to aid the man, and in the process forgets his own troubles. . . . Judas is the down-and-outer *par excellence,* and has nothing to look forward to either in life or in death. With absolutely nothing to gain from it, he makes the instinctively humane gesture and tries to protect the suffering man. That is why Wright has chosen to canonize him—not because he has lived a pure life but because he is a man, fallible like all men, who redeems his unspeakable act of betrayal through an act of kindness. Judas thus is presented as the archetypal good man who does indeed make mistakes. And Wright does more than empathize with him; he identifies with him and tells the story from his point of view. This is the key poem to understanding James Wright's love for humanity and for the outcast. It is a brilliant poem, a sonnet of great dramatic power.

The poems in Wright's first two volumes, then, are generally too literary, too subservient to the poems and poets of the past. At the same time, it must be recognized that Wright handles the traditional forms with considerable skill, sometimes with brilliance. There are many fine poems here, poems which anticipate both stylistically and thematically the later work. Still, we must admit that Wright had not yet found his voice in these early books, that his own distinctive style, though emerging, had not yet appeared.

The Branch Will Not Break (1963), Wright's happiest book, is mostly concerned with nature, especially with the landscape of western Minnesota. The book's title indicates its major affirmation—the faith that nature will endure and continue to sustain man. (pp. 16-17)

Wright's new aesthetic involves a loosening of form, a movement away from the heavy domination of meter, rhyme, and rhetoric toward rhythmical sparseness and verbal simplicity. . . .

The function formerly served by regular form in Wright's poems now comes to be served by his images, by his use of what has been called the "deep" or the "subjective" image. This "new" way of perceiving and recording has its origins in surrealism, and shares with that movement an interest in the subconscious mind. (p. 19)

Wright is not a surrealist poet, though he does use many of the techniques of surrealism. I would place him in a middle-ground, somewhere between the poles of surrealism and rationalism. The poetry of surrealism too often can be unintelligible to most readers as the poem records what the poet discovers on a quick, associational trip through the deeper regions of his mind. Wright has definitely liberated his imagination from the strict confines of logical, rational thought, but his poems retain, nevertheless, something of a logical structure. A good illustration of all this is the poem "Miners." The title indicates the subject and is an important guidepost, for without it we might quickly become lost in the poem's oblique imagery—the title provides, in other words, the rational key to the poem. The first of the poem's four sections goes like this: "The police are probing tonight / for the bodies / Of children in the black waters / Of the suburbs." The stanza is illusive and seems to have little to do with the title. The drowning of the children is metaphorical —that they drown in "the suburbs" indicates that their death is spiritual rather than physical. The suburbs, further,

are not localized; they could be anywhere in America. The "black waters" might be taken to suggest the mines, and one explanation of the stanza could be: these are the children of miners, living in suburbs and destined to become miners themselves someday; thus they are trapped in a hopeless life and might be said to be "drowned." The police serve two functions: first, their probing adds a realistic detail to the stanza; second, they represent an enemy, the hostility of the real world, through their implicit function as an arm of the establishment which exploits the miners.

The second stanza is somewhat more specific, centering on the process of the search for the bodies and localizing the setting in southern Ohio. . . . The third stanza, however, is the central one, for it turns directly to the miners themselves and their hopelessness. . . . There, stated in clear and accurate detail, is the life of the miner. Of course he doesn't literally knock on the door of a tomb [as the poem seems to state], though the poem gains power from the possibility that a miner could dig into a grave. Rather, the imagery suggests the inevitable death wish of the miner, caught as he is in a hopeless situation.

The final stanza completes the portrait of the miner's family by turning to his wife: "Many American women mount long stairs / In the shafts of houses, / Fall asleep, and emerge suddenly into tottering palaces." Even their dreams, the only really positive element in their lives, are precarious, as their dream palaces totter. The imagery of the poem is fascinating: all the settings, the "black waters," the mine, the "shafts of houses," and the "tottering palaces" suggest the grave. And it is evident, from the way he writes of the suburban children and American wives, that Wright is not speaking just of coal miners here; his comments expand to include, seemingly, most of mankind. . . . I take this to be one of Wright's more surrealistic poems, and I mean my discussion of it to stand as an illustration of his 'surrealist' method in general. (pp. 20-1)

The Branch Will Not Break is Wright's nature book, suffused with the desire to escape from the world of man into the world of nature. The speaker in these poems, as in all of Wright's poems, is a harried and haunted man, a man who feels out of place in society, perhaps in the world. Nature in *The Branch Will Not Break* gives him sustenance, acceptance, resurrection, even pronounces a benediction upon him in some poems. The central poem with regard to the use made here of nature is "A Blessing," which comes very near the end of the volume. It is a remarkable poem, one which attempts to achieve a miracle. . . . [The] poem ends: "Suddenly I realize / That if I stepped out of my body I would break / Into blossom." This is the moment of the supreme consecration of man by nature in Wright's poetry, and the key to the happiness of this volume. It is a peak not again reached in the later poetry.

The Branch Will Not Break is an important book in contemporary American poetry, probably the most successful importation of the methods of modern French and Spanish surrealism that we have. It is also a courageous book—by changing his aesthetic so radically, Wright was taking the chance of confusing and alienating his audience. It is courageous too because of the psychological risks it takes—the journey into the interior of the mind which is part of surrealism is a dangerous trip. . . . (p. 22)

Shall We Gather at the River is both Wright's best book

and his darkest, desperate and despairing. It is a unified work, more a sequence of poems than a collection of individual lyrics, which is what the other volumes remain. The poems are united through their narrator, a harried and haunted man, the outcast tamed poet or vice versa, and are located in the present—Minneapolis and the Mississippi River mostly—and the past—the Ohio River and the area in which Wright grew up. The poems set in the present establish a horrible and constantly threatened existence, from which the speaker attempts to escape into the past. But what he finds there is mostly death. Where the escape from a hostile environment in *The Branch Will Not Break* was made to nature, here it is made in the direction of death—and this difference indicates the greatly contrasting moods of the two books.

The book can be divided roughly into three parts, with a prologue and an epilogue. The first part, encompassing the nine poems from "The Minneapolis Poem" through "Before a Cashier's Window in a Department Store," establishes the persona of the speaker as an outcast and details his way of life at the bottom of society. The second part, eight poems from "Speak" through "Listening to the Mourners," consists of attempts to escape this situation, primarily in the present. In the third, and most important, section, eighteen poems from "Youth" through "Poems to a Brown Cricket," the speaker, dissatisfied by the movements in part two, returns to the countryside of his youth and, through memory, reconstructs its events. The division is mine, not Wright's, and is far from perfect. . . . (pp. 22-3)

Psychology and mythology come together in Wright's use of the river. Freud tells us that water is to be associated with both birth and death, as man is born on a literal flood of water, remembers this, and subconsciously associates water both with the pre-birth state of death-like semi-consciousness and with death itself. Wright knows Whitman's poetry well, and in "Out of the Cradle Endlessly Rocking" Whitman makes just this three-fold connection: the waves of the sea fall with the rhythm of the rocking cradle (also the rhythm of the heart beat), associating water with birth, and the word the waves whisper is "death, death, death." Mythology gives us the rivers Lethe, across which souls soon to be born are carried, and Styx, across which Charon carries these same souls after death—so again water is associated with both birth and death, the cycle of life. Add to this the ancient metaphor of the river as life, and you have the materials for understanding James Wright's use of the river. (p. 26)

The many drownings in Wright's poems, from *The Green Wall, Saint Judas,* and [*Shall We Gather at the River*] especially, now take on greater significance; the poems are full of people who have drowned in the Ohio. The dead, the subject of death, the river, and the drowned all come together in Jenny, who becomes increasingly important as the book progresses. The speaker centers his search for some kind of happiness in her, his great love, and it is the fact that she is dead that gives the book its despairing darkness. (p. 27)

The power of this book is at least partially ascribable to its unity, the fact that it is almost one long poem rather than a series of short ones. . . . The other thing that makes me rate *Shall We Gather at the River* highest among Wright's books is the depth of its theme. In his large use of the quest and the river, encompassing birth and death, Wright

touches something very deep in all of us. The book has truth because we all suffer, we all are searching for love, we all feel nostalgia for the settings and affections of the past. . . . [By] using materials often associated with the collective unconscious, Wright has touched a responsive chord in us all.

The best of the "New Poems" are the long ones that Wright has increasingly taken to writing in recent years. One of their titles gives us a clue to the structural notion which lies behind them: "A centenary Ode: Inscribed to Little Crow, Leader of the Sioux Rebellion in Minnesota, 1862." We could probably define the modern ode as a long, loosely constructed poem, often consisting of variations on or around a theme. Other poems of this variety which stand out here are "A Secret Gratitude" and "Many of Our Waters: Variations on a Poem by a Black Child." . . . [This] form seems to be becoming a characteristic mode for Wright. . . . The question is really one of structure rather than style as such. The style of these poems is essentially that of the poems of *Shall We Gather at the River*—a more mature, more highly perfected version of the 'surrealistic' style of *The Branch Will Not Break*. (pp. 28-9)

The form . . . of Wright's longer poems is open, and things get into them on the basis of simple association. It makes for a fluid and exciting art form. (p. 31)

Though the "New Poems," at least by contrast with *Shall We Gather at the River,* tend as a section towards disunity, their general drift and their placement makes a fitting climax to the *Collected Poems*. Throughout the first four books there is a constant search, within a basically hostile world, for love. The protagonist-seeker is an outcast, separated from love and equanimity by society and the fact of death. The first two volumes could be said to be introductory: pervaded by mortality, alienation, and generally lacking in love, they could not be called joyful. *The Branch Will Not Break* provides a happy interlude, an escape from the hostile universe of the other volumes. But *Shall We Gather at the River* forcefully proves that the happiness was only temporary and the search for love again takes over in a hostile world. Though the world remains generally hostile in the "New Poems," the search for love finally has a successful resolution.

Wright has placed two of his new poems at the front of the book, where they serve as a prologue. "The Quest" seems to have been placed there in recognition of the implicit quest, the search for love, that carries us through the collected volume. . . . The quest here is for love, and it is successful. The most positive of the "New Poems" are several love poems—and they are among the most positive in Wright's work generally. Their predominance here seems to indicate a successful end to the book-long quest of the protagonist-speaker—it ends in the discovery and celebration of a real love.

The section ends on a remarkable note in the poem "Northern Pike," a note which indicates the fulfillment of the quest in spite of everything. . . . There is an attitude of acceptance, a feeling that, in spite of man's continuing cruelty and the general hostility of the world, somehow things in the speaker's world have reached a long-desired balance. The poem and the book appropriately end with these lines: "There must be something very beautiful in my body, / I am so happy." (pp. 31-2)

Peter A. Stitt, "The Poetry of James Wright," in The Minnesota Review *(© 1972 by* The Minnesota Review*), Spring, 1972, pp. 13-32.*

COR van den HEUVEL

There is a universality in Wright's work not only in subject matter but in form and technique as well. He is a classicist in the broad sense of the word. A craftsman who can put to use the traditional elements of his art while at the same time exploring new means of expression. In subject matter, his work encompasses both the outer world of planets and horses, grass and stars, and the inner world of the mind and heart which seeks to relate to the inner worlds of others.

His first book [*The Green Wall*] was devoted mostly to groundwork—mastering traditional forms. It appealed mainly to academic critics. Though the poems revealed some awareness of the human condition, the doorway to the human heart was opened only a crack—and the wonders of existence were barely tapped. The demands of the traditional forms in some cases resulted in an awkwardly elaborate facade of rhyme and meter through which a stilted sentimentality came on stage to talk of dead hounds and whores. But in many of the poems the language was expertly handled and in some cases the form began to take a less restricted shape—though the iambics might still drum their tum-te-tums too insistently upon the ear.

In his second book, *Saint Judas*, the forms retained a strictness, but there seemed to be a freedom of language within them—a more natural speech—so that the rhymes and meter did not obtrude on the senses but rather provided a subtle music to the sense. And, too, Wright began to express in earnest his concern for the downtrodden—the rejected and suffering members of humanity—which some of his friends and critics feel is the most important and characteristic element in his work. . . .

In "At the Executed Murderer's Grave," Wright's pity, though it first excludes the dead murderer—"I do not pity the dead, I pity the dying,"—ultimately includes him, for we are all criminals one way or another in our grasping after love. . . . (p. 164)

Death—"Earth is a door I cannot even face"—and Love—the terrible beauty that causes pain and suffering as well as joy—are the two poles of the [above] poem. The poet stands in the middle torn by the immense incomprehensibility of the two—and by pity for himself, and by extension for the rest of mankind, all caught in the web of life strung upon them.

Wright is concerned as deeply with the other emotions as well. Hate plays a major role in a number of poems as the poet vents his rage at the cruelty and stupidity of our world. (p. 165)

In his next book, *The Branch Will Not Break*, the outer universe poured into Wright's poetry with a magic immediacy that led many to think the poet had undergone a violent metamorphosis. The language became simpler and more natural—with a haunting beauty. Here is "In Fear of Harvests":

It has happened
Before: nearby
The nostrils of slow horses
Breathe evenly,
And the brown bees drag their high garlands,
Heavily,
Toward hives of snow.

The words and images work like a magic incantation to dispel, if only for a moment, the fear of death. Death appears (or fades) in the perspective of a vivid sense of continuing life and the round of the seasons, and seems almost desirable—transformed by the wonder of the world of which it is an essential part. The language and the images have that simple beauty characteristic of Japanese haiku, somehow becoming an actual presence on the page. (p. 166)

[Before] *Branch* was published Wright started his "association" with *The Fifties* (later *The Sixties*). Some of the enigmatically beautiful new poems later to appear in *Branch* first appeared in that magazine. About this time, the magazine also began its series of translations of modern European and South American poets. . . . The influence of these foreign poets [especially Georg Trakl, whose poetry Wright translated,] . . . seemed to bring a new tone to Wright's work, a simplicity and depth of language and image—and cryptic silences where, "far off, the shopping centers empty and darken," or "flashlights drift over dark trees."

Whatever the influences (for one can see where the poet feels a kinship with ancient Chinese poets as well as modern Spanish or German ones), Wright has used them to find his own individual voice.

But it is a voice that grew out of his earlier books also—it was not a veering off into a totally new direction. For Wright was always moving in the direction of a more simple and immediate language. Even the imagery had its precursors. It awaited enrichment or fruition, of course, but the seedlings can be found here and there even in *The Green Wall*. For example, in that book there are these two lines from "She Hid in the Trees From the Nurses":

Now far away the evening folds
Around the siloes and the hill.

In *Branch* this "basic" image is enriched (by the distillation of simplicity—which even extends to the spelling), and touched with new magic:

A long sundown.
Silos creep away toward the west.
("In Memory of a Spanish Poet")
(pp. 166-67)

In his next book, *Shall We Gather at the River*, Wright returned from the infinite spaces to be found in leaves and stones to stand with the hurt and downtrodden of humanity again. . . . The experience [of *Branch*], I believe, enabled him to come back with deeper powers of compassion and love—a new intensity of feeling for that mortal life which struggles to catch a glimpse of the eternal—and a greater skill in his craft. (pp. 167-68)

Branch constituted an important development in Wright's work (and it is still my favorite). There was a great advance in technical proficiency as well as a dazzling blossoming of images. Before *Branch* the lines would sometimes gurgle and choke on their syntax as they were squeezed into the molds of rhyme and meter. With *Branch* there was a "sea change" in language, speech pattern, imagery, and tone—it was now plain American speech heightened to a strange beauty by the imaginative powers and craftsmanship of a man who had worked long and hard to learn the secrets of his art. The rhythms were balanced to fit their images, thoughts, and feelings—and the poems rounded into a complete form of their own with neither a word too little or too much. While the language had become sharp and clean as sunlight in a mountain stream, the images presented startling shapes from a shadowy primeval mist, or the mysteriously clear and tangible presences of simple existence like the breathing of horses.

I now feel that this was a further development of Wright's art and experience of life, rather than a sudden freakish change of character. It was another dimension of human experience, and it will continue to enrich his work, but it is not the primary concern of his art (as, for example, it seems to have been with some of the Japanese haiku masters— what I mean is the infinite in a grain of sand, eternity in a grass blade's moment of dawn and dew). His *primary* concerns—and I think in these two things his work has been consistent—is to achieve a *superhuman* facility with speech in order to embody the *human* spirit.

His subject matter has, of course, varied, but the most common subject with which Wright has taken his stand for the human spirit has been with those who suffer more than the rest of us. . . . (p. 168)

Wright sees life neither as "pretty pictures," nor as an ugly meaningless smear—he sees its horror and its beauty even in its smallest manifestations. . . . (p. 170)

> *Cor van den Heuvel, "The Poetry of James Wright," in* MOSAIC: A Journal for the Study of Literature and Ideas *(copyright © 1974 by the University of Manitoba Press; acknowledgment of previous publication is herewith made) Vol. VII, No. 3 (Spring, 1974), pp. 163-70.*

R. J. SPENDAL

[The central conflict of "Lying in a Hammock at William Duffy's Farm in Pine Island, Minnesota" is] the opposition between an impulse to change and failure or inability to do so. The speaker is aware from the beginning that he has "wasted" his life. Each of the poem's major images depicts his frustrated impulse toward change. The last lines suggest that as the evening of his life approaches the speaker resigns himself to a permanent state of irresolution. To "lean back" is to give up; this hardly seems the posture of aroused insight.

The butterfly, a traditional symbol of metamorphosis, indicates at the outset the speaker's concern with change. However the conventional meaning of the image is undercut by several details: "bronze" suggests rigidity; sleep denies to the butterfly any possibility of consciously determined movement; and "Blowing like a leaf" implies a lack of volitional strength—a leaf is easily swayed. The house in line 4 conveys a sense of achievement and security easily associated with a life well-led; but the house is empty and it belongs to William Duffy rather than the speaker. . . . Lastly, the chicken hawk "looking for home" symbolizes the speaker's own quest for fulfillment; but the bird only "floats," he does not vigorously and resolutely pursue his

search. By now the speaker too has yielded to a life of floating as he lies back in his hammock. It is too late in the day for difficult decisions, too dark for movement. The point of the many temporal and spatial references in the poem is that they suggest a movement and direction which, ironically, continue to be absent from the speaker's life. And the poem is haunted by absences: the butterfly is unconscious; the house is empty; the cows and horses are not physically present; the hawk, like the speaker, is absent from his home.

The speaker's divided state of mind is further reflected in the binary character of much of the poem's imagery: "two pines" . . . and, at least by implication, the two points between which the speaker's hammock is strung. The theme of irresolution is also conveyed through structure. The winged creatures at beginning and end have conventional associations with aspiration and the will to change, while the quadrupeds of the middle section symbolize the weight of reality, life conducted at the level of exigency (eating and excreting). The poem, like the speaker, is thus equally divided between the conflicting claims of character renewal and brute subsistence. With a little imagination one can even see the butterfly and hawk lifting the poem at each end while the cows and horses bow it in the middle—the shape of a man lying in a hammock. This structural image supports what the poem's other details have already revealed: the speaker is a victim of blunted purpose, hopelessly suspended between alternate courses of action. (No. 64)

> *R. J. Spendal, in* The Explicator *(© copyright, 1976, by The Explicator Literary Foundation, Inc.), May, 1976.*

HUGH KENNER

James Wright, of Ohio, has been to Vienna, to Verona, to Sirmio, never forgetting Ohio, which sounds as sweet as any of them. Of Verona's Adige he writes,

> This is another river
> I can still see flow by.
>
> The Ohio must have looked
> Something like this
> To the people who loved it
> Long before I was born.

It must, it must; though in an unexpectedly weak book ["To a Blossoming Pear Tree"] this poet who has shown strength in the past is making little effort to reach for the feel of that "must have."

The present collection goes better when anecdotal material can carry itself. Wright was waiting for a bus in the cold, and a young Sioux with a hook for a hand was good to him. . . .

> Did you ever feel a man hold
> Sixty-five cents
> In a hook,
> And place it
> Gently
> In your freezing hand?

We can imagine how *that* was. The language isn't surgically clean, just clean enough to convey the incident; that seems to be the neutral quality James Wright is after now, content to be carried by his matter, anecdotal matter with nostalgic auras. (pp. 12-13)

Hugh Kenner, in The New York Times Book Review *(© 1978 by The New York Times Company; reprinted by permission), February 12, 1978.*

RICHARD HOWARD

[The poems in Wright's *To A Blossoming Pear Tree* are concerned with the] mythology of the insulted and injured to be located alike in southern Ohio and in the poet's body ("helpless and miserable / dreaming itself / into an apparition of loneliness"). And they exploit that mythology with the insolence of utter conviction. But so deeply is the poet identified with something which has happened to him outside the poem that he cannot be bothered, or even begged, to make it into a coherence within the poem. . . . The divine event is a *deja vu;* it is, it has always been, as Wright says, "a secret of blossoms we had no business / to understand, only to remember." (One figures here is the source of Wright's new apostrophe, the object of his attentions and the subject of his *askesis:* blossoming.) Hence there is a particular *stimmung* (he has translated Theodor Storm, Trakl and, most recently, Hesse) of James Wright's past, which we remember, which we recognize . . . and we note certain clues toward what is dimly apprehended as a sort of Ohio Osiris Complex in the last book, *Two Citizens:* the sense of disintegration in dark waters, the embrace of a tree, and a resurrection ("I rose out of my body so high into / that sycamore tree that it became / the only tree that ever loved me"). But my sense, my suspicion of Wright's legend of himself as the Torn God was confirmed by no more than scattered limbs, perhaps appropriately—"wound after wound, I look for / the tree by the waters"—and in the arrogance of these disjunct, choking poems there are but glimpses of what I divined to be gathering on the farther shore, far indeed, the other side of "that water I rose from." . . .

Chastened, cautious now ("Saguaro, you are not one of the gods"), and a little dimmed from—perhaps *by*—his old exaltations, his peerless apocalypse (in which of course the entire earth found its death and rebirth inside the poet's own body, conceived as infinite and eternal), James Wright addresses himself, loyal still to his plain chant, his ground bass, to those energies and impulses in nature which are effervescent, fecund and even prodigal. Fifteen years ago, this was his identification:

> Suddenly I realize
> That if I stepped out of my body I would break
> Into blossom.

By a characteristically sensitive enjambment, Wright thus indicated both the breaking *and* the blossoming. But now, in the tormented title poem which confronts, which invokes these same energies and impulses, a discrepancy, an alienation is powerfully mourned; there is no release into ecstasy, merely its notation as otherness, and the human humiliation. . . . (p. 22)

The poems in Wright's lovely new book are all . . . attestations—diffident yet explicit, careful yet fervent, defeated yet proud—of disjunction, of negation, of (we must say it) failure in his vast project. If he were to succeed, after all, we should not have the poems at all. We should have silence. But he has failed, and the confession of his failure ("a half-witted angel drawling Ohioan / in the warm Italian rain") constitutes his new book, its resonance greatly enlarged by the poems about Italy, the region around Verona in particular: "It is all right with me to know that my life is only one life. I feel like the light of the river Adige. By this time, we are both an open secret". . . . No American poet is so consistent as Wright, so consigned to his peculiar, beautiful doom. The further nuance here is of course the exchange of the ruined American midlands (and the repugnant American public mentality) . . . for the Italian locus, the places and objects of Verona which afford the poet, which furnish him, his apocalyptic transformations not more easily or more readily, but more ripely; it is here in Italy that the asseveration is most richly to be made the

> . . . it was hard to name
> Which vine, which insect, which wing,
> Which of you, which of me . . .

Something in his own country has the more painfully cast James Wright out of his own body, and the moments when he finds himself, when he *comes to,* as we say, are more likely to be elsewhere, abroad:

> I am sitting contented and alone in a little park near the Palazzo Scaligeri in Verona, glimpsing the mists of early autumn as they shift and fade among the pines and city battlements on the hills above the river Adige. The river has recovered from this morning's rainfall. It is now restoring to its shapely body its own secret light, a color of faintly cloudy green and pearl.

Now surely such perceptions can be made back home, but there is some functions of the self which is available to Wright *over there* and only so: the function is one of transformation, which he has gainsaid among the strip-mines and the scrap-iron, or which has gainsaid him. "What can I do to join him," Wright asks about the garter snake baking on a rail, and it is his very question, the interrogation proposed to a condition where being can be shared or participated in more broadly, more fully. The blossoming pear tree is no longer to be found in Wright's own veins and vesicles. The wonder of the book named for this tree is that he has put away any bitterness, any *ressentiment* about the collapse of the eager transaction as it was reported in so many other poems, so many earlier books. There is nothing to do but sit still and look very closely, very carefully at what is in front of your eyes, his eyes; the acknowledgement of the separate life, the contours which are not shared but merely shards, fragments of a unity, a totality inaccessible even to wishing—this acknowledgement makes for a poetry which, by immense repudiations, has come to accept itself, has resigned itself (what else is prose but the resignation of poetry, the submission to an element which makes not stay against that ebbing tide?) to a constatation of being which he cannot become, or rather a becoming he cannot be; call it an acceptance of mortality rather than a god's estate, of death rather than eternal life. As James Wright asks (in prose): "What color is a hungry shadow?" (pp. 22-3)

Richard Howard, "James Wright's Transformations," in New York Arts Journal *(copyright © 1978 by Richard W. Burgin), February-March, 1978, pp. 22-3.*

Cumulative Index to Critics

Abbey, Edward
Robert M. Pirsig **6**:421

Abbott, John Lawrence
Isaac Bashevis Singer **9**:487
Sylvia Townsend Warner **7**:512

Abeel, Erica
Pamela Hansford Johnson **7**:185

Abel, Lionel
Samuel Beckett **2**:45
Jack Gelber **6**:196
Jean Genet **2**:157

Abernethy, Peter L.
Thomas Pynchon **3**:410

Ableman, Paul
Mervyn Jones **10**:295

Abrahams, William
Elizabeth Bowen **6**:95
Hortense Calisher **2**:97
Herbert Gold **4**:193
Joyce Carol Oates **2**:315
Harold Pinter **9**:418
V. S. Pritchett **5**:352

Ackroyd, Peter
Brian Aldiss **5**:16
Martin Amis **4**:19
Miguel Ángel Asturias **8**:27
Louis Auchincloss **6**:15
W. H. Auden **9**:56
Beryl Bainbridge **8**:36
James Baldwin **5**:43
John Barth **5**:51
Donald Barthelme **3**:44
Samuel Beckett **4**:52
John Berryman **3**:72
Richard Brautigan **5**:72

Charles Bukowski **5**:80
Anthony Burgess **5**:87
William S. Burroughs **5**:92
Italo Calvino **5**:100; **8**:132
Richard Condon **6**:115
Roald Dahl **6**:122
Ed Dorn **10**:155
Margaret Drabble **8**:183
Douglas Dunn **6**:148
Bruce Jay Friedman **5**:127
John Gardner **7**:116
Günter Grass **4**:207
Mac Donald Harris **9**:261
Joseph Heller **5**:179
Mark Helprin **10**:261
Russell C. Hoban **7**:160
Elizabeth Jane Howard **7**:164
B. S. Johnson **6**:264
Pamela Hansford Johnson **7**:184
G. Josipovici **6**:270
Thomas Keneally **10**:298
Jack Kerouac **5**:215
Francis King **8**:321
Jerzy Kosinski **10**:308
Doris Lessing **6**:300
Alison Lurie **4**:305
Thomas Mc Guane **7**:212
Stanley Middleton **7**:220
Michael Moorcock **5**:294
Penelope Mortimer **5**:298
Iris Murdoch **4**:368
Vladimir Nabokov **6**:358
V. S. Naipaul **7**:252
Joyce Carol Oates **6**:368
Grace Paley **6**:393
David Pownall **10**:418, 419
J. B. Priestley **9**:441

V. S. Pritchett **5**:352
Thomas Pynchon **3**:419
Peter Redgrove **6**:446
Judith Rossner **9**:458
May Sarton **4**:472
David Slavitt **5**:392
Wole Soyinka **5**:398
David Storey **4**:529
Paul Theroux **5**:428
John Updike **7**:488; **9**:540
Gore Vidal **8**:525
Harriet Waugh **6**:559
Jerome Weidman **7**:518
Arnold Wesker **5**:483
Patrick White **4**:587

Adamowski, T. H.
Simone de Beauvoir **4**:47

Adams, Alice
Lisa Alther **7**:14

Adams, Leonie
John Crowe Ransom **4**:428

Adams, M. Ian
Juan Carlos Onetti **10**:376

Adams, Percy
James Dickey **7**:81

Adams, Phoebe-Lou
Beryl Bainbridge **5**:40
Dashiell Hammett **5**:161
David Jones **7**:189
Jerzy Kosinski **6**:285
Yukio Mishima **9**:385
Berry Morgan **6**:340
Joyce Carol Oates **6**:374
Reynolds Price **6**:426
João Ubaldo Ribeiro **10**:436
Christina Stead **8**:500

Adams, Robert M.
Edward Dahlberg **7**:63
Robert M. Pirsig **4**:404
Severo Sarduy **6**:485

Adams, Robert Martin
John Barth **10**:24
Jorge Luis Borges **10**:66
Anthony Burgess **10**:90
T. S. Eliot **10**:171
William H. Gass **2**:154
José Lezama Lima **10**:321
Flann O'Brien **10**:363
Alain Robbe-Grillet **10**:437
Angus Wilson **2**:472

Adelman, Clifford
John Berryman **3**:71

Adler, Dick
Ross Macdonald **1**:185

Agar, John
Jonathan Baumbach **6**:32
Laurie Colwin **5**:107

Aggeler, Geoffrey
Anthony Burgess **2**:86; **5**:85

Agius, Ambrose, O.S.B.
Edward Dahlberg **7**:64

Ahearn, Kerry
Wallace Stegner **9**:509

Ahrold, Robbin
Kurt Vonnegut, Jr. **3**:501

Aiken, Conrad
William Faulkner **8**:206

Aiken, David
Flannery O'Connor **10**:365

Aiken, William
David Kherdian 6:281

Alazraki, Jaime
Pablo Neruda 2:309; 7:261

Alderson, Sue Ann
Muriel Rukeyser 10:442

Aldiss, Brian
J. G. Ballard 3:33

Aldridge, John W.
James Baldwin 4:42
Donald Barthelme 2:39
Saul Bellow 2:49, 50
Louis-Ferdinand Céline 7:47
John Cheever 3:105
John Dos Passos 4:131
James T. Farrell 4:157
William Faulkner 3:150
William Gaddis 3:177; 6:193
Joseph Heller 5:177
Ernest Hemingway 3:231, 233
James Jones 3:261
Jerzy Kosinski 2:231
Alison Lurie 5:260
Norman Mailer 1:193; 2:258
Mary McCarthy 3:327, 328
Wright Morris 3:342
John O'Hara 2:323
Katherine Anne Porter 3:392
Philip Roth 4:459
Alan Sillitoe 3:447
William Styron 3:472
John Updike 2:439
Robert Penn Warren 1:356
Eudora Welty 2:461
Colin Wilson 3:536
Edmund Wilson 2:474
P. G. Wodehouse 2:478

Alegria, Fernando
Jorge Luis Borges 2:71

Alexander, John R.
Robinson Jeffers 2:215

Alexander, Michael
Donald Davie 5:113
Ezra Pound 7:336

Alexander, William
Carl Sandburg 4:463

Alexandrova, Vera
Mikhail Sholokhov 7:420

Algren, Nelson
Clancy Sigal 7:424

Allen, Bruce
Richard Adams 5:6
Julio Cortázar 5:110
Stanley Elkin 6:168
John Gardner 8:236
Thomas Keneally 5:212
Kenneth Koch 5:219
Peter Matthiessen 7:211
Iris Murdoch 6:347
Joyce Carol Oates 6:369
Manuel Puig 5:355
John Sayles 10:460
Isaac Bashevis Singer 6:509
Paul West 7:524
Patrick White 5:485

Allen, Dick
Margaret Atwood 2:20
Wendell Berry 6:61
Hayden Carruth 7:40

Paul Goodman 2:169
Thom Gunn 6:221
Richard F. Hugo 6:245
Philip Levine 2:244
George Oppen 7:281
Judith Johnson Sherwin 7:414

Allen, Gay Wilson
Carl Sandburg 10:447

Allen, Henry
Robert M. Pirsig 4:403

Allen, Walter
A. Alvarez 5:17
Kingsley Amis 1:5
Saul Bellow 1:30
Elizabeth Bowen 1:40
Paul Bowles 1:41
Truman Capote 1:55
Ivy Compton-Burnett 1:61
James Gould Cozzens 1:66
Edward Dahlberg 1:71
John Dos Passos 1:79; 8:181
Lawrence Durrell 1:85
James T. Farrell 1:98; 8:205
William Faulkner 1:101
E. M. Forster 1:104
John Fowles 4:170
William Golding 1:120
Henry Green 2:178
Graham Greene 1:132
L. P. Hartley 2:181
Ernest Hemingway 1:142
Richard Hughes 1:149
Aldous Huxley 1:150
Christopher Isherwood 1:155
Pamela Hansford Johnson 1:160
Doris Lessing 1:173
Richard Llewellyn 7:206
Bernard Malamud 1:197
John P. Marquand 2:271
Carson McCullers 1:208
Henry Miller 1:221
Wright Morris 1:231
Iris Murdoch 1:234
P. H. Newby 2:310
Flannery O'Connor 1:255
John O'Hara 1:260
William Plomer 4:406
Anthony Powell 1:277
Henry Roth 2:377
J. D. Salinger 1:298
William Sansom 2:383
C. P. Snow 1:316
John Steinbeck 1:325
William Styron 1:330
Allen Tate 2:427
Robert Penn Warren 1:355
Evelyn Waugh 1:358
Rebecca West 7:525
Angus Wilson 2:471

Allen, Ward
Donald Davidson 2:112

Allsop, Kenneth
J. P. Donleavy 6:139
Thomas Hinde 6:238

Alonso, J. M.
Rafael Alberti 7:11
Jorge Luis Borges 9:117

Alpert, Hollis
Daniel Fuchs 8:220
Budd Schulberg 7:402

Alter, Robert
S. Y. Agnon 4:11
Yehuda Amichai 9:23
John Barth 9:71
Donald Barthelme 8:49
Saul Bellow 3:48, 49
Jorge Luis Borges 2:76; 6:94
John Hollander 8:298
Jerzy Kosinski 2:232
Norman Mailer 3:312
Bernard Malamud 3:320, 321
Claude Mauriac 9:366
Elsa Morante 8:402
Vladimir Nabokov 2:302; 8:414
Hugh Nissenson 4:380
Flann O'Brien 7:269
Manuel Puig 10:420
Thomas Pynchon 9:443
Raymond Queneau 10:429
Alain Robbe-Grillet 6:468
Earl Rovit 7:383
André Schwarz-Bart 4:480
J.I.M. Stewart 7:465
John Updike 2:444
Kurt Vonnegut, Jr. 8:531
Elie Wiesel 3:526

Altieri, Charles
Robert Creeley 2:107

Alvarez, A.
John Berryman 2:58; 3:65
Albert Camus 4:89
E. M. Forster 1:109
Dashiell Hammett 3:218
Zbigniew Herbert 9:271
Miroslav Holub 4:233
Philip Larkin 3:275
Robert Lowell 3:300
Hugh Mac Diarmid 4:309
Norman Mailer 3:312
Sylvia Plath 2:335; 3:388
Jean Rhys 4:445
Jean-Paul Sartre 4:475
Edith Sitwell 9:493
Aleksandr I. Solzhenitsyn 7:436
Patrick White 3:521
Elie Wiesel 3:527
Yvor Winters 4:589

Amacher, Richard E.
Edward Albee 1:5

Amado, Jorge
João Ubaldo Ribeiro 10:436

Ambrose, Stephen E.
Cornelius Ryan 7:385

Ambrosetti, Ronald
Eric Ambler 9:20

Ames, Evelyn
J. B. Priestley 5:351

Amis, Kingsley
Ray Bradbury 10:68
Ivy Compton-Burnett 1:60
Leslie A. Fiedler 4:159
Philip Roth 1:293
Arnold Wesker 3:517

Amis, Martin
J. G. Ballard 6:27
Peter De Vries 7:77
Bruce Jay Friedman 5:127
Ernest J. Gaines 3:179
John Hawkes 7:141

Iris Murdoch 4:367
Vladimir Nabokov 8:412
Philip Roth 6:475

Amory, Cleveland
Rod McKuen 1:210

Anderson, David
Albert Camus 4:89, 90
William Golding 3:197, 198
Jean-Paul Sartre 4:477

Anderson, David C.
L. E. Sissman 9:491

Anderson, Elliott
Vladimir Nabokov 3:354

Anderson, H. T.
Erich Segal 10:467

Anderson, Jack
Philip Levine 4:286
George MacBeth 2:252

Anderson, Jervis
James Baldwin 8:41

Anderson, Michael
Edward Bond 6:85

Anderson, Patrick
Ward Just 4:266

Anderson, Quentin
Vladimir Nabokov 3:351

Anderson, Reed
Juan Goytisolo 10:244

André, Michael
Robert Creeley 2:107

Andrews, Peter
Michael Crichton 6:119
Arthur Hailey 5:157
Irving Stone 7:471

Annan, Gabriele
Simone de Beauvoir 4:47
Heinrich Böll 9:111

Annan, Noel
E. M. Forster 4:166

Ansorge, Peter
Sam Shepard 6:495

Appel, Alfred, Jr.
Vladimir Nabokov 1:240; 2:300

Apple, Max
John Gardner 10:222

Arendt, Hannah
W. H. Auden 6:21

Armes, Roy
Alain Robbe-Grillet 4:449

Armstrong, William A.
Sean O'Casey 1:252; 9:407

Aronson, James
Donald Barthelme 1:18
Saul Bellow 1:33
James Dickey 1:73
John Fowles 1:109
John Knowles 1:169
John Updike 1:345
Eudora Welty 1:363

Arpin, Gary Q.
John Berryman 10:48

Ascherson, Neal
György Konrád 10:304
Tadeusz Konwicki 8:327
Milan Kundera 4:278

Tadeusz Rózewicz 9:465
Yevgeny Yevtushenko 1:382

Ashbery, John
A. R. Ammons 2:13
Elizabeth Bishop 9:89

Ashton, Dore
Octavio Paz 10:392

Ashton, Thomas L.
C. P. Snow 4:504

Asinof, Eliot
Pete Hamill 10:251

Aspler, Tony
William F. Buckley, Jr. 7:36
William Gaddis 8:226

Astrachan, Anthony
Vladimir Voinovich 10:509

Atchity, Kenneth John
Jorge Luis Borges 2:71
James Jones 3:261
Robert Penn Warren 4:581

Atheling, William, Jr.
Isaac Asimov 3:17
Arthur C. Clarke 1:58
Harlan Ellison 1:93
Robert A. Heinlein 1:139; 3:227

Atherton, Stan
Margaret Laurence 6:290

Atkins, John
L. P. Hartley 2:182

Atkinson, Brooks
Elmer Rice 7:361

Atkinson, Michael
Robert Bly 10:58

Atlas, James
Samuel Beckett 6:37
Marie-Claire Blais 6:82
J. V. Cunningham 3:122
Alan Dugan 6:144
Paul Goodman 4:198
Randall Jarrell 6:261
Galway Kinnell 5:217
W. S. Merwin 5:287
John O'Hara 6:386
Kenneth Rexroth 6:451
Laura Riding 7:375
Delmore Schwartz 4:478
L. E. Sissman 9:490
James Tate 2:431

Atwood, Margaret
Marie-Claire Blais 6:80
Susan B. Hill 4:227
Erica Jong 6:267
A. G. Mojtabai 5:293
Adrienne Rich 3:429
Audrey Thomas 7:472

Auchincloss, Eve
R. K. Narayan 7:257

Auchincloss, Louis
Katherine Anne Porter 7:316

Aucouturier, Michel
Aleksandr I. Solzhenitsyn
7:432

Auden, W. H.
Joseph Brodsky 4:77
Loren Eiseley 7:90
Chester Kallman 2:221

J. R. R. Tolkien 1:336
Andrei Voznesensky 1:349

Auster, Paul
John Ashbery 6:14
John Hollander 8:300
Laura Riding 7:375
Giuseppe Ungaretti 7:484

Avant, John Alfred
Eleanor Bergstein 4:55
Gail Godwin 5:142
Gayl Jones 6:266
José Lezama Lima 4:291
Joyce Carol Oates 6:371, 373
Tillie Olsen 4:386
Patrick White 5:486

Axelrod, George
Gore Vidal 4:556

Axelrod, Steven
Robert Lowell 2:249

Axelrod, Steven Gould
Saul Bellow 6:60

Axthelm, Peter M.
William Golding 10:232

Ayer, A. J.
Albert Camus 9:152

Ayo, Nicholas
Edward Lewis Wallant 10:515

Ayre, John
Austin C. Clarke 8:143
Mavis Gallant 7:110
Mordecai Richler 5:378

B. D.
Sylvia Townsend Warner 7:511

Baar, Ron
Ezra Pound 1:276

Backscheider, Nick and Paula
Backscheider
John Updike 5:452

Backscheider, Paula and Nick
Backscheider
John Updike 5:452

Baer, Barbara L.
Harriette Arnow 7:16
Christina Stead 5:403

Bailey, O. L.
Eric Ambler 6:2
Dick Francis 2:142
George V. Higgins 4:223
Maj Sjöwall 7:501
Mickey Spillane 3:469
Per Wahlöö 7:501

Bailey, Paul
Gabriel García Márquez 3:180
Nadine Gordimer 10:239
Yasunari Kawabata 2:223
Brian Moore 3:341
James Purdy 2:351
Philip Roth 3:437
Muriel Spark 5:400
David Storey 2:426
Gore Vidal 6:550
Tennessee Williams 7:544

Bailey, Peter
Nikki Giovanni 2:165
Melvin Van Peebles 2:447

Bair, Deirdre
Samuel Beckett 6:43

Baird, James
Djuna Barnes 8:49

Baker, A. T.
A. R. Ammons 5:30

Baker, Carlos
Ernest Hemingway 6:234

Baker, Donald W.
Edward Dahlberg 7:63

Baker, Houston A., Jr.
James Baldwin 1:16
Arna Bontemps 1:37
Sterling Brown 1:47
W. E. B. Du Bois 1:80
Ralph Ellison 1:95; 3:145
Leon Forrest 4:163
Langston Hughes 1:149
LeRoi Jones 1:163
Ann Petry 1:266
Ishmael Reed 2:369; 6:449
Jean Toomer 1:341
Richard Wright 1:380

Baker, Howard
Caroline Gordon 6:206
Katherine Anne Porter 1:273

Baker, James R.
William Golding 3:200

Baker, Roger
Beryl Bainbridge 4:39
John Bueil 10:81
Paula Fox 8:217
Janet Frame 3:164
John Hawkes 1:139
Jerzy Kosinski 1:172
Larry McMurtry 3:333
Harold Robbins 5:378
Herman Wouk 9:580
Rudolph Wurlitzer 2:483
Helen Yglesias 7:558

Balakian, Anna
André Breton 9:132
René Char 9:164

Baldanza, Frank
Alberto Moravia 2:293
Iris Murdoch 1:235
James Purdy 2:350; 4:424;
10:421

Baldeshwiler, Eileen
Flannery O'Connor 1:255

Baldwin, James
Alex Haley 8:259
Norman Mailer 8:364

Bales, Kent
Richard Brautigan 5:71

Ballard, J. G.
Philip K. Dick 10:138
Robert Silverberg 7:425

Balliett, Whitney
Richard Condon 4:105
Clancy Sigal 7:424

Ballif, Gene
Jorge Luis Borges 6:87
Vladimir Nabokov 6:351
Alain Robbe-Grillet 6:464
Nathalie Sarraute 8:469

Ballstadt, Carl
Earle Birney 6:78

Bambara, Toni Cade
Gwendolyn Brooks 2:81

Banning, Charles Leslie
William Gaddis 10:210

Barber, Michael
Gore Vidal 4:557

Barbera, Jack Vincent
John Berryman 8:88

Barbour, Douglas
Rudy Wiebe 6:566

Barclay, Pat
Robertson Davies 7:72

Bargad, Warren
Amos Oz 8:436

Barge, Laura
Samuel Beckett 10:34

Barghoorn, Frederick C.
Aleksandr I. Solzhenitsyn
4:508

Barker, A. L.
Edna O'Brien 5:311

Barker, Frank Granville
Margaret Drabble 10:163
J. B. Priestley 9:442

Barker, George
Brian Aldiss 5:14

Barksdale, Richard K.
Gwendolyn Brooks 5:75

Barnes, Clive
John Bishop 10:54
Lawrence Ferlinghetti 2:134
Simon Gray 9:240
Arthur Kopit 1:170
Tom Stoppard 1:328
Michael Weller 10:525
Lanford Wilson 7:547

Barnes, Harper
James Tate 2:431

Barnes, Julian
Richard Brautigan 5:72; 9:124
James Clavell 6:114
Len Deighton 7:76
B. S. Johnson 6:264
Pamela Hansford Johnson
7:184
G. Josipovici 6:270
Richard Llewellyn 7:207
Vladimir Nabokov 6:359
Joyce Carol Oates 9:402

Barnes, Regina
James T. Farrell 4:158

Barnouw, Dagmar
Doris Lessing 6:295

Barnstone, William
Jorge Luis Borges 6:93

Barnstone, Willis
Jorge Luis Borges 9:120

Baro, Gene
Auberon Waugh 7:512

Baron, Alexander
Bernard Malamud 2:268

Barrenechea, Ana María
Jorge Luis Borges 1:38

Barrett, Gerald
Jerzy Kosinski 10:305

CRITIC INDEX

Barrett, William
Samuel Beckett 2:48
Albert Camus 2:99
Arthur C. Clarke 4:105
William Faulkner 3:154
Ernest Hemingway 3:238
Hermann Hesse 2:191
Alain Robbe-Grillet 2:377
Leon Uris 7:491

Barry, John Brooks
T. S. Eliot 6:165

Barry, Kevin
John Berryman 6:65

Barthes, Roland
Raymond Queneau 5:357

Bartholomay, Julia A.
Howard Nemerov 6:360

Bassoff, Bruce
William H. Gass 8:244

Batchelor, John Calvin
Mark Helprin 10:262

Batchelor, R.
Ardré Malraux 9:353

Bates, Evaline
Ezra Pound 3:397

Bates, Graham
Pär Lagerkvist 7:198

Bateson, F. W.
W. H. Auden 6:24
John Gardner 2:151

Bauer, William
John Buell 10:82

Bauke, J. P.
Jakov Lind 4:292

Baumann, Michael L.
B. Traven 8:520

Baumbach, Jonathan
Truman Capote 8:132
Ralph Ellison 1:95
John Hawkes 4:212
Norman Mailer 4:318
Bernard Malamud 1:197, 199
Mary McCarthy 5:275
Wright Morris 1:232
Flannery O'Connor 1:256
Grace Paley 6:393
J. D. Salinger 1:299
William Styron 1:330
Peter Taylor 1:333
Edward Lewis Wallant 10:511
Robert Penn Warren 1:355

Bayley, John
W. H. Auden 2:27, 28
Anthony Burgess 4:85
D. J. Enright 8:203
Robert Lowell 4:296
Anthony Powell 10:417
Aleksandr I. Solzhenitsyn
4:511; 7:444; 10:479

Bazarov, Konstantin
Ivo Andrić 8:20
Heinrich Böll 3:76
James A. Michener 1:214
Aleksandr I. Solzhenitsyn
2:411; 10:483

Beacham, Walton
Erskine Caldwell 8:124

Beards, Virginia K.
Margaret Drabble 3:128

Beatie, Bruce A.
J. R. R. Tolkien 3:477

Beauchamp, Gorman
E. M. Forster 10:183

Beauchamp, William
Elizabeth Taylor 4:541

Beck, Marilyn
Rod McKuen 1:210

Becker, Lucille
Georges Simenon 2:398, 399;
8:488

Becker, Lucille F.
Louis Aragon 3:14

Bedient, Calvin
A. R. Ammons 8:13
W. H. Auden 2:27
Samuel Beckett 1:24
Leonard Cohen 3:110
Edward Dahlberg 7:67
Donald Davie 10:120
Louise Glück 7:119
John Hawkes 4:215
Joseph Heller 5:178
Geoffrey Hill 5:184
Daniel Hoffman 6:243
Ted Hughes 2:202; 4:235
David Ignatow 7:182
Thomas Kinsella 4:271
Philip Larkin 5:228
Robert Lowell 3:303
George MacBeth 5:264
James Merrill 8:381
Joyce Carol Oates 2:314; 3:362
Octavio Paz 4:398
Jon Silkin 6:498
R. S. Thomas 6:532
Charles Tomlinson 4:545, 547
Mona Van Duyn 7:499
Robert Penn Warren 10:523
Richard Wilbur 9:568
James Wright 5:520

Beer, Patricia
W. H. Auden 6:19
Eleanor Hibbert 7:156
Alice Munro 10:357
Peter Redgrove 6:447

Beichman, Arnold
Arthur Koestler 1:170
Anthony Powell 3:400

Beja, Morris
Lawrence Durrell 4:145
William Faulkner 3:153
Nathalie Sarraute 4:466

Belgion, Montgomery
André Malraux 4:334

Belitt, Ben
Jorge Luis Borges 2:75
Robert Lowell 4:297
Pablo Neruda 1:247

Bell, Bernard
William Styron 3:473

Bell, Bernard W.
Jean Toomer 4:550

Bell, Gene H.
Jorge Luis Borges 9:118

Alejo Carpentier 8:135
Vladimir Nabokov 6:360

Bell, Ian F. A.
Ezra Pound 10:404

Bell, Millicent
Margaret Atwood 2:19
Peter De Vries 2:113
Eugenio Montale 7:231
John O'Hara 2:325

Bell, Pearl K.
Martin Amis 4:20
John Ashbery 6:12
Beryl Bainbridge 4:39
James Baldwin 4:40
Saul Bellow 8:70
Marie-Claire Blais 6:81
Louise Bogan 4:69
William F. Buckley, Jr. 7:35
Eleanor Clark 5:106
Arthur A. Cohen 7:51
Len Deighton 7:76
William Faulkner 6:177
Paula Fox 2:140
Nadine Gordimer 5:146
Juan Goytisolo 5:149
Günter Grass 4:206
Graham Greene 3:214
Joseph Heller 5:180
George V. Higgins 7:157
Maureen Howard 5:189
Ruth Prawer Jhabvala 8:311
Charles Johnson 7:183
Diane Johnson 5:199
Uwe Johnson 10:284
James Jones; 10:291
Milan Kundera 4:277
John Le Carré 5:232
Alison Lurie 4:307
Peter Matthiessen 5:275
John McGahern 5:281
A. G. Mojtabai 9:385
V. S. Naipaul 7:254
Amos Oz 5:335
Cynthia Ozick 7:288
Walker Percy 8:438
Anthony Powell 3:403
J. F. Powers 8:447
Ishmael Reed 6:448
Adrienne Rich 6:459
Jill Robinson 10:439
Anne Sexton 6:494
Alix Kates Shulman 10:475
Stephen Spender 5:402
Mario Vargas Llosa 6:546
Patrick White 3:523

Bell, Vereen M.
E. M. Forster 1:107
Ted Hughes 9:281

Bellamy, Joe David
Sam Shepard 4:490
Kurt Vonnegut, Jr. 4:564

Bellman, Samuel Irving
Saul Bellow 8:81
Jorge Luis Borges 6:91
Jerome Charyn 5:103
Leonard Cohen 3:109
Stanley Elkin 6:169
William Faulkner 3:152
Leslie A. Fiedler 4:160, 161
Bruce Jay Friedman 3:165

Ernest Hemingway 3:234
Jack Kerouac 3:263, 264
Meyer Levin 7:205
Bernard Malamud 1:197; 3:320,
325
Saul Maloff 5:271
Wallace Markfield 8:380
James A. Michener 5:288
Harry Mark Petrakis 3:382
Philip Roth 3:435
John Updike 3:487
Elie Wiesel 5:490

Beloff, Max
Paul Scott 9:477

Beloof, Robert
Stanley J. Kunitz 6:285
Marianne Moore 4:360

Bender, Marylin
Alix Kates Shulman 2:395

Bendow, Burton
Grace Paley 4:393

Benedikt, Michael
Galway Kinnell 2:230
Richard Wilbur 3:532

Bennett, Joseph
Anthony Hecht 8:266

Benson, Jackson J.
Ernest Hemingway 6:232
John Steinbeck 9:517

Benstock, Bernard
William Gaddis 3:177
Flann O'Brien 7:270
Sean O'Casey 5:317

Benston, Alice N.
W. S. Merwin 2:276

Bentley, Allen
Morris L. West 6:564

Bentley, Eric
Robert Penn Warren 8:536
Herman Wouk 9:579

Bentley, Joseph
Aldous Huxley 1:152

Berets, Ralph
John Fowles 3:163

Berger, Charles
Olga Broumas 10:77

Bergin, Thomas G.
Salvatore Quasimodo 10:429

Bergman, Andrew C. J.
Peter Benchley 4:53
Guy Davenport, Jr. 6:124

Bergmann, Linda S.
Ronald Sukenick 4:531

Bergonzi, Bernard
Kingsley Amis 2:6, 9
W. H. Auden 6:22
John Barth 3:39
Paul Bowles 2:79
Anthony Burgess 2:85
Donald Davie 10:123
Nigel Dennis 8:173
Richard Fariña 9:195
John Fowles 2:138
Paula Fox 2:139
B. S. Johnson 6:262
Doris Lessing 3:283

Iris Murdoch 2:297
Flann O'Brien 4:383
Anthony Powell 3:400
Thomas Pynchon 3:408
Alain Robbe-Grillet 4:447
Andrew Sinclair 2:401
C. P. Snow 4:501
Evelyn Waugh 1:357; 3:510
Angus Wilson 2:473

Berkson, Bill
Frank O'Hara 2:320
Jerome Rothenberg 6:477

Berlin, Isaiah
Aldous Huxley 3:254

Berman, Susan K.
Fredrica Wagman 7:500

Bermel, Albert
Ed Bullins 1:47
Jean Genet 10:227
Christopher Hampton 4:211

Bernays, Anne
Alice Adams 6:1

Berner, Robert L.
Alan Paton 10:388

Bernetta (Quinn), Sister Mary, O.S.F.
Allen Tate 4:539

Bernikow, Louise
Muriel Rukeyser 6:479

Berns, Walter
Daniel J. Berrigan 4:57

Bernstein, Burton
George P. Elliott 2:131

Berrigan, Daniel
Horst Bienek 7:28

Berry, Wendell
Hayden Carruth 4:94

Berryman, John
Saul Bellow 10:37
Ernest Hemingway 10:270

Bersani, Leo
Julio Cortázar 2:104
Jean Genet 2:158
Norman Mailer 8:364
Alain Robbe-Grillet 1:288
Robert Wilson 7:551

Berthoff, Warner
Norman Mailer 3:313
Iris Murdoch 3:345
Vladimir Nabokov 3:352
Muriel Spark 3:464
Edmund Wilson 2:475; 3:538

Bespaloff, Rachel
Albert Camus 9:139

Bessai, Diane
Austin C. Clarke 8:142

Besser, Gretchen R.
Julien Green 3:205

Bessie, Alvah
Norman Mailer 3:319

Bester, Alfred
Isaac Asimov 3:16
Robert A. Heinlein 3:227

Bester, John
Kenzaburō Ōe 10:372

Bethell, Nicholas
Aleksandr I. Solzhenitsyn 7:441

Betsky, Celia
Max Apple 9:32
Harriette Arnow 7:15
Don DeLillo 10:135
Doris Lessing 10:315

Betsky, Celia B.
A. Alvarez 5:19
Margaret Drabble 2:119
John Hawkes 4:217
Iris Murdoch 4:370

Bevan, A. R.
Mordecai Richler 5:377

Bevan, Jack
Arthur Gregor 9:253

Bevington, Helen
Louis Simpson 4:500

Bewley, Marius
A. R. Ammons 2:11
John Berryman 2:56
C. Day Lewis 6:128
Thomas Kinsella 4:270
Hugh MacDiarmid 2:253
Sylvia Plath 2:335
Herbert Read 4:440
Charles Tomlinson 2:436

Bezanker, Abraham
Saul Bellow 1:32
Isaac Bashevis Singer 3:454

Bianco, David
James Purdy 10:426

Biasin, Gian-Paolo
Leonardo Sciascia 8:473

Bidart, Frank
Robert Lowell 9:336

Bien, Peter
Yannis Ritsos 6:462

Bienstock, Beverly Gray
John Barth 3:41

Bier, Jesse
James Thurber 5:434

Bigger, Charles P.
Walker Percy 8:440

Bigsby, C. W. E.
Edward Albee 9:6, 9
Arthur Miller 10:342

Binns, Ronald
John Fowles 4:171

Binyon, T. J.
Eric Ambler 9:21

Birnbaum, Milton
Aldous Huxley 3:255; 4:239

Birstein, Ann
Iris Murdoch 4:370

Bishop, Ferman
Allen Tate 2:428

Bishop, Lloyd
Henri Michaux 8:390

Bishop, Tom
Jean Cocteau 8:145
Julio Cortázar 2:103
Raymond Queneau 5:359
Claude Simon 9:482

Black, Campbell
Isaac Bashevis Singer 6:507

Black, Cyril E.
André Malraux 1:203

Blackburn, Sara
R. V. Cassill 4:95
Rosalyn Drexler 2:120
Jim Harrison 6:225
Alan Lelchuk 5:244
David Madden 5:266
Michael McClure 6:316
Toni Morrison 4:365
Marge Piercy 3:384
Alix Kates Shulman 2:395
Gillian Tindall 7:473
David Wagoner 5:474
Fay Weldon 6:562

Blackburn, Tom
Kingsley Amis 2:6

Blackmur, R. P.
E. E. Cummings 8:154
John Crowe Ransom 5:363
Allen Tate 4:536

Blaha, Franz G.
J. P. Donleavy 4:125

Blake, George
John Cowper Powys 9:439

Blake, Patricia
Aleksandr I. Solzhenitsyn 1:319; 7:439

Blake, Patricia and Max Hayward
Andrei Voznesensky 1:349

Blake, Percival
Leonardo Sciascia 8:474

Blakeston, Oswell
Michael Ayrton 7:19
Gabriel García Márquez 3:180
P. G. Wodehouse 2:480

Blamires, David
David Jones 2:216, 217; 4:260

Blassingame, Wyatt
Harriette Arnow 7:15

Blaydes, Sophia B.
Simon Gray 9:242

Blazek, Douglas
Robert Creeley 2:107
W. S. Merwin 5:286
Diane Wakoski 4:573

Bleikasten, André
Flannery O'Connor 10:366

Blish, James
John Brunner 10:77

Bliven, Naomi
Louis-Ferdinand Céline 4:103
Andrea Giovene 7:117
Eugène Ionesco 6:257
Anthony Powell 7:343

Bloch, Adèle
Michel Butor 8:120
Pär Lagerkvist 7:200

Blodgett, E. D.
D. G. Jones 10:285
Sylvia Plath 3:388

Blodgett, Harriet
V. S. Naipaul 4:375

Bloom, Harold
A. R. Ammons 5:25; 8:14; 9:26
John Ashbery 4:23; 9:41
W. H. Auden 6:16
Saul Bellow 6:50
Jorge Luis Borges 6:87
James Dickey 10:141
Allen Ginsberg 6:199
John Hollander 8:301, 302
Philip Levine 9:332
Robert Lowell 8:355
Archibald MacLeish 8:363
James Merrill 8:388
Howard Moss 7:249
W. D. Snodgrass 10:478
Robert Penn Warren 8:539

Bloom, Robert
W. H. Auden 1:10

Blotner, Joseph L. and Frederick L. Gwynn
J. D. Salinger 1:295

Blow, Simon
Isaac Bashevis Singer 6:510

Bluefarb, Sam
Bernard Malamud 1:196; 9:350
John Steinbeck 5:407
Richard Wright 3:546

Bluestein, Gene
Richard Fariña 9:195

Bluestone, George
Nelson Algren 10:5

Blumenfeld, Yorick
Yevgeny Yevtushenko 1:382

Bly, Robert
A. R. Ammons 5:28
Robert Lowell 4:297

Blythe, Ronald
Erica Jong 6:267
Alice Munro 6:341
Joyce Carol Oates 6:368
David Storey 8:506

Boak, Denis
André Malraux 4:330

Boardman, Gwenn R.
Yasunari Kawabata 2:222
Yukio Mishima 2:286

Boatwright, James
Paul Horgan 9:278
James McCourt 5:278
Gore Vidal 6:549
Robert Penn Warren 1:356

Boatwright, John
Walker Percy 8:438

Bode, Carl
Katherine Anne Porter 7:318

Bodo, Maureen
Gore Vidal 10:504

Boe, Eugene
Christina Stead 2:421

Boeth, Richard
John O'Hara 2:324

Bogan, Louise
W. H. Auden 1:9
W. R. Rodgers 7:377

Bohner, Charles H.
Robert Penn Warren 1:354

Bok, Sissela
Vladimir Nabokov 1:245

Boland, John
Brian Aldiss 5:15
John Dickson Carr 3:101
Richard Condon 4:106
Harry Kemelman 2:225
Michael Moorcock 5:293

Bold, Alan
Robert Graves 1:130

Bolger, Eugenie
Hortense Calisher 8:125
José Donoso 4:130

Bollard, Margaret Lloyd
William Carlos Williams 9:571

Bolling, Douglass
E. M. Forster 9:206
Doris Lessing 3:290
Rudolph Wurlitzer 4:598

Bolton, Richard R.
Herman Wouk 9:580

Bondy, François
Günter Grass 2:173

Bone, Robert A.
James Baldwin 1:15
Arna Bontemps 1:37
W. E. B. Du Bois 1:80
Ralph Ellison 1:95; 3:142
Langston Hughes 1:147
Zora Neale Hurston 7:171
Ann Petry 1:266
Jean Toomer 1:341
Richard Wright 1:378
Frank G. Yerby 1:381

Boni, John
Kurt Vonnegut, Jr. 5:465

Booth, Martin
John Matthias 9:361

Booth, Philip
Randall Jarrell 1:159
Louis Simpson 7:426

Borges, Jorge Luis
Adolfo Bioy Casares 4:63

Borinsky, Alicia
Manuel Puig 5:355

Borkat, Robert F. Sarfatt
Robert Frost 9:222

Borroff, Marie
John Hollander 2:197
Denise Levertov 2:243
William Meredith 4:348
James Merrill 2:274

Bosley, Keith
Eugenio Montale 7:229

Bosmajian, Hamida
Louis-Ferdinand Céline 3:103

Boucher, Anthony
C. Day Lewis 6:128
Patricia Highsmith 2:193
Harry Kemelman 2:225
Mary Stewart 7:467
Julian Symons 2:426

Bouise, Oscar A.
Eleanor Hibbert 7:155
Per Wahlöö 7:501

Boulton, James T.
Harold Pinter 6:406

Bouraoui, H. A.
Nathalie Sarraute 2:385

Bourjaily, Vance
Philip Roth 9:460

Boutelle, Ann E.
Hugh MacDiarmid 2:253

Boutrous, Lawrence K.
John Hawkes 3:223

Bowen, Barbara C.
P. G. Wodehouse 10:538

Bowen, John
Arthur Kopit 1:171

Bowering, George
Margaret Atwood 2:19
Margaret Avison 2:29
Earle Birney 4:64
D. G. Jones 10:288
Margaret Laurence 3:278
A. W. Purdy 6:428
Mordecai Richler 5:374
Audrey Thomas 7:472

Bowering, Peter
Aldous Huxley 4:237

Bowers, A. Joan
Gore Vidal 8:526

Bowers, Marvin
L. E. Sissman 9:491

Bowie, Malcolm
Yves Bonnefoy 9:114

Bowles, Gloria
Diane Wakoski 7:505

Bowles, Jerry G.
Craig Nova 7:267

Bowra, C. M.
Rafael Alberti 7:7

Boyd, Blanche M.
Renata Adler 8:5

Boyd, Robert
James Purdy 2:350

Boyers, Robert
Saul Bellow 3:57
Alan Dugan 6:143
Witold Gombrowicz 7:125
Robinson Jeffers 2:214; 3:258
Arthur Koestler 6:281
Robert Lowell 8:349; 9:336
Adrienne Rich 7:364
Theodore Roethke 8:457
W. D. Snodgrass 2:406
Gary Snyder 2:406
Richard Wilbur 6:569

Boyle, Kay
James Baldwin 1:15
Tom Wicker 7:534

Boyle, Ted E.
Brendan Behan 1:26

Boyle, Ted E. and Terence Brown
Kingsley Amis 2:6

Bradbrook, M. C.
T. S. Eliot 1:91; 2:130

Bradbury, Malcolm
Ivy Compton-Burnett 10:109
John Dos Passos 8:181

E. M. Forster 4:167; 10:180
John Fowles 3:162; 4:172
William Gaddis 8:227
Thomas Hinde 6:240
Aldous Huxley 4:244
Iris Murdoch 4:367
C. P. Snow 4:505
Muriel Spark 2:418
Lionel Trilling 9:531
Evelyn Waugh 8:543
Angus Wilson 5:513

Bradford, M. E.
Donald Davidson 2:111, 112
William Faulkner 1:102; 3:155
Allen Tate 2:429

Bradford, Melvin E.
Walker Percy 3:381

Bradford, Richard
James Kirkwood 9:319

Bradford, Tom
Ray Bradbury 10:69

Bradley, Sculley
Robert Frost 3:169

Brady, Charles A.
David Kherdian 6:281

Brady, Patrick
Albert Camus 9:147

Bragg, Melvyn
E. M. Forster 2:136

Braine, John
Richard Llewellyn 7:207
Fay Weldon 9:559

Brater, Enoch
Samuel Beckett 6:42; 9:81

Braudy, Leo
John Berger 2:54
Thomas Berger 3:63
Richard Condon 4:107
Norman Mailer 1:193; 8:368

Braun, Julie
Philip Roth 4:453

Braybrooke, Neville
Graham Greene 1:130
François Mauriac 4:337

Brée, Germaine
Samuel Beckett 10:27
Jean Cocteau 1:59
Jean-Paul Sartre 7:397

**Brée, Germaine and
Margaret Otis Guiton**
Louis Aragon 3:12
Albert Camus 1:54
Louis-Ferdinand Céline 1:57
Jean Cocteau 1:59
Georges Duhamel 8:186
Jean Giono 4:183
Julien Green 3:203
André Malraux 1:202
François Mauriac 4:337
Raymond Queneau 2:359
Jules Romains 7:381
Jean-Paul Sartre 1:306

Breit, Harvey
James Baldwin 2:31

Brendon, Piers
Donald Barthelme 5:53
Rosalyn Drexler 2:119

Daphne du Maurier 6:146
Robert Penn Warren 4:582

Breslin, James E.
T. S. Eliot 6:166

Breslin, Jimmy
Gore Vidal 8:525

Breslin, John B.
C. S. Lewis 6:308
Tom McHale 5:281
Wilfrid Sheed 10:474

Breslin, Patrick
Miguel Ángel Asturias 8:28

Bresnick, Paul
James Purdy 10:425

Brewster, Dorothy
Doris Lessing 1:173

Brickell, Herschel
Harriette Arnow 7:15

Brickner, Richard P.
Anthony Burgess 2:86
Jerome Charyn 8:136
Frederick Forsyth 2:137
Herbert Gold 7:120
Cormac McCarthy 4:341
Vladimir Nabokov 3:355
Harry Mark Petrakis 3:383
Muriel Spark 3:465
Richard B. Wright 6:581

Bridges, Les
Mickey Spillane 3:469

Bridges, Linda
Donald Barthelme 5:55
Georges Simenon 8:487

Brien, Alan
Kingsley Amis 2:6
Alan Ayckbourn 8:34
John Osborne 5:333
Harold Pinter 6:418
Tennessee Williams 8:547

Brignano, Russell Carl
Richard Wright 4:594

Brinnin, John Malcolm
John Ashbery 6:12
Allen Ginsberg 6:201
Galway Kinnell 1:168
Sylvia Plath 1:269
William Jay Smith 6:512

Bristol, Horace
Pearl S. Buck 7:33

Brivic, Sheldon
Richard Wright 9:585

Brockway, James
Beryl Bainbridge 10:16
Angela Carter 5:102
J. P. Donleavy 4:126
Mavis Gallant 7:111
Penelope Gilliatt 10:230
Julien Green 3:205
Susan B. Hill 4:228
Piers Paul Read 10:435
Muriel Spark 5:399; 8:495

Brodsky, Joseph
Eugenio Montale 9:388

Brogan, Hugh
Mervyn Peake 7:301

Brombert, Victor
St.-John Perse 4:398

Bromwich, David
Conrad Aiken 5:10
A. R. Ammons 9:28
Hayden Carruth 10:100
Robert Frost 9:266
John Hawkes 4:216
John Hollander 5:187
Richard Howard 7:167
Doris Lessing 3:288
Penelope Mortimer 5:299
Iris Murdoch 3:348; 6:347
Howard Nemerov 9:394
Robert Pinsky 9:416
Anne Sexton 10:467
Charles Simic 9:479
Stevie Smith 8:492
Muriel Spark 3:465
Paul Theroux 5:427
Elie Wiesel 3:528

Bronowski, J.
Kathleen Raine 7:352

Brooke, Jocelyn
Elizabeth Bowen 1:39

Brooke, Nicholas
Anne Stevenson 7:462

Brooke-Rose, Christine
Ezra Pound 7:328

Brooks, Cleanth
Randall Jarrell 1:159
Marianne Moore 10:347
Walker Percy 6:399
Allen Tate 4:539

Brooks, Ellen W.
Doris Lessing 3:284

Brooks, Peter
Alain Robbe-Grillet 1:287

Broome, Peter
Robert Pinget 7:306

Brophy, Brigid
Kingsley Amis 2:5
Simone de Beauvoir 2:42
Hortense Calisher 2:95
Ivy Compton-Burnett 3:111
Jean Genet 2:157
Patricia Highsmith 2:192
Henry Miller 2:281
Françoise Sagan 3:443; 6:482
Georges Simenon 2:397
Elizabeth Taylor 2:432
Evelyn Waugh 3:509

Brophy, Brigid, Michael Levey, and Charles Osborne
William Faulkner 1:102
W. Somerset Maugham 1:204

Broughton, Panthea Reid
William Faulkner 6:175
Carson McCullers 4:345

Brown, Ashley
Caroline Gordon 6:204, 206
Allen Tate 2:428

Brown, Calvin S.
Conrad Aiken 3:4

Brown, Clarence
Czeslaw Milosz 5:292
Vladimir Nabokov 1:242

Brown, F. J.
Arthur Koestler 3:271
Alberto Moravia 2:293
Mario Puzo 1:282
Muriel Spark 2:417

Brown, Frederick
Louis Aragon 3:13
Jean Cocteau 1:60

Brown, Harry
Hollis Summers 10:494

Brown, Ivor
J. B. Priestley 2:346

Brown, John Russell
John Arden 6:8
John Osborne 5:332
Harold Pinter 6:408, 413
Arnold Wesker 5:482

Brown, Lloyd W.
Imamu Amiri Baraka 3:35
Langston Hughes 10:281

Brown, Merle E.
Kenneth Burke 2:88

Brown, Robert McAfee
Elie Wiesel 5:493

Brown, Rosellen
Margaret Atwood 8:28
Tim O'Brien 7:272
May Sarton 4:471
Judith Johnson Sherwin 7:414
Diane Wakoski 4:572

Brown, Russell M.
Robert Kroetsch 5:221

Brown, Ruth Leslie
John Gardner 2:151

Brown, T.
Louis MacNeice 10:323

Brown, Terence and Ted E. Boyle
Kingsley Amis 2:6

Brown, William P.
John Brunner 10:78

Browning, Preston M., Jr.
Flannery O'Connor 3:367

Brownjohn, Alan
Dannie Abse 7:1
Donald Davie 5:115
C. Day Lewis 6:128
Geoffrey Grigson 7:136
Seamus Heaney 7:148
Thomas Kinsella 4:270
Philip Larkin 5:226
George MacBeth 9:340
Anthony Powell 7:341
Louis Simpson 7:428

Brownjohn, Elizabeth
Philip Larkin 5:227

Broyard, Anatole
Saul Bellow 2:52
José Donoso 8:179
Jules Feiffer 8:217
Penelope Gilliatt 10:229
Günter Grass 2:172
Jerzy Kosinski 10:307
Bernard Malamud 2:266
Philip Roth 3:436
Françoise Sagan 9:468
Nathalie Sarraute 8:473
Mark Schorer 9:473

Georges Simenon 8:488
John Updike 2:440; 9:539

Bruccoli, Matthew J.
John O'Hara 3:370

Brudnoy, David
James Baldwin 2:33

Brukenfeld, Dick
Joyce Carol Oates 3:364

Brumberg, Abraham
Aleksandr I. Solzhenitsyn 4:514

Brustein, Robert
Edward Albee 3:6, 7
Jean Anouilh 1:6
James Baldwin 4:40
Brendan Behan 1:26
Jack Gelber 1:114
Jean Genet 1:115
Joseph Heller 3:228
Rolf Hochhuth 4:230
William Inge 1:153
Eugène Ionesco 1:154
Arthur Miller 6:330
John Osborne 5:332
Harold Pinter 1:266; 3:385, 386
Ronald Ribman 7:357
Jean-Paul Sartre 4:476
Murray Schisgal 6:489
Peter Shaffer 5:386
Tom Stoppard 3:470
Ronald Tavel 6:529
Jean-Claude Van Itallie 3:492
Gore Vidal 4:552, 553
Peter Weiss 3:514
Arnold Wesker 5:482

Bryan, C. D. B.
Julio Cortázar 2:103
Craig Nova 7:267

Bryant, J. A., Jr.
Eudora Welty 1:361; 5:480

Bryant, Jerry H.
James Baldwin 8:41
John Barth 2:36
Saul Bellow 2:52
William S. Burroughs 2:91
Joseph Heller 3:228
James Jones 3:261
Norman Mailer 2:260
Bernard Malamud 2:266
Carson McCullers 4:344
Toni Morrison 4:366
Flannery O'Connor 2:317
Walker Percy 2:333
Thomas Pynchon 2:353
Ayn Rand 3:423
John Updike 2:441
Kurt Vonnegut, Jr. 2:452
John A. Williams 5:497

Bryant, Rene Kuhn
Thomas Berger 8:83
Heinrich Böll 6:84
John Fowles 6:187
Paula Fox 8:219
John Hersey 7:154
Doris Lessing 10:316
James A. Michener 5:291

Bryden, Ronald
Peter Barnes 5:49
Doris Lessing 6:299

Peter Nichols 5:306
David Storey 4:529
Paul West 7:525

Buchanan, Cynthia
Norman Mailer 2:263

Buchen, Irving H.
Carson McCullers 10:334

Buchsbaum, Betty
David Kherdian 6:280

Buck, Philo M., Jr.
Jules Romains 7:378

Buckle, Richard
John Betjeman 2:60

Buckler, Robert
Elia Kazan 6:274

Buckley, Priscilla L.
Eric Ambler 6:4

Buckley, Vincent
T. S. Eliot 3:138

Buckley, William F., Jr.
William F. Buckley, Jr. 7:35
Aleksandr I. Solzhenitsyn 4:511
Tom Wolfe 2:481

Buechner, Frederick
Annie Dillard 9:178

Buell, Frederick
A. R. Ammons 8:17

Buffington, Robert
Donald Davidson 2:112
John Crowe Ransom 4:430, 437

Bufkin, E. C.
Iris Murdoch 2:297
P. H. Newby 2:310

Buitenhuis, Peter
Harry Mathews 6:314
William Trevor 7:475

Bunnell, Sterling
Michael McClure 6:321

Bunting, Basil
Hugh MacDiarmid 4:313

Burbank, Rex
Thornton Wilder 1:364

Burgess, Anthony
Kingsley Amis 1:6; 2:8
James Baldwin 1:16
Samuel Beckett 1:23; 3:44
Saul Bellow 1:31
Elizabeth Bowen 1:40; 3:82
Bridgid Brophy 6:99
William S. Burroughs 1:48
Albert Camus 1:54
Louis-Ferdinand Céline 7:46
Agatha Christie 1:58
Ivy Compton-Burnett 1:62
Lawrence Durrell 1:87
T. S. Eliot 3:139
E. M. Forster 1:107
Jean Genet 1:115
Penelope Gilliatt 2:160
William Golding 1:121
Günter Grass 1:125
Henry Green 2:178
Graham Greene 3:207
Joseph Heller 1:140
Ernest Hemingway 1:143; 3:234
Aldous Huxley 1:151

Christopher Isherwood 1:156
Pamela Hansford Johnson 1:160
Arthur Koestler 1:169; 3:270
John Le Carré 9:326
Colin MacInnes 4:314
Norman Mailer 1:190
Bernard Malamud 1:199; 3:322
Mary McCarthy 1:206
Henry Miller 1:224
Iris Murdoch 1:235
Vladimir Nabokov 1:244; 3:352
Flann O'Brien 1:252
J. B. Priestley 2:347
Alain Robbe-Grillet 1:288
J. D. Salinger 1:299
William Sansom 2:383
Alan Sillitoe 1:307
C. P. Snow 1:317
Muriel Spark 2:416
John Wain 2:458
Evelyn Waugh 1:359; 3:510
Angus Wilson 2:472
Edmund Wilson 3:538

Burgess, Charles E.
William Inge 8:308

Burhans, Clinton S., Jr.
Joseph Heller 3:230
Ernest Hemingway 8:283
Kurt Vonnegut, Jr. 8:530

Burke, William M.
John A. Williams 5:497

Burkom, Selma R.
Doris Lessing 1:174

Burnett, Michael
James Thurber 5:440

Burns, Alan
Ann Quin 6:442
C. P. Snow 1:317

Burns, Gerald
W. H. Auden 4:33
John Berryman 6:62, 63
Austin Clarke 9:169
Seamus Heaney 7:147
Robert Lowell 5:256
Frank O'Hara 5:324
Charles Olson 5:328
Ezra Pound 5:348
Gary Snyder 5:393
William Stafford 4:520

Burns, Stuart L.
Jean Stafford 4:517

Burns, Wayne
Alex Comfort 7:52,53

Burnshaw, Stanley
James Dickey 10:141

Burroughs, Franklin G.
William Faulkner 3:157

Burrow, J. W.
Aldous Huxley 3:254
J. R. R. Tolkien 3:482

Burroway, Janet
James Leo Herlihy 6:235

Busch, Frederick
J. G. Farrell 6:173
John Hawkes 7:140
Alice Munro 10:356
Paul West 7:523

Bush, Roland E.
Ishmael Reed 3:424

Butscher, Edward
John Berryman 3:67
John Gardner 3:185
Jerzy Kosinski 6:282
James Wright 5:519
Rudolph Wurlitzer 4:598

Butt, John
Carlos Fuentes 10:208

Byers, Margaret
Elizabeth Jennings 5:197

Byrd, Max
Jorge Luis Borges 6:93
Peter De Vries 10:136

Byrd, Scott
John Barth 1:17

Cahill, Daniel J.
Jerzy Kosinski 2:232

Calas, Nicholas
André Breton 9:125

Calder, Angus
T. S. Eliot 2:128

Caldwell, Joan
Audrey Thomas 7:472

Caldwell, Stephen
D. Keith Mano 2:270

Calisher, Hortense
Yukio Mishima 2:289
Vladimir Nabokov 1:246
Christina Stead 5:403

Callahan, John
Michael S. Harper 7:138

Callahan, John F.
Alice Walker 5:476

Callahan, Patrick J.
C. S. Lewis 3:297
George MacBeth 2:251
Alan Sillitoe 1:308
Stephen Spender 2:420

Callan, Edward
W. H. Auden 1:9, 11
Alan Paton 4:395

Callendar, Newgate
Eric Ambler 4:18
Isaac Asimov 9:49
William Peter Blatty 2:64
James Jones 3:262
Harry Kemelman 2:225
Emma Lathen 2:236
Georges Simenon 2:399
Mickey Spillane 3:469
Vassilis Vassilikos 8:524
Donald E. Westlake 7:528, 529

Callow, Philip
Andrew Sinclair 2:400

Cambon, Glauco
Robert Lowell 8:348
Eugenio Montale 7:224
Giuseppe Ungaretti 7:482

Cameron, Ann
Tom Robbins 9:454

Cameron, Julia
Judith Rossner 6:469

Campbell, Gregg M.
Bob Dylan 6:157

Cannella, Anthony R.
Richard Condon 10:111

Cansler, Ronald Lee
Robert A. Heinlein 3:227

Cantor, Peter
Frederic Raphael 2:367

Capitanchik, Maurice
E. M. Forster 2:135
Yukio Mishima 6:338

Caplan, Lincoln
Frederick Buechner 6:103

Caplan, Ralph
Kingsley Amis 1:6

Capouya, Emile
Albert Camus 2:98
Robert Coover 7:57
Paul Goodman 7:129
James Leo Herlihy 6:234
Ignazio Silone 4:493
Aleksandr I. Solzhenitsyn 1:320

Capp, Al
Mary McCarthy 5:276

Caputo-Mayr, Maria Luise
Peter Handke 8:261

Caram, Richard
Anne Stevenson 7:463

Carew, Jan
George Lamming 2:235

Carey, John
Lawrence Durrell 4:147
Richard Eberhart 3:135
William Empson 8:201
D. J. Enright 4:155
Doris Lessing 6:292
John Updike 7:489

Carey, Julian C.
Langston Hughes 10:278

Cargill, Oscar
Pearl S. Buck 7:32

Carne-Ross, D. S.
John Gardner 3:185
Eugenio Montale 7:222

Carpenter, Bogdana and John R. Carpenter
Zbigniew Herbert 9:274

Carpenter, Frederic I.
Robinson Jeffers 2:212

Carpenter, John R.
Greg Kuzma 7:196
John Logan 5:255
James Schevill 7:401
Gary Snyder 2:407
Diane Wakoski 2:459
Charles Wright 6:580

Carpenter, John R. and Bogdana Carpenter
Zbigniew Herbert 9:274

Carr, John
George Garrett 3:190

Carroll, David
Chinua Achebe 1:1

Carroll, Paul
John Ashbery 2:16
Robert Creeley 2:106
James Dickey 2:116

Allen Ginsberg 2:163
Frank O'Hara 2:321
W. D. Snodgrass 2:405
Philip Whalen 6:565

Carruth, Hayden
A. R. Ammons 9:30
W. H. Auden 1:11
John Berryman 2:56
Earle Birney 6:75
Charles Bukowski 5:80
Cid Corman 9:170
Robert Creeley 8:153
J. V. Cunningham 3:121
Annie Dillard 9:177
Robert Duncan 2:122
Loren Eiseley 7:91
Clayton Eshleman 7:97, 98
Robert Frost 10:198
Jean Garrigue 8:239
Arthur Gregor 9:251
H. D. 8:256
Marilyn Hacker 9:257
John Hollander 8:301
Richard Howard 7:166
David Ignatow 7:174, 175, 177
Denise Levertov 8:346
Philip Levine 2:244
Robert Lowell 4:299; 9:338
W. S. Merwin 8:390
Josephine Miles 2:278
Howard Nemerov 2:306
Charles Olson 9:412
Robert Pinsky 9:417
J. F. Powers 1:280
Kenneth Rexroth 2:370
Reg Saner 9:468
Anne Sexton 2:390; 4:484
Gilbert Sorrentino 7:448
Diane Wakoski 2:459; 4:574
Theodore Weiss 8:545
Louis Zukofsky 2:487

Carson, Katharine W.
Claude Simon 9:485

Carter, Albert Howard, III
Italo Calvino 8:126
Thomas McGuane 7:213

Carter, Angela
Thomas Keneally 5:210

Carter, Lin
J. R. R. Tolkien 1:339

Carter, Paul
Eugenio Montale 9:387

Carter, Robert A.
Arthur Gregor 9:253

Cary, Joseph
Eugenio Montale 7:223; 9:386
Giuseppe Ungaretti 7:482

Casebeer, Edwin F.
Hermann Hesse 3:245

Caserio, Robert L.
Gilbert Sorrentino 7:449

Casey, Carol K.
Eleanor Hibbert 7:156

Caspary, Sister Anita Marie
François Mauriac 4:337, 338

Casper, Leonard
Flannery O'Connor 6:375

Cassill, R. V.
Mavis Gallant 7:110
Thomas Hinde 6:241
Irwin Shaw 7:413
Wilfrid Sheed 2:393
Christina Stead 2:422

Catinella, Joseph
Christopher Isherwood 1:157
Joel Lieber 6:311
Bernard Malamud 1:201

Causey, James Y. and Jacob Ornstein
Camilo José Cela 4:95

Caute, David
Jean Genet 5:137
Lionel Trilling 9:531

Cavan, Romilly
Derek Walcott 4:574

Cavitch, David
William Stafford 4:521

Cawelti, John G.
Mario Puzo 6:430
Mickey Spillane 3:468

Caws, Mary Ann
André Breton 2:81; 9:125

Caws, Mary Ann and Sarah Lawall
Yves Bonnefoy 9:113

Cecchetti, Giovanni
Eugenio Montale 7:221

Cecil, David
Aldous Huxley 3:252

Cerf, Bennett
John O'Hara 2:324

Chace, William M.
Ezra Pound 4:415

Chaillet, Ned
Athol Fugard 9:232

Chamberlain, John
Mary McCarthy 3:326

Chamberlin, J. E.
Margaret Atwood 8:28
George MacBeth 5:265
W. S. Merwin 3:338
Charles Tomlinson 4:547; 6:535, 536
David Wagoner 5:475

Chambers, Ross
Samuel Beckett 9:77

Chametzky, Jules
Isaac Bashevis Singer 1:313

Chankin, Donald O.
B. Traven 8:517

Chapin, Katherine Garrison
Allen Tate 4:536

Chaplin, William H.
John Logan 5:253

Chapman, Raymond
Graham Greene 1:133

Chapman, Robert
Anthony Burgess 4:83
Ivy Compton-Burnett 3:112

Chappell, Fred
George Garrett 3:191
Richard Yates 7:554

Charters, Ann
Charles Olson 5:326

Charters, Samuel
Robert Creeley 4:117
Robert Duncan 4:142
Larry Eigner 9:180
William Everson 5:121
Lawrence Ferlinghetti 6:182
Allen Ginsberg 4:181
Charles Olson 5:329
Gary Snyder 5:393
Jack Spicer 8:497

Charyn, Jerome
Kōbō Abe 8:1
Martin Amis 9:26
R. H. W. Dillard 5:116
Elizabeth Jane Howard 7:165
James Purdy 10:424
Judith Rossner 9:457
Jerome Weidman 7:518
Kate Wilhelm 7:538

Chase, Richard
Saul Bellow 1:27

Chasin, Helen
Alan Dugan 6:144
May Sarton 4:472

Chassler, Philip I.
Meyer Levin 7:205

Chazen, Leonard
Anthony Powell 3:402

Cheatwood, Kiarri T-H.
Ayi Kwei Armah 5:32

Cheever, John
Saul Bellow 10:43

Cheney, Brainard
Donald Davidson 2:112
Flannery O'Connor 1:254

Cherry, Kelly
John Betjeman 10:53

Cherry, Kenneth
Vladimir Nabokov 8:413

Chesnick, Eugene
John Cheever 7:48
Nadine Gordimer 7:133
Michael Mewshaw 9:376

Chester, Alfred
Terry Southern 7:454

Cheuse, Alan
John Gardner 5:132
André Schwarz-Bart 4:480

Chevigny, Bell Gale
Tillie Olsen 4:387

Chiari, Joseph
Jean Anouilh 8:23
Jean Cocteau 8:144

Chomsky, Noam
Saul Bellow 8:81

Christ, Ronald
Jorge Luis Borges 2:70, 73; 4:75
José Donoso 8:178
Gabriel García Márquez 3:179
Pablo Neruda 5:301; 7:260
Octavio Paz 3:375; 4:397; 6:398
Manuel Puig 5:354
Mario Vargas Llosa 9:542

Christgau, Robert
Richard Brautigan 9:124

Churchill, R.C.
P. G. Wodehouse 10:537

Cifelli, Edward
John Ciardi 10:106

Ciplijauskaité, Biruté
Gabriel García Márquez 3:182

Cismaru, Alfred
Simone de Beauvoir 2:43
Marguerite Duras 6:149
Eugène Ionesco 9:289

Cixous, Helen
Severo Sarduy 6:485

Claire, Thomas
Albert Camus 9:150

Claire, William F.
Allen Tate 9:521
Mark Van Doren 6:541

Clancy, William
Brian Moore 7:234

Clapp, Susannah
Caroline Blackwood 9:101
Seán O'Faoláin 7:274
George MacBeth 9:340
David Plante 7:308

Clark, John R.
Doris Betts 6:69
Alan Sillitoe 1:308

Clarke, Gerald
Gore Vidal 2:449
P. G. Wodehouse 2:480

Clarke, Loretta
Paul Zindel 6:587

Claudel, Alice Moser
David Kherdian 9:317

Clausen, Christopher
T.S. Eliot 10:171

Clayton, John Jacob
Saul Bellow 6:50

Clements, Robert J.
Pablo Neruda 2:308
Irving Stone 7:469
Vassilis Vassilikos 4:551

Clemons, Walter
Lisa Alther 7:12
James Baldwin 5:43
Peter Benchley 8:82
E. L. Doctorow 6:133
J. G. Farrell 6:173
Joseph Heller 5:176, 182
George V. Higgins 7:158
Maureen Howard 5:189
G. Cabrera Infante 5:96
Erica Jong 4:263
Milan Kundera 4:276
Doris Lessing 6:302
Alison Lurie 4:305
Ross Macdonald 1:185
James McCourt 5:278
Carson McCullers 1:210
Vladimir Nabokov 6:354
Donald Newlove 6:364
Joyce Carol Oates 2:316; 3:363
Flannery O'Connor 2:317
Grace Paley 4:391
Robert M. Pirsig 4:403
Manuel Puig 5:354
Adrienne Rich 6:458
Isaac Bashevis Singer 3:456

Raymond Sokolov 7:430
Tom Wicker 7:534
Richard B. Wright 6:582

Clemons, Walter and Jack Kroll
Saul Bellow 6:55

Clifford, Gay
Stanley Middleton 7:221

Clifford, Paula M.
Claude Simon 9:485

Clinton, Farley
William Safire 10:447

Clucas, Humphrey
Philip Larkin 5:227

Clurman, Harold
Edward Albee 2:2; 5:14
Jean Anouilh 3:12
Fernando Arrabal 2:15; 9:41
Alan Ayckbourn 5:37; 8:35
Samuel Beckett 2:47; 6:33
Ed Bullins 1:47; 5:83
D.L. Coburn 10:108
E. E. Cummings 8:160
Brian Friel 5:129
Jean Genet 2:158
Bill Gunn 5:153
Christopher Hampton 4:211, 212
Rolf Hochhuth 4:230
William Inge 8:308
Eugène Ionesco 4:250
Preston Jones 10:296
Terrence McNally 4:347; 7:217, 218
Mark Medoff 6:322
Arthur Miller 1:218; 6:335
Jason Miller 2:284
Clifford Odets 2:320
John Osborne 5:330
Miguel Piñero 4:402
Harold Pinter 6:405, 410, 415, 419
David Rabe 4:426; 8:450, 451
Terence Rattigan 7:355
Peter Shaffer 5:388
Sam Shepard 6:496, 497
John Steinbeck 5:408
Tom Stoppard 1:327; 4:526; 5:411; 8:501
David Storey 5:417; 8:505
Gore Vidal 2:450
Richard Wesley 7:519
Thornton Wilder 6:573
Tennessee Williams 2:465; 5:500, 504; 7:545
Lanford Wilson 7:549

Cluysenaar, Anne
László Nagy 7:251
Jon Silkin 6:498

Coale, Samuel
Jerzy Kosinski 3:273; 6:284
Alain Robbe-Grillet 6:468

Cocks, Jay
Harold Pinter 3:388

Coe, Richard N.
Jean Genet 1:117
Eugène Ionesco 6:251

Coffey, Warren
Kurt Vonnegut, Jr. 3:494

Cogley, John
Dan Wakefield 7:502

Cogswell, Fred
Earle Birney 1:34

Cohen, Arthur A.
Joseph Brodsky 4:77
Cynthia Ozick 3:372

Cohen, Dean
J. P. Donleavy 1:76

Cohen, Larry
Jules Feiffer 2:133

Cohen, Nathan
Mordecai Richler 5:371

Cohn, Dorrit
Alain Robbe-Grillet 1:289

Cohn, Ruby
Edward Albee 1:4; 2:4
James Baldwin 2:32
Imamu Amiri Baraka 2:35
Djuna Barnes 4:43
John Dos Passos 4:133
Lawrence Ferlinghetti 2:134
John Hawkes 4:215
Kenneth Koch 5:219
Arthur Miller 2:279
Harold Pinter 6:405
Tennessee Williams 2:465

Colby, Rob
Olga Broumas 10:76

Cole, Barry
Ann Quin 6:442

Cole, Laurence
Jean Rhys 2:372

Cole, William
Charles Causley 7:42
Alex Comfort 7:54
Richard Condon 10:111
Louis Simpson 7:429
R. S. Thomas 6:531

Colegate, Isabel
Susan B. Hill 4:227
Joyce Carol Oates 6:369

Coleman, Alexander
Pablo Neruda 2:309
Nicanor Parra 2:331

Coleman, Sister Anne Gertrude
Paul Vincent Carroll 10:95

Coleman, John
Jack Kerouac 2:227
Leon Uris 7:490

Coles, Robert
Shirley Ann Grau 4:208
Kenneth Koch 8:324
Cormac McCarthy 4:343
Muriel Rukeyser 10:442
William Stafford 7:461
William Styron 1:331
James Wright 3:544

Collier, Carmen P.
Pearl S. Buck 7:32

Collier, Eugenia
James Baldwin 2:33
Melvin Van Peebles 2:447

Collier, Michael
Delmore Schwartz 10:463

Collier, Peter
Earl Rovit 7:383

Collings, Rex
Wole Soyinka 5:397

Collins, Harold R.
Amos Tutuola 5:443

Collins, Ralph L.
Elmer Rice 7:360

Commager, Henry Steele
MacKinlay Kantor 7:194

Compton, D. G.
Samuel Beckett 3:47
Frederick Buechner 2:84
John Gardner 2:151
Bernard Kops 4:274
Vladimir Nabokov 6:352
Frederic Prokosch 4:422

Conarroe, Joel
John Berryman 8:91
Richard Howard 7:167
Howard Nemerov 2:307
Anne Sexton 2:391
W. D. Snodgrass 2:405

Condini, Nereo
Eugenio Montale 7:230
Isaac Bashevis Singer 6:511
Tom Wolfe 9:579

Conley, Timothy K.
William Faulkner 9:200

Conn, Stewart
Anne Stevenson 7:463

Connell, Evan S., Jr.
Simone de Beauvoir 2:43
James Dickey 2:116
Wilfrid Sheed 2:392

Connelly, Kenneth
John Berryman 1:34

Conner, John W.
Nikki Giovanni 4:189

Connolly, Cyril
Ernest Hemingway 6:225
Louis MacNeice 4:315
Ezra Pound 4:408, 414

Conquest, Robert
Ezra Pound 7:334
Aleksandr I. Solzhenitsyn
2:413; 4:513

Conroy, Jack
Charles Bukowski 2:84

Contoski, Victor
Robert Duncan 2:123
David Ignatow 7:175
David Kherdian 6:281
Marge Piercy 6:403
Charles Simic 9:480

Conway, John D.
Paul Vincent Carroll 10:98

Cook, Albert
Djuna Barnes 4:43
André Malraux 4:327

Cook, Bruce
Kingsley Amis 8:11
James Baldwin 3:32
Heinrich Böll 6:84
William S. Burroughs 1:49
Evan S. Connell, Jr. 4:109

Gregory Corso 1:64
Robert Duncan 1:83
Allen Ginsberg 1:118
Lillian Hellman 8:281
Marjorie Kellogg 2:224
Thomas Keneally 5:211
Jack Kerouac 1:166
Jerzy Kosinski 1:171
Ross Macdonald 2:256
Norman Mailer 1:193
Brian Moore 7:235
Charles Olson 1:263
Ezra Pound 1:276
Budd Schulberg 7:403
Irwin Shaw 7:413
Georges Simenon 2:399
Gary Snyder 1:318
Arnold Wesker 5:484
William Carlos Williams 1:372

Cook, David
Camara Laye 4:283

Cook, Reginald L.
Robert Frost 1:111

Cook, Roderick
Harry Mathews 6:314
Berry Morgan 6:340

Cooke, Michael G.
Gayl Jones 9:308
George Lamming 4:279
Joyce Carol Oates 9:403
Jean Rhys 4:445
William Styron 1:331
John Updike 2:443
Alice Walker 9:558
Robert Penn Warren 4:581

Cookson, William
David Jones 4:260
Hugh MacDiarmid 4:310

Cooley, Peter
Ted Hughes 2:201

Coombs, Orde
James Baldwin 8:40

Cooper, Arthur
Richard Adams 5:5
Richard Condon 6:115
Michael Crichton 2:109
J. P. Donleavy 6:142
Ward Just 4:266
John Le Carré 3:281
James A. Michener 5:290
Wright Morris 7:245
Ishmael Reed 6:450
Philip Roth 2:378
Irwin Shaw 7:414
David Storey 5:417
Gore Vidal 6:549
Fay Weldon 6:563

Cooper, Philip
Robert Lowell 4:300

Cooperman, Stanley
W. S. Merwin 1:212
Philip Roth 3:438

Coover, Robert
José Donoso 4:127
Carlos Fuentes 8:224

Core, George
Edna O'Brien 8:429
Seán O'Faoláin 7:273

John Crowe Ransom 2:364;
5:366
William Styron 1:331
Allen Tate 4:537
William Trevor 9:529

Corke, Hilary
John Cheever 3:106

Corn, Alfred
John Hollander 8:302
Boris Pasternak 7:300
Reg Saner 9:469

Cornwell, Ethel F.
Samuel Beckett 3:45
Nathalie Sarraute 8:471

Corodimas, Peter
Ira Levin 6:305

Corr, Patricia
Evelyn Waugh 1:356

Corrigan, Matthew
Charles Olson 5:328

Corrigan, Robert W.
Edward Albee 5:11
John Arden 6:9
Saul Bellow 6:51
Friedrich Dürrenmatt 8:196
Michel de Ghelderode 6:197
Arthur Miller 1:218
John Osborne 5:332
Harold Pinter 6:417
Thornton Wilder 5:494

Corrington, John William
James Dickey 1:73
Marion Montgomery 7:233

Cortázar, Julio
Jorge Luis Borges 8:102

Cortínez, Carlos
Octavio Paz 10:393

Corwin, Phillip
Kay Boyle 5:67

Cosgrave, Patrick
Kingsley Amis 3:8
Robert Lowell 4:300
Georges Simenon 3:452

Cott, Jonathan
Bob Dylan 6:156

Cotter, James Finn
Robert Bly 10:62
Mark Van Doren 6:542

Cottrell, Robert D.
Simone de Beauvoir 8:58

Covatta, Anthony
Elio Vittorini 6:551

Coveney, Michael
Athol Fugard 5:130
Sam Shepard 6:496

Cowan, Louise
John Crowe Ransom 5:363
Allen Tate 2:431
Robert Penn Warren 6:555

Cowan, Michael
Norman Mailer 8:371

Cowley, Malcolm
Conrad Aiken 10:3
Pearl S. Buck 7:31
E. E. Cummings 3:118
John Dos Passos 4:135

William Faulkner 8:210
Robert Frost 4:173
Doris Lessing 6:303
John O'Hara 2:325
Ezra Pound 4:407
James Thurber 5:430

Cox, David
Wilfrid Sheed 4:489

Cox, Kenneth
Hugh MacDiarmid 4:311
Ezra Pound 4:413
C. H. Sisson 8:490
Louis Zukofsky 7:562

Coxe, Louis
David Jones 2:217
Anne Sexton 2:391

Coyne, J. R., Jr.
Fredrick Forsyth 5:125
E. Howard Hunt 3:251

Coyne, John R., Jr.
Dick Francis 2:142
Ward Just 4:266
Donald E. Westlake 7:528
Tom Wolfe 2:481

Coyne, P. S.
Wilfrid Sheed 2:395

Coyne, Patricia S.
Kingsley Amis 3:10
Erica Jong 4:265
Joyce Carol Oates 9:402
Morris L. West 6:564

Craft, Robert
Aldous Huxley 5:193

Craft, Wallace
Eugenio Montale 7:230

Craib, Roderick
Bernard Malamud 3:322

Craig, Patricia
Edna O'Brien 8:429

Craig, Randall
Jean Genet 2:160
Robert Shaw 5:390
Sam Shepard 4:489
E. A. Whitehead 5:489

Crain, Jane Larkin
Caroline Blackwood 9:101
Sara Davidson 9:175
Lawrence Durrell 6:153
Bruce Jay Friedman 5:126
John Gardner 5:134
Gail Godwin 8:248
Shirley Ann Grau 9:240
Milan Kundera 4:276
Alan Lelchuk 5:244
Doris Lessing 6:299
Grace Paley 4:394
Walker Percy 6:401
Kathleen Raine 7:353
C. P. Snow 6:518
Muriel Spark 5:398
Mario Vargas Llosa 6:545
Gore Vidal 4:555
David Wagoner 5:474
Sol Yurick 6:583

Crankshaw, Edward
Aleksandr I. Solzhenitsyn
1:319

Creagh, Patrick
Giuseppe Ungaretti 7:484

Creeley, Robert
Robert Duncan 4:141
William Everson 5:121
Robert Graves 6:210
Charles Olson 5:326
Ezra Pound 3:395
William Stafford 4:519
William Carlos Williams 5:507
Louis Zukofsky 4:599

Crews, Frederick C.
Shirley Ann Grau 4:207
Philip Roth 2:379

Crews, Harry
Elliott Baker 8:39

Crichton, Michael
Frederick Forsyth 2:136
Kurt Vonnegut, Jr. 3:495

Crick, Francis
Michael McClure 6:319

Crick, Joyce
Michael Hamburger 5:159

Crinklaw, Don
John Gardner 3:186

Crinkley, Richmond
Edward Albee 2:3

Crist, Judith
Harry Kemelman 2:225

Crowder, Richard
Carl Sandburg 1:300

Crowson, Lydia
Jean Cocteau 8:148

Cruise O'Brien, Conor
Jimmy Breslin 4:76
Graham Greene 3:214
Seamus Heaney 7:149

Cruse, Harold W. and Carolyn Gipson
W. E. B. Du Bois 2:120

Cruttwell, Patrick
Iris Murdoch 2:296
Patrick White 7:529

Cruttwell, Patrick and Faith Westburg
Adolfo Bioy Casares 4:64
Jerzy Kosinski 3:274

Cuddon, J. A.
Peter De Vries 2:114
James Purdy 4:423
Frederic Raphael 2:367
Claude Simon 4:497

Culbertson, Diana and John A. Valley
Alberto Moravia 7:243

Culler, Jonathan
Walker Percy 8:439

Cumare, Rosa
Flann O'Brien 5:317

Cunliffe, Marcus
Irving Stone 7:469

Cunliffe, W. Gordon
Günter Grass 1:126
Uwe Johnson 10:283

Cunningham, Laura
Richard Price 6:427

Cunningham, Valentine
Louis Auchincloss 6:15
John Barth 5:51
Donald Barthelme 3:43
Alejo Carpentier 8:134
Len Deighton 4:119
Shusaku Endo 7:96
Frederick Forsyth 5:125
Mervyn Jones 10:295
Anna Kavan 5:206
William Kotzwinkle 5:220
Mary Lavin 4:282
Colin MacInnes 4:314
Stanley Middleton 7:220
Yukio Mishima 4:358
Vladimir Nabokov 3:355
Hans Erich Nossack 6:364
David Plante 7:307
Françoise Sagan 9:468
William Sansom 6:484
Paul Theroux 8:513
Gillian Tindall 7:474
Ludvík Vaculík 7:495
Harriet Waugh 6:559
Arnold Wesker 5:483
Patrick White 4:587

Currie, William
Kobo Abe 8:2

Curtis, Anthony
J. B. Priestley 5:351

Curtis, C. Michael
Sara Davidson 9:175
Annie Dillard 9:179

Curtis, Jerry L.
Jean Genet 10:224

Curtis, Simon
Donald Davie 5:113
Seamus Heaney 7:151

Cushman, Jerome
Jascha Kessler 4:270

Cushman, Keith
Mark Shorer 9:474

Cutler, Bruce
Louis Simpson 7:428

Cutter, William
S. Y. Agnon 4:15

Czajkowska, Magdalena
Tadeusz Rózewicz 9:463

Dabney, Lewis H.
William Faulkner 6:174

Dacey, Philip
Arthur Gregor 9:255

Dahlie, Hallvard
Brian Moore 1:225; 7:237
Alice Munro 10:357

Daiches, David
W. H. Auden 1:8
Saul Bellow 3:55
Elizabeth Bowen 1:39
Ivy Compton-Burnett 1:60
C. Day Lewis 1:72
T. S. Eliot 1:89
William Empson 3:147
Christopher Fry 2:143
Robert Graves 1:126
Henry Green 2:178

Aldous Huxley 1:149
Hugh MacDiarmid 2:252
Louis MacNeice 1:186
Bernard Malamud 3:323
Henry Roth 6:473
Edith Sitwell 2:403
Stephen Spender 1:322
Evelyn Waugh 1:356

Daiker, Donald A.
Hugh Nissenson 4:381

Dale, Peter
John Berryman 2:58
Basil Bunting 10:84

Dalton, Elizabeth
Vladimir Nabokov 1:245
John Updike 1:344

Dame, Enid
Chaim Potok 7:322

Dana, Robert
Yukio Mishima 2:286

Dangerfield, George
Rayner Heppenstall 10:272

Daniel, John
Ann Quin 6:441
Isaac Bashevis Singer 6:507

Daniel, Robert W.
W. D. Snodgrass 10:478

Daniels, Robert V.
Larry Woiwode 10:540

Danielson, J. David
Simone Schwarz-Bart 7:404

d'Arazien, Steven
Hunter S. Thompson 9:528

Dardess, George
Jack Kerouac 5:213

Darrach, Brad
George V. Higgins 4:224
Joyce Carol Oates 2:313
Ezra Pound 7:336
Irving Stone 7:471

Dauster, Frank
Gabriel García Márquez 3:182

Davenport, G.
J. R. R. Tolkien 3:482

Davenport, Gary T.
Seán O'Faoláin 7:275

Davenport, Guy
Michael Ayrton 7:17
Beryl Bainbridge 8:36
Thomas Berger 8:82
Wendell Berry 8:85
Frederick Buechner 2:82
Paul Celan 10:101
Louis-Ferdinand Céline 3:104
Evan S. Connell, Jr. 4:110
Joan Didion 1:75
J. P. Donleavy 4:124
Miroslav Holub 4:233
Charles Olson 6:388; 9:412
Nicanor Parra 2:331
Chaim Potok 2:338
James Purdy 2:350
J.I.M. Stewart 7:466
Harriet Waugh 6:560
Richard Wilbur 6:569
Louis Zukofsky 2:487; 4:599;
7:560

CRITIC INDEX

Davidon, Ann Morrissett
Simone de Beauvoir 8:57
Grace Paley 4:391
Gore Vidal 4:557

Davie, Donald
A. R. Ammons 5:30
John Berryman 8:87
Austin Clarke 6:112
Michael Hamburger 5:159
Anthony Hecht 8:267
John Hollander 8:299
Galway Kinnell 5:217
John Peck 3:377

Davies, R. R.
Joanne Greenberg 7:135
Diane Johnson 5:198
William Sansom 6:482

Davies, Russell
Richard Condon 8:150
Joan Didion 8:177
Francis King 8:321
William Trevor 9:528

Davis, Charles T.
Robert Hayden 5:68

Davis, Deborah
Julio Cortázar 5:109

Davis, Fath
Toni Morrison 4:366

Davis, George
George Lamming 2:235
Clarence Major 3:320

Davis, Hope Hale
John Cheever 8:140

Davis, L. J.
Richard Condon 4:106
Peter De Vries 7:78
Stanley Elkin 4:153
Leon Forrest 4:163
Lois Gould 4:200
Hannah Green 3:202
John Hersey 2:188
Stanley Hoffman 5:184
James Jones 10:291
William Kennedy 6:274
Ira Levin 6:307
John O'Hara 2:324
J. F. Powers 8:448
Philip Roth 2:379
Françoise Sagan 6:481
Ronald Sukenick 4:531
J. R. R. Tolkien 8:516
Vassilis Vassilikos 8:524
Richard B. Wright 6:582

Davis, M. E.
José María Arguedas 10:10

Davis, Paxton
Eric Ambler 9:18
George Garrett 3:189

Davis, Rick
Richard Brautigan 9:125
Richard Condon 10:111

Davis, Robert Gorham
Saul Bellow 2:49
John Dos Passos 1:78
William Styron 3:472

Davis, Robert Murray
Evelyn Waugh 1:359

Davison, Peter
Robert Creeley 8:151
Robert Frost 4:175
John Hollander 8:298
Galway Kinnell 2:229
Denise Levertov 8:345
Sylvia Plath 2:337
Anne Sexton 8:482
William Stafford 7:460

Davy, John
Arthur Koestler 1:169

Dawson, Helen
David Storey 4:529

Day, A. Grove
James A. Michener 1:214

Day, Douglas
Robert Graves 1:127

Day, James M.
Paul Horgan 9:278

Deane, Seamus
Seamus Heaney 7:150

Debicki, Andrew P.
Claudio Rodríguez 10:439

De Bolt, Joe and Edward L. Lamie
John Brunner 8:110

deBuys, William
Paul Horgan 9:279

Decancq, Roland
Lawrence Durrell 8:191

de Charmant, Elizabeth
Giorgio Bassani 9:74

Deck, John
Harry Crews 6:17
Henry Dumas 6:145
J. G. Farrell 6:173
Michael Moorcock 5:294
John Seelye 7:406

Dector, Midge
Leon Uris 7:491

Deedy, John
J. P. Donleavy 4:123

Deemer, Charles
Renata Adler 8:7
John Cheever 3:108
Peter Handke 5:165
Bernard Malamud 3:324

Deen, Rosemary F.
Randall Jarrell 6:259
Galway Kinnell 3:268

De Feo, Ronald
Martin Amis 4:21
Beryl Bainbridge 8:37
Thomas Bernhard 3:65
William S. Burroughs 2:93
José Donoso 4:128
William Gaddis 6:195
Gabriel García Márquez 2:149;
  10:216
John Gardner 5:131, 134
Graham Greene 6:219
John Hawkes 1:138
Dan Jacobson 4:255
Jerzy Kosinski 1:172
Iris Murdoch 6:345
Howard Nemerov 6:360
Sylvia Plath 1:270
Anthony Powell 3:404

James Salter 7:388
Gilbert Sorrentino 3:461
William Trevor 7:477
John Updike 5:460
Angus Wilson 5:514

Degenfelder, E. Pauline
Larry McMurtry 7:213

Degnan, James P.
Kingsley Amis 2:10
Roald Dahl 1:71
Wilfrid Sheed 2:394

de Jonge, Alex
Aleksandr I. Solzhenitsyn
  9:506

Dekker, George
Donald Davie 8:166

Dekle, Bernard
Saul Bellow 1:32
E. E. Cummings 1:69
John Dos Passos 1:80
William Faulkner 1:102
Robert Frost 1:111
Langston Hughes 1:148
John P. Marquand 2:271
Arthur Miller 1:219
John O'Hara 1:262
J. D. Salinger 1:300
Upton Sinclair 1:310
Thornton Wilder 1:366
Tennessee Williams 1:369
William Carlos Williams 1:371

Delany, Paul
A. Alvarez 5:19
Margaret Atwood 4:24

de Laurentis, Teresa
Italo Calvino 8:127

Delbanco, Nicholas
Frederick Busch 10:93
Graham Greene 9:251

Deligiorgis, Stavros
David Kherdian 9:318

Della Fazia, Alba
Jean Anouilh 1:7

Delong-Tonelli, Beverly J.
Fernando Arrabal 9:36

Demarest, Michael
Michael Crichton 6:119

DeMaria, Robert
Diane Wakoski 2:459

Dembo, L. S.
Charles Olson 2:327
George Oppen 7:283
Louis Zukofsky 2:488

DeMott, Benjamin
Margaret Atwood 2:20
James Baldwin 2:32
Jorge Luis Borges 2:70
T. S. Eliot 2:127
Russell C. Hoban 7:162
Doris Lessing 2:240
Henry Miller 2:283
Philip Roth 9:462
John Updike 5:459
Kurt Vonnegut, Jr. 2:453

Dempsey, David
Terry Southern 7:454

Deneau, Daniel P.
Hermann Hesse 3:249
Jakov Lind 1:178
Alain Robbe-Grillet 4:449

Denne, Constance Ayers
Joyce Carol Oates 6:372

Denney, Reuel
Conrad Aiken 1:3

Dennis, Nigel
Louis-Ferdinand Céline 1:57
Robert Pinget 7:305
E. B. White 10:531

Dennison, George
Paul Goodman 4:197

DeRamus, Betty
Joyce Carol Oates 3:364

Deredita, John
Pablo Neruda 7:257
Juan Carlos Onetti 7:278

Der Hovanessian, Diana
David Kherdian 6:280

Dessner, Lawrence Jay
Mario Puzo 6:429

Detweiler, Robert
John Updike 2:442

Deutsch, Babette
W. H. Auden 2:21
Louise Bogan 4:68
E. E. Cummings 3:116
T. S. Eliot 2:125
William Empson 8:201
Robert Frost 3:171
Jean Garrigue 8:239
H. D. 3:217
Marianne Moore 2:290
St.-John Perse 4:398
Ezra Pound 2:339
Kathleen Raine 7:351
John Crowe Ransom 2:361
Theodore Roethke 3:432
Carl Sandburg 4:463
Edith Sitwell 2:402
Stephen Spender 2:419
Allen Tate 2:427
Richard Wilbur 9:568
William Carlos Williams 2:466

DeVault, Joseph J.
Mark Van Doren 6:541

Devert, Krystyna
Hermann Hesse 2:189

DeVitis, A. A.
Graham Greene 1:133

Devlin, John
Ramón Sender 8:478

De Vries, Peter
James Thurber 5:429

Devrnja, Zora
Charles Olson 9:412
Charles Simic 9:478

Dewsnap, Terence
Christopher Isherwood 1:156

Dick, Bernard F.
William Golding 1:120
John Hersey 2:188
Iris Murdoch 6:342
Mary Renault 3:426

Stevie Smith 8:492
Gore Vidal 4:558

Dick, Kay
Simone de Beauvoir 4:48

Dickey, Chris
Kurt Vonnegut, Jr. 5:470

Dickey, James
Conrad Aiken 1:3
John Ashbery 2:16
John Berryman 1:33
Kenneth Burke 2:87
Stanley Burnshaw 3:91
Hayden Carruth 4:93
E. E. Cummings 1:68
J. V. Cunningham 3:120
Robert Duncan 1:82
Richard Eberhart 3:133
William Everson 1:96
Robert Frost 1:111
Allen Ginsberg 1:118
David Ignatow 4:247
Robinson Jeffers 2:214
Galway Kinnell 1:167
James Kirkup 1:169
John Logan 5:252
Louis MacNeice 1:186
William Meredith 4:347
James Merrill 2:272
W. S. Merwin 1:211
Josephine Miles 1:215
Marianne Moore 1:226
Howard Nemerov 2:305
Charles Olson 1:262; 2:327
Kenneth Patchen 1:265
Sylvia Plath 2:337
Herbert Read 4:439
Theodore Roethke 1:290
May Sarton 4:470
Anne Sexton 2:390
Louis Simpson 4:497
William Jay Smith 6:512
William Stafford 4:519
Allen Tate 6:527
Robert Penn Warren 1:352
Theodore Weiss 3:515
Reed Whittemore 4:588
Richard Wilbur 3:531
William Carlos Williams 1:370
Yvor Winters 4:590

Dickey, R. P.
Lawrence Ferlinghetti 6:183
Robert Lowell 5:258

Dickey, William
Daniel J. Berrigan 4:56
Hayden Carruth 7:40
James Dickey 2:115
William Everson 5:121
W. S. Merwin 2:277
George Oppen 7:281

Dickins, Anthony
Vladimir Nabokov 2:304

Dickinson, Hugh
Eugène Ionesco 6:250

Dickstein, Lore
Gail Godwin 8:247
Judith Guest 8:254
Sue Kaufman 3:263
Judith Rossner 6:469
Isaac Bashevis Singer 3:456

Dickstein, Morris
John Barth 7:24
Donald Barthelme 6:29
R. P. Blackmur 2:61
Daniel Fuchs 8:220
John Gardner 3:184
Philip Roth 4:454
Rudolph Wurlitzer 2:484

Didion, Joan
John Cheever 8:137
Doris Lessing 2:240

Diez, Luys A.
Juan Carlos Onetti 7:280

Dillard, Annie
Evan S. Connell, Jr. 4:109

Dillard, R. H. W.
W. S. Merwin 8:389
Vladimir Nabokov 2:304
Colin Wilson 3:537

Dillingham, Thomas
Susan Fromberg Schaeffer 6:488

Dillon, David
John Hawkes 4:218
Wallace Stegner 9:509

Dillon, Michael
Thornton Wilder 6:571

Dimeo, Steven
Ray Bradbury 3:85

Dinnage, Rosemary
Isak Dinesen 10:152
Doris Lessing 6:303

Di Piero, W. S.
John Ashbery 4:22
John Hawkes 9:269

Dirda, Michael
John Knowles 10:303

Ditsky, John
John Hawkes 2:186
Erica Jong 8:313
Joyce Carol Oates 2:316

Dix, Carol
Martin Amis 4:20

Dixon, John W., Jr.
Elie Wiesel 3:527

DiZazzo, Raymond
Robert L. Peters 7:303

Djilas, Milovan
Aleksandr I. Solzhenitsyn 2:408

Dobbs, Kildare
Margaret Laurence 3:278
Alice Munro 6:341

Dobie, Ann B.
Muriel Spark 2:416

Dodsworth, Martin
Robert Bly 2:65
Donald Davie 8:163
James Dickey 2:115
Marianne Moore 2:291

Doerksen, Daniel W.
Margaret Avison 4:36

Dohmann, Barbara and Luis Harss
Jorge Luis Borges 2:69

Julio Cortázar 2:101
Gabriel García Márquez 2:147
Juan Carlos Onetti 7:276
Juan Rulfo 8:461
Mario Vargas Llosa 3:493

Dollen, Charles
William Peter Blatty 2:64
Paul Gallico 2:147
N. Scott Momaday 2:289

Donadio, Stephen
John Ashbery 2:19
Richard Fariña 9:195
Sandra Hochman 3:250

Donahue, Francis
Camilo José Cela 4:97

Donahue, Walter
Sam Shepard 4:491

Donaldson, Scott
Philip Roth 1:293

Donnard, Jean-Hervé
Eugène Ionesco 6:249

Donnelly, Dorothy
Marge Piercy 3:384

Donoghue, Denis
A. R. Ammons 9:27
W. H. Auden 3:24
Saul Bellow 2:51
Marie-Claire Blais 2:63
Kenneth Burke 2:88
Austin Clarke 9:167
C. Day Lewis 6:129
T. S. Eliot 2:126
John Fowles 10:188
William Golding 3:196
Shirley Ann Grau 4:209
Graham Greene 9:250
Anthony Hecht 8:269
Paul Horgan 9:278
Randall Jarrell 1:160
Robert Lowell 4:295
James Merrill 2:274
W. S. Merwin 2:277
Marianne Moore 2:291
Ezra Pound 2:340
Philip Roth 6:476
Christina Stead 2:422
Allen Tate 6:527; 9:521
Charles Tomlinson 2:437
Lionel Trilling 9:530
Derek Walcott 2:460
Anne Waldman 7:507
Robert Penn Warren 4:579
Rebecca West 7:525
William Carlos Williams 2:467

Donovan, Josephine
Sylvia Plath 3:390

Dooley, D. J.
Earle Birney 6:71

Dooley, Dennis M.
Robert Penn Warren 10:517

Doubrovsky, J. S.
Eugène Ionesco 6:247

Douglas, Ellen
Flannery O'Connor 6:381
May Sarton 4:471

Douglas, George H.
Edmund Wilson 2:477

Dowling, Gordon Graham
Yukio Mishima 6:337

Downer, Alan S.
Thornton Wilder 5:495

Doxey, William S.
Ken Kesey 3:267
Flannery O'Connor 3:368

Doyle, Mike
Irving Layton 2:236
A. W. Purdy 6:428
Raymond Souster 5:395, 396

Doyle, Paul A.
Paul Vincent Carroll 10:96
James T. Farrell 8:205
MacKinlay Kantor 7:195
Seán O'Faoláin 1:259; 7:273
Evelyn Waugh 1:359

Drabble, Margaret
Michael Frayn 3:164
Philip Larkin 8:333; 9:323
Iris Murdoch 4:367
Muriel Spark 8:494

Drake, Robert
Reynolds Price 3:405
Eudora Welty 5:478

Driver, Christopher
Yukio Mishima 4:357

Driver, Tom F.
Jean Genet 1:115
Arthur Miller 1:215; 2:279

Druska, John
John Beecher 6:49

Dryden, Edgar A.
John Barth 5:52

Duberman, Martin
Ed Bullins 1:47
Laura Z. Hobson 7:163

Duberstein, Larry
Joel Lieber 6:312

Dubois, Larry
William F. Buckley, Jr. 7:34
Walker Percy 8:445

Duffey, Bernard
W. H. Auden 4:35
Jack Kerouac 1:66

Duffy, Martha
James Baldwin 4:41
Jean Cocteau 1:59
Joan Didion 1:75
Nikki Giovanni 2:164
Lillian Hellman 4:221
D. Keith Mano 10:328
Tom McHale 5:281
Grace Paley 4:393
Walker Percy 2:334
Sylvia Plath 2:336
Judith Rossner 6:470
Patrick White 3:523

Duhamel, P. Albert
Flannery O'Connor 1:253
Paul Scott 9:477

Duncan, Erika
William Goyen 8:251
Anaïs Nin 8:425

Duncan, Robert
John Wieners 7:536

Dunlop, John B.
Vladimir Voinovich 10:509

Dunn, Douglas
Giorgio Bassani 9:77
John Berryman 4:62
George Mackay Brown 5:78
Donald Davie 5:115
Lawrence Durrell 4:147
D. J. Enright 4:156; 8:203
Geoffrey Grigson 7:136
John Hawkes 7:141
Seamus Heaney 7:150
Erica Jong 6:268
Sylvia Plath 5:339
William Plomer 4:407
Peter Redgrove 6:446
Jon Silkin 6:499
Anne Stevenson 7:463
Charles Tomlinson 6:534
Andrew Young 5:525

Dupee, F. W.
Kenneth Koch 5:218
Robert Lowell 3:299
Bernard Malamud 3:321
W. S. Merwin 3:338
John Osborne 5:330
J. F. Powers 4:418

Dupree, Robert
Allen Tate 6:525

Durbin, Karen
Eleanor Clark 5:107

Durgnat, Raymond
Ann Quin 6:442

Durham, Frank
Elmer Rice 7:363

Durham, Philip
Dashiell Hammett 3:218

Durrant, Digby
Caroline Blackwood 6:80
Julia O'Faolain 6:383

Durrell, Lawrence
George Seferis 5:385

Du Verlie, Claude
Claude Simon 4:497

Dwyer, David J.
Mary Renault 3:426

Dyson, William
Ezra Pound 1:276

Dzwonkoski, F. Peter, Jr.
T. S. Eliot 6:163

Eagle, Herbert
Aleksandr I. Solzhenitsyn
9:504
Ludvík Vaculík 7:495

Eagle, Robert
Alberto Moravia 7:244
Flann O'Brien 4:385

Eagleton, Terry
George Barker 8:45
Donald Davie 8:162
Thom Gunn 6:221
Seamus Heaney 7:150
William Plomer 8:447
Stevie Smith 8:491
Maura Stanton 9:508
Charles Tomlinson 6:535
Andrew Young 5:525

Eastman, Fred
Marc Connelly 7:55

Eaton, Charles Edward
Robert Frost 9:225

Eberhart, Richard
Djuna Barnes 8:48
Archibald MacLeish 3:310
Ezra Pound 7:324
Kenneth Rexroth 2:370

Echevarría, Roberto González
Julio Cortázar 10:114
Carlos Fuentes 10:209
Severo Sarduy 6:486

Eckley, Grace
Edna O'Brien 5:312

Eddins, Dwight
John Fowles 10:183

Edel, Leon
Lawrence Durrell 1:85
William Faulkner 1:100
Ernest Hemingway 10:265
Alain Robbe-Grillet 1:286
Nathalie Sarraute 1:303

Edelstein, Arthur
William Faulkner 1:102
Janet Frame 6:190
Jean Stafford 7:458
Angus Wilson 2:472

Edelstein, J. M.
Patricia Highsmith 2:193

Edelstein, Mark G.
Flannery O'Connor 6:381

Edenbaum, Robert I.
Dashiell Hammett 3:219
John Hawkes 2:185

Eder, Richard
Edna O'Brien 8:430

Edinborough, Arnold
Earle Birney 6:70

Edmiston, Susan
Maeve Brennan 5:72

Edwards, C. Hines, Jr.
James Dickey 4:121

Edwards, Michael
Donald Davie 5:114
Charles Tomlinson 4:547

Edwards, Sharon
Jessamyn West 7:522

Edwards, Thomas R.
Lisa Alther 7:14
Kingsley Amis 8:12
James Baldwin 4:41
Donald Barthelme 8:49
Frederick Buechner 2:83
Charles Bukowski 2:84
Anthony Burgess 5:88
John Cheever 7:48
Evan S. Connell, Jr. 4:108
Stanley Elkin 4:153
Leslie A. Fiedler 4:161
Paula Fox 2:140
John Gardner 2:151; 5:133
Gail Godwin 8:248
Herbert Gold 4:193
James Hanley 8:266
James Jones 10:293
Jerzy Kosinski 2:233

George Lamming 2:235
Norman Mailer 2:264
Harry Mathews 6:616
Peter Matthiessen 7:211
Thomas McGuane 3:330
Leonard Michaels 6:324
Brian Moore 7:237
Ishmael Reed 2:368
Philip Roth 3:437
André Schwarz-Bart 2:389
Hubert Selby, Jr. 2:390
Wilfrid Sheed 4:488
John Updike 5:460
Derek Walcott 4:576
Tom Wolfe 1:375

Eggenschwiler, David
Flannery O'Connor 6:378
William Styron 5:419

Egremont, Max
Seán O'Faoláin 7:276
Anthony Powell 7:341; 9:438
Gillian Tindall 7:474
Ludvík Vaculík 7:496

Ehre, Milton
Aleksandr I. Solzhenitsyn
2:412

Ehrenpreis, Irvin
John Ashbery 6:13
W. H. Auden 9:58
Geoffrey Hill 8:293
Donald Justice 6:272
Robert Lowell 1:180; 8:353
George Oppen 7:285
John Updike 5:455

Eisen, Dulcie
Ronald Tavel 6:529

Eisenberg, J. A.
Isaac Bashevis Singer 1:310

Eisinger, Chester E.
Arthur Miller 6:331

Elias, Robert H.
James Thurber 5:431

Elizondo, Salvador
Octavio Paz 3:376

Elkin, Stanley
Frederick Forsyth 2:136

Elliott, George P.
Jean Giono 4:187
Robert Graves 2:176
Norman Mailer 3:317
Susan Sontag 10:485
David Wagoner 3:507

Elliott, Janice
Patricia Highsmith 2:193
Aleksandr I. Solzhenitsyn
1:321

Elliott, Robert C.
Ursula K. Le Guin 8:341

Elliott, William I.
Shusaku Endo 7:95

Ellis, James
John Knowles 1:169

Ellison, Harlan
Barry N. Malzberg 7:208

Ellison, Ralph
Richard Wright 9:583

Ellmann, Mary
John Barth 2:39
Vladimir Nabokov 1:244
Joyce Carol Oates 3:364
Aleksandr I. Solzhenitsyn
1:321
Michel Tournier 6:538
Rebecca West 7:526
Vassily S. Yanovsky 2:485

Ellmann, Richard
W. H. Auden 9:55
Giorgio Bassani 9:76
Samuel Beckett 2:47

Elman, Richard
William Bronk 10:73
Frederick Busch 10:91

Elman, Richard M.
Charles Bukowski 9:137
Hannah Green 3:202
Jack Spicer 8:497
Hunter S. Thompson 9:526
Rudolf Wurlitzer 2:482

Elon, Amos
Yehuda Amichai 9:22

Elsom, John
Alan Ayckbourn 5:35
Samuel Beckett 6:43
Edward Bond 6:85
Michael Frayn 7:108
Sam Shepard 6:496
Tom Stoppard 5:412
E. A. Whitehead 5:488

Elstob, Peter
Len Deighton 4:119

Emanuel, James A.
Langston Hughes 1:147

Emerson, O. B.
Marion Montgomery 7:232

Emerson, Stephen
Gilbert Sorrentino 7:450

Emmons, Winfred S.
Katherine Anne Porter 1:273

Engel, Bernard F.
Marianne Moore 1:227

Engel, Marian
Penelope Gilliatt 2:160
Margaret Laurence 3:278
Joyce Carol Oates 6:372
Françoise Sagan 6:481
Michel Tournier 6:537

Enright, D. J.
John Ashbery 9:49
Heinrich Böll 3:74
Anthony Burgess 4:80
Stanley Burnshaw 3:90
James Clavell 6:114
Lawrence Durrell 6:151
Witold Gombrowicz 4:195
Günter Grass 2:271; 4:202
Robert Graves 2:175
Hermann Hesse 3:243
Randall Jarrell 9:296
Yasunari Kawabata 5:206;
9:316
Milan Kundera 9:321
Philip Larkin 3:276
Doris Lessing 3:282
Czeslaw Milosz 5:291

Yukio Mishima 4:353
Vladimir Nabokov 3:352
V. S. Naipaul 4:371
Ezra Pound 3:395
Stevie Smith 3:460
C. P. Snow 9:496
Muriel Spark 3:463
John Updike 2:439

Enslin, Theodore
George Oppen 7:281

Eoff, Sherman H.
Jean-Paul Sartre 1:303
Ramón Sender 8:477

Ephron, Nora
Erich Segal 3:447

Epstein, Joseph
E. M. Forster 4:165
Joseph Heller 5:174
Alan Lelchuk 5:241
Aleksandr I. Solzhenitsyn
2:409
Stephen Spender 5:402
Edmund Wilson 2:477; 8:551

Epstein, Lawrence J.
Elie Wiesel 5:493

Ericson, Edward, Jr.
Thornton Wilder 10:533

Ericson, Edward E., Jr.
C. S. Lewis 6:310
Aleksandr I. Solzhenitsyn
4:509

Erlich, Victor
Joseph Brodsky 6:96

Eron, Carol
John Hawkes 4:218

Eskin, Stanley G.
Nicholas Delbanco 6:130

Esslin, Martin
Arthur Adamov 4:5
Edward Albee 2:4; 9:10
John Arden 6:5
Samuel Beckett 1:24; 4:52;
6:33, 44
Friedrich Dürrenmatt 4:139
Max Frisch 3:167
Jack Gelber 1:114
Jean Genet 1:117
Günter Grass 4:201
Graham Greene 9:250
Rolf Hochhuth 4:231
Eugène Ionesco 1:154; 4:252
Arthur Kopit 1:170
Slawomir Mrozek 3:344
Robert Pinget 7:306
Harold Pinter 1:268; 6:407, 414
Neil Simon 6:506
Peter Weiss 3:515

Estess, Sybil
Elizabeth Bishop 9:95

Ettin, Andrew V.
James Merrill 2:273

Evans, Don
Ed Bullins 5:82

Evans, Eli N.
James Dickey 7:86

Evans, Fallon
J. F. Powers 1:279

Evans, Oliver
Paul Bowles 1:41

Evans, Robley
J. R. R. Tolkien 3:478

Evarts, Prescott, Jr.
John Fowles 2:138

Evett, Robert
Terrence McNally 7:219
Lanford Wilson 7:548

Ewart, Gavin
William Sansom 2:383

Eyster, Warren
James Dickey 1:74

Fabre, Michel
James Baldwin 3:31
Chester Himes 2:195

Fadiman, Edwin
Laura Z. Hobson 7:163

Faery, Rebecca B.
Richard Wilbur 9:570

Fahey, James
Evan S. Connell, Jr. 4:109

Falck, Colin
A. Alvarez 5:16
John Berryman 2:55
William Empson 3:147
Geoffrey Grigson 7:136
Thom Gunn 6:220
Seamus Heaney 7:149
Ted Hughes 9:280
Philip Larkin 3:275, 276
Robert Lowell 2:245; 5:256
George MacBeth 9:340
Anne Sexton 8:483
Charles Tomlinson 2:436

Falk, Signi
Tennessee Williams 1:367

Falke, Wayne
Kenzaburō Ōe 10:372
John Updike 5:453

Fallis, Laurence S.
Ruth Prawar Jhabvala 4:259

Fallowell, Duncan
Giorgio Bassani 9:77
John Berger 2:54
William Peter Blatty 2:64
Robert Coover 3:114
Mark Helprin 7:152
Ruth Prawar Jhabvala 8:312
Jerzy Kosinski 3:274
Iris Murdoch 4:368
Tim O'Brien 7:272
Seán O'Faoláin 7:274
Mervyn Peake 7:303
David Plante 7:308
Françoise Sagan 9:468
James Salter 7:388
Hubert Selby, Jr. 2:390
Terry Southern 7:454
Muriel Spark 3:465; 8:493
Auberon Waugh 7:514

Fandel, John
E. E. Cummings 3:120

Fanger, Donald
Aleksandr I. Solzhenitsyn
1:319

Farrell, James T.
Ben Hecht 8:269

Farrell, John P.
Richard Wilbur 3:532

Farwell, Harold
John Barth 5:50

Farwell, Ruth
George Mackay Brown 5:77

Farzan, Massud
Ahmad Shamlu 10:469

Faulks, Sebastian
Yasunari Kawabata 9:316

Fawcett, Graham
Anthony Burgess 8:111

Featherstone, Joseph
Katherine Anne Porter 3:392

Feaver, William
Michael Ayrton 7:19

Feder, Lillian
Conrad Aiken 5:8
W. H. Auden 4:33, 34, 35
George Barker 8:43
Samuel Beckett 6:37
T. S. Eliot 6:160
Robert Graves 6:210
Ted Hughes 9:281
Robert Lowell 4:301
Ezra Pound 3:396; 4:414

Federman, Raymond
Samuel Beckett 9:79

Feied, Frederick
John Dos Passos 1:80
Jack Kerouac 1:166

Feifer, George
Aleksandr I. Solzhenitsyn
7:444

Fein, Richard J.
Robert Lowell 3:304

Feingold, Michael
Dannie Abse 7:2
Athol Fugard 9:235
John Guare 8:252, 253
Peter Handke 8:263
John Hopkins 4:234
Ira Levin 3:294
Miguel Piñero 4:401
Tennessee Williams 7:544

Feinstein, Elaine
Gail Godwin 8:247
William Golding 2:169
Nadine Gordimer 3:202
George MacBeth 5:265
Mary McCarthy 3:329
Grace Paley 6:339
Christina Stead 5:403

Feirstein, Frederick
Robert Graves 2:177

Feld, Michael
John Updike 2:445

Feld, Rose
Jack Spicer 8:497

Feld, Ross
Paul Blackburn 9:98
Tom Wolfe 9:578

Feldman, Anita
Irwin Shaw 7:412

Feldman, Irma P.
Helen Yglesias 7:558

Feldman, Morton
Frank O'Hara 2:322

Felheim, Marvin
Ben Hecht 8:272
Carson McCullers 1:208
Eudora Welty 1:361

Felstiner, John
Pablo Neruda 1:247; 2:309;
5:302

Fender, Stephen
John Sayles 10:462

Fenton, James
W. H. Auden 6:18
Giorgio Bassani 9:76
Douglas Dunn 6:148
Charles Tomlinson 6:534

Ferguson, Alan
Ivo Andrić 8:20

Ferguson, Frances
Robert Lowell 4:302

Ferguson, Suzanne
Djuna Barnes 3:36
Randall Jarrell 2:209

Fernandez, Jaime
Jun'ichiro Tanizaki 8:511

Ferrari, Margaret
Marge Piercy 6:402

Ferrer, Olga Prjevalinskaya
Eugène Ionesco 6:256

Ferrier, Carole
Diane Wakoski 7:505

Ferry, David
Theodore Roethke 1:291

Fetherling, Doug
Mordecai Richler 3:431

Feuer, Kathryn B.
Aleksandr I. Solzhenitsyn
7:445

Feuser, Willfried F.
Chinua Achebe 7:6

Fickert, Kurt J.
Friedrich Dürrenmatt 4:139

Fiedler, Leslie A.
John Barth 3:38
Saul Bellow 1:27, 31; 3:48
Leonard Cohen 3:109
Bob Dylan 3:130
William Faulkner 1:101; 3:149
Allen Ginsberg 2:162; 3:193
John Hawkes 3:221
Ernest Hemingway 1:143;
3:232, 233
John Hersey 7:153
Randall Jarrell 1:160
Robert Lowell 2:246
Norman Mailer 3:311
Bernard Malamud 9:341, 351
Henry Miller 2:282
Alberto Moravia 2:293
Wright Morris 1:232
Vladimir Nabokov 1:239
Ezra Pound 7:329
John Crowe Ransom 2:363
Mordecai Richler 5:375
Henry Roth 6:470

CRITIC INDEX

CRITIC INDEX

Robert Penn Warren 4:579
Richard Wilbur 3:530
Herman Wouk 1:376

Field, Andrew
Vladimir Nabokov 1:242
Yevgeny Yevtushenko 1:382

Field, George Wallis
Hermann Hesse 1:147

Field, Joyce and Leslie Field
Bernard Malamud 9:348

Field, Leslie and Joyce Field
Bernard Malamud 9:348

Fields, Beverly
Anne Sexton 2:391

Fields, Kenneth
J. V. Cunningham 3:121
Robert Lowell 4:299
N. Scott Momaday 2:290
Marya Zaturenska 6:585

Filer, Malva E.
Julio Cortázar 10:117

Fincke, Gary
Ben Hecht 8:271

Finger, Louis
John Le Carré 9:326

Finholt, Richard
James Dickey 10:142

Finkle, David
John Fowles 9:215

Finley, M. I.
Michael Ayrton 7:17

Finn, James
François Mauriac 4:339
P. G. Wodehouse 2:480

Firchow, Peter
Aldous Huxley 8:305

Fireside, Harvey
Andrei Sinyavsky 8:489, 490

Firestone, Bruce M.
Anthony Burgess 10:89

Fisch, Harold
Aharon Megged 9:374

Fischer, John Irwin
Brosman, Catharine Savage
9:135

Fisher, Emma
John Berryman 10:47

Fisher, William J.
William Saroyan 8:466

Fitzgerald, Robert
Seamus Heaney 7:151

Fitzlyon, Kyril
Aleksandr I. Solzhenitsyn
1:321

Fixler, Michael
Isaac Bashevis Singer 1:311

Flaherty, Joe
Richard Brautigan 9:124

Flamm, Dudley
Robert M. Pirsig 4:404

Flanders, Jane
Katherine Anne Porter 10:396

Flanner, Janet
André Malraux 4:326

Fleischer, Leonard
John A. Williams 5:496

Fleishman, Avrom
John Fowles 9:210

Fleming, Robert E.
John A. Williams 5:496

Fleming, Thomas J.
Ira Levin 6:305

Fletcher, John
Uwe Johnson 5:201
Kamala Markandaya 8:377
Jean-Paul Sartre 7:398

Flint, R. W.
A. R. Ammons 8:15; 9:29
Irving Feldman 7:102
Anthony Hecht 8:267
Randall Jarrell 1:159
Karl Shapiro 8:486

Floan, Howard R.
William Saroyan 1:301

Flood, Jeanne
Brian Moore 5:294

Flora, Joseph M.
Vardis Fisher 7:103
Günter Grass 6:209
J. E. Wideman 5:490
Nancy Willard 7:539

Flower, Dean
Hubert Selby, Jr. 8:477
Helen Yglesias 7:559

Flowers, Betty
Donald Barthelme 5:56

Fontenot, Chester J.
Alex Haley 8:260

Foote, Audrey C.
Anthony Burgess 4:81
Nathalie Sarraute 2:386
Christina Stead 5:404
Mary Stewart 7:468

Foote, Timothy
W. H. Auden 3:26; 6:24
Anthony Burgess 5:89
Peter De Vries 2:114
John Gardner 3:187
John Le Carré 5:232
V. S. Pritchett 5:352
Aleksandr I. Solzhenitsyn
4:516
Tom Stoppard 4:525
Tom Wolfe 2:481

Ford, Richard J.
Hermann Hesse 2:189

Forrest, Alan
W. H. Auden 3:27
Mario Puzo 2:352

Fortin, René E.
Boris Pasternak 7:296

Foster, David W.
Camilo José Cela 4:96

Foster, David William
Jorge Luis Borges 3:78; 6:89
Julio Cortázar 10:118
Ernesto Sábato 10:445

Foster, John Wilson
Seamus Heaney 5:170
Brian Moore 1:225

Foster, Richard
Norman Mailer 1:190; 8:365

Foster, Ruel E.
Jesse Stuart 1:328

Fowlie, Wallace
Michel Butor 8:119
René Char 9:158
Jean Genet 5:135
Henri Michaux 8:392
Anaïs Nin 4:378
Jules Romains 7:379

Fox, Hugh
William Carlos Williams 5:509

Fox-Genovese, Elizabeth
William Gaddis 8:226

Frakes, James R.
Nelson Algren 4:17
Wendell Berry 4:59
Bruce Jay Friedman 5:127
Patricia Highsmith 2:194
Stanley Hoffman 5:185
Diane Johnson 5:198
Michael Mewshaw 9:376
Muriel Spark 2:418
Richard G. Stern 4:522

Francescato, Martha Paley
Julio Cortázar 10:116

Frank, Armin Paul
Kenneth Burke 2:89

Frank, Joseph
Djuna Barnes 8:47
André Malraux 4:327
Aleksandr I. Solzhenitsyn
7:443

Frank, Sheldon
Margaret Laurence 6:289
Hans Erich Nossack 6:365

Frankel, Haskel
Bruce Jay Friedman 3:165
Muriel Spark 2:417
Peter Ustinov 1:346
Charles Webb 7:514

Franklin, Allan and Paul M. Levitt
Jorge Luis Borges 9:116

Franklin, H. Bruce
J. G. Ballard 3:32

Fraser, G. S.
Basil Bunting 10:86
Robert Creeley 1:67
C. Day Lewis 6:127
Nigel Dennis 8:172
Lawrence Durrell 4:145
Jean Garrigue 2:153
Randall Jarrell 9:296
Robert Lowell 2:249
W. S. Merwin 1:214
C. P. Snow 4:502
Gary Snyder 1:318
Louis Zukofsky 1:385

Fraser, John
Louis-Ferdinand Céline 1:56;
4:102
Yvor Winters 4:592; 8:552

Fraser, Kathleen
Adrienne Rich 3:429

Fredeman, W. E.
Earle Birney 6:72

Freedman, Ralph
Saul Bellow 1:29
Hermann Hesse 1:146

Freedman, Richard
Hortense Calisher 2:96
Dick Francis 2:142
Lois Gould 4:199
S. J. Perelman 9:416
P. G. Wodehouse 5:517

Fremantle, Anne
W. H. Auden 1:10
Auberon Waugh 7:513

Fremont-Smith, Eliot
Richard Adams 4:6
Martin Amis 4:20
Max Apple 9:33
Louis Auchincloss 4:31
E. L. Doctorow 6:132
Lawrence Durrell 6:152
Gael Greene 8:252
Joseph Heller 5:173
Lillian Hellman 4:221
Marjorie Kellogg 2:223
Jascha Kessler 4:269
Arthur Koestler 3:271
Jerzy Kosinski 1:172
John Le Carré 9:327
Alan Lelchuk 5:243
Norman Mailer 4:322
James A. Michener 5:289
Richard Price 6:426
Philip Roth 4:453, 455
Alix Kates Shulman 10:476
Gore Vidal 6:54
Irving Wallace 7:510
Patrick White 3:524

French, Philip
Jorge Luis Borges 4:75
Truman Capote 8:132
Graham Greene 3:212; 6:220

French, Robert W.
Joyce Carol Oates 1:251

French, Warren
William Goldman 1:123
R. K. Narayan 7:254
James Purdy 2:349
J. D. Salinger 1:297
John Steinbeck 1:324; 5:406
Thornton Wilder 1:366

Friar, Kimon
Yannis Ritsos 6:463
Vassilis Vassilikos 8:524

Friedberg, Maurice
Aleksandr I. Solzhenitsyn
1:319; 7:435

Friedenberg, Edgar Z.
Hermann Hesse 2:190

Friedman, Alan
William S. Burroughs 5:93
John Gardner 7:112
Yukio Mishima 4:357
Amos Oz 8:435
Ishmael Reed 2:367
André Schwarz-Bart 2:389
Elie Wiesel 3:528

Friedman, Alan J. and Manfred Puetz
Thomas Pynchon 6:434

Friedman, Alan Warren
Saul Bellow **8**:69
Lawrence Durrell **1**:87
Bernard Malamud **8**:375

Friedman, Jack
Wendell Berry **4**:59
José Lezama Lima **4**:290

Friedman, John
William Eastlake **8**:200

Friedman, Melvin J.
Bruce Jay Friedman **5**:127
Eugène Ionesco **6**:256
André Malraux **4**:333
R. K. Narayan **7**:255
Flannery O'Connor **1**:253
Isaac Bashevis Singer **1**:313

Friedman, Norman
E. E. Cummings **1**:69
David Ignatow **7**:174

Frohock, W. M.
Erskine Caldwell **1**:51
James Gould Cozzens **4**:113
John Dos Passos **1**:77
James T. Farrell **1**:97
William Faulkner **1**:99
Ernest Hemingway **1**:141
André Malraux **4**:324
John Steinbeck **1**:323
Robert Penn Warren **1**:351

Frost, Lucy
John Hawkes **3**:223

Fruchtbaum, Harold
Loren Eiseley **7**:90

Fryer, Jonathan H.
Christopher Isherwood **9**:292

Fuchs, Daniel
Saul Bellow **3**:62

Fuchs, Vivian
Thomas Keneally **10**:299

Fulford, Robert
Brian Moore **3**:340
Mordecai Richler **3**:429
Philip Roth **3**:435

Fuller, Edmund
Paul Bowles **1**:41
Frederick Buechner **4**:80
James Gould Cozzens **1**:65
James Jones **1**:161
Jack Kerouac **1**:165
Alan Paton **4**:395
J. R. R. Tolkien **1**:335
Herman Wouk **1**:375

Fuller, Elizabeth Ely
Isak Dinesen **10**:150

Fuller, John
Thom Gunn **3**:215
Randall Jarrell **2**:208
William Plomer **4**:406
Ann Quin **6**:441
Kathleen Raine **7**:353
Jon Silkin **6**:499
Andrew Young **5**:523

Fuller, Roy
W. H. Auden **3**:25
Aldous Huxley **5**:192
Stephen Spender **2**:420
Lionel Trilling **9**:530

Fulton, Robin
Pär Lagerkvist **10**:313

Furbank, P. N.
E. M. Forster **4**:165, 168
Uwe Johnson **10**:284
Gore Vidal **4**:556

Fussell, B. H.
Peter Taylor **4**:543

Fussell, Edwin
Wendell Berry **6**:61
Hayden Carruth **7**:40

Fussell, Paul
Thomas Keneally **8**:318

Fussell, Paul, Jr.
Karl Shapiro **4**:486

Fytton, Francis
Paul Bowles **2**:78

Gadney, Reg
George V. Higgins **7**:158
Patricia Highsmith **2**:194
Ross Macdonald **2**:257
Alistair MacLean **3**:309

Gaines, Richard H.
Chester Himes **2**:196

Gaiser, Carolyn
Gregory Corso **1**:63

Galassi, Jonathan
John Berryman **6**:63
Robert Duncan **2**:123
Robert Graves **6**:212
Seamus Heaney **7**:147
Randall Jarrell **9**:297
Eugenio Montale **7**:231
Howard Nemerov **9**:396

Galbraith, John Kenneth
William Safire **10**:446

Gall, Sally M.
Eleanor Lerman **9**:329
Charles Wright **6**:580

Gallagher, D. P.
Adolfo Bioy Casares **8**:94
Jorge Luis Borges **6**:88
Gabriel García Márquez **8**:230
G. Cabrera Infante **5**:96
Pablo Neruda **7**:257
Octavio Paz **6**:394
Manuel Puig **10**:420
Mario Vargas Llosa **6**:543

Gallagher, David
G. Cabrera Infante **5**:95
Manuel Puig **3**:407

Gallagher, Michael
Shusaku Endo **7**:95

Gallant, Mavis
Simone de Beauvoir **4**:48
Louis-Ferdinand Céline **7**:46
Günter Grass **4**:205
Vladimir Nabokov **2**:303

Galler, David
Ted Hughes **2**:198
Howard Nemerov **2**:307

Galligan, Edward L.
Georges Simenon **1**:309

Galloway, David D.
Saul Bellow **3**:51, 55
Stanley Elkin **4**:152

Dan Jacobson **4**:253
J. D. Salinger **3**:445
William Styron **3**:473
John Updike **3**:486

Gannon, Edward, S.J.
André Malraux **4**:326

Gant, Lisbeth
Ed Bullins **5**:82

Ganz, Arthur
Harold Pinter **6**:416

Ganz, Earl
John Hawkes **1**:139
Flannery O'Connor **2**:318

Gardner, Erle Stanley
Meyer Levin **7**:203

Gardner, Harvey
Jimmy Breslin **4**:76

Gardner, John
Saul Bellow **10**:44
Anthony Burgess **2**:84
Italo Calvino **8**:129
John Fowles **9**:215
William H. Gass **1**:114
John Knowles **4**:271
Brian Moore **8**:395
Charles Newman **8**:419
Walker Percy **8**:442
Philip Roth **2**:379
Patrick White **9**:567
Larry Woiwode **6**:578

Gardner, Peter
John Hersey **9**:277

Gardner, Philip
D. J. Enright **4**:155
Philip Larkin **5**:230

Garebian, Keith
Patrick White **9**:563

Garfitt, Roger
George Barker **8**:46
Joseph Brodsky **6**:96
Robert Creeley **4**:118
Douglas Dunn **6**:148
Geoffrey Grigson **7**:136
Anna Kavan **5**:206
Reiner Kunze **10**:310
Philip Larkin **8**:332
George MacBeth **5**:263
László Nagy **7**:251
Julia O'Faolain **6**:383
Peter Porter **5**:346
Thomas Pynchon **3**:418
Peter Redgrove **6**:445
C. H. Sisson **8**:490
Anne Stevenson **7**:462
Derek Walcott **4**:575

Garis, Leslie
Doris Lessing **6**:302

Garis, Robert
Herbert Gold **4**:191
Anthony Powell **3**:400

Garnick, Vivian
Toni Morrison **10**:355

Garrard, J. G.
Aleksandr I. Solzhenitsyn
2:411; **9**:503

Garrett, George
John Cheever **3**:107

Sue Kaufman **8**:317
Wright Morris **3**:342

Garrigue, Jean
Marianne Moore **1**:228

Garson, Helen S.
John Hawkes **9**:268

Gasque, Thomas J.
J. R. R. Tolkien **1**:337

Gass, William H.
Donald Barthelme **3**:43
Jorge Luis Borges **3**:76
Robert Coover **3**:113
Vladimir Nabokov **3**:351
J. F. Powers **1**:281
Philip Roth **3**:437
Isaac Bashevis Singer **3**:454
Susan Sontag **10**:484

Gassner, John
Edward Albee **3**:6, 7
Jean Anouilh **3**:11, 12
Samuel Beckett **3**:44, 45
Brendan Behan **8**:63
Lillian Hellman **4**:220
William Inge **8**:307
Eugène Ionesco **4**:250
Archibald MacLeish **3**:310
Arthur Miller **6**:330
John Osborne **5**:330
Harold Pinter **3**:386
Thornton Wilder **5**:495
Tennessee Williams **5**:498, 500

Gates, David
Samuel Beckett **9**:83

Gathorne-Hardy, J.
Vladimir Nabokov **3**:354

Gavin, William
Auberon Waugh **7**:514

Gayle, Addison, Jr.
Gwendolyn Brooks **1**:46

Geddes, Gary
Raymond Souster **5**:395

Geering, R. G.
Christina Stead **2**:423

Geherin, David J.
Joan Didion **8**:173

Geismar, Maxwell
Nelson Algren **4**:16
John Beecher **6**:48
Saul Bellow **1**:27
James Gould Cozzens **1**:66
John Dos Passos **1**:77
William Faulkner **1**:100
Nadine Gordimer **5**:146
Ernest Hemingway **1**:142
John Hersey **1**:144
Norman Mailer **1**:187
Henry Miller **4**:350
Henry Roth **6**:471
J. D. Salinger **1**:295
William Styron **1**:329
Leon Uris **7**:490
Herman Wouk **1**:376

Gelfant, Blanche H.
Yasunari Kawabata **9**:316
Jack Kerouac **5**:213
Jean Stafford **7**:459

Gellatly, Peter
C. Day Lewis 6:128

Gelpi, Albert
Adrienne Rich 6:457

Geltman, Max
Arthur Koestler 8:325
Ezra Pound 5:349; 7:338

Geng, Veronica
Nadine Gordimer 5:148

George, Diana L.
Lionel Trilling 9:532

George, Michael
J. B. Priestley 5:350

Gerald, John Bart
Robert Lowell 3:302
Robert Stone 5:411

Gerould, Daniel C.
Tadeusz Różewicz 9:463

Gerrard, Charlotte F.
Eugène Ionesco 9:286

Gerstenberger, Donna
Iris Murdoch 6:348

Gertel, Zunilda
José Donoso 4:128
Juan Carlos Onetti 7:278

Giannaris, George
Vassilis Vassilikos 8:524

Gibbs, Beverly J.
Juan Carlos Onetti 10:374

Gibbs, Robert
Margaret Avison 2:29

Gibian, George
Aleksandr I. Solzhenitsyn
7:447

Gibson, Donald B.
James Baldwin 3:32
Imamu Amiri Baraka 5:46
Ralph Ellison 3:143
Langston Hughes 5:19

Giddings, Paula
Margaret Walker 1:351

Gide, André
Pär Lagerkvist 7:199

Gidley, Mick
William Faulkner 3:156

Gifford, Henry
Marianne Moore 4:361

Gilbert, Sandra M.
Jean Garrigue 8:239
Sandra Hochman 8:297
Diane Johnson 5:200
Kenneth Koch 8:323
Eleanor Lerman 9:329
Anne Sexton 4:484
Kathleen Spivack 6:521
Diane Wakoski 9:554

Gilbert, W. Stephen
Peter Handke 5:163
J. B. Priestley 5:350
David Storey 5:416

Gilbert, Zack
Leon Forrest 4:164

Giles, Mary E.
Juan Goytisolo 10:243

Gill, Brendan
Edward Albee 5:12
Alan Ayckbourn 5:36; 8:34
John Bishop 10:54
Anne Burr 6:104
D. L. Coburn 10:107
Noel Coward 9:172, 173
Charles Gordone 1:125
Bill Gunn 5:152
John Hopkins 4:233
James Kirkwood 9:319
Preston Jones 10:296
Ira Levin 6:306
David Mamet 9:360
Terrence McNally 7:219
Arthur Miller 6:334
Peter Nichols 5:307
Clifford Odets 2:319
John O'Hara 6:385
Ronald Ribman 7:358
William Saroyan 8:468
Murray Schisgal 6:490
Peter Shaffer 5:386
Neil Simon 6:505
John Steinbeck 5:408
Tom Stoppard 4:526; 5:413;
8:504
David Storey 2:424
Gore Vidal 2:449
Tennessee Williams 5:503;
8:548
Lanford Wilson 7:547
Robert Wilson 7:550

Gillen, Francis
Donald Barthelme 2:40

Gillespie, Robert
Eric Ambler 6:2
John Le Carré 9:326
Jorge Luis Borges 6:91

Gilliatt, Penelope
Samuel Beckett 4:49
Noel Coward 9:172
Joe Orton 4:387

Gilman, Harvey
Howard Nemerov 6:362

Gilman, Richard
Richard Adams 4:7
Edward Albee 5:10
John Arden 6:6
Imamu Amiri Baraka 5:44
Donald Barthelme 2:40
Saul Bellow 6:49
J. P. Donleavy 6:140
Bruce Jay Friedman 5:126
William H. Gass 2:154
Jack Gelber 1:114; 6:196
Graham Greene 6:214
Eugène Ionesco 6:249
Kenneth Koch 5:218
Norman Mailer 2:260; 8:367
Michael McClure 10:331
Arthur Miller 6:326, 327
Sean O'Casey 5:319
Harold Pinter 6:405, 406, 410
Reynolds Price 6:424
John Rechy 7:356
Philip Roth 3:438
Robert Shaw 5:390
Neil Simon 6:502
John Updike 2:440
Tennessee Williams 5:499

Gilsdorf, Jeanette
Robert Creeley 4:118

Gindin, James
Kingsley Amis 2:4
Saul Bellow 3:54
Truman Capote 3:100
Margaret Drabble 10:165
E. M. Forster 3:160
John Fowles 10:189
William Golding 2:165; 3:198
Rosamond Lehmann 5:238
Doris Lessing 2:238
Iris Murdoch 2:295; 3:347
John Osborne 2:327
Philip Roth 3:436
Alan Sillitoe 3:447, 448
David Storey 2:423; 4:528
John Wain 2:457
Angus Wilson 2:470; 3:534

Gingher, Robert S.
John Updike 5:454

Gingrich, Arnold
Chester Himes 2:196

Ginsberg, Allen
Jack Kerouac 2:228

Giovanni, Nikki
Alice Walker 5:476

Gipson, Carolyn and Harold W. Cruse
W. E. B. Du Bois 2:120

Girson, Rochelle
Peter S. Beagle 7:25

Gitlin, Todd
James Baldwin 2:32
Robert Bly 2:66
Bob Dylan 4:150
Paul Goodman 7:130
Denise Levertov 2:243
Marge Piercy 3:383

Gitzen, Julian
Robert Bly 10:56
Seamus Heaney 5:172
Ted Hughes 4:237
Denise Levertov 5:250
Peter Redgrove 6:446
R. S. Thomas 6:531
Charles Tomlinson 2:437; 4:548

Givner, Joan
Katherine Anne Porter 7:319;
10:398
Eudora Welty 5:479

Glasser, William
J. D. Salinger 8:464

Glassman, Peter
Shirley Ann Grau 9:240

Glatstein, Jacob
Marianne Moore 4:358

Gleason, Judith Illsley
Chinua Achebe 7:3

Gleason, Ralph J.
Nelson Algren 10:7
Bob Dylan 6:156

Gleicher, David
Margaret Atwood 3:19

Glen, Duncan
Hugh MacDiarmid 4:311

Glendinning, Victoria
Melvyn Bragg 10:72
Anthony Burgess 5:87
Angela Carter 5:101
Roald Dahl 6:122
Chester Himes 7:159
Russell C. Hoban 7:160
Elizabeth Jane Howard 7:164
Françoise Sagan 9:468
Alan Sillitoe 6:500
J. I. M. Stewart 7:466

Glenn, Jerry
Paul Celan 10:102, 104

Glicksberg, Charles I.
Arthur Adamov 4:6
Albert Camus 1:52
Jean Genet 5:136
Hermann Hesse 3:244
Aldous Huxley 3:254
Eugène Ionesco 9:288
Robinson Jeffers 3:260
André Malraux 1:201

Glimm, James York
Thomas Merton 3:337

Glover, Al
Michael McClure 6:320

Glover, Elaine
John Fowles 6:188
Nadine Gordimer 7:131
Joseph Heller 8:279
Tim O'Brien 7:271

Glover, Willis B.
J. R. R. Tolkien 1:340

Goddard, Donald
Lothar-Günther Buchheim
6:102

Godshalk, William L.
Kurt Vonnegut, Jr. 3:500

Godwin, Gail
Beryl Bainbridge 5:39
Julien Green 3:205

Goitein, Denise
Nathalie Sarraute 10:457

Gold, Herbert
Richard Condon 10:111
John Dos Passos 4:136
Aleksandr I. Solzhenitsyn
2:409
Terry Southern 7:454
Gore Vidal 6:550

Gold, Ivan
George V. Higgins 10:273
Paul Horgan 9:279
John Updike 2:440
Helen Yglesias 7:558

Goldberg, Steven
Bob Dylan 6:154

Golden, Robert E.
Thomas Pynchon 3:409

Goldensohn, Lorrie
Ira Sadoff 9:466
Maura Stanton 9:508

Goldfarb, Clare R.
Aleksandr I. Solzhenitsyn
7:443

Goldman, Albert
Bob Dylan 3:130

Goldman, Mark
  Bernard Malamud 1:197

Goldman, Michael
  Joyce Carol Oates 3:361

Goldman, William
  Ross Macdonald 1:185

Goldsmith, Arnold L.
  John Steinbeck 9:515

Goldsmith, David H.
  Kurt Vonnegut, Jr. 4:562

Goldstein, Laurence
  David Ignatow 4:248
  Adrienne Rich 7:372
  James Wright 3:541

Goldstein, Malcolm
  Thornton Wilder 1:365

Goldstein, Richard
  Bob Dylan 3:130

Goldstone, Richard H.
  Thornton Wilder 6:574

Golffing, Francis
  Salvatore Quasimodo 10:429

Gömöri, George
  László Nagy 7:251

Goodheart, Eugene
  Cynthia Ozick 3:372
  Theodore Roethke 1:292
  John Seelye 7:405
  William Carlos Williams 5:510

Goodman, James
  George Seferis 5:385

Goodman, Paul
  Ernest Hemingway 1:144

Goodman, Robert L.
  David Kherdian 6:280

Goodman, Walter
  Thomas Berger 8:83

Goodrich, Norma L.
  Jean Giono 4:187

Goodstein, Jack
  Alain Robbe-Grillet 2:376

Goodwin, Michael
  John Brunner 10:80

Goodwin, Stephen
  Walker Percy 2:335
  Peter Taylor 1:334

Gordimer, Nadine
  Chinua Achebe 3:2
  V. S. Naipaul 4:372
  James Ngugi 3:358

Gordon, Andrew
  Ishmael Reed 2:368

Gordon, David J.
  Herbert Gold 4:192
  William Golding 1:122
  Uwe Johnson 5:200
  Brian Moore 1:225
  Vladimir Nabokov 1:245
  Tom Stoppard 1:328

Gordon, Jan B.
  Richard Adams 5:4
  John Braine 3:86
  Doris Lessing 6:292
  Iris Murdoch 3:349

Gornick, Vivian
  Paula Fox 2:140
  Lillian Hellman 8:282
  Grace Paley 4:391

Gossett, Louise Y.
  Flannery O'Connor 1:256

Gossman, Ann
  Lawrence Durrell 1:87

Gottfried, Martin
  Lanford Wilson 7:547

Gottlieb, Annie
  Henry Bromell 5:74
  Louis-Ferdinand Céline 4:104
  Lois Gould 10:241
  Charles Johnson 7:183
  Tillie Olsen 4:386

Gottlieb, Elaine
  Isaac Bashevis Singer 6:507

Gould, Jean
  Elmer Rice 7:363

Goulianos, Joan Rodman
  Lawrence Durrell 8:193

Goyen, William
  Anaïs Nin 4:379

Goytisolo, Juan
  Carlos Fuentes 10:204

Graff, Gerald
  Donald Barthelme 6:30
  Saul Bellow 6:54
  Stanley Elkin 6:169
  Norman Mailer 8:372

Graham, Desmond
  Jorge Luis Borges 8:103
  Philip Larkin 5:229
  Eugenio Montale 9:388

Graham, John
  John Hawkes 3:221
  Ernest Hemingway 3:236
  Gibbons Ruark 3:441

Graham, Kenneth
  Richard Adams 5:5
  Laurens van der Post 5:463

Grande, Brother Luke M., F.S.C.
  Marion Montgomery 7:232

Grant, Annette
  Shirley Ann Grau 4:209

Grant, Damian
  W. H. Auden 6:17
  Seamus Heaney 5:172
  Sylvia Plath 2:337
  Peter Porter 5:347

Grau, Shirley Ann
  William Goyen 8:250
  Marion Montgomery 7:233

Graver, Lawrence
  Samuel Beckett 6:40
  Doris Lessing 2:242
  Carson McCullers 1:209
  Iris Murdoch 3:347
  Muriel Spark 2:417
  Paul Theroux 8:513
  William Trevor 7:475

Graves, Robert
  Yevgeny Yevtushenko 1:382

Gray, James
  Pearl S. Buck 7:32
  Jules Romains 7:381

Gray, John
  Paul Bowles 2:79

Gray, Paul
  Lisa Alther 7:12
  Samuel Beckett 6:44
  Adolfo Bioy Casares 8:94
  Vance Bourjaily 8:104
  Jimmy Breslin 4:76
  William F. Buckley, Jr. 7:35
  Alex Comfort 7:54
  Evan S. Connell, Jr. 6:116
  Peter De Vries 7:78
  Thomas M. Disch 7:86
  John Gardner 5:132
  William H. Gass 8:246
  Russell C. Hoban 7:160
  Maureen Howard 5:189
  Elia Kazan 6:274
  Peter Matthiessen 5:274
  V. S. Naipaul 7:253
  Seán O'Faoláin 7:274
  Cynthia Ozick 7:288
  Reynolds Price 6:425
  Robert Stone 5:409
  John Updike 5:457
  James Welch 6:561
  Fay Weldon 6:562

Gray, Paul Edward
  John Fowles 1:109
  Iris Murdoch 1:236
  Joyce Carol Oates 1:251
  Eudora Welty 1:363

Gray, Ronald
  Heinrich Böll 9:112

Greacen, Robert
  W. H. Auden 3:25
  Samuel Beckett 4:50
  Margaret Drabble 2:117
  Bernard Kops 4:274
  Doris Lessing 3:287
  Harold Robbins 5:378
  Isaac Bashevis Singer 3:457
  Vassilis Vassilikos 4:551

Grebanier, Bernard
  Thornton Wilder 1:365

Grebstein, Sheldon Norman
  Ernest Hemingway 3:235
  John O'Hara 1:261

Green, Alan
  Peter De Vries 3:126
  Michael Frayn 3:164

Green, Benny
  John Fowles 6:186
  Brian Moore 7:238
  John O'Hara 6:383

Green, Gerald
  Thomas Berger 3:63

Green, Martin
  E. L. Doctorow 6:138
  B. S. Johnson 6:263
  J. D. Salinger 1:298

Green, Randall
  John Hawkes 4:217
  Aleksandr I. Solzhenitsyn 4:512

Green, Robert J.
  Athol Fugard 9:233

Greenberg, Martin
  Reiner Kunze 10:310

Greene, Daniel
  Don L. Lee 2:237

Greene, George
  Paul West 7:522

Greene, James
  Eugenio Montale 9:388

Greene, Robert W.
  Raymond Queneau 10:430

Greenfeld, Josh
  Philip Roth 2:378
  Paul Zindel 6:586

Greenfield, Jeff
  Dan Wakefield 7:503

Greenman, Myron
  Donald Barthelme 6:29

Greenway, John
  Norman Mailer 2:262

Greenya, John
  Budd Schulberg 7:403

Gregor, Ian and Brian Nicholas
  Graham Greene 6:214

Gregory, Hilda
  Joyce Carol Oates 1:251; 2:315
  Mark Strand 6:522
  Nancy Willard 7:540

Gregory, Horace and Marya Zaturenska
  Laura Riding 7:373

Greider, William
  William Safire 10:447

Greiner, Donald J.
  Djuna Barnes 8:48
  Frederick Busch 10:91
  John Hawkes 1:138; 4:213; 7:145
  Kurt Vonnegut, Jr. 3:499

Grella, George
  Ian Fleming 3:158

Griffin, Robert J.
  Cid Corman 9:169

Griffith, Albert J.
  Carson McCullers 1:209
  Peter Taylor 1:334; 4:542
  John Updike 5:455

Grigsby, Gordon K.
  Kenneth Rexroth 1:284

Grigson, Geoffrey
  Robert Lowell 3:302
  Kathleen Raine 7:351

Griswold, Jerry
  Ken Kesey 3:268

Groden, Michael
  William Faulkner 9:198

Gropper, Esther C.
  Hermann Hesse 2:189; 3:244

Gross, Barry
  Arthur Miller 10:344

Gross, Beverly
  Jonathan Baumbach 6:32
  Saul Bellow 2:52

B. H. Friedman 7:109
Peter Spielberg 6:514

Gross, Harvey
T. S. Eliot 6:161
André Malraux 4:335
Ezra Pound 4:414

Gross, Theodore L.
J. D. Salinger 1:300

Grosskurth, Phyllis
Margaret Atwood 2:20

Grossman, Edward
Simone de Beauvoir 2:44
Saul Bellow 8:80
Thomas Berger 3:63
Heinrich Böll 3:75
Joseph Heller 5:181
Doris Lessing 3:287
Vladimir Nabokov 3:355
Kurt Vonnegut, Jr. 5:466

Grossman, Joel
Philip Roth 9:459

Grossvogel, David I.
Julio Cortázar 10:112

Groth, Janet
John Cheever 8:136

Groves, Margaret
Nathalie Sarraute 4:470

Grumbach, Doris
Simone de Beauvoir 4:49
Kay Boyle 5:66
Hortense Calisher 8:124
Arthur A. Cohen 7:50
Joan Didion 8:175
E. L. Doctorow 6:131
Stanley Elkin 4:154
Susan B. Hill 4:288
Maureen Howard 5:188
Alison Lurie 4:307
Cormac McCarthy 4:342
Mary McCarthy 5:276
A. G. Mojtabai 9:385
Brian Moore 5:297
Penelope Mortimer 5:299
Julia O'Faolain 6:383
Judith Rossner 9:457
J. R. Salamanca 4:461
May Sarton 4:471
Clancy Sigal 7:425
Anne Tyler 7:479
Nancy Willard 7:538, 539
Sol Yurick 6:584

Guerard, Albert J.
Donald Barthelme 5:53
Jerome Charyn 5:103
John Hawkes 2:183; 3:222

Guerrard, Philip
Mervyn Peake 7:301

Guicharnaud, Jacques
Eugène Ionesco 6:254
Jean-Paul Sartre 1:304

Guimond, James
Gilbert Sorrentino 3:461

Guiton, Margaret Otis and Germaine Brée
Louis Aragon 3:12
Albert Camus 1:54
Louis-Ferdinand Céline 1:57
Jean Cocteau 1:59

Georges Duhamel 8:186
Jean Giono 4:183
Julien Green 3:203
André Malraux 1:202
François Mauriac 4:337
Raymond Queneau 2:359
Jules Romains 7:381
Jean-Paul Sartre 1:306

Gullason, Thomas A.
Carson McCullers 4:344
Flannery O'Connor 1:259

Gullon, Agnes
Pablo Neruda 7:260

Gunn, Edward
Djuna Barnes 4:44

Gunn, Thom
David Ignatow 7:173
Howard Nemerov 9:393
Louis Simpson 7:426, 427

Gurewitsch, M. Anatole
William Gaddis 6:195

Gurko, Leo
Ernest Hemingway 6:226
John P. Marquand 10:331
Edward Lewis Wallant 5:477

Gussow, Mel
Ed Bullins 1:47
Charles Gordone 1:125

Gustafson, Richard
Reg Saner 9:469

Gwynn, Frederick L. and Joseph L. Blotner
J. D. Salinger 1:295

Gyurko, Lanin A.
Julio Cortázar 5:108; 10:112

Haas, Joseph
Jerome Weidman 7:517

Haberl, Franz P.
Max Frisch 9:218

Hack, Richard
Kenneth Patchen 2:332
Colin Wilson 3:537

Hadas, Pamela White
Marianne Moore 10:348

Haenicke, Diether H.
Heinrich Böll 6:83
Paul Celan 10:101
Friedrich Dürrenmatt 8:194
Max Frisch 9:217
Günter Grass 6:207
Uwe Johnson 5:201
Reiner Kunze 10:310
Anna Seghers 7:408

Haffenden, John
John Berryman 10:45

Haft, Cynthia
Aleksandr I. Solzhenitsyn 7:435

Hagopian, John V.
James Baldwin 1:15
William Faulkner 3:157
J. F. Powers 1:282

Hague, René
David Jones 7:189

Hahn, Claire
William Everson 5:122
Jean Garrigue 8:239

Hale, Nancy
Jessamyn West 7:522

Hales, David
Berry Morgan 6:340

Halio, Jay L.
William Gaddis 10:212
John Gardner 10:220
Ernest Hemingway 6:230
Mary McCarthy 5:276
Isaac Bashevis Singer 1:314; 6:509
C. P. Snow 6:517
Aleksandr I. Solzhenitsyn 7:434
Alice Walker 5:476

Hall, Donald
Allen Ginsberg 3:195
Rod McKuen 3:333
Marianne Moore 4:362

Hall, James
Saul Bellow 3:50
Elizabeth Bowen 3:82
William Faulkner 3:152
Graham Greene 3:207
Iris Murdoch 2:296
J. D. Salinger 3:444
Robert Penn Warren 4:577

Hall, James B.
Mario Puzo 1:282

Hall, Joan Joffe
Wendell Berry 4:59
Marie-Claire Blais 6:81
Shirley Ann Grau 4:210
Ursula K. Le Guin 8:342
Robert Stone 5:410
John Updike 5:458

Hall, John
Gary Snyder 1:318

Hall, Linda B.
Carlos Fuentes 8:222
Gabriel García Márquez 10:214

Hall, Richard W.
Ezra Pound 5:348

Hall, Stephen
R. H. W. Dillard 5:116

Haller, Robert S.
Alan Sillitoe 6:500

Halliday, Mark
Eleanor Lerman 9:329

Halpern, Daniel
David Wagoner 5:475

Hamill, Pete
Seán O'Faoláin 7:272
Leon Uris 7:492

Hamill, Sam
Greg Kuzma 7:197

Hamilton, Alice and Kenneth Hamilton
Samuel Beckett 10:31
John Updike 2:443; 5:449

Hamilton, Ian
Kingsley Amis 2:6
Robert Lowell 2:246; 4:303
Louis MacNeice 4:317

Hamilton, Kenneth and Alice Hamilton
Samuel Beckett 10:31
John Updike 2:443; 5:449

Hamilton, Mary and Diane Roman
Paul Vincent Carroll 10:98

Hamilton, William
Albert Camus 1:52
Paul Goodman 7:128

Hammond, John G.
Robert Creeley 8:151

Hammond, Jonathan
Athol Fugard 9:229

Handa, Carolyn
Conrad Aiken 10:1

Hanna, Thomas L.
Albert Camus 9:143

Hannah, Barry
William Eastlake 8:200

Hanne, Michael
Elio Vittorini 9:551

Hansen, Arlen J.
Richard Brautigan 3:90

Hansen, Olaf
Peter Handke 10:259

Harder, Worth T.
Herbert Read 4:443

Hardie, Alec M.
Edmund Blunden 2:65

Hardin, Nancy S.
Margaret Drabble 3:129

Hardin, Nancy Shields
Doris Lessing 6:297

Harding, D. W.
Roy Fuller 4:178

Hardison, O. B., Jr.
Larry McMurtry 7:215

Hardwick, Elizabeth
Renata Adler 8:6
Doris Lessing 3:285
Marge Piercy 3:383
Alexsandr I. Solzhenitsyn 10:480

Hardy, Barbara
A. Alvarez 5:18

Hardy, Melody
Arthur C. Clarke 4:105

Hare, David
Ngaio Marsh 7:209

Hargrove, Nancy D.
T. S. Eliot 6:165

Harold, Brent
Vladimir Nabokov 6:356

Harper, Howard M., Jr.
John Barth 1:18
Saul Bellow 1:33
Jerzy Kosinski 1:172
Vladimir Nabokov 1:245
Philip Roth 1:293

Harper, Michael S.
Robert Hayden 9:269

Harper, Ralph
Eric Ambler 4:18

Harrington, Michael
Theodore Roethke **3**:433

Harris, Jane Gary
Boris Pasternak **10**:382

Harris, Leo
Ngaio Marsh **7**:209
Julian Symons **2**:426

Harris, Lis
Truman Capote **3**:100
Grace Paley **4**:392

Harris, Marie
Marge Piercy **6**:403

Harris, Michael
Thomas Berger **5**:60
John Gardner **5**:133

Harris, Wilson
George Lamming **4**:279
V. S. Naipaul **4**:374

Harrison, Barbara Grizzuti
Ruth Prawer Jhabvala **4**:257
Iris Murdoch **6**:343

Harrison, Jim
Larry McMurtry **2**:272

Harrison, Keith
John Berryman **3**:69

Harrison, Tony
Lorine Niedecker **10**:360

Harss, Luis and Barbara Dohmann
Jorge Luis Borges **2**:69
Julio Cortázar **2**:101
Gabriel García Márquez **2**:147
Juan Carlos Onetti **7**:276
Juan Rulfo **8**:461
Mario Vargas Llosa **3**:493

Hart, Jeffrey
E. L. Doctorow **6**:136
Auberon Waugh **7**:514

Hart, John E.
Jack Kerouac **3**:264

Harte, Barbara
Janet Frame **3**:164

Hartley, George
Philip Larkin **5**:230

Hartman, Geoffrey
Ross Macdonald **2**:257

Hartman, Geoffrey H.
A. R. Ammons **2**:13
André Malraux **9**:358

Hartt, Julian N.
Mary Renault **3**:426

Hartung, Philip T.
Budd Schulberg **7**:402

Harvey, David D.
Herbert Read **4**:440

Harvey, G. M.
John Betjeman **10**:52

Harvey, Lawrence E.
Samuel Beckett **9**:80

Harvey, Robert D.
Howard Nemerov **2**:306

Hasley, Louis
Peter De Vries **1**:72
Joseph Heller **5**:173

S. J. Perelman **3**:381
E. B. White **10**:526

Hass, Robert
Robert Lowell **9**:336

Hassan, Ihab
John Barth **2**:36
Samuel Beckett **1**:23
Saul Bellow **1**:29
André Breton **2**:81
Frederick Buechner **4**:79
William S. Burroughs **2**:91
Truman Capote **1**:55
J. P. Donleavy **1**:75
Ralph Ellison **1**:94
Jean Genet **2**:159
Allen Ginsberg **2**:164
Herbert Gold **4**:190
Ernest Hemingway **3**:237
Norman Mailer **1**:188, 189; **4**:319
Bernard Malamud **1**:195, 196
Carson McCullers **1**:207, 208
Henry Miller **1**:222
Vladimir Nabokov **1**:239
Alain Robbe-Grillet **2**:375
J. D. Salinger **1**:296; **3**:446
Nathalie Sarraute **2**:385
Jean Stafford **7**:455
William Styron **1**:330

Hassett, John J.
José Donoso **4**:129

Hatch, Robert
Anne Burr **6**:104

Hatfield, Henry
Günter Grass **2**:173

Hauck, Richard Boyd
Kurt Vonnegut, Jr. **5**:465

Haugh, Robert
John Updike **7**:489

Hauptman, Ira
John Buell **10**:81

Hausermann, H. W.
Herbert Read **4**:438, 439

Haverstick, S. Alexander
John Knowles **4**:271

Hawkes, John
John Barth **10**:21
Flannery O'Connor **1**:254

Haworth, David
Morris L. West **6**:563

Hay, Samuel A.
Ed Bullins **5**:83

Hayes, Brian P.
Joyce Carol Oates **1**:252

Hayes, E. Nelson
J. R. Salamanca **4**:461

Hayes, Noreen and Robert Renshaw
J. R. R. Tolkien **1**:336

Hayman, David
Louis-Ferdinand Céline **7**:42

Hayman, Ronald
Robert Duncan **7**:88
Robert Frost **4**:174
Allen Ginsberg **6**:198
Arthur Miller **6**:331

Charles Olson **5**:327
Anne Sexton **4**:482
David Storey **5**:414
Charles Tomlinson **4**:544

Haynes, Muriel
Shirley Ann Grau **4**:208
Lillian Hellman **4**:222
Thomas Keneally **5**:210

Hays, Peter L.
Henry Miller **9**:379

Hayward, Max and Patricia Blake
Andrei Voznesensky **1**:349

Hazo, Samuel
John Berryman **2**:57

Hazzard, Shirley
Jean Rhys **2**:371
Patrick White **3**:522

Headings, Philip R.
T. S. Eliot **1**:91

Healey, James
Catharine Savage Brosman **9**:135
Michael Casey **2**:100
Leonard Cohen **3**:110

Heaney, Seamus
David Jones **7**:187

Hearron, Thomas
Richard Brautigan **5**:68

Heath, Jeffrey M.
Evelyn Waugh **8**:543

Heath, Susan
Martin Amis **9**:25
John Hersey **7**:154
Yasunari Kawabata **5**:208
John Knowles **4**:272
Yukio Mishima **6**:337
Anaïs Nin **4**:379
V. S. Pritchett **5**:353
Kurt Vonnegut, Jr. **3**:503

Heath, William
Paul Blackburn **9**:100

Hecht, Anthony
W. H. Auden **2**:22
Ted Hughes **2**:198
James Merrill **2**:273
Marianne Moore **2**:291
Howard Nemerov **2**:306
L. E. Sissman **9**:489
Richard Wilbur **9**:570

Heckard, Margaret
William H. Gass **8**:244

Heffernan, Michael
Albert Goldbarth **5**:143
Gibbons Ruark **3**:441

Heidenry, John
Agatha Christie **6**:110
Robert M. Pirsig **4**:405

Heilbut, Anthony
Stanley Elkin **9**:191

Heilman, Robert B.
Edward Albee **5**:11
Max Frisch **3**:168
Harold Pinter **3**:386

Heims, Neil
Paul Goodman **4**:198

Heiney, Donald
Jean Anouilh **8**:22
Alberto Moravia **2**:294
Elio Vittorini **9**:546, 548

Heller, Amanda
Max Apple **9**:32
John Cheever **8**:138
Don DeLillo **8**:171
Joan Didion **8**:175
William Gaddis **6**:194
Mark Helprin **7**:152
Leonard Michaels **6**:325
Larry Woiwode **6**:579

Heller, Michael
William Bronk **10**:75
Cid Corman **9**:170
George Oppen **7**:284
Charles Reznikoff **9**:449

Helms, Alan
John Ashbery **2**:18
Robert Bly **10**:61
Philip Levine **4**:287

Hemenway, Robert
Zora Neale Hurston **7**:170

Hemmings, F.W.J.
Mary Stewart **7**:467

Henault, Marie
Peter Viereck **4**:559

Henderson, Tony
Patricia Highsmith **4**:226

Hendin, Josephine
John Barth **3**:42
Donald Barthelme **6**:28
Richard Brautigan **1**:45
William S. Burroughs **5**:92
Janet Frame **2**:142
John Hersey **2**:188
Marjorie Kellogg **2**:224
Robert Kotlowitz **4**:275
Doris Lessing **3**:286
Michael McClure **6**:316
Joyce Carol Oates **6**:371; **9**:404
Flannery O'Connor **6**:375
Thomas Pynchon **6**:436
Hubert Selby, Jr. **1**:307; **4**:482
Paul Theroux **5**:427
John Updike **9**:536
Kurt Vonnegut, Jr. **4**:569

Hendrick, George
Jack Kerouac **2**:227
Katherine Anne Porter **1**:273

Henighan, T. J.
Richard Hughes **1**:149

Henkel, Wayne J.
John Knowles **4**:272

Henkels, Robert, Jr.
Raymond Queneau **10**:430

Henninger, Francis J.
Albert Camus **4**:93

Henry, Avril
William Golding **10**:237

Henry, Gerrit
W. S. Merwin **5**:287

Hentoff, Margaret
Paul Zindel **6**:586

Hentoff, Margot
Joan Didion **8**:174

CRITIC INDEX

Hentoff, Nat
Paul Goodman 4:197
Colin MacInnes 4:314

Hepburn, Neil
Rayner Heppenstall 10:273
Thomas Keneally 5:211; 10:299
Tim O'Brien 7:272
David Plante 7:308
William Sansom 6:484
William Trevor 7:477
John Updike 7:489
Fay Weldon 9:559

Herbold, Tony
Dannie Abse 7:2
Michael Hamburger 5:159

Hernlund, Patricia
Richard Brautigan 5:67

Herr, Paul
James Purdy 2:347

Herrera, Philip
Daphne du Maurier 6:147

Hertzel, Leo J.
J. F. Powers 1:281

Hesse, Eva
Ezra Pound 7:329

Hesseltine, William B.
MacKinlay Kantor 7:194

Hewes, Henry
Edward Albee 2:2
Ed Bullins 5:84
Günter Grass 2:173
Terrence McNally 7:216
David Rabe 4:425
Peter Shaffer 5:388
Tom Stoppard 4:524
Melvin Van Peebles 2:447
Gore Vidal 2:450
Tennessee Williams 2:465

Heyen, William
Robert Bly 5:61
Louise Bogan 4:68
John Cheever 3:106
E. E. Cummings 3:118
James Dickey 2:117
Richmond Lattimore 3:278
Denise Levertov 1:177
Hugh MacDiarmid 2:253
Arthur Miller 6:336
Theodore Roethke 3:433
Anne Sexton 6:491
Neil Simon 6:503
W. D. Snodgrass 6:513
William Stafford 4:520
John Updike 3:485
Richard Wilbur 3:533
William Carlos Williams 2:468

Heymann, Hans G.
Horst Bienek 7:29

Heywood, Christopher
Peter Abrahams 4:1

Hickey, Dave
B. H. Friedman 7:108

Hicks, Granville
Louis Auchincloss 4:30; 9:52,
53
James Baldwin 2:31
Peter S. Beagle 7:25
James Gould Cozzens 1:66

Shirley Ann Grau 4:207
Elia Kazan 6:273
Ken Kesey 6:277
Meyer Levin 7:204
Bernard Malamud 1:200
Harry Mathews 6:314
Katherine Anne Porter 7:312
Reynolds Price 3:404, 405
Ann Quin 6:442
Kurt Vonnegut, Jr. 2:451
Auberon Waugh 7:514
Herman Wouk 1:376

Hicks, Granville and Jack Alan Robbins
Louis Auchincloss 4:28
Herbert Gold 4:189
Flannery O'Connor 1:258

Highet, Gilbert
Henry Miller 1:224
Ezra Pound 1:276

Highsmith, Patricia
Georges Simenon 2:398

Hill, Donald L.
Richard Wilbur 3:530

Hill, Helen G.
Norman Mailer 4:321

Hill, Susan
Daphne du Maurier 6:146

Hill, William B.
Peter De Vries 10:137

Hill, William B., S.J.
Paul Gallico 2:147
Bernard Malamud 5:269
Anthony Powell 10:417
Muriel Spark 2:418

Hilliard, Stephen S.
Philip Larkin 9:323

Himmelblau, Jack
Miguel Ángel Asturias 8:25

Hinchliffe, Arnold P.
Edward Bond 6:86
Harold Pinter 1:267

Hinden, Michael
John Barth 3:41

Hindus, Milton
Louis-Ferdinand Céline 1:56

Hingley, Ronald
Aleksandr I. Solzhenitsyn
1:319; 4:515; 7:445
Andrei Voznesensky 1:349

Hinz, Evelyn J.
Anaïs Nin 1:248; 4:377

Hinz, Evelyn J. and John T. Teunissen
Doris Lessing 6:293

Hipkiss, Robert A.
Ernest Hemingway 3:242

Hippisley, Anthony
Yuri Olesha 8:433

Hirsch, Edward
Geoffrey Hill 8:296

Hirsch, Foster
Ernest Hemingway 1:144
Mary McCarthy 3:328
Tennessee Williams 5:505

Hirt, Andrew J.
Rod McKuen 3:332

Hislop, Alan
Jerzy Kosinski 2:233
Wright Morris 3:344
Frederic Prokosch 4:422

Hitchcock, George
Diane Wakoski 7:503

Hitrec, Joseph
Ivo Andrić 8:19

Hjortsberg, William
Angela Carter 5:101
Rosalyn Drexler 2:120

Hoagland, Edward
Erskine Caldwell 8:123
William Saroyan 8:468; 10:454

Hochman, Baruch
S. Y. Agnon 4:12
Isaac Bashevis Singer 1:312

Hodgart, Matthew
Kingsley Amis 5:23
V. S. Pritchett 5:353

Hodgart, Patricia
Paul Bowles 2:78

Hoeksema, Thomas
Ishmael Reed 3:424

Hoerchner, Susan
Denise Levertov 5:247

Hoffa, William Walter
Ezra Pound 2:343

Hoffman, Daniel
A. R. Ammons 2:11
W. H. Auden 2:25
Richard Eberhart 3:133, 134
Ted Hughes 2:198
Robert Lowell 2:247

Hoffman, Frederick J.
Conrad Aiken 1:2
James Baldwin 1:15
Samuel Beckett 1:21
Saul Bellow 1:30
John Dos Passos 1:79
James T. Farrell 4:157
William Faulkner 1:100
John Hawkes 4:212
Ernest Hemingway 1:142
Katherine Anne Porter 1:272
Theodore Roethke 3:434
Philip Roth 4:451
John Steinbeck 1:325
Robert Penn Warren 1:353

Hoffman, Michael J.
Henry Miller 1:224

Hoffman, Nancy Y.
Anaïs Nin 4:380
Flannery O'Connor 3:369

Hogan, Robert
Paul Vincent Carroll 10:97
Arthur Miller 1:216
Elmer Rice 7:361

Hoggart, Richard
W. H. Auden 1:9
Graham Greene 6:217

Hokenson, Jan
Louis-Ferdinand Céline 9:152

Holahan, Susan
Frank O'Hara 5:324

Holbert, Cornelia
Kenzaburō Ōe 10:373

Holden, Anthony
Rayner Heppenstall 10:272

Holden, David
Piers Paul Read 4:445

Holden, Jonathan
Nancy Willard 7:540

Holder, Alan
Robert Lowell 5:256

Holder, Stephen C.
John Brunner 8:107

Holland, Bette
Eleanor Clark 5:106

Holland, Robert
Marilyn Hacker 9:258

Hollander, John
A. R. Ammons 2:12
Howard Moss 7:247

Holman, C. Hugh
John P. Marquand 10:328
Robert Penn Warren 4:576

Holmes, Carol
Joseph McElroy 5:279

Holmes, Charles S.
James Thurber 5:439, 441

Holmes, John Clellon
Jack Kerouac 2:227

Holmes, Kay
Emma Lathen 2:236

Holroyd, Michael
William Gerhardie 5:139

Holzinger, Walter
Pablo Neruda 9:396

Hood, Stuart
Aleksandr I. Solzhenitsyn
1:319

Hope, Christopher
Nadine Gordimer 5:147
Louis Simpson 9:486
Derek Walcott 9:556

Hopkins, Crale D.
Lawrence Ferlinghetti 10:174

Horn, Carole
Caroline Blackwood 6:80

Horowitz, Michael
Jack Kerouac 5:214

Horowitz, Susan
Ann Beattie 8:54

Horton, Andrew S.
Ken Kesey 6:278
John Updike 7:487

Horvath, Violet M.
André Malraux 4:332

Hosking, Geoffrey
Vladimir Voinovich 10:507

Howard, Ben
Loren Eiseley 7:92
Marilyn Hacker 5:155
Anne Sexton 6:494

Howard, Jane
Maxine Kumin 5:222

Howard, Leon
Wright Morris 1:232

Howard, Maureen
Donald Barthelme 8:50
Jorge Luis Borges 1:38
Paul Bowles 2:79
Isak Dinesen 10:150
Margaret Drabble 2:117;
  10:163, 165
Peter Handke 8:261
Lillian Hellman 8:281
Doris Lessing 6:301
Toni Morrison 10:356
Philip Roth 1:292
John Updike 9:537
Kurt Vonnegut, Jr. 1:347
Tennessee Williams 1:369

Howard, Richard
A. R. Ammons 2:12; 5:24
John Ashbery 2:17, 18
W. H. Auden 2:26; 3:23
Imamu Amiri Baraka 10:18
Marvin Bell 8:67
Robert Bly 5:61
Millen Brand 7:29
Gregory Corso 1:63
James Dickey 7:79
Irving Feldman 7:102
Paul Goodman 7:128
Daniel Hoffman 6:244
John Hollander 5:185
Uwe Johnson 5:201
Galway Kinnell 5:215
Kenneth Koch 5:219
Denise Levertov 5:245
Philip Levine 5:251
John Logan 5:252, 254
William Meredith 4:348
James Merrill 2:274
W. S. Merwin 2:277; 5:284
Howard Moss 7:249
Frank O'Hara 5:323
Sylvia Plath 5:338
Adrienne Rich 3:428
Raphael Rudnik 7:384
Gary Snyder 5:393
William Stafford 7:460
Allen Tate 4:538
Mona Van Duyn 3:491
David Wagoner 5:473
Robert Penn Warren 6:557
Theodore Weiss 3:516
James Wright 5:518; 10:547
Vassily S. Yanovsky 2:485

Howard, Thomas
Frederick Buechner 2:82

Howe, Irving
James Baldwin 3:31
Saul Bellow 3:49, 60; 8:79
Louis-Ferdinand Céline 3:101
James Gould Cozzens 4:111
Ralph Ellison 3:141
William Faulkner 3:151
Paula Fox 2:139
Robert Frost 3:170
Daniel Fuchs 8:221
James Hanley 8:265
Ernest Hemingway 3:232
György Konrád 4:273
Jerzy Kosinski 1:171
Norman Mailer 3:311

Bernard Malamud 8:376
Octavio Paz 3:377
Sylvia Plath 1:270; 3:391
Ezra Pound 2:344
Philip Roth 2:380; 3:440
Delmore Schwartz 10:466
Ignazio Silone 4:492, 494
Isaac Bashevis Singer 1:311
Lionel Trilling 9:533
Edmund Wilson 3:538
Richard Wright 3:545; 9:585

Howell, Elmo
Flannery O'Connor 3:369

Howlett, Ivan
John Osborne 5:333

Hoyem, Andrew
Larry Eigner 9:180

Hoyenga, Betty
Kay Boyle 1:42

Hoyt, Charles Alva
Bernard Malamud 1:196
Muriel Spark 2:414
Edward Lewis Wallant 5:477

Hubert, Renée Riese
André Breton 2:80
Alain Robbe-Grillet 4:449
Nathalie Sarraute 4:470

Hubin, Allen J.
Michael Crichton 6:119
Harry Kemelman 2:225

Huebner, Theodore
Anna Seghers 7:408

Hughes, Carl Milton
Chester Himes 4:229
Ann Petry 1:266
Richard Wright 1:377
Frank G. Yerby 1:381

Hughes, Catharine
Edward Albee 2:3; 9:6
Samuel Beckett 2:47
Daniel J. Berrigan 4:57
Ed Bullins 5:82
D. L. Coburn 10:108
Allen Ginsberg 2:164
Charles Gordone 4:199
Rolf Hochhuth 4:232
James Kirkwood 9:320
Mark Medoff 6:323
David Rabe 4:427
Robert Shaw 5:391
Michael Weller 10:526
Tennessee Williams 2:466;
  5:502

Hughes, Daniel
John Berryman 3:70

Hughes, Dorothy B.
Donald E. Westlake 7:528

Hughes, James
Louis Auchincloss 9:53

Hughes, John W.
Dannie Abse 7:1
John Ashbery 2:17
W. H. Auden 2:26
John Ciardi 10:106

Hughes, Olga R.
Boris Pasternak 7:297

Hughes, R. E.
Graham Greene 1:131

Hughes, Ted
Sylvia Plath 1:270
Clancy Sigal 7:423

Hughson, Lois
John Dos Passos 4:136

Hugo, Richard
Theodore Roethke 8:458

Hulbert, Debra
Diane Wakoski 4:572

Hume, Kathryn
C. S. Lewis 6:308

Humphrey, Robert
William Faulkner 1:98

Hunt, Albert
John Arden 6:5

Hunter, Kristin
Ann Beattie 8:55

Hurren, Kenneth
Samuel Beckett 6:43
Christopher Fry 2:144
John Hopkins 4:234
Peter Nichols 5:306
Harold Pinter 6:418
Peter Shaffer 5:388
Neil Simon 6:505
Tom Stoppard 4:527
David Storey 5:415

Hussain, Riaz
Philip K. Dick 10:138

Hutchens, John K.
P. G. Wodehouse 2:481

Hux, Samuel
John Dos Passos 8:182

Huxley, Julian
Aldous Huxley 3:253

Hyde, Lewis
Vicente Aleixandre 9:18

Hyde, Virginia M.
W. H. Auden 3:23

Hyman, Stanley Edgar
W. H. Auden 2:22
James Baldwin 2:32
Djuna Barnes 3:36
John Barth 2:35
Truman Capote 3:99
E. E. Cummings 3:117
T. S. Eliot 6:159
William Faulkner 3:152
Janet Frame 2:141
Bruce Jay Friedman 3:165
William Golding 2:168
Ernest Hemingway 3:234
Norman Mailer 2:258
Bernard Malamud 2:265
Wallace Markfield 8:378
Henry Miller 2:283
Marianne Moore 2:291
Vladimir Nabokov 2:299
Flannery O'Connor 1:257
Seán O'Faoláin 7:273
J. F. Powers 4:419
James Purdy 2:348
Thomas Pynchon 2:353
John Crowe Ransom 2:363
Alain Robbe-Grillet 2:374

J. D. Salinger 3:444
Isaac Bashevis Singer 3:452
John Steinbeck 5:405
Jun'ichiro Tanizaki 8:510
John Updike 2:440
Yvor Winters 4:589
Herman Wouk 9:579

Hynes, Joseph
Graham Greene 9:244
Evelyn Waugh 3:511

Hynes, Samuel
W. H. Auden 1:11; 3:24
C. Day Lewis 10:130, 131
T. S. Eliot 10:172
E. M. Forster 3:161
William Golding 1:122
Graham Greene 6:219
Louis MacNeice 4:317; 10:326
Stephen Spender 5:401; 10:488
J. I. M. Stewart 7:464

Ianni, L. A.
Lawrence Ferlinghetti 2:133

Idol, John
Flannery O'Connor 3:366

Ignatow, David
Denise Levertov 8:347
George Oppen 7:282
Diane Wakoski 7:506

Irele, Abiola
Chinua Achebe 7:3

Irwin, John T.
George P. Elliott 2:131
David Ignatow 7:177
Louis MacNeice 1:187
Thomas Merton 3:336
William Jay Smith 6:512
David Wagoner 3:508
Theodore Weiss 3:517

Irwin, Michael
Isak Dinesen 10:149
John Updike 9:539

Isaac, Dan
Isaac Bashevis Singer 3:453
Elie Wiesel 5:493

Isbell, Harold
John Logan 5:253

Ishiguro, Hidé
Yukio Mishima 9:384

Italia, Paul G.
James Dickey 10:139

Itzin, Catherine
Jack Gelber 6:197

Iwamoto, Yoshio and Dick Wagner
Yukio Mishima 9:381

Jackson, Angela
Henry Dumas 6:145

Jackson, Blyden
Gwendolyn Brooks 5:75
Robert Hayden 5:169
Langston Hughes 5:191
Margaret Walker 6:554

Jackson, Ester Merle
Tennessee Williams 7:540

Jackson, Joseph Henry
Irving Stone 7:468

CRITIC INDEX

CRITIC INDEX

Jackson, Richard L.
Ramón Gómez de la Serna 9:239

Jackson, Robert Louis
Aleksandr I. Solzhenitsyn 7:446

Jacobs, Nicolas
David Jones 4:261

Jacobs, Rita D.
Saul Bellow 10:42

Jacobs, Ronald M.
Samuel R. Delany 8:168

Jacobsen, Josephine
Arthur Gregor 9:256
Daniel Hoffman 6:242
David Ignatow 4:249
Denise Levertov 3:293
James Schevill 7:401
Mona Van Duyn 7:498

Jacobson, Dan
D. J. Enright 4:155
Andrei Sinyavsky 8:490

Jacobson, Irving
Arthur Miller 6:333; 10:345

Jacobus, Lee A.
Imamu Amiri Baraka 5:46

Jaffe, Dan
A. R. Ammons 2:12
John Berryman 2:57
Gary Snyder 2:406
Hollis Summers 10:493

Jaffe, Harold
Peter S. Beagle 7:26
Kenneth Rexroth 2:369

Jahiel, Edwin
Marguerite Duras 6:150
Antonis Samarakis 5:381
Vassilis Vassilikos 4:552

Jahn, Janheing
Camara Laye 4:282

James, Clive
W. H. Auden 3:28
John Betjeman 6:66
Lillian Hellman 8:280
Philip Larkin 5:225, 229
John Le Carré 9:327
Norman Mailer 3:317
Aleksandr I. Solzhenitsyn 7:436
Yvor Winters 8:553

James, Stuart
James A. Michener 5:290

Jameson, Fredric
Larry Niven 8:426

Janeway, Elizabeth
Pamela Hansford Johnson 7:184
Jessamyn West 7:519

Janeway, Michael
Anne Tyler 7:479
Tom Wicker 7:533

Janiera, Armando Martins
Kobo Abe 8:1
Jun'ichiro Tanizaki 8:510

Jarrell, Randall
Conrad Aiken 3:3

W. H. Auden 2:21
Elizabeth Bishop 1:34; 4:65
R. P. Blackmur 2:61
Alex Comfort 7:54
E. E. Cummings 3:116
Robert Frost 1:109; 3:169
Robert Graves 1:126; 2:174
David Ignatow 7:173
Robinson Jeffers 2:213
Robert Lowell 1:178; 2:246
Josephine Miles 1:215
Marianne Moore 1:226; 2:290
Ezra Pound 2:340
John Crowe Ransom 2:361
Theodore Roethke 3:432
Muriel Rukeyser 6:478
Carl Sandburg 4:462
Karl Shapiro 4:485
Christina Stead 2:420
Richard Wilbur 3:530
William Carlos Williams 1:369; 2:467

Jebb, Julian
Alison Lurie 5:259

Jefferson, Margo
Beryl Bainbridge 5:39
Rosalyn Drexler 6:142
Nadine Gordimer 7:133
Elizabeth Jane Howard 7:164
Gayl Jones 6:265
V. S. Naipaul 7:253
Juan Carlos Onetti 7:280

Jelenski, K. A.
Witold Gombrowicz 7:123

Jellinck, Frank
Rex Stout 3:472

Jenkins, Cecil
André Malraux 4:336

Jenkins, David
A. R. Ammons 5:28

Jennings, Elizabeth
Robert Frost 3:171

Jervis, Steven A.
Evelyn Waugh 1:359

Jochmans, Betty
Agatha Christie 8:142

John, Roland
Stanley J. Kunitz 6:287

Johnson, Abby Ann Arthur
Penelope Gilliatt 10:229

Johnson, Ann S.
David Garnett 3:188

Johnson, Colton
Anthony Kerrigan 6:276

Johnson, Curtis
Guy Davenport, Jr. 6:125

Johnson, Diane
Don DeLillo 8:172
Joan Didion 8:176
Nadine Gordimer 5:147
Erica Jong 8:315
Doris Lessing 3:286; 10:316
Toni Morrison 10:355
Joyce Carol Oates 3:361
Jean Rhys 6:453
Muriel Spark 3:465
Gore Vidal 10:502
Paul West 7:524

Johnson, Douglas
Louis-Ferdinand Céline 7:45
Claude Mauriac 9:367

Johnson, Greg
John Updike 9:538

Johnson, Halvard
Gary Snyder 1:318

Johnson, James William
Katherine Anne Porter 7:311

Johnson, Kenneth
Richard Wilbur 6:570

Johnson, Marigold
Bernard Malamud 3:324

Johnson, Richard
W. H. Auden 2:26

Johnson, Richard A.
Turner Cassity 6:107
Anthony Hecht 8:268
Delmore Schwartz 2:387

Johnston, Arnold
William Golding 3:198

Johnston, Dillon
Austin Clarke 6:111
Albert Goldbarth 5:143
Seamus Heaney 7:147

Johnstone, J. K.
E. M. Forster 3:160

Jonas, George
Margaret Atwood 3:19

Jonas, Gerald
Isaac Asimov 9:49
Samuel R. Delany 8:168, 169
Ursula K. Le Guin 8:343
Barry N. Malzberg 7:209
Larry Niven 8:426
Kate Wilhelm 7:538

Jones, A. R.
Sylvia Plath 9:430

Jones, Alun R.
Eudora Welty 1:362; 2:460

Jones, Bernard
John Cowper Powys 9:441

Jones, Brian
Howard Nemerov 2:306

Jones, D. A. N.
Ed Bullins 1:47
John Fowles 6:184
Mervyn Jones 10:295

Jones, D. Allan
John Barth 5:52

Jones, D. G.
Earle Birney 6:76
Anne Hébert 4:219
Irving Layton 2:237

Jones, Edward T.
John Updike 3:487

Jones, Ernest
Budd Schulberg 7:403

Jones, Granville H.
Jack Kerouac 2:226

Jones, John Bush
Harold Pinter 9:418

Jones, Louisa E.
Raymond Queneau 10:431

Jones, Richard
L. P. Hartley 2:182
Anthony Powell 7:346

Jones, Robert F.
James Jones 3:262

Jones, Roger
Saul Bellow 10:39

Jong, Erica
Sara Davidson 9:174
Doris Lessing 3:287
Anne Sexton 4:483; 8:484
Eleanor Ross Taylor 5:425

Joost, Nicholas and Ann Risdon
T. S. Eliot 9:190

Jordan, Clive
Martin Amis 4:19
Dan Jacobson 4:253
G. Josipovici 6:271
Yukio Mishima 4:356
Thomas Pynchon 6:432
Gillian Tindall 7:473
Ludvík Vaculík 7:494
Kurt Vonnegut, Jr. 4:567

Jordan, Francis X.
Gore Vidal 10:501

Jordan, June
Millen Brand 7:30
Nikki Giovanni 2:165
Zora Neale Hurston 7:171
Gayl Jones 9:306
Marge Piercy 6:402

Joseph, Gerhard
John Barth 1:17

Josipovici, Gabriel
Saul Bellow 3:54
Vladimir Nabokov 3:353

Judson, Jerome
John Ciardi 10:105

Jumper, Will C.
Robert Lowell 1:178

Justus, James H.
John Berryman 4:60
John Crowe Ransom 4:431
Karl Shapiro 4:487
Robert Penn Warren 4:578, 582

Kabakoff, Jacob
Aharon Megged 9:375

Kabatchnik, Amnon
William F. Buckley, Jr. 7:36

Kael, Pauline
Norman Mailer 3:315

Kahn, Lothar
Arthur Koestler 3:271
Jakov Lind 4:293
André Schwarz-Bart 4:479
Peter Weiss 3:515
Elie Wiesel 3:527

Kakish, William
Peter Hundke 10:260

Kalem, T. E.
Edward Albee 2:2; 5:12
Kingsley Amis 3:8
Samuel Beckett 2:47
Ed Bullins 5:84
Anne Burr 6:104
Friedrich Dürrenmatt 4:141

Jules Feiffer 8:216
Robert Graves 2:177
Bill Gunn 5:152
John Hopkins 4:234
Ira Levin 3:294
Terrence McNally 7:217
Jason Miller 2:284
Peter Nichols 5:307
Sean O'Casey 5:319
Murray Schisgal 6:490
Neil Simon 6:506
Isaac Bashevis Singer 6:511
Aleksandr I. Solzhenitsyn
 1:321
Tom Stoppard 4:526
David Storey 2:424, 425; 4:530
Thornton Wilder 6:572
Tennessee Williams 7:545
Robert Wilson 7:550

Kalstone, David
A. R. Ammons 2:12
John Ashbery 2:17
John Berryman 3:69
A. D. Hope 3:250
Philip Levine 5:250
James Merrill 2:273, 275
James Schuyler 5:383

Kameen, Paul
Daniel J. Berrigan 4:57
Robert Lowell 3:303

Kamin, Ira
Charles Bukowski 9:137

**Kane, Patricia and Doris Y.
Wilkinson**
Chester Himes 7:159

Kanfer, Stefan
Jerzy Kosinski 6:285
Terrence McNally 7:218
Brian Moore 7:237
Isaac Bashevis Singer 3:453;
 6:510
John Steinbeck 5:408

Kanon, Joseph
Louis Auchincloss 4:29
Daphne du Maurier 6:147
Penelope Gilliatt 2:160
Jacqueline Susann 3:475
John Updike 2:444

Kantra, Robert A.
Samuel Beckett 3:46

Kaplan, Johanna
Dan Jacobson 4:254
Cynthia Ozick 7:287

Kaplan, Sydney Janet
Doris Lessing 6:296

Kapp, Isa
Jascha Kessler 4:269
Grace Paley 4:394
Philip Roth 4:459

Karimi-Hakkak, Ahmad
Ahmad Shamlu 10:470

Karl, Frederick R.
Samuel Beckett 1:20
Elizabeth Bowen 1:40
John Braine 1:43
Ivy Compton-Burnett 1:60
Lawrence Durrell 1:83
William Golding 1:119
Henry Green 2:178

Graham Greene 1:132
L. P. Hartley 2:181
Joseph Heller 1:140
Christopher Isherwood 1:155
Pamela Hansford Johnson
 1:160
Doris Lessing 1:173, 175
Iris Murdoch 1:233
P. H. Newby 2:310
Anthony Powell 1:277
William Sansom 2:383
C. P. Snow 1:314, 315, 316
Muriel Spark 2:414
Evelyn Waugh 1:357
Angus Wilson 2:471

**Karl, Frederick R. and Marvin
Magalaner**
E. M. Forster 1:103
Aldous Huxley 1:150

Karlen, Arno
Edward Dahlberg 7:62

Karlinsky, Simon
Vladimir Nabokov 1:241; 2:305
John Rechy 7:357
Aleksandr I. Solzhenitsyn
 2:408
Yevgeny Yevtushenko 1:382

Karp, David
Meyer Levin 7:203

Kasack, Wolfgang
Aleksandr I. Solzhenitsyn
 7:434

Kasindorf, Martin
Christopher Hampton 4:212

Kattan, Naim
Mordecai Richler 5:373

Katz, Claire
Flannery O'Connor 6:379, 380

Katz, Jonathan
Albert Goldbarth 5:144

Kauffmann, Stanley
Edward Albee 2:3; 5:11, 14
Fernando Arrabal 2:15; 9:41
Alan Ayckbourn 5:37
John Berryman 3:69
Ed Bullins 7:36
Anthony Burgess 2:86
D. L. Coburn 10:108
E. L. Doctorow 6:133
Athol Fugard 5:130; 9:230
Peter Handke 5:164
James Leo Herlihy 6:234
James Kirkwood 9:319
Jerzy Kosinski 1:171; 2:233
Arthur Miller 2:280
Henry Miller 4:350
Peter Nichols 5:307
Hugh Nissenson 9:399
Edna O'Brien 3:365
John O'Hara 2:325
Miguel Piñero 4:402
Harold Pinter 3:386, 387; 6:417
David Rabe 4:425, 426; 8:450
Terence Rattigan 7:356
James Salter 7:387
André Schwarz-Bart 2:388
Irwin Shaw 7:412
John Steinbeck 5:408
Tom Stoppard 4:527

Gore Vidal 2:450
Kurt Vonnegut, Jr. 2:452
Tennessee Williams 5:504;
 7:545
Robert Wilson 9:576

Kaufman, Donald L.
Norman Mailer 2:263

Kaye, Howard
Yvor Winters 4:593

Kaysen, Xana
Jerzy Kosinski 10:309

Kazin, Alfred
Renata Adler 8:7
James Baldwin 1:13
Brendan Behan 1:25
Saul Bellow 1:28; 3:61
Jane Bowles 3:84
Paul Bowles 1:41
William S. Burroughs 5:91
Albert Camus 2:97
Louis-Ferdinand Céline 9:158
John Cheever 3:108
James Gould Cozzens 4:116
E. E. Cummings 8:155
Joan Didion 3:127
Lawrence Durrell 1:83
Ralph Ellison 1:93; 3:146
Frederick Exley 6:170
Gabriel García Márquez 2:149
William H. Gass 8:240
Paul Goodman 4:195
Graham Greene 1:131
Ernest Hemingway 3:242
David Ignatow 4:249
Jack Kerouac 1:165
Alan Lelchuk 5:241
Robert Lowell 1:179
Norman Mailer 1:187
Bernard Malamud 1:194; 3:326
Wallace Markfield 8:379
John P. Marquand 2:271
Mary McCarthy 3:329
Carson McCullers 4:345
Vladimir Nabokov 3:356; 8:418
V. S. Naipaul 4:373; 9:393
Joyce Carol Oates 2:313; 3:363
Flannery O'Connor 1:259;
 3:370
John O'Hara 1:260; 3:371
Walker Percy 2:334
Ann Petry 1:266
Katherine Anne Porter 3:393
Ezra Pound 1:274
J. F. Powers 1:279
Thomas Pynchon 3:419
Kenneth Rexroth 1:284
Philip Roth 1:292
J. D. Salinger 1:295, 296; 3:446,
 458
Karl Shapiro 4:484
Isaac Bashevis Singer 1:310;
 3:457; 9:487
C. P. Snow 1:314
Aleksandr I. Solzhenitsyn
 2:410; 4:515
Peter Taylor 4:543
Paul Theroux 8:514
John Updike 3:488; 9:538
Kurt Vonnegut, Jr. 3:505
Robert Penn Warren 1:352;
 4:582
Edmund Wilson 2:475

Keane, Patrick
Galway Kinnell 5:216

Kearns, Edward
Richard Wright 1:379

Kearns, Lionel
Earle Birney 6:77

Keates, Jonathan
Jorge Luis Borges 6:94
John Fowles 10:187
John Hersey 7:155

Keating, Peter
Erica Jong 8:315

Keefe, Joan
Flann O'Brien 10:362

Keenan, Hugh T.
J. R. R. Tolkien 1:336

Keene, Donald
Yukio Mishima 2:287; 4:354
Jun'ichiro Tanizaki 8:509

Keeney, Willard
Eudora Welty 1:361

Keith, Philip
J. E. Wideman 5:489

Keller, Jane Carter
Flannery O'Connor 3:365

Kellman, Steven G.
Aharon Megged 9:374

Kellogg, Gene
Graham Greene 3:208
François Mauriac 4:339
Flannery O'Connor 3:365
J. F. Powers 4:419
Evelyn Waugh 3:511

Kelly, James
Irwin Shaw 7:411

Kempton, Murray
Gore Vidal 4:554

Keneas, Alex
Ira Levin 6:305

Kenefick, Madeleine
Gayl Jones 6:265
Cynthia Ozick 7:290

Kennard, Jean E.
Anthony Burgess 10:86
William Golding 10:233
Joseph Heller 8:275
James Purdy 10:421

Kennebeck, Edwin
Terry Southern 7:453

Kennedy, Andrew K.
John Arden 6:10
Samuel Beckett 6:46
T. S. Eliot 6:166
Harold Pinter 6:419

Kennedy, Dorothy Mintzlaff
Raymond Federman 6:181
Howard Nemerov 6:363

Kennedy, Eileen
Penelope Gilliatt 10:230

Kennedy, John S.
John Steinbeck 1:323

Kennedy, Ray
Joseph Wambaugh 3:509

Kennedy, William
Thomas Bernhard 3:64

Robertson Davies 2:113
Don DeLillo 10:134
Gabriel García Márquez 8:232
John Gardner 7:111
Joseph Heller 5:179
Elia Kazan 6:273
William Kotzwinkle 5:219
Peter Matthiessen 7:211
Mordecai Richler 5:378

Kennedy, X. J.
A. R. Ammons 2:13
Edward Dahlberg 7:62
Eleanor Lerman 9:328
James Merrill 2:275

Kenner, Hugh
W. H. Auden 2:29
Robert Bly 10:62
John Dos Passos 8:182
Ernest Hemingway 8:285
Marianne Moore 4:360
Vladimir Nabokov 6:357
George Oppen 7:283, 285
Ezra Pound 2:345; 4:412; 7:325
Richard G. Stern 4:522
William Carlos Williams 2:469
James Wright 10:546
Louis Zukofsky 7:561, 562

Kenney, Edwin J., Jr.
Iris Murdoch 6:345

Kent, Cerrulia
Laura Z. Hobson 7:164

Kent, George E.
James Baldwin 1:15
Gwendolyn Brooks 1:46
Chester Himes 4:229

Kermode, Frank
W. H. Auden 2:25
Beryl Bainbridge 8:37
Samuel Beckett 2:46
T. S. Eliot 2:126, 128
E. M. Forster 10:178
William Golding 2:167, 169
Nadine Gordimer 10:240
Graham Greene 6:215
Peter Handke 5:165
Henry Miller 2:282
Iris Murdoch 2:298
Philip Roth 3:440
Muriel Spark 2:414, 415, 418

Kern, Edith
Samuel Beckett 2:47

Kern, Robert
Gary Snyder 9:500

Kernan, Alvin B.
Philip Roth 4:453
Evelyn Waugh 1:358

Kerr, John Austin, Jr.
José Rodrigues Miguéis 10:341

Kerr, Walter
Charles Gordone 1:124
Harold Pinter 1:267
Neil Simon 6:503
Michael Weller 10:526

Kerrane, Kevin
Robert Coover 7:59

Kerrigan, Anthony
Jorge Luis Borges 4:74; 9:115

Kerr-Jarrett, Peter
Octavio Paz 6:397

Kessler, Edward
Daniel Hoffman 6:242
Charles Wright 6:580

Kessler, Jascha
A. R. Ammons 5:28
Imamu Amiri Baraka 2:34
Charles Bukowski 5:79
James Dickey 7:79
Loren Eiseley 7:91
Irving Feldman 7:101
Lawrence Ferlinghetti 10:174
Robert Graves 2:176
Sandra Hochman 8:297
Ted Hughes 2:201
June Jordan 5:203
Anthony Kerrigan 4:269
György Konrád 10:304
Don L. Lee 2:238
Thomas Merton 3:335
Octavio Paz 10:388
Karl Shapiro 8:485
Muriel Spark 8:492
Robert Penn Warren 4:578
Louis Zukofsky 7:560

Kettle, Arnold
John Berger 2:55
Ivy Compton-Burnett 3:111
E. M. Forster 3:159
Graham Greene 3:206
Aldous Huxley 3:252

Keyser, Barbara Y.
Muriel Spark 8:494

Kherdian, David
Philip Whalen 6:565

Kidder, Rushworth M.
E. E. Cummings 8:161

Kieffer, Eduardo Gudiño
Jorge Luis Borges 9:117

Kiely, Robert
Maeve Brennan 5:73
Hortense Calisher 2:96
Michael Frayn 7:106
Gabriel García Márquez 2:148
William H. Gass 2:155
Bernard Malamud 3:323

Kiernan, Robert F.
John Barth 3:42

Killam, G. D.
Chinua Achebe 1:1

Killinger, John
Fernando Arrabal 9:37

Kilroy, Thomas
Samuel Beckett 3:45

Kimball, Arthur G.
Yasunari Kawabata 9:309

Kindilien, Glenn A.
Saul Bellow 10:44

King, Bruce
Nadine Gordimer 10:240
Ruth Prawer Jhabvala 8:312
V. S. Naipaul 9:392

King, Charles L.
Ramón Sender 8:479

King, Francis
Aldous Huxley 5:193

King, Thomas M.
Jean-Paul Sartre 7:394

Kinkead, Gwen
Penelope Gilliatt 2:161

Kinney, Jeanne
Carson McCullers 4:344

Kinsella, Anna M.
Alberto Moravia 7:242

Kinsella, Thomas
Austin Clarke 6:111

Kinzie, Mary
Jorge Luis Borges 2:73

Kirby, Martin
Walker Percy 8:440

Kirby-Smith, H. T., Jr.
Elizabeth Bishop 4:66
Arthur Gregor 9:254

Kirk, Elizabeth D.
J. R. R. Tolkien 1:341

Kirk, Russell
Ray Bradbury 10:68

Kirkham, Michael
Charles Tomlinson 4:543

Kirsch, Robert
Jascha Kessler 4:270

Kitchin, Laurence
Arnold Wesker 5:481

Kizer, Carolyn
Ted Hughes 2:201

Klaidman, Stephen
Juan Goytisolo 5:150

Klappert, Peter
Daniel Mark Epstein 7:97
Kathleen Spivack 6:520

Klein, Marcus
Saul Bellow 1:29
Ralph Ellison 1:94

Kleinberg, Seymour
Isaac Bashevis Singer 3:458

Klemtner, Susan Strehle
William Gaddis 10:212

Kliman, Bernice W.
Philip Roth 3:438

Klinkowitz, Jerome
Imamu Amiri Baraka 5:45
Donald Barthelme 3:43; 5:52;
6:29
Jonathan Baumbach 6:32
Erica Jong 6:269
Jerzy Kosinski 3:272
Flann O'Brien 7:269
Gilbert Sorrentino 3:462
Ronald Sukenick 3:475; 4:530
Kurt Vonnegut, Jr. 1:348;
3:500; 4:563

Kmetz, Gail Kessler
Muriel Spark 8:493

Knapp, B. L.
Marguerite Duras 6:151

Knapp, Bettina Liebowitz
Jean Anouilh 8:24
Jean Cocteau 8:145
Georges Duhamel 8:187
Jean Genet 1:116

Robert Pinget 7:305
Nathalie Sarraute 8:469

Knapp, James F.
T. S. Eliot 6:163
Delmore Schwartz 2:387

Knapp, John V.
John Hawkes 7:145

Knelman, Martin
Harold Pinter 9:421
Mordecai Richler 5:377

Knieger, Bernard
S. Y. Agnon 8:8

Knight, Damon
Isaac Asimov 3:16
Ray Bradbury 3:84
Robert A. Heinlein 3:224

Knight, G. Wilson
John Cowper Powys 7:347

Knight, Karl F.
John Crowe Ransom 4:428

Knight, Susan
Frederick Busch 7:38
John Gardner 3:186
József Lengyel 7:202

Knoll, Robert E.
Ezra Pound 3:398

Knopp, Josephine
Elie Wiesel 5:491

Knowles, A. Sidney, Jr.
Marie-Claire Blais 2:63
Frederic Prokosch 4:421

Knudsen, Erika
Elisaveta Bagryana 10:11

Kobler, Turner S.
Rebecca West 7:526

Koch, Kenneth
Frank O'Hara 2:322

Koch, Stephen
Hermann Hesse 3:243
Reynolds Price 6:425
Nathalie Sarraute 8:472
Christina Stead 5:404
Gore Vidal 4:554

Koenig, Peter William
William Gaddis 10:209

Koethe, John
John Ashbery 2:17; 3:15
Sandra Hochman 3:250
Theodore Weiss 3:517

Kolodny, Annette and Daniel
James Peters
Thomas Pynchon 3:412

Kolonosky, Walter F.
Vladimir Voinovich 10:508

Koltz, Newton
Wright Morris 3:343
Patrick White 3:524

Korg, Jacob
Bernard Malamud 2:269

Korges, James
Erskine Caldwell 1:51

Korn, Eric
Philip K. Dick 10:138
Rayner Heppenstall 10:272
Judith Rossner 9:457

Claude Simon 9:482
Gore Vidal 10:502

Kornfeld, Melvin
Jurek Becker 7:27

Kosek, Steven
Kurt Vonnegut, Jr. 4:569

Kostach, Myrna
Rudy Wiebe 6:566

Kostelanetz, Richard
R. P. Blackmur 2:61
Ralph Ellison 3:141
Ezra Pound 2:344

Kotin, Armine
Jean Arp 5:33

Kott, Jan
Andrei Sinyavsky 8:488

Kozol, Jonathan
Marjorie Kellogg 2:223

Kramer, Aaron
Stanley J. Kunitz 6:287

Kramer, Hilton
Donald Barthelme 8:50
E. L. Doctorow 6:137
Robert Lowell 8:357
Archibald MacLeish 8:362
Mary McCarthy 5:276
L. E. Sissman 9:492
Robert Penn Warren 8:538

Kramer, Peter G.
William Goyen 5:149

Krance, Charles
Louis-Ferdinand Céline 9:153

Kraus, Elisabeth
John Hawkes 7:146

Krickel, Edward
James Gould Cozzens 1:67
William Saroyan 1:302

Kriegel, Leonard
T. S. Eliot 6:166
Günter Grass 2:172
James Jones 10:293
Iris Murdoch 1:234
Ezra Pound 7:333
Harvey Swados 5:423
Edmund Wilson 2:475

Krim
James Jones 10:290

Kroll, Ernest
Peter Viereck 4:559

Kroll, Jack
Edward Albee 2:1
Jean Anouilh 3:12
W. H. Auden 3:27
Alan Ayckbourn 5:36
Ed Bullins 1:47
Anne Burr 6:103, 104
Rosalyn Drexler 2:119
Frederick Exley 6:171
Jules Feiffer 8:216
Jean Genet 2:158
John Guare 8:253
Bill Gunn 5:152
Ted Hughes 2:200
Stanley J. Kunitz 6:286
Ira Levin 6:306
David Mamet 9:360
Terrence McNally 7:218

Mark Medoff 6:322
Arthur Miller 2:280; 6:334
Jason Miller 2:284
Rochelle Owens 8:434
Miguel Piñero 4:402
Terence Rattigan 7:355
Jonathan Reynolds 6:451
Ronald Ribman 7:358
Murray Schisgal 6:490
Neil Simon 6:504
Tom Stoppard 5:414
David Storey 2:424, 426
Kurt Vonnegut, Jr. 2:452
Lanford Wilson 7:548

Kroll, Jack and Walter Clemons
Saul Bellow 6:55

Kroll, Steven
Irvin Faust 8:215
Thomas McGuane 3:330
Dan Wakefield 7:503
Irving Wallace 7:510

Krutch, Joseph Wood
Erskine Caldwell 8:122
Elmer Rice 7:360

Krzyzanowski, Jerzy R.
Tadeusz Konwicki 8:325

Kuczkowski, Richard
Susan Sontag 10:485

Kuehl, Linda
Doris Lessing 3:282
Iris Murdoch 3:345
Marge Piercy 3:384
Muriel Spark 2:417
Eudora Welty 5:479

Kunitz, Stanley
John Berryman 8:86
Robert Creeley 8:152
Robert Frost 9:223
Jean Garrigue 8:240
H. D. 8:255
Robert Lowell 9:334
Marianne Moore 8:397; 10:346
Theodore Roethke 8:458

Kustow, Michael
Arnold Wesker 3:519

Kyle, Carol A.
John Barth 9:65

Laber, Jeri
Aleksandr I. Solzhenitsyn
2:411; 4:514

La Charite, Virginia
René Char 9:167

Lafore, Lawrence
Irving Wallace 7:509

LaFrance, Marston
Evelyn Waugh 1:358

Lahr, John
Arthur Kopit 1:171
Joe Orton 4:388
Harold Pinter 6:411
Sam Shepard 4:491

Lally, Michael
Charles Bukowski 9:138
Larry Eigner 9:182
Kenneth Koch 8:323
Howard Moss 7:249
Anne Sexton 6:493

Lambert, Gavin
Agatha Christie 8:142
John O'Hara 6:384

Lambert, J. W.
Edward Albee 2:4
Alan Ayckbourn 5:35
Peter Barnes 5:50
Edward Bond 4:70; 6:84
A. E. Ellis 7:95
Michael Frayn 7:108
Athol Fugard 5:130
John Osborne 2:328
Sam Shepard 6:496
Tom Stoppard 3:470; 5:413
David Storey 2:425; 4:530
Arnold Wesker 3:518

Lamie, Edward L. and Joe De Bolt
John Brunner 8:110

Lamming, George
Ishmael Reed 3:424
Derek Walcott 4:574

Lamont, Rosette C.
Fernando Arrabal 9:35
Eugène Ionesco 1:155; 6:252,
256; 9:287

Lamport, Felicia
S. J. Perelman 5:337

Landess, Thomas
Thomas Merton 1:211

Landess, Thomas H.
John Berryman 2:60
Caroline Gordon 6:205
William Meredith 4:349
Marion Montgomery 7:234
William Jay Smith 6:512
Allen Tate 4:540
Mona Van Duyn 3:491
Eudora Welty 1:363
James Wright 3:541

Lane, James B.
Harold Robbins 5:379

Lanes, Selma G.
Richard Adams 4:9

Langbaum, Robert
Samuel Beckett 9:85
E. M. Forster 1:107

Langlois, Walter
André Malraux 9:355

Lardner, John
Irwin Shaw 7:409

Lardner, Susan
György Konrád 10:305
Joyce Carol Oates 9:404
Wilfrid Sheed 2:393

Larkin, Joan
Hortense Calisher 4:88

Larrabee, Eric
Cornelius Ryan 7:385

Larrieu, Kay
Larry Woiwode 10:542

Larsen, Anne
Lisa Alther 7:11
Leonard Michaels 6:325

Larsen, Eric
Charles Newman 8:419

Larson, Charles
Hyemeyohsts Storm 3:470

Larson, Charles R.
Peter Abrahams 4:2
Chinua Achebe 5:1
Ayi Kwei Armah 5:31
Leslie A. Fiedler 4:163
Camara Laye 4:284
Kamala Markandaya 8:377
Peter Matthiessen 7:210
V. S. Naipaul 7:253
R. K. Narayan 7:255
James Ngugi 7:263
Simone Schwarz-Bart 7:404
Raymond Sokolov 7:430
Wole Soyinka 5:396
Amos Tutuola 5:445
James Welch 6:561

Lasagna, Louis, M.D.
Michael Crichton 2:108

LaSalle, Peter
J. F. Powers 8:448

Lask, I. M.
S. Y. Agnon 4:10

Lask, Thomas
David Ignatow 7:177
Ross Macdonald 1:185
Georges Simenon 8:486
W. D. Snodgrass 2:405

Laska, P. J.
Imamu Amiri Baraka 10:21

Lasson, Robert
Mario Puzo 2:352

Latham, Aaron
Jack Kerouac 2:228

Latrell, Craig
Harold Pinter 9:421

Lattimore, Richmond
John Berryman 2:59
Jorge Luis Borges 2:73
Edgar Bowers 9:121
Joseph Brodsky 6:97
Michael Casey 2:100
Alan Dugan 6:144
Daniel Hoffman 6:243
Vladimir Nabokov 8:407
Adrienne Rich 7:364
L. E. Sissman 9:491

Laughlin, Rosemary M.
John Fowles 2:138

Laurence, Margaret
Chinua Achebe 7:3

Laut, Stephen J., S.J.
John Gardner 10:220

Lavers, Annette
Sylvia Plath 9:425

Lavers, Norman
John Hawkes 2:186

Lavine, Stephen David
Philip Larkin 8:336

Lawall, Sarah and Mary Ann Caws
Yves Bonnefoy 9:113

Lawler, Daniel F., S.J.
Eleanor Hibbert 7:156

Lawless, Ken
J. P. Donleavy 10:155

Lawrence, D. H.
Edward Dahlberg 7:61
Ernest Hemingway 10:263

Lawson, Lewis A.
William Faulkner 3:153
Flannery O'Connor 1:255

Lazarus, H. P.
Budd Schulberg 7:401

Leahy, Jack
David Wagoner 5:474

Leal, Luis
Juan Rulfo 8:462

Learmont, Lavinia Marina
Hermann Hesse 2:191

Leary, Lewis
Lionel Trilling 9:534

Leavitt, Harvey
Richard Brautigan 5:67

Lebowitz, Alan
Ernest Hemingway 1:144

Lebowitz, Naomi
Stanley Elkin 4:152
E. M. Forster 4:166
J. F. Powers 1:279

LeClair, Thomas
John Barth 7:23
Saul Bellow 6:53
Anthony Burgess 1:48
Jerome Charyn 5:103; 8:135
Don DeLillo 10:135
J. P. Donleavy 1:76; 4:124;
   6:141; 10:154
Stanley Elkin 6:170; 9:190
John Gardner 8:236
John Hawkes 7:141, 144
Joseph Heller 8:278
Walker Percy 6:400
David Plante 7:307
Thomas Pynchon 6:435
Tom Robbins 9:454
Ronald Sukenick 6:523
Harvey Swados 5:420

LeClercq, Diane
Patricia Highsmith 2:194
Susan B. Hill 4:226
William Sansom 6:483

Ledbetter, J. T.
Mark Van Doren 6:542

Lee, Dennis
A. W. Purdy 6:428

Lee, Don L.
Nikki Giovanni 4:189
Conrad Kent Rivers 1:285

Lee, James W.
John Braine 1:43

Leeds, Barry H.
Ken Kesey 6:278
Norman Mailer 1:191
D. Keith Mano 2:270

Leeming, Glenda
John Arden 6:9

Leer, Norman
Bernard Malamud 8:374

Leffland, Ella
Lois Gould 10:242

Lehan, Richard
Walker Percy 2:332
Wilfrid Sheed 2:392
Susan Sontag 1:322

Lehman, David
David Ignatow 7:182
Charles Reznikoff 9:449
Ira Sadoff 9:466

Lehmann, John
Edith Sitwell 2:403

Lehmann-Haupt, Christopher
Michael Crichton 2:109
Rosalyn Drexler 2:119
Pete Hamill 10:251
Charles Newman 2:311

Leib, Mark
Sylvia Plath 3:389

Leibowitz, Herbert
Robert Bly 2:66
Jean Garrigue 2:153
Robert Lowell 4:297
Josephine Miles 2:278
Kenneth Rexroth 6:451
Theodore Roethke 3:434
Delmore Schwartz 2:388
Isaac Bashevis Singer 3:453
W. D. Snodgrass 2:405
Gary Snyder 5:395
Mona Van Duyn 3:492
William Carlos Williams 9:574
Edmund Wilson 3:540

Leibowitz, Herbert A.
Frank O'Hara 2:321

Leigh, David J., S.J.
Ernest Hemingway 6:233

Leiter, Robert
Janet Frame 6:190
Nadine Gordimer 7:132
Cormac McCarthy 4:342
Jean Rhys 6:453
Clancy Sigal 7:424
Larry Woiwode 10:541

Lejeune, Anthony
Paul Gallico 2:147
Anthony Powell 7:345
P. G. Wodehouse 2:480

LeMaster, J. R.
Jesse Stuart 8:507

Lemay, Harding
J. R. Salamanca 4:461

Lemmons, Philip
Brian Moore 8:396
William Trevor 7:478

Lemon, Lee T.
Kenneth Burke 2:87, 89
Louis-Ferdinand Céline 3:105
Guy Davenport, Jr. 6:124
Judith Guest 8:254
Jack Kerouac 5:213
Jerzy Kosinski 10:306
Joyce Carol Oates 6:369
John Rechy 1:283
C. P. Snow 4:503
Patrick White 5:485
Yvor Winters 4:591

Lensing, George
James Dickey 4:120
Robert Lowell 1:183
Louis Simpson 4:498
Louis Zukofsky 1:385

Lenski, Branko
Miroslav Krleža 8:329

Lentfoehr, Sister Therese
David Kherdian 6:281

Leonard, John
Lisa Alther 7:12
Saul Bellow 6:56
John Cheever 3:107; 8:139
Joan Didion 1:74
Doris Lessing 3:285
Alison Lurie 4:306
Larry McMurtry 2:271
Thomas Pynchon 3:414
Wilfrid Sheed 2:393

Lernoux, Penny
Mario Vargas Llosa 9:544

LeSage, Laurent
Robert Pinget 7:305

Leslie, Omolara
Chinua Achebe 3:2

Lessing, Doris
Kurt Vonnegut, Jr. 2:456

Lester, Julius
Henry Dumas 6:146

Lester, Margot
Dan Jacobson 4:256
Hugh Nissenson 9:400

Le Stourgeon, Diana E.
Rosamond Lehmann 5:235

Levensohn, Alan
Christina Stead 2:422

Levenson, J. C.
Saul Bellow 1:29

Levenson, Michael
Herbert Gold 7:121
Tom McHale 5:282
John Updike 5:460

Levertov, Denise
David Ignatow 7:173
John Wieners 7:535

Levey, Michael, Brigid Brophy,
and Charles Osborne
William Faulkner 1:102
W. Somerset Maugham 1:204

Levi, Peter
David Jones 4:261
George Seferis 5:384

Levi, Peter, S.J. and Robin
Milner-Gulland
Yevgeny Yevtushenko 1:381

Leviant, Curt
S. Y. Agnon 4:12
Jakov Lind 4:292
Isaac Bashevis Singer 3:453
Elie Wiesel 3:530

Levin, Bernard
Aleksandr I. Solzhenitsyn
   7:436

Levin, Dan
Yasunari Kawabata 2:223

Levin, Elena
Yevgeny Yevtushenko 1:382

Levin, Martin
Brian Aldiss 5:14
Taylor Caldwell 2:95
Austin C. Clarke 8:143
George Mac Donald Fraser
   7:106
Paul Gallico 2:147
Natalia Ginzburg 5:141
William Kotzwinkle 5:220
Richard Llewellyn 7:207
John McGahern 5:280
Alice Munro 6:341
Craig Nova 7:267
J. B. Priestley 2:347
Ann Quin 6:441
Jean Rhys 2:371
Judith Rossner 6:468
Terry Southern 7:452
David Storey 4:530
Jesse Stuart 8:507
Hollis Summers 10:493
Elizabeth Taylor 4:541
Fredrica Wagman 7:500
P. G. Wodehouse 2:479; 5:516
Louis Zukofsky 2:487

Levin, Meyer
Elmer Rice 7:358
Henry Roth 6:472

Levin, Milton
Noel Coward 1:64

Levine, George
John Gardner 7:113
Paul Goodman 2:171
Juan Carlos Onetti 7:279
Thomas Pynchon 3:414

Levine, June Perry
Vladimir Nabokov 6:352

Levine, Paul
Truman Capote 1:55; 3:99

Levine, Suzanne Jill
Severo Sarduy 6:486
Mario Vargas Llosa 6:547

Levitt, Morton P.
Michel Butor 3:92
Claude Simon 4:495

Levitt, Paul M. and Allan Franklin
Jorge Luis Borges 9:116

Levitzky, Sergei
Aleksandr I. Solzhenitsyn
   4:507

Levy, Francis
Thomas Berger 3:64
Ruth Prawer Jhabvala 4:257

Levy, Paul
Roald Dahl 6:122
Doris Lessing 6:301

Lewald, H. Ernest
Ernesto Sábato 10:446

Lewis, C. S.
J. R. R. Tolkien 1:336

Lewis, Janet
Caroline Gordon 6:206

Lewis, Paula Gilbert
Gabrielle Roy 10:440

Lewis, Peter Elfed
Marvin Bell **8**:65
Ruth Prawer Jhabvala **8**:313

Lewis, R. W. B.
Graham Greene **1**:131
André Malraux **4**:328
John Steinbeck **9**:512

Lewis, Robert W.
Edward Lewis Wallant **10**:516

Lewis, Robert W., Jr.
Ernest Hemingway **1**:142

Lewis, Stuart
Bruce Jay Friedman **3**:166

Lewis, Theophilus
Neil Simon **6**:502, 503

Lewis, Tom J.
Stanislaw Lem **8**:344

Lewis, Wyndham
Ezra Pound **7**:322

Ley, Charles David
Vicente Aleixandre **9**:10

Lhamon, W. T., Jr.
Anthony Burgess **5**:89
Bob Dylan **6**:158
John Gardner **3**:187
William Kennedy **6**:275
Joseph McElroy **5**:280
Robert M. Pirsig **4**:405
Thomas Pynchon **3**:412
Kurt Vonnegut, Jr. **4**:568

Libby, Anthony
William Carlos Williams **2**:470

Libby, Marion Vlastos
Margaret Drabble **5**:117

Liberman, M. M.
Katherine Anne Porter **1**:274;
7:318
Jean Stafford **4**:517

Lieber, Joel
Lois Gould **4**:199

Lieber, Todd M.
Ralph Ellison **3**:144
Robert Frost **9**:221
John Steinbeck **5**:406

Lieberman, Laurence
Rafael Alberti **7**:10
A. R. Ammons **2**:11
John Ashbery **9**:44
W. H. Auden **2**:28
John Berryman **1**:33
James Dickey **1**:73; **2**:115
Arthur Gregor **9**:252
Anthony Hecht **8**:268
Zbigniew Herbert **9**:271
Richard Howard **7**:165
Galway Kinnell **1**:168
Stanley J. Kunitz **6**:286
W. S. Merwin **1**:212; **3**:338
Howard Moss **7**:248
Howard Nemerov **2**:307
John Peck **3**:378
Kenneth Rexroth **2**:371
W. D. Snodgrass **2**:405
William Stafford **4**:520, 521
Mark Strand **6**:521
Theodore Weiss **3**:517
Reed Whittemore **4**:588

Lifton, Robert Jay
Albert Camus **2**:99
Kurt Vonnegut, Jr. **2**:455

Lima, Robert
Jorge Luis Borges **6**:88
Ira Levin **6**:306
Colin Wilson **3**:538

Lindberg-Seyersted, Brita
Bernard Malamud **9**:343

Lindborg, Henry J.
Doris Lessing **6**:299

Lindfors, Bernth
Chinua Achebe **7**:4

Lindner, Carl M.
Robert Frost **3**:175
James Thurber **5**:440

Lindop, Grevel
John Berryman **3**:66
Bob Dylan **4**:148

Linehan, Eugene J., S.J.
Taylor Caldwell **2**:95
Irving Wallace **7**:509

Lingeman, Richard R.
Erich Segal **10**:466

Lipsius, Frank
Herbert Gold **7**:121
Bernard Malamud **2**:268
Henry Miller **2**:283
Thomas Pynchon **6**:434

Listri, Pier Francesco
Allen Tate **6**:525

Little, Roger
St.-John Perse **4**:400

Littlejohn, David
James Baldwin **5**:40
Imamu Amiri Baraka **5**:44
Samuel Beckett **2**:45
Jorge Luis Borges **2**:68
Gwendolyn Brooks **5**:75
Lawrence Durrell **4**:144
Jean Genet **2**:157
John Hawkes **2**:183
Robert Hayden **5**:168
Joseph Heller **3**:229
Chester Himes **7**:159
Langston Hughes **5**:190
Robinson Jeffers **2**:214
John Oliver Killens **10**:300
Henry Miller **2**:281, 283
Ann Petry **7**:304
J. E. Wideman **5**:489
Richard Wright **9**:583

Littler, Frank
Nigel Dennis **8**:173

Lloyd, Peter
Leonardo Sciascia **9**:476

Locke, Richard
Donald Barthelme **8**:52
Thomas Berger **8**:83
Heinrich Böll **3**:73
John Cheever **8**:139
Joan Didion **8**:175
John Le Carré **5**:233
Vladimir Nabokov **2**:303; **8**:418
Thomas Pynchon **2**:356
John Updike **1**:345; **9**:540

Lockerbie, D. Bruce
C. S. Lewis **1**:177

Lockwood, William J.
Ed Dorn **10**:159

Lodge, David
Kingsley Amis **2**:10
William S. Burroughs **2**:92
Graham Greene **1**:134; **3**:206
Ted Hughes **2**:199
Norman Mailer **4**:321
Alain Robbe-Grillet **4**:447
Wilfrid Sheed **2**:394

Logan, John
E. E. Cummings **3**:117

Lomas, Herbert
Roy Fuller **4**:179
John Gardner **7**:115
Paul Goodman **4**:196
John Hawkes **7**:143
Robert M. Pirsig **6**:421
Ezra Pound **3**:398

Long, Robert Emmet
Ernest Hemingway **3**:237
Edmund Wilson **8**:550

Longley, Edna
Douglas Dunn **6**:147
Seamus Heaney **5**:170

Longley, John Lewis, Jr.
Robert Penn Warren **1**:355

Loprete, Nicholas J.
William Saroyan **10**:457

Lorch, Thomas M.
Edward Lewis Wallant **10**:512

Lorich, Bruce
Samuel Beckett **6**:34

Lowell, Robert
W. H. Auden **1**:9
John Berryman **2**:57
Randall Jarrell **2**:207
Stanley J. Kunitz **6**:285
Allen Tate **4**:535

Lowenkron, David Henry
Samuel Beckett **6**:40

Lucas, John
Ezra Pound **7**:332

Lucey, Beatus T., O.S.B.
Daphne du Maurier **6**:146

Luchting, Wolfgang A.
José María Arguedas **10**:9
José Donoso **4**:126, 127
Gabriel García Márquez **2**:150
Mario Vargas Llosa **10**:496

Lucid, Luellen
Alexsandr I. Solzhenitsyn
10:480

Lucid, Robert F.
Ernest Hemingway **6**:232
Norman Mailer **4**:323

Lucie-Smith, Edward
Sylvia Plath **9**:424

Luckett, Richard
Anthony Powell **7**:339
Robert Penn Warren **6**:555
Edmund Wilson **3**:540

Ludwig, Jack
Bernard Malamud **2**:269

Ludwig, Linda
Doris Lessing **6**:301

Lueders, Edward
Jorge Luis Borges **2**:72
George MacBeth **2**:252

Lukacs, John
Aleksandr I. Solzhenitsyn
7:438

Lumley, Frederick
Terence Rattigan **7**:354

Lumport, Felicia
Jessamyn West **7**:520

Lurie, Alison
Richard Adams **5**:7
Iris Murdoch **3**:348

Luschei, Martin
Walker Percy **3**:378

Lustig, Irma S.
Sean O'Casey **9**:411

Luttwak, Edward
Bernard Malamud **3**:325

Lynch, Dennis Daley
William Stafford **7**:462

Lynch, Michael
Richard Howard **7**:168
Michael McClure **10**:332

Lyne, Oliver
Ted Hughes **9**:282

Lynen, John F.
Robert Frost **1**:110

Lyon, George W., Jr.
Allen Ginsberg **3**:194

Lyon, Melvin
Edward Dahlberg **1**:72

Lyons, Bonnie
Margaret Atwood **8**:33
Henry Roth **2**:378; **6**:473
Delmore Schwartz **10**:463

Lyons, Eugene
Walker Percy **6**:399
John Updike **3**:486

Lyons, Gene
Peter Benchley **8**:82
Len Deighton **7**:75
John Hersey **9**:277
Elia Kazan **6**:274
George MacBeth **9**:340
Irving Wallace **7**:510
Robert Penn Warren **8**:540
Richard Yates **7**:555

Lyons, John O.
Vladimir Nabokov **1**:241

Lytle, Andrew
Allen Tate **4**:535

MacAndrew, Andrew R.
Yuri Olesha **8**:430

Macaulay, Jeannette
Camara Laye **4**:285

Macauley, Robie
R. P. Blackmur **2**:51
Patrick White **9**:566

MacBrudnoy, David
George Mac Donald Fraser
7:106

MacDiarmid, Hugh
Ezra Pound 4:413

Macdonald, Dwight
James Gould Cozzens 4:111
Philip Roth 1:293

Macdonald, Rae McCarthy
Alice Munro 10:357

Macdonald, Ross
Nelson Algren 10:8
Dashiell Hammett 5:160

MacInnes, Colin
James Baldwin 1:14

MacIntyre, Alasdair
Arthur Koestler 1:170

Maciuszko, George J.
Czeslaw Milosz 5:292

Mackay, Barbara
Imamu Amiri Baraka 10:19
Ed Bullins 7:37
James Kirkwood 9:319

MacKinnon, Alex
Earle Birney 6:79

Macklin, F. Anthony
Gore Vidal 2:449

MacLeish, Archibald
Ezra Pound 3:399

MacLeish, Roderick
Eric Ambler 6:3
Richard Condon 8:150
Len Deighton 7:74
George V. Higgins 4:224

Macnaughton, W. R.
Ernest Hemingway 8:286

MacShane, Frank
Jorge Luis Borges 2:76
Edward Dahlberg 1:71
W. S. Merwin 1:212
Pablo Neruda 9:399

MacSween, R. J.
Ivy Compton-Burnett 10:110

Madden, David
James M. Cain 3:96
William Gaddis 1:113
Wright Morris 1:230; 3:343

Maddocks, Melvin
Richard Adams 4:7
Kingsley Amis 2:7, 8
John Beecher 6:48
Heinrich Böll 3:75
Paul Bowles 2:78
J. P. Donleavy 6:142
Ernest J. Gaines 3:179
John Gardner 2:152
Joseph Heller 5:176
Thomas Keneally 5:209, 212
Doris Lessing 2:239; 6:298, 303
Bernard Malamud 2:267
Thomas Pynchon 2:354
Piers Paul Read 4:444
Philip Roth 4:456
Cornelius Ryan 7:385
Angus Wilson 3:536

Magalaner, Marvin and Frederick R. Karl
E. M. Forster 1:103
Aldous Huxley 1:150

Magid, Nora L.
Mordecai Richler 9:450

Magliola, Robert
Jorge Luis Borges 10:68

Magner, James E., Jr.
John Crowe Ransom 4:431

Mahlendorf, Ursula
Horst Bienek 7:28

Mahon, Derek
Austin Clarke 9:168
Donald Davie 10:125
John Le Carré 5:233
József Lengyel 7:202
Brian Moore 8:394
Edna O'Brien 8:429

Maida, Patricia D.
Flannery O'Connor 10:364

Mairowitz, David Zane
Edward Bond 6:86

Maitland, Sara
Flann O'Brien 5:314

Majdiak, Daniel
John Barth 1:17

Majeski, Jane
Arthur Koestler 8:324

Majkut, Denise R.
Bob Dylan 4:148

Major, Clarence
Ralph Ellison 3:146

Malanga, Gerard
Anne Waldman 7:508

Malin, Irving
Frederick Busch 7:39
Hortense Calisher 4:87
Eleanor Clark 5:105
B. H. Friedman 7:109
John Hawkes 4:217
Joseph Heller 5:182
Ken Kesey 6:278
Carson McCullers 4:344
Flannery O'Connor 2:317
Walker Percy 8:445
James Purdy 2:347
Muriel Spark 5:398; 8:496
Peter Spielberg 6:519
Harvey Swados 5:421
Elie Wiesel 5:490

Malkin, Lawrence
Harold Pinter 6:418

Malko, George
Frederick Buechner 4:80

Malkoff, Karl
Kenneth Rexroth 1:284
Theodore Roethke 1:291
May Swenson 4:533

Mallalieu, H. B.
John Gardner 7:116
Pablo Neruda 7:261
David Pownall 10:419

Mallet, Gina
Iris Murdoch 1:237
Tennessee Williams 7:545

Malley, Terrence
Richard Brautigan 3:88

Maloff, Saul
Nelson Algren 4:18
Louis Auchincloss 4:30
Heinrich Böll 9:110
Frederick Busch 7:38
Edward Dahlberg 7:68
Ernest Hemingway 3:236
Milan Kundera 9:321
Norman Mailer 2:264
Vladimir Nabokov 6:356
Flannery O'Connor 3:365
Clifford Odets 2:319
Sylvia Plath 2:336
Philip Roth 3:435; 4:455
Alan Sillitoe 1:307
Calder Willingham 5:512

Maloney, Douglas J.
Frederick Exley 6:171

Mandel, Siegfried
Uwe Johnson 5:200

Mandelbaum, Allen
Giuseppe Ungaretti 7:481

Mander, John
Günter Grass 6:208

Mangelsdorff, Rich
Michael McClure 6:318

Mangione, Jerry
Andrea Giovene 7:116

Mann, Golo
W. H. Auden 3:29

Mann, Jeanette W.
Jean Stafford 7:458

Manning, Olivia
Sylvia Townsend Warner 7:511

Mano, D. Keith
Richard Adams 4:9
J. G. Ballard 3:34
Thomas Berger 5:60
Daniel J. Berrigan 4:58
Jorge Luis Borges 2:71
John Cheever 3:108
Evan S. Connell, Jr. 6:117
Peter DeVries 10:136
J. P. Donleavy 4:125
Irvin Faust 8:214
William Gerhardie 5:140
James Hanley 3:221
Joseph Heller 5:180
George V. Higgins 4:224
B. S. Johnson 6:263, 264
Erica Jong 8:315
Vladimir Nabokov 2:301
Hugh Nissenson 9:400
John O'Hara 2:325
Philip Roth 4:458
William Saroyan 10:456
Alexander Theroux 2:433
John Updike 2:444; 5:456
Patrick White 3:525
Tennessee Williams 7:546

Manso, Susan
Anaïs Nin 8:424

Marcello, J. J. Armas
Mario Vargas Llosa 10:499

Marcotte, Edward
Alain Robbe-Grillet 6:467

Marcus, Adrianne
Jon Silkin 2:395
William Stafford 4:520

Marcus, Greil
Wendell Berry 8:85
E. L. Doctorow 6:134
John Sayles 10:460
Raymond Sokolov 7:431
Robert Wilson 9:576

Marcus, Mordecai
William Everson 1:96
Robert Frost 9:224
Ted Hughes 2:203
Bernard Malamud 1:199

Marcus, Steven
William Golding 2:165
Dashiell Hammett 10:252
Bernard Malamud 2:265
Irving Stone 7:470

Marguerite, Sister M., R.S.M.
Eleanor Hibbert 7:155

Mariani, John
Aleksandr I. Solzhenitsyn
7:440

Mariani, Paul
Robert Penn Warren 8:536
William Carlos Williams 9:572

Marill-Albérès, René
Jean-Paul Sartre 1:304

Marius, Richard
Frederick Buechner 4:79

Markmann, Charles Lam
Julien Green 3:205
Joyce Carol Oates 2:313

Markos, Donald
Hannah Green 3:202

Markos, Donald W.
James Dickey 1:74

Markow, Alice Bradley
Doris Lessing 6:297

Marks, Mitchell
Frederick Busch 7:38

Marowitz, Charles
Ed Bullins 1:47
John Osborne 5:331
Tom Stoppard 1:327

Marranca, Bonnie
Peter Handke 8:261; 10:256

Marsh, Pamela
Agatha Christie 1:58

Marshall, Donald
Stanislaw Lem 8:343

Marshall, Tom
Margaret Atwood 8:29
P. K. Page 7:292

Martin, Graham
Roy Fuller 4:177

Martin, Jay
Robert Lowell 1:181

Martin, Robert A.
Arthur Miller 10:346

Martin, Robert K.
Richard Howard 10:274

Martin, Wallace
D. J. Enright 8:204

Martinez, Z. Nelly
José Donoso 8:178

Martz, Louis L.
Robert Creeley 1:67
X. J. Kennedy 8:320
Robert Lowell 1:181
Joyce Carol Oates 9:403
Robert Pinsky 9:417
Ezra Pound 1:276
Reg Saner 9:469
Jon Silkin 2:396
William Stafford 4:521
John Wain 2:458

Martz, William J.
John Berryman 1:34

Masinton, Charles G.
J. P. Donleavy 10:153

Maskell, Duke
E. M. Forster 1:108; 9:203

Mason, Ann L.
Günter Grass 4:204

Mason, Michael
Donald Barthelme 8:53
George V. Higgins 10:273

Massingham, Harold
George Mackay Brown 5:76

Mathewson, Rufus W., Jr.
Boris Pasternak 7:299
Mikhail Sholokhov 7:421
Aleksandr I. Solzhenitsyn 7:441

Mathewson, Ruth
Alejo Carpentier 8:134
Joan Didion 8:176
J. P. Donleavy 10:154
Margaret Drabble 8:184
Paula Fox 8:219
Christina Stead 8:500
Robert Penn Warren 8:540

Matlaw, Myron
Alan Paton 10:387

Matthews, Charles
John Hawkes 2:183

Matthews, J. H.
André Breton 2:80

Matthews, T. S.
Edmund Wilson 8:551

Matthias, John
Elizabeth Daryush 6:123
Michael Hamburger 5:158
David Jones 7:189
Anne Stevenson 7:463
R. S. Thomas 6:530

Maurer, Robert
A. Alvarez 5:17
Robertson Davies 7:73
José Donoso 8:180
MacDonald Harris 9:258
Pablo Neruda 9:398
Clancy Sigal 7:425

Maurer, Robert E.
E. E. Cummings 8:155

Mauriac, Claude
Samuel Beckett 2:44
Albert Camus 2:97
Henry Miller 2:281
Alain Robbe-Grillet 2:373

**Nathalie Sarraute 2:383
Georges Simenon 2:396**

Maurois, André
Aldous Huxley 3:253
Jules Romains 7:381

Maury, Lucien
Pär Lagerkvist 7:198

Maxwell, D. E. S.
Brian Friel 5:128

May, Derwent
Nadine Gordimer 5:145
Alison Lurie 4:305
Tadeusz Różewicz 9:463
Louis Simpson 9:485

May, John R.
Kurt Vonnegut, Jr. 2:455

May, Keith M.
Aldous Huxley 4:242

Mayer, Hans
Friedrich Dürrenmatt 4:140
Witold Gombrowicz 4:193
Günter Grass 4:202
Jean-Paul Sartre 4:473

Mayhew, Alice
Graham Greene 1:134
Claude Mauriac 9:363

Maynard, Robert C.
Alex Haley 8:259

Mayne, Richard
Saul Bellow 8:70
J.I.M. Stewart 7:465

Mazzaro, Jerome
Elizabeth Bishop 9:88
David Ignatow 7:175, 178
Randall Jarrell 6:259
Robert Lowell 4:295, 298
Joyce Carol Oates 3:359
Ezra Pound 4:417
John Crowe Ransom 2:366
W. D. Snodgrass 6:514
William Carlos Williams 5:508

Mazzocco, Robert
John Ashbery 3:15
Chester Kallman 2:221
Philip Levine 5:251
William Meredith 4:348
Anne Sexton 6:492
Eleanor Ross Taylor 5:426
Gore Vidal 6:548

McAleer, John J.
MacKinlay Kantor 7:195
Alain Robbe-Grillet 10:438

McAllister, Mick
Michael McClure 6:319

McAuley, Gay
Jean Genet 10:225
Peter Handke 10:254

McCabe, Bernard
Wilfrid Sheed 10:474

McCaffery, Larry
Donald Barthelme 5:55
William H. Gass 8:242

McCahill, Alice
Elizabeth Taylor 2:432

McCall, Dorothy
Jean-Paul Sartre 7:388

McCarthy, Colman
P. G. Wodehouse 5:516

McCarthy, Harold T.
Henry Miller 9:377
Richard Wright 3:545

McCarthy, Mary
William S. Burroughs 2:90
Ivy Compton-Burnett 3:112
Vladimir Nabokov 2:301
J. D. Salinger 3:444
Nathalie Sarraute 2:384

McClain, Ruth Rambo
Toni Morrison 4:365

McClatchy, J. D.
A. R. Ammons 5:31
Louise Glück 7:119
Richard Howard 7:167
Robert Lowell 8:355
James Merrill 6:324
Robert Pinsky 9:417
Sylvia Plath 5:346
Ira Sadoff 9:466
Maura Stanton 9:507
Diane Wakoski 7:504
Robert Penn Warren 6:557
Theodore Weiss 8:546
Charles Wright 6:581

McClellan, Edwin
Yukio Mishima 6:338

McClelland, David
Flann O'Brien 5:315

McConnell, Frank
John Barth 7:25
Saul Bellow 6:54
John Gardner 7:115

McConville, Edward
John Sayles 10:461

McCullough, Frank
George Garrett 3:189

McDaniel, Richard Bryan
Chinua Achebe 7:6

McDonald, James L.
John Barth 2:38

McDonald, Susan S.
Harriet Waugh 6:560

McDonnell, Jane Taylor
Galway Kinnell 2:230

McDowell, Frederick P. W.
John Braine 1:43
Lawrence Durrell 1:87
E. M. Forster 1:107; 10:181
Doris Lessing 1:175
Iris Murdoch 1:236
Frederic Raphael 2:366
Muriel Spark 2:416

McDowell, Robert E.
Thomas Keneally 10:298

McElroy, Joseph
Samuel Beckett 2:48
Italo Calvino 5:99
Vladimir Nabokov 2:304

McElroy, Wendy
Gabriel García Márquez 10:217

McEvilly, Wayne
Anaïs Nin 1:248

McFadden, George
Robert Lowell 9:333

McGann, Jerome
Robert Creeley 2:106; 8:151
David Jones 7:188
X. J. Kennedy 8:320
Eleanor Lerman 9:331

McGann, Jerome J.
Turner Cassity 6:107
Daniel Mark Epstein 7:97
A. D. Hope 3:251
Donald Justice 6:272
Muriel Rukeyser 6:479
Judith Johnson Sherwin 7:415

McGilchrist, Iain
W. H. Auden 9:57

McGinnis, Wayne D.
Kurt Vonnegut, Jr. 8:529

McGinniss, Joe
George V. Higgins 4:222

McGregor, Craig
Bob Dylan 4:148

McGuane, Thomas
Richard Brautigan 1:44
John Hawkes 2:185

McGuinness, Frank
Kingsley Amis 1:6
Andrew Sinclair 2:400

McHale, Tom
Diane Johnson 5:198
D. Keith Mano 2:270
J. F. Powers 8:447

McInerney, John
John Knowles 10:303

McInerny, Ralph
Anthony Burgess 4:80

McKenzie, Alan T.
John Updike 5:452

McKinley, Hugh
Anthony Kerrigan 6:275

McKinnon, William T.
Louis MacNeice 10:324

McLay, C. M.
Margaret Laurence 3:278

McLellan, Joseph
Donald Barthelme 8:52
John Berryman 8:90
Arthur Hailey 5:156
Robert Heinlein 8:275
George V. Higgins 10:274
John Sayles 7:399
J.R.R. Tolkien 8:515

McLeod, A. L.
Patrick White 7:531

McMahon, Joseph H.
Jean-Paul Sartre 7:389

McMahon-Hill, Gillian
Russell C. Hoban 7:161

McMichael, James
May Sarton 4:471

McMullen, Roy
Nathalie Sarraute 2:385

McMurtry, Larry
Vardis Fisher 7:103
Ward Just 4:265

CRITIC INDEX

McNeil, Nicholas J., S.J.
Eleanor Hibbert 7:156

McNelly, Willis E.
Ray Bradbury 10:70
Robert Heinlein 8:274
Kurt Vonnegut, Jr. 2:452

McPheeters, D. W.
Camilo José Cela 4:98

McPherson, Hugo
Mordecai Richler 5:374

McPherson, William
Margaret Atwood 8:30
Paula Fox 8:218
John Gardner 8:235
Maxine Kumin 5:222
John Updike 5:457

McSweeney, Kerry
V. S. Naipul 9:391
Anthony Powell 9:435

McWilliams, Dean
Michel Butor 3:94
Marguerite Duras 3:129

**McWilliams, Nancy R. and Wilson
C. McWilliams**
John Steinbeck 5:405

**McWilliams, Wilson C. and Nancy
R. McWilliams**
John Steinbeck 5:405

Meades, Jonathan
Simone de Beauvoir 2:43
Jorge Luis Borges 1:39; 3:77;
4:74
Louis-Ferdinand Céline 3:105
Iris Murdoch 2:297
Vladimir Nabokov 2:302; 3:354
Alain Robbe-Grillet 1:289;
2:376; 4:448
Kurt Vonnegut, Jr. 2:455

Meckier, Jerome
Evelyn Waugh 3:512

Medawar, Peter
Arthur Koestler 6:281; 8:324

Meeter, Glenn
Kurt Vonnegut, Jr. 4:566

Megaw, Moira
W. H. Auden 6:24

Megged, Aharon
S. Y. Agnon 4:14

Meiners, R. K.
James Dickey 7:81
Robert Lowell 1:182
Delmore Schwartz 2:387
Allen Tate 4:536

Meinke, Peter
W. H. Auden 6:20
John Beecher 6:48
John Dos Passos 4:136
H. D. 8:256
Marilyn Hacker 5:155
Ted Hughes 4:236
Philip Levine 5:250
Howard Nemerov 2:307
Muriel Rukeyser 6:478
Anne Sexton 4:483
Diane Wakoski 7:504
Robert Penn Warren 6:555
Charles Wright 6:579

Mellard, James M.
Bernard Malamud 1:198
François Mauriac 9:367
Kurt Vonnegut, Jr. 3:504; 4:565

Mellor, Isha
Sol Yurick 6:583

Mellors, John
Martin Amis 4:20
Louis Auchincloss 6:15
Beryl Bainbridge 10:17
Thomas Berger 5:60
Caroline Blackwood 9:101
Melvyn Bragg 10:72
Angela Carter 5:102
Peter De Vries 7:77
Shusaku Endo 7:96
John Fowles 6:188
John Hawkes 7:141
Mark Helprin 10:260
Dan Jacobson 4:253
Ruth Prawer Jhabvala 8:312
G. Josipovici 6:270
Bernard Malamud 5:269
Stanley Middleton 7:219
Yukio Mishima 4:357
Alberto Moravia 7:244
Iris Murdoch 4:369
Julia O'Faolain 6:382
V. S. Pritchett 5:353
Piers Paul Read 4:444; 10:435
William Sansom 6:484
Nathalie Sarraute 10:460
Penelope Shuttle 7:422
Alan Sillitoe 6:499
Wole Soyinka 5:398
Richard G. Stern 4:523
David Storey 8:504
Ludvík Vaculík 7:495
Charles Webb 7:516
Patrick White 5:485

Mellown, Elgin W.
Jean Rhys 2:373
John Wain 2:458

Melly, George
Jean Arp 5:33

Melville, Robert
Herbert Read 4:438

Mendelson, David
Eugène Ionesco 6:255

Mendelson, Edward
John Berryman 4:61
Thomas Pynchon 3:415; 6:439

Mengeling, Marvin E.
Ray Bradbury 1:42

Mercer, Peter
John Barth 9:61

Mercier, Vivian
Samuel Beckett 6:38
Harry Crews 6:118
J. P. Donleavy 4:125
E. M. Forster 2:135
George V. Higgins 4:222
Aldous Huxley 5:193
Iris Murdoch 4:368
Raymond Queneau 5:360
Alain Robbe-Grillet 6:465
Nathalie Sarraute 4:466
Claude Simon 4:496

Meredith, William
John Berryman 2:59; 3:68
Anthony Hecht 8:268
Robert Lowell 2:248
Muriel Rukeyser 10:442

Merideth, Robert
Norman Mailer 1:192

Merivale, Patricia
Vladimir Nabokov 1:242

Merkin, Daphne
Chaim Potok 7:321

Merrill, Reed B.
William H. Gass 8:245

Merrill, Robert
Kurt Vonnegut, Jr. 8:534

Merrill, Thomas F.
Allen Ginsberg 1:118

Mersand, Joseph
Elmer Rice 7:359

Mersmann, James F.
Robert Bly 5:62
Robert Duncan 4:142
Allen Ginsberg 4:182
Denise Levertov 5:247
Diane Wakoski 7:507

Merton, Thomas
Albert Camus 1:52
J. F. Powers 1:281

Mesher, David R.
Bernard Malamud 9:346

Mesic, Michael
James Dickey 4:121
Chester Kallman 2:221

Mesnet, Marie-Béatrice
Graham Greene 3:210

Metcalf, Paul
Charles Olson 9:413

Metzger, C. R.
Lawrence Ferlinghetti 10:176

Mewshaw, Michael
Jonathan Baumbach 6:31
Doris Betts 3:73
Robertson Davies 7:74
William Eastlake 8:200
B. H. Friedman 7:108
Robert F. Jones 7:192
David Slavitt 5:391
Raymond Sokolov 7:430
Peter Spielberg 6:519
Paul Theroux 5:427

Meyer, Ellen Hope
Erica Jong 4:264
Joyce Carol Oates 2:315

Meyer, Thomas
Lorine Niedecker 10:360

Meyers, Jeffrey
E. M. Forster 3:162; 4:169
Doris Lessing 2:241
André Malraux 4:333

Mezey, Robert
Jerome Rothenberg 6:478
Gary Snyder 9:498

Michaels, Leonard
John Barth 2:37
Jorge Luis Borges 2:77
Dashiell Hammett 5:160

Peter Handke 8:264
Erica Jong 8:314
Bernard Malamud 3:324
Vladimir Nabokov 8:417

Michener, Charles T.
Anthony Powell 3:402; 7:343

Middlebrook, Diane
Allen Ginsberg 6:199

Mihailovich, Vasa D.
Miroslav Krleža 8:330

Milch, Robert J.
Chaim Potok 2:338

Miles, William
Langston Hughes 1:148

Milford, Nancy
Louise Bogan 4:69

Millar, Margaret
Daphne du Maurier 6:146

Miller, Baxter
Langston Hughes 10:282

Miller, David
Michael Hamburger 5:158

Miller, James E., Jr.
William Faulkner 6:180
J. D. Salinger 1:298

Miller, Jane
Simone Schwarz-Bart 7:404

Miller, Jeanne-Marie A.
Imamu Amiri Baraka 2:35
Gwendolyn Brooks 1:46; 4:78
Charles Gordone 4:198

Miller, Karl
Martin Amis 4:21
Paula Fox 8:218
Ted Hughes 4:236
Dan Jacobson 4:256
Hugh MacDiarmid 2:254
Flann O'Brien 5:316
Anne Roiphe 9:456
Michel Tournier 6:538

Miller, Neil
Julio Cortázar 2:103

Miller, Nolan
Henry Bromell 5:73

Miller, Stephen
Zbigniew Herbert 9:272

Miller, Tom P.
William Stafford 4:521

Miller, Vincent
T. S. Eliot 9:182

Millgate, Michael
James Gould Cozzens 4:114
John Dos Passos 4:133

Mills, James
George V. Higgins 4:222

Mills, Ralph J., Jr.
Yves Bonnefoy 9:112
René Char 9:160
Richard Eberhart 3:134, 135
David Ignatow 7:174, 179
Maxine Kumin 5:222
Denise Levertov 2:243; 3:293
Philip Levine 4:287
Kathleen Raine 7:351
Theodore Roethke 1:291
Anne Stevenson 7:462

Millstein, Gilbert
Irvin Faust 8:215

Milne, Tom
John Osborne 5:330

Milne, W. Gordon
John Dos Passos 4:134

Milner-Gulland, Robin
Andrei Voznesensky 1:349

Milner-Gulland, Robin and Peter Levi, S.J.
Yevgeny Yevtushenko 1:381

Milosh, Joseph
John Gardner 10:220

Milton, Edith
Beryl Bainbridge 10:17
Frederick Buechner 9:136
Alan Sillitoe 10:477

Milton, John R.
Vardis Fisher 7:105
N. Scott Momaday 2:290

Milton, Joyce
Jules Feiffer 8:217

Milun, Richard A.
William Faulkner 6:177

Mindlin, M.
Yehuda Amichai 9:22

Minogue, Valerie
Alain Robbe-Grillet 10:437
Nathalie Sarraute 10:458

Mirsky, Mark J.
John Hawkes 7:145

Mirsky, Mark Jay
Samuel Beckett 6:38
Anthony Burgess 4:83
Günter Grass 4:205
Flann O'Brien 5:314
Manuel Puig 3:407

Mitchell, Julian
Ivy Compton-Burnett 10:110

Mitchell, Juliet
Norman Mailer 1:192

Mitchell, Marilyn L.
John Steinbeck 9:516

Mitchell, W.J.T.
Hubert Selby, Jr. 4:481

Mitchison, Naomi
W. H. Auden 9:57

Mitgang, Herbert
Giorgio Bassani 9:75
Leonardo Sciascia 9:475

Mittleman, Leslie B.
Kingsley Amis 8:11

Miyoshi, Masao
Yasunari Kawabata 9:311

Mizener, Arthur
James Gould Cozzens 4:115
John Dos Passos 4:133
Anthony Hecht 8:266
Anthony Powell 10:408
James Thurber 5:439
Edmund Wilson 2:475

Mo, Timothy
Jennifer Johnston 7:186
John Le Carré 5:234
Colin MacInnes 4:315

Wilfrid Sheed 4:489
Harriet Waugh 6:559

Moers, Ellen
Lillian Hellman 2:187

Mojtabai, A. G.
Yasunari Kawabata 5:208
Thomas Keneally 5:211
Richard Yates 8:555

Mok, Michael
Aleksandr I. Solzhenitsyn 2:409

Mole, John
Louis Simpson 7:428
R. S. Thomas 6:530

Molesworth, Charles
John Berryman 2:56; 8:89
Ted Hughes 4:236
Galway Kinnell 3:269
Anne Sexton 8:483
Charles Tomlinson 4:548

Molloy, F. C.
John McGahern 9:370

Moloney, Michael F.
François Mauriac 4:337

Momberger, Philip
William Faulkner 6:179

Monagan, John S.
Anthony Powell 7:342

Monas, Sidney
Aleksandr I. Solzhenitsyn 4:511

Monegal, Emir Rodríguez-
See Rodríguez-Monegal, Emir

Monet, Christina and Michael Zilkha
Mark Medoff 6:323

Monguió, Luis
Rafael Alberti 7:8

Monogue, Valerie
Harold Pinter 6:404

Monsman, Gerald
J. R. R. Tolkien 1:339

Montagnes, Anne
Brian Moore 5:297

Monteiro, George
Bob Dylan 4:149
Robert Frost 4:174; 10:199
Ernest Hemingway 6:231

Montgomery, Marion
T. S. Eliot 6:163
Robert Frost 10:195
Flannery O'Connor 1:258

Montgomery, Niall
Flann O'Brien 7:269

Moody, Michael
Mario Vargas Llosa 9:544

Moorcock, Michael
Angus Wilson 3:535

Moore, Brian
Robertson Davies 2:113

Moore, D. B.
Louis MacNeice 4:316

Moore, Harry T.
Arthur Adamov 4:5
Kay Boyle 5:65

John Dos Passos 4:132
E. M. Forster 1:106
Herbert Gold 4:190
Eugène Ionesco 4:252
James Jones 3:262
Meyer Levin 7:204
Henry Miller 4:350
Alain Robbe-Grillet 2:374
Nathalie Sarraute 2:384
Georges Simenon 2:397
Claude Simon 4:494
John Steinbeck 5:405

Moore, Honor
Marilyn Hacker 5:156
June Jordan 5:203

Moore, Hugo
Hugh MacDiarmid 4:311

Moore, Jack B.
Frank Yerby 7:556

Moore, John Rees
James Baldwin 2:31
Samuel Beckett 10:29
J. P. Donleavy 1:76; 4:124
Robert Penn Warren 6:558

Moore, Marianne
Ezra Pound 7:322
Edith Sitwell 9:493

Moore, Maxine
Isaac Asimov 9:49

Moore, Richard
George Garrett 3:192

Moore, Stephen C.
John Cheever 7:49
Robert Lowell 3:301

Moorman, Charles
J. R. R. Tolkien 1:337

Moramarco, Fred
John Ashbery 4:22; 9:42
Robert Creeley 1:67
David Ignatow 7:181
Galway Kinnell 2:229
W. S. Merwin 1:213
James Schevill 7:401

Moran, Ronald
Wendell Berry 4:59
Robert Creeley 4:117
David Ignatow 4:248
Marge Piercy 6:402
Louis Simpson 4:498
James Tate 6:528

Morello-Frosch, Marta
Julio Cortázar 2:104
Gabriel García Márquez 3:183

Morgan, Edwin
John Berryman 10:47
Eugenio Montale 9:387

Morgan, Ellen
Doris Lessing 3:288

Morgan, John
Günter Grass 6:209

Morgan, Robert
Geoffrey Hill 8:294

Morgan, Speer
Dan Jacobson 4:256

Morley, Patricia A.
Patrick White 7:529

Morley, Sheridan
Terence Rattigan 7:354

Morris, Alice
Christina Stead 2:422

Morris, C. B.
Rafael Alberti 7:9
Vicente Aleixandre 9:12

Morris, Christopher D.
John Barth 7:23

Morris, H. H.
Dashiell Hammett 10:253

Morris, Harry
Louise Bogan 4:68
James Dickey 1:73
Jean Garrigue 2:154
John Hollander 2:197
George MacBeth 2:251
Louis Simpson 4:498

Morris, Ivan
Yasunari Kawabata 2:222

Morris, Jan
Laurens van der Post 5:464

Morris, John N.
Donald Justice 6:271
Adrienne Rich 7:370
Mark Strand 6:521
Nancy Willard 7:539
Charles Wright 6:580

Morris, Robert K.
Anthony Burgess 4:81; 5:86
Lawrence Durrell 4:146
John Fowles 6:189
James Hanley 5:167
Doris Lessing 6:290
Olivia Manning 5:271
Anthony Powell 1:278; 3:404; 7:345
V. S. Pritchett 5:354
C. P. Snow 6:515
Thornton Wilder 6:578

Morris, Wesley
John Crowe Ransom 4:433

Morris, Wright
Ernest Hemingway 1:141

Morrison, Blake
Donald Davie 10:124

Morrison, J. M.
Hugh MacDiarmid 2:254

Morrison, John W.
Jun'ichiro Tanizaki 8:509

Morrison, Theodore
Robert Frost 1:111

Morrissette, Bruce
Alain Robbe-Grillet 1:287

Morrissey, Daniel
John Updike 7:488

Morrow, Lance
John Fowles 6:187
Erica Jong 8:314
Yasunari Kawabata 5:208
James A. Michener 5:290
Yukio Mishima 4:356, 358

Morse, J. Mitchell
Kingsley Amis 2:6
James Baldwin 2:32
Bruce Jay Friedman 3:165

CRITIC INDEX

Joanne Greenberg 7:134
Jakov Lind 2:245
Mary McCarthy 1:207
Vladimir Nabokov 2:299
Peter Weiss 3:514

Morse, Samuel French
W. H. Auden 6:18
Margaret Avison 2:29
John Berryman 3:65
Robert Lowell 3:301
Louis Zukofsky 1:385

Mortimer, John
James Thurber 5:433

Mortimer, Penelope
Elizabeth Bishop 9:89
Nadine Gordimer 7:132
Fay Weldon 6:562

Moscoso-Gongora, Peter
José Lezama Lima 10:319

Moser, Gerald M.
José Rodrigues Miguéis 10:340

Moses, Edwin
Albert Camus 9:148

Moskowitz, Moshe
Chaim Grade 10:248

Mosley, Nicholas
J. P. Donleavy 10:155

Moss, Howard
W. H. Auden 6:20
Elizabeth Bishop 1:35; 9:91
Elizabeth Bowen 1:41; 3:84
Graham Greene 6:217
Flann O'Brien 1:252
Katherine Anne Porter 1:272
Jean Rhys 6:454
Nathalie Sarraute 1:302
Eudora Welty 2:463

Moss, Leonard
Arthur Miller 1:217

Moss, Robert F.
Lawrence Durrell 6:153
John O'Hara 6:384

Moss, Stanley
Stanley J. Kunitz 6:286

Mossman, Elliott
Boris Pasternak 10:382

Motley, Joel
Leon Forrest 4:164

Mott, Michael
A. R. Ammons 8:15
Geoffrey Grigson 7:135
David Jones 7:186

Mottram, Eric
Fielding Dawson 6:126
Michael McClure 6:317
Arthur Miller 1:218
Gilbert Sorrentino 7:449
Diane Wakoski 4:572

Mount, Ferdinand
Peter Handke 10:257

Movius, Geoffrey H.
William Carlos Williams 9:575

Moynahan, Julian
Louis Auchincloss 9:54
Frederick Buechner 9:137
Anthony Burgess 8:113

J. P. Donleavy 4:126
Jack Kerouac 2:228
Ken Kesey 6:277
Tom McHale 3:331
Brian Moore 3:341; 8:394
Seán O'Faoláin 7:274
Anne Roiphe 9:455
Wilfrid Sheed 10:472
James Tate 2:431

Mozejko, Edward
Elisaveta Bagryana 10:13

Muchnic, Helen
Mikhail Sholokhov 7:418, 421
Aleksandr I. Solzhenitsyn
9:507

Mudrick, Marvin
Donald Barthelme 2:39
William S. Burroughs 2:90
E. M. Forster 2:135
John Fowles 2:137
Jerzy Kosinski 2:231
Doris Lessing 2:239
Norman Mailer 1:192
Bernard Malamud 1:200
Vladimir Nabokov 3:355
Joyce Carol Oates 2:314
Nathalie Sarraute 2:384; 4:468
David Wagoner 3:508

Mudrovic, Mike
Claudio Rodríguez 10:440

Mueller, Lisel
Robert Bly 1:37
Louise Glück 7:118
Michael S. Harper 7:138
Jim Harrison 6:223
Anthony Hecht 8:268
W. S. Merwin 1:212
Marge Piercy 6:401
Peter Viereck 4:559
Alice Walker 6:553
Reed Whittemore 4:588

Muggeridge, Malcolm
Paul Scott 9:478

Muller, Gilbert H.
William Faulkner 8:212

Müller-Bergh, Klaus
José Lezama Lima 4:288

Munk, Erica
Martin Duberman 8:185

Murchison, John C.
Jorge Luis Borges 2:71, 75

Murchison, W., Jr.
John Dickson Carr 3:101

Murchland, Bernard
Albert Camus 2:97
Jean-Paul Sartre 7:396

Murdoch, Charles
John Glassco 9:236

Murillo, L. A.
Jorge Luis Borges 4:70

Murphy, Richard
Philip Larkin 5:231

Murr, Judy Smith
John Gardner 10:219

Murray, Atholl C.C.
David Jones 7:188

Murray, Edward
Samuel Beckett 6:35
William Faulkner 6:176
Ernest Hemingway 6:229
Eugène Ionesco 6:251
Arthur Miller 6:327, 332
Alain Robbe-Grillet 6:466
Tennessee Williams 5:501

Murray, Jack
Alain Robbe-Grillet 1:287

Murray, John J.
Robert Penn Warren 4:579

Murray, Michael
Edward Albee 2:3

Murray, Michele
Paula Fox 2:140
Susan B. Hill 4:227
Robert Kotlowitz 4:275
Pär Lagerkvist 7:200
Mary Lavin 4:282
Grace Paley 4:392

Murray, Philip
Aldous Huxley 3:256

Murtaugh, Daniel M.
Marie-Claire Blais 4:67
Wilfrid Sheed 2:393

Mus, David
T. S. Eliot 2:129

Musher, Andrea
Diane Wakoski 7:505

Muske, Carol
Jon Anderson 9:31

Myers, Robert J.
Lothar-Günther Buchheim
6:100

Myrsiades, Kostas
Yannis Ritsos 6:463

Nadeau, Maurice
Louis Aragon 3:13
Simone de Beauvoir 1:19
Samuel Beckett 1:22
Michel Butor 1:49
Albert Camus 1:54
Louis-Ferdinand Céline 1:56
Jean Genet 1:115
Jean Giono 4:185
Raymond Queneau 2:359
Alain Robbe-Grillet 1:288
Françoise Sagan 3:444
Nathalie Sarraute 1:303
Jean-Paul Sartre 1:305
Claude Simon 4:495

Naiden, James
Lorine Niedecker 10:360

Naipaul, Shiva
Miguel Ángel Asturias 8:27
José Donoso 4:130

Naipaul, V. S.
Jorge Luis Borges 2:77
Jean Rhys 2:372

Nance, William L., S.M.
Katherine Anne Porter 7:314

Nardin, Jane
Evelyn Waugh 8:544

Naremore, James
Philip Larkin 5:226

Nassar, Eugene Paul
Ezra Pound 7:335

Nathan, George Jean
Noel Coward 9:171
Terence Rattigan 7:353
Elmer Rice 7:359

Navarro, Carlos
Jorge Luis Borges 3:79

Navasky, Victor S.
Meyer Levin 7:204

Nazareth, Peter
James Ngugi 7:266

Needleman, Ruth
Octavio Paz 3:375

Neimark, Paul G.
Agatha Christie 1:58

Nelson, Howard
Robert Bly 10:54

Nelson, Hugh
Harold Pinter 6:413

Nelson, Joyce
Kurt Vonnegut, Jr. 4:562

Nelson, Raymond
Chester Himes 2:196

Nemerov, Howard
Conrad Aiken 3:4
Kingsley Amis 2:5
Djuna Barnes 3:36
Kenneth Burke 2:89
James Dickey 4:120
Harry Mathews 6:315
Marianne Moore 4:359
Howard Moss 7:247
Kathleen Raine 7:353

Nettelbeck, Colin W.
Louis-Ferdinand Céline 3:103

Nevins, Francis M., Jr.
Ellery Queen 3:421
Rex Stout 3:471

Nevius, Blake
Ivy Compton-Burnett 1:62

New, William H.
Margaret Avison 4:36
Robertson Davies 7:73
Simon Gray 9:241

Newberry, Wilma
Ramón Gómez de la Serna
9:237

Newlin, Margaret
Sylvia Plath 3:389

Newlove, Donald
Peter Benchley 4:53
Joseph Brodsky 4:78
Thomas Kinsella 4:271
W. S. Merwin 5:287
J. D. Salinger 8:463

Newman, Charles
Saul Bellow 6:59
Sylvia Plath 9:421
Philip Roth 4:457

Newman, Christina
Brian Moore 8:395

Newman, Michael
W. H. Auden 6:25

Nichol, B. P.
Earle Birney 6:76

Nicholas, Brian and Ian Gregor
Graham Greene 6:214

Nichols, Stephen G., Jr.
John Hawkes 3:221

Nicol, Charles
Kingsley Amis 5:22
Brigid Brophy 6:100
Anthony Burgess 5:90
Peter De Vries 7:77
Dashiell Hammett 5:162
John Hawkes 4:218; 7:144
Milan Kundera 9:320
Norman Mailer 4:323
Vladimir Nabokov 1:244
Kurt Vonnegut, Jr. 3:504; 8:534

Niemeyer, Gerhart
Aleksandr I. Solzhenitsyn
7:439

Nightingale, Benedict
Alan Ayckbourn 5:35
Edward Bond 4:70
A. E. Ellis 7:93
Michael Frayn 7:107
John Hopkins 4:234
David Mercer 5:284
Peter Nichols 5:305, 306
John Osborne 5:333
J. B. Priestley 5:350
Neil Simon 6:504
Tom Stoppard 5:412
David Storey 5:415
E. A. Whitehead 5:488

Nissenson, Hugh
Chaim Potok 2:338; 7:321

Nitchie, George W.
Robert Lowell 8:350
George MacBeth 2:251
Marianne Moore 8:397

Noble, David W.
James Baldwin 4:40

Nokes, David
Michael Mewshaw 9:377

Nolan, Paul T.
Marc Connelly 7:55

Noland, W. Richard
Elliott Baker 8:38

Nomad, Max
Ignazio Silone 4:493

Norris, Leslie
Andrew Young 5:525

Norwood, W. D., Jr.
C. S. Lewis 1:177

Novak, Michael Paul
Robert Hayden 5:169

Novak, William
Grace Paley 6:391
Susan Fromberg Schaeffer
6:488

Novick, Julius
Edward Albee 9:10
John Bishop 10:54
Simon Gray 9:242
David Mamet 9:360
David Rabe 4:425
Tom Stoppard 4:525; 8:504

David Storey 8:505
Tennessee Williams 8:548

Nyabongo, V. S.
Alice Walker 6:554

Nye, Robert
Brigid Brophy 6:98
E. M. Forster 3:162
David Garnett 3:189
Graham Greene 3:214
Bernard Malamud 5:269
Anthony Powell 3:402
John Cowper Powys 7:349
William Sansom 6:483
Penelope Shuttle 7:422

Oates, Joyce Carol
Harriette Arnow 2:14
James Baldwin 5:42
Frederick Busch 7:38
James M. Cain 3:95
Robert Coover 7:58
Robert Creeley 8:152
Roald Dahl 1:177
James Dickey 7:83
Joan Didion 8:175
Margaret Drabble 2:118; 5:117
James T. Farrell 4:158
Janet Frame 2:141
Gail Godwin 5:142
William Goyen 8:250
Jim Harrison 6:224
Maxine Kumin 5:222
Philip Larkin 8:337
Mary Lavin 4:282
Doris Lessing 2:241
Philip Levine 4:286, 288
Bernard Malamud 3:323
Berry Morgan 6:339
Alice Munro 6:342
Iris Murdoch 1:237
Vladimir Nabokov 2:304
Charles Newman 2:312; 8:419
Flannery O'Connor 1:258
Sylvia Plath 2:338; 5:340
Philip Roth 4:454
Anne Sexton 6:492
Elizabeth Taylor 2:433
Peter Taylor 1:335
Paul Theroux 8:512
William Trevor 9:529
John Updike 2:441
Fay Weldon 9:559
Eudora Welty 1:363
Richard Yates 7:554

Oberbeck, S. K.
Kingsley Amis 2:7
Frederick Forsyth 5:125
John Hawkes 1:137
John Hersey 7:154
Norman Mailer 2:264
Joyce Carol Oates 2:315
Georges Simenon 2:398
Kurt Vonnegut, Jr. 3:502

Oberg, Arthur
John Berryman 4:66
Galway Kinnell 3:270
Greg Kuzma 7:197
Philip Levine 2:244
John Matthias 9:362
Joyce Carol Oates 6:367
Anne Sexton 4:482

Mona Van Duyn 7:498
Derek Walcott 9:556

O'Brien, James H.
Liam O'Flaherty 5:321

O'Brien, John
Gilbert Sorrentino 7:450

Obuchowski, Mary Dejong
Yasunari Kawabata 9:316

O'Connell, Shaun
Marjorie Kellogg 2:224
Gilbert Sorrentino 7:447

O'Connor, Garry
Jean Anouilh 8:24

O'Connor, John J.
Lanford Wilson 7:547

O'Connor, Mary
Caroline Gordon 6:203

O'Connor, William Van
Kingsley Amis 1:5
Donald Davie 5:113
D. J. Enright 4:154
Elizabeth Jennings 5:197
Philip Larkin 3:275
Iris Murdoch 1:234
Ezra Pound 1:275
John Wain 2:458

O'Daniel, Therman B.
Ralph Ellison 1:95

O'Doherty, Brian
Flann O'Brien 5:314

O'Faolain, Julia
Beryl Bainbridge 10:15
Mark Helprin 10:260
Edna O'Brien 5:311
Isaac Bashevis Singer 9:489

Ogunyemi, Chikwenye Okonjo
Toni Morrison 10:354

O'Hara, J. D.
Kingsley Amis 8:11
Donald Barthelme 5:54
Ann Beattie 8:54
Samuel Beckett 6:39
Jorge Luis Borges 2:77
Kay Boyle 5:66
Anthony Burgess 5:86, 88
Louis-Ferdinand Céline 4:103
Roald Dahl 6:121
Edward Dahlberg 7:71
Lawrence Durrell 6:152
George V. Higgins 4:223
José Lezama Lima 4:288
Vladimir Nabokov 1:246
Judith Rossner 6:469
C. P. Snow 9:498

O'Hara, T.
Derek Walcott 4:575

O'Hara, Tim
Ronald Sukenick 4:531

Ohmann, Carol B.
Muriel Spark 2:414

Ohmann, Richard M.
Pär Lagerkvist 7:199

O'Keeffe, Timothy
Patrick White 3:521

Olderman, Raymond M.
John Barth 3:40

Peter S. Beagle 7:26
Stanley Elkin 4:153
John Hawkes 3:222
Joseph Heller 3:229
Ken Kesey 3:266
Thomas Pynchon 3:411
Kurt Vonnegut, Jr. 3:505

Oldsey, Bernard S. and Stanley Weintraub
William Golding 2:167

Oliphant, Dave
Albert Goldbarth 5:143

Oliver, Edith
Ed Bullins 5:83; 7:36
Anne Burr 6:103
John Guare 8:253
Christopher Hampton 4:211
Mark Medoff 6:322
Rochelle Owens 8:434
Terence Rattigan 7:355
Jonathan Reynolds 6:451
Sam Shepard 6:497
Tom Stoppard 3:470; 4:525
Derek Walcott 2:460
Richard Wesley 7:518

Oliver, Raymond
Arthur Gregor 9:255

Oliver, Roy
Arthur A. Cohen 7:51

Olmert, Michael
Philip Roth 4:452

Olney, James
Chinua Achebe 1:2
Loren Eiseley 7:92

Olsen, Gary R.
Hermann Hesse 6:238

Olshen, Barry N.
John Fowles 9:210

Olson, David B.
Robert Penn Warren 10:518

Olson, Lawrence
Yukio Mishima 2:288

Olson, Toby
Diane Wakoski 7:505

Onley, Gloria
Margaret Atwood 4:25

Opdahl, Keith
Saul Bellow 3:51

Oppenheimer, Joel
Philip Roth 4:457
William Saroyan 10:456

Ormerod, Beverley
Édouard Glissant 10:230

Ormerod, David
V. S. Naipaul 4:371

Ornstein, Jacob and James Y. Causey
Camilo José Cela 4:95

O'Rourke, William
Rosalyn Drexler 2:120
Craig Nova 7:267

Orr, Leonard
Richard Condon 4:107

Orth, Maureen
Bob Dylan 3:130

CRITIC INDEX

Ortiz, Gloria M.
  Pablo Neruda 7:260

Orwell, George
  Alex Comfort 7:52
  Graham Greene 6:216

Osborn, Neal J.
  Kenneth Burke 2:87

Osborne, Charles, Brigid Brophy,
and Michael Levey
  William Faulkner 1:102
  W. Somerset Maugham 1:204

Osborne, David
  Albert Camus 2:99

Ostriker, Alicia
  Ai 4:16
  Cid Corman 9:170
  Alan Dugan 2:121
  Paul Goodman 7:131
  Anne Waldman 7:508

Ostroff, Anthony
  Donald Justice 6:271
  Kathleen Spivack 6:520
  Mark Van Doren 6:542

Ostrom, Alan
  William Carlos Williams 1:370

Ostrovsky, Erika
  Louis-Ferdinand Céline 4:98

Otten, Anna
  Heinrich Böll 2:66
  Michel Butor 8:120
  Alain Robbe-Grillet 6:467;
   8:453
  Nathalie Sarraute 2:386
  Claude Simon 4:497

Oviedo, José Miguel
  Mario Vargas Llosa 10:497, 500

Owen, Carys T.
  Louis-Ferdinand Céline 9:155

Owen, I. M.
  Robertson Davies 7:72

Owens, Iris
  Lois Gould 4:200

Owens, Rochelle
  Diane Wakoski 7:505

Ower, John
  Mordecai Richler 9:451
  Edith Sitwell 9:494

Ower, John B.
  Edith Sitwell 2:404

Ownbey, Steve
  George V. Higgins 10:273
  Georges Simenon 8:486

Owomoyela, Oyekan
  Chester Himes 7:159

Ozick, Cynthia
  Saul Bellow 10:43
  Frederick Buechner 2:83
  Hugh Nissenson 4:380

Pace, Eric
  Joseph Wambaugh 3:508

Pacernick, Gary
  Millen Brand 7:30

Pachter, Henry
  Paul Goodman 7:129

Pachter, Henry M.
  Hermann Hesse 6:236

Pack, Robert
  James Schevill 7:400

Packard, Nancy H.
  Grace Paley 6:393

Page, James A.
  James Baldwin 3:32
  Ralph Ellison 3:145
  Richard Wright 3:546

Palevsky, Joan
  Isak Dinesen 10:148

Palmer, Eustace
  Chinua Achebe 7:5
  James Ngugi 7:265

Palmer, Penelope
  Charles Tomlinson 6:536

Palmer, R. Roderick
  Haki R. Madhubuti 6:313
  Sonia Sanchez 5:382

Panshin, Alexei
  Robert A. Heinlein 3:224

Panter-Downes, Mollie
  John Le Carré 9:327

Parameswaran, Uma
  Derek Walcott 9:557

Parente, Diane A.
  James Dickey 10:142

Parente, William J.
  Alexsandr I. Solzhenitsyn
   10:479

Parisi, Joseph
  X. J. Kennedy 8:320
  Mark Van Doren 6:543

Park, Clara Claiborne
  Brigid Brophy 6:99
  Richard Wilbur 9:568

Parkhill-Rathbone, James
  C. P. Snow 1:317; 6:518

Parkinson, Thomas
  Robert Lowell 1:179, 180
  Gary Snyder 1:317

Parr, J. L.
  Calder Willingham 5:510

Parrinder, Patrick
  Philip K. Dick 10:138
  B. S. Johnson 9:302

Parsons, Ann
  William Carlos Williams 2:469

Parsons, Thornton H.
  John Crowe Ransom 2:364

Paschall, Douglas
  Theodore Roethke 3:434

Patten, Brian
  Isaac Asimov 3:17
  Kurt Vonnegut, Jr. 3:504

Patten, Karl
  Graham Greene 1:131

Paul, Sherman
  Paul Goodman 1:123
  Boris Pasternak 7:295
  Edmund Wilson 1:373

Paulin, Tom
  John Fowles 10:189
  Jerzy Kosinski 10:308

Pawel, Ernst
  Heinrich Böll 2:67; 9:109
  Hermann Hesse 2:192
  Jakov Lind 2:245

Payne, Robert
  Yuri Olesha 8:432
  Boris Pasternak 7:292

Paz, Octavio
  Elizabeth Bishop 9:89
  André Breton 9:129
  Alexsandr I. Solzhenitsyn
   10:478
  William Carlos Williams 5:508

Pearce, Richard
  Saul Bellow 8:72
  John Dos Passos 8:181
  John Hawkes 9:266
  Henry Roth 6:473

Pearson, Gabriel
  John Berryman 2:55

Pearson, Norman Holmes
  Ezra Pound 2:340

Peavy, Charles D.
  Hubert Selby, Jr. 1:306

Peden, William
  James Baldwin 8:40
  Doris Betts 6:70
  Ed Bullins 7:37
  John Cheever 7:49
  Laurie Colwin 5:108
  James T. Farrell 8:205
  Shirley Ann Grau 9:240
  Chester Himes 7:159
  Langston Hughes 10:281
  Grace Paley 6:392
  Ann Petry 7:305
  William Saroyan 8:468
  Irwin Shaw 7:411
  Isaac Bashevis Singer 6:509
  Jesse Stuart 8:507
  Tennessee Williams 5:502

Peel, Marie
  John Osborne 2:329
  Peter Redgrove 6:445, 446
  Penelope Shuttle 7:423
  Alan Sillitoe 3:448
  David Storey 2:425
  R. S. Thomas 6:531

Pelli, Moshe
  S. Y. Agnon 8:8

Penner, Allen R.
  Alan Sillitoe 1:308

Peppard, Murray B.
  Friedrich Dürrenmatt 1:81

Percy, Walker
  Walter M. Miller, Jr. 4:352
  Marion Montgomery 7:232
  Eudora Welty 1:362

Perera, Victor
  Miguel Ángel Asturias 3:18

Perez, Gilberto
  Beryl Bainbridge 10:16
  Alan Sillitoe 10:477

Pérez Firmat, Gustavo
  José Lezama Lima 10:319

Perkins, David
  Ezra Pound 3:397
  Carl Sandburg 10:449

Perlberg, Mark
  Larry Eigner 9:181
  Michael S. Harper 7:138
  George Oppen 7:285

Perloff, Marjorie G.
  John Berryman 2:59
  Ed Dorn 10:156
  Clayton Eshleman 7:99
  Thom Gunn 3:216
  Ted Hughes 2:204; 4:235
  Richard F. Hugo 6:244
  Erica Jong 6:270
  Galway Kinnell 2:230
  Denise Levertov 2:243
  Robert Lowell 1:181
  Frank O'Hara 2:322; 5:325
  Sylvia Plath 9:432
  Ezra Pound 10:400
  Adrienne Rich 7:369
  Françoise Sagan 6:482
  Mark Van Doren 10:496
  Mona Van Duyn 3:492
  Diane Wakoski 7:504
  John Wieners 7:537
  James Wright 3:542, 544

Perrick, Eve
  Ira Levin 3:294

Perrine, Laurence
  John Ciardi 10:105

Peterkiewicz, Jerzy
  Witold Gombrowicz 4:195
  Alain Robbe-Grillet 4:447

Peters, Daniel James and Annette
Kolodny
  Thomas Pynchon 3:412

Peters, Robert
  Charles Bukowski 5:80
  Clayton Eshleman 7:99
  Michael McClure 6:316
  Anne Waldman 7:508

Peters, Robert L.
  Hollis Summers 10:493

Peterson, Clarence
  Wilfrid Sheed 2:392

Petrie, Paul
  A. Alvarez 5:16

Pettingell, Phoebe
  Donald Hall 1:137
  Philip Levine 9:332
  Robert Lowell 8:353

Pettit, Philip
  J. R. R. Tolkien 3:483

Pevear, Richard
  A. R. Ammons 3:10
  Charles Causley 7:42
  Richmond Lattimore 3:277
  Denise Levertov 3:292
  Hugh MacDiarmid 4:313
  James Merrill 3:334
  Pablo Neruda 5:301
  George Oppen 7:286
  Ezra Pound 2:343
  Louis Zukofsky 7:563

Peyre, Henri
Simone de Beauvoir 1:19
Albert Camus 1:53
Louis-Ferdinand Céline 1:57
René Char 9:162
Georges Duhamel 8:186
Jean Giono 4:185
Julien Green 3:203
André Malraux 1:201
François Mauriac 4:338
Raymond Queneau 5:358
Alain Robbe-Grillet 4:446
Jules Romains 7:383
Nathalie Sarraute 4:464
Jean-Paul Sartre 1:305
Claude Simon 4:494

Pfeiffer, John R.
John Brunner 8:105

Phelps, Donald
Fielding Dawson 6:125
Gilbert Sorrentino 7:451

Phelps, Robert
Dan Wakefield 7:502

Phillips, Allen W.
Octavio Paz 3:376

Phillips, Delbert
Yevgeny Yevtushenko 3:547

Phillips, Norma
Alan Sillitoe 6:501

Phillips, Robert
Hortense Calisher 8:125
Arthur A. Cohen 7:52
James T. Farrell 4:158
Allen Ginsberg 6:199
William Goyen 5:148, 149
Richard Howard 10:275
Robert Lowell 4:303
Bernard Malamud 3:325
Carson McCullers 4:345
Brian Moore 7:239
Patrick White 4:586

Phillips, Steven R.
Ernest Hemingway 3:241

Pick, Robert
Frank Yerby 7:556

Pickering, Sam, Jr.
Anthony Powell 7:338
P. G. Wodehouse 5:517

Pickering, Samuel F., Jr.
Joyce Carol Oates 6:369

Pickrel, Paul
Sylvia Townsend Warner 7:511

Picon, Gaëtan
Michel Butor 8:119
Albert Camus 9:144
Henri Michaux 8:392

Piercy, Marge
Margaret Atwood 3:20
Margaret Laurence 6:289
Alice Walker 9:557

Pigaga, Thom
John Hollander 2:197

Piggott, Stuart
David Jones 4:261

Pinckney, Darryl
Gayl Jones 9:307
Richard Wright 9:585

Pinkerton, Jan
Peter Taylor 1:333

Pinsker, Sanford
Bernard Malamud 3:322
Isaac Bashevis Singer 3:454
John Updike 7:489

Pinsky, Robert
John Berryman 8:93
Ted Hughes 9:282
Philip Levine 9:332
Theodore Roethke 8:461
Raphael Rudnik 7:384

Pittock, Malcolm
Ivy Compton-Burnett 10:108

Plummer, William
Jerzy Kosinski 10:306

Poague, Leland A.
Bob Dylan 6:156

Pochoda, Elizabeth Turner
Tadeusz Konwicki 8:327
Alan Lelchuk 5:245
Joyce Carol Oates 6:373

Podhoretz, Norman
James Baldwin 1:13, 14
Saul Bellow 1:28
Albert Camus 1:52
J. P. Donleavy 1:75
George P. Elliott 2:130
William Faulkner 1:98
Paul Goodman 1:123
Joseph Heller 1:139
Thomas Hinde 6:239
Jack Kerouac 1:165
Norman Mailer 1:188
Bernard Malamud 1:194
Mary McCarthy 1:205
John O'Hara 1:260
Philip Roth 1:292
Nathalie Sarraute 1:302
John Updike 1:343
Edmund Wilson 1:372, 373

Poggioli, Renato
Eugenio Montale 7:221

Poirier, Richard
John Barth 3:40
Saul Bellow 8:74
Jorge Luis Borges 3:77
T. S. Eliot 3:140
Robert Frost 4:176; 9:226
Lillian Hellman 4:221
Norman Mailer 2:263, 265;
3:314; 4:322
Vladimir Nabokov 6:354
Thomas Pynchon 2:355; 3:409
William Styron 3:474
Gore Vidal 4:553
Rudolph Wurlitzer 2:482; 4:597

Poland, Nancy
Margaret Drabble 5:118

Pollitt, Katha
Margaret Atwood 8:30
Sandra Hochman 8:298
James Purdy 10:425
Anne Tyler 7:479

Ponnuthurai, Charles Sarvan
Chinua Achebe 5:3

Pontac, Perry
Miguel Piñero 4:401

Pool, Gail
Anne Sexton 10:468

Poore, Charles
Wilfrid Sheed 2:392

Popkin, Henry
Albert Camus 9:145

Porter, Katherine Anne
Ezra Pound 7:325

Porter, M. Gilbert
Saul Bellow 2:54; 8:72

Porter, Peter
Stevie Smith 3:460

Porter, Raymond J.
Brendan Behan 8:64

Porter, Robert
Milan Kundera 4:276

Porterfield, Christopher
Kingsley Amis 2:8
Christopher Fry 2:143
Ted Hughes 2:199
Donald E. Westlake 7:528

Poss, Stanley
John Hollander 8:301
P. H. Newby 2:310
Adrienne Rich 7:370
Theodore Roethke 8:460
Nancy Willard 7:539

Potok, Chaim
Paul West 7:523

Potoker, Edward Martin
Judith Rossner 9:456
Ronald Sukenick 6:524

Potts, Paul
George Barker 8:43

Pouillon, Jean
William Faulkner 8:208

Povey, John F.
Chinua Achebe 1:1; 7:6
Cyprian Ekwensi 4:151

Powell, Anthony
Evelyn Waugh 3:513

Powell, Neil
Thom Gunn 3:216

Power, K. C.
Michael McClure 6:321

Pratt, Annis
Doris Lessing 3:288; 6:292

Pratt, John Clark
John Steinbeck 1:326

Pratt, Linda Ray
Sylvia Plath 3:390

Pratt, William
John Berryman 10:45
Joseph Brodsky 6:97

Prescott, Orville
Michael Ayrton 7:17
J. I. M. Stewart 7:466
Robert Penn Warren 8:543

Prescott, Peter S.
Alice Adams 6:1
Richard Adams 4:7
Eric Ambler 6:3
Kingsley Amis 3:8
Martin Amis 4:20
Donald Barthelme 5:54

William Peter Blatty 2:64
Vance Bourjaily 8:104
Kay Boyle 5:65
Richard Brautigan 5:71
Lothar-Günther Buchheim
6:101
Anthony Burgess 5:85
Michael Crichton 6:119
Robertson Davies 7:73
Len Deighton 7:75
Don DeLillo 8:171
Peter De Vries 7:78
John Dos Passos 4:137
Lawrence Durrell 6:151
Leslie A. Fiedler 4:161
John Fowles 6:186
Michael Frayn 3:165
Nadine Gordimer 5:146
Graham Greene 3:213
Lillian Hellman 4:221
George V. Higgins 4:223
Russell C. Hoban 7:161
Dan Jacobson 4:254
Diane Johnson 5:198
Robert F. Jones 7:193
Thomas Keneally 8:318
William Kennedy 6:275
Jerzy Kosinski 6:285
John Le Carré 5:232, 234
Doris Lessing 2:241
Peter Matthiessen 5:274
Cormac McCarthy 4:341
John McGahern 5:280
A. G. Mojtabai 9:385
Brian Moore 7:236
Toni Morrison 4:365
Penelope Mortimer 5:299
Joyce Carol Oates 6:374
Flann O'Brien 5:314
Reynolds Price 6:425
Philip Roth 2:378; 4:455; 6:475
Isaac Bashevis Singer 3:458
Aleksandr I. Solzhenitsyn
4:516
Muriel Spark 5:399
Robert Stone 5:409
Harvey Swados 5:422
Paul Theroux 5:428
Michel Tournier 6:537
William Trevor 7:478
John Updike 5:455, 458
Gore Vidal 4:554
Jessamyn West 7:521
Patrick White 3:524
P. G. Wodehouse 5:515
Larry Woiwode 6:579
Richard Yates 7:555

Presley, Delma Eugene
John Fowles 3:163
Carson McCullers 4:346

Press, John
John Betjeman 6:67
Philip Larkin 8:339
Louis MacNeice 4:316

Price, Derek de Solla
John Brunner 10:80
Ursula K. Le Guin 8:343

Price, James
Martin Amis 9:26
Beryl Bainbridge 8:37
Caroline Blackwood 9:101
Margaret Drabble 8:184

Price, Martin
  Marjorie Kellogg **2**:224
  Iris Murdoch **1**:236; **3**:349
  Joyce Carol Oates **1**:251
  Nathalie Sarraute **4**:469
  C. P. Snow **1**:317
  David Storey **4**:530
  Angus Wilson **5**:514

Price, R. G. G.
  Kingsley Amis **2**:7
  Paul Bowles **2**:78
  L. P. Hartley **2**:182
  Elizabeth Taylor **2**:432

Price, Reynolds
  William Faulkner **1**:102; **3**:151
  Graham Greene **3**:212
  Toni Morrison **10**:355
  Walker Percy **8**:442
  James Welch **6**:560
  Eudora Welty **2**:463

Priebe, Richard
  Wole Soyinka **3**:463

Priestley, J. B.
  T. S. Eliot **3**:135
  William Faulkner **3**:150
  Ernest Hemingway **3**:232
  Ezra Pound **3**:394

Prigozy, Ruth
  Larry McMurtry **3**:333

Primeau, Ronald
  John Brunner **8**:109

Prince, Peter
  Martin Amis **4**:19
  Charles Bukowski **5**:80
  Anthony Burgess **4**:84
  John Fowles **6**:184
  Thomas Keneally **5**:210
  Alice Munro **6**:341
  David Pownall **10**:419
  Piers Paul Read **4**:444
  Philip Roth **3**:439

Pringle, John Douglas
  Hugh MacDiarmid **4**:312

Pritchard, William
  John Berryman **3**:72
  Anthony Burgess **4**:84
  Thomas Pynchon **3**:418
  Richard G. Stern **4**:523

Pritchard, William H.
  Dannie Abse **7**:1
  Margaret Atwood **3**:19
  Wendell Berry **8**:85
  John Berryman **8**:90
  Henry Bromell **5**:74
  Anthony Burgess **1**:48
  Donald Davie **8**:162, 163
  John Fowles **9**:214; **10**:189
  Allen Ginsberg **3**:195
  Robert Graves **2**:177
  Marilyn Hacker **9**:257
  John Hollander **5**:187
  Ted Hughes **9**:281
  Richard F. Hugo **6**:244
  Alan Lelchuk **5**:245
  Denise Levertov **2**:242
  Philip Levine **2**:244
  Robert Lowell **1**:184
  Louis MacNeice **4**:316
  Iris Murdoch **8**:406

  Vladimir Nabokov **3**:353
  Howard Nemerov **6**:363
  Anthony Powell **7**:339
  Kenneth Rexroth **2**:369
  Adrienne Rich **3**:427; **6**:459
  Susan Fromberg Schaeffer **6**:489
  Aleksandr I. Solzhenitsyn **4**:510
  Kathleen Spivack **6**:520
  Robert Stone **5**:410
  May Swenson **4**:532
  Elizabeth Taylor **2**:433
  John Updike **3**:487
  Richard Wilbur **6**:571
  James Wright **3**:544
  Rudolph Wurlitzer **4**:597
  Richard Yates **7**:556

Pritchett, V. S.
  Simone de Beauvoir **4**:48
  Samuel Beckett **4**:50
  William Golding **2**:168
  Juan Goytisolo **5**:151; **10**:245
  Norman Mailer **2**:262
  Vladimir Nabokov **6**:356
  Flann O'Brien **10**:364
  Aleksandr I. Solzhenitsyn **1**:320
  Paul Theroux **8**:513
  James Thurber **5**:433
  Gore Vidal **8**:529

Procopiow, Norma
  Marilyn Hacker **5**:155
  Eleanor Lerman **9**:329
  Anne Sexton **4**:483

Proffer, Carl R.
  Aleksandr I. Solzhenitsyn **9**:506

Pronko, Leonard C.
  Eugène Ionesco **1**:154

Pryce-Jones, Alan
  Michael Ayrton **7**:16
  John Betjeman **6**:69
  Italo Calvino **5**:98
  Vladimir Nabokov **1**:246

Pryse, Marjorie
  Helen Yglesias **7**:558

Puckett, Harry
  T. S. Eliot **10**:167

Puetz, Manfred
  John Barth **9**:72

Puetz, Manfred and Alan J. Friedman
  Thomas Pynchon **6**:434

Pugh, Anthony R.
  Alain Robbe-Grillet **4**:450

Purcell, H. D.
  George MacDonald Fraser **7**:106

Purdy, A. W.
  Earle Birney **6**:73

Pyros, J.
  Michael McClure **6**:320

Quennell, Peter
  Robert Graves **6**:210

Quigly, Isabel
  Pamela Hansford Johnson **1**:160

Quinn, Sister Bernetta, O.S.F.
  Alan Dugan **2**:121
  David Jones **4**:259
  Ezra Pound **4**:416; **7**:326
  William Stafford **7**:460
  Allen Tate **4**:539
  Derek Walcott **2**:460
  See also Bernetta (Quinn), Sister Mary, O.S.F.

Quinn, James P.
  Edward Albee **5**:11

R
  David Jones **4**:259
  Arthur Koestler **6**:281
  Aleksandr I. Solzhenitsyn **4**:506

Raban, Jonathan
  A. Alvarez **5**:18
  Kingsley Amis **8**:11
  Beryl Bainbridge **5**:40
  John Barth **1**:17
  Saul Bellow **1**:32
  Stanley Elkin **6**:169
  Nadine Gordimer **5**:145
  Erica Jong **4**:265
  Mary McCarthy **1**:207
  John McGahern **9**:369
  Stanley Middleton **7**:220
  Brian Moore **1**:225
  Iris Murdoch **4**:369
  Vladimir Nabokov **6**:359
  Jean Rhys **6**:456
  Richard G. Stern **4**:523
  William Trevor **7**:476

Rabassa, Gregory
  Gabriel García Márquez **3**:180

Rabinovitz, Rubin
  Kingsley Amis **5**:20
  Samuel Beckett **6**:40, 41
  Norman Mailer **5**:267
  Iris Murdoch **1**:235; **2**:297
  C. P. Snow **4**:500
  Angus Wilson **5**:512

Rabinowitz, Dorothy
  Beryl Bainbridge **8**:36
  Elliott Baker **8**:40
  Giorgio Bassani **9**:77
  Maeve Brennan **5**:72
  Anthony Burgess **5**:88
  Hortense Calisher **4**:87; **8**:124
  John Cheever **3**:107
  Lois Gould **4**:201
  Peter Handke **5**:165
  Mark Helprin **7**:152
  Dan Jacobson **4**:254
  Ruth Prawer Jhabvala **4**:256, 257; **8**:311
  Robert Kotlowitz **4**:275
  Mary Lavin **4**:281
  Doris Lessing **2**:241
  Meyer Levin **7**:205
  Brian Moore **7**:237
  Wright Morris **3**:344
  Edna O'Brien **5**:312
  John O'Hara **6**:384
  Grace Paley **4**:392
  S. J. Perelman **5**:337
  Philip Roth **3**:437
  Anne Sexton **10**:468
  John Updike **2**:445
  Gore Vidal **4**:553

  Dan Wakefield **7**:503
  Joseph Wambaugh **3**:509
  Harriet Waugh **6**:560
  Arnold Wesker **5**:482

Rabkin, Gerald
  Derek Walcott **9**:556

Rachewiltz, Boris de
  Ezra Pound **7**:331

Rackham, Jeff
  John Fowles **2**:138

Rader, Dotson
  Hubert Selby, Jr. **4**:481
  Yevgeny Yevtushenko **3**:547

Radford, C. B.
  Simone de Beauvoir **4**:45, 46

Radin, Victoria
  Sara Davidson **9**:175

Rafalko, Robert
  Eric Ambler **9**:22

Rafalko, Robert J.
  Philip K. Dick **10**:138

Raffel, Burton
  J. R. R. Tolkien **1**:337

Ragusa, Olga
  Alberto Moravia **2**:292

Rahv, Betty T.
  Albert Camus **9**:148
  Alain Robbe-Grillet **8**:451
  Nathalie Sarraute **8**:469
  Jean-Paul Sartre **7**:395

Rahv, Philip
  Saul Bellow **2**:50
  T. S. Eliot **2**:126
  Ernest Hemingway **3**:231
  Arthur Miller **2**:278
  Delmore Schwartz **10**:462
  Aleksandr I. Solzhenitsyn **2**:411

Raine, Craig
  Harold Pinter **6**:419

Raine, Kathleen
  David Jones **2**:216; **7**:191
  St.-John Perse **4**:399
  Herbert Read **4**:440

Rainer, Dachine
  Rebecca West **7**:525

Ramras-Rauch, Gila
  S. Y. Agnon **4**:14

Ramsey, Paul
  Robert Bly **5**:62
  Edgar Bowers **9**:121
  Hayden Carruth **10**:100
  Larry Eigner **9**:181
  Eleanor Lerman **9**:328
  W. S. Merwin **5**:286
  Howard Nemerov **9**:394

Ramsey, Roger
  Friedrich Dürrenmatt **4**:140
  Pär Lagerkvist **10**:311

Rand, Richard A.
  John Hollander **5**:187

Randall, Dudley
  Robert Hayden **5**:168
  Margaret Walker **6**:554

Randall, Julia
  Howard Nemerov 2:308
  Gabrielle Roy 10:441

Ranjbaran, Esmaeel
  Ahmad Shamlu 10:469

Ranly, Ernest W.
  Kurt Vonnegut, Jr. 2:453

Ransom, John Crowe
  Randall Jarrell 1:159
  Allen Tate 4:535

Ransom, W. M.
  Galway Kinnell 3:268

Raphael, Frederic
  Michael Frayn 7:107
  Jakov Lind 4:293

Rascoe, Judith
  Laurie Colwin 5:107

Rasi, Humberto M.
  Jorge Luis Borges 2:74

Ratner, Marc L.
  William Styron 5:418

Ratner, Rochelle
  Clayton Eshleman 7:100

Ray, Robert
  James Baldwin 2:34
  J. I. M. Stewart 7:466

Raymond, John
  Georges Simenon 3:449

Raynor, Vivien
  Evan S. Connell, Jr. 6:115
  Iris Murdoch 3:348
  Edna O'Brien 3:364

Rea, Dorothy
  Auberon Waugh 7:514

Read, Forrest, Jr.
  Ezra Pound 7:327

Read, Herbert
  Allen Tate 4:535

Real, Jere
  Peter Shaffer 5:388

Rebay, Luciano
  Alberto Moravia 7:239

Rechnitz, Robert M.
  Carson McCullers 1:209

Reck, Rima Drell
  Louis-Ferdinand Céline 7:44

Redding, Saunders
  Shirley Ann Grau 4:208
  Richard Wright 1:377

Redfern, W. D.
  Jean Giono 4:186

Reed, Diana
  J. G. Ballard 6:28

Reed, Ishmael
  Chester Himes 2:195

Reed, John
  Arthur Hailey 5:156

Reed, John R.
  William Dickey 3:127
  D. J. Enright 4:155
  Daniel Hoffman 6:243
  John Hollander 8:302
  Richard Howard 7:169; 10:276
  James Merrill 8:388

Charles Reznikoff 9:450
  David Wagoner 3:508
  Philip Whalen 6:566

Reed, Peter J.
  Kurt Vonnegut, Jr. 3:495

Reed, Rex
  Tennessee Williams 2:464

Reedy, Gerard
  C. S. Lewis 6:308

Reeve, Benjamin
  Grace Paley 4:393

Reeve, F. D.
  Joseph Brodsky 6:98
  Aleksandr I. Solzhenitsyn
    1:319

Regan, Robert Alton
  John Updike 5:454

Regier, W. G.
  W. H. Auden 3:22
  Michael Benedikt 4:54
  Howard Nemerov 9:395
  Pablo Neruda 5:305
  Francis Ponge 6:423

Reibetanz, John
  Philip Larkin 8:334

Reichek, Morton A.
  Chaim Grade 10:249

Reid, Alastair
  Jorge Luis Borges 2:73
  Pablo Neruda 5:302

Reilly, Robert J.
  C. S. Lewis 3:298
  J. R. R. Tolkien 1:337; 3:477

Reiter, Seymour
  Sean O'Casey 5:319

Remini, Robert V.
  Gore Vidal 8:526

Rendle, Adrian
  Tom Stoppard 3:470

Renek, Morris
  Erskine Caldwell 8:123

**Renshaw, Robert and Noreen
Hayes**
  J. R. R. Tolkien 1:336

Resnik, Henry S.
  Richard Fariña 9:195
  Wilfrid Sheed 2:392

Rexine, John E.
  Vassilis Vassilikos 4:552

Rexroth, Kenneth
  Robert Creeley 4:116
  Robert Duncan 1:82; 2:123
  T. S. Eliot 2:127
  William Everson 1:96
  Allen Ginsberg 2:164; 3:193,
    194
  William Golding 3:196
  Paul Goodman 2:169
  Robinson Jeffers 2:211
  Denise Levertov 1:175; 2:243;
    3:292
  W. S. Merwin 2:278; 3:338
  Henry Miller 1:219
  Marianne Moore 2:292
  Kenneth Patchen 2:332
  Laura Riding 3:432

Muriel Rukeyser 6:478
  Carl Sandburg 1:300; 4:463
  Isaac Bashevis Singer 3:452
  Edith Sitwell 2:403
  Gary Snyder 2:407
  Jean Toomer 4:548
  Philip Whalen 6:565
  William Carlos Williams 1:371;
    2:469
  Yvor Winters 4:594

Reynolds, R. C.
  Larry McMurtry 7:215

Reynolds, Stanley
  Anna Kavan 5:205
  Robert Penn Warren 4:582

Rhoads, Kenneth W.
  William Saroyan 10:455

Rhodes, Joseph, Jr.
  W. E. B. Du Bois 2:120

Rhodes, Richard
  Chester Himes 2:194
  MacKinlay Kantor 7:196
  Wilfrid Sheed 2:394

Ribalow, Harold U.
  Meyer Levin 7:205
  Henry Roth 6:471
  Arnold Wesker 3:518

Ribalow, Menachem
  S. Y. Agnon 4:10

Rice, Edward
  Thomas Merton 3:337

Rice, Julian C.
  LeRoi Jones 1:163

Rich, Adrienne
  Jean Garrigue 8:239
  Paul Goodman 2:170
  Robert Lowell 3:304
  Robin Morgan 2:294
  Eleanor Ross Taylor 5:425

Rich, Alan
  Alan Ayckbourn 8:34
  Jules Feiffer 8:216
  Simon Gray 9:241
  John Guare 8:253
  Preston Jones 10:297
  Tom Stoppard 8:501, 503
  Tennessee Williams 7:545
  Lanford Wilson 7:549

Rich, Nancy B.
  Carson McCullers 10:336

Richards, Lewis A.
  William Faulkner 3:153

Richardson, D. E.
  Catharine Savage Brosman
    9:135

Richardson, Jack
  John Barth 3:39
  Saul Bellow 8:71
  T. S. Eliot 9:182
  Jack Kerouac 2:227
  Arthur Miller 2:280
  Vladimir Nabokov 2:300
  Peter Shaffer 5:389
  Tom Stoppard 4:527

Richie, Donald
  Yukio Mishima 2:288; 4:357

Richie, Mary
  Penelope Mortimer 5:300

Richler, Mordecai
  Ken Kesey 3:267
  Bernard Malamud 2:267
  Alexander Theroux 2:433

Richman, Sidney
  Bernard Malamud 1:198

Richmond, Jane
  E. L. Doctorow 6:131
  Thomas McGuane 3:329

Richmond, Velma Bourgeois
  Muriel Spark 3:464

Richter, David H.
  Jerzy Kosinski 6:283

Richter, Frederick
  Kenzaburō Ōe 10:373

Ricks, Christopher
  Giorgio Bassani 9:75
  Samuel Beckett 2:48
  Charles Causley 7:41
  Robert Creeley 2:108
  Nadine Gordimer 7:131
  Marilyn Hacker 5:155
  Geoffrey Hill 8:293
  Richard Howard 7:167
  Galway Kinnell 5:217
  Robert Lowell 1:181; 9:335
  Louis MacNeice 1:186
  Reynolds Price 6:423
  Christina Stead 8:499
  John Updike 1:346
  Robert Penn Warren 6:556
  Patrick White 4:586

Riddel, Joseph N.
  C. Day Lewis 10:125

Rideout, Walter B.
  John Dos Passos 4:131
  Randall Jarrell 2:207
  Norman Mailer 4:318
  Henry Roth 2:377

Ridley, Clifford A.
  Julian Symons 2:426

Ries, Lawrence R.
  William Golding 10:239
  Ted Hughes 9:283
  Anthony Powell 9:439
  Alan Sillitoe 10:476

Righter, William
  André Malraux 4:329

Riley, Clayton
  Charles Gordone 1:124

Rinzler, Carol Eisen
  Judith Rossner 6:469

Risdon, Ann and Nicholas Joost
  T. S. Eliot 9:190

Ritter, Jess
  Kurt Vonnegut, Jr. 4:563

Riva, Raymond T.
  Samuel Beckett 1:25

Rivera, Francisco
  José Donoso 4:129

Rizza, Peggy
  Elizabeth Bishop 4:66

Rizzardi, Alfredo
  Allen Tate 4:538

CRITIC INDEX

CRITIC INDEX

Robbe-Grillet, Alain
  Samuel Beckett 10:25
Robbins, Jack Alan and Granville Hicks
  Louis Auchincloss 4:28
  Herbert Gold 4:189
  Bernard Malamud 1:200
  Flannery O'Connor 1:258
Roberts, David
  R. V. Cassill 4:94
Roberts, Thomas J.
  Italo Calvino 8:129
Robinson, Jill
  Alice Adams 6:2
  Anna Kavan 5:206
Robinson, Robert
  Saul Bellow 6:54
Robinson, W. R.
  George Garrett 3:190
Robson, Jeremy
  W. H. Auden 4:33
  Leonard Cohen 3:110
Rockwell, John
  Peter Handke 5:164
Rodgers, Audrey T.
  T. S. Eliot 6:162, 166
Rodman, Selden
  Carlos Fuentes 10:207
Rodrigues, Eusebio L.
  Saul Bellow 3:56; 6:52
Rodríguez-Monegal, Emir
  Jorge Luis Borges 2:72; 3:80
  Gabriel García Márquez 3:183
  Juan Carlos Onetti 7:276, 279
Rodriguez-Peralta, Phyllis
  José María Arguedas 10:8
Rodway, Allan
  Samuel Beckett 4:51
  Tom Stoppard 8:502
Rogan, Helen
  Maeve Brennan 5:73
  John Gardner 5:134
  Jennifer Johnston 7:186
  Irving Wallace 7:510
Rogers, Del Marie
  Reynolds Price 6:423
Rogers, Linda
  Margaret Atwood 4:27
  Angus Wilson 5:515
Rogers, Michael
  Peter Benchley 4:54
  John Gardner 3:188
  Piers Paul Read 4:445
Rogers, Thomas
  Vladimir Nabokov 6:358
  Tom Stoppard 1:328
Rogers, W. G.
  Pearl S. Buck 7:33
  Joanne Greenberg 7:134
Rogoff, Gordon
  David Mamet 9:361
Rohlehr, Gordon
  V. S. Naipaul 4:372
Rohter, Larry
  Carlos Fuentes 8:223

Rollins, Ronald G.
  Sean O'Casey 9:409
Rolo, Charles J.
  Pär Lagerkvist 7:198
  Irwin Shaw 7:411
Roman, Diane and Mary Hamilton
  Paul Vincent Carroll 10:98
Romano, John
  Ann Beattie 8:56
  Frederick Busch 10:92
  Joyce Carol Oates 9:406
  Sylvia Plath 5:342
  Gore Vidal 10:501
Rome, Florence
  Muriel Spark 3:465
Ronge, Peter
  Eugène Ionesco 6:249
Root, William Pitt
  Sonia Sanchez 5:382
  Anne Sexton 4:483
Rorem, Ned
  Paul Bowles 2:79
  Tennessee Williams 5:502
Rose, Ellen Cronan
  Doris Lessing 6:300
Rose, Ernst
  Hermann Hesse 1:145
Rose, Lois and Stephen Rose
  J. G. Ballard 3:33
  Arthur C. Clarke 4:104
  Robert A. Heinlein 3:226
  C. S. Lewis 3:297
  Walter M. Miller, Jr. 4:352
Rose, Marilyn
  Julien Green 3:204
Rose, Stephen and Lois Rose
  J. G. Ballard 3:33
  Arthur C. Clarke 4:104
  Robert A. Heinlein 3:226
  C. S. Lewis 3:297
  Walter M. Miller, Jr. 4:352
Rose, Willie Lee
  Alex Haley 8:260
Rosen, Norma
  Paula Fox 8:218
Rosen, R. D.
  James Tate 6:528
Rosenbaum, Ron
  Richard Condon 4:106
Rosenberg, Harold
  André Malraux 4:334
  Anna Seghers 7:407
Rosenblatt, Roger
  Renata Adler 8:5
  Ludvík Vaculík 7:496
  Thornton Wilder 6:572
Rosenfeld, Alvin H.
  Herbert Gold 7:122
  Jakov Lind 4:293
Rosengarten, Herbert
  Margaret Atwood 8:33
Rosenthal, David H.
  Louis-Ferdinand Céline 7:45
  Austin C. Clarke 8:143
  Nicanor Parra 2:331

Rosenthal, Lucy
  Hortense Calisher 2:96
  Richard Llewellyn 7:207
  Sylvia Plath 2:336
  Alix Kates Shulman 2:395
Rosenthal, M. L.
  Yehuda Amichai 9:25
  A. R. Ammons 2:13
  Imamu Amiri Baraka 2:34;
    10:19
  John Berryman 2:56
  John Betjeman 2:60
  Kay Boyle 1:42
  John Ciardi 10:105
  Austin Clarke 6:110
  Robert Creeley 2:105
  E. E. Cummings 1:68
  James Dickey 2:115; 7:81
  Robert Duncan 2:122
  T. S. Eliot 2:125
  D. J. Enright 4:155
  Robert Frost 1:110
  Allen Ginsberg 1:118; 2:162
  Paul Goodman 1:124; 4:196
  Jim Harrison 6:223
  Ted Hughes 2:197; 9:280
  X. J. Kennedy 8:320
  Galway Kinnell 1:168
  Thomas Kinsella 4:270
  Philip Larkin 3:275, 277
  Denise Levertov 2:242
  Robert Lowell 1:179; 2:247
  George MacBeth 2:251
  Hugh MacDiarmid 2:253
  W. S. Merwin 1:211
  Marianne Moore 1:226
  Charles Olson 2:326
  Robert L. Peters 7:304
  Sylvia Plath 2:335
  Ezra Pound 1:274; 7:332
  Kenneth Rexroth 1:283
  Theodore Roethke 3:432
  Delmore Schwartz 2:387
  Anne Sexton 2:391
  Karl Shapiro 4:484
  Charles Tomlinson 2:436
  Reed Whittemore 4:588
  William Carlos Williams 1:370
Rosenthal, R.
  Paula Fox 2:139
Rosenthal, Raymond
  Edward Dahlberg 7:66
  Tennessee Williams 8:547
Rosenthal, T. G.
  Michael Ayrton 7:20
Roshwald, Miriam
  S. Y. Agnon 8:9
Ross, Alan
  Kingsley Amis 2:7
  Alberto Moravia 7:244
Ross, Gary
  Margaret Atwood 4:27
Ross, James
  Reynolds Price 6:426
Ross, Morton L.
  Norman Mailer 1:192
Rossi, Louis R.
  Salvatore Quasimodo 10:427

Rosten, Norman
  James Tate 2:431
Roszak, Theodore
  Paul Goodman 2:170
Roth, Philip
  Edward Albee 9:1
  Saul Bellow 6:52
  Norman Mailer 5:268
  Bernard Malamud 5:269; 8:376
  J. D. Salinger 8:464
  Fredrica Wagman 7:500
Rothberg, Abraham
  Graham Greene 3:211
  Gary Snyder 9:499
  Aleksandr I. Solzhenitsyn
    4:507; 7:437
Rothman, Nathan L.
  Frank Yerby 7:556
Rothstein, Edward
  Agatha Christie 8:141
Roudiez, Leon
  Michel Butor 8:114
  Claude Mauriac 9:363
Routh, Michael
  Graham Greene 9:246
Rovit, Earl H.
  Saul Bellow 1:31; 8:71
  Ralph Ellison 1:93
  John Hawkes 2:184
  Norman Mailer 8:372
  Bernard Malamud 1:195
Rowan, Louis
  Diane Wakoski 7:506
Rowan, Thomas
  J. F. Powers 1:281
Rowley, Peter
  Paula Fox 2:139
  John Knowles 4:272
Rowse, A. L.
  Flannery O'Connor 2:318
Ruark, Gibbons
  Andrei Voznesensky 1:349
Ruben, Elaine
  Maureen Howard 5:189
Rubenstein, Roberta
  Margaret Atwood 8:31
  Doris Lessing 6:303; 10:316
Rubin, Louis D., Jr.
  William Faulkner 1:101
  Carson McCullers 10:338
  John Crowe Ransom 4:428;
    5:365
  Carl Sandburg 10:450
  Susan Sontag 10:484
  William Styron 3:473
  Allen Tate 9:523
  Robert Penn Warren 1:353;
    4:577
  Eudora Welty 1:361
Rubins, Josh
  Agatha Christie 6:108
Rueckert, William
  Wright Morris 7:245
Rupp, Richard H.
  John Updike 1:343

Ruskamp, Judith S.
Henri Michaux 8:392

Russ, Joanna
Robert Silverberg 7:425
Kate Wilhelm 7:537

Russell, Charles
John Barth 7:22
Richard Brautigan 9:123
Jerzy Kosinski 6:284
Vladimir Nabokov 6:353
Ronald Sukenick 6:523

Russell, John
André Malraux 9:357
Anthony Powell 3:402

Ryan, Frank L.
Daniel J. Berrigan 4:56
Anne Hébert 4:220

Ryan, Marjorie
Diane Johnson 5:198

Ryf, Robert S.
Henry Green 2:179
B. S. Johnson 9:299
Doris Lessing 10:313
Vladimir Nabokov 6:353
Flann O'Brien 7:268

Ryle, John
Mark Helprin 10:261

Saal, Hubert
Irwin Shaw 7:411

Sabiston, Elizabeth
Philip Roth 6:475
Ludvík Vaculík 7:497

Sabri, M. Arjamand
Thomas Pynchon 3:417

Sacharoff, Mark
Elias Canetti 3:98

Sadoff, Dianne F.
Gail Godwin 8:247

Säez, Richard
James Merrill 6:323

Sagar, Keith
Ted Hughes 2:203

Sage, Lorna
Olga Broumas 10:76
Erica Jong 6:267
Vladimir Nabokov 8:412

Sage, Victor
David Storey 8:505

Said, Edward W.
R. P. Blackmur 2:61
Paul Goodman 2:169

Sainer, Arthur
Martin Duberman 8:185
Simon Gray 9:242
Michael McClure 6:317
Miguel Piñero 4:401

St. John-Stevas, Norman
C. S. Lewis 6:308

Sakurai, Emiko
Kenzaburō Ōe 10:374

Sale, Roger
Kingsley Amis 5:22
Saul Bellow 6:61
Thomas Berger 8:84
Frederick Buechner 2:83; 6:103

Anthony Burgess 5:87
Frederick Busch 10:94
Agatha Christie 8:141
Richard Condon 8:150
Robertson Davies 7:72
E. L. Doctorow 6:135
Margaret Drabble 2:118, 119;
8:183
George P. Elliott 2:131
Frederick Exley 6:172
Leslie A. Fiedler 4:162
B. H. Friedman 7:109
Paula Fox 2:141
Herbert Gold 7:121
Witold Gombrowicz 7:122
Dashiell Hammett 5:161
John Hawkes 4:214
Mark Helprin 10:261
Maureen Howard 5:188
Ken Kesey 6:278
John Le Carré 5:234
Alan Lelchuk 5:240
Doris Lessing 2:239, 242;
6:299, 304
Alison Lurie 4:306
Ross Macdonald 2:255
David Madden 5:266
Norman Mailer 2:261; 4:319
Peter Matthiessen 7:212
Iris Murdoch 8:404
Tim O'Brien 7:271
Grace Paley 6:392
J. F. Powers 8:447
Richard Price 6:427
Judith Rossner 6:470
Philip Roth 2:381; 6:476
Andrew Sinclair 2:400
Isaac Bashevis Singer 9:487
Robert Stone 5:410
Paul Theroux 5:428
J. R. R. Tolkien 1:338
Mario Vargas Llosa 6:547
Kurt Vonnegut, Jr. 8:532
David Wagoner 5:475
Larry Woiwode 10:541

Salisbury, Harrison E.
Aleksandr I. Solzhenitsyn
4:511

Salomon, I. L.
Robert Duncan 4:142

Salter, D. P. M.
Saul Bellow 2:53

Salzman, Jack
John Dos Passos 4:138
Jack Kerouac 2:229
Tillie Olsen 4:386

Sampley, Arthur M.
Robert Frost 1:112

Sampson, Edward C.
E. B. White 10:529

Samuels, Charles Thomas
Richard Adams 4:7
Donald Barthelme 3:43
Lillian Hellman 2:187
Christina Stead 2:421
John Updike 1:344; 2:442
Kurt Vonnegut, Jr. 2:454

Sanborn, Sara
Anthony Burgess 4:84
Rosalyn Drexler 6:143

Alison Lurie 4:305
Joyce Carol Oates 3:363

Sandars, N. K.
David Jones 4:260

Sandeen, Ernest
R. P. Blackmur 2:62

Sanders, David
John Hersey 1:144; 7:153

Sanders, Ed
Allen Ginsberg 4:181

Sanders, Frederick L.
Conrad Aiken 3:5

Sanders, Ivan
György Konrád 4:273; 10:304
Milan Kundera 4:278
József Lengyel 7:202
Amos Oz 8:436

Sanders, Peter L.
Robert Graves 2:176

Sandler, Linda
Margaret Atwood 8:29, 30

Sanfield, Steve
Michael McClure 6:320

Sargent, David
Robert Wilson 9:576

Saroyan, Aram
Kenneth Koch 8:323
Anne Waldman 7:508

Saroyan, William
Flann O'Brien 10:362

Sarris, Andrew
Norman Mailer 3:315
Wilfrid Sheed 4:487

Sartre, Jean-Paul
William Faulkner 9:197
Jean Genet 2:155

Sayre, Nora
Iris Murdoch 1:236
Anne Roiphe 3:434
Elizabeth Taylor 2:432
Kurt Vonnegut, Jr. 3:502

Sayre, Robert F.
James Baldwin 1:15

Scaduto, Anthony
Bob Dylan 4:148

Scannell, Vernon
Randall Jarrell 9:298
George MacBeth 9:341

Scarbrough, George
James Schevill 7:400

Scarf, Maggie
Susan Sontag 10:487

Schaap, Dick
Mario Puzo 2:351

Schaefer, J. O'Brien
Margaret Drabble 5:119

Schafer, William J.
David Wagoner 3:507

Schapiro, Leonard
Aleksandr I. Solzhenitsyn
7:440

Schatt, Stanley
Langston Hughes 10:279

Isaac Bashevis Singer 3:459
Kurt Vonnegut, Jr. 1:348; 4:560

Schechner, Richard
Eugène Ionesco 6:253

Scheerer, Constance
Sylvia Plath 9:432

Schickel, Richard
Louis Auchincloss 9:54
Joan Didion 1:75
Alan Lelchuk 5:242
Ross Macdonald 1:185
Thomas Pynchon 2:358
Peter Shaffer 5:387

Schier, Donald
André Breton 2:81

Schjeldahl, Peter
Paul Blackburn 9:100
André Breton 2:80; 9:129
James Schevill 7:400

Schlueter, June
Arthur Miller 10:346

Schlueter, Paul
Pär Lagerkvist 7:201
Doris Lessing 1:174; 3:283
Mary McCarthy 1:205

Schmerl, Rudolf B.
Aldous Huxley 3:255

Schmidt, Michael
Donald Davie 8:165
George MacBeth 2:252
Jon Silkin 2:396

Schmitz, Neil
Donald Barthelme 1:19
Richard Brautigan 3:90
Robert Coover 3:113; 7:58
Thomas Pynchon 6:435
Ishmael Reed 5:368; 6:448

Schneck, Stephen
Richard Brautigan 1:44
LeRoi Jones 1:162

Schneidau, Herbert N.
Ezra Pound 4:408

Schneider, Duane
Anaïs Nin 1:248

Schneider, Elisabeth
T. S. Eliot 3:140

Schneider, Richard J.
William H. Gass 8:240

Schoenbrun, David
Cornelius Ryan 7:385

Scholes, Robert
Jorge Luis Borges 10:63
Lawrence Durrell 8:190
John Hawkes 9:262
Ishmaél Reed 5:370
Kurt Vonnegut, Jr. 2:451; 4:561

Schorer, Mark
Truman Capote 3:98
Lillian Hellman 4:221
Carson McCullers 4:344
Katherine Anne Porter 7:312

Schott, Webster
Richard Adams 5:6
Louis Auchincloss 4:31
W. H. Auden 2:25
Donald Barthelme 2:41

Saul Bellow 8:69
William Peter Blatty 2:63
Vance Bourjaily 8:103
James Clavell 6:113
Robert Coover 7:57
Michael Crichton 2:108
John Gardner 10:223
Ira Levin 6:305
Larry McMurtry 2:272
Sylvia Plath 2:338
Raymond Queneau 10:432
Philip Roth 3:436
Georges Simenon 2:398
Harvey Swados 5:421
Elio Vittorini 6:551
Jessamyn West 7:520
Tennessee Williams 5:506

Schraepen, Edmond
William Carlos Williams 9:575

Schramm, Richard
Philip Levine 2:244
Howard Moss 7:248

Schreiber, Jan
Elizabeth Daryush 6:122

Schreiber, LeAnne
Jerome Charyn 8:135

Schroth, Raymond A.
Norman Mailer 2:261; 3:312

Schulder, Diane
Marge Piercy 3:385

Schuler, Barbara
Peter Taylor 1:333

Schulman, Grace
Richard Eberhart 3:134
Pablo Neruda 5:302
Octavio Paz 6:395
Adrienne Rich 3:427
Mark Van Doren 6:541
Richard Wilbur 9:569

Schulz, Max F.
John Barth 9:68
Norman Mailer 1:190
Bernard Malamud 1:199
Kurt Vonnegut, Jr. 1:347

Schwaber, Paul
Robert Lowell 1:184

Schwartz, Delmore
Randall Jarrell 1:159

Schwartz, Edward
Katherine Anne Porter 7:309

Schwartz, Howard
David Ignatow 7:178

Schwartz, Kessel
Vicente Aleixandre 9:15
Adolfo Bioy Casares 8:94
Gabriel García Márquez 10:215
Juan Rulfo 8:462

Schwartz, Lloyd
Elizabeth Bishop 9:93, 97

Schwartz, Lynne Sharon
Beryl Bainbridge 5:40
Natalia Ginzburg 5:141
Alix Kates Shulman 10:475
Fay Weldon 9:560

Schwartz, Nancy Lynn
Jill Robinson 10:438

Schwartz, Paul J.
Samuel Beckett 6:41
Alain Robbe-Grillet 8:453

Schwartz, Ronald
Miguel Delibes 8:169

Schwarzbach, F. S.
Thomas Pynchon 9:443

Schwarzchild, Bettina
James Purdy 2:349

Schwerner, Armand
Diane Wakoski 7:506

Scobbie, Irene
Pär Lagerkvist 10:312

Scobie, Stephen
John Glassco 9:237

Scobie, W. I.
Melvin Van Peebles 2:448
Derek Walcott 2:459

Scofield Martin
T. S. Eliot 9:186

Scott, Alexander
Hugh MacDiarmid 4:310

Scott, Carolyn D.
Graham Greene 1:130

Scott, J. D.
Andrew Sinclair 2:400

Scott, Nathan A., Jr.
Richard Wright 1:378

Scott, Peter Dale
Mordecai Richler 5:372

Scott, Tom
Hugh MacDiarmid 4:309
Ezra Pound 4:413

Scott, Winfield Townley
David Ignatow 7:173
Louis Simpson 7:426

Scott-James, R. A.
Edith Sitwell 9:493

Scouffas, George
J. F. Powers 1:280

Scruggs, Charles W.
Jean Toomer 4:549

Scruton, Roger
Sylvia Plath 5:340

Scupham, Peter
W. H. Auden 6:16
Robert Graves 6:211
H. D. 8:257
David Jones 4:262

Searle, Leroy
Dannie Abse 7:2
Erica Jong 4:264

Searles, Baird
Anna Kavan 5:205

Searles, George J.
Joseph Heller 8:279

Seaver, Richard
Louis-Ferdinand Céline 1:57

Seay, James
James Wright 3:543

Seebohm, Caroline
Kamala Markandaya 8:377

Seed, David
Isaac Bashevis Singer 9:487

Seelye, John
Donald Barthelme 2:41
Norman Mailer 3:316
Marge Piercy 3:383
James Thurber 5:439
David Wagoner 5:474

Segal, Lore
Joan Didion 1:75

Segovia, Tomás
Octavio Paz 3:376

Seib, Kenneth
Richard Brautigan 1:44

Seiden, Melvin
Vladimir Nabokov 2:302

Selby, Herbert, Jr.
Richard Price 6:427

Seligson, Tom
Hunter S. Thompson 9:527

Sellin, Eric
Samuel Beckett 2:47

Selzer, David
Peter Porter 5:346

Sena, Vinad
T. S. Eliot 6:159

Seymour-Smith, Martin
Robert Graves 1:128

Shadoian, Jack
Donald Barthelme 1:18

Shands, Annette Oliver
Gwendolyn Brooks 4:78, 79
Don L. Lee 2:238

Shannon, James P.
J. F. Powers 1:279

Shapcott, Thomas
Frank O'Hara 2:323
W. R. Rodgers 7:377

Shapiro, Charles
Meyer Levin 7:203
David Madden 5:265
Joyce Carol Oates 3:363
Anthony Powell 1:277
Harvey Swados 5:420
Jerome Weidman 7:517

Shapiro, David
Hayden Carruth 10:100
X. J. Kennedy 8:320

Shapiro, Jane
Rosalyn Drexler 6:143

Shapiro, Karl
W. H. Auden 1:8; 3:21
T. S. Eliot 3:136
Rod McKuen 1:210
Henry Miller 4:349
Ezra Pound 3:394
William Carlos Williams 5:506

Shapiro, Paula Meinetz
Alice Walker 6:553

Sharpe, Patricia
Margaret Drabble 10:162

Shattan, Joseph
Saul Bellow 8:80

Shattuck, Roger
Jean Arp 5:32
Saul Bellow 6:57
Alain Robbe-Grillet 2:376

Shaw, Irwin
James Jones 10:290

Shaw, Peter
Robert Lowell 8:351
Hugh Nissenson 9:400

Shaw, Robert B.
A. R. Ammons 3:11
W. H. Auden 2:26
Wendell Berry 8:85
Stanley Burnshaw 3:91
James Dickey 2:117
Robert Duncan 7:88
Allen Ginsberg 6:201
John Glassco 9:236
Richard Howard 7:166
David Ignatow 4:248
Philip Larkin 8:338
William Meredith 4:348
Adrienne Rich 6:457
Raphael Rudnik 7:384
Charles Simic 6:501; 9:479
Allen Tate 2:430
Mark Van Doren 6:541
Marya Zaturenska 6:585

Shea, Robert J.
Budd Schulberg 7:403

Shear, Walter
Bernard Malamud 1:197

Shechner, Mark
Tadeusz Konwicki 8:328

Sheed, Wilfrid
Edward Albee 1:4
James Baldwin 1:16; 8:42
Robert Coover 7:58
Robert Frost 1:110
William Golding 1:121
Joseph Heller 5:182
James Jones 1:162
Norman Mailer 1:193; 4:320
Terrence McNally 7:216
Arthur Miller 1:217
Alberto Moravia 2:292
Iris Murdoch 1:236
John Osborne 1:263
Walker Percy 2:332
Neil Simon 6:503
William Styron 1:330
John Updike 1:343
Kurt Vonnegut, Jr. 1:347
Evelyn Waugh 3:512
Arnold Wesker 3:518
Tennessee Williams 1:369
Tom Wolfe 2:481

Sheehan, Donald
John Berryman 1:34
Richard Howard 7:166
Robert Lowell 1:181

Shelton, Austin J.
Chinua Achebe 7:4

Shelton, Frank W.
Robert Coover 7:60
Ernest Hemingway 10:269

Shepard, Paul
Peter Matthiessen 5:273

Shepherd, Allen
Reynolds Price 3:405, 406
Robert Penn Warren 1:355

Sheppard, R. Z.
Louis Auchincloss 4:30

Saul Bellow 6:55
William Peter Blatty 2:64
Lothar- Günther Buchheim
  6:101
Anthony Burgess 5:85
Peter De Vries 2:114
E. L. Doctorow 6:133
Alex Haley 8:260
James Leo Herlihy 6:235
Dan Jacobson 4:254
Bernard Malamud 2:266
S. J. Perelman 5:338
Ishmael Reed 5:370
Harvey Swados 5:422
Michel Tournier 6:537
Mario Vargas Llosa 6:545
Gore Vidal 6:548
Paul West 7:523

Sherwood, Terry G.
Ken Kesey 1:167

Shinn, Thelma J.
Flannery O'Connor 6:375
Ann Petry 7:304
William Saroyan 10:452

Shippey, Thomas
Lothar- Günther Buchheim
  6:100

Shivers, Alfred S.
Jessamyn West 7:520

Shorris, Earl
Donald Barthelme 2:42
John Gardner 3:184
William H. Gass 2:155
Thomas Pynchon 3:414

Shorter, Eric
Alan Ayckbourn 5:36

Shoukri, Doris Enright-Clark
Marguerite Duras 3:129

Showalter, Elaine
Mary McCarthy 3:329

Showers, Paul
Peter De Vries 2:114
John Seelye 7:407

Shuman, R. Baird
William Inge 1:153
Clifford Odets 2:318, 320

Shuttleworth, Martin
Christina Stead 2:421

Shuttleworth, Paul
Leon Uris 7:492

Sicherman, Carol M.
Saul Bellow 10:37

Siegel, Ben
Saul Bellow 8:78
Bernard Malamud 1:195
Isaac Bashevis Singer 1:313

Siegel, Paul N.
Norman Mailer 5:266

Siemens, William L.
Julio Cortázar 5:110

Sigal, Clancy
Kingsley Amis 3:9; 5:22
Melvyn Bragg 10:72
Alan Sillitoe 3:448

Siggins, Clara M.
Taylor Caldwell 2:95

Lillian Hellman 4:221
Saul Maloff 5:270

Silbajoris, Rimvydas
Boris Pasternak 10:387

Silenieks, Juris
Édouard Glissant 10:231

Silet, Charles L. P.
David Kherdian 9:317, 318

Silkin, Jon
Geoffrey Hill 5:183

Silverstein, Norman
James Dickey 7:81

Silvert, Conrad
Peter Matthiessen 7:210

Simenon, Georges
Georges Simenon 3:451

Simmons, Ernest J.
Mikhail Sholokhov 7:416, 420

Simon, John
Edward Albee 2:1; 5:13
Alan Ayckbourn 8:34
Peter Barnes 5:49
Samuel Beckett 3:47
Ed Bullins 5:84; 7:36
Anne Burr 6:104
Martin Duberman 8:185
Jules Feiffer 2:133
Lawrence Ferlinghetti 2:134
Athol Fugard 9:230
Frank D. Gilroy 2:161
Charles Gordone 1:124
Bill Gunn 5:153
Christopher Hampton 4:211
Lillian Hellman 8:281
William Inge 8:308
Arthur Kopit 1:171
Ira Levin 3:294
Robert Lowell 4:299
Norman Mailer 2:259; 3:316
Terrence McNally 4:347;
  7:217, 218, 219
Mark Medoff 6:321, 322
Arthur Miller 2:279, 280; 6:335
Jason Miller 2:284, 285
Joe Orton 4:387
John Osborne 2:328
Rochelle Owens 8:434
S. J. Perelman 5:337
Harold Pinter 3:386, 387
David Rabe 8:449, 451
Jonathan Reynolds 6:452
Murray Schisgal 6:490
Peter Shaffer 5:387, 389
Ntozake Shange 8:484
Sam Shepard 6:497
Neil Simon 6:506
John Steinbeck 5:408
Tom Stoppard 3:470; 4:525,
  526; 5:412; 8:504
David Storey 4:528; 5:415, 417
Ronald Tavel 6:529
Melvin Van Peebles 2:448
Gore Vidal 2:450; 4:554; 10:503
Derek Walcott 2:460
Peter Weiss 3:513
Michael Weller 10:526
Thornton Wilder 10:535
Tennessee Williams 2:464;
  5:501; 7:544; 8:549
Robert Wilson 7:550, 551

Simonds, C. H.
Joan Didion 1:74

Simpson, Louis
Robert Bly 2:65
James Merrill 8:380
Kenneth Rexroth 2:370
W. D. Snodgrass 2:405

Sinclair, Dorothy
Erich Segal 10:467

Singh, G.
Eugenio Montale 7:223, 226
Ezra Pound 2:342, 344; 7:334

Sinyavsky, Andrei
Robert Frost 4:174

Sire, James W.
C. S. Lewis 1:177

Sisk, John P.
J. F. Powers 1:280

Sissman, L. E.
Kingsley Amis 2:7; 5:22
Martin Amis 4:21
Jimmy Breslin 4:76
Michael Crichton 6:119
J. P. Donleavy 4:126
J. G. Farrell 6:174
Natalia Ginzburg 5:141
Joseph Heller 8:278
Dan Jacobson 4:255
Thomas McGuane 3:329
Tom McHale 3:332; 5:282
Brian Moore 7:237
Anne Roiphe 3:434
John Updike 2:441
Evelyn Waugh 3:513
Fay Weldon 6:563
Edmund Wilson 2:478

Sisson, C. H.
H. D. 8:257

Skau, Michael
Lawrence Ferlinghetti 10:177

Skelton, Robin
Anthony Kerrigan 6:276
Dorothy Livesay 4:294

Skodnick, Roy
Gilbert Sorrentino 7:448

Skow, Jack
John Gardner 5:132
Robert Graves 2:176

Skow, John
Richard Adams 5:5
Richard Brautigan 3:86
Arthur A. Cohen 7:52
Richard Condon 4:107; 6:115
Julio Cortázar 5:109
Robertson Davies 2:113
Lawrence Durrell 6:152
Charles Johnson 7:183
Robert F. Jones 7:193
Sue Kaufman 3:263
Yasunari Kawabata 5:208
Milan Kundera 4:277
John D. MacDonald 3:307
Iris Murdoch 4:370
Vladimir Nabokov 6:354
Harold Robbins 5:379
Susan Fromberg Schaeffer
  6:488
Irving Stone 7:471
Kurt Vonnegut, Jr. 4:568

Morris L. West 6:564
Patrick White 3:525

Slater, Candace
Salvatore Espriu 9:193

Slaughter, Frank G.
Millen Brand 7:29

Slavitt, David R.
Ann Quin 6:441

Slethaug, Gordon E.
John Barth 2:38

Slonim, Marc
Mikhail Sholokhov 7:415, 418
Aleksandr I. Solzhenitsyn
  1:320

Sloss, Henry
Richard Howard 10:276
James Merrill 8:381, 384
Reynolds Price 3:406
Philip Roth 1:293

Smith, A.J.M.
Earle Birney 6:74
P. K. Page 7:291

Smith, Barbara
Ishmael Reed 6:447
Alice Walker 6:553

Smith, Dave
Harry Crews 6:118
Albert Goldbarth 5:144
Louis Simpson 7:429

Smith, David E.
E. E. Cummings 8:158

Smith, Grover
Archibald MacLeish 8:359

Smith, H. Allen
Jacqueline Susann 3:476

Smith, Janet Adam
Richard Adams 4:8
J. R. R. Tolkien 2:435

Smith, Liz
Truman Capote 8:133

Smith, Maxwell A.
Jean Giono 4:184
François Mauriac 4:340

Smith, Michael
Rosalyn Drexler 2:119
Anthony Kerrigan 6:275
Tom Stoppard 1:327
Robert Wilson 7:549

Smith, Raymond J.
James Dickey 10:141

Smith, Roger H.
John D. MacDonald 3:307

Smith, William Jay
Louis MacNeice 4:315

Smyth, Paul
Derek Walcott 4:575

Sniderman, Stephen L.
Joseph Heller 3:230

Snodgrass, W. D.
Theodore Roethke 8:455

Snow, C. P.
Norman Mailer 4:322

Snow, George E.
Aleksandr I. Solzhenitsyn
  4:507

Snow, Helen F.
Pearl S. Buck 7:33

Snowden, J. A.
Sean O'Casey 9:406

Sokel, Walter Herbert
Heinrich Böll 9:102

Sokolov, Raymond A.
E. L. Doctorow 6:132
Dan Jacobson 4:254
Gayl Jones 6:265
Thomas Keneally 8:319
József Lengyel 7:202
John Sayles 7:400

Solomon, Barbara Probst
Juan Goytisolo 5:151
João Ubaldo Ribeiro 10:436
Mario Vargas Llosa 10:500

Solotaroff, Theodore
Saul Bellow 1:33
Paul Bowles 1:41
Anthony Burgess 1:48
William S. Burroughs 1:48
Albert Camus 9:146
Alex Comfort 7:54
George P. Elliott 2:130
John Fowles 6:185
Herbert Gold 7:120
Paul Goodman 1:123
Günter Grass 1:125
Stanislaw Lem 8:344
Bernard Malamud 1:196, 200
Henry Miller 1:219
Flannery O'Connor 1:256
Katherine Anne Porter 1:271
V. S. Pritchett 5:352
James Purdy 2:348
Philip Roth 4:451
Jean-Paul Sartre 1:304
Hubert Selby, Jr. 8:474
Susan Sontag 1:322
Vladimir Voinovich 10:508
Richard Wright 1:377
Richard Yates 7:553

Somer, John
Kurt Vonnegut, Jr. 4:566

Somers, Paul P., Jr.
Ernest Hemingway 8:283

Sonnenfeld, Albert
Heinrich Böll 9:107

Sonntag, Jacob
Amos Oz 8:435
Isaac Bashevis Singer 3:456
Arnold Wesker 3:519

Sontag, Susan
James Baldwin 4:40
Albert Camus 4:88
Paul Goodman 2:170
Rolf Hochhuth 4:230
Eugène Ionesco 4:251
Nathalie Sarraute 4:465
Jean-Paul Sartre 4:475

Sorrentino, Gilbert
Paul Blackburn 9:99
Robert Creeley 2:106
Robert Duncan 2:122
William Gaddis 8:227
Charles Olson 2:327
John Wieners 7:535, 536
Louis Zukofsky 7:563

Soule, Stephen W.
Anthony Burgess 5:90

Sourian, Peter
Albert Camus 2:98
Eleanor Clark 5:105
Jack Kerouac 2:227
William Saroyan 8:468
Vassilis Vassilikos 4:552

Southerland, Ellease
Zora Neale Hurston 7:171

Southern, David
Michael McClure 6:320

Southern, Terry
John Rechy 1:283

Southworth, James G.
E. E. Cummings 3:115
Robert Frost 3:168
Robinson Jeffers 3:257
Archibald MacLeish 3:309
Laura Riding 7:373

Souza, Raymond D.
Octavio Paz 10:392
Ernesto Sábato 10:444

Spacks, Patricia Meyer
Kingsley Amis 5:24
Nicholas Delbanco 6:130
Hannah Green 3:202
Joseph Heller 5:183
Jennifer Johnston 7:186
D. Keith Mano 10:328
Alberto Moravia 2:294
Iris Murdoch 6:347
Anne Sexton 8:483
Andrew Sinclair 2:402
Muriel Spark 2:419; 5:400
Peter Spielberg 6:520
J. R. R. Tolkien 1:336
Elio Vittorini 6:551
Eudora Welty 2:464
Paul West 7:524
Patrick White 4:587

Spann, Marcella
Ezra Pound 4:413

Spanos, William V.
Yannis Ritsos 6:460

Spaulding, Martha
Kamala Markandaya 8:377
J. R. R. Tolkien 8:516

Spears, Monroe K.
W. H. Auden 2:22
John Berryman 2:57
James Dickey 2:116
T. S. Eliot 2:127
Ted Hughes 2:199
David Jones 2:217
Madison Jones 4:263
Robert Lowell 2:248
Ezra Pound 2:342
John Crowe Ransom 2:366
Karl Shapiro 4:487
Allen Tate 2:430
Robert Penn Warren 1:355;
  4:579

Spector, Ivar
Mikhail Sholokhov 7:420

Spector, Robert D.
William Bronk 10:73
Robert Duncan 7:87

D. J. Enright 4:156
David Ignatow 7:174
Kenneth Rexroth 2:371

Speer, Diane Parkin
Robert Heinlein 8:275

Spence, Jon
Katherine Anne Porter 7:320

Spencer, Benjamin T.
Edward Dahlberg 7:70

Spencer, Jack
André Schwarz-Bart 2:388

Spencer, Sharon
Djuna Barnes 3:38
Jorge Luis Borges 3:77
Julio Cortázar 3:114
Carlos Fuentes 3:175
Anaïs Nin 4:376
Alain Robbe-Grillet 4:448

Spendal, R. J.
James Wright 10:546

Spender, Stephen
A. R. Ammons 2:12
W. H. Auden 3:25, 27
Robert Graves 2:177
Thom Gunn 3:216
Ted Hughes 2:200
Aldous Huxley 3:253; 5:192;
  8:304
Philip Levine 4:287
James Merrill 3:335
W. S. Merwin 3:340
Eugenio Montale 7:225
Elsa Morante 8:403
Sylvia Plath 9:429
William Plomer 4:406
James Schuyler 5:383
Gore Vidal 2:450; 8:527
James Wright 3:541

Spiegel, Alan
Jean-Paul Sartre 7:398

Spiegelman, Willard
John Betjeman 10:53
Richard Howard 7:169
James Merrill 8:384
Adrienne Rich 7:370

Spieler, F. Joseph
Robert Wilson 9:577

Spilka, Mark
Ernest Hemingway 10:263
Doris Lessing 6:300
Erich Segal 3:446

Spitz, Robert Stephen
Pete Hamill 10:251

Spivack, Kathleen
Robert Lowell 2:248

Spivey, Herman E.
William Faulkner 6:176

Spivey, Ted R.
Conrad Aiken 5:9
Flannery O'Connor 1:255

Sprague, Rosemary
Marianne Moore 4:362

Spurling, Hilary
Anthony Powell 10:417

Spurling, John
Peter Barnes 5:50
Samuel Beckett 6:42

Peter Benchley 4:54
Francis King 8:322
David Mercer 5:284
Yukio Mishima 9:384
Peter Nichols 5:308
David Plante 7:307
Peter Shaffer 5:388
Elie Wiesel 5:491

Squires, Radcliffe
Caroline Gordon 6:204
Randall Jarrell 6:260
Frederic Prokosch 4:420
Allen Tate 2:429; 4:540

Stade, George
Kingsley Amis 8:10
E. E. Cummings 3:119
E. L. Doctorow 6:132
John Gardner 3:186
Robert Graves 1:129
Jerzy Kosinski 3:272
Alan Lelchuk 5:243
Joseph McElroy 5:279
Jean Rhys 6:452
Wilfrid Sheed 4:488
Muriel Spark 2:416
John Updike 5:458
Kurt Vonnegut, Jr. 3:501

Stafford, Jean
James A. Michener 5:289
Paul West 7:523

Stafford, William
Millen Brand 7:29
Loren Eiseley 7:93
David Kherdian 6:280
Kenneth Rexroth 2:370
Louis Simpson 7:427
Theodore Weiss 8:546

Stallknecht, Newton P.
Amos Tutuola 5:445

Stambolian, George
Sam Shepard 4:490

Stampfer, Judah
Saul Bellow 6:60
Philip Roth 6:476

Stanford, Ann
May Swenson 4:533

Stanford, Derek
Earle Birney 4:64
Robert Creeley 2:106
C. Day Lewis 1:72
Lawrence Durrell 4:147
Aldous Huxley 5:192
Elizabeth Jennings 5:197
Hugh MacDiarmid 4:313
Louis MacNeice 1:187
William Plomer 4:406
Stephen Spender 1:322; 2:419
Yevgeny Yevtushenko 3:547

Stanford, Donald E.
Caroline Gordon 6:202
Marianne Moore 4:364
Ezra Pound 10:407
Allen Tate 2:430
Yvor Winters 4:591

Stange, Maren
Susan Sontag 10:486

Stankiewicz, Marketa Goetz
Slawomir Mrozek 3:345

Stanlis, Peter L.
Robert Frost 3:174

Staples, Hugh B.
Randall Jarrell 6:261
Robert Lowell 2:246

Stark, John
Jorge Luis Borges 8:94
E. L. Doctorow 6:131
William Gaddis 8:228
Vladimir Nabokov 8:407

Stark, John O.
John Barth 7:22

Starr, Kevin
E. L. Doctorow 6:136
John Dos Passos 8:181

Starr, Roger
Anthony Powell 3:403

Stasio, Marilyn
Anne Burr 6:105
John Hopkins 4:234
Terrence McNally 4:346, 347
Jason Miller 2:284
David Rabe 4:426
Melvin Van Peebles 2:448
Murray Schisgal 6:491

States, Bert O.
Harold Pinter 6:412

Stavrou, C. N.
Edward Albee 5:12

Stefanile, Felix
William Bronk 10:73

Stegner, Page
Vladimir Nabokov 1:239

Stein, Benjamin
Joan Didion 8:177

Stein, Charles
Jerome Rothenberg 6:477

Stein, Robert A.
J. V. Cunningham 3:122

Steinberg, M. W.
Robertson Davies 7:72
Arthur Miller 1:215

Steiner, Carlo
Giuseppe Ungaretti 7:483

Steiner, George
Jorge Luis Borges 2:70
C. Day Lewis 6:126
Lawrence Durrell 4:144
Paul Goodman 7:127
Graham Greene 6:220
Aldous Huxley 5:194
Thomas Keneally 8:318; 10:298
Robert M. Pirsig 4:403
Jean-Paul Sartre 7:397
Aleksandr I. Solzhenitsyn
4:516
John Updike 5:459
Patrick White 4:583

Stepanchev, Stephen
John Ashbery 2:16
Imamu Amiri Baraka 2:34
Elizabeth Bishop 4:65
Robert Bly 2:65
Robert Creeley 2:105
James Dickey 2:115
Alan Dugan 2:121
Robert Duncan 2:122

Jean Garrigue 2:153
Allen Ginsberg 2:162
Randall Jarrell 2:208
Robert Lowell 2:247
W. S. Merwin 2:276
Charles Olson 2:325
Kenneth Rexroth 2:369
Karl Shapiro 4:485
Louis Simpson 4:498
William Stafford 4:519
May Swenson 4:532
Richard Wilbur 6:568

Stephens, Donald
Dorothy Livesay 4:294
Rudy Wiebe 6:567

Stephens, Martha
Richard Wright 1:379

Stephens, Robert O.
Ernest Hemingway 3:239

Stephenson, William
James Dickey 4:122

Stepto, Robert B.
Michael S. Harper 7:139

Stern, Daniel
Paul Bowles 2:79
Joanne Greenberg 7:134
Marjorie Kellogg 2:223
Jakov Lind 4:292
Bernard Malamud 3:324
Chaim Potok 2:339
Ann Quin 6:441
Paul West 7:523
Elie Wiesel 3:529

Stern, David
Robert Kotlowitz 4:275
Amos Oz 5:334

Sterne, Richard C.
Octavio Paz 10:391

Sterne, Richard Clark
Jerome Weidman 7:517

Stetler, Charles
James Purdy 4:423

Stevens, Peter
A. R. Ammons 8:14
Margaret Atwood 4:24
A. W. Purdy 3:408

Stevens, Shane
John Rechy 7:356

Stevens, Wallace
Marianne Moore 10:347

Stevenson, Anne
Elizabeth Bishop 1:35

Stevenson, David L.
James Jones 3:260
Jack Kerouac 2:226
William Styron 1:329

Stevenson, Patrick
W. R. Rodgers 7:377

Stevick, Philip
Donald Barthelme 8:53
William S. Burroughs 5:93
William H. Gass 8:247
Jerzy Kosinski 6:283
Jean Stafford 4:518
Kurt Vonnegut, Jr. 5:465

Stewart, Corbet
Paul Celan 10:102

Stewart, Harry E.
Jean Genet 10:225

Stewart, John L.
John Crowe Ransom 2:362

Stewart, Robert Sussman
Heinrich Böll 2:67

Stiller, Nikki
Louis Simpson 9:486

Stilwell, Robert L.
A. R. Ammons 3:10
Sylvia Plath 1:269
Jon Silkin 2:395
James Wright 3:540

Stimpson, Catharine R.
Marge Piercy 6:403
J. R. R. Tolkien 1:338

Stineback, David C.
Allen Tate 9:525

Stinson, John J.
Anthony Burgess 4:82

Stitt, Peter A.
John Berryman 10:46
Louis Simpson 7:429
Robert Penn Warren 10:519
James Wright 10:542

Stock, Irvin
Saul Bellow 2:50
Mary McCarthy 1:206

Stocking, Marion Kingston
Galway Kinnell 1:168
Gary Snyder 1:318

Stokes, Eric
Kamala Markandaya 8:378

Stoltzfus, Ben F.
Alain Robbe-Grillet 1:285

Stone, Elizabeth
John Fowles 9:213
John Gardner 8:234

Stone, Laurie
Max Frisch 9:217
Anaïs Nin 8:423
Anne Roiphe 9:455

Stone, Robert
Peter Matthiessen 5:274

Stoneback, H. R.
William Faulkner 8:213

Storch, R. F.
Harold Pinter 6:409

Story, Jack Trevor
C. P. Snow 6:517

Stouck, David
Marie-Claire Blais 2:63
Hugh MacLennan 2:257

Stowers, Bonnie
Hortense Calisher 4:88
Saul Maloff 5:271

Stratford, Philip
Graham Greene 6:212

Straub, Peter
Michael Ayrton 7:19
Beryl Bainbridge 8:36
James Baldwin 4:43
J. G. Ballard 3:35
Donald Barthelme 3:44
Brian Glanville 6:202

Hermann Hesse 6:237
Jack Kerouac 3:266
Francis King 8:321
Margaret Laurence 6:290
Olivia Manning 5:273
Thomas McGuane 7:213
Michael Mewshaw 9:376
James A. Michener 5:291
Anaïs Nin 8:419
Joyce Carol Oates 9:402
Flann O'Brien 4:385
Simone Schwarz-Bart 7:404
Isaac Bashevis Singer 6:509
Richard G. Stern 4:523
John Updike 5:457
Morris L. West 6:563

Street, Douglas O.
Lawrence Ferlinghetti 6:183

Strehle, Susan
John Gardner 10:218

Strout, Cushing
William Styron 5:420

Strozier, Robert M.
Peter De Vries 7:78
S. J. Perelman 5:337
P. G. Wodehouse 5:517

Struve, Gleb
Vladimir Nabokov 1:241

Struve, Nikita
Aleksandr I. Solzhenitsyn
7:433

Stuart, Dabney
Ted Hughes 2:201

Stubblefield, Charles
Sylvia Plath 1:270

Stubbs, Jean
Julio Cortázar 2:102
Daphne du Maurier 6:147
George Garrett 3:193
Eleanor Hibbert 7:155
Anaïs Nin 8:421

Stubbs, John C.
John Hawkes 1:138

Stubbs, Patricia
Muriel Spark 3:466

Stumpf, Thomas
Hayden Carruth 7:41
Daniel Mark Epstein 7:97
Ishmael Reed 5:368
Muriel Rukeyser 6:479

Stupple, A. James
Ray Bradbury 10:69

Sturgeon, Theodore
Isaac Asimov 3:16
Michael Crichton 2:108
Barry N. Malzberg 7:208

Sturrock, John
Peter De Vries 3:125
Gabriel García Márquez 8:233;
10:217
Alain Robbe-Grillet 8:454

Styron, William
Terry Southern 7:453

Suderman, Elmer F.
John Updike 2:443; 3:488

Sukenick, Lynn
Doris Lessing 3:288

Anaïs Nin 8:421
   Robert L. Peters 7:303

Sukenick, Ronald
   Rudolph Wurlitzer 2:483

Sullivan, Anita T.
   Ray Bradbury 3:85

Sullivan, Jack
   Richard Condon 8:150
   Paul Horgan 9:279
   J. B. Priestley 9:442

Sullivan, Kevin
   Flann O'Brien 5:316
   Sean O'Casey 5:320

Sullivan, Mary
   B. S. Johnson 6:262
   William Sansom 6:483
   Fay Weldon 6:562

Sullivan, Nancy
   May Swenson 4:534

Sullivan, Rosemary
   Marie-Claire Blais 6:81

Sullivan, Ruth
   Ken Kesey 6:278

Sullivan, Tom R.
   William Golding 8:249
   Michel Tournier 6:538

Sullivan, Victoria
   Saul Bellow 8:76

Sullivan, Walter
   Donald Barthelme 1:19
   Saul Bellow 8:81
   Guy Davenport, Jr. 6:124
   Margaret Drabble 8:184
   William Golding 2:166, 168
   Graham Greene 6:219
   Bernard Malamud 1:200
   Joyce Carol Oates 6:368; 9:405
   Flannery O'Connor 2:317
   John O'Hara 6:385
   Jean Rhys 6:456
   Alan Sillitoe 6:501

Sullivan, Wilson
   Irving Stone 7:470

Sullivan, Zohreh Tawakuli
   Iris Murdoch 6:346

Sultan, Stanley
   Ezra Pound 7:331

Suter, Anthony
   Basil Bunting 10:83, 84

Sutherland, Donald
   Rafael Alberti 7:10
   Octavio Paz 10:389
   St.-John Perse 4:399
   Francis Ponge 6:422

Sutherland, Stuart
   Peter De Vries 10:137

Sutton, Walter
   Allen Ginsberg 4:181
   Robert Lowell 4:303
   Thomas Merton 3:336
   Marianne Moore 4:364
   Ezra Pound 3:395

Swados, Harvey
   David Ignatow 4:249

Swenson, May
   Robin Morgan 2:294

Anne Sexton 2:392
   W. D. Snodgrass 2:406

Swift, Pat
   George Barker 8:44

Swigg, Richard
   E. M. Forster 9:209
   Philip Larkin 9:324

Swigger, Ronald T.
   Raymond Queneau 2:359

Swinden, Patrick
   C. P. Snow 4:503

Swink, Helen
   William Faulkner 3:154

Sykes, Christopher
   Aldous Huxley 4:244; 8:303

Sykes, S. W.
   Claude Simon 9:483

Symons, Julian
   Eric Ambler 4:18
   W. H. Auden 2:28
   John Berryman 2:59
   John Dickson Carr 3:101
   John Cheever 8:140
   Agatha Christie 6:107; 8:140
   C. Day Lewis 6:129
   Len Deighton 4:119
   Friedrich Dürrenmatt 4:141
   Ian Fleming 3:159
   Roy Fuller 4:178
   Dashiell Hammett 3:219
   Lillian Hellman 4:222
   Patricia Highsmith 2:193; 4:225
   Chester Himes 4:229
   John Le Carré 3:282
   John D. MacDonald 3:307
   Ross Macdonald 3:307
   Mary McCarthy 3:326
   Henry Miller 2:281
   Ellery Queen 3:421
   Laura Riding 3:431
   Georges Simenon 3:451; 8:487
   Louis Simpson 4:498
   Maj Sjöwall 7:501
   C. P. Snow 4:500
   Mickey Spillane 3:469
   Rex Stout 3:471
   Per Wahlöö 7:501
   Robert Penn Warren 4:577
   Patrick White 3:523
   Angus Wilson 3:536

Syrkin, Marie
   Henry Roth 6:472

Szanto, George H.
   Alain Robbe-Grillet 1:288

Szogyi, Alex
   Lillian Hellman 2:187

Szporluk, Mary Ann
   Vladimir Voinovich 10:504

Tabachnick, Stephen E.
   Conrad Aiken 5:9

Talbott, Strobe
   Aleksandr I. Solzhenitsyn
      4:516

Taliaferro, Frances
   Nadine Gordimer 5:147
   Tom McHale 5:283

Tallman, Warren
   Mordecai Richler 3:430

Tanner, Stephen L.
   Ernest Hemingway 8:288

Tanner, Tony
   John Barth 1:17; 2:37
   Donald Barthelme 2:40
   William S. Burroughs 2:92
   William Gaddis 3:177
   John Gardner 2:152
   John Hawkes 2:185; 7:143
   Ernest Hemingway 10:266
   Norman Mailer 1:189
   Bernard Malamud 2:267
   James Purdy 2:351; 4:422
   Thomas Pynchon 6:430, 432
   Susan Sontag 1:322
   John Updike 2:445

Tarn, Nathaniel
   William H. Gass 1:114

Tarshis, Jerome
   J. G. Ballard 3:34

Tate, Allen
   John Crowe Ransom 2:363;
      5:364
   Eudora Welty 1:362

Tate, Robert S., Jr.
   Albert Camus 1:54

Tatham, Campbell
   John Barth 1:18
   Raymond Federman 6:181
   Thomas Pynchon 2:354

Taubman, Robert
   Cynthia Ozick 7:287

Tavris, Carol
   Kate Wilhelm 7:538

Taylor, Clyde
   Imamu Amiri Baraka 5:47

Taylor, F. H. Griffin
   George Garrett 3:192
   Robert Lowell 1:181
   Theodore Weiss 3:516

Taylor, Henry
   Marvin Bell 8:64
   Irving Feldman 7:103
   X. J. Kennedy 8:319
   Howard Nemerov 6:363
   Flannery O'Connor 1:258
   James Wright 5:521

Taylor, Jane
   Galway Kinnell 1:168

Taylor, John Russell
   John Arden 6:4
   Alan Ayckbourn 5:34
   Edward Bond 4:69
   David Mercer 5:283
   Peter Nichols 5:305
   Joe Orton 4:388
   Terence Rattigan 7:354
   Robert Shaw 5:390
   Tom Stoppard 4:524
   David Storey 4:528
   E. A. Whitehead 5:488

Taylor, Lewis Jerome, Jr.
   Walker Percy 6:399

Taylor, Mark
   W. H. Auden 3:27
   John Berryman 3:72
   Tom McHale 5:282
   Walker Percy 3:378

Earl Rovit 7:383
   Edmund Wilson 8:550
   Richard Yates 8:555

Taylor, Michael
   Gillian Tindall 7:474

Temple, Joanne
   John Berryman 3:72

Temple, Ruth Z.
   Nathalie Sarraute 1:303; 2:386

Tenenbaum, Louis
   Italo Calvino 5:97

Tennant, Emma
   J. G. Ballard 6:28
   Italo Calvino 5:100
   Thomas Hinde 6:242
   Penelope Mortimer 5:298

Terbille, Charles I.
   Saul Bellow 6:52
   Joyce Carol Oates 6:371

Teresa, Vincent
   Mario Puzo 2:352

Terrien, Samuel
   Fernando Arrabal 2:15

Terry, Arthur
   Vicente Aleixandre 9:17
   Salvador Espriu 9:192
   Octavio Paz 10:393

Teunissen, John T. and Evelyn J.
Hinz
   Doris Lessing 6:293

Therese, Sister M.
   Marianne Moore 1:229

Theroux, Paul
   Frederick Buechner 2:83
   Anthony Burgess 5:89
   John Cheever 7:48
   Peter De Vries 3:126; 7:76
   Lawrence Durrell 6:151
   George MacDonald Fraser
      7:106
   Nadine Gordimer 5:147
   Shirley Ann Grau 4:209
   Graham Greene 3:213
   Ernest Hemingway 6:229
   Susan B. Hill 4:226
   Erica Jong 4:264
   John Knowles 4:272
   Milan Kundera 4:276
   Mary McCarthy 5:277
   Yukio Mishima 4:356
   Brian Moore 3:341; 7:236
   V. S. Naipaul 4:373, 374; 7:252
   Cynthia Ozick 7:288
   S. J. Perelman 9:415
   Jean Rhys 2:372
   David Storey 4:529
   Peter Taylor 4:542
   Kurt Vonnegut, Jr. 5:470

Thiher, Allen
   Fernando Arrabal 9:33
   Louis-Ferdinand Céline 4:101

Thody, Philip
   Albert Camus 4:91
   Jean-Paul Sartre 4:476

Thomas, Carolyn
   David Jones 7:191

Thomas, Clara
   Margaret Laurence 3:281

Thomas, D. M.
John Matthias 9:362

Thomas, David
James Baldwin 5:43

Thomas, David P.
Christopher Isherwood 1:157

Thomas, M. Wynn
Katherine Anne Porter 10:394

Thomas, Peter
John Betjeman 6:65
Robert Kroetsch 5:220

Thompson, Eric
T. S. Eliot 2:125

Thompson, John
John Berryman 3:71
Irving Feldman 7:102
Natalia Ginzburg 5:141
Joseph Heller 5:176
Robert Lowell 9:338
Amos Oz 5:335

Thompson, Leslie M.
Stephen Spender 10:487

Thompson, R. J.
John Hawkes 4:214
Mary Lavin 4:282

Thompson, Toby
Bruce Jay Friedman 5:126

Thomson, George H.
J. R. R. Tolkien 1:335

Thorburn, David
Renata Adler 8:7
Ann Beattie 8:57
Judith Guest 8:254
Norman Mailer 3:315
Thomas Pynchon 3:416

Thorp, Willard
W. D. Snodgrass 2:404

Thorpe, Michael
Doris Lessing 3:291

Thurman, Judith
Joyce Carol Oates 6:374
Jean Rhys 6:456
Laura Riding 7:374

Thwaite, Anthony
W. H. Auden 6:24
Charles Causley 7:41
Douglas Dunn 6:148
Geoffrey Grigson 7:136
Seamus Heaney 7:147
David Jones 7:187
R. K. Narayan 7:256
C. P. Snow 4:503

Tillinghast, Richard
James Merrill 2:274
Adrienne Rich 3:427

Timms, David
Philip Larkin 5:223

Tindall, Gillian
Louis-Ferdinand Céline 7:45

Tindall, William York
Samuel Beckett 1:22

Tinkle, Lon
Hollis Summers 10:493

Tisdale, Bob
John Hawkes 4:215

Tobias, Richard C.
James Thurber 5:435

Tobin, Patricia
William Faulkner 3:155

Tobin, Richard L.
Lothar-Günther Buchheim
6:101

Todd, Richard
Renata Adler 8:4
Louis Auchincloss 9:54
Donald Barthelme 8:49
Saul Bellow 6:55, 61
Thomas Berger 3:64
Eleanor Bergstein 4:55
Vance Bourjaily 8:104
E. L. Doctorow 6:138
Bruce Jay Friedman 5:126
John Hawkes 4:216
Sue Kaufman 8:317
William Kotzwinkle 5:220
Cormac McCarthy 4:343
Walker Percy 8:443
Marge Piercy 6:402
Robert M. Pirsig 6:420
Judith Rossner 6:470
John Updike 7:489
Kurt Vonnegut, Jr. 3:501
Richard Yates 7:555

Toliver, Harold E.
Robert Frost 4:175

Tomalin, Claire
Beryl Bainbridge 10:15
Charles Newman 2:311
Paul Theroux 5:427

Tonks, Rosemary
Adrienne Rich 3:428

Toolan, David S.
Tom Wicker 7:535

Torchiana, Donald T.
W. D. Snodgrass 2:404

Totten, Nick
Beryl Bainbridge 8:37
Heinrich Böll 9:111
Gail Godwin 8:249
James Hanley 8:265
Francis King 8:322
Iris Murdoch 8:405
Vladimir Nabokov 8:417
David Pownall 10:419
Piers Paul Read 10:434

Towers, Robert
Renata Adler 8:4
John Cheever 8:138
Stanley Elkin 9:191
John Gardner 8:233
Larry McMurtry 7:214
Walker Percy 8:444
Anthony Powell 9:435
Philip Roth 9:461
James Salter 7:387
Wilfrid Sheed 10:473
Paul Theroux 8:512
Kurt Vonnegut, Jr. 8:533
Rebecca West 9:562

Toynbee, Philip
Arthur Koestler 1:170
Mordecai Richler 5:375

Trachtenberg, Alan
Henry Miller 4:351
Tom Wolfe 9:578

Tracy, Honor
Graham Greene 3:206

Tracy, Phil
Kingsley Amis 3:9

Traschen, Isadore
William Faulkner 9:201

Treece, Henry
Herbert Read 4:437

Treglown, Jeremy
Tom Robbins 9:454

Trickett, Rachel
James Purdy 2:349
Andrew Sinclair 2:401
Wallace Stegner 9:508
Angus Wilson 2:473

Trilling, Diana
Aldous Huxley 8:304
Irwin Shaw 7:410

Trilling, Lionel
E. M. Forster 1:104
Robert Graves 2:174

Trimpi, Helen P.
Edgar Bowers 9:121, 122

Trodd, Kenith
Andrew Sinclair 2:400

Trotter, Stewart
Jean Genet 5:137
Graham Greene 6:220

Trowbridge, Clinton
John Updike 2:442

True, Michael
Daniel J. Berrigan 4:58
Paul Goodman 2:169

Truscott, Lucian K.
Bob Dylan 3:131

Tsuruta, Kinya
Shusaku Endo 7:96

Tucker, Carll
Imamu Amiri Baraka 10:19
Ed Bullins 7:37
Jules Feiffer 8:216
Richard Howard 7:169
Robert Lowell 9:338
Archibald MacLeish 8:363

Tucker, James
Anthony Powell 7:338; 10:409

Tucker, Martin
Chinua Achebe 3:1
Cyprian Ekwensi 4:152
Nadine Gordimer 3:201
Ernest Hemingway 3:234
Jerzy Kosinski 1:172
Bernard Malamud 3:322
James Ngugi 3:357
Cynthia Ozick 7:287
Alan Paton 4:395
William Plomer 4:406
Wole Soyinka 3:462
Amos Tutuola 5:443
Laurens van der Post 5:463

Tunney, Gene
Budd Schulberg 7:402

Turco, Lewis
Robert Hayden 9:270

Turin, Michele
Alix Kates Shulman 10:476

Turnbull, Martin
François Mauriac 4:340

Turnell, Martin
Graham Greene 1:134

Turner, Darwin
Alice Walker 9:558

Tuttleton, James W.
Louis Auchincloss 4:29

Tyler, Anne
Marilyn French 10:191
Lois Gould 10:241
Sue Kaufman 8:317
Thomas Keneally 10:299
Alix Kates Shulman 10:475
William Trevor 7:478

Tyler, Ralph
Richard Adams 5:5
Agatha Christie 6:109
S. J. Perelman 9:416
Jean Rhys 6:455

Tyms, James D.
Langston Hughes 5:191

Tyrmand, Leopold
Witold Gombrowicz 7:124

Tytell, John
Jack Kerouac 3:264

Unger, Leonard
T. S. Eliot 1:90

Unterecker, John
Lawrence Durrell 1:84
Ezra Pound 4:415
Kenneth Rexroth 2:370

Updike, John
Michael Ayrton 7:20
Ann Beattie 8:55
Samuel Beckett 6:45
Saul Bellow 6:56
Jorge Luis Borges 8:100
Italo Calvino 5:101; 8:130
Albert Camus 9:149
John Cheever 7:50
Julio Cortázar 5:109
Don DeLillo 10:135
Margaret Drabble 8:183
Daniel Fuchs 8:221
Witold Gombrowicz 7:124
Günter Grass 2:172; 4:206
Ernest Hemingway 8:285
Ruth Prawer Jhabvala 8:312
Gayl Jones 6:266; 9:307
Erica Jong 4:263
Jerzy Kosinski 6:282
Alberto Moravia 7:243
Wright Morris 7:245
Iris Murdoch 6:344
Vladimir Nabokov 2:301;
3:351; 6:355; 8:414, 415, 416,
417
R. K. Narayan 7:256
Flann O'Brien 7:269, 270
Robert Pinget 7:306
Raymond Queneau 5:359, 362
Alain Robbe-Grillet 8:452
Françoise Sagan 6:481

Simone Schwarz-Bart 7:405
Muriel Spark 5:400
Christina Stead 8:499, 500
James Thurber 5:433
Anne Tyler 7:479
Sylvia Townsend Warner 7:512
Edmund Wilson 8:551

Uphaus, Robert W.
Kurt Vonnegut, Jr. 5:469

Urang, Gunnar
C. S. Lewis 3:298
J. R. R. Tolkien 2:434

Uroff, Margaret D.
Sylvia Plath 3:391

Usborne, Richard
MacDonald Harris 9:261

Usmiani, Renate
Friedrich Dürrenmatt 8:194

Vaizey, John
Kingsley Amis 5:22

Valgemae, Mardi
Jean-Claude Van Itallie 3:493

Valley, John A. and Diana Culbertson
Alberto Moravia 7:243

Van Brunt, H. L.
Jim Harrison 6:224

van Buren, Alice
Janet Frame 2:142

Vande Kieft, Ruth M.
Flannery O'Connor 1:258
Eudora Welty 1:360

Vandenbroucke, Russell
Athol Fugard 9:230

van den Haag, Ernest
William F. Buckley, Jr. 7:34

van den Heuvel, Cor
James Wright 10:545

Vanderbilt, Kermit
Norman Mailer 3:319
William Styron 3:474

Vanderwerken, David L.
Richard Brautigan 5:69

Van Doren, Mark
John Cowper Powys 7:346

Van Duyn, Mona
Margaret Atwood 2:19
Adrienne Rich 3:427
Anne Sexton 2:391

Vansittart, Peter
Piers Paul Read 10:436

Vargas Llosa, Mario
Gabriel García Márquez 3:181

Vargo, Edward P.
John Updike 7:486

Vendler, Helen
A. R. Ammons 2:14
Margaret Atwood 8:29
John Berryman 3:68; 10:46
Elizabeth Bishop 9:90
Olga Broumas 10:77
Hayden Carruth 7:41
E. E. Cummings 3:119
D. J. Enright 8:203
Allen Ginsberg 2:163; 3:195

Louise Glück 7:118
Seamus Heaney 7:152
John Hollander 5:187
Richard F. Hugo 6:245
Randall Jarrell 9:295
Erica Jong 4:263
Haki R. Madhubuti 6:313
Mary McCarthy 3:328
James Merrill 2:275
Howard Moss 7:250
Joyce Carol Oates 3:361
Frank O'Hara 5:323
Octavio Paz 4:397
Adrienne Rich 7:367
Irwin Shaw 7:414
Allen Tate 2:429
Charles Tomlinson 6:535
Diane Wakoski 7:504
Robert Penn Warren 10:525
Charles Wright 6:581

Verani, Hugo J.
Juan Carlos Onetti 7:277

Vernon, John
Michael Benedikt 4:54
James Dickey 7:82
David Ignatow 4:247
James Merrill 3:334
W. S. Merwin 1:213

Verschoyle, Derek
Rayner Heppenstall 10:271

Vickery, John B
John Updike 5:451

Vickery, Olga W.
John Hawkes 4:213

Vidal, Gore
Louis Auchincloss 4:31
Italo Calvino 5:98
John Dos Passos 4:132
E. Howard Hunt 3:251
Norman Mailer 2:265
Henry Miller 2:282
Yukio Mishima 2:287
Anaïs Nin 4:376
John O'Hara 2:323
Alain Robbe-Grillet 2:375
Aleksandr I. Solzhenitsyn 4:510
Susan Sontag 2:414
Tennessee Williams 7:546

Vilhjalmsson, Thor
Gabriel García Márquez 2:150

Vintcent, Brian
Marie-Claire Blais 4:67
Anne Hébert 4:220

Viorst, Judith
Lois Gould 10:243

Vogel, Dan
William Faulkner 6:177, 178
Arthur Miller 6:333
Robert Penn Warren 6:556
Tennessee Williams 5:504

Volpe, Edmond L.
James Jones 1:162

Vonalt, Larry P.
John Berryman 3:66; 4:60
Marianne Moore 1:230

Von Hallberg, Robert
Charles Olson 6:386

Vonnegut, Kurt, Jr.
Joseph Heller 5:175

Voorhees, Richard J.
P. G. Wodehouse 1:374

Vopat, Carole Gottlieb
Jack Kerouac 3:265

Wade, David
J. R. R. Tolkien 2:434

Wade, Michael
Peter Abrahams 4:2

Waggoner, Hyatt H.
E. E. Cummings 3:117
Robert Duncan 2:122
T. S. Eliot 2:127
Robert Frost 3:173
H. D. 3:217
Robinson Jeffers 2:214
Robert Lowell 3:300
Archibald MacLeish 3:310
Marianne Moore 2:292
Ezra Pound 2:341
John Crowe Ransom 2:363
Theodore Roethke 3:432
Carl Sandburg 4:463
Karl Shapiro 4:485
Richard Wilbur 3:532
William Carlos Williams 2:468

Wagner, Dave
Robert L. Peters 7:303

Wagner, Dick and Yoshio Iwamoto
Yukio Mishima 9:381

Wagner, Geoffrey
R. P. Blackmur 2:61

Linda Wagner
Diane Wakoski 9:554

Wagner, Linda Welshimer
William Faulkner 1:103
Ernest Hemingway 6:231
Denise Levertov 1:176; 5:247
Philip Levine 9:332
Diane Wakoski 9:555

Wain, John
William S. Burroughs 5:91
Edward Dahlberg 7:66
C. Day Lewis 6:127
Günter Grass 2:173; 4:202
Michael Hamburger 5:158
Ben Hecht 8:270
Ernest Hemingway 3:233
Aldous Huxley 5:192
Flann O'Brien 4:383
C. P. Snow 4:500

Wainwright, Andy
Earle Birney 6:77

Wainwright, Jeffrey
Ezra Pound 7:332

Wakefield, Dan
Harvey Swados 5:422
Leon Uris 7:490

Wakoski, Diane
Clayton Eshleman 7:98
David Ignatow 4:248
John Logan 5:255
Robert Lowell 4:304
Anaïs Nin 4:377
Jerome Rothenberg 6:477

Walcott, Ronald
Hal Bennett 5:57, 59
Charles Gordone 4:199

Walcutt, Charles Child
James Gould Cozzens 4:114
John O'Hara 1:262

Waldmeir, Joseph
John Updike 5:450

Waldron, Randall H.
Norman Mailer 3:314

Waldrop, Rosemary
Hans Erich Nossack 6:365

Walker, Alice
Ai 4:16
Flannery O'Connor 6:381
Derek Walcott 4:576

Walker, Carolyn
Joyce Carol Oates 3:360

Walker, Cheryl
Adrienne Rich 3:428
Robert Penn Warren 6:558

Walker, Robert G.
Ernest Hemingway 8:287

Walker, Ted
Andrew Young 5:523

Wallace, Michele
Ntozake Shange 8:485

Wallenstein, Barry
Ted Hughes 2:200

Waller, Claudia Joan
José Lezama Lima 10:317

Waller, G. F.
Paul Theroux 8:514

Walsh, Chad
Robert Bly 2:66
Robert Graves 6:212
Ted Hughes 2:197
Philip Larkin 5:228
Archibald MacLeish 3:311
Howard Nemerov 2:306
Jerome Weidman 7:517

Walsh, William
Earle Birney 6:78
R. K. Narayan 7:254
Patrick White 3:521; 4:583, 584; 7:532; 9:567

Walsten, David M.
Yukio Mishima 2:286

Walt, James
Ward Just 4:266
John O'Hara 6:385
J. R. Salamanca 4:462

Walter, James F.
John Barth 10:22

Walters, Jennifer R.
Michel Butor 3:93

Walters, Margaret
Brigid Brophy 6:99

Walton, Alan Hull
Colin Wilson 3:537

Ward, A. C.
W. H. Auden 1:8
Samuel Beckett 1:21
Edmund Blunden 2:65
Ivy Compton-Burnett 1:62

Noel Coward 1:64
T. S. Eliot 1:90
E. M. Forster 1:104
Christopher Fry 2:143
Robert Graves 1:128
Graham Greene 1:132
Aldous Huxley 1:150
W. Somerset Maugham 1:204
Iris Murdoch 1:234
J. B. Priestley 2:346
Edith Sitwell 2:403
C. P. Snow 1:316
Evelyn Waugh 1:358
Arnold Wesker 3:518
P. G. Wodehouse 1:374

Ward, David E.
Ezra Pound 1:275

Ward, J. A.
S. J. Perelman 9:414

Ward, Margaret Joan
Morley Callahan 3:97

Warkentin, Germaine
A. W. Purdy 3:408

Warner, Edwin
Jorge Luis Borges 2:71

Warner, John M.
John Hawkes 3:223

Warner, Jon M.
George MacBeth 5:263

Warner, Rex
E. M. Forster 1:105

Warnke, F. J.
Richard Yates 7:553

Warnock, Mary
Brigid Brophy 6:98
Iris Murdoch 8:404

Warren, Robert Penn
James Dickey 10:140
Eudora Welty 1:362

Warsh, Lewis
Richard Brautigan 3:86

Warshow, Robert
Arthur Miller 1:215

Washburn, Martin
Richard Adams 4:7
Anthony Burgess 4:84
Nicholas Delbanco 6:129
John Gardner 3:187
Lois Gould 4:200
Juan Goytisolo 5:150
Günter Grass 4:206
Dan Jacobson 4:255
György Konrád 4:273
Denise Levertov 3:293
Alison Lurie 4:306

Washington, Mary Helen
Alice Walker 6:554

Washington, Peter
Seamus Heaney 7:149
Stevie Smith 8:491

Wasserman, Debbi
Murray Schisgal 6:490
Sam Shepard 4:489
Tom Stoppard 4:525
Richard Wesley 7:519

Waterman, Andrew
John Matthias 9:361

Waterman, Arthur
Conrad Aiken 3:5

Waters, Chris
Tim O'Brien 7:271

Waterston, Elizabeth
Irving Layton 2:236

Watkins, Floyd C.
Robert Frost 9:219
Ernest Hemingway 3:239

Watkins, Mel
James Baldwin 2:33
Simone Schwarz-Bart 7:404
Alice Walker 5:476

Watson, J. P.
J. R. R. Tolkien 2:434

Watt, Ian
John Fowles 2:137

Watts, Harold H.
Aldous Huxley 1:151
Ezra Pound 7:323

Watts, Richard
Lanford Wilson 7:548

Waugh, Auberon
Michael Ayrton 7:18
James Leo Herlihy 6:235
Elizabeth Jane Howard 7:164
Tom Robbins 9:453
Gillian Tindall 7:474
William Trevor 7:476
P. G. Wodehouse 5:516

Way, Brian
Edward Albee 9:2

Weales, Gerald
Edward Albee 9:4
Beryl Bainbridge 4:39
Elizabeth Bowen 6:95
Ivy Compton-Burnett 1:63
J. P. Donleavy 4:123
John Hawkes 4:139; 4:213
Robert Lowell 4:299
Norman Mailer 3:319; 4:319
Bernard Malamud 1:201
Mark Medoff 6:322
Arthur Miller 1:218
Harold Pinter 9:420
James Purdy 2:348; 4:422
David Rabe 4:427
Ronald Ribman 7:357
Peter Shaffer 5:390
Sam Shepard 4:489
Wole Soyinka 3:463
Tom Stoppard 1:327; 8:502
David Storey 2:424
James Thurber 5:430
Robert Penn Warren 1:356
Thornton Wilder 10:536
Tennessee Williams 1:368;
2:466

Weatherhead, A. Kingsley
Robert Duncan 1:82; 7:88
Marianne Moore 4:360
Charles Olson 1:263
Stephen Spender 1:323
William Carlos Williams 1:371

Weathers, Winston
Par Lägerkvist 7:200

Webb, Phyllis
D. G. Jones 10:285

Weber, Brom
Thomas Berger 5:60
Edward Dahlberg 7:69
Bernard Kops 4:274
C. P. Snow 4:503
John Updike 2:442

Weber, Ronald
Saul Bellow 1:32

Webster, Grant
Allen Tate 2:427

Webster, Ivan
James Baldwin 4:43
Gayl Jones 6:266

Weeks, Brigitte
Marilyn French 10:191
Iris Murdoch 8:405

Weeks, Edward
Margaret Atwood 4:25
Jorge Luis Borges 1:39
Lothar-Günther Buchheim
6:102
Pearl S. Buck 7:33
Daphne du Maurier 6:147
Loren Eiseley 7:91
Yasunari Kawabata 5:208
Peter Matthiessen 5:273, 275
Iris Murdoch 6:344
Vladimir Nabokov 6:357
André Schwarz-Bart 4:480
Irwin Shaw 7:413
Mikhail Sholokhov 7:418
Joseph Wambaugh 3:509
Jessamyn West 7:519
Herman Wouk 1:377

Weigel, John A.
Lawrence Durrell 1:86

Weightman, John
Alan Ayckbourn 5:37
Simone de Beauvoir 4:49
Albert Camus 2:98
Louis-Ferdinand Céline 4:100
Marguerite Duras 6:149
A. E. Ellis 7:94
Jean Genet 5:136, 139
André Malraux 9:359
Peter Nichols 5:308
Francis Ponge 6:422
Alain Robbe-Grillet 2:377
Nathalie Sarraute 4:468, 469
Jean-Paul Sartre 9:473
Tom Stoppard 5:412
David Storey 5:416
Gore Vidal 4:555

Weinberg, Helen
Saul Bellow 2:53
Herbert Gold 4:192
Norman Mailer 2:261
Philip Roth 4:452

Weinberger, G. J.
E. E. Cummings 8:160

Weinfield, Henry
Gilbert Sorrentino 7:448, 449

Weintraub, Stanley
C. P. Snow 9:497, 498

Weintraub, Stanley and Bernard S. Oldsey
William Golding 2:167

Weisberg, Robert
Stanley Burnshaw 3:92

Randall Jarrell 2:211
Richmond Lattimore 3:277

Weiss, Theodore
Donald Davie 5:115
Ezra Pound 10:405

Weiss, Victoria L.
Marguerite Duras 6:150

Welburn, Ron
Imamu Amiri Baraka 2:35
Don L. Lee 2:237
Dudley Randall 1:283

Wellek, Rene
R. P. Blackmur 2:62
Kenneth Burke 2:89

Weller, Sheila
Ann Beattie 8:55
Gael Greene 8:252
Diane Wakoski 7:507

Wellwarth, George
Arthur Adamov 4:5
Edward Albee 2:1
John Arden 6:8
Samuel Beckett 2:46
Brendan Behan 8:63
Friedrich Dürrenmatt 4:138
Max Frisch 3:166
Jean Genet 2:157
Michel de Ghelderode 6:197
Eugène Ionesco 4:251
Bernard Kops 4:274
John Osborne 2:327
Harold Pinter 3:385
Arnold Wesker 3:518

Welty, Eudora
Elizabeth Bowen 6:94
Annie Dillard 9:175
E. M. Forster 3:161
Ross Macdonald 2:255
Patrick White 5:485

Wernick, Robert
Wright Morris 3:343

Wertime, Richard A.
Hubert Selby, Jr. 8:475

Wescott, Glenway
Katherine Anne Porter 7:313

Wesling, Donald
Ed Dorn 10:157

West, Anthony
Yehuda Amichai 9:22
Leonardo Sciascia 9:474
Sylvia Townsend Warner 7:512

West, Paul
Miguel Ángel Asturias 3:18
Michael Ayrton 7:18
Samuel Beckett 2:48
Earle Birney 6:72
Heinrich Böll 3:74
Michel Butor 8:113
Louis-Ferdinand Céline 1:57
Evan S. Connell, Jr. 4:108
Julio Cortázar 2:103
Guy Davenport, Jr. 6:123
José Donoso 4:127
Gabriel García Márquez 10:215
John Gardner 2:150
William Golding 1:122
Peter Handke 5:166
MacDonald Harris 9:261

Uwe Johnson 5:202
Jakov Lind 2:245
Charles Newman 2:311
Sylvia Plath 1:271
André Schwarz-Bart 2:389
Robert Penn Warren 1:353

West, Ray B.
Katherine Ann Porter 1:272

Westbrook, Max
Saul Bellow 1:30
William Faulkner 1:101
Ernest Hemingway 1:143
J. D. Salinger 1:299
John Steinbeck 1:326
Robert Penn Warren 1:355

Westbrook, Perry D.
Mary Ellen Chase 2:100

Westbrook, Wayne W.
Louis Auchincloss 4:30

Westburg, Faith and Patrick
Cruttwell
Adolfo Bioy Casares 4:64
Jerzy Kosinski 3:274

Westlake, Donald E.
Gael Greene 8:252

Weston, John
Paul Zindel 6:586

Wetzsteon, Ross
Charles Gordone 1:124
May Sarton 4:472

Whedon, Julia
Penelope Gilliatt 2:160

Wheeler, Charles
William Safire 10:447

Wheelock, Carter
Jorge Luis Borges 2:76; 3:81;
4:72; 6:90
Julio Cortázar 5:109

Wheelock, John Hall
Allen Tate 4:536

Whichard, Nancy Winegardner
Patrick White 4:583

Whicher, Stephen E.
E. E. Cummings 3:116

Whissen, Thomas R.
Isak Dinesen 10:144, 149

Whitaker, Jennifer Seymour
Alberto Moravia 7:243

Whitaker, Thomas R.
Conrad Aiken 3:3

White, E. B.
James Thurber 5:432

White, Edmund
John Ashbery 6:11
Edward Dahlberg 7:65
Thomas M. Disch 7:87
Lawrence Durrell 6:153
Jean Genet 5:138
Russell C. Hoban 7:161
Yasunari Kawabata 5:207
Marjorie Kellogg 2:224
José Lezama Lima 4:290
Harry Mathews 6:315
Yukio Mishima 4:355
Howard Moss 7:248
Vladimir Nabokov 2:304
James Schuyler 5:383

Gore Vidal 8:527
Tennessee Williams 5:503

White, Gertrude M.
W. D. Snodgrass 10:477

White, Jean M.
Dick Francis 2:143
Ross Macdonald 3:308
George Simenon 2:398
Maj Sjöwall 7:502
Per Wahlöö 7:502
Donald E. Westlake 7:529

White, John
Michael Ayrton 7:18

White, John J.
MacDonald Harris 9:259

White, Patricia O.
Samuel Beckett 1:25

White, Ray Lewis
Gore Vidal 2:448

White, Victor
Thornton Wilder 10:536

White, William Luther
C. S. Lewis 3:295

Whitehead, James
Jim Harrison 6:224
Stanley J. Kunitz 6:287
Adrienne Rich 3:427
Gibbons Ruark 3:441

Whitehead, John
Louis MacNeice 1:186

Whitman, Ruth
Adrienne Rich 6:459
Anne Sexton 6:494

Whittemore, Reed
Allen Ginsberg 2:163
James Kirkwood 9:320
Charles Olson 2:326
Tom Robbins 9:453

Whittington-Egan, Richard
Truman Capote 8:133
Rayner Heppenstall 10:272

Wickes, George
Henry Miller 1:221
Anaïs Nin 1:247

Widmer, Kingsley
John Dos Passos 4:133
Leslie A. Fiedler 4:160
Herbert Gold 4:191
Henry Miller 1:220

Wiegand, William
J. D. Salinger 1:295
Jerome Weidman 7:516

Wiegner, Kathleen
Diane Wakoski 9:555

Wiersma, Stanley M.
Christopher Fry 2:144; 10:202

Wiesel, Elie
Chaim Grade 10:246

Wieseltier, Leon
Yehuda Amichai 9:24
Elie Wiesel 3:529

Wiggins, William H., Jr.
John Oliver Killens 10:300

Wilcox, Thomas W.
Anthony Powell 7:341

Wilde, Alan
Christopher Isherwood 1:156;
9:290

Wildgen, Kathryn E.
François Mauriac 9:368

Wilding, Michael
L. P. Hartley 2:182
Jack Kerouac 5:215
Christina Stead 2:422, 423

Wildman, John Hazard
Mary Lavin 4:281
Joyce Carol Oates 6:367
Reynolds Price 6:423

Wilhelm, James J.
Ezra Pound 4:418

Wilkinson, Doris Y. and Patricia
Kane
Chester Himes 7:159

Willard, Nancy
Pablo Neruda 1:246
J.R.R. Tolkien 8:515

Willett, Ralph
Clifford Odets 2:319

Williams, David
Christina Stead 2:423

Williams, Hugo
Horst Bienek 7:29
William S. Burroughs 5:92

Williams, John
Henry Miller 1:223

Williams, Jonathan
Richard Brautigan 3:87
Rod McKuen 3:333
Anne Sexton 4:482

Williams, Lloyd
James Ngugi 7:262

Williams, Miller
Donald Davidson 2:111
John Crowe Ransom 4:434
Hollis Summers 10:493
Andrei Voznesensky 1:349

Williams, Raymond
Aleksandr I. Solzhenitsyn
2:407

Williams, Richard
Allen Ginsberg 6:201
Richard Wilbur 6:568

Williams, Sherley Anne
James Baldwin 3:32
Imamu Amiri Baraka 3:35;
10:20
Ralph Ellison 3:144
Haki R. Madhubuti 6:313

Williams, Tennessee
William Inge 8:307

Williams, William Carlos
Marianne Moore 10:348

Williamson, Alan
Jon Anderson 9:31
Robert Bly 5:65
Galway Kinnell 5:216
Robert Lowell 4:304
Gary Snyder 5:394
James Wright 3:541; 5:519, 521

Willis, Ellen
Bob Dylan 3:131

Willis, J. H., Jr.
William Empson 3:147

Wills, Garry
Thomas Keneally 5:210
Vladimir Nabokov 3:356

Wilner, Eleanor
Adrienne Rich 7:369

Wilson, Angus
Kingsley Amis 3:9
L. P. Hartley 2:181

Wilson, Colin
Jorge Luis Borges 3:78

Wilson, Douglas
Ernest Hemingway 3:241

Wilson, Edmund
W. H. Auden 2:21; 4:33
Marie-Claire Blais 2:62; 4:66
Morley Callaghan 3:97
John Dos Passos 4:130
Anne Hébert 4:219
Hugh MacLennan 2:257
Katherine Anne Porter 7:309
Aleksandr I. Solzhenitsyn
2:407
J. R. R. Tolkien 2:433
Angus Wilson 2:470

Wilson, J. C.
Wright Morris 7:246

Wilson, Jane
Andrew Sinclair 2:401

Wilson, Keith
David Kherdian 6:280

Wilson, Milton
Earle Birney 6:74, 75

Wilson, Reuel K.
Tadeusz Konwicki 8:328

Wilson, Robley, Jr.
Daniel J. Berrigan 4:56
Richard Howard 7:165
Philip Levine 4:285

Wimsatt, Margaret
Margaret Atwood 3:19
Graham Greene 3:208

Winch, Terence
W. S. Merwin 8:388, 390
Flann O'Brien 10:363

Windsor, Philip
Aleksandr I. Solzhenitsyn
7:441

Winegarten, Renee
Ruth Prawer Jhabvala 4:258
Bernard Malamud 3:324; 8:375
André Malraux 1:203
Grace Paley 6:392

Winehouse, Bernard
Conrad Aiken 10:2

Wing, George Gordon
Octavio Paz 3:376

Winks, Robin W.
Len Deighton 7:75

Winter, Thomas
Anthony Burgess 4:81

Winters, Yvor
Robert Frost 10:192

Wintz, Cary D.
Langston Hughes 10:279

Wisse, Ruth R.
Saul Bellow 8:68
Chaim Grade 10:246
Cynthia Ozick 7:289

Wistrich, Robert
A. E. Ellis 7:93

Witt, Harold
Conrad Aiken 1:4

Wixson, Douglas Charles, Jr.
Thornton Wilder 10:531

Woiwode, L.
John Cheever 3:107

Wolcott, James
William F. Buckley, Jr. 7:35
Peter Handke 10:255
Wilfrid Sheed 10:472
Gore Vidal 8:528

Wolf, Barbara
Yukio Mishima 2:288; 6:338

Wolf, William
Gordon Parks 1:265

Wolfe, G. K.
Kurt Vonnegut, Jr. 3:495

Wolfe, George H.
William Faulkner 9:203

Wolfe, H. Leslie
Laurence Lieberman 4:291

Wolfe, Peter
Richard Adams 5:6
A. Alvarez 5:20
Maeve Brennan 5:72
Laurie Colwin 5:108
Jakov Lind 1:177
Walker Percy 2:333
Mary Renault 3:425
Charles Webb 7:515
Patrick White 3:522

Wolff, Geoffrey
Frederick Buechner 2:83
Arthur A. Cohen 7:52
Julio Cortázar 3:115
J. P. Donleavy 6:140
George P. Elliott 2:131
Paula Fox 8:217
John Gardner 2:152
James Jones 3:261
Jerzy Kosinski 1:171; 3:272;
6:282
D. Keith Mano 2:270
Peter Matthiessen 5:273
Wright Morris 7:247
Donald Newlove 6:363
Ezra Pound 2:342
Thomas Pynchon 2:356
Isaac Bashevis Singer 3:456

Wolfley, Lawrence C.
Thomas Pynchon 9:444

Wolheim, Donald A.
Isaac Asimov 1:8
Ray Bradbury 1:42
Arthur C. Clarke 1:59
Harlan Ellison 1:93
Philip Jose Farmer 1:97
Edmond Hamilton 1:137
Robert A. Heinlein 1:139
Clifford D. Simak 1:309
A. E. Van Vogt 1:347
Kurt Vonnegut, Jr. 1:348

Wolitzer, Hilma
Richard Yates 8:556

Wolkenfeld, J. S.
Isaac Bashevis Singer 1:311

Wood, Charles and Karen Wood
Kurt Vonnegut, Jr. 4:565

Wood, Karen and Charles Wood
Kurt Vonnegut, Jr. 4:565

Wood, Michael
Miguel Angel Asturias 3:18
John Barth 2:37
Donald Barthelme 2:41
John Betjeman 6:66
Adolfo Bioy Casares 4:63
Elizabeth Bishop 9:95
Jorge Luis Borges 2:72
Anthony Burgess 8:112
Italo Calvino 8:131
Evan S. Connell, Jr. 6:116
Julio Cortázar 2:105
Lawrence Durrell 6:153
T. S. Eliot 10:169
Stanley Elkin 4:154
William Empson 8:201
Carlos Fuentes 8:225
John Gardner 5:131; 8:235
Juan Goytisolo 5:150
Judith Guest 8:253
John Hawkes 4:219
Seamus Heaney 7:147
Erica Jong 4:264
Stanislaw Lem 8:345
José Lezama Lima 4:289
Norman Mailer 3:316
Thomas McGuane 3:330
A. G. Mojtabai 9:385
Brian Moore 8:395
Berry Morgan 6:340
Vladimir Nabokov 2:303
Pablo Neruda 5:303
Hans Erich Nossack 6:365
Joyce Carol Oates 2:316
Grace Paley 4:392
Octavio Paz 4:396
Ezra Pound 2:345
Anthony Powell 3:403
Manuel Puig 3:407
Thomas Pynchon 2:357
Raymond Queneau 10:432
Philip Roth 4:456
Severo Sarduy 6:487
Isaac Bashevis Singer 3:459
Muriel Spark 5:399; 8:495
Charles Tomlinson 6:534
John Updike 2:445
Mario Vargas Llosa 6:546
Gore Vidal 8:525
Kurt Vonnegut, Jr. 3:503
Eudora Welty 2:463
Angus Wilson 3:535
Rudolph Wurlitzer 2:483

Wood, Peter
Peter De Vries 2:114
Alberto Moravia 2:293

Wood, Susan
Penelope Gilliatt 10:230

Wood, William C.
Wallace Markfield 8:380

Woodcock, George
Earle Birney 6:71, 75
Louis-Ferdinand Céline 9:158
Jean Genet 5:138
Denise Levertov 5:246
Hugh MacDiarmid 2:255
Brian Moore 1:225; 3:341
Herbert Read 4:441
Kenneth Rexroth 2:370, 371
Mordecai Richler 5:375

Woodfield, J.
Christopher Fry 10:200

Woods, Crawford
Ross Macdonald 3:308
Isaac Bashevis Singer 3:457
Hunter S. Thompson 9:526

Woods, William C.
Lisa Alther 7:13
Leon Uris 7:492

Woods, William Crawford
Jim Harrison 6:225

Woodward, C. Vann
William Styron 3:473

Wooten, Anna
Louise Glück 7:119

Worsley, T. C.
Stephen Spender 10:488

Wrenn, John H.
John Dos Passos 1:77

Wright, David
C. Day Lewis 6:126

Wright, George T.
W. H. Auden 1:10
T. S. Eliot 3:137

Wright, James
Richard F. Hugo 6:244

Wunderlich, Lawrence
Fernando Arrabal 2:16

Wyatt, David M.
Ernest Hemingway 8:288
Robert Penn Warren 8:541

Wylder, Delbert E.
William Eastlake 8:198

Wymard, Eleanor B.
Annie Dillard 9:177

Wyndham, Francis
Caroline Blackwood 6:79

Yagoda, Ben
Margaret Drabble 10:164

Yannella, Philip R.
Pablo Neruda 5:301

Yardley, Jonathan
Chinua Achebe 3:2
Kingsley Amis 2:8
Hal Bennett 5:59
Wendell Berry 4:59; 6:62
Doris Betts 3:73
Frederick Buechner 6:102
Harry Crews 6:117, 118
Peter De Vries 7:77
James Dickey 2:116
Frederick Exley 6:171
William Faulkner 3:158
Brian Glanville 6:202
James Hanley 5:167, 168
Jim Harrison 6:224
John Hersey 9:277
George V. Higgins 7:157
Diane Johnson 5:199
Madison Jones 4:263
Ward Just 4:266
Thomas Keneally 8:319; 10:299
John Knowles 4:271; 10:303
Bernard Malamud 2:267
Saul Maloff 5:271
Cormac McCarthy 4:342
A. G. Mojtabai 5:293
Toni Morrison 4:365
Walker Percy 3:381
Piers Paul Read 4:444
J. R. Salamanca 4:462
John Seelye 7:406
Wilfrid Sheed 2:394; 4:488
Thomas Tryon 3:483
Jerome Weidman 7:518
Eudora Welty 2:462
Tom Wicker 7:533
Calder Willingham 5:511, 512

ya Salaam, Kalumu
Nikki Giovanni 4:189

Yates, Donald A.
John Dickson Carr 3:100

Yates, Norris W.
Günter Grass 4:203
James Thurber 5:433

Yenser, Stephen
Robert Lowell 3:305
James Merrill 3:335
Robert Penn Warren 8:537, 540

Yglesias, Helen
Ludvík Vaculík 7:494

Yglesias, Jose
Christina Stead 2:421
Mario Vargas Llosa 6:547

Yglesias, Luis E.
Pablo Neruda 7:262; 9:398

Yoder, Edwin M.
MacKinlay Kantor 7:195

Yohalem, John
Richard Brautigan 5:70
James McCourt 5:277
Charles Webb 7:516

Young, Marguerite
Mark Van Doren 10:495

Young, Peter
Andrei Voznesensky 1:348

Young, Thomas Daniel
John Crowe Ransom 4:433, 436

Young, Vernon
W. H. Auden 2:28
George Mackay Brown 5:77
J. V. Cunningham 3:121
William Dickey 3:126
Lawrence Ferlinghetti 6:183
John Hollander 2:197
Richard F. Hugo 6:245
Laurence Lieberman 4:291
Robert Lowell 5:258
Pablo Neruda 1:247
Nicanor Parra 2:331
Yannis Ritsos 6:464
Jon Silkin 2:396
Maura Stanton 9:508
James Tate 2:432
Diane Wakoski 2:459; 4:573

CRITIC INDEX

Zak, Michele Wender
Doris Lessing **6**:294

Zaller, Robert
Anaïs Nin **4**:377

Zatlin, Linda G.
Isaac Bashevis Singer **1**:312

Zaturenska, Marya and Horace Gregory
Laura Riding **7**:373

Zavatsky, Bill
Ed Dorn **10**:157

Zehr, David E.
Ernest Hemingway **8**:286

Zeik, Michael
Thomas Merton **3**:337

Zeller, Bernhard
Hermann Hesse **2**:190

Zilkha, Michael and Christina Monet
Mark Medoff **6**:323

Zimmerman, Eugenia N.
Jean-Paul Sartre **9**:472

Zimmerman, Paul
R. K. Narayan **7**:256

Zimmerman, Paul D.
E. M. Forster **2**:135
Lois Gould **4**:199

Zinnes, Harriet
Robert Bly **1**:37
Robert Duncan **1**:83
Anaïs Nin **4**:379; **8**:425
Ezra Pound **3**:399
May Swenson **4**:533, 534
Mona Van Duyn **7**:499

Ziolkowski, Theodore
Heinrich Böll **2**:67; **6**:83

Hermann Hesse **1**:145, 146; **3**:248
Hans Erich Nossack **6**:364

Zivanovic, Judith
Jean-Paul Sartre **9**:470

Zivkovic, Peter D.
W. H. Auden **3**:23

Zivley, Sherry Lutz
Sylvia Plath **9**:431

Zolf, Larry
Mordecai Richler **5**:376

Zucker, David
Delmore Schwartz **10**:464

Zuckerman, Albert J.
Vassilis Vassilikos **4**:551

Zuger, David
Adrienne Rich **7**:372

Zweig, Paul
Richard Adams **5**:6
A. R. Ammons **5**:29
John Ashbery **2**:18
William Dickey **3**:126
Clayton Eshleman **7**:100
John Hollander **5**:186
David Ignatow **7**:181
Kenneth Koch **8**:322
Philip Levine **4**:286
Leonard Michaels **6**:325
Czeslaw Milosz **5**:292
Vladimir Nabokov **3**:354
Pablo Neruda **5**:303
George Oppen **7**:284
Charles Simic **6**:502
William Stafford **7**:461
Diane Wakoski **4**:571
James Wright **3**:542

Cumulative Index to Authors

Abe, Kōbō **8**
Abrahams, Peter **4**
Abse, Dannie **7**
Achebe, Chinua **1, 3, 5, 7**
Adamov, Arthur **4**
Adams, Alice **6**
Adams, Richard **4, 5**
Adler, Renata **8**
Agnon, S(hmuel) Y(osef) **4, 8**
Ai **4**
Aiken, Conrad **1, 3, 5, 10**
Albee, Edward **1, 2, 3, 5, 9**
Alberti, Rafael **7**
Aldiss, Brian **5**
Aleixandre, Vicente **9**
Algren, Nelson **4, 10**
Alther, Lisa **7**
Alvarez, A(lfred) **5**
Ambler, Eric **4, 6, 9**
Amichai, Yehuda **9**
Amis, Kingsley **1, 2, 3, 5, 8**
Amis, Martin **4, 9**
Ammons, A(rchie)
  R(andolph) **2, 3, 5, 8, 9**
Anderson, Jon **9**
Andrews, Cecily Fairfield
  See West, Rebecca **7, 9**
Andrić, Ivo **8**
Anouilh, Jean **1, 3, 8**
Antschel, Paul
  See Celan, Paul **10**
Anthony, Florence
  See Ai **4**
Antoninus, Brother
  See Everson, William **1, 5**
Apple, Max **9**
Aragon, Louis **3**
Arden, John **6**
Arguedas, José María **10**

Armah, Ayi Kwei **5**
Arnow, Harriette **2, 7**
Arp, Jean **5**
Arrabal, Fernando **2, 9**
Ashbery, John **2, 3, 4, 6, 9**
Asimov, Isaac **1, 3, 9**
Asturias, Miguel Ángel **3, 8**
Atwood, Margaret **2, 3, 4, 8**
Auchincloss, Louis **4, 6, 9**
Auden, W(ystan) H(ugh) **1, 2, 3, 4, 6, 9**
Avison, Margaret **2, 4**
Ayckbourn, Alan **5, 8**
Ayrton, Michael **7**
Bagryana, Elisaveta **10**
Bainbridge, Beryl **4, 5, 8, 10**
Baker, Elliott **8**
Baldwin, James **1, 2, 3, 4, 5, 8**
Ballard, J(ames) G(raham) **3, 6**
Baraka, Imamu Amiri **2, 3, 5, 10**
  See also Jones, (Everett)
  LeRoi **1**
Barker, George **8**
Barnes, Djuna **3, 4, 8**
Barnes, Peter **5**
Barondess, Sue Kaufman
  See Kaufman, Sue **3, 8**
Barth, John **1, 2, 3, 5, 7, 9, 10**
Barthelme, Donald **1, 2, 3, 5, 6, 8**
Bassani, Giorgio **9**
Baumbach, Jonathan **6**
Beagle, Peter S(oyer) **7**
Beattie, Ann **8**
Beauvoir, Simone de **1, 2, 4, 8**
Becker, Jurek **7**
Beckett, Samuel **1, 2, 3, 4, 6, 9, 10**
Beecher, John **6**

Behan, Brendan **1, 8**
Belcheva, Elisaveta
  See Bagryana, Elisaveta **10**
Bell, Marvin **8**
Bellow, Saul **1, 2, 3, 6, 8, 10**
Benchley, Peter **4, 8**
Benedikt, Michael **4**
Bennett, Hal **5**
Berger, John **2**
Berger, Thomas **3, 5, 8**
Bergstein, Eleanor **4**
Bernhard, Thomas **3**
Berrigan, Daniel J. **4**
Berry, Wendell **4, 6, 8**
Berryman, John **1, 2, 3, 4, 6, 8, 10**
Betjeman, John **2, 6, 10**
Betts, Doris **3, 6**
Bienek, Horst **7**
Bioy Casares, Adolfo **4, 8**
Birney, (Alfred) Earle **1, 4, 6**
Bishop, Elizabeth **1, 4, 9**
Bishop, John **10**
Blackburn, Paul **9**
Blackmur, R(ichard) P(almer) **2**
Blackwood, Caroline **6, 9**
Blais, Marie-Claire **2, 4, 6**
Blake, Nicholas
  See Day Lewis, C(ecil) **1, 6**
Blatty, William Peter **2**
Blixen, Karen
  See Dinesen, Isak **10**
Blunden, Edmund **2**
Bly, Robert **1, 2, 5, 10**
Bogan, Louise **4**
Böll, Heinrich **2, 3, 6, 9**
Bond, Edward **4, 6**
Bonnefoy, Yves **9**
Bontemps, Arna **1**

Borges, Jorge Luis **1, 2, 3, 4, 6, 8, 9, 10**
Bourjaily, Vance **8**
Bowen, Elizabeth **1, 3, 6**
Bowers, Edgar **9**
Bowles, Jane **3**
Bowles, Paul **1, 2**
Boyle, Kay **1, 5**
Bradbury, Ray **1, 3, 10**
Bragg, Melvyn **10**
Braine, John **1, 3**
Brand, Millen **7**
Brautigan, Richard **1, 3, 5, 9**
Brennan, Maeve **5**
Breslin, Jimmy **4**
Breton, André **2, 9**
Brodsky, Joseph **4, 6**
Bromell, Henry **5**
Bronk, William **10**
Brooks, Gwendolyn **1, 2, 4, 5**
Brophy, Brigid **6**
Brosman, Catharine Savage **9**
Broumas, Olga **10**
Brown, George Mackay **5**
Brown, Sterling **1**
Brunner, John **8, 10**
Buchheim, Lothar-Günther **6**
Buck, Pearl S(ydenstricker) **7**
Buckley, William F(rank), Jr. **7**
Buechner, (Carl) Frederick **2, 4, 6, 9**
Buell, John **10**
Bukowski, Charles **2, 5, 9**
Bullins, Ed **1, 5, 7**
Bunting, Basil **10**
Burgess, Anthony **1, 2, 4, 5, 8, 10**
Burke, Kenneth **2**
Burnshaw, Stanley **3**

Burr, Anne 6
Burroughs, William
  S(eward) 1, 2, 5
Busch, Frederick 7, 10
Butor, Michel 1, 3, 8
Cabrera Infante, G(uillermo) 5
Cain, James M(allahan) 3
Caldwell, Erskine 1, 8
Caldwell, Taylor 2
Calisher, Hortense 2, 4, 8
Callaghan, Morley 3
Calvino, Italo 5, 8
Camus, Albert 1, 2, 4, 9
Canetti, Elias 3
Capote, Truman 1, 3, 8
Carpentier, Alejo 8
Carr, John Dickson 3
Carroll, Paul Vincent 10
Carruth, Hayden 4, 7, 10
Carter, Angela 5
Casares, Adolfo Bioy
  See Bioy Casares, Adolfo 4
Casey, Michael 2
Cassill, R(onald) V(erlin) 4
Cassity, (Allen) Turner 6
Causley, Charles 7
Cela, Camilo José 4
Celan, Paul 10
Céline, Louis-Ferdinand 1, 3, 4,
  7, 9
Char, René 9
Charyn, Jerome 5, 8
Chase, Mary Ellen 2
Cheever, John 3, 7, 8
Christie, Agatha 1, 6, 8
Ciardi, John 10
Clark, Eleanor 5
Clarke, Arthur C(harles) 1, 4
Clarke, Austin 6, 9
Clarke, Austin C(hesterfield) 8
Clavell, James 6
Coburn, D(onald) L(ee) 10
Cocteau, Jean 1, 8
Cohen, Arthur A(llen) 7
Cohen, Leonard 3
Colwin, Laurie 5
Comfort, Alex(ander) 7
Compton-Burnett, Ivy 1, 3, 10
Condon, Richard 4, 6, 8, 10
Connell, Evan S(helby), Jr. 4, 6
Connelly, Marc(us) 7
Coover, Robert 3, 7
Corman, Cid (Sidney
  Corman) 9
Cornwell, David
  See Le Carré, John 3, 5, 9
Corso, (Nunzio) Gregory 1
Cortázar, Julio 2, 3, 5, 10
Coward, Noel 1, 9
Cox, William Trevor
  See Trevor, William 7, 9
Cozzens, James Gould 1, 4
Creeley, Robert 1, 2, 4, 8
Crews, Harry 6
Crichton, (John) Michael 2, 6
Cummings, E(dward)
  E(stlin) 1, 3, 8
Cunningham, J(ames)
  V(incent) 3
Dahl, Roald 1, 6
Dahlberg, Edward 1, 7
Dannay, Frederick
  See Queen, Ellery 3

Daryush, Elizabeth 6
Davenport, Guy, Jr. 6
Davidson, Donald 2
Davidson, Sara 9
Davie, Donald 5, 8, 10
Davies, (William) Robertson 2,
  7
Dawson, Fielding 6
Day Lewis, C(ecil) 1, 6, 10
Deighton, Len 4, 7
Delany, Samuel R. 8
Delbanco, Nicholas 6
Delibes, Miguel 8
DeLillo, Don 8, 10
Dennis, Nigel 8
Destouches, Louis-Ferdinand
  See Céline, Louis-
  Ferdinand 1, 3, 4, 7, 9
De Vries, Peter 1, 2, 3, 7, 10
Dick, Philip K(indred) 10
Dickey, James 1, 2, 4, 7, 10
Dickey, William 3
Didion, Joan 1, 3, 8
Dillard, Annie 9
Dillard, R(ichard) H(enry)
  W(ilde) 5
Dinesen, Isak 10
Disch, Thomas M(ichael) 7
Doctorow, E(dgar)
  L(awrence) 6
Donleavy, J(ames) P(atrick) 1,
  4, 6, 10
Donoso, José 4, 8
Doolittle, Hilda
  See H(ilda) D(oolittle) 3, 8
Dorn, Ed(ward) 10
Dos Passos, John 1, 4, 8
Drabble, Margaret 2, 3, 5, 8, 10
Drexler, Rosalyn 2, 6
Duberman, Martin 8
Du Bois, W(illiam) E(dward)
  B(urghardt) 1, 2
Dugan, Alan 2, 6
Duhamel, Georges 8
Dumas, Henry 6
du Maurier, Daphne 6
Duncan, Robert 1, 2, 4, 7
Dunn, Douglas 6
Duras, Marguerite 3, 6
Durrell, Lawrence 1, 4, 6, 8
Dürrenmatt, Friedrich 1, 4, 8
Dylan, Bob 3, 4, 6
Eastlake, William 8
Eberhart, Richard 3
Eigner, Larry (Laurence
  Eigner) 9
Eiseley, Loren 7
Ekwensi, Cyprian 4
Eliot, T(homas) S(tearns) 1, 2,
  3, 6, 9, 10
Elkin, Stanley 4, 6, 9
Elliott, George P(aul) 2
Ellis, A. E. 7
Ellison, Harlan 1
Ellison, Ralph 1, 3
Empson, William 3, 8
Endo Shusaku 7
Enright, D(ennis) J(oseph) 4, 8
Epstein, Daniel Mark 7
Eshleman, Clayton 7
Espriu, Salvador 9
Everson, William 1, 5

Evtushenko, Evgeni
  See Yevtushenko,
  Yevgeny 1, 3
Exley, Frederick 6
Farigoule, Louis
  See Romains, Jules 7
Fariña, Richard 9
Farmer, Philip Jose 1
Farrell, J(ames) G(ordon) 6
Farrell, James T(homas) 1, 4, 8
Faulkner, William 1, 3, 6, 8, 9
Faust, Irvin 8
Federman, Raymond 6
Feiffer, Jules 2, 8
Feldman, Irving 7
Ferguson, Helen
  See Kavan, Anna 5
Ferlinghetti, Lawrence 2, 6, 10
Fiedler, Leslie A(aron) 4
Fisher, Vardis 7
Fleming, Ian 3
Forrest, Leon 4
Forster, E(dward)
  M(organ) 1, 2, 3, 4, 9, 10
Forsyth, Frederick 2, 5
Fowles, John 1, 2, 3, 4, 6, 9, 10
Fox, Paula 2, 8
Frame, Janet 2, 3, 6
Francis, Dick 2
Fraser, George MacDonald 7
Frayn, Michael 3, 7
French, Marilyn 10
Friedman, B(ernard) H(arper) 7
Friedman, Bruce Jay 3, 5
Friel, Brian 5
Frisch, Max 3, 9
Frost, Robert 1, 3, 4, 9, 10
Fry, Christopher 2, 10
Fuchs, Daniel 8
Fuentes, Carlos 3, 8, 10
Fugard, Athol 5, 9
Fuller, Roy 4
Gaddis, William 1, 3, 6, 8, 10
Gaines, Ernest J. 3
Gallant, Mavis 7
Gallico, Paul 2
García Márquez, Gabriel 2, 3,
  8, 10
Gardner, John 2, 3, 5, 7, 8, 10
Garnett, David 3
Garrett, George 3
Garrigue, Jean 2, 8
Gass, William H(oward) 1, 2, 8
Gelber, Jack 1, 6
Genet, Jean 1, 2, 5, 10
Gerhardi, William
  See Gerhardie, William 5
Gerhardie, William 5
Ghelderode, Michel de 6
Gilliatt, Penelope 2, 10
Gilroy, Frank D(aniel) 2
Ginsberg, Allen 1, 2, 3, 4, 6
Ginzburg, Natalia 5
Giono, Jean 4
Giovanni, Nikki 2, 4
Giovene, Andrea 7
Glanville, Brian 6
Glassco, John 9
Glissant, Édouard 10
Glück, Louise 7
Godwin, Gail 5, 8
Gold, Herbert 4, 7
Goldbarth, Albert 5

Golding, William 1, 2, 3, 8, 10
Goldman, William 1
Gombrowicz, Witold 4, 7
Gómez, de la Serna, Ramón 9
Goodman, Paul 1, 2, 4, 7
Gordimer, Nadine 3, 5, 7, 10
Gordon, Caroline 6
Gordone, Charles 1, 4
Gould, Lois 4, 10
Goyen, (Charles) William 5, 8
Goytisolo, Juan 5, 10
Grade, Chaim 10
Grass, Günter 1, 2, 4, 6
Grau, Shirley Ann 4, 9
Graves, Robert 1, 2, 6
Gray, Simon 9
Green, Hannah 3
  See also Greenberg, Joanne 7
Green, Henry 2
Green, Julien 3
Greenberg, Joanne 7
  See also Green, Hannah 3
Greene, Gael 8
Greene, Graham 1, 3, 6, 9
Gregor, Arthur 9
Grieve, C(hristopher) M(urray)
  See MacDiarmid, Hugh 2, 4
Grigson, Geoffrey 7
Guare, John 8
Guest, Judith 8
Gunn, Bill 5
Gunn, Thom(son) 3, 6
H(ilda) D(oolittle) 3, 8
Hacker, Marilyn 5, 9
Hailey, Arthur 5
Haley, Alex 8
Hall, Donald 1
Hamburger, Michael 5
Hamill, Pete 10
Hamilton, Edmond 1
Hammett, (Samuel) Dashiell 3,
  5, 10
Hampton, Christopher 4
Handke, Peter 5, 8, 10
Hanley, James 3, 5, 8
Harper, Michael S(teven) 7
Harris, MacDonald 9
Harrison, Jim 6
Hartley, L(eslie) P(oles) 2
Hawkes, John 1, 2, 3, 4, 7, 9
Hayden, Robert 5, 9
Heaney, Seamus 5, 7
Hébert, Anne 4
Hecht, Anthony 8
Hecht, Ben 8
Heiney, Donald
  See Harris, MacDonald 9
Heinlein, Robert A(nson) 1, 3, 8
Heller, Joseph 1, 3, 5, 8
Hellman, Lillian 2, 4, 8
Helprin, Mark 7, 10
Hemingway, Ernest 1, 3, 6, 8,
  10
Heppenstall, (John) Rayner 10
Herbert, Zbigniew 9
Herlihy, James Leo 6
Hersey, John 1, 2, 7, 9
Hesse, Hermann 1, 2, 3, 6
Hibbert, Eleanor 7
Higgins, George V(incent) 4, 7,
  10
Highsmith, (Mary) Patricia 2, 4
Hill, Geoffrey 5, 8

Hill, Susan B. 4
Himes, Chester 2, 4, 7
Hinde, Thomas 6
Hiraoka, Kimitake
 See Mishima, Yukio 2, 4, 6, 9
Hoban, Russell C(onwell) 7
Hobson, Laura Z(ametkin) 7
Hochhuth, Rolf 4
Hochman, Sandra 3, 8
Hoffman, Daniel 6
Hoffman, Stanley 5
Hollander, John 2, 5, 8
Holt, Victoria
 See Hibbert, Eleanor 7
Holub, Miroslav 4
Hope, A(lec) D(erwent) 3
Hopkins, John 4
Horgan, Paul 9
Howard, Elizabeth Jane 7
Howard, Maureen 5
Howard, Richard 7, 10
Hughes, (James) Langston 1, 5,
 10
Hughes, Richard 1
Hughes, Ted 2, 4, 9
Hugo, Richard F(ranklin) 6
Hunt, E(verette) Howard 3
Hurston, Zora Neale 7
Huxley, Aldous 1, 3, 4, 5, 8
Ignatow, David 4, 7
Inge, William 1, 8
Innes, Michael
 See Stewart, J(ohn) I(nnes)
 M(ackintosh) 7
Ionesco, Eugène 1, 4, 6, 9
Isherwood, Christopher 1, 9
Jackson, Laura Riding
 See Riding, Laura 3, 7
Jacobson, Dan 4
Jarrell, Randall 1, 2, 6, 9
Jeffers, Robinson 2, 3
Jennings, Elizabeth 5
Jhabvala, Ruth Prawer 4, 8
Johnson, B(ryan) S(tanley) 6, 9
Johnson, Charles 7
Johnson, Diane 5
Johnson, Pamela Hansford 1, 7
Johnson, Uwe 5, 10
Johnston, Jennifer 7
Jones, D(ouglas) G(ordon) 10
Jones, David 2, 4, 7
Jones, Gayl 6, 9
Jones, James 1, 3, 10
Jones, (Everett) LeRoi 1
 See also Baraka, Imamu
 Amiri 2, 3, 5, 10
Jones, Madison 4
Jones, Mervyn 10
Jones, Preston 10
Jones, Robert F(rancis) 7
Jong, Erica 4, 6, 8
Jordan, June 5
Josipovici, G(abriel) 6
Just, Ward 4
Justice, Donald 6
Kallman, Chester 2
Kantor, MacKinlay 7
Kaufman, Sue 3, 8
Kavan, Anna 5
Kawabata, Yasunari 2, 5, 9
Kazan, Elia 6
Kellogg, Marjorie 2
Kemelman, Harry 2

Keneally, Thomas 5, 8, 10
Kennedy, Joseph Charles
 See Kennedy, X. J. 8
Kennedy, William 6
Kennedy, X. J. 8
Kerouac, Jack 1, 2, 3, 5
Kerrigan, (Thomas) Anthony 4,
 6
Kesey, Ken 1, 3, 6
Kessler, Jascha 4
Kherdian, David 6, 9
Killens, John Oliver 10
King, Francis 8
Kinnell, Galway 1, 2, 3, 5
Kinsella, Thomas 4
Kirkup, James 1
Kirkwood, James 9
Knowles, John 1, 4, 10
Koch, Kenneth 5, 8
Koestler, Arthur 1, 3, 6, 8
Konrád, György 4, 10
Konwicki, Tadeusz 8
Kopit, Arthur 1
Kops, Bernard 4
Kosinski, Jerzy 1, 2, 3, 6, 10
Kotlowitz, Robert 4
Kotzwinkle, William 5
Krleža, Miroslav 8
Kroetsch, Robert 5
Kumin, Maxine 5
Kundera, Milan 4, 9
Kunitz, Stanley J(asspon) 6
Kunze, Reiner 10
Kuzma, Greg 7
Lagerkvist, Pär 7, 10
Lamming, George 2, 4
Larkin, Philip 3, 5, 8, 9
Lathen, Emma 2
Lattimore, Richmond 3
Laurence, (Jean) Margaret 3, 6
Lavin, Mary 4
Laye, Camara 4
Layton, Irving 2
Le Carré, John 3, 5, 9
Lee, Don L. 2
 See also Madhubuti, Haki
 R. 6
Lee, Manfred B(ennington)
 See Queen, Ellery 3
Le Guin, Ursula K(roeber) 8
Lehmann, Rosamond 5
Lelchuk, Alan 5
Lem, Stanislaw 8
Lengyel, József 7
Lerman, Eleanor 9
Lessing, Doris 1, 2, 3, 6, 10
Levertov, Denise 1, 2, 3, 5, 8
Levin, Ira 3, 6
Levin, Meyer 7
Levine, Philip 2, 4, 5, 9
Lewis, C(ecil) Day
 See Day Lewis, C(ecil) 1, 6
Lewis, C(live) S(taples) 1, 3, 6
Lezama Lima, José 4, 10
Lieber, Joel 6
Lieberman, Laurence 4
Lima, José Lezama
 See Lezama Lima, José 4
Lind, Jakov 1, 2, 4
Livesay, Dorothy 4
Llewellyn, Richard 7
Llosa, Mario Vargas
 See Vargas Llosa, Mario 3, 6

Lloyd, Richard Llewellyn
 See Llewellyn, Richard 7
Logan, John 5
Lowell, Robert 1, 2, 3, 4, 5, 8, 9
Lurie, Alison 4, 5
MacBeth, George 2, 5, 9
MacDiarmid, Hugh 2, 4
MacDonald, John D(ann) 3
Macdonald, (John) Ross 1, 2, 3
MacInnes, Colin 4
MacLean, Alistair 3
MacLeish, Archibald 3, 8
MacLennan, (John) Hugh 2
MacNeice, Louis 1, 4, 10
Madden, David 5
Madhubuti, Haki R. 6
 See also Lee, Don L. 2
Mailer, Norman 1, 2, 3, 4, 5, 8
Major, Clarence 3
Malamud, Bernard 1, 2, 3, 5, 8,
 9
Maloff, Saul 5
Malraux, (Georges-) André 1,
 4, 9
Malzberg, Barry N. 7
Mamet, David 9
Manning, Olivia 5
Mano, D. Keith 2, 10
Markandaya, Kamala
 (Purnalya) 4, 7, 9
Markfield, Wallace 8
Markham, Robert
 See Amis, Kingsley 1, 2, 3, 5,
 8
Marquand, John P(hillips) 2, 10
Márquez, Gabriel García
 See García Márquez,
 Gabriel 2, 3
Marsh, (Edith) Ngaio 7
Mathews, Harry 6
Matthias, John 9
Matthiessen, Peter 5, 7
Maugham, W(illiam) Somerset 1
Mauriac, Claude 9
Mauriac, François 4, 9
McCarthy, Cormac 4
McCarthy, Mary 1, 3, 5
McClure, Michael 6, 10
McCourt, James 5
McCullers, (Lula) Carson 1, 4,
 10
McElroy, Joseph 5
McGahern, John 5, 9
McGuane, Thomas 3, 7
McHale, Tom 3, 5
McKuen, Rod 1, 3
McMurtry, Larry 2, 3, 7
McNally, Terrence 4, 7
Medoff, Mark 6
Megged, Aharon 9
Mercer, David 5
Meredith, William 4
Merrill, James 2, 3, 6, 8
Merton, Thomas 1, 3
Merwin, W(illiam)
 S(tanley) 1, 2, 3, 5, 8
Mewshaw, Michael 9
Michaels, Leonard 6
Michaux, Henri 8
Michener, James A(lbert) 1, 5
Middleton, Stanley 7
Miguéis, José Rodrigues 10
Miles, Josephine 1, 2

Miller, Arthur 1, 2, 6, 10
Miller, Henry 1, 2, 4, 9
Miller, Jason 2
Miller, Walter M., Jr. 4
Milosz, Czeslow 5
Mishima, Yukio 2, 4, 6, 9
Mojtabai, A(nn) G(race) 5, 9
Momaday, N(avarre) Scott 2
Montale, Eugenio 7, 9
Montgomery, Marion 7
Montherlant, Henri de 8
Moorcock, Michael 5
Moore, Brian 1, 3, 5, 7, 8
Moore, Marianne 1, 2, 4, 8, 10
Morante, Elsa 8
Moravia, Alberto 2, 7
Morgan, Berry 6
Morgan, Robin 2
Morris, Wright 1, 3, 7
Morrison, Toni 4, 10
Mortimer, Penelope 5
Moss, Howard 7
Mrozek, Slawomir 3
Munro, Alice 6, 10
Murdoch, (Jean) Iris 1, 2, 3, 4,
 6, 8
Nabokov, Vladimir 1, 2, 3, 6, 8
Nagy, László 7
Naipaul, V(idiadhar)
 S(urajprasad) 4, 7, 9
Narayan, R(asipuram)
 K(rishnaswami) 7
Nemerov, Howard 2, 6, 9
Neruda, Pablo 1, 2, 5, 7, 9
Newby, P(ercy) H(oward) 2
Newlove, Donald 6
Newman, Charles 2, 8
Ngugi, James 3, 7
Nichols, Peter 5
Niedecker, Lorine 10
Nin, Anaïs 1, 4, 8
Nissenson, Hugh 4, 9
Niven, Larry 8
Nossack, Hans Erich 6
Nova, Craig 7
Oates, Joyce Carol 1, 2, 3, 6, 9
O'Brien, Edna 3, 5, 8
O'Brien, Flann 1, 4, 5, 7, 10
O'Brien, Tim 7
O'Casey, Sean 1, 5, 9
O'Connor, (Mary) Flannery 1,
 2, 3, 6, 10
Odets, Clifford 2
Ōe, Kenzaburō 10
O'Faolain, Julia 6
O'Faoláin, Seán 1, 7
O'Flaherty, Liam 5
O'Hara, Frank 2, 5
O'Hara, John 1, 2, 3, 6
Olesha, Yuri 8
Olsen, Tillie 4
Olson, Charles 1, 2, 5, 6, 9
Onetti, Juan Carlos 7, 10
O'Nolan, Brian
 See O'Brien, Flann 1, 4, 5, 7
Oppen, George 7
Orton, Joe 4
Osborne, John 1, 2, 5
Owens, Rochelle 8
Oz, Amos 5, 8
Ozick, Cynthia 3, 7
Page, P(atricia) K(athleen) 7
Paley, Grace 4, 6

AUTHOR INDEX

Parks, Gordon 1
Parra, Nicanor 2
Pasternak, Boris 7, 10
Patchen, Kenneth 1, 2
Paton, Alan 4, 10
Paz, Octavio 3, 4, 6, 10
Peake, Mervyn 7
Peck, John 3
Percy, Walker 2, 3, 6, 8
Perelman, S(idney) J(oseph) 3, 5, 9
Perse, St.-John 4
Peters, Robert L(ouis) 7
Petrakis, Harry Mark 3
Petry, Ann 1, 7
Piercy, Marge 3, 6
Piñero, Miguel 4
Pinget, Robert 7
Pinsky, Robert 9
Pinter, Harold 1, 3, 6, 9
Pirsig, Robert M(aynard) 4, 6
Plaidy, Jean
    See Hibbert, Eleanor 7
Plante, David 7
Plath, Sylvia 1, 2, 3, 5, 9
Plomer, William 4, 8
Ponge, Francis 6
Porter, Katherine Anne 1, 3, 7, 10
Porter, Peter 5
Potok, Chaim 2, 7
Pound, Ezra 1, 2, 3, 4, 5, 7, 10
Powell, Anthony 1, 3, 7, 9, 10
Powers, J(ames) F(arl) 1, 4, 8
Pownall, David 10
Powys, John Cowper 7, 9
Price, (Edward) Reynolds 3, 6
Price, Richard 6
Priestley, J(ohn) B(oynton) 2, 5, 9
Pritchett, V(ictor) S(awden) 5
Prokosch, Frederic 4
Puig, Manuel 3, 5, 10
Purdy, A(lfred) W(ellington) 3, 6
Purdy, James 2, 4, 10
Puzo, Mario 1, 2, 6
Pynchon, Thomas 2, 3, 6, 9
Quasimodo, Salvatore 10
Queen, Ellery 3
Queneau, Raymond 2, 5, 10
Quin, Ann 6
Quoirez, Françoise
    See Sagan, Françoise 3, 6, 9
Rabe, David 4, 8
Radvanyi, Netty Reiling
    See Seghers, Anna 7
Raine, Kathleen 7
Rand, Ayn 3
Randall, Dudley 1
Ransom, John Crowe 2, 4, 5
Raphael, Frederic 2
Rattigan, Terence 7
Read, Herbert 4
Read, Piers Paul 4, 10
Rechy, John 1, 7
Redgrove, Peter 6
Reed, Ishmael 2, 3, 5, 6
Renault, Mary 3
Rexroth, Kenneth 1, 2, 6
Reyes y Basoalto, Ricardo
    Eliecer Neftali
        See Neruda, Pablo 1, 2, 5, 7, 9

Reynolds, Jonathan 6
Reznikoff, Charles 9
Rhys, Jean 2, 4, 6
Ribeiro, João Ubaldo 10
Ribman, Ronald 7
Rice, Elmer 7
Rich, Adrienne 3, 6, 7
Richler, Mordecai 3, 5, 9
Riding, Laura 3, 7
Ritsos, Yannis 6
Rivers, Conrad Kent 1
Robbe-Grillet, Alain 1, 2, 4, 6, 8, 10
Robbins, Harold 5
Robbins, Tom 9
Robinson, Jill 10
Rodgers, W(illiam) R(obert) 7
Rodríguez, Claudio 10
Roethke, Theodore 1, 3, 8
Roiphe, Anne 3, 9
Romains, Jules 7
Rossner, Judith 6, 9
Roth, Henry 2, 6
Roth, Philip 1, 2, 3, 4, 6, 9
Rothenberg, Jerome 6
Rovit, Earl 7
Roy, Gabrielle 10
Rózewicz, Tadeusz 9
Ruark, Gibbons 3
Rudnik, Raphael 7
Rukeyser, Muriel 6, 10
Rulfo, Juan 8
Ryan, Cornelius 7
Sábato, Ernesto 10
Sadoff, Ira 9
Safire, William 10
Sagan, Françoise 3, 6, 9
Salamanca, J(ack) R(ichard) 4
Salinger, J(erome) D(avid) 1, 3, 8
Salter, James 7
Samarakis, Antonis 5
Sanchez, Sonia 5
Sandburg, Carl 1, 4, 10
Saner, Reg(inald) 9
Sansom, William 2, 6
Sarduy, Severo 6
Saroyan, William 1, 8, 10
Sarraute, Nathalie 1, 2, 4, 8, 10
Sarton, (Eleanor) May 4
Sartre, Jean-Paul 1, 4, 7, 9
Sayles, John 7, 10
Schaeffer, Susan Fromberg 6
Schevill, James 7
Schisgal, Murray 6
Schorer, Mark 9
Schulberg, Budd 7
Schuyler, James 5
Schwartz, Delmore 2, 4, 10
Schwarz-Bart, André 2, 4
Schwarz-Bart, Simone 7
Sciascia, Leonardo 8, 9
Scott, Paul 9
Seelye, John 7
Seferis, George 5
Segal, Erich 3, 10
Seghers, Anna 7
Selby, Hubert, Jr. 1, 2, 4, 8
Sender, Ramón 8
Sexton, Anne 2, 4, 6, 8, 10
Shaffer, Peter 5
Shamlu, Ahmad 10
Shange, Ntozake 8

Shapiro, Karl 4, 8
Shaw, Irwin 7
Shaw, Robert 5
Sheed, Wilfrid 2, 4, 10
Shepard, Sam 4, 6
Sherwin, Judith Johnson 7
Sholokhov, Mikhail 7
Shulman, Alix Kates 2, 10
Shuttle, Penelope 7
Sigal, Clancy 7
Silkin, Jon 2, 6
Sillitoe, Alan 1, 3, 6, 10
Silone, Ignazio 4
Silverberg, Robert 7
Simak, Clifford D(onald) 1
Simenon, Georges 1, 2, 3, 8
Simic, Charles 6, 9
Simon, Claude 4, 9
Simon, (Marvin) Neil 6
Simpson, Louis 4, 7, 9
Sinclair, Andrew 2
Sinclair, Upton 1
Singer, Isaac Bashevis 1, 3, 6, 9
Sinyavsky, Andrei 8
Sissman, L(ouis) E(dward) 9
Sisson, C(harles) H(ubert) 8
Sitwell, Edith 2, 9
Sjöwall, Maj
    See Wahlöö, Per 7
Slavitt, David 5
Smith, Florence Margaret
    See Smith, Stevie 3, 8
Smith, Stevie 3, 8
Smith, William Jay 6
Snodgrass, W(illiam)
    D(eWitt) 2, 6, 10
Snow, C(harles) P(ercy) 1, 4, 6, 9
Snyder, Gary 1, 2, 5, 9
Sokolov, Raymond 7
Solwoska, Mara
    See French, Marilyn 10
Solzhenitsyn, Aleksandr
    I(sayevich) 1, 2, 4, 7, 9, 10
Sontag, Susan 1, 2, 10
Sorrentino, Gilbert 3, 7
Souster, (Holmes) Raymond 5
Southern, Terry 7
Soyinka, Wole 3, 5
Spark, Muriel 2, 3, 5, 8
Spender, Stephen 1, 2, 5, 10
Spicer, Jack 8
Spielberg, Peter 6
Spillane, Mickey 3
Spivack, Kathleen 6
Stafford, Jean 4, 7
Stafford, William 4, 7
Stanton, Maura 9
Stead, Christina 2, 5, 8
Stegner, Wallace 9
Steinbeck, John 1, 5, 9
Stern, Richard G(ustave) 4
Stevenson, Anne 7
Stewart, J(ohn) I(nnes)
    M(ackintosh) 7
Stewart, Mary 7
Stone, Irving 7
Stone, Robert 5
Stoppard, Tom 1, 3, 4, 5, 8
Storey, David 2, 4, 5, 8
Storm, Hyemeyohsts 3
Stout, Rex 3
Strand, Mark 6

Stuart, Jesse 1, 8
Styron, William 1, 3, 5
Sukenick, Ronald 3, 4, 6
Summers, Hollis 10
Susann, Jacqueline 3
Sutton, Henry
    See Slavitt, David 5
Swados, Harvey 5
Swenson, May 4
Symons, Julian 2
Tanizaki, Jun'ichiro 8
Tate, (John Orley) Allen 2, 4, 6, 9
Tate, James 2, 6
Tavel, Ronald 6
Taylor, Eleanor Ross 5
Taylor, Elizabeth 2, 4
Taylor, Peter 1, 4
Tertz, Abram
    See Sinyavsky, Andrei 8
Theroux, Alexander 2
Theroux, Paul 5, 8
Thomas, Audrey 7
Thomas, R(onald) S(tuart) 6
Thompson, Hunter S(tockton) 9
Thurber, James 5
Tindall, Gillian 7
Tolkien, J(ohn) R(onald)
    R(euel) 1, 2, 3, 8
Tomlinson, (Alfred) Charles 2, 4, 6
Toomer, Jean 1, 4
Tournier, Michel 6
Traven, B. 8
Trevor, William 7, 9
Trilling, Lionel 9
Tryon, Thomas 3
Tutuola, Amos 5
Tyler, Anne 7
Ungaretti, Giuseppe 7
Updike, John 1, 2, 3, 5, 7, 9
Uris, Leon 7
Vaculík, Ludvík 7
van der Post, Laurens 5
Van Doren, Mark 6, 10
Van Duyn, Mona 3, 7
Van Itallie, Jean-Claude 3
Van Peebles, Melvin 2
Van Vogt, A(lfred) E(lton) 1
Vargas Llosa, Mario 3, 6, 9, 10
Vassilikos, Vassilis 4, 8
Vidal, Gore 2, 4, 6, 8, 10
Viereck, Peter 4
Vittorini, Elio 6, 9
Voinovich, Vladimir 10
Vonnegut, Kurt, Jr. 1, 2, 3, 4, 5, 8
Voznesensky, Andrei 1
Wagman, Fredrica 7
Wagoner, David 3, 5
Wahlöö, Per 7
Wain, John 2
Wakefield, Dan 7
Wakoski, Diane 2, 4, 7, 9
Walcott, Derek 2, 4, 9
Waldman, Anne 7
Walker, Alice 5, 6, 9
Walker, Margaret 1, 6
Wallace, Irving 7
Wallant, Edward Lewis 5, 10
Wambaugh, Joseph 3
Warner, Sylvia Townsend 7

AUTHOR INDEX

Warren, Robert Penn 1, 4, 6, 8, 10
Waugh, Auberon 7
Waugh, Evelyn 1, 3, 8
Waugh, Harriet 6
Webb, Charles 7
Weidman, Jerome 7
Weiss, Peter 3
Weiss, Theodore 3, 8
Welch, James 6
Weldon, Fay 6, 9
Weller, Michael 10
Welty, Eudora 1, 2, 5
Wesker, Arnold 3, 5
Wesley, Richard 7
West, Jessamyn 7
West, Morris L(anglo) 6
West, Paul 7

West, Rebecca 7, 9
Westlake, Donald E(dwin) 7
Whalen, Philip 6
White, E(lwyn) B(rooks) 10
White, Patrick 3, 4, 5, 7, 9
Whitehead, E. A. 5
Whittemore, (Edward) Reed 4
Wicker, Tom 7
Wideman, J(ohn) E(dgar) 5
Wiebe, Rudy 6
Wieners, John 7
Wiesel, Elie(zer) 3, 5
Wilbur, Richard 3, 6, 9
Wilder, Thornton 1, 5, 6, 10
Wilhelm, Kate 7
Willard, Nancy 7
Williams, John A(lfred) 5
Williams, Tennessee 1, 2, 5, 7, 8

Williams, William Carlos 1, 2, 5, 9
Willingham, Calder 5
Wilson, Angus 2, 3, 5
Wilson, Colin 3
Wilson, Edmund 1, 2, 3, 8
Wilson, John Anthony Burgess
   See Burgess, Anthony 1, 2, 4, 5, 8, 10
Wilson, Lanford 7
Wilson, Robert 7, 9
Winters, Yvor 4, 8
Wodehouse, P(elham) G(renville) 1, 2, 5, 10
Woiwode, Larry 6, 10
Wolfe, Tom 1, 2, 9
Woods, Helen Ferguson
   See Kavan, Anna 5

Wouk, Herman 1, 9
Wright, Charles 6
Wright, James 3, 5, 10
Wright, Richard 1, 3, 4, 9
Wright, Richard B(ruce) 6
Wurlitzer, Rudolph 2, 4
Yanovsky, Vassily S(emenovich) 2
Yates, Richard 7, 8
Yerby, Frank G(arvin) 1, 7
Yevtushenko, Yevgeny 1, 3
Yglesias, Helen 7
Young, Andrew 5
Yurick, Sol 6
Zaturenska, Marya 6
Zindel, Paul 6
Zukofsky, Louis 1, 2, 4, 7

AUTHOR INDEX

Appendix

THE EXCERPTS IN CLC-10 WERE REPRINTED FROM THE FOLLOWING PERIODICALS:

Agenda
America
American Literature
The American Poetry Review
The Anglo-Welsh Review
The Antigonish Review
The Antioch Review
Arcadia
Ariel
Arizona Quarterly
The Atlantic Monthly
Best Sellers
Book World—The Washington Post
Books Abroad
Books and Bookman
Booklist
BooksWest
boundary 2
Canadian Literature
Canadian Slavonic Papers
Catholic World
The CEA Critic
The Centennial Review
Chicago Review
Commentary
Commonweal
Comparative Literature
Comparative Literature Studies
The Connecticut Review
Contemporary Literature
Contemporary Review
Criticism
Critique: Studies in Modern Fiction
The Dalhousie Review
Diacritics
Éire-Ireland
Encounter
English Language Notes
English Studies
Essays in Criticism
Essays in Literature
The Explicator
Extrapolation
Folio
Forum for Modern Language Studies
French Review
French Studies
The Georgia Review

Harper's
Hispania
The Hollins Critic
The Hudson Review
The International Fiction Review
The Iowa Review
Italian Americana
Japan Quarterly
The Journal of Irish Literature
Journal of Modern Literature
Journal of Spanish Studies: Twentieth
   Century
Judaism
Kansas Quarterly
Keystone Folklore Quarterly
L'Esprit Créateur
The Listener
London Magazine
The Los Angeles Times
The Michigan Quarterly Review
The Midwest Quarterly
The Minnesota Review
Mississippi Quarterly
Modern Drama
Modern Fiction Studies
The Modern Language Review
Modern Poetry Studies
MOSAIC
Mother Jones
Ms.
The Nation
National Review
New Boston Review
The New England Quarterly
The New Leader
The New Republic
The New Review
New Statesman
New York Arts Journal
New York Magazine
The New York Review of Books
The New York Times
The New York Times Book Review
The New Yorker
The Ontario Review
Paideuma
Parnassus: Poetry in Review
Partisan Review

Paunch
Phylon
Plays and Players
Ploughshares
Plural
Poetry
PN Review
Prairie Schooner
Psychology Today
Publishers Weekly
Renascence
Review
Rolling Stone
Romance Notes
Russian Literature Triquarterly
Salmagundi
Saturday Review
Scandinavian Studies
Sewanee Review
Shenandoah
South Atlantic Quarterly
The Southern Humanities Review
The Southern Literary Journal
Southern Review
The Southern Review
Southwest Review
The Spectator
Stand
Studies in Black Literature
Studies in Short Fiction
Studies in the Twentieth Century
Symposium
The Texas Quarterly
Time
The Times Literary Supplement
TriQuarterly
Twentieth Century Literature
The Village Voice
Virginia Quarterly Review
Virginia Woolf Quarterly
Voyages
West Coast Review
West Coast Review of Books
The Western Review
World Literature Today
World Research INK
Yale French Studies
The Yale Review

THE EXCERPTS IN CLC-10 WERE REPRINTED FROM THE FOLLOWING BOOKS:

Adams, M. Ian, Three Authors of Alienation: Bombel, Onetti, Carpentier, *University of Texas Press, 1975.*

Adams, Robert Martin, AfterJoyce: Studies in Fiction After "Ulysses," *Oxford University Press, 1977.*

Allen, Gay Wilson, Carl Sandburg, *University of Minnesota Press, 1972.*

Amis, Kingsley, New Maps of Hell: A Survey of Science Fiction, *Harcourt, 1960.*

Arpin, Gary Q., The Poetry of John Berryman, *Kennikat, 1978.*

Axthelm, Peter M., The Modern Confessional Novel, *Yale University Press, 1967.*

Baumbach, Jonathan, The Landscape of Nightmare: Studies in the Contemporary American Novel, *New York University Press, 1965.*

Berryman, John, The Freedom of the Poet, *Farrar, Straus, 1976.*

Blodgett, E. D., Poets and Critics: Essays from "Canadian Literature," *Oxford University Press, 1974.*

Bradbury, Malcolm, ed., Forster: A Collection of Critical Essays, *Prentice-Hall, 1966.*

Clareson, Thomas D., ed., Voices for the Future: Essays on Modern Science Fiction Writers, *Vol. 1, Popular Press, 1976.*

Cowley, Malcolm, And I Worked at the Writer's Trade: Chapters of Literary History, *Viking Penguin, 1978.*

Cox, James M., ed., Robert Frost: A Collection of Critical Essays, *Prentice-Hall, 1962.*

Daemmrick, Horst S., and Haenicke, Diether H., eds., The Challenge of German Literature, *Wayne State University Press, 1971.*

De Bolt, John, ed., The Happening Worlds of John Brunner, *Kennikat, 1975.*

Doyle, Paul A., Paul Vincent Carroll, *Bucknell University Press, 1971.*

Finholt, Richard, American Visionary Fiction: Mad Metaphysics as Salvation Psychology, *Kennikat, 1978.*

Friedman, Melvin J., ed., Samuel Beckett Now, *University of Chicago Press, 1970.*

Gallagher, D. P., Modern Latin American Literature, *Oxford University Press, 1973.*

Gilman, Richard, Common and Uncommon Masks: Writings on Theatre 1961-1970, *Random House, 1971.*

Hadas, Pamela White, Marianne Moore: Poet of Affection, *Syracuse University Press, 1977.*

Holman, C. H., John P. Marquand, *University of Minnesota Press, 1965.*

Hynes, Samuel, The Auden Generation: Literature and Politics in England in the 1930s, *Viking Penguin, 1977.*

Johnson, Ira D., and Johnson, Christine, Les Americanistes: New French Criticism on Modern American Fiction, *Kennikat, 1978.*

Kennard, Jean E., Number and Nightmare: Forms of Fantasy in Contemporary Fiction, *Archon Books, 1975.*

Kermode, Frank, Puzzles and Epiphanies: Essays and Reviews, *Chilmark, 1962, Routledge and Kegan Paul, Ltd. 1962.*

Kirk, Russell, Enemies of the Permanent Things: Observations of Abnormity in Literature and Politics, *Arlington House, 1969.*

Kunitz, Stanley, A Kind of Order, A Kind of Folly, *Atlantic-Little, Brown, 1975.*

Mizener, Arthur, The Sense of Life in the Modern Novel, *Houghton Mifflin, 1964.*

Riddel, Joseph N., C. Day Lewis, *Twayne, 1971.*

Ries, Lawrence R., Wolf Masks: Violence in Contemporary Poetry, *Kennikat, 1977.*

Robbe-Grillet, Alain, For a New Novel: Essays on Fiction, *Grove Press, 1965.*

Rosenthal, M. L., The Modern Poets: A Critical Introduction, *Oxford University Press, 1960.*

Sampson, Edward C., E. B. White, *Twayne, 1974.*

Shapiro, Charles, ed., Twelve Original Essays on Great Novels, *Wayne State University Press, 1958.*

Spurling, Hilary, Invitation to the Dance: A Guide to Anthony Powell's "Dance to the Music of Time," *Little, Brown, 1978.*

Stevens, Wallace, The Necessary Angel, *Knopf, 1951.*

Tanner, Tony, The Waves of Wonder: Naïvety and Reality in American Literature, *Cambridge University Press, 1965.*

Tomlinson, Charles, ed., Marianne Moore: A Collection of Critical Essays, *Prentice-Hall, 1970.*

Tucker, James, The Novels of Anthony Powell, *Columbia University Press, 1976.*

Weeks, Robert P., ed., Hemingway: A Collection of Critical Essays, *Prentice-Hall, 1962.*

Whissen, Thomas R., Isak Dinesen's Aesthetics, *Kennikat, 1973.*

Williams, William Carlos, Selected Essays, *New Directions, 1948.*

Winters, Yvor, The Function of Criticism: Problems and Exercises, *Swallow Press, 1957.*